ISBN 978-1-5285-3148-1
PIBN 10940809

1 MONTH OF
FREE
READING

at

www.ForgottenBooks.com

By purchasing this book you are
eligible for one month membership to
ForgottenBooks.com, giving you
unlimited access to our entire
collection of over 1,000,000 titles via
our web site and mobile apps.

To claim your free month visit:

www.forgottenbooks.com/free940809

HANSARD'S

PARLIAMENTARY DEBATES,

THIRD SERIES:

COMMENCING WITH THE ACCESSION OF

WILLIAM IV.

50° VICTORIÆ, 1887.

VOL. CCCXIV.

COMPRISING THE PERIOD FROM

THE TWENTY-SIXTH DAY OF APRIL 1887

TO

THE THIRTEENTH DAY OF MAY 1887.

FIFTH VOLUME OF THE SESSION.

LONDON:

PUBLISHED BY CORNELIUS BUCK & SON,

AT THE OFFICE FOR " HANSARD'S PARLIAMENTARY DEBATES,"

22, PATERNOSTER ROW. [E.C.]

1887.

TABLE OF CONTENTS

TO

VOLUME CCCXIV.

THIRD SERIES.

VOL. CCCXIV.   [THIRD SERIES.]   [*b*]

TABLE OF CONTENTS

ORDERS OF THE DAY.

——o——

TABLE OF CONTENTS.

TABLE OF CONTENTS.

TABLE OF CONTENTS.

TABLE OF CONTENTS.

ORDERS OF THE DAY.

Criminal Law Amendment (Ireland) Bill [Bill 217]—COMMITTEE —ADJOURNED DEBATE [THIRD NIGHT]—

Order read, for resuming Adjourned Debate on Amendment proposed to Question [26th April], "That Mr. Speaker do now leave the Chair," for Committee on the Bill :"—Question again proposed, "That the words proposed to be left out stand part of the Question : "—Debate *resumed* 251

After long debate, Question put :—The House *divided;* Ayes 341, Noes 240 ; Majority 101.

    Division List, Ayes and Noes 298

Main Question put, and *agreed to :*—Bill *considered* in Committee; Committee report Progress; to sit again *To-morrow.*

Incumbents of Benefices Loans Extension Act (1886) Amendment Bill [*Lords*] [Bill 230]—

Order for Second Reading read 303

Moved, "That the Debate be now adjourned,"—(*Mr. T. M. Healy :*)— Question put, and *agreed to :*—Second Reading *deferred* till *To-morrow.*

Bankruptcy Offices (Sites) (*re-committed*) **Bill** [Bill 243]—

Bill *considered* in Committee [*Progress 20th April*] 303

After short time spent therein, Bill *reported,* without Amendment ; to be read the third time *To-morrow.*

Truck Bill [Bill 109]—

Bill *considered* in Committee [*Progress 20th April*] 304

After short time spent therein, Committee report Progress; to sit again *To-morrow.*

MOTIONS.

Fishing in Rivers Bill—*Ordered* (*Mr. Broadhurst, Mr. Arnold Morley, Mr. Bernard Coleridge*); *presented,* and read the first time [Bill 244] 308

Juvenile Offenders Bill—*Ordered* (*Mr. Secretary Matthews, Mr. Stuart-Wortley*); *presented,* and read the first time [Bill 245] 308

                                                      [1.15.]

TABLE OF CONTENTS.

LORDS, FRIDAY, APRIL 29.

COMMONS, FRIDAY, APRIL 29.

PRIVATE BUSINESS.

———o———

QUESTIONS.

———o———

ORDERS OF THE DAY.

——o——

TABLE OF CONTENTS.

PUBLIC PETITIONS.

—o—

QUESTIONS.

—o—

TABLE OF CONTENTS.

TABLE OF CONTENTS.

MOTION.

———o———

ORDERS OF THE DAY.

———o———

MOTIONS.

———o———

TABLE OF CONTENTS.

COMMONS, WEDNESDAY, MAY 4.

ORDERS OF THE DAY.
—o—

MOTIONS.
—o—

TABLE OF CONTENTS.

LORDS, THURSDAY, MAY 5.

COMMONS, THURSDAY, MAY 5.

PRIVATE BUSINESS.

QUESTIONS.

TABLE OF CONTENTS.

ORDERS OF THE DAY.

—o—

TABLE OF CONTENTS.

TABLE OF CONTENTS.

ORDERS OF THE DAY.

——o——

TABLE OF CONTENTS.

COMMONS, MONDAY, MAY 9.

VOL. CCCXIV. [THIRD SERIES.] [*c*]

TABLE OF CONTENTS.

COMMONS, TUESDAY, MAY 10.

QUESTIONS.

COMMONS, WEDNESDAY, MAY 11.

PRIVATE BUSINESS.

TABLE OF CONTENTS.

TABLE OF CONTENTS.

TABLE OF CONTENTS.

TABLE OF CONTENTS.

WITHDRAWAL OF MOTION.

—◦—

ORDERS OF THE DAY.

—◦—

TABLE OF CONTENTS.

TABLE OF CONTENTS.

ORDERS OF THE DAY.

—o—

Criminal Law Amendment (Ireland) Bill [Bill 217]—

Bill *considered* in Committee [*Progress 11th May*] [SEVENTH NIGHT] .. 1820
After long time spent therein, Committee report Progress; to sit again upon *Tuesday* next.

TABLE OF CONTENTS.

COMMONS.

—◆—

NEW MEMBER SWORN.

THURSDAY, APRIL 28.

For *the Borough of Taunton*—Honble. Alfred Percy Allsopp.

NEW WRITS ISSUED.

MONDAY, MAY 2.

For *Cornwall* (*St. Austell Division*), *v.* William Copeland Borlase, esquire, Chiltern Hundreds.

FRIDAY, MAY 6.

For *Cork* (*North-East Cork Division*), *v.* Edmund Leamy, esquire, Steward or Bailiff of Her Majesty's Three Chiltern Hundreds of Stoke, Desborough, and Bonenham, in the County of Buckingham.

HANSARD'S
PARLIAMENTARY DEBATES,

IN THE

SECOND SESSION OF THE *TWENTY-FOURTH PARLIAMENT* OF THE

UNITED KINGDOM OF *GREAT BRITAIN* AND *IRELAND*,

APPOINTED TO MEET 5 AUGUST, 1886, IN THE FIFTIETH

YEAR OF THE REIGN OF

HER MAJESTY QUEEN VICTORIA.

FIFTH VOLUME OF SESSION 1887.

HOUSE OF LORDS,

Tuesday, 26th April, 1887.

MINUTES.] — PROVISIONAL ORDER BILLS —
First Reading—Local Government * (70).
Second Reading—Metropolitan Police * (65).

DEFENCES OF THE EMPIRE—COLONIAL
DEFENCE.—QUESTION.

VISCOUNT SIDMOUTH asked the
Under Secretary of State for the
Colonies, When the new regulations
relating to employment and remuneration of naval and military officers serving
in the Colonies will be laid on the Table;
and whether copies would be supplied
to Members of the Colonial Conference?
THE UNDER SECRETARY OF
STATE (The Earl of ONSLOW), in reply,
said, he regretted that some unavoidable
delay had been caused in the prepara-

VOL. CCCXIV. [THIRD SERIES.]

tion of these Papers by the fact that the
printer had mixed them up with some
Papers relating to another subject, and
it had taken some time to eliminate
them. They were now, however, in a
satisfactory shape and would be sent
immediately to the printer, and it was
hoped that they would be ready on,
Wednesday. With regard to the request
that the Papers should be placed in the
hands of Members of the Colonial Conference, he had to inform the noble
Viscount that this has been done, the
Paper containing the regulations having
been circulated among them, and they
had expressed their satisfaction with the
arrangement entered into by Her Majesty's Government, which they said had
brought about a change which they had
long desired, and which would be of
great service and benefit to the Colonies.

House adjourned at a quarter before
Five o'clock, to Thursday next,
a quarter past Ten o'clock

B

HOUSE OF COMMONS,

Tuesday, 26th April, 1887.

MINUTES.]—WAYS AND MEANS—*considered in Committee—Resolutions* [April 25] *reported.*
PRIVATE BILL *(by Order)—Second Reading—* Howat's Divorce.*
PUBLIC BILLS — *First Reading* — Customs and Inland Revenue * [241].
Second Reading—Metropolis Management Acts Amendment (Westminster) * [208], *referred to Select Committee on* Metropolis Management Acts Amendment (No. 2) * [166].
Committee—Criminal Law Amendment (Ireland) [217] [*First Night*], *debate adjourned.*
Committee—*Report*—Quarries * [58-239] ; Police Force Enfranchisement * [17-240].
Third Reading — Customs Consolidation Act (1876) Amendment * [155], and *passed.*
PROVISIONAL ORDER BILLS — *Ordered — First Reading* — Commons Regulation (Ewer) * [237] ; ¡Commons Regulation (Laindon) * [238].
Second Reading — Local Government (Highways)* [224]; Local Government (Poor Law) * [226]; Local Government (Poor Law) (No. 2) * [227].

QUESTIONS.

—o—

POOR LAW (ENGLAND AND WALES)— HALIFAX BOARD OF GUARDIANS— THE DIETARY.

MR. J. E. ELLIS (Nottingham, Rushcliffe) asked the President of the Local Government Board, Whether the following is a correct extract from a letter of the Local Government Board to the Halifax Board of Guardians, of December, 1886 :—

"I am directed by the Local Government Board to acknowledge the receipt of your letter of the 1st instant, applying for their sanction to the proposal of the Guardians of the Halifax Union to allow the children in the workhouse a dinner of rice pudding with treacle on Fridays, in lieu of the bread and cheese dinner now prescribed for them on that day. I am directed to request that the Board may be informed what quantities of rice pudding and treacle the Guardians propose to prescribe for each class of children, and, at the same time, what will be the quantities of each ingredient used in the preparation of a pound of rice pudding ; "

and, if so, whether he will state the reason why it appears necessary to the Local Government Board thus to fetter the discretion of the representatives of the ratepayers with respect to the ingredients of a pound of rice pudding ?

THE PRESIDENT (Mr. RITCHIE) (Tower Hamlets, St. George's), in reply, said, the effect of the letter was correctly stated in the Question. The particulars seemed to be of rather a minute character ; but the question was a larger one—namely, whether the Local Government Board should exercise any control or supervision over the dietary of workhouse inmates ? When any change in such dietary was proposed it was necessary that, in the first instance, the Board should be made acquainted with the fact.

EDUCATION DEPARTMENT (ENGLAND AND WALES) — LLANELLY BOARD SCHOOL.

MR. STANLEY LEIGHTON (Shropshire, Oswestry) asked the Vice President of the Committee of Council on Education, Whether his attention has been called to a request from the School Board of Llanelly (Brecon), for the sanction by the Education Department of an enlargement of the Board School ; whether it is a fact that in the Voluntary and Board Schools of the district, taken together, more than sufficient accommodation is available for the children ; and, whether, under such circumstances, the Department is empowered, by the Education Act, to require or to sanction the provision of unnecessary school accommodation at the expense of the ratepayers ?

THE VICE PRESIDENT (Sir WILLIAM HART DYKE) (Kent, Dartford): The Question to which my hon. Friend refers is merely one of adding a classroom, which both the Board and the Inspector of the district think necessary for the proper organization of the school. Moreover, the Department are not satisfied that there is a sufficiency of accommodation in the existing schools ; and, under all the circumstances, it would be unusual to refuse to sanction the Board's proposal.

LOCAL GOVERNMENT BOARD—AUDIT OF MUNICIPAL ACCOUNTS.

MR. STANLEY LEIGHTON (Shropshire, Oswestry) asked the President of the Local Government Board, Whether the audit of municipal accounts is conducted by auditors chosen and appointed by the municipalities themselves and the ratepayers ; whether any complaints have reached the Local Government Board in reference to the manner in which the audits have been made ; and, whether he will consider the expediency of providing for an independent audit through a Board of Auditors unconnected with local interests?

THE PRESIDENT (Mr. RITCHIE) (Tower Hamlets, St. George's): Municipal accounts are audited by auditors appointed by the Mayor and elected by the burgesses. Representations have, no doubt, been made more than once to the Local Government Board on this question; but, while the existing arrangement can hardly be regarded as satisfactory, the Government cannot hold out hopes that they will introduce a measure which shall take away from municipal boroughs the powers they at present exercise in this matter.

BURMAH (UPPER)—ATTACKS UPON OUTPOSTS.

MR. BRADLAUGH (Northampton) asked the Under Secretary of State for India, Whether it is true, as stated in *The Calcutta Press* of March 19, that the Reports from Burmah were then very unsatisfactory; whether raids by Burmans upon British outposts continued, and in some recent ones the police stations were burnt, the telegraph wires cut, and some of the policemen killed; whether the Lingadaw post was attacked in great force; whether numerous petty actions are also reported, showing that the pacification of the country is far from being established; and, whether the whole of the population of Mandalay, without exception, have refused to pay the House and Land Tax?

THE UNDER SECRETARY OF STATE (Sir JOHN GORST) (Chatham): The Reports from Burmah, which have been received by the Secretary of State, are not unsatisfactory. Attacks on outposts have taken place in some parts of the country. We have news of one station having been burnt, and one telegraph wire having been cut; but not of any policemen having been killed in any recent attack. Lingadaw was attacked on March 11 by 300 dacoits, who were beaten off with heavy loss to themselves and none to the defenders of the post. In order to pacify the country it has been necessary to break up the bands of dacoits, and in this operation many petty actions have necessarily taken place. No information has reached the Secretary of State that the population of Mandalay has refused to pay the House and Land or any other Tax.

MR. BRADLAUGH asked, whether the hon. and learned Gentleman could give the House any information as to the news telegraphed to the newspapers about Burmah yesterday and to-day?

SIR JOHN GORST said, he had not seen the newspaper reports in question, and he was not able to give any information on the subject?

HARBOURS—DOVER HARBOUR—THE ADMIRALTY PIER.

SIR EDWARD WATKIN (Hythe) asked the Secretary to the Board of Trade, If he will lay upon the Table a Return of the names, salaries, and duties of the officers and men employed by the Board of Trade at the Admiralty Pier at Dover, which is under the charge of that Board?

THE SECRETARY (Baron HENRY DE WORMS) (Liverpool, East Toxteth): With the unimportant exception of the names of individuals, the information asked for by the hon. Baronet is given at page 51 of the Civil Service Estimates now before Parliament. The expense of printing a separate Return appears unnecessary.

CHINA—THE OPIUM DUTY—ORDINANCE OF THE HONG KONG LEGISLATURE.

MR. KING (Hull, Central) asked the Secretary of State for the Colonies, What is the nature of the provisions of an Ordinance, which it is understood has been recently introduced into the Hong Kong Legislature, for the purpose of assisting the Chinese authorities in the realization of the duty on opium imported into China?

THE SECRETARY OF STATE (Sir HENRY HOLLAND) (Hampstead): It would be difficult to state the provisions of the Bill in the limits of an answer to a Question; but the hon. Member can see the Bill, if it would not be inconvenient to him to come to the Colonial Office. Shortly, it is a measure for preventing the import or export of raw opium in quantities of less than one chest, and for restricting the possession of similar opium in smaller quantities in other hands than those of the opium farmer, and for preventing junks leaving at night under any circumstances, which they can now do, but only if specially authorized. The Bill met with opposition in the Council, and the final result is not yet known.

IRELAND—THE CATTLE TRADE—THE RATHDOWN UNION—PLEURO-PNEU-MONIA.

MR. MURPHY (Dublin, St. Patrick's) asked the Chief Secretary to the Lord Lieutenant of Ireland, If he is aware that the Guardians of the Rathdown Union, at a meeting held on the 12th instant, passed the following Resolution:—

"That no cattle from North or South Dublin Unions be admitted into the Rathdown Union for any purpose whatever, except for slaughter, for the space of 12 months; cattle now in the show yard at Ballsbridge to be exempted from this order;"

whether he is aware that the dairy cattle for supplying Dublin with milk are, to a large extent, fed on the grass lands in Rathdown Union; and, whether he will take any steps in reference to the Resolution, which, if put in force, must seriously affect the supply of milk to Dublin, and inflict injury both on dairy keepers and on those who let grazing in Rathdown Union?

THE PARLIAMENTARY UNDER SECRETARY (Colonel KING-HARMAN) (Kent, Isle of Thanet) (who replied) said: A Regulation to the effect stated has been made by the Guardians of the Rathdown Union, in pursuance of their powers as a Local Authority. It was obviously made with a view to protect their Union from the introduction of pleuro-pneumonia by cattle brought from Dublin dairies. It is believed that in previous years the grass lands in the Union have been, to a considerable extent, used by these cattle. Before asking the intervention of Government with respect to any such Regulation, the proper course is for any persons feeling aggrieved thereby to submit their objections to the Local Authority, who have full power to alter or modify their Regulations.

MR. J. W. BARCLAY (Forfarshire) asked the Chancellor of the Duchy of Lancaster, Whether he can inform the House what steps the Irish Government have taken to prevent cattle suffering from pleuro-pneumonia being taken outside the Dublin infected district for shipment?

COLONEL KING-HARMAN (who replied) said: The Irish Government cause all cattle found to be suffering from pleuro-pneumonia to be slaughtered

Sir Henry Holland

without delay. All cattle in the Dublin infected district are required to be branded, and their shipment has been prohibited by an Order of the Privy Council which came into force on the 22nd instant. As I stated yesterday, in the case of one dairy 41 cows were slaughtered, and at another dairy 21, both being suspected of being infected with pleuro-pneumonia.

POOR LAW (ENGLAND AND WALES)—ELECTION OF GUARDIANS—FULHAM PARISH.

MR. DE LISLE (Leicestershire, Mid) asked the President of the Local Government Board, If he can explain how it happened that, in the parish of Fulham, at the recent election of Guardians, no voting papers were furnished in some cases to duly qualified ratepayers, who were thus precluded from voting; and, whether this omission would annul the election; and, if so, whether Her Majesty's Government will make inquiry into the alleged defects of the said election before the Guardians exercise any of their legal functions?

THE PRESIDENT (Mr. RITCHIE) (Tower Hamlets, St. George's): The Board have communicated with the Returning Officer, and they learn from him that there were upwards of 8,000 voting papers for the parish of Fulham, and that in two instances only had complaints been made to him that voting papers had not been delivered. In those cases the names had not been marked in the Rate Book by the overseers as names of persons entitled to vote. The Regulations of the Local Government Board, with the view of meeting cases of accidental omission, provide that a person to whom a voting paper has not been duly delivered on the day fixed for the delivery shall be entitled to receive a voting paper, on application to the Returning Officer, for the purpose of recording his vote. The Board have received a communication from one of the candidates, in which three cases are specified, where it is alleged that voting papers were not delivered; but assuming that this is established, it would not, in the opinion of the Board, render the election invalid; and, so far as this allegation is concerned, the Board see no sufficient reason for directing an inquiry.

ARMY (AUXILIARY FORCES) — THE
VOLUNTEERS — THE CAPITATION
GRANT.

MR. THORBURN (Peebles and Selkirk) asked the Secretary of State for
War, Whether the Volunteer Forces
Capitation Grant, remitted to Volunteer
Regiments this month, and earned by
drills done by them from 1st November,
1885, to 1st November, 1886, is a payment to re-imburse them for expenses
incurred by them during that period, or
is a payment to meet expenditure from
1st November, 1886, to 1st November,
1887; and, if the latter, what portion of
it will fall to be returned to the War
Office in the event of a regiment being
disbanded or resigning, say, on the 1st
June of this year?

THE SECRETARY OF STATE (Mr.
E. STANHOPE) (Lincolnshire, Horncastle): The Capitation Grant is to
meet current expenses which may be
expected to accrue before a further
grant is made. The case put by the
latter part of the hon. Member's Question is hypothetical; but I may say that,
considering the period which would have
elapsed since the Returns on which the
grant was made, repayment of the money
would not be claimed.

REPUBLIC OF SOUTH AFRICA (TRANSVAAL)—FLOGGING OF NATIVE
WOMEN.

SIR ROBERT FOWLER (London)
asked the Secretary of State for the
Colonies, Whether his attention has
been called to an article in *The Transvaal
Advertiser*, giving details of the cruel
flogging of a Native woman by order of
a Landdrost in the Transvaal, and
stating that it was within her knowledge that six other women had been
flogged with the cat-o'-nine-tails in the
"tronk" at Pretoria; and, whether, as
these barbarous acts are a violation of
the agreement entered into with the
Republic of South Africa, Her Majesty's
Government will remonstrate with the
authorities at Pretoria?

THE SECRETARY OF STATE (Sir
HENRY HOLLAND) (Hampstead): I have
not myself seen the account referred to
by my right hon. Friend, which, if
true, describes circumstances of great
brutality; but Her Majesty's Government have no right to interfere. The

Article 18 of the Convention of Pretoria
of 1881, under which it would have been
the duty of the British Resident to call
the attention of the Transvaal authorities to such cases of ill-treatment of
Natives, was omitted from the Convention of London of 1884, and there has
been, therefore, no violation of the
agreement referred to.

CELEBRATION OF THE JUBILEE YEAR
OF HER MAJESTY'S REIGN — THE
SERVICE IN WESTMINSTER ABBEY.

MR. LABOUCHERE (Northampton)
asked the First Commissioner of Works,
Whether the House will have an opportunity to pronounce an opinion upon the
Estimate of the expenditure connected
with the Jubilee Service in Westminster
Abbey, before that expenditure has been
incurred; whether it is correct, as stated
in the Press, that all materials employed
in erecting galleries, &c., will become
the property of the Dean and Chapter;
whether any Estimate has been made of
the expenditure that would be required
were the Jubilee Service to take place in
St. Paul's Cathedral; and, if so, whether
it would be less than that which is contemplated in Westminster Abbey; and,
whether all seats will be reserved, or
whether any portion of the Abbey will
be thrown open to the public; and, if
so, what portion?

THE FIRST COMMISSIONER (Mr.
PLUNKET)(Dublin University): The Estimate will, I hope, be laid upon the Table
within a few days; but it may, and probably will, be necessary to incur some expense before the Vote can be taken. It
is not proposed that the materials employed in erecting galleries, &c., shall
become the property of the Dean and
Chapter. No accurate Estimate of the
cost of holding the Service in St. Paul's
has been made; but, judging from the
precedent of the Thanksgiving Ceremony
on the occasion of the recovery of the
Prince of Wales, the cost would be about
the same as that of a ceremony in Westminster Abbey. The arrangements with
regard to the distribution of seats will
be in the hands of the Lord Chamberlain; and I have no doubt that he will,
as in former similar cases, provide, as
far as possible, for the representation of
all classes and interests of the people.
The admission will, I presume, be by
ticket.

Mr. LABOUCHERE: Do I understand that the Estimates will be voted before the Service takes place?

Mr. PLUNKET: The Estimate will be laid on the table as soon as possible; but I cannot undertake to say that none of the expense will be incurred before the Vote is passed.

Mr. LABOUCHERE: Will the Vote be taken before the ceremony?

Mr. PLUNKET: I hope so, certainly.

'THE BOARD OF TRADE JOURNAL"—ADVERTISEMENTS.

Mr. MONTAGU (Tower Hamlets, Whitechapel) asked the Secretary to the Board of Trade, Under what authority, and on what precedents, advertisements are now inserted in *The Board of Trade Journal*, in competition with private enterprize?

The SECRETARY (Baron HENRY DE WORMS) (Liverpool, East Toxteth): The arrangement for inserting advertisements in *The Board of Trade Journal* was, as is usual, made by the Stationery Office by the authority of the Treasury, and in this case with the concurrence of the Board of Trade. The Board of Trade are informed that there are precedents for inserting advertisements in publications issued by the Government.

WAYS AND MEANS—THE FINANCIAL RESOLUTIONS—STAMP DUTIES—COMPANIES—COMPOSITION FOR TRANSFERS.

Mr. MONTAGU (Tower Hamlets, Whitechapel) asked Mr. Chancellor of the Exchequer, Whether Companies electing to pay annually 1s. per cent on their capital would be allowed to convert their fully paid shares into certificates to bearer, thus avoiding the trouble as well as the expense of transfers?

The CHANCELLOR OF THE EXCHEQUER (Mr. GOSCHEN) (St. George's, Hanover Square): Yes, Sir. I consider it will be one of the advantages of the plan.

WAR OFFICE (ORDNANCE DEPARTMENT)—THE COMMITTEE ON DEFECTIVE CUTLASSES AND BAYONETS—THE EVIDENCE.

Mr. HANBURY (Preston) asked the Secretary of State for War, When the Evidence of the Committee on Defective Cutlasses and Bayonets will be issued to Members?

The SECRETARY OF STATE (Mr. E. STANHOPE) (Lincolnshire, Horncastle): The Committee on Naval Cutlasses appointed their own Secretary, and I have not yet received from him the evidence taken by the Committee. I understand that it is under revision, and I will do my best to hurry on its production.

PREVENTION OF CRIME (IRELAND) ACT, 1882—EXAMINATIONS UNDER SECTION 16.

Mr. ANDERSON (Elgin and Nairn) asked the Chief Secretary to the Lord Lieutenant of Ireland, If he could state in how many cases were witnesses examined under the powers conferred by Section 16 of "The Prevention of Crime Act, 1882;" in respect of what offences were they examined; and, in how many cases were convictions obtained on such examinations?

The PARLIAMENTARY UNDER SECRETARY (Colonel KING-HARMAN) (Kent, Isle of Thanet) (who replied) said: The hon. Member has given no Notice of his Question; and I could not give him a complete answer without inquiries which would occupy some time, and for which he has afforded no opportunity. The official records immediately at my disposal show, however, that during the existence of the Crimes Act 114 inquiries were held under Section 16, and that one-third of these inquiries resulted in prosecutions. The classes of offence in respect of which the inquiries were held were chiefly murder, conspiracy to murder, manslaughter, firing at the person, attacking houses, killing or maiming cattle, and other crimes of violence, besides injury to property, intimidation, and writing threatening letters.

Mr. ANDERSON: Will the right hon. and gallant Gentleman grant a Return?

Colonel KING-HARMAN: It would be an exceedingly difficult Return to make out; but if the hon. Gentleman will put upon the Paper, or communicate to me, exactly what he wants, I will do my best to meet his wishes.

Mr. SEXTON (Belfast, W.) asked, if the right hon. and gallant Gentleman included in the enumeration the Tubbercurry conspiracy case, in which 11 men were kept in Sligo Prison for a month, and in which a prolonged inquiry was held, resulting in an acquittal?

COLONEL KING-HARMAN asked the hon. Member to give Notice of the Question.

IRISH LAND COMMISSION—JUDICIAL RENTS—RETURNS.

MR. J. E. ELLIS (Nottingham, Rushcliffe) asked the Chief Secretary to the Lord Lieutenant of Ireland, When the Returns of Judicial Rents for the months of January, February, and March last will be distributed?

THE PARLIAMENTARY UNDER SECRETARY (Colonel KING-HARMAN) (Kent, Isle of Thanet) (who replied) said: The distribution of Parliamentary Papers does not rest with the Irish Government; but I have no doubt the Returns for January and February, which were presented on the 12th instant, will be distributed without delay. The March Return has not yet been received from the Land Commissioners; and, the Question being down without Notice, I have been unable to make inquiry with respect to it.

TRADE AND MANUFACTURE —"THE SWEATING SYSTEM."

MR. ESSLEMONT (Aberdeen, E.) (for Mr. CONYBEARE) (Cornwall, Camborne) asked the Secretary of State for the Home Department, Whether the Government will consider the advisability of appointing a Royal Commission to inquire into the "Sweating System," or take other steps to remedy the grievances alleged to be caused by the system?

THE UNDER SECRETARY OF STATE (Mr. STUART-WORTLEY) (Sheffield, Hallam) (who replied) said: I understand the hon. Member's Question to relate to the alleged employment in tailoring work for excessive hours and inadequate wages, and under insanitary conditions, of Jewish and other foreigners in the East of London and in some large towns. The Secretary of State has been advised by the Chief Inspector of Factories that the grounds for these allegations, and the causes and extent of such breaches or evasions of the Factory Act as do take place, are so well ascertained that no advantage would be gained by any special inquiry. Prosecutions for breaches of the Factory Act have been instituted whenever sufficient evidence was obtained; and I have directed that the vigilance of the Inspectors shall be in no way relaxed.

WAR OFFICE—THE TWO ARMY CORPS —ORGANIZATION.

MR. HENNIKER HEATON (Canterbury) asked the Secretary of State for War, Lord Wolseley having announced that the organization of two Army Corps is complete, If he will issue, as a Parliamentary Paper, the statement of this organization, in order that the taxpayer may see what he is at last getting for his money?

THE SECRETARY OF STATE (Mr. E. STANHOPE) (Lincolnshire, Horncastle): I shall have no objection to give some details of the composition of our two Army Corps.

MERCHANT SHIPPING ACT, 1876— DENMARK—DECK CARGOES.

MR. CALDWELL (Glasgow, St. Rollox) asked the Secretary to the Board of Trade, Whether intimation has been sent to the Danish Government that the conditions of "The Merchant Shipping Act, 1876," applicable to foreign merchant vessels, are now to be applied to Danish vessels; and, whether a similar intimation has been sent to any other, and, if so, to what other Governments?

THE UNDER SECRETARY OF STATE FOR FOREIGN AFFAIRS (Sir JAMES FERGUSSON) (Manchester, N.E.) (who replied) said: A Circular Letter has been addressed by the Foreign Office to the Governments of all Maritime States on the subject of deck cargoes brought to the United Kingdom during the winter months, and informing them that if the provisions of the Merchant Shipping Act, 1876—which prohibit certain deck loads and limit others—are infringed, prosecutions will be instituted for the recovery of the penalties incurred.

THE PRIMROSE LEAGUE, BOURNEMOUTH — THE CRIMINAL LAW AMENDMENT (IRELAND) BILL.

MR. CAREW (Kildare, N.) asked the First Lord of the Treasury, Whether it is true that, in a letter addressed to the Bournemouth Habitation of the Primrose League on Saturday last, he, through his Secretary, used the following words:—

"Mr. Smith feels the necessity of passing the Crimes Bill through its different stages as speedily as possible, so as to put an end to the tyranny and coercion of the loyal and peaceful peasants of Ireland by the National League, and to secure the punishment of these dastardly and cowardly assassins;"

and, whether he means to convey by this expression that there is a connection between the National League and assassination?

THE FIRST LORD (Mr. W. H. SMITH) (Strand, Westminster): I have not seen the letter to which the hon. Gentleman refers; but I am, of course, responsible for the acts of my Secretary. He informs me that the letter to which the hon. Gentleman refers contained the reference to "dastardly and cowardly assassins," and that his reference to "dastardly and cowardly assassins" applied to those men who had been guilty of grave offences in Ireland against the peace of the country and against poor and unoffending persons.

MR. SEXTON (Belfast, W.): May I ask whether, seeing that the language of the letter is correctly quoted, it does establish direct relations between the League and dastardly and cowardly assassins? I wish, further, to ask whether the right hon. Gentleman has any objection to address a fresh letter to the Bournemouth Habitation of the Primrose League for the purpose of removing the false impression under which they have been placed?

MR. W. H. SMITH: I am not prepared to accept the statement that this is an accurate representation of the letter of my Secretary. I have not seen the letter, but I shall take care to look at it.

MR. E. ROBERTSON (Dundee): I wish to ask another Question with reference to a statement in *The Standard* of this morning to the effect that a letter has been addressed to a Tiverton Conservative Working Men's Club in which the following words are used by the right hon. Gentleman:—

"The Government will resolutely carry its measure into effect in spite of the unconstitutional obstruction of the Gladstonians and the avowed enemies of England."

I beg to ask the right hon. Gentleman whether that report is correct; and, if so, when such alleged unconstitutional

Mr. Carew

obstruction as that complained of occurred? Also, who are "the avowed enemies of England" with whom he associates the Gladstonian Members in such obstruction; and, lastly, whether he, the Leader of this House, will in future take note at the time of what he deems to be obstruction before denouncing it to persons outside the House who have no knowledge of the facts?

MR. W. H. SMITH: The hon. and learned Member quotes a letter which he states to be my letter. I did not write the letter. It was written, no doubt, by one of my Secretaries.

MR. E. ROBERTSON: The paragraph states that the letter was written by the right hon. Gentleman.

MR. W. H. SMITH: That is inaccurate, as a good many statements of that kind are inaccurate. [*Cries of "The Times!"*] I did not write the letter, and I have not seen the letter; but I am not prepared to say that the purport of the letter is that from which I desire to withdraw. I am entitled, Sir, as hon. Gentlemen are entitled, to have my own opinions as to the character and result of the proceedings in Parliament? and the discussions may, in my judgment, have arrived at a point where obstruction may have arisen from them. Whether it is unconstitutional obstruction or not depends entirely on the judgment of Parliament, the judgment of hon. Gentlemen who may express that opinion, and the judgment of hon. Gentlemen who differ from it; but I may say this for myself—that I think the Records of Parliament have seldom presented, if they have ever presented, a condition of affairs such as that at which we have now arrived, under which the Public Business of the country has been delayed and frustrated, and the public interests have suffered. Whether that be an unconstitutional obstruction or not is for the country and for the public to decide. I am asked whether the epithet about the "avowed enemies" of England is one which I am prepared to acknowledge. I do not wish, Sir, to apply epithets if it is possible to avoid them; but if hon. Gentlemen avow themselves to be the enemies of England, it is, I think, not altogether undesirable that that fact should have attention drawn to it. I am again asked whether, as Leader of the House, I will call attention to obstruction when I deem it to be obstruction? I will as far as, in my judgment, it is wise and advisable to do so, and I shall seek to exercise the powers which the House has put in the hands of Members of the House in order to prevent that obstruction; but I must have regard to the fact that, by repeatedly drawing attention to obstruction, I may be myself also contributing to that terrible evil which I am afraid threatens the Parliamentary institutions of this country.

MR. E. ROBERTSON: The right hon. Gentleman has not given a direct answer to my second Question—Who are the avowed enemies of England? I will put it in another form, and I will ask him who are the Members of this House to whom he refers as having avowed themselves to be enemies of England?

MR. W. H. SMITH: Sir, I refer the hon. and learned Gentleman to the columns of *United Ireland*. I have not wished to name hon. Members. [*Cries of* "Name, name!" *and* "No cowardly reserve!"] No; I will not do so. ["Oh!"]

An hon. MEMBER: We defy you to do so.

MR. SPEAKER: Order, order!

MR. W. H. SMITH: If the hon. and learned Gentleman refers to the pages of *United Ireland* and other Nationalist organs, I think he will find that I am justified in what I say.

MR. T. P. O'CONNOR (Liverpool, Scotland): I wish to ask the First Lord of the Treasury——

MR. SPEAKER: Order, order! Mr. De Lisle.

MR. DE LISLE (Leicestershire, Mid), not being present,

CRIME AND OUTRAGE (IRELAND)—AGRARIAN OUTRAGES.

MR. DILLON (Mayo, E.) said, he wished to ask the Chief Secretary to the Lord Lieutenant of Ireland a Question in reference to the following Notice of Motion:—

"Dr. Kenny—Crime (Ireland) (Agrarian Outrages)—Return, by Provinces (a), and Counties (b), of Agrarian Outrages in Ireland, reported by Royal Irish Constabulary, for the year ending 31st December, 1886, and continued to date, giving the following particulars relating thereto:—Number; date of offence; constabulary district or sub-district; name and rank of officer in charge of district or sub-district; name or names of person or persons injured or otherwise affected by outrage; description of outrage; short details of same; whether any person was arrested for commission of same; and, if so, name or names of persons arrested; name of any person made amenable, *i.e.*, brought to trial; tribunal before which made amenable; result of proceedings."

This Return was placed upon the Paper last week, and it was again placed upon the Paper for this evening. He noticed it was blocked by one of the Government Whips. As he understood, this Return was taken almost verbatim from the Return laid upon the Table of the House by Mr. Forster in 1881 before he moved for the Coercion Act of that year. The Question he wished to put to the Chief Secretary was, Whether the Government objected to have such a Return furnished to the House now; and, if so, why?

THE CHIEF SECRETARY (MR. A. J. BALFOUR) (Manchester, E.), in reply, said, he believed that communications had already been made to the hon. Member (Dr. Kenny), in whose name the Motion stood, and that the purport of those communications was that they had no objection to give a Return which would substantially give all the facts asked for in this Return, which, in their opinion, bore upon the subject now before the House. The Return on the Paper did not correspond with that furnished by Mr. Forster. It differed from it in many important particulars. The Government were quite prepared to give a Return without particulars as regards names, which they believed might be injurious to individuals in Ireland. But with that exception he was prepared to give a Return in the form in which Mr. Forster gave it in 1881.

MR. DILLON: Would the right hon. Gentleman give us some indication of the form in which he will be prepared to give the Return?

MR. A. J. BALFOUR: I may be wrong; but I believe an intimation on the subject was given to the hon. Member for South Cork (Dr. Kenny) yesterday.

MR. T. P. O'CONNOR (Liverpool, Scotland): I wish to ask the right hon. Gentleman the First Lord of the Treasury, whether, having regard to the importance which attaches to utterances in his name from the position which he at this moment happens to occupy in this House, he will take care to read all the letters sent in his name in future—

["Order, order!"]—or to employ a Secretary——

MR. SPEAKER : Order, order !

ORDERS OF THE DAY.

——o——

CRIMINAL LAW AMENDMENT (IRE-
LAND) BILL.—[BILL 217.]

(*Mr. A. J. Balfour, Mr. Secretary Matthews, Mr. Attorney General, Mr. Attorney General for Ireland.*)

COMMITTEE. [FIRST NIGHT.]

Order for Committee read.

Motion made, and Question proposed, "That Mr. Speaker do now leave the Chair."—(*Mr. A. J. Balfour.*)

MR. R. T. REID (Dumfries, &c.), in rising to move, as an Amendment—

"That this House declines to proceed further with a measure for strengthening the Criminal Law against combinations of tenants until it has before it the full measure for their relief against excessive rents in the shape in which it may pass the other House of Parliament,"

said : Mr. Speaker, in the ordinary course the Amendment which stands in the name of the hon. Member for the Poplar Division of the Tower Hamlets (Mr. Sydney Buxton) would have pre-cedence of mine; and I am fully aware that, in rising to address the House now, I am only doing so in consequence of the courtesy of the hon. Member, for which I beg to thank him. The right hon. Gentleman the Leader of the House has, in answer to Questions which have been put to him to-night, expressed a strong opinion as to the conduct of some Mem-bers in this House in relation to obstruc-tion. I wish the right hon. Gentleman to endeavour, as I believe he desires to do, to deal justly with all Members of the House. If the right hon. Gentle-man could realize for himself the extent of feeling which exists on this side of the House in regard to this Bill, I am sure he would see that we should be failing in our duty if we do not do all that lies in our power, if not to persuade hon. Gentlemen opposite—which I am afraid would be a hopeless task—at least, to persuade some of those Gentlemen who call themselves and believe themselves to be Liberals, that they are supporting a Bill destructive of all Liberal policy in Ireland. I believe that this Bill, which is called a "Bill for the Pre-vention of Crime in Ireland," will really be more productive of crime than

Mr. T. P. O'Connor

almost any other measure which has been passed by this House for many years. It is a Bill directed against combinations ; it is essentially a Bill against combinations, and the first thing that will happen will be that political combinations will be made the subject of attack. Now, Sir, there never has been, I believe, in history any instance in which political combinations have been made the subject of attack which has not been succeeded by those terrible secret societies that have made so disastrous a figure in the past history of Ireland. If you suppress the open National League, which now holds open meetings and publishes its deliberations, you will soon have in its place the re-introduction of those secret societies which the Na-tional League has set its face against, and has suppressed. So far as political combinations are concerned, against which the action of this Bill is intended to be directed, I maintain that it is of no more use to attempt to eradicate the sentiment of nationality, or whatever hon. Members may choose to call it, than to attempt to extract the brine from the English Channel. The feeling is so deeply seated — it has been cherished so long in the hearts of the people, and it has survived so many great trials—that I feel it is quite hopeless to endeavour to eradi-cate the Home Rule aspirations that now exist. Passing from political com-binations to agrarian combinations, it is further desired and intended to put down agrarian combinations in such a way that no body of men will be able to act together. The clauses of the Bill are of such a character that I believe the right hon. Gentleman the Chief Secre-tary for Ireland (Mr. A. J. Balfour) can hardly appreciate how severe they are ; the language is so wide, the net is so large, and the meshes are so small. Indeed, however it may appear at first sight, and even where the words of a section may seem to preclude the misuse of power, in order to prevent any misapprehension of the stringent character of the Bill, hon. Members will find, in the Definition Clause, language which leaves the mea-sure so drastic that I can scarcely believe the right hon. Gentleman fully appre-ciates the effect of his own proposals ; and this stringent measure is to be applied by Resident Magistrates for the purpose of putting down agrarian combinations. Now, Sir, let me suppose, for a moment, that the right hon. Gentleman may succeed in putting down agrarian combinations, and that the provisions of the Bill are used in such a way that the tenants cannot combine, either under the Plan of Campaign, or in any way more moderate or more legitimate in the way of combination, to bring pressure to bear upon their landlords. At the present time the tenants have some protection in the publicity which attends evictions; because, when a writ of ejectment is executed, the British public is made acquainted with it. There is, generally, a large crowd present, and although I do not, in the least, sympathize with any violence which may take place when the crowd is disposed to resist the execution of the law, still it is an evidence of the open and avowed hostility of the people to these evictions. But all this is to be changed. Ejectments are, in future, to take place not in any open way, so that they would come home to the minds and consciences of the people of Great Britain when the account is received, but by means of a written notice, which can be sent without any public display at all. The other and the chief means of protection they have had has been the Boycotting of an evicted farm. Boycotting an evicted farm is a very old practice in Ireland, and mention of it will be found in the old books which relate to the Irish agrarian question. The result of this Bill will be to prevent any farm from being Boycotted, even where an eviction has been most cruel, harsh, and oppressive. No doubt there may be hon. Gentlemen opposite who think that that is a good object. It is one of the things for which the Bill has been introduced; but what will be the position of the tenants when the Bill is passed? If this Bill has the effect which is desired, the tenants will be reduced to such a position that they will become the absolute slaves of the landlords; they will be unable to move a hand or foot, in any direction, for the purpose of protecting themselves; and if it be the case that there are harsh and cruel landlords in Ireland, and that there are many honest tenants who cannot pay their judicial rents, what is the inevitable result the right hon. Gentleman must expect? The Government must be aware that throughout the history of Ireland the one great cause of agrarian outrage has been evictions. It is notorious that that is so; and I find among the Papers which were circulated only this morning a Return for the last quarter ending the 25th of March, some facts in which, I think, will be rather suggestive to the right hon. Gentleman. The right hon. Gentleman will recollect that he named certain counties as being counties within which he proposed to apply this measure. Well, Sir, let me see what have been the evictions in some of those counties. In the County of Kerry, which is the worst of all the counties described by the right hon. Gentleman, in the three months ending March 25, 1886, there have been no less than 1,766 persons evicted; in the next worst of these counties, and also a county mentioned by the right hon. Gentleman —namely, the County of Mayo, there were 489 evictions; the next worst county is the County of Cork, and in that county there were no less than 341 evictions in the West Riding, and 272 in the East Riding. That, also, was one of the counties referred to by the right hon. Gentleman. I might enlarge upon this point, for I find that the next worst county is Limerick, and that, also, is one of the counties referred to by the right hon. Gentleman. What do these statistics show? Why, that the five counties in which the largest number of evictions are to be found are also five of the seven counties to which the right hon. Gentleman referred as being counties in which there has been exceptional crime. Does not the right hon. Gentleman himself, with his knowledge of history, and his recollection of what has uniformly taken place in Ireland, admit that if the tenants are to be put under the heels of the landlords, it must necessarily lead to a considerable increase of outrages? Knowing the history of the relations between outrages and evictions, can the right hon. Gentleman doubt that that must be so? I quite agree that if justice demanded it, if it were really fair and just, these men should be forced to pay their rents— that is, where the failure to pay was owing to their own fault. If they can pay, and will not pay, I am ready to admit that no fear of the commission of outrage ought to affect the minds of the Government. It is perfectly clear that men who are perfectly able to pay their rent,

First Night.]

and who refuse to do so by reason of desiring to take advantage of a state of lawlessness for the purpose of getting rid of their legal obligations, deserve no sympathy, and I, for one, profess no sympathy whatever for them. But, Sir, is not this a matter upon which the right hon. Gentleman should satisfy himself before he puts in the hands of the landlords such powers as are contained in this Bill, for we all know how the landlords are likely to use them. Before enacting these provisions, should he not satisfy himself that there is no likelihood of their being abused, and that the refusal to pay rents arises from a dogged determination to break contracts, instead of an absolute inability to pay the rents? I think I shall be able to show the right hon. Gentleman, beyond all doubt, that the position in which these tenants are who are to be placed in the condition I have described, without a remedy or any resource against their landlords, is that they positively cannot pay their rents; that their inability, as far as it goes, is an inability arising from poverty and misery and from utter distress, and not from a wish to have recourse to those factious measures of which the Orange Party and the Castle Party are apt to accuse the members of the National League. What is the real position of the tenants? To the information contained in the Blue Book, which has been so often referred to in the course of this debate, there is a most useful Appendix, which gives a Table supplied by the Registrar General, in which he gives the financial position of the tenants of Ireland, and puts before the country a picture which, if true, goes far to explain the existence of distress and even of disorder in Ireland. The Registrar General says that in 1881 the estimated total value of the crops in Ireland was £46,000,000 odd ; in 1885 it was £35,000,000; and in 1886 it had been reduced to £31,000,000. I ask the House to consider what a fall that represents ; and £46,000,000 is by no means a high value for the crops of Ireland in average years, for I find that some years ago it was as high as £53,000,000. The Registrar General refers to the total value of live stock in the same years. In 1881 it was £50,000,000; in 1885, £43,000,000 ; and in 1886, £41,000,000. Now, Sir,

Mr. R. T. Reid

the Report of the Royal Commission gives a great deal of information in addition. It points not only to the fall of prices, but to the gradual deterioration of the soil. It states that since 1879 much of the tenants' capital has disappeared ; that the cost of cultivation has also greatly increased. It states, further, that the withdrawal of credit by the banks and others has left the farmers in a position of very great difficulty. That that is the condition in which the tenants find themselves placed at the present moment it is impossible to doubt. No one who impartially reads the evidence given before the Royal Commission—and I believe there are many hon. Gentlemen on the other side of the House who desire to do so—can come to any other conclusion from these figures, and from other facts borne out and strengthened by the opinion of almost every witness examined by the Commission, than that the non-payment of rent is due to the fact that the tenants are really unable to pay. The Commissioners tell us that whatever combinations there may have been have had their source and encouragement in the fact that the tenants have really been unable to pay, and that they have been driven to enter into combinations because they had no other means of protecting themselves. There is one paragraph in the Report of the Commissioners which I think has not been referred to. At all events, if it has, I should like to refer again to two sentences contained in it. The Commissioners say—

"It has been said that these combinations only exist for the purpose of obtaining equitable reductions of rent. In some cases that may be true, and the refusal of some landlords of any abatement may explain much that has occurred ; but the evidence shows that those tenants farmers, who have joined many of these combinations, constituted themselves the sole judges of what is an equitable rent."

Well, that is true, under the Plan of Campaign ; but, at the same time, it is also true that in September last the hon. Member for the City of Cork (Mr. Parnell) brought in a Bill, under which an equitable rent would not have been fixed by the tenants themselves, but by an impartial tribunal to which he was willing to submit the question. It is true, as is stated in the Report of the Commission, that these combinations exist, and that the Commissioners recommend that they should be put down; but what is proposed to be done in the case of those landlords whose refusal to grant any abatement "may explain much that has occurred." It seems to me altogether hopeless to trust to the effect of any appeal to those gentlemen. Everyone knows—and I speak from information gained by conversations with both Conservatives and Liberals—that there are a certain handful of landlords in Ireland who have never acted towards their tenants as hon. Gentlemen opposite are in the habit of acting towards theirs; but who have been systematically rapacious and unjust towards the poor people who are under their control. No one can deny that; and I want to know, when the great powers of this Bill are granted under the authority of the Parliament of this country, what provision is to be made to meet the case of those landlords, be they few or be they many, whose rapacity has been a disgrace to the country for many years past, and who still exist to cause future trouble, disorder, and crime? In 1880 I well recollect that the late Mr. W. E. Forster made an appeal to the landlords after the Compensation for Disturbances Bill had been thrown out. What was the result of that appeal? It was addressed to deaf ears; it had no effect whatever. Evictions were not only continued, but increased; and, as a consequence, crime also increased, notwithstanding that the Bill of 1881 was passed to check it. Only last autumn, the noble Marquess the Member for Rossendale (the Marquess of Hartington) also made a similar appeal. No one was in a condition to make a stronger appeal than the noble Marquess. He is a great Irish landlord himself—the greatest, I believe, of the Irish landlords, and he is in a position of authority—I do not say it offensively—in connection with the present Government. The Government take his advice, and look largely for support to his great influence, and the position of authority he holds with many hon. Members who sit on this side of the House. With all the weight of that authority, he made an appeal last autumn to the Irish landlords, and what was the result? The appeal was altogether disregarded, and the trouble which arose last winter in Ireland is almost exclusively due to the perversity of a certain number of landlords. What is really wanted, and what might really settle this difficulty, and I believe make it absolutely unnecessary to pass the ferocious clauses of this terrible Bill, is this—that there should be really a fair rent as it was intended, by the Act of 1881 there should be. Let me quote again a few sentences—not more than five or six—from the well-known evidence of Sir Redvers Buller before the Royal Commission. I know that much of it has been quoted already. I am not going to weary the House by reading the whole of it over again; but I have extracted what I may call aphorisms worthy of being printed in letters of gold from the evidence of that distinguished officer. He says—

"My view of the country is this—that the majority of the tenants meant to pay their rents, and where they could pay they did pay them; but the rents have been too high. I do think that they are too high."

Again, he proceeds to say—

"I think it was the pressure of a high rent which produced the agitation and consequent intimidation against the payment of rent. I think—and I feel it very strongly—that in this part of the country you can never have peace, unless you create some legal equipoise or legal equivalent to supply the want of freedom of contract which now exists between landlord and tenant."

Again, he says—

"You have got a very ignorant and poor people, and the law should look after them, instead of which the law only looks after the rich. That, at least, appears to me to be the case."

He further said—

"I propose that there should be a Court of Assessors of a permanent character for each county or district, or parts of one or more counties, which should have power, when applied to by a landlord or tenant, to raise or lower rents, on the basis of present prices and the rents paid for the past five years."

He then says that it would be desirable to put a very strong coercive power on the bad landlord. Hon. Members must recollect that the Royal Commission have testified their opinion as to the inability of the tenants to pay the rents, although there is not one of them who holds the opinions I do, or is in any sense a Nationalist. Yet all of them, except one, recommend a revision of the judicial rents. A heavy responsibility will rest upon the Government, if they take the course of denuding the tenants of all means of combination, deprive them of the sympathy of the public, and, at the same time, leave them to the mercy of landlords, who are merciless in their dealings with their tenants. If that is to be done, in face of the warning we have derived from past experience as to the increase of outrages springing from evictions, and in face of the solemn warnings given to the Royal Commission by Sir Redvers Buller and the advice he has given, I cannot help thinking that the right hon. Gentleman the Chief Secretary will incur a very heavy responsibility indeed. The first fruits of coercion will be evictions; from evictions may arise—I hope it will not be the case—murder, treason, privy conspiracy, and rebellion. That is the course which has been followed in Ireland in the past, and I deeply fear that the same course will be followed in the future, if the Government persist in their present policy. Then it is said that a Bill has been introduced which proposes to offer a remedy. I am aware that I am not allowed, in opposing the present Bill, to refer in detail to the provisions of that measure; but this I think I am entitled to say—that we should most unquestionably be wanting in our duty if we allowed a permanent Bill of the character of that which is now before the House to pass into law, without providing, at the same time, the most conclusive safeguards against its misapplication, and for the protection of the tenants against excessive rents. As I have said, I do not wish to enter into the provision of the Relief Bill in detail, and I am not going to do so; but I want to point out what would be the position of the tenant, supposing even that both of these Bills should become law. What would be the position of a tenant who is under a legal obligation to pay a practically unjust rent, and whose position is such that he cannot obtain any indulgence from his landlord? Upon that point I only propose to say a few words, for the purpose of illustrating what the position of the tenant would be under such circumstances. I am taking the case of a man who cannot pay—the case of a man against whom there is an unjust fixed rent, either judicial or otherwise—and what I say in regard to that case is this—the proposals which I have heard of from the Government practically give the ten-

ants no relief at all. The tenant whose rent exceeds £50 a-year cannot possibly obtain relief, nor can he get relief if he has means in his power, either by borrowing or by obtaining assistance from his children towards the payment of the rent, or from any other source; but even if he succeeds in getting over these preliminary difficulties, the relief which is afforded to him is no relief at all. It is not suggested that his rent should be lower, and all the wretched man could do in regard to any proposal I have yet heard of is to make himself a bankrupt and reduce himself to the position of a serf. He is then obliged to come under the orders of a Bankruptcy Court, and when the bankruptcy has been concluded he will be a fortunate man, indeed, if he is reinstated in his holding. It must be recollected that it is not proposed to confer anything as a right upon this unfortunate man. He is subject to whatever terms may be imposed upon him by the Judge, and in many cases he will, in all probability, impose such terms as the landlord may think fit to suggest. Now, this proposal of the Government, which, I presume, will come, before long, under the notice of this House, assuming it to be passed in its absolute integrity, will, I affirm, speaking as a lawyer, upon what credit I have to lose for legal acumen, be absolutely worthless as a protection. It would not keep one man on his holding by right, nor would it secure him the slightest abatement of his rent; but it would leave him absolutely at the mercy of his landlord, qualified by such terms as the County Court Judge may think fit to grant. We all know the terms which are likely to be put forward when a man is destitute. When he is on the eve of being turned out of his holding the agent would appear at his elbow day after day, and say—"Why don't you purchase?" That has been attempted already, and there is the strongest proof of it to be found in the evidence before the Commissioners. Mr. M'Carthy's evidence has been quoted. I do not intend to read it; but I will summarize it in the shortest way. I am, however, using M'Carthy's own words in the short summary I give. He stated that the operation of the Act has been hindered by the unwise attempts which have been made on the part of some of the land agents to coerce the tenants into pur-

Mr. R. T. Reid

chasing at prices which the Land Commissioners consider unfair, and that pressure was exercised by telling the tenant that he must either sign the contract of purchase or go out. What will be the effect of the Bill of the Government? I do not assert that it is their intention—because the right hon. Gentleman the Chief Secretary, speaking at Ipswich, denied it—that the intention of the Government is in any way to force on the provisions of the Purchase Bill. I am only speaking of the effect of the proposals of the Government. [*Cries of* "Oh!"] I am speaking now of Lord Ashbourne's Act, which is at present in force, and I assert that the real effect of this Bill will be to force the tenant into such a position that he will have no alternative between going out on the roadside, or purchasing on such terms as the landlord may feel inclined to give him. It is not only coercion, but beggary for the Irish tenant; and, so far as the British taxpayer is concerned, the effect will be to shuffle off upon the shoulders of our constituencies rotten estates in Ireland which are not worth one-half of the sum we shall be called upon to pay for them. I protest against these proposals, because I am confident the result will be a large and heavy loss to the British taxpayer. I do not believe that the Chief Secretary for Ireland would willingly impose that burden upon the country; but I believe that many persons behind him would be delighted to do so, and would be only too glad to see their friends thrust out of the position which they occupy and the whole burden placed on the shoulders of the British taxpayer. I am afraid that the Government cannot appreciate the full effect of their proposals, and I am bound, as a lawyer, to assert—although it may appear presumptuous on my part to do so—that there is no protection whatever in this Bill for the honest tenant who cannot really pay the rent. The protection afforded is absolutely worthless, and I am satisfied that it will be proved to be so when it is brought to the test. I therefore feel it my duty to resist this Bill as a matter of justice to the unfortunate people of Ireland, where, at the present moment, there is so much misery and destitution prevailing. I hope that we shall not be invited to proceed to the Committee stage of the Bill, as we were

invited to proceed to the second reading stage, with allusions and charges such as were imported in the earlier debates, and which were made and circulated at a most admirably chosen time against the hon. Member for Cork (Mr. Parnell) and other hon. Gentlemen sitting below the Gangway. Now, Sir, I remember that substantially the same charges were made in 1883 by the late Mr. W. E. Forster, who did not shelter himself behind *The Times* newspaper. Mr. Forster came forward, and took upon himself the responsibility of making the charges; they were denied, and two years afterwards the noble Lord the Member for South Paddington (Lord Randolph Churchill) entered into political relations with the gentlemen against whom the charges were made. And not only so, but the hon. Member for Cork himself was called into council by Lord Carnarvon, the Lord Lieutenant of Ireland, who evidently thought he was doing nothing wrong in associating with the hon. Member. Much as I differ from the noble Lord the Member for South Paddington, and Lord Carnarvon also, I know them to be men of intelligence and honour, and I altogether decline to accept any of those statements until they have been completely proved. That is the position which I think it is incumbent upon every hon. Member to take up. But let me suppose, for the sake of argument, that every word of these charges is true—assuming that the hon. Member for Cork, in 1882, wrote a letter which was most infamous if he did write it, and—hon. Gentlemen I hope will excuse me for using this hypothesis—that hon. Gentlemen associated in 1882 with people of a murderous character; but is that any reason why in 1887—five years afterwards —the House should pass a Bill of this ferocious nature for the purpose of taking away the liberties of Ireland? I feel it to be the duty of hon. Members who speak upon this Bill to take an opportunity of saying something in reference to the charges and the manner in which they have been used. I believe it is almost unprecedented in Parliamentary history, at a critical stage of a Bill, at a time when political passion runs high, that accusations should be repeated which were made three years ago, and thrown at the heads of hon. Gentlemen sitting either upon this or any other side of the House. I beg to enter my em-

[*First Night.*]

phatic protest against such a course, and I hope that the Government, upon whom a heavy responsibility lies, will, for the sake of the honour and integrity of the House, undertake that the charges shall be made specifically, and that they will discountenance proceedings which I think wholly unbecoming the honour and reputation of the House. I have now stated to the House the general reasons which induce me to oppose this Bill. I do not intend to resist it myself by any resort to means of obstruction; but although I may not speak again against it, I hope that other hon. Gentlemen will do so, and that they will not cease to dwell upon the iniquity of the proposals now made by Her Majesty's Government; that they will not cease to protest against the cruel injustice which is being perpetrated against the Irish people, contrary, I believe, to many of the pledges which hon. Gentlemen gave at the last Election, in forcing this Bill upon Ireland against the wishes alike of Ireland and Great Britain.

Mr. SHAW LEFEVRE (Bradford, Central), in rising to second the Amendment, said, he was anxious to ask the House to pause, before proceeding further with this Bill, until the Government were able to lay before the House the policy with which they proposed to accompany coercion. Since the Bill had been read a second time they had had important developments of the Government policy "elsewhere," and they were able to see how their remedial measure was likely to be received by their own supporters. One-half of that measure could not pass in its present form; it was repudiated by the landlords and tenants of Ireland; and it was certain that it would not be passed in its entirety by the House of Lords. He asked the House, therefore, to wait until it saw what would be the substitute for the remedial measure of the Government. The measure before the House was originally propounded mainly as a Bill to prevent crime; but as the discussion went on further important objects were revealed. The noble Marquess the Member for Rossendale (the Marquess of Hartington), in a very menacing speech, told the country that the object of the Bill was to put down the revolutionary Party, and that until we put down that Party it was absolutely impossible finally

Mr. R. T. Reid

to deal with the agrarian question, or even to think of giving to Ireland that small modicum of self-government which he would be willing to grant. Again, only a few days ago the noble Marquess the Prime Minister (the Marquess of Salisbury) had distinctly declared that the object of the Bill was to put down combinations by tenants; and he had gone on to say that unless the House of Lords and the Government passed some remedial measure it would be totally impossible to expect the country to accept a Bill intended to put down combinations among tenants. The ground upon which this Coercion Bill was based was the prevalence of crime in Ireland; but, putting aside agrarian offences, at no time had Ireland been so free from crime as she was at present. Was there any hope of putting down agrarian crime by means of a purely coercive measure? The experience of the last 86 years showed that coercive measures, unless coupled with full remedial measures, had no effect upon agrarian crime. Then, again, experience showed that agrarian crime had very little relation with political agitation. Thus, during the agitation in favour of Roman Catholic Emancipation, and during O'Connell's agitation in favour of Repeal, there had been very little agrarian crime. Indeed, it had been said at those times that the total absence of crime was a most serious symptom. The fact was that agrarian crime had its origin in a totally different state of things, such as in economic causes, in bad seasons, and in times of great agricultural depression from low prices or otherwise, when harsh and ignorant landlords exacted the uttermost farthing of rent that they could squeeze out of their tenants —these were the causes which brought the people to despair and crime. In 1833, when the great tithe war was going on, there was a great deal of agrarian crime. At that time, in the middle of the discussions on coercion, Lord Palmerston, writing to his brother, said—

"By what sweeping majorities this reformed House of Commons is passing the most violent Coercion Bill ever passed into law! It is a real *tour de force*; but then it will be followed by remedial measures. There is this difference between our case and that of the Metternich and the Pope. We coerce as they do, but we redress grievances as they do not."

["Hear, hear!"] An hon. Member

opposite cheered that. No doubt the hon. Member thought, as Lord Palmerston did, that the remedial measure was very satisfactory. But he might perhaps remind the hon. Member that the House of Lords threw out the remedial measures. There was, therefore, little difference between the English Government and that of Metternich and the Pope. It was quite possible that, following the same analogy, the present House of Lords might not pass a remedial measure at this moment which would be satisfactory or sufficient for the purpose. But the House of Lords passed the coercion measure; and the following year the Lord Lieutenant of Ireland was obliged to report to the Home Secretary of the day that agrarian crime had greatly increased in Ireland. The same thing had happened when extreme coercive measures had been again resorted to. The passing of the Coercion Bill in 1833 was followed by an increase in crime from 17,000 to 21,000 in the following year; and it was not until Lord Melbourne, two years later, adopted a different policy—that of substituting remedial measures altogether for coercion—that agrarian crime in Ireland began to diminish. Lord Melbourne, speaking in 1837, alluding to the change of policy with regard to that country which he had brought about, said that he did not believe in coercion, because the odium and the obloquy which it brought upon the Government fatally weakened the power of the Administration in preserving law and order. Later, again, agrarian crime enormously increased after the potato famine of 1846; and coercion was again in 1847 resorted to; but it did not succeed in putting down crime. Crime increased under it from 32,000 in 1847, to 40,000 in 1848, and it was not till favourable seasons returned that agrarian crime diminished. Coming later to 1881, when the lamented Mr. Forster introduced a very severe Coercion Act, accompanied by a strong remedial measure, Mr. Forster told the House of Commons that the Bill would be directed against village ruffians, and not against political agitators. In spite of that Act, agrarian crime increased. He believed that the reason why the Land Act failed to stop agrarian crime was that a great number of the Irish tenants were encumbered by arrears, and could not go into the Land Court. In

the following year a remedial measure was passed dealing with arrears, at the same time that another Coercion Act was passed through the House. The smaller tenants were relieved. His firm and confident belief was that the reduction of crime after 1882 was not due to the Coercion Act of that year, but to the remedial measures of that year—namely, the Arrears Act, which was one of the most beneficial pieces of legislation ever passed. He was quite prepared to admit that there was some increase of agrarian crime at the present time, but it was not serious. [Mr. W. E. GLADSTONE: Hear, hear!] It was not serious as compared with past times. He agreed that it was and should be the object of them all to get that agrarian crime reduced within the narrowest proportions. That would not be done by coercive measures; but only by remedial measures carried out in a satisfactory manner. The remedial policy of the Government could be divided into two main parts; the first being that which related to the leaseholders, which had given satisfaction throughout the country; and, indeed, it was a reflection upon Parliament and a great pity that the Bill giving leaseholders the benefit of the Land Act was not passed long ago. The other half of the remedial policy of the Government was not so satisfactory. In fact it had given great dissatisfaction to the class for whom it was intended. The relief intended by that part of the policy of the Government could only be given through the medium of the Bankruptcy Court; and, looking broadly at that policy, it appeared to him to be absurd and altogether out of relation to the demands of the Irish people. It had been scouted equally by landlords and by tenants. If he were a landlord, he should be more frightened at that part of the policy of the Government than at any measure which had been suggested by the hon. Member for Cork (Mr. Parnell). On the other hand, the tenants were not contented. He believed it was generally feared throughout Ireland that that policy, if carried out, might have the effect of demoralizing the smaller tenants, while it might not give a remedy to the better class of tenants, who would not like to allow themselves to be made bankrupts, when perhaps they had some savings left in the savings' banks. He confidently believed that the measure could not pass into law, and that it must be radically changed. It was, in his view, incapable of amendment, and the Government must substitute for it some other and totally different remedial policy. One of the first clauses which they would have to consider in Committee on the Bill was Clause 2, giving greater power against combinations of tenants, withdrawing such cases for the first time from juries and putting them under the jurisdiction of Resident Magistrates, who were merely the creatures of the Government. He asked the House whether it was reasonable or right that they should be called upon to discuss the clause until they had the full policy of the Government before them in the shape in which the House of Lords would pass the remedial Bill. The clause would put great power into the hands of the landlords, and he feared its adoption would induce the House of Lords rather to favour the interests and strengthen the hands of the landlords than to generously deal with the reasonable demands of the Irish tenants. Unfortunately, the history of the House of Lords in regard to remedial legislation for Ireland had not been satisfactory in the past. Time after time over a long period it had thrown out important measures dealing with the Irish Land Question, and hardly a measure of the kind had ever come before it which it had not seriously injured. A great deal of the agrarian trouble which had occurred in Ireland had been due to the successive actions of the House of Lords upon those agrarian Bills. When one looked at the composition of the House of Lords on Irish Questions one was not altogether surprised. They had been leavened and prejudiced by that infusion of Irish Peers who looked at those questions only from one point of view. Remedial measures of an agrarian kind for Ireland ought not to be introduced in the House of Lords, but in the House of Commons, where alone were the means of ascertaining the real wants and wishes of the Irish people through their Representatives. If they passed the coercive clauses before the Lords considered their remedies, what hope could there be that they would produce an effective remedy? If the measure, when it came down into that House, was amended in accordance with the views of the Irish people, what hope had they that the Lords would

accept their Amendments? The only security they could possibly have that the remedial measure would be sufficient and satisfactory, was by refusing coercion till a measure that was sufficient for the purpose was passed by the House of Lords; and in order to secure this object, he asked the House to refrain from going into Committee until they knew what form the remedy would take. He would only say, in conclusion, that the utterances of the Prime Minister in "another place" showed an utter misconception and want of appreciation of the position and desires of the Irish tenants; and that he did not understand the principle on which the Land Act of 1881 was passed, and on which an amendment and readjustment of the judicial rents was now demanded. Speaking in "another place," Lord Salisbury said—

"It is the landlord's right to get his rent as long as the tenant can pay ; it is the landlord's right to change the tenant if he can find a tenant who can derive better produce from the farm. As long as he restricts himself within these two rights, no one can accuse him of being harsh and unreasonable."

He (Mr. Shaw Lefevre) entirely denied this view of the landlord's position. It was founded on an entire misconception of the Land Act of 1881. That Act established and recognized a dual ownership in the land; it gave legal sanction to the tenant's interest, and put his right on an equal footing with that of the landlord. Nothing could be clearer than this—that, from the point of view of equity and justice, the landlords in Ireland were not justified in insisting upon their rights to the total extinction of the tenants' interest and property in their holdings. If, since the Land Act was passed and the judicial rents were fixed, an entire change had occurred in the conditions—if prices of agricultural produce had fallen so that the continuation of the same rent for the remainder of the 15 years involved the total extinction of the tenants' interest and reduced them to the position of tenants at a rackrent—then every principle of justice required a revision of the terms of the Land Act. He would urge the House, then, not to part with its control over this question, not to pass this tremendous weapon to put down combinations, until it was satisfied that a remedial measure sufficient for the purpose and adequate to provide a remedy.

Mr. Shaw Lefevre

against agrarian crime was laid before it. In conclusion, he would ask the House to listen to the opinion of Sir Robert Peel, whom hon. Members opposite would admit to have been one of the greatest statesmen of the present century, and who had probably more experience of Coercion Bills than any man in his generation. Speaking in 1833, on Lord Grey's Coercion Bill, he said—

"He had always dreaded measures of coercion, for he feared that, while their effect for good would be temporary, they would leave behind them a rankling wound of which the soreness would be long felt. There was a great risk that coercive measures would relax the energy of the ordinary law, and widen the breach between the richer classes, for whose protection they were framed, and the poorer classes, for whose punishment they were intended."

There never had been a Coercion Bill of which it could be more truly said than this—that it was intended for the protection of the rich and for the punishment of the poor. By keeping their hands clean now they might obtain from the House of Lords possibly a more satisfactory remedial measure than was now before it. If, on the other hand, they passed the Coercion Bill in its present shape—and passed it before the other House had determined what the final shape of the remedial measure would be—his confident belief was that that remedial measure would turn out to be a nullity and a sham; whereas the Coercion Bill would be one of the harshest and most severe and comprehensive that had ever been passed through Parliament. He begged to second the Amendment of his hon. and learned Friend the Member for Dumfries.

Amendment proposed,

To leave out from the word "That" to the end of the Question, in order to add the words "this House declines to proceed further with a measure for strengthening the Criminal Law against combinations of tenants until it has before it the full measure for their relief against excessive rents in the shape in which it may pass the other House of Parliament,"—(*Mr. R. T. Reid,*)

—instead thereof.

Question proposed, "That the words proposed to be left out stand part of the Question."

THE CHIEF SECRETARY FOR IRELAND (Mr. A. J. BALFOUR) (Manchester, E.) said, no one who carried his recol-

lection back to the four weeks of prolonged debate that had already taken place on the broad principles of this Bill would be surprised at the signs of weariness and slackness that prevailed in the House, and those signs were not confined to one portion of the House, for they were as obvious on the Benches below the Gangway opposite as in any other quarter of the House.

MR. T. P. O'CONNOR (Liverpool, Scotland): Will the right hon. Gentleman give me the opportunity of stating why there are not so many Irish Members sitting here as on ordinary occasions? They are not in their places because they are at the present time addressing meetings being held throughout England to protest against this very Bill we are discussing.

MR. A. J. BALFOUR, continuing, said, that, under ordinary circumstances, he should not have thought it necessary for any Member of the Government to enter again upon the well-worn path of this debate; but perhaps it would be hardly consistent with the courtesy due to the position of the Gentlemen who brought forward this Amendment, and to the moderation which characterized their remarks, if he did not rise to reply. The hon. and learned Member (Mr. R. T. Reid) who had brought forward Motion expressed the hope that the subjects of acute controversy raised in the course of the debate on the second reading would not be revived. He joined with the hon. and learned Gentleman in that hope; but the hon. and learned Gentleman had scarcely, in some remarks that he made, taken the course best calculated to realize his hope. Speaking on behalf of the Government, he could assure the House that he should do nothing which could justify any hon. Gentleman in prolonging a debate which, in the opinion of the Government, had already proceeded long enough. The right hon. Gentleman the Member for Central Bradford (Mr. Shaw Lefevre) had given the House an historical disquisition with a view of showing that the only effective method of putting down crime was by means of remedial legislation. But after the Land Bill of 1860—which was described as a Landlords' Bill—though it merely applied to Ireland principles recognized in most civilized countries of the world—Ireland was freer from agrarian crime than at any time since Returns of agrarian crime had been prepared. In 1865, before the remedial legislation of the Liberal Party, before the Land Act of 1870 and the Land Act of 1881, the total number of agrarian crimes was 86 —a figure lower than the difference between the agrarian crimes of 1885 and 1886, which was described as inappreciable. He had already endeavoured to explain to the House that the Returns of agrarian crime were so made out that many crimes which had reference to the disturbed state of the country, and which were of a nature aimed at by this Bill, nevertheless did not appear in the Returns, as the police did not deem them to come within the category of "agrarian" offences. Thus midnight raids for arms would not, in all cases, be described as agrarian.

MR. EDWARD HARRINGTON (Kerry, W.) said, they would come under the head of "attacks on dwelling-houses."

MR. A. J. BALFOUR said, they might or they might not. But last year there were 72 cases of firing into dwelling-houses, and of these only 43 were put down as agrarian, and there were 402 cases of malicious injury to property, and only 150 were classed as agrarian.

MR. EDWARD HARRINGTON said, this was due to the Belfast riots.

MR. A. J. BALFOUR said, the Belfast riots might possibly account for some of the cases that were not classed as agrarian. Then there were 165 cases of killing, cutting, and maiming cattle, and only 73 were classed as agrarian. He mentioned this to show that there were certain classes of offences which were connected with the state of the country and which were not classed as agrarian crime.

MR. DILLON (Mayo, E.): Will the right hon. Gentleman inform the House on what principle the police classed an offence as agrarian? This is a very important point.

MR. A. J. BALFOUR said, the police only returned an offence as agrarian where they could trace a close connection between it and matters with regard to land. Therefore, offences which arose out of the disturbed condition of the country were not classed as agrarian.

MR. DILLON asked how the police had, for instance, classified the murder of Curtin, which had no connection with the agrarian question?

Mr. A. J. Balfour

MR. A. J. BALFOUR said, he was not quite sure, but he did not think this had been set down as agrarian. This he knew, however—that the lamentable case to which he alluded on Friday, where two unfortunate girls were shot in a raid for arms, was not classed as agrarian crime, and yet that was as much due to agrarian discontent as if it had been the result of a most cruel eviction. This fact should be borne in mind in studying the Returns of agrarian crime. He also desired to point out that, as he read the figures, the increase of the ordinary serious crime throughout Ireland, excluding the Metropolitan district, was at least as great in proportion as the increase of agrarian crime. The hon. and learned Member who moved the Amendment attacked the Irish landlords in very severe terms. [Mr. R. T. REID: Not all.] Well, he had attacked a large and important section of them. The hon. and learned Member declared that it was the duty of the landlords to reduce the rents of their tenants in precise proportion to the fall in prices, and to other circumstances affecting the value of the land in Ireland. Well, it was his (Mr. A. J. Balfour's) opinion also that that was the duty of Irish landlords; but it did not lie in the mouths of hon. Gentlemen opposite to declare that it was their duty, for in 1881 the Party opposite deliberately turned the landlords into rent-chargers and mortgagees, and consequently it did not become Members of that Party to say to the landlords—"You ought to act as if we had never limited your immemorial rights." Of course, he was not to be understood to mean that the landlords ought to act up to the strict letter of the rights conferred upon them in 1881. On the contrary, he thought that every Irish landlord would be acting rightly and wisely for himself, his order, his tenantry, Ireland and the Empire, if he were to revise in a generous spirit and according to the necessities of the time his contracts with his tenants, even if those contracts had been imposed upon him by right hon. Gentlemen opposite. The hon. and learned Member asked—"What is to be done when by this Coercion Bill you will have conferred upon the landlord these immense powers for the enforcement of his rent?" But what "immense powers" did the Bill give? At the most it would enable the landlord to use those legal powers which the Party opposite had themselves conferred upon him. Was that so monstrous a result of legislation that they ought to shrink from it with horror? That the Government earnestly desired to prevent anything in the nature of harsh eviction was amply proved by the legislation which they had introduced in "another place." The hon. and learned Member said that there were at present two checks upon landlords—namely, publicity and Boycotting. In reference to the first of these, the hon. and learned Member appeared to suppose that, under the Land Bill of the Government, a landlord would be able to evict his tenants without any publicity at all—without the presence of those immense crowds of excited people which the hon. and learned Member deemed so valuable for the protection of the tenants' interests. But the hon. and learned Member was in error. It was perfectly true that a landlord would be able to turn a tenant into a caretaker without any parade; but if he should wish to evict the tenant, to turn him out of his holding on to the wayside, the same concourse of people would have the opportunity of assembling, and, as now, the services of the police might unhappily be required. Thus, all those "tragic circumstances" which the hon. and learned Member thought so valuable would continue to remain part of the ordinary procedure at evictions. The hon. and learned Member declared that eviction was the cause of crime, and argued that, because in counties where the number of evictions was highest the number of crimes was also highest, the evictions must be the cause of the crimes. He did not deny that in certain cases evictions might result in crime; but he asserted most emphatically that intimidation, and some of those combinations which met with so much favour from the hon. and learned Member, were the causes of eviction. Over and over again it happened that where a settlement would otherwise be come to between landlord and tenant on amicable terms, the organization which the hon. and learned Member defended stepped in and said that the settlement must not take place, and thus deprived the landlord of every means of exacting the smallest fraction or fragment of his legal rights, excepting by the extreme method of eviction.

Mr. W. REDMOND (Fermanagh, N.) asked if the right hon. Gentleman would be good enough to give a single instance of such action on the part of the organization to which he referred? [*Cries of* "Order!"]

Mr. SPEAKER said, that the Question of the hon. Member appeared to be an argument in the guise of a Question.

Mr. R. T. REID wished to say that if any organization interfered to prevent a man from paying an honest rent, he was sure it would have no sympathy from him.

Mr. A. J. BALFOUR said, that he knew that the hon. and learned Member had no sympathy with crime; but he thought that the policy which the hon. and learned Member recommended would have the effect of fostering that very crime which he desired to see repressed. He now came to the second check mentioned by the hon. and learned Member —namely, Boycotting. What conclusion could be drawn from the Amendment and speech of the hon. and learned Member except that he regarded Boycotting as a very good method by which to remove any harshness which might exist in connection with the working of the Irish Land Act? What other conclusion could be drawn except that he preferred that this monstrous and iniquitous system of Boycotting—this system of punishment inflicted by an irresponsible tribunal on innocent men and women—should go on rather than that the landlord should be put in a position to exercise those legal rights which the legislation of the right hon. Member for Mid Lothian had conferred upon him? He now came to the consideration of the specific grievance which the hon. and learned Member alleged that the Irish people had. This grievance was that the judicial rents fixed before 1883 were between 12 and 14 per cent too high. That was the grievance which ought, in the opinion of the hon. and learned Member, to induce the Government to allow intimidation, Boycotting, outrage, and crime to go on unchecked. Could there be a more extravagant notion? The extent of the grievance was that the judicial rents fixed during 1881, 1882, 1883, and perhaps 1884 ought to be

[[First Night.]

revised. It seemed to him that the position was absurd when viewed in the light thrown upon it by statistics. There had been 1,102 evictions for nonpayment of rent in the six months ending on the 31st of March last. In only 254 of these cases had judicial rents been fixed. In the remaining 848 cases judicial rents had never even been applied for. [An Irish MEMBER : Leaseholders.] No; they could not make them out to be leaseholders—there might be here and there one. The great majority of those 848 might have stayed their evictions if they had applied to the Land Court for fair rents to be fixed. Why did they not do so? [An hon. MEMBER: Arrears.] They might have applied to the Land Court and had the evictions stayed till the Court had settled the rent. Was not that a conclusive proof that if the hon. and learned Gentleman had his way, and the Government had carried out that policy which the hon. and learned Gentleman said they were incurring a grave responsibility by not carrying out, the condition of the Irish tenantry would not be remedied, except to a small and even infinitesimal amount? Compare the tender mercies of Gentlemen opposite with the policy of the Government. They had occupied themselves in denouncing the Land Bill brought forward in " another place." He was not going to discuss the provisions of that Bill. But it was framed by the Government in a far larger and more liberal spirit than appeared to animate the breasts of Gentlemen opposite, and its benefits would not be confined to an insignificant fraction of the Irish tenantry. The Government did not simply desire to prevent harsh and improper evictions in those cases in which judicial rents had been fixed before 1885, but approached the question in a larger spirit. He was not going to pronounce an opinion whether the clauses of that Bill, especially the Relief Clauses, were or were not unworkable. He did not deny their extreme complexity. The framing of those clauses was a matter of great difficulty and anxiety to the Government, and to deal with the question at all would tax the ingenuity of any Government. But the reason was that the land system of Ireland had been so tinkered and boggled by the Party opposite that it was

Mr. A. J. Balfour

in a state of hopeless and inextricable confusion. That wonderful system of 1881, which was to remedy the wrongs of Ireland, had now so utterly and hopelessly broken down at the first strain put upon it, that the difficulties of a Government which attempted to reform it were almost greater than the ingenuity of man could overcome. That alone was the cause of any objections which might be raised by Gentlemen opposite to these particular clauses of the Bill now before the House of Lords. Now, what was the meaning of the hon. and learned Gentleman's Amendment? It was that the House declined to proceed further with a measure for strengthening the Criminal Law until it had seen the provisions of a Bill introduced into the other House. But had not the Government pledged themselves that before the Crimes Bill left that House the House should see the measure before the House of Lords? Was that not enough? [*Cries of* "No!"] Why was it not enough? It was that hon. Gentlemen opposite meant to delay the passing of the Crimes Bill to the utmost of their power, and for that end he could not conceive a more ingenious plan than the one proposed. The House would have the opportunity of rejecting the Land Bill on the third reading if they were dissatisfied with the form in which it left the House of Lords. But it was not enough. It was not merely that the Crimes Bill should be thrown out if the Land Bill were not satisfactory, but that it should be strangled by excessive debate if the Land Bill were satisfactory. Gentlemen opposite were never tired of imputing sinister motives to the Government. The right hon. Member for Newcastle (Mr. John Morley), before the Land Bill was introduced into the House of Lords, said that their object was to exact unjust rents from the tenants. The accusation had ceased even to be plausible since the introduction of the Bill in the House of Lords. But the hon. and learned Gentleman said that the Crimes Bill was intended to compel the Irish tenants to pay excessive rents.

MR. R. T. REID said, that in consequence of the right hon. Gentleman's speech at Ipswich he had distinctly disclaimed making such an imputation. He was in the habit of accepting the assurances of Gentlemen opposite.

MR. A. J. BALFOUR said, he entirely accepted the hon. and learned Gentleman's statement; but he was puzzled to know how hon. Members could go on talking about Bills which they had never seen. They had discussed the Crimes Bill before they had seen it, and their criticisms had been refuted by the event; and now they had been discussing a Land Purchase Bill which was not even before the House of Lords. The hon. and learned Member, following the right hon. Member for Mid Lothian, was now imputing to the Government the monstrous intention of passing the Crimes Bill in order to compel Irish tenants to pay more for their land than it was worth. How did the right hon. Gentleman know what the Land Purchase Bill was to be? By what gift of prophecy did he know the provisions of a Bill which was still in embryo? The Government could not accede to this Amendment, which was obviously intended to delay the Bill. They denied, and had always-denied, that it was intended by the Bill to interfere with the relations of landlord and tenant. This was a Bill to put down crime, and crime could not wait to be put down until they had a Bill with regard to Irish land. It was not conflicts between landlord and tenant in which they desired to interfere, it was not combinations they desired to crush; but it was crime which would be tolerated in no other country on the earth, which ought not to be tolerated in Ireland, and which the Government, as far as in them lay, did not mean to tolerate 24 hours longer than the Forms of this House rendered absolutely necessary.

MR. W. E. GLADSTONE (Edinburgh, Mid Lothian) said, he had not the least intention of entering into the debate as regards the polemical considerations with which the speech of the right hon. Gentleman naturally bristled, although if he did he would be compelled to meet many of the allegations of the right hon. Gentleman with a direct negative; but with reference to what he might call the parenthetical part of the right hon. Gentleman's speech, when he was speaking of agrarian crime, it would be of great use to the House if the right hon. Gentleman would favour them with some Memorandum containing information as to the rules and principles upon which agrarian crime was distinguished by the police in Ireland. He was not blaming the police; but this information would guide the judgment of the House. There was another question arising directly out of a statement which he understood the right hon. Gentleman to have made outside the walls of the House. The statement was thus reported —

"In 1870, when Mr. Gladstone brought in his Coercion Bill, if a band of 30 men went about posting up threatening notices threatening some man with outrage and Boycotting if he carried out one of the ordinary avocations of life, the 30 men who did that counted as 30 offences. Now they are counted as one."

That statement must have been in some sense true or the right hon. Gentleman would not have made it. He understood that by the changes which had been made, comparisons of figures between that period and the present were entirely vitiated. He wished, therefore, to know whether the right hon. Gentleman would be kind enough to let the House have a distinct account in the form of a Memorandum of any change in the method of reckoning agrarian offences since any date the right hon. Gentleman thought it convenient to fix, in order that they might know how far they could rely on the comparison of figures which were absolutely vital to the formation of any sound judgment on this question?

MR. A. J. BALFOUR said, he should be most happy to have a Memorandum prepared, explaining the principle on which the police distinguished between agrarian and other offences. He believed the only change that had been made was between 1868 and 1870. It was not made by a Conservative Government, and he believed the right hon. Gentleman would find the effect of it in the statistics themselves. If the right hon. Gentleman looked at the figures for the year he would find an explanatory foot-note. He had accurately described what the method used to be, and the result as to certain crimes was extremely misleading.

MR. W. E. GLADSTONE said, that there might be a note of the kind somewhere, but he had carefully examined the Papers, and he had seen nothing which dealt with the question. It would be extremely desirable that the right hon. Gentleman should favour them with such a statement as he had mentioned.

[First Night.]

MR. A. J. BALFOUR said, that it should be done.

VISCOUNT WOLMER (Hants, Petersfield) said, he was pleased at being able for the first time in the course of these debates to agree with a large part of the speech which had been made by a brother Liberal who, unhappily, was divided from him on this Irish Question. The hon. and learned Member had, however, confused together what appeared to be two aspects of the question. The major question was how Ireland was to be governed in the future; the minor question had reference to the relations between landlord and tenant in Ireland. The hon. and learned Member had told the House how deeply he and those who agreed with him felt on the subject of this proposal of the Government; and he put this fact forward as a justification for straining the Forms of Parliament almost to the breaking-point in their endeavour to prevent the Bill from passing. There were other questions on which men felt very strongly, but that was no reason why they should endeavour to stop the whole machinery of the Government of the country. To his mind it was absolutely necessary to separate the two branches of this question. First of all, however, he would deal with that part of it which was more immediately touched by the Amendment of the hon. and learned Member for Dumfries (Mr. R. T. Reid), which had laid before the House in terms with which he very largely agreed the duty of that House towards that part of the tenantry of Ireland who wished to pay their rents, but who were not in a position to do so. The hon. and learned Member added that he had no sympathy with tenants who could pay a just rent and who would not pay it. But he omitted to lay before the House the fact that the whole action of the Plan of Campaign, and of the hon. Member for East Mayo (Mr. Dillon), was to confound in one great system of repudiation the two classes of tenants. One of the main duties of the Government of any civilized country was to insist that such separation should be made — that by the action of such a Bill as that now before the House the tenant who would repudiate a just contract should be made to fulfil that contract, and that, by the action of some such Bill as had been introduced in "another place," the honest tenant should be protected from eviction. To the measure now before the other House, both the hon. and learned Member for Dumfries and the right hon. Gentleman the Member for Bradford (Mr. Shaw Lefevre) had been a little unfair. They could not be in a position to pronounce upon that measure till it had left the House of Lords and they knew the shape in which it would be presented to the House of Commons. But there was a point which they could take hold of, and that was the declaration of the Prime Minister, who laid it down as an axiom of the Government that the land war in Ireland must be made to cease; and that it could not be made to cease as long as it was in the power of certain landlords, enemies of their class and of their country, to inflict upon men who could not pay punishments which were only merited by those who sheltered themselves under the wings of the hon. Member for East Mayo in his attempts to protect the other class of tenants. Liberal Unionists held that their primary duty was to maintain the Union; but in supporting the Government in their action for this purpose, they intended to put the utmost pressure they could upon them to pass such an Act as would put an end to the unjust and barbarous evictions. Before passing away from this branch of the subject, he could not help alluding to the Land Purchase Bill brought in last year by the right hon. Gentleman the Member for Mid Lothian. The bases of that Bill were the rents which were now denounced as unjust. He was waiting for an informal vote of thanks to the Liberal Unionists for protecting the right hon. Gentleman's reputation and the country from such an act as that. Then, it was said that the Liberal Unionist Members voted against the Bill of the hon. Member for the City of Cork (Mr. Parnell), which, it was alleged, would have had the effect already which the Government now intended to produce by the Bill introduced in the House of Lords. But the hon. Members who made that accusation against the Unionist Party were demanding for Members from Ireland a totally exceptional treatment from that which was given to English and Scotch Members. When the Scotch Members brought forward the question of the crofters the right hon. Gentleman appointed a Royal Commission, and would not legislate until he had received its report. What was sauce for a Scotchman was sauce in a similar case for an Irishman. The accusation had been very freely levelled against the Party which had the honour to follow the noble Lord the Member for Rossendale (the Marquess of Hartington) and the right hon. Gentleman the Member for West Birmingham (Mr. J. Chamberlain), that they were supporting what was called a Coercion Bill, having been returned as anti-coercionists. [Mr. COSSHAM: Hear, hear.] He would ask the hon. Member for Bristol to turn to the speeches of those who agreed with him and to the columns of *The Daily News* and other Liberal newspapers, and he would find that they raised the cry of "Conciliation *versus* Coercion," and said to the electors—"Do not vote for any Unionist Members, because you will be voting for coercion." Did any Home Ruler deny that his Party devoted their energies to putting the issue of conciliation *versus* coercion? [Mr. GLADSTONE: Hear, hear.] The right hon. Gentleman acknowledged that was his point. [Mr. GLADSTONE: No, no.] He was sorry if he had misunderstood the speeches of the right hon. Gentleman; but that was the whole object of the Home Rule Press, from *The Daily News* down—or up, he did not know which to call it—to *The Nation* in Ireland. That was the point which was always being put forward. Yet now it was asserted by the same Party that at the last Election the country never had the question of coercion brought before it at all. The real point now at issue was contained in this principle—"Are you going to govern Ireland by or against and in spite of the National League?" Some hon. Gentlemen around him, headed by the right hon. Member for Mid Lothian, had determined that Ireland should be governed by the National League. The country had determined that Ireland should not be governed by the National League, and that being so, it was absurd to turn round on Liberal Unionists and say that they had abandoned all their traditions in their endeavour to beat the National League. The Home Rule Liberals had entered into a partnership with the League, and could not dissociate themselves from the deeds of the League. They were told of an increasing roll of Irish crime; they heard of multitudes of victims of outrage who dared not give

evidence against those who had outraged them; and they had heard read the charges of Judges announcing that in their opinion law had almost ceased to exist in many parts of the country. It was acknowledged on all hands that the jury system in Ireland was at a deadlock. In the Report of the Cowper Commission also, not only did the Commissioners press upon the Government the necessity for the maintenance of law and order, but nobody could take up that Report in an impartial spirit without reading of acts which made his blood curdle with rage and indignation at such things being allowed in a civilized country. In the face of all that, the House was told that there was in Ireland a sort of semi-divine calm; and when hon. Members came down to that House and declared it to be their duty to support a Government which would repress that state of things they were told they were interfering between the poor and the rich. They were interfering between the poor and the rich—between the poor Irish tenants and that rich tyrant the National League. [*Home Rule cheers.*] Yes; there were other riches than money could give, and he doubted whether many men had more power given by the possession of gold than was given to members of the National League as heads of the local Courts. The hon. and learned Member for Dumfries in his most moderate and useful speech said he thought it his duty to enter his protest as an English gentleman and a Member of that House in a matter of certain accusations made in the public Press. He was going to follow in the hon. and learned Member's footsteps— he trusted with the utmost care—because he also felt it his duty to state his view on that question. A charge had been made than which none other more foul or more terrible could be conceived; it had been denied point-blank by the hon. Member for Cork (Mr. Parnell). In that case *The Times* had been guilty of a most foul and malignant perjury, libel, and forgery. Ought a Member of that House to sit down under such an accusation levelled against a Member of that body? Was any Member of that House to be liable to similar accusations? The right hon. Member for Mid Lothian had said, and had justly said, that the burden of proof lay upon *The Times* and not that of disproof upon the hon.

[First Night.]

Member for Cork. [*Home Rule cheers.*] Yes; but there was only one way of setting that machinery in motion. In an action for libel *The Times* would either have to give in at once or else file a plea of justification, and on that plea the whole burden of proof would rest on *The Times*. *The Times* would have to prove that the denial of the hon. Member for Cork was a false denial; *The Times* would have to prove that the letter was genuine and not a forgery, and if *The Times* failed to prove that—and he could think of few things more difficult to prove—not only would the hon. Member for Cork gain enormous damages, not only would he ruin his chief journalistic foe, but he would deal a deadly blow at the influence of the Unionist Party. The hon. Member for Cork had everything to gain and nothing to lose by such a course; and if, in the face of that, he did not commence that action, which he undertook to say no Member of the Liberal or Conservative Parties would fail to take under similar circumstances, then he ventured to say that the people of this country were not to be blamed if they drew conclusions very unpalatable to the National League in Ireland; and Members of that House were not to be blamed if, in their position as trustees of this country, they refused more than ever to give into the hands of a man who would not take such measures to clear himself as were open to him, the care of those most delicate relations between our country and his which would result from the passing of any such Bill as that proposed by the right hon. Member for Mid Lothian.

MR. EDWARD HARRINGTON (Kerry, S.) said, the noble Viscount who had just sat down (Viscount Wolmer) was one of those who made himself the mouthpiece of attack against Irish Members, but granting that the 86 Members for Ireland had come red-hot from a convict prison, their election to the House only showed that the wrongs of the Irish people were such that in spite of that the people determined to send them to Parliament to expose their grievances. He feared that the common principles of decency and honour were being subverted. Ideas on such subjects must have changed since the time when the denial of a Gentleman whose word had never been proved untrue would be taken anywhere, and much more so

that of an hon. Member of that House. In former times that word was taken without question; but, now, there were "insinuating doubts" thrown against it. If this sort of thing was continued and it suited hon. Members opposite to insist upon and repeat, in the insinuating and offensive methods they adopted, the charges they brought against hon. Members on that side of the House, he would not say that those who sat on those Benches would be answerable always for the temper in which they might meet those charges. Those charges were insults and calumnies which in former times would have been met in a very different manner from that adopted [now-a-days. The right hon. Gentleman the Chief Secretary for Ireland (Mr. A. J. Balfour) had found great fault with the Amendment of the hon. and learned Member for Dumfries (Mr. R. T. Reid), but he (Mr. E. Harrington) thought that, judging from past experience of Bills introduced in the House of Lords, the Amendment was quite justified. He did not think the right hon. Gentleman the Chief Secretary had been dealing very fairly by the House in the matter of the statistics of agrarian outrages. During the quarter ending March 31 last, the total number of agrarian outrages in Ireland was 241; but of these 118 consisted of threatening letters. Dealing with evictions in Kerry, he showed that in the quarter ending the 30th of June, 1886, 187 families, numbering 1,206 persons, were evicted; in the succeeding quarter 207 families, embracing 1,274 persons, were evicted; while in the last quarter 306 families, numbering 1,706 persons, were evicted. Since the beginning of the agitation—or rather the depression in agriculture which has given rise to the agitation—there had been evicted in Kerry 14,000 persons. This meant that one out of every eight or nine persons in the agricultural population of the county had been evicted. There was no need for him to indicate what a continual and irritating cause of crime these evictions must be. He was far from palliating either crime or outrage, but it was the duty of the Irish Members to plainly tell the Government what was the cause of the crime and outrage, and to ask them to make an honest endeavour to get at the root of the evil. It was easy to represent the

Irish Members as defending crime and outrage, but that was doing them a gross injustice. They hoped and believed that the near future history of their country would vindicate their action from other such odious aspersions. They were as anxious as any other section of the House that crime and outrage should be put down in Ireland; but their experience of every coercive measure which had been passed for that purpose showed that those measures were invariably directed against political offenders; while in many instances criminals were either allowed to go scot-free or such unfair means were taken to obtain their conviction that, when convicted, they were made objects of popular sympathy—a state of things highly inimical to that proper respect for the law which should exist among the people of any country. That Crimes Bill the Government now wished to pass before they carried their remedial measures, and the working of it, it should be remembered, was to be intrusted to the hands of the Resident Magistrates, a body of men who were practically the offshoots and dependents of the landlord class, and all whose interests were bound up with the maintenance of rents at their present exorbitant level. He insisted that the National League had exercised a humanizing influence in checking secret societies, which would undoubtedly have developed if the tenants had been left unprotected against the landlords. The League consisted of determined, outspoken men, who faced the tyrants, and told them their opinion of them, and everything that the League had done was as open as the day. Were it not for the League, crime would have been rampant; but to the League crime was repugnant, as it was to all honest and fearless men. If the Government would now come forward with their "large proposals" for the settlement of the Irish Land Question, there would be no need for this Bill. On an investigation into the nature of the claims which had been returned as having been dealt with by Grand Juries, arising out of malicious injuries, he found that those put forward by the Land Corporation of Ireland were practically adjudicated upon by Grand Juries consisting of its own shareholders; and it had put forward claims for cattle which it had afterwards been found had strayed upon the farms of its own members, prematurely assuming that the cattle had been stolen by Moonlighters. One thing put down as malicious injury was the firing of grass; whereas nothing was more common than to set fire to it for the purpose of obtaining an improved growth, and it was within the bounds of possibility that some of the claimants who had obtained compensation had themselves set fire to the grass for the purpose of improving it. The real difficulty of getting at the truth in these matters was that there were so many men concerned in the unjust administration of the law who were related to landlords, or were in some way identified with the interests of the landlords. He gave warning that, if this Bill passed into law, he should go back to his constituency, and, while endeavouring to keep the people within the lines of the law, would take every opportunity of resisting the oppression and tyranny which the Bill would impose upon the people, and he should not be afraid to take the consequences. He felt that he had not put the House to any inconvenience by addressing it, because the House had obliged him by absenting itself; but if hon. Members would not listen to what Irish Members had to say, the Irish people had the ear of the country, which was now open to the tale of misery which they had to tell.

Mr. J. E. ELLIS (Nottingham, Rushcliffe) said, he thought those who had followed the discussion on the Bill before the House would have come to the conclusion that the arguments on the other side of the House very much resolved itself into two heads. Hon. Members asserted, in the first place, the desirability of maintaining law and order in Ireland; and they then occupied themselves with recriminations against right hon. Gentlemen on the Front Opposition Bench for the part they took in 1881-2. On the latter point he agreed very much with the Member for Glasgow (Mr. E. R. Russell). There were many Members on that side of the House who cared very little what course was taken by the Liberal Party, at the head of which was the right hon. Gentleman the Member for Mid Lothian in 1881 and 1882. The circumstances had changed in almost every respect, and he understood that the right hon. Gentleman, and those who were associated with him, had

[First Night.]

entirely changed their policy in this matter. It had been admitted by the right hon. Member for Derby (Sir William Harcourt) that the old policy had failed, and the Liberal Party had turned back on it for ever. Then, as to the first assertion, as to the necessity for restoring law and order in Ireland; the memories of those who used that argument to so wide extent as they did must have rather failed them on this matter. This Bill was a distinct fulfilment of a pledge given in the Queen's Speech at the beginning of the Session, and he would venture to recall the attention of the House to the Speech, which clearly referred to this Bill and its introduction. That Speech pointed out very clearly the relation between such disorder as existed in Ireland and the conflict between landlords and tenants in that country. Her Majesty, in the Speech, said that grave crime was less in Ireland; but she went on to say that the relations between the owners and the occupiers of land in certain districts had been seriously disturbed, and further, that—

"Organized attempts to excite the latter class against the fulfilment of their legal obligations was made."

And then we were told that our attention would be called to reforms in legal procedure. It was clear that in these reforms were contemplated, not in regard to the general maintenance of law and order, but the suppression of the "organized attempts" to which Her Majesty had previously referred. The "legal obligations" of the Queen's Speech meant nothing more nor less than "rent." The Land Court in Ireland had decided, and Lord Cowper's Commission asserted, that the rent of land in Ireland was much greater than it should be; and that being so, it followed, as Mr. Knipe, the dissentient Commissioner on the Cowper Commission, and also Sir Redvers Buller, said, that the combinations which this Bill was intended to suppress were the salvation of the people. He had heard, with great astonishment, some references to the land legislation of the right hon. Member for Mid Lothian in 1881. The noble Lord the Member for Rossendale said that the law in regard to the occupation of land in Ireland was more favourable to the tenant than in almost any country he

knew. That might be; but it was not more favourable than the circumstances demanded, seeing that in Ireland the tenant had created the value of that for which he was asked to pay rent. The Land Act of 1881 had turned out a partial failure, because the advice of the hon. Member for Cork was not listened to then, as it also, unfortunately, was not listened to last September. Had it been, we should now have been in a better position. Since the introduction of this Bill, the conduct of the Government in withholding statistics and information which were requisite to support their assertions, and the case they tried to make out in its favour, had been almost unprecedented in Parliamentary history. Such figures as had been meagrely doled out to the House, not only did not support, but contradicted some of the assertions made. The Chief Secretary had told them in his speech on the second reading that statistics showed that agrarian crime was in excess as compared with previous years. The facts were the other way; for whereas there were 279 cases of agrarian crime in the last quarter of 1885, there were only 166 in the last quarter of 1886. In the first quarter of 1886 the number of agrarian crimes was 256, and in the first quarter of 1887 it was 241. These figures showed clearly that agrarian crime was not increasing, as was asserted, but was diminishing. But this was not the only instance in which the Government had shrunk from, or been unable to make good, their assertions. The First Lord of the Treasury made an assertion that juries would not convict in Ireland. Thereupon he (Mr. J. E. Ellis) placed on the Paper a Notice of Motion for a Return showing the number of cases in which juries had so failed to convict; but when he asked the right hon. Gentleman to consent to the production of this Return, he was told that there were no official records. But, if there were no official records, why should the right hon. Gentleman have told the House in such an off-hand way that juries would not convict? In the same way, he had put on the Paper a Motion for a Select Committee to investigate the truth of the anecdotes told by the Chief Secretary in support of his case on behalf of the Bill; but, although the hon. Member for Cork had said that he would refer the statements he had made to a ·

Select Committee, the Chief Secretary (Mr. A. J. Balfour) declined to do so. He (Mr. J. E. Ellis) protested against such conduct on the part of the Government when so grave a matter was at stake. The debate on the Bill had amply demonstrated that the disorder and dissatisfaction in Ireland were mainly due to evictions and to the treatment of the tenants by the Irish landlords. Lord Dufferin, speaking of the landlords of Ireland, in the House of Lords, said, in the year 1845—

"There are those possessing property in Ireland, in whose honour, in whose sense of justice, in whose compassion, I, for one, have no confidence whatever."

That was strong language to use of any class of men; but he believed it was amply justified by the conduct of the Irish landlords during the time of the great famine from 1845 to 1847. Further, he believed the words of Lord Dufferin were true of many of the landlords of Ireland at the present moment; and the Land Act of 1881 was an evidence that the Irish landlords could not be trusted to deal fairly by their tenants without the intervention of the law. Now, what was going on in Ireland at the present time? The evictions in 1885 affected 15,423 persons; in 1886, 19,473. In the first quarter of 1885, 3,446 were evicted; 1886, 3,447; 1887, 5,040, making a total of more than 400 a week, or 20,000 per annum; and the right hon. Member for Mid Lothian had justly said that in certain circumstances eviction meant a sentence of death. The evictions at Glenbeigh were simply a sample of what took place. One need go no further than that for an explanation of the disorder at present existing in that country. He observed that the number of homicides in Ireland in 1886 was 10; who could tell in how many of the 20,000 cases of evictions the word "homicide" justly applied? The real fact was that this Bill was intended to crush the National League, and so to leave the tenants at the mercy of the landlords by making evictions less noticeable. He had examined the constitution of the National League as laid down in the address to their fellow-countrymen of the hon. Member for Cork and his Colleagues, dated October, 1882, and with the permission of the House, he should like to quote it. It was as follows:—

"The necessity of close organization, for the purpose of concentrating and giving a definite direction to the National energies, is universally felt. It has been forced upon public attention by the encroachments upon popular rights, which have been going on in all directions since the power of union among the people was relaxed. The landlord combination for the purpose of breaking the spirit of the Irish tenant; the dismay which the present scale of judicial rents has created among applicants to the Land Courts; and the confiscation of tenants' property that is being effected wherever disorganization has crept in render it more necessary now than ever that the Irish tenantry should be re-united in vigilant and lawful association, for the purpose of protecting themselves from injustice, and for seeking that full measure of land law reform which alone can secure them against the perils of halting legislation. From the farming classes the desire for organized effort has extended to the labourers, whose miserable condition has been so long disregarded, and to the artizans, who see in the spirit evoked by a great National combination, a power which can nourish our decaying native industries with millions of money, now annually drained away into foreign markets.

With all these incentives to organization, the Irish National League unites a programme of social and political reform, which will gradually transfer all local power and patronage from privileged strangers into the hands of the people, and so fortify them for the work of National Self-Government, which is the inspiration of all our struggles. The National Conference has, with the most hearty unanimity, embodied these principles in the programme of the Irish National League. It remains for you now, in your various districts, to give immediate and practical effect to these resolutions; so that from the formation of local branches, the League may be able to proceed to the election for the Central Council, and may be able to offer to every section of the Irish people the power and protection which organization and discipline alone can ensure."

He submitted that there was nothing in that address of a treasonable or reprehensible character. He felt bound to condemn the language of the Chief Secretary for Ireland with reference to the National League, as reckless and random assertions tending to lower the dignity of the House. The right hon. Gentleman said—

"We cannot forget that the League leans a part upon those dark, secret societies which work by dynamite and the dagger, whose object is anarchy, and whose means are assassination."

This was a serious charge, and when they remembered by whom it was made, he thought they were justified in asking for proof. He (Mr. J. E. Ellis) could not but contrast this statement with the speech of Lord Spencer, to which he listened with so much pleasure, at Newcastle on September 21, 1886, in which that noble Lord explicitly severed the Representatives of the Irish people from the faintest complicity in or knowledge of crime or outrage. On the subject of the letter in *The Times*, the signature of which was attributed to the hon. Member for Cork, he took diametrically the opposite view to that taken this evening by the noble Lord (Viscount Wolmer). He accepted the emphatic disclaimer of the hon. Member for Cork, and he believed the English people would accept it. It seemed to him that in such a matter they should require as strict an adhesion to the laws of evidence as would be observed in a Court of Justice; and he must say that the conduct of the noble Lord the Member for Rossendale (the Marquess of Hartington), in launching serious charges against the hon. Member for East Mayo (Mr. Dillon), and then sheltering himself behind an anonymous journal, was what he should not have expected from him. The Chancellor of the Exchequer, in a speech in that House, had said that what the Government had to do was to attempt to break down the oppression under which the people of Ireland were suffering, and to enable them to protect themselves against the self-constituted Dictators of the country. That was the fallacy which underlay the whole argument. Hon. Members below the Gangway were no more self-constituted Dictators of Ireland than the right hon. Gentleman was the self-constituted Dictator of St. George's, Hanover Square, and they sat in that House by as unquestionable a title as any Member of it. No proof had been given in that House that the National League was built up in the way that had been asserted. The Chief Secretary for Ireland told them that it prevented settlements between landlord and tenants, but when challenged he had been unable to show that that was so. The source of the strength of the National League lay in the conviction of the people of Ireland that to it they owed their salvation. A policy of exasperation had been entered upon in the last week or 10 days, which consisted of vilifying the characters of Irish Members in that House. This attempt to preserve the Union by forged letters in newspapers and rancorous abuse would fail as it deserved to. This Amendment asked that they should have the

Mr. J. E. Ellis

full measure for relief before them before they went on with the consideration of a measure for strengthening the Criminal Law against combinations of tenants. The Prime Minister himself had said that the two Bills were sister Bills, and that the one was the complement of the other. For his own part he had not much confidence in the remedial measure put forward by the Government. *The Times* recommended it to the Conservative Party and their allies on the ground that it would save landlords the expense of having to go to the Court at Dublin. They had been almost threatened again that evening by the Chief Secretary for Ireland with regard to the length of this debate; but he could assure the right hon. Gentleman that this charge of Obstruction had not the slightest terrors for him; he knew that he had the support of his constituents against this Bill, and on that side they would continue to do their duty in this matter. It was because he believed that this Bill contained within it a grave danger to the peace of Ireland, and that it would postpone that for which they all hoped and which they earnestly desired, the better government of that country, that he offered it his resolute and uncompromising opposition.

MR. WALLACE (Edinburgh, E.) said, he considered the Amendment a reasonable one. It was perfectly conceivable that, if some adequate measure of relief with respect to Irish rents were placed before them, and they were certain that it would pass into law, the House might become convinced that there would be no necessity for further proceeding with this strengthening of the Criminal Law. He admitted, for himself, that he was not very hopeful of any such measure being placed before them by the Government, because, from the character of the remedial measure which they had proposed "elsewhere," he despaired of their being able to put it into such a shape that it could be hopefully regarded by the House. He could not see how the proposal of bankruptcy, as the highway to success, had the promise of success. It struck him as very much like as if they were told that to knock a man down was the best way to set him on his legs. He had never himself observed an operation of that kind successful. Still, they were bound to look upon it as possible that some measure of a hopeful character might be put before them; and he was satisfied that unless they had the assurance that some effectual measure of remedy against the evil of excessive rent, now undeniably existing in Ireland, was to accompany this measure of coercion, it would add infinitely to the amount of misery at present endured by the Irish people, and to the amount of hostility with which English rule was already regarded. He was satisfied that this measure, under such circumstances, would produce an immense amount of oppression. The Home Secretary and the Chief Secretary for Ireland had both stated that the Bill was aimed at crime alone, and not at combinations of tenants for the purpose of reducing unjust rents; but if it made those combinations crimes, their statement was a mere quibble. All the liberty the Home Secretary, by the Bill, would leave for combinations of tenants, was the liberty to express an opinion, or hold a sort of academic discussion with regard to the rents that they would like to pay for their land; and if they took any steps to carry that opinion into practical effect, and bring it to bear with any practical aim upon their landlord, then, according to the law as it had been laid down by the Queen's Bench in Ireland, they involved themselves at once in a criminal conspiracy. He held that all combinations for any purpose whatever that would be of any practical use, would be stamped by the Bill as criminal, and every person who engaged in them would be exposed to very severe punishment. It was said that there were no new crimes created by the Bill; but he was certain that several of the combinations aimed at had never yet been pronounced to be criminal by any English or Irish tribunal. Whether these were new crimes or not, it was perfectly certain that the sort of tribunal which was to be erected in Ireland for the purpose of dealing with so delicate a matter of jurisprudence, would manufacture new crimes. There was plenty of material in the Bill to enable the two Resident Magistrates to make a great many new crimes. There were, at all events, artificial crimes that were perpetuated by the proposed legislation. In connection with trade disputes in England, the test of criminal combina-

tion was the criminality or innocence of the act when done by an individual. What was allowable in industrial matters and in the case of artizans should be equally allowable in the case of agrarian disputes as between landlords and tenants. What was innocent in the case of individual tenants, ought also to be innocent in the case of a combination of tenants. If a combination among tenants who desired a reduction of rents should be held to be illegal under this Bill, as he feared it would, the Government could not escape the charge of having created or perpetuated an artificial crime. A law having such results could not fail to cause passionate resentment in the people of Ireland; and their irritation would certainly not grow less when they considered the character of the tribunal which was to be intrusted with the enforcement of the law. Instead of trial by jury, they were to be subjected to the arbitrary authority of Resident Magistrates. The Irish people would feel that they were being under what they regarded as English usurpation and English despotism; for now, when they had, by the return of 86 Nationalist Members, given unequivocal expression to their desire for Home Rule, he failed to see how anyone who believed in the principle that a country ought to be governed in accordance with the will of its people could look upon the perpetuation of the direct rule of this country in Irish home affairs as anything less than a usurpation and a tyranny. At the very moment when they felt this usurpation most keenly, the Irish people were to be deprived of the traditional safeguard against Government tyranny. In support of the proposal to suspend trial by jury in certain cases, it was alleged that jurors were in sympathy with crime. He did not believe, however, that jurors could ever really be in sympathy with crime. The right way to state the proposition was, to say that jurors felt antipathy for the Government who prosecuted the perpetrators of crime; and the true inference to be drawn from what was called the failure of the jury system in Ireland was, not that the jury system had broken down, but that the system of anti-Irish Government for Ireland had broken down. The more startling the failure of juries to support the Government in the prosecution of undoubted crime, the clearer

[First Night.]

was the proof of antagonism between the people whom those juries represented and the Government. In such circumstances it was not the jury system that ought to be abolished, but the system of government, in order that a Government more in harmony with the mind and will of the Irish people, should be substituted for that at present in power. If it were true that juries were terrorized by the National League, then all that was required was as much strengthening of the law as would procure the conviction and punishment of that offence and no more. If this sort of legislation were pressed forward, there would be an evil done to others besides the Irish nation. The appeal which was made to the English people in order to secure the enactment of this measure, would have a demoralizing effect. It was an appeal to the worst passions of the English people. They were a generous people, but they had their faults; and they were extremely jealous lest it should be said that they were unable to keep down any nation with whom they had once been in hostile conflict. The question which was now being put to the English people was this—"Will you allow yourselves to be put down by this contemptible Irish nation?" The Bill appealed to the worst side of the English character, and would, so far as successful, be more injurious to England than to Ireland. The conquest of Ireland by England might be an easy task; but the self-conquest of England, in matters where justice and right were concerned, was a more difficult, but a more brilliant and useful victory. That victory, the Government were doing their best to prevent, and leading the English nation onwards and downwards on the path of pride, injustice and oppression. Fully believing that the measure they were pressing upon the House was one of that nature, he cordially supported the Amendment.

MR. MUNDELLA (Sheffield, Brightside): Mr. Speaker, the Amendment which has been moved by the hon. and learned Member for Dumfries (Mr. R. T. Reid), in a speech marked by great ability and great moderation, invites this House to declare that it will not—

"Proceed further with a measure for strengthening the Criminal Law against combinations of tenants until it has before it the full measure for their relief against excessive rents in the

shape in which it may pass the other House of Parliament."

It has been said by hon. Gentlemen opposite, and by the noble Lord the Member for the Petersfield Division of Hants (Viscount Wolmer) behind me, that in moving this Amendment we are straining the powers of Parliament to the utmost and almost to the verge of breaking. The noble Lord has only had a short experience of this House, or otherwise he would have known that important measures of this kind are almost invariably met on the stage of going into Committee by some Amendment or other. This is the more necessary in the case of a measure which touches—as this does—the liberties of 5,000,000 of people. It is not to be expected that a Bill which will surround the whole of the Irish people with a network of legal machinery of a technical and even of a dangerous character can be prosecuted through this House with the facility of a Turnpike Bill; and it is too much to ask that a Bill of that character should be passed without discussion. Her Majesty's Government have already allowed four or five speeches— some of them marked by very great ability—to be made from this side of the House without any reply. I remember, on a former occasion, that such a policy was designated "a conspiracy of silence," although it was not, fortunately, a conspiracy punishable under the provisions of this Bill. Now, I do not think that such an Amendment as this ought to be met with a conspiracy of silence. I am bound to say that as far as the right hon. Gentleman the Chief Secretary for Ireland (Mr. A. J. Balfour) is concerned his answer was full, and that he replied to my hon. and learned Friend with the courtesy which uniformly characterizes him. But we have had from no other Member of the Party opposite any reply to the rest of the speeches which have been addressed to the House to-night. Now, Sir, what is the position in which we stand? We have practically two measures before us— perhaps not exactly before us; but, at any rate, in our minds; one of them is actually before us, and with the provisions of the other we are perfectly well acquainted. One of them purports to be a measure against crime, whereas the other purports to be for the relief of tenants from excessive rents. Now, if the speech of my hon. and learned Friend proved anything, it proved two things—namely, that a repressive measure would only tend to aggravate and increase crime, whereas the measure which is intended for the relief of the tenants will altogether fail. Moreover, we have been assured in this House that the repressive measure is intended to be pressed through both Houses of Parliament with all its pristine severity. [*Cheers.*] Hon. Gentlemen opposite cheered that statement. They rejoiced in the severity of the proposed amendment of the Criminal Law in Ireland; but we have no guarantee as to the condition into which the measure of relief will come down to this House, or as to the character it is likely to assume when it passes through Parliament. I think the difficulty of discussing these two measures apart must be obvious to every hon. Member; but it is impossible not to connect them together in our minds, because the Prime Minister said that he considered these two Bills as sister Bills, one being the complement of the other. Why, I would ask, is a Coercion Bill to be a complement of a Relief Bill for the Irish tenants? The right hon. Gentleman the Chief Secretary has answered that the object of the Bill we are now discussing is the prevention of crime. But another contention is that effectual relief given to the Irish tenants will render all repressive legislation unnecessary. What is it that is at the root of the present condition of Ireland? The noble Lord the Member for Petersfield spoke of the character of the Irish landlords. He thought that we had dealt with them with great severity. Now, I do not feel at liberty to reflect' on the Irish landlords in the severe strain which they have been reflected upon by other and higher authorities elsewhere. Let me bring to the notice of the right hon. Gentleman opposite the statement which was made in respect of the condition of Ireland, and the character of the Irish landlords on the highest authority no later than Friday last in the House of Lords, " With one or two exceptions," said a noble Earl in "another place "— " he distinctly stated that until very recently landlords did not make improvements on the land; that the tenants made them, and when they were made their rents were raised. He attributed the present condition of Ireland to the fact that the landlords, in other respects an admirable race of men "—[it was not stated what those other respects were]—" were undoubtedly bad landlords."

That is not the language of any supporter of the right hon. Gentleman the Member for Mid Lothian (Mr. W. E. Gladstone), nor is it the statement of an Irish Member, nor of those Bashi-Bazouks to whom the right hon. Gentleman the Chancellor of the Exchequer (Mr. Goschen) made reference in his Edinburgh speech. It is the statement of one of your own witnesses, for these are the words of Earl Cowper, speaking in his place in the House of Lords within the last few days, and nothing so strong has ever been said by anybody on this side of the House. Indeed, no language has been used which is so sweeping and so condemnatory as the words of the noble Lord. He says that until very recently the landlords made no improvements on the land, and that when improvements were made by the tenants the rents were immediately raised, or, in other words, that the landlords confiscated the property of the tenants. Then he attributed the present condition of Ireland to the fact that the landlord class in Ireland, who in other respects were a most admirable race of men, were undoubtedly bad landlords. The noble Lord went on to say that—

" The future hope of the country lay in protecting the tenants in the possession of their improvements."

Now, let us consider, for a moment, if that is the condition of Ireland, and if such a condition lies at the root of the deplorable state of things in that country, why it is that Her Majesty's Government should insist on passing through this House a Coercion Bill of unexampled severity, and give us no guarantee that their measure of relief will be one that is at all adequate to the requirements of justice. On the contrary, the very measure of relief which was recommended by Lord Cowper's Commission Her Majesty's Government have distinctly put aside, and refuse to act upon. Let me remind hon. Gentleman opposite that of all the Viceroys of Ireland now living Lord Cowper is the only one who is opposed to the principle of a domestic legislature for Ireland. All others have, more or less, given in their adhesion to that proposition. Remember further that he is the ally of the Government, the Chairman of their own Royal Commission, and yet he expresses his own conviction after serving for long months in Ireland, and after examining witnesses, whose evidence is to be found in that ponderous Blue Book; and he goes still further, because, while he has declared that the present agrarian condition of Ireland is so bad, he has also declared the Government to be a hateful bureaucracy. This is the declared opinion of one of the leading Members of the Unionist Party in terms which, if coming from a Liberal, would be regarded as tolerably strong. Now, Sir, with respect of the Land Bill, we ask whether it will remedy the evils which now exist, or whether it will not prove to be altogether inadequate to cope with them. We recognize that, so far as the leaseholders are concerned, it offers a substantial boon to them; but they only form one-fourth of the tenants of Ireland. To the rest it is a cruel mockery. I think the right hon. Gentleman the Chief Secretary can derive very little consolation from the debates which have taken place on this subject, because I believe that the whole of the Government measure has been condemned, almost in the strongest terms, by all those who have spoken upon it—whether friend or foe. Surely the only proper and sensible way of carrying out the recommendation of your own Commission, was to reduce excessive rents by submitting the claims of the tenants to the Land Commission which originally fixed the rents. But what is the course proposed to be taken? Instead of doing that you substitute the most stupid and heartless provisions that were probably ever submitted to Parliament. You refuse to reconsider or to revise the rents until the tenant is reduced to bankruptcy, yet you throw over what your own witnesses have said. Sir Redvers Buller tells you—

"I feel very strongly that you can never have peace unless you create some legal equipoise, or some equivalent."

You do not propose to supply any such equivalent; but you give to the County Court Judge an indirect and temporary power of revising rents; but that power extends only to bankruptcy; and the thrifty, solvent, and honest tenant must pay unjust rents until his little savings are gone. I cannot conceive anything more likely to demoralize the tenants of

Mr. Mundella

Ireland than such a provision. You declare that the thrifty tenant must go on until his savings are exhausted before he can hope for a reduction, whereas the unthrifty and dishonest man can go at once to the Bankruptcy Court and hope to get a reduction of rent. In a case of bankruptcy, we can understand that the Judge should decide how far the bankruptcy was due to the tenant's own conduct; but when the bankruptcy arises from bad seasons—it may be from bad farming—you put into the Bill more extraordinary provisions than have ever been inserted in any other measure ever brought before the House. If the rent exceeds £50 there is to be no relief whatever for the tenant. If his rent is only £49 he may hope for a reduction; but if it happens to be £51 he is entirely outside all chance of it, and is practically beyond the reach of the law. If, from any course whatever, he is able to pay—it may be from his children's earnings, or from some supplementary industry—he must pay as long as his means hold out. If the landlord does not proceed by way of ejectment, but by distress, the tenant can get no relief whatever. If he becomes a bankrupt he may obtain relief.

MR. SPEAKER: I must remind the right hon. Gentleman that he is violating one of the Rules of this House, which is that no hon. Member is entitled to discuss the provisions of a measure which is now before "another place."

MR. MUNDELLA: I am much obliged to you, Sir, for your reminder, and I shall, of course, at once bow to your ruling; but I was about to point out that the remedial proposals of Her Majesty's Government appear to be framed not so much to do simple justice to the Irish tenants as to satisfy the conscience of the English constituencies. I may ask what is the justification for this Coercion Bill of the Government? I do not believe that the settlement of the agrarian question will, of itself, put an end to Irish discontent. But there are other questions which lie deeper than the mere agrarian question. Above all, there is the National Question, and the question of the Local Self-government of the Irish people. Those questions this House will have to deal with sooner or later, and it is the duty of the Government to satisfy the wishes of the Irish people in that direction before they strike at their liberties. We maintain that there is nothing in the present state of crime in Ireland to justify the demand for this Bill. The right hon. Gentleman the Chief Secretary to-night, for the first time, has endeavoured to make out a case for it—I do not think very successfully—and I am sorry that I was not in the House when my hon. Friend the Member for the Rushcliffe Division of Nottinghamshire (Mr. J. E. Ellis) gave to the House, as I understand, a complete, searching, and thorough refutation of the statements made by the right hon. Gentleman the Chief Secretary. But we had a series of authoritative statements on the subject before the right hon. Gentleman opposite took Office—leading up to the time at which he did take Office—which ought to satisfy the House that there is no plea for coercion. On Lord Mayor's Day, the 9th of November last, the Prime Minister stated that the state of things in Ireland had decidedly improved, that outrages were diminished, and that order was being much better maintained. Later than that, the late Chief Secretary (Sir Michael Hicks-Beach)—whose absence from this House I am sure we all regret, and especially the cause of it—stated that during the previous six months outrages had diminished by one-half compared with what they were in the six months before. The right hon. Gentleman added that a better feeling prevailed between landlords and tenants than had existed for many years. Then, again, we come down to the Queen's Speech, and in that Speech it was stated that although there were grave crimes, more or less, in Ireland, those grave crimes were much fewer. We had also a very definite utterance from the noble Lord the Member for South Paddington (Lord Randolph Churchill) as recently as February last. The noble Lord said—

"I see nothing unsatisfactory, always speaking comparatively, and nothing alarming in the present state of Ireland. There has been a good deal of disorder and violent speaking; but the hopeful future of Ireland is that, in spite of all the prophecies of hon. Gentlemen opposite, the country is now perfectly free from crime."

The noble Lord made subsequent references to the state of Ireland which were still stronger—comparing Ireland to a horse which was badly ridden, and declaring that unless it was better ridden in future it might throw its rider. It is quite true that the right hon. Gentleman the Chief Secretary has, in all his speeches, laid much stress upon the prevalence of Boycotting. I am one of those who look upon Boycotting as a great evil — a practice which entails much suffering, and is very hard to endure; but we have the authority of the Prime Minister for saying that Boycotting is not a question which comes within the Crimes Act. The Prime Minister distinctly stated that the Crimes Act could not affect Boycotting, seeing that that is an offence which cannot be dealt with by legislation. It is altogether a matter of local public opinion, and it is impossible to put an end to it by repressive legislation. Well, Sir, this Bill —the Bill we have now under consideration—is really a measure directed against combination, and some of us know what it is to deal with the laws which affect combinations of this kind. It is aimed at combinations, both agrarian and political. We have had some experience of the law of conspiracy in this country when it has been administered by a judge and jury, but it would be nonsense to allow the law of conspiracy—a most technical and complex question—to be administered by the Irish Resident Magistrates. Let us for a moment consider who these Resident Magistrates are. They are the servants of the Executive Government, obeying the orders and asking for orders from Dublin Castle. They are not independent Judges; they are not in any way in the position of Stipendiary Magistrates in England; they are not men trained to the law. I have an authority on that matter which states that a couple of years ago there were in Ireland about 90 Stipendiary Magistrates, of whom 35 were military men, 22 were ex-constabulary officers, two were ex-constabulary clerks, and of the remainder 19 held only temporary appointments terminable at the will of the Viceroy. I would appeal to any man who has any knowledge or experience of the administration of the law whether it is reasonable that we can leave the law of conspiracy and intimidation to be administered by men who, if lawyers, are lawyers without experience, who probably never had to deal with a conspiracy case in their lives, and who if soldiers are without the requisite knowledge. But, at the same time, I would rather deal with soldiers because I am satisfied that they would be men of common sense, and of good feeling, and would be less likely to come to an unjust decision than men possessed with a smattering of legal and technical knowledge, especially if these Resident Magistrates are to administer the law without the assistance of a jury. I conceive that if the law of conspiracy and the law of intimidation are to be administered without a jury in Ireland by the Resident Magistrates the liberty of the Irish people is actually gone. We find how difficult it has been, even with a Judge and jury, to obtain justice for trades unions, and those of us who fought the Trades Unions Bill had a long and painful experience of the manner in which the Stipendiary Magistrates, and even the Judges of the Superior Courts, strained the law of conspiracy, and condemned men to long periods of penal servitude for some act which was then illegal, but which is legal to-day. And now some of the most difficult branches of the law are to be confided to the Irish Resident Magistrates, who are for the most part military men or ex-constabulary officers. Surely if there is to be combination at all, either agrarian or political combination, it is better that it should be open than secret. There is nothing, in my opinion, so dangerous as to suppress combination. All attempts to suppress combination in all ages and in all countries have been negatived by secret conspiracy and crime. What does the examination of history teach us with regard to the suppression of combination? You had secret societies in the Middle Ages, you have had the Carbonari in Italy, and you have now the Nihilists in Russia. Wherever you attempt to suppress combination you will have secret conspiracy and crime. I think it is flung in our teeth that we have become demoralized by association with hon. Members who belong to the National League. I have had some experience of secret combinations, and I am by no means prepared to reproach those who are fighting for freedom of association with being sympathisers with crime. I know that when I first came into this House in 1868 and moved to abolish the Criminal Law Amendment Act, in order to give freedom of association to the working classes of this country—from 1868 to 1875 those of us who took part in that movement were constantly reproached with sympathy with outrage and crime. Noble Lords and right hon. Gentlemen—some who are now in "another place," and others who are at present in this House—reproached me when I introduced this measure for being in sympathy with the Sheffield ratteners. It was stated that I wanted to obtain impunity for the Sheffield rattening, but after the Royal Commission sat in 1874, what did Lord Cross, who was then Home Secretary, do? He took up the very Bill we had introduced for seven years running, and which had been rejected year after year in this House; and he passed a measure which is practically the Magna Charta of the associated members of the working classes of this country. What has been the result? Why, that from that day to this there has never been so little outrage, so little illegality, and so little that employers could complain of in connection with the trade unions of the country. The country is now free from the bad feeling which used to exist between employer and employed, and the relations between the working classes and their employers are more satisfactory in this than any other country in the world. This result has been brought about by sanctioning the association of workmen in unions for their own protection. It was not obtained by repressive legislation, but by legislation of a relaxing character. With respect to the question of coercion, I must make reference to a great name which has been constantly used by certain Gentlemen to defend their position in supporting a Coercion Bill. The noble Lord the Member for Petersfield stated that when we went to the country at the last Election we reproached them with being coercionists, and he says that, therefore, as we told them that they would inevitably be driven to coercion, the result was that they were returned in order that they might support coercive measures. No greater mistake can be committed than that. The noble Lord forgot to tell us that almost every hon. and right. hon. Gentleman opposite, and every Liberal Unionist who came into the House, denied that coercion was an alternative of the measure of last year. We knew perfectly well that if you rejected that measure coercion was inevitable; and I am afraid that this Bill will

Mr. Mundella

not be the "be all" and "end all" of your coercion policy. It is said with respect of Lord Salisbury's speech, that his 20 years of firm government pointedly alluded to coercion. Every hon. Gentleman opposite denied that assertion, and said that coercion was the furthest thing from their thoughts; and that it was only a horrible Liberal Government that would dream of introducing coercion. Great names have been introduced into this House in defence of a Coercion Bill. Hon. Gentlemen on that side of the House, and some hon. Members on this side, are very prone to shelter themselves under the great name of the right hon. Gentleman the Member for Birmingham (Mr. Bright)—they never fail to quote him, when they can, in defence of coercion. They remind me of some of those early Florentine Masters whose works we sometimes see in Italy, and which depict some great saint covering under his mantle a number of peccant souls of all races, all ages, and all creeds. The right hon. Gentleman the senior Member for Birmingham has now the advantage of being quoted on Conservative platforms by hon. Gentlemen who have denounced him all their lives, and have denounced all his works. I should like to know how far they are prepared to follow him in anything except the restriction of the liberty of the Irish people? And so it is with regard to some of our Unionist Liberal Friends. The hon. Member for Inverness (Mr. Finlay) quoted Lord Macaulay, and read an extract from a speech delivered by Lord Macaulay in 1833, in justification of the vote he was about to give. But what were the circumstances under which Lord Macaulay made that speech in 1833? The hon. Gentleman made no statement to show the condition of crime in the country at that time; but Lord Macaulay said that in one county alone, within a few weeks, 60 murders and assaults with intent to murder and 600 burglaries had occurred. He added that, since the previous summer, the slaughter in Ireland had exceeded that of a pitched battle—

"Talk of civil war," he said, "I would rather have lived in any of the civil wars we have had in England during the last 200 years than in some parts of Ireland at the present moment."

Yes, Sir; but is there anything like that state of things to-day in Ireland? The House has been told that, during the past year, there have been 10 homicides in Ireland; whereas Lord Macaulay spoke of 60 murders or assaults with intent to murder in one county alone. Lord Macaulay made another speech in 1844, which the hon. Member for Inverness did not quote; and when he quoted my right hon. Friend the senior Member for Birmingham he showed his willingness to quote him when defending himself from a charge of desiring to impose a restriction upon civil liberty; but when the question of religious liberty, or any other question in connection with which my right hon. Friend has taken a foremost place, comes to the front, I think the hon. Member for Inverness will be found a long way in the rear. Now, I say that, if you pass this Bill, you cannot stop short with the coercive provisions it contains; you must carry the coercion further. At the risk of wearying the House with another quotation, I must read a few lines from a speech of your Predecessor, Sir, in the Chair you now occupy. No shrewder man ever occupied that Chair, none more benevolent, none more honourable. Lord Hampden said—

"The Union as now established has been only maintained through Coercion Acts repeatedly passed by Parliament against the will of the Irish people, and without coercion such a Union could not be maintained."

But he goes further, and says—

"It has been difficult, as I can testify, to carry on the Business of the House of Commons in the face of 40 discontented Members; it will be still more difficult to do so in the face of the larger contingent of 86 discontented Members. It can be done, no doubt; the House of Commons is omnipotent; but this can only be attained by the exercise of coercive laws, not only outside the House against the people of Ireland, but inside the House against the Representatives of Ireland."

We are told that the American people are against you, and that it is in view of the Irish vote. [*Cries of* "No, no!"] I trust that right hon. Gentlemen opposite will be more awake to the facts of the case some day. The best of the American people, as far as I know them —and I know a good deal of them—are against you. I know many of the men who have taken part in the meetings which have been held throughout the United States, and especially in the New England States, and I know that the feeling of the American people is against this Coercion Bill. When I see the names of the leading episcopal clergy of the United States, and such names as those of Russell Lowell, Wendell Holmes, and Senator Hoare, and hundreds of others, I know that they are our best friends, not only in America, but in the world, and that the whole of the enlightened and intelligent sentiment of America is against this Bill. [*Cries of* "No!"] I say yes. You may shut your eyes to the fact; but the time is coming when we must recognize the fact that we are face to face with a difficulty which is not confined to our own shores. Some day or other we shall experience a rude awakening from our determined attitude and our determination to put our foot on the liberties of the Irish people. It was towards the close of the last century, in the course of one of the greatest speeches he ever delivered in this House, that Mr. Burke, in speaking of conciliation with America, referred to the success of the English government in Ireland. He said that for 500 years we had accomplished nothing by means of our arms; but that, having given a Constitution and Parliament to Ireland, that country had become the glory and the strength of Britain. A long time has passed since any hon. Member of this House of Commons has been able to rise in his place and speak of Ireland being the glory and the strength of Britain. On the contrary, she has become our weakness and our shame, and if we are to maintain our position in the councils of the world, if we are to be a strong and united Empire, and to have that real union about which hon. Members opposite speak so much, and I am afraid think so little, we must endeavour to make Ireland our friend, and make her once more the glory and strength of our country.

Mr. DILLON (Mayo, E.): Of all the remarkable speeches which have been delivered in the course of these debates by the new governors of Ireland, I think the speech of this evening is the most remarkable. In that speech the right hon. Gentleman the Chief Secretary for Ireland (Mr. A. J. Balfour) complained of the many weeks of debate already devoted to what he called the broad principles of this Bill. But I will take leave to point out that the debate, as a rule, has not been devoted to the broad principles of the Bill, because those broad principles, in point of fact, have yet to be debated mainly in Committee.

Mr. Mundella

The debate has been devoted to the question, which I venture to say has certainly not been more than adequately discussed, of the circumstances and the condition of Ireland which were brought forward as the justification for the introduction of this Bill. Before referring in detail to the speech of the right hon. Gentleman the Chief Secretary, I wish to direct the attention of the House to two statements made by the right hon. Gentleman this evening, and of which, I think, immediate notice should be taken. In the first place, the right hon. Gentleman the Chief Secretary has once more reiterated that this Bill is to put down crime. Now, I want to know, however, whether on this point the House is to believe the Chief Secretary or the Prime Minister? The other night the Prime Minister delivered a speech containing an authoritative exposition, which I presume we are bound to accept, of the policy and object of the Government, and he most distinctly stated, in language which, if not always prudent, is at least always clearly and distinctly understood, that this Bill is not to put down crime, but to put down certain combinations in Ireland. He emphasized the words "certain combinations," in order to show that what the Government have in view are combinations which are at present known to exist in that country. Lord Salisbury says—

"Our position is that this land war must cease. We have offered to the other House of Parliament a measure, not without hesitation, in order to put a stop to certain combinations. But surely we are not unreasonable in saying that, when we have asked for exceptional measures in order to put a stop to these combinations, some check should be put upon the action of landlords who exasperate their tenants and keep alive such combinations."

I wish to know whether the House is to accept the declaration of the object of the Government from the Prime Minister or from the right hon. Gentleman the Chief Secretary? I most distinctly say that the Irish people are bound to come to the conclusion that the Prime Minister more frankly and more truthfully declares the object and policy of the Government in this measure—that it is not a measure to stop certain combinations which are known to exist in that country. The second declaration of the right hon. Gentleman the Chief Secretary was to the effect that the Government distinctly pledge themselves, and will even give security to the House, that before this Bill is passed into law, or even leaves this House, another measure will be passed by the House of Lords which will secure the tenants of Ireland from an unjust use of power which this Bill will place in the hands of the landlords. I am astonished how any right hon. Gentleman responsible for the government of Ireland can come before this House after what has occurred during the past two weeks and make such a statement as that. We are at least entitled, before we give credence to such a statement, to ask where is the measure of which the right hon. Gentleman was speaking? Because it is certainly not the measure now before another House of Parliament. I have examined the Land Bill of the Government and I have read it, and I think it cannot be repudiated too often by those who take an interest in the welfare of Ireland, and are authorized to speak on behalf of the Irish people. In the name of the tenants of Ireland, I absolutely and utterly repudiate that measure, and I declare that their position would be made worse, instead of better, if that measure were passed into law. That measure bears on it the mark of coming from men who are totally and disgracefully ignorant of the condition of the country which they undertake to legislate for; and it will be only adding yet another stone to the mighty monument of the wretched and broken-down attempts of the English Parliament to legislate for the people of Ireland. It is a fact beyond the possibility of denial that that measure has been met in Ireland with a chorus of disapproval and rejection that is wholly unprecedented in regard to any measure ever proposed for that country, and it is exceedingly difficult to say whether the Irish landlords or the Irish tenants condemn it in the most strong and violent terms. I myself went over to Ireland, and remained there a fortnight, having travelled in the North and other parts of the country; but I did not find that there was a single individual, whether landlord, or land agent, or tenant, who approved of it except the hon. Member for South Tyrone (Mr. T. W. Russell). Yet it has been introduced as a reason for allowing the further progress of the Coercion Bill to put down crime in Ireland. I should like to know where the measure really is

which is to afford protection to the Irish tenants? The tenants declare, through every means they have of making their voice reach Parliament, that the measure now before the other House of Parliament affords them no shadow of protection or of hope, because the whole method of the Bill is calculated to render it entirely worthless, as I shall presently show. Now, Sir, the right hon. Gentleman the Chief Secretary for Ireland stated, at the very outset of his speech, that the Government wish to pass such a measure as will enable them so far to restore law and order in Ireland that the landlords may use the power you give them — pointing over to these Benches. What power could he mean but the one—that law and order should be so far restored in Ireland that the landlords should be able to exact the judicial rents? There was no meaning whatever in what the right hon. Gentleman said, unless he meant to place the landlords of Ireland in that position. The right hon. Gentleman went on to say that the whole amount of our grievance is that the judicial rents fixed before the beginning of 1886 were 12½ per cent too high. I listened with pain and astonishment to the right hon. Gentleman's remarkable assertion, and I was surprised to find that the Government should have taken so little pains to study the evidence as to come down here, at this stage of the proceedings, and inform the House that the whole grievance of the Irish tenants is that the judicial rents have been fixed 12½ per cent too high. Let me refer the right hon. Gentleman to the Report of the Cowper Commission, which is signed exclusively by landlords. What does Lord Cowper say? He uses these words, and they are most remarkable—

"Although we admit that it is undesirable to disturb an arrangement which it was understood would be permanent, yet we cannot put aside the necessities of the Irish tillage farmers; to compel the Irish farmers to sell their working stock in order to pay rent would be fatal to their future prosperity; and should prices continue on the present low scale it would become absolutely necessary to revise the rents judicially fixed prior to the beginning of 1886."

The Commissioners say they cannot put aside the necessities of the Irish farmers; but the right hon. Gentleman the Chief Secretary is prepared to put aside altogether the recommendations of the Commissioners. I contend that, strong as these words are, and they are not all the Government have to go upon, the position of the Government is entirely untenable. I maintain, however, that even these words, strong as they are, utterly inadequately represent the present condition of the Irish farmers. Let me turn, for one moment, to the evidence of the chief valuer of the Irish Land Commission—Mr. Gray—a Yorkshireman, whose appointment upon the Commission was, I believe, received from the outset with the greatest possible dissatisfaction by the tenants of Ireland. What does Mr. Gray say? He was asked by Lord Cowper—

"When you talked of two or three years ago, you had no doubt in your mind, the existence of a period of depression?"

Mr. Gray said—

"I certainly had not; for my part, I thought we had gone through the worst, and I looked forward to the revival of trade. My idea was that there was more to be expected from a revival of trade than from legislative measures."

He was asked if he thought the farming had fallen away in one district in Ireland more than another, and his reply was, that in some districts it had been reduced to a very low pitch, and he added, that they all knew that if the land did not grow a greater amount of produce than in a state of nature, no one could live upon it. He was then asked to give an idea of the fall in the value of farms, and he said that the question was one which he had some difficulty in answering. He had seen some farms in the South and West which he could not see afforded any means of living at all, and in reference to such farms he should say that there was a fall of at least 100 per cent. That is the evidence of the chief valuer of the Irish Land Commission—Mr. Charles Gray. And yet the right hon. Gentleman the Chief Secretary says that his object in this Bill is to give the landlords the opportunity of exacting the rights you have conferred upon them, and to restore a sufficient degree of law and order in Ireland to enable them to exercise and exact those rights. I have already shown what that may result in, and I could show a great deal more if time permitted. I have given an indication of what the real condition of affairs in Ireland is in the opinion of men who are in a position to judge, and whose evidence is absolutely untainted

Mr. Dillon

by any suspicion of partiality towards the Nationalist · Party. Let me turn now to the reductions of rent which have been made on the estates of certain gentlemen to whom I alluded on a previous occasion—namely, the reductions recently made on the estates of Mr. Arthur Murrough Kavanagh, Lord Castletown, and Lord Courtown. I quote them from the last Return of the reductions of judicial rents, and I give them for three reasons—first, because these gentlemen are representative gentlemen; secondly, that it is proof of the necessity of making reductions, although they were only made after a desperate fight in court; and, thirdly, because all three of them wrote to *The Times* the next day, not denying any of the facts, but saying that they intended to appeal as they considered they had been unjustly treated. I will first read the amount of the reductions to show what the condition of affairs must have been. I believe these estates may be taken as typical of many others; secondly, I propose to point out who it was who made the reductions; and lastly, I shall point out that the weight of evidence completely refutes the allegation of these landlords that they were marked out for vengeance by the friends of the National League. On the estate of Lord Courtown the rent of one farm was reduced from £15 8s. 6d. to £8, on another from £67 to £38, on a third from £16 to £8 15s., and on a fourth from £28 to £14 15s. On the estate of Mr. Arthur Murrough Kavanagh the rent on one farm was reduced from £14 to £7 15s., on another from £2 to 12s. 6d., and on a third from £17 17s. to £8 a-year. Upon the estate of Lord Castletown the rent of one farm was reduced from £21 to £14, of another from £33 to £19, of another from £28 to £13, or less than one-half. and upon another from £428 to £380. I quoted these figures a fortnight ago, and the Irish landlords affected by the statement in their defence asserted that the Government Commissioner had acted as our agent, and had marked them down for public vengeance. Now, I will answer that charge. Who was the Commissioner? The gentleman who made the reductions was Mr. Robert Reeves, one of the Sub-Commissioners, himself a County Clare landlord, and a member of a Conservative family. Yet hon. Members opposite have the coolness and audacity to suggest in defence of their conduct that Mr. Reeves acted under our instructions, and marked them down for vengeance. So much for the landlords, and the way they are likely to act towards their tenants if you give them additional power. I will conclude the question of the action of the landlords by quoting a short passage from the evidence of Mr. Edward W. Power—the agent of Lord Clancarty —on whose estate the present Plan of Campaign is enforced. The evidence of Mr. Power was given before the Cowper Commission, and in regard to it I would paraphrase the saying—"Would that mine enemy would write a book," by another—"Would that mine enemy or his agent would only consent to give evidence." Mr. Power stated that he did not think the allegations as to the poverty of the tenants and their inability to pay had any existence generally; but as the Leaders of the Government had appealed to the landlords to give reductions to the tenants last winter, Lord Clancarty felt himself obliged to offer some temporary abatement to show that he had done all that he could. He added, that if the tenants did not pay they deserved no further consideration. He had told Lord Clancarty years ago that if the Government would only assist them the landlords would get their rents. Was there ever such a frank acknowledgment in regard to the policy of the Government in assisting the landlords to put pressure upon the tenants? And this Gentleman also thought that the Government had acted unfairly in going about beseeching the Irish landlords to give reductions of rent to their Irish tenants. I think that, under these circumstances, I am entitled to assume, that if this Bill is passed it will be used by the Irish landlords in the sense in which the right hon. Gentleman the Chief Secretary says that the Government desire to pass it— that is to say, that it will be used by the landlords to exact the rights that are still left to them, and which they often speak of as very slight. It will be used by them to recover rents the Government Commission have declared to be impossible, and destructive of the prosperity of the country if they were attempted to be recovered. This power is to be placed in their hands to enable them to put down all combination among the tenants to refuse to pay

exorbitant rents. In endeavouring to illustrate and justify his argument, the right hon. Gentleman the Chief Secretary fell back on the old and often exploded statement about the cause of evictions in Ireland and the number of evictions. He endeavoured to show that the number of tenants who have been evicted has been exceedingly small; and he then went on to state that crime was not the result of evictions, but that intimidation and crime produced evictions. With regard to the assertion in reference to the smallness of the number of tenants evicted, a more utterly deceptive statement could not possibly be brought before the House. It is perfectly true that the greater number of tenants who were evicted in Ireland up to the 1st of January last were non-judicial tenants, but the right hon. Gentleman, in making his statement, has taken no account whatever of the effects of the pressure put by the Government on estates in Ireland on which great reductions were made last autumn to judicial tenants, and the pressure, also, by which we succeeded in obtaining large reductions. That is only a portion of the case, because the eviction of the judicial tenants is only now commencing. The judicial tenants got some relief from the Land Courts, and would naturally not be the first to break down. They are now, however, rapidly falling into arrear, and, if necessary, I could convince hon. Members that the condition of things that exists with regard to judicial tenants all over Ireland, and especially in the Province of Ulster, can hardly be exaggerated. What is the condition of things on many of the estates in Ulster? Evictions are now becoming frequent; but that is not the worst. On many of the large estates, like the Downshire estates and the Wallace estates, it is found that many of the tenants have fallen into arrear. But what is the course of action usually adopted on a large estate? A man is not evicted at once when he ceases to pay rent, but he is allowed to go on falling into arrear for four, five, or six years before a writ of ejectment is issued against him, because the landlord knows that he has the security of the tenant right; and it frequently happens that by keeping up a continual pressure and threatening to evict, the tenant is induced to give up his holding, and dispose of his tenant right. There-fore a condition of things does exist at this moment in the Province of Ulster of the utmost gravity, so far as the future of the people and the general prosperity of the country are concerned. If you find that on a large estate a con-siderable portion of the tenants are fall-ing rapidly into arrear, and are threat-ened with eviction, you will have to face a very serious condition of things. Very recently—only about 10 days ago — I chanced to be in the County of Down, in the very heart of the Downshire estate. In the town of Banbridge I found that the number of ejectment processes for hear-ing was 78 in one session, and of these only six were defended. That is a most portentous and extraordinary fact, and this is taking place, too, in a district where there has been no suspicion of agitation on the part of the National League. These 72 undefended eject-ment processes have occurred, as I stated, in a district where there never has been any agitation at all ; and I have been as-sured by those who know the country that this is only a picture, not alone of the condition of the Downshire Estate and the Wallace Estate, but of the sur-rounding estates. Many of these men have been waiting and hoping for relief year after year, and yet this Bill affords them no prospect of relief whatever. I have gathered from evidence to which it was impossible to shut my eyes or doubt, that if no relief be given, the tenants of Ulster will, within a very short time, be in the same condition as the tenantry of the West and South of Ireland, and will be compelled to have recourse to the same methods for relieving their dis-tress. [*Laughter.*] I am afraid that the hon. Gentleman opposite who laughs may find it anything but a laughing matter when the crisis comes. I am in-formed that the tenantry of the Duke of Abercorn, of Lord Castlereagh, and of Sir Richard Wallace have met already and have threatened agitation. At every single meeting we had on the estates I have mentioned, the Plan of Campaign was alluded to with cheers, and was threatened to be used against the land-lords if they did not accede to the wants of the tenants. I have no doubt that the Members from Ulster have in their mind's eye this fact, that this movement, if not dealt with at once, will be much more difficult to deal with in the future.

Mr. Dillon

I can, therefore, easily understand their anxiety to get the Bill through, to enable them to deal with combinations of ten-antry in Ulster. I believe—I am firmly convinced—that if this Bill were per-mitted to go through the House rapidly, we should have no security whatsoever that any measure will be passed through either this or the other House giving protection to the tenants, or that this measure will not be used as an instru-ment of coercion by the landlords. What did the right hon. Gentleman the Chief Secretary say as the only consolation he could afford us regarding the other Bill—even on his theory that the Bill in its present shape, or under Amendments which have been foreshadowed, will give protection to the tenants? He said—

"Hon. Gentlemen will have an opportunity of rejecting the Coercion Bill on the third read-ing should the other Bill, when it comes to this House, not satisfy them."

Not satisfy whom ?—the majority of this House. But do the Irish tenants be-lieve that they can trust their interests and look for protection to the majority of this House? They have, unfortu-nately, more evidence than is necessary to convince them that that protection means simply no protection whatsoever. Now, I wish to say a word with refer-ence to the contention the Chief Secre-tary put forward repeatedly in the course of his speeches in these debates, that evictions have not been the cause of crime, but, on the other hand, intimida-tion and crime and outrage has been the cause of the evictions. Sir, I utterly and absolutely deny that statement; and, furthermore, I say that there is not a shadow of foundation for it. What are the facts of the case ? I have here with me a summary which I got drawn up the other day—a complete analysis —of all the cases in which I was instru-mental in getting the weapon of combi-nation—namely, the Plan of Campaign, put into operation in Ireland. It is to that weapon the right hon. Gentleman alludes, when the right hon. Gentle-man speaks of "intimidation, crime, and outrage." The number of estates on which the Plan of Campaign has been used is 75. It is difficult to say exactly the number of families affected by it; but I should think the number would be 30,000 or 40,000. Well, on the whole of these 75 estates on which we have used the weapon, with the single exception of that of the Marquess of Lansdowne, no evictions have taken place; and I can point to hundreds of families who unquestionably would have been evicted but for the Plan of Campaign. There would have been wholesale evictions. The case of the Marquess of Lansdowne's clearances is the only case of real eviction in the whole of Ireland which can be traced to the operations of the Plan of Campaign or to combination, and even in that case a great many families who have been evicted will be back in their homes before the end of the week. There is no foundation, then, for the statement of the Chief Secretary. On the contrary, when we turn to the Returns of eviction, we find that in those places where the League is weakest, and where the Plan of Campaign has not been put in force, evictions have raged with the most unchecked fury. In the County of Kerry we find that on not one estate has the Plan of Campaign been adopted. It was tried in the case of one estate, and did not prove successful—that is to say, the tenants did not fall into the combination. In the County of Kerry there were 303 evicted within the past three months—more than four times as many as in any other county in Ireland; and Kerry is the only county in the South of Ireland in which I have not operated. I would pursue that argument throughout the whole of Ireland, and so strongly do the figures work out, that you might almost say that evictions have been numerous in Ireland in inverse ratio to the numbers of families that have been banding together in the Plan of Campaign. So that there is not a shadow or a shade of foundation for the statement that evictions are due to intimidation or combination amongst the tenants. The exact reverse is the case, and I challenge any English Member to go over to Ireland, in the next Vacation, to make investigations on the spot, and to see if I am not speaking the absolute truth. There is another point I would refer to. When the right hon. Gentleman was endeavouring to make out a case for this Coercion Bill, he alluded to the condition of the County of Mayo; and, although he has not alluded to that at any length again to-night, I cannot resist saying a word as

to that, for two reasons—first of all, because he described that county as being in a particularly disorderly and tumultuous state. He used the words of a learned Judge who declared, at the last Mayo Assizes, that the condition of Mayo differed in a very small degree, if at all, from a condition of civil war. The second reason I desire to refer to the subject is because Mayo is the county I represent. Furthermore, I desire to point to this matter as a typical instance of the reliability of statements extracted from the charges of Judges, upon which the right hon. Gentleman the Chief Secretary confessed he chiefly based his case for this Bill. We were told this county was in a condition, as well as I recollect the words, little, if at all, differing from civil war. Now, I have here some facts relating to the condition of Mayo, which I think will surprise hon. Members of this House. I have, first of all, the evidence of Mr. Francis Blackburn Henn, Resident Magistrate, who resides in Ballina, and has under his charge the police of the northern part of Mayo. He was examined before the Royal Commission in October last, and this was the evidence he gave. He was asked—"How are rents being paid in your district?" His reply was—"I must say satisfactorily." After some considerable cross-examination, Lord Cowper said—

" Your district seems to be in such a satisfactory state, that I do not think I have anything more to ask you."

" Yes, satisfactory," said Mr. Henn, "I am glad to say." That is the testimony of the Resident Magistrate, the head of the police in the Northern Division of the County of Mayo, a county, recollect, that we are told is in a state little, if anything, differing from civil war. I can speak positively for the Eastern Division of Mayo, and I can say that it has not been for many years in a condition of greater freedom from crime than it is in at present. With the exception of one serious riot at Charlestown last spring, there has been absolutely no crime, disorder, or interference with law for the whole of the winter and spring. I turn to the statistics of crime in Mayo, and it takes away my breath to lay them side by side with the speech of Judge Lawson, in making his charge in the month of April. The report of agrarian outrages in the County of Mayo, from the 1st January to 31st March, 1887, shows that the total agrarian offences for the first three months of this year were 12, of which seven were threatening letters, leaving five outrages in a county with a population of 230,000 human beings. These are the statistics for the three months—Murder and manslaughter, none; firing at the person, none; attempts to murder, none; conspiracy to murder, none; assaults on the police, none —and this in a county which is in a state of civil war—for three months, no assault on the police; aggravated assault, one; assaults on bailiffs or process-servers, none—and if there is any division in which the Irish people are inclined to indulge, if they are at all disorderly, it is assaults on bailiffs and process-servers, who are to them about the most obnoxious individuals in the country; and if you want to know whether the country is absolutely and phenomenally quiet, you would ask whether there have been any assaults on bailiffs and process-servers—robbery, none; taking or holding forcible possession, one; intimidation, otherwise than threatening letter, none. That is in a county where intimidation so reigns, that no man, according to the learned Judge, is safe, and the ordinary operations of the law are prevented. No officer of the law was assaulted—neither police, process-server, nor bailiff, nor was any man intimidated, according to the Police Report for these three months. I leave it to any fair-minded man to judge what kind of credence is to be given to Judges' charges, when we have the evidence of Official Returns that this is the state of things. When I heard the Chief Secretary talk about the condition of Mayo, I hardly knew what to make of it, because it is a county I represent, one I frequently reside in, and one which I know to be more peaceable than any district with which I am acquainted in England. I alluded to Mayo a little aside from the main part of my argument, because I think it is almost like throwing water on a drowned rat to try and make any further case against the Government, so far as this Bill is based on crime. The Government only base their case on five counties, and this is one; and I, therefore, contend that having shown that the actual condition of one of the counties is a condition of peace and quiet, it is sufficient to dispose entirely of the other four. The Chief

Mr. Dillon

Secretary declared that the object of the Bill was to enable landlords to get the few rights that were left to them by the late Government, and that, to my mind, condemned his Bill, not only from one point of view, but from the point of view of every honest and liberal and kindly man in England.

MR. A. J. BALFOUR: I am sorry to have to interrupt the hon. Gentleman; but he has made that assertion four or five times. I never said that.

MR. DILLON: I have made the assertion several times I confess, because I consider it of enormous importance. I took down the right hon. Gentleman's words at the time. If he withdraws them, of course——

MR. A. J. BALFOUR: I do not withdraw what I said. In what I said, I was arguing upon the statement of the right hon. Gentleman opposite, and I said, on his statement, that was the result.

MR. DILLON: That certainly alters the matter. It slightly alters the character of the statement; but still, I think, from the statement of the Prime Minister, I am entitled to assume that that is the object of the Government. His contention that the grievance which we complained of, and put forward as a reason for not passing this Bill until we were secure of the removal of that grievance, was utterly insignificant, as argument for the delay of a measure of this character shows to me that he must still be completely ignorant of the real condition of affairs in Ireland. I say again, at the risk of repetition, that it would be difficult, in my mind, to use language to exaggerate the position of the Irish farmers; and I say, that the grievance which we complain of, and which, putting aside altogether the question of the right of self-government, on the Unionist theory, we are entitled to get remedied by this House, one of the greatest and most vast that a people can suffer from. It is a grievance touching the lives and the existence of great multitudes of our people. It is a grievance—and, remember, this has been stated before—which has reached such a pitch that it has now become actually intolerable. What is the condition of things in Ireland to-day? You have tens of thousands—I am not sure that I should be incorrect if I said you have 100,000 families in Ireland, who are face to face with absolute desperation—who are face to face with desperation, and see in the Land Bill of the Government, no prospect, nor any promise of relief from their present position, who are told, that in order even to seek relief from that Bill—a hope of relief which I know will be absolutely delusive—they must exhaust their means, and do what, in spite of all the hard words that are used towards Irish tenants, they still consider a disgrace—namely, become bankrupt and slaves to the County Court Judge, and plunge themselves into what is hateful and dreadful to every agricultural tenant in the world—the meshes of the law. I say these people are in such a condition that they ought to excite the compassion and sympathy of every Government in the world. The population of Ireland at the present moment is flying from the country at a rate unparalleled in its history. So great and so terrible is the effect of the depression, and so gloomy is the prospect, that though our population has sunk by 250,000 within the last five, seven, or eight years—a thing unknown in any other country in Europe—and, at the present moment, all the ships that the Liverpool lines can put on, carry away our young people—the best blood of Ireland—as they crowd into the ports seeking the means of emigration. The heart of Ireland is sick and weary of waiting, and if you pass this Bill, and, at the same time, give the people such a measure of relief, such a contemptible mockery as the Bill which has originated in "another and a suitable place," the people of Ireland will turn away in absolute despair, and take refuge, some of them in America, and those who have the courage to remain at home in the only thing they have hope in—namely, combination in some shape or another; and if you do not allow them to combine openly, of course they will do so in secret.

MR. FLYNN (Cork, N.): I rise to support the Amendment of the hon. and learned Gentleman the Member for Dumfries (Mr. Reid), and I must say, at the outset, I am surprised that we have had nothing like an adequate reply to the question, why this drastic measure should go into Committee. I think we had a right to expect some sort of reply to the Amendment which has been placed on the Paper. The hon. Gentleman the Member for East Mayo (Mr. Dillon), just

before resuming his seat, drew the attention of the House to the present alarming condition of Ireland. Ireland is in such a condition at the present moment that she does not require coercive measures; she is in such a condition as to require prompt and immediate remedial measures of the largest and most extensive application. My hon. Friend has alluded to the emigration which is taking place from Ireland, and I contend that it is a blot upon English statesmanship of to-day that this emigration should occur. It is a disgrace to the Legislature of this country to find that, at the present moment, while the people of Ireland—the young people of Ireland—are hurrying from their native land, unable to find homes or employment, this Parliament should be engaged in passing measures, not to remedy their condition and improve the resources of the country, not to make the land one in which employment can be found, but in seeking to repress Constitutional agitation, and in putting an end to liberty. It is a sad, sorry, and sickening sight. Hon. and right hon. Gentlemen on the Front Treasury Bench may, from the attitude of their superior knowledge, sneer at and "pooh, pooh" the evidences of sympathy with Ireland which come from all parts of the civilized world; but the criticisms of the civilized world are passed upon the proposals of the Government, because all countries are now in possession of the facts that are occurring here. Within the last few weeks, Queenstown, which is the principal Irish port for emigration, has been black with people, not old and apparently broken-down people, but with decently clad young men and young women, who, under a happier and any normal condition of things, ought to be able to find employment at home, and ought to be able to contribute to the development of the industries of Ireland. Sir, the Government seek to deny that this measure has any connection with the collection of excessive rents; but we say that is the very spirit and essence of the Bill now before the House. And, Sir, we will prove that, not by declamatory remarks, not by soaring into the realms of imaginative figures, into which the right hon. Gentleman the Chief Secretary so often soars, but by a hard reference to solid facts—with reference to the Report of the Royal Commission that the Govern-

[First Night.]

ment themselves appointed. Sir, I think that Members on this side of the House are perfectly justified, before going into this case, in laying before the House the fact that Lord Cowper's Commission was, in its composition and appointment, a Commission undoubtedly of landlords. We are also justified in laying stress on the fact that the only Member of the Commission who was not either in profession or in sympathy, identified with the landlord interest, was a Liberal Unionist, who has presented a Report to which the Government has paid not the slightest attention; and to which they attach not the smallest importance. Sir, the right hon. Gentleman the Chief Secretary seemed to be inclined to-night not to agree with the statement that outrages and disorder proceed as naturally as any cause follows effect from eviction and rack-renting in certain districts in Ireland. But Returns which have been placed in the hands of Members lately show most conclusively that we have only to refer to the figures, which illustrate the present condition of the most rack-rented county in all Ireland, and that is Kerry, to prove our case. Undoubtedly, Kerry swells to a very large and undue proportion the list of outrages. In the Returns lately to hand, we find that in the quarter ending 31st of March last, out of 1,007 evictions, that unhappy county furnished 306, or, practically, one-third. Thirty per cent of the evictions which have taken place, therefore, in all Ireland in the present quarter, or the quarter just ended, took place in that county, and the evictions which took place in that county were more than half, more than 57 per cent of those that occurred in the entire wide Province of Munster. We say these figures establish to the mind of every reasonable man a clear and distinct connection between evictions and outrage. Let us turn to that which illustrates the present condition of the tenantry with regard to rent. I observe that at the last sitting of the Kerry and Clare Sub-Commission a large number of cases were brought on for hearing. The right hon. Gentleman the Chief Secretary for Ireland stated this evening—and I do not know from what source he draws his information—that the Reports show that there was a fall of about 12½ per cent in the price of agricultural produce.

The Cowper Commission reported that there was a fall of 18½ per cent. Last week the average reductions made in the rents by the Sub-Commission were from 50 to 60 per cent. In one case— Captain Fagan, landlord; Tim Minahan, tenant—the old rent was £33 10*s*., and it was reduced to £16—that is to say, the tenant had been paying, in the estimation of the Commissioners, 100 per cent over the value of his farm. I have other cases here of a similar kind. On Lord Kenmare's estate several cases were adjudicated upon, and the reductions made averaged from 35 to 50 per cent. What do these figures show? They show that the rack-renting in Kerry has exceeded all belief, and it was not until it was proved by figures before the Sub-Commission that the real state of the case became known. A large number of evictions have taken place in Kerry, and it does seem to me the Government are taking a most unwise course, if they are sincere in their desire to restore law and order, in introducing a measure of this kind in the face of circumstances of the nature I have described. Sir, in the course of this evening's debate, the National League has been referred to as a fruitful source of intimidation; and I should like to be allowed for a few moments—and it will only be for a few moments—to refer to a case in my own constituency, which illustrates where evidence has been given before the Cowper Commission with regard to these cases of Boycotting and intimidation, how groundless the majority of such cases are. In discussing the question, Sir, a few nights ago, the hon. and gallant Gentleman the Member for North Armagh (Colonel Saunderson) referred to the case known as the Troy case in my constituency. He referred to it at considerable length from what I have heard. I was not present when he spoke; but from the report I have seen of his speech, it is evident he drew his information from those very veracious pamphlets published by a body known as the Irish Loyal and Patriotic League. He referred to this case of Troy, and seemed to make great capital out of it. He stated that this man Troy had been Boycotted through the agency of the National League— that he had been subjected to all sorts of intimidation, that his horse had been poisoned, and that he had been violently

Mr. Flynn

ejected from a meeting at Liscarrol, which he had attended for the purpose of making public his grievance. I should like to lay all the facts before the House in a few words. In the first place, this alleged case of Boycotting arose from the fact that there was a family dispute between this man Troy and the real owner of a farm. Troy had, under false pretences, got possession of the farm, until the children of the owner, who was a lunatic, came of age—or rather until the eldest son of the then lunatic came of age. The consideration for which Troy obtained possession of the farm was the payment of £100. When the young man came of age, £100 was offered to Troy, and he was expected to relinquish the farm; but he distinctly declined to do so. Thereupon, very naturally, a large number of the neighbours and friends sympathized with this young man—whose name was Burke. They said that Troy had acted unfairly and dishonestly, and to my mind they had a perfect right to take the course which they then adopted. They refused to have any communication with Troy—they refused to hold any intercourse with him until he consented to do what they required. They required him to make honest restitution. It was said, in the course of the hon. and gallant Gentleman's speech, that this man's horse was poisoned, but that was not the fact. The horse died from overwork, and when the charge was brought before the branch of the National League in the district, they offered to pay the expense of a veterinary surgeon, in order that the question might be examined into further. I have, in my possession, a letter written by the landlord of this very farm, concerning which this great dispute arose—this dispute of which the hon. and gallant Member made such a flourish of trumpets a few nights ago. The landlord says that the man who claims the farm is his tenant, and that he is anxious that he should pay his rent. The hon. and gallant Gentleman referred in strong language to the fact that this man Troy attended a public meeting for the purpose of making his grievance known to the public and speaking from the platform, and that he was violently ejected from the platform. But the truth of the matter is, that Troy attended at the meeting, and having hired a number of ruffians and primed

them with drink, he actually assaulted the Chairman of the meeting; instead of his being the injured party, he was the cause of the meeting being broken up. I do not wish to trouble the House with accounts of this kind, my desire being simply to show on what substantial grounds alleged cases of Boycotting are brought forward to show how terrible is the state of crime existing in Ireland. I referred a moment ago to the recent reductions in rents in Kerry; and I have here a Report issued within the last few days by the Sub-Commission which sat for the purpose of revising them. I find that the reductions range from 55 to 60 per cent. If this Bill passes, unaccompanied by remedial legislation of a character very different from that which is before the other House, I ask what will be the actual condition of the vast majority of the tenants? It is obvious that these people, because they cannot pay their rents, and have fallen into arrears, will be evicted wholesale; and I say that the passage of this Bill into law will put a premium on evictions, and render impossible any attempt at accommodation on the part of the tenants; thus, instead of tending to the restoration of law and order, its effect will be exactly opposite. It will make matters far worse than they now are by adding a keen sense of irritation to that of injury, under which the Irish people at present labour. We are told that this measure is to be accompanied by a remedial measure now being proceeded with in "another place." It is not competent to us to discuss the details of that remedial measure; but from what we have seen of it, I think that the effect of it will be to drive tenants to seek salvation from ruin. We are told a humorous story of persons who committed suicide to save themselves from slaughter; and I think the Irish tenants must seek ruin by the Bankruptcy Court before they can hope for any relief from the present intolerable condition of things. I hold that not to be an inaccurate version of the legislation proposed in "another place;" and I can only say that the Irish Representatives, unless the Bill be largely altered and improved in several respects, will be forced to offer it every opposition in their power, and, in doing so, they will be simply discharging their duty to the people of Ireland. I am sorry to see that, at the present time, evictions are

[First Night.]

very numerous in Ireland; and if the Government would pay attention to the Report of their own Commission, if they would pay attention to the work at present going on in the Sub-Commissioners' Courts all over Ireland, they will be compelled to acknowledge that these evictions are unjust, and that a Bill, such as this before the House, will tend to heighten that injustice. We have heard a great deal of the sacredness of judicial rents. Now, I find that, in the past week, over 200 persons were evicted on an estate in Queen's County, because of the non-payment of rents; but when I compare those rents with a valuation founded on the present state of things, they are 50 per cent, and in some few cases 60 per cent, in excess. What relief do you offer these men? None whatever, until they become bankrupts. When the measure I have referred to comes before this House we shall be at liberty to go into it, and prove to the satisfaction of the House how illusory are its provisions, and how utterly powerless they are to deal with the state of things now existing in Ireland. The rents are admitted to be too high, and yet the Government will not carry out the recommendations of their own Land Commission. Do they seriously imagine that, by placing more power in the hands of Resident Magistrates, and almost absolute power in the hands of the Lord Lieutenant of Ireland, they can remedy a state of things such as has been shown to exist? Why, it is an insult to the common sense of the country to say so. Mr. Knipe, who is a distinguished dissentient from the other Commissioners, made a Report, to which I think this House ought to pay considerable attention. We must remember that he is not a landlord, but a large tenant farmer having practical knowledge of land; and he recommends, not that you should introduce coercive measures, or amend the Criminal Law for the purpose of putting down combinations or organizations; but that you should shorten the judicial term, and that you should deal, through the Courts, at once with judicial rents which are admittedly too high. This Bill will only tend to introduce a greater state of exasperation than exists at present; and I cannot see how any responsible Government or Party of politicians cannot, in the present state of things, find no better

Mr. Flynn

remedy than this Bill, added to a promise of remedial legislation of the character to which reference has been made. I trust the House will pause before it goes into Committee on this Bill. I know, however, that any words I can offer will have very little weight with the Government or their supporters. No matter how much we recall to their minds the speeches they formerly made against coercion, they seem callous on the subject, and proof against all such reminders. We, however, on these Benches are not the keepers of their consciences, and I shall not pursue that subject any further. I have not the honour of knowing the hon. Member for the Houghton Division of Durham (Mr. Wood); but I assure all Liberals who supported him at the recent Election that at every meeting in the Division he was against coercion, and made it one of his strongest points on the platforms last summer. I ask hon. Gentlemen opposite to bear in mind that it is no light task which the Government undertook when, in defiance of the 86 Representatives whom the Irish people have sent to this House, they persist in forcing on them this measure. We, at least, claim to know Ireland's wants better than the Government, and, certainly, better than their supporters; but it seems, nevertheless, that our voices are to be drowned and our protests disregarded. This is the first time that the great bulk of the Liberal Party have been opposed to coercion. I am sick of the argument used with reference to the position of the Liberal Party in this respect, and I do not see the utility, at this stage of the proceedings, of bandying across the floor of the House charges of inconsistency as to what was done in 1871 and 1882. The Liberal Party acknowledge that they have turned their back on the hateful policy of coercion; and, in doing so, they have taken a statesmanlike course. While the debate on the Procedure Rules was going forward in this House, there was one argument which repeatedly came from the other side, on the question of the Conservative advocacy of the closure. Hon. Gentlemen opposite said—"We know much better now; four or five years have passed, and we are in a better position to judge." This is exactly the argument which the Liberal Party are entitled to use with reference to the present proposals of the Government. Coercion has been tried, and, notwithstanding what has been said by the right hon. Gentleman the Member for West Birmingham (Mr. J. Chamberlain), it has failed. Is it sufficient for the Government that it should realize the aspiration of Lord Cowper, in seeking to drive discontent beneath the surface? If so, is it a condition of things which any Government could look upon as satisfactory, or a condition of things which any great political Party in the country will be glad to see maintained? I contend that discontent ought not to exist, and considerations of public duty and safety have sunk to a very low ebb, when the highest ideal which the Government can propose to Parliament and the country is, that they should drive discontent below the surface, and overthrow all Constitutional agitation in Ireland. The Government profess to be very indignant when they are accused of designing by this Bill to repress lawful combination. But what else do you mean? You entrust all the powers of the Bill to the Lord Lieutenant, who is to say what is or is not a dangerous association; and you entrust the punishment of members of such associations to Resident Magistrates who are dependent on the Lord Lieutenant for their position, pay, and promotion. Considering the gravity of the position in Ireland, and the far-reaching nature of these proposals, I am entitled to recall the fact that the Lord Lieutenant of Ireland has but recently escaped from a severe controversy with his own tenants, and that it is exceedingly probable, unless he alters the tone he adopted a short time ago, that he may be engaged in litigation with them. Can he be said to be an impartial judge in cases of this character? We cannot forget that the hon. and gallant Gentleman who has recently found a resting-place on the Front Treasury Bench (Colonel King-Harman) is a convicted rack-renter. I do not want, more than is necessary, to cast the right hon. and gallant Gentleman's misfortunes in his face; but we have a right to prove that those who are anxious for the passing of this measure are themselves interested, to a large extent, in the suppression of all combinations of the Irish people against rack-rents. We ask the Government to pause in the steps they are taking; and, at the same time, remind them that they would not be able to pass this measure at all were it not for the support of some Members who sit on the Opposition Benches. But, Sir, under happier conditions, we should ask the Government to pause—we would ask them to reflect on the futility of the step they are taking. I would warn them, Sir, if they hope by the provisions of this Bill, no matter how stringently administered, to break down what we call the national spirit of the Irish people, that they are greatly and grossly mistaken. If they hope to terrorize or intimidate the Representatives of the Irish people from defending their lawful and just rights in all possible events, they are equally mistaken; and they are most mistaken of all, Sir, when they think that they add to the happiness of the Irish people, or to the strength of this Empire, or to the strength of the Union, by a measure so ill-omened, and a policy so mistaken.

Motion made, and Question, "That the Debate be now adjourned,"—(*Mr. Handel Cossham,*)—put, and *agreed to.*

Debate *adjourned* till *To-morrow.*

POLICE FORCE ENFRANCHISEMENT BILL.—[BILL 17.]

(*Mr. Burdett-Coutts, Sir Henry Selwin-Ibbetson, Mr. Whitmore, Mr. Radcliffe Cooke, Sir Albert Rollit, Mr. Howard Vincent, Lord Claud Hamilton, Colonel Laurie.*)

COMMITTEE.

Bill *considered* in Committee.

(In the Committee.)

MR. WHITMORE (Chelsea): I wish to say two or three words in support of a clause which I desire to add to the Bill. I have drawn up the provision with the view of meeting a difficulty which I think must arise in the operation of the Bill. It has been held, in the case of soldiers who otherwise would be entitled to vote, that if they had been absent from their qualifying premises in the course of their duty, and if, in attempting to return home, they would be committing a breach of a legal obligation, that by that fact they would be disqualified and ousted from the Register. I think the same legal doctrine should apply to policemen; and as it must often be the case that they must be compelled to absent themselves, in pursuit of their legal duties, from their qualifying premises in many ways, I think that to meet the possible difficulty it would be well to insert this clause—

" A person otherwise entitled to be registered as a voter at Parliamentary elections in respect of the occupation of a dwelling-house shall be deemed an inhabitant occupier thereof as tenant, notwithstanding his temporary absence therefrom and in the execution of duty as a police officer during a part of the qualifying period not exceeding four months."

I beg to move the insertion of that clause in page 1, after line 11.

New Clause (Registration in case of temporary absence of police officer on duty,) — (*Mr. Whitmore*,) — *brought up,* and read the first time.

Clause read a second time, and *added* to the Bill.

Bill *reported;* as amended, to be considered upon *Monday* next, and to be *printed.* [Bill 240.]

MOTIONS.

COMMONS REGULATION (EWER) PROVISIONAL ORDER BILL.

On Motion of Mr. Stuart-Wortley, Bill to confirm the Provisional Order for the regulation of Ewer Common, situated in the parish of Alverstoke, in the county of Southampton, in pursuance of a Report of the Land Commissioners for England, *ordered* to be brought in by Mr. Stuart-Wortley and Mr. Secretary Matthews.

Bill *presented,* and read the first time. [Bill 237.]

COMMONS REGULATION (LAINDON) PROVISIONAL ORDER BILL.

On Motion of Mr. Stuart-Wortley, Bill to confirm the Provisional Order for the regulation of Laindon Common, situated in the parish of Laindon, in the county of Essex, in pursuance of a Report from the Land Commissioners for England, *ordered* to be brought in by Mr. Stuart-Wortley and Mr. Secretary Matthews.

Bill *presented,* and read the first time. [Bill 238.]

METROPOLIS MANAGEMENT ACTS AMENDMENT (WESTMINSTER) BILL.

Read a second time, and *committed* to the Select Committee on the Metropolis Management Acts (No. 2) Bill.

Ordered, That all Petitions against the Bill, presented not later than three clear days before the sitting of the Committee, be referred to the Committee ; and that such of the Petitioners as pray to be heard by themselves, their Counsel, or Agents, be heard against the Bill, and Counsel heard in support of the Bill.

Ordered, That it be an instruction to the Committee that they have power to consolidate

Mr Whitmore

this Bill and the Metropolis Management Acts Amendment (No. 2) Bill into one Bill.

WAYS AND MEANS.

CUSTOMS AND INLAND REVENUE BILL.

Resolutions [April 25] *reported,* and *agreed to.*

Ordered, That it be an Instruction to the Gentlemen appointed to prepare and bring in a Bill upon the Resolution reported from the Committee of Ways and Means on the 22nd day of this instant April, and then agreed to by the House, that they do make provision therein, pursuant to the said Resolutions.

Bill *presented,* and read the first time. [Bill 241.]

House adjourned at One o'clock.

HOUSE OF COMMONS,

Wednesday, 27th April, 1887.

MINUTES.] — PRIVATE BILL (*by Order*) — *Third Reading*—West Lancashire Railway, and *passed.*

PUBLIC BILLS — *Ordered* — *First Reading* — Education (Scotland) Acts Amendment (No. 2) * [242].

Second Reading—Mining Leases (Cornwall and Devon) * [146], *referred to Select Committee on* Stannaries Act (1869) Amendment * [147].

Report of Select Committee—Bankruptcy Offices (Sites).*

Committee— Criminal Law Amendment (Ireland) [217] [*Second Night*], *debate further adjourned.*

PRIVATE BUSINESS.

WEST LANCASHIRE RAILWAY BILL (*by Order.*)

THIRD READING.

Order for Third Reading read.

Motion made, and Question proposed, "That the Bill be now read the third time."

MR. WOOTTON ISAACSON (Tower Hamlets, Stepney): Since I last had the honour of addressing the House in opposition to this Bill I have received a number of letters from the first preference shareholders denying in the strongest terms the paragraph in the Circular that was sent out by the solicitors of this Railway Company, stating that they had a majority of three-fourths of the first and second preference shareholders in support of this Bill. I find, Sir, that the second preference shares are held in great part by the Chairman, for which the Company received no consideration whatever, and £66,000 has been paid in direct violation of the Companies Acts. The directors are personally responsible for this, and, as a matter of fact, the proceeding is what one may term, in every sense of the word, diametrically opposed to the interest of the public. This £66,000 is included in the £168,000 owing by the Company. At the meeting where it was stated that the first and second preference shareholders gave their consent to the issue of this new stock, it appears that the first preference shareholders were not in attendance at all, and that the resolutions at the meeting were actually carried by the Chairman's vote for the second preference shares. There is another matter to which attention should be drawn, and that is, at the annual, or rather at the half-yearly meeting, only the ordinary shareholders had the power of voting, and the first and second preference shareholders had no power whatever. On these grounds, in addition to what I stated on the last occasion, I implore the House not to give its consent to the passing of this Bill. If it does, it will be giving its consent to the passing of a Bill under which the British public cannot, under any circumstances, see their money back, whatever they subscribe to the amount required. On the last occasion, as the House will remember, I was interrupted by the hon. Gentleman the Member for Hythe (Sir Edward Watkin) and the hon. Member for Devonport (Mr. Puleston), who held a sort of brief from the solicitors of the Company. He also supported the Bill in a manner——

MR. PULESTON (Devonport): I should like to know whether the hon. Gentleman is in Order in saying that I held a brief from the solicitors of the Company. I explained in the House exactly what my position was in the matter, that I had no interest in the Bill direct or indirect; nor do I know the shareholders.

MR. SPEAKER: The hon. Member will withdraw the expression.

MR. WOOTTON ISAACSON: By all means. I had no wish to say anything hurtful to the hon. Gentleman's feelings; but I did feel a little surprised that the hon. Member should come forward and support the Bill when neither of the hon. Members whose names are on the back of it—namely, the hon. Gentleman the Member for Preston (Mr. Hanbury) and the hon. Gentleman the Member for Southport

(Mr. Curzon)—did so. I thought it extraordinary that the defence of the Bill should be left to the hon. Member for Devonport, who knows nothing about the case. I certainly felt that he was hardly the right Member to support a Bill of this kind. For myself, I have only one motive in trying to get this Bill thrown out, and that is the public good. In opposing the Bill I am only doing what I am sent here for. I only hope the House will see the necessity of not supporting the Bill, and will not permit it to be read a third time.

MR. PULESTON (Devonport): The hon. Gentleman, just before he sat down, said he was opposing the Bill for the public good, and that in the course he is taking he is only discharging a duty he was sent here to perform. Well, what right had he to attribute other motives to other hon. Members? As I have said, I have no interest in this matter either directly or indirectly. I came here understanding that the Bill was unopposed. The Chairman of Committees, on the last occasion, gave strong reasons why the Bill should pass, and he explained fully, that though certain conditions were in the Bill it was left to the Company to decide whether they would accept those conditions or not. So that by no possibility can the Bill have an injurious effect upon anyone concerned. It was explained fully that the personal interest the hon. Gentleman has in the railway was not touched —that his priority was not to be interfered with in any way. The hon. Gentleman has no title whatever to come here and claim the virtue of supporting or opposing a Bill in which he is personally interested as "a public duty," and then attribute to an hon. Member, who has no interest whatever in the matter, interested motives. I never heard such an argument in this House. When I opened my remarks on the last occasion I took pains especially to express regret that I felt myself in opposition to the hon. Gentleman—a courtesy which I supposed he would have appreciated. So much for that. I must say it seems to me a very unusual course for the hon. Member to oppose the Bill again, seeing that on the last occasion he did not get a single hon. Member to support him, and you ruled, Sir, that he could not vote on the Bill, but that there was nothing to prevent him from speaking in opposition to it. Not a single Member got up to say a word in his behalf, everyone else, including the Chairman, in explaining the provisions, holding that the Bill was to support a valuable public enterprise, give public value to that which had not hitherto been able to pay, and giving powers to a Company to proceed with a work, which I believe to be a great public improvement. One party, I understand, has put something like £500,000 into the Company, and I think the owners of such an investment are entitled to have such provisions in a public measure as will enable them to be recouped, if it is possible to recoup them without injury to the public interest. I believe that that can be done by this Bill, not only without injury to the public interest, but with great advantage to the part of the country through which the railway will pass. I hope, in view of the strong expression of the House the other day, in view of the speech of the Chairman of Committees, who told us, when the Bill was discussed, that it remained with all those interested to say whether they accept the provisions of the measure or not, and in view also of the unusual course pursued for the second time by the hon. Member for Stepney, that the House will pass this Bill.

Sir JOSEPH PEASE (Durham, Barnard Castle): I have no intention of rehearsing the debate of last Thursday a second time over. I am sure the House sympathizes with the hon. Gentleman opposite, who has got an investment he does not like. That is obvious.

Mr. WOOTTON ISAACSON: Pardon me. I am prepared to sink the whole of my investment for the public good.

Sir JOSEPH PEASE: I am sure the hon. Gentleman's conduct will be appreciated by the debenture holders in this unfortunate railway. Having got this Bill, we, in the House of Commons, have got to see — I have no personal interest in the matter—that the best thing is done for those who, like the hon. Gentleman, have invested money in this unfortunate railway. The shareholders, in general meeting assembled, by a large majority—in person and proxy—agreed to this Bill, which does the best that can be done for the undertaking. They still have it in their power to do what they like with their

own property under this Bill, which does not affect the 8,400 of first debentures which the hon. Gentleman holds. Their priority is established, and nothing this Bill can do will rob him of the position he holds in the Company. Indeed, the Bill will improve his position, as I am informed there are £163,000 of floating liabilities. I am told that many of the creditors have agreed to take the second debenture stock—not the first, but the second—rather than press their claims, many of which would come in front of the first debentures. What are we to do for the best in connection with this railway? They say—"Pass this Bill; issue this second class of mortgages, put them in front of the preference and ordinary shares, in order that the thing may be put in a proper financial position so far as it can be under the unfortunate circumstances that have surrounded its birth. As the hon. Gentleman opposite has said, this railway may be good or may be bad, and may have been got up under circumstances of which some of us might not approve; but there it is on the ground. Parliament has sanctioned it, and it is a connecting link between Liverpool and Blackburn. I have studied it on the map, and it seems to me that the only way to carry out the object in view is to accede to the arrangements contained in this Bill. I feel that the hon. Gentleman's position will be secured by the common interest of the Company, and I trust he will not press his opposition further.

Mr. WOOTTON ISAACSON: May I be permitted to say a few words. The hon. Gentleman (Mr. Puleston) has entirely misunderstood my position. I have never for a moment taken my investment into consideration. I have been prepared to sink my own interest from the beginning, and when the solicitors approached me I never would allow them to mention the amount I had invested. I said I would have no interview with the solicitors, because I felt that what I was doing was for the public good. I said I felt that the issue of this stock was contrary to necessity, and that the poor investors and preference shareholders would lose their money. I wish to say ——

Mr. SPEAKER: The right of the hon. Gentleman to speak is limited strictly to a personal explanation.

Question put, and *agreed to.*

Bill read the third time, and *passed.*

ORDERS OF THE DAY.

———

CRIMINAL LAW AMENDMENT (IRE-
LAND) BILL.—[BILL 217.]

(*Mr. Arthur Balfour, Mr. Secretary Matthews,
Mr. Attorney General for Ireland.*)

COMMITTEE. ADJOURNED DEBATE.

[SECOND NIGHT.]

Order read for resuming Adjourned
Debate on Amendment proposed to
Question [26th April], "That Mr.
Speaker do now leave the Chair," for
Committee on the Bill.

And which Amendment was,

To leave out from the word "That" to the
end of the Question, in order to add the words
" this House declines to proceed further with a
measure for strengthening the Criminal Law
against combinations of tenants until it has
before it the full measure for their relief against
excessive rents in the shape in which it may
pass the other House of Parliament,"—(*Mr.
Robert Reid,*)

—instead thereof.

Question again proposed, "That the
words proposed to be left out stand part
of the Question."

Debate *resumed.*

MR. HANDEL COSSHAM (Bristol,
E.) said, he classified the supporters of
the Bill into four—the old Tory Party,
who, opposing all remedial legislation
for Ireland, held that all misery could
be redressed by coercion; the growing
section of the Tory Party who were in
touch with the democracy, and were not
indisposed to homœopathic doses of remedial legislation along with coercion;
those Liberal Unionists who believed in
the same mixture more largely composed
of remedial measures; and the section
who followed the right hon. Gentleman
the Member for West Birmingham (Mr.
Joseph Chamberlain), and who believed
in remedial legislation in equal quantities with coercion. To the first class of
those he mentioned he made no appeal,
and would briefly say that the history
of the world was strewn with the wrecks
of Empires whose Governments depended
wholly upon force. He appealed to the
noble Marquess the Member for the
Rossendale Division of Lancashire (the
Marquess of Hartington) and those who

were sincere in their declarations to use
pressure upon the Government in favour
of remedial legislation should support
the Amendment, for if this Bill once
passed from the control of the House,
all power of pressure on the Government
was gone. All the Amendment asked
was that the progress of the Bill should
be suspended until the House had before it those remedial measures without
which the right hon. Gentleman the
Member for West Birmingham and
others had declared they would not
support a Coercion Bill. He would
watch with great interest to see whether
the right hon. Gentleman would put his
old principle of Radicalism in practice
by supporting this Amendment. Then
he would expect the noble Lord the
Member for South Paddington (Lord
Randolph Churchill), who belonged to
the Radical section of the Tory Party,
to vote for this Amendment also. The
Amendment put into words that which
Liberal Unionists and moderate Conservatives had expressed as their desire.
The object of this Bill was to prevent
combination among the tenants of Ireland. By the Amendment the right of
the tenants to combine was claimed, and
in the name of common sense, justice,
and fair play, why should they not combine for common interest, just as workmen in this country and elsewhere also
combined for a common and lawful purpose? He was a large employer of
labour, and he never objected to the
workmen of this country combining to
obtain the best wages they could get.
The landowners of this country had combined, to a very large extent, for the
promotion of rack-rents. The House of
Lords, he might say, was a large landlord combination for the promotion of
their own interests. There was combination amongst lawyers and parsons,
and if they and the landlords and workmen were allowed to combine for the
promotion of their own interests, why
not the tenants of Ireland also? This
kind of legislation had always been dangerous; but it was more dangerous now
than ever. In the plainest way and compelled by evidence, they could not ignore
Lord Cowper's Commission had declared
that Irish rents were 20 per cent too high,
and how could Liberal Unionists support a Bill that would put into the landlord's hands the power of enforcing
rents their own Commission had de-

clared unjustifiable. Believing in Government by and for the people he had always opposed coercion, and had he sat in the House should have voted against the Bill of 1882. In the speeches of the right hon. Gentleman the Chief Secretary for Ireland (Mr. A. J. Balfour) there was the ever-recurring phrase "Law and order." It would not do to force a measure of this kind on Ireland without giving reasons for it, and he asserted that the Government were not only treating their Liberal Unionist Friends, but the House at large, with scant courtesy when they refused to answer the arguments urged against the passing of the measure by Opposition speakers. He did not believe in the efficacy of this legislation. He was in favour of the principle, "Government by the people for the people." Coercion of Ireland now would be as disappointing as it had been in the past, because we were attempting to govern the country against the will of the people. Why was it that the Irish people were not so loyal and law-abiding as the population in other parts of the Kingdom? Because the people of Ireland did not believe in the laws under which they lived, and in the making of which they had no part. Their laws were made for the rich against the poor, according to Sir Redvers Buller. Give the people of Ireland a voice in their legislation, and the people would be as loyal as any other; but their patriotism demanded opposition to laws forced upon them against their will. Personally, he believed in the men who tried to reform the world, not in the men who tried to crush it; and he reminded right hon. and hon. Gentlemen opposite that the Founder of Christianity was put to death under what was called "law and order" in those days for opposing the laws under which He lived. Would a Tory Government never learn from history? Let them look back on the Tory policy of a century ago, which lost the American Colonies and saddled this country with an expenditure of £180,000,000. Let them also remember how the same policy of coercion in recent history drove Canada to the verge of rebellion and farther from law and order than Ireland was now. That same policy of force was defeated when it was applied to Canada, else had the Dominion been also lost to us. No lack of illustrations were there

Mr. Handel Cossham

in history of the disastrous results of force. The only danger to the Union in Ireland was the danger of carrying that Coercion Bill. In his opinion, the only danger to the union between this country and Ireland was the carrying of that Coercion Bill and for the English Government to continue governing the Irish people against their will. He trusted that the Liberal Unionists would check the Government in the course they were pursuing, and he invited that section of the Liberal Party and the House generally to reconsider their position with regard to coercion, which the Amendment now before it gave them the opportunity of so doing. For every £1 of rent which was collected for the landlords of Ireland the British taxpayers had to pay £2 or £3; and as soon as the democracy came to understand that they would make short work of the present Government and their coercion.

Mr. J. W. PLUNKETT (Gloucestershire, Thornbury) said, as a new Member, he claimed the indulgence of the House. He did not propose to follow the hon. Gentleman the Member for East Bristol (Mr. Handel Cossham) in the speech which he had read to the House from beginning to end.

Mr. HANDEL COSSHAM: I never read a speech in my life.

Mr. J. W. PLUNKETT, said, he apologized to the hon. Member. He had been going to add that he had the corresponding advantage of knowing the hon. Member's speech by heart. He did not believe that the time had come when the English people, whose flag waved over territories in every part of the world, should have to confess that they were not able to rule their oldest and nearest Possession. He hoped once for all they had got rid of Ministers who had given way to intimidation. On Monday last the hon. Member for East Bristol made a speech in which the right hon. Gentleman the Member for Mid Lothian (Mr. W. E. Gladstone) was compared to a huge rock. He (Mr. J. W. Plunkett) had compared the right hon. Gentleman to a quarry, because there were persons who thought they could get nothing out of him except by blasting and explosions. The explosion at Clerkenwell had led to the Disestablishment of the Irish Church; and who then could say what might not be got out of the right hon. Gentleman by making use of the resources of modern civilization? It was difficult to understand what were Liberal opinions, because if he during the Elections of 1885 had suggested that the Liberal Party was in favour of Home Rule for Ireland he would not have been allowed to say anything more until he had withdrawn such a glaringly improbable accusation; but since that time Liberal opinions had changed. The hon. Member for the Auckland Division of Durham (Mr. Paulton), who had spoken strongly against this Bill, knew nothing of that country—indeed, he believed that the hon. Member was never there. The right hon. Gentleman the Member for Mid Lothian (Mr. W. E. Gladstone) had undertaken on more than one occasion to give peace to Ireland, but while doing so he had to be guarded by policemen, until he came to the conclusion that there ought to be an amputation—or Home Rule. The remedies of the right hon. Gentleman had failed because there were persons interested in keeping the sore open, and no one could have suspected that while applying them the doctor was contemplating the possibility of amputation being ultimately necessary. Lord Russell had almost anticipated the present Bill, because he said that juries were fit only for countries in which the people were friends of the law, that in Ireland it was difficult to find a jury which dared to do its duty, that he would adopt the Scotch plan, and make it penal to reveal how jurymen voted. And Lord Russell added that the Irish people were under two different and repugnant systems of law, one enacted by Parliament and enforced by the Courts, and the other concocted in the whisky shop and enforced by the assassin. When hon. Members opposite called this Crimes Bill coercion, he ventured to say that if they could bring over to England the system against which this measure was directed there was not an Englishman who would not go down upon his knees and pray for such a Bill as this. It had been alleged that a great number of Conservative candidates had got into Parliament at the late General Election because they promised not to vote for coercion. He denied that he had been returned because he had declared against coercion at the last Election. On the contrary,

he owed his return to his declaration that he would support the Party of no surrender to crime and outrage. He had stated himself on that occasion that the coercion referred to would affect no honest man, but only criminals, but that there was another coercion, that of the National League against those who wished to carry on their honest pursuits, and that England would not have done her duty until the lives, liberty, and property of every man, woman, and child in Ireland were secure under the authority of the Queen. The Dissentient Liberals had been accused of ratting. Well, the interesting rodent referred to in this allusion was supposed to desert a sinking ship, and he thought if a man had been sailing under the Union Jack and suddenly found that the skull and crossbones of the pirate had been hoisted instead, he had a perfect right to desert the ship, and the sooner it sank the better. A right hon. Gentleman who might have been on the Woolsack—but fortunately he and his friends had got the sack without the wool—had said that it was not our first duty to enforce a law if that law was unjust. But who was to decide whether a law was just or unjust? When the right hon. Gentleman the Member for Derby (Sir William Harcourt) issued an edict as to the flogging of little boys, it was not enforced, not because it was unjust, but because it was against the law of England. When the right hon. Gentleman passed his own Coercion Act, it was not a just law in the opinion of those against whom it was to be applied. The right hon. Gentleman had not given us any means of defining who were to be the arbiters as to whether a law was just or unjust. The Parnell Manifesto issued in November, 1885, was most venomously directed against the Liberal Party. A more crushing condemnation of Liberal policy could not have been written than was then issued by the Nationalist Party. Yet now those two Parties were allies. Doubtless, to some extent, dates had to be considered; but there must have been a great and radical change on one side or the other to bring about this alliance. Then, which Party had changed, which had swung round? It was very important that the fact should be known. Had the Irish Nationalists modified their demands and course of action; or, rather, had the Liberal Leaders suddenly changed their

[Second Night.]

views? When hon. Members below the Gangway opposite pretended to call for justice and freedom for Ireland, the English people had a right to inquire what justice and freedom they themselves allowed to their countrymen who differed from them, and upon whom they had placed their heel. The result of such inquiries showed that there were the hardest tyranny and the most crushing system of terrorism for all those who refused to obey the dictates, or dared to oppose the National League; and he was confident that the English people, with this knowledge, would never consent to the lives, liberties, and property of the Irish people being handed over to the inventors of Boycotting and the wire-pullers of the National League. The object of the Bill was to prevent such an undesirable consummation, and, under those circumstances, it would receive his hearty and cordial support.

MR. A. E. PEASE (York): The speech to which we have just listened is one advocating the measure now before the House, and we might naturally expect the hon. Member, being the heir to a large estate in Ireland, to take the landlord's view of that measure. In the remarks I have to make, I shall take somewhat an opposite view to that which he has taken. It is as evident in the face of this proposed measure as it has been made clear in the course of this debate, that the objects of the Bill are not merely the repression of crime, but the suppression of a political association called the National League and the prevention of combination amongst tenants to defend themselves against the exactions of rack-renting landlords. During the whole course of the debate Members opposite have tried to strengthen their case and prejudice that of the Opposition to this Bill by alleging a connection between Members on this side of the House with criminal associations, and illegal conspiracies in America and elsewhere. If it can be shown not only that this alleged connection is founded on the flimsiest evidence, but also that hon. Members opposite are endeavouring to protect by this measure a class of men who are responsible for more numerous outrages and more serious crimes than the Fenians or the dynamitards, then the case of the Government will be correspondingly weakened. We maintain that this measure will be

Mr. J. W. Plunkett

used to prevent the use of those weapons by which alone the Irish tenants can protect themselves against the exactions of unjust landlords; and I wish to point out that during the last 50 years the Irish landlords, or rather a section of Irish landlords, have been responsible for atrocities before which the deeds of the worst Fenian conspirators pale. I agree entirely with what was said by a noble Lord last night that that section of the Irish landlords have been a curse to the Empire, to their country, and to their class; but if the Irish people are prejudiced by the existence of a body of men who take violent courses in America, and, perhaps, also in Ireland, on the same ground we cannot be surprised that the Irish landlords are compromised by the doings of a section of their body. I should like to point out this difference between the horrible crimes committed by the Fenian and other illegal associations, and the crimes committed by a section of the Irish landlords. I suppose that the most extreme denunciator of these conspirators will admit that there might have been some small ground of provocation on their side; but the Irish landlords who have acted cruelly towards their tenants have acted wantonly against their own tenantry—a class of people whom it was their duty to protect—against the helpless and wretched people who were unable to look to other protectors, and should have had a claim on their sympathy and humanity. It is by such Acts as the one before the House that we have supported the Irish landlords in their acts of cruelty and power, and we believe that these Acts will encourage them, as some of the expressions that have fallen from hon. Gentlemen in this Parliament must encourage them, in their exacting courses. I should like to remind the House of a sentence that fell from a Member of this Government during the Session of last autumn, which, I think, was a direct encouragement to Irish landlords to evict their tenants. I know that the late Chief Secretary for Ireland was active, but not in conformity with the policy here laid down—he did his best to protect the Irish tenants. The sentence to which I allude was this—

" If there are any persons in this House who think that there should be any interference by the Government with the right of landlords to recover land in the event of the non-payment of rent they fall into a grave and serious error."

Now we believe this Bill to be a new penal law intended to brand the Irish people permanently as a subject race, and we believe identification is the policy we should pursue with respect to Ireland. But there can, as Mr. Grattan said, be no identification between the oppressor and the oppressed, the conqueror and the conquered, and we believe it is by very different means that we must attach the Irish people to the Imperial Government. I am about to deal with the behaviour of a section of the Irish landlords during the present generation. I think it is only by bringing before the public in this House the actual facts of what may be termed the land law in Ireland that has come down to this day, that the people of this country can understand how the whole body of Irish landlords are compromised in the eyes of the Irish people. I shall have to trouble the House with a considerable number of extracts with regard to the conduct of the Irish landlords during the last 50 years. I shall remind the House of the condition of the Irish people during the famine, how the Irish people were then plunged into distress such as never afflicted any other country in the world, and I shall ask what, when the Irish were suffering in this manner, was the conduct of the Irish landowners? I am aware that there were many bright and noble exceptions to the general behaviour of this class to their tenantry. But if we read the Reports of the Government Inspectors during the years 1847 to 1852, and if we read the evidence of the Relief Commissioners and the Select Committee on the Poor Laws, we shall see what was the conduct of the landlords towards their tenants, and I think I am justified in dwelling on the conduct of the landlords during the famine, because it is in times of national distress and when the nation is in extremities that we can rightly judge of the qualities of those who should have influence for good with the people. During 1849 there were 90,440 evictions, and in 1850 there were 104,163 evictions. I mean by "evictions" evicted persons rendered homeless. Here is a Report from the Ballina Union, on the 5th of February, 1848.

Sir Robert Hamilton, the Inspector, wrote—

"The cabins of the people are miserable. Bad as they are, the proprietors and lessees are rapidly depriving them even of this shelter. One proprietor lately unroofed upwards of 80 cabins at Mullaghroe in one day. The village of Cornboy, in the Belmullet Division, in which 150 persons were relieved last winter, has also been unroofed, and everywhere the demolition of homes is steadily going forward. Upwards of one-third of the cabins in the district are unroofed. . . . The people are miserably clothed, their appearance is frightful, especially the children, many of whom are little better than living skeletons. I found five out of one family which had been ejected out of Mullaghroe lying on the roadside last Wednesday near the workhouse; they were carried into it by my orders, but, I fear, only to die."

Then Mr. W. J. Hamilton, another Government Inspector, writes in March of the same year—

"In some localities it is to be feared that the heartless conduct of Mr. Walsh has brought many persons to a premature grave. . . . The same system of evictions is still going on, and I cannot as an eye-witness to the terrible results of it without expressing my horror of the barbarous manner in which many poor persons have been treated. . . . Mr. Lyons is following Mr. Walsh's example."

As to the position of some of these landlords I will quote from one report of Sir R—— Routh to Mr. Trevelyan, in 1847, in reply to an enquiry as to the incomes of the landowners from land in the Skibbereen Union—

"Lord Carbery	- -	£15,000	per year ;
R. H. H. Becher	- -	4,000	„
Mr. Newman	- -	4,000	„
Rev. S. Townsend	- -	8,000	„
Sir W. R. Becher	-	10,000	„
The O'Donovan	-	2,500	„

and so on ; and he asks—

"Ought such destitution to prevail with such resources ? "

Commissary General Hewetson reported for his district—

"Too many places similarly situated ; landlords either absent, or, though present, as well as committees, not sufficiently active. It is not right I should be called upon to urge what is their duty to perform, but so it is."

Then, Captain Kennedy, writing in July, 1848, says—

"I frequently travel 15 miles without seeing five stacks of grain of any kind—all threshed and sold. Rent has seldom or ever been looked for more sharply or levied more unsparingly than this year. Of the proprietors there are but few resident. I cannot speak of their means. I only know that there has not been any amount of poor rate levied in their Union seriously to injure them, no more than any man of common

[*Second Night.*]

humanity ought voluntarily to bestow in disastrous times."

From Castlerea, Mr. Auchmuty wrote to a similar effect; while Captain Kennedy, on May 7th, 1849, wrote—

"As soon as one horde of houseless and all but naked paupers are dead, or provided for in the workhouse, another wholesale eviction doubles the number, who, in their turn, pass through the same ordeal, wandering from house to house or burrowing in bogs or behind ditches, till, broken down by privation or exposure to the elements, they seek the workhouse or die by the roadside. The state of some districts in this Union baffles description. Sixteen houses, containing 21 families, have been levelled in one small village in Killard Division, and a vast number in the rural parts of it. Notwithstanding that fearful, and, I believe, unparalleled numbers have been unhoused in this district within the year, probably 15,000, it seems hardly credible that 1,200 more have had their dwellings levelled within a fortnight."

In his Report on King's County, Mr. Fitzgerald says—

"I do not know any landlords, with the exception of Lord Rosse, and another small proprietor, who have taken any means to enable their poor tenants to sow their lands. There are other proprietors who act like the besiegers of a town in starving them out—"cant" their cows to-day and get the tenants on the relief list to-morrow."

Captain Kennedy, in June, 1848, says—

"The misery attendant on these wholesale and simultaneous evictions is frequently aggravated by hunting these ignorant, helpless, creatures off the property from which they, perhaps, have before wandered five miles. It is not an unusual occurrence to see 40 or 50 houses levelled in one day, and orders given that no remaining tenant or occupier should give them even a night's shelter. I have known some ruthless acts committed by drivers and sub-agents, but no doubt according to law however repulsive to humanity: wretched hovels pulled down where the inmates were in a helpless state of fever and nakedness, kept by the roadside for days. As many as 300 souls—creatures of the most helpless class—have been left houseless in one day."

Colonel Clarke, replying in regard to the Kenmare Union, said—

"And yet it cannot be doubted that upwards of 1,000 dwellings have been levelled to the ground in this Union within the last 12 months, and the unfortunate, starving inmates thrown on the cold world with no shelter."

Mr. McKie, reporting on the Galway Union, said—

"The encouragement given to people to locate themselves in these wretched districts, so long as they could pay rent without a thought as to their moral or physical condition, has led to a mass of destitution."

I have extracts of other Reports all to a like effect, but I will not weary the House by reading them. Here is the evidence given before the Select Committee on Poor Law in 1849, by Captain Douglas Labalmondiere. In answer to a question he said—"There has been a great number of houses thrown down in the Union." "By whom?" he was asked. "By the landlords, the proprietors." "After the inmates left them?" "Some after they had gone to the workhouse, and others previously." Colonel Vandeleur, giving evidence with respect to another Union, after stating that there had been a large number of evictions in his district, said—

"In fact, the evictions extended to all classes, from the smallest to the largest occupiers. In that Union a very small proportion left their houses voluntarily; the houses were generally levelled."

Asked—"Is that a modern practice in your neighbourhood?" he replied, "The practice has been invariable." Captain Lang, in his evidence before the same Committee, said—

"Independent of the failure of the potato crops, the first most prominent cause is that which must strike any observer long and intimately acquainted with the state of Ireland in general—namely, the reckless and improvident mismanagement of landed property, the imprudence and want of foresight of the proprietors."

Captain Gordon reported respecting the 40s. freeholders that they had been created for a political purpose—

"And when the encouragement of the class of tenants ceased to be an object, they were gradually evicted."

Captain Kennedy said—

"It is beyond a doubt that 12,000 to 13,000 persons have been evicted within the year."

He was speaking of the Kilrush Union only; and asked to state the precise causes of the destitution, he said—

"Simply want of employment and wholesale evictions. The destitution in this Union is a mighty and fearful reality. A great portion of the people are all but naked."

I should like to dwell for a moment on the question as to what number of landlords have acted in this way towards their tenants. I find that in respect to the Kilrush Union the following is the official Return concerning evictions:—

"During the first quarter of 1848, on Sir John Reed's property, 17 or 19 houses were tumbled on one day; on Mr. McDonnell's property, 22 houses; since January 1st, Mr. Roughan's property, 8 houses; since January 1st, Mr. O'Dwyer's property, 14; Mr. Carew's

Mr. A. E. Pease

property, 11; Mr. Stackpole's property, 14; Mr. Crowe's property, 24; in Moryarter, more than 220 houses."

And I find it reported that "30 or 40 cabins are frequently levelled in a single day. The inmates crowd into neighbouring ones till disease is generated, and they are then thrown out without consideration or mercy. The relieving officers thus find them and send them to the hospital when beyond medical aid." Mr. Hamilton, reporting in 1848 to the Commissioners, said—

"Colonel Kirkwood's estate in Binghamstown is held by a middleman (Mr. Lyons), who has removed nearly all the occupying tenants holding under him. I understand Mr. Lyons is a wealthy man, but I believe he does not purpose cultivating his lands this year."

As to the manner in which evictions are carried out, I will read an extract from the sworn deposition of Pat Broderick. Broderick said—

"After which, Mr. Walsh's son directed that we should not leave a single house without levelling, and that he did not care one damn where the people went to. The next day we accordingly went and levelled as many houses as we could. We were occupied in the same manner for three or four succeeding days."

Sir Thomas Ross, referring to the eviction of 30 families from Lord Ventry's property, in the Dingle Union, said—

"And the unfortunate people, amounting in all to 150 persons, were exposed for several nights on the roadside."

Mr. St. George, one of the proprietors in the Galway Union, was asked to explain the evictions on his estate, when he said—

"Several persons have been dispossessed, but I am informed no act of inhumanity has been perpetrated in the removal, unless in the most urgent cases."

He seemed to think that in what he considered urgent cases it was quite justifiable to resort to inhuman treatment. Now, as to the way the people were employed, Captain Haynes, of Tipperary, reported that—

"There is a disinclination on the part of landlords and farmers to employ the people, except on their own terms—1s. and 1s. 2d. a week."

And it was considered justifiable to refuse the people relief if they refused to accept such wages. I must apologize for wearying the House with references to the condition of the tenantry, and the action of the landlords during the Irish famine. I will pass to more recent

times; but first of all let me read what the senior Member for Birmingham (Mr. John Bright) said as to the conduct of the Irish landlords and their agents at the time of the famine. The right hon. Gentleman, in 1849, said—

"When law refuses its duty, when Government denies the right of the people, when competition is so fierce for the little land which the monopolists grant to cultivation in Ireland, when, in fact, millions are scrambling for the potato, these people are driven back from law, and from the usages of civilization, to that which is termed the 'law of Nature,' and if not the strongest, the laws of the vindictive; and in this case the people of Ireland believe, to my certain knowledge, that it is only by these acts of vengeance, periodically committed, that they can hold in suspense the arm of the proprietor, of the landlord, and the agent, who, in too many cases, would, if he dared, exterminate them."

But *The Times* is an authority to which hon. Gentleman opposite look for a confirmation of their political views, and, perhaps, they would like to know what this authority said in 1852, in 1860, and at a later date, in regard to the conduct of the Irish landlords. In 1852, *The Times* said— "The name of an Irish landlord stinked in the nostrils of Christendom." In 1860, *The Times*, referring to the evictions on the part of Lord Plunkett, the Protestant Bishop of Tuam, said—

"There remains a hideous scandal. A Bishop had better sit down and die or cast himself on the charity of his diocese than figure to the world in the unseemly character of a wholesale evictor, collecting red armies and black armies, and pulling down houses over the heads of their aged and long-settled occupants. We hedge round the Bishop with a propriety which makes large demands upon us, and make some demands upon him. We cannot help feeling that the crowbar comes under this class of restrictions. We may not always bear in our minds the imaginary crozier, but at least we expect an open palm and a gentle pressure, not a heave at the crowbar, followed by falling thatch and crumbling masonry, out of which some poor old couple escape into the vast around."

The hon. Member read the description given of an eviction in the county of Westmeath by Dr. Nulty, now Catholic Bishop of Meath:—

"Seven hundred human beings were driven from their homes on this one day. There was not a shilling of rent due on the estate at the time, except by one man. The Sheriff's assistants, employed on the occasion to extinguish the hearths and homes of those honest, industrious men, worked away with a will at their awful calling until evening fell. At length an incident occurred that varied the monotony of the grim and ghastly ruin which they were

[*Second Night.*]

spreading all round. They stopped suddenly and recoiled—panic-stricken with terror—from two dwellings, which they were directed to destroy with the rest. They had just learned that typhus fever held those houses in its grasp, and had already brought death to some of their inmates. They therefore supplicated the agent to spare these houses a little longer; but he was inexorable, and insisted that they should come down. He ordered a large winnowing-sheet to be secured over the beds in which the fever victims lay—fortunately they happened to be delirious at the time—and then directed the houses to be unroofed cautiously and slowly. I administered the last Sacrament of the Church to four of these fever victims next day, and—save the above-mentioned winnowing-sheet, there was not then a roof nearer to me than the canopy of heaven. The scene of that eviction day I must remember all my life long. The wailing of women, the screams, the terror, the consternation of children, the speechless agony of men, wrung tears of grief from all who saw them. I saw the officers and men of a large police force who were obliged to attend on the occasion, cry like children. The heavy rains that usually attend the autumnal equinoxes descended in cold, copious torrents throughout the night, and at once revealed to the houseless sufferers the awful realities of their condition. I visited them next morning, and rode from place to place, administering to them all the comfort and consolation I could. The landed proprietors in a circle all round, and for many miles in every direction, warned their tenantry against admitting them to even a single night's shelter. Many of these poor people were unable to emigrate. After battling in vain with privation and pestilence, they at last graduated from the workhouse to the tomb, and in little more than three years nearly a fourth of them lay quietly in their graves."

In 1882 Sir George Trevelyan said—

"At this moment, in one part of the country, men are being turned out of their houses actually by battalions, who are no more able to pay the arrears of these bad years than they are to pay the National Debt. In three days (in Connemara) 150 families were turned out, numbering 750 persons. It was not the case that these poor people belonged to the class of extravagant tenants. They were not whisky drinkers; they were not in terror of the Land League."

[The hon. Member also quoted from Irish newspapers of 1883.] Hon. Members opposite sometimes appeal in order to strengthen their political case against our side to General Gordon. Now, this gentleman, writing to *The Times*, in December, 1880, said—

"I call your attention to the pamphlets, letters, and speeches of the landlord class as a proof of how little sympathy or kindness there exists among them for the tenantry. No half-measure Acts, which left the landlord with any say to the tenantry of these portions of Ireland, will be of any use. They would be rendered, as past Land Acts in Ireland have been, quite abortive, for the landlords will insert clauses to do away

Mr. A. E. Pease

with their force. Any half-measures will only place the Government face to face with the people of Ireland as the champions of the landlord interest."

We maintain that that is exactly what the present measure is doing. The Government would be bound to enforce their decision, and with a result which none can foresee, but which certainly would be disastrous to the common weal. In January last *The Times* said—

"The evictions at Glenbeigh, County Kerry, are still being carried out from day to day. Yesterday, after a tenant named Reardon was evicted, it was represented to the agent that the tenant's infant child was dying, and its mother begged a shelter for it for the night; but the agent refused, and ordered the bailiffs to nail up the door. The poor woman cried bitterly, and laid the dying child in the pigstye in the yard, and tried to procure straw for a bed there."

I shall not take up the time of the House by referring to the eviction scenes which have been more or less strikingly brought before the country during the last 12 months. We know that the cases of which details have been given are only samples of hundreds and thousands of similar cases that have taken place in Ireland. During the last quarter 1,042 families, including 5,190 people, have been evicted, that is at the rate of 20,000 people a-year, or 400 a-week. We maintain that this measure will encourage the Irish landlords in these courses. This measure is, on the face of it, for the suppression of the National League, that League which Sir Redvers Buller has said is the only thing the Irish people have to look to for help. While these horrible evictions are being enacted year after year, very few expressions of sympathy have escaped the lips of hon. Gentlemen opposite. I know hon. Gentlemen upon Government Benches do feel the iniquity of many of the evictions and wish to stop them. I wish they could see that a Bill like this will only encourage the worst class of Irish landlords in the evil courses they have hitherto pursued. I should like, whilst upon this point, to state what I regard as the worst part of the measure before the House. To whom is the administration of this Bill to be intrusted? The present Lord Lieutenant of Ireland, who is a member of a secret society—I refer to the Orange Society. [Lord ARTHUR HILL: No, no.] I believe the Lord Lieutenant is a member of the Orange Society? [Lord ARTHUR HILL:

No.] Well, I will withdraw the statement if it is incorrect. [Mr. M. KENNY: The hon. and gallant Member for the Isle of Thanet (Colonel King-Harman) is.] Certainly, the Lord Lieutenant is associated, both politically and socially, with those who are members of that secret society, and who are supporting this measure for the suppression of an association, the National League, which is opposed to the Orange Society, and a measure for the taking from the hands of the Irish tenantry one of the few weapons they have for defending themselves. I do not know whether the rumour is correct or not, that the right hon. and learned Gentleman the Attorney General for Ireland is about to be raised to the Judicial Bench in Ireland. I do not for a moment wish to say anything that would cast a shadow on the character of the right hon. and learned Gentleman as an impartial and honourable Member of this House; but I say that his appointment to the Bench will be as unfortunate before the people of Ireland as the appointment of the right hon. and gallant Gentleman opposite (Colonel King-Harman) to the Office of Under Secretary to the Lord Lieutenant. The present Lord Grey, writing the other day to *The Times*, described the coercion of 1881 as cruel, unjust, and useless. The noble Lord did not say that at the time. However, I believe that many Liberals who, like Lord Grey, are supporting this measure, will in seven years' time denounce it as one useless, cruel, and unjust. When charges of a most serious nature are brought against hon. Members on this side of the House with regard to their connection with illegal and criminal associations, we have a right to see what sort of men have associated with the Party on the other side of the House. I think I have shown that a section of the Irish landlords have been morally as criminal in their dealings with the Irish tenants as any society of conspirators or tenants have been to them. The connection between hon. Members opposite and the landlord class has been far more close than any connection between hon. Members on this side of the House and criminal associations. I agree with Mr. Sismondi, the great historian and political economist, when he said that the Irish landlords had shaken the very foundations of society by making the laws of property in the country unendurable. I also agree with Mr. Burke who said that—

" When men are kept as being no better than half-citizens for any length of time, they will be made whole Jacobins."

If this measure is passed into law, you will take away the privileges of citizenship from a large number of Irishmen, and thereby drive them into courses of revolution and anarchy. I have great pleasure in supporting the Resolution of the hon. and learned Member for Dumfries.

MR. M. J. KENNY (Tyrone, Mid) said, the Amendment before the House was founded on the action of the Liberal Government in 1882, when they introduced their Bill for the repression of crime in Ireland, accompanied with a Bill wiping out arrears of rent, which was the question believed to be the cause of the disturbances at the time in Ireland. The precedent established by the Liberal Government in 1882 was this—the Crimes Bill was introduced on the 11th May, and was read a first time on Monday, and on the following Thursday the Arrears of Rent Bill was introduced by the then Chief Secretary for Ireland, now Sir George Trevelyan. The stages of these Bills were taken successively, so that the Bill for wiping out arrears of rent in Ireland became law practically at the same time that the Bill for the repression of crime became law. If that was the case in 1882, how much stronger, he asked, was the reason why remedial measures should, if not precede, at least accompany in the different stages any measure for the repression of crime. The Crimes Bill of 1882 was a panic-stricken piece of legislation. It immediately followed the Phœnix Park assassinations, and consequently the temper of the House and of the country was so aroused that coercion was deemed an absolute necessity, and any attempt to govern Ireland at the time, without the aid of these extreme criminal laws, would have been met with the greatest opposition by the Tory Party. Not only did that repressive legislation immediately follow the Phœnix Park assassinations, but at the time the condition of Ireland was, in comparison with the condition of Ireland now, excessively disturbed. There were in that year a great number of outrages of many kinds in Ireland, many times more numerous than the outrages attributed to Ireland within the past 12 months, and the circumstances of the case were eminently favourable to a policy of coercion, while he contended that there was nothing in the condition of Ireland to-day to justify for a moment the introduction of such a stringent Coercion Bill as they were now considering. Turning to the remedial measures of the Government, he might remind the House that there was no distinct assurance, notwithstanding Lord Salisbury's recent statement, that the Government would resign if their remedial Bill was not accepted, inasmuch as the Government had not stated that they would reject vital amendments. Then there was no guarantee as to the condition in which that Bill would leave the other House of Parliament. This was the first time that any great Bill dealing with the agrarian system in Ireland had not been introduced into the House of Commons in the first instance. The only exception was the Land Purchase Bill of Lord Ashbourne; but that measure was limited in scope by Parliament, and it had been still more limited in operation; so that it could hardly be called an exception. He claimed that any legislation dealing with the Land Question should have been originated in the House of Commons. After the rejection of the Bill of the hon. Member for Cork last year, the Government appointed a Commission, consisting of two landlords, one Irish and the other English, an eminent political economist and agriculturist, and an Irish County Court Judge, who was himself also a landlord and a "shoneen," or impecunious landlord. The Commission was to act as a jury on the condition of affairs with regard to land in Ireland; but he asked could any fair-minded man describe it as a fair jury when three of its members were partizans of one party, and only one a partizan of the opposite party? That was a packed jury if ever there was one. Yet this packed Commission, in spite of their prejudices, and in spite of the evident reluctance of Lord Milltown and other Members, issued a report distinctly in favour of the tenants' case, and altogether against the landlord party in Ireland. He attached the greatest weight to the Report of Mr. Knipe, the only member of the

Mr. M. J. Kenny

Commission who had anything like personal or practical acquaintance with the condition of the tenant farmers in Ireland. Mr. Knipe gave very instructive figures from the return of Dr. Grimshaw, the Registrar-General, showing that the value of grain had fallen from 63,000,000 in 1855, to 31,000,000 in 1886, and that the value of live stock had fallen within the last five years—from 1881 to 1886—from 50,000,000 to 41,000,000. The depreciation in the value of farm produce was more than double the rent in Ireland, and yet, in spite of this extraordinary collapse, the farmers were expected to pay now the rents they had contracted for in prosperous times. In 1881 the reductions made in Ulster rents averaged 25 per cent, and in the other parts of Ireland 17 or 18 per cent. But now the Sub-Commissioners felt constrained to make reductions of 50 per cent, and in some cases even more. The Chief Secretary, displaying an ignorance which absolutely unfitted him for the post he held, asked why tenants did not go into the Land Courts. One reason was, that owing to enormous rack-rents, the tenants were in arrears, and if they went into the Court, the landlord would turn them out on the roadside for the arrears. Then there was the question of turbary, which in Ulster had become a burning question. Immediately after the assessment landlords almost universally began to charge rent for rights of turbary which had hitherto been rent free, and in this way raised rents to their former level. An ex-Sub-Commissioner, in his evidence before Lord Cowper's Commission, stated that in Ulster the only illegal combination was that of the landlords to defeat the operation of the Land Act of 1881. Then Mr. Knipe, who was a Conservative and had been an ardent supporter of the hon. and and gallant Member for North Armagh (Colonel Saunderson), basing his opinion not only on his own knowledge, but also on the evidence of General Buller, had pronounced strongly against any measure of coercion. Declaring the opinions of many Protestants of Ulster, he warned the Government that coercion would only aggravate existing evils. The coercion which General Buller advised was a court of equity which would have "a certain amount of coercive power on a bad tenant and a very strong coercive power on a bad landlord." The fact was that the Bill was not directed against crime—there was not a single clause which would tend to put down or assist in the detection of crime—but to repress political associations. The Bill also incorporated and revived the odious Whiteboy Acts of former generations, which were passed when there was tenfold more violence and turbulence in the country than existed at the present day, and it gave the Lord Lieutenant an even greater power of suppressing meetings than was given by those Acts, inasmuch as they contained definitions of what constituted an illegal meeting, whereas, in this Bill there were no such definitions; but the Lord Lieutenant was empowered to proclaim any meetings he chose, and could imprison with hard labour for three months anyone who offended against such a proclamation. There was one very ingenious clause which provided that any person who knowingly and voluntarily supplied horses, arms, and ammunition, for the purpose of assisting at a meeting of any persons assembling for an unlawful purpose would be liable under this Bill to six months' hard labour. And how could that be construed? It could be construed that any man who supplied a horse and cart to convey persons to an eviction would be liable to imprisonment even although he were not present himself. Who were the men who would administer this Act—an Act, be it remembered, that would be put into operation mainly in disputes between landlord and tenant? He did not wish to refer to the extraordinary, anomalous, and unprecedented appointment of the Under Secretary for Ireland (Colonel King-Harman), who was bound by every tie personal, family, and otherwise to the landlord party. He had heard of a Minister without a portfolio, but he had never heard of a Minister without a salary. The Under Secretary, besides being Under Secretary, was an Irish landlord owning a large property, and he had been getting rents paid to him far in excess of what he was entitled to—the average reduction on his rents, as was shown by the Blue Book, amounted to something like 38 per cent. Whereas this gentleman was entitled to only 62s. on the average he had, under the terror of eviction, got 100s. from his unfortunate tenantry. In some cases, the reduction was 70 per cent. Was it fair or proper that such a

man—a man who might be in conflict with his own tenants—should be appointed to advise the Chief Secretary, who would advise the Lord Lieutenant when to put this Act into operation? Similar reductions had been made all over Ireland. Hon. Members who were connected with the land in Ireland were apt to talk about dishonesty on the part of tenants; but he wanted to know whether there were not many instances on the other side in which cases of restitution might not fairly be raised? Within the last three months there had been only one case of murder in County Kerry, and no other case of homicide. Yet during that time 5,000 persons had been turned out of their homes on the highway, and that fact, he thought, constituted a much greater moral offence than the one murder of which the other side had made so much. He maintained, although he would not palliate for a moment the enormity and heinousness of wilful murder, that the person who was responsible for turning out those men on the highway was an infinitely worse criminal than the man who took one human life. Fully half of those 5,000 persons belonged to the County Kerry. Was it a mere accidental occurrence that the most disturbed county in Ireland should be the County of Kerry? It was on the lines of the amendment that the House ought to proceed, and not on the lines sketched out by the Government. If the Government set itself to try their remedial measures, and if the remedial measures were suitable and sufficient, they would find that that would be enough in itself to put an end to outrage, and that there would not be the slightest necessity for the practical suspension of the Constitution in Ireland. The continuance of the Liberal Unionists in their present course would, he believed, insure the extinction of so-called Unionism, and secure at the next Election an overwhelming declaration in favour of the policy of the right hon. Member for Mid Lothian.

Sir JOSEPH PEASE (Durham, Barnard Castle) said, the House was so kind to him, on the occasion of the second reading of that Bill, in listening to what he had to say against the measure, that he should only trouble it that afternoon with a very few figures, which he desired to lay before the House, and, if possible, by the means of the Press,

[*Second Night.*]

before the country. It did seem to him that the House had been singularly destitute of any practical information as to why they should pass that Bill. He must also say, he did not think the House, at that moment, was being very handsomely treated by Her Majesty's Government, for he never recollected any previous instance in which, when an important measure brought forward by the Government was under discussion, that, even on a Wednesday afternoon, the House was left without a single Representative of that Government on the Front Government Bench. For one Cabinet Minister to appear on that Bench for a few moments that afternoon, had been the one honourable exception to the scant courtesy with which the House had been treated. He desired to call the attention of the House to the Return which had been laid on the Table at the instance of his right hon. Friend the Member for Newcastle-on-Tyne (Mr. John Morley), and which purported to give the aggregate number of the agrarian offences during the last six or seven years. In 1880, according to that Return, there were 2,585 of these offences; in 1881, 4,439; 1882, 3,433; in 1883, 870; in 1884, 762; in 1885, 914; and in 1886, 1,056; while up to March, 1887, they were 241, being on a lower average than previous years. These figures showed how small was the amount of agrarian crime upon which the Bill was based. The Home Secretary referred lately to the Return for March, and in doing so had made the most he could of it. He (Sir Joseph Pease) wanted to call particular attention to the fact that the Bill could not be based on the March Return. Leave was given to introduce the Bill on the 21st of March last, when, of course, the March Return could not have been in the hands of the Government. The Bill must have been before the Cabinet even before the Return of crime for February of this year was complete; and, therefore, January crime of this year could only have been considered when the Bill was framed. What was the state of the country, according to the Return of crime for the quarter ending December of last year? In the Quarter ending December last, there were 11 offences against life and limb—namely, three of firing at the person, one of aggravated assault, four of assault on life, and three

of assault on bailiffs—and there was no murder, manslaughter, assault with intent to murder, poisoning, conspiring to murder, or assault on the police. In the previous Quarter, ending September, there were 306 offences compared with 264 in the Quarter ending September, 1885. But it was not right to consider the Returns without excluding the threatening letters. That reduced the number of offences from 264 to 122 in the Quarter ending September, 1885; from 279 to 143 in the Quarter ending December; from 256 to 115 in the Quarter ending March, 1886; from 297 to 146 in the June Quarter; from 306 to 177 in the September Quarter; from 166 to 80 in the December Quarter; and from 241 to 118 in the last March Quarter. In the face of these figures, how could the Government ask for this penal legislation? The figures were lowest in the December Quarter, on the Returns for which this Bill must be mainly founded; and the next lowest Returns were those for March last. He maintained that there was hardly ever a Return which had come out of Ireland during the time he had been in Parliament which was so satisfactory as regarded crime. These were strong, but strange facts, and he presented them to the House as conclusive against any need for the Bill so far as statistics could possibly prove. He did not know how it was, when the Government found those tremendous facts against them, that they came to the House and asked for such severe penalties to be put upon the people of Ireland. He desired now to call the attention of the House to the evictions which had taken place in Ireland in the December Quarter of 1885; 369 families, representing 1,818 persons, were evicted when the crimes other than threatening letters were 143. In the corresponding Quarter of 1886, 666 families, representing 3,458 people, were evicted and turned destitute into the roads and streets; and yet the crimes only numbered 80—this renewed evictions and crime of the last Quarter of 1885, from when there was no coercion and no attempt at coercion, to the last Quarter of 1886, when there was the strongest possible reason to believe coercion would be attempted. He thought the condition of things in the latter period showed wonderful forbearance on the part of the people of Ireland. He did not say they were not right and just in so acting; but he thought the fact ought to be generally known. Now, he came to the first quarter of the present year, when crime had risen to 115 cases, independent of threatening letters. In the quarter of this year ending March 31st, one of the worst, coldest, and most inclement winter quarters we had had in this country for many years, the Irish landlords had evicted, and turned out into the roads and streets, 1,042 families, representing 5,190 people. Under such circumstances, an increase of crime could not be surprising; but it had been very slight, and taking the whole of the last seven Quarterly Returns, he found that crime was lowest at the end of the last quarter of 1886. Those were facts which he wanted the country to understand, although, when hon. Gentlemen who supported the Government said they did not rely upon criminal statistics, but on the general state of the country, he thought it was right that they should turn to these facts to see what was the general state of the country. In the face of them, he repeated, why should they put such terrible penalties upon the people of Ireland? Conspiracy, too, was often no crime. He was not an advocate of Boycotting; but he had known others besides the Irish resort to that practice. He could recollect the time when the whole of the anti-slavery Party in this country Boycotted the West India planter; and when no West Indian grown sugar was allowed to enter his father's house. It was the same at Manchester and other places, where strong anti-slavery feeling prevailed. He now came to some figures which were still more curious. When he was told that people would not prosecute in Ireland, and that juries would not convict in that country, he wanted to know what evidence there was of this? In England and Wales, according to the Return for the year 1885, there were in that year 43,962 indictable offences committed. In those cases, 19,207 persons were apprehended, or 43·6 per cent. In London alone in that year there were 14,502 indictable offences, for which only 4,993 offenders were brought to justice. These were striking figures; but what was the case in Ireland, where it was said the Queen's writ did not run, and persons were not brought to justice? Why, in the year 1885, in

Ireland, in 52 per cent of the indictable offences committed, persons were apprehended. That was a very important fact, and upset a great deal which had been said about the non-detection of crime in Ireland. In England, of the 43 per cent apprehended for indictable offences, 26 per cent were discharged before trial, and of those tried by juries 77 per cent were convicted, and 22 per cent were acquitted. What was the state of Ireland in 1885? There were 6,961 indictable offences, 43,594 persons apprehended; 1,394 discharged; 2,155 tried; 73.5 per cent convicted, and 26.5 per cent discharged. The figures showed, in the long run, that the difference in Irish as compared with English crime which was not convicted, was only 1·76 per cent, as in England only 24 per cent of the indictable offences committed reached punishment, and in Ireland 22.75 per cent of these offences were punished. Those were the facts which he wished to emphasize to the House and the country, if he could. He had waited in vain to hear some of the facts concerning cases in which juries had refused to convict, and in which people had refused to prosecute. Yet he had shown, from the criminal statistics of England and Ireland, that the number of cases in which juries had convicted were nearly the same, the only difference being between the two countries that in England 77 of those tried were convicted, and in Ireland 73½ per cent; but when they came to the total of crime committed, and the convicted and punished, they found there was only a difference of 1·76 per cent against Ireland. He had already expressed his views on the Bill, so far as he desired to do so; and he had not risen for the purpose of delaying the Bill, but he was very anxious that the facts which necessarily had a bearing upon the measure should be put before the House and the country.

COLONEL HUGHES-HALLETT (Rochester) said, that nothing new had been introduced respecting the Bill in the debate that afternoon. He did not expect to introduce anything new himself after so many nights' debate; for the House had reached the stage of weariness of which the right hon. Gentleman (Mr. A. J. Balfour) had spoken last night, and which an English poet had described as—

" A weariness beyond what assoc feel
  Who tread the circuit of the cistern wheel."

He thought the hon. Gentleman who had just spoken (Sir Joseph Pease) had given them some interesting statistics; but he had mentioned no practical reasons why the Government should not have introduced the measure. He had added no new arguments; but that was not surprising. There was, however, one thing which would not be controverted. Amid the conflict of argument between both sides of the House on that question one fact had come out into bold prominence, and that was that the condition of Ireland at the present moment required the immediate and earnest consideration of Her Majesty's Government. ["Hear, hear!" *from the Opposition.*] The crucial point, no doubt, was in what direction that consideration should tend. Whatever was the cause of the discontent in Ireland he did not believe that the question of reductions of rent or evictions was the real and legitimate reason. Hon. Gentlemen opposite thought that what were called "remedial measures" should receive their first attention; but if it were conceded that it was manifest, on the one hand, that discontent and distress existed in Ireland, it must be admitted, on the other hand, that, to a certain extent, crime, disorder, and lawlessness were dominant there; and hon. Members who advocated the application of remedial measures in the first place appeared to forget that it was absolutely necessary, before they could apply remedies to a disease, that the disease should have arrived at a stage at which the remedies could be efficacious. In his humble judgment remedial legislation was the natural consequence of the legislation that was first required to restore a civilized country to the condition of civilized life. The cancer of disorder having broken out in the body politic of Ireland, that cancer had to be cut out before they could usefully apply the remedies which would restore health and soundness to the National Constitution. The first condition of any true cure for the ills of Ireland was the re-establishment of order and respect for the law, so that honest, industrious, and peaceable citizens should be able to pursue their daily avocations without fear of injury to their lives and property. It was in order to re-establish

Colonel Hughes-Hallett

and enforce in Ireland the elementary conditions of every civilized community that the Government had brought in the present Bill. Hon. Members below the Gangway opposite could not fairly complain if the Government took a leaf out of their book. Imitation was the sincerest flattery; and even hon. Members —Home Rulers—must concede that the National League coerced— [*Home Rule cries of* "No!"]—well, hon. Members might take a different view of Boycotting and the proceeedings of Captain Moonlight to that which was held in this country; but it was none the less the fact. They talked of the Bill as a drastic Coercion Bill; but the principles of the National League, it must be conceded, were principles of coercion. ["No, no!"] When, for example, the tenant who could pay was not allowed to pay the judicial rent fixed by the Land Act of 1881, on pain of being Boycotted or outraged, he asked, was that not coercion of the worst kind? To his mind, the question for the House and the country to decide was which form of coercion should be in force—the coercion of the National League and its forms of intimidation and outrage, or the coercion necessary to enforce order and obedience to the law of the land. That Bill only proposed the coercion, or in other words the punishment, of criminals in Ireland, whether they were guilty of Boycotting, intimidation, outrage, or assassination, precisely as they were coerced or punished in England, Scotland, and every other civilized country. That Bill had been denounced as a most cruel and tyrannical measure; but it was not one whit more harsh or more severe than the Crimes Act of 1882. The Act of 1882 contained powers of arrest, of imprisonment without trial, and of suppression of newspapers, and other powers which either did not exist at all in the present Bill, or only existed in a modified form. It had been argued that Her Majesty's Government had shown no sufficient reason for the introduction of this measure, and that they had only put forward a few isolated cases of crime. He ventured, however, to say that the foundation for this measure was not merely isolated cases of crime, but the broad and general system of intimidation, terrorism, and outrage which had prevailed so long in Ireland, which no Government could permit to go on, and which was the outcome of the National League, the apostolic successor of the Land League, with reference to which the right hon. Gentleman the Member for Mid Lothian (Mr. W. E. Gladstone) had said that crime dogged its steps with fatal precision, and that, for the first time in the history of Christendom, a body of men had arisen in Ireland who were not ashamed to preach the doctrine of public plunder. He (Colonel Hughes-Hallett) was surprised at the extraordinary change which had taken place in the opinions of the right hon. Gentleman the Member for Mid Lothian and Lord Spencer. He was not surprised at the changes in the views of the right hon. Member for Derby (Sir William Harcourt), because they were only consistent with his character. To his mind the land agitation in Ireland had sprung from a sort of hatred not against landlords *quâ* landlords, but was due really to hatred of England, and thus the Irish landlords were attacked for the reason that they were at one and the same time the existing owners of the soil and the supporters of the Union. Under the cloak of that hatred an attack was made upon the landlords because they were the friends of England, and, to use the words of the hon. Member for Cork, the props of English power in that country. He had been surprised to hear two ex-Chancellors of the Exchequer speak of hon. Members below the Gangway as representing five-sixths of the Irish people. It was true that if they divided 86 by 103, they would arrive at about that proportion; but if they took the figures of the number of voters at the Election of November, 1885, they would see that out of 741,913 electors only 296,960 voted for the hon. Member for Cork and his supporters. [Mr. JUSTIN M'CARTHY (Londonderry); How many were unopposed?] In the face of these figures he was amazed that it should be asserted that hon. Members below the Gangway represented five-sixths of the people of Ireland, when, in fact, they represented little more than one-third. Her Majesty's Government refused to allow the remaining two-thirds in Ireland to be coerced by that third part; they simply asked for protection for Her Majesty's subjects in Ireland against terrorism of various kinds, and on the ground that Courts of Justice were paralyzed and juries did

not dare to convict on account of the intimidation that was being exercised. The right hon. Gentleman the Member for Mid Lothian had, on one occasion, alluded to the Crimes Act of 1882 as a Protection Bill. So was the Bill of 1887. It sought to protect the honest, the loyal, and the true from injury and from interference with their rightful business, and to bring to justice the outrage-monger and the assassin, with whom he could hardly suppose that hon. Members opposite would sympathize. But it was argued that crime and outrage would not diminish under this Bill. They had diminished under the Act of 1882. In the half-year ending in June, 1882, the number of crimes had been 2,567, and in the half-year ending on December 30, 1882, they had dropped to 836. Why should there not be a similar diminution now? The Bill would give that individual freedom which all were entitled to enjoy who were true to Queen, Government, and country.

MR. THEODORE FRY (Darlington): Sir, the hon. and gallant Gentleman who has just sat down (Colonel Hughes-Hallett) has found fault with the figures that have been quoted in the course of this debate, and he added that he did not see much in those figures. Well, it strikes me that the hon. and gallant Gentleman is one of those who thinks very little of statistics, and I believe that if the Angel Gabriel came down and declared that they were true the hon. and gallant Gentleman would still adhere to the opinion that they proved nothing. The hon. and gallant Gentleman says that he has not changed his mind since he was before the electors of Rochester. That may be so. But I doubt very much if he promised that he would vote for a Coercion Bill like that now before the House. If he did make such a promise, he is almost an unique Member of his Party, for from Lord Salisbury, even down to the humblest of his followers in this House, the country was told that the Conservative Party was against coercion, and that they had not the slightest intention of voting for coercion for Ireland.

COLONEL HUGHES-HALLETT: If the hon. Member will do me the honour to look over my speeches some pleasant Sunday afternoon, he will find that I never made any such promise. On the contrary, I said that suppression of the

National League was one of the first things that the Government ought to undertake in the settlement of the Irish Question.

MR. THEODORE FRY: I accept the statement of the hon. and gallant Gentleman, which shows that he is a speckled bird among his friends, for he is almost the only one among them who has not given promises against coercion. I believe that the minority and not the majority who voted on the second reading of the Coercion Bill represented the highest percentage of public feeling out-of-doors on the subject. Having had no opportunity hitherto of giving more than silent opposition to the measure now before the House, I wish, on the present occasion, to support most strongly the Amendment of the hon. and learned Member for Dumfries (Mr. R. T. Reid). Her Majesty's Government have admitted most fully the need of remedial measures, and the overwhelming case made out on behalf of the tenants against unjust rents and barbarous evictions, and the demand that the second measure shall be laid before us before the first is passed, is only consistent with the most simple rule of justice. I may remind the House that the Government of the right hon. Member for Mid Lothian had dealt with coercion and remedial measures at the same time. Lord Salisbury's Administration, however, does not adopt this course. There can be but one reason why the Amendment is objected to, and it is because the Government know well the Bill now under discussion in "another place" will utterly fail to satisfy the wishes of those who sit on this side of the House. One great fallacy pervades the argument presented in favour of the Coercion Bill, and that is that those who support it are the only Members of this House who wish that law and order should prevail in Ireland. They take the whole credit for this pious wish, and choose to stigmatize us with desiring a very different state of affairs. Every Member, whether belonging to the Liberal Party or representing Irish constituencies, is as anxious as the Chief Secretary that law and order should prevail, and that crime should cease from one end of the land to the other, not only in Kerry, but in Belfast as well. The only question is how this object can be best attained, whether by Coercion Bills of the deepest hue, or by giving to

Ireland such a system of government as will win respect and sympathy. The difference between us is this, that Her Majesty's Government profess that by some magical influence which they possess their measure will succeed in making Ireland contented and happy, whilst 85 or 86 similar measures have failed already to effect that object; but do they really believe that now, when Irish sentiment in favour of Home Rule is stronger than ever it was, and constitutionally expressed as it has never been before, and is growing day by day—do they think that they are going to succeed? They know as well as we do, and probably they say so in sealed houses, that this measure will be a hopeless and ignominious failure. I do not mean that it will fail to fill the prisons of Ireland, that it will still further tend to exasperate the Irish nation; but it will fail, as all its predecessors have failed, to produce happiness and contentment, and to make a lasting friendship and peace between the two nations. The only new feature connected with it, as compared with its forerunners, is that it is to last for ever. Those who arranged the Union in 1800 thought it would last for ever; but there is no "for ever" in politics. This Bill carries its death-warrant in itself. It cannot last, because it is the offspring of injustice and despair. It is a child born of fears, and nourished by distrust. The simplest axioms of true liberty and Constitutional government are still, as they have been, at variance with Tory principles, which never change, though they at times do attempt to alter the reforms of Liberal Governments. The promoters of this measure may rest assured that at the next General Election, come when it may, the death-knell of this measure will be rung, and this idol which they are about to set up will be shattered into a thousand pieces. The only vote I ever gave in this House which I regret was the one in favour of the last Coercion Bill. I gave it because crime then was very much greater than it is now, and the remedial measures promised by our great Leader were very different. But, besides this, we have grown wiser, and some of us have studied more closely this great Irish Question, and, aided by the expression of the wishes of the Irish people, have determined to try a more excellent way, a way which those who refuse to take accept a responsibility

Colonel Hughes-Hallett

which they will one day find has been
not only useless, but mischievous. Some
of us, too, have seen the poverty-stricken
tenants turned out of their homes in the
bitterest of weather, and mothers and
children turned out on the roadside.
We have seen houses destroyed by the
torch or the crowbar; we have seen the
deeds which tend to cause crime, and to
make that crime undiscovered; and we
are determined, so far as we can, to
assist in the passing of laws in the
future which shall contribute to promote
friendship between the two nations, laws
which, founded upon justice, may last
for ever.

MR. J. ROWLANDS (Finsbury, E.)
said, the dreariness of the debate was
accounted for by the fact that the Government proposed coercive legislation
without showing that there was any
ground for it in the increase of crime in
Ireland; and the weakness of the case
for the Bill was shown by the irrelevant
topics introduced into the speeches made
in support of it. It was absurd to say,
as the hon. and gallant Gentleman the
Member for Rochester (Colonel Hughes-
Hallett) had said, that the Irish Nationalist Members did not represent the
feelings of the people of Ireland. It
could not be honestly asserted that the
four seats of Dublin held by Members
of the Nationalist party, and the share
which they had in representing Belfast,
had been secured by means of intimidation. A great deal had been said
about the Report of that majority of the
Royal Commission, and he submitted
that if that Report had had the weight
which it ought to have carried with it in
that House no Coercion Bill would have
been introduced, because it showed that
there was no justification for such
a measure. But there was another
Report, which the Government appeared
to have lost sight of. The Government
themselves appointed to a seat on the
Commission a gentleman—Mr. Knipe—
who was a practical man, so far as the
case of the tenant farmers was concerned, and who had some knowledge of
the condition of things which the Commission had to investigate. Mr. Knipe
made a separate Report, in which he
stated that rents were not being paid
out of earnings, but out of sums which
tenants had accumulated to meet emer-
gencies in their families and to provide
for their declining years; and he further

contended that the Report of the majority did not represent the severity of
the situation, and that coercive legislation would not only fail to secure
tranquillity, but would seriously aggravate present difficulties. He complained
that the Government had disregarded that
Report, but he promised them that the
country should know all about it. It had
been said that the Whiteboy Acts were
after all not so very drastic. They were,
however, so drastic that if they were
enforced in England every organization
in the country could be swept away.
As one who believed strongly in the
advantages of organization, he objected
to placing in the hands of the Lord
Lieutenant the power of suppressing all
organizations; and he should do his
utmost to oppose this Bill. Reference
had been made to the alleged letter of
the hon. Member for Cork (Mr. Parnell),
which *The Times* had recently published.
The noble Lord the Member for Hampshire (Viscount Wolmer) asserted that
the hon. Member for Cork had no course
open to him other than to commence
legal proceedings against *The Times*.
But every man should be deemed innocent until those who had made a
charge proved it, and he protested, as a
poor man, against the theory that it was
the duty of a Member of Parliament to
embark on the expense of legal proceedings to rebut charges that might be
made against him. There were poor
men in that House against whom
slanders might be hurled, and were they
to be held to lie under the stigma of
them unless they were prepared to enter
upon an expensive action in order to
defend their character? It was an entire
reversal of what had always been understood as legal justice in this country.
It was for the people who made a charge,
whatever it might be, to prove it. With
regard to the Bill, he hoped that the Government would give some further
justification for it before the House was
asked to proceed to the Committee stage.
Those who opposed the Bill believed
that it was most ill-advised, and that
the only plan was to take the Irish
people into our confidence, and give up
attempting to govern Ireland as a conquered country.

MR. FENWICK (Northumberland,
Wansbeck) said, it might be as well to
remind the Tory Members of their
alliance with the Parnellite Members

when the Liberal Government, in 1885, proposed to re-enact certain provisions of the Crimes Act of 1882. Hon. Gentlemen opposite had not been careful to read all that had then fallen from the Leaders of their own Party, or they would have been aware that the Bill which was now before the House had been severely criticized by the noble Lord the Member for South Paddington (Lord Randolph Churchill), who, until recently, has held a responsible position in that Party. In 1885, the noble Lord, addressing a meeting at Bromley-by-Bow, criticized the provisions of the Act which was then in operation, especially the provision for the change of venue. The noble Lord, on that occasion, told his hearers that the position which the Liberal Party had taken up in their proposal to renew the Crimes Act amounted to this, that the peasantry of Galway were so ignorant and brutal, and sympathized so much with crime, that none of them could be tried in Galway, but must be taken away to Dublin and Belfast. He (Mr. Fenwick) admitted that if the noble Lord had also added the Old Bailey, London, he would very justly and accurately have described the provisions in this Bill for the change of venue. Those peasants were not to be tried now by a jury selected from the peasant class, but by a jury drawn from the upper classes, and composed of Protestants. That speech was made by the noble Lord a few days before the fall of the Government of the right hon. Member for Mid Lothian. The more carefully the provisions of the present Bill were considered by hon. Members, and by the country generally, and the more those hon. Gentlemen who supported the Bill were induced to make speeches in its favour, the more clearly and distinctly would its real character be revealed. The Government, so far as he understood, had entirely abandoned the plea of excessive crime in Ireland, and for the simple reason that there was not in Ireland such excessive crime as to warrant such a measure as was now proposed for the acceptance of the House. If the Government had been more honest, they would have distinctly told the House at first what they and their supporters had since stated—that the Bill was not intended to deal with crime and outrage, but was intended to strengthen a certain political faction in Ireland, to strike at

Mr. Fenwick

a political organization, and to suppress the National League. He would remind hon. Gentlemen opposite that the National League was an organization created by the free and spontaneous wish of five-sixths of the Irish people. The Liberal Unionists, who had undertaken to keep the Government in power until they had passed such a Bill as this, ought, he thought, to impress on the Government the necessity of extending their Bill, not only to the National League, but also to the Primrose League, and the Orange organization in Ireland. ["Hear, hear!"] An hon. Gentleman on the Ministerial side of the House said "hear, hear," to that; but the Primrose League, in his (Mr. Fenwick's) opinion, was as gigantic an organization for Boycotting and intimidation as ever the National League was. On the principle that "he takes from me my life who takes from me the means by which I live," hon. Gentlemen opposite, and those associated with the Primrose League, were as guilty as those who were said to be associated with the hon. Member for Cork (Mr. Parnell) in the perpetration of outrages. Perhaps the House would permit him to give an example of what he meant— an incident which he thought would be within the memory of some hon. Gentlemen in this House. This was a case of Boycotting which came under his own observation, and for the authenticity of which he was prepared to vouch. A gentleman of middle age, intelligent, and industrious, at the Election of 1885 took the chair at a meeting held in support of the Liberal candidate in his Division. His employer at that time was the Tory candidate; and without any other reason being assigned than the fact that he had the courage of his convictions, and had come forward to speak out those convictions on a public platform, and urged his fellow-workmen to support the Liberal candidate, he received notice to leave his employment, and for three long months he was Boycotted in that district, and not a single employer would give him an hour's work. He would now turn for a few minutes to a speech that was delivered last night by the noble Lord (Viscount Wolmer). He (Mr. Fenwick) had read somewhere of "the courage that shuts its eyes, and blindly rushes on to its own destruction." The speech of the noble Lord evidently showed the courage of despair. The noble Lord said that the real point at issue was whether Ireland should be governed by the National League or against and in spite of the League. "We," said the noble Lord—meaning the Liberal Unionists, for they were really the Party who were in power, though the Conservatives were in receipt of the emoluments of Office—"intend to beat the National League." More resolute men than the noble Lord had endeavoured to rule Ireland by repression and coercion, and their efforts had proved futile, and it would yet be found that this attempt to govern Ireland by coercion would fail. The policy of the Government stood condemned before the country. ["No, no!"] There was not a single town of any importance in the country where a free spontaneous meeting could be held in favour of the policy that was now proposed by the Government. ["Oh, oh!"] He was surprised that hon. Gentlemen opsite seemed to question that statement. Why, the Government had already been compelled to manufacture resolutions at headquarters, and to send them down to the branches of the Primrose League in the country, suggesting that meetings should be held in a hole-and-corner fashion, and that resolutions of support and sympathy should be sent to Lord Salisbury. He would read to the House the copy of the Circular sent round to the members of the Primrose League in the country. The Circular was as follows:—

"Dear Sir or Madame,—I am desired to request that you will, without delay, suggest to your Habitation to pass a resolution expressing confidence in Lord Salisbury, and approval of his Irish policy. Such resolution should be forwarded to the Grand Council at the earliest possible moment, and it is important that the resolution should be noted in the local press. I append a form which has been approved—'That this meeting views with indignation the systematic obstruction which the Government is receiving in its endeavours to carry out its fundamental duties of securing the lives, liberties, and property of Her Majesty's subjects, and begs to assure Lord Salisbury of its unabated confidence in his policy, and its entire approval of the proposed amendment to the Criminal Law, by which the system of intimidation and illegal conspiracy now rampant in Ireland can be crushed.'"

He (Mr. Fenwick) would venture to repeat that the Tory Party could not, in any town of importance in this country, secure a majority of votes in favour of

such a resolution as that. The noble Lord the Member for Petersfield (Viscount Wolmer) said that the Government had declared that the land war in Ireland must cease; but how was it to be brought to an end? By the suppression of the National League? By enacting laws in favour of the rich against the poor? By making it illegal for the tenants in Ireland to combine in order to secure just reduction of excessive rents? It was in this way that the Government intended to put down the land war in Ireland. The noble Lord also went on to say that the Judges in Ireland had pronounced against the system of terrorism that reigned in Ireland; but he (Mr. Fenwick) held in his hand a resolution that was passed by the Grand Jury of the County of Cork, representing the division of Bantry and Skibbereen. This was the declaration of the Grand Jury after Judge Fergusson had congratulated them on the present state of the division. The Grand Jury spontaneously passed a resolution condemning the Coercion Bill as unnecessary and un-Constitutional; so that if, on the one hand, there were Irish Judges who declared that a state of terrorism existed in Ireland, there were, on the other hand, other Judges who had spoken strongly and directly as to the peaceful condition of the country. The noble Lord the Member for South Paddington (Lord Randolph Churchill) had stated that Ireland, at present, was particularly free from exceptional crime. The absence of crime seemed to be the reason why the Government had brought in their Coercion Bill. The Government had appointed a Royal Commission to ascertain whether unjust rents were charged in Ireland or not. That Commission, which had been selected by the Government itself, had now reported unfavourably as to the excessive rents that were being charged; yet now the Government were, in reality, throwing away the Report of their own Commission. They refused to act upon the recommendations of the Commissioners. It was in keeping with the whole policy and traditions of the Tory Party to undertake to enact laws that would suppress the poor in favour of the rich. In the face of this, it was an insult to the Irish people for the Government to talk of bringing in remedial measures for the tenants. The noble Lord the Member for Petersfield (Viscount Wolmer) resented the charge that was being brought against those Liberal Unionists who were supporting a Bill for Coercion, and immediately proceeded to lay down this principle, that the Home Rule Liberals in the House of Commons had entered into a partnership with the National League, and that it was impossible for the Liberal Home Rulers to dissociate themselves from the deeds of the League ; on the same principle it might be said the Liberal Unionists had entered into a partnership with the Tory Government in order to suppress the liberties of the Irish people, and it would be impossible for the Liberal Unionists to dissociate themselves from the evil consequences that might follow from such a mad policy as the Government were now bent on pursuing. He had no hesitation in saying that this Bill would prove as complete a failure as the coercion policy that had been pursued in the past. The only just and proper way to restore law and order in Ireland, and to make the Irish people respect the law, was by the Government setting itself immediately to repeal unjust laws, and bring in sound remedial measures. They could only permanently restore law and order in Ireland when they had brought the law into harmony with the desires of the Irish people. Until that was done, he maintained the task undertaken by the Government was hopeless; and they would never succeed until they had removed the repression under which the Irish people was now compelled to live.

Mr. W. F. LAWRENCE (Liverpool, Abercromby) said, he was able to controvert the statement made by the hon. Member who had just spoken, that there was not an important town in England in which a spontaneous public meeting could be held in favour of the Irish policy of the Government. So far from that being the case, he would state that on Easter Monday, in the City of Liverpool, there was a large open-air meeting got up and spoken to by working men strongly endorsing the present action of Her Majesty's Government. A great deal had been said making comparisons between the action of Boycotting in Ireland and the action of the Primrose League. He would only say in regard to that, that whatever Boycotting the Primrose League might have been guilty

Mr. Fenwick

of, it had never had the sanction of crime to support it. That was the difference between Boycotting and the action of the Primrose League. He thought such Amendments as they were now discussing were merely red herrings drawn across the track to divert them from the true question, which was the question of the Union and the integrity of the country. Hon. Members below the Gangway were fond of talking about protecting the agricultural interest, but their Leader had stated in a historic phrase that he would never "have taken his coat off" to promote the interests of the Land Question, but it was for a very different purpose he was working. The real question before the House was who should govern Ireland —the responsible and Constitutional Government of the country or the National League ? And how were they to best govern Ireland, united as the two countries were, and yet unequal in their circumstances ? What they wished was, to govern Ireland with the minimum of friction and to give her equal liberty and equal justice with England. A great deal had been said about the increase in the number of evictions since last November; but what about the Plan of Campaign ? Had that not caused the increased evictions ? [" No, no ! "] He was sure that it was as certain as it could possibly be that the initiation of the Plan of Campaign had been the cause of much increased eviction. With regard to the depreciation in the value of land which had been referred to, that was hardly to be wondered at when the attention of the cultivators was distracted from their land to political agitation and Moonlighting ; and as for the scarcity of money, its cause might be traced to the pockets of the promoters of that agitation. It had been said that the Government were going to reduce the Irish people to a state of half-citizenship. He did not think the Bill would have that effect; but it certainly would restrict some of the liberties they at present enjoyed— for instance, that of maiming and torturing dumb animals. But he had yet to learn that such cruelty was consistent with the rights and duties of whole citizenship. The right hon. Member for the Brightside Division of Sheffield (Mr. Mundella) said the day before that the Government were more intent on trying measures which were consonant with the English conscience, but had less regard to justice to Ireland. He was quite content that any measure which the Government brought in should harmonize with the conscience of the English people, because he was sure the conscience of the English people would never go wrong; but justice to Ireland could not be separated from justice to England. The conscience of the English people saw that the safety of·the mass of the people was the highest law, and they said that the majority of the people of these islands were entitled to say how these islands were to be governed. The first duty of the Government was the maintenance of law and order, and nobody had held up that duty more strongly in the past than the right hon. Member for Mid Lothian (Mr. W. E. Gladstone). It was said that we ought to be guided by the opinion of the majority in Ireland; but could that be carried to its full extent? Would it be said that if the majority in Ireland demanded separation or to be united with the American Republic we should give way? For his part, he would do his utmost to discourage all such vain hopes. The Whiteboy Acts had been described as monstrous; but they were at present in force, and yet the country could not be governed even with them, and the reason was that the juries of the country had been demoralized by the amenities of the Land League. Lord Macaulay had been quoted to prove that the Union had been supported by Coercion Acts, and it had been said that there had been 85 Acts passed since the Union. That, he believed, was not true; only 40 had been passed, the other 45 being passed by the so-called independent Irish Parliament. During the time of the Irish Parliament the relations of the two Parliaments were very much strained by such a subject even as a Regency Bill. Hon. Members seemed to lose sight of the fact that England and Ireland must remain united, and that the only question which concerned thinking men was which process would keep them together with the least friction to both of them. Something had been said about the enlightened and intelligent opinion of America being against the Government on the question. He did not attach much importance to that statement, because he did not think the opinion of America had very often been on the side of the Mother Country. Was it not the fact that the intelligent and enlightened opinion of America was also in favour of driving a coach and six through the Treaty of 1818. He also bore in mind the Alabama Claims, and as long as the surplus amount paid for those claims remained in the pockets of Americans he did not attach much importance to that intelligent and enlightened opinion. He thought the less attention England paid to the opinions expressed outside the better she would get on.

MR. MAHONY (Meath, N.) said, that the right hon. Gentleman the Chief Secretary for Ireland (Mr. A. J. Balfour) has said that it was necessary to pass this Bill in order to secure the fair working of a Land Purchase Bill for Ireland. That appeared on the face of it to be an extraordinary statement. It amounted to this—that a Land Purchase Bill was to be passed on behalf of the Irish tenants, which was to be of such a character as to require a Coercion Bill to ram it down the throats of the Irish people. They had already a Land Purchase Act in Ireland, and they were told that the National League were doing their best to prevent its working. He denied that *in toto*. If hon. Members would turn to the evidence of a large land agent in the County Kerry (Mr. George Sands), given before the Cowper Commission, they would see that he stated that the prominent Nationalists in his locality did everything they could to bring about a settlement between landlord and tenant on a property with which he was connected, and that the result was that the estate was sold. There was no opposition to the sale on the part of the National League. On the contrary, they did everything they could to assist in carrying it out. And why? Because the terms which the landlord was willing to accept were fair terms. What the National League had been trying to do, and had done, was to prevent the tenants, under pressure from the landlords, agreeing to purchase upon terms they could not possibly carry out in the future. He thought that they wanted some Bill to prevent the landlords bringing unfair pressure upon the tenants to make them purchase. General Buller had referred to the landlords' pressure, and had said that some counteracting pressure was required. But the Government did not propose to give them that. But landlords in Ireland had been able to bring pressure to bear in order to make their tenants agree to purchase their holdings on unfair terms ; and the Land Commissioners had, in 434 cases, involving the amount of £317,000, refused to sanction the terms agreed òn between the landlord and the tenants under the Land Act. What did that mean ? It meant that, in the present state of Ireland, before open combination amongst the tenants was put down by the Bill, the landlords in Ireland had been able to force their terms of purchase on the tenants. In 67 other cases, the Land Commissioners had reduced the total amounts of purchase from £61,000 to £50,000, a reduction of 22 per cent. These facts showed that, even without the Coercion Acts, the landlords had powers to compel tenants to accept their terms, and that in these cases there was not sufficient security, taking the joint interest of the landlord and the tenant together. What they wanted was a Bill to prevent the landlords from bringing unfair pressure to bear on the tenants ; but the Government only proposed to put down the legitimate combination among the tenants in Ireland, and they told them that that was necessary in order to allow their remedial measures to work. All he could say was, that if, in the face of the cases which he had brought forward, they brought in a Purchase Bill, and rammed it down the throats of the Irish people with a Coercion Act, the Irish people would be justified in repudiating it at the first opportunity, and he should certainly advise them to do so. If people were forced to accept certain terms, they would repudiate them whenever they got the opportunity. The Chancellor of the Exchequer had asserted that tenants were able to pay in many cases of evictions, and that these evictions had been got up by the National League. He thought it was a disgraceful thing that that assertion should be made, after it had been absolutely denied and after the evidence given by General Buller. There was one clause permitting tenants to make application to the Court for their own bankruptcy. That clause was an utter sham ; but there were other clauses in the Bill which were not shams, and

Mr. Mahony

were not meant to be shams, and those were clauses for the relief of the landlords. The Bankruptcy Clause enabled the landlord to make all his tenants bankrupt, and then there was the clause to render evictions easy. The Chief Secretary told the House that he did not press his case of statistics. He (Mr. Mahony) should think not, indeed. Then the Chief Secretary gave them a number of Judges' charges—extra-judicial utterances of which they in Ireland knew very well the worth. Last night, the hon. Member for East Mayo (Mr. Dillon) tore that portion of the case into rags. With regard to the system of abuse to which their opponents were now having recourse, *The Times* was only at its old work. In 1843 it had attacked Mr. Cobden, with regard to the supposed attempt to murder Sir Robert Peel ; and there was a strange similarity between the article in which that attack had been made and those which they had seen in that paper lately, and he thought the result would be the same. The great movement in which Mr. Cobden was then engaged was not in the slightest degree impeded by the action of *The Times,* and neither would the movement which the Parnellites were engaged in. Theirs was the cause of justice, and as such it was certain to succeed.

Motion made, and Question, "That the Debate be now adjourned,"—(*Mr. T. P. O'Connor,*)—put, and *agreed to.*

Debate *further adjourned* till *To-morrow.*

DUKE OF CONNAUGHT'S LEAVE BILL.

(*Mr. William Henry Smith, Mr. Secretary Stanhope, Sir John Gorst.*)

[BILL 228.]   SECOND READING.

Order for Second Reading read.

Mr. DILLWYN and Sir JOHN SWINBURNE rose simultaneously and objected.

THE FIRST LORD OF THE TREASURY (Mr. W. H. SMITH) (Strand, Westminster): I hope that the objection will not be persisted in, and that the second reading will be allowed to be taken. [*Cries of* "Order!"] I may point out that the Duke of Connaught, during his absence from India, will receive no salary whatever. By an arrangement this Bill is rendered necessary, and should be passed without delay, in order to enable His Royal

Highness to leave India without vacating his command. [*Renewed cries of* "Order!"] I appeal to hon. Members—[*Further cries of* "Order!"]

MR. SPEAKER: If any hon. Member objects that is sufficient to block the Bill.

Second Reading *deferred* till *Tomorrow.*

QUESTION.

THE MAGISTRACY (IRELAND)—RESIDENT MAGISTRATES—RETURN AS TO PROFESSIONS, QUALIFICATIONS, &c.

MR. E. ROBERTSON (Dundee) asked the First Lord of the Treasury, in the absence of the Chief Secretary for Ireland, Whether he could give any information as to the promised Return concerning the professional qualifications and antecedents of Resident Magistrates in Ireland?

THE FIRST LORD OF THE TREASURY (Mr. W. H. SMITH) (Strand, Westminster), in reply, said, that not having had Notice of the Question, he was not in a position to give an answer; but he would communicate at once with the Chief Secretary, and, if possible, reply to-morrow.

MOTION.

EDUCATION (SCOTLAND) ACTS AMENDMENT (NO. 2) BILL.

On Motion of Mr. Buchanan, Bill to amend the Education (Scotland) Acts, 1872 to 1883, *ordered* to be brought in by Mr. Buchanan, Mr. James Campbell, Mr. Edward Russell, Mr. Esslemont, Mr. Preston Bruce, Mr. Lacaita, and Mr. Donald Crawford.

Bill *presented*, and read the first time. [Bill 242.]

House adjourned at ten minutes before Six o'clock.

HOUSE OF LORDS,

Thursday, 28th April, 1887.

SHEFFIELD CORPORATION WATER BILL.

THIRD READING.

Order of the Day for the Third Reading, read.

Moved, "That the Bill be now read 3ª." —(*The Earl of Derby.*)

THE EARL OF WEMYSS, in rising to move, as an Amendment, that the Bill be read a third time that day six months, said: My Lords, In pursuance of the Notice I have given, I now move that this Bill be read a third time this day six months; and I may say I have put that Notice on the Paper at the request of several noble Friends of mine who take a deep interest in this question. I should not for one moment have thought of putting such a Notice on the Paper if the Bill had been a Water Bill of the ordinary character; but, so far from that, the Bill comes to us from a Committee of your Lordships' House, recommended, not as a Bill of ordinary character, but recommended to your Lordships' adoption upon grounds of public policy. Now, my Lords, this Bill which is so recommended involves a novel principle, and the public policy which is to be found in this Bill is neither more nor less than this—the substitution of a municipal monopoly in the matter of water supply—the compulsory substitution of a municipal monopoly for private enterprize. Now, my Lords, the Committee do not assert, or in any way say, that the Water Company, which for many years has provided water to Sheffield, has been in any way wanting in its duty. They do not say the Company have been guilty of providing an insufficient supply, or accuse them of overcharges, or of providing impure water. So far from that, in consequence of the way in which this Company has dealt with Sheffield in the matter of its water supply, the Committee of your Lordships' House say that they hope the Company will be liberally treated when it comes to a question as to what sum is to be paid to them if this compulsory power is given to the Corporation. Now, my Lords, I think it is possible that an attempt may be made to induce your Lordships to assent to this Bill, which, I venture to say, contains a very novel and, I think, very dangerous and hurtful principle, on the ground that the purchase of works of an existing private enterprize only applied to a locality—that it only applies to Sheffield—and that, therefore, not being a general Bill, your Lordships may agree to pass a measure. Supposing such an argument is used? It is an argument with which your Lordships, by this time, ought to be familiar. It is an old friend with a new face and with a new name; but still it is the old argument of exceptional legislation. Well, my Lords, we know how—when exceptional legislation is passed in favour of any case—the evil grows. Noble Lords who come from other places besides Ireland know how evil principles introduced into legislation under the guise of exceptional circumstances have spread to Scotland; and they are showing themselves in the Metropolis in reference to leaseholds. Therefore, I wish your Lordships to treat this question—as I think it should present itself to your Lordships—as a great question of principle, and to treat it, not in its local, but in its general application. My Lords, I have very much doubt, if this Bill is passed, whether Sheffield will be greatly benefited by its becoming law. It so happens that other Corporations besides Sheffield have dealt with water, as they have with gas, in the United Kingdom for many years; and although these Corporations have prospered in their dealings with gas, yet they have failed and lost money in their dealings with water. For instance—and I believe they themselves admit it—the Manchester Corporation, who took up the water supply of Manchester in the year 1858, have, up to the present time, lost £110,000. The town of Bury—a town with which my noble Friend who was Chairman of this Committee (the Earl of Derby) is connected — that Town Council also took up the supply of water, and it has lost £3,000 in so doing; and your Lordships must remember that these are losses which came upon the rates generally. They are made up by

extra charges on the borough funds, which applies to people who, in many cases, do not benefit by the water. Therefore, my Lords, it is not always Corporations who are successful in their trading, and although they have succeeded in gas, they have failed in water; and I very much doubt whether the town of Sheffield will, under this Bill, be better supplied with water than it has been by the private enterprize of the Water Company, which it is now intended compulsorily to abolish. With reference to the trading by Corporations, I should like to ask why they should be confined to gas and water? Gas is not such a necessity of life as bread or clothing; and, that being so, why should not Corporations—if they are to become traders—deal in clothes, and keep tailors' shops? Why should they not keep bakers' shops and butchers' shops, and deal in anything which is necessary to life? Why should they not keep a great store like the Army and Navy Stores in London? This Bill is brought before your Lordships as a compulsory Bill. My objection to this Bill is that its compulsory character is now for the first time introduced into this kind of legislation; and I ask, if it is to be applied to gas and water, why should it not apply to all other necessaries of life? Then we shall come to this pass, that no man in the City of London, nor in this free country, will be able to live, move, or have his being without being under some sort of government or local inspection as to his private business. That is what it will come to under this proposed system of legislation. But, my Lords, I will admit, for the sake of argument—I do not admit it otherwise—that this Bill will confer a benefit on the town of Sheffield. Even admitting that, for the sake of argument, I still ask your Lordships, on the very ground upon which this Bill is submitted to your Lordships—namely, on the ground of public policy—on these broad grounds, and on that broad principle, I invite your Lordships not to consent to the third reading of this Bill. My Lords, what will be the effect of passing a compulsory measure of this kind? It will entitle the Corporation of Sheffield to take forcible possession—I do not care whether they pay fair compensation or not—it will entitle them to take forcible possession of works which they have not created, but which were

The Earl of Wemyss

croated by private enterprize. That necessarily must discourage private enterprize; and what has private enterprize done for this country? Why everything. It is private enterprize that has given us canals; it is private enterprize that has given us railways; it is private enterprize that has given us gas, electric lighting, and the telephone; it is private enterprize that puts, not only part of the country in communication with another by means of railways and telegraphs, but which by telegraphs put the Empire into connection with the Colonies and our Indian Possessions. All that is the result of private enterprize. At the present moment the greatest engineering work which has ever been undertaken in this age of engineering skill—the Forth Bridge, in which many noble Lords in this House take an interest—that is entirely the result of private enterprize. It was private enterprize which cut the Isthmus of Suez, and which is cutting the Isthmus of Panama; and, above all, do not forget this, that it was private enterprize, and nothing else, which gave us our Indian Empire, and practically our Colonial Empire. Well, my Lords, I say in countries such as ours it is essential that nothing shall be done for the benefit of any local town or for any other reason which can interfere with the great principle of independent and private enterprize. Macaulay, in the third chapter of his History, referring to the progress that this country had made in the hundred years before he wrote, said it was due mainly to the confidence and security which was afforded to property in this country and that which was created by industry, energy, or by self-denial. Whether that property was created by, and remains the property of, individuals, or whether it is aggregated into the property of Companies, the principle is the same; and I ask your Lordships to take care how you deal with that principle in this House. Above all other Assemblies, your Lordships' House ought to be looked upon as the guardian of the questions involved in this great principle. What is the secret of all this successful private enterprize? It is, as Macaulay says, confidence and security with reference to property. If you take away confidence and security, what hope can there be that there will be private enterprize in the future as there has been in the past?

If, whenever a Company is prosperous, a municipality may cast its eye—a covetous eye—upon it, and come to Parliament to buy, even though they are not disposed to sell, there will be an end to all confidence. It has been well said by Sir Frederick Bramwell—the most able engineer, and brother of the distinguished Lord who bears the name—that Government trading, whether local or imperial, was fatal to progress and to the national prosperity. If your Lordships wish for an example how unwise State interference is you have it in a Bill which has passed or is passing through your Lordships' House—I mean the Electric Lighting Bill. In 1882, an Electric Lighting Bill was brought in by the Government of the day, which empowered the Government at the end of 14 years to take possession of the property of Electric Lighting Companies without giving compensation on taking the business on as a going concern, but treating it as an old marine store, and simply at the end of 14 years paying for the plant as old iron. The time was extended when that should happen from 14 to 20 years. That Bill was passed in 1882, and what has happened? All enterprize in electric lighting was absolutely and entirely stopped and killed by these compulsory powers which the Government proposed to take. So last year, electric lighting being at a standstill, a Bill was brought in and submitted to a Committee of your Lordships' House, which proposed to extend the 20 years when the Government could come in to 40 years. The Bill which is now passing through your Lordships' House is based on that extended period. That is a most pregnant instance of the evil of compulsory interference with private enterprize, and it is because I feel that it is in the cause of public policy, it is on the ground—the sole ground—of public policy, that I ask your Lordships to refuse to pass this Bill. There is one point which must have struck your Lordships, and to which I have not referred; and that is that it is always right and customary for your Lordships to support the decision of a Committee of your own House. Now, my Lords, that is a general proposition which no sane man in your Lordships' House, and no sane man in the other House of Parliament, would for one moment venture to dispute. While I was a Member of the

House of Commons, and since I have been a Member of your Lordships' House, whenever a decision of a Committee has been attempted to be overthrown, I have always given my vote in favour of the decision of the Committee. I think we ought to be grateful to noble Lords who give their time to these Committees, and it is only under most exceptional and most peculiar circumstances that your Lordships, or the other House, should be asked not to give effect to the views of the Committee. Now, if this had been a simple question between two Private Bills promoted by the Corporation and the Water Company in the ordinary course, with no new principle involved, I should not have ventured to have given this Notice, and I should have been considered extremely foolish if I had done so. But this is entirely a different case. Although there were attempts made to prove before the Committee that there was a precedent for this Bill of the Corporation, if I am rightly informed the Chairman of the Committee did not think much of the precedents adduced, and the promoters were advised to go on to other points and not to attempt to prove their case by precedents. It is well they were so advised, for no precedent exists for their Bill. I say this Bill is novel in principle, wholly unprecedented in character, and, for the first time, it imposes upon a Company the possibility—a certainty in this case—that they would have to part with their property at whatever sum the arbitrators chose to fix. This is a question wholly outside any question which is ordinarily referred to a Committee of your Lordships' House. Indeed, my Lords, I say that it never could have been your Lordships' intention that five Members of this House—no matter how able, no matter what their record of Parliamentary experience may be—should, upon the question of a Private Bill, introduce into legislation a great and novel principle which may strike at the very roots of enterprize and the commercial prosperity of the nation, which lives upon the security of property which has been created by private enterprize. I maintain that a principle such as that ought not to be passed in your Lordships' House on the third reading of a Private Bill, but ought, if required, to be taken up by the Government, and take its place in a general measure

brought in by the responsible Government. I hope, my Lords, that your Lordships will not pay attention to the arguments about supporting the decisions of Committees, but will support me in my Motion for the rejection of this Bill.

Amendment *moved*, to leave out ("now") and add at the end of the Motion ("this day six months.")—(*The Earl of Wemyss.*)

THE EARL OF DERBY, in rising to support the Bill, said, that neither he nor any of the noble Lords who considered the Bill in Committee had any sympathy whatever with the Socialistic ideas of which his noble Friend on the Cross Bench (the Earl of Wemyss) was so much afraid. They were not enemies of property or of private enterprize. The Committee in question had devoted 14 days to the consideration of the Bill, and whilst he sympathized to a great extent with the noble Earl, he could not forget that there were many undertakings which could be better managed by public authorities than by private enterprize; and this matter of water supply appeared to be one of them. The state of things at Sheffield was as follows. There were two Bills before the Committee, one promoted by the Corporation and the other by the old Water Company at Sheffield, which had for many years supplied the borough. In 1864 it sustained a great disaster owing to the bursting of the principal reservoir, and it then came to Parliament for relief, and obtained power to levy for 25 years an increased water rate. This power would expire in 1889, and the Company, in the Bill which they recently promoted, sought to make it perpetual. Then came the Bill promoted by the Sheffield Corporation, in which they sought to take the water supply into their own hands. They were supported by the great bulk of the ratepayers, the voting having been something like 21,000 for, and 3,000 against. The Committee, after hearing the arguments *pro* and *con* in favour of the higher scale of rates, came to the conclusion that the Sheffield Water Company's request was not a reasonable one, and that it ought to be rejected; and the only alternatives were to allow the Company to go on supplying the water on the old rate or to transfer to the Corporation the powers of supplying the water. The Committee were influenced in their decision by the fact that the sanitary arrangements of Sheffield were unsatisfactory, and that to be made satisfactory they required to be carried out on a wider scale; and also by the fact that the water supply was in the North of England generally in the hands of the municipal authorities. They therefore resolved to transfer the powers of water supply to the Sheffield Corporation, and made provision upon a very generous basis for the purchase of the Company's undertaking. He had little doubt that the present shareholders in the Sheffield Water Company would in reality be much better off by the purchase of their property, than they would have been by going on with their undertaking on the reduced scale of rates, which was all they would have been entitled to after 1889.

Lord GRIMTHORPE said, what they had to consider was how their decision would be looked at hereafter. The record would be only that in the case of a Company, absolved twice from the charge of negligence, their works should be sold compulsorily, on the ground of public policy. If he were still at the Bar, and were representing a Corporation, he should know what use to make of that record. He learned in 1864 that the Company had reduced their maximum charges in 1853, believing that their prosperity and that of Sheffield would go on increasing. They said that since that time the great calamity of the landslip and flood had come upon them and upon the town, and on application to Parliament they were granted increased rates for 25 years. The Chairman of the Committee, and he (Lord Grimthorpe) himself, thought that by the end of that period things would have come round, and the Company thought so also. They were all wrong; and the real fact was that the dividends had been continually going down, notwithstanding the additional rates. There was no doubt that if these rates were stopped the Company would have no dividends at all. They could now prophesy after the event, and it was clear that the company were asking for nothing unreasonable in asking for the rates, which were still below the original ones, for a purer period than 25 years, and there could be no doubt that if the Committee that would have seen in 1864 how things

would turn out, that they would be granted a longer period. In his opinion, the present Committee must have miscarried in their calculations, in supposing they were giving fair and liberal terms. If the Company in 1853 had kept up their old rates instead of decreasing them they would never have had to come to Parliament, and would have been able to pay a dividend notwithstanding the calamity. The Corporation had issued a paper of reasons for the purchase of the undertaking. The paper said that it was a generally admitted axiom that water-works should be in the hands of Corporations, as they were more economically worked. That was not the general result of experience. Mr. Burdett, secretary to the Loan Department of the Stock Exchange, read a paper on municipal finance some two years ago, and showed in it that out of 38 Corporations' books it was evident that upon the whole they lost upon their water-works. They borrowed at $3\frac{1}{2}$ per cent, and did not receive as much in return as they paid in interest. It was absolutely wrong to say that Corporations could manage these undertakings more economically than Companies could. The latter paid dividends, and the former did not make enough to pay the lowest common rate of interest. The noble Earl (the Earl of Derby) said the ratepayers by a large majority were in favour of the Bill. They always were, because they did not understand economics. He admitted that when a Corporation and a Company came to Parliament for rival Bills for water-works, it had been the practice to prefer the Corporation. No harm was done to anybody under those circumstances; but the present case was one of buying on very unfair terms. The only case approximating to it was that of Middlesborough. In that case the Company were charged with supplying very bad and insufficient water, being restricted in the quantity they could take from the Tees. The result was that the works passed out of the hands of the Company into the hands of the Corporation, and that Corporation, which had been so sensitive when they got the Bill 11 years ago, had not done a stroke of work yet, or had done it very recently if at all. That was the only case of straightforward compulsory purchase founded on the alleged misconduct of a Company. At Birmingham the Company agreed to sell their works to the Corporation in 1851. The Corporation went on for 2½ years before they thought of acting upon the agreement, and then Mr. Chamberlain persuaded them to purchase the undertaking. They inserted in the Bill a provision for 20 years' purchase. The Committee declined to pass the clause, and eventually 29 years' purchase was agreed upon. Was that a good thing for the town? It gratified the town, and there was no doubt that the time would come when it would be a good thing for the town if the Company were otherwise to go on raising more capital with a high dividend, which, however, could easily be prevented. The Corporation also said, in the paper of "Reasons in Favour of Third Reading" which they had issued, that it was not a fact, as stated by the opponents of the Bill, that Parliament had ever refused to sanction the purchase of the works by the Corporation, and they enlarged upon that point. They seemed to have forgotten that in their own Petition against the Company's Bill this year they had said exactly the opposite. They said that they had several times endeavoured to effect such transfer. They tried it in 1864, and the Committee were of opinion that the Corporation had not made out a sufficient case for compulsory purchase. The Corporation said, first of all, that they were going to proceed upon particular local grounds, and not on public policy, and then they issued that paper which, from beginning to end, argued the case upon grounds of public policy. A worse case of issuing misleading statements he had never seen. Nobody would suffer in an ordinary case of purchase by arbitration. In this case the Company would suffer by being ruined, and every shareholder would feel it. The ratepayers would gain by the transfer, because they would get for nothing these works which cost a million and some odd pounds. As to the assertion about public policy, he had shown that every precedent contradicted it, and so does the only public Act on the subject. It would have been perfectly easy for the framers of the Public Health Act to have provided that it should be lawful for any Corporation to buy the water works on arbitration terms. They were authorized to buy water rights—a totally

Lord Grimthorpe

different thing—from the persons possessing them, but they were very carefully excluded from buying water works compulsorily, especially on such terms as these, which practically told the arbitrator to treat the Company as insolvent after 1894. He could not see any grounds for passing the Bill.

LORD BALFOUR said, at one time, in consequence of his connection with the Local Government Board, which he represented, he had had his attention called to some provisions in the Bill; but those matters were all arranged. Whilst looking into those matters he was brought into contact with the promoters of the Bill, and had an opportunity of learning how matters really stood. The mistake in the paper of reasons as to Parliament having never refused to sanction the transfer of the works had crept in through the death of the late Town Clerk. It was discovered by a gentleman in the office of the agents who circulated the paper, but too late, as the paper had been sent to all the Peers. He was sure his noble Friend did not intend to imply that the Corporation had made wilful mis-statements. It would not have been of any use to have made an attempt to mislead the House, as the Chairman of the Committee was also the Chairman of the Committee which refused to sanction the transfer, and it would not have passed unnoticed. The noble Lord's contradiction of the statement in the paper proved that this was no new question for the people of Sheffield, and that they had had ample time to make up their minds on the question, and the majority which had been quoted by the noble Earl in favour of the purchase was the more significant for that fact. It was the result of no catch vote, but the deliberate vote of the people of the town. He did not think it was just of the noble Lord to say that the Company could be bought for nothing at the end of a certain number of years. He thought the Company was placed in an exceptionally favourable position for going before an arbitrator, and the Select Committee had gone out of its way to say that the terms should be fair and liberal, and that was a most important point on behalf of the Company when they got before the arbitrator, as he hoped they would do if Parliament passed the Bill. A great deal of discussion had gone on about the propriety of Local Authorities managing gas and water works. They were not there to discuss the general question any more than the Committee upstairs. They had to decide whether the Bill should be allowed to pass. The noble Lord said that the Corporation would not be able to make a dividend—a Corporation ought not to make enough to pay a dividend—if it did, it showed that the water was not supplied at the lowest possible rate; and so far from that being an argument against Corporations purchasing these undertakings, it was all the other way. He was quite sure that he would carry the House with him if he said that if it had not been for the expressions of the Committee about public policy, they would never have known about the matter at all. There was another point he would like to allude to, and that was that the noble and learned Lord behind him (Lord Grimthorpe) seemed to imply that Sheffield was a decaying place. He was, however, informed that so far from that being the state of the case, the population of Sheffield had increased since 1864 by 100,000.

LORD GRIMTHORPE said, that he pointed out that the receipts from water had considerably decreased, and that he, therefore, supposed such was the case.

LORD BALFOUR, continuing, said, the noble Earl (the Earl of Wemyss) urged that Sheffield would not benefit by the transfer. He (Lord Balfour) wished to point out that the vote taken in the town resulted in 21,936 being in favour of the change, and only 3,785 against—a very conclusive decision as to the Sheffield feeling in the matter. The noble Earl, again, had complained that local circumstances had not been sufficiently stated for the passing of the Bill. Well, he (Lord Balfour) submitted that if they were to hear all the local circumstances, that would be discussing the question upon its merits, which was undesirable in the House. As to the local circumstances, he thought they might trust a Committee which sat 15 days, and have every confidence that the decision arrived at was a just one. In conclusion, he wished to say that if the noble Earl was so anxious that a Corporation should never be allowed to purchase compulsorily under any circumstances, the right time to have stated that would have been on the occasion of

the second reading, and not on the third, when the parties had been put to such an amount of expense. If action against the Bill were necessary to be taken now, the proper course would obviously have been to move for its re-committal, and if their Lordships now passed the third reading the Bill would still have to go before the other House, when the objectors to it could again be heard.

THE DUKE OF ARGYLL said, he could not quite agree with the noble Lord (Lord Balfour of Burleigh) who had just sat down, when in the earlier part of his speech he said that he should vote for it purely as a Local Bill, and not take the question of public policy into consideration. He thought, on the contrary, that important considerations of public policy were involved in the question, and wished to explain to his noble Friend that in the interest of those general and abstract principles of which he was so powerful an advocate, he hoped that House would not refuse their sanction to read the Bill a third time. One contention was that valuable private property should not be taken by Public Authorities compulsorily to the sacrifice of private interests. He recognized the importance of the principle, and if this Water Company had been a great and thriving concern he should not take the view he did. The speech of his noble Friend opposite, however, proved that the Water Company's position was one which might be practically described as one of bankruptcy. The noble and learned Lord (Lord Grimthorpe) stated that it was not in a position to earn any dividend whatever; and, further, that even under the favourable recommendations of the Committttee, the Company would benefit little or nothing by the compulsory sale. But, at any rate, he relieved their minds from the fear which his hon. Friend on the Cross Benches (the Earl of Wemyss) had sought to instil, which was that they were ex-appropriating a valuable property in Sheffield. The Company, however, unless it obtained new powers, had no valuable property whatever. It came to Parliament and asked for new powers, and surely they had a right to inquire into the matter. They were not bound to give them new powers, and they must look at the whole question as one of public policy as to whether the powers should be granted. That ground of objection had been entirely removed. They were all agreed in one sense or another, and there ought to be some reform in local government in this country. He confessed, however, he was one of those who had been alarmed at the way in which every community was being stimulated to go in for Home Rule. Heaven only knew—or rather "the other place" only knew—what were the powers which leading politicians would not give to local governing bodies. It looked almost as if the power of life and death, and the power of taxation, were to be given over to local governments. He thought that this was a real danger, and that the public mind ought to be disciplined upon the matter. Looking at it in that light, therefore, he considered that it was of the highest importance that Sheffield should not be refused a privilege which she so manifestly asked for. The Company itself was practically non-existent, and they had to consider the question as that of a great city desiring the management of its own wants. He could conceive nothing more likely to exaggerate that feeling in favour of local government than Parliament refusing to great cities any of the legitimate powers they ought to possess. He agreed that it was an argument in favour of Corporations having control of water works that in their hands they did not pay large dividends. The use of water was now so intimately connected with sanitary arrangements that it was most important that the water supply should be in the hands of the Local Authority. Many places had taken over the management of their own water supplies; and Glasgow had done the same thing at enormous expense, but with infinite benefit to its inhabitants, and he firmly believed that such matters derived great advantage by being in the hands of municipal government instead of those of private companies.

Lord BRAMWELL said, he felt it his duty to oppose the third reading of this Bill. The case before them—that of a Company with an undertaking—was not like the common case of a portion of land being wanted without which a scheme could not be carried into execution. Everyone would admit that, however reluctant the man might be to have his land taken, it must be acquired on the ground of public policy. This, however, was a very different thing. Here

the scheme was completed. The Water Works Company were in possession of their water works, which their Act of Parliament gave them power to construct, and it was now proposed to take it from them and to give them compensation. Well, as to that, the noble and learned Lord opposite (Lord Grimthorpe) stated that the Company would not be better off when their property was taken from them, and they received the compensation. At any rate, they said—"Let us be the judges, and leave us alone." The first consideration, therefore, their Lordships had to look at was—did they think it a desirable thing when persons had embarked their capital in an enterprize of this description that anybody unless for the most urgent reason in the world should have the right to say to them—"Now, we shall put a value on your porperty and take it from you, giving you that value for the possession of it?" Was it desirable that when any scheme was propounded requiring capital that those subscribing should be told—"You go into this speculation subject to this, that it may be taken from you at a certain value?" It was a singular thing, but if it was so beneficial to the Water Company shareholders, they were a most ungrateful and unwise set, for he did not find that the value of the shares had risen in the market since. He was sorry to differ from the noble Earl (the Earl of Derby); but he understood him to say that from the discussion on the Company's Bill, the Committee learned that they could not carry into execution those matters which were necessary for the welfare of the Company at Sheffield, and the noble Duke who had just sat down (the Duke of Argyll) used the expression that they were coming for further powers. They were not coming for further powers, except to raise their revenue for the purpose of augmenting their dividend, which had been a small one; but they did not admit, and it was not proved, that their situation was such that they could not do everything that the people of Sheffield had a right to expect. He was told that was so, and he believed that in the reasons given by the Corporation it was not suggested that the means of the Company were not such as that they could do everything which the Corporation could do if the property was transferred to them. All the Company asked was something to enable them to augment their dividend. For these reasons, there was no good cause why their property should be taken from them if they were unwilling to part with it. It was urged that the ratepayers were the best judges of what they wanted, and these were of opinion that the service would be better and cheaper. Well, he did not see how the Corporation could work it more cheaply than the Water Company, and if they paid the Water Company a fair price, it followed that the ratepayers would have as much to pay for their water as they were now doing. It was obvious that if the Corporation could work the affair more cheaply, it would have to pay a fair price, and they must in time charge the ratepayers accordingly. It was said that a great many Corporations had the control of the water supplies. Well, a great many more, on the other hand, had not, and he did not understand that those who had not were worse off than where the power rested in the Corporation; and, he felt perfectly satisfied that it was impossible, in concerns of this sort, that they could be managed as well as by private enterprize. In conclusion, he asked them in a case such as this, where the promoters of an undertaking were unwilling to part with it, whether it was in accordance with public policy to ask Parliament to pass a Bill to compel them to sell that undertaking?

THE CHAIRMAN OF COMMITTEES (The Duke of BUCKINGHAM and CHANDOS) said, from the position he held in the House as the Chairman of Committees, he desired to say a few words, as questions might arise whether the decision of a Committee of their Lordships' House had been given in accordance with the merits of the case placed before them, or whether considerations had been brought in which were not involved in the case before them. He happened to preside over a Committee in 1864, before which the Sheffield Water Company promoted a Bill, and in which they were authorized to make certain charges for 25 years. The 25 years had nearly expired; but at the time the Bill passed, neither the promoters, nor the Corporation, nor the Committee could foresee changes which in such a time had come over Sheffield, nor the expenses which would come on the Water Company. Now, in the pre-

sent Session of 1887, two Bills had been promoted and placed before a Committee. That Committee had negatived the Preamble of the Water Company's Bill, the principal point of which was to perpetuate the charges which, in 1864, had been limited to 25 years. The Committee had, on the other hand, passed the Preamble of the Bill promoted by the Corporation for the compulsory purchase of the Water Company's rights. The Committee, in announcing their decision, had placed on record certain reasons which influenced them in that decision, and it was practically only the statement of those reasons which had caused the debate on the question as to whether the Bill should be read a third time. There was no doubt that many who read the decision and the statement of reasons given by the Committee might consider that, bearing in mind the failure to prove improper management on the part of the Company, as stated by the Committee—they might think that the Committee had travelled beyond their province in negativing the Company's Bill upon the question of public policy. There was no doubt that it was of the greatest importance that there should be full confidence in the decisions of the Select Committees appointed to consider Private Bills. That confidence, he believed, existed universally; but occasionally, no doubt, questions might arise, as had arisen that night; and if the decision to be given that night was a final decision, if that was the second House the Bill had been before, instead of the first House, it might have been a question whether it would not be well to recommit both Bills and refer them to another Committee. But in this case it was not a final decision which the House was asked to give that night. If the Bill was read a third time it would be submitted to "another place," and be subjected there to close scrutiny. Before a Committee of the other House both parties, for and against the Bill, could take full advantage of the questions which had been raised before the Committee of their Lordships' House, and the discussion that night in their Lordships' House. The decision of their Lordships' Committee or of their Lordships' House could be reviewed, reversed, or altered in any way which, in the view of the Committee of the other House of

Parliament, the justice of the case might require. In view of the fact that the decision that night would not be final, and that the Bill—if read a third time—would go down to be carefully investigated elsewhere, he certainly thought their Lordships would do well to read the Bill a third time, and pass it on in the ordinary course for further investigation.

THE EARL OF MORLEY said, he must confess that when he came to the House, having only seen the reasons which the Committee gave for passing the Bill, he felt very strongly in favour of the Amendment of the noble Earl (the Earl of Wemyss). The decision of the Committee, as stated in their reasons, appeared to be based entirely on questions of public policy, which it seemed to him should be decided in a general way and not on a Private Bill. But the noble Earl on the Front Bench (the Earl of Derby) had based the defence of their decision entirely upon local and special grounds, which had been ascertained after careful inquiry, and on that ground he should be unwilling to dispute the decision at which the Committee had arrived.

LORD DENMAN said, he felt no hesitation in voting against the third reading of this Bill. No blame had ever been cast on the management of the Water Company, which, living near, he would certainly have heard of. The promoters of this Bill promised cheapness and a supply for water-closets; but the Company's Bill would last on to 1890, and, as to cheapness, nothing could be worse than creating sewer-gas by water-closets. The death of the Earl of Chesterfield, at Scarborough, and the dangerous illness of the Prince of Wales were caused by it. Inquiry should be made as to the Chinese system and the Flemish plan of manuring, and as to the Rochdale system, instead of expensive manures being bought to maintain fertility of land without permanently enriching it. He would not pass the Duke of Portland's Bill for artificial manures, as described by *The Nottingham Journal*, on large farms on Sherwood Forest, on any consideration. He believed over-peopled countries could be fed by our restoring to the earth what we took from it.

The LORD CHANCELLOR was about to put the Amendment, when—

The Duke of Buckingham and Chandos

THE EARL OF WEMYSS said, he was satisfied with the protest he had made, and would not divide the House, but would ask leave to withdaw the Amendment.

Amendment (by leave of the House) *withdrawn*.

Original Motion *agreed to*.

Bill read 3ª; and *passed*, and sent to the Commons.

TITHE RENT-CHARGE BILL.

(The Marquess of Salisbury.)

(NO. 54.) SECOND READING.

Bill read 2ª (according to Order).

EARL DE LA WARR, in rising to move that the Bill be referred to a Select Committee, said, that he did so wishing to submit to their Lordships whether the questions which were dealt with in it did not require more information than their Lordships were probably in possession of, and whether important interests which were involved in the changes proposed in this measure did not demand more attention and consideration than could be given in the ordinary course of a Bill in passing through that House. He believed he was not wrong in saying that it was not unusual in such cases to refer the Bill to a Select Committee. This Bill was not one of an ordinary character. In the first place, it involved great and fundamental changes. The principle of tithe, as their Lordships knew, was that it was a charge upon the produce of land, and the same principle was adhered to by the commutation of 1836, when tithe in kind was commuted for a rent-charge depending upon the average prices of corn, wheat, barley, and oats in the last seven years. But this Bill instead of dealing with the tithe rent-charge as a liability upon the produce of land made the owner of the land personally liable for it, so that he "may be sued for such arrears as for a simple contract debt." This was a fundamental change of very serious importance entirely altering the nature of tithe or tithe rent-charge as a tenth of the produce of land, and converting it into a debt for which the landowner was personally liable, instead of the owner of tithe rent-charge having as now the power of distress upon the occupier of land. Instead of this, if this Bill passed, he would have power through the Law Courts to seize any personal property of the landowner. Then he would further beg to call their attention to the fact that in this Bill, so far as he could see, there was no provision whatever for a re-adjustment of the tithe rent-charge in consideration of the great fall in the value of agricultural produce since the commutation in 1836. The tithe of an acre of corn land about that time would have been worth probably not less than 40 per cent more than it was at the present time. The commutation of tithe into rent-charge was made upon some such basis. About that time also we were growing in this country about 16,000,000 or 17,000,000 quarters of wheat annually, while according to the reports of the harvest of 1886 the quantity grown was only about 7,000,000 quarters. He could not see in this Bill any recognition whatever of facts such as these. Then they had to consider what would be the effects of this Bill with regard to existing contracts of tenancy. It was true that there was in this Bill a clause (5) dealing with this question, and it might be easy to say, as in this clause, that the "tithe rent-charge shall be added to the rent." But he thought their Lordships would understand that at the present moment of almost unprecedented depression this was more easily said than done, and that while they were, perhaps, relieving the tithe-owner from the difficulty of collecting it they would simply be throwing the burden upon the landowner, whose only remedy would be to increase the rent in proportion, and thus the tenant occupier would be in no way benefited. Then there was the question of redemption. It was true that there was a clause (7) for allowing redemption at 20 years' purchase, but it did not afford any facilities for doing so. He believed that by a well-considered scheme of redemption the value of land would be raised, and the landowner would therefore be better able to make easy arrangements with his tenants until the land, after a term of years, became entirely freed from the rent-charge. He trusted that the noble Marquess (the Marquess of Salisbury) would, by consenting to the appointment of a Select Committee, afford the opportunity of a fuller consideration of the question—which was already one of no little friction and uneasiness—the diffi-

culties of which, would not, he believed, in any way be removed by the Bill in its present shape or by Amendments in a Committee of the Whole House without further evidence and information.

Moved, "That the Bill be referred to a Select Committee."—(*The Earl De La Warr*.)

THE PRIME MINISTER AND SECRETARY OF STATE FOR FOREIGN AFFAIRS (The Marquess of SALISBURY) said, his impression was—and it had been increased by the speech of the noble Earl (Earl De La Warr)—that this was not a simple Bill. The matters dealt with in this Bill, such as whether the liability for tithe should be placed on the landowner, whether the question of the original valuation of the tithe should again be raised, and other points, involved questions of principle which could best, he thought, be discussed in this House, and if the Bill was referred to a Select Committee, as the noble Earl suggested, there would, he feared, be a danger of that occurring which occurred with regard to the Church Patronage Bill, that was, that when the Bill came back the House might take an entirely different view from the Committee. Some words which his noble Friend dropped seemed to indicate that he intended not a Select Committee in the ordinary sense, but a Select Committee which should receive evidence. This would mean that the Bill could not possibly be proceeded with further this Session. In view of the earnest expressions of desire for the passing of the Bill which he had received from the clergy in various parts of the country, he should be loth to do anything to deprive them of such hope as they could cherish of getting the Bill passed in the present year. He quite admitted that they might not be successful, because Business had not proceeded with great rapidity in the House of Commons. Still, they ought to do all they could ; but if they referred the Bill to a Select Committee to take evidence, their chance would be very small. Therefore, so far as his own opinion went, he should not consent to the Bill going to a Select Committee.

THE ARCHBISHOP OF CANTERBURY said, he thought the clergy owed the noble Marquess a debt of great gratitude for the care and skill with which he had endeavoured to meet the very great difficulties raised by the Bill. He should be glad to see those difficulties minutely examined; but, at the same time, he was most loth to propose anything which might in the slightest degree impede the progress of the Bill or run counter to the judgment of the noble Marquess as to the best way of discussing it. He had seen it stated that there was great opposition to this Bill on the part of the clergy, but he had no knowledge of such opposition; on the contrary, he had received much favourable criticism upon it, and that very afternoon he had received from an excellent body that gave great attention to matters of this kind —the Church Defence Association—an intimation that they would consider it little short of a disaster if the Bill were hindered or dropped. Though perhaps more suitable for discussion in Committee, he desired to mention two points on which he had received a great number of communications. The first was contained in Clause 2, which provided that an allowance of 5 per cent was to be made to the landowners who paid their tithe punctually within three months. He did not think that would be a fair arrangement. There were many landowners who had always themselves, and not through tenants, paid their tithe in full, and who did not desire that 5 per cent should be handed over to themselves. At present he knew of many more who were already making arrangements to pay their own tithe without any thought of discount. In none of these cases could the simple withdrawal of 5 per cent from its owners be a just act. Again, a large number of the clergy collected their tithe in full without any cost to themselves. The reason assigned for this deduction of 5 per cent by the landowner was that it would compensate him for his risk, trouble, and expense. But the landowner's risk ought to be nothing, and it could not be computed. The trouble was only the trouble of paying his just debts, and the expense would be much less than the expense incurred in its collection by the tithe-owner, since the landowner could collect the tithe with his rents. Nor did he think that such reduction of 5 per cent would be any inducement to unwilling owners to pay their tithe in time. There was a general impression that the number of the tithe-payers was very much greater than the number of the land-

owners, and that it would therefore be a great saving of trouble to the clergy to collect it from the latter instead of from the former. An investigation had now been held on this point. Two parishes in each of five counties had been taken, and in these ten parishes it was recently found that whereas the tithe-payers numbered 883, the landowners were 704; so that the difference was not nearly so great as had been commonly supposed. He hoped to be excused for dwelling for a moment on this point, as, besides its immediate bearing, it had a general interest. In order to verify the above result, which excited some surprise, six other counties were similarly examined, and with the same results. He might state as a still more general expression of the facts, and in corroboration of the minor inquiries, that for the total amount of tithe rent-charge paid to the Ecclesiastical Commissioners, the tithe-payers numbered 58,000 and the landowners 37,000. Of course, in considering the pacific effects of this measure, which he trusted would be very considerable, it must be taken into consideration that a great many of the tithe-payers were also landowners. The second point of difficulty to which he desired to call the attention of the House was the 7th clause, which made it compulsory upon the tithe-owner to surrender his tithe rent-charge to the landowner at 20 years' purchase. It was not well, he thought, to draw this hard-and-fast line, for the value of the tithe rent-charge was determined by variable elements—namely, the corn averages, and also the rating, which in different places varied from $7\frac{1}{2}$ per cent to 25 per cent. These and other circumstances made great differences in the number of years' purchase which would represent the value of different rent-charges; for example, compare Norham, where there is one owner and one payer, with Haxey, where there are 804 payers, and where there would be 428 payers if owners paid, it is evident that Norham is worth many more years' purchase than Haxey would be. He suggested that the Bill should be amended by the insertion of a proviso that the payment for the tithe should be "not less" than 20 years' purchase. He believed that if it were determined that not less than 20 years' purchase should be given the question of the purchase of the tithe by the landowner would in most cases be settled amicably. For landowners and titheowners who should be unable to agree between themselves simple arbitration ought to be established by reference to the Land Commissioners. But to fix once for all a certain price to be paid to the tithe-owners on all estates in all parts of the country, whether payers were many or few, and without regard to such varying elements as rating and corn charge, would be as fallacious as it would be to fix now the price of Consols 10 years hence.

THE EARL OF SELBORNE said, he did not see any necessity for the Bill being referred to a Select Committee. There were points in the Bill which could be better dealt with by the House than by a Select Committee. The matters to which the most reverend Prelate (the Archbishop of Canterbury) had drawn attention would, he hoped, receive careful consideration. The Act of 1836 clearly made tithes a charge upon the landlords, but by contract the tenants in many cases, if not generally, had paid them. It was clear, in point of reason and justice, that the clergy ought not to be prejudiced in their rights in consequence of the contracts between landlords and tenants which had changed the mode of defraying the charge, and that the clergy ought not to be forced into deplorable collisions with their parishioners merely because landlords had made certain arrangements with their tenants and the tenants misunderstood the whole position. The question between the landlord and the tenant was merely one of rent, with which the clergyman ought not to have anything to do ; and it was unreasonable that his only remedy for a charge which the law had laid upon the landlord's interest in the land should be by distress, or for want of a sufficient distress, upon the goods of the tenant. There was one additional point to which he desired to direct attention. The power of distress was taken away by the Bill. That he considered a good thing. But it was necessary to provide some substitute, and he suggested that in cases where the tithe could not be otherwise obtained some simple means should be provided of getting from the County Court an attachment upon the landlord's rent due, or to become due, from the tenant. The tenant would simply be served with

notice of the landlord's default and directed to pay so much of the rent to the titheowner. This, he contended, would be a simple way of doing justice unaccompanied by any annoying circumstances.

THE EARL OF KIMBERLEY said, with reference to the clause providing for the return of 5 per cent to the landlords who made prompt payment, the remedy which the law had given to the tithe-owner was the power to distrain on the land on which the tithe rent-charge was fixed, and if the landowner was made personally liable, something was given to the Church which it had not before, and something ought to be paid by the Church for the privilege. The tithe-owner ought not to obtain this advantage without paying something for it. He did not attach much importance to the redemption clauses. Tithe had fallen to 85, and many competent judges thought it would fall still lower, to 75 or even 70. Thus the inducement to landowners to redeem was not very great. All turned, it seemed to him, upon a question of policy—was it or was it not to the advantage of the Church to promote those redemptions ? If it were thought to be of advantage to promote those redemptions, unless they offered liberal terms they would have no redemptions. He was inclined to think that there were parts of the country where redemption would be advantageous to the Church. There were other parts where he was not aware that any difficulty had yet arisen, and therefore the Church might feel easy with regard to the tithes. They had, however, all seen in some parts of the country what seemed to indicate much more serious difficulties hereafter ; and, therefore, he thought the Government had done well in putting into the Bill what they thought were the terms of redemption likely to be accepted, though he himself doubted whether those terms were likely to be accepted.

THE BISHOP OF LONDON said, it should be remembered that if something was to be given to the Church, something was to be taken away from it, because, although they might say the remedy of distraint was of a very odious kind, yet there could be no doubt it was exceedingly effectual, as proved by the rareness with which it had been found necessary to resort to it. As to the remedy against the owner, he might be found very difficult of access, whereas there was no difficulty whatever in finding out where to distrain and what to distrain upon. There was a large amount of land charged with tithe in the diocese of London which was rapidly becoming building land, and 25 years' purchase was readily given by the owner for the tithe. In such cases it would not be fair that the incumbents should lose five years' purchase of their tithe. The Bill gave the landlord power to redeem at any time, but no corresponding power was given to the titheowner. Of course the landowner in these circumstances would choose his own time for redemption, while the titheowner had no such choice of time. If there were a power of compulsory redemption, some other mode should be adopted than that of fixing a hard - and - fast rule of 20 years' purchase. Some experienced body, such as the Land Commissioners, should have power to decide.

THE UNDER SECRETARY OF STATE FOR THE COLONIES (the Earl of ONSLOW) said, that it was the intention of the Act of 1836 to make tithe a landowners' question. But the remedy being given by distraint against the tenant, landlords invariably made arrangements with their tenants to pay the tithe. The noble Earl who moved the Amendment (Earl De La Warr) said that the effect of the Bill would be that landlords would have to raise their rents. But with respect to existing contracts the landlord would be entitled to add the tithe to the rent, and no fresh contract would have to be entered into. The landowner ought to be considered as well as the tithe-owner. If this Bill passed, the remedy would be not against the goods on a particular farm, but against all the estate, real and personal, of the landlord, and therefore he thought there should be some *quid pro quo* given up by the tithe-owner. As a rule the landlords of England were at the present time far too impoverished to be anxious to redeem the tithe rent-charge at 25 years' purchase. Only in rare cases was a landlord in a position to find the money for the purpose of redeeming the tithe rent-charge, and it would be hard to compel him to find with great difficulty a considerable sum of money for the purpose of redemption. He believed this measure would have the effect of smoothing away a very serious difficulty.

It gave a simpler remedy against a more solvent person, and it removed, at the same time, a great many hardships.

THE DUKE OF MARLBOROUGH said, he felt bound to say, in the interest of many of those who were loyal supporters of the Government, and who were as anxious as the noble Marquess to see this Tithe Question settled, that the Bill failed in many respects to meet their wishes. Many of the provisions of the Bill would require very serious consideration in Committee. He contended that in dealing with the question of tithes, they ought to go on the basis of the value of produce, and not on the basis of the value of the land. The views which he wished to put before the House were shared by many who, like himself, were supporters of the Government. They considered that a 5 per cent reduction would not meet the exigencies of the case, and they likewise considered that 20 years' purchase of the average tithe would not in any way render it possible for the redemption to take place. The present net annual value of the tithe was £64, and it was impossible to suppose that any landowner would buy at 20 years' purchase. The only prospect of success for such a measure was that some scheme of gradual purchase should be rendered possible. The agricultural interest would certainly not be satisfied, and it was evident that some modification would be required not only in the interest of the landlord, but also in the interest of the tenant. There was no protection to the tenant that he would not be forced to pay the tithe, in case the landlord defaulted; on the other hand, there was no protection to the landlord that if he paid, he would be able to recover his rent in the case of annual tenants.

EARL STANHOPE (for Earl DE LA WARR) asked leave to withdraw the Motion to refer the Bill to a Select Committee. He desired to add two words respecting the Bill. In his opinion, it was most desirable, in the interests of the Church, that tithes should be paid directly by the landlord. Had time allowed of it, he could have pointed out how easily teinds were paid in this way in Scotland, and also under what Acts these payments were regulated. As to the recovery of tithes, he thought that if the remedy of distress were given up, there was no alternative but that of

The Bishop of London

giving the tithe-owner a right of personal action. Three years ago, he (Earl Stanhope) had brought forward a Tithe Bill which was founded on this same principle, because there seemed to be no other ready means to promote the object in view. As to redemption, he should prefer an easier means provided by which the principal and interest of the rent-charge might be discharged in a certain number of years. In the 7th section of the Irish Church Act Amendment Act, there was a Proviso to this effect, and he now begged to give Notice that he would move a similar clause when the Bill went into Committee.

LORD EGERTON OF TATTON desired to confirm, to the fullest possible extent, what had been said by the most rev. Prelate as to the view taken by the clergy of this Bill. He had the honour of presiding that day over a representative body of clergy and laity, and a resolution was passed by it unanimously—

"That the Government Bill now before the House of Lords is recognized as a friendly attempt to meet the difficulties of the present crisis, and while regarding the Bill as capable of improvement in points of detail, it considers it deserving of the support of Churchmen, and earnestly trusts that every effort may be made to pass it without delay."

With regard to the remission of 5 per cent to landowners, he thought that some better reasons than he had as yet heard should be given for it. A large number of landowners in the North of England now paid the tithe, and he did not see why they should receive a remission of 5 per cent for doing that which the Act of 1836 always contemplated that they would do. This Act had been for many years favourable to the landowner and he must take the rough and the smooth together, and be prepared at the present time to make some sacrifices. He hoped the Government would persevere with the Bill as a fair solution of a difficult question.

EARL FORTESCUE heartily thanked Her Majesty's Government for bringing in the Bill. It would be a great relief to the clergy to be freed from bickerings connected with the present mode of collecting the tithe.

THE MARQUESS OF SALISBURY hoped their Lordships would be able to come to some agreements in Committee. He was glad to find that the House had generally agreed to accept the measure, though several points of detail, no doubt, required to be carefully looked into. The 5 per cent raised a thorny question; but he was not without hope that some adjustment might be found. He should be glad to facilitate advances for tithe redemption, which undoubtedly could not be carried out without some assistance of that kind; but, whether in the present state of the national finances it could be done, he did not know. At all events, he should be glad to facilitate it. With regard to the question raised by the noble Duke (the Duke of Marlborough), he had a distinct opinion that the landowner had no case whatever. His impression was, that if anyone had to complain it was the tithe-owner. The whole fall had been in the price of grain, and he very much doubted if there had been any fall at all in the price of green crops, or of stocks. That made it all the worse for those who came into the arrangement of 1836. If there was any case at all, it was on behalf of the clergy, and not against them. That, however, was a matter which could not be mixed up with the present Bill. If it was to be dealt with at all it must be by a separate measure.

Motion (by leave of the House) *withdrawn*.

Bill *committed* to a Committee of the Whole House on *Friday* the 13*th of May* next.

SUPREME COURT OF JUDICATURE (IRELAND) BILL.—(No. 63.)

(*The Lord Privy Seal, Earl Cadogan.*)

THIRD READING.

Order of the Day for the Third Reading read.

Moved, "That the Bill be now read 3ª." —(*The Lord Privy Seal.*)

LORD DENMAN, in moving, as an Amendment, that the Bill be read a third time that day six months, said: If the creation of more than four Courts became necessary, after the abolition of Chiefs, he hoped that, at least, each Court might have separate entries of causes—to begin at No. 1 in each, only to be transferred to other numbers, when each list might be finished. On Circuit two Chiefs often went together, and took part in the general business. And there was no need to abolish the Courts of Common Pleas and of Exchequer. He (Lord Denman) had been associated by statute — as a man of knightly degree—to the Lord Chief Justice of the Courts of King's Bench and of Queen's Bench, and the days of sitting could not be named till his appointment was known. At first, it took two years to bring a cause into Court— remanets produced an enormous income. The late Marshal and Associate had boxes made for the parchment records, and called them his "corn-bins;" whilst, since then, his successor, from his predecessor's determination to clear off arrears, became so great a loser, that if ever he had a horse which he had improved, he could not keep him or sell him, and was obliged to give him away. The noble Lord on the Woolsack had a horse at livery standing next to his, and both owners gave away their animals. He had not been able to put horses together lately with the noble Lord; but he hoped by August 5, when the Women's Suffrage Bill would come on, to have his continued support.

Amendment *moved*, to leave out ("now") and add at the end of the Motion ("this day six months.")—(*The Lord Denman.*)

On Question that ("now") stand part of the Motion?

Resolved in the *affirmative*.

Original Motion *agreed to*.

Bill read 3ª accordingly, and *passed*.

NAVY—SHIPS OF WAR—FAILURES OF DESIGN AND CONSTRUCTION—H.M.SS. "WARSPITE," "IMPERIEUSE," AND "COLOSSUS."

QUESTION.   OBSERVATIONS.

VISCOUNT SIDMOUTH asked Hei Majesty's Government, Whether they intend to institute any inquiry respecting the circumstances which have occasioned several of the recently constructed vessels of Her Majesty's Navy to fail in fulfilling the purposes for which they were originally designed? He referred in particular to the *Impérieuse* and *Warspite*, declaring that they were incapable of carrying more than enough coal for two days' steaming at full speed, that they had had their masts taken out of them, and that they would not carry the heavy guns it was originally intended to put into them. Those ships were admitted failures; and he desired to know, whe-

ther the Government would take the same course with regard to them that they had taken in connection with the bent swords and bayonets, and issue a searching inquiry into the matter. He also wished to know, Whether the alterations considered necessary in the steering arrangements of Her Majesty's ships *Ajax* and *Agamemnon* had proved satisfactory? The blame for the system which had produced such mischievous and expensive results to the country, so far as he could make out, was due to a most pernicious act on the part of a former First Lord of the Admiralty, Mr. Childers, who procured an Order in Council, by means of which the decision on the whole question of the construction of ships was taken away from the Board of Admiralty, and vested between the Chief Constructor and the First Lord of the Admiralty.

LORD ELPHINSTONE (A LORD in WAITING) said, that the Question was put in a different form from that of which the noble Viscount (Viscount Sidmouth) had given him private Notice. The information asked for was of a very technical character, but he was, on behalf of the Admiralty, anxious to give all that he could in answer to Questions which might be put to him. With reference to the *Warspite* and the *Impérieuse*, these ships were designed in 1881, but not launched till 1884. Had the original weights been adhered to the ships would have come out as designed, but during the three years occupied in construction several improvements were effected in naval ordnance and many alterations made in the weights originally intended to be carried. Quickfiring guns and the latest designs in machinery were introduced, and the ships' complements increased, all of which added very considerably to the weights. Then, again, the original weight of coal to be carried was 400 tons. Although she has a coal-carrying capacity for 1,130 tons the present Board had decided that they should carry 900 tons. The consumption of coal when the vessel was going at full speed, would, however, lessen the draught by 4in. each day, and the daily consumption of provisions would still further lighten the draught. Of the *Admiral* class, the *Collingwood* was the only ship completed, and if the full weights that she was capable of carrying were on board, she would be 7¼ inches deeper than was intended, bringing the top of the armour belt within 1 foot 10½ inches of the water line. In this case also, however, there would be a daily decrease of draught of 4in. The noble Viscount wished for an inquiry—an inquiry into what? Into the reason why the ships in question had failed to fulfil the purpose for which they were originally designed. The reason was well known; it was that different weights were put into the ships over and above the legend weights. The alteration in procedure and the new regulations contained in the Appendix of the Statement of the noble Lord the First Lord of the Admiralty (Lord George Hamilton) would prevent the repetition of any of the alleged defects or miscalculations to which allusion had been made. The Government did not therefore propose to institute any inquiry. Then the noble Viscount had called attention to Mr. Childers's Order in Council of 1869, and asked how far that Order implicated the First Lord and the Chief Constructor. The Chief Constructor was answerable to the Controller, to whom it referred. The Controller was to be responsible to the First Lord of the Admiralty for so much of the business as referred to the material of the Navy—that was to say, building, repair of ships, guns, and naval stores. With regard to the *Impérieuse* and the *Warspite*, as a matter of fact the general principles of these two ships had been discussed and approved by the entire Board of Admiralty of 1881, but how far the Board have been consulted as to the details of additional weight, &c., he was unable to say. He did not know whether the noble Viscount had read the debate on the Naval Estimates in the other House, but if he had he might have noticed that Lord Charles Beresford, one of the Lords of the Admiralty, speaking on the very subject of that Order in Council, said that it was not in force at the present moment. In the Appendix to the Naval Estimates the noble Viscount would find the following words:—

" 1. Cases having recently been brought to the notice of my Lords in which the immersion of a ship when complete for sea will be seriously and prejudicially affected by reason of introduction during construction of additions and alterations to the hull, machinery, complement, armament, &c., the procedure hereafter defined is to be strictly observed. 2. When a design for a ship is required, the Controller will furnish the Board with a general idea of the class of vessel required. 3. The Controller will, after conferring with the First Naval Lord, and obtaining his written approval as to the speed, armament, complement, and sail power, if any, instruct the Director of Naval Construction to prepare a sketch design for consideration, embodying such features as may have been decided upon by the First Naval Lord and the Controller. 4. The Director of Naval Construction, after conferring with and obtaining the opinion in writing of the Director of Naval Ordnance and the Engineer-in-Chief as to the armament and machinery respectively, is to prepare a sketch which shall be submitted to the Controller, who will bring the same before the Board. 5. If the sketch design is generally approved by the Board, orders will be given by the Controller that the design is to be worked out in detail, or modified with a view to its ultimate adoption. (The sketch design will be prepared in accordance with the following Board Minute of September 21, 1886, relating to load draught.) 6. The Director of Naval Construction will, in consultation with the Director of Naval Ordnance and Engineer-in-Chief, complete the design and submit it with a full and careful description of the expected qualities and capabilities of the ship for the concurrence of the Controller, by whom it will be sent to the secretary for circulation to the several members of the Board, before being considered at a Board meeting. After a design has been approved by the Board, and has received the Board's stamp, not any alteration or addition either in hull, machinery, armament, complement of men, boats or stores, or other details, shall be permitted without the concurrence of the Board. 7. The Controller shall be responsible that not any deviation from the designs approved by the Board shall take place which would in any way affect the immersion of the ship when completed for service.") — *Board Minute, February 15, 1887.*)

He thought that he had answered all the Questions put to him by the noble Viscount.

THE EARL OF NORTHBROOK said, that, as the noble Viscount (Viscount Sidmouth) had alluded to the Board of Admiralty which had been in Office while he (the Earl of Northbrook) was First Lord of the Admiralty, he wished to make a few remarks on what had been said. With regard to what he had said about the *Impérieuse* and the *Warspite*, he thought the noble Viscount had been very much misinformed when he described them as failures. The noble Lord (Lord Elphinstone) had explained the facts of the case, and he (the Earl of Northbrook) would refer the noble Viscount to a paper which had been read at the Institution of Naval Architects by Sir Nathaniel Barnaby, going into the whole of the circumstances connected with the alteration of the weights of the *Impérieuse* and *Warspite.* The subject was of too technical a character to be usefully or profitably discussed in the House; but he challenged the noble Viscount to answer Sir Nathaniel Barnaby's paper. The slight increased immersion of these ships had been caused by alterations made during their progress, and had greatly improved them as fighting ships. These alterations had been in the machinery and in the armament of the ships, the armament being heavier than at first designed, and the machinery having been much improved. He would point out that within the last three or four years great changes had been effected in the construction of marine steam engines; and it was absolutely necessary, if the Admiralty wished to have the most powerful ships that could be put afloat, to utilize all these improvements in machinery. Therefore the Board of Admiralty of that time would not have been fit to hold their posts if, through any technical or pedantic adherence to the original designs, they had failed to take advantage of any improvement that had been made in the last few years. Lord George Hamilton had written in a Report which was upon their Lordships' Table, that, with the exception of being more deeply immersed, the *Impérieuse* had fully realized the expectations of her designers, and that she was one of the most powerful ironclad cruisers afloat. The statements of the noble Viscount, therefore, were not borne out by those best qualified to speak on the subject. With regard to Sir Nathaniel Barnaby and the Constructing Staff of the Admiralty, it was only due to that distinguished public servant to say publicly, as one under whom Sir Nathaniel Barnaby had served, that he thought that the country was greatly indebted to that gentleman for the ability with which he had designed the more recent types of fighting vessels for Her Majesty's Navy. He believed that those who had paid attention to naval affairs of late years, for the most part, attached as great importance to the element of speed in ironclads as to any other quality which these ships possessed; and if there was one point more than any other on which they might feel satisfaction, it was that all the ships that had recently been designed had on their trials realized a greater speed than was expected. The *Impérieuse* and *Warspite*

The Earl of Northbrook

had realized 17 knots instead of 16; the same satisfactory result had been shown in the ships of the *Admiral* class; and in the *Sanspareil* and *Renown*, he believed the speed would be at least a knot greater than that calculated in the original designs. For this the greatest credit was due to Mr. James Wright, the chief engineering adviser of the Admiralty, for the sound and practical advice which he had given with respect to contracts made for the machinery of Her Majesty's ships, by which they had been able to take advantage of the great improvements which had been introduced in marine engines during the last five or six years. The noble Viscount had said something about the constitution of the Board of Admiralty. He (the Earl of Northbrook) did not intend to go into that thorny question at that hour of the evening; but he would say that, during the whole time he had been at the Admiralty, there had been the fullest and freest opportunity given to the Naval Lords of the Admiralty to express their views as to the construction of ships, and that it was not the case that he, as a civilian, had in any way endeavoured to push forward his own private opinions upon that technical subject against those of his professional advisers.

MARKETS AND FAIRS (WEIGHING OF CATTLE) BILL. [H.L.]

A Bill to amend the law with respect to weighing cattle in markets and fairs—Was *presented* by The Earl of Camperdown; read 1ª. (No. 72.)

House adjourned at a quarter past Eight o'clock, till To-morrow, a quarter past Ten o'clock.

HOUSE OF COMMONS,

Thursday, 28*th April*, 1887.

MINUTES.]—NEW MEMBER SWORN—Honble. Alfred Percy Allsopp, *for* the Borough of Taunton.
PRIVATE BILLS (*by Order*)—*Considered as amended* —Great Eastern Railway.
Lords Amendments considered — Belfast Main Drainage, *debate further adjourned.*
PUBLIC BILLS — *Ordered* — *First Reading* — Fishing in Rivers* [244]; Juvenile Offenders* [245].

Committee—Criminal Law Amendment (Ireland) [217] [*Third Night*] — L.P. ; Truck [109]—R.P.
Committee—Report—Bankruptcy Offices (Sites) (*re-comm.*) * [243].

PRIVATE BUSINESS.

———o———

BELFAST MAIN DRAINAGE BILL
(*by Order*).
LORDS' AMENDMENTS.   [ADJOURNED DEBATE.]

Order read, for resuming Adjourned Debate on Question [7th April], "That the Lords Amendments be now considered."

Question again proposed.

Debate *resumed*.

MR. SEXTON (Belfast, W.): I have to move that the Motion to take into consideration the Lords' Amendments to this Bill be postponed. I may remind the House that the object of the Bill is to legalize a scheme for the construction of main drainage works, the execution of which will cost the people of the town of Belfast £500,000 sterling, and render them liable to an annual taxation of £25,000 for 35 years to come. The public debt of the town of Belfast already amounts to £750,000, and involves an annual taxation of £45,000 for the repayment of principal and interest. The local taxation of the town has become so heavy that it is the subject of great and bitter complaint among the working classes, who say that the system of taxation pursued by the Town Council for some years has been of such a nature as to impose a grievous burden upon them, and to require careful consideration. When this Bill was before the House last year, I was not then one of the Members for Belfast; but, as an Irish Member, I took an interest in this community, and I felt it my duty to point out that the municipal government of Belfast is of so anomalous a nature as to render it undesirable that this scheme should be proceeded with until the people of Belfast obtain more control over the expenditure of their own money. The population of the town is upwards of 220,000, and there are more than 30,000 Parliamentary voters, but the municipal voters only number some 5,000 ; so that 25,000 householders in the borough are shut out from any share in its municipal

government who, if the borough were situated in England or Scotland, would have a share in the government of the town. I have here a statement made by Dr. Graham, one of the aldermen of the borough, who calls attention to these facts, and points out that, as a necessary consequence, the people are powerless. He says that a great majority of the inhabitants are opposed to the present ill-conceived main drainage scheme. There are five wards in the town, and at the last election for the Cromac Ward it was decided to make the drainage scheme a test question. Dr. Graham reluctantly consented to stand as an alderman, and he was returned by a majority of 3 to 1. The resolution under the scheme has been unanimously passed at a public meeting, and no public meeting has been held or could be held in its favour. The Town Council have preferred to send up a deputation to coach up Members in regard to the Bill ; they dare not submit their proposal to a public meeting. I may say that I have received a telegram from the Lagan Pollution Committee, expressing a hope that I may succeed in overthrowing the Bill to-night, and intimating that a Petition, signed by more than 1,000 persons, will be presented this evening against the measure.

Message to attend the Lords Commissioners ;—

The House went ;—and being returned ;—

MR. SPEAKER *reported* the *Royal Assent* to several Bills.

BELFAST MAIN DRAINAGE BILL
(*by Order*).

Question again proposed, "That the Lords' Amendments be now considered."

MR. SEXTON resumed his speech. The hon. Member said : When the interruption of our proceedings took place I was engaged in summing up the case of the Corporation of Belfast, and I have fortified myself with documents which show that a great body of the ratepayers of Belfast are at present excluded from any voice in the municipal government of the town. When the Bill was before the House last year I pressed the case strongly upon hon. Members, and the House was sensible of the justice of the case I urged—namely, that this large expenditure, amounting to £500,000, should be left in the hands of the people of Belfast themselves, and that the Bill should not be legalized until the householders are admitted to the same franchise as that which prevails in every borough in England and Scotland. The House agreed, at my instance, to insert a clause in the Bill for the purpose of extending the municipal franchise. That clause was Clause 80. When the Bill went up to the House of Lords the Examiners of the Committee of Standing Orders reported that the Standing Orders had not been complied with. The ground upon which they so reported was that there had been no advertisement intimating to the people of Belfast that such a provision would be contained in the measure. The Town Council had not given notice of any intention to insert a provision extending the municipal franchise to the whole of the now excluded householders. How could they have given such notice, seeing that they had no such intention when they introduced the Bill? The Corporation is elected by a very small fraction of the ratepayers, and it is hardly likely that they would consent to any reform which would mean danger to their own power. They do not approve of this clause; they opposed its insertion to the utmost of their power, and the clause, in the end, was inserted altogether against their will. At the time the Examiners reported that the Standing Orders had not been complied with the Committee of Standing Orders took a very extraordinary course. They might have moved that the Standing Orders should be suspended and have allowed the Bill to proceed, or they might have refused to suspend the Standing Orders, and the Bill would have been rejected. The course they took, however, was to insist on the observance of the Standing Orders, and, nevertheless, to declare that the Bill might proceed provided the obnoxious clause was struck out. I am glad to see the hon. Gentleman the Chairman of the Committee of Ways and Means (Mr. Courtney) in his place, and I want to know from him whether these Standing Orders are not intended to protect the communities from improper action on the part of the promoters of Private Bills. In this instance the Standing Orders have been applied in order to deny and defeat

Mr. Sexton

the right of this House to introduce a special provision into a Private Bill. I maintain, with all humility, but with firmness, that the House of Lords have no Constitutional right to use any Standing Order of theirs to prevent the House of Commons from exercising its undoubted function of making any alteration it may like in a Private Bill. The Standing Orders are directed against the promoters of Private Bills, and were never intended to be exercised against the Privileges of this House. Indeed, the House of Lords, in this very case, have broken their own Standing Orders, because they have inserted a provision in reference to the rating of a Public Company which was not inserted in the Bill originally. In so doing they have violated the Standing Orders of their own House. Now, the clause which has been struck out by the House of Lords was, in my opinion, indispensable to the Bill, and I cannot, as an Irish Representative, and still less as one of the Members for Belfast, assent to the passing of the measure unless the clause is reinstated. The people of Belfast are already taxed most heavily for local purposes. This Bill authorizes the expenditure of £500,000, and it will impose a burden upon the ratepayers of 1s. 6d. in the pound for 35 years to come. I maintain that it is not only unsatisfactory, but intolerable, to throw these burdens upon them until they are admitted to their full share of the municipal franchise which they would enjoy if Belfast were a borough in England or Scotland. I, therefore, ask the House to agree to postpone the consideration of the Lords' Amendments, and especially of that which relates to the striking out of this clause, until the House has had an opportunity of considering the question of the extension of the municipal franchise. There are already three Bills before the House which have that object in view. One of them stands in the name of my hon. Friend the Member for North Kildare (Mr. Carew), another is in the name of the hon. Baronet the Member for Mid Armagh (Sir James Corry), and there is a third in the name of the hon. Member for North Belfast (Mr. Ewart). Each of these proposes to effect the purpose I have in view, although the last of the three is for the extension of the municipal franchise in Belfast alone. Now, I claim that I am only making a reasonable demand when I ask that this Bill should be put back until Parliament has decided whether it will pass any of these three Bills. I have never heard before in this country that the House of Lords has used its Standing Orders in order to limit the rights and Privileges of this House. I challenge any hon. Member to cite a case, and I should be surprised to hear it seriously maintained that the House of Lords possesses this power. Moreover, I would point out that all Parties in this House are now vieing with each other to promote a rational system of local self-government. If this clause is to be rejected, what becomes of all the protestations we have heard? The House has now before it the demand of two of the Members for Belfast; for I believe I am correct in saying that I am supported by the hon. Member for East Belfast (Mr. De Cobain). There have been Petitions presented from public meetings and the inhabitants, and a great majority of the Irish Representatives, without distinction of Party, are in favour of the principle of this clause. What becomes of the protestations which have been made by hon. Members on all sides of the House as to their desire to extend a system of local self-government, if they insist on saddling the expenditure of £500,000 upon the ratepayers of Belfast, and refuse them any share in the control of their own affairs? There is another ground also why the consideration of the Lords' Amendments should be postponed. Since the Bill came before the House a Royal Commission has sat and considered the social condition of Belfast. That Commission has made several recommendations which, I believe, have been adopted in their main principles by the Government. One of them is that the Law of Compensation for Malicious Injury in the town of Belfast shall be amended. By a cunning contrivance of the Town Council, in a former year, a person maliciously injured can claim no compensation. The Royal Commissioners recommended that Belfast should be placed, in this respect, on the same footing as the rest of Ireland, and that a person maliciously injured should have the right of claiming compensation out of what is called the General Purposes Rate. That, however, is the very rate which will have to provide the money for executing the drainage works autho-

rized by this Bill. The General Purposes Rate will be saddled with the payment of £25,000 a-year; and I warn the Government that if they allow this Bill to pass in its present shape, they will find that the General Purposes Rate will be mortgaged beyond the power to provide for any other object, and no funds will be left out of which compensation can be paid for malicious injury to persons or property. I, therefore, think that before the Bill is allowed to pass the Government should formulate their proposals in this respect. There is also another point. The Royal Commissioners have recommended a large increase of the local police force of Belfast. I assume from what I have heard that the increase will be something like 200 or 300 constables. The local contribution for that purpose will have to be paid out of the General Purposes Rate; but if the General Purposes Rate be mortgaged for the purposes of this Bill, there will be nothing left for the support of an additional police force. Every hon. Member knows that the maintenance of a proper police force in Belfast—a town where the peace has been so often disturbed—is a matter of much wider importance than the passing of this Bill. Therefore, I contend that we ought not to consent to pass the Bill, or to consider the Amendments introduced into it in the House of Lords, until we have before us the proposals of the Government for an increase of the police force of Belfast, and until we see in what manner and from what funds the cost of that additional force is to be defrayed. To-day the only proposal I make is that the consideration of the Lords' Amendments shall be postponed until the people of Belfast have been consulted, and, in the meantime, I hope and expect that we may have before us the recommendations of the Government in regard to the Law of Malicious Injury and the increase of the police force. I trust that the Government will agree that this measure shall not be pressed forward until we are in complete possession of that information. I am supported, as I have said, by the public opinion of the town of Belfast. No Petition has been presented in favour of the Bill; no public meeting has been held in favour of it. On the contrary, the Bill has been pushed through by contrivance and stealth; and I am here to say that if the

House of Commons, in the face of its protestations that it desires the people of Ireland to have a full and rational local self-government, decides upon pressing this Bill forward, much difficulty may be experienced in collecting the rates levied under it. For my own part, I should advise my constituents not to pay the increased rates until they have been admitted to a share in the municipal government of the town, so as to prevent in the future the jobbery which has been committed in the past. I beg to move that the consideration of the Lords' Amendments be postponed until the 28th of July.

MR. SPEAKER: Does any hon. Member second that Motion?

MR. T. W. RUSSELL (Tyrone, S.): It very rarely happens that I am able to agree with the hon. Member for West Belfast (Mr. Sexton) in public affairs; but feeling, as I do, that the general case, not against this Bill, but for the adjournment, is exceedingly strong, I very cordially second the Amendment he has moved Now, I do not presume the merits or the demerits of the Belfast Main Drainage Bill. It may be a very good Bill; it may be one that is entirely necessary for the welfare of the town. I do not presume to settle that question; but I say most emphatically that, at this time of day, it is absolutely absurd for a town of 250,000 inhabitants to be governed by 5,000 or 6,000 ratepayers. That is the case I make against going further with this Bill at present. I shall be told, no doubt, that there is a Bill before the House for the purpose of extending the municipal franchise in Belfast. Well, there are a good many Bills before the House for one purpose or another, which I am afraid will not get much further than this House, and I have some idea that the Municipal Franchise Bill is not being pressed forward with so much ardour as to insure its being passed this Session. If this Bill is allowed to pass, I am not sure that the prospect of carrying a Municipal Franchise Bill will not be very much impeded. Holding, as I do, that this House ought not to commit the town of Belfast to the expenditure of £500,000 without the inhabitants of that town being consulted, I think we shall do wisely if we refuse to go further with this Bill at present and adopt the Motion of the hon. Member

Mr. Sexton

ber for West Belfast. Fortunately, we have had some indication of what the feeling of that town is. The hon. Member for West Belfast read out from a Circular which most hon. Members received to-day the result of a municipal election in the town, which was fought upon this single issue—the result being that a highly popular Member of the Town Council was ousted from the Corporation and from the Aldermanship which he filled by a gentleman who stood on this issue alone. That shows, I think, how strong the public feeling is. As the hon. Member for West Belfast has pointed out, there has been no public meeting in favour of this Bill. There have, however, been several against it; and I hold in my hand a Petition, signed by more than 1,000 of the most respected inhabitants of Belfast, for presentation at the proper time to-day. In view of these facts, and having regard to the enormous expenditure which is contemplated under this Bill, I think the House will act wisely in giving the people of Belfast a chance of settling these important questions for themselves.

Amendment proposed, to leave out the word "now," and at the end of the Question to add the words " upon this day three months."—(*Mr. Sexton.*)

Question proposed, "That the word ' now ' stand part of the Question."

MR. EWART (Belfast, N.): I hope that the House will reject the Amendment of the hon. Member for West Belfast (Mr. Sexton) and will allow the measure, which is one of the utmost importance to the health and prosperity of the inhabitants of Belfast, to proceed. I cannot help thinking that the course which is taken in regard to this Bill is one which is almost unprecedented. I think I am not overstating the case when I say that this Bill has been discussed, as mentioned, during the last and present Parliament no less than ten times, and on every occasion the hon. Member for West Belfast has opposed it, both in season and out of season, with the result of keeping back most useful and beneficial improvements connected with Belfast. Not only has he done so, but he has repeated that course on the present occasion. The reasons which the hon. Member has given for objecting to the Bill are not accurate. He has told the House that if the Bill is passed it will involve the expenditure of £500,000. In that statement the hon. Member is inaccurate.

MR. SEXTON : Not at all.

MR. EWART: The cost will be £300,000 and not £500,000, as has been stated, and the charge for interest and the Sinking Fund will not exceed £12,000 a-year. Perhaps I may be allowed to supplement the statement of the hon. Member by giving the history of this Bill. The Bill was introduced in the last Parliament, and upon the second reading the hon. Member proposed an instruction to the Committee, directing them to assimilate the Irish franchise to that which exists in England. The Motion of the hon. Member was rejected by the House, and the Bill was referred to a Special Committee on police and sanitary Bills, of which the hon. Member himself and an hon. Member sitting near him were Members. The Bill passed through that Committee, and came down again to this House. Upon the Report the hon. Member again proposed that the House should deal with the question of the franchise, and on the 21st of June last the Motion was brought before the the House, when most hon. Members had not returned from the holidays, and a clause was carried which had the effect of staying the further progress of the Bill. Ultimately the Bill was carried over until this Session, and it was passed with the clause proposed by the hon. Member. It then went to the House of Lords, and in a Committee of that House the Bill was opposed by certain ratepayers of Belfast. Their opposition was fully heard there; but, nevertheless, the Bill comes down here without the clause originally inserted in it at the instance of the hon. Member for West Belfast. The hon. Member has referred to the small number of municipal voters in Belfast as compared with those upon the Parliamentary register. I do not dispute the fact; but one would suppose, from the speech of the hon. Member, that the blame for that condition of things is attributable to the Town Council of Belfast. Now, they are in no way whatever to blame for it; they have their existence under the Irish Municipal Corporations Act, and the franchise is the same in the borough of Belfast as it is in all other boroughs in Ireland.

MR. SEXTON: No; it is not the same in Dublin.

MR. EWART: I say the same as in all other boroughs in Ireland. Dublin, the metropolis, is no doubt an exception. I also admit that the franchise is higher than it is in England, although I am unable to say why the distinction was drawn by Parliament. It is beyond my recollection; but the Corporation of Belfast are in no way responsible for the franchise as it is. The hon. Member is very impatient to have the franchise altered; but I would remind the House that, although the 'hon. Member has been for a good many years a Member of this House, he has not on any single occasion, that I can remember, proposed to make an alteration in the existing franchise.

MR. SEXTON: Yes; every year.

MR. EWART: Personally, I am in favour of the assimilation of the municipal franchise in Ireland to the municipal franchise in England, and there are two Bills before the House, at this moment, which deal with that subject. I should be very happy to give my support to any measure which proposes to extend the municipal franchise in the sense I have spoken of. With regard to the Bill of my hon. Friend the Member for Mid Armagh (Sir James Corry), I must say that the Friends of the hon. Member for West Belfast have not dealt very fairly with that measure, because I find that it is blocked by the hon. Member for Mid Cork (Dr. Tanner). I think that fact throws some light on the proceedings which I need not further enter into. The hon. Member for West Belfast has referred to the fact that the Municipal Corporation of Belfast is onesided. I do not know why the hon. Member should find fault with the Town Council of Belfast for that. It is, I believe, the case that in every borough and city in England the majority try to get their own members returned. The very same thing has happened in the City of Dublin and the City of Cork, and the municipal elections which take place at the close of the year in England are looked upon as being quite as much a political index as a General Election. I regret very much that that should be so, because I should like to see the Town Council representing the opinion of the inhabitants free and unfettered of both

Parties in the Irish boroughs and in the Irish cities. The hon. Member has, on more than one occasion, referred to the misdeeds of the Corporation of Belfast. Well, I have been for 35 years more or less intimately acquainted with the working of the Belfast Corporation, and for 24 or 25 years I was a member of it. I can bear my testimony that a more exemplary, a more economical, a more earnest, and a more painstaking Corporation does not exist in the United Kingdom; and their management of the municipal affairs of Belfast has been a credit to the town. And now, Sir, with regard to the Motion of the hon. Member. He proposes that the consideration of the Bill shall be further postponed. The works which it contemplates are most important to the health and prosperity of Belfast. The course pursued by the hon. Member has already had the effect of delaying the execution of these works for one year, and if the Motion he now makes is carried, it will still further delay those works for another year. It is necessary to commence the first operations by making an outfall into the harbour, and that can only be done during the summer. Therefore, if this Motion is carried, the execution of the works will be practically delayed for another year. I think the constituents of the hon. Gentleman will be in no way obliged to him for the efforts he has made to obstruct the execution of works so very much desired. The hon. Member complains of the burden of taxation in Belfast. Let me tell the House that as regards the small class of houses—the workmen's houses —the rating comes to 5s. 4d. in the pound, and upon the larger description of houses to 6s. 6d., while in regard to the model Corporation, of which the hon. Gentleman is a member—the Corporation of Dublin—the taxation is no less than 9s. 7d. in the pound.

MR. BIGGAR (Cavan, W.): I rise for the purpose of supporting the Motion of my hon. Friend the Member for West Belfast (Mr. Sexton). The hon. Gentleman the Member for North Belfast (Mr. Ewart), who has just sat down, says that he is extremely anxious to see the municipal franchise extended in the town of Belfast. It is somewhat strange, I think, that he should be so very anxious to have the franchise for municipal purposes extended in that borough,

and yet that he should always have voted against the Motions which have been made by my hon. Friend for the extension of the municipal franchise. The real fact is that that Motion has invariably been opposed by hon. Members opposite when it has been brought forward in this House, and the hon. Gentlemen who have opposed my hon. Friend have continually protested against the extension of the municipal franchise. The hon. Member for North Belfast does not seem to remember that year after year the Irish Party have brought forward Bills in this House in favour of the extension of the municipal franchise in the Irish boroughs, and that he himself and others who act with him have uniformly voted against them. I do not know how the hon. Gentleman can reconcile his conduct with the statement he has just made to the House; but, even on the merits of the Bill, I very much doubt whether it would be of advantage to the people of Belfast to pass it in its present shape. That, however, is not the question now before the House; but the question is that the consideration of the Lord's Amendments be postponed until the 28th of July in order to give full time for the passing of a Bill for the extension of the municipal franchise. I would appeal to the hon. Gentleman and his Friends to give facilities for the progress of that Bill, and if that is done I will promise them, on behalf of my hon. Friends, that this Bill will get through its remaining stages without the slightest trouble or difficulty, and those in charge of the Bill will have ample opportunity of getting the costs they have incurred charged upon the ratepayers. The hon. Member has made reference to the fact that the municipal franchise in Belfast is an exceedingly narrow one; but he overlooked the fact that no public meeting has been held in the borough of Belfast in favour of this Bill. Nor did he allude to the fact that Dr. Graham, who belongs to the Tory Party, recently fought one of the wards of Belfast on the single issue whether this Bill should pass, and carried his election by a majority of three to one. Under these circumstances, I think it comes with a very bad grace from one of the Representatives of Belfast that he should get up in his place in this House to oppose a Motion, especially when the

Mr. Ewart

Motion is not directed against the Bill, but simply asks that its consideration shall be postponed until an opportunity has been afforded for carrying out such reforms as these Gentlemen themselves profess to have at heart.

SIR JAMES CORRY (Armagh, Mid): The hon. Member for Cavan (Mr. Biggar) has taken very good care, in the remarks he has made, not to support the suggestion which the hon. Member for West Belfast (Mr. Sexton) has thrown out, the reason being that he fully understands the question, and that he is more intimately acquainted with it than the hon. Member for West Belfast. The hon. Member for West Belfast has stated that if the recommendations of the Royal Commissioners are carried out the expense will have to be defrayed out of the General Purposes Rate. That is not so; because if it is necessary to levy a rate in order to carry out the recommendation of the Commissioners for the extension of the police force, the expense will fall upon the Police Rate, and not upon the General Purposes Rate. The hon. Member for West Belfast has been informed by a Member of the Corporation that he was elected upon this question; but, as far as I am aware, the election took place upon a totally different question. As a matter of fact, it was a personal question between the Gentleman who was elected and another gentleman, and the provisions of this Bill had nothing to do with the contest. The hon. Member says that, as regards the ratepayers, they have not had a sufficient opportunity for expressing their opinion on this question. My hon. Friend the Member for North Belfast (Mr. Ewart) has referred to the taxation of Belfast, and contrasted it with that of Dublin. I look upon that as a question of considerable importance. The small householders I may say, who include the artizans, pay a less rate than those who occupy a larger house property, and the result is that, so far as the taxation of the artizans of Belfast is concerned, they only pay 5s. 4d. in the pound, while those of Dublin pay 9s. 7d. in the pound. I think that shows that the Corporation of Belfast have been much more economical in the public works they have carried out than the Corporation of Dublin. Indeed, I am happy to say, that the works they have

executed will compare most favourably with any which have been carried out in Dublin. The House has been reminded that there is down upon the Paper a Bill, with which my name is associated, for the extension of the municipal franchise. I have the fullest intention of carrying out the proposals contained in that Bill, and if the measure itself had not been blocked by the hon. Member for Mid Cork (Dr. Tanner), I might have obtained the second reading of it before now. If the right hon. Member for Mid Cork will remove the block I will avail myself of every opportunity of pressing the Bill forward. It is impossible, however, under the half-past 12 o'clock Rule to bring forward the Bill so long as the block remains. With regard to the present measure, I hope the House will proceed at once to consider the Lords' Amendments, because the Bill is of a most pressing nature, and it is felt that it will be impossible to continue much longer the existing sanitary arrangements.

THE CHAIRMAN OF COMMITTEES (Mr. COURTNEY) (Cornwall, Bodmin): I have risen thus early in the debate in order to make a suggestion. The hon. Member for West Belfast (Mr. Sexton) has, however, touched upon one point which it is necessary I should refer to. He has stated that the House of Lords, acting under their Standing Orders, refused to permit the insertion of a clause which had been included by this House in the Bill. He has, consequently, condemned the action of the House of Lords, as an interference with the liberty of the House of Commons. May I remind the hon. Member, that I urged at the time that clause was introduced here, that it was totally irregular, and contrary to the spirit, even if not the letter, of our own Standing Orders. For my part, I cannot see that that there is any ground for the accusation which has been made by the hon. Member against the House of Lords, who have simply defended the interests of outside persons who had received no notice of the intention of the promoters of the Bill to make such a provision. But I think we may altogether put aside the hon. Member's ground for complaint, because I find that the hon. Gentleman himself does not attach very much weight to it. As I understand, he admits that if the Municipal-

Franchise Bill should become law, so that the ratepayers of Belfast would be included in it, he would then have no objection to the Bill going forward which contemplates the execution of these works. The way in which the matter stands is this—the hon. Baronet the Member for Mid Armagh (Sir James Corry) has introduced a Bill which he declares his desire to push forward with due celerity, and the hon. Member for West Belfast has expressed his intention to support the Bill. It is now blocked by what I am afraid I must call the indiscriminate action of the hon. Member for Mid Cork.

MR. SEXTON: That has simply been done in order to insure the discussion of the Bill at a reasonable hour.

MR. COURTNEY: Yes; but it is impossible to insure the discussion at a reasonable hour, and really no discussion is necessary. I am sure the hon. Member for West Belfast will agree with me in that remark, seeing that the question is one which has been discussed in this House over and over again, and which is now accepted in principle by both sides of the House. I would, therefore, suggest that, instead of deferring the consideration of this Bill for three months, the hon. Member should allow the present Motion to be withdrawn, and move that the further consideration of the Bill be deferred until the 24th of May. In the meantime, the block which now stands against the Municipal Franchise Bill might be withdrawn, and that Bill could be passed through this House with the full hope that it may receive the assent of the other House, and there would then remain no obstacle to the progress of this Bill. In that case, these drainage works would be able to go forward, and the summer would not be lost. Therefore, I trust that the Motion will be withdrawn, and the Bill be postponed until the 24th of May, the hon. Member for West Belfast using his influence, in the meantime, to secure the withdrawal of the block against the Municipal Franchise Bill. If that course is pursued, the whole question with regard to both Bills might be satisfactorily disposed of.

MR. M. J. KENNY (Tyrone, Mid): The suggestion which has been made by the hon. Gentleman the Chairman of Ways and Means (Mr. Courtney) renders it unnecessary for me to refer at all to

the particular merits or demerits of the Bill now before the House. I think I may state that, acting on the suggestion of the hon. Gentleman the Chairman of Ways and Means, my hon. Friend the Member for West Belfast (Mr. Sexton) will be prepared to modify his Motion in the direction indicated, and will take measures, so far as the Members of our Party are concerned, to secure that no further opposition shall be offered to the passage through the House of the Bill for the extension of the Municipal Franchise in Ireland. I may say, however, as an extenuation of this proceeding, that at the end of last year we had a Bill for the extension of the Municipal Franchise of Ireland before the House; but it was blocked all through the Session by the hon. Member who now sits for North Antrim (Sir Charles Lewis) and some other hon. Members on that side of the House. The result was that it was virtually defeated. We are prepared, in compliance with the suggestion of the hon. Gentleman the Chairman of Ways and Means, to take a very different course as far as we are concerned, and we will promise to give every assistance in our power to the passage through this House of the Municipal Franchise Bill. At the same time we are in this position that we have no guarantee that there may not be an adverse decision in "another place." If we allow the proposed Main Drainage Bill to go through without this clause, the Municipal Franchise Bill may be defeated in the House of Lords, and the defeat itself may be procured by the negotiations of hon. Members here. If that should be the case, we should then be placed in a worse position than that which we now occupy. All we are anxious for is that when the Main Drainage Bill comes into operation in Belfast the whole of the ratepayers of the Town of Belfast should have a voice in the control of the works. That is our only object, and this clause was inserted in the Bill in order to secure that the people of Belfast should have the right of exercising the municipal franchise. Under the circumstances, I think it was a reasonable and fair clause to insert in the Bill now under discussion; and I would suggest to the hon. Gentleman the Chairman of Ways and Means whether a clause may not be put in this Bill to delay its operation

Mr. Courtney

until such time as the ratepayers of Belfast may obtain the right of exercising municipal votes.

SIR CHARLES LEWIS (Antrim, N.): I have only risen for the purpose of distinctly stating to the House, after the speech of the hon. Gentleman the Chairman of Ways and Means (Mr. Courtney), that if nobody else moves the rejection of the Municipal Franchise Bill, I shall do so.

MR. JOHNSTON (Belfast, S.): I may say that the promoters of this Bill, having carefully considered the suggestion of the hon. Gentleman the Chairman of Ways and Means (Mr. Courtney), find themselves unable to accept it. A very great delay has already taken place in carrying out these very necessary improvements in Belfast, and the unsanitary condition of the River Lagan at the present time is such that even *The Northern Whig*, in a recent issue, calls upon the promoters of the Bill to ask the House to pass the measure through all its remaining stages without further delay. The hon. Member for West Belfast (Mr. Sexton) has referred to the municipal franchise as it already exists in Ireland. If the friends of the hon. Gentleman had not already blocked the Bill which has been introduced by the hon. Baronet the Member for Mid Armagh (Sir James Corry), that measure would probably have passed through this House, and would only have awaited the sanction of "another place." I think I ought to mention that the Bill for the extension of the municipal franchise in Ireland, which stands in the name of the hon. Baronet the Member for Mid Armagh was brought in at the suggestion of the late Chief Secretary for Ireland — the right hon. Gentleman the Member for West Bristol (Sir Michael Hicks-Beach). It was impossible, as the right hon. Gentleman told the hon. Member for Mid Armagh, that the Government, in addition to all their other public engagements, could take charge of a Bill for the extension of the municipal franchise. But the right hon. Gentleman added that he was prepared to give it the support of the Government, in order that the inequality which at present exists between England and Ireland in regard to the municipal franchise, so far as the Parliamentary boroughs are concerned, should be remedied and done away with. Perhaps

I may be pardoned if I state to the House that I myself have always been an earnest advocate for the extension of the municipal franchise in Ireland. At all the various elections I have had the honour of contesting and of always winning in Belfast, I have ever advocated that measure. Belfast, I think, will compare favourably in regard to the character of its government, the nature of its improvements, and its present financial and mercantile position, with the Metropolis of Ireland, which has a very peculiar Corporation ruling its affairs at the present moment. I venture to ask the House to resist any further delay in the progress of the Main Drainage Bill, and not to allow the summer to pass without the commencement of these most necessary works, which have been proved to be so much needed in the great and important town of which I have the honour to be one of the Members.

MR. T. C. HARRINGTON (Dublin, Harbour): I will not trespass long upon the time of the House; but it becomes my duty—as the Representative of a Division of the Metropolis of Ireland to which the hon. Member has referred—to defend it from the aspersions he has endeavoured to cast upon it. If the rates of the City of Dublin are higher than the rates of the City of Belfast, the blame must not be attributed to the Nationalist Corporation of Dublin, but to those who, for years, had the government of Dublin in their hands, and who for various purposes voted away the money of the ratepayers. We have at present this anomalous condition of things in regard to that city, that the most valuable property in it has been given away as grants to Tory gentlemen in the past, and that that property is constantly increasing in value without the ratepayers of the city deriving the least benefit from it. If the hon. Gentleman will make an inquiry as to the manner in which the Pembroke Estate was voted away by a Tory Corporation, for the annual present of a goose at Christmas, I think he will get some information as to the manner in which the municipal powers were administered during the time his Party had the administration of the Corporate affairs of Dublin in their hands. As to the suggestion which has been made by the hon. Gentleman the Chairman of Ways and Means (Mr. Courtney), I must say that those who are promoting this Bill have absolutely left themselves without any argument whatever in asking the House to consider the Lords' Amendment. They profess to be anxious for the extension of the municipal franchise in Belfast. There are as many as three Bills before the House for that purpose at this moment; but it is notorious that they have themselves been doing all they can to prevent those Bills from coming forward for discussion. They are now, to-day, endeavouring to rely on a mere accidental block which my hon. Friend the Member for Mid Cork (Dr. Tanner), in a moment of mistaken zeal, placed against the Bill of the hon. Baronet opposite. They have had full opportunity, time after time, of voting for the extension of the municipal franchise, but, time after time, they have refused to do so. Now, Sir, if the suggestion which has been made by the hon. Gentleman the Chairman of Ways and Means were adopted, and the promoters of the Bill are really anxious that the general body of ratepayers should have some control over the extraordinary expenditure upon which the Corporation of Belfast is about to enter, and those hon. Gentlemen will accept the proposal of the hon. Gentleman the Chairman of Ways and Means, we, on our part, are prepared to assent readily to the adoption of the Lords' Amendments. I cannot say that the suggestion of the hon. Gentleman the Chairman of Ways and Means has been at all treated in the most gracious manner by hon. Members opposite, seeing that the hon. Member for North Antrim (Sir Charles Lewis) has given Notice that whatever course may be taken in reference to the block which now stands against the Municipal Franchise Bill, he intends to move the rejection of the measure. I repeat, on behalf of my hon. Friend the Member for West Belfast, that he and his Friends who sit on this side of the House are perfectly prepared to adopt the suggestion of the hon. Gentleman the Chairman of Ways and Means, and if the proposal they are anxious to pass be rejected the citizens of Belfast will then know to whom it is that they are indebted for the delay in proceeding with the Main Drainage Bill.

MR. SEXTON: I wish to say that, with the leave of the House, I am

Mr. T. C. Harrington

quite willing to accept the proposal of the hon. Gentleman the Chairman of Ways and Means. Of course, any suggestion coming from the hon. Gentleman occupying the position he does carries with it more than ordinary authority.

MR. SPEAKER: Does the hon. Member withdraw his Amendment in favour of the proposal made by the hon. Gentleman the Chairman of Ways and Means?

MR. SEXTON: Yes.

Amendment *withdrawn*.

Main Question again proposed.

MR. COURTNEY: I beg now to move that the consideration of the Lords' Amendments be postponed until the 24th of May. [An hon. MEMBER: The 24th of May would be a very inconvenient day.]

MR. COURTNEY: Then I will substitute the 20th of May.

Motion made, and Question proposed, "That the Debate be adjourned till the 20th of May."—(*Mr. Courtney*.)

THE CHIEF SECRETARY FOR IRELAND (Mr. A. J. BALFOUR)(Manchester, E.): I hope the House will be careful as to the course it takes. I am under the impression that, although a compromise was suggested by the Chairman of Ways and Means, that compromise was not actually accepted. The compromise itself consists of two parts—first, that the block shall be withdrawn from the Bill dealing with the municipal franchise; and next, that the Gentlemen in charge of the Main Drainage Bill should consent to its postponement. Both parts of the compromise will require the assent of hon. Members in this House. The first part requires the assent of those who have blocked the Franchise Bill, and the other requires the consent of hon. Members who are in charge of the present Bill. If I understand correctly what fell from the hon. Member for North Antrim (Sir Charles Lewis), he does intend to oppose the Municipal Franchise Bill, whether the block is withdrawn or not. I gather from the remarks of the hon. Member for Mid Tyrone (Mr. Kenny), that he asks the Government to give facilities for taking the Municipal Franchise Bill, in the event of the block being removed. I am afraid I cannot give any pledge of that kind which might involve the delay of Public Business. All I rose for was to remind the House that, while certain hon. Members on that side of the House appear to think that an arrangement has been arrived at, I do not understand that arrangement to have been accepted by the hon. Baronet below the Gangway.

MR. FLYNN (Cork Co., N.) : I wish to invite the attention of hon. Members to one important consideration, and that is that my hon. Friend the Member for West Belfast (Mr. Sexton) and the hon. Member for East Belfast (Mr. De Cobain), who both of them represent working men constituencies, are opposed to the provisions of this Bill. I am informed that a large meeting of the ratepayers of Belfast was held on Monday evening, to condemn the Bill, and that a resolution submitted to that meeting was passed with only three dissentients. I am further informed that the hon. Member for East Belfast, who is deeply interested in the Bill in his representative capacity, and who knows a good deal more of it than most hon. Members in this House, is very anxious to be present in the House when the measure is under discussion. I believe that a second Petition against the Bill has been placed in the hands of the hon. Member for South Tyrone (Mr. T. W. Russell) ; and, under these circumstances, especially considering the fact that two out of the four hon. Members who represent Belfast are decidedly opposed to the passing of the Bill in its present form, I ask the House to say whether the compromise suggested by the Chairman of Ways and Means is not a reasonable one, and one which hon. Members opposite ought to accede to without the slightest hesitation ? In the event of that compromise not being adhered to, I would urge my hon. Friend the Member for West Belfast to oppose the Bill in its present stage as far as he possibly can. The action of the Government and of hon. Members opposite is most unreasonable, and it affords a convincing proof, to my mind, that their anxiety for the passing of any Bill for the municipal franchise in Ireland is of a very lukewarm character indeed.

Question put.

The House *divided :* — Ayes 192 ; Noes 177 : Majority 15.—(Div. List, No. 96.)

MR. SPEAKER : To what day ?

MR. SEXTON : The 20th of May.

Debate *further adjourned* till *Friday* 20th May.

GREAT EASTERN RAILWAY BILL.
(*by Order*).
CONSIDERATION.

Order for Consideration, as amended, read.

Motion made, and Question proposed, "That the Bill be now considered."

MR. PENROSE FITZGERALD (Cambridge) : I rise for the purpose of moving the Amendment which stands in my name on the Paper with regard to this Bill—namely—

"That with respect to all the Clauses relating to Coldham Common, Cambridge, the Bill be re-committed to the former Committee on the Bill."

My reason for moving the Amendment is entirely connected with the clauses which relate to Coldham Common at Cambridge. The Great Eastern Railway Company propose to take the new part of their line through this Common, which is quite close to a very populous part of the borough of Cambridge—a Common much used for the purposes of recreation by the inhabitants, both poor and rich. At the present moment this Common is very largely used, but taking in view the increase of population and other circumstances, it is likely to be still more largely used than it is at present, and, therefore, it is desired that the clauses to which I object should be referred back to the Committee for further consideration. The Bill itself is an Omnibus Bill, and it is no part of my wish to destroy the useful parts of the measure which are unconnected with this Common. All I desire is to reserve to the inhabitants of the borough the right to enjoy this open space which is so near to them. The Common is also largely used by the Volunteers, who form one of the first and most efficient battalions of Volunteers in the Kingdom. The rifle butts are upon this Common, and I believe, from what I know of the locality, that if the existing butts are removed there will be no possibility of finding any other position which will be suitable. The line which the Great Eastern Railway Company propose to make goes straight through the middle of the range. An attempt

has been made to come to an arrangement with the Railway Company ; but
that arrangement, I am sorry to say, has
fallen through, and it now only rests
with me, on the part of the poorer portion of the inhabitants of the borough of
Cambridge, to move that the consideration of these clauses be referred back to
the Committee. I am quite aware it
will be said that the War Office do not
see any reason to oppose this Bill. Now,
at the commencement of this contention
we received a letter from the War Office
which induced us to believe that they
intended to oppose the Bill ; but it now
appears that the War Office have made
up their minds not to oppose the measure. I presume that since that time the
War Office have seen good reason to
change their minds. One of my reasons
for objecting to the proposed removal
of the butts is that in all probability
we shall be unable to get the Government Inspector to pass the new range.
There will, therefore, be no range at all,
and if there is no range, this must lead
to the disbandment of this regiment of
Volunteers. I know it will be urged
that the owners of the land behind these
butts are identical with the owners of
the land which it is proposed to substitute ; but my answer to that contention is, that as we do not know where the
proposed new butts would be placed it
is impossible to say who the owners of
the land behind them may be. There
have been numerous Petitions presented
against these clauses. The Mayor and
Corporation of Cambridge do not believe
that if the House refer the Bill back to
the Committee, any material damage
will be done to the Great Eastern Bill.
The Railway Company have only to extend the proposed line to the right or the
left of the present site, and by paying
for the land they can obtain all the
siding which they say are necessary for
the purposes of the Bill. We object to
their taking this Common, which is the
property of the town of Cambridge, and
which is held on trust by the Corporation. The evil of allowing Common
rights to be interfered with by Railway
Companies has been shown in many
instances — such as Barnes, Tooting,
and Wandsworth Commons. In those
cases we can see for ourselves the effect
of allowing a railway to pass through
the middle of a recreation ground.
Under these circumstances, I propose

Mr. Penrose Fitzgerald

that the clause of the Bill, as regards
Coldham Common, should be referred
back to the former Committee on the
Bill.

Amendment proposed,

To leave out the words "now considered,"
in order to add the words "re-committed to
the former Committee with respect to all the
Clauses relating to Coldham Common, Cambridge."—(*Mr. Penrose Fitzgerald.*)

Question proposed, "That the words
'now considered' stand part of the
Question."

Mr. HANBURY (Preston): As I
was the Chairman of the Committee
who considered this Bill I desire at once
to put before the House what were the
views of the Committee in regard to this
portion of the Great Eastern Railway
Bill. In the first place, it was a thoroughly representative Committee, and
the Members of it were the hon. Member for the Tewkesbury Division of
Gloucestershire (Sir John Dorington),
the hon. Member for the Forest of Dean
(Mr. T. Blake), the hon. Member for
North Sligo (Mr. P. M'Donald), and
myself. Upon this question we were all
unanimous, and I did expect that the
hon. Member for Cambridge (Mr. Penrose Fitzgerald) would have been able
to bring before the House some better
arguments than he has done to justify
the throwing out of this portion of the
Bill. It is not to be supposed that we
passed these clauses giving power to the
Railway Company to interfere with
Coldham Common on light grounds. We
went into the question thoroughly, and we
were convinced of the absolute necessity
of the Railway going over the Common,
or of not making the proposed station
at all. The Great Eastern Station at
Cambridge, at the present moment, is
one of the most inconvenient in the
Kingdom. All the trains run in on one
side, and as there is a considerable
amount of traffic there is great danger in
carrying on the ordinary work of the
line. The Company are going to spend
£100,000 on the improvement of the
station, and that fact may be put in the
scale as an advantage conferred on the
population of Cambridge against the
small disadvantage which they would
suffer from the railway being allowed to
go across the Common. Cambridge is a
great place for changing trains, and
there is a heavy traffic over no less than

three different lines, and it is absolutely necessary if this traffic is to be carried on properly, that there should be a siding constructed about 1,200 yards in length. The Committee thought at first that that was a very unusual length; but we found on inquiry that there are already sidings 2,300, and even 2,700 yards long. As I have said, we went into the matter thoroughly. We tried to avoid the necessity of crossing this Common, but we found that if the people of Cambridge were to derive any advantage whatever from this station, it was absolutely essential that this portion of the Bill should be carried out. I quite agree with the hon. Gentleman, and especially with those hon. Gentlemen who belong to the Commons Preservation Society, that the Common land of this country ought to be protected in every possible way, more particularly when it is contiguous to our great towns where there is hardly sufficient breathing space already; but if there is one place in the world where the outcry for the preservation of Commons ceases to have any material or practical force, it is Cambridge, where the Corporation themselves possess no less than 300 acres of common ground, and where there are already a considerable number of open spaces belonging to the Colleges and other Institutions. So far as open spaces are concerned, very little damage will be done by this Bill to the people of Cambridge. After all, what the Railway Company propose to do is simply to take away three acres from a Common of 100 acres in extent, and in place of those three acres the Committee have insisted upon the Railway Company providing another three acres immediately adjoining this Common. I am therefore of opinion that the rights of the public have been protected in every way. Ample provision has been made for preservation and footpaths, and for enabling the cattle to pass under the railway when the line is constructed. We are told that the construction of the line will interfere with the amusements of the people of Cambridge. Now, one of the Members of the Committee went over to Cambridge in order to obtain information for himself upon that point; and, on visiting the spot, instead of finding the Common full of people, there was hardly anybody there at all. This was only about a fortnight ago. I

maintain that, in the first place, Coldham Common is not going to be diminished by a single inch. The people of Cambridge will have exactly the same amount of space provided for them which they now enjoy. I have shown that it is not a place which is used for the recreation of the townspeople. Will the fact that it is intersected by a railway interfere with the right of pasturage? In order to guard against any interference of that kind we have made provision by which there will be no difficulty whatever either for passengers or cattle to pass from one side of the line to the other. One part of the line will be upon the level, and the other part will be in a cutting; but ample provision is made both for the accommodation of passengers and cattle. Provision is also made for a cricket ground; but one of the Town Councillors of Cambridge told us that there is absolutely no cricket played there at all. So far as the recreation of the people is concerned, the only persons who are really interested in this Common, in connection with playing games upon it, are some 60 members of the University, who have the use of the Common from the Corporation for nothing, and play golf upon it. They are the only persons who can possibly suffer by the severance of the Common, and surely if they want a golf ground they are able to provide one at their own expense. In the first place, the ground is very bad for the purpose, and the result is, as I have said, that there are only about 60 members of the University who belong to the Golf Club. I deny, however, that the interests of 60 members of the University of Cambridge should interfere with a great public improvement like this. We have been told by the hon. Member for Cambridge that the construction of this line will interfere with the rifle range. If that is so, how is it that the War Office, which at first opposed the Bill, now find that there is no necessity for opposing it? The fact is, that the rifle range can easily be removed to another place some 20 yards to the left. The Railway Company have proposed to remove the butts, and to incur every expense in acquiring new ones. There will be no difficulty in so doing, because the land is the property of the same owners whose land is now fired over. Further than that, I am told that the Volunteers have no right to shoot over those persons ground at all. Therefore, they cannot possibly be in any worse position, if they have to move their butts for some 20 yards to the left of the position which they now occupy, and no damage whatever can be done to the rifle corps by anything we have sanctioned with regard to this Common. I have shown that the Common will not be damaged to any extent whatever; and I trust that, on account of the accommodation to the town of Cambridge, the Bill will be passed. The people of Cambridge themselves do not oppose the Bill, and the only opponents, as a matter of fact, are the 60 members of the University, who now enjoy it as a golf ground. I trust that the House will not be led away by any false sentiment, but will support the unanimous decision of the Committee.

MR. SHAW LEFEVRE (Bradford, Central): As chairman of the Commons Preservation Society, to which the hon. Member for Preston (Mr. Hanbury) has alluded, I wish to say why I am prepared to support the Amendment which has been moved by the hon. Member for Cambridge (Mr. Penrose Fitzgerald). Until a few years ago Parliament was very careless as to railways going through Commons, and several of the best Commons we had in the neighbourhood of the Metropolis—such as Wandsworth, Barnes, and Tooting—have been seriously injured by being intersected by railways in the manner now proposed. During the last 20 years the Society to which I belong have, by their action, been able to prevent any case of this kind from occurring within easy reach of London, or in any populous part of the country. Anyone going down to Barnes or Tooting Common will see for himself the effect of intersecting those Commons by railways. It is impossible to prevent the destruction both of the beauty and unity of a piece of common land if you allow a railway to intersect it on the level, as is seen in the cases I have mentioned. The hon. Member for Preston thinks that no damage will be done because the Railway Company propose to give up to the town another three acres of land, which is the amount of land actually proposed to be taken; but that is not the point. The evil is done by intersecting the Common and cutting it in half. I have not risen to oppose this

Bill without having satisfied myself that a very serious injury is certain to be done in this case. I have been down to Coldham Common, and, having carefully inspected it, I came to the conclusion that a great public evil would result from the adoption of this proposal. Coldham Common is close to the town of Cambridge—indeed, it is within 100 yards. That part of the town is growing rapidly. Cambridge itself has a population of more than 35,000, and although there are other Commons, this is one which is much resorted to for purposes of recreation. I do not put the question on the ground of the rifle range; but I put it on the general ground of the evil of allowing the common to be destroyed by being intersected in this manner. I dare say that arguments will be brought forward on behalf of the Railway Company to show that the land is necessary for their proposed sidings. We always hear arguments of that kind in such cases; but I must confess that I never listen to them. I invariably refuse to listen to them, because I know that, as a rule, if a proposal of this sort is rejected by Parliament the Railway Company invariably find some other mode of carrying out their object. I should have opposed this Bill on the second reading if it had not been for the fact that it was an Omnibus Bill, and I thought it was scarcely fair to oppose the second reading on a ground of this kind, which applies only to a portion of it. The Bill has now been before a Select Committee, and I am sorry that the Committee should not have had more regard to the interests of the public. So far, however, as questions of this kind are concerned, I think they are better fought out in a full House than in a Committee. I feel confident that if the House adopt the Motion of the hon. Member for Cambridge, and send the Bill back to the Committee, the Railway Company will be able to obtain what they want in some other way, without inflicting serious injury upon the public. There are two ways of avoiding this Common—one is by making a divergence before the Common is reached, and the other by going beyond it. There is no necessity whatever for destroying this Common; and I will as the House to remember that an injury of this kind once inflicted can never be undone. It is upon this ground that I have opposed

Mr. Hanbury

other cases; and I venture to hope that the House will adopt the same course in this instance, and will refer the Bill back to the Committee.

Lord CLAUD HAMILTON (Liverpool, West Derby): As one of the Members in charge of the Bill, I should like to say one or two words in reply to what has fallen from the right hon. Gentleman the Member for Central Bradford (Mr. Shaw Lefevre). The right hon. Gentleman has not pointed out to the House the present condition of the station at Cambridge. It is on one side of a siding, extending over a quarter of a-mile, into which the trains of four separate Railway Companies, who have running powers, are taken. The Great Eastern Railway Company have long contemplated, in consequence of the danger to the passengers and the inconvenience to the travelling public generally, the necessity of remodelling the station. Hitherto, for financial and other reasons, they have been unable to do so; but now the financial position of the Company has greatly improved, and they believe that they are able to make these improvements on a proper and adequate scale. They have presented this Bill with that object. They instructed their engineer to prepare plans, and, in doing so, they requested him, if possible, to avoid passing over Coldham Common; but, after giving the matter every consideration, the engineer found that it was impossible to do this. It was necessary for the accommodation of the through traffic, as well as for the local wants of Cambridge, to take in this bit of Coldham Common to which reference has been made. The right hon. Gentleman says—"Why not stop short of Coldham Common?" The reason is that if the line were to turn off short of Coldham Common, it would pass on a level crossing through the proposed new goods siding of the Great Eastern Railway, and would, consequently, be attended with great danger, not only to the lives of the railway *employés*, but of the travelling public. I do not believe for a moment that the Board of Trade would ever sanction such a railway scheme. It would certainly be quite contrary to anything they have heretofore sanctioned. The Company believe that it is absolutely essential to go through Coldham Common in order to make the great

improvements proposed at Cambridge Station. The right hon. Gentleman has drawn attention to the injury done to the Commons at Tooting, Wandsworth, and Barnes, by allowing them to be intersected by railways; but I would ask the right hon. Gentleman this question—how many people do you find upon Tooting, Wandsworth, and Barnes Commons when you go there? It is a place of resort for hundreds of human beings every hour of the day; but if you go to Coldham Common you will find nothing there but skylarks and a few head of cattle. Coldham Common is not used by the people of Cambridge for the purpose of recreation. There are other Commons in the neighbourhood of Cambridge closer to the town, and are much used; but Coldham Common, from its peculiar position, is not used for the purpose of recreation at all, and there are very few people to be found upon it for any purpose whatever. As a matter of fact, it is only used for the grazing of cattle and for playing the game of golf and for rifle practice, for which ample accommodation will be afforded under the proposed changes. The most important part of the matter, however, is the evidence which has been given before the Committee by the Engineer of the Railway Company, to the effect that it is quite impossible to make the proposed improvements in connection with Cambridge Station without taking these three acres of ground, in substitution for which the Company give three acres elsewhere. Under these circumstances, I trust the House will reject the Amendment.

The POSTMASTER GENERAL (Mr. Raikes) (Cambridge University): It is not without reluctance that I rise to take part in this discussion, or to depart from the usual practice of refraining from entering into questions which have already been considered by a Select Committee upstairs. I listened with great interest and attention to the statement of the hon. Member for Preston (Mr. Hanbury), who was Chairman of the Committee upon this Bill, which satisfied me that, at all events, the matter received very attentive consideration. I must also say that I do not go the whole length of my right hon. Friend opposite (Mr. Shaw Lefevre) in his general opposition to all schemes for dealing with commons. I think that every one of these cases is worth being heard on its own merits, and that it is a mistaken policy to meet with unscrupulous opposition every scheme which may be submitted to Parliament for utilizing common land, whether for a railway, or any other purpose. But this case, I am bound to say, is a very flagrant case on the part of a Railway Company to wrest a portion of a common from the public. There is a large and growing population in that part of the borough of Cambridge contiguous to the Common now proposed to be dealt with. We have been told by my hon. Friend the Member for Preston that there are other commons in Cambridge. That is quite true; but, has as been pointed out already in the course of this debate, such commons are not convenient for the poorer inhabitants for the purpose of pasturage, and as to there being other open land within the boundaries of the borough of Cambridge, it might just as well be said that it would be reasonable to run a railway through Hyde Park because there is an open space in Berkeley Square. This Common is one which the Mayor and Corporation of Cambridge, who represent a population of between 40,000 and 50,000, have expressed an earnest desire to retain in its present state. It has been pointed out that this Common, so far from being confined to skylarks and the grazing of cattle, at present is used as a rifle ground for the Volunteers; and it has further been pointed out that it is used by a golf club, consisting of members of the University. I have no wish to ask for the members of the University any other advantages or facilities for recreation than would be accorded to the general body of the public; but I do not see that because they happen to be members of the University that should be any reason why they should not be listened to. On the whole, I cannot help thinking that the Great Eastern Railway Company will be able to find some other way of approaching their railway station at Cambridge, and if this part of their scheme is rejected by the Committee, I have no doubt that their engineer will find some other way of improving the station without trespassing upon Coldham Common. I have no doubt that when the Company come back to Parliament in a future Session

Mr. Raikes

they will have found some method of getting over the difficulty. I speak with all due deference, because I certainly do not share the pronounced views of the Commons Preservation Society; but I never remember a stronger case than the present for resisting the attempt of a great Railway Company to deprive the public of an important part of one of their recreation grounds, which, at the present moment, is employed for valuable public purposes.

Mr. T. BLAKE (Gloucester, Forest of Dean): As a Member of the Select Committee to whom this Bill was referred, I can corroborate everything that has been said by the hon. Member for Preston (Mr. Hanbury), who was Chairman of the Committee, in reference to this Common. I may say, for myself and the other Members of the Committee, that we endeavoured most strongly to ascertain whether the proposed alterations and improvements at Cambridge Station could be carried out without touching this Common. The evidence of the engineer was that he had tried in every possible way to avoid touching Coldham Common, but had found it utterly impossible to do so in view of the improvement of the station accommodation, and at present no train can come in from the Newmarket line without danger. At present an experienced official, distinguished by a badge worn on his arm, called a "pilot," has to be sent out to meet every train and to bring it into the station. The Great Eastern Company now propose to construct a double section, with docks for the various trains, and to lay down a number of other lines. The Board of Trade will not sanction trains running across these lines, and the only way to avoid danger to the traffic is to take this portion of Coldham Common. The station is now a quarter of a mile long, and any person coming in from Norwich is required to walk that distance; whereas, if the scheme now before the House is passed, the Company propose to run all trains properly into the station. On Tuesday week I went down to Cambridge specially to inspect this Common. It was a very fine day, and I went down to the Common, which is about a mile and a quarter from the central Post Office in the town. I found that the only persons on the common were two lads, whereas all the other commons and open spaces were, at the same time, being used by a considerable number of persons of all ages. I was told that the Common is chiefly used for grazing cattle, and that it is not unusual to find 200 or 300 head of cattle upon it. The Company propose, if they are permitted to make use of the Common, to give an equal number of acres close adjacent to the Common, and with reference to the rifle range, I cannot see that there would be any difficulty, or that the Volunteers would be in any degree injured, if it were slewed round as suggested, or otherwise altered, as the Bill proposes. The Bill in no way seriously interferes with the rifle range. In the interests of the public, generally, and of the inhabitants of the district in particular, the Committee came to the unanimous conclusion that it would be of great convenience to the town of Cambridge if these works were carried out, and that there would be very little injury to the Common, seeing the purposes for which it is used. I do not think it is necessary that I should go further into the reasons which induced the Committee to pass the Bill. Our inquiry extended over a period of three weeks, and we took more than 500 pages of evidence. We were most patient in hearing all the evidence that could be submitted to us; we heard counsel on both sides, and I am satisfied that we came to a right and proper conclusion.

MR. P. M'DONALD (Sligo, N.): I feel it my duty to call the attention of the House to what the real facts of the case are in connection with this Bill. I had the honour to be one of the four Members to whom this Bill was referred; and, in the first place, I will express my full and entire concurrence in all that has been stated by my hon. Friend the Member for Preston (Mr. Hanbury), who was Chairman of the Committee. He has stated—and his statement has been confirmed by my hon. Friend who has just sat down, that we gave to this Bill the fullest consideration. We sat for three whole weeks, for five days in each week, considering all the bearings of the case. We took into our careful consideration every point relating to the Bill that was submitted to us either by the promoters or the opponents; and I am pleased to be able to inform the House that we were unanimous in the conclusion to

which we arrived. The question that has been raised as regards Coldham Common is one that has not, I believe, been fairly put before the House. It is not a question of robbing the public, or depriving them of their right to an open space. If it were so, I should have been one of the last to support any scheme of the kind. On the contrary, I should have entered my strongest and most strenuous protest in opposition to it. But the matter was one of an entirely different kind, and related solely to the accommodation and convenience of the public. The present railway requirements at Cambridge are such that the existing station accommodation is altogether insufficient. I went fully into the consideration of the case. I had no interest in the Bill either one way or the other. Being an Irish Member, I was able to look upon the question from a purely conscientious or public point of view, and I am obliged to say that I entirely concurred with the conclusion at which the Chairman and other Members of the Committee arrived. The railway accommodation at Cambridge is totally inadequate to the requirements of that town. There is only one siding, and consequently it is not only exceedingly inconvenient, but very often dangerous, to the general public to carry on the traffic. It is most desirable that an extension of the station arrangements should be made. The engineer of the Great Eastern Company gave evidence to the effect that he had tried every possible means of finding a suitable extension, but was unable to find any without going through this Common. As regards the Common itself, I have already said that I should be opposed to any encroachment upon the rights of the people; but in this case there is no encroachment, inasmuch as there is an equivalent provided. An equal extent of land adjoining the Common is to be added to the Common in substitution for that which is taken away by the railway, consequently, there is no deprivation; and, under the circumstances, I do not consider that the public have any reason to complain. In my opinion, the opposition which has been raised to this part of the Bill is merely drawing a red herring across the track. To talk of the public interest involved in the preservation of the Common, as compared with the necessity for making adequate provision for the requirements of the travelling public, is absurd. I believe the only object with which such remarks have been made has been to put my hon. Friends who sit on these Benches in a position which may induce them to arrive at an erroneous conclusion. If there was any intention to deprive the public of their rights, I should be the first to object; but being thoroughly acquainted with the provisions of the Bill, I shall support it and vote against the Amendment.

MR. BRYCE (Aberdeen, S.): I only rise for the purpose of saying one word on this subject as an eye witness. Two years ago this Common was threatened by another Railway Company, and being shortly afterwards in Cambridge, I visited and examined Coldham Common. I found that, so far from being a mile and a quarter from the town of Cambridge, it is within a few hundred yards of the houses and town. I have a map in my hand which shows how the town has extended towards the Common. This is one of the poorest and most growing parts of the town, and the the Common will soon be bordered by houses. Under these circumstances, I hope the House will consent to refer the Bill back to the Committee. Everyone who has taken part in discussions of this kind knows that whenever an engineer wants to obtain possession of a particular piece of ground, whether it is common land or otherwise, he always protests that there is no other way of carrying out the work; but when that ground is refused his ideas undergo a change, and he discovers some other expedient.

Question put.

The House *divided:*—Ayes 101; Noes 237: Majority 136.—(Div. List, No. 97.)

Question proposed, "That the words 're-committed to the former Committee with respect to all the Clauses relating to Coldham Common' be there added."

THE PRESIDENT OF THE LOCAL GOVERNMENT BOARD (MR. RITCHIE) (Tower Hamlets, St. George's): I ask the permission of the House to be allowed to interpose only for a few moments. I think my intervention may have the effect of saving the time of the House. There are some Amendments on the Paper in the names of the hon. Member for South-East Essex (Major

Mr. P. M'Donald

Rasch), the hon. Member for South-West Ham (Major Banes), and the hon. Member for North-West Ham (Mr. Forrest Fulton), in reference to the market rights proposed to be conferred by the Bill upon the Great Eastern Railway Company. I imagine that if the Motion now before the House is carried, those hon. Members will be unable to move their Amendments; and, therefore, what I propose to do is to ask the House to assent to an Amendment to the Motion, which, I think, will, in all probability, secure the object these hon. Gentlemen have in view. I do not agree with the Amendments the hon. Gentlemen have put down; but I do agree in the object which, as I take it, they desire to secure. This Bill confers upon the Railway Company certain market rights—the power of levying certain market rates and tolls in connection with the markets both at Stratford and Bishopsgate. I should be very sorry indeed if the House were to put any impediment in the way of conferring these powers on the Railway Company, or that anything should be done which would have the effect of closing the market at Stratford. It has been open now for some years, and it is greatly valued by the inhabitants of that district. When the question came before the House the other day in reference to the market rights and tolls, we discussed the propriety or otherwise of the market rights being in the hands of the public authority rather than in the hands of any private person. I stated then, what I state now, that while the market rights are held exclusively, they should be held, not by private persons, but by the public authority. As far as I understand the market rights proposed to be conferred by this Bill, they form part of the question which the House, a short time ago, referred to a Royal Commission. The Bill proposes to confer them upon the Railway Company, to the exclusion of the Corporation of West Ham, or of any other public body whatever, and in order to prevent any claim for vested rights from being set up hereafter in favour of the Company under the provisions of this Bill, I propose to ask the House to consent to a further reference to the Select Committee, so that they may be instructed to insert in the Bill provisions which will lay down distinctly that in the event of a market authority being set up, either in the one place or the other, and being desirous of purchasing either of these markets, the Railway Company shall have no power whatever to ask for compensation for the rights conferred by this Bill. What, therefore, I propose is to add to the Amendment which is now before the House these words—

" And in order to consider Clauses to provide that in the event of a public authority being appointed a market authority for the district in which the proposed markets are situated, and being empowered to acquire existing markets, no compensation for the market tolls, rates, and charges granted in this Bill shall be payable to the Railway Company."

Amendment proposed to the said proposed Amendment—

To add at the end thereof the words, "And in order to consider Clauses to provide that, in the event of a public authority being appointed the market authority for the district in which the proposed markets are situated, and being empowered to acquire existing markets, no compensation for the market tolls, rates, and charges granted under the Bill shall be payable to the Railway Company."—(*Mr. Ritchie.*)

Question proposed, " That those words be there added."

Mr. BRADLAUGH (Northampton): I do not wish to occupy the time of the House unduly in a matter of Private Business, and I am very much indebted to the Government for taking the action they have, which is certainly an affirmation, as I understand it, of the principle adopted by the House the other evening —if not in words, certainly in spirit. But there were one or two words which fell from the right hon. Gentleman which seem to me to go a little further than the Amendment he suggests. I maintain that market rights, if given to anybody at all, with power to make regulations and levy tolls, ought not to be given to a Railway Company who have a monopoly of the carriage to the place where the market is held. By giving them these powers, there is a possibility of making it an altogether exclusive market, and this difficulty is hardly met by the Amendment, which is very fair as far as it goes. The Amendment meets one phase of what the House has affirmed; but the doctrine was also affirmed by the general consent of the House that encouragement should be given to the sending of produce from any place to where the market is held. As I understand the Market Clauses

of this Bill they will have an opposite effect. The interest of a Railway Company is to have as large a tonnage rate as possible for long distances, and not to develop the interest of the neighbourhood. It, therefore, requires some other words in the Amendment to provide for the development of that which, at the present moment, it is possible for the Railway Company to destroy. As a matter of fact, Railway Companies do destroy districts close at hand by charging through rates at a very low price. Perhaps the House will forgive me if I mention an instance of this to show how the interests of different constituencies may be affected. Some time ago I happened to be in Cornwall, and I was told that a Redruth gentleman, who had a great admiration for the hon. Member for the Camborne Division of Cornwall (Mr. Conybeare), desired to supply the constituents of that hon. Gentleman with a drinking mug ornamented with the likeness of the hon. Member. [*A laugh.*] If I am wrong, perhaps the hon. Member will correct me; but I think I am right in my facts. The gentleman I refer to had the likeness admirably executed in Staffordshire, but the work itself was done in Germany, because the Railway Companies brought the stuff—I am not speaking of the likeness — cheaper from Germany to Camborne at such a low rate that it was cheaper than it would have been if it had been brought from Staffordshire, and the consequence was that the people of Staffordshire were robbed of the employment they would otherwise have had but for the unfair handicapping of the Railway Companies. I would, therefore, ask the Government to affirm both of the principles which I understood the House to adopt. I desire to thank the Chairman of the Committee, who examined the clauses of the Bill, for the valuable overhauling which they gave to the charter rights as they stood. I only suggest that the Government should go further and prevent the Railway Companies from giving undue preference to produce brought from long distances, to the destruction of the trade in the neighbourhood in which the markets are situated.

Mr. FORREST FULTON (West Ham, N.): Sir, I think I have some reason to complain of the action of the right hon. Gentleman the President of the Local Government Board. Without the slightest Notice to me, representing, as I do, a borough which is most interested in this matter, and without, as far as I know, the smallest intimation to my hon. Friend who represents the other Division of the borough of West Ham (Major Banes), in this House, at the eleventh hour, at a quarter past 6 this afternoon, the right hon. Gentleman the President of the Local Government Board presents an entirely new matter to the consideration of the House, and protects himself by the observation that, forsooth, it was through indifference that we have not proceeded with the Motions which stand in our name on the Paper. If the right hon. Gentleman had applied his mind to the other Motions on the Paper, he would have seen that we have not proceeded with those Motions advisedly and properly, because it had been intimated to us through a high authority of this House that as this is an Omnibus Bill it was undesirable and even would be unfair to move that the Bill should be considered on this day six months. Therefore, in pursuance of that intimation, we placed further Notices on the Paper, confining our opposition exclusively to that part of the Bill to which alone we desire to offer opposition—namely, the Market Clauses. If the right hon. Gentleman will refer to the Notices of Motion, he will find a Notice set down as No. 5, in my name; but, of course, I could not bring it on until the Motion of the hon. Member for Cambridge had been disposed of. I desire to say that I have not the smallest hesitation as to the course I propose to take in regard to the Notice which stands in my name. I have not the smallest intention of withdrawing the Notice from the Paper. It seems to me that it involves a question of the greatest possible importance. If this House is going to pass the Bill, in the form in which it now stands, it will absolutely stultify the decision at which it arrived the other day on the Motion of the hon. Member for Northampton (Mr. Bradlaugh), when the Government consented to grant a Royal Commission for the purpose of inquiring into the whole question of market rights and tolls. By the Bill which is now under consideration, it is proposed to confer upon the Great Eastern Railway Company statutory market rights and tolls in the borough

Mr. Forrest Fulton

of West Ham, which, above all others, a Railway Company is least likely to carry out satisfactorily. I know that the House is naturally very reluctant to interfere with the proceedings of a Private Bill Committee who have thoroughly considered the matter; but when the Bill was before the Committee they were not aware that this House was going to consent to the appointment of a Royal Commission to inquire into the whole subject. I think, that, at any rate, we ought to have the opinion of the borough of West Ham, and I certainly have some knowledge of what that opinion is. The right hon. Gentleman says that the inhabitants of that borough are in favour of this market. Now, I do not believe for one moment that if these clauses are struck out, this market will cease to exist. It is a mere "bogey" on the part of the Great Eastern Railway Company. They have no intention of discontinuing this market. The only reason for inserting these provisions in the Bill is that the Company have been involved in litigation with an individual who claims to have certain market rights, and who threatens them with an action unless some sort of protection is given him. He further threatens to shut up this market, as he has already succeeded in shutting up Bishopsgate Market.

Mr. SPEAKER: Order, order! I must remind the hon. and learned Gentleman that the whole subject-matter of this Bill is not before the House. The specific point is the question of the re-committal of the Bill in respect of certain proposed clauses, and if the Bill is re-committed, it will necessarily have to come down to the House again, and the hon. Member will then be in a position to move, when the Bill re-appears in the House, the Motion which is now standing in his name on the Paper.

Mr. FORREST FULTON: Of course, if that is so, I do not desire to trouble the House any further. I am quite satisfied with the understanding that I shall have an opportunity of bringing this matter forward at a later stage.

Mr. HANBURY: As a Member of the Committee, I should be glad, and I think my Colleagues on that Committee will be glad, to accept the proposition of the right hon. Gentleman the President of the Local Government Board. We have already made provision in the Bill that no rights which are conferred upon the Company should prevent other markets from being made. The rights we have given to the Railway Company in connection with this market are totally different from those which have been given by the charter granted to Mr. Horner. We have conferred no rights of that kind whatever. As to the suggestion of my hon. Friend the Member for Northampton (Mr. Bradlaugh), I think there is something in what he says; but it is a matter which is also carefully guarded in the Bill. But then there arises a further point which is rather in favour of the people who live in contiguity to those markets—namely, that they should have facilities afforded to them against the introduction of produce from a distance. I do not quite agree with my hon. Friend, for this reason—one of the main points which induced us to give these powers to the Railway Company for establishing a market was the fact that London, at the present moment, is entirely dependent for its perishables upon a supply which is drawn from a very small area indeed; and, as the population increases, it is becoming more and more difficult to get an adequate supply from this small district, and, consequently, the prices go up. Mr. Clare Sewell Read, a gentleman whose name is well known in this House, gave evidence before us, and he represented that it was of the utmost importance that a supply should be obtained from longer distances. On the one hand, we have farmers at a distance, who are longing to bring up their produce to the Metropolis, but who find it necessary to wait until they can get proper market accommodation; and, on the other hand, we have the people of this part of London looking anxiously for an increased supply. We consider it desirable to bring the two into more immediate communication; and if there is any Railway Company which ought to be given this power, it is undoubtedly the Great Eastern Company, which draws its supplies from a purely agricultural district, which has its terminus in the midst of the poorest part of London, and which is in a position to supply them with everything they can require. Subject to these observations, I entirely support the proposals of the right hon. Gentleman.

Mr. PICKERSGILL (Bethnal Green, S.W.): I desire to say a word or two upon this question, because one of the markets it is proposed to establish is situated in the midst of the constituency I represent. I only desire to say that I am opposed as strongly to the establishment of the Bishopsgate Market as the hon. and learned Member for West Ham (Mr. Forrest Fulton) is to the establishment of the market at Stratford, and that, so far as the proposition of the right hon. Gentleman the President of the Local Government Board is concerned, it does not disarm the opposition which I intend to offer to the Bill.

MAJOR RASCH (Essex, S.E.): With the greatest deference, I cannot agree to the proposition which has been submitted to the House by the right hon. Gentleman the President of the Local Government Board. I oppose these clauses in the interest of my constituents, the farmers and market gardeners of South-East Essex. If these provisions should pass, my belief is that the position of my constituents will be much worse than it is now.

Mr. SPEAKER: The hon. and gallant Member will have an opportunity of renewing his opposition to the Bill, and of raising that question, when the Bill comes back from the Committee.

MAJOR BANES (West Ham, S.): I wish to endorse what has been said by the hon. and learned Member for North West Ham (Mr. Forrest Fulton), that up to this moment we had no idea this proposition was about to be made by the right hon. Gentleman the President of the Local Government Board. I had hoped that an understanding would be come to; and, on behalf of the Corporation of West Ham, I may say that they have done all they possibly could to bring about an understanding with the Railway Company on the principle enunciated by the right hon. Gentleman, that Local Authorities are the proper persons to exercise these rights on behalf of the public; and, having reference to the fact that the House had sanctioned that principle by its decision on the Motion of the hon. Member for Northampton (Mr. Bradlaugh) on Market Rights, I had hoped that some arrangement of this kind might have been come to without any necessity for troubling Parliament. On behalf of the Corporation of West Ham, I must say that we have great reason for opposing this market on many grounds. In justice to the Corporation, I can show that they are quite unanimous in the feeling they entertain that the grant of these market rights as they at present stand in the Bill will not only be detrimental to the producer, but to the general public, who are the consumers. May I ask you, Mr. Speaker, whether it is possible to move that an Instruction be given to the Committee to leave out these clauses altogether?

MR. SPEAKER: It would be incompetent for the hon. and gallant Member to do that now. The Instruction would require Notice.

MR. BURDETT-COUTTS (Westminster): I wish, Sir, to ask for your instruction upon a similar point. We, who are opposing this Bill, oppose it because we believe that market rights should not be granted to a Railway Company, and we know that the granting of these rights to the Great Eastern Railway will destroy the other markets and give the Company a monopoly of market rights in the East End. I wish to ask you whether, by re-committing the Bill to the former Committee, with a reference to the clause which has been mentioned by the right hon. Gentleman the President of the Local Government Board, and without any reference to the clauses conferring market rights on the Great Eastern Railway Company, we are not in some sense confirming the judgment of this House in favour of those market rights? [*Cries of* "No!"]

THE CHAIRMAN OF COMMITTEES (Mr. COURTNEY) (Cornwall, Bodmin): It seems to me that there is some little uncertainty as to what has happened, and what is going to happen. The House has decided to re-commit the Bill in respect of particular clauses. The Bill must, therefore, come back again from the Committee, when the whole question of the Market Clauses can be considered by the House. The right hon. Gentleman the President of the Local Government Board proposes—

"In the event of a public authority being appointed a market authority for the district in which the proposed markets are situated, and being empowered to acquire existing markets, no compensation for the market tolls, rates, and charges granted in this Bill shall be repayable to the Railway Company."

That is a matter to be considered by the Committee, and to be determined on its merits. When the Bill comes back the whole question of the Market

Major Banes

Clauses can be brought under the consideration of the House.

COLONEL MAKINS (Essex, S.E.): I understand, Sir, from your ruling, that it is not competent to enter into the question of market rights generally?

MR. SPEAKER: I understand that the Amendment of the right hon. Gentleman is, in substance, that if a public authority be appointed the authority in connection with these markets, such authority shall not be entitled to obtain compensation for the market tolls, rates, and charges granted in the Bill—that the acquirement of market property shall not give any kind of right to compensation in the event of such market tolls or rates being affected by subsequent legislation.

COLONEL MAKINS: This is how I understand the case to stand, and it is the way in which we believe it to be provided for in the Bill. In order to make it more abundantly certain we have acquiesced in this reference to the Committee. I shall not, therefore, take up the time of the House in defending the action of the Company, by giving any details with regard to the market, seeing that the question will have to be gone into again. At the same time, I would ask the House not to allow judgment to go by default, because we are not able now to state our case in reply to the observations which have fallen from the hon. Members for West Ham (Mr. Forrest Fulton) and Northampton (Mr. Bradlaugh). I shall be quite prepared, at the proper time, to justify the course which has been taken by the Railway Company.

Question put, and *agreed to.*

Main Question, as amended, put.

Ordered, That the Bill be re-committed to the former Committee with respect to all the Clauses relating to Coldham Common, Cambridge, and in order to consider Clauses to provide that, in the event of a public authority being appointed the market authority for the districts in which the proposed markets are situated, and being empowered to acquire existing markets, no compensation for the market tolls, rates, and charges granted under the Bill shall be payable to the Railway Company.

SUTTON DISTRICT WATER BILL
(*by Order*).
CONSIDERATION.

Order for Consideration read.

MR. CUBITT (Surrey, Mid): As some of the clauses it is intended to propose in this Bill appear on the Paper to-day for the first time, I presume that the usual course will be followed which is taken in reference to opposed Bills, and that the consideration will be postponed until to-morrow.

Consideration, as amended, *deferred* till *To-morrow.*

QUESTIONS.

——o——

ADMIRALTY—EXAMINATIONS IN SEA-MANSHIP OF MIDSHIPMEN FOR RANK OF LIEUTENANTS.

MR. CRAIG-SELLAR (Lanarkshire, Partick) asked the First Lord of the Admiralty, Where, and by whom, the examinations in seamanship of Midshipmen for the rank of Lieutenants are conducted; what is the system pursued by the examiners; and what steps are taken to secure uniformity in the granting of certificates; and, whether, looking to the fact that the " class " awarded has a serious effect upon the future careers of the officers, the recommendation of the Committee on the Education of Naval Executive Officers (1885), that the seamanship examination should be for a " pass " certificate only, and not for a " class," as at present, is to be carried out in future?

THE FIRST LORD (Lord GEORGE HAMILTON) (Middlesex, Ealing): The seamanship examinations are conducted by three Captains, who are nominated by the Commander-in-Chief on each Station, whenever an officer's time for examination has arrived. There is a form supplied to the examining officers detailing the various points for examination, and showing the full number of marks to be awarded for each subject. This form is universal throughout the Service, and the examinations are everywhere conducted on the same principles. It is impossible to obtain absolute uniformity in any series of examinations; but it is believed that the system in force insures, as far as is possible, even results. It is true that the Committee on the education of Naval Executive Officers recommended a " pass " examination in seamanship; but they did not propose to abolish the " class " examination in that subject, but merely to defer it till a later period. An experiment was tried for some years of establishing at Portsmouth one set of

examining officers for the whole Service; but it was found to be unsatisfactory, and was abandoned, and the previous system was reverted to, and is now in operation. The manner in which the Committee proposed to give effect to their recommendation concerning the seamanship examination was found to be so impracticable that it has not been adopted; but the Admiralty have called upon the Admirals in command of the Mediterranean and Channel Squadrons to report in what way, in their opinion, the present examination may be improved upon, and their Reports, when received, will be carefully considered.

BANKRUPTCY — COSTS OF ADMINISTRATION.

MR. BRADLAUGH (Northampton) asked the Secretary to the Board of Trade, Whether his attention has been called to the exceedingly large costs and charges often incurred in the administration of bankrupts' estates; and, whether the Government can take any action in the matter?

THE SECRETARY (Baron HENRY DE WORMS) (Liverpool, East Toxteth): The cost of administration of bankrupts' estates, as shown by the Board of Trade Reports presented to Parliament, has largely decreased, as compared with those incurred under the Act of 1869 more especially in the case of estates administered by Official Receivers; but it cannot be denied that excessive costs are still incurred recklessly, and without any corresponding benefit to creditors, in some cases where the administration had been conducted by non-official Trustees and Committees of Inspection appointed by the creditors. The control exercised by the Board of Trade over the costs incurred by such Trustees is chiefly limited to seeing that they have been legally incurred, and securing that the creditors are furnished with proper information on the subject. The Official Receiver is precluded by the Bankruptcy Act from acting as Trustee under adjudications where the assets exceed £300; but the desirability of taking steps for the modification of this provision is under consideration. The Government are not, however, prepared to take any action which would interfere with the power of creditors to appoint a non-official Trustee where they deem it advisable to do so.

POST OFFICE (ENGLAND AND WALES) "OFFICIAL PAID" LETTERS — RE-DIRECTION.

Mr. BRADLAUGH (Northampton) asked the Postmaster General, Whether letters stamped "official paid" are exempted from all charge for re-direction; whether letters stamped "paid" are subjected to the ordinary charge for re-direction; whether many letters and packets, sent out by and for the Imperial Institute, have been re-directed and delivered without charge for such re-direction; and, whether he can now state the date at which the quarterly account was opened for the Imperial Institute with the Post Office; how much appears to the debit of the account; and how much has been actually paid?

The POSTMASTER GENERAL (Mr. RAIKES) (Cambridge University): The answer to the first and second paragraphs of the hon. Member's Question is in the affirmative. The paying account for the Imperial Institute was only opened on the 31st of January last, so that the first quarter has not yet expired; but the account will be rendered as soon as the month expires, and payment will be demanded. There have been cases of re-direction of letters within the same delivery which, as in the case of ordinary correspondence, require no extra fee, and no cases have yet come to notice of re-directions to addresses beyond the free delivery. A careful check on the postage will be kept, and a special and distinct stamp will be used in lieu of the present one, which will greatly facilitate the object in view.

ADMIRALTY—THE "PRIMROSE BALL" AT VENTNOR—THE COASTGUARD.

Mr. BRADLAUGH (Northampton) (for Mr. LABOUCHERE) (Northampton) asked the First Lord of the Admiralty, Whether his attention has been called to the fact (as stated in a local newspaper) that, at a ball at Ventnor last Thursday, called the Primrose Ball,

"Thanks to the help of the Coastguard, who are always ready to help in these festive arrangements, the display of bunting was pretty in the extreme;"

and, whether Coastguards are permitted to take an active part in hanging halls with flags (some of which probably are public property) on the occasion of Primrose festivities?

The FIRST LORD (Lord GEORGE HAMILTON) (Middlesex, Ealing): Any help in hanging flags that was rendered by the Coastguardmen on the occasion of the Primrose Ball at Ventnor was unconnected with their public duties, and done in the time at the men's disposal. The Coastguard not infrequently assist in the decorations for local festivities, and I am glad that they should do so. None of the flags used were public property.

WAR OFFICE—PROMOTIONS IN THE ROYAL ENGINEERS.

Mr. BRADLAUGH (Northampton) (for Mr. LABOUCHERE) (Northampton) asked the Secretary of State for War, Whether he is aware that, by a Royal Warrant of 22nd January, 1887, a Corporal of the Royal Engineers has been promoted to Company Sergeant Major, over the heads of Sergeants of many years standing, and also that junior Sergeants have been promoted to Company Sergeant Major over senior Sergeants; and, whether it is intended to reinstate in their former position of seniority those Sergeants who have been superseded?

The SECRETARY OF STATE (Mr. E. STANHOPE) (Lincolnshire, Horncastle): My answer to the first part of the Question of the hon. Member is "Yes;" and to the second, that it is not intended to reinstate these Sergeants. The Warrant to which he refers has simply extended to the Royal Engineers provisions which have been in force for the other arms since 1882. It applies only to Volunteer Instructors.

PARLIAMENT—"OFFICES OF PROFIT UNDER THE CROWN"—DISQUALIFICATIONS UNDER THE 6TH ANNE.

Mr. HENRY H. FOWLER (Wolverhampton, E.) asked Mr. Attorney General, Whether the Secretaries to the Treasury and the Admiralty, the Under Secretaries of State, and the Parliamentary Secretaries of the Board of Trade and of the Local Government Board, have not been qualified to sit in Parliament by special legislation declaring them "capable of being elected and sitting and voting in the House of Commons;" and, whether there is any instance, since the Statute of 6 *Anne*, of the creation of an Office tenable by a

Member of Parliament, except under the authority of an Act of Parliament passed on the creation of such Office?

THE ATTORNEY GENERAL (Sir RICHARD WEBSTER) (Isle of Wight): To answer the Question fully would require a treatise. The Offices mentioned in the first part of the right hon. Gentleman's Question are all Offices of profit, and the Statutes referred to were passed to enable the holders to sit in Parliament, notwithstanding that they held Offices of profit. The Secretaries to the Treasury and the Admiralty and two of the Under Secretaries of State did not receive their qualification to sit in Parliament by special legislation; but were by express proviso excluded from the general words of the Statute 15 *Geo.* II., c. 22, which might otherwise have disqualified them; while the Secretaries of the Board of Trade and of the Local Government Board, being holders of new Offices of profit, were by the Statutes creating those Offices enabled to sit in Parliament. The right of the Crown to create new Ministerial Offices—not being Offices of profit—is undoubted, and is stated in books of the highest authority, to which I shall be pleased to refer the right hon. Gentleman; and the only limitation on such right is that such new Offices shall be without fee or reward, and not inconsistent with the Constitution or prejudicial to the subject. The instances of the creation of an Office tenable by Members of Parliament without Statute are not common; because, as a rule, profit is attached to Offices. But there are cases recorded, and I may call the right hon. Gentleman's attention to the case of Lord Middleton, in the year 1717.

MR. HENRY H. FOWLER: What was the Office held by Lord Middleton?

SIR RICHARD WEBSTER: It was that of Lord Justice in Ireland.

MR. SEXTON (Belfast, W.): Would the hon. and learned Gentleman have any objection to making a public reference to one or two of the works of authority which he mentioned?

SIR RICHARD WEBSTER: *Chitty's Prerogatives of the Crown*, which is a book of the highest authority, 40 or 50 years old; and *Comyn's Digest*, which the House will recognize as being of high authority. Indeed, I may say that this opinion is in accordance with all the recognized traditions of the last 100 years, and is also in accordance with the opinion of the Law Officers of the Crown for a very long time.

MR. CHILDERS (Edinburgh, S.) asked, was the hon. and learned Gentleman aware that the additional Under Secretaries appointed during the past 20 years were appointed under a special Statute?

SIR RICHARD WEBSTER said, he was quite aware of it, and he thought he had so stated.

MR. W. E. GLADSTONE (Edinburgh, Mid Lothian): The question being one of great interest, will the hon. and learned Gentleman, in a supplemental answer, give us now, or at a convenient time, a Return of the instances in which this power has been exercised since the case of Lord Middleton—Lord Middleton of the House of Commons?

SIR RICHARD WEBSTER said, he was sorry he could not oblige the right hon. Gentleman at the present moment. He was willing to give all the information possible; but he could not answer that offhand. [MR. GLADSTONE: At a future day?] Yes. There certainly was an instance either of a Queen's Counsel or a Queen's Serjeant who, being appointed to that Office, which was newly created for him, did not vacate his seat, on the ground that he had in his patent the fact that he should have neither fee nor reward. He wished to make himself quite clear. There was no distinction between an Office of profit and a place of profit. It had been throughout recognized that in order to create disqualification it must be an Office of profit or a place of profit; and the view that there was no distinction between a place of profit and an Office of profit had been, as far as he knew, invariably recognized by the Law Officers of successive Governments.

ROYAL IRISH CONSTABULARY—CONSTABLE KENNEDY, CO. MONAGHAN.

MR. JOHNSTON (Belfast, S.) asked the Chief Secretary to the Lord Lieutenant of Ireland, If a Constabulary Court of Inquiry was held on 12th May, 1886, at Glasslough, County Monaghan, to inquire into a charge made against Constable Kennedy by two brothers, M'Gonnell, for using party expressions; whether six respectable witnesses, one of them a policeman, swore that Kennedy never used the alleged expressions whether, of the three witnesses for the prosecution, one has had to leave the country for an assault, while another was dismissed from Sir John Leslie's employment for using disloyal expressions; what has been the result of the Court of Inquiry; and, will the evidence taken at the investigation be laid before the House?

THE PARLIAMENTARY UNDER SECRETARY (Colonel KING-HARMAN) (Kent, Isle of Thanet) (who replied) said: The statements in the first paragraph are substantially correct. Three witnesses, considered reliable, proved the offence against the policeman. One of those witnesses has left the country; but not for the reason stated. The constable was found guilty, and removed to another county.

WAYS AND MEANS—THE FINANCIAL RESOLUTIONS—THE CARRIAGE TAX —APPLICATION TO THE METROPOLIS·

MR. WEBSTER (St. Pancras, E.) asked Mr. Chancellor of the Exchequer, In what way will the Metropolitan ratepayer be relieved by the proposed grant in aid of local taxation from the receipts of the Carriage Tax, as there is no Imperial grant in aid of the maintenance of public roads within the area comprised in the Metropolis Management Act, 1855?

THE CHANCELLOR OF THE EXCHEQUER (Mr. GOSCHEN) (St. George's Hanover Square), in reply, said, that the grant made was simply in respect of the roads that came under the Act of 1870, and the roads repaired by the Justices as main roads. There were very few roads of this kind within the Metropolitan area, although there were some that would be affected.

| BUSINESS OF THE HOUSE—COAL MINES REGULATION BILL.

MR. J. E. ELLIS (Nottingham, Rushcliffe) asked the Secretary of State for the Home Department, Whether, as the Second Reading of the Coal Mines Regulation Bill was taken after a quarter before Six o'clock on Wednesday, 13th April, he will undertake that the Motion to go into Committee shall be made at such a time as will afford an opportunity for debate upon the Bill?

THE UNDER SECRETARY OF STATE (Mr. STUART - WORTLEY)

Mr. Johnston

(Sheffield, Hallam) (who replied) said: Yes, Sir; the Secretary of State will undertake that the facilities for discussion asked for by the hon. Member shall be given.

In reply to Mr. FENWICK (Northumberland, Wansbeck),

MR. W. H. SMITH stated that, although the Bill was put down for Monday next, it would not be taken on that day.

INDIA—THE HINDOO LAW OF MARRIAGE—INFANT MARRIAGES.

MR. J. G. TALBOT (Oxford University) asked the Under Secretary of State for India, Whether the attention of Her Majesty's Government has been called to a recent case in India, referred to in a letter signed "F. M. M." in *The Times* of the 21st April; and, whether Her Majesty's Government are prepared to take such measures as will prevent for the future the enforcement of infant contracts of marriage by English law, framed for entirely different conditions of society?

THE UNDER SECRETARY OF STATE (Sir JOHN GORST) (Chatham): I must refer to an answer which I gave to a Question on this subject on March 18. I then stated that as the case might be the subject of appeal, the consideration of the expediency of legislation would, in the opinion of the Secretary of State, be premature. The case is now, I believe, under appeal; and while the legal proceedings are still pending, the Secretary of State adheres to the opinion already expressed.

INDUSTRIAL SCHOOLS (IRELAND)— THE CAPPOQUIN INDUSTRIAL SCHOOL, WATERFORD.

MR. PYNE (Waterford, W.) asked the Chief Secretary to the Lord Lieutenant of Ireland, If the Cappoquin Industrial School is the only one for boys in the County or City of Waterford; if the school is certified for 50 boys only, although it has accommodation for 70; if it is a fact that the County and City of Waterford have over 200 children in industrial schools, some at long distances from Waterford from want of accommodation; and, if, under those circumstances, he will reconsider his decision, and give a grant for the 70 children to the Cappoquin School?

The PARLIAMENTARY UNDER SECRETARY (Colonel King-Harman) (Kent, Isle of Thanet) (who replied) said: The Cappoquin School is certified only for the accommodation of boys under 10 years of age, and an enlargement of the certificate would not enable the managers to receive children of other classes. I am unable to say with certainty how many Waterford children may be inmates of schools in other parts of Ireland; but the sum presented for by the Grand Juries of the City and County, if the allowance is 2s. per head, would make the number 174. That number, of course, includes boys over 10, and girls who could not in any case be accommodated in the Cappoquin School. I regret I cannot hold out any hope of an enlargement of the certificate in this case. It was specially considered a few months ago by the late Chief Secretary (Sir Michael Hicks-Beach), who was mainly influenced in his decision by the consideration that difficulty has been found in procuring vacancies in senior schools for boys who have to be removed from junior schools like that at Cappoquin on reaching the age of 10, and that difficulty would be increased by compliance with the suggestion of the hon. Member.

TRADE AND COMMERCE—COMMERCIAL TREATY WITH FRANCE.

Mr. WEBSTER (St. Pancras, E.) asked the Under Secretary of State for Foreign Affairs, Whether the negotiations entered into for the renewal of the Cobden Treaty with France, which lapsed in 1882, failed owing to the opposition of France; and, whether the Government now propose to again enter into negotiations with the French Government for the renewal of a Commercial Treaty with that country for a fixed term?

The UNDER SECRETARY OF STATE (Sir James Fergusson) (Manchester, N.E.): The negotiations for the conclusion of a new Treaty to take the place of the Cobden Treaty of 1860 failed owing to the divergence of the views of the two Governments. In the main, Her Majesty's Government represented the desire of British manufacturers that the existing duties should be lowered, while the French Customs authorities desired the substitution of specific for *ad valorem* duties. The pro-

ceedings are fully stated in the Correspondence laid before Parliament in 1882 (Commercial No. 9). There is no reason now to believe that any good result would be obtained by a proposal on our part to renew the negotiations. The public sentiment in France and in the French Legislature is more than ever in favour of fostering native industry and protecting home trade. England and France reciprocally grant to the trade of each other under their domestic legislation the benefit of treatment as of the most favoured nation.

WAYS AND MEANS—THE FINANCIAL RESOLUTIONS—THE DUTY ON TOBACCO.

Mr. BROADHURST (Nottingham, W.) asked Mr. Chancellor of the Exchequer, If he can now inform the House whether the reduction of the duty on tobacco will take immediate effect, so as to prevent the great loss to the workpeople engaged in the cigar-making trade which will ensue if the reduction does not take effect till the 21st May; and, if not, whether he will give rebate on all tobacco leaf taken out of bond between now and the 21st May?

The CHANCELLOR OF THE EXCHEQUER (Mr. Goschen) (St. George's, Hanover Square): I see the hon. Member's Question refers to great loss to the workpeople in the cigar-making trade which will result if the reduction of duty does not take place till the 21st May. I cannot understand why this should be the case. There is no reason, in the change of duty, why any cigar manufacturer having tobacco in stock should not continue to carry on his manufacture as usual. But I am informed that a number of these manufacturers either have discharged, or are going to discharge, their workpeople, rather than take fresh tobacco out of bond while the higher duty is still in force. I should be sorry to think that many manufacturers would adopt so harsh a course, especially in view of the great boon about to be bestowed upon them, as to discharge their workpeople rather than continue to pay the present rate of duty on the comparatively small amount of raw material necessary to keep them employed till the 21st. The hon. Member will easily understand that it is impossible for me, in so serious a matter, and one affecting so many interests, to change the day originally fixed for the reduction of duty. But I am considering whether some steps may not be taken to put a stop to the mischief which the hon. Member's Question directly contemplates, and I am not without hope that means may be found to prevent the threatened discharge of workpeople.

THE UNITED STATES—THE LIQUOR TRAFFIC.

MR. E. ROBERTSON (Dundee) asked the Under Secretary of State for Foreign Affairs, If he will endeavour to obtain, through the Government of the United States, or the separate State Governments, Reports showing the various methods of regulating the liquor traffic adopted in the different States of the Union, and their effect, particularly with reference to the amount of revenue derived from what is termed the "high licence" system, and to the comparative efficacy of that system and the system of total prohibition?

THE UNDER SECRETARY OF STATE (Sir JAMES FERGUSSON) (Manchester, N.E.): Inquiries will be made of Her Majesty's Minister at Washington whether the Returns desired by the hon. Member can be readily procured. I cannot undertake to promise them, until it is ascertained whether they would entail much expense and special labour.

EDUCATION DEPARTMENT (SCOTLAND) — THE GARNETHILL AND HUTCHESON SCHOOLS IN GLASGOW.

MR. CALDWELL (Glasgow, St. Rollox) asked the Lord Advocate, Whether Garnethill Public School, under the Glasgow School Board, situate in the North-Western District of Glasgow, has both a primary and a separately manned and equipped secondary department; whether Garnethill Public School, in addition to possessing the advantages of contributions from the local rates, is placed on the list of State-aided schools and is in receipt of Government grant for both its departments; whether Hutcheson Schools, in the Southern District of Glasgow, have been erected at the sole expense of charity funds bequeathed for the poor, and are managed and maintained under a scheme of the Educational Endowment Commis-

Mr. Goschen

sioners, approved of by the Scotch Education Department and by Parliament, at a cost to the charity funds of several thousand pounds annually, over and above what is received for school fees; whether Hutcheson Schools have both a primary and a secondary department; and, whether the Scotch Education Department will place Hutcheson Schools on the list of State-aided schools in Scotland, entitling them to participate in the Government grant?

THE LORD ADVOCATE (Mr. J. H. A. MACDONALD) (Edinburgh and St. Andrew's Universities): While a higher class public school is defined by the Education Act, the distinction between a primary and a secondary department is not defined either by that Act or by the Scotch Code; and my Lords are unable, therefore, to say whether the organization of the Garnethill School corresponds to the hon. Member's description. The instruction in respect of which the school has been inspected and grants paid is such as is embraced by the Scotch Code. The organization of the Hutcheson's Schools, and any claims which these schools may be able to make to participate in the Parliamentary grant, can only be judged by their Lordships when the managers of these schools decide to prosecute such a claim, and when the necessary particulars called for by the Department in connection therewith are furnished.

SCOTLAND—HOLIDAYS FOR THE AGRICULTURAL POPULATION.

MR. THORBURN (Peebles and Selkirk) asked the Lord Advocate, Whether Her Majesty's Government will take steps to secure certain holidays for the agricultural population in Scotland, at all events equivalent in number to those lost to them by the abolition rapidly taking place of fast days and fair days, hitherto held as non-working days or holidays?

THE LORD ADVOCATE (Mr. J. H. A. MACDONALD) (Edinburgh and St. Andrew's Universities): Her Majesty's Government cannot pledge itself to take steps to secure holidays for the agricultural population of Scotland. Such matters must be regulated by local requirements and circumstances, and would be more properly dealt with by Local Boards, which it is hoped may soon be established.

EGYPT—THE MIXED TRIBUNALS AT ALEXANDRIA—REMOVAL OF A MEMBER.

MR. BADEN-POWELL (Liverpool, Kirkdale) asked the Under Secretary of State for Foreign Affairs, Whether one of the Foreign Members of the Mixed Tribunals at Alexandria has been lately removed from his post; and, if so, what was the reason for his removal, and who was responsible for his appointment?

THE UNDER SECRETARY OF STATE (Sir JAMES FERGUSSON) (Manchester, N.E.): One of the Foreign Members of the Mixed Tribunals at Alexandria has lately resigned, but is reported to have withdrawn his resignation. The Foreign Judges in Egypt are appointed by the Egyptian Government on the recommendation of the countries to which they belong.

POST OFFICE—TRUSTEE SAVINGS' BANKS.

MR. BARTLEY (Islington, N.) asked the Postmaster General, Whether no depositor in the Trustee Savings' Banks can insure his or her life, or buy a deferred annuity in the Post Office, unless he or she either first closes his or her Trustee Savings' Bank account, or forfeits his or her savings?

THE POSTMASTER GENERAL(Mr. RAIKES) (Cambridge University): The facts, as stated by the hon. Member, are correct. The Savings' Bank Act, 1882, requires a person who wishes to insure or purchase an annuity through the Post Office to open an account in the Post Office Savings' Bank, and a previous Act prohibits one person from having a direct interest in more than one Savings' Bank account. The same Act of 1882 applies, however, to the Trustee Savings' Banks; and therefore a depositor in the Trustee Bank can apply for a contract to the bank in which he is a depositor.

LAW AND JUSTICE (SCOTLAND)—CASE OF —— FERRIE, AT HAMILTON.

MR. MASON (Lanark, Mid) asked the Lord Advocate, Whether a man named Ferrie was sentenced to 30 days' imprisonment at Hamilton, on 9th April last, for breach of the peace; whether he had been in prison for 60 days' previous to trial; whether it is the law that he could only have been sentenced to 60 days' imprisonment if he had been sent to summary trial at once; and, whether, considering that, seeing the sentence would appear to have been a heavy one, he will advise his release now?

THE LORD ADVOCATE (Mr. J. H. A. MACDONALD) (Edinburgh and St. Andrew's Universities): The facts are as stated by the hon. Member. The offence was a serious one. The man Ferrie behaved with great violence and obstinacy. After a poker which he was brandishing in the street had been with difficulty taken from him, and when he was allowed to go, he re-appeared with a pair of tongs, and again acted with such violence that it was only after a severe struggle that he could be arrested and locked up. It was, in all probability, because of the long detention before trial that Crown Counsel finally ordered him to be tried summarily, it being thought that a sentence not exceeding 60 days, in addition to the 60 days already suffered, would be sufficient. I am not of opinion that three months in prison is at all an excessive punishment in the circumstances, and could not advise any remission.

EGYPT—THE SUAKIN-BERBER RAILWAY.

MR. SHEIL (Meath, S.) asked the Surveyor General of the Ordnance, in reference to the cost and distribution of the plant of the Suakin-Berber Railway, Whether the "storing" of a large portion of this plant at Woolwich consists in leaving rails, engines, carriages, and trucks to rot and decay in the open air in a lonely spot on the Plumstead Marshes?

THE SURVEYOR GENERAL (Mr. NORTHCOTE) (Exeter): Of this railway plant the rails are properly stacked in the open, as is usual. The engines are under cover, and, having been thoroughly overhauled and repaired, are in better condition than when they left Suakin. The carriages and trucks are standing on rails in the open; they are kept in good order ready for use.

MR. CONYBEARE (Cornwall, Camborne): What is to become of them?

MR. NORTHCOTE: As I stated the other day, some of the rails are to be used in the construction of military railways; but a large proportion of the stock is to be sold.

BURMAH—THE POLICE.

MR. SHEIL (Meath, S.) asked the Under Secretary of State for India, Whether he is aware that police officers in Burmah, some of whom have seen active service and have acquired the Burmese language, have been superseded by men from India of shorter service and lower grade; whether the Inspector General of Police, Lower Burmah, has represented to the Government the injustice that has been done to his junior officers; and, whether the Government of India will take into consideration the grievances complained of?

THE UNDER SECRETARY OF STATE (Sir JOHN GORST) (Chatham): The Secretary of State has no information whatever on the subject referred to. As a matter of course, any grievances complained of will be duly considered by the proper authorities in India.

LITERATURE, SCIENCE, AND ART— PUBLICATION OF THE ICELANDIC SAGAS.

MR. LYELL (Orkney and Shetland) asked the Secretary to the Treasury, When the Rolls edition of the Icelandic Sagas will be published; whether the whole work has long since been finished, and the greater part of it been in type for several years; whether its publication is now awaiting an introduction by the editor, Sir George Dasent; and, whether he will take steps to secure the speedy issue of a work that has already been so long delayed?

THE SECRETARY (Mr. JACKSON) (Leeds, N.): There appears to have been an unreasonable delay in the publication of these volumes. I understand, however, that the first two volumes will be published in June. I will see if I can do anything to secure the speedy issue of the remainder. The delay appears to be due to the fact that the manuscript of a translation and an introduction to be furnished by Sir George Dasent have not yet been supplied.

PREVENTION OF CRIME (IRELAND) ACT, 1882—RETURNS.

MR. ANDERSON (Elgin and Nairn) asked the Chief Secretary to the Lord Lieutenant of Ireland, Will the Government grant the Return as to Preliminary Inquiries under the Prevention of Crime (Ireland) Act, 1882, on the Paper for Friday?

THE PARLIAMENTARY UNDER SECRETARY (Colonel KING-HARMAN) (Kent, Isle of Thanet) (who replied) said: All the information that can be given has already been furnished to the hon. Member in my reply to his Question of a few days since. The Government cannot give the Return asked for, as they have no official records which will enable them to do so. Some of the magistrates who held the inquiries are dead, or have left the Service.

EVICTIONS (IRELAND)—THE SKINNERS' ESTATE, NEAR DRAPERSTOWN, CO. DERRY.

MR. M'CARTAN (Down, S.) asked the Chief Secretary to the Lord Lieutenant of Ireland, with reference to the recent evictions on the Skinners' Estate, near Draperstown, County Derry, Whether he will state the amount of expenses incurred in sending the 250 policemen, County Inspector, District Inspectors, Divisional Magistrate, and Resident Magistrates from their different stations to and from the scene of the evictions; the expenses incurred by them during their stay in the neighbourhood; and, the amount paid for cars and other vehicles employed by them in connection with these evictions?

THE PARLIAMENTARY UNDER SECRETARY (Colonel KING-HARMAN) (Kent, Isle of Thanet) (who replied) said: I am unable, at present, to state the expenses incurred in affording the Sheriff such protection as would insure him freedom from molestation in the discharge of his duty; but I may observe that the labour of collecting such information is considerable, and no public advantage is gained by furnishing the particulars requested.

MR. M'CARTAN asked, when the right hon. and gallant Gentleman would be able to give this information to the House, as it was of some importance?

COLONEL KING-HARMAN said, the importance of such information was a matter of opinion; but he had already mentioned that he did not see that any great advantage was to be gained by it.

PORTUGAL AND ZANZIBAR — THE INTERNATIONAL DELIMITATION COMMISSION.

MR. F. S. STEVENSON (Suffolk, Eye) asked the Under Secretary of State for Foreign Affairs, Whether the nego- tiations between Portugal and Zanzibar have resulted in an amicable settlement; whether Portugal accepts the decision of the International Delimitation Commis- sion, and of the London Conference, relative to the boundaries of the terri- tory constituting the dominions of the Sultan of Zanzibar; and, what is the amount of the losses sustained by Bri- tish subjects in consequence of the re- cent hostilities?

THE UNDER SECRETARY OF STATE (Sir JAMES FERGUSSON) (Man- chester, N.E.): Portugal and Zanzibar have appointed Special Commissioners to discuss the question of boundary. The Portuguese Commissioner, Senhor Capello, the well known African traveller, is understood to have sailed from Lisbon on the 18th instant. The captured vessel *Kilwa* will be restored to the Sultan. Portugal has not accepted the conclu- sions of the International Delimitation Commission, so far as they affect her claims to the territory in dispute. The amount of losses of British subjects in consequence of the recent hostilities has not yet been reported.

ADMIRALTY—COLONIAL DEFENCES— TORPEDO BOATS FOR SINGAPORE.

MR. DE LISLE (Leicestershire, Mid) asked the First Lord of the Admiralty, When the three first-class torpedo boats, which have been detailed for the protec- tion of the Singapore Harbour and Coal- ing Station, will be sent to their destina- tion?

THE FIRST LORD (Lord GEORGE HAMILTON) (Middlesex, Ealing): No first-class torpedo boats have been de- tailed for the protection of Singapore Harbour and Coaling Station. There are two of these boats at Hong Kong, and it is intended to send out four more. [Mr. DE LISLE: And none at all to Hong Kong?] No. The armoured ship *Orion* is at the present time stationed at Singapore.

THE ROYAL COMMISSION ON THE LAND LAW (IRELAND) ACT, 1881, AND THE PURCHASE OF LAND (IRE- LAND) ACT, 1885—ALLEGED "COOK- ING" OF THE REPORT.

MR. CONYBEARE (Cornwall, Cam- borne) asked the Chief Secretary to the Lord Lieutenant of Ireland, Whether

his attention has been called to a para- graph in *The Pall Mall Gazette* of the 26th instant, headed *Cooking the Cowper Com- mission's Report*, which purports to give a letter from Mr. W. Sinclair, of Strabane, to *The Dublin Express*, complaining that portions of his evidence had been omitted from the Blue Book, and that the proofs of his evidence had never been sent to him for correction; whether the above statements are correct; why Mr. Sinclair was not enabled to correct the proofs of his evidence, and why portions of his evidence were omitted; whether any, and which, of the other witnesses were treated in a similar manner; and, whe- ther the Government intend to publish an Appendix to the Blue Book contain- ing all the passages so omitted from the evidence of different witnesses?

THE PARLIAMENTARY UNDER SECRETARY (Colonel KING-HARMAN) (Kent, Isle of Thanet) (who replied) said: The Irish Government has no- thing whatever to say to the matters re- ferred to by the hon. Member. Reports of Royal Commissions do not pass through their hands.

PALACE OF WESTMINSTER—VENTILA- TION OF THE PRIVATE BILL COM- MITTEE ROOMS.

MR. HOWORTH (Salford, S.) asked the First Commissioner of Works, If his attention has been called to the bad state of the ventilation of the Private Bill Committee Rooms; whether he is aware that in the present Session the Town Clerk of Sheffield caught cold in one of the Committee Rooms and died soon afterwards; whether he is aware that Members have often to protect them- selves from draughts by wearing their hats and covering their legs with their overcoats; whether it has come to his knowledge that Members, counsel, wit- nesses, and others continually complain of the discomfort to which they are ex- posed; and, whether he will take steps to improve the ventilation of the Com- mittee Rooms upstairs?

THE FIRST COMMISSIONER (Mr. PLUNKET) (Dublin University): I had not received any complaints as to the bad state of ventilation in the Private Bill Committee Rooms until I saw my hon. Friend's Question on the Paper, nor had I heard of the painful circum- stances alleged in the second paragraph. Of course, I shall inquire further into the subject; but I am assured that there is an attendant of the Ventilation Department, whose duty it is to be always in the neighbourhood of the Committee Rooms, and to report any such complaints if made to him.

ARMY—THE CAMERON HIGHLANDERS.

MR. FINLAY (Inverness, &c.) asked the Secretary of State for War, Whether there is any foundation for the rumour that it is in contemplation to abolish the distinctive name of the "Cameron Highlanders," or to convert the regiment into a battalion of Foot Guards; and, whether, in view of the universal dissatisfaction which would be caused in Inverness-shire and Scotland generally, any such change will be persisted in ?

THE SECRETARY OF STATE (Mr. E. STANHOPE) (Lincolnshire, Horncastle): There is no intention at present to change in any way the name or the status of the Cameron Highlanders.

THE MAGISTRACY (IRELAND)—RETURN OF RESIDENT MAGISTRATES.

MR. HENRY H. FOWLER (Wolverhampton, E.) asked the Chief Secretary to the Lord Lieutenant of Ireland, When the Return with respect to Resident Magistrates in Ireland, ordered on the 31st March, will be laid upon the Table of the House?

THE PARLIAMENTARY UNDER SECRETARY (Colonel KING-HARMAN) (Kent, Isle of Thanet) (who replied) said : This Return was presented on the 18th instant.

BORNEO—THE SULTAN OF BRUNEI.

ADMIRAL COMMERELL (Southampton) (for Admiral MAYNE) (Pembroke and Haverfordwest) asked the Under Secretary of State for Foreign Affairs, Whether the Government have received a telegram from the Sultan of Brunei begging that Her Majesty's Government will pay no attention to any representations they may receive from the Rajah of Sarawak, or other people, regarding the affairs of Brunei, Limbang, and Putong, but await the arrival of his (the Sultan's) letter ; and, whether this telegram came through the regular official channel, the Consul General, or direct from the Sultan ; and, if direct, whether Her Majesty's Go-

Mr. Plunket

vernment are aware of any reason for its being so sent ?

THE UNDER SECRETARY OF STATE (Sir JAMES FERGUSSON) (Manchester, N.E.) : A telegram was received through the Colonial Office on the 1st of March from a merchant in London, to whom it had been sent from Singapore, stating that the Sultan of Brunei had requested him to represent to the Secretary of State to suspend action in regard to complaints from the Government of Sarawak or others against him, and that the Sultan had explained matters by mail. The probable reason why this message did not come through the regular official channel is that the Sultan believed that the Consul General had made complaints of him. That, however, was not the case. The letter indicated in the telegram has now arrived, and is being translated.

PUBLIC BUSINESS —THE LOCAL GOVERNMENT BILL—LEGISLATION.

MR. F. S. STEVENSON (Suffolk, Eye) asked the First Lord of the Treasury, Whether the Local Government Bill, promised by the Chancellor of the Exchequer, will be introduced in the House of Commons or in "another place ; " and, whether questions relating to allotments and to the management of local charities will come within the scope of that Bill, or form the subjects of separate measures ?

THE FIRST LORD (Mr. W. H. SMITH) (Strand, Westminster): The Local Government Bill will be introduced in this House as soon as the state of Public Business will permit. The question as to allotments will be dealt with in a separate Bill. The management of local charities will not come within the scope of the Local Government Bill, except in those cases where the charities are administered by the Local Authorities.

THE REVISED STATUTES—ISSUE OF A NEW AND CHEAPER EDITION.

MR. HOWELL (Bethnal Green, N.E.) asked the First Lord of the Treasury, Whether the Government have considered the propriety of issuing a new and cheaper edition of the Revised Statutes, corrected up to date, as promised by the Chancellor of the Exchequer in the Second Session of

1886, and by the First Lord of the Treasury early in the present Session; whether the Government have arrived at any decision on the subject; and, if so, whether they are in a position to communicate such decision to the House; and, whether he can state to the House the probable price at which a complete set will be obtainable in the event of such publication?

THE FIRST LORD (Mr. W. H. SMITH) (Strand, Westminster): The question of a cheap edition of the Statutes has been under the consideration of the Statute Law Revision Committee, and they have submitted to the Treasury the following proposals:—That a revised edition of the Statutes be undertaken, of convenient size, to be published volume by volume as revision is completed; that the work be commenced at once, in which case the first volume can probably be brought out this year. The Committee believe that such an edition could be supplied at a price not exceeding eight guineas for the complete set. We have had these recommendations under consideration at the Treasury, and are about to give our sanction to the proposals of the Committee.

MR. MUNDELLA (Sheffield, Brightside) asked, whether the claims of the Government as to copyright would come under consideration?

MR. W. H. SMITH said, that was under the consideration of the Law Officers of the Crown at the present moment. It was necessary to see that the copyright belonging to the nation should be preserved; but all matters of importance were published by the newspapers.

MR. MUNDELLA wished to know if the copyright of the Revised Code, published by teachers for their own use, was retained by the Government?

MR. W. H. SMITH: Obviously, a publication of that kind is never interfered with by the Government.

LAW AND JUSTICE (ENGLAND AND WALES) — OATHS AND AFFIRMATIONS—THE OATHS BILL.

MR. BRADLAUGH (Northampton) asked the First Lord of the Treasury, Whether, at Liverpool City Sessions on Saturday last, the Recorder refused the oath and affirmation of W. A. Newcomb as a juror, Mr. Newcomb having applied to affirm on the ground that he was a

person without religious belief; whether on Monday, at an inquest at Wood Green, Mr. Wynne Baxter, the Coroner, accepted the affirmation of Mr. Oates as a juror, although Mr. Oates had stated that he was without religious belief; whether he is aware that similar instances of conflict, as to acceptance and rejection of affirmation by jurors without religious belief, are constantly occurring in the Queen's Bench Division of the High Court of Justice, and before Coroners; and, whether, under these circumstances, the Government can afford any facilities for taking the opinion of the House on the Second Reading of the Oaths Bill, which, during the whole of the present Session, has been persistently blocked?

THE FIRST LORD (Mr. W. H. SMITH) (Strand, Westminster): I have no personal knowledge of the cases quoted, nor am I aware that similar cases of conflict are of constant occurrence. In the present state of Public Business, it is not possible for me to give facilities for any measure that is not a Government Bill.

MR. BRADLAUGH: Can the right hon. Gentleman influence Gentlemen who sit behind him to withdraw their block to the Bill?

MR. W. H. SMITH: I have no power to do that.

IRISH LAND LAW BILL.

MR. DILLON (Mayo, E.): I wish to ask the First Lord of the Treasury, If he will kindly state what day the Irish Land Law Bill will be set down for second reading?

THE FIRST LORD (Mr. W. H. SMITH) (Strand, Westminster): I am not aware of the precise day; but will inquire and tell the hon. Member to-morrow.

CRIMINAL LAW AMENDMENT (IRELAND) BILL.

MR. SEXTON (Belfast, W.) asked the First Lord of the Treasury, Whether, in the event of the debate on the Amendment of the hon. and learned Member for Dumfries (Mr. Reid) closing that night and the Speaker leaving the Chair, the Government would immediately put down Progress for Monday next, so as to allow hon. Members a day or two for the purpose of considering the numerous Amendments on the Paper?

THE FIRST LORD OF THE TREA-SURY (Mr. W. H. SMITH)(Strand, West-minster): I may say that it will not be possible for the Government to accede to the suggestion of the hon. Gentleman. There has been great delay—I do not say unnecessary delay, because I wish to refrain from using any language which would create an unpleasant feeling on the other side of the House—but the House must feel, and everyone must feel, that the time already occupied in the discussion of this measure has been unprecedented. The Government are ready to proceed without any delay whatever, and the measure will be taken to-morrow.

MR. CONYBEARE (Cornwall, Camborne) asked whether it was a fact that the First Lord of the Treasury had arranged that there should be only four speeches that night?

MR. W. H. SMITH: Hon. Gentlemen must be aware that it is not in the power of the Leader of the House to make any such arrangement. It is a question within the discretion of the House itself.

ORDERS OF THE DAY.

—o—

CRIMINAL LAW AMENDMENT (IRE-LAND) BILL.—[BILL 217.]

(*Mr. Arthur Balfour, Mr. Secretary Matthews, Mr. Attorney General for Ireland.*)

COMMITTEE. ADJOURNED DEBATE.

[THIRD NIGHT.]

Order read for resuming Adjourned Debate on Amendment proposed to Question [26th April], "That Mr. Speaker do now leave the Chair," for Committee on the Bill.

And which Amendment was,

To leave out from the word "That" to the end of the Question, in order to add the words "this House declines to proceed further with a measure for strengthening the Criminal Law against combinations of tenants until it has before it the full measure for their relief against excessive rents in the shape in which it may pass the other House of Parliament,"—(*Mr. Robert Reid,*)

—instead thereof.

Question again proposed, "That the words proposed to be left out stand part of the Question."

Debate *resumed.*

MR. E. BECKETT (York, N.R., Whitby) said, he was aware that to interpose in a debate already protracted beyond the limits of fair discussion could not be justified without some special reason. He thought that the House would admit that special reason was provided in the information bearing on certain passages of great importance which had lately occurred in the House, and to which he proposed to refer. He might say that the Amendment before the House might have been dictated by the Chicago Convention. He would ask hon. Members opposite whether they would make the maintenance of law dependent on remedial measures in all cases? Supposing that bread riots broke out in the streets of London, that the streets were torn up and barricades erected, where they to wait until their grievances were inquired into before the rioters were suppressed? When the Socialist riots broke out in London, and they were not immediately suppressed, the then Home Secretary received a considerable amount of blame for not having foreseen and prevented them, and he took precautions to prevent their recurrence. It was obvious that these riots must be suppressed without delay, and the grievances which were then complained of had not been redressed until this day, although they were, he maintained, quite as serious in their character as the Irish grievances which were complained of. The Amendment, if carried, would be a piece of class legislation, and it aimed at protecting one class, the tenants of Ireland; but the other classes subject to the tyrannies of the National League would be absolutely at the mercy of that organization. An hon. Member opposite had said: Supposing the positions were reversed, how would the inhabitants of this country like to live under the Crimes Act? That argument could be made to act both ways. The National League viewed the system of intimidation in Ireland with complacency, because they were the authors and not the victims of it; but if the positions were reversed, and if hon. Members in the House were subjected to the outrages perpetrated in Ireland, they would be the first to cry out against the National League and demand its immediate suppression. No one could deny that intimidation existed in Ireland, and that Boycotting was prevalent. Hon. Gentlemen opposite, and especially the right hon. Gentleman (Mr. John Morley), had asserted that Boycotting could not be put down. If they had followed the course of politics in America, they would know that Boycotting had been imported into America from Ireland among other things from that country which the Americans did not like. It had been taken cognizance of by the American tribunals, and a judgment was recently given in the highest Court in America which denounced Boycotting very plainly. Judge Brown, of the United States Circuit Court, asserted—

"That all combinations and associations designed to coerce men to become members, or to interfere with, obstruct, vex, or annoy them because they are not members, and all associations designed to interfere with the perfect freedom of employers in the proper management of their business, or to dictate the terms upon which their business shall be conducted by threats of injury or loss by interference with their property or traffic, &c., are illegal combinations, and all acts done in furtherance of such intentions and accompanied by damage are actionable."

That seemed to be broad and full, but the most significant part of the decision was probably the sentence which stated that—

"The acts mentioned are not only illegal, rendering the defendants liable in damages, but also misdemeanours at Common Law as well as by Section 168 of the Penal Code"

of New York State. That was to say, the power to enforce the right which every individual possessed to labour where and when he would, and to conduct his business without let or hindrance, and to enjoy his property free from loss or interference from others, was a part of the great unwritten law which was the heritage of all civilized people. What was Boycotting but interference with the rights of others; and how were they to deal with that interference? The right hon. Gentleman (Mr. John Morley) said, with reference to such interference—

"Where ways of living interfere with the lawful rights of others it is necessary to force the dissidents, however strong may be their conscientious sentiments."

That was what the Government proposed to do. America had acted on the principle thus laid down, and had very swiftly, sharply, and sternly repressed Boycotting; and, as a consequence, it had almost ceased there. What the

Americans had done, we in Ireland could do; and that, in his opinion, was a sufficient answer to those who maintained that Boycotting could not be put down by law. Boycotting was inflicted in most cases for the payment of rent. The action of the National League had stripped rent of its moral sanction. The National League never punished a man for not paying his rent; it visited all its pains and penalties on those who paid their rents. The pages of the Report of the Cowper Commission teemed with evidence to that effect. Mr. Kavanagh said—

"To prevent the payment of rent is the first and most important principle in the policy of the League, because it is the shortest and most direct course to bring landlords and tenants into collision."

It was objected that this Bill was permanent. But it need not be permanent unless Ireland chose. At any moment she could shake herself free from its shackles, and stand from under its incubus. Having done its work, the Bill would be removed into the background, and it was hoped that the sense of its perpetual presence would have a good effect. It differed from all previous Coercion Bills in that it had the forms and nature of law. Not many people had seen the handcuffs, the felon's cell, or the gallows; but the knowledge that they existed went a long way to deter people from doing wrong. In the same way, it was hoped that that Bill would prevent people committing outrages which the Bill was destined to punish. Even if the Bill was permanent, it was directed against an organization which sought to be permanent, and which sought to establish its rule by resting it upon the pillars of disorder and disaffection. No attempt to improve Ireland would be effectual until the League was put down. He was supported in that contention by the authority of *The Irish World*, which said, on January 20, 1886—

"Just now 'law and order' in Ireland—that is, landlordism and police rule—are having a pretty rough time of it. 'Legal obligations,' in other words rent paying, cannot be said to be very much attended to. A cable despatch tells us that three-fourths of the Irish farmers are refusing to pay even judicial rents, hence the danger to 'law and order,' and the absolute need, from a British point of view, of stamping out the League."

It was said that the League had better

bo left alone, because it was using its influence to restrain outrages. But that was just where the danger lay. If the Land League could restrain outrages it could also create them. If it could put down crime it could also keep up crime. If crime expanded and contracted at the orders of the League, it showed the League had power to go outside the Constitution—a power which could not co-exist with the authority of that House, and which ought to be taken from them. The House was aware that charges of a very serious nature had been made against hon. Gentlemen opposite. Those charges had been stigmatized by the hon. Member for East Mayo (Mr. Dillon) as false and most criminal in character. He was not going to question the denial which had been given by the hon. Member for Cork—

" For Brutus is an honourable man ;
    So are they all—all honourable men.''

But the evidence on which the charges rested had not been disproved; and, therefore, we were compelled to have some faith in them, and there was a growing conviction of their truth. So far, the serious charges made by *The Times* had only been met by a denial from the hon. Member for Cork. Therefore, it was important to inquire what that denial was worth. Against charges supported by evidence there was only the word of the hon. Member for Cork, and therefore the value of his word became of the most enormous importance. His credibility affected not only the fate of that Bill, but the whole fate of the movement. He proposed to refer to some things which had occurred in the career of the hon. Member for Cork in 1883, in America, in order to test his credibility.

MR. DILLON (Mayo, E.): I do not know whether it is worth while to call the hon. Member to Order ; but I wish to ask whether he is in Order in entering upon an argument to prove that a denial made by another hon. Member is not worthy of credence ?

MR. SPEAKER : It would not be competent for the hon. Member to call in question the denial of the hon. Member for Cork ; but, as I understood the hon. Member, he accepted that denial.

MR. T. M. HEALY (Longford, N.): No, no !

MR. E. BECKETT said, he had expressly accepted the denial of the hon.

Mr. E. Beckett

Member for Cork. In 1880 the hon. Member for Cork went to America to organize the movement which had resulted in the Chicago Convention, and he and his Colleagues were severely criticized by the American papers, and notably by *The New York Herald*, for attempting to stop relief flowing to the Irish people through any channel that was not consulted by them. That paper denounced their conduct, and then correspondence fastened on the hon. Members the charge of refusing relief, out of funds subscribed in America, to persons in Ireland merely because they had paid their rent. On February 1, 1880, *The New York Herald* published a letter from its Dublin correspondent, stating that—

" At a meeting of the Balla Tenants' Defence Association, held on Sunday, January 18, 1880, for the purposes of considering some cases of destitution in the neighbourhood and granting relief among the applicants, were some tenant farmers, occupiers of holdings of from five to ten acres, who were in a state of great misery. The president of the association, Mr. J. A. Walsh, having learned that some of these men had paid rent, proposed that no relief should be given to any man who had paid rent, and this was carried by a majority.''

The Balla Association was formed under the direct auspices of the hon: Member for Cork in November, 1879, and affiliated with the Land League of Mr. Davitt. The hon. Member for Cork, who was in Washington when the letter from Dublin was published in *The New York Herald* of February 1, wrote to that journal on February 3, 1880, in these terms—

"I have received no information as to the occurrence alleged by your correspondent at Balla, and am not disposed to believe that any such resolution has been passed by the local committee. Balla, however, has recently been the scene of a very cruel eviction, and it is just possible that the local committee, in a fit of exasperation, may have taken some steps calculated to give colour to the accusation made against them. I have cabled for information, and will let you have it as soon as possible.''

On February 4 the hon. Member for Cork sent from Washington to *The New York Herald* a communication received by him from the executive committee in Dublin declaring that—

" No such resolution had been passed at Balla or elsewhere, and denying that relief had been refused to rent-paying tenants.''

The New York Herald published this on February 7, with the following editorial comments—

"We have found Mr. Parnell not over-careful as to the accuracy of all he says against those he may regard as adversaries. Considerations of the untrustworthiness of the information received by Mr Parnell prevent our accepting as final the denial he has received from Ireland of the account of the proceedings of the Balla Committee, as hitherto reported by our correspondent. Our correspondent's statement was impartial and without prejudice."

On February 8, 1880, *The New York Herald* published a despatch, dated Dublin, February 7, from its correspondent, to this effect—

"The report of the meeting of the Balla Tenants' Defence Association is entirely correct. Messrs. Egan and O'Sullivan and Biggar were not present. *The Herald's* informant, who is the correspondent of the Dublin *Times* and *Freeman's Journal*, was present, and took part in the meeting. Both *The Times* and *The Freeman's Journal* of January 20 say that about 100 almost starving heads of families attended the meeting and made application for relief, as it was understood that some money had been received by the League. Mr. J. A. Walsh, the president, being informed that rent had been paid by many of the applicants, proposed that no relief should be granted them. This was carried by a majority."

The report was published in newspapers throughout the kingdom from January 20, and has remained uncontradicted to the present moment. That showed that *The Times* was not the only paper which found it necessary and easy to maintain important assertions in face of the denial of the hon. Member for Cork. There was another passage he would like to quote to the House. In an interview published in *The New York Herald* on January 2, 1880, the day after his arrival in America, the hon. Member for Cork used this language—

"In 1847 the Queen of England was the only Sovereign in Europe who gave nothing out of her private purse to the starving Irish. The Czar of Russia gave, and so did the Sultan of Turkey, but the Queen gave nothing."

This extraordinary slander upon the Queen reached England, and was publicly contradicted by the noble Lord the Member for South Paddington (Lord Randolph Churchill), who stated that Her Majesty had contributed £2,000 in 1847 to the relief of the starving Irish. This communication was cabled to America and published in *The New York Herald*, where it elicited from the hon. Member for Cork, not a frank avowal of the gross injustice he had done to Her Majesty, but a letter so remarkable that he would quote it verbally, and leave it

to the judgment of the House and country. On Monday, February 20, 1880, the hon. Member for Cork published this letter—

"In reference to Lord Randolph Churchill's contradiction of my statement, that the Queen gave nothing to relieve the sufferers from the famine in 1847, I find that I might have gone still further, and have said with perfect accuracy not only that she gave nothing, but that she actually intercepted £6,000 of the donation which the Sultan desired to contribute to the Famine Fund. In 1847 the Sultan had offered a donation of £10,000, but the English Ambassador at Constantinople was directed by Her Majesty to inform him that her contribution was to be limited to £2,000, and that the Sultan should not, in good taste, give more than Her Majesty. Hence the net result to the Famine Fund by the Queen's action was a loss of £6,000."

In that letter the hon. Member for Cork betrayed his knowledge of the fact that the Queen had given £2,000. Instead of confessing his error he aggravated the original falsehood of which he had been guilty, and imparted to it a most malignant character by piling on the top of it the monstrous concoction just read to the House.

Mr. T. M. HEALY rose to Order. He wished to ask if the hon. Gentleman was justified in saying "he had aggravated the falsehood of which he had been guilty," referring to the hon. Member for Cork?

Mr. DILLON wished to ask, further, whether the hon. Member opposite was in Order in attributing to the hon. Member for Cork that he had been guilty of a monstrous falsehood? The hon. Member opposite had been arguing for the last 20 minutes, in the teeth of the Speaker's ruling, that the hon. Member for Cork was capable of, and had frequently been convicted of, falsehood, with the object of showing that his statement in the House last week was false.

Mr. SPEAKER: I must remind the hon. Member that to attribute falsehood to another hon. Member of this House is unparliamentary. The hon. Member is entitled to enter into an argument founded upon facts and to draw inferences from those facts; but he must not directly accuse an hon. Member of falsehood.

Mr. SHIRLEY (Yorkshire, W.R., Doncaster): Sir, I wish to take your opinion on another point. May I ask whether the hon. Gentleman, in discussing details of the proceedings of the hon.

Member for Cork in America, is speaking relevantly to the particular question before the House?

MR. SPEAKER: I have not thought proper to interfere, up to this point, with the hon. Member; but if he accuses any hon. Member of falsehood I have no doubt that he will withdraw the expression, and he ought to withdraw it.

MR. E. BECKETT said, that he had not directly accused the hon. Member for Cork of falsehood. He had merely left the House to draw their own inferences from certain facts. [*Cries of* " Order! " *and* "Withdraw! "]

MR. T. M. HEALY: The word, distinctly, was "falsehood."

MR. SPEAKER: I must ask the hon. Member to withdraw the expression that he used of another hon. Member—that he was guilty of falsehood. I have already said that the hon. Member is entitled to use arguments and to draw such inferences from facts as he chooses; but his observations must be couched in Parliamentary form and expressed in Parliamentary language. [*Cries of* "Withdraw! "]

MR. E. BECKETT said, he understood that he used the word "concoction." [*Cries of* "No, no!" *and* "Falsehood."] If he had used the word falsehood with regard to the hon. Member for Cork he asked leave to withdraw it; he meant concoction. What was the essence of the charge which had been made against the hon. Member for Cork by *The Times?* The charge was that the Parnell movement was a foreign conspiracy, invented by felons and traitors, fed by foreign funds, and carried on by a systematic combination of agitation, terrorism, and murder, and that the Irish Party had, through certain of its accredited Members, been in constant touch and sympathy with the Queen's enemies. That charge, taken as a whole and in detail, could not be refuted by hon. Members opposite; certainly it had not been refuted. *The Irish World* of January 30 stated plainly that Ireland's mission was not to promote the union of the two countries, but to destroy the Pirate Empire—referring to the British Empire, and to strive to accomplish that end in and out of that House—to play a double game, which should be more or less Constitutional in that House and illegal out of it. This double character was plainly revealed in *The Times* letter.

Mr. Shirley

This had been confessed by the hon. Member for Cork in words which were published the day after his arrival in New York, and which had never been repudiated or disavowed by him. The hon. Member for Cork had been accompanied on Board the *Scythia* by the hon. Member for East Mayo and the authorized correspondent of *The New York Herald*. On the day after their arrival at New York, in January, 1880, *The New York Herald* contained an account setting forth the hon. Member's views of the situation in Ireland and his own proposed action. The hon. Member for Cork said—

" A true revolutionary movement in Ireland should, in my opinion, partake of both a Constitutional and an illegal character. It should be both an open and a secret organization, using the Constitution for its own purposes, but also taking advantage of its secret combinations."

Accepting the hon. Member's denial of the authorship of the letter which had appeared in *The Times*, he left it to the House to judge whether precisely such a letter might not have been written in precisely such circumstances by a man adopting the views and methods which had been avowed by the hon. Member for Cork. When asked if Mr. Davitt, who had accompanied him from Dublin to Queenstown, was not a leader of the Fenians, the hon. Member for Cork replied that he did not believe him to be a leader or to have control of the organization. By that statement the hon. Member for Cork betrayed a knowledge of Fenianism rather extraordinary in the face of his declaration the other night, when the hon. Member said—

" I said it was absolutely untrue to say that the Irish National League or the Parliamentary Party had ever had any communication whatever, direct or indirect, with the Fenian organization in America or this country. I further said I did not know who the leaders of the Fenian organization of this country or America were."

It would be strange if the hon. Member for Cork, who was the first President of the Land League, had not some knowledge of the Fenian organization and the Fenian leaders, considering that the Land League was started by a Fenian, and that it had been mainly supported by Fenian funds. The Fenians at first looked coldly upon the movement. It was accepted by a certain section of that body with the reservation that the temporary support rendered by them to a Constitutional movement should not in any way be considered a surrender of the ultimate appeal to physical force. But the Fenians would not give their support for nothing, and if the Constitutional movement failed, the Nationalists were pledged beforehand to Fenian methods, and Fenian methods were criminal methods. In the same conversation, the hon. Member for Cork, when asked if he was a Fenian, said—"No; I could not belong to an illegal society." Certainly he could not. He understood this so well that he excused the Fenians for their distrust of previous Parliamentary Leaders. The hon. Member for Cork, in reference to this subject, said—

"The leaders of the Fenian movement do not believe in Constitutional action, because it has always been used in the past for the selfish purposes of its leaders. There was a strong objection by the Fenians to our Parliamentary action for the same reason. And, indeed, if we look at the action of the Irish Parliamentary Party since the Union, there is ample justification for the views of the physical force party."

The Irish Party admitted that Sheridan acted as their agent, their tried and trusted agent, one of the leading spirits of the Land League, and yet they contended that they know nothing against him. The hon. Member for East Mayo, referring to a speech Sheridan made on the 1st of August, 1880, had said—

"Mr. Sheridan was known to the people, and had long association with the physical force party."

MR. DILLON (Mayo, E.) said, he was glad of the opportunity for making a correction. What he had said was that Sheridan was known to have been associated at one time with the physical force party, but that at the meeting referred to Sheridan said—

"I have now joined a Constitutional movement, and if that Constitutional movement fails I shall return to my own ways."

The Irish Nationalist Party, however, hoped that Mr. Sheridan would have no occasion to return to his old ways.

MR. E. BECKETT said, that, according to the statement of the hon. Member for East Mayo, Mr. Sheridan had never abjured the physical force party.

MR. DILLON: He did.

MR. E. BECKETT said, that Mr. Sheridan had stated that he was always ready to return to the physical force party. [*Cries of* "No!"] At all events, the National League did not appear to regard his former connection with the physical force party as a disqualification. [Irish MEMBERS: Certainly not.] Perhaps it was rather a recommendation in their eyes. How curiously that sentiment coincided with the sentiment in *The Times* letter. What was the physical force party? They were men who believed in the use of all the destructive machinery of modern science, and in illegal as being better—that was, being more effectual—than legal methods for accomplishing their objects. The hon. Member for East Mayo, referring to the man who sent $5 for bread and $20 for lead, said—"These were men who belonged to the physical force party in America, as most of our people there did." It was people of this way of thinking who supplied the funds of the National League. The truth was that the people of England must recognize the fact that they were face to face, not with the Irish people, but with the Irish in America, who were the real masters and paymasters of those Irish Representatives who came into that House to shout and to interrupt the Business of the country, but who were mere puppets in the hands of foreigners. [*Cries of* "Oh, oh!"]

MR. SPEAKER: The hon. Member describes hon. Members as coming here for purposes of interruption. This is not a Parliamentary expression, and I ask the hon. Member to withdraw it.

MR. E. BECKETT said, he would withdraw the expression. The real strength and power of this movement existed across the Atlantic. As Lord Beaconsfield some time ago said—"The movement is not in London or in Dublin, but it is in New York." Remedial measures were useless until we had convinced the Irish Party in America that their threats were idle, their efforts useless, their money thrown away, and that England refused to bow to their yoke. The whole character of the movement was reflected in its leaders. The hon. Member for Cork was not an Irishman, but an Irish-American. He had marked himself out from all previous Parliamentary Leaders, and his movement was marked out from all previous Parliamentary movements, and we must recognize the true character of this movement if we were to be prepared to overcome the National League and its criminal organization in Ireland. He would only add, in conclusion, that he had endea-

\oured to show two aspects of the character of the hon. Member for Cork—first, that his word could not be relied on; and, secondly, that he had given countenance and support to illegal methods and to the physical force party; and he now left the matter to the judgment of the House.

Mr. J. NOLAN (Louth, N.) said, he thought the attack which the hon. Member for the Whitby Division of York had just made on the hon. Member for Cork might be passed over with the contempt it deserved. The hon. Member for Cork had, in his place in that House, denied in unmistakable terms the calumnies which had been uttered against him, and that ought to be sufficient for hon. Members. He thought the hon. Member had made a great mistake in directing attention to the conduct of the landlords of Ireland, who were not ashamed during the famine years to take from the starving tenants the money which was sent for their relief from across the Atlantic. That money, subscribed at that time by the generous-hearted people of England and by other parts of the world, was diverted by the dominant class in Ireland from the objects for which it was given; and while the unfortunate tenants were perishing of hunger by the wayside, the members of that class were growing fat and rich on that money. As to the hon. Member's reference to the physical force party of some years ago, and his effort to trace a connection between the utterance of that party and the action of the Nationalist Party at the present time, he thought the House would agree that they were altogether out of date. The action taken by the right hon. Member for Mid Lothian (Mr. W. E. Gladstone) had effected a considerable change in the opinions and sentiments of the great majority of the people who had a few years ago looked forward to physical force as the only remedy for the evils of Ireland. Very strong and just grounds had been shown for rejecting the Bill. The Government had utterly failed to show any case for urgency; it had been proved that crime was not abnormal in Ireland, and serious doubts had been thrown on the accuracy of even the few statistics which the Government had laid before the House. Apart from the justice of the case, the Bill ought to be rejected on the ground of experience alone, for it

was an indisputable and important fact that coercion in Ireland had always failed in the past. He asserted that the Government had not only ignored the recommendations of the Royal Commission which they had appointed to consider the social condition of Ireland, but this Bill was in direct opposition to those recommendations. The feeling in Ireland, not confined to any particular Party, was very strong against the passing of this Bill. The majority of the Irish Members in that House had often been attacked; but he would say of the minority that they were simply the Representatives of the landlord class, who from first to last had been at the bottom of all the difficulties between the people of Ireland and of England. The Irish landlords had been spoken of in that discussion on the other side as the very props of the British Government in Ireland; but if, in America, there were at the present moment a very large body of Irishmen bitterly opposed to the British Government, it was only because they had been driven there by the bad landlords of their native country. The same landocracy had in former times driven large numbers of Irishmen to seek service in the Armies of Spain, Austria, and France, in whose ranks they had been brought to fight against the armed forces of Great Britain. He could quote authorities to show that the way in which the landlords had treated the people in Ireland within living memory was nothing new. In 1718, an English Churchman, the Bishop of Derry, after a journey through the country, gave a deplorable picture of the extreme wretchedness of the people under their rack-renting landlords. Lord Clare, who was certainly not a Nationalist, said that in his time the lower orders in Munster were in a state of oppression not to be equalled in any other part of the world. Since the Union, other impartial witnesses had testified to the extortionate character of the Irish landlords and the misery which their rapacity inflicted on the people. He would appeal to the Government to pause before proceeding with this drastic Bill, which the people of Ireland believed to be aimed at their Constitutional liberties. The measure, if passed into law, would only increase the difficulties of the Government; and it would be met, not by armed resistance, but by

Mr. E. Beckett

passive resistance, which the Government would find as difficult to overcome.

MR. R. G. WEBSTER (St. Pancras, E.) said, he believed that to the vacillating policy which was followed in Ireland during the years 1880-5 we owed the exceptional circumstances of the present day. The only remedy which the right hon. Member for Mid Lothian had ever conceived was an alteration of the laws affecting landlords and tenants; but the sequel had shown that both the Acts of 1870 and 1881 had been gigantic failures. He would remind the House that even before the Union it was found necessary by the Parliament on College Green to pass repressive measures to control the Irish people. The policy of the present Government, if they were but allowed to restore law and order in Ireland, would be the same as that of Lord Beaconsfield after the suppression of the Fenian insurrection by the Duke of Abercorn—namely, a policy directed to the development of the resources of the country. That the Bill before the House was imperatively needed he had no doubt. Crimes had increased in Ireland, juries refused to return verdicts, and the Judges, most of whom had been appointed by the right hon. Member for Mid Lothian himself, had almost unanimously described the prevalent lawlessness as unprecedented. They had heard a great deal in that House about Irish landlords. He would like to tell Irish Nationalist Members that, in consequence of their action in Ireland he, sitting on a London Board of Guardians, had had to relieve the wives of Irish landlords, in the district of St. George's Hanover Square, from absolute starvation. He thanked God he was not an Irish landlord. If people in London did not pay their rents they had to suffer eviction; and he saw no reason why, if they would not pay rent in Ireland, they should not be evicted. Speaking as the result of long experience of the Metropolis, he could assure the House that there was no sympathy amongst any class with the operations of the League; but that, on the contrary, there was a very prevalent desire that the laws of the Queen should be rehabilitated in Ireland. He believed also that the people of England hoped that the Government would do everything in their power to support law and order in Ireland. Personally, he would not object to the provisions of the Bill being applied to the whole of the United Kingdom, because they would not affect law-abiding subjects. The Bill, if it became law, would, in his opinion, put a stop to the fearful condition of things which now existed, and would leave room for measures of useful legislation which would promote industry and benefit all classes of people alike in Ireland; and, order being restored, the country would become prosperous and happy.

MR. T. P. O'CONNOR (Liverpool, Scotland) said, he was sorry that the inhabitants of London had had the burden thrown upon them of relieving Irish landlords; but he was not sorry that the people in the Hanover Square district had had to pay out of their pockets something towards the relief of aristocratic paupers. There were two classes of paupers in England. Some of these were the friends of the hon. Gentleman who had just sat down, belonging to the landlord class; but there were several thousand paupers belonging to the Irish tenant class, who had been driven out of Ireland owing to the land laws, which the Party on the Ministerial side of the House had supported, and who had been a burden to the English taxpayers. Pauperism in England was the strongest proof of the folly of the policy of the Conservative Party. With regard to the Amendment, he wished to say that he thought the complaints as to the debate being prolonged were rather unjust. He proposed to lay before the House several reasons why it appeared to him that they had not debated this Bill at one hour's length more than they were justified in doing by the circumstances of the case. In the first place, he must say that it was a new doctrine, even on the part of the Tory Party, that debates on repressive legislation should be confined within narrow limits. Sir Robert Peel, the greatest Leader the Tory Party ever had, laid down more than once in speeches proposing repressive legislation, that it was a thing that should be resorted to only in the last extremity, after long delay, and that a full, and ample, and prolonged amount of discussion was justified upon such questions. Furthermore, he (Mr. T. P. O'Connor) thought the Government themselves had supplied them with

[*Third Night.*]

the strongest and most unanswerable argument in favour of their debating the present Bill at considerable length, and he would go further—he thought the debate on even the present stage had been largely justified, in fact had been made absolutely necessary, by the conduct and by the words of the Government themselves. He was going to make allusion to a speech which had always been referred to by more than one speaker in this House—the words were used in "another place," and he would tell the House when he had read them the orator by whom they were used. In the speech to which he referred it was declared that in Ireland there was not only combined resistance to rent; but there was, also, combined eviction on a wholesale scale. It was said that one of the results of this combined and wholesale eviction was to drive the tenants of Ireland to the verge of madness, and it was further declared that, in consequence of the wholesale eviction on the one hand and wholesale resistance to rent on the other, there was a state of war in Ireland to which the Government had determined to put an end. Well, that was as dark and portentous a picture of the state of Ireland as could be drawn by any Member on these Benches. They have the statement that there was wholesale eviction, and that there was an approach almost to civil war, and that the tenantry of Ireland was driven to the verge of madness. What did that statement imply? If that were a correct picture of the state of Ireland— and nobody could doubt the correctness of the picture—it was clear that some great and even gigantic remedy was required to put an end to such a state of things. The state of things was extreme. The remedy for that state of things must be extreme also. This speech spoke of two Bills—the Bill now before the House and a Bill which had been introduced in "another place," and the speaker used these remarkable words with regard to these Bills—

" We consider these two Bills as sister Bills. They are the complement of each other."

Here these two Bills were put in direct association, in extreme and close interdependence, and that was the position they take up. He said that this Bill and another Bill to which he would only refer very casually were inter-dependent, and that he had a right to keep these Bills so

Mr. T. P. O'Connor

to speak neck and neck, so that one might not leave the House until the other was ready to accompany it or to almost immediately follow it. The Amendment declared that the House declined to proceed further with the measure for strengthening the Criminal Law against combinations of tenants until it had before it the full measure for their relief against excessive rents in the shape in which it might pass the other House of Parliament. He submitted that the speech from which he had quoted was the strongest argument in favour of the contention expressed in this Amendment, because it imposed upon the House in the face of a terrible state of things the solemn duty of saying whether the Government had provided a sufficient remedy. The Bill ought not to be allowed to leave the House until the remedial measure had been made to assume a form in which it would be effectual. They had the coercive measure in all its full details; but the remedial measure was not in a happy state, as in a certain portion of it the Government had announced their willingness to accept Amendments. The Bill was, in fact a blank sheet of paper on which the friends and foes of the Bill were invited to write their record. Most of its provisions were protested against on all sides, or have yet to be filled in by the Opposition and the Ministers of the Crown. The Coercion Bill was a hostage to this House for the remedial Bill. They were asked to part with the hostage before they had received the consideration, and the Government must think them rather more ingenuous and confiding people than they were if they supposed that without protest they would give them the powers they asked for before they had the least conception what the remedial measure was going to be. They were justified also in prolonging that debate on account of the circumstances which had attended the introduction and further stages of the Bill. The House had absolutely no information before it when the discussion began, and information was throughout doled out with a grudging and procrastinating hand. The Leader of the Opposition was promised statistics, but neither on the first nor on the second reading were they vouchsafed, and there were some details which had been asked for but were still not forthcoming. The Home

Secretary had brought forward a striking argument and made a great impression by referring to statistics which he had written before him, and which he stated discovered an enormous increase in crime. But the House was not in possession of those statistics until yesterday morning, some time after the second reading had been carried. This conduct of the Government was in striking contrast to the procedure of Mr. Forster in 1881, who at the outset gave the House the fullest details, even to the minutest and most petty particulars. They would therefore be justified in continuing the present discussion till they had extracted every single fact and circumstance on which the Government rested their case. With the exception of the Chief Secretary's speeches the debate had been practically all on one side. He had that day read through every one of the Chief Secretary's speeches. The right hon. Gentleman had an elegant literary style, so that a perusal of his speeches was not altogether an unmitigated evil. The right hon. Gentleman had produced only four cases on behalf of his contention that trial by jury broke down, and that none of these cases supported the case of the Government. One was an assault in Roscommon, the case of Clark the maltster. Although it was stated that there was a miscarriage of justice in that case, the statement rested only on the authority of the Crown Solicitor, the notorious Bolton, and was contradicted by the evidence of a barrister present at the trial, who said that the evidence was extremely confused. Then there was the case of Fitzgerald and Donovan, which had nothing to do with political or agrarian questions, and was only such a mishap as might happen in England. Then there was the alleged assault upon a woman who was proved to be a disreputable person. And the only accusation brought against the National League was that of illegal action on the part of a branch in Sligo, which was immediately dissolved. The cases brought forward in support of the Bill were bogus cases which had all been shattered, and not one of which had stood the test of examination. Then as to the charges of the Judges, upon which the Chief Secretary relied for the first and second reading of the Bill. The right hon. Gentleman had quoted

the charge of Mr. Justice Lawson as to the state of the County of Mayo to the effect that it approached as nearly to rebellion as anything short of civil war could do. But what were the statistics of crime in Mayo, a county with 230,000 inhabitants? During the last quarter the outrages were 12 in all, of which seven were threatening letters, and not one of the remaining five was of a serious character. Of murder, manslaughter, firing at the person, conspiracy to murder, assault on the police, assault on bailiffs and process-servers there were none, and that was in a county where the condition of things was stated to be little short of civil war. He thought that English officials would be delighted if they could point to such a state of things among a similar population in England. He did not blame the Chief Secretary for his inaccuracies. The right hon. Gentleman was a Scotchman, perhaps he was never in Ireland till he went over to take the oaths of Office, and when talking of Irish affairs he was as much astray as he (Mr. T. P. O'Connor) would probably be in the intricacies of the theology of the right hon. Gentleman's native land. But the difference between them was this—the Chief Secretary had the arrogance of his ignorance, whereas he (Mr. T. P. O'Connor) had the modesty of his. The right hon. Gentleman grew worse every day, and in time his primordial ignorance would be transformed into invincible ignorance. The right hon. Gentleman also founded the argument for his Bill upon previous Coercion Acts which had been passed by the Liberal Party; but the position of the Liberal Party now was not approval of past Coercion Acts or satisfaction at their results. In fact, their experience of the evil consequences of coercion in the past was the strongest argument against a policy of coercion for the future. The Chief Secretary had spoken of the Coercion Bill of 1866, and said that there was but a small amount of agrarian crime at that time. But was not the right hon. Gentleman aware that at that time a large proportion of the people of Ireland were in a state of almost open rebellion, many of them had arms in their hands, and there were risings in various parts of the country? Then the right hon. Gentleman referred to the Coercion Bill of 1870. But the whole case of the Government then was that there was a great increase, a recrudescence, of crime as compared with former years. The other night the right hon. Gentleman attacked the remedial legislation of the Liberal Party; but if it had not been for that legislation Ireland would now be in open rebellion, as it was in 1866. Again, the right hon. Gentleman said that after 1860 Ireland was free from crime. That circumstance was due, however, partly to the terrible emigration, and partly to the fact that between 1860 and 1865 there was a large amount of political crime, because the Fenian organization was at work. Such was the glorious state of things which the right hon. Gentleman spoke of as the blessed harvest that came of the legislation of 1860. He never entered upon the subject of Irish crime without a feeling of humiliation and also of exasperation, because he thought Ireland was treated in a manner in which no other country in the world was treated. Supposing that he had a ubiquitous police, most of whose time was spent in docketing and ticketing and summing up every single offence committed in this country, what a terrible and grim total might he not present of the crime of the people of England! Many of the crimes enumerated in Mr. Forster's Blue Book were of a trivial character. One of the so-called crimes consisted of a small wooden gate, the property of a nobleman, being taken off its hinges and broken. In another case several panes of glass were maliciously broken in the windows of an unoccupied house, and in a third a barrel of coal-tar was maliciously spilt. If he (Mr. T. P. O'Connor) went among the docks in the Scotland Division of Liverpool, where his own constituents lived, and enumerated crime in that way, Liverpool could be represented as a little hell upon earth. But this was the way in which the totals of crime were made out in Ireland, in order to blacken the character of his country. The statistics recently produced were the strongest evidence against the case of the Government. When the Home Secretary last addressed the House in support of this Bill he made the first successful speech he had delivered in the House. No doubt the right hon. Gentleman would make many other successful speeches, for he knew of no man who was better qualified than the

right hon. Gentleman to talk on every side of a political question. The Home Secretary produced an effect on the House by quoting the statistics of crime in the first quarter of the present year. The right hon. Gentleman stated that the number of agrarian crimes was 241 in that quarter, whereas in the last quarter of 1866 the number was 166. But the right hon. Gentleman made a false and unfair comparison, as he ought to have compared the figures for the first quarter of this year with those for the corresponding quarter of last year. The number of crimes in Ireland during the first quarter of the present year was 241, and in the corresponding quarter of last year 256, showing a decrease in the more recent period. In the second quarter of last year the number was 297, and in the third quarter 306. Only in the last three months of 1866 were there fewer crimes than in the quarter just passed, the number being 166, and that was because the late Chief Secretary and the Plan of Campaign were both compelling the suspension of evictions. It was said that there was no connection between evictions and crime; but the truth was that evictions were dogged by crime. During the September quarter of last year there were 306 crimes, and the number of persons evicted was 5,685. There were only 166 crimes in the December quarter, and it was because the persons evicted had decreased to 3,669. In the first three months of the current year the increase of the number of evicted persons to 5,190 was accompanied by an increase of crimes to 241. He was not going to read the noble Lord the Member for Rossendale (the Marquess of Hartington) a lecture upon good taste, although from his adoption of anonymous slanders lately he might stand in need of such a lecture, but at all events he ought to consult with his brother Leaders of the Tory Party for the purpose of maintaining something like harmony between his and their views with regard to the object of this Bill. Sometimes it was said that the object of the measure was to put down crime, but did the Chief Secretary in using that expression mean by crime murder or the wilful upsetting of a pot of coal-tar? Again, it was said that the Bill was intended to put a stop to certain combinations—that was to say, it was to prevent tenants from

Mr. T. P. O'Connor

defending themselves against their landlords. The Leader of that House had declared that the object of the Bill was to put an end to the sufferings of the Irish tenantry, who were being ground down and coerced by the National League. But the National League was a voluntary association. [*Cries of* "No."] If it was not a voluntary association why did the Government propose to put it down by force? The National League was the creation of and the emanation from the Irish people, and, according to the evidence of the Governments own witnesses, was looked upon by the Irish tenantry as their salvation. The noble Lord the Member for Rossendale had declared that the Bill was not levelled against political combinations, but the fact was that it was aimed at putting down the Irish Party in that House. The noble Lord himself had said that until that Party was put down it would be impossible for the Conservative Party, or the Liberal Unionist Party, or any other Party, to work out a solution of the Irish difficulty by providing for self-government in Ireland. It was clearly the object of the Tory Party to obtain the power of inflicting six months' imprisonment upon their political opponents. The noble Lord had admitted that from 1880 to 1885 he had been in conflict with the Irish Nationalist Party in that House, with the result that the Irish Party had increased from 45 in number to 86. When he heard the noble Lord promulgating his exploded nostrums and his defeated and discredited policy it reminded him of the observation, "With how little wisdom is the world governed!" One effect of the Bill was to confound persuasion with intimidation. He desired to call attention to the emigration which had taken place within the last four weeks, which showed that the policy of the Government was already having its disastrous results. During that period 9,236 persons had left Ireland, and the number was increasing. The reason was that the Government, between threatened eviction and threatened coercion, were making Ireland intolerable to the Irish people. He would show the House the genesis of the dynamite party. In 1863 *The Times* wrote—

"Eighty thousand persons—chiefly young men and women—have left Ireland, mostly for

ever. They have gone with money in their pockets, with strong limbs and stout hearts, and they have left behind the aged and the weak."

They left with tears in their eyes and curses for the Government in their hearts. *The Saturday Review*, commenting on that emigration, said of a letter addressed to the right hon. Member for Mid Lothian (Mr. W. E. Gladstone) by Archbishop John of Tuam—"He sighs for the departing items of assassination and murder;" and again, "'Ireland,' he said, 'is relapsing into a desert tenanted by lowing herds instead of howling assassins." Here those people were all grouped together as howling assassins. That was the language used by leading English journals, and it was little wonder that those men when they reached America listened willingly to the malignant counsels of the dynamite party. The same policy was being pursued now. Instead of seeing any progress they saw reaction; instead of advance they saw a going back to the very worst features of the perfectly infernal period of suffering. The roads in Ireland were thick with crowds of Irishmen and Irishwomen leaving the shores of Ireland for ever. If these men and women thought that the present Government and the present policy represented the English people and represented English opinion, he should tremble for the future of those Irishmen and Irishwomen when they landed in America; but he called upon the Liberal Party, he called upon the right hon. Member for Mid Lothian, and upon the masses of the English people, to stand between the Government and the Irish people, to continue protesting against the policy that already was producing such disastrous results, and tell these people that if they left Ireland in tears, and by the policy of the Government, they left in spite of the efforts of the Liberal Party, and in spite of the efforts of the English people. He asked the Liberal Party and the English people to extend to the Irish people their sympathy and assistance, and in that way he hoped that, even out of the suffering and terrors of the present time, there might not come the old harvest of hate, but a new and better epoch of sympathy and attachment between the people of England and the people of Ireland.

THE CHANCELLOR OF THE DUCHY OF LANCASTER (Lord JOHN MAN-

[*Third Night.*]

NERS) (Leicestershire, E.): The hon.
Gentleman the Member for the Scotland Division of Liverpool (Mr. T. P. O'Connor) has at some length passed in review the recent debates upon this Bill, and he has been good enough to criticize all that has passed. When he concluded his eloquent speech, and appealed to the Liberal Party to adopt a course of policy which would put an end to the great emigration which is going on in Ireland, which emigration he described as having originated with the Land Act of 1860, I could not help remembering that the Land Act of 1860, to which he attributed so much of the recent, and even the present, miseries of Ireland, was an act of the Liberal Party. And when he called to mind that in the present year thousands of people are emigrating from Ireland, I could not help calling to mind that the Land Act under which they are emigrating was also an Act of the Liberal Party. It strikes me as not a little remarkable that the two great instances which the hon. Gentleman brought forward as the real causes of emigration from Ireland must both be attributed to the action not of hon. Gentleman on this side of the House, but of the great Liberal Party to whom he addressed his impassioned appeal. But I will do justice to the hon. Gentleman, he made an attempt to do what many hon. Gentlemen who have preceded him in debate have not attempted to do — namely, to defend the Amendment which we are now discussing. It is most remarkable that until the hon. Gentleman's speech no attempt—no serious attempt—has been made to vindicate this Amendment, which I do not hesitate to say is one of the most extraordinary, one of the most exceptional, and one of the most unjustifiable Amendments with which a Government measure was ever encountered. It is open to more objections than any Amendment I can remember. It is—

"That this House declines to proceed further with a measure for strengthening the Criminal Law against combinations of tenants until it has before it the full measure for their relief against excessive rents in the shape in which it may pass the other House of Parliament."

Well, Sir, one would imagine from this Amendment that the Bill against which it is directed is a Bill for strengthening the Criminal Law against combinations

Lord John Manners

of tenants. [Sir WILLIAM HARCOURT: "Hear, hear!"] The right hon. Gentleman the Member for Derby ironically cheers that. What does the title say? That it is—

"A Bill to make better provision for the prevention and punishment of crime in Ireland, and for other purposes relating thereto."

The Amendment entirely overlooks the main portion of the objects of the Bill, and gives a totally different construction to its very title. The hon. and learned Gentleman the Member for Dumfries (Mr. R. T. Reid), in vindicating his extraordinary Amendment, stated that it has been alleged in "another place" that this measure and the measure now before the other House of Parliament are a complement one of the other— that they are, in fact, sister Bills—and he contended, therefore, that it is as impossible, as it would be unwise, for this House to part with this Bill until it has the other Bill from the House of Lords. Suppose the House of Lords accepted the view of the hon. Gentleman that one Bill is dependent upon the other. Suppose the House of Lords were to say these Bills are complements one of the other, and we will pass a Resolution that we will not send the Bill now in the House of Lords to the House of Commons until we have received the Bill now in the House of Commons. What would be the position of Parliament?—a complete deadlock. Yet that is a natural conclusion to be drawn from the Amendment itself, and from the support it has received from the hon. Gentleman opposite; and I am bound to say that, in my opinion, the House of Lords, if they were to pass such a Resolution, would have a great deal more to say for themselves than the House of Commons would have if it accepted this extraordinary Amendment. And for this reason, pass what measures you may for improving the condition of land tenure in Ireland, pass any remedial measures you please, until you have restored peace, tranquillity, order, and legality in Ireland, every one of your remedial measures must fail. Well, my right hon. Friend the Chief Secretary to the Lord Lieutenant of Ireland (Mr. A. J. Balfour) has distinctly declared that until the Bill to which reference has been made has come down from the House of Lords he would take care that this Bill did not leave this House, so that if that is really the object which the hon. and learned Gentleman the Member for Dumfries and those who agree with him have in view, their object is attained. Why, therefore, should this long debate have taken place, why should impassioned appeals be made to the great Liberal Party, and why should the retrospect of all previous failures of Irish remedial legislation have occupied our time to-night? Then the hon. Gentleman the Member for the Scotland Division of Liverpool complained very much about statistics. The statistics which have been given are statistics exactly in the same form as those given by our Predecessors in Office. We have followed precisely the course adopted by them, with, perhaps, one exception. In 1882, when the right hon. Gentleman the Member for Derby proposed the most drastic and the most Draconian measure upon the question of crime ever introduced into this House, he produced no statistics at all. We have followed previous precedents, and we have produced statistics, as soon as they were furnished to us, to the House, and that is my answer to the complaint of the hon. Gentleman the Member for the Scotland Division of Liverpool. Again, the hon. Gentleman made a very elaborate attack upon the noble Marquess the Member for Rossendale (the Marquess of Hartington). I believe there is no Member of this House who can defend himself better than the noble Marquess, and therefore I have no intention of attempting that work of supererogation. But I notice that the hon. Gentleman complains that the noble Marquess has said this is a Bill to put down crime, and not to interfere with the combinations of tenants. I entirely agree with the noble Marquess that this is a Bill to prevent crime in the first instance, if it be possible, to detect crime in the second instance, if the first object is not attained, and to punish crime in the third place. These are the main objects of the Bill. If there be criminal conspiracies, why then criminal conspiracies will come under the purview of the measure. What struck me as very extraordinary was that the hon. Gentleman the Member for the Scotland Division of Liverpool seemed to assume all through his speech that because the Bill is directed against criminal conspiracies, it is there-

fore directed against the political organization to which he belongs. Well, Sir, there is an old saying very well known, "If the cap fits it is not our fault." It is the hon. Gentleman who has fitted the cap on his own head.

MR. T. P. O'CONNOR: I am very sorry to interrupt the noble Lord, but I should like to say that what I said was that the Bill was directed against combinations and especially against the National League. I said so on the authority of a letter written by the right hon. Gentleman the First Lord of the Treasury (Mr. W. H. Smith).

LORD JOHN MANNERS: Any letter which the right hon. Gentleman the First Lord of the Treasury has written will, I am sure, contain nothing but good sense. But to return to the phraseology of the Bill, I find "criminal" always inserted as the adjective before the substantive "conspiracy," and that constitutes the whole difference between us. If the hon. Gentleman thinks that combinations of tenants to do lawful things in a lawful manner are to be crushed under this Bill, he labours under a very great mistake. If combinations are formed to carry out illegal objects in a criminal manner, no doubt this Bill will, as we hope, tend very materially to check and to put down illegal and criminal combinations of that kind. These are the two portions of the Bill. The Amendment takes one of them, twisting it in a most extraordinary manner, and entirely omits all reference to the other, which is the putting down of crime and outrage. Now, Sir, in a former debate the right hon. Gentleman the Member for Mid Lothian (Mr. W. E. Gladstone), whom I have the pleasure to see before me, stated that in order to justify the introduction of a measure of this kind it was necessary to show that there was an exceptional state of crime and outrage in the country, and he did me the honour to quote some observations of mine delivered in the month of June last. I do not blame him for doing so; but the right hon. Gentleman extracted one very short sentence, and without regard to the context fixed his own construction upon it. What I really said was this:—

"We are told, if you do not accept these schemes, you must fall back upon a permanent system of what is called coercion, and I think that among the many wise sayings of old Samuel

[*Third Night.*]

Johnson there was no saying wiser than that in which he advised his friends to clear their minds of cant. Let us on this subject of coercion clear our minds of cant, and let us see what it means. What does coercion in this sense mean? It means the repression by exceptional measures of exceptional crime and exceptional outrage, and therefore if there be no exceptional crime and no exceptional outrage, there will be no exceptional repressive legislation."

That was my statement; and now we say that there is exceptional crime, exceptional outrage, exceptional disorganization of the whole social machine in Ireland, and, therefore, we produce this exceptional legislation. But if that is not justification enough, I will most respectfully refer the right hon. Gentleman to a speech he delivered just three months before these observations of mine were made. The right hon. Gentleman was trying to make out a case for the great political revolution which he was endeavouring, but endeavouring in vain, to make this House accept, and amongst the other reasons he assigned, I find this. Speaking on the 8th of April of last year, the right hon. Gentleman said—

" In the first place, with certain exceptions for the case of winter juries, it is impossible to depend in Ireland upon the finding of a jury in a case of agrarian crime according to the facts as they are viewed by the Government, by the Judges, and by the public, I think, at large. That is a most serious mischief, passing down deep into the very groundwork of civil society. . . . . Finally, Sir, it is not to be denied that there is great interference in Ireland with individual liberty in the shape of intimidation."— (3 *Hansard* [304], 1040.)

Then he referred to the lapse of the Crimes Act, and added—

" The return to the ordinary law, I am afraid, cannot be said to have succeeded. Almost immediately after the lapse of the Crimes Act Boycotting increased fourfold. Since that time it has been about stationary; but in October it had increased fourfold, compared with what it was in the month of May."—(*Ibid* 1043.)

Then we have the right hon. Gentleman, just 12 months ago, announcing that the groundwork of Irish society was undermined, that there were exceptional outrages; and so despondent was he as to the social condition of Ireland, that he appealed to the House of Commons to virtually repeal the Union in order to get to the bottom of the terrible state of things which existed, according to him, in Ireland in April of last year. Well, but what do our ridiculed statistics show? They show that in the year 1886 there were at least 100 more cases

Lord John Manners

of agrarian crime than there were in 1885, the period of crime to which the right hon. Gentleman must have been referring when he gave that melancholy description of the state of Ireland in April last. Therefore, Sir, I say that, according to the facts, figures, and statements which have been placed before the House by my right hon. Friend the Chief Secretary to the Lord Lieutenant of Ireland (Mr. A. J. Balfour), our case is proved by the admissions of the right hon. Gentleman the Member for Mid Lothian ; and if I were a counsel addressing a learned Judge and jury, I would probably resume my seat with the quotation I have made from the right hon. Gentleman's speech, and say, " My Lord and gentlemen, our case is before you." Now, I notice that Lord Cowper's Commission has been constantly cited during these debates, and great importance is attached by hon. and right hon. Gentlemen opposite to any recommendation of the Commissioners which they think will sustain them in their opposition to this just and necessary measure. I observe, however, that Lord Cowper's Commission, after they have recommended a variety of measures which they think would tend to the amelioration of the condition of Ireland, conclude with this remarkable paragraph :

" But while recommending certain changes in the law which circumstances have rendered necessary for the present relief of the tenants, it is right that we should also press, in the interest of all classes, the maintenance of law and order, which has in several parts of the country been grievously outraged. In the absence of that security which ought to be enjoyed in every civilized community, capital is discouraged, enterprise and industry are checked, and it is impossible that any country can thrive or any healing measures be devised which will add much to its prosperity."

Those are the concluding parts of that portion of the Report of Lord Cowper's Commission which deals with the remedial proposals for Ireland, and I think that the hon. Gentleman the Member for the Scotland Division of Liverpool (Mr. T. P. O'Connor), who has dilated with such unction on the emigration which is now setting in from the shores of that unhappy country, ascribing the whole of it to the action of the ruined landlords of Ireland, might ask himself this question. Do none of these poor people leave their native homes in consequence of the paralysis of industry, the flying away of capital, the loss of employment occasioned by the ruin of landlords, the entire absence of all industrial enterprize, the shutting up of many sources of employment, which heretofore were open to them? Can he or any man deny that many of these sources of mischief are owing to the action of that very body to which it is his pride to belong? No, Sir; unless capital can be induced again to visit Ireland, until industry can reap its just reward, until employment of various kinds can again be found for the great masses of the Irish people, until new sources of industry can be opened to Ireland's sons, until those latent industrial resources which Ireland undoubtedly possesses, but which, as it seems to me, since the days of Lord George Bentinck have attracted very little attention in this House, are cultivated and developed, I hear that whatever laws relating to land in Ireland are passed, emigration will continue, but it will not be the fault of the pauperized and ruined landlords of Ireland. Now, the right hon. Gentleman the Member for the Brightside Division of Sheffield (Mr. Mundella) favoured us on Tuesday night with a very solemn warning upon the condition of Ireland. He warned us that there was a great movement in the United States of America, that even respectable people had joined it, and I think he went so far as to say he himself was personally acquainted with an Episcopal clergyman who did not at all approve of this measure. I must say, I think this Episcopal clergyman of the United States would probably be devoting his energies and his intellect to more useful purposes, if he were to attend to the affairs of the United States, than in informing the right hon. Gentleman what his views are of a measure which he probably has never seen, and which, if he had seen, most unquestionably he would not understand. I do not at all like, I confess, to hear right hon. Gentlemen who have held high Office, referring in this House in the manner in which the right hon. Gentleman did to what he is pleased to call the opinion of the respectable people of the United States. I think the respectable people of every country had much better attend to the affairs of their own country and let us, poor benighted Englishmen, manage the concerns of that great Empire which we have inherited from a long line of an-

cestors, and which we hope to hand down unimpaired to a remote posterity. Well, now, I will ask right hon. Gentlemen opposite to think for a moment what views the respectable people of the United States would have taken, if when they were in the midst some years back of their severe secession struggle, if the Mayors, Councilmen, and even Episcopal clergymen of England had come together and passed resolutions denouncing the conduct of one or other of the great parties in the United States. [An hon. MEMBER: We did.] Yes; but the only one of any weight who expressed an opinion on the subject, was the right hon. Gentleman the Member for Mid Lothian.

MR. W. E. GLADSTONE (Edinburgh, Mid Lothian): The noble Lord is imputing to me that of which he has never informed himself. He is probably not aware that my statement on that subject has been published in America itself, and I received from the American Government itself a most satisfactory letter in regard to it.

LORD JOHN MANNERS: Precisely so; that shows that what I stated was strictly correct. The right hon. Gentleman expressed an opinion, it was published in America, and he received a letter in regard to it. [Mr. W. E. GLADSTONE: What opinion?] An opinion with reference to the formation, not only of an Army and Navy, but of a Nation, by Jefferson Davis. Well, now, Sir, we are told very often that the tale of crime in Ireland is not sufficient to justify the Bill we have introduced. It is said there have only been 12 or 13 murders in the last 15 months. If there had been a few more murders and a few more violent outrages, why, then something might be said—according to the opinion of hon. Gentlemen opposite—for a Bill of this nature. That is not the view Her Majesty's Government take on this great and important question. They think that it is much better to interfere while crime—though very serious and though advancing—has not reached the height it did in 1880, before the right hon. Gentleman opposite introduced his repression Bill. We think it infinitely better to bring forward a measure now when, critical as is the condition of many counties in Ireland, deep, according to the right hon. Gentleman, as is

[*Third Night.*]

the disorganization which is prevalent in Ireland, there is still time to hope we may, by a combination of remedial measures of this sort, and remedial measures of another sort, clear away the organized terrorism, intimidation, Boycotting, and crime which have made the lives of peaceable, honest, loyal, and law-abiding citizens almost intolerable. That is my answer to the plea for further delay. I say that the Government did try—when they came into Office last year—to rule Ireland and administer her affairs without any exceptional legislation. I admit, with the right hon. Gentleman, that the attempt has failed; and admitting the failure of that attempt, what was the plain and bounden duty of the Government? Surely it was, as soon as they had satisfied themselves that that attempt had failed, to come forward and produce to the House of Commons that measure which they thought essential for the restoration of peace, tranquillity, order, and happiness to Ireland. We recognize the enormous difficulties which we have to face in the attempt we are making. We see opposite to us the late trusted Ministers of the Crown arrayed in opposition to a measure to restore peace and tranquillity to Ireland. We are aware of the immense weight which attaches to their opinion. We know the enormous obstacles which stand in our way; but, Sir, we know this—we know that we are discharging a plain and simple duty. We know that we have the support of this House of Commons, which, as the right hon. Gentleman was kind enough to point out in one of his numerous letters, is the product of universal household suffrage; we know by the large Majorities which have sent this Bill forward from one stage to another that we enjoy the confidence of the House in respect to this measure, and we are firmly convinced that behind this House of Commons—so recently in touch with the householders of this country—we have the support of the vast majority of the people of England. Having put our hands to the plough, we do not intend to draw them back until this House shall have finally decided upon, as we hope in the affirmative, this measure for the restoration of law and order, peace and happiness in Ireland, and we confidently appeal to the hon. Members of this

Imperial Parliament to sustain and encourage us in our determination and resolve.

MR. JOHN MORLEY (Newcastle-on-Tyne): Mr. Speaker, the noble Lord (Lord John Manners) who has just sat down has reproached us on this side of the House with having regard to the opinions that are held in foreign countries as to the policy which the Government are now pursuing. I can remember very well that, in the last Parliament, the noble Lord and his Friends were constantly taxing Her Majesty's then Government with their disregard of the opinion of foreign countries, and showing how they were sacrificing the name and reputation of Parliament and the country in the eyes of civilized Europe. And then, Sir, I should like to ask the noble Lord whether he considers the opinion of Canada the opinion of a foreign country. It cannot have escaped the noble Lord's attention that the Legislature of Canada has, within the last few hours, voted something like four to one in condemnation of the policy which Her Majesty's present Government are pursuing towards Ireland. But the noble Lord has pronounced this Amendment to be one of the most extraordinary that he has ever, during his prolonged Parliamentary experience, come into contact with. He read the Amendment, and the point with which he found fault was that the Amendment describes the measure now before the House as a measure for strengthening the Criminal Law against combinations of tenants. But, Sir, we have a very good authority for that description of the measure in a passage from a speech quoted only a few minutes ago by the hon. Gentleman the Member for the Scotland Division of Liverpool (Mr. T. P. O'Connor). It was the Prime Minister himself who, not very long since, said—"We have offered to the other House"—that is, the House of Commons—"a measure in order to put a stop to certain combinations," which is the very allegation made in this Amendment. I fail, therefore, to see why the noble Lord should, on that ground, find the Amendment so extraordinary. Well, then the noble Lord went on to ask why, if we have a right to insist upon seeing what is called the sister measure to this Coercion Bill, the other House of Parliament might not, with equal reason, insist upon seeing our Coercion Bill, before they part with their so-called remedial measure? Why, the answer to that is a very obvious one. We are very doubtful, in this House, in what shape, with what efficacy, your so-called remedial measure will come down from "another place;" they have no doubt in what shape you will send up your Coercion Bill. We have no security that we shall get a Land Bill after our heart; but they have very good reason to expect that they will get a Coercion Bill after their heart. This is my answer to that point raised by the noble Lord. The noble Lord dwelt at great length upon the flying away of capital from Ireland, and one among the other objects which he ascribed to the present measure was, he said, the keeping of capital in Ireland. I do not believe there is any subject upon which grosser fallacies are current than upon this matter of capital; we have very good evidence, and the Irish landlords know that they have had only too much English capital. I think we shall find that this is so, if we consider what the amounts of the Irish mortgages during the last fifty or more years have been. Experts say it is almost impossible to measure the sum; but Mr. Giffen has done all he could to find out the amount, and he puts it at £50,000,000, or about one-third of the value of Irish rents. Well, take that for one fact, and take the other fact which I ventured to bring before the notice of the House when I spoke on the Motion of Urgency made by the right hon. Gentleman the First Lord of the Treasury (Mr. W. H. Smith)—namely, that, according to the evidence of Mr. Hussey, the Irish landlords have not control of more than one-fifth of their revenue, the other four-fifths going away in no small proportion to the mortgagees. Has capital done them so much good that they need seek more? What you need in Ireland is not to prevent capital flying away—you do not want more capital on these terms; what you want is not to prevent capital flying away, but to prevent labour flying away. This is a Bill which will end—my hon. Friend the Member for the Scotland Division of Liverpool has shown that it is already operating—in the direction of driving away the thews and sinews of Ireland, which would do much more for that country than English capital. The noble

Lord taxed us, as I think the right hon. and learned Home Secretary (Mr. Matthews) did at an earlier stage of the Bill, with great inconsistency, because the right hon. Gentleman the Member for Mid Lothian (Mr. W. E. Gladstone), when he introduced the Home Rule Bill last year, described the condition of Ireland as profoundly unsatisfactory, indeed, as leaving almost everything to be desired. We are now asked how it is that, having, a year ago, taken what the noble Lord has spoken of as so melancholy a view of the state of social order in Ireland, we now resist their measure for dealing with social disorder. We do not deny for a moment now, any more than we did a year ago, that the state of social order in Ireland is profoundly unsatisfactory; but we say it is not unsatisfactory in the way and under the conditions which can be measured by criminal statistics. What we said was, and what we still say, is, that you must go deeper than a mere attempt to suppress the symptoms; you must get to the root of the malady. Our measure may, or may not, have been the right way of getting at the root of the malady; but what we say of your present measure is, that it is not an attempt to go to the root of this deplorable state of affairs. By way of illustrating the social disorder in the country, you assert that jurors will not convict because they are intimidated by the National League. ["Hear, hear!"] You say "hear, hear," and you argue that, if Parliament will allow you to suppress the National League, intimidation will cease, and jurors will give verdicts. There was a Committee of the House of Lords, referred to by the First Commissioner of Works (Mr. Plunket) the other night, and I am surprised that it has not been referred to more often in the course of these debates—Lord Lansdowne's Committee on Irish Jury Laws, in 1881. I will only read one very short passage. It is from the evidence of a certain Mr. Kelly, Queen's County, who was chairman of County Clare, and he, in answer to a question put to him by Lord Lansdowne, or Lord Cairns—I forget now which—says—

"The class from which jurors are taken in Ireland are perfectly convinced that the way to put a stop to offences connected with the land is not by punishment; they are perfectly convinced that the proper mode of putting an end to such offences is that the landlord should not

[Third Night.]

take proceedings calculated to provoke them. The verdict of ' not guilty ' does not mean that the man is not guilty of the act, but that he should not be punished for it. They do not appreciate their real duty as jurors; they think their duty is to decide, not whether the accused did the act, but whether he ought to be punished for it."

Of course, I am not going, for a moment —hon. Gentlemen opposite will not suspect me of it—to sympathize with that view, or defend it; but unimpeachable evidence of this kind, of which I think I can give the House dozens of other instances, does show that the malady, which we all admit, does not arise from intimidation, but from a wide-spread popular sympathy with the offenders. Now, Sir, I turn from the noble Lord's (Lord John Manner's) speech to the speech of the right hon. Gentleman the Chief Secretary for Ireland (Mr. A. J. Balfour), in answer to the hon. and learned Mover of the Amendment (Mr. Reid). The right hon. Gentleman complained that the debate had been too long already, and he deprecated this discussion. Sir, I have not taken part in the debates on the Bill since the Bill was introduced; and, therefore, I hope I shall escape the lash of the right hon. Gentleman (Mr. W. H. Smith) and his Secretary. I maintain that the Government have themselves to thank for the prolongation of this debate. What I mean by that is that, in the first instance, they presented their case—I say this with all respect to the Chief Secretary— in so slovenly, so loose, and so unbusinesslike a manner that we had, as the hon. Gentleman the Member for the Scotland Division of Liverpool (Mr. T. P. O'Connor) has said, to extort information from them step by step and day by day. Why, the right hon. Gentleman the Chief Secretary gave us scarcely any figures at all when he introduced the Bill. I think none whatever. Then it was felt that that was rather strong, and the Home Secretary (Mr. Matthews), two or three nights afterwards, got up and gave us figures, but they were figures from a Return which was not before the House. The right hon. and learned Gentleman the Attorney General for Ireland (Mr. Holmes) also based a very plausible argument, as to the condition of Kerry, upon Returns which were not before the House. It was impossible for us satisfactorily to discuss the proposals of the Government, supported by

Mr. John Morley

these arguments, until we were able for ourselves to gauge and to test the statements on which these proposals were founded. The case of statistics has, as is admitted now by the right hon. Gentleman the Chief Secretary, broken down.

MR. A. J. BALFOUR: I never admitted that it had broken down.

MR. JOHN MORLEY: Of course, I never meant to say that the right hon. Gentleman was so ingenuous as to say that the case had broken down; but what was his attitude a few nights ago? First of all, he said—"We do not base our case upon the statistical Returns of crime." Then the Home Secretary and the Attorney General for Ireland said— " Oh! by the way, there are some statistics of crime which are of great importance." Then, two nights ago, the Chief Secretary, when the statistics were proved, in the minds of all men of impartial judgment and of experience of Irish statistics to be not in the least degree alarming, said—

" The Returns of agrarian offences, I must inform the House, are not complete Returns, and the Constabulary do not include in them all those offences which are connected with the disturbed state of Ireland."

MR. A. J. BALFOUR: I made that statement when I introduced the Bill.

MR. JOHN MORLEY: I am bound to say that I speak with reserve when I say that I doubt whether that is a correct account of the Constabulary Returns. I doubt very much—the right hon. and learned Gentleman the Attorney General for Ireland can easily put me right if I am wrong—whether the Chief Secretary for Ireland is strictly right in this matter. For example, the right hon. Gentleman (Mr. Balfour) said that the Curtin murder was not returned as an agrarian crime; I venture to doubt it.

MR. A. J. BALFOUR: I said the Return of outrages did include the attack made upon the two girls for speaking to policemen. I said I was not certain whether the Curtin case was returned. I have since inquired, and I find it was not returned as an agrarian crime.

MR. JOHN MORLEY: I spoke from memory. [MR. A. J. BALFOUR: Hear, hear.] But, in any case, the observations of the right hon. Gentleman have diminished the effect of the particular statistics that have been given, because he said that the agrarian Returns were not complete. Well, now, just as the figures have shifted, so has the account of the objects of the Bill shifted. We are not clear, and we are less clear than ever, after the speech of the noble Lord (Lord John Manners), what is the object of this Bill. We were, first of all, told that the Bill was a Bill against crime, and we were told the other night again by the Chief Secretary, in words that have already been quoted this evening, that it is not combination that the Government desire to crush, but it is crime. [Mr. A. J. BALFOUR: Hear, hear!] The Chief Secretary adheres to that; but when it was found that no great case was being made out upon the state of crime, that ground was given up, and it was attempted to justify the proposals of the Bill on the ground of the general disturbance of the country. We were told, in so many words, that the Bill was one aimed against combinations, and now we are told that it is not aimed against combinations. ["No, no!"] Yes; we are assured first that it is, and then that it is not. I say that the House is left in a state of complete confusion even now as to what the real object of the Bill is. We shall endeavour, in Amendments, to test the object of the Bill; we shall endeavour to find out, by the response which the Government give to Amendments put down to the Bill, whether they really mean to confine the operation of the Bill to the suppression of crime, or whether they mean to extend it to combinations. Sir, if the Government mean to confine the operation of the Bill to the suppression of crime, why do they incorporate the Whiteboy Acts? And, Sir, I think we have some reason to complain of the Government for not answering, in any way, the urgent request of my right hon. Friend the Member for Mid Lothian that the clauses of the Whiteboy Acts, which they intend to incorporate in the 2nd section of the Bill, should be set out in the Bill. My right hon. Friend pressed that, and I think that if any hon. Gentleman, even on that side of the House, will take the trouble to read in the Paper laid before the House some of the provisions which it is proposed to include, he will be of opinion that the Whiteboy Clauses ought to be set out in all their naked ugliness in the body of the Bill itself. I am not going, at this hour of the night (12 o'clock), to weary the House by going through these Whiteboy Clauses; but there are one or two of them I should like to call the attention of the House to, because they show better than any vague words of Ministers used in the course of the debate what the effect and the operation of the Bill will be. Now, one of the Whiteboy Clauses is that—

"If anybody appears with any badge, dress, or uniform not usually worn by him or her, or assumes any political name or denomination not usually assumed by His Majesty's subjects upon lawful occasions."

I do not know whether that description will or will not cover Orangemen; the hon. Member for South Belfast (Mr. Johnston) does not always wear a dress or uniform, and does not always assume a particular name and denomination not usually assumed by Her Majesty's subjects. If anyone answering to that description—

"Shall appear by day or night to the terror of His Majesty's subjects—[*Ministerial cheers*] —he shall be liable, under the Bill, to be brought before two Resident Magistrates, and to suffer six months' imprisonment."

You cheer ironically the words "to the terror of His Majesty's subjects," and you argue that if people assemble to the terror of Her Majesty's subjects they ought to be amenable to punishment. I do not much differ with you upon that point; but I say of that, as I do of the argument of the noble Lord about criminal conspiracies, it is not what is to the terror of Her Majesty's subjects, it is not what is a criminal conspiracy, but it is what two Resident Magistrates shall think to be to the terror of Her Majesty's subjects or a criminal conspiracy. That is the secret of the whole Bill. It will be remembered that in the so-called Peterloo massacre the firing of the soldiers upon the multitude then assembled for a purely political object, and, as all of us in every part of the House now think, an object perfectly harmless, was held to be justifiable by the Judges, on the ground that the meeting was one calculated to conduce to the terror of His Majesty's subjects. And now there is one other clause from the many others which I should like to particularly mention—

"If any person shall print, or knowingly circulate, or deliver any notice, letter, or message tending to excite to a tumultuous meeting or unlawful combination, he shall be liable to be punished."

That, again, is a combination plainly unlawful — a combination indubitably unlawful; and I have no doubt the offenders might very well be brought before the magistrates and punished. But here, again, the same criticism applies. It is what two Resident Magistrates shall believe and define to be an unlawful combination; and I do hope that, if these clauses are to be put into the Bill, even this House of Commons will have enough of the old spirit of English liberty and English justice left in it to strike them out. A great deal has been said about the power conferred upon Resident Magistrates by these clauses. They are to have absolute discretion in putting down meetings, and absolute discretion as to the imprisonment of editors and proprietors of disagreeable newspapers. I think the best lawyers in the House will agree that that is the effect of these clauses. Now, I wish to read one passage of a letter which has not been noticed in this debate, but which will give Parliament an idea of the position of Resident Magistrates during the operation of a Coercion Bill. Mr. Clifford Lloyd is not a gentleman whose testimony will be suspected of being unduly hostile to the Government; but what did he write to the newspapers a little time ago? I will read a short passage from a letter of his. He said—

"It is this primary duty of Government— I mean the duty of keeping law and order— that the Lord Lieutenant has never been able to perform, and for this reason—that every tendency of the Castle system is to concentrate authority within its walls, and to remove from judicial officials every sense of responsibility. When the strain comes, such a system invariably breaks down. The state of confusion to be witnessed at Dublin Castle during the Land League disturbances can hardly be imagined. Telegrams came pouring in from all parts of the country announcing murders, attacks by armed parties, risings, riots, and acts of treason; and there were demands from magistrates for police and troops, and requests for instructions in reference to events which had generally passed before the instructions arrived. I have before me nine telegrams received by a Resident Magistrate during the course of one day concerning his movements on the following day with police and troops, and each of the nine telegrams contained orders in opposition to those previously issued."

And Mr. Clifford Lloyd then goes on to say what Lord Cowper and Mr. Forster

Mr. John Morley

did to try and alter that state of things. They issued instructions to the Resident Magistrates for preserving life, securing property, and for maintaining law and administering the law. Well, you have there, therefore, evidence of two things —first of all, that the Resident Magistrates are not likely, supposing there should come troublous times in Ireland again, to have their minds in the condition for deciding nice judicial questions; and, secondly, they are not at all unlikely, in spite of the announcement —I am sure the sincere announcement —of the right hon. Gentleman the Chief Secretary, to apply to Dublin Castle for instructions in reference to administering the law; and I think that, at least from the Parliamentary Under Secretary (Colonel King-Harman), they are very likely to receive them. Sir, I should like to make one or two very brief remarks upon the Chief Secretary's observations regarding the remedial measure in "another place." The right hon. Gentleman said—"Our Bill in the House of Lords shows that we wish to stay evictions." My noble Friend the Member for Hampshire (Viscount Wolmer) said, the other night, that the Liberal Unionists would not vote for this measure unless they felt sure that the Government were going to bring in a measure to stop what he called "barbarous evictions." Now, the right hon. Gentleman the Chief Secretary, in answering the arguments advanced in support of the Amendment by the hon. and learned Gentleman the Member for Dumfries, said—

"It is quite true that in the last resort, if the landlord reduces the tenant to the status of a caretaker, the popular excitement connected with evictions will come off in exactly the same way at the expiry of the six months' notice as it comes off now."

That is, no doubt, true; the caretaker will have to be turned out, precisely as the tenant will have to be turned out, the only difference being that the caretaker will be turned out by the landlord's bailiff and the tenant by the Sheriff. But think how the 4th clause will operate. That clause enables the landlord to substitute service of a notice for that process which is connected with so much odium, violence, and uproar at evictions. Does anyone seriously doubt that landlords finding this restraint upon evictions removed—this restraint of public danger and odium—finding that they can gain their ends without all these drawbacks, a number of eviction processes will be taken out by way of notice which would never have been undertaken if the public proceedings had had to go on as under the present system? Of course, I am quite aware that the effect may be to give you six months of peace—to give you peace during the six months while the notices are running; and this six months' peace will be convenient to you. But it will be a hollow and treacherous peace, because, at the end of the six months, you will find your last state worse than the first. The landlords will have issued a multitude of notices, and the tenants will have been lulled into a sense of comparative security, and will not have made the efforts they otherwise would have made for reasonable settlement. Therefore, I say the Government Bill shows, not, as the right hon. Gentleman thinks, that they wish to stay evictions—though I have no doubt they do wish to do that—but shows that they wish to stay evictions for six months. At the end of the six months I venture to predict you will have a greater crop than ever you have had of those violent expulsions to which the right hon. Gentleman referred rather cynically the other night. Another point the right hon. Gentleman made has been repeated several times in the course of these debates. The right hon. Gentleman said—

"Why do not tenants, if they are placed in circumstances of such distress, go into the Courts, as they can, and get relief under the Land Act?"

Why, has the right hon. Gentleman never heard of arrears—that the tenants have arrears hanging round their necks in enormous numbers, and that these arrears prevent them from going into Court and getting the relief Parliament intended them to have? If the right hon. Gentleman has read the Blue Book containing the account of the proceedings of Lord Cowper's Commission, he will have seen that a Mr. John Cunningham, of Donegal, was asked by Lord Milltown—

"Are they afraid to go into Court, for fear the landlord will deprive them of the right of turbary?"

And his answer was—

"Yes; and a good many people are afraid to go into Court, lest they should be deprived of the right of grazing."

Lord Milltown again said—

"I have heard before now that it prevents a great number."

Whereupon Mr. Cunningham said—

"A great number; I have seen them leave the Court in large numbers, rather than go on with their cases."

I think that when the right hon. Gentleman knows more of Ireland, he will admit that is one of the poorest arguments that could possibly have been used in answer to the case put forward by my hon. and learned Friend the Member for Dumfries. Another point which the right hon. Gentleman made was one which has been referred to tonight by the hon. Member for the Scotland Division of Liverpool (Mr. T. P. O'Connor), and by the noble Lord the Member for East Leicestershire (Lord John Manners), and I wish to refer to it from a point of view which has not occurred after all to either of those Gentlemen. The right hon. Gentleman referred to the Land Act of 1860. The noble Lord missed the point of our comment on the references of the Chief Secretary to the Land Act of 1860, and he said, in that spirit of recrimination which has so much marked these debates, and with so little effect—"Oh! but that Act came from the Liberal Party." I do not care whom it came from. The point is, that the right hon. Gentleman the Chief Secretary expressed his approval and admiration of the Act of 1860. [Mr. A. J. BALFOUR: I never did.] Why, you said the Land Act of 1860 contained principles which were accepted by all the countries in the civilized world. Surely that is an expression of approbation? I know the right hon. Gentleman does not just now think a great deal of the civilized world.

MR. A. J. BALFOUR: I wish to explain. I said that the Land Act of 1860 applied in Ireland the principles of land legislation which are habitually professed in all civilized countries. You have adopted a Land Act which does not follow those principles. I expressed no opinion.

MR. JOHN MORLEY: If that is not an expression of approbation, I should like to know what it is! And I should like to ask the right hon. Gentleman whether there is not a difference between the condition of landed property in other parts of the civilized world, and the way in which it has been worked in Ireland? Is there any other part of the civilized world where the main value of land has been created out of the tenants' own industry? I would approve the principle of the Act of 1860, if it were applied in countries such as our own, where tenants have not made improvements. The point is important; because the right hon. Gentleman is the Representative of the Irish Government, and he will have something to say upon remedial legislation, on the strength of which the Liberal Unionists are going to support the Government. What is the principle of the Act of 1860? It is that the relations between landlord and tenant should be pure relations of contract, and in no sense relations of tenure. The principle of the Act is that the hiring of land is just as much a transaction founded on trade principles as the chartering of a ship, or the hiring of a street cab. [" Hear, hear!" *from the Ministerial Benches.*] Those Gentlemen who cheer that statement, at all events, approve the principle. Are they going, in their remedial legislation, to act upon that principle? The Act of 1860 was the climax—the high-water mark—of what I call English legislation for Ireland—I mean legislation enacted in a midnight ignorance of Irish usage, of the history of Irish land, and of the whole body of the economic and agricultural conditions of Ireland. That measure came after the Encumbered Estates Act, and the two together are proof positive of the unfitness of this Parliament to deal with the Irish Land Question, whether upon the footing of contract or on the footing of tenure. As to the years between 1860 and 1870, which the right hon. Gentleman thought were remarkably free from crime, I do not know whether they were free from crime; but whether or not, I make this remark—that they were years of incessant discontent, of growing agitation, and of increasing alarm and terror in the minds of the tenants. Therefore, if the legislation of 1860 and its principle is going to be accepted in any degree whatever by the Government, all I can say is that they will find themselves, as I think, in the most lamentable case. I should like to allude to a remark which has been made constantly in the course of these debates by all conversant with the facts, that you must settle the Land Question first, and when you settle that the political question will disappear. The right hon. Gentleman the First Lord of the

Treasury has told us that the Government have a Purchase Bill in an advanced state of preparation. Well, Sir, I am for a Purchase Bill also, and I believe that you will have no settlement in Ireland until there has been a great increase in the number of peasant owners. But you will not get a large increase in the number of peasant owners in a hurry. It will be—I do not care what your Purchase Bill may be—a very slow process indeed, and you will not be able to deal with the real root of the evil by a Purchase Bill at all. I venture to predict, having had opportunities for talking with Irish land experts of the best and largest experience on this subject, who all agree in this—that a Purchase Bill, and the principle of purchase alone, will be absolutely ineffectual in dealing with the great problem of the congested districts. It is absolutely certain, too, that purchase and the transformation of small tenants into owners of land will not get rid of the political difficulty. Again, no Purchase Bill, unless it is a Bill of such enormous magnitude as my imagination refuses to conceive, can do away with the necessity of lowering rents. Your purchase scheme will, undoubtedly, force down rents. Suppose two farms situated side by side, of equal value, and each rented at £100 a-year, and suppose that the landlord of one of them sells under your Bill—the tenant's rent will fall from £100 to £78 or £75. Is it in human nature that if this occurs to one man, his neighbour will be content to pay the same rent as before? It cannot be but that, if you reduce the rent of one tenant by 22 or 25 per cent, the other will not rest until he has got a similar advantage. This question of the reduction of rents is, therefore, entirely independent of the fall in prices, and depends wholly on the fact that the credit of the Imperial Exchequer has been introduced into the question, and the consequent low rate at which money can be borrowed. I honestly regret that the Government have taken the course which they have seen it their duty to take in bringing in this Bill, instead of introducing the Bills which the First Lord of the Treasury has foreshadowed, one of which he said was before the House of Lords and the other in an advanced state. If I were to judge this policy from the point of view of right hon. Gentlemen opposite, I should find it as condemnable as

Mr. John Morley

I should if it came from ourselves. I should go about the question in an entirely different way. You agree that the Irish tenants have grievances, and that the land system in Ireland needs to be dealt with. You have got your remedies. Why did you not bring them in two months ago, or one of them at least? Why did you not bring them in on the 21st of March, instead of introducing this disastrous and ill-omened measure? Sir, I have often been taxed with thinking more highly of the power of the hon. Member for Cork (Mr. Parnell) than it deserves; but I venture to say that, if the two Bills which you have for relieving the immediate needs of the Irish tenants, if they were good Bills, had been first introduced, I do not believe the hon. Member for Cork would have been able, and I do not believe he would have been inclined, to keep back such a boon from the great mass of those in Ireland who returned him and 85 other Members to this House. We do not believe that Land Bills will settle the Irish Question; but you do. We do not believe that the Irish tenants are burning to throw off the yoke of the hon. Member for Cork and the National League; but you do. If I held those opinions, the very thing I should have done would have been to press on agrarian remedies, and to abstain from coercion. Coercion will have the inevitable effect—and I believe you know it in your hearts as well as we know it — by reason of the traditions and the strongest passions in Ireland, of throwing the whole sentiment of the country against your remedial legislation, and giving new strength to what you are pleased to consider a lawless organization. I think there are many of your Irish friends who will tell you, if you ask them their real opinion, though not in debate, that the effect of this Bill must be to throw new strength of popular opinion on the side of the hon. Member for Cork and the National League. You think you can put down the National League. What did Lord Spencer say? [*Cries of* "Oh!" *and laughter.*] Yes; but Lord Spencer knows a great deal more of this matter than any of us, and I would rather take Lord Spencer's knowledge of Ireland, and of the Executive Government in Ireland, than that of the hon. Gentleman who laughs. Lord Spencer said that—

"The suppression of the National League might seem to be a very easy thing to do; but it would be one of the most gigantic tasks that any statesman could undertake. The National League in three of the four Provinces was bound up with the people of the country. It had supporters in every village and every town in the country; and even in Ulster the National League existed, and returned a majority of Members for that Province. To put down the League was a herculean task for any Government. We all knew the difficulties there were when Lord Cowper and Mr. Forster tried to put down the Land League; but I will venture to say that the difficulties will be very much greater if any Government should attempt to put down by force the National League."

You have gone in for a Coercion Act because you think it is the easiest thing to do. Your Purchase Bill will, perhaps, involve you in a very considerable quarrel with the British taxpayer; your Tenants' Bankruptcy Bill has already got you into very considerable trouble with your landlord friends. Measures of that kind test the resources of statesmanship. Anybody can pass a Coercion Bill. But it is not anybody who can undo the mischief which Coercion Bills have often done, and which this Coercion Bill will do more than any of the others. It is because we believe that it will do none of the good which you anticipate, and that it will do enormous and irreparable mischief at a critical moment in the relations between England and Ireland, that we protest against it, and shall continue to protest against it at every point.

Question put.

The House *divided*:—Ayes 341; Noes 240: Majority 101.

AYES.

Agg-Gardner, J. T.	Beadel, W. J.
Ainslie, W. G.	Beaumont, H. F.
Allsopp, hon. A.	Beckett, E. W.
Allsopp, hon. G.	Beckett, W.
Amherst, W. A. T.	Bective, Earl of
Anstruther, Colonel R. H. L.	Bentinck, Lord H. C.
Anstruther, H. T.	Bentinck, rt. hn. G. C.
Ashmead-Bartlett, E.	Bentinck, W. G. C.
Baden-Powell, G. S.	Beresford, Lord C. W. de la Peer
Baggallay, E.	Bethell, Commander G. R.
Bailey, Sir J. R.	
Baird, J. G. A.	Bickford-Smith, W.
Balfour, rt. hon. A. J.	Biddulph,'M.
Balfour, G. W.	Bigwood, J.
Baring, Viscount	Birkbeck, Sir E.
Barnes, A.	Blundell, Colonel H. B. H.
Barry, A. H. Smith-	
Bartley, G. C. T.	Bond, G. H.
Bates, Sir E.	Bonsor, H. C. O.
Baumann, A. A.	Boord, T. W.
Beach, W. W. B.	Borthwick, Sir A.

[*Third Night.*]

Bridgeman, Col. hon.
F. C.
Bright, right hon. J.
Bristowe, T. L.
Brodrick, hon. W. St.
J. F.
Brookfield, A. M.
Brown, A. H.
Bruce, Lord H.
Burdett-Coutts, W. L.
Ash.-B.
Burghley, Lord
Caldwell, J.
Campbell, Sir A.
Campbell, J. A.
Campbell, R. F. F.
Chamberlain, R.
Chaplin, right hon. H.
Charrington, S.
Churchill, rt. hn. Lord
R. H. S.
Clarke, Sir E. G.
Cochrane-Baillie, hon.
C. W. A. N.
Coddington, W.
Coghill, D. H.
Colomb, Capt. J. C. R.
Commerell, Adml. Sir
J. E.
Compton, F.
Cooke, C. W. R.
Corbett, A. C.
Corbett, J.
Corry, Sir J. P.
Cotton, Capt. E. T. D.
Cranborne, Viscount
Cross, H. S.
Crossley, Sir S. B.
Crossman, Gen. Sir W.
Cubitt, right hon. G.
Curzon, Viscount
Curzon, hon. G. N.
Dalrymple, C.
Davenport, H. T.
Davenport, W. B.
Dawnay, Colonel hon.
L. P.
De Lisle, E. J. L. M.
P.
De Worms, Baron H.
Dickson, Major A. G.
Dimsdale, Baron R.
Dixon, G.
Dixon-Hartland, F. D.
Donkin, R. S.
Dorington, Sir J. E.
Dugdale, J. S.
Duncan, Colonel F.
Duncombe, A.
Dyke, right hon. Sir
W. H.
Eaton, H. W.
Ebrington, Viscount
Edwards-Moss, T. C.
Egerton, hon. A. J. F.
Egerton, hon. A. de T.
Elcho, Lord
Elliot, hon. A. R. D.
Elliot, Sir G.
Elliot, G. W.
Ellis, Sir J. W.
Elton, C. I.
Evelyn, W. J.

Ewart, W.
Ewing, Sir A. O.
Eyre, Colonel H.
Farquharson, H. R.
Feilden, Lt.-Gen. R. J.
Fellowes, W. H.
Fergusson, right hon.
Sir J.
Field, Admiral E.
Fielden, T.
Finch, G. H.
Finch-Hatton, hon. M.
E. G.
Finlay, R. B.
Fisher, W. H.
Fitzgerald, R. U. P.
Fitzwilliam, hon. W.
J. W.
Fitz-Wygram, Gen.
Sir F. W.
Fletcher, Sir H.
Folkestone, right hon.
Viscount
Forwood, A. B.
Fowler, Sir R. N.
Fraser, General C. C.
Fry, L.
Fulton, J. F.
Gardner, R. Richard-
son-
Gathorne-Hardy, hon.
A. E.
Gathorne-Hardy, hon.
J. S.
Gedge, S.
Gent-Davis, R.
Gibson, J. G.
Giles, A.
Gilliat, J. S.
Godson, A. F.
Goldsmid, Sir J.
Goldsworthy, Major-
General W. T.
Gorst, Sir J. E.
Goschen, rt. hn. G. J.
Gray, C. W.
Green, Sir E.
Greenall, Sir G.
Greene, E.
Grimston, Viscount
Grotrian, F. B.
Grove, Sir T. F.
Gunter, Colonel R.
Gurdon, R. T.
Hall, A. W.
Hall, C.
Halsey, T. F.
Hamilton, right hon.
Lord G. F.
Hamilton, Lord C. J.
Hamilton, Lord E.
Hamilton, Col. C. E.
Hamley, General Sir
E. B.
Hanbury, R. W.
Hankey, F. A.
Hardcastle, E.
Hardcastle, F.
Hartington, Marq. of
Hastings, G. W.
Heathcote, Capt. J. H.
Edwards-
Heaton, J. H.

Herbert, hon. S.
Hermon-Hodge, R. T.
Hervey, Lord F.
Hill, right hon. Lord
A. W.
Hill, Colonel E. S.
Hill, A. S.
Hoare, S.
Hobhouse, H.
Holland, right hon.
Sir H. T.
Holmes, rt. hon. H.
Hornby, W. H.
Houldsworth, W. H.
Howard, J.
Howorth, H. H.
Hozier, J. H. C.
Hubbard, rt. hn. J. G.
Hubbard, E.
Hughes, Colonel E.
Hughes-Hallett, Col.
F. C.
Hulse, E. H.
Hunt, F. S.
Hunter, Sir W. G.
Isaacs, L. H.
Isaacson, F. W.
Jackson, W. L.
James, rt. hon. Sir H.
Jarvis, A. W.
Jennings, L. J.
Johnston, W.
Kelly, J. R.
Kennaway, Sir J. H.
Kenrick, W.
Kenyon, hon. G. T.
Kenyon-Slaney, Col.
W.
Kerans, F. H.
Kimber, H.
King, H. S.
King-Harman, Colonel
E. R.
Knatchbull-Hugessen,
H. T.
Knightley, Sir R.
Knowles, L.
Lafone, A.
Lambert, C.
Laurie, Colonel R. P.
Lawrance, J. C.
Lawrence, Sir J. J. T.
Lawrence, W. F.
Lea, T.
Lechmere, Sir E. A. H.
Lees, E.
Legh, T. W.
Leighton, S.
Lewis, Sir C. E.
Lewisham, right hon.
Viscount
Llewellyn, E. H.
Long, W. H.
Low, M.
Lowther, hon. W.
Lowther, J. W.
Lubbock, Sir J.
Lymington, Viscount
Macartney, W. G. E.
Macdonald, right hon.
J. H. A.
Mackintosh, C. F.
Maclean, F. W.

Maclean, J. M.
Maclure, J. W.
M'Calmont, Captain J.
M'Garel-Hogg, Sir J.
M.
Makins, Colonel W. T.
Malcolm, Col. J. W.
Mallock, R.
Manners, rt. hon. Lord
J. J. R.
March, Earl of
Marriott, rt. hn. W. T.
Maskelyne, M. H. N.
Story-
Matthews, rt. hn. H.
Maxwell, Sir H. E.
Mayne, Admiral R. C.
Mildmay, F. B.
Mills, hon. C. W.
Milvain, T.
More, R. J.
Morrison, W.
Mount, W. G.
Mowbray, rt. hon. Sir
J. R.
Mowbray, R. G. C.
Mulholland, H. L.
Muncaster, Lord
Muntz, P. A.
Murdoch, C. T.
Newark, Viscount
Noble, W.
Northcote, hon. H. S.
Norton, R.
O'Neill, hon. R. T.
Parker, hon. F.
Pearce, W.
Pelly, Sir L.
Penton, Captain F. T.
Pitt-Lewis, G.
Plunket, right hon. D.
R.
Plunkett, hon. J. W.
Pomfret, W. P.
Powell, F. S.
Price, Captain G. E.
Puleston, J. H.
Quilter, W. C.
Raikes, rt. hon. H. C.
Rankin, J.
Rasch, Major F. C.
Reed, H. B.
Richardson, T.
Ridley, Sir M. W.
Ritchie, rt. hn. C. T.
Robertson, J. P. B.
Robertson, W. T.
Robinson, B.
Ross, A. H.
Rothschild, Baron F.
J. de
Round, J.
Royden, T. B.
Russell, Sir G.
Russell, T. W.
Salt, T.
Sandys, Lieut.-Col. T.
M.
Sclater-Booth, rt. hn.
G.
Sellar, A. C.
Selwin-Ibbetson, rt.
hon. Sir H. J.

Selwyn, Captain C. W.
Seton-Karr, H.
Shaw-Stewart, M. H.
Sidebotham, J. W.
Sidebottom, T. H.
Sidebottom, W.
Smith, rt. hn. W. H.
Smith, A.
Spencer, J. E.
Stanhope, rt. hon. E.
Stanley, E. J.
Sutherland, T.
Swetenham, E.
Sykes, C.
Talbot, J. G.
Taylor, F.
Temple, Sir R.
Theobald, J.
Thorburn, W.
Tollemache, H. J.
Tomlinson, W. E. M.
Tottenham, A. L.
Townsend, F.
Trotter, H. J.
Tyler, Sir H. W.
Verdin, R.

Walsh, hon. A. H. J.
Waring, Colonel T.
Watson, J.
Webster, Sir R. E.
Webster, R. G.
West, Colonel W. C.
Weymouth, Viscount
Wharton, J. L.
White, J. B.
Whitley, E.
Whitmore, C. A.
Wiggin, H.
Wilson, Sir S.
Winn, hon. R.
Wodehouse, E. R.
Wolmer, Viscount
Wood, N.
Wortley, C. B. Stuart-
Wright, H. S.
Wroughton, P.
Yerburgh, R. A.

TELLERS.

Douglas, A. Akers-
Walrond, Col. W. H.

NOES.

Abraham, W. (Glam.)
Abraham, W. (Limerick, W.)
Acland, A. H. D.
Acland, C. T. D.
Allison, R. A.
Anderson, C. H.
Asher, A.
Asquith, H. H.
Atherley-Jones, L.
Austin, J.
Balfour, rt. hon. J. B.
Barbour, W. B.
Barran, J.
Biggar, J. G.
Blake, J. A.
Blake, T.
Blane, A.
Bolton, J. C.
Bolton, T. D.
Bradlaugh, C.
Bright, Jacob
Bright, W. L.
Broadhurst, H.
Bruce, hon. R. P.
Bryce, J.
Buxton, S. C.
Byrne, G. M.
Cameron, C.
Cameron, J. M.
Campbell, Sir G.
Campbell, H.
Campbell-Bannerman, right hon. H.
Carew, J. L.
Chance, P. A.
Channing, F. A.
Childers, right hon. H. C. E.
Clancy, J. J.
Cobb, H. P.
Cohen, A.
Coleridge, hon. B.
Colman, J. J.
Commins, A.

Condon, T. J.
Connolly, L.
Conway, M.
Conybeare, C. A. V.
Corbet, W. J.
Cossham, H.
Cox, J. R.
Cozens-Hardy, H. H.
Craig, J.
Craven, J.
Crawford, D.
Crawford, W.
Cremer, W. R.
Crilly, D.
Crossley, E.
Deasy, J.
Dillon, J.
Dillwyn, L. L.
Dodds, J.
Ellis, J.
Ellis, J. E.
Ellis, T. E.
Esslemont, P.
Evershed, S.
Farquharson, Dr. R.
Fenwick, C.
Ferguson, R. C. Munro-
Finucane, J.
Flower, C.
Flynn, J. C.
Foley, P. J.
Foljambe, C. G. S.
Forster, Sir C.
Forster, Sir W. B.
Fowler, rt. hon. H. H.
Fox, Dr. J. F.
Fry, T.
Fuller, G. P.
Gane, J. L.
Gardner, H.
Gaskell, C. G. Milnes-
Gilhooly, J.
Gill, H. J.
Gill, T. P.
Gladstone, rt. hn. W. E.

Gladstone, H. J.
Grey, Sir E.
Haldane, R. B.
Hanbury-Tracy, hon. F. S. A.
Harcourt, rt. hn. Sir W. G. V. V.
Harrington, E.
Harrington, T. C.
Hayden, L. P.
Hayne, C. Seale-
Healy, T. M.
Holden, I.
Hooper, J.
Howell, G.
Hoyle, I.
Hunter, W. A.
Illingworth, A.
Jacoby, J. A.
James, hon. W. H.
James, C. H.
Joicey, J.
Jordan, J.
Kay-Shuttleworth, rt. hon. Sir U. J.
Kennedy, E. J.
Kenny, C. S.
Kenny, J. E.
Kenny, M. J.
Kilcoursie, right hon. Viscount
Lacaita, C. C.
Lalor, R.
Lane, W. J.
Lawson, H. L. W.
Leahy, J.
Leake, R.
Lefevre, right. hon. G. J. S.
Lockwood, F.
Lyell, L.
Macdonald, W. A.
MacInnes, M.
M'Arthur, A.
M'Cartan, M.
M'Carthy, J.
M'Carthy, J. H.
M'Donald, P.
M'Donald, Dr. R.
M'Ewan, W.
M'Kenna, Sir J. N.
M'Lagan, P.
M'Laren, W. S. B.
Mahony, P.
Maitland, W. F.
Mappin, Sir F. T.
Marum, E. M.
Mason, S.
Mayne, T.
Menzies, R. S.
Molloy, B. C.
Montagu, S.
Morgan, rt. hon. G. O.
Morgan, O. V.
Morley, rt. hon. J.
Mundella, right hon. A. J.
Murphy, W. M.
Neville, R.
Newnes, G.
Nolan, Colonel J. P.
Nolan, J.
O'Brien, J. F. X.

O'Brien, P.
O'Brien, P. J.
O'Connor, A.
O'Connor, J. (Kerry)
O'Connor, T. P.
O'Doherty, J. E.
O'Hanlon, T.
O'Hea, P.
O'Kelly, J.
Palmer, Sir C. M.
Peacock, R.
Pease, Sir J. W.
Pease, A. E.
Pease, H. F.
Pickard, B.
Pickersgill, E. H.
Picton, J. A.
Playfair, rt. hon. Sir L.
Plowden, Sir W. C.
Portman, hon. E. B.
Potter, T. B.
Powell, W. R. H.
Power, P. J.
Power, R.
Priestley, B.
Provand, A. D.
Pugh, D.
Pyne, J. D.
Quinn, T.
Rathbone, W.
Redmond, W. H. K.
Reed, Sir E. J.
Reid, R. T.
Rendel, S.
Richard, H.
Roberts, J.
Roberts, J. B.
Robertson, E.
Roe, T.
Roscoe, Sir H. E.
Rowlands, J.
Rowlands, W. B.
Rowntree, J.
Russell, Sir C.
Samuelson, Sir B.
Schwann, C. E.
Sexton, T.
Shaw, T.
Sheehan, J. D.
Sheehy, D.
Sheil, E.
Shirley, W. S.
Smith, S.
Stack, J.
Stanhope, hon. P. J.
Stansfeld, right hon. J.
Stepney-Cowell, Sir A. K.
Stevenson, F. S.
Stuart, J.
Sullivan, D.
Sullivan, T. D.
Summers, W.
Swinburne, Sir J.
Talbot, C. R. M.
Tanner, C. K.
Thomas, A.
Tuite, J.
Vivian, Sir H. H.
Waddy, S. D.
Wallace, R.

[*Third Night.*]

Wardle, H.
Warmington, C. M.
Watt, H.
Wayman, T.
Whitbread, S.
Will, J. S.
Williams, A. J.
Williamson, J.
Williamson, S.
Wilson, C. H.
Wilson, H. J.

Winterbotham, A. B.
Woodall, W.
Woodhead, J.
Wright, C.
Yeo, F. A.

TELLERS.
Marjoribanks, rt. hon.
E.
Morley, A.

Main Question put, and *agreed to.*

Bill *considered* in Committee; Committee report Progress; to sit again *To-morrow.*

INCUMBENTS OF BENEFICES LOANS EXTENSION ACT (1886) AMENDMENT BILL [*Lords*].—[BILL 230.]

(*Mr. Secretary Matthews.*)

SECOND READING.

Order for Second Reading read.

MR. T. M. HEALY (Longford, N.): I do not think the Bill should be read at this hour (1.45 A.M.) without some explanation. I beg to move the adjournment of the debate.

Motion made, and Question, "That the Debate be now adjourned,"—(*Mr. T. M. Healy,*)—put, and *agreed to.*

Second Reading *deferred* till *To-morrow.*

BANKRUPTCY OFFICES (SITES) (*re-committed*) BILL.—[BILL 243.]

(*Mr. D. R. Plunket, Mr. Jackson.*)

COMMITTEE.

Bill *considered* in Committee.

(In the Committee.)

Clauses 1 to 9, inclusive, *agreed to.*

Clause 10 (Exemption from operation of 18 & 19 *Vict.*, c. 122).

DR. TANNER (Cork Co., Mid): Before we dispose of Clause 10 I wish to move that you, Mr. Courtney, do report Progress, and ask leave to sit again. I think we are going through with the Bill at an inordinate rate.

Motion made, and Question proposed, "That the Chairman do report Progress, and ask leave to sit again."—(*Dr. Tanner.*)

THE FIRST COMMISSIONER OF WORKS (Mr. PLUNKET) (Dublin University): This Bill is now passing through what I may almost call a formal stage. The alterations which are being made are purely formal.

DR. TANNER: There is no material alteration made in the Bill?

MR. PLUNKET: No.

MR. T. M. HEALY (Longford, N.): We have heard a great deal about the Examiners. Did this Bill go before them?

MR. PLUNKET: Yes.

MR. T. M. HEALY: Were the notices published?

MR. PLUNKET: All the important Amendments.

Clause *agreed to.*

Remaining Clauses *agreed to.*

Bill *reported*, without Amendment; to be read the third time *To-morrow.*

TRUCK BILL.—[BILL 109.]

(*Mr. Bradlaugh, Mr. Warmington, Mr. John Ellis, Mr. Arthur Williams, Mr. Howard Vincent, Mr. Esslemont.*)

COMMITTEE.   [*Progress 20th April.*]

Bill *considered* in Committee.

(In the Committee.)

Clause 1 (Short title) *agreed to.*

On the Motion of Mr. STUART-WORTLEY, the following Amendment made:—

In page 1, line 5, at end, insert "the Act of the session of the first and second years of the reign of King William the Fourth, chapter thirty-seven, intituled 'An Act to prohibit the payment in certain trades of wages in goods or otherwise than in the current coin of the realm' (in this Act referred to as the principal Act), may be cited as 'The Truck Act, 1831,' and that Act and this Act may be cited together as the Truck Acts 1831 and 1887, and shall be construed together as one Act."

Clause, as amended, *agreed to.*

Clause 2 (Application of principal Act to workman as defined by Employers and Workmen Act, 1875).

On the Motion of Mr. STUART-WORTLEY, the following Amendments made:—In page 1, line 6, leave out from "the," to "principal" in line 7; and in line 9, after "ten," insert—

"And the expression 'artificer' in the principal Act shall be construed to include every workman to which the principal Act is extended and applied by this Act."

On the Motion of Mr. DONALD CRAWFORD, the following Amendment made:—

In page 1, line 9, after "ten," insert "except a servant in husbandry."

Clause, as amended, *agreed to.*

Clause 3 (Workman to be entitled to advance of portion of wages).

Amendment proposed,

In page 1, line 11, leave out from beginning of Clause to "take," in line 17, and insert ".the wages of a workman, whether he had paid according to the work done, or according to the time during which he is employed, shall accrue due and be payable as follows (that is to say):—

(a.) The wages shall accrue due weekly or at such intervals of time less than a week as may be provided by the contract;

(b.) The wages shall, save as hereinafter mentioned, be payable and paid weekly or within seven days after the end of the week in which they accrue due, or at such intervals of time of less than a week as may be provided by the contract;

(c.) The contract may provide for the payment at the time at which the wages would otherwise be payable under this section of a part only, not being less than seventy-five per cent of the wages accrued due; and in such case the residue, if any, shall be paid within one week of the ascertaining of such residue, or within such less time as may be provided by the contract;

(d.) The amount of wages due at the end of any week or other less interval shall be calculated, if the workman is paid according to the work done, in proportion to the work done during that week or interval, and if he is paid according to the time during which he is employed, in proportion to the time during which he has been employed during that week or interval;

(e.) Where wages which have accrued due, but are not yet payable, are paid in advance, no profit, discount, or interest shall be charged on such advance.

(2.) The employer shall comply with this section, and shall not."—(*Mr. Stuart-Wortley.*)

Question proposed, "That the words proposed to be left out stand part of the Clause."

MR. BRADLAUGH (Northampton): I would propose that we should pass this Amendment down to the word "contract" in Sub-section "b." The hon. Member for Preston (Mr. Tomlinson) wants to propose some alteration, and I pledged myself to him to move to report Progress, so that it would not be necessary to raise the point to-night.

MR. TOMLINSON (Preston): I would ask that the Committee should report Progress now.

MR. BRADLAUGH: I would appeal to the hon. Member to let us take the Amendment down to the word "contract." We shall not then touch the point he wants to raise; and I desire to get through as much of this Bill as we can to-night.

MR. TOMLINSON: I should like to have a further opportunity of considering the clause, which greatly differs from the one in the Bill. It was generally understood that we should not proceed beyond a certain point to-night.

MR. BRADLAUGH: I think the hon. Gentleman is in error in saying that there is a difference between this clause and that originally drafted. I am grateful to the Government for the re-drafting, which, I think, is a great advantage. I would point out to the hon. Member that the question of a payment at a certain period of a percentage of the wages that have accrued due can be raised after we have disposed of Sub-section "b."

THE CHAIRMAN: I would point out that if the Question before the Committee is carried, and the words proposed to be left out are left out, and words are inserted only so far as the word "contract," the clause will not make sense—the words inserted will not run with those that follow. The words must run on to the end.

MR. BRADLAUGH: Then I move, Sir, that you do report Progress.

Motion made, and Question proposed, "That the Chairman do report Progress, and ask leave to sit again."—(*Mr. Bradlaugh.*)

MR. T. M. HEALY (Longford, N.): Before that is put, Sir, I should like to ask the Government if there is any reason why this Bill should not extend to Ireland? The original Bill did extend to Ireland. I think it was an excellent measure. Before this Bill comes on for consideration again, I think we should have a distinct understanding that it will apply to Ireland.

MR. C. T. D. ACLAND (Cornwall, Launceston): I should like to ask the hon. Member for Northampton (Mr. Bradlaugh) whether he intends to press the application of the Bill to the whole of England? because in the Stannaries Acts Amendment Bill there is provision for the continuation of the custom of fortnightly and monthly payments with which this Bill would interfere. As that Bill is going to be considered by a Select

Committee, I shall be obliged to ask that the hon. Gentleman will agree to an Amendment excepting the Stannaries altogether from the Bill. If it is permissible, I should be glad if the hon. Member will give me an answer on this point.

MR. BRADLAUGH: I ask that Progress may be reported at this point, because it is clear it will be useless to try to pass half the clause, and to try to discuss half of it, as it will not be in Order to do as I at first proposed. I should be glad to extend the Bill to Ireland, but, unfortunately, the original Act does not so extend; and, so far as I am concerned, I am bound by the original Act. As to extending the measure to the whole of England, there is no objection that I can see. There are objectionable practices in Cornwall that I think it is desirable to put a stop to, if possible.

MR. CONYBEARE (Cornwall, Camborne): I am aware that the hon. Gentleman the Member for the Launceston Division of Cornwall (Mr. C. T. D. Acland) is interested in this matter—as I am myself, having a Bill of my own before the Committee. I desire to give the miners as much as they can wish for, and if they can derive any advantage from this Bill I shall be glad.

THE ATTORNEY GENERAL FOR IRELAND (Mr. HOLMES) (Dublin University): In reference to the question put by the hon. and learned Member opposite (Mr. T. M. Healy), I wish to say that the difficulty in the way of applying the Bill to Ireland is as stated by the hon. Member for Northampton. The original Bill extends to Great Britain only; and if legislation of this kind is to apply to Ireland, the Bill will have to be materially added to. Before the measure comes before the Committee again I will consider the question now raised, and see if it will be possible to extend the Bill to Ireland.

MR. BRADLAUGH: In the original Act there are words which declare that the Act shall only apply to Great Britain. If those were repealed, then everything would be easy.

MR. HOLMES: It would require more than that.

THE ATTORNEY GENERAL (Sir RICHARD WEBSTER) (Isle of Wight): I desire to say that I propose, in Subsection "b," to strike out the words "or within seven days after the end of

Mr. C. T. D. Acland

the week in which they accrue due." If there is any objection to that, or if there are districts where it is desired that wages should be paid other than weekly, we shall be glad to consider it. We have thought it would be well to leave the word "weekly" in the clause, so that the Committee may make what alteration it likes. When we are again in Committee on the Bill I shall move that the words to which I have alluded be struck out.

MR. T. M. HEALY: The insertion of the words "in this Act and the principal Act shall apply to Ireland" would be all the alteration necessary to meet our wishes in this matter. The words of the principal Act are singular—"That this Act shall apply to that part of Great Britain and Ireland called Great Britain."

MR. C. T. D. ACLAND: There are special circumstances attending the payment of Cornish miners that do not apply to other miners. We intend to bring before the Committee considering the Bill to which I referred the best evidence we can get from the miners themselves.

COLONEL BLUNDELL (Lancashire, S.W., Ince): It will be a serious thing to abolish fortnightly pays——

THE CHAIRMAN: That is irrelevant to the Motion before the Committee.

MR. T. M. HEALY: I beg to give Notice that I shall put a Question to the right hon. and learned Gentleman opposite as to the proposal to extend the Bill to Ireland before allowing Progress to be made at the next Sitting.

Question put, and *agreed to.*

Committee report Progress; to sit again *To-morrow.*

FISHING IN RIVERS BILL.

On Motion of Mr. Broadhurst, Bill to declare the Law relating to Fishing in Rivers, *ordered* to be brought in by Mr. Broadhurst, Mr. Arnold Morley, and Mr. Bernard Coleridge.

Bill *presented,* and read the first time. [Bill 244.]

JUVENILE OFFENDERS BILL.

On Motion of Mr. Secretary Matthews, Bill to amend the Law relating to Juvenile Offenders, *ordered* to be brought in by Mr. Secretary Matthews and Mr. Stuart-Wortley.

Bill *presented,* and read the first time. [Bill 245.]

House adjourned at a quarter after One o'clock.

HOUSE OF LORDS,

Friday, 29th April, 1887.

MINUTES.]—Public Bills—*First Reading*—Registration of Dogs in the Metropolis * (73).
Report—Railway and Canal Traffic * (60-74).
Provisional Order Bill — *Third Reading* — Metropolitan Police * (65), and *passed*.

THE CANADIAN PACIFIC RAILWAY—LINE OF ROYAL MAIL STEAMERS FROM VANCOUVER CITY TO HONG KONG, CHINA, AND JAPAN.

MOTION FOR PAPERS.

The Earl of HARROWBY, in rising to ask, What course was intended to be taken by Her Majesty's Government respecting the proposals of the Canadian Government to establish a line of first-class Royal Mail steamers between the Pacific terminus of the Canadian Pacific Railway at Vancouver City and Hong Kong, China, and Japan, and to move for Papers, said, that the Question of which he had given Notice arose out of the completion of that very great work the Canadian Pacific Railway. Many Englishmen in the present day had large interests in our Colonies; but he might state that he had nothing personally to do with any Canadian matter in any way whatever. The reason why he felt a very keen interest in this subject was that when he first came into the House of Commons in 1857 he had sat for many weeks on the Hudson's Bay Committee, under the Presidency of his lamented Friend the late Lord Iddesleigh. The question had been whether the Hudson's Bay Charter should be continued or not, and they had decided that the Hudson's Bay rule should be abolished and its territory thrown open to colonization and civilization. He had also had all the confidential Papers on the subject before him in the first Cabinet of his noble Friend the present Prime Minister. He would ask their Lordships to remember that this great Canadian Pacific Railway formed one of the most interesting stories in the modern history of nations. It had created quite a revolution in the Dominion of Canada; and as an instance of that he might mention that a journey which occupied Lord Wolseley and his men 76 days to accomplish, between Toronto and Fort Garry, when he put down the Riel rebellion, could now be performed with the greatest comfort and ease in two days. In fact, this railway was, perhaps, the greatest revolution in the condition of the British Empire that had occurred in our time. He was quite sure that the people of England did not appreciate what a tremendous revolution the creation of that railway had already effected, and would effect in the future. What had that railway actually effected? It had brought the Pacific Ocean within 14 days of the English Coast. Vancouver City, the terminus of the line, could only be reached before that in between two or three months. Suddenly, when this line was completed, they found themselves not only in telegraphic communication with Vancouver, but within 14 days' reach of that vast ocean. He would ask their Lordships to consider what was this British Columbia with which that railway had brought them into immediate connection. There had been a general feeling that its natural fate must lead to its drifting into the great American Union, as they had had little hope of seeing that wonderful railway completed across the Continent. What was this British Columbia, of which Vancouver promised to be the centre? It had 450 miles of coast, a climate of singular merit, excellent fisheries, the most magnificent timber, and a soil suited for every kind of cereal, while gold lay concealed below the soil. It had the only good coal supply on the North Pacific, and possessed a good dry dock. It was true that the entrance to the Strait was commanded by land belonging to America; but there was a channel, admirably suited for large ships, with an average depth of 100 fathoms, which could be made impregnable at small cost. In comparing the time taken to go to Yokohama, Hong Kong, and Shanghai by the best steamers under the new contract for 1888, he found that from England by the Peninsular and Oriental route, *viâ* Suez and Brindisi, to Hong Kong, took from 33 to 37 days, and by the Canadian Pacific Railway from 32 to 35 days; to Shanghai by the Peninsular and Oriental route 37 to 42 days, by the Vancouver route 32 days; to Yokohama by the Peninsular and Oriental route 41 to 45 days, by Vancouver 27 days. By the Cape the time taken to go to Bombay was 31 days, by Vancouver 38 days; to Singapore by the Cape 32 days, by Vancouver 32 days; to Brisbane by the Cape 28 days, by Vancouver 27; to Fiji by the Cape 32 days, by Vancouver 27 days. These were important figures, as showing that if we were barred from the Cape route or the Suez Canal we should have an excellent third alternative route. The Suez route was as precarious as any route could be, and it might be a matter of the gravest difficulty to prevent it from being stopped up. By the Cape route we might have to run the gauntlet of a considerable number of hostile foreign stations if we were at war with either France or Germany. A third great line of communication would, therefore, in case of war, be of infinite value to the whole of the Imperial interests. Beyond that, if this line were once taken up as a great naval line, there must soon follow a line of submarine telegraph from Vancouver to our Australian Colonies. He had always felt that the country was not sufficiently alarmed as to the danger of our having in time of war our great telegraph lines seriously interfered with. Our communications with India were very much at the mercy of Turkey, and those with China at the mercy of Russia and France; it was, therefore, most desirable that every means of independent communication should be secured. Lord Dufferin had stated—

"That the effect upon the Native mind of English troops reaching India from the East as well as from the West would be enormous."

Canada had already done its part nobly in this matter, and the enterprize that it had shown was highly creditable. Canada was only constituted a Dominion in 1867, and in 1870 and 1871 Hudson's Bay and Columbia were admitted. It was only in 1881 that the Canadian Pacific Railway Act was passed, and the construction of some 2,500 miles of railway commenced. According to the contract the work was to be completed by May, 1891; but such was the energy displayed that the last rail was laid in November, 1885. The cost to the Canadian Government was over £24,000,000, and £1,000,000 a-year had to be imposed by way of taxation to meet this cost. This wonderful railway was one of the

The Earl of Harrowby

most remarkable engineering feats of which he had ever heard, and it was only right that in a great Assembly like that they should express their admiration of it. It was a magnificent undertaking, which redounded to the honour of the Canadian people, and with which the names of Sir John Macdonald, Sir George Stephen, and Sir Charles Tupper would ever be associated. In October, 1885, when Lord John Manners was Postmaster General, the Post Office invited tenders for a fortnightly service to begin in February, 1888, between Vancouver, Yokohama, and Hong Kong, to cross the Pacific at the rate of 10½ to 11 knots an hour. The Canadian Pacific Railway sent in a tender for a fortnightly service between Vancouver, Yokohama, and Hong Kong at an average speed of 14 knots, which was the highest rate ever contracted for ocean voyages. The Company undertook to build under Admiralty supervision vessels of first-class type capable of steaming 18 knots, adapted for the conveyance of troops, and also for conversion at short notice into armed cruisers; to carry the Japan and China mails between the Atlantic port and Vancouver free of charge, to carry troops on service between the Atlantic port and Hong Kong at absolute cost, and to carry war materials and Government stores across the Continent at absolute cost. The subsidy which they asked from the British Government was £100,000 a-year. Mr. Holt also sent in a tender for an 11 knots an hour service, and he required £108,000 a-year. He could not believe that the Government would really reject a proposal to take possession of the Pacific by means of a great line of mail steamers set floating under the auspices of our venturous Canadian brethren. To have in the Pacific five first-rate steamers ready for conversion at any moment into armed cruisers could not fail to result in a saving of expenditure during war scares. During the Russian war scare in 1885 Mr. Gladstone's Government chartered as armed cruisers in the Pacific for six months nine vessels for £333,000, and only one of them could attain the minimum speed of the proposed Canadian Pacific ships; whilst some of them were absolutely useless for purposes of war. Then £1,000,000 was also spent to charter transports, many of them being intended for the Pacific. If the proposals which came from Canada were accepted armaments for the vessels could be kept at Vancouver on the one side and at Hong Kong on the other, so that it would take but a very short time to prepare them to meet an enemy. It might be asked— "Has Canada done her share in this matter of grave Imperial importance?" The reply was that Canada's work with respect to the railway was very great; but she had shown her readiness to go further by advertising for steamers sufficiently speedy to cover the distance between England and Canada in six days. He held that Canada was doing her part of the work nobly. Let England beware lest procrastination on her side resulted in her being forestalled by Germany or Japan. The Government of Japan was quite ready to move in the matter, while some years ago the North German Lloyd Company made inquiries as to whether they would have a chance of opening up this route. He invited the House to consider the difference of opening up the vast commerce of China, Japan, and Australia to British ships representing the Royal Mail Service, and, on the other hand, having those great commercial stations in the hands of the Germans and the Japanese. If it were said that England could not at present afford the subsidy, he would answer— "Economize where you rightly can; if necessary save the money devoted to the new Admiralty and War Offices; cease to buy works of art; cease decorating your parks; but do not postpone acquiring control over this great Pacific line." When the line should have been established the extension of communication with China, Japan, and the Australian Colonies must be most beneficial. The best way to meet the existing depression of trade was to strike out and obtain more frequent communication between England and new markets of the world. We wanted a sense of complete stability —a sense that war would be avoided— and by putting these armed cruisers into the hands of enterprizing Canada we should do more to convince the nations of the world that we were strong than by any other means. With Royal Mail steamers as cruisers in disguise—for that was really what the proposal meant— they would do more towards the peace of the world than by any other device of which they could think. In the

world of politics, he feared, there was a tendency to shrink from those great responsibilities of Empire which were crowding in upon us. This tendency, however, had not yet made itself manifest among the people, who would, he believed, agree with him that we ought to follow at sea the example set by the old Roman Empire upon land, and to establish great lines of communication between the scattered portions of the Empire. He felt sure that by taking the course he had advocated the Prime Minister, who was as anxious for federation as anybody could be, would do what was most likely to lead to the practical realization of the idea.

Moved, "That there be laid before this House papers respecting the proposals of the Canadian Government to establish a line of first class Royal Mail steamers between the Pacific terminus of the Canadian Pacific Railway at Vancouver City and Hong Kong, China, and Japan."—(*The Earl of Harrowby.*)

LORD BRABOURNE said, he was anxious to add a few words to the statement so ably made by his noble Friend upon a subject which he considered of paramount importance. By this Canadian route they would not only obtain regularity and speed, but they would be able to establish with distant countries and with our distant Dependencies communications which would be entirely in British hands, or in the hands of those who had British interests at heart. So far as Canada was concerned, he had the good fortune to have enjoyed the friendship of Canadian statesmen, and especially of Sir John Macdonald, perhaps the greatest Colonist who had ever presided over a British Colony; and he was certain that the wish of Canada, in making the proposals under consideration, was that she might afford greater support to the Mother Country. As Canada was our oldest Colony, so she was the Colony which for the longest period had evinced devoted loyalty to the Mother Country and her institutions. What had Canada now done? With a comparatively small population she had expended an enormous sum in the construction of that Pacific Railway, which was one of the wonders of the age. No doubt, one of her objects had been the consolidation of her own strength and the development of her own resources, but she had other objects in view, and mainly that of incroasing the power of Great Britain and binding herself by still closer ties to the fortunes of the Empire. Canada, indeed, deserved well of England and of Englishmen, and it would be cause for great regret if anything should prevent the Mother Country from responding to the appeal which the Dominion had made. He (Lord Brabourne) well knew the position of the Government with regard to expenditure. They had rigid censors of expenditure whom they were bound to regard; but this matter was not one which the Government could refuse to entertain on the ground of economy. Though the enterprize might not be re-munerative immediately, at a future time it would very probably repay us ten-fold or twenty-fold. But whether or no this was likely to be the case, he urged upon the Government to receive with favour a proposal, the acceptance of which, while gratifying Colonial feeling, would, he confidently expected, lead to the direct and material advantage of Imperial interests.

THE UNDER SECRETARY OF STATE FOR THE COLONIES (The Earl of ONSLOW) said, he did not propose to follow the noble Earl in his remarks about the advantages of the Canadian and Pacific route; but he could assure him that the Government highly appreciated, in these days, when all the Colonies were stirring themselves with such patriotism towards providing their own defences, the contribution which Canada had made to the defence and unity of the Empire. It was no small achievement for a Colony with less than 5,000,000 people to have contributed £25,000,000 for the construction of a trans-continental railway for the benefit of the Empire. The subject dealt with by the proposal of the noble Earl had been under the consideration of two Committees. The first Committee dealt with it almost entirely from the point of view of commercial and postal advantage, and they were unable to recommend the adoption of the proposal that Her Majesty's Government should contribute £100,000 a-year for a tri-weekly service to Hong Kong. It was found that the mails which went from this country to China and Japan did not bring into the Imperial Exchequer more than some £22,000 a-year. The second Committee considered it in its strategical aspect, and the opinions which were

Lord Brabourne

elicited before that Committee from naval officers were not entirely and un-mistakably in favour of the proposal. He was bound to say, however, that the opinions of the military officers who were consulted pronounced, he thought without exception, in favour of the proposal. The matters with which those two Committees dealt chiefly concerned the defence of the Empire, and were more or less of a confidential nature; it would not, therefore, be advisable that the Papers should be presented to Parliament. Since these Committees had reported the subject had assumed a somewhat different aspect. It had been proposed that instead of a tri-weekly there should be a fortnightly service for the same contribution, and that the ships should be built according to Admiralty requirements as to speed, construction, and capacity as armed transports. But the Government did not see their way to so large a proposal. Since then a further proposal had been made—namely, that the service, provisionally at any rate, should be monthly, and that Her Majesty's Government should make a contribution of £60,000 a-year. Upon receipt of that communication a telegram was addressed to the Canadian Government inquiring whether they were prepared to assist in contributing towards this subsidy. At first it was understood that the Canadian Government declined to make any contribution whatever. Since then, however, a further communication had been received in which the Canadian Government had expressed their willingness to make some contribution from Canadian funds, and that proposal was at the present moment under the consideration of Her Majesty's Government. The noble Earl would, therefore, see that he was not entirely accurate in stating that a decision had already been taken upon the subject by Her Majesty's Government. The Canadian Pacific Company had, he believed, already taken some steps for placing the service in an efficient condition, and he was informed that three ships of the Cunard Company had left Liverpool, and were now on their way to Vancouver with the object of being placed on the service. He assured the noble Earl that the subject was receiving, and would continue to receive, the most careful attention of Her Majesty's Government, and that as soon as a decision was arrived at Papers would be laid before Parliament; but, until the matter was finally settled, he could not present the Papers moved for by the noble Earl.

THE EARL OF CARNARVON said, he supported as far as he could the admirable, clear, and statesmanlike statement of his noble Friend who brought this question forward. There was every reason why the Government should accept the suggestions of his noble Friend, because, as he understood from his noble Friend the Under Secretary, the original subsidy asked of the Government for the Pacific service was £100,000 ; but this sum had been reduced to £60,000, and ultimately even to £45,000, with a monthly service. That was a comparatively trifling sum, but the expenditure would bring great benefits with it. He doubted, however, whether the saving of the £15,000 on the £60,000 or the £40,000 on the £100,000 was worth making if it involved a monthly instead of a fortnightly service. But he would accept the monthly service, in the hope that it would ultimately lead to a fortnightly service, and that a large and profitable commerce would grow up between Vancouver and China and Japan. He would add nothing to the well-deserved eulogy which his noble Friend had pronounced on the Canadian Pacific Railway, so admirable in its conception, in its construction, and in its completion. The service which it was proposed should be established consisted of three parts. First, there was the steamer service between England and Canada, which was to be carried on in swift vessels subsidized by the Canadian Government; secondly, there were fast trains across the Continent; and, lastly, there was the service in the Pacific Ocean which they were now discussing. Now, there were five distinct Imperial and commercial advantages which would arise from the establishment of this route. First, a rapid through postal and passenger route to the East; secondly, before long a complete and independent British telegraphic line ; thirdly, rapid and cheap transport for troops and stores across the Continent to our Eastern Possessions, it being part of the bargain that troops and stores should be carried at cost price ; fourthly, as his noble Friend had pointed out, the establishment of a third route to the East in addition to

the Suez Canal, which in time of war might easily be blocked, and to the Cape route, which was wholly undefended. This third route, moreover, was entirely through British territory. Fifthly, the ships to be constructed for the Pacific service were to be constructed so as to serve as cruisers. He heartily concurred in this last provision, which was one of the recommendations of the Defence Commission, whose opinion it was that the exigencies of a great war could only be met by arming our merchant vessels as cruisers. He also understood that the service had been guaranteed for efficiency by one of the largest commercial houses in this country, whose name he would not mention as he had not seen it in print. He would only say further on this point that they must bear specially in mind that since this Canadian Pacific Railway had been completed the whole character of the docks at Esquimault had undergone a material change. Those docks had now been finished, and a great deal of Imperial money had been spent upon them. There was now at Esquimault a dock which was capable of receiving the largest of our ships. In addition to that guns and armaments might be sent there, and the House must bear in mind that Vancouver Island was the only coaling station we possessed in that part of the world. There was only one other point which he would add to his noble Friend's admirable statement. For several generations this country had pursued a continuous course of policy with regard to Canada, and large sums had been expended in the construction of roads and railways for military purposes. The great Canadian Pacific Railway had now been completed, and he submitted that it would be a misfortune to stop here when we were in sight of the goal which we had been striving for so many years to attain. His noble Friend had referred to a delicate subject to which he would only allude briefly ; but it was right that their Lordships should fully understand that if we did not establish our claim to this great maritime highway—if we did not meet the Dominion on this particular question—the service would fall into the hands of another European Power. They must not think that others would be equally negligent of their obvious interests. If that were so the direct advantages which must flow from the establishment of the service would be lost to us, and would be transferred to others ; and, worse than that, another foreign influence would and must be established in the Pacific Ocean. However, he would not dwell further upon that point ; but he hoped Her Majesty's Government would weigh it carefully. The establishment of a commercial line of steamers for Vancouver would also give a footing to the commerce of the South Pacific. He trusted, therefore, that Her Majesty's Government would come to the conclusion that this was a good bargain, commercially, at the present time, and that it would be a great misfortune if this opportunity were allowed to slip.

THE EARL OF DUNRAVEN said, he could not let this debate go by without expressing how deeply he sympathized and agreed with all that had fallen from the noble Earl who had brought this Motion forward. He had only just come up from the country, and, therefore, he had not the advantage of hearing all that he said ; but from what he did hear he was convinced that he went very fully and fairly into the most important points connected with this important subject. His noble Friend the Under Secretary of State for the Colonies had told them that the Government were giving this matter their serious consideration. He believed he had heard these words many times before from various Governments. As a general rule, when he had heard those words he had found the results of that consideration had been nothing. He trusted that in this case, seeing the great importance of the subject, the result would be entirely different. On the commercial aspect of the case it was difficult to speak ; but he would point out to their Lordships how it might be under-rated. The great importance of it was to this country that the material prosperity and well-being of Canada should be increased. Canada was a good customer of ours. We had a large trade with the Dominion, and anything that increased the power of producing their goods must be of great advantage to the manufacturing interest of this country. It was impossible to say how far this line of steamers would increase the prosperity of Canada ; but he begged their Lordships to remember that so great was the advantage of the Northern

route, and so much nearer did it approach to Vancouver Land, that there could be no question that a large contributing trade would take place if Vancouver was connected by steamers with Shanghai and Hong Kong. It was impossible to give an estimate of what value this trade might be ; but it would probably be very great. The most important aspect undoubtedly was that it would be an alternative line to our Eastern Colonies, and he did not think it was possible to over-estimate the value of this line from that point of view. The noble Earl the Under Secretary of State for the Colonies had told them that all the military authorities he had consulted were in favour of the line, and most of the naval authorities also. That appeared to him a strong and almost unanswerable argument for subsidizing this line of steamers. The value of it from an Imperial point of view could be understood by every-one, as the Suez Canal route would not be available during hostilities. The route they were now considering would be entirely on British territory on land or water, where vessels conveying goods could not be harassed from the opposition of, any foreign Power ; that was an advantage which was very great. He did not think it was a question as to whether this line was worth £40,000 a-year, £50,000 a-year, or £60,000. The question this country had to consider was, whether, if a line of steamers were established between British North America and our Possessions in the East, it was worth the reasonable sum of money they were asking. The fact that it would be available by first-class steamers steaming 18 knots, capable of carrying troops, capable of being armed at a moment's notice—provided armaments were ready, as he supposed they would be—the value of such a force as that to this country could not be over-estimated. The great expense at which the country was placed was commented upon by the noble Earl—a vast amount of shipping was absolutely wasted. A Bill subsidizing this line of steamers, as had been promised, would be a great saving to the country ; and it ought not to be looked upon as a matter of expense, but, on the contrary, as a great economy. There could be no question that in periods of danger a first-class line of steamers would be of great value to the country, and that the country would get value for their money. What could be the value of these steamers to the country in the event of war it was impossible for him to estimate. He did not think it possible for anyone to put it down in pounds, shillings and pence. The Dominion of Canada had done all in their power to connect the Mother Country with the East and the Southern Colonies, and he would express his own opinion and many others most strongly, that no ordinary consideration ought to be allowed to stand in the way of this country doing what remained to be done, and put the last link in the chain and complete the line of communication between the East and this country. It was not a matter that ought to be looked at from the narrow view of economy. The possible advantages to the country were enormous; the possible advantages from a commercial point of view were very large; and he sincerely trusted that in considering this question Her Majesty's Government would not allow themselves to be influenced by small considerations at the present, but that they would consider the great advantages from a commercial point of view in the future.

EARL GRANVILLE said, that when he was at the Colonial Office about a year ago, he had examined carefully into the matter. He did not undervalue the objection on principle of the Treasury, nor those of some of the naval authorities, against some of the statements made as to the advantages in case of war; but he had come to the conclusion that on the whole it was a thing which ought to be done, subject to some conditions as to detail. The question was again referred to a Committee, which was still investigating the matter when he left Office. He was very glad to hear the Under Secretary say, in regard to what had happened since, that there was some likelihood of a satisfactory arrangement of that question by the Government.

THE EARL OF HARROWBY said, he must express his gratification at the announcement that Her Majesty's Government were still considering the matter. He thought that everybody had understood that the scheme proposed by the Canadian Government was entirely declined. He must take exception to one or two statements of his noble Friend the Under Secretary. He said Her Majesty's Government thought the question too large.

If that thing was worth doing at all, it was a very large question indeed. It was much better to leave it alone than deal with it in that spirit. They had to assist in keeping up that feeling of patriotism which was now so strong in the Colonies. They had also to meet the difficulties of our growing population, which pressed upon the means of employment, while at the same time those means of employment were becoming less and less plentiful. The Government had to assist not only from a sentimental point of view, but had to meet the very dangerous condition the country was coming to. He should look with the very gravest apprehension on any proposal to cut down the number or character of the ships. If this country wanted to dominate the Pacific they must be bold in that matter and approach it in such a way as would impress the nations of the world. If they did it in a poor or petty spirit they would defeat the object they had in view and leave the position open to more enterprising nations than ourselves.

Motion (by leave of the House) *withdrawn.*

REGISTRATION OF DOGS IN THE METROPOLIS BILL.

BILL PRESENTED. FIRST READING.

LORD MOUNT-TEMPLE said, he was induced to call attention to the regulations for the prevention of rabies and hydrophobia, because they occasioned great annoyance to people of all classes, and particularly to the poor, who appreciated the companionship of their four-footed friends more vividly than the upper classes, who had more human friends in the country. These regulations were without any effective adequate results. The opposition of public opinion in London had emancipated the dogs from the gagging of their jaws, which was now inflicted in many districts of the country. In one county one dog suspected of rabies ran about biting men, boys, and sheep, and was killed. The dog did not injure the men or the boys, but called forth an order in Council to gag every other dog in the county for a long, indefinite period. He drew away the police from their important duties to watch for unmuzzled dogs in the roads, and to summon innocent persons to be punished because their dogs jumped over a garden fence into a highway to bark at the police. Muzzling was a barbarous blunder, and a failure. The rabid dogs could not be muzzled, for their impulse was to seek solitude or darkness in the early stages of the disorder, and the few that were muzzled had such violent strength that they tore off the muzzles with their paws. Nature had provided a preliminary period of incubation between the early stages and the complete outburst of the disorder, during which the dog ought to be kept in confinement, and be killed if the rabies became manifest. So the only dogs that were muzzled were the innocent and healthy dogs. He considered the present method of muzzling both injurious to the dogs and inefficient for the purpose of preventing the spread of the disease. The principle upon which he had proceeded in framing his Bill was to place a responsibility upon the owner of the dog, who should have presented to him such a statement of the premonitory symptoms of rabies as were set forth in one of the Orders issued by the Agricultural Department of the Council. In addition to the present register of persons who had paid the dog-tax and obtained a licence, there ought to be a register of the dogs themselves as well as of the owners. When the tax was paid he proposed that there should be given to the owner of the dog a badge bearing a number, which should be placed on the collar of the animal. This number being registered could always be seen, and if a dog was found wandering about in the streets or roads without a collar, it would be *primâ facie* evidence that the animal was ownerless, when it might be taken up by the police. The Bill did not propose to interfere with any of the existing police regulations, but placed it within the power of the authorities to adopt the method of registration he had described and placing the responsibility upon the dog owner as an alternative for the muzzle. This would obviate the great amount of cruelty which was inflicted by the animals having to wear muzzles which did not fit them. A small amount of expense would be thrown upon the costs of the Police, but that would be more than covered by the gain to the Exchequer of the great increase of the Dog Tax, when an obligation had been enforced upon every owner of a dog to obtain a license. It was probable that the tax was not actually received at present from more than half the persons who kept dogs. This Bill was restricted

to the Metropolis, where the most efficient organization of police was found, but it might be afterwards extended all over England.

Bill to amend the Metropolitan Streets Act, 1867, and to provide for the compulsory registration of dogs over the age of six months in the Metropolis—*Presented* The Lord MOUNT-TEMPLE).

THE LORD PRESIDENT OF THE COUNCIL (Viscount CRANBROOK) said, he was very willing that every feasible means whereby a dangerous disease might become less prevalent, if not stamped out altogether, should be adopted, but he was not prepared to admit that the muzzle had been so painful and ineffective as the noble Lord believed. In 1885 rabies rose to so great a height in the Metropolis that one veterinary surgeon alone had no less than 77 cases before him; besides which 28 people died in and close to London from hydrophobia. Now, after the police regulations with regard to the muzzling of dogs, or leading them by a string, were put in force, the number of cases in the Metropolis fell to two, and that, he submitted, was a strong indication that the police rules had done a great deal to mitigate the disease. Rabies being a disease only communicated by saliva, it was a remarkable fact that in certain parts of the country where the people kept fighting dogs the disease was constantly prevalent. Looking abroad he found that in Berlin rabies and hydrophobia formerly prevailed to a very great extent, and for nine years the whole of the dogs in the City were put in muzzles, and so rigidly was the law carried into effect that during the whole of that period not one human being was attacked by hydrophobia. Nor did he believe himself that the muzzle was injurious to the dog. At the present moment there was the remarkable case of the deer in Richmond Park, among which rabies had broken out. That outbreak must be due to some afflicted dog having bitten one or more deer, these in turn communicating the malady by the saliva from one to another, because they might be seen tearing their own flesh, the others then coming and licking the place where the flesh had been torn away, the result being that a number of the deer had had to be put to death, and the others put under control lest the disease should spread. He would not seek to interfere with the noble Lord laying his Bill on the Table, because he would be glad to have advantage taken of every method by which this painful disease might be prevented. The whole subject was one in which the more they could come to accurate conclusions the better; but he was sure, from the reports made to him, that the best authorities were strongly of opinion that the disease might be stamped out altogether by a system of muzzling being universally adopted and carried out for a sufficient length of time.

The Earl of KIMBERLEY said, that he was not an enemy of dogs, but he was a greater friend of men, and he agreed with the noble Viscount that there was no real objection to the use of the muzzle. He could not understand why people allowed their fondness for their dogs to go so far that, because of the suffering which they said was inflicted on dogs by muzzling, they were prepared to run the frightful risk of spreading the disease or, at least, of preventing its mitigation. He was thoroughly convinced from what he had heard that if proper precautions were taken for a sufficient time we should practically get rid of the disease. Even taking the lowest ground, the consequence of such steps would be that they would relieve the whole dog race from a frightful torture. He hoped that both in the Metropolis and throughout the country the authorities would not be deterred by the outcry of those who did not like to see their pet dogs in what they considered a painful position from carrying out such regulations.

Bill read 1ª. (No. 73.)

FRIENDLY SOCIETIES—THE INDEPENDENT MUTUAL BRETHREN FRIENDLY SOCIETY—REPORT OF THE CHIEF REGISTRAR.

OBSERVATIONS.

The Duke of MARLBOROUGH said, he rose to call the attention of the Lord Chancellor to the Report made to the Chief Registrar of Friendly Societies in the case of the "Independent Mutual Brethren Friendly Society," containing grave charges of misapplication of the Society's funds on the part of the persons mentioned in the Report, which Report had been laid on the Table of that House, and had been the subject of much comment in the public Press;

and to ask his Lordship whether he intended to take any action in the matter, with the view of having such charges investigated; and whether the Public Prosecutor had been instructed to take the necessary steps to have the parties implicated brought to justice; and, secondly, whether Her Majesty's Government intended to bring in a Bill for the more effectual prevention of such practices in future, and for the protection of provident people of the working class and their widows and orphans from similar frauds. He was glad to see that the Chancellor of the Exchequer the other night had stated that it was the desire of Her Majesty's Government to deal with this question. There was nothing more remarkable at the present time than the fact that the principle of thrift and economy was growing very largely among the people of this country, as shown by the spread of friendly societies in the last few years, and the enormous sums invested in the Post Office and other savings banks. As Her Majesty's Government had undertaken grave and important functions, it was, therefore, more necessary that these matters of private enterprize should be controlled by the action of the Legislature. He wished to call their Lordships' attention to one fact in the Report made in 1885 with regard to the society to which he had alluded. The Trustees had already been prosecuted by the Registrar-General for not fulfilling the conditions laid down by the Act of Parliament. The Registrar General had informed him that these were matters of perpetual occurrence. The large Friendly Insurance Companies were governed by an Act of Parliament which gave the Registrar General no control over them. An Insurance Company, which was really composed of a small body of Directors, and which had intrusted to it such enormous sums derived from a number of small subscriptions, was an institution which ought to be rigidly controlled by Parliament. Year after year these poor persons who had set aside their savings had done so by depriving themselves of certain pleasures, and, after years of saving, they were liable to see this fund lost through the rascality or improvidence of others.

Lord GREVILLE said, the noble and learned Lord on the Woolsack would confer a great benefit on the poor, if by legislation he could protect them against the dishonest practices of which they were now frequently the victims.

THE LORD CHANCELLOR (Lord HALSBURY) said, he did not think that the noble Duke had at all exaggerated the importance of this subject. The difficulty of legislation on such a point, however, was that there was a desire to leave something to the independent action of these societies, to permit them to establish themselves in a way conformable to their own wishes, subject to what might be called State control to prevent fraudulent practices. It might be —he did not say that it was so—that the State control was not sufficiently strong to accomplish that object; but it would be very undesirable to take away from those societies all control over themselves. With regard to the particular case to which the noble Duke had called attention, he hoped he would be excused if he refrained from referring to its particulars, as the matter was now before the Public Prosecutor, and it would, therefore, not be desirable or right for him to discuss the case. It certainly was a very sad one, and, whatever the legal result of the investigation now proceeding might be, he might say that if the state of the law were such that such practices as these were beyond its reach, then the state of the law urgently demanded reform.

RAILWAY AND CANAL TRAFFIC BILL.
(The Lord Stanley of Preston.)

(NO. 60.) REPORT.

Amendment *reported* (according to Order).

Clause 5 (Sittings of Commissioners).

On the Motion of The Lord STANLEY of PRESTON, the following Amendment made:—

In clause 5, page 3, line 6, at end of clause, insert as a fresh sub-section—"If the President of the Board of Trade is satisfied either of the inability of an appointed Commissioner to attend at the hearing of any case, or of there being a vacancy in the office, and in either case of the necessity of a speedy hearing of the case, he may appoint a temporary Commissioner to hear such case, and such Commissioner, for all purposes connected with such case, shall, until the final determination thereof, have the same jurisdiction and powers as if he were an appointed Commissioner. A temporary Commissioner shall be paid such sum by the Commissioner so unable to sit, or, if the office is vacant, out of the salary of the office, as the President of the Board of Trade may assign."

Lord Greville

On the Motion of The Lord STANLEY of PRESTON, the following Amendment made:—After clause 5 insert—

(Appointment of additional judge.)

"It shall be lawful for Her Majesty, having regard to the business required by this Act to be transacted by the ex officio Commissioners, and to the proper transaction of the business of the superior court in England, to appoint an additional judge of such court, and from time to time to fill any vacancy in such judgeship, and the law relating to the appointment and qualification of the judges of such superior court to their duties and tenure of office, to their precedence, salary, and pension, and otherwise, shall apply to any judge so appointed under this section, and a judge so appointed under this section shall be attached to such division or branch of the court as Her Majesty may direct, subject to such power of transfer as may exist in the case of any other judge of such division or branch."

Clause 15 (Appeals on certain questions to superior court of appeal).

LORD GRIMTHORPE moved an Amendment with the object of allowing appeals from the decisions of the Commissioners upon questions of fact. He argued that one could never make sure that on a first hearing the full merits of a case would be understood. When the point had been raised in Committee, he was told that Railway Companies were monopolists and rich and that their opponents would be poor. He could not, however, admit that this was a true view of the case.

Amendment *moved*, in page 6, lines 1 and 2, to leave out the words (" upon a question of fact or.")—(*The Lord Grimthorpe.*)

THE LORD CHANCELLOR (Lord HALSBURY) said, that matters of fact were usually decided by a jury or an inferior Court, unless they had reason to believe there was a miscarriage of justice. The general principle of law was that upon questions of fact there ought to be no appeal.

On Question, That the words proposed to be left out stand part of the Bill? Their Lordships *divided*:—Contents 36; Not-Contents 14: Majority 22.

Resolved in the *negative*.

On the Motion of The Lord STANLEY of PRESTON, the following Amendment made:—

In page 6, line 11, after (" may ") insert (" draw all such inferences as are not inconsistent with the facts expressly found, and are necessary for determining the question of law, and have all such powers for that purpose as if the appeal were an appeal from a judgment of a superior court ").

PART II.—TRAFFIC.

THE EARL OF CRAWFORD, in moving that the following clause be inserted as the first of the Traffic Clauses:—

"The maximum toll, rate, or charge contained in every existing Act of Parliament relating to railways and canals in the United Kingdom shall include the charges for station accommodation, use of sidings, and wharves; and no railway or canal company shall be entitled to make any additional charges therefor, excepting in all cases where a specific charge in respect of such matters, or either of them, is expressly authorised by such existing railway or canal Act,"

said, as representing the traders, they did not much object to all terminal charges, as some of them were fair; but those were protected in the latter part of his clause. At the present hour the Railway Companies could erect a large station and apportion the price of the station over the traffic, so as to pay the interest on the outlay upon the station. The traders objected to this. No such power was contemplated in the earlier Acts of Parliament. It was never intended that they should charge, not only for the line, but also for the stations. It was not so many years ago that terminal charges were unknown in this country. The idea of the charges came from America, where the Companies merely constructed an iron road, and then built the stations as private speculations, recouping themselves for their outlay by terminal charges. At a comparatively recent date the practice of terminal charges was introduced into this country. He had considerably modified his former proposal, yielding largely to the Railway Companies, and hoped that his clause, as amended, might be accepted by Her Majesty's Government.

Amendment *moved*,

In page 7, line 26, after ("Part II.— Traffic.") insert new clause—"The maximum toll, rate, or charge contained in every existing Act of Parliament relating to railways and canals in the United Kingdom shall include the charges for station accommodation, use of sidings, and wharves; and no railway or canal company shall be entitled to make any additional charges therefor, excepting in all cases where a specific charge in respect of such matters, or either of them, is expressly authorised by such existing railway or canal Act."—(*The Earl of Crawford*.)

LORD BRAMWELL said, he did not object to the clause, but thought the first portion of it was unnecessary, inasmuch as under the existing law a Railway Company could not make terminal charges unless it were empowered to do so by a special Statute.

LORD HENNIKER said, that he thought the noble and learned Lord (Lord Bramwell) was wrong on this point to some extent. No doubt the law had always been laid down as he had said—namely, that maximum rates included terminals. This, however, had all been reversed by a recent case—Hall's case—and the law was now in a very unsatisfactory condition. The decision in this case was not really on the merits, but as to whether an appeal would lie from the Divisional Court. By an accident, the Railway Commissioners were the only inferior Court from which an appeal to the highest Court did not lie; and so the judicial decisions and the law, as established for many years, was reversed on a technical point. He was of opinion, therefore, that the present position of the question was most unsatisfactory, and that, as the present law was by no means clear on the subject, this clause ought to be added to the Bill.

LORD GRIMTHORPE remarked, that some Companies had the power to charge terminals while others had not, and where they had the power they ought to keep it.

THE PRESIDENT OF THE BOARD OF TRADE (Lord STANLEY of PRESTON) said, he could not accept the clause which the noble Earl proposed to introduce. A change had taken place since the first days of railways. It was at first supposed that Railway Companies were merely owners of the way; but they became carriers, and then other duties were assumed by them. Having pointed out other considerations, they finally said that whatever was necessary for the use of the Railway as carriers should be covered by the carriage rate, and whatever fell within the exception might be the subject of special charge. If Railway Companies provided accommodation of a character or extent far beyond that required for the actual traffic, then the terminal charges were not to be considered with reference to the cost, but with reference to the accommodation really necessary. The question of terminal charges was to be considered by the Railway Companies in framing their schedules, which they would have to submit to the Board of Trade; the parties would be heard on both sides, and he believed that in many cases perfectly fair arrangements would be come to. Those schedules and rates would be embodied in Bills which would come before Parliament in the usual manner, and in dealing with which the fullest opportunity of being heard would be afforded to the parties. He hoped his noble Friend would not press his Amendment, which he could not assent to.

Amendment *negatived*.

Clause 22 (Revised classification of traffic, and schedule of rates).

On the Motion of The Lord STANLEY of PRESTON, the following Amendment made:—

In page 7, line 35, at end of line insert ("In the determination of terminal charges of any railway company regard shall be had only to the expenditure reasonably necessary to provide the accommodation in respect of which such charges are made, irrespective of the outlay which may have been actually incurred by the railway company in providing that accommodation").

Clause 23 (Undue preference in case of unequal rates and charges, and unequal service performed).

THE EARL OF JERSEY moved, in page 9, line 34, to insert the words "except in the case of foreign goods." In support of his Amendment, he referred to the differential charges given by the Companies in favour of foreign and colonial beef as against home beef from Liverpool to London. This difference, it was argued, was necessary in order to secure the traffic in the interest of the public; but it was a great hardship that the producers in this country should find themselves placed in competition with foreigners who did not pay the same rates and taxes, and who had frequently a bounty besides. He could not look upon the arrangement in any other light than as unfair preference. It was contrary to the principles of fair trade, if not even contrary to common sense; and it was certainly highly injurious to the home trade. He hoped the noble Lord would have some regard to the interest of the home trade, and not permit the Railway Companies to give this preference to foreigners.

Amendment *moved*, in page 9, line 34, after ("may") to insert ("except in the case of foreign goods").—(*The Earl of Jersey*.)

THE PRIME MINISTER AND SECRETARY OF STATE FOR FOREIGN

Lord Stanley of Preston

AFFAIRS (The Marquess of SALISBURY) said, he could assure his noble Friend that it had been the great object of the Government to mitigate and do away with the grievances to which he had called attention. They had taken great pains in the wording of this clause, and they certainly thought they had attained the result at which his noble Friend aimed in the Amendment he had proposed. He did not in the least differ from the noble Lord in the inference he drew from the illustration he had given. He thought great injury had been done to British trade in various articles by the inequality of railway rates. But he wished to call the noble Lord's attention to some words at the end of the clause, which appeared to him to make all the difference. The noble Lord would observe that the wording of the clause was this—that if there was a difference in the treatment of British goods or foreign goods, which was the case submitted by the noble Lord, the burden of proof would be on the Railway Company to show that no undue preference existed, and they were to be allowed to show that an undue preference did not exist. In certain cases—and this was what his noble Friend objected to—where this lower charge and difference of treatment were necessary for the security of the traffic in respect of which they were given, it might not be an undue preference. He wanted his noble Friend to observe that there were two most important qualifications which, it seemed to him, would utterly prevent the occurrence of those cases to which the noble Earl had very justly taken objection. There were two safeguards in the clause; in the first place, the Commissioners were only to do this so far as they thought reasonable, and then the larger one, that the Railway Company might only do it to secure the traffic in the interests of the public. They could not do it merely to swell their own receipts and make their dividends larger; they must show that there was a distinct public interest in carrying traffic from, say, Liverpool to London by rail instead of by sea. He hoped the noble Lord would not press his Amendment, because if consumers once got the idea that, in consequence of legislation which they considered in favour of the agricultural interest, wheat was made dearer, they would find such a state of things as would be very difficult to cope with. What they desired was fairplay for the British producer, without any suspicion that they were asking for Protection. There were many people ready enough to fix that stigma upon them. By the noble Lord's Amendment foreign goods were to be placed on a distinctly lower level than home goods.

THE EARL OF JERSEY : No ; on the same level.

THE MARQUESS OF SALISBURY : No, no. There was a special provision given in the case of home goods, which the noble Lord struck out in the case of foreign goods. It would be impossible, with those words, to disclaim the repeated charge of Protection which would be infallibly made against them. He would make no promise; but the Government were very much disposed to see whether they could not, in the Amendment of the noble and learned Lord (the Earl of Selborne), find some further security for the grievance complained of by his noble Friend. If any further security could be got, it must be through some legislation of the kind. He earnestly hoped the noble Lord would not stamp the Bill with the opprobrium of Protection by moving the insertion of his Amendment.

THE EARL OF JERSEY said, he disclaimed any idea of Protection, but only desired to point out that at present American and other foreign goods were placed on the English market on more favourable terms than those of the English producer.

LORD BRAMWELL said, the only effect of putting higher rates on foreign goods would be that they would come by sea to London at higher cost, and the price of meat to the consuming classes in London would be higher than it was now. Railway Companies did not charge those rates out of any love for foreigners, but because they were the best rates they could get without driving the trade from Liverpool to London. To adopt the clause would be as much Protection as possibly could be. What right has Parliament to take away this right from Railway Companies without compensation ?

THE EARL OF CAMPERDOWN did not agree with the noble and learned Lord who had just sat down. He hoped this matter would go to a Division.

EARL FORTESCUE said, the noble and learned Lord had conclusively shown that, owing to the preferential rates accorded by the Railway Companies to foreign produce, the price was artificially brought down below that at which that produce could be profitably conveyed by sea to the port of sale. These preferential rates constituted a practical bounty on foreign as against English produce, and were, therefore, in his opinion, distinctly opposed to the principles of Free Trade. We censured foreign Governments for giving bounties to their subjects ; but that was less objectionable than giving bounties, as we thus did, to foreigners.

On Question ? Their Lordships *divided* :—Contents 11 ; Not-Contents 23 : Majority 12.

CONTENTS.

Bath, M.	Ravensworth, E.
Beauchamp, E.	Harlech, L.
Camperdown, E.	Hartismere, L. (*L.*
[*Teller.*]	*Henniker.*)
Fortescue, E.	Sinclair, L.
Jersey, E. [*Teller.*]	Wigan, L. (*E. Crawford and Balcarres.*)
Lindsay, E.	

NOT-CONTENTS.

Halsbury, L. (*L. Chancellor.*)	Elphinstone, L.
	Foxford, L. (*E. Limerick.*) [*Teller.*]
Salisbury, M.	Harris, L.
	Hopetoun, L. (*E.*
Mount Edgcumbe, E.	Hopetoun.)
(*L. Steward.*)	Kintore, L. (*E. Kintore.*) [*Teller.*]
Powis, E.	
Waldegrave, E.	Lyttleton, L.
	Poltimore, L.
Balfour of Burley, L.	Stanley of Preston, L.
Brabourne, L.	Tweeddale, L. (*M. Tweeddale.*)
Bramwell, L.	
Burton, L.	Winmarleigh, L.
Colville of Culross, L.	Wynford, L.
Denman, L.	

Resolved in the *negative*.

On the Motion of The Lord STANLEY of PRESTON, the following Amendment made :—After Clause 23, insert the following Clause :—

(Extension of enactments as to undue preference to goods carried by sea.)

" The provisions of section two of the Railway and Canal Traffic Act, 1854, and of any enactment amending and extending that section, shall apply to traffic by sea in any vessels belonging to or chartered by any railway company, in the same manner and to the like extent as they apply to the land traffic of a railway company."

On the Motion of The Lord STANLEY of PRESTON, the following Amendment made :—In page 10, leave out Clause 25, and insert the following Clause :—

(Classification table to be open for inspection. Copies to be sold.)

" (1.) The book, tables, or other document in use for the time being containing the general classification of merchandise carried by goods train on the railway of any company, shall, during all reasonable hours, be open to the inspection of any person without the payment of any fee at every station at which merchandise is received for conveyance, and the said book, tables, or other document as annually revised shall be kept on sale at the principal office of the company at a price not exceeding one shilling.

"(2.) The company shall within one week after application in writing made to the secretary of any railway company by any person interested in the carriage of any merchandise which have been or are intended to be carried over the railway of such company, render an account to the person so applying in which the charge made or claimed by the company for the carriage of such merchandise shall be divided, and the charge for conveyance over the railway shall be distinguished from the terminal charge (if any), and if any terminal charge is included in such account the nature and detail of the terminal expenses in respect of which it is made shall be specified.

"(3.) Every railway company shall publish at every station at which merchandise is received for conveyance, a notice, in such form as may be from time to time prescribed by the Board of Trade, to the effect that such book, tables, and document touching the classification of merchandise and the rates as they are required by this section and section fourteen of the Regulations of Railways Act, 1873, to keep at that station, are open to public inspection, and that information as to any charge can be obtained by application to the secretary or other officer at the address stated in such notice.

"(4.) Any company failing to comply with the provisions of this section, shall, for each offence, and in the case of a continuing offence for every day during which the offence continues, be liable, on summary conviction, to a penalty not exceeding five pounds."

Bill to be read 3ª on *Thursday* next ; and to be *printed* as amended. (No. 74.)

House adjourned at half past Eight o'clock, to Monday next, a quarter before Eleven o'clock.

HOUSE OF COMMONS,

Friday, 29th April, 1887.

MINUTES.] — PRIVATE BILLS (*by Order*) — Second Reading — Wolverhampton Corporation (No. 2).
Considered as amended—Sutton District Water.
PUBLIC BILLS — *Ordered — First Reading* — Tramways (War Department) * [246].
Second Reading—Incumbents of Benefices Loans Extension Act (1886) Amendment [230];

Private Bill Legislation [107], *debate adjourned.*
Select Committee—Truro Bishopric and ‾ Chapter Acts Amendment * [205] ; Sir John St. Aubyn, Mr. Charles Acland, and Mr. Stuart-Wortley *nominated* Members.
Committee—Criminal Law Amendment (Ireland) [217] [*First Night*]—R.P.
Third Reading — Bankruptcy Offices (Sites) * [243], and *passed.*

PRIVATE BUSINESS.

SUTTON DISTRICT WATER BILL
(*by Order*).

CONSIDERATION.

Bill, as amended, *considered.*

MR. ARTHUR O'CONNOR (Donegal, E.) : If I am in Order, I desire to move, in the temporary absence of the hon. Member for North Camberwell (Mr. Kelly) the new clause which he has placed upon the Paper, and in the drafting of which I may say I have been personally concerned.

MR. SPEAKER : It is not competent for the hon. Gentleman to move a new clause in the absence of the hon. Member in whose name it stands.

GENERAL GOLDSWORTHY (Hammersmith) moved the following new clause : In page 5, after Clause 8, to insert Clause 8a—

(" If authorised capital for any year not raised, the amount may be made up.")

"If in any year or years the Company have not issued capital to the full amount hereinbefore prescribed in relation to such year or years, they may in any subsequent year issue, in addition to the amount prescribed for such year, such amount of capital as shall be sufficient, together with the amount then raised, to produce in manner aforesaid twenty thousand pounds in respect of the first two years following the passing of this Act, and five thousand pounds in respect of every subsequent year then expired : Provided, That the Company shall not in any one year (after the first two years following the passing of this Act) issue any greater amount of capital than shall be sufficient to produce ten thousand pounds."

New Clause,—(*General Goldsworthy,*) —*brought up,* and read the first time.

Motion made, and Question, "That the said Clause be now read a second time," put and *agreed to.*

MR. CUBITT (Surrey, Mid) : I may remind the House that the insertion of this clause was conditional on certain Amendments being inserted on the Motion of the hon. Member for Bermondsey (Mr. Lafone). The hon. Member has not moved those Amendments.

Mr. LAFONE (Southwark, Bermondsey): I am quite prepared to move them.

Mr. SPEAKER: Does the hon. Gentleman propose to move his Amendment in substitution of the new clause which has just been proposed?

Mr. LAFONE: I refer to the Proviso which stands in my name.

The CHAIRMAN of WAYS and MEANS (Mr. COURTNEY) (Cornwall, Bodmin): I understand that this new clause depends upon a certain other thing being done.

Motion and Clause, by leave, *withdrawn.*

Mr. LAFONE (Southwark, Bermondsey): I have now to propose to insert the following Proviso, in page 4, line 3, after "1871" :—

"Provided also, that if the Company, in exercise of the powers conferred upon them under or by virtue of the Act of 1871, or section 12 of "The Waterworks Clauses Act, 1847," abstract, or in any way interfere with, any water now supplying any wells in use, or which would supply any wells sunk before the passing of this Act, but not in use on the premises belonging to the South Metropolitan District Schools, the Company shall be for ever bound to sell all water supplied by them to the said schools at the rate of sevenpence per 1,000 gallons."

I rise with great unwillingness to move the Proviso which stands in my name, because I am aware that it is an unusual step to take. There are, however, very peculiar circumstances connected with the case. I represent the Sutton District School Authorities, and I may say that if the House passes this Bill, in its amended form, those authorities will have to face the prospect of having the water supply, which they now receive from the wells which they have sunk, at great expense, taken from them. This protecting clause will prevent that possibility. They are now using at least 500,000 gallons of water per week, and they have an agreement with the existing Sutton Water Company for a supply of water under certain conditions. They have recently built a new school at Banstead, which is also in the Sutton Water Company's District; but it is necessary to raise the water for the Banstead school to a much higher level than at Sutton, and the expense of doing so is of course increased. I am told, however, that the new supply authorized by this Bill will have to be raised, in certain cases, some 80 or 90 feet higher than the level of Banstead School. Negotiations have been going on for some time, and the Sutton School Authorities have been exceedingly anxious to prevent any discussion in this House. They have, however, found it absolutely necessary to protect the interests of the schools and the children intrusted to their charge by obtaining the insertion of some clause such as that which I have placed on the Paper. The negotiations have proceeded as far as this, that, with the consent of the House, the Water Company are prepared to make an alteration in the clause to provide that they shall be bound to sell for ever the water supplied by them to the South Metropolitan District Schools, at the rate of 7½d. per 1,000 gallons; but we are not satisfied with this. The Company are asking for large concessions, and they are acquiring very largely extended powers for the supply of water all over the district. They propose to take powers which will enable them to draw water from a very wide area, and when their works are completed they will be able to largely increase their supply. We are afraid that when these powers are fully carried out a large portion of our supply will be taken away from us, and that we shall be practically at the mercy of the Sutton Water Works Company. That is a state of things which we have no desire to see brought about, nor do we intend to submit to it quietly. The Company propose to supply us at the same rate as their other customers, but that is not what we want at all. We want a great deal better terms, just as a manufacturer is able to attain better terms in the Metropolitan District. We are quite ready to give the Water Company a fair and reasonable price for the water supplied to us, but nothing more. We are by far the largest consumers of water in this district, and we think that we ought to have special advantages. I have no wish to detain the House, but I think I ought to mention the position in which the managers of this school found themselves placed. They had no idea what the provisions of this Bill were, but as soon as they discovered that the Bill would materially interfere with their rights and privileges, they gave instructions that it should be opposed. Since then they have tried to negotiate outside the House so as to prevent, if possible, any obstruction to the progress of Public Business here. They have, however, found it impossible to come to an amicable settlement, and with the permission of the House I will move this Proviso, merely altering the figure six to seven.

Amendment proposed,

In page 4, line 3, after "1871," insert the words "Provided also, that if the Company, in exercise of the powers conferred upon them under or by virtue of the Act of 1871, or section 12 of 'The Waterworks Clauses Act, 1847,' abstract, or in any way interfere with, any water now supplying any wells in use, or which would supply any wells sunk before the passing of this Act, but not in use on the premises belonging to the South Metropolitan District Schools, the Company shall be for ever bound to sell all water supplied by them to the said schools at the rate of seven pence per 1,000 gallons."—(*Mr. Lafone.*)

Question proposed, "That those words be there inserted."

MR. CUBITT (Surrey, Mid): I am sorry, on the part of the promoters of this Bill to be obliged to oppose the Amendment which is brought forward by my hon. Friend the Member for Bermondsey (Mr. Lafone). I think that hon. Gentlemen who have listened to him will see how highly technical the Amendment is. Whether the rate should be 6*d.* or 7*d.* or any other figure is really not a question which can be entertained by this House. It is altogether a question of evidence, and I am afraid that my hon. Friend and the Sutton District Authorities must suffer for having lost the proper opportunity of going before the Select Committee to whom the Bill was referred. Indeed, I believe that an Amendment of this kind is contrary to the spirit of our Standing Orders. This Bill has been for a long time before the House. It was read a second time before Easter, and an unusual indulgence was given to the opponents who represent the Local Authorities of the district. In the end, however, the Petition against the Bill was withdrawn, and the Bill passed as an unopposed measure, before the Chairman of Committees. That course having been taken, I contend that it is now too late in the day for the hon. Member to come down with a clause of this kind which it is quite impossible to discuss in a full House, seeing that it deals with a considerable amount of technical matter. Let me remind the

Mr. Lafone

House that this Water Company does not supply a small parish, but it includes within the limits of its supply a very extensive district. Hon. Members will therefore see that the question of a remunerative price for supplying certain schools is not one which can be easily decided. I hope that the House will at once reject the Amendment of my hon. Friend.

MR. ARTHUR O'CONNOR (Donegal, E.): It is quite true that this Bill passed as an unopposed Bill before the Chairman of Committees. It is equally true that when the real facts of the case were known to the House, the House readily consented to the re-committal of the Bill in order that its merits should be fully considered. Now, what are the facts in regard to this Bill? The Local Authorities of the district were so far from being fully represented before the Committee, that they were only represented by the Local Board, which consists of 12 members, composed to a considerable extent of persons who have a personal interest in the Water Company. Of the total number there are no less than four whose personal interests are directly opposed to their duty as representatives of the Local Authority. One of them, Mr. Moore, is a Director of the Water Company, and also a member of the Local Board. Three other members of the Local Board were also shareholders in the Company, and I believe it is a fact that they transferred their shares a short time ago in order that they might be able to take part in the matter without rendering themselves liable to penalties hereafter. Under these circumstances, I am afraid that an efficient representation of the views of the local people was practically prevented from being heard before the Committee. In fact, it is pretty plain that the representation before the Select Committee was not what it ought to have been, seeing that the opposition to the Bill was not persisted in. This is all of a piece with previous proceedings. The Company propose to raise extra capital, but their real object is to put money practically into the hands of the shareholders. No body of persons are more interested in this Bill than the District Schools, which are represented by the hon. Member who moved the Amendment. I trust that in coming to a decision, hon. Members will recollect what the past proceedings of this Company had been, and will not be induced to give way to the Water Company, and for the sake of the interests of certain shareholders to sacrifice the interests of the District Schools.

The CHAIRMAN of COMMIT-TEES (Mr. Courtney) (Cornwall, Bodmin): The hon. Member who has just sat down has stated matters which have no relevance to the question now before the House. That question is to insert a proviso requiring that water should be supplied at a fixed rate. I submit that it is impossible for the House to consider any Amendment of that kind. The price to be paid for a water supply by a particular school or by anybody else must depend upon a variety of circumstances which cannot be investigated in a full House. It is impossible for this House to consider Questions of this kind in detail. If they were to do so, they would render the work of our Committees upstairs impossible. No such investigation could be carried on in a full House with any security that adequate justice was being done to the parties. I would, therefore, advise the House to resist the insertion of any Amendment of this kind.

Mr. KELLY (Camberwell, N.): The School Managers are the largest rate-payers of Sutton; but it was scarcely possible for them to expend the heavy sum which would have been necessary if they had opposed this Bill in Committee. The School Authorities only ask that in event of their wells being deprived of water by the operations of the Water Company they should get their own water supply back again at the lowest possible rate. I think that it is a reasonable and a proper thing to ask. The Water Company are to take the water which, at the present moment, is in the possession of the District School Authorities, and all the School Authorities desire is that it shall be sold back to them again at the lowest possible rate.

Question put.

The House *divided:*—Ayes 85; Noes 150: Majority 65.—(Div. List, No. 99.)

Mr. KELLY (Camberwell, N.): There are some Amendments which stand in my name upon the paper, and I am anxious to ascertain from my right hon. Friend the Member for Mid Surrey (Mr. Cubitt) how

far he is disposed to accept them. In order to ascertain that I beg to move in Clause 8, page 5, line 29, to leave out the word "mortgage," and insert the word "mortgages."

Amendment proposed, in Clause 8, page 5, line 29, to leave out the word "mortgage," and insert the word "mortgages."

Question proposed, "That the word 'mortgage' stand part of the Clause."

Mr. CUBITT: I have no objection to the Amendment.

Amendment *agreed to.*

Amendment proposed,

In Clause 8, page 5, line 32, after the word "pounds" insert "nor shall the Company create and issue in any subsequent year any greater amount of mortgages, debenture stock, or preference or ordinary shares or stock than shall be sufficient to produce in the aggregate, including any premium which may be obtained thereon, the sum of five thousand pounds."—(*Mr. Kelly.*)

Question proposed, "That those words be there inserted."

Mr. CUBITT: I was prepared to accept this Amendment, provided the new clause proposed by the hon. Member had been inserted; but that clause has been passed over, and therefore I am afraid I must oppose the Amendment.

Mr. KELLY: May I say that I was prevented from moving the clause which stands in my name simply by a desire to save the time of the House? I understood from my right hon. Friend that if the opponents of the Bill agreed to the insertion of the promoters' clause, he was willing to accept these Amendments. I am afraid that I have now lost the opportunity of moving the new clause which stands in my name; but I am perfectly ready, if it will be in Order, to ask the House to insert that clause.

Mr. COURTNEY: Perhaps I may suggest a way of getting over the difficulty, if any real difficulty exists. The hon. Member for Camberwell proposes to insert a clause, and I understand that the Water Company are willing to assent to its insertion. The difficulty may be got over by moving the clause as a Proviso. If the Amendment is accepted, the hon. Member can then propose as a further Amendment, which would run "provided always, &c."

Mr. KELLY: I understood that my right hon. Friend the Member for Epsom was willing to accept all my Amendments, provided the promoters' new clause were inserted.

Mr. COURTNEY: I appealed to the hon. Member to know whether he was ready to allow this Proviso to be accepted if the new clause were inserted, and I understood him to reply in the affirmative. The two depend upon each other, and can be accepted together.

Mr. KELLY: In order that I may not unnecessarily occupy the time of the House, I may say that I will agree to the proposal of the hon. Member.

Question put, and *agreed to.*

Mr. KELLY moved, in page 5, after Clause 8, to insert Clause A—

"If in any year or years the Company have not issued capital to the full amount hereinbefore prescribed in relation to such year or years, they may in any subsequent year issue, in addition to the amount prescribed for such year, such amount of capital as shall be sufficient, together with the amount then raised, to produce in manner aforesaid twenty thousand pounds in respect of the first two years following the passing of this Act, and five thousand pounds in respect of every subsequent year then expired: Provided, That the Company shall not in any one year (after the first two years following the passing of this Act) issue any greater amount of capital than shall be sufficient to produce ten thousand pounds."

Question, "That those words be there inserted," put, and *agreed to.*

Mr. KELLY moved, in Clause 15, page 7, line 7, to leave out "one hundred," and insert "fifty."

Amendment *agreed to.*

Mr. KELLY moved, in the same clause, line 9, to leave out the words—

"Requiring notice of the amount of such reserved price shall be sent by the Company in a sealed letter to the Board of Trade not less than twenty-four hours before the day of auction or last day for the reception of tenders as the case may be, and such letter may be opened after such day of auction or last day for the reception of tenders, and not sooner, and provided that no priority of tender shall be allowed to any holder of shares or stock in the Company."

Question, "That the words proposed to be left out stand part of the Clause," put, and *negatived.*

Mr. KELLY moved, in Clause 17, line 27, after "advertise," to insert the words—

"With a declaration of the minimum price at which such shares or stocks would be sold."

Question, "That those words be there inserted," put, and *agreed to.*

Bill to be read the third time.

QUESTIONS.

BURIAL ACT — FEES—THE VICAR OF LONG COMPTON.

Mr. COBB (Warwick, S.E., Rugby): asked the Secretary of State for the Home Department, Whether the Rev. Samuel Rogers, the Vicar of Long Compton, in Warwickshire, on 25th January, 1887, refused, shortly before the hour appointed for the funeral, to bury the body of Richard Bateman, a churchman and parishioner, unless extra fees, amounting in the whole to £1 0s. 6d. were previously paid to him; whether, in consequence of the Vicar's conduct, the body was, upon the following day, taken in a farmer's dogcart to Todenham, in Gloucestershire, and there interred by the Vicar of that parish without charging any fee; whether, recently, the same Rev. Samuel Rogers demanded and received from three poor orphan lads 15s. for fees for the burial of their mother; and, whether, under the Burials Acts, the Vicar was justified in demanding such fees before the funeral, or more than the ordinary burial fees; and, if not, whether any communication will be made to the Vicar by the Home Office?

The UNDER SECRETARY of STATE (Mr. STUART-WORTLEY) (Sheffield, Hallam): The Secretary of State has received a letter from the Vicar, who distinctly assures him that he did not refuse to bury the person named; but the wife on being told by the clerk that the usual fees must be paid at the church, of her own accord had the body removed to another church for burial. In the case of the three orphans referred to, no demand whatever was made for fees; but the eldest of them came to the vicarage and paid 15s., of which half was returned to him by the Vicar, who also helped the family in other ways. The Vicar seems to have done nothing that constitutes an infringement of the Burials Acts, nor is it clear that he demanded more than the fees warranted by custom in his parish.

FISHERIES (SCOTLAND)—WHITE HER-
RING FISHERY, WICK AND PUL-
TENEYTOWN.

MR. MACDONALD CAMERON
(Wick, &c.) asked the Lord Advocate,
Whether his attention has been called
to complaints that the Trustees of the
Hemprigg's Estates, and the British
Fishery Society, acting through their
agents, have from time to time prevented
the fishermen of Wick and Pulteneytown
from drying and mending their nets on
and otherwise using the foreshore and
forelands for the space of 100 yards
above the highest high water mark, in
accordance with the rights conferred
upon people engaged in the white herring fishery, by Section 11 of the Act 11
Geo. IV. c. 31; and, whether the Government have considered whether the
Act applies to such cases as these?

THE SOLICITOR GENERAL FOR
SCOTLAND (Mr. J. P. B. ROBERTSON)
(Bute) (who replied) said, the Lord Advocate had been informed by the Chairman of the Carthnenshire Fisherman's
Association that he had attended every
meeting of the association since it was
formed, and that he never heard of any
such complaints as those referred to by
the hon. Member against either the
Hemprigg's Trustees or the British
Fishery Society, or their agents; and
that, so far as the fishermen are concerned, there is no ground for any such
complaint in any action of the above-
named Trustees or Society. The agent
for the Hemprigg's Trustees also informs the Lord Advocate that no such
complaint has ever been made to them.

MR. MACDONALD CAMERON
gave Notice that he would bring in a
Bill to amend the Act of Geo. IV.

LAW AND JUSTICE (SCOTLAND)—SEND-
ING DEEDS FOR ADJUDICATION BY
POST.

MR. J. C. BOLTON (Stirling) asked
the Lord Advocate, Whether he will
arrange that the privilege now enjoyed
by solicitors resident in Glasgow of
sending by post direct to the Solicitor
of the Board of Inland Revenue "deeds
for adjudication," without the intervention of an Edinburgh agent, shall be
extended to solicitors in all other towns
in Scotland?

THE SOLICITOR GENERAL FOR
SCOTLAND (Mr. J. P. B. ROBERTSON)

(Bute) (who replied) said, the privilege
had already been conceded to four other
large towns besides Glasgow; but it
could not be extended to all other towns
in Scotland without an increased cost
for staff. In order to systematize the
arrangement, it was necessary to keep
forms of schedules, &c., in towns where
the concession was made, so as to prevent an undue amount of clerical labour
in Edinburgh. If this were to be applied
to all towns it would entail increased
expense; but if it were shown that any
particular town had a ground for coming
within the arrangement, by reason of
the number of deeds sent up annually
for adjudication, the Board of Inland
Revenue would be glad to consider the
case on a written statement being submitted to them.

MR. J. C. BOLTON asked, if the
privilege would be extended to the town
of Stirling?

MR. J. P. B. ROBERTSON said, he
thought it would be necessary that some
specific application should be made in
order to entitle the authorities to grant
such a request.

BANK OF ENGLAND—THE ISSUE DE-
PARTMENT — THE GOVERNMENT
DEBT.

MR. MACDONALD CAMERON
(Wick, &c.) asked Mr. Chancellor of
the Exchequer, Upon what terms the
debt to the Issue Department of the
Bank of England of £11,015,000 is controlled, and the loss or gain to the Exchequer by its continuance?

THE CHANCELLOR OF THE EXCHE-
QUER (Mr. GOSCHEN) (St. George's,
Hanover Square): I do not quite understand what the hon. Member means
by the word "controlled." If he means
by that on what terms the money is borrowed, it is a permanent 3 per cent loan,
so that, as compared with Consols, there
is neither loss nor gain to the Revenue
by its continuance.

MR. MACDONALD CAMERON:
May I ask what are the terms?

MR. GOSCHEN: Three per cent.

MR. MACDONALD CAMERON:
Why is it?

MR. GOSCHEN: It is by Act of
Parliament, and it is a loan on the same
terms as the general Funded Debt of the
country—namely, 3 per cent; but I understand that if this loan were dealt with,
it would involve dealing with the whole

charter of the Bank of England. The origin of the loan is very complicated; but I shall be glad to give the hon. Member, either publicly or privately, any further information he may desire.

EDUCATION DEPARTMENT(SCOTLAND) —ELECTIONS OF SCHOOL BOARDS— CUMULATIVE VOTING.

MR. SHIRESS WILL (Montrose, &c.) asked the Lord Advocate, Whether, in view of the objection generally entertained in Scotland to the principle of the cumulative method of voting at elections of School Boards, and seeing that the next triennial elections of such boards throughout Scotland will recur next year, the Government will facilitate, so far as in their power, the progress of the School Board Elections (Scotland) Bill, now before the House, by which it is proposed to abolish that method of voting in Scotland; and, whether the Government will themselves introduce a measure with that object?

THE SOLICITOR GENERAL FOR SCOTLAND (Mr. J. P. B. ROBERTSON) (Bute) (who replied) said, the Bill referred to by the hon. Member is not confined to the point of the cumulative method of voting. It is true that some of the points raised in the Bill may be matters of general agreement, and while the Government would be glad to deal with these, they fear that at present it will be difficult to give facilities for passing a Bill affecting the cumulative vote, which has already been under the consideration of, but has not been the subject of a report from, a committee of this House, and regarding which widely different views are held in various quarters.

ARMS (IRELAND) ACT—EMERGENCY CARETAKER.

MR. HAYDEN (Leitrim, S.) asked the Chief Secretary to the Lord Lieutenant of Ireland, Whether an emergency caretaker, named Hebron, in charge of a farm near Athleague, in the County of Roscommon, was convicted at two Petty Sessions Courts recently, at Coolderry, of having arms in a proclaimed district, and of having assaulted the police; and, whether these offences are included in the list of crimes presented to Parliament in support of the Coercion Bill?

THE PARLIAMENTARY UNDER SECRETARY (Colonel KING-HARMAN) (Kent, Isle of Thanet) (who replied) said: Assuming that this Question has reference to the case of Richard Horan, I find that he and his father and brother are caretakers for the landlord of some Boycotted land, and are tenants on the estate, not emergency men. Horan was recently fined for a trifling assault on a constable who was taking from him a gun for which he had no licence. The gun belonged to his brother, who was duly licensed. He was also fined for carrying the gun without a licence. These offences are not included in the Outrage Returns.

THE MAGISTRACY (IRELAND)—CORONER FOR WESTMEATH.

MR. D. SULLIVAN (Westmeath, S.) asked the Chief Secretary to the Lord Lieutenant of Ireland, Whether, on the death Mr. P. Connell, a former Coroner for one of the two Divisions of the County of Westmeath, no appointment of a successor was made; whether, although Mr. Fetherstonhaugh, the other Coroner, has now been dead nearly two months, no writ for the election of a successor to one or both has yet been issued; and, whether it is intended to have a Coroner or Coroners appointed for Westmeath?

THE PARLIAMENTARY UNDER SECRETARY (Colonel KING-HARMAN) (Kent, Isle of Thanet) (who replied) said: On the death of Mr. P. Connell the two Coronerships were united into one, and Mr. Fetherstonhaugh, the then existing Coroner, became Coroner for the whole County of Westmeath. The order of the magistrates which was made in 1878 did not make provision, by some oversight, for future arrangements; and, therefore, it became necessary to go through certain legal preliminaries before the appointment could be made. Those preliminaries are now in course of process, and as soon as they are completed the writ for the new election will be issued.

THE COLONIES—COLONIAL STATISTICS—ANNUAL REPORTS.

COMMANDER BETHELL (York, E.R. Holderness) asked the Secretary of State for the Colonies, Whether, upon further consideration, and having in view the great importance to people in this country of an authentic and easily accessible source of information as to the state and progress of the various Colonies, he would have any objection to requesting the Governors of the self-governing as well as other Colonies to furnish an Annual Report of the countries over which they respectively rule?

THE SECRETARY OF STATE (Sir HENRY HOLLAND) (Hampstead): In the self-governing Colonies the Ministers are responsible for the preparation of the Annual Reports on those Colonies, and it would not be desirable to require the Governors of those Colonies to furnish their own Report in addition. The Colonial Government Reports are very full and able; and although they are too voluminous to reprint here as Parliamentary Papers, a form in which they would not be very accessible to the general public, I will endeavour to make arrangements for placing them as soon as they are received in the Libraries of the Houses of Parliament.

ARMY—THE COMMISSARIAT AND TRANSPORT CORPS.

CAPTAIN M'CALMONT (Antrim, E.) asked the Secretary of State for War, Whether it is true, as stated in several of the Service Journals, that no more Quartermasters are to be appointed in the Commissariat and Transport Corps; and, if so, whether he will, in allotting commissions under the new scheme, consider the claims of many of the conductors, who have rendered long and valuable services, and whose departmental knowledge would thus be of advantage to the State; whether it is intended, under the new scheme, to continue the practice of passing all recruits for the Commissariat through the mounted branch; and, whether he has any information to show that such practice tends to discourage the enlistment of persons best suited for the duties of the department?

THE SECRETARY OF STATE (Mr. E. STANHOPE) (Lincolnshire, Horncastle): Quartermasters will continue to be appointed to the Commissariat and Transport Corps as the demands of the Service require. It is not intended to discontinue the practice of imparting to all recruits some instruction in riding, as occasions constantly arise when the men of the corps are required to be mounted. I may add, however, that the course is by no means severe, and no difficulty is experienced in obtaining recruits for the corps, which is at present above its establishment.

INLAND REVENUE — PAYMENTS TO THE LEGACY AND SUCCESSION DUTY DEPARTMENT.

MR. WINTERBOTHAM (Gloucester, Cirencester) asked the Secretary to the Treasury, Whether it is the fact that while payments to the Legacy and Succession Duty Department at Somerset House are allowed to be made from the country by cheques through the post, yet similar payments due from residents within the Metropolitan Postal District are required to be made by personal attendance at Somerset House; if so, whether he will give the necessary orders to allow the same facilities to all alike of remitting through the post, and put an end to a system which is alleged to entail waste of time to dwellers in the Metropolitan area and to the Controller's Office?

THE SECRETARY (Mr. JACKSON) (Leeds, N.): The facts are as stated. The personal attendance contributes very largely to the expeditious and accurate examination of the accounts; and, taken as a whole, is a convenience both to the Department and to the public, by preventing delay and unnecessary correspondence. I am not prepared, therefore, to recommend an alteration of the system.

INDIA (BENGAL)—MANUFACTURE AND SALE OF STRONG DRINK.

MR. S. SMITH (Flintshire) asked the Under Secretary of State for India, Whether the Government of India intend to grant the prayer in the Petition addressed to them by 4,000 of the inhabitants of Oolooberia, urging that the out still system for the sale of spirits should not be introduced there, on the ground that it has caused "vice, drunkenness, and poverty" wherever established?

THE UNDER SECRETARY OF STATE (Sir JOHN GORST) (Chatham): No information has been received by the Secretary of State that any such Petition has been received by the Government of India.

PRISON REGULATIONS (IRELAND)— THE REV. MATTHEW RYAN.

MR. FINUCANE (Limerick, E.) asked the Chief Secretary to the Lord

Lieutenant of Ireland, If his attention has been directed to a paragraph in *The Freeman's Journal* of last Tuesday, which stated that—

"The Rev. Matthew Ryan was visited on the previous day by his brother and a Mr. Rafferty, Dublin, to whom he presented his photograph, which the Governor of the gaol detained;"

and, whether the Prison Regulations enable a Governor to do this; and, if so, will the Government consider the desirability of relaxing these Rules in the case of first-class misdemeanants?

THE PARLIAMENTARY UNDER SECRETARY (Colonel KING-HARMAN) (Kent, Isle of Thanet) (who replied) said : The ordinary Rules of the Prison were observed on the occasion referred to. It is not intended to make any alterations in those relating to first-class misdemeanants.

MR. T. M. HEALY (Longford, N.): But is the statement true that the photographs were detained?

COLONEL KING-HARMAN : I understand that the Rules of the prison are against any photograph or communication of that nature being passed between prisoners and visitors.

EDUCATION DEPARTMENTS (INDIA)—
DIRECTORSHIPS OF PUBLIC INSTITUTIONS.

SIR ROPER LETHBRIDGE (Kensington, N.), asked the Under Secretary of State for India, Whether the Government of India recognises the preferential claims of officers of the Graded Educational Departments to the appointments of Director of Public Instruction in the various Indian Provincial Administrations; whether, on the occasion of the last vacancy in the Directorship of Public Instruction in the North Western Provinces, a junior covenanted civilian was appointed to the post, in supersession of all the educational officers of the Department; whether Mr. J. C. Nesfield, M.A., of Merton College, Oxford, Inspector of Schools in Oudh, had formerly served with credit as Acting Director of Public Instruction in Burma, and subsequently as Director of Public Instruction in Oudh; whether, on the amalgamation of Oudh with the North Western Provinces, Mr. Nesfield had been reduced from the grade of Director of Public Instruction to that of Inspector of

Mr. Finucane

Schools, for the convenience of the Government; and, whether Mr. Nesfield was one of the educational officers recently superseded; and, if so, for what reason?

THE UNDER SECRETARY OF STATE (Sir JOHN GORST) (Chatham): The facts referred to in the Question are substantially as stated. A discretion is, however given to the Local Government to depart from the general rule when the interests of the Public Service require it; and in the exercise of this discretion Mr. Nesfield and others were passed over.

INDIA (BENGAL)—PAY OF NATIVE OFFICIALS.

SIR ROPER LETHBRIDGE (Kensington, N.) asked the Under Secretary of State for India, Whether the rule that Natives of India, when appointed to posts usually held by Europeans, should draw only two-thirds of the pay of their appointments, has operated in Bengal in such a way as to inflict a pecuniary fine on two Native officers, who have recently been promoted from the subordinate educational service to the superior or graded educational service for exceptional merit and ability; and, with reference to the statement of the late Under Secretary of State on the subject, on the 23rd February, 1886, whether the Government of India has taken any measures to carry out the instructions of the Secretary of State?

THE UNDER SECRETARY OF STATE (Sir JOHN GORST) (Chatham): The Secretary of State is not aware of any specific cases in Bengal where the rule has operated in the manner described. The instructions of the Secretary of State on the subject have been referred by the Government of India to the Public Service Commission.

PARLIAMENTARY ELECTIONS — HABITATION OF THE PRIMROSE LEAGUE, BIRMINGHAM.

MR. P. STANHOPE (Wednesbury) asked the Secretary of State for the Home Department, Whether his attention has been called to the meeting of the Walsall Primrose League on 26th April last, at which statements were authoritatively made by Lady Sawyer, in reference to the Habitation of the Primrose League of the Ladywood District of Birmingham—namely, that—

"In connection with her Habitation there was also a sewing society which made up garments which were distributed to the very poor of the town through the visitors,"

and that, as a consequence,

"this Habitation had been engaged in three contests already, and had been successful in each;"

and, whether, in view of these statements, he will direct inquiries to be made as to the legality of the operations of the Primrose League Habitation of the Ladywood District of Birmingham, in connection with the three elections referred to?

THE UNDER SECRETARY OF STATE (Mr. STUART-WORTLEY) (Sheffield, Hallam) (who replied) said: The Secretary of State has seen no report of the proceedings referred to or of the statements quoted. The Secretary of State does not consider it to be within the province of the Home Department to institute inquiries into alleged malpractices in connection with elections, for which the law provides a sufficient remedy.

PUBLIC BUSINESS—EMPLOYERS' LIABILITY BILL.

MR. BRADLAUGH (Northampton): asked the Secretary of State for the Home Department, When the Employers' Liability Bill, promised by the Government last Session, and again promised this Session, will be introduced; and, what has caused the delay in the introduction?

MR. ARTHUR O'CONNOR (Donegal, E.) asked the Secretary of State for the Home Department, Whether the Government have abandoned their intention to introduce a Bill to amend the Employers' Liability Act; and, if not, on what date he proposes to introduce it; and, how soon the Bill may be expected to be in the hands of Members?

THE UNDER SECRETARY OF STATE (Mr. STUART-WORTLEY) (Sheffield, Hallam) (who replied) said: It is the intention of the Government to introduce an Employers' Liability Bill at the earliest possible date. I hope it will be in the hands of Members in the course of next or the following week. Considering the present state of Public Business no advantage would have been gained by its introduction at an earlier period of the Session.

AGRARIAN OUTRAGES (IRELAND)— THE RETURN.

DR. KENNY (Cork, S.) asked the Chief Secretary to the Lord Lieutenant of Ireland, Whether he will grant the Return as to Agrarian Outrages in Ireland, in the form adopted by the late Mr. Forster in 1881, standing on the Paper for Monday next?

THE PARLIAMENTARY UNDER SECRETARY (Colonel KING-HARMAN) (Kent, Isle of Thanet) (who replied) said: It has been already intimated to the hon. Member that he can have the Return omitting the names of the persons injured.

DR. KENNY: What is the objection to Column 3, which is the only one which would give us any accurate information to enable us to test the Return?

COLONEL KING-HARMAN: The objection is that giving the names of the persons injured would subject them to further molestation.

DR. KENNY: May I ask the right hon. and gallant Gentleman, whether he is of opinion that the danger is greater now than it was in 1880, when Mr. Forster gave these particulars?

MR. SPEAKER: Order, order! That is a matter of opinion, and cannot form the subject of a Question.

MR. T. M. HEALY (Longford, N.): May I ask the right hon. and gallant Gentleman, whether the names were given in the Returns furnished by Mr. Forster and the details of the outrages?

COLONEL KING-HARMAN: In the Returns of Mr. Forster the names were given.

HIGH COURT OF JUSTICE—QUEEN'S BENCH DIVISION—DELAY OF CAUSES.

MR. NORRIS (Tower Hamlets, Limehouse) asked Mr. Attorney General, Whether he can give any reason for the Court presided over by Mr. Justice Grove, in the Queen's Bench Division, not sitting on Wednesday and Thursday the 20th and 21st instant, thus preventing the case of the "Gaslight and Coke Company v. the Vestry of St. George's, Hanover Square," being proceeded with after the first day of hearing, and causing considerable inconvenience as well as pecuniary loss to both parties?

THE ATTORNEY GENERAL (Sir RICHARD WEBSTER) (Isle of Wight):

Tho case referred to in the hon. Member's Question was postponed, because it was necessary to form a special Court to hear a case which had been adjourned from the preceding sittings in consequence of the difficulty of forming the necessary Court. The postponement was unavoidable, and no serious inconvenience was thereby occasioned.

LAW AND JUSTICE (IRELAND)—THE JURY SYSTEM—RETURN OF JURORS AND VOTERS.

MR. T. M. HEALY (Longford, N.) asked the Chief Secretary to the Lord Lieutenant of Ireland, Why the small Return, showing comparatively the number of jurors and voters in each county in Ireland, ordered last month, has not been presented, and if it will be available before the Jury Clauses of the Coercion Bill are likely to come on?

THE PARLIAMENTARY UNDER SECRETARY (Colonel KING-HARMAN) (Kent, Isle of Thanet) (who replied) said: This Return is in course of preparation, and will probably be ready for presentation next week.

MR. DE LISLE (Leicestershire, Mid) asked the Speaker, whether "the Coercion Bill," as given in the Question, was the proper designation of the Bill now before the House?

MR. SPEAKER: The proper and official title ought to have been the Criminal Law Amendment (Ireland) Bill.

An Irish MEMBER: "Coercion Bill!"

MR. SPEAKER: Order!

LOCAL GOVERNMENT (IRELAND) — SUPPLY OF WATER TO RATHMINES.

MR. P. M'DONALD (Sligo, N.) asked the Chief Secretary to the Lord Lieutenant of Ireland, If it is a fact that there is no supply of water through the greater part of Rathmines township except for a few hours in the morning; whether the new waterworks, which were to have been finished a year ago, are still far from completion; and, whether, in consequence, he will, as President of the Local Government Board, order steps to be taken to provide a proper supply of water to the township?

THE PARLIAMENTARY UNDER SECRETARY (Colonel KING-HARMAN) (Kent, Isle of Thanet) (who replied) said: I am informed that an ample supply of the present water is given to

Sir Richard Webster

the township, the quantity considerably exceeding 40 gallons per head per diem of the population. It is expected that the works will be completed this year, while the extended statutable period does not expire until towards the end of the following year. The Local Government Board do not, therefore, consider that there is any necessity for their interference in the matter.

INDIA (MADRAS)—VIOLATION OF THE CIVIL SERVICE COVENANT.

MR. BUCHANAN (Edinburgh, W.) asked the Under Secretary of State for India, Whether he has any information that Mr. C. G. Master, Member of the Council of Madras, was, in 1885 and for several years preceding, proprietor of a tea and cinchona estate at Ootacamund, which was worked by him for commercial purposes, in violation of the Civil Service Covenant; whether Mr. Master is still owner of the estate in question; and, if not, when, and to whom, it was transferred; whether he is aware that Mr. H. E. Stokes, Chief Secretary to the Madras Government, and Mr. J. H. Garstin, Member of the Board of Revenue, Madras, are shareholders in the North Travancore Land Planting and Agricultural Society (Limited); whether the holding of shares in such a Company is a contravention of the Civil Service Covenant, and of the direct instructions of the Secretary of State and Government of India; and, whether the Secretary of State will institute an inquiry into these and other alleged breaches of the Covenant that have recently occurred in the Madras Service?

THE UNDER SECRETARY OF STATE (Sir JOHN GORST) (Chatham): The information in the possession of the Secretary of State is that the land in question consisted of 50 acres appurtenant to Mr. Master's dwelling, partly planted with tea and cinchona trees; that it was not worked for commercial purposes, but that in 1885 a sale of cinchona seedlings was made to Mr. Master's son, which was censured by the Government of India as a trading transaction. The Government of India issued orders in 1885 positively forbidding the cultivation by Government officials, for purposes of profit, of tea and cinchona on lands connected with their dwellings. I do not know whether Mr. Master is still the owner of the land in question.

My answer to the third paragraph is, Yes; but it is not contrary to the rules for a civilian to be a shareholder in such a Company, provided he takes no part in the management. The matters referred to have already been fully inquired into and dealt with by the Government of India and the Secretary of State.

BUSINESS OF THE HOUSE—THE NEW RULES OF PROCEDURE.

MR. BROADHURST (Nottingham, W.) asked the First Lord of the Treasury, Whether he can state to the House when he intends to proceed with the remainder of the Rules of Procedure, or, if he cannot see his way to deal with the whole of them, whether he will press forward the one dealing with the rearrangement of the hours of meeting and rising of the House?

THE FIRST LORD (Mr. W. H. SMITH) (Strand, Westminster) : In the present state of Public Business it is impossible for me to state when the House may resume the consideration of the Rules of Procedure; but with regard to the particular Rule to which the hon. Member refers, I can only say that if it is the general wish of the House that the discussion of the Rule should be taken at a late hour in the evening, and without involving any prolonged debate, I would endeavour to meet the wish of the House, and it would give me great pleasure to do so.

IRISH LAND LAW BILL.

MR. DILLON (Mayo, E.) asked the First Lord of the Treasury, When the Irish Land Law Bill would be put down for Committee in the other House?

THE FIRST LORD (Mr. W. H. SMITH) (Strand, Westminster): I am sorry I have no information on the point; but I will inquire, and inform the hon. Member.

ORDERS OF THE DAY.

——o——

CRIMINAL LAW AMENDMENT (IRELAND) BILL.—[BILL 217.]

(*Mr. A. J. Balfour, Mr. Secretary Matthews, Mr. Attorney General, Mr. Attorney General for Ireland.*)

COMMITTEE.   [FIRST NIGHT.]

Bill *considered* in Committee.

(In the Committee.)

PRELIMINARY INQUIRY.

Clause 1 (Inquiry by order of Attorney General).

MR. MARUM (Kilkenny, N.) : I beg to move, as an Amendment, in the first section, in line 6, to insert after the word "where" the words "grounded upon a sworn information," or the latter word only, in regard to this Amendment. I may say that it formed the subject matter of very considerable discussion in the Grand Committee upon law, which sat some years ago. That was a very strong Committee, and included among its Members the present Lord Chancellors of England and Ireland, the present Solicitor General, Sir Michael Hicks-Beach, &c. After considerable discussion, the Committee determined on inserting these words, and it was the right hon. and learned Gentleman the Member for Bury (Sir Henry James) who proposed that the initiation of proceedings should be upon a sworn information. There are several precedents for the initiation of such proceedings upon a sworn information. I find that the 14 & 15 *Vict.* c. 93 requires a sworn information, and I find, also, that in the Peace Preservation Act of 1870 the initiation is required to be upon sworn information. The Crimes Prevention Act of 1882 likewise puts the initiation of proceedings upon a sworn information ; and, lastly, in the Criminal Law Amendment Bill of 1885, it was likewise required that the initiation should be by sworn information. These appear to me to be important precedents, and the only precedent I can discover for the omission is in the 46th *Vict.* c. 3 (Explosive Substances Act), which was passed at a time when it may be said that we were legislating in a panic. That Act authorizes the proceedings to be taken by the Executive without being initiated by sworn information. That Act, however, was not intended to form part of our permanent legislation ; and I maintain that, as it is intended to make this Bill a portion of the permanent legislation of the country, we ought not to be guided by a precedent which was set in a time of panic. With reference to the person who is to have the initiation of the proceedings, it is put forward here as being the Attorney General—that is to say, the Executive, and not any judicial authority.

That proposal I also consider to be objectionable.

THE CHAIRMAN: Order, order! The hon. and learned Member must confine himself to his Amendment, which only provides that the proceedings shall be grounded upon a sworn information.

MR. MARUM: The matter before the Committee is, I understand, the initiation of the proceedings. It is at present provided that it should be at the instance of the Attorney General, and my objection is that it should be by the Attorney General instead of some judicial authority—namely, a magistrate. As the section stands, a Member of the Executive may come forward and in that way take action without the interposition of any judicial functionary whatever. In point of fact, the Attorney General may proceed to order the magistrates to take such and such steps. Now, I think it altogether undesirable to mix up the judicial with the Executive functions. I do not propose to enter into the whole scope of the section now; but I consider it necessary to point out that this is the first attempt to connect the Executive with the judicial function, and that the Attorney General is to take the initiatory proceeding.

THE CHAIRMAN: Order, order! The hon. and learned Member must confine himself distinctly to the Amendment he is proposing. He is not entitled to enter into a second Amendment, but must confine himself to the one he is moving.

MR. MARUM: Then I beg leave to move the Amendment which stands in my name upon the Paper. It provides that the Attorney General shall only take action upon a sworn information.

Amendment proposed, in page 1, line 6, after "where," insert "grounded upon a sworn information."—(*Mr. Marum.*)

Question proposed, "That those words be there inserted."

THE CHIEF SECRETARY FOR IRELAND (Mr. A. J. BALFOUR) (Manchester, E.): The Government have no objection to the principle of the Amendment proposed by the hon. and learned Gentleman the Member for North Kilkenny (Mr. Marum). The clause, I apprehend, follows closely upon a former precedent. A somewhat similar Amendment has been put down in different forms by several hon. Members, including the

right hon. Gentleman the Member for East Wolverhampton (Mr. Henry H. Fowler), and the hon. and learned Member for Elgin and Nairn (Mr. Anderson). We do not think that the words proposed by the hon. and learned Member for North Kilkenny are the best, and we prefer those which are suggested by the hon. and learned Member for Elgin and Nairn.

MR. MARUM: I have no objection to withdraw the Amendment.

MR. CHANCE (Kilkenny, S.): I do not see how the Amendment of the hon. and learned Member for Elgin and Nairn can be inserted, unless the Amendment of the hon. and learned Member for North Kilkenny is passed in the first instance.

THE CHAIRMAN: Order, order! It is the second Amendment, which stands in the name of the hon. and learned Member for Elgin and Nairn, that is in question.

THE ATTORNEY GENERAL FOR IRELAND (Mr. HOLMES) (Dublin University): The Amendment referred to by my hon. and learned Friend the Member for Elgin and Nairn (Mr. Anderson) is this, to leave out—

"The Attorney General for Ireland believes that any offence to which this section applies has been committed in a proclaimed district,"

with the view of inserting—

"A sworn information has been made that an offence to which this section applies has been committed in a proclaimed district, the Attorney General for Ireland, &c."

That is the Amendment suggested by the hon. and learned Member for Elgin and Nairn, and it is similar to that of the right hon. Gentleman the Member for East Wolverhampton, whose Amendment, however, is of a double character. The right hon. Gentleman proposes to omit the words "where the Attorney General believes that" in order to make the section read—

"Where a sworn information has been made that any offence to which this section applies has been committed in a proclaimed district, he may direct a Resident Magistrate to hold an inquiry," &c.

MR. T. M. HEALY (Longford, N.): Perhaps I may be allowed to make a suggestion. It does appear to me that if we accept these words, they will carry with them a number of other words to which objection is entertained—for instance, the word "offence." The clause, as it stands, is somewhat curiously worded. In the first instance, it speaks of "an offence," and then it goes on to speak of such offence as "a crime," which is absurd. If the Amendment of the hon. and learned Member for Elgin and Nairn (Mr. Anderson) is affirmed as it is proposed, it will carry the words "offence committed in a proclaimed district," and will thereby prevent the discussion from taking place which I desire to raise. I would suggest that the right hon. Gentleman the Chief Secretary for Ireland (Mr. A. J. Balfour) should bring up a Proviso at the end of the clause to provide that this step shall only be taken on a sworn information. The acceptance of the Amendment now would commit the Committee at once to several debatable points. I strongly object to the insertion in the clause of the word "offence" in one part of it, and of "crime" in another, with no words to provide that the offence shall be an indictable offence.

SIR GEORGE CAMPBELL (Kirkcaldy, &c.): This section relates to a preliminary inquiry. The object of it is to enable an inquiry to be held into certain circumstances in order to ascertain whether the offence has been committed or not. A man may say he has been robbed or assaulted, and the question is whether he has been robbed or assaulted at all. This section is only to cover a preliminary investigation in order to ascertain what the facts of the case are.

THE ATTORNEY GENERAL (Sir RICHARD WEBSTER) (Isle of Wight): If the Amendment of the hon. and learned Member for Elgin and Nairn (Mr. Anderson) is carried, it will then be open for any hon. Member to deal with the word "offence" by any other word contained in it. The words which the hon. and learned Member for Elgin and Nairn proposes to substitute for the words—

"The Attorney General for Ireland believes that any offence to which this section applies has been committed in a proclaimed district."

are these—

"Where a sworn information has been made that an offence to which this section applies has been committed in a proclaimed district, the Attorney General for Ireland may direct," &c.

If this Amendment is agreed to, the Committee will then have accepted the principle of the Amendment which stands in the name of the right hon. Member for East Wolverhampton (Mr. Henry H. Fowler). The proceedings are to depend on a sworn information, and the question to which the hon. Member for North Longford (Mr. T. M. Healy) has called attention can then be raised.

THE CHAIRMAN: It could not be raised after the Amendment is carried. The first proposal will be to leave out certain words, and the next proposal will be to insert certain other words. A Motion might then be made to amend the words proposed to be inserted, and in that way the question desired to be raised by the hon. and learned Member for North Longford (Mr. T. M. Healy) could be submitted to the Committee.

MR. ANDERSON (Elgin and Nairn): I think the difficulty could be met by adopting the words I intend to propose in the first instance as an Amendment to the Amendment of the hon. and learned Member for North Kilkenny (Mr. Marum)— namely, to add "that an offence to which this section applies has been committed in a proclaimed district." The Committee could then take up my Amendment which stands No. 2 on the Paper. I propose to move the insertion of these words, if I am in Order in doing so, after the word "where."

THE CHAIRMAN: The question before the Committee at this moment is the Amendment of the hon. and learned Member for North Kilkenny. The hon. and learned Member proposes, as I understand, to move an Amendment to that Amendment. The hon. and learned Member will be perfectly regular in moving his Amendment.

MR. ANDERSON: Then I beg to move the Amendment which stands in my name on the Paper.

Amendment proposed, in page 1, line 6, as an Amendment to Mr. Marum's Amendment, add the words "that an offence to which this section applies has been committed in a proclaimed district."—(*Mr. Anderson.*)

Question proposed, "That the words proposed to be added to the proposed Amendment," be there inserted.

MR. CHANCE: I think a little confusion may arise in regard to this Amendment. The Amendment of the hon. and learned Member for North Kilkenny (Mr. Marum) would make the section read "where grounded upon a sworn in-

[*First Night.*]

formation," and the words of the hon. and learned Member for Elgin and Nairn (Mr. Anderson) would not run after that. I would propose to insert after "where," and before the Amendment of my hon. and learned Friend the Member for North Kilkenny, the word "upon." But it would be necessary for the hon. and learned Member for Elgin and Nairn to withdraw his Amendment in the first instance.

Mr. HENRY H. FOWLER (Wolverhampton, E.): My Amendment, I think, would get rid of both of these difficulties. My Amendment is to leave out the words "the Attorney General believes," and to insert the words "a sworn information has been made." The section would then read—

"Where a sworn information has been made that any offence to which the section applies has been committed," &c.

We should then arrive at the point raised by the hon. and learned Member for North Longford (Mr. T. M. Healy) in the next line.

Mr. A. J. BALFOUR: I think that the course suggested by the right hon. Gentleman would probably be the best.

Mr. ANDERSON: Then I beg to withdraw the Amendment I have proposed to the Amendment of the hon. and learned Member for North Kilkenny.

Amendment, by leave, *withdrawn.*

Mr. MARUM: I also beg to withdraw my Amendment.

Amendment, by leave, *withdrawn.*

Mr. HENRY H. FOWLER: I have now to move, in line 6, after "where," to leave out the words "the Attorney General for Ireland believes," in order to insert the words "a sworn information has been made."

Amendment proposed, in page 1, line 6, after "where," leave out "the Attorney General for Ireland believes."— (*Mr. Henry H. Fowler.*)

Question proposed, "That the words proposed to be left out stand part of the Clause," put, and *negatived.*

Question, "That the words 'a sworn information has been made' be there inserted," put, and *agreed to.*

Mr. T. M. HEALY: I beg to move, as an Amendment, in line 7, to omit the word "offence," and insert the word

"crime." If hon. Members will look at the 11th line, they will find that the words there are "such crime." I think it is altogether objectionable that it should be called an offence in one portion of the section, and a crime in another. More than that, I think the Government ought to make up their mind at this early stage of the Committee's proceedings what it is exactly that is to be inquired into. In all other cases it has been an indictable offence; and I observe that when the Grand Committee on Law and Procedure dealt with the question, Mr. Cecil Raikes and Sir John Gorst—who I presume are the present Members of Her Majesty's Government —took precisely the stand that I am now taking. In the Standing Committee on Law and Procedure, Mr. Raikes, in the case of the Bill of the right hon. and learned Member for Bury (Sir Henry James), thought it should only apply to treason and murder. I think that it is most desirable to fix what the provisions of the Bill are to be. If the Government will omit the word "offence," they can put in "murder" or "manslaughter," or anything else they like. But it seems to me that in this respect we should follow, to some extent, the Crimes Act of 1882.

Amendment proposed, in page 1, line 7, to leave out the word "offence," in order to insert the word "crime."—(*Mr. T. M. Healy.*)

Question proposed, "That the word 'offence' stand part of the Clause."

Mr. HOLMES: I wish to point out that the final paragraph of the clause defines the offences to which the section applies as "felony, misdemeanour, and any offence punishable under this Act." The discussion on the point raised could more conveniently be taken when we reach that part of the clause. I suggest that the most reasonable plan to adopt would be to alter the word "crime" in another part of the clause, and make it "offence."

Sir WILLIAM HARCOURT (Derby): I dare say what the right hon. and learned Gentleman the Attorney General for Ireland (Mr. Holmes) has said is true; but the question as to what crimes this clause may be applied to may be raised later. It is true that there are variations in the language employed— there is sometimes one offence, and

Mr. Chance

sometimes several offences. The offences under this Act may be extremely small, and I think it is very important to follow similar proceedings in the past. The examination provided by the clause should be restricted to crimes such as those at the bottom of page 3—murder or manslaughter, attempt to murder, and aggravated crimes of violence against the person. In other cases the preliminary examination has, I believe, been confined to offences where a man might be arrested without a warrant, and that would clearly exclude altogether such phraseology in this clause as the word "offence." The right hon. and learned Attorney General for Ireland proposes to alter "crime" into "offence," so as to make the section apply to the smallest possible contraventions of the Act. Now, I think if we are to have one particular word in the Act, it ought to be one which would only apply to the worst offences, and in that case the word ought to be "crime."

Mr. T. M. HEALY: I have moved to omit the word "offence;" and as to the suggestion of the right hon. and learned Attorney General for Ireland (Mr. Holmes) that is the very thing I object to. It is one of the drafting tricks which we are accustomed to, but which, I think, ought to be put an end to. Words have been put in to hide what the Government are going to do, until we reach the end of the clause. The draftsman in this case has evidently been on the watch to insure the carrying of the provision before the Committee know what they may have committed themselves to. I want the Committee to understand what it is they are committing themselves to. Let me take the case of unlawful seizure. If my hon. Friend the Member for East Mayo (Mr. Dillon) were to commit that offence after the Act is passed, he could be had up before a magistrate and examined as to the state of his banking account, and asked all sorts of questions in reference to it. What I want to provide is that the clause should only be extended to major offences, such as would be indictable—as crime. If we pass a clause, and allow this principle to be carried, before the Committee have an opportunity of understanding what it is they are doing, having thus agreed to the major part with a light heart, it can be made to apply to the general crimes

under Section 2. I want the Committee to understand, before they proceed further with the clause, what it is to which the Government propose to apply Section 2. This is the proper time for making the Committee clearly comprehend that this iniquitous clause is not to apply to any but major crimes in the Crimes Act. In the Crimes Act of 1882 there were distinct exceptions, and when the Criminal Code Bill was before the Grand Committee on Law and Procedure I find that Mr. Cecil Raikes proposed that there should only be a preliminary inquiry under that Bill with regard to indictable offences. Indeed, Mr. Raikes proposed to omit the words "indictable offences" in order to insert "treason—felony and murder." If the clause is carried, as it now stands, a magistrate may be called upon to make a preliminary investigation into charges affecting the Press. For instance, an objectionable article may have been inserted in *United Ireland* or some other Irish newspaper, and it will be possible to bring every printer's devil before a Resident Magistrate and compel him to give up the entire secrets of the office with the liability of a month's imprisonment if the questions put to him are not answered. The Committee should understand now, before going a step further, what it is that the Government really mean by this clause. Now is the time to decide the question.

Sir RICHARD WEBSTER: The Government have not the smallest objection to the discussion being taken at once. The only question was, whether it would not be better to take it on another clause. For my own part, I think the observations which have been made by the right hon. Member for Derby (Sir William Harcourt) make it necessary that the discussion should be taken now. If we insert the word "crime" we must adhere to the word "crime" throughout, and I would submit to the Committee that "offence" is the proper word to use. I cannot believe that the right hon. Gentleman has risen to express his regret, and to apologize for the Act of 1882, and I may say that this clause is substantially founded on Sub-section 1 of the 16th clause of the Act of 1882. The words of that sub-section are these—

"For the purposes of this section any felony or misdemeanour, or any offence against the

Act, with the exception of offences expressed in Sections 10 and 11, are treated as crimes."

Sections 10 and 11 relate to illegal meetings, and to the arrest of persons found out of doors at night in suspicious circumstances. To every person in a proclaimed district who took part in a riot or unlawful assembly, who took or held forcible possession of a house, or committed an aggravated assault upon a constable, bailiff, process-server, or any other officer of the law in the execution of his duty—to every person who took part in the proceedings of an unlawful association, except those offences which were dealt with in Sections 10 and 11 the inquiry clause was applied. It will thus be seen that the Act of 1882 was made to apply, not only to crimes and misdemeanours, but to various other offences under the Act. I submit to the Committee that it is necessary and wise, for the purpose of a preliminary inquiry, to include offences as well as murder, manslaughter, &c. Her Majesty's Government are strongly of opinion that the proper word to insert in this place is "offence," and if a discussion is to take place at all it had better take place now.

Sir. WILLIAM HARCOURT: It does not appear to me that the analogy between this Bill and the Act of 1882 is well founded—and for two reasons. We are now, first of all, establishing a permanent law, and, therefore, we must look at the law in a different frame of mind and deal with it altogether in a different manner from that in which we might be disposed to deal with a temporary law. We are wholly departing from the principle laid down in the Criminal Code Bill of 1883—namely, that these preliminary examinations should not be applicable except to the graver offences. That is a distinct and fundamental principle. I say nothing on the subject of the Scotch law, because my hon. and learned Friend the Member for Elgin and Nairn (Mr. Anderson) completely smashed up the argument of the hon. and learned Solicitor General for Scotland (Mr. J. P. B. Robertson) the other night on that subject, and proved that this principle, which some hon. Members had assumed to be the every day usage of the Scotch Courts, was, in point of fact, hardly ever employed. You are now going to establish a permanent law for Ireland, and

Sir Richard Webster

yet this is the kind of preliminary examination you propose to enact. It was said the other night that the popular impression in this country is that this is a Bill against crime. Now, the people of this country know what crime is; and by crime they do not mean the small offences which may be disposed of by a magistrate — certainly not such small offences as will fall within the scope of this Bill. If we are to have an inquiry into all these offences, I believe it will be possible to bring up every man in Ireland. The whole population is to be subjected at once to the operation of the Bill, not upon the allegation that some murder, or arson, or burglary, or serious crime has been committed, but upon the assumption that a person may be connected with some combination or other. The Bill is also made applicable to the whole of the Whiteboy Acts under Clause 2; and when hon. Members come to the consideration of those Whiteboy Acts, they will see that they apply to all public meetings. Every one of these Whiteboy Acts give to the magistrate the power of dealing with any public meeting which he chooses to regard as being to the terror of the public. Now, it has been laid down by a very high authority, indeed —which authority was quoted by my right hon. Friend the Member for Newcastle-upon-Tyne (Mr. John Morley)— what a meeting is which is to the terror of the public. Lord Eldon has declared that numbers constitute force, that force constitutes terror, and that terror constitutes illegality. Therefore, a numerous meeting will necessarily be an illegal meeting, and will constitute terror to the public. Therefore, the doctrine of the Government amounts to this—that it is to be at the option of any Resident Magistrate in Ireland to consider every man who attends a public meeting, where there may be no force or intimidation used at all, guilty of attending an illegal meeting—such, for instance, as a meeting in favour of Parliamentary reform, which, under this definition, may be declared by the great lights of the law to be an illegal meeting. Anybody who takes part in such a meeting, either before or after the fact, may be subjected to a criminal examination. This is one of the tests by which the intentions of the Government can be judged. They allege that this is a Bill against serious crime and against serious crime alone, and that it is not aimed at combinations or political meetings. Now, I maintain that, within the purview of this Bill, it will touch all of those things. Therefore, let us come to some clear understanding with the Government whether this preliminary inquiry is to be devoted to a *majora crimina* or not. If the Government say that it is only to be applied to serious crime, then we shall know where we are and what is the value of all the assertions which have been made. That is my first point. But, then, in the Act of 1882, by the 1st sub-section, there was, as the hon. and learned Attorney General (Sir Richard Webster) has mentioned, an exception in Clause 10. That section related to illegal meetings; but the Government make no such exception here. They deal with the whole of the Whiteboy Acts which apply to meetings. Let us know whether or not these examinations are to be applied to what may be alleged to be illegal meetings of every kind all over Ireland. Is every man who may be alleged to have taken part in a public meeting to be liable to be subjected to this preliminary examination, seeing that it will be an offence under this Bill? I maintain that this clause is not in accordance with the Act of 1882, which specially excluded the application of the Act to public meetings. Do the Government accept the proposition that the provisions of the Bill are to be confined to grave crimes?

MR. A. J. BALFOUR: I accept at once the challenge the right hon. Gentleman has thrown down. He tells us that this Bill to begin with is to be treated in a different fashion from his own Bill, because his Bill was an exceptional and temporary Bill, whereas this Bill is to become part of the permanent law of Ireland. The right hon. Gentleman might have remembered that this Bill, so far from applying to all Ireland for all time, is only to be a law for that part of Ireland which, in the opinion of Parliament and of the Government which depends for its existence on Parliament, requires it.

An hon. MEMBER: Not the opinion of Parliament; only that of the Lord Lieutenant.

MR. A. J. BALFOUR: The right hon. Gentleman went on to say that the people of this country are under the impression that this Bill deals with crime, and that by crime is meant serious crime. But if Her Majesty's Government was in fault, the Government of which the right hon. Gentleman was a Member were not less in fault when he brought in the Bill of 1882. His own Bill dealt with crimes quite as trivial as this Bill deals with. The right hon. Gentleman argues that if the word "offence" is retained the preliminary inquiry might apply not only to the *majora crimina*, but to the Whiteboy offences. His own Bill applied to the Whiteboy offences. In Sub-section I of the 16th Section of the Act of 1882, it was stated that offences for the purposes of this section meant any felony or misdemeanour. As a matter of fact, offences under the Whiteboy Acts are at this moment quite apart from this Bill, both felonies and misdemeanours. The right hon. Gentleman should have got up his Irish law before criticizing the Bill. A preliminary inquiry under the Act of 1882 did apply to Whiteboy offences, in horror of which the right hon. Gentleman now holds up his hands. Let me explain, broadly, to the Committee what the opinion of the Government is. We adhere to the word "offence" and object to the substitution of the word "crime," or any limiting word of that kind, because we are clearly of opinion—and in this, I believe, we are following the precedent set by the Government of which the right hon. Gentleman was a Member—that if it be proper and worth while to give the magistrate summary jurisdiction for any species of offence, it is also worth while to give him the necessary power for discovering by whom the offence has been committed. I can perfectly understand hon. Gentlemen thinking that we have included in the Bill a great deal too many offences; but there will be an opportunity of discussing that question in the later stages of the Bill. It will be in the power of any hon. Member to move Amendments as to the Whiteboy Acts. But we cannot withdraw from the broad principle we have laid down, that if it is worth while giving summary jurisdiction to the magistrates for dealing with offences, it is also worth while to give them means for discovering the offenders.

SIR WILLIAM HARCOURT: The clause as it stands will apply to illegal meetings. In the Act of 1882 the application of the power to illegal meetings was excepted, and the question I wish to put to the Chief Secretary is this—Does he mean to apply this preliminary inquiry to illegal meetings which were expressly excepted from the Act of 1882?

MR. A. J. BALFOUR: I think the right hon. Gentleman rests his case on a wrong basis. The Act of 1882 did include illegal meetings under the Whiteboy Acts.

SIR WILLIAM HARCOURT: Clause 10 of that Act excluded illegal meetings; but the right hon. Gentleman makes no exception in the present Bill. The Whiteboy Acts are expressly incorporated in this Bill, and I ask him whether he means to do that which the Act of 1882 did not do—that is, to apply this preliminary examination to illegal meetings?

MR. HOLMES: By our present Bill the Government propose to do precisely what was done with regard to this point by the Act of 1882. It is quite true that in the Act of 1882 there was an exception, and that there is no such clause in the present Bill; but that is because the section to which such exception applied is not to be found in the Bill. As far as I have been able to ascertain, the only provision in the Act of 1882 with regard to public meetings, was a clause which, for the first time, empowered the Lord Lieutenant, if he believed that any public meeting was calculated to endanger the public peace, to proclaim such meeting, and declared that if, after such Proclamation, persons attended such meeting and did not disperse when ordered to, they would be guilty of an offence. There was nothing in either the Whiteboy Acts, nor is there anything in this Bill corresponding to that provision.

SIR WILLIAM HARCOURT: I beg the right hon. and learned Gentleman's pardon; but I think that he misunderstood me. I have here the Whiteboy Acts, and in Clause 7 of the Act, passed in 1775-6, I find these words—

"If any person . . . . wearing any particular badge, dress, or uniform not usually worn by him, her, or them, upon his, her, or their lawful occasions, or assuming any particular name or denomination not usually assumed by His Majesty's subjects upon their lawful occasions, shall rise, assemble, or appear by day or by night to the terror of His Majesty's subjects, every person so offending," &c.

Sir William Harcourt

A meeting under such circumstances is an illegal meeting, or

"If anybody shall incite to any riot, tumultuous meeting, or unlawful combination or confedracy."

That also is an offence under this Bill. Then, again, it is an offence—

"If any person or persons shall knowingly print, write, post, publish, circulate, send or deliver, or cause or procure to be printed, posted, circulated, sent or delivered any notice or message exciting, or tending to incite any riot, tumultuous or unlawful meeting, or assembly, or unlawful combination or confederacy, or threatening any violence, injury, or damage upon any condition, or in any event or otherwise to the person or property real or personal of any person whatever, or demanding any money, arms, weapons or weapon, ammunition, or any other matter or thing whatsoever, or directing or requiring any person to do, or not to do, any act, or to quit the service or employment of any person."

Now, here are three separate classes of offences under the Whiteboy Acts which apply to public meetings, and which will become offences under this clause. The preliminary investigation will apply to all of them. Our proposal in the Act of 1882 was not to apply this preliminary investigation to any offence connected with the holding of a public meeting. No doubt the second clause of the Act provided that if such meeting was held after it had been specifically prohibited, the holding of such meeting or assembly, was to be dealt with as a public offence. There is more than one clause in this Bill which is aimed at public meetings, and I want to know, when we come to deal with that question, how far the right of public meeting is struck at by the Bill. In particular, I want to know at the commencement of the consideration of the clauses of the Bill, whether the Government propose to lay down the principle contained in the Act of 1882, that these preliminary investigations are not to apply to offences connected with public meetings.

MR. HOLMES: The principle laid down by the Act of 1882 was this—that meetings prohibited by the Lord Lieutenant were unlawful. It was then for the first time declared to be the law that if the Lord Lieutenant believed that any meeting was calculated to interfere with or endanger the public peace, he could proclaim it; and if, after such proclamation any person took part in such meeting, he was guilty of an offence.

That was for the first time made law by that Act. There is nothing corresponding to it in any of the Whiteboy Acts, and nothing corresponding to it in the present Bill. It is quite true that the Act of 1882 did not incorporate the Whiteboy Acts. We have no doubt done so, but they were existing at the time the Act of 1882 passed, and there could be a preliminary investigation as to any offence committed against them. Preliminary investigations, as a matter of fact, were held.

MR. T. M. HEALY: When?

MR. HOLMES: In 1882, 1885, and 1886 there were several preliminary investigations under the Whiteboy Acts.

MR. T. M. HEALY: Never.

MR. HOLMES: There is nothing whatever in the Act of 1882 which lays down any principle as to public meetings except that they might be prohibited by proclamation, and that provision is not contained in the present Bill. The right hon. Gentleman the Member for Derby says that it is directed against combinations and associations. I entirely differ from him. I maintain that there were clauses in the Act of 1882 which were directed against associations, and that in this respect the two measures are precisely parallel.

MR. CHANCE: I must express the greatest surprise at the way in which this controversy has been carried on by the occupants of the Treasury Bench. I do not propose to characterize it as I feel inclined to do, because I am afraid that the language I might use would not be considered Parliamentary. The Government say that the preliminary investigation is to be applied in order to discover cases of unlawful assembly, and they add that the Act of of 1882 was just as bad, because the same powers existed under it. But they entirely overlook the fact that Sub-section I. of Clause 16 of the Act of 1882 provides that only felony, murder and misdemeanour shall be inquired into by a preliminary process, and that the holding of public meetings is not made subject to such preliminary investigation. The hon. and learned Gentleman the Attorney General (Sir Richard Webster) has been asked if that is true or not, and he says distinctly and emphatically that it is not true, because if hon. Members will read the section, they will find that there are general words which cover

public meetings. Section 16 of the Act of 1832 gives this power in all cases of misdemeanor. Unlawful assembly is undoubtfully a misdemeanor under the Whiteboy Acts, and if the Section ended there, such power would exist in the case of such of such assemblies; but if hon. Members read to the end of the Section, they will find that the general words are restricted by the exemption contained in Sections 10 and 11 of offences connected with illegal meetings. There may be a distinction between the case of illegal meetings and unlawful assemblies, although what the distinction is I do not know, and I cannot see how any any hon. Member on the Treasury Bench can get up and raise any question as to the extent of the powers conferred upon the Executive by the Act of 1882. The right hon. Gentleman the Chief Secretary for Ireland (Mr. A. J. Balfour) says that this is not to be permanent law, but that it will depend entirely upon the action of the Lord Lieutenant. ~ I congratulate him on his ingenuousness in defending so wide a word as "offence," by telling us that the application of the section is to rest altogether upon the action of the Lord Lieutenant. In point of fact, he asks the House to hand over all its duty in regard to the definition of the law to the Lord Lieutenant of Ireland, and to enable him to say what the cases are in which it shall be applied. I do not understand that this is to be part of the ordinary law of the United Kingdom, or that it is to be applied to England, so that the law in one part of the Kingdom will be altogether different from what it is in another, and the definition of it in Ireland will be left entirely in the hands of the Lord Lieutenant. Now, I hold that it is the duty of Parliament to define the law, and to take care that no judicial weapon shall be used unjustly or unfairly. Nevertheless, we are told in the most common-place language, from the Treasury Bench, that it is almost a virtue on their part to provide that the definition of what the offences are which are to be dealt with by the provisions of this Bill shall altogether depend upon the action of the Lord Lieutenant. The right hon. and learned Attorney General for Ireland, in the remarks he made, did not go through all the provisions of the Act of 1882. If he had done so, he would have found that there are several provisions in this measure which are not at all similar to those in the Act of 1882. He says that offences under the Whiteboy Acts could be made the subject of preliminary investigation. Undoubtedly they could; but what followed? In that case the persons charged with an offence were not sent before two Resident Magistrates, but were to be charged before a jury. There are some other examples. Take the case of conspiracy. One of the sections of this Bill enables a preliminary investigation to take place in a case of constructive criminal conspiracy. Under that Bill it is undoubtedly the fact that what is perfectly lawful for one man to do would become unlawful if two men did it. Under this Bill such an unlawful act is subject to punishment, but before the offence fructifies into a crime, the Lord Lieutenant can put the Act in force in order to discover the secret minds of the two men. Having tortured them, and compelled their wives and children to criminate them, the Government can then proceed against them for criminal conspiracy before two Resident Magistrates. On this point, I have another reason why the word "offence" should not be retained in the clause. The preliminary investigation may be used not only against the prisoner charged with the offence, but also against a witness. If the witness happens to go back on what he may have previously said, it is possible for the prosecuting counsel to produce his depositions, to confront the witness with them, and to make use of them in cross-examination. There was one occasion, in Cork, before Judge O'Brien, when a man was absolutely convicted upon depositions used in that way.

Mr. HOLMES: I can assure the hon. Gentleman that that will not be the fact. This legislation would never be used at any time for such a purpose.

Mr. CHANCE: But it can be used for the purpose of cross-examination; and I defy the right hon. and learned Gentleman to say that under this section, as it is now drawn, a statement made by a witness may not be used against such witness to cross-examine him in order to show that he is going back on his own evidence. I say, most respectfully, that I do not care one straw what the intentions of the Government may be, because I feel that their intentions will be of no account in the

case of a man being brought up and treated to six months with hard labour. I could give plenty of reasons to show that the word "offence" is a most improper one to use in the section. Agreement to demand a certain abatement of rent would, under this Bill, be held to be a criminal conspiracy. A landlord could go up to Dublin Castle with certain depositions in his pocket, and he would produce pretty good evidence that there must have been some agreement between his tenants to demand an abatement of rent. Thereupon the Government would send down some gentleman to inquire into the facts of the case, and all these proceedings may be utilized against tenants in bankruptcy. I am told that a great question of principle is to be settled here. I distinctly deny it; and whether the word "offence" is inserted in the clause or not, I am afraid that when we come to the end of the section we may find that the term is used in a still more objectionable manner.

Mr. R. T. REID (Dumfries, &c.): I do not think the argument, whether a provision of this nature was inserted in the Act of 1882 or not, has really anything to do with the question. If it was an error to insert it in that Act that is certainly a reason why we should not repeat the error now. The point seems to me to be that you are giving this power of inquisition in regard to all offences under the Act. This measure applies to offences on an unprecedented scale. The 1st sub-section of the 2nd clause provides—

"Any person who shall take part in any criminal conspiracy to compel or induce any person or persons either not to fulfil his or their legal obligations, or not to let, hire, use, or occupy any land, or not to deal with, work for, or hire any person or persons in the ordinary course of trade, business, or occupation; or to interfere with the administration of the law,"

may be precluded in any district which the Lord Lieutenant may have thought proper to proclaim. That is simply a renewal of the inquisition in a most formidable form. I can quite understand putting down crime where something serious has been done, and I can perfectly understand that it may be desirable to get at the root of a criminal conspiracy, but to enact the power of making an inquisition into matters of this kind is to place the most unlimited

Mr. Chance

powers and authority in the hands of the Executive Government.

SIR GEORGE CAMPBELL: It seems to me that this clause 1, if properly used and limited, is a most excellent clause, and I have no desire to see it confined to proclaimed districts. I believe that it is at the present moment the law of Scotland and of India and other countries, and it ought to be the law of all countries. At the same time, the law in Scotland and India is not applied to minor offences, it is applied to major offences only, and not to minor offences. I therefore hope that the Government will impose some reasonable limitations upon it, and will be prepared to specify what the offences are to which it is to be applied. I certainly hope the principle will be adopted that it is to be applied to major offences only.

MR. DILLON (Mayo, E.): We have now got into Committee upon the Bill, and we have not been allowed to be long left in the dark as to the real object of the measure. The Amendment moved by my hon. and learned Friend the Member for North Longford (Mr. T. M. Healy) raises an important and broad principle—one which has been discussed all through the debate—namely, what are the object and purpose of the Bill. We are now led to believe, by the action of the Government, that the putting down of and dealing with crime is not the object of the Bill, but that it is something totally different; and we can now see that the Prime Minister and his view of firm government are to prevail in the policy of the Treasury Bench. Hon. Gentlemen much more learned in the law than I can pretend to be have dealt with the legal aspect of the question; but I wish to draw the attention of the House to a practical view of the matter, and to consider what will probably be the action of the Resident Magistrates in Ireland when they have such powers as this clause proposes to confer on them. It has been stated by a great Statesman that the happiness and contentment of the people will not depend so much on the letter of the law as it does upon the spirit and manner in which the law is enforced. It may be true, and I believe it is true, that with certain modifications the principle of this clause has long been the law of Scotland; but there cannot be the slightest doubt that if the Scotch Law Officers had chosen to abuse the powers intrusted to them the law would soon have become intolerable, and the people of Scotland would not have submitted to it. The law referred to, in Scotland, however, is not to be compared with the power proposed to be given by this clause. I have said that if such powers were placed in the hands of the Scotch Law Officers for any other purpose than detecting major offences, the Scotch people would not tolerate them for a single hour; and the officer who abused the power would be summarily dismissed, because he is responsible to the people. But you have always to remember that you are dealing with an Irish Bill; that you are placing power in the hands of men who hate the Irish people, over whom the people have no control, and who would abuse the powers intrusted to them with absolute impunity, and in spite of the people. On that ground alone the Irish Members are justified in closely scrutinizing the powers proposed to be placed in the hands of the Executive Government, because—as I have pointed out—we have to deal with a body of men who are hostile to the Irish people. We know, from experience, what has been done in the past, and, therefore, we are entitled to ask what is likely to be done under this Bill. It is perfect moonshine to talk to us about such provisions having been contained in the Act of 1882. I believe this Bill is much worse than the Act of 1882, although, at the same time, I admit that the Act of 1882 was exceedingly bad. Indeed, the very men who passed the Act of 1882 are, I believe, prepared to admit now that it was a most severe and improper Act. In a letter written by Sir George Trevelyan, the other day, he states, on the part of those who were principally intrusted with the carrying out of the provisions of that Act, that it was always the desire of the Government to confine its operations to the detection of crime, and not to apply it to political organizations. Nothing can be more intolerable and degrading than the provisions of the present measure; and yet the full power of the measure may be enforced in very trivial cases if the principle be affirmed by leaving in the word "offence," instead of substituting "crime." There is not a single man in Ireland, if he does not happen to be a Conservative in politics, who may not be brought up under this Bill and examined as to every detail of his private life. Can anybody conceive anything more odious or more repugnant to the spirit of English life and English law ? Let me give a case which occurred about three months ago. In the County of Limerick a local bench of magistrates, acting on their own motion, unquestionably broke the law, and going far beyond their powers, sent persons to prison illegally; but they were, unfortunately, too poor to resist the magistrates. The occurrence happened at a place called Drumcolla, and the charge was that a meeting had taken place at a private house which was alleged to be a meeting of the National League, and witnesses were examined as to what took place in that private house. Those who were members of the National League, one and all, refused to give information. I have carefully inquired into the case, and I am perfectly convinced, from the little knowledge of law I possess, that the magistrates had no right to press the matter further. It occurred, however, at the time when the Plan of Campaign had been declared to be illegal. The men who were summoned declined to give evidence on the ground that they might incriminate themselves; but the magistrates committed several of them to gaol, and remanded them time after time because they refused to answer questions, notwithstanding that their ground of refusal was the fear of incriminating themselves. I maintain that in the course they took the magistrates distinctly broke the law ; but the men were too poor to proceed against them. If this Bill becomes law, this power will be exercised all over Ireland. Any policeman may go and swear his belief that there has been an illegal meeting, and that is exactly what will occur if this section is passed. He will go to the nearest magistrate and swear an information. In regard to a private meeting, at which there are one or two priests present, you may have them summoned before a magistrate, together with all the other people who were present, and everybody knows that, whatever criminal Act you may pass, you will not be able to get an Irishman, in such a case, to give you any information whatever. Therefore, you are placing in the hands of the Government the power of putting in force a law which

Mr. Dillon

will practically suspend the Act of Habeas Corpus, because nothing will induce these men to give evidence upon the sworn information of some police constable. You may sweep into prison whole bodies of men whose only crime will be a refusal, as a point of honour, to give evidence. I have not the smallest doubt that will be the operation of the Bill when it becomes an Act, and it is the way in which it will be used if it is not controlled in principle by the insertion of the word "crime." As it stands, it may, for example, be used for imprisoning any number of men for no other reason than refusing to give evidence, or refusing on oath to retail the private conversation which may have taken place around the dinner table. As I have said, you are giving the Government a power tantamount to suspending the Habeas Corpus Act, because this operation can be repeated over and over again, and there is nothing to insure that any man may not be kept in prison for an indefinite time. Under these circumstances, I hope that the Committee will adopt the Amendment.

Mr. BRADLAUGH (Northampton): Unless the Government are very desirous of prolonging the discussion on this Bill, I do not quite understand why they should oppose the Amendment of the hon. and learned Member for North Longford (Mr. T. M. Healy), to leave out the word "offence" and insert "crime." I understood the hon. and learned Gentleman the Attorney General to say that that Amendment will not change the operation of the Bill. If so, why does he exclude it ? If it is not clear to his mind, and he does not agree with it, why should he insert the word "crime" in line 11 of the same clause ? In line 11 the words are not "such offence," but "such crime." How is it that that which is an offence in line 7 becomes crime in line 11 ? Unless there is a different meaning, how is it that the word "offence" becomes "crime" in a subsequent part of the clause ? Why should it not be described as "such offence," if the Government interpret the word "offence" to have the same meaning as "crime?" If both words mean the same thing, what are we fighting about ? Either the contention of the Government is absurd, or they are trying to induce the Committee to vote two different things within the limits of the same clause. I do not presume to have the requisite knowledge to enable me to interpret legal terms in Ireland; but I presume that even in Ireland, language has the same definite meaning as it has in other parts of Her Majesty's Dominions, and if you have in a penal clause an "offence" defined as a "crime" in another part of it, I cannot understand why the Government should object to use the same descriptive words four lines before which they use four lines after. There may be a subtle and hidden meaning in this definition; and, if so, the Committee ought to know what it is. There is evidently a distinction of meaning in the mind of the right hon. and learned Attorney General for Ireland (Mr. Holmes), and I do not think there is any Member of the House who is more capable of discriminating between different words than the right hon. and learned Gentleman. I doubt, however, whether he quite understands the definition he has drawn. I myself would suggest that the word ought to mean crime, and crime of a felonious character. If it is intended to mean something else, the difference should be made very clear. At present it seems to me that the Government are trying to land the Committee in a maze, and unless there is some subtle meaning which has not yet been brought out, I hope the Government, by accepting the Amendment, will prevent the Committee from being engaged in a long and unsatisfactory discussion upon the clause.

MR. A. J. BALFOUR: The hon. Member for Northampton (Mr. Bradlaugh), who has just sat down, has spoken under a misapprehension. The Government are quite ready to admit that the Bill would be much better drafted if the word "offence" were used in line 11 instead of "crime." But we do not admit that there is any distinction to be drawn in law between the word "offence" and the word "crime." The right hon. Gentleman the Member for Derby (Sir William Harcourt) got up very early in the discussion and talked of the vital principle which is here raised, and said it was the business of the Government to declare whether they meant to limit the operation of the section to what he called "graver crimes," or not, I, in the clearest language I could command, said that it was intended to apply the section to every offence that is punishable under

this Bill. Therefore, I deny that there is any obscurity in the policy which the Government have enunciated.

SIR WILLIAM HARCOURT: I should like to know how far the statement of the right hon. Gentleman goes. The title of the Bill is, that it is a Bill to—

"Make better provision for the prevention and punishment of Crime in Ireland, and for other purposes relating thereto."

That is the statement of the object of the Bill which has gone forth to the country. The Committee are now to understand, however, that this is not the intention of the Bill.

MR. A. J. BALFOUR: No.

SIR WILLIAM HARCOURT: The word crime is to be struck out of the Bill on the ground of better drafting. The country, I think, will understand what is meant by the better drafting of the Bill. The Committee are really now getting to the bottom of the Bill. We have had half-a-dozen statements of the object of the Bill. We see now what the Bill is not. It is not a Bill for the punishment of crime; it is a Bill for applying penalties by Resident Magistrates to new offences created by the Bill. Our first Amendment should be in the Preamble of the Bill, because if the word "crime" is to disappear everywhere in the Bill, it ought to disappear in the Preamble. Now that the Committee have got clearly at the hand of the Government, their first proceeding ought to be to make the title of the Bill correspond with its intentions. They ought to say that it is a Bill for summary proceeding by men who are not lawyers, and for inflicting for ever on the whole of the Irish people penalties for certain offences. [*Cries of* "No, no!"] But I say Yes; because you may have every man brought up under this clause, whether he is guilty or not. It applies to every man in Ireland. Every landlord who does not get the whole of his rent can have every one of his tenants brought up before a Resident Magistrate, who may be a half-pay captain, and require the whole of his previous life to be inquired into. We have now got the real meaning of the Bill. Something has been said about the Scotch Law; but I should like to ask the hon. and learned Gentleman the Solicitor General for Scotland (Mr. J. P. B. Robertson) how many instances he has known personally in his experience of the Scotch Law, of a power of this kind being used in Scotland. I have not had much experience of the Scotch Law; but I believe that if an inquiry of this kind were necessary in Scotland, it would be conducted by the Procurator Fiscal, who is a lawyer, before the Sheriff, who is a high judicial officer, and who would only allow questions to be put according to law. That is a very different thing from holding an inquiry before a Resident Magistrate. I think the Committee ought clearly to understand the position to which we have now got. We have got rid of crime altogether in the larger parts of the Bill. It is a Bill for summarily proceeding against everybody who is suspected of knowing something about somebody who will not let, hire, use, or occupy any land. Of course the Committee know what that is meant for. That is the real thumbscrew. It used to be employed in Scotland. I do not know whether the Government propose to re-introduce the ancient method here; but it seems to be the "boot" which is to be applied by the landlords to all the tenants of Ireland. It is the method by which the provisions of the Bill are to be applied, and it is to be applied by all the employers of labour in Ireland to persons who do not come strictly within the definition of the Trades Union Act. Everybody who may be suspected of having made an agreement with anybody else, not to work for, or hire, or purchase from another in the ordinary business of trade, may be summoned before a Resident Magistate and examined. Therefore, this Bill touches the whole population of Ireland—not the criminal population at all, but people in their social relations—who may do anything inconvenient to the landlord class. That is the real meaning of the Bill. And now we come to the fact whether this exceptional preliminary proceeding is to be confined to crime, and we are told, "Oh, dear! not at all." It is to apply to all anti-landlord offences. Those are the things to which it is to be applied. I say that the English people never would have endured such a proposal as that for a single moment. My contention is that this procedure should be strictly limited to offences for which a man could be arrested by warrant, and not to a case where a man is unwilling to continue to farm a particular piece of land at a high rent. The preliminary investigation ought not to affect minor offences, but

Sir William Harcourt

should apply to crime only. It must be clearly understood that it is to be applied to offences which are not included in the Criminal Code, and that it would not be tolerated for a single moment in England.

Mr. ANDERSON: I only desire to say a word on the question upon a point which has already been mentioned. The word "crime" certainly appears to me to be a most important one as it appears in this clause. What I wish particularly to mention is that the power which it is proposed to introduce into the section is alleged to exist in the Scotch Law; and some hon. Members have had circulated among them documents which profess to lay down what the Scotch Law is. I have one from the Patriotic Union, which says, among other things, that this particular section, and other parts of the Bill, are taken from the Scotch Law. Now, Sir, the learned Counsel, who appears to have been consulted by the Patriotic Union, appear to be very much in the dark as to what the Scotch Law on the subject really is. I believe that a power of this kind has not been put in force within the memory of any person practicing at the present moment at the Scotch Bar. I would ask the right hon. and learned Lord Advocate (Mr. J. H. A. Macdonald), or the hon. and learned Solicitor General for Scotland (Mr. J. P. B. Robertson), whether, in his professional experience, he has ever known this power to be put in force with regard to any offences, serious or otherwise. There is no response. I have taken some trouble to inquire into the subject, both by research and by gathering information as to the experience of Scotch lawyers, and I can find no instance recorded in which a power of this kind has been exercised with regard to any class of offence. One of the great objects of our Criminal Procedure is that everything should be public and open; but here we have something which, to my mind, is worse than what we read of in the dark ages. It is certainly as bad as any inquisition. I have heard from the right hon. and learned Gentleman the late Lord Advocate (Mr. J. B. Balfour) that an impression exists in Scotland that there is such a law; but it is only an impression; and lawyers very often get impressions which are very mistaken and erroneous. When you are, in a Committee of the House of

Commons, introducing into the Public Law of Ireland a subject of this serious and inquisitorial character, I think you require something more definite than the mere impression of a right hon. Gentleman, even so eminent as the right hon. and learned Gentleman the Lord Advocate of the late Liberal Government. There is a sort of idea that the power has been put in force in some cases of grave importance — such as treason, murder, or something of that kind. That seems to be the idea; but the opinion is unanimous that, in regard to minor offences, the exercise of such a power is a thing entirely unheard of. Everybody is agreed that any attempt by the Procurator Fiscal or the Sheriff to put such a power in force, except in the case of a crime of the utmost gravity, would not be permitted. Therefore, I think the Committee ought, in regard to this word "offence," to test the question, and let it be understood in the country what the proposal means. I hope it will be made clear and distinct that it is not the law of Scotland. I am quite sure of this—that if you were now to attempt to introduce this proposal into Scotland, and to give the Sheriff or the Procurator Fiscal the power of inquiry in regard to every political agitation, you would have the same difficulty which I imagine you will have in Ireland. You would not be able to manage the people of Scotland, who could not submit to it for a moment. Therefore, I venture to urge upon the Committee that the proposed attempt of the Government to introduce into the Bill a principle which is not to put down crime, but to place it in the power of every Resident Magistrate, assisted by, I presume, the Attorney General for Ireland, whose name is used in the section to conduct a preliminary investigation into offences of a trivial character, is a power which ought not to be placed in the hands of any Government.

MR. T. P. O'CONNOR (Liverpool, Scotland): I regard this Amendment as a test Amendment in every sense of the word. It tests the meaning of the Bill, the intentions of the Government, and the sincerity of some hon. Gentlemen who are called Liberal Unionists on this subject. I think the speech we have just heard throws a flood of light on the whole question. I quite agree with the hon. and learned Gentleman (Mr. Anderson) that there has been no

argument which has done so much for the Bill of the Government as the argument that this clause is only a reproduction of a provision which exists in the Scotch law. Let me make this frank confession to my hon. and learned Friend— that until I heard his speech I was under the impression that this is a power which is used almost every week in Scotland. The intricacies of the law are often trying to an English lawyer; but they are much more intricate to an Irish layman like myself; and I confess that the general impression among Irishmen, and even among Englishmen, has been that whenever a grave crime was committed in Scotland, such as murder or attempt to murder, the ordinary, popular, and usual mode of procedure was a preliminary investigation of this kind to begin with. I now find that I have been labouring under a complete delusion, and that this power has never, within the memory of man, been employed in Scotland at all. I was rather astonished to see the hon. and learned Solicitor General for Scotland (Mr. J. P. B. Robertson) sitting quietly on the Treasury Bench while one of the principal proposals of the Government for the support of the Bill was being removed without any attempt to defend it. I was somewhat disappointed at the speech of the hon. Member for Kirkcaldy (Sir George Campbell). Because a particular law happens to be good for Scotland or England it does not necessarily follow that it would be good for Ireland, and that it is not to be inquired into. The excellence of a law depends largely upon the administration of the law, and I implore the Committee, in considering any proposal under this or any other Bill, not to lose sight of the fact that the administration of the law, whether good or bad, in England or Scotland, is subject to the control of public opinion, while in Ireland it is entirely independent of public opinion. I will not go into questions of controversy; but there is this fundamental distinction between Irish administration and English and Scotch administration—that the latter is more or less in sympathy with the people, whereas in Ireland the administrators of the law are not only out of sympathy with the people, but are in a hostile camp. I want to bring home, as clearly as I can to English and Scotch Members, how a law like this will work in Ireland.

Let me take one point. The right hon. Gentleman the Chief Secretary for Ireland (Mr. A. J. Balfour) has several times laid stress upon the fact that this extraordinary law is only to come into operation in districts which have been proclaimed by the Lord Lieutenant. The right hon. Gentleman was perfectly candid in his statement. He is under the impression that this is really an effective and honest safeguard against the abuse of the power. Let me bring to the recollection of the right hon. Gentleman a fact which he must remember if I only jog his memory. My hon. Friend the Member for East Mayo (Mr. Dillon) was imprisoned under Mr. Forster's Coercion Act in 1881. That exceptional law was only applicable to a district which had been proclaimed. We all thought that a district would only be proclaimed when there existed within it a large and widespread amount of crime, which would render it liable to disturbance. But what happened? The City of Dublin was proclaimed. But in the City of Dublin there were no offences against the ordinary law; no agrarian crime existed; and, although there was disturbance going on in several other parts of Ireland, there was none in Dublin. When Mr. Forster was brought face to face with this Proclamation he was perfectly candid and honest in his answer. He said, in the course of debate, that the reason for proclaiming the City of Dublin was that the speeches of my hon. Friend the Member for Tipperary (Mr. Dillon)—for he represented Tipperary then—were delivered mainly in the City of Dublin, and that Dublin had been proclaimed in order to enable him to imprison my hon. Friend. I would ask the right hon. Gentleman if that fact does not effectually dispose of his idea that the necessity of proclaiming a district has anything to do with the wide-reaching application of the Bill? Many allusions have been made to the Crimes Act of 1882. I am not going to be the apologist of that Act. I objected to it strongly, and I opposed its administration strongly after it came into operation. Under that Act there were some gross and terrible cases of hardship and injustice. There was the case of my hon. Friend the Member for Westmeath, now Member for the Harbour Division of Dublin (Mr. T. C. Harrington). My hon. Friend was put in gaol for

having delivered a speech in which he was supposed to have intimidated the tenant farmers of the County of Westmeath, and a few weeks afterwards he was elected as the Representative of the very farmers he was accused of having intimidated. At the same time, I wish to declare that these cases of the employment of the Crimes Act of 1882 for political purposes and against political opponents were isolated cases, and they stand out in bold relief against the shameful abuse of the administration of the Crimes Act of 1882 for other purposes. We have the testimony of Lord Spencer and Sir George Trevelyan, that they were mainly concerned in the administration of that Act, and I have now given you the testimony of an opponent of the Act. Lord Spencer and Sir George Trevelyan are perfectly justified in their claim that the Crimes Act was used against serious crimes, and not against political offences. But we found that juries were unfairly selected, and that verdicts was got in some cases which were not entitled to moral consideration; but our opposition to them did not hurt the course of law and order. That, however, does not alter the fact that the crimes proceeded against under the Crimes Act were crimes of murder, attempt to commit murder, and other grave crimes. Are we to compare the employment of the Crimes Act against a man who is accused of murder with the provisions of a Bill like this, which, by the confession of the Government, is intended to be employed against political opponents and agrarian combinations? [An hon. MEMBER: No.] I am glad that I have got that contradiction. I think it was the hon. and learned Member for North West Ham (Mr. Forrest Fulton) who said "No."

MR. FORREST FULTON (West Ham, N.): The hon. Gentleman is entirely in error; I said nothing.

MR. T. P. O'CONNOR: No; I am told it was the hon. Gentleman the Under Secretary of State for India.

THE UNDER SECRETARY OF STATE FOR INDIA (Sir JOHN GORST) (Chatham): No; I said nothing.

MR. T. P. O'CONNOR: I must say, Mr. Courtney, that this is one of those occasions where silence, like discretion, is the better part of valour. I was saying that there was what almost amounts to a confession on the part of the Govern-

Mr. T. P. O'Connor

ment that the Bill is to be used against political opponents. If the Bill is intended to be directed against crime—such serious and grave crimes as murder and attempt to murder—if it is intended to be used only against crime, why do not the Government accept the Amendment, and insert the word "crime"? Why do they stand by the word "offence?" I will tell the Committee why. It is because it has a wider and broader meaning than the word "crime"—because "offence" implies political action, social action, individual action, and agrarian action; and all those things the Government mean to arm themselves with a perfect armoury of weapons to put down. Let me tell you how this will work. There are two parish priests at present in prison in Ireland—Father Keller and Father Ryan—because they have refused to answer certain questions in the Court of Bankruptcy. Father Keller is in prison now under the jurisdiction of the Judge of a Superior Court in Ireland; but if he had refused to put himself under the jurisdiction of the commonest Resident Magistrate he can be, when this Bill becomes an Act, put in prison by a man who belongs to the most dastardly class who ever coerced, or shamed, or disgraced a country. See how this will work. The 5th subsection of Clause 2 applies the Bill to—

"Any person who, by words or acts, shall incite, solicit, encourage, or persuade any other person to commit any of the offences hereinbefore mentioned."

If I write an article in a newspaper encouraging the tenants of the Marquess of Clanricarde to ask for a reduction of 25 per cent of rent—a much smaller reduction than the Judges of the Land Court have made, for there has been a singular revelation within the last few weeks in this respect—namely, that the Judges of the Land Court in Ireland have more heavily mulcted the landlords than the Plan of Campaign sought to do; but if I, as a writer in a newspaper, write an article to persuade the tenants to ask for a reduction of 25 per cent of rent, I am guilty of an offence under Section 2 of the Bill. I can be hauled before one of these Irish Resident Magistrates, and if I refuse to give evidence I can be sent to prison for month after month for 1 *l.* or 18 months—just as long as the Resident Magistrate

thinks it necessary to keep me in prison for terrorizing Her Majesty's subjects. Nevertheless, the right hon. Gentleman the Chief Secretary has the face to declare that the Bill is not levelled against the combination of tenants to secure abatements of rent. I can only put down the right hon. Gentleman's statement to invincible ignorance. I say that we are now testing the *bona fides* of the Government and of the Liberal Unionists, and not even among our most sanguine anticipations could we have imagined that, as early as the second line of the Bill, the Government would have exposed their whole hand, and shown that this Bill is a great network and machinery for putting down all political combination and all social and agrarian movements.

Mr. J. B. BALFOUR (Clackmannan, &c.): As in the course of this discussion appeals have repeatedly been made as to the law of Scotland, I desire, as a Scotch lawyer, to say a few words as to the practice there. What I have to say, however, is rather of a negative than a positive character. It is that, although I have for a considerable number of years taken part in the administration of the Criminal Law in Scotland, I do not recollect of any case in which the power now in question has been exercised—I mean, of course, the power of putting on oath and examining persons with regard to a crime in respect of which no one had been put under charge. While in the text-books it is stated that that power exists—and I have no reason to doubt that it does exist—the Committee may gather some indication of the manner in which it is viewed by those whose duty it is to administer the Criminal Law of Scotland when I say that I am unable to recall any instance in which, in my experience, it has been exercised. I do not say that in some very grave and exceptional case it might not be right to exercise it; but to make it a normal and ordinary part of the Criminal Law would be wholly contrary to the spirit in which that law is now generally administered. I may add that if it were proposed to extend or apply the exercise of that power to the case of what may be called petty offences, I feel perfectly certain that such a thing would never be assented to by any Lord Advocate, or tolerated in Scotland for a single day. If I am asked as to the manner in which such a power would be exercised, I should find it difficult to give a definite answer, because I have no experience of its having been put in force; but I should say that it would only be exercised subject to careful precautions and safeguards. An inquiry on oath in regard to a crime with which no one was charged would only be held in the presence of a magistrate who was a lawyer, such as the Sheriff; and he would, no doubt, disallow the examination of any person who was not a competent witness, and decline to permit any questions to be put which would not be competent questions in a Court of Law. I cannot imagine, in an investigation of this kind, that there would be greater latitude of inquiry than would be permitted in the case of an ordinary witness in open Court. I may add that there are various provisions in this clause which strike me as open to grave objection. I do not propose to go into any details just now; but one appears to me to be so objectionable that I have put down an Amendment to it. [*Cries of* "Order!"] I am not going to discuss that Amendment now; but I was merely going to indicate the mode in which the provisions of the Bill are proposed to be carried out. Further, the Bill is directed against many things which are not crimes at all. At all events, it is, in my opinion, clear that many of the so-called "offences" specified are not criminal offences according to the law of Scotland. As an example of the objectionable proposals of the Bill, I may mention the one by which it is intended to enact that the usual protection which exists as a safeguard for a witness shall be done away with, and that he is to be called upon to answer questions which may criminate himself. As I have said, there seem to me, and to my hon. and learned Friend near me the Member for the Elgin Burghs (Mr. Asher), that there are a great many things struck at by this Bill which, according to the law of Scotland, would not be crimes at all. I am not going to anticipate the discussion upon Clause 2; but our opinion is clear that many of these things against which that clause is directed would not be even offences in Scotland. Historically, I am unable to find that the power in question has ever been put in force in Scotland, except in the case of crimes of a grave description; at all events, I am sure that it

Mr. J. B. Balfour

would never be used as a means of pursuing what may be termed a fishing inquiry into matters of the character specified in Clause 2—a kind of inquiry which, if permitted, might involve every person in a whole parish or country side being summoned and interrogated on oath in regard to the action of his friends and neighbours in regard to matters not criminal. When you come to such charges as combination, you at once get into a maze from which it is impossible to say that any man can escape, and every man may be examined as a possible witness against his neighbour. I do not believe that in Scotland such a law so administered would ever be tolerated. I owe an apology to the House for speaking somewhat hypothetically in regard to the rules of Scotch law and practice in pursuing inquiries by way of examination on oath where no one has been put under charge; but my justification must be that I am without actual experience of the power in question having been put in practice, although I believe that the power does technically exist.

Dr. COMMINS (Roscommon, S.): Having heard from the highest authority what the law of Scotland is, it is quite as well to see what the law of England is in regard to the words "offence" and "crime" introduced here. They appear to have been introduced in gross ignorance of their meaning. The 1st sub-section of the clause says—

"Where the Attorney General for Ireland believes that any offence to which this section applies has been committed in a proclaimed district, he may direct a resident magistrate to hold an inquiry under this section, and thereupon such resident magistrate may, although no person may be charged before him with the commission of such crime, sit at a police court or petty sessional court-house, or police station, and examine on oath concerning such offence any witness appearing before him, and may take the deposition of such witness; and, if he see cause, may bind such witness by recognizance to appear and give evidence at the next petty sessions, or when called upon, within three months from the date of such recognizances."

Now, there is a well-known A B C book on English law—*Blackstone*—who says of the acts punishable by Criminal Law, that they are divided into two categories—crimes and offences; that crimes are indictable offences only, whereas offences in a broader sense include everything not indictable. There are two technical words which, in a work by one of the highest Constitutional writers on the law, have their true technical meaning given to them. The hon. and learned Gentleman the Attorney General (Sir Richard Webster) argued as though the two words are synonymous, and I am sorry that there should be such gross ignorance. In an Act of Parliament it is probable that the first word used will be held to govern all the rest of the clause; and, therefore, the word "crime," which appears in the section later on, will most likely be interpreted to mean an "offence." In that sense it may be made applicable to the most trivial matters; and let me see what such trivial offences may be. There is "conspiracy to combine" to induce anybody not to fulfil his legal obligations. Whether that is a crime at all I hardly know. It is certainly not a crime under the English law. Nevertheless, it is one of the offences under this Bill. Two persons seen speaking in the street may be suspected by a shopkeeper or a landlord of conspiring to put the Plan of Campaign in force, so far as the landlord is concerned, or to Boycott the shopkeeper. For this offence, of trying to induce any person to do anything contrary to the Act, anyone speaking energetically to a friend may be accused of contemplating Boycotting, and on such an accusation may be subjected to a preliminary examination. The result must be that it will not be safe for two persons to speak together in the street. If they are seen to do so they may be subjected to the proceedings sanctioned by this clause. This, I think, shows the wide scope of the Bill, and how its provisions may be made to apply to the ordinary relations of life. It is not enough to say that such and such is the intention of the framers of the Bill. The intentions of the framers of the Land Act were set at defiance in the famous case of "Adams v. Dunseath." A law must be interpreted according to its words, and not according to the intentions of its promoters. When this Bill is passed it will be all in vain for any person in Ireland to say it was the intention of the Chief Secretary for Ireland and of the right hon. and learned Gentleman who is in charge of the Bill, the Attorney General for Ireland, that the Bill should not be applied to minor offences, but to indictable offences. We

have really nothing to do with the intentions of these right hon. Gentlemen. The word "offence" is a well-known word. An offence is anything punishable by either fine or imprisonment, and the Act must be applied according to the rules governing the administration of law. That would be so if the gentlemen who have to apply the Act were learned in the law, if they were men without prejudice, if they did not now form a portion of the very class who are intended to be armed with this Act as a means of oppressing another class. If it is the intention of the Government that "offence" is only to mean crime which is punishable by indictment, they have absolutely no alternative but to substitute the word "crime" for the word "offence." There is evidence in every line of the Bill of a covert intention on the part of the Government. The Bill is more dangerous than it pretends to be. There is a dagger under the cloak. I ask the Government to remove this impression by expunging the word "offence," and substituting the word which will give effect to what they say is their intention.

MR. T. M. HEALY: I should like to submit a few considerations to the First Lord of the Treasury (Mr. W. H. Smith). The right hon. Gentleman knows a good deal about newspapers and the Law of Libel. Suppose I write an article in a newspaper, and that article is declared, under this sub-section, to be an incitement to crime. The Government will then be entitled to examine everybody in the newspaper office, down to the printer's devil, as to who wrote the article. Of course, all the newspaper *employés* will refuse to answer, and then you will practically stop the issue of the newspaper by the operation of this Bill. There are such things as Smith's bookstalls, through which this article inciting to crime may be circulated. Suppose this Act is made perpetual; that a Liberal Administration come into Office with their views as to how the Act ought to be used; that they summon everybody supposed to be connected with the publication of the article, and examine them as to whether they published it or not; that they get admissions, and use those admissions afterwards for the purpose of an examination before two Resident Magistrates — you may have the entire machinery of the right hon. Gentleman's business dislocated. Is that a reasonable thing?

Mr. JOHNSTON (Belfast, S.) : Is the hon. and learned Gentleman aware that there are none of Smith's bookstalls in Ireland? They belong to Charles Eason and Son.

Mr. T. M. HEALY : I thought the hon. Gentleman would be guilty of some grotesque interruption. I put it to the Government that it is the liability to these acts we object to. They may say, of course, that they do not intend it; but their intentions are nothing to us. There is a landlord in Ireland called Colonel King-Harman; we sometimes hear of him in this House. He meets the landlords in the Kildare Street Club. If a landlord does not get his rent, he may suggest to the right hon. Gentleman the Chief Secretary (Mr. A. J. Balfour)—or to Colonel King-Harman, a gentleman connected with the Irish Government—that it is desirable to hold an inquiry. The magistrate who puts the questions is the judge of whether they are relevant or not. He may ask a witness if his children have got the small-pox, and if he declines to answer he may be sent to prison for contempt of Court. There is no restriction of any kind, sort, or description upon this Bill or its operation. The man who administers the Act is the man who puts it into force. The man who orders the inquiry, along with the Attorney General for Ireland, is the judge of whether the case which is inquired into is a crime or not. Everything depends upon the individual initiative of some gentleman connected with the landlord Administration of Ireland. The Government say—"You had this power in the Crimes Act." I say— "You had nothing of the kind, and if you had, it is one thing to trust a landlord Administration, and another thing to trust a Liberal Administration." As a matter of fact, we did not trust the Liberal Administration, and no taunts thrown from the Benches opposite will affect our movements. If we are between two millstones we are hurt, no matter who grinds them. The point is this — that in the Crimes Act you had nothing of this description. You may have had inquiries into Boycotting and assaults on bailiffs and cases of that kind; but there was nothing about the letting of farms or land, or Whiteboy offences. We are told there

was; but my hon. Friend the Member for South Kilkenny (Mr. Chance) has shown that that was not so. The distinction is to be seen in this way—How did you apply the law when you applied it to yourselves? How did you frame the law when you were making it applicable to the Three Kingdoms? When the Criminal Code Bill was before the Grand Committee in 1883, the right hon. and learned Gentleman the Member for Bury, then Attorney General (Sir Henry James), proposed it should include indictable offences; but Mr. Cecil Raikes, the Postmaster General in Her Majesty's present Administration, was not satisfied to have it confined to indictable offences, but proposed to leave out the words "indictable offences," and insert "treason, treason felony, or murder." If that was good Tory doctrine in 1883, as applied to the three countries, what are we to say now? This is a Bill which may be used by a Liberal as well as a Tory Administration. Hon. Gentlemen opposite think themselves perfectly safe at the present moment; but when a Liberal Government comes in, I shall enjoy what theologians have called morose delectation if I see this Act put into operation against the Party opposite, and Gentlemen connected with the Orange Society and the landlord Party given a little touch of the things to which we have been constantly subjected. And, mind you, that is the mistake you are making. You are legislating for all time. You think you are going to last all time, which, in my opinion, is rather an error, to put it extremely mildly. I put it to the hon. Gentleman (Mr. Johnston) who interrupted me a moment ago, and who blocked the Arms Bill last year, because he thought a Home Rule Government was coming into power, how he would like, under a Liberal Administration, to have his house in Rathmines invaded, himself arrested and dragged before a Petty Sessional Court? This kind of thing may be done if it is suspected that a witness is not going to attend to give evidence. I could suspect the hon. Gentleman (Mr. Johnston) was not going to attend the Court, have him sent to prison, and kept there as long as I liked; he would have to wait my time. This was how matters were worked by men like Plunkett in 1882. I think the English people would be fools to adopt such

Mr. T. M. Healy

a provision as this. What is the effect of this provision? If I were a Resident Magistrate, and I thought certain acts were crimes, I could, by any kind of false representation—by sworn information, for instance—get his permission to hold an inquiry. Sworn informations need not be in writing. Is that so or not? [No reply.] At any rate, there are plenty of sworn informations which are not in writing; the right hon. and learned Gentleman will not deny my statement. Well, I could come to him, possibly when he has left the Kildare Street Club, where he has been cogitating with landlords down the country, and by any kind of false representation get his permission to hold an inquiry, and, of course, as no one would answer, the entire tenantry could be sent to gaol for contempt of Court. You say you are anxious to put down crime. Very well, take care that you get the means of putting down crime. If this clause passes in its present shape, and is thus applicable to small offences, it is very probable the leaders of the people will recommend the people not to answer to any of the summonses. You cannot indict a nation. Your gaols will only hold 5,000 persons. You will have the entire population refusing to give you any assistance. While the discovery of murder and other serious crime is desirable, you will, by the way in which you use this Bill in regard to petty offences, raise such a prejudice that the people will refuse *en masse* to come to Court, and take the alternative of going to prison. What we ask is not very much. We ask that this provision should be limited in its operation. We ask that men should not be asked about things that really do not concern the Government. We ask that petty offences should be excluded from the operation of the Act. We ask you to confine the Act to serious and grave crime, such as murder, manslaughter, maiming, and the like. I can only say of this clause that if you get it without such limitation, you will get a clause which will be able to do serious mischief in the sense of creating dissatisfaction and disaffection, without enabling you to detect and punish crime.

MR. CLANCY (Dublin Co., N.): In debating this question, some hon. Gentlemen seem to have gone on the assumption that the clause now under discussion is borrowed from the law of Scotland. It may appear very presumptuous in an Irishman to interfere with Scotchmen in this matter; but I venture to say a word or two, and if I am wrong I can be corrected. I say that this is not the law of Scotland at all. The law of Scotland is different to this in several important particulars. It is worth while inquiring what these particulars are. In Scotland you must have before you have the secret inquiry—the Star Chamber inquiry, which is proposed by this Bill—a public trial before the Sheriff. That is a most important provision. The Procurator Fiscal in Scotland, on being called upon by any private person——

THE CHAIRMAN: Order, order! The discussion has taken a very wide range; but it is out of Order to enter into the details of the legal procedure in Scotland.

MR. CLANCY: I was naturally led to suppose, from preceding speeches, that I might be allowed to explain that the power given by this clause cannot be exercised in Scotland. I hope some other opportunity will be afforded of showing how the matter really stands. At present I will content myself by deliberately re-asserting that this is not the law of Scotland at all. Now, a remark was made by the right hon. Gentleman the Chief Secretary (Mr. A. J. Balfour) to which attention ought to be drawn. The right hon. Gentleman said a safeguard against the abuse of this power would be found in the fact that the power would be exercised under the supervision of Parliament. Now, if that were the case, there might be some safeguard and some protection for witnesses and accused persons in Ireland; there might be some chance of their being treated justly. But we know very well what will take place. We know well, from actual experience, that when an appeal is made to this House from the authorities in Ireland we shall be denied a hearing, and shall be told that this is no place for reviewing the judgments of the Irish tribunals. This power will not be exercised even by the Lord Lieutenant. Sometimes the Lord Lieutenant may be a person quite incompetent to understand Acts of Parliament. I have only to refer to the present case —the case of the Marquess of Londonderry. Everyone knows that he is something very like a nincompoop——

THE CHAIRMAN: I must ask the hon. Gentleman to respect the dignity of this House.

MR. CLANCY: I will withdraw the expression if you desire it, Mr. Chairman, and say that everyone knows that the Marquess of Londonderry is a man of such meagre intellect that he is not able to write his replies to the addresses presented to him, and that he is not able, and never will be able, to understand an Act of this sort. The result will be that the persons who will practically investigate these charges, in the first instance, will be the political companions of the landlords of Ireland, the intimates and associates of the landlords of the country; such persons, for instance, as the Parliamentary Under Secretary for Ireland, who has the strongest possible reason for thinking that the worst crime that can be committed is to cease paying rent. The Parliamentary Under Secretary for Ireland (Colonel King-Harman) has already suffered by a reduction of rent, effected in the Land Courts, to the extent of 50 per cent; and, therefore, it is not unlikely that when he receives a communication stating that a combination exists against the payment of rent he will be inclined to regard the act of combination as an offence within the meaning of this Act, and he will be backed up by the whole corps of Crown solicitors in every part of Ireland, most of whom are of the landlord class, and all of whom have got into their offices by back-stairs intrigues, exercised by persons of the landlord class. The result will be that the most trivial offences will be regarded as crimes, and prosecuted as such. I say that if this Act were exercised under the supervision of Parliament, or under the supervision of a competent man like Lord Spencer, who had intelligence of his own to apply to these matters, and not under Viceroys like the present Tory Viceroy, we might have some ground to expect that there would be no abuse of these powers. Exercised as these powers will be by landlord understrappers of all sorts and degrees, prejudiced to the last against any combination against landlords, these powers will become an infamous engine of tyranny, and as such ought to be resisted, and will be resisted. No man in Ireland will answer any question put to him on such sub-jects; he will be prepared to go into gaol and stay there as long as necessary rather than submit to "Star Chamber" inquiries directed against acts which are not crimes, and conducted by agents of the Government who are simply partizans of the landlord class.

COLONEL NOLAN (Galway, N.): Mr. Courtney, I think it is agreed on all hands, even by the Government who are bringing in this clause, that what is proposed is a very severe inquisition. At the end of the clause I find that an offence is defined to be a misdemeanour. Everything, therefore, that is a misdemeanour can be brought within the Act, which I maintain is a very severe course of proceeding, and one quite unknown to the English law. I should like to put a few questions to one of the Legal Authorities of the Irish Government. I had intended to put them to the Attorney General for Ireland (Mr. Holmes), but I see he is not in his place. Perhaps the hon. and learned Solicitor General for Ireland (Mr. Gibson) will be kind enough to inform us what are misdemeanours? I have no doubt the hon. and learned Gentleman is quite capable of explaining the law of Ireland; and, therefore, I should be extremely glad if he will give us the benefit of his advice on this subject. Perhaps I may be allowed to help the Solicitor General for Ireland in the matter by suggesting to him a few cases, and asking him whether they are misdemeanours, and whether, consequently, they come under this section of the Bill? Take, for example, poaching. It may be argued that poaching, under any circumstances, is a misdemeanour. My own belief is that some cases of poaching are misdemeanours, and others are not; but I should like a little information upon the point. [*Laughter.*] I see that the hon. Member for South Belfast (Mr. Johnston) smiles. Now, I will mention one subject upon which he is a very good authority—namely, that of fisheries. ["Oh!"] Yes; I had the honour of working with him as a Colleague upon the Fishery Commission, and I must say he was certainly one of the most valuable and able Colleagues I ever had. I would like to ask him whether he considers salmon poaching in any case a misdemeanour; and, if so, are not a large number of people constantly committing a misdemeanour, and would it be wise to apply such stringent provisions as these in such a matter? Then there is the case of cutting sea-weed. I do not say that that ought not to be considered an offence, but it certainly is not that class of offence to which we ought to apply this very severe mode of proceeding. An enormous number of people, probably 200,000 or 300,000, are affected; and, therefore, I should like to know whether the cutting of sea-weed is to be considered a misdemeanour? If so, will this clause be applied to the enormous number of cases of contested rights which are continually occupying the Petty Sessional Courts in the coast districts of Ireland? Again, I should like to ask the Irish Law Officers whether offences against the Excise are misdemeanours—whether all of them, or some of them, are misdemeanours? I should like to know whether the distillation of whisky, without a proper licence, or without the intention of paying duty, is to be considered a misdemeanour? I do not think we want to strengthen the hands of the Excise to that extent; I mean that the House has always, as a rule, kept the police and the jurisdiction of the Courts as much as possible free from the Excise Office. I cannot help thinking that this Act may be availed of by the Excise Authorities, and that a very great evil will result therefrom. The offences against the Excise are extremely numerous. No doubt, the cases of distillation of whisky without licence are the most numerous; but there are many other offences against the Excise, such as not reporting concerning malt, and the other articles which are used in distilleries. These offences may be considered misdemeanours. It is as well we should receive some information upon the point from the Law Officers of the Crown. There are other cases which I know, judging from my Petty Sessional experiences, are of frequent occurrence. I wish to have regard to all offences that come before Petty Sessions, and I want to know can this Act be applied to them? Because, if so, you are instituting an enormous machinery, and very severe machinery, for dealing with the large number of Petty Sessional offences. Let us take, again, offences against the Sunday Closing Act. They are misdemeanours. It may be wrong to sell whisky or beer on Sundays; but I do not think this Act ought to be applied

to such cases. I do not know whether harvesting, or the making of hay on Sunday, is a misdemeanour in Ireland. I should like to get some information on that point from the Irish Law Officers of the Crown; because, if that is a misdemeanour, a very large number of people will be affected. There is one thing which I believe is a misdemeanour in Ireland. I believe it is actually a misdemeanour to celebrate Divine Service in Ireland with locked doors. I have been informed, on very high legal authority, that this is considered a very severe offence in Ireland. It was constituted an offence under some old Act—I do not know whether it is one of the Whiteboy Acts, but I do know it has never been repealed. It is necessary we should know whether this Act is to be put in force against such breaches of the law. These are a very few instances of what may be regarded as misdemeanours. I could, of course, cite many others. For instance, the non-vaccination of a child, the many offences against sanitary law, such even as the non-whitewashing of a house when it has been ordered. These are all matters which ought to be expressly excluded from the operation of this Act. There are cases of driving cattle upon other people's land. These cases are continually cropping up before Petty Sessions. I wish to know if such cases as these are misdemeanours; because, if so, you are putting a totally new class of machinery in force for the offences which I may say are of daily occurrence in Ireland. There are, in fact, an enormous number of misdemeanours. There is one, and a very important one. We ought to be told whether the taking or cutting of turf under any circumstances is a misdemeanour, because that will affect one-half of the population. I do not say that the people are right in cutting turf; but if they offend in this direction, there ought to be a civil action against them. Certainly, the machinery of this Act ought not to be put in force in such cases. I have mentioned about one-half or two-thirds of the classes of cases which usually come before Petty Sessions in Ireland, and I desire to know whether I am wrong in supposing that all these cases, or nearly all of them, are misdemeanours which may be brought within the purview of this Bill? If I am right in my supposition, surely it is

[First Night.]

necessary the Law Officers of the Crown should give us some pledge that they will so amend the definition of the word "offence" that it shall not include some, at any rate, of the cases I have enumerated.

MR. FORREST FULTON (West Ham, N.): It appears to me the Committee has got into a state of the most inextricable confusion about a very simple matter. The word "offence" is one which is perfectly well understood by lawyers. The word "offence," which we are now discussing in line 2, Clause 1, is used in its generic sense—that is to say, it includes offences punishable by indictment and offences punishable on summary conviction, and in this sense the word "offence" is synonymous with the word "crime" used in the Preamble. In Section 5 you see the word "offence" used in both senses, in its generic sense and in its specific sense. In line 11 the word "crime" appears. That is clearly a draftsman's error. If the right hon. Gentleman the Member for Mid Lothian will look at the section he will see I am right. He will see that the word "crime" is used there in the same sense as the word "offence" in the second line of the paragraph. Now, it must be manifest that this is not the proper place to consider such an Amendment as this. When we come to Sub-section 5 we may well consider whether the offences to which the section is to apply should be limited to those punishable by indictment only. I think this may be a very important subject for discussion, but that it should not be brought up now, but when Sub-section 5, which defines what offences shall be subjected to these inquisitorial powers, is reached. I think, however, the Committee will see that the word "offence" is properly used in the line now under discussion.

MR. W. E. GLADSTONE (Edinburgh, Mid Lothian): I am very glad the hon. and learned Gentleman (Mr. Forrest Fulton), who has risen to lend the weight of his authority to the Government, thinks this clause requires amendment, so that the power it gives cannot be applied to all misdemeanours.

MR. FORREST FULTON: I said it might very well be the subject of argument, when we come to Sub-section 5, whether that should be so or not.

MR. W. E. GLADSTONE: If the hon. and learned Gentleman thinks it

might be the subject of argument, I conclude he sees some argument which might be used in favour of the proposition. He thought he was assisting the Government by suggesting it might be well to entertain the question of restricting the operation of this clause; but, in other respects, the hon. and learned Gentleman, whose aid is, undoubtedly, most valuable, is flatly in contradiction with the right hon. Gentleman the Chief Secretary for Ireland (Mr. A. J. Balfour). The hon. and learned Gentleman commented upon the generic and specific sense of the word "offence," and the difference in meaning between the word "crime" and the word "offence." Yes; but the right hon. Gentleman the Chief Secretary has expressly declared that in the view of the Government there is no distinction. [Mr. A. J. BALFOUR: Hear, hear!] The hon. and learned Gentleman will see that he has, to a certain extent, wasted his pains, because he has established a flat contradiction on the verbal point between the right hon. Gentleman and himself. Now, we have been debating this Amendment for two and a-half hours. We often hear complaints of the time that is occupied in the discussions upon this Bill. Who is the person responsible for occupying the time? We assert that, in this Amendment, we have a most important object. To us it amounts pretty nearly to a question of principle. Is that the case with the Government? No; for the Government say there is no difference whatever between crime and offence. If that is the case, what is the definition of obstructive debate? The definition of obstructive debate is that we occupy the time of the House in arguing for that which is not material. It is not obstructive debate for any Gentleman to occupy the time of the House in arguing for that which is, in his view, is material. That is the exact description of the position of the two Parties in this House. I do not understand why the Government do not at once accede to this Amendment. It is an important Amendment, in our view; and if, from the point of view of the Government, crime and offence are the same thing, why should they oppose the great majority of the lawyers who have spoken, the great weight of legal authority, and the wishes of a large portion of the House, and the mass of the Irish

Colonel Nolan

Members, in a matter where the Government thought there was no important principle at stake? I must say I think, in such a matter as this, the Irish Representatives are entitled to some very small and infinitesimal share of consideration. The Chief Secretary for Ireland says it would be better drafting if, in a subsequent line—I think the 11th—we substituted the word "offence" for "crime." But I can tell the right hon. Gentleman he must expect that, when we come to the 11th line, we shall make the best fight in our power for the retention of the word "crime." We are not going, under the pretext of better drafting, to part with the word "crime," which we think valuable, in order to substitute for it the word "offence.' If crime and offence are equivalent, which is the contention of the Government, then they ought at once to accede to the Amendment. If, on the other hand, crime and offence are not equivalent, then it is a most extraordinary thing that in the framing of this Bill, and in finding a title for it, they should describe it as "a Bill to make better provision for the prevention and punishment—not of offences in Ireland—of crime in Ireland." The whole argument in favour of this clause—and a very weighty argument it has been on many points—is derived from the case of Scotland. My hon. and learned Friend the late Solicitor General for Scotland (Mr. Asher) has, I think, declared in this House, and is prepared to declare again, that he has never known that power to be used. My right hon. and learned Friend the late Lord Advocate (Mr. J. B. Balfour) has also declared that, in Scotland, he has never known that power to be used. Another hon. and learned Gentleman, speaking from a Bench behind me (Mr. Anderson), has made a similar declaration in still broader terms. The hon. and learned Solicitor General for Scotland (Mr. J. P. B. Robertson) has been distinctly challenged on the question, and has not replied; he has sat here under the most pointed challenge, and has not replied. If the hon. and learned Gentleman did reply, I do not imagine he would be able to overcome such a statement as has been made by my hon. and learned Friends. So far as I have been able to gather the effect of the various declarations, especially of Scottish lawyers, on this matter, there appeared to be some doubt whether in some extreme case, on some very particular occasion, and at some very indefinite period, this power might have been used. But that is the only distinct glimpse we can have of it as a practical power. It is plain that, for all practical purposes, it is not used, and that if it ever were used, it would be used in the case of very heavy and serious crime. Well, now, if that is so, what is the application of this Scottish argument to the case before us? In Scotland, as we have seen, this is not an instrument of ordinary application. Is it the purpose of the Government, under the plea of equal legislation which you profess, to bring this power into the Irish law, to place it in the same position which it occupies in the law of Scotland? No; you are intending to use it for totally different purposes, and on an unlimited number of different occasions. In Scotland it is applied by persons of legal authority and education. The Government are going to give it for cases where it will be under the superintendence and control of persons not having legal authority and education. But what is more important is this—and I must confess I have never had the advantage of hearing the case discussed so fully as upon this occasion—the impression made upon my mind as a listener is this—that while it may be useful and wise to retain a power of this kind in the system of Scottish jurisprudence, it is a power only suited to countries where the people are in thorough sympathy with the law, and where the Administrative Body is not alienated and estranged from the people. The question is, *primâ facie*, that we are going to carry it into a country-where, from our mismanagement, the people are not in sympathy with the law, and where, as the necessary result of that unhappy state of things, the Administrative Body is not in sympathy with the people. Now, that being the state of the case, you are going to take this almost obsolete power from the Scottish law, and carry it into England—no, not into England; for I have a sufficiently good opinion of the hon. and learned Gentleman (Sir Richard Webster), who now occupies the Office of Her Majesty's Attorney General, to believe that he would be the first man to offer a stern and stout resistance to such a proposal—

[*First Night.*]

but in Ireland, and you are going to give this power for daily use by persons, the majority of whom have no legal knowledge or skill in the management of affairs. Besides that, you are going to apply this power to a set of cases for the use of which it has never been dreamt of, and for that purpose to bring in the word "offence," which in your unofficial, un-judicial letter *obiter dictum* of debate, may be said to be synonymous with "crime," but which your own independent supporter behind you has told you is not synonymous with crime. As the Bill stands, it is not one for the punishment of crime, but one for erecting into crime a multitude of acts which are not crimes under the present law. It is the intention of the Opposition seriously to struggle to restrict the effects of this clause, and all the powers given under it, to crimes of the most serious character, and to erect an effectual barrier between any plan of conspiracy, I may say, on the Treasury Bench to extend the application of this power beyond serious crimes. The right hon. Gentleman (Mr. A. J. Balfour) has told us that there are many innocent conspiracies; and, therefore, I am making no charge against the Government in saying that there is probably a conspiracy on the Treasury Bench on this subject to carry by numbers what they are unable to justify by argument. In my opinion, the Government have shown no adequate grounds to justify their refusal to accept this Amendment, and the discussion upon it has now occupied two and a-half or three hours.

THE SOLICITOR GENERAL FOR SCOTLAND (Mr. J. P. B. ROBERTSON) (Bute): I should not presume to reply to a Member of the House of such eminence and authority as the right hon. Gentleman (Mr. W. E. Gladstone) were it not that he threw out a direct challenge to me. That challenge was accompanied by the prediction that any reply I could offer would be of the utmost futility and inutility. I almost fear that the right hon. Gentleman has invited my participation in the debate for other purposes than that I may make a solid contribution to this discussion. But I will answer the right hon. Gentleman's challenge. The question which is immediately before the Committee is, whether there should be any distinction between classes of offences when it is

proposed to confer this power on the Executive in Ireland. I say, as a matter of law, the authorities in Scotland who represent public prosecutions have that power; and, what is more, the right hon. and learned Gentleman the Member for Clackmannan (Mr. J. B. Balfour), who, after much persuasion, was induced to rise to say something which might sound rather like a contradiction of what I have said, was obliged to admit that my proposition is absolutely accurate, and that, by the law of Scotland, this power is invested in the Public Prosecutor. It was said, by way of answer to the present proposal, that, as a matter of fact, the power is seldom exercised. I think my right hon. and learned Friend the Member for Clackmannan will agree with me when I say that there have been instances, within living memory, in which precognition on oath has been resorted to where no one was under charge; but that proceeding has been sparingly used.

MR. T. P. O'CONNOR (Liverpool, Scotland): What is your authority? [*Cries of* "Order!"] Will the hon. and learned Gentleman give us his authority?

MR. J. P. B. ROBERTSON: I am speaking on a matter requiring great precision of statement, and I am adopting moderate language which will commend itself to the judgment of my hon. and learned Friends opposite. The right hon. Gentleman the Member for Mid Lothian, in discussing this Amendment, has used phraseology which is eminently adapted, not to elucidate, but to confuse this question. He has persistently spoken of the system, and has asked whether this system is in use. What does the right hon. Gentleman mean by that? Does he mean the system of the preliminary private examination into facts by a magistrate—[Mr. W. E. GLADSTONE: Certainly not.]—I beg the right hon. Gentleman's pardon; but I have not completed my proposition—backed by powers of imprisonment against recalcitrant witnesses, and backed by the power of putting witnesses on oath when that is necessary? That, I think, is a fair and accurate description of the system embodied in this clause. That system, I assert, is the present law of Scotland; but I agree entirely with the guarded statement of my right hon. and learned Friend (Mr.

J. B. Balfour) that the examination upon oath in a preliminary inquiry of witnesses before anyone is charged is an uncommon occurrence; and I quite accept what my right hon. and learned Friend said—namely, that he has not known it occur in practice—nor have I in my experience. [*Opposition cheers.*] But I think hon. and right hon. Gentlemen opposite ought, before they indulge in such exuberant rejoicings, to condescend to notice that this admits that these powers, by the law of Scotland, are at the disposal of the authorities when required; and if they have not been exercised, it is merely because the circumstances of Scotland do not necessitate their being put in force. They have found a lodgment in the Scottish law, in order to meet the exigencies of a less settled state of society, and they were exercised in Scotland when the requirements of society compelled it. If it is necessary now, owing to the requirements of Ireland, to put such powers in force, they will be put in force, and if not, they will not. But the right hon. Gentleman (Mr. W. E. Gladstone), and those who have spoken from the opposite Benches, have introduced another confusion into their statement which completely destroys the force of the arguments they have used. They have said that the power of examining on oath before a charge is made against an individual has never been used except in the case of a grave charge. Again, I accede to that; but the gravity of an offence is measured by its danger to the community. There is no limitation to this law in Scotland, except what the customs of society have placed round the land; there is no distinction of offences to which this power may be applied; the limitation in the use of it is merely owing to our happy circumstances. My proposition is not, and never has been—the right hon. Gentleman knows it as well as anyone else—that this is a daily practice in the law of Scotland. I never said so; but I have said that the main scope and features of the system are settled in the Constitutional Law of Scotland. My right hon. and learned Friend opposite (Mr. J. B. Balfour) will allow that, in not very ancient memory, there have been cases where witnesses have been examined on oath where there was a charge made. I will go farther, and

say that my right hon. and learned Friend has done that himself. Why is it witnesses are not put on oath at preliminary inquiries where no person is charged, and that the power of imprisonment is not resorted to? It is because the community is willing to give evidence. You do not require to hold preliminary inquiries, and to put on oath people who are prepared to speak fairly and frankly the truth about a crime. The question is not whether these weapons are in daily use in Scotland, but whether they are at the command of the State if the exigencies of society require them. Before closing my remarks, I may be permitted to call the attention of the right hon. Gentleman the Member for Mid Lothian to certain words which seem to me to most admirably describe the state of things which calls for remarks of this kind—

"As impunity for crime was the great curse and plague of the disturbed districts of Ireland at the present moment, and as that impunity depended upon the difficulty of obtaining evidence, it was proposed to put any person who might be able to give evidence to no other inconvenience than might result from rendering them liable to be examined before there was a defendant. That was the sole distinction between the existing law and that which the Government proposed. He thought the majority of the House would consider, under the circumstances of Ireland, that if they were to have a Bill of this kind at all, it was not an unreasonable demand to make. It went to the root of the mischief with which they were dealing."

These are the words of the right hon. Gentleman, and they seem to me to justify completely what is proposed now. No argument is needed to convince the constituencies, if that is what was intended by the impassioned observations of the right hon. Gentleman, of what is already well known in England to be the case about Scotland, and what is in Scotland perfectly notorious. The purpose of this Bill is to put into effect means for obtaining information for the detection of crime; and if they have the sanction of the precedent of Scotland, as I think is undoubtedly the case, that will commend itself to what is not the least law-abiding, and, according to the right hon. Gentleman, is one of the most intelligent portions of Her Majesty's Dominions.

MR. ASHER (Elgin, &c.): Mr. Courtney, I think the Committee is now in a position to form a very clear opinion as to how far the action of the Government is justified by the law of Scotland. My hon. and learned Friend (Mr. J. P. B. Robertson) had considerable reluctance in adding his contribution to this debate; and I think it is pretty plain, from what my hon. and learned Friend has said, that there is no foundation whatever in the law of Scotland for the attitude of the Government with reference to this particular Amendment. I understood my hon. and learned Friend not materially to dissent from the view of the Scottish law and practice which has been stated from this side of the House. We have never disputed that, according to the letter of the Scotch law, a power does exist to examine upon oath in the course of a preliminary inquiry, even when no one is under charge; but we have asserted that, in the experience of my right hon. and learned Friend (Mr. J. B. Balfour) and myself, as Law Officers for Scotland, we did not remember any case in which the power had been exercised, and we are now in a position to say that the experience of the hon. and learned Gentlemen opposite, who are now the Law Officers for Scotland, has been the same. I was anxious to hear what my hon. and learned Friend (Mr. J. P. B. Robertson) would say with regard to the law of Scotland as applicable to this particular Amendment. What is the Amendment we have been considering for the past few hours? It is whether this power of preliminary inquiry, when no one is under charge, is to be given in the case of a crime only, or in the case of an offence. Now, as has been pointed out, there is no substance in the discussion which has taken place, unless a crime is something different to an offence, and it is perfectly evident that the Government are resisting this Amendment because they intend to make this inquisitorial power applicable, not merely to that which is known to the law as a crime, but also to that which is to be created into a statutable offence by the clauses of this Bill. My hon. and learned Friend has not suggested either that it is, or that it ever was, the law of Scotland—even the letter of the law—that inquisitorial power on oath should be applicable to anything but crime. It is impossible, in considering the Amendment, not to have in view what are the offences created by this Bill. We say, distinctly, that it is proposed to make a great many things offences

Mr. Asher

under this Act which certainly, in the minds of Scotch lawyers, are not crimes at all. The hon. and learned Gentleman the Solicitor General for Scotland did not attempt to deal with that portion of the speech of the late Lord Advocate (Mr. J. B. Balfour), in which he distinctly stated that, after careful consideration, he had come to the conclusion that many things would, under this Bill, be made statutable offences which are not crimes according to that law. In that opinion of my right hon. and learned Friend I cordially concur, and my hon. and learned Friend opposite does not dissent from that view. To these statutable offences you are going to apply this inquisitorial power. I am bound to say that when one looks at the subject-matter of these offences, and sees how they are interwoven with the social relations of the people in a variety of ways—for instance, in regard to the taking of land or a house, or the employment of a tradesman—one must come to the conclusion that to give power of this kind in such cases is nothing but to set up a Court of Inquisition from which no man is safe. I believe that there is not, and there never was, in the law of Scotland, a power of this kind applicable to that which is not crime, but a mere statutable offence of the nature contemplated in this Bill. It seems to me the Committee may safely assume, by the admissions of lawyers on both sides of the House, that, in so far as this Amendment is concerned, the argument with which the right hon. Gentleman the Chief Secretary for Ireland justifies this clause of the Bill—namely, its analogy to the law of Scotland, has no weight whatever; but that, on the contrary, if the Government's object is to assimilate the law of Ireland to that of Scotland with reference to preliminary inquiries, this power should not be made applicable to anything but crime, and the Amendment ought, therefore, to be accepted.

MR. MOLLOY (King's Co., Birr): When the hon. and learned Gentleman the Solicitor General for Scotland (Mr. J. P. B. Robertson) rose to answer the arguments of the right hon. Gentleman the Member for Mid Lothian (Mr. W. E. Gladstone), to disgrace him in the opinion of this Committee, he was loudly cheered by all the Members of the Tory Party opposite, and I began to think that perhaps there was some chance of the right hon. Gentleman being beaten by the Solicitor General for Scotland. But of all the speeches we have heard upon this Amendment, the worst speech is that of the Solicitor General for Scotland, and I will explain why I call it the worst speech. I do not say it was not oratorically clever; but it was not straight, and I will prove my statement. The hon. and learned Gentleman endeavoured to show that the right hon. Gentleman the Member for Mid Lothian was wrong in his arguments; he described what the law would be in Ireland under this clause, and then he endeavoured to induce the Committee to believe that that which had existed in Scotland was identical to that which is about to be enacted for Ireland. During his remarks he made use of the words " the prevention of crime in Scotland." That was a bad argument, and a bad argument involves a bad speech. By a quibble of words you endeavour to deceive your hearers, and support an argument which you must admit was not a just argument. It was the crime in Scotland the hon. and learned Gentleman laid stress upon. That is begging the whole question. The argument of hon. Gentlemen upon this side of the House is founded upon the word "offence," and I think I am entitled to say the hon. and learned Gentleman's speech was not quite as fair as we are entitled to expect from a Gentleman holding the high position in this House of Solicitor General for Scotland. Again, the hon. and learned Gentleman endeavoured to persuade the Committee, by a quotation from a speech of the right hon. Gentleman the Member for Mid Lothian (Mr. W. E. Gladstone), that this law, which exists in Scotland in a modified form, was some time since put into force. When he was challenged from these Benches, he did not give a single example of this power being used in Scotland. Does he mean to say that the statement of the late Lord Advocate was correct or incorrect? The late Lord Advocate stated that this law was never put into force in Scotland, and the Solicitor General for Scotland rose to show that it was. Can he show that? I ask, is it fair to endeavour by a quibble to lead the Committee to believe that what is now proposed for Ireland is identical with what exists in Ireland when that is not so. I do not wish to

be discourteous; but I think, without being so, I am justified in saying the speech of the Solicitor General for Scotland was not worthy of him, and was not a straight speech. Who is to put this clause of the Bill or of the Act, if it passes, into force? The Attorney General for Ireland. Now, who is the Attorney General for Ireland? He sits upon the Treasury Bench there, and under this Bill a great deal depends upon his belief. We have had some beliefs of the right hon. and learned Gentleman. We have his beliefs about four or five times in a week. Let me give some examples of his beliefs. He believes, for instance, the statement of the right hon. Gentleman the Chief Secretary for Ireland (Mr. A. J. Balfour), that the County of Mayo is bordering upon civil war. That is his belief, and yet it has been proved conclusively in this House, by statistics from your judicial authorities in Ireland, that Mayo is, in fact, more peaceful than any county of England. Now, what is the opinion of the right hon. and learned Gentleman of the Irish Members? He has expressed it in this House upon several occasions, and anyone who examines the speeches of the right hon. and learned Gentleman will find that his belief is that every Irish Member should be imprisoned. Let me go a step further, and ask who the Attorney General for Ireland is? Is he an independent Member of the Government? Has he even been an independent Member of the Government? Has he not simply carried out the instructions of the Government night by night? Is he not as much a counsel holding a brief when he sits on that Bench, as he is when he goes into Court? And yet he is a Member of the Government which declares that everything in Ireland is wrong; that every act done by the people of Ireland is an offence, meaning, of course, a crime; that nothing in Ireland is honest; that the starving peasantry are dishonest when they cannot pay their rent— yet this is the Gentleman who has the power, upon his belief, based upon his instructions from the Government, to put this clause into effect in Ireland. We can form a very good opinion of the class of cases and evidence which will be sufficient to satisfy the Attorney General that he ought to put this inquisitorial power into effect. Now, who are they

[First Night.]

who are to be entrusted with the carrying out of this Act ? The Resident Magistrates. Speaking, the other day, at a meeting in the country, I described one of the Resident Magistrates of Ireland, who happens to be one——

THE CHAIRMAN: Order, order! The hon. Gentleman is going through the clause almost word by word. The Question before the Committee is, whether the word "crime" or the word "offence" should be employed.

MR. MOLLOY: I was going to show that the Resident Magistrates are totally unfit to exercise the legal functions conferred upon them by this Bill; but I will not pursue the point. I shall have plenty of opportunities of doing that at later stages. Now, as to an offence, I will deal with the Attorney General for Ireland's belief of what is an offence. We saw an hon. and learned Gentleman (Mr. Forrest Fulton) rising from the opposite Benches with an anxious desire to support the Government. We heard his description of an offence, and we have received from the Treasury Bench some very vague definition of an offence. But is there, in this Bill, any limitation to the word offence ? Will the Attorney General for Ireland get up and say there is any limitation of any sort whatever to the word offence ?

MR. HOLMES: Yes, there is; in the final section of this clause.

MR. MOLLOY: The right hon. and learned Gentleman will have an opportunity of explaining the matter fully. We are aware that the Whiteboy Acts are to be included in this Bill, and I say distinctly, and I challenge contradiction, that there is practically no limitation to the word "offence." It means nothing more than this—that any act which may be disagreeable to the Government, or which may not be generally approved of by the Government, becomes under this Bill an offence. I hope the Attorney General for Ireland, who was so quick to rise a few moments ago, will explain this point when he rises hereafter. "Offence," practically, has no limitation whatever, and the passing of this Act means that Parliament will put it into the power of the Attorney General for Ireland, not even an independent Member of the Government, and of the Resident Magistrates of Ireland, to hold inquisitorial examinations into every act, private or otherwise, of every person in Ireland. Now, that is the real definition of the word "offence" as used here, and I challenge denial from the Attorney General for Ireland. It is because of the wideness of the word "offence" that I have so serious and strong objection to its retention here. I and my hon. Friends are bound to insist upon this Amendment, and to do all we can to put such limitation upon the clause as will compel the judicial authorities in Ireland to be honest in the exercise of the powers to be conferred upon them

MR. D. CRAWFORD (Lanark, N.E.): So much reference has been made to the Scotch law that I should like to refer to an analogy which has not been pointed out as yet. From the time my hon. and learned Friend the Solicitor General for Scotland spoke a week ago, and from the time the right hon. Gentleman the Chief Secretary for Ireland (Mr. A. J. Balfour) referred to the subject of the Scotch law, we all on this side of the House have been distinctly under the impression that it was asserted and alleged that this power of examining witnesses upon oath, when no charge was made against anybody, is a matter of common practice in Scotch law. That is the point which we traverse. That is the point which I understand the right hon. Gentleman the Member for Mid Lothian (Mr. W. E. Gladstone) to contradict, and not to question whether any description of preliminary inquiry such as prevails in Scotland is, or is not, a good thing in itself. Now, I think it is established on the authority of my legal Friends on this side of the House that this power of examining witnesses upon oath, when no person is to be under charge, has never been exercised within the memory of living man. We have that on the best legal authority on this side of the House, and we have it on the tardy admission of the hon. and learned Solicitor General for Scotland. I think I am justified in saying that this feature in the Scotch system is an obsolete one, and that my hon. and learned Friend has not pointed out a true analogy to the present proposal in the Scotch Criminal Law. Now, I think it is possible to point to one. Under the Scotch law the offences of arson, rape, and robbery are still capital offences, unless the law has been changed recently. I have

Mr. Molloy

taken part in many criminal cases, and my recollection is that these are still capital offences, and that the Judge has no alternative but to pronounce sentence of death upon the prisoner, unless the Lord Advocate, or the Advocate Deputy who is prosecuting, stays the application of the law. I ask whether hon. Gentlemen opposite are ready to apply that law to Ireland or to England? I do not deny that it would be congenial to the spirit of the Bill if it were to make a great variety of offences punishable by the penalty of death. But I hardly think the Government will be bold enough to make such a proposal. As enough has been said upon this question, I am not going to detain the Committee further than to say that I have submitted what appears to me to be a true analogy, and that it is an unfair and misleading argument to urge that an obsolete Scotch law may be applied in Ireland.

Question put.

The Committee *divided:*—Ayes 157; Noes 120: Majority 37.—(Div. List, No. 100.)

DR. COMMINS (Roscommon, S.): I propose to insert in line 7, after the word "committed," the words "after the passing of this Act." The wording of the clause is—

"Where the Attorney General for Ireland believes that any offence to which this section applies has been committed. . . . "

The object of my Amendment is very clear; because, as the clause stands at present, it will be quite open to magistrates to open inquiry into offences committed years ago. The result of that will be that you will induce probably an amount of false swearing in connection with crimes that were unable to be proved at the time; it will also give an amount of insecurity to society that will be perfectly intolerable, besides giving a fresh start to the manufacture of spurious offences for the purpose of harassing honest men. In a subsequent section that error seems to be avoided; for instance, it provides that summary jurisdiction shall apply only to a person who shall commit the offence after the passing of the Act. The present section, however, says nothing as to when the offence, about which inquiry is made, shall have been committed. If the Government mean to leave it open to institute inquiries

into offences committed last year, four years, or seven years ago, then, of course, they will oppose my Amendment; but, if not, then I can conceive no reason why it should not be accepted. It interferes in no way with the clause, either in respect of grammar or sense, and cannot, in any way, impair the legal meaning of the Act.

Amendment proposed, in page 1, line 7, after "committed" insert "after the passing of this Act."—(*Dr. Commins.*)

Question proposed, "That those words be there inserted."

THE ATTORNEY GENERAL FOR IRELAND (Mr. HOLMES): Our intention is that the provision should apply to offences although they may have been committed before the passing of this Act.

MR. T. M. HEALY: Now we have it out—retrospective legislation.

MR. HOLMES: I do not hesitate to say that any Government that did not think it necessary to introduce a clause of this kind, having regard to the state of affairs in Ireland, would be nothing less than culpable. The clause creates no new principle whatever; its object is to procure that evidence which in most other countries can be procured with considerable facility for the purpose of detecting crime. We are all aware that in Ireland there have been some very serious crimes — some very dreadful crimes — committed in the last few months, which remain undetected, and in order that they may, if possible, not escape detection, the Government bring in this Bill. The hon. Member for South Roscommon (Dr. Commins) has drawn attention to the fact that in a subsequent clause the drafting is different. It is different, of course, because the Bill provides there for a different procedure, and it is reasonable and proper that drafting should correspond. But when we are dealing with the detection and of crimes——

MR. T. M. HEALY: Offences.

MR. HOLMES: Which are crimes— [*Cries of* "Offences!" *and* "Look at the Bill!"]—these crimes——

MR. T. M. HEALY: Offences, offences!

THE CHAIRMAN: I must ask the hon. and learned Member for North Longford to cease his remarks.

MR. HOLMES: To detect these crimes it is necessary that the Bill should be retrospective, and for that there is abundant precedent. In the Act of 1870 there was a similar provision, and also in the Act of 1882, both being retrospective; and I remind hon. Members that if the clause in the latter Act had not been of a retrospective character the murderers of the Phœnix Park would not have been discovered. In 1883 an Act was carried almost unanimously which dealt with dynamite explosions, and that also was retrospective. Therefore, it seems to me that nothing can be more proper than to make this clause retrospective, and I am glad that the hon. Member for South Roscommon has drawn attention to the fact. It is said that it is retrospective with regard to those offences which are made crimes for the first time under the Bill. [*Laughter*.]

MR. T. M. HEALY: You said there were no new ones.

DR. COMMINS: You have let it out unawares. [*Cheers*.]

MR. HOLMES: I am sorry to see that hon. Gentlemen opposite are very much confused in their ideas. If there be any new offences created under this Bill, and I deny that there are—[*laughter*, and "No, no!"]—these cannot be affected at all by the retrospective character of the clause. That cheer of hon. Members was, therefore, premature, and if they had listened for a moment they would have seen the folly of it.

MR. T. M. HEALY: I am sure that the Committee is delighted with the ingenuousness and candour of the right hon. Gentleman's reply. We have been all the evening on the question of the difference between offence and crime, and the Government have adhered to the word "offence," but as soon as we propose this Amendment we get the word crime over and over again, and we are reminded of the murders in the Phœnix Park. We have it here that the Government intends to do what the law of England has always looked upon with abhorrence—to go into stale treasons. It is the Plan of Campaign which sticks in the throats of the Government. We know that the right hon. Gentleman gave his famous opinion on the Plan of Campaign; we know he said there was a way in which it could be dealt with; we know that he instructed his police to seize the money; we know that he put our hon. Friends on trial, and that he

did not get the money because he did not know where it was; but now he is going into matters which occupied his attention last November and December, and thinks to have every one up at the beck of men like King-Harman and Tottenham. [*Cries of* "Order!"] I am not speaking of them in the capacity of Members of this House.

THE CHAIRMAN: The hon. Gentlemen are referred to in connection with the present Bill. The hon. Member must speak in accordance with Parliamentary usage.

MR. T. M. HEALY: I have yet to learn that it is not a fact that there are such landlords in Ireland as King-Harman and Tottenham, and I say that I have a right to refer to them typically. We now know what the Government mean. We have now, for the first time, learnt that the Act is to be retrospective; and we know that the Government have refused to define the crimes which can be committed under the Act. The hon. Member for North Antrim (Sir Charles Lewis) will perhaps be surprised to hear that the Bill deals with bribery and corruption, and that even election proceedings can be gone into. Under the circumstances, I ask what is more monstrous than that the Government should pretend that the Act creates no new crimes, and that any matter may be gone into which has occurred during the last 20 years. I ask if there is to be any limit at all. Even Mr. Forster put a limit into his Bill. In connection with murder, manslaughter, or moonlighting, no possible complaint against the drafting of the Bill can be made. But the right hon. Gentleman speaks of new offences, and I venture to think that the result of the Bill will be that from the day it becomes law, if it ever does, you will not be able to get evidence of any crime, however hideous and abominable it may be. The word will be passed. ["Hear, hear!"] I am glad the hon. Gentleman says "Hear, hear," because it shows that we can pass the word. You propose to smash up the National League, but perhaps even from the prison cell will issue the voice of intimidation—the voice of the suppressed National League which you have tried to stifle by this Bill—and from one end of the country to the other you will not get a single man to come forward. ["Hear, hear!"] The hon. Baronet opposite cheers that statement. That too shows the forces you are playing with, and I tell the Government that by this clause which they think is so innocuous they are putting their hand into a hornets' nest, and they will be stung before they get it out. Now, I put this to any sensible man, such, for instance, as the Parliamentary Under Secretary for Ireland (Colonel King-Harman), a man whom we know to have no prejudices against Nationalists. I put it to him as a Member of the Goment, whether or not it is their object by the machinery of this clause to put down crime. We may quarrel with the clause, but it is our interest as much as it is the interest of the Government to put a stop to the terrible crimes which have occurred in Ireland and in England; it is our interest to put down and to detect crimes, not only because of their moral guilt, but because we are aware of the immense prejudice which they raise; but is it not the interest of the Government not to prejudice the entire population of Ireland against the Bill, who will know that it is directed not against crimes, but against offences political and agrarian? I think the Government have begun very badly. I have no doubt that by certain odds they may push forward the Bill; but I say it is a serious thing for Her Majesty's Government, in face of the opposition of five-sixths of the Irish Representatives and the greater portion of the Liberal Party, to give no recognition to the arguments which we put forward. Are we to get no concession from the Government? We have had none as yet, but I hope the Government will see their way not to allow themselves to be misled by the representatives of reactionary landlords with regard to the retrospective portion of the Bill. The hon. Gentleman the Attorney General for Ireland (Sir Richard Webster) is the representative of the landlords, and although I have the greatest respect for his abilities, to his opinion on a political matter I would not attach a feather's weight, because he is simply the landlords' mouthpiece. This result of going retrospectively into this matter will be that you will have Ireland a seething sea of discontent and disorder. You will probably order inquiry under this clause into the Plan of Campaign; a witness will refuse to give evidence, and like the first policeman who resigned the other day, he will be followed by many more. The first imprisonment under this Act will be the keynote of this state of things. I warn the Government to walk with circumspection, and if they wish to make practical use of the measure let them begin well. They have not begun well. They propose to go into stale matters. Let them by all means go into murders and cases of manslaughter, maiming, and serious offences of that character; but, with regard to the new offences which the right hon. Gentleman has admitted will be created, I would warn them to take another course, because I should not have the smallest hesitation in getting up on the first available platform and seeking the first available plank bed by telling my countrymen to refuse to attend these summonses.

MR. T. C. HARRINGTON (Dublin, Harbour): I must confess, after the declaration of the right hon. Gentleman the Attorney General for Ireland (Mr. Holmes), as to the serious crimes which he said had been committed in Ireland, that I could not help thinking it most unfortunate that the late Chief Secretary for Ireland (Sir Michael Hicks-Beach) should have been absent from the House before this Bill was brought in. We had a statement from him a short time before he resigned his Office—he said to his constituents that the state of Ireland left little or nothing to be desired. But that right hon. Gentleman who was then responsible for the state of the country, and who was able to say this of the state of Ireland, has been stowed away by the Government. But what are the difficulties that are to be obviated by this Bill? Does the right hon. Gentleman think seriously that by going back on offences that have been committed in Ireland—petty offences, for he asks powers with regard to these as well as serious offences—he will be contributing anything to the maintenance of law and order in Ireland? Is it not more likely that he will disturb even the present state of the country, and make it worse than it is at the present time? I was astonished at the statement of the right hon. Gentleman, that the Phœnix Park murderers would never have been brought to justice if it had not been for the retrospective character of the Act of 1882. This has been the statement over and over again; but the very contrary is the fact. All the circumstances of the murder were known to the authorities in Ireland long before the Act passed through the House, and long before inquiry was held. Everything which the provision in the Act could bring to light was already known. Again, the right hon. Gentleman stated that this clause cannot be retrospective with regard to new offences. But I think he has overlooked the fact that up to the present time it has not been made punishable that men should refuse to give evidence on the ground that he might incriminate himself. I regret that the right hon. Gentleman the Attorney General for Ireland is not in his place; but he has stated to the House that in regard to new offences the provisions of the Act are not retrospective. I would have liked to call his attention to the 3rd sub-section, which says that a witness examined under this section shall not be excused from answering any question on the ground that the answer thereto may criminate, or tend to criminate, himself; but that any statement made by any person in answer to any question put to him on any examination under this section shall not, except in the case of an indictment or other criminal proceeding for perjury, be admissible in evidence against him in any proceeding, civil or criminal. But the words "in any proceeding against him for perjury" announce that examination may take place with regard to offences committed before the Act, and that his answer may be given as evidence against him, and he may be punished even if it tend to criminate him. There would be no opposition to the adoption of a clause of this kind if we had a reasonable limitation; but if it is the intention of the Government to go back on petty offences that may have been committed in Ireland and drag private citizens before them for the purpose of inquiry, we are entitled to oppose it in every way. I repeat, for my part, that if there were a reasonable limitation, I would not for one moment object to the provision being embodied in the Act— if it were applied only to serious crimes —but if you apply it to political purposes and Party purposes, and in order to assist Irish landlords in getting the unjust rents which have been recently condemned by the Sub-Commissioners

Mr. T. C. Harrington

in Ireland, I shall strongly oppose it. The hon. Member for North Longford (Mr. T. M. Healy) has referred to the recent trial of the Member for East Mayo (Mr. Dillon) and others for the adoption of the Plan of Campaign, and that since that time the very demand made by the tenants have been justified by the Sub-Commissioners, and more than justified, because, while the tenants only demanded a reduction of 30 per cent, the average abatement made by the Sub-Commissioners amounts to 35 per cent. This is one of the offences, no doubt, to which it is the intention of Her Majesty's Government to apply the provisions of this Act. So far as we are concerned, we have no reason to dread any use they may make of the Act; but we have a deep and vital interest in the peace of the country, and I maintain that, so far as the maintenance of peace, and the maintenance of law and order, the application of these provisions to petty offences will plunge the country into a state of ruin, and that right hon. Gentlemen opposite will have most to regret the difficulties they have created by their adoption. Everyone having the slightest acquaintance with Ireland knows how the provisions of the Act of 1882 have been worked. The Government are most anxious to get the provisions of the Act of 1882; but all I can say is that even when the administration of Ireland was in the firm grip of Lord Spencer, the Act of 1882, in spite of his best efforts, was used by his officials for Party purposes. At that time we had the clauses relating to secret inquiry and other clauses of the Bill administered in a way that any Government would be ashamed of. Even now if it is not the intention of the Government to limit this section, they will find that their partizans in Ireland will be too strong for them; and if they are not stronger than the right hon. Gentleman the Attorney General and his subordinates, I can understand the amount of difficulty and trouble in store for them. We had cases in Ireland under the secret clauses of the Act of 1882 where inquiries were instituted, and persons were summoned who could not by any means be brought into connection with the offence that had been committed; yet they stated publicly, after their examination, that they had been examined in respect of circumstances which could not possibly have any connection with the offence. I have no doubt that if that was the case in the past, the same magistrates would make very unsatisfactory use of the powers given in this Act, and especially if they believe that the Government will protect them in any lawlessness which they may perpetrate.

MR. CHANCE (Kilkenny, S.): My hon. Friend, in support of his very reasonable Amendment, pointed out that the clause was retrospective; and the right hon. Gentleman the Attorney General for Ireland (Mr. Holmes) replied that there was nothing unreasonable in that, inasmuch as it enables you to discover and punish crime. His statement was perfectly reasonable; but I want to ask the right hon. Gentleman if he seriously contends that this section does not create new crimes retrospectively. I think he will find that it does create new crimes with respect to old offences and punishes persons for them. I admit at once that where new offences are made by the Act it is obviously not to the interest of the Government that they should be punished unless committed after the passing of the Act. Now, I call the attention of the right hon. Gentleman to the 2nd and 3rd sub-section of this clause. Under the 2nd sub-section any witness declining to answer any question put to him is liable to be committed to gaol for contempt of Court, as for declining to give evidence on an indictable offence. I point out that, up to the present, no witness is compelled to answer any question tending to criminate himself; but going to the 3rd section, I find that it can be applied to any witness who refuses to answer a question on that ground. That is distinctly a new offence. I suppose that we may be told that punishment for contempt of Court is not punishment for an offence; but if a man is sent to gaol for a number of years for contempt it will not be a great stretch of language to term that a serious offence. A man declines to incriminate himself with respect to an old offence, and he is sent to gaol—that is creating a new offence in respect of an old offence. I am told that if we read further we shall see that—

"Any statement made by any person in answer to any question put to him on any examination under this section shall not, except in the case of an indictment or other criminal proceeding for perjury, be admissible in evidence against him in any proceeding, civil or criminal."

Well, obviously, all this is mere quibble. A man, for instance, may say that he collected rent, gave a receipt and paid the rent into a bank; the Government gets the facts, goes to the cashier of the bank and questions him. It is clear that in this case the witness has been compelled to give the Government a weapon that may be very unfairly used against him. His evidence may also be used against him on a charge of perjury. In this way, on three points the Government raise new crimes on old offences. Does the Bill then recommend itself to any sensible Member of this House?

DR. KENNY (Cork, S.): From the fact that a portion of this clause is to be retrospective in its operation, we may gather that the whole object of inquiry is to make it possible to punish Irish Nationalists for acts done in the past which hitherto have not by law been regarded as crimes. Unless the Amendment of my hon. Friend the Member for South Roscommon (Dr. Commins) be accepted, it is qui e possible that my hon. Friend the Member for East Mayo (Mr. Dillon) will come under this particular clause. It is impossible to persuade any Irish or English Member that the acts of my hon. Friend were criminal acts; but under the Bill, as it stands, the Government can now say that the acts of my hon. Friend were done in a proclaimed district, and are offences under the Act. As my hon. Friend has just very successfully shown, the operation of the clause will make *ex post facto* inquiry into acts which have not been punishable for the purpose of dealing with them under the Bill. This discussion has shown the importance of the previous discussion which has taken place on the word "offence," and how necessary it is that the Government should define the meaning of the term in this Bill, because they would then have to show that the operation of the clause is to crime only, to which, of course, we could not object. But they have refused to make any definition of the word "offence." They stick to that term, although the right hon. Gentleman the Attorney General for Ireland (Mr. Holmes) did not push it to great length in his reply. There is no limitation proposed to the application of the clause; and although, as far as I and my Colleagues are concerned, we have no fear of any act of ours being inquired into, yet transactions may be brought up which occurred 10 or 15 years ago. The whole object of the Bill is to create the state of feeling which the Government will say was smouldering in Ireland when they brought forward the measure. We shall advise our countrymen not to reply to inquiries under this Act. On every opportunity I have in Ireland I shall call on them not to reply. We do not wish to create bitterness of feeling; but there are men outside the lines of the political movement who will not harken to our advice, and the Government, having made them, will have to deal with them. I trust that the alternative words proposed by the hon. Member for South Roscommon will be accepted by the Government.

MR. STANSFELD (Halifax): I must express my surprise, seeing the number of lawyers on the Front Bench opposite, that no one of them has thought it right or has felt himself called on to rise in reply to the speech of the hon. Gentleman the Member for South Kilkenny (Mr. Chance). That hon. Member raised a number of questions of great importance, upon which, I think, we ought to have had some expression of opinion from hon. Gentlemen opposite. I am bound to say I heard the speech of the right hon. Gentleman the Attorney General for Ireland (Mr. Holmes) with the deepest regret and with some surprise. I have been accustomed to look upon the science of law as a noble science, and to think that the adepts in it have some respect for it. I have been accustomed to think that these Gentleman have a sound idea as to what constitutes law, and are not persons likely readily to take part in the passing of measures which have none of the characteristics of law. I say that this clause has none of the characteristics of law. [*Laughter.*] If hon. Gentlemen think it proper to meet that statement with derision I can easily prove what I say, though it will compel me to address the House at greater length than I desired. The clause we are discussing is peculiar in this respect—that it will not make any change until the fiat of the

Dr. Kenny

Lord Lieutenant is issued. The Bill is simply a catalogue of arbitrary powers, which you leave the Lord Lieutenant to enforce as a political partizan; but I must not travel far on that road. I must confine myself to the first clause. I will put the case in this way—I have a right to say this. If you bear in mind the relation between the 2nd and 6th and 7th clauses, you will see that it will be possible, under the 1st clause, to inquire into the speech or writing of any Irish Member of Parliament, or any Irish contributor to the Press, who in times past, however distant, has spoken in approval of these things which we call the Plan of Campaign and the National League; and I want to know whether the Government really think it decent, and think it worth their while, to take such a power in this clause? Is it not enough to start from the date of the passing of this measure? What possible advantage can they gain by raking up the past? Surely, as a matter of policy, there should be some limit to a proceeding of this kind. I do not think, even if the Committee pass the clause, the Government will find it to their advantage to put it in operation in that way; but I call on them to say whether they desire to be invested by the House of Commons with such an extraordinary power as this? But the hon. and learned Gentleman has put another case, which requires an answer from the Law Officers of the Crown. He has shown that when an inquiry takes place with reference to an offence which may not be an offence under this Act— an offence committed, or supposed to be committed, before the passing of this Act—and a witness refuses to give evidence with regard to it, he will practically commit an offence under this Act. That, surely, requires an answer. ["Hear, hear!"] "Hear, hear" from the right hon. Gentleman the Attorney General; but his argument is this— "We do not create an offence; we do not take power to punish an old offence." But you do the same thing. You inquire into an old offence, not being an offence under this Act, and you punish the man who refuses to criminate himself by giving evidence which may tell against himself. So that a new offence is linked with the old one. You say such a man is safe because his statement cannot be brought in evidence against him; but my hon. and learned Friend showed conclusively that you compel the man to furnish you with evidence, and put you on the track of evidence, with which you can confront him on subsequent indictment; and, therefore, practically speaking, you do take power here of a retrospective character to enable you to bring within the operation of the law a man who would not otherwise be under it. Is it worth while to do this—is it a decent proceeding? One of the best known and most thoroughly recognized principles of Criminal Law is that it ought not to be *ex post facto* and retrospective; and I must express my amazement at that which I see with great regret—namely, that amongst the number of distinguished lawyers opposite, there is not one who, for the sake of his profession and the science to which he belongs, will rise up and protest against being made responsible for the establishment of the new legal principle involved in this clause, the object of which is so much of a Party character—I do not mean as between the two Parties in this House, but I mean that you have made up your minds that there is an Irish Party you are determined to subjugate, and you take powers in this Act in order that you may subjugate it. I think we are at least entitled to some explanation, in regard to this matter—to some defence from the Government.

THE SOLICITOR GENERAL (Sir EDWARD CLARKE) (Plymouth): The right hon. Gentleman who has just sat down has said that the clause now proposed has none of the characteristics of law; and he has asked the Government whether they think it decent and think it worth while to propose such a clause to the House. Well, I have a very substantial answer to that question, and I say that the clause has the characteristics of law, that it is exactly the same in its scope, intention, and operation as the sections with regard to procedure which are constantly passed in all the Acts which go through this House. I would point out that this clause is the same as the clauses which have appeared in three Acts of Parliament for which the right hon. Gentleman has been himself responsible—whether by active advocacy, by the support of his vote, or by silent acquiescence in this House, I do not care. In one way or other, he has been responsible

for three Acts of Parliament in which sections of the same kind as this were put, which have had what he has called a retrospective effect, but the effect of which was not truly retrospective.

MR. STANSFELD: What Acts?

SIR EDWARD CLARKE: The Acts of 1870, 1882, and 1883. In each one of these cases a clause was contained in the Bill, and passed through the House, corresponding to the one now under consideration, and without any such limitation as is proposed by the right hon. Gentleman. He asks if this proposal is decent. I think I have satisfactorily answered his question by reference to action he himself sanctioned in times gone by.

MR. STANSFELD: I must interrupt the hon. and learned Gentleman. I was not responsible for one of these Acts.

SIR EDWARD CLARKE: If the right hon. Gentleman tells me that in 1870—when, I think, he was a Member of the Government—he did not sanction the Act that was passed, of course I retract my statement at once. As for the Acts of 1882 and 1883, he was, at any rate, a Member of the House when they were passed——

MR. STANSFELD: Yes.

SIR EDWARD CLARKE: And what I said was that the right hon. Gentleman was responsible for the Acts that were passed; and that, either by speech, vote, or silent acquiescence, he was, therefore, a party to the passing of this clause. Of course, I have not had time to refer to the record of the votes which were given in the House at that time. That, I think, sufficiently answers the right hon. Gentleman's question as to whether this is decent. Now, then, I come to the question as to whether it is worth while to pass this clause. If the House of Commons had put in such a limitation as the right hon. Gentleman now suggests, it would be giving impunity to offences—it would be exempting any offences which might be committed before the actual passing of this Act from that machinery of detection which the Committee has thought it desirable to adopt. Truly speaking, there is no retrospective character in this at all. [*Laughter.*] No; properly so speaking, there is no retrospective character in it at all; and what is provided is this—that from the time that this Bill passes, and gets the Royal Assent, there will be

[First Night.]

put in operation a machinery deemed necessary for the detection of crime. That machinery will operate from the time the Act passes, but, of course, will be applicable to crime, whether it has been successfully completed before the time the Act receives the Royal Assent or not. Why is it that we are desiring to pass this Bill at all? It is because the offences to which it refers are in daily operation in different parts of Ireland; and it would be preposterous to ask the House of Commons to tie its hands and say, by putting in this Amendment, that everything that one might succeed in doing before the time the Bill becomes law should be exempt from the operation of the measure. No answer was given to the speech of the hon. and learned Gentleman the Member for South Kilkenny (Mr. Chance), for the reason—and I say it with all respect to the hon. and learned Gentleman—that it was perfectly clear to our minds that there was nothing at all in that speech. The hon. and learned Member said the Bill creates a new offence, and deals with an offence committed before the passing of the measure. There is no foundation for that statement whatever, and if the hon. and learned Gentleman will only read the clause through from end to end, he will see that there is not.

Mr. CHANCE: I did not say that. What I said was, you use an old offence to compel a new and unconstitutional crime, and then say the clause is not retrospective. If by reason of an old offence you compel a man to commit a new offence, the section is clearly retrospective. Owing to what he did before, you oblige him to commit a new offence and punish him for it.

Sir EDWARD CLARKE: Language seems to have lost its accustomed meaning. The hon. and learned Gentleman says you use an old offence in order to make a man commit a new offence.

Mr. CHANCE: Precisely.

Sir EDWARD CLARKE: But you do not make him commit an offence at all. From the time this Act has passed, if this clause is adopted there will be a certain procedure for inquiry into and investigation of crime, and if a man is called up under that procedure——

Mr. CHANCE: To criminate himself.

Sir EDWARD CLARKE: If a man is called up he is asked certain questions

as to what has taken place. He may, if he likes, refuse to answer those questions. If he does, he will be punished for that refusal. ["Hear, hear!"] Yes, for refusal to answer. That refusal will be an act done after the passing of this measure. Or he may, if he feels himself in conscience coerced to commit a crime at all, choose to commit perjury, and then he will be punished for perjury; but the perjury will be committed after the Act has passed. There will be no obligation on anyone to commit that offence. I may say that it was only in consequence of the serious importance with which the observations of the right hon. Gentleman the Member for Halifax (Mr. Stansfeld) seemed to invest this matter that I rose to make this explanation.

Mr. STANSFELD: The hon. and learned Gentleman the Solicitor General has spoken of the Acts of 1870, 1882, and 1883. 1 wish to state precisely my responsibility with regard to every one of these Acts. With regard to the Act of 1870, I had some responsibility of an official character, as I was a Member of the Government, though not of the Cabinet; but it must be remembered that in those days Coercion Bills were not permanent. [*Laughter.*] Yes; that makes all the difference in the world. My argument is this. These Bills were not permanent Bills; they were passed with almost universal consent, and, as a matter of fact, close attention was not given to them by every Member of the Government. [*Cries of* "Oh, oh!"] This is really the truth. Anyone who has been in Office knows that it is perfectly impossible for a man to keep himself perfectly alive to all the Business in the hands of his Colleagues when his time is so much taken up with the consideration of his own Bills, and with the management of the Business of his Department. I accept the official responsibility I have described, and no more. With regard to the Acts of 1882 and 1883, I had no official responsibility for them at all, as I was not a Member of the Government, and I was prevented by circumstances of a private nature from attending much at the House. I think the hon. and learned Gentleman opposite will accept this explanation.

Colonel HUGHES (Woolwich): I am glad the question as to whether or not this measure will be retrospective has been raised. I think the point should be stated in the Bill in express terms, so that there can be no doubt as to the construction to be placed on the provisions. Looking at Section 1, which relates to Proclamations having to be issued before the Act can come into force, we see these words—the Lord Lieutenant may—

" By Proclamation declare the provisions of this Act which relate to proclaimed districts, or any of those provisions, to be in force within any specified part of Ireland as from the date of the Proclamation, or any later date specified in the Proclamation."

I should have thought that, after the Proclamation of a district, Section 1 would come into operation. The words in Section I., as they stand, run—

" Any offence to which this section applies has been committed in a proclaimed district."

I should have read that "in a proclaimed district after it has been proclaimed." I am told that it means "committed in a proclaimed district before or after it has been proclaimed." I wish to see the interpretation which has been put upon this by the right hon. and learned Attorney General for Ireland (Mr. Holmes) made clear. The meaning ought to be made perfectly clear if we are going to pass a new law in consequence of the old law being insufficient. I agree that it should be retrospective. I have no desire to give leave and licence for the commission of offences up to the time when the Bill becomes law; but I think the intention of the Act should be clearly set forth. I also think that if there is to be a distinction made between crime and offence—between any of the crimes mentioned in Section 2 and Section 4—that also should be clearly defined in the Bill and should not be left a matter of argument. If we in this House do not know what the Bill means, and the extent of the litigation which it may involve, I think, if ony for the guidance of the Courts, it is essential that the definitions of the measure should be clear and precise. We should be very careful to make the meaning of the words "committed in a proclaimed district" clear, because, as I have said, I should have thought they meant "committed in a proclaimed district after the proclamation of the district," and I do not want any more inefficient prosecutions.

MR. CHANCE: I regret that I cannot thank the hon. and learned Gentleman the Solicitor General (Sir Edward Clarke) for having extended any very conspicuous courtesy to me. I may, at least, thank him for this—namely, for having in his observations pretty clearly shown to the House that he was not prepared to meet the point that I raised, and that he was able to evade it by a series of those discreet generalities which are better suited for the Old Bailey, at which he is such a distinguished practitioner, than for the High Court of Parliament. What I said was simply this, that a small offence committed before the passing of this Act will be made a lever for forcing a man into the commission of a new offence, and that when that new offence has been committed the man may be imprisoned for an indeterminate period. That is my case, pure and simple. I am met by this statement, that the clause does not compel a man to commit this new offence. But I pointed out that if he declines to criminate himself he commits an offence punishable by indeterminate imprisonment, and that is a pretty good description of an offence in a despotic country. A man will have the option either to criminate himself or to hand over to the Crown evidence against himself which will lead to his conviction for some other offence. That is not a reasonable position in which to put a man, or a reasonable way to deal with the Commission of an offence before the passing of the Act. It is the introduction of the despotic idea into the law. It is an entirely new suggestion that a new unconstitutional, un-English punishment should be attached to an old offence. I defy the hon. and learned Gentleman opposite to point out a case where a retrospective offence has been punished by a new penalty. An old offence is to be used here as a nest egg for the creation of a new offence.

MR. DILLON (Mayo, E.): It seems to me there is one aspect of this question which has been overlooked. As well as I can understand it the position of the Government now is that an offence under the Act, committed in a district before it is proclaimed, even before the Act is passed, can be made the subject-matter of one of these inquiries. But a most important consideration arises with

[First Night.]

respect to this. There cannot be a shadow of a doubt that there are matters made offences in this Bill which, in the eyes of the majority of the people of Ireland, are not only not offences at all, but meritorious acts. That is the very essence of the Bill that we complain of. It is a fact beyond denial—the Government will not attempt to deny it—that many of the offences under this Bill, before the passing of the Bill, have not been in the consciousness of the vast majority of the people of Ireland offences or crimes at all, but have been acts committed openly, of which they have not been in the least ashamed. That is a matter of most vital import to the question at issue. What do the Government propose to do? A thing which no just Legislature has never done in history, to make or pass a law that constitutes certain actions or proceedings offences which are not only not really offences, but which, in the minds of the people for whom you are legislating, are meritorious acts in which they openly and proudly engaged in the face of day. That, to my mind, is one of the greatest grievances to which you can subject a people; because what will be the effect of it? You will institute an inquiry into some of the operations that I myself have been engaged in carrying on; you will institute an inquiry into certain meetings in private houses, at which I have been present, or in which associates and comrades of mine have taken part; we, unquestionably, shall refuse to come up to give evidence in your Courts, and as a consequence we shall be found guilty of crime and put into prison. Can anything be conceived more unjust, more scandalously unjust, than creating, *ex post facto*, certain things crimes which were not believed to be crimes by the people who committed them, which are not crimes, and which no law that you can make will induce the people to consider as crimes, and then punishing people under the machinery established by this Act because they will not betray confidences, repeat conversations, and turn themselves into informers in the face of their own people? Now, I contend that the effect of that will be, in the first place, to bring the law in Ireland into greater disrepute than it is at present. In my opinion, the great task that lies before any Executive or Go-

vernment in Ireland is not at all as much to enforce the law as to try and get the people into sympathy with the law. You cannot do that, and you cannot enforce the law when the law does not recommend itself to the public conscience, and to imagine that you will improve the condition of Ireland by passing a provision like this, which not only will fail to recommend itself to the consciences of the people, but will revolt their consciences, seems to me the greatest act of fatuity in which a Government could engage. It seems to me that, from their own point of view, they should be cautious to avoid passing laws which seem to be the infliction of gross injustice on the people. This provision, if it is passed, will, to my mind, avail the Government nothing whatever. There is no grave crime at present prevailing in Ireland—with the exception of one or two cases which the Government have failed to prove—and, therefore, in that respect there is a very marked and wide difference between the condition of affairs prevailing in that country now and that which prevailed at the time of the passing of the Act of 1882. There is the greatest possible difference. In the year 1882 we struggled and protested against any retrospective action in that measure. But there cannot be the slightest doubt that the condition of things which prevailed in Ireland at that time was as widely different from the condition of things that prevails to-day as one thing can be from another. I recollect that when the Act of 1882 was being discussed in this House, several most desperate and atrocious murders took place in Ireland. There was the murder of Mr. Burke and the dragoon who was guarding him, and several other most terrible murders. The Government said they could not discover the perpetrators of these murders, and one of the objects of their Act was to investigate these matters. But that is not the object now. At the present moment the Government have nothing to go upon with respect to combinations which are open and not secret, and it ought not to be forgotten that any investigation of this kind will fail to unravel or discover them. There is nothing to show that any widespread combination for the perpetration of any serious crime has been the cause of this Bill. My contention is, having regard to past and present transactions in Ireland, that it

Mr. Dillon

cannot be the honest intention of the Government to discover or to track out crime, but that this provision is to be used for the purpose of imprisoning men for refusing to give evidence against their comrades, and in that way, as I understand it, by an underhand and mean dodge to suspend the Habeas Corpus Act, as in 1881. I cannot doubt that the clause, if it is put in force, will be put in to effect in the spirit in which the Government are now contending; that it means, simply and solely, the suspension of the Habeas Corpus Act as against the people engaged in the movement against unfair rents in Ireland, who will be summoned to give evidence, and upon their refusal to say what is required of them, will be forthwith imprisoned.

MR. WARMINGTON (Monmouth, W.): It has been supposed by an hon. Gentleman that something is now proposed which will have operation throughout Ireland. But that is not the case. The section will have operation only in what is called a proclaimed district. A district cannot be proclaimed until after the passing of the Act, and consequently it is impossible that an offence contemplated by the Bill can be committed in a district until it is proclaimed; and, further, it cannot be proclaimed until the Proclamation has been issued. Of course, however, that does not get rid of the difficulty as to what is the effect of the section. There is the other question as to what the effect ought to be; it is a very difficult one, and upon that I hope the Government will give attention to what has been said on this side of the House. It has been urged, over and over again, by those who are Representatives for Ireland, that they do not desire that there should be any difficulty in the way of inquiry into any real or grave crime; that is to say, they have no objection to the application of this power which is of Scotch origin, to the same purposes as those to which it has been applied in days past. But what do the Government propose to do? They propose to apply this section to every conceivable offence under the Criminal Law. I challenge the Attorney General for Ireland to get up and say that there is any offence known to the law to which this section will not apply, because he has taken care not to limit the word "offence." He has defined it by saying that it shall apply to every felony, mis-demeanour, and offence made punishable in this Act. The consequence is that as soon as the Act is passed it will be put into force against political offences. There is nothing to prevent that. If a political libel has been published in Ireland he will be able to examine the editor to get evidence whereon he may found a criminal indictment against the writer. It is said that these are not crimes against which the Act is to be made use of. Why then, do the honest thing and define the crimes in terms by which you really intend to abide. If you mean to make the Act retrospective make it so in clear terms.

MR. O'DOHERTY (Donegal, N.): I reply to the right hon. Gentleman the Attorney General for Ireland, by saying that the offences which he says the Bill does not apply to are punishable under the clause which we are now discussing. I say nothing about indictable offences which are to be tried by a Judge and jury in the ordinary way, as the right hon. and learned Gentleman said, and nothing about the machinery under the section relating to the trial of persons by jury. But I altogether object to trial by Petty Sessions Courts of agrarian offences. The right hon. and learned Gentleman knows that those Courts are, to a large extent, composed of landlords and land agents; and are we to understand that the sheep is to be given up to be tried by wolves?

THE CHAIRMAN: The hon. Member is wandering from the point now before the Committee, which is, whether the words "after the commencement of this Act" shall be inserted.

MR. O'DOHERTY: I have referred to two classes of trials—trial by Judge and jury, and trial by Petty Sessions Courts, to the latter of which I especially desire to call the attention of the Attorney General for Ireland. I say that the offences committed before the passing of the Act are manifestly those to which the Act ought not to apply, and I submit that my argument was perfectly in order. [*Cries of* "Order!"] The Chairman, at any rate, is much more lenient to me than hon. Members opposite. In discriminating between these offences, the only thing there is to rely upon is the discretion of the Attorney General for Ireland. No doubt the clause provides that he must be satisfied on oath that an offence has been com-

[First Night.]

mitted, and then he must exercise his discretion as to whether he shall direct his officer to go down and inquire into it. I have no doubt that it will occur that the case will be tried by a tribunal by which the public and I would have no confidence that justice would be done. Why does not the right hon. and learned Gentleman take care to say that agrarian offences shall be not tried by the tribunal proposed.

THE CHAIRMAN: The hon. Gentleman is not confining himself to the point before the Committee to which I directed his attention—namely, that as to the insertion of the words "after the commencement of this Act."

MR. O'DOHERTY: I will then call attention to another point— the machinery of the clause. This is not the machinery of the Act of 1870 or 1882. In those cases, if a man refused to give evidence he was only liable to the ordinary penalties of refusing to give evidence on trials; but, now, he will be liable to all penalties he would be liable to in the case of an indictable offence. As far as I can see, there remains nothing now but the discretion of the Attorney General to prevent the most insignificant misdemeanour being inquired into by such cumbrous and terrible machinery as this.

MR. BRADLAUGH: I am glad to find myself in accord with the proposition put forward by the hon. and learned Gentleman the Solicitor General —namely, that the English language has lost its meaning in this House. The Solicitor General, who always argues with exceeding clearness, says there should be power to examine witnesses as to offences which are being now committed; and that the offence of refusing to give an answer, or a false answer, would be the new offence within the meaning of the Act. Then if that be the meaning of the Act in the minds of the Government, it is clear that it is not the meaning of the word, and that it has not the same meaning as that which it bears in ordinary books. It was pointed out by one hon. Gentleman who supports the Government that the operation of the clause was limited to any offence committed in a proclaimed district, and I think I see some approval on the part of the Attorney General for England, which induces me to think that that is the correct view of the meaning of the

Mr. O'Doherty

words. But it appears now that the meaning of "proclaimed in the future" is the same thing "proclaimed in the past." I must be excused for saying that that is a lesson in English which I got for the first time to-night.

MR. EDWARD HARRINGTON (Kerry, W.): I believe it will be found that the attempts to work this Act will, in a great measure, tend to impair what is supposed to be the intention of the Act. If you confine this investigation to the discovery of indictable offences— offences of a serious nature, which are included in the meaning of the word crime, the proposal, in my opinion, would be a fair and reasonable one, and you would have a larger majority than you will have under present conditions. But that is clearly not the intention of the Government. Let us not mince matters. We assert, and in this we are corroborated, that your whole purpose in putting this Bill forward is the maintenance of rents in Ireland at their present figure. For that purpose, you will dive into matters political and semi-political; and in that connection I say that when my hon. Friend near me referred to acknowledged agrarian crime, he did not mean crimes which might appear as agrarian in the statistics, but, as they are called, agricultural offences. These are the things you want to investigate. With regard to the working of the Act, what will happen is this —If you bring a guilty man before you, and he commit perjury — [*Cries of* "Order!"]—I do not think I am out of Order. I am dealing with the inquisitorial clause, and with regard to its retrospective operation I think it would be well that a line should be drawn, and that we should not place it in the power of every local despot or intriguer to investigate political or semi-political matters. If you do, the result will assuredly be that you will make it respectable to refuse to give evidence. The most respectable men in Ireland will thus be the first to be brought before these tribunals.

MR. LOCKWOOD (York): If it had not been for the explanation of the hon. and learned Solicitor General I think there would have been no doubt as to the construction to be put upon this section. My hon. and learned Friend says the section makes the Bill retrospective with regard to three classes of offences—felony, misdemeanour, and any offences punishable under the Act. Now, with regard to the third class, I think that may be left out of consideration; but with regard to the other two—felonies and misdemeanours—I understand that he claims that, in respect of these, this Act is retrospective.

SIR EDWARD CLARKE: I said it was not truly retrospective, but dealt with procedure after the passing of the Act.

MR. LOCKWOOD: That is a distinction which may have some meaning in the mind of my hon. and learned Friend, but I should say it is a distinction which may be said to make no difference whatever with regard to what I have said. We want to be informed upon this point—whether the felonies and misdemeanours that the clause will deal with are those which have been committed in a proclaimed district? I did not gather from the statement of the hon. and learned Solicitor General that he was speaking of the felonies and misdemeanours which are committed in a proclaimed district only. If that was his meaning, I hope he will say so; because, if they are to be offences committed before the district is proclaimed, then the words of the Amendment become necessary.

THE ATTORNEY GENERAL (Sir RICHARD WEBSTER) (Isle of Wight): I wish to point out that the intention of the Government is that this inquiry in a proclaimed district may be made in reference to crimes which have been before committed. That was said at the commencement of this discussion, before we had the advantage of the attendance of my hon. and learned Friend the Member for York (Mr. Lockwood). We are now discussing whether the words "after the passing of this Act" are to be inserted or not. We do not say that a district ought to be proclaimed because crime is going to be committed—the point is, that where crimes have been committed there will be a difficulty in getting evidence as to those crimes; and, therefore, as in the Act of 1882, so in this Act, there will be the means of getting evidence with reference to them, whether they have been committed before or after the Proclamation. I must say that it would be simply stultifying ourselves, if we did not make provision against what has taken place before. If there is any

doubt on the matter, we will put in words to make the meaning perfectly clear.

MR. ANDERSON (Elgin and Nairn): I imagine that this is the first time in the history of the House of Commons that the Attorney General of a Government has got up and defended a measure which is to make a penal act retrospective. [Sir RICHARD WEBSTER intimated dissent.] The hon. and learned Gentleman seems to dissent from that. But his remarks have no other meaning; for he says that the Government only mean the Act to be retrospective in a proclaimed district; but he forgets that many of the acts to which this Bill are to apply are not now offences. Therefore, when you proclaim a new district, you create new offences; and when you create new offences as you do by this Act, you make the Criminal Law retrospective. And you do so for this reason—because it is clear that persons will then be capable of being examined as to matters which are now understood to be innocent combinations. You propose then to have up and examine persons—it may be Members of this House—as to acts which may have taken place at this moment. That is indeed your object. The Solicitor General (Sir Edward Clarke), in the language which he used, veiled that purpose with some amount of subtlety, but the Attorney General has not disguised it. He said, in effect, "We intend to make the National League responsible for every act done before the beginning of this Act; we mean to hit the Plan of Campaign," and it may be that hon. Members near me may be attacked. When new offences of this kind are created, I am astonished to hear the Attorney General defend the making retrospective a provision of this serious and drastic character. I cannot, indeed, understand the conduct of the Government. Before the Attorney General spoke, the purpose of the Government was not clear; but now it is clear, and we shall, on this side of the House, all divide with great satisfaction in favour of the Amendment, for the purpose of protesting against a practice unknown to the Criminal Law of England—that of making an Act of so serious a character retrospective.

MR. T. C. HARRINGTON (Dublin, Harbour): The speech of the hon. and learned Attorney General for England casts additional light on what we are doing by passing this Act. During the discussion of this measure, up to the present time, we have been told repeatedly that there is a safeguard as to the application of the provisions of this measure held out to the House, in the fact that the Lord Lieutenant will exercise discretion as to issuing Proclamations to put the Act in force. But the speech of the Attorney General now shows that it is not merely as to crimes that may occur after the passing of this Act, but with also as to offences that may have been committed in past years before the Act comes into force, that the Lord Lieutenant will exercise his discretion in proclaiming a district. That does away with the safeguard supposed to be offered to the House in asking them to rely on the discretion of the Lord Lieutenant in proclaiming a district. For, as the matter is now explained, the Lord Lieutenant is to proclaim a district because offences were committed there last October, or in the course of last year or the year before, and an inquiry is then to be instituted into those offences—that is to say, into offences which were not offences at the time they are said to have been committed, but have been for the first time created offences by the issue of the Lord Lieutenant's Proclamation of the district. I say that you will thus set up an instrument of extraordinary and unparalleled tyranny in the districts which may be proclaimed. This might be all very well if you wished to inquire into serious crimes. We have no objection to have an inquiry as to serious crimes. But if the Lord Lieutenant proclaims a district for one offence, he proclaims it for all; and the provision which gives him power to have an inquiry does in effect, as I have already said, create new offences.

VISCOUNT WOLMER (Hants, Petersfield): I would beg to remind the Committee, after what has fallen from the hon. Member for Elgin, that if the clause in the Act of 1882, which corresponds to the clause under discussion, had not existed, the perpetrators of the Phœnix Park murders would never have been discovered.

MR. MAURICE HEALY (Cork): The Committee has been for some time discussing the question whether the operation of this measure will be retrospective; but I can assure hon. Members that the Act will be administered in Ireland by tribunals who will have no doubt on the point. This Act will be administered by Resident Magistrates, and they will have no difficulty at all in construing the Act in the sense which the Government have declared that they intend it to bear. The draftsman who has drawn the Bill so skilfully drawn it so as to suggest to hon. Members who read it that this clause is not in fact intended to be retrospective, or to affect offences committed before the passing of the Act; while the Government know that any Court or Body of Resident Magistrates to whom the administration of the Act may be handed over will not have the smallest difficulty in construing it as retrospective. In discussing the Amendment before the Committee, we are in considerable embarrassment from the necessity of making a distinction between crimes which we understand to be crimes, and of other offences which are known in this Bill as "offences." For the purpose of considering the effect of my hon. Friend's Amendment, you must divide crimes into three categories. You have, first, crimes, such as murder, manslaughter, and arson, which everyone in the House and in England knows to be crimes. Secondly, there are crimes of a political or quasi-political character And, in the third place, you have the class of offences known as offences against this Act. As to the first class—such as murder, manslaughter, and arson—I do not think there will be any difference of opinion in any quarter of the House. The position we take up is this. We are unwilling to have this Star Chamber inquiry at all. We say that it is not necessary, and that it will do no good. But if you are determined to have a judicial inquiry of the character contemplated, and, with that view, pass this clause, then I do not think it can be argued that it should not apply to crimes of that character whether committed before or after the passing of the Act. But as to political or quasi-political offences, they stand in a totally different position and, certainly, this clause should not be made retrospective as to offences of that kind. The Government have sustained a series of mishaps during the past 12 months in dealing with combinations in Ireland. They have instituted a series of prosecutions for the

Mr. T. C. Harrington

purpose of putting an end to these combinations, and we know what has come of them. We know that, in some cases, the prosecutions were abortive; that in other cases, these prosecutions came to an issue only to be decided by the jury in favour of the defendants; and that in a third class of prosecutions, the proceedings have resulted in the disagreement of the jurors. How will any fairminded and intelligent man get up and defend the proposition that the Government, having failed in these prosecutions, having brought my hon. Friends near me before a jury, and having lamentably failed in the prosecution—are now to take powers in this Act to renew these prosecutions, and that under the section we are now discussing they are to hold Star Chamber inquiries, are to bring up any witnesses they choose, are to examine tenants, members of the National League, and perhaps even Members of this House, and are then, with the evidence so obtained, to attempt to renew these prosecutions? The Government may attempt to defend that action; but I do not think that action of that kind will commend itself to any reasonable being, and I should be surprised to hear any hon. Member in any quarter of the House rise and defend any proceeding of that kind. Then take another class of cases, that of political libel. Is it to be contended that it is fair or reasonable that the Government should have power under this clause to ransack the old files of *United Ireland*, or any other Nationalist papers, to select any articles they may think liable to prosecution, to hold Star Chamber inquiries as to articles—I do not know how many years old, for there is no restriction as to time in this clause—and to bring the real or supposed writer of those articles before Resident Magistrates with the disadvantage of having arrayed against him the exceptional and extraordinary powers conferred by this clause? I do not think that is fair play, or that it is dealing in a fair and reasonable manner with political opponents, and I shall be surprised if action of that kind commends itself to the good sense and good feeling of the House or of the mass of the English people. Now, I come to the third class of offences I have mentioned. As to these offences the Government, as I understand, admit the reasonableness of our position. One Gentleman tells us

that there are no offences created by the Act; and the right hon. and learned Attorney General for Ireland tells us that there are certain offences newly created, but that this clause will not be retrospective as to these; and the right hon. and learned Gentleman tried to show that the clauses are so drawn that the Act only applies to offences committed after the passing of the Act. But I would point out that that is no answer to our argument on this point. The position of the Government in regard to these clauses is, as I understand, that they do not create new offences, but merely introduce a new procedure, and that the whole effect of these clauses is to enable these offences to be tried summarily by Resident Magistrates. But we object to that. And even assuming that the Bill, as drawn, would not warrant the Government in holding inquiries for the purpose of obtaining evidence to prosecute persons before Resident Magistrates for offences committed before the passing of the Act, there is nothing in the Bill to prevent the Government from holding inquiries as to such offences, and then prosecuting the persons, who are said to have committed them, before a Judge and jury. The whole contention of the Government as to this matter is, that the Summary Jurisdiction Clauses are not retrospective; but the only effect of that is that crimes cannot be tried summarily; but there is, as I have said, nothing to prevent the holding of a Star Chamber sort of inquiry, followed by the trial of the accused, not before two Resident Magistrates, but by a change of venue, either in England or in some other district in Ireland. Now, we contend that this should not apply to offences of a political character. Gentlemen opposite get up and declaim about the terrible crimes of murder and Moonlighting committed in Ireland. On the other hand, if we propose to restrict the Bill to crimes of this character, the Government then say that the Bill is not intended to be confined to them. The practical conclusion of the Government is, therefore, much wider than the premisses from which it is supposed to follow. I think the Amendment before the House is a most proper one. It is a most intolerable grievance that, as regards articles in *United Ireland*, and offences committed in the execution of the Plan of Campaign, the Government should be permitted to hold Star Chamber inquiries under this measure, and thus bring to punishment offences committed before the passing of the Act. I appeal to hon. Members on both sides to give us fair play in this matter. As regards political offences, this clause should certainly not be retrospective.

MR. ASQUITH (Fife, E.): It is with unaffected diffidence that I differ from the right hon. and learned Gentleman the Attorney General for Ireland on the construction of a section of an Act of Parliament for which he has a parental responsibility. But if it had not been for the confident opinion he has expressed in a different sense, I should not have entertained a doubt that this clause applies only after the date of the Lord Lieutenant's Proclamation. What are the words of the clause? They are that—

"Where a sworn information has been made that any offence to which this section applies has been committed in a proclaimed district."

I ask, how an offence can be committed in a proclaimed district until that district has been proclaimed? And then, let me call attention to the language of the 5th clause, which deals with the Proclamation of a district, and provides that—

"The Lord Lieutenant . . . may from time to time . . . by Proclamation, declare the provisions of this Act which relate to proclaimed districts, or any of those provisions, to be in force within any specified part of Ireland, as from the date of the Proclamation: and the provisions of this Act which are mentioned in the Proclamation shall, after the said date, be in force within such specified part of Ireland, and that part of Ireland shall be a proclaimed district within the meaning of the provisions so mentioned."

At what date, then, does a district become a proclaimed district? Either from the date of the Proclamation, or from some date specified in the Proclamation. I ask, then, how an offence can be said to have been committed in a proclaimed district until after the Proclamation which brings that district to the status of a proclaimed district? Then this section is declared to apply to offences to which, in the later part of the clause, the section is said to apply. Now, look at the 5th sub-section of the clause. It runs as follows:—

"The offences to which this section applies are any felony or misdemeanour, and any offence punishable under this Act."

Mr. Maurice Healy

On that I make two observations. In the first place, the language of that sub-section is clearly in favour of the construction that this Act creates an entirely new category of crimes. There are only two classes of indictable offences known to the English law—felonies and misdemeanours. And, therefore, the latter words of this sub-section can only apply to offences created by this Act, and made by it for the first time punishable. Next, let us look to the first part of the clause, and see how it would work out, according to the Attorney General's construction. According to my hon. and learned Friend, a preliminary inquiry may be held as to any offence, whether committed before or after the Proclamation of a district. If so, an inquiry may be held, under the 5th sub-section, as to an offence which becomes punishable for the first time under this Act. That is to say, you take power to inquire into an offence which was not a crime when it was committed, but became a crime by the Proclamation of the Lord Lieutenant making the district in which it was committed a proclaimed district. By the construction put on this clause by the hon. and learned Attorney General, he does, by his own admission, a thing which no Act can be presumed to do—that is to create retrospective offences and enable an inquisitorial investigation to be instituted into them, although they were not offences at the time they were committed. I say that if the hon. and learned Attorney General meant by this clause to convey the meaning he has suggested, then the language which he used as a vehicle for his meaning has failed of its effect. But I admit that the language he has used is so equivocal as to render it necessary to insert in the clause words which shall prevent Resident Magistrates in Ireland from giving a retrospective effect to it, and for that reason I shall support the Amendment. But I think my hon. Friend (Dr. Commins) has been too liberal to the Government in this matter. He says, in his Amendment, "after the commencement of this Act." Now, the incriminating offence may be done after the commencement of the Act, but before the issue of any Proclamation by the Lord Lieutenant. I would, therefore, propose that he should change the wording of the Amendment, so as to make it run "committed in a proclaimed district, after the district has been proclaimed." That, I think, would meet the fair and legitimate requirements of the case.

SIR HENRY JAMES (Bury, Lancashire): I can understand the position of my hon. and learned Friend and other hon. Gentlemen sitting on this side of the House. Of course, they object to this clause. They objected to it on the second reading of the Bill; and, objecting to it, they are acting wisely in endeavouring to minimize its effect. But, in spite of the objections raised to the clause, the Bill has been read a second time. The question now is, how the intention of the majority is to be carried out; for I suppose the Committee will not allow this intention to be defeated, although the manner of giving effect to it is, of course, open to criticism. The Amendment before us refers not only to offences which may be created by the Bill, but to all felonies and misdemeanours; and the effect of the Amendment, if it were carried, would be that, although a great deal of crime were found to exist in a district—and until it has been so found to exist the Lord Lieutenant cannot proclaim the district —there would be no power to inquire into this past crime, and this clause would be perfectly inefficacious as to crimes committed in the past. Why is the clause not to apply to offences that have been committed in the past, and only to apply to those committed in the future? Suppose this Bill comes into operation upon, say, the 31st of August, and great crime is found to have existed in a certain district in September and October, and the district is proclaimed on account of that crime, yet it is said that the detection of the crime is not to take place because of its being anterior to the Proclamation. My hon. and learned Friend the Member for East Fife (Mr. Asquith) says this was never done in any Act of Parliament before. Why, it was done *totidem verbis* in the Act of 1882 in respect of felonies, misdemeanours, and offences created under that Act. With one exception, the Bill framed by my right hon. Friend the Member for Derby (Sir William Harcourt) was, in its 16th clause, exactly the same as the provision we are now discussing. The words are entirely the same. I may be wrong, but I think that when the Bill of the right hon. Gentleman was under discussion an Amendment was moved similar to that now under the consideration of the Committee. The suggestion of the hon. and learned Gentleman the Member for East Fife, or his first criticism as to a proclaimed district, is against himself; because if he is right that the clause as framed will only refer to districts after they are proclaimed, he stands as the friend, the candid friend, of the Government, pointing out that this provision is insufficient for its purpose and requires strengthening. Will the hon. and learned Gentleman agree to the insertion of words to make it perfectly clear that the clause shall apply to districts before they are proclaimed? I should say that on this point my hon. and learned Friend is hypercritical. The district and the county will be the same though it may not have been proclaimed. The clause speaks of the geographical area, and when it mentions a proclaimed district it means the district or county in which the offence has been committed. But do not let us waste time over this question. As I understand the hon. and learned Member for East Fife, he agrees with the Government, and wants to correct the drafting of the Act of 1882. We thought it was right at the time; we thought we were making the Act what you call retrospective and quite safe and sure; but, as I say, we need not waste much time in argument as to this drafting if the hon. and learned Gentleman wishes to make the clause retrospective. The question as to whether the retrospective principle should apply to offences existing under the measure makes the matter much more serious and important. I presume there is no substantial objection to the principle being applied to felonies and misdemeanours; but when we come to the definitions I would ask the Government whether they think it desirable to make it refer to offences under the Act, because, really and truly, except the offence under Clause 7, which does not become an offence until the district is proclaimed, there would be nothing which would be affected by foregoing the principle. Therefore, I think it would be well to humour my hon. and learned Friend in this matter, and, confining the retrospective action of the clause to felonies and misdemeanours, reconsider the question of applying it to offences under the Act.

Sir WILLIAM HARCOURT (Derby): We are very much indebted to my right hon. and learned Friend (Sir Henry James), because, though he came in like a lion, he went out like a lamb. He began with a vehement and rhetorical denunciation of everybody sitting on these Benches, and ultimately conceded that his distinguished pupil was perfectly right, and that what the hon. and learned Gentleman the Member for East Fife (Mr. Asquith) proposed was a thing which, in fairness, should be allowed. Let us recognize, then, the advice given to the Government by one of their main supporters. We are going to get some good out of the Liberal Unionists after all. Of course, this is the whole keystone of the position, that the offences under this Act should be struck out of this examination or inquiry by a Resident Magistrate. That they should be struck out is the advice that my right hon. and learned Friend has given, and, therefore, we have got the main part of what we are contending for. I am surprised that my right hon. and learned Friend's memory is beginning to fail. He talked to us of the Act of 1882. It so happened that when my right hon. and learned Friend spoke I was just looking at the discussion which took place on this clause in the Act of 1882. Though I worked the labouring oar in the passing of that Act, when we came to legal points I received valuable assistance from my right hon. and learned Friend, who was then Attorney General. He seems to have entirely forgotten what occurred in 1882. The clause in the Act of that year was not *totidem verbis* with the clause in this Bill, and if my right hon. and learned Friend had been in the House as I have been since 5 o'clock he would have heard the matter discussed over and over again, and he would have had his recollection freshened. He would have seen that the two clauses differ on this very point on which the argument turns, because the clause in the Act of 1882 took especial care to except from the operation of the Act all those provisions in which anything like a new offence was created. That is the very gist of the new arrangement, and the consequence is that my right hon. and learned Friend's contention is strictly in accordance with the Act of 1882 ; and, therefore, the statement of the right hon.

and learned Gentleman (Sir Henry James) on the subject of the clause of 1882 might have been entirely spared. I am glad that the right hon. and learned Gentleman—even if by a circuitous and singular route—has come to the conclusion to which I have adverted. If the Government take his wise advice and will strike out from the operation of this clause all words as to offences under the Act, and will take the advice of their other learned advisers who spoke earlier in the debate from below the Gangway, and strike out the word "misdemeanour," we shall have got this section into working order. I think the independent supporters of the Government have tendered useful advice, and I hope it will be carried out.

THE CHIEF SECRETARY FOR IRELAND (Mr. A. J. BALFOUR) (Manchester, E.): The right hon. Gentleman the Member for Derby (Sir William Harcourt) who has just spoken has forgotten something. He says that under the Act of 1882 there was no inquiry into crimes created by the Act.

SIR HENRY JAMES: That was not the case.

MR. A. J. BALFOUR: No; there were other clauses that created offences which came under the Act. This was one provision—

"Every person who knowingly is a member of an unlawful association as defined by this Act, or takes part in the operations of an unlawful association as defined by this Act, or of any meeting thereof, shall be guilty of an offence against this Act."

And if a person was guilty of an offence against the Act, and there was no special exemption made in favour of that offence, there was an inquiry. So that although the right hon. Gentleman, as he himself said, "worked the labouring oar," that process does not appear to have imprinted upon his memory any great recollection of the provisions of the measure. [Sir WILLIAM HARCOURT dissented.] I give the right hon. Gentleman a copy of his handiwork (handing him a copy of the Act). The present clause in the Bill differs in no respect from the 9th clause of the Bill of the right hon. Gentleman opposite except in this only, that we limited the operation of our clause to the proclaimed district, and he did not. If any objection lies against our clause as differing from the right hon. Gentleman's clause, it is only in so far as we lay down safeguards, and he did not. The right hon. and learned Gentleman the Member for Bury (Sir Henry James) pointed out that if the criticism of the hon. and learned Gentleman the Member for East Fife is carried, the Amendment now before us will be useless. But we do not hesitate to say that we do believe that the Amendment really substantially is required to carry out the intention of hon. Gentlemen below the Gangway opposite. We do not agree that that intention should be carried out. We are distinctly of opinion that after a district has been proclaimed there ought to be the power of making such inquiry into crimes committed before the Proclamation as to enable us to discover the perpetrator of these crimes. [An hon. MEMBER: Offences!] Well, offences or crimes. I need hardly point out that the contention of some hon. Gentlemen that offences, if there are any created by this Act, will only be offences after the Act is passed, and after the district in which these offences are committed is proclaimed; and, of course, with regard to such offences, the Amendment now before us is entirely irrelevant and will have no effect. I hope the discussion we have now had is sufficient. [*Cries of* "Oh, oh!"] Well, we have discussed the subject for three hours. The principle we have adopted in this clause is one which has been adopted by successive Governments and by successive Houses of Parliament. If I am to discuss the value of this clause, perhaps I might read a quotation from the right hon. Gentleman opposite (Sir William Harcourt) when he was defending a clause of exactly similar import. In introducing a provision of this kind in the Explosives Act of 1883 he used these words—

" It is a clause which was originally in the Peace Preservation (Ireland) Act "—that is, the Act of 1881—" it was re-enacted by this House in the Prevention of Crime Act of last year; and it has proved of singular efficacy, because it was by its use "—its retrospective use, I may interpolate—" that the Phœnix Park murders were traced. . . . . . Therefore this clause is one of the most essential and important clauses of the Bill."—(3 *Hansard*, [277] 1848.)

Well, Sir, the right hon. Gentleman has changed his opinion on a great many questions connected with the go-

vernment of Ireland, and I do not in the least wish to reproach him with that now; but there is one subject on which, I presume, he has not changed his opinion. I presume he is as desirous now as he was in the year 1883 that if crime—anything like the crime which occurred in the Phœnix Park—exists in Ireland machinery shall be at hand by means of which that crime shall be detected.

MR. T. M. HEALY: I should like to ask the right hon. Gentleman the Chief Secretary for Ireland (Mr. A. J. Balfour), as he seems to be so familiar with these Acts, and with the necessity of a Proclamation for putting the clauses in operation, what district he will proclaim for the purpose of inquiring into conspiracy? Take the Plan of Campaign. That was a "conspiracy" for which hon. Gentlemen, Members of this House, were indicted. They were alleged to have made speeches, one in Galway, one in Limerick, one in Dublin, one in Sligo, one in Monaghan, and one in Cork—one at the Giants' Causeway, and another at Cape Clear. Some English Members may not be familiar enough with Irish geography to know what that means; but I ask the right hon. Gentleman the Chief Secretary, who knows all about Ireland, and who will, naturally, take the point at once, what district he would proclaim in order to have an inquiry into such a case as this? You may change your venue as much as you like; but where would you hold your inquiry for this conspiracy, which "spreads like a cancer," as we have heard from hon. Gentlemen opposite? What district would you proclaim for the purpose of holding that inquiry? That is the real way to test this matter. I defy the Government to do it unless they proclaim the whole of Ireland. I see the right hon. and learned Gentleman the Member for Bury (Sir Henry James) in his place, and I am thankful that he should have made a practical suggestion, though, as he will have observed, the Government have not taken the slightest notice of that suggestion. The right hon. Gentleman the Chief Secretary has not noticed the speech of the right hon. and learned Gentleman the Member for Bury. The right hon. and learned Gentleman recommends the suggestion we have been making all along. Inquire into as many murders or serious crimes as you like, or take power to do it—although some hon. Members will not have the word "crime"; I suppose they wish now to speak of the Phœnix Park "offence"—for we must speak by the card now, since the speech of the right hon. Gentleman the Chief Secretary. Take power to deal with these serious "offences;" but with regard to what the hon. and learned Gentleman the Attorney General (Sir Richard Webster) admits to be a new crime, what is going to happen? The right hon. and learned Gentleman the Member for Bury was very much twitted during the passage of the Corrupt Practices Act on certain points, and I would ask him whether in this matter there is not an implied repeal of the Corrupt Practices Act? [*Cries of* "No!"] I think so. I would remind him that if he refers to the 49th section, he will see that everything under that measure is felony or misdemeanour. You can inquire into all these felonies and misdemeanours, no matter when they occur. Take the case of bribery at Taunton—suppose Taunton were in Ireland—or the case of Londonderry, the late Member for which place has been made a Baronet by Her Majesty's Government for having been unsuccessful in practising "offences." I say it would be impossible, in spite of the provisions of the Corrupt Practices Act, once you get this clause passed, to hold an inquiry into Election matters—I will not say "crimes," but "offences." The Corrupt Practices Act says, notwithstanding the provisions of 15 & 16 *Vict.* c. 57, the Election Commissioners

" shall not make any inquiry concerning elections that have taken place prior to the passing of this Act."

I have a distinct recollection that when this Act was being passed the right hon. Gentleman the Postmaster General (Mr. Raikes) twitted the right hon. and learned Gentleman the Member for Bury in a most unhandsome manner, saying that this was to protect the corruption of Taunton—for which borough the right hon. and learned Gentleman then sat—and making some most personal allusions. Fortunately, however, Taunton is not in Ireland. But I say that it would be possible in all electoral matters, after the passing of this Act, to go back, and this is an implied repeal of the 49th section of the Corrupt Practices Act.

Mr. T. M. Healy

Furthermore, if you are going to use this Act for the purpose of any crime, no matter when committed, remember it is to be said to the credit of the right hon. and learned Gentleman the Member for Bury that he certainly acted in that matter with great consideration to the House. I moved an Amendment, when his Bill was under discussion, to the effect that none of the provisions of the Crimes Act were to apply, and what happened? Why, in the 69th section we find these words—

" No person shall be tried for any offence against this Act, committed under any of the provisions of the Prevention of Crime (Ireland) Act, 1882."

If the Prevention of Crime Act were in existence you would not want this Bill, and the provision to which I refer would be in force. The least, therefore, we can ask the Government is that they should adopt some provision similar to that which formerly operated, and with which the Government were perfectly content. [*Interruption.*] The hon. and learned Attorney General interrupts: He has not given the same attention to this Bill as was given by the right hon. and learned Gentleman the Member for Bury to the measure of the right hon. Gentleman the Member for Derby, though that right hon. and learned Member was as much against Home Rule as any hon. Gentleman opposite. The right hon. and learned Gentleman, in a Statute which did not refer to coercion, which was only a Corrupt Practices Act, providing for extraneous and non-coercive matters, provided that the Crimes Act should not be availed of. Is it reasonable when you are dealing with "terrible conspiracies," with "frightful outrages,"and "offences against women," about which you write through your private secretaries, and which make the hair of the Primroser stand on end, that you should be legislating retrospectively against these new "offences" which you are creating in this measure? Deal with the new offences when you create them if you like, but with nothing of a stale nature. The right hon. and learned Gentleman the Member for Bury says the measure necessarily will have an *ex post facto* operation. I challenge him to say whether his Criminal Code Bill would have had a retrospective operation? [Sir HENRY JAMES: Yes.] Here is the Bill, which would come into law some time in 1883, and which, naturally, would speak from the sign manual of Her Majesty. According to that measure—

"Any justice who has reason to believe that any offence has been committed within the limits of his jurisdiction"

could have that jurisdiction the moment this Act had passed and not before. No doubt he got his jurisdiction the moment he received Her Majesty's Commission for all other purposes, but he could not have held inquiries into criminal matters until the Act passed. [*Laughter.*] Let me tell the hon. and learned Gentleman the Attorney General that though he may laugh now for the purpose of leading a number of Gentlemen who know nothing of these-matters into the Lobby, if he were arguing in some place where those who would have the decision of the matter understood what they were called upon to decide he would not be so much inclined to smile. Under the circumstances, I do think it reasonable that the suggestion of the right hon. and learned Gentleman the Member for Bury, at least, should be adopted. The Government are obtaining the support of the Liberal Unionists in the passing of the Bill, then let them give effect to the opinion of the Liberal Unionists. Let them pass this clause for felonies and misdemeanours, but do not allow what you call "incitements to Boycotting," "incitements to joining the Plan of Campaign," agreements not to take a farm, agreements not to buy tea or sugar from a particular person—do not allow these " crimes " which, admittedly, have not been offences, and will not be offences until this Bill is passed, to be made the subject of inquiry until they are committed in the future. The Liberal Unionists in this matter should insist upon having effect given to their opinions. They should not allow the Government to avail themselves of their support in one place and then deride their opinions in another. The Tory Party by itself, even if it were 100 stronger than it is now as a homogeneous Party, could never pass such a Bill as this—would never attempt to do it. It is the support of such Gentleman as the right hon. and learned Gentleman the Member for Bury, the right hon. Gentleman the Member for West Birmingham (Mr. Joseph Chamberlain), and the noble Marquess the Member for Rossen-

dale (the Marquess of Hartington)—it is the support of these Gentlemen that is putting violence into the Tory Party. The Tory Party would not dare by themselves to face this English House of Commons with such a Bill as this. [*Laughter.*] No, Sir; they would rather make an alliance with the hon. Gentleman the Member for Cork (Mr. Parnell); they would rather send Lord Carnarvon to interview that hon. Member to find out his opinions; and I venture to think that if there were a Tory Government in power, and Lord Carnarvon had consulted the hon. Member upon such a point as the passage of this section, some deference would be paid to his opinion. But, yet, here you have the noble Marquess and the right hon. and learned Gentleman the Member for Bury supporting the Government just as my hon. Friend the Member for Cork might have been supporting them, and surely when they give their opinion some deference ought to be paid to it. The same deference ought to be paid to it as would have been paid to the opinion of the hon. Member for Cork when Lord Carnarvon met him in the drawing-room of an hon. Member opposite, whose name I could mention, but I will not. I do think the time has arrived when right hon. Gentlemen opposite should give us some concession of a substantive character with regard to this matter. Any serious crime you want to inquire into you can inquire into with all your hearts. But as regards newly created offences, I do ask the right hon. and learned Gentleman the Member for Bury, as he is giving the Government the benefit of his support, to insist upon due weight being given to his opinions by Her Majesty's Government.

Mr. DILLON: The action of the Government to-night is, I am afraid, likely to prolong the debate to a very considerable extent. Some hours ago we moved from these Benches a reasonable and fair Amendment; but no single Member of the Government has met us in a fair way from the time this discussion started until now. Over and over again those hon. Members on the other side, who have stood up, have referred to old worn-out topics, such as the discovery of the Phœnix Park murders and other crimes discovered and punished under the Act of 1882. I pointed out at an early stage of the debate — as also did other hon. Members—that we were not objecting to retrospective action in reference to inquiries affecting murders or serious crimes; but when we had two hours ago made that clear beyond all question, the noble Viscount the Member for Petersfield (Viscount Wolmer), who is distinguished for his love for the Irish people, started up on these Benches and said he desired to remind this House that the Phœnix Park murders would not have been discovered had it not been for the retrospective action of the clauses of the Act of 1882. The noble Lord was followed in that parrot cry by every Member who stood up on the Benches opposite; and, finally, the right hon. and learned Gentleman the Member for Bury (Sir Henry James) made a most extraordinary statement, for he said that no district in Ireland could or would be proclaimed by the Lord Lieutenant unless and until a large and serious amount of grave crime prevailed in it. Will any hon. Member representing the Government stand up and give us a pledge to that effect? If any one will, I will undertake, on behalf of the people of Ireland, to say that no district will be proclaimed under this Act at all. The right hon. and learned Member for Bury made that extraordinary statement; but I noticed that no hon. Gentleman on the Front Bench opposite attempted to say a single word on that subject. We know perfectly well that the week after this Act has passed into law, a large district of Ireland—every district, in fact, in which the people are making any resistance to the payment of rent—will be instantly proclaimed. We complain of inaction on the part of the Government, or of this, that instead of replying to the arguments addressed to them from these Benches, they persistently give the go-by to everyone of these arguments, and reply to arguments not addressed to them at all, which they merely set up for the purpose of overthrowing. The right hon. Gentleman the Chief Secretary for Ireland, when he last addressed the Committee, what did he say? The right hon. and learned Gentleman the Attorney General for Ireland (Mr. Holmes) had, at an earlier period of the discussion, pointed out that the new crimes that were especially created by this Bill would not become crimes until a district was proclaimed, and that,

Mr. Dillon

therefore, no inquiry would be held with regard to them. That is true; but that is not what we are complaining of. What we are complaining of is that conspiracy, intimidation, and the various offences under the Whiteboy Acts, all of which are crimes already in Ireland, but which are, by this Act, to be shifted from their ordinary Courts of Procedure into the Courts of Summary Procedure, will form a net so vast and wide-reaching and narrow in its meshes that the entire population of Ireland can, under the interpretation which it will be possible to put upon these offences, be caught in it. Read the Whiteboy Acts to observe what are offences in law, and the House will see it will not be necessary to institute inquiries in every portion of Ireland in order to bring the whole population into this net, and that it will not be necessary to have recourse to these new offences at all. Read the charge of the Judge in my trial in Dublin, and the House will see what is the law as laid down by Mr. Justice Murphy; read the charge of Lord Fitzgerald in "The Queen *v.* Parnell," in 1881, and it will be seen that it will be impossible to enter into a political controversy which may have for its results pecuniary injury or loss to any class of the community without exposing you to the Law of Conspiracy as interpreted by a Judge or a partizan magistrate. The greatest abuses can arise under this Law of Conspiracy if you have not the protection of a jury who will give to the law a Constitutional interpretation. I say the Law of Conspiracy, as laid down by these Judges and the new offences laid down by this Bill, are almost unnecessary, because, in the present social condition of Ireland, it would be impossible to have any political association whatever, except an association to further the views of the Executive, that would not be swept into the net of a conspiracy prosecution; and the result of that—and what we complain of, and the Government must understand it, though they have made no effort to meet us in argument up to the present—is that under this clause, after the Act has passed and the Proclamations are issued, the Government may proceed to inquire into offences which are not under this Act, but were made before this Act was passed. Inquiries may take place, and the result may be to imprison me and all who have been working with me, because we refuse to swear against our fellows. Suppose I were brought up before a Magistrates' Court in one of the proclaimed districts, and were questioned as to what I had said to a man in reference to the working of the Plan of Campaign, do you think I should reply? And if you took up 40 or 50 priests, and questioned them in the same way, do you think they would reply? Of course they would do nothing of the sort. I say that until the Committee put a proviso in the Bill tying the hands of the Government for such conduct, we are entitled to say that they deliberately look to this clause as a means of imprisoning men because they cannot, in honour, consider themselves free to give evidence before such Courts of Inquiry as may be created under this Bill. I ask this Committee, is it reasonable, and I would say to the Government is it a prudent course for them to adopt, to utterly refuse to meet us in argument on this question, and to refuse to go into this practical and important question whether they will administer the measure in this way, or will not, and why, if they do not intend to do so, they do not put in some proviso which will bar them from that course? I heard the hon. and learned Attorney General for England (Sir Richard Webster) making use of suppositions that we have had *ad nauseam*. I heard him declare that we must go upon the supposition that this Bill will be fairly administered; but we remember that plea being put forward by the late Mr. Forster. I do not deny that when Mr. Forster put forward that plea he meant what he said; but when he went over to Ireland, and found himself in the hands of the permanent officials of the Castle, it would have taken 10 Mr. Forster's to resist the pressure put on him. Whereas he pledged himself, night after night, that the Bill would be used only against village ruffians and criminals, and laughed to scorn the idea that Members of this House would find themselves imprisoned under the Act. The measure was not in operation six weeks before I found myself under lock and key. [An hon. MEMBER: Hear, hear!] "Hear, hear!" says an hon. Gentleman. I do not deny—I never doubted—that there are many Members on the Benches opposite who consider that the fittest

place for me and for many hon. Gentlemen around me would be under lock and key in Ireland. I never questioned that; but what I ask is that there should be honesty in the debates in this House. Do not tell this House and the country that you are introducing Bills to deal with criminals in Ireland, and then, when the Bill is passed, and, under false pretences, the consent of this House has been procured for it, turn it to uses which hon. Members and Members of the Government gave their word of honour it would not be put to. I want, at least, to know this—that whatever measures are introduced against the people of Ireland, they will be introduced honestly and straightforwardly; that we shall be told that they intend to suspend the Habeas Corpus—and they will be able to do that with perfect ease under the provisions of this Bill. I ask that the Government will tell us what they mean to do, and will not get up and say—"We do not mean to suspend the Habeas Corpus; no man can be punished under this Act unless he is a criminal; no man can be punished under this Act unless he gets a fair trial," and so on. I have heard it said that, under the provisions of this Bill, I and hundreds who have worked with me, and stood by me in the operations of a legal organization, can be imprisoned and held in prison because we will refuse to say what was stated to us in confidence and honour; and I say that until the Government give us a pledge—and not only do that, but put it in the shape of a proviso that will tie their hands against the pressure that will be put on them in Ireland—we are entitled to say that they are knowingly and wittingly taking these powers knowing that they will use them.

MR. MOLLOY (King's Co., Birr): The hon. and learned Member for North Longford (Mr. T. M. Healy), who has just sat down, is justified in all that he has said to-night. To every argument that has been addressed from this side of the House to the Government to-night the parrot answer has invariably been given—"Do you, or do you not, wish to give us power to put down murder and other serious crime?" Speaker after speaker on this side has declared, in most emphatic terms—"We do not object to your taking powers to search out serious crime." The question they put is not our point; it is begging the whole question. It is deceiving the Committee when hon. Gentlemen get up from the Tory Benches and continually make this claim, saying—" You are refusing to give us power to put down serious crime." Let it be clearly understood that that is not our intention. It has not been the intention of any hon. Gentleman on this side during the whole of the debate. Our contention is a totally different one, and the right hon. and learned Gentleman, from whom we expected very little assistance indeed— even he, in his speech, got up and pointed out this difference, and suggested to the Government that they ought to introduce such an Amendment as would meet our case. Now, Sir, the right hon. Gentleman the Chief Secretary for Ireland (Mr. A. J. Balfour) has been indulging in these phrases all the evening. He cannot rise in his place to speak to any Amendment but he uses the words "murder" and "attempt to murder," and "other serious crime," though they have no more to do with the argument that we are engaged in than if we were to discuss a question of foreign policy. I think the right hon. Gentleman opposite said—of course, I mean the last time he favoured us with his opinions, of which he is very chary— that everything that is not an offence now will not be an offence under this Act, punishable under this Act. I think I accurately stated what he said. He does not deign to give me any reply, therefore I assume that his silence gives consent. I think his statement is not correct, and I will point out how it is not. There are combinations of tenants in Ireland now some of which, according to lawyers, may be illegal; but there are others which, according to almost the entire legal opinion, are not legal acts and are not offences. It has been stated in the course of the last two or three days from the Government Benches that there may be combinations of tenants with a view to obtain reductions of rents which are perfectly legal. It is no offence now for these combinations to take place. But when this Act passes, will these combinations be legal or illegal? Why they will be made illegal at once by some authority under the Bill. Inquiries will take place by the Resident Magistrates, and does any one in the House suppose for a moment that the Resident Magistrates, without

Mr. Molloy

any legal training or knowledge, will be able to discriminate as between the legality or illegality before the passing of the Act and the legality or illegality after the passing of the Act? Of course no distinction will be made by these gentlemen, and under this Bill acts that are now perfectly legal, according to the best authorities that have been admitted in the course of the last few days, will become illegal under this Act. The statement of the right hon. Gentleman was a very brief one, and it was to the effect that such a thing could not take place, and that nothing that is now a legal act could be inquired into. I think I have shown that the statement he makes is wrong, as he would find if he were not in such a hurry, and would carefully consider the matter and examine into the facts. It is perfectly illusory for the right hon. Gentleman to make these statements to the House, for it is clear to everyone who has given any consideration to the matter that acts that are now legal can be treated under this Act as illegal, and, though permitted before the passing of the Act, will be punished under the powers of the Act.

Dr. KENNY (Cork, S.): The Government, I expect, will begin to accuse us of obstruction; but the real obstructionists are the Treasury Bench, who are endeavouring to defeat the just and solid arguments we are advancing against this clause as it stands, and in favour of the hon. and learned Gentleman the Member for South Roscommon (Dr. Commins), by a conspiracy of silence The right hon. and learned Gentleman the Member for Bury (Sir Henry James) made to the Government a very reasonable proposition; but, as has been pointed out, they have thrown overboard that statement, and will not listen in any way to his suggestion. I think we could not have a better example of their *bona fides* than this. If they had a *bona fide* intention of applying this Star Chamber Clause only to investigations into crime, no one on these Benches would have any objection; every speaker on this side has said so. But it is clear the Government have an *arrière pensée* as to this power, and that they do intend to apply the clause to the investigation of acts which were committed or took place before the passage or inception of this Bill at all when they get the Lord

Lieutenant to do what he is certain to do at their bidding—namely, proclaim any district. I am going to make a suggestion, which I think will put the *bona fides* of the Government to a complete test. I would suggest to my hon. and learned Friend the Member for South Roscommon that he should withdraw his Amendment on the Government undertaking to put at the end of the clause certain words which will carry out the object we have in view. I propose this to meet the difficulties which have arisen in the course of the debate. Of course, my objection to the whole clause still stands, and I shall still object to it, no matter how the Government amend it. The Government will by brute force carry it against us, as they have carried the Bill against us; but I would endeavour, by this Amendment, to make them make an honest, a fair, and open use of it. They should not, I contend, obtain these powers under one pretext, and then apply them to a different state of things altogether. The suggestion I would make is this— that my hon. and learned Friend the Member for Roscommon should withdraw his Amendment on the Government undertaking to add at the end of the clause these words—

"Provided always, no such inquiry shall be held into the commission of any offence"—or "act" would, perhaps, be more correct— "committed or done before the passing of the Act where such offence is one which is made an offence by the passing of this Act, and is included in those to which the Summary Jurisdiction Clauses of the Act apply."

That will, I think, test their *bona fides* perfectly well, for this reason — we object to their holding inquiries into acts which took place before the passing of the Act, which acts are not crimes in any sense of the word; we object to their inquiring into combinations—lawful and legal combinations—of tenants for the purpose, for instance, of refusing to pay an exorbitant rent until they get a just abatement, or such an abatement as operations on other estates have shown to be necessary and just— such an abatement as that obtained at Loughrea, where the result of combination on the part of the tenants was to induce the Marquess of Clanricarde, one of the most notoriously bad landlords in Ireland or out of it, to make an allowance to the distressed tenants, the rents being for a time retained under the

Plan of Campaign. Under this Act, after such an operation has occurred, the Lord Lieutenant can have an inquiry held — if the Government do not act straightforwardly in the matter — and can take the hon. Gentleman the Member for East Mayo (Mr. Dillon), or any one in this House who happens to go over to Ireland and take part in these operations, and examine them before this inquiry, and when these Gentlemen and the tenants refuse—as undoubtedly they will refuse—to answer any questions on the subject, the magistrates can put them into prison, suspend their liberties indefinitely or as long as they please, and then the Government may say to this House and to this country— "What a peaceful country we have made of Ireland; this has been a most beneficent Act, and has put down all manner of crime!" That, we hold, would be a dishonest use of the Act; and though the right hon. Gentleman the Chief Secretary for Ireland (Mr. A. J. Balfour) may be sincere in saying that he does not intend that the Act shall operate in that way, we say that it would take a much stronger man than he to resist the pressure which the landlords of Ireland will bring to bear upon the Executive in that country when they find that their rents are not being paid, and which cannot be paid under existing circumstances. In a short time the right hon. Gentleman may find himself forced into the position he now repudiates, and then he will see himself discredited like many of his Predecessors in the position he now holds. It has been said that the Chief Secretaryship for Ireland has been the grave of many political reputations, and the right hon. Gentleman may himself experience this disagreeable truth if he does not take care, in matters like this, to save himself from the possibility of being discredited.

MR. ILLINGWORTH (Bradford): I can well imagine that some would have this discussion confined to legal Gentlemen in this House; but I think that laymen in this House, at any rate on this side of it, have a very important duty to discharge. They have to listen and watch with the greatest anxiety and intelligence what is to be the scope of this measure, what powers are to be given to the Government, and how these powers are likely to be exercised in Ireland. We have had a debate now for over two hours as to the real meaning of this 1st section. We know very well that the measure is without limit prospectively, and we have ascertained from the right hon. and learned Attorney General for Ireland (Mr. Holmes), and from the hon. and learned Attorney General for England (Sir Richard Webster), that retrospectively —as to time—the Act is to be without any limit whatever. We seemed as if we were approaching an understanding by the friendly interference of the right hon. and learned Member for Bury (Sir Henry James) a short time ago; and at one moment, when the right hon. Gentleman the Chief Secretary was speaking, I really thought he was inclined to take hold of the suggestion—I might almost have said the mandate—of the right hon. Gentleman. The Government, knowing that the keystone of the arch is on this side of the House, cannot refuse to pay attention to the views of the right hon. and learned Gentleman as a Liberal Unionist. I do not hesitate to give the Liberal Unionists some credit in this matter. They have some merits of Liberalism left in them, and they must be anxious for the share of responsibility which will fall on their shoulders. I do not wonder at the right hon. and learned Gentleman intervening thus early in the debate, and attempting to give such a character to this measure as will not stamp it with infamy when it becomes an Act of Parliament. I venture to think we have not heard the last word from the Government; therefore, in sitting down, I would move, Sir, that you do report Progress and ask leave to sit again. If that Motion is accepted, the Government will then be in a position on Monday to say in a full House, and with the concurrence of the House, that the machinery of the Act shall apply to murder and offences approaching murder without any limitation whatever, but that it shall not include misdemeanours—that to any point beyond serious crime it shall be limited prospectively, so as to have no effect whatever unless a district has been proclaimed, and the offence should have been committed after the passing of the Act. If the clause we are discussing is passed in its present shape, and it is used for the purpose of stifling political discussion in Ireland, it may bring about an alarming state of things. We shall have a Star Chamber in existence again.

Mr. Illingworth

There has been no defence made for this clause by the other side of the House; and I consider the Irish Party will be justified in withstanding to the utmost any such scheme as has been indicated from the other side—by which new offences are set up and will be punished retrospectively in Courts of Summary Jurisdiction. I beg, Sir, to move that you do report Progress, and ask leave to sit again.

Mr. CONYBEARE (Cornwall, Camborne): I am very glad indeed that my hon. Friend the Member for Bradford (Mr. Illingworth) has moved to report Progress, because it is desirable in this discussion that we should give right hon. Gentlemen opposite time to think. I observe that hon. and right hon. Gentlemen over there do not seem capable of saying much in this House; but, perhaps, they think all the more, and in the hope that their thoughts may be productive of some good result, I think we should facilitate their operations if we occasionally moved to report Progress and so gave them a little additional time. It is very unfortunate that, on great and important questions such as we are now discussing, we should not have some advantage from the robust intelligence I see before me on the Front Ministerial Bench, and from the keen and philosophical attainments which sit beside it. There is an old saying of Juvenal's, I think, that knowledge is worth nothing unless you can impart it to others. I am afraid that the truth of that maxim is being illustrated by Her Majesty's Government, though they seem to think that knowledge is an excellent thing to be bottled up and kept to themselves. If they have any arguments, I think it would be well that they should let us know what they are. If they have no arguments—which is more likely to be the case—the sooner the country knows that the better it will be, because the sooner the country will see the honesty of those who are now misrepresenting them. When the Motion now moved has been fully discussed and disposed of, I may have something further to say on the clause before the Committee ; but as I have been away for a portion of the evening, I am desirous of asking the Government, before they proceed further, what the exact position of affairs is, because I have been unable to gather from hon. Members on this side of the House what is the exact question under discussion. No one appears to know exactly, and, that being so, we are likely to get rather mixed in our ideas, and not to succeed in pursuing a regular and orderly course. I sincerely trust, without pressing the matter any further, Her Majesty's Government will accede to this Motion for reporting Progress, not because it is a comparatively late hour, but because the matter has been now under discussion the whole evening. It is well understood that there are some important Bills coming on—measures which are of great interest generally—and it is only fair that we should have some opportunity of considering them before we are thoroughly exhausted. We have to discuss the important provisions of the Truck Bill, and those of the Merchant Shipping Act Amendment Bill, and we ought to do that before we get into the small hours of the morning. On these grounds, Sir, I second the Motion for reporting Progress.

Motion made, and Question proposed, "That the Chairman do report Progress, and ask leave to sit again."—(*Mr. Illingworth.*)

THE FIRST LORD OF THE TREASURY (Mr. W. H. SMITH) (Strand, Westminster): Mr. Courtney, regard for the order and regularity of debate does not permit me to refer to the observations of the hon. Gentleman who has just sat down. But, Sir, with reference to the remarks which fell from the hon. Member for West Bradford (Mr. Illingworth), I wish to point out that the House has been discussing for nearly four hours the Amendment of the hon. and learned Member for Roscommon (Dr. Commins), and that Amendment has been repeatedly answered from this Bench, although hon. Members who were not in the House at the time may not have heard those answers, for the House is much fuller now than it was.

An hon. MEMBER : The right hon. and learned Member for Bury (Sir Henry James) was not answered.

MR. W. H. SMITH : We, who sit on this Bench, have a responsibility, no doubt ; but it is no part of our duty to obstruct the progress of the measure which we desire to pass through the House. Answers having been given re-

peatedly, it is not, from the point of view of the Government, our duty to repeat them over and over again ; and, under these circumstances, it is impossible for me to consent to the Motion for reporting Progress. We must, therefore, ask the Committee to make real Progress, as this is a measure of very great importance, after such ample discussion as has been given to the proposal before the Committee.

MR. JOHN MORLEY (Newcastle-on-Tyne): The right hon. Gentleman the First Lord of the Treasury forgets that the Amendment now under consideration was not moved until nearly 10 o'clock.

MR. A. J. BALFOUR: Half-past 8 o'clock.

MR. JOHN MORLEY: The right hon. Gentleman (Mr. W. H. Smith) says that Her Majesty's Government have answered all the questions and arguments laid before them. May I point out to him that one most important suggestion was made by my right hon. and learned Friend the Member for Bury (Sir Henry James) ? Can the right hon. Gentleman give us any assurance that that suggestion shall be considered by the Government ? Because I think that such an assurance would probably facilitate the progress of the Bill.

MR. A. J. BALFOUR : I think the right hon. Gentleman opposite (Mr. Morley) is under some misapprehension as to when the discussion of this Amendment commenced. I imagine he was not here at the beginning of the discussion, which began at half-past 8 o'clock. He now accuses us of not having given some reply to the suggestion of the right hon. and learned Gentleman the Member for Bury (Sir Henry James). The reason why we have not done so is that that suggestion, though very important, and deserving of every consideration, especially considering the quarter from which it comes—[*Ironical cheers from the Opposition Benches*]—the importance of the position which the right hon. and learned Gentleman occupies—important, if for no other reason, because the right hon. and learned Gentleman was one of those who took no small part in the enactment of the Bill of 1882—I say the reason why we have not given a detailed answer to his suggestion is, that it is not relevant to the Amendment now before the Committee. ["Oh, oh!" *and laughter.*] I hear hon. Gentlemen laugh loudly, and, I presume, ironically, at that. Perhaps they are not aware of what it is that the Amendment now before the House refers to. It refers to the retrospective, or so-called retrospective, character of the investigations which this clause sets on foot. The suggestion of the right hon. and learned Member for Bury, so far as I understood it, was that the last few words at the end of Sub-section 5 should be omitted.

Sir HENRY JAMES: No; I said you should limit the powers under which the clause is to be made retrospective.

Mr. A. J. BALFOUR: Well, I accept the correction of the right hon. and learned Gentleman. It is, perhaps, relevant to the observation made by the right hon. Gentleman the Member for Newcastle-on-Tyne (Mr. John Morley). I now understand that the suggestion put forward is this—that any offence punishable under this Bill—that is to say, any offence created by this Bill, if such there are—shall not be subject to retrospective investigation. Well, Sir, the Government would accept that suggestion at once, if they thought it was not amply carried out by the form of the Bill as it stands. As we understand it—and I do not think the right hon. and learned Gentleman will doubt the interpretation as I put it upon the clause—the clause, as it stands now, does not, I think, give any power to admit of retrospective investigation into an act which was not a crime before the passage of the Bill, or until the Bill becomes law. I therefore do not believe that we could make the Amendment suggested, without introducing a contradiction in terms into our Bill. But I will, at all events, give this pledge to the House—that if the right hon. and learned Gentleman, on reflection, thinks the clause, as it stands, does not carry out this intention, which we have over and over again expressed to-night from this Bench, and which it is our desire should be carried out, we will introduce words into the Bill which will carry it out in the clearest possible manner.

Sir WILLIAM HARCOURT (Derby): Then I suppose, under these circumstances, the right hon. Gentleman will not object to report Progress? It seems an unkind suggestion to say that my

right hon. and learned Friend the Member for Bury (Sir Henry James) speaks "without reflection," and I imagine, from my long knowledge of him, that he never speaks without reflection, and that he has naturally reflected upon this subject, which is a very important one, and has not made his suggestion to the Committee without reflection. Why, then, the right hon. Gentleman opposite (Mr. Balfour) should say my right hon. and learned Friend will do something "on reflection," I confess I do not understand; and if time for reflection be wanted by anybody, I should think it is rather wanted on the part of the Government than on that of my right hon. and learned Friend. If the Government will take time for reflection, and see how they can make their Bill square with the suggestion of my right hon. and learned Friend, and carry out that which is clearly consistent with justice and with the principles of law, we shall be able to get on with the Bill. Under these circumstances, I would say that the right hon. Gentleman the Chief Secretary for Ireland has made out the strongest possible argument in favour of the Motion which is now before the Committee.

Sir HENRY JAMES: I think my right hon. Friend (Sir William Harcourt) has acted rather ungraciously towards the Government. A Motion has been made to report Progress in order to obtain an answer to a suggestion for which I am responsible. An answer has been given, and there will be no occasion to act upon that answer until we come to Sub-section 5, line 12, where the words, if necessary, should be inserted. Why, then, should we report Progress? I say we ought not. I will not get into conflict with my right hon. Friend. I cannot help looking back to what went on five years ago, when we were associated together in carrying a similar measure; and I cannot help thinking of what my right hon. Friend would have said then if any Motion similar to the one before us now had been made when we were engaged in passing the Crimes Act of 1882.

Mr. T. M. HEALY: We all know how very soon lovers' quarrels are made up. No sooner was there any ripple in the wave than the right hon. and learned Gentleman the Member for Bury (Sir Henry James) at once gave way to the Government. I do say that in a matter of this kind, on which the whole peace of Ireland depends, whether we report Progress or not, it is most desirable that this matter should be made clear. The right hon. and learned Member for Bury has made a suggestion which his friends the Government are unable to entertain at the moment. On a second thought he has been recommended to take time for reflection. The Government think that the alteration he suggests is not needed. The first intimation made by the right hon. Gentleman the Chief Secretary for Ireland to the right hon. and learned Gentleman the Member for Bury was that his speech was altogether out of Order, and had nothing whatever to do with the point immediately before the Committee. That was the first unkind suggestion. The second was, that he spoke without reflection. To us, who will have to bear the infliction of this Bill, it is very edifying to see these altercations between the two Front Benches; but I would point out that, whichever way the lash falls, it always cuts us. We take very little interest in the academic quarrels of right hon. Gentlemen on the two Front Benches; but what we want to know is, whether the Government will give us a promise to give this matter an independent consideration, with the view of providing that the Bill shall apply retrospectively only to serious crimes, and not to offences such as those dealt with by the other sections? I will make a suggestion, which may lead to this Motion for Progress being withdrawn. The sooner this Bill is brought into operation in all its naked horror, the sooner Englishmen will realize its effects; and, therefore, I make a suggestion with a view to the withdrawal of the Motion for reporting Progress. The Government say their intentions are so and so. As the Bill will be administered, when passed, not by lawyers, but by Resident Magistrates, will the Government have any objection to insert a provision, under which those Resident Magistrates may have quoted to them, as authoritative, the words used by the Government, as reported in *Hansard?* Lawyers have to refer to text books and cases; but when you deal with men who are not lawyers. and who are nothing better than gentlemen of the Captain Plunkett type, then you ought to have references to *Hansard* to show what the Act is really intended

for. If the Government would agree to that, this Motion for reporting Progress might be withdrawn; because then we might say to Captain Plunkett and other magistrates of the same stamp— "When the Bill was before Parliament the Chief Secretary for Ireland said so and so;" or—"The First Lord of the Treasury said so and so;" and by that means we might have a proper legal decision in these matters. I am in favour of making progress with the measure, and placing it on the Statute Book; but I would like to see everything decent and in order; and as the Government have admitted a flaw in the Bill, perhaps they will give us a pledge that they will accept the suggestion of the right hon. and learned Member for Bury, and exclude the retrospective operation of the clause from all cases but serious crimes. The Motion for Progress might then be withdrawn, and we might—I will not say pass the whole of the Bill to-night —but sit a little longer upon it, at all events.

DR. COMMINS: There is one thing that should be put to the Committee— one thing which is necessary for us to know—and that is, what is the intention of the Government by this Bill; or, what are we to understand by this section of the Bill? Have they made up their minds? If not, the very best thing to do is to give them a little time to make up their minds. The effect of the Amendment is clear enough—nobody has any doubt about that—but what is the intended effect of the thing to be amended? What is that? For there all the difficulty lies. The right hon. and learned Attorney General for Ireland (Mr. Holmes) started up, at the very beginning of this discussion, to say that he could not accept the Amendment, because it was the intention of the Government that the Bill should have a retrospective effect. Is that their intention with regard to all classes of crimes and offences? because I confess that the meaning of the Bill is not very clear in that respect. If the Bill is intended to have a retrospective effect, it would have been fairer to have said so, as in the Act of 1882. But then it was rather puzzling, after the declaration of the right hon. and learned Attorney General for Ireland, to hear the hon. and learned Solicitor General for England (Sir Edward Clarke) say that the section, as it stands, has no retrospective effect whatever. I think it would be a very useful thing if these two hon. and learned Gentlemen could be got to agree as to their interpretation of the Bill, and as to which of the accounts given to the Committee is the correct one. Well, we have also had a third account given as to what it is that the Government intend by the Bill, and as to what is the operation of the clause. The hon. and learned Attorney General for England (Sir Richard Webster) has a different version; because he told us that the clause was intended only to have a retrospective effect from the date of Proclamation. That is a third interpretation of the clause which we are trying to amend. Then we come to still other interpretations; but I will not quote them all. There have been a variety of them, all differing as to what it is that we are actually discussing. The right hon. and learned Member for Bury gave us a different version. If this discussion is to be profitable at all, it is desirable that we should have some authoritative declaration of the intention of the clause, and of what the Government intend to effect by it. Are we to have retrospective investigation into crimes of a grave character, and not into minor offences; or is there to be no distinction? If that matter were once settled, we might, perhaps, go on. I cannot help congratulating the Committee upon the better tone and feeling which have lately been displayed in the discussion. Well, I hope that the Government will see their way to the exhibition of a better spirit when they come to deal; not with the words of the Bill, but with the substance of it; and in order that they may have time for reflection, and to reconsider their own disagreement as to the drafting of the Bill and its effect, I cordially support the Motion for reporting Progress.

Mr. ILLINGWORTH: I should not have risen again, Mr. Courtney, had it not been for a few words which fell from the Leader of the House (Mr. W. H. Smith). I can quite appreciate his sense of responsibility and anxiety for the progress of Public Business, and that feeling excuses me for saying that I have no less anxiety for the efficiency of the House of Commons than he has. But, Mr. Courtney, I should like to observe that when the right hon. Gentleman assured the Committee that

Dr. Commins

every important point had been answered hours ago by right hon. Gentlemen on the Treasury Bench, I think he went altogether wide of the mark; and in proof of that I would refer to the fact that when the Chief Secretary for Ireland (Mr. A. J. Balfour) rose in his place to reply to the appeal which had been made to him, he, himself, showed that he did not understand the suggestion of the right hon. and learned Member for Bury (Sir Henry James), and when the right hon. and learned Member set him right as to what was the real significance of that suggestion, why, then, he replied by hinting that the right hon. and learned Member for Bury should also take time for reflection, and that if, upon reflection, the right hon. and learned Gentleman was not satisfied that the section, as it stands, really did nothing more than he desired, then the Government would give an understanding that they would alter the clause. No doubt, that is a great compliment to pay to the right hon. and learned Gentleman the Member for Bury, and if the matter be left to any one influential individual in this House I do not know anyone more competent than he to come to a conclusion upon it; but I do not understand that he will undertake the task, or that he would be likely to discharge it to the satisfaction of all the Members from Ireland. There are 24 or 25 Orders of the Day, and this is a Government night. I did not propose that we should report Progress at an untimely hour; but I think—now that we have been discussing this Bill from 5 o'clock until half-past 12—it is only reasonable that we should turn to something else. I cannot, therefore, withdraw my Motion.

SIR WILLIAM HARCOURT: I have a suggestion to make, Mr. Courtney, that I hope will help us, and perhaps solve the difficulty into which the Committee has got upon this Amendment. It has been suggested by the Government, as well as by my right hon. and learned Friend the Member for Bury, that the proper time to deal with this matter is when we come to the end of the clause, on Sub-section 5. Well, it is quite plain that the Government are disposed to make some alteration in this Sub-section 5, at the end of the clause, in conformity with the suggestion made by my right hon. and learned Friend the Member for Bury; and if that be so, it is far better that we should have the advantage of knowing what that alteration will be. Now, if the hon. and learned Member for Roscommon (Dr. Commins) will withdraw his Amendment at this stage, we may then discuss this matter in the fuller light which has been thrown upon it. ["Oh, oh!" *and laughter.*] I do not know why hon. Members should laugh. I am endeavouring to make a suggestion to save the time of the Committee. If my hon. and learned Friend will withdraw his Amendment, we shall then be in a position to know what are the alterations which the Government are prepared to make at the suggestion of my right hon. and learned Friend the Member for Bury, and then we can deal with the question in a thoroughly satisfactory manner when we come to Sub-section 5, at the end of the clause. If that is done, it appears to me that it will make our path easier; but, otherwise, we shall go to a Division without really knowing what is the decision of the Government in the matter. I hope my hon. and learned Friend will withdraw his Amendment, and we shall then be able to discuss this matter.

Question put.

Dr. COMMINS and Mr. CHANCE rose together—[*Cries of* "Order!"]

MR. CHANCE: I am entitled to address the Chair.

THE CHAIRMAN: The Question was put before the hon. Member rose.

MR. CHANCE: No, Sir.

THE CHAIRMAN: And strangers were ordered to withdraw.

MR. CHANCE: No, Sir.

MR. ARTHUR O'CONNOR (Donegal, E.): Mr. Courtney, this is my first —[*Cries of* "Order!" *and* "Name!"] From my personal observation, I say my hon. Friend rose to address the Committee before the Question was put. [*Cries of* "Order!"] The hon. Member then resumed his seat, and speaking with head covered, said: From my personal observation—[*Cries of* "Order!"]

THE CHAIRMAN: Order, order! Mr. Arthur O'Connor, on a point of Order.

MR. ARTHUR O'CONNOR (still seated, and with head covered): I can say, Mr. Courtney, from my personal observation, that my hon. Friend had

risen to address the Chair before you put the Question.

MR. JUSTIN M'CARTHY (also seated, and with head covered): I can speak from the same personal observation. I saw my hon. Friend rise to do that.

THE CHAIRMAN: I regret that there should be any misapprehension in the matter; but I am afraid it is now impossible to correct it.

The Committee *divided*:—Ayes 158; Noes 241: Majority 83.—(Div. List, No. 101.)

Amendment again proposed.

SIR RICHARD WEBSTER: I am very anxious, in a few words, to repeat the explanation I have already given, and I would submit to the Committee that, upon this particular point we have had so long under discussion, we might really now take a Division. The Amendment is to add the words "committed after the passing of this Act." I do not for the moment consider what the clause purports to include; but the suggestion was, by those who supported the Amendment, that everything — felonies, misdemeanours, or offences under the Act — should not be included unless committed after the passing of the Act. It is clear the Government could not accept these words; and, in fact, hon. Members below the Gangway have now admitted that they do not wish felonies and misdemeanours to be affected by the Amendment; they are agreed that the clause should apply to felonies and misdemeanours committed before the passing of the Act; therefore, I would point out to the Committee that on the particular question whether there should be this limitation the Committee is ready to go to a Division. Upon the other point, the point of difference between the right hon. and learned Gentleman the Member for Bury (Sir Henry James) and ourselves, our view is distinctly this— that inasmuch as the offences to which this section applies include felonies and misdemeanours, it is clear that felonies and misdemeanours, whether committed before or after the passing of this Act, may be inquired into. Our view also in respect to offences punishable under this Act, inasmuch as they would not be offences until a district is proclaimed, is in accord with that of the hon. Member for East Fife (Mr. Asquith)—there is no offence to inquire into until the district is proclaimed. That is the strict and true meaning of the section, and no Amendment is necessary. But I put it to the Committee whether the question of limiting the clause to after the passing of the Act should not now be decided after four hours' discussion?

MR. DILLON: So far as we are concerned we have no desire to stand between the Committee and a Division; but at the same time, before we proceed to divide, I wish to point out that, in my opinion, the delay that has occurred is entirely due to the way in which we have been met. Nobody can deny, after the statement of the hon. and learned Attorney General (Sir Richard Webster), that a serious practical question is raised by the Amendment we have been discussing. We have complained constantly that we were not met in debate in a clear and specific way. I must repeat, before we proceed to a Division, that the complaint we made at the outset, and repeated again and again during the discussion, was never met. We did not complain strongly of this inquiry being made retrospective in respect to felonies and serious crimes; but we complained of the retrospective action not in regard to crimes in a proclaimed district, but to crimes or offences of a lesser character, like combination or unlawful confederation, which are offences before this Act is passed at all, and, therefore, so far as the Act is concerned, would be treated as felonies or serious crimes. Now, I understand the Government will introduce words that will define their position in this regard. I trust we are correct when we make the assumption that we have it from the Government that they will place words on the Paper defining the position they will take up in this regard, so that the Committee will have an opportunity of considering that position before we proceed any further. On this assumption I have no objection to a Division now.

MR. T. M. HEALY: It is well we should understand the position if we allow this discussion to close. The matter is clear so far as the speech of the right hon. Gentleman the Attorney General goes—that is, that the Government believe that the words of the section are clear, though we do not. Very well. Believing that their meaning is

clear, they will undertake to make their meaning clear to us from their view. We do not ask them to adopt our meaning, but that they will introduce words to remove all ambiguity. More we do not ask now—though we may afterwards press them to make it wider—than to introduce words making their meaning clear to us.

MR. A. J. BALFOUR: Well, we do not believe that is necessary. We believe the wording of the clause absolutely clear as it stands; but, if there is any doubt about it, we are willing to introduce words to remove it.

DR. COMMINS: It is evident that the Government have not made their meaning clear to their own followers, for there have been arguments from them against the retrospective action of the clause, and they have not been answered yet. At any rate, I hope they will make their meaning clear.

MR. JOHN MORLEY: I understand that the Chief Secretary says he intends to affix the same meaning to the words as is desired on this side. The Government do not think that additional words are necessary. But still, as a doubt exists, they will not object to the insertion of words to satisfy our desires and their own wishes?

MR. A. J. BALFOUR: If we can add words conveying our meaning and not making the clause nonsensical. Surplusage there will be; but, however, we will not object to that. But I hope it is understood what we do mean; I hope there is no doubt about that. The clause is to apply to existing crimes; the retrospective action is to apply to existing crimes, not to such crimes—if such there be—as are created by this Act.

MR. T. P. O'CONNOR: Just let me ask a question on this point, that we may have the matter clear and avoid misunderstandings and complications later on. The contention of the Attorney General is that no offences under this Act can become offences until the Act comes into operation in a proclaimed district. The contention of my hon. Friend near me (Mr. Dillon) is that there is a large number of offences under this Act, and, to a certain extent, created by the Acts which already come under existing legislation, as, for instance, the Whiteboy Acts. My hon. Friend says you have altered the method of dealing with these

Sir Richard Webster

offences that are dealt with under existing laws. We want to limit the retrospective action of the clause to serious agrarian crimes, and that is what I understand the right hon. Gentleman to accept?

MR. A. J. BALFOUR: All existing crimes, felonies, and misdemeanours under the existing law may have this retrospective power applied to them.

MR. DILLON: What we want is this. —We want the Government to place on the Paper words that will define what they consent to do, and that will raise the issue. We will postpone discussion until then, if the Government will promise to place such words on the Paper? It is clear, I think, that the Chairman will allow the subject to be raised, and so we postpone discussion of the matter.

MR. T. C. HARRINGTON: I should like to be allowed to make a suggestion. I will not occupy the time of the Committee, and I think the right hon. Gentleman will allow it is worth attention. If he really wishes the clause to be effective, for the purpose of procuring evidence, then I caution him that the sooner he makes up his mind to draw a distinction between graver offences and lighter offences the better for himself and his Government. If the retrospective action of the clause is to apply to inquiries into lighter offences, the result will be that every person who is summoned before the inquiry, if he does not go to gaol, will be regarded as an unpopular man. If you make it applicable to lighter offences—small offences, not crimes in the ordinary sense of the word —you defeat the very object you pretend to have in view.

MR. JOHN MORLEY: I suppose, after what has passed—after what has fallen from the right hon. Gentleman the Chief Secretary and the hon. Member for East Mayo (Mr. Dillon)—the hon. and learned Member for South Roscommon (Dr. Commins) will withdraw his Amendment.

MR. ARTHUR O'CONNOR: May I ask when the words the Government propose to place on the Paper will be in the hands of Members?

MR. A. J. BALFOUR: They shall be put down on Monday.

DR. COMMINS: After what has passed, I will, with the leave of the Committee, withdraw my Amendment.

THE CHAIRMAN: Is it your pleasure the Amendment be withdrawn? ["No, no!"]

MR. T. P. O'CONNOR: I really would appeal to the Ministry to use some of their influence with their followers to allow the Amendment to be withdrawn. I am sure they are bound to do so by the pledges they have given to this side of the House. Fairly and frankly—I give them all credit for it— they have undertaken to meet us when the question arises. They will prejudice the consideration of this question if there be any foregone conclusion; and I think there will be a foregone conclusion if a Division is taken on the Amendment of my hon. Friend, which will put us in a very unfair and prejudiced position. I appeal to right hon. Gentlemen to allow the Amendment to be withdrawn. [*Cries of* "No, no!"] I do not appeal to hon. Gentlemen behind the Treasury Bench; I appeal to a somewhat higher order of intelligence. I appeal to the right hon. and learned Gentleman, who has met us in a fair spirit, not to mar the attitude he has taken up.

SIR RICHARD WEBSTER: With regard to the appeal of the hon. Member, and the words which will be put down on Monday, may I point out again to hon. Members that the Amendment proposed would limit the clause in regard to felonies and misdemeanours to those committed after the passing of the Act. It is necessary, at any rate, to have the decision of the Committee that felonies and misdemeanours are subject to the clause.

MR. HENRY H. FOWLER: The hon. and learned Gentleman takes a rather unusual view of the matter. We have been discussing the Amendment for a considerable time. The Government say the clause means one thing, the Opposition say it means another. The right hon. and learned Gentleman the Member for Bury (Sir Henry James) makes a suggestion that appears to be acceptable to a large section on both sides, and the Government say they will consider that suggestion; while maintaining the principle that the action of the clause shall be retrospective for felonies and misdemeanours, they are willing it shall be prospective for other offences that are created by the Act. Then the usual course is to withdraw the Amendment in dispute, and let the question be fairly raised upon the new words when they are before us. The hon. and learned Gentleman the Attorney General (Sir Richard Webster) says he wants a definite decision that the words of the clause shall have a retrospective application so far as felonies and misdemeanours are concerned. Yes; but we contend, and this is why the Amendment is urged, that the words will carry us much further than he wishes us to go. When we are trying to come to a workable understanding, I am afraid it will not tend to the progress of Business to insist upon a decision on the Amendment now.

MR. W. H. SMITH: We have no desire to avoid coming to a workable conclusion; but, as the right hon. Gentleman is well aware, if the Amendment is withdrawn on this occasion, it will be perfectly open to hon. Gentlemen to raise the same question over again—that is to say, another five hours may be added to the same period already spent on this question. We gave our interpretation at first, and contend it is the correct one. It is only now that hon. Gentlemen accept the limited interpretation we contend is the right one; and we, therefore, say that the proper result of this discussion is that it should be accepted by the Committee in the sense we present it. We also add, if there is any question in their minds which we contend there ought not to be, that new offences will not be within the retrospective action of the clause, then we will bring down words on Monday to make that perfectly clear. That being so, we must, in the interest of Business, ask that the Amendment be negatived, so that the whole question may not be renewed at our next Sitting. If the words we shall present are not satisfactory, then it will be perfectly open to the Committee to reject or amend those words.

MR. CHANCE: I want to point out distinctly the attitude the Government have taken up. We have never objected to this power being given in the fullest manner, retrospective and prospective, for the discovery of grave crimes and the punishment of criminals; but we do object to all offences being included—we object to its application to the offence of conspiracy. Speaking of this offence

Mr. Henry H. Fowler

of conspiracy, Mr. Justice Stephen says—

"There is no doubt that plausible reasons may be found to declare it a criminal offence to combine to do anything which, in the opinion of the Judge, is politically or socially dangerous."

Well, the offence of conspiracy has hitherto been tried before a Judge and jury, and you have a great safeguard, yet you have the opinion of Justice Stephen brought out distinctly, that there is danger in leaving to the Judge the power of declaring the Law of Conspiracy. But, under this Act, the power will be given to Resident Magistrates appointed by the Castle, dismissed by the Castle, and dependent for their pensions on the certificate of the Chief Secretary that they have served him with diligence and fidelity. While allowing them to declare combinations criminal, you will enable them to create new offences; you will enable them to get evidence as to old transactions which no Judge and jury would have punished, if you allow the retrospection to apply to misdemeanours. You will hand over such cases to be tried on such evidence for what would be really new criminal offences, in the opinion of two Castle officials. We desire to prevent that being done. We decline to allow the Act to be made retrospective, so that it may be made to apply to offences to be created by it. If we allowed the Government to take a decision on this point, the result would be that they would say, when the end of the 1st section is reached, it has been decided to include conspiracy and misdemeanour in the retrospective action of the Act. We desire to prevent that, and if we have to discuss it for the next few hours we will do our best to prevent it.

MR. DILLON: I think the whole of the delay this evening has been caused by the way in which the Government have met us. After the last Division on the Motion to report Progress, I made a proposal with a desire to come to an arrangement to end the discussion. I endeavoured to point out to the Government that while we did not desire to raise any further debate upon the question of the retrospective action of the clause with regard to felonies, yet, with respect to misdemeanours, we did distinctly say that the issue had not been sufficiently debated to allow a decision to be taken. And I distinctly understood the Government to say—"We are willing to put on the Paper words which will raise this question again, and enable the House, without having its hands tied, to come to an understanding as to what crimes or offences they would allow the clause to be retrospective in its action." But now the Government endeavours to tie our hands. Evidently, on the question of misdemeanours, a point of the greatest possible moment rests, and the Government must have known that that was the question I wished to raise. I myself was put on my trial in Dublin for misdemeanour; and on that occasion the question of the combination of the Plan of Campaign was struck at by the Government. If they make this clause retrospective with regard to misdemeanours, they will be taking to themselves power to imprison all of us in Ireland for things we have done long before this Act was spoken of. Is it fair play towards a Party like ours to insist on a decision being taken on that important point at so late an hour in the night? I admit it would be fair play enough, if the question had been debated; but it has not been debated. You cannot call it a debate, when one side has for some time been putting forward its case, and the other side of the Committee have never attempted to reply. We have not had the question we put answered by a single Member on the Government Benches. I have been compelled to repeat our case over and over again; no hon. Member from that side of the House has even pretended to answer whether it is intended to use this clause retrospectively in regard to misdemeanours, and we, therefore, have a right to think it is intended to use it in such a way as to expose myself, and others who have worked with me in Ireland, to imprisonment for refusing to give evidence before the tribunals to be constituted. I understood that the Government were willing to leave that matter to be raised on Monday; in that case, we should be willing to have this Amendment withdrawn. But when I said that under such circumstances we would not press the Amendment to a Division, it never occurred to me the Government would try to bind our hands on the matter by forcing a decision.

MR. ARTHUR O'CONNOR: It is complained that this Amendment has been discussed at considerable length; but I appeal to the fair sense of the Committee whether there is not ample explanation for that in the fact that, after it was moved, a very startling revelation was made by the Government that the Bill, as drafted, would have a retrospective effect? Such an announcement as that would naturally lead to prolonged discussion. What is the proposal of the Government as we have heard it from the hon. and learned Attorney General? He says it is necessary that the Government should obtain a declaration from the Committee by means of a Division taken on the Amendment of the hon. and learned Member for Roscommon (Dr. Commins), to the effect that, at any rate as regards felonies and misdemeanours, the retrospective character of the Bill should not be limited. If the Division is taken on the Amendment with the object which the hon. and learned Attorney General has described, the decision will be operative, not only with regard to felonies and misdemeanours, but also with regard to everything covered by the word "offence." The position of the Government is perfectly untenable, for it will bring within the Act many things. which the House has no suspicion of. Let us look at some of the proceedings punishable as felonies and misdemeanours under the Whiteboy Acts. Here is one—if any person shall send, or cause to be sent, any notice or message directing or requiring any person to do, or not to do, any act, any person so offending shall be liable—to what? To transportation or imprisonment. There is the penalty of felony; at any rate, that is a misdemeanour. That is the kind of offence—sending a message to do or not to do any act is the kind of offence with regard to which you are to give these Resident Magistrates summary jurisdiction. I am perfectly certain there is not a Member of this House outside the Cabinet, excepting, possibly, the noble Marquess the Member for Rossendale (the Marquess of Hartington), who had the least suspicion the Act was intended to give such powers as these to these men. It does appear to me unreasonable on the part of the Government to force a Division on the Amendment; it does seem to me to be unfair to ask the Committee to proceed with the consideration of this clause until we have before us the express words which the Government propose to add to the clause.

Mr. J. BRYN ROBERTS (Carnarvonshire, Eifion`: I wish to point out that, to my mind, both sides of the Committee seem to have misconceived the importance of either withdrawing or negativing these words. I think it is practically unimportant. It is clear that the view taken by the Government is incorrect. The hon. and learned Attorney General stated that he wished to have these words negatived, in order to affirm that the Act, as regards felonies and misdemeanours, should be retrospective. If these words are negatived, they will not affirm that; they will only affirm that certain offences which are not defined, and which will not be defined until the 5th section comes under consideration, will come under the retrospective action of the Act. There will be nothing to prevent any Member of the House proposing later on that the retrospective portion of the Act shall only apply to, say, murder and larceny; and, if that were carried, not even all felonies would come under the purview of the section. It appears to me immaterial to the Government whether or not the Amendment is withdrawn; and it also appears to me equally immaterial to hon. Members below the Gangway whether or not it is negatived.

Mr. T. M. HEALY: I agree. I am quite ready to go to a Division on the matter. It does not matter a button whether the Amendment is negatived or withdrawn. If hon. Gentlemen opposite have not the courtesy to allow us to withdraw it, we do not wish the Committee to be troubled with a Division, although, as far as we are concerned, we are ready to take one. I never heard anything more extraordinary than the doctrine laid down by the First Lord of the Treasury. It sounds like an extract from a comic opera to suggest that the passing of this Act makes a distinction between a felony and misdemeanour. The Bill has entirely misled both sides of the House. Now, Sir, I wish to point out one thing. In this Act you are incorporating the provisions of the Petty Sessions Act, so that you can compel a witness to produce books, accounts, and documents, as he may required; and refusal to do so will con-

stitute misdemeanour. The right hon. and learned Attorney General for Ireland is the person who is to set this law into operation. He has, from his point of view, been atrociously libelled in regard to his action relative to the Plan of Campaign. If this Bill is to be retrospective, he can issue a summons compelling the editor of *United Ireland* of bring into Court his account books and papers to be examined with reference to libels on him; and he can inquire fully into the Plan of Campaign. I ask the Committee—Are we unreasonable in asking that there should be some definite and restrictive words upon that point? Now, the noble Marquess is the real prop of the Government in this business, and I ask him, if we are unreasonable in saying that when the operation of the Plan of Campaign has already been made the subject of criminal inquiry, and in regard to which a jury containing six Protestants has disagreed, it should not be made the subject of an inquisition under this Act? I do not think we are; and for the Members of the Government to complain that time has been wasted is nonsense. I say it has been usefully spent. If the Act is passed in this form, do not suppose for one moment that you will get any information out of me, or that if you summon me to give evidence I will attend. I tell you plainly I will not. I am only using our case for the purposes of illustration. We do not disguise the mutual hatred between us and you. Every time I hear an expression of hatred from that side of the Committee I am ready to pay it back with redoubled interest. But I am here arguing on behalf of the people of Ireland—on behalf, not of myself, but for a large number of men who are not inclined to go to gaol for refusing to show their books and papers—people whose time is valuable to them, and I do ask the Government is it unreasonable that we should ask, in regard to ancient matters of history, in relation to stale old matters affecting the Plan of Campaign, that they should be definitely excluded? The word misdemeanour seems to sound sweetly in the ears of hon. Members opposite, in the same way as Mesopotamia did to the old lady. It may be a very trifling matter; but where can you draw the line? There is the forged letter in *The Times;* there is the Boycotting at the

Mr. Arthur O'Connor

bookstalls; they are misdemeanours according to our view of the law; but, of course, we cannot expect it to be endorsed by hon. Gentlemen opposite. Do not let us be misled by words; let us deal with serious crime. If the Government will let us raise the question of misdemeanour at a later stage, I see no objection to a Division being taken. If they will not agree to that, then let us argue the matter an hour or two longer. It makes very little difference to us. You, Sir, to whose ruling I have always been able to give my intellectual as well as Parliamentary adhesion, because they always seem founded on common sense and reason——

THE CHAIRMAN: Order, order!

MR. T. M. HEALY: Very well, I will say nothing more about that. I cannot see how we are later on to be precluded from raising this question.

MR. A. J. BALFOUR: There can be no doubt that, at a later stage of this Bill, the question whether misdemeanours are to be included will be open to discussion. There is no question about that. It does not turn on the decision on this Amendment. But, at the same time, we think it very desirable to come to a decision on it, and if hon. Gentlemen will allow it to be negatived the question raised by it will be settled. That question does not relate to misdemeanours; it is a question whether retrospective action of every kind should be excluded, and hon. Gentlemen below the Gangway opposite can surely have no objection to a final decision on that point being come to. The question they desire to raise can be discussed in the fullest manner later on.

Amendment *negatived*.

MR. T. M. HEALY: Before the Motion to report Progress is made I wish to ask a question. The Government, by accepting the Amendment of the right hon. Gentleman the Member for East Wolverhampton, have agreed to the omission of certain words. I wish to ask if there are means of raising a question as to those omitted words?

SIR RICHARD WEBSTER: I think the acceptance of the Amendment of the right hon. Gentleman the Member for East Wolverhampton will not preclude the Amendment of the hon. Member for Dublin City being taken in its order.

Motion made, and Question, "That the Chairman do report Progress, and ask leave to sit again," put, and *agreed to*.

Committee report Progress; to sit again upon *Monday* next.

INCUMBENTS OF BENEFICES LOANS EXTENSION ACT (1886) AMENDMENT BILL [*Lords*].

(*Mr. Secretary Matthews.*)

[BILL 230.]　　SECOND READING.

Order for Second Reading read.

Motion made, and Question proposed "That the Bill be now read a second time."

Motion made, and Question proposed, "That the Debate be now adjourned." —(*Mr. Arthur O'Connor.*)

THE UNDER SECRETARY OF STATE FOR THE HOME DEPARTMENT (Mr. STUART-WORTLEY) (Sheffield, Hallam): The object of the Bill is to get rid of a trifling error in an Act passed in the last Session of Parliament by the right hon. Gentleman opposite the Member for Edinburgh (Mr. Childers). I trust, therefore, that the hon. Member (Mr. Arthur O'Connor) will allow it to go on.

MR. T. M. HEALY (Longford, N.): Last night I asked that the Bill should be postponed, and that the block should be withdrawn. I think it is perfectly harmless.

Question put.

The House *divided*:—Ayes 80; Noes 137: Majority 57.—(Div. List, No. 102.)

Original Question put, and *agreed to*.

Bill read a second time, and *committed* for *Monday* next.

PRIVATE BILL LEGISLATION BILL. (*Mr. Craig Sellar, Sir Lyon Playfair, Mr. Howorth, Mr. John Morley, Mr. Arthur Elliot.*)

[BILL 107.]　　SECOND READING.

Order for Second Reading read.

MR. CRAIG SELLAR (Lanarkshire, Partick), in rising to move that the Bill be now read a second time, said: The opposition to this Bill has, I believe, been withdrawn; and I believe that the principle of the measure is approved by hon. and right hon. Gentlemen on the two Front Benches, and supported by the vast majority of hon.

Members on both sides of the House. It deals with an old question. The subject has been for nearly 50 years before this House, and this Bill for more than two years. What I wish to do to-night is to ask the House to allow the Bill to be read a second time and then referred to a Select Committee. I shall be willing, if that course be followed, to undertake not to proceed with the consideration of the Bill during this Session. The proposals of the measure would, however, be thrashed out upstairs, and we should know what the House really thought on the subject. I should then be prepared, in another Session, to bring in the Bill as amended by the Select Committee. The object of the measure is to carry out the recommendations of the Committee upon Procedure of last Session, which Committee recommended that arrangements should be made to relieve the House of the work done by the Private Bill Committees. I need not, at this hour, enter more minutely into the matter; but I hope the House will consent to read the Bill a second time, and then refer it to a Select Committee. I beg to move the second reading.

Motion made, and Question proposed, "That the Bill be now read a second time."—(*Mr. Craig Sellar.*)

Mr. T. M. HEALY (Longford, N.): Mr. Speaker, I am really surprised at what I may call the superb hardihood of the hon. Gentleman (Mr. Craig Sellar) in proposing, at this hour of the morning, to take the second reading of a Bill of more far-reaching importance than, perhaps, any measure, except the Criminal Law Amendment (Ireland) Bill, introduced this Session. I observe, on the back of the Bill, the name of the right hon. Gentleman the Member for Newcastle-on-Tyne (Mr. John Morley). Of course, I am very sorry to have to oppose any measure to which he lends the high sanction of his name; but, for my part, Sir, to use an expression of the late Mr. Henley, who said that when he could no longer oppose a Bill he would lie on his back and cry "Fudge," I will give my most strenuous opposition to this Bill, even to ejaculating "Fudge." It is proposed to refer Irish Private Bills to a Committee of Irish Judges. Why, we would die fighting that proposal. We say this of the tribunals of

the House of Commons—that as long as we are compelled to come to Westminster, there is not a fairer body for dealing with Private Bills than a Committee upstairs. We think that great injustice was done lately in proposing to destroy our best buildings in Dublin by carrying out a certain undertaking; but, as far as fair play and impartiality go, we have the fullest confidence in the integrity of the Private Bill Committees upstairs. But I would rather give authority in these matters to the most corrupt body in the most corrupt constituency in this country than give it to a committee of Irish Judges. We have had bitter experience of such a tribunal under the Labourers' Act and the Tramways Act. To compel us to go before them, to compel the Irish advocates to go before them, to be sneered at and insulted by them, is a thing to which I, for one, will never give my consent. I tell the hon. Member for Partick (Mr. Craig Sellar) that, if he were to practise before these men, he would be the last in the world to make such a proposal as this. We can go to the Committees upstairs, and our arguments will be listened to. Politics are not concerned there as they are in the House. I am not speaking of political matters, but of waterworks, gasworks, and things of that kind. But to give the Irish Judges the powers of a Select Committee! I think that no one who has lived in Ireland, except a Liberal Unionist, would venture to propose such a thing. To my sorrow, I have been before three Judges, in the miserable matter of providing a labourer's cottage, and I will tell the House what was said by Lord Ashbourne. It was proved before him, by the Local Government Board Inspector, that a stream ran through the house of the unfortunate labourer. What did Lord Ashbourne say to him? "Oh, my poor man," he said, "you appear to be enjoying very good health." When the Inspector proved that a stream was running through the house, the present Lord Chancellor of Ireland sneered at the unfortunate official, and attempted to brow-beat him. We made a great mistake when we changed the Labourers' Act, so as to have cases arising under it heard before the Judges. We have been taught a very severe lesson by that mistake, and one which will not be lost on us. I beg to move that the debate be now adjourned.

Motion made, and Question proposed, "That the Debate be now adjourned." —(*Mr. T. M. Healy.*)

MR. HUNTER (Aberdeen, N.): Mr. Speaker, this Bill applies also to Scotland, and contains provisions which are of a most extraordinary character. I second the Motion for Adjournment. I must protest, as I have protested before and shall always continue to do, against important Business of this kind being brought on at so late an hour. I shall not detain the House by making a speech; but I think, under the circumstances, everyone will admit the reasonableness of the Motion.

SIR JOSEPH PEASE (Durham, Barnard Castle): I agree very cordially with what has fallen from the hon. Member who has just sat down. Whatever this Bill may be, it is an important measure, and it is too late to be taken up at this time of the night. But my hon. Friend in charge of the Bill (Mr. Craig Sellar) has entirely misrepresented— although most unintentionally on his part—the position of the House towards this Bill. I had the honour of opposing the measure two years ago, and the House agreed with me in condemning its principle. I think that the numbers who voted were 58 for the Bill and 150 against it, so that there was a majority of nearly three to one against the principle it contains. The Bill proposes to send to three Commissioners, to be paid £3,000 a-year each, all the Private Business that now goes before Select Committees. There are other provisions of a similar character that require the utmost consideration. The measure, of course, would apply to Gas Works, Water Works, and Railways, and all Private Bills, and it raises questions of the utmost importance. And it is proposed that the Bill shall be, after the second reading, referred to a Select Committee, as if the principle was agreed to. I should not mind referring the whole question of Private Bill legislation to a Select Committee; but I cannot agree to the Motion for the second reading, and shall certainly oppose it.

THE FIRST LORD OF THE TREASURY (Mr. W. H. SMITH) (Strand, Westminster): I venture to ask the hon. Gentleman opposite (Mr. Craig Sellar) whether he will not, under all the circumstances of the case, consent to the adjournment of the debate? It is obvious that considerable difference of opinion prevails as to the principle of the Bill; and, looking at the lateness of the hour we have now reached, it does not seem advisable that we should go on discussing the question. I shall remain, however, of opinion that the measure itself is one that ought to be considered very carefully by the House, and that it could be very advantageously threshed out by a Select Committee. I am sure that the hon. Baronet who has just spoken (Sir Joseph Pease) fully admits the importance of the question. The hon. and learned Member for North Longford (Mr. T. M. Healy) has objected to the jurisdiction of the Irish Judges; but that is a question which would be very properly considered by a Committee. However, under all the circumstances, I trust the hon. Member for Partick will consent to the adjournment of the debate until a day when sufficient consideration can be given to the Bill.

MR. JOHN MORLEY (Newcastle-on-Tyne): I entirely concur in the observations which have just fallen from the right hon. Gentleman the First Lord of the Treasury; I hope my hon. Friend will consent to the adjournment of the debate. I may say that I entirely agree with the hon. and learned Member for North Longford as to the undesirableness of submitting these questions to a tribunal of Irish Judges; but not entirely for the reasons which my hon. Friend stated. I think that many advantages could be gained if the proposal, which is one of great importance, were previously threshed out in a Select Committee, and I wonder—I merely throw this out as a suggestion for the consideration of the right hon. Gentleman—whether it would not be worth while for the Government, independently of the action of my hon. Friend (Mr. Craig Sellar), to move for the appointment of a Select Committee. A Committee so appointed would be able to do all that my hon. Friend's proposal could effect. In the meantime, whilst cordially approving of the principle of the Bill, I hope my hon. Friend will consent to the adjournment.

MR. CRAIG SELLAR: I thank my hon. and right hon. Friends for the kind way in which they have spoken of my proposal, and shall act as they suggest. In reference to the suggestion of my right hon. Friend the Member for New-castle-on-Tyne (Mr. John Morley), I may say that if the Government would con-sent to the appointment of a Select Committee on this subject, I should be glad to move that the Order for the second reading of my Bill be discharged. I propose to adjourn the second reading until next Friday.

MR. ILLINGWORTH (Bradford, W.): I think that as a general principle we are entitled to protest against any attempt on the part of hon. Members at getting through the second reading of Bills of the first magnitude and of the most far-reaching importance, by giving undertakings that they will be-have in the best manner when they get their proposal before a Select Committee. Whenever this question of Private Bill legislation is dealt with, it must be by a responsible Government. I protest against the attempt which has been made to smuggle through the second reading stage, without discussion, a Bill of the first magnitude, and the very principles of which are not understood by many Members of the present House of Commons.

Question put, and *agreed to.*

Debate *adjourned* till *Friday* next.

M O T I O N S
——o——

TRAMWAYS (WAR DEPARTMENT) BILL.

On Motion of Mr. Northcote, Bill to facilitate the construction of Tramways by Her Majesty's Principal Secretary of State for the War De-partment; and for other purposes connected therewith, *ordered* to be brought in by Mr. Northcote, Mr. Edward Stanhope, and Mr. Brodrick.

Bill *presented*, and read the first time. [Bill 246.]

TRURO BISHOPRIC AND CHAPTER ACTS
AMENDMENT BILL [H.L.] [*Lords*].

Sir John St. Aubyn, Mr. Charles Acland, and Mr. Stuart-Wortley were *nominated* Members of the Select Committee on the Truro Bishopric and Chapter Acts Amendment Bill [*Lords*].

House adjourned at half after Two o'clock till Monday next.

HOUSE OF LORDS,

Monday, 2nd May, 1887.

———

MINUTES.]—PUBLIC BILL—*First Reading*—Bankruptcy Offices (Sites) * (76).

INDIA (THE NORTH-WESTERN FRON-TIER)—THE QUETTA RAILWAY.

QUESTION.

THE EARL OF KIMBERLEY asked the Secretary of State for India, Whe-ther the Pishin Valley Railway was yet open for public traffic; and, if not, when it would be?

THE SECRETARY OF STATE FOR INDIA (Viscount CROSS): My Lords, there are two railways to Quetta, both starting from Sibi, on the North-Western Frontier system. The Bolan route is now quite completed, and traffic is work-ing on it throughout. On the Sind-Pishin route the rails have already been linked through; but the line is not yet opened for traffic. I hope that the railway will be opened shortly.

ISLANDS OF THE SOUTH PACIFIC—THE NEW HEBRIDES.

QUESTION.   OBSERVATIONS.

THE EARL OF HARROWBY, in rising to call attention to the condition of affairs in the New Hebrides, and to ask, What course is proposed to be taken with refer-ence to this important subject by Her Majesty's Government? said, he desired to draw the attention of the House to the continued presence of French soldiers in the Islands of the New Hebrides, although there stands on record a diplo-matic understanding between France and England that neither Power should do anything in contravention of the inde-pendence of the Islands. He submitted that the subject was an important one from three points of view. In the first place, it was important from the Native point of view; secondly, from the Im-perial and Australian point of view; and thirdly, and still more important, because if it was the fact that French troops were still in occupation of these Islands, the sanctity of all International engage-ments was called in question, or, rather, would be called in question, if such an occupation was sanctioned by the Government of France. He could not but believe that it was the rashness or over-zeal of Local Authorities which had kept French troops in the Islands, for unless he had strong evidence to the contrary, he should be very unwilling to suppose that the French Government would, for one moment, take the line of showing such complete disregard of International undertakings. The presence of the French troops was a clear breach of the International engagement, and if it were likely to be sanctioned by the Government of France a serious breach would occur. The Islands, he might remind their Lordships, were discovered in the first instance by Captain Cook, and under the Charter of 1840 they were included in the Colony of New Zealand. They consisted of about 30 Islands, extending over a length of ocean of about 400 miles North and South. They were extremely rich, were more healthy than the rest of the Pacific Islands, and contained several valuable harbours. The population, numbering from 100,000 to 150,000, were rapidly becoming civilized, and the story of their civilization and Christianization by the Reformed Presbyterian Church of Scotland was one of the most creditable in our history. So far as any European language went English was the only tongue known in the Islands, and the feeling of the Natives towards English people was exceedingly friendly. In every Island an Englishman might go about unarmed, though he did not know that quite the same could be said with regard to other nationalities. Australia was especially interested in these Islands from their proximity to her shores, and she was in a panic lest they should become the home of the relapsed criminals from France. In quite recent times both France and Germany had shown their appreciation of the strategic and commercial importance of the group. He thought we had a right, when we found those Islands civilized entirely by British enterprize, Christianized by Scotch enterprize, and wholly British in feeling, to protest against their being handed over to any other country. France, of course, would like to have the Islands for a labour supply to her Colony of New Caledonia. That labour question in the Pacific was one of the most terrible blots in our modern civilization. A French Admiral who had held a high position in the

Government recently stated in the Senate that the labour that France got from the New Hebrides was simply another form of downright slavery, and that might be accepted as undoubtedly true. In the French Chamber it had been announced that New Caledonia could not take more convicts, and that it would be well if she could get them over to the New Hebrides. Anything more pitiable than such a result he could not imagine. What was the legal position now between France and England as to the New Hebrides? Lord Derby wrote to the Colonial Office in February, 1878, inclosing a letter from the French Ambassador, calling attention to articles in Australian newspapers advocating the annexation of the New Hebrides to the British Crown, and stating that though the French Government did not attach great importance to this annexation movement, still, as they themselves had no intentions with regard to that group, they would be glad to have an assurance to that effect from Her Majesty's Government. Lord Derby informed the Colonial Office that he proposed, if they concurred, to inform the French Ambassador that Her Majesty's Government had no intention of proposing any measures to Parliament with a view of changing the condition of independence which the New Hebrides then enjoyed. The Secretary for the Colonies concurred in this answer. As time went on the feeling in favour of annexation became stronger and stronger in Australia, and alarmed the French Government. A commuication was made to Her Majesty's Government that the Government of the Republic felt it their duty to ascertain whether the Declarations of 1878 still remained as valid in the opinion of Her Majesty's Government as in that of France, as otherwise they would feel it their duty to insist on the maintenance of the existing state of things. In a despatch to Lord Lyons, the noble Earl who was then at the head of Foreign Affairs (Earl Granville) had said that the Agreement of 1878 was considered by Her Majesty's Government to be perfectly valid. On the 31st of August, 1883, the English Chargé d'Affaires informed Lord Granville that he had left at the French Foreign Office a *note verbale* to this effect. Lord Derby, when at the Foreign Office, had assured the Australian

Colonies that no proposal for the annexation of the New Hebrides would be entertained without consulting the Australian Colonies, and also without securing conditions satisfactory to those Colonies. When the noble Earl opposite (the Earl of Rosebery) had been Foreign Secretary an offer had been made by France to give up the transportation of relapsed criminals if she might take the New Hebrides. That was refused by the Australian Colonies on being consulted, and the noble Earl had then informed the French Government of that refusal. There the matter rested; but in June, 1886, without any formal annexation on the part of France, or without the Central Government at Paris being in any way connected with the matter, French troops were placed on the Island. From a letter which he had received from a well-known Scotch gentleman at Melbourne, he understood that the French still occupied a military station and were erecting what appeared to be permanent buildings, and putting up wooden sheds either for convicts or for additional troops. He had had another letter, dated December 6, 1886, from another Scotch gentleman at Havannah Harbour, Exatè, stating that on June 1 a military post had been established in that harbour with over 100 French Marines, and immediately afterwards a similar post had been established at Port Sandwich. He thought that these letters would justify him in bringing this matter before their Lordships' House, as it was a matter which ought to be decided quickly one way or another. The Government had shown no undue pressure in the matter, and, on the other hand, he believed that the Central Government in France had in no way been committed to this infraction of the Treaty. It might be said that this occupation had been rendered necessary on account of outrages; but he had made inquiries, and had found that no serious cases of outrage had been brought home to the inhabitants of the New Hebrides. As often as not what were called outrages were the result of the abominable system of labour trade which prevailed in those parts, and which had done more to set the Natives of the Islands against the Whites than anything which could be done. He would, therefore, implore Her Majesty's Government, in the interests of the Natives, in the interests of our Australian Colonies, in the interests of our Imperial and commercial obligations, but, above all, in the interest of the sacredness of good faith in public International Agreements, to take up this matter and bring to a termination the French occupation. As Germany had recently shown, there was no need for any sense of wounded pride, and no humiliation, in an admission on the part of a great nation that it had done a wrong act.

THE PRIME MINISTER AND SECRETARY OF STATE FOR FOREIGN AFFAIRS (The Marquess of SALISBURY): My noble Friend (the Earl of Harrowby) has made a very interesting speech, and I only feel very great regret that it is not in my power to give him in return anything nearly so valuable or so interesting. The truth is, I heard with some dismay my noble Friend go from point to point on matters which have been laid before the House, and I have very little indeed to add to what he has said. My noble Friend will understand that there are matters which he has discussed, and which he has a perfect right to discuss, but into which it would not be right for me to follow him. For example, I could not examine the motives which induced the French Government to attach value to the New Hebrides, and the same reason likewise precludes me from examining into motives which have induced the Australian Colonies to look upon these Islands with exceptional interest. There is no doubt of the International state of the case—that France and England have engaged to each other not to annex the New Hebrides, and there is no doubt that at this moment the French Government is in occupation of these Islands; but that they have assured us, in tones whose earnestness and sincerity we have no right to doubt, that they have no intention of permanently occupying those Islands; and, therefore, no definite character ought to be attached to their proceedings. They have informed Her Majesty's Government that they have been obliged to take the step they have taken, solely in consequence of the outrages which have occurred. There have been outrages—we do not quite know how many; but, undoubtedly, certain persons in 1885 were killed, and several others wounded and attacked. The position of the French Government is that

The Earl of Harrowby

as soon as satisfactory arrangements can be made by which the peace of the Islands can be maintained, and Europeans can be preserved from danger of outbreak, they would be glad to withdraw their troops. Her Majesty's Government have made proposals for the purpose of carrying this object into effect. These proposals have not been rejected, neither have they been absolutely accepted. Under the pressure of political events which have happened internally and externally upon France during the last six months, the negotiations have not gone on with that rapidity which we should like to see. We have, upon more than one occasion, called attention to the delay, and the French Government have always assured us that they were prepared to make proposals, and I believe that the French Ambassador is likely to make a communication of some importance in the course of the present week. I can make no further answer, except to assure my noble Friend that I am as fully sensible as he is of the sacredness of the International engagement which prevents both France and England from occupying these Islands of the New Hebrides, and Her Majesty's Government have no intention of departing on their side from the engagement.

THE EARL OF ROSEBERY said, he was far from urging on the Government to take any other course than they had taken, and he did not doubt that the noble Marquess the Prime Minister had kept that course adequately in view and had expressed his opinion to the French Government; but he was sure the answer would cause great disappointment in the Australian Colonies and among those in this country who were interested in the question. Could the noble Marquess state whether there were any ships of war in the vicinity of the New Hebrides? He should be glad to learn that the British ships of war which were at the New Hebrides last May were still there, and whether there was any force representing our interests in the Islands. That was a matter of some importance, as showing that we attached weight to the question.

THE MARQUESS OF SALISBURY said, he could not answer the Question without Notice. It was his impression that some of Her Majesty's ships had been there from time to time. There was, however, no permanent station there, and whether there were any ships there at this present moment he could not say.

THE EARL OF CARNARVON said, no one in England who had followed these matters closely, and no one in Australasia, could avoid regretting its present position, or could regard the present state of things as satisfactory. With regard to these Islands an understanding had, so far back as 1840, been come to between this country and the French Government that their independence should be respected. In 1858 a definite agreement to this effect was entered into, and that agreement had for years been recognized by successive English Governments and by the French Government. Now, however, after several years of *pourparlers* on the subject the French flag was to be found flying there. It was difficult to reconcile this with the amiable theory set up by his noble Friend (the Earl of Harrowby) who introduced the subject that it might be the indiscreet act of some agent or imprudent officer on a foreign station. He was sorry that this was not the only case of this nature which had arisen. There was another group of Islands, well known to Colonists and mariners—the Society group—one of which formed the subject in 1847 of a distinct reciprocal agreement between this country and France that its independence should be respected. Yet for at least five or six years the French flag had been flying upon it, notwithstanding all protests and complaints that had been received on the subject. At the great distance England was from these Islands and the scene of these transactions, and owing to attention being diverted at home by the multiplicity of political questions, matters had been occurring in the South Pacific which often escaped our attention, but which to the great Colonies were questions of life and death. He did not make any charge against the French Government—or even a complaint—it was, perhaps, very creditable to French policy and foresight; but if their Lordships took a map and referred to the present state of things in the Eastern part of the South Pacific, they could not fail to be struck with the enormous amount of the recent French annexations. Tahiti, for instance, which some years ago nearly led to a collision between the two countries, was till lately under French protection. Recently the protectorate had been converted into sovereignty. Similarly the Society Islands, Rapa, the Austral group, and the mass of the Islands that went by the name of the Lower Archipelago had, in recent years, been annexed. The desire for territory, and the wise foresight which looked to the opening of the Panama Canal, accounted partly for what had taken place. Turning from the East to the West Pacific, where Australian interests mainly lay, a similar state of things existed. In the West Pacific there was the great French Colony of New Caledonia, peopled by convicts; there were the Loyalty Islands, and, if the New Hebrides were by any accident transferred to the jurisdiction of France, there would stretch a great block of intervening Islands between Australia and Fiji—all under the French flag—and which might be described as our outpost on the other side. Whatever might be thought of these things in this country, no Australian would, or could, or ought to regard the prospect without a feeling of considerable anxiety. He could not say what were our precise relations with other countries with which we came into contact in the Pacific. No one who was not in Office could exactly tell. But he had no reason to believe these relations were otherwise than satisfactory. About three years ago their Lordships might remember that an important agreement was come to between this country and Germany by which the two Governments agreed to delimit their jurisdiction—their spheres of influence it would be more correct to say—in the South Pacific. The result of this had been that, so far as Germany was concerned, the chances of friction had been very much lessened. He would throw out for the consideration of Her Majesty's Government the suggestion whether some such understanding might not be arrived at with France as regarded the same seas. The noble Earl pointed out strong reasons why this matter should be satisfactorily settled without delay. There were two special reasons for this. It was a question that closely affected the natives of the South Pacific. He (the Earl of Carnarvon), about 1876 and 1877, was the author of two Acts which created the Office of High Commissioner with jurisdiction to deal with all cases of outrage on natives, especially such as arose out of the labour

The Earl of Carnarvon

traffic. Those Acts had done great good, but they had not altogether attained their object. It was not possible for the British Government to give the High Commissioner jurisdiction over foreigners, or natives, in any but British Islands. He earnestly recommended the Prime Minister to consider whether some amendment of the existing state of things, which allowed a large part of the criminal and uncivilized community in those quarters to escape jurisdiction, could not be come to by the consent and co-operation of foreign Powers. There used to be a mixed Slave Trade Court which worked very well in the Slave Trade days; and he believed this Slave Trade Commission—which, as he said, formerly existed—might contain a suggestion for a precedent. There was another reason which rendered the settlement of the matter urgent—namely, the Recidivist question in New Caledonia. That was a very large and important question, and one that had moved the Australian public mind to its lowest depths. Until this question of the New Hebrides—with which it was connected—should have been settled it would remain, he feared, a burning question, containing in itself the germs of future anxiety, trouble, and possible danger.

EARL GRANVILLE: I rise to express my gratification that, being in Office, the noble Marquess (the Marquess of Salisbury) seems to think that there is some weight in the principle which I was in the habit of asserting, that an answer should not be hastily given without Notice to Questions relating to important foreign affairs. There is still this difference between us, however. When I laid down that principle I adhered to it, and did not answer Questions until after Notice; whereas the noble Marquess, after enunciating the principle, has really told us how the matter stands to which the Question put to him refers. There is certainly no one more anxious than I am to avoid causing any feelings of unnecessary excitement between our great neighbours the French and ourselves. The proof of this is, that when we first received the news of the landing of French troops in the New Hebrides, and considered the advisability of sending immediately ships of war to the scene, we hesitated to do so, lest it should cause unnecessary irritation. A short time afterwards, however, on getting further information, we agreed that it was desirable to send British ships, not as a menace or in any spirit of hostility, but in order to put the two countries on the same footing. Since then, as far as I know, the occupation has been consistently disowned by the French Government, who have always given us assurances that they do not desire the occupation of the New Hebrides, and that they intend to adhere to the International agreement. Last year the noble Earl near me repeated that assurance, which he had recently received from the French Government. But now that this French occupation of the shore had gone on, not only for weeks and months, but for more than a year, a change in our policy, and a reversal of the order that ships shall be on the spot, may exercise an unfavourable impression, especially on the Colonial mind. I am glad, therefore, to hear from the noble Marquess that he is about to receive an important communication from the French Government. In conclusion, let me say that no one can desire more heartily than myself that the communications between the Governments may lead to a really satisfactory result for the French nation, ourselves, and our Colonial fellow subjects.

NAVY—POSITION OF LIEUTENANTS—RETIREMENT.

QUESTION. OBSERVATIONS.

LORD SUDELEY, in rising to call attention to the present system of retirement in the Navy, and to the block which at present exists in the Lieutenants' List; and to ask, Whether the Admiralty propose to take any steps to improve the position of lieutenants? said, that he did not wish to cast any blame on the retirement scheme of 1870. In fact, he looked upon it as a settled charter which could not be altered, and which had, on the whole, worked very well. Their Lordships, doubtless, remembered the state of the retirement list of all ranks before 1870, the endless confusion that existed, the number of retirement lists with separate letters of the alphabet to each, and the perfect block of promotion. Year by year feeble attempts were made to overcome the difficulties that surrounded the question; but it was not

until 1870 that any considerable attempt was really made to grapple with them. The general result had been very satisfactory, and he was glad to find that the calculations made by Mr. Childers as to cost had been fully borne out. Mr. Childers said that the cost of the executive officers (including navigating officers) on non-effective pay would rise for a few years and then gradually diminish. This had been the case. In 1870-1 the cost was £337,798; in 1875-6 the cost was £456,185; and in 1887-8 it was to be £341,540. One great principle of the scheme was that there were to be young officers on all the lists, and with that object Mr. Childers gave a high retired pay. Unless that principle was kept up, the greatest advantage of the whole scheme would disappear. He wished to call attention to the state of the lieutenants' list, because he thought the time had arrived when some special help must be given to that list, so that the wheels of the retirement scheme might be made to work smoothly. In the lieutenants' list a block which was not foreseen had arisen, and the average age was getting older year by year. If the Admiralty did not act promptly very great discontent might result, and probably so much pressure would be exercised upon the Naval Authorities that they would find it impossible to resist a large inflation of the upper lists, in order to give what was called a "flow of promotion." That there was grave discontent among the lieutenants, who were the backbone of the Service, no one could deny. The total number of lieutenants and navigating officers now authorized was 1,000. It was thought in 1870 that it would be possible to keep the number down to 600, with 200 for navigating duties, making a total of 800, but in 1879 it was found necessary to raise the number by another 200. It had not yet been found practicable to get the list up to the authorized number. There were still only 873 lieutenants, and he believed that it would be seven or eight years before the entries as naval cadets would make it possible for the full number to be reached. The annual average number of promotions was only about 23, and it was only possible for two lieutenants out of nine ever to be promoted. This constituted the great cause of complaint; because the list was below its authorized numbers it had been impossible to allow any special retirements. In 1871 there were 79 lieutenants of over 10 years' seniority; in 1879 there were 150; in 1883 there were 193; and in April, 1887, there were no less than 279, or nearly one-third of the entire list. Now, it was well known that when a lieutenant had over 10 years' seniority he had arrived at an age when—unless he had a prospect of promotion within the next two or three years—he was bound to become more or less discontented and unsettled. What was specially wanted in the Navy was that the lieutenants' list should be kept young and efficient. At present it was perfectly clear that the list during the next few years would get considerably older, with the very greatest disadvantage to the Service in general. When a lieutenant became over 12 years' seniority he knew that he could never reach the higher grades of the Service, but would, even if promoted, have to be retired either as commander or captain. It was absolutely necessary also that young men should be selected for promotion to commanders, as otherwise the age would be raised in every rank, and there would be constant expensive retirement. A pamphlet had lately been published, which he understood had been approved by nearly all the lieutenants on the list, pointing out very fairly their complaints in respect to promotion, position, and pay. He was told that it was contemplated to increase the commanders' list slightly. If that were done because of the requirements of the Service, it would be a wise course; but if it were done merely in order to facilitate promotion, much as he desired to benefit the lieutenants, the result would be most disastrous. The captains' and commanders' lists must be small, and an attempt to increase them, except for the requirements of the Service, would do away with the main features of the retirement scheme of 1870, and there would be no stop to it. In respect to promotion, the lieutenants seemed to desire that certain special regulations should be enacted in their favour, so that every man might have a certainty of promotion to commander. On this point he could not go with them, as they asked what it was impossible to concede. In framing the scheme of 1870, Mr. Childers laid this down very clearly. He stated—

Lord Sudeley

" No lieutenant should be deemed to have a moral right to promotion ; but promotion from his rank or that of commander was to be purely by selection on account of efficiency and prospective usefulness. The idea of promotion from that rank merely to enable a good flow to be secured was absolutely rejected."

So soon as there were a sufficient number on the list, the only way in which the matter could be dealt with was by allowing the optional retirement at an earlier age, of, say, from 32 to 35, to all lieutenants who found that from various causes they were not likely to obtain promotion. At present no man had the right to retire until he was 40 years of age, and although the Admiralty had obtained an Order in Council to enable them to allow officers to retire younger that power was not known in the Service. It would be far better that officers should be allowed to leave at a period when there was some prospect of their being enabled to obtain a livelihood in other professions, and it would be far more economical that you should retire men young than that you should retire men from age when captains and commanders at much higher rates. Some inducement ought to be offered to officers to accept this optional retirement, and if £100 were given in addition to the present retirement it would be found to work. A man of 32 to 35 ought to be able to retire upon about £200 a-year as a minimum. It was supposed under the present scheme that a lieutenant could retire at about £300 a-year. Although this was true under special circumstances if he held on until he was 45, no one had succeeded in obtaining so high an amount; and, as a matter of fact, the average rate of retirement was only about £150. As regarded the question of position, there could be no doubt that during the last few years there had been changes in the relative rank of officers of the civil branches which had placed them higher in many ways than the lieutenants. With respect to pay, a considerable change might be made at a very small expense. In the "Lieutenants' Pamphlet" this matter was stated very clearly. The pay of the ordinary lieutenant was the same now as it was in the year 1841—namely, 10s. a-day, the only difference being an increase of 2s. per day after ten years' service. This rate was small even in 1841; but it was absurdly small when one considered the highly-trained scientific officers of the present day. Forty-seven years ago a lieutenant had to be a thorough seaman, efficient in the command of men, and possessed of a general knowledge of gunnery, but he was not supposed to do much more. Now, he was required to be not only a thorough seaman, but a competent scientific officer, able to manage huge and unwieldy ironclads; well acquainted with engines, hydraulic gunnery, and torpedoes in all their branches; able to command a naval brigade on shore, to navigate and pilot his vessel, and to have a general knowledge of International Law. Some increase, therefore, ought to be made in the pay which was given 45 years ago. No doubt it was urged that extra allowances were given besides this 10*s.* a-day for definite qualifications, and this was certainly true for trained officers, principally instructors, at from 2*s.* 6*d.* to 3*s.* 6*d.* a-day. This was merely special pay for special work, and the average lieutenant's pay remained the same—namely, 10*s.* a-day. He found that there were 58 gunnery officers, 34 torpedo, and 137 senior lieutenants receiving these special allowances for this special work. It was sometimes urged that there was an unlimited supply of naval cadets forthcoming, and therefore there was no necessity to raise the pay of lieutenants. This was a most unfair argument to use, because a boy of 14 did not calculate what he had to look forward to. In 1841 a lieutenant was the best paid officer of that rank, and now in 1887 he was the worst paid. In 1841 lieutenants received 10*s.* a-day; in 1887, 10*s.*, rising to 12*s.*; in 1841, masters received 7*s.* a-day; in 1887, 12*s.*, rising to 22*s.*; in 1841, assistant surgeons received 7*s.* a-day; in 1887, 11*s.* 6*d.*, rising to 27*s.*; in 1841, chaplains received 8*s.* 9*d.*; in 1887, 12*s.*, rising to 22*s.*; in 1841, naval instructors received 7*s.* a-day; in 1887, 12*s.*, rising to 22*s.*; and in 1841, paymasters received 7*s.* a-day; in 1887, 12*s.*, rising to 22*s.* The lieutenants asked that progressive pay should be given, as had been done in every other branch. They proposed that the extra 2*s.* which was now given when they had 10 years' seniority should be given at eight years instead, and a further 2*s.* when they had served 11 years. This increase would, he believed, only cost about £10,000, and if it brought

with it moderate contentment it would be cheaply purchased. The lieutenants who were of 10 years' seniority had, with their junior service, actually been 20 years in the service. Let their Lordships think what it must be to a man to find himself with no chance of promotion before him after this service, and to have to remain a lieutenant until he was 40 years old on £216 a-year. We had at the Admiralty at the present moment a Board who were eminently fitted to deal with the subject, and Admiral Sir Anthony Hoskins, who had special charge of the Department, was one of our most able and distinguished Admirals, and one who had the interests of lieutenants most thoroughly at heart. He had consulted several great authorities on the suggestion he had made, and they all agreed. Perhaps there was no one who had given greater attention to the subject of retirement than Admiral Colomb, and had worked out the most copious statistics on the subject. He most cordially concurred in the plan of optional retirement at an early age and increased pay. Mr. Childers allowed him to say that he also quite approved an optional retirement at an early age. There was much more that might be said on the subject; but he thought he had said enough to show that the lieutenants' list was in a most unsatisfactory condition. For many years the numbers would be short, and, in consequence, it would be impossible to do so much either in retirement or by promotion year by year. In consequence the number of senior men would greatly increase, which would be a serious evil, not only to the lieutenants themselves, but to the Naval Service generally. The only possible alleviation at present that he could see open was a small progressive increase of pay, and a promise of optional retirement in the future. He ventured to say that this was a serious matter. The lieutenants were, as he had already said, the backbone of the Service. It was from this list that all our captains and commanders had to be selected, and whatever was hurtful to and detrimental to this body of officers must work with most disastrous effect on those who would command our ships. An officer in the Navy required special consideration. Life at sea was surrounded with perils and dangers which only those who had gone through them could thoroughly appreciate. When one thought of the years spent in different seas under the strictest discipline, far removed from the joys and happiness of home life, continually undergoing long night watches and monotonous voyages, it was impossible for the severest critic not to have a deep feeling of sympathy for these gallant officers, and to be most anxious that any feeling of discontent as to their pay and position should be speedily removed. Of this he was quite certain—that we had now a picked body of lieutenants, men imbued with the finest sense of honour and with the deepest devotion to their duties; and if the prayer of the petition which the lieutenants had put forward in their pamphlet was not entertained, he thought it would be one of the greatest mistakes that it would be possible to make. He trusted that the noble Lord who represented the Admiralty would be able to give a satisfactory reply.

THE EARL OF BELMORE said, he wished to say a few words on the case which had been so clearly stated by the noble Lord who had just sat down (Lord Sudeley). The small increase of pay which was made three years ago was in consequence of his having brought this subject before the notice of their Lordships in 1883. He then asked that 1*s.* a-day extra pay might be granted to officers of eight years' standing and upwards. The noble Earl who was then First Lord of the Admiralty (the Earl of Northbrook) was not able to do anything in that year, but in the following year he provided for an increase of 2*s.* a-day to all lieutenants of 10 years' standing and upwards. That increase gave great satisfaction then, but he thought the time had now arrived when something more ought to be done, and he agreed with his noble Friend that the request of the lieutenants, as far as the increase of pay was concerned, should be acceded to. He did not intend to offer any observations upon this question of retirement or choice of cabins, as he was not an authority upon those subjects, not having had the advantage of serving in the Navy. But there was no doubt but that the position of the lieutenants was much more unfavourable now than it was, say, 20 years ago. To show this, he would mention two matters within his own observation. When he went to Australia, he found, on his arrival at

Lord Sudeley

Sydney, six ships on the station. Three were commanded by commanders; the other three were corvettes, commanded by post captains—one of these captains was the Commodore. He was then only about 40, having been appointed when 39. He had been posted at 26. Another, the late Admiral Hope, who had been flag lieutenant to Admiral Corry in the Baltic, had been made a captain at 32. The third, now Admiral Lyons, had become a captain at 27. But it might be said that two of those officers had had war service in the Black Sea during the Crimean War; whilst the third, as he had said, had been a flag lieutenant. He would, therefore, take another case. In 1866 the Duke of Somerset, who was then First Lord of the Admiralty, brought out a new Warrant for the promotion of commanders, and 31 were, as it were, by a single stroke of the pen, promoted on June 11, who had been serving, probably, in all parts of the world. As a very near relation of his own was amongst the number, the matter had the more impressed itself on his memory. Of these 31 officers, only four were over 40 years of age; one was 51, three were 40, or between that and 50. The remaining 27 were between 30 and 40. The junior of these—not in age, but in standing—had five and a-half years' standing as a commander. Their average age was between 37 and 38. These men were made post captains. Nowadays, a lieutenant would be rather fortunate to be made a commander at 32 or 33, and 37 would not be a bad average of age for that rank. He thought that the lieutenants had a very strong case; and he felt sure that his noble Friend the First Lord of the Admiralty would give the matter his careful consideration, and do all he could for them consistently with the requirements of the Chancellor of the Exchequer.

LORD ELPHINSTONE (A LORD in WAITING) said, he must, in the first place, take the opportunity of thanking his noble Friend (Lord Sudeley) for having so fully and so courteously explained the question he intended putting. He was not surprised at his calling attention to the subject, for it was one in which he knew his noble Friend took a deep interest, and he also remembered the very active and prominent part he took in the other House of Parliament when the question of naval retirement was under discussion in 1870 and 1873. The Admiralty were keenly alive to the matter. The problem how to insure a steady and an uniform flow of promotion through the various ranks of the Naval Service was one that successive Boards of Admiralty had for many years been endeavouring to solve. And he could assure his noble Friend that the present Board were as anxious to find a solution as he was himself. He would endeavour to show the causes which had led to the present state of the lieutenant's list. It was unnecessary to refer to the earlier schemes of retirement, or to any anterior to that of 1870, when Mr. Childers, then First Lord of the Admiralty, re-organized the list and introduced his retirement scheme, which, with slight modifications, was the present scheme of naval retirement. Mr. Childers's object was to reduce the list, first, by a compulsory age retirement, and, secondly, by giving such an increase to the retiring pension as would not only induce officers to retire but would make them contented to do so. Two hundred and seventy officers accepted that retirement. Three years afterwards, in 1873, Mr. Goschen, who succeeded Mr. Childers as First Lord, still further increased the retiring pension, as it was found that officers were not retiring as quickly as it was hoped and expected that they would do. About 170 officers accepted the new retirement. Under the scheme of 1870, Mr. Childers desired that the numbers should be only sufficient for the actual requirements of the Service with reference to employment and not as outlets for promotion. He therefore fixed the number of admirals at 60, captains at 150, commanders at 200, and lieutenants at 600. But, fully recognizing the difficulty, or rather the absolute impossibility, of passing 600 lieutenants into a list of only 200 commanders, he increased the retiring allowance, and gave what was considered an adequate and a liberal compensation for loss of promotion. He saw, in fact, that it was quite out of the question to hope to pass every young officer who entered the Service through the various grades until he became an admiral. He therefore said, in effect— "If I am unable to promote you, I will at any rate give you a fair money compensation when you retire." He spoke

in the presence of a noble Earl opposite who was a Lord of the Admiralty at that time. He would correct him if he was wrong, but he said that the very essence of the retirement scheme of 1870 was that, where an officer could not be promoted—and it was perfectly clear that all could not be promoted—they should be liberally compensated on retirement. In 1875 the number of admirals was increased to 68, of captains to 175, of commanders to 225; and in 1879 the lieutenants' list was increased to 800. Now, if a difficulty existed in 1870, when 600 lieutenants had to be squeezed into a list of 200 commanders, that difficulty was the greater when 800 lieutenants had to be squeezed into a list of 225 commanders. In the same year —1879—it was determined that the masters or navigating line should be abolished, and that the duties of navigating should be undertaken by the lieutenants. The navigating line was gradually to die out, and the number of lieutenants was gradually to increase until it reached its maximum of 1,000, which it would do in about six years. Anyone who had followed him through the figures he had given would readily understand the cause of the present state of the lieutenants' lists, and the limited possibilities of those officers rising to the rank of commander. The noble Lord opposite had referred in terms of well-merited praise to lieutenants as a class. He echoed every word. He yielded to no one in his admiration of their zeal and ability, and of the way they had set themselves to keep pace with the altered conditions of the Service and of the requirements of the times; and he sympathized with them in the difficulty they experienced in obtaining that promotion which they naturally looked to as their reward. He said more. He said that the Admiralty sympathized, and sympathized deeply, especially with the senior and deserving officers for whom no promotion was to be found. The commanders' list stood at present at 225. The Admiralty, finding that they could usefully employ a larger number of commanders, proposed to increase that number by the addition of seven yearly, until the maximum of 270 was reached, and they were in communication with the Treasury upon the subject. This addition to the commanders' list would, to a certain extent, benefit the lieutenants.

At present two out of nine obtained commander's rank. If the proposed change were carried out, two out of seven would obtain their promotion. In former times the number was about one in every 15. The noble Lord opposite proposed that lieutenants should be allowed to claim their retirement after 10 years' service as lieutenants. Under the existing regulations a lieutenant might claim his retirement with the rank of commander at the age of 40; but, were his noble Friend's suggestion carried out, a lieutenant would be entitled to claim his retirement at the age of from 30 to 35, at the very time when his services could be least dispensed with, and his experience was most valuable, and irrespective of the requirements of the Service at the time. At the present moment there were 875 lieutenants on the active list; and if this suggestion were carried out no less than 243, or more than one-fourth, could claim their retirement. Take this case. There were 88 lieutenants serving in the Mediterranean, 19 of whom were over 10 years' seniority; therefore, nearly one-fourth could insist upon retirement. Under the Order in Council of 1870 lieutenants could retire at any time, with the consent of the Admiralty, no matter what their seniority might be. The Admiralty were the best judges as to the present requirements of the Service, and they were and must be the sole judges as to the prospective requirements of the Service. To them, and to them alone, must be left the option of consent or non-consent to the application of an officer wishing to retire at an age under that fixed by the Order in Council of 1870. The Admiralty had no wish to compel any officer to serve against his will, nor was it to the interests of the Service that any reluctant or discontented officer should be retained whose services could properly be dispensed with, but so long as the lieutenants' list was below the proper strength and there were no officers available on half-pay, as was the case as present, they were bound to refuse applications to retire before the age established by the Order in Council of 1870, save in very exceptional cases. With regard to the suggestion that lieutenants should receive an increase of 2*s.* a-day after eight years' seniority, with a further increase

Lord Elphinstone

of 2*s.* after 12 years' seniority, instead of as, at present, 2*s.* after 10 years, he must remind his noble Friend that the actual amount received by a very large proportion of the lieutenants was greater now than at any former time, and that out of 875 lieutenants no less than 337 were in receipt of additional pay, varying from 1*s.* a-day to a possible 8*s.* as first lieutenant and gunnery lieutenant of a rated ship. He could only repeat that the Admiralty were fully alive to the matter. They were desirous of taking such steps as were feasible to improve the position of the lieutenants without departure from the principles laid down by the Order in Council of 1870, and they were giving the matter their fullest, their serious, and their most earnest consideration.

THE EARL OF CAMPERDOWN said, he was at the Admiralty in 1870 and was familiar with the terms of the Order in Council of that year. This question of promotion and retirement was a question which had always been occupying the attention of the Admiralty, and would continue to occupy their attention so long as the Admiralty existed. When in 1868 Mr. Childers had this question of promotion and retirement brought under his notice the evils of the system had reached a very high pitch. The condition of things then was altogether different from that which now prevailed. The references that evening had been confined to one rank of officers; but with regard to the other ranks there had been an enormous block on the captains' list, and the same remark applied to other classes of officers. The principle which Mr. Childers applied consistently to every rank in the Navy was this. In the first place, he reduced the number; in the next place, he laid down the principle that in future establishments of each rank should be in proportion to the number of officers whom it was found impossible to employ, and not in reference to the number of other lists. He believed that principle to be a most important one, and he trusted that the Admiralty would never give it up. But beyond that Mr. Childers recognized that it would be impossible to promote all the officers of the various ranks, and therefore for the first time he instituted a very large and liberal scale of retirement. He would undertake to say that the scale of retirement in the Navy would compare very favourably indeed with that of any other Service either in this country or any other. It was quite true that it was perfectly impossible to promote 1,000 lieutenants with a list of some 250 commanders, and therefore their Lordships must at once recognize the absolutely certain fact that a large number of lieutenants never could be promoted, and by no scheme that ingenuity could devise would it be possible to effect that object. Well, then, what were the Admiralty to do? It must give them an adequate retiring allowance. That was a matter which rested entirely with the Admiralty, and their Lordships must look to the Admiralty to do that which was right. With regard to the proposed addition to the list of commanders, he did not, of course, profess to be able to judge how much employment there was for the commanders; but he hoped the Admiralty would exercise a very diligent scrutiny in this regard and take care not to create more commanders than they could find employment for, because that could only add eventually to the numbers of the discontented. It would be useless and prejudicial to the Service to make an addition to the commanders' list simply as a sort of sop to the lieutenants in the hope that by promoting a few just now they might allay the discontent owing to the necessary want of employment. His noble Friend had spoken of the inadequate pay of the lieutenants; but he omitted, to notice certain allowances which they received, and it must not be supposed that the pay was on the same footing as in 1841. Again, the proposition that a lieutenant should have an absolute option of retiring at the age of 32, as suggested by his noble Friend (Lord Sudeley)—considering that for five years, from 13 to 18, the country educated naval officers, and that at the latter age their services really commenced—was surely one that was not advanced in a serious manner; at all events, he did not believe it was one which the country was likely to accept. He thought that there was no Naval Service in the world in which the officers were treated more liberally than the British.

VISCOUNT SIDMOUTH said, he could not agree that an adequate scheme of retirement would meet the necessity of the case. An officer who was still a lieutenant at the age of 35 was placed in an entirely false position, for he could not find any possible pursuit on shore. In the interests of the Service it was not so much a question of money as of early promotion or of the officer being allowed to retire at an age when he might find some employment on shore. He remembered Lord Palmerston saying that the great object of the Military and Naval Services was promotion and not pay, and he hoped the Admiralty would give their attention, not so much to the subject of increased remuneration of officers as to their early promotion when lieutenants. He would now take the opportunity to ask the Question standing in his name with regard to interpreters. The number of officers qualified as interpreters was very much below that which was found in almost any other Navy in the world. There were about 90 officers of various ranks who are qualified so to act. Out of those not above 16 or 18 were qualified in French, only four in German, and about two in Italian. All the rest were officers qualified in Eastern languages which might or might not be extremely useful, but certainly not so much in the Naval Service as a thorough knowledge of the leading European languages. In the German Service there was hardly an officer who was not a thorough English and French scholar, and the same might be said with regard to Russia. Every Russian officer not only spoke excellent English, but was also thoroughly conversant with French, and most with German. He therefore wished to know whether the Admiralty would give further encouragement to the junior classes of Naval officers to qualify themselves to act as interpreters.

THE EARL OF NORTHBROOK said, he wished to express his entire concurrence in the expressions which had been made use of with regard to the high merits of the large class of lieutenants. There was no branch of the gallant and distinguished service which deserved more encouragement than the lieutenants of the Navy. It had constantly been a subject of great regret to successive First Lords of the Admiralty that they were unable to grant promotion to a great many of this class, whose claims they thoroughly acknowledged. He approved of the policy which the noble Lord opposite had told them the Admiralty were about to follow. If it could be done with a due regard to the interests of the public service, he thought it was wise to increase the number of commanders and thereby give additional promotion to lieutenants. It would not be to the advantage of the Service if the commanders' list was to be largely increased without additional employment being found for them; but, owing to the amalgamation of the navigating officers with the lieutenants, and the increase in the number of small vessels, he believed that such employment might be found. He thought that the Admiralty were right in effecting the change gradually. The responsibility must naturally rest upon the Admiralty, and he could entirely confirm what had been said with regard to Sir A. Hoskins, to whose particular branch this question referred, and in whose hands this matter was placed. For this reason he, for his own part, felt great confidence in the view which the Admiralty had taken of this matter, and he trusted that the proposals which the noble Lord had told them were about to be made would receive the assent of all the authorities concerned, because they would give considerable encouragement to the older lieutenants on the list, by holding out a greater prospect of promotion, which they wanted more than increased pay or speedier retirement from the Service.

LORD ELPHINSTONE said, that he always received his instructions from the Admiralty before he answered Questions which were placed on the Paper, and his answer to the Question of the noble Viscount (Viscount Sidmouth) was that the Admiralty fully appreciated the desirability of the junior officers acquiring a knowledge of foreign languages, and their attention had been called to the matter in connection with the *Britannia* course of instruction, but the Admiralty did not propose to hold out any hope of further pecuniary inducement.

LAND IMPROVEMENT (IRELAND).

MOTION FOR A PAPER.

THE EARL OF BELMORE said, he rose to call attention to the question of improvements made on their estates by owners of land in Ireland; and to move for a Return in tabular form of—I.

Totals of Loans by the Board of Public Works in Ireland for land improvement made between 1847 and 1881 inclusive to owners of land for (*a*) Erection of farmhouses and offices; (*b*) Labourers' cottages; (*c*) Drainage, reclamation, and improvement of lands; II. Totals of Loans between the same years to Drainage Boards; III. and IV. Similar Returns since 1881. He was impelled to move for this Return in consequence of the statements made in the debate on the second reading of the Irish land Bill by his noble Friend Earl Cowper, who had been both Lord Lieutenant and also President of the late Royal Commission, and whose utterances therefore commanded such attention, and had been, indeed, since quoted in another place against the landlords by a late Minister. His noble Friend had then rather astonished him by saying that the impression left upon his mind by the inquiries he had made — whilst presiding over the Royal Commission — was that except upon as many estates as one could count upon one's fingers, the landlords had not been in the habit of making in any expenditure upon their estates, and that in cases where the tenants had effected improvements it had been a general custom with the landlords to raise the rents. He had only one word to say with regard to the latter point, and he would say that first of all. He had no doubt read of such cases in the Press, and he had heard of one single case of late years on the part of a gentleman who was now dead, but he denied that the practice was a general one. With regard to the question of expenditure, he entirely dissented from the statement of the noble Earl. He was prepared to admit that in former days it was not the custom for landowners to spend money upon their estates. But to take the case of the North of Ireland, which had been settled by the plantation of Ulster in the reign of James I.—which was a colonizing scheme—it was governed by the rules of the Plantation, and one of the most important provisions of that system was the giving very long leases for lives or for other long terms, which grew into a custom. Upon that he did not believe much improvement was made until the middle or end of the last century. They gathered from the

The Earl of Northbrook

very interesting account given of a tour by Mr. Arthur Young in Ireland in 1776, that an extensive system of overcropping then prevailed among the tenants. That clearly showed that no agricultural value could have been added to the land at that time or, indeed, for a very long time afterwards. He believed that in the latter part of the last century landlords were alive to the desirability of the maintenance of their estates, and by way of illustration he might say that he had in his possession the counterpart of a lease granted by the first Earl of Belmore in 1795, in which, in addition to rent, the tenant was bound to make some 56 yards of fences every year, and plant trees along them, during the term of a lease for three lives, or else pay 8*s*. extra a year. Further, he had to build two farmhouses or cottages or pay a small penalty. When the lease fell in all these improvements were to belong to the landlord, and all this was fully understood by the tenant. He always maintained that the landlord paid for the improvement by taking a smaller rent for the farm than he otherwise would have taken if he had to pay separately for the improvements made. The tenant was thus paid for his improvement by the long lease of his farm at a low rent. In modern times the landlords had spent large sums of money in improving their estates. There were some estates which, no doubt, his noble Friend had in his mind's eye when he spoke of landlords who did not make all the improvements themselves. But these, which were generally known as the English managed estates, were very exceptional, probably not more than five. There were landlords who had spent in improvements large sums obtained from the Board of Works, which sums could be shown in a Return made to Parliament. It was impossible on some estates to show how much had been spent on home farming, or how much upon improving the estate, but there was no doubt that in the aggregate it amounted to a very large sum of money. But besides that, there was another very large source of expenditure which it was impossible almost to get at—namely, the money paid for timber and slates allowed to tenants by landlords in many parts of the country. He understood that there had been a very large expenditure in that direction

by the late Duke of Abercorn, in addition to a large amount of loans borrowed from the Board of Works. The late Earl of Caledon also had, he had heard, made a large outlay in improvements on his estates after the famine time. He therefore felt that it was extremely unfair that landlords who had made sacrifices in this way should be condemned, as they had been condemned by implication in the statement of his noble Friend (Earl Cowper). He quite admitted that his noble Friend had a perfect right to form his own opinion. But in moving for this Return of money spent on their estates by improving landlords between the years 1848 and 1881, he wished to show their Lordships that the great bulk of the landlords in Ireland did not neglect the duties of their position, and spent large sums in providing for the welfare of their tenantry. He believed that some expenditure had been made since 1881, and he, therefore, included a head for such, in his Motion, and also for loans made to Drainage Boards, the interest of which would be paid partly by tenants and partly by landlords.

Moved, That there be laid before this House Return, in tabular form, of—

"I. Totals of Loans by the Board of Public Works in Ireland for land improvement made between 1847 and 1881, inclusive, to owners of land for

(a) Erection of farm houses and offices;

(b) Labourers' cottages;

(c) Drainage, reclamation, and improvement of lands:

II. Totals of Loans between the same years to Drainage Boards:

III. and IV. Similar Returns, since 1881."— (*The Earl of Belmore*.)

THE LORD PRIVY SEAL (Earl CADOGAN) said, there was no objection on the part of the Government to the Return being given for which the noble Earl moved. It should be laid on the Table as soon as possible.

EARL COWPER said, that as reference had been made to some observations of his he desired to say a few words. He was exceedingly sorry if he gave any cause for annoyance or dissatisfaction to any noble Lords in that House. His remarks on the point referred to were quite unpremeditated, and were called forth by the speech of the noble Duke (the Duke of Argyll) who, speaking the same night earlier in the debate, had found fault with the

Land Act of 1881 on the ground that it stopped all improvements on the part of landlords. In answering that argument of the noble Duke, he pointed out that he did not believe that improvements as a rule were made by the landlords—that they were, in fact, usually made by the tenants, and that the only plan was to encourage tenants to make improvements, and to protect such improvements when made. He qualified his remarks by saying that "until recently" one could count on one's fingers the Irish estates on which improvements were made by the landlords. He was very glad that the Government had granted the Return, as he felt sure that the improvements which had been made by the landlords ought to be known to the public generally. In the course of the inquiry, which with the other members of the Commission, he recently made in Ireland, the question was often put as to the difference between the net and the gross income of an estate, and the difference was usually represented at 15 per cent. In some cases it was put at 20 per cent. This included agency and rates, and was very much less than was the case upon English estates. He would appeal to any noble Lord present to state whether he was not under the mark in saying that in one form or another fully one-half of the nominal income went back upon the land. In the case of a friend of his own, the owner of 70,000 acres, the carefully-kept accounts of the estate showed that in 22 years no less than £930,390 had been expended on the land and in improvements. In the face of those figures he thought he was justified in saying that as a rule improvements had been made in Ireland by the tenant, and in many cases the rent had been raised upon such improvements. Members of that House who were Irish landlords could not be taken as typical of the class of Irish landlords. Many landlords in Ireland had, owing to the improvidence of their ancestors, been placed in very straitened circumstances, and cases of rents being raised on improvements made by the tenant certainly had frequently occurred. As he had said, he should be glad to see this Return furnished, so that it might be shown what landlords had done in this matter. He fully realized that Irish landlords were at the present time,

Earl Cowper

owing to no fault of their own, in a very difficult position. Many of them were trying to do their duty under very adverse circumstances, and he was sorry if he said anything that caused offence to them.

THE EARL OF ERNE said, he was sorry that the noble Lord had not withdrawn the statements more fully than he had done. Such statements, coming from one who had filled the high position of Viceroy, and who lately presided over an important Royal Commission in Ireland, could not fail to unduly prejudice public opinion against the Irish landlords in the settlement of the Irish Land Question, which now could not be very far distant. He merely rose to express his regret that this was not done, and to give one reason why Irish landlords could not improve their estates in the way that English landlords did, and that was the immense number of small holdings that existed on most of them. He had taken some figures on the subject from a Return which had been made to their Lordships' House. From this Return it appeared that there were 660,000 agricultural holdings in Ireland. Of these 415,000, or nearly two-thirds, were under £10 rental, and of these 215,000 were under £5 rental, while the average value of the holdings in that country was only £13 and a fraction each. Now, under these circumstances, was it possible for Irish landlords to improve their estates in the same way as English landlords? Nevertheless, the Irish landlords had spent large sums of money on improvements, as can be shown by the statistics asked for; and, in addition, had given very large remissions of rent to their tenants to aid them in making them. He believed that in many cases these improvements, which had been made with money given by the landlord, had been confiscated by the Sub-commissioners when fixing the judicial rents.

THE DUKE OF ARGYLL said, that the speech of his noble Friend (Earl Cowper) failed to show that the criticisms which he had recently passed on the Act of 1881 were ill founded. His noble Friend said that it was the object of that Act to secure to the tenant the benefit of his improvements. Of that object of the measure he entirely approved. But he must point out that the promoters of the measure also intended to secure to the landlords a fair share of the benefits of the improvements made by them. By the proviso at the end of Section 5 permission was given to increase the rent of a holding, subject to a statutory term in respect of capital laid out by the landlord on improvements. This proviso, in fact, allowed free contract between landlord and tenant in a material particular. Unfortunately, the provision was rendered worthless by the rule that at the expiration of every 15 years a tenant might ask for a revision of his rent. Fifteen years was not in itself a sufficiently long term to secure the repayment of capital spent on improvements and interest thereon, and as the rent might be revised at the end of that term, the landlord could not be certain that his improvements would be paid for. There was no probability whatever, under the Act of 1881, that a landlord would effect any improvements on the land held by his tenants, for he could not be sure that he would ever recover the capital spent upon them. That was the great defect of the Act. With reference to the question of raising rent on a tenant's improvements, he would like to know whether those who condemned the practice so vehemently disapproved what were called "improvement leases." In England leases of that kind were common. A tenant was granted a lease at a low rent in consideration of the improvements which he might affect, and at the end of a given period the rent could be raised. Surely there could be no objection to a contract of that sort. As to the Return which had been asked for, he feared that it would not cover the whole ground. It would not present any estimate of the amount of assistance given by landlords to the small tenantry in the improvement of their cottages. Landlords often contributed slates, wood, and lime—in other words, all that cost money—towards the improvement of thatched cottages, while the tenants only contributed the labour. If the system of landowning was to continue in Ireland, some means ought to be taken to encourage landlords to lay out capital on the land. Modifications ought to be introduced into the Act of 1881 for the purpose of rendering unassailable bargains made by landlords with their tenants with a view to the improvement of the land. In the absence of such modifications landlords would not expend a single farthing. He could conceive no greater calamity than that the whole rental of a country should be withdrawn out of the fund which, in happier circumstances, would be available for agricultural purposes. In Ireland there was still a vast field for the introduction of agricultural improvements, a great portion of the country being absolutely unreclaimed. He trusted that some system would be devised under which landlords would be encouraged to make improvements.

THE EARL OF BELMORE said, in reply, that the noble Earl (Earl Cowper) had, in making his comparison between what he thought the small expenditure of Irish landlords, with the large amounts spent by English ones, entirely omitted to notice the very valuable tenant-right interest of the Irish farmers in their farms, which, of course, the English ones, who did not make improvements, did not acquire. To make a fair comparison this should be taken into account.

Motion *agreed to*.

House adjourned at a quarter past Seven o'clock, till To-morrow, a quarter past Ten o'clock.

HOUSE OF COMMONS,

Monday, 2nd May, 1887.

MINUTES.]—NEW WRIT ISSUED—*For* Cornwall (St. Austell Division), *v.* William Copeland Borlase, esquire, Chiltern Hundreds.

SELECT COMMITTEE—Saving Life at Sea, *appointed* and *nominated·*

PRIVATE BILL (*by Order*)—*Second Reading* — Walton-on-Thames and Weybridge Gas.

PUBLIC BILLS—*First Reading*—Solicitors (Ireland) * [247].

Select Committees—Butter Substitutes * [48], *nominated;* Merchandise Marks Act (1862) Amendment * [142]; Mr. Lane *disch.;* Mr. Peter M'Donald *added.*

Committee—Criminal Law Amendment (Ireland) [217] [*Second Night*]—R.P.; Colonial Service (Pensions) * [155]—R.P.; Truck * [109]—R.P.

Committee—Report—Accumulations * [31].

Considered as amended—Third Reading—Police Force Enfranchisement * [240], and *passed.*

PROVISIONAL ORDER BILL—*Second Reading*—Local Government (Ireland) (Limerick Water) * [236].

———o———

WALTON - ON - THAMES AND WEY-
BRIDGE GAS BILL (*by Order*).

SECOND READING.

Order for Second Reading read.

Motion made, and Question proposed,
" That the Bill be now read a second
time."

MR. BRADLAUGH (Northampton):
I beg to move as an Amendment, that
the Bill be read a second time on this
day six months. The Bill is now very
materially altered in the character
of its provisions. It is a Bill for the
extension of the capital of the Company and the extension of the district
which is to be supplied. Since my
Notice of opposition was put on the
Paper, the promoters have abandoned
the larger portion of the district which,
at first, they asked power to supply with
gas. They have also abandoned several
exceedingly objectionable clauses of the
Bill, and they have reduced the amount
of capital which they asked Parliament
to sanction. I cannot help thinking that
it is a great pity this House should be
called upon at all to deal with so paltry
a question as that which is now involved.
The Bill asks for power to take over two
or three small districts at some considerable distance from their source of
supply, but with scarcely any population, and districts which are already
supplied with gas by a Limited Liability
Company. There is really no reason
whatever why the promoters should
come to this House for the powers they
now seek. They originally sought to
enlarge their capital by £50,000, and
they proposed to pay a sum of £15,000
for the Gas Works they then proposed
to take over. They have now, in the
face of the opposition which was raised
to the Bill, abandoned their intention of
taking over the greatest portion of those
works; but they, nevertheless, ask for
power to raise an increased capital to
the extent of £30,000; and they propose
to pay something less than £2,700 for
the purchase of certain works which
they say they want at Cobham. There
can be no excuse whatever for asking
for a large amount of additional capital,
so far as the ordinary works of this Gas
Company are concerned. They have
already a very much larger amount of

capital than any other Company of a
similar nature in proportion to the
amount of gas they manufacture. As a
matter of fact, this Company has, at the
present moment, a capital three times in
excess of those Companies which have
similar work to execute. Its capital is
50 per cent, at least, above that of any
other Company whose returns I have
been able to examine, and who are doing
a similar business. The inhabitants of
the district, who are the consumers of
the gas supplied by the Company, complain that they are now charged 5s. per
1,000 feet for the gas they get from the
Company; and they contend that the
Company have no right to attempt to
supply other places, the population of
which altogether is under 2,500, when
the result is likely to be an increase in
the price of the gas at present supplied
to them. I hardly know how far the
House will feel it right to consider
seriously an application of this kind;
but I think it is most monstrous that a
Bill should be lodged, and the bulk of
the clauses which were objectionable
having been abandoned, the Company
should still ask Parliament to authorize
them to raise an addititinal capital of
£30,000, when all they say they want
to lay out is a sum of £2,700 in the purchase of some other works where the
gas is now charged at the rate of 6s. per
1,000 feet, they charging 5s. per 1,000
feet themselves. It is said that they
have not sufficient capital to enable
them satisfactorily to continue their
existing supply. Propably one reason
for that is that the Company have been
carrying on a coal business, by which
those who oppose the Bill allege they
have lost money. That is a business
which does not fall within the scope of
the powers of a Gas Company at all;
and I submit that they ought not
to have any Parliamentary authority
for carrying it on. I am loth; to
occupy the time of the House with a
matter which is really much too small
for the dignity of a Parliamentary discussion. It may be urged that it is a
matter which could be best settled in a
Committee upstairs; but my point is
that a question of such trivial importance ought not to be submitted to a
Committee at all. In fact, the Bill is
an impertinence in the face of the
House. I beg to move that the Bill be
read a second time upon this day six
months.

MR. CONWAY (Leitrim, N.) seconded the Amendment.

Amendment proposed, to leave out the the word "now," and at the end of the Question to add the words, "upon this day six months."—(*Mr. Bradlaugh.*)

Question proposed, "That the word ' now' stand part of the Question."

MR. KIMBER (Wandsworth) : I hope the House will not consider that the hon. Member has made out any justification for not allowing this Bill, in the usual course, to go before a Committee, where all the details may be fairly considered. The course which the hon. Member is taking is, I think, entirely opposed to the ordinary Rules which govern the proceedings of this House and its Standing Orders. I believe it will be in the power of the promoters of the Bill to show, by the clearest evidence, if it is referred to a Select Committee, that the hon. Member has altogether disregarded the facts of the case. He asserts that the Company propose to acquire the power of raising an excessive amount of capital. Surely, that is one of those questions which the House by its Standing Orders has intended should be relegated to Committees. The Bill itself has already passed the Standing Orders. I am informed that in this respect the provisions of the Bill have been subjected to the scrutiny of the usual authorities before whom such Bills go, and they are satisfied that it is entitled to go before a Committee. At all events, it is only fair that the Company which has expended all its original capital in the execution of works ought to be allowed to raise something in addition in order to enable them to carry on those works satisfactorily. I noticed in the remarks of the hon. Member, that he stated nothing to show that this additional capital is not required.

MR. BRADLAUGH : Will the hon. Member pardon me. I think I did show that, because I said that other Companies are carrying on similar works upon one third, or 50 per cent less capital than has already been granted to this Company for the amount of gas they manufacture.

MR. KIMBER : I admit that it is quite possible to pick out a bad case; but I do not think it is fair to select one or two of the worst cases that can be picked out for comparison. The hon.

Member has been good enough to give me a list of Private Bills of this nature, but I am supplied by the promoters with a list of a good many which tell the other way, and I think I should be able to show a great many instances in which Gas Companies have received the sanction of Parliament to a much larger extention of capital than is asked for in this case. Indeed, I have a list of other Companies which shows just the contrary result. In this case, there is very good reason why the House should not interfere in preventing the Company from raising the additional capital they ask for. The hon. Member has himself admitted that if this Bill is granted the cost of gas to the consumer of the district the Company propose to supply will be very considerably reduced. At the present moment, I believe their charge is 4s. 9d. per 1,000 feet.

MR. BRADLAUGH : Five shillings per 1,000 feet is the price set down in their statement.

MR. KIMBER : Less discount—the actual price is, I believe, 4s. 9d. per 1,000 feet. I would also put this to the House, that the whole of the capital authorized by the Bill is actually to be raised without the payment of any premium to the shareholders. The whole of the new capital is to be put up to auction, and if a premium is paid that premium will not go into the pockets of the shareholders. These are, however, matters of detail with which I am almost ashamed to trouble the House. I would only add, that, upon my own responsibility, I can give the assurance that if the Bill is passed the public will derive great advantage from it. If any hon. Member will take the trouble to examine the Bill, and view it upon its merits, I am satisfied he will arrive at the conclusion that it will compare favourably with any other legislation of the same class, and that it is fairly entitled to be submitted to the investigation of a Select Committee.

DR. TANNER (Cork Co., Mid): I should like to say one or two words with regard to this Bill. When it first came before this House for second reading it contained a number of provisions which I looked upon as objectionable, and I gave Notice of opposition to it. Since then I have had time to inquire into various points upon which, in the first instance, I was not satisfied, and the result of the investigation was to induce me to withdraw that opposition. What I did then I am prepared to support now, and if the House come to a Division it will afford me a certain amount of pleasure to support the second reading of the Bill, having found out that I was wrong in having opposed it in the first instance.

THE CHAIRMAN OF WAYS AND MEANS (Mr. COURTNEY) (Cornwall, Bodmin): This Bill appears now in a very different form from that in which it was originally introduced, and it is promoted for a widely different object. Under these circumstances, I think the House ought to act in accordance with the principle which usually guides it, and allow the Bill to go before a Select Committee upstairs, by whom its details will be fairly considered.

Question put.

The House *divided*:—Ayes 135; Noes 70: Majority 65.—(Div. List, No. 103.)

Main Question put, and *agreed to.*

Bill read a second time, and *committed.*

PUBLIC PETITIONS COMMITTEE.

Leave given to the Select Committee on Public Petitions to make a Special Report:—

Special Report *brought up*, and read as followeth:—

Public Petitions Committee.
Special Report.

Since the Special Report made by your Committee to the House on the subject of the alleged fictitious or forged signatures to the Petition from Haggerstone, in favour of the London Coal and Wine Duties Continuance Bill, other Petitions in favour of the said Bill have been presented, the signatures to which appear to your Committee to be also fictitious or forged, and that, previous to the presentation of the Petition from Haggerstone, there were other Petitions relating to the same subject which excited suspicion.

SIR CHARLES FORSTER (Walsall): Perhaps it will suit the convenience of the House if I state the course we propose to adopt under the altered circumstances of the case. Since I presented the Report from the Committee on Public Petitions on Monday last, the matter has assumed a much more serious aspect. We cannot doubt, from the information we have received, that frauds of the most barefaced and extensive character have been perpetrated against the authority and privileges of Parliament. Under

these circumstances, the Committee on Public Petitions are prepared to accept the suggestion of the hon. Member for Northampton (Mr. Bradlaugh), that a thorough searching and exhaustive inquiry should be instituted into the matter. The Committee are prepared to institute that inquiry themselves; and, therefore, I have to move that the Order for resuming the Adjourned Debate on the Special Report of April 25 be discharged. At the same time, we think that it would not be wise for the House to part with the Petition. All I can say is, that I regret that this necessity should have arisen; but we shall endeavour to discharge, to the best of our ability, any duty which the House may impose upon us. I beg to move, after the discharge of the Order—

"That the Report be referred back to the Committee, with an Instruction that they do inquire into the circumstances under which, and the parties by whom, the names appearing on the Petition referred to were thereunto appended."

Motion made, and Question proposed,

"That the Report be referred back to the Committee, with an Instruction that they do inquire into the circumstances under which, and the parties by whom, the names appearing on the Petition referred to were thereunto appended."—(*Sir Charles Forster.*)

MR. BRADLAUGH (Northampton): I think that the words which have fallen from the Chairman of the Select Committee on Public Petitions fully justify the action I took last week in moving the adjournment of the debate. I was then of opinion that if the Order that the Petition should lie on the Table was then discharged, the House would have lost its hold upon that Petition. I hoped that the Committee might be able to do something to identify the person who had forged the Petition and the signatures attached to it, and to identify further the person who had employed him to forge the signatures. If I am right in my conjecture, the gentleman—if that be the proper term by which to designate him—who employed the person who forged this Petition is a gentleman whose name will appear whenever the Committee which is now sitting upstairs makes its Report with reference to the chargest against the Corporation of the City of London. He is the gentleman whose name appears in the City Accounts. I am not at

Dr. Tanner

liberty, Sir, as you decided last week, to refer to any of the evidence which has been given before the Committee upstairs. My mouth is closed in that respect; but I am entitled to say that I am speaking now of a gentleman whose name appears in the City Accounts as having been employed by the Special Committee which is now taking action to obtain the renewal of the Coal and Wine Dues. I am sure that I shall be able, and that the Committee on Public Petitions will be able, to ascertain that there are several Aldermen and members of the Corporation of London who have expressed an opinion that the obtaining of signatures by the payment of money is a praiseworthy proceeding under the circumstances. I believe the Committee will be able to ascertain that within the last three and a-half months one gentleman alone has received more than £400 from the City of London for procuring such Petitions. In addition to the particular Petition reported on last week, I believe the Committee will be able to ascertain that there have been other Petitions presented every signature of which is forged. One of them, I am told, contains such signatures as Sir Michael Hicks-Beach, Joseph Biggar, and W. H. Smith, of the Strand. Of course, it may be that at the address which is given of "the Strand" there is another Mr. W. H. Smith, or otherwise that signature will certainly turn out to be a forgery. It may be that "Joseph Biggar," described as a pork merchant, is not the hon. Member of that same name who has a seat in this House, or otherwise that also will turn out to be a forgery. If I am rightly informed, the Committee on Public Petitions will be able to ascertain that one of these Petitions which have been presented purports to be signed by no less than 13 race horses. I believe that the hon. Baronet the Member for the University of London (Sir John Lubbock) has paid some attention to the development of mind in animals; but this is a new phase in that development, which has never come within my experience before. I do not think, however, that the matter is one upon which I ought to jest. The whole subject of Petitioning to this House is one which requires to be dealt with as a question of exceeding gravity. I undertook, four years ago, if an inquiry were granted on a Petition in which I was very much interested, to prove that the signatures of children of two, three, four, and six months old had been attached to a Petition; and, even allowing for the spread of education since the Act of 1870, it certainly requires a strong effort of imagination to suppose that those signatures were genuine. The right of petitioning this House ought to be regarded as a right, and a duty exercised by citizens with a view of bringing before this House matters which they cannot otherwise bring forward; but if the canvassers for Petitions are to be paid for obtaining signatures, the whole thing is rendered corrupt at once. In many instances, I am afraid, means have been resorted to for manufacturing signatures, and the whole matter of petitioning has been reduced to a monstrous absurdity. I thank the Committee on Public Petitions for the action they have taken in the matter; and I believe that this is a very proper Petition upon which to take that action. I should not have interposed last week if it had not been that I wished to prevent the Chairman of the Committee on Public Petitions from contenting himself with passing the matter over by merely moving the discharge of the Order directing the Petition to lie on the Table, because I was anxious to see that in a case of this kind, where a deliberate fraud has been perpetrated on this House, the persons who have been guilty of that fraud should, if possible, receive the punishment they deserve. I trust that the Committee will have power to examine witnesses on oath, so that they may be prosecuted if they give false evidence, and that they shall also have power to send for persons and papers. I trust, further, that the Committee will not be content with the punishment of the tools, but that they will bring to the knowledge of the House those by whom such tools have been employed, so that they also may be punished.

MR. WEBSTER (St. Pancras, E.): There is no one who more deplores than I do the fact that any Petition presented to this House should not be what it purports to be—namely, the Petition of the individuals whose names are attached to it. It must, however, be apparent to the House, as has been alleged by the hon. Member for Northampton (Mr. Bradlaugh), that not only are Petitions got up on this particular subject upon one side which purport to be signed by persons who have not really signed them, but there is every reason to believe that in this instance there have been Petitions of a similar nature presented against the continuance of the Coal and Wine Dues. I would, therefore, express a hope that the inquiry of the Committee may be extended to all Petitions which may have been presented on this subject, and that the parties may be represented by counsel. I certainly think that the Committee on Public Petitions should be required to examine—and carefully to examine—all the Petitions which have been presented against the Coal and Wine Dues as well as those which have been presented in favour of their continuance. Perhaps I may be allowed to mention a fact which occurred only on Wednesday last. On that day all the Metropolitan Members were flooded with Petitions against the Coal and Wine Dues. It appears that an individual named John Lloyd, who resides at Lancaster House, Savoy, and was at one time, and I believe is at present, the Secretary of the Municipal Reform League, was the collector of these Petitions, and I think some step ought to be taken to ascertain the character of those Petitions. Probably the Petitions to which I refer are called into existence by some organization—may be of coal merchants, or of gas company proprietors, or of some league of London Municipal Reformers. I trust that this inquiry will take place, and that it will be a searching one. I, for one, do not in the slightest degree deprecate its taking place; but I think it ought to be an equitable inquiry, and that it should deal with the allegations which have been made all round. I would, further, express a wish that the Committee also include within the inquiry, how it has happened that certain political meetings which have been held in the Metropolis have been recently broken up? All I can say is that at very many meetings I have addressed in London I have curiously enough recognized a small knot of the same faces and heard the same noisy voices who have done their utmost to disturb the proceedings, but have not succeeded in their object owing to the good sense of the majority of the audience. All that I ask is that the inquiry, when it takes place, shall not be confined to one side, but that it shall include the facts equally on the one side and the other. With regard to the hon. Member for Northampton, the constituency he represents appears to be a very lucky one, seeing that the two hon. Members who represent it are not only able to attend to the wants of the 50,000 inhabitants of that town, but have ample time to devote to the affairs of other people.

MR. BRADLAUGH: Perhaps the the hon. Member will excuse me for reminding him that I am a citizen of London.

MR. WEBSTER: I presume that the hon. Member speaks in this House not as a citizen of London, but as a Member of Parliament. [Mr. BRADLAUGH: Hear, hear.] I would venture again to express a hope that the Inquiry which, I presume, will be entered into, will be an inquiry all round, and that the Committee will carefully investigate not only how the Petitions in favour of the continuance of the Coal and Wine Dues have been got up, but also how the Petitions against almost every municipal institution in the Metropolis have been got up.

MR. HOWELL (Bethnal Green, N.E.): It seems to me that the matter before the House is the Petition which has been called in question by the Committee on Public Petitions, and not whether some other Petitions which may have been presented to the House are of a similar character. I say this without any fear as to the result of any investigation which may take place. I trust that the Committee will be able to arrive at a satisfactory conclusion as to who has paid for the getting up of these Petitions, and who has been at the bottom of the bogus meetings which have been held in the Metropolis in favour of the renewal of the Coal and Wine Dues.

MR. DONALD CRAWFORD (Lanark, N.E.): As a Member of the Committee on Public Petitions I should like to say, in reference to one observation which fell from the hon. Member for East St. Pancras (Mr. Webster) that at the meeting of the Committee to-day a decision was arrived at that the Inquiry should embrace the Petitions both for and against the continuance of the Coal and Wine Dues.

Mr. Webster

MR. BRADLAUGH: Perhaps the House, by its indulgence, will permit me to say that as the hon. Member for East St. Pancras has pledged himself to a knowledge of fictitious signatures attached to Petitions presented on the other side he will feel it his duty to attend the inquiry of the Committee and give evidence.

Question put, and *agreed to.*

Motion made, and Question proposed, "That the Order [25th April] for resuming the Adjourned Debate on the Special Report of the Select Committee on Public Petitions be discharged."— (*Sir Charles Forster.*)

Question put, and *agreed to.*

Motion made, and Question proposed, "That the Committee have power to send for persons, papers, and records." —(*Sir Charles Forster.*)

MR. TOLLEMACHE (Cheshire, Eddisbury): I understand that the Petition has been referred back to a Committee which already exists, and of which three form a quorum. I would suggest that in an important matter of this kind the quorum should be increased to five.

MR. SPEAKER: If it is the pleasure of the House that the quorum should be increased, the House has the power of increasing it.

VISCOUNT LYMINGTON (Devon, South Molton): I am certainly of opinion that it is of the utmost importance that the Committee should have the power to examine witnesses on oath.

Question put, and *agreed to.*

Order, That three be the quorum of the Committee, read, and *discharged.*

Ordered, That five be the quorum.

QUESTIONS.

WAR OFFICE (ORDNANCE DEPARTMENT) — DEFECTIVE WEAPONS— THE CITY OF LONDON ARTILLERY.

MAJOR RASCH (Essex, S.E.) asked the Secretary of State for War, Whether the swords served out to the City of London Artillery are in the condition in which they were originally issued, and that, consequently, the explanation given of the failure of the Infantry bayonets, owing to structural alteration, does not apply to them; whether the worthlessness is due to their manufacture from an improper material — namely, Bessemer steel; and, who had the contract for; and, who passed these swords?

THE SURVEYOR GENERAL OF THE ORDNANCE (Mr. NORTHCOTE) (Exeter) (who replied) said: The sword bayonets of which the City of London Artillery are in possession are in the condition, so far as pattern is concerned, in which they were originally issued. No structural alteration has been made in them. An inspection of these sword bayonets is now in progress; and until it is completed it is impossible to say by whom these particular weapons were made, and who passed them. The manufacture of sword bayonets of the pattern referred to commenced in 1854, and went on till 1876. Large numbers were obtained from contractors at home and abroad, and many were made at Enfield. Those made at Enfield were all of "Firth's steel;" and the specification for those obtained by contract required that they should be of the best cast steel.

In reply to Mr. HANBURY (Preston),

MR. NORTHCOTE said: The Report as to sword bayonets has not yet been received; but we are pressing for it. With reference to intrenching tools, it appears that a number of ordinary shovels issued to the 2nd Battalion of the East Kent Regiment were recently broken while being used by the troops. Opinions differ materially as to whether the usage to which these shovels were subjected was fair or otherwise. They have been returned into store; and the Inspector General of Fortifications has been requested to assist in thoroughly investigating the question.

THE PUBLIC FUNDS—PROPORTIONATE HOLDERS.

SIR EDWARD WATKIN (Hythe) asked Mr. Chancellor of the Exchequer, If he can state what proportion the individual and joint holding (or personal holding) in the public funds bears to the personal holding of Trustees, excluding Government, Saving Banks, and other impersonal trust holdings?

THE CHANCELLOR OF THE EXCHEQUER (Mr. GOSCHEN) (St. George's, Hanover Square): It is not possible to give the information asked for. The Bank of England do not recognise trusts, and have no means of distinguishing between personal holdings and the holdings of Trustees.

LAW AND POLICE (SCOTLAND)—OUTRAGES AT DUTHIL, INVERNESS-SHIRE.

MR. FRASER-MACKINTOSH (Inverness-shire) asked the Lord Advocate, Whether he has received information of continued outrages, supposed to be instigated by persons in authority in the neighbourhood, being lately committed against the peace and comfort of the parish minister of Duthil, in Inverness-shire; and, whether a neutral and unbiased investigation has been, or will be, instituted?

THE LORD ADVOCATE (Mr. J. H. A. MACDONALD) (Edinburgh and St. Andrews Universities): I received a letter from the minister of Duthil some weeks ago, and at once ordered an inquiry, the result of which was communicated to me last week. Nothing of the nature of an outrage occurred on the occasion to which the letter referred. Some parties in the parish celebrated the result of a litigation, in which the minister of Duthil was on the losing side, by lighting a bonfire on a farm half a mile from his residence, and firing shots from guns at the same place; a torchlight procession was formed, which marched along the public road past the house in which Mr. Bain lives, cheering as they went. Nothing occurred calling for the interference of the Lord Advocate.

ROYAL IRISH CONSTABULARY—CONSTABLE JOSEPH BENNETT.

MR. M'CARTAN (Down, S.) asked the Chief Secretary to the Lord Lieutenant of Ireland, Whether Constable Joseph Bennett, who, in August last, took a gun out of Waterford Street Barrack, Belfast, and discharged it at some persons at the corner of Cullingtree Road, thereby injuring one of them, is still doing duty at Belfast; whether he was made a prisoner at the time, and detained in barracks, with a view of placing him on his trial; and, whether he has been yet tried, or has been punished in any way for the serious offence then committed?

THE PARLIAMENTARY UNDER SECRETARY (Colonel KING-HARMAN) (Kent, Isle of Thanet) (who replied) said, this constable did, during the disturbances at Belfast in August last, fire

Mr. Goschen

upon a stone-throwing mob without orders. He was not arrested, but was placed under supervision, on the advice of the medical officer, as it was quite clear from his demeanour that he was not accountable for what he had done. He has not since then performed any duty, and has been at intervals under detention as a lunatic. He is about to be discharged from the Constabulary as unfit for further service.

LITERATURE, SCIENCE AND ART—REPRODUCTION IN FAC-SIMILE OF ANCIENT MSS. — WELSH MANUSCRIPTS.

MR. BOWEN ROWLANDS (Cardiganshire) asked the Secretary to the Treasury, Whether sums of money have been granted from time to time out of the Estimates, towards reproducing in fac-simile, and publishing, some of the most important of the ancient MSS. of England, Scotland, and Ireland; and, whether the Government will consent to give similar encouragement towards reproducing and publishing ancient Welsh MSS?

THE SECRETARY (Mr. JACKSON) (Leeds, N.): It is the fact that between 1864 and 1884 sums of money have been provided, from time to time, in the Estimates, towards reproducing in fac-simile and publishing some of the most important of the ancient manuscripts of England, Scotland and Ireland. It was found in 1884 that nearly £10,000 had been spent in the preceding 10 years on this work, while the receipts from sales were only £1,850. In view of this evidence of lack of public interest in the work, and for other reasons, the publication was discontinued; and I do not think that I can hold out any hope that a recommencement of the work will be made in favour of Welsh manuscripts.

POST OFFICE (IRELAND)—COMMUNICATION BETWEEN SKIBBEREEN AND BALTIMORE.

MR. GILHOOLY (Cork, W.) asked the Postmaster General, Whether, in view of the fact that an industrial school at Baltimore, County Cork, is to be immediately opened, and that increased mail accommodation is required in the district, he will consider the desirability of having a mail car running daily throughout the year between Skibbereen and Baltimore?

THE POSTMASTER GENERAL (Mr. RAIKES) (Cambridge University) in reply, said, that the mail car between Skibbereen and Baltimore already ran daily during the fishing season—that was to say, from the middle of March to the middle of July. During the remainder of the year the service was by rural postmen. He would cause further inquiry to be made into the question of continuing the daily car service throughout the year; but he thought it well to mention that, when the question was last considered, the correspondence was not sufficient to warrant the additional cost of such an arrangement.

MERCHANT SHIPPING—THE LOO ROCK, BALTIMORE HARBOUR.

MR. GILHOOLY (Cork, W.) asked the Secretary to the Board of Trade, Whether, in view of the fact that the Loo Rock, at the entrance to Baltimore Harbour, County Cork, is a serious and dangerous obstruction, he will consider the advisability of having it removed?

THE SECRETARY (Baron HENRY DE WORMS) (Liverpool, East Toxteth): The Loo Rock is within the limits of Baltimore Harbour, and is under the jurisdiction of the Baltimore and Skibbereen Harbour Commissioners, who, by a Provisional Order confirmed by Parliament in 1884, have power to deepen and improve the harbour and its entrance. The Board of Trade have no jurisdiction in the matter.

ADMIRALTY—MARINE AND ARMY PENSIONS (BANDSMEN).

CAPTAIN PRICE (Devonport) asked the Secretary to the Admiralty, Whether a Marine pensioner is not allowed to serve in a band on board one of Her Majesty's Ships, without giving up his pension, whereas an Army pensioner is allowed to do so; whether he is aware that recently three bandsmen (pensioners) applied for service on board H.M.S. *Royal Adelaide*; that two of these were pensioners from the Marines, and known to the bandmaster as good musicians, whilst the third was a line bandsman; that the two Marines were unable to serve without giving up their pensions, whilst the Army pensioner was engaged, and is now serving and receiving his pension in addition to his pay; and, whether there are several

other cases of a similar kind; and what is the reason for this difference of treatment between the Marines and the Line?

THE SECRETARY (Mr. FORWOOD) (Lancashire, Ormskirk): The entry of Marine pensioners as bandsmen, or in other ratings, is quite exceptional. As a rule, the terms offered in such cases involve a surrender of pension while receiving full naval pay; but it is quite optional on the part of the pensioner to accept or refuse the proposals. In respect to the band of the *Royal Adelaide*, two Marine pensioners declined the terms proposed. An Army pensioner has joined the band, and does, as I am informed, continue to receive his pension from the War Office. I do not know of any other cases of a similar kind.

ARMY (AUXILIARY FORCES)— THE VOLUNTEER CAPITATION GRANT.

MR. HOWARD VINCENT (Sheffield, Central) asked the Secretary of State for War, If, having regard to the representations he has received as to the difficulties which would be entailed on the Volunteer Force if the capitation grant was made solely dependent on the attainment of an advanced standard in musketry, he has decided to adopt the recommendation of the recent Committee, and give an increased grant of 5s. in respect of those Volunteers who succeed in passing into the second class, without depriving those who are efficient in all other respects of the present grant of 30s.?

THE SECRETARY OF STATE (Mr. E. STANHOPE) (Lincolnshire, Horncastle): I have given full consideration to the representations made by various deputations from the Volunteer Force on the subject of the Capitation Grant, and I have been specially struck by one point which was urged upon my attention. It was represented that if the whole grant were dependent upon proficiency in musketry, Volunteer corps would sustain a loss in respect of uniform supplied to recruits who turned out very indifferent shots; and it was pointed out that there must always be a certain percentage of every battalion who cannot be brought up to the requisite standards I have, accordingly, obtained the consent of the Treasury to the following arrangements for Infantry Volunteers (the conditions as to the others remaining as stated in my Memorandum) :—In the first year of a Volunteer's service he will earn the full grant of 35s. on condition that he is efficient, and hits the target 12 times in 60 shots; but in later years he will not earn this grant at all unless he is at least a second-class shot. If, however, he remains efficient in drill, although not up to the second-class standard of musketry, he will be granted, for not more than two consecutive years, a capitation allowance of 10s. After the two consecutive years all capitation will cease unless the Volunteer becomes a second-class shot.

NATIONAL EDUCATION (IRELAND)— TEACHERS—RESTRICTIONS ON RESIDENCE.

MR. FLYNN (Cork, N.) asked the Chief Secretary to the Lord Lieutenant of Ireland, Whether a young man who holds the position of national school teacher in Ireland is prohibited, by a Rule of the Commissioners of Education, from residing in the house of his father, who may happen to hold a publican's licence; and, if so, whether he will consider the desirability of altering such Regulation?

THE PARLIAMENTARY UNDER SECRETARY (Colonel KING-HARMAN) (Kent, Isle of Thanet) (who replied) said: Under a Rule of the Commissioners teachers of National Schools are especially forbidden to keep public-houses, or houses for the sale of spirituous liquors, or to live in any such house. The Irish Government agree with the Commissioners that it would be very undesirable to make any alteration in this Regulation.

MR. T. M. HEALY (Longford, N.): May I ask the right hon. and gallant Gentleman will the same Rule be made to apply to magistrates?

COLONEL KING-HARMAN: The hon. and learned Member must put the Question on the Paper.

INDIA—REPORT OF THE COMMISSION ON THE PUBLIC CIVIL SERVICE.

MR. KING (Hull, Central) asked the Under Secretary of State for India, Whether the Public Service Commission, which was presided over by Sir Charles Aitchison, and has recently taken a vast amount of evidence, was originally ap-

Mr. E. Stanhope

pointed simply to take evidence on the question of the admission of natives to certain branches of the Civil Service; whether the evidence taken was permitted, in effect, to embrace the entire question of a re-construction of the Civil Service of India, and among them the Uncovenanted Service; what number of representatives of the Uncovenanted Service were appointed on the Commission, and how many members of the Covenanted Service, and how many natives respectively, acted on the inquiry; and, when the Report of the Commission is expected to be ready?

THE UNDER SECRETARY OF STATE (Sir JOHN GORST) (Chatham): The objects of the Public Service Commission were originally defined in a Resolution of the Government of India, dated October 4, 1886. The statement implied in the Question is substantially correct. The Secretary of State has no official knowledge of the evidence taken; and is, therefore, impossible to express any opinion as to the correctness of the statement implied in the second Question. The Commission originally appointed consisted of six members of the Covenanted and one of the Uncovenanted Civil Service; six Natives, one of whom is a High Court Judge; and three other members, one of whom is Sir Charles Turner, late Chief Justice of Madras. By a Resolution of March 8, 1887, the Commission has been re-constituted for the purpose of more detailed inquiry, and I am unable to say when the Report may be expected.

LITERATURE, SCIENCE, AND ART— THE ANCIENT LAWS OF IRELAND.

MR. T. P. GILL (Louth, S.) asked the Chief Secretary to the Lord Lieutenant of Ireland, Whether anyone is at present editing the Ancient Laws of Ireland; and, if so, who?

THE PARLIAMENTARY UNDER SECRETARY (Colonel KING-HARMAN) (Kent, Isle of Thanet) (who replied) said: Professor Atkinson, LL.D., Professor of Sanskrit and Comparative Grammar, and Lecturer on Celtic in the University of Dublin, is at present engaged on this work, under the direction of the Commissioners for the Publication of the Ancient Laws and Institutes of Ireland.

LAW AND JUSTICE (IRELAND)—THE CASE OF ROBERT COMERFORD, BELFAST.

MR. M'CARTAN (Down, S.) asked the Chief Secretary to the Lord Lieutenant of Ireland, with reference to the case of Robert Comerford of Belfast, Whether the Lord Lieutenant recently received a Memorial praying for the release of Comerford; and, whether he will state what answer has been given to the Memorialists?

THE PARLIAMENTARY UNDER SECRETARY (Colonel KING-HARMAN) (Kent, Isle of Thanet) (who replied) said: Yes, Sir; and the Lords Justices decided that the law must take its course.

MR. M'CARTAN asked whether the matter would not be re-considered, in view of the fact that Comerford got in Ireland 29 months' imprisonment with hard labour for the commission of an offence the punishment for which in England could not exceed six months, and in view of the fact that he had now been over three months in gaol?

COLONEL KING-HARMAN considered it was quite sufficient that this Question had been referred to the Lords Justices, who were a more competent authority on legal matters than he was.

THE MAGISTRACY (ENGLAND AND WALES) — THE HELSTON BENCH — SENTENCE ON EDWARD WHITE.

MR. CONYBEARE (Cornwall, Camborne) asked the Secretary of State for the Home Department, Whether his attention has been called to the case of Edward White, who was on Saturday last sentenced by the magistrates of Helston to one month's imprisonment with hard labour on a charge of embezzling moneys amounting to about 10s.; whether the prisoner had been employed as a workman on a farm, and to supply with milk twice a-day some 100 customers, at amounts ranging from one halfpenny and upwards; whether he was unable to read or write; whether the evidence showed that the accounts between the prisoner and his employer had been left by the latter to depend on the prisoner's memory; that the prisoner explained the discrepancies complained of in such accounts as due

to default in his memory; that some of the accounts in dispute in the prosecutor's books were marked as paid in his own handwriting, though he denied having received the money; that all the witnesses for the prosecution testified to the prisoner's honesty; and the prosecutor himself admitted that his conduct was good while in his employ; whether the sentence of the Court was received with prolonged hissing and cries of shame; whether he will inquire into the case, with a view to the mitigation or remission of the sentence; whether it is the fact that the Town Clerk accompanied the magistrates when they retired to consult about their decision on the case; whether the prosecutor was until recently the managing clerk in the said Town Clerk's office; whether the prosecutor's brother at present acts in that capacity; and, whether both brothers gave evidence in the case?

THE SECRETARY OF STATE (Mr. MATTHEWS) (Birmingham, E.), in reply, desired to point out to the House the inconvenience of hon. Members putting into Questions a large number of details, and a vast number of facts that only partially represented what took place in investigations before magistrates. In the case of Edward White, to which the hon. Member's Question referred, he had been sentenced to a month's imprisonment for embezzling 10s. belonging to his employer. White was engaged by a farmer to deliver milk, receiving small sums in payment, and he had not accounted for his receipts. The Justices were unanimous in their decision, and he was not prepared to interfere with the sentence, or order a fresh inquiry.

POOR LAW (IRELAND)—ELECTION FOR AN ELECTORAL GUARDIAN—TUAM UNION.

COLONEL NOLAN (Galway, N.) asked Mr. Attorney General for Ireland, Whether the Returning Officer was correct in holding bad a nomination paper in the Tuam Union, in an election for an Electoral Guardian, because the nominator had signed himself Patrick O'Neill, his name on the rate book being Patrick Neill, but he being generally known by the former designation; and, if a nomination paper should be held bad in another Electoral Division of the same Union, because the date was written the 2nd day of February, 1887, instead of the 2nd day of March, 1887?

THE ATTORNEY GENERAL FOR IRELAND (Mr. HOLMES) (Dublin University), in reply, said, he had been informed that the objections had been brought before the Local Government Board based upon the matters to which the Question referred, and these objections were being investigated. The Local Government Board was, by Act of Parliament, the authority for deciding questions of this character; and he would not feel himself at liberty to offer any opinion on the matter of law.

CUSTOMS BOARD—OFFICERS OF THE PORT OF LONDON.

MR. FORREST FULTON (West Ham, N.) asked the Secretary to the Treasury, Whether his attention has been drawn to an Order of the Board of Customs, under date 22nd February, 1887, abrogating the privilege accorded from time immemorial to the officers of Customs in the Port of London of communicating with each other by means of the official bags; and, whether he can explain the necessity for this restriction?

THE SECRETARY (Mr. JACKSON) (Leeds, N.): It came to the knowledge of the Board of Customs that letters and documents which had no relation to public official business were frequently sent in the official bags to different parts of the Port of London. An order was, therefore, issued that no documents were to be sent in the bags unless they related to public official business. The Board see no reason for altering their decision.

POST OFFICE SAVINGS BANK—LIMITS OF DEPOSITS—LEGISLATION.

MR. HOWELL (Bethnal Green, N.E.) asked the Postmaster General, If he is in a position to state whether the Government are prepared to introduce a Bill with the view of affording increased facilities for depositors in the Post Office Savings Banks?

THE POSTMASTER GENERAL (Mr. RAIKES) (Cambridge University): I am already in communication with the Chancellor of the Exchequer upon the subject to which the hon. Member refers. At present, however, I have hardly, as yet, received that sufficient evidence of a

Colonel Nolan

desire on the part of hon. Members to support a measure to carry out the changes suggested to which I alluded in my reply to the hon. Member for East Donegal (Mr. A. O'Connor) on February 17 last.

INDIA — DISTRIBUTION OF PRIZE MONEY FOR THE CAPTURE OF JHANSI.

MR. E. ROBERTSON (Dundee) asked the Under Secretary of State for India, Whether any further distribution of prize money for the capture of Jhansi is likely to be made?

THE UNDER SECRETARY OF STATE (Sir JOHN GORST) (Chatham): The whole of the prize captured at Jhansi has been already distributed.

POST OFFICE (IRELAND) — NOTICES AND POLITICAL CARTOONS.

MR. JOHNSTON (Belfast, S.) asked the Postmaster General, If he is able to give any further information concerning the display of *Freeman's Journal* cartoons, side by side with Post Office notices, in the joint office of the Post Office and *Freeman's Journal*, Rathmines Road, Dublin; if there are other suitable places in Rathmines for a Post Office besides *The Freeman's Journal* office; whether the Post Office has, till recently, been held in various shops in the locality; and, if any steps have been taken to prevent the display of political cartoons side by side with postal notices?

THE POSTMASTER GENERAL (Mr. RAIKES) (Cambridge University): In answer to a previous Question from the hon. Member, I stated that I had been unable to ascertain that in the Rathmines Road Receiving Office cartoons of *The Freeman's Journal* had been exhibited side by side with Post Office notices. It has since been ascertained that, inside the shop and close to the shop door, there is a raised screen on which cartoons have been exhibited, and sometimes, but not always, Post Office notices as well. Of this I informed the hon. Member in a letter I wrote to him on Thursday last; and I further informed him that explicit instructions had been given that, under no pretence whatever, were Post Office notices and cartoons to be again posted side by side. In Rathmines there are, no doubt, other places suitable for a Post Office besides the shop in which it is now held. During the last four years the Post Office has been removed only once—namely, from No. 86A, in Rathmines Road, where the accommodation was insufficient, to the present convenient premises at No. 95. I may add that by the kindness of my hon. Friend I have had the pleasure of inspecting the cartoons, and it does not appear to me to be in any degree more offensive than ordinary caricatures; and the likenesses of my right hon. Friend the Chief Secretary for Ireland and the noble Marquess at the head of the Government were, I thought, remarkably good.

FRANCE—ARREST OF MR. AUGUSTUS HARE, AT EMBRUN.

Mr. NOBLE (Hastings) asked the Under Secretary of State for Foreign Affairs, Whether he can give the House any information about the arrest of Mr. Augustus Hare, at Embrun, France, on 22nd instant, and complained of by him in a letter to *The Times* of 29th instant?

Mr. CAVENDISH BENTINCK (Whitehaven) also asked the Under Secretary of State for Foreign Affairs, Whether he has seen a letter addressed to *The Times* newspaper, under date 27th April, by Mr. Augustus J. C. Hare, stating that the authorities at Embrun, in France, had refused to accept his British passport as an identification, "because it was not dated in the present year;" and, whether it is necessary for British subjects travelling abroad to renew their passports every year?

The UNDER SECRETARY of STATE) (Sir JAMES FERGUSSON) (Manchester, N.E.) : I have read Mr. Hare's letter in *The Times* of the 29th ultimo. No complaint has, however, been received at the Foreign Office from him; but should any such complaint be made it will be at once inquired into. Ordinary passports for English travellers in France were abolished by the Emperor Napoleon, and we have never been informed that they were required, except temporarily during the Franco-German War. When passports are issued by the Secretary of State they hold good for an unlimited time, as far as Her Majesty's Government are concerned; but we are not aware how long their validity is recognized by the authorities of foreign

countries. When inquiries on this point are made at the Foreign Office it is customary to suggest that the holder of the passport, before setting out on his journey, should apply for a *visâ* to his passport from the Diplomatic or Consular authority of the country which he proposes to visit. A notice was inserted in *The London Gazette* of May 11, 1886, warning all travellers in France that under the provisions of a recent French law, "making sketches, drawings, or plans, in the vicinity of a fortress," rendered persons liable to fine and imprisonment. I can express no opinion upon the case, of which I know nothing, except from Mr. Hare's published letters.

Mr. CAVENDISH BENTINCK : Are we to understand that in future it will be necessary, for the purpose of identification, for English travellers in France to have their passports *visâd*?

Sir JAMES FERGUSSON : I have no reason to believe that it is necessary for ordinary travellers; but I need not remind the House that in some countries there is some susceptibility about making drawings; and I think in the Eastern part of France just now that is only natural. At any rate, English gentlemen cannot be too careful in providing themselves with every safeguard against arousing suspicion.

LAW AND POLICE (ENGLAND AND WALES)—SENTENCE ON RIOTERS AT THE MARYLEBONE POLICE COURT.

Mr. PICKERSGILL (Bethnal Green, S.W.) asked the Secretary of State for the Home Department, Whether his attention has been drawn to the sentences of six months' imprisonment with hard labour passed on seven men by Mr. De Rutzen, at the Marylebone Police Court, on the 27th instant; whether Mr. De Rutzen is correctly reported to have stated, that he had intended to send the defendants for trial by a jury, but yielded to the application of Mr. Poland, the Counsel for the Treasury, to deal with the cases summarily; whether the defendants were charged with "riotous conduct and inciting the crowd to commit a breach of the peace," but were dealt with for assaults on the police; and, whether Mr. De Rutzen stated that one of the men was "the instigator of all the mischief;" and, if so, whether, at all events as regards the other six defendants, he will consider the advisability of mitigating the sentences passed upon them?

THE SECRETARY OF STATE (Mr. MATTHEWS) (Birmingham, E.): My attention has been called to the sentences. The seven defendants were charged with assaulting the police in the execution of their duty, as well as with riotous conduct and inciting to riot. Mr. Poland did suggest that they should be dealt with summarily on the charge of assault, and Mr. De Rutzen stated that he had no objection to that course, although, otherwise, he should have committed the defendants for trial. Mr. De Rutzen stated that the sentence of six months' imprisonment with hard labour was not too heavy for any of the defendants, and that it was wholly inadequate in the case of Williams, whom he designated as the leader and the person most to blame. I therefore see no reason for mitigating the sentences, against which an appeal lies. Notice of appeal has already been given on behalf of two of the defendants—Williams and Pole.

MR. JOHN MORLEY (Newcastle-upon-Tyne) asked whether the prosecution had the sanction of the Home Office?

MR. MATTHEWS: I have really not considered the question. There were several charges on the sheet; and the magistrate exercised his discretion as to whether he would convict on the graver or the lighter charge. I have not even considered whether the evidence before Mr. Poland warranted him in dropping the charge of inciting to riot.

MR. JOHN MORLEY: Are we to understand that no Minister in this House is responsible for the action of Mr. Poland?

MR. MATTHEWS: I am really not aware of the facts of this question, or how the prosecution came about. There might have been a police prosecution, or a private prosecution; Mr. Poland was not instructed from the Treasury. I will, however, inquire, and inform the right hon. Gentleman if he wishes to know.

MR. LABOUCHERE Northampton): Pending this appeal, will these men be kept in prison?

MR. MATTHEWS: The law will follow its usual course.

Mr. Pickersgil l

OPEN SPACES (METROPOLIS) — THE CHURCHYARD BOTTOM WOOD, HORNSEY.

MR. J. ROWLANDS (Finsbury, E.) asked the hon. Member for the Epping Division of Essex, Whether means can be devised by the Ecclesiastical Commissioners for preserving for ever, as a public recreation ground for the population of North London, the Churchyard Bottom Wood, comprising 51½ acres, in Hornsey; and, whether, according to a Parliamentary Survey of 1647, it forms part of the "Woods and Waste" of the Manor of Hornsey, and is one of the few remaining portions of the old Middlesex Forest?

SIR HENRY SELWIN-IBBETSON (Essex, Epping): Gravel Pit Wood of 70 acres is already dedicated to the public as a gift by the Commissioners under a special Act obtained by agreement with the Corporation of London; and while prepared to sell the Church Bottom Wood, as shown by the offer made to the Local Board, they are not prepared to make any further gift. The Wood in question formed no part of the "waste" of the Manor of Hornsey, but was part of the Episcopal demesne land, and has been granted out on beneficial lease by the Bishops of London since the early part of the 17th century.

INDIA—HINDOO MARRIAGE LAW— THE PUNJAB CIVIL CODE.

MR. COZENS-HARDY (Norfolk, N.) asked the Under Secretary of State for India, Whether he is aware that in the Punjab Civil Code there is an express enactment that the Court · shall not compel either party to complete a child marriage against his or her will; whether similar enactments are in force in other parts of India; and, whether the Government are willing to assimilate the law in Bombay to the law in the Punjab in this respect?

THE UNDER SECRETARY OF STATE (Sir JOHN GORST) (Chatham): There was such a provision in the Punjab Civil Code; but that Code ceased to have the force of law in 1872. I am not aware that similar enactments are in force in other parts of India; and as to the rest of the Question I refer to the answer given to a similar Question on Friday.

MERCHANT SHIPPING — RUSSIAN
BILLS OF HEALTH AT
CONSTANTINOPLE.

MR. CONYBEARE (Cornwall, Camborne) asked the Under Secretary of State for Foreign Affairs, Why it is that German and Norwegian steamers can obtain Russian bills of health at Constantinople to the Black Sea ports on Sundays, while no British steamers are allowed that privilege; and, whether he will make inquiries or representations with a view to getting the same privileges accorded to British ships which are enjoyed by those of foreign nations?

THE UNDER SECRETARY OF STATE (Sir JAMES FERGUSSON) (Manchester, N.E.): Inquiries on the subject have been addressed to Her Majesty's Embassy at Constantinople, and, if necessary, representations will be made.

TRADE AND COMMERCE—STRIKE OF SHIPBUILDERS AT BELFAST.

MR. SEXTON (Belfast, W.) asked the Chief Secretary to the Lord Lieutenant of Ireland, Whether it is true, as reported, that 6,000 *employés* of the Belfast shipbuilders are on strike; whether there is any cause in dispute except a claim on the part of the *employés* to have their wages paid every week, instead of every fortnight, as at present; and, whether the Government will consider of some means of bringing the dispute to a friendly termination, in view of the provision of the Truck Bill for weekly payment of wages?

THE PARLIAMENTARY UNDER SECRETARY (Colonel KING-HARMAN) (Kent, Isle of Thanet) (who replied) said: It appears that there is at present a dispute between the shipbuilders and their *employés* at Belfast on the subject of the existing system of paying wages. The Irish Government, while trusting that an amicable settlement will be come to, have no power to interfere in the matter.

MR. SEXTON: I beg to ask the Secretary of State for the Home Department, whether he has any objection to despatch an Inspector to Belfast, with the view of seeing whether a friendly arrangement could be come to?

THE SECRETARY OF STATE (Mr. MATTHEWS) (Birmingham, E.) was understood to ask for Notice of the Question.

GREENWICH HOSPITAL—INVESTMENT OF FUNDS.

SIR SAMUEL WILSON (Portsmouth) asked the Civil Lord of the Admiralty, What additional income will be available during the present year on account of the recent changes in the investment of the funds of the Greenwich Hospital; and, whether the additional income will be devoted to providing pensions for seamen of the Royal Navy?

MR. ASHMEAD-BARTLETT (CIVIL LORD) (Sheffield, Ecclesall): In the Greenwich Hospital Estimates for the present financial year an additional sum of £2,651 is provided for pensions to seamen and marines and for their widows and children. Further, the addition of £5,000 made last year to the actual expenditure on these pensions will be maintained. The full benefit to be derived from recent efforts to re-invest the funds of Greenwich Hospital will not be realized during the present year.

POST OFFICE—CONVEYANCE OF MAILS TO TASMANIA AND NEW ZEALAND.

MR. HENNIKER HEATON (Canterbury) asked the Postmaster General, At what rate per letter was, or will be, paid to the Shaw, Savill, and Albion Steamship Company, for conveyance of Mails per S.S. *Coptic,* which left Plymouth for Tasmania and New Zealand on the 23rd instant, and what rate was charged to the public per letter to Tasmania and New Zealand; and, is he aware that the steamers of this Company sail once a month, and make the passage in 38 days?

THE POSTMASTER GENERAL (Mr. RAIKES) (Cambridge University): The usual ship letter gratuity of 1*d.* per letter has been paid to the commander of the *Coptic* for the mails which were put on board that ship at Plymouth on the 23rd of April for conveyance to Tasmania and New Zealand. The charge made to the public was 6*d.* per letter, which is uniformly the rate charged by all routes to Australasia, under a Treasury Warrant dated February, 1880. I am aware that the steamers of the Shaw, Savill, and Albion Steamship Company sail once a month. They make the passage to Tasmania, as I am informed, in from 39 to 44 days, and to New Zealand in from 44 to 49 days. I may, perhaps, add that no letters are sent by these private steamers other than such as are specially so superscribed by the senders, and that the number is very limited. If this course were not taken the Colonies would suffer the injustice of being deprived of a portion of their postage by the regularly subsidized mail packets which they now maintain themselves at considerable loss to the Colonial Revenues.

MR. HENNIKER HEATON: Arising out of that answer, am I to understand that though the British Post Office only pays 1*d.* per letter for the conveyance of these letters by fast and regular steamers to Australasian ports, the charge of 6*d.* per letter is made to the public?

MR. RAIKES: I have already answered that Question.

POST OFFICE — NEWSPAPERS FOR INDIA AND THE COLONIES—NON-DELIVERY.

MR. HENNIKER HEATON (Canterbury) asked the Postmaster General, Whether about 25,000 newspapers, &c., for India and the Colonies are posted and not forwarded every year; in what manner are they destroyed; and, if any are sold as waste paper?

THE POSTMASTER GENERAL (MR. RAIKES) (Cambridge University): The exact yearly number of newspapers posted for India and the Colonies and stopped, either on account of insufficient payment of postage or of non-compliance with the conditions laid down by the Act of Parliament, cannot be stated; but it is thought that the number is not over-stated by the hon. Member for Canterbury—25,000. Such of the stopped newspapers as bear the names and addresses of the senders are returned to them. The rest are consigned to the Stationery Office as waste paper, and are, I believe, sold.

SCOTCH FISHERY BOARD—TRAWLING IN THE MORAY FIRTH.

MR. ANDERSON (Elgin and Nairn) asked the First Lord of the Treasury, Whether the Scotch Fishery Board have recommended that trawling be prohibited in the Moray Firth; and, when a bye-

Mr. Raikes

law will be made carrying out such recommendation? The hon. Member also asked, Whether the First Lord of the Treasury can state why it is that an Order published on the 18th April was not known to the Scottish Office at the end of last week?

THE LORD ADVOCATE (Mr. J. H. A. MACDONALD) (Edinburgh and St. Andrew's Universities) (who replied) said: With regard to the subsequent Question of the hon. Member, I have to say that if this Question had been put to someone connected with the Scotch Department on the previous occasion when it appeared on the Paper, it would possibly have been answered on the day on which it had been asked. The Scotch Fishery Board have made a bye-law prohibiting trawling in the Moray Firth within certain specified limits. This bye-law has been duly advertised, and will, on the expiry of the statutory period, be transmitted to the Secretary for Scotland fo confirmation.

MR. ANDERSON: I should like to ask the First Lord of the Treasury, whether the Government will appoint someone who will really represent the Scotch Department in the House?

THE FIRST LORD (Mr. W. H. SMITH) (Strand, Westminster): The hon. Gentleman has not been long in this House; but he is probably aware that the Lord Advocate does represent the Scotch Department in the House.

IRISH LAND LAW BILL.

MR. DILLON (Mayo, E.) asked, When the next stage of the Irish Land Law Bill would be taken in the House of Lords?

THE FIRST LORD OF THE TREASURY (Mr. W. H. SMITH) (Strand, Westminster): The 12th of May.

BUSINESS OF THE HOUSE—CUSTOMS AND INLAND REVENUE BILL.

MR. BARTLEY (Islington, N.) asked Whether the First Lord of the Treasury could state on what day this Bill would be taken; and, whether he would so arrange that it would come on at an hour which would give an opportunity for discussing the important subjects of local taxation and local finance?

THE FIRST LORD (Mr. W. H. SMITH) (Strand, Westminster): I am not able to say. It depends on the progress of Business.

PRIVILEGE—MR. HOLMES AND "THE TIMES" NEWSPAPER.

MR. T. M. HEALY (Longford, N.): I rise, Sir, for the purpose of calling the attention of the House to a matter which I conceive to be a question of Privilege. I refer to certain statements which appeared in *The Times* newspaper on Saturday last reflecting on a right hon. and learned Member of this House in connection with the discharge of his functions in this House as a Member of the House. I will only read a small portion of the article. The words of which I complain are these—

"Common sense surely prescribed scrupulous adhesion to precedent in all non-essential matters; but common sense seems to be the very last quality that enters into the drafting of an Act of Parliament. After the sworn information was settled Mr. Healy pounced upon the use of the word 'offence' in one line to indicate the thing called a crime in another. It is a small matter, perhaps; but anybody, except a draftsman of a Bill, would have taken one word or the other and stuck to it, were it only as a matter of symmetry. On this question of offence or crime an excited wrangle took place. It might very likely have taken place all the same had the Government held uniform language in the Bill; but they would, at all events, have occupied a more logical and consistent position. Then a little later the Attorney General for Ireland filled the Parnellites with exultation by blundering into something which looked very like an admission that the Bill creates new crimes. Every candid person, of course, knows what that maladroit official wanted to say, and ought to have said—namely, that the Procedure Clause of the Bill applies improved methods of detection to crimes committed before its passing; but does not punish as a crime any act that was not a crime when committed. But then they are not candid persons with whom the Government have to deal; and one of the Irish Law Officers floundering helplessly among his own confused ideas and ill-chosen phrases was a spectacle which filled the Parnellites with the wildest delight."

It seems to me, Mr. Speaker, that it might be a painful matter for the right hon. and learned Member for the University of Dublin (Mr. Holmes) to have to draw attention himself to so gross an attack upon him.

MR. SPEAKER: Order, order! I consider that the hon. and learned Gentleman is trifling with the House. I conceive that there is no question of Privilege arising out of these words. The Clerk will now proceed to read the Orders of the Day.

ORDERS OF THE DAY.

CRIMINAL LAW AMENDMENT (IRELAND) BILL.—[BILL 217.]

(Mr. A. J. Balfour, Mr. Secretary Matthews, Mr. Attorney General, Mr. Attorney General for Ireland.)

COMMITTEE. [*Progress* 29th *April.*]

[SECOND NIGHT.]

Bill *considered* in Committee.

(In the Committee.)

PRELIMINARY INQUIRY.

Clause 1 (Inquiry by order of Attorney General).

MR. T. M. HEALY (Longford, N): The Amendment which I propose to move is one which has reference to the application of this Bill by means of a Proclamation. It seems to me that we ought to know from the Government exactly to what portions of Ireland they intend to apply the measure. At the present moment we know that Ireland, with two or three exceptions, is peaceful and orderly, and my Amendment is to omit the words "in a proclaimed district." The clause, as it stands, says that—

"Where the Attorney General for Ireland believes that any offence, to which this section applies, has been committed in a proclaimed district, he may direct a Resident Magistrate to hold an inquiry."

Now, I assert that the County of Kerry, the City of Londonderry, and the town of Belfast are the only places where offences, which might be brought under this Bill, have been committed during the last 12 months, and I think we are entitled to know from the Government exactly what the districts are which they have in their mind. We all know that Belfast has been the scene of bloody riots, almost bordering on civil war, for which, practically, no person has yet been brought to justice. We also know that in regard to the City of Derry the hon. Baronet the Member for North Antrim (Sir Charles Lewis) was petitioned against and unseated; and although he was not mentioned in the Report of the Election Judges as having been personally guilty of corrupt practices, several of his supporters were reported. We know, further, that in the County of Kerry there have been several crimes committed. What I want to know is whether the Government will

[*Second Night.*]

tell us exactly what portions of Ireland they conceive this Bill ought to be made applicable to, because, in my judgment, if these words are allowed to remain in the clause without some qualification, what might happen is this. The Government might proclaim the whole of Ireland outside the Province of Ulster; and, whenever any Catholics are murdered in Ulster, as usually takes places in the month of July, no Proclamation would be issued, and the stringent provisions of the Act would not be put in force. It, therefore, seems to me that we ought to know from the Government exactly what the districts of Ireland are which they propose to proclaim under this Bill. We know that in very recent years, under the Crimes Act, a murder of a most brutal character was perpetrated on a Catholic in Ulster, Philip M'Guire, but no inquiry was held, and the perpetrator escaped the consequences of his crime. Then, again, in the City of Derry, although the Government were represented there on a recent occasion by a learned Queen's Counsel, and an investigation was held into certain charges of bribery and corruption which had taken place in that city, and which led to the unseating of the Member who had been returned to represent it in Parliament, the Government have never since made the slightest attempt to make use of the information brought to their notice, nor has the Public Prosecutor pursued an investigation into the corrupt practices which took place at that election. The Government have simply allowed the whole matter to drop. Now, it seems to me that if the provisions of this Bill are to be honestly administered, and were I, unfortunately, to come under its provisions, we should find some gentleman occupying some distinguished position in connection with the Government who would be eager to prosecute me. I am, therefore, induced to ask what the regions of the country are which the Government intend to occupy, and whether the Bill, when it becomes an Act, is to be put in force in Kerry and Clare, while Belfast and Londonderry are to be exempted? Let us know, at any rate, what are the districts which are to be proclaimed, and what counties are to be proclaimed. What are the districts to which the Government propose to apply this measure? In order to give the Government an op-

portunity of answering the question, I will move that the words "in a proclaimed district" be struck out of the clause; and if that is done, I shall then propose to move to insert the words "Kerry, Londonderry, and Belfast," and I shall give my reasons for including the two latter places.

Amendment proposed, in page 1, lines 7 and 8, leave out the words "in a proclaimed district."—(*Mr. T. M. Healy.*)

Question proposed, "That the words 'in a proclaimed district' stand part of the Clause."

THE CHIEF SECRETARY FOR IRELAND (Mr. A. J. BALFOUR) (Manchester, E.): The hon. and learned Gentleman has asked for information which he is perfectly well aware it is not in the power of the Government to give. We have laid down from the beginning that we mean the provisions of this Bill to apply to those parts of Ireland, and those parts of Ireland only, where the existence of such crime may be found to exist as will justify its application. The hon. and learned Gentleman asks me now to leave out the words "in a proclaimed district," and to insert in the Bill other words to bind the Government as to the districts in which the Act will be put into operation. The hon. and learned Member must see that that Amendment and the consequent Amendment are inconsistent with the whole scope of the measure.

MR. T. M. HEALY: I am certainly surprised that the right hon. Gentleman has not thought fit to tell us whether Belfast is to be proclaimed or not. There have been more people killed and wounded in Belfast in the last six months than in all the rest of Ireland during the last six years. A Royal Commission, appointed by the Government themselves, has inquired into the matter so far as Belfast is concerned, although no attention has been paid to their recommendation. I want to know if the Catholics of Ireland are to go unprotected when this Bill is passed; and whether it is to be applied only in the interests of the landlord party? I shall certainly press for information in regard to Belfast. There is in that town a large body of people with arms in their hands who have committed murder and outrage, but have been acquitted with applause in an open Court. Although, in one instance, a soldier and a policeman were killed, and in a second a policeman was seriously wounded, no person has, as yet, been hanged. I wish to know whether, under the circumstances, the Government consider that we ought to allow our co-religionists in the North of Ireland to be killed and wounded by their friends with impunity? I think we are fairly entitled to know what parts of Ireland are to be proclaimed under this Bill; and whether in that blood-stained region of Belfast, where 30 people have been killed, Her Majesty's troops shot at, and members of the Constabulary murdered, the criminals are to escape scot free?

MR. A. J. BALFOUR: What the hon. and learned Member has a right to know, and what I will at once tell him, is that the Government will exercise perfect impartiality between different creeds and different parts of Ireland.

MR. DILLON (Mayo, E.): The right hon. Gentleman the Chief Secretary has informed the Committee that the Act is not intended to apply to any part of Ireland except where crime exists. [Mr. A. J. BALFOUR: And disorder.] The right hon. Gentleman did not use the word "disorder" in his speech. It may be said that there was disorder in Mayo when the tenants would not pay Lord Dillon's rents. The right hon. Gentleman says that the provisions of the Bill will be applied impartially. This is not the first time nor the twentieth that we have listened to declarations of that character. When the Act of 1881 was being adopted in this House, the late Mr. Forster, who, I venture to feel, was quite as much entitled to credence as the present Chief Secretary for Ireland, declared over and over again that the Act was not to be applied in Ireland, unless necessity required its application. But what happened? Before the Act had been in force for a month, it was applied in the City of Dublin for the purpose of arresting me. There was no disorder or crime there. It has never been pretended that there was agrarian disorder, because it could not be said that there was anybody who happened to hold farms in the City of Dublin. Dublin was utterly free from disorder of any kind. Nevertheless, Dublin was proclaimed for the sole object of arresting certain Members of Parliament. We know from experience when Acts of this kind are passed, that, notwithstanding the declarations of the Government at the time, the powers which such Acts give will be used unscrupulously by the Executive. The Chief Secretary has said that the provisions of the Bill will not be applied to any part of Ireland until there is such an amount of crime as to justify its application. Will the Chief Secretary take the trouble to look over the condition of Ireland, and say what are the districts in Ireland in which, at present, he considers there is a sufficient amount of crime to justify the application of such a measure at all? Is it not true that outside the Counties of Kerry, Clare, and Western Limerick absolute peace prevails in Ireland? I think we are in a position to make a tremendously strong case against taking away the liberties of the whole people of Ireland, and leaving them at the mercy of the Executive Government, because in a remote corner of the country there is a state of disorder. The Amendment of my hon. and learned Friend raises a most important issue. I think we have a right to protest test that because in a remote corner of the country there is a state of disorder we ought to take away the liberty of the whole nation. I have here the quarterly Returns of crime and outrage in Ireland for the last two quarters, and I find that in the Province of Ulster the crimes, leaving out of view threatening letters, were exactly six from September up to December. In the Province of Leinster, the largest and most populous Province in Ireland, the number of crimes for the winter quarter was eight in the whole Province. Is it not a monstrous thing that you should pass a Bill, which is to apply potentially to the whole of Ireland, when a condition of things exists as to absence from crime in regard to which you cannot find a parallel for years? In the Province of Connaught, in the same quarter, there were 29 crimes, excluding threatening letters; and, although that is not as favourable a condition of things as in Ulster and Leinster, it nevertheless shows an absence of crime which has been unparalleled for years. In those three Provinces there does not exist a shred of crime in justification for

[Second Night.]

a measure like this, and yet the Government are proposing to place in the hands of the Executive of Ireland a power to apply this Bill to all those Provinces—to three-fourths of the population of Ireland, who have been free from crime for years past. I come now to the Province of Munster, and the condition of things there is this—In Munster, excluding threatening letters, there were 44 serious crimes; but, deducting the outrages in Kerry and Clare, there were about 13 in the whole Province. Those were the figures of the winter quarter. I come now to the quarter ending with March 31, and in reference to both quarters I contend that an unanswerable case exists for exemption from the provisions of a Bill like this. I think the Government are bound to stand up and show that some case exists for such a sweeping measure before they can hope to get the consent of the Committee to it. In other measures which have been passed by Parliament, the provisions of the Act have been confined to special districts in Ireland. Take the case of Westmeath. Disturbances had existed there; but did the Government seek to include the whole population of Ireland? Nothing of the sort. They showed that a bad condition of things prevailed in Westmeath, and they passed the Westmeath Act. Why should we not have now a Kerry and Clare Act? The last quarter's Returns show a slight increase, but a very trifling increase, over the previous quarter, which has not usually been the case, and which is, undoubtedly, to be attributed to the change in the policy of the Government in reference to Ireland. Instead of putting pressure on the landlords, as they did in the winter quarter, with excellent results, the Government entirely changed their policy, and the consequence was that there was a considerable increase in the number of evictions. In the Province of Ulster the number of serious crimes during the last three months was 10. When I call them "serious crimes" I ought to tell the Committee that many of them were of an absurdly trivial character. In the Province of Leinster there were 21, and when I look down the column of serious crimes included in this Return, I find that such crimes as murder, conspiracy to murder, firing at the person, and assaulting the police, are all absolutely blank. The crimes included

in the Return are almost all of a trifling character, a good many of them consisting of injury to property. As the Government absolutely refuse to give us any information as to the nature of the crimes described under the head of injury to property, we can only conjecture that they are absolutely of the same character as the injury to property specified in the Blue Book of 1881. There is already standing on the Notice Paper a Motion for a Return of crime and outrages; but the Government have blocked it. In Leinster I cannot find that within the last three months there have been more than seven or eight outrages of a serious character. In the Province of Connaught, during the same period, there were about 38; but several of the counties were absolutely free from serious crime. In the Province of Munster, outside the three counties I have already named, other than threatening letters, the outrages numbered 26. In the three counties of Kerry, Clare, and Limerick, they numbered 48; but if those three counties are eliminated from the Return I maintain that the condition of Ireland is such as not to afford a shadow or shred of excuse for this Bill. I contend that the Government are bound to act on the precedent of the Westmeath Act, and to confine the operation of their Bill, at any rate at this stage, to the three counties in which there does happen to have been this small modicum of excuse for it.

MR. W. H. K. REDMOND (Fermanagh, N.): I hope my hon. and learned Friend the Member for North Longford (Mr. T. M. Healy) will press this Amendment and force it upon the Government, or, possibly, we may have a repetition of what occurred under the Coercion Act of 1881. By that Act, certain districts were proclaimed in Ireland, where there was certainly not a sufficient amount of crime to warrant their being proclaimed at all. Districts were proclaimed then not for the purpose of putting down crime, but for the purpose of putting down political agitation. In the County of Wexford the Return of crime made in 1881 showed that there had been 56 outrages in that county, and upon that Return Mr. Forster had the county proclaimed; but it is an important fact that when the Return came to be analyzed it was found that, leaving threatening letters out, there were not more than eight or nine of what might be called crimes in the whole county. Nevertheless, that county was proclaimed, because the Government wanted to do then what they want to do now—not so much to put down crime or outrage, as to attack their political opponents and to put down political demonstrations. The Chief Secretary has mentioned crime and disorder. What does the right hon. Gentleman mean by disorder? It does not take a vivid imagination to picture what may be considered disorder in the eyes of the Irish Executive and their officials. Disorder, in their eyes, may be the holding of political meetings, the delivery of political speeches, and the carrying on of the National movement generally. That is what the right hon. Gentleman means by disorder, and it is evidently what he is anxious to recognize by this Bill. That it is agitation he desires to put down is evident from the fact that he refuses to state to what district the Government propose to apply this Coercion Act in Ireland. I maintain that it is impossible for the Government to prove that there are more than two or three districts throughout the whole of Ireland where crime is in existence to such an extent as to warrant coercion, or the application of any exceptional law. Whatever hope the Government may have of inducing the people of this country to support them in coercing districts where crime unfortunately does prevail, I trust they will not have the sympathy of the country when they are endeavouring to put upon the whole of Ireland a severe and arbitrary measure of coercion which is not warranted by the existing state of crime. The right hon: Gentleman, in reply to my hon. and learned Friend, said that while he could not accept the Amendment he would give an assurance that the Bill would be impartially administered. We, unfortunately, judging by the experience of the past, cannot accept the assurance of the right hon. Gentleman, or of the Government of Ireland, as a sufficient guarantee that this Bill, if it is enacted for the whole country, will be impartially administered. I represent a district in the Province of Ulster which is most happily free from crime; but, still, it is a district where Orangeism extensively prevails, and out of the 84 magistrates of the county 82 of them

are persons who, if not actually Orangemen, still are in distinct and avowed sympathy with the Orange Organization. I could give many other instances, and I hope, in the course of a few days, to put a question as to the administration of justice on the part of certain magistrates in the County of Fermanagh. I could cite instance after instance where, in the most flagrant possible manner, the magistrates have put justice altogether aside, and have given their decisions directly in sympathy with the spirit of the Orange Organization. Surely this is proof enough that it will be most outrageous, and even fatal, to place a Bill of this description in the hands of Resident Magistrates with Orange sympathies all over the country. The right hon. Gentleman has given us an assurance that this Bill will be used impartially in the Catholic districts of the South, and in the turbulent Orange districts in the North. A right hon. Gentleman who is not now a Member of this House, but who formerly held the position of Chief Secretary to the Lord Lieutenant, wrote a letter a short time ago to the newspapers, in which, from the knowledge he obtained during the time he held the Office of Chief Secretary, he gives his opinion as to how this Bill will be used. He does not hesitate to express a strong opinion as to the character of the men who compose the Executive Government in Ireland, and who would practically have the sole administration of this Bill. The right hon. Gentleman to whom I refer—Sir George Trevelyan—cannot be accused by hon. Members who sit on the other side of the House, and who represent Irish constituencies, of any desire to exaggerate the facts of the case. I would ask the Committee to look at this Amendment, not from the Irish Members' point of view; do not let them be influenced by what we say, but let them take the words of Sir George Trevelyan, who, with his practical experience of the Office of Chief Secretary and of the working of a Coercion Bill in Ireland, has given his testimony that it will be impossible for the Government to administer the Bill impartially among Orange partizans of such notoriety as the right hon. and learned Attorney General for Ireland (Mr. Holmes), and the right hon. and gallant Gentleman the Parliamentary Under Secretary

(Colonel King-Harman). These are some of the reasons which induce us to look with the greatest alarm and suspicion on the attempt of the Government to saddle the whole country with a Coercion Bill, and these are the reasons which have actuated my hon. and learned Friend in proposing this Amendment. We ask the Government to say distinctly, before the Bill leaves the House, to what districts of Ireland its provisions are to be applied, and to give some guarantee that Orange rowdyism and Orange crime will be put down in the North of Ireland, just as much as any crime which happens to be in existence in the South of Ireland. I cannot possibly conceive that a more reasonable request could be made by the Irish Representatives in this House than the request which they now make —that instead of saddling the whole of the country, which is admittedly free from crime, with this Coercion Bill, the Government, if they are intent on passing coercion at all, should content themselves with passing it upon those districts in the South and North of Ireland where, unfortunately, crime and outrage do prevail. As has been pointed out already, there has been more blood shed, more outrage, more lawlessness, and more real disorder in the Orange districts of the North of Ireland than in any number of districts in the South and West, and without the same provocation. If the Chief Secretary wishes to make the country believe that the Government are serious in their attempt to put down crime, he will rise in his place and say that they will rest satisfied with proclaiming those districts in which crime does prevail, and that they will not attempt to coerce or proclaim an entire country for the misdeeds of a few portions of that country. The Irish Representatives, whether Protestant or Catholic, protest against this infamous attempt to impose a law of this kind upon the people of all the constituencies; and I believe that if every Member representing an Irish constituency in this House were to protest in the same way against his constituents, who are free from crime, being coerced, he would only be discharging his duty towards the constituents who have sent him here to defend their liberties.

Mr. E. ROBERTSON (Dundee): I would suggest to the right hon. and

Mr. W. H. K. Redmond

learned Attorney General for Ireland (Mr. Holmes) that he might make a concession to the hon. and learned Member for North Longford (Mr. T. M. Healy). The Attorney General is the person who will put the provisions of this Bill into operation, and he knows, if anybody knows, what the districts are in which it will be necessary to enforce the Act. He knows, if anybody knows, what the districts are, if this Bill had already become law, in which he would feel it his duty to give the Resident Magistrates the power of putting this 1st clause in motion. What I would suggest that the right hon. Gentleman should do now is that he should name or insert by name in the Bill these specific districts which he says require the operation of the Act, and that he should do so without prejudice to the general power of proclamat on contained in the Bill. By doing so he would lose nothing whatever which the Bill proposes to give him; but he would enable the House to judge, from the list he would submit, how that impartiality which the Chief Secretary has promised in regard to the application of the Bill is likely to be exercised. If the right hon. and learned Gentleman will be pleased to name the places which he says require the application of such an Act, the House will then be able to see whether the list he gives is a fair and impartial list or not. If it is fairly impartial, the House will then be able to prognosticate the spirit and manner in which the Act is likely to be carried out.

Mr. LABOUCHERE (Northampton): The only reply which the Chief Secretary has vouchsafed to the hon. and learned Member for North Longford (Mr. T. M. Healy) is that he has already explained the scope and spirit of the Bill. Now, as far as I can see, the scope and spirit of the Bill are aimed at crushing out the Nationalists, and allowing the Orangemen to do precisely as they like. An Orangeman may commit murder, but a Nationalist may not grin through a horse collar. The Chief Secretary has given a pledge that the Bill will be administered impartially; but by whom is it to be administered? It is to be administered by gentlemen who, if they wish to be so or not, cannot be impartial, so bound up are they with the Orange faction in Ireland. They have their feelings so strongly on the side of the Orange faction, that they cannot and will not be impartial. Who is to be the judge whether the Administration is impartial or not? They themselves, in a proclaimed district, are to be the judges of their own impartiality. The hon. and learned Member for North Longford claims that the Bill should be limited in its operation to those parts of Ireland where there is a certain amount of crime. You limit the Bill to Ireland; you do not apply it to the whole of the United Kingdom, and yet you are always telling us that there is no distinction between Ireland and the United Kingdom. Surely your reason for limiting the operation of the Bill to Ireland is because there is exceptional crime in existence there, and none in the United Kingdom. Therefore, you ought to limit the Bill to those parts of Ireland where you assert that exceptional crime prevails. The reason why I have risen now is this—whenever one of the right hon. Gentlemen on the Treasury Bench gets up and speaks upon the Bill, he always enlarges the scope of it. We were told that the Bill was directed against crime. We are now told that it is a Bill against crime and disorder. I always imagined that disorder could only be proved by the fact that there is crime; but the right hon. Gentleman implies that there is some distinction between crime and disorder. Before going further, I think we ought to understand from the right hon. Gentleman—I am sorry to disturb the sleep of the just in which he is indulging—but I think we ought clearly to understand what he means by disorder, irrespective of crime. We do not know under what conditions the district may be proclaimed by the Lord Lieutenant. We had some idea that he might take a right or a wrong view; but we thought he would only proclaim a district where there was a considerable amount of crime. We are now told that he will not only proclaim a district where there is crime, but one in which there is only disorder. The vague distinction which has been used by the right hon. Gentleman is a most important one, and before we pass this clause we ought to understand clearly on what conditions, and on what conditions alone, Her Majesty's Government intend to use the provisions of the Bill.

Mʀ. JOHNSTON (Belfast, S.): I ask the indulgence of the Committee for a very few moments. I rise for the purpose of replying to the observations which have been made upon the Orange Organization and upon the City of Belfast by the hon. and learned Member for North Longford (Mr. T. M. Healy). I think that the attack which has been made upon the City of Belfast by the hon. and learned Gentleman ought not to be allowed to be passed over in silence by anyone who has the honour of representing that constituency. The constituency which I represent has had nothing to do with any of the disturbances which have occurred in Belfast; but I cannot sit quietly here and hear the members of the Orange Society characterized as "blood-stained." I know we are accustomed to hear the Orange Organization calumniated.

Tʜᴇ CHAIRMAN: Order, order! It would not be relevant to the Amendment now before the Committee to discuss the question of the Orange Organization.

Mʀ. JOHNSTON: I did not propose to discuss the Orange Organization at all, nor have I any desire to say anything further. I only wish to repudiate the calumnious charges which have been made against the Orange Society by the hon. and learned Member for North Longford and the hon. Member for North Fermanagh (Mr. W. Redmond). Having done so, I will now resume my seat.

Mʀ. EDWARD HARRINGTON (Kerry, W.): I trust the Committee will appreciate the anxiety of the hon. Gentleman to protect the Orange Organization.

Mr. JOHNSTON: I rise to Order. I wish to know whether, having been called to Order myself, and having obeyed the ruling of the Chair, the hon. Member is regular in continuing the discussion?

Tʜᴇ CHAIRMAN: The hon. Member must confine himself to the Amendment before the Committee.

Mʀ. EDWARD HARRINGTON: The object of the Amendment is to limit the application of the Bill to certain districts in Ireland. As representing one of the counties which come within the category of disturbed districts, I think I am taking a proper position when I invite the Government to name that county in the Bill in order that the causes of its disturbed condition may be investigated and, if possible, removed. I have no objection to see crime punished; but I think it is only justice to ask, concurrently with the Proclamation of a district and the punishment of crime, that the application of the provisions of this Bill should be limited to those districts where disturbance and disorder have prevailed. If Her Majesty's Government are desirous of getting at the root of the disorder in these disturbed districts, I think it will be found that it is attributable to the aggravated forms of injustice to which the tenants and others in those districts have been perpetually subjected. I thank the Chief Secretary for the word "disorder" which he has introduced into the discussion. It raises a new issue altogether, and I should like to know what meaning is attached, in the mind of the right hon. Gentleman and Her Majesty's Government, to the use of that word "disorder?" We have from the beginning announced plainly, fairly, and above-board, that we have no objection to the Bill reaching crime in Ireland; but what we do object to is, that the Government should take a partizan and political view of what they are pleased to call "disorder," but which relates to transactions which it has been found necessary from time to time to resort to in order to prevent a worse and more general description of disorder. What we are afraid of is that the Government may direct the operations of their Bill towards that description of disorder, while they allow more serious forms of crime to escape scot-free. Hon. Members ought not to dismiss altogether from their minds the important facts brought forward by my hon. Friend the Member for East Mayo (Mr. Dillon) as to the condition of the counties in which the right hon. Gentleman the Chief Secretary asserts that there is a state of disorder and lawlessness. My hon. Friend showed that there has been scarcely a single crime committed from boundary to boundary during the time covered by the Chief Secretary's statement. There is no use in mincing the matter. I will, however, endeavour to keep within the observance of Parliamentary Forms; but we believe that, from the highest to the lowest, the public officials of Ireland are saturated with Orange prejudices and with landlord antipathies to the people, and that,

Mr. Edward Harrington

consequently, there will be a scandalous maladministration of this Bill, which will not be limited at all in its evil effects by any assurance of impartiality that may given by the Chief Secretary. We place no value upon the right hon. Gentleman's assurances. His own mind may be of a more even character. Perhaps he is not so intimately associated with Orangemen and the landlord class in Ireland. Over and over again the same assurances have been given; but as long as Dublin Castle is Dublin Castle; so long as the Resident Magistrates get their instructions generally from Dublin Castle, stating the character of the persons they are to try, and virtually directing them what to do—so long as that system of government prevails in Ireland, it is in vain to depend upon any assurances, however sincere they may be at the time of their utterance in this House. I think there is now a distinct issue raised on this Amendment, and before we proceed further with the debate I think the Committee ought to insist upon some interpretation on the part of the Government of what meaning they attach to the word "disorder." Does the Chief Secretary mean to say that the County of Mayo is in a state of disorder, and that this Bill will be applied to that county? Is he unwilling to lay down a cast-iron rule that the Bill is only to apply to certain districts in Ireland? What we want to know from the Government is, whether they will tell us, taking Ireland as it is now, if the Bill were passed to-night, to what districts they would seek to apply it to-morrow? Surely that is not asking too much. The Government say they want to put down exceptional crimes — such as murder, firing into houses, mutilation of cattle, and Moonlighting. Are they of every-day occurrence in Ireland? If this Bill were now passed; if all opposition ceased at once; if we grant to the Government the whole measure, will they tell us, in return, what the districts of Ireland are to which, in their present condition, they would apply the provisions of this Bill?

COLONEL HUGHES (Woolwich): I think it is most important that we should have regard to the words we are discussing. The Amendment proposes to leave out the words "in a proclaimed district." But the speeches which have been made referring to those words have not made the matter at all clear. The words "in a proclaimed district," as they are applied in the section, have reference to where the offence is committed. On Friday the attention of the Government was called to the specific construction that might be placed on this phrase as limiting the clause to offences committed in a proclaimed district after the district has been proclaimed. I understood the Attorney General for England to say that if there were any doubt as to the meaning of these words the Government would look into the matter, and, if necessary, change them. The junior Member for Northampton (Mr. Bradlaugh), and others, also asserted that these words are meant to apply to offences committed in a proclaimed district after a district has been proclaimed under the Act. It has been proposed by the hon. and learned Member for North Longford (Mr. T. M. Healy) that the words "in a proclaimed district" should be struck out, in order to insert the names of three counties. I quite agree that those words ought to be struck out, but not for the purpose of inserting the names of three counties. Such a course would prevent the provisions of the Bill from being applied to any other part of Ireland in the future except those three counties. It would be very bad legislation to put down the mischief and crime which may arise in three counties, and to leave all the rest of Ireland open to the operation of the National League. My objection to the words as they stand is, that they would limit the operation of the Bill to offences committed after the passing of the Bill, and after a district had been proclaimed. It has been clearly declared by the Government that the Bill is intended to apply to crimes which have already been committed, and offences which have already taken place, but which have not yet been discovered, and I understand that an inquiry is to be made into past offences as well as into future offences. Therefore, I take it that these words will have to be struck out, and I was in hopes that some Member of the Government would state how it is intended to correct what appears to me to be a verbal inaccuracy. I understand the phrase to mean that "where the Attorney General for Ireland believes that any offence to which

this section applies has been committed." Then, taking out the words "in a proclaimed district," he may direct a Resident Magistrate to hold an inquiry under this section. If the clause were altered in that way, it would apply to every district now proclaimed, and to every district which may be proclaimed hereafter. It appears to me that we are really dealing with a verbal inaccuracy, and I think it would greatly facilitate the understanding of the discussion of this Bill if hon. Members would have a copy of the measure actually in their hands at the time the discussion is going on.

MR. CLANCY (Dublin Co., N.): The hon. and gallant Gentleman has devoted the greater part of his speech to an explanation of what everybody in the House understood. He objects to any limitation of the clause, and, no doubt, would prefer to see it very much extended. The right hon. Gentleman the Chief Secretary has asked us to trust to the impartiality of the Executive in carrying out the provisions of the Bill. Now, we refuse to trust to the Government, or to their impartiality. We cannot do so. The Government is a Government of partizans, and the latest accession to the ranks of the Ministry shows that the Government are partizans, and also Orange partizans. The Parliamentary Under Secretary for Ireland is a member of every landlord organization in Ireland. He is a member of the Orange Society; he has advised the Orangemen of Ireland, in a remarkable speech, to keep their hands upon the trigger. I presume that the opportunity for doing so will arise under this Bill. At the present moment there is ample evidence in our hands that the Government now engaged in the administration of the law in Ireland is a landlord Government to the backbone and spinal marrow. The right hon. Gentleman the Chief Secretary tells us to trust to the impartiality of the Executive. What happened at the last Winter Assizes? In Sligo, when Catholic peasants evicted from the Clanricarde estates were indicted, not a single Catholic was placed upon the jury; but in Omagh no one but an Orangeman was set to try the Orange rioters of Belfast. It is an undoubted fact that the Government in the West of Ireland packed juries to convict Nationalist prisoners; whereas, in the North of Ireland, they refused not only to pack juries, but to exclude the most notorious and well-known partizans from the jury-box. Under such circumstances, to endeavour to induce us to believe in their impartiality is to endeavour to impose upon our credulity. Take, again, the attitude of the Government on the subject of Boycotting. When the Boycotting is committed in Ulster by Orangemen we do not hear a word about it. Take the case of the Rev. Mr. Macaulay — a Presbyterian Home Rule minister. Mr. Macaulay is a venerable man, who has done great service to religion in his district. He has not only been subjected to Boycotting, but has been subjected to outrage. His property has been destroyed by the action of Orange partizans; but the Government have refrained from condemning either the Boycotting or the outrage. Indeed, they have gone to the extent of refusing to post up in the police barracks of the country notices offering a reward for the discovery of the perpetrators of the outrage on his church. The reverend gentleman offered a reward himself; but this Government of impartiality, which denounces Boycotting in Munster, Leinster, and Connaught, which weeps bitter tears for imaginary cases of Boycotting like that of the midwife, has not a word to say as to the Boycotting, intimidation, and violence practised towards the Rev. Mr. Macaulay. How are we to trust a Government like that? There is another illustration I should like to bring under the notice of the Committee. We have heard within the last few weeks a good deal of condemnation of Irish juries, and of verdicts which they have either found or refrained from finding when the Crown have desired to secure a verdict of guilty. The jurymen have been held up as men who have wilfully disregarded their oaths; but we have not heard a word of a remarkable case which occurred a short time ago in the County of Fermanagh. In that case, some Orangemen were brought before a local Bench of Magistrates which was entirely composed of Orangemen. They were charged with firing with intent to kill at a body of Nationalists. Of course, in the view of Orangemen that is no crime at all, or next to none. Nevertheless, the Crown considered it so grievous an offence that they had the offenders brought before

the local magistrates. The charge was completely proved, but the Orange magistrates set the culprits scot-free, declaring that there was no stain upon their character. The Attorney General had this matter brought under his attention, and he himself deprecating the gross partizanship displayed by the local Bench of Magistrates, and directed a re-hearing of the case. The result, however, was the same, and the magistrates acquitted these men once more, although they were plainly guilty of a most heinous crime.

THE CHAIRMAN: The hon. Gentleman is clearly wandering from the Question before the Committee in commenting upon the conduct of a local Bench of Magistrates.

MR. CLANCY: I was trying to make good my charge against the Government that we can have no confidence in their impartiality.

THE CHAIRMAN: The hon. Gentleman has himself pointed out, in the case to which he was referring, that the Attorney General for Ireland had acted impartially.

MR. CLANCY: I was proceeding to remark, Sir, that, notwithstanding the action of the Attorney General, Her Majesty's Government took no further steps in the matter, but disregarded the plain duty they had to peform in the most disgraceful manner. They might, if they could have done nothing else, have dismissed those Justices from the Commission of the Peace, but they did absolutely nothing to mark their disapproval. I cannot understand the equity of an arrangement by which, no matter how heinous an Orange offence is, it goes altogether unpunished; whereas, for the commission of the most trivial offence, a Nationalist is severely punished. I refuse to trust to a Government of that kind. I assert that the Government is a Government of partizans from top to bottom. The Lord Lieutenant of Ireland is a member of the Orange Party. If there is anything Lord Londonderry understands, although I do not think he understands much, he comprehends the principles and rules of the Orange Society, of which, I believe, he is a Past Master. The Parliamentary Under Secretary for Ireland is a sworn member of the same Body, and he is convicted in this Blue Book—in the evidence given before the Cowper Commission—of having robbed his tenants in the most disgraceful manner.

THE CHAIRMAN : The hon. Member must not speak of a Member of this House in those terms.

MR. CLANCY : Well, then, I would put the matter this way—that the Parliamentary Under Secretary has had his rents reduced by 54 per cent, and that he has been convicted by the Land Courts in Ireland of having fleeced his tenants to that extent; and, no doubt, he would have continued to get these iniquitous rents if the Land Court had not stepped in. I am not permitted to characterize conduct of this sort as I deem right, but I know what is said of it out-of-doors.

THE CHAIRMAN : The hon. Member is clearly irrelevant. He is not referring to anything which attaches to the conduct of the right·hon. Gentleman as a Member of the Government.

MR. CLANCY : I am referring to the antecedents of the right hon. and gallant Gentleman, and I say we fully expect him to pursue in Office the policy which he has pursued when out of Office. I think it would be ridiculous to ask the people of Ireland, or any Member of the Irish Party, to regard other than as partizans in the highest degree a Government composed of such men as the Parliamentary Under Secretary for Ireland.

COLONEL HUGHES : I rise to Order. I want to know whether, upon the words "in a proclaimed district," the hon. Member is in order in entering into the conduct of individuals?

THE CHAIRMAN : The Question, "in a proclaimed district," involves the use of the discretion of the Government. I understand that the hon. Member is speaking of the trust which ought to be reposed in the Government.

MR. CLANCY : I am impugning the impartiality and *bona fide* of the professions of the Government. I maintain from its connections, and from its acts in this House and in the country, it will remain a partizan Government to the end, as it has been in the past. By a subsequent part of this Bill, the Lord Lieutenant is to proclaim districts in conjunction with the Irish Privy Council. I am told that the Judges do not take part in these administrative acts, although they are Members of the Privy Council; but that they put their signatures to Proclamations merely as a matter of form, being required to do so

as Members of the Privy Council. But there are men in Ireland who do take an active part in the business. Who are they? Here, again, we come upon the Parliamentary Under Secretary for Ireland (Colonel King - Harman) who is a Member of the Privy Council. [*Cries of* "Order!"] I believe I am entitled to speak of the right hon. and gallant Gentleman by his name as a Member of the Privy Council. Then there is another Gentleman, Mr. Arthur Mac Murrough Kavanagh, the head of the I. L. P. U., and a man who also has had his rents cut down very considerably within the last few weeks. Then there is The O'Conor Don, another convicted rack-renter, who is not now a Member of this House, and, therefore, I may speak of him as I really feel. These are the gentlemen who, acting in conjunction with Lord Londonderry, will have the power of putting the provisions of this Bill in force. I say that it is ridiculous and preposterous to expect, for a moment, impartiality from a Body of this kind, composed of Lord Londonderry, the Parliamentary Under Secretary for Ireland, who has had his rents reduced by 54 per cent, Mr. Arthur Mac Murrough Kavanagh, who has robbed his tenants time out of mind, and The O'Conor Don, who has done likewise. I therefore protest against giving to the Executive in Ireland any discretionary power whatever. We believe that the Bill will be used solely for landlord and Orange purposes; we believe that Orange outrages in Ulster, however heinous they may may be, will go unpunished, and that the slightest offences perpetrated in other parts of Ireland by persons supposed to be Nationalists, will be made the ground for applying to those districts this most atrocious Bill, which I hope the Liberals and Radicals of this country will do their best to stop before it proceeds further.

The PARLIAMENTARY UNDER SECRETARY for IRELAND (Colonel King-Harman) and Mr. GLADSTONE rose together. The right hon. Member for Mid Lothian gave way.

THE PARLIAMENTARY UNDER SECRETARY FOR IRELAND (Colonel KING-HARMAN) (Kent, Isle of Thanet) : I thank the right hon. Gentleman for allowing me to make a brief personal explanation. I have no desire to say anything in regard to the Bill on its clauses. The matter of my rents has been repeatedly called in question by hon. Gentlemen below the Gangway opposite, and it is simply in order that the House may understand the real state of the case that I rise to make a few remarks. I have been accused of being a rack-renter. I think that the House knows generally what is the meaning of Griffith's valuation. That valuation was made in the year 1854, at a time when prices in Ireland were lower than they are now. It was avowedly made by Sir Richard Griffith 25 per cent below the letting value of the land—[*Cries of* "No!"]—and it was distinctly stated that it was made as a basis of rating, and not of rent. In 1881, a large body of my tenants came to me, and asked to have their rents reduced to Griffith's valuation. I was then able to point out to them what I wish now to point out to the House—that in 1881 the rents on a very large property were within £100 of Griffith's valuation, which, as I have stated, was 25 per cent below the letting value of the land, and I had no opportunity, even if I had desired it, afterwards of raising the rents. If, in 1881, I was able to show that my rents were 25 per cent below the letting value, I can hardly be called a rack-renter.

MR. T. M. HEALY: Are you an Orangeman?

MR. W. E. GLADSTONE (Edinburgh, Mid Lothian): I apprehend that, although the courtesy of the Committee has permitted the right hon. and gallant Gentleman to make a personal explanation, I am not expected to say a word on the subject of that explanation, because it would be abusing the patience of the Committee to attempt to do so. But I desire to refer to the Motion under discussion, and likewise to one or two points which have arisen in that course of the debate—to the important suggestion which has been made, and the demands which have been preferred in the course of the debate. Now, with respect to the Amendment, I would venture to make this observation. The words in the clause are "in a proclaimed district," and I find that they occur again and again before any power to proclaim a district is given. That may, or may not be good drafting of a Bill, or it may have been better to have

given power to proclaim before anything was said about a proclaimed district. It is, however, too late now to rearrange the clauses of the Bill; but I think it would not be satisfactory to the Committee to have a discussion of this nature raised again and again on the term "a proclaimed district" each time it arises. I would suggest whether it is convenient to proceed with the discussion on this basis. Assuming that this is a Bill which is to go through Committee, it is probable that there may be something in the nature of a power of proclaiming particular districts, and that the hon. and learned Member for North Longford himself recognizes. The words "in a proclaimed district" are in the nature of limiting words, and the simple omission of them would leave a power applicable to the whole of Ireland. Would it not, therefore, be best to leave the words "proclaimed district" at present, and when we come to the proclamation of districts in Clause 5, and the definition of the powers given to the Lord Lieutenant, then to raise the points which may be properly raised as to the conditions on which the Proclamation should take place? Other matters have occurred which I think require notice. The hon. and learned Member for North Longford has demanded from the Chief Secretary for Ireland to know whether Belfast is to be included in the proclaimed districts, and the right hon. Gentleman considered that he gave a sufficient answer when he said that all districts would be treated on a principle of perfect impartiality. I own that, after what has occurred, that answer is insufficient. The right hon. Gentleman himself has referred to particular parts of Ireland as being parts of Ireland the condition of which justified their inclusion in the present Bill. He described them, I think, as including one third of the area of Ireland, and the hon. Member for Cork (Mr. Parnell) said they included only one-sixth of the population. After that was done, and Clare, Kerry, and other counties had been pointed at as requiring the action of a Bill of this kind, it became perfectly lawful, regular, and legitimate to ask whether Belfast was in contemplation. The hon. Member for South Belfast (Mr. Johnston) has, with great propriety, felt it to be his duty to say something on behalf of his constituents, and he has said what is to be regarded with credence, that the bulk of the people of Belfast regard the outrages in that town with horror. Is there not exactly the same thing in other districts? Are we not bound to make the same presumption with respect to persons who have not been guilty of crime and outrage in the districts which it is proposed to proclaim? If the apology is good for Belfast it is good for other places. Well, there is no doubt the conduct of certain persons in Belfast has stained the character of Ireland more than it has been stained by conduct in any other part of Ireland. Therefore, it is perfectly fair to ask what is the view the Government take of the case of Belfast. I shall never call this Bill a Bill for the repression of crime, for that is a most untrue description; but I suppose that crime is included in the purview of the Bill, and, if so, I think that hon. Gentlemen sitting for Irish constituencies are quite justified in pressing for some explanation as to the scope of the Bill, and what view the Government take of the state of things in Belfast—a state of things which, from recent accounts, has not even yet reached its long wished for and right determination. Another point I wish to notice is the further explanation given by the Chief Secretary to-night of the scope of the Bill. It was a small Parliamentary incident which might not be noticed in any report of the debate, but which it is well to record. When the hon. and learned Member for North Longford spoke of the Bill as a Bill for the repression of crime the right hon. Gentleman the Chief Secretary for Ireland called across the Table, enlarging that description, "crime and disorder." Now, that is a very important fact. We have heard that crime and offences are synonymous, to the great surprise of many persons in this House; but now we know from the mouth of the right hon. Gentleman himself that he is not satisfied with the description which has been given of the Bill—that it is a measure for the repression of crime. We now know from his mouth that it is something else, which, although it may be bad and evil in itself, is not crime, but is, nevertheless, included in the scope of the Bill. Of course, the right hon. Gentleman can retract what he has said; but I wish to notice the words of the right hon. Gentleman as a full jus-

tification for the protest which has been made. When the Bill was originally introduced there was a disputable proposition—namely, that the Bill was directed, not simply against crime, but that it did include something which is not now crime, and did aim at connecting it with offences with a view of establishing a certain state of things in Ireland. I accordingly support the demand that we should know what view the Government take in regard to the case of Belfast. I see the noble Lord the Member for Leicestershire (Lord John Manners) in his place. I see that he has defined the purpose of a Coercion Bill as a Bill only to be proposed in the case of exceptional crime and outrage. In Belfast there is, undoubtedly, exceptional crime and outrage—[*Cries of* "No!"]—and I think we ought to know whether occurrences such as these in Belfast are what are not within the purview of the Bill. We do not want to be answered by the reply, "we cannot tell whether this state of Belfast will be continued." There may be perfect tranquillity in Belfast; but that is equally true of all the other parts of Ireland specially referred to. Therefore, I hope the Government will throw a little light upon the subject. I think that the general question intended to be raised by the Amendment certainly requires full discussion.

LORD RANDOLPH CHURCHILL (Paddington, S.): The suggestion the right hon. Gentleman has made as to the most convenient time for the Committee to discuss the question of the proclaimed districts is, I think, an admirable one; but he has greatly destroyed the value of that suggestion—that is to say, its practical value, for the purpose of bringing this discussion on, by raising two points which might easily be developed into points of great controversy, and lead to protracted discussion. I will venture, on one of those two points, to make a few remarks. The right hon. Gentleman found fault with the Chief Secretary for using and suggesting the word "disorder."

MR. W. E. GLADSTONE: Adding it to crime.

LORD RANDOLPH CHURCHILL: Yes; but, at the same time, the right hon. Gentleman has distinctly made himself a party to the insinuation which has been freely developed from below the Gangway, that the Government intend to apply this Bill to the South and South-West of Ireland, leaving Ulster free from the operation of the Bill. I wonder the right hon. Gentleman could not see that the use of the word "disorder" in connection with crime will bring Belfast under the operation of the Bill. The right hon. Gentleman has totally destroyed the value of the suspicion which he laid the Government open to by the attack he has made upon them for having added the word "disorder." There have been riots and disorder in Belfast—[Mr. CLANCY : Murder.]—there have been riots and disorder in Belfast, mostly of a serious character, and undoubtedly accompanied with loss of life—[Mr. CLANCY : Murder.] — accompanied by offences which may be regarded as murder; but the law has been asserted and vindicated in Belfast by Belfast juries.

MR. T. M. HEALY: Has anyone been hanged?

LORD RANDOLPH CHURCHILL : I say that law and order have been restored in Belfast, and a great number of the rioters have been brought to justice. Many persons have been convicted, and one of them who was accused of murder was convicted of the crime of manslaughter and sentenced, I think, to a number of years penal servitude. The son of the same man would have been convicted had it not been proved that he was innocent. These men were tried, and it cannot be asserted that they did not get a fair trial, nor can it be asserted in regard to the riots in Belfast that the ends of justice have been in any way defeated. The law has been asserted in Belfast as well as it could have been asserted in any other great town in the United Kingdom where popular passion and excitement run high. Yet the right hon. Gentleman the Leader of the Opposition seriously contended, and asked the Committee to believe, that there is no analogy whatever between the deplorable riots which have taken place in Belfast and the Moonlighting which have taken place in Kerry—Moonlighting outrages for the Commission of which not one single person has been made amenable.

An hon. MEMBER : That is not true.

Lord Randolph Churchill

LORD RANDOLPH CHURCHILL : Will the right hon. Gentleman assert that the juries in the North of Ireland have failed to do their duty in regard to the cases of disorder which have occurred in Belfast? [*Cries of* " Yes! "] Those cases are of a totally different character, and I am surprised that the right hon. Gentleman should gravely stand up and compare the diabolical outrages which have even been denounced by hon. Gentlemen below the Gangway in Kerry, Galway, Clare, and parts of Limerick and Cork with the riots in Belfast? Are they to be put on the same footing as the riots which constantly occur in Belfast, but which are invariably suppressed and put down, and which are invariably followed by the ends of justice being vindicated? It is a most deplorable thing that the right hon. Gentleman should use all his great influence, and his great abilities to confuse and mislead the Committee, and by pitting the diabolical outrages in the South against the Party riots in Belfast, that he should attempt to condone and apologize for such outrages.

MR. T. M. HEALY : The noble Lord the Member for South Paddington, who has just sat down, very naturally feels somewhat sore on the subject of Belfast. Of course we have been told that " Ulster will fight, and Ulster will be right." I have not risen, however, for the purpose of entering into any historical incidents in the career of the noble Lord. I wished to correct him in regard to a matter of fact as to the way in which law and order are administered in Ireland. We have been told by the noble Lord that law and order have been as well administered in Belfast as in anywhere else throughout the whole world, and yet we remember that some 300 or 400 people have been maimed for life, 35 murdered, and that not one single person has been hung, and only some two or three have been punished. The noble Lord complains, and the same calumny has been repeated by a right hon. Gentleman in a region which is not easily accessible in this House—namely —the Islands of Orkney and Skye—the noble Lord complains that the murderers of the Curtins and others have not been brought to trial and punishment in Kerry. The Government allow these lies and calumnies to go forth when the right hon. and learned Gentleman the Attorney General for Ireland (Mr. Holmes) at the present moment can jingle in his pocket the guineas which he got for convicting those persons. So far from that statement being true, I assert, as a matter of fact, that within the last six months whole batches—I believe to the number of 40—of the Kerry Moonlighters have been brought to trial, and 20 within my own knowledge were convicted at the last Winter Assizes. And yet, the right hon. Gentleman the Attorney General for Ireland says, that as far as he is aware, there has not been a single Moonlighter convicted in Kerry.

THE ATTORNEY GENERAL FOR IRELAND (Mr. HOLMES) (Dublin University): As far as I am aware, there has not been a single Moonlighter convicted in Kerry. It was only by changing the venue to the County of Cork that convictions were obtained.

MR. T. M. HEALY: The right hon. and learned Gentleman may mislead the Committee; but he cannot mislead me. The right hon. Gentleman has said that there was a change of venue. There was no change of venue at all. What happened was this. The ordinary law enables the Government to transfer the trials of certain persons at the Winter Assizes to certain places. I know the City of Cork jurors, and I say this, that persons who convicted these Moonlighters were Nationalists almost to a man. Furthermore, I declined brief after brief and refused to defend these men, although some of them may possibly have been innocent. No Nationalist member of the Irish Bar defended them, and they were convicted. These facts are as well known to the Government as they are to us. Furthermore, when a Conservative Administration was last in Office, Lord Salisbury boasted in the House of Lords of the success of the Government in these transactions. Lord Spencer retorted that it was by means of Winter Assizes, and Lord Salisbury replied "Yes; but it was by the ordinary law."

LORD RANDOLPH CHURCHILL: That was in 1885.

MR. T. M. HEALY: Yes; and in 1886 as well, and it was under the ordinary law. Contrast this with what has happened, on the other hand, in Ulster. The right hon. and learned Attorney General himself knows well that, as a matter of fact, he denounced the Tyrone juries, and said that they were worse than those of Kerry. I challenge him to contradict that statement. The right hon. and learned Gentleman is always a straightforward and honourable opponent, and I observe that he does not contradict that assertion. What happened was this—the Walkers were put on their trial. There was no Winter Assize in Belfast; but, at the Tyrone Assizes, Judge Lawson, who, God knows, is no friend of ours, told the jury as plainly as possible that they were perjuring themselves, that they could not convict the prisoners of manslaughter, although they were willing to bring in a verdict to that extent, but that the offence was one of murder. Time after time the jury came back into Court; but they refused to convict, and then the Government transferred the trial back to Belfast—back to the scene of the labours of these prisoners on the Shanklin road. They did it in spite of the Report of the Commission which is contained in the Blue Book, and now before the House—a Commission presided over by one of the English Judges, supported by an Irish Queen's Counsel —Mr. Delapore Trench—and subscribed to by Mr. McHardy, a member of an Orange Society. That Report states—

"We are sorry to add that certain persons, having great influence in Belfast, thought proper, at various periods during the riots, to indulge in language, written and spoken, well calculated to maintain excitement at a time when all men of influence should have tried to assuage it. Mr. Cullen, the Divisional Magistrate of Ulster, and others, laid before us certain specimens of these utterances, some of which we print in Appendix D, and which speak for themselves. We feel it our duty to draw special attention to a letter of the 4th day of August, 1886, written by Mr. De Cobain, Member of Parliament for one of the Divisions of the town—a letter the publication of which the Mayor of Belfast most properly brought under the notice of the Government. Another cause of the continuance of the riots was the unhappy sympathy with which, at certain stages, the well-to-do classes of Protestants regarded the proceedings of the rioters. At one stage of the riots it seemed as if the greater part of the population of the Shankhill district united against the police. This is the more to be regretted, as it was on all sides admitted that no more valuable aid could have been given to the police than that afforded by respectable and influential people of the localities in which the troubles arose."

In illustration of this charge the Commission called special attention to a

[*Second Night.*]

letter published by Mr. De Cobain, which was brought under the notice of Government; but, from that day to this, no attempt has been made to deal with the origin of these riots. It was with that Report staring them in the face that responsible and influential persons in Belfast sided with the rioters that the right hon. and learned Gentleman the Attorney General for Ireland sent these Walkers back to be tried in Belfast. He did so well knowing in his heart that these men would not be convicted, because they were Orangemen. I assert this as a fact—that no Orangeman in Ireland has ever yet been convicted on a trial for murder. I will give an instance to show the manner in which this particular trial was "rigged." The trial took place when Her Majesty's late Government were in Office, and the right hon. Gentleman the Member for Newcastle-upon-Tyne (Mr. John Morley) was Chief Secretary for Ireland. In the ordinary course, Mr. Walker, the Liberal Attorney General, and The M'Dermot, the Liberal Solicitor General, would have had the conduct of the trial, which ought to have gone naturally to the Summer Assizes. But the Liberal Government were likely to leave Office, and, therefore, it was arranged to have the prisoners returned for trial at a time when the right hon. and learned Gentleman the present Attorney General for Ireland (Mr. Holmes), and the hon. and learned Gentleman the present Solicitor General for Ireland (Mr. Gibson), would be the Law Officers of the Crown. Whereas, in the ordinary course, the trial would have been conducted by Mr. Walker and The M'Dermot; it was so arranged that the men were returned for trial at a time which was too late for the Summer Assizes in Belfast. If this fact is not within the knowledge of the right hon. and learned Gentleman the Attorney General, I can assure him that it is notorious to the Bar of Ireland. Without the slightest necessity for that remand, the case was remanded so as to throw off the trial until the following Assizes. In moving my Amendment, I referred to the state of Derry. I presume that bribery and corruption will be an offence under this Act, seeing that is a misdemeanour. Now, the grossest bribery and corruption were proved to have prevailed in the City of Londonderry at the last General Election, when the hon.

Baronet who now sits for North Antrim (Sir Charles Lewis) was returned. It has been asserted that everyone connected with the candidature of the hon. Baronet, when the inquiry was about to take place, fled from Derry, and no summons could be served upon them. One or two of them were fortunately dragged up; but no person to my knowledge, although gross corruption was clearly established, has been prosecuted in connection with these charges, nor was even an attempt made to ascertain where these men were. The recognized agents of the hon. Baronet—the whole gang of them — were shown to be absolutely steeped in corruption; but not one of them has been punished. The Crown Prosecutor sat in Court mute, and yet the Election was given in favour of my my hon. Friend (Mr. Justin M'Carthy) on a single charge of bribery. Of course, my hon. Friend could have gained no advantage from continuing the investigation; but the whole burden of going on with it, and probing it to the bottom, rested with the Government. In Belfast the Government took a different course, and prosecuted an unfortunate cripple; but in Derry, where the bribery was of a most extensive character, every individual concerned in it got away absolutely unscathed. I have now explained the reasons why I have proposed this Amendment; but the moment I heard the right hon. Gentleman the Leader of the Opposition (Mr. W. H. Smith) suggest that it would come in better at a later period, I rose to offer to withdraw the Amendment. Of course, the noble Lord the Member for South Paddington (Lord Randolph Churchill) naturally desired to make an explanation and to continue the debate, and, therefore, I gave way. If the Government desire that the Amendment should be withdrawn, I have no objection to withdraw it; but I hope they will take advantage of the opportunity, in order to give the Committee some explanation in regard to the points which have been raised. For my own part, I accept the suggestion of the right hon. Gentleman the Member for Mid Lothian (Mr. W. E. Gladstone), and after this explanation I am quite ready to withdraw the Amendment.

MR. HOLMES: The Committee will not be surprised, after the speech which has been delivered by the hon. and

Mr. T. M. Healy

learned Member for North Longford (Mr. T. M. Healy), that even at the risk of continuing the discussion for some little time longer, I should desire to say a few words. I will ask the permission of the Committee to commence my observations by an allusion to myself personally. It has been said more than once, in the course of this and other discussions, that I am an Orange partizan. I wish to assure the House, at the very commencement of my remarks, that there is probably no hon. Member of this House less connected in any way with Orangeism than I am. I am not an Orangeman, nor have I had any connection of any kind, either by family or otherwise, with that society. It so happens that, as I believe, I am not even personally acquainted with three Orangemen, save and except hon. Members of this House, some of whom, for aught I know, may be Orangemen.

An hon. MEMBER: What of Colonel King-Harman?

MR. HOLMES: I may say, further, that in the course of my career I have often taken opportunity publicly to express my strong abhorrence of these party demonstrations, which, in my opinion, both on one side and the other, have been highly detrimental to the prosperity and happiness of the North of Ireland. I trust the Committee will excuse my having, under the circumstances, made this personal reference. The hon. and learned Member for North Longford has stated that it was by the operation of the ordinary law in the South of Ireland that the Kerry Moonlighters were brought to justice. I took the liberty of interrupting him, because the statement he made was not precisely in accordance with the facts. As far as my knowledge goes, there has not been a single instance, in the last three or four years, of a Kerry Moonlighter having been convicted in Kerry. No doubt, at the Winter Assizes in 1885, there was a large number of Kerry Moonlighters convicted in the City of Cork. The hon. and learned Member says that they were convicted under the provisions of the ordinary law, but the hon. and learned Member will bear in mind that that only arose from the circumstance of the offences having been committed at a particular season of the year, and, therefore, the trial was trans-

ferred from one county to another. But I would ask, whether, if the Government is of opinion, from past experience, that it is necessary to have the venue changed from one county to another, they are not justified in asking the legislature to make an alteration in the law? Would not an alteration in the law be justified if under the present law a man who committed an offence in February or May got scot free, whereas if the offence had been committed in September or October, he would probably have been convicted at the Winter Assizes? It is to meet this difficulty that the Government asked the House to enable a change of venue to be made.

An hon. MEMBER: To the Old Bailey.

MR. HOLMES: In regard to the Winter Assizes, in the year 1886, the hon. Member for North Longford is wrong when he states that 40 Moonlighters were convicted in the City of Cork.

MR. T. M. HEALY: I did not say so —I said 20.

MR. HOLMES: It is not for me to criticize the action of Cork juries, but I believe that there was nothing like an extensive conviction of Moonlighters at those Assizes.

Mr. T. M. HEALY: Will the right hon. and learned Gentleman tell the Committee how many persons were tried, and how many were convicted?

MR. HOLMES: I cannot go through the cases individually now. All I assert is that the number of Moonlighters convicted at the Cork Winter Assizes was very small. I now come to the observations which the hon. and learned Member has made in reference to the Belfast riots. In the first place, I may say that the hon. and learned Member is under a serious misapprehension as to the facts of the case. He says that not more than six or seven of the rioters were successfully prosecuted. I can inform the hon. and learned Member that by summary conviction more than 100 were brought to justice, and, at the Winter Assizes, about 66 were convicted and sentenced to heavy penalties. Therefore, it is a misrepresentation of the facts to say that only about six of the rioters were brought to justice. The hon. and learned Member proceeded to say that the results of this Winter Assizes at Tyrone were unsatisfactory, and that I myself declared that Tyrone juries were worse than Kerry juries. The hon. and learned Member seems to imagine that because I listened to that allegation and remained silent, that, therefore, I assented to it. Now, I always think that when an hon. Member is making a series of statements it is better to wait for a proper opportunity of reply instead of throwing out interjectional observations. Not only did I never make such a statement, but no such idea ever occurred to my mind. I have stated over and over again that the juries at the Tyrone Winter Assizes did their duty with wonderful fairness and impartiality. There were three serious cases of murder tried at the Tyrone Assizes. In one case—the case of a Catholic indicted for a wilful murder committed in Lurgan—there was no doubt whatever that the offence was wilful murder, but the question was whether the prisoner was the person who committed it or not. The charge was one of murdering a Protestant during an Orange demonstration. The Tyrone jury acquitted the prisoner.

MR. T. M. HEALY: Did the jury disagree with the Judge's charge? What was the name of the man?

MR. HOLMES: It was the first case heard, and it was immediately before Donelly's case. Donelly was not tried for wilful murder at all. The case I refer to was a case of murder, and the sole question, as I have already stated, was whether the prisoner committed the murder or not.

An hon. MEMBER: The name of the prisoner was Hart.

MR. HOLMES: I presume the hon Member does not suppose that I have any intention to misrepresent the facts of the case. I was in Court myself, and it cannot be supposed that for a moment I would represent that the result of my case was different from what it actually was. As I have said, the verdict in that case was one of acquittal, the prisoner charged being a Catholic, and the charge being one of murder. The second case was that of the murder of Head Constable Gardner. What occurred in that case was this—the jury disagreed. I was under the impression when I read the depositions in connection with the case that there was a substantial case, but when I heard the evidence given

in Court it seemed pretty clear to me that there had been a mistake on the part of the constable who identified the prisoner. This prisoner was subsequently acquitted, and one of the most distinguished judges on the Irish Bench—Lord Justice Fitzgibbon—on the second trial, which took place at Belfast, said that it was impossible for the jury to come to any other conclusion. That was one of the cases in which the jury disagreed at the Winter Assizes. The third case was the only case, as far as I am aware, which occurred at the Winter Assizes at Tyrone in which there was a failure of justice. It was the case of the elder Walker, who was indicted for the murder of a soldier named Hughes. The jury stated that they were willing to find a verdict of manslaughter, but they refused to find a verdict of murder. Now, I admit that in that case the jury ought to have found a verdict of murder on the admitted facts, and that was the only case tried at the Tyrone Assizes in which there was any failure of justice whatever. Catholic rioters were acquitted and convicted, and Protestant rioters were again and again convicted. I believe that more than 40 were convicted and sentenced to suffer punishment. I wish to impress these facts upon the Committee that in one or two cases where a Catholic was put upon his trial, and where there seemed hardly to be a doubt as to the proof of the offence, yet the jury yielded to the persuasion of counsel, and he was acquitted. Having read the informations that were laid against the prisoners, and all the depositions, I have had a full opportunity of knowing whether the juries did their duty or not, and I am sure that if the hon. and learned Member for North Longford had had the same advantage he would agree with me that the only single failure of justice during those trials, which extended over three weeks, was the case to which I have referred—namely the case in which the elder Walker was placed on his trial for murder, and in which the jury refused to convict him of anything but manslaughter. Although it has been charged against the Government that the Walkers were tried at Belfast, I can assure hon. Members that the honest desire was that they should not be tried there. But it was impossible to prevent it. I myself had a strong objection to that course being taken in

Mr. Holmes

consequence of · the excitement under which the people of Belfast were labouring at the time. In face of the fact that on former occasions Belfast rioters were tried before Belfast juries, and that the juries did their duty, and that we could not make out a case under the existing law to induce the Court of Queen's Bench to change the venue, we came to the conclusion that it was impossible for the Crown to remove the case elsewhere. I admit, however, that if we had had in force an Act of Parliament such as we now ask the House to pass, the case would have been tried with a different venue. The charge is that the conduct of this prosecution was taken out of the hands of the Law Officers of the Crown under the Liberal Government by delay, and placed in the hands of the Law Officers of the present Government. But, Sir, if the prisoners had been returned for trial at Belfast it would have been absolutely necessary for the Law Officers to have had the case tried at Belfast at the time the riots were going on; and the Law Officers who represented the Government of that day did go down to Belfast for the purpose of conducting these and certain other cases—other cases connected with the riots which had previously been returned for trial. But what did they do? They applied to the Court that each of the cases should stand over to the Spring Assizes upon the ground that the excitement was such that it was impossible to get a fair trial. [Mr. CHANCE: The Court of Queen's Bench made the order, then.] But something more with reference to that— the Law Officers of the Crown, although they applied that the case should stand over to the Spring Assizes, did certainly not seem to be of opinion that when that excitement had cooled down the case could not be properly tried at Belfast. In one of the most serious cases they gave an undertaking that the man should be tried in the County of Down. It is right for me to say that, according to my recollection, justice was done in this case by a County Down Magistrate at the Spring Assizes. [*Interruptions.*] I always make it a rule, while hon. Gentlemen are speaking, to abstain from interrupting them, knowing that I have the right to reply to their statements afterwards. It is very difficult while interruptions take place for anyone but the speaker himself to hear what he is saying, and the effect of the interruptions which have unfortunately been made may be that the reply I have made on the charges of the hon. Gentleman has not been so clear to the minds of some as I desire that it should be. I have now gone through the case of the hon. and learned Member for North Longford (Mr. T. M. Healy). Speaking in the hearing of the Chief Secretary for Ireland, with whom it will rest, I say that if such a state of things as existed in the past existed in Belfast after the passing of this Act, the Government of the day would have ·no hesitation in applying the Act in Belfast in the same way as they would in Kerry. During the 18 months that I have been responsible for criminal prosecutions in Ireland, as far as I am aware, I have not shown the slightest difference as between one party and another. With regard to the action of the Bench of Magistrates in Fermanagh, I did in that case all that it was possible for me to do. In the case of the man whom they would not return for trial, I took steps to have the case investigated a second time, and I regret to say that the result was the same; but my power ended there. The same thing occurred more than once in the South of Ireland, and I took the same course; but again with the same result. If we had had this Bill in force we should have got the persons charged summarily dealt with. But whether it be in Fermanagh or Kerry, I pledge myself that I will not make any difference between one party and another as long as I have this Act to administer.

MR. T. M. HEALY (Longford, N.): The right hon. Gentleman has informed us that so far as he is concerned he will make no difference between parties. On Friday last he stated, and even boasted, that this Act would be retrospective. The Government will have the fullest power of investigation under this clause, and they have already stated that they are looking out for evidence with regard to the Belfast riots. I ask whether, with regard to the crimes committed in the district and which are undetected, the Government really intend to break up the Orange Organization and put it down. That is the subject and purport of my inquiry. The right hon. Gentleman, however, has confined himself to dealing with general matters, on which, of course, it is difficult to make any reply. But let

[*Second Night.*]

me say that the action of the Tyrone juries as reported in the public Press, and described by Justice Lawson, has been of the most disgraceful character. The right hon. Gentleman knows very well in the case of the Donellys, who acted in defence of their own houses, that Justice Lawson charged for acquittal, that the jury refused to agree and the man was tried again; whereas, if the jury had done their duty, the men would have been acquitted. The right hon. Gentleman said he could have taken no other course than that which he took in Walker's case. But, Sir, the right hon. Gentleman has only to go to the Court of Queen's Bench to get them to do all he wants. Am I to be told that the most servile and corrupt Court in Ireland——
[*Cries of* " Order ! " " Withdraw ! "]

THE CHAIRMAN : The hon. and learned Gentleman knows that he must not speak in that way of Courts of Justice. [*Cries of* " Withdraw ! "]

MR. T. M. HEALY : I shall of course withdraw it in this House. When I leave the House I shall speak in the same way. I say that the Court of Queen's Bench in Ireland has never refused any application on the part of the Crown. If the Crown makes a motion it is always granted.

MR. HOLMES : I think I can say that my recollection is that out of five or six applications on behalf of the Crown the motion was refused in every case but one or two.

MR. T. M. HEALY : Will the right hon. Gentleman tell us when those applications were made ?

MR. HOLMES : Twenty years ago.

MR. T. M. HEALY : I admit that it was so at that time. I am referring to the last seven or eight years, and I ask the right hon. Gentleman to give a single instance where the Court of Queen's Bench has refused the motion of the Crown. The only case that I remember was in the case of the " Crown *v.* Boyd." That is the only instance which the right hon. Gentleman can give. I assert that there was a distinct connivance on the part of Her Majesty's Government to cause disorder at Belfast, and I will give as an instance the case of the Orangeman tried for the Monaghan murder, who was caught almost redhanded in the act; who fired the shot, and who, because his mother got up and swore that he fired the revolver before he left

Mr. T. M. Healy

the house, was acquitted. In Belfast you have no necessity to resort to the system of change of venue. You have there your juries ready to hand, and, therefore, Orangemen escape and Catholics are always convicted. We know that has always happened. We ask the Government, with the Report in the Blue Book staring them in the face, whether they intend to put down the Orange disorder in the North as they have stated they will do in the case of agrarian disorder in the South. That is the object of this debate, and I take it we are entitled to an answer on that point. The Government have refused pratically to give any information as to the districts to which this clause will be applied. I am, however, willing to accept the suggestion of the right hon. Gentleman the Member for Mid Lothian (Mr. W. E. Gladstone) to postpone to a later day the exertion of pressure on that point.

THE CHIEF SECRETARY FOR IRE-LAND (Mr. A. J. BALFOUR) (Manchester, E.) : I hope we may now consider that this episode, which, however important it may be, is hardly relevant to the question before the Committee—especially as the hon. Member has accepted the suggestion of the right hon. Gentleman the Member for Mid Lothian—has terminated. The hon. and learned Member who moved this Amendment having accepted the suggestion of the right hon. Gentleman opposite—that the debate should be raised on a later stage of the Bill, I presume that, in doing so, he speaks for those Gentlemen who are sitting near him. I do not intend to reply to the statement of the right hon. Gentleman the Member for Mid Lothian as I should certainly have done had I followed him in debate, except in a very few words. There is no intention on the part of the Government, and there is no power, to extend the meaning of the Bill beyond the words which are laid down within its four corners. The reason why I used the word " disorder " was because it appeared to me at the time that which would best convey my meaning to the House. There are many Members who talk as if Boycotting and intimidation were not crimes. To say to them that the Bill only dealt with crime would, therefore, have been misleading. No one can maintain that they do not constitute disorder; and this is why I added that word to my description of the objects of the measure.

MR. DILLON (Mayo, E.): So far as Members on these Benches are concerned the Amendment has been withdrawn. The discussion which has arisen, as far as I can judge, is entirely owing to the action of the noble Lord the Member for South Paddington (Lord Randolph Churchill).

Amendment, by leave, withdrawn.

Original Question again proposed.

MR. MAURICE HEALY (Cork): The Government ask for this power with reference to crime in Ireland because they allege that evidence with regard to the Commission of crime is, for some reason or other, withheld. Now, I am of opinion that before you give power to the Attorney General to institute the inquiry provided for by the section, he should be satisfied, in the words of the Amendment I am about to move, that, "Owing to intimidation, or other improper cause, evidence in connection with such offence had been withheld." We say that before this power is given, granting the inquiry to be necessary, we should have some guarantee that the machinery placed in the hands of the officials shall not be abused to the harm of individuals. There can be no doubt that an Act of Parliament should be put into words which the Government think clearly embody their meaning, and, therefore, if they have no wish to cause harm to individuals, but only to reach cases where evidence is withheld through intimidation, they can have no objection to the insertion of these words. All we ask is that in the clause it shall be provided that the Attorney General shall not have power to set the provision in motion unless he has satisfied himself that proof exists which makes it necessary to institute the inquiry. The clause is not limited to any class of crimes, it includes all; but we know that a multitude of the cases of ordinary crimes arise as distinct from agrarian crime. No one contends, in those cases, that there is any indisposition to come forward and give evidence, and no one has implied that it exists; and, on the other hand, it has been admitted that the Attorney General should not be able to order inquiry unless he has proof that it ought to be held for the reason assigned. For these reasons, I hope the

Government will accept the very reasonable Amendment which I now beg to move.

Amendment proposed,

In page 1, line 8, after "district," insert "and that, owing to intimidation, or other improper cause, evidence in connection with such offence has been withheld."—(*Mr. M. Healy.*)

Question proposed, "That those words be there inserted."

THE ATTORNEY GENERAL (Sir RICHARD WEBSTER) (Isle of Wight): I can, in a few words, state why it is impossible for Her Majesty's Government to accept this Amendment. I cannot think that the hon. Gentleman remembers that on Friday night we agreed to insert words providing that a sworn information shall be made before the Attorney General for Ireland takes action under the provisions of the Bill. The hon. Gentleman wishes us to say now that the Attorney General shall not act unless he is satisfied that, owing to intimidation or other improper cause, information has been withheld. It amounts to this, that however impossible it may be to obtain evidence, the Attorney General would not be able to act unless he had some evidence before him. The provision with regard to the sworn information will operate as a sufficient safeguard against the powers of the clause being applied where intimidation does not exist. We certainly cannot, for these reasons, assent to the Amendment of the hon. Member for Cork.

MR. MAURICE HEALY: All my Amendment asks is that the information contain a sworn statement that evidence has been withheld through intimidation or other improper cause. It would not be exceedingly unreasonable that before the Attorney General for Ireland could institute an inquiry under the section he should hold a preliminary inquiry. What my Amendment provides is that the Attorney General shall be satisfied, not merely that the offence has been committed, but that a state of things has arisen such as the Government admit to be an indispensable preliminary to the proper use of the powers contained in this clause—that the information which sets the Attorney General in motion shall not merely contain a verification of the fact that an offence has been committed, but shall also contain an allegation made on the sworn testimony of some person on whom he can rely as to the state of things in the district— that owing to intimidation evidence cannot be obtained.

Amendment proposed,

In page 1, line 8, after "district," insert "and that, owing to intimidation or other improper cause, evidence in connection with such offence has been withheld."—(*Mr. Maurice Healy*.)

Question proposed, "That those words be there inserted."

THE ATTORNEY GENERAL (Sir RICHARD WEBSTER) (Isle of Wight): It is impossible for Her Majesty's Government to accept the Amendment, seeing that it has already been provided that the Attorney General is only to take action under the provisions of the Bill in cases where an information has been sworn, which will operate as a sufficient safeguard against those provisions being extended to places where intimidation does not exist.

SIR CHARLES RUSSELL: I do not think that my hon. and learned Friend the Attorney General (Sir Richard Webster) has done full justice to the arguments advanced in favour of this Amendment or to the Amendment itself. The Government do not propose, as I understand, that this is to be a provision which is to be put in operation in every case. They propose it as a provision which they say is necessary on account of several difficulties which are specified. The difficulties are alleged to be in getting evidence on account of people being intimidated, and the Amendment proposes that instead of this being a clause which might, if the Attorney General for Ireland gets a sworn information, apply generally, it shall be restricted to a class of specified cases in regard to which there has been a failure to get evidence. That, I understand, is the argument in support of the Amendment; and the hon. and learned Gentleman the Attorney General endeavoured to meet that by saying this is not workable at all, and is not necessary, because the clause provides, by the Amendment to which the Government agree, that there shall be sworn information. That is no answer to the objection made, and which this Amendment puts forward—

Mr. Maurice Healy

namely, that this sworn information should disclose something more than the commission of an offence, and that all the clause provides is that there shall be a sworn information to the effect that an offence has been committed to which this section applies. Now the section applies, not merely to offences punishable under this Act specifically, but it applies also to felonies and misdemeanours, which means all felonies, and all misdemeanours, and all offences under this Act. If the sworn information, according to the provision of the section, disclosed the existence of those special grounds upon which this particular clause is to operate, and which will be put forward as justification, that would be another matter; but it does nothing of the kind. The sworn information, according to the provision as it now stands and specifies, need not contain anything to show that there are any exceptional circumstances whatever within the district proclaimed which prevent evidence being obtained—which shows that intimidation or anything else prevails to prevent evidence being forthcoming. My hon. and learned Friend the Attorney General has not quite met that contention. I quite agree with the criticism he made upon the wording of the Amendment itself; it would be better if the Amendment ran—"Owing to intimidation or other causes evidence in connection with such offences is not forthcoming."

SIR RICHARD WEBSTER: Mr. Courtney, I want to say a few more words upon this Amendment. It is well the Committee should understand exactly the view the Government take. This clause is to apply to proclaimed districts. The right hon. Gentleman the Member for Mid Lothian (Mr. W. E. Gladstone) has referred to-night to the fact that we may have to discuss what districts shall be proclaimed. Her Majesty's Government will not proclaim any district without cause; they will not proclaim a district unless there are circumstances which make it right for such an inquiry to be held into the terrorism under which the people are living. Therefore, the fact that the clause is limited to a proclaimed district in itself implies that there is a state of circumstances under which it is desirable an inquiry should be held. My hon. and learned Friend the Member for Hackney says that, in addition to that, there should be something like a statement, with the sanction of an oath, that there is intimidation or some other improper cause which prevents evidence in connection with particular offences being forthcoming. In our view, it would not be a right precaution or safeguard to throw around this remedial measure which we think most desirable. I do not want to go now into cases in which these inquiries have been held, and held with advantage to the public in the past; but we certainly do think that, once a district is proclaimed, once the responsible Government has said the condition of a district is such that it ought to be proclaimed, and that this section ought to apply, the discretion should be left to the Executive, to the Attorney General for Ireland, subject only to this precaution—that he shall, before putting the section into operation, be satisfied, on sworn information, that an offence has been committed. The Government cannot agree to the Amendment, nor can we agree to the substance of it, because we consider it would unduly limit the power of the Executive which is responsible for proclaiming the district.

MR. CHANCE (Kilkenny, S.): It is needless for me to say that we cannot admit the validity of the arguments of the hon. and learned Gentleman (Sir Richard Webster). The case the hon. and learned Gentleman has made against the Amendment is simply this. No district will be proclaimed until the Executive Government has come to the conclusion that a state of general terrorism exists in the district. Then the hon. and learned Attorney General maintained that if terrorism does exist in a district, it is reasonable that the Executive power should abandon the ordinary law and resort to extreme powers such as those contained in this Bill. There is a certain lameness in that argument, because the hon. and learned Attorney General would have us believe that, because there is general intimidation in a district, there is general sympathy with every form of crime in the district. Greatly as Conservative Members of this House have maligned Ireland, I do not think any one of them will say that every description of crime is considered lightly in Ireland. I think that the real reason why the Government should, in the pursuance of their present policy,

decline to accept this Amendment is a very simple one indeed. They desire to use 'this weapon, not as a weapon to obtain evidence in cases where it has been withheld, or where it has not been forthcoming, but as a weapon to persecute people in Ireland at the bidding of any Member of the Privy Council, or, what is equivalent, any landlord member of the Constitutional Club. Although they could find plenty of land agents, and others who would be willing to swear anything, they decline to put the tender consciences of these individuals to the test of showing that there is some difficulty in obtaining evidence. The Government desire, on the mere allegation that a crime has been committed in a district, to put this section into force. Under this section as it stands, it will be perfectly competent for the Attorney General for Ireland, on receiving sworn information that an offence has been committed, to order an inquiry, to drag up men even from outside the district, and, if they refuse to answer any question put to them, run them into gaol. I think this Amendment is extremely reasonable. The foundation of this section is that evidence is not forthcoming. We have heard a great deal of the good intentions of the Government; but when they are asked to embody their good intentions in the Bill they refuse. I am forced to the opinion that they intend to use this section at the bidding of any landlord in any district to torture, imprison, and ruin the people.

MR. O'DOHERTY (Donegal, N.): I think the hon. and learned Gentleman the Attorney General (Sir Richard Webster) is a little astray in thinking that this clause is applied to witnesses in proclaimed districts only. That is not so. A witness may be summoned from outside a proclaimed district, if the district in which he resides adjoins any county, part of which is proclaimed. A little area may be proclaimed, and three or four counties may abut upon it. This is a witness's section, putting witnesses to very serious inconvenience, and I think I may fairly say to real torture. It is their case which is to be considered, and not the case of criminals. If the hon. and learned Attorney General really does mean to confine the operation of the section to witnesses in a proclaimed district, it will be absolutely necessary that the section should undergo some alteration. Now, if the Government think that they cannot get men to give a formal opinion, that evidence is not forthcoming on account of the intimidation which prevails, they are grievously mistaken as to the quality of the men they have supporting them in Ireland. They will have no such difficulty. But if this Amendment is accepted, there will be a chance of some one amongst the Government's supporters being honest enough not to swear up to the mark. I am well acquainted with what the effect in many cases of similar provisions to this is, and I do say that unless some precaution of this sort is taken, the same thing which occurred to my knowledge under the Crimes Act will occur again. If the Government do not accept some Amendment, confining in some way the operation of this section, undoubtedly it will be made the vehicle of very considerable oppression. I did not rise to detain the Committee at any length; but I thought it necessary to point out that this is a witness's clause, that it is the case of witnesses that is to be considered, and that the hon. and learned Attorney General for England is quite mistaken if he thinks witnesses are protected by the Proclamation of the Lord Lieutenant.

Mr. ANDERSON (Elgin and Nairn): I venture to think that, so far, the Government have not appreciated the immense importance of this Amendment. We have already seen, from the discussion, that the clause has been drafted in great haste and with a very great want of care. It is rather curious that, in an important Bill of this kind, such blunders should have been committed in the first few lines, occasioning, as they do, greater discussion in the Committee. The hon. and learned Attorney General (Sir Richard Webster) has already admitted the faultiness of the clause by accepting the Amendment as to sworn information. The Amendment now proposed does not carry the safeguard very much further, but its adoption will make people feel safer. The object of having a sworn information was to prevent an abuse of this very extraordinary provision, and I cannot conceive any Criminal Law which ought to be surrounded with greater safeguards than this. This clause simply amounts

to the introduction into the Irish Criminal Law of the Inquisition. It is the first time that it has been introduced permanently into that law. I should like to hear what the hon. and learned Attorney General would say, if it were to be proposed to introduce permanently such an Inquisition into the Criminal Law of this country. What is it that is demanded? It is proposed, and I think most reasonably proposed, that not only should there be a sworn information, but that there should be some inquiry made beforehand—before the sworn information is laid—that there is difficulty in getting evidence. We have not had any information from the Government as to the cases in which similar power, under the Act of 1882, was put into execution. The great danger of a clause of this kind is that it may be used for purposes other than the detection of crime. I can well imagine some unscrupulous official—however guarded you are, it is impossible not to have such people about you—using this power with the greatest cruelty. Now, what were the cases in which inquiries took place under the Act of 1882? We have been told that inquiries took place in 119 cases. I asked in how many cases the inquiries were held after examination? That is a most pertinent inquiry from the very point of view of this Amendment. We are entirely left in the dark on that subject. I think that if an answer had been given, we should have found that out of these 119 cases, probably half of them never ought to have been investigated. I suppose the discussion of this Amendment will take up some time, and that presently the Government will say we are obstructing the Committee. But I cannot understand any more important Amendment being proposed than this, and I cannot understand any Government who have really at heart the introduction of a measure which shall be an improvement to the Criminal Law not desiring that a provision of this kind shall be as little harsh and as little distasteful as possible. I think it is the duty of the Committee to insist upon this Amendment.

Sir WILLIAM HARCOURT (Derby): I really think that this is one of the points upon which the Government might very well have met the proposals that have been made from this side of the House. I cannot think that the hon. and learned Attorney General (Sir Richard Webster) has fully answered the points raised by my hon. and learned Friend the Member for Hackney (Sir Charles Russell). First of all, the hon. and learned Attorney General says that if a district is proclaimed, it follows, as a matter of course, that this power should come into operation. In answer to that, you say that it is not at all a necessary consequence, that there may be reasons quite apart from the difficulty of obtaining evidence which might lead to the proclamation of a district. The right hon. and learned Gentleman the Attorney General for Ireland (Mr. Holmes) has already, this afternoon, told us that with reference to the Kerry Moonlighters he had no difficulty whatever in obtaining evidence and convictions. The men were tried at Cork. Well, but you might have proclaimed both Kerry and Cork, and yet you would have had no difficulty in obtaining the conviction of the men. There is another thing the hon. and learned Attorney General (Sir Richard Webster) has not remarked. He spoke as if this clause only operates in the proclaimed district. That is not so. The moment you have got a district proclaimed, and the offence sworn to upon information, you may force every man in Ireland to attend to give evidence—under this clause upon the mere suggestion that a man belonging to Antrim, Tyrone, Dublin, or elsewhere, knows something about what has happened in Kerry, you may subject him to this exceptional form of examination. The hon. and learned Attorney General has made no observation in answer to that point; therefore, it is quite plain that the operation of this clause is a far wider one than that of the mere proclaimed district. In point of fact, every man in Ireland is subjected to the operation of the clause. It is quite obvious that this is not a small question, but a very large question. What objection can there be to meeting hon. Members in this matter? I am quite certain that if this clause referred to England, we should not feel the difficulty about it we do now. We know very well that in England this clause would not be put into operation unless there were some very strong reasons for it, and that there would be confidence in the administration of the clause. We know that, justly or unjustly, that feel-

ing, generally speaking, would not exist in the greater part of Ireland; therefore, it is necessary to give satisfaction to all reasonable demands. Let me ask what is demanded? You are asked, first of all, that a sworn information should be made as to the crime. The Government admit that—a very proper admission. Well, what objection can you have, having that sworn information, that it should be sworn that you cannot get evidence? You have plenty of people at your command. Having admitted there should be sworn information as to crime, why should you object to having sworn information that a state of things exists which makes it impossible to get evidence without resorting to this section? You cannot, it seems to me, by the adoption of this Amendment impede seriously the administration of justice; whereas, on the contrary, it will give an appearance, at all events, which will satisfy people that this clause, stringent as it is, will not be applied unless there is particular reason for its application. The present proposal seems to be so reasonable that I cannot understand the objection of the Government to accept it.

SIR RICHARD WEBSTER: Mr. Courtney, it certainly is difficult to speak in moderate language when one has to deal with the class of observations the right hon. Gentleman the Member for Derby (Sir William Harcourt) favours the House with when criticizing the proposals of Her Majesty's Government. I have not the slightest objection to meeting fair criticism in the House, and I am perfectly willing, if I am wrong, to admit I am wrong, or if I feel I have put forward something I cannot support, to say so at once. I have been very much surprised that the right hon. Gentleman, who has for years been known, not only to this House, but to England and the world, as a great jurist, who has been a Law Officer of the Crown, who for many years practised the science of the law, should put such arguments before us as he has done during the course of these debates. I do not want to refer to matters that have gone before, on the second reading of the Bill, although I may have to do so on some future stage of the debate; but we heard a great many arguments on Friday last from the right hon. Gentleman in reference to the distinction be-

[Second Night.]

tween the word "offence" and the word "crime," which were answered conclusively by his own Bill of 1882 and by the Preamble of the Bill of 1882.

SIR WILLIAM HARCOURT : Will you read that?

SIR RICHARD WEBSTER : I will with the very greatest pleasure. I will accept the invitation of the right hon. Gentleman. He told us the other night there was a broad distinction between "offence" and "crime"—that "offence" was a mild offence.

THE CHAIRMAN : The discussion is now travelling very wide of the Amendment.

SIR RICHARD WEBSTER : I am sorry, Sir, that I somewhat irregularly accepted the invitation of the right hon. Gentleman. I must go into the question on another occasion. I will now deal with what he has said to-night on this particular Amendment. He has suggested that, in respect to this clause, there should be some such precaution set round the action of the Attorney General as that there should be a sworn statement that, owing to intimidation, or some other cause, evidence is not forthcoming. I wonder whether he remembers the section of his own Bill? Was there, in the Bill of 1882, any precaution of this kind? [Sir WILLIAM HARCOURT : No.] The right hon. Gentleman says "no." Why did he not say so when he was addressing the Committee? Why did he not tell the Committee what was the distinction between 1882 and the present time?

SIR WILLIAM HARCOURT : I will tell the hon. and learned Gentleman. The distinction between 1882 and the present time is the difference between the condition of Ireland at that time and now. [*Cheers.*]

SIR RICHARD WEBSTER : Sir, it is most extraordinary the right hon. Gentleman should think that can pass muster in this House. I am not dealing with the applause which comes from below the Gangway. The right hon. Gentleman's point is that, although in a particular procla med district you cannot get evidence, in some other parts of Ireland you can get evidence with perfect ease, and that, therefore, you ought to put some safeguard round the person who has to put the Act in force. Our clause is certainly justified by the 16th section of the Bill of 1882. By that

section there was exactly similar power given to the Resident Magistrates of Ireland. Although I have no objection to the right hon. Gentleman swallowing his own words as often as he likes, I think that when he attacks this Bill and those who have framed this Bill, and when he insists upon precautions being inserted in this clause, he should, at least, tell us why precautions are required now and why they were not required in 1882. That is not all. Has England ever been proclaimed? Has it ever been necessary to bring in a Crimes Bill for England? Yet, what did the right hon. Gentleman do in the Explosives Bill of 1883—a year later? I do not suppose he remembers it—at any rate, it is very convenient to be able to forget all your own legislation, all your own speeches, all your own arguments, when what you wish to do is to make a Party opposition. I have noticed as a most curious thing that the right hon. Gentleman quotes everybody except himself, and yet there is nobody who has made more powerful speeches on these and kindred subjects than the right hon. Gentleman. I am not going to read the section, but I remind the right hon. Gentleman, and I inform the House, that in the Explosives Act of 1883 there was a section of a much more stringent character than that under discussion, for it said that in every part of the United Kingdom, without affidavit, without any person being charged, without a search warrant being obtained, or anything else, an inquiry of this kind may be set on foot. Neither the Bill of 1882 nor the Act of 1883 made provision for sworn information at all.

MR. T. M. HEALY : The Act of 1882 does.

SIR RICHARD WEBSTER : I am obliged for the correction. The Act of 1882 does, but the Explosives Act of 1883 does not. Of course I cannot hope to convince right hon. and hon. Gentlemen opposite who are of the character of mind possessed and enjoyed by the right hon. Gentleman the Member for Derby; but, at any rate, when we are looking at this clause, and to the proviso that it is thought desirable to enact, I think we may fairly appeal to the House not to go back to a second reading discussion of this Bill. It is idle to suggest that the difference between this clause and the Act of 1882 is to be found in the

Sir Richard Webster

condition of Ireland now and the condition of Ireland then. Once given that
the Preamble of the Act of 1882 was
proved, then Clause 16 of that Act becomes a proper clause—once given that
the Preamble of this Bill is proved, then
this clause that we are discussing is
proved. All I can say is, that willing
as I am, and willing as Her Majesty's
Government are to consider fairly suggestions for carrying out the Preamble
of this Bill, we do object to Amendments
being made, supported by right hon.
Gentlemen opposite, which are totally at
variance with the principles of the Bill,
and at variance with the principles which
he has accepted in measures of his
own. I must say we are driven to the
conclusion that the right hon. Gentleman
does not wish to facilitate the debate
when he makes speeches like that which
we heard from him just now.

SIR CHARLES RUSSELL : We are
only at the beginning of what will be a
long discussion in Committee; and I am
sorry that the hon. and learned Gentleman the Attorney General (Sir Richard
Webster) who, as we all know, is a very
amiable man, should lose his temper,
as it will prevent the Bill being discussed in a fair and judicial spirit. I
must say that my right hon. Friend the
Member for Derby (Sir William Harcourt) spoke in a very calm manner, and
without making any attack or any offensive observations upon anyone. He gave
his reasons, which appeared to me to be
very solid reasons, in support of this
Amendment in a very temperate way,
and his reasons were well worthy of
consideration. If they are answered,
they should be answered in the spirit
in which they were delivered. The
hon. and learned Attorney General, in
answering the arguments of my right
hon. Friend—if answer it can be called,
because his style of meeting the case is
worn threadbare—has referred to the
Act of 1882. Well, as far as I am individually concerned, I disapproved of
the Act of 1882, and I voted against it,
and spoke against it, just as I am voting
and speaking against this Bill; but my
right hon. Friend near me was well
founded in calling attention to the different state of things that existed in Ireland
then, though I do not think his observations justified the measure passed in that
year. But to meet this argument my hon.
and learned Friend the Attorney General

says, that once it is granted upon the
second reading that the principle of a Bill
is proved, then the necessity for the provisions of that Bill follows the proof of
that Preamble. He says this is the case
in regard to the Bill of 1882—so he says
that the Preamble of the Bill now under
discussion is proved, the proving of the
provisions of the Bill also follows. But
my hon. and learned Friend fails to see
a marked distinction between the two
cases. There was a Preamble to the
Act of 1882, and it was—

"That whereas by reason of the action of
secret societies and combinations for illegal
purposes in Ireland, the operation of the ordinary law has become insufficient for the repression and prevention of crime, and it is expedient to make further provision, &c."

Well, I turn to the Bill which my hon.
and learned Friend the Attorney General
regards, I presume, with something like
parental fondness. What is its Preamble? Where is it to be found? It
is not to be found; there is no Preamble
at all. This is the title of the Bill—

" A Bill to make better provision for the prevention and punishment of crime in Ireland,
and for other purposes relating thereto ;"

and straightway it goes on to the enacting part. There is no Preamble whatever. I would call the hon. and learned
Attorney General's attention to another
distinction between the Act of 1882 and
the Bill under discussion. In the first
place the Act of 1882 was not proposed
to be incorporated in the permanent
general Criminal Law of the country.
It was avowed as a temporary measure,
as legislation to meet a temporary condition of things. That Bill was put forward to meet an exceptional case, but
the present Bill of the Government is
part of what is to be their permanent
policy for the management of the affairs
of Ireland. It is not put forward as
necessary to meet a sudden emergency,
to grapple with some exceptional outbreak of crime. The measure is not
resorted to as a "hateful expedient,"
because it could not be avoided
in the nature of things; but it is
to be regarded for the future as part
of the Tory policy for the government of
Ireland. There is another point in the
speech of the hon. and learned Attorney
General to which I would like to refer.
Clause 16 of the Act of 1882 expressly
excluded from its operation a subject
which this Bill relates to, and which will

be found, as we contend, liable to great abuse. Under the 16th section of the Act of 1882, all matters relating to illegal assemblies were excluded.

SIR RICHARD WEBSTER: No, no!

SIR CHARLES RUSSELL: Section 16 provided that where a sworn information had been made that an offence had been committed, any magistrate could summon a person to appear before him, though no one was charged with the offence. If my hon. and learned Friend will look at the 1st sub-section of that Section 16, in the Act of 1882, he will find that an offence for the purpose of that section means—

"Any felony or misdemeanour, and also any offence against this Act, with the exception of the offences specified in Sections 10 and 11."

Now, the offence specified in Section 10 is the case of illegal meetings; while Section 11 deals with the question of the arrest of persons found out at night under suspicious circumstances.

SIR RICHARD WEBSTER: Section 10 deals with meetings prohibited by the Lord Lieutenant as being dangerous to the public peace and safety. Section 8, Sub-section 1, makes it an offence to take part in any riot or unlawful assembly.

SIR CHARLES RUSSELL: I did not say that riot was not within the provisions of that Act.

SIR RICHARD WEBSTER: You said unlawful assembly was excluded.

SIR CHARLES RUSSELL: I gave references to Sections 10 and 11; but perhaps I ought to have said illegal meetings. I thought I had said so, and I think I did. So much for the answer, or rather the attempted answer, of my hon. and learned Friend opposite to the speech of my right hon. Friend near me. I do not think the attempt was at all a successful one. My right hon. Friend says that it would be possible under this section, unless some safeguard is introduced such as is contemplated in this Amendment, to summon persons from any part of Ireland for the purpose of giving evidence with reference to a crime committed in any other part of Ireland; and it is not too much to say that this exceptional power, which even the Government themselves have not sought to justify, except by reference to special circumstances which prevent evidence being forthcoming on the ground of intimidation, ought to be safeguarded by

showing the existence of these causes as justification for the provision. My hon. and learned Friend the Attorney General complains of the opposition to this Bill, and seems to insinuate, without stating it, that this Amendment is of an obstructive character; I deny that it is obstructive; but I do not hesitate to say that I look upon this Bill as mainly and essentially a bad Bill, and that I think it will work mischief; and, thinking that, I feel I should fail in what I consider to be my duty if I did not, so far as I could, resist it and where unsuccessful in resistance endeavour, to the best of my power, to get safeguards introduced into it.

MR. W. REDMOND (Fermanagh, N.): I rise for the purpose of supporting the Amendment of the hon. Member for Cork (Mr. Maurice Healy). I do so because this clause, like the whole of this detestable Bill—which is more detestable to hon. Members for Ireland than it can be to anyone else—provides for what I may call a Star Chamber examination of the people in Ireland. With regard to the hon. and learned Gentleman the Attorney General (Sir Richard Webster), I may say that he is setting a very bad example to Irishmen here by falling into a temper without provocation. If there are men in any section or quarter of this House who ought to be excused for getting into a temper on this Bill, or who have reason on their side for getting into a temper over this Bill, it certainly should be, to my mind, the Representatives of the people of Ireland. I would, therefore, advise the hon. and learned Gentleman not to give way to that restiveness under criticism of this Bill, and not to copy the style of the right hon. Gentleman the Chief Secretary for Ireland (Mr. A. J. Balfour) when dealing with matters affecting Ireland. The Amendment of the hon. Member for Cork simply provides that no person shall be arrested and brought before this inquisition unless there is sworn information to the effect that this is the only way of getting evidence to convict. But the Government mean by this secret inquiry—and they cannot get out of the situation in any other way—that there is intimidation abroad in the district that prevents evidence of the offences being given and causes evidence to be withheld. All the Amendment asks is that a clause might be inserted, or a line might be inserted, in the Bill providing that before men are brought into this Star Chamber to be examined on whatever matter the magistrate likes—it shall be proved before this action is taken that there is intimidation in the district with regard to the crime upon which the person is called upon to give evidence. I do not think anything more reasonable could be proposed in this House. The refusal of the Government to accept this Amendment, to my mind, will be interpreted by the Irish people into a belief that the Government do not want so much to inquire about crime in these secret courts of inquiry in particular places in Ireland, but that they want to have power to examine in secret men of all kinds and descriptions on whatever subjects they may be interested in, or with regard to any matter which the landlords of the district may be interested in. I can conceive nothing more likely than that, in a district where some sort of offence has occurred, men in that neighbourhood for their own purposes trying to get evidence upon a certain matter, will accuse a number of leading politicians in the place and have them brought before the secret court or inquisition, and have them questioned on matters concerning the relations of landlords and tenants. The Bill may be also used in this way. The local landlords and the local magnates may find political agitation in their district very unpleasant, and they in conjunction with the Castle Authorities may wish to get their opponents out of the way.

THE CHAIRMAN: The hon. Gentleman is discoursing at large. He must confine himself to the principle of the Amendment before the Committee.

MR. W. REDMOND: What I was endeavouring to do was to show that if the safeguard contained in the Amendment is not accepted it may be possible for the Government Authorities to have men brought before these secret courts of inquiry on the pretence of their having some knowledge of crime in the neighbourhood, but in reality for the purpose of extracting information on subjects of quite a different nature— information on matters concerning the interests of the landlords. We know what has been done in Ireland, and the Amendment of my hon. Friend, as I take it, is framed for the purpose of providing that no person shall be called

before the secret court of inquiry except persons likely to give evidence in regard to crime, and who would not otherwise give evidence. Now, I do not see why——

THE CHAIRMAN: The hon. Gentleman does not appear to have comprehended the Amendment, to which he is not speaking. The Amendment requires that "it shall be stated that owing to intimidation or other improper cause evidence is not forthcoming."

MR. W. REDMOND: I should wish, Sir, to be in Order, and what I was trying to argue when you interrupted me was that as the Amendment provides that there shall be evidence to prove that evidence cannot be got with regard to an offence in consequence of intimidation. This Amendment is only a safeguard that the court of inquiry will only be called into requisition in cases where it is absolutely clear that the usual mode of getting evidence has failed, or is not available. I do not think that it is at all unreasonable that the Government, before they seek to get evidence in this demoralizing way, in this unconstitutional manner, shall be required to have exhausted all other legitimate methods of getting evidence, and that they shall be in a position to prove before calling this Star Chamber method into play, that it is not possible to obtain evidence in the ordinary course. The refusal of the Government to accept this simple Amendment is nothing more than another proof added to those which they have already given, that they intend not only to give us coercion in Ireland, but to force whatever kind of coercion they like down our throats without any regard to our representations or inclinations in the matter.

MR. BRYN ROBERTS (Carnarvonshire, Eifion): The hon. and learned Gentleman the Attorney General (Sir Richard Webster) has delivered three speeches in opposition to the Amendment without advancing a single argument against the substance of that Amendment. The first time he addressed us he simply objected to the wording of the Amendment as implying a preliminary inquiry which could not have taken place. That was a mistake which was disposed of by the hon. and learned Gentleman the Member for Hackney (Sir Charles Russell), who pointed out that the word "forthcoming" should be substituted for "withheld." When the hon. and learned Gentleman the Attorney General got up a second time the only objection he advanced was that this section would not be put in operation except in a proclaimed district, and that that was safeguard enough. It was then pointed out that that was not a safeguard, inasmuch as the Lord Lieutenant could proclaim a district whenever it appeared to him necessary, and without any crime whatsoever existing. Then the third speech of the hon. and learned Gentleman the Attorney General was to the effect that there was a similar section inserted in the Act of 1882. It therefore comes to this, that the hon. and learned Attorney General supposes that there was some reason against such an Amendment discoverable in 1882, which in his opinion is not discoverable now because he has not stated it now. If there is a reason against it now why does not the hon. and learned Gentleman state it? And if there is no objection to it, and we assume so in the absence of argument, why not have the Amendment in the Act? Probably there was some objection to it in 1882 which is not now stated. The only reason why this section should be adopted at all is that there may be some difficulty in obtaining evidence. Will it be for one moment suggested that this section should be put into operation except on this ground? If this section should not be put into operation except on this ground, why not enact that it shall not be put into operation except on this ground? What is the objection to this enactment? The ground upon which the Act of 1882 was enacted was that there was a serious state of crime then existing in Ireland, and therefore the ostensible ground for it was the unusual amount of crime and disturbance; but it has been expressly stated that this measure has not been brought forward or based on statistics of crime. If this is so, then there is all the more apprehension that the Bill may be used for political purposes—much more ground for this apprehension than there was in the case of the Act of 1882. It has been stated—and I think it has been stated by a Cabinet Minister—that the object of this Bill is to put down the National League in Ireland. It is therefore only reasonable that Irish Members should be jealous as to the application of this Act, and should be careful

Mr. B. Roberts

to see that safeguards should be inserted so as to prevent its being illegitimately used against political opponents, and not for the purpose of repressing crime. I could mention cases in this country where it would be very convenient for us Liberals to have such a power as that contained in this clause; but it would be a bad thing to give such a power to us. There are cases of Boycotting by the Primrose League, which it would be convenient for us to have the power of inquiry into under cover of investigating matters of crime. It would be very advantageous to us to be able to investigate all the operations and workings of the Primrose League. It would be convenient for us to find out how the practice of Boycotting had been applied to shopkeepers, and how the system had been worked by the landlords, who are stated to have given their farms entirely to Church people and Conservatives. It is because it would be possible to abuse powers of this kind and to use them for these illegitimate purposes, that we wish to have the security guaranteed by this Amendment put into the Act. We wish to provide that the only ground upon which the power conferred by the clause in question could be put into operation shall be that of the difficulty of obtaining evidence. Another illegitimate reason for putting this power into operation would be the ascertaining the defence of a prisoner while putting him upon his trial, and without eliciting evidence in his favour. I do not say the Act would be used in this way; but it is only reasonable that we should take precautions to prevent such a thing, and that we should see that this section shall not be put into operation for any purpose except that contemplated by the Legislature when the clause was added to the Act.

MR. P. J. POWER (Waterford, E.): The clause the hon. Member for Cork (Mr. Maurice Healy) wishes to press upon the attention of the Committee is for the protection of witnesses from the insults they would be subjected to if the clause passed in its present form without this safeguard. When the hon. and learned Gentleman the Attorney General for England (Sir Richard Webster) rose to answer the arguments in favour of this Amendment and to answer the right hon. Gentleman the Member for Derby (Sir William Harcourt), we expected that he would demolish those arguments, or, at any rate, that he would endeavour to deal with them. The hon. and learned Gentleman rose in such a heat, however, that he probably lost control of himself. At any rate, I think that everyone will admit that he did not touch the arguments adduced by the right hon. Gentleman in favour of this Amendment, and I think we cannot do better in discussing this measure than to avoid as far as possible the heated method in which the hon. and learned Gentleman addressed himself to the matter. He said that the first information, which merely stated on oath that the crime had been committed, was sufficient, and that the Amendment of my hon. Friend the Member for Cork (Mr. Maurice Healy) was quite unnecessary. Well, Sir, the information on oath that a crime has taken place does not in the least touch the difficulty which the hon. Member for Cork wishes to guard against. The information on oath, as the Bill at present stands, is to state that a crime has taken place; but this does not meet the difficulty which my hon. Friend wishes to lay before the Committee. I think that in dealing with all the provisions of this Bill and with the Amendment, the Committee ought to devote great and serious attention to this matter, because it is now proposed that the terms of this drastic Coercion Bill are to be perpetual. Hitherto, when it has been the duty of any Government to propose a Coercion Act, the measure has always been limited to a certain period; consequently, when we are asked to pass a drastic Coercion Act, not for a period, but in perpetuity, it behoves hon. Gentlemen to be careful to safeguard the interests of the people whom they ask this House to coerce. We on these Benches would wish very much to have some other statement from the Treasury Bench besides that of the hon. and learned Gentleman the Attorney General, in which some reasons might be conveyed to us for rejecting this moderate proposal. The hon. and learned Gentleman the Attorney General did not condescend to give us any reasons for rejecting the Amendment. Now that we see other legal Gentlemen sitting on the Treasury Bench, we have a right to appeal to them on this matter, and I think the least one of them could do would be to rise and give us something, at any rate,

in the nature of a reason against this proposal.

MR. CLANCY (Dublin Co., N.): It seems to me that the arguments in favour of this Bill, and in favour of every clause of it, and the grounds upon which every Amendment proposed from these Benches is rejected are that the clauses of this measure are similar to the clauses in the Act of 1882, as if the Act of 1882 were the perfection of legislation, as if that Act were a just measure required by the necessities of the case. Hon. Gentlemen on the opposite side of the House, of course, do not agree with us; but there is not an Irish Member on these Benches—and I fancy there are now a good number of English Members in agreement with us—who did not regard the Act of 1882 as one of the most infamous measures ever submitted to Parliament. We contended then, and we contend now, that it was not required by the necessities of the day, and that there were provisions in that Act which were simply a disgrace to England, the only thing to be said for it being that it was not so bad as this Bill, and perhaps not quite so bad as some of the great Coercion Bills which preceded it. The answer to the argument that the clause was in the Bill of 1882, is, that two wrongs do not make a right. The argument that the clause was in the Bill of 1882, and that, therefore, without any other suggestion or argument, it is to be taken as a just proposal, is, to my mind, a most preposterous and ridiculous proposition, which would never be listened to for a moment in any Assembly except one prepared to carry this Bill through, whether it be right or wrong. With regard to the taunts which have been addressed to the right hon. Gentleman the Member for Derby (Sir William Harcourt), in regard to his having "swallowed his principles," I should like to know who have most "swallowed their principles" — the Liberal Party, or the Party on the other side who declared, in 1885, that coercion was unnecessary — the Party who coquetted with the Nationalists through the Lord Lieutenant, and who said, if they were supported by the Irish vote, they would go in for Home Rule. The idea of the hon. and learned Attorney General taunting the right hon. Gentleman the Member for Derby with having forgotten his principles is an evidence of an audacity that I should not have thought Members of this House capable of, if I had not evidence of it before my own eyes. What is the reason for rejecting an Amendment like this? Do Ministers really want this House to understand that they want this power of secret inquiry even when witnesses are forthcoming? Perhaps they do. But if they do not, why is it that they have not avowed it up to the present time? One of the pretences upon which they justify this Bill is that evidence is not forthcoming to convict criminals; but when they reject an Amendment of this kind, they confess that they want an inquisitorial power—that they want to confer upon the Executive in Dublin Castle power to act—not upon any sworn or trustworthy information which can be submitted to them—but that they want to act upon the information of Irish landlords, who will sneak up the back stairs of the Castle to confer with them in whispers in order to induce them to protect their interests. The Government want to act upon the whispers of ruffians and villians of this description. This Act would not be so bad if it were not for the fact that it will be used to advance the iniquitous cause of these landlords—these sneaking creatures who hate their countrymen, and who want to deprive them of all the liberty that a free people should possess. Again, it would be all right if these people to whom I am referring had not in Dublin Castle a sympathetic Executive. What will render the absence of this Amendment more than ordinarily unjust is that in Dublin Castle the rack-renting landlords will find sympathy from top to bottom. In Dublin Castle what every one of them whispers will be received as Gospel, and the oaths of the people, in contradiction of such whispers, will be treated as nought. This is what will render this provision, and will render every other provision of the Bill, so exceedingly dangerous. I cannot too strongly impress upon the House this feature of the case, and I hope every opportunity will be seized to make it plain to the English people that this Bill is to be worked, not by an impartial Executive, but by one that is thoroughly partizan, and is determined to be partizan, and will continue to be partizan so long as it can find support in this country.

Mr. Clancy

MR. EDWARD HARRINGTON (Kerry, W.): I make no apology for addressing the Committee upon this Amendment at this period, because I think I speak with some authority upon this question—authority derived from my own criminal knowledge and experience, I myself having undergone imprisonment, accompanied with the luxuries of prison clothes and oakum-picking, for six months under a measure of this kind. When complaints and recriminations are bandied from one side of the House to the other, to me they are not very convincing. I was much struck by an observation of an hon. Friend of mine the other night. Speaking of the readiness with which different Governments adopted a coercive policy for Ireland, he said that whether it was the upper or the nether millstone that did the grinding—whether the Coercion Act was a Liberal or a Tory one—still we were ground all the same. With reference to this Amendment, even if we cannot get our views accepted, still we will stand in the position of making a reasonable demand in regard to every line of the Bill, leaving to the Government the onus of refusing those demands. What do we ask now? We ask, in this Amendment, that where a crime is committed that these ridiculous powers of secret inquisitorial investigation shall not be granted unless there is some reason to believe that an offence has been committed, and that, owing to intimidation, the evidence in connection with it is not forthcoming. I think that is a very fair and a very proper proposition. I had not the advantage of hearing the speech of the hon. and learned AttorneyGeneral (Sir Richard Webster); but it has been reported to me from these Benches, that in that speech he said practically nothing, and that he only indulged in a *tu quoque* argument with the right hon. Gentleman the Member for Derby (Sir William Harcourt). I think we have a right to claim that some Member of Her Majesty's Government shall stand up and tell us what they want by this Bill. Do they want to put down crime? We give them very large power to do that. Do they want where crime has been committed to bring prisoners to justice? You have power to do that in the existing law, and where you have not we give it to you in this Bill, and we concede full power to bring criminals to justice. But you say you want power to examine witnesses—either for or against the accused—secretly. I think this is an unconstitutional demand. It is one that ought to be given only on very solid grounds, and until you have shown that some very great necessity exists for it, you have not a leg to stand on. If intimidation is rife in Ireland, it must be very easy for you to prove it—and that is all we ask for in the Amendment—that you shall prove that crime is rife in a district before you ask for powers of secret inquisition—that you shall show that the people are unwilling to come forward to give evidence against criminals. If you do not do that, it is monstrous to ask for these powers. What will happen at these secret inquiries? Why, the Resident Magistrates—men who have no legal knowledge, except such as will satisfy the present Lord Lieutenant of Ireland—and I am of opinion that it is a very meagre amount of legal knowledge that will satisfy him—such Resident Magistrates may put to witnesses any questions they like. They may ask a man whether the moon is made of green cheese, and where, for certain philosophical or other reasons, the witness declines to answer the question, they may send him to prison for an indefinite period. Magistrates, it is said, have at the present time power to commit a person for not giving an answer, but that is not so much the question. The question really is the amount of power the magistrate is to have to originate inquiries. His legal knowledge, or the construction of his mind, may not be perfect—and yet, under the Act, you are going to have no check upon him. On that question, if it is to be asked, he himself is the sole judge and the only authority to commit the witness if he refuses to answer. Bearing always in mind the serious fact that in a disturbed district a person who goes before a tribunal and comes out in a mysterious way is set down, more or less, as a marked man, I think you should grant to us that there shall be proof that in those districts there is such intimidation as warrants you in taking the powers under the clause. We only ask that, before you take to yourselves power of bringing every man, woman, and child into the secret chamber of the magistrate—before you take power to examine them on every act of their lives, every act of association and intimacy — you should prove, not merely that there has been crime committed in the district, but that you should also prove that the state of disorganization is such that the people do not sympathize with the law, and that they are willingly shielding the criminal, and that evidence is not forthcoming. I say we have a right to insist, within the prescribed limits of debate here, that there should be an answer to this argument from the Government Bench. Why is it the Government will not answer these words? Let them stand up and tell us why they refuse to insert the provision which my hon. Friend proposes, that this secret inquiry shall only take place when it is proved that there is need for it. We want it proved that there is sympathy with the criminal, not before you punish crime, but before you adopt this secret method of procedure. I think we are entitled to an answer on that point, and that before we get much further we shall obtain it.

Notice taken, that 40 Members were not present; Committee counted, and 40 Members being found present,

MR. COX (Clare, E.) said: I cannot understand why the Government do not accept the Amendment of my hon. Friend the Member for Cork (Mr. M. Healy). It seems to me that the Amendment is a very reasonable one—that the Attorney General should be satisfied that, owing to intimidation or other improper cause, evidence has been withheld before this mysterious inquiry is instituted. It is very easy for the Government to prove that intimidation exists, if it does exist; and we consider that this clause should be safeguarded by the Amendment of my hon. Friend, which will do something to remove from the minds of Members of this House and the people of Ireland the impression that the Bill is aimed at the political opponents of the Government, and not at crimes?

MR. MURPHY (Dublin. St. Patrick's): I think, in refusing the Amendment of my hon. Friend, the Government are themselves responsible for the delay which may take place in discussing this point further this evening. The Government ought, in my opinion, readily to admit an Amendment which, while it

[*Second Night.*]

explains their meaning, is some measure of protection that this clause shall not be put in force improperly. The fact that there has been intimidation can very easily be explained, and I cannot understand why the Government persist in refusing to accept our proposal intended to secure that this provision shall be fairly worked.

Mr. M. J. KENNY (Tyrone, Mid): As far as I can judge, the position of the Government on this point is that they have, by refusing to accept this Amendment, smashed their whole argument for the passage of the Bill. It is really on the prevalence of intimidation throughout the whole of Ireland that their argument for the Bill is based. If intimidation and undue influence exist all through Ireland, as has been contended by the Government for the last four or five weeks, the words proposed to be introduced by my hon. Friend would have no practical effect whatever on the working of the Act; because although the words may seem to be a limitation of the powers of the clause, if the contention of the Government is correct, there would be no limitation in practice. The words amount to this, that the Attorney General for Ireland shall satisfy himself that, owing to intimidation or improper influence, evidence has been withheld. I need not point out that if intimidation is so widespread as the Attorney General for Ireland says it is, the introduction of the words would not act as a real limitation of the powers in this Bill. But the right hon. Gentleman knows very well, and everyone connected with the Government knows, that there is no such thing as general intimidation, except that exercised by the landlords. The original contention of the Government is fallacious in every respect, and they are aware that under examination it entirely falls to pieces. We ask that the Government should satisfy themselves that they have proof that there is intention to interfere with the ends of justice before they resort to the measure which is proposed; and I say it would be an abuse of government in this or any other country were that precaution not taken. In Scotland this species of inquiry is only applied to cases of major crime; whereas in Ireland it is proposed to be applied to every crime constituted by this Bill. I do not see why the Govern-

ment should refuse to accept this Amendment, unless, as I have pointed out, they have utterly given up the whole case on which they found the Bill. Of course, if they have abandoned their position, then I admit that they are consistent in rejecting the Amendment. What has been our experience? We know that a clause similar to this was applied in Ireland to the persecution of many innocent persons by the permanent Heads of Departments. They are the same to-day as they were then, with the exception of Sir Robert Hamilton, who has been run out simply because he was a moderate man, and his place has been taken by a military person, who will probably be replaced by the Under Secretary for Ireland (Mr. King-Harman), or some notorious and rabid Orangeman. The clause will be in the hands of the permanent officials. It is because of that, and because it will not be applied to the honest detection of serious crime, but to the purpose of continuing excessive rents in Ireland and to purposes even more unjust, that we wish to insert these words; and it is because the Government have no intention whatever of asking for this clause for the purpose of detecting real crime, but for defeating their political opponents by these underhand means, that they refuse to accept it.

Mr. CHANCE (Kilkenny, S.): We have been discussing this clause at very considerable length, and although this Amendment has been spoken against by eminent lawyers on the Treasury Bench, I wish to state that no really intelligent reason has been given for declining to accept this Amendment. It was the Attorney General for England who struck the key note, that we should have unlimited confidence in the Lord Lieutenant, and that when he proclaimed a district the mere fact that this was done was conclusive evidence that everyone in the district was a rascal or assassin. I have pointed out, that although a district may be disturbed or proclaimed, it does not follow that the people in that district would have sympathy with all crime. The sworn information might disclose crime or offences which every individual in the district might reprobate, and under the clause the Attorney General would be in a position to drag everybody in the county before a magistrate, if they do not give as much evidence as is wanted.

That is a very alarming state of things. But they were not satisfied with ending there; they harked back to the old Crimes Act of 1882, and asserted that similar powers were included in that Act. Now there is a very great distinction between the provision of the Act of 1882 and the provision of this Bill as to the procedure for setting on foot this special inquiry. In the Act of 1882 you will find that this inquiry is set on foot by sworn information made and handed to any Resident Magistrate, and then the Act goes on to say that upon the sworn information the Resident Magistrate might summon and examine witnesses whom he believes to be material witnesses concerning the offence. I need not point out to the five eminent legal Gentlemen now sitting on the Treasury Bench what the meaning of "may" is here. A Resident Magistrate is a judicial functionary, and you say he may do certain acts, which means that he shall. In 1882, upon the information of any individual the Resident Magistrate really should call before him any material witnesses whom he found within his jurisdiction. The position in this Act is entirely different, because here the information is to be handed to the Attorney General, a gentleman who is not a judicial functionary, but who will have it in his discretion to say whether he shall or shall not direct the Resident Magistrate to hold an inquiry. I also desire to point out the distinction as to the method of proclaiming a district. Now, in the Act of 1882, we find that a Proclamation could only be made upon specific allegations that there had been crime and outrage. But in this case it will be in the power of the Lord Lieutenant to proclaim any district upon no allegation whatsoever, but upon his own opinion that it would be wiser and better for the district to be proclaimed. Not having the safeguard as to the power of proclamation we are entitled, I think, to have the safeguard we now suggest. It has been argued *ad nauseam* that this Bill is necessary owing, first, to the existence of crime; and, secondly, to the existence of widespread demoralization and intimidation. If intimidation does exist, and if this clause is only necessary for intimidation, surely it would be only common sense and reason not to put this clause into force until you

have got at least one individual to swear there is widespread intimidation. I do not think that it is a real safeguard that some individuals should be called upon to swear. I have no doubt that you will find scores of land-agents, bailiffs, emergency men, and members of the Irish Patriotic Union who will most readily swear there is a widespread intimidation, but at least we should have this safeguard, that if they do swear they can be pilloried in this House and the public Press as liars and scoundrels. The least we are entitled to ask is that when this clause, which gives most drastic powers, is put into force, we should have some individual charged with the responsibility of putting it into force, some individual whose name would be before the public, and who could be dealt with in the public Press and in this House. The Government do not desire that; they desire that some gentleman, slinking about the Constitutional Club, should say to the Attorney General— "There are a number of tenants who are not paying their rents, and an inquiry ought to be held." If these powers of secret inquiry were given to men like Plunkett, there is not the slightest doubt they would be used most drastically. That is what we desire to prevent. We desire that any proceedings putting this section into force must be taken in the light of day. If the Government has any real belief in the existence of intimidation they can have no objection whatever to accept this Amendment. They will not accept it, however, and why? Because they know there is no real intimidation in the country. What did Inspector Davies, of Castleisland, one of the worst districts in Ireland, say before Lord Cowper's Commission? He said—

"Intimidation is very rife, but there are only two persons who are seriously interfered with owing to it."

It is quite evident the Government mean to use these powers against their political opponents, and this Amendment, at any rate, has had the good effect of showing the falsity and the hollowness of the arguments put forward on a previous occasion in favour of this Bill. One by one we have seen their arguments torn to shreds; our observations will go to the public, and we have no fear but what the public

[*Second Night.*]

will deal between us fairly and justly. For that reason I hope the debate to-night will be continued until the Government give us some more honest, more straightforward, or, at least, intelligible answer to this Amendment.

Dr. COMMINS (Roscommon, S.): The object of this Bill, or of this clause, is the detection of crime. Let us see what grounds the Government can have for refusing this Amendment. We contend that however good the evidence of the Government may be, however much the framers of this Bill may have directed it against crime, it will be used for other purposes; for the purpose of collecting debts, for the purpose of intimidation, the very thing they say now it is to remedy —for the purpose of intimidating, especially the peasant class, and for the purpose of breaking up combinations, whether economic, social, or political, rather than for the purpose of the detection of crime. We are told we must have unlimited confidence in the honour of the Lord Lieutenant or the Attorney General for Ireland. Of course, where a Constitutional Government exists, not only in form but in reality, there is unlimited confidence in the honour, integrity, and patriotism of the Executive from the highest to the lowest branch of it. But the very fact that there is that confidence in the Executive, and in the honour of the servants of the Executive, does not prevent their power being hedged around by the law in every way, so that if they should go wrong there should be a check preventing them going far wrong. However you may trust the administration of the Executive, you should have checks to prevent them going wrong. I want to know why it is the Government object to have this check upon the improper and unconstitutional use of these very drastic powers which it is proposed to grant to the Attorney General for Ireland and to the Resident Magistrates? Let us see how these powers may be used. The clause may apply to an offence of any kind, the pulling down of a garden wall, or the burning of four or five pennyworth of hay, cattle trespassing on the highway—anything may be considered an offence, and dealt with under this clause. Wherever it is wanted to interfere with the organization of the people, wherever it is wanted to put on the screw so as to enforce the collection of rents, wherever it is wanted

to get at the secrets of the tenants, an offence will be ready to turn up. There are people in Ireland who will create offences—a person who wants to put this section in motion has nothing to do but to write a threatening letter to himself and nail it up on his own door—as one man was caught in the act of doing—and then go to the Resident Magistrate the next morning and claim that this clause shall be enforced. Let us take an ordinary case of crime. As the Bill stands at present, unless there is some check against the abuse of this power, it may be used, although the police in the neighbourhood, and the Resident Magistrates in the neighbourhood, may have ample evidence as to who has committed a particular offence. There is nothing to prevent a sworn inquiry being held with the sole object of exercising a terrorism over the whole people of a neighbourhood. I cannot see what loss or damage would be done to the administration of the law by the small delay which the adoption of the precautions recommended would entail. It would be a delay in the interest of justice, fair play, and the good name and the good character of the neighbourhood, and would conduce to no mischief whatever, or in any way prevent the detection and the final punishment of crime. There is another consideration which I wish to advance. The whole history of Irish agrarian crime brings out the fact very prominently that agrarian crimes are not committed by the persons residing in the neighbourhoods where the crime is committed. Every Special Commission reveals that Castleisland is acknowledged to be one of the most disturbed districts of Ireland; but even there, if we may judge from previous agrarian disturbances, it is quite possible that the offences which have been committed have been committed by people from a distance, by people coming, possibly, 50 or 60 miles. In a case of that sort let us see what an advantage it would be to have some breathing time. Let the authorities make inquiries, and see whether or not there is reason to suppose that the real criminals were people belonging to the proclaimed districts. Suppose—and the supposition is not only a feasible one, but a very likely one in a great many instances to be correct—suppose the man who maimed cattle, or fired into a house, came from a

Mr. Chance

considerable distance, what would be the result? For an offence of which every person in the district would be innocent, the district would be subjected to this inquisitorial proceeding, which would spread terror among innocent men and do nothing to detect crime.

THE CHAIRMAN: I have failed for some time to see the connection of the hon. Member's remarks with the Amendment before the Committee.

DR. COMMINS: I did not think my arguments were going too wide, Mr. Courtney; but I will, of course, bow to your decision. I was just about to point out one evil that would follow from the non-adoption of this Amendment. It is this, that it will be in the power of the evil-disposed of any neighbourhood to turn on this inquisition with all its persecutions and invidious accessories upon a perfectly innocent district. Under these circumstances, I submit that this Amendment is a very proper one, and unless it is adopted, or something equivalent to it is adopted, the efficiency of the Act will be greatly curtailed.

Question put.

The Committee *divided:*—Ayes 110; Noes 206: Majority 96.—(Div. List, No. 104.)

MR. HENRY H. FOWLER (Wolverhampton, E.): I would propose, on page 1, line 8, to leave out "he," and insert "the Attorney General for Ireland." This is a small consequential Amendment.

Amendment proposed,

In page 1, line 8, leave out "he," in order to insert "the Attorney General for Ireland."—(*Mr. Henry H. Fowler.*)

Question, "That the word proposed to be left out stand part of the Clause," put, and *agreed to.*

Question, "That those words be there inserted," put, and *agreed to.*

MR. T. M. HEALY (Longford, N.): There is another consequential Amendment. I want to know what is to become of the word "may?" It seems to me that there was some little protection for us in these words as they originally stood; but now, as the clause is altered, it may not be necessary even for the Attorney General to have his inner consciousness satisfied. The moment he gets this power, he may act. I do not

know where the words would now follow, but it seems to me that the Attorney General should have satisfied himself that this thing is clearly the case. "May" is always read in these Acts as "shall," and the word "may" will be taken as mandatory. I think I am right in that. That being so, the moment the sworn information is laid, the Attorney General will be bound, as I understand it, to direct this inquiry. I think it would be well to insert, instead of "may," the words "the Attorney General, if he is satisfied or thinks fit, may," leaving it to the personal decision of the right hon. and learned Gentleman. I do not think that is too much to ask. Therefore, I trust the Government, now or on the Report stage, will give us some guarantee that the words I have proposed shall be substituted.

MR. A. J. BALFOUR: We think the word "may" covers the contention of the hon. and learned Gentleman opposite; but we have no objection to add after the word "may," "if he think fit," if the hon. and learned Member desires it.

Amendment proposed, in page 1, line 8, after "may," insert "if he think fit."—(*Mr. T. M. Healy.*)

Question, "That these words be there inserted," put, and *agreed to.*

MR. MAURICE HEALY: I think the decision the Committee has just come to, rejecting the Amendment which was under discussion for some time, makes this Amendment I now propose still more necessary. We in this part of the House consider, when Parliament confers on an Irish Executive such enormous powers as those contained in this section, that some form of restriction ought to be imposed with the object of giving protection to the general public living in Ireland against an abuse of these powers. Now, the Committee has just decided that it will not require that before the Attorney General puts this machinery into motion some credible person shall have sworn in effect that there is some necessity for the exercise of the powers contained in the clause. The Committee having come to that decision, it appears to me to be more and more necessary that this matter should not be left on the unchecked initiative of the Irish Attorney General, an individual who, necessarily,

[*Second Night.*]

from his origin and Office, is more or less of a partizan, and that before he can move in the matter he should have the authority and sanction of some judicial tribunal in Ireland. I, therefore, propose that, instead of leaving this power to the mere initiative of the Irish Attorney General, leaving it to him to institute this inquiry or not, as he thinks fit, that the matter should rest with no official of that kind, but should rest with one of the constituted Courts of Ireland, to whom the Attorney General should apply, in the first instance, with the object of obtaining its sanction before he puts the machinery given by this section into operation. Now, I quite concede that if we on this side of the House were able to look upon the provisions of this Bill from the same point of view as Gentlemen sitting on the Front Treasury Bench, that none of these restrictions and none of these protective provisions, which we are now endeavouring to insert, would be necessary. I quite concede that if we could look upon the Irish Executive, and on their *employés* in Ireland, with the same confidence and the same opinions generally as Gentlemen sitting on the Treasury Bench, the proposals we are now making would be groundless; but, unfortunately, we do not share the confidence in themselves and their officials which the Government seem to entertain. When we get up and move Amendments to this Bill we are told that the powers contained in this clause and in this Bill will not be abused. We are told by the Irish Secretary that this Act will be exercised impartially. We are told that these powers will be used equally towards all sections of the community, and that they will not be used to harass or oppress any individual or any Party in Ireland. We know from experience, unfortunately, however, that whatever may be in the minds of the officials in this House who give us these declarations, that when the Act comes into force and these powers can be put into effect in Ireland, the hands that wield them are not those of the officials who give us these pledges in this House, but are those of the permanent officials in Ireland, who are utterly unamenable to Parliamentary criticism, and over whom we have no sort of check. It is all very fine for the Irish Secretary to tell us that this Act will be administered im-

partially. I have no doubt in the world that when he says that he means it, and I have no doubt if he personally supervises every little detail of Irish administration, that, perhaps, we would have some hope that the Act would be well administered; but we know perfectly well that the Irish Secretary is, except on matters of policy, the mere mouthpiece of the Irish Administration. We know that, in all matters of detail, and that in regard to all practical working of the Executive Government in Ireland, the permanent officials in Ireland hold the strings, and it is their hands which run the machine. We know very well that the Irish Secretary has little more to do than to defend their action in this House when it is impeached on the Irish Benches. That being so, we must be excused if we refuse to accept the declarations of the Irish Officials in this House; and if this Act is going to be administered impartially, in the same unhesitating system as, perhaps, hon. and right hon. Gentlemen might expect, well, we have our own ideas as to how this Act is going to be wielded. We derive those ideas not from any speculative opinions of our own, but from the experience of several past Coercion Acts which have been enforced in Ireland during the past half-dozen years; and we shall, therefore, have to act on the opinions formed on our past experience rather than on the declarations made from the Front Tory Bench—declarations made in this instance, as they have been made in the past by Gentlemen occupying the same position, only to be disregarded when the check of the Parliamentary Session ceases to operate, and the officials in Ireland get the Act into their hands to work it. That being so, we have to look out for some check on the action of the Irish Attorney General; and I do not think, whatever may be the opinion of the Government on the policy of the Amendment itself, that if we are to seek a check of this kind it is suggested that any more reasonable check can be imposed than that which I have proposed in the Amendment—namely, the sanction of a Superior Court to an inquiry of this kind before it is held. Well, now, we may be told that the Irish Attorney General may be safely entrusted with the powers which will be conferred upon him by this clause, and that he is not likely to abuse

Mr. Maurice Healy

these powers. We may be told that so important a functionary as the Attorney General for Ireland is not likely to be swayed by passion or influenced by prejudice, and that he may be relied upon fairly and impartially to exercise the powers granted by this section. But, before we can accept that view of the matter, we must examine into some of the past actions of the present Attorney General. Let me take a case. Let me suppose that a particular offence has been committed in Ulster, and let me suppose that it seems good to the Irish Nationalists to hold a meeting in that part of Ireland. Supposing that a declaration on the part of the Nationalists to hold that meeting is met by a declaration on the part of the Orangemen that they will also hold a meeting, a counter demonstration likely to lead to disturbance; and suppose they carry out their declaration, and the Orangemen do hold their meeting; and suppose, in consequence of such action, that policemen and other people are shot down, and outrages in various forms are committed by the Orangemen. Let us suppose that some lives are lost in consequence of such action on the part of these people. What comes of this when we look at the action of the Attorney General in a case of this kind, when we remember what has been the action of the present Attorney General in a cognate matter? We know that when a contingency of that kind arose before that the Irish Attorney General, who no doubt did not hold Office at that time, but who had held Office, and who may hold Office again—we know that, so far from condemning, as he should have done, the action of the Ulster Orangemen, he declared when, in consequence of this action one unfortunate man lost his life at the hands of the police, that the blood of this young man lay on the head of Lord Spencer, who was then Lord Lieutenant of Ireland. What I say is this, that officials who speak, and think, and act as the present Attorney General acted in cases of that kind should not have confidence reposed in them—we cannot feel confidence that such enormous powers as those contained in this section will be fairly and impartially worked if conferred upon them. Therefore it is more and more necessary, before an official of that kind gets into his hands the tremendous machinery

that this clause will place at his disposal, he should first obtain the authority and sanction of one of the constituted tribunals of the land on a case made by him for the purpose. It is all very well for the Attorney General to get up and tell us in this House that he is not an Orangeman, and that he has never known an Orangeman. Why, of course the right hon. and learned Gentleman is not an Orangeman. If he were, he would seriously stand in the way of his promotion. No Government with any decency could appoint an Orangeman as a Judge, and therefore the fact that the right hon. and learned Gentleman is not an Orangeman does not tell at all in this matter. The question is—has he or has he not Orange sympathies? And we believe, judging from statements out of his own mouth, that he has such sympathy, and that holding such sympathy he cannot in any sense be regarded by us as anything but a partizan, a party man holding strong views on matters of public policy, and not at all to be regarded in the light of a judicial functionary. Now, can any objection be taken to the change I put in with regard to the judicial authority? I do not propose that the Attorney General shall ask the sanction of any hostile body. I do not propose that he shall have to get the sanction of any body of persons who are likely to look with disfavour upon any proposal he makes. I propose that the veto on his action should be vested in the Judges of the land—gentlemen whose praises right hon. Gentlemen on the Treasury Bench are never tired of sounding, and against whom as the persons wielding this authority no objection can be urged with any degree of decency from that quarter of the House. If the Attorney General for Ireland can make out a proper case for the exercise of the powers of this section there can be no possible contention that the Courts of Justice in Ireland, in whom my Amendment would vest a veto on this question, would in any way throw obstacles in the way of the right hon. and learned Gentleman, or make the administration of this section difficult. The Judges, as we must assume in a matter of this kind, would be exceedingly likely to view with favour and to assist and facilitate in every way the action of the right hon. and learned Gentleman on this point of setting this machinery in motion, and in that aspect of the matter, at any rate, no conceivable objection can be taken to the form of the Amendment. That being so, I would really press on the Government the propriety of considering whether this or some Amendment conceived in a similar spirit should not be accepted. Looking at the matter from every point of view, I, myself, cannot suggest any valid reason or objection which could be urged against my proposal. It cannot be urged that the application to a Court would in any way prejudice the Attorney General, or would in any way tend to militate against the success of the inquiry that was afterwards held. All that the Amendment proposes to do is to require that before the right hon. and learned Gentleman sets these enormous powers in motion, he should go to a Court of Justice and make out his case, and that the Judges of the High Court should judge whether the holding of such an inquiry is a necessary or a proper thing to do. Now, it was urged in reply to the case we endeavoured to make out from the last Amendment I proposed to the House that the mere fact that a district had been proclaimed by the Government was of itself a *prima facie* proof that inquiries, such as this section proposes to hold, were a necessity, and that it might be necessarily inferred from the fact that a district had been in that manner proclaimed, that an offence was committed in that district, that it was unlikely or impossible that evidence would be forthcoming to convict the person charged with the offence and to bring him to justice. Let me point out what I pointed out before, that however just that argument is as to the offences that might be likely as it is alleged to excite sympathy amongst certain classes of the population, that no such case can be made out against offences of a non-agrarian character. It cannot be contended that if somebody's pocket is picked, or somebody's house is broken into by burglars, or some other offence of that kind is committed, that the inference will be that it has been done by a Moonlighter, and that the act is accompanied with agrarian sympathies. It cannot be alleged that in a case of that kind, free from the taint of an agrarian character, there would be the smallest obstacle thrown in the way of getting evidence by the people, and it

cannot be alleged that a person concerned in a matter of that kind—that is to say, any person made the victim of an offence of that kind, would have the smallest hesitation in coming forward to give evidence. That being so, is it not in the highest degree oppressive to confer on an irresponsible official like the Attorney General power to make an inquiry under this section in a case of this kind? It would not be of the smallest advantage to hold such an inquiry, and no results of a useful character could possibly follow. Hold your inquiry by all means in cases where you have reason to think that from intimidation or other possible cause, that which you fear is likely to happen—namely, that evidence will not be forthcoming; but, unless you can make out a case of that kind, and unless it can be shown that there is some hesitation on the part of persons coming forward to give evidence, or, unless it is shown that there is combination amongst the people against coming forward to bring offenders to justice, I hold that it is inexpedient to hold inquiries of this kind. We have been frequently referred to the Scotch law. We have been referred to it as a justification of the present proposal of the Government, and we are told that when powers of that kind exist in Scotland, in the Scotch law, it is not an unreasonable thing for these powers to exist in respect of Ireland. Well, it has been shown very effectually that that is not a valid argument, and that this power, even if it really exists, is not practically in operation in Scotland. But that consideration is not relevant to the Amendment I am moving. What is relevant is that under the Scotch law, as I understand, and as I have been able to obtain information, the proceeding is strictly analogous to the proceeding I propose in the present Amendment. As I understand it, before this process can be put in force in Scotland, the authority of some judicial officer has to be obtained. No inquiry can be held without such sanction. No official in Scotland has taken on himself the complete and absolute power of holding an inquiry of this kind without regard to the sanction of any judicial Court. As I understand it, in Scotland, before you can use this power of holding a secret inquiry, you have to obtain the sanction of some constituted Court of Law. You have to obtain that sanction on a case made out for the purpose. When it is said, therefore, that in passing this clause the Government are only extending to Ireland legislation which already exists in Scotland, and that this Amendment of mine is not necessary, we may retort— "If you wish to give us this law, give it to us as it exists in Scotland. Do not give us your version of it. Do not give us the Scotch law diluted through the mind of the Attorney General, altered to suit the wishes of the Government." If the Government wish to obtain the benefit of their argument derived from the Scotch law, let us, at least, in Ireland have the protection which the Scotch law gives to the Scotch people. Let this power be vested in the Executive in Ireland as it is in Scotland; let the law do for us in Ireland what it does for you in Scotland; take this power out of the hands of irresponsible officials and vest it in a Court of Justice. I have very little hope that the Government will accept this Amendment having regard to the manner in which Amendments are uniformly received from this quarter of the House, no matter how they are moved, or by what arguments they are supported—I have no great hope that they will be disposed to view this Amendment with any exceptional favour or with any more favour than they have extended to other Amendments. But I do appeal to hon. Gentlemen who permit themselves to be influenced by the declarations of the Government to the effect that the proposal they are making in this clause is simply to extend to Ireland a law which already exists in Scotland—I do appeal to them to see, when Scotch procedure is transferred to Ireland, that it is carried out as it is in Scotland, and that the same protection shall be given to us in Ireland that the Scotch public have in Scotland under that law as it exists there. It has been pointed out, and has been pointed out very properly, that the persons we are seeking to protect by this Amendment of ours are not the persons who commit the offences, but are witnesses against whom these powers may be used oppressively. We have had, as I have already pointed out, some experience of the way in which Irish officials act in matters of this kind, and when we study the action of the local magistrates in the

exercise of those powers conferred upon them by the Crimes Act, we cannot come to any other conclusion than that these powers were abused in many instances. They were wantonly set in motion, and, in nine cases out of ten, their being set in motion led to no possible good result. That being so, we do ask that before powers of this kind are again placed in the hands of these gentlemen, that the Legislature shall at any rate impose some small check on the action of those officials, and that this House shall be satisfied before they hand over these powers to the Irish Executive that some protection is provided for the benefit of witnesses against whom the powers may be oppressively used. It has been pointed out that the powers may be used not only against witnesses living in a proclaimed district, but against witnesses living outside that proclaimed district; in fact, against witnesses living anywhere in Ireland; and this being so, I ask is it unreasonable that before the Irish Attorney General shall be allowed to put these powers in force, he shall at any rate go before a competent authority and get the sanction of that authority for what he is going to do. If we could be even satisfied that the Attorney General himself would investigate every case before putting these powers in motion, we might in that case be content with whatever protection his personal supervision could give us; but we know very well that the Attorney General in this matter will simply act on the unchecked suggestion of the local magistrates or other local officials who put him in motion. We know that the duties of the Attorney General are such that it would be out of his power to investigate every case that came before him and to make the proper inquiries before he puts these powers or any other powers into operation. We know very well that the Attorney General has simply to take the word of the permanent officials in Ireland, and that in issuing his fiat for the holding of an inquiry of this kind we shall not have in reality the authority of the Attorney General at all, but the authority of some magistrate in the country who had set him in motion. We ask that that should not be allowed, and that if the Attorney General wants these powers, he should go to a tribunal who can investigate his demand and inquire for themselves whether there is any necessity for the exercise of these powers, and whether it is or is not expedient that they should be granted. We say that, in asking for that, we are asking for very little indeed; and I contend that if these powers should be handed over without check or control to the permanent officials in Ireland, this House should have some other check to give protection to the persons who may be arrested and harried by the exercise of these powers. I beg to move the Amendment which stands in my name.

Amendment proposed,

In page 1, line 8, after "may," insert "apply to the High Court for an order directing an inquiry under this section, and thereupon the Court may, if satisfied that an offence has been committed as aforesaid, and that owing to intimidation or other improper cause, evidence in connection with such offence has been withheld, make an order accordingly, and may."—(*Mr. Maurice Healy.*)

Question proposed, "That these words be there inserted."

THE SOLICITOR GENERAL (Sir EDWARD CLARKE) (Plymouth): The hon. Gentleman has thought it necessary to make a somewhat long speech in support of his Amendment; but I think I shall be able in a very few words to show the Committee that it is an Amendment that we cannot be reasonably asked to accept. It is proposed in this Amendment that application shall be made to the High Court for an order directing an inquiry under this section, and that if the Court is satisfied that an offence has been committed and that evidence is withheld, they may make an order accordingly. It is on these two conditions —namely, that an offence has been committed, and that owing to intimidation or other improper cause, evidence is being withheld—being proved to its satisfaction that the Court is to make an order. It will be observed that provision has already been made by an Amendment requiring sworn information to strengthen this case. Sworn information is now required, and that sworn information will be the only information upon which a Court or anybody can be satisfied that an offence has been committed, so that the precaution the hon. Member desires to take is already taken. And then as to the other point—where there is intimidation or other improper cause and evidence in connection with the offence is being withheld, the matter

has been discussed and decided already this evening. The Committee have refused to require that the Attorney General shall have before him proof that owing to intimidation it is impossible to obtain evidence. It would be most unreasonable now, I say, that a Court should be required to find satisfactory evidence which the Committee decided about an hour ago the Attorney General should not require before taking action. I would like to point out to the Committee as the matter stands now, how generally unreasonable and contrary to the object of this Bill this Amendment would be. In the first place, the Amendment would be no real safeguard to anybody. The application to the Court is an *ex parte* application. It must be. There is no person to whom any notice can be given. No person can appear before the Court to show cause against the order asked for, and, therefore, it would be an *ex parte* matter, on affidavits that have been previously before the Attorney General with regard to this point. The only effect would be that there would be delay in consequence of having to make the application to the Court, and there would be of necessity the publication of the information which had come to the knowledge of the Attorney General—a publication which would have the effect of possibly preventing the detection of the crime which it is the very object of the clause to detect. The hon. Gentleman is quite mistaken in believing that in Scotland any application has to be made to a Court of law. No such application is necessary there. Therefore, the whole of the quarter-of-an-hour which the hon. Member devoted in his speech to that point—namely, the argument that in this matter Ireland should be treated on the lines of the Scotch law—was wasted with an argument which had no foundation in fact. Therefore, on these grounds I trust the House will not assent to the Amendment moved by the hon. Gentleman, and the substance of which has either been already decided, or if accepted would be hostile to the Bill.

MR. HALDANE (Haddington): I venture to dissent wholly from the view of the Solicitor General. I think there is a great deal to be said in favour of this Amendment. And though I support it on grounds somewhat different from those of the hon. Gentleman who has moved it, I support it on grounds which appear to me to be quite sufficient. The speech of the Solicitor General only shows how entirely the Lord Advocate has neglected what would seem to have been his duty—namely, the duty of informing right hon. and hon. Gentlemen who sit upon the Front Bench what is the nature of the law of Scotland upon this point. It should have been shown to them that the Attorney General in England, and the Attorney General in Ireland, occupy a wholly different position to that of the Lord Advocate in Scotland. If the Lord Advocate in Scotland is not a judicial functionary, at least he is a *quasi*-judicial functionary. He certainly exercises a control over criminal proceedings which is wholly unknown to the spirit of English and Irish jurisprudence—a control which is of a judicial nature; and what I understand this Amendment to propose is to distribute the power vested in an executive functionary in Scotland, sitting in what is really a distinct judicial capacity—in the capacity of having a control over the criminal proceedings of the country—what I understand this Amendment to propose is to distribute this power between the Attorney General and the High Court in such a way as will really bring the proposition into accord with what is the law in Scotland. What is the function of the Attorney General for Ireland? So far from his being a *quasi*-judicial official he is a mere litigant, pursuing accused persons in a spirit of hostility. I give every credit to the Attorney General for Ireland for desiring to do his duty. I feel confident he will do that duty in a fair spirit; but in asking that the Committee should give such powers to him as are proposed by the Government, I would point out that the Committee will be sanctioning powers of a character wholly different from those vested in the Lord Advocate for Scotland. There is another consideration which surely should have weight with us. This is a power to be exercised though no person is charged with any offence. Will the Lord Advocate get up and say that he has been accustomed to allow inquiries of this kind to take place without any person being charged? Will he get up and say that there is a single case in the recent

history of Scotch law in which a roving Commission has been given to search for the purpose of getting up evidence for the trial into the consciences of all kinds of men, to search into the consciences of men who are charged with no crime, and are brought forward for no offence, but are simply told they must attend and give evidence? In Scotland it is a case of merely giving evidence, but here it is proposed that evidence should be given upon oath for purposes wholly different from those known in Scotland. That is the case put forward, and we are asked to give legislative sanction to what is wholly unknown in Scotland. I certainly think that this Amendment should receive the support of Members on this side of the House; first, because it is a proposal simply to vest in a Court and the Attorney General in Ireland powers which will be properly so jointly vested, and which are vested in Scotland in a similar manner in a judicial functionary; secondly, because the power proposed to be given by the Bill is a power far wider than that conferred upon any functionary in Scotland; and, thirdly, because the case we have got here is a case in which it will be possible to take evidence for the purposes of the brief on the trial, and make use of that evidence when it is taken in a way for which there is no precedent either in the law of Scotland, or, so far as I know, any other system of civilized jurisprudence.

MR. CHANCE: I think the speech of the Solicitor General is a sufficient example of the danger of allowing any Law Officer of the Crown to form an opinion upon a matter without presenting an affidavit before a Superior Court. The hon. Member for Cork (Mr. M. Healy) addressed the Committee for 30 minutes, during the greater portion of which time the Solicitor General was either sleeping, pretending to be asleep, or engaged in sneering at the hon. Gentleman; and then he gets up and says he proposes, in a few words, to completely demolish the case of my hon. Friend. He proceeds to do it—to his own satisfaction clearly. He says my hon. Friend's arguments are wholly inadmissible, because the Court must be satisfied that an offence has been committed, and that intimidation is rampant in a district. But the Government, who have introduced the Bill, have laid it down that they require this Bill and this power because these offences have been committed, and because intimidation has been rampant; but they decline to submit to any judicial tribunal any evidence to show that the contention on which they are getting rid of the liberties of the country is true in any single case. Why should not the Court be satisfied that an offence has been committed? "Oh," says the Solicitor General, "because we have already provided that the Attorney General for Ireland is not to be set in motion except on a sworn information." But that is a fallacy. What would satisfy the Attorney General for Ireland would not satisfy a division of the High Court. Anyone who has practised in the Court of Chancery knows very well that that Court often refuses to act on affidavits which have been settled by eminent counsel to their satisfaction. The learned Solicitor General's second point is that the Committee have just refused to require that the Attorney General should have proof that intimidation or other improper cause exists whereby evidence is withheld, and that it would be unreasonable that the High Court should require that which the Committee has decided the Attorney General should not require. In this argument he is also guilty of a fallacy. We refuse to make a condition precedent to any motion by the Attorney General that sworn information as to intimidation should be afforded; but it is quite another thing here, for the reason that we are considering what the Court should demand before granting power to hold an inquiry. For these reasons I do not think that the defence made for the clause by the Solicitor General holds good. We are now considering the question of the position of the Law Officers of the Crown. We have given individuals, without a shred of representative authority, power to make and unmake the law in particular localities; and now we are asked to go a step further, and destroy the distinction between the Executive and judicial authority; and we have, for the first time, a partizan Law Officer sitting on that Bench opposite responsible for the policy of the Government, with power to apply a law which never before could be applied to any individual, no matter how humble, except by a competent judicial authority

Mr. Chance

standing between the people and the Crown. It may be considered nothing to take this step now, and make the Resident Magistrates the mere servants of the Executive, or of a particular Party; but it seems to me to involve a large principle. It seems to me this House would do well to consider whether it is wise to depart from the old principle that the Executive shall depend on the judicial tribunals when it seeks to put the law into force, and whether it is wise to give to a political Party the power of creating a political force to deal with political offenders, and to punish people at its own will.

MR. A. R. D. ELLIOT (Roxburgh): I am satisfied, from all I have heard, that hon. Gentlemen below the Gangway on this side of the House have been misinformed on the subject of that part of the Scotch law which bears an analogy to the proposal in this clause. I come from Scotland and am familiar with the working of this law, and seeing that these preliminary inquiries are constantly occurring there, that we hear no complaints with regard to them, and that there is nothing extravagant in the principle, I am surprised that hon. Members should be startled at the proposal of the Government. I see that these inquiries are to be guarded in this clause in the most careful manner, and are only to be allowed when an offence has been committed. An inquiry will not take place whether an offence has been committed or not, but only when the Attorney General believes that such an inquiry should be held. In Scotland such a preliminary inquiry takes place when the Procurator Fiscal, who may be no more than a solicitor in a country town, thinks fit to initiate it. Supposing a haystack has been burnt down. It is not necessary that there should be a suspicion of arson against a particular individual, but this local legal official can institute an inquiry to find out how the thing occurred. If it has been an accident, well and good; but he investigates the matter in order to ascertain whether or not a crime has been committed, and he does that in 99 cases out of 100, off his own bat, so to speak, because he is Procurator Fiscal of the district. He examines witnesses on oath before the Sheriff, where the oaths and depositions are taken, or in his own office. The inquiry is not necessarily one to be followed up by a committal and a trial. The Procurator Fiscal goes round and collects evidence behind the back of the accused—if there is an accused. If there is an accused he is arrested, but is not made acquainted with any of the evidence the Procurator is collecting against him. He is put in prison to await his trial, and is not even allowed to have the advice of a solicitor until the depositions collected by the Procurator Fiscal, whether sworn to or not, have gone before a magistrate, who says whether or not a committal shall take place. It is not until the committal has taken place on the evidence so obtained that the accused is allowed to say a word in his defence. This is the everyday system in Scotland. It is difficult to understand how hon. and right hon. Gentlemen can be serious when they come down to the House of Commons and say that something new and startling is being done in this Bill when a system quite as strong was introduced five years ago, and was about to be renewed three years ago by the right hon. Gentleman sitting below me (Mr. W. E. Gladstone). This is a proposal to introduce the usual system of preliminary inquiry, known to all of us in Scotland, into the Criminal Law of Ireland. I know that in most cases in Scotland it is not thought desirable to take evidence on oath, but in some cases it is. But when we come to look at what is being done, the whole question comes to this—whether or not a preliminary inquiry should be introduced, at the instance of an official representative of the Crown. That is the whole gist of the question. Whether in one case out of 100 evidence may or may not be taken on oath is a very minor matter indeed. The question is whether an official, representing the Crown, should be allowed to collect evidence on oath, and afterwards use it against an accused. I think the exaggerated and fictitious view which has been taken on this matter of preliminary inquiry, will astonish the people of Scotland, who are thoroughly accustomed to investigations of this sort.

MR. W. E. GLADSTONE (Edinburgh, Mid Lothian) : I am quite certain that though my hon. and learned Friend (Mr. A. R. D. Elliot) undertakes to speak with the greatest confidence for the people of Scotland, the opinions of the hon. and learned Member are not in consonance with the feelings of the people of Scotland on any question with regard to the relations of the people of England and the people of Ireland. All I know of the people of Scotland and of their relations with their Representatives in this House gives me the impression that it would be impossible to resort to a worse authority than my hon. and learned Friend to ascertain the opinions of the people of Scotland. Sir, then the hon. and learned Member says that provisions similar to these were passed five years ago, and were about to be renewed three years ago ; but he entirely overlooks that which we take to be a fundamental and essential difference in this matter—namely, that whatever provisions were framed five years ago were directed exclusively against crime, whereas our contention, confirmed as we believe by the language of the Government, is that this is not a Bill for dealing with crime. ["Oh, oh!" *and laughter.*] I really cannot have my mind influenced by outcries of that kind. I know that the Bill has been otherwise described by right hon. Gentlemen opposite, but I do not appreciate the force of their description. I know that reliance is placed upon it much more than upon the speech of the right hon. Gentleman, from which I gather that, in the view of the Government, this is not a Bill for dealing with crime. The right hon. Gentleman will correct me if I need correction—but I am afraid correction will not help the matter in the least—when I say that this Bill is not exclusively or mainly a Bill for the purpose of dealing with crime, but for the purpose of dealing with acts that are not crime, but which now, for the first time, are going to be made crime. That is, in our view, the fundamental difference between the proposal made five years ago and the present proposal. I do not mean to say that I should be ready to renew the proposal of five years ago. [*Ministerial laughter, and* "Hear, hear!"] No; I am not ready to renew it, and for the reason that I am perfectly convinced, as the House is perfectly aware from the declarations of last year, that this method of coercion only aggravates the evils which it seeks to cure, and that there is another method totally distinct that is a wise and prudent one to pursue. But my hon. and learned Friend has given

Y 2   [*Second Night.*]

us his account, forsooth, of the law of Scotland. He was greatly surprised at the opinions expressed on this side of the House. Well, Sir, surprise is one of those feelings of which everyone has at his command an unbounded quantity. He can produce it according to the occasion. I, like my hon. and learned Friend, have an abundant stock of surprise in me which I expend, from time to time, as occasion offers, and I reciprocate the feeling of my hon. and learned Friend. My hon. and learned Friend's account of the law and practice in Scotland is in diametrical contradiction to that given by the late Solicitor General for Scotland. He says he is familiar in Scotland by daily usage with this practice, whereas the late Solicitor General for Scotland told us that the practice was not in operation. The distinct statement of the hon. and learned Solicitor General for Scotland—a statement which did the greatest credit to his legal acuteness and impartiality—was, that the precognition in Scotland, though purely voluntary, was, as he said, backed by this power which was never exercised. The power of examination on oath, conducted by legal authority on the part of the Government without compulsion, and applicable to a country where the law and the people are in sympathy, is a thing so different from that now proposed that all the ingenuity of my hon. and learned Friend, and all his faculty for speaking on behalf of the people of Scotland, will not induce us to accept the account which he has laid down in flat contradiction to the late Solicitor General for Scotland.

Mr. HUNTER (Aberdeen, N.): I have lived many years in Scotland, and I have never heard of any such practice as that mentioned by the hon. and learned Gentleman (Mr. A. R. D. Elliot) of an inquiry on oath being held by a Procurator Fiscal when no person is accused. The right hon. Gentleman the Chief Secretary for Ireland stated that Scotland was happy and free because she possessed this law; but I say that we are happy and free in Scotland because we possess no such law. I admit there are some statements in old books on the law in Scotland which are exceedingly vague; and I think that Members from Scotland have come to be of opinion, having regard to the statement of the right hon. Gentleman, that the time has come when the law in Scotland should be reduced to a

Mr. W. E. Gladstone

more clear form than it is in at present. Suppose the members of the Farmers' Alliance, which is the nearest approach we have in Scotland to the National League in Ireland, were to be examined by the Procurator Fiscal with reference to the transactions of the society. I will tell hon. Gentlemen opposite that every Scotchman worthy of the name would tear the notice in pieces and throw it into the fire. It is utterly untrue that anything exists in Scotland which can in any way be compared to this system of inquiry which is proposed for Ireland. An inquiry of a preliminary character by the Procurator Fiscal into crimes would in Scotland, as in every other country, receive the support of those who have any evidence to give; but this proceeding is entirely of a voluntary character, notwithstanding the assertions in the books on the Scotch law. If the Lord Advocate contradicts me on that point, let him produce any case] where, no person being accused, people have been compelled to come forward and give evidence. I say let the Government rest their case on any grounds they please, but do not let them vilify the fair name of Scotland by accusing us of having in operation any such law as this.

Mr. HALDANE: In order to get rid of the difficulty pointed out by the Solicitor General, I propose to move an Amendment to the present Amendment, by adding after "the High Court" the words, "or to a Judge thereof in Chambers."

Amendment proposed to the said proposed Amendment, in line 1, after the words "High Court," to insert the words "or to a Judge thereof in Chambers."—(*Mr. Haldane.*)

Question proposed, "That those words be there inserted."

Mr. T. M. HEALY: I intend to put forward an Amendment, that the law under this section in Ireland shall be the same as the law in Scotland, and then to claim the entire vote of the Scotch Party on this side of the House. I have not the smallest doubt that it will be accepted at once by hon. Gentlemen opposite. The Solicitor General for England dwelt largely on the fact that publicity in this country was necessary; but what the Solicitor General stood upon most was that this is an *ex parte* application, and that it would be a mere "*pro formá*" proceeding—absolutely needless. Has the right hon. Gentleman read the 4th section of this Act which deals with the change of venue, and that in connection with Section 3 the words are—

"Where an indictment for a crime committed in a proclaimed district has been found against a defendant, or a defendant has been committed for trial for such crime, and a trial is to be at a Court of Assize for any county in a proclaimed district, or at a Court of Quarter Sessions for any county or borough in a proclaimed district, the High Court on application by or on behalf of the Attorney General for Ireland, and upon his certificate that he believes that a more fair and impartial trial can be had at a Court of Assize in some county to be named in the certificate, shall make an order as of course that the trial shall be had at a Court of Assize in the county named in the certificate."

The words are "of course." I am astonished that the Solicitor General should get up and say that we have not read the Bill. Let him presume on the ignorance of his own Party; but, so far as we are concerned, we have both read and understand the Bill. We ask that he should transfer the words from the 4th section to the 1st, and we ask no more. There is no doubt that the High Court, or a Judge thereof, would make the order when applied to "as of course;" but the necessity of the Attorney General having to apply for the order would, at any rate, give the protection of publicity. Let us reverse the state of things. Supposing the Home Rule Government in Ireland were endeavouring to smash up the Orange Party and were proceeding to put them down, how would the hon. and gallant Member for North Armagh thunder against giving us this power without reference to the High Court? You say that this is the law under the Act of 1882. I say that nothing is more absurd, and that of all the flagitious statements this is the foremost. The Act of 1882 said that the magistrate should not summon anybody who was not believed to be capable of giving material evidence. There is nothing in this Bill of that kind. What is the intention here? Why, anybody knows that it is intended to prevent the tenants entering into combination. We will take Lord Clanricarde, or the estates of the King-Harmans, the Smith-Barrys, or Tottenhams. One of these landlords will go to the Government and say—"There is a combination against our estates;

have up the ringleaders; examine and cross-examime them; put them on the rack, and if they refuse to answer you can give them a week or two of imprisonment;" you will not get the information, but they will be put in prison. But the right hon. Gentleman cannot go with such a story as that to the High Court. We propose to substitute for the action of the right hon. and learned Gentleman, who will go with the landlords of the country as long as he is a Member for Dublin University, the action of the Court of Queen's Bench. Now, as the Court of Queen's Bench will always accede to any proposal made by the Attorney General there ought to be no objection to this Amendment. We are only asking the protection which, under Section 3, you give us yourselves. Why do you compel the Attorney General to go to the High Court if his Motion is to be granted "as of course?" Why do you compel him to waste the tax-payers money? You compel him to go before the High Court, in order that the High Court and the public generally may be satisfied that there is a fair case before this power is granted. The Government have said that the law in Scotland is the same as the provision under this clause. The Lord Advocate, who, I believe, has written a book on the subject, and who is probably the most learned man whom Scotland sends to this House, has, however, never ventured to open his mouth in support of that statement. The right hon. and learned Gentleman knows too much to do that; he is too learned a man for Her Majesty's Government, when they can get the hon. and learned Member for Roxburghshire (Mr. A. R. D. Elliot) to defend their position. I ask English Members, if they had the same apprehensions for their country as we have for ours, whether they would not compel the Attorney General to go to the High Court before this power is exercised? I trust the Government will not persist in rejecting every Amendment which comes from these Benches. I believe their intention is to show the country that their Bill is so splendidly drafted that it needs no Amendment; but the Bill is badly drawn; and I say that it is unfair to refuse every Amendment we propose on the pretence that the Bill has been beautifully drafted by the Attorney

[Second Night.]

General, and does not require to be
amended. I say that we, in Ireland,
are entitled to some consideration, even
at the hands of the Tory Party, and that
if Irish Members are to come into this
House at all, you must, at any rate,
listen to the voices of those who are
really acquainted with the state of facts
in Ireland.

Question put, and *agreed to.*

Amendment further amended, by inserting, in line 2, after the word
" Court," the words " or Judge."

Question proposed,

" That the words ' apply to the High Court,
or to a Judge thereof in Chambers, for an
order directing an inquiry under this section,
and thereupon the Court or Judge may, if satisfied that an offence has been committed as aforesaid, and that, owing to intimidation or other
improper cause, evidence in connection with
such offence has been withheld, make an order
accordingly, and may,' be there inserted."

MR. DILLON (Mayo, E.): It has
been stated as one reason for not accepting this Amendment that it would interfere with the discovery of crime. How
the application to the High Court of
Justice could interfere with the discovery
of crime is beyond the grasp of my apprehension. The Solicitor General
stated that this Amendment was perfectly unnecessary. What difficulty is
there in inserting it? If it be unnecessary, and can do no harm to the Bill,
while at the same time it satisfies us,
why not agree to it and put an end to
this discussion? I think the Government ought to have that amount of
confidence in the High Court in Ireland,
which would be shown by submitting
these cases to it. Certainly our experience of that Court is not of such a high
character as to make us much value the
effect of this Amendment; but we regard
it as likely to be some check on the action of the Attorney General for Ireland. When I was held to bail last
winter the prosecution was founded upon
affidavits, which were sworn by certain
sub-inspectors of police; I defended myself on that trial, and I directed the attention of the Judge to those affidavits,
and to the fact that Clarke swore to a
number of things that he could not have
known of his own knowledge. The
Judge stated that he considered that
two of the affidavits were illegal, and

that he dismissed them from his mind
before giving judgment. This is a
case exactly in point. What we contend is this—that the Attorney General shall be compelled to produce
affidavits which will show something to
justify his demands, and which shall be
in legal form; and that these affidavits
shall not be drawn up in Dublin Castle
in the shape which the Government
want, and sworn to without the person
making them taking the trouble to read
them. In the case I mention it turned
out that two of the affidavits referred to
were on old forms used against the hon.
and learned Member for North Longford
two years ago. The form was sent down,
and Mr. Flower swore to it without considering whether he was in a position to
swear to it or not. We want to prevent
that practice which is going on in Ireland continually. The reason why we
ask that this Amendment should be accepted is because the Attorney General
would be assumed to go before Court
with a decently sworn information; and
it may be hoped that the Judges would
ascertain whether the person swears to
facts within his knowledge, or which he
reasonably believes were true. I repeat
that, if the Government consider this
Amendment formally to be unnecessary,
there is no use in refusing to accept the
Amendment, which pleases us, and does
the Bill no harm.

MR. BRADLAUGH (Northampton):
I understand the Solicitor General for
England to object, first, that this Amendment might be destructive to the object
sought to be attained, and, in the next
place, that it would involve delay. Is
it possible to imagine that it would
cause any delay at all? There would be
always some Judge acting at Chambers,
which gets over the objection that the
Court is not always sitting, and also
provides for avoiding publicity if it be
necessary to avoid it. I should have
thought that the Attorney General
would have been glad of the protection
which this clause would give him
against any chance of being supposed
to be acting unjustly. I am sure that if
this were a matter relating to England,
the English Attorney General, having
to take the initiative, would only be too
glad to put upon another tribunal the
responsibility of deciding what had to
be done. I trust the Government will
not cause a further occupation of the

time of the Committee by resisting an Amendment which cannot do harm if they mean to do right, and which cannot be otherwise than acceptable to hon. and learned Members sitting on the Treasury Bench. Of course, if these investigations are not aimed at crime, then I can understand the Attorney General would object to go to the High Court of Justice with a case which that Court would treat as deserving ridicule. If the investigation is aimed at grave cases, there is no reason why the Attorney General should not submit it to that high tribunal—indeed, he should be glad of having an opportunity of doing so. I trust that if it is only to palliate English feeling the Government; will agree to this Amendment.

MR. W. REDMOND (Fermanagh, N.): The hon. and learned Gentleman the Solicitor General (Sir Edward Clarke), in the course of his remarks on this Amendment, complained rather unjustly that this Amendment should be proposed. I think that when it comes to be understood how great is the aversion which this part of the Bill creates in the minds of Irishmen, it will not be very wonderful that a great deal of time is spent in these discussions. There is not a clause in the whole of this Bill, as I have already said, that is more distasteful and detested than this, which provides for secret Courts of Inquiry to be conducted by Resident Magistrates, who are men totally out of sympathy with the great bulk of the people. The right hon. and learned Attorney General for Ireland (Mr. Holmes) will not accept this Amendment, simply and solely because he wants to have the right upon his own authority of causing the establishment of these Courts of Inquiry, of giving these powers to Resident Magistrates, without having his reasons made public. There can only be one reason possible for refusing to delegate this matter to the judgment of the High Court. That reason is that the Government fear that, in a great many cases, the High Court would refrain from establishing these inquiries, and giving Resident Magistrates these powers where the Attorney General would not hesitate to do so. The conduct and action of the Government in this matter goes to confirm the suspicion which the Representatives of Ireland have had all along with regard to this Bill—namely, that it is not a measure to put down crime in the country, but that, on the contrary, it is a measure the powers of which are directed against the organization and the movement of the people for their self-preservation against landlords. If these Courts of Inquiry were only required to put down crime, would it not be to your advantage that the existence of crime and the necessity for these Courts should be made as public as possible, and brought before the High Court of Ireland, so that the people of this country might have your statements in support of this Bill fortified, and that you might be able to show to the people of this country that you really had grounds for proposing this Bill containing, as it does, most extraordinary coercive powers? But right hon. Gentlemen on the Treasury Bench do not court inquiry. They do not accept the Amendment to delegate the establishment of these tribunals to the High Court, simply because they are afraid that in a great many cases the High Court, not being so partizan as many members of the Executive in Ireland, would decide that there were no grounds for establishing these Courts of Inquiry, and so that by even the Courts of Ireland the necessity which you say exists for coercion would be disproved, and you would be further discredited in the eyes of the people. I hope sincerely my hon. Friend (Mr. M. Healy) will press this Amendment; I hope that, line by line and word by word, if possible, every portion of this clause will be contested here before it is allowed to become law, because there is no clause in that Bill that is more unconstitutional, more tyrannical, more unjustifiable, and more detestable to the people of Ireland than this 1st clause of your measure, whereby you propose to give to Resident Magistrates, to half-pay officers, retired and shelved police officers, men who are never in sympathy with the people, men who are allies of the landlord class of the country—whereby you propose to give to such men the power of terrifying and bullying in secret unfortunate men on every conceivable subject which may come into their heads, without ever having any report made of the proceedings. I maintain that such a provision is infamous in itself; it has been proved more infamous every minute in this discussion

[*Second Night.*]

by the action of the Government in refusing to allow the slightest ray of public opinion to fall on their proceedings, and in the keeping for the Attorney General, and, I suppose, for the Chief Secretary for Ireland, and that late Orange functionary, the new Parliamentary Under Secretary (Colonel King-Harman)—in keeping for these men the power of life and death almost over the Irish people unimpaired. You are afraid to appeal to the High Court; you are afraid to let any public light fall on these affairs; you want to have it all worked by your chosen instruments, by your Attorney General, by your Parliamentary Under Secretary, men who, Sir George Trevelyan and others have declared, are unfit to have the control of the lives and liberties of the Irish people.

THE FIRST LORD OF THE TREASURY (Mr. W. H. SMITH) (Strand, Westminster): Mr. Courtney, I rise to move that the Question be now put.

Motion made, and Question proposed, "That the Question be now put."—(*Mr. W. H. Smith.*)

Question put accordingly.

The Committee *divided*:—Ayes 257; Noes 135: Majority 122.

AYES.

Agg-Gardner, J. T.
Ainslie, W. G.
Amherst, W. A. T.
Anstruther, Colonel R. H. L.
Ashmead-Bartlett, E.
Baggallay, E.
Bailey, Sir J. R.
Baird, J. G. A.
Balfour, rt. hon. A. J.
Balfour, G. W.
Baring, Viscount
Barry, A. H. Smith-
Bartley, G. C. T.
Bass, H.
Bates, Sir E.
Baumann, A. A.
Beach, W. W. B.
Beadel, W. J.
Beaumont, H. F.
Beckett, W.
Bective, Earl of
Bentinck, rt. hn. G. C.
Bentinck, Lord H. C.
Beresford, Lord C. W.
De la Poer
Bethell, Commander G. R.
Biddulph, M.
Bigwood, J.
Birkbeck, Sir E.
Blundell, Col. H. B. H.

Bond, G. H.
Bonsor, H. C. O.
Boord, T. W.
Borthwick, Sir A.
Bridgeman, Col. hon. F. C.
Bright, right hon. J.
Brodrick, hon. W. St. J. F.
Brookfield, A. M.
Bruce, Lord H.
Burdett-Coutts, W. L. Ash.-B.
Burghley, Lord
Caine, W. S.
Campbell, Sir A.
Campbell, J. A.
Chamberlain, R.
Chaplin, right hon. H.
Charrington, S.
Clarke, Sir E. G.
Coghill, D. H.
Commerell, Adml. Sir J. E.
Compton, F
Cooke, C. W. R.
Corbett, J.
Corry, Sir J. P.
Cotton, Capt. E. T. D.
Cranborne, Viscount
Cross, H. S.
Crossman, Gen. Sir W.

Curzon, Viscount
Dalrymple, C.
Davenport, H. T.
De Lisle, E. J. L. M. P.
De Worms, Baron H.
Dickson, Major A. G.
Dimsdale, Baron R.
Dixon, G.
Dixon-Hartland, F. D.
Dorington, Sir J. E.
Dugdale, J. S.
Duncan, Colonel F.
Duncombe, A.
Ebrington, Viscount
Elcho, Lord
Elliot, hon. A. R. D.
Elliot, Sir G.
Elliot, G. W.
Elton, C. I.
Ewart, W.
Ewing, Sir A. O.
Feilden, Lieut.-Gen. R. J.
Fellowes, W. H.
Fergusson, right hon. Sir J.
Fielden, T.
Finch, G. H.
Finch-Hatton, hon. M. E. G.
Finlay, R. B.
Fisher, W. H.
Fitzgerald, R. U. P.
Fitzwilliam, hon. W. J. W.
Fitz-Wygram, General Sir F. W.
Forwood, A. B.
Fowler, Sir R. N.
Fraser, General C. C.
Fry, L.
Gathorne-Hardy, hon. A. E.
Gathorne-Hardy, hon. J. S.
Gedge, S.
Gent-Davis, R.
Gibson, J. G.
Giles, A.
Gilliat, J. S.
Goldsmid, Sir J.
Goldsworthy, Major-General W. T.
Gorst, Sir J. E.
Goschen, rt. hon. G. J.
Gray, C. W.
Grimston, Viscount
Grotrian, F. B.
Gunter, Colonel R.
Gurdon, R. T.
Hall, A. W.
Hall, C.
Halsey, T. F.
Hambro, Col. C. J. T.
Hamilton, right hon. Lord G. F.
Hamilton, Lord E.
Hamilton, Col. C. E.
Hanbury, R. W.
Hanbury-Tracy, hon. F. S. A.
Hankey, F. A.
Hardcastle, F.

Heath, A. R.
Heathcote, Capt. J. H. Edwards-
Herbert, hon. S.
Hermon-Hodge, R. T.
Hervey, Lord F.
Hill, right hon. Lord A. W.
Hill, Colonel E. S.
Hill, A. S.
Hoare, S.
Hobhouse, H.
Holland, rt. hon. Sir H. T.
Holloway, G.
Holmes, rt. hon. H.
Hornby, W. H.
Hozier, J. H. C.
Hughes-Hallett, Col. F. C.
Hulse, E. H.
Hunt, F. S.
Hunter, Sir G.
Isaacson, F. W.
Jackson, W. L.
Jardine, Sir R.
Jarvis, A. W.
Johnston, W.
Kelly, J. R.
Kenrick, W.
Kenyon, hon. G. T.
Kenyon-Slaney, Col. W.
Kimber, H.
King, H. S.
King-Harman, right hon. Colonel E. R.
Knightley, Sir R.
Lafone, A.
Lambert, C.
Laurie, Colonel R. P.
Lawrance, J. C.
Lawrence, Sir J. J. T.
Lawrence, W. F.
Lea, T.
Legh, T. W.
Leighton, S.
Lewis, Sir C. E.
Lewisham, right hon. Viscount
Long, W. H.
Low, M.
Lowther, hon. W.
Lowther, J. W.
Macartney, W. G. E.
Macdonald, rt. hon. J. H. A.
Maclean, J. M.
M'Calmont, Captain J.
Makins, Colonel W. T.
Malcolm, Col. J. W.
Mallock, R.
Manners, right hon. Lord J. J. R.
Marriott, right hon. W. T.
Matthews, rt. hon. H.
Maxwell, Sir H. E.
Mayne, Adml. R. C.
Mills, hon. C. W.
Morgan, hon. F.
Morrison, W.
Mount, W. G.

Mr. W. Redmond

Mowbray, rt. hon. Sir
  J. R.
Mulholland, H. L.
Muntz, P. A.
Murdoch, C. T.
Newark, Viscount
Noble, W.
Northcote, hon. H. S.
O'Neill, hon. R. T.
Paget, Sir R. H.
Parker, hon. F.
Pearce, W.
Polly, Sir L.
Penton, Captain F. T.
Pitt-Lewis, G.
Plunket, right hon.
  D. R.
Plunkett, hon. J. W.
Pomfret, W. P.
Powell, F. S.
Price, Captain G. E.
Quilter, W. C.
Raikes, rt. hon. H. C.
Rankin, J.
Rasch, Major F. C.
Reed, H. B.
Ridley, Sir M. W.
Ritchie, rt. hon. C. T.
Robertson, J. P. B.
Robertson, W. T.
Ross, A. H.
Round, J.
Russell, T. W.
Salt, T.
Sandys, Lieut-Col. T.
  M.
Saunderson, Col. E. J.
Sclater - Booth, right
  hon. G.
Sellar, A. C.
Selwin - Ibbetson, rt.
  hon. Sir H. J.

Shaw-Stewart, M. H.
Sidebottom, T. H.
Sidebottom, W.
Smith, rt. hon. W. H.
Smith, A.
Spencer, J. E.
Stanhope, rt. hon. E.
Stanley, E. J.
Stewart, M.
Swetenham, E.
Talbot, J. G.
Taylor, F.
Temple, Sir R.
Thorburn, W.
Tollemache, H. J.
Tomlinson, W. E. M.
Tottenham, A. L.
Townsend, F.
Trotter, H. J.
Walsh, hon. A. H. J.
Waring, Colonel T.
Webster, Sir R. E.
Webster, R. G.
West, Colonel W. C.
Weymouth, Viscount
Wharton, J. L.
White, J. B.
Whitley, E.
Whitmore, C. A.
Winn, hon. R.
Wodehouse, E. R.
Wolmer, Viscount
Wood, N.
Wortley, C. B. Stuart-
Wright, H. S.
Wroughton, P.
Yerburgh, R. A.

TELLERS,

Douglas, A. Akers-
Walrond, Col. W. H.

NOES.

Abraham, W. (Lime-
  rick, W.)
Acland, A. H. D.
Allison, R. A.
Asquith, H. H.
Barbour, W. B.
Beaumont, W. B.
Biggar, J. G.
Blake, J. A.
Blake, T.
Blane, A.
Bolton, J. C.
Bradlaugh, C.
Broadhurst, H.
Bruce, hon. R. P.
Buxton, S. C.
Campbell, H.
Campbell-Bannerman,
  right hon. H.
Carew, J. L.
Chance, P. A.
Childers, rt. hon. H.
  C. E.
Clancy, J. J.
Cobb, H. P.
Cohen, A.
Coleridge, hon. B.
Commins, A.
Connolly, L.

Conway, M.
Conybeare, C. A. V.
Cossham, H.
Cox, J. R.
Cozens-Hardy H. H.
Craig, J.
Craven, J.
Crawford, D.
Cremer, W. R.
Dillon, J.
Dillwyn, L. L.
Ellis, T. E.
Esslemont, P.
Fenwick, C.
Finucane, J.
Flower, C.
Flynn, J. C.
Foley, P. J.
Foster, Sir W. B.
Fowler, rt. hn. H. H.
Fox, Dr. J. F.
Gaskell, C. G. Milnes-
Gilhooly, J
Gill, H. J.
Gill, T. P.
Gladstone, rt. hn. W.E.
Gladstone, H. J.
Grey, Sir E.
Haldane, R. B.

Harcourt, rt. hon. Sir
  W. G. V. V.
Harrington, E.
Hayden, L. P.
Hayne, C. Seale-
Healy, M.
Healy, T. M.
Holden, I.
Hooper, J.
Hunter, W. A.
Illingworth, A.
James, C. H.
Joicey, J.
Jordan, J.
Kay-Shuttleworth, rt.
  hon. Sir U. J.
Kennedy, E. J.
Kenny, C. S.
Kenny, M. J.
Lawson, H. L. W.
Leahy, J.
Lefevre, rt. hn.G. J. S.
Lockwood, F.
Macdonald, W. A.
M'Cartan, M.
M'Carthy, J.
M'Donald, P.
M'Kenna, Sir J. N.
M'Lagan, P.
M'Laren, W. S. B.
Marum, E. M.
Mason, S.
Molloy, B. C.
Morgan, O. V.
Morley, rt. hon. J.
Murphy, W. M.
Nolan, Colonel J. P.
Nolan, J.
O'Brien, J. F. X.
O'Brien, P.
O'Brien, P. J.
O'Connor, A.
O'Connor, J. (Kerry.)
O'Connor, J. (Tippry.)

O'Connor, T. P.
O'Doherty, J. E.
O'Hanlon, T.
O'Hea, P.
O'Kelly, J.
Paulton, J. M.
Pickard, B.
Picton, J. A.
Pinkerton, J.
Powell, W. R. H.
Power, P. J.
Power, R.
Pyne, J. D.
Quinn, T.
Redmond, W. H. K.
Roberts, J. B.
Robinson, T.
Rowlands, J.
Russell, E. R.
Sexton, T.
Sheehan, J. D.
Sheehy, D.
Sheil, E.
Shirley, W. S.
Stack, J.
Stansfeld, rt. hon. J.
Stevenson, F. S.
Stuart, J.
Sullivan, D.
Sullivan, T. D.
Tanner, C. K.
Tuite, J.
Wallace, R.
Wardle, H.
Warmington, C. M.
Whitbread, S.
Will, J. S.
Williams, A.

TELLERS,

Marjoribanks, rt. hon.
  E.
Morley, A.

On the numbers being announced—

COLONEL NOLAN (Galway. N.), rising in his place, said: Mr. Courtney, I rise to a point of Order.

THE CHAIRMAN: If the hon. and gallant Gentleman wishes to address the Committee during a Division he must do so in the usual manner.

COLONEL NOLAN (resuming his seat, and speaking with head covered): I desire to know, Sir, whether it is in Order for a number of hon. Members in the "Aye" Lobby to stand at the glass door and hoot hon. Members going to divide in the other Lobby?

THE CHAIRMAN: Of course, such conduct was disorderly.

Question put, "That those words be there inserted."

The Committee divided:—Ayes 142; Noes 261: Majority 119.—(Div. List, No. 106.)

[Second Night.]

Mr. MAURICE HEALY: I now move to insert in this clause, after the word "may," in line 8, the following words:—"By warrant in writing under his hand."

Mr. HOLMES: I would suggest that the expression "by warrant" is a purely technical expression, and that the words "by writing under his hand" would be better.

Mr. MAURICE HEALY: I do not think the form suggested by the right hon. and learned Gentleman would be so good as that which I have proposed; but if he is of opinion that it would be better, I will not press my Amendment as against his.

Amendment, by leave, *withdrawn.*

On the Motion of Mr. HOLMES, the following Amendment made:—In page 1, line 8, after "may," insert "by order in writing under his hand."

Mr. MAURICE HEALY: I have now to move another Amendment which stands in my name, and which I desire to see inserted, because, otherwise, I think there is reason for suspecting that the clause may be used for improper purposes. I propose, therefore, to move that in Clause 1, page 1, line 8, after the word "may," there should be inserted these words—"Provided that no person has been made amenable for such offence." If this safeguard be not granted, the Crown may, when a person is in custody charged with an offence, make use of this section to bring his witnesses into a police station and subject them to a course of secret cross-examination, merely with the object of getting at the prisoner's defence. The right hon. and learned Gentleman the Attorney General for Ireland is aware that in civil matters, where a person is entitled to interrogatories, he is not permitted by the rules which have to be observed to ask questions relating solely to the defence that is to be set up; and all I ask is—whether by means of this Amendment in its present form, or by some other Amendment which may better meet the view of the right hon. and learned Gentleman—that something analogous to the practice followed in civil cases may be also established in criminal cases coming under the operation of this Bill. I should state, in order that the Committee may not think the evil which I wish to guard against is a purely imaginary one, that I have known cases, even under the existing

law, in which the Crown Prosecutor has improperly endeavoured to extract from the witnesses for the prisoner what the prisoner's defence was to be. Of course, there is no such machinery under the existing law as is set up by this clause; but the power that is resorted to is that which is given by the Winter Assizes Act, whereby the Crown is compelled to pay the expenses of the witnesses, this provision, innocuous and beneficial as it would otherwise be, having been frequently used for the purpose of making a contract with the witnesses for the defence, and then with the object of improperly seeking to extract from the witnesses what is the defence set up on behalf of the prisoner. It may be contended that where a prisoner is innocent this can do him no harm; but we say that what is good law and good sense in civil cases ought to be so in criminal cases. We all know that in civil cases no such proceeding as I desire to prevent in criminal cases is allowed, notwithstanding that there is the fullest power to administer interrogatories, the object being to prevent the interrogatories being addressed to the ascertainment of the defence. I may add that I have no particular attachment to the wording of the Amendment as it stands in my name; but I regard the point to which it relates as an essential one, and, therefore, I ask the Committee to adopt this proposal.

Amendment proposed, in page 1, line 8, after "may," insert "provided that no person has been made amenable for such offence."—(*Mr. Maurice Healy.*)

Question proposed, "That those words be there inserted."

Mr. HOLMES: As I understand what the hon. Member for Cork means by the insertion of the words of his Amendment, it is that, where a man has been arrested for any offence, the investigation intended by the clause shall not take place. This is not an Amendment which the Government can possibly accept. The hon. Gentleman hardly seems to understand what is meant by the word "amenable."

Mr. MAURICE HEALY: The meaning I put on the word "amenable" is being arrested, or charged with an offence by being summoned upon a specific charge.

Mr. HOLMES: If that is the hon. Member's view, I repeat that it is quite impossible for the Government to accept his Amendment. It frequently happens that a great number have been engaged in the commission of a particular offence; and if in such a case any one of those persons were arrested, the investigation would, according to the Amendment, be checked altogether. If the hon. Gentleman means that if a man is summoned the magistrate is not to hold an inquiry unless that particular person is present, and unless the evidence is directed against that particular person, the Government cannot possibly accept such a proposal. Why, a bogus summons might be issued against a certain person, and then no one could be required to give evidence. The Government desire to afford all proper protection to individuals; but the hon. Gentleman must see that it is impossible for them to go to the extent he proposes.

MR. CHANCE: The Committee has already had evidence of the claim put forward by the right hon. Gentleman the First Lord of the Treasury (Mr. W. H. Smith) to shut up the proceedings of this House, and it may be that in this claim a large number of hon. Members seated on the opposite Benches fully concur, and are of opinion that this discussion has already gone to too great a length for them. Those hon. Gentlemen may, however, be told—and if they do not know it already they ought to be told, if they have any glimmering of intelligence at all—that the debates which are being conducted on this side of the House are not being carried on with any hope of moving either their minds or their hearts. They are being conducted with another object entirely. They are being conducted with the object of explaining the provisions of this infamous measure to the public, in order that the public may sooner or later send hon. Gentlemen opposite who are promoting the measure to the political perdition they merit. Of course, the right hon. and learned Attorney General for Ireland (Mr. Holmes), who is at the present moment hovering between the Treasury and the Judicial Bench, meets us with the regular *non possumus* to which he is accustomed, and the reason why he does this is sufficiently plain. He has stated that if any person is charged with the commission of a criminal offence, the effect of the adoption of this Amendment would be to prevent the extraordinary power of investigation conferred

by this clause from being exercised. The right hon. and learned Gentleman seems to disregard the fact that when a person is arrested the ordinary power of examining witnesses comes into force, and persons may be sent for from any part of the Kingdom and put upon their oath, and if they decline to answer any reasonable question put to them they may be sent to gaol. But we have now got to a further stage. We understand that the extraordinary powers of this Bill are to be so employed that they are not to be relied upon for the mere purpose of supplementing the ordinary provisions of the law, but that when even the ordinary magistrates are not staunch enough to carry out the behests of the Government, then, whether a person accused of an offence has been arrested or not, a tribunal may be sent down armed with these extraordinary powers. As the section stands without this Amendment, although a person may have been arrested and made amenable, the Crown officers would be enabled to ransack the whole country for witnesses, and send them to gaol if they failed to give such answers to the questions put to them as might be deemed desirable. We know very well who and what the Resident Magistrates are, and that it will be a very simple matter to send one down with a roving commission to catch witnesses for the defence in any particular case, and send them to gaol for four, five, or six months for having given unsatisfactory answers when interrogated, so that, when a prisoner has been got hold of, his witnesses may be safely kept on one side. We are told that we do not understand the meaning of the word "amenable." Let me call to the recollection of hon. Gentlemen opposite that when statistics were being used to defame the juries of Ireland, it was their Chancellor of the Exchequer who showed that prisoners had been made "amenable" in a large number of cases, and that in a very small number of instances were they convicted.

MR. T. M. HEALY: I do not think the Committee need debate this question at any serious length, as it is almost hopeless to point out and demonstrate the objectionable nature of the course being taken by the Government. I would simply put this one question to the right hon. and learned Attorney General for Ireland—would the right hon.

and learned Gentleman consider it fair, supposing. for instance, I were being put upon my trial for murder, and I had, say, 10 witnesses for my defence, that all those 10 witnesses should be examined by a process of private inquiry, and everything relating to my defence gone into, so that he might be furnished with full particulars on the subject in his brief? But I will take another case. Let us apply this argument to the Maamtrasna case, or the Huddy case, in both of which everybody who was called on to give evidence spoke the Irish language. All of them were Irish-speaking witnesses, and they were all extremely poor. Not one of these could be brought up to Dublin to give evidence at the cost of the prisoners, and their names had to be furnished to the Crown Solicitor in order that they might be brought to Dublin at the expense of the Government; and of all the mean things I ever heard of the meanest would probably be this—that when these wretched peasants were brought to Dublin from the West of Ireland, and the Crown Solicitor had got their names, they should be taken into a room at the Castle and there pumped under this section of the Crimes Bill, and their statements taken down and furnished to the Attorney General in his brief. Such a thing would be odious and hateful, and could not have been done in France during the worst days of Napoleon. And yet this is what is proposed to be done in the Jubilee year of Her Most Gracious Majesty. There is not a pickpocket in England whose witnesses would be subjected to such treatment as this. Well may we ask, is this the way Her Majesty's Government are going to treat us? A prisoner may be guilty, but the law assumes him to be innocent. The duty of proving his guilt lies with the prosecution. Everything connected with the defence will, under this clause, be in the hands of the Government, who will very carefully conceal the depositions made against a prisoner by their own witnesses. I say, if you are going to fight us in Ireland like this, you had better proclaim martial law at once. We hear that the Government have been very much troubled in these matters. Why should they not insert a simple little clause that would enable them to do as they please? This would simplify matters everywhere, and would

Mr. T. M. Healy

very much simplify them to the right hon. Gentleman the First Lord of the Treasury (Mr. W. H. Smith). Here we put before the Committee an Amendment on which the Committee might do one of two things. They might say either let the Government inquiry be suspended until the accused person has been arrested, or they might provide some safeguard when he has been arrested against the witnesses being subjected to secret examination, so that they might not be thumb-screwed by George Bolton and Company. The Government may object to our Amendment, but they know very well what is at the bottom of it. Do not let them take these verbal objections about being made amenable. Is that candour? Is that the way in which they ought to treat fair-minded opponents? Yes; we, at all events, give fair battle and use plain language, if necessary, such as can be understood even by the Tory Party below the Gangway; and we say it is unreasonable to ask us to submit to a system which throws the entire defence of the prisoner, because of his poverty, into the hands of the Crown, and which asserts that by whatever steps the Government plan must be followed.

Colonel NOLAN (Galway, N.): I rise, Sir, to suggest to the right hon. Gentleman the First Lord of the Treasury (Mr. W. H. Smith) the desirability of reporting Progress. It is most unusual to go on after half-past 12 with any important Bill, and I would point out to the right hon. Gentleman that by applying the closure to-night he has got through more Business than he might have expected to get through. The Committee has had the advantage of hearing the opinions of hon. Members on both sides upon the Scotch law, and on many other important points. According to the right hon. Gentleman's own Rules, we are to adjourn every night at half-past 12 o'clock, and it is now a quarter to 1. There is a long Bill on the Paper which will take at least a quarter of an hour, even if there is no other Business to be disposed of. I, therefore, beg to move to report Progress.

Motion made, and Question proposed, "That the Chairman do report Progress, and ask leave to sit again."— (*Colonel Nolan.*)

MR. W. H. SMITH: It is not, Sir, in my power to assent to the Motion of the hon. and gallant Gentleman. The hon. and gallant Gentleman says we have made great progress this evening. I am unable to agree with him, and I am sure that very few hon. Members in the House will agree with him. The progress made this evening is, in my opinion, progress which will not reflect credit on this House. We have disposed of nine Amendments out of 140 of which Notice has been given on the 1st section of the Bill. Under these circumstances, I must ask the Committee to sit for some time longer.

MR. T. M. HEALY: I think my hon. and gallant Friend will be unwise to press a proposal of this kind, and I hope he will withdraw it. But I think we are entitled to some answer from the Government as to the Amendment. The fact that we got no answer naturally drove my hon. and gallant Friend to make the Motion for reporting Progress. I am quite prepared to go on with this discussion, provided that we are treated with even Tory courtesy. I hope my hon. and gallant Friend, on receiving some reply, will withdraw his Motion.

MR. CONYBEARE (Cornwall, Camborne): I do not care much whether the hon. and gallant Gentleman withdraws his Motion or not; but I am of opinion, whatever the opinions of hon. Gentlemen opposite may be, that we have sat here quite long enough discussing this Bill. [*Laughter.*] If we are not allowed to express our opinions, at any rate we can register them; and I shall venture to express my opinions until the right hon. Gentleman the First Lord of the Treasury (Mr. W. H. Smith) brings down his extinguisher again. My reason for supporting the Motion placed before the Committee is that there are several important Bills coming on. At any rate, there is one measure—the Truck Bill of my hon. Friend the Member for Northampton (Mr. Bradlaugh)—which we have been promised should come on this evening. We cannot give due attention to the various provisions connected with that Bill if we prolong the discussion upon this measure through the early hours of the morning. Of course, the right hon. Gentleman the First Lord of the Treasury gets up whenever anything is said from this side of the House with the remark that in his opinion this, that, and the other is not right, and that to his intense regret he finds it his painful duty to oppose us. In this he reminds me more than anything else of a celebrated character of Charles Dickens, whose name, I think, was Pecksniff. All I can say is that if the right hon. Gentleman will be so perverse— [*Cries of* "Order!"] Well, when hon. Gentlemen opposite sit in the Chair they will be able to rule me out of Order—not before. As the right hon. Gentleman the First Lord of the Treasury never will listen to a single word we say, I, for my part, shall have the greatest pleasure in making him walk through the Division Lobbies.

COLONEL NOLAN: I am quite willing to withdraw my Motion; but I trust that when the Amendment is disposed of, the Government will consent to report Progress.

Motion, by leave, *withdrawn.*

Amendment again proposed.

MR. HOLMES: I can assure the hon. and learned Member for North Longford (Mr. T. M. Healy) that it was not from any discourtesy to him, or any desire not to answer his observations, that I did not rise again to reply. But I had already stated that this Amendment could not possibly be accepted. As far as I heard the hon. and learned Gentleman, he did not contest that. He went upon another point, and asked me whether I considered it fair that the Government should adopt the machinery provided by this clause in the case he mentioned. I think it would be unfair, but I do not see how any Amendment introduced here could provide against such a case. Nobody can say who a prisoner's witness will be. I have heard Judges say over and over again that nobody ought to describe a witness as a witness for the Crown or a witness for the prisoner, because a witness ought to be absolutely impartial and to give his evidence truly. If an investigation takes place under this section the persons who will be brought before the magistrates are persons who are supposed to know something of the matter. No one can tell up to the time when the trial takes place who will call the witnesses. But the Crown will not willingly adopt this provision for the purpose of extracting a prisoner's

[*Second Night.*]

case from those who may be his witnesses. I most willingly give that assurance.

Mr. MAURICE HEALY: The right hon. and learned Gentleman the Attorney General for Ireland (Mr. Holmes) is not correct in saying that the case respecting a misuse of the clause for the purpose of extracting a prisoner's case from his witnesses has not been made out. That was the ground on which I submitted the Amendment to the Committee. The arguments I ventured to address to the Committee have not, I think, been answered by the right hon. and learned Gentleman. It is very easy for him now to get up and tell us that this clause, if passed, will not be used in the manner we suggest; but will he be willing—I do not care whether he takes my words or uses words of his own—to introduce a declaration into the Bill, whether in the form of a Proviso or otherwise, that the clause shall not be misused in the manner which I have described? The right hon. and learned Gentleman says it is impossible to distinguish between those who may be witnesses for the prisoner and those who may be witnesses for the Crown. I venture to tell him that there is no such impossibility. I will put a very common case to him. Let us take it that the prisoner's defence is an *alibi*. The prisoner's witnesses in such a case could not be persons who could possibly prove the Crown case. The witnesses who would prove the Crown case would be parties who witnessed the commission of the offence or knew something about it. Those who would be called to prove the *alibi* could not possibly be witnesses for the Crown. I quite grant that in certain cases it is quite conceivable that it would be difficult to draw a distinction between witnesses for the Crown and witnesses for the defence; but that difficulty arises in every civil case. If the right hon. Gentleman's observations are true of criminal cases they are equally true of civil cases; but, notwithstanding this, the Courts of Law have no difficulty in administering the law so as to prevent the misuse of that process of the judicial system which might otherwise enable one party to improperly get hold of the case of the other party. I will ask the right hon. Gentleman again whether he will be willing to give effect to the promise he has given here, and to make

Mr. Holmes

it binding on his successor when he himself is sitting on the Judicial Bench? Will the right hon. and learned Gentleman introduce words into the Bill to carry out the pledge he has given that the powers granted by this section shall not be improperly used for the purpose of getting at witnesses for the defence?

Mr. PICTON (Leicester): The right hon. and learned Attorney General for Ireland (Mr. Holmes) has plainly admitted that under the clause, as it is proposed to pass it, cases of gross unfairness may possibly arise, and all the guarantee he offers against the occurrence of such cases of unfairness is that the Government do not intend that such things should happen.

Mr. HOLMES: I beg the hon. Member's pardon. I did not for a moment admit that, under the clause as it stands, it would be possible at all for unfairness to arise; but what I said was, that it would be grossly unfair to use the power for the purpose of extracting the prisoner's case. I did not say this would be possible.

Mr. PICTON: Well, we understand from the right hon. and learned Gentleman that it will be possible, in certain cases, that a witness who would testify for the prisoner may be examined in secret on oath, and have the whole of his testimony extracted from him. Well, Sir, I think that a very grave scandal would arise under such circumstances. What should we think in this country if a man who was lying in gaol accused of a certain offence had his witnesses examined on oath by the prosecution without his knowledge, and without anyone who represented him being present? I think we should consider that the days of Stuart tyranny had come back, and that we should be ready to rise in rebellion. I thought that the power conferred by this clause was to be used, in cases where no one was accused, in order to ascertain the origin of particular crimes, and that when an accused person was forthcoming it would sink into abeyance, and the ordinary procedure would be adopted. Under the circumstances, unless we have some fair answer to the appeals which have been made from this quarter of the House, I feel that we shall be responsible for a grave infraction of all the principles of justice if we do not contest this clause.

MR. M. J. KENNY: When the right hon. and learned Attorney General for Ireland (Mr. Holmes) said that he had made no admission that this clause might be used for the purpose of getting hold of the case of a prisoner, he was technically right; but when he said that it would be grossly unfair so to use it, he practically admitted that it could so be used. We cannot, Sir, accept any promise such as the right hon. and learned Gentleman has made. The right hon. and learned Gentleman, at the present time, is, as it were, suspended between the House of Commons and a seat on the Judicial Bench; and when he has gone from here, which I believe will be in a very short time, we shall have a new set of officials, who will not be in any way bound by what he promises, and who will, in the most ready manner, repudiate any responsibility for the statements made by their Predecessors. The fact is, that the Government seem to be determined to play against every prisoner with loaded dice. They will only have their own case, and the means of securing the fullest evidence against every prisoner; but they are providing means for securing, in advance, the evidence of witnesses for the defence. They are also providing themselves with machinery to tyrannize over, persecute, and intimidate the witnesses for the defence. These things have been done before by a set of men who will be at the game again in a few months —that game in which they are such practised adepts. They know how to go into prisoners' cells and to tell them that there are in the next cells persons who will come forward as witnesses against them. They understand the process of manufacturing cases for the purpose of getting men out of the way. There are men whom they want to get out of the way now, and they will do it in the same way as they have done it before. We want something more than a mere assurance from the right hon. and learned Attorney General for Ireland that the powers conferred by this clause will not be used for preventing fair trials taking place in Ireland. If this clause passes into law in its present shape, the Government will have an absolute power to conduct any criminal proceedings they like. The hon. Member for Leicester (Mr. Picton)

spoke of the Stuart days. It will be worse than that. The Government will be able to carry on their trials in a more abominable way than in the worst days of Irish misgovernment. It would be infinitely more honest and honourable for them to say at once that this is what they intend. Even if the Amendment of my hon. Friend the Member for Cork (Mr. Maurice Healy) be accepted, I doubt whether it will afford sufficient protection. It would, however, do something towards affording prisoners the chance of a fair trial in Ireland; and therefore it ought to be accepted in a reasonable spirit. If the pledges which the right hon. and learned Attorney General for Ireland is so profuse in giving to the Committee are anything more than mere empty words, I would ask the right hon. and learned Gentleman and the Government why they have not introduced a clause which would embody the real opinions and give us effective safeguards against the taking away of the lives and liberties of men in Ireland, whose lives and liberties ought to be secured? The Government have given us no effective assurance of their sincerity. I want to know from the English Law Officers why they have not shaped the clause in such a way that, whilst giving the Government the liberty they claim to secure evidence against prisoners, it would afford prisoners an assurance that their witnesses would not be seized upon, persecuted, tortured, and thrown into gaol, so that they may be forced to give such evidence as the Government desire, or to withhold such evidence as the Government do not wish them to give?

DR. COMMINS: The longer the discussion of this Bill proceeds the more we become aware of the depths of what I might almost call the chicanery to which its framers have descended. Practically, it is not denied that, after a prisoner is committed—I will not use the expression "made amenable," as right hon. Gentlemen on the Treasury Bench seem to have forgotten its meaning—it will be open to the Attorney General for Ireland, unless some such Amendment as this is carried, to bring before two magistrates appointed by him every witness whom he may imagine to know something in favour of the prisoner. He may get their evidence, hand it over to the prosecution, and

[Second Night.]

exercise such pressure upon them as may prevent them coming forward at the trial, or may lock them up in gaol until the trial is over. It is not denied that such things are possible. The hon. and learned Member for North Longford (Mr. T. M. Healy) has given an instance of such a course being pursued. We need not, however, have any instance, because it is clear that it can be followed; and, unless the Government intend to use this power for some such purpose, I do not see why they seek to obtain it. When they are driven into a corner they say—"Oh, you must trust to us. We do not intend to do anything of the kind." Well, that has been the plea of despotism and injustice all the world over. We cannot trust to their good intentions. We know where good intentions lead to. A large number of good intentions have gone to that place from the Treasury Bench, and a large portion of its foundation has a Treasury odour about it. My hon. Friend the Member for Cork (Mr. Maurice Healy) has given instances, such as the case of an *alibi*, in which the witnesses for the defence may not know anything at all about the charge against the prisoner. There are other cases in which it would be still more dangerous to tamper with witnesses for the defence. A good many crimes of violence will be dealt with under this measure, and a good many cases of assault upon the police and upon bailiffs. We know that in all these cases the guilty party is, as as a rule, the person who begins, so that you have only to keep out of the road the person who knows who began the quarrel, in order to put it in the power of an Emergency man, or a policeman, to attack anybody he thinks fit. If the offending party can keep out of the way any looker-on who can say who commenced the dispute, he can have it all his own way, and will be able to half-kill a man first and send him to gaol afterwards. This is the power given by this Bill; this is the power we are asked to entrust to the right hon. and learned Gentleman the Attorney General for Ireland on his promising that it will not be abused. We cannot trust anybody with such powers, and if they are forced from us we must expose them thoroughly, and let the English people see what the provisions of this Bill really amount to.

Dr. Commins

MR. JOHN MORLEY (Newcastle-on-Tyne): I regret, Sir, that the right hon. and learned Attorney General for Ireland (Mr. Holmes) has not seen his way to give a more specific and definite pledge to meet the very reasonable objections urged by the hon. and learned Member for North Longford (Mr. T. M. Healy). I think there is no doubt—and I do not understand the Attorney General for Ireland to deny it—that under the clause as drawn very great and serious abuses may arise. I have some recollection of what took place under the late Act, and I think that hon. Gentlemen below the Gangway are not wrong in saying that some abuses occurred two or three years ago. I, for one, shall certainly vote for the Amendment. As, however, the arguments have now been stated, and the Government remain obdurate, a Division might as well be taken without delay.

MR. CONYBEARE: Mr. Courtney— [*Cries of "Divide!"*] I may remind hon. Members opposite that I have not yet spoken on a single Amendment. I was going to urge, on behalf of the Amendment before the Committee, that the very argument which the right hon. and learned Attorney General for Ireland has advanced against the proposal proves our contention, which is that the Government under this clause will be able to get at, and to tamper with the witnesses of an unfortunate prisoner. The right hon. and learned Gentleman has said that it is wholly unfair to get hold of witnesses and to deal with them in the manner which, as has been stated on this side of the House, has been adopted. That very intimation, as was pointed out, appears to me to convey the necessary inference that there is a possibility of these things occurring under this clause. But I go further, and say that, according to the argument of the Attorney General for Ireland himself, those deplorable consequences must ensue, because the right hon. and learned Gentleman said, in answer to the hon. and learned Member for North Longford, that when the preliminary inquiry was taking place it would not be known who the witnesses would be. Now, that being so, I submit that the first effect of these persons being summoned and interrogated and subjected to the rack and the thumb-screw will be to pollute the source of justice from the outset. People who may, or may not, be witnesses for the prisoner will be got hold of, and, before you can tell whether they will or will not be witnesses for the defence, will be subjected to all the interrogations and racking inquiries which will be permissible under this Act. I said you would be submitting them to the rack and the thumb-screw. It is quite true. I do not mean that even this Government will introduce physical torture again. But I would point out that there are other means of torture. [*Ministerial ironical cheers.*] Well, in the case of persons who have more sensitive nerves than hon. Gentlemen opposite, there are other means of torture far worse than the thumb-screw, or the boot, or the rack. I maintain—and I shall endeavour to make right hon. Gentlemen on the Treasury Bench appreciative of my contention through the method of the Division Lobbies, if that course should be necessary—that under this clause, as it at present stands, the Government will do all they can to get hold of witnesses and compel them to answer under the threat of longer or shorter periods of imprisonment. This, in fact, is an abominable effort on the part of the Government to endeavour to manufacture evidence for the purpose of bolstering up cases which would be scouted out of Court if left to stand or fall on their merits. It is most monstrous that witnesses should be capriciously subjected to this inquisition and mental rack and torture, which is only worthy of the most iniquitous tyranny of the Middle Ages. I confess that I wonder that even a Tory Government can be so far degenerate as to assent to a clause which unrestrictedly permits the tampering with witnesses and with their evidence to the prejudice of the unfortunate prisoners. To me it is perfectly evident, and even on the very argument of the right hon. and learned Gentleman the Attorney General for Ireland (Mr. Holmes) himself, it is completely fair and just that the disgraceful evil which this Amendment of my hon. Friend (Mr. M. Healy) aims at counteracting—and which will necessarily ensue should the clause become law—should be cut out from this Bill which the Government has brought in with the object of suppressing the Constitutional liberties of the Irish people.

MR. CHANCE: We have been often told, Sir—and told with an assurance which is a scandal in the face of the little basis of fact which is behind the statement—during the course of this debate that the procedure proposed in this Bill of the Government is in many points similar, if not identical, to the procedure which is the admitted practice under the law of Scotland. Now, Sir, I have taken the trouble to consult authorities in this matter, and I find that in this volume—*Hume on Crime*—the procedure in the Scotch Courts is laid down in this manner—that after the libel is raised all intercourse between the Crown and the witnesses for the prisoners is forbidden and prohibited expressly. This prohibition is what we desire to create by the Amendment which is under the consideration of this Committee. In these circumstances I find it—I must necessarily find it—very difficult to understand what is the exact position in argument, and in common sense, of those Gentlemen who tell us, over and over again, that the clause against which the Amendment is directed is the same as a provision contained in the Scotch law, and make a strong effort to justify themselves on this false ground, in their desire to retain to the Government the right to torture and interfere with the witnesses for the defence—the witnesses for prisoners against whom the prosecutors are already prejudiced. Surely, Sir, we do not ask too much when we look for some explanation of unreasoning belief and conduct of this sort.

SIR JOHN SWINBURNE (Staffordshire, Lichfield): I think, Sir, considering the many alterations which it will be now necessary to make in this measure, that it should be presented to the Members of the Committee in a clearer form. I would like to learn from the Government whether, in consequence of these numerous alterations which have taken place, it is their intention to have the Bill reprinted for Members' convenience?

MR. A. J. BALFOUR (Manchester, E.): I think that surely the hon. Member (Sir John Swinburne) will remember that up to this moment the Committee has got through exactly three lines and a half of the measure, and I would ask him to accept as reasonable that under these circumstances the Government think it too much to ask, and quite unnecessary, that this Bill should be re-printed at present.

Question put, and *agreed to.*

Committee report Progress; to sit again *To-morrow.*

COLONIAL SERVICE (PENSIONS) BILL.
(Sir Herbert Maxwell, Sir Henry Holland, Mr. Jackson.)

[BILL 158.] COMMITTEE.

Bill *considered* in Committee.

(In the Committee.)

DR. TANNER (Cork Co., Mid): I want to say, Sir, that it appears to me that, at this early hour of the morning, the Committee should not proceed with this measure. Certainly, there are a great number of Amendments down for consideration; but, really, I think that the Movers are not prepared at such an hour to go into them. I trust that the Government will believe that I am only right in asking that they should be con-sidered some other day—that, in fact, the whole discussion on this Bill should be postponed until some more fitting occasion and opportunity. I hope that Ministers in charge of the measure will see their way to accede to my request, and allow it to be taken at some future period at a more convenient hour than half-past 1 in the morning, after the stress of a severe and straining debate. If hon. Gentlemen opposite are unable to fall in with my views on the matter, I must tell them that it will be my very painful duty to move to report Progress.

SIR HERBERT MAXWELL (A LORD of the TREASURY) (Wigton): I hope that the hon. Gentleman (Dr. Tanner) will allow this Bill to be pro-ceeded with, for I think that the Amend-ment standing in his name is hardly very serious—in fact, the measure might well be advanced until some serious Amendment is reached. So far as I am able to understand, there are none of the Amendments marked on the Paper which are amendments of vital importance. It seems to me that all the Amendments are merely suggestions of improvements on the phraseology of the Bill; and I would put it to the hon. Member that, in these circumstances, we might very well go on with the measure.

DR. TANNER: I am afraid I am unable to agree with the hon. Gentle-

Mr. A. J. Balfour

man's (Sir Herbert Maxwell's) view of the matter; but I will meet him thus far—that is, if the hon. Gentleman is willing to come to a compromise—that if he so desires, I will be content to go on as far as the end of Clause 2 of the measure. However, I want him clearly to understand that I certainly cannot proceed any further than that.

Clauses 1 and 2 severally *agreed to.*

Clause 3 (Provision as to pensions under 28 & 29 *Vict.* c. 113, and 35 & 36 *Vict.* c. 29).

MR. T. M. HEALY (Longford, N.): As to this measure, Sir, I want to say that I think the Government have no right—not a bit—to make the entire of these pensions a charge on the Con-solidated Fund, if that, as I understand it, is what they propose to do.

SIR HERBERT MAXWELL: I am afraid that the hon. and learned Gentle-man (Mr. T. M. Healy) does not quite understand what is proposed to be done. The whole charge will not be laid on the Consolidated Fund. It is provided in the clause that the pensions for Colonial service shall be paid out of Colonial funds, and the Imperial out of Imperial funds.

Committee report Progress; to sit again *To-morrow.*

ACCUMULATIONS BILL.—[BILL 31.]
(Mr. Cozens-Hardy, Mr. Bryce, Mr. Haldane.)

COMMITTEE.

Bill *considered* in Committee.

(In the Committee.)

MR. T. M. HEALY (Longford, N.): I do not know whether this measure applies to Ireland; but my impression is that it does not, and I should like to ask the hon. Member for North Norfolk (Mr. Cozens-Hardy) which is the case? In the event of it being limited to this country, I would suggest to him that it would be very advisable if he could see his way to extend the mea-sure, so that Ireland might have the benefit of it.

MR. COZENS-HARDY (Norfolk, N.): As a matter of fact, this Act will apply to Ireland, limiting accumulations, exactly as in England.

Bill *reported;* as amended, to be con-sidered upon *Wednesday.*

POLICE FORCE ENFRANCHISEMENT
BILL.—[BILL 240.]

(*Mr. Burdett-Coutts, Sir Henry Selwin-Ibbetson, Mr. Whitmore, Mr. Radcliffe Cooke, Sir Albert Rollit, Mr. Howard Vincent, Lord Claud Hamilton, Colonel Laurie.*)

CONSIDERATION. THIRD READING.

Bill, as amended, *considered.*

MR. D. CRAWFORD (Lanark, N.E.): I object, Sir, to the 6th clause of this Bill in point of form.

MR. T. M. HEALY (Longford, N.): I presume, since the Government has given us their pledge in this House not to extend this Bill to Ireland, we may rely that they will not violate the promise.

Bill read the third time, and *passed.*

TRUCK BILL.—[BILL 109.]

(*Mr. Bradlaugh, Mr. Warmington, Mr. John Ellis, Mr. Arthur Williams, Mr. Howard Vincent, Mr. Esslemont.*)

COMMITTEE. [*Progress 28th April.*]

Bill *considered* in Committee.

(In the Committee.)

Clause 3 (Workmen to be entitled to advance of portion of wages).

MR. BRADLAUGH (Northampton): I wish to appeal to the hon. Gentleman the Member for the Hallam Division of Sheffield (Mr. Stuart-Wortley) to withdraw his Amendment, in order that the Committee may be able to postpone the clause, and to go on with the undisputed clause.

THE UNDER SECRETARY OF STATE FOR THE HOME DEPARTMENT (Mr. STUART-WORTLEY) (Sheffield, Hallam): If the Committee will allow me, I desire to withdraw the Amendment which I have moved on the clause.

Amendment, by leave, *withdrawn.*

Clause 4 *omitted.*

Clause 5 (Order for goods as a deduction from wages illegal).

On the Motion of Mr. STUART-WORTLEY, the following Amendments made :—In page 2, line 1, leave out to " in any," in line 8 ; in line 9, leave out from " workman " to last " the," and insert " for the recovery of his wages ;" in line 10, leave out from " entitled to any goods," in line 11, and insert " any set-off or counter claim in respect of ;" in line 12, leave out " such," and after " direction," insert " of the employer or any agent of the employer ;" in line 13, leave out from " otherwise " to end of Clause, and insert—

" And the employer of a workman, or any agent of the employer, or any person supplying goods to the workman under any order or direction of such employer or agent, shall not be entitled to 'sue the workman for or in respect of any goods supplied under such order or direction.
" Provided that nothing in this section shall apply to anything excepted by section twenty-three of the principal Act."

MR. CONYBEARE (Cornwall, Camborne): I do not know if we are to have a reprint of the Bill ; in its amended form it is quite impossible to follow these alterations.

MR. STUART-WORTLEY: I can supply the hon. Member with a reprint to-morrow.

MR. BRADLAUGH : I have considered the wording very carefully.

THE ATTORNEY GENERAL (Sir RICHARD WEBSTER) (Isle of Wight): The Amendments are to avoid the necessity of striking out the clause altogether. Perhaps the hon. Member will follow my reading of the clause as it will stand in its amended form.

[Clause read.]

Clause, as amended, *agreed to.*

Clause 6 (Wages to be paid in pay office).

On the Motion of Mr. STUART-WORTLEY. Clause *struck out* of the Bill.

Clause 7 (No contracts with workmen as to spending wages at any particular shop, &c.)

On the Motion of Mr. STUART-WORTLEY, the following Amendments made :—In page 2, line 20, leave out from " shall " to " a condition," in line 24, and insert " directly or indirectly, by himself or his agent, impose as ;" line 25, leave out " such artificer or ;" line 25, leave out " or shall," and insert—

" Any terms as to the place at which, or the manner in which, or the person with whom, any wages or portion of wages paid to the workman are or is to be expended, and no employer shall by himself or his agent ;"

line 26, leave out " artificer or ;" line 27, leave out from " of " to end of line, and add—

" The place at which, or the manner in which, or the person with whom, any wages or portion of wages paid by the employer to such workman, are or is expended, or fail to be expended, and in any action by a workman for wrongful dismissal, the violation of any terms prohibited by this section, or the failure of a workman to spend his wages, or any portion thereof, at any place or in any manner or with any person shall not be a justification for his dismissal."

Mr. CONYBEARE : I do not wish to oppose the clause, or impose any obstacle to the passage of the measure generally ; but there is a question I should like to bring before the notice of the Committee, though, perhaps, it will be considered at a later stage of the Bill, for I understand the hon. Member for Wednesbury (Mr. P. Stanhope) has to-night placed an Amendment on the Paper. It is a point that seems to be cognate to matters in this clause, and that is the action of employers who have been known to make deductions from workmen's wages to pay the entrance fee and subscriptions to political clubs.

Mr. BRADLAUGH : My hon. Friend will allow me to explain ; that point will be raised by a new clause later. Notice of the clause has been given by the hon. Member for Wednesbury. We are purposely avoiding all contentious clauses to-night.

Mr. CONYBEARE : I am entirely satisfied.

Clause, as amended, *agreed to.*

Clause 8 (Jurisdiction and recovery of penalties).

On the Motion of Mr. STUART-WORT-LEY, Clause *struck out* of the Bill.

Clause 9 (Penalties and expenses in Scotland).

On the Motion of Mr. STUART-WORT-LEY, Clause *struck out* of the Bill.

Clause 10 (Artificer to be paid in cash, and not by way of barter, for articles made by him).

On the Motion of Mr. STUART-WORT-LEY, the following Amendments made :— In page 3, line 7, leave out to " under," and insert—

" Where articles are made by a person at his own home, or otherwise, without the employment of any person under him except a member of his own family, the principal Act and this Act shall apply as if he were a workman, and the shopkeeper, dealer, trader, or other person buying the articles in the way of trade were his employer, and the provisions of this Act, with respect to the payment of wages, shall apply as if the price of an article were wages earned during the seven days next preceding the date at which any article is received from the workman by the employer.

" This section shall apply only to articles."

In page 3, line 12, leave out from " materials " to end of Clause, and insert—

" Where it is made to appear to Her Majesty the Queen in Council that, in the interests of persons making articles to which this section applies in any county or place in the United Kingdom, it is expedient so to do, it shall be lawful for Her Majesty, by Order in Council, to suspend the operation of this section in such county or place, and the same shall accordingly be suspended, either wholly or in part, and either with or without any limitations or exceptions, according as is provided by the Order."

Clause, as amended, *agreed to.*

On the Motion of Mr. STUART-WORT-LEY, Clauses 11, 12, and 13 severally *struck out* of the Bill.

Motion made, and Question proposed, " That the Chairman do report Progress, and ask leave to sit again."—(*Mr. Stuart-Wortley.*)

SIR RICHARD PAGET (Somerset, Wells) : I should like to have an assurance that the Bill will be reprinted. Is it proposed to re-commit the Bill?

Mr. STUART - WORTLEY : This Committee stage is not yet finished. There are several new clauses to move, and it is, I think, unusual to reprint a Bill until Committee is finished.

Mr. BRADLAUGH : There will be nothing gained by reprinting the Bill now ; these clauses do not contain contested matter.

Mr. F. S. POWELL (Wigan) : I think it will be convenient for the Committee to have it reprinted before proceeding further. I say this with no hostility to the Bill whatever.

THE ATTORNEY GENERAL (Sir RICHARD WEBSTER) : We have had a few copies reprinted, and I dare say there will be copies to spare for those hon. Members who desire to have them.

Mr. TOMLINSON (Preston) : The Committee, of course, understand that Clause 3 stands over : it is postponed simply.

Question put, and *agreed to.*

Committee report Progress ; to sit again *To-morrow.*

TRUCK [EXPENSES].

Considered in Committee.

(In the Committee.)

Resolved, That it is expedient to authorise the payment, out of moneys to be provided by Parliament, of any Expenses that may be incurred by the Inspectors of Factories and Mines, under the provisions of any Act of the present Session to amend and extend the Law relating to Truck.

Resolution to be reported *To-morrow.*

MOTIONS.

BUTTER SUBSTITUTES BILL.

Ordered, That the Select Committee on Butter Substitutes Bill do consist of Eighteen Members:—Mr. Sclater-Booth, Sir Richard Paget, Mr. Maclure, Mr. Charles Gray, Mr. James William Lowther, Lord Elcho, Colonel Eyre, Mr. Egerton Hubbard, Mr. Jacob Bright, Sir Henry Roscoe, Mr. Edward Russell, Mr. Walter M'Laren, Mr. Colman, Mr. Hoyle, Mr. Gurdon, Mr. Matthew Kenny, Mr. Conway, and Mr. Hooper *nominated* Members of the Committee, with power to send for persons, papers, and records.

Ordered, That Five be the quorum.

SAVING LIFE AT SEA.

Committee *appointed*, "to inquire into the existing Laws and Regulations regarding Boats, Life Buoys, and other Life Saving Gear required to be carried by British Merchant Ships, and to report what, if any, amendments are required therein."

Ordered, That the Committee do consist of Seventeen Members:—Lord Charles Beresford, Mr. Macdonald, Sir Edward Birkbeck, Mr. Hoare, Mr. Howard Vincent, Mr. Donkin, Captain Price, Sir James Corry, Sir Charles Palmer, Viscount Kilcoursie, Mr. Bruce, Sir William Plowden, Mr. Menzies, Mr. Thomas Sutherland, Mr. Taylor, Mr. Richard Power, and Mr. Thomas Gill *nominated* Members of the Committee, with power to send for persons, papers, and records.

Ordered, That Five be the quorum.—(*Baron Henry De Worms.*)

House adjourned at Two o'clock.

HOUSE OF LORDS,

Tuesday, 3rd *May*, 1887.

MINUTES.]—PUBLIC BILLS—*First Reading*—Police Force Enfranchisement * (77) ; County Courts Consolidation * (78).

MALTA—CHANGES IN THE CONSTITUTION.—QUESTION.

EARL DE LA WARR asked Her Majesty's Government, Whether they can give any information with regard to the time when the proposed Constitutional changes in the Government of Malta will be carried into effect; and whether such information will be in possession of the Maltese constituencies before the next General Election? He asked for this information understanding that the Council of Government had been dissolved.

THE UNDER SECRETARY OF STATE FOR THE COLONIES (The Earl of ONSLOW) said, it was the fact that the Council of Government in Malta had been dissolved; and, inasmuch as it was necessary that a period of three months should elapse before the election of the new Council, it had been thought desirable to take steps, as soon as possible, to enable the constituencies of Malta to consider the new scheme of proposed Constitutional changes. He should hope to be able to lay Papers on the subject, including a despatch written to the Governor of Malta describing the proposed changes, on the Table in the course of a day or two, and they would be in the possession of the constituencies of Malta in ample time before the next election took place.

ISLANDS OF THE SOUTH PACIFIC—THE NEW HEBRIDES.

EXPLANATION.

THE PRIME MINISTER AND SECRETARY OF STATE FOR FOREIGN AFFAIRS (The Marquess of SALISBURY): The noble Earl opposite (Earl Granville) read me a little lecture last night on my imprudence in not following my own rule by refusing to answer a Question where no Notice has been given. I fully admit that his lecture was entirely deserved, because it turns out that I confessed to sins which I had not committed. It appears that my impression was correct. There is a war ship of the Royal Navy at the New Hebrides, and there has been for some time.

COUNTY COURTS CONSOLIDATION BILL [H.L.]

A Bill to consolidate the County Court Acts —Was *presented* by The Lord Chancellor ; read 1ᵃ. (No. 78.)

House adjourned at half past Four o'clock, to Thursday next, a quarter past Ten o'clock.

HOUSE OF COMMONS,

Tuesday, 3rd May, 1887.

MINUTES.]—PUBLIC BILLS — *Ordered* — *First Reading*—Tramways and Public Companies (Ireland) Acts Amendment * [252].
Committee—Criminal Law Amendment (Ireland) [217] [*Third Night*]—R.P.; Truck [109]—R.P.
Committee—*Report*:— Quarries (*re-comm.*) [239]; Colonial Service (Pensions)[158-251].
PROVISIONAL ORDER BILLS — *Ordered* — *First Reading* — Gas and Water * [248]; Gas * [249]; Water * [250].

NOTICE OF MOTION.

ARMY (AUXILIARY FORCES) — THE VOLUNTEERS — THE CAPITATION GRANT.

MR. HOWARD VINCENT (Sheffield, Central): In consequence of the disastrous financial effect the decision announced yesterday as regards the Capitation Grant by my right hon. Friend the Secretary of State for War will have upon corps of Volunteer Infantry, I beg to give Notice that I shall take the earliest possible opportunity of moving—

"That, in the opinion of this House, the adoption in their entirety of the Recommendations of the recent Committee is absolutely essential to the welfare and stability of the Volunteer Force, and that for the Government to punish Volunteers efficient in drill, but unable, owing to accidental circumstances, to come up to an arbitrary standard of shooting, by deprivation of two-thirds of the grant heretofore allowed, involving a fine to individuals or corps of twenty shillings per annum, and by practical dismissal, after two failures, is impolitic in the interests of the Country, and unjust to those who sacrifice much time and money to submit themselves to training for National defence."

QUESTIONS.

INDIA—THE GUNPOWDER FACTORY AT MADRAS.

MR. MALLOCK (Devon, Torquay) asked the Under Secretary of State for India, Whether the Government of India has ordered the Gunpowder Factory at Madras to be closed; and, whether the Madras Government has applied to the Secretary of State for India to cancel this order; and, if so, whether he will be able to accede to the application made by the Madras Government?

THE UNDER SECRETARY OF STATE (Sir JOHN GORST) (Chatham): The Government of India have ordered the Gunpowder Factory at Madras to be closed, and the Madras Government have applied to the Secretary of State for India to cancel that order. The matter is now under consideration.

POST OFFICE (IRELAND) — POSTAL BUSINESS AT BALLYSHANNON.

SIR CHARLES LEWIS (Antrim, N.) asked the Postmaster General, Whether he has received a largely-signed Memorial from inhabitants of Ballyshannon; whether he has inquired into the foundation of the complaint made, as to the premises of the present Postmaster being unsuitable for the business and the convenience of the public; and, if he shall find it advisable, whether he will take steps to secure that the postal business shall be conducted in a more suitable and convenient situation?

THE POSTMASTER GENERAL (Mr. RAIKES) (Cambridge University): I have received the Memorial referred to, and inquiry has been made on its subject by the District Surveyor. The Ballyshannon Office being vacant, the opportunity will be taken to remove it from the Mall, where it has been for some years, and place it in a more convenient position. I think no reasonable objection can be taken to the proposed site; for, although Mr. Mitchell's premises are in the south side of the town, they are within a few minutes' walk of the principal business establishments. A letter box will be placed in the main street at the corner of the Mall.

MERCHANT SHIPPING—SAVING LIFE AT SEA — THE LINE-THROWING GUN.

MR. HOARE (Norwich) asked the Secretary to the Board of Trade, Whether any Report has been received on the use of the line-throwing gun as a means of saving life at sea; and, if not, whether the Board of Trade will institute an inquiry with the view of ascertaining how far the gun is suitable for wreck service, either on sea or from the land?

THE SECRETARY (Baron HENRY DE WORMS) (Liverpool, East Toxteth): Several Reports have been received respecting the line-throwing gun referred to by the hon. Member, one of which refers to experiments made specially at Shoeburyness. These Reports will be laid before the Select Committee which is appointed to inquire into the subject of means for saving life at sea.

POOR LAW (IRELAND) — VOTING PAPERS IN THE BANTRY UNION.

MR. GILHOOLY (Cork, W.) asked the Chief Secretary to the Lord Lieutenant of Ireland, Whether information has reached him that, at the scrutiny of votes for the Glenlough Electoral Division of the Bantry Union, two voting papers purporting to have been signed by Ellen Kingston and Cornelius Brien were proved to be forgeries, and were recognized by the Returning Officer of the Bantry Union as papers that were left at the lodge of Mr. J. E. Barrett, J.P.; whether two genuine papers were also taken at the houses of Ellen Kingston and Cornelius Brien; whether the numbers on the forged papers were altered; if Constable Kavanagh acted in accordance with his duty in collecting at the house of the parties above mentioned more voting papers than he distributed; whether he had taken voting papers at a distance from some of the houses where he distributed them, and from persons other than the occupiers, and in some cases against their wishes; and, whether an inquiry will be held as to the manner in which Constable Kavanagh, of Durrus, discharged his duties at the recent Poor Law elections of the Bantry Union?

THE PARLIAMENTARY UNDER SECRETARY (Colonel KING-HARMAN) (Kent, Isle of Thanet) (who replied) said: The statements in the first two paragraphs of this Question appear to be substantially correct. The Returning Officer reports that the number on one of the forged papers seems to have been altered, but not on the other. He is of opinion that the constable collected at the houses of the persons named only the papers that he had previously left at the respective houses. I am unable to reply to the fifth paragraph, which contains general statements; but if the hon. Member is still of opinion that the constable acted improperly in the discharge of this duty, and that he will be so good as to communicate with me as to any particular alleged irregularities, further inquiry shall be made.

MR. T. M. HEALY (Longford, N.): Have the Government made any inquiry with regard to the forger of the papers?

COLONEL KING-HARMAN asked for Notice of the Question.

MR. T. M. HEALY: Surely that is a matter which refers to the Criminal Law of the country, and ought to be attended to by the Government.

COLONEL KING-HARMAN: In that case I must refer you to the Law Officers of the Crown.

MR. T. M. HEALY: I wish to ask the right hon. and learned Gentleman the Attorney General for Ireland, whether he will take any steps to punish the parties who forged these voting papers?

THE ATTORNEY GENERAL FOR IRELAND (Mr. HOLMES) (Dublin University) said, that he had never heard of the matter before, and, of course, must make inquiries.

LUNATIC ASYLUMS (IRELAND)—USE OF THE COLD PLUNGE BATH AS A PUNISHMENT.

MR. W. J. CORBET (Wicklow, E.) (for Dr. KENNY) (Cork, S.) asked the Chief Secretary to the Lord Lieutenant of Ireland, with reference to the case of "Lamb v. Ashe," tried recently before the Recorder of Dublin, Will he state under what Rule of Privy Council, or Order of Lunacy Department, the use of cold plunge bath is permitted as a punishment for lunatics; whether any Rule was made by Privy Council, or Order issued by Lunacy Department, forbidding the use of the cold plunge bath for such a purpose, on the occasion of the trial for the homicide, in 1872, of a lunatic, named Danford, in the Limerick Asylum, of an attendant in that institution, who was alleged to have caused Danford's death by submersion in a cold plunge bath; and, whether, on that occasion, the Resident Medical Superintendent was forced to resign his office for having permitted the use of the cold plunge bath in Danford's case, and for subsequently partly obliterating the reference to the occurrence in the daily statement book?

THE PARLIAMENTARY UNDER SECRETARY (Colonel KING-HARMAN) (Kent, Isle of Thanet) (who replied) said: The Privy Council Rule relied on by Dr. Ashe for ordering the cold plunge bath as a punishment for lunatics is No. 49 of the Special Rules for Dundrum

Asylum, or No. 79 for ordinary district asylums, both being in identical terms. This Rule recognizes the use of the cold bath as a punitive measure, but with certain safeguards, requiring that it shall be administered only under the express direction of either of the medical officers and in the presence of an attendant or servant. No special Rule or Order was issued after the death of Danford forbidding the use of the cold bath. As regards the case of the Limerick Resident Medical Superintendent, which relates to some 15 years ago, the Government of the day found that he had committed several irregularities both before and after the death of Danford, and they felt it to be their duty to call upon him to resign. However, as already explained to the House, the circumstances of the Dundrum and Limerick cases are quite dissimilar. I may add that the Irish Government have recently decided that the use of baths for punitive purposes is objectionable, and they have given an order for their discontinuance.

INDIA—THE MAHARAJAH DHULEEP SINGH.

SIR GEORGE CAMPBELL (Kirkcaldy, &c.) asked the Under Secretary of State for India, If Maharajah Dhuleep Singh is now drawing any allowance from the Indian Government; and, what is his position?

THE UNDER SECRETARY OF STATE (Sir JOHN GORST) (Chatham): The Maharajah Dhuleep Singh is not himself at present drawing any allowance from the Indian Government, he having some months ago refused to do so. A portion of his stipend is being paid, with his consent, to the Maharanee and her family. If the latter part of the Question refers to his geographical position, I do not know; but his legal and political position is altogether unaltered.

ADMIRALTY—IMPURE WATER SUPPLY TO HER MAJESTY'S SHIPS AT MALTA.

MR. NORTON (Kent, Tunbridge) asked the Secretary to the Admiralty (with reference to the supply of impure water to Her Majesty's ships at Malta, resulting in a serious outbreak of enteric fever), Whether any further Report

on the subject has been received from the Naval authorities at that port; and, if so, will he lay it upon the Table?

THE SECRETARY (Mr. FORWOOD) (Lancashire, Ormskirk): As requested by my hon. Friend, I have inquired further into this question; and I find, from a Report just received from Malta, that prior to the year 1885 occasional testings of the water in the tanks took place. Subsequently, however, to December, 1885, a monthly analysis of the water has been instituted; and if any tank is found to contain water unfit for drinking it is run off, and the tank thoroughly cleaned out. The Report from Malta is somewhat lengthy; but I shall have much pleasure in showing it to my hon. Friend, if he would like to see it.

NATIONAL EDUCATION (IRELAND)—
SCIENCE AND ART DEPARTMENT—
RESULTS FEES.

MR. FLYNN (Cork, N.) asked the Chief Secretary to the Lord Lieutenant of Ireland, Whether it is a fact that the Commissioners of National Education in Ireland refuse to pay results fees to teachers for passes obtained by pupils in "physical geography," in cases in which the Science and Art Department have paid for passes obtained by the same pupils in "physiography" within the previous six months; and, whether he is aware that the Science and Art Department considers the two subjects as different, and pay for passes in "physiography," though the Board of National Education have previously paid for passes in "physical geography" obtained by the same pupils within six months previous?

THE PARLIAMENTARY UNDER SECRETARY (Colonel KING-HARMAN) (Kent, Isle of Thanet) (who replied) said: The Commissioners of National Education understand that the general subject of physiography embraces physical geography; and they accordingly decline, under their Rules, to pay results fees for physical geography when the pupils are enrolled in physiography classes under the Department of Science and Art within the six months preceding the results examination. I am not aware what the practice of the Science and Art Department is with regard to this matter; but the Commissioners of National Education must clearly be bound by their own Regulations.

CIVIL SERVICE COPYISTS—THE
TREASURY MINUTE.

MR. FLYNN (Cork, N.) asked Mr. Chancellor of the Exchequer, Whether he will consider the advisability of amending the Treasury Minute of December last, relating to Civil Service Copyists, so far as to enable "registered service" to count in lieu of "actual service" for bonus, and also for gratuity on retirement, and service on the Census of 1881 to be reckoned in favour of writers whose names were retained on the Register during the period of such service; and, whether he will extend the £7 a-year retiring gratuity to any period of service without limit, and allow parts of years to be proportionately paid for, as in the case of pensions to members of the permanent service of the Crown?

THE CHANCELLOR OF THE EXCHEQUER (Mr. GOSCHEN) (St. George's, Hanover Square): Copyists are only employed as required. When there is no employment for them in a Government Office they frequently obtain employment elsewhere; but their names are retained on the Register of the Civil Service Commissioners. The Government cannot allow time during which no service is rendered to the Government to count for pension or gratuity. No application that service on the Census of 1881 may count in favour of copyists who were retained on the Register of the Civil Service Commissioners during the period of such service has been before me. I do not know, therefore, the circumstances of the case, and I am unable to express an opinion with respect to it. I am not prepared to grant gratuities without limit. The Treasury, in fixing a limit, follows the lines of the Rules applied to the whole Departmental writers. It is not the case that the Superannuation Acts allow broken parts of years to count for pension.

NAVY — CLYDE BRIGADE OF THE ROYAL NAVAL ARTILLERY VOLUNTEERS.

MR. BUCHANAN (Edinburgh, W.) asked the First Lord of the Admiralty, Whether he is aware that the Clyde Brigade of the Royal Naval Artillery Volunteers has no facilities for acquiring the gunnery practice on shore enjoined by General Order, No. 5,981, of 18th October, 1886, as necessary to enable the men to earn the Government grant; and, whether, in view of the fact that this valuable force, numbering 140 men and officers, will have to be disbanded if they cannot earn the Government grant, he will consider the possibility of allowing them, at any rate for this year, of going through their drill on board the gunboat *Forrester*, at present stationed on the Clyde? The hon. Gentleman also asked, whether, the *Forrester* having left the Clyde, the Government would arrange to have another gunboat stationed there?

THE FIRST LORD (Lord GEORGE HAMILTON) (Middlesex, Ealing): Directions were given last week that the Clyde Brigade might drill on the gunboat *Forrester*, then lying off Greenock. The hon. Gentleman had sent him a telegram stating that the *Forrester* had since then left for Glasgow. He had no information on the subject; but would make inquiries. Speaking generally, the Government were most anxious to afford all facilities to the Royal Naval Artillery Volunteers to train and drill; but there would be some difficulty in permanently stationing a gunboat at each place, as they were rather short of these vessels at present. He would, however, inquire and see what could be done.

POST OFFICE (IRELAND)—IMPROVED SERVICE IN THE NORTH OF IRELAND.

MR. M'CARTAN (Down, S.) asked the Postmaster General, with reference to the increased mail accommodation required between Belfast, Newtownards, and Downpatrick, Whether he has received a Memorial from the Town Commissioners of Downpatrick, urging the necessity of improved service; whether he will state the amount for which the Belfast and County Down Railway Company propose to give the increased accommodation required; and, whether he will mention what is the amount which the Treasury offers to give to the Railway Company for such additional service?

THE POSTMASTER GENERAL (Mr. RAIKES) (Cambridge University), in reply, said, that, as he had informed the hon. Member in reply to his Question of April 25, he had entered into further negotiations with the Belfast and County

Down Railway Company respecting the improvement of the mail service. Negotiations of this kind could not be concluded in a day; and while they were proceeding. Questions as to the terms offered or demanded were more likely to prevent than to facilitate a settlement.

Mr. M'CARTAN: May I ask the right hon. Gentleman when these negotiations are likely to conclude? They have now been going on for some months, and the people are kept out of the required accommodation.

Mr. RAIKES: I can assure the hon. Member that no effort on my part has been wanting to bring them to a conclusion.

LAND LAW (IRELAND) ACT (SUB-COMMISSIONERS).

Dr. FOX (King's Co., Tullamore) asked the Chief Secretary to the Lord Lieutenant of Ireland, When it is probable a Sub-Commission will sit to hear land cases from the Edenderry Union, which have already appeared twice on the list?

The PARLIAMENTARY UNDER SECRETARY (Colonel KING-HARMAN) (Kent, Isle of Thanet) (who replied) said: The Land Commissioners report that the Leinster Sub-Commission recently sat in the County of Kildare and the King's County, in which counties Edenderry Union is situate; and that the next sitting cannot be held until the Sub-Commission has made the circuit of the remaining counties of the Province, which will probably be in the autumn of this year.

ARMY—MILITARY PRISONS—REPORT ON DISCIPLINE AND MANAGEMENT (1885).

Sir ROBERT FOWLER (London) asked the Secretary of State for War, What steps have been taken to remedy the defects pointed out in the Report on the Discipline and Management of the Military Prisons (1885)?

The SECRETARY OF STATE (Mr. E. STANHOPE)(Lincolnshire, Horncastle): The suggestions of the Inspector General of Prisons, to which my hon. Friend refers, have been under the consideration of a Committee, whose Report has only been received about 10 days ago. I have myself only seen it to-day; and, therefore, have not yet been able to decide

Mr. Raikes

how far its recommendations can be carried out.

EGYPT — SIR HENRY DRUMMOND WOLFF'S MISSION—THE MILITARY OCCUPATION.

Mr. DILLON (Mayo, E.) asked the Under Secretary of State for Foreign Affairs, Whether his attention has been directed to the following paragraph, which appeared in *The Observer* of 1st May:—

"The report that Sir Drummond Wolff has proposed to fix a term of five years for the continuance of our military occupation of Egypt is calculated, if taken by itself, to create an erroneous impression. We have reason to believe that the proposed engagement to withdraw our troops at the close of 1892 is coupled with two conditions. The first is that nothing is to occur in the interval to necessitate the continuance of our occupation, a necessity of which we are to remain the sole judges; the second is that in the event of our withdrawal we are to be authorized by the Sultan to return at our own good will to Egypt, to the exclusion of any other Power, and even of Turkey herself, if there should be any renewal of internal disorders, or any such default in the payment of Egyptian liabilities as might give rise to European intervention;"

and, whether this is a correct statement of the proposals made to the Porte by Sir Henry Drummond Wolff; and, if not, whether he will state to the House what are the exact nature of these proposals?

The UNDER SECRETARY OF STATE (Sir JAMES FERGUSSON) (Manchester, N.E.): I must once more ask the House to excuse me from making such a statement as the hon. Member asks for. Negotiations with the Porte in regard to Egypt are proceeding; and Parliament will be informed of their nature and result, as soon as this can be done consistently with the public interests.

THE CURRENCY—ISSUE OF COPPER COINS.

Mr. J. ROWLANDS (Finsbury, E.) asked Mr. Chancellor of the Exchequer, Whether the authorities of the Mint will issue copper coins to meet the scarcity created by the withdrawal from circulation of the French coins?

The CHANCELLOR OF THE EXCHEQUER (Mr. GOSCHEN) (St. George's, Hanover Square): Yes, Sir; English bronze coin is being issued as usual. The Mint has an ample supply to meet the demands occasioned by the withdrawal of the French coins from circulation. It may interest the House to know that about £6,000 worth of French bronze coins have been received, and that it is anticipated that the total amount withdrawn from circulation will not exceed £12,000. The Mint have in hand English bronze coin to nearly twice this amount.

LAW AND POLICE—SOCIALIST MEETINGS — INSTRUCTIONS TO THE POLICE.

MR. CUNNINGHAME GRAHAM (Lanark, N.W.) asked the Secretary of State for the Home Department, If the Police have special instructions to break up Socialist meetings, or if they act on their own authority in so doing?

THE UNDER SECRETARY OF STATE (Mr. STUART-WORTLEY) (Sheffield, Hallam) (who replied) said: No, Sir; the police have received no special instructions of the kind.

MR. CUNNINGHAME GRAHAM asked, whether London would be included among the proclaimed districts?

[No reply.]

LAW AND JUSTICE (ENGLAND AND WALES) — PUBLIC PROSECUTIONS— THE SOLICITOR TO THE TREASURY.

MR. PICKERSGILL (Bethnal Green, S.W.) asked the Secretary of State for the Home Department, Who is the Minister of the Crown responsible for instructions given by the Solicitor to the Treasury to Counsel in a prosecution conducted by the Treasury; whether Mr. Poland, in his application to the magistrate at the Marylebone Police Court, to withhold from a jury the cases of the seven defendants charged before him with riotous conduct, was acting by the direction of a Minister; and, whether his intention to make such application was officially communicated to any Minister? The hon. Member said, he would further ask, whether the Home Secretary desired to withdraw the statement that Mr. Poland was not instructed by the Treasury; also, whether he was aware that five of the defendants, who were not Socialists, were most anxious to appeal, but were prevented doing so owing to the amount of bail—namely, two sureties in £50 each; and, whether, having regard to the position in life of the persons, such bail was not oppressive?

THE UNDER SECRETARY OF STATE (Mr. STUART-WORTLEY) (Sheffield, Hallam) (who replied) said: The first of the hon. Member's supplementary Questions is covered by the answer I am about to give to the Question on the Paper; and of the second I shall require Notice. The Question on the Paper does not discriminate between the functions of the Treasury Solicitor, as such solicitor, and his functions as Director of Public Prosecutions. In his latter capacity, he may act either on his own motion or on the instructions of some particular Department. When he acts simply as Solicitor to the Treasury, he acts under the authority of the Minister who instructs him. In this particular case, the usual application was made by the Commissioner of Police for the authority of the Secretary of State for the employment of counsel, and the authority was accordingly given. Such an application is always acceded to, as a matter of course, when the case is one of difficulty, and instructions are formally given through the Treasury Solicitor. When once instructions have been given, it is not the practice for a Minister of the Crown to interfere with the conduct of the case, and he did not do so in this instance. Nor, as a rule, does the Treasury Solicitor interfere with the discretion of counsel in a prosecution of this sort, and the Secretary of State did not so interfere in this case. In the particular line pursued by Mr. Poland, he was not acting under the direction of a Minister. Nor, as far as the Secretary of State is aware, did he communicate his intention to any Minister.

LAW AND POLICE (ENGLAND AND WALES)—DISTURBANCES AT KENNINGTON.

MR. CONYBEARE (Cornwall, Camborne) asked the Secretary of State for the Home Department, Whether his attention has been drawn to the accounts of the disturbance at Kennington, on Sunday morning last, contained in *The Standard* of the 2nd instant, and in letters from eye-witnesses published in *The Pall Mall Gazette* of the same date, and whether those reports are correct; whether, in consequence of the previous disturbance of a Socialist meeting by the "Primrose Society," a Socialist had applied to the Lambeth Police Court for protection, and that Chief Inspector Chisholm had thereupon

"informed the magistrate that in order to stop these disturbances neither party would be permitted to hold these meetings;"

whether it is a part of the duties of the police, and, if so, since when, and by what authority, to deny to any section of the community their right to hold a public meeting; and, whether he will cause an inquiry to be made into the circumstances leading to the disturbance, and the action of the police?

THE UNDER SECRETARY OF STATE (Mr. STUART-WORTLEY) (Sheffield, Hallam) (who replied) said: The Secretary of State has not seen the particular newspaper reports referred to; but he is informed by the Chief Commissioner of Police that it is not a fact that a Socialist applied to the Police Court for protection, or that the Inspector made use of the words quoted. It certainly would be no part of his duty to make any such statement, or to volunteer any statement as to what the future action of the police might be. The Secretary of State sees no reason to make any further inquiry into the matter, which is now the subject of proceedings before a magistrate.

CHINA—THE CONVENTION—BRITISH TRADE WITH THIBET.

SIR ROPER LETHBRIDGE (Kensington, N.) asked the Under Secretary of State for Foreign Affairs, with reference to the Convention concluded between the British and Chinese Governments, as the result of Mr. Colman Macaulay's Mission to Pekin, What was the nature of the concessions promised by China in the interests of British trade with Thibet; what progress has been made by the Chinese Government in fulfilling its promises; and, whether all the Papers on the subject will be laid before Parliament?

THE UNDER SECRETARY OF STATE (Sir JAMES FERGUSSON) (Manchester, N.E.): The agreement with China in regard to trade with Thibet will be found in Article 4 of the Burmah Convention (China No. 5, 1886). As I stated in answer to a Question by my hon. Friend the Member for Central Leeds (Mr. G. W. Balfour) on the 7th of March, Her Majesty's Government entertain no doubt that the Chinese Go-

Mr. Conybeare

vernment will fulfil their engagements under the Convention. There are no Papers that can be laid before Parliament at present.

SIR ROPER LETHBRIDGE asked, whether the House was to understand that China had hitherto made no progress in fulfilling her promises?

SIR JAMES FERGUSSON said, that he was not aware that any steps had yet been taken to open up trade with Thibet; but Her Majesty's Government certainly relied upon the fulfilment of the obligations entered into by China.

WAYS AND MEANS—THE FINANCIAL RESOLUTIONS—THE TOBACCO DUTIES.

MR. HOOPER (Cork, S.E.) asked Mr. Chancellor of the Exchequer, Whether he is aware that the process of manufacture, as carried on by the Irish roll tobacco manufacturers, necessitates each manufacturer having a stock of at least three to four weeks supply always on hand; and, if so, whether he would make provision whereby such manufacturers would be enabled to continue to keep their *employés* at work without heavy loss to them? The hon. Gentleman also asked, whether the Chancellor of the Exchequer had anything to add to the information he gave with reference to the cigar manufacturers?

MR. J. ROWLANDS (Finsbury, E.) (for Mr. BROADHURST) (Nottingham, W.) asked Mr. Chancellor of the Exchequer, Whether he can now state what, if any, arrangements he has made with regard to the Duty on tobacco, in order to prevent the threatened and great displacement of labour in the cigar-making trade?

THE CHANCELLOR OF THE EXCHEQUER (Mr. GOSCHEN) (St. George's, Hanover Square): Yes, Sir; I am aware that the roll tobacco manufacturers must have a stock of three or four weeks' supply on hand, and I have to inform the hon. Gentleman that the month has been given to allow the manufacturers an opportunity to reduce their stocks to the lowest possible limit. This arrangement was made entirely in the interest of the roll manufacturers, and it was never expected that they would entirely cease working; and there is no reason why they should incur any loss by continuing to work, as they need not reduce their prices till their stocks on the 21st of May are exhausted. Having ascertained that the cigar manufacturers stood in a different position from the rest of the trade as regards the disposal of their stocks, and could be treated separately without injustice to its other branches, I have, with a view to avoiding a threatened wholesale discharge of workpeople—while demurring to its necessity—made arrangements by which, under strict precautions against abuse, and under careful supervision, the cigar manufacturers might clear between this and the 21st of May so much tobacco as they would work up in the time, and obtain a rebate of 4*d.* per lb. upon it at the end of the period.

MR. HOOPER asked, could the Chancellor of the Exchequer see any objection to extending that privilege to the case of Irish roll manufacturers?

MR. GOSCHEN said, he was afraid that was impossible, though he should be glad to do it.

MR. HOOPER asked, would the right hon. Gentleman have any objection to receive a deputation on the subject? In face of the information repeatedly given, that the livelihood of so many persons was threatened for a period, would the right hon. Gentleman consider the justice of allowing a rebate of 4*d.* on all stocks held at the 21st instant?

MR. GOSCHEN said, if it was desired, of course he would receive a deputation; but he demurred entirely to the statement that it was necessary for the manufacturers to discharge their workmen during these three weeks. When the duty was raised 4*d.* per lb. the manufacturers had precisely the same amount of advantage as they now allege to have of disadvantage; and he could not conceive that great firms would discharge workmen who had served them permanently on account of the small loss that might be incurred during the three weeks by taking out the tobacco at a higher duty.

TRADE AND COMMERCE—STRIKE OF SHIPBUILDERS AT BELFAST.

MR. SEXTON (Belfast, W.) asked the Secretary of State for the Home Department, Whether he will send one of the Inspectors of Factories, or some other competent person, to Belfast, to inquire and report whether the good offices of the Government can be carefully employed to bring about a settlement of the dispute which has resulted in a strike of 6,000 shipyard *employés?*

THE UNDER SECRETARY OF STATE (Mr. STUART-WORTLEY) (Sheffield, Hallam) (who replied) said : So far as Inspectors of Factories are concerned, the practice has always been to prohibit their interference in any trade disputes between masters and workmen; and the Secretary of State thinks it would be undesirable to deviate from this practice. Nor does he think that the Government could undertake to tender their good offices for the settlement of any such dispute, or to send any person to inquire into the matter.

EVICTIONS (IRELAND)—LORD GRANARD'S ESTATE, CO. LONGFORD—NOTICE TO THE BOARD OF GUARDIANS.

MR. T. M. HEALY (Longford, N.) asked the Chief Secretary to the Lord Lieutenant of Ireland, How many notices of eviction have been served by Lord Granard on the Board of Guardians respecting his Drumlish (County Longford) property; is it the fact that the Government have sent some 100 police to the spot; and, could he state whether any of those families threatened with eviction have only recently been relieved by public charity?

THE PARLIAMENTARY UNDER SECRETARY (Colonel KING-HARMAN) (Kent, Isle of Thanet) (who replied) said, that owing to the short Notice which had been given of the Question he was unable to supply any information.

MR. T. M. HEALY: These evictions are going on to-day, and these people are starving.

MR. DILLON (Mayo, E.): I wish to ask the Chief Secretary to the Lord Lieutenant of Ireland a Question of which I have given him private Notice —namely, Whether his attention has been directed to the fact that evictions on a vast and increasing scale are being carried out in Ireland; whether the practice adopted by the Irish Executive during the administration of his Predecessor of inquiring into the merits of those evictions, and remonstrating with the landlords when their action seemed to be harsh and unjust, is still adhered to; and, whether, in view of the Report of Lord Cowper's Commission, the Government would hold out some hope to the House that a stay will be put upon evictions in Ireland until after this House shall have had an opportunity of considering the Relief Bill now before the House of Lords?

THE CHIEF SECRETARY (Mr. A. J. BALFOUR) (Manchester, E.): I have only just got the hon. Gentleman's Question on my arrival in the House. My attention has not been called to the fact that evictions are going on on an increasing scale. With regard to the Question which he asks me, whether I shall continue what he alleges to be the policy of my Predecessor in inquiring into the merits of each case, and putting pressure upon the landlord according to the results of that inquiry, without giving an opinion of how far that is the most judicious course to be pursued by the official responsible for the government of Ireland. I have to say that it is our opinion the proper method of dealing with evictions in Ireland is by legislation; and if hon. Gentlemen will consent to pass the Bill now before the House within any period at all approaching in its length the period which has on similar occasions been taken previously by other Parliaments, the Bill now before the House of Lords will be able to pass through all its stages in this House in time, I believe, to prevent any suffering resulting from the evictions to which the hon. Gentleman has alluded.

MR. T. M. HEALY: I wish to ask the right hon. Gentleman, whether he himself any longer gives attention to Irish Questions? I, Mr. Speaker, placed a Question on the Paper with regard to evictions on Lord Granard's property, where the people had been recently fed by public charity, and where they are now absolutely starving. Are we to be left to the tender mercies of an Irish rack-renter; or will the right hon. Gentleman himself give some attention to the Questions that we put, and give us something like his mediation between us and this rack-renter? I beg to ask the right hon. Gentleman, has his attention been called to the Question put by me with regard to evictions on Lord Granard's estate, and in which I asked whether 100 police are at the present moment engaged in evicting men who were lately the subject of State charity, and who are at present starving, and which Ques-

Mr. Dillon

tion was treated with contempt by the Irish rack-renter?

MR. A. J. BALFOUR: I understand that the Question now put has been already answered by my right hon. and gallant Friend the Under Secretary (Colonel King-Harman).

BOYCOTTING AND INTIMIDATION (IRELAND) — CIRCULAR LETTER TO THE CHIEFS OF POLICE.

DR. TANNER (Cork Co., Mid) asked the Chief Secretary to the Lord Lieutenant of Ireland, Whether it is true, as reported, that the Hon. Captain Plunkett has addressed a Circular Letter to the County Inspectors and District Inspectors of Constabulary in his Division, requiring lists of Boycotting and intimidation cases in their respective commands since last September, with mention of what evidence would be available in the event of it being decided to institute prosecutions in individual instances; and, whether Captain Plunkett is acting on orders received from the Executive in issuing the alleged Circular; and, if so, what was the date of its issue?

THE PARLIAMENTARY UNDER SECRETARY (Colonel KING-HARMAN) (Kent, Isle of Thanet) (who replied) said: I am not aware whether the Circular Letter referred to has been issued by Captain Plunkett; but it is not at all improbable that it has, as it is the duty of Divisional Magistrates in Ireland to obtain local Reports, both for their own information and that of the Executive, on all matters affecting the peace of their districts.

MOTION.

PRIVILEGE (MR. DILLON AND "THE TIMES" NEWSPAPER).—RESOLUTION.

[FIRST NIGHT.]

SIR CHARLES LEWIS (Antrim, N.): Sir, I very much regret, but I feel it to be my duty to call the attention of the House to what I consider to be a grave Breach of Privilege. I hold in my hand *The Times* newspaper of yesterday. It contains a charge of wilful and deliberate falsehood against an hon. Member of this House, not only in his capacity as a Member of this House and his duty as a Member, but specifically in a speech which he made in this House on the 22nd of last month. It is expressly by no inference, but by direct challenge, that the charge is brought against his conduct as a Member of this House, in the debates of this House, and the charge against him in this journal is, that he has deliberately, and of his own knowledge, made false statements when he was dealing in this House with a statement made by another and a noble Member. It is in regard to that statement, and to no other, that I desire to draw the attention of the House to what I conceive to be a most grave and serious matter. In order to make the matter thoroughly understood, it will only be necessary for me to remind the House that the noble Marquess the Member for Rossendale (the Marquess of Hartington), some days previously to the 22nd of last month, made an explanation with reference to certain statements of the hon. Member for East Mayo (Mr. Dillon), which had been made some days before in debate. The noble Marquess entered into a long explanation as to the groundwork of the charges made against, among other persons, the hon. Member for East Mayo. What followed was this. On the 22nd of last month the hon. Member for East Mayo gave a long and deliberate explanation in detail in answer to the statements which had been previously made by the noble Marquess. Now, Sir, what has happened has been this. It will only be necessary to read three extracts from the article which appears in *The Times* newspaper of yesterday, and which is headed " Parnellism and Crime," " Mr. Dillon "—who I need not point out to the House is the hon. Member for East Mayo—" and P. J. Sheridan." The first extract to which I invite the serious attention of the House is in these words—

" Mr. Dillon, M.P., has attempted upon two several occasions within the last few days to excuse his own connection and that of his brother Members of Parliament with P. J. Sheridan, Invincible, dynamiter, and assassin. We propose to test his statements as a sample of Parnellite testimony. We shall show that nearly all Mr. Dillon's material allegations are demonstrably and flagrantly false, and that Mr. Dillon might readily have informed himself of their falsehood had he chosen so to do. Mr. Dillon's defence amounts to this—that Sheridan refrained from murderous conspiracy while actually in Mr. Dillon's employment, and that the Nationalist Party hope he will 'have no occasion' to return to the ways of Fenianism, because they intend to realize the ends of Fenianism themselves. We shall prove that the assertion of fact is false, and the hope groundless; that Sheridan did plot murder while he was an acknowledged Land League agent; and that he ostentatiously recanted the abjuration which he is said to have made and publicly proclaimed himself a relapsed dynamiter."

I pass over all the detailed evidence, or alleged evidence, which intervenes between that statement and the next statement, which I consider to be a Breach of the Privileges of this House.

MR. SPEAKER : I must remind the hon. Member that he proposes to bring before the House a question of Privilege, which is a definite matter; and the question of Privilege which I understand he is going to raise is an article which appeared in *The Times* newspaper with reference to the hon. Member for East Mayo. I do not think that the hon. Baronet is entitled to review the whole of a preceding debate upon a question which refers to a specific article in a newspaper which appeared yesterday, and which contains the charge which I understand he is about to deal with as a question of Privilege.

SIR CHARLES LEWIS: With submission to you, Sir, I am now reading at this moment from the newspaper article.

MR. SPEAKER: The hon. Baronet spoke of a previous debate in this House in which the noble Marquess the Member for Rossendale and the hon. Member for East Mayo took part.

SIR CHARLES LEWIS: I speak with submission. I was not using any words of my own; I was reading from *The Times*. [*Cries of* "Go on!" " Read on!" "Read away!"]

MR. SPEAKER: Order, order!

SIR CHARLES LEWIS: I will now, Sir, in order to put myself right with you, Sir, read verbatim, if I may be allowed, and entirely and slavishly from the article—

" The material parts of this statement are absolutely irreconcilable with Mr. Dillon's story. Mr. Dillon says that Sheridan's connection with the 'constitutional organization' ceased upon his arrest, and was never renewed. Ford, on the contrary, declares that Sheridan resumed 'his usual labours of speaking and organizing' on his release, and continued them until Mr. Parnell's arrest; that, thereupon, he helped to transfer the headquarters of the League to Paris, and from thence 'carried on the work through the Ladies' Land League and other agencies' until May or June of 1882. Ford's narrative was written a comparatively short time after the transactions it relates; he had no apparent object in falsifying it. He had Sheridan himself at his elbow to supply the information. Fortunately, we are not driven to choose between the word of Mr. Dillon and the word of Patrick Ford and P. J. Sheridan. The testimony of the latter is corroborated, and the testimony of the former is refuted, by the unanswerable evidence of contemporary papers."

I come now to the climax of the article, and that which contains the gravamen of the whole charge on which I shall base my Motion. The article says, in conclusion—

"Our present business, however, is not to prove that Sheridan is a murderer and a contriver of murders, or even to show that he organized murderous conspiracies when a paid agent of the 'constitutional organization' and a trusted member of the Land League Executive. We have treated certain episodes in this scoundrel's career in, perhaps, tedious detail, to demonstrate once for all the incredible falsehood and effrontery of Parnellite apologists. We have examined an elaborate explanation made by one of the most respected of Mr. Parnell's lieutenants from his place in Parliament, and we have shown that it is a tissue of gross and palpable falsehoods."

MR. T. M. HEALY (Longford, N.): I rise to Order. I wish to ask you, Sir, whether the hon. Baronet must not conclude with a Motion? Of course, this is a question of Breach of Privilege, and we are entitled to know whether he intends to conclude with a Motion.

MR. SPEAKER: The hon. Baronet is compelled to conclude with a Motion, as he has raised a question of Privilege.

SIR CHARLES LEWIS: I have not the slightest hesitation in saying that I intend to take the invariable course, which is to ask that this article should be read by the Clerk at the Table; and upon this article I shall make a Motion. I will proceed with the extract—

"Whether Mr. Dillon was or was not conscious that the statements he was making were untrue is a point of little public moment. But it is right and necessary that the world should know that 'the Bayard of the League' has given an entirely fictitious account of a series of important transactions in which he himself and several of his leading Colleagues in the House were principal actors. We are reduced to this alternative—Mr. Dillon either refrained from all serious efforts of recollection and inquiry, and recklessly palmed off upon the House as ascertained facts within his personal knowledge a mass of confused, inaccurate, and unexamined memories, or he deliberately told the House a detailed story which he knew to be untrue. In either case several of his Colleagues must have known that his statements were unfounded."

Sir Charles Lewis

Now, Sir, the course which I thought it proper to pursue, under the circumstances, was to write this letter to the hon. Member for East Mayo, which was delivered to him, I believe, about midday or early this afternoon — "Sir Charles Lewis presents his compliments to Mr. Dillon"—[*Laughter.*] I do not see why, in this case, I should disregard the ordinary courtesies of life—

"Sir Charles Lewis presents his compliments to Mr. Dillon, and begs leave to draw his attention to an article in *The Times* charging him with deliberate and intentional untruth in his explanatory speech delivered in the House of Commons on the 22nd ultimo. It is the intention of Sir Charles Lewis to bring this matter before the House as a grave Breach of Privilege; but should Mr. Dillon, as the gentleman chiefly and primarily concerned, desire to introduce the subject in vindication of his own character, Sir Charles Lewis will, on receiving an intimation to that effect, make way for Mr. Dillon, provided it is done to-day. Sir Charles Lewis reserves to himself the right to read this letter to the House."

[*Laughter and ironical cheers.*] Well, Sir, I will make no remark upon the cheers which have proceeded from the other side of the House than this—that if hon. Members of this House, when a charge of wholesale and wilful falsehood is made against an hon. Member in connection with his conduct in the course of debate, think that it is a matter of no importance, I venture to disagree with them. In these extracts which I have read there is no possible evasion or escape from the result that a Member of this House is charged with having uttered a wilful and deliberate falsehood in the course of debate, with the intention to deceive the House. It is not necessary for me to repeat over again the extraordinarily strong language used in this article. Every gentleman is the guardian of his own honour. It is not for me to suggest what course any Member of this House should take; but what I venture to say is this—that never in the history of this Parliament have such charges been made in any public channel of communication such as the *The Times* newspaper, and have been passed without notice being taken of them. But while every man is the guardian of his own honour, this House ought to be the guardian of its own honour; and though certain persons may say that such charges, made with such circumstantial surroundings and detail, do not require to be noticed, and only deserve the contempt of hon. Members against whom they are made, I venture to say that this House ought to take notice of them, and in whatever light it may regard the character of an hon. Member as a politician, is bound to take up this article and to resent the assault made upon the character of its Members, unless it can be justified and proved at the Bar of the House. I am not going to detain the House any longer on this occasion; but I shall have to make a Motion afterwards. I wish now to move, in the ordinary course, that the extracts from this article be read at the Table.

Complaint made to the House by Sir Charles Lewis, Member for North Antrim, of certain passages in *The Times* of the 2nd of May :—

The said Paper was delivered in, and the passage complained of read, as followeth :—

"Our present business, however, is not to prove that Sheridan is a murderer and a contriver of murders, or even to show that he organized murderous conspiracies when a paid agent of the ' Constitutional Organisation,' and a trusted member of the Land League Executive. We have treated certain episodes in this scoundrel's career in perhaps tedious detail, to demonstrate once for all the incredible falsehood and effrontery of Parnellite apologists. We have examined an elaborate explanation made by one of the most respected of Mr. Parnell's lieutenants from his place in Parliament, and we have shown that it is a tissue of gross and palpable falsehoods. Whether Mr. Dillon was or was not conscious that the statements he was making were untrue, is a point of little public moment. But it is right and necessary that the world should know that ' the Bayard of the League' has given an entirely fictitious account of a series of important transactions in which he himself and several of his leading Colleagues in the House were principal actors. We are reduced to this alternative—Mr. Dillon either refrained from all serious efforts of recollection and inquiry, and recklessly palmed off upon the House, as ascertained facts within his personal knowledge, a mass of confused, inaccurate, and unexamined memories, or he deliberately told the House a detailed story which he knew to be untrue. In either case, several of his Colleagues must have known that his statements were unfounded. The party sat exulting by, and endorsed the fabrication."

SIR CHARLES LEWIS said : I now beg to move that the publication in *The Times* newspaper of the 2nd of May, of the article headed " Parnellism and Crime," is a Breach of the Privileges of this House.

MR. MUNTZ (Warwickshire, Tamworth): I beg to second the Motion.

Motion made, and Question proposed,

"That the publication in *The Times* newspaper of the 2nd of May, of the article headed ' Parnellism and Crime,' constitutes a breach of the Privileges of this House."—(*Sir Charles Lewis.*)

MR. CHILDERS (Edinburgh, S.): As a point of Order, I beg to submit that, according to the ruling in Sir Erskine May's book, it is necessary, in the first place, that the hon. Baronet should state the name of the printer and publisher whom it is desired to bring before the House?

SIR CHARLES LEWIS: I do not know whether this is the proper time for doing that; but I may say that the name of the printer is George Edward Wright.

An hon. MEMBER: Who is the publisher ?

MR. LABOUCHERE (Northampton): And the proprietor ?

MR. SPEAKER: With reference to what has fallen from the right hon. Gentleman the Member for East Edinburgh (Mr. Childers), I may say that the first step is that the Motion be put, "That this constitutes a Breach of Privilege." It is for the House to decide that question, and also what further steps ought to be taken.

MR. DILLON (Mayo, E.): Must that Motion be decided before anyone is entitled to address the House ?

MR. SPEAKER: I will put the Motion first, and then any hon. Gentleman will be entitled to address the House. The Question is, "That the publication in *The Times* newspaper of the 2nd of May, of the article headed ' Parnellism and Crime ' is a Breach of the Privileges of the House."

MR. DILLON : Mr. Speaker, I have not, so far as I am concerned personally, the slightest objection to urge against this Motion. As far as I am personally concerned, I welcome it, and I have only one objection against it, and that is, that it will inevitably lead to a great deal of waste of the time of the House. Before I make any observations on the charge levelled at me by the hon. Baronet, I would like to ask you, Sir, a few questions as to the course of procedure, of which I confess I am entirely ignorant. I want to know what course this debate will take, and whether, in the event of its being determined that this is a Breach of Privilege, and that the printer be had up before the Bar of the House, at what stage it will be most convenient for me to make a detailed reply to these charges, inasmuch as I only read them carefully for the first time about an hour ago, it will be necessary to have a little time to look into these detailed statements. Therefore, I ask you, Sir, what is the usual course of procedure, as it may be more convenient to answer these statements at some other period than the present? Before I sit down, having asked that question, I have only to say, with regard to the course adopted by the hon. Baronet, that I was under the impression that your ruling, Mr. Speaker, on the occasion lately when the hon. Member for West Belfast (Mr. Sexton) brought forward an analogous case, was that it was not open to us to bring forward attacks made in the newspapers as questions of Privilege; and I may add that it has been my practice, since I became a Member of this House, to abstain from trespassing upon the time of the House, or wasting its time by noticing the repeated attacks of newspapers, which I have always treated with contempt.

MR. SPEAKER: With regard to the questions put to me by the hon. Member for East Mayo, I may tell him, in the first place, that I have not seen the article in any detail until it was shown to me not long ago. As to the exact Procedure in the case it is this. I have put the Motion to the House that the words contained in the article constitute a Breach of the Privileges of the House. That, of course, will be for the House to decide, and if the House decides that a Breach of Privilege has been committed, a Motion may be made that certain persons do attend at the Bar of this House. But, as the hon. Member says, he is not prepared at this moment to enter into a detailed statement in reference to these charges made by *The Times* newspaper, and read to-day by the hon. Baronet the Member for North Antrim, the debate can be adjourned; and I need not say that if it is adjourned it will retain the same place and privilege of priority as it does at the present moment. With regard to the other question, there is no analogy whatever between the case brought forward by the hon. Member for West Belfast and the case now before the House.

Mr. Dillon

THE FIRST LORD OF THE TREASURY (Mr. W. H. SMITH) (Strand, Westminster): I wish to state that I was entirely unaware of the intention of the hon. Baronet the Member for North Antrim (Sir Charles Lewis) to raise this question until I came down to the House. It appears to me, Sir, that the course which you have suggested is the proper course to take, as the hon. Member for East Mayo (Mr. Dillon) has stated that he has not had an opportunity to consider fully the details of the charges made in *The Times* newspaper, which have been read by the hon. Baronet the Member for North Antrim. He has indicated his desire—I think I am correctly interpreting him—to make a statement to the House with reference to them.

MR. DILLON: The right hon. Gentleman has misunderstood me. The difficulty I felt myself placed in was this—that I did not know exactly what position to take up with regard to the Motion. I distinctly stated that I did not wish to postpone the matter. If the House decides that it is a Breach of Privilege and directs that the offender be brought to the Bar, I am perfectly prepared to face *The Times* newspaper, but I do not intend—I have no desire to enter into any personal statement or defence. The reason I asked the question was that if it is decided that this is a Breach of Privilege, and if you bring the printer and publisher of *The Times* newspaper to the Bar of this House I am quite prepared to enter into a statement. But I have no desire to do so unless it is declared that this is a Breach of Privilege.

MR. W. H. SMITH: I have no desire to enter into the question whether the matter constitutes a Breach of Privilege or not. I understand that it is an open question; it is for the House to determine whether the statement contained in this newspaper article which has been read by the hon. Baronet constitutes a Breach of Privilege or not. But there are questions of fact involved, and questions of fact ought not to be argued without Notice and without consideration by this House. I should venture to think that the best course, under all the circumstances of the case, is that we should adjourn the debate. [*Cries of* "No, no!"] Well, Sir, the hon. Member has himself expressed a desire to have some time to look into the matter. I deprecate that the time of the House should be unnecessarily wasted by any unnecessary debate or consumption of the time of the House. If it be the wish of the House to consider at once questions of which we have had no notice whatever, I should not seek to interfere with that decision; but I think it would be more fair and reasonable to all parties, to the hon. Member himself, and to the hon. Baronet behind me, and more suitable to the serious questions involved in the statements made to the House, if further time should be allowed for consideration. I therefore beg to move that the debate be now adjourned.

Mr. T. M. HEALY: Of all the un-reasonable propositions I have ever heard made in this House, the attempt of the right hon. Gentleman the First Lord of the Treasury (Mr. W. H. Smith) to shunt this debate is the most un-reasonable. The hon. Baronet the Member for North Antrim (Sir Charles Lewis) has made a series of charges against the hon. Member for East Mayo, founded upon statements which have appeared in *The Times* newspaper, and which he says form a Breach of the Privileges of this House, whatever the hon. Member for East Mayo might say with regard to them. Supposing that a man says that I am a murderer. That may or may not be so, but any statement made by me that I am not a murderer would make it less a Breach of the Privileges of this House. The House assumes, as a matter of course, that every one of its Members, including the hon. Baronet, is an honourable man, and therefore any statement made by the hon. Member for East Mayo in no way affects the question whether the charges form a Breach of the Privileges of this House or not. A statement of this character the House can decide upon its merits, bearing in mind what is due to the dignity of the House, and if the House declares that the charges form a Breach of its Privi-leges, then will come the time for my hon. Friend the Member for East Mayo to make his reply, and the House will deal with the charges in a proper manner —whatever that manner may be. But surely the House is now in a position to decide whether a series of libellous statements affecting character form a Breach of Privilege or not. The last time the hon. Baronet called the attention of the House to a Breach of Privilege

was when he complained of a statement in *The World* that he wore a white waistcoat.

SIR CHARLES LEWIS: The hon. and learned Member is not correct. I never brought that under the notice of the House as a Breach of Privilege.

Mr. T. M. HEALY: It is a very con-venient thing for the hon. Baronet to have forgotten the fact, but if he has forgotten it I have not.

SIR CHARLES LEWIS: Will the hon. Member favour me with the year, the month, and the day when I did so.

MR. T. M. HEALY: If the hon. Baronet can give us the year, the month, and the day, and the other particulars of his charges against my hon. Friend, I will also supply him with the particulars he asks for. The Motion of the right hon. Gentleman the First Lord of the Treasury for the adjournment of the House is most unreasonable. We ought to know from the right hon. Gentleman whether he intends that the time of the House should be wasted by one of his own Party, apparently with his own con-nivance, and why, after having allowed a supporter, without a single word of protest, to advertise *The Times*, and to give Mr. John Walter the step in the Peerage which he desires, he should then, having allowed the hon. Baronet to give a poisonous stab which may or may not be suited to certain natures, he comes down, and instead of moving the closure—which is more in his line—he should, in order to save the time of the House, move the adjournment of the debate. I must say, that for the right hon. Gentleman to take such a course is, at least, most unreasonable. The right hon. Gentleman must have known what was going to take place, and if he wished to have saved the time of the House he should have made an appeal to the hon. Baronet at the proper time; but, having allowed the hon. Baronet to bring the matter forward, the least he can do is to allow the debate to proceed some little way; but instead of doing that the right hon. Gentleman makes a Motion, knowing that, in accordance with the strict rule of the House, every speaker is compelled to confine himself strictly to the question of the adjournment of the debate. I ask the right hon. Gentleman to withdraw the Motion for the adjournment of the debate. As yet I have not had an op-portunity of reading *The Times*, but copies can soon be obtained, and I shall be happy to do so. Let the Motion be withdrawn, let us get a copy of this, and then the charges can easily be digested, and we shall be able to dispose of them in a proper manner. I do not ask that each of the 670 Members should be supplied with a copy; one will be sufficient. I certainly think the right hon. Gentleman ought to withdraw the Motion. These charges have been made by an hon. Member whom the right hon. Gentleman the First Lord of the Treasury has lately promoted to the rank of a Baronet; and it has been distinctly stated by the hon. Baronet that they have been made in the interests of the House, and in the interests of Her Majesty's Government. [*Cries of* "No!"] Surely, the hon. Baronet is a faithful follower of Her Majesty's Government --he has been epauletted by them, and elevated into one of their recognized champions. Under the circumstances, I must say that the Government are taking a most unfair course towards the Irish Party. If a Motion of this kind is accepted, what will the supporters of the Government do? They will go to the country and crow, and pretend that we wanted an adjournment—that we are anxious to shelve these charges. We are not anxious to shelve them. We are anxious to deal with them when they are brought forward in a proper manner. When the extracts from the article in *The Times* were read at the Table, there was such a constant "buzz" in the House that we were unable to hear what the words were. We heard the name of " P. J. Sheridan " mentioned, but we have heard that name pretty frequently. We presume it was a repetition of the old and stale charges, and we are perfectly ready to deal with them. Any statement *The Times* may have to make against my hon. Friend the Member for East Mayo will not affect the House at large. Any statement my hon. Friend may make will not affect his Colleagues. I, therefore, think that the right hon. Gentleman has been most ill-advised in the course which he has taken in moving the adjournment of the debate, which is practically giving the traditional day's start to the liar which is always of so much advantage in a lie. When these charges are brought forward in a proper way in this House, the Irish Members will be as they have usually been as

Mr. T. M. Healy

able to face them as the hon. Baronet was unable to face the charge of corruption at Derry.

MR. DILLON : I am bound to resist to the best of my ability the Motion for the adjournment of the debate. The right hon. Gentleman the First Lord of the Treasury seems to have completely misunderstood the few words I addressed to you, Sir, in regard to the course of procedure upon the action which has been taken by the hon. Baronet. These charges were made against me in *The Times* newspaper, and, as I stated on a previous occasion in this House, I should never, as far as I am concerned, think of wasting five minutes of the time of this House on any charge which *The Times*—or any other newspaper of that class—might bring against me. But when an hon. Member of this House takes upon himself to write the letter which he has done. I can only say that if he had not brought this Motion I should have directed your attention, Sir, to it as being a gross breach of courtesy and good breeding, if not of the Privileges of this House, because the letter plainly charges me with deliberate falsehood, and with cowardice to boot, and then having written that letter—a most improper letter for any Member of the House to write to another—he comes down to this House and practically repeats the charges by the Motion he has made. I am, therefore, entitled to demand—although I am only an humble Member of this House—I am entitled to demand, at the hands of the Government, that that charge shall be brought to an issue here without further delay, and that the country and the supporters of the hon. Member opposite shall not be told to-morrow that I played the part of a coward here to-day; and as I am charged by the hon. Baronet with being, and that I shrank from facing this issue or requested any delay. That would be an utterly false statement of my position. My position is this—I deliberately say that the two columns which appear in *The Times* are calumnies, base and atrocious calumnies, and are deliberate, malicious, and abominable misrepresentations of the truth. I am prepared to face the printer and publisher of *The Times* at any moment, and more especially when he is brought here by the vote of this House, and to prove that he is himself—that which he charges me with being—a foul and cowardly liar. I seek no time to make my defence, but I deny the right of the hon. Baronet to put me on my defence until he brings my accuser to that Bar, when a Motion of this kind is made. The reason, Sir, that I asked for your instructions in the matter was that I did not wish to place myself in the position of opposing this Motion. I support the Motion. I want the printer of *The Times* there at that Bar. And if he be brought there I shall prove to conviction that he is as base and as cowardly a liar as he wishes to make me out to be.

THE CHAIRMAN OF WAYS AND MEANS (Mr. COURTNEY) (Cornwall, Bodmin): I take part in this debate with great reluctance, and I think I may be permitted to do so if I say at the out-set that I do so as *amicus curiæ*, and in order to suggest, if possible, to the House what I think ought to be done. The hon. Baronet the Member for North Antrim (Sir Charles Lewis) has read certain extracts from a newspaper, and the hon. Member for North Longford says—"We have not seen these extracts from *The Times.*" I understood, Sir, that even you, in the incidental remarks you made, said that you had not seen them in detail. They are not only fresh to you, but I believe that very few hon. Members have been able to study them closely. The extracts have doubtless been read at the Table; but I venture to say, with the greatest respect to our able Clerk, that the reading of them at the Table did not convey any accurate knowledge to the House of the contents of the article. As the vast majority of the Members of the House have not care-fully studied those articles, it would be extremely dangerous to the character of the House as a tribunal seeking to do right between all the parties concerned, not only hon. Members of the House, but persons outside, to proceed to decide the question whether the articles are not a Breach of Privilege. Upon that ground, I, therefore, suggest that the Motion for the adjournment of the de-bate should be agreed to, and that the debate should be adjourned until Thursday next, the latest day to which it would be adjourned. I do not make that suggestion because I think that the hon. Member for East Mayo desires to put aside these charges. It must be admitted that he has made a most eloquent pro-

test. Between now and Thursday hon. Members can have the article in their hands, and have an opportunity of con-sidering it. If the House does, on Thursday, come to the conclusion that the article is a libel and a Breach of the Privileges of the House, I have no doubt that the House will not hesitate to follow up the consequences of that con-clusion—one of which, I apprehend, would be bringing the offender of the Privileges of the House before the Bar of the House. The hon. Member for East Mayo will not be injured in any degree by the delay. I think the cha-racter of the House requires that such a delay should occur before the House proceeds with a matter which involves the examination of an article which may be new to many hon. Members. I may further say, in support of postponement, that, on hearing the article read, I saw a manifest discrepancy—I do not know whether it is important or not—between the article and what the hon. Member appears to have thought he has found in the article. I mention that as an illustration of the necessity for appealing to hon. Members, and especially to those who are, and may, justifiably and pro-perly, be excited by the article being brought before this Assembly, to agree to an adjournment, so that we may approach, in a proper temper, the exa-mination and the consideration of the article on Thursday next.

LORD RANDOLPH CHURCHILL (Paddington, S.): I rise, Sir, for the purpose of giving what humble support I may to the remarks of the hon. Mem-ber for Bodmin (Mr. Courtney) who has just sat down. I feel that the Motion which the right hon. Gentleman the Leader of the House (Mr. W. H. Smith) has made is, in all the circumstances of the case, the wisest Motion that could be made, not only on the ground that it would be very convenient to hon. Mem-bers to have the opportunity of examin-ing with care the passages complained of, but also on the ground that the House of Commons, at the present day, cannot, I imagine, be too careful in guarding against the multiplication of questions of Privilege. It appears to me that we should not hastily or rashly come to the conclusion that a claim to bring any matter before this House as a question of Privilege is necessarily a Breach of the Privileges of the House, or a matter with which the House of Commons only can deal. There are other matters which might be examined which, undoubtedly, would be Breaches of Privilege, and which only the House could deal with; but there are other matters which the House of Commons had better leave to the Courts of Law. In so far as Breaches of Privilege partake of the nature of libel upon individuals, they are matters which, I think, the House of Commons should be chary of entertaining. The House of Commons cannot afford any adequate remedy to a person injured by a libel such as that which is complained of now. Suppose you had the printer and publisher of a libel at the Bar of the House, there is no penalty you could inflict upon him beyond imprisonment; but, suppose the printer and publisher of *The Times* has been guilty of a libel, is proceeded against in a Court of Law, and is convicted by a jury, then the penalty may be inflicted which may be of a most severe character. Therefore, what I would impress upon the House is this— we ought to be most careful not to admit that it is in the power of any newspaper to publish statements about hon. Members of the House of such a character as may at any moment produce a privileged interruption to our ordinary Business. That seems to me to be the danger involved in this matter. If you admit the right of *The Times* to make statements against a Member in respect of the debates of this House which are to be met subsequently at the Bar of the House, it is in the power of any newspaper to seek notoriety by writing libellous attacks upon Members of the House and being brought to the Bar to support them. Therefore, I advocate adjournment because I am anxious that those who have experience of the practice of the House, such as the right hon. Gentleman the Leader of the Opposition (Mr. W. E. Gladstone), and others, should examine the matter, and see whether, even if the statements complained of are libellous, they are still matters which ought to be treated as a Breach of the Privileges of the House. It is with no wish to decide partially as between one side and the other that I am anxious that the Motion of the Government should be agreed to. The liberty of the Press is so important, and has been so extended, that the House of

Lord Randolph Churchill

Commons should be most careful, in such a grave matter, not to take any false or hasty step.

MR. SEXTON (Belfast, W.): The noble Lord the Member for South Paddington (Lord Randolph Churchill) has suddenly grown astonishingly timid and circumspect. He himself has not been ashamed in recent speeches in this country, when he was not face to face with us, to avail himself of the currency of these scandalous and miserable charges for the sake of gaining a Party advantage. The right hon. Gentleman the Chief Secretary to the Lord Lieutenant of Ireland (Mr. A. J. Balfour), the Minister responsible for the affairs of our country, has not been ashamed to refer, in express terms, to the charges which are the subject of debate, and to give them the advantage of the further currency to be obtained by his political position, and the expression of his opinion that they were well founded. For some time past Gentlemen of the first position in this House have, from time to time, in various forms of language more or less direct, given countenance and currency to charges of this kind. The noble Lord the Member for South Paddington is not ashamed to endeavour to place us in a position of further disadvantage by obtaining delay. Sir, we have been pursued for years by moral assassins. Our position in this country has been rendered painful, and in this House has been rendered most intolerable, and it is becoming a question necessary for us to consider whether it can be any longer endured. It is, at a moment like this, not ashamed of reaping advantage from these charges, the noble Lord comes up and endeavours to induce the House to consent to further delay—at a time when an hon. Member from whom we never expected a friendly turn — the hon. Member for North Antrim (Sir Charles Lewis)—has made an apparently successful effort in the direction in which our efforts were unsuccessful. I will remind you. Sir, that when we put Questions from this side of the House with reference to *The Times* you, Sir, informed us that you could not allow the matter to be raised without a Notice of Motion being put upon the Paper.

MR. SPEAKER : Order, order ! I never informed the right hon. Gentleman or the House to that effect. After the first article had appeared in *The Times*, the question was put to me whether I regarded that as a matter of Privilege, and I laid down the limits of a question of Privilege, and I said, that, in my opinion, no question of Privilege had arisen; but, subsequently, some weeks after the appearance of the first article, I used these words—"I am far from saying that questions of Privilege have not arisen."

MR. SEXTON: I am sure, Sir, that you will understand that I am not intending to call in question your ruling. But only a few days ago I called your attention, Sir, to the fact that the hon. Member for Cork (Mr. Parnell) had, in a speech in this House, declared that the forged letter in *The Times* was a vindictive and a barefaced forgery. I called your attention to the fact that since that declaration hon. Members of this House had declared that the letter was Mr. Parnell's letter. Upon that occasion you ruled that I was not entitled to raise the question as a matter of Privilege.

MR. SPEAKER: The matter is one of very great importance, and I feel bound again to interrupt the hon. Gentleman. The distinction between the two cases is this. I laid it down the other day as a case of presumptive Privilege, that an attack had been made upon an hon. Member for his conduct in this House. The article, as far as I gathered from the words read by the hon. Baronet, went to this effect—that a statement made by an hon. Member in his place in this House was false. I do not wish to repeat the expressions that were used; but it was that charge which constituted the whole gravamen, and it was that which, in my opinion, constituted a question of Privilege, which I do not think it my duty to forbid being brought under the notice of the House. Whether it is a Breach of Privilege it is for the House to decide and not for me.

MR. SEXTON: I did not intend to refer to the matter in any critical spirit as to the ruling of the Chair; but I wished to point out that on other occasions similar questions have arisen that we have more than once—indeed, on many occasions—endeavoured in this House to call the attention of *The Times* and other calumniators as a Breach of Privilege; but up to the present moment we have not succeeded in doing so.

Therefore I am thankful and glad that the hon. Baronet the Member for North Antrim has made the Motion he has made to-day, and I address the House as a supporter of that Motion. I join my hon. Friend the Member for East Mayo in resisting the Motion of the right hon. Gentleman the First Lord of the Treasury which, Sir, I declare to be from the moment it was made discreditable to the Government, and the adoption of which will be dishonourable to the House. I heard with infinite surprise the speech of the hon. Gentleman the Chairman of Ways and Means (Mr. Courtney.) He said that the language of the article had not been distinctly heard; but who wants distinctly to hear it? Does it contain anything new? Have we not been exposed to these charges for months and years? Does anyone doubt the nature of them? Hon. Members may not have heard the exact words read by the hon. Baronet, or by the Clerk at the Table; but does not everyone in the House know that the hon. Member for East Mayo has been accused by this infamous print—*The Times*—of having stated in this House what he knew to be a deliberate falsehood. If that statement is not a Breach of the Privileges of this House, I do not know what can be. Does anyone need to go beyond the title of the article "Parnellism and Crime?" The article asserts that there is a direct association between a body of the Members of this House and breakers of the Criminal Law of the country. The very title of the article constitutes a Breach of Privilege. What plea is raised for delay? The allegations against the hon. Member for East Mayo are definite, numerous, and specific, and my hon. Friend is ready to make his reply. Why should the reply of my hon. Friend be judged to be necessarily antecedent to the declaration of the House upon the question of Privilege? Do you think you will entrap my hon. Friend into an elaborate defence of himself until you take the publisher of *The Times* by the throat and bring him to the Bar of this House. I speak in your presence, Sir, and subject to your correction; but I speak with great confidence, and I say that the question of Privilege is not concerned with the sufficiency of the reply to be made to this attack. The essence of Privilege lies in the nature of the charge, without reference to the reply. You have no right either to call on my hon. Friend to make his reply or to ask for delay in reference to his reply because, by the mere fact of your allowing this Motion to be made, you have given an indication of your opinion. Judging from former precedents set by yourself and other Speakers, you would not have allowed the Motion to be made unless you conceived that a question of Privilege had arisen. The House has to that extent obtained your direction. Now, the simple question raised by the Motion of the hon. Baronet the Member for North Antrim is attempted to be evaded by the Queen's First Minister in this House, the right hon. Gentleman the Leader of the House of Commons, the chief custodian of the collective honour of this Chamber, by a Gentleman who is not ashamed to allow his secretary to write letters to Primrose Leagues.

Mr. SPEAKER: The Motion before the House is the adjournment of the debate, and the hon. Member is now introducing irrelevant and extraneous matter.

Mr. SEXTON: I maintain that it would have been far more decent on the part of the right hon. Gentleman the First Lord of the Treasury if he had abstained from intervening in the debate an obstructive and evasive Motion. I contend, Sir, that the Breach of Privilege is complete, and I challenge any hon. Member, or any hon. and learned Member, to say, especially in view of your recent ruling, that any newspaper is entitled to say of a Member of this House that he has been guilty of wilful and deliberate falsehood. My hon. Friend has replied to *The Times*, and we are ready to reply to *The Times*. The House will know what to think of this game of moral assassination which is now being played in this country, when I tell hon. Members that for two days I have been waiting under a subpœna to be called in a criminal case, but the parties went to a jury without daring to call me. I wish they had called me, and placed me upon the table, because I think that if that had been done even the hon. Baronet would not have had the hardihood to make the Motion he has made to-day. We have in various ways endeavoured to bring our opponents and calumniators to book.

We have hitherto failed to do so in this House, and we have good reason for believing that there is no effectual justice to be obtained outside the House. Now, Sir, a Member of this House, who is a supporter of the Government, has thrown down the challenge—we have heard a good deal lately about challenges that have been thrown down and have not been taken up—and now, Sir, we take up his challenge. What will the noble Marquess the Member for Rossendale (the Marquess of Hartington) do? What will the right hon. and learned Gentleman the Member for Bury (Sir Henry James) do? What will be done in this Motion by this Party in the House of Commons, who have in various ingenious and indirect forms of language, in an attempt to fasten this fault upon us, challenged us to take up the gage? Will they assist us to take up the gage which has been thrown down? The Government have a majority here. They can carry the Motion that this article of *The Times* is a Breach of Privilege. If they carry that Motion, the further result of which the noble Lord the Member for South Paddington (Lord Randolph Churchill) seems to think would be indefinite and uncertain, the printer and publisher of *The Times* would be called upon to appear at the Bar and make a statement to the House, and if he refused to make it, or if that statement were unsatisfactory, this House would be bound in defence of its Member to order an inquiry into the matter. That, Sir, is the step we desire. Will the gentlemen of England—at least, those who have a spark of manhood or chivalry in them—assembled in this House, determine now whether any longer a Party of Irishmen, who have laboured painfully and arduously for many years for the advancement of the liberties of their countrymen, are to sit here isolated at the mercy of every ruffian who calls himself the editor of a newspaper. We ask you as gentlemen, as public men, as men united by the common tie of humanity, to let a Committee of this House be formed; let any Committee be formed which fairly represents the Parties in this House; let it be a Committee on which the Government have a majority; but, at any rate, let a Committee of this House be formed where we shall not be defeated by the jugglery of a Sheriff or the criminality of jurors, and then let *The Times*

Mr. Sexton

or any other newspaper bring along its battalions of forgers and of liars. We should soon bring this miserable jugglery to an end, and expose the wretched extremity of a Party which, finding that it can no longer, on a basis of fair play, maintain itself before the people, has resorted to the devices of the garotter and the Thug. Only give us a tribunal of this House, and humble as we are—helpless as we are here—and powerful as are our opponents—unscrupulous as they are, we shall prove, Sir, that for no greater crime than that we have stood up as honest men, and as men who claim to have some courage in defence of the political rights and liberties of our people, we have been pursued by a system of moral assassination, the most shameful, and the most unscrupulous the world has ever known.

MR. CHAPLIN (Lincolnshire, Sleaford): I sympathize with the desire which has been expressed by the hon. Member for West Belfast (Mr. Sexton), who has just sat down, to meet this charge without further delay, making allowance for the natural warmth which has been displayed. I altogether fail to see what they have to complain of. The hon. Member for West Belfast says that it does not matter in the least what this article contains, and that the name itself —"Parnellism and Crime"—is sufficient to constitute a reason for prosecuting this debate without any adjournment. But I must remind the hon. Member that this is not the first article that has appeared, and which has been described as "Parnellism and Crime." These articles have been published now for many days; and during that time hon. Members opposite have thought it unnecessary to take any notice of them. [*Cries of* "No, no!" *and* "Hear, hear!"] At any rate, no action has been taken upon them, and I confess I do not understand why it is so absolutely necessary to proceed with this debate now, without an adjournment for a single day. Now, Sir, we are asked to decide whether certain statements in *The Times* newspaper constitute a Breach of the Privileges of this House; and it seems to me that in so grave and serious a matter as that it is only reasonable and right that the House of Commons should arrive at a calm, judicial, and deliberate action. If we are to come to such a decision in this case, it is absolutely necessary that we should all have a complete understanding and knowledge of the statements complained of. I happen to be in the same position as the right hon. Gentleman the First Lord of the Treasury. [An hon. MEMBER: Oh, dear no!] Perhaps I may be allowed to state my view without interruption on a matter which I regard as most serious. I am in the same position as the hon. Gentleman the Chairman of Committees (Mr. Courtney), and of the hon. and learned Member for North Longford (Mr. T. M. Healy), both of whom appear to have had no Notice that it was intended to bring the question before the House. The hon. and learned Member for North Longford says that he had never seen this article.

MR. T. M. HEALY: I beg the right hon. Gentleman's pardon. I said that I had never read it.

MR. CHAPLIN: Speaking for myself, and I believe for many other hon. Members of this House, I may say that I, for one, have had no sufficient opportunity of studying these articles, and I have no adequate knowledge of what they contain. I was unable to hear what it was that was read by the Chief Clerk at the Table. That being so, how is it possible for the House to arrive at a conclusion upon this subject when the majority of hon. Members at this moment do not know what the articles contain? Under these circumstances, I think, Sir, that it is absolutely necessary that the debate should be adjourned.

MR. BRADLAUGH (Northampton): I, Sir, intend to vote against the adjournment of this debate, and I desire respectfully to submit to the House my reasons for that vote. The right hon. Gentleman who has just spoken (Mr. Chaplin) has asked what disadvantage it can be to hon. Members on this side of the House to have an adjournment? Well, I will tell him, speaking only for the Radical Members, and not for the Irish Members, for none of whom I have any right to speak, the objection urged to the adjournment is that outside this House these matters are repeated at nearly every meeting as reasons for carrying a Bill now before the House, which I regard as one of monstrous stringency, and I do not desire in any way to co-operate with anyone in securing such delay as will aid in the circulation of unfair charges. What is the question we are

[First Night.]

asked to discuss? The question is, Is the statement submitted by the hon. Baronet the Member for North Antrim (Sir Charles Lewis) a Breach of Privilege? And if his translation of that statement is correct, no more distinct Breach of Privilege could be submitted. His translation, and I took down his words carefully, was that the article in *The Times* charged the hon. Member for East Mayo (Mr. Dillon) with wilful and deliberate falsehood in a statement which he had made to this House. If that be not a Breach of Privilege, nothing can be. I understood the hon. Gentleman the Chairman of Committees (Mr. Courtney) to suggest that there was a discrepancy between the language read by the hon. Baronet and the interpretation he placed upon it; but knowing the legal acuteness of the hon. Baronet, and knowing that in a grave matter of this kind he must have carefully considered every word, I feel sure that the hon. Baronet, when he made himself the guardian of somebody else's honour, as well as constituting himself for to-day the guardian of the honour of this House, took pains not to give one shade of interpretation to the statement graver than it deserved. But the suggestion of the noble Lord the Member for South Paddington (Lord Randolph Churchill) is that this House ought to be very careful how it gets into a quarrel with the Press.

LORD RANDOLPH CHURCHILL : I said nothing of the kind.

MR. BRADLAUGH : I am always unlucky in understanding the noble Lord. We sometimes seem to attach different meanings to the same words. I understood the noble Lord to say that, at any rate, whatever might be the judgment of the House as to this particular article, the one reason why the House should not deal with it was that it only had the power of imprisonment. I have not had the long experience in Parliament which the noble Lord has had, but I have had occasion more than once to examine the Records of the House, and I can refer him from memory to cases in which the House has done more than put into prison those whom it has declared to have been guilty of a Breach of Privilege. That, however, is entirely an outside question, and I only deal with it in order to remind the noble Lord that his memory is not always accurate upon matters of this kind.

Mr. Bradlaugh

What attack upon a Member is to be regarded as a Breach of Privilege if an attack like this is not? What is the excuse for the adjournment of the debate? The truth of the question is another matter, to be dealt with in another way and at another time. There can be no excuse for saying that this debate has been raised from this side of the House for the obstruction of any measure that is before the House; but it has been raised by a favoured supporter of the right hon. Gentleman the First Lord of the Treasury (Mr. W. H. Smith). I cannot imagine that he would have been so disloyal to the Party to which he belongs as to raise it without some consultation with, or communication to, the chief of that Party whom he is anxious to serve. The question having been raised, I venture to appeal to every English Radical—and I have no right to appeal to any others—to give us their votes against the adjournment, as a declaration to the world outside, that they will be no parties to putting into the hands of speakers at Conservative meetings weapons which, even if real, ought not to be used in order to expedite a Bill which is directed against the liberties of a nation, and which will be used for no other purpose.

SIR WILLIAM HARCOURT (Derby): I do not desire to criticize the course which the right hon. Gentleman the First Lord of the Treasury has taken in suggesting the adjournment of this debate. Certainly, the ground upon which he based that suggestion was that he thought that the hon. Member for East Mayo might require time to consider the matter. But that evidently is not the case. The hon. Member for East Mayo and his Friends have demanded that this matter should be considered and determined at once. Well, Sir, in the time that I have sat in this House I have heard a good many cases of Breach of Privilege brought before the House, but, generally speaking, the House of Commons has very wisely decided not to encourage Motions of that kind. It is perfectly plain that Motions of that kind might be multiplied to any extent. There are hundreds of papers in this country which write almost every day things which almost everyone of us, if he chose, might treat as a Breach of Privilege. I may say that I, myself, when I read them very frequently, find myself libelled, and if I chose I might treat it as a Breach of Privilege. But, Sir, there is a peculiarity in this case which I never recollect happening in any other. It has generally been left to the hon. Member himself or his Friends to determine how far he thinks observations of that character worthy of his notice or not. I think that every man who is a wise man takes no notice of that sort of attack, and depends upon his own character for his defence. But we have here—made as a Party Motion—a Motion by an hon. Member who cannot even make the plausible pretext that he does it in defence of the person who is attacked, but who uses the Motion, instead of defending the individual or the House, as a means of personal attack upon another hon. Member. That is an unparalleled situation with regard to a Motion of Privilege. It comes forward and it is presented to the House, though ostensibly as a Motion against *The Times*, in reality as a Motion in favour of *The Times*. It is brought forward by the hon. Baronet the Member for North Antrim (Sir Charles Lewis) as an accusation against the hon. Member for East Mayo (Mr. Dillon). It is using a question of Breach of Privilege, under the shallow pretence of vindicating the hon. Member for East Mayo, and of vindicating the character of the House, for the sake of making what is really and substantially an attack upon the honour of the hon. Member for East Mayo across the Table of this House. Everybody knows that this is the real character of the transaction. It is a charge of falsehood advanced by the hon. Member for North Antrim, under cover of *The Times* newspaper, against another hon. Member of this House. It is so brought forward as stated in the letter which the hon. Member for East Mayo has read. The hon. Member for North Antrim says—

"*The Times* newspaper says that you have deliberately stated in the House of Commons that which is false; I advance that authority, and call upon you to meet it."

[*Cries of* "No, no!"] I think that it will appeal to the candid judgment both of this House and of people outside the House whether that is the true character of the transaction. Therefore, Sir, we are in the presence of something different altogether from a question of Breach of Privilege. It is a charge—a scarcely veiled charge of falsehood advanced by one Member of the House against another, and the Member against whom the charge is brought—on behalf of himself and his friends—demands instant redress. I cannot understand how the House can hesitate for a moment with regard to this demand. If they had said that this charge required time to meet it, everybody in this House would have granted the delay. But they do not demand that delay; they demand that the House shall, in some form or another, give redress, either against *The Times*, which has been used as a stalking horse in this case, or against the hon. Member who has used that stalking horse in this House. One consequence of the course that has been taken will be that when any hon. Member of this House has a hostile feeling against another, he will read every paragraph concerning him in any newspaper, and call upon you, Sir, to deal with it as a question of Privilege. It will be the institution of a new form of obstruction; the time of the House will be taken up every night by having to consider comments in every London or Provincial newspaper upon the conduct of some hon. Member, and whether they constitute a Breach of Privilege. This matter is brought forward by the hon. Baronet the Member for North Antrim, one of the principal Irish supporters of the right hon. Gentleman the First Lord of the Treasury, and we must deal with it as it arises. We all know the manner in which Irish Members have been treated upon this question—how they have been taunted with their unwillingness to meet these charges. These charges have been publicly advanced on the responsibility of a Member of this House, and then when they ask to be allowed to meet them they are refused a decision of the House upon the question. Do you doubt that, according to Parliamentary precedent, to say that a Member of this House has either deliberately stated that which is untrue, or recklessly forbore to know whether it was untrue or not, I do not care what form the charge may take—does anyone doubt that, according to the strict form of Parliamentary precedent, that is a Breach of Privilege? That being so, and considering the circumstances, I quite admit the difficulty in which Gentlemen on the Front Bench opposite are placed; but that is due to their own supporters. The House has nothing to do with that. The position we have got to deal with is this. We have a charge of great gravity and great magnitude advanced in this House, and we have a demand made by the Gentlemen implicated in it that instant measures should be taken to meet those charges. I do not see how we can refuse that demand. Therefore, I do not complain of the spirit in which the right hon. Gentleman the First Lord of the Treasury originally suggested the adjournment; but as it is quite plain that the ground on which he was induced to make it has not been borne out by the attitude and language of the hon. Member for East Mayo, I hope that, in the circumstances, he will not press this Motion, but will allow the House to come to a decision.

THE ATTORNEY GENERAL (Sir RICHARD WEBSTER) (Isle of Wight): Mr. Speaker, I have no wish at all to find fault with the observations of the right hon. Member for Derby (Sir William Harcourt), except upon one point, to which I shall refer in a moment; but there were two statements made below the Gangway opposite which I must be allowed to deal with, and to deal with in the most emphatic manner. One hon. Member said that this Motion has been made with the connivance of the right hon. Gentleman the First Lord of Treasury (Mr. W. H. Smith), or some other Member of Her Majesty's Government. Another hon. Member in the same quarter said that this Motion would not have been made without consultation with Her Majesty's Government. Now, the right hon. Gentleman the First Lord of the Treasury stated distinctly, not half an hour ago, that until he came down to this House he had no notice of it, and he also stated that until then he had no idea that it was going to be made. I think that, under those circumstances, it is going a little too far to suggest that the Motion was made with the connivance of my right hon. Friend the First Lord of the Treasury. It is, I think, at all events, probable, that if any intimation had been given that such a Motion was to be made such communication in the ordinary way would have been made to myself. All I can say is that until I came down to the House, and heard the hon. Baronet actually making his statement, I had

Sir William Harcourt

not the slightest idea of it; and I believe I may say that there was no single Member of the Government who ever connived at, or was consulted upon, this question. I trust that that denial will be sufficiently explicit. I am sure that the right hon. Gentleman the Member for Derby had no intention of doubting the word of my right hon. Friend. If there was a misunderstanding under which the right hon. Gentleman the First Lord of the Treasury moved the adjournment, it was one in which I also shared with regard to the wish of the hon. Member for East Mayo. I understood him to say that he had not read *The Times* article, and that he himself was not unfavourable to some delay. We thought, I dare say wrongly, that the hon. Member for East Mayo was not fully aware of the charges which had been made against him, and that it would suit his convenience to have the matter deferred.

MR. DILLON: As the hon. and learned Member has not stated what I actually said, I think I ought to repeat what I did say. I said, Sir, that I wanted from you information as to the course of Procedure in matters of this kind. What I had in my mind was this, that the House would decide whether the publisher of *The Times* would be brought up at the Bar or not, and that I ought to reserve my statement until such time as he was brought to the Bar.

SIR RICHARD WEBSTER: I thought he had indicated that he had not read the article. Of course, I at once accept his statement, but the point I was coming to is this, and it is one which I wish the House to consider. Hon. Gentlemen opposite appear to be under a misapprehension; they appear to think that if the printer or publisher was brought to the Bar that he could enter into a justification of the charges that have appeared in *The Times*, and could prove the truth of what has been written. But he can do nothing of the kind. If the House decides that it is a Breach of Privilege, it decides it in the absence of the printer. The printer or publisher may then be brought to the Bar. The matter may then be considered, and perhaps punishment inflicted on him; but no statement as to the truth of the charges is permissible from him. Therefore, although I can appreciate the desire of the hon. Member for East Mayo to disprove and meet with emphatic and specific denial the charges that have been made against him, yet I must point out that that cannot be done with the printer at the Bar.

MR. DILLON : What I really wanted was information. I was under the impression that there would be a debate upon the question whether the printer should be punished or not, and I wanted to know whether there would be a suitable time to enter at length into the nature of these charges.

SIR RICHARD WEBSTER: I am speaking now of what the position of the printer would be—the alleged libeller. The hon. Member for East Mayo has spoken of him as a cowardly liar, and I do not wonder at it; because the charges are very grave and serious. It is quite plain that the printer at the Bar would have no opportunity of proving whether the charges that have been made are true. The adjournment of this debate will, at any rate, not alter the position of the House with regard to the question, and if the hon. Member for East Mayo desires at once to make a statement, or later on, I do not suppose that the House would put any obstacles in the way of his so doing. The House must remember that this question of Privilege is an exceedingly difficult one. The right hon. Gentleman the Member for Derby says that there is no doubt that this is a case of Privilege. I cannot say so. I cannot give an opinion so rapidly as he, or in so off-handed a way. I do not think that this is by any means a clear case. I think it is a case that ought to be very carefully considered before the House decides upon it; and I ask the House to remember that it has been over and over again laid down that a question of Privilege is so delicate a matter that it ought never to be approached without deliberation. If the hon. Gentleman the Member for East Mayo desires to make a statement now, I think he ought to be allowed to do so ; but the question whether the printer should be summoned to the Bar ought not, I think, to be decided without extreme deliberation and care, so as to see that no mistake is made. On behalf of the Government, I disclaim the least intention or desire to postpone this question for Party motives, or for the reasons suggested by the hon. and learned Member for North Longford (Mr. T. M. Healy). Whether we were under a misapprehension or not the Motion for adjournment was made as the best way of dealing with the matter, and the observations of the hon. Gentleman the Chairman of Ways and Means, as well as those of the right hon. Member for Derby, show that they were under the same impression. The issue before the House being whether the House should determine the matter now or two or three days hence, I think that, subject to the right of the hon. Member for East Mayo to make an explanation now if he desires, the House would act more wisely if it resolved to proceed with calmness and deliberation, and accede to the Motion for the adjournment.

MR. LOCKWOOD (York): I should have thought there was only one person who ought to be consulted with regard to the Motion of the right hon. Gentleman the First Lord of the Treasury. There appears to have been some uncertainty as to the observations addressed to the House, in the first instance, by the hon. Member for East Mayo (Mr. Dillon), but that uncertainty has now been removed, and I am surprised that the Motion for adjournment is still persisted in. My hon. and learned Friend the Attorney General (Sir Richard Webster) has pointed out that the course proposed by the Motion of the hon. Baronet the Member for North Antrim (Sir Charles Lewis) would not really give the hon. Member for East Mayo an opportunity for meeting the charges in *The Times* as he wishes to do; but the Motion has been made by a supporter of the Government—the chosen Friend and ally of the Government — and it was received with favour on the opposite side of the House. [*Cries of* "No, no!"] Well I did not notice any marks of dissent; but do not suppose that, for a single moment, I am desirous of throwing any doubt on any statement which has been made by my hon. and learned Friend. The hon. Baronet who made the Motion has recently been promoted by his Party, and there is indeed some regret that he was not promoted even to a higher sphere, which might have removed the Government from the unpleasant position in which he has placed them now. No doubt the matter cannot be disposed of to-night; but the hon. Member for East Mayo has the right to

[First Night.]

at once defend himself against the charges brought against him, and, at any rate, advance that defence one stage to-night. The reason given by the right hon. Gentleman the First Lord of the Treasury for this Motion was based on a misunderstanding of the observations that were made by the hon. Member for East Mayo; but, notwithstanding that this ground has now been removed, my hon. and learned Friend the Attorney General has attempted to justify it on other grounds. We have heard from the hon. Gentleman the Chairman of Ways and Means (Mr. Courtney), and from the noble Lord the Member for South Paddington (Lord Randolph Churchill), that there is a doubt whether there is a question of Privilege involved in this matter at all. [Mr. COURTNEY dissented.] Then I withdraw that remark, as far as it applies to the hon. Gentleman the Chairman of Ways and Means, but I certainly misunderstood the effect of the observation he made. The noble Lord the Member for South Paddington certainly expressed a doubt whether this is a question of Privilege or not, and I think it very strange that these doubts should only have arisen after it was found that the hon. Member for East Mayo was anxious to take up the challenge which was thrown down.

SIR RICHARD WEBSTER: Will my hon. and learned Friend pardon me. The right hon. Gentleman the First Lord of the Treasury distinctly said, in reference to the Motion, that it was doubtful as to whether this was a question of Privilege at all.

MR. LOCKWOOD: I did not hear the right hon. Gentleman express that doubt. [*Cries of* "Oh, oh!"] I trust that hon. Members opposite believe, at any rate, that I am speaking honestly. I say that I certainly did not hear the right hon. Gentleman say so. If I had done so I should not have included him in the observation I made just now. I should have said—and I do not think it would be an unfair observation to make—that the right hon. Gentleman, in moving the adjournment of the debate, was, in fact, asking for time, because he was not quite sure that the action of the hon. Baronet the Member for North Antrim had not placed the Government in an uncomfortable position. As I have said, if I had heard the observation—referred to by my hon. and learned

Friend—made by the right hon. Gentleman I certainly should not have included him, and I wish to assure him that it was not a wilful act on my part. Perhaps I may be allowed to conclude the few observations I venture to make by appealing to the House whether, as the hon. Gentleman the Member for East Mayo has said, that, so far as the House is concerned, he begs the House to advance his defence by one step, at least, to-night —I appeal to the House whether, under those circumstances, it is desirable to insist upon the adjournment of the debate? We have heard a great deal lately about challenges having been thrown down. A challenge has been thrown down to-night—a challenge which, I understand, is aimed at the hon. Member for East Mayo. [Sir EDWARD CLARKE: No.] I do not say that the hon. and learned Gentleman the Solicitor General (Sir Edward Clarke) threw the challenge down. I was not addressing the hon. and learned Solicitor General. I was referring to the cheers with which the Motion of the hon. Baronet was received. I may have been mistaken even in this. At any rate, I will go so far as to say that no one ventured to rise on that side of the House to find fault with the Motion of the hon. Baronet. Under these circumstances, I ask the House to reject the Motion for adjournment, and to give the hon. Member for East Mayo an opportunity of meeting the charges which have been made against him at the earliest possible moment.

MR. JUSTIN M'CARTHY (Londonderry): Mr. Speaker, I hope the House will not consent to allow a day or an hour to pass without declaring this matter a Breach of Privilege, and allowing inquiry to be instantly made. We have been told over and over again that we do not court inquiry. Even to-night, as an instance of the looseness of the accusations which have been made against us, I may call attention to the fact that the right hon. Gentleman opposite said that, although charges have been levelled against us again and again, we have never sought any opportunity of refuting them. Now, Mr. Speaker, as my hon. Friend the Member for West Belfast (Mr. Sexton) has stated in his speech, he has himself, on more than one occasion, endeavoured to obtain a chance in this House of raising the whole of this subject as a question of Privilege, but he has failed. The hon. and learned Gentleman the Attorney General (Sir Richard Webster) has endeavoured to limit what the House can do when a man is brought to the Bar of this House charged with a Breach of Privilege. I think that much more can be done than the hon. and learned Gentlemen seems to think. The man accused can be heard in his own defence at the Bar of the House, he can be heard by counsel by the permission of the House; he can bring up every statement, and sustain any charge he has alleged, in his own defence, and elaborately substantiate the whole of his case if he thinks fit, against the person he has accused, and then when he has withdrawn from the Bar, it is competent for the House to go into the whole question. I, therefore, take it that the course which the House is now asked to pursue will give the fullest chance of sifting these charges to the bottom. I was glad to hear one statement made by the Attorney General—namely, that the Government have not connived at this singular proceeding on the part of the hon. Baronet the Member for North Antrim (Sir Charles Lewis). I was glad, also, to hear the hon. and learned Gentleman declare it as his opinion—and it is my opinion too—that when a hon. Member of this House declares that certain statements which have been made against him are untrue, his disclaimer ought to be believed. The Attorney General said, in the course of his speech, that we cannot consider this subject now, because many Members have not read the particular article in question; and he added, the moment after, that this article is only one of a series of articles, all written with the same purpose, and form part of a combined charge. But if that be so, surely we do not want to read the whole of these two columns of print in order to know that a Breach of Privilege has been committed. We know that in this article an hon. Member of this House is accused of downright falsehood, uttered in his place in this House; and, surely, if there is any Breach of Privilege at all, that is a Breach of Privilege of the most gross and scandalous nature. The noble Lord the Member for South Paddington (Lord Randolph Churchill) is anxious that there shall be no undue encroachment on the time of the House. There was a season in the career of the noble Lord when he was not so anxious about saving the time of House. The noble Lord said that if we admit that this was a question of Privilege, we should be inundated with similar cases in the future. As if this case does not altogether stand by itself; as if, at any former time, the same series of charges have been made, day after day, against Members of this House. I trust that a time may never come in the history of this honourable House when such charges shall again be made, and when the same attempt shall be made by the Government to prevent their being brought to an issue. Now, Sir, I confess that I am not fond of bringing newspaper writers and publishers to the Bar of this House, nor am I fond of appealing to the judgment of the House in defence of my own character, or the personal character of my Friends. If this were merely a personal question, and if it concerned only the men abused and their personal friends, I would say to my Friends, "Let it pass; let us take no notice of it; let us trust to time for the vindication of our character, and to the fair future judgment of this House." For myself, I may say that after a tolerable long and not obscure, not, perhaps, altogether undistinguished career in literature here among you, I find myself charged, day after day, with being the patron and hirer of murderers. Yet, did I stand alone, I should take no action; and if anyone were to ask me if I was guilty of these crimes, I should refuse to give him any manner of answer whatever —I should refuse to reply to the charge knowing that better men than myself have been maligned and slandered. But it is no longer a personal question. These calumnies are being used for a Party purpose to aid the passing of a most odious Bill, and, if possible, to stem the rising tide of English opinion in favour of the legislative independence of Ireland. These are the purposes for which these accusations are made in the newspapers; and the First Lord of the Treasury, who drives, I am told, a roaring trade in this literature of the pest-house, does not think it wrong or beneath his dignity to stand up in this House to endeavour, by an evasive Motion, to prevent us from vindicating our characters and our cause at the earliest possible moment. We court inquiry. We not only court inquiry, but we insist upon it. We say that this House has no right to allow these charges to be made day after day against a number of its Members, and not to endeavour to interfere, in order that justice may be done. We appeal to any tribunal in this House—to any Committee of English Gentlemen whatever. I say for myself, that I should be willing to go before a Committee composed of Members of this House most bitterly opposed to me in political opinion; believing them to be English Gentlemen, I should submit our case to them cheerfully and fearlessly. Then I say that the Government have no right to press this evasive Motion to-night, and to take away from us the earliest opportunity, even although the Motion proceeds from so strange a source. Let the Government put all small arguments and sophistry aside. We at last have got a chance that an inquiry may be held; and we demand that it shall be held by the House itself. I hope there is no man of honour in this House who will go into the Lobby in support of the Motion for adjournment.

MR. LABOUCHERE (Northampton): When the hon. and learned Attorney General got up, he told us that the Motion for adjournment was made by the First Lord of the Treasury under a misunderstanding. That misunderstanding having been cleared up, I was surprised that the hon. Gentleman did not go on to say that the Motion, having been made under a misunderstanding, would be withdrawn. The Government, however, determined to persist in it. The right hon. Gentleman based his whole argument in favour of adjournment on the statement that the publisher of *The Times* could not speak at the Bar in his own defence. Surely, that could only be an argument against the original Motion, and not an argument for adjournment, because a discussion carried on day after day will not alter the fact that the publisher of *The Times*, when called to the Bar, could not speak in his own defence.

SIR RICHARD WEBSTER: I said that the publisher might not prove the charges.

MR. LABOUCHERE: As a matter of fact, he might. There have been similar cases before. There happens to be an hon. Member of this House who chanced to be in a similar position—the hon. Member for Cardiff (Sir Edward Reid).

The hon. Member was once brought up to the Bar, and the Speaker asked the hon. Member what he had to say; and the hon. Member, I believe, had a good deal to say in his defence. Then, in the last Parliament but one, my hon. Friend and Colleague in the representation of Northampton (Mr. Bradlaugh) was called before the Bar two or three times, and he was asked each time, whether he had anything to say; and, with the consent of the House, was permitted to speak. Of course, if the Attorney General means that the publisher of *The Times* could not appear at the Bar with a whole train of witnesses, that is possible, I cannot contradict him. But are we to understand that the conduct of hon. Members opposite has been all swagger? They have persistently told us, over and over again, that some action ought to be taken by hon. Members below the Gangway on this side of the House with reference to the accusation of *The Times;* but when those hon. Members express their readiness to answer the challenge, the Party opposite say—" Oh, no; it cannot be allowed, because the publisher of *The Times* cannot come here with a large number of witnesses." Where were those witnesses when the case which took place yesterday and to-day was heard in the Royal Courts of Justice? After all his swagger, the defendant in that action could not produce one single witness in support of his charges; and an intelligent English jury have awarded the plaintif £500. Another point of the Attorney General was an objection to the course proposed on this side of the House, that a Division should be taken at once. The hon. and learned Gentleman says that when a Breach of Privilege is alleged in this House, the matter is never decided on the spot. I have here a case proving the contrary. Mr. Mitchell Henry in May, 1881, alleged that a letter written by Mr. Patrick Egan, and published in *The Freeman's Journal,* was a Breach of Privilege, and then and there the letter was decided to be a Breach of Privilege. The right hon. Member for the Sleaford Division of Lincolnshire (Mr. Chaplain) and several other hon. Members on the other side of the House say that they do not exactly know what is the character of the article to which attention has been drawn, and that they want time for the purpose of reading it. I will quote three lines from the article which constitute by themselves a gross Breach of Privilege. These are the lines which I wish to read—

"We have examined an elaborate explanation made by one of the most respected of Mr. Parnell's lieutenants from his place in Parliament, and we have shown that it is a tissue of gross and palpable falsehoods."

We need not go any further. If that is not a Breach of Privilege, I really cannot conceive what will amount to an offence of that kind. It is very clear why the First Lord of the Treasury, the noble Lord the Member for South Paddington, the right hon. Gentleman the Member for the Sleaford Division of Lincolnshire, and several Unionist Gentlemen have tried to put off the issue that has been raised. It is because they do not know what the case of *The Times* is; they want to gain time to consult the editor of *The Times.* If we put it off until Thursday, they will go hot-handed to their ally to ask him whether he will allow his publisher to come to the Bar, and whether he really has a case which will bear investigation in this House. If the editor of *The Times* answers their question in the affirmative, they will return to this House quite ready to vote for inquiry; but if he replies in the negative they will vote against it, for they cannot afford to run counter to his wishes. We are not the subservient followers of *The Times.* I do not suppose that anyone of us in this part of the House cares one brass farthing what *The Times* says. [Lord RANDOLPH CHURCHILL: Nor what *Truth* says. An hon. MEMBER: Or *The Daily News.*] Yes; we do care what *The Daily News* says. But we do not care what *The Times* says, except, as Mr. Cobden once said, that we are glad when we are opposed by *The Times,* because that is the first step towards carrying a measure. We all regard the present course as a course of shirk and evasion on the part of the Government, and I am perfectly convinced that the country will regard it in the same light.

SIR CHARLES LEWIS: As I have been repeatedly referred to in the course of the debate, I think, for my own sake, I am entitled to ask the House to listen to me for a few minutes. It ought to be known generally by all younger Members that no Notice of this Motion

could have been given according to the Rules of the House. If I had not taken the course which I took, but had left the matter over until to-morrow or Thursday, it would have been too late to deal with it as a matter of Privilege. It was absolutely necessary to act to-day or not at all. I wrote first to the hon. Member for East Mayo (Mr. Dillon), who has chosen to put an interpretation on my letter to which I will only say that it is directly opposed to its proper interpretation. I thought I was doing a fair and gentlemanly thing in giving him ample notice of the course which I intended to pursue, and in giving him, if he desired it, the opportunity of mentioning the matter himself. In the next place, there have been a variety of suggestions made by the right hon. Member for Derby (Sir William Harcourt) with his usual recklessness—["Order, order!"]—that this Motion was brought forward by me in connivance with the Government.

SIR WILLIAM HARCOURT: I never said anything of the kind. I never suggested for a moment, after the right hon. Gentleman (Mr. W. H. Smith) said that he knew nothing about it, that he did know anything about it. On the contrary, I said particularly that we had no reason to complain of the course which the Government took.

MR. T. M. HEALY: It was I who said it, and I apologize for it, and withdraw the remark. I had seen the private secretary of the late Chief Secretary for Ireland (Sir Michael Hicks-Beach) leave his seat, and sit behind the hon. Baronet (Sir Charles Lewis) when he was making his Motion, until he had concluded, and he afterwards returned to his seat behind the First Lord, as if he was prompting him.

SIR CHARLES LEWIS: What I first did, Sir, was to write to yourself. I took care that the letter should be delivered early in the day; but, by some misfortune in your household, it did not get delivered until you were in the Chair. The next thing I did was to inform the First Lord of the Treasury that I intended to bring on this Motion without consulting anyone. From first to last I acted in the matter as I intended to act, thoroughly independently of any Member of the Government. I know these Motions are always inconvenient to those who sit on the Front Bench; and just because I knew there would be an effort and a desire on the part of those in authority not to have this question brought forward, and because I thought it essential to the interests of the country and the dignity of this House and of those who desire to see law and order established in Ireland, I acted, from first to last, with perfect independence, and on my own deliberate judgment I have made this Motion, and those who know my character will not think I am going to run away from it.

MR. DILLON: The last time the hon. Member made a Motion in this House he did run away from it.

SIR CHARLES LEWIS: I have not the slightest intention of screening myself under the Motion for Adjournment. I am quite prepared to let it take its usual and regular and legitimate course, and I shall not flinch for one moment from making the next ordinary consequential Motion. Now, what has happened since? I am delighted to hear the reiterated promises from that side of the House, that if the editor or publisher of *The Times* is made to stand before that Bar, they are anxious and greedy for an opportunity of proving their defence. I am delighted to hear it. It is the first symptom of any desire on their part to take up the challenge. ["No, no!"] Inasmuch as I made this Motion on my own authority, so far as the House will allow it, I shall pursue it on my own authority, and I shall give my vote against the adjournment, and not flinch for a moment from the position which I have taken up. The hon. Member for East Mayo has departed from his original position, and he is now anxious to have the matter investigated. I shall be no party to stand between him and a full inquiry. I have nothing more to say; but I deny emphatically that when I introduced this matter I made any charge of my own against the hon. Member for East Mayo. Rightly or wrongly, I took the view that it would be disgraceful to this House if these charges of wilful and deliberate untruth and wilful misrepresentation did not meet with condemnation and punishment on one side or the other. Although it may be unpleasant to have such a matter introduced, I believe it was essential that it should be disposed of, and I shall not flinch from following it to its legitimate conclusion.

Sir Charles Lewis

MR. W. E. GLADSTONE (Edinburgh, Mid Lothian): I think the hon. Baronet (Sir Charles Lewis) has exercised a wise discretion in stating that if this matter goes to a Division he will vote against the adjournment; but I still hope there need be no Division. I was greatly disappointed when the hon. and learned Attorney General rose and sat down without announcing to the House that, in the circumstances and the development which the question had received since the Motion of the First Lord of the Treasury, the Government were prepared to withdraw the Motion. My right hon. Friend near me (Sir William Harcourt), without making any charge against the right hon. Gentleman or the Government, endeavoured to urge that appeal, and I wish, further, to press that appeal on the Government. But if that appeal is made in vain, I must, for one, put in a negative to the Motion for Adjournment. I make no complaint whatever of the conduct of the First Lord of the Treasury. I think many Members shared his impression —although it was an erroneous impression —that the hon. Member for East Mayo had signified his desire, more or less, that further time would not be disagreeable to him, although he made no request upon the subject. But since the right hon. Gentleman spoke that impression has been altogether removed, and the hon. Member for East Mayo and his Friends have protested against the adjournment. The hon. Gentleman has made a protest against the adjournment, and he has been joined in that protest by the Mover of the Motion. The main part of the Attorney General's speech was an argument not against the immediate proceedings, but against the whole proceedings of the House in these matters. He said you will call the individual to the Bar, that individual will have no opportunity of making any adequate defence, and the House itself also will be limited in its methods of procedure. Every word used by the Attorney General on this subject is an argument, as the hon. Member for Northampton (Mr. Labouchere) said, on the Main Question, and not on the adjournment. It was an argument against proceeding in the matter at all. It was a speech which ought to be made on Thursday next, if the adjournment is carried, and not on the Motion for Adjournment. The Attorney General did not confine himself to that. I think he read a passage from Sir Erskine May.

SIR RICHARD WEBSTER: It was from Mr. Disraeli's speech on Dr. Kenealy's case.

MR. W. E. GLADSTONE: That is not an authority on Parliamentary Procedure like that of Sir Erskine May; but I admit that it is entitled to every attention. The time for proceeding with care and deliberation is, when you have developed matter to consider. I am sure the hon. and learned Attorney General will not deny that the general Rule of the House is, when a Motion is made respecting a Breach of Privilege, to proceed with it and decide it at once. If there are doubts in the case as to its being a Breach of Privilege, let us consider what these doubts are, because the First Lord of the Treasury seemed to have a doubt in his own mind on the subject. There can be no doubt at all about this. Even those who may not have read the whole of the article know that we have here an article against a Member of Parliament containing a charge of wilful and deliberate falsehood in the discharge of his duty as a Member for the purpose of deceiving the House. I am never anxious to touch upon a question of Privilege; but if there be such a thing as a Breach of Privilege at all, surely a charge of wilful and deliberate falsehood committed in the performance of Parliamentary duties constitutes a Breach of Privilege. If there are any doubts on the subject, how are we to clear them up between now and Thursday? The question is one which needs only to be stated, and that view is unquestionably supported by the regular course of the House on these occasions, which, subject to a few exceptions, has been to come to an immediate decision, although in cases where it was supposed that an apology was likely to be made, or upon other special grounds, delay has been sometimes granted. The necessity for an inquiry arises only on the subsequent stages. The Attorney General seems to think that the mode of proceeding is necessarily limited to some statement by the printer at the Bar, who would not be a competent person to explain and defend the statements of a leading article. But that is not so. Not only will it be in his power to make such

defence as he can, but I am not certain —though I will not enter on the question, for it is not a material point—I am not certain that the House is tied up, if it should think fit in the exercise of its discretion, to afford to such person the assistance of counsel. And that is not all. The hon. and learned Attorney General has overlooked a much more material fact which is distinctly referred to in the statement of Sir Erskine May. Sir Erskine May says—

"On his appearance at the Bar he is examined and dealt with according as the explanations of his conduct are satisfactory or otherwise, or as the contrition expressed by him for his offence conciliates the displeasure of the House."

That is not the termination of the proceedings. Sir Erskine May goes on to state—

"If there be any special circumstances arising out of a complaint of a Breach of Privilege it is usual to appoint a Select Committee to inquire into them, and the House suspends its judgment until their Report has been presented."

I submit to the Government, with great respect, on that supposition, that the whole contention of the Attorney General as to the unsatisfactory nature of the process disappears. Either in this House, at the Bar of the House, or in a Select Committee, there is, and will be, full power of examining the whole matter. So much for the substance of the proceeding. On the question of delay I have but one word to say. I feel the embarrassment of a case of this kind, which is entirely unusual in character and circumstances. It is the first case which I recollect in which a Motion has been made for taking notice of a Breach of Privilege by a Member who makes the Motion—and this, I think, will not be denied, and I do not wish to make any imputation beyond that—by a Member who makes the Motion in a sense hostile to the person against whom the Breach of Privilege has been committed. There is no doubt about that. The circumstance of the hon. Member for East Mayo and his Friends in this House being placed in a peculiar position gives them a very peculiar right of appeal to this House. Their position would have been one thing, had they taken notice of this Motion; it is another thing when the Motion itself is a challenge to every one of them; because the hon. Member for

2 B 2

East Mayo, although he is made the subject of the severest charges, is, at the same time, described as one of the most respected of Mr. Parnell's "lieutenants," so that those who sit around him are not allowed to escape. Under these circumstances, an appeal has been made by those who are termed the Irish Party, no doubt with some warmth, and no doubt with the introduction of topics which are not entirely within our immediate purview; such accusations—and systematically the subjects of such accusations—are entitled to speak with warmth, or at any rate, must be excused when they do speak with warmth. I have no such excuse, and I hope I have made my appeal to the right hon. Gentleman in a way which can give him no cause to complain. It appears to me that the development of the case since he spoke amply warrants his withdrawal of the Motion, and I trust he will withdraw it. Before this Assembly, as an Assembly of English Gentlemen, on behalf of the parties who are accused of the basest and vilest offence that can be committed by Members of Parliament against the House of Commons, and who call for an immediate trial, I say that it is impossible to resist their appeal.

THE SOLICITOR GENERAL (Sir EDWARD CLARKE) (Plymouth): Mr. Speaker, of course it is with great diffidence that I venture to address the House on a matter of this kind after the right hon. Gentleman, who has had so long an experience of the conduct and Business of the House; but I do, notwithstanding the right hon. Gentleman's speech, ask the House to consider whether he has not himself stated ample reasons for having an adjournment, in order that the question, the gravity of which he pointed out, may receive some further consideration? There is not the smallest desire on this Bench, or on this side of the House, to refuse hon. Gentlemen below the Gangway opposite the fullest opportunity in the House of meeting the damaging accusations which have been made against them. I do not think there is anyone on this side of the House who has not listened with some sympathy to some of the expressions, at all events, which have been used by Members below the Gangway on that side of the House. This Motion did not proceed from the Government,

Mr. W. E. Gladstone

nor was it brought before the House by any supporter of theirs in concert with the Government. The question is, whether the House shall at once proceed to say that it is a Breach of Privilege, or whether the discussion shall take place on Thursday next? If this had been a technical or an unimportant question, the Government would have been glad to get rid of it, instead of resuming it on another night. But it is a question of the greatest possible seriousness. My hon. Friend the Member for the Bodmin Division of Cornwall (Mr. Courtney) has pointed out that, although it is usual for the House to deal with these matters promptly, yet in this case the House is called upon to deal with it when hon. Members have not an accurate knowledge of what they are dealing with. The Motion for Adjournment was made upon an understanding that it was the desire of the hon. Member for East Mayo. That has since turned out to be erroneous; but is that fact a justification for withdrawing the Motion for Adjournment? The House is dealing with an important question of law, and cannot be governed either by the desire of the hon. Member or the desire of the hon. Baronet the Member for North Antrim. There is one matter which has never been referred to in the course of this discussion. The statement in *The Times* which has been read, and upon which this Motion is founded, purports to be an answer to something which was stated in the House by the hon. Member for East Mayo. In the House of Commons the hon. Member said a statement which had appeared in *The Times* was a false statement. *The Times* repeats the statement, and retorts the charge of falsehood. That is suggested to be a Breach of the Privileges of this House. The right hon. Gentleman said he thought this was a question to be dealt with at once. I think, however, there is very grave doubt, indeed, whether this is a Breach of the Privileges of the House; and it is most important that those who are called upon on the other side of the House to assist the judgment of the House in deciding so grave a question as this should have time to consider, and to prepare themselves to discuss this very important matter. The Rules with regard to Privilege in this House have been much altered and limited as compared with what they were formerly, and it is a most serious thing for the House to take upon itself to declare that, whenever a Member denies the truth of a statement in a newspaper, if that paper re-asserts its statement, any Member may bring it before the House as a matter which affects its Privileges. There is another reason which the right hon. Gentleman has given to the House for dealing hastily with the matter. It has been pointed out that, according to the ordinary course of proceedings in this matter, the printer of *The Times* would be brought to the Bar of the House, not to enter into the question whether his statement was true or not—because the House would have already decided that, whether it was true or not, the making of that statement was a Breach of Privilege —but he would be brought to the Bar to receive the sentence for the offence which the House had already adjudged him to have committed. The hon. Member for Northampton (Mr. Labouchere) spoke of the case where a Member of the late Government was brought to the Bar in consequence of a letter or a pamphlet he had written with regard to the naval administration. I remember the circumstances of that case well; for that was the first time I was within these walls, though I witnessed the scene from another part of the House from that in which I am now. No justification was made on that occasion. The hon. Gentleman—now the Member for Cardiff (Sir Edward Reed)—stood at the Bar and apologized humbly to the House for his offence, and then withdrew, in order that the House might pronounce its judgment. But, that being the case, the right hon. Gentleman has made another suggestion as to the further action of the House in this matter. He has suggested that a Select Committee should be appointed to inquire into the matter. That suggestion makes the matter still more serious, and still more deserving of deliberation.

MR. W. E. GLADSTONE : That would be a later stage. I simply read from Sir Erskine May's book.

SIR EDWARD CLARKE: I know it is a later stage. I can read Sir Erskine May's book as well as the right hon. Gentleman. I had the page before me as he read the passage. His suggestion is in answer to the statement of my hon. and learned Friend the At-

torney General, who pointed out that the appearance of the printer of *The Times* at the Bar of the House would be an appearance to receive sentence, and not to contest the facts in question. In answer to that the right hon. Gentleman says—" You can appoint a Committee." ["Hear, hear!" *from the Irish Members.*] A Committee of the House of Commons to consider this matter would be as inadequate a tribunal in its powers, in its results and action, and in the conduct of its proceedings, as could be possibly appointed to examine a charge of this gravity; and I venture to submit that it would be, in my opinion, a serious error in judgment on the part of the House to look forward to any such discussion on a question with which other tribunals are far more competent to deal than the House of Commons, and which are always open. I wish to point out that those considerations with which the right hon. Gentleman dealt are considerations which show the great gravity of the matter with which the House is dealing now, and which I, therefore, submit make it only reasonable that an adjournment should take place for a day or two, in order that we may recur to that question which must at some time be discussed fully—namely, the question whether, in fact, there has been a Breach of the Privileges of the House.

MR. WHITBREAD (Bedford): Sir, I regret very much that I have not heard the whole of this debate; but I have heard a good deal of it, and enough, I think, to justify me in asking leave to address to the House a few sentences—and they shall be very few— on this subject. The gist of the speech of the hon. and learned Gentleman who has just sat down is this—that if a newspaper attacks an hon. Member of this House, and that hon. Member denies the charges made against him, and says they are false, and if then the newspaper, in a further article, retorts the charge of falsehood, it is in the option of the newspaper to choose the Court, and this House will, *primâ facie,* believe the word of the newspaper, and disregard the word of its own Member. Now, just consider for a moment how this thing has been brought about. I am quite aware of the danger and inconvenience of bringing these questions of Privilege forward. I do not want to see editors of newspapers or their printers called to the Bar of this House; but this is a case which must be judged of in connection with its surrounding circumstances. An ordinary charge of falsehood on the part of a newspaper I think we might very well ignore; but what are the surrounding circumstances of the case? I never remember, I never read, more dreadful accusations, repeated over and over again, brought into this House more than once, dwelt upon by some of the most respected and honoured Members who sit on these Benches, as if they were accusations which had a basis of truth in them, and which must be met. These are circumstances which render the case a peculiar one, and which justify us in acting upon charges made by a newspaper which we could afford, in other cases, to disregard. But one word more. Consider how this case has been brought forward in point of time. *The Times* newspaper said that it was in possession of this information, I think, for many months. That information was carefully suppressed until the right time and the right moment to launch it. Then, over and over again, those hon. Members who sit below the Gangway— the Representatives of Ireland—were challenged to place themselves before an English jury. They have not done so, and the charges were repeated again. And I say, now that you have selected the Court, you were not satisfied with the charges being made, and with reiterating them on every public platform. You treated them as true, because they were not met before a jury in England; and at last you have brought them into this Court. You have appealed unto Cæsar, and unto Cæsar you should go. Have you omitted to do anything—have the opponents of hon. Members from Ireland omitted any single step—which could give those hon. Members something like an extra claim on the honour of this House? You have assumed the truth of the charges; you have not forborne to repeat them, and to point out that they have not been answered. They offer you an opportunity now upon the spot, and without delay. I trust, Sir, that both the Party sitting here and the Party sitting opposite will act in this matter as I believe every single Member of them would do if the case were submitted to him alone.

Mr. Whitbread

THE LORD MAYOR OF DUBLIN (Mr. T. D. SULLIVAN) (Dublin, College Green): Sir, as my name has been mentioned in the article in *The Times* which has been the subject of the present discussion, I wish to say that I join heartily and cordially in the challenge which has been thrown down by my hon. Colleagues to the editor and publisher of that paper to come before this tribunal, and make good their charges against us. I am amazed, Sir, to find that any hesitancy whatever is shown on the other side of the House in accepting the challenge that we now make to them. I should have thought that they would have closed immediately with any offer of that kind. All their pretences must be false and fraudulent, if they do not accept readily and heartily the proffer which we make to them to bring this question before a tribunal the honour of which stands beyond impeachment. I say that it is very well to challenge Irish Members to test this question in a Court of Law. There is not a man here who does not know that the findings of a Court of Law are not always what they ought to be—that they are not always consonant with the merits or the truth of the case. We all know that jurors are liable to be influenced by clever statements, by inflammatory addresses, and by false representations; but we are willing to meet these charges before a higher and better tribunal, as I trust it will always be regarded, the tribunal of a Committee of this House itself. Will these charges rest, forsooth, on the high authority of *The Times* newspaper? And if hon. Gentlemen opposite believe a tithe of these accusations against hon. Members who sit upon these Benches, I ask them should they not be eager to seize the first opportunity of dissociating themselves from the Gentlemen who represent Ireland in this House, and who sit on these Benches? I am astonished to find this appeal urged for delay, and I wonder whether this appeal for delay is not merely an electioneering trick, as I am much inclined to think it is, or whether it arises from a fear to have the accusations tried before so high and impartial a tribunal as I believe a Committee of this House would be. As one of those persons whose names are mixed up in this article in *The Times*, and who are branded to some extent by these accusations, I want to express my readiness to do anything I can to bring these charges to an immediate and a satisfactory trial. And I will only say, in conclusion, that whatever murderers, or assassins, or rebels there may be in Ireland, a very large share of the responsibility rests on *The Times* newspaper itself. I can tell the House that the favourite maxims and quotations of the assassins and dynamiters are drawn from the articles of *The Times*, and from certain writings of Mr. James Anthony Froude. I know that when O'Donovan Rossa wishes to make a strong case for his doctrines and opinions, he has recourse to the articles which have appeared in *The Times* newspaper. I know of my own knowledge that not only incitements to rebellion, but apologies for assassination, have from time to time appeared in *The Times*, and I will produce them at the proper time, if necessary, before the House of Commons. I will only repeat that I cordially join in the challenge thrown down by my hon. Colleagues, and I claim that these charges shall be brought to as speedy and immediate a trial as they can be before a Committee of this House.

SIR HENRY TYLER (Great Yarmouth): I hope, Sir, that the Motion for Adjournment will be withdrawn. I believe that Motion was made, in the first instance, inadvertently, in consequence of a misapprehension as to a part of the statement of the hon. Member for East Mayo, and I believe that if it had not been for that misapprehension the Motion would never have been made. But as it has been made I think it should now be withdrawn. I do so because these are charges which are not now made for the first time, but which have been made for weeks, and even for months, and which have only now culminated in the article which has been produced to this House. These charges have to be sifted — the matter has somehow to be fought out, and in consequence of the Motion of the hon. Member for North Antrim the opportunity has at length arrived for dealing with them. Hon. Members below the Gangway opposite have not sought this opportunity, and they have not, as many Members on this side think, been sufficiently active in seeking other opportunities; but, as this opportunity has

been afforded, I think it ought to be embraced at once, and I see no reason for delaying the matter. It is just as simple as that two and two make four. An hon. Member of this House has been accused over and over again, and especially in the article now before us, of stating falsehood in debate in his place in this House, and of wilfully stating falsehoods. If that be not a Breach of Privilege, I cannot conceive how there can be such a thing as a Breach of Privilege at all. Therefore, I shall not support the Motion for Adjournment, but shall vote at once for this being held to be a Breach of Privilege.

Question put.

The House *divided*:—Ayes 213; Noes 174: Majority 39.

AYES.

Amherst, W. A. T.
Anstruther, Colonel R. H. L.
Anstruther, H. T.
Baden-Powell, G. S.
Baggallay, E.
Bailey, Sir J. R.
Baird, J. G. A.
Balfour, rt. hon. A. J.
Balfour, G. W.
Barnes, A.
Barry, A. H. Smith-
Bartley, G. C. T.
Barttelot, Sir W. B.
Beach, W. W. B.
Bentinck, W. G. C.
Beresford, Lord C. W. de la Poer
Bethell, Commander G. R.
Bigwood, J.
Birkbeck, Sir E.
Blundell, Colonel H. B. H.
Bond, G. H.
Bonsor, H. C. O.
Boord, T. W.
Borthwick, Sir A.
Bristowe, T. L.
Brodrick, hon. W. St. J. F.
Brookfield, A. M.
Brown, A. H.
Burghley, Lord
Campbell, J. A.
Campbell, R. F. F.
Chamberlain, R.
Chaplin, right hon. H.
Charrington, S.
Churchill, rt. hn. Lord R. H. S.
Clarke, Sir E. G.
Cochrane-Baillie, hon. C. W. A. N.
Coddington, W.
Coghill, D. H.
Compton, F.
Cooke, C. W. R.

Corbett, J.
Corry, Sir J. P.
Courtney, L. H.
Cranborne, Viscount
Cross, H. S.
Cubitt, right hon. G.
Dalrymple, C.
De Lisle, E. J. L. M. P.
De Worms, Baron H.
Dixon, G.
Dixon-Hartland, F. D.
Dorington, Sir J. E.
Dugdale, J. S.
Duncombe, A.
Ebrington, Viscount
Edwards-Moss, T. C.
Elcho, Lord
Elliot, hon. A. R. D.
Elton, C. I.
Ewart, W.
Ewing, Sir A. O.
Feilden, Lt.-Gen. R. J.
Fellowes, W. H.
Fergusson, right hon. Sir J.
Finch, G. H.
Finch-Hatton, hon. M. E. G.
Finlay, R. B.
Fisher, W. H.
Fitzgerald, R. U. P.
Fitzwilliam, hon. W. J. W.
Fletcher, Sir H.
Forwood, A. B.
Fowler, Sir R. N.
Fraser, General C. C.
Fry, L.
Gathorne-Hardy, hon. A. E.
Gathorne-Hardy, hon. J. S.
Gedge, S.
Gibson, J. G.
Godson, A. F.
Goldsworthy, Major-General W. T.

[*First Night.*]

Gorst, Sir .J E.
Goschen, rt. hn. G. J.
Gray, C. W.
Greenall, Sir G.
Greene, E.
Grimston, Viscount
Grotrian, F. B.
Gunter, Colonel R.
Hall, A. W.
Hall, C.
Halsey, T. F.
Hambro, Col. C. J. T.
Hamilton, right hon.
  Lord G. F.
Hamilton, Col. C. E.
Hamley, Gen. Sir E.B.
Hanbury, R. W.
Hankey, F. A.
Hardcastle, F.
Heath, A. R.
Heaton, J. H.
Herbert, hon. S.
Hermon-Hodge, R. T.
Hervey, Lord F.
Hill, right hon. Lord
  A. W.
Hill, Colonel E. Ş.
Hingley, B.
Hoare, S.
Holland, right hon.
  Sir H. T.
Holloway, G.
Holmes, rt. hon. H.
Hornby, W. H.
Hozier, J. H. C.
Hughes, Colonel E.
Hunt, F. S.
Isaacs, L. H.
Isaacson, F. W.
Jackson, W. L.
Jarvis, A. W.
Jennings, L. J.
Johnston, W.
Kelly, J. R.
Kennaway, Sir J. H.
Kenrick, W.
Kenyon - Slaney, Col.
  W.
Kimber, H.
King, H. S.
King - Harman, right
  hon. Colonel E. R.
Knatchbull-Hugessen,
  H. T.
Lafone, A.
Laurie, Colonel R. P.
Lawrence, W. F.
Lea, T.
Lechmere, Sir E. A. H.
Legh, T. W.
Lethbridge, Sir R.
Lewisham, right hon.
  Viscount
Long, W. H.
Low, M.
Lowther, hon. W.
Macartney, W. G. E.
Macdonald, right hon.
  J. H. A.
Maclean, F. W.
M'Calmont, Captain J.
M'Garel-Hogg, Sir J.
Malcolm, Col. J. W.

Mallock, R.
Manners, rt. hon. Lord
  J. J. R.
Marriott, rt. hn. W. T.
Maxwell, Sir H. E.
Mayne, Admiral R. C.
Mildmay, F. B.
More, R. J.
Morgan, hon. F.
Morrison, W.
Mowbray,rt.hn.SirJ.R.
Muntz, P. A.
Murdoch, C. T.
Noble, W.
Norris, E. S.
Northcote, hon. H. S.
Norton, R.
Paget, Sir R. H.
Pearce, W.
Pelly, Sir L.
Penton, Captain F. T.
Pitt-Lewis, G.
Plunket, rt. hn. D. R.
Powell, F. S.
Puleston, J. H.
Quilter, W. C.
Ritchie, rt. hn. C. T.
Robertson, J. P. B.
Robinson, B.
Ross, A. H.
Round, J.
Russell, Sir G.
Sandys, Lt.-Col. T. M.
Sellar, A. C.
Selwin - Ibbetson, rt.
  hon. Sir H. J.
Selwyn, Captain C. W.
Sidebottom, T. H.
Sidebottom, W.
Smith, right hon. W.
  H.
Spencer, J. E.
Stanhope, rt. hon. E.
Swetenham, E.
Talbot, J. G.
Temple, Sir R.
Theobald, J.
Thorburn, W.
Tomlinson, W. E. M.
Townsend, F.
Verdin, R.
Vernon, hon. G. R.
Waring, Colonel T.
Webster, Sir R. E.
Webster, R. G.
Weymouth, Viscount
Wharton, J. L.
White, J. B.
Whitley, E.
Wiggin, H.
Wilson, Sir S.
Wodehouse, E. R.
Wolmer, Viscount
Wood, N.
Wortley, C. B. Stuart-
Wright, H. S.
Wroughton, P.
Yerburgh, R. A.
Young, C. E. B.

TELLERS.

Douglas, A. Akers-
Walrond, Col. W. H.

NOES.

Abraham, W. (Lime-
  rick, W.)
Acland, A. H. D.
Anderson, C. H.
Asquith, H. H.
Atherley-Jones, L.
Barbour, W. B.
Barran, J.
Biggar, J. G.
Blake, J. A.
Blake, T.
Blane, A.
Bolton, J. C.
Bright, W. L.
Bruce, hon. R. P.
Cameron, C.
Campbell, H.
Carew, J. L.
Chance, P. A.
Channing, F. A.
Childers, right hon. H.
  C. E.
Clancy, J. J.
Clark, Dr. G. B.
Cobb, H. P.
Commins, A.
Connolly, L.
Conway, M.
Conybeare, C. A. V.
Corbet, W. J.
Cossham, H.
Cox, J. R.
Cozens-Hardy, H. H.
Craig, J.
Craven, J.
Crawford, W.
Cremer, W. R.
Crossley, E.
Dillon, J.
Dodds, J.
Ellis, T. E.
Esslemont, P.
Farquharson, Dr. R.
Fenwick, C.
Ferguson,R.C.Munro-
Finucane, J.
Flower, C.
Flynn, J. C.
Foley, P. J.
Forster, Sir C.
Forster, Sir W. B.
Fowler, rt. hon. H. H.
Fox, Dr. J. F.
Gilhooly, J.
Gill, H. J.
Gill, T. P.
Gladstone, rt. hn.W.E.
Gladstone, H. J.
Grove, Sir T. F.
Haldane, R. B.
Harcourt, rt. hn. Sir W.
  G. V. V.
Harrington, E.
Hayden, L. P.
Hayne, C. Seale-
Healy, M.
Healy, T. M.
Holden, I.
Hooper, J.
Hunter, W. A.
Illingworth, A.
Jacoby, J. A.

James, hon. W. H.
James, C. H.
Joicey, J.
Jordan, J.
Kay-Shuttleworth, rt.
  hon. Sir U. J.
Kennedy, E. J.
Kenny, C. S.
Kenny, M. J.
Labouchere, H.
Lalor, R.
Lawson, H. L. W.
Leahy, J.
Lefevre, right hon. G.
  J. S.
Lewis, T. P.
Lockwood, F.
Macdonald, W. A.
Maclean, J. M.
Mac Neill, J. G. S.
M'Cartan, M.
M'Carthy, J.
M'Carthy, J. H.
M'Donald, P.
M'Ewan, W.i
M'Kenna, Sir J. N.
M'Lagan, P.
M'Laren, W. S. B.
Mappin, Sir F. T.
Marum, E. M.
Maskelyne, M. H. N.
  Story-
Mason, S.
Molloy, B. C.
Montagu, S.
Morgan, O. V.
Morley, rt. hon. J.
Mundella, right hon.
  A. J.
Murphy, W.M.
Newnes, G.
Nolan, J.
O'Brien, J. F. X.
O'Brien, P.
O'Brien, P. J.
O'Connor, A.
O'Connor, J. (Kerry)
O'Connor, J. (Tippry.)
O'Connor, T. P.
O'Doherty, J. E.
O'Hanlon, T.
O'Hea, P.
O'Kelly, J.
Parker, C. S.
Pickard, B.
Pickersgill, E. H.
Picton, J. A.
Pinkerton, J.
Playfair, rt. hon. Sir
  L.
Plowden, Sir W. C.
Powell, W.R. H.
Power, P. J.
Power, R.
Price, T. P.
Priestley, B.
Pugh, D.
Pyne, J. D.
Quinn, J.
Redmond, W. H. K.
Reid, R. T.
Roberts, J.

Roberts, J. B.
Robinson, T.
Rowlands, J.
Rowlands, W. B.
Rowntree, J.
Russell, Sir C.
Russell, E. R.
Russell, T. W.
Sexton, T.
Shaw, T.
Sheehan, J. D.
Sheehy, D.
Sheil, E.
Sinclair, W. P.
Smith, S.
Stack, J.
Stanhope, hon. P. J.
Stansfeld, right hon. J.

Sullivan, T. D.
Summers, W.
Swinburne, Sir J.
Tanner, C. K.
Thomas, A.
Tuite, J.
Tyler, Sir H. W.
Wallace, R.
Warmington, C. M.
Wayman, T.
Whitbread, S.
Will, J. S.
Wilson, H. J.
Wilson, I.
Winterbotham, A. B.
Woodall, W.
Wright, C.

TELLERS.

Stepney - Cowell, Sir A. K.
Stuart, J.
Sullivan, D.

Marjoribanks, rt. hon. E.
Morley, A.

MR. T. M. HEALY : What day?

MR. W. H. SMITH : Thursday.

Motion made, and Question proposed, " That the Debate be adjourned till Thursday."—(*Mr. W. H. Smith.*)

MR. SEXTON (Belfast, W.): Mr. Speaker, I beg to move that this matter be set down for to-morrow. I think the Government will be ready to admit, after the Division the House has just taken—considering that the number on one side was 174, and the number on the Government's side 213, and that the House has defeated the immediate discussion of the question by only a very slight majority—that there is a great and substantial body of opinion in favour of immediately proceeding with this matter. I think the Government will admit that, after the small majority the Division has given them, we have a right to demand at their hands that the discussion shall proceed to-morrow. I beg to make a Motion to that effect; and I ask you, Sir, what will be circulated in the Papers to-morrow? Certain passages from *The Times* article were read by the hon. Member for North Antrim (Sir Charles Lewis). Another extract was read by the hon. Gentleman the Member for Northampton (Mr. Labouchere). As the article in *The Times*, from beginning to end, contains foul and libellous charges, and as passages cannot be specified and advantageously separated from each other, I think we have a right to claim at the hands of the House that the whole of the article should be circulated with the Papers to-morrow.

MR. SPEAKER : The ordinary course of procedure is that I should officially direct that only that portion of the article which was read at the Table of the House should be put upon the Votes. I do not know whether the hon. Gentleman (Mr. Sexton) heard it read ; but a certain portion of the article was read by the Clerk at the Table. It is competent for the hon. Gentleman to move that the whole of the article be printed in the Votes.

MR. SEXTON : I move, Sir, that the whole of the article be read now, so that it can be printed and circulated to Members.

MR. SPEAKER : The Question before the House is on what day the adjourned debate shall take place.

Amendment proposed, to leave out the word " Thursday," and insert the word " To-morrow."—(*Mr. Sexton.*)

Question proposed, "That the word ' Thursday ' stand part of the Question."

MR. W. H. SMITH : I fully recognize that right hon. Gentlemen below the Gangway have to demand that this question should be reconsidered and disposed of by the House as speedily as possible; but I am unable to admit that in the Division just taken the majority for the adjournment was of so minute a character as to require that the question should be taken up instantly. In moving the adjournment of the debate, my object was to give the House an opportunity of weighing and considering the statements put before it. I confess I was also moved by the statement which was put before it, in the first instance, by the hon. Member (Mr. Dillon) ; and I was also influenced by the fact that those who sit on both sides of me are in doubt as to whether a Breach of Privilege has really been committed. In so grave a matter affecting hon. Gentlemen below the Gangway, affecting the Privileges of this House, affecting the practice of this House, I think we ought not to act precipitately, or do anything without due and proper consideration. The hon. Member (Mr. Sexton) has moved that the matter be considered to-morrow. If I could receive any assurance that the matter would be disposed of to-morrow, and not talked out, there would be a disposition on the part of the Government to accede to the views of

[First Night.]

the hon. Member. Considering the gravity of the question, I hope the House will consent to the adjournment to Thursday, the day to which a Motion of this character would, under ordinary circumstances, be deferred. At the same time, I wish it to be understood that I am not opposing the Motion for Wednesday upon any light ground. I am anxious that a decision should be taken as soon as possible.

MR. JOHN MORLEY (Newcastle-on-Tyne): I should like to remark that the right hon. Gentleman has rather changed his ground. When the right hon. Gentleman moved the adjournment of the debate, we all understood, and it has been repeated in the course of the discussion that his motive—[Mr. W. H. SMITH: One of them.] I did not understand there was more than one motive—namely, to give the hon. Member for East Mayo (Mr. Dillon) an opportunity for preparing his answer. I do not want to labour that point, I simply mention it in passing. Now, the right hon. Gentleman says that the Motion that this is a Breach of Privilege may be talked out to-morrow. Why, Sir, right hon. Gentlemen opposite have shown they are not at all shy in using the instrument they possess for closing debate. [Mr. W. H. SMITH dissented.] The right hon. Gentleman shakes his head, as if he would reproach me for making an unjust charge. Why, then, did you ask for urgency for Procedure? It was to arm yourselves with a particular instrument, and, as I say, you have on two occasions in the course of the discussion on the Criminal Law Amendment (Ireland) Bill shown that you are not shy in using it. I cannot understand, when you have taken up so much of the time of the House, and put aside so much of the other Business of the House in order to arm yourselves with this weapon, you now take up a position which implies that five or six hours' debate on this topic will not be sufficient to sift it to the bottom. We have not the least desire —hon. Members below the Gangway have not the least desire—to postpone the discussion, or to prolong it. On the contrary, it was you, to-night, who were for prolonging it. Why, what else has this Division been about? Sir, there is no kind of reason for supposing that if the question comes on to-morrow, it will not be finished to-morrow. I shall certainly

support the Amendment of my hon. Friend (Mr. Sexton).

MR. DILLON: I think I am entitled to make a strong appeal to the Government that they should bring this question to an issue as soon as possible. My position is perfectly clear in the matter. I wish this House to come to a decision on the question whether a Breach of Privilege has been committed or not before I make any statement at all. I wish to know whether the editor of *The Times* is to be brought to the Bar or not? I am anxious the House should order the editor of *The Times* to appear at the Bar. Sir, I think I am entitled, from the peculiar position in which I have been placed, to make an almost irresistible appeal to the Government not to postpone or delay the decision on this matter. It is monstrous to hold that there can be any difficulty in arriving at a decision on the question. The truth or falsehood of the charges made by *The Times* is not anything to the point at issue. The question is a simple one, which has been over and over again decided immediately it was raised in this House; and to argue that when, to-morrow, every Member of this House will have delivered to him with the Votes the charges complained of, he cannot, before he comes down to the House; make up his mind whether a Breach of Privilege has been committed or not, is to my mind the grossest absurdity. Therefore, I think an act of the greatest injustice and unfairness to me personally, and to those around me, would be committed if a decision on the question were postponed. To my mind, the discussion to-morrow ought to be concluded within an hour. I intend to contribute no speech to the debate, and I do not think my Colleagues will speak at any length. The issue is simple, and we shall invite the House to come to a decision as soon as possible. I desire to remind the House that the debate to-night was not on the question whether a Breach of Privilege had been committed, but on the Motion for the adjournment of the debate. Had it been on the question of Breach of Privilege, so far as my Friends or myself go, you might have settled it in an hour. This is all I have to say on the question. With all the earnestness I can command, I appeal to the Government, as a matter of fairness, as a duty they owe to the humblest

Mr. W. H. Smith

Member of this House, that they will allow no delay to intervene, beyond what is necessary consequent upon the Division we have just taken, between now and the settlement of the one question whether a Breach of Privilege has been committed or not. When that question is settled, I shall allow them to fix whatever day they like upon which the editor of *The Times* shall appear at the Bar. They may suit their own convenience in the matter; and it may be one, two, three, or four days hence I shall be prepared to meet him whenever he comes. The question is whether he is ready to meet us, or whether he is not? I say that any further attempt to postpone the settlement of the question will be treated by us—and I think there is manliness enough still left in England to treat it—as a cowardly and base attempt to avoid the issue on the part of the men who have played a cowardly part in pursuing with horrible slanders men who, you must remember, are not in their own country, men who are not amongst friends, and who are taken at a sore and terrible disadvantage in dealing with a great organ like *The Times*. I only ask you, Sir, to inform us in what way the question that the whole of the article, and not simply the parts read at the Table, should be circulated in the Votes to-morrow, can be best raised?

MR. SPEAKER: The best course will be for an hon. Gentleman to move, when the debate is resumed, that the whole of the article be laid on the Table.

MR. DILLON: I beg to point out to you, Sir, that that will deprive hon. Members of the opportunity of reading the whole of the article to-morrow in their Papers, to which I attach great importance.

MR. SPEAKER: I can only deal with the parts of the article read. I cannot direct to be put upon the Votes anything more than the hon. Baronet the Member for North Antrim (Sir Charles Lewis) handed to the Clerk to be read.

MR. W. H. SMITH: I rise at once to respond to the strong appeal which has been made by the hon. Gentleman (Mr. Dillon). I understand the right hon. Gentleman the Member for Newcastle-upon-Tyne (Mr. John Morley), and the hon. Member for East Mayo (Mr. Dillon), to distinctly give their assurance that the debate on the Main Question, if taken to-morrow, will be settled without delay. My desire is to give the House only sufficient time to form an accurate opinion on the facts of the case. I have no wish whatever to stand between the hon. Gentleman and his wish to obtain the judgment of the House upon the question which has been raised; and therefore, on the distinct understanding which I take it has been conveyed, I will consent to the adjournment of the debate until to-morrow instead of till Thursday. It is hardly necessary for me to refer to the observation of the right hon. Gentleman the Member for Newcastle-upon-Tyne as to the closure. I am sure he would hardly suggest that I should enforce the closure on a question of Privilege, when the character and reputation of hon. Members below the Gangway are concerned.

MR. SPEAKER: Perhaps the best course would be to say, in reply to the appeal of the hon. Member for East Mayo (Mr. Dillon), that I will take it upon my own authority to have the whole article referred to by the hon. Baronet (Sir Charles Lewis) printed and circulated with the Votes.

MR. T. M. HEALY: Mr. Speaker, it is as well there should be no misunderstanding as to the proceedings to-morrow. We do not understand that we are to come down to-morrow at 12 o'clock, in order that the Government should oppose the Motion of the hon. Baronet (Sir Charles Lewis); we do not understand that the Government mean to come down to the House and ask us to go to a Division at once. What we understand is, that the Government mean to make some proposition to-morrow. We certainly cannot agree to any course like this, that the Government should come down to-morrow and say—"We have scrutinized the article referred to by the hon. Baronet the Member for North Antrim; we cannot see anything in it in the nature of a Breach of Privilege; we oppose the Motion; and we will compel you, in virtue of the pledges you gave last night, to take an instant Division." I will consent to no such course as that. I should like to know exactly what the Government means; because, after all, the pledges of the Members of the Government and of their supporters have to be strictly scrutinized when we know that the hon. Baronet the

[First Night.]

Member for North Antrim (Sir Charles Lewis) said, in the most distinct manner, he was going to oppose the Motion for Adjournment, and then abstained from voting altogether. I invite the Government to let us know now what they mean. Let us not patch up an arrangement to-night which will result in further misunderstanding to-morrow. I shall be no party whatsoever to coming down here at 12 o'clock to-morrow to hear the right hon. Gentleman (Mr. W. H. Smith) say that he cannot agree to the Motion, and then to our being compelled to take a Division there and then. I beg to remind the Government that to-night supporters of the Government are to pass a Resolution demanding from us an inquiry into this subject. I see that the following Motion is to be moved by the hon. and gallant Gentleman the Member for North Armagh (Colonel Saunderson), and seconded by the hon. Gentleman the Member for the Loughborough Division of Leicestershire (Mr. De Lisle)—

"That in the opinion of this meeting the grave charges of complicity with crime, and of association with those who advocate the use of dynamite and assassination which have been publicly brought against leading Members of the Parnellite Party, and supported by unrefuted evidence, require from that Party and from their Radical allies definite and public disproof."

That Motion is to be made to-night, at a great meeting to be held in support of the Government in St. James's Hall, with a Member of the Government—Mr. Ashmead Bartlett—in the Chair. Under these circumstances, to ask us to come down to-morrow—to that be the understanding—and simply hear the opinion of the Government, is, to say the least, reasonable. We ask that this Motion should be gone into fully to-morrow. It is not extraordinary to ask that this matter should be properly and fully gone into, and at once. Seeing that 85 or 86 Members of the House are affected, what does it matter whether an hour or two hours of the time of the House be taken up with a grave question that involves the honour of so large a body of Members of the House, involves almost the question of the passing of the Bill now before the House, and the question, later on, of the legislative independence of our country? I ask the Government, under all these circumstances, to let us know exactly what it is they mean by saying we shall not amplify debate to-

morrow. If the Government agree to the Motion, I shall not open my mouth to-morrow, and I do not suppose that any of my hon. Friends will; we will sit as silent as statues. I certainly do think we are entitled to have a clear explanation from the Government as to their intentions.

Mr. W. H. SMITH: I can only speak again with the indulgence of the House. I thought I was distinct, clear, and candid in what I said just now. I said that I and my hon. and learned Friends around me had our doubts as to whether or not these statements constitute a Breach of the Privileges of this House. I made no disguise of what we thought; but no doubt it will be my duty, when I come down to the House to-morrow, to state the distinct opinion of the Government upon that question; and when I invite hon. Gentlemen to come to an early decision on the question, I certainly do not request them to take the opinion of the Government without question or controversy. I am acting in good faith with them, and I believe they are acting in good faith with me; I will, so far as I am able to do so, afford them every facility to obtain it. All we ask is that the House will not continue the discussion after Wednesday.

Sir WILLIAM HARCOURT: I quite understand what the right hon. Gentleman says. He does not ask for an undertaking that the proposal of the Government shall not be debated, but that every effort shall be fairly made to close the debate before 6 o'clock, when a Division shall be taken. Of course, one cannot but foresee that if the Government were to oppose the Motion there would be a long debate. What my right hon. Friend the Member for Newcastle-u. wished to convey (Mr. John Morley) of the House, there that, on this side long the debate, if the desire to pro-Government is to suppposition of the It is quite plain, because the Motion. all be in accord. Of course we should bers below the Gangway a hon. Members very difficult and unfair posed in a their accuser has left the H. Even hon. MEMBER: He did not vo. [An his declaration that he never] After from a Motion he has now away House. That is the manner t the these grave accusations against which are

Mr. T. M. Healy

dealt with; and surely this is a reason in itself why this question should come to instant decision. I think that the House will agree that this discussion should be taken on Wednesday, and not on Thursday.

MR. ILLINGWORTH (Bradford, W.): I think the House will be well advised if it refuses to have its hands tied as to the course of the debate to-morrow. If it be a question of Privilege that is to be raised, surely the House of Commons ought to take its own time within which it will debate the question, and settle it in a manner that will be satisfactory to the majority of the Members of the House. The right hon. Gentleman the Leader of the House (Mr. W. H. Smith) seemed to be horrified at the suggestion of the right hon. Gentleman the Member for Newcastle-upon-Tyne (Mr. John Morley) that the closure might be used to-morrow; but the right hon. Gentleman is even anticipating the closure, because he wants to make terms before to-morrow comes, and before the House of Commons knows what the position of the Government upon this question is, that the House will not, under any possible circumstances, carry the discussion of the subject over to-morrow. If the Government like to take up a position which will be satisfactory to the House at large, it is evident the debate cannot occupy any great length of time; but if they shrink from affording hon. Gentlemen from Ireland ample opportunity of discussion, I, for my part, should feel justified, upon the statement of the Leader of the House (Mr. W. H. Smith), that this is one of the gravest questions which can possibly be raised, in assisting hon. Gentlemen below the Gangway in carrying the debate over till Thursday. I quite agree with the hon. and learned Member for North Longford (Mr. T. M. Healy) that it would be altogether premature to determine now at what time the debate should close to-morrow.

Question put, and *negatived*.

Question, "That the word 'To-morrow' be inserted," put, and *agreed to*.

Main Question, as amended, put.

Ordered, That the Debate be adjourned till *To-morrow*.

ORDERS OF THE DAY.

—o—

CRIMINAL LAW AMENDMENT (IRE-LAND) BILL.—[BILL 217.]

Mr. A. J. Balfour, Mr. Secretary Matthews, Mr. Attorney General, Mr. Attorney General for Ireland.)

COMMITTEE. [*Progress 2nd May.*]

[THIRD NIGHT.]

Bill *considered* in Committee.

(In the Committee.)

PRELIMINARY INQUIRY.

Clause 1 (Inquiry by order of Attorney General).

MR. CHANCE (Kilkenny, S.): Mr. Courtney, I desire to move to the 1st clause of this Bill an Amendment, which I hope will not be characterized by any Member of the Government as obstructive, or as an unsubstantial one. The Amendment will make a very grave alteration in the Bill—one which certainly ought to be made. I will admit there may possibly be, on the part of right hon. Gentlemen opposite, some iota of a desire to maintain law and order, or what they consider to be law and order; but it seems to me there are many ways in which that should be done. Unfortunately, we differ from some people as to the method of maintaining law and order. Some people think that will most probably be done by allowing noble Lords to travel about disturbing the districts through which they go; and other gentlemen think it may best be done by circulating, for a pecuniary consideration, enormous numbers of the gross and abominable libels which have been referred to in the House to-night. There is another way in the opinion of some people, and that is the exercise of powers such as those created by this clause. Now, I think it is but reasonable that there should be some precaution provided that the tribunal with such extraordinary powers as are given by this clause, which it is proposed to set up over the Irish people, should be constituted of persons who will have some sort of claim to a character for independence and impartiality. What is it that the Government propose to do by this clause? They propose to give to a certain tribunal very large powers. They propose that this

[*Third Night.*]

tribunal should have power to examine any person it likes; to examine that person secretly; to compel that person to criminate himself or herself; and they propose that this tribunal shall have unlimited power to commit to gaol, for any reason the tribunal thinks fit, any person whom it may choose to call before it, whether that person is a material witness or not. Therefore it is that we ought to scrutinize very carefully the constitution of this tribunal. We find it is to be constituted of one Resident Magistrate. Now, I believe there is before the House, though it has not yet been circulated, a statement showing the previous occupation of the Resident Magistrates of Ireland. That statement proves very effectually that the Resident Magistrates are gentlemen who are thoroughly unfit to be trusted with any large judicial powers, or, indeed, with any powers at all. Out of 76 magistrates 58 are half-pay officers, and only 9 lay any claim to legal training. Now, the 6 & 7 *Will.* IV. c. 13, s. 13, shows that the Resident Magistrates of Ireland are perfectly dependent upon the Lord Lieutenant; he appoints them, and has the power to remove them at his will and pleasure. The 16 & 17 *Vict.* c. 60, s. 2, provides that before one of these gentlemen can secure a superannuation allowance he must obtain a certificate from the Chief Secretary to the Lord Lieutenant that he has served him " with diligence and fidelity." My proposition is to substitute for these individuals a permanent Law Officer of the county—the Crown Solicitor or Sessional Crown Prosecutor acting before the County Court Judge— to assimilate the provision of this section to the Scotch law, of which we have heard so much. I propose to leave out the words from "direct," in page 1, line 8, to " and," in line 9, and to insert—

" The Crown solicitor or sessional Crown prosecutor of the county in which such crime is alleged to have been committed, to summon and examine witnesses before the county court judge of such county touching the commission of such crime."

I need hardly point out that under the clause, as it is framed at present, an inquiry will be held before a single Resident Magistrate, at the orders of the Castle; that this gentleman is not only to be prosecutor and examining counsel, but also Judge; that he is to ask questions, and to decide whether the questions

Mr. Chance

are proper or not; and that he is to have full power to send to gaol. In Scotland a permanent Judge is at the head of the Court, and protects the witnesses. We hear a great deal of the tyranny of the French law in the matter of preliminary examination; but, according to the French law, a Judge is appointed every three years to hold preliminary inquiries. This Judge retains his character and status as a permanent Judge of the Civil Tribunal, and when his term of office is at an end he goes back to the Civil Tribunal. He is an independent Judge, and not appointed to hold office at the pleasure of somebody else. He protects the witness from being called upon to criminate himself. And what power has this permanent Judge? It may surprise hon. Gentlemen to know that the only power he has is to commit a witness to gaol for 10 days, or to fine him 100 francs. If hon. Gentlemen have the slightest desire that this Act shall be administered fairly, or shall, in the slightest degree, have any right to command the confidence of the people of Ireland, I imagine they ought to accede to my Amendment. I appeal even to the most rabid Tory to recollect that no good can possibly be served by setting up such an infamous tribunal as that proposed. The people will decline to appear before such a tribunal; they will dare it, and they will be right. If the object of hon. Gentlemen sitting on the Treasury Bench is to detect crime and outrage, that object will be best attained by establishing a tribunal which will have some semblance at least of independence and impartiality. I beg to move the Amendment which stands in my name.

Amendment proposed,

In page 1, line 8, to leave out from the word " direct " to the word " and," in line 9, in order to insert the words " the Crown solicitor or sessional Crown prosecutor of the county in which such crime is alleged to have been committed, to summon and examine witnesses before the county court judge of such county touching the commission of such crime."—(*Mr. Chance.*)

Question proposed, "That the word ' a ' stand part of the Clause."

THE ATTORNEY GENERAL FOR IRELAND (Mr. HOLMES) (Dublin University): The proposition that there shall be an inquiry has been confirmed by the Committee in more than one Division, and the question we have now to decide is what tribunal is to carry on the examination. Let me say, in the first instance, that I do not profess to understand the law of Scotland, and that I have not read, and do not care to read, anything about the French law. I prefer to take the analogy of the English law, and preliminary inquiry is a thing very well known to English law. It has existed in England for a considerable period, and there are in this country certain officers who are entrusted with the duty of holding preliminary inquiries. Who are these officers? They are the magistrates. [Mr. CHANCE: With the prisoner charged.] The person who is employed to take depositions as an initial step to a criminal prosecution is the magistrate. It seems to me a most reasonable thing that this duty should be entrusted to the magistrates. In the observations he has made, the hon. Gentleman (Mr. Chance) has referred to the judicial duties of magistrates. The taking of depositions is not regarded as a judicial duty at all. It has been laid down again and again by the Supreme Courts that that is a magisterial duty as distinguished from a judicial duty. The taking of depositions is one of the ordinary functions of a Justice of the Peace. It is constantly performed by every Justice of the Peace both in England and in Ireland. The duty is far more important than the duty a magistrate is called upon to perform under this Bill, because the depositions now taken may be used in evidence against the prisoner, and, further, they may be used against the very person who is giving evidence. The House having confirmed the proposition that we are to have in certain parts of Ireland the taking of evidence before a person is charged, why not leave the inquiry to the same class of functionaries who have at present the right to take depositions? This section is not being enacted for the first time. It has been enacted on various occasions. In 1870 it was enacted, and then this power was given to any ordinary Justice of the Peace. In 1882 it was enacted, and then power was given, in the very terms we have incorporated in the present clause, to the Resident Magistrates. It was enacted again as part of the permanent law of England in reference to a particular class of crimes, and power was given to any ordinary Justice of the Peace. The

hon. Member has said that Resident Magistrates in Ireland are not persons who can be expected to administer this clause in a proper and fair way. Every day Resident Magistrates are performing far more important duties than that proposed to be cast upon them. They are taking depositions which can be used as evidence not merely against the prisoner, but also against the person who makes them. We are not extending in any way the functions of Resident Magistrates; and it must be borne in mind that all the present Resident Magistrates have not been selected by a Tory Government at all, but that a large number of them were appointed by the Government of Earl Spencer. Well, now, everyone knows that some of the best magistrates to be found have really had no previous training in the law. As a matter of fact, if you go through the Magistracy of England you find that the greater number of them are men who have made themselves acquainted with magisterial duty by study. That being so, the hon. Gentleman makes the totally novel proposition—a proposition for which no analogy can be found in the Common Law of any country—that the witnesses should be taken before County Court Judges. Now, as a matter of fact, I venture to say that out of all the County Court Judges in Ireland probably there are not five who have ever taken a deposition. It forms no part of their duty now; it never did; and to ask them to enter upon a duty they have never performed while Resident Magistrates would seem to be most unreasonable. Besides, County Court Judges sit at specified periods; they have four Sessions a-year, each of which lasts for a little more than a month. Is it suggested that they should increase the number of their Sessions? Now, the hon. Member began by saying that he hoped no Member of the Government would suggest that this was an obstructive Amendment. I do not mean to make such a suggestion; but I will take the opportunity of calling hon. Members' attention to this—that although we have had legislation on this subject again and again—we had it in 1870, in 1882, and again in 1883—I am not aware that on any one of those occasions was a proposition of this kind ever made or suggested. Therefore, this is a very novel proposition, and it certainly does not commend itself to my judgment. In conclusion, I will merely say that as the clause stands there are three protections in regard to the initiation of this preliminary inquiry. First of all, there is to be sworn information; then the Attorney General may or may not act upon this information; and, thirdly, the Resident Magistrate may or may not hold the inquiry.

MR. T. M. HEALY (Longford, N.): Unless the right hon. and learned Gentleman the Attorney General for Ireland spoke for the purpose of consuming time, he might, seeing that there are scarcely any Members of his own Party in the House, and that he was practically speaking to us, have used arguments relative to what we have addressed to him. The Attorney General for Ireland knows very well that he did not touch upon a single point in the speech of my hon. Friend (Mr. Chance). The right hon. and learned Gentleman began by saying that Resident Magistrates and magistrates generally have always been accustomed to take depositions. So they have; but under what considerations? When a person is charged, and when witnesses come up voluntarily and in open Court to make the depositions. We complain that some Cavalry man, or some gentleman connected with the Navy or the Militia or Horse Marines, should have power to take up anybody he pleases, and subject him to an inquisition in his own private room, as was done in one case in Dublin. To tell us that Resident Magistrates have always been acting in the way proposed by this Bill is to tell us a thing that is not. It is absurd for the right hon. and learned Gentleman to use an argument of that kind. Again, he said he knew nothing about Scotch law, and did not want to know anything about French law. I think it would be a little better —anyhow, he would be none the worse— if he did know something about French and Scotch law. It would be no burden to him. He is not so overburdened with a knowledge of the British law that he cannot stand a little further enlightenment. He says he does not know anything at all of French law. What was the point raised by my hon. Friend (Mr. Chance)? The point was, that in a country where serious crimes have proceeded at a most extraordinary and an abominable rate, the most you can

do to a person who refuses to answer your questions is to imprison him for 10 days, or to fine him 100 francs. It is proposed in this Bill to give the power to keep such a man in gaol for ever. In France the Judge who presides at the preliminary inquiries is appointed for three years, while in Ireland the Resident Magistrates, who are recruited mainly from the Cavalry, the Artillery, the Militia, or the Marines, are appointed by the Lord Lieutenant, and may be dismissed at a moment's notice. Then, again, my hon. Friend pointed out what happens in Scotland; but the Attorney General for Ireland disposes of the subject by saying he knows nothing about Scotch law. Then he tells us that these provisions were proposed before, and no objection was taken. They were proposed at a time when the great majority of the Irish people were disfranchised, when we had not had the experience of Mr. Curran and Mr. George Bolton, when witnesses were not dragged up and sentenced to long terms of imprisonment. I see my hon. Friend the Member for Tipperary (Mr. J. O'Connor) in his place. He was sent to gaol for a fortnight under a clause like this. Why? Because he would not answer irrelevant questions. This is a very nice power to put into the hands of half-pay Cavalrymen and Militiamen. Another argument used by the Attorney General was that County Court Judges in Ireland only sit six months in the year. If I were to bring forward a Motion to reduce the salaries of these gentlemen, on the ground that they only sit six months a-year, I should be told they sit all the year round. The Motion does not mean that the County Court Judge is to sit at Sessions. The Judge can by order take these depositions within his county at any time, whether in or out of Session; and all that we desire is that gentlemen learned in the law should at least be provided to take part in this inquiry. My hon. Friend said that some of them are barristers. Well, no doubt that is so; but what sort of barristers? Take the case of the one most recently appointed. I will ask the Committee to judge of the sufficiency of the legal knowledge of this gentleman by the amount of salary he is receiving. The Solicitor General for Ireland appointed him for making Primrose League speeches during the General

Mr. Holmes

Election. This gentleman went over to Ireland as a Liberal Unionist. He had formerly been a Sub-Commissioner appointed under the Administration of the right hon. Gentleman the Member for Mid Lothian (Mr. W. E. Gladstone), and, like many of the crawling barristers of the Irish Bar, when he has got all he can get from a person, the moment the right hon. Gentleman went out of power, like a miserable cur, went and bit the hand that had fed him. So this gentleman, having no legal business, went over during the General Election and made speeches for the evening, and so successful was he in his undertaking that he was appointed by the present Administration as a Resident Magistrate; and what does the Committee think is the magnificent salary that this gentleman with a sufficiency of legal knowledge receives—why £450 per annum. These are the kind of men, these wastrels of the Legal Profession whom you get as magistrates when you depart from your usual practice of appointing Militiamen and ex-Army captains. For my own part, I would rather be tried by a military man, even a Militiaman, than by one of the wastrels of the Irish Bar appointed by the Government for doing Liberal Unionist work at the General Election. The County Court Judges receive something like £1,200 a-year, and have a fair amount of legal training; and I submit that it would be infinitely preferable to make these gentlemen the authority under this clause. But that reasonable demand is met by a disdainful negative by the Attorney General for Ireland. Of course, the Government did not deal at all with one argument of my hon. Friend, an argument I myself addressed to the Chief Secretary in the form of a Question in this House. I refer to the point of the tenure of office of these Resident Magistrates. This Return which my hon. Friend has read to the House is most amusing, for it gives you almost the pedigrees of these gentlemen like those of racehorses, and here you have every one of them marked "tenure of office—pleasure." So, therefore, this law is to be made permanent in our country; and whereas the great principle ever since the English Revolution has been that men of this kind are not to be appointed by pleasure, you get a class of men to whom you pay £420 a-year

in Ireland, and hold them in their office subject to your pleasure. No doubt, you will be able to get men to carry out the provisions of this Bill, men without much professional character, for £420 a-year, men who, for them, are in a state of starvation; but you cannot get decent men to do work of this kind. It is dirty work, or may be made dirty work by gentlemen who may stoop to all sorts of discreditable devices to please. We say that if these inquiries are to be conducted at all, they should not be conducted by gentlemen who will stoop to discreditable devices. Seeing that the entire principle of the English Judiciary is that it should be permanent, it is too bad that you should hold over these Stipendary Magistrates the alternative of being sent about their business if they refuse to do your dirty work. It is too bad that these distinguished gentlemen should have before them the prospect of dismissal—the fear of being sent back to the Four Courts when their practice, if they ever had any, is at an end, and that you send back those half-pay cavalry gentlemen who no longer find employment in the Army to seek other occupation. We protest against these gentlemen having held over them the alternative of dismissal or carrying into effect what we maintain are the tremendous penalties of this measure. The fear of this discussion is that we Irish Members are told that we are wanted here, that our presence here is needful to secure the happiness of England and Ireland; we are told that all we have to do is to stay here and argue in a proper manner, and that we shall be listened to. We are told that our arguments will always be listened to with intense pleasure and intense interest, and that if we only put them reasonably and state them with moderation—and moderation is a quality which, for my part, I always condemn and never indulge in—our arguments will not only be listened to, but will be carried into practical effect. These hypocritical pretences ought to be dropped. Why do you not frankly refuse our requests, and say to us— "We won't argue with you; we are going to pass this Bill on the *sic volo sic jubeo* principle." I should infinitely prefer that method on the part of the Government to speeches such as that we have just heard from the right hon.

and learned Gentleman the Attorney General for Ireland, whose arguments are really a negation and debauchery of debate.

Notice taken, that 40 Members were not present; Committee counted, and 40 Members being found present,

Mr. MOLLOY (King's Co., Birr): The answer given by the Attorney General for Ireland on the Amendment of my hon. Friend, if it prove nothing else, certainly proves the versatility of the right hon. and learned Attorney General's powers of argumentation. It was only last night that the right hon. and learned Gentleman drew attention to the Scotch law to support the introduction of this clause into this Bill—in order to induce the Committee to assent to the clause as it then stood—but, Sir, when dealing with the question of the Scotch law to-night upon the point where the Scotch law was absolutely against the arguments of the Government, the right hon. and learned Gentleman took up the extraordinary ground of saying that he himself knew nothing whatever about the Scotch law. As I say, it was only last night that he was arguing upon another Amendment that what was proposed in the clause existed in Scotland. He was not even correct in his facts last night, because under the Scotch law the person who has the power of inquiry is a judicial person— it is a person of judicial training, and the right hon. and learned Gentleman failed altogether to see that our objection to the clause as it now stands, is that these enormous powers are to be put into the hands of persons totally unqualified to exercise them. Then the right hon. and learned Gentleman went on to give us a learned dessertation on the powers of the magistrates at the present time, both in Ireland and in England; and, if there was anything in his argument, it amounted to this, and this only, that the powers proposed to be given to the Resident Magistrates in Ireland under these clauses, are powers that they have at the present moment. That is an extraordinary argument for a Gentleman in the position of the Attorney General for Ireland to use, when it is proposed to confer these new and extraordinary powers upon these gentlemen. It seems to me that the right hon. and learned Gentleman failed altogether to

Mr. T. M. Healy

grasp the object and meaning of this Amendment, and I hope that presently the Solicitor General for Ireland, who is in his place, will get up and make some show of argument, at any rate, in opposition to our proposal. Here are powers of a most extraordinary nature being conferred upon Resident Magistrates in Ireland, and the Amendment that we propose is an Amendment that I should have thought the Government would have been most ready to assent to. It is not an Amendment which will limit their powers in any sense, but it is an Amendment for securing that those powers shall be exercised, as the Government are never tired of telling us they will be exercised, in a judicial and fair spirit. We do not believe either in the judicial power or the fair spirit of the Resident Magistrates of Ireland. Of course, we object to these powers altogether, and, for the matter of that, to the whole Bill; but what we want to see in this clause is, that when granting these powers, we should take precautions to see that they shall be exercised with some fairness and some show of justice. The Crown Solicitor and Sessional Crown Prosecutor in Ireland, the functionaries named in this Amendment, are men of legal training. They may be good, bad, or indifferent; but, at any rate they are men of legal training, and are able to understand the bearings of a legal case, and to conduct the case; but the Resident Magistrates of Ireland are as unable and unfit to conduct such inquiries as either you or I, Sir, would be to conduct the operations of a balloon. I beg your pardon, Mr. Courtney, perhaps you might be able to manage a balloon; but I am quite sure that I should not. Who are these Resident Magistrates? We have heard a list of them read out to-night. They are half-pay colonels, quarter-pay captains, and no-pay lieutenants of the Army. What sort of men are they? I will mention one case which has come under my own observations, and, for obvious reasons, I will not mention the gentleman's name. I will tell the Committee what I know about one of those gentlemen to whom the Government are about to entrust the enormous powers of this clause. I was asked to give the gentleman a recommendation, and I told him that if I did he would not get the appointment. He arrived in this country after military service abroad. He was noted in the service as one of the best gentlemen riders they had, and was also noted as being the best pigsticker in India. He came back to this country, and with that desire for larger resources that all gentlemen from India seem to have, he applied at once for a position as Resident Magistrate in Ireland. As I say, he came to me and asked me to help him, and I have given the reason why I did not intervene on his behalf. I did not want to injure him. I said to him, you have not the faintest possible chance of obtaining this position, and he replied, "Oh, yes, I have. One of our chaps is already in." This, Sir, is literally true. I have heard it said by officials in this House that no one is appointed to the Resident Magistracy who has not been tested beforehand. Hon. Gentlemen will remember that statement having been made by Governments in this House for the past five or six years. Well, at any rate, this gentleman on returning from India applied for the post of Resident Magistrate, and in three days he got it. I will not say whether he is in that position still or not, because I do not wish to particularize him. Here is a man, a particularly good rider, who had won several races and was in possession of several valuable cups. He was a good pigsticker, but he knew no more about the law than a child. He knew little about his own country, he had gone straight from College into the Army, he had seen a long period of service in India, he came home, and three days afterwards was appointed Resident Magistrate in Ireland. Is it astonishing, Sir, that we have no confidence in such men as these? I am not speaking of this gentleman's honesty or general character, but this Committee is about to put most enormous powers into the hands of these men, and it is childish for the Attorney General for Ireland to say that these powers are now exercised in this country and in Ireland. It is nothing of the kind, and the Attorney General for Ireland knows it perfectly well. The powers that ordinary Justices of the Peace have now are limited powers. The powers in the law as it exists are governed by traditions and practice, and are not in any way to be compared with the enormous powers to be placed in the hands of these men. What are these powers? It is not neces-

sary that a crime should have been committed; it is not necessary that an offence should have been committed; but if somebody believes that something is wrong—a very general statement—any one of these gentlemen, the pigsticker, for instance, receives a mandate from the Attorney General for Ireland and holds an inquiry. The right hon. and learned Gentleman said—"I have power under this Bill to instruct them to make this inquiry; but the Resident Magistrates are quite an independent body of gentlemen, and they can refuse to make the inquiry if they like." I should like to see my friend the pigsticker refusing to obey the mandate of the right hon. and learned Gentleman, seeing that he is holding his office during pleasure. No, Sir, I imagine that he would hold the inquiry. What would he inquire into? Into crime? No, no crime has been committed. As to some offence? No, for no offence has been committed. He makes a roving inquiry into whatever he chooses. Let us look a little further. An independent magistrate in this country when there has been some unfortunate being evicted from his holding, or when he has his furniture taken away by the Sheriff, does not go down to the scene of the proceedings at the head of 50 or 100 policemen. When there is a riot in the street the independent magistrates of this country do not go round and take part in it; but in Ireland the Stipendiary Magistrates do these things. You may find them commanding a whole army of police, and mixing themselves up with military enterprises against some miserable starving tenant, who is to be evicted. The Stipendiary Magistrate in Ireland is in charge of everything of this kind. He may go out into the street, and perhaps through his indecision, his folly, or his want of patience and consideration when the people are in a state of excitement, makes it infinitely worse than it would otherwise have been. He may go then from the street into his study, which for the nonce is called a Court of Justice, and he may summon before him anyone he likes and may cross-examine them as he chooses. There are several of these gentlemen who have acted as agents of the landlords, and several of them are related to landlords. I should like to know if it is fair to ask these men to hold these inquisitorial inquiries, or whether it is fair to give them the power to do so, and whether it is fair to give them the power to cross-examine some unfortunate tenant or other or any number of tenants, he himself being interested in the collection of rents in that district? But under this Bill it is to such men as these that you give these powers. I will take an example, the case of a Resident Magistrate in Ireland whom the Government appointed, and whom they were uncommonly glad to get rid of again—a gentleman who was sent out to Egypt, and who was turned out of there, and who was sent elsewhere and has had to be relieved of his duties in every quarter of the world in which he has been placed—I allude to Mr. Clifford Lloyd. I will not appeal to young Members of the House because they will not have, probably, a sufficient acquaintance with the debates which have taken place in recent years to follow me closely upon this point; but I will ask old Members of this House who have followed the course of these debates, and have followed the career of this gentlemen in his judicial wanderings all over the globe—I will ask them whether anyone will say that the powers under this Bill are powers which should be given to such a man as Mr. Clifford Lloyd? Why, the right hon. and learned Gentleman the Attorney General for Ireland himself will not get up and say that Mr. Clifford Lloyd is a person to be intrusted with these powers, and the right hon. and learned Gentleman took part in the debates which were held some time ago with regard to this Gentleman's conduct.

THE ATTORNEY GENERAL FOR IRELAND (Mr. HOLMES): No, no.

MR. MOLLOY: At any rate, the right hon. and learned Gentleman read the debates.

MR. HOLMES: No, I did not.

MR. MOLLOY: Then I am sorry the right hon. and learned Gentleman did not pay more attention to his duties; because we were constantly discussing this question, and I am unable to imagine—

MR. HOLMES: I had not the honour of a seat in the House when the debates concerning the conduct of Mr. Clifford Lloyd took place.

MR. MOLLOY: No doubt the right hon. and learned Gentleman was not in the House when Mr. Clifford Lloyd was in Ireland and when the debates immediately affecting him took place; but the right hon. and learned Gentleman must remember that very many references have been made to Mr. Clifford Lloyd in this House quite recently. At any rate, will anyone say that Mr. Clifford Lloyd is a person to whom the inquisitorial powers of these clauses should be intrusted? Will anyone say that Mr. Clifford Lloyd is the sort of gentleman to whom a roving commission should be given to ask such questions as he chooses on any occasion? We want these powers to be exercised fairly. No one can say that the demand we make in this Amendment is one that limits the powers of the Resident Magistrates. It does not tend to that at all. We want these powers to be exercised with fairness and justice, and we contend that it is impossible for your Militiamen and Yeomanrymen and your relics of foreign service to conduct such inquiries as are contemplated in the clause with anything like fairness. Then let us go a little further into the interesting duties of these *quasi*-judicial functionaries in Ireland. Stipendary Magistrates here when they are in a difficulty, what do they do? Do they come to the Home Secretary for instructions? I should like to hear what the Home Secretary would say to one of them if he did. Are they responsible to the English Attorney General? Certainly not. Well, but what do the Resident Magistrates in Ireland do? They go regularly to Dublin Castle, and take their instructions from the Chief Secretary. If the Chief Secretary should not happen to be at the Castle, they come over to this country to take their instructions from him as to how they are to conduct their business. We are asked to look on the powers contained in this clause as if they were to be conferred on Stipendiary Magistrates in this country; but it is impossible to have the same confidence in the Resident Magistrates in Ireland. Can anyone feel confidence in the judicial fairness of a man who holds his position at the discretion of the Lord Lieutenant, who acts as a policeman, and very often as a riotous policeman—who goes to the Chief Secretary and gets his instructions originally from Dublin Castle? Is this a man to whom judicial powers should be given? Would you dare to give these powers to any such class of men in this country, or in any other part of Her Majesty's Dominions, except perhaps in India, where

Mr. Molloy

very curious things happen. I would venture to say that in all the Acts passed in this House in time of difficulty such powers were never given to a body of men subject to the will of a particular Minister as those you propose to give to the Resident Magistrates in Ireland. I fail to see what objection there can be on the part of Her Majesty's Government to this clause if all they want is that these powers shall be exercised, and exercised fairly. What objection can they have to putting these powers into the hands of men who are capable of exercising them because of their judicial office and capacities? If you had said in your Bill that Resident Magistrates should have the power, but that no Resident Magistrate should sit without having somebody of judicial training by his side, I could understand it. I should say— "Well, you wish to keep up the powers of your Resident Magistrates in Ireland; but you are willing to take such precautions as will prevent the miscarriage of justice or a misuse of these powers." But you do not do that. The Chief Secretary says that the Government will take care to see that the Resident Magistrates who exercise these powers shall have some legal knowledge. That, again, is a childish observation to make on the part of the Government; because the powers are not limited to any section of Resident Magistrates, but are given to all of them. There are no words of limitation in the clause as to the exercise of his powers by the Attorney General. You will not take the commonest precautions to see that the work that these magistrates have to do shall be honestly and judicially done; but you ask the House and the country to grant these powers to a body of men to whom you cannot point a parallel in any other portion of the three Kingdoms. I say you ask this country to do it; and, unfortunately, this country is altogether ignorant on these points, although we are endeavouring, and, I think, with some success, to give them a little knowledge now. For these reasons I strongly support the Amendment, and I hope the Solicitor General for Ireland will deal with this question, not as the Attorney General for Ireland did, by stating that the powers to be conferred upon the Resident Magistrates will be similar to powers exercised by magistrates in this country, but will answer the objections I have en-

deavoured to put before the Committee —these reasonable objections which we entertain to placing these powers in the hands of a political body.

MR. JAMES STUART (Shoreditch, Hoxton): It is especially necessary for our case against the clause in this Act that it should be distinctly understood what is the character of the Resident Magistrates in Ireland. Now, I do not intend to traverse in any sense the ground that has been gone over already. We have had from an hon. Member who spoke before the dinner hour, a list of the Resident Magistrates at the present time in Ireland, and I think I am right in saying that in this list we find that 59 out of the 76 are military men in one form or other. But I just wish to call the attention of the Committee to the statutable position of these magistrates. They are appointed under an Act of 6 & 7 *Will.* IV., but I do not intend to weary the Committee with quotations from that Act. I only desire to refer to the continuing or Amendment Act, 16 & 17 *Vict.* c. 60, in which their position is clearly indicated, because it is provided that they shall receive their pensions or their retiring allowance or superanuation on a certificate of deligence and fidelity which is to be given to them, and then there occurs a provision that whereas magistrates, that is Resident Magistrates, are not under the order or control of the Inspector General of Constabulary, and as therefore he has frequently no knowledge of their diligence and fidelity, it is therefore provided that in the case of the superanuation of magistrates who thus cannot receive a certificate from the Inspector General of Constabulary, such certificate is to be given by the Secretary to the Lord Lieutenant. It is clear from this, and also from the clause in the other Act in which it is stated that magistrates hold office during the pleasure of the Lord Lieutenant or of the Governor or Governors, that Resident Magistrates are officially under the direction of the Government and of the Castle in that country. But, Sir, I want to call attention to this fact, and also that the whole of the justification that has been given or attempted to be given, as far as I can make out for this preliminary inquiry indicated in Section I., has been that it is the existing law in Scotland; and I know that before this Bill came before the House in its Committee stage

I, and I presume other Members of the House, read a pamphlet from some Liberal Unionist source or else from the Loyal and Patriotic Union, in which it is stated that our opposition to the preliminary inquiry to be established by this Bill was utterly condemnable, because what we are condemning already existed in Scotland, which is one of the freest countries under the sun. But the preliminary inquiry proposed differs vitally from the law of Scotland, and what I want to observe is this, that the Amendment which is now proposed has for its object to make this preliminary inquiry somewhat more in accordance with the procedure in Scotland. The procedure in Scotland is in no sense, so far as I understand it, similar to the preliminary inquiry as it is proposed by the Government, but were this clause inserted there would be a certain amount of similarity in respect, at any rate, of the Court appealed to. The Attorney General for Ireland, I think, said that in this country or in Ireland there was no such thing as having a County Court Judge to perform such duties. Sir, there is no such thing either in this country or in Ireland as this preliminary inquiry, and if we go to Scotland where such an inquiry—in a very different form, but still an inquiry of this kind—does exist, we there find that the corresponding individual to the County Court Judge is exactly the person before whom such an inquiry takes place, because the Sheriff and the Sheriff's substitute practically occupies that position, and the Crown Solicitor in Ireland is the answering official to the Procurator Fiscal in Scotland; and I take it, therefore, that the argument on which this clause is presented to the House requires the insertion of this Amendment to make that argument at all hold water. I have only one other remark to make in respect of these Resident Magistrates, and that is that in Scotland you give the whole preliminary inquiry into the hands of a competent legal authority. In Ireland, you propose to give it into hands that are not competent in regard to legal matters. The Bill contains evidence within itself, that the authorities to whom you are going to entrust these powers are not competent legal authorities. Let us turn to the 11th clause and to the 6th paragraph. We there find—it is on page 7—that the Court of Summary Juris-diction is defined as being, in other parts of Ireland than the Metropolis—

"Two Resident Magistrates in Petty Sessions, one of whom shall be a person of the sufficiency of whose legal knowledge the Lord Lieutenant shall be satisfied."

Well, it is evident from that you try to safeguard the character of such a Court by providing that care shall be taken that at any rate one of the Resident Magistrates who sit on it shall have a competent legal knowledge. It is as obvious as the day, that that means that these Gentlemen in general have not this legal knowledge; but if you turn to this preliminary inquiry proposed by the Bill you will find that it is provided that it is to take place before a single Resident Magistrate. Now, these Resident Magistrates, as you admit in the very clauses of this Bill, are not competent, by the possession of legal knowledge, to form a Court of summary jurisdiction under this Bill; therefore they are not competent for the inquiry which you say is similar to that of Scotland. One more remark, and I have done. This Bill appears to me, and to many others, to be a Bill which puts everything into the hands of the Executive, and which overrides, wherever it can, the ordinary legal process. I do not wish to criticize any other clause than that before the Committee; but here, for instance, we find that practically the whole of this preliminary inquiry is in the hands of that Executive. We object to that position. We object to placing the whole Criminal Procedure of Ireland in the hands of the Executive Government, which is an English Government, and is represented largely by English and Scotch Gentlemen sitting on the opposite Benches. Our desire in supporting this Amendment is that we shall, if possible, separate the Executive from the Judicial authority and restore something of regular Criminal Procedure which is burst up and abandoned, article by article, in this Bill. We find here, in fact, as in many other things, the Tory Government and the Conservative Party are about to play like a bull in a china shop with the ancient principles of the Constitution under which we live.

MR. J. O'CONNOR (Tipperary, S): I desire to express my regret that the greater number of the Party opposite do not feel it to be their duty to be present during this discussion—the discussion of this very important Amendment. I also must express my regret that the Government see their way to accept any of the checks and safeguards that have been proposed from this side of the House from time to time during the discussion of this Bill. I believe it would be very advantageous for the Government if they accepted this Amendment, because they will have to defend in the future the administration of this very stringent Act, and they ought to know by this time with what vigour any complaint with regard to the administration of the Act will be urged by the Representatives of Ireland. They ought to know, from the character of those who will have to administer the Act— they ought to suspect, at least, how often they will be called upon to defend action that will not be consistent with the intention of this House in passing this stringent law. The proposal of the Government in the present measure differs somewhat from the Act of 1882. In carrying out the Act of 1882, the Government had to appoint Special Resident Magistrates to carry it out. They appointed, in Dublin, a man of such wide experience and such legal knowledge as Judge Curran. They appointed Mr. Hall in the South of Ireland. He was not a lawyer, he was not a retired solicitor, he was not a friend of the landlords—he was a promoted policeman, he was a man who had some knowledge of the administration of the law. I am not saying that he was the best possible person; but, at any rate, he was better than many of the magistrates who will have to administer this Bill. As to the statements of the Attorney General for Ireland, with regard to the present magistrates taking depositions, it must be borne in mind that they are assisted in their daily functions by Clerks of the Peace who are gentlemen of wide experience. I believe that the Resident Magistrates in the discharge of their duties have the assistance of men of great experience; but that will not be the case under this Act. [The ATTORNEY GENERAL for IRELAND (Mr. Holmes): Oh! yes; that will be the case.] Now, I have a book on Scotch law which states that in these cases the ordinary rules of evidence as regards the examination of witnesses should be followed; but the magistrates putting this Act in operation will not be supposed to do

that. At one time I resisted the operation of the clause in the Act of 1882; I resisted it up to the point of refusing to be sworn. Now, why was I brought before the Court at all? The officials of the district knew well that I had no sympathy whatever with the case they were investigating. The officials in that part of the country and the officials of Dublin no doubt well knew that I had delivered a speech a few days before I was summoned, in which I denounced in vigorous language the acts that had been done. They must have known that I could give no material evidence in the case they were investigating, and I hold that it ought to be the object of the Law Officers to get material evidence with regard to the matter under investigation. Well, the first question which the magistrate will put to the person coming before him may not be relevant to the case, and it is possible that the individual may not think it right to answer it; and the magistrate will be able to say that he is the best judge of the questions to be asked. I protested that I was right in not answering certain questions, and the magistrate said— "How dare you, Sir, make terms with the law?" The conspiracy under investigation might have involved 30 or 40 persons; yet I was the 201st person brought before that Court of Inquiry. Men were brought before it who had severed their relations with politics long before, and were asked questions relating to matters that had taken place years previously. When I declined to answer, the magistrate held out to me the prospect that I should go to prison. I elected to go to prison. But, before we reached that point, the magistrate tried, by threats and bullying, to overcome my resolution. He did not try the whisky inducement referred to tonight; but, when I declined to be sworn, he suggested that I should leave the country—that I should leave my business and my family and my country, because I would not please him. This was one of the Resident Magistrates appointed to carry out the law. I hold that I am as good a citizen as he is, and I maintain that I respect the law of the land as much as anyone in the country, from the Lord Lieutenant down to the ordinary policeman; and yet that man had the audacity, under the Act of Parliament, to suggest that I should leave the country. This is why we propose to introduce checks and safeguards against the improper administration of such a stringent Act as this. But returning to that inquiry. Having failed by bulling and threats to compel me to submit to his terms, he tried to force me to do so by other means. I looked round the apartment, and what did I see? There was a detective with a revolver in his hand at full cock. I bade him put it aside, and he did so, but the magistrate did not tell him to do that. By every force of terror the magistrate tried to compel me to submit to examination, but I refused. I think it was a dishonourable position to be placed in at all, and I thought the Act was being used, in the first place, for a purpose to which it ought not to be applied; and, in the second place, I thought I should do better to incur the penalty under the Act than submit to the dishonourable terms imposed. Now, what effect had this treatment with regard to the Act of Parliament? Had it the effect of gaining for it any additional respect? No, Sir, my conduct drove back the Crimes Act in Ireland, because, shortly afterwards, the Executive could not get men to be sworn at all, and the half-a-dozen inquiries going on at the time were closed up in a fortnight. Men accepted the penalty of imprisonment rather than have to submit to the terms imposed by the magistrate. This will occur again, and I advise young men in Ireland, if the Government do not accept the checks which we propose, to decline to be sworn, and to go to prison— to resist the Government who are prosecuting their political opponents to the extent of trying to get them to leave the country. This advice will be followed, I have no doubt, by the young men of the country; and I say no matter how you pass this Act of Parliament it will prove to be a failure. The Scotch law, to which reference has frequently been made, provides that it should be stated to the person brought forward what is the charge on which he is brought up for examination. No such statement will be made, according to my experience, by the Resident Magistrates in Ireland. Again, by the Scotch law, it is also to be stated to the person to be examined that he is not obliged to make any statement unless he pleases or answer any question. That is what the

Scotch law requires, but this Act does not provide for any such protection of the witnesses. The magistrates will say that they are the best judges of what questions should be put, and if any protest be made by the person under examination he will be threatened with imprisonment. In my own case, when I was brought up a second time for examination I was sent back to prison, and if it had not been for the action taken in this House, I should have remained there until the expiration of the Act of Parliament, passing 22 out of the 24 hours in a cell 12 feet by six feet. Therefore, I hold that if the Government desire to get material evidence under this Act they will accept this Amendment and others that have been proposed on this side of the House. The successful operation of this Act will greatly depend on the confidence that will be excited in the minds of the people with regard to its administration. It will be absolutely necessary, in order to its proper administration, that men should be appointed to carry out its provisions who have some knowledge of the law, and who have some respect for the law, because I maintain that such men as Captain Plunkett, and many others like him in Ireland, have no respect whatever for the law. I know the private sentiments of the persons of whom I am speaking, I know their temper, and I know that they will bring to their judicial functions minds warped by prejudice and a determination to crush the people by hook or crook. I believe the Government will consult their convenience in future if they accept this Amendment—if they put the administration of the law in the hands of lawyers who have some respect for it, and who have some regard for the Constitution, for these Resident Magistrates in Ireland have no respect for the Constitution because they do not understand the Constitution. Their education and training has been altogether against the proper understanding of the Constitution. Therefore, I say that the Government will do well to place the administration of this very stringent Act of Parliament in the hands of men in whom they have confidence, and in whom also the people will have some amount of confidence. They will consult their convenience by doing that, because the other course on which they seem bent,

Mr. J. O'Connor (Tipperary)

and the obstinacy which seems to characterize them in their dealings with suggestions made on this side of the House, will lead to a considerable amount of inconvenience and heart-burning in future, for they will have to defend acts which will not bear strict investigation; they will have to defend many false and many erroneous interpretations of the Bill now under consideration and about to become the law of the land. I have had bitter experience not only of the Crimes Act, but of most other Coercion Acts passed for what is called the better Government of Ireland. I have no desire to see the people driven to a state of exasperation. I have no desire to endure those physical sufferings in the future which I have endured in the past; but, if it should come to that, I shall not shirk them. I shall be in my place in Ireland to contend against the wicked administration of this Act of Parliament, because many acts of Parliament designed for the good of Ireland have been wickedly administered by those in whom the Government of the day have had confidence. It is in the best spirit, therefore, that I now offer these suggestions to the Government. I have drawn from my experience in doing so. I cannot discuss the question from a legal point of view—that has been already done by those on these Benches who are well qualified to deal with it. The duty will be imposed on us to see that the Act, if it becomes law, is administered in a fashion which will press as lightly as possible on the people of Ireland; and I have no doubt that the Government will have often to defend the action of the administrators of the law—the Resident Magistrates and others. The law will perhaps be put in operation against Members of this House. However that may be, any improper administration of the Act which may result from refusing to admit the very reasonable Amendments proposed on these Benches, will bring such a storm about their ears as to make the Government regret the course they have taken.

MR. CLANCY (Dublin Co., N.): It is obvious that in the matter of coercion in Ireland the Government are going from bad to worse. It is worth noting the progress that has been made from the hesitating, halting provisions in earlier Coercion Bills to the cynical perfections of the present proposals. The section of the Act of 1870, which established secret inquiries, provided that any Justice of the Peace might open an inquiry. That was bad enough, considering the character of the County Magistrates in Ireland, three-fourths of which body consist of members of the landlord class; but, in the Act of 1882, by the 16th section, it was enacted that these inquiries should be held by a Resident Magistrate in the district in which the crime was committed. That was a distinct advance. It was found, on investigation, that the unpaid magistrates were not quite dependent enough on the Government of the day, and it was felt that some more dependent officials ought to be employed for carrying out this provision of the Act. But that was not enough for the framers of the present Bill. This Bill provides that any Resident Magistrate may hold these inquiries. How will that work? The Government will look out for some men of exceptional experience in hunting out crime, and their choice will fall, in all probability, on some person like French, or one engaged in the Detective Department. Everyone knows that French was in the highest repute when he was in the Constabulary, where he stood at the head of the Detective Department. He was the man employed by the Government of the day to hold inquiries in various parts of the country, and was, as he said, "often obliged to work things close up to the wind."

THE CHAIRMAN (Mr. COURTNEY) (Cornwall, Bodmin): I fail to see the relevancy of the observations which the hon. Member is now making to the Question before the Committee.

MR. CLANCY: I was trying to point out that such a man might be appointed for the purpose of administering this section.

MR. COURTNEY: According to my view, that is not relevant.

MR. CLANCY: I was endeavouring to show that the Government might select persons, who were engaged, like French, in hunting up crime by more than questionable devices.

MR. COURTNEY: That would be totally out of Order.

MR. CLANCY: Well, I will leave that point, and suggest that some members of the Irish Bar should be substituted for the Resident Magistrates, and I cannot see why a proposal of this character should not be accepted. Surely the County Court Judges can furnish a sufficient number of men for the purpose of the Government. There must be among them suitable persons—they are nearly all of them connected with the landlords, and they are all experienced in holding Courts of Inquiry already. Between these men, and the half-pay officers, who have always been, and will be, mere creatures of the Government, there is the widest possible difference. The County Court Judge is not dependent for his salary or the continuance of his office on Her Majesty's Government, and the profession of the Bar has after all some effect in producing a sense of honour among its members which is entirely absent from the class of half-pay officers. This proposal, if it were adopted, would have the effect of assimilating, to some extent, the law of Ireland to the law of Scotland. The law of Scotland is this, that the inquiry must be carried out by a judicial authority. It seems to me that this is a point which has been overlooked. Now, I am open to correction if I am wrong; but I believe I am right in saying that, in the first place, no inquiry can be held like this in Scotland unless there is an an accused person, and, secondly, that it cannot be put in operation except by order of a judicial officer. We now ask that the inquiry should be conducted by judicial officers, and it seems to me that we have a perfect right to make this request, because the very worst construction only can be put upon the intentions of the Resident Magistrates.

COMMANDER BETHELL (York, E.R., Holderness): I shall be glad if Her Majesty's Government can see their way to mentioning the qualifications which may be desirable in the gentlemen who will administer this part of the Bill. I speak from my experience as an officer, and while I think substantial justice is done, yet I should be disposed to say that difficult cases are not always satisfactorily or easily dealt with, and I assume that that arises from the fact those gentlemen who have had to administer the law were men without judicial experience. I should have been glad if the Government could have seen their way, in some degree, to make a concession to Gentlemen on the other side of the House in this matter. I am

Mr. Clancy

disposed to think that it would give greater confidence in the administration of these powers, if people with some knowledge of the law had been directed to administer them.

Mr. MAURICE HEALY (Cork): It would have been interesting to know how the hon. and gallant Gentleman who has just sat down is going to vote on this question. Notwithstanding the Platonic regret expressed about the absence of safeguard from this clause, we shall not be surprised to find the hon. and gallant Gentleman voting in the ranks of the majority. I think the Amendment before the House is the most important we have had yet to deal with. Hitherto we have had Amendments of a very important nature; but up to the present time I venture to say we have only touched a fringe of the matter, and that the pith and marrow of the question is the character of the tribunal to which the Government intend handing over these inquiries. Our opinion is that not only has the Government selected a bad class of officials for holding these investigations, but that if they were to rack their brains to find out the worst class of persons they could not have hit upon a class better suited to their purpose than that of the Resident Magistrates. We have heard what that official's duties and obligations are as defined by Act of Parliament. We know, Sir, what hostage to fortune this official is obliged to give before he can merit reward; we know that, when a Resident Magistrate in Ireland at the close of his judicial career claims the pension which most public officials enjoy, he has, as a preliminary, to go to his masters in Dublin Castle and obtain from the Chief Secretary a certificate that he has served him with diligence and fidelity, these being the words which are to be found in the Act of Parliament. We can imagine the cold reception which one of these officials would get if his acts as Resident Magistrate, and if the political views and sentiments expressed by him at any time, did not meet with favour in the sight of the Chief Secretary. We have further heard, Mr. Courtney, what the general character of the class from which Resident Magistrates in Ireland are drawn is. We have seen it proved from the figures supplied to us by the Government that the vast majority of Resident Magistrates are not legal gentlemen, are not men trained in the law, are not men who have any special knowledge of legal subjects, but are, in the proportion, I think, of 59 to 17, half-pay officers or gentlemen in some way connected with the Military Services in this country. Well, Sir, that is not enough. I ask you whether the Irish Resident Magistrates are drawn from the people, are they drawn from the classes who, in Ireland, may be supposed to be in sympathy with the masses of the people? We know that is not the case; we know that, on the contrary, the office of Resident Magistrate is a rest, a *refugium peccatorum*, that that office is the reward which every broken down half-pay officer, which every younger son or younger brother of an Irish landlord or Peer looks forward to when he cannot eke out his means in any other way. I venture to say that if the Return which is before the House could be still further supplemented, we should find that even a still larger proportion of that body than is indicated by the figures I have mentioned is connected directly or indirectly with the landlord class, a class whom we all know have for the last half-dozen years been engaged in deadly conflict with the mass of the people to whom these gentlemen are to mete out law under this section. What is the next fact we have to meet? What has been the relation existing between Resident Magistrates in Ireland and the people, and the politicans of Ireland for the past half-dozen years? There is not one of these officials, certainly not one prominent among them, who has not on some occasion or other come into violent conflict with some public man, with the National League organization, or with some of the prominent members of it. We know that one of the most important duties which these gentlemen have or had to fulfil under the Crimes Act was the duty of dispersing public meetings, and we know that in discharging that duty they over and over again came into violent, and I must say in some cases physical, conflict with Irish politicians who were conducting the national movement. That being so, I ask, is this this the class of officials to whom the Government ought to hand over the enormous powers conferred by this section? The Government themselves admit in this Bill that for the adminis-

tration of some of its provisions, at least, some legal knowledge is required. Then they go on to provide for the holding of a Court of Summary Jurisdiction; they make this concession to public opinion and to our views—they require that one of the magistrates composing that Court shall be a gentleman possessed of some degree of legal knowledge. I assert, Sir, that if it is important that one of the magistrates composing the Court of Summary Jurisdiction should be a person having legal knowledge, it is ten times more important that the official who holds the proposed Star Chamber inquiry should be a person similarly qualified. It is said by the right hon. and learned Attorney General for Ireland (Mr. Holmes) that nothing of this sort is required, that any magistrate will be sufficient to administer the powers conferred under this section, because, as he says, any magistrate has power to take depositions. We will be content to limit the powers of this section to the powers of taking depositions; but is it not the case of the Government that something more than the taking of depositions is required. If all that they want is the taking of depositions, they have that power already, and this section is not necessary. We know very well that the duty of the magistrate who holds a Court under this section will not be merely to take depositions, but to hold a species of inquisition; to endeavour to rack from willing or unwilling witnesses information on any and every conceivable subject which the Attorney General may hand to him for investigation, and that the duties to be performed by the magistrate presiding in this Star Chamber Court will be duties as different as any can be from the mere duty of taking depositions. No, Mr. Courtney, the proceedings which will go on in the secret Courts, into which the Press cannot peep for the purpose of retailing what takes place, upon which, as the section at present stands, there will be no sort of check—the proceedings of these courts will resemble, not the ordinary proceedings of any Court of Law, but will resemble—and I should say considerably exceed—the proceedings which go on at a drum-head court martial. I have never been present at a drum-head court martial, but I can very well understand that that class of proceedings would be

[Third Night.]

far more congenial to the captains and colonels from whom the Irish Resident Magisterial Bench is recruited than the ordinary proceedings which takes place in a Court of Law. I wish now to advance another argument on this subject, and it is one which I do not think has been hitherto brought to the notice of the Committee. We have had some experience in Ireland of the exercise of these powers in the past; we all know that for three years under the Crimes Act this power to hold secret investigations was given to the Executive in Ireland, and was largely exercised by them. And what, I ask, was the lesson which these inquiries taught? Why, that in the one case where the duty of holding an inquiry was handed over, not to a Resident Magistrate, but to a competent member of the Irish Bar, namely—in the case where a secret investigation was held in Dublin into the Phœnix Park assassinations, and in that case only was a secret inquiry successful. In no other case out of the enormous number of secret inquiries held all over Ireland have the proceedings resulted successfully. Let us consider the case of Kerry, taking into consideration the state of that country about the time when the Crimes Act was passed. In no part of Ireland was the necessity for these secret inquiries greater, assuming that inquiries of this character are necessary at all. A small district of Kerry, the distance round Castleisland, had been disgraced by probably more crime than had been committed in any other, I will not say equal area of Ireland, but I might almost say in all the rest of Ireland taken together. What happened in Kerry? The Government, instead of acting as they did in Dublin, instead of appointing a competent person, a barrister or lawyer, to hold a secret inquiry, sent down Captain Plunkett and other gentlemen of that character. These men held inquiry after inquiry, they brought up witness after witness, the inquiries were spread over weeks and even months, and what was the result? Absolutely nothing. In no single case did the inquiries held in Kerry lead to the bringing of a single criminal to justice; whereas, in the one case where they appointed Mr. Curran, a gentleman who is now a County Court Judge, the inquiry was eminently successful. Well, what happened in Kerry is not the only instance of the failure

of these inquiries. Several murders had been committed in or about the district of Loughrea, and the Government sent down a Resident Magistrate to hold inquiries there. As in Kerry, the Resident Magistrate failed, as he will always fail wherever duties other than those of a bludgeon man are cast upon him. If the Government found their action in this matter on the experience drawn from the administration of the Crimes Act, they will find in that experience the strongest argument for taking away from Resident Magistrates the powers conferred by this section, and handing them over either to the County Court Judges, or to some other competent persons. My hon. Friend the Member for South Kilkenny (Mr. Chance) has already drawn attention to the fact that by this Amendment he has brought the proposals of the Government more in consonance with the Scotch law, upon which law the Government chiefly rely in making this proposal. I do not intend to dwell upon that aspect of the matter. The only argument addressed to the Committee against the proposal of my hon. Friend is that the duties which this section creates are duties of a character foreign to those which are ordinarily discharged by County Court Judges. Well, of course, we know that that is so; we know perfectly well that up to the present time County Court Judges in Ireland have not been called upon to discharge such duties as are contemplated by this section. But that is no argument against the Amendment of my hon. Friend; the power created by this section is altogether a new power, it has never existed before except in the one case of the Crimes Act, where, as I have pointed out, it failed when it was administered by Resident Magistrates to whom it is now proposed to hand over the administration of it, and it succeeded in the one case in which it was handed over to a County Court Judge. The proposal to hand over this power to County Court Judges is a novel one; but so are the powers contained in the Bill we are now discussing, and if the Amendment is to be condemned on the ground that the proposal contained in it is a novel one, I fear that in using that argument the Government are using one which will tell with deadly effect against many other of the proposals of this Bill. I ask that the Government should give us some undertaking that if they will not accept the Amendment of my hon. Friend they will, at any rate, do something that will in some way provide that the officials to whom they hand over the tremendous powers created by this clause shall be persons competent to administer these powers intelligently, and who can be relied upon to administer the Bill impartially. I am sure my hon. Friend is not particularly wedded to the form in which he has proposed his Amendment. He would be glad to welcome any concession in the direction of his Amendment, and I think the least we can ask is that in some form or other the Government will acknowledge the wisdom of the Amendment. The point of the Amendment is one deserving the attention of the Government and of the Committee, and I think we are justified in debating the Amendment until we receive some concession at the hands of the Government.

THE ATTORNEY GENERAL (Sir RICHARD WEBSTER) (Isle of Wight): I do not intend to repeat what has already been said by my right hon. and learned Friend the Attorney General for Ireland (Mr. Holmes); but I desire to say what the Government consider it well to do in regard to this matter. We do intend to accept the Amendment of the right hon. Gentleman the Member for Wolverhampton (Mr. H. Fowler) which appears upon the Paper lower down—namely, to insert in Clause 1, line 8, after the word "magistrate," the words "of whose legal knowledge the Lord Chancellor shall be satisfied."

SIR WILLIAM HARCOURT (Derby): I do not know whether it arises upon this Amendment; but can the Government let us know to-night the nature of the other Amendments they have undertaken to propose on the subject of the retrospective action of the Bill?

SIR RICHARD WEBSTER: Probably the right hon. Gentleman is unaware that the Amendment he particularly mentions already stands upon the Paper of Amendments.

MR. M. J. KENNY (Tyrone, Mid): I think we might have been induced to have accepted the Amendment of the right hon. Gentleman the Member for Wolverhampton (Mr. Henry H. Fowler), if we had not had an opportunity of studying the extraordinary Return which has been read by my hon. Friend the Member for South Kilkenny (Mr. Chance) this evening, and which gives an account of the qualifications and previous callings of the Resident Magistrates of Ireland. After having read that Return, it is perfectly clear to us that the Lord Chancellor of Ireland could not by any possibility reasonably satisfy himself of the legal knowledge of these gentlemen, for the simple reason that they have no legal knowledge whatever. I observe a most remarkable fact in connection with that Return, that there is a distinction made in it between barristers and practising barristers. There are about three barristers and two practising barristers given in the Return. I think that is the amount that the Profession of the Law contributes to the Resident Magistracy of Ireland. There are some other interesting items of information to be gained by a perusal of this Return. The main body of the magistrates of Ireland are half-pay officers, or men of that class—there are 59 of such men out of a total of 76 Resident Magistrates. We have just listened to a most interesting speech from the hon. and gallant Gentleman the Member for the Holderness Division of York (Commander Bethell). The hon. and gallant Gentleman has pointed out the general inability of men unacquainted with law, or men of military or *quasi*-military connection, to adjudicate on any questions in which legal points are of necessity raised. I contend there is no point of criminal practice in which a man's knowledge of law should be more thorough than the point in connection with the testing of evidence in criminal cases. It requires a man to have a considerable amount of practical knowledge and to be acquainted with the proceedings in Court, before he can possibly be qualified to sit and adjudicate on questions in connection with the exactness, or otherwise, of the evidence of persons brought before him. The whole character of this clause, the whole power which it is proposed to confer under it, is a power of so wide and so far-reaching a character that it is impossible for us to consent to it without opposition. We cannot consent for a moment to powers such as are provided for in this clause being conferred upon the Resident Magistrates of Ireland. We have unfortunate experience of the way in which these inquiries have been held under previous Acts; we know

well the power that was exercised under
the Coercion Act of 1882 by Mr. Clifford
Lloyd and persons of his class in Ireland; we know that men were brought
before Resident Magistrates, examined
time after time, committed and re-committed to prison, and kept in gaol for
months at a time. We know that secret
inquiries were held with a view of extracting information, and with no success; we know that when that was done
the political officials of the Crown in
Ireland were of a Liberal tendency, and
we can very well expect what will be
done when not only the permanent
officials of Ireland, but most of the political officials for the time being, are of
an Orange hue. The permanent officials
have always been Orangemen; but this
is almost the first time we have had
avowed Orangemen in high political
positions. Take, for instance, the Parliamentary Under Secretary to the Lord
Lieutenant (Colonel King-Harman). Not
long ago he went to Rathmines, and
was rapturously applauded when he said
he was just after joining the Orange
Society. It is men of this class who are
to be entrusted with this enormous
power. We know that when a Resident
Magistrate acts at all fairly, he is at once
marked out on a Report of the local
police for the censure and condemnation
of the Government in Dublin. I can
give instances which have come within
my own knowledge when men, having
acted fairly, men, having decided in a
way which did not suit the tastes of the
Sub-Inspectors and County Inspectors
of Ireland, were watched and degraded,
and sometimes dismissed. There was
such a case in 1883. A Mr. Perry,
a Resident Magistrate in Ireland,
had attended a meeting and read a proclamation suppressing it; but his conduct on the Bench was extremely fair,
and he refused to convict on every petty
charge brought before him by the police.
Shortly afterwards he was turned out of
the Resident Magistracy; but he has
been re-appointed, I think, by the Tory
Government, and sent to the most remote
part of West Mayo—namely, Belmullet.
Captain West was censured, too, because
he would not do what was required of
him by the police; and I need not refer
to the case of Mr Butler, who was sent
to a remote portion of Kerry because he
would not do the bidding of the Government. The Government deal with these

men who do not suit their views as
ordinary men deal with their enemies—
they give them no quarter whatever.
These men are appointed by the Lord
Lieutenant, and are dismissed at pleasure; the result is that they are in the
same moral condition that Judges of
England were in 200 or 300 years ago,
who were dependent for their continuance in office upon the will of the King
for the time being. We know exactly
what the conduct of such Judges as
Judge Jefferies was. If the condition of
the Judges was so excessively corrupt,
what must be the present condition of
these officials who are dependent for
their places upon the will of the Lord
Lieutenant for the time being? It is a
monstrous thing to propose that the
liberties of the great body of the Irish
people should be intrusted to such men.
We know that under this clause inquiries will be constantly held, that Resident Magistrates will be sent about from
place to place to hold inquiries, and
that the whole country will be agitated,
disturbed, and terrorized by these constant inquisitions; no such thing as personal safety or personal liberty existing
in the country. The right hon. and
learned Attorney General for Ireland
(Mr. Holmes) has been again harping
on the depositions. He assumes, because the depositions are taken in
private, that the Court of Inquiry
should also take place in private. The
only persons whose depositions are
taken in private are persons who know
that they know something about the
facts they are being examined upon;
and they cannot be examined under the
cognate clause in the law of Scotland,
and compelled to give evidence to criminate themselves. In the present Bill
there is no such safeguard. A man can
be compelled to give evidence upon any
question put to him; and when men
have refused to answer questions, on the
ground that it would criminate themselves, the magistrates have taken upon
themselves to say that the answer they
would give would not be of an incriminating character, and because the witnesses would not then answer, they have
been committed for contempt of Court
and kept in prison a month at a time.
If that sort of thing can happen under
the law as it stands, what would it be
under a law that gave magistrates absolute power to put any question they liked

to witnesses, and that, not in open Court, but in a secret Court where a man may be intimidated — where those poor peasants may be frightened out of their lives by one of these military swash-bucklers? We know the kind of men these Resident Magistrates are—these half-drunken swaggering *botheens*, the scorn of the people, and the most demoralizing influence in the country. We know who these gentlemen are—taken from the most demoralizing class which has afflicted the countries of Europe. I think we are bound at every stage of the discussion of this clause to resist as far as we possibly can the crea-tion of a Statute which will place such absolute powers and such absolute dis-cretion in the hands of the Resident Magistrates; and I think that if the Government have any real regard for personal liberty—and they are very fond of talking about the terrorism of the National League—they would not pass a law which will place such absolute power in the hands of irresponsible persons, but would give some security to people who are to be examined in Courts of Law that they shall not be compelled, under pain of imprisonment, to make statements which would crimi-nate themselves, and lead to the convic-tion of their friends who were guilty of no crime at all.

MR. W. A. MACDONALD (Queen's Co., Ossory): I believe no class of men could be chosen more incapable to dis-charge the important duty sought to be placed upon them by this clause than the Resident Magistrates of Ireland. And what is the reason of this? It is not that I believe that gentlemen who belong to the military profession are less honourable, according to their code of honour, than barristers would be, but because I conceive that there is no kind of training in the world which can be given to men so unsuitable to make them civil magistrates as a military training. Now, have had personal ex-perience of those gentlemen—not in the sense that I myself have suffered from them, which might be supposed by some hon. Gentlemen in this House to create in my mind a bias against them—but because I have been very closely asso-ciated with a case which was tried by one of those military Resident Magis-trates, and at which I was present; and the circumstances were such that I declare positively in this House that nothing would induce me to give evi-dence at a secret inquiry of this kind before these men. Now, I will briefly explain to the Committee my experience. Some years ago I was living in the South of Ireland, and there was a servant of mine who had been assaulted by a policeman. My ser-vant was a Roman Catholic, and the policeman was a Protestant. I took a great deal of interest in the case be-cause I believed the woman's statement, and I thought it was my duty to do all in my power to secure that justice should be done. Accordingly I engaged legal assistance for her, and did all I could to see that she obtained fair and just treat-ment. I went to the Court on the day that I supposed that the case would come on—the Petty Sessions Court of the place. That case did not come on, but a case somewhat connected with it did, and I am bound to say I was amazed by what I witnessed in that Court on that occasion. One of these military Resident Magistrates—I have no objection to give his name—it is Captain Hatchell—his name was read out in the list by the hon. Gentleman who moved the Amend-ment—well, this gentleman placed him-self in that Petty Sessions Court, with his back to the fire, and carried on the proceedings in the way that, I venture to say, would not for a moment be tolerated in an English Court. One man came forward as a witness. He had been a soldier—I happened to know something of the man. He gave his evidence exactly in the same way as he ordinarily expressed himself. There was nothing hard, nothing insulting or offensive in the man's manner at all; and this military Resident Magistrate actually threatened to send him to gaol if he would not give his evidence in what he was pleased to term "a more respectful manner." Al-together I was strongly impressed with the idea that it was absolutely impossi-ble to obtain .justice from this magis-trate, and so firmly was I convinced of this that I wrote to a number of the ordinary Justices of the Peace in my neighbourhood, telling them generally of my want of confidence, and request-ing them to come and see that justice would be done at the next meeting of the Court, when I knew this case would come on. I received a letter from one

[*Third Night.*]

of these magistrates, in which he stated that he had intended to be present, even if he had not received my letter, and that he regretted that I had been driven to make the application. Well, the next time the case did come on, and there was a full Bench of magistrates. Then the military gentleman of whom I have been speaking learned to behave himself, being restrained by the other Justices ; and everything was done in an ordinary and Constitutional way, and the policeman was fined. The Resident Magistrate, however, showed his bias before the case was finally disposed of. He said—" I will not agree to that," when it was proposed by the other magistrates that costs should be given to my servant for the assault that had been committed upon her. I think anybody with a fair mind must have been pained when he heard the list read out by the hon. Gentleman who proposed the Amendment, when one after another of these Resident Magistrates were described as military men. What do they know about law ? What can they know about law ? I say that generally they know nothing about the law, and still less about justice ; and I say it is simply monstrous, if you will consider the character of the inquiry you propose to give them power to hold, and the duties you propose to impose upon them —it is simply monstrous that this power should be placed in their hands. Why, Sir, it is not a question of taking depositions. Surely some knowledge of the law is necessary if men are to be able to ask impertinent questions. Now, the proposal which has been made to us— which is called a concession on the part of the Government—is an utterly worthless and unsatisfactory concession. In fact, there is no concession at all. The Lord Chancellor, we are told, is to take care that this power is to be given to Resident Magistrates who have a knowledge of the law. But where will you find in the list that has been read out to us Resident Magistrates who possess a knowledge of the law ? They do not possess it ; and unless we have a distinct assurance and security from the Government that an entirely new class of Resident Magistrates will be created, in whom the Lord Chancellor can have confidence, because they possess a knowledge of the law, the concession of the Government will be absolutely futile.

Mr. W. A. Macdonald

Well, I wish to say that, in my judgment, a genuine concession in this matter is called for, not only from the point of view of the immediate interests of the Government, but on account of their ultimate interests, if they are to secure that this section is to be worked. Already the Government may have seen in this House ominous signs that should lead them to consider that probably this section will not be worked at all. Already we have heard that the word may be passed that no one in Ireland ought to give information at all at these tribunals. If this is done, what becomes of your law ? And I consider that if you are sensible men, you will modify your clause in such a way that these objectionable features—which make it reasonable, and, as I think, right, that the people should be advised not to give evidence—will be removed, so that you may get the information which you require under this section. I will only say, in conclusion, that it is proposed by this Amendment to give this power to the Crown Solicitor—a man who has experience in examining witnesses before the County Court Judge. Now, is there any man of fair mind who really believes that this matter will be so well and so fairly done by a Resident Magistrate as it would be done by a Crown Solicitor in the presence of a County Court Judge ? Why, the County Court would be a check on the Crown Solicitor if he asked questions not pertinent to the inquiry ; and the County Court Judge is a man in whom the Government have special confidence. They have such confidence in him that they are absolutely going to put a Bankruptcy Clause in the Bill, which is now before the House of Lords, into his hands, to be worked by him. What does that mean ? Why, it means this—that they believe that there is no authority in Ireland more generally respected than the County Court Judge ; and I say, without fear of contradiction, that there is no authority in Ireland so little respected as the Resident Magistrates, whose characters I have attempted to describe to this House.

MR. EDWARD HARRINGTON (Kerry, W.): I desire to point out very briefly—as I believe this is a subject upon which many Members desire to speak—that there is no real guarantee in the provision of the right hon. Gentleman. He says, as a substitute for what we ask, that the County Court Judge will be the tribunal before whom this secret inquiry will take place, and that we shall get a little later on a promise that the magistrates who will work this clause will be men in whose legal knowledge the Lord Lieutenant has sufficient confidence. But the legal knowledge of the Lord Chancellor himself might be called into account by some of my hon. Friends learned in the law. The Attorney General may be the king of hearts, and the Lord Chancellor may be the knave of spades, and so on. It gives us no guarantee at all; and I put it on a stronger basis when I say that out of 76 magistrates at present on the list you have 59 of them who, on their own showing, according to their own proud boast, are military men who do not know the law. Why these gentlemen would consider it a disgrace to their military training to know anything about the law. And even after you take these 59 gentlemen out, there is not one amongst them who has a practical acquaintance with the law. It is out of that residue that the Lord Chancellor has to appoint men of whose "legal knowledge" he shall be sufficiently assured. No doubt it is true that in a few instances you have appointed barristers to these positions, but in these cases you have appointed a paltry class of men who have been continually at the back-stairs of Dublin Castle—gentlemen who have not been able to make their living by honest effort, and who have been continually begging Members, night after night, in the Lobby of the House, for God's sake to get them something to do. Take the last appointment—Mr. Cecil Roche. How does he look upon his duty as a magistrate? Why, I know a case in which a young men's society held a meeting on a publican's premises, hung out a banner and created a disturbance. The publican came before this magistrate and gave evidence. He stated that he had asked these young men to take in the banner when the police called his attention to it. The banner was put out again unknown to him. For this offence Mr. Cecil Roche inflicted upon the man the full penalty of the law, notwithstanding that it was his first offence, and that he had hitherto borne an irreproachable character, and conducted his

house in a satisfactory manner, and notwithstanding also that he was ignorant of the offence committed. The magistrate who gave a decision of that exceptional severity was a short time afterwards called upon to decide a case where a young man, the son of a bailiff, who had been already 24 times in gaol, had stabbed a man in the street, and he inflicted a fine of 25s. upon him. I say that the people of Ireland cannot have an atom of confidence in such a man. Give us your half-pay captains, nay, give us half-pay corporals, in preference to such a man as that. When we use the expression half-pay captains, I should like, speaking for myself, and without consulting any of the Members of the Party to which I belong, I should like to ask hon. Gentlemen opposite to understand that we mean no reflection whatever upon gentlemen who have at any time served their country. We ourselves should be proud if the condition of the law in our country were such that if we had any military ability in us we might have an opportunity of exercising it. I say that we realize that there are many reasons which compel gentlemen to resign their military careers for private life, or for the civil service of their country. At the same time, there are a large number of these gentlemen who, as has been pointed out, being unable to advance themselves in the Army, or Navy, or Yeomanry, or Militia, while drawing from the State the half-pay they are entitled to, supplement it by being creatures of Dublin Castle. I made a challenge in a full House—though there were not so many Members present as there are now—and I now make the same challenge in Committee, and I hope I shall attract the attention of the two right hon. and learned Gentlemen putting their heads together over the way—on the subject of the latest case of the transfer of Resident Magistrates from one place to another — Mr. Butler, the brother of General Butler, who was removed from the county of Kerry. He was a man the Irish people have no reason to cherish a very warm affection for. He has done his duty strictly and severely. But we have always found that whenever he has had any duty to discharge, although his action has been characterized by severity, yet he has always shown a desire to ascertain the truth and to harmonize his decrees with justice even when those decrees have gone against us. A number of men were brought before him charged with resisting the officers of the law in one of the houses that was burned at Glenbeigh. Will the Committee believe it, that these houses were burned down without the eviction being in one single instance legally carried out; and, therefore, as a matter of fact, the burning of these houses was an incendiary act? The Sheriff himself was not present, nor was the Sheriff's representative, but a young sprig of the aristocracy—the Sheriff's clerk—went and carried out this act upon his own authority. The Solicitor for the defence of these men charged with resisting the officers of the law—who was a gentleman—whose legal knowledge could not be questioned—placed this fact before the magistrates; and on a demurrer by the two legal gentlemen representing the Crown to plead anything but justification for that state of affairs, the magistrates dismissed the case against the prisoners. What did that decision mean? Why, that the evictions were illegal. What did the Government subsequently do? Remember that, when the magistrates gave their decision, the two solicitors representing the Crown gave no reason why, the case should not be dismissed, either because they had no reason or would not condescend to give it. When asked for a reason, they said, in a defiant tone—" Your worships can do what you like," which I translate, " Your worships can dismiss the case if you dare." They did dismiss the case—two local magistrates. Mr. Butler was for the dismissal, Mr. Considine was not. The latter has been transferred to a place near his own property near Dublin, within easy reach of the fashion and comfort of the metropolis; whilst the other gentleman, Mr. Butler, has been sent to a dreary district in the wild part of the country. Mr. Butler was taken out of an easy district at a personal pecuniary loss of £200 a-year, and transferred to one of the most difficult districts in Ireland. I state that in the presence of a representative of Dublin Castle, and I ask, will he sit silently by while such an accusation is brought against it, however humble may be the individual who brings it. I charge them with having punished a

magistrate because he had acted according to his convictions and according to law; and I therefore ask them how can they expect us to withdraw this Amendment and rely upon their opinion of the sufficiency of the legal knowledge of those who have to administer the law? If I do not proceed further with this point it is not because I have not a number of instances which I could give to the Committee. I will mention another for the edification of the Committee. It is one that I have spoken about and written about frequently. It is an instance that took place in Kerry—a case that occurred before a gentleman brought from the North of Ireland, and who had never known the county before. The magistrate admitted to someone in the trial that they had marked a man for the purpose of making him inform against a number of others. I say I have spoken and written about these things, and yet the magistrate in question has never dared to contradict what I say. Two magistrates went into Tralee Gaol and brought this informer along, and the prisoner who was to be identified was put, as a matter of form, among three or four prisoners. In the first place, this man was a little taller than any of the others, and it would have been easy to know him for that reason alone. But to make assurance doubly sure, while passing the other men who were not in gaol for the same crime, it is alleged to me that the magistrates distinctly walked along the gravel, and when they reached the man they wished identified they walked on the grass. I have made that statement in the paper I conduct in the district. It was a libel, if not true; but yet no one has had the courage to proceed against me for it. A little later, however, one of the printers in my employ did a foolish thing, and these magistrates brought him up and gave him six months' imprisonment. The way these Acts are carried out in Ireland is a disgrace to Her Majesty's Government — these things were a disgrace during the Liberal Government — because the mainspring of all the evil action which takes place is Dublin Castle. We see that, in order to strengthen this system, another of the most notorious of the rack-renters of Ireland canonized and installed in Dublin Castle. I can see, in the remarks of the hon. and learned

Mr. Edward Harrington

Attorney General, nothing to make us waive our support to this Amendment.

MR. FLYNN (Cork, N.): I think we are justified in asking for some further assurance on this matter than we have yet had. We have a full knowledge of the Resident Magistrates in Ireland; we know the class from which they are drawn; we know their antecedents; we know their conduct in connection with the administration of the law; and, therefore, we strenuously support the Amendment which my hon. Friend the Member for South Kilkenny (Mr. Chance) has put before the Committee. We wish to make it plain to the Committee why we require from the Government a larger and more satisfactory assurance in the direction in which this Amendment tends. A Return has been read by the hon. Member for South Kilkenny as to the number of Resident Magistrates in Ireland, their professions and their position. Out of 76 Resident Magistrates, we find that 59 are not lawyers at all; they are men who have had no connection whatever with the law in the past, no legal training, and who cannot be suggested to have judicial minds. It will not satisfy us, and it ought not to satisfy this Committee, that the Lord Chancellor should give his approval to all or any of these 59 Resident Magistrates, and therefore recommend them as competent to carry out this stringent clause. Out of 17 Resident Magistrates said to be lawyers, only a small number are men who have had any legal training whatever, and who are entitled to administer a law of this kind or deal with matters in which niceties of evidence are likely to arise. But I ask the attention of the Committee to a matter of which I have specific and particular knowledge. It is in connection with the Resident Magistrates in the County of Cork. I find that out of six Resident Magistrates in the County of Cork, two of these are half-pay officers—gentlemen who have served in the Army 21 years; that two of them are Constabulary Officers and that one is a barrister-at-law. But barrister-at-law in this case does not mean a practicing barrister. I ask the attention of the Committee particularly to the point that in the County of Cork not one of these six magistrates, to whom will be intrusted the administration of this very

important clause, is a man to whom English Members would willingly entrust in England the carrying out of a clause of this stringent and drastic character. We do not propose to carry the discussion on this Amendment further. We have given, and we have evidence to prove to the satisfaction of independent and unbiassed Members of the Committee, that there is a necessity for something in the direction in which this Amendment goes; and if the Government do not meet us, we know very well that the public in Ireland and in England will modify this clause in the direction of legality and justice.

Question put.

The Committee *divided* :—Ayes 258; Noes 176: Majority 82.—(Div. List, No. 108.)

MR. MAURICE HEALY (Cork): The Government having refused to accept the Amendment of my hon. Friend the Member for South Kilkenny (Mr. Chance), it only remains to be seen whether we can carry out our object by another Amendment to which we ask the Government to agree. The Government have refused to inquire into the legal knowledge of the Resident Magistrates, and my object is to secure a court which in some measure will be fit to hold inquiry. The Resident Magistrates have no legal knowledge, and there is not half-a-dozen out of the whole 76 who would be considered by the Lord Chancellor as competent to conduct these inquiries. The Amendment I propose will not render the clause cumbersome in any way, our only object being to secure its proper administration. I insist and I press it on the Committee, that something is required for the protection of persons who are likely to come under the operation of the clause beyond what would be afforded by a Court of one Resident Magistrate; and I appeal to the Government to accept the Amendment which I now beg to move.

Amendment proposed, in page 1, line 8, after "a" to insert a "Court consisting of two or more."—(*Mr. Maurice Healy.*)

THE CHIEF SECRETARY FOR IRELAND (Mr. A. J. BALFOUR) (Manchester, E.): I think the hon. Member for Cork (Mr. Maurice Healy) will see that this is an Amendment which certainly the Government cannot accept. There is no precedent whatever for requiring two magistrates to be present when such an inquiry is made, and there is no analogy to the proposal as far as I know of in any previous Act in which the provision for secret inquiry exists. To require that the Court should consist of two Resident Magistrates is to throw an enormous burden on the judicial forces at the disposal of the Crown. You not only require a magistrate in the Court of the district, but you require another magistrate not to assist, but to sit by and check him. I think it will be seen that this proposal of the hon. Member would not afford any safeguard or protection in the matter, and while it would be of no advantage in that direction, it would impose a great burden on those responsible for the administration of justice. I trust the hon. Member will not think it necessary to press his Amendment, and that he will allow the Committee to proceed at once to the Amendment of the right hon. Gentleman the Member for East Wolverhampton (Mr. Henry H. Fowler). The Government have intimated their intention to accept that, and when it is disposed of we shall be in a position to proceed with the rest of the clause.

Mr. T. M. HEALY (Longford, N.): I think it will be well perhaps to adopt the suggestion of the right hon. Gentleman, and go on to the Amendment of the right hon. Member for East Wolverhampton. For my part, I have no objection to that course being taken, but I urge the Government to say, that if we abandon this Amendment they will consider this most important point. Suppose a question is asked, and it is said not to be germane to the inquiry; suppose the magistrate says that it is, we ask if you will give us an appeal from the magistrate. If you will, we will abandon this Amendment. You have two Judges in the case of Election Petitions, and in every case of summary jurisdiction you have two magistrates who have to agree. I think nobody should be sent to gaol except on the warrant of two magistrates. If the point I have mentioned is conceded by the Government the objections to the clause on this head be met. This is our seek to provide that the conduct magistrates;

but we want to provide that the magistrate who sends a man to gaol shall not be the magistrate who conducts the inquiry. I trust the Government will agree to the Amendment I have myself placed upon the Paper to deal with this point. This is a different case from that of ordinary depositions. A man may be asked a question here which will commit him with reference to matters outside the inquiry; he may be asked questions as to whether his children go to school, the state of his banking account, whether he owns or rents land, and I contend that all these question are of a nature to which a witness should not be subjected. Let it be borne in mind also that a man may be committed to prison over and over again for refusing to answer questions wholly immaterial to the issue. For these reasons, I think that the decision of more than one magistrate should be had before a man is sent to prison under this clause.

THE CHIEF SECRETARY FOR IRELAND (Mr. A. J. BALFOUR) (Manchester, E.): There is no necessity that this suggestion should be carried out. Under the existing law a man may be examined in private. He may be asked an improper question, and he might be committed to prison for refusing to answer it. If he were committed, however, he has his remedy at law, and he has that remedy also under our Bill. We see no reason why that should not be a sufficient safeguard in dealing with this particular point of obtaining evidence, and we are reluctant to encumber the clause by introducing safeguards which are unnecessary.

Mr. T. M. HEALY: The right hon. Gentleman has not referred to my Amendment. The Magistrates' Protection Act gives absolute immunity to magistrates, however improper the questions asked may be. If the right hon. Gentleman will repeal, for purposes of this Act, the provisions of the Magistrates' Protection Act, then, of course, I will agree to the withdrawal of the Amendment. By the Act I have referred to the magistrates are protected in any amount of illegality they may commit. Of course, the Attorney General will tell us that that is not so; but if you bring an action against a magistrate, the Judge will rule that this is a matter for him and not for the jury to decide. I have an Amendment on that point also; and if the right hon. Gentleman will accept that Amendment, or give some assurance of concession on the point to the Committee, we shall allow the matter to pass. But we have no remedy whatever, and no one knows that better than the right hon. and learned Gentleman the Attorney General for Ireland.

THE ATTORNEY GENERAL FOR IRELAND (Mr. HOLMES) (Dublin University): I do not agree altogether with the hon. and learned Gentleman as to the provisions of the Magistrates' Protection Act. It is only when a magistrate is acting within his jurisdiction that the Act affords protection to the magistrate.

MR. BRADLAUGH (Northampton): Will the right hon. and learned Attorney General for Ireland say whether there is to be any record of questions put by the magistrates and refused to be answered, which will enable the High Court to express an opinion upon the question? Because, otherwise, a man would be helpless if he were committed for refusing to answer; and unless the commitment shows what it was he refused to answer, it would be impossible that he could raise the question at all. Perhaps the right hon. Gentleman the Chief Secretary for Ireland (Mr. A. J. Balfour) will permit me to add that there is a difference between taking a deposition under the ordinary law and this procedure. In the case of ordinary indictment magistrates may take depositions in their private rooms, the person against whom it is made being present with his solicitor. It is only the reporters and the public who may be excluded in the case of an indictable offence. Of course, where summary cases are taken in open Court under Statute the analogy does not hold. Unless some provisions are taken such as I have suggested, the man is absolutely defenceless against illegality.

MR. HOLMES: The Government are prepared to accept any reasonable Amendment, and there is one Amendment on the Paper which will meet the objections that have been raised on this point by providing that a shorthand note should be taken of everything which occurs in the examination. A similar Amendment was proposed in 1882; but it was not accepted, owing to the difficulty of providing shorthand writers. Shorthand writers are now more numerous, and the Government will see their way to providing that there shall be a correct transcript of everything that occurs.

MR. MAURICE HEALY (Cork): I quite admit the importance of the concession which the right hon. and learned Gentleman makes; but, unfortunately, I do not see that it is one which has a large bearing on the Amendment. I understand the action of the Court of Secret Inquiry would be that a witness is summoned before the Court; he considers that a question is improper and refuses to answer it, and then the power given by this section comes into force, and the witness may be committed. But what will happen is this—a witness is committed for contempt of Court; and, therefore, the Attorney General will see that the reasoning with which he endeavours to convince the Committee that this Amendment is needless does not really apply. As I understand the law, when a witness has been committed for contempt of Court the magistrate will make out a warrant; he will state in it that the witness has been asked a proper question and that he has refused to answer it, and that he is committed to gaol. I think that warrant will be conclusive, because no Court will be able to go behind it and investigate the statement, and in that way the witness will have no sort of defence whatever. It is all very well to say that you will allow the evidence to be taken down in shorthand; but what is the use of that if, when it is taken down, it will be of no value when application is made for the decision of a Court of Law? If I am right on this point I think the right hon. and learned Gentleman the Attorney General for Ireland will admit that, as long as such a warrant as I have described remains in force, it will not be competent for the party against whom the warrant is made out to bring any action on account of the injury done to him. It is a principle of our Courts of Law that a poor man imprisoned under any legal process can bring an action in respect of any illegality in putting that provision into force. He must first set aside the order of the Court committing him to prison; and what I am pointing out is that as long as the warrant is regarded by the Court as final and conclusive, it is quite idle for any purpose germane to this Amendment to promise that the evidence shall be taken down in shorthand, because it would not be open to the party aggrieved to use that evidence in any superior Court for the purpose of inducing that Court to quash the warrant under which he is committed. I, therefore, submit to the right hon. and learned Gentleman the Attorney General for Ireland that his promise is not material to the question. We want that there should be some power of reviewing the action of Resident Magistrates under this clause; we want that there shall be a check on the action of the magistrate who commits a man to prison for refusing to answer any question put to him. Until a concession on that point is made I respectfully urge that the taking down of evidence in shorthand is simply delusive.

Mr. BRADLAUGH (Northampton): The statement of the right hon. and learned Gentleman the Attorney General for Ireland (Mr. Holmes), although very satisfactory, as far as it went, did not, in my opinion, meet the case, because if there is a warrant simply for committal for contempt no Court will go behind to examine what the contempt is. Therefore, it will be necessary for the Government that they should undertake that the warrant shall allege the specific offence of refusing to answer a particular question, such question being set out verbatim, and not the general offence of contempt.

The ATTORNEY GENERAL for IRELAND (Mr. Holmes) (Dublin University): I agree on the point of law with the hon. Member with regard to the superior Courts; but the argument does not apply to the warrant of an inferior Court, in which the specific grounds for its issue must be stated.

Mr. T. M. HEALY: Will the right hon. and learned Gentleman provide that in the Act? If so, we will withdraw the Amendment. Can anything be fairer than that?

Mr. HOLMES: I have no objection whatever.

Mr. T. M. HEALY: Then we withdraw the Amendment.

Amendment, by leave, *withdrawn*.

Mr. HENRY H. FOWLER (Wolverhampton, E.): The object of the Amend-

Mr. Maurice Healy

ment which I beg to move is to secure that the official responsible for seeing that the Act is carried out is a trained lawyer.

Amendment proposed, in page 1, line 8, after "magistrate," insert "of whose legal knowledge the Lord Chancellor shall be satisfied."—(*Mr. Henry H. Fowler.*)

The ATTORNEY GENERAL for IRELAND (Mr. Holmes) (Dublin University): The Government are willing to accept the words of the Amendment that the Lord Chancellor shall be satisfied with the legal knowledge of the magistrate. I cannot, however, undertake that all the magistrates will be trained lawyers, as that would involve the question as to what constitutes a trained lawyer.

Mr. T. M. HEALY (Longford, N.): How are we to understand that these persons are competent persons? If the right hon. and learned Gentleman will say these men will be either barristers or solicitors, I shall withdraw my opposition. The right hon. and learned Gentleman will not do that. It is by the refusal of these reasonable proposals that the debate is prolonged. What is the meaning of the term "a man of legal knowledge?" Is Captain Plunkett a man whose legal knowledge is to satisfy the Government? The term legal knowledge is very vague. Are we to have men who have proved their legal knowledge by examination? You cannot appoint a Civil Service writer at 10*d*. an hour who has not passed an examination. Are we to be told that the men who are to have power of unlimited imprisonment are to be men with whose legal knowledge the Lord Chancellor is satisfied, and no more? We know that the Lord Chancellor is a very civil man, and that he will not want to compel these men to undergo an examination. I ask the Committee whether it is not the fact that this Amendment has been met in form and refused in substance? Let the right hon. and learned Attorney General for Ireland say, at least, that these shall be men who have at least been called to the Bar. It is not saying much of a man that he has been called to the Bar. I have been called to the Bar myself. I do not profess to have much legal knowledge, and my experience has been pretty much confined to

" eating the dinners ;" but, however, let the Government provide that there shall be some smattering of the law in these men. If the Government will not accept that proposal, it simply shows that in agreeing to the Amendment of the right hon. Gentleman the Member for East Wolverhampton they are keeping their promise to the ear and breaking it to our hopes.

MR. HENRY H. FOWLER (Wolverhampton, E.) : Knowledge of the law is not a matter of inspiration or revelation, and my contention is that the Lord Chancellor should be satisfied that the Resident Magistrate has had such an amount of legal training and acquired such an amount of legal knowledge as would render him competent for the discharge of his duties. I did not move my Amendment in the spirit in which the right hon. and learned Gentleman the Attorney General for Ireland has accepted it. The right hon. and learned Gentleman seems to regard the qualification of legal knowledge as a purely perfunctory matter. I desire that the Resident Magistrate shall be a competent lawyer, such as the Lord Chancellor, in the discharge of his official duty, would be responsible to this House for appointing to carry out this important provision.

MR. ANDERSON (Elgin and Nairn): The Amendment of the right hon. Gentleman the Member for East Wolverhampton (Mr. Henry H. Fowler) undoubtedly means that the person appointed shall possess legal qualification and experience; and I am certain that had the hon. and learned Gentleman the Attorney General for England (Sir Richard Webster) been present, he would not have dissented from the view taken by the right hon. Gentleman. The right hon. and learned Attorney General for Ireland (Mr. Holmes) distinctly stated a short time ago that the Government accepted the Amendment, on page 16, of the right hon. Gentleman the Member for East Wolverhampton. I confess that I was disarmed by what I thought to be a reasonable proposal of the right hon. and learned Attorney General for Ireland on behalf of the Government. I read the words of the Amendment on the Paper in the sense given to them by the right hon. Gentleman the Member for East Wolverhampton, and I think that no words can be clearer than those which say that the magistrate shall be a person of whose legal knowledge the Lord Chancellor shall be satisfied. What can they mean except that the person appointed to discharge this duty is to have legal knowledge to the satisfaction of the Lord Chancellor ? That, of course, means that he is to be a person of some legal qualification and legal experience, and it is perfectly surprising to hear the right hon. and learned Attorney General for Ireland taking up the position which he now assumes. I should wish the hon. and learned Gentleman the Attorney General for England to be sent for, because I am sure that he would not agree with the course taken by the Government. I venture to think that this is another example of the surprising action of the Government, and I hope that some hon. Member will get up and ask the Government to state whether they mean what the right hon. and learned Attorney General for Ireland says they mean, because, without the meaning which is attached to the Amendment by the right hon. Gentleman the Member for East Wolverhampton, this Amendment is of no use. I have here a Return, not yet printed, as to the legal qualifications of the Resident Magistrates. I will read a portion of it. Here is one gentleman, aged 28 when he obtained his appointment ; former vocation none ; salary £425, which is raised—perhaps for his extraordinary ability and knowledge of the law—to £550. Do the Government mean to say that when they accepted the Amendment of the right hon. Gentleman the Member for East Wolverhampton they meant that the Lord Chancellor was to be satisfied with a person of that capacity ? Another magistrate is on this list, whose qualification is that he has been an officer in the Grenadier Guards. I have known officers in the Guards—they are very charming persons; but I deny that they have any legal knowledge. Here is another gentleman, aged 39 ; he was a civil engineer and has served in the Militia. The hon. Member for North Longford (Mr. T. M. Healy) has stated that being called to the Bar and having eaten a certain amount of dinners, is not a very substantial or good qualification; but that qualification would seem to be thought a very sufficient one, if I may judge from one of the entries in the Return from which I am reading. It is

[Third Night.]

stated of one Resident Magistrate—Mr. Considine—that he is 35 years of age, that he was High Sheriff of Limerick in 1881, and that he kept all his terms for the Bar, and, I suppose, ate all his dinners with great punctuality; but that, for family reasons, he was not called to the Bar. Well, it would be a very interesting inquiry to find out what the family or other reasons were why this gentleman was not called to the Bar, but became a Resident Magistrate at a salary from the State of £500 a-year. But, Sir, this is really turning a very serious matter into a burlesque. The right hon. Gentleman the Chief Secretary to the Lord Lieutenant may smile, but you are really dealing with a serious matter. [*Laughter.*] I do not think the Government appreciates the seriousness of this enactment as they ought to do. You are going to hand over powers never dreamt of before to young gentlemen who, for family reasons, were not called to the Bar. Is that a thing that is fair or reasonable, or even decent? We heard last night a good deal from the Government as to the waste of time in the opposition to this Bill; but the persons who are wasting time now are the Government themselves. This is a question which should never have been raised by the Government. I hope that the hon. and learned Gentleman the Attorney General for England is here, and that we shall hear from him if he intends to stand by the Amendment in the sense in which it was originally understood to have been accepted by the Government?

THE CHIEF SECRETARY FOR IRELAND (Mr. A. J. BALFOUR) (Manchester, E.): When I heard the speech of the right hon. Gentleman opposite I was greatly astonished, because he attributed to the hon. and learned Gentleman the Attorney General for England views which he never entertained. We discussed the question when we were going over the Amendments on the Paper. But I have since had an opportunity of consulting the hon. and learned Attorney General, and he says that he never used the words the right hon. Gentleman put into his mouth. He never thought of saying that these Resident Magistrates should be either barristers or solicitors. I am both disappointed and astonished at the manner in which this concession on the part of the Government has been re-

ceived. An Amendment was put on the Paper by the right hon. Gentleman the Member for East Wolverhampton (Mr. Henry H. Fowler). We accepted that Amendment, although no provision to the like effect was contained in the Act either of 1870 or 1882. We have put it into this Act for the first time, and have thus introduced into this measure a limitation never thought necessary by any previous Government. The hon. and learned Member for Elgin and Nairn (Mr. Anderson), however, talks as if the phrase "sufficiency of legal knowledge" was here used for the first time in Bills of this kind. But he has either not read the Act of 1882 or he forgets its provisions, for in that Act there was a clause requiring the Lord Lieutenant to certify the legal knowledge of one of the magistrates who was to exercise jurisdiction with respect to charges of offences against that Bill. Well, how did Lord Spencer carry out the Crimes Act? Did he interpret that clause as meaning that one magistrate must be a barrister? He did not. I appeal to Gentlemen opposite who admire the manner in which Lord Spencer carried on the government of Ireland; and I would ask them to inquire either of Lord Spencer, or of any Gentleman there connected with the Government of Ireland, whether it was not then the fact, and is not the fact now, and has not always been the fact in Irish history that some of the best magistrates in Ireland have not been barristers or people who have gone through a legal training. And it is not unnatural that it should be so. It is easy enough to get barristers for £400 a-year to do your work. But it is not so easy to get a successful barrister, and the result is that if you insist on having barristers at salaries of £400 or £500 a-year, you will not get the pick of the profession, and, probably, you will not get such efficient men as if you look in other walks of life for men of sound sense, of a certain amount of legal knowledge, and of good character. Such men as these will carry out the work you want them to perform far better than the inefficient barristers you would secure at the salaries I have mentioned. I have now shown that the interpretation hon. Members opposite would put on the words of the Amendment is not that which was put by Lord

Spencer upon similar words in the Act of 1882; and that the construction which we put on those words is one to which we must adhere if the Act is to be properly worked by the magistrates of Ireland.

MR. JOHN MORLEY (Newcastle-upon-Tyne): I should like to begin by an emphatic repudiation of the proposition that we are in any degree bound on this side of the House by the precedent of 1882.

MR. A. J. BALFOUR: I never said that the right hon. Gentleman was bound by the precedent of 1882. What I appealed to was the interpretation of that Act by Lord Spencer.

MR. JOHN MORLEY: But this Act is not going to be administered by Lord Spencer. And I will frankly confess that, even if it were, I am not sure that I should take a different line from that which I now take. I was not in the House at the time the Act of 1882 was passed. I hope that if I had been I should have objected to a great many clauses of that Act; but, be that as it may, I think the time has come when the Government must give the House some better argument in favour of their proposals than that this or that provision was in the Act of 1882. We maintain that the whole condition of Ireland and the circumstances with which we are dealing, are fundamentally different from what they were then. It cannot be denied that the manner in which the right hon. Gentleman the Attorney General for Ireland (Mr. Holmes) has explained the sense in which he has accepted the Amendment has taken the value out of his concession. I quite admit the difficulty of insisting that the gentleman to whom this power is given must be always a barrister or a solicitor. The mere fact of a gentleman being a barrister does not necessarily ensure to the Lord Lieutenant or the Lord Chancellor that he is possessed of legal knowledge and experience. I shall, therefore, propose—and I believe the right hon. Gentleman will assent to the Amendment—to insert "after legal knowledge" the words "and legal experience." The Amendment will then run—"Of whose legal knowledge and legal experience the Lord Chancellor shall be satisfied." I know that will still leave the proposal open to some objection, but I think it would, as

amended, prescribe an extra caution, and would give us an extra safeguard in these proceedings.

Amendment proposed to the said proposed Amendment to insert after "legal knowledge" the words "and legal experience."—(*Mr. John Morley*).

Question proposed, "That those words be there inserted."

THE ATTORNEY GENERAL FOR IRELAND (Mr. HOLMES) (Dublin University): I understand that the right hon. Gentleman opposite has admitted that it would be extremely difficult, under all the circumstances, always to get a barrister or solicitor as the Resident Magistrate acting under this clause; and, indeed, that the fact of a gentleman being called to the Bar or being a solicitor, would be but a small guarantee of his possessing legal knowledge. Therefore, I understand he concedes that the Resident Magistrate might not be either a barrister or a solicitor. That was what I meant to convey, in order to prevent any misapprehension in the observations I made a short time ago; but I did not mean to convey that this clause should be dealt with in a perfunctory manner, or that the Lord Chancellor would dream of being satisfied with a person, unless he possessed real legal knowledge. It is very difficult for a person to possess legal knowledge without having legal experience, and that being so I see no objection to the Amendment of the right hon. Gentleman. Therefore, I am ready to accept the Amendment; but if I had accepted the Amendment of the right hon. Member for East Wolverhampton (Mr. H. H. Fowler) without giving the explanation that a Resident Magistrate acting under this clause need not be a barrister or a solicitor I should have misled the House.

Question put, and *agreed to.*

Amendment proposed,

In page 1, line 8, after "magistrate" insert the words "being a person of the sufficiency of whose legal knowledge and legal experience he shall be satisfied."—(*Mr. Maurice Healy.*)

Question proposed, "That those words be there inserted."

MR. O'DOHERTY (Donegal, N.): The words of the Amendment are, "legal knowlege and experience." Does that mean knowledge of the law, and experience of its practice? Will the Attorney General for Ireland accept the Amendment with that meaning? [After a pause.] The right hon. Gentleman does not answer.

THE ATTORNEY GENERAL FOR IRELAND (Mr. HOLMES) (Dublin University): I have answered the question frequently.

MR. J. O'CONNOR (Tipperary, S.): I should have proposed a previous Amendment on the Paper if I had not understood that there was to be a substantial concession with regard to the Amendment of the right hon. Gentleman the Member for East Wolverhampton (Mr. H. H. Fowler). I should have proposed that there should be associated with the Resident Magistrate a gentleman of legal knowledge. However, that is past and gone; and now we must take the Amendment as it stands. In the first instance, and as the Amendment first stood, I thought, after the remarks of the Attorney General for Ireland, that the supposed concession of the Government was no concession at all. I am glad to find that the Government have, however, accepted an Amendment upon the original Amendment; but still, even in its amended state, it is open to objection. It is quite possible and easy to find in Ireland gentlemen who are not barristers or solicitors, but who are, nevertheless, well acquainted with the practice of the law. Let me mention one—Mr. Huntley, of Cork, who might well be elevated to the Bench. Mr. Huntley is a man who has written on the practice of the Petty Sessions Court and of Justices of the Peace. He is a man of very high character, and would command general confidence. But I hold, at the same time, that the Government have it now in their power to promote from the ranks of the police such a man as Mr. Horn, who they will say possesses some knowledge of the practice of the law, and thereby they will fulfil the conditions of this Amendment. If they do not accept this Amendment in its entirety, we shall have a disagreeable state of affairs to meet—that of having this clause administered by certain officials like Captain Plunkett, and men of that stamp. I think, therefore, that it would be for the benefit of the Government if they accepted the Amendit its entirety. [An hon. MEMBER: They

have.] Well, if they have, I have nothing further to say.

MR. T. M. HEALY (Longford, N.): After what has transpired, I think we can go on to another Amendment. I am not even now satisfied that this Amendment, as accepted by the Government, is more than a show on their part. But, so far as it goes, it is now clear; and, therefore, I think we may go on.

Question put, and *agreed to.*

COLONEL NOLAN (Galway, N.): I rise to point out to the Government the necessity for reporting Progress. I am sure that even the most greedy of the Conservatives will be satisfied with the progress we have made, for we have swept away a whole page of Amendments. We had a very late night last night, and we are going to have an early, and perhaps an excited, Sitting tomorrow. And let it be recollected that we have made the progress I have mentioned in spite of a Motion made at the beginning of the evening by a Conservative Member. The Member for North Antrim (Sir Charles Lewis) took up a great deal of time in the early part of the evening; but since then, and as I have said, in spite of that, the Committee have done a great deal of work, and made great progress, and therefore I hope that the Government will now consent to report Progress.

Motion made, and Question proposed, "That the Chairman do report Progress, and ask leave to sit again."— (*Colonel Nolan.*)

THE CHANCELLOR OF THE DUCHY OF LANCASTER (Lord JOHN MANNERS) (Leicestershire, E.): The hon. and gallant Member says that we have made great progress. We have certainly made some progress; but some of the Amendments which stand immediately next on the Paper are almost consequential Amendments upon that to which we have just agreed. I should propose that we should proceed with those Amendments, and then we will agree to report Progress.

COLONEL NOLAN (Galway, N.): On that understanding I will withdraw the Motion for reporting Progress.

Motion, by leave, *withdrawn.*

MR. MAURICE HEALY (Cork): Of course, the two first Amendments

Mr. O'Doherty

standing in my name immediately after the one we have just agreed to are disposed of by the discussion we have had. I, therefore, come to the third Amendment standing in my name, the wording of which I shall have to alter, having regard to the Amendments already accepted on the clause. I shall move it in this form—"And being a magistrate for the county or place in which such offence was committed." This, I think, will make the clause run grammatical. Now, I need not debate on the subject of that Amendment. The clause as it stands, without the Amendment, would enable the Government to select their Resident Magistrate from any part of Ireland. If an offence, for instance, were committed at Cork, they might send a magistrate from Belfast, or *vice versâ*. That would, I think, be very objectionable. There are Resident Magistrates in Ireland whom it might be convenient for the Government to send on a roving commission all over the country. But that would be a very inconvenient course for others than the Government. In moving this Amendment, I can refer to the precedent of the Crimes Act. Under the Crimes Act, a magistrate empowered to hold an inquiry under that Act was required to be a magistrate having jurisdiction in the place where the inquiry was held. And in the Criminal Code Bill introduced by the Government some years ago, the magistrate to hold an inquiry under the clause corresponding to this was required to be a magistrate having jurisdiction in the place where the inquiry was held. The Government will, I think, see that it would really be very inconvenient if they were to have the power to select any one of the staff of 80 Resident Magistrates and send him all over the country. If there is to be an inquiry of this kind, let it be held by a magistrate on the spot. Of course, there might be cases in which Members of the Government might say—"We cannot entrust this case to a Resident Magistrate on the spot because, having regard to the terms of the Amendments we have accepted, the magistrate must be competent in point of legal knowledge to hold an inquiry; but the Resident Magistrate on the spot is not a person with the sufficiency of whose legal knowledge the Lord Chancellor would be satisfied." But it must be remembered that a Resident Magistrate has a general jurisdiction over half-a-dozen counties. There is hardly a single Resident Magistrate whose jurisdiction would be confined to a single county, and, therefore, no difficulty of that kind would arise because it is inconceivable that within the range of two or three counties over which the jurisdiction of a Resident Magistrate would extend, there should not be found a single magistrate of whose legal knowledge the Lord Chancellor would not be satisfied. I will therefore propose to amend the clause in the manner I have mentioned.

Amendment proposed,

In page 1 line 8 after "satisfied" insert the words—"and being a magistrate for the county or place in which such offence was committed."—(*Mr. Maurice Healy*.)

Question proposed, "That these words be there inserted."

THE ATTORNEY GENERAL FOR IRELAND (Mr. HOLMES) (Dublin University): The Amendment cannot be accepted. It is true that in the Act of 1882 the words "of the county or place" were inserted, but then there was not in that Act the qualification of a magistrate —in reference to the holding of an inquiry —which we have now introduced into this Bill. The Lord Chancellor will desire that one of these inquiries should be conducted by a magistrate possessing the best knowledge and the highest qualifications attainable; and for the purpose of securing that end it may be necessary to bring a magistrate from a distance. Considering the qualification for a magistrate conducting one of these inquiries, which we have inserted in the Bill, I do not think the choice of such a magistrate should be restricted.

MR. T. M. HEALY (Longford, N.): I recollect Sir George Trevelyan stating, as Chief Secretary to the Lord Lieutenant, that it was the intention of the framers of the Crimes Act, that no person would be employed in a judicial inquiry under it who was not a person of legal knowledge. That was not a provision of the Act, but it was a pledge given by the Government of the day. Then in the Criminal Code Bill, which was proposed by a former Government, and went to a Grand Committee, it was provided that the magistrate holding one of these inquiries should be a magistrate having jurisdiction in the place where it is held.

[Third Night.]

And I attach considerable value to such a provision. A magistrate having jurisdiction in the place where the inquiry is held, would be less likely than a stranger to be influenced by outside stories. He would also be less likely to ride rough-shod over the people than he would be if he did not live there or live amongst them. If a man lives in a county his great desire must needs be to get on well and without friction with the people by whom he is surrounded and with whom he mixes. He is less likely than a stranger to the district to be imposed on by the police, or to send people lightly to gaol merely as it is said, for the sake of example. Magistrates who live amongst the people of a district and ride to hounds there are anxious not to come too directly into collision with the people; and for my own part I would much rather have a magistrate who rides to hounds in the district where he has jurisdiction, than a magistrate who rides to hounds in some other district at a distance from it. I would not, however, advise my hon. Friend to go to a Division on this Amendment; but I trust that in view of the fact that the Criminal Code Bill of 1883 contained this provision the Government will keep it in view, and act as far as possible in accordance with it.

Question put, and *negatived*.

Amendment proposed, in page 1, line 10, after " may," insert " if he so think fit."—(*Mr. Marum.*)

Question, " That these words be there inserted," put, and *agreed to*.

Motion made, and Question, " That the Chairman do report Progress, and ask leave to sit again,"—(*Mr. T. M. Healy,*)—put, and *agreed to*.

Committee report Progress; to sit again *To-morrow*.

QUARRIES (*re-committed*) BILL.—[BILL 239.]
(*Mr. Thomas Blake, Mr. Conybeare, Mr. Burt, Mr. Cobb, Mr. Abraham (Glamorgan).*)

COMMITTEE.

Bill *considered* in Committee.

(In the Committee.)

Amendment made.

Bill *reported*.

MR. T. M. HEALY (Longford, N.): I observe that this Bill does not extend to Ireland, and as I find it has been re-committed, I wish to ask if the exclusion of Ireland was duly considered?

Mr. T. M. Healy

THE UNDER SECRETARY OF STATE FOR THE HOME DEPARTMENT (Mr. STUART-WORTLEY) (Sheffield, Hallam): I believe so; but I have no knowledge of it myself.

MR. T. M. HEALY: I will ask the question of the hon. Member for the Forest of Dean Division of Gloucester?

MR. BLAKE (Gloucester, Forest of Dean): The exclusion of Ireland was duly considered.

MR. T. M. HEALY: I do not like to move that the Bill should apply to Ireland, as I am not sufficiently acquainted with the circumstances of our quarries; but I would like to ask whether the hon. Gentleman has considered the whole of the case of Ireland?

MR. BLAKE: I had communications from several Irish Members that the Bill would be opposed if it was proposed to extend it to Ireland.

Bill, as amended, to be considered *To-morrow*.

COLONIAL SERVICE (PENSIONS) BILL.
(*Sir Herbert Maxwell, Sir Henry Holland, Mr. Jackson.*)

COMMITTEE. [*Progress 2nd May.*]

Bill *considered* in Committee.

(In the Committee.)

Clause 4 (Mode of computing superannuation allowance to be granted in certain cases).

Amendment proposed, in page 2, lines 16 and 17, leave out, "profits of his employment," and insert "salary and emoluments of his office."—(*Sir Herbert Maxwell.*)

Question proposed, " That the words ' profits of his employment ' stand part of the Clause."

DR. TANNER (Cork Co., Mid): I wrote to ask the hon. Baronet who has charge of the Bill what he actually means by this Amendment, "profits of his employment," and "salary and emoluments of his office." I should think these words are very nearly synonymous, and I should say that when any of these colonial officers is drawing pay from any office he holds under the Government in any of the various Colonies under consideration, that he would frequently get advantages which are of a pecuniary nature, and which are profits; and I think these would come under the form of profits which would pay him better than if they came under this Amendment. I should like to know why the hon. Baronet proposes to introduce this Amendment, instead of retaining the words "profits of his employment.

SIR HERBERT MAXWELL (A LORD of the TREASURY) (Wigton): I would submit to the hon. Gentleman that these words more clearly express, and in more technical language, that which was intended by the first drafting of the Bill. It is an improvement in drafting, that is all.

MR. M. J. KENNY (Tyrone, Mid): But it makes different sense. The difference between the original and the new drafting is this—that the pension could only be calculated in the existing drafting on the profits derived from the office; but under the new drafting, it is calculated upon the gross salary received, and that is very different. A man may receive salary as a Governor of a Crown Colony, which may include the expense of the Government of his house, and so on, and a variety of other things which are by no means a profit to him, and so far as I can gather, the pension would be calculated, not on the net salary, but upon the gross salary of such an official; and, therefore, it might lead to abuses. I have read this Clause 4 very carefully; but I see that the new words it is proposed to introduce makes the clause quite different, and, to my mind, most objectionable.

SIR HERBERT MAXWELL: I think if the hon. Member will read the new clause which I propose to insert instead of Clause 3, and will read that, in conjunction with Clause 4, he will find that the maximum pension is included, and every safeguard is taken that the pension shall bear the proper proportion to the joint services of the Governor.

Question put, and *negatived.*

Amendment *agreed to.*

Clause, as amended, *agreed to.*

Clause 5 (Application of 28 & 29 *Vict.* c. 113, and 35 & 36 *Vict.* c. 29, to High Commissioner of Cyprus).

MR. M. J. KENNY (Tyrone, Mid): I rise for the purpose of moving the omission of this clause; and I hope the Committee will pay some attention to it. This is a clause to include in the category of Colonial or ex-Colonial

Governors, the High Commissioner of Cyprus. The Island of Cyprus means a net loss to this country of £35,000 a-year—that is to say, there was voted out of the Consolidated Fund, to make good the loss occasioned by having the island, something like £35,000 a-year. There may be any number of High Commissioners of Cyprus, as the island is a healthy place; but I want to point out that the High Commissioners may die off, or to avoid the danger of so dying off, some may be disposed to run away from their appointments, and thus get this pension. When we come to consider the loss which this island is already to the taxpayers of this country, I think it extremely unreasonable we should be called upon to contribute something like £1,000 a-year, or two-thirds of the salary of the High Commissioner of the Island of Cyprus, and thus increase the tax already placed upon the taxpayers of this country, owing to the inability of the inhabitants of Cyprus to pay sufficient taxes for the administration of the island. Cyprus is by no means a Colony, in the ordinary sense of the term, and if this is to go on, we do not know where it is to stop. I should like to know for what reasons the Government have come forward and included this clause in the Bill; I should like to know how many of these ex-Commissioners there are to whom it is proposed this Bill shall apply; and to have some estimate as to what may be the ultimate cost of including this clause.

THE SECRETARY OF STATE FOR THE COLONIES (Sir HENRY HOLLAND) (Hampstead): Of course, I do not propose to go into the question as to whether it was desirable to take Cyprus under our care; but we have got it, and we administer it as a Crown Colony. We are bound to do so, and the consequence is we are bound to have an Administrator there. It follows that if we are to get a good Administrator, we must deal with him in the same way as with Governors of other Colonies, and reward him accordingly. The only object of this section is to bring the Administrators of Cyprus into the same position as the Governors of other Colonies. Cyprus is not, in the strict sense, a Colony; but it is governed as a Crown Colony. In respect of the other question which the hon. Gentleman asks, may I state the first Governor of Cyprus was Lord Wolseley, who has no pension as such Governor. The next Governor, Sir Richard Biddulph, was one who has likewise no pension, and the present Governor, Sir Henry Bulwer, has not retired from the service; therefore there has been, at present, no Governor at Cyprus enjoying a pension. If the hon. Member is right in saying it is a healthy place, he may hope the Administrators may live for some time before retiring, and will, therefore, not require pensions for any length of time.

MR. M. J. KENNY: I merely wanted to ask whether those gentlemen who have been High Commissioners would, supposing the Bill were now law, be entitled to receive a pension; and whether any existing law would enable them to retire on a pension?

SIR HENRY HOLLAND: No, Sir; there is no such law.

DR. TANNER (Cork Co., Mid): When I first entered Notice of opposition to this Bill, I had sincere doubts as to the course I ought to pursue. Naturally, I am an unsuspicious person, and I have found that I am of too confiding a nature; but when I found this clause in the Bill, I, of course, strongly objected to it. Owing to my ignorance of the technicalities as to the entering of notice of opposition to certain clauses in regard to certain points to which I object, I unfortunately made a mistake in dealing with it. I can now, however, very easily see the reason why the Government have shown an inordinate amount of anxiety about this Bill; it is in order to protect their properties in this veritable white elephant—the Island of Cyprus. The Island of Cyprus, we all know, is one of those very undesirable subjects about which there is great doubt whether it was of any use whatever, or likely to be of any protection to this country. It weighs upon this country in every possible way, and tends rather to promote a *casus belli* in connection with other countries; and, what is further, we see that the Government are trying to make a Colony of it. It has been stated by the right hon. Gentleman (Sir Henry Holland) that hitherto it has not been considered a Colony; and, accordingly, it is proposed to make provision for the Governors of the Island similar to the provision made for the Governors of other Colonies connected with the British Empire. What are the

Government doing now? They know the difficulties that beset them on all sides in connection with the occupation of Cyprus and the suspicion of Continental Governments, and they are now trying to get in this thin end of the wedge for carrying out their policy of peace without honour in connection with this Island. Consequently, I shall take upon myself to move the omission of the clause, and I shall oppose it by every means. I sincerely hope I may get assistance in disputing this insidious attempt of the Government to press the Bill through always at this late hour of the night.

MR. MAURICE HEALY (Cork): I confess I am at a loss to understand the terms in which this clause is drawn. The right hon. Gentleman states that no past Governors of this Island can be entitled to pensions.

SIR HENRY HOLLAND: They will be entitled to pensions for services; but not for service in the Island only.

MR. MAURICE HEALY: Not entitled to pensions *quâ* Governors of Cyprus for all practical purposes, for the purposes of this section, they are not entitled to pensions at all. That being so, I want to know why the draftsman has drawn the clause, so that it will apply to persons who have ceased to be Governors of the Island before this Act is passed, as well as those who cease to be Governors after the passing of the Act? The two persons who have been Governors—Lord Wolseley, and another gentleman whose name I did not catch—what is the object of taking power to give them pensions if they are not entitled to them? The right hon. Gentleman has not explained that. The section is made retrospective, although the Colonial Secretary says there is no necessity to make it retrospective. At least, he should explain what seems the very peculiar framing of the section.

MR. CHANCE (Kilkenny, S.): I think I must move to report Progress, for this is no time to take a discussion on such a Bill. I recollect, when Cyprus was taken in charge, there was a great parade of intended improvements in administration, and it was said though this would involve some charge upon this country at first, later on that charge would be reimbursed. But now we have the Government coming for money—

sponging on the taxpayers of this country—by a clause that, I think, requires a closer scrutiny than it can receive at this hour. As my hon. Friend (Mr. M. J. Kenny) has pointed out, not only have we the statement that no High Commissioner who has served previously to the passing of the Act is entitled to a pension, but we have here words that distinctly bring those gentlemen within the meaning of the Act entitling them to pensions. The words of the clause would apply to Lord Wolseley and the other gentleman not named. We should like more detailed information, and I feel constrained to move to report Progress.

Motion made, and Question proposed, "That the Chairman do report Progress, and ask leave to sit again."—(*Mr. Chance.*)

SIR HENRY HOLLAND: I hope the hon. Gentleman will not persist with this Motion. I am sorry if I have not explained the point, which seemed a very small one. This is not a question as to the general expenditure of Cyprus.

MR. CHANCE: You are asking for money.

SIR HENRY HOLLAND: We have Cyprus on our hands. We have not the Sovereignty, but we have to govern it as we govern a Crown Colony. We must have a Governor, and surely no one can doubt that service as Administrator of Cyprus should be on the same footing as the administration of a Crown Colony? In respect to the point raised by the hon. Member for Mid Cork (Dr. Tanner), it is, as I said before, not a question whether the Governors, who in the past have done their duty in the Island, should be pensioned for it, but that service there may be counted in with services entitling to a pension. I really hope, after this explanation, we may go on with the Bill of which we have passed the most material part.

DR. TANNER: I hope my hon. Friend (Mr. Chance) will press his Motion. In addition to the points I have urged, it has been clearly shown that the two preceding Governors of Cyprus have managed their affairs in so good a manner that, beside being Governors, they have enjoyed many other honorariums. They have held other posts, they were officers of high military rank. The first High Commissioner, Lord Wolseley, was a general in the Army, and enjoyed

many subsidies that accrued to him from that position. I do not understand why the Treasury Bench, and, notably, the right hon. Gentleman who has the Bill in charge, press the measure with such pertinacity? Possibly, it is because they are a Conservative Government nominally, and consequently consider that Cyprus is specially under their care. The Island was first acquired by a Conservative Government, and they feel bound, in every possible way, to pay in an inordinate and exorbitant way such officers as they may promote to high office in the Island.

SIR ROBERT FOWLER (London): I believe it is the fact that Sir Henry Bulwer, the present High Commissioner, served for many years in Natal, and I presume the clause is only that he, and others in like position, may not lose the advantage of service in different parts of the world.

SIR HERBERT MAXWELL: The hon. Member for Mid Cork (Dr. Tanner) has expressed his opinion that a Tory Government press on the Bill, because it contains provisions for the benefit of Governors of Cyprus, in whom he supposes the Government are specially interested; but I may remind him that the Bill was drafted by our Predecessors in Office.

MR. M. J. KENNY: If all the Governors of Cyprus were like those of the past I do not know that I should care to criticize this clause. I do not exactly know the salary of the High Commissioner—I suppose some £2,000 or £3,000 a-year. But what would be possible under the clause is that persons holding minor appointments, not gentlemen of Lord Wolseley's rank and character, might be suddenly thrust into this position, and have their pensions calculated upon the high rate of pay attached to the office, and by that means a fraud would be perpetrated upon the taxpayers. If we have an undertaking that such things would not be done, probably my hon. Friend (Mr. Chance) would withdraw his Motion.

SIR HENRY HOLLAND: I can only give the assurance that no Government would appoint to a place like Cyprus a man not competent for the duties of this important position. The object of the Bill is to secure good men for the post, putting them in the same position as regards pensions as other

Governors. The new clause, as the Committee will see, limits the amount of pension to two-thirds of the amount of the salary and emoluments. I trust hon. Members will now allow us to proceed.

MR. ILLINGWORTH (Bradford, W.): I hope the hon. Gentleman (Mr. Chance) will consent to withdraw his Motion. I quite agree with the right hon. Gentleman (Sir Henry Holland) that there should be no distinction, so far as the Governor is concerned, in consequence of the policy under which Cyprus was occupied. Under the conditions we obtained the Island, we are bound to administer it.

MR. CONYBEARE (Cornwall, Camborne): That is quite true; but is not the responsibility shared with the Turks, and should not the Turks pay a share?

SIR HENRY HOLLAND: A certain subsidy is, by Convention, paid to Turkey; the surplus accrues to this country, and the administration is ours.

MR. CONYBEARE: But with a loss of £25,000, whence is the surplus to come?

MR. MAURICE HEALY: I do not think my point has been met. I agree that it is quite reasonable that Governors of Cyprus should be entitled to have their time in Cyprus allowed in calculating the period for earning a pension, and if that was all the clause effected, I should not oppose it. But my objection is, that this section does a great deal more than that. It does not confine itself with enabling the Government, when pensioning those gentlemen who have served as Governors of Cyprus, to to take into account the time served as Governors of Cyprus, it empowers the Government to give pensions simply for service as Governor of Cyprus. It bears that interpretation; but I venture to say the proper way to carry out the object said to be in view, is not to draw the section in this retrospective manner, but to add a Proviso somewhat in this form—

"Provided always, That in the case of any person who has served as Governor of Cyprus in calculating his time of service, the time of service as Governor of Cyprus shall be taken into consideration."

SIR HENRY HOLLAND: It has reference to the present Governor, now acting as such.

MR. CHANCE: I am willing to withdraw my Motion on condition that the "Report" stage is taken at a reasonable hour, and after a reasonable interval of time.

SIR HENRY HOLLAND: Yes; certainly.

Motion, by leave, *withdrawn.*

Clause *agreed to.*

Clause 6 (Definition of permanent Civil Service of a Colony).

Amendment proposed, in page 2, lines 35 and 36, to leave out the words "or superannuation allowance."—(*Sir Herbert Maxwell.*)

Question proposed, "That the words proposed to be left out stand part of the Clause."

MR. M. J. KENNY (Tyrone, Mid): May I ask, would service in a self-governing Colony be calculated in fixing pensions in the term of service of those who subsequently held office as Governors of a Crown Colony?

THE SECRETARY OF STATE FOR THE COLONIES (Sir HENRY HOLLAND) (Hampstead): The sum he receives from a Colony, and is entitled to receive, will be deducted from the pension he receives in respect to work in Cyprus or anywhere else.

MR. M. J. KENNY: That is not exactly a satisfactory answer. I object to persons who hold office conferred on them by a Colonial Government, practically an independent Government, claiming the time they have so served, together with the term served under the Imperial Government. I think there should be a limitation in Clause 6 to the term in a Crown Colony only to prevent abuses that might arise.

SIR HENRY HOLLAND: I would call the hon. Member's attention to Clause 2 as amended, which provides that the Treasury shall determine the portion of the payment from the Consolidated Fund, or moneys voted by Parliament, and that there shall be no payment therefrom in respect of any employment in the permanent Civil Service of a Colony. The Imperial taxpayer will not be called upon to pay for pensions in respect to service in a self-governing Colony.

DR. TANNER (Cork Co., Mid): Then there can be no harm in defining that. If you introduce the word in line 35 "of any Crown Colony" that would meet the object.

Sir Henry Holland

THE CHAIRMAN: That is not the Amendment under discussion.

Question put, and *negatived.*

Amendment *agreed to.*

Clause, as amended, *agreed to.*

New Clauses—

On the Motion of Sir HERBERT MAXWELL, the following Amendment made:— In page 2, leave out Clause 3, and insert the following Clause :—

(Provision for pensions.)

"A person shall not receive by way of pension, under the Colonial Governors (Pensions) Acts, 1865 and 1872, an amount which, together with any pension for service in the permanent Civil Service of the State or of a Colony, exceeds the sum of £1,000 a-year, or two-thirds of the salary and emoluments of his office in that service, whichever is greater. But his pension under the said Acts shall not be reduced by reason of his pension in respect of the said service being an emolument within the meaning of section 7 of 'The Colonial Governors (Pensions) Act, 1865.' "

On the Motion of Sir HERBERT MAXWELL, the following Amendments made:—In page 2, after Clause 6, insert the following Clauses:—

(Provision against double pensions.)

"A person shall not receive a pension under the Colonial Governors (Pensions) Acts, 1865 and 1872, or this Act, and also under section 12 of 'The Superannuation Act, 1859.' "

(Explanation of terms.)

"The expressions 'permanent Civil Service of the State,' 'permanent Civil Service of Her Majesty,' and 'permanent Civil Service of the Crown,' are hereby declared to have the same meaning, and this Act and any enactment relating to salaries and pensions shall be construed accordingly.

"In this Act 'pension' includes superannuation allowance."

Bill *reported;* as amended, to be considered upon *Tuesday* next, and to be *printed.* [Bill 251.]

TRUCK BILL.—[BILL 109.]

(Mr. Bradlaugh, Mr. Warmington, Mr. John Ellis, Mr. Arthur Williams, Mr. Howard Vincent, Mr. Esslemont.)

COMMITTEE. [*Progress 2nd May.*]

Bill *considered* in Committee.

(In the Committee.)

Clause 3 (Workmen to be entitled to advance of portion of wages).

Motion made, and Question, "That the Clause be postponed,"—(*Mr. Bradlaugh,*)—put, and *agreed to.*

New Clause—

(Servant in husbandry.)

"Nothing in the principal Act or this Act shall render illegal a contract with a servant in husbandry for giving him food, drink, a cottage, or other allowances or privileges in addition to money wages as a remuneration for his services,—(*Mr. Stuart-Wortley,*)

—*brought up,* and read the first time.

Motion made, and Question proposed, "That the Clause be read a second time."

MR. C. T. D. ACLAND (Cornwall, Launceston): I hope the Government will be inclined to accept the Amendment I have to move to this new clause, which is to insert after the word "drink," the words "not being alcoholic." I am not especially anxious for the word "alcoholic," if "intoxicating" will suit the Government better, though there is some difference between the two. My point is that in some parts of England—certainly in the West, and, I believe, in other parts of the country—labourers have, by contract, to receive part of their wages in intoxicating liquor, and this custom has been found to be exceedingly detrimental to the labourers themselves and the health of their families. One result of taking home part of their wages in liquor is that, having more than they care to drink themselves, children of tender age at home learn to drink this liquor, often of the roughest and worst possible kind. Besides that, when a farmer has produced, by accident or carelessness, an inferior liquor of an intoxicating character which he cannot sell in the ordinary way, he passes it off in payment to his labourers. I have known this happen; and I have known a farmer decline to engage a man who would not accept part of his wages in liquor; and I have also known labourers, who have been imprisoned for being intoxicated, complain that they could not get employment unless they accepted liquor as part of their wages. It seems to me that hardly any argument is required to establish the reasonable nature of the Amendment I propose.

Amendment proposed, in line 2, after "drink," insert "not being alcoholic." —(*Mr. C. T. D. Acland.*)

Question proposed, "That those words be there inserted."

2 E

MR. C. W. GRAY (Essex, Maldon): This Amendment is a very important one; too important to go into at this time in the morning. I shall strenuously oppose it; but I should prefer to urge my argument at a more convenient time. I will now move to report Progress.

Motion made, and Question proposed, "That the Chairman do report Progress, and ask leave to sit again."—(*Mr. C. W. Gray.*)

MR. BRADLAUGH (Northampton): I will not oppose the Motion to report Progress. I only proposed to take these clauses on the understanding that they were not opposed.

SIR JOSEPH PEASE (Durham, Barnard Castle): I would call attention to the state of this Bill, one of the most puzzling Bills, in its present form, I have ever had to deal with. The Government Amendments are larger than the original Bill; and when you come to look at these Amendments with the original Bill, you have the greatest difficulty in finding what is the real state of the proposals before the House. I am told that it is contrary to our practice, at this stage, to move that the Bill be reprinted; but might I suggest to the Government that a Paper might be circulated showing the effect of their Amendments upon the Bill? If such a Paper could be circulated from the Home Office, it would be of the greatest convenience to hon. Members interested in the Bill.

MR. CONYBEARE (Cornwall, Camborne): I should like to know when the Government will consent to taking this measure at some reasonable time? The 3rd clause has now been postponed several times, because it contains contentious matter, and now we have the new clause postponed, because of a small, though not unimportant, Amendment of the hon. Member for Launceston (Mr. C. T. D. Acland). If we are always to be put off until 2 in the morning, there is no hope of our getting forward with the Bill. I would appeal to the Government to fix the Bill for some hour when there would be reasonable prospect of making progress with it.

THE UNDER SECRETARY OF STATE FOR THE HOME DEPARTMENT (Mr. STUART-WORTLEY) (Sheffield, Hallam): As to what fell from the hon. Baronet (Sir Joseph Pease), he only describes that which necessarily arises when the Government, friendly to the progress of a Bill, is obliged to amend it; but I shall be able to place in his hands a reprint of the Bill, and I have a few copies for hon. Members who desire them.

MR. BRADLAUGH: I am very much indebted to the Government for the pains they have taken to make this a practical measure. I make no complaint whatever of what the Government have done. I am sure they are actuated by the desire to make it a good Bill.

MR. CONYBEARE: I make no complaint. I only appeal to the Government to give us some assurance that the Bill will be taken at a time when we can make progress with it.

MR. MUNDELLA (Sheffield, Brightside): It is very inconvenient for Members to sit here for three or four nights in expectation of the Bill, and then to find immediately we reach a crucial Amendment that Progress is to be reported. I should be glad to know if the Government would agree to bringing the Bill on at an hour when we can deal with this important Amendment, and which, though it is opposed, the best agricultural authorities are in favour of?

MR. CONYBEARE: I must press my appeal upon the Government. I do not think we are being treated in a friendly manner. I, perhaps, may not expect to be treated in a friendly manner by the Government; but I may claim a little courtesy when I repeat the appeal that has been endorsed by the right hon. Gentleman (Mr. Mundella) that the Bill should be taken at a reasonable time.

MR. STUART-WORTLEY: Hon. Members must be aware that it is not a matter in which we have any discretion. It is not our Bill, and it is not in our power to bring the Bill on at an early hour.

MR. CONYBEARE: I contend it is in the power of the Government to make such arrangements that other Business might cease at an earlier hour.

MR. MUNDELLA: I only ask that facilities should be given to the Bill after the main Business of the evening is disposed of. To-night, for instance, the Government were engaged upon Business of their own, when they might have allowed this Bill to come on. On some other night it might come on after other Business is disposed of, say, at 1 o'clock. If that is not done, I should oppose the Motion to report Progress.

MR. FINCH-HATTON (Lincolnshire, Spalding): May I say the Bill might have come on an hour earlier, had not hon. Members chosen to engage in a desultory discussion upon Cyprus.

MR. CHANCE (Kilkenny, S.): The discussion to which the hon. Gentleman refers did not occupy 20 minutes. He could not have been in the House during the discussion, and I would advise him in future, before hazarding such a statement, to look at the clock.

MR. FINCH-HATTON: That is exactly what I did.

MR. C. T. D. ACLAND: There can be no difficulty in providing facilities on another occasion; and if there is not a promise to give them, I really must divide against the Motion to report Progress.

THE SECRETARY TO THE TREASURY (Mr. JACKSON) (Leeds, N,): The hon. Member is surely most unreasonable. It is within his recollection that the hon. Member most interested (Mr. Bradlaugh) has, in the most frank manner, said he makes no complaint whatever against the Government, who have shown their friendly spirit towards the Bill. I am sure hon. Members will see, having regard to the time and the hour at which we meet again to-morrow, it is not unreasonable to report Progress if a long discussion is anticipated, and the Government are not to blame in acceding to a Motion to which the hon. Member for Northampton has himself assented. The Government will give every possible facility to further the progress of the Bill, as they have hitherto. If to-night another Bill has had precedence, it was because it was a small measure necessary to be passed, and it was not supposed would be met with opposition. However, that Bill is now out of the way, and the Government will deal with this Bill in a friendly spirit, and with a desire to co-operate with the hon. Member in making it a good measure.

MR. MUNDELLA: Still the hon. Gentleman does not undertake that, on the next occasion, it shall come on before other Government Business that may happen to be on the Paper.

MR. CHANCE: I think the case of the right hon. Gentleman the Member for the Brightside Division of Sheffield is rather stronger than he thinks, when he intimates his intention of opposing the adjournment of the debate. When another Bill was before the House I made a similar Motion; but I withdrew it on being informed that an intimation had been made by someone on the Government side of the House that, if the discussion on it was strangled, the opposed clauses of this Bill would be taken. Although by no means satisfied with that intimation, I withdrew my Motion; and yet, when the Government have had the advantage of getting their Bill through, they will not now do something towards getting these clauses taken. I do not think there is any serious objection to this clause. Only one hon. Member has opposed it, and I do think we might as well make an end of it, and thus secure a substantial advance with the Bill.

MR. CONYBEARE (Cornwall, Camborne): I am opposed to going on with this Bill. I have great respect for the Financial Secretary to the Treasury; but when he talks of the friendliness of the Government towards this Bill, and of the satisfaction of the hon. Member for Northampton (Mr. Bradlaugh), we understand, as far as the House is concerned, that no facilities have been afforded by the Government. All the Amendments have been arranged outside the House; but the contentious matter must be postponed to some other night. We have a right to press for some assurance from the Government that when the Bill comes on next time it shall be at such a reasonable hour as will enable us to make some progress with the contentious part of the Bill; otherwise, it will go on night after night, until it comes to be included in the "Massacre of the Innocents."

MR. BRADLAUGH: For my part, I can assure the House that I will put the Bill down as often as I can.

Question put, and *agreed to.*

Committee report Progress; to sit again upon *Thursday.*

MOTIONS.

GAS AND WATER PROVISIONAL ORDERS BILL.

On Motion of Baron Henry De Worms, Bill to confirm certain Provisional Orders made by the Board of Trade under "The Gas and Water Works Facilities Act, 1870," relating to Caterham and District Gas, Sunbury Gas, and Stowmarket Water, *ordered* to be brought in by Baron Henry De Worms and Mr. Jackson.

Bill *presented*, and read the first time. [Bill 248.]

GAS PROVISIONAL ORDERS BILL.

On Motion of Baron Henry De Worms, Bill to confirm certain Provisional Orders made by the Board of Trade under "The Gas and Water Works Facilties Act, 1870," relating to Bedford Gas, Long Melford Gas, Musselburgh Gas, Penmaenmawr Gas, and Portsea Gas, *ordered* to be brought in by Baron Henry De Worms and Mr. Jackson.

Bill *presented*, and read the first time. [Bill 249.]

WATER PROVISONAL ORDERS BILL.

On Motion of Baron Henry De Worms, Bill to confirm certain Provisional Orders made by the Board of Trade under "The Gas and Water Works Facilities Act, 1870," relating to Beverley Water, Freshwater and Yarmouth Water, Hoylake and West Kirby Water, Poole Water, and West Lulworth Water, *ordered* to be brought in by Baron Henry De Worms and Mr. Jackson.

Bill *presented*, and read the first time. [Bill 250.]

TRAMWAYS AND PUBLIC COMPANIES (IRELAND) ACTS AMENDMENT BILL.

On Motion of Colonel Nolan, Bill to amend the Tramways and Public Companies (Ireland) Acts, *ordered* to be brought in by Colonel Nolan, Mr. James O'Brien, Mr. Foley, and Mr. Sheehy.

Bill *presented*, and read the first time. [Bill 252.]

House adjourned at ten minutes after Two o'clock.

HOUSE OF COMMONS,

Wednesday, 4th May, 1887.

MINUTES.] — SELECT COMMITTEE — Sunday Postal Labour, *nominated.*

PUBLIC BILLS—*Resolutions in Committee—Ordered — First Reading* — Limited Partnerships * [254]; Partnership Law Consolidation and Amendment * [255].

Ordered—First Reading—Registration of Firms* [253]; Temporary Dwellings * [256].

Second Reading—Hares Preservation [4], *debate adjourned.*

Third Reading — Accumulations * [31]; Quarries * [239], and *passed.*

Withdrawn—Herb and Ginger Beer Makers' Licence [16].

PROVISIONAL ORDER BILLS—*Second Reading*— Commons Regulation (Ewer) * [237]; Commons Regulation (Laindon)* [238].

PARLIAMENT — PROCEDURE — HERB AND GINGER BEER MAKERS' LICENCE BILL.

SECOND READING. BILL WITHDRAWN.

MR. H. S. WRIGHT (Nottingham, S.): I wish to put a Question to you, Sir, on a point of Order. Since the first reading, early in the Session, of the Herb and Ginger Beer Makers' Licence Bill, of which I had charge, I have been informed that no Bill connected with Revenue can be brought in by a private Member. The object of this Bill being to grant licences to the makers of these non-intoxicating beverages upon the payment of certain sums according to rental, I beg to ask whether I should be in Order in moving the second reading, which has been set down for to-day?

MR. SPEAKER: The Bill which is referred to by the hon. Gentleman is a Bill which bears the title of "The Herb and Ginger Beer Makers' Licence Bill," whereby the hon. Gentleman proposes to impose an Inland Revenue Duty on certain non-intoxicating beverages. It is impossible for the hon. Member to bring in a Bill of that nature. It would be necessary that such a Bill should be introduced in Committee of the Whole House on the recommendation of a Minister of the Crown. Does the hon. Member move the discharge of the Order?

MR. H. S. WRIGHT: I do, Sir.

Motion made, and Question, "That the Order for the Second Reading of 'The Herb and Ginger Beer Makers' Licence Bill' be read and discharged,"—(*Mr. H. S. Wright,*)—put, and *agreed to.*

Order *discharged.*

Bill *withdrawn.*

PARLIAMENT—PRIVILEGE—THE CASE OF SIR EDWARD (THEN MR.) REED IN 1863.

PERSONAL EXPLANATION.

THE SOLICITOR GENERAL (Sir EDWARD CLARKE) (Plymouth): I wish, Sir, to ask the indulgence of the House with regard to a matter of personal explanation as to something I said yesterday evening in addressing the House with reference to the hon. Member for Cardiff (Sir Edward Reed). In the course of his speech the hon. Member for Northampton (Mr. Labouchere) referred to an incident which took place 24 years ago in this House, when the hon. Member for Cardiff, not then a Member of this House, was called to the Bar of the House. In speaking of it afterwards as an incident I remembered, I find I used the words "was brought to the Bar in consequence of charges he had made with regard to naval administration." The hon. Gentleman the Member for Cardiff has been good enough to call my attention to a letter on which a formal Motion of Breach of Privilege was made, and that letter was not one which attacked naval administration, but was one addressed to a Member of the House, saying—

"I call upon you to say why you made this false and libellous statement against me in your place in Parliament, and on what grounds you justify it. I beg to say I have not sought the post at the Admiralty, and I think when an hon. Member puts forward the claims of his supporter, he ought to do so without subjecting me to personal abuse in a place where I can have no opportunity of answering him."

Sir, it is not accurate to say that the article contained charges with regard to naval administration; but it contained the words I have just read, and I am obliged to the hon. Member for Cardiff for giving me an opportunity of expressing my regret that, in dealing with the matter which occurred so long ago, I was guilty of an inaccuracy.

Sir EDWARD REED (Cardiff): I am obliged to the hon. and learned Gentleman for having made this explanation. I was naturally anxious not to have it supposed that I was ever brought to the Bar of this House for having made accusations against the naval administration, because the greater part of my political life has been spent in making complaints against bad naval administration. I was brought to the Bar of this House 24 years ago for having written a letter to a Member of this House about something which fell from him in this House.

ORDERS OF THE DAY.

PRIVILEGE (MR. DILLON AND "THE TIMES" NEWSPAPER).—RESOLUTION.

ADJOURNED DEBATE. [SECOND NIGHT.]

Order read, for resuming the Adjourned Debate on the Question, 3rd of May—

"That the publication in the 'Times' newspaper of the 2nd of May, of the article headed 'Parnellism and Crime,' constitutes a breach of the Privileges of this House."—(*Sir Charles Lewis.*)

Question again proposed.

Debate *resumed.*

THE FIRST LORD OF THE TREASURY (Mr. W. H. SMITH) (Strand, Westminster): You have intimated to me, Sir, that I have no right to address the House, having exhausted that right by speaking on the Main Question yesterday; but, Sir, I think I may throw myself on the indulgence of the House to fulfil the engagement I entered into last evening to state to the House the view the Government take of the course which the House should adopt in the present circumstances. Sir, the Government have given very grave consideration to the Motion made by the hon. Member for North Antrim (Sir Charles Lewis); they have given also very grave consideration to the statement made by hon. Gentlemen opposite below the Gangway. The Government recognize the demand of those hon. Members for an inquiry into the facts or allegations contained in the complaint made by the hon. Member for North Antrim. They had to consider what course it is befitting the House to take to meet those charges and allegations. Sir, after having given very full consideration to the arguments which were advanced yesterday, and to the facts of the case as they are contained in the Paper brought before the House, they have come to the conclusion that the allegation that the publication in *The Times* newspaper is a matter constituting a Breach of the Privileges of this House is not sustained by precedent, nor is it sustained by the facts of the case as they are disclosed in the complaint itself. Sir, in making that statement I should not presume to do so upon my own responsibility only. It is my duty to ask the opinion and to take the advice of those who are competent to give an opinion upon the law as well as the facts of the case, and I have taken that opinion and I have asked for that advice. But, Sir, it is impossible to be indifferent to the demands made by hon. Gentlemen below the Gangway. They ask for an inquiry; not only did the hon. Member for West Belfast (Mr. Sexton) ask for it in impassioned language last night, but the hon. Member for East Mayo (Mr. Dillon) demanded an inquiry. The proposal made is that this publication shall be voted by the House to be a Breach of the Privileges of this House; and, if that Motion is carried, the necessary result is that the printer will be summoned to the Bar of the House, that a Breach of the Privileges of this House will be voted upon and determined before any inquiry into the allegations contained in the article complained of has taken place. This, Sir, I venture to think, is a very serious fact for the House of Commons to consider. We, in the exercise of our own privilege, our own authority, and our own power, are asked to determine that a Breach of Privilege has been committed, before any inquiry is instituted into the circumstances upon which this Breach of Privilege is founded. I admit, Sir, that hon. Gentlemen below the Gangway have perpetually denounced the statements which are made; but there has been, they will admit, no such inquiry as that which they now demand into the facts of the case, into the allegations against which their denials are placed. Hitherto there has only been a denial of those allegations. The proposal, as I understood hon. Gentlemen below the Gangway, was that a Committee should be appointed to inquire into these allegations. Now, Sir, during the time I have been in this House the practice of the House has been to divest itself, as far as it is possible to do so, of any judicial duty. It has been felt, and held, Sir, that this House, constituted as it is, is unfit to enter upon the careful discharge of a duty which ordinarily falls upon a Court of Justice—to ascertain facts, to determine whether allegations as between one side and another are correct, and carefully and exhaustively to consider all that can be urged on the other side of a disputed question of great moment and gravity. We have felt it right even with regard to Election Petitions to transfer to a judicial body the decision of questions deeply affecting the honour, character, and reputation of this House and of parties in this House; and we have felt that even in so small a matter as whether a Gentleman should retain a seat or not retain a seat in this House, it is not judicially able to decide a question of that character. Still more do I consider the House, or a Committee of the

House, unfit to consider the questions of very great gravity which must be referred to a Committee, if a Committee of Inquiry is entertained upon the subject involved in this debate. The decision, therefore, that the Government has come to in this matter is that, acknowledging the gravity of the circumstances, acknowledging the claims of hon. Gentlemen below the Gangway to have the matter fully and impartially investigated, it is the duty of this House, and it is the duty of the Government, to afford them every possible facility for that investigation in a manner which will conduce at once to the honour of this House and to the determination of the questions which are involved. We, therefore, shall propose to hon. Gentlemen who now demand an inquiry that the Attorney General, coupled with any Queen's Counsel whom they may select, shall be instructed to prosecute the parties—[An hon. MEMBER: A proposal worthy of the Government.]—whose conduct is complained of. It is alleged that false and scandalous libels have been levelled against the hon. Member for East Mayo, and he has denounced these libels in the strongest possible language in this House. We regard the circumstances of sufficient moment, and it is our duty to endeavour to solve the question at the earliest possible moment, and by a method which will command the approval, as we believe it will satisfy the consciences, of the people of the United Kingdom. With the assistance of the hon. Member himself, with the assistance of counsel whom he may himself select in the direction of a prosecutor, as has been done in former cases, such a prosecution may be instituted as will determine the question as between the newspaper and the hon. Member without in the slightest degree involving the dignity or the honour of this House. The question is before us in the shape of a Motion that the article complained of is a Breach of the Privileges of the House. I will once more draw the attention of the House to the fact that we shall be determining upon matters which are alleged *seriatim* to be capable of proof, as to which I express no opinion whatever, and desire to express no opinion whatever, and as to which I believe this House to be absolutely incapable of forming a judgment. We shall be affirming the proposition that an editor of and a writer in a news-

Mr. W. H. Smith

paper, or any proprietor of a newspaper, who may deem it to be his duty to make statements which he alleges he has power to sustain in a Court of Law, is to be brought to the Bar of this House; and, without the previous inquiry necessary to ascertain the truth or falsehood of the allegation, is to be treated as an offender against the Privileges of this House. I think, Sir, therefore, that such a proceeding would be absolutely inconclusive, and would be unworthy of the dignity and of the honour of this House. It would be one which this House would be unwilling to adopt. It is a course which I should be unwilling to invite any of my Colleagues to adopt, if they were subjected to charges as painful and serious as those to which the hon. Member has been subjected. Therefore it is that I hope the House will, on a Motion to be made by one of my hon. or right hon. Friends sitting near me, accept the course which the Government have thought it their duty to indicate.

MR. T. P. O'CONNOR (Liverpool, Scotland): Mr. Speaker, we on this side of the House may be shocked and disgusted, but we are not surprised, at the course the right hon. Gentleman has suggested. We did not require the short interval that has elapsed since last night to be certain of the fact that the Government, having spread these charges broadcast over the country, would skulk from the only course in which they can be met. Sir, I am no friend of the Government or of *The Times;* but I must say, bitterly as I am opposed to them, I think that Christian charity would make one feel some commiseration for the position of humiliation and degradation in which they are placed. What is the proposal of the Government? In the first place, their statement is this—that a charge of falsehood against a Member of this House, with regard to words used in this House, is not a Breach of the Privileges of this House; the charge that an hon. Member makes a statement which is a deliberate falsehood is not a question which, in the opinion of the right hon. Gentleman the nominal Leader of the House, affects the honour and dignity of the House. But that is not the only statement which has been made against my hon. Friend. The statement is made that he was in association and in combination with assassins, and that when he denied that statement he was

guilty of deliberate falsehood. And the Leader of the House is so conscious of the honour and dignity of the House that he thinks the House is not called upon to declare a Breach of Privilege the charge of false denial of association and intimacy and combination with murderers. I had no high expectation of the manner in which the right hon. Gentleman would fulfil the duties of Leadership in this House—duties which have hitherto been fulfilled by men of a very different type; but I must say that I am more than surprised at the degradation to which he has already brought the House. Now, what is the proposal of the right hon. Gentleman? His proposal is a collusive action at law against *The Times* newspaper with a co-plaintiff who has been making the same charges as the defendant. Above all others, by whom is that statement made? The right hon. Gentleman, besides being Leader of the House, is a man of business, a prosperous man of business. Business is honourable or dishonourable according to the manner in which it is conducted. But the right hon. Gentleman is a man of business whose chief stock-in-trade is the publication and sale of the very newspaper and of the very libels of which this complaint is made. I have here a copy of *The Times* containing some of these libels, and this copy was bought at one of W. H. Smith and Sons' bookstalls, so that the right hon. Gentleman is the vendor of the libels, and is an interested—a deeply interested—party in the case. The man himself who publishes and propagates the criminal libel is the man, forsooth, who is going to take the action for criminal libel. Did anybody ever hear in their lives of any such proposition made, and made with an assumption of fair play and of reason and justice—that two men who should be in the dock together should part company, and that one should go from the dock into the position of plaintiff, and that we should be taken in by a collusive action of this kind? Sir, we reject the proposal. We reject it as a proposal which is unfair, which is unjust, which is unprecedented, which is collusive. Now, Sir, let me say what the position of the Government is with respect to this matter. There is scarcely a Gentleman on these Benches —[*Ministerial cries of* "Hear, hear!" *and laughter*]—I say there is scarcely a

[*Second Night.*]

Gentleman on the Benches opposite who has not made himself a partner and fellow-conspirator of the libellers against whom we now protest.

MR. DE LISLE (Leicestershire, Mid): I rise to a question of Order. [*Cries of* "Sit down!" *and* "Order!"] The hon. Member for Mid Cork (Dr. Tanner), standing below the Bar, has said of us sitting on this side of the House, that we are a "damned lot of Cads." ["So you are!" *and cries of* "Order!"]

MR. SPEAKER: I must direct the Clerk to take those words down. Has the hon. Member for Mid Cork anything to say in reply?

DR. TANNER (Cork Co., Mid) (who had moved from the Bar to the Bench below the Gangway) said: Sir, in the first place, the hon. Member for a Division of Leicestershire has made a mistake, as I never used the word "damned." In the second place, when my hon. Friend said—"There is scarcely a Gentleman on these Benches," Gentlemen on that side laughed and sneered, and I certainly did say that those who laughed in that way were cads; and so they are, and I wish to reiterate the expression in the strongest possible way.

MR. SPEAKER: The hon. Member has said he reiterates the expression. His remarks must not be allowed to pass without notice. I must order him to withdraw, and to apologize to the House for having used that expression.

DR. TANNER: Certainly; if you wish me to do so, I will withdraw it. But I must ask you, Sir, to call upon the hon. Member to apologize for what he has done and to withdraw his sneer.

MR. SPEAKER: The hon. Member is not to dictate to me what I am to do. I called upon the hon. Member to withdraw and apologize. I understand that he does both—that he withdraws the expression and expresses his regret to the House for having used it.

DR. TANNER assented by raising his hat.

SIR TREVOR LAWRENCE (Surrey, Reigate): I wish to say that I distinctly heard—[*Cries of* "Order!"]

MR. SPEAKER: Order, order! The matter has now closed. I must remark that complaints are made to me about expressions used out of my hearing of which I should certainly take notice if I had heard them. I will appeal to hon.

Gentlemen on both sides of the House to be careful of giving expression to any observations which are likely to cause pain to any other hon. Member. I call upon Mr. T. P. O'Connor.

The following is the entry in the Votes:—

Mr. de Lisle, Member for Mid-Leicestershire rose to Order, and stated that Dr. Tanner, Member for Mid-Cork, standing below the Bar, had called the Members sitting near Mr. de Lisle on the right side of the House "a damned set of Cads."

Mr. Speaker directed the words to be taken down by the Clerk, and called on the honourable Member for Mid-Cork to resume his place. The words were taken down accordingly.

Mr. Speaker called on Dr. Tanner to offer an explanation regarding the words taken down.

Dr. Tanner stated that he had not used the word "damned," but, in the course of his explanation, repeated the rest of the words complained of.

Mr. Speaker called upon Dr. Tanner to withdraw the words and to apologise to the House for having used them.

Whereupon Dr. Tanner withdrew the words and made his apology to the House.

MR. T. P. O'CONNOR: To whom are we asked to trust our fortunes in an action against *The Times?* We are asked to give our cause into the custody of a body of men scarcely one of whom has not made himself a partner and a sponsor for the libels in *The Times?* Is it not notorious that for the last three weeks the main burden of the arguments of the Government in support of their policy is the libels of *The Times?* Is there a single hon. or right hon. Gentleman of any importance on those Benches who has addressed the country during the last three or four weeks who has not made the libels of *The Times* the burden of his discourse? The right hon. Gentleman the Chief Secretary to the Lord Lieutenant went down to Ipswich, took the opportunity to advertise *The Times*, and as far as he dared suggested and insinuated his belief in the libels. It is in this way that the libels in *The Times* have been advertised, and the slanders of *The Times* propagated, and those who have advertised and backed up the slanders are now to be the guardians of the honour of those who have been libelled. The noble Lord the Member for South Paddington (Lord Randolph Churchill) has acted as the aid and assistant of the Government in refusing the only proper sort of inquiry which ought to be taken against the libels of *The Times*. Everybody knows that whenever there is an unfair attack to be made against a political opponent the noble Lord is only too ready to seize the opportunity of rushing in and making it. Political vituperation is the capital upon which the noble Lord has traded throughout his whole political life. The noble Lord also has advertised the libels of *The Times*. Every single opponent of the rights of Ireland in this House has taken up the libels of *The Times*. It has become a Party issue, a political weapon, and the very men who wield this poisoned dagger against us are now, forsooth, the Gentlemen who are to stand between our accusers and us. The right hon. Gentleman says the House of Commons is not a fit tribunal for this inquiry. I suppose he meant to suggest that another tribunal would be more suitable. Well, Sir, I declare to the right hon. Gentleman that the reason he dreads the tribunal of the House of Commons is because of the certainty of the verdict, and the reason he prefers the other tribunal is because of the uncertainty of the verdict. [*Ministerial cries of* "No!"] The right hon. Gentleman does not want to play a fair game. He has invited us to the struggle, and when we have accepted the invitation, given with so much braggadocio throughout the country, the reply of the right hon. Gentleman is to invite us to a game in which the dice are loaded and the cards are marked. Why does the right hon. Gentleman want to take this case from the tribunal of the House of Commons and bring it into a Court of Law? It is because he knows that, owing to legal technicalities, to quibbles, and collusive action—for collusive action is certain in this case—owing to legal technicalities, owing to quibbles and cranks, the main and clear issue will be obscured from the public, and especially from the ignorant and prejudiced portion of the public, because it is upon ignorance and prejudice that the right hon. Gentleman relies. We, on the other hand, want to have the case tried in a court of honour by gentlemen. ["Oh, oh!" *and a laugh*.] In that court of honour we invite you to

take part, and if you laugh at my statement that a court of honour, consisting partly of you, would not be a court of gentlemen, I shall not dispute it with you, but shall leave it to yourselves. How would the case stand if it were tried before a Committee of this House? A Committee of this House would confine the case to the real issue. A Committee of this House would not be confused by quibbles, or indulge in dishonest appeals to passion. A Committee of this House would have the facts fair and square before them, and upon those facts they would come to an issue. But now the right hon. Gentleman invites us to a tribunal in which he knows that, however fair the tribunal might endeavour to be, the questions at issue might be twisted and turned by technicalities of the law and the ingenuity of counsel, and in which we, the accused, are to have our accusers as the defenders of our honour. The country now will be able to decide between the Party opposite and us. The challenge given to us has been taken up by us, and the men who gave the challenge with all the courage, before the fight, of Bob Acres, exhibit the prudence of that historic gentleman when the opportunity comes for testing their courage.

SIR WILLIAM HARCOURT (Derby): I must appeal to the indulgence of the House on this occasion, like the right hon. Gentleman opposite, in order to say what I think of the course proposed by the First Lord of the Treasury. One thing, I think, cannot be denied, and that is that it is a course entirely inconsistent with the general and traditional proceedings of this House in matters of this character. The right hon. Gentleman stated that the House, in proceedings of this character, concludes the matter by a Motion that a Breach of Privilege has been committed. That is not the fact. The question of Privilege in this House, according to the old traditional practice of the House of Commons—followed, I believe, by every Leader of the House down to the present moment—has been, I take it, that when some charge against the honour or conduct of a Member of this House is made by speech or writing outside the House, *primâ facie* that statement is an offence against this House. This House does not inquire of the printer or of the speaker who is standing at the

Bar whether the statements complained of are true or not—that has never been done. For instance, let me put this case—supposing a charge of corruption were made against a Member of this House sitting on a Committee, or against a right hon. Gentleman sitting upon that Bench as a Minister of the Crown. What is the traditional course of proceeding which has been followed by the House in such a case? It is to call the author of the charge to the Bar of the House. The House has not to decide whether the charge is unfounded, but whether it is *primâ facie* an offence against the House to have made such a charge. That is the course which I have witnessed pursued by the Predecessors of the right hon. Gentleman as Leaders of this House. I have seen it done by Mr. Disraeli, sitting in his place on that Bench, and by other Leaders of the House of Commons. I am afraid, however, that to make an appeal to the right hon. Gentleman founded on the practice of his Predecessors is not a strong appeal. We appealed upon a former occasion to the practice pursued by Sir Robert Peel; but the right hon. Gentleman said he did not think much of that precedent. Therefore, I do not think it would be of much avail to refer the right hon. Gentleman to the practice pursued by Mr. Disraeli, or by other Leaders of the House who have occupied the position which the right hon. Gentleman now occupies. But the view taken by the House of Commons has always been, that when a charge has been made against the honour of its Members, it is *primâ facie* a matter for the judgment of this House. I will give an example. A charge of corruption has been made. Is it true to say that the House of Commons is incapable of examining such a charge? Has that been the view of previous Leaders of this House? Where such charges have been made they have called the persons who made the charges to the Bar; they have appointed Committees to inquire into these charges, and have proceeded in the manner which those inquiries justified and the circumstances of the cases required. That has been the traditional practice of the House of Commons; we are going to break that traditional practice. We are going to overthrow the whole claim of the House of Commons to vindicate the cha-

racter of its Members; we are going to state, for the first time, that the House of Commons is incapable of inquiring into the conduct of its own Members. Such an allegation has never been made before by any Leader of the House of Commons. It is contrary to the constant practice which of recent years has been pursued. And why is this breach of the traditions of the House to be made? Against whom is this breach of the traditions of the House to be made? Why, it is against the Irish Members. You have selected them as the first example in which to refuse the protection of the Parliament of the United Kingdom—the protection that has been granted by every other Parliament, and by every other Leader of the House to every Member of the English House of Commons. I do not say it is your intention to refuse this protection in the present instance—I have no right to speculate as to what your intention is, but I can say that it is the natural consequence of your acts, and of the spirit in which you proceed, that people will come to the conclusion that your object is to treat the Representatives of Ireland in a different manner from that in which you would treat Representatives of England or of Scotland who had been placed in a similar position. If the result of your conduct should be to make it impossible for Members from Ireland to discharge the duty which is imposed upon them in this House, because they do not receive the fair and ordinary and traditional treatment that has been given to every other Member of the House of Commons, that would be the natural and legitimate conclusion from the course you are now pursuing. I should have thought that, in the existing circumstances, you would have been most careful, if there was to be a departure for any reason from the ancient and traditional usage of the Parliament of England, that you should not have selected an Irish Member, in order to make him the object of that new course of procedure. Well, now, what is the course of proceeding that is proposed? As I say, those Members are entitled by prescriptive right and by the traditions of Parliament to an inquiry by Parliament into charges affecting their honour. That has been the practice of the House of Commons; that has been the usage of the great

Sir William Harcourt

Leaders of the House of Commons. They have never refused such a claim when it has been made by the humblest amongst the Members of this House, and yet that is the claim which you refuse to-day. Well, I say, what is it you propose to substitute in its place? You propose to substitute in its place a prosecution by the Attorney General. I wonder that you did not order the Member for North Antrim (Sir Charles Lewis) to undertake the case. This proposal of the Government is the natural sequel to the transaction of yesterday. We had a proposal to vindicate the character of a Member—a proposal in counterfeit—from the hon. Member for North Antrim. I think hon. Members and people out-of-doors will be able to form their own judgment as to the true character of that proposal. Well, that proceeding is followed by the present proposal—that a prosecution should be conducted by the Attorney General. That seems to be a very natural corollary to the proposal of yesterday. The two transactions seem to be one and the same, conceived in the same spirit, and proposed with the same object—exactly on a par, I think, with each other. How can you expect that parties concerned can have any confidence in such a course? If the matter went before a Committee of the House of Commons, the Government would command a majority of that Committee. Well, that would be no disadvantage to you in the objects you are prosecuting. At all events, then the proceedings would have been under the control and within the knowledge of this House. The evidence would not have been in the hands of what I cannot but call a hostile party. What is the principle on which prosecutions by the Attorney General are conducted? Does any man conduct a prosecution—does any man, does any responsible Government, instruct an Attorney General to conduct a prosecution when he does not, when they do not, believe in the guilt of the parties prosecuted? I say that any Government that instructs the Attorney General to prosecute any person where there is not a *primâ facie* belief and conviction of the guilt of the party, does a most unconstitutional and improper act. To instruct the Attorney General to prosecute a prisoner when you are satisfied of your belief in his innocence is not a prosecution, but a persecution;

therefore, before you institute proceedings, you must have formed an opinion —which opinion you declined to form on the *primâ facie* case of Privilege—that the party indicted has done something wrong. You say that, without examination into the matter, you cannot tell whether what has been done is wrong or not; therefore, you will not conduct the ordinary proceeding, but you will conduct an extraordinary proceeding, and order a prosecution upon a matter upon which you have no opinion as to whether the party prosecuted has done anything wrong or not. The one proceeding is absolutely inconsistent with the ground upon which you have rested your refusal to do the other. A prosecution involves in itself, or ought to involve on the part of the Government, the recognition of a principle upon which all such prosecutions have hitherto been conducted—namely, that the Government is satisfied that there is good reason to believe that the person prosecuted is guilty. But if you are satisfied of that, what is your objection to examining the prisoner at the Bar of the House? The two proposals are absolutely inconsistent. Here you have a prosecution proposed to be initiated on behalf of a Government, every one of whose Members, I think, have intimated that, so far from believing that the parties to be prosecuted have done anything that is wrong, believe that they have done perfectly right—that they have brought charges which, if not absolutely proved, are probably well founded. That is the situation; that is the state of mind of the Government which is to be charged with this prosecution which is to vindicate the hon. Member for East Mayo. All I can say is, that if you think that this would be esteemed and considered by anybody a fair trial, I do not agree in that view. I believe that the question, urged as it was yesterday by the hon. Member for North Antrim, followed as it has been by the proposal now made, to put the case of the hon. Member for East Mayo into what cannot be regarded as other than hostile hands, will be considered an extremely poor substitute for that justice which has hitherto been granted to Members of the House of Commons by English Parliaments from generation to generation. Some right hon. and hon. Members on this side of the House may take what course they

[*Second Night.*]

like upon this matter; but all I can say for myself is, that I must protest against this proposed breach of the traditions of Parliament. I do not say that there have been no cases in which prosecutions have been instituted; but there have been no cases in which prosecutions have been instituted under circumstances such as these. There have been no cases of prosecution by a Government which, on the face of it, has expressed sympathy with the parties to be prosecuted. No instances that the Attorney General can produce of prosecutions ordered will stand on any analogical ground with this at all; and, therefore, the Attorney General will in vain refer to proceedings of that character. The recent practice of the House of Commons—the practice for a great many years has been totally different—has been to give to its own Members the protection of a fair and impartial inquiry by its own body. That is what the hon. Member for East Mayo has demanded—I think justly demanded—and that is what the Government has refused.

THE SOLICITOR GENERAL (Sir EDWARD CLARKE) (Plymouth) : Mr. Speaker, I rise to move as an Amendment to the Motion now before the House—

" That this House declines to treat the publication of the article headed ' Parnellism and Crime' in *The Times* of the 2nd of May as a Breach of the Privileges of the House."

I shall endeavour, Sir, to support that Amendment by some reasons which I hope, whether they commend themselves to the acceptance of right hon. and hon. Gentlemen opposite or not, will, at all events, be acknowledged to deserve the consideration of the House. I am sure it will be understood that I speak upon this matter at this time with a feeling of very deep personal responsibility. My hon. and learned Friend the Attorney General and I, holding the positions which we now occupy, are responsible for our advice on matters of law, including the Rules and Practice of Parliament, to the Government as Members of which we have the honour to serve. [" No, no!"] Yes; to that Government as Members of which we have the honour to serve. We are bound—I say for myself, and I am sure also that I can say for my hon. and learned Friend—when a question of this kind arises to address

Sir William Harcourt

ourselves to it with reference strictly to legal considerations. I say for myself, and I am sure I can say for my hon. and learned Friend, that in the opinion which we intimated last evening, early in the evening, to the Leader of the House, and in the opinion which, after very careful consideration, we definitely gave to the Government some hours later, we have been utterly careless of Party or political results. [*Laughter.*] I think that when I make that assertion in the House the majority of the House, at all events, will give me credit for making it honestly. Now, Sir, there is only one observation I should like to make at this moment on the speech of the right hon. Gentleman who has just addressed us. I will deal presently with the question of the character of the prosecution which it is suggested might be instituted, and with the difficulties that exist in the way of the management and conduct of such prosecution. But at the present moment I want to refer to a sentence in which the right hon. Gentleman said that this proposal resembles the " transaction " of yesterday, and that the country and the House will understand the nature of the proceedings. Well, Sir, I quite agree, and I hope the country and the House will thoroughly understand the nature of these proceedings. But I do not think the right hon. Gentleman ought to have used the word " transaction," which is a word which has been used habitually for the purpose of pointing to some contract or arrangement which was absolutely repudiated by the right hon. Gentleman the Leader of the House yesterday in terms which were accepted at once by the right hon. Gentleman opposite. I think he might have refrained from using a word which carries with it the imputation which that word implies.

SIR WILLIAM HARCOURT : I did not use the word in that sense.

SIR EDWARD CLARKE : I am very glad it was not intended to use the word " transaction " in the sense I have referred to, for everyone will know that no arrangement was made. But with regard to the country and the House understanding the real meaning of the Motion of yesterday, I think we most of us understood it and deeply regretted that such a Motion should have been made. There was not a syllable of applause or cheering from these Benches when the Motion was made by the hon. Baronet. So far as I know, it was made by the hon. Baronet without the consent—for consent was not asked—of any of the other Members on this side of the House ; and he will excuse me if I say frankly now before the House, as I said the moment I heard the Motion, that I deeply regret that it should have been made. [*Ironical cheers from the Irish Members.*] Yes ; I deeply regretted that such a Motion had been made, because I did not think it was in accordance with Parliamentary precedent, nor with a fair exercise of the rights of Parliament with regard to matters of this kind, that a Motion should be made which in form was an attack upon the editor or the writer in *The Times,* but which in substance appeared to be an attack in the House, not on *The Times* newspaper, but on the hon. Member for East Mayo. I thought then, rightly or wrongly, that upon that ground the Motion was objectionable, and on that ground I regretted it ; but with regard to the political or Party aspects of the matter, we have entirely neglected, so far as our opinion is concerned, what the results may be. I am quite sensible of the weight of the observations which have been presented to the House by hon. Members below the Gangway opposite. I am quite sensible of the use they will make, and that they are entitled to make, of this incident. I am quite sensible of that fact. [*Laughter.*] Hon. Members are surprised that I should be, but I am sensible of that fact, although that had nothing whatever to do with the responsibility of the Law Officers of the Crown when yesterday evening, on this Motion being made, they were asked to express an opinion upon it. Yesterday, speaking for the Government, I expressed grave doubt as to whether what had taken place was, according to the custom and practice of the House, a Breach of Privilege of the House upon which we ought to exercise that exceptional power of bringing to the Bar of the House, and sending to imprisonment, those who offend against our Privileges. I am glad that we had an adjournment, although the adjournment yesterday was strongly protested against. I am glad we had an adjournment, because it has given me an opportunity of going through, as far as time permitted me, every reference and precedent I could

lay my hands on with regard to this matter. I have carefully searched the precedents of the House of Commons, and if the right hon. Gentleman the Member for Derby is right in what he has just said, that there has been a long and constant and unbroken line of precedents in favour of the appointment of a Committee to consider the truth of a matter of this kind, all I can say is ——

SIR WILLIAM HARCOURT : I said recent practice was in favour of that course.

SIR EDWARD CLARKE : Well, then, the recent practice. I thought, however, that the right hon. Gentleman gave a larger scope to his statement ; but I would rather be tiresome than incorrect. But if there is a recent practice to that effect, and of course a recent practice by which we ought to be bound, and from which our present action may be denounced, and fairly denounced, as an unwarrantable departure, all I can say is that I have been extremely unfortunate in not finding any record of that practice. My belief that no such practice exists is strengthened by the fact that the right hon. Gentleman, after making that statement to the House, did not condescend to support it in any way by precedents. But before I address myself to the serious question here involved, I would ask the indulgence of the House whilst I refer to the last debate that took place in this House on a question of Privilege. It was in the month of February, in the year 1880, when Sir Charles Russell—not the Sir Charles Russell we all know and respect so well, but the Sir Charles Russell who used to sit for Westminster—complained before this House that in a placard published and signed by Mr. Plimsoll, he had been denounced as guilty of inhuman and degrading conduct in blocking a Bill in this House. Sir, the Motion was made that this placard should be considered a Breach of Privilege on Tuesday evening, the 17th of February, and with the full concurrence of the Members of the Liberal Party, who were then led in this House by the noble Marquess the Member for Rossendale (the Marquess of Hartington), that debate was adjourned from Tuesday to Friday in order that the House might have time to consider the matter. [Sir WILLIAM HARCOURT here made some interruption.] The right hon. Gentleman had better not disagree with me, because I have the book before me, and I am going to quote some of his own words. Sir, that debate was adjourned from Tuesday, the 17th of February, to Friday, the 20th of February. On Friday, the 20th, the most valuable speech made in the course of the debate was made by the right hon. Gentleman the Member for Derby, who had in the interval prepared himself to discuss the question; and he alluded to a complaint made by the hon. Member for West Norfolk that the consideration of the question before the House had been delayed by the adjournment. The right hon. Gentleman defended that delay, and quoted a precedent in favour of it. He said—

"He would next call the attention of the House to another case of very great importance, which occurred in 1844, when a charge of a most odious character was brought by Mr. Ferrand against Sir James Graham—a charge which was unquestionably and undeniably false—that of using his influence, with other Members of the House, to obtain from an Election Committee a false and fraudulent Report. It was impossible to make an accusation more odious or unfounded; and he should like to observe, in reply to the hon. Member for West Norfolk (Mr. Bentinck), who complained that the consideration of the question before the House had been delayed, that that was precisely the course which had been advocated by Sir Robert Peel in 1844. Sir Robert Peel then said that the case was one which ought not to be disposed of in a hurry, ridiculous as the charge was, and unanimous though the feeling of the House might be that it was without foundation. A decision, Sir Robert Peel,"—

["Hear, hear!"] I am glad we are all in accord about it now—

"who was in favour of the public discussion of the conduct of Members of Parliament, and even of Cabinet Ministers, contended could not be arrived at on the question without establishing an important precedent; and, therefore, it was desirable, before coming to any such decision, to look back at the records which were within the House. Considering the great Constitutional question involved, Sir Robert Peel went on to urge 'the necessity of perfectly free discussion, and the risk that a feeling of indignation might prompt the House to adopt some sudden course which it might afterwards regret. Hon. Members, in their individual capacity, ought to have the means of seeing what had, in similar circumstances, been done in past times, and be afforded an opportunity of deliberating as to what ought to be done in the present. That, he thought, was a sufficient answer to what had fallen from the hon. Member for West Norfolk."—(3 *Hansard*, [250] 1116-7.)

Well, the adjournment that was here decided upon was precisely what we asked for yesterday, and what the House granted.

Sir Edward Clarke

DR. COMMINS (Roscommon, S.): That was all settled yesterday.

SIR EDWARD CLARKE: I have tried to do what the right hon. Gentleman did with great success and with great effect upon the House in 1880—namely, to look back to the precedents. I find that on February 17 Sir Charles Russell had moved that the words constituted a Breach of the Privileges of the House. On February 20 (Friday) Mr. Plimsoll apologized for the use of the words, and thereupon the Chancellor of the Exchequer (Sir Stafford Northcote) proposed a Resolution which declared the words to be a Breach of the Privileges of the House. [Mr. T. M. HEALY: Hear, hear!] There is still danger. The Resolution proceeded to say that the words were a Breach of the Privileges of the House; but, considering that the accusation had been withdrawn, the House did not think it necessary to take further steps in the matter. But the right hon. Gentleman in his speech resisted the declaration that it was a Breach of the Privileges of the House, and he quoted three precedents to support him in a protest he made against the House passing a Resolution which declared them to be a Breach of Privilege. I say the right hon. Gentleman quoted three precedents. He referred to the question in 1844, when Mr. Ferrand made the charge against Sir James Graham. He said—

"But did the House of Commons, he would ask, in 1844, decide that a Breach of Privilege had been committed? No; although the charge brought against Sir James Graham had neither been proved nor withdrawn, Sir Robert Peel would not allow so dangerous a precedent to be set; but he made a Motion to the effect that Sir James Graham and the other Members named, having denied in their places the truth of the allegations made against them, and Mr. Ferrand having declined to substantiate his charges, the House was of opinion that those charges were wholly unfounded and calumnious, and did not affect in the slightest degree the honour or the characters of the Members in question. There was in all that not a word about Privilege, for Sir Robert Peel was alive to the danger of passing such a Resolution as that which the Chancellor of the Exchequer now proposed. He would not permit the House of Commons to set so mischievous an example, and put such a restraint on the public discussion of the conduct of Members of Parliament. There was also another case—the Abercromby case—to which he might refer, which occurred in 1824, when Lord Eldon denounced in the Court of Chancery a Member of the House as having been guilty of falsehood. The matter was brought before the House as a question of Privilege and was debated at great length. Some very eminent persons were in favour of pronouncing the language of Lord Eldon a Breach of Privilege; but Mr. Canning and Mr. Peel were opposed to that course, and a majority of the House supported the view which they took."

Now, I ask the House to notice this, and I beg that I may be understood—though it will be a great honour to me—as adopting the language of the right hon. Gentleman and incorporating it in my speech—

" Those were the three great precedents on the subject; and it was clear from them that, in recent times, the House of Commons had not shown itself willing to invoke the shield of Privilege for the purpose of defending its Members from public criticism. If he were to quote ancient precedents, which the Chancellor of the Exchequer had very wisely declined to entertain, a rule would, no doubt, be found to the effect that there could be no criticism upon any act of a Member of Parliament in reference to his Parliamentary conduct; and if they chose to act upon the principle of Privilege as laid down in Parliamentary precedent, to speak of a man's vote, even to publish his speech or his vote, or to criticize his vote, was a Breach of Privilege. That was the only principle, if a rigorous course was to be adopted, on which the House could stand. All the rest was a question of degree. It was a question of adjectives, and as regarded the adjectives of the hon. Member for Derby "—

there seems to have been a former Member for Derby who used that argument—

" they were withdrawn, and they had no place in the Resolution of the Chancellor of the Exchequer. What they were asked to affirm was, that criticizing and condemning the conduct of an hon. Member of that House was a Breach of Privilege. That was how he understood the Resolution."—(*Ibid.* 1117-8.)

That was how the House understood the Resolution, and how the noble Marquess the Member for Rossendale understood it, and all the Liberal Members who were then in the House went into the Lobby to the number of 116—I think it was—against that Resolution. Though I do not follow it at length this most valuable speech, which I respectfully commend to the perusal and attention of the House, I should like to refer to one more passage.

MR. ILLINGWORTH (Bradford): Will the hon. and learned Gentleman give us the numbers on the other side?

SIR EDWARD CLARKE: Certainly; but I did not conceive that it was relevant—182 voted in favour of it. [*Laughter.*] Hon. Gentlemen will do me justice in this matter. I do not misapprehend the question as to whether that binds us in this case or not; I am only for a moment referring to it in order to get the valuable authority of the right hon. Gentleman opposite for some propositions in this matter. He went on to say—

" The question was, whether the House was to declare that printed placards—nothing was said about the character of the language in them, which might be the most respectable—reflecting upon the conduct of an hon. Member of that House, constituted a Breach of the Privileges of Parliament. It seemed to him that, in passing such a Resolution as that before them, the House would be striking a fatal blow at liberty of speech. If, for instance, an hon. Member were to make a speech denouncing another hon. Member for obstruction, was the Member so denounced to come forward and to appeal, under the protection of the Chancellor's Resolution, to the protection of the House ? It was too late in the day for the House of Commons to employ the engine of Privilege to smother public criticism upon the conduct of hon. Members. He did not say the Chancellor of the Exchequer had such an intention; but that would be the effect of his Resolution. If a Member of the House used language offensive to another Member, there were other ways of obtaining a withdrawal of, and redress for, the language. If he refused to withdraw that language, as in the case of Mr. Ferrand, then the Member whose conduct was impugned might be vindicated by the unanimous opinion of the Members of that House. But when they drew this old and rusty sword of Privilege for purposes of this character, then he believed that the House would be embarking in a course which would land it in immense embarrassment, and in which he saw no end of difficulty. There would be nothing to prevent its enforcing the new doctrine of Privilege against every newspaper and every election placard."—(*Ibid.* 1119-20.)

I am sure the House will not think that I require to make an apology for having quoted this speech. But now let me turn to the question that the Law Officers advising the Government had to consider, and upon which, having advised the Government, they are prepared very respectfully to advise the House. The fact is, that what the right hon. Gentleman called the doctrine of Privilege is a doctrine that the House of Commons is a Court, that it is like other Courts of Justice, and that it has the same power of compelling regularity, order, and decency in its proceedings as other Courts of Justice have, and that it has the power, which other Courts of Justice have, of taking up and dealing with accusations made against hon. Members of this House when they are acting in the service of the House. We will suppose that a Chairman of a Committee of this House, a Committee to which the House had delegated some of its judicial functions, was charged with corruption in his Office. There is no doubt whatever that that would be a contempt of the House, and would be a Breach of the Privileges of the House. If an attack be made upon the Speaker of the House, who represents the highest authority here, then the House has not been in the habit of leaving it to the Speaker by personal action to vindicate himself of the charge; but the House had resented, sometimes punished by its own action, and sometimes—and I think more often—referred the question to the tribunals where alone a question of this kind can properly be discussed. I am sure that hon. Gentlemen will make allowance for the shortness of time which has elapsed since the last Sitting of the House in which to go through the long range of precedents affecting matters of Privilege. I have done my best. I have not found, and I do not believe anyone can find, an instance of the House of Commons exercising its direct punishment by committal to prison of a person for an accusation made by him against a Member of the House of Commons, which was not directly an accusation of corruption or of misfeasance in a vote given in the House of Commons, or was not an attempt to coerce or intimidate him in his action in the House of Commons. I ask the House, and I ask the hon. Member for East Mayo, to look frankly at the case we have got here. There is no accusation here against an hon. Member of the House for corruption, or that any act that he has done as a Member of the House has been in any way tainted. What happened was this. An accusation of personal misconduct, if I may be allowed to use that general phrase—accusations of personal misconduct, not in the House, but outside the House, were made against the hon. Member for East Mayo; and in the course of debate in this House the noble Marquess the Member for Rossendale (the Marquess of Hartington) quoted from statements which had been made in regard to the hon. Member for East Mayo, and upon being asked to substantiate the statements he had quoted, the noble Marquess said he had taken the statements from *The Times* newspaper, and he did not put his own authority at the back of them. Thereupon the hon. Member for East Mayo denounced *The Times* in unmeasured language, and I will not say

that that language was not entirely justified by the feeling which possessed the hon. Member at the time. He denounced *The Times* for having told a falsehood about him. Upon this, *The Times* says that the falsehood is not with *The Times*, but with the hon. Member for East Mayo. That is what the House has now got to deal with, and if it should be found that through carelessness——

Mr. DILLON (Mayo, E.): As the hon. and learned Gentleman has appealed to me across the floor of the House, I think it right to say that while I do not intend—indeed, it would not be proper of me to enter into the debate—I think it right, in justice to myself, to state that I consider the hon. and learned Gentleman's statement to be extremely inaccurate.

Sir EDWARD CLARKE: I am very sorry it should be so. I was endeavouring, at all events, to state fairly what had taken place, and I really think that if the hon. Member for East Mayo would follow me step by step he would admit there is no inaccuracy. Let me just put the case again. The statements which had appeared in *The Times* with regard to the hon. Member for East Mayo were statements not as to something he had done in the House, but statements in which it was alleged that, at a particular time, some years ago, he was in communication—in habitual and common connection, I think the words were—with several persons whose character it was suggested the hon. Member must have known was bad. That was the accusation made. Then, in this House, the noble Marquess the Member for Rossendale (the Marquess of Hartington) quoted some statements on the subject in debate; and the hon. Member for East Mayo got up, I think, the next day, and made a most positive denial of the statements. Thereupon followed this article in *The Times*. If I have been at all inaccurate I am extremely sorry; I hope there is no inaccuracy. But now I do want to ask the House to consider —and this is what I was going on to say—that it may be by accident—I do not think it has been through carelessness—that I have overlooked some precedent which might be found in the Books, and which might justify the taking of immediate action by the House of Commons in the sense of punishment by imprisonment—[*Cries of* "No!"]—of a person who has made a libellous statement. I beg your pardon; it is a question of punishment. If the House of Commons decides that this matter is a Breach of Privilege, the person guilty of that Breach of Privilege would be brought to the Bar of the House of Commons, and, unless an apology or retractation was made, or satisfaction given to the House, that person would be ordered into custody. [*Cries of* "No!"] Well, all I can say is that that is the only power that the House of Commons has exercised beyond the power of reprimand, and there is no case whatever in which any other power has been exercised by the House of Commons for a very long time past except that of ordering persons into custody. [An hon. MEMBER: A Select Committee.] A Select Committee? When, yesterday afternoon, I said a word about a Committee, the right hon. Gentleman the Member for Mid Lothian (Mr. W. E. Gladstone) quite justifiably said—"Oh, that is an ulterior step." It is an ulterior step, and I will come to it. I hope the House will not think my speech has been inordinately long if it is lengthened by observations of this kind. Now, I venture to say that I believe that no case is to be found in the records of Parliament in which the House of Commons has committed a man to custody as being guilty of a Breach of Privilege for such a statement or such an act as is now alleged, and, if I have missed one, I can only say I feel surprised and sorry to hear it. Now, just let me say this. The foundation of the jurisdiction of this House, in regard to Privilege, is that it shall be upon an interference with the House itself, or with the conduct and action of a Member of the House. Of course hon. Gentlemen know that this question of the right of the House of Commons to commit for contempt has been brought under judicial decision, and in the case of "Burdett *v.* Abbot," the matter was largely discussed, and judgment was given by Lord Ellenborough and other Judges in that case. It was held that the House of Commons was entitled to commit for Breach of Privilege because it was a Court, and it was further held that the House of Commons was entitled to judge of its own Privileges, and that, if it judged of its own Privileges and com-

mitted a person for Breach of Privilege, no Court existing in this country could inquire whether that jurisdiction had been properly exercised or not. And I submit to hon. Gentlemen opposite, who, though they may be deeply interested in the political issue which is connected with this matter, are yet, I hope, far more deeply interested in the position the House of Commons and the attitude the House of Commons should take in regard to the question of Privilege—I submit to them that this is an occasion on which they can well remember and can give great weight to the words of the right hon. Gentleman opposite (Sir William Harcourt) which I have already read. I will not trouble the House by reading extracts from law books, and I hope the House will do me the justice to acknowledge that I do not very often address it in a tone as if I were arguing a legal question unless the necessity of the case compels me to do so. But all the early precedents put the matter upon this ground, that it must be for contempt of the House or interference with a Member of the House, as a Member of the House; there has been no such interference here. There is an allegation that an hon. Gentlemen in this House was guilty of falsehood, no corruption is alleged, nor is anything alleged which has been in past cases considered to be a Breach of Privilege by the House of Commons which justifies the exercise of its own authority. Now, there are some cases in which the House of Commons has taken another course. In the case of Sir Francis Burdett, a Committee was appointed to consider the Privileges of the House of Commons and the course which ought to be taken in regard to them. That Committee sat in the year 1810, and presented a Report which will be found in the first volume of *Hatsell's Precedents*. In their Report the Committee, speaking of commitment for libel, say it—

"Tends to excite public misapprehension and disaffection, endangers the freedom of debates and proceedings in Parliament, and requires most prompt interposition and restraint. The effect of immediate punishment and example is required to prevent the evils necessarily arising from this offence, which evil would be much less effectually guarded against by the more dilatory proceedings of the ordinary Courts of Law. Nevertheless, upon some occasions the House of Commons has proceeded against persons committing such an offence by direct prosecution or by addressing His Majesty to direct them, as appears by the precedents collected in the appendices."

Now, in the appendices there is a list of the cases in which the House of Commons has dealt with the question of libel upon its Members. These cases run down to about the year 1800. Turning to Appendix B, I find that since 1697, there have been 12 cases in which the House of Commons has dealt with libels upon the House of Commons or any of its Members, by ordering a prosecution in a Court of Law. [Sir CHARLES RUSSELL: By address.] It is the same thing, it is an address for a prosecution. These cases come down to the year 1810, and I am unable to find examples at all since 1810 in regard to the action of the House of Commons in matters of this kind. There are very few cases of newspaper libel upon Members of the House of Commons. There appear to have been three in the year 1821, which will be found in the 112th Volume of the Commons Journal, and it is interesting to notice what became of these three cases. The first was the case of *The Morning Chronicle*, which was brought before this House in the month of February, 1821, for a Breach of Privilege. It was alleged that a false statement had been made as to the way in which Members gave their votes. A Motion was made that Lambert, the printer, should attend at the Bar. An adjournment was moved and defeated; the Previous Question was moved, and then the Previous Question and the Motion were both withdrawn and the House took no step in the matter whatever. On the 8th of May, in the same year, the publication *John Bull* was charged with having published a false and scandalous libel on a Member of the House and in Breach of the Privileges of the House, and the assertion was that a Member of the House, under a threat made by the son of a person whom he had attacked, had made a speech in apology, and made it intentionally in so low a tone that it could not be heard. In that case proceedings were taken. The printer attended at the Bar, and eventually Henry Fox Cooper—looking to the date, 1821, and that name, I think it is probable there was a great deal of popular feeling in the House—who with the printer were committed to Newgate ; but I find no record of what was done with

Sir Edward Clarke

them afterwards. On the 10th of May, in the same year, *The Times* was attacked, and a Motion was made that an article in *The Times* was a Breach of the Privileges of the House as a misrepresentation of what passed in the House during the speech of a Member of the House. A Motion was made that the printer, Bell, should attend at the Bar of the House, and in that case, as in the case of *The Morning Chronicle*, the House took no action. Well, now, Sir, I have given the House my judgment, and so far as I can the result of my examination of the precedents. But let me point out to the House another matter——

MR. COBB (Warwick, S.E., Rugby): May I ask the hon. and learned Gentleman——

MR. SPEAKER: If the hon. and learned Gentleman the Solicitor General does not give way the hon. Member cannot intervene.

SIR EDWARD CLARKE: I hope it will not be thought discourteous in me if I do not give way, but if I answer interpolated questions it interferes with the current of the attention of the House. Well, now, it has been suggested that a Committee is the ordinary and proper course or the usual course of dealing with questions of Privilege. Upon that point I should like to quote an authority which hon. Gentlemen below the Gangway on that side of the House will at once recognize. The case took place in 1879 in regard to the Committee upon the High-level Bridge — the case of Grissell and Ward. Some statements had been made to a Committee of this House as to the conduct of certain persons who were interested in the proceedings of that Committee, and containing the suggestion of possible corruption against some Members of the Committee. The Committee came to the House and asked that an inquiry should be made. There was no inquiry after the persons were brought to the Bar of the House, the inquiry took place before the persons were brought to the Bar of the House, before the House had decided whether it would order them to attend at the Bar of the House. That is as different as possible from this case; but in the course of the debate objection was taken to the appointment of a Committee, and the objection was taken by the hon. Member —I do not know what constituency he then represented, so I may be pardoned calling him by name—Mr. Parnell. The hon. Member for Cork (Mr. Parnell) was then a Member of the House, and he took objection to the appointment of a Committee, and he said—

" There are just two precedents for referring a question of Privilege to a Committee, and only two precedents, as far as I can discover, and they are not precedents which govern the present case. On the 18th of February, 1575, a Committee was appointed to examine the matter touching the case of Hall's servant. That matter was treated as a question of Privilege. Also, on the 3rd of December, 1601, a complaint was made to the House of an information having been exhibited by the Earl of Huntingdon in the Star Chamber against Mr. Belgrave, a Member. The matter was referred to a Committee of Privileges, who reported upon the 17th of December. But we have no precedent at all for the Report of a Select Committee which complains to the House of a Breach of Privilege against itself of a most offensive character— there is no precedent whatever for sending such a Report to a Select Committee. On the contrary, all the precedents go in the direction of showing that these matters have always been considered by the House at once, and decided upon as a matter of Privilege."—(3 *Hansard*, [247] 1883-4.)

I believe the hon. Member was perfectly right in his statement that since the year 1601 there has been no precedent for appointing a Committee on a question of this kind. Now let me go to a further point. The Committee which it is proposed now to appoint is entirely new and unsupported by any precedent given in the book that we regard as authoritative. In that book, which I remember Mr. Disraeli telling me to study very carefully and deliberately, Sir Erskine May's, and in which there is that sentence with which the right hon. Gentleman the Member for Mid Lothian (Mr. W. E. Gladstone) fortified his argument yesterday in suggesting that a Committee of the House should be appointed, there are only two references to instances in which the appointment of a Committee took place—one being a case in regard to an Election Petition, and the other the case of " Grissell and Ward," which I have shown to be one of an entirely different character from this. And, I believe, Members of the House will search in vain in the records of Parliamentary Procedure from the oldest time to find the case of a Committee appointed to inquire, as between an hon. Member in this House and his accuser outside the House, whether the hon. Member or his accuser had been guilty of telling a false-

hood or not. Let me tell the House why Parliament would have been very unwise in adopting such a course. The suggestion appears now to be to bring someone to the Bar of the House on the ground that the action of that person constitutes a Breach of the Privilege of the House. The question is, whether an hon. Member of the House has told a falsehood. [An hon. MEMBER : In the House.] In the House, certainly ; but in reference to his personal conduct, unconnected with his position as Member of the House ; and the question is, whether that matter should be referred to a Committee of the House. The suggestion appears to be that, having brought a person to the Bar of the House, that a Committee of the House should be appointed which should act in a judicial capacity, and enter upon a question which, above all others, if it is to be decided at all, ought to be decided by the calmest and most impartial tribunal which it is possible to have. If I wanted demonstration of the monstrous character of this proposal, I should find it in the language which the right hon. Gentleman the Member for Derby (Sir William Harcourt) just now used. The right hon. Gentleman positively pointed to this side of the House, and said— " Every one of you have expressed your opinion tacitly, or in words, that this charge is true ; " and he went on to say—" You will be able to name the majority of the Committee." Why, Sir, I am not challenging the fact ; but what does that statement come to ? It comes to this—that at the very outset of the proceedings, while the House is considering how best to have a fair and impartial arbitrament in a matter of the gravest importance, the Committee which it is suggested should sit upon that matter is denounced beforehand —[*Cries of dissent and cheers*]—by the right hon. Gentleman who supports it, on the ground that it will be nominated by those who will be pledged to one conclusion. Sir, I would appeal to all Members of this House who are desirous of dealing justly and calmly with a serious question, whether what has occurred in this House to-day, and the cheers we have heard from different parts of the House are not a demonstration that the appointment of a Committee by this House would be a means absolutely insufficient for dealing with this question? Just see what would happen. This Committee would be sitting; it would not have all the opportunities and all the powers possessed by a Court of Law. ["Yes!"] Those Gentlemen who say "Yes" are not very familiar with Courts of Law. There would be no control over a Committee of the House of Commons—a Committee composed of ardent partizans. [Mr. T. M. HEALY: The Government would have a majority.] The Government would have a majority! Does not the hon. Gentleman see that by interposing that observation he is strengthening the argument I am using? [Mr. T. M. HEALY: We are not afraid.] We know now, by the declarations which have come from both the Front Bench opposite and below the Gangway, that if that Committee were to arrive at a decision hostile to the hon. Member for East Mayo, it would at once be denounced as a packed Committee. Just let me suggest to the House what I am sure every hon. Member will feel to be a real and practical view with regard to this matter. Assume that a Committee is appointed; assume that after a long struggle as to what was relevant and what irrelevant, the Committee had taken all the evidence and was going to consider its judgment — does anyone doubt that that Committee would come to the House with two Reports, that there would not be a Report of the majority and a Report of the minority? It is obvious that that is the conclusion at which we must arrive, from the very fact that the suggestion has been made from below the Gangway that Members there do not trust Members on this side of the House.

MR. T. M. HEALY (Longford, N.): We said the very contrary. You have no right to say that.

SIR EDWARD CLARKE: I think no one who has heard the speeches delivered can doubt that at the end of the investigation such would be the case.

MR. DILLON (Mayo, E.): I rise to Order. The hon. and learned Gentleman is attributing to us a statement which all my hon. Friends, together with myself, utterly repudiate. I understand it is customary in debate to accept the repudiation of hon. Members.

SIR EDWARD CLARKE: If that is really the sentiment of the hon. Member below the Gangway, and I do not doubt that it is, it is rather a pity that

Sir Edward Clarke

the observations I have referred to have been made.

MR. T. M. HEALY: Who made them? Who made them? [*Cries of* "Order!"]

MR. SPEAKER: It is irregular for the hon. Member for North Longford to interrupt the speech of the Solicitor General. Order, order!

MR. T. M. HEALY: A deliberate charge has been made against us, that we stated that we would not trust a Select Committee formed by hon. Gentlemen opposite. That statement is made on the Solicitor General's responsibility. I say we are entitled to know who it was that said this thing.

SIR EDWARD CLARKE: I think it was the hon. Member for West Belfast (Mr. Sexton), who, I think, called out just now the words "You have a majority."

MR. SEXTON (Belfast, W.): I claim the right of explanation. I did not use those words; if I had, they would not have affected my position. I said yesterday distinctly that, although the Government would have a majority on the Select Committee, yet I would regard that tribunal with confidence.

SIR EDWARD CLARKE: I wish to recall to the recollection of the House to further observations that have been made below the Gangway. The hon. Member for the Scotland Division of Liverpool (Mr. T. P. O'Connor) has made a speech in which, with very strong language, he has assailed the Government, and denounced the Government, for its action in this matter of taking action against *The Times*, and he has suggested that nobody can trust to a prosecution conducted by the Government. I am very glad to know that this speech is beyond the reach of interference now; because it has already been sent to the printers, and hon. Members who did not hear it can refer to it for themselves. If hon. Members will refer to it, they will find that it is a denunciation of the Government for making a dishonest proposal with regard to the prosecution of a writer in *The Times*, or the printer, and a suggestion that nobody could trust to a prosecution conducted under the circumstances.

MR. DILLON (Mayo, E.): The hon. and learned Gentleman has made use of a form of expression with regard to me which I cannot allow anybody to make use of unchallenged in this House. After listening to our statement, which was made in good faith, he said that he was glad that the speech of my Colleague had gone to the printers. That is as much as to say I have told a lie. I call for his explanation or withdrawal.

Sir EDWARD CLARKE having risen, there were repeated cries of " Withdraw ! "

MR. DILLON : Sir, I rise again to Order. I wish to ask whether you heard the statement I have alluded to, and whether you rule that an hon. Member is entitled in that way to insinuate that another hon. Member is not to be trusted on his word ?

MR. SPEAKER : I did not hear that the hon. and learned Gentleman said anything of the sort. I understand the hon. and learned Gentleman to say that the words uttered were now in print, and could be, therefore, verified beyond dispute.

SIR EDWARD CLARKE : I hope I may be allowed to say that I am extremely sorry if, for one moment, I have been led into expressions which suggested any improper reflection upon, or hurt the feelings, of the hon. Member opposite. But I meant no more than this— that if, owing to the flush and excitement of debate, with Members coming in and going out, some hon. Members had not heard the speech of the hon. Member for the Scotland Division of Liverpool, I was glad that the speech had gone to the printers, because it could be referred to in print to justify the interpretation I put upon it. I cannot recite the whole of that speech at this moment; but, putting an interpretation upon it, I suggest that if hon. Members have an opportunity of reading it, it will justify what I say. I trust hon. Members will believe that I had no intention or desire of reflecting upon them in the way which they seem to suppose. Sir, I have pointed out to the House that the procedure by Committee, as I submit, would be absolutely contrary to the whole course of Parliamentary precedent; that it would be to invent a new procedure altogether —and I have pointed out that the proceedings of a Committee on this subject and the result would hardly be satisfactory. I should like now to say a few words as to the question of prosecution, and as to the suggestion of the Leader

of the House. What we find in *Hansard* is this—that there have been 12 cases during a certain number of years in which the House of Commons has ordered a prosecution. Of course, directly that question of prosecution arose, we knew perfectly well that hon. Members below the Gangway opposite would not be satisfied with a prosecution conducted exclusively by the present Attorney General and Solicitor General; and, if they will allow me to say so, they are perfectly justified in taking that objection. If a prosecution is to take place, I agree that they ought to be represented in that prosecution by persons in whom they have entire confidence, not only in the sense of believing that those persons are thoroughly acquainted with the law, and will try to do their duty in the case, but also in the sense of believing that they have some sympathy with them in the action they are taking. Hon. Members below the Gangway may be sure that there is not the slightest desire on the part of the Attorney General or myself to interpose ourselves as the instruments of the prosecution in this matter. There was a little while ago a case in which a similar, but not so great a difficulty arose. It was, I think, in the last Parliament that the junior Member for Northampton (Mr. Bradlaugh) was ordered by the House to to be prosecuted, notwithstanding the Resolution of the Government, and notwithstanding that it was felt that my hon. and learned Friend the Member for Bury (Sir Henry James), who had been supporting the hon. Member for Northampton in his action, ought not alone to conduct that prosecution, and the consequence was that the present Lord Chancellor, then sitting on the Front Opposition Bench, was associated with the Attorney General in the conduct of that case, and, as I know, took a very active and diligent part in the framing of that indictment and in the subsequent proceedings. Hon. Members below the Gangway will, perhaps, allow me to say that I do not think that this proposal for a prosecution by the House, or under the order of the House, is one that can fairly or properly be entertained, except on the Motion of the the hon. Member for East Mayo. But if he, or any Friend of his, with regard to these circumstances, which are exceptionally grave, moves that the House

[*Second Night.*]

should order that a prosecution be instituted, although I think that in accordance with the Rules and precedents of the House it would be right that the Attorney General should be nominally associated with the prosecution, the House may be quite certain that the whole conduct of that prosecution would be left to such persons as they might nominate; and I am not speaking merely of the counsel who would appear in Court, but also with regard to the solicitors who would make preparations for the trial. If hon. Members ask the House of Commons that the proceedings may be of this nature, the Government will interpose no objection; and that was the proposal of the right hon. Gentleman the Leader of the House. I hope the House will forgive me for having trespassed so long upon its attention. Even if I strain its indulgence, I wish to say two or three words upon the general subject. The question of the Privilege of the House of Commons and the right of the House of Commons to exercise its own power for the punishment of persons who have assailed Members of Parliament is an extremely serious one. In 1880 the noble Lord the Member for Rossendale (the Marquess of Hartington), who then led the Liberal Party, said the whole course of the House of Commons in recent times had been in the direction of relaxing, and not of straining the Rules of Privilege. We live in times when a question of this kind is extremely serious; and I hope that, disentangling it from the immediate excitement and passion of the day, we may be able to consider calmly what the position is which the House of Commons is called upon to take up. If an hon. Member were to say that an attack had been made upon him in such a manner or in such circumstances that it could not be met in the ordinary way in which an attack would be met by a gentleman who was not a Member of this House, there might be some ground for the appeal made by hon. Members opposite. But that has never been said by hon. Members below the Gangway—[*Cries of* "Yes!"]—no appeal has been made to the House—[*Cries of* "Yes!"]—no spontaneous appeal—[*laughter*]—the interruptions of hon. Members again bring me into conflict with them. In this case the accusation which is made is made by a responsible person, by a person who can

be dealt with in the ordinary Courts of Law. [*Laughter.*] Certainly he can. All the Courts of Law are open to the hon. Member, and all the machinery of the law is at the disposal of the hon. Member, and I venture to say that, after what has taken place, if one of these hon. Members below the Gangway opposite would go into a Court of Law to complain of and seek redress for an attack of this kind, it would be the defendant and not the plaintiff who would have to fear the prejudice and sentiment of a jury. [An hon. MEMBER: It is false, and you know it is.] But the House of Commons is asked to extend its practice with reference to this matter, to extend it in a dangerous direction, to institute a form or proceeding hitherto unknown in its history, and to do this when a prompt and far more effectual remedy can be obtained in those Courts of Law which are open to all the subjects of the Queen. It is my sincere hope that the House of Commons will never stretch the Law of Privilege one inch beyond its established limit. Its extension may have been necessary in other times and circumstances; but, situated as we are, I fear that such an extension would be a dangerous one, and I feel that it would not be justified by the circumstances which the House has now before it.

Amendment proposed,

To leave out from the word "That" to the end of the Question, in order to add the words "this House declines to treat the publication of the article headed 'Parnellism and Crime' in *The Times* of the 2nd of May as a Breach of the Privileges of this House."—(*Sir Edward Clarke*.)

Question proposed, "That the words proposed to be left out stand part of the Question."

MR. ILLINGWORTH (Bradford, W.): Sir, in the very long and learned speech to which we have just listened from the Solicitor General, I think an attempt has been made, not to vindicate the rights and privileges of this House which have always been claimed as a protection of its members against slander, but rather to transfer the jurisdiction of the House to a tribunal which, as the matter stands at present, can by no means be satisfactory. To my judgment, the feeling in the country which has been evoked by the charges originally made in *The Times*, and so industriously circulated by a very large proportion of the Conservative Party among its most pro- minent and more obscure Members, is such that the House of Commons is the only tribunal to which can be submitted the calm and temperate consideration of the great question which has been under discussion yesterday and to-day.

Notice taken, that 40 Members were not present; House counted, and 40 Members being found present.

MR. ILLINGWORTH said: I was urging that this question has proceeded so far, and that public opinion in the country has been inflamed to such an extent that if justice is to be found in any tribunal whatever it must be sought in that of the House of Commons. The Solicitor General gave us to understand that even in this House the state of Party feeling was such, and that such was the intensity of feeling on this side of the House, that justice could not be looked for from a Committee composed of Members on both sides selected by the Party opposite. But the hon. Mem- ber for East Mayo, who is most pro- minently affected by this charge, has declared from his place in this House— and he has been joined by other hon. Members—that he would be perfectly satisfied with a tribunal of the House of Commons. If that be so, the objection of the hon. and learned Gentleman prac- tically falls to the ground. The Soli- citor General points out that an ordinary tribunal of the country—a common jury or a special jury empanelled in London, would be a tribunal to which this case with some hope of justice might be sent; but even supposing that on any London jury 11 men take the view that this is an unfounded charge against my hon. Friend the Member for East Mayo —and that there was one dissentient juryman—I want to know where would be the justice of exposing an hon. Member to the enormous and crushing expenditure that would be incurred; what would be the satisfaction of his knowing that there were 11 jurymen in his favour and one dissentient? I be- lieve there is so much sense of dignity and fairness among the Members of this House, that if it is necessary that a Com- mittee of the House should be appointed, a Committee would be found who would deal with the case as impartially, and far more so, perhaps, than any other tribunal to which it could be submitted. It is not denied that Parliament must,

in certain circumstances, interfere to pro- tect its Members, however humble, from gross and scandalous charges. The So- licitor General has urged that where a Committee has been ordered there was some individual charge of corruption against a Member of this House. Now, I hold that the charge under which the hon. Member for East Mayo and some of his Colleagues are lying is infinitely graver than any charge of individual corruption. Last night, if I read cor- rectly, the report of the speech of the right hon. Gentleman the Member for West Birmingham, who referred to the charges which appeared in *The Times* a short time ago, he said that if those charges remained unrebutted the hon. Member for Mayo would be unfit for association with Members of this House. I feel that there is such a weight and seriousness in the imputation under which the hon. Member suffers at the present moment, that I believe the House will not refuse to appoint a Committee to investigate the matter. We have happily an increasing number of Members in this House who have found their way there not by the length of their purses, but by the estimation in which they are held by their consti- tuencies; and supposing *The Times*, or any other paper, happens to fix a colossal slander on some of these work- ing-class Members, I want to know what redress there is for Members of the House not having the advantage of deep purses in struggling against charges which may be utterly false, if the House abandons its traditional right of protect- ing its Members under such circum- stances. I think the House will not hesitate to throw its protection over one of its Members, however humble he may be, if it should see that the necessities of the case demand it. There has in this case undoubtedly been a very serious Breach of Privilege committed; the most serious charges have been made; they are persisted in, and they are adopted by the whole Conservative Party. If that is so, I think the House will agree in supporting the claim made by the hon. Member for East Mayo, and insist that the printer of *The Times* shall be produced at the Bar of this House. With regard to the independ- ence of a London jury, let me ask whe- ther *The Times* newspaper and those who seek to screen themselves behind it would like this trial to take place in

[*Second Night*]

Ireland. Suppose the venue were changed from London to Cork, would *The Times* think that substantial justice were done to it in that case? Sir, I think *The Times* would have just ground of complaint against such a course being taken. But the hon. Member for East Mayo would have just such a feeling of insecurity in his case being before a London jury at the present moment. We have lately had charges brought against the Corporation of the City of London; they have been investigated by a Committee of the House, and there has never been a breath or hint given to imply that the Committee appointed was not in any way competent to deal with that matter. With regard to this view, if it be taken in the present case, I believe that the House itself would name a Committee whose Members would abandon all feeling and prejudice, and enter upon the inquiry with but one desire—namely, to reach the truth. I do not pretend to go into the merits of the charges brought against the hon. Member for East Mayo and his Colleagues. The preliminary question in which we are engaged is as to whether the House of Commons shall take into its own hands the appointment of a tribunal in order that the impartial investigation which this case demands may be secured for the hon. Member for East Mayo. So far as the statement of the Solicitor General is concerned, that we are all on one side or the other of this question, I do not see how we should escape from that if we were to transfer the case to another tribunal in the country. With regard to the proposal that the assistance of the Attorney General and Solicitor General should be given to my hon. Friend in the conduct of the case, I must say that the suggestion is surrounded by the gravest suspicion, and I do not hesitate to say that if this House refuses the appointment of a Committee, my hon. Friend should trust to time to do him that justice which the House denies him. Therefore, Sir, I shall give my vote against the Amendment of the Solicitor General, and I trust this discussion will proceed so far that there will remain no doubt as to whether a Breach of Privilege has been committed, and as to whether the House will declare itself totally unfitted for the grave duty of inquiry into the matter.

Mr. Illingworth

MR. SYDNEY BUXTON (Tower Hamlets, Poplar): I do not think that the Leader of the House is bound to take his opinion from the legal point of view, affecting, as it does, the character of a Member of the House of Commons. In discussing a question of this kind, we are entitled to consider it as laymen and not as lawyers. The Solicitor General (Sir Edward Clarke) stated that there is no precedent for the proposal now made. Now, I think that even some of the cases he quoted showed there was a very considerable precedent for the proposal now made—namely, that this attack upon the hon. Member for East Mayo (Mr. Dillon) is a Breach of the Privileges of this House. But if there be no precedent, it seems to me that this attack is of such a nature that it is high time we created a precedent; because, Mr. Speaker, if this attack, which is now made on a Member of this House, is not a Breach of the Privileges of this House, it seems to me that none of us have any possible protection in our action as Members of this House, or for any statements which we make from our places in this House. What is the accusation which we believe is a Breach of Privilege? It is simply this. My hon. Friend the Member for East Mayo denied certain statements which the noble Lord the Member for Rossendale (the Marquess of Hartington) had made in this House, and what we complain of is that *The Times* asserts that my hon. Friend falsely denied the statements that were made. If a newspaper, especially a newspaper of the reputation of *The Times*, is entitled to attack an hon. Member, and to say he has made wilful and false statements in the exercise of his duty as a Member of this House, if that is not a Breach of Privilege, it is not possible that a Breach of Privilege can be committed. The Solicitor General, in order to prove his point, quoted at considerable length passages from a speech of the right hon. Gentleman the Member for Derby (Sir William Harcourt); but it appears to me that the words which the right hon. Gentleman used towards the end of his speech completely knocked away the ground from under the Solicitor General. My right hon. Friend the Member for Derby said that the whole question of Breach of Privilege is a question of "degree." That, surely, is the point before us this afternoon;

and we believe that the limit has been passed — though it is a very grave matter to consider a question of Privilege, and to bring a printer or editor up to the Bar we believe that the limit on this occasion has been passed, and that we are entitled to consider this a Breach of Privilege. The Government themselves and the Solicitor General himself, in the Amendment he has moved, do not deny that this is a Breach of Privilege; but they prefer to look another way, and to pretend that they do not see it. The Solicitor General tried in his speech to prove that better and more substantial justice would be done by means of a criminal prosecution, conducted by the Attorney General on the part of the hon. Gentleman the Member for East Mayo, than would be done if the matter were referred to a Select Committee impartially chosen from Members out of the different Parties in this House. But I think we ought to remember that the question we want to decide is not so much whether the editor or printer of *The Times* shall receive punishment as to clear the character of the hon. Members below the Gangway, and especially that of my hon. Friend the Member for East Mayo from the aspersions that have been made. No doubt, if, while doing that, they could also have the satisfaction of imprisoning and fining the editor of *The Times* there would be an additional advantage. But that is not the point before the House of Commons. The House of Commons does not very much care whether the editor of *The Times* is punished or not. What it does desire to find out is whether hon. Members in this House have or have not been guilty of the charges made against them. Now, the Solicitor General says that if you refer the matter to a Select Committee, the Select Committee will inevitably disagree on the points submitted to them. But if a Select Committee of this House disagreed on such a question as this, surely a jury is all the more likely to disagree, and, Mr. Speaker, there is all the difference in the world in regard to the position of my hon. Friends below the Gangway between the disagreement of a jury and that of a Select Committee. If the matter is referred to a jury, one obstinate or prejudiced man can prevent a verdict being given, and the world at large would never know how many of the jury were for a conviction and how many against it. Even by disagreement a jury could blast the reputation of the hon. Member for East Mayo and his Colleagues; whereas, in a Select Committee, we can weigh brains as well as count noses, and if there is a division of opinion in a Select Committee, we shall have, as the Solicitor General says, a majority Report and a minority Report, and we Members of the House and the public at large will be able to see how far the evidence has proved the case of *The Times*, or how far hon. Members below the Gangway stand acquitted. Therefore, I assert that there is no comparison at all in a matter of this kind between the justice of a criminal prosecution and a reference to a Select Committee. There is just this other matter, that the Attorney General is to conduct the prosecution. Now, in a Select Committee each side would be able to choose their own unprejudiced counsel; but if my hon. Friend (Mr. Dillon) goes into a Criminal Court with the Attorney General as his counsel he will go into Court with one hand tied behind him. No Member of the House would for a moment say that the Attorney General would not do his duty in the matter to his fullest ability; but, after all, the Attorney General is but human. He is a Member of a Conservative Government, he is a Colleague of those who have been denouncing hon. Members below the Gangway up-hill and downdale, and it is quite impossible that after what he has said, he can go into Court really believing that hon. Members below the Gangway are innocent of the charge made against them. It seems to me, therefore, that if we decide on a criminal prosecution in this matter, and if we direct the Attorney General to go into Court to conduct the prosecution, that whoever may be the Queen's Counsel associated with him, the hon. Member for East Mayo will not have the ghost of a chance of obtaining a fair verdict. We ought to remember, also, that we are now in the middle of passing a Criminal Law Amendment Bill for Ireland, and that, judging from the letters of the Private Secretary to the Leader of the House (Mr. W. H. Smith), this Bill is directed solely and wholly against the National League. Is it

[*Second Night.*]

likely, therefore, that my hon. Friend the Member for East Mayo, one of the most prominent members of the National League, is going to direct the Attorney General to conduct his prosecution, and to place in the hon. and learned Gentleman's hands, as he necessarily must, all the documents belonging to the National League? Of course not. Owing to the action of the hon. Baronet the Member for North Antrim (Sir Charles Lewis), who, having got his Baronetcy, does not particularly care whether the Government like him or not, the Government have been landed in a position of considerable difficulty. Their friends have digged a pit, and the Government, instead of the Irish Members, have fallen into it, and they must get out of it the best way they can. I think the country will judge to-morrow whether the Government do desire to have this question cleared up in the only possible way.

SIR CHARLES RUSSELL (Hackney, S): I hope I shall not ask in vain for the indulgence of the House for a short time while I address myself to some of the topics dealt with in the speech of my hon. and learned Friend the Solicitor General (Sir Edward Clarke). I say, in all sincerity, that the speech of my hon. and learned Friend was an exceedingly able speech; but I must beg leave to add to that observation that by far the greater part of the topics with which he dealt, those to which he devoted the greatest amount of his ingenuity and of his earnestness, were not the topics which are directly germane to the point before us; and, further, while the Solicitor General broadly asserted that this was no case of Breach of Privilege at all, he has had at the end of his speech a Resolution put into his hand which does not so assert, but merely that the House declines to treat it as a Breach of Privilege. Let me remind the House of the position in which the matter stands. The hon. Baronet the Member for North Antrim brought to the attention of the House a publication which, in his judgment, was a Breach of the Privileges of the House, and, having done so, he proposed the Motion that the House should declare that such publication was a Breach of the Privileges of the House. I hope hon. Members will not forget what, I think, has been so often forgotten in the course of the debate upon this matter, that this is not a

question of an individual Member, nor an offence against an individual Member merely, but it is an offence against the House perpetrated in the shape of a libel, or an alleged libel, upon one of its Members. You recollect the course that was followed yesterday—the right hon. Gentleman the Leader of the House moved, as it was thought at first, under a misapprehension of the views of the hon. Member for East Mayo, that the debate should be adjourned; but finally, when his misconception was removed, he persisted in the Motion for Adjournment. To-day the right hon. Gentleman announced that the Government, having meanwhile considered the matter, and acting upon the advice of their Legal Advisers, have come to the conclusion that this is not a question of Breach of the Privileges of the House at all, and now we have the Resolution that the publication in question is not one which properly can be treated by the House as an invasion of its Privileges. The House will, therefore, observe that the Motion which is now moved by my hon. and learned Friend the Solicitor General, at the instance of the Government, is not a Motion to pass to the other Business of the House, but it is a Motion which, if carried—and I beg the earnest attention of hon. Members upon that side of the House as upon this—it is a Motion which, if carried, will be understood by the country to express the opinion of this House that an imputation—than which it is difficult to conceive any grosser—that an imputation conveyed against an hon. Member, not only in relation to his character as a Member of this House, but in relation to his actual conduct in this House, is not a matter to be treated by this House as a question of Privilege. The consequences of this Resolution of the Government, if carried, certainly seem to me to be serious. Now, on what ground is this course sought to be pursued? Let me say, in passing, that I agree with what was said by my right hon. Friend the Member for Edinburgh (Mr. Childers) last night, when he pointed out that the precedents of late years justified as an initial step in proceedings of this kind the summoning of the supposed offender to the Bar of this House. That has been the course followed in recent years; but the course the Government take is not based upon any objection to the particular course which has been pursued here, and I am bound to say that they have met the Motion of the hon. Baronet the Member for North Antrim (Sir Charles Lewis) point blank by asking this House to decline to treat the article in question as a Breach of the Privileges of this House. The right hon. Gentleman (Mr. W. H. Smith) did not, the House will have observed, express any opinion of his own as to whether this was or was not a Breach of the Privileges of this House. He sheltered himself, or fortified himself—I am not using the phrase in any invidious sense—behind the opinion of those who are responsible for legal advice to the Government. I am exceedingly sorry to find myself in conflict with the legal opinion, upon a matter of this kind, of my hon. and learned Friends whom I greatly respect on the other side of the House; but I must say, with deliberation, and I think I shall be supported by legal Gentlemen on this side of the House, who, I hope, will make their opinions heard in this House, when I say that there is no justification in any text-book, or in the works of any writer on Constitutional Law, that I am aware of, for the distinction which the Solicitor General sought to draw between the different kinds of imputations of misconduct upon hon. Members, some of which would and some would not be Breaches of Privilege, and I hope the Attorney General, who probably will take part in this debate later on, will be able to throw some light on the subject. I maintain the criteria are two and only two. They are, is the charge sufficiently serious to deserve notice from the House, and does it refer to an hon. Member in his character and conduct as a Member? Now, what is this publication? What is the charge against the hon. Member for East Mayo? It is, that in his place in this House, and for the purpose of misleading and deceiving this House, he was guilty of a deliberate falsehood; and my hon. and learned Friend the Solicitor General admitted so much, but proceeded to argue that there are no precedents which show any proceedings on the part of this House treating imputations upon its Members in their character and conduct as Members of this House as Breaches of Privilege, except in cases

of corruption, misfeasance, or coercion, or intimidation. What does my hon. and learned Friend mean by misfeasance? Does my hon. and learned Friend gravely ask the House to say that a charge of corruption against an hon. Member is a more serious matter than a charge of deliberate falsehood? After all, bad as the offence of corruption is, and warped as the hon. Member's mind affected by it would be in the discharge of his duty, it cannot equal a deliberate falsehood put forward for the purpose of deceiving this House, which is in itself a dereliction of duty and a very grave offence against all decency and all propriety. Now I think that precedents show a list of serious cases where there was not an allegation of corruption, where there was not misfeasance, whatever that means in this particular connection, in which the House has taken steps in the matter. First of all, I will call attention to the fact that in the Appendix to *Hatsell's Precedents*, which was published in the beginning of the present century, and beginning with cases as far back as the time of Elizabeth, there is a very large enumeration of cases of reflections, aspersions, libels, and so on, upon the House, and upon individual Members in relation to their conduct in the House. In none of those cases do I find the slightest trace of a distinction drawn such as my hon. and learned Friend the Solicitor General refers to. But I will cite a case which seems to me to be very much to the point on this matter. It is the case of Mr. Gray Bennett against the *John Bull* newspaper, which is to be found recorded. My hon. and learned Friend referred to the case, but did not draw attention to the point I desire to refer to. The case is recorded in the 76th Journal of the House, and it occurred in 1821. It was a case in which Mr. Gray Bennett, in a speech in this House, was supposed to have made an injurious reflection upon the Lord President of the Council. The newspaper referred to this fact, and, referring to the further fact that Mr. Gray Bennett had apologized for the aspersion he had made, went on to say that he only made the apology because a stalwart and courageous son of the President of the Council had waited upon him and delivered a challenge to him, and that when he expressed the apology in the House he

[*Second Night.*]

expressed it in so low a voice that it did not reach a considerable portion of the Representatives of the Press, and so did not get the publication it deserved. I want to know was that corruption, was that misfeasance, under what head does that come? Well, I find that in that case the printer and publisher was summoned before the House, the article was treated as a Breach of the Privileges of the House, and the Motion was made that the printer and publisher should be sent to the Tower. There was a Division as to whether he should be sent to the Tower or to Newgate, and it was ultimately decided that he should be sent to Newgate. I am not sure whether there was not another person brought up and sent to prison, because of the prevaricating way he answered the questions addressed to him; but that is no matter. Is that not a case in which it can neither be alleged that there was corruption nor misfeasance on the part of the publisher? Yet so jealous was the House at this time of the reputation of its Members that instant proceedings were taken, and the offending publisher was sent to and detained for some time in prison. Another case I desire to refer to, that of Mr. Clive. This case, which will be in the recollection of some hon. Members of the House, arose in 1858. Mr. Clive had been a Member of a Private Bill Committee, and the charge against him was that he had been guilty of partiality, and it was suggested he might also have had corrupt motives. This debate is instructive for another reason, and it is this. The right hon. Gentleman the Leader of the House said it was most unfair, by the proceeding of the hon. Baronet the Member for North Antrim (Sir Charles Lewis) to stigmatize *The Times* newspaper before *The Times* newspaper had had an opportunity of being heard. ["Hear, hear!"] I notice that some hon. Member assents to that argument at the present moment. I beg to point out to the Leader of the House, and to the hon. Gentlemen who take that view, that no such thing is involved in the proper mode of proceeding in this case, that the House will not proceed to condemn *The Times* newspaper, or be committed to any particular course, until *The Times* newspaper, if called on to appear, has taken its course, and either confessed or apologized, or stated

Sir Charles Russell

that it stands by its article, and is prepared to substantiate it. That was the course which was followed in the case I have mentioned—I mean the case of Mr. Clive. It came before the House, and the offending publisher and some others implicated were called before the House. The publisher was not prepared to withdraw the aspersions made in the article, and declined to give the names of those who had furnished him with the information contained in the article. Upon that the House came to the conclusion that the article was a scandalous libel, that the proprietor had been guilty of a Breach of Privilege of the House, and he was ordered into custody and sent to prison. The discussion which took place on the appearance of the offending parties at the Bar, shows that if proveable justification were alleged, the matter would be referred for inquiry to a Committee. There is another case to which I should like to call attention. It has an important bearing upon the question, which is wider in its import, I take leave to say, than the Leader of the House seems to suppose. It is considered by the Leader of the House, and by my hon. and learned Friend the Solicitor General, that this is simply a question of whether notice is to be taken of the matter with a view to the punishment or otherwise of *The Times*. That is not the only ground on which the House has acted, and will act, in defence of the character of its Members. If there were no question of *The Times* in the case, and no idea of calling *The Times* to account at the Bar of this House, still it would be within the competence of this House, and within the right and proper discharge of the duty of the Leader of this House, apart altogether from any question of charge against a particular publisher, to see that some means were taken by this House so that the matter should be inquired into, and, if necessary, by a Committee of this House. Now I will refer, by way of illustration, to a precedent supported by what will be admitted by all Members of this House to be very high authority—I mean Lord John Russell. It was a case in which an imputation had been made against a number of Irish Members—against the whole Irish Party in the House at that time—of corruption. That imputation had been circulated in *The Times*—it was not circulated, perhaps, inside the House, but elsewhere — and it had also got voice through statements of some Members of the House. On the 7th of February, 1854, Mr. Butt rose for the purpose of calling the attention of the House to something which he thought they would consider concerned the character, not only of some Members, a large section of the House, but of the House itself. He proceeded to complain that the article was a Breach of our Privileges, and moved that it be read by the Clerk at the Table, and that afterwards it be referred to a Committee of Privileges to inquire into the charges in question, and to report thereon. Now, this is the part of the article in *The Times* which was read to the House—

" We have satisfied the theory of the Constitution. . . . . But we have not succeeded in obtaining a body of Representatives which an Irishman would look upon with satisfaction, or an Englishman without dismay. In the name of Constitutional Government, we may be permitted to ask, what does a section of Irish Members represent beyond the embodied wish of some hundreds of needy men to obtain place, salary, power ? "

The present Irish Party are free, as far as I know, from that imputation. The Clerk at the Table, having read the article, and the House having declared it to be a Breach of the Privileges of the House, Mr. Butt moved that a Committee of Privileges be appointed to inquire and report upon the allegation contained in the article. According to the right hon. Gentleman's (Mr. W. H. Smith's) theory, that course was unfair to *The Times;* it was prejudicing *The Times* before it was heard. I think the words he used were—" Stigmatizing most unfairly the conduct of *The Times* newspaper." I say that this is an aspect of the case which has not been dealt with by my hon. and learned Friend, and has not been presented to the mind of the House as it ought to be—namely, that wholly apart from the question of taking any step to vindicate the Privileges of this House against any particular offender against them, there is a wider and more important ground for taking action. I maintain that when, from any quarter, a serious charge against the honour and character of any of its Members has been made, and publicly brought, as in this case, to the notice of the House by an hon. Member, and in no friendly spirit, it is the duty of the House, and the primary duty of the Leader of the House, to see that the House shall take action to elucidate the matter. It cannot—it ought not to pass it by. What did Lord John Russell say on that occasion ? He said—

" The House cannot feel the slightest doubt or hesitation in the propriety of assenting to the Motion of the hon. and learned Member for Youghal. It is due to the honour of Parliament, to the character of the Government, and to the character of those Irish Members who have been included in that sweeping denunciation to which the hon. and learned Gentleman has called our attention. . . . . If such offers were made, I trust the Committee will ascertain from whom they proceeded, and to whom they were addressed—in short, that they will inquire into all the particulars and details connected with the transaction."—(3 *Hansard*, [130] 327-8.)

Well, now, I think I have shown that there are precedents for action by this House, apart from the particular specification of causes to which my hon. and learned Friend referred. I say that there is not a single precedent to support the Solicitor General's contention, and there is not, I again say, a trace of authority that I am aware of, in any Constitutional writer for drawing a distinction as to the character of the imputations, provided the imputations themselves are grave and are made in reference to the conduct in Parliament of Members of this House. The distinction must, therefore, be taken to be an unreal and an unsound one. My hon. and learned Friend referred to some other cases, and why he referred to them I do not really know. Take the Ferrand case. It is perfectly true that no ultimate proceedings were taken in that case Why ?· Because the charge was not persisted in, and there was an express Motion carried in this House relieving the Member concerned from the imputation. In the case of " Grissell and Ward," the Solicitor General pointed out that there was a Committee before there was a Resolution. I am not at this moment concerned in arguing in the least which should come first ; what I am arguing is that, whether you are going to proceed against *The Times* or not, this, upon the face of it, is a grievous imputation on a Member of this House in his character of a Member of this House, and in relation to his conduct in this House, and that this

[*Second Night.*]

itself constitutes a Breach of the Privileges of this House. Do hon. Gentlemen recollect one remarkable case, which has not been yet referred to, the case of Mr. Whittle Harvey; because it shows how jealous is the House of Commons, in ordinary circumstances, where English or Scotch Members are concerned, of the honour of its Members. There was actually referred to a Committee of this House, among other things, the decision of the question whether the verdict of a jury, some 20 years before, was a right and proper verdict. Now, let me point out and meet the grounds upon which the suggestion of further inquiry by Parliament is resisted. It seems to me that my hon. and learned Friend, and those who take the same line with him, are jumping before they come to the stile. The question is not now whether a Committee shall be appointed to inquire, but whether, aye or no, this House is to pass by this publication, and say to the world that it is not such an imputation upon a Member of this House as to constitute such a Breach of the Privileges of the House as to demand the notice of the House. But more. My hon. and learned Friend says a Committee of this House is an unfit tribunal. I am bound to examine my hon. and learned Friend's argument on that point. My hon. and learned Friend said that Parliament was not fit properly to perform judicial functions. But it does perform various judicial functions, and, through its Committees, it has for years performed them, and a Committee has been the machine by which charges against Members—as these shown—have been dealt with. My hon. and learned Friend went on to say that it would be no satisfaction to hon. Members below the Gangway to have a Committee appointed according to the Rules of the House; because hon. Members on that side, who have a majority, and who will have a majority in the Committee, have practically acquiesced in those charges. I think my hon. and learned Friend does injustice to the Members below the Gangway and to his own Friends on that side of the House. I think most unjust, most unfair things have been said in public by hon. Members on the other side of the House on the subject of the charges against hon. Members below the Gangway; but I,

Sir Charles Russell

for one, decline to believe that if the responsibility was to be thrown on them of being judges in this matter, hon. Members on that side of the House, sobered by a sense of responsibility, would not be able to overcome even their intense prejudices. Hon. Members below the Gangway have declared—and I should be surprised if they had not—that they believe, however strong and virulent your prejudices may be, when you have the sense of responsibility as a judge put upon you, each one of you will be able to rise superior to your prejudices and to look at and try the matter honestly and fairly. What is the alternative? The alternative suggested is a trial by criminal prosecution. I ask my hon. and learned Friend the Attorney General, who will follow me—I am sure he will desire to be quite candid in the matter —whether he thinks that a criminal prosecution for a political libel is a likely course by which to vindicate the character of an aspersed man? Does not my hon. and learned Friend know that the Judges—the highest on the Bench—although they recognize that, according to the existing law, a libel may be treated as a violation of the Criminal Law, have again and again declared against the institution of criminal proceedings in relation to libels upon particular individuals? In other words, a man who institutes criminal proceedings for libel, in 99 cases out of 100, goes into Court handicapped. If this be true of any libel, how much stronger the argument against the institution of criminal proceedings for a political libel. Moreover, the person accused, who might be able to throw an important light upon the question in dispute, would have his mouth closed. Now, I want to draw the attention of the House to a point which has not been noticed as yet during the progress of this discussion. It has been suggested by the Leader of the House, and by the hon. and learned Gentleman opposite, that the Government are willing to institute a criminal prosecution of *The Times* newspaper for libel upon their own responsibility, provided the hon. Member for East Mayo (Mr. Dillon) desires they should do so.

SIR EDWARD CLARKE: What I said was that the Government will consent to a Motion that the House should institute a prosecution.

SIR CHARLES RUSSELL : That practically amounts to the same thing ; it gives it even greater solemnity. But what business has this House, what business has the Attorney General or the Government to have anything to do with the prosecution of *The Times* unless this touches a matter of Privilege ? I want the Attorney General to tell us what justification there would be for either the House or the Government to take any part in the prosecution, unless the article which is complained of touches closely the matter of Privilege. Your own suggestion of an alternative course, shows clearly you have no faith in the argument of the Solicitor General that this is not a Breach of Privilege. I think there are some other reasons which can be urged against this course. I do not speak of the delay. I do not speak about the prejudice which will exist, but I will remind my hon. and learned Friend that while I have as strong an opinion as any man of the honesty and the integrity of English jurymen, we cannot conceal from ourselves that there are politicians to be found in English juries, just as there are politicians with strong views among the Members of this House appointed upon Committees. In justification of the view I take upon this question, I should like to read to the House one passage from a very grave Constitutional writer. Mr. Hallam, speaking of the House, says—

"The majority are bound to respect and indeed have respected, the right of every Member, however obnoxious to them, on all questions of Privilege, even in a case most unlikely to occur—that of libel. It would be unjust if a patriotic legislator, exposed to calumny for his zeal in the public interest, should necessarily be driven to the troublesome and uncertain process of law when the offence so manifestly affects the real interests of Parliament and of the nation."

That is not the argument of an excited politician. Now, Sir, these are some of the reasons why I submit that the House ought not to consent to the Amendment which has been proposed by the Solicitor General. I speak with strong feeling in this matter. If this House, by affirming the Amendment the Government propose, say that this is not a Breach of the Privileges of this House, or is not to be declared to be such, I want to know what accusation in the future will be said to be a Breach of Privilege ? Is this House going to give

up practically the defence of the honour of its Members, by a mode which, although, perhaps liable to some abuse in times of political excitement, has, on the whole, had a useful and salutary effect ? We must not overlook the fact that the newspapers of to-day dictate to this House how it shall conduct its Business. They dictate to hon. Members what they shall say and what they shall not say. They even lay down hard and fast lines as to when a debate is to begin, and when it shall terminate. They even presume to advise the Leader of the House when he should invoke that new instrument of Government, the closure, which is now at his disposal. All that the House can afford to disregard, but it cannot treat with contempt, it cannot afford to treat with contempt, an accusation of this kind deliberately made, deliberately persisted in, and brought pointedly before the attention of the House, and in a hostile sense by an hon. Member. I am not going to discuss the question of the prudence or otherwise of the action of the hon. Member for North Antrim (Sir Charles Lewis). I have no doubt that those amongst whom he sits, and those on the Front Government Bench, heartily wish he had been somewhere else than in his place yesterday. But the matter is now before the House ; and it has been so pointedly brought to the attention of the Government, that they must deal with it ; and if they deal with it in the way this Amendment proposes it should be dealt with, I say a fatal blow will be dealt against that power of protection which this House has in past times been able to invoke for the defence of the character of the House itself, and for the defence of the character of its Members. But, above all, there is one consideration which is present to my mind, and which ought to be present to the mind of hon. Members on the other side of the House ; it is the position in which hon. Members below the Gangway stand. They are a minority in this House. Their conduct has been gravely impugned ; there has been no opportunity, so far as this House is concerned, of having this matter looked into until it was brought to the attention of the House by the hon. Member (Sir Charles Lewis) in the form of a Motion such as that before us on this occasion. It is due to hon. Members below the

Gangway, it is due to you who have spoken so bitterly of hon. Members below the Gangway, you who have so little charity in your hearts in considering their conduct and their position —it is due to them and to yourselves, as a matter of fair play, that an opportunity should be given for inquiry. Is there one hon. Member opposite who will say that if a similar charge had been made against—let me say the right hon. Gentleman the Member for Sleaford (Mr. Chaplin), whom I see opposite, or any other hon. Member sitting on that side of the House—they would not have felt bound to give that hon. Member an opportunity of meeting, as the precedents of the House entitle him, the charge before a Committee of this House?

LORD RANDOLPH CHURCHILL (Paddington, S.): I do not know whether I should be saying anything repugnant to the general sentiment of the House of Commons if I ventured to express an imagination which has occurred to my mind, that the House would regret if this most interesting and most important discussion fell too much into the hands of lawyers. The right hon. and learned Gentleman (Sir Charles Russell) has made a most able speech to the House, and has criticized with great minuteness and great research the variety of cases which has been dealt with, with equal minuteness, equal research, and equal, if not greater ability, by the hon. and learned Gentleman the Solicitor General (Sir Edward Clarke). But I do not think the matters which are before the House can be entirely decided by legal analysis, and I will venture, if it is not inconvenient to the House, to offer a few observations which occur to me, as one who has for some years followed the proceedings of this House, and who has, on more than one occasion, assisted in discussions of this character. I will own there was one feature in the close of the remarks of the right hon. and learned Gentleman (Sir Charles Russell) which struck me with surprise, as illustrating the extraordinary change which the present state of politics seem to have brought upon the minds of Members, and that was that the right hon. and learned Gentleman, in his character of a great Liberal lawyer—I might almost say, judging from the tone of his remarks, a great Radical lawyer—should

Sir Charles Russell

assail with much animosity the liberty of the Press. The hon. and learned Gentleman said that the Press presumes to comment in such and such manner upon matters which occur in our daily life here. I make no further remark on that subject.

SIR CHARLES RUSSELL: I used the word "dictate."

LORD RANDOLPH CHURCHILL The hon. and learned Gentleman does not contest the fact that he used the word "presume." I only thought it was very remarkable that a great Liberal and Radical lawyer should speak of the presumption of the Press. And then in the very sentence with which the hon. and learned Gentleman concluded his speech—I shall be sorry if I do not represent him rightly—he spoke as if the Party on this side of the House were deliberately refusing an inquiry into matters which are not occupying the House. I do not think that was either a legal or judicial statement. We are refusing no inquiry. The difference which separates us from hon. Gentlemen opposite is this—that we differ as to the form of the inquiry. There is nothing unreasonable in that. We, on these Benches, entertain the opinion that an inquiry purely judicial would best elicit the truth as to this grave matter. Hon. Gentlemen opposite prefer that there should be another form of inquiry. But I will return to that matter before I conclude my remarks. I would like to bring the House, if possible, from all the complicated arguments of the two legal Gentleman who have addressed us to the real nature of the Motion before us. The hon. Baronet the Member for North Antrim (Sir Charles Lewis) has moved that certain matters constitute a Breach of the Privileges of the House, and the Solicitor General has moved that these matters do not constitute a Breach of the Privileges of the House. Perhaps I should be mis-describing the Solicitor General's Motion if I used those words. His Motion is different, for it is—

" That this House declines to treat the publication of the article headed 'Parnellism and Crime' in *The Times* of the 2nd of May, as a Breach of the Privileges of this House."

I say with much frankness and candour that, from a technical point of view, no sane or reasonable person would entertain the slightest doubt that in this case there has been a Breach of the Privilege of the House of Commons. There is no doubt about that; but there have often been serious theoretical Breaches of the Privileges of the House of Commons which the House has declined to treat as Breaches of Privilege, and no one can better inform the House on that matter than the present Leader of the Opposition. I do not know where you can lay down any hard-and-fast line for the conduct of the House under circumstances of this kind. But I should think that something like this would not be far from the truth—that where the House has seen other remedies for this particular evil than to exert its authority it does not exert it. Where it has seen other remedies more perfect, more rapid —["Oh, oh!"]—well, I am only trying to state the position of affairs—more justifiable, and more satisfactory than the action of its own authority, it has preferred those remedies. I could illustrate that to the House even in my own short political experience. If you take the case, in 1844, of Mr. Ferrand, who made imputations against a Committee of the House of Commons, or if you take the case of Mr. Grissell, who also endeavoured to corrupt a Committee—["No, no!"]—yes; that was the allegation—he represented that he was able to corrupt a Committee of the House—if you take these cases the House will see that there was, literally, no other remedy open to the House except that it should act on its own authority. There was nothing a Court of Law could take notice of; and, similarly, Mr. O'Connell, when he was summoned before the House for stating that Committees of the House of Commons were in the habit of deciding Election Petitions corruptly, made no allusion to individuals. He made a general statement; and, obviously, the House was obliged to act for itself, for there was no other remedy open to it. But this case is quite different. Here certain Members of the House of Commons are undoubtedly aggrieved, and through those Members the House of Commons as a body is aggrieved. But the Members so aggrieved have a far more perfect remedy than that of putting the authority of this House into action—namely, that of resorting to the ordinary tribunals of the country, and proving the falsity of the libels which have aggrieved them, and by using all the authority of those tribunals

to bring upon the offenders the most severe penalties. Well, I do not think I have given an incorrect history of this question of Privilege nor of the methods of treating them adopted by the House, nor do I think I have spoken in a manner at all opposed to common sense. But a variety of other considerations arise which may have somewhat of a Party character, but which we cannot altogether put out of view. Hon. Gentlemen below the Gangway opposite have manifested extraordinary excitement over the action of the hon. Baronet the Member for North Antrim, and they have declared that they welcome and grasp at the particular form of Parliamentary investigation suggested by the hon. Baronet, and they have charged all those who do not agree with them with a desire to evade the investigation of the matters that are at issue. But I ask hon. Members opposite, would this matter have been brought before the House of Commons at all if it had not been for the action of the hon. Member for North Antrim? ["Yes!"] I have no information upon that point. It is certain that if the hon. Baronet the Member for North Antrim had not brought the question before us yesterday, it would not have been brought before us.

MR. SEXTON (Belfast, W.): I endeavoured to bring the matter before the House, but unsuccessfully.

LORD RANDOLPH CHURCHILL: The hon. Member could not have endeavoured to bring *The Times* article of May 2 before the House. I understand the circumstance he wished to call attention to occurred some time ago.

MR. SEXTON: The forged letter.

LORD RANDOLPH CHURCHILL: Exactly; I am not speaking of the forged letter; I am speaking of the present matter. I want to know if we can have any assurance from hon. Gentlemen opposite that this matter would have been brought before the House but for the action of the hon. Member for North Antrim? Hon. Members have spoken in terms of severe comment of the right hon. Gentleman the Leader of the House. The hon. Member for the Scotland Division of Liverpool has spoken of my right hon. Friend in terms which, I believe, are repudiated by everybody outside his own immediate circle of friends. Many of us may have legitimately differed from my right hon. Friend in political matters, and may not have agreed with the counsels he has given the House; but until the hon. Member spoke this afternoon there has never yet been the smallest difference of opinion that the whole career of the right hon. Gentleman has been an honour to the House of Commons.

MR. T. P. O'CONNOR: I rise to make a personal explanation. I think the noble Lord, if he undertakes to repeat the charges I made, ought to repeat them correctly, and ought not to attribute to me charges I did not make. My statement was this. The right hon. Gentleman the Leader of the House offered to institute a prosecution against *The Times* through the Attorney General, and my answer to that was that the right hon. Gentleman, in his character outside the House, was *particeps criminis* with *The Times* in propagating the very libels we complain of.

LORD RANDOLPH CHURCHILL: I utterly decline to accept any contradiction from the hon. Member. I heard the hon. Member's speech, and I am perfectly sensible, as was everybody else who heard him on this side of the House, of the insinuations which the hon. Member conveyed when he referred to the Leader of the House, and I am glad to have the opportunity of expressing what I believe to be the feeling of the entire House that those insinuations are unjustifiable. But what are we to expect when the hon. Member proceeded to compare the Courts of Justice in this country to marked cards and loaded dice—when he thinks it legitimate to speak in that way of Courts of Justice which have an unstained record of more than 1,000 years? When we have such statements made—when we have our Courts of Justice compared to people who cheat and gamble—when we hear accusations of that kind from below the Gangway opposite, I think the First Lord of the Treasury can afford to pass by the hon. Member's remarks. I come now to the remarks—the very legitimate remarks — made by the hon. and learned Gentleman who last addressed the House. He said it was the duty of the Leader of the House to afford protection to every Member of the House—to get the House into a groove which would afford protection to every Member. How could

the Leader of the House be in the least aware, from the conduct of hon. Gentlemen opposite, that it was their desire that this matter should be brought before the House? What indication have they given of any desire that public notice should be taken of this matter? When the charge is brought against the Leader of the House that he has not dealt with this case, I may retort and say that surely the protection of hon. Members below the Gangway opposite is a matter that more concerns the Leader of the Opposition. He it is who is concerned with the honour of his followers. It concerns, and seriously concerns, the Leader of the Opposition in more ways than one, for it was the direct opinion and hope of the country that when he assumed the Leadership of the movement for the repeal of the Union, that that movement would at once assume——

MR. W. E. GLADSTONE (Edinburgh, Mid Lothian): I never assumed any such Leadership.

LORD RANDOLPH CHURCHILL: The right hon. Gentleman is splitting hairs when he denies that he assumed the Leadership of the movement for the repeal of the Union. [*Cries of* "No, no!" *and* "Withdraw!"] That movement is invariably designated as a movement for the repeal of the Union. What I say is this—that where there is any indication of an injury being sustained by hon. Gentlemen below the Gangway, if the duty of protecting them falls upon anyone, it does not fall upon the First Lord of the Treasury, but on the Leader of the Opposition. I say that he and the whole of his Party are much more concerned than we are, or than the House of Commons is, in relieving hon. Gentlemen below the Gangway opposite—who form so large a part of the right hon. Gentleman's following—from imputations which, if they are true, are likely to deprive them of all political credit. Now, Sir, the hon. and learned Gentleman who has just sat down was extremely anxious that we should measure ourselves as the House of Commons against *The Times* newspaper—that we should have the printer up at the Bar of the House, and appoint a Select Committee to inquire into the conduct of the prisoner, and that if certain things are proved that he should be punished. Does the hon. and learned Gentleman really think that would be a safe or a judicious course for the House to take? I can quite understand that there may have been days when the Privileges of the House, which have proved so formidable against Monarchical and arbitrary power, might have been thought useful against the growing power of the Press; but I cannot conceive that, in the present day, anyone can argue seriously, with any hope of success, that the House of Commons can measure itself against the Press. The Press of England is far more powerful than the House of Commons, and there is only one power I know of that is greater than the Press, and that is the power of the Courts of Law. [*Laughter.*] I see that the hon. Member for Sunderland (Mr. Storey), who is, I believe, himself not unconnected with the Press, joins with those who laugh. The Courts are extremely powerful, and can punish, and even suppress, newspapers.

MR. STOREY (Sunderland): We only suppress newspapers in Ireland.

LORD RANDOLPH CHURCHILL: There is no law in Ireland I know of at the present moment, and there is none proposed to be made, that can do that. There is no law, with the exception of the law which the right hon. Gentleman the Leader of the Opposition (Mr. W. E. Gladstone) passed, which can suppress newspapers. There is no law that I know of which is going to be enacted to this end.

MR. STOREY: Will the noble Lord do me the justice of permitting me to say that that was a law which I opposed?

LORD RANDOLPH CHURCHILL: What I was pointing out was this—that there was no law in Ireland, except the one which the right hon. Gentleman the Member for Mid Lothian passed, which gave the power to suppress newspapers, and there is no law before the House proposed to be enacted which gives the power. I was asking hon. Members opposite what are the powers of the House of Commons against *The Times?* I say absolutely they are *nil.* You might possibly, if you wish, commit the printer of *The Times* — [*Cries of* "The publisher!"]—the publisher and the printer of *The Times* to the Clock Tower or Newgate; but the moment the House is prorogued they are liberated. You cannot inflict any fine. I think for more

than 100 years the House has renounced all attempts to inflict fines. You have absolutely no power against the Press of England, Ireland, or Scotland. You are absolutely powerless; and yet the hon. and learned Gentleman the ex-Attorney General invites us, in contra-distinction to the course proposed by the Government, to embark in a contest with the Press of the country, in which we must inevitably get the worst of it. Not only should we get the worst of it, but it is a course which will not elicit what we want to arrive at—namely, the truth of these matters. Now, Sir, let us consider the idea which is greatly favoured by hon. Gentlemen opposite, and in regard to which they consider they are very much aggrieved because we will not adopt it. Hon. Gentlemen opposite consider the proper mode of meeting this matter is to summon the printer of *The Times* to the Bar of the House, and then appoint a Select Committee. I do not altogether agree with the view of the hon. and learned Gentleman the Solicitor General (Sir Edward Clarke) that it was necessary immediately to send the printer of *The Times* to prison. He would, in the first place, be heard at the Bar; and then he would be told to attend again on a certain day, and meanwhile the investigation would take place. But hon. Gentlemen advocate the appointment of a Select Committee for the purpose of investigating all these matters, and pronouncing who is guilty of having made false statements for the purpose of influencing public opinion. May I ask the House to examine this matter a little more closely. Take, for instance, the composition of the Committee. How do you propose to constitute it? It is said that the Government would have a majority on the Committee. Hon. Gentlemen are very generous now in their appreciation of the noble and chivalrous motives which actuate the Government; but suppose the Government majority took a view opposed to that of the other section of the Committee, I imagine there is no imputation of baseness and corruption which would not be brought against the Government. But I want to go further. You admit that the Government have a majority; will the Members of the Irish Party be on that Committee? [*Cries of* "Yes!"] Then, in the whole history of jury-packing, they have never brought forward an instance which gave me a more vivid idea of controlling the tribunal beforehand than by placing upon that Committee Representatives of the Irish Nationalist Party.

Mr. DILLON (Mayo, E.): No one said that at all.

Lord RANDOLPH CHURCHILL: I understand the hon. Member for East Mayo, who very often shows an acute perception of what is justice and what is a common-sense view, is against placing on the Committee any Member of the Irish Party?

Mr. DILLON: I do not think that is a fair way of proceeding. That question has not arisen, and the opinion has not been expressed from these Benches. I am ready at the proper time to express my opinion; but to put an expression of opinion into the mouths of hon. Members is certainly a very curious proceeding.

Lord RANDOLPH CHURCHILL: "The question has not arisen." That is exactly the point. You may not wish to look at the question which will arise; but I ask the question because it is of vital importance that it should be determined. It is a matter which the hon. Member for East Mayo, who leads the Irish Party for the moment in the absence of the hon. Member for Cork (Mr. Parnell), says he has not considered, and is at the present moment unable to give an opinion upon.

Mr. DILLON: I said nothing of the sort. The noble Lord said—[*Cries of* "Order!"]

Mr. SPEAKER: I understand the hon. Member to rise to a point of Order.

Mr. DILLON: I speak on a point of Order. Sir, I have not the least desire to interrupt the noble Lord. He stated that I had not made up my mind on the point. I said nothing of the sort; I said I had not expressed my opinion on the matter, but that I was ready to do so.

Lord RANDOLPH CHURCHILL: I will no longer incur the displeasure of the hon. Member—after the unfavourable interruptions of hon. Gentlemen I will do nothing further to call forth their displeasure; but it is clear that the composition of the Committee is a matter of first-class importance, and the matter of first-class importance in that composition is the representation of the Irish Party. If the Irish Nationalist Members are on the Committee, it is instantly exposed to the suspicion that there are Members on it who have made up their minds beforehand; and if they are not, then its decision is valueless in the eyes of the Irish Party. But that is not enough in criticism of the proposal of hon. Gentlemen opposite as against the Government proposal. There is another question. What are the powers of the Committee to be? We all know what the powers of the Law Courts are. · If this matter is investigated in a Court of Law, there will be examination and cross-examination of witnesses; the evidence will be sifted by approved rules—rules well-known and understood, which cannot be transgressed, and which have been made in the interest of justice. But what are the powers of a Committee of the House of Commons? Now, imagine a Committee of the House of Commons endeavouring to investigate the truth of these allegations. On every question where a difference of opinion arose as to whether certain matters ought to be inquired into or not, the room would be cleared, and a Party Division would take place—a distinctly Party Division. Suppose, as was suggested, that the hon. Member for Cork (Mr. Maurice Healy) was asked certain questions involving a certain line of examination, the room would be cleared, the Committee would vote, and if the Government had a majority the Committee would decide that the hon. Member for Cork should be asked the questions. What view would be taken of such a line by the Nationalist Party? But another question arises—would the Committee have before it counsel? Now, I know of no case until the other day where a Select Committee of the House of Commons, appointed to investigate matters of this kind, had the aggrieved parties and the plaintiff's parties represented by counsel to cross-examine witnesses and address the Committee. Is there any precedent? Obviously, if *The Times* and those who support it cannot be represented by counsel, and cannot call witnesses, the investigation would be a perfect farce. But if, on the other hand, they could call witnesses and cross-examine, will hon. Gentlemen contend that the Committee is as fit to control counsel and sift evidence as the Judges of the Courts are? Put it as you like, you must arrive at the conclusion that the Committee is hopelessly incompetent to investigate such matters as these. I am aware that a very curious precedent was set by the House the other day—set, I think, by the House very lightly—in a case affecting the Corporation of the City of London. I was astonished when I saw what was done. There it was agreed, apparently without much discussion or the production of precedents, that the Corporation should be represented practically by counsel, and that the other side should be represented by persons who were as good as counsel. But what I want to know is this—I invite an expression of opinion on the point, either from the Front Benches opposite or from hon. Members below the Gangway—do hon. Gentlemen opposite contemplate that in an investigation by ·a Committee counsel should appear, and that the investigation should be as similar as possible as that in the Courts of Law? That is a point of great importance. I maintain that if there is to be such an investigation, then hon. Members had far better go before a Court of Law, because it would be a far superior form of investigation to that of a Committee of the House of Commons; and if they do not, and if it is said that counsel shall not be heard for *The Times*, then I say that the inquiry is a farce. I have stated—I think, not at too great length—two practical objections connected with the composition of the Committee and the powers of the Committee, which I feel confident, on examination, will be fatal to the inquiry. I must point out that there is ·nothing in the least inconsistent in this suggestion of the Government—that there should be a prosecution by the Attorney General—with the Motion before the House. If the House should come to the conclusion—not altogether an irrational one—that it will not treat this question as a question of Breach of Privilege, because it would involve the House in a conflict with the Press, which would lead to the result of the spectacle of the powers of the House of Commons being weaker than those of the Press—it places hon. Gentlemen opposite in the position, and leaves it with them in their discretion, and in the name of the House of Commons, to take proceedings. [*Laughter.*] That is a

very important matter. What is the object of the Government after all, laugh at it as you like? The Government offer this. They say that if hon. Gentlemen choose to make a Motion to the effect that a prosecution should be instituted by the Crown—formally in the name of the Crown, but in reality by hon. Members' own functionaries—against the authors of the libel, that Motion will come on as a matter of Privilege, will take precedence of all other Business, and, as far as the Government are immediately concerned, will be immediately agreed to. What is that but offering to hon. Gentlemen as fair and as impartial a tribunal for the investigation of those libels as the British Constitution can furnish? The Courts of Law have not worked badly for English justice in the past. The Court did not work badly for English justice, or for Irish justice, in the case of Mr. Brenon against Mr. Ridgway. The Government·offer to the Irish Nationalist Party, who are the aggrieved persons, at the cost of the country, the employment of any counsel they may like to name, and of any firm of solicitors they have confidence in, and to bring into this country, free of expense, any witnesses whom they think it necessary to produce; and they say that in that way they believe the truth will be arrived at, and if *The Times* is proved to have libelled grossly and outrageously the character of hon. Gentlemen opposite, then not only will *The Times* and those who are responsible for it have to suffer the severest penalties which the Criminal Law of this country can impose, but also the character of hon. Gentlemen opposite will have been cleared in a manner in which the House of Commons itself is powerless to clear it, and justice, which, after all, ought to be and is, I believe, the very essence of the British Parliament and of the British character, will have been aimed at and will have been done.

MR. DILLON : I have listened with attention to the speech of the noble Lord the Member for South Paddington (Lord Randolph Churchill); or rather, I should say, I have listened to only a portion of it, not the whole, which was characterized, as usual, with the very greatest ability and subtlety. I do not propose to follow that speech into all its details, because I think it is one which ought to be considered carefully and

[Second Night.]

answered by others at a further stage of this debate, and because to do so would compel me to speak at much greater length than I propose to do with other matter before me. I will content myself by alluding to two matters which were touched upon in the speech of the noble Lord. He alluded, as I fully expected he would, to the case of Mr. Brenon against Mr. Ridgway as an example of how confidently we might look to an English Court of Law and an English jury as a fair tribunal; but he omitted to state to the House that counsel for Mr. Brenon very properly pointed out to the jury that Mr. Brenon had been publicly expelled from our organization in Ireland; that he was a bitter and persistent enemy of ours; and that there was read in the Court, for the purpose of influencing the mind of the jury, an atrocious lampoon written by Mr. Brenon upon the hon. Member for Cork (Mr. Parnell), and, of course, these matters were taken into consideration. Mr. Brenon's character, before he obtained that verdict, was cleared to the mind of the jury of the stain that he was in any way connected with or bound up with the Nationalist cause in Ireland, and it was shown that, on the contrary, purged from all connection with our work, he was one of our bitterest and lowest enemies. So much for the argument of Brenon and his verdict. The other point alluded to by the noble Lord was, that it would be impossible to constitute out of this House a Committee which would judge fairly and honourably in this matter. Now, Sir, that is a contention to which I utterly demur. I will not follow the noble Lord in all the turnings and twinings of his argument; but I say that I utterly decline to accept the proposition that it would not be perfectly easy to constitute out of this House such a Committee as would be accepted by us and all sections of the House as an impartial Committee. At all events, will the noble Lord not consider this point—that we who are parties chiefly interested, we who are in difficult circumstances, and a small minority in this House, and until recently a miserable minority in this country, we at least have some right to be consulted as to the tribunal before which we seek to lay our case? Every argument used by the noble Lord and by the hon. and learned Solicitor

Mr. Dillon

General (Sir Edward Clarke) goes to show —what? Not that the Committee would be prejudiced in our favour, but unfair in a sense unfavourable to us, and yet we are willing to go before it. I now come to the speech delivered by the hon. and learned Solicitor General at the opening of the debate. He, in speaking on behalf of the Government, made the statement that no hon. Member of this House had appealed to the House, and stated that he had been assailed under peculiar circumstances, and that the redress open to every ordinary citizen was not open to him. Now, I contend that that accurately describes the condition of the case. That was precisely the statement I made—that I and my hon. Friends around me had been assailed; that the case was not an ordinary case; and that we considered the ordinary remedies open to the citizens of this country were not open to us; and it is for this reason, and precisely for this reason, that we have made our appeal that the case should be heard, if it is heard at all, before a Committee of this House. What are the circumstances of the case? We have been assailed now with what I may fairly describe as a conspiracy for malignant persistency, unparalleled in this country since the days of Titus Oates, and just as in the days of the Popish Plot the Catholics of England had no redress from the ordinary tribunals of the country, so has the Press of this country lashed the popular mind into such a fury against us and the cause which we represent, that I have no hesitation in saying that we are not on an even footing with the ordinary citizen, and that, owing to the action of our assailants and the Press of the same way of thinking in politics, it would not be just or fair to ask us to face these assailants in a Court of Justice in England. Why, consider what has happened in this country for the last six years. For six years we have struggled in this House in defence of a cause which has been almost universally unpopular in this country. For six years the voice of every leading politician in England has been raised over and over again in denunciation of us and our movement. For six years all the leading newspapers in England, with very few exceptions, have held us up to public odium in this country, denouncing our motives, and in every way inflaming the public mind against us. During that period of six years I myself have twice been imprisoned—twice I have stood my trial for criminal conspiracy, and three times have I been arrested by the police. Undoubtedly, all these facts would be used to prejudice the mind of the public in England against us; and although I am not ashamed of these facts, can any honest man stand up in this House and say that in the minds of a law-abiding people like the English, who have not known the difficulties and the troubles of our country, these facts that I have been three times arrested by the police and have been twice imprisoned would not be used to prejudice the mind of the jury against me and to make out that I was a criminal? And that is not all; for at this very moment the Leaders of two great political Parties are engaged day by day, and week by week, in denouncing us from public platforms in every portion of England as criminals, and worse than criminals; and are we to be told that under those circumstances our case is on all fours with that of the ordinary private citizen who seeks redress? I say that a more untruthful and monstrous proposition was never put forward. It is because Gentlemen opposite and the Government know that they have so inflamed the passions of a large section of the people of England against us that our position would be cruelly unfair in a Court of English Law in endavouring to defend ourselves. It is for that reason they refuse us the mode of redress which we ask for and seek to drag us into a position in which we would be taken at a disadvantage. And when we come to the position of the defendant, what would be our standing in the case? We, who are strangers, not among our own people, are asked to take action against the mightiest and wealthiest newspaper in London. Who would be sitting on the jury to try the issue? The readers of *The Times*. The men who day by day for all these years have read as regularly as the sun has risen the articles written to prove that we were all associates of murderers and assassins; and are we to be told that here, in London, among a population which has been prejudiced against us and inflamed by this very paper that we are called upon to prosecute, we would stand on an equal ground with *The Times* and be sure of a fair and impartial verdict? The reasons why I personally—

and I speak now entirely for myself—decline, and shall decline, to enter into any legal proceedings against *The Times* are these. Nothing on earth will induce me to do it. [*Ministerial laughter.*] I say to the men who laugh that it is a cowardly thing to taunt me for saying so. They have sought—trusting to the strength of their position in fighting a battle which, to me and those who sit around me, is a battle far dearer than life—to place us in a position where we have not a chance. They seek to fight us with our hands tied. Sir, the reason why I decline, and shall decline, to take any legal proceedings against *The Times* are these—first of all, because I am convinced that there is not a shadow of a chance of a verdict; secondly, because I believe that, in the view of all the circumstances to which I have alluded, the real issues would be obscured and hidden from the public by the most irrelevant matter, and by the speeches and denunciations of counsel; and, thirdly, because, believing as I do that the real issues to be determined are very few and exceedingly small, I desire to bring this matter to the most speedy decision possible, and I believe that for a case of this nature a Committee of Gentlemen in this House is a much more competent and suitable tribunal than any Court of Law in this country. I feel convinced that the motives of the Government in adopting the course they now propose is, that they have convinced themselves that *The Times* newspaper has no case on which it would dare go before the Committee of this House, and, like the cowardly calumniator that it is, it slinks away from the opportunity that has been freely offered it of substantiating its charges if it can do so. Sir, we have heard of a lowly animal dwelling in the sea whose mode of defence is this—that when it sees an enemy approaching it emits clouds of dirt, and makes the water muddy, so that its enemy cannot see where it is. Now that *The Times* has the opportunity offered of coming before a Committee of English gentlemen here—and, as far as I am personally concerned, I am willing to leave my case—I speak for myself alone—to a Committee on which no Irishman will sit—*The Times* shrink, like that lowly animal, into its hole, having received full warning that we shall not attempt to pursue it into that hole,

[*Second Night.*]

knowing as we do perfectly well it would emit such a cloud of dust and dirt that the public would lose sight of the real issues. Now, I have pointed out already that really the only substantial objection to a Committee that has been urged by the noble Lord the Member for South Paddington and the hon. and learned Solicitor General is that such a Committee might be held to be prejudiced against us, and it has also been said that when the Committee had decided we should turn round and denounce it. I think I am in the recollection of the House that that is really the only substantial point. It is said, forsooth, that if the Committee decided against us we should turn on them and denounce them as partizans! I should like to leave it to the judgment of any impartial person, whether Conservative or Liberal, what would be our position before the country, if, after a Committee of the House had decided by a large majority against us on this issue, we took refuge in denouncing them as partizans? Do the noble Lord and the hon. and learned Solicitor General wish to put forward this proposition—that their estimate of English gentlemen has sunk so low as to believe that in an issue of this nature, affecting the honour—I may almost say the political existence—of men who sit with them in this House, they think they would vote on strictly Party lines? Do they mean that the Conservatives would all vote against us, and the Liberals would all vote for us? Though I am strongly opposed to Conservatives, I take no such view. There may be men on those Benches who would take such a shocking and dishonourable course as to shut their eyes to the plainest evidence that could be laid before them; but my confidence is such that I am prepared, without the slightest hesitation or the least fear, to go before a Committee constituted of English Liberals, English Unionists, and English Conservatives, and I do not expect that the Division would be on strictly Party lines. Surely, as I have said already, we who are in a small minority; we whose political existence is threatened by this ferocious persecution; we, who are the attacked and the admittedly weaker Party, have a right, or it used to be always considered so in matters of this character, to a voice in the selection of the tribunal. Does *The Times* take up the position

along with the Government that it is not possible to find a Committee of this House to investigate this matter? I do not believe that any Member of the Government has yet really taken up that position. Now, I would ask the House to listen to a declaration of vast importance, to which the noble Lord did not refer. He took upon himself to speak for the Press of England. He took the Press of England under his wing; but he said nothing about *The Standard* newspaper, for which he has no great affection. *The Standard* newspaper is not a paper devoted to the Irish Nationalists. It is more entitled than he is to speak for the Press of England, and what does *The Standard* say? It says to-day that as beyond all question we have "appealed to Cæsar," we have a right to be heard by this House. If the noble Lord wants the opinion of the Press of England, I give him the opinion of the greatest and most influential of the daily Conservative Press of England. There is the opinion of that great paper. It does not appeal to the House not to interfere with the Press. On the contrary, it says that after the debate of yesterday, there can be no doubt we are entitled to demand at the hands of the House the Committee we press for. I stated yesterday that I did not intend to make any long statement in reply to *The Times* article till the issue has been decided whether it is a Breach of Privilege or not. I mean to adhere to that statement. If the House had decided to bring forward the printer of *The Times*, I should be perfectly prepared to meet the charge in detail in any shape or way the House might desire. But I can see no object to be gained by replying to that statement of *The Times* now by getting up time after time and replying to the last statement of *The Times*, wasting the time of the House, and arriving at no definite conclusion. If I spent an hour in replying to-day, there would be three columns in *The Times* to-morrow proving what I said was false, and then the House, if willing, might set itself the task of listening to the hon. Baronet the Member for North Antrim (Sir Charles Lewis) one day, and to me the next, until even the House of Commons would get weary of *The Times*. I do not, therefore, intend to go at any length into the reply to these charges. I will only say one or two

Mr. Dillon

sentences on the matter. In looking over the article everyone must observe that there are two classes into which the charges made may be divided. There is the class of positive assertion and of innuendo and insinuation, and I say that a more monstrous and infamous system of calumny cannot be pursued by a public journal than the system of insinuation and innuendo. Anyone reading through this article will see that there is hardly a single direct assertion of any consequence whatever on which an action could be founded; but the article is studded with carefully and skilfully constructed insinuations, conveying to the mind of the British public impressions which are not directly stated at all; and the argument throughout is constructed in that fashion. I say that the man who sits down and deliberately writes for the purpose of destroying a public man's character, not by direct and honest and straight assertion of facts, which can be proved or disproved, but by a series of insinuations out of which he can wriggle when he is brought to book, is little better than a murderer and an assassin himself. Such sentences as this occur over and over again. I will not take up the time of the House by reading more than one—

"We shall prove that Sheridan did plot murder while he was an acknowledged Land League agent, and that he ostentatiously recanted the abjuration which he is said to have made, and publicly proclaimed himself a relapsed dynamiter"—

the insinuation being that before I employed Sheridan as an agent he had been a dynamiter. What else does that sentence mean if not that? Anyone who knows Irish history knows that long before the breaking up of that association dynamite was never heard of in Irish politics. The insinuation throughout the first two paragraphs is that I knew him to be a murderer, an assassin, a dynamiter before I employed him. And when you go through the thing you find there is not even an attempt to prove one of these allegations. That is the character of the whole document. If you pick out of that document all the direct assertions they are absolutely worthless. But it bristles with innuendos without an attempt to substantiate them; but which the British public, who do not study Irish history, and have no

time or inclination for the details of this matter, will swallow. The public will swallow the poison thus put in their mouths. This thing has been going on for months and years, and for months and years *The Times* has denounced the cause in which we believe, and also the people of Ireland, with a malignity unparalleled, as I believe, in the history of journalism. There is no common case, for here we have one of the wealthiest and most powerful journals of the world, trusting in its great position, in its wealth, and in its great influence, which has pursued and is pursuing with an unsparing hate a small Irish Party, and the cause for which we struggle. And why? Because we have committed the unpardonable sin in the eyes of the English *Times*, the sin which *The Times* never forgives—because we have dared to stand up against wealth and authority on behalf of an oppressed and trampled people. For that reason, and for no other, a decree has been registered in Printing House Square that we, the Irish Party, must be exterminated and hunted to our political death. For that reason, and for no other, they are determined to get us into such a position that they can bring to bear upon us the full force of the influences which they command. For that reason they are determined to destroy us, because they hope and believe that in our ruin would be involved the ruin of the cause of Irish freedom and Irish nationality, and of the suffering people whom we represent in this House.

MR. CLANCY (Dublin Co., N.): The noble Lord the Member for South Paddington (Lord Randolph Churchill) commenced his speech by making some comments on the remarkable changes of mind which he said had taken place on the part of some Members of this House. But, perhaps, he himself has shown the most remarkable changes of mind of which an instance is to be found either inside or outside the House of Commons, and I would draw attention to the fact that even on the very question which is now before the House the noble Lord has changed his mind within the last fortnight. Speaking, a few days ago, at Nottingham, he retailed these atrocious calumnies from *The Times*, though, following the example of the noble Marquess the Member for Rossendale (the Marquess of Hartington), he would not himself, indeed, take the responsibility of endorsing them. He said—

"I make myself no party to these accusations. All I say is, that they are brought. I leave the matter there, but I do not know that it will rest there. It may—"

And, now, this is the sentence to which I wish to draw the particular attention of the House—

"It may even be necessary for the House of Commons independently of the action of the Irish Party, to take action, and to endeavour of its own independent authority to clear the House of Commons, as a body, from the charges made against a section of the House, which undoubtedly re-act upon the whole House of Commons."

Now, that was spoken at Nottingham not ten days ago. It brought down the house. It was delivered amidst the loud cheers of a large packed audience of Tories in Nottingham. Everybody there expected, I venture to say, that the noble Lord himself would, some day or other, move for the precise Committee which is now demanded in this House; and, certainly, nobody who was at that meeting, I will further venture to say, would ever have expected, that when the Motion was made by some other Member, the noble Lord would be one of the most prominent in objecting to it. He was very courageous at Nottingham; but now his courage has oozed out at his fingers' ends. Now, when we accept the challenge which the House of Commons has offered, he stands up as one of the most conspicuous opponents of the course he recommended not ten days ago. What conclusion are we to draw from that? If he does not now seize hold of the opportunity which we offer him, and which he indicated himself in the speech from which I have quoted—I hope I shall not be un-Parliamentary in saying so—but in face of the extract I have read from his speech, I can have no hesitation in saying that, in my opinion, he was trying to humbug the people of Nottingham and the people of England. What is the course of the Government to-day? It is very remarkable. My hon. Friend the Member for the Scotland Division of Liverpool (Mr. T. P. O'Connor) referred to this suggested prosecution as a collusive action. Sir, I think there was more ground for that remark than has yet been manifested to the House, when I call the attention of the House to the fact that the course now suggested by the Government is the

Mr. Clancy

very plan suggested this morning by *The Times*. The criminal has got behind the ear of the Judge, and the Judge has disgraced himself by listening to his suggestions. We are invited to trust to a public prosecution, in preference to an investigation by a Committee, and we are treated to long and elaborate disquisitions on legal points and precedents as if they were the all-important matters in the case. Legal subtleties and principles and precedents reaching back for centuries are trotted out in this House as if the mention of them settled the whole case. We are invited to go upon narrow limits and small lines and mere technicalities, when a question of honour is involved, and when it has been recognized, again and again, that the House of Commons is the best judge of all to recognize such questions as those and to decide them. It seems to me that there is no comparison whatever between a Committee of this House and a Court of Law for dealing with a matter like this. What we want to do is to get to the bottom of this question. What we want to do is to get out every fact, to enable everybody who has anything to say upon this question to have his say. That cannot be done in a Court of Law, where everybody would be tied down by legal rules of evidence. What we want to get in would not be allowed to get in there; and, on the other hand, counsel would be allowed to make various statements, both of fact and comment, which would not be allowed in a Committee upstairs. But in a Committee upstairs everybody who has any evidence to give of any sort whatever would be listened to. No rules of evidence would stand in the way of the reception of that evidence, and nobody would be entitled to say, after it was all over, that the whole case was not presented to the Committee. The fact has been greatly insisted on that a prosecution is offered to us. But we could have instituted one ourselves. I do not see, therefore, the value of the concession of the Government. Do hon. Members mean to say that we cannot institute a prosecution ourselves? Why, I thought the challenges of the Tory Press and of the Tory Party, for the last few weeks, distinctly challenged us to go into a Court of Law of our own motion; and now, forsooth, they offer us a prosecution when we decline one, and pretend that they are thereby offering us something which we could not otherwise have. They offer to conduct it for us, too, at the public expense. All I can say as to the question of payment is, that I think the acceptance of Government money in England or Ireland is not a part of the programme of the Irish Party. If we go into a Court of Law we will pay our own expenses, and not touch Government money in England, which no Member of the National Party would dare to touch in Ireland. What is the position of the Government now? I hope the people of England will appreciate that position. They are challenged now, by a series of statements which cannot be misrepresented, to go before a Committee, practically of their own selection; they are challenged to go before a Committee on which their Party will have a majority; and if they do not accept that challenge, the people of England will come to the conclusion that they cannot even trust Members of their own Party to decide upon this case. I am not surprised that they will not. All the evidence of the last few weeks, and the speeches of various Members of the Government, point clearly to the fact that they, at all events, whatever may be said of their Party, want to create the impression that they, at least, believe in the truth of the accusations made against hon. Members on this side of the House. The hon. Member for West Surrey (Mr. Brodrick) has distinctly expressed his belief in the genuineness of the forged letter. I think the Chief Secretary for Ireland (Mr. A. J. Balfour) has also expressed his belief in the truth of these charges; and, if I am not misinformed, that very impartial Gentleman who spoke on behalf of the Government a little while ago (Sir Edward Clarke), and who offered us a perfectly impartial trial in a Court of Law, himself expressed at Taunton last week, again and again, the basest insinuations against the Irish Party. I call upon the hon. and learned Solicitor General to repudiate that assertion, if it be untrue. My challenge is, that again and again in the course of the Taunton Election he made insinuations, if not express declarations, to the effect that the serious charges in *The Times* were well founded.

THE SOLICITOR GENERAL (Sir EDWARD CLARKE) (Plymouth): I do not know that it is convenient to rise and interrupt a Member; but after this direct challenge I may be permitted to say that when I was speaking at Taunton I expressed a strong opinion with regard to the abstinence of those against whom the charges had been made from bringing them to public test and solution; but I did not go beyond that.

MR. CLANCY: The whole drift of the remarks of the hon. and learned Gentleman were adverse to the Irish Party on the question, and he and his Party circulated a *fac simile* of the forged letter. I am astonished at the attitude now taken up by him, and I will venture to say that if he went down to Taunton next week, and stated to the people there that he had publicly repudiated here what he stated there a week ago, he would not get so favourable a reception; and if the Election were to take place over again, probably his *protégé* who was last week returned for Taunton would not get so many votes as he then did. The position of the Government is this. There is a fair challenge which we have made again and again, both in this House and out of it, to go before a Committee of this House. The Government decline now to accept it, and the conclusion which we come to, and, I believe, the conclusion which the people of England will come to, is that so little do they believe in their own case, and so little do they believe in the case of *The Times*, that they cannot trust even the Members of the Conservative Party to decide it.

MR. HUNTER (Aberdeen, N.): This is the first time I have ever known it asserted that the person who gave the challenge was the person who had the choice of the weapons. I have always understood that, according to the code of honour, it is the person who receives the challenge who has the choice of weapons. Now, Sir, the noble Lord the Member for South Paddington (Lord Randolph Churchill) has made one admission, and I call the attention of the House to that admission. He has admitted that this publication in *The Times* is a Breach of Privilege. If it is a Breach of Privilege, it is within the jurisdiction of this House to punish that Breach of Privilege; and there exist, therefore, two concurrent and independent remedies for this alleged wrong. The Government say—"We will not give you that remedy to which, as Members of this House, you are entitled; and we refer you to that remedy which you can obtain for yourselves without any assistance from us." Now, Sir, every Member of this House is liable to libel, both in his public and in his private capacity; and, so far as a libel is made upon a Member in his private capacity, it is not reasonable or just that the power of this House should be invoked for his protection. But when the libel arises out of his public capacity—when the libel arises out of his conduct in this House—it is not just nor right that he should be deprived of the ancient and Constitutional remedy which is provided for a question of Privilege. Now, Sir, I admit that in the days that are gone by, this House has interfered in cases of Privilege in which it would not be wise for it to interfere now; but, in answer to the challenge of the hon. and learned Solicitor General, let me bring to the attention of the House one single case which shows the views that were entertained of the jurisdiction of this House—its unquestionable jurisdiction —which will throw some light upon the question now before the House as to whether this is a Breach of Privilege. These authorities, ancient though they be, are binding and conclusive. Now, Sir, I find that in one case in which this House was concerned—and a case of mere verbal slander, not of libel or of written statement—it was said in a coffee-house that Sir Peter Rich, a Member of this House, was " the first Popish Knight King James had made," and that he was " a rogue and rascal." These were words of a slightly defamatory character, and they were not spoken in relation to any business before the House of Commons; but, nevertheless, this House held a Committee of Inquiry to examine into the matter; and the House, being satisfied that these words had been used, committed the gentleman who had used them to prison under the usual jurisdiction of the House. There are numerous other cases from that time down to the present. Let me refer for one moment to a case which was brought before the House in 1880— the case of Mr. Plimsoll. The hon. and learned Gentleman the Solicitor General (Sir Edward Clarke) quoted from that debate some observations which were made by the right hon. Gentleman the

Member for Derby (Sir William Harcourt), and he will forgive me for saying that he did not quote those expressions with exact fulness, because he did not bring to the notice of the House what was the real point to which the observations of the right hon. Gentleman the Member for Derby were directed. There was no question ever raised that Mr. Plimsoll was guilty of a Breach of Privilege, because he had published a placard in which the conduct of an hon. Member of this House was referred to as " degrading and inhuman." These were offensive epithets, and only offensive epithets—they were not nearly so bad as the words in *The Times*—and it being admitted on all sides that the hon. Member for Derby (Mr. Plimsoll) had been guilty of a Breach of the Privileges of this House, the only question that was before the House was what notice the House would take of it. A Motion was made in this House that it should be declared a Breach of Privilege, and it was contended by the right hon. Gentleman the Member for Derby (Sir William Harcourt) that, although it was a Breach of Privilege, the House should not take further notice of the case. And why? Because the hon. Member for Derby (Mr. Plimsoll) had apologized for the words he had used. Having apologized for the words he had used, there existed no reason for bringing the penal jurisdiction of the House into operation. But, in that case, some of the friends of Her Majesty's Government took a very different view from the view which they take now. It is quite true that the person offended was a Conservative and an English Member; but I trust the day will never come when less justice will be done to a Radical Member or to an Irish Member than to a Conservative Member or an English Member; and by a large majority it was declared that, in the opinion of this House, the conduct of the hon. Member for Derby (Mr. Plimsoll), in publishing printed placards denouncing the part taken by two Members of this House was a Breach of Privilege; but the House, having regard to the withdrawal by the hon. Member of the expressions used, was of opinion that no further action on its part was necessary. In that debate the Conservative Party took a very different view of the question of Privilege from that which we have heard them express to-day in this

Mr. Hunter

House. The then Attorney General (Sir John Holker), taking a strong view of the question of Privilege as it affected the question before the House, said there could be no doubt as to what the law of Parliament was upon the subject, for it was laid down with the greatest clearness in the work of Sir Erskine May, which was the great authority upon Parliamentary law. He went on to show that the law as there laid down was that to print or publish any books or libels reflecting on the proceedings of the House, or on any Member for his services in the House, was a high violation of the rights and Privileges of the House of Commons, and then the hon. and learned Gentleman quoted the Resolution of 1699, declaring that to publish the names of Members, or reflect upon them, or misrepresent their proceedings in Parliament was a Breach of Privilege, and that to print or publish any books or libels was a high violation of the rights and Privileges of Parliament. Sir John Holker went on to say that that was a very distinct enunciation from the Parliament of that day, and it was the law to which he gave his adhesion. Reference was made in that debate to another case, where a very highly respected Judge, now Lord Justice Lopes, was made the subject of a Motion for Breach of Privilege in the House of Commons; and all that the then Mr. Lopes had said with respect to the Irish Members was that they were "a disreputable Irish band." The only objectionable word that he used was the word "disreputable," and I am sure the House will agree with me in saying that that was a very mild and a very harmless expression compared with the torrent of precise and abusive epithets which *The Times* has thought fit to employ. Therefore, if it was a Breach of Privilege to use the word "disreputable," then, *à fortiori*, it is a Breach of Privilege for *The Times* to employ the language it has used. What did Mr. Disraeli say with reference to that Breach of Privilege? He said—

"I am not here to deny that it is a Breach of Privilege to speak of any Members of this House in their capacity as such in terms which imply disgrace, or, as the hon. Gentleman said, calumny."—(3 *Hansard*, [222] 330.)

What happened in that case? Why, Mr. Lopes apologized, and withdrew the language he had used; and, consequently, nothing further was done in the matter. But there never was any doubt that words of that character were an invasion of the rights of the House and a Breach of Privilege. Now, Sir, there was another case to which I may refer for a moment—a case which occurred on the 16th of April, 1878—when Mr. O'Donnell, then a Member of this House, brought forward, as a matter of Privilege, some remarks made against him by a paper called *The Globe*, and the words which he brought up were these—

"The facts are too clear to be contradicted with any chance of success, and we do not do Mr. O'Donnell's intelligence the injustice to suppose that he followed with one grain of belief the loathsome parable which he obtruded upon the House."—(3 *Hansard*, [239] 1400.)

In that case, the right hon. and learned Member for Bury (Sir Henry James) contended that *The Globe* had not gone beyond the limits of fair criticism, and justified his denial of the remedy of Privilege expressly on this ground—that the words did not constitute a libel. If the words had constituted a libel, then, in his opinion, they were a Breach of the Privileges of the House; but he stated that they were words which no Judge would for one moment hold to be of the nature of a libel, and, therefore, they would not amount to a Breach of Privilege. Therefore, by implication, if they had amounted to a libel, they would have been a Breach of Privilege. What I should like to know is this. It being an undoubted fact that *The Times* has been guilty of a Breach of the Privileges of this House according to all the cases, I should like to know why the hon. Member who suffers from the conduct of *The Times* is not to have his remedy in this House? It is said he has another remedy. Well, that is true. In almost every case of Breach of Privilege that has ever occurred there is a concurrent jurisdiction in the case, and I may refer to one or two words used by Lord Ellenborough in his judgment in the leading case upon the subject, in which he shows that the nature of that remedy in Parliament is that it is a concurrent remedy, and not, as was suggested by the noble Lord the Member for South Paddington (Lord Randolph Churchill), an exclusive or separate remedy. Dealing with the question of

[Second Night.]

relief outside the House, Lord Ellenborough asked—

"Whether it was consistent with the dignity of such Bodies as the House of Commons, and, what was more, with the immediate and effectual exercise of their important functions, that they should wait for the comparatively late result of a prosecution in the ordinary Courts of Law for the vindication of their Privileges from wrong and insult? Therefore," he said, "by the necessity of the case, the principles of human reason seemed to require that such Bodies, constituted for such purposes, and exercising such functions as they did, should possess the powers which the history of the earliest times showed them, in fact, to possess and use."

Now, Sir, this being a clear case of Breach of Privilege, if Parliament is not to interfere to uphold its rights on behalf of the hon. Member for East Mayo (Mr. Dillon), it is very difficult to see in what case it could interfere at a future time; and the ground upon which Lord Ellenborough specially based his judgment—the delay and dilatoriness of the proceedings of a Court of Justice—is a ground which will always continue to exist. Now, Sir, I was surprised, above all things, to hear the noble Lord the Member for South Paddington say that a Committee of this House was not a tribunal which could be trusted in a matter of personal honour. If a Committee of this House cannot be trusted, how are you going to trust a jury? I think it was once stated by a right hon. Gentleman who is a Member of this House that if you were to take the first 658 men who passed through Temple Bar you would have as good a House of Commons as you obtain by the process of selection which now exists; but I never heard anybody say that if you take the first batch of men from a jury list you would have a better House of Parliament than you have now. It is the greatest possible reflection upon Members of this House to say that they are not capable of forming a jury. The noble Lord has a great admiration for Courts of Law. It may be that persons who are not, by their connection, brought closely into intimate relations with the administration of the Law Courts are very often great lawyers; but I utterly deny that any verdict of a jury can have, or ought to have, the weight of a decision of a Committee of this House fairly appointed. There is this advantage in having a Committee—that this question would be brought to an immediate test; but how long it would

be before the Courts of Law would decide it no one can tell. Months, I believe, would elapse before the final decision was given. There would have to be a Commission to examine witnesses in America, and I have no doubt *The Times* would be successful in keeping the trial over for a very considerable period. There is another remark which I feel bound to make, although it may be very distasteful to many hon. Members. I can only look at the position of the Irish Members from the position which I must imagine Scotch Members might have been in under similar circumstances if it happened that there was a Scotch Party analogous to the Irish Party, and that that Party, unfortunately, was brought into collision with the Tory majority in an English House of Commons, and that Scotch Members were treated with the libels and the ribaldry which were common about 160 years ago. Hon. Members who are acquainted with the history of that time must know that precisely the same kind of remarks, and libels of the same kind as the insults now levelled at Irishmen, were formerly levelled at Scotchmen, and I dare say that the compliments were returned with interest. But, Sir, if such a case were to arise, and if the Leader of the Scotch Party were insulted and libelled by an English newspaper, I confess that, for my part, I should be very unwilling indeed, and would be no party to allowing the question of the honour of the Leader of the Scotch Party to be tried before an English jury. I think it was Lord Russell who said, in relation to one of our contracts with the United States, that every nation is the guardian of its own honour. The Irish nation is the guardian of the honour of Irishmen; and it seems to me that they are under an obligation, and that it would be a very questionable proceeding if they were to allow themselves, by any gibes or insults, to be drawn out of the straight path in pursuing their political welfare. I would like to mention another reason before I sit down. These insults and these libels are published with a clear and distinct purpose. The libels are not even sincere. The man who wrote in *The Times* that the hon. Member for East Mayo (Mr. Dillon) had uttered a gross falsehood knew, when he wrote those words, that he did not believe them. It is impossible to

Mr. Hunter

read that article without seeing that these allegations are insincere—that it is simply a case of the rhetorical piling up of agony—a simple throwing of mud in the face of hon. Gentlemen in the hope of drawing them into litigation, and drawing a red herring across the scent, and so drawing away the attention of the public from the great question before the House. The hon. Member is not really attacked. The whole thing is a mere instrument used hypocritically for the purpose of taking away the freedom and independence of the Irish people. Sir, we understand it all. We know perfectly well that the hon. Member for East Mayo is incapable of telling a lie. I should say it is very likely I might even say the same thing of the writer in *The Times*. But we know what it all means. It is simply an application of the old and stale story, "No case—abuse plaintiff's attorney." I tell hon. Members and I tell *The Times* that it may lie, but it cannot deceive—the artifice is too obvious; and, therefore, I trust that whatever may be said or done hon. Members here will not allow themselves to be drawn and inveigled into a needless and useless and miserable litigation.

Mr. W. E. GLADSTONE and Mr. A. E. GATHORNE-HARDY rose together; the latter giving way—

MR. W. E. GLADSTONE (Edinburgh, Mid Lothian) said : Sir, I will not stand for more than a single moment between the hon. Member and the House; but I think it would, perhaps, be for the convenience of the House if I were to state what, in the very complex assemblage of questions that we have now before us, and with a view to a clear issue, it is my intention to propose in case this question goes to a Division, and in case the Motion of the hon. and learned Solicitor General be carried, which would displace the present words of the Main Question in order to substitute other words, when the Motion of the hon. and learned Gentleman the Solicitor General becomes the Main Question I shall propose the following Amendment :—

"To leave out all the words after the word 'House,' in order to add the following words—'is of opinion that an inquiry should be made by a Select Committee into the charge of wilful falsehood in a speech made in this House,

brought in an article published in *The Times* newspaper of the 2nd of May, against John Dillon, Esquire, Member for East Mayo.'"

I will not say a word more, but simply give that Notice.

THE FIRST LORD OF THE TREASURY (Mr. W. H. SMITH) (Strand, Westminster) : I would suggest that the right hon. Gentleman should put that Amendment at once.

MR. W. E. GLADSTONE : I think I should be involved in the confusion of which I complain if I were to adopt that course. I confess I am a little surprised at the suggestion of the right hon. Gentleman.

THE SOLICITOR GENERAL (Sir EDWARD CLARKE) (Plymouth) : Might I ask the indulgence of the House to explain ? The right hon. Gentleman has just given Notice that, in the event of my Amendment becoming a substantive Motion, he proposes to move the Amendment which he has just read out. The question that my right hon. Friend the Leader of the House suggested was whether it would not be possible now to substitute the Motion I have made for the original Motion, in order that we may address ourselves to-morrow to the discussion of the right hon. Gentleman's Amendment.

MR. W. E. GLADSTONE : I have no power to do that, but I will so far as this—so far as rests with me I will certainly endeavour to promote a decision as early as possible to-morrow upon the question now before the House, in order that we may approach the Amendment of which I have just given Notice.

MR. A. E. GATHORNE-HARDY (Sussex, East Grinstead) : Sir, I do not rise to prolong this debate, and in the few remarks I have to make I shall not reach the time for closing the debate. My object in rising is simply to reply to the plain and simple challenge which has been thrown out by the hon. and learned Gentleman (Sir Charles Russell) who was Attorney General in the late Government. The hon. and learned Gentleman threw out a distinct challenge to Gentlemen who sit on this side of the House. He asked us to state whether, if this accusation were made against the right hon. Gentleman the Member for the Sleaford Division of Lincolnshire (Mr. Chaplin) or against some other Member of our Party, we would not have acted

[*Second Night.*]

in a different manner from the way in which we have acted on this question. Well, Sir, all I can say is that if that accusation was correctly levelled at us, any Committee formed, or partially formed, on our side of the House would be a most unfit tribunal to decide this question; but, for myself, I may say that I would most unquestionably have treated the matter in precisely the same manner as I propose to treat the question upon the present occasion. It is my deliberate opinion that this House would be unwise in stretching the question of Privilege, and I believe we should do well if we should establish a direct precedent that where there is at the present moment another remedy for the question raised as Privilege it should be decided by the ordinary tribunals, and in the ordinary way. I simply answer the appeal and the challenge put before us by stating that unquestionably I should have acted with regard to any Gentleman in any quarter of the House in the same way that I am acting now. The hon. and learned Gentleman referred to the Committees which have previously sat for the purpose of deciding what may be called judicial questions, and he dealt specially with the question of electoral corruption and of seats in this House, which the House has deliberately transferred from its own Members to a judicial tribunal, Mr. Speaker, I venture to ask hon. Gentlemen in every quarter of the House whether they would desire to go back to the old practice—whether the change which has been made in that practice has not been of the greatest advantage? I venture to say that no change has ever been more beneficial, or has acted more fairly, than the transfer to the Judges of the realm of the jurisdiction over seats in this House. There is much more that I would like to say; but, as I said when I began, I do not mean to speak up to the period when our debates conclude, and having replied to the challenge which has been thrown out I am satisfied to resume my seat, having, I hope, answered the question which I believe to have been thrown out in good faith, and which I think demanded an answer from some independent source.

MR. BRADLAUGH : I beg, Sir, to move the adjournment of the debate.

Mr. A. E. Gathorne-Hardy

Motion made, and Question, "That the Debate be now adjourned,"—(*Mr. Bradlaugh,*)—put, and *agreed to.*

Debate *adjourned* till *To-morrow.*

HARES PRESERVATION BILL.

(*Colonel Dawnay, Sir John Lubbock, Lord Elcho, Mr. Dillwyn, Sir Albert Rollit, Mr. Beach, Mr. Staveley Hill.*)

[BILL 4.] SECOND READING.

Order for Second Reading read.

Motion made, and Question proposed, "That the Bill be now read a second time."—(*Colonel Dawnay.*)

MR. T. M. HEALY (Longford, N.): This question about hares and rabbits is one which it is not possible to discuss at the end of a Wednesday Sitting.

COLONEL DAWNAY (York, N.R., Thirsk): I rise to Order. The Bill does not include rabbits.

MR. T. M. HEALY: Well, I will give the hon. and gallant Gentleman the benefit of the rabbits; but, as it deals with the important question of hares, I would say it is undesirable that a measure of this character should be dealt with at this hour of the evening. I am sure that the hon. and gallant Gentleman, knowing all he does about hares, will feel that a question so important as this could not be adequately discussed in two or three minutes. Now, hares may be looked at from various points of view. Of course, you can course hares; but, in my opinion, the best way to treat a Bill respecting hares is to prevent it from passing, and on this ground, that we have always found Gentlemen connected with the landed Party in England anxious to prevent poor people from having those advantages which they ought to have by nature, but are prevented by law from possessing. The state of the Game Laws is already in a sufficiently involved and complicated position without the addition to the long list of Statutes of fresh Acts of Parliament on this very complicated and difficult subject. I must, therefore, complain of the hon. and gallant Gentleman for imposing a trivial question like this upon our minds, when our minds are occupied with greater subjects. I think we should come with calmness to discuss the question of hares.

I think a day like this should be sacred from any sporting subject.

It being a quarter of an hour before Six of the clock, the Debate stood adjourned till *To-morrow.*

LIMITED PARTNERSHIPS BILL.

Considered in Committee.

(In the Committee.)

Resolved, That the Chairman be directed to move the House, that leave be given to bring in a Bill to establish Limited Partnerships.

Resolution *reported:—* Bill *ordered* to be brought in by Sir Bernhard Samuelson, Mr. Shaw, Mr. Seale-Hayne, and Sir Frederick Mappin.

Bill *presented,* and read the first time. [Bill 254.]

PARTNERSHIP LAW CONSOLIDATION AND AMENDMENT BILL.

Considered in Committee.

(In the Committee.)

Resolved, That the Chairman be directed to move the House, that leave be given to bring in a Bill to consolidate and amend the Law of Partnerships.

Resolution *reported:* — Bill *ordered* to be brought in by Sir Bernhard Samuelson, Mr. Shaw, Mr. Seale-Hayne, and Sir Frederick Mappin.

Bill *presented,* and read the first time. [Bill 255.]

MOTIONS.

——o——

REGISTRATION OF FIRMS BILL.

On Motion of Sir Bernhard Samuelson, Bill for the Registration of Firms, and of persons carrying on business under names or styles other than their own, *ordered* to be brought in by Sir Bernhard Samuelson, Mr. Shaw, Mr. Seale-Hayne, and Sir Frederick Mappin.

Bill *presented,* and read the first time. [Bill 253.]

TEMPORARY DWELLINGS BILL.

On Motion of Mr. Elton, Bill to provide for the Registration and Regulation of Vans and other vehicles used as temporary Dwellings, *ordered* to be brought in by Mr. Elton, Mr. Burt, Mr. Caine, Mr. Matthew Kenny, and Colonel Makins.

Bill *presented,* and read the first time. [Bill 256.]

SUNDAY POSTAL LABOUR.

Ordered, That the Select Committee on Sunday Postal Labour do consist of Seventeen Members:—The Committee was accordingly *nominated* of,—Mr. Baggallay, Mr. G. Cavendish Bentinck, Mr. Channing, Dr. Clark, Mr. Dixon-Hartland, Mr. Finucane, Mr. Gedge, Mr. E. Harrington, Mr. Howorth, Sir John Kennaway, Mr. Marriott, Sir Edward Bates, Mr. Pickard, Mr. Storey, Mr. Quilter, Mr.

John Roberts, Mr. Henry Wilson:—With power to send for persons, papers, and records:

Ordered, That Five be the quorum.—(*Dr. Clark.*)

House adjourned at five minutes before Six o'clock.

HOUSE OF LORDS,

Thursday, 5th May, 1887.

————

MINUTES.]—PUBLIC BILLS—*First Reading*—Accumulations * (81) ; Quarries * ; Lunacy Districts (Scotland) * (82).

Third Reading—Railway and Canal Traffic (74), and *passed.*

PROVISIONAL ORDER BILL — *Second Reading*—Local Government * (70).

AFGHANISTAN—REPORTED DISTURBANCES.—QUESTION.

THE EARL OF FIFE : I wish to ask the noble Viscount the Secretary of State for India, Whether it be true, as reported from India, that the Khyber Pass is now held by tribes who are fighting against the Ameer of Afghanistan ; and, if that be the case, whether that interferes with the arrangements of the Indian Government for keeping open the Pass?

THE SECRETARY OF STATE FOR INDIA (Viscount CROSS) : All reports that are received from Afghanistan, unless they are authenticated by positive information from the Viceroy, are to be discounted to a certain extent. Numerous reports have been spread abroad, I think, of a mischievous character, and many of them have turned out to be untrue. With regard to the Question of the noble Earl, I have to say that the Viceroy is in constant communication by telegraph with me, and if anything of importance takes place, he invariably sends me word the moment he hears of it. Up to the present moment I have received nothing whatever from the Viceroy as to the disturbances in the Khyber Pass ; but when I saw this subject referred to in the newspapers I thought it so important that I sent a special telegram to the Viceroy regarding it. To that telegram I have not yet received any answer; but I expect one to-morrow, when I may be able to give a reply to the noble Lord's Question.

2 H

RAILWAY AND CANAL TRAFFIC BILL.

(The Lord Stanley of Preston.)

(NO. 74.)   THIRD READING.

Moved, "That the Bill be now read 3ª."
—*(The Lord Stanley of Preston.)*

Motion *agreed to.*   Bill read 3ª.

On Question, "That the Bill do pass?"

On Motion of The Earl of SELBORNE, the following Amendment made:—In Clause 25, page 11, line 19, after ("made") insert—

("Provided that the court of commissioners shall have power to direct that no higher charge shall be made to any person for services in respect of goods carried over a less distance than is made to another person for similar services in respect of the same description and quantity of goods carried over a greater distance on the same line of railway.")

Further Amendment made.

Bill *passed,* and sent to the Commons.

LUNACY DISTRICTS (SCOTLAND) BILL. [H.L.]
' A Bill to make provision for altering and varying lunacy districts in Scotland—Was *presented* by The Marquess of Lothian ; read 1ª. (No. 82.)

House adjourned at Five o'clock, till To-morrow, a quarter past Ten o'clock.

———

HOUSE OF COMMONS,

Thursday, 5th May, 1887.

———

MINUTES.] — PRIVATE BILLS *(by Order)*— *Second Reading*—Flamborough Head Tramways.*
Third Reading—Sutton District Water, and *passed.*
PUBLIC BILLS — *Committee* — First Offenders *(re-comm.)* [189]—R.P. ; Truck [109]—R.P.
PROVISIONAL ORDER BILLS — *Ordered* — *First Reading*—Tramways (No. 1)·* [257].
Report—Local Government (Poor Law) *[226] ; Local Government (Poor Law) (No. 2)* [227] ; Local Government (Highways) * [224].

———

PRIVATE BUSINESS.
—o—

SUTTON DISTRICT WATER BILL
(by Order).

THIRD READING.

Order for Third Reading read.

Motion made, and Question proposed, "That the Bill be now read the third time."—*(Mr. Dodds.)*

MR. KELLY (Camberwell, N.) in rising to move—

"That the Bill be re-committed to the former Committee, with respect to two new Clauses (rates at which water is to be supplied for domestic purposes) and (Duty to public accounts),"

said : I do not apologize for proposing the recommittal of the Bill, because from the point of view which I take of this measure, I consider it of the greatest importance that the circumstances of the case should be fairly stated to the House. It cannot be stated, as a matter of fact, that this Bill has ever been before a Committee in any proper sense, nor has there been any opportunity afforded for those who are most interested in it to oppose it. The Bill was undoubtedly sent to a Committee, but those whose rights were endangered had no opportunity of appearing before that Committee, I feel bound to notice shortly the reason why the ratepayers were not represented before the Committee. A Resolution was proposed at a meeting of the Local Board of Sutton for the presentation of a Petition, asking that the ratepayers should be allowed to oppose the Bill. That Resolution was resisted by the Water Company, but was carried, and a Petition was accordingly presented to the House of Commons ; and the House allowed the ratepayers to come in. If nothing further had been done, there would have been no discussion upon this Bill, except in Committee. But an extraordinary and unwarrantable action was taken by the Water Company through one of their Directors by several of their shareholders. At a subsequent meeting of the Local Board, the Resolution authorizing the Local Board to oppose the Bill was rescinded by a majority of 1.

SIR TREVOR LAWRENCE (Surrey, Reigate) : I rise to Order. I wish to know, Sir, whether the hon. Member is entitled, in discussing a proposal to re-commit this Bill for the purpose of inserting certain new clauses, to enter into the general question of the Bill itself.

MR. SPEAKER : The hon. Gentleman proposes to re-commit the Bill for the purpose of inserting new clauses, and the discussion must be confined to the new clauses which he proposes to insert.

MR. KELLY : I wish to confine myself strictly to your ruling, Sir ; but it will be impossible to argue the question whether the Bill should be re-committed or not, unless I am able to state the reason why the Bill was not opposed before the Select Committee, as it certainly ought to have been. I venture to think I am in Order, and I propose to be very brief in my remarks. I say that the Resolution of the Local Board to oppose this Bill was rescinded by a majority of 1.

SIR TREVOR LAWRENCE : I beg again to rise to Order. The hon. Member, Sir, is entirely disregarding your ruling.

MR. SPEAKER : I have not heard yet what the point is which the hon. Member desires to raise. The clauses which he proposes to insert, if the Bill is re-committed, relate to the rates at which water is to be supplied for domestic purposes, and the duty of the Company to publish accounts.

MR. KELLY : I am obliged to give reasons for proposing the insertion of these clauses. Unless I can satisfy the House that the ratepayers of Sutton have been shut out from a hearing before the Committee by what I conceive to be most unfair and unwarrantable action on the part of the Water Company, I do not see how I can justify the course I am now taking. I may say at once that I should have shrunk from troubling hon. Members with the matter at all unless I had felt satisfied that corrupt influence had been used to shut out the ratepayers from being represented before the Committee. I hope then that I am not doing wrong when I repeat again that the Motion rescinding the Resolution to oppose the Bill was passed by a majority of 1. I wish to call the attention of the House to the fact that in the majority which voted to rescind the Resolution there was one Director and two large shareholders of the Water Company. Consequently, gentlemen who had been elected to protect the interests of the ratepayers, voted against those interests, and prevented the Bill from being properly discussed before a Committee. In the interests of the ratepayers, having, I trust, satisfied the House that the ratepayers were improperly shut out on that occasion, I would venture to say one word as to the principle which usually guides the deliberations of this House in reference to Private Bills. The Water Company is now coming

here to ask for powers to double their capital, and they are asking for very extraordinary powers which are now never conceded in any modern Bill, and as far as I know are not conferred upon any Water Company. I do not think it is ever found now that the words "Annual rack rent and valuation" are introduced into a Bill, and if any Company happens to come here which possesses that right it is generally exorcised from the provisions of their Bill. Of course it is our duty to revise whatever power may have been improperly or wrongly conferred upon a Company, and to revise them in the interests of the ratepayers, so that they may be made just and right. This House has done that over and over again, and has even gone a great deal further. I will only call the attention of the House to the case of the Vauxhall and Southwark Water Company. They were required not only to do what I ask a Committee to do in this case, but a great deal more, because that Company was compelled to put by a certain sum of money to provide the payment of interest upon capital. I ask for nothing of that kind here. There was another point then raised. It was made competent for the ratepayers, as has been provided successfully in other cases, to secure that the maximum of 10 per cent profit should be reduced to 7 per cent. A provision of that kind is not asked for now. This Company is entitled to pay 10 per cent, and more than that, they are further allowed to pay back dividends for a great number of years up to 10 per cent. The Sutton Water Company now come before the House to ask for power to raise new capital. I do not for a moment mean to say that they ought not to be allowed to raise new capital, but what I do say is that they ought only to be allowed additional capital on condition of paying due regard to the wants and interests of the ratepayers. Our complaint is that in asking for fresh capital the Company propose to obtain it upon a different principle from that which has guided the House in other cases, and therefore I propose that—

"From and after the passing of this Act the Company shall be entitled, in the case of a supply of water for domestic purposes to any private dwelling house or part of a private dwelling house, to charge only at a rate per centum not exceeding five pounds per centum on the net rateable value upon which the assessment to the poor's rate is computed in the parish or district where such dwelling house is situate: Provided always, That the Company may charge for a supply of water which cannot be supplied by gravitation from any of their reservoirs, seven pounds ten shillings per centum per annum on the net rateable value of the premises supplied ; " and " That the Company shall publish half-yearly a full statement of its income and expenditure from all sources whatsoever, together with full particulars of its capital account in two local newspapers in the district supplied by the Company."

I have called attention to the fact that the words contained in the Company's Act are "Annual rack-rent and valuation." My contention is that in accordance with the principle which has guided recent legislation in regard to Water Companies these words "Annual rack-rents and valuation" should be altered into "Annual rent and annual valuation." I maintain that those words come strictly within the ruling of the case of Dodds against the Grand Junction Company, when the highest tribunal in this country held that the words of the Act did not mean the annual gross value but the annual net value. I have only very little more to say. If the right hon. Gentleman the Member for the Epsom Division of Surrey (Mr. Cubitt) is prepared to contend that this application is not made in the interests of the ratepayers of Sutton. I would point out to the House that the right hon. Gentleman places himself in this singular position, that he is arguing that the ratepayers of Sutton are anxious to pay a great deal more for their water supply than they ought to pay. I think that will be a very difficult proposition to establish to the satisfaction of the House. I will only point out, in conclusion, that I am simply asking for the re-committal of the Bill in reference to these clauses, and I trust I have satisfied the House that it is owing to the unscrupulous action of those who are directly interested in stifling the voice of the ratepayers that this question was not discussed in Committee at the time it ought to have been discussed. I venture to think that if I have established that allegation the House will really have no option but to consent to the re-committal of the Bill in order that these clauses may be considered and dealt with.

Amendment proposed,

To leave out the words "now read the third time," in order to add the words "re-committed to the former Committee with respect to

Mr. Kelly

two new Clauses (Rates at which water is to be supplied for domestic purposes) and (Duty to publish accounts)."—(*Mr. Kelly.*)

Question proposed, "That the words 'now read the third time' stand part of the Question."

MR. CUBITT (Surrey, Mid) : I am sorry, Sir, on behalf of the promoters of the Bill that I am compelled again to trouble the House upon this question. I hardly ever remember a case in which an ostensibly unopposed Bill has been so deliberately opposed in all its stages except in the proper place—namely, before a Select Committee of this House. I do not wish to detain the House by entering into the technical question which the hon. Member for North Camberwell (Mr. Kelly) has introduced, but I must protest against the words "unscrupulous action," as applied to certain Members of the Local Board of Sutton. I would point out to the House that the Sutton Water Company is purely a Local Company, and that a great many of its shareholders, who live in the locality, have no other object than that of benefiting the ratepayers. It so happens that some of them are members of the Local Board, but it also happens that after the Bill had been read a second time the House treated all those who were interested in the matter with special indulgence. The opponents went before the Committee on Standing Orders, and obtained additional time to enable them to oppose the Bill before a Select Committee. Before the Committee sat the various questions in dispute were settled with the Local Board, and the Local Board withdrew all their opposition. The result was that this measure, instead of being referred to an ordinary Select Committee, went, as an unopposed Bill, before the Committee presided over by the Chairman of Ways and Means. Having made that explanation I am bound to say that I think this is a question which cannot be entertained by the House in this way. It is a somewhat strange thing that, although this Bill has been debated on three or four separate occasions in this House the particular clauses which the hon. Member now moves never appeared upon the Paper until a few days ago, nor was the question raised at all until the Bill had been read a second time ; and, therefore, I think it would be a very singular course to take to refer the Bill back again to a Committee. I believe that the Committee over which the Chairman of Ways and Means presides would not be competent to deal with such questions as those which are raised in these new clauses. The question is one which relates to the percentage to be paid to the shareholders, and would require to be considered upon evidence which the Committee on Unopposed Bills is not competent to take. I, therefore, hope to have the authority of the Chairman of Ways and Means for opposing the unusual course which the hon. Member for North Camberwell now proposes to take.

SIR CHARLES LEWIS (Antrim, N.): I may say that I have a considerable property interest in Sutton, but I have no connection with this Water Company. I wish, however, to point out that it would be a serious matter if, in regard to this Bill, we were to adopt a mode of procedure, which is altogether unusual. It seems to be thought now that after a Private Bill has been read a second time and considered by a Select Committee, it should be subjected to opposition on the Report stage, or upon the third reading. This is a case of that kind. All these matters have been gone into since the Bill was brought before the House, and now an attempt is made to re-open the whole question. I must say that it appears to me that unless we consent to depart altogether from the ordinary Rules and practice of the House with reference to Private Bill Legislation we ought to pay no attention to the proposal which is now made. At the same time, I am perfectly ready to admit that these clauses are very reasonable if they had been brought before the Committee at the proper time, and under proper circumstances. I must, however, strenuously resist this attempt upon the part of the hon. Member for North Camberwell to alter the practice and spirit which has hitherto guided our Private Bill Legislation.

MR. COGHILL (Newcastle - under-Lyme): I would remind the House that there was a long contest in the Law Courts over this particular question of the rateable value. Having had that question thoroughly ventilated I think Parliament would stultify itself if it omitted to put the words proposed by the hon. Member into this Bill. I also support the proposal of the hon. Member in the interest of the shareholders of this Company, because there are numerous instances in which Water Companies have been known to behave with lavish extravagance towards the water consumers. In more than one case they have provided the consumers with altogether extraneous articles, such as eels and other solid matter, which ought, in the interests of the shareholders, to have been charged for, and they ought not to have been allowed to make these gratuitous presents to the consumers without receiving payment for them. No doubt, the Company have a right to be paid for what they supply to the consumers of water; but I am afraid that their customers very much object to this extraneous matter and these foreign substances being supplied to them at all. I feel bound, on this occasion, to support, cordially, the Motion of the hon. Member.

THE CHAIRMAN OF COMMITTEES (Mr. COURTNEY) (Cornwall, Bodmin): The hon. and learned Member who has just spoken (Mr. Coghill) has treated the question in a somewhat abstract fashion, without reference to the particular objections which have been urged against the Bill. I am not going to enter into the questions which have been submitted to the House by the hon. Member for North Camberwell (Mr. Kelly). The case is this. This is a Motion for the third reading of a Private Bill. If the Bill had gone before an opposed Committee, the questions now raised by the hon. Member for North Camberwell in which the hon. and learned Member behind me (Mr. Coghill) feels interested could have been argued and decided there; but the Local Authorities who might have brought these questions before the Select Committee failed to take the necessary steps for doing so. And now, upon the third reading, it is desired to have the whole matter sent back to the Committee, in order to do that which could have been done in the first place if the opponents of the Bill had taken the proper steps for enforcing what they say they now desire. The proposal of the hon. Member for North Camberwell is to send the Bill back to the same Committee; but I venture to say that the same Committee would not undertake this duty. It is a duty which can only be undertaken after hearing evidence. It is altogether new matter, which only an unbiased Committee could possibly decide after hearing evidence. If the House sends the Bill back to the Committee on Unopposed Bills we shall only have to report that the case is not one that can be entertained by us, and we shall find it necessary to ask the House to treat it as an opposed Bill, and to appoint a Committee to consider the matter. It is very unfortunate that the opponents, by their own *laches*, should have lost their opportunity of contesting the Bill. Allow me to point out that, although the House will probably affirm the third reading of the Bill, it has yet to go before another House, and if the opponents have no opportunity before the House of Commons they may be able to obtain one for opposing the Bill "elsewhere;" and in that case the questions now raised can be fully fought out in a Committee of the House of Lords. The whole matter can then be fully investigated and decided. I hope the House will refuse to enter into the merits or demerits of the particular proposals now made in respect of these clauses, and will simply insist upon reading the Bill a third time.

Mr. RADCLIFFE COOKE (Newington, W.): Perhaps the hon. and learned Gentleman who spoke from the Opposition Benches (Mr. Coghill), will allow me to remind him that some of the substances he has mentioned as having been found in the Metropolitan water supply are not foreign substances at all. I only rise, however, to say that if this Bill is referred back to the Committee, the opponents of the measure will be in no better position than they were when the Bill was considered on a previous occasion, because I understand that neither the hon. Member for North Camberwell, nor any person on his behalf, nor any person on behalf of the oppressed ratepayers of Sutton, will be able to go before that Committee to support the clauses which the hon. Member wants the Committee to insert. Under these circumstances, it does appear to me that the hon. Gentleman has a very bad case. I think it would be rather hard for the House to re-commit the Bill for the purpose of having a matter considered which it is quite impossible to get properly considered, even if the Bill is referred back to the Committee.

Mr. R. CHAMBERLAIN (Islington, W.): I have only one word to say. The

Mr. Courtney

hon. Gentleman the Chairman of Ways and Means said the third reading ought to be passed, because no opposition was offered to the provisions of the Bill when it was before the Committee. The hon. Member for North Camberwell (Mr. Kelly), however, has stated that the Local Board of Sutton passed a Resolution that a Petition against the Bill should be presented, praying that they might be allowed to oppose the Bill in Committee, and that this Resolution was subsequently rescinded by a majority of 1 only. Certainly, if, as has been alleged, the majority who rescinded the Resolution included a Director and certain shareholders of the Sutton Water Company who did not scruple to vote against the interests of the ratepayers, I think that is a matter which justifies the hon. Member in asking for the re-committal of the Bill. If this fact is accurately stated, it is quite evident that the present consumers were prevented from being properly represented when the Local Board came to their final decision. I think we ought to receive some explanation of this circumstance from those who are now supporting the Bill, in order to show whether or not the Local Board abstained from opposing the Bill under such peculiar and objectionable circumstances.

Question put.

The House *divided*:—Ayes 192; Noes 102: Majority 90.—(Div. List, No. 109.)

Main Question put.

Bill read the third time, and *passed*.

QUESTIONS.

DOMINION OF CANADA—THE "MOLLY ADAMS"—DEPOSITION OF CAPTAIN JACOBS.

Mr. GOURLEY (Sunderland) asked the Secretary of State for the Colonies, If he will be good enough to inform the House of the nature of the reply received from the Canadian Government relative to the deposition of Captain Jacobs, of the *Molly Adams*, dated 12th November, 1886; and, whether he can account for the delay which has arisen in not receiving an earlier reply to the despatch sent to the Marquess of Lansdowne by Mr. Secretary Stanhope, on the 27th December last, regarding this vessel?

THE SECRETARY OF STATE (Sir HENRY HOLLAND) (Hampstead): The general nature of the reply recently received from the Canadian Government shows that the statements of Captain Jacobs are in some particulars quite incorrect, and in others are so exaggerated as to give an entirely misleading account of the occurrence. With regard to the delay, the Marquess of Lansdowne, in expressing his regret at the delay which has occurred in sending a reply, said—

"Some time was taken in collecting the evidence embodied in the Reports which accompanied the Minute of the Privy Council of the Dominion (and are enclosed in his despatch); and the occurrence of the General Election for the Federal Parliament to some extent interrupted the course of business in the Public Departments, and increased the delay."

RAILWAYS (IRELAND)—GREAT SOUTHERN AND WESTERN RAILWAY COMPANY.

MR. LEAHY (Kildare, S.) asked the Secretary to the Board of Trade, Whether it is a fact that the Great Southern and Western Railway Company, at Moorhill and Canny Court on the Baltinglass Extension Line, acquired possession of a plot of land from the tenants of the locality for the purpose of erecting a flag station at that point, which is very much needed, where six roads converge each leading to populous districts; whether the Railway Company are now offering this ground so received for that special purpose for sale, and whether, if the land is sold, it will be impossible to erect a station there, thereby inflicting a continuation of the present inconvenience to over 300 residents who have memorialized against the sale of this land; and, whether the Board of Trade will take steps to prevent this alleged injustice being carried out, or cause the sale of this land to be stayed until the inhabitants have an opportunity of opposing this action on the part of the Great Southern and Western Railway Company?

THE SECRETARY (Baron HENRY DE WORMS) (Liverpool, East Toxteth): The Board of Trade are informed by the Great Southern and Western Railway Company, that it is not a fact that they had any intention of erecting a station at Moorhill and Canny Court, on the Baltinglass Line, and they did not acquire any land for such a purpose.

THE MAGISTRACY (IRELAND)—DERRY-GONNELLY PETTY SESSIONS.

MR. W. REDMOND (Fermanagh, N.) asked Mr. Attorney General for Ireland, Whether he is aware that, on the night of the 14th July last, a party of Nationalists on their way home from a demonstration held in Derrygonnelly, County Fermanagh, were fired at, as alleged, by an Orangeman named James Kerr at a place called Dromore, near Derrygonnelly; whether the said James Kerr was prosecuted by the Crown at Derrygonnelly Petty Sessions on Friday, 30th July, 1886, for this offence, when the following witnesses, John Gallagher, John M'Glone, and Patrick Cox, swore in the most positive manner that they distinctly saw James Kerr fire three shots in quick succession at them; whether the majority of the magistrates on the Bench refused informations against Kerr, and whether any of the magistrates so refusing are friends of the accused; whether the Attorney General, on reading the evidence taken before the magistrates, ordered a new trial; whether, when the Crown Solicitor for Fermanagh (Mr. Alexander), by order from the Attorney General, brought up the case a second time before the magistrates at Derrygonnelly Petty Sessions on the 26th November, 1886, the magistrates on the Bench refused to accede to the order made by the Attorney General; whether two of the magistrates were from another Petty Sessions district, and is it true that one of them never sat at Petty Sessions in Derrygonnelly previous to the hearing of the charge preferred against James Kerr; is it a fact that the Crown had three additional witnesses to examine in this case, and that the magistrates refuse to hear them; why was a new trial ordered, and on what grounds did the Attorney General recede from the order he made for a new trial; and, will he order a fresh trial, or explain the reason why he declines to do so?

THE ATTORNEY GENERAL FOR IRELAND (Mr. HOLMES) (Dublin University): Proceedings were taken by the police at the time, and under the circumstances mentioned in the Question. Some witnesses supported, while others rebutted, the charge by direct evidence, and the Bench refused to send the accused for trial. On reading the papers, I thought it possible that the Justices had fallen into the same mistake as the hon. Gentleman seems to have done in his Question, and that they had regarded the proceedings as a trial, and not as a preliminary investigation with a view to trial. I accordingly directed the Sessional Crown Solicitor to have fresh summonses issued, and the case brought forward again. This was done; but although some further evidence was forthcoming, the Justices declined to alter their former ruling, or to re-open the inquiry, and I have no power to interfere further. I would add that it is not to be understood that Justices have not considerable discretion as to sending a case for trial, or that the magistrates exercised this discretion improperly in the case; but I thought that they ought to have an opportunity of further considering it. I am unable to give the information asked for as to the composition of the Bench.

Mr. W. REDMOND asked, whether the attention of the right hon. and learned Gentleman had been directed to the language used by Mr. Carson, one of the magistrates on the occasion, to the effect that the action of the Attorney General ordering a new trial was shameful and an insult to the Bench, and that the Bench would not review again their former decision at the beck of any official; whether the right hon. and learned Gentleman thought that proper language for a magistrate to use towards the Representative of Her Majesty's Government in Ireland; and, whether he had directed the attention of the Lord Chancellor to it?

Mr. HOLMES said, he had no power to order the magistrates to alter their decision.

Mr. W. REDMOND: Does the right hon. and learned Gentleman not consider the language of Mr. Carson an insult to him?

Mr. SPEAKER: Order, order!

FISHING PIERS AND HARBOURS (IRELAND) — PIER AT ARDMORE, CO. WATERFORD.

Sir GUYER HUNTER (Hackney, Central) asked the Chief Secretary to the Lord Lieutenant of Ireland, Whether the Government are in a position to grant the prayer of a Petition made by the fishermen and residents of Ardmore, in the County of Waterford, to

Mr. Holmes

the Lord Lieutenant of Ireland, in 1866, for the erection of a pier or breakwater, necessary for the protection of the numerous boats engaged in the fishing industry of that place, and towards which private subscriptions to a considerable amount were promised, and a substantial baronial grant passed about three years ago; whether, owing to the absence of some such protection, much poverty prevails among the fishermen; and, whether the able-bodied are, as a consequence, emigrating to America?

The PARLIAMENTARY UNDER SECRETARY (Colonel KING-HARMAN) (Kent, Isle of Thanet) (who replied) said: This case has been brought under the notice of the Commission on Irish Public Works, who will consider it, together with other similar cases. The Royal Commissioners propose to visit the Coast next month, and will visit Ardmore. The police are not aware that much poverty exists among the people there, or that the emigration is exceptional.

POST OFFICE — MID-DAY MAILS BETWEEN BRISTOL AND SOUTH WALES.

Mr. L. FRY (Bristol, N.) asked the Postmaster General, Whether he can now state when arrangements for carrying the mid-day mails between Bristol and South Wales, through the Severn Tunnel, will come into operation; and, if not, what is the reason for the delay?

The POSTMASTER GENERAL (Mr. RAIKES) (Cambridge University): The Post Office is still in communication with the Railway Company in reference to the conveyance of the local mails between Bristol and South Wales by the Severn Tunnel Line; and endeavours will be made to bring the matter to an early conclusion.

POST OFFICE—MAIL STEAMERS IN THE NORTH OF SCOTLAND.

Mr. McDONALD CAMERON (Wick, &c.) asked the Postmaster General, Whether he will give orders that at least the contract rate of speed of 10 knots an hour should be maintained by the Mail Steamers in the North of Scotland?

The POSTMASTER GENERAL (Mr. RAIKES) (Cambridge University): The Question of the hon. Member probably refers to the Orkney Mail Packet, respecting which I have received other representations. The contract requires vessels to be provided capable of steaming at a rate of not less than 10 knots an hour; but there must often be occasions when, from adverse circumstances of wind and weather, that speed cannot be maintained. I will, however, have inquiry made as to the recent performance of the service.

SEA-FISHING BOATS (SCOTLAND) ACT, 1886.

MR. McDONALD CAMERON (Wick, &c.) asked the Lord Advocate, Whether he is aware that the Sea-Fishing Boats (Scotland) Act of 1886, which was passed on the 26th of June of that year, has not yet become operative, in consequence of the Orders in Council provided for by the Act not having been issued, or if issued, not having been transmitted to the Collectors of Customs; and, whether he can say when these Orders will be transmitted to the Collectors of Customs?

THE LORD ADVOCATE (Mr. J. H. A. MACDONALD) (Edinburgh and St. Andrew's Universities): The Order in Council was passed on the 7th of March, without which the Act was inoperative. But I understand from the Board of Customs that elaborate instructions had to be prepared for the guidance of the Collectors of Customs in administering the Act. The final proof of these instructions were sent by the Board of Customs to the Stationery Office on April 2nd for printing, but the requisite copies have not yet been received by them from that Department. Every expedition, however, will be used, in order that the instructions may be in the hands of the Collectors of Customs as soon as possible.

LABOURERS (IRELAND) ACT — COTTAGES IN THE BANDON UNION.

MR. HOOPER (Cork, S.E.) asked the Chief Secretary to the Lord Lieutenant of Ireland, What is the cause of the delay that has occurred in forwarding the Board of Guardians of the Bandon Union the Provisional Order for the erection of labourers' cottages in that Union?

THE PARLIAMENTARY UNDER SECRETARY (Colonel KING-HARMAN) (Kent, Isle of Thanet) (who replied) said: Petitions having been lodged against the Order, it cannot become absolute until confirmed by an Order in Council. The Law Officers have settled the preliminaries, and the matter will be before His Excellency in Council in a few days.

HARBOUR AND PASSING TOLLS ACT, 1861.

MR. R. W. DUFF (Banffshire) asked the Secretary to the Treasury, If he will lay upon the Table of the House the amended conditions (specifying rate of interest, &c.) on which loans will be made for harbour improvement, under the Harbour and Passing Tolls Act of 1861?

THE SECRETARY (Mr. JACKSON) (Leeds, N.): Yes, Sir; I will lay the Treasury Minute on this subject on the Table very shortly.

HOUSE OF COMMONS—DEFICIENT VENTILATION IN THE VOTE OFFICE.

DR. TANNER (Cork Co., Mid) asked the First Commissioner of Works, Whether his attention has been called to deficient ventilation in the Vote Office; whether he will have the electric lighting apparatus introduced in lieu of the four antiquated gas jets at present in use; and, whether the existing arrangements have been proved to be injurious to the health of the officials?

THE FIRST COMMISSIONER (Mr. PLUNKET) (Dublin University): I am afraid it is true that the Vote Office is inconveniently small, and that at times when much crowded the ventilation is not very good; but I have not, I am glad to say, heard that the existing arrangements have proved injurious to the health of our excellent officials in that Office. I fear there will be considerable difficulty in mending the matter; but I will consult with Dr. Percy as to what can be done as to substituting electric for gas lighting. The difficulty is that the plant for our electric lighting is already strained to the utmost.

LITERATURE, SCIENCE, AND ART— ROYAL COMMISSION ON HISTORICAL MANUSCRIPTS — WELSH MANUSCRIPTS.

MR. T. E. ELLIS (Merionethshire) asked the Secretary to the Treasury, Whether he will submit to the Royal Commission on Historical Manuscripts the desirability of appointing a competent Welsh scholar to inspect and calendar the collections of manuscripts in Wales?

THE SECRETARY (Mr. JACKSON) (Leeds, N.): I am informed by the Historical Manuscripts Commission that they have at present no application before them for an inspection of Welsh manuscripts from any possessor of such documents. They are quite prepared at any time, so far as other work on hand and the funds at their disposal will allow, to undertake the inspection of any Welsh manuscripts of historical value brought under their notice; but no special appointment of an Inspector of such manuscripts could be made.

IRISH LAND LAW BILL—"M'CONKEY *v.* ROBERTSON."

MR. T. M. HEALY (Longford, N.) asked Mr. Attorney General for Ireland, Do the Government intend to avail themselves of the opportunity afforded by their Land Bill to remedy the hardship resulting from the decision of "M'Conkey *v.* Robertson" in the Court of Appeal, whereby tenants who have sublet even the smallest portion of their land, for labourers cottages or otherwise, are deprived of the benefit of the Land Act of 1881; has his attention been called to the report in *The Freeman's Journal* of May 2, of the case of Sarah Keating, tenant, Captain George Bolton, landlord, which was an appeal by the landlord from the decision of the Sub-Commissioners, on the ground that the tenant was not in occupation of the holding in respect of which the fair rent was fixed within the meaning of the Land Act of 1881; and as to which the Court stated—

"That it was for the Legislature to decide whether such a state of things should continue, but they were bound by the decision of ' M'Conkey *v.* Robertson,' and accordingly they should dismiss this originating notice on that ground;"

and whether, in view of the fact that the leaseholders, who are now to be admitted to the benefit of the Act of 1881, have nearly all labourers cottages erected on their lands, the Government will take care that such technical " subletting " shall not be allowed to defeat the intentions of Parliament?

THE ATTORNEY GENERAL FOR IRELAND (Mr. HOLMES) (Dublin University), in reply, said, he had seen

Mr. T. E. Ellis

the report, and could not concur with the view taken of the result of the case of M'Conkey and Robertson. That certainly was not a decision of the Court that to let even the smallest portion of the holding would deprive the tenant of the benefit of the Land Act, although one of the Judges threw out some such suggestion.

MR. T. M. HEALY: I would like to say that the Question which appears on the Paper is a very different Question from that which I desired to put to the right hon. and learned Gentleman.

CRIME AND OUTRAGE (IRELAND) — THREATENING LETTERS — GEORGE HEWSON.

MR. CONWAY (Leitrim, N.) asked the Chief Secretary to the Lord Lieutenant of Ireland, Whether an emergency man, named Lennox, in the employment of George Hewson, of Dromahair, County Leitrim, was charged, in the early part of April, at Drumkeerin, with writing threatening letters; whether the said letters were directed respectively to his employer and to himself; whether Lennox personally complained to the police; whether police asked to be furnished with copies of letters by Lennox, with the result that Lennox was charged with being the writer of the originals; whether a *primâ facie* case was made out by the police against Lennox; whether his employer declined to proceed against him, with the result that, on the 15th April, 1887, Lennox was discharged; whether the Government will take up the prosecution; and, whether the so-called threatening letters were reported by the police, and formulated in the return of crime for the quarter ending 31st March, 1887?

THE PARLIAMENTARY UNDER SECRETARY (Colonel KING-HARMAN) (Kent, Isle of Thanet) (who replied) said: Lennox, who is not an emergency man, but a caretaker, employed by Mr. Hewson, reported to the police that he had received a threatening letter. The letter was addressed to himself. No letter was received by Mr. Hewson. The police tested Lennox's handwriting, and came to the conclusion that he had probably written the letter. The evidence, however, was not sufficient to establish a case; and, under the circumstances, Lennox was discharged. Mr. Hewson had nothing whatever to do with the case, which was entirely in the hands of the police. The case occurring near the end of the quarter, was at first included in the Return of Outrages for that quarter; but, as the result of the subsequent investigation, steps were taken to cancel the record, a note of which will appear in the April Return.

LAW OFFICERS OF THE CROWN—NON-CONTENTIOUS BUSINESS.

MR. SYDNEY BUXTON (Tower Hamlet's, Poplar) asked the Secretary to the Treasury, In how many instances, during the years 1884, 1885, and 1886, the opinion of the Attorney General was obtained in cases of non-contentious business?

THE SECRETARY (Mr. JACKSON) (Leeds, N.): The opinion of the Attorney General and Solicitor General was obtained in non-contentious business in 1884 in 350 cases; in 1885, in 405 cases; in 1886, in 360 cases. These figures do not include consultations, or the numerous cases in which the opinion of the Attorney General or Solicitor General has been taken by the various Departments of the State by means of personal inquiry, or informal letter; nor do they include cases decided by the Attorney General as to licences in mortmain, or cases referred to him for direction under the Public Prosecutions Act, nor hearings under the Patent Act.

POST OFFICE — PAYMENT TO THE AUSTRALIAN GOVERNMENT ON ACCOUNT OF POSTAGES 1879-85.

MR. HENNIKER HEATON (Canterbury) asked the Postmaster General, What were the sums paid to the Australian Governments on account of postages collected in the United Kingdom on Australian Mails during the years 1879, 1880, 1881, 1882, 1883, 1884, and 1885?

THE POSTMASTER GENERAL (Mr. RAIKES) (Cambridge University): The sums paid to the Governments of the Australasian Colonies on account of postage collected in the United Kingdom on correspondence sent in Australasian mails during the years mentioned by the hon. Gentleman were as follows:—In the year 1879, £56,722; 1880, £36,757; 1881, £34,750; 1882, £38,209; 1883, £39,911; 1884, £42,374; 1885, £50,515. I have to apologize to the House for wasting its time by the presentation of statistics like these in a form which cannot be of any use to the public.

MR. HENNIKER HEATON said, his reason for asking the Question was that a contract was about to be signed for 10 years, thus closing the door to all reform. It was absoluely necessary for him to ask these Questions, as the preparation of the Returns might occupy the officials at the Post Office five or six months.

PUBLIC MEETINGS — INTERFERENCE BY THE POLICE.

MR. LABOUCHERE (Northampton) asked the Secretary of State for the Home Department, Whether his attention has been called to the fact that a peaceable meeting was being held in Kennington last Sunday, when Inspector Chamberlain called upon those taking part in it to break up, because a mob calling themselves the Primrose Society were advancing with hostile intent, and, upon his orders not being complied with, directed the police to break up the meeting; and, whether peaceable meetings, which do not interfere with traffic, are not to be permitted in the streets, if the Primrose Society or any other Association contemplate breaking them up?

THE UNDER SECRETARY OF STATE (Mr. STUART-WORTLEY (Sheffield, Hallam) (who replied) said: The Commissioner of Police informs me that Inspector Chamberlain did not call upon the meeting held in Kennington last Sunday to break up, and that he did not direct the police to break it up. The mere contemplation of violence by Primrose Societies gives to the police no additional powers of interference with peaceable meetings.

CELEBRATION OF THE JUBILEE YEAR OF HER MAJESTY'S REIGN—THE SERVICE IN WESTMINSTER ABBEY.

MR. LABOUCHERE (Northampton) asked the First Commissioner of Works, Whether he has had his attention called to a letter in *The Pall Mall Gazette*, from Archdeacon Farrar, in which it is stated that the Dean and Chapter of Westminster Abbey intend to present to the Abbey Restoration Fund the value of all the materials used for the contemplated Jubilee Service; whether these materials will belong to the Dean and Chapter, or be sold for the account of the Treasury; and, whether, at the contemplated service, the claims of every class of the community to tickets will be fully recognized? The hon. Member explained that since putting the Question on the Notice Paper he had received from Archdeacon Farrar a communication in which he stated that his letter was written under a misconception. Therefore, he would not ask the first two portions of the Question; but he would supplement the third part by inquiring when the additional Estimate for the ceremony at Westminster Abbey was to be in the hands of hon. Members, as it was ordered to be printed on April 20, and had not yet been presented to the House?

Mr. COBB (Warwick, S.E., Rugby) asked the First Commissioner of Works, Whether, at the Queen's Jubilee Thanksgiving Service in Westminster Abbey, on 21st June, seats will be apportioned to the Members of both Houses of Parliament, to representatives of the Army, Navy, Civil Service, Church, Law, Colonies, India, and numerous other Bodies and persons selected to represent the nation, and the space for other spectators will be extremely limited; whether the ceremony is to be of a National character; and, whether seats will be apportioned to members of the various Nonconformist Bodies, Working Men's Clubs, Trades Unions, Friendly Societies, Miners Associations, Industrial and Provident Societies, the Agricultural Labourers Union, and other Associations throughout the country with which the working classes are connected, so that all classes and interests of the people may be represented in proportion, as far as possible, to their numbers?

The FIRST COMMISSIONER (Mr. PLUNKET) (Dublin University): I hope the Estimate will be laid on the Table early next week. As to the second part of the Question, and in answer to the Question by the hon. Member for Warwickshire, the ceremony is intended to be national. The Lord Chamberlain will have exclusive control of the admission to the Abbey on the occasion; and, he proposes, he tells me, to follow as nearly as possible the precedent of the arrangements on the occasion of the

Mr. Labouchere

Thanksgiving Service at St. Paul's Cathedral for the recovery of the Prince of Wales, and which were understood to have given satisfaction at that time. I have no doubt that all classes of the people will, as far as possible, be properly represented.

Mr. H. J. WILSON (York, W.R., Holmfirth): I wish to ask, in connection with these Questions, whether any Nonconformist ministers have been, or will be, invited to take part in this national ceremony?

Mr. PLUNKET: I cannot go into the details of the arrangements. I have no doubt that the Lord Chamberlain, as far as he can, will endeavour to secure that all classes of the people shall be properly represented on the occasion.

RUSSIA — IMPRISONMENT OF MR. ROBINSON, A BRITISH SUBJECT.

Mr. JOICEY (Durham, Chester-le-Street) asked the Under Secretary of State for Foreign Affairs, If he has yet received any Report from Sir Robert Morier, the British Representative at St. Petersburg, as to the case of Mr. Robinson, a British subject, who, after having been imprisoned by the Russian Government for eight months without trial, for infringing its Passport Regulations, was sentenced to four months' imprisonment; whether he is aware that Robinson was kept in prison before trial without any advice being given by the Russian Authorities to the British Embassy or Consulate; whether he is aware that the sentence was passed on Robinson on the 4-16th December last, and that the Russian Procureur General announced that the term of imprisonment would not begin till January 24th —February 5th, 50 days after the sentence was passed, although Robinson had been in prison so many months without trial; whether Robinson has already been in prison more than four months since sentence was passed; and, if so, whether his detention now is illegal; and, whether, under these circumstances, he will wire instructions to Sir Robert Morier to press for the immediate release of Robinson?

THE UNDER SECRETARY OF STATE (Sir JAMES FERGUSSON) (Manchester, N.E.): Sir Robert Morier has sent the reply on the case received from the Russian Government. Robinson was arrested for having a false passport. Until he could be tried, he was imprisoned under a provision of the law as a vagabond for being without a permit of residence. Sentence was passed on him on the 4-16th of December. It was communicated to him on the 18-30th, from which date the legal interval of 15 days was allowed for appeal. The operation of the sentence began on the 2-14th January, and has not expired. He was condemned to expulsion on its termination. It is not the practice, when foreigners are arrested for infractions of the law, to inform their Embassies or Consulates. There appears to have been nothing illegal in the procedure.

WAYS AND MEANS—THE FINANCIAL RESOLUTIONS — THE TOBACCO DUTIES—SCOTCH ROLL TOBACCO.

Dr. CAMERON (Glasgow, College) asked Mr. Chancellor of the Exchequer, Whether his attention has been called to the exceptional position of the roll tobacco trade in Scotland, and the fact that, owing to the length of time required for the manufacture of Scotch roll tobacco, a large number of operatives have been dismissed, in anticipation of the reduction in duty on the 21st instant; and, whether, to prevent the loss and hardship thereby caused, he will consider the propriety of granting, in the case of the Scotch roll tobacco trade, a similar concession to that granted to the cigar manufacturers?

The CHANCELLOR of the EXCHEQUER (Mr. Goschen) (St. George's, Hanover Square): My attention has been called to the position of the roll tobacco trade in Scotland; but I understand that there is a great difference in the position of different manufacturers, even in Scotland, in the sense of the hon. Member's Question. While representations have come to me from some parts of Scotland, I have had none from others; and I must repeat what I have said before in this House—that the month for the reduction of duty was specially arranged in the interest of the roll tobacco manufacturers. There are, I am aware, some special cases where there is more difficulty than in others, owing to the longer period over which the manufacture extends; but in these cases there are also special circumstance which, in my judgment, render it easier for the manufacturers to recoup their loss. I regret that any operatives should have been temporarily dismissed, owing to the reluctance of the manufacturers to incur a loss for two or three weeks by taking out at the higher duty the small amount of additional tobacco necessary for their work during a week or two, a loss a part of which, at all events, I should think they could have recouped; but I do not see my way to make a change which, while giving relief to some, would be regarded as a breach of faith by others. I did not make the concession to the cigar manufacturers till I had ascertained at a deputation, in which gentlemen from various parts of the country, I think including Scotland, were present, that the case of the cigar manufacturers could be distinguished from that of the rest of the tobacco trade, and was not on all fours with it.

Dr. CAMERON asked, whether the Chancellor of the Exchequer was not aware that the loss incurred by roll tobacco manufacturers in Scotland would be infinitely heavier than the loss incurred by cigar manufacturers?

The CHANCELLOR of the EXCHEQUER said, he had endeavoured to ascertain from the deputation that had waited upon him whether the case of the cigar manufacturers was on all fours with other cases, and there appeared to be a unanimous view that there was a difference.

Mr. HOOPER (Cork, S.E.) asked, whether on the deputation the whole of the tobacco manufacturers in Ireland were represented?

The CHANCELLOR of the EXCHEQUER said, that he did not know that there was on the deputation a gentleman from Ireland; but there was a gentleman from Scotland. He was extremely sorry that inconvenience should be caused to a small portion of the trade by a boon which he thought the whole of the trade recognized as satisfactory in itself; but he was afraid that in all cases of a change of duty there was some inconvenience felt in some quarters. Having given full weight to the representations made to him by the deputation, he was afraid he must close the door upon any further concession.

SOUTH PACIFIC—TONGA—
MR. B. LEEFE, THE BRITISH CONSUL.

MR. W. H. JAMES (Gateshead) asked the Secretary of State for the Colonies, Whether his attention has been called to a letter in *The Sydney Morning Herald*, in which the writer, Mr. Duncan Campbell, states that Mr. B. Leefe, the British Consul at Tonga, informed the Roman Catholic priests who waited upon him, that—

"The King was perfectly justified in persecuting the people who were not of his religion, and in forcing them to turn over to his religion;"

and, whether the Consul, in giving such advice, was acting in accordance with his instructions?

MR. ATKINSON (Boston) asked the Secretary of State for the Colonies, If his attention had been called to the report of doings in Tonga, given by *The Pall Mall Gazette* of the 3rd instant; and, whether he has any further intelligence from Tonga?

THE SECRETARY OF STATE (Sir HENRY HOLLAND) (Hampstead) : I have seen the letter referred to by the hon. Member; but the passage to which he alludes is in a letter signed "A. W. Mackay," written, as we gather, at the request of Mr. Moulton, who is the chief Wesleyan minister in Tonga. Owing to the excitement prevailing in the Island at the time, it seems necessary to accept with reserve statements from either side. The despatches as yet received do not in any way confirm the report of Mr. Leefe's alleged language, of which I should venture to doubt the accuracy. It is necessary to await the Report of Sir Charles Mitchell, who reached Tonga on the 27th of March, and proposed to send a telegraphic summary of his Report as soon as practicable. This answer will, I think, cover Question 41, put by the hon. Member for Boston.

ACCOUNTANT GENERAL'S DEPART-
MENT — GREENWICH HOSPITAL
BRANCH.

MR. W. H. JAMES (Gateshead) asked the First Lord of the Admiralty, Whether the Office of Superintendent of the Greenwich Hospital Branch of the Accountant General's Department was lately abolished, the occupant of the Office receiving a gratuity of £1,500,

and a pension of £566 13s. 4d.; whether, soon after, the appointment was resuscitated, the title of "Director" being substituted for that of Superintendent; and, whether it is true, that a salary of £1,000 per annum is now attached to the Office, although, in 1879, Sir Robert Hamilton, in his Report on the Re-organization of the Admiralty, stated that the duties could be performed by a principal clerk, at a salary of £600 a-year?

THE FIRST LORD (Lord GEORGE HAMILTON) (Middlesex, Ealing) : The Office of Superintendent of the Greenwich Hospital Branch of the Accountant General's Department was abolished in 1885, in accordance with the proposals of the Committee on Greenwich Hospital, and the pension and gratuity mentioned were awarded to the holder of the Office, who had served more than 40 years. The appointment has not been resuscitated; but, on the recommendation of the Committee, the Office of Director of Greenwich Hospital was created, with a direct responsibility for the whole of the business of Greenwich Hospital, which had hitherto been divided between two officers. A salary of £1,000 a-year is attached to the new Office, as recommended by the Committee. In the Report of the Committee on the re-organization of the Admiralty in 1878, of which Sir Robert Hamilton was a member, there is no recommendation of a change in the position or salary of the then existing Office of Superintendent of the Greenwich Hospital Branch. It may be added that under the new system the cost of management has been largely reduced.

NAVY—H.M.S. "AJAX" — COMPENSA-
TION FOR INJURIES.

MR. LABOUCHERE (Northampton) asked the First Lord of the Admiralty, Whether the finding of the Court of Inquiry in respect to the injury done by H.M.S. *Ajax* firing shells into houses in the Firth of Clyde will be laid upon the Table of the House; and, what is the amount of the claims made for compensation by persons whose property was injured on that occasion?

THE FIRST LORD (Lord GEORGE Hamilton) (Middlesex, Ealing) : Except in special cases when the Court has been directed not to sit with closed doors, it has been the practice to treat the Reports of Courts of Inquiry as confidential, and I propose to adhere to this practice. The claims for compensation amount to £390.

ARMY — SOLDIERS AT POLITICAL MEETINGS — THE ROYAL IRISH REGIMENT AT GOSPORT.

MR. LABOUCHERE (Northampton) asked the Secretary of State for War, Whether he is aware that a number of soldiers of the Royal Irish Regiment, now quartered at Gosport, took part at a Unionist meeting at Portsmouth on 29th April, and conducted themselves in a disorderly manner, their proceedings being thus described in the local Press—

"Great uproar, which was increased by the throwing of something by a private of the Royal Irish Rifles, who was seated in the front row of the gallery. A body of soldiers belonging to the Royal Irish Rifles, some seamen, and a body of civilians made for the platform, and, cheering defiantly, formed a bodyguard round Private Hanna;"

and, whether he will give orders for more strictly enforcing the Regulation forbidding soldiers in uniform from taking part at political meetings?

THE SECRETARY OF STATE (Mr. E. STANHOPE) (Lincolnshire, Horncastle): I have made inquiry into this matter, and find that the report in the local Press gives a very inaccurate account of what occurred. There were some eight or nine men of the Royal Irish Rifles at the meeting in question; but they were quite orderly, and did not begin any disturbance. But an attack was made on the platform by a mob of roughs in order to break up the meeting, and the soldiers, on a call been made from the platform for assistance, joined in restoring order. The General Officer commanding has already taken steps to call attention to the instruction in the Queen's Regulations as to soldiers attending political meetings in uniform.

DR. TANNER (Cork Co., Mid) asked, whether the soldiers in question were paid, as were the roughs the other night at St. James's Hall, for tearing the coats off the backs of those who expressed disapprobation?

MR. SPEAKER : Order, order!

BOSTON ELECTION PETITION—MR. FYDELL ROWLEY.

MR. FINCH (Rutland) asked Mr. Chancellor of the Exchequer, with re-

ference to the case of Mr. Fydell Rowley, Whether he is aware that Mr. Fydell Rowley was scheduled to the Report of the Election Commissioners, and has not been found guilty of bribery; and, whether, under the circumstances, Mr. Rowley is disqualified from filling the office of High Sheriff?

THE CHANCELLOR OF THE EXCHEQUER (Mr. GOSCHEN) (St. George's, Hanover Square): In reply to the hon. Gentleman, I have to say that I am aware that Mr. Rowley was scheduled to the Report of the Boston Election Commissioners as having been guilty of bribery at the Election of 1880. I have only superficial information of the subsequent proceedings; but I believe that a prosecution was instituted against Mr. Rowley, and his case tried at Lincoln in 1881, when the jury failed to agree. The question whether, in these circumstances, Mr. Rowley is or is not disqualified from filling the office of High Sheriff is rather for a lawyer to pronounce on than myself.

LAW AND JUSTICE—SOUTHAMPTON BOROUGH POLICE COURT—EXCLUSION OF THE PUBLIC.

MR. CONYBEARE (Cornwall, Camborne) asked the Secretary of State for the Home Department, Whether his attention has been called to a report, in *The Hampshire Independent*, of certain proceedings at the Southampton Borough Police Court on Friday, 29th April, from which it appears that, upon a man of respectable dress and appearance being placed in the dock, and before any charge had been preferred against him, the solicitor of the prosecutor claimed from the magistrates, and obtained from them, permission to exclude all reporters of the Press, as well as the public generally, and refused to allow them even to hear the charge of which the prisoner was accused; whether such report is correct; whether it is the fact that the accused had commenced proceedings in the Divorce Court, that his case was set down for hearing in the cause list of Friday the 29th ultimo, and that, on the previous day, he was arrested at the instance of one of the co-respondents; whether it is the right, and, if so, under what law or authority, of a prosecuting solicitor in any case to insist that the reporters of the Press should not be informed of the charge to be brought against a person in open Court; and, whether the magistrates were right in acceding to the application of the prosecuting solicitor, and refusing to the reporters even to hear the charge made against the accused; and, if so, by virtue of what authority have local magistrates this power of hearing cases *in camera*, which the Judges of the High Court decline to exercise?

THE UNDER SECRETARY OF STATE (Mr. STUART-WORTLEY) (Sheffield, Hallam) (who replied) said, the accused person was charged with an unnatural offence. On the application of the solicitor for the prosecution the Court was ordered to be cleared; and, acting on the discretionary powers vested in them by the 19th section of 11 & 12 *Vict.* c. 42, the Court was cleared. The case was remanded until Friday; and the offence being an indictable one, the magistrates could only have taken depositions of witnesses.

MR. CONYBEARE: My question was as to the refusal to allow the reporters of the public Press to remain.

MR. STUART-WORTLEY: Reporters, Sir, are members of the public.

MR. CONYBEARE: I think I have a right to press for an answer to the last part of my Question.

MR. STUART-WORTLEY: I have quoted the section under which the Justices cleared the Court. It would not be proper for me to express any opinion on their action regarding the application for a remand.

MR. CONYBEARE: In my opinion this is a question of such importance that I shall call further attention to it.

METEOROLOGY—STORM WARNINGS— MR. B. A. COLLINS.

MR. HENNIKER HEATON (Canterbury) asked the Secretary to the Board of Trade, Has his attention been drawn to an invention by Mr. B. A. Collins, the object of which is to obtain from the Atlantic, westward of the British Islands, hourly observations of the barometer, so that the area of an approaching storm may be defined in time to warn navigators of its probable density, and thereby serve to preserve life and property along our coasts; if so, what action is to be taken to test its value?

THE SECRETARY (Baron HENRY DE WORMS) (Liverpool, East Toxteth):

The Board of Trade have received no other communication on the subject of this invention than that addressed to them by the hon. Member himself. The hon. Member's letter has been referred to the Meteorological Department; but their Report has not yet been received.

NAVY—WRECK OF H.M.S. "ESCORT."

MR. R. W. DUFF (Banffshire) asked the first Lord of the Admiralty, If he can give the House any information concerning the loss of H.M.S. *Escort* off Malta on the 28th April; whether it is true that three lives were lost on that occasion; whether it is correct that the *Hellespont* Government tug, sent out to rescue the crew of the *Escort*, returned to Malta without having accomplished that object, and that the crew of the *Escort* who were saved owed their lives to the exertions of Maltese fishermen; and if he can explain these circumstances to the House?

THE FIRST LORD (Lord GEORGE HAMILTON) (Middlesex, Ealing): The dockyard tug *Escort*, when returning to Valetta Harbour on a dark and squally night, ran on the Monsciar Reef and was wrecked, with the loss of three lives. The *Hellespont* tug, that had come out from the harbour to succour the *Escort*, finding that there was no hope of saving the ship, and that the heavy breakers prevented her getting near enough to the wreck to save the crew, returned to the harbour for a lifeboat. In the meantime, three Maltese fishing boats put off to the wreck from Marsa Scala; and though unable to get alongside, they succeeded in approaching sufficiently near to enable certain of the crew to reach them by swimming. Great credit is due to Inspector of Police Salvatore Cassar and the crews of the Maltese boats for the courageous manner in which they effected the rescue of the shipwrecked men.

PUBLIC MEETINGS — SALVATIONIST OR SOCIALIST MEETINGS AND THE POLICE.

MR. CUNNINGHAME GRAHAM (Lanark, N.W.) asked the Secretary of State for the Home Department, Whether, without previous intimation or formality, an Inspector of Police, in London, is allowed to disperse a Salvationist or Socialist meeting?

THE UNDER SECRETARY OF STATE (Mr. STUART-WORTLEY) (Sheffield, Hallam) (who replied) said : An Inspector of Police has the same powers with respect to Salvation or Socialist meetings that he has with respect to any other meetings that are likely to produce obstruction or a breach of the peace, or which are held for an unlawful purpose. It would depend upon the circumstances of each case whether any, and what, previous intimation to disperse should be given by the police officer.

MR. CUNNINGHAME GRAHAM asked, whether any breach of the peace, or obstruction of traffic, was caused in recent instances where Inspectors interfered ; and whether a man, by becoming a Salvationist or a Socialist, forfeited his right as a British citizen to the right of free speech, and the holding of public meetings ?

MR. STUART-WORTLEY replied that the question whether or not there was obstruction must become the subject of inquiry before a magistrate with regard to a criminal charge arising out of the proceedings.

MR. JAMES STUART (Shoreditch, Hoxton) asked, whether the hon. and learned Gentleman would lay on the Table of the House the instructions under which the police acted in dealing with meetings in open spaces in London ?

MR. STUART-WORTLEY asked for notice of the Question.

MR. CUNNINGHAME GRAHAM : I beg to say that, the answer being entirely unsatisfactory, I will repeat the Question to-morrow.

EVICTIONS (IRELAND)—EVICTIONS ON LORD GRANARD'S ESTATE, CO. LONGFORD—NOTICE TO GUARDIANS.

MR. T. M. HEALY (Longford, N.) asked the Chief Secretary to the Lord Lieutenant of Ireland, How many notices of eviction have been served by Lord Granard on the Board of Guardians respecting his Drumlish (County Longford) property ; is it the fact that the Government have sent some 100 police to the spot ; and, could he state whether any of those families threatened with eviction have only recently been relieved by public charity ?

THE PARLIAMENTARY UNDER SECRETARY (Colonel KING-HARMAN) (Kent, Isle of Thanet) (who replied) said : It appears that the number of families to be evicted on the Drumlish estate was 41. Notices of eviction were duly served on the relieving officer. Two hundred police were ordered to protect the Sheriff. The persons to be evicted have not been at any time in receipt of relief from the rates of the union ; but they are represented to be in very poor circumstances. The Government are informed that the agents, the Messrs. Roe, have openly stated that it is not the landlord (Lord Granard), but the mortgagees of the estate who have pressed the matter to the extreme of eviction.

MR. CONYBEARE (Cornwall, Camborne) : Are these Messrs. Roe the same as the agent at Glenbeigh ?

COLONEL KING-HARMAN : I do not know.

MR. T. M. HEALY : I did not mean to cast any reflection on Lord Granard, but only to get at the facts ; but as the right hon. and gallant Gentleman has stated that it is the mortgagees who are responsible, will he give us the names of the agents and mortgagees ?

COLONEL KING-HARMAN : The agents' names I have already stated. The mortgagees are Maynooth College.

MR. T. C. HARRINGTON (Dublin, Harbour) : Might I ask the right hon. and gallant Gentleman whether it was the same agents who recently burned the houses at Glenbeigh ; and, whether Her Majesty's Government will take steps to prevent them from burning the houses of these people also ?

COLONEL KING-HARMAN : I have already stated that I do not know. [*Cries of* "They are !"] The hon. and learned Gentleman can put the Question down.

MR. T. M. HEALY : May I ask the right hon. and gallant Gentleman, does he mean to convey that the authorities of Maynooth College, a Catholic Institution, where priests are educated, are responsible for these evictions ?

COLONEL KING-HARMAN : That is a matter which does not come within my knowledge. What I stated was that the agents had publicly stated that it was at the instance of the mortgagees, and not of Lord Granard, that these evictions had taken place.

MR. T. M. HEALY : This is a matter which ought to be cleared up. The right hon. and gallant Gentleman has now let it go before the public that it is owing to the action of the authorities of

Maynooth College that these evictions have taken place. I wish to ask him does he adhere to that statement, or does he withdraw it or qualify it?

MR. CHANCE (Kilkenny, S.): With the permission of the House, may I be allowed to state that I am the solicitor to Maynooth College and its Trustees, and there is not a particle of truth in the allegation.

COLONEL KING-HARMAN: I most carefully refrained from mentioning the names of the mortgagees. I mentioned the names of the agents. The hon. and learned Gentlemen asked me the names of the mortgagees, and I stated that I had been informed it was Maynooth College.

MR. T. M. HEALY: I ask the right hon. and gallant Gentleman, is the Government acquainted with all these cases of eviction, and does it not make itself acquainted with the names of the agents in each case, the ground of the eviction, and everything appertaining to the circumstances; and I ask him now, will he give us the names of the agents in these cases who are evicting these 40 families, who admittedly are poor and practically starving. Can he give us the names of the mortgagees for whom these agents are acting?

COLONEL KING-HARMAN: I have already given the name of the agents, the Messrs. Roe; and of the mortgagees, Maynooth College.

MR. T. M. HEALY: Does the right hon. and gallant Gentleman state that the Messrs. Roe, the Glenbeigh evictors and the burners of the houses, are acting for Maynooth College in this matter?

MR. SPEAKER: Order, order!

POST OFFICE — CARRIAGE OF THE AMERICAN MAILS FROM LONDON TO QUEENSTOWN.

MR. HENNIKER HEATON (Canterbury) asked the Postmaster General, What is the estimated cost of the carriage of the American mails from London to Queenstown and *vice versâ*; are any mails put on board the regular mail steamships at Liverpool for America; and, if so, what price per lb. is paid for these letters and newspapers, &c.; what price is paid from Queenstown to America for letters and newspapers; and, what is the estimated difference in the cost of conveyance of mails, if they were all sent from Liverpool to the United

Mr. T. M. Healy

States in place of from Queenstown, judging by the weight sent last year?

THE POSTMASTER GENERAL (Mr. RAIKES) (Cambridge University): I think the House will bear me witness that I have spared no pains to gratify the quotidian curiosity of the hon. Member. But I think he might before this have learnt more consideration for a Public Department than is shown by a six hours' notice of a Question requiring considerable statistical inquiry. If he will put it down for some day next week I will endeavour to answer it.

MR. HENNIKER HEATON said, the Question was one which could be answered in half-an-hour.

IRELAND—BELFAST—STRIKE OF SHIPWRIGHTS.

MR. M'CARTAN (Down, S.) (for Mr. SEXTON) (Belfast, W.) asked the Chief Secretary to the Lord Lieutenant of Ireland, If he will obtain from the Constabulary in Belfast, and communicate to the House, and report on the cause and extent of the existing strike among the shipyard *employés*, and the probable effect of its prolonged duration upon the peace and order of the town? In connection with the Question, I would also ask, whether the right hon. Gentleman is not aware that there appeared in the Belfast morning papers of yesterday a letter from Mr. M'Blain, member of a large shipbuilding firm, in which he states that 19-20ths of the workmen at present on strike are sober, industrious, and regular in their hours of work, and that it is a serious grievance to them not to receive their wages weekly?

THE PARLIAMENTARY UNDER SECRETARY (Colonel KING-HARMAN) (Kent, Isle of Thanet) (who replied) said: Sir, I have not seen the letter referred to. With regard to the Question on the Paper, it appears that the only subject in dispute is a demand on the part of the workmen to be paid their wages weekly instead of fortnightly, as at present. There are about 6,000 workmen concerned in the movement.

POST OFFICE—CONVEYANCE OF FOREIGN AND COLONIAL MAILS, 1866.

MR. HENNIKER HEATON (Canterbury) asked the Postmaster General, The estimated amount of money received as postage in England for the conveyance of Foreign and Colonial Mails during the year 1866?

THE POSTMASTER GENERAL (Mr. RAIKES) (Cambridge University): There are no records from which an answer to the hon. Member's Question could be framed.

MR. HENNIKER HEATON gave Notice that on the Estimates he would call attention to the Post Office scandal, that no accounts were kept of the money thus received.

MR. T. C. HARRINGTON (Dublin, Harbour) asked whether, in view of the answer of the Postmaster General, the Goverment intended to appoint an assistant Posmaster General?

MR. SPEAKER: Order, order!

Subsequently,

MR. HENNIKER HEATON explained that, by a curious error, 1866 had been printed in his last Question instead of 1886.

MR. RAIKES said, he had answered the Question on the Paper to the best of his ability. If the hon. Gentleman wished to give Notice of another Question he should be happy to answer it.

THE MAGISTRACY (IRELAND) — THE AHADILLANE BENCH OF MAGISTRATES.

DR. TANNER (Cork Co., Mid) asked Mr. Attorney General for Ireland, Whether two emergency men, named respectively Daniel Falvey and Timothy Buckley, were brought before the Ahadillane Bench of Magistrates, Captain Stokes, R.M., presiding, on last Wednesday, the 27th April, and charged with attacking the dwelling house of a farmer, named Edmond Twohig, at Donoughmore, on the 25th of last March; whether the charge was substantiated by several witnesses; whether it was also sworn that Buckley, on the occasion in question, drew a revolver, and Falvey called on him to fire upon Twohig and his young daughters; whether, notwithstanding the evidence adduced, Captain Stokes, R.M., although stating "the outrage should not have been committed," refused to send the case forward for trial; whether the other magistrate, Mr. Charles Lynch, disagreed with this decision, saying, "that such downright blackguardism should not go unpunished; whether the

emergency man Falvey was confined in the Upton Reformatory for five years for breaking into a dwelling house; and, whether he will call the attention of the Lord Chancellor to the case?

THE ATTORNEY GENERAL FOR IRELAND (Mr. HOLMES) (Dublin University), in reply, said, the information he possessed did not bear out the statements made by the hon. Gentleman in his Question.

DR. TANNER: May I ask the right hon. and learned Gentleman, whether the words I have put down in the Question as being used by the magistrates which were reported in the local newspapers are not absolutely correct; and, whether, again, it was not sworn by two or three witnesses that this man Buckley drew a revolver, and that Falvey called to fire upon Twohig and his two young daughters? I will ask the right hon. and learned Gentleman also a point which I inserted in the Question; but which I find has been removed from the Paper——

MR. SPEAKER: Order, order! The hon. Gentleman is, therefore, not entitled to ask it.

MR. HOLMES said, he was informed that there was no truth in the story, and he could only repeat what he had previously stated. In regard to much of what the hon. Member observed he had no information.

DR. TANNER: Of course, I shall repeat this Question.

ROYAL IRISH CONSTABULARY—BOYCOTTING AND INTIMIDATION—RETURNS BY THE POLICE.

DR. TANNER (Cork Co., Mid) asked the Chief Secretary to the Lord Lieutenant of Ireland, whether it is true, as reported, that the Hon. Captain Plunkett has addressed a Circular Letter to the County Inspectors and District Inspectors of Constabulary in his Division, requiring lists of Boycotting and intimidation cases in their respective commands since last September, with mention of what evidence would be available in the event of it being decided to institute prosecutions in individual instances; and, whether Captain Plunkett is acting on orders received from the Executive in issuing the alleged Circular; and, if so, what was the date of its issue?

THE PARLIAMENTARY UNDER SECRETARY (Colonel KING-HARMAN) (Kent, Isle of Thanet) (who replied) said: No such Return as the one alluded to has been called for by Captain Plunkett, so far as the Executive are aware of. It has been the practice for a considerable time past for the Divisional Magistrate to submit to Government monthly Returns of persons "Boycotted," and other matters affecting the peace of their districts. This is probably the origin of the newspaper paragraph, which the Government believe to be in all other respects without foundation.

CIVIL SERVICE WRITERS—THE BONUS SCHEME.

SIR SAMUEL WILSON (Portsmouth) asked Mr. Chancellor of the Exchequer, Why the services of Civil Service writers, previous to 1870, are not to be allowed to count under the recent Bonus Scheme, for increase of pay, the same as allowed to clerks and all other Civil servants; and, whether the Treasury will re-consider the question, so that all the actual services of the Civil Service writers may be duly recognised?

THE CHANCELLOR OF THE EXCHEQUER (Mr. GOSCHEN) (St. George's, Hanover square): The Minute of the Treasury of December last, to which the hon. Member refers, related only to copyists upon the General Register of the Civil Service Commissioners. This General Register created a new class of copyists, and the Minute, therefore, only refers to service rendered in that class of copyists, and not to possible antecedent service in some other capacity. No circumstances have been brought to my notice which make me think it necessary to re-consider the Minute.

LAW AND POLICE — PERSONAL SEARCHES BY THE POLICE.

MR. PICKARD (York, W.R., Normanton) asked the Secretary of State for the Home Department, Whether he has made inquiry into the case of the police searching the men and boys at the Hoyland Silkstone Colliery, Yorkshire, as reported in *The Barnsley Independent* of April 2nd; and, if so, whether he will state under what legal authority the police acted in searching the persons of these men and boys?

THE UNDER SECRETARY OF STATE (Mr. STUART-WORTLEY) (Sheffield, Hallam) (who replied) said: The Secretary of State has obtained a Report from the Chief Constable on the subject, who informs him that in consequence of an application received from the official liquidator of the colliery three sergeants and one constable were sent to the pit, a breach of the peace being anticipated, while search was made among the men for percussion caps. This search was instituted in consequence of a pistol loaded with powder and ball, but without percussion cap, having been found under suspicious circumstances, after violence and threats had been used by some of the men against the underviewer, in a corf of dirt which had been brought from the pit. The Secretary of State understands that the police were only present, while the search itself was conducted under the personal direction of the manager, who considered that he had the right to make it under the Rules of the colliery, and it was made purely out of consideration for the safety of the miners, the pit being liable to fire. The Secretary of State does not see that anything was done to call for his interference.

LAW AND POLICE—THE SALVATION ARMY.

MR. T. D. BOLTON (Derbyshire, N.E.) asked the Secretary of State for the Home Department, Whether his attention has been called to the case of five members of the Salvation Army, who have been sentenced to seven days' imprisonment for holding a meeting at Eckington in Derbyshire, this being the first occasion upon which they had appeared before the magistrates; whether information has reached him that one of the prisoners, the captain of the Army, is in a very bad state of health, and will be seriously injured by his imprisonment; and, whether he will inquire into the case with a view to a remission of the sentence?

THE UNDER SECRETARY OF STATE (Mr. STUART-WORTLEY) (Sheffield, Hallam) (who replied) said: The Secretary of State has telegraphed for information as to the facts of this case, and has also sent for a Medical Report from the prison authorities. The latter has just come by telegraph, and states that—

" One of the Salvation Army men is not robust, but is not ill, and not likely to suffer from the short imprisonment ; " and that the " rest are in good health."

INTERMEDIATE EDUCATION BILL FOR WALES—CHARGE OF £300,000.

MR. RICHARD (Merthyr Tydvil) asked the First Lord of the Treasury, Whether the Intermediate Education Bill for Wales, which has been introduced by the hon. Member for the Denbigh Boroughs (Mr. Kenyon), has been introduced with the sanction or approval of Her Majesty's Government ; and, whether the proposal it contains for charging a sum of £300,000 on the Consolidated Fund has been made with any understanding that it will be favourably considered by Her Majesty's Government?

THE FIRST LORD (Mr. W. H. SMITH) (Strand, Westminster): The Bill has been prepared on the sole responsibility of the hon. Members whose names are on the back of the Bill ; and while Her Majesty's Government have great sympathy with the object sought to be promoted by those hon. Members, they have not yet considered the provisions of the measure, nor have they any information as to the extent to which it is supported by hon. Members for Wales. It must be obvious that no understanding exists as to the proposed grant of public money.

BUSINESS OF THE HOUSE—COAL MINES REGULATION BILL.

In reply to Sir JOHN SWINBURN (Staffordshire, Lichfield),

THE FIRST LORD OF THE TREASURY (Mr. W. H. SMITH) (Strand, Westminster) said, that under the conditions in which they were now placed with respect to Public Business, it was impossible for him to name a day for the Committee stage of the Coal Mines Regulation Bill.

ORDERS OF THE DAY.

PRIVILEGE (MR. DILLON AND "THE TIMES" NEWSPAPER).—RESOLUTION.

ADJOURNED DEBATE. [THIRD NIGHT.]

Order read, for resuming Adjourned Debate on Amendment proposed to Question [3rd May],

" That the publication in *The Times* newspaper of the 2nd of May, of the article headed ' Parnellism and Crime,' constitutes a Breach of the Privileges of this House."—(*Sir Charles Lewis.*)

And which Amendment was,

To leave out from the word "That" to the end of the Question, in order to add the words " this House declines to treat the publication of the article headed ' Parnellism and Crime ' in *The Times* of the 2nd of May as a Breach of the Privileges of this House,"—(*Mr. Solicitor General,*)

—instead thereof.

Question put, "That the words proposed to be left out stand part of the Question."

The House *divided*:—Ayes 218 ; Noes 297 : Majority 79,—(Div. List, No. 110.)

Question proposed,

" That the words ' this House declines to treat the publication of the article headed " Parnellism and Crime " in *The Times* of the 2nd of May as a Breach of the Privileges of this House ' be there added."

MR. BRADLAUGH (Northampton): The Motion which stood before the House a few minutes ago, asks the House to declare the article published and circulated amongst the Members to be an article which, in the opinion of this House, constituted a Breach of Privilege. The House has decided to omit those words ; but it has not yet expressed any opinion as to whether or not the article in question does constitute a Breach of Privilege. Curiously enough, the House is not even asked by the Government to declare any such opinion. It is only asked to abstain from expressing an opinion. The Amendment which has been moved by the hon. and learned Solicitor General is an Amendment which asks the House to decline to treat the publication of the article headed " Parnellism and Crime " as a Breach of the Privileges of this House. It is, to say the least, curious that the Government have not taken upon themselves the responsibility of facing what is the real issue, and that it should seek to evade a declaration upon this grave matter by simply asking the House to decline to express an opinion. I can understand why the House is merely asked to "decline." It is because every precedent which could have been brought before the House would be to the effect that such an article as the one we have before us has always been held to be a

[*Third Night.*]

Breach of the Privileges of this House whenever the House has been asked to express an opinion upon it. There are cases, which I will deal with presently, in which the House has refrained from expressing any opinion at all. But it is for the Government to say why it is that they now ask the House to "decline." I am in a position of some difficulty, because I find myself obliged, respectfully, to disagree with the First Lord of the Treasury and the Government as to what are the precedents, and I think I shall be borne out by the highest authorities in this House. I also feel some difficulty in finding myself bound to differ from the hon. and learned Solicitor General both as to law and precedent. When I come to examine them I hope the House will not think me impertinent in that remark. The question is one which I have been compelled to consider during the last six years, and I have had exceptional opportunities of studying it afforded to me. I have heard many views on the subject, both accurate and inaccurate. I have been subjected personally to the criticisms of the Lord Chancellor, the late Lord Chancellor and the right hon. and learned Gentleman the Member for Bury (Sir Henry James), and if I err to-night it will not be from want of reflection in the opinion I am about to express. I have had the additional advantage of hearing some of the doctrines propounded by legal tribunals within this House which have a right to express an opinion. Now, the first question which I propose to ask the House is— What kind of libels have been repeatedly treated by the House as Breaches of Privilege? The matter is shortly stated, in very much better words than I could employ, by the late Sir Erskine May, who says in his book, at page 100—

"Libels upon Members have been constantly punished, but to constitute a Breach of Privilege they must concern the character or conduct of Members in that capacity."

If the article we have to consider does not come within that definition it is utterly impossible that anything could. It is a direct imputation— a grave imputation, if not true—and one of the most scandalous imputations it is possible to conceive against the character and conduct of one Member specially named and of a number of other Members associated with him, as being parties guilty of deliberate falsehood,

Mr. Bradlaugh

with intent to deceive this House during its debates. I will only quote one sentence from the article itself. It says—

"We have examined an elaborate explanation made by one of the most respected of Mr. Parnell's lieutenants from his place in Parliament, and we have shown that it is a tissue of gross and palpable falsehoods."

If that stood alone, surely it is a Breach of Privilege. But the article goes on to say—

"Mr. Dillon either refrained from all serious efforts of recollection and inquiry, and recklessly palmed off upon the House, as ascertained facts within his personal knowledge, a mass of confused, inaccurate, and unexamined memories, or he deliberately told the House a detailed story which he knew to be untrue. In either case, several of his Colleagues must have known that his statements were unfounded. The Party sat exulting by and endorsed the fabrication."

If this be not a Breach of the Privileges of this House, it is utterly impossible to conceive any kind of article which can constitute such a Breach of Privilege. It is perfectly true that the First Lord of the Treasury has committed himself to the statement, that it is not sustained by precedent that such a matter as this constitutes a Breach of Privilege. I have, at various times, had occasion carefully to examine every precedent. Lest I might have failed in my memory I went through the whole of them again last night, having advantage of the brief I used against the right hon. and learned Gentleman the Member for Bury when I last had an opportunity of discussing the question for some days with him, and I can find no such precedent. I do not believe, and I say it with all respect to the First Lord of the Treasury, that any such precedent exists. I am sure he has spoken what he believes; but I think he has been deceived by those who have not paid the close attention to precedents that they ought to have done. I am corroborated in this, if corroboration were needful, by the very high authority of the late Leader of the House, who last night expressed himself more distinctly than I should like to do, and with more emphasis than I dare use. The noble Lord the Member for South Paddington (Lord Randolph Churchill) said, that from a technical point of view, no sane or reasonable person would say that in this case there has not been a Breach of Privileges of the House. Of course, the noble Lord is better acquainted with his Colleagues than I am, and has a better right to express an opinion upon their sanity or reasonableness than I can possibly have. The noble Lord may think there is some meaning in the word "technical." [Lord RANDOLPH CHURCH-HILL (Paddington, S.): Yes.] Then the noble Lord thinks it is possible to charge a man with being a murderer "technically," with being a liar "technically," and that it is possible to charge a number of persons with wilfully endorsing a deliberate falsehood for the purpose of deceiving the House "technically." I do not doubt that the noble Lord is a better judge of technicalities than I am myself. I only understand the ordinary English applicable to a matter of this kind. My experience — an experience which the noble Lord did much to help me to, and for which I shall be ever grateful—does not enable me to understand the introduction of the word "technical" by an English Gentleman into the discussion of a question of this kind. Assuming that it is impossible to deny that this is a Breach of the Privileges of this House, is there sufficient reason for the House to shrink from treating it as such? The First Lord of the Treasury says there is. The reason why he asks the House to decline to say whether or not this is a Breach of Privilege, is because he says the Government have proposed an alternative for an expression of opinion by the House—namely, that there shall be an inquiry into this matter, conducted by the Attorney General, assisted by some Queen's Counsel, which inquiry shall assume the form of a criminal prosecution against the publisher of _The Times_. I do not know whether the right hon. Gentleman has considered that such a course would give an express advantage to the publisher of _The Times_ and put the hon. Member for East Mayo (Mr. Dillon) to a distinct disadvantage. I am glad to see the Attorney General in his place, because he, at any rate, will appreciate the point I am about to submit. If the Amendment of the Solicitor General is carried, it could be given in evidence on the trial of the indictment against the publisher of _The Times_, to show that for some reason, which may or may not be given, the House has declined to consider this grave and scandalous charge and infamous imputation a Breach of Privilege, and the jury would be influenced by that—influenced

to the extent of disagreeing; influenced to the extent of giving the defendant the benefit of the doubt, which every counsel claims for his client in a criminal proceeding. If this were a cunningly invented device for influencing the jury—which I am sure it is not—it could not have been more adroitly contrived. If the Government had used the weight of their authority and of those who will follow them into the Lobby to declare these articles a Breach of Privilege, then their proposal would have been a logical one, and it would have been proper to come to the House for the direction of the Attorney General to prosecute the person who in the opinion of the House has been guilty of a gross Breach of Privilege, by publishing abominable and scandalous charges which are not true, and ought to be punished with a heavier punishment than the House could inflict by a mere fine or sessional imprisonment. It is well known that this newspaper has been industriously engaged for some weeks in circulating a tissue of statements with the view of influencing the passing of a particular Bill rather than the advancement of any matter of truth. If I were to judge matters by what is happening outside the House, I should be inclined to think that the Government do desire to influence the jury; because I find hon. Gentlemen who vote with them, and over whom they have influence, in their addresses to the country, using language which must certainly reach the ears of all who are likely to be jurymen, to excite a prejudice which must tell against the Members of the Irish Party and in favour of the publisher of _The Times_ whenever the matter is submitted to the consideration of a jury. In his speech yesterday, the Solicitor General used some words, which I will trouble the House with for a moment. The hon. and learned Gentleman said—

" We are bound, when a question of this kind arises, to address ourselves to it with reference strictly to legal considerations."

I understood the hon. and learned Gentleman to say that he said that, after consultation with his hon. and learned Colleague the Attorney General—[The SOLICITOR GENERAL (Sir Edward Clarke) (Plymouth) assented.] I am right in that. Why, then, did not two such acute men as himself and the Attorney General advise the Government that

⌊ _Third Night._ ⌋

they were putting *The Times* in a position of advantage, because, legally, this Resolution could be given in evidence before a jury? [The ATTORNEY GENERAL (Sir Richard Webster) (Isle of Wight) dissented.] Surely the hon. and learned Gentleman does not remember the proceedings commenced in the name of the Attorney General against the junior Member for Northampton, in which a whole bundle of Resolutions of the House were admitted in evidence in a Trial at Bar on a criminal information, and pressed, despite the objection of the defendant in that case that they were not admissible in evidence against him. They not only formed part of the proceedings, but in summing up to the jury, the Court sitting at Bar, and not with a single Judge—the Court, composed of three Judges of high eminence—commented upon the fact. I am not aware that there is any possible distinction to be drawn between a Trial at Bar and a trial on criminal information in the High Court of Justice, or the Central Criminal Court on indictment. I challenge the Attorney General to show that there is a shadow of ground for any such distinction. Then, if the Law Officers knew this, a grave responsibility rests upon them. I do not wish to use hard words, for I am assured of the high honour and ability of the hon. and learned Gentlemen; but it looks as if they have neglected that consideration for Party purposes, so that the Government might not be defeated in this crisis—a crisis which they have themselves provoked by the persistent course of circulating these very libels in their own speeches, so that a verdict against *The Times* would mean a verdict against nearly every individual Member of the Government as well. It would not only be a verdict against *The Times*, but, to adopt the words of the noble Lord the Member for South Paddington, it would be "technically" to condemn the Government. Another reason given by the Solicitor General for not treating this as a question of Privilege is one in which I find myself utterly in disagreement with the hon. and learned Gentleman, so utterly in disagreement that I must read his words, for fear of misrepresenting him. The Solicitor General said that he had not had time to examine the long range of precedents which

had been referred to, but that he had done his best. He then proceeded to say—

"I have not found, and I do not believe anyone can find, an instance of the House of Commons exercising this power of punishment by committal to prison of a person for an accusation made by him against a Member of the House of Commons which was not directly an accusation of corruption or a misfeasance in a vote given, or which was not an attempt to coerce and intimidate him in his actions in the House of Commons."

Well, I would undertake to find at least a dozen. I will, however, only give one, an old and well-known precedent, because I am afraid that I shall exhaust the patience of the House long before I have done with this matter. I am surprised that the Solicitor General should not have found a precedent, because he has mentioned the case of "Burdett *v.* Abbott," a case which I had the honour to hear quoted by the right hon. and learned Gentleman the Member for Bury, some half-a-dozen times or so, when I was before a Court. It will be found reported in the 14th volume of *East's Reports*, in which every precedent bearing upon this question down to the year 1811 has been carefully collected. I do not know whether the hon. and learned Attorney General, or those who hold consultation with the Solicitor General about precedents, went back beyond 1811; but I may say that precedents from thence to 1839, including that of "Burdett *v.* Abbott," were re-collected in the case of "Stockdale *v.* Hansard," which will be found in 9 "Adolphus and Ellis." I have those precedents here, and none of them bear out the contention of the hon. and learned Solicitor General. I will give one which annihilates his contention completely. The hon. and learned Solicitor General has dealt with the case of Sir Francis Burdett. I excuse the hon. and learned Gentleman's ignorance, especially from the short time he has had to study the matter, but he might have had the advantage of the assistance of a number of legal Gentlemen who are at present Members of this House. Undoubtedly he would have had more complete information if he had had an opportunity of studying the matter from the same point of view as I have had myself. The hon. and learned Gentleman, I say, referred to the case of Sir Francis Burdett. Now Sir Francis Burdett was

Mr. Bradlaugh

voted guilty of a Breach of Privilege as the author of an address to his constituents, and of an article in *Cobbett's Register*. I do not intend to weary the House by quoting these papers at length. Hon. Members will find them verbatim in the 16th volume of *Hansard's* 1st series, pages 138 to 173. That libel was declared to be a gross Breach of the Privileges of this House. Sir Francis Burdett was committed to prison for its publication, and Lord Ellenborough, in the Court of Queen's Bench, held that Sir Francis Burdett had been properly found guilty, but neither his address to his constituents, nor the article in *Cobbett's Register* contained one solitary ingredient of those which the hon. and learned Solicitor General had said is specifically necessary before the House would commit anyone to prison. If we had not had the hon. and learned Solicitor General's assurance that he had consulted his hon. and learned Colleague, and that they had both carefully reflected upon the matter, one might have thought that they had been content with some more modern edition of a work on Privilege, and had not troubled themselves to go into any of these matters at all. What does the hon. and learned Solicitor General say the ingredients are that are necessary before this House declares that there has been a Breach of Privilege? In the first place, there must be a direct accusation of corruption; that is not the case in this instance. Secondly, an accusation of misfeasance in giving a vote; that does not exist here. Thirdly, an attempt to intimidate or coerce the House; that is not here. There never was a more careful—there probably could not be a more learned—paper than that which was issued in the name of Sir Francis Burdett. I do not mean to imply that it was not his own composition; but the noble Lord knows how often he himself has to rely on matters which are searched out for him. It is a careful argument by Sir Francis Burdett against the power of the House to commit to prison Mr. John Gale Jones, who was declared by the House to have been guilty of contempt towards it. There is not a suggestion that the House acted corruptly; nor is there a suggestion that any Member of the House voted corruptly. There is no allegation of any unfair grounds or motives—no

suggestion of intimidation or coercion. Every one of the ingredients which the hon. and learned Solicitor General specifically named are wanting in this case. If the exigencies of debate permitted, I would undertake to quote precedents by the dozen; but I maintain that one unanswered case is as good as a dozen when the allegations which have been made are so completely disposed of. I do not deny that the House has a perfect right to do what the Government now asks it to do—namely, to decline to deal with the matter, and to decline to express an opinion on it, even though it be a Breach of Privilege. But I would submit respectfully to the House that the class of cases in which the House has so declined is a class of cases to none of which does this belong. The House has sometimes declined when the case has been too trivial to be dealt with as a Breach of Privilege, and it has more than once declined when it has known that the charge has been withdrawn and apologized for. Ferrand's case was referred to by the hon. and learned Solicitor General. In that case, the person accused declined to substantiate his charges, and the House was of opinion that the charges were totally unfounded and calumnious, but that they did not affect in the slightest degree the character of any Member of the House. Do any of those circumstances apply to this case? I do not see how the hon. and learned Solicitor General, in dealing with Ferrand's case, could have felt its applicability, seeing that it was dismissed as a calumnious matter. In this case, there can be no pretence that the charges can be dismissed as trivial; and, secondly, the accuser in this case does not decline to substantiate the charges. As far as I understand, the publisher of *The Times* says—"I am ready to substantiate my charges, and I want an opportunity of substantiating them." [*Cries of "*Hear, hear!" *from the Ministerial Benches.*] "Hear, hear!" hon. Members opposite say. They agree to that; then Ferrand's case does not apply to this case. The hon. and learned Solicitor General has quoted, in the course of his very able speech, cases as precedents for the course the Government propose to take. The hon. and learned Gentleman said—

"The junior Member for Northampton, in the last Parliament but one, was ordered by the House to be prosecuted, notwithstanding the fact that the Government had taken his part in the proceedings that led to the prosecution; and it was felt that the hon. Member for Bury, who had been supporting the hon. Member for Northampton in his action, ought not alone to conduct that prosecution; and, accordingly, the present Lord Chancellor, then sitting on the Front Opposition Bench, was associated with him in the conduct of the case, and took a very active and diligent part in the framing of the indictment and in the subsequent proceedings."

I think I remember, when I had the pleasure of sitting over there (pointing to the Benches beneath the Gallery) seeing the hon. and learned Solicitor General in his place listening to the debate which then occurred; and he must be aware that it was suggested by Members of his own Party that a prosecution conducted against myself by the right hon. and learned Member for Bury might be a collusive prosecution.

SIR EDWARD CLARKE: No.

MR. BRADLAUGH: Will the noble Lord the Member for South Paddington say no?

LORD RANDOLPH CHURCHILL (Paddington, S.): Certainly.

MR. BRADLAUGH: I thought the noble Lord would. I have refreshed my memory on this matter, and I propose to read to the House the exact words of the noble Lord, which, I think, will justify the statement I have just made. In vol. 284 of *Hansard*, page 659, the following words occur in the speech of the noble Lord the Member for South Paddington:—

"There is no doubt that the Attorney General will be instructed by the Government to commence a more or less friendly and collusive action against Mr. Bradlaugh."

The noble Lord not only suspected the honour of the right hon. and learned Member for Bury, but he absolutely suggested that even a Court of Law might not be fair. Now, let me say that in the series of conflicts in which I have been engaged, I never allowed myself to make any such suggestion, nor has anything ever occurred in my life to justify me in making such a suggestion against any Law Officer of the Crown. But, Sir, not only did the noble Lord the Member for South Paddington say that —and those who are sitting round him cheered the statement—but he absolutely suggested that the Court itself might not be fair. The noble Lord expressly selected, in one speech, the Lord

Chief Justice of all England, and said that the political views of that Judge expressed themselves too much in his judgment. I see the noble Lord does not say anything as to that. If he did, I would refer to *Hansard*, vol. 278, page 479, in which the noble Lord suggested that a Court might be biased on other considerations than the evidence before it. That is in *Hansard*.

LORD RANDOLPH CHURCHILL: I am not responsible for *Hansard*.

MR. BRADLAUGH: I myself have not the same knowledge of "technicalities" as the noble Lord possesses; but I certainly should not have permitted myself, even inside or outside of this House, to have made such a suggestion. I am quoting from *Hansard*, where the noble Lord objects to proceedings against me in a Court of Law, on the ground that even Courts of Law might be biased by "the demonstrations in my favour." [Lord RANDOLPH CHURCHILL dissented.] The noble Lord shakes his head; but again I say it is in *Hansard*. In order that there might be no doubt on the matter, I obtained the speech of the noble Lord from the Library when I entered the House. But that is not all. So much did the noble Lord feel that our highest Courts of Justice might be corruptly influenced, that he permitted one-third of the Party he then led to rise in its place in this House and challenge the composition of the Court which was to try me on an information by the Attorney General, the verdict carrying with it the collateral consequence of an offence that was a misdemeanour. Upon that issue the noble Lord permitted an appeal to be made to the Government that one Judge should not be allowed to sit on the trial. That appeal was made in the noble Lord's presence without one word of objection from him. On the contrary, immediately afterwards the noble Lord made an appeal to the Government to know whether the Judges who took part in the trial were to include any more ex-Liberal Attorney Generals. [Lord RANDOLPH CHURCHILL nodded.] Just so; but it appeared that in 1884 the noble Lord was of opinion that a Court of Law was not a fair tribunal. [Lord RANDOLPH CHURCHILL dissented.] Perhaps it may not be quite correct to say that the noble Lord was of that opinion. I am always ready to be corrected by the noble Lord. He was

Mr. Bradlaugh

not of that opinion. He only said so. It was probably only a technical difference, which I trust the House will excuse my pressing. Now, every prosecution by the Attorney General might have been a collusive proceeding in 1884. What has occurred to prevent it from being less possible that it might be a collusive proceeding now? The proceedings in 1884 were only aimed at making one humble individual a bankrupt; but in this case the Court would have to deal with a charge of murder against certain hon. Members, because an accessory before the fact is guilty of murder. Does the noble Lord think that that is a technical distinction? I hope the noble Lord will appreciate the point. An accessory before the fact in a case of murder is guilty of murder himself, and an accessory after the fact is not much less guilty. Will you put these proceedings into the hands of the Attorney General, who, you say, may be influenced by political considerations, having regard to the fact that upon the result of these proceedings the fate of the Government would depend? You have used the Parnell letter; you have used these charges against Mr. Dillon and others in order to win votes at elections and to stimulate the flagging spirits of the Liberal Unionists; and right hon. Gentlemen and noble Lords have thought it right to appeal to these charges as grounds for deciding an issue with which they have had no connection. I regret to have occupied the time of the House so long. I only wish to make one further remark in argument, now that I have disposed of the facts of the noble Lord the Member for South Paddington. The noble Lord, in his speech to the House last night, stated what he considered to be the only difference between Gentlemen sitting upon this side of the House and Gentlemen sitting upon that side. He said—" The sole difference which separates us is as to the form of the inquiry." Now, what are the two forms of inquiry? They are inquiry by law, and inquiry by a Select Committee of this House. The noble Lord, in 1884, was against inquiry by a Court of Law, he is now for it. He was in favour of an inquiry by a Committee of this House—[Lord RANDOLPH CHURCHILL dissented.] The noble Lord shakes his head. I often sympathize with the noble Lord. I am perfectly sure of his thorough accuracy; but I often

think he must forget the matter which has been prepared for him by other hands. Now, the speech to which I wish to refer was only delivered some 16 days ago. I admit that, to the noble Lord, 16 days is a very long time indeed; but during those 16 days something may have happened showing a glimmering of an opening which before seemed closed, and which may have induced him to see matters in a different light. The noble Lord, with that freedom of speech which always characterizes him, and which I can only try painfully to imitate on occasions when I have to reply to him—the noble Lord, speaking at Nottingham, if he is correctly reported, and I am convinced he is, although he may say there is the same blunder which has crept into the reports of *Hansard*—the noble Lord the Member for South Paddington, speaking at Nottingham about the accusations against the Irish Members, was generous enough to say that he made himself no party to them. That was the act of a loyal man; but he spoilt it later on by advising his audience to buy the pamphlet. It was not enough to say that he would make himself no party to the accusation; but he went on directly afterwards to point out where it is, how it is to be got, and what the facilities are for obtaining it. The noble Lord is reported in *The Times* to have said—

" Now, are we to give over the government of Ireland? How can we abstain from suppressing the authority in Ireland of these men who are accused of such crimes and such criminal practices, and who are unable to prove their innocence? I make myself no party to these accusations. All I say is that they are brought. I leave the matter there. I do not know that it will rest there. It may be necessary even for the House of Commons, independently of the Irish Party, to take action and to endeavour on its own independent authority to clear the House of Commons as a body from the charges against a section of the House of Commons which undoubtedly must reach upon the character of the whole House of Commons. But upon that point I say nothing. I have brought it before you, I advise you to buy this pamphlet, and read it and circulate it."

LORD RANDOLPH CHURCHILL: I hope the hon. Member will pardon me for interrupting him; but the hon. Member is quite mistaken in saying that I was for the Committee and against the Court 16 days ago, and I must point out that almost the entire portion of my speech which was devoted to this matter was taken up with trying to prove that the only course open to the Irish Members was a resort either to an English, Irish, or Scotch Court of Law. I certainly did allude to the possibility of the House of Commons taking some action, but that was only thrown out as a possible *ultima ratio.*

Mr. BRADLAUGH: The noble Lord need not fear that I shall be offended by his interrupting me. When I have had the same training as the right hon. and learned Member for Bury, I shall probably get used to the noble Lord's regard for technicalities, and the very strong view he takes for himself. I may say at once that it is not the views of the noble Lord which I am dealing with. I do not know what they may be; I am only dealing with the noble Lord's words. I have taken the sentence as reported in *The Times.* I have taken a complete sentence; I have introduced nothing into it, and if the noble Lord did not mean what he said, it is a pity he said it. I thought I had expressed myself very clearly when I said that a few days ago the noble Lord was in favour of a Select Committee. I did not say that 16 days ago, he was in favour of a Committee as against a Court of Law. What I say is that the noble Lord, as reported in *Hansard*, was against a Court of Law in 1884, and in favour of a Committee 16 days ago. I read a passage from the speech of the noble Lord in which he expresses a strong opinion that there should be an independent inquiry in a Committee of the House of Commons on its own Motion. I do not know whether, technically, I am right or not; but the noble Lord certainly intimated that in his opinion it might be necessary for the House of Commons to institute an inquiry altogether independent of the views of the Irish Members. Am I to understand from the noble Lord that his words do not mean what they say? If, in the mind of the noble Lord, they have some other meaning, I shall be glad to accept it, and I should then know how to deal with his views as well as with his words. I am afraid that I have trespassed too long on the time of the House. I only desire, speaking now for a large number of earnest Radicals outside this House, who are pained and grieved beyond measure by these shocking measures which are being used as political weapons, and resorted to by every suppor-

ter of the Government, to state what the view is which they take of this matter. It is an absurd suggestion that the Attorney General, who, in this House, has voted that the charges constitute a grave and scandalous libel, and although they embody the foulest charges which can be made against a Member of Parliament, should go into a Court of Law and ask English jurymen to declare by their verdict that what he has said by his vote is not true.

Lord RANDOLPH CHURCHILL: I did not wish to interrupt the hon. Gentleman while he was addressing the House, but I hope the House will permit me to make a personal explanation. The hon. Gentleman has quoted remarks of mine out of *Hansard*, which I am alleged to have made in 1884. Now, at that time, my speeches were greatly compressed by *Hansard*—["Oh, oh!"]— as is invariably the case with private Members of Parliament. I appeal with confidence to hon. Members who have personal experience of the fact that the speeches of private Members are not fully reported, whether a report thus condensed and compressed, as is usual in *Hansard*, can be taken as a true and faithful representation of what one has really said. Right hon. Members are hardly in a position to judge of that matter, seeing that their speeches are generally reported verbatim. But I must also point out that the quotations that have been made do not in the least apply to my present position in the matter now under the consideration of the House. I never thought, or even dreamt, and I will call the right hon. and learned Gentleman as a witness, of saying that the right hon. and learned Member for Bury, who was Attorney General at the time referred to, could be capable of collusion in an action at law. What I meant to point out was that the course which the Government proposed to take would render them open to the charge of collusion. [*Cries of* "Oh!" *and* "Order!"] I am entitled to make a personal explanation. It is very odd that hon. Gentlemen opposite are ready to hear everything that is said against me, but object to receive any explanation, and that their sense of justice—["*Cries of* "Go on!"] What I wish to point out now is, that the Government of that day, in consequence of the representation of some hon. Mem-

Lord Randolph Churchill

bers who sat below the Gangway, associated in the case of a Queen's Counsel belonging to the Party opposed to them, in order to obviate any such accusation as I pointed to as possible. Consequently, the action of the Government of that day, taken, as it was, after representations had been made to them, formed a precedent for the course which the Government of the present day are following.

MR. BRADLAUGH: May I ask for the indulgence of the House in order that I may say that I quite accept the explanation of the noble Lord, and I can corroborate his statements as to the compression of his speeches; because I once unguardedly used an expression which I heard from his lips, but which I could not find in *Hansard* when I went to look for it. Therefore I am perfectly sure that he is correct in that remark; the only difficulty I have is to imagine how any process of compression could have put words on record which were never spoken.

SIR WILLIAM HARCOURT (Derby): I have no desire to trespass on the time of the House, except for a few minutes. I wish to make a few remarks with reference to a statement made by the hon. and learned Solicitor General yesterday. I can only account for that statement on the ground of the extraordinary brief time—to refer to his brief plea—which he had at his disposal for examining into the Question before the House. A statement more inconsistent with the real facts of the cases to which he referred it would be impossible to conceive. The First Lord of the Treasury stated very positively that in his opinion these words in *The Times* were not a Breach of Privilege, and the hon. and learned Solicitor General rose to support, in an elaborate argument, the doctrine altogether new to me, in a broadly stated proposition that the words contained in *The Times* article are not a Breach of Privilege. He cited a speech of mine in support of that view. Now, that speech, so far from making any such allegation, had a precisely contrary effect. I said from the first to the last that the proceedings of Mr. Pilmsoll, to whose case the hon. and learned Gentleman referred, did constitute a Breach of the Privileges of this House. I stated that in the most distinct manner; therefore all that the hon. and learned Solicitor General said

upon that point falls to the ground. I can only presume that he had not had time to read the books from which he professed to quote; but as, in this matter, it is important that there should be no misunderstanding, I will read what I did say in answer to the Attorney General of that day (Sir John Holker). I said—

" For anyone to take any notice whatever of the conduct of a Member of Parliament in the discharge of his duty in the House, or to comment in any terms whatever upon such conduct, or upon his speeches or votes in the House, is a Breach of Privilege."

Therefore, to assert that I argued that the words complained of in Mr. Plimsoll's case were not a Breach of Privilege is to assert exactly the opposite of what I really did say. Let me say, in a few words, that the case of Mr. Plimsoll was this. He had used words attributing inhuman conduct to a Member who had blocked a Bill in which we all know he was much interested. The case was brought before the House as a Breach of Privilege, and Mr. Plimsoll apologized for his conduct. I contended, and I was supported by the noble Marquess the Member for Rossendale (the Marquess of Hartington), then the Leader of the Opposition, by the right hon. Gentleman the senior Member for Birmingham (Mr. John Bright), and by the whole Opposition—I contended not that it was a Breach of Privilege, but that, as Mr. Plimsoll had made amends to the House, the matter should not be proceeded with further, and I moved the Previous Question, which was an admission that the case was a Breach of Privilege. Therefore anything more contrary to the representation of the hon. and learned Solicitor General of what I said, I cannot conceive. Now, what was the course taken by the Conservative Government? They held that it was of such supreme importance to maintain the doctrine that animadversion on the conduct of a Member of the the House by people outside could not be permitted, that, although Mr. Plimsoll had made amends, they declined to vote for the Previous Question, and declared the case to be a Breach of Privilege. The present Leader of the House has acted in direct opposition to the precedents set by all his Predecessors. He has acted in the teeth of the precedents set by Sir Stafford Northcote in the case of Mr. Plimsoll, and by Mr. Disraeli in the case of Mr. Justice Lopes. To the case of Mr. Lopes, the Solicitor General did not refer, although he might have done so with advantage. What was the case? Mr. Lopes made a speech at a political dinner, in which he said—

" What was the present position of the Liberal Party in the House of Commons? They were deserted by their Chief; they were allied to a disreputable Irish band whose watchword in the House was Home Rule or the repeal of the Union."

Those words were brought before the House as a Breach of Privilege. Did Mr. Diraeli, as Leader of the Conservative Party, say that they were not a Breach of Privilege? No; on the contrary, he said it was the duty of the House to take due notice of such language, and to affirm, in the most distinct manner, that if the words were not apologized for they would be voted a Breach of Privilege, and that action would be taken in accordance with such vote. That was the course taken by Mr. Disraeli with reference to the conduct of one of his own supporters, who is now Mr. Justice Lopes. And what happened? As might have been expected, Mr. Lopes apologized to the House for the language he had used, and therefore the course which was taken on a subsequent occasion was followed; the Previous Question was moved. The Solicitor General says that charges of this kind are not a Breach of Privilege; Sir Stafford Northcote and Mr. Disraeli said that they were, and that it was the bounden duty of the House to take cognizance of them as such, and be proceeded with further in the absence of apology. I therefore repeat my assertion that— probably from hurry—the hon. and learned Gentleman has not had time to read the reports of those cases. [Sir EDWARD CLARKE: Yes; I did read them.] Neither in Mr. Plimsoll's nor in Mr. Lopes' case was there any denial, for one moment, that a Breach of Privilege had been committed, and that, if not apologized for. it ought to be punished. There has hitherto been no Leader of the House of Commons who has taken a different view of these matters, and I have a strong opinion that if this had not been the case of an Irish Member the course pursued by all former

Sir William Harcourt

Leaders of the House would have been pursued now. Nobody who has looked into the facts of this case ought to dispute for a single moment that, by the law of Parliament, this is a Breach of Privilege. Why was the Previous Question moved in the cases I have referred to? Because an apology had been given and an amend had been made. Has *The Times* newspaper made an amend or an apology? In both of the previous cases it was pointed out that it was the bounden duty of the House of Commons to assert the Privileges of the House when they were attacked in a manner not half so violent or in so poisonous a manner as in this instance, and yet we have a Conservative Government, in the teeth of all precedents, calling upon the House to declare that this is not a Breach of Privilege. I only rose to state these facts in entire contradiction to the statements which have been made by the hon. and learned Solicitor General.

MR. W. E. GLADSTONE (Edinburgh, Mid Lothian): I rise to submit to the House a proposition which, I believe, it is desired to make the principal subject of discussion to-night. I will say with respect to it, in the first instance, that I have confined it in point of scope to the subject-matter of this debate. I have heard that many Members are of opinion that a Committee, if appointed, ought to examine into a broader field and into a larger mass of charges which have been brought against Irish Members. But that is not a matter which I should be justified in placing before the House, at any rate, at the present stage. It does not grow out of the case produced by the hon. Baronet the Member for North Antrim (Sir Charles Lewis). That was restricted— absolutely restricted—to the case of the hon. Member for East Mayo (Mr. Dillon), and, feeling the enormous importance of the issue that is before us, I am desirous that that issue should be clear; and, whatever may be said at a future stage, in case the House should be content to accept my Amendment, I do not think that, at the present stage, it would have been warrantable in me to entertain the idea of enlarging that Amendment. I must take the liberty of making a few remarks upon the speech of the noble Lord the Member for South Paddington (Lord Randolph

Churchill) with regard to matters of which, it appears to me, the introduction into his speech was wholly needless and perfectly gratuitous. He laid down the doctrine that it was more my business than the business of the Leader of the House to afford protection to the hon. Member for East Mayo. Of course, the insinuation thereby conveyed was that the Member for East Mayo and I were identical in our political position. [*Ministerial cries of* " Hear, hear ! "] I perfectly understand that; but it would have been better that this insinuation should have been broadly stated. But what I want to point out is that the noble Lord has evidently not the smallest conception of the capacity in which the Leader of the House interferes in cases of this kind. The Leader of the House is the protector of the whole House, and every Member sitting on these Benches and on the Benches below the Gangway has the same right to appeal to him as any Member who sits behind him. I have no such capacity. I have no right to protect anybody further than might accrue to any Gentleman according to the place he might occupy, and the part he has taken in this matter. The hon. and learned Gentleman understands, I am glad to say, the position I laid down. It is impossible to allow the remarks of the noble Lord to pass without protest, and I hope, if he notices the subject again, he will speak in a different manner. The noble Lord also spoke in the same gratuitous way, and introduced—God knows we have enough of disputable matters—introduced other disputable matters without the least necessity. He spoke of the time since I had assumed the Leadership of the repeal of the Union. The noble Lord is perfectly aware that I have never done anything of the sort. He understands that there is the broadest distinction between what I have proposed and the repeal of the Union. He thinks not. He is at liberty to argue the contrary; but he is not at liberty to say that I have made myself the Leader of the repeal of the Union, because that is a gross misstatement. I understand why the noble Lord used the expression. I perfectly understand why the noble Lord does not speak of Home Rule, but of repeal of the Union. The noble Lord knows there is a future before him, and that the noble Lord should

call our plan " repeal of the Union " would not be at all wonderful if he did so in future contingencies, when other plans of Home Rule may be found convenient to be proposed; and it may be convenient also to fall back upon a course of previous assertions that he objected to a repeal of the Union, but does not object to any Home Rule which is not repeal of the Union. I apologize to the House for this digression. Now, Sir, yesterday we had before us at least five questions of the greatest importance, perfectly distinct from one another, any one of which might, I apprehend, have been the subject of an important separate debate. The first was whether the article in *The Times* constituted a Breach of Privilege; the second was whether, even if a Breach of Privilege, it was to be treated as a Breach of Privilege by this House, for that is a totally different matter. The third was, whether it was the duty of the Irish Party to go into a Court of Law. The fourth was, whether a Committee ought to be appointed; and the fifth was, whether there should be a prosecution. Now, Sir, I admit that the most conclusive reasons against the decision of the House have, in my opinion, been given this evening by the hon. Member for Northampton (Mr. Bradlaugh), and my right hon. Friend sitting near me (Sir William Harcourt), why this matter should be regarded and treated as a Breach of Privilege. I admit sorrowfully that the Division which has been taken disposes of that question. It is a most serious and formidable decision at which the House has arrived. I believe it to be without precedent. A charge— an incrimination of the very highest degree and quality which incrimination can possibly reach—has been made against a Member of this House. That Member has appealed to this House to intervene and make itself a party. [*Cries of* " No ! " *from the Ministerial Benches.*] MR. DILLON (Mayo, E.): Certainly he does.

MR. W. E. GLADSTONE: Yes; by supporting the Motion of the hon. Baronet (Sir Charles Lewis). If the House declares this to be a Breach of Privilege, it thereby intervenes and gives the means by which the matter can be settled. Therefore, I do not understand how it is possible to raise a doubt on this subject. He does so; and under what circumstances? He does it as a Member of the minority, constantly assailed and denounced indoors and out-of-doors. He does it as a Member of the minority, which is challenged to do it by a Member of the Party opposite—by a supporter of the Government—by a Gentleman doubtless acting not in communication with the Government, but at the same time a very favoured supporter, who has recently received at their hands such a mark of honour as is the token of their confidence, and such as constitutes a great distinction. It is also, Sir, a minority which represents a nation. [*Cries of* "No!"] Will the hon. and gallant Gentleman opposite wait? I am going to explain my meaning, although the fact seems to me to be indisputable. Has the House of Commons represented England in times past? If it has, by what majority? Has there never been a minority in this House? Is it not the majority which represents the nation? When in the House of Commons have you had such a majority speaking for the nation—so large a majority against so small a minority as is the case in Ireland now? That, it seems to be, is not an arguable matter—it is indisputable; and in the Parliamentary sense, no candid man can for a moment deny that the Party to which I refer represents a nation. [*Cries of* "No!"] There never has been a majority so large. If they do not represent a nation, then the English nation has never been represented within the walls of this House. It appears to me that the House should really consider its position in this matter, and not too severely try the patience of the Irish people. It is a strong measure —it is a most unfortunate measure— that there should be a going back upon the protection heretofore afforded by this House to its Members, at the very same moment that your sense of duty leads you to think it necessary to inflict upon the Irish people, by a Coercion Bill, and by a permanent Coercion Bill, a brand of perpetual dishonour, and when the impression has gone abroad among men's minds that with large portions of this House there are two measures of justice —one for Irish Members of the Irish Party, and the other for all other Members who do not belong to that Party. Two of the five questions I have referred to are, in my judgment, disposed of. I may greatly regret it, considering the

Mr. W. E. Gladstone

circumstances under which they have been disposed of, and I entreat the House to consider a little before they add to the gravity of the decision at which, unhappily, the House has already arrived. Now, Sir, the three questions that remain are—first, ought the Irish Members to go into a Court of Justice? And after all that has been said I feel it necessary to say some words more upon the subject, and to suggest reasons which appear to me, if the Irish Members think fit to urge them, to entirely deprive us of the right to complain if they decline to carry the matter to a Court of Law. The first of the reasons which they allege against the course is the delay it would entail. Will any Gentleman venture to say at what period sentence would be obtained? I will not enter into details, because those acquainted with legal questions would do so far better. From all that I have heard of the proceedings of the Courts of Law, I believe that most serious delay might, and probably would be the result, of going to such a Court. Well, then, with regard to the composition of the Court what are we to say? The noble Lord (Lord Randolph Churchill) last night, with extraordinary rashness, gave a general acquittal of all the Judges of all the Courts of England, and a general eulogy upon the record of 1,000 years. The noble Lord is not apparently aware that, within the present century, very serious questions have been raised with respect to the conduct of eminent Judges in English Courts of Justice. I agree with the noble Lord that we ought not to leave this question entirely in the hands of lawyers, and that other Members ought to take part in it. If we do take part in it, it is in order that we may bring to bear upon these debates the results of our Parliamentary experience and historical knowledge; but to manufacture history which is not true, and will not bear examination, is a course with respect to which I should say, if it is to be pursued, we had better leave the matter altogether in the hands of lawyers. Has the noble Lord ever heard of Lord Ellenborough? Does he know the opinion pronounced upon him by his brother Judge and biographer, Lord Campbell. ["Oh, oh!"] The Solicitor General sneers.

Sir EDWARD CLARKE: I did not sneer; I laughed at the idea.

MR. W. E. GLADSTONE : The Solicitor General laughs at the name of Lord Campbell. Lord Campbell stated that in the case of Lord Dundonald the conduct of Lord Ellenborough was severely censured, not only by the vulgar, but by men of education on both sides, and that he had the greatest misgivings himself as to his own conduct in the affair—so much so, that he says it drew upon the Lord Chief Justice a considerable degree of public obloquy, causing very uneasy reflections in his own mind. I know not how that is, but it shows that various questions of that kind arose in connection with different judgments. Entirely differing with the noble Lord, I believe myself that all Judges now upon the Bench might be trusted perfectly. But there is one Judge now upon the Bench who came down from the Bench to take part in regard to the great Irish Question more violent than has been taken almost by any layman I can remember. And if one of these Gentlemen sitting below the Gangway says it is excusable in him to feel some mistrust in such a case, though I should not feel such mistrust myself, yet I must say that I understand that mistrust. Well, then, we are told that it is absolutely certain that they would get a verdict. Is it, Sir, so certain that a verdict would be got? Is it so certain that when the House declines to treat these allegations as a Breach of Privilege, departing from all its usages, that a verdict would be got? [*Ministerial cries of* " Oh ! "] I will show that by-and-bye. I am about to tell an anecdote concerning myself, which, I think, is to the point with regard to the certainty of getting verdicts against newspapers in cases wherein a public man attempts to restrain the liberty of newspapers to comment on his conduct or his language. Thirty years ago, nearly, I had the honour of serving Her Majesty for a short time as High Commissioner in the Ionian Islands. At that time the people of the Ionian Islands, who had, I think, little or nothing in the way of a practical grievance to complain of, were, notwithstanding, possessed with an intense sentiment of nationality, and this sentiment of nationality, which had determined them to accept nothing except the union with their own blood and race, was treated by a portion of the Press of this country, and especially by a portion of the Metropolitan Press, with unmeasured and bitter contempt. It was continually said—

"Who are these miserable Ionians that desire to join themselves to an equally miserable set of people in Greece instead of welcoming the glory of being attached to a great Empire ?"

Well, when I was in the Islands, a certain course was taken by the Assembly, and it happened that the same newspaper, *The Times* newspaper, had an article to this effect—

"The Ionian Assembly has been committing treason, and the Queen's Commissioner has been helping them to commit treason."

I have no avidity for going into a Court of Law. I do not share the views of the hon. and learned Solicitor General on the great felicity of litigants, though I know that most lawyers have those ideas. At the same time, when I saw a plain and clear charge of treason made against myself, I felt that it was a case of unwarrantable licence, and that I must prosecute *The Times.* I came home immediately after; I took the best advice in my power; I consulted legal friends of great character. I cannot recall now all their names, but one of them was Mr. Wortley, father of my hon. Friend opposite. I consulted also my own professional adviser, Mr. James Freshfield; and anyone who remembers him will recollect that he was almost at the head of the entire Legal Profession. Every one of those gentlemen said to me—" Do not do it." They did not question that it was written down that I had aided the Assembly in committing treason. They said—" Do not do it, for you cannot depend upon getting a verdict." I should have come into Court without any particular prejudice against me further than might be raised on the special case. But I am of opinion that in this case there is in the mind of a portion of the public a gross and cruel prejudice. I am not of opinion that that is the only difficulty in getting a verdict. In my own case, it was not to gross prejudice, or any prejudice at all, that my advisers referred to when they positively protested in such terms that I was unable to persist, and induced me to acquiesce in the publication of this monstrous charge. It was this—that juries have a just and proper prejudice in favour of the liberty of the Press;

and that, helped on by counsel, who know perfectly well how to bring in everything irrelevant and everything invidious—in the strict exercise of their duty, and I am not finding fault with them at all—by mixing up together the more or less legimate elements that might operate upon their minds—I say that, if I were a juryman, it would take very much indeed to make me give a verdict in restraint of the liberty of the Press. Such being the case, I cannot, for my own part, think that it is very unreasonable if Gentlemen of the Nationalist Party, in the condition in which they stand, are not more forward to go into a Court of Law. I think their apprehensions are reasonable apprehensions. I do not wish to charge perjury or anything of the sort; but it is impossible to efface from the mind of a juryman the belief that he is more or less concerned in the merits and character of the law he is administering, and when a great object like the liberty of the Press is in view, he has an immense and a just reluctance to do anything that can possibly be construed into a disposition to restrain it. Therefore, I cannot think we are entitled in the least degree to complain of hon. Members below the Gangway, or of the hon. Member for East Mayo, when he declines to commit himself to the mercies or the chances of a Court of Law in a case like this. Without any reflection against British jurisprudence in general, the chances of a verdict which my advisers in my case saw were uncertain 25 or 30 years ago would be very much more slender in the present case. Well, Sir, that being the case with regard to the Irish Members, we now come to the two remaining questions. It is said by hon. Members opposite that there are two modes of proceeding, and that the only difference is as to the mode of inquiry. Well, Sir, I am bound to say that one mode of proceeding is open to us according to reason and according to precedents, and I shall proceed to contend that the precedents adduced by the hon. and learned Gentleman the Solicitor General are perfectly and entirely valueless for the purposes for which he was urging them. In point of fact, he himself omitted from his speech what was necessary as an essential element and broad foundation of his proposition that a prosecution was an allowable course. But the hon. and learned Gen-

tleman made assertions with regard to Parliamentary Committees, which I think it only fair to him that I should recite as I take them from the report of his speech. He said there had been no precedents since 1601 for a Committee of this kind. That is the first proposition. [Sir EDWARD CLARKE: On a similar case.] It would be to invent a totally new procedure. The second proposition is that it would be to institute a form of proceeding hitherto unknown in this country. These are the propositions to which the hon. and learned Gentleman committed himself. Well, with regard to a similar case, we all know what similar circumstances came to mean in the Acts relating to railways—namely, that they might make different charges "in similar circumstances." The word "similar" is capable of very various interpretations; but what I wish to contend now is this—not that there was a gentleman named Dillon in some case, not that the same words were used in the same case which I am going to adduce, but because I believe they are the most extraordinary words, and, as far as I know, the most unparalleled ever used against a Member of Parliament. I am going to contend that in similar cases, and in far weaker cases, it has been the established practice of the House of Commons, if they so thought fit, to proceed by Committee. After contending that the course of appointing a Committee is conformable both to reason and precedent, I will also contend, and I think I shall be able to show, that the course of procedure proposed by the hon. and learned Solicitor General is not conformable either to the one or to the other. But I must notice that the appointment of a Committee has a great merit to begin with of being an extremely prompt method of bringing this question to an issue. These things have been done again and again, and in no case has great or inconvenient delay occurred. I contend that a Committee is a perfectly competent tribunal, and not, as the noble Lord said, a ridiculously incompetent tribunal, to determine the question whether a Member of this House has, or has not, been guilty of gross and wilful falsehood in certain statements.

LORD RANDOLPH CHURCHILL: That was not my point. I did not say that. I said that a Committee would be

Mr. W. E. Gladstone

hopelessly incompetent to investigate all the charges which have been brought against hon. Members by *The Times* newspaper.

MR. DILLON (Mayo, E.): What are the charges?

MR. W. E. GLADSTONE: I am very glad, and I thank the noble Lord for his explanation, for he has not said that a Committee would be hopelessly incompetent to deal with a case of this kind. If we were to say so, we should be pronouncing a very severe verdict on what I call the established practice and Procedure of the House of Commons. But what is there in the nature of the case to prevent Gentlemen practised in business, men of long experience in this House, men some of them lawyers with all the knowledge derived from the science of the law, others of them having a wide and varied experience, and all of them acting under the public eye, each of them liable to have his conduct and his vote freely discussed and considered; what is there in the nature of the case, what is there in the character of the body charged with the legislative responsibilities of the greatest deliberative assembly in the world, what is there in the character of a few competent gentleman judiciously selected by this body to prevent them from being able to discharge duties which 12 common jurors or 12 special jurors will be perfectly competent to perform? I venture to think that, on the contrary, such a Committee is the body most competent to deal with such an assumption. It would be a different matter if we were proposing that proceedings should be taken with a penal or vindictive view. There, I admit, you might take exception, and probably if the Committee in the course of its inquiries came upon matter which made the Committee believe that a penal character ought to be given to the proceedings, the Committee would refer the matter to the House; and the House would consider whether penal proceedings ought or ought not to take place. But for the examination of a question that is not penal, I contend that a Committee is a most proper and competent tribunal. Let us see now whether the broad doctrines of the hon. and learned Solicitor General can be sustained. I contend that there is not a syllable of them which can be sustained. I hope my proposition is broad enough; and I

hope that he will show by an examination of such partial precedents as I have been able to look into, that as to the substance of the matter my doctrines falls beyond the reason and justice of the case. The hon. and learned Gentleman was very much indisposed to allow the similarity of the case of Mr. Grissell to be urged, pointing out that the inquiry was held prior to the calling of the parties to the Bar of the House. That circumstance seemed, in his mind, to determine the whole matter as to similarity. That is not a question of substance at all. The matter was examined by a Committee, and the House took notice of that examination and proceeded to act upon it as far as it thought fit, but as the hon. and learned Gentleman contends that in point of form and order, it was different from this, I will not proceed further with that case. I take the case of Mr. Butt in 1884. I say that that case proves that not only this Committee ought to be granted, but that upon far weaker and far narrower grounds this House has declined to reject the appeal of its Members for protection by the House. And I challenge the examination of what I say, word for word, by the Law Officers of the Crown, who, by the way, have been so kind as to assume in this case on behalf of the Government the responsibility in a way which I certainly never experienced. I say that this is not a similar, it is a much stronger case, and that it would be almost an abuse of words to say that it is similar. I beg that the hon. and learned Gentleman will examine this proposition in regard to the case of Mr. Butt. I say that everything that was done in the case of Mr. Butt is an argument, and an argument applying with ten times more force, for conceding that the case of the hon. Member for East Mayo is one that you should take notice of and proceed upon. What was the allegation made in the case of Mr. Butt? It was that there was a party of Gentlemen in this House—I do not know that it is worth while to quote the exact words—but a party of Gentlemen who were extremely hungry for place, salary, and pension. That was the whole breadth of the allegation. [Sir RICHARD WEBSTER: Corruption.] The hon. and learned Gentleman says corruption. Well I will not dispute that if the hon. and learned Gentleman says it is so. It was an allegation that there was a greediness for a place, salary, and pension. I must say that the hon. and learned Solicitor General has established in his own mind a scale of offences, and a scale which appears to me to be totally irrational. According to him to accuse a man of giving a wrong vote is a matter to be taken notice of. To accuse a man of bribery or corruption, is a Breach of Privilege that must be taken notice of; but to accuse a man of deliberate and wilful lying is a minor matter, and I ask the House to take notice of that. Now, I say that instead of being a minor matter, the charge of wilful and deliberate falsehood in the discharge of your duty in this House, is the highest, the gravest, the blackest charge that can be brought. I cannot distinguish, Sir, between the speeches of a man and the actions of man in this House. In this House speech is action. The work of this House is done by speech, and to offend in the point of truth in the performance of duty in debate, by wilful and deliberate falsehood is the highest of all offences that can be committed. Why is corruption a grave offence? Because it may lead you to act falsely here. But this is a case where you do act falsely in the performance of your duty, where, in reasoning with the House and professing to assist it in its work, you deliberately tell it what you know to be falsehoods, and attempt to mislead the House. I say this, because in Mr. Butt's case it is intimated that it was said the Members attacked were open to corruption. But what said Lord John Russell in that case? I do not think the hon. and learned Solicitor General will say that to charge men with being greedy of place is worse than to charge them with being guilty of wilful and deliberate falsehood. To say a Member is greedy of place may imply that he is in a condition in which he is liable to be corrupted. Well, Lord John Russell, as Leader of this House, at once accedes to the proposal for inquiry. He does not raise a doubt upon it; no doubt is raised upon it in any quarter of the House, and yet it was comparatively a very slender basis on which to found proceedings. And it proved to be a slender basis, for when the House had so far given satisfaction to the wish of Mr. Butt, a Committee was appointed without a dissentient voice, not for a penal, but for a protec-

tive purpose, and Mr. Butt finally desisted from further pursuing the matter, being satisfied with the end he had attained. But later on Mr. Butt was personally the object of a charge which amounted to corruption. That was in 1858. The case was brought before the House on petition, and the petition charged Mr. Butt with the receipt of money for conducting the case of Ali Moorad Khan. What was the course then taken by the House? Mr. Roebuck brought forward the matter; a Committee was proposed, and was at once appointed, consisting of seven Members, to investigate the charge. The noble Lord the Member for South Paddington (Lord Randolph Churchill) found a difficulty about advocate Members of the House sitting on a Committee in the present case. That I believe is also an established practice of the House, and two advocate Members were appointed to sit on the Committee of 1858 to which I am referring. But observe that the allegation there went much beyond the allegation of 1854. It was an allegation in a petition of personal corruption. There was no vindictive proceeding. It was a simple question of protecting the House assailed in the character of one of its Members, and a Committee was at once appointed by the House for the purpose of examining into the allegation. The hon. and learned Solicitor General has not taken any notice of that case. I contend that that is a weaker case than the present one, for I say that the charge of falsehood, wilful and deliberate falsehood in debate is a higher charge even than that of pecuniary corruption. There is another case—a case which is of some interest to me, because I was myself so far concerned in it that I was a Member of the Committee that was appointed, and that was the case of Mr. Whittle Harvey, which was very briefly mentioned by my hon. and learned Friend the late Attorney General (Sir Charles Russell). That case happened in the year 1834. Mr. O'Connell made a Motion to the effect that there should be an inquiry into the practice of the Inns of Court, in regard to applications for admission to those Inns. Mr. Whittle Harvey had been rejected by the Inn to which he sought admission. Objection was taken to the terms of the Motion by Sir James Scarlett, Lord Althorp, and others. It

Mr. W. E. Gladstone

- was amended by consent into a Motion for inquiry into the circumstances of the rejection of Mr. Whittle Harvey by the Benchers. Now, I call the particular attention of the House to that case, and to the manner in which it was received. The Motion in the form in which I have quoted it—the amended form that is for an inquiry by a Committee—was adopted unanimously by the House. No objection was taken to it, and Lord Althorp used words which I wish I had heard fall from the right hon. Gentleman the present Leader of the House. He said—

"With respect to the Amendment, after what has passed in the House, and feeling, as he must, that if the hon. Member for Colchester claimed an inquiry at their hands, it was but justice to grant him the required investigation, he, for one, would not raise the least objection to it."—(3 *Hansard*, [23] 934.)

The hon. Member, by the Vote he has given has claimed inquiry at your hands. I will come presently to the question whether you are now offering an inquiry. I contend that you are not. I shall come to that by-and-bye. He claims inquiry, and the hon. and learned Gentleman will say he is granted an inquiry. But what was the object of that Committee? The object of that Committee, if I remember aright, was to examine whether the verdict of the jury given 20 years before, which affected the moral character of Mr. Harvey—whether it was a verdict worthy of credence, or a verdict given in error. What must be the feeling of the House of Commons with regard to the right of Members to demand its protection, if a man like Lord Althorp, in the presence of Sir James Scarlett, without a word of objection from him, was ready to grant a Committee for such a purpose as that, "because," as Lord Althorp said, "it was claimed by the hon. Member, and was but justice to him?" That is what I mean by saying that certainly the circumstances are not in each particular alike, but infinitely stronger, and that every step taken by the House of Commons on every former' occasion constitutes an argument, *a fortiori*, of a resistless kind for acceding to the wish of the hon. Member. It may be said that that was a bad precedent, established by the House on that occasion. I cannot enter into the question, but the more a proceeding is open to objection on ac-

count of hopeless difficulties connected with inquiry, the stronger is the argument fortified by the cases in respect of Parliamentary principle which establishes that the House has placed itself traditionally under a moral obligation to accede to demands of this kind. Well, now we are told there is no difference between us about inquiry. The only difference is about the kind of inquiry. Let me say a few words about the proposal of the Government. The proposal of the Government is this—that when an incrimination of the very highest order, and I defy the hon. and learned Solicitor General to deny that the charge of wilful falsehood is an incrimination of the very highest order, has been made against one of its Members, and he demands an inquiry you refuse him—apparently you, the legal advisers of the Government, or at all events the hon. and learned Gentlemen the Attorney General and Solicitor General—who are acting by voluntary action, for which I think their Colleagues must feel very much obliged, you refuse the Committee; but you offer that if the hon. Member for East Mayo will accept it the public purse shall be brought into play against a private undertaking in order to examine whether the charges made against the hon. Member are libellous or not. And that this is to be done—the public purse is to be opened and a private undertaking is to be assailed. You may tell us that *The Times* is rich and powerful, but the precedent you are making will not depend upon wealth and power. You are going thus to open the public purse and to put the Attorney General and his myrmidons in motion. [*Cries of* " Oh, oh ! "] Do not suppose that I am not going to say anything unfair in that respect, and the expression is an unhappy one ; because besides these myrmidons there will be a great number of independent counsel with their myrmidons. But this is all to be done, and to be done—mark my words—for the first time in history. [Sir RICHARD WEBSTER : Ten precedents.] Well, I know your 10 precedents and they are not worth 10 brass farthings. They are worth a great deal less than 10 brass farthings because they are perfectly irrelevant, or if they are relevant they are relevant against you and show that this proceeding ought not to be entertained. For my part, I do not care what

[*Third Night.*]

it is that the hon. Member for East Mayo may be offered or accepts. I do not care whether he accepts your proposal. I, for my part, will oppose it as an utterly unwarrantable and unprecedented proceeding. My affirmation would be this—and I think I can make it good—there never has been such a proceeding without a declaration by the House of a positive or presumable offence. The House has never set in motion the Attorney General without making itself a party in the case. I challenge contradiction from the hon. and learned Solicitor General. The hon. and learned Gentleman unhappily omitted all reference to this point. He said, I will give you 10 cases anterior to the year 1810. I believe so far as my researches go they are anterior to 1795; that is not very important. There were 10 cases in which prosecutions were ordered. Will the hon. and learned Gentleman give me one single case in which there was a prosecution without a previous condemnation by the House of the thing for which there was to be a prosecution? If that is so what is the value of the precedents you give? Every one of these 10 precedents condemns the hon. and learned Gentleman, and goes to show that he must—if he appeals to precedent—interpose the prior judgment and the prior declaration of the House. My contention is this, and although I speak with reserve as my opportunities of inquiry are limited, and I do not presume to dogmatize—but, so far as I have ever known, and so far as I can learn, the House in these matters has two modes of Procedure. Its course has always been marked by a high sentiment of honour—by that high sentiment of Parliamentary honour which proves to us, or has proved to us until the present occasion, that the age of chivalry is not altogether dead, for this House has ever had a chivalrous sympathy with its own Members in cases relating to their own characters, and has felt that their characters were parts of its own possession and character. It has two methods of proceeding, one of them penal and the other protective. Do not let these be confounded. It is only by confusing the issues that you can hope to establish anything like a case, and by adducing precedents which are altogether against you. When the proceeding is penal the House takes one of two courses.

Mr. W. E. Gladstone

It either proceeds by exercising its own powers, or it proceeds by putting the law in motion directly or through the Attorney General for the purpose of a prosecution. That is one course. The other course is when the proceeding is protective. Now, when it is protective, I believe that I am justified in saying that the usual course has been the appointment of a Committee. You may tell me there was in 1844 the case of Mr. Walter Ferrand, but then in that case there was no defence. There was no case. The whole thing was given up. What did the House do? It passed a most severe condemnation in protection of the character of its own Member, and yet I am not sure that the charges even then unfortunately made by Mr. Ferrand, a gentleman who was considered to be intemperate in the language which he used in this House, although through a long life he enjoyed the highest respectability and the affection of his friends—I am not sure that even those charges, rash and extravagant as they were, came up to the extraordinary height of the accusations made against the hon. Member for East Mayo. The House passed a Resolution to protect him, and I have given already five other cases, one of them objected to by the hon. and learned Solicitor General, in which, for the protection of the characters of Members, Committees were appointed without difference of opinion. That I believe to be a true statement of the general basis of the proceedings of the House in these matters, and therefore I affirm there is a total want of the slightest approach to a precedent for that which the Government are now proposing. I will at once abandon my ground if the hon. and learned Gentleman can produce a case and a prosecution ordered by the House without a previous condemnation by the House. Let him give me a contradiction in one word across the Table, and I will at once yield the point. He has had more time now, and his hon. and learned Friend the Solicitor General has been doing his best, and no more competent persons could apply themselves to the task. According to my mind, and my accusation is established by the invincible silence of the opposite Bench, there has been no case where the House has used the public purse to promote the purpose of private litigation without making itself a party in the case by pronouncing a preliminary judgment upon the matter which is to be considered. In a case of this kind, in my opinion, when you prove what has been the former practice of the House, you have gone a great way towards proving your whole case, because the practice of the House in these matters has been deeply considered from time to time by the most competent of its Members, and there has grown up a system, the result of reflection and experience; and it is reflection and experience that in this case we appeal to when we speak of the precedents before us. But I do not speak of the precedents before us alone. It appears to me that the reason of the case is so strong that I cannot conceive how it can be resisted. Perhaps it would be well, as to some of these cases which I have taken out at random, that I should show what the proceedings were, whether in cases of libel against the House or against its Members. In Volume 43, page 215, of the Journals of the House, there is the case of Sir Elijah Impey respecting a certain pamphlet or certain writings which contained a scandalous libel of this House and its Members, and thereupon they made an address for a prosecution. In page 232 of the same volume of the Journals there is the case of Warren Hastings. A pamphlet was published containing passages highly disrespectful to the House, and upon that the House proceeded to make an address for a prosecution. In the 44th volume of the Journals, page 463, again in the case of Warren Hastings, and where the newspaper in question was *The World*, the House voted—

"That the pamphlet contains matter of a scandalous and libellous nature reflecting on the Proceedings of the House."

Thereupon a prosecution was ordered. I am not aware, Sir, and I think it is pretty plain, that the hon. and learned Solicitor General is not at variance in this essential particular. Will he tell me it is not an essential particular; will he tell me that this House would adopt a wise course or a warrantable course in ordering prosecutions at random in matters in regard to which it has no information? In the first place, as respects the course of action. Has the hon. and learned Gentlemen reflected upon the use which the counsel defending the hon. Member for East Mayo would be justified in making of the proceedings the hon. and learned Gentleman now proposes? That counsel would show that in every case it had been the practice of the House to make itself a party by pronouncing its own judgment, and only then instituting or requiring a prosecution. He would show that in this case the House has forborne to pronounce an opinion. He would say— "Gentlemen of the jury, the House has not forborne without a reason for forbearing, and I leave it to you to consider what that reason is." But, Sir, in principle is it tolerable that the House should pursue such a course? I protest against such a use of public authority, and such a use of public money, and such a departure from the fixed traditions of the House. In what capacity do you go into Court? You are going to have a public prosecution of *The Times* newspaper. Who is the prosecutor? The House of Commons is the prosecutor, and the House of Commons as prosecutor says nothing upon the merits of the case. Is that a tolerable state of things; is it just towards the party incriminated; have you a right to put him on his trial unless you believe there is a case for a trial; is it just to the character of the House itself? Either, Sir, you believe in the justice of the prosecution that you have ordered to be instituted, and if you believe in it, well, so far you are pre-judging the case —that is unavoidable; or you do not believe in it. If you go into Court pretending to ask from that Court sentence that a libel has been committed, and while you pretend to ask it, you carefully avoid pronouncing that opinion which your Predecessors always have pronounced. What is it but collusion of the grossest character, unworthy of those who, I think in error, though I have no doubt with upright intention, advise it; unworthy of those who seem disposed to receive the advice, and who, in my opinion, seem condemned to the adverse judgment of both the public and posterity? I confess that it is with surprise I see Her Majesty's Government taking the present course. I think it will not be complained of me that I have not been sufficiently plain in my proposition. I do not wish to mislead the House; I do not wish unnecessarily to occupy the time of the House. I have dwelt very greatly upon the question of

[Third Night.]

precedents as applicable to my own proposition; I have dealt more upon it as applicable to the proposition of the Government. In order that I may not waste time, I have asked whether I am wrong in my statement of the facts. I have every reason to believe, from my own examination, and much more I think from the silence of the Law Officers of the Crown, that I am not wrong in my statement of the facts. Well, under these circumstances, I can only say I hope and I believe that I have not said what is offensive in respect to the Government. I have endeavoured to make a fair and straightforward appeal to them. I think they are pursuing a most dangerous course in other matters in respect to Ireland, and likewise in this matter. It may be allowed that in other matters affecting Ireland they are covered to a wonderful degree by the unhappy action of hon. Gentlemen on this side of the House, who are giving them their support. But this is a case in which they will not receive quite the same shelter from that concurrence and co-operation; and I do hope, Sir, that while there is yet time, they will reconsider the views which they have adopted, and that upon grounds of reason, and upon grounds of precedent, they will grant the Motion which I now proceed to move; and that they will not exclude from their view the grave international controversy which is now raised, and the pressure they are putting upon the Irish nation by their proposals for placing Irishmen permanently upon a footing of inequality and inferiority to their fellow-subjects, under the pretext of a Legislative Union; and that in this matter, at least, they will take care to give them justice, and full justice—aye, even if it were necessary, indulgent justice, where their honour and character are concerned.

Amendment proposed, to the proposed Amendment,

To leave out all the words after the word "House," in order to add the words "is of opinion that an inquiry should be made, by a Select Committee, into the charge of wilful falsehood, in a speech delivered in this House, brought in an article published in the 'Times' newspaper, of the 2nd May, against John Dillon, esquire, Member for East Mayo."—(*Mr. W. E. Gladstone.*)

Question proposed, "That the words proposed to be left out stand part of the proposed Amendment."

Mr. W. E. Gladstone

THE ATTORNEY GENERAL (Sir RICHARD WEBSTER) (Isle of Wight): Mr. Speaker, I am unwilling that there should be delay of any kind between the powerful speech we have just heard from the right hon. Gentleman the Member for Mid Lothian (Mr. W. E. Gladstone), and whatever reply I, with my less experience, may be able to make to him. I quite admit that the statement of the right hon. Gentleman has been perfectly straightforward, and that he has put the issues in the clearest possible way. I will endeavour, though I cannot hope, of course, to interest the House so much, to answer his speech as fairly as I possibly can. Sir, whatever may have been the criticisms upon our conduct, which have been addressed to us by the right hon. Gentleman the Member for Mid Lothian and the right hon. Gentleman the Member for Derby (Sir William Harcourt), my hon. and learned Friend the Solicitor General (Sir Edward Clarke) and I feel the great responsibility of our position, and we do not shrink from supporting the opinion which we were bold enough to express requesting a little more time for consideration. We do not hesitate to support our opinion by argument. We have but one advantage over the right hon. Gentleman the Member for Mid Lothian, and that is that both of us are very considerably younger than he. I have no other advantage whatever in addressing this House; but it is a great satisfaction to me, and I am sure it is a great satisfaction to my hon. and learned Friend the Solicitor General, and I say it advisedly, to find that with the greatest ability that can be brought to bear upon this question, the ability of the right hon. Gentleman the Member for Derby, of my hon. and learned Friend the Member for Hackney (Sir Charles Russell), and to-night of the right hon. Gentleman the Leader of the Opposition (Mr. W. E. Gladstone), we still are able to stand up and maintain that our position in this House—that our opinion in this House with regard to the course which should be adopted—is practically unquestioned by those on the other side of the House. [*Laughter.*] I maintain that our position has not been assailed—not been successfully assailed. Now, what I want to do is to address to the House the reasons which we have for our opinion. I do not wish to say there is no doubt about the proposition; but I wish to support the position taken up by the hon. and learned Solicitor General and those who have spoken on this side of the House by fair argument, I trust couched in moderate and respectful language, to the right hon. Gentleman the Member for Mid Lothian, and to show that our position has not been successfully assailed. Now, I in no way quarrel with the five propositions with regard to this matter which the right hon. Gentleman the Member for Mid Lothian has laid down. I agree with him with the first two propositions as to Breach of Privilege, and I wish to examine as closely as I can the statements he made upon the other three. He will remember—and the House will remember—that towards the close of his speech he referred to what I may call the discussion prior to the moving of his own Amendment, and pointed out the reasons why the Irish Members should not go into Court. I will, before I sit down, venture to deal with one or two of his arguments, and with one or two which were raised by hon. Gentlemen opposite before he spoke. Now, as to the right hon. Gentleman's last three propositions, I must say that some of the right hon. Gentleman's observations as to whether the Irish Members ought to go into Court struck me as being such that he could scarcely hope they would for a moment really engage the serious attention of this House. Why, Sir, he spoke about the delay which would occur if the Irish Members were to go into a Court of Law. I will deal with that question before I sit down. Now, Sir, upon the question of delay of trial let me point out that this charge against the hon. Member for East Mayo (Mr. Dillon) is not the first charge of the kind that has been levelled against the Irish Members. It is the repetition, or rather the application to him—I am speaking now of general charges, not of the particular one referred to by the hon. Baronet the Member for North Antrim (Sir Charles Lewis)—it is but a repetition of more grave charges, even more serious charges made against the hon. Member for Cork (Mr. Parnell) and other Members of the Party who sit below the Gangway opposite. When was the first publication of these slanders? and I will so call them, for they are slanders if they are not true and are not justified.

These allegations are gross slanders if they are not true, and not one single word shall fall from me to express a contrary opinion. When were these slanders first issued to the public? This House remembers that the articles on "Parnellism and Crime" began to be issued on the 7th of March in this year, very nearly two months ago. The right hon. Gentleman the Member for Mid Lothian has said that by the vote given to-night the hon. Member for East Mayo has appealed to the House to intervene in his behalf. Sir, I must say, after the utterances of the hon. Member for East Mayo in the speech he made in reply to the noble Marquess the Member for Rossendale (the Marquess of Hartington), who quoted some statements made in *The Times*, it does seem to me somewhat strange to interpret the vote of to-night into an appeal to the House to take action in his behalf in respect to this charge. If it were necessary that this action should be taken, if it were necessary some grave action should be taken to enable hon. Members below the Gangway rightly and properly to perform their duties to the House, how is it that not one single step in that direction has been made by any hon. Member below the Gangway either in or outside of this House? But, Sir, I will deal specifically with the reasons given by the right hon. Gentleman the Member for Mid Lothian. I must say that, knowing what I do of the opinion of the legal profession, and of the opinion of the literary world in regard to the criticisms of Lord Campbell—I refer not to his position as a Judge, but as a biographer—I am perfectly astonished at the position assumed by the right hon. Gentleman; Lord Campbell has since passed away; but it is notorious that it has been said of him that his criticisms and biographies upon his Predecessors were not just. It is strange that Lord Campbell should be the only authority with regard to the English Judicial Bench that the right hon. Gentleman should have laid before the House. I have to make my observations in the absence of the right hon. Gentleman the Member for Mid Lothian. I do not complain of that, because I cannot expect him to stay in the House to listen to me, though I have noticed that more than once we have been obliged to reply to him in his absence. Still I cannot help asking the

[*Third Night.*]

House and the country to observe that this is the only criticism on the Judicial Bench the right hon. Gentleman has been able, notwithstanding the assistance of those around him, to extract from the records of history or otherwise with respect to the conduct of Judges. I cannot see what was the force of the right hon. Gentleman's remarks with regard to the English Judicial Bench, unless he intended to suggest, nay, more, to insinuate, that there would not be a fair trial. I am aware that it is perfectly true that the right hon. Gentleman did say that in making the quotation from Lord Campbell he did not suggest that any of the Judges on the Bench at the present time would not do his duty; but still the whole tenour of his remarks upon this part of the case was that he approved of the course adopted by the hon. Member for East Mayo, because he thought there were reasons why he could not fully trust the English Judicial Bench. All I can say is this—and I do not speak only because I have worked in the despised Profession of the Law for a great many years, or because I have been brought in contact with every one of Her Majesty's Judges — that their public life, their fearless conduct, their determination to express their opinions, even against popular feeling, has shown that they are men who are determined to do their duty. I maintain that it is a sad thing that a Gentleman in the position of the right hon. Gentleman the Member for Mid Lothian should intimate that there is any one of Her Majesty's subjects, either English, Scotch or Irish, who would not get, not only justice, but protection against any popular feeling if his case were tried before any one of Her Majesty's Judges. Sir, the second reason given by the right hon. Gentleman is amusing. It appears we have elicited a fact most interesting in the history of the right hon. Gentleman. I think he said that in the year 1859 he consulted Mr. James Freshfield, a member of a legal firm of great eminence—the right hon. Gentleman said, with perfect justice, Mr. James Freshfield was one of the most distinguished members of his branch of the Legal Profession—respecting a charge of libel upon him. The right hon. Gentleman did not tell us more about the libel except that he was accused of treason. Now, if the real sting of the libel was that the right hon. Gentleman

had been guilty of treason and treasonable practices towards Her Majesty the Queen, I do not believe that there is any Solicitor of standing who would have advised him not to go into court.

Mr. W. E. GLADSTONE: As the hon. and learned Gentleman has thought it worth while to allude to the matter, may I state what, to the best of my recollection, occurred. I spoke from memory; but I wish to state as precisely as I can that which occurred, and to repeat what I stated a few moments ago which I think was quite accurate. The charge was primarily against the Ionian Assembly, upon which it was the custom of the time to pour unmeasured contempt. In the article it was said—

"It is as usual, committing treason, and Her Majesty's Commission is assisting and sharing in the treason."

The advice given to me—I wish I could recollect all those who gave it, but I have mentioned two persons—was given to me in the most positive and absolute manner.

Sir RICHARD WEBSTER: I do not question in the least what the right hon. Gentleman says, but I think that his explanation only bears out my observation. I know that in a matter of this kind I ought to be very careful what words I use. I am weighing my words, and I say that if the charge made against the right hon. Gentleman really amounted to treason, I do not believe that Mr. James Freshfield or any other eminent legal gentleman would have hesitated to tell him to go into Court. It seems to me perfectly clear from his statement, most candidly made to us, that a charge was made against the Ionian Government, or whatever the body was, that it was suggested that the right hon. Gentleman the First Commissioner had been party to whatever had been done; but that the real construction to be put upon the article was that it it did not amount to one of treason, but simply to a criticism upon the right hon. Gentleman's conduct as a pu l c man, which, as has been pointed out by many eminent Judges, public men are obliged to undergo. But does the right hon. Gentleman mean the House to understand that the charge, such as is related to us after a lapse of 30 years, approaches in the smallest degree the charges which have been made against hon. Members below the Gangway.

MR. W. E. GLADSTONE: It is not so bad.

SIR RICHARD WEBSTER: Sir, I should have hesitated, even though I am, according to the right hon. Gentleman, fond of introducing irrelevant matter, I should have hesitated to say " not so bad."

MR. W. E. GLADSTONE: I meant the charge against me was not so bad.

SIR RICHARD WEBSTER: Clearly it was not nearly half as bad. I was just saying that I am, according to the right hon. Gentleman, one of the persons fond of introducing irrelevant matter. I notice this because I want to prepare the House for the three reasons of the right hon. Gentleman why the Irish Party should not go into Court. The right hon. Gentleman's third reason was that lawyers are always in the habit of introducing irrelevant matters of prejudice or otherwise, which irrelevant matters are intended to divert the attention of the juries and Judges to such an extent that they are unable to do justice to a case of libel brought before them. The observations of the right hon. Gentleman upon this point were cheered; but I do not think there are many lawyers in the House who would like to attach their names to a written opinion endorsing such a statement as that. Mr. Speaker, I recognize to the full the gravity of the charges — not this particular charge under discussion; but the charges which have been made against the hon. Gentleman the Member for East Mayo, and the other Members of the Party with whom he associates—and it is because these charges, if unfounded, are scandalous; it is because, if these charges are founded upon doubtful testimony, it is monstrous and outrageous to suggest that the Irish Party dare not go to law, because they will not get justice in the tribunal. The right hon. Gentleman the Member for Mid Lothian admits that the charges against a Party are worse by far than a charge made against an individual. The more clear that is made the better. Now, the second proposition of the right hon. Gentleman was supported in a way which makes it more easy for me to deal with it, because I am able to rely, not upon any language of my own, but upon the strong judgment, to a great extent, of this House. I repeat what the hon. and learned Solicitor General said yesterday.

Whatever may be the criticisms of this House upon the opinion of my hon. and learned Friend, I may be allowed to say that I feel that this House is very much indebted to the hon. and learned Solicitor General for the reasons he laid before the House. Now, Sir, in the course of his speech, which I listened to with the greatest admiration, my hon. and learned Friend the Solicitor General said to propose a Committee in a case in which there had been a libellous attack made upon an hon. Member of the House, which libellous attack the libeller was prepared to justify, is without precedent. After a careful examination of the subject by my hon. and learned Friend the Member for Hackney, after a careful examination of it by the right hon. Gentleman the Member for Mid Lothian, I re-assert our position, and I say, without the slightest fear of contradiction, that the publication being admitted, the authorship of the publication being admitted, the application of the article to the hon. Member for East Mayo, to the hon. Member for Cork, and others, not being denied, this House never has granted —and I go further—this House never ought to grant a Committee upstairs. I need hardly tell the House that, at a moment's notice, I had to express an opinion on this matter. I did so with diffidence and hesitation. I felt unable to assume the confidence which was, undoubtly, felt by the right hon. Gentleman the Member for Derby in the positive opinion he expressed. Perhaps I was wrong; but it did occur to me that my position required me to give opinions which I could justify. Whatever may be said by hon. Members below the Gangway as to Law Officers of the Crown giving legal opinions to please the Government, or from Party motives, I challenge hon. Members of the House to say that of me. I may make mistakes —I do not claim infallibility, and it is possible that I may be mistaken—but if I should stoop to give this House a legal opinion from Party motives I should be unworthy to occupy this place for a single instant. I think that the suggestion of the hon. Gentleman the Member for the Scotland Division of Liverpool (Mr. T. P. O'Connor) as to opinions given for Party purposes is one that I need not devote much attention to. I listened with great attention to the powerful and interesting speech of the hon.

[*Third Night.*]

and learned Member for South Hackney (Sir Charles Russell). He, too, had spent the best part of his time in seeking for precedents, and trying if he could find out something. We were naturally afraid that we might have overlooked some material case, and that he might have found out something that we had failed to discover. It was a relief to me when I found that he sat down, not only not contesting our position, but supporting it, and frankly admitting—for he is always frank—that he had no instance in point. He said that, as he had no precedents at hand, the House ought to make a precedent. I shall have occasion to notice one case of extreme importance brought forward by the hon. and learned Member for South Hackney in the course of my answer to the speech of the right hon. Gentleman the Member for Mid Lothian. I want to dispose of the cases which have been mentioned by the right hon. Gentleman, though not exactly in the order he followed. I will take his last case first. The right hon. Gentleman attached immense importance to the case of Whittle Harvey. I invite the attention of the House to the statement of that case as reported in the Third Series of *Hansard*, Vol. 23, and I submit to any hon. Gentleman, whether lawyer or layman, that the case of Whittle Harvey has not the slightest application to the case now before the House. The right hon. Gentleman opposite (Mr. Childers) is going to answer me, and I hope, when he does, he will deal with the substance of my argument on this point. What are the facts? In the Whittle Harvey case a Petition—I think two Petitions—were presented to the House by 500 members of the constituency which Whittle Harvey represented—it was Colchester, I think—asking that an inquiry might be directed by the House as to the mode of admitting persons to practise at the Bar. That is to say, the jurisdiction of the House was invoked in a matter of great public interest. That Petition was supported by hon. Members, and accordingly the House, considering that the way in which persons were called to the Bar was of sufficient public importance to warrant an inquiry, directed that a Committee should be appointed for the purpose of inquiring into the matter. It had nothing in the world to do with the House as a House of Commons; but

Whittle Harvey happened to be a person whose application to be called to the Bar had been rejected by the Members or Benchers of his Inn, and accordingly an inquiry was entered upon as to the circumstances of the refusal. The consequence was that an investigation was held extending over some months. Now, I ask the House what this case of compliance with a Petition presented to the House in the ordinary course of Business has to do with a case of libel? I should weary the House if I were to give instances in which inquiries were directed on the mere Motion of hon. Members. Members in cases where they have got up Petitions. But I must say that whatever may have been the course pursued by the House with regard to inquiry in a particular instance, there is no analogy whatever between the case now before the House and the case of an inquiry into that which was a matter of public interest with relation to a Member of the House on a Petition presented by his constituents. I will give right hon. and hon. Gentlemen opposite all the information at my disposal on the case to which I have referred; because, if any answer can be given to the distinction I have pointed out to that case and the case at present under consideration, it would only be right that they should have the opportunity of giving it. I pass now to the case of Grissel and Ward, in 1879—though it was not really relied on by the right hon. Gentleman. In that case there was an allegation of corruption, or of a power to corrupt, in relation to a Member of a Private Bill Committee upstairs, and the inquiry was not for the purpose of considering whether a Breach of Privilege had been committed, but of ascertaining the facts. A Committee was appointed to inform itself, and to inform the House, whether there was or was not any truth in the charge made against a Member of a Select Committee upstairs as a Member in the service of this House. I appeal to the House, at least to those hon. Members who are good enough to listen to me at this unusual hour (8.40 P.M.), whether there is any analogy between that and the one case before the House? Another case was cited by the hon. and learned Member for South Hackney, which is certainly well worthy of the consideration of the House. It is a direct authority, as showing that at times when the course now suggested

Sir Richard Webster

might have been pursued by the House, it was not pursued. A charge was made against Mr. Clive of corruption, as Member of a Select Committee upstairs. It was made by Washington Wilkes. That was undoubtedly a case in which a charge was made against an hon. Member of the House, in the service of the House, in his capacity as Chairman of a Railway Bill Committee. When the printer was called to the Bar, he declined to withdraw the charge, except to the extent of publishing the denial of Mr. Clive; and he asserted the truth of the charge. There was an express occasion on which, if it had been the practice of the House to inquire into the truth of charges against Members of the House by Select Committees, that course would have been suggested. But it was not suggested by anybody that there should be a Select Committee to inquire into the truth of the libel. On the contrary, the House, regarding it as a Breach of Privilege, by virtue of its powers, without inquiring into the truth of the charge, without dealing with the question of justification or otherwise, even though the man protested the truth of the libel, he was sent off to prison. [*Opposition cheers.*] Hon. Gentlemen cheer. Will they be so good as to remember that the suggestion for a Committee was originally made by the right hon. Gentleman the Member for Mid Lothian, after reading a passage from Sir Erskine May, which he has not quoted again to-night? That case has no reference whatever to the case we are discussing, in which it is suggested that the function of the Committee should be brought into play, after the printer has been called to the Bar of the House, for the purpose of establishing the truth or falsehood of the libel. There is not a shadow of foundation in precedent for the exercise of any such authority, for the point which I desire to make is that on the very occasion when, as the right hon. Gentleman suggests, the appointment of a Committee to inquire would have been the proper course, no Committee was suggested, nor was anything of the kind done.

MR. MAURICE HEALY (Cork): Was the inquiry refused?

SIR RICHARD WEBSTER : There was no suggestion made by anyone that there should be an inquiry.

MR. MAURICE HEALY: The printer was asked to name his informant, and he refused.

SIR RICHARD WEBSTER : The hon. Member has not done me the courtesy to listen to my remarks. The printer was asked if he would withdraw the charges, but he said he would not, and that he was prepared to prove the truth of the charges. He would not give up the name of his informant, but that does not weaken the strength of my argument. No inquiry was asked for; there was none suggested by any one. Now, I have dealt with the Whittle Harvey case, the Grissel and Ward case, and the Clive case. I thank the right hon. Gentleman for having quoted Mr. Butt's case in 1854, because I do not wish for any stronger argument in my favour. The allegation made in that case—which may be found in *Hansard*, Vol. 130—was that a section of Irish Members represented nothing beyond the embodied wish of some hundreds of needy men to obtain place, salary, and position. In effect the charge was one of open corruption. The hon. and learned Solicitor General did not suggest, nor do I for a moment suggest, that if a charge of corruption is made a Select Committee should not be appointed. No one has ever suggested that. My hon. and learned Friend has stated in language as clear as could be used that that was a case in which a Committee would be appointed, and he drew the clearest distinction between such a case, and that we are now considering. But what happened? Does the appointment of that Committee offer any inducement to adopt the same course? I wonder how many hon. Members have taken the pains to examine the Report of that Committee, and see what testimony the experience of that Committee gives us to the desirability of pursuing the same course when persons wish to clear themselves of charges of crime. I will deal first with the question of the delay which the right hon. Gentleman the Member for Mid Lothian says must necessarily be involved by the Government proposal. The right hon. Gentleman adverted to the promptitude and expedition with which the matter could be disposed of before a Select Committee of this House. But in Mr. Butt's case the Select Com-

[Third Night.]

mittee, which was appointed on the 7th of February, did not make its report until the 19th of June, a period of more than four months. But that is not all. Was the Report of that Committee satisfactory? The Committee reported that they had been obliged so to extend their inquiries us to investigate matters of "idle gossip and of groundless scandals"; and they added that in their opinion—

"No investigation by a Committee with the powers which has been entrusted to them could be satisfactory,"

Am I wrong, therefore, in saying that I am glad the right hon. Member for Mid Lothian cited Mr. Butt's case? Am I wrong in pointing out that if he wished us to act in this matter as he has proposed, and as he deems would be prudent he should at least have informed us as to the success of the operation in former cases. Moreover, prior to the Report of the Committee there were 18 or 19 divisions, upon most of which there was a difference of opinion among the Members of the Committee, some of whom were Gentlemen of great experience. The difference of opinion was displayed in a most remarkable manner, and the consequence was that scarcely any result was arrived at. Therefore, not only was the inquiry conducted by that Committee unsatisfactory, but the Committee themselves were obliged to confess their inability to conduct such an inquiry in an efficient manner. Hon. Members may flatter themselves that for certain purposes a Committee would be most desirable. I would say one word about that. Still, dealing with the question of delay, I want to know what is going to happen if this Committee is appointed? In that case, even if the Committee were to sit two or three days a week, it would be impossible for them to make their Report before the expiration of three or four months. The right hon. Gentleman the Member for Mid Lothian has dwelt upon the time that the matter would take to try in a Court of Law, but all that I can say is this, that as the noble Lord the Member for South Paddington—and several others who spoke on this side of the House have pointed out—if a prosecution were directed by this House on the Motion of an hon. Member the trial of the case would be expedited, as means would be taken to enable it to be

Sir Richard Webster

tried promptly, and it might be brought to a satisfactory conclusion one way or the other within a quarter of the time it would take a Select Committee to come to a conclusion. I have only one more precedent to cite. It is a curious one, and it is one which I think the House will be glad to have before it. I have said that during the whole course of the time to which reference has chiefly been made—that is to say, during the last 50 or 60 years—there has been no instance in which an allegation made by a newspaper regarding a Member, except in the cases where the charges have been made against Members of improper conduct in their service to the House —Members of Committee or Members in some other official capacity—has been referred to a Select Committee of this House. I want to know why the House should not be informed as to what occurred in the case of Mr. O'Donnell. This point was raised in the case of Mr. O'Donnell, which occurred in 1878, and the Report of which is to be found in the 239th Vol. of *Hansard*. The charge was made in *The Globe* newspaper on the 16th of April, 1878, in relation to the murder of the Earl of Leitrim, that Mr. O'Donnell had made certain statements in the House in which he had not a grain of belief, and that he had suggested certain reasons, certain motives, which might have operated towards the palliation of the commission of that murder. It is said that nothing worse can be attributed to an hon. Member in his place in this House than falsehood. Well, I am not saying that that is not a grave charge; but I say that looking back to the way the House has dealt with these cases it never has looked upon the charge of falsehood in speech as one of those matters calling for its interference. I am not going to quote all the opinions of those Gentlemen who took part in the discussion to which I refer, but I commend those speeches to the attention of the House. I will read some of the observations of Sir Stafford Northcote on this case in 1878. The Motion having been made " That the said article of *The Globe* is a Breach of the Privileges of this House," Sir Stafford Northcote, the then Chancellor of the Exchequer said—

" I confess, Sir, that though I listened as well and attentively as I could to the article just read by the Clerk at the Table. I was not able to follow the whole of it; but it appears to me that it was an article upon the question of Ribbonism, and upon the agrarian system in Ireland, and that it had special reference to the recent tragedy, the murder of Lord Leitrim, and that the object and tenour of the article was to attribute the murder to the system to which the writer refers. Undoubtedly, there appeared to be a sentence in the course of the article in which reference was made to the speech of the hon. Member for Dungarvan the other night, and the apparent intention of the writer was to set aside the explanation suggested by the hon. Member as being one which it would hardly be, in the opinion of the writer, inconsistent with the intelligence of the hon. Member to suppose he had believed to be the true explanation. I do not understand that the tenour of the article is one that can be described as a Breach of the Privileges of this House, and I believe the proper course to adopt, attention having been called to this matter by the hon. Member, and the House having heard the article read, would now be—if the House takes the same view as I do—namely, that it was in the nature, for the most part, of an argument upon the general subject of Ribbonism, and that the sentence so introduced, and which is specially complained of, was one of a casual character—that the House had better adopt the Amendment which I am about to propose, which is—'That the House do now proceed to the Orders of the Day.'"—(3 *Hansard*, [239] 1400-1.)

MR. CHILDERS (Edinburgh, S.): Read the opinion of my right hon. and learned Friend the Member for Bury (Sir Henry James).

SIR RICHARD WEBSTER: I have often endeavoured to be in two places at once; but I have never tried to make two speeches at once. Will the right hon. Gentleman have a little patience. Sir Henry James, speaking on the same occason, said—

"He had no doubt that the right hon. Gentleman the Chancellor of the Exchequer might have been quite right in one sense in taking the conciliatory course which he had indicated; but if the Motion of the right hon. Gentleman, simply to proceed with the Orders of the Day, were accepted, it would be thought that he agreed, to some extent, with the Motion that the article complained of was a Breach of Privilege, and that he wished to avoid coming to a determination upon it. It appeared to him (Sir Henry James) that the article was no Breach of Privilege at all, and he desired to point out to the Chancellor of the Exchequer that the course which he had followed—however advisable from a conciliatory point of view—might be taken as conveying a *quasi*-admission that the House regarded the article as a Breach of Privilege. He (Sir Henry James) had always understood that a Breach of Privilege of that description consisted in a writer having libelled a Member of that House in his capacity as a Member of Parliament, and that the House did not regard criticism, unless it was libellous in relation to the House generally."—(*Ibid.* 1401-2.)

I say that that is the test that has been laid down over and over again that, in matters of libel published outside, a Breach of Privilege is not supposed to be committed unless the libel is against the House generally, against a Member in his official capacity, or against some considerable section of the House. I again submit—and upon this point I challenge contradiction—that there is not, from the beginning to the end of these precedents, extending over the last 50 or 60 years, one single case in which a libel upon a private Member of this House, otherwise than in respect of his service in this House, has been treated by this House as a question of Breach of Privilege. Of course, I do not mean to say that if you go back 100 or 150 years you may not find precedents of that kind in plenty. The noble Lord the Member for South Paddington is taunted with having called this a technical Breach of Privilege; and, no doubt, in the days of the Long Parliament it was held to be a Breach of Privilege to publish the way in which a Member of the House had voted, and most arbitrary and wicked practices were resorted to to stop the publication of the proceedings of the House. If we are to hold that imputations of deliberate falsehood on the part of hon. Members constitute a Breach of the Privileges of this House, I do not think that we need go very far back to find newspapers which have committed such Breaches of Privileges every week during the past few years. I pass now from the question of Privilege. I have pointed out that neither the right hon. Gentleman the Member for Derby, the right hon. Gentleman the Member for Mid Lothian, nor anyone else has been able to show a precedent for a Committee of Inquiry. I have pointed out that the cases they refer to were cases in which Committees could rightly and properly have been granted on other grounds. There have been Committees of the House, and investigations ordered by the House, in order to ascertain what the facts were; but neither directly nor indirectly, when a man has stood at the Bar to justify a libel, or prove the truth of an allegation, have the circumstances been inquired into by a Select Committee. I now pass to that which is, perhaps, the gravest and most serious point in this discussion, and that is the one which is raised by the offer which Her Ma-

[*Third Night.*]

jesty's Government have made to pursue a certain course if they are directed to do so by the Order of this House on request being made by any of those Members who are desirous of having their character cleared from these charges. In dealing with this branch of the subject, I must express my regret that the right hon. Member for Derby is not in his place, and the hope that he will read what I am about to say; and, if it be possible for him to do so, to answer at some time or other my observations. I am not speaking now, as it was suggested rather significantly I had done the other night, "under the influence of temper." I am not in the habit of allowing temper at any time to interfere with what I have to say; I say I feel, and I feel deeply, what has been said by the hon. Member for the Scotland Division of Liverpool, by the right hon. Member for Derby, and, lastly, but of course more weighty than all, by the right hon. Member for Mid Lothian. What was said by the right hon. Member for Mid Lothian a few minutes ago? He said that it was collusion of the grossest character. He said that for Her Majesty's Government to suggest there should be a prosecution carried on in the way proposed would be collusion of the grossest character, such as would be a disgrace to Her Majesty's Government. [*Opposition Cheers.*] Those sentiments are cheered! I will examine in a few moments whether there is one single grain of justice in those imputations. Sir, I will quote from *The Times* report of the speech of the hon. Member for the Scotland Division of Liverpool—and I know the report is correct. He said—

"What is the proposal of the right hon. Gentleman? It is a collusive action at law against *The Times* with a co-plaintiff who has been making the same charges as the defendant."

And he goes on to say—

"The right hon. Gentleman does not want to play a fair game. He has invited us to the struggle, and when we have accepted the invitation, then he asks us to come to a game in which the dice are loaded;"

and the hon. Member replied to that invitation, that no honourable man would be a party to a proposition such as that which was made. [*Cheers.*] I hope that those who hear me, and those who may read what I am saying, will judge between the one side and the

Sir Richard Webster

other and will note those cheers. Sir, Her Majesty's Government have made this proposition, because this is not a case in which we think the House ought to interfere as a Breach of Privilege. We think it would be unwise, having regard to the course of events which has lately taken place, for the House to regard this libel upon a private Member—as a Member distinguished from a Member in the service of the House —as a matter which the House ought to interfere with as a matter of privilege; but in order that it may be shown that we do regard the position of hon. Members below the Gangway opposite—that we do wish to give them an opportunity of having the best investigation possible, we have intimated that, if any hon. Member moves for it, the Government will not resist a prosecution on behalf of the House, and in the name of the Attorney General, in order that justice may be done and the truth ascertained. What is the reply? The reply is "This is collusive. You wish the Attorney General, who sympathizes with the slanders, to be the prosecutor." Sir, I will not pause to refer to my own utterances. Nobody can say I have said anything with regard to the justice or the truth of those affairs. All I can say, is that if the man who made those statements is not in a position to prove them, he is not worthy to be an editor a single minute longer. I should be the last man to judge a Member on the allegation of a newspaper editor. But we have this to consider. It is suggested that Her Majesty's Government intended to take the course proposed, in order that there might not be a conviction; that is the suggestion, and it is perfectly amazing that that suggestion should be made by an hon. Gentleman supported by the hon. Members below the Gangway opposite. I do not wonder that in their position they feel bound to make such imputations, though I think they might have made them in a less drastic way. But I cannot understand an hon. Gentleman saying, that because the name of the Attorney General is used it is a collusive trial. Did the hon. and learned Gentleman the Member for Hackney, whose successor I am, and who filled the post of Attorney General with greater ability and power than I am able to do—did he support that statement? To his honour, he said not one word in support of it. Let me just tell the House what are the functions of the Attorney General. I allow or direct proceedings in my own name, of a great many of which, in the course of the year, I have not the slightest knowledge whatever. Private solicitors and counsel are engaged, and I know nothing whatever of the matter. It is well known that though the name of the Attorney General is used in suits of all kinds, criminal as well as others, he has nothing to do with them personally. The most absurd and complete misrepresentation of our position is made, when it is suggested that Her Majesty's Government wish their Attorney General or their Solicitor General to take part in the prosecution, and that I should allow my name to be used. I hear an hon. Member say—"The use of your name is 'loaded dice!'"

MR. CONYBEARE (Cornwall, Camborne): I merely made a *sotto voce* remark. All that I meant was, that if the hon. and learned Member's name was to be used in the way suggested, that would give an unfair advantage to the Crown, and, in my opinion, might be likened to the use of loaded dice.

SIR RICHARD WEBSTER: I think the hon. Member is himself a member of the Bar. Yet the hon. Member stands up in this House and says that because the Attorney General of England allows his name to be used in order that there should be a party on the record capable of instituting a prosecution, this is giving a false colour and importing " loaded dice " into the proceedings. I will appeal to any member of the Bar of Ireland, and to every hon. Member of this House — even the greatest Radical—whether that is not a scandalous imputation? Sir, the position is simply this—that if this House were to order a prosecution, because of that my name must be used, but the solicitor would be the solicitor instructed by the hon. Gentleman who might wish to prosecute, and the counsel would be of his own choosing—it might be the hon. and learned Member for South Hackney (Sir Charles Russell). Does he play with "loaded dice?" Would hon. Members venture to suggest that a prosecution conducted by that hon. and learned Member who sympathizes with them on political matters would not be properly conducted? Are there

no members of the English Bar who are sufficiently skilful and sufficiently honourable to be able to conduct this case? Sir, I leave that gross slander upon the Profession of which I am, for the moment, the unworthy representative, and the grosser slander upon the action of Her Majesty's Government, to recoil upon the heads of those who make them. Sir, I have waited, and waited in vain, in the hope that the right hon. Member for Derby might favour me with his presence, if but for three minutes. I am going to point out that not only has the right hon. Member for Mid Lothian made a suggestion which we indignantly repudiate, but that the right hon. Member for Derby has done worse. In this House yesterday he said, among other things, that if I allowed a prosecution which I did not believe in, I should be guilty of gross misconduct and do an un-Constitutional act. But, Sir, all that the Attorney General has to be satisfied of in directing or sanctioning a prosecution for libel is that a libel has been published, and nothing else; and that a libel has been published in the present instance is beyond controversy. It is a positive fact that the only thing which need be put before him to get his sanction for a prosecution is *The Times* article; and does anyone suggest that I should not allow my name to be used in an action when I saw a libel had been committed against a Member of the House? Therefore, the suggestion that I must be satisfied as to the truth or falsehood of the accusation is utterly be ond the point. The right hon. Member for Derby made this accusation, but did not stop to hear the speech of the Solicitor General—he left about the middle of it. He went to Southampton; and last night he made a speech, and I will give an extract from it. I cannot say whether it is true; but if the right hon. Gentleman denies the accuracy of what I read, I will withdraw it. I quote from a local paper, whose reports are usually very accurate. I wish the right hon. Gentleman would cross that little silver streak, and make that speech in a constituency not very far from Southampton. [*Cries of* " Order!" *and* "That is a threat!"]

MR. EDWARD HARRINGTON (Kerry, W.): I should like to ask whether the hon. and learned Gentleman is in Order, when speaking of the right hon. Gentleman the Member for Derby as delivering a speech, in saying he wishes he had crossed a silver streak to repeat it—meaning to hold out a threat?

SIR RICHARD WEBSTER: The hon. Member forgets I have the honour to represent that place.

MR. EDWARD HARRINGTON: Yes; that is the point.

SIR RICHARD WEBSTER: The right hon. Member for Derby is reported to have said—

"They offered that the honour of Mr. Dillon and his Colleagues should be taken charge of by the Attorney General and Her Majesty's Government"—

this, when my hon. and learned Friend the Solicitor General had stated that they might employ any counsel they chose—

"Had Mr. Dillon and his Friends accepted that offer, there is little doubt that Mr. Dillon, in the arms of Sir Richard Webster, would fare very much as Little Red Riding Hood did when she was confided to the charge of her grandmother."

And this is the language of the right hon. Gentleman! This is the language of the Gentleman who has been Solicitor General—who was almost leader of the Bar! I say that this address, by a man fresh from the House of Commons, to a public audience, insisting that Her Majesty's Government only wanted to get up a bogus prosecution for the purpose of enabling *The Times* to prove the truth of the libel under colour of a prosecution which should be collusive—I say it is a scandalous accusation against the Government.

MR. E. ROBERTSON (Dundee): Will the hon. and learned Gentleman excuse me for interrupting him? I heard the statement of the right hon. Gentleman the First Lord of the Treasury yesterday, and I distinctly understood him—[*Cries of* "Order!"] Are we now to understand that the right hon. Gentleman's proposal is that the name of the Attorney General should be used only nominally, and not, as we understood yesterday, that he should conduct the prosecution with two other counsel?

SIR RICHARD WEBSTER: I am very much surprised at the statement of the hon. and learned Member, who is also a member of the Bar. Did he, or did he not, listen to the speech of the hon. and learned Solicitor General? The hon. and learned Solicitor General yesterday, in this House, within 20 minutes after the right hon. Gentleman the Member for Derby had spoken, said that, so far as I was concerned, I should have nothing to do with the prosecution, but that my name would simply be used formally, as counsel. In addition to that, the Treasury Solicitors will have nothing in the world to do with it; and any solicitor hon. Members below the Gangway choose to employ can conduct the case for them. If this kind of statement is to be made by members of my own Profession, let them have the honesty to read the speeches in *The Times*. The speech of the hon. and learned Solicitor General is in black and white in *The Times* of to-day, and I say there is not one single Member of this House who listened to the hon. and learned Solicitor General who could have thought for a moment that Her Majesty's Government wished actively to interfere with this prosecution. We simply want to show that money shall be no obstacle; that the Irish Members shall have perfectly fair play, and that if it is a case in which action ought to be taken, it shall be taken in such a way as to do the fullest justice to all parties. Sir, I must apologize for trespassing so long upon the time of the House; but there is one aspect of this case which must not be forgotten. Hon. Gentlemen below the Gangway seem to set but slight store on the chance of getting a verdict; but do they remember that the principal witnesses in the prosecution will be themselves? Do they remember that the hon. Member for East Mayo, and other Members of the Party to which he belongs, can go into the witness-box, and make their statements upon oath, and subject themselves to cross-examination? Do they attach no value to the publicity of evidence—evidence given, not by order of Parliament, but as a matter of right? Everything that hon. Members say in the witness-box will come out before the public——

MR. MAURICE HEALY: You would say we would swear anything.

SIR RICHARD WEBSTER: These interruptions, at any rate, show that this power, which will be open to hon. Members below the Gangway who wish these charges to be disproved—namely, the power of going into the witness-box and subjecting themselves to cross-examination—is a power to which they do not seem to attach much value. If a public man is aspersed, if a libellous charge is brought against hon. Members, they should be anxious to go into the box to refute it. The right hon. Gentleman the Member for Mid Lothian told us that when, 30 years ago, a charge, though only a doubtful charge, of treason was brought against him, he was burning with desire to go into the box and clear himself. I wish to know why that burning desire does not rest in the breasts of hon. Gentlemen below the Gangway? It is idle, Sir, to suggest that justice cannot be done in this country. Has this country fallen so low that scandalous libels are to be committed, and that Judges and jurors are to have their minds so warped that justice cannot be obtained? If that is the case, why do you allow your Courts to exist at all? Why do you allow lawyers and a legal system so corrupt and so liable to mislead you to continue any longer? Why do you allow these lawyers to remain at large? That kind of argument, Sir, will do very well for those who desire to adopt the suggestion that Her Majesty's Government is not honest and straightforward, but it will not do with the country. Now, Sir, I have dealt with the three propositions of the right hon. Gentleman the Member for Mid Lothian. I have also immediately dealt with the question of precedents, and with the question of how far the Committee could go; and I appeal to the majority of the House—I appeal to that majority which the right hon. Gentleman said does represent the United Kingdom—I appeal to that majority to say, Aye or No, which is the honourable and satisfactory course. We do not consider that this is a case—the House has expressed its opinion that this is not a case—in which the old weapon of Privilege should be invoked in order to punish some writer who may have libelled or who may have slandered some Member of this House, not being a servant of the House, there being full remedies open to that Member in the Courts of Law. It has been pointed out over and over again that the main argument in favour of Breach of Privilege is because there is no other remedy. It has been pointed out that Breach of Privilege is directly analogous to contempt of the Courts of Law, and that it is necessary to punish it in order that the proceedings of the House may go on

without let or hindrance. These libels have rested over the heads of hon. Members below the Gangway for many weeks—I might almost say for many months. These hon. Members have not moved hand or foot to deal with them, and if they are so exceedingly anxious to clear themselves let them think better over it and commence this prosecution. At any rate, the House will not be misled in this matter. The Motion was made by the hon. Baronet the Member for North Antrim, as we have distinctly stated, and as it is now admitted by right hon. Gentlemen opposite, without the concurrence or wish of, and certainly without consultation with, Her Majesty's Government. That Motion, however, has been made. It has raised an important question. On the one side there is the absolute necessity of not allowing the freedom of the Press to be interfered with, while on the other hand there is, of course, the necessity that the dignity of this House should not be interfered with, and that the power of hon. Members to do their duty shall not be impaired; but can anybody have the slightest doubt that if these are matters to be inquired into at all, the Courts of Law are the proper tribunals in which they ought to be dealt with, where there is a calm and judicial atmosphere, and where there are men who have for years been accustomed to deal with questions of this kind? And I appeal, also, on behalf of British juries, and maintain that if these charges are shown to be scandalous and invented, the Courts of Justice and Her Majesty's Judges will deal out with no stinting hands the punishment that ought to be awarded to the authors of these libels.

MR. CONYBEARE: Owing to an unfortunate whisper of mine I am afraid that the hon. and learned Attorney General (Sir Richard Webster) derived the impression that I was making a personal attack upon him. Now, I wish at the very outset of my remarks to assure him that I had not the slightest intention of referring to him in the matter. I think that will at once be obvious, and I am only sorry that the hon. and learned Gentleman should have put the construction he did upon two words which I used. I have too much respect for the hon. and learned Attorney General to suggest that he could be capable of conduct which he repudiated repeatedly in the course of his remarks with such emphasis. But when I say that I think I am justified by the spirit of the remarks which were made not only by the right hon. Gentleman the Member for Mid Lothian (Mr. W. E. Gladstone), but by the hon. Member for the Scotland Division of Liverpool (Mr. T. P. O'Connor). The substance and the gist of the allegation on this side of the House was this— hon. Members on this side object to the proposal of the Government and to proceedings which they suggest would be open to the interpretation of being a collusive action, and which might, metaphorically speaking, be open to the remark that they were playing with loaded dice. It is perfectly obvious, I think, that no personal charge is contained in the remarks which have come from this side of the House ; and I repeat that I have not the slightest intention to attribute dishonest conduct to the hon. and learned Attorney General personally. But I must consider for one moment what is the position of the Government in this matter. The right hon. Gentleman the First Lord of the Treasury (Mr. W. H. Smith) yesterday afternoon used these words—

" We therefore propose to hon. Gentlemen below the Gangway who now demand an inquiry that the Attorney General, coupled with any Queen's counsel whom they may select, shall be instructed to prosecute the parties whose conduct is complained of."

Now, I submit, in the absence of any further explanation, that the right hon. Gentleman the First Lord has distinctly justified us in maintaining as we do that the object of this proposal on the part of the Government was that the Law Officers of the Crown should take an active part in the prosecution which the Government wishes to institute. We are told by the hon. and learned Attorney General that that is not so, and that, so far from his having anything to do with the matter as counsel in the case, his name is to be used simply in a formal manner, just as it is used in hundreds of cases referred to in which, as Law Officer of the Crown, he is made a party to proceedings of which he knows nothing and of which he has never heard. I say that makes the case very much worse, and still more justifies us in saying that the unfair conduct on the part of the Government resembles a game played with loaded dice ; because if the Government

do not intend to take part in this prosecution of theirs—if their Law Officer of the Crown is simply to be added in a formal manner as a party to this prosecution—what reason can possibly be suggested for such an unprecedented proposal as that, except that they wish to throw all the weight of the Crown influence on the side of the Government for the purpose of implying and conveying to the minds of those who might have to decide the case that the whole of the influence of the Crown and its Law Officers was to be, and would be, on the side of those whom they were pretending to assist in this prosecution, while in reality it would be on the side of *The Times*, which would be made the criminal party ? The Government have identified themselves so thoroughly by many observations which have fallen from its Members and by the repeated accusations of their supporters on both sides of the House ; they have so made these odious charges their own that we may be pardoned for believing that the interposition of the Law Officers of the Crown as such can only have one object —namely, to convey to the minds of the jury, who would be infallibly brought to this conclusion—that it was a prosecution in which the Government was not on the side of the party they were supposed to be assisting, but of the party which had championed their cause day after day, week after week, and month after month, by disseminating these odious calumnies, forgeries, and slanders through the length and breadth of the land. I think the proposal that the Attorney General should take up this position only makes the matter worse. I should like to make one or two observations upon the case set out by the hon. and learned Attorney General, and some remarks relative to the method in which this matter has been brought before the House. It is quite clear, from what has transpired to-night, and from the arguments which have fallen from the right hon. Gentleman the Member for Mid Lothian and others, as well as from the argument of the hon. and learned Attorney General, that there is a conflict of precedents in this case ; and if that be so, I submit that it would be better to follow that which has been the traditional policy and custom of the House rather than to depart by a hair's breadth from that custom and introduce proceed-

Mr. Conybeare

ings which, at any rate, must be regarded as novel in the extreme, if they are not wholly indefensible. The hon. and learned Attorney General went on to argue that the matter affected only one Member of the House ; that it does not affect a section of the House or the House itself. I hope I am not misrepresenting the hon. and learned Attorney General, who, I regret, is not in his place; but, if I understand his argument, it amounted to this—that if these libels affected not an individual Member, but a number of Members, then there would be a Breach of Privilege—not otherwise. I maintain, in opposition to this argument, that the libels placed before the House in the articles which appeared in *The Times* do not apply to the hon. Member alone, but to the whole body of his associates. The three first lines of this article are by themselves perfectly sufficient to bear out that contention—

"Mr. Dillon, M.P., has attempted upon two several occasions within the last few days to excuse his own connection and that of his brother Members of Parliament with P. J. Sheridan, Invincible, dynamiter, and assassin. We propose to test his statements as a sample of Parnellite testimony."

No words can be used in a more general sense as indicating the whole body of the Nationalists—

"We shall show that nearly all Mr. Dillon's material allegations are demonstrably and flagrantly false, and that Mr. Dillon might readily have informed himself of their falsehood had he chosen so to do."

That is one passage; there is another passage at the bottom of page 12, in which we read—

"We have treated certain episodes in this scoundrel's career in, perhaps, tedious detail, to demonstrate once for all the incredible falsehood and effrontery of Parnellite apologists."

That, Sir, may apply not only to Members from Ireland, but also to Members from England, because there are plenty of us on this side of the House who certainly might, without any stretch of the imagination, be termed Parnellite apologists; and it appears to me that there might be based on the statement an argument that this is a libel affecting directly other than hon. Members from Ireland, in fact, hon. Members from Great Britain as well—

"We have examined an elaborate explanation made by one of the most respected of Mr. Parnell's lieutenants from his place in Parliament,

and we have shown that it is a tissue of gross and palpable falsehoods. Whether Mr. Dillon was or was not conscious that the statements he was making were untrue is a point of little public moment. But it is right and necessary that the world should know that 'the Bayard of the League' has given an entirely fictitious account of a series of important transactions in which he himself and several of his leading Colleagues in the House were principal actors. We are reduced to this alternative—Mr. Dillon either refrained from all serious efforts of recollection and inquiry, and recklessly palmed off upon the House, as ascertained facts within his personal knowledge, a mass of confused, inaccurate, and unexamined memories, or he deliberately told the House a detailed story which he knew to be untrue. In either case, several of his Colleagues must have known that his statements were unfounded. The Party sat exulting by, and endorsed the fabrication."

Now, the few words I last read amply justify us in asserting that the honour of the whole Party from Ireland is at stake, and that it is idle to talk about this not being a Breach of Privilege because it affects, forsooth, only one individual. Then on the following page we read—

"So far as we are concerned, it is perfectly immaterial whether he does or does not take the obvious and only method by which the accusation can be disposed of. Within the House of Commons his denial is conventionally accepted, because debate could not go on were the House, as a whole, to adopt the methods and manners of Mr. Parnell's Party, who give the lie direct to any speaker with whom they disagree."

There you have a charge of direct and wilful falsehood against every Member of the Party who represent our Irish fellow-citizens. Again, there is, towards the end of the second letter, on page 14, this passage—

"Mr. Dillon has stood in public estimation somewhat apart from the rank and file of his Party. His honesty has been vouched for, if we mistake not, by some prominent Members of the Opposition who have not ventured, in the case of his Colleagues, upon quite such thorough-going advocacy. The public can now judge what amount of confidence can be reposed in Mr. Dillon's assertions, and from that they can infer how much importance attaches to the asseverations of Gentlemen who have not attained to the dignity of the 'Bayard of the League.'"

From that we are asked to infer that the chivalrous "Bayard of the League," the hon Member for East Mayo, is, as *The Times* terms him, a liar, and his Colleagues, being below him in the scale of gentlemanly conduct, are liars to whom a great many unmentionable epithets might be applied. I will go one step further, and venture to argue

[*Third Night.*]

that the charges which are at issue in this case are not merely contained in the one charge of direct and wilful falsehood on the part of the hon. Member for East Mayo. These charges against the whole of the Irish Party affect us directly; and if they affect us directly as Members representing other parts of the Empire than Ireland, I say that this shows more than ever that this is a case of Privilege, and ought to be treated by this House as such. We have this accusation brought against Members representing Ireland—namely, that they knowingly associated with murderers and assassins, and I argue that that charge against these hon. Members directly affects every one of us who, knowing that they are, as *The Times* asserts, the associates of assassins, choose to sit here and associate ourselves with them. It seems to me that if we are to follow the new code of aristocratic morality laid down by the noble Marquess the Member for Rossendale (the Marquess of Hartington); and if, as English Gentlemen, we are to adopt the course, which, I hope, we Commoners will not be in a hurry to imitate from these Noblemen—if we are to assume, as a principle in our jurisprudence and code of honour in this country, that every ruffian who chooses to bring an impudent charge against an innocent man is to be treated as having proved that charge, and the maligned one is to be treated as a criminal until the charge has been disproved, there are but two alternatives open to us. We must either expel all the Gentlemen representing Ireland whose conduct is thus so contaminating to ourselves—we must ask them to dissociate themselves from us, or we must, by some forcible means, dissociate ourselves from them—or else we must treat this matter as a question of Privilege, and we, every one of us, must be prepared to take it up and do our best to ascertain, by the means recommended by the right hon. Gentleman the Member for Mid Lothian (Mr. W. E. Gladstone), whether there is any foundation for these charges or not. That, Sir, appears to me a logical conclusion from the attitude taken up by our opponents. They say that these hon. Gentlemen are abominable altogether, because they have associated, at one time or another, with those whom they knew, or ought to have known,

Mr. Conybeare

had their hands red with blood. How is it, in that case, that we ourselves are not tarred with the same brush; how is it that, night after night, Tories, Radicals, and Liberal Unionists come and sit alongside of these hon. Gentlemen, and yet refuse the only means which is open to us, as a House of Commons, of either disproving these charges or getting rid of the contaminating society of these hon. Gentlemen? I understood the argument of the hon. and learned Gentleman the Attorney General to be that there never was a case in which, where the libeller denied his guilt, or, in other words, maintained the truth of the libel, there was an inquiry. Is not the conclusion from that argument this—that if there is no dispute, there can be no necessity for an inquiry? The hon. and learned Attorney General quoted, with great triumph, Clive's case—a case in which the printer was sent to prison, and in which, he said, no Committee of Inquiry, such as the right hon. Gentleman the Member for Mid Lothian proposes in this case, was appointed. But why was the printer sent to prison? Why was there no inquiry in that case? Because the printer came to the Bar of the House, in obedience to the summons, and persisted in his charge. I have not been able to go into all the precedents which have been quoted. I have no myrmidons at my command who can wade through dusty tomes and law books. I have not the assistance which the hon. and learned Attorney General is able to command; and I merely take account of the actual statement of fact which he himself made to the House a short time ago. That statement clearly shows that there was no inquiry in Clive's case, because there was no dispute whatever. The printer came to the Bar of the House, was guilty of what may be called brazenefaced effrontery, which I should not b-surprised if the editor of *The Times* displayed under similar circumstances, persisted in repeating the charge, and refused to make obeisance to the House, and to apologize for the fault of which he was accused. The next argument used by the hon. and learned Attorney General with which I shall deal was that a question of Privilege can only arise if it affects a Member of Parliament in the service of the House. I want to ask the hon. and learned Attorney General how he makes out that this charge against the hon. Member for East Mayo and his Colleagues does not affect them in the discharge of their service as Members of this House? The hon. and learned Attorney General seemed to think that a great deal depended upon the question whether a Member who is libelled is sitting on a Select Committee upstairs, or whether he is merely speaking as a Member on the floor of this House. I maintain that if any distinction is to be drawn at all, it is a far greater Breach of Privilege to reflect upon a Member of this House when, as the chosen spokesman of his constituents, he is delivering a message which he believes in his conscience he is bound to deliver on the floor of this House, than when he is simply engaged in the transactions of a Private Bill Committee—when he is simply asked to determine some petty question connected with the building of gasworks or the construction of a railway. Such service, important as it is, is far and away less dignified and important than the duties of Members on the floor of this House. Now, if that is so, I want to know how anyone can maintain for a moment that a libel of any kind made against an hon. Member when sitting as a Member of a Select Committee is not a tenfold greater Breach of Privilege directed against him when sitting, or speaking, or voting in this House? But, Sir, I will not labour that point, but proceed to make a passing remark upon an argument about which a great deal has been said—as to the reasons why Members from Ireland should distrust the possible result of a trial, if they instituted a trial, against *The Times* newspaper. I do not wish to say much upon this point, because it has been already amply dealt with by hon. Members, and especially by the right hon. Gentleman the Member for Mid Lothian; but some of us on this side of the House have seen enough of trials—and especially of political trials—to be assured that the proverbial uncertainty of the law is doubly uncertain when there is any possibility of political bias creeping into the minds of those who have to decide the issues. I am not preferring a charge against either Judges or jury; but I say that, after the sedulous propagation of these forgeries and libels against hon. Members from Ireland, it

would be almost a miracle if you could find 12 men, either special or petty jurors, in this country who would not be, to some extent, tinged with political bias, unconsciously it might be, but still sufficiently so to make a miscarriage of justice more than an uncertainty. The hon. and learned Gentleman the Attorney General was very severe upon the right hon. Gentleman the Member for Mid Lothian for having, as he thought, aspersed the character of the Judges. Well, I am a humble Member of the Learned Profession to which the hon. and learned Attorney General belongs; but I have not attained to the same eminent position he has done, and therefore I may be a little more careless than he of the aspersions, or the supposed aspersions, on the heads of the Profession, or the Judges of this country, amongst whom, I have no doubt, the hon. and learned Attorney General hopes one of these days to be numbered. But I have only to say upon this point that the observations of the right hon. Gentleman the Member for Mid Lothian scarcely bore the construction of aspersion upon the Judges of this country which the hon. and learned Attorney General sought to make out. What did the right hon. Gentleman say? He did not make reckless or indefinite charges against the Judges. I was sitting here when he spoke, and I remember that he distinctly said this—" Supposing one particular Judge—a Judge who has identified himself in the most violent manner with the Party opposed to hon. Members from Ireland — were to try the case ? " Of course, we all knew that the right hon. Gentleman was referring to Sir Fitzjames Stephen. We all know what took place in Ireland some few years ago, when Chief Justice May identified himself in the same violent and prejudiced manner, against the Nationalist Party. We all know that, owing to his violent language, and to the attitude he had taken up, Chief Justice May either was not allowed to, or did not venture to, conduct certain trials. I should hope it would be the same in this country, but we have no guarantee that it would be. We know how our arrangements are made with reference to the trial of causes, and I do not see that there is any guarantee whatever that Sir Fitzjames Stephen, whom hon. Members from Ireland have, owing to his declarations, very good reason to distrust, would not be appointed the Judge to try what might be to them a question of life and liberty, if not of death. Now, one other remark I should like to make with reference to the question of a trial. A great deal was made by the hon. and learned Attorney General as to the question of delay. He took that up as one of his first arguments, and argued strongly against the right hon. Gentleman the Member for Mid Lothian, and tried to prove, from one of the cases in which a Select Committee had been appointed, that the delay would be far greater in the case of a Select Committee reporting to this House than it would be in the case of a trial in our Courts of Law. I can only say the hon. and learned Gentleman the Attorney General must be exceptionally fortunate in the despatch of his professional business if he feels warranted in making this statement, because the case which he cited to show the inordinate delay on the part of a Select Committee only occupied, at most, a few months—I think four or five months. In the case he cited the Select Committee was appointed early in February, and had reported in the beginning of June. Now, we know perfectly well that when you once bring a case in the Courts of Law it goes on year after year. Fortunately, the delays in our Courts are not as great as formerly. But what happened in the case of "Brenon *v.* Ridgway," tried only the other day, Ridgway being, as we all know, the representative of *The Times* itself? In that case the trial did not come on for eight months. Mr. Brenon had to wait all these months before he could get his case before the Law Courts. Will the hon. and learned Gentleman the Attorney General tell me it would be possible for him to exercise his authority in pressing forward a case of this kind, so as to have it advanced before its proper order in the cause list? If that is the object for which the assistance of the Crown's Law Officers is to be invoked in this proposed prosecution, it does not reflect credit on their position, because anything more unfair to the general body of suitors in this country than that the hon. and learned Attorney General should seek to advance before its proper time a prosecution proposed in order that grave personal charges

against hon. Members from Ireland should be inquired into it is difficult to conceive. If an action were instituted to-day against *The Times*, there is every probability that we should have to wait, especially in the face of the coming Long Vacation, until next year, and probably later, before it could be brought before the Courts, and then possibly the verdict might be of a most unsatisfactory character. The whole of the hon. and learned Attorney General's impassioned appeal at the end of his oration was intended to make the country believe that hon. Members from Ireland are not anxious to have this matter settled; and he taunts them with not having moved before in this matter. The memory of the hon. and learned Gentleman must be very short. I was here in this House on an early day this Session when the hon. Baronet the Member for the Cockermouth Division of Cumberland (Sir Wilfrid Lawson) brought this matter before the House. It was not the precise words of this article he complained of, but it was a most abominable libel upon hon. Members from Ireland. He brought the matter forward as a question of Privilege. And then it will be within the recollection of the House that the hon. Gentleman the Member for West Belfast (Mr. Sexton) has on two occasions brought this matter, in one form or another, before the House. To say, again, that hon. Members of the Nationalist Party object to be sworn and examined—and that is the only reason that has been assigned why they do not institute a prosecution against *The Times*—is monstrous. When the Attorney General was referring to one case as a precedent, some hon. Members upon these Benches drew his attention to the fact that to-day witnesses are allowed to be sworn before Select Committees, and hon. Members from Ireland have expressed a very urgent and anxious desire that they should have an opportunity of bringing this matter before a Select Committee of this House. It is perfectly well understood by hon. Members opposite — they have admitted it themselves—that witnesses can be examined upon oath by Select Committees; and yet the Attorney General wants us and the country to believe that it is because the Irish Members are afraid of meeting these charges on their oaths that they dare not attack *The Times* newspaper in the Law Courts of this country. The whole argument advanced against my hon. Friends falls completely to the ground. Now, Sir, what were the concluding remarks of the Attorney General? He spoke of the antiquated weapon of Privilege, an expression of that kind which I venture to think is somewhat derogatory to the House so far as its traditions and Rules are concerned in the matter of Privilege—such an expression might have been expected from some spirits on this side of the House who are usually supposed to be rather revolutionary in their tendencies; but to hear a Law Officer of the Crown, a Law Officer of the Tory Party, a man who certainly, from his position, would be expected to have the greatest reverence for precedent, and who, owing to the Conservative instincts which, I am sure, possess him most thoroughly, ought to have an infinitely stronger love for all that is old and respected and conventional in the proceedings of this House—to hear this Gentleman speak of the antiquated weapon of Privilege fills me with amazement. Greatly as I am in favour of getting rid of all obnoxious and useless fictions which have no sense and no spirit of utility in them, I am not disposed, as the Attorney General is, judging from what he says, to throw away this antiquated weapon of Privilege. I believe that if you do get rid of Privilege, you will deprive the House of Commons in the future of one of its most important, one of its most valued, and one of its most cherished rights and powers. To say that when we take up a question which affects the honour and dignity, not only of one Member but of many Members of this House, we take up an antiquated weapon which should no longer be used, is to say that which ought not to be allowed to go unchallenged. I desire now for one moment to take up the challenge which the hon. Baronet (Sir Charles Lewis), who introduced this matter, threw out to us. I do so because I really feel some commiseration for the Government in the miserable plight in which they find themselves placed. When I recollect that the same hon. Baronet played the Tory Government of Mr. Disraeli, in the year 1875, the same trick, which one would have thought could only be the effort of some malicious opponent, I really think that the

Government deserve to be pitied for having such a candid friend at their elbow to be constantly leading them into difficulties. The hon. Gentleman appears in this matter to have made but a poor requital to those who have made him the latest ornament of the British Baronetage —["Oh!"]—well, is he not an ornament?—in bringing this matter before the House, and leading to the waste of a whole week of the time which the Government declare to be most essential to the carrying out of their policy. Probably, Sir, the best way in which hon. Members opposite can make a return for the obligation under which they are to the hon. Baronet will be to transplant him to another sphere of action altogether. I am sure that we on this side of the House ought to endeavour to requite him in some way, for certainly we have had much more to be thankful to him for his efforts, his chivalrous efforts, on behalf of his political opponents in this matter, than those on that side of the House. Well, what was the challenge which the hon. Baronet made? He said—"Those who sit opposite to me and know my character will not think that I am going to run away from the Motion which I have placed before the House." I certainly do know something of the character of the hon. Baronet, and all I can say is that, knowing what I do of his character, I should not be surprised at anything he did in the way of running away from his guns. My estimation of the hon. Baronet, based, I am sorry to say, on a longish experience of him, was amply justified and corroborated by the fact that almost immediately after he had made that declaration he did run away from his guns. I think that it is only proper when an hon. Member in the position of the hon. Baronet gets up and, under the cover of championing the cause of others, makes a deliberate attack upon the honesty and honour of several Members on this side of the House, it should be clearly understood what manner of man it is who makes the attack; and I want to place before the House this fact—that but a few days ago, on the 30th of last month, I think, this same hon. Baronet was charged publicly in the Press with action which I will forbear to characterize, but which the House will, perhaps, permit me to describe by reading from an affidavit published in the newspapers

[Third Night.]

and a copy of which I hold in my hand. The defendant in this case says—

"I brought actions both in England and the United States against the said C. E. Lewis and others, in which I charged that over 50,000,000 dollars of bonds of the New York, Pennsylvania, and Ohio Railroad Company were illegally issued, of which only a small proportion of the proceeds were applied to the purposes of said Railway Company — such bonds for 50,000,000 dollars being issued in preference to the share capital of that Company of which I am the owner of 20,000,000 dollars, and thus crushing the value of the same. The said shares, and all other shares in said Company, to the amount of 45,000,000 dollars, being illegally registered on the said Railway Company's books in the name and as the property of the said Lewis and his colleagues, thus giving them absolute control of said railway, and preventing me and other shareholders from exercising legal control over affairs of said Company."

That is a distinct charge, and I think I may say a very strong charge, against the honour of a Member of this House. It is, at least, as strong a charge, made on oath, as the charge made in *The Times*, which is not made on oath—as these forgeries and libels which are published against the Irish Members. Here we have a charge, not only made on the sworn evidence of the person who made that affidavit, but we have the utterances on the same subject of a former Member of this House—namely, Lord Bury. He made references to these same matters in a public speech at a public meeting, in 1886. These charges against the hon. Baronet have never been answered yet. He comes down to this House, and taunts the House, or, rather, hon. Members on this side of it, with not taking action to clear their characters from charges of a most serious kind by the anonymous writers in *The Times*. What did Lord Bury say on the occasion to which I have referred? Quoting a passage from the Report on this Railway Company—the Atlantic and Great Western Railway Company —made by Sir James Allport, he said—

"The nominal capital has been increased since 1871 from 60,000,000 to 124,500,000 dollars, or possibly to 132,500,000 dollars; and here, speaking to an assembly of proprietors of this railroad, I come to a point which, I think, has been insufficiently considered. Sir James Allport and Mr. Swarbrick say of this increase of 64,500,000 dollars, or possibly 72,500,000 dollars, ' We have only been able to trace 8,500,000 dollars that can by any possibility have added to the value of the property.' "

Mr. Coryb are

It is charged against the hon. Baronet —and this is the gravamen of the charge against the hon. Baronet, and what he has to meet—that in his position as trustee connected with this line of railway he fraudulently registered the share capital in his own name; that he issued $40,000,000 of first mortgage bonds; that in that way he swamped the original shareholders; and that of the whole amount of money invested only £500,000 sterling was spent on the railway. As we are to-night dealing with quotations from *The Times*, it may be interesting to know what *The Times* had to say upon this subject. It said, on May 13, 1886—

"Their trustees appear to have gone mad with delight in squandering the resources of the proprietors. Not one penny which had been obtained by these had ever reached the Company."

I say these are grave charges. I go into these matters because I know something about them. I was plaintiff in a Chancery suit, which was rendered necessary through the adroitness and legal skill of the hon. Baronet; and one of the objects of that suit, of which I was, unfortunately, so long a plaintiff, was to prevent this same hon. Baronet from putting into his pocket some £40,000 belonging to his *cestuis que trust*. When, therefore, the hon. Baronet taunts hon. Members on this side of the House——

MR. J. W. LOWTHER (Cumberland, Penrith): Is the hon. Member, Sir, speaking to the subject before the House?

MR. SPEAKER: The charges the hon. Member is now bringing against another hon. Member of this House have nothing whatever to do with the Question before the House. They are not relevant to the subject of the debate.

MR. CONYBEARE: Of course, I bow to your ruling, Sir. I stated at the commencement of my remarks on this subject that I was taking up the challenge of the hon. Baronet, which was to the effect that those who knew his character would not think that he would do so-and-so, or that he was going to do so-and-so. I thought that when he deliberately challenged us as to his character, we had a right to consider what his character really was. As, however, you rule, Sir, that further reference to these matters is out of Order, I shall not, of course, presume to pursue the subject further. I can only say this—that I have deliberately stated on many occasions, and I repeat it now, that if ever a Tory Government were to offer to place the hon. Member for North Antrim in a position of trust in the Government of this country, I should at once place a Notice of Motion on the Order Book of this House to the effect that it would be improper to place this hon. Member in any such position.

MR. GEDGE (Stockport): It seems to me that in the discussion of the matters before the House we have, to a certain extent, lost sight of the main issue. We have two proposals before us— one is that the House should pass an opinion on the question whether *The Times* article is or is not a Breach of Privilege on the part of the editor or printer of that newspaper, and the other is whether the House will or will not appoint a Select Committee to examine into the charge brought by the editor of *The Times* against the hon. Member for East Mayo. I think we are apt to forget that the real charge brought by *The Times* newspaper is not whether or no he spoke what is not true either knowingly or recklessly, or whether that speech of his, which was a denial of certain charges brought against him by that newspaper, was a false or true denial. The important point is not whether *The Times* called the denial false, or whether to say so is a Breach of Privilege; but it is whether the charges brought against the hon. Member were true or not true, and the question is how can the truth of these charges be best ascertained. From that point of view, it seems to me to be our best course is to vote for the Resolution of the Solicitor General. Now, as to the main point before us, this Resolution states that it is inexpedient for us to treat this matter as a Breach of Privilege. The right hon. Gentleman the Member for Derby (Sir William Harcourt) has tried to be severely sarcastic upon the present Law Officers of the Crown, because they seemed to assume to themselves that upon them lay the burden of advising the Government upon matters of this kind, and the right hon. Gentleman gave us to understand that when he was Solicitor General nothing of the kind occurred. Sir, I was familiar with the right hon. Gentleman's career as a member of the Bar up to the time of his becoming Solicitor General, and I am not at all surprised that when he became Solicitor General the Government of the day were not in the habit of consulting him upon such matters. They only followed the example of solicitors, members of my own profession, because I can assure the House that up to the time when the right hon. Gentleman became Solicitor General his name did not appear in a single report of a case in the Law Courts. I can quite understand, therefore, that the Government did not trouble to take the right hon. Gentleman's advice on matters of law. [*Cries of* " Question !" *and* " Order !"] I am not aware that I have said anything against Order. I am testing the value of the right hon. Member's sneer at the Solicitor General. With regard to the question of Privilege, the point seems to me to be this—has the hon. Member for East Mayo been, by the charge brought against him, in any way debarred from acting his proper part as a Member of this House ? Has he been prevented from doing his duty as a Member of Parliament, and has he been prevented from speaking freely ? Sir, I think not. It seems to me that there has been a duel between the hon. Member and *The Times*, in which hard language has been used on both sides. That newspaper brought very grave charges, indeed, against the hon. Member and his political associates, and adduced much evidence in support of those charges. They were scattered broadcast through the land for several weeks and the hon. Member took no notice of them ; but when these charges were repeated in this House, on the authority of that newspaper, by the noble Lord the Member for Rossendale (the Marquess of Hartington) the hon. Member for East Mayo in the strongest language gave the lie direct to the newspaper. *The Times* repeated the accusation, qualifying the charge of untruth with the alternative that the hon. Member might have spoken recklessly and not wilfully, and *The Times* challenged the hon. Member to enable it to prove its case in the Law Courts by bringing an action against the paper. Well, under these circumstances, is it for the hon. Member to say—" I am a Member of Parliament, and you are only a newspaper ; you are not to retort on me, because I occupy a higher position than you ; if you place your word against mine, I shall take advantage of my position and come down upon you as a matter of Privilege?" It seems to me that such an attitude on the part of the hon. Member does not show an excess of courage. It appears to me to bear some resemblance to the line of conduct pursued by the woman who, having scratched a man's eyes out, bitterly complained of his turning round upon her and using his fists, and shrieked out, "What a shame to strike a woman!" For myself, I do not see why anyone should interfere between the two—they should fight it out together. Let us consider what the effect of calling the conduct of *The Times* a Breach of Privilege would be? Would it assist the hon. Member in establishing the truth of his denial? Not at all. It is not even a step towards the ulterior step of appointing a Select Committee, because the Resolution of the right hon. Gentleman the Member for Mid Lothian (Mr. W. E. Gladstone) proposes to appoint this Committee of Inquiry though the House shall not have declared the conduct of *The Times* newspaper to be a Breach of the Privileges of the House. So that the result of treating this as a matter of Privilege will be this—you would bring the printer or the publisher of *The Times* to the Bar of the House. If he were for one moment to attempt to justify the libel, and say to the House— "It is true I brought certain accusations and certain grave charges against the hon. Member for East Mayo, but my allegations were true;" if he did that, I believe that the House would hold that it was only an aggravation of his original offence, and would not listen to his plea. The House would have up the printer and the publisher, who are technically liable for a technical Breach of Privilege and imprison them, while the real culprits, the editors and the writers in *The Times*, would go on repeating the offence to the end of the chapter. Therefore, the hon. Gentleman would gain nothing by having this matter treated as a Breach of Privilege. No step would have been taken in vindication of his character. But then it is said that such a course would be a step towards the ulterior settlement of this question. But such a step I maintain can be taken without proceedings of the kind. What is the proposal? That we shall inquire into a charge of wilful falsehood—it is limited to that point only. The charge has

regard to one particular allegation— namely, that the hon. Member for East Mayo had continued the employment of a man or men when he knew them to be guilty of very abominable crimes. But if the hon. Member were to bring an action against *The Times* newspaper for these libels, then he would not be limited, as he would be before a Select Committee, to the investigation of that one matter. He might bring into Court all the many charges which have been brought against himself and his Colleagues for a long time past, and if *The Times* failed to substantiate them all it would have to pay the penalty. Therefore, his position before a Court of Law, I maintain, would be infinitely better than that he now seeks were he successful in obtaining it. I listened yesterday to the speech of the hon. Member for East Mayo with great attention. I felt that if he was an innocent man, the heart of every innocent man ought to go out to him in warm sympathy, and that even if the allegations made against him were true, yet taking into consideration the circumstances of his position, the earnestness of his advocacy of the cause he represents, the difficulties he has had to encounter, and the materials which he has had to work with, we ought all to feel for him if he has been betrayed into some act of indiscretion. I felt this that he had a reputation once, and if he has lost that reputation through excess of sympathy with that cause we ought all to feel for him. I therefore, as I say, listened very attentively to the speech he made in order that I might make up my mind as to the right view of the position in which he stands. His speech was not an impromptu speech, but was premeditated. Though he said he did not intend to reply to the charges which had been brought against him, or to enter into the debate, when some time after he took part in the debate I noticed that he made his speech from copious notes; therefore the hon. Member's decision was careful and deliberate. He gave us three reasons why he declined to go— and never would go—to a Court of Law to vindicate his character. His first reason was this—"There is not a shadow of a chance of my obtaining a verdict, for the jury will have read *The Times* and will be prejudiced against me." His second reason was—"The real issues will be obscured and hidden from the pub-

Mr. Grdjo

lic by the introduction of irrelevant matter, and by the denunciations of counsel;" and his third reason for declining to go into Court and demanding a Committee of Inquiry was—"I desire a speedy decision." Well, Sir, I hope to show in the course of a few moments, if I am allowed the indulgence of the House, that each one of these reasons as used in support of his objection to taking his case before a Court of Law applies with tenfold more force against carrying that case before a Select Committee of the House. Take his first point, that there would not be the shadow of a chance of his obtaining a verdict from a jury who were readers of *The Times*, and would be prejudiced against him. I ask whether Members of a Select Committee of this House would not consist of men who habitually read *The Times*? I would ask whether it is not likely that a great many special jurymen confine themselves to penny papers, including *The Standard*, which has been referred to as taking the side of the hon. Gentleman? I would say that many men of the jury class are what we call arm-chair politicians, who trouble themselves very little indeed about politics until politics are forced on their attention. I would say that in the case of a trial before a Court of Law a dozen men would be selected all of whom would desire to give a verdict according to their oaths; but how would it be with us? They are non-combatants; we are in the thick of the fight. We are all politicians and Party men; we are fighting the battles of politics and Party every day — there is not one of us who does not hold a strong opinion on matters of politics. Therefore, to take a jury from our body—*à fortiori* are we not more likely to be prejudiced—I do not say we should be; but are we not more likely to be prejudiced than the ordinary jury selected in the usual way in a Court of Law? Then with regard to the hon. Member's second point, which is that the real issues will be obscured and hidden from the public by the introduction of irrelevant matter into the case, and by the denunciatory speeches of counsel, let us just look at the difference on this point between the two tribunals. In the one case the hon. Gentleman would go before a jury presided over by one Judge, or possibly in a great case of this kind by three—gentlemen of the highest legal and judicial training and experience— and would not these three Judges take care to keep out irrelevant matter? Would they not very soon put a stop to all gratuitous denunciations in the speeches of counsel—would they not at once recall these gentlemen to the issues before the Court if they caught them wandering from the point? There would be direct issues to lay before the Judges, and the jury and all would combine to keep counsel and witnesses closely to these issues. The Judge would control counsel, would exclude extraneous matter and those denunciations which the hon. Member seems to fear; he would tell the jury that they had but one issue to try according to their oaths on the evidence before them, and in that way would the verdict be given. The evidence given would be legal evidence—no hearsay evidence. The hon. Member for the County of Dublin desires that everyone who could throw a light on this matter should have a hearing. Probably that course would be allowed before a Select Committee, and a pretty time the investigation would take. Before a Select Committee you would have no presiding Judge. You would have a large body of gentlemen taking strong views upon political questions, and when it became necessary to settle a point of Order or Procedure, it would be necessary to have the room cleared in order that the matter might be decided by a vote— perhaps a Party vote. There would be little chance of excluding irrelevant matter. In a Court of Law the burden of proof would lie on the defendant, and as the fact of the publication of the libel would be proved, it would rest with the defendant to show justification. That would be very much in favour of the plaintiff, as also would the fact that in a Court of Justice you would be confined to strict legal evidence. *The Times* newspaper would have to prove up to the hilt all the charges it has made, or there would be a verdict against it. All this I maintain is in favour of the hon. Gentleman. The third reason why the hon. Gentleman desires the case to be investigated by a Select Committee, rather than a Court of Law, is that he is anxious to have a speedy decision. He thinks he would be more likely to get a speedy decision from a Select Committee than from a Court of

[Third Night.]

Law. Well, Sir, there are two parts of a trial in which delay may occur. Delay takes place in preparing a case for trial and getting up evidence, and it also takes place in the conduct of a trial. I would contrast the two proceedings on these points. Before a trial in Court a Commission can be issued to America or elsewhere to examine witnesses; but no such Commission can issue from this House. If you go to a Court of Law you can have persons summoned to give evidence, interrogatories can be administered, and various applications can be made and questions put. I am speaking now of proceedings before a Civil Court. There can be no doubt as to the question of rapidity being in favour of proceedings before the Court of Law. As I say, you can get evidence by Commission or otherwise before a Court of Law, but you cannot do that before a Committee of Inquiry. Then the Committee would sit intermittently. You would adjourn from time to time for the purpose of obtaining evidence. You would adjourn for the convenience of Members, and possibly for the convenience of witnesses, and all this can only be done by debate and division; but when you come to the actual trial itself, and your evidence is all got together, the Court of Law would sit *de die in diem* every day until the case was settled. That would not, however, be the case with an inquiry before a Select Committee. It would probably sit three or four hours a day two or three times a week, and we know perfectly well, from the nature of the inquiry that would have to be made, that these sittings would continue for weeks and months. And then, in the end, the verdict of a jury must be given on oath and be unanimous. It is subject to appeal if anything has gone wrong in the conduct of the case; but the verdict of a Committee of Inquiry would be by a majority, and even beforehand every possible verdict which could be given has been stigmatized as a Party verdict. As the hon. Member for Poplar said—"Brains will be counted as well as noses." Such a verdict will convince nobody, or certainly not those who sympathize with the hon. Member; it will be, like the last chapter of *Rasselas,* "a conclusion in which nothing is concluded." For all these reasons, I think it would be much better that this case

Mr. Gedge

should be taken before a Court of Law, and not be inquired into by a Committee of this House, which must be extremely unfit to undertake a trial of this sort. Then there is another point to consider. If you get a verdict against *The Times* in a Court of Law, *The Times* would meet with condign punishment, and a tremendous blow will be struck in favour of the hon. Member and his Party; but if a Committee of this House find a verdict one way or the other the defeated party would go scot free and simply abuse the tribunal and point to the Report of the minority as justifying all that had been done. Then it is pleaded—and I think some weight should be given to the plea—that the hon. Gentleman is challenged, and that, being challenged, he ought to have the choice of weapons. No doubt, you ought to follow that course in a duel, or in a proceeding which affects only the character of the two persons interested; but that is not the case here. In civil actions the plaintiff selects the tribunal, and I never heard, in criminal matters, that the choice of the Court was given to the accused. I do not wonder at the hon. Gentleman opposite deciding in favour of a Committee, because it must be obvious to everyone that if he loses he can impugn the verdict as worthless; but, if he wins, his triumph will indeed be magnificent, because he can say—"I have obtained a verdict from a body, the majority of which is composed of my opponents." He can gain everything in the one way, while he can lose nothing in the other. But the hon. Member for East Mayo is not the only person to be considered in this case, nor are he and *The Times* newspaper the only parties interested. There is the country, which, through its Representatives, wishes to know the truth. The right hon. Gentleman the Member for Mid Lothian (Mr. W. E. Gladstone) laid down a very strong proposition just now—namely, that this House had never, in any similar case, allowed a prosecution of this kind to take place without there first being a Resolution upon the Minutes condemning the article under consideration. Earlier in the debate it was urged that the fact of our not passing a Resolution stating that this is a Breach of Privilege, or of our passing a Resolution declining to treat it as a question of Privilege, will be brought before the jury if the case is taken into a Court of Law, and will have the effect of prejudicing their minds. It is said that, under these circumstances, a jury could not be trusted to find a verdict in favour of the hon. Member for East Mayo. I should have thought that it would have been much more likely to prejudice the jury if a Resolution were brought before them showing that the House had already judged the question and condemned the newspaper. Then, indeed, you might look in vain for a fair trial for the defendant newspaper. But what right had the right hon. Gentleman the Member for Mid Lothian to suppose that in this case the House would depart from its former precedents and not pass a right and proper Resolution? Why, it is evident that when the hon. Member for East Mayo or any of his Friends bring forward a Resolution the Attorney General and Solicitor General, and the Government generally, will ask that that Resolution should be couched in right and proper terms. The Resolution must say that it has been brought to the notice of the House that *The Times* newspaper has published an article reflecting upon the veracity of a Member of this House, and that, therefore, the House will direct a prosecution by the Attorney General. All the virtuous indignation of the right hon. Gentleman the Member for Mid Lothian has thus been thrown away. Hon. Members of this House, as representing the country—which is, after all, the most important party in this matter—are bound to see, not that this man is charged or that that man is charged, or that the other man is defended, or that our privileges are protected, but that the truth is elicited in this matter. This country has a right to expect that its Legislative Assembly shall not convert itself into a judicial tribunal; and to require that we shall do all in our power to take care that this great question of fact, which affects not only unimportant Members of this House, but also some most conspicuous Members amongst us, and the conduct of a great Party struggle of almost unparalleled importance, shall be determined, not by a Select Committee, which will be reasonably suspected of partizanship, but by that High Court of Justice to which every subject is amenable, than which there is no more upright tribunal in the world. The country has a right

to demand that this great question shall not become the play of Party, as it is only too likely to be if referred for consideration to a Select Committee of this House. For these reasons, I shall oppose the Amendment of the right hon. Gentleman opposite.

MR. CHILDERS (Edinburgh, S.): Sir, in French history there was a critical day which went by the name of the " Day of Dupes." I wonder by what name this debate will be known in our history; possibly that of a " Debate of Shams." The first sham was the proposal of the hon. Baronet (Sir Charles Lewis) to adopt a Resolution with which he could have no sympathy, and this is met by the Government by an offer which they know perfectly well will not be accepted for a moment. The Attorney General was very indignant at this sham offer being called illusory, and appeared to take it as a personal reflection on him. [The ATTORNEY GENERAL (Sir Richard Webster): Collusive.] Well, illusory and collusive; but I can say for those sitting near me that by any such expression it was never intended to impute anything dishonourable or improper to the hon. and learned Gentleman. We called the action of the House collusive if it should direct a prosecution of *The Times*, when it was perfectly well known that there was no wish on the part of the House that any such prosecution should take place. If the word I have used has been supposed to convey any personal reflection on the Attorney General I withdraw it at once. I wish to direct the few remarks which I desire to make to the main question, whether it is proper that the House should direct Mr. Attorney General to take proceedings against *The Times* newspaper, or whether it should, by means of a Committee, make inquiry into the facts that have been alleged as to the conduct of this House of one of its Members. That, Sir, is the plain position. My right hon. Friend the Member for Mid Lothian (Mr. W. E. Gladstone) stated and re-stated, and applied, I think, all the earlier part of his speech to, the argument that the House of Commons has never ordered a prosecution without a previous Resolution alleging and condemning the offence for which the prosecution was to be instituted. My right hon. Friend urged that in very strong and clear language, and brought conclusive proof of it before the House. I noticed when my right hon. Friend was speaking that there was much agitation among Gentlemen on the opposite side of the House. There was a collection of books brought in from the Library; there were communications between the First Lord of the Treasury and the Chancellor of the Exchequer and the Law Officers of the Crown; there was a reference again to certain other books which were brought into the House during the right hon. Gentleman's speech; and when my right hon. Friend made that challenge in unmistakable terms, we had a right to expect that the Attorney General, in his reply, would deal with this statement and argument. But not one single word fell from the Attorney General in reply to that argument of the right hon. Gentleman the Member for Mid Lothian, which was the cardinal argument in his speech. I lay special emphasis on this, because there are many in the House now who were not present during my right hon. Friend's speech, or during the speech of the Attorney General. My right hon. Friend said, I repeat, that the House never ordered a prosecution without a previous Resolution alleging and blaming the offence for which the prosecution was to be instituted; and he then argued that if the House were now to order a prosecution, as suggested, it would be going against the precedents of the last 300 years. Clearly, then, some good reason should be given if the House was now asked to take such a course. Now, I say that it was the duty of the Attorney General to meet that argument; he might have met it by a negative, or in some way parried it; it was the main argument of my right hon. Friend, but not a word fell from him in reply. Therefore, we must take the proposition of my right hon. Friend to be established, and that the course which he advises to be taken now is absolutely the right course, because neither in respect to great things or to small, to libels or to Breaches of Privilege, the House has ever ordered a prosecution to take place without first alleging what the offence is. The Attorney General, on the other hand, says that the House has never appointed a Select Committee in a case of libel upon the House, or upon a body of the Members or upon an individual Member,

Mr. Childers

where the libeller was ready to justify. That is an extraordinary doctrine, altogether opposed to the facts of Parliamentary history. The House has appointed Select Committees on charges against Members over and over again, and justification has been frequently attempted; but what the Attorney General might have said is that the House has frequently exercised its discretion either to appoint a Committee, or proceed on the evidence actually before them at the time; and where the evidence has been plain, the House has acted on the assumption that a Breach of Privilege has taken place, and punished the individual, allowing the record to stand on the Journals of the House, or, at the last moment, accepting an apology. The argument of the hon. and learned Gentleman, therefore, falls to the ground. But I should like to meet one or two other objections which have been taken to inquiry into this case by a Select Committee, taken by the Attorney General, the Solicitor General, and the noble Lord the Member for South Paddington (Lord Randolph Churchill). One of those objections is that any Committee must be composed of ardent partizans; and that, therefore, you could not have from a Committee so constituted a judicial verdict. I deny that altogether. My humble opinion is, that although we in this House, like anyone else, have our prejudices on political subjects, the moment we are appointed as Members of a Select Committee, to inquire into any questions referred to us, we do our utmost to throw aside those prejudices. That is the history of a long series of Committees, some on purely political questions. It may be said that when the question has been one about the seat of a Member, before these matters were transferred to a judicial inquiry on the spot in some cases Party feeling has been evinced; but in the great majority of cases that has not been so, and that was not the reason for transferring the trial to a local Court. I remember in my own time more than one case in which a Member was unseated when the great majority of the Committee were of his political opinions; and it is of common notoriety that, where serious personal questions have been involved, the Committees of this House have been thoroughly impartial, or if there have been one or two Members disposed to be carried away by personal feelings the great majority of the Committee have been impartial. The next argument put forward by the Attorney General was this — that a Committee of this House dealing with a question of this kind would be dilatory and uncertain in its proceedings. Of its uncertainty the hon. and learned Gentleman gave a hypothetical instance; but of its dilatoriness he gave a precise instance, which is within my recollection. The hon. and learned Gentleman spoke of Mr. Grissell's case, and he said that occupied a long time.

THE ATTORNEY GENERAL (Sir RICHARD WEBSTER) (Isle of Wight): Oh, no; the case which I mentioned when the Committee was appointed in February, and reported in June, was Mr. Butt's case, not Mr. Grissell's case.

MR. CHILDERS: I beg pardon. The hon. and learned Gentleman spoke of the two cases in the same breath, and I thought that he referred to the case of Mr. Grissell. In that case, the offence appears to have been committed at the end of June, or on the 1st of July, and the whole matter was concluded on the 16th of July. But, except the single instance of Mr. Butt's case, I do not remember any Committee having acted in a case of this kind otherwise than promptly. The rule with Committees of this kind is that they sit from day to day, and it must have been a most exceptional instance if it has been thought necessary to make a long postponement. That is the well-established rule for the last 30 years. In at least 20 cases to which I have referred of Committees of this kind dealing with personal questions the sitting has been from day to day, and the decision has been arrived at without the least delay. The one case given by the Attorney General of dilatoriness may, therefore, be opposed by 20 cases in which no delay has taken place. But then the noble Lord the Member for South Paddington (Lord Randolph Churchill) brought a most strange charge against the action of these Committees, for he said that the machinery for examining and cross-examining witnesses was wanting, and that the appointment the other day in a particular Committee of two Gentlemen of special experience to take evidence—one on one side and one on the other—was anomalous, novel,

and, in fact, a very dangerous innovation. Now, the noble Lord probably has not had time to refer to the well-known practice of the House in days past; but I have done so, and I find that it has been the regular practice of the House, on the occasions when Committees have been appointed on personal questions, to appoint two Members, either directly or through the Committee of selection—one on one side and one on the other—whose functions were to examine witnesses, without the power of voting. The case of Mr. Stonor, which is exactly in point, is notorious; and in that case Mr. Moore and another Member were appointed to examine witnesses—one on one side and one on the other—without the right of voting. Again, there is the case of Mr. Butt, who was accused of improper conduct with reference to services rendered in Parliament to an Indian Prince. That case was referred to a Committee, on which two Members of the House were appointed to examine witnesses only. Then, in the case of the Leeds Bankruptcy Court inquiry, in 1865, the Lord Advocate and Mr. Bovill were appointed extra Members of the Committee, to examine witnesses without the right of voting; and again, in the case of the School Inspector's Reports in 1864 which led to the resignation of Mr. Lowe, the then Lord Advocate and the present Lord Salisbury were appointed special Members of the Committee without the power of voting—simply to examine witnesses. The noble Lord, therefore, is entirely mistaken in thinking that this Committee, were it appointed, could not have two Members of the Legal Profession sitting on it for the purpose of examining witnesses. Even where the House has not thought fit to appoint additional Members there are numerous cases where counsel have been allowed to be employed for the purpose of examining witnesses in personal inquiries without being Members of the Committee. I was myself concerned in a case which occurred in 1859. I presented a Petition alleging conduct inconsistent with honour on the part of a Member, admitting that I had been guilty of a Breach of Privilege; and · my Petition was referred to a Select Committee, and in aid of that Committee two lawyers—one on one side and one on the other—were appointed to examine witnesses. I think no one else asked questions except the Chairman, and the Committee in due time arrived at the decision which, I am happy to say, was in my favour. Therefore, the practice of Committees of this kind has, undoubtedly, been to appoint two Members belonging generally to the Legal Profession expressly for the purpose of examining witnesses, without the power of voting, or to allow Counsel to be heard. This objection, therefore, falls to the ground. There is, however, one case precisely in point which I think has not been mentioned. It is that of a Member charged with Breach of Privilege in the form of slander of other Members who would undoubtedly have been convicted, either by a Select Committee or directly by the House, but in all probability by a Select Committee, if he had not taken the proper steps in the matter and cleared himself. That is the case of Mr. Lopes, who in 1875 was complained of for having in the country spoken of certain Irish Members as a "disreputable Irish band in alliance with the Liberal Party." Those words, although spoken so far back as in December, were brought before the House when it met in February. A Motion was made that the words were a Breach of Privilege, and the Leader of the House and of the Party to which Mr. Lopes belonged said that, unless the hon. Member apologized, it would be their duty to act towards him as one guilty of a Breach of Privilege. The words of Mr. Lopes would have been the subject of inquiry by a Select Committee; but he rose immediately and, admitting that he used the words, fully apologized for having used them; and the Leader of the House said that he was of opinion that justice had been done. All the precedents, then, are against the doctrine of the Attorney General. I put it to the House, in connection with the argument of the Attorney General, that there has been no case in which it has been made clear that a Breach of Privilege has been committed in the form of language used by the Press, or words spoken against a Member of this House, or a body of Members, in which the House has not itself taken action, and there is not a single case in which the House has, without a previous decision, remitted a matter for trial by a Court of Law. Therefore, if we are going to act

from precedent, I do not think there can be any doubt that this new doctrine set up by the Attorney General ought to be disregarded, and that the old doctrine which the House has always followed ought to be acted upon in the present case. It seems to me, however, that this is far too important a subject to be argued simply on precedent of rule and custom. I think we ought to look at the practical question before us. Now, what is the position of this question? An hon. Member of this House, whom, I think I may say, we all respect, has been accused in the columns of a very influential newspaper of having lied in this House. He has been accused of wilful falsehood in a speech delivered in this House in answer to a Member of this House. Charges had been brought against him, which charges he analyzed, and it is on the answer he gave to those charges, and for that answer, that he has been accused of wilful falsehood. Let us ask what we ourselves should feel if such language had been applied to our friends or ourselves? Should we not urge that, the charge having been made with reference to a speech made in this House, the investigation of its propriety should be carried on amongst ourselves—*in foro domestico*—and should we not shrink from the suggestion to send a brother Member against whom such an accusation is made to a tribunal outside the House? I could understand if the hon. Member for East Mayo had said—"I have lost confidence in the fairness of the House," if he were under the belief that a Select Committee would be a partial and prejudiced tribunal—that it might be a question whether or not we should abandon our established practice. But the hon. Member for East Mayo, being a Member of a body equal to one-eighth of the House, powerful in its position as representing the Irish people, and yet in the aggregate not strong as compared with the whole House, comes to us and says—"I am perfectly satisfied that there should be an inquiry by a Committee of the House; I am satisfied that if the House will appoint that Committee, the moment it is appointed Members would be prepared to put aside all Party feeling and to do me justice. Whatever may be the personal feelings of Members, I am convinced that those feelings will disappear when they occupy the judicial position of Members of a

Mr. Childers

Select Committee." Well, Sir, I say, that being so, and the appeal being that of the hon. Member himself, that we ourselves should judge him in this important matter, I say that the country will never understand why we should reject the hon. Member's appeal, and insist on sending him to the judgment of a tribunal which the hon. Member feels would be under a heavy prejudice against him, the members of which—I am not speaking of the Judge, of course, but of the jury—would be under the influence of the enormous prejudice which at this time exists in London against the hon. Member and his Friends, and with regard to whom I think I may justly say he cannot be assured of securing an impartial verdict. [*Cries of* "No!"] An hon. Member says "No!" but if that hon. Member were in this position himself, and had been exposed during the last two years to the attacks which the great majority of the people of London have directed against the hon. Member for East Mayo, I think he would very much prefer the judgment of a Committee of this House to the judgment of a London jury. Therefore, both on the grounds of custom and precedent, on the ground of the Rules which we have laid down for ourselves during the last 300 years, but still more on the grounds of fairness to the hon. Member for East Mayo and his Friends, we should, however specious may be the arguments of the Attorney General, absolutely, of course, without prejudice, give the hon. Member for East Mayo the tribunal for which he asks. I say that, if we wish to do what is fair, we should adopt the Amendment of my right hon. Friend, and appoint a Select Committee, leaving it to the Committee of Selection to choose grave and impartial persons fairly representing all Parties in the House, from which I feel confident that a conclusive and fair judgment would come.

MR. CHAPLIN (Lincolnshire, Sleaford): Mr. Speaker, at an earlier period of the evening the noble Lord the Member for South Paddington (Lord Randolph Churchill) was subjected to elaborate onslaughts from the hon. Gentleman the junior Member for Northampton (Mr. Bradlaugh) on the one hand, and from the right hon. Gentleman the Member for Mid Lothian (Mr. W. E. Gladstone) on the other hand. The right hon. Gentleman the Member for Mid Lothian commenced his speech this afternoon by repudiating the statement of the noble Lord that the right hon. Gentleman had constituted himself the Leader of the Party for the repeal of the Union; but shortly afterwards he closed his observations by complaining that grave international questions had been raised between Ireland and England by the course Her Majesty's Government had pursued. I want to ask this question. How is it possible that there could be international questions between Ireland and England, unless the noble Lord was justified in his supposition that there must be in the policy of the right hon. Gentleman something he contemplates in the nature of a repeal of the Union? Sir, the hon. Member for Northampton (Mr. Bradlaugh) attacked with great bitterness and careful elaboration former statements of the noble Lord. I am not concerned to dwell at any length on that attack to-night. I know no human being either inside this House or beyond its walls who is more perfectly able to defend himself than the noble Lord, and he will have ample opportunities of replying to the hon. Member for Northampton. I do not desire to dwell upon that subject to-night, further than to say this—that when the noble Lord rose and stated how utterly untrustworthy were the speeches contained in *Hansard* made by private and independent Members, as reliable evidence of what they have absolutely stated in this House, I can only say that, from my own personal experience on many occasions on that subject, I am able to endorse everything that fell from the noble Lord. Now, the right hon. Gentleman the Member for Mid Lothian has somewhat narrowed the issues which are raised by this discussion. He began by pointing out that in the first instance five points of grave importance have been raised by the Amendment of my hon. and learned Friend the Solicitor General (Sir Edward Clarke). Now, it seems to me that after the decision this evening there are only two practical questions before the House, and they are—whether the inquiry which it seems all sections of the House are agreed ought to be made should be prosecuted by a Committee of this House, or whether there should be a prosecution in a Court of Law. The right hon,

Gentleman has suggested that the inquiry should be conducted by a Select Committee. Her Majesty's Government, on the other hand, have offered, if hon. Members desire it, to give them every facility and assistance for a prosecution in a Court of Law. The right hon. Gentleman pointed out many objections to a prosecution in a Court of Law. First of all, he said it was likely to lead to very considerable delay, and he argued that the proceedings by a Committee must necessarily and naturally be much more speedily disposed of than they would be in a Court of Law. I wish to make this observation, that earlier in the Session charges were made against certain hon. Members of this House, and those charges were referred to the deliberation of a Select Committee. They were made on the 18th of March last. We are now approaching the middle of May, and I am not aware that any Report whatever has been made by this Committee, nor do I understand there is any immediate prospect of that Report being presented. I am referring to the Committee which sat on the charges made against the Corporation of London. Well, then, the right hon. Gentleman expressed great doubts as to whether a fair verdict could be obtained in a Court of Law; and those doubts, so far as I can gather from his speech, were shared, in no small degree, by the right hon. Gentleman the Member for South Edinburgh (Mr. Childers), who has just sat down. But how did the right hon. Gentleman the Member for Mid Lothian support them? I must say I thought his case was a rather weak one, when he was absolutely obliged to go back 30 years to the case of the Ionian Islands as the only illustration he could adduce at the present time in support of the argument he made to-night. Now, while the right hon. Gentleman was doubtful as to the possibility of obtaining a verdict in a Court of Law, or as to the merits of a prosecution undertaken in that way, he was perfectly clear that there were no objections which could be advanced to an inquiry by a Committee. "There is only one mode," he said, "according to reason and according to precedent by which this inquiry ought to be conducted." "The Committee," he said, "would be the most perfectly competent tribunal;" and then he asked this question—

. *Mr. Chaplin*

"What is there in the nature of this case to make a Committee unable to discharge a duty which you say any common jury or special jury is perfectly competent to discharge?"

Well, I will give the right hon. Gentleman, in a moment, one or two objections which occur to me. I am not going now into the question of precedent. I do not profess that I am sufficiently versed in precedent on this question to entitle me to express an opinion; but I rather agree with the right hon. Gentleman opposite (Mr. Childers) that we ought not to be absolutely guided by precedent on this question. Now, the right hon. Gentleman the Member for South Edinburgh (Mr. Childers) said the principal argument adduced by the right hon. Gentleman the Member for Mid Lothian against the institution of a prosecution is, that no prosecution has ever been ordered by this House unless the House has previously expressed an opinion upon it. I understand that was the main contention of the right hon. Gentleman. I do not know how that may be; but even admitting, for the sake of argument, he is right, what I want to point out to the House and the right hon. Gentleman is that the case which is now before us is absolutely in itself without any precedent whatever. Why, Sir, there is no case of Breach of Privilege on record that I am aware of in regard to which the Parliamentary and political interest of every single section of Members of this House was vitally and deeply concerned. But that is the case on the present occasion. There is no question or doubt about that. I want the House to consider how that circumstance affects the proposals which have been made for a Committee. For the purposes of an inquiry of this nature there are, in my humble opinion, two conditions which are absolutely essential. In the first place, the tribunal must be thoroughly impartial, so far as it is possible to obtain impartiality. In the second place, if the tribunal is to be a Committee of this House, it ought to be fairly representative of every section of Members in the House. I propose to show that in this case it is absolutely impossible that either one of these conditions can be fulfilled. For all practical purposes there are at the present time four different Parties in this House. There is the Party which supports the Government; there is the

Party which supports the right hon. Gentleman the Leader of the Opposition (Mr. W. E. Gladstone); there is the Party which follows the noble Lord the Member for Rossendale (the Marquess of Hartington); there is the Party of Irish Members who follow the hon. Member for Cork (Mr. Parnell); and what I say is that the political and Party interests of each and all of these four different sections are deeply—in some cases I might almost say vitally—concerned in the decision of the question now before us. Take the case of the Government. Suppose for a moment that these charges should be substantiated. What would be the effect upon Her Majesty's Government? Why, of course, it would enormously facilitate the passing of the Bill which is now before the House. [*Opposition cheers.*] Those cheers are the best illustration I could possibly receive of the justice and force of my argument. The substantiation of these charges would enormously facilitate the passing of the Bill, which the Government have said over and over again is vital to their interests. Well, the same argument applies, of course, but in a minor degree, to the Party which follows my noble Friend the Member for Rossendale. What is the position of hon. Gentlemen who sit below the Gangway opposite? They are the parties who are actually incriminated by these charges, and, of course, it is more vital to them—it is more important to them than to any other section of this House—that the verdict of any Committee should be in their favour. But if that is the position of hon. Gentlemen below the Gangway, how does it affect the right hon. Gentleman the Member for Mid Lothian and his Friends? Why, just suppose for a moment what would be the effect upon the Party who follow hon. Gentlemen who sit on the Front Bench opposite if, unhappily, such charges as these should be proved to be true, if it should be shown that the right hon. Gentleman and his Friends had accepted the alliance, and are relying on the support of men who were proved to have associated, for their own political purposes, either with murderers or men who had conspired to murder. Why, Sir, it would be the destruction, the absolute destruction, of their political reputation, and, unless I much mistake the temper of the English people at the present time, it would mean their absolute political extinction for the future. Sir, I have as much respect for the impartiality of the House of Commons, and for the honour and integrity of its Members, as any person who has the honour of a seat in this Assembly; but I know that human nature is human nature after all, and with such tremendous issues at stake as these, I ask the House of Commons—Is it possible to suppose that any Members belonging to either of the four sections could be placed on any Committee to decide these issues, who, however insensibly it might occur, could help being biased, to some extent, by their political passions and their political feelings? Is it possible that any Committee you could select could be as impartial as they ought to be, or as all of us should desire? I have offered to the House some reasons which justify me in saying that the first of the two conditions which I have laid down cannot be fulfilled, and is not likely to be fulfilled in the present case. But what was the second condition? It was that every section of Members in the House must be fairly represented upon this Committee. There we are met at once with the difficulty which was pointed out by the noble Lord the Member for South Paddington (Lord Randolph Churchill) last night, and that difficulty consists in this—that if hon. Gentlemen opposite, or any of their Friends representing them, were placed upon that Committee, you would, in consequence of the terms of the articles which are the subject of this debate, be actually putting the accused on the tribunal which is to decide whether they are innocent or whether they are guilty. Hon. Gentlemen opposite tell us now that they would be perfectly satisfied to leave the decision to a Committee on which they were not represented; and, if I recollect aright, the hon. Member for East Mayo (Mr. Dillon) was exceedingly indignant last night with my hon. and learned Friend the Solicitor General, because he ventured to question the hon. Gentleman's views on that point. The hon. Gentleman was very wrath with the hon. and learned Solicitor General, because he said that happily a speech made earlier in the evening by the hon. Gentleman the Member for the Scotland Division of Liverpool (Mr. T. P. O'Connor) had

[*Third Night.*]

been sent to the Press, and his impression of that speech could be verified on a subsequent occasion. I have taken the trouble to read the report of the speech of the hon. Gentleman the Member for the Scotland Division of Liverpool, and I am bound to say it bears out to the letter the impression it made on the hon. and learned Solicitor General and me, and corresponds with the notes I took of the speech when it was delivered. I want to call the attention of the House to this—that we are constantly told by hon. Gentlemen opposite that they are burning with a desire to submit their case to a Committee of this House, and that they will be perfectly satisfied with a Committee on which they are not represented. I do not wish to question their sincerity, but I cannot help making this observation—that it does seem to me, if that is really their desire, most passing strange that in spite of the letter of the hon. Baronet the Member for North Antrim (Sir Charles Lewis), who made this Motion, and his direct invitation to the hon. Member for East Mayo to take proceedings himself, the hon. Gentleman actually declined to take any initiative in the matter.

Mr. DILLON: I explained fully at the time the reason why I did so. I said I have always abstained, and always will abstain, from invoking the protection of the House against newspapers; but that when a challenge was given by another Member I was prepared to accept it.

Mr. CHAPLIN: I hope the explanation of the hon. Member is wholly satisfactory to himself. But, Sir, in support of what I was saying as to the willingness of hon. Gentlemen opposite now to leave the decision of this matter to a Committee on which they are not represented, I desire to call attention to one sentence in the speech delivered by the hon. Gentleman the Member for the Scotland Division of Liverpool last night. The hon. Gentleman said—

" Every single opponent of the Irish Party " —that means, I suppose, all the hon. Gentlemen on this side of the House—" has taken up the libels of *The Times*. They have become a party, a political weapon, and the very men who wield this poisoned dagger are now, forsooth, the Gentlemen who stand between our accusers and us ! "

That is the complaint which was made last night. What is the charge which is made against the Government to-day?

Why, that the very men who wield this poisoned dagger, forsooth, are not to be constituted their judges on this occasion ! Sir, we desire to judge no man. For myself, I can say this—that as a Member of the House of Commons I am bound to assume that any other Member of the House of Commons—and in this case I do assume it—is innocent until he is proved to be guilty. But I cannot shut my eyes to the extreme gravity of the situation in which both hon. Gentlemen opposite, and the House of Commons as a whole, are placed ; and if I am asked, as I was asked last night pointedly by the hon. and learned Gentleman the late Attorney General (Sir Charles Russell), what course I, for instance, would have taken if similar charges had been made against me in this House, this is my reply—wherever the truth could be most closely sifted, wherever the inquiry could be most searching and the investigation most complete, wherever justice was most certain—[Mr. DILLON: A great chance we should have in the City of London.]—wherever the absence of Party and political passion is most assured, and most certainly at the present time that would not be in the House of Commons, there I would demand, nay, more, I would insist on being heard in my defence, and on being heard without delay. And that is the course, if I may presume to say so, which hon. Members below the Gangway opposite, if they are innocent, as I assume them to be, and if they are not afraid of meeting inquiry, would do well, and would do wisely, even at the eleventh hour, in my humble opinion, to adopt.

Mr. R. T. REID (Dumfries, &c.): I heard with satisfaction from the right hon. Gentleman the Member for the Sleaford Division of Lincolnshire (Mr. Chaplin) the statement that he would assume the innocence of hon. Members from Ireland until their guilt had been proved. I wish the same language and the same spirit had been exhibited, not only by hon. Gentlemen sitting opposite, but by some hon. Gentlemen on this side of the House, who have not hesitated, in my judgment, most cruelly to prejudice the issue in any proceedings that may be taken in this matter. I do not intend to speak very long to-night, and I do not intend to dwell upon the precedents, because I think they have been thoroughly dealt with, and because I am aware that there is not likely to be a concurrence of opinion in regard to precedents. *Quot homines, tot sententiæ.* But this is not a case of precedent at all. We have to determine whether or not hon. Gentlemen who have been maligned with a degree of savageness and pertinacity almost unexampled in the political warfare of the last half-century are to be afforded an opportunity in this House, the first Assembly of English Gentlemen, of clearing their character from the stain cast upon it. The hon. and learned Gentleman the Attorney General (Sir Richard Webster) showed in his speech great sensitiveness in regard to imputations that he conceived had been made against him as to the exercise of his official duty. I did not understand that such imputations were made. I do not believe that the Attorney General would be guilty of any dishonourable conduct; but I thought that the style—the manner—of some taunts he levelled against hon. Gentlemen coming from Ireland scarcely accorded with the sensitiveness he himself exhibited when he imagined imputations were made against himself. Now, the purpose for which I wish to say a few words to-night is to state why I believe that Irish Gentlemen are perfectly warranted in declining to accept the criminal prosecution suggested. The occasion of the proceeding, to begin with, is not an ordinary occasion. It is not a question between *The Times* newspaper and hon. Gentlemen. It is a question which has been discussed for many weeks and months, one may say for years, involving charges which have been taken up by Gentlemen like the noble Lord the Member for Rossendale (the Marquess of Hartington) and diligently advertised by them, charges which have been repeated on many platforms within the past two or three weeks, charges involving issues of the gravest possible national importance; for although I do not think they ought to bear upon it, they undoubtedly do bear upon the great political question that is vexing the country at this moment. Under these circumstances, the object of the inquiry ought to be to ascertain the strict truth—not merely as it affects *The Times* newspaper—but to let us, who sit in this House, know whether the men who sit beside us are to be stamped with infamy as asso-

ciates with cruel murderers, or are the victims of calumnies, and as such entitled to the sympathy and support of all honest men. When that is the nature of the question which has to be determined there are some essential conditions to a full and fair inquiry. One of them is, that the burden of proof ought to be thrown upon the shoulders of those who make the accusations. Another is, that all the sources of information should be opened and revealed for the inspection of the Court which has to determine this important matter. It is another condition that if, short of complicity with guilt, there has been a want of judgment, a carelessness in estimating the character of other men or in the selection of associates in common work, the exact measure of the fault, if fault there be, ought to be ascertained and decided in open day. And, beyond all that, it is necessary there ought to be no delay in coming to a conclusion, because delay of justice in such a case as this is equivalent to a denial of justice. I think we ought also to bear in mind that the accused in this case are also accusers. They say there has been a deliberate conspiracy to ruin them for political purposes; they say there is an attempt to vilify their character in order to plunder the liberties of their country, and they demand to know who are the real movers behind these scenes of iniquity. For this purpose it is essential that the editor of *The Times* with his informants, with his assistants, in the making and publishing of these charges, should be brought before the tribunal in order that we may learn how these remarkable revelations had their origin, why it is they were not sooner divulged, and why they have been divulged at so opportune a moment? I do not think the House would dispute the truth of these general propositions, and I propose, shortly, to apply them; and I desire to say that in my humble judgment these essential conditions would not be fulfilled by a criminal trial in which these gentlemen should be prosecutors. The burden of proof, to begin with, would be shifted from the defendants—from *The Times*, on to the shoulders of those who have been slandered. ["No!"] I say the burden of proof unquestionably would be cast on the shoulders of those who have been slandered. The Judge would undoubtedly direct the jury, if he knew

[*Third Night.*]

anything at all about law, that if they had any doubt—[*Laughter.*] · I assume the Judge would know about the law, and I was not, perhaps, very rightly referring to the doubts expressed by hon. Gentlemen opposite and suggesting that perhaps all of them are not so well acquainted with the matter as the Judges would be. It is quite certain that not only would the burden of proof be on the prosecution, but that the natural presumption arising from human compassion for men placed in a dock on a criminal charge would be doubly felt in the case of the representatives of a great public organ, which for many years has been held in high esteem in this country; and if hesitation from that ground arose, who can question that the jury, saturated with the prejudice which has been instilled into them by all the newspapers nearly of the country, would gladly seize the occasion to relieve themselves from the burden of finding a verdict of guilty on a criminal charge. Yet a verdict of acquittal· in those circumstances would be equivalent to a verdict of condemnation of Gentlemen who are sitting here in this House. Again, Sir, in a criminal prosecution all the sources of information would not be truly and honestly available. On the day of the trial the prosecution would be wholly ignorant of the materials the defence would have under their control. Some document, whether forged or otherwise, might be sprung upon them at the last moment, which at the time they could not, without having recourse to investigation and inquiry in remote countries, be able either to expose or explain. Or some witness of infamous character might be brought forward for the purpose of testifying to some falsehood, and it would require long search in remote corners of the earth to find out and trace the infamy of his character, or to show how untrustworthy and unreliable he was. Under those circumstances, who could doubt that the jury might well believe—for an adjournment under these circumstances could not take place—who would doubt that the jury might well find a verdict in favour of persons charged in a criminal case, and that that verdict would be treated, and naturally treated, as a verdict of condemnation against these Gentlemen? But, further than that, I can understand why the apologists of *The Times* desire this form

of inquiry. The defendants themselves —the editor, the printer, the writers— would not go into the witness-box, and would not be liable to cross-examination. It would be impossible to ascertain where these remarkable stories had their origin. The whole object of the defendants' counsel would be to avert a conviction. The defendants would not be endeavouring to take part in an impartial inquiry. It would be impossible to call them as witnesses—those in the dock would be able to say they could not present themselves as witnesses; and the result is that the matter which these gentlemen, who in their turn are accusers, most earnestly desire to find out, and which I desire to find out, would not and could not possibly be ascertained by this method of inquiry. If *The Times* wants to avoid having the sources of its information investigated, there is no method of avoiding it better than going into the dock, where they will not be exposed to that kind of inquiry. Again, if it appeared even that some gentlemen had accepted with too little inquiry the aid of men of bad character, of whom they had themselves no suspicion, it might well be that the jury would find a verdict in favour of the defendants; not because of the guilt of the prosecutors, but because the defendants acted in good faith. That, also, would be construed by the public as a condemnation of the conduct of hon. Gentlemen. But, it is said—"Why should not some action be brought?" Anyone who knows what an action in such a case would mean will not require to ask that question. An action with all the preliminary proceedings, an action with Commissions to all parts of the world—to America and elsewhere—extending over a period of at least 12 or 18 months, would result in this, that the trial could not take place for 18 months or two years, and in the meantime these Gentlemen, who are as much entitled to the consideration of this House, if it be a House of the first Gentlemen in Europe—these Gentlemen, who are as much entitled to the consideration of the House as any body of Members who have to work among us, who sit among us, and who have to go through the painful duties which they have to encounter in their labours—these Gentlemen in the meantime would rest under the stigma—the unremoved imputation —of crime from which they cannot have an opportunity of purging themselves. Under these circumstances it seems to me that there are strong reasons why many of us in friendly council, if we were asked by any other friend, would recommend that such proceedings should not be chosen, if any reasonable alternative existed. It is not a fair trial; but, far beyond that, it is not a proper method of investigation of that which we wish to see investigated. It would burke that part of the inquiry in which hon. Gentlemen are accusers, and would be an unsatisfactory trial of that part in which they are accused. As regards a Committee of this House, I am surprised to hear the right hon. Gentleman (Mr. Chaplin) say—I was surprised to hear it from the right hon. Gentleman—that he doubted—appeared to doubt—that in this House of Commons you could find 12 or 13 men of honour who would put aside all interest and Party affection, and truly try a question so deeply affecting Members of this House. I, Sir, have a very different opinion of the House of Commons, and I can say this for the right hon. Gentleman, differing from him as I do—that if I was in like case with these hon. Gentlemen, I would gladly leave to the decision of the right hon. Gentleman himself and 12 others such as him the responsibility of dealing with the matter. He has not done justice to himself. He has not done justice to Gentlemen who are sitting behind him; and I am very sorry indeed that he, perhaps in a rhetorical flight or an unguarded moment, should have led to the opinion that he thinks so low of the House of Commons that there are not 12 or 14 honest men to be found in it.

MR. CHAPLIN: The hon. and learned Member will allow me to explain. I adhere most strictly to every word I said; and I assure him it was not in an unguarded moment that the words fell from me. What I desired to convey to the House was this—and I thought I had conveyed it—that this being such a tremendous issue as regards the Party interest of every section of Members in this House, it would be next to impossible that an inquiry could be conducted by Members of this House without their being insensibly biased in their judgment.

MR. R. T. REID: I think the right hon. Gentleman has merely re-stated in other words, and better words than mine, what I have stated I thought he had said. But I will pass from the subject. I am sorry the right hon. Gentleman is obdurate in his opinion of the House, and I can only say that I am able to take a higher estimate of the right hon. Gentleman and his Friends than he seems to take himself. This Committee would, at all events, be prompt. It would begin, or it might begin, its labours in the course of a week. It would be composed of such elements that it is impossible for hon. Gentlemen opposite to complain as far as they are concerned. The hon. Member for East Mayo (Mr. Dillon) says he is content that it should consist of English and Scottish Members alone, and that it should consist of a majority of Members from the other side of the House. How is it possible, if the purpose is to enable the Members who are charged to confront their accusers — how is it possible to deny that the matter should be sent to a tribunal so constituted? The tribunal would have the power of cross-examination, the power of sifting to the bottom the whole of the truth or untruth of these charges; and, more than that, the Committee would have the power of investigating what were the sources of authority on which *The Times* newspaper made these charges—who were the persons behind it—who are the men who have fabricated and forged —as I believe they have forged—these documents, and palmed them off on *The Times*. In that way there would be satisfaction given to both sides; whereas the method that is proposed by the Government appears to me to give satisfaction to neither. Sir, it is not merely that these are reasons, in my humble opinion, sufficient to lead the House to grant this inquiry, and to appoint this Committee; but these are also some of the opinions and some of the objections entertained by the hon. Gentlemen themselves to the proposal of the Government. They object to the tribunal which the Government propose. They come forward, being accused of such offences as no man I suppose within living memory in this House has ever been accused of; and they say, and I say, that if there is a spark of honour, a spark of chivalry in this House, it is due to them, strangers, almost friendless in this country, to give them the

[*Third Night.*]

inquiry they ask for. [*Laughter.*] I observe the hon. and gallant Gentleman opposite (Colonel Saunderson) laughs at my description of hon. Members below the Gangway on this side as strangers and almost friendless. The hon. and gallant Gentleman is not a stranger; but the hon. and gallant Gentleman in this House, I am sorry to say, seems to take more interest in finding fault with his own countrymen, and attacking his own countrymen, than in anything else, and that in a way that I should be sorry to see any countryman of mine do. I suppose we may pretty well know what part the Unionist Liberals are going to take in this Division. The Unionist Liberals seem to me to worship with blind devotion the fetish called the " Union of the Unionist Party," and I am afraid that under that flag they are going to ally themselves with Gentlemen who have like themselves—and not worse I admit — denounced other Members outside and inside this House; they are going to exhibit to the country at large this spectacle—that having repeated these charges in this House, and repeated them outside this House, when the men charged ask for an inquiry by impartial persons—for that you will not dispute so far as the composition of the Committee is concerned—they have not the courage to face those whom they have accused. What will be said in the country of this debate and its result? To my mind the result is a foregone conclusion. It is not much use in giving argument to Liberal Unionists. I am afraid it is a foregone conclusion; but what will be said about it in the country? [*Ministerial cheers.*] Yes; I will tell you what will be said in the country. It will be said that for a considerable time Conservatives and Liberal Unionists went about the country denouncing on public platforms brother Members as guilty of crimes which ought to be punished by the halter or the scaffold. It will be said that they did not mean to bring this matter to the test of an inquiry, but that a bungling Member of their Party brought the matter to the front without reckoning on the consequences; and that, after dilatory suggestions, the Government endeavoured to evade the consequences. It will be said that they have been lacking in that spirit of English fair play which has hitherto been

Mr. R. T. Reid

recognized and practised; that they have put forward subtle arguments, and left to their Attorney General and Solicitor General to find out technical defences where there were not any honest answers. I have stated what I believe will be said and deeply felt in the country. I do not believe the right hon. Gentleman who is Leader of the House deserves the censures which have been passed upon him from this side of the House. I believe the right hon. Gentleman wishes to do right; but I am sorry to say that I think he has been overruled by others. I wish the right hon. Gentleman, whom we respect, would put his own honest mind to this matter, and would ask what would his feeling be in a case of this kind if any man accused him of much less than these men are attacked for. If any man attacked him, and he wanted to have a Committee of Inquiry, and if he found that hon. Gentlemen of different political opinions were opposing him and finding arguments against him, I am afraid he would feel a little bitter too; and, under those circumstances, he ought to make some allowance for the feelings of hon. Gentlemen and what they have said in regard to himself. I would only say this in conclusion—that I would far rather forego that enormous Party advantage which we Liberals shall reap from this transaction—I would far rather forego that than I would do what I believe to be really dangerous to the true interests of the United Kingdom and of Ireland—namely, to encourage and give ground for the opinion in Ireland—aye, and it will spread to England and Scotland too—that in this House of Commons there is one method of justice for Englishmen and Scotchmen, and another and a different one for Irishmen.

MR. PAULTON (Durham, Bishop Auckland): I will not, Sir, at this time of the night (12.20) detain the House for more than a very few minutes; but I wish just to put forward one point that I do not think has yet been touched upon. The right hon. Gentleman the Member for the Sleaford Division of Lincolnshire (Mr. Chaplin) stated—and I was very glad to hear him say it— that all Parties were agreed that some inquiry should be made into this matter. On that statement I maintain the right hon. Gentleman should vote for the

Amendment of the right hon. Gentleman the Member for Mid Lothian, for this reason—that the Irish Members have declared that they will not resort to an action in a Court of Law. I say nothing as to the wisdom or unwisdom of the course which they have decided to pursue. That is not my argument. It does not concern the point I wish to make; but I will incidentally venture to remark that I think they are as much justified, in their position, in doubting the fairness of the judgment which they might receive at the hands of a Court of Law, as hon. Gentlemen opposite are justified in asserting that a Committee of this House would not give a fair and impartial inquiry. That being so, my point is that the Irish Members, having decided that they will not resort, for reasons which may or may not be good, to an action in a Court of Law, if hon. Gentlemen on that side of the House wish that an inquiry should be held, they must vote for this Motion, or they will have no inquiry at all. It appears to me, Sir, that this is a test as to whether hon. Gentlemen on the other side of the House wish for any inquiry or not. I should be very sorry to say anything which should wound the feelings of hon. Members on the other side; but I must confess that their conduct in this matter does give some ground, at any rate, for suspicion that their object in the action they have taken is not the desire which I think all Members of this House should hold—namely, to vindicate the character of hon. Members in this House. It appears to me, Sir—I hope I may be wrong, and I should wish to be corrected by the voices of hon. Members if I am wrong—but it does not appear to me that they would be altogether pleased if the result of this investigation should prove that these charges are, as I believe them to be, wholly and entirely false and unjustifiable. I am not very much surprised that this debate has turned so much upon legal points. My hon. and learned Friend who has just spoken said that, in his opinion—and he is a good judge—the question before us ought not to be decided merely on legal points; but I am not surprised, Sir, that the Party opposite have sought to escape by what I may call a legal quibble from the difficulty in which they have been placed by the extreme action of the hon. Baronet (Sir Charles Lewis). Hard things have been said on both sides of the House of the hon. Baronet; but I will venture to say this of him—that I think he has, at any rate, some claim to patriotism, for although I know nothing of his motives—I may not have a high opinion of them; but it is not necessary for me to express it—of his conduct I may certainly say it would appear to be somewhat of a patriotic kind, for he has sacrificed his Party to what I will venture to say will be for the benefit of his country. And, Sir, besides the legal points upon which this debate has to a great extent turned, the main contention of hon. Members opposite has been that we must be very chary of incurring the danger of stretching what I may call the doctrine of Privilege. I venture to think that the danger in this case is not that we should strain the doctrine of Privilege, but that we should unduly restrict it. I most fully concur in the words which have fallen from my hon. and learned Friend who preceded me in this debate, that in the interests of fair play it is astonishing to us who sit on this side of the House, as English Gentlemen, that hon. Members opposite—that any Party in this House—should have dreamt of hesitating for one single instant as to what their action would be in this matter. I am not going to detain the House by repeating arguments which have been already used, but I certainly wish to emphasize one point—namely, that if hon. Members do wish an inquiry at all they must vote for this Motion, and I most sincerely hope and trust that they will show that their desire has been throughout this matter—and I am bound to say that so far we have had but little ground for thinking so—to maintain the honour and the dignity of this Assembly, in whose Members we all have an equal interest and an equal concern.

CAPTAIN PRICE (Devonport): I beg to move the adjournment of the debate.

Motion made, and Question proposed, "That the Debate be now adjourned." —(*Captain Price.*)

MR. T. M. HEALY (Longford, N.): Before this debate is adjourned I should like to ask Her Majesty's Government a question with reference to procedure tonight. I observe the first Order after

[Third Night.]

this is the Criminal Law Amendment (Ireland) Bill—Committee. I presume that at this hour of the night (12.25) it is not intended to go on with a Bill of that character. If it were intended I should think it would be most unusual and most unfortunate; and, furthermore, I wish to have it distinctly understand that, as far as we are concerned, nothing that we have done in this business has in any way tended to delay the bringing forward of this measure. I believe, as far as I understand, the Government cannot blame us for the delay that has taken place, and, of course, they do not do so. Then I observe the next Order on the Paper is the Duke of Connaught's Leave Bill. I should like to ask Her Majesty's Government is it intended to bring on that measure to-night, because I think, before we agree to this Motion, we should receive an understanding exactly what the course of the Government is with regard to the Amendments on the Paper. I do hope the Duke of Connaught will be able to come home to Her Majesty's Jubilee, because it is a most important thing that the whole family should be present at that time; and, for my part, I should be extremely sorry that his military duty should detain the illustrious Duke. I should like to say that it is important on a measure of this kind that we should have a distinct understanding in advance from Her Majesty's Government; and, therefore, I appeal to the Government to say, before we agree to this Motion, what it is they exactly desire to do. [*Laughter.*] I do not know what the Lord Advocate is laughing at. I hope he is not laughing at my allusions to the illustrious Duke of Connaught. I must say, Sir, that I do think when Members of the Government, on an occasion so important as the present, meet with jeers——

Mr. SPEAKER: Order, order! The Question before the House is the adjournment of the debate. The hon. and learned Gentleman is now discussing other matters on a Motion for the adjournment of the debate.

Mr. T. M. HEALY: I apologize to you, Sir, and to the House for having ventured to go from the straight line of debate, and I will simply confine myself to asking Her Majesty's Government whether they intend on an evidence of this kind, when all our minds

Mr. T. M. Healy

are greatly exercised with the important matter which has been before us, asking the House to debate the Crimes Bill in Committee, or the Duke of Connaught's Leave Bill, each of which forms a large subject of inquiry in itself? I think the hour of half-past 12 is hardly the time when Bills of this kind should be brought on. There is an important Truck Bill on the Paper, and others in addition to that—the Merchant Shipping Bill, for instance—each of which—at any rate, as far as the Truck Bill is concerned—should be brought on. I hope we shall have an answer from the Government.

THE FIRST LORD OF THE TREASURY (Mr. W. H. SMITH) (Strand, Westminster): I regret that my hon. and gallant Friend has moved the adjournment at so early an hour; but, as he has done so, the Government will not oppose his Motion. I do not think that the importance of debate will be much emphasized by its further continuance, when it has already lasted the greater part of three days. The hon. and learned Member opposite (Mr. T. M. Healy) asked me what Business we propose to take this evening. We are indebted to him for the fact that we cannot proceed with any opposed Business, as it is now after half past 12. Probably, if the Motion for Adjournment had been made at an earlier hour in the evening, the hon. and learned Gentleman would not have found it necessary to take part in the discussion. I suppose he is not aware of the fact that a communication was made to the hon. Member for Northampton (Mr. Bradlaugh), earlier in the evening, to the effect that it was the intention of the Government to afford every facility in their power for the further progress of the Truck Bill. That Bill will be the only measure of any importance that will be proceeded with this evening.

Mr. ARTHUR O'CONNOR (Donegal, E.): Might I ask the right hon. Gentleman if the Government propose to give any assistance in furthering the Merchant Shipping Act (1854) Amendment (No. 2) Bill?

Mr. W. H. SMITH: It will not be taken this evening, as far as the Government are concerned.

Question put, and *agreed to.*

Debate *further adjourned* till *To-morrow.*

FIRST OFFENDERS (*re-committed*)
BILL.—[BILL 189.]

(*Mr. Howard Vincent, Lord Randolph Spencer Churchill, Sir Henry Selwin-Ibbetson, Mr. Hoare, Mr. Addison, Mr. Hastings, Mr. Lawson, Mr. Molloy.*)

COMMITTEE.   [*Progress* 14*th April.*]

Bill *considered* in Committee.

(In the Committee.)

Clause 1 (Power to court to release upon probation of good conduct, instead of sentencing to imprisonment).

Amendment proposed,

In page 2, line 10, to leave out all after "will" to "report," in line 11, and insert, "if required, appear before the court, or some specified future court, to answer privately or otherwise."—(*Mr. Howard Vincent.*)

Question proposed, "That the words proposed to be left out stand part of the Clause."

Mr. T. M. HEALY (Longford, N.): I must say that the words, "privately or otherwise," are, in my opinion, most objectionable; and I am greatly surprised that the Government should be willing to allow such words to be inserted. Why, in the case of a juvenile's first or second offence, should we introduce expressions of this character, which are repugnant to our ideas of justice? If juveniles get drunk or pick pockets, why are we to provide that they shall appear before the Court "privately or otherwise?" Why should they not take their chance like anybody else who commits an offence? I do say that such a provision is most objectionable. The juvenile may be a sprig of the aristocracy. The offences of juveniles of that class commit generally take the form of breaking windows, or getting drunk, or something of the kind. Why should the investigation of such a case be made "privately or otherwise?"

Mr. HOWARD VINCENT (Sheffield, Central): Perhaps the hon. and learned Member will allow me to explain that the words, "privately or otherwise," do not apply to the arraignment for a first offence before the magistrate, but to the appearance made after the offender has been out on probation. In such circumstances, it would be exceedingly hard upon him that his name should appear in the papers as having been a second time before the magistrate when he may

have been behaving himself well since his release on probation.

Question put, and *negatived*.

Question proposed,

"That the words, 'if required,' appear before the court, or some specified future court, to answer privately or otherwise,' be there inserted."

Mr. T. M. HEALY (Longford, N.): It is, of course, a pity that there should be any controversy respecting a measure which we admit to be humanely intended, and which is proposed with the best intentions. But I must say this— that the magistrates who will have to carry out this measure belong chiefly to the class of gentlemen who sit on the Benches opposite, and not to the class who sit on these Benches. The Lord Chancellor of Ireland is engaged, at the present moment, in wiping off from the Bench every magistrate who has any sympathy with us. We, therefore, object to giving to magistrates any invidious powers which will enable them to dispose of cases differently in regard to their own class than they would do in regard to other classes. I think that the Gentlemen opposite, who are in charge of this Bill, ought to meet us in this matter, and ought to take no strong opinion in regard to it. I think that the hon. Member for the Hallam Division of Sheffield (Mr. Stuart-Wortley), the Under Secretary of State for the Home Department, is placed in a difficult position in regard to opposing any Amendment brought forward by his Colleague (Mr. Howard Vincent) in the representation of Sheffield. I do not say that they are either of them biased by the fact that they are Colleagues in the representation of the same town; but that there is, perhaps, more communication existing between them than between two ordinary Members. At all events, I beg to move the omission of these words, "privately or otherwise."

Amendment proposed to the proposed Amendment, to leave out the words "privately or otherwise."—(*Mr. T. M. Healy.*)

Question proposed, "That the words proposed to be left out stand part of the proposed Amendment."

Mr. HOWARD VINCENT (Sheffield, Central): If the hon. and learned Member objects to the inclusion of these words, I will not press for their retention. At the same time, I should like to say that this matter has been very carefully thought out. I may, perhaps, be allowed to explain, in regard to the number of Amendments in my name, that after the second reading of the Bill my right hon. and learned Friend the Home Secretary (Mr. Matthews) authorized the Parliamentary Counsel to consider with me how the measure could be improved, and it is only after long consultation with him that these Amendments have been placed on the Paper. I may say that I have this evening received a letter from the Minister of Justice in New Zealand, stating that a similar measure to this proposed by me has been unanimously adopted by the Legislature has been working well for some months, and that it has already saved the Colony a considerable sum in prison expenses.

THE UNDER SECRETARY OF STATE FOR THE HOME DEPARTMENT (Mr. STUART-WORTLEY) (Sheffield, Hallam): I think it better that the words which the hon. and learned Gentleman proposes to omit should be left in the clause. The object of the measure is to enable juvenile offenders to take advantage of the means provided for reformation, and to remove the stigma of the original conviction where an intention has been shown to do better in the future. I hope the hon. Member will see that it will be well not to omit the words to which he has raised an objection. Of course, to say that these words must not go into the clause is to say that we cannot trust magistrates anywhere. We must trust the magistrates.

MR. T. M. HEALY: Sir, this is one of the curses of a United Parliament. When applying a Bill to all three countries, you are under the disadvantage of speaking about countries you do not understand. But still, as I do not wish to prejudice those admirable young gentlemen, the first offenders of England, if the hon. Gentleman the Member for the Central Division of Sheffield (Mr. Howard Vincent) will consent to leave out these words now, I shall be willing on the Report stage, when we shall be able to consider the Bill as a whole, to give my attention to the re-introduction of the words.

SIR JOSEPH PEASE (Durham, Barnard Castle): I hope the hon. Gentle-

Mr. Howard Vincent

man (Mr. Howard Vincent) will keep these words in the Bill. If they are omitted, a juvenile offender who has behaved himself properly since his first offence will be liable to have the disgrace of a second public appearance before the magistrates cast upon him.

MR. F. S. POWELL (Wigan): It seems to me that the retention of the words is almost necessary, in order to make the Bill what it is intended to be. The object of allowing the first appearance to be made privately is to exempt the young offender from the stigma of a public appearance, and to prevent his being branded as a criminal and a felon. Unless these words are retained, the whole of the section will become either mischievous or surplusage; because a magistrate will never make use of the power conferred on him by the clause, and, if he does, it will be an act, not of kindness, but of great severity to the young offender. For the sake of my hon. Friend the promoter of the Bill, in his errand of mercy to the young offenders, I hope these words will not be omitted.

MR. CHANCE (Kilkenny, S.): The objection we take to this provision is that, whilst we consider it perfectly reasonable that an offender who has been allowed to remain out of prison should be called up afterwards to answer for his subsequent conduct, we do not think that the greater number of the magistrates ought to be trusted with the discretionary power to call one offender up publicly and another privately. I understand the contention to be that an offender ought not to have cast upon him the stigma of a second appearance. If so, why retain the power of calling them up a second time at all? Would it not meet the case to strike out the words "or otherwise," so that all should have to come up privately? If this were done, the object of the promoters of the Bill would be served, and the magistrates would have no power to make invidious distinctions. I trust that my hon. and learned Friend (Mr. T. M. Healy) will withdraw his Amendment to the proposed Amendment, and then move to leave out the words "or otherwise."

MR. T. M. HEALY: I am quite willing to accept that suggestion. Let us have them all examined privately, and I shall be quite happy. What I object to is allowing a magistrate to make fish of one and flesh of another.

Amendment to the proposed Amendment, by leave, *withdrawn.*

MR. T. M. HEALY then moved to amend the proposed Amendment by omitting the words "or otherwise."

Amendment proposed to proposed Amendment, to leave out the words "or otherwise."—(*Mr. T. M. Healy.*)

Question, "That the words proposed to be left out stand part of the proposed Amendment," put, and *negatived.*

Amendment, as amended, *agreed to.*

On the Motion of Mr. HOWARD VINCENT, the following Amendment made:—Page 2, line 15, to leave out from "exceed" to end of line 18.

Amendment proposed, in page 2, after line 19, add the following sub-sections:—

1 (3.) "The authority to whom an offender is required by the court to notify his residence, or report himself, shall be either an authority which is bound to obey the orders of the court or an authority which consents to undertake the duties imposed on it under this section.

(4.) "It shall be the duty of any such authority—

(a.) To make, if required, a report to the court, or to some specified future court, as to the conduct of the offender since his release ;

(b.) To report immediately to the court, or to some court of summary jurisdiction, any breach of the conditions with which the authority was concerned ; and

(c.) In the event of any breach of any such condition, to take or assist in taking such steps as may be necessary for bringing the offender to justice." — (*Mr. Howard Vincent.*)

Question proposed, "That those sub-sections be there added."

MR. T. M. HEALY: Sir, there is an immortal expression which is supposed to have come from a transpontine theatre —"We don't expect grammar, but you might join the flats." In the House of Commons we do expect grammar. The way in which one of the sub-sections is put is as follows:—"The authority to whom an offender is required by the court to notify his residence," and so on, "shall be either an authority which." An authority cannot be both "who" and "which," and if it be "who" it cannot be also "it." It seems to me that the hon. Members for Sheffield, one of whom is a Member of the Government, and the other of whom has been a distinguished official, might, at the least, have consulted Lindley Murray, and have made the sub-section read properly. That is all I have got to say about this Amendment.

THE CHAIRMAN: Does the hon. and learned Member propose an Amendment ?

MR. T. M. HEALY: I beg to move the omission of the word "whom" in the first line, and the insertion, instead thereof, of the word "which."

Amendment to the proposed Amendment *agreed to.*

DR. TANNER (Cork Co., Mid.): I really think, Sir, that after my hon. and learned Friend has pointed out in such an efficient way the faulty manner in which these Amendments have been drafted the time has come at which to report Progress. I think that Progress should be reported, in order that another measure, which will be of infinitely more service to the public, and one which is looked forward to by many people, may be gone on with.

Amendment, as amended, *agreed to.*

On the Motion of Mr. HOWARD VINCENT, the following Amendments made:—In page 2, line 20, leave out sub-section (3); line 23, after "excuse," insert "(proof whereof shall lie on him);" line 24, after "conditions" insert "of his recognisance;" same line, leave out "imposed upon him on his release;" and in line 28, after "released," insert "and order his recognisance to be forfeited."

Amendment proposed,

In page 2, line 30, after "jurisdiction," insert "and the term 'authority' includes any person or body of persons, official or otherwise, required or consenting to undertake the duties of an authority under this section."— (*Mr. Howard Vincent.*)

Question proposed, "That those words be there inserted."

MR. T. M. HEALY: This appears to be an Amendment of very great importance, and I shall beg the hon. Member in charge of the Bill to state clearly to the Committee what it is exactly that is proposed. In this section the term "court" implies a Court of Summary Jurisdiction, and it is now proposed to insert a provision that "authority" shall include—

"Any person or body of persons, official or otherwise, required or consenting to undertake the duties of an authority under this section."

That appears to me to involve something absolutely foreign and novel to our

Criminal Law. I confess that at the first blush I do not understand it, and I, therefore, will not pronounce upon it until the hon. Member for the Central Division of Sheffield (Mr. Howard Vincent) explains what it means. At present I look upon it with repugnance, as I think it unusual and, unless it can be explained, dangerous.

Mr. HOWARD VINCENT: I am glad of the opportunity of explaining to the hon. and learned Member the meaning of this provision. I think that many cases might occur in which it might be very beneficial to appoint as the authority the Secretary or Manager of a Discharged Prisoners' Aid Society a clergyman, or a priest, or some other non-official person having knowledge of the individual, and means of assisting him to obtain an honest livelihood, without exercising undue control over his movements. Any such undue control might hinder the offender from gaining his livelihood. As to the expression, "official or otherwise," it might possibly occur that a police superintendent, or some other person under the orders of the Court, would be able to exercise the duties of an authority under the section. I hope the hon. and learned Gentleman, however, will understand that it is exceedingly desirable not to make it a question of police supervision. That is distinctly cut out of the Bill in every shape and form. The great object of the measure is to enable private persons to come before the Court and say to the magistrate—"This is a first offender. I know his history, and if the Court will suspend its judgment on him and look over this offence, I shall be able to make him a respectable member of society."

Mr. CHANCE: I think this provision is extremely objectionable. I regard this also as a proposal to make flesh of one person and fish of another, because, under it, one offender may have to report himself at a police station and another to his own father. That is what we object to. We think it invidious, and we think it too large a power to give to an unpaid magistrate.

Mr. HOARE (Norwich): I think it is desirable that we should, as far as possible, provide for relieving these first offenders from being placed under police supervision. At present magistrates, in dealing with a case, are often applied to

by some person in whom they have confidence, and, rather than send a first offender to prison, allow that person to be responsible for placing him in a reformatory. If that can be done on the present occasion, I hope the Committee will approve of the work being left in trustworthy hands.

Mr. RADCLIFFE COOKE (Newington, W.): It is an extremely dangerous principle, in my opinion, to leave it to a lot of amateurs to say what persons who have been convicted shall be allowed quietly to merge into the honest, peaceable population, and be heard of no more. Who are these authorities, these "officials or otherwise," these bodies of persons—who may be priests, clergymen, women, perhaps secretaries of institutions, and the like, persons wholly unacquainted with our forms of law, who will have to report as to the conduct of persons of whom they may know very little? And if they report in the contrary direction—adversely, that is—what is to happen then? I consider the whole of this Bill—this part of it especially—to be a most abominable piece of amateur legislation. Instead of being an Act of mercy—as an hon. Friend beside me called it—it is an Act of the greatest hardship towards those whom, apparently, my hon. Friend (Mr. Howard Vincent) wishes to benefit. I intend to move the rejection of the clause at the proper moment. That is all I have to say with regard to this mischievous Amendment.

Mr. T. M. HEALY: I wish the hon. Gentleman opposite (Mr. Howard Vincent) could see his way to omit this provision. These young offenders will have to report themselves to somebody. But we know very well that if we introduce such a system as is now proposed, the amateur inspector will grow neglectful. Suppose any offender agreed to report himself to me, does anybody suppose that I should take care to look after his record? Certainly not. Then how much less will the clergyman and the village doctor? Everybody must commit his first criminal offence some time. The most hardened offenders have to make a beginning. Well, then, in London, where the magistrates are not to be imposed upon, he will, perhaps, be looked after. But in the country he will, perhaps, learn the 100th Psalm, or something of that sort, and the village clergyman will send a good report at once. We all know that it is the most astute and the most dangerous offenders who play off most successfully upon the parson and such people. Suppose the parson's wife makes out such a young gentleman's report, what sort of guarantee have you got? You are about to introduce a system into the English Criminal Law absolutely unknown before. I look upon it as a curious innovation, and I think the Committee would be well advised to put some limit upon its operation. Let the Act remain in force, say, for two years and no longer, and then it might be put into the Continuance Bill for a year or two longer, if it was found to be working fairly. I look upon the Bill with great suspicion, I must say, even though emanating from the hon. Gentleman opposite (Mr. Howard Vincent). I would ask the hon. Gentleman to throw overboard this "old nobility," so to speak—that is to say, the unpaid magistrates and others, who do not look with too tender an eye even upon juvenile offenders.

MR. HOWARD VINCENT: I do not wish to press this Amendment against the general wish of hon. Gentlemen; but I would point out, in justification of it, that the most successful man of to-day in dealing with these discharged prisoners is one of these very unofficial members—I mean Mr. Wheatley, the secretary of St. Giles's Mission, who has been enabled for many years to do much good in that way.

MR. RADCLIFFE COOKE: Yes; but that is all done now. When a prisoner is discharged, there is nothing to prevent that discharged prisoner being taken care of by friendly societies and friendly persons. That is done now; and if my hon. Friend (Mr. Howard Vincent) had practised in a Criminal Court, he would have seen, as I have constantly seen, the gentleman of whom he speaks before the Court. He would have heard Judges hesitate to decide, until they had heard what this gentleman had to say; and not until Mr. Wheatley had told the Judge whether the prisoner would be benefitted by his discharge or not, is any decision come to. If all this can be done now, I do not see what is the use of this Bill at all.

MR. CHANCE: We have already decided that a first offender is to report

himself to some authority—either an official or an amateur. Now, we must have some definition of what an amateur authority is. It would be idle to withdraw this Amendment, and leave that point undecided.

SIR RICHARD PAGET (Somerset, Wells): I am desirous of pointing out the great difficulty in which we shall be involved if this Amendment is withdrawn. I would beg the Committee to remember that when the Bill was first introduced there was no such authority, and the Bill was taken exception to on the ground that the supervision of first offenders would, under it, necessarily be by the police. I, for one, distinctly object to dealing with first offenders in this way; and that is the reason, I take it, that the Bill has been altered to its present shape, and the word "authority" introduced. The whole object of this Bill is, instead of punishing first offenders by sending them to prison, to provide for their release and supervision, so that you are bound to introduce some new authority; and even if this Amendment be withdrawn, you must introduce some provision that the authority shall be duly recorded and defined. These persons are, for the first time, invested with statutory power, and it will be necessary to provide that, in the case of any person accepting an appointment under this Bill, there should be some record of the fact.

THE UNDER SECRETARY OF STATE FOR THE HOME DEPARTMENT (Mr. STUART-WORTLEY) (Sheffield, Hallam): I quite recognize the difficulties which have been pointed out by some hon. Gentlemen; but the House has placed itself in its present position by deciding the general principle of the Bill on the second reading—namely, that first offenders shall not be sent to prison, but be subjected to friendly supervision. I may say there is no existing machinery known by which that can be carried out. I think, however, that if this Amendment is withdrawn, we may safely leave it to be discovered by the Court whether this or that body of persons is qualified by public opinion to undertake these duties, which, be it remembered, is simply the duty of making a periodical report. They are bound to make sworn reports, but that is the extent of their duty.

MR. CHANCE: But that is not the whole duty. Under Sub-section 3, the amateur authority is to take steps, or assist in taking steps, to bring the offender to justice in certain circumstances. And suppose, after a bad report, the first offender is committed, what is to prevent him finding an enterprising country attorney who will bring an action against the amateur authority for false imprisonment? It is absolutely necessary that before you give this amateur authority power to do what no one else can do without a warrant, that you should define who this amateur authority shall be.

MR. BRADLAUGH (Northampton): I beg to suggest that Progress be reported. I think it would facilitate the eventual settlement of the question.

MR. CHANCE: I beg to move, Sir, that you report Progress. There is evidently very great difference of opinion on this important point, and I do not think we can be expected to thresh the matter out fully and satisfactorily at this point.

Motion made, and Question, "That the Chairman do now report Progress, and ask leave to sit again," — (*Mr. Chance,*)—put, and *agreed to.*

Committee report Progress; to sit again upon *Monday* next.

TRUCK BILL.—[BILL 109.]

(*Mr. Bradlaugh, Mr. Warmington, Mr. John Ellis, Mr. Arthur Williams, Mr. Howard Vincent, Mr. Esslemont.*)

COMMITTEE. [*Progress 3rd May.*]

Bill *considered* in Committee.

(In the Committee.)

New Clause—

(Servants in Husbandry.)

"Nothing in the principal Act or this Act shall render illegal a contract with a servant in husbandry for giving him food, drink, a cottage, or other allowances or privileges in addition to money wages as a remuneration for his services,"

—*brought up,* and read the first and second time.

MR. C. T. D. ACLAND (Cornwall, Launceston): As there is now a larger attendance of hon. Members than when I moved this Amendment on Tuesday, I should like to state to the Committee what the object of the Amendment is—

namely, that it shall not be possible to force upon any agricultural labourer that he should receive part of his wages in liquor—a custom which exists now in many parts of England. Occasionally, farmers, or agricultural employers, refuse to employ men who do not wish to take, and are not willing to take, as part of their wages a supply of intoxicating liquor. I know that I shall be largely supported by many persons, both inside and outside this House, when I say that this is a grievance which ought to be remedied. I do not know of any way of remedying it, if we allow a contract to be considered legal under which a servant in husbandry can be found drink as a part of his wages. I wish to insert, after the word "drink," the words "not being alcoholic," though, if the Committee think it better, I am willing to withdraw the word "alcoholic," and substitute the word "intoxicating." It has been said that if this Amendment is accepted, those who have been accustomed to work on this system will be very much injured. I do not think any consideration of that kind ought to blind us to the exceeding inexpediency of a custom which induces men to consume drink when otherwise they would not have done so. I do not wish to limit the power of farmers to give their labourers that which they can give them cheaper than the men could get it elsewhere—such as oatmeal, barley-meal, and so on—these things can do them no harm ; but we know that the provision of intoxicating drinks very often causes the labourer to get into trouble. It is for the sake of the labourers, as well as for the sake of the farmers who are interested in the well-being of their labourers, that I move this Amendment.

Amendment proposed, in line 2, after "drink," insert "not being alcoholic." —(*Mr. C. T. D. Acland.*)

Question proposed, "That those words be there inserted."

THE ATTORNEY GENERAL (Sir RICHARD WEBSTER) (Isle of Wight): This Amendment is essentially a matter for the Committee to express its opinion upon, and Her Majesty's Government do not wish in any way to dictate to the Committee. When this matter was before the original Committee, the question of the agricultural labourer was expressly excluded from its Report. If the Committee thinks that the hon. Member (Mr. C. T. D. Acland) has laid before it sufficient information to enable it to decide the question that these words should be inserted, then, of course, the Committee will give its opinion. But, at the same time, I would add that I am told it is by no means clear whether the agricultural labourers, in some parts of the country, who have been accustomed to have cider and beer, would regard this Amendment in a favourable light. Whether or not the Committee thinks that temperance would be promoted by the proposed arrangement is another question. I only want to point out that whilst the object of the Bill is to insist that wages shall be paid in money and not in kind, that bargains of the kind which have been referred to by hon. Members opposite—so much pork, so much skimmed milk, and so on—shall not be forced upon the labourer, it is quite clear that the clause gives no addition to wages. It does not prevent those things being given, on the other hand, and it is for the Committee to say whether it has sufficient information before it to warrant the exclusion of gifts of alcoholic or intoxicating liquor.

MR. BRADLAUGH (Northampton): As the hon. and learned Attorney General (Sir Richard Webster) has said, this is essentially a matter for the Committee to decide. But I would wish to point out to my hon. Friend (Mr. C. T. D. Acland), that if the representations made to me are correct, the words "not being alcoholic" exclude every description of herb beer, which, I presume, is not the desire of the Mover of the Amendment. For my own part, I quite accept the interpretation of the hon. and learned Attorney General, that there is no desire on the part of the promoters of this Bill to do anything but prevent the payment of wages in anything but in money.

MR. C. W. GRAY (Essex, Maldon): The hon. Member who moved this Amendment (Mr. C. T. D. Acland) said his object was to prevent farmers forcing drink upon their labourers in lieu of a money payment for their labour. But the Amendment goes very much further than that. I am quite in accord with the hon. Member that farmers should not be allowed to force beer upon their labourers; but I do not agree that we want such an Amendment as this. I would point out to the Committee that it upsets many agreements customary in many English counties — agreements which, I am sure, are entered into freely and willingly by the agricultural labourers themselves. I would point out also to the hon. Member that, if his Amendment were carried, the consequence would be that if I have a particularly strong piece of clover or of tares to be cut, and I offer my men 5s. or 6s. an acre, and they say—"That is a very strong piece, master; we will do it if you will give us some beer to boot," we should be prevented by this Amendment from coming to any arrangement of that sort. On a farm there are constantly "odd jobs," as we call them, cropping up, which have to be met by a pint of beer, and it is much better that they should be met by a pint of beer fresh from the farmer's cellars. [*Laughter.*] Hon. Members want to ridicule my argument before they have heard it. Will they tell me that a pint of beer fresh from the farmer's cellars is not better for the men than beer got from a public-house, which has been carried about all through a long and, probably, hot day? For the convenience of the men themselves, and in the interests of temperance, I say it is a good deal better. If farmers and labourers were accustomed to enter into bargains which were set forth in written terms, then this Amendment might act fairly well. But all the farmer's contracts with his men are merely verbal agreements. If I find one evening that the bullocks or the sheep have broken accidentally into one of my fields, and say to Tom or Dick—"Go and put them out, and if you call at the house to-morrow you shall have a pint of beer," by this Amendment, I should be putting myself in the position of having broken the law. [Mr. C. T. D. ACLAND: Hear, hear!] The hon. Member says "Hear, hear!" If he objects to that, I entirely disagree with him. There is a good old custom in many parts of the country under which, on Sunday mornings, the stock-men are allowed to come to breakfast in the farmer's kitchen, and, if they are not teetotallers, they have a pint of beer given them with it. That would also be illegal according to this Amendment. There are many other cases which I might allude to. A load of corn has to be loaded or unloaded; the men have extra hard work. and they prefer a pint of beer to 2d. or 3d.

in coppers. Speaking for the Eastern Counties, I am sure if the men had an opportunity of expressing their opinion on this Amendment, they would, almost to a man, vote against it. It is not necessary for me to take up the time of the Committee longer. If the hon. Member really wants only to prevent farmers forcing beer upon their labourers in lieu of money, that point would be secured by inserting, after the word "services," the words "provided that in accepting such return for such services, the servant is a willing party to such contract." But this Amendment goes much further than that, and I am sure it will be objected to by nearly every labourer in the Eastern Counties.

MR. RADCLIFFE COOKE (Newington, W.): I am sorry to say I have a farm in Herefordshire, and to the labourers on that farm I give cider, following a custom that has obtained in that county from time immemorial. It is the drink of the county, and there can be no better drink for human beings than good cider. In the course of their work, agricultural labourers sometimes get thirsty, and there is no better drink to quench that thirst than cider. This Amendment is proposed by the son of a Baronet; and when an Amendment of this kind is suggested by one of the upper classes, it finds support from hon. Baronets, like the hon. Members for Barnard Castle (Sir Joseph Pease) and Cockermouth (Sir Wilfrid Lawson), and others, who really have no experience whatever of the wants and feelings of the agricultural classes. Probably, hon. Gentlemen who promote this Amendment, when they do a day's hard work on the moors in Scotland, or over the turnip fields of England, they find they want something to drink, and consume claret, and all sorts of fine things, at their luncheon; but what is the agricultural labourer of Herefordshire to have with his luncheon if he may not have this excellent cider? His wife makes him some miserable tea— tea of the commonest, coarsest description, bought at the village shop, a beverage that hon. Gentlemen have never ventured to try. Or, I have heard it suggested by some rabid teetotallers, let them mix oatmeal and water in a bucket, and drink that, as if they were animals, not human beings. As an alternative to their miserable tea, the

labourers of Herefordshire may have water. Now, water, as is well known, is a most dangerous liquid to drink, contaminated, as it often is, by the percolation of sewage into wells. In country cottages, too, it often happens that the labouring classes find a difficulty in getting water for washing, let alone for drinking. I do not suppose hon. Gentlemen who promote this Amendment know anything of the turbid liquid that labourers have to put up with. Naturally, the Hereford man takes cider; it is a practice that has been in vogue from time immemorial, and it is a drink that does a man no harm whatever. I do not say you cannot get drunk on cider, but you must drink a great deal of it to do so. In another point of view, this Amendment is objectionable. We do make a little profit sometimes from agriculture—not much; and in the county I am speaking of, we make a little profit from the sale of cider. It is true, however, that there are persons so abandoned that they, by this drink, make a profit also as regards its consumption in the surrounding districts. They come from Gloucester, Shropshire, and Worcester to buy this drink to give their labourers; and so the producers make a little money that way. Do you grudge us this one of our little sources of profit, hon. Gentlemen and Baronets who will not drink cider? You, when you wish to slake your thirst, order hock, claret, Burgundy, and other expensive drinks, when you would be better advised if you ordered cider. I could supply you with it, and assure you it is a first-class drink. There is no reasonable ground for this prohibition. We have always been in the habit of giving cider on our farms; and if you say we shall not do so from this time forth, wages will remain exactly the same; though the men will feel the deprivation, they will be glad to stay. Practically, the cider is a gift to them, and a custom farmers are not likely to interrupt. Unless this House intervenes in this improper way, they will continue to supply this drink—a better drink than anything else that can be obtained.

MR. FINCH - HATTON (Lincolnshire, Spalding): At the risk of being stigmatized as a Baronet by my hon. Friend, I must say that I quite sympathize with the speech, though not with

Mr. C. W. Gray

the Amendment, of the hon. Member opposite (Mr. C. D. T. Acland). He said it was possible, as matters now stood, to force upon agricultural labourers, against their will, drink instead of wages. Now, I go with the hon. Member in his wish to remove that possibility ; and if his Amendment of the clause did that only, I should support him ; but, as an hon. Member said just now, the speech does one thing, but the Amendment does quite another thing. As hon. Members are aware, this proposal makes it illegal to give alcoholic drink at all as part of a contract. Now, if we go into the minutiæ of farming, my experience bears out that of the hon. Member who has spoken near me, and I might as well expect my thrashing machine to work without oil, as to expect to get an extra amount of work done in an emergency without a glass of beer. It is this glass of beer that often gets over just the turning point of a difficult day's work, in a manner satisfactory to both labourer and employer, and neither is the worse for the giving or receiving it. I trust the hon. Member will see his way to accept the Amendment suggested from below the Gangway, which will carry out the spirit of his speech, and prevent this being made a condition of employment against the will of the agricultural labourer. On the other hand, I may remind the Committee that the same hon. Member (Mr. C. T. D. Acland) has a Bill dealing with this special question, and I think it would be much better to leave this point to be dealt with as a matter of principle in such a Bill, than to attempt to deal with it thus by a side wind. I make the admission from experience of the constituency I represent, that public opinion is making strides in the direction of it being undesirable that wages should be given in beer, to the extent it has been ; but I believe that public opinion will be crushed and held back by any premature attempt of the Committee to introduce a provision of this kind, interfering unnecessarily with freedom of contract. It would be in harmony with the spirit of the speech of the hon. Member for Launceston, if the arrangement were legal where both parties agree.

MR. BRADLAUGH (Northampton): I do not wish to abridge this very interesting discussion, but I would point out that whether the clause stands with or without the Amendment, does not affect the matter at all. Intoxicating drink can equally be given, whether the Amendment is inserted or not. Having said that, it will be seen that this discussion, however interesting, has no legal value whatever.

MR. CREMER (Shoreditch, Haggerston): I will not follow the discussion on the qualities and relative merits of beer and cider, as to which hon. Members who have spoken are probably better judges than I. The hon. Member opposite (Mr. Gray) has, however, made the statement that agricultural labourers prefer to be rewarded with beer instead of money ; but that does not square with the experience I have gathered from a long residence among the agricultural population. I think Hodge is too acute, and knows better than to accept a pint of very small beer in lieu of the pence referred to. The opportunity is scarcely ever offered him to decide between 3d. and a pint of very small beer. I would suggest to the hon. Member to make the experiment the next time, when Hodge performs similar labour. Let him offer 3d. with one hand, and the pint of small beer with the other, and I think he will find that Hodge has a very great appreciation of the value of the two forms of remuneration. The hon. Member for West Newington (Mr. Radcliffe Cooke) referred to the quality of the water in agricultural villages, and I am unfortunately able to bear him out in his description. I have been in the cottages of labourers, and unfortunately compelled to drink the wretched water which is provided the labourers by the squires and landlords of the kingdom. I have frequently seen the water fetched from ponds in the neighbourhood of cottages, no wells having been provided by the landlords. I do not say the object was to drive the labourers to the public-house ; but that has been the effect. I have seen water brought into the cottages from the ponds full of life ; and this is the water the labourers and their families have to drink. The hon. Member for West Newington is perfectly correct in his description of the fluid that a large proportion of the agricultural labouring class are compelled to drink, through the shameful neglect of the landlords and farmers. My object in rising, was however, to ask the hon. Member, who has charge of the Bill (Mr. Bradlaugh), whether the clause has reference exclusively to out-door servants?

MR. BRADLAUGH: It extends to all persons to whom the Employers and Workmen's Act extends. All their wages are to be paid in current coin of the Realm. This discussion only applies to gifts in addition to that, and does not affect the principle.

MR. CREMER: I am glad to have that explanation. I will not occupy time further than to suggest to the hon. Member who brought forward this Amendment, that he should substitute the word "intoxicating" for "alcoholic," it would then shut out the possibility of contention in regard to herb beer, ginger beer, and other beverages which are said to contain some alcohol, in relation to which there has been considerable discussion, especially in the Midland Counties. The word "intoxicating" would get rid of the difficulty.

MR. C. T. D. ACLAND: I shall be glad to withdraw the word "alcoholic" and substitute "intoxicating."

Amendment, by leave, *withdrawn.*

Amendment proposed, in line 2, after the word "drink," to insert the words "not being intoxicating."—(*Mr. C. T. D. Acland.*)

Question proposed, "That those words be there inserted."

MR. FENWICK (Northumberland, Wansbeck): From a very lengthened experience of the working classes, I can say that those who oppose the introduction of the words of my hon. Friend (Mr. C. T. D. Acland) do not do so in the interest of the working classes. From my own experience, I can testify to the great injury done to the working classes by giving them alcoholic drink. Nothing tends more to the demoralization of the working classes than taking intoxicating drink; and I have no doubt that those who are first to give such drink lay the basis of the demoralization and degradation of the class and their families, and will be the first, when labourers show signs of intoxication, to dismiss them from employment. I would like to inform the hon. Gentleman opposite (Mr. Finch-Hatton), who talked about a field of clover being hard work, that wages sweeten labour, and he will find

Mr. Cremer

that labourers will prefer to have the price of the beer to having the beer itself. No man who knows the evils drink has wrought will hesitate about rather giving money value for services, encouraging the labourer to hold the principles of temperance and sobriety. Within my own experience I have known cases where persons have been engaged to do work, for which part payment was given in drink, and when this was refused the wages were reduced. This is is a thing that ought not to be tolerated; we should do all that lies in our power to encourage the labouring classes to become sober and thrifty, and there is no greater enemy to thrift than the habits of drinking intoxicating drink.

THE SECRETARY TO THE LOCAL GOVERNMENT BOARD (Mr. W. H. LONG) (Wilts, Devizes): I am anxious as a county Member to express my sympathy with the view of the hon. Member who moved this Amendment (Mr. C. T. D. Acland). It is, we must all allow, very desirable in the interests of labourers and farmers that, as much as possible, the practice should be stopped of paying wages in any degree in liquor. But while I accept that view, I must point out that the Amendment goes considerably beyond that view, upsetting a custom that has existed for a considerable time, and which has been accepted by labourers themselves under conditions where it was not carried out to the detriment of the labourers. There are cases, if we accept the authority of those who have spoken from the other side, where labourers have been encouraged to drink to excess, and everybody will deplore that; but I think those who are cognizant of the habits of agricultural labourers will agree with me that it is not to the interest of the farmer, any more than it is to that of the labourer, that the latter should drink to excess. But whatever may be said by the hon. Member who has just spoken (Mr. Fenwick), those having experience of farming operations well know that there are times when the assistance of beer, in moderation and of good quality, stimulates the men to get through quickly with a piece of work in a way that the payment of money afterwards would not effect. I mention that as a fact within my personal experience. If the result of Amendment would be to prevent the farmer or the employer from forcing upon his men alcoholic liquor, when they would prefer to have money, then I should be glad to vote for it; but as it goes so far beyond that, and will, if carried, prevent any payments in kind, even where such are the accepted customs of the country I must vote against it.

MR. BRADLAUGH: I may say again, the adoption of the words will not have that effect.

An hon. MEMBER: The clause will merely prohibit the giving drink as part of a contract. In cases referred to on the other side, in which it was thought to be an advantage to give drink to stimulate men to further exertion, this clause will not interfere. The clause simply says that parties shall not enter into a contract, by which a servant shall receive intoxicating drink as part of his wages; but it does not in any way interfere with the giving of drink to labourers on an occasion of special service under trying conditions.

DR. CLARK (Caithness): I do not understand why the hon. Member (Mr. Stuart-Wortley) should have moved this clause, which allows drink, as one of the terms of a contract by which a man may be hired.

THE CHAIRMAN: The hon. Member will remember the question is the Amendment of the clause.

DR. CLARK: The hon. Member, in altering the word from "alcoholic" to intoxicating, has not made a scientific change. It is the alcohol only that is intoxicating; I think, however, it would be unwise to allow the clause to stand, for it will permit a farmer to pay part of his wages in drink. As there are a great number of labourers who are not drinkers of beer or cider, or, even in my own country, of whisky, they will be compelled to accept lower wages practically not taking part in drink. It cannot be too often repeated that if, instead of taking beer and cider, that are the causes of disease and premature death, a man took cocoa and other beverages that do not intoxicate and do not cause disease, he would have a healthier, longer life. Total abstainers live longer than even moderate drinkers. I support the Amendment now; but I shall oppose the clause as being altogether unnecessary.

MAJOR RASCH (Essex, S.E.): Because I represent an agricultural constituency, I feel bound to oppose the Amendment of the hon. Member for Launceston (Mr. C. T. D. Acland), and I am certain its adoption will be prejudicial to agricultural interests. We pay our agricultural labourers £7 10s. in money to £1 5s. in black beer; and the result of the Amendment of the hon. Gentleman will be, that farmers will have to give up that old-established custom, and if they pay their men in money entirely, the men will be driven to buy beer at a higher price at the pothouse. Surely, the hon. Member does not suppose he is going to make agricultural labourers teetotallers by Act of Parliament.

SIR WALTER FOSTER: It is desirable that we should have this one point cleared up by an authoritative statement from the hon. and learned Attorney General—namely, Will this Amendment prevent the gift of drink? I strongly support the remarks that have been made from below the Gangway by the hon. Member for Caithness (Dr. Clark), for the fallacies supported by the other side cannot receive contradiction too often. There is no advantage in the use of alcoholic liquors for the purpose stated. Alcoholic liquor does not give strength, and no man works the better, or the longer for it. This has been practically proved in the Army, and the fact has been demonstrated over and over again by physiologists. It will be a great advantage to the labourer and his family if we carry this Amendment. If a man is paid in money even so small a sum as 1d. or 2d., that money will go to benefit the family, instead of being used for the gratification of an appetite that ought not to be encouraged.

THE ATTORNEY GENERAL (Sir RICHARD WEBSTER) (Isle of Wight): In answer to the Question asked, I can only repeat what the hon. Member for Northampton (Mr. Bradlaugh) has already said—that the clause, as it stands, does not touch the question of simple gifts of drink. It allows the farmer to make the contract for payment, partly in money and partly in food, drink, or a cottage or residence. The Amendment moved prevents the drink being of an intoxicating character; but gifts as an incentive to extra exertion would be outside the clause altogether.

Question put.

The Committee *divided:*—Ayes 112; Noes 101: Majority 11.—(Div. List, No. 111.)

Motion made, and Question proposed, "That the Clause, as amended, stand part of the Bill."

DR. CLARK (Caithness): If the spirit of this measure is to be carried into effect, Sir, I think that this clause is unnecessary. I should like to see its spirit carried out thoroughly and fully towards agricultural as well as other labourers. As the hon. and learned Member for North Longford (Mr. T. M. Healy) has pointed out, the conditions prevailing in the Three Kingdoms are very different, circumstances suitable for persons in one place may do harm if applied in another district. Still, if the English agricultural labourer is not yet prepared for the full application to his case of the principle of this Act, I will not press my objection. I do, however, strongly object to the application of this clause to Scotland.

An hon. MEMBER: Before the clause is finally agreed to, may I suggest to the hon. Member for the Hallam Division of Sheffield (Mr. Stuart-Wortley) the desirability of further amending it, by adding the words "or fuel?" I think it would be an advantage if he would do so.

THE CHAIRMAN: Order, order! It is now too late to propose an Amendment to the clause.

Question put, and *agreed to.*

Clause *added* to the Bill.

On the Motion of Mr. STUART-WORTLEY, the following New Clauses *agreed to,* and *added* to the Bill:—

(Offences.)

"If any employer or his agent contravenes or fails to comply with any of the foregoing provisions of this Act, such employer shall be guilty of an offence against the principal Act, and shall be liable to the penalties imposed by section nine of that Act, as if the offence were such an offence as in that section mentioned.

(Fine on person committing offence for which employer is liable, and power of employer to exempt himself from penalty on conviction of the actual offender.)

"(1.) Where an offence for which an employer is, by virtue of the principal Act or this

Sir Richard Webster

Act, liable to a penalty has in fact been committed by some agent of the employer or other person, such agent or other person shall be liable to the same penalty as if he were the employer.

"(2.) Where an employer is charged with an offence against the principal Act or this Act he shall be entitled, upon information duly laid by him, to have any other person whom he charges as the actual offender brought before the court at the time appointed for hearing the charge, and if, after the commission of the offence has been proved, the employer proves to the satisfaction of the court that he had used due diligence to enforce the execution of the said Acts, and that the said other person had committed the offence in question without his knowledge, consent, or connivance, the said other person shall be summarily convicted of such offence, and the employer shall be exempt from any penalty.

"When it is made to appear to the satisfaction of an inspector of factories or mines, or in Scotland a procurator fiscal at the time of discovering the offence that the employer had used due diligence to enforce the execution of the said Acts, and also by what person such offence had been committed, and also that it had been committed without the knowledge, consent, or connivance of the employer, then the inspector or procurator fiscal shall proceed against the person whom he believes to be the actual offender in the first instance without first proceeding against the employer.

(Recovery of penalties.)

"Any offence against the principal Act or this Act may be prosecuted, and any penalty therefore recovered in manner provided by the Summary Jurisdiction Acts, so, however, that no penalty shall be imposed on summary conviction exceeding that prescribed by the principal Act for a second offence.

(Procedure in England. Prosecution.)

"(1.) It shall be the duty of the inspectors of factories and the inspectors of mines to enforce the provisions of the principal Act and this Act within their districts so far as respects factories, workshops, and mines inspected by them respectively, and such inspectors shall for this purpose have the same powers and authorities as they respectively have for the purpose of enforcing the provisions of any Acts relating to factories, workshops, or mines, *and all expenses incurred by them under this section shall be defrayed out of moneys provided by Parliament;*

(Application of penalties.)

"(2.) In England all penalties recovered under the principal Act and this Act shall be paid into the receipt of Her Majesty's Exchequer, and be carried to the Consolidated Fund."

New Clause—

(Procedure in Scotland.)

"In Scotland—

"(1.) The procurators fiscal of the sheriff court shall, as part of their official duty, investigate and prosecute offences against the principal Act or this Act, and such prosecution may also be instituted in the sheriff court at the instance of any inspector of factories or inspector of mines;

"(2.) All offences against the said Acts shall be prosecuted in the sheriff court,"—(*Mr. Stuart-Wortley,*)

—*brought up*, and read a first time.

Motion made, and Question proposed, "That the Clause be read a second time."

DR. CLARK: I think that these provisions require consideration, at any rate as far as the county I represent is concerned. In many places there, the Procurator Fiscal acts as the agent or factor of the landlord. The Procurator Fiscal is the official directed to investigate breaches of the law. Is he to investigate offences committed on the property for which he is agent? Somebody else surely ought to do that.

MR. BRADLAUGH: That has already been provided for, by enacting in another part of the clause that the prosecution may also be instituted by the Inspector of Factories, or the Inspector of Mines.

Question put, and *agreed to.*

Clause *agreed to*, and *added* to the Bill.

On the Motion of Mr. STUART-WORTLEY, the following Clause *brought up*, and read a first and second time.

(Definitions.)

" In this Act, unless the context otherwise requires,—

The expression ' Summary Jurisdiction Acts' means, as respects England, the Summary Jurisdiction Acts as defined by the 'Summary Jurisdiction Act, 1879;' and, as respects Scotland, means the Summary Jurisdiction (Scotland) Acts, 1864 and 1881, and any Acts amending the same:

Other expressions have the same meaning as in the principal Act."

Amendment proposed,

In line 5, to add—" The expression ' Truck ' shall mean the payment of wages in goods or otherwise than in the current coin of the realm."—(*Mr. Tomlinson.*)

MR. D. CRAWFORD (Lanarkshire, N.E.): I should like to know the opinion of the hon. and learned Attorney General upon this. So far as I know, the word " Truck " does not occur either in the principal Act or in this Bill. While the proposed definition may be correct enough as a sort of rough definition of truck, various enactments both in the principal Act and in this Bill

go considerably beyond prohibiting the payment of wages other than in the current coin of the Realm. For instance, the Act prohibits any stipulation by which wages are to be spent in any particular way.

THE ATTORNEY GENERAL (Sir RICHARD WEBSTER) (Isle of Wight): My impression is, that there is no objection to the clause; but it was only put on the Paper this morning. I do not think the definition will interfere with any express enactment with regard to particular contracts in the principal Bill. I think the definition is not objectionable.

MR. TOMLINSON (Preston): I think is is very desirable to have this definition.

Amendment *agreed to.*

Clause, as amended, *agreed to*, and *added* to the Bill.

Committee report Progress; to sit again *To-morrow.*

MOTION.

———o———

TRAMWAYS PROVISIONAL ORDERS (NO. 1) BILL.

On Motion of Baron Henry De Worms, Bill to confirm certain Provisional Orders made by the Board of Trade, under " The Tramways Act, 1870," relating to Birmingham Central Tramways (Extension), Bristol Tramways, Burnley and District Tramways (Extension), Macclesfield Tramways, Oldham, Ashton-under-Lyne, Hyde, and District Tramways, West Metropolitan Tramways, and Weymouth Tramways, *ordered* to be brought in by Baron Henry De Worms and Mr. Jackson. [Bill *presented*, and read the first time.[Bill 257.

House adjourned at twenty-five minutes after Two o'clock.

———————

HOUSE OF LORDS,

Friday, 6th May, 1887.

———

MINUTES.]—PUBLIC BILL—*Second Reading* — Customs Consolidation Act (1876) Amendment (71).

THE COLONIAL CONFERENCE— FRANCE AND THE NEW HEBRIDES.

QUESTION. OBSERVATIONS.

THE EARL OF ROSEBERY : I rise to ask the Under Secretary of State for the

Colonies, a Question of which I have given him private Notice. It refers to the report of the proceedings of the Colonial Conference which appeared in *The Standard* this morning. It is a very interesting and detailed account of what took place, and I shall be glad to learn, if the noble Earl thinks fit to tell me, whether it is authentic or not? In the next place, I wish to know if, in view of the somewhat premature publication, it is proposed to give us the real and actual papers with regard to what has actually taken place in the Conference? I do not know what the authenticity of *The Standard's* account may be; but, at any rate, it seems to me very desirable that having had four columns of the proceedings of the Colonial Conference published in that newspaper some more authoritative account should be supplied to both Houses of Parliament. I do not ask for all the somewhat spicy details published in *The Standard*—the interview, for instance, of the Prime Minister with the Colonial Representatives; but, we are deeply interested in the question, and, of course, we should be glad to have as much detail as possible. There is one point in connection with the account which I will ask your Lordships' permission to say a word or two about. There is a proposition with regard to a compromise with which my name is associated—that in exchange for the cession of the interests of the Government and this country in the New Hebrides, the French Government will undertake not to send convicts to the Pacific. That proposition was officially made to me, but not by me; and I wish to state most distinctly that it is the only connection I have with it, and that the idea of calling it a proposition made by me is one which I wish most distinctly to repudiate.

THE UNDER SECRETARY OF STATE FOR THE COLONIES (the Earl of ONSLOW): My Lords, the account of the proceedings at the Colonial Conference which appears in *The Standard* substantially represents what took place. At the same time, however, it is inaccurate in some important details, and it is so incomplete as to give a misleading impression of the conclusion arrived at as to some of the most important subjects which were discussed. I might especially refer to the subject mentioned by the noble Earl, the New Hebrides, as to

The Earl of Rosebery

which there is no report whatever of the very able speeches which were delivered by one of the Representatives of New Zealand, in favour of the proposals made by Her Majesty's Government before the Conference. I believe I am not inaccurate in saying, that there was ultimately a general disposition expressed on behalf of the delegates present to accept as satisfactory the action of Her Majesty's Government. We are most anxious to lay on the Table of both Houses of Parliament, at the earliest possible date, a full account and report of the proceedings at the Conference. Some of these are already in print, and others are in the printers' hands; but, before they can be presented, the noble Earl will understand that it will necessarily take some short time for the different delegates to revise the reports, in order that they may be in every respect accurate. As soon as that is done, after the conclusion of the Conference, which will be early next week, Papers will be laid before Parliament giving a complete account of both the subjects and the details of the discussions at the Conference. Whether they may be spicy or not, they will be placed in the hands of your Lordships to pronounce an opinion upon.

THE EARL OF ROSEBERY: Will the Papers contain reports of the speeches of the delegates?

THE EARL OF ONSLOW : The reports will be, in the case of most of the discussions, verbatim.

CUSTOMS CONSOLIDATION ACT (1876) AMENDMENT BILL.

(*The Lord Brabourne.*)

SECOND READING.

Order of the Day for the Second Reading, read.

LORD BRABOURNE, in moving that the Bill be now read the second time, said, its object was to remove the unfair regulation which made every person on board a ship on which smuggled goods were found, liable to the penalties for smuggling. The Bill proposed that the liability should only accrue in case it could be shown that the person charged was concerned in or privy to the illegal act. The measure had passed the other House of Parliament without opposition.

Moved, "That the Bill be now read 2ª."
—(*The Lord Brabourne.*)

Motion *agreed to;* Bill read 2ª accordingly, and *committed* to a Committee of the Whole House on *Monday* next.

AFGHANISTAN—REPORTED DISTURBANCES.

MINISTERIAL STATEMENT.

THE SECRETARY OF STATE FOR INDIA (Viscount CROSS): Yesterday, in answer to the Question of a noble Earl whom I do not now see in his place (the Earl of Fife) I promised that I would lay before your Lordships to-day any information that I might have received from the Viceroy with regard to the reported disturbances in Afghanistan. In accordance with that promise, the information I have to give to your Lordships is this—The intelligence received from the Viceroy to-day does not confirm the report referred to by the noble Earl in his Question of yesterday. No fighting is reported as having occurred in the neighbourhood of the Khyber Pass, though it appears that an engagement took place on the 12th ultimo between the Ameer's troops and the tribes in the Hotak country, in which both sides are said to have claimed the advantage. There is no reason, however, to believe that the Ameer is not holding his own, as well as the Pass.

House adjourned at half past Four o'clock, to Monday next, a quarter before Eleven o'clock.

HOUSE OF COMMONS,

Friday, 6th May, 1887.

MINUTES.]—NEW WRIT ISSUED—*For* Cork (North - East Cork Division), *v.* Edmund Leamy, esquire, Steward or Bailiff of Her Majesty's Three Chiltern Hundreds of Stoke, Desborough, and Bonenham, in the County of Buckingham.

PUBLIC BILLS — *Second Reading* — Municipal Corporations Acts (Ireland) Amendment (No. 2) [176].

Committee—Truck [109]—R.P.

Report—Metropolis Management Acts Amendment (No. 2) * [166] and Metropolis Management Acts Amendment (Westminster) * [208], *consolidated into* Metropolis Management (Battersea and Westminster) * [258].

Withdrawn—Private Bill Legislation * [107].

PROVISIONAL ORDER BILLS—*Third Reading*— Local Government (Highways) * [224]; Local Government (Poor Law) * [226]; Local Government (Poor Law) (No. 2) * [227], and *passed.*

MOTION.

NEW WRIT.

MR. SHEIL (Meath, S.) moved—

"That a new Writ be issued for the election of a Member to serve in the present Parliament for the North-Eastern Division of the County of Cork in the room of Edmund Leamy, Esquire, who, since his election, has accepted the Stewardship of the Chiltern Hundreds."

MR. E. STANHOPE (SECRETARY of STATE for WAR): I should like to ask the hon. Gentleman who has made this Motion at what time the hon. Member accepted the Chiltern Hundreds?

MR. SHEIL: I cannot say with absolute certainty; but I think it was in the month of September last.

Motion *agreed to.*

QUESTIONS.

RAILWAY COMPANIES—FREE PASSES FOR MEMBERS OF PARLIAMENT.

MR. SHIRLEY (Yorkshire, W.R., Doncaster) asked the Secretary to the Board of Trade, Whether arrangements can be made with the various Railway Companies so that Members of Parliament may be carried over all lines free of expense, as in Australia and other countries?

THE SECRETARY OF STATE FOR WAR (Mr. E. STANHOPE) (Lincolnshire, Horncastle) (who replied) said: In answer to the hon. Member, I have to say that the Board of Trade have no power whatever to interfere with any arrangements the Railway Companies may wish to make with regard to the issue of free passes on their line.

POOR LAW (IRELAND)—THE MASTER OF THE ARMAGH WORKHOUSE.

MR. BLANE (Armagh, S.) asked the Chief Secretary to the Lord Lieutenant of Ireland, If the Local Government Board, of which he is President, refused to sanction the appointment of a person as Master of the Armagh Workhouse on account of having been decreed for seduction before Judge Gamble in 1886; whether, notwithstanding the refusal of the Local Government Board to sanction the appointment, the Guardians passed a Resolution again requesting them to give their approval, and enclosing testimonials; and, whether the Government will take serious consideration of the matter?

THE PARLIAMENTARY UNDER SECRETARY (Colonel KING-HARMAN) (Kent, Isle of Thanet) (who replied) said: The Local Government Board have finally declined to sanction this appointment, and the Guardians have ordered advertisements to be published for a new election. With respect to the addition to the Question of which the hon. Member has given private Notice, I find that the testimonials did include one from the Rev. Dr. Smyth in the terms described. It must, however, be borne in mind that that testimonial was given some weeks before the matter reflecting on the moral character of Mr. Brooks had gained publicity, and the probability is that the rev. gentleman was quite unaware of it.

THE MAGISTRACY (IRELAND)—BLACK-LION PETTY SESSIONS—ARREST OF JOHN KEANY.

MR. BLANE (Armagh, S.) asked the Chief Secretary to the Lord Lieutenant of Ireland, Whether Sergeant John Grimley arrested a man named John Keany, on the 19th March last, on the charge of drunkenness, and kept him confined in the lockup for fully eight hours; whether, on the charge being investigated at Blacklion Petty Sessions (County Cavan), on the 18th instant, before Messrs. W. C. Bracken and Phibs Nixon, J.P.'s, five witnesses, including the constable who assisted at the arrest and the barrack orderly, swore that Keany was perfectly sober, and had no appearance of drink on him at the time of his arrest; whether, notwithstanding this evidence for the defence, the presiding magistrates marked in the case "no rule;" whether this sergeant has been removed from the district; and, if so, for what reason; whether a Report complaining of his conduct on the occasion of his making the arrest referred to was sent by a respectable man named M'Keon, stationmaster on the Sligo, Leitrim, and Northern Counties Railway; and, will the Government institute an inquiry into the case?

Mr. Blane

THE PARLIAMENTARY UNDER SECRETARY (Colonel KING-HARMAN) (Kent, Isle of Thanet) (who replied) said: The facts are substantially as stated in the Question. The magistrates considered that Keany must have been more or less under the influence of drink, having regard to the quantity which it was admitted he had taken; and they were of opinion that the sergeant fully believed such to be the case when he made the arrest. In view of the contradictory evidence given, they decided upon marking "no rule." The sergeant has been transferred in the interest of the Public Service, but in no way connected with this case. M'Keon did complain to the district officer, who thought it proper to wait for the sworn evidence in the case, and when it was marked "no rule," he considered further steps unnecessary.

POOR LAW (IRELAND) — BELFAST BOARD OF GUARDIANS—GRATUITIES TO OFFICIALS.

MR. BLANE (Armagh, S.) asked the Chief Secretary to the Lord Lieutenant of Ireland, If the attention of the Local Government Board has been directed to the proceedings of the Belfast Board of Guardians on the 19th instant, when £10 was voted to Mr. James C. Neeson, acting clerk of the Union, for his services as Returning Officer in the room of the clerk of the Union who was ill, and £4 to Mr. Joseph W. Robb, sub-clerk, who assisted Mr. Neeson on the occasion; does the clerk receive £50 annually for the discharge of the duties of Returning Officer, let there be contested elections or not; does this sum form part of his salary or a bonus, and is it paid from Imperial or local funds; was there a deputy appointed to discharge Mr. Neeson's ordinary duties, and at what remuneration and how long engaged; and, have the Local Government Board sanctioned the payment of the moneys to Messrs. Neeson and Robb?

THE PARLIAMENTARY UNDER SECRETARY (Colonel KING-HARMAN) (Kent, Isle of Thanet) (who replied) said: Yes, Sir; the Local Government Board are aware of this case, the facts of which are substantially as represented in the Question. The salary attached to the office of Returning Officer is £50 a-year. It is payable in addition to the salary of the Clerk of the Union, and like that salary is chargeable to the poor's rate of the Union at large. A temporary assistant clerk was appointed, at the rate of 25*s.* a-week, to discharge the ordinary duties of Mr. Neeson while he acted as Clerk and Returning Officer. The payment of the amounts voted to Messrs. Neeson and Robb has not yet been sanction by the Local Government Board, as a Notice of Motion has been given by one of the Guardians to have the question of remuneration re-considered.

POST OFFICE (IRELAND)—DETENTION OF SUMMONSES AT BLACKROCK.

MR. BLANE (Armagh, S.) asked the Chief Secretary to the Lord Lieutenant of Ireland, Whether complaints have reached him, in connection with a case recently tried between Mr. Edward Little, cab owner, and the Postmaster of Blackrock, that the subpœnas issued by Mr. Gerald Byrne, Mr. Little's solicitor, to the witnesses for the defence, which were posted on the 14th April and should have been delivered that evening, were not delivered until the afternoon of the 16th, on which day the case was tried, and that in consequence of the nonappearance of these witnesses the Postmaster won the case; and, whether he will cause an inquiry to be made into this alleged detention of summonses in the Post Office?

THE PARLIAMENTARY UNDER SECRETARY (Colonel KING-HARMAN) (Kent, Isle of Thanet) (who replied) said: No such complaint appears to have been received by the Irish Government. In the case of any alleged irregularities on the part of Post Office officials, the proper course is for the person feeling aggrieved to communicate with the Postmaster General.

CHURCH ESTATES COMMISSIONERS— VACANT LAND, BREAM'S BUILDINGS, CHANCERY LANE.

MR. CHANNING (Northampton, E.) asked the right hon. Baronet the Member for West Essex, as an Ecclesiastical Commissioner, Whether the Church Estates Commission, in 1879, pulled down the dwellings of about 1,000 poor people, on land near Bream's Buildings, Chancery Lane; whether this land has, since 1879, lain desolate, and paid neither rent nor rates; whether the Commissioners will now let or sell the land for artizans' dwellings, under "The Housing of the Working Classes Act, 1885," section 11, sub-section 2, at a reasonable rate for the purpose; whether the Commissioners will consider the advisability of passing a rule that in no case should more than 15 families of the working classes be evicted at one time from land of the Ecclesiastical Commission, without previous notice in writing to every Bishop and other Ecclesiastical Commissioner, and a Return presented to both Houses of Parliament; and, whether, until the said land is built upon, the Ecclesiastical Commissioners will allow the land to be used as a playground for the children of the neighbourhood?

SIR HENRY SELWIN-IBBETSON (Essex, Epping): In 1879 the land in question came into the possession of the Ecclesiastical Commission on the expiring of the leases. It was covered with small tenements of a miserable description and occupied by a dense population, living in degraded circumstances and having a considerable admixture of the criminal classes. They may have numbered 1,000 persons. The Ecclesiastical Commissioners, in co-operation with the Metropolitan Board of Works and the City Commissioners of Sewers, took steps for clearing this area as circumstances permitted, and formed a new street there. Negotiations have been going on for some time for letting the land; and, as regards a portion, they are likely to come to a successful issue almost immediately. The value of the land, owing to its proximity to the Law Courts, renders it unsuitable for the erection of workmen's dwellings; but the Commissioners have offered land the other side of Fetter Lane at a much lower price for the purpose. They have from time to time sold or let on building leases upwards of 20 sites in the Metropolis for the erection of workmen's dwellings. The number of the tenements for which such sales or lettings were designed to provide may be taken at 2,000. The Commissioners have never evicted as many as 15 families of the working classes at one time from their property; and as they see no reason why they should do so in the future they are not prepared to make any new Rule on the subject. The Kyrle Society have been in communication with the Commissioners with reference to a temporary occupation of the land pending its appropriation for building purposes.

WAR OFFICE (ORDNANCE DEPARTMENT) — SMALL ARMS — THE METFORD RIFLES.

COLONEL HUGHES-HALLETT (Rochester) asked the Surveyor General of the Ordnance, Whether the Metford rifle barrel has been officially recommended for adoption in the place of the reversed ratchet barrel as issued to the Army experimentally; and, if so, the date of the recommendation; and, whether any decision has been arrived at with respect to the Metford barrel; and, if not, when a decision may be expected?

THE SURVEYOR GENERAL OF ORDNANCE (Mr. NORTHCOTE) (Exeter): On the 5th of January last the Special Committee on Small Arms recommended that the Metford system of rifling should be adopted for Her Majesty's Service; and on the 18th of February the Secretary of State for War intimated to that Committee, when giving instructions as to magazine arms, that the question of rifling had been determined in favour of the Metford system.

EDUCATION DEPARTMENT (SCOTLAND) — THE GAELIC LANGUAGE.

DR. CAMERON (Glasgow, College) asked the Lord Advocate, Whether any of the Inspectors of the Department of Scotch Education in Argyllshire speak or understand Gaelic; and, if not, whether the Department will consider the expediency of making some arrangement for the inspection of the Gaelic-speaking districts of that county, which will enable the provisions of the Scotch Code for the encouragement of that language to be taken advantage of?

THE LORD ADVOCATE (Mr. J. H. A. MACDONALD) (Edinburgh and St. Andrew's Universities) : One of the Inspectors in Argyllshire is qualified to conduct the examinations in Gaelic for the grant under the Scotch Code, should any application for examination in Gaelic be made. No such examination has been applied for hitherto.

VACCINATION ACTS — DISTRESS WARRANT AT KETTERING.

MR. CHANNING (Northampton, E.) asked the Secretary of State for the

Home Department, Whether his attention has been called to the circumstances attending the recent execution of a distress warrant on Edward Johnson, of Kettering, for non-payment of a fine under the Vaccination Acts; whether it is a fact, as reported, that the police in carrying out the distress removed a harmonium for which £8 had been paid, and which was valued at £5; whether, in reply to a question from Mrs. Johnson, the police stated that they were taking the harmonium to the police station; and, in reply to a question from Mrs. Johnson as to when and where the harmonium would be sold, the Inspector replied—

"I don't know when nor where, nor can I tell you any more about it. Here is the receipt for it; that is enough for you;"

whether the Inspector, after placing the harmonium in the conveyance he brought with him, at once drove away with it to an auction sale at Crasford, four miles off, where the harmonium was immediately sold for the sum of £2; whether the action of the police, in thus removing an article seized under a distress warrant, and refusing information as to time and place of sale, was within their powers under the existing law; and, whether, under these circumstances, he will make some representation to the Local Bench of Magistrates to prevent any similar occurrences?

THE UNDER SECRETARY OF STATE (Mr. STUART-WORTLEY) (Sheffield, Hallam) (who replied) said: I have received a Report from the Chief Constable as to the circumstances of this distress. Johnson was unable to inform the police what he had paid for the harmonium, but said that he valued it at £4 or £5, and requested the police to take the harmonium rather than any other chattels. The Inspector did tell Mrs. Johnson that he could not inform her where the harmonium would be sold. He took it to the police-station, and from thence, in consequence of some excitement among the neighbours which led him to fear a disturbance, he took it to an auction sale at Crasford, where it was sold for £2. Assuming that the distress was otherwise regular—and I am assured that it was—I am not aware that the law requires the police to give information as to the time and place of sale. I will cause inquiry to be made of the magistrates to ascertain

Sir Henry Selwin-Ibbetson

whether the statutory period of five days intervened between the making of the distress and the removal of the harmonium.

ADMIRALTY—DOCKYARDS — HAULBOWLINE.

MR. JOHN O'CONNOR (Tipperary, S.) asked the First Lord of the Admiralty, Whether it is intended to proceed with the erection of the coaling wharf at Haulbowline Docks; whether he will urge the docks engineer to put the piling machinery in repair before the summer arrives, when the machinery will be required; and, whether any of the shipwrights employed at Haulbowline are under notice to be discharged by the 1st June?

THE FIRST LORD (Lord GEORGE HAMILTON) (Middlesex, Ealing): Yes; it is intended to proceed with the work at Haulbowline, and all the machinery required for the purpose will be put in order. Three shipwrights are under notice to be discharged on the 1st of June.

COMMISSIONERS OF WOODS AND FORESTS—CROWN RENTS IN WALES.

MR. KENYON (Denbigh, &c.) asked the Secretary of State for the Home Department, Whether the Commissioners of Woods and Forests are now exacting a Crown rent from Mr. Wynne, of Peniarth, County Merioneth, without being able to prove the lands out of which the said rent issues, though it has been clearly pointed out to them that the said rent should issue out of an adjoining farm, the property of another owner; and, whether he is aware that cases of this kind are constantly occurring in different parts of Wales, and that great and general dissatisfaction is expressed at the administration of this Office in the Principality?

THE SECRETARY TO THE TREASURY (Mr. JACKSON) (Leeds, N.) (who replied) said: The rent supposed to be referred to is an ancient manorial rent of 1s. 6d. per annum, charged on a property recently acquired by Mr. Wynne. The rent has heretofore been paid by the owner of the same premises certainly for 50 years, and the Commissioners of Woods are advised that Mr. Wynne is now liable for it; but further inquiries are being made. Cases of disputed liability for ancient fee farm and other

Crown rents not unfrequently occur, and occasion much trouble and expense to the Commissioners of Woods. Two or three landowners, whose predecessors have paid Crown rents for generations, have within recent years repudiated their liability, and put the Commissioners to the expense of not only making local inquiries, but also Record searches in order to prove their title. I am not aware of any dissatisfaction with the administration of the Office.

EXTRAORDINARY TITHE RENT-CHARGE—THE CAPITAL VALUE.

MR. STANLEY LEIGHTON (Shropshire, Oswestry) asked the Secretary of State for the Home Department, Whether the Land Commissioners, appointed under the authority of "The Extraordinary Tithe Rent-Charge Redemption Act, 1886," have not yet certified the capital value of the Extraordinary Tithe Rent-Charge in any parish; and, whether, until such certificate has been made out, the Extraordinary Tithe Rent-Charge will be assessable under Section 4 of 49 & 50 *Vict.* c. 54, according to the same methods of calculation as were used before the said Act was passed?

THE UNDER SECRETARY OF STATE (Mr. STUART-WORTLEY) (Sheffield, Hallam) (who replied) said: The Land Commissioners have not yet made a certificate in respect of any parish. The hon. Member will learn from the Commissioners' Report, recently presented, that the labour thrown upon the Commissioners by the Act of last year has been heavy, and that a great many preliminary investigations have been, and still remain to be, made. Nevertheless, the Commissioners report that they will endeavour to complete the carrying out of the Act soon after the close of the current financial year. The answer to the hon. Member's second Question depends upon what is to be considered the proper construction of the 4th section of the Extraordinary Tithe Redemption Act of last year, as to which it would not be proper for me to offer an opinion.

HONG KONG—PUNISHMENT OF FLOGGING.

MR. POWELL WILLIAMS (Birmingham, S.) asked the Secretary of

State for the Colonies, Whether the flogging of prisoners in Hong Kong, which had been abolished under Sir John Pope Hennessy's administration, has been re-introduced with the consent of the Secretary of State; and, whether it is a fact that the day after the Legislature of Hong Kong had passed an Ordinance permitting flogging, 24 Chinese prisoners were flogged in Hong Kong Prison for mere prison offences, by order of Mr. Mitchell Innes, a junior Civil servant, who is at present acting as Governor of the gaol?

THE SECRETARY OF STATE (Sir HENRY HOLLAND) (Hampstead): In the new set of Prison Regulations for Hong Kong, passed last year, a Regulation was included restoring to the Superintendent of the gaol the power of sentencing prisoners in his own authority to corporal punishment not exceeding 12 strokes of the rattan in cases of mutiny, incitement to mutiny, personal violence, repetition of threatening language, or any act of insubordination requiring to be suppressed by extraordinary means. Each case of the exercise of such power to be reported to the Governor. The power was restored upon the Superintendent of the gaol reporting that without it he could not safely introduce certain prison reforms, which included reduction of diet, the existing diet having been considered as much in excess of the requirements of health. The Superintendent considered that any such changes were likely to lead to mutiny among the Chinese prisoners, which would require to be promptly quelled. The Regulation was recommended by a Special Commission, with one dissentient, and by the acting Governor, and was approved by my Predecessor in December last. On January 31, the reduction in diet having been brought into force on January 20, a mutiny broke out, and the Acting Superintendent (Mr. Mitchell Innes) ordered 54 out of 135 mutineers to receive 12 strokes each; subsequently, after an inquiry before the Superintendent and a Police Magistrate, under a power which has never been suspended, 11 of the ringleaders were sentenced to 18 strokes. The Governor appointed a Special Committee to inquire into what had happened; and they reported that the action of the Acting Superintendent was necessary, and justified by the cir-

Mr. Powell Williams

cumstances. The Acting Governor reports that latterly there has been a decline both in the number of prisoners and in that of prison offences.

MR. CHANNING (Northampton, E.): Cannot Her Majesty's Government recommend any alternative punishment instead of flogging?

SIR HENRY HOLLAND said, there were alternatives; but flogging was considered necessary in certain cases.

IRISH LAND COMMISSIONERS—SITTINGS IN WICKLOW.

MR. BYRNE (Wicklow, W.) asked the Chief Secretary to the Lord Lieutenant of Ireland, Why the Land Commissioners have not sat in the County of Wicklow in March or April this year, as they have done in previous years, for the purpose of fixing fair rents; whether it is a fact that tenant farmers, who have served originating notices on their landlords long since, have to wait unusually long periods to have a fair rent fixed; and, whether the Sub-Commissioners, who are announced to be at the Court House of Shillelagh on the 9th May instant, to fix rents of plots of land for labourers' cottages in that Union, could then fix fair rents for tenants in the district?

THE PARLIAMENTARY UNDER SECRETARY (Colonel KING-HARMAN) (Kent, Isle of Thanet) (who replied) said: That the Land Commissioners report that there is no fixed time in the course of a year for the sitting of a Sub-Commission in any particular county. The last sitting in County Wicklow was in August, 1886, and all the cases then listed for hearing were disposed of, with the exception of seven, which had to be adjourned for legal reasons. There has been no unusual, or unavoidable, delay in hearing Wicklow cases. It would not be practicable to carry out the suggestion in the last paragraph of the Question. The Sub-Commission referred to consists of two members only, the legal member being with difficulty spared for one day from his work of fixing fair rents in the County Louth, and it will have a special delegation to dispose of labourers' cottage cases under the provisions of the Labourers' Acts. The circumstances would not, therefore, admit of its being employed in fixing fair rents.

ROYAL IRISH CONSTABULARY—PAR-
LIAMENTARY QUOTA FOR TIP-
PERARY, NORTH RIDING.

MR. P. J. O'BRIEN (Tipperary, N.)
asked the Chief Secretary to the Lord
Lieutenant of Ireland, Whether at any
time the Parliamentary quota of the
Police Force for the North Riding of the
County of Tipperary was fixed at 309
men; if so, up to what date, and, on
what ground has the quota been since
reduced to 266 men, and the district in
consequence charged for extra police?

THE PARLIAMENTARY UNDER
SECRETARY (Colonel KING-HARMAN)
(Kent, Isle of Thanet) (who replied) said:
Up to July, 1882, the free quota of the
North Riding of the County of Tipperary
was 309 men. At that date the quin-
quennial revision was carried out, and
this number was reduced to 259 men;
but in August, 1885, on a distribution
of the force under 48 *Vict.*, c. 12, this
number was increased to 266 men. At
these distributions the number fixed for
this county was that to which it was entitled on considerations of area, population, and conformation as applied to
counties generally. The only extra force
now in the Riding is 43 men, appointed
by the Lord Lieutenant pursuant to
Section 13 of 6 & 7 *Will.* IV., c. 13, to
districts declared by Proclamation to be
in a state of disturbance. There are no
extra men appointed at the request of
the magistrates to this county for ordinary duty.

MR. JOHN O'CONNOR (Tipperary,
S.): May I ask the right hon. and gallant Gentleman when this declaration
of disturbance was made?

COLONEL KING-HARMAN: I must
ask the hon. Member to give me Notice
of that. I have not got the information yet.

CONTAGIOUS DISEASES (ANIMALS)
ACT — IMPORTATION OF CATTLE
FROM IRELAND.

SIR JOHN SWINBURNE (Staffordshire, Lichfield) asked the Vice President of the Committee of Council on
Agriculture, What steps Her Majesty's
Government have taken to prevent the
possibility of cattle which have been
in contact with cattle suffering from
pleuro-pneumonia in or near the City of
Dublin from being landed in Great
Britain?

THE CHANCELLOR OF THE DUCHY
(Lord JOHN MANNERS) (Leicestershire,

E.): Her Majesty's Government have
not taken any steps to prevent the landing in Great Britain of cattle from any
part of Ireland; but as a result of correspondence on the subject, the Irish
Government have passed an Order,
with the object of preventing the ex-
portation of animals from certain districts in or near Dublin in which pleuro-
pneumonia is known to exist. The correspondence is now complete, and will
be laid before Parliament.

ADMIRALTY—THE DOCKYARDS—DIS-
CHARGE OF WORKMEN.

COLONEL HUGHES-HALLETT
(Rochester) asked the First Lord of the
Admiralty, On what principle it has been
determined that men shall be selected
for discharge in the reduction now being
made at Chatham and in other Royal
Dockyards; whether the selection is left
entirely in the hands of the officers in
command of those Dockyards, or arranged by the Admiralty; and, whether
any regard is paid to length of service;
and, if so, what length of service constitutes a claim to continued employment?

THE FIRST LORD (Lord GEORGE
HAMILTON) (Middlesex, Ealing): It will
probably be convenient that I should
quote the Dockyard Regulation with
regard to the discharges of men from the
Royal Dockyard—

"When a reduction is ordered to be made in
any department of the Yard, particular care is
to be taken that, without favour or partiality,
such persons are discharged as, by the Report
of their respective superiors and the inspection
of the Superintendent, may be found from age,
infirmity, and inability to be the least fit for
their respective situations."

I can only add that the Admiral Superintendents are most careful in supervis-
ing the lists of men whom it is proposed
should be discharged. It should be
understood that the only men discharged
are the hired men, whose engagements
render them liable to discharge at seven
days' notice. Not being entitled to
pension, their pay is higher than that of
the men on the Establishment.

CAPTAIN PRICE (Devonport): May
I ask whether there are any officials at
the Admiralty who examine into these
cases one by one to see that the Regulations are carried out?

LORD GEORGE HAMILTON: No,
Sir; it is the duty of the Admiral Superintendents.

WAR OFFICE—PROMOTION OF CAPTAINS—THE AMENDED WARRANT—THE JUBILEE YEAR.

COLONEL HUGHES-HALLETT (Rochester) asked the Secretary of State for War, Whether, having regard to the amended warrant of 1st January last, which practically stops the promotion of captains to the rank of major until the two second lieutenant colonels and supernumerary majors in territorial regiments have been absorbed, he will, on the occasion of this Jubilee year of Her Majesty's reign, take into consideration the case of captains of 18 years' full pay service, whose prospects have been prejudiced by the Warrant alluded to, by recommending them to Her Majesty for a step of brevet rank, provided they are proposed for that step by their superiors?

THE SECRETARY OF STATE (Mr. E. STANHOPE)(Lincolnshire, Horncastle): I am not prepared to accept the suggestion in my hon. Friend's Question. Promotion to the rank of major is mainly regimental, and considerable inequality in the rate of promotion is, therefore, inevitable. There are a few captains of 18 years' service; but, as a rule, promotion has of late years been so rapid that very few captains have even nearly approached the period for compulsory retirement. Now that that period has been postponed for five years, it is hoped that all deserving officers in the rank of captain will be promoted, notwithstanding that promotion will be for a time retarded by the recent alterations of establishment.

WAYS AND MEANS—THE FINANCIAL RESOLUTIONS—THE TOBACCO DUTY.

DR. CAMERON (Glasgow, College) asked Mr. Chancellor of the Exchequer, Whether he has considered the possibility of equitably obviating the loss and dislocation of trade occasioned by the reduction of the Tobacco Duty in the case of manufacturers dealing in classes of tobacco requiring several weeks for their production, by granting tobacco manufacturers generally, as was done under similar circumstances in the case of beer brewers, a drawback on their stocks in hand at the date of the reduction?

THE CHANCELLOR OF THE EXCHEQUER (Mr. GOSCHEN) (St. George's, Hanover Square) : The case of the maltsters and brewers on the one hand and tobacco manufacturers on the other, as regards the claim for drawback, are entirely different. In 1880 the duty was transferred from malt to beer, which was not a simple remission, as in the case now before us; and the drawback on malt was allowed because the repeal of the duty took effect from October 1, 1880, the very day on which the Act repealing the duty came into operation. In the case of tobacco, time has been given for manufacturers to get rid of their stocks.

BUSINESS OF THE HOUSE—THE COAL MINES, &c. REGULATION BILL.

MR. W. CRAWFORD (Durham, Mid) asked the Secretary of State for the Home Department, If he will promise not to take the next stages of the Coal Mines, &c., Regulation Bill after midnight, on any night, so as to give time for discussion?

THE UNDER SECRETARY OF STATE (Mr. STUART-WORTLEY) (Sheffield, Hallam) (who replied) said: We adhere to the pledge given on April 28 as to the next stage. In the interests of the progress of the Bill, I had rather not name any hour after which any stages will not be taken.

OPEN AIR MEETINGS (METROPOLIS)—INSTRUCTIONS TO THE POLICE.

MR. JAMES STUART (Shoreditch, Hoxton) asked the Secretary of State for the Home Department, Whether he will lay upon the Table of the House a Copy of the Instructions under which the Metropolitan Police are authorized to act in respect of public meetings held in open spaces in the Metropolis?

THE UNDER SECRETARY OF STATE (Mr. STUART-WORTLEY) (Sheffield, Hallam) (who replied) said, except a General Police Order which has been public property for many years, and the substance of which is that the police are not to interfere with persons attending political meetings unless especially ordered by the Commissioner, there are no General Instructions upon which the police are authorized to act in respect of public meetings in open spaces. Each case must depend on its own particular circumstances, and must be left to be dealt with according to the discretion of the Chief Commissioner.

FINANCE, &c.—THE BUDGET OF 1883—EXTINCTION OF THE NATIONAL DEBT.

MR. MACDONALD CAMERON (Wick, &c.) asked Mr. Chancellor of the

Exchequer, with reference to the Budget of 1883, which created, by means of the Chancery Stock, an annuity of £2,674,000 for 20 years, and, by means of the Savings Banks Stock, three annuities of £1,200,000 each, to expire in 5, 10, and 15 years, and an annuity of £700,000 for 20 years, absorbing the £5,130,000 falling in in 1885, If he would explain to the House what effect the present Budget will have in delaying the extinction of the National Debt, as then agreed to by Parliament?

THE CHANCELLOR OF THE EXCHEQUER (Mr. GOSCHEN) (St. George's, Hanover Square) : The Question hardly admits of being clearly answered orally. It is proposed to lay a Paper now in preparation explaining the exact effect of the Debt proposal, and showing the amount by which the repayment of the Debt is arrested, as compared with the arrangement made in 1883.

WAR OFFICE—DEFECTIVE WEAPONS.

MR. HANBURY (Preston) asked the Secretary of State for War, Whether, in view of the fact disclosed before the Committee which recently took evidence on the subject of defective weapons, the Government have come to a decision as to what officials are responsible for the manufacture and issue of defective weapons to the men of Her Majesty's Navy; what action it is proposed to take to punish such officials ; and, what steps the Government intend to take to prevent the recurrence of such scandals at the War Office without the responsibility for them being traced home to any particular official ? The hon. Member remarked that the Question had been altered at the Table, and he was not responsible for the somewhat illogical form in which it appeared upon the Paper.

THE SECRETARY OF STATE (Mr. E. STANHOPE) (Lincolnshire, Horncastle) : Looking at the very great importance of the questions raised by my hon. Friend, I hope the House will grant me its indulgence if I reply at somewhat greater length than is usual. The conclusion which it seems to me is to be drawn from the Report of the Cutlass Committee is that the conversion of the cutlasses was mainly responsible for their becoming inefficient arms. The pattern was got out, tried on board the *Excellent*, and approved in 1871, and the responsibility for the pattern must be shared between Sir John Adye, Director General

of Artillery; Colonel Dixon, Superintendent at Enfield ; Captain Hood, Director of Naval Ordnance; and Captain Boys, captain of the *Excellent*. But the fault lay also in the mode in which the conversion was carried out in 1874, and the evidence appears to point to the responsibility being shared between Sir John Adye, Director of Artillery; Colonel Fraser and Colonel Close, Superintendents at Enfield ; and Mr. Perry, foreman of the works. I do not attempt to apportion the responsibility. The Committee appointed to investigate the matter has not done so. And, looking to the fact that all these transactions occurred 12 or 13 years ago, and all these officers have been changed, I am not inclined to undertake a duty which the Committee, with full knowledge of all the circumstances, has not been able to accomplish. But what is much more important is that the system should be put on a proper footing. Everybody admits that the present Heads of the Ordnance Department cannot be held responsible for blunders made long before their time; and I personally know that they are doing their best to make a recurrence of them impossible. But, although I have the fullest confidence in General Alderson, the present Director of Artillery and Stores—and I am sure that opinion will be largely shared by others —something more is required. It is to give full confidence to the public that weapons and stores issued to the Army and Navy are fit for the service for which they are required, and also to give confidence to contractors that the goods supplied by them will be subjected to an impartial trial. And although it would not be proper on my part to propose a detailed scheme until I have before me the Reports of the Royal Commission and of the Earl of Morley's Committee —both shortly expected—I will state to the House frankly my own conclusion. In my opinion, nothing can adequately restore full public confidence except an examination entirely independent of the Manufacturing Departments of the Government. Independent test appears to me to be the right solution, and I hope I may be supported by the House in establishing it. There is one other point closely connected with this question which the House will, perhaps, allow me to mention. I have been convinced that the financial control at present exercised over one or two of these Departments of the War Office is insufficient, and not continuous. This is an opinion expressed some time ago in this House by my hon. Friend the Surveyor General of the Ordnance, and I think he is quite right. The Departments to which I refer are not, under the constitution of the War Office, subject to the control of the Financial Department; their Heads are appointed for five years; and their Parliamentary Chiefs changed with every Government. Let them work as hard as they can—and to their hard work and efficiency I gladly bear testimony—they cannot make this system satisfactory. And I am prepared, as soon as the inquiries now being conducted are concluded, to make proposals to the Treasury for establishing a permanent financial control. I have only now to thank the House for allowing me to make so long a statement on a matter of grave importance.

WAYS AND MEANS—THE FINANCIAL RESOLUTIONS—THE TOBACCO DUTY —EFFECT ON THE MANUFACTURE IN IRELAND.

MR. MURPHY (Dublin, St. Patrick's) asked Mr. Chancellor of the Exchequer, Whether it has been represented to him that the process of tobacco manufacture in Ireland occupies a period of from three to five weeks, whereas the system of manufacture in England allows the leaf to be converted into consumable tobacco in five or six days; whether representations have reached him from the Irish manufacturers that, in view of the proposed reduction of duty, they would suffer a grievous loss if they continued manufacturing at the present time, as in consequence of the competition of English tobacco (manufactured under different conditions) they could not charge the difference in duty to the public; whether, to avoid this loss, they have had to cease manufacturing, thereby throwing out of employment for the next three weeks about 2,000 people in Ireland; whether, as the result of a conference with the tobacco trade, on which there was no Irish representative, the Chancellor of the Exchequer made certain arrangements in relief of cigar manufacturers; and, whether he will favourably consider the question of affording some similar relief to the Irish trade, either by way of drawbacks on stocks held on the 21st May, or otherwise?

Mr. E. Stanhope

COLONEL NOLAN (Galway, N.) also had the following Question on the Paper:—To ask Mr. Chancellor of the Exchequer, Whether he is aware that a large number of workers in Irish tobacco factories are now disemployed, as a result of the change in the Tobacco Duties proposed in his Budget; and, whether, having regard to the concession made to the cigar manufacturers to prevent similar discharges of workmen, he will re-consider the position of the Irish trade, with a view to allowing a resumption of work on terms that would not eventually affect the Revenue?

THE CHANCELLOR OF THE EXCHEQUER (Mr. GOSCHEN) (St. George's, Hanover Square): I will answer this Question and that of the hon. Member for North Louth (Colonel Nolan) together. Representations have been made to me in the sense indicated in the first three Questions of the hon. Member for Dublin; but I cannot admit that I consider that the Irish manufacturers have proved their case. I can only repeat the substance of my former answers. I do not admit the necessity for discharging workmen; nor can I admit the right of manufacturers on any change of duty to put the pistol at the breast of a Minister, and to declare that they will dismiss their workmen unless certain concessions are made to them. I deny that it is proved that they cannot recoup themselves to a certain extent for the payment of the higher duty during a few weeks. I repeat that it would be a breach of faith to the rest of the trade, and an injustice to those who have taken out tobacco at the higher rate of duty on the strength of my declaration that I would not reduce the duty till the 21st instant. Besides, the amount cleared since the Budget Statement has been very considerable. Operations have been conducted on the strength of a month's grace for the sale of stocks. Retailers as well as manufacturers may have made their arrangements; and, accordingly, I feel there is no option for me but to decline to agree to any further change. It was not in consequence of representations made to me by the manufacturers that I made the concession as regards the cigar trade. The concession was made as the result of other inquiries which I set on foot, which showed me that the two branches of the trade could not with justice be treated alike.

MR. T. M. HEALY (Longford, N.) inquired, whether the right hon. Gentleman would be able to take the Customs and Inland Revenue Bill before Whitsuntide?

MR. GOSCHEN: I hope that it will be taken before Whitsuntide.

MR. T. M. HEALY said, he would take the opportunity, when the Bill was before the House, of calling attention to the gross injustice with which Ireland had been treated.

MR. GOSCHEN: Representations have been made to me from Scotland as well as Ireland. No injustice whatever has been done to Ireland.

LAW AND JUSTICE—THE LAW COURTS AND THE PUBLIC PRESS—CORONERS' INQUIRIES.

MR. CONYBEARE (Cornwall, Camborne) asked Mr. Attorney General, Whether it is the usual practice, either in the Courts of Quarter Sessions or of Assize or in the Superior Courts, to withhold from the Reporters of the Public Press, upon the motion of any party, all information as to the name of the person charged, and the nature of the offence of which he is accused; and, whether there is any Statute or rule of Law giving such power either to Magistrates or to Coroners; and, if not, whether such action as that of the Magistrates at Southampton, and of the Coroner, Mr. Vulliamy, in Suffolk, in excluding the Press before any charge has been advanced against an accused person is legal?

THE ATTORNEY GENERAL (Sir RICHARD WEBSTER) (Isle of Wight): In proceedings by indictment it is the practice to read out in open Court to the prisoner the bill found against him by the Grand Jury, or the material part thereof, and to take his plea thereon. Thus, everybody in the Court is informed of the name of the person charged, and of the nature of the accusation. Before magistrates the practice is regulated by 11 & 12 *Vict.* c. 42, and the proceedings may be in private. It has been a subject of controversy whether a Coroner's Inquest ought necessarily to be a public proceeding; but the weight of authority seems to be decidedly in favour of the view that a Coroner has an absolute discretion to exclude whom he will. There is no Statute regulating the practice on Coroner's Inquests as far as regards the presence of reporters.

BUSINESS OF THE HOUSE—LONDON CORPORATION (CHARGES OF MALVERSATION) — REPORT OF THE SELECT COMMITTEE — AGRICUL-TURAL HOLDINGS BILL, &c.—COAL MINES, &c. REGULATION BILL.

MR. BRADLAUGH (Northampton) asked the First Lord of the Treasury, Whether, in the event of the Select Committee on the charges against the Corporation of the City of London reporting next Monday, he will afford facilities on an early day after Whitsuntide for the discussion of that Report?

MR. CHANNING (Northampton, E.) asked the First Lord of the Treasury, Whether, in view of the continued and disastrous depression of agriculture, and, in view of the probable occupation of the whole time of the House of Commons for some months to come by the affairs of Ireland, and, in view of the improbability of the proposal to constitute a Grand Committee on Agriculture being reached, he will consent to give facilities for reading a second time the Agricultural Holdings Bill and other Bills relating to agricultural tenancies, and to refer them without delay to a Select Committee, so that it may be possible, before the close of this Session, to pass some measure to promptly relieve and permanently improve the position of the tenant farmers of England and Wales?

SIR JOHN SWINBURNE (Staffordshire, Lichfield) asked the First Lord of the Treasury, Whether, in view of the assurance of the Secretary of State for the Home Department, on Thursday, 28th April, that opportunity should be given for discussion on going into Committee on the Coal Mines, &c. Regulation Bill, and of the fact that the Bill stands on the Orders for Monday 9th May, he will mention an hour after which the Motion to go into Committee on this Bill will not be made?

THE FIRST LORD (Mr. W. H. SMITH) (Strand, Westminster): The Government and myself are most anxious that the House should, as quickly as possible, revert to the ordinary Rules and Regulations for the conduct of Public Business, which give to private Members certain days of the week for their Motions and Bills. But, as I have already informed the House, the several stages of the Criminal Law Amendment (Ireland) Bill will be taken on every day for which is is set down in preference to other Business. The Government feel it to be absolutely necessary that that Bill should be disposed of with the greatest possible rapidity, consistent with the due consideration of its provisions. We are aware of its gravity and importance, and therefore we admit that these provisions ought to be carefully examined. But it must be in the power of hon. Gentlemen opposite who desire to forward their own measures—the importance of which I do not deny —and the consideration of Motions which they desire to submit to the House—it must be largely within their power to facilitate the efficient but not the excessive discussion of the measure before the House. When that Bill is disposed of I hope it will be in the power of the Government to facilitate the progress of other measures which they consider of great importance.

Mr. CHILDERS (Edinburgh, S.) asked, on what day the Budget Bill would be taken? The right hon. Gentleman, in answer to a Question some days ago, said that it would be taken in 10 days.

Mr. W. H. SMITH: I said not before 10 days. I hope it will be possible to take it on Thursday; but I am not able to say so absolutely. I will give a positive answer on Monday.

Mr. BRADLAUGH asked, if the right hon. Gentleman would give a pledge that, after the legislation for Ireland was disposed of, he would give a day for the discussion of the Report of the Committee on the charges against the London Corporation?

Mr. W. H. SMITH said, the hon. Gentleman would understand that he was quite unable to give any pledge with regard to the conduct of Public Business until they knew what progress was made with Public Business now before the House, to which they attached great importance.

Mr. BRADLAUGH said, he did no ask that any particular day should be fixed; but that the right hon. Gentleman should, at his own convenience, give a day for the discussion of the Report.

Mr. W. H. SMITH: I will give an answer to the hon. Member when I have seen the Report. I am most anxious to facilitate the conduct of Business, and the discussion of measures and Motions in which hon. Members on the other side take an interest; but I am sure the hon. Member will see that it is scarcely reasonable to ask me to enter into an engagement with regard to a Report not yet adopted by the Committee, and not yet before the House.

Mr. BRADLAUGH: In consequence of the answer of the right hon. Gentleman, I beg to give Notice that, in the event of his being unable to give an assurance that the Government will afford a date, I shall take such a course as is in my power directly the Report is on the Table to secure that discussion.

In answer to Sir JOHN SWINBURNE,

Mr. W. H. SMITH: said, he understood there was a general acquiescence in the House in the desirableness of passing the Coal Mines, &c. Regulation Bill, and an engagement on the part of the Government to afford time for its discussion, but he could not undertake to fix any particular hour. He would consult, as far as possible, the convenience of hon. Members; but, under the conditions in which they were now placed, it must be obvious to the hon. Baronet and hon. Gentlemen interested in seeing such measures passed that opportunities as they occurred must be taken advantage of.

Mr. T. M. HEALY asked, whether the House was distinctly to understand that Thursday next was to be the day for the Budget Bill? He also wished to know, whether the subject of the treatment of the Irish tobacco manufacturers had been before the Government as a whole, or had it been confined to the Chancellor of the Exchequer?

Mr. W. H. SMITH said, he had given an answer to the right hon. Gentleman opposite (Mr. Childers) as to the discussion of the Budget Bill. The Chancellor of the Exchequer was a Member of the Government, and his answer must be taken as the answer of the Government.

In reply to Mr. CHANNING,

Mr. W. H. SMITH said, the Government were as conscious of the depression in agriculture, and as desirous as the hon. Member of doing whatever was in the power of the Government and of Parliament to relieve it; but a question of the kind he had submitted was of such a general character that it was really out of his power to make any promise on the subject.

THE COLONIAL CONFERENCE—REPORT OF THE PROCEEDINGS IN "THE STANDARD."

MR. PAULTON (Durham, Bishop Auckland) asked the Secretary of State for the Colonies, Whether the account in *The Standard* to-day of the proceedings of the Colonial Conference had been published with the authority of the Colonial Office; and, whether it was correct?

THE SECRETARY OF STATE (Sir HENRY HOLLAND) (Hampstead): I much regret that this account of the proceedings of the Conference, which is inaccurate in many particulars and very incomplete, has appeared in *The Standard*. It has no official authority, and has not been sanctioned by the Colonial Office. I have made, and am making, inquiry into the matter. I may add that at the earliest opportunity I shall, with the full assent of the Delegates, present a revised account of all the proceedings and papers, except such as are of a strictly confidential nature.

MR. T. M. HEALY (Longford, N.) asked, whether there was any truth in the statement in *The Standard* that one of the most important of the Australian Delegates said that the Marquess of Salisbury's speech might very well have come from a French Premier?

SIR HENRY HOLLAND: It is not correct.

ORDERS OF THE DAY.

PRIVILEGE (MR. DILLON AND "THE TIMES" NEWSPAPER).—RESOLUTION. ADJOURNED DEBATE. [FOURTH NIGHT.]

Order read, for resuming Adjourned Debate on Amendment to the proposed Amendment to the Question [5th May],

And which Amendment was,

After the first word "That" in the Main Question, to add the words "this House declines to treat the publication of the article headed ' Parnellism and Crime' in *The Times* of the 2nd of May as a Breach of the Privileges of this House."—(*Mr. Solicitor General.*)

Amendment proposed to the proposed Amendment—

To leave out all the words after the word "House," in order to add the words " is of opinion that an inquiry should be made, by a Select Committee, into the charge of wilful falsehood, in a speech delivered in this House, brought in an article published in *The Times* newspaper, of the 2nd of May, against John Dillon, esquire, Member for East Mayo,"—(*Mr. Gladstone*,)

—instead thereof.

Question again proposed, "That the words proposed to be left out stand part of the said proposed Amendment."

Debate *resumed*.

CAPTAIN PRICE (Devonport), said, if the House would kindly indulge him a few minutes, he would venture not to traverse old ground, but to make a suggestion which had not yet been made in the course of that debate. Before doing that he should like to make two observations upon something which fell from the hon. and learned Member for Dumfries (Mr. R. T. Reid.) That hon. and learned Gentleman made a great point about the delay which probably would occur if the hon. Gentlemen opposite— the Nationalists—accepted trial by Jury, and he understood the hon. and learned Member to say that the reason why there would be delay was because it would be necessary to bring persons from distant parts to give evidence in support of or against the charges that were made. But if they had an inquiry of any kind, or an inquiry by a Committee of the House, were there to be no witnesses? If there were to be no witnesses brought from any part of the world to give evidence, what was the good of having an inquiry at all? He thought the argument entirely broke down. Then there was another point to which the hon. and learned Gentleman alluded. He spoke a good deal upon the question as to whether there was likely to be any prejudice on the part of Members composing the Select Committee. He did not know of any precedent brought forward which really bore upon the case. One case was brought to their notice by the right hon. Member for Mid Lothian, the case of Mr. Henry Lopes, who, they were told, had brought a charge against a section of the Members of that House. He called them a band of disreputable Members, or something of the kind. The right hon. Gentleman argued that the Members of the Select Committee appointed to inquire into the case would be in no way prejudiced. But if Mr. Henry Lopes had brought specified charges against a Party of hon. Members in that House, and a Select Committee was appointed, that would have been a very different matter, and he (Captain Price) challenged anybody to say there would not have been considerable risk of Party prejudices influencing the Committee appointed to inquire into those charges. He wished now to make a suggestion which he thought would be acceptable to all parties. The House and the country were demanding that there should be an inquiry into the matter, and he thought the House and the country would not be satisfied until there was a full and impartial investigation. Two proposals had been made —one, that the hon. Members who were affected by it should take the case into the Law Courts, and there try it, but that proposal was practically dead—because the hon. Members opposite would not have it. They utterly repudiated it, and distinctly said they would not have anything to do with the proposal, and it was beyond the power of the House to force them to it. Then there was another proposal. It was that the question should be relegated to a Select Committee of the House. He said for all practical purposes that was dead also. [*Cries of* " No!"] An hon. Gentleman said " No; " but the Division on the question was about to take place, and did hon. Members opposite think that the House was going to agree to the proposal of the right hon. Member for Mid Lothian ? [*Cries of* " No!"] Then he said for all practical purposes it was dead. If he might use a common phrase, all was over but the shouting, and the shouting was to take place by-and-bye in the Division Lobby. With respect to the first proposal, he did not mean to say that the effects of that proposal were dead. The very fair offers that had been made to the hon. Gentlemen opposite, and the way in which they had rejected those offers, were not forgotten by the country, and would not be forgotten by the country; but he said that the two proposals which had been before the country so long were practically dead and buried. Would the country look with satisfaction upon that state of things? He ventured to say it would not. He (Captain Price) was anxious, as other Members of the House were, that an inquiry should take place, and he would venture to suggest that a Royal Commission should be appointed to go thoroughly into the case. [*Laughter from the Irish Benches.*] Hon. Gentlemen

Captain Price

opposite scouted the idea of a Royal Commission. [*Cries of* " No!"] He was sorry for it.

Mr. DILLON (Mayo, E.): Who is scouting the idea?

CAPTAIN PRICE said, it appeared to him that when he made the suggestion it was scouted by the hon. Gentlemen opposite.

MR. T. C. HARRINGTON (Dublin, Harbour): You have no authority to offer it.

CAPTAIN PRICE said, he had no authority to make the offer; but he merely suggested it is an independent Member. He thought hon. Members appeared to scout it. He regretted that upon that day, of all others, when the mind of every Member of that House must be carried back to the dreadful event which cast a stain upon the fair fame of Ireland, that hon. Gentlemen should throw any obstacle in the way of a free, a fair, and impartial inquiry into that matter. He thought it would be advisable, and relieve them of all their difficulties, if a Royal Commission were appointed to go into the subject. He did not know whether there were any precedents for that proposal ; but he ventured to say that not one single precedent had been quoted which had gone on all fours with the case before the House. That was the very nature of Parliamentary precedent. What they had to look to in precedents were not details, but whether the general principle involved was in any way analogous to the question they were considering. What was the principle of the question under discussion now ? The principle appeared to him to be this—it was necessary that a strict, complete, and impartial inquiry should be made into the gross and scandalous charges brought against a body of public men. He thought he could give the House a case in which a Royal Commission was appointed by Parliament on a Motion that it was necessary that a strict, complete, and impartial inquiry should be made into the gross, and it might be scandalous, charges brought against a body of public men in Jamaica about 20 years ago. Great excitement existed in this country. It was understood by people that the coloured inhabitants of Jamaica had risen in rebellion against the authority of the Queen. There was a small and noisy Party in the House—though he thought results justified their noise—who demanded that an inquiry should be made into certain charges brought against the Representative of the Queen and certain military officers in the Colony. The charges were that they had used great severity and cruelty in suppressing the disturbance. A Royal Commission was appointed, and he was not altogether wrong in saying that when the Commission sailed from these shores there were very few people who did not anticipate a termination in favour of the Governor and officers employed in Jamaica. What happened? The Royal Commission did its duty as honest Englishmen, and sent in a Report which censured the men whose conduct they had been sent out to inquire into. Was there no analogy between that case and the present? If, under such circumstances as those he had mentioned, a Royal Commission could be appointed free from prejudice in such exciting times as those, was it not possible for a Royal Commission of English gentlemen now to deal fairly and honestly with a question like that which now oppressed them? It might be said that if a Royal Commission might be expected to act without prejudice, why not a Select Committee? He submitted that the cases were entirely different. A Select Committee would be composed of Members of the House, while a Royal Commission would consist of gentlemen selected from outside those walls. The hon. Member for the Tower Hamlets (Mr. Buxton) said the other day that the country could count brains as well as noses. He supposed the hon. Member meant that all the Liberals would be " brains," and all the Conservatives "noses." He should like, also, to refer to one other case—he referred to the Sheffield Commission. In that case the members of the Commission felt that they were not competent to cross-examine witnesses so well as members of the Legal Profession, and permission was accorded them by Parliament to appoint three barristers of over 10 years' standing to cross-examine witnesses, and upon the evidence thus elicited the Commission reported. Why should not that course be followed now? It was necessary that a full and complete inquiry should be made into the matters now under the consideration of the House, and he ventured to put forward the suggestion he

had made. He was one of those who, whatever he might think as to the probabilities of the case, felt it was incumbent upon him to treat these charges as not yet proven, and to regard hon. Gentlemen opposite as innocent men in every respect. He did not say that the result of such an inquiry as he proposed would be to exonerate the hon. Members concerned; but, at all events, if the result of an inquiry should be to show that those charges were well founded, then he thought the country would know how to estimate the agitation now going on in Ireland and England, and what to think of the men with whom the Member for Mid Lothian and his Colleagues proposed to entrust the destinies and liberties of the Irish people.

SIR HENRY JAMES (Bury, Lancashire): Sir, if I followed my inclination, I should leave to others more competent than I the task of offering guidance to the House upon this matter. I must confess that I thought this Motion in its inception was not such as ought to be received with favour by this House. It is a back-handed Motion. I do not conceive for a moment that this Motion—pretended to be brought forward in the interests of the Members of this House whose conduct is most in question, but really meant to attack those hon. Members—is calculated to enhance the character or honour of this House. If this precedent is followed, the time of this House may be occupied by Motions the object and intention of which will be to attack and not to defend hon. Members. But, Sir, this proposition has now been changed in its aspect. The Motion has been made, and the House has disagreed with it. It is no longer a question between the hon. Baronet the Member for North Antrim (Sir Charles Lewis) and the hon. Member for East Mayo (Mr. Dillon); it is not even a question now between the hon. Member for East Mayo and *The Times* newspaper; the question with which this House has to deal is one in which this House, and every individual Member of this House, must bear the responsibility. This Motion has been discussed, and not unnaturally discussed, in a Party spirit, and Party views have been presented from both sides of this House. If that were the only result of this debate my inclination would have been to take no part in it; but subjects have been referred to and statements have been made which I think ought not to be passed by in silence, and against some of those assertions and some of those views I hope I shall be allowed to make a most respectful protest. There are some of the institutions of this country which might well have been spared even in the extraordinary heat of Party conflict, and it is with sincere regret that many Members of this House have heard the assertions which have been made upon high authority — upon the highest authority — in relation to the administration of justice in this country. These statements were not intended for this House alone, nor only for this country, but for countries outside; and strangers and foreigners will be told that that institution to which we have often pointed with so much pride, the security of justice in trial by jury, has fallen so low that in the highest quality that jurymen ought to possess —impartiality—owing to circumstances of political excitement they will be deficient, and that jurors will be governed by prejudice and political views. I seek to make practical denial that this is the case in this country. Sir, it would be satisfactory, when such suggestions are made, that even one single instance should be given in proof of the assertion that is so presented to the House. I would ask my hon. and learned Friend the Member for Hackney (Sir Charles Russell) if he can state any instance in which a trial was prejudiced by political feeling entering the jury-box and preventing a fair trial? I would ask him whether he knows of any case where a jury have ever gone wrong in this country because of political influence? [*Ironical Home Rule cheers.*] I hear some hon. Members express dissent. This debate is not yet over, and I challenge any hon. Member who may reply to me to point to a single case where there has been a false verdict given owing to political feeling. [Mr. T. C. HARRINGTON (Dublin, Harbour): What about the Manchester trials?] What are the instances on the other side? My hon. and learned Friend the Member for Hackney, when he as Law Officer represented the Government, had to prosecute the Socialists in this Metropolis when they were charged with causing riots which resulted in the breaking of shop windows and the stealing and destroying of the property of London

tradesmen. Those men were tried by a jury of London tradesmen, who could have no sympathy with any of them. My hon. and learned Friend brought all his great powers of advocacy to bear in endeavouring to obtain a conviction against those men, and yet every one of them was acquitted. Let me take one more instance. It was my duty to prosecute two electioneering agents for corrupt practices. They were placed on their trial, and a jury was empannelled who were the personal and political friends of both those men. Sir, as far as I recollect, no juror was challenged, and that jury convicted those two agents politically acting with them and their personal friends. It was only necessary to remind that jury of their oath and the honour of their oath and they did not hesitate. I can produce instance after instance of this kind; but I look in vain in my own practical experience for any instance to the contrary; and I ask my hon. Friends upon what ground this charge is made of partiality in our juries? Now, I have said that this charge was made on the highest authority. It was made by the right hon. Gentleman the Member for Mid Lothian (Mr. W. E. Gladstone), who reminded the House of an incident in his political life. A charge of treason was preferred against him in his capacity as High Commissioner of the Ionian Islands, and the right hon. Gentleman said that he was advised by the late Mr. James Freshfield and Mr. James Stuart-Wortley that if he instituted a prosecution an impartial verdict could not be obtained from a jury. But there might be other reasons why that advice was given, and I hope I have the sanction of my right hon. Friend to call attention to what the words were. I believe the facts of the case were as follows :—On January 27, 1859, in the Ionian National Assembly, a Member named Danderlo said—

" I propose the union of the Seven Islands with Greece, and that a Memorial be presented by the Assembly to the Queen, and that through Her Majesty the other Powers be also called upon to accept our proposal."

On this it was resolved—

" That the Assembly of the Seven Islands proclaim that the sole and unanimous will of the Ionian people has been and is the union of all the Seven Islands with the Kingdom of Greece."

The right hon. Gentleman had just assumed authority as the Lord High Commissioner, and upon this Resolution being

Sir Henry James

communicated to him he sent back an answer pointing out that the form of proceeding was irregular, and containing the phrase "the Assembly has, through inadvertence, deviated from the Constitution," and he suggested the regular mode of expressing the desire of the Assembly. Upon this *The Times* wrote an article which contained these words, the only passage in which, I believe, the word "treason" is in any way used—

"Lord Clyde did not tender his assistance to put into the most plausible shape the Manifesto of the Queen of Oude, nor did the English Commanders in North America offer their assistance to Congress in 'framing their Declaration of Independence. But Mr. Gladstone's is a mind that delights in balancing between alternatives, and rather than a treasonable resolution should not be made in a workmanlike manner he is willing to lend a hand to it himself."

I am bound to say on those facts that anyone who was competent to advise the right hon. Gentleman would have given him the advice he actually received, utterly irrespective of the question whether a jury would convict or not. It would be absurd to say that article could be twisted into an accusation that the right hon. Gentleman had been guilty of levying war against the Queen. I know that the right hon. Gentleman made a full declaration that in his own mind he believed that every English Judge would be perfectly impartial; but he referred to the conduct of Lord Ellenborough in Lord Dundonald's case in 1814, and stated that he was severely censured by Lord Campbell. I will pass the question whether Lord Campbell was always an impartial biographer, especially when his contemporaries were the subject of his labours; but even Lord Campbell said in relation to that case that Lord Ellenborough, in the whole of the proceedings connected with the trial, was undoubtedly actuated by an earnest desire to do what was right. If this is the only record that can be brought against the impartiality of our Judicial Bench—if this is all that can be said against the administration of the law, difficult and onerous as it is, I must confess that our Bench need not be very much ashamed. Juries and Judges have been criticized, and, speaking of counsel at the Bar, my right hon. Friend said that they would exercise their power for

introducing invidious and irrelevant matter. Now, Sir, I was sorry to hear that statement.

MR. W. E. GLADSTONE (Edinburgh, Mid Lothian): Will you allow me to speak, Sir. The right hon. and learned Gentleman has conveyed an idea of my intention, which was also conveyed by the Attorney General last night, totally contrary to what I meant. I had in my mind certainly the most splendid piece of forensic eloquence, perhaps of all eloquence, known to the history of the century—a wonderful and well-known passage of Lord Brougham's, wherein he described the duty of counsel engaged in defending his client in a criminal prosecution, and said—

"He has no right to look to the right or to the left or to any consequence or any consideration except the defence of his client."

Now, Sir, it was in regard to the defence of his client and not to the general disposition of counsel to introduce invidious and irrelevant matter that I spoke. Such a charge, in my opinion, would be the most absurd that could be conceived.

SIR HENRY JAMES: I can assure my right hon. Friend that I am most anxious not to misrepresent him, and I am sure he has only truly explained what was in his thoughts, though he made no reference to Lord Brougham in his speech. Yes; I recollect those words of Lord Brougham. My right hon. Friend heard them; I heard them too. Such words were uttered—perhaps repeated—on an occasion almost worthy of historic record. My right hon. Friend will recall the scene, when the orators of two generations sat side by side in the old Hall of the Middle Temple, when Berryer, as the guest of the Bar of England, sat by the side of Lord Brougham. Surely, too, my right hon. Friend must recall how, when Lord Brougham used those words, he who was the most entitled to speak on behalf of the Bar of England sprang to his feet and protested against that saying, declaring that that was not the duty of counsel, but that it was their duty to fight with the weapons of a warrior and not with the dagger of an assassin. I am certain my right hon. Friend will recollect, even after this interval of 20 years, how that protest was accepted, and how the cheers from the assembled members of the Bar rang

[*Fourth Night.*]

out in that old' Hall of the Middle Temple. And I declare from my conscience that I believe these words of Sir Alexander Cockburn have been, and are now, the guiding words of every member of the Bar. Now, Sir, I would ask to be allowed to touch on one or two other subjects. My hon. and learned Friend the Member for Dumfries (Mr. R. T. Reid) yesterday spoke of the impossibility of obtaining redress by legal proceedings on account of the delay of the law, and he said that it would take at least 18 months or two years before the trial could take place. I entirely dissent from that statement. If a prosecution is undertaken by the Attorney General it has, on the claim of the Attorney General, precedence of other causes, and I will undertake to say that the case could be tried within six weeks from the day it is instituted. It has also been said that no trial can fairly take place before a jury, because it would be pointed out to the jury that by a Resolution of this House the House had refused to treat this libellous matter as a Breach of Privilege, and the hon. Member for Northampton pressed this point upon the House. It is, no doubt, perfectly true that Resolutions of this House are admissible in evidence. When the hon. Member for Northampton brought an action against the Serjeant-at-Arms for having imprisoned him, the Serjeant-at-Arms pleaded that he had done so by the order of a Resolution of the House. Therefore, of course, that Resolution was admissible in evidence, to justify the acts of the Serjeant-at-Arms, and was produced. Resolutions of the House were also produced and put in evidence, when the proceedings were instituted against the hon. Member for sitting and voting without having taken the oath, against him. But, Sir, there is this necessity before a Resolution of the House can become admissible in evidence—it must be relevant to the issue to be tried; and I say that if this prosecution for libel were instituted there would be no power to introduce the Resolution of the House, because it would not be relevant to any issue. I hope with regard to the points of justice, impartiality, fairness, delay, and the Resolutions of this House, I have now cleared the way. I next come to the question of whether a Committee of this House is a better tribunal for trying the issue before us than a jury. It

has been said that a jury is an unfitting tribunal, because the individual and personal responsibilities of each juror are not known, and because the jurymen themselves are not known. I do not agree to that. I am not sure that in important trials the names of every juryman are not published in the newspapers, and very often the particular way in which they gave their opinion in their private chamber while consulting as to the verdict they should give appears in the newspapers, and is thus put before the public. Every individual juryman takes an oath to perform his duty according to his conscience, and I believe they will perform that duty. Now what is to be said as to the alternative offered by the Government? My hon. and learned Friend the Member for Hackney spoke a few evenings ago, and said—"When we become Members of a Committee we discard all Party prejudices and forget our political views." It must not be forgotten, however, we have not only to judge ourselves, but other people have to judge us; and I must say, after some years' experience in the House, having associated with a great many Members of the House, and having applied some self-examination, I do not think that we are better than other people. Why, if we are always just in a Committee Room, is it to be said that in a jury-box jurymen are not just? If my right hon. Friend's Amendment were carried, and there is a Committee to try this question, your conduct and words will be—as my right hon. Friend has said—subject to review and censure. That is a prospect which is rather appalling; and I do not know who will be the Member of this House who will wish to serve on that Committee. Do his duty as he will, there will always be two sides taken with regard to the question; and if, as is said, this is a Party question, you will have two different platforms, and who will escape that review and censure? It has lately been said on this side of the House that political capital has been made by the whole of the Party opposite out of these charges. You are willing to make these men your judges; what will be said of their impartiality if judgment goes against you? Again, have not Members on this side said that these charges were vile calumnies? On Wednesday last we heard a powerful voice—so powerful that its echoes **must** have been heard in the neighbourhood of the New Forest, and belonging to one who for many reasons, should sit as a Member of such a Committee ; and he, before he has heard a single word of the evidence, declares these charges to amount to a foul and malicious calumny. We cannot put ourselves on such a high pedestal of justice and impartiality. I am very unwilling to quote precedents, and there is only one set of precedents which I will touch upon. The right hon. Gentleman the Member for Mid Lothian referred to them, and asked a question with respect to them from the Law Officers of the Crown. Out of that set of 10 precedents, which appear in the *Appendix to Hatsell*, in only two was there a previous declaration that the offence was a Breach of Privilege, and in the other eight a Resolution was moved that a libel had been written. [Sir WILLIAM HARCOURT: False and scandalous libel.] I understand that the offer of the Government was that a Resolution should be moved that the charges in question constituted a libel. ["No, no!"] I say that that was the offer made by the Attorney General. My right hon. Friend says that the Resolution in previous cases was that the charge was a "false and scandalous libel." But you are asking for a fair trial, and if the House is asked to vote this a false and scandalous libel, that is hardly the course a fair trial should take. I will refer to one other precedent— namely, the case of Mr. Whittle Harvey. The question of Privilege there arose in the form of a Motion to inquire into the manner in which certain voluntary bodies, the Inns of Court, conducted their proceedings. Objection having been taken to the form of the Motion, it was altered into a Motion to inquire into the conduct of Mr. Whittle Harvey. That gentleman said that he had been refused admission by one of the Inns of Court on the ground of a verdict in a trial 10 years before, and he asked that a Committee should decide whether that verdict was a right one or not. If this is to be put before us as a valuable precedent, I can only say that the rusty sword of Privilege is becoming a bent and broken weapon. Nothing should make this House into a Court of Inquiry into private and professional life. Now, what is the case before us ? It is, I think, a case outside all precedents. It is a case of first impression. *The*

Times newspaper made a statement in an original article, in the first instance, in relation to the communications that passed between certain Members of this House and some objectionable persons. In the course of debate reference was made to that article by the noble Marquess the Member for Rossendale (the Marquess of Hartington), and on April 21 and 22 the hon. Member for East Mayo (Mr. Dillon) dealt with that article. But the article had not, I believe, referred to him by name or otherwise in relation to anything that had occurred in this House. The hon. Member asserted, in language intended to be emphatic, that the charges contained in the article were wicked and cowardly lies, and *The Times* then said the hon. Member stated what was grossly untrue ; and on this statement of facts we are now asked to supersede the ordinary tribunals of the country and deal with it ourselves as a Breach of Privilege. And so, if a Member chooses to come to this House and say that a charge against him is false, the result is to be that the newspaper must either submit by its silence to the charge of having said what was false, or if it has the courage to say "we repeat our statement," it then commits an offence against this House, and has the opportunity taken away from it of appearing and vindicating itself before a Court of Justice. Now, I have to call the attention of the House to what really is the question before it. A charge is made ; and those against whom it is made deny it, and say—"If you venture to contradict us we shelter ourselves within the Privilege of this House."

MR. DILLON : I listened patiently to the right hon. and learned Gentleman before interrupting him ; but he has not treated me fairly in his statement. He accuses me of appealing to this House against a newspaper for simply saying that it was right and I was wrong. I never did anything of the sort. I never appealed to the House until the statements in the newspaper were made use of by the noble Marquess and by another Member in order to assail me in this House. I have said over and over again that I never did and never would appeal to this House to protect myself against any newspaper.

SIR HENRY JAMES : I do not think I have stated anything contrary to what the hon. Member has just said. I never

[*Fourth Night.*]

stated that he had appealed to this House, and I did state that the noble Marquess had called attention to the charges in *The Times* article. I quite admit that the hon. Member himself has not asked for this Committee, and I cannot see where I have committed any error of fact. If the hon. Member follows me closely, I think he will see that I am perfectly accurate. In a question such as this, where a point of Privilege is raised, we ought to be very careful as to what we do; and we must be quite certain that we are right before we take a step which involves that someone shall be summoned before us as if he had committed a wrong. This question of Privilege is like the entrance to a quarrel, and ought to be most carefully considered before it is entered upon. I trust it is with something like impartial judgment that I have come to this conclusion. [*Parnellite laughter, and cries of* "Oh, oh!" *and loud Ministerial cheers.*] Yes, perhaps you may be right. Your dissent rebukes me. You mean that in such matters I cannot be impartial. Perhaps not. Then how can I act as an impartial judge in a Committee Room? Hon. Gentlemen on this side of the House will not believe in the possibility of any one of us being impartial, and yet they believe in our fitness to sit upon a Committee whose first quality should be perfect impartiality. I do believe that if we were now to travel out of the ordinary course, and interfere with the course that can be taken by every person aggrieved by libel, and ondeavour to erect a tribunal from within our own ranks to try this issue between subject and subject, we should be entering upon a career and setting a precedent which would produce most evil consequences.

Mr. T. M. HEALY (Longford, N.): Sir, we now know for the first time what foreigners and others must think of the House of Commons. Every possible subject under the sun may be the object of an Inquiry by a Select Committee; but when 86 of your Members are charged with complicity in assassination, in dynamite plots, and treasons against the Queen, and in every form of political, and moral, and human villany, then, Sir, there is no question whatever to be referred to a Select Committee of this House. I must say, Mr. Speaker, that I was highly edified by the speech of the right hon. and learned Gentleman

Sir Henry James

who has just sat down (Sir Henry James). I understand there is a form of prayer in the Church of England—I do not profess to speak accurately of its rites—that at a certain period of the service the congregation get up, and, beating their breasts, say—"Oh, I am a very great sinner!" I may be entirely in error; but it does not affect my argument, because, Sir, we now understand the Uriah Heep attitude of the right hon. and learned Gentleman when he says that the Members of this great Assembly, who have been selected with the greatest care by 30,000,000 of your population for their fitness to discharge the functions of statesmen, to sift all the niceties of questions of diplomacy and to touch upon all great questions of legislation, have professed themselves by a majority of votes to be unfit and incapable of inquiring into the career and conduct of 86 of their own Members. This proposition is so amusing that while the right hon. and learned Gentleman was speaking I sent for a list of the subjects considered by the Select Committees of this House. I find, Sir, that in the present Session amongst subjects you thought worthy of inquiry are town holdings, butter substitutes, railway and canal Bills, police pensions, police and sanitary regulations, the rating of machinery, War Office sites, and the Bishopric of Truro. Therefore every possible question under the sun is worthy of inquiry by your Members except the character of one-eighth of the entire body of this House. Now, let me say plainly at the outset that, so far as we are concerned as Irishmen, we do not care one brass farthing, or a pinch of snuff, whether you give us this Inquiry or not. We have not asked for the Inquiry originally, but charges having been made we say not only do we not shrink from the Inquiry, we court the Inquiry; and if we are asked why do we get up now to demand this Inquiry—why did not we demand it when the charges first appeared in the newspapers? Our answer is plain. If we got up too early it would be denounced as obstruction, it would be said that we were availing of these charges, that we were raising a question of Privilege with the object of preventing the progress of the Business of the House, and that we had no real desire for the Inquiry. But when an hon. Member not of our Party thinks it worth his while to move in this matter, we say we embrace the opportunity afforded us; and I must say, Mr. Speaker, that I have been greatly surprised at the way in which this House has treated this question. Either you believe these charges or you do not; either you believe you can prove them or you do not; either you believe *The Times* can prove them or you do not; and surely if you can prove them you would be delighted to ruin us. If you believe they would be proved, how unworthy you must be for the position you occupy. If you believe there is no solid ground for these charges, how mean and contemptible must be your characters. How wretched and loathsome must be the political character of Gentlemen who go from Primrose Lodge to Primrose Habitation catching votes by poisoning the public mind against the Representatives of those whom you are pledged to call your fellow-subjects, stirring up strife and hatred and enmity, and some of you making profit out of it too. But when we seize you by the throat and say —"Now, Messrs. W. H. Smith and Co., you have your opportunity, now you can ruin for all time, or practically for our lifetime at least, this Irish movement, this Home Rule Question, and ruin with it the Liberal allies who are, thank God, coming to our assistance." Now that they are afforded that opportunity, Messrs. W. H. Smith and Co. slink into their holes. Now that you are challenged to use the machinery which this House gives us to put to the test those foul and atrocious calumnies levelled against us, you shrink from doing it. But you do offer us a tribunal. The right hon. and learned Member for Bury (Sir Henry James) began his speech with a challenge—he challenged the right hon. Gentleman the Member for Hackney (Sir Charles Russell) to give one single instance of any political trial in which a British jury failed to do its duty. Now, Sir, it is not for me to attack British juries. We have in this Bill before the House a proposal to change the venue of Irish trials to England, and we have protested against any Irishman being put upon his trial before a British jury; and let me tell the right hon. and learned Member for Bury this—when he asks for a single instance where political prejudices were concerned, where a British jury failed to do its duty. I will give him the most notorious instance of all, which no Englishman can dare to forget, even

though you are often graciously pleased to forgive yourselves. I refer to the matter known in Ireland as the Manchester martyrdom. [*Ironical laughter.*] The Irish Secretary laughs—he will not laugh before I am done—the right hon. Gentleman does not seem to be acquainted with Irish matters, and much less with political questions which have arisen in England. What happened at that Manchester trial? Five men were put on trial on a charge of wilful murder, and five men were instantly convicted. No sooner was the verdict found than the 40 reporters who were engaged at the trial signed a Memorial to the Home Secretary, declaring that the man M'Guire was undoubtedly innocent. M'Guire was proved to have served on board a British warship somewhere in the British Channel on the day the prison van was attacked at Manchester, and M'Guire was released after being sentenced to death on the verdict of a British jury. Why does not the Irish Secretary sneer now? Sir, the right hon. and learned Member for Bury invites us to take our case before a London jury. Are we likely to do that in the present state of political feeling? Why, Sir, you can hardly go into a railway carriage that you do not see gentlemen reading their *Globe*, or their *St. James's Gazette*, or *Times*, and wishing that the rope were round our necks, and saying this, too, though knowing some of us. Why, Sir, I over heard not long ago a Member of this House, on the platform of Westminster Bridge Station saying—"I wish we had them like rats in a pit, with a terrier at their throats. [*Cries of* "Name, name!"] I do not know the names of all the Members of this House. I do not know the names of more than 100 Members, and I do not want to know more. But the parties I refer to were three Members of this House who left the House before me, and were waiting for the last train at Westminster Bridge, and I heard them with my own ears. I do not blame these Gentlemen at all—it is natural when they are fed on this stuff that they should feel so. I do not make a complaint of these men or say they were right or wrong; but I point to it as showing the state of feeling amongst Parties in this country. This matter does not affect us all—it affects you—it affects this House. Gross charges of murder, and assassination, and trea-

[*Fourth Night.*]

son, and every form of political and social villainy have been made against 86 Members of this House, and the inquiry, the right hon. and learned Member for Bury suggests, is an inquiry before a British jury. The right hon. and learned Member for Bury in his speech said one very remarkable thing —he said he would not prejudice a trial of this question by the House declaring in advance that it was a libel.

SIR HENRY JAMES: I object to the House declaring in advance that it is a false, scandalous, and malicious libel.

MR. T. M. HEALY: The right hon. and learned Gentleman refuses to declare in advance this to be a false, scandalous, and malicious libel. He refuses, he says, on the ground that it would prejudice the jury; but in every instance where a prosecution of this kind has been ordered by this House the declaration has always been made in advance, and the right hon. and learned Member for Bury, out of the fund of his learning and his great authority, reserves himself when the Irish character is at stake—and when Irishmen are on their trial—he refuses to do for Irishmen that which, in every other instance, this House has always done for even its humblest British Member. We can now, Sir, accurately gauge and estimate the nature of the Liberal Unionist Party. We have heard of the saying—so far as the English in Ireland were concerned— that they were more Irish than the Irish themselves. I would say of the right hon. and learned Member for Bury and the noble Lord the Member for Rossendale (the Marquess of Hartington) beside him that they are more Tory than the Tories themselves, because the Tory party only went the length of saying that they would not declare this a Breach of Privilege because they had some technical reason for not doing so; but though no Member of the Party would accept the offer to prosecute the editor of the paper, the right hon. and learned Member for Bury wants the House to guard itself against this—not to prejudice a British jury; and he wants it not to do what every House of Commons would have done, and that is to declare in advance of sending it to a jury that it was a scandalous, a false, and a malicious libel. In every case this House has been like a grand jury who passes a Bill of indictment, and passes it down to a petty

Mr. T. M. Healy

jury to examine it in its details, and the right hon. and learned Gentleman the Member for Bury—the future Lord Chancellor of England—wants the procedure in this matter to be departed from in the case of the 86 Irish Members whose characters are at stake. We thank the right hon. and learned Gentleman, but we are told to go before a British jury. There are Members of the House willing so to humiliate themselves in the face of their constituencies as to profess that they are more incompetent and more incapable of finding out the truth or the falsehood of this political matter than 12 shopkeepers of the City of London. Really, from the way in which the right hon. and learned Member for Bury talked about 12 shopkeepers you would think they were angels without wings. You would think that the wind of politics had never ruffled their souls—that they are absolutely pure and free from all political taint; that at Temple Bar, once you pass the Dragon or Griffin, I forget which, you are in some empyrean where human frailty suddenly disappears. But I take a different view. I say that the 12 commonest Members of this House—I will even say the 12 Orange Members of this House, with the pious Catholic Member for Loughborough Division (Mr. De Lisle) as foreman of the panel—would be more competent to deal with this matter than any jury outside these walls. It is said that the House does not possess sufficient powers. The Attorney General for England stated in his most interesting and able speech—but completely illusory as I think—that former charges were made against some Irish Members, and the matter ended unsatisfactorily, because the Committee declared they had no power to summon witnesses and examine them upon oath. But a measure has been passed for the purpose of giving the Committee that power, and not only can the Committee summon witnesses, but they can ask them leading questions; they can be cross-examined up and down and made to produce documents and dates, and the Committee could introduce matters which would not be permitted as relevant by any Judge before a jury; and yet, with all these opportunities for a full investigation, the House is asked to decline, and say, "Oh, we are unworthy." I must say that this opinion of unworthiness comes very well from Gentlemen who, while they say they are unworthy to investigate this matter, think themselves worthy to decide the Irish international question, to vote upon it, and speak upon it, and upon Imperial and Colonial questions, who think themselves capable of doing anything, except what any petty jury of London could do. I should just like to say that though the charges in *The Times* refer to a period five years ago, they were never brought forward by the Liberal Party, or by Lord Spencer, whom we attacked daily at the time. I have nothing to confess in reference to those attacks; so far as my part in them is concerned I am not ashamed of them, for they were conscientious on my part; but I have this to say—that I regret we did not in those days recognize that Lord Spencer was acting conscientiously also. Very well; but Lord Spencer was hunting down criminals in Ireland with complete success. We were here in this House attacking his Party, including the right hon. Gentleman the Member for Mid Lothian, quite as fiercely, but, I think, a little less fiercely, than we are attacking the Party opposite. If there was any body of men who had the power as well as the interest to crush the Party with which I am associated, it was Lord Spencer and his Colleagues, if they could have proved us to have had any connection with crime. Furthermore, they had a power which you say is an invaluable power, and which you, through getting the House of Commons to pass the closure against us, have been trying to acquire for yourselves—they had the power of secret inquiry. Although investigations had been carried on for days and weeks and months by the most secret inquiries into all these matters which are now agitating the English mind—that was five years ago—was any Irish Member summoned before the secret inquiry? The records are still in existence under the thumb, I presume, of the Irish Secretary. He has only to go to Dublin Castle and turn up the shorthand notes of everything in connection with it—the murders and every other form of outrage which was committed with regard to which secret inquiries had been held. If the Irish Secretary turns up these secret inquiries and examines into all that the witnesses swore—and God knows you can get plenty of informers at any time, for a

small trifle, just as *The Times* can purchase forged letters for a small trifle. Let him publish the result of his secret inquiries — give them to *The Times*. Let them have every word that had been given in evidence, publish them from first to last, and we will give you our answer. Why do not you do that? That, at any rate, you can do, as your English gentlemen think themselves obliged in honour and honesty to make the speeches they do. Sir, if this House by a majority refuses us the inquiry we demand, I say this—that the honour of the British gentleman will be placed on a level with that of an Indian Thug, and, for my part, I would rather be an Indian Thug, meeting my victims in the open, than a British gentleman, who, when these charges have been denied, and when you are afforded the fullest opportunity of investigating them, declines the investigation, but repeats the charges. But, Sir, we are told that this is a narrow issue, and this is a mere technical question, whether a man has been called a liar or not. Is there a man who uses these arguments and does not know how worthless they are? Will they deceive the public outside? Naturally the right hon. Member for Mid Lothian has dealt with the matters which grew out of the Motion of the hon. Baronet the Member for North Antrim; but what is it, I ask, that gives actuality and life to this debate? Is it the question of whether my hon. Friend the Member for East Mayo has been called a liar by *The Times?* You know very well that it is not. You know very well that is the merest *Nisi Prius* special pleading. You know that it is the Irish representation which is on its trial; and the Irish representation challenges you to the combat; and they tell you that they stand on no technical reference, such as is made naturally and necessarily by this Motion, but that if you have any specific charges against any man on these Irish Benches, bring them forward and we shall meet them; and after that you can go and snivel at your Primrose gatherings. You tell us that we are standing on technicalities. It is you who are standing on technicalities; and what is more, you know it. Oh! but as to this British jury, I would remind the House what took place on a recent trial before a London jury. A creature who, from our point of view, is a contemptible person—Mr. Brenon—a man who had all the qualifications that commend themselves to the Tory Party, who was expelled from the Land League for having made infamous charges of immorality against the doctors of Merrion Square, in Dublin, which, as the noble Lord opposite will recognize, is the leading square inhabited by medical men—the most gross charges of immorality—in one of your congenial English society papers—*Mayfair*—I believe it is since dead. It was too gross even for the Tory Party. This gentleman had, in addition to that, issued an address as a Conservative candidate for Gloucester. He had written to *The Times*, in which he assailed my hon. Friend the Member for Cork and every man of his Party in the most infamous and scurrilous terms. Some persons wrote a pamphlet—I have not read the pamphlet—in which this person was described as a dynamiter and assassin and everything of the kind, and I am told that this was the part congenially relied upon by the hon. and gallant Gentleman the Member for North Armagh (Colonel Saunderson). Very well. He went before a British jury, and no sooner was the jury empannelled than it was common gossip in this House that there were seven Tories on the jury. That was instantly known about three hours after the jury was empannelled. What did they do with that man? They gave him £500, the other side—the defendant's—refusing to enter into one tittle of evidence to show that this unfortunate creature was really guilty, or that there was any foundation whatsoever for the loathsome libels made upon him. If £500 damages was considered sufficient atonement and satisfaction by a British jury for a Conservative anti-Land League assailant of ours, what chance would we have? It appears to me that anything more infamous than the treatment of Brenon by the defendant Ridgway, who published the lampoon, has never been heard of. He libelled and lampooned him in the most infamous and scandalous manner, and he did not bring forward one shred or tittle of evidence. I think of all the modern scandals in modern London trials the shamefully inadequate verdict towards this man was one of the worst. As far as I am, concerned, I do not intend to trouble the House at any greater length beyond saying this—that *The Times* news-

paper, which has printed these libels, is a newspaper about which we were assailed for not bringing an action. It is only when in the House that I see *The Times*. Only three times in my life have I bought a copy of the paper. The paper which the most of us read every morning is *The Standard*. I speak for myself. I always find it a frank and honest opponent, and I much prefer it to the lukewarm Liberalism of the other newspaper—*The Daily News*. *The Times*, as a newspaper power, we look upon with contempt. The circulation, I understand, had fallen to about 20,000 when these libels came on. [Lord RANDOLPH CHURCHILL: Nearer 90,000.] There was a meeting, as I understand, of the proprietors to see if they could not give it a fillip, and by means of this forgery they raised it up to 50,000. Its advertising circulation has fallen off; and, so far as Ireland is concerned, with the exception of two or three landlords, I do not suppose a dozen copies of the newspaper are sold. So far, therefore, as its attacks upon us are concerned, we do not care one pinch of snuff; but if they are worthy of being inquired into, why do you not inquire into them? You sell them, and it is a very remarkable fact—I do not state it as a fact within my own knowledge, but it has been stated in an English newspaper—that on the day they published this " Parnell letter," by some mysterious means a double or treble supply had been ordered in advance over all the bookstalls of the right hon. Gentleman opposite. There was a special placard at all his bookstalls. A further instance of the decadence of *The Times* is that it has lately to adopt the method of all the other morning papers, and take to placards. As I have said, this is a matter that concerns you. *The Times'* infamies do not touch us. *The Times* has recently taken to misreporting our speeches; and if you will read the work done by the gentlemen in the Gallery who represent it at the present moment, you will find the most ingenious misrepresentations of what we say in this House transferred into the columns of *The Times* newspaper. Its Irish reputation has been blasted by the confessions of the Irish Secretary. I am referring especially to the Millstreet outrages. It has upon its staff as chief writer an Irish Orangeman named Wilson, and this Mr. Wilson recently obtained the dismissal of

Mr. T. M. Healy

the Cork reporter, who had supplied the news to *The Times* for over 20 years, simply because of his account of the Glenbeigh outrages. This Cork reporter was likewise the local correspondent of *The Dublin Daily Express*, on which he had served also for 20 years; and this Mr. Wilson, who got this man dismissed for his account of the Glenbeigh outrages, got him at the same time dismissed from *The Dublin Daily Express*, on which the Dublin correspondent of *The Times* works, and instead of this gentleman was appointed a brother-in-law of Mr. Wilson's on *The Cork Constitution*, a paper run, as anybody who will take up the list of its shareholders will see, almost entirely by land agents and landowners. And it is this man from Cork who is pumping in the sewage into *The Times*. So far as his accounts of bogus outrages from Munster go also, they are contradicted in this House and proved to be lies by the confessions of the Irish Secretary. *The Times* still prints them, after contradiction, in its weekly edition, and they are still circulated as Gospel truth by the pamphleteers of the I. L. P. U., and by Mr. Bellow, the pamphleteer of Gloucester. Now, Englishmen, if they like, can conduct this campaign against Ireland by means of falsehood. So far as Irishmen are concerned, as I have said, the matter touches us not; but it touches the Liberals; it touches them, because if this campaign is to be conducted by calumny, and allowed to go on uncontradicted, the Liberal Party will be charged with sympathy and complicity with outrages. It is on that ground we support the demand that has been made for an inquiry into these matters. It is not that our virtue or our character is affected. If all England—aye, and if all the Colonies to boot—wrote us down as knaves and scoundrels, so far as I am concerned, thanks be to God, it would not affect me one hair's breadth, and no more would it affect the faithful people who stand behind us. We have fought their cause; we have fought their battle; we have fought it in season and out of season, caring not what you think about us; caring not what happened to us; caring not what may be the censure of all your authority. We look to them, and your opinion we disregard as the idle winds. Our characters are known in Ireland—known too,

I may say, to the priests and bishops of the country, who, I venture to say, would not allow their Church to be stained with an alliance with criminals or murderers. We appeal from beyond this House to the people outside—we appeal to the English people outside, who are not entirely tarred with prejudice or with hate. We believe that at their hands our motives will receive proper recognition. We appeal, above all, to other nations that love liberty, and leaving you and your leading newspaper, which did not hesitate to succour and support the Stepniaks, the Gallengas, and the Mazzinis—we ask other nations outside to look upon our characters, to look upon our career, and say whether they can see in them justly judged anything half or one tithe as bad—if anything were bad—as was done in the struggle for freedom of Poland, of Austria, and of Greece or Italy? Our people in Ireland have sent us here not to curry favour with anybody. We have never —even our worst enemies will not say it of us—we have never fawned upon you; we have never sought for the favour of your great men. Some of your great men, thank God, have by reason of their greatness given us their sympathy. We won that sympathy by argument, by fair fight, by logic, and by reason—we won it, so far as we have won any course or way into the hearts and consciences of fair-thinking men, we have won it simply on the ground of reason and of justice. We, the Irish Party of this time, will not last for ever—the Irish cause will remain—and if you succeeded, as you will not succeed, in taunting us with sympathy or complicity with dynamiters or assassins—if you succeeded in damaging our Party, aye, in chaining our bodies, or destroying it—you would still have the Irish nation in Ireland and beyond the seas to reckon with. We are ephemeral, our cause endures—it will endure—and you, as your fathers before who have sought to prejudice us by a cloud of infamy and misrepresentation, you have been baulked and been defeated, and the Irish nation, by bound after bound, leaps this very moment into the full noontide light of freedom and of prosperity.

Colonel SAUNDERSON (Armagh, N.) said, the hon. and learned Member for North Longford (Mr. T. M. Healy) had announced that he would not de-

liver a speech of an impassioned character, and immediately proceeded to
say that he had got his opponents by
the throat. If the speech were not impassioned, he should be sorry to be in
the neighbourhood of the hon. and
learned Member when he was really in
an impassioned mood. The hon. and
learned Member had appealed to the
English people; but, as far as he (Colonel
Saunderson) could make out, the appeal
was to all Englishmen who did not happen to be upon a jury panel. Then the
hon. and learned Gentleman said that if
his body or the bodies of his friends
were made away with, they had across
the Atlantic those to whom he would
appeal, and that sentiment was applauded by the right hon. Gentleman
the Member for Mid Lothian. "Destroy us; we have still got Patrick
Ford." He (Colonel Saunderson) did
not wish, on that occasion, to make an
impassioned speech. He did not wish
to arouse any angry feeling; but he
desired to say a few words in explanation of the vote which he intended to
give against the appointment of a Committee. He intended to oppose it on
two grounds—first, because he did not
think a Committee was necessary; and,
secondly, because he thought that if a
Committee were appointed, it would not
have the effect which the right hon.
Member for Mid Lothian (Mr. W. E.
Gladstone) desired. The right hon. Gentleman, in introducing his Amendment,
brought forward several instances with
which he did not intend to deal. But
he thought that the instances adduced
were not applicable to the present case.
In the instances mentioned by the right
hon. Gentleman the characters of hon.
Members of that House were assailed,
but the Party passions of the House of
Commons were not inflamed. In the
present case the character of an hon.
Member was assailed; but, as the right
hon. Gentleman truly observed, something more was at stake than the character
of the hon. Member for East Mayo (Mr.
Dillon). He could quite understand
why the right hon. Member for Mid
Lothian wished, as far as he could, to
whitewash that portion of his followers
who had supplied him with a policy.
They were the backbone of his Party;
but he wanted to point out to the right
hon. Gentleman that if he carried his
Amendment, he would succeed in white-

washing, not the whole backbone, but
only one of the vertebræ. The Motion
of the right hon. Gentleman strictly
limited the action of the proposed Committee. The scope of the Committee
was entirely bounded by the terms of
the Amendment, and the right hon.
Gentleman had confined it absolutely
to the allegation made in only one of
the articles which appeared in *The Times*
—the article which had directly accused
the hon. Member for East Mayo of telling
a falsehood in the House of Commons.
The right hon. Gentleman spoke of that
article as being a very terrible one, as
undoubtedly it was. He said that it
was unparalleled, and the gravest and
blackest charge that could be brought
against a Member of Parliament; but
surely the right hon. Gentleman must
be aware that blacker and graver charges
than that had been brought against hon.
Members. He did not know whether
the right hon. Gentleman ever read *The
Times*—probably he did not; but the
right hon. Gentleman could not get
over the fact that his noble Friend the
Member for Rossendale (the Marquess
of Hartington), in the House of Commons, quoted a series of articles which
made definite charges against certain
Members of the Party led by the right
hon. Gentleman; that those charges
were publicly stated here in the House
of Commons, and that they were of a
far graver character than simply accusing
the hon. Member for East Mayo of telling a falsehood. Hon. Members were
stated to be in direct trade and traffic
with murderers and dynamitards and
assassins. He considered that to be a
far graver charge than charging a man
with uttering a falsehood in the House
of Commons. As to whether these statements were true or not, he did not express an opinion.

Mr. T. P. O'CONNOR: Then why
do you repeat them?

Colonel SAUNDERSON said, he
would tell them in a moment. What
they said was this—that against a certain
body of Members in that House allegations of the gravest character, involving
their character as Members of the House
of Commons, had been brought, and
that they remained practically unchallenged. The right hon. Gentleman the
Member for Mid Lothian was suddenly
awakened to the necessity of taking
action in that matter. These grave and

terrible charges could not be brought against a Member of this House, the right hon. Gentleman at length thought, without action being taken in the shape of the appointment of a Committee. But in former times the right hon. Gentleman was asleep. He had himself ventured to point out in that House long ago—[An hon. MEMBER: Ridgway's pamphlet.] The hon. Gentleman was quite mistaken. He had himself quoted from a speech of the hon. Member for Cork (Mr. Parnell), in which the hon. Member for Cork accused Members of the late Government of having, by suborning witnesses, procured the condemnation of men whom they knew in their hearts to be innocent. That was a worse accusation than any that had been made against hon. Gentlemen below the Gangway opposite. He could not well conceive a graver charge to be made against Members of the Government than that of employing men to suborn witnesses in order to procure the condemnation of men whom they knew to be innocent. Yet those were the accusations that were levelled against Lord Spencer and Sir George Trevelyan; but the right hon. Gentleman opposite, as far as he was aware, never got up in the House as Prime Minister and proposed that a Select Committee should be appointed to inquire into those most cruel charges that were levelled against friends of his own. But the right hon. Gentleman had now thoroughly awakened, and he proposed that a Committee should be appointed to examine into certain charges that had been made against a Member of his Party. Great difficulty would attend the composition of such a Committee. He believed it was usual, although not necessary, for the Mover of the Committee to have a place on it himself. Would the right hon. Gentleman decline to serve on that Committee? The right hon. Gentleman made no sign.

MR. W. E. GLADSTONE: I will consider it.

COLONEL SAUNDERSON: Would the right hon. Member for Derby consent to serve on the Committee? Would he consider it? [Sir WILLIAM HARCOURT assented.] For himself (Colonel Saunderson), if he happened to be summoned on a jury to try a man for a capital offence, and if he were publicly to state before he was summoned on the panel that he

believed the accused person to be guilty, he should be ordered by the counsel for the prisoner to stand by. Well, that was just the case of both of those right hon. Gentlemen. The allegations made in *The Times* on which the right hon. Gentleman rose to take action occurred in the year 1881. In the year 1881 the right hon. Gentleman was Prime Minister, and in that year he put the hon. Member for East Mayo in gaol; in that year he went to various parts of the country, and in eloquent terms he proclaimed the Party which he now led to be a Party that were marching through rapine to the disintegration of the Empire; he described them as leaders of an organization whose steps were tracked by blood, murder, outrage, and crime; and he said they were engaged in a pilgrimage of spoliation and plunder. If hon. Gentlemen below the Gangway opposite succeeded in getting that Committee, they must order both of those right hon. Gentlemen to stand by. But how would the Committee be composed? Some hon. Gentlemen below the Gangway had said they would consent to its being exclusively composed of Members of the Conservative Party, but they were not all agreed upon that point. The hon. Member for East Mayo said he would be satisfied with that arrangement; but the hon. Member for the Scotland Division of Liverpool would not be satisfied.

MR. T. P. O'CONNOR: I never expressed an opinion on the point. I would ask whether the hon. and gallant Gentleman is entitled to attribute to me an opinion which I never expressed?

COLONEL SAUNDERSON said, that if the hon. Member would only be patient he would read from his speech. He knew too well the kind of battle he had to fight to indulge in random assertion. If the Committee was to be exclusively composed of Members chosen from the Conservative side, he presumed the Leader of the House (Mr. W. H. Smith) would have something to say to its formation; and the hon. Member for the Scotland Division of Liverpool, two days ago, speaking of his right hon. Friend who would have to choose the Committee, said—

" I had no great expectation of the manner in which the right hon. Gentleman would fulfil his duties of Leadership, but I am more than surprised at the degradation to which he has already brought this House."

[*Fourth Night.*]

In the eyes of the hon. Member for the Scotland Division of Liverpool, his right hon. Friend the Leader of the House had degraded the House; and yet would the hon. Member be willing to allow a packed Committee, chosen by a degraded person, to try his case? It was not very hard to understand why hon. Gentlemen below the Gangway were so anxious—or, at any rate, said they were anxious—to get a Committee. He could perceive from their speeches that they would go all over the country, and say that they came forward in the House of Commons and demanded the appointment of a Committee, and it was refused. He did not know whether the hon. Member for East Mayo was now in the House; but he was about to broach subjects that intimately related to the hon. Member. Why should there be a necessity for a Committee to examine the allegations that had been made by *The Times* when *The Times* gave them the proofs on which those allegations were made? [*Cries of "Oh!" and cheers.*] He would not say they were good proofs, nor would he express an opinion; but no one could deny that they had, in the paper furnished to each hon. Member, the whole case set forth. They had the statements there made by *The Times*, which gave the authority on which it made the allegation that the hon. Member for East Mayo had told a falsehood in that House. Let the hon. Member for East Mayo get up in the House, go through these statements *seriatim*, and deny their truth. There was no one in the House who would not accept his denial. They did not want a Committee for the hon. Member to give the lie to those statements. The noble Lord the Member for Rossendale made some statements in the House some time ago on an article from *The Times;* and the hon. Member for East Mayo got up and said very emphatically that they were slanderous lies. But *The Times* then went on to show that it had grounds for the assertions that it had made; and he would point out how the case was put by that paper, which was placed in the hands of hon. Members after all to be made use of, although as yet but little use had really been made of it. The hon. Member for East Mayo first denied that P. J. Sheridan had any connection with murderous crimes when he was under the hon. Member's authority.

The Times showed that Mr. Sheridan was engaged absolutely in organizing murders when he was under the authority of the hon. Member. Then the hon. Member for East Mayo went on and denied that Sheridan had ever had any connection with the Land League organization since the 1st of April, 1881. That was a distinct statement. Then *The Times* went on to cite *The Freeman's Journal*. He did not know whether the proprietor of *The Freeman's Journal*, the hon. Member for St. Stephen's Green Division of Dublin (Mr. Dwyer Gray), was now in his place; but he wanted to know, if that was not true, why the hon. Gentleman allowed that untruth to appear in his paper? If the hon. Member for East Mayo would get up and distinctly state that those facts which were put in that paper were untrue, he, for one, would never say a word more about it. Though the hon. Gentleman might think him a very unfair man, he would never quote a statement which the hon. Member for East Mayo said distinctly was untrue. He was quite ready to admit, though he differed so much from the hon. Member, that he had no right whatever to reject his distinct statement as to a matter of fact of that kind. He would just read what was set forth in the paper which was before the House. The hon. Member for East Mayo, in contradicting the noble Marquess the Member for Rossendale (the Marquess of Hartington), stated that Mr. Sheridan never had any connection with the Land League after the 1st of April, 1881. Now, in *The Freeman's Journal* of October 13, 1881, there was announced a citizens' meeting to be held at the offices of the Central League. The meeting was duly held. The chair was taken by Mr. Charles Dawson, M.P., Lord Mayor - Elect. Among those present, said *The Freeman's Journal* next day, were Messrs. J. Dillon, M.P., J. G. Biggar, M.P., J. O'Kelly, M.P., G. M. Byrne, M.P., H. J. Gill, M.P., T. D. Sullivan, M.P., R. H. Metge, M.P., E. D. Gray, M.P., and P. J. Sheridan, of Tubbercurry (ex-suspect). Would the hon. Member for East Mayo get up in the House and, without the trouble of appointing a Committee, simply tell them that *The Freeman's Journal* had no right and no grounds to make that assertion? If he did, he, for one, certainly would never quote that as a fact. But the

Colonel Saunderson

hon. Member had never stated in the House that *The Freeman's Journal*, when it made that statement, uttered a falsehood. Then, further on, *The Times* said that *The Freeman's Journal* described the events of "the memorable afternoon of Saturday," when a meeting of the Executive of the League was held in the Imperial Hotel, Sackville Street, and was attended by Mr. T. D. Sullivan, Mr. Biggar, Dr. Kenny, and Mr. Sheridan, of Tubbercurry. [At this point Mr. DILLON, who had hitherto been absent, entered the House.] He was glad the hon. Member for East Mayo was in his place. He asked him not to wait for any Committee, but to get up there and then and deny these allegations in *The Times*. The hon. Member had stated that he had ceased to associate with Sheridan in April, 1881; but *The Times* showed, from Irish papers, that he met Sheridan at a meeting of the Central League long after. That appeared in *The Freeman's Journal*. Now, he wanted the hon. Member to stand up and say whether that was true or not.

MR. DILLON (Mayo, E.) said, he thought the time was come when the House should get away from these personal discussions. He, for one, should be no party to them any longer. He had offered to enter into these charges fully before a Committee of that House, and he was ready to do so. But if they were asked to go on exchanging the lie with hon. Members of that House or with newspapers outside, he, for one, should not do so any longer.

COLONEL SAUNDERSON said, he had no wish to exchange the lie, and he should not wish to insult the hon. Member. But he said that this was a fact which must be taken notice of by that House. In the hands of every hon. Member was a copy of the allegation, and the dignity of a Member, and the dignity of the House, required the hon. Member to meet on the floor of the House this accusation against his fair fame and honour as a Member should——

MR. DILLON said, he must appeal to the Speaker whether, with these repeated challenges across the floor of the House, the debate could be expected to be conducted in an orderly fashion? He had already denied it altogether.

MR. SPEAKER: I think there is much force, in the point of view of Order, in what has fallen from the hon. Mem-

ber for East Mayo. The Question before the House is a comparatively narrow one. It is, first, whether there is a Breach of Privilege; and, secondly, whether a Committee should be appointed to inquire into certain allegations in the newspaper. I do not think this is the time in this House to try that case, or to make charges on one side or to answer them on the other. It might lead to disorder, and I may point out that if the House thinks fit to appoint the Committee, then would be the time for the inquiry, and then would come the time for charges to be made and met.

COLONEL SAUNDERSON: The right hon. Gentleman the Member for Mid Lothian had insinuated that Judges were not to be trusted, and Home Rule Members did not believe in jurors. Then there was the alternative remaining of a Committee, and the Committee would deal with the one allegation only. Its decision would be worthless, and hon. Members would not scruple to say the Committee was prejudiced. Lastly, there was the course indicated by the Government, of which he could not say he altogether approved. The reputations of hon. Gentlemen were of infinite value to themselves, but he doubted if the British public wished to pay some thousands to sustain that reputation. The hon. Member for Dumfries (Mr. R. T. Reid) had accused him of having from time to time hinted accusations against his fellow-countrymen. Personally, he had not a particle of animosity against any Member of the Nationalist Party— [Mr. T. M. HEALY: Nor have we for you.]—were it not for the fact that it was proposed to hand over the destinies of his country and the framing of her laws to hon. Gentlemen opposite. He did not wish to rake up memories they all wished buried in oblivion; but so long as it was proposed to hand over their destinies to the keeping of hon. Gentlemen opposite it was a duty he owed to the people he represented, who trusted him as others trusted hon. Members opposite, to point to the records of their past, showing that they gave no hope of a successful and prosperous future for Ireland.

MR. HENRY H. FOWLER (Wolverhampton, E.) said, the right hon. and learned Member for Bury (Sir Henry James) seemed to have the most unlimited faith in English Judges, English juries, and in the Bar. Well,

[*Fourth Night.*]

he agreed with him about the Bench of the day and about the Bar, but he declined altogether to believe in the infallibility of English juries, and that was one if not the main issue they had to try. He asked the right hon. and learned Member for Bury if he had forgotten the case of Lord Cochrane, the verdict in whose case, after the greatest injustice and indignity had been inflicted, was reversed by public opinion. If he wanted an illustration of the fallibility of English juries it was not necessary to go so far back. Two or three years ago there was a 45 days' trial. The jury found a verdict which the Judge sympathized with, and which "society" concurred in; but the man on whose evidence it was obtained was now suffering imprisonment as a convict on the ground that he was a fraudulent impostor. How many hundred times had the Attorney General and the Solicitor General applied to the Court above to set aside verdicts on the ground that they were contrary to the evidence? And yet they were asked to lay down absolutely that a special jury of London or Middlesex was less likely to err than a Committee chosen from Members of the House. It was not necessary to contend that juries would act corruptly or unfairly, although the probabilities were that a jury would not be so fair as a Committee of this House. As to Members of a Committee being necessarily chosen from the sections of the House, and therefore politically interested in the decision of the Committee, where would jurymen be found who would not be identified with the same sections? In this respect hon. Members of the House were just as likely to be fair and impartial as jurors were. The right hon. and learned Member for Bury had carefully guarded himself against saying that there had not been a Breach of Privilege. The hon. and learned Solicitor General, in looking up precedents as far as time allowed, had worked remarkably well; but he had strangely omitted the last precedent and the last occasion that the question of Privilege was formally brought before the House. It was raised by the Leader of the Conservative Party—Sir Stafford Northcote—who asked the House to say by its vote that the senior right hon. Member for Birmingham (Mr. John Bright) had committed a Breach of Privilege in making a charge against

Mr. Henry H. Fowler

the Conservative Party. History repeated itself, for it was a similar charge to that now made. The charge then was that the Conservative Party were—

"Found in alliance with the Irish rebel Party, the main portion of whose funds for the purposes of agitation came directly from the avowed enemies of England and whose oath of allegiance was broken by general consent."

Sir Stafford Northcote said—

"The right hon. Gentleman has charged the Conservative Party, in language which is very clear, with being in alliance with a rebel Party. This is language to which it is utterly impossible that hon. Members of this House can, on whatever side they sit, listen without demanding some explanation and some satisfaction for such extraordinary observations."—(3 *Hansard*, [280] 803.)

Sir Stafford Northcote moved that they should be regarded as a Breach of the Privileges of this House, and a Division was taken. There was not a man now in the Government and then in the House who did not vote that it was a Breach of Privilege. The Division List contained the names of the First Lord and both the Secretaries to the Treasury, the First Lord of the Admiralty (Lord George Hamilton), and the Civil Lord to the Admiralty (Mr. Ashmead-Bartlett), the Secretary of State for the Colonies (Sir Henry Holland) and even that of the hon. and learned Solicitor General (Sir Edward Clarke). That Division meant that it was a Breach of the Privileges of the House to say that the Conservative Party were in alliance with Irish rebels. But now it was affirmed that it was not a Breach of Privilege to say that the Irish Party were in alliance with murderers and assassins. Whatever the first was, it was a political offence and this was a moral offence; that was an indiscretion and this was a crime. The same men who formerly said it was a Breach of Privilege to make such a charge, not by name against anyone, but against a Party as a whole, now said it was not in accordance with precedent to treat as a Breach of Privilege the charge that a Member had told a lie to the House in his capacity of a Member of the House, and that his Colleagues sat by and were accomplices with him in the fabrication, and that all were in league and associated with some of the vilest criminals of the United States.

In asking the House to decline to treat this as a Breach of Privilege, the hon. and learned Solicitor General must take one of three grounds. He must either say that, although technically it was, substantially it was not, a Breach of Privilege; or, secondly, although technically and substantially it might be a Breach of Privilege, it was too trivial to be taken notice of; or, thirdly, that it was justifiable on the ground of its truth. The hon. and gallant Gentleman the Member for North Armagh (Colonel Saunderson) read the part of the article which served his purpose; but he did not read that which constituted the *gravamen* of the charge. The right hon. and learned Member for Bury treated the matter as if it was a simple conflict of testimony, one man saying, "You are a liar," and the accused retorting, "You are another," and the House of Commons being asked to decide who spoke the truth. But that was not so. It was a serious matter, affecting not only the hon. Member for East Mayo (Mr. Dillon) and the position of the Irish Members, but also the character of the House itself. The first article said—

"Sheridan's direct complicity in this particular conspiracy, to murder at a time when he was Mr. Dillon's acknowledged agent, acting upon Mr. Dillon's instructions, was established beyond all controversy in the course of these same trials."

There was a distinct charge that the hon. Member for East Mayo's instructions were being given at the time when Sheridan was engaged in a particular conspiracy to murder. Then there was the statement which had been repeatedly read to the House that the hon. Member for East Mayo, in his place in the House, had uttered a tissue of gross and palpable falsehoods. But the last sentence of the article had not been read to the House. It was this—

"In either case — whether he recklessly palmed off on the House as ascertained facts within his personal knowledge a mass of confused, inaccurate, and unexamined memories, or he deliberately told the House a detailed story which he knew to be untrue—several of his Colleagues must have known that his statements were unfounded. The Party sat exulting by, and endorsed the fabrication."

What was the comment? It was this—

"The letter has now come to be regarded, as we always intended it should be, as a part of a long series of statements founded upon unquestionable evidence, and indisputably connecting Mr. Parnell and the rest of the 'Constitutional agitators' with associations for the perpetration of outrages and murder."

It was added that the first article—

"Demonstrates what is the main point in connection with the general question that the most solemn, passionate, and detailed denials by Members of the Parnellite Party can be, and are, offered to the House of Commons and the country when there is not a scrap of fact to support them."

And the article wound up with this—

"The Parnellite Party are proved to be the close associates of murderers, and are also shown to be conspicuously destitute of that quality which Englishmen rightly prize above all others as the indispensable foundation of character."

That was one of the gravest charges ever brought against any Member of that House. The rule which his right hon. Friend the Member for Derby (Sir William Harcourt) wisely laid down in 1880 was that that House was not to take notice of questions of criticism—that criticism was not a Breach of Privilege. But this was not a charge of criticism; it was a charge which affected the character of 86 Members of the House; it affected the character of the Liberal Party. He was glad the right hon. Gentleman the Chancellor of the Exchequer (Mr. Goschen) took that down. He (Mr. Henry H. Fowler) repeated it. The Liberal Party had been held up to scorn as the associates of men who did not scruple to commit the vilest of crimes. The Liberal Party had a character at stake. He went further and said the House of Commons had a character at stake. If these men were guilty of what *The Times* charged them with they ought to be expelled from the House. And how could the Liberal Party vindicate themselves except by the Constitutional precedents and practice of the House, by inquiry within the House into charges of misconduct by Gentlemen within the House? *The Times* had singled him out as one of the associates of those criminals. If he knowingly associated himself with men guilty of those crimes he deserved to be expelled. The hon. Member for North Armagh was pleased to designate this as a narrow and contracted issue, saying that all that could be inquired into was simply the truth or falsehood of the statements of the hon. Member for East Mayo. Would the hon. and gallant Gentleman be surprised to hear that

[*Fourth Night.*]

there was a disposition on the part of hon. Members below the Gangway that the inquiry should have a much wider range? Since he had begun speaking one of the Irish Party had sent him a telegram received from the hon. Member for Cork (Mr. Parnell) stating that he was quite willing the inquiry should extend to the forged letter. That was a challenge which the Government were bound to meet. What was the objection to granting the Committee? He had shown that the House itself was the only complete judge of its own character, and it had invariably exercised disciplinary jurisdiction over the conduct of its own Members. The noble Lord the Member for South Paddington (Lord Randolph Churchill) urged two objections, one to the composition of the Committee, and the other to its powers. Now, he (Mr. Henry H. Fowler) had himself some experience of Courts of Law, and some experience of Committees of that House; he had been before them; he had sat on them; and he would repeat that a Select Committee of the House of Commons was the fairest tribunal which could possibly be had. There were men sitting there who could name at once Members who were known to be utterly incapable of discharging improperly any judicial functions, men whose lives had been spent in that House, whose characters were part of its character, who had raised the reputation of the House, and were they to be supposed incapable of trying whether a letter was a forged letter or not? The noble Lord's second objection was that the Committee would not have power to make the investigation properly. But there was no power which Courts of Law possessed which the House of Commons did not possess. It could examine on oath; it could send for persons and papers; it could enforce attendance, and go over the whole range of inquiry far better than a Court of Law. The hon. and learned Gentleman the Solicitor General had talked of the promptitude with which a Court of Law could deal with the matter. We had had recently many instances of the length of time which Courts of Law had taken in trying the cases which came before them. There was no higher authority in that House on a question of law than the hon. and learned Member for Dumfries (Mr. R. T. Reid), and he had stated distinctly that in criminal proceedings in

a Court of Law it would be impossible to cross-examine the printer, publisher, or editor of *The Times*, and without such cross-examination it would be absolutely impossible properly to investigate this case. The hon. and learned Solicitor General had said that there was no precedent for the case. He agreed with the hon. and learned Gentleman that there was no precedent. There never had been during the 600 or 700 years of the history of this Parliament such grave charges brought against Members of Parliament. The persons who brought the charges said they were prepared to substantiate them, but the course proposed by the Government was without precedent. They refused to declare that a Breach of Privilege had been committed, and they refused a Committee of Inquiry into such grave charges brought against hon. Members for their conduct in the House. The noble Lord the Member for South Paddington had said that there was something higher than Parliament, higher than Courts of Law. There was something higher than both; there was a Court which could be appealed to from a decision of Parliament or of a Court of Law, and that higher tribunal was the constituencies of the country. He knew how the House would decide to-night. One of the Members of the triumvirate who held the destinies of the House indicated which way the House would go. But there would be an appeal, and the hearing of that appeal had already commenced. The Conservative Press, the Unionist Press had discerned that the instinct of fair play which was one of the dominant factors in the formation of English public opinion—was already resenting, and would hereafter resent in louder tones, the refusal of a Parliamentary inquiry into the most serious charges affecting the character, the morality, and the political life of the Leaders any section of that House. He ventured to say in no spirit of defiant boast, but from profound conviction, that the majority of that night would hereafter deeply regret not on Party, but on higher, grounds that they declined to take the most obvious, the most Constitutional, and the most expeditious mode of defending Parliament against one of the gravest assaults which had ever been made upon the honour and the dignity of the House of Commons.

Mr. Henry H. Fowler

MR. MAC INNES (Northumberland, Hexham) said, the real question before the House was, did they or did they not desire that an inquiry should be held into the truth or falsehood of this inquiry? They had all listened with great interest to many able and eloquent speeches from lawyers on both sides of the House upon the question of precedent and Privilege, but possibly an ordinary layman might be excused if he came to the conclusion that on matters of precedent and Privilege there was a great deal to be said on both sides; and though it might appear unseemly for any Member sitting in the House to speak lightly of precedent and Privilege, yet he would venture to say that many hon, Members in the House, and certainly a very large number of the public outside the House, were not nearly so much interested in ingenious disquisitions on precedent and Privilege as they were in the main question—was there or was there not to be an inquiry into the truth or falsehood of these accusations? It was said that we were all agreed that there should be an inquiry, and that the only question about which there was any difference of opinion was whether the inquiry should be made in the Courts of Law or before a Committee of that House; but with all due respect, he ventured to say that that was not the case—that at least was not the question upon which the House had to decide, because the question as to the settlement of the matter in the Courts of Law had already been decided. To bring about an inquiry in the Courts of Law the initiative must be taken by the hon. Member for East Mayo (Mr. Dillon), and that hon. Member had told the House fairly, frankly, and most distinctly what his course would be—and had given very clearly his reasons—and whether they might or might not agree with the hon. Member for East Mayo that was not the question before the House. He must say that he (Mr. MacInnes) thought the Member had undue apprehensions with regard to the matter, but though he did not share the hon. Member's feelings he could understand and respect them. The hon. Member had told the House plainly that he would not take any action in the Courts of Law, but he had offered with equal frankness to submit his case to a Special Committee of the House of Commons. A great many allusions had been made to the fact that Irish Members had been somewhat slow in bringing these serious accusations which had been made against them before the House of Commons, and he admitted that it was a matter of deep regret that they did not sooner take action in the matter; but it was not for him to inquire into the motives which actuated hon. Members in the course which they thought it wise and prudent to pursue in a matter which so deeply affected themselves. It was sufficient for him to know that the Irish Members now courted the fullest inquiry; and every fair-minded man must have rejoiced to see as the debate had proceeded how the scope of the inquiry had been widened and extended. That night it had been still further expanded by the speech of the hon. and learned Member for North Longford (Mr. T. M. Healy), who stated that not only were the Party willing that the conduct of the hon. Member for East Mayo should be considered by a Committee of the House, but the whole conduct of the Party which had been impugned—and he thought the country would hear with great satisfaction of the telegram from the hon. Member for Cork (Mr. Parnell), unreservedly putting his case before a Special Committee of the House, if only the House would appoint such a Committee. A great deal had been said about the proceedings before a Committee, and it was abundantly clear if there was an inquiry, whatever the tribunal before which it took place, there would be a great deal of criticism of the proceedings before the tribunal, and of its decision, whatever it might be; but he asked if that were any reason for stifling inquiry? because at this moment they had only one avenue of inquiry open to them, and if they refused to grant a Committee they would in effect stifle inquiry, whatever they might say to the contrary. The question, therefore, for the decision of the House was—Did they want an inquiry or did they not? It had been said that the Government had done all that was needful, and that it rested with the hon. Member for East Mayo to take advantage of the proceedings they offered to initiate. But, as the right hon. Member for East Wolverhampton (Mr. Henry H. Fowler) eloquently expressed

[*Fourth Night.*]

it, they were all interested in this matter, and he was astonished to hear hon. Members opposite declare that it was a matter which only affected the character of the hon. Member for East Mayo. Hon. Members opposite, when they voted, as he feared they would vote, in large numbers against this Amendment, were really voting on a foregone conclusion that there should be no inquiry. Hon. Members on his side of the House, on the other hand, who were going to follow the right hon. Gentleman the Member for Mid Lothian (Mr. W. E. Gladstone), had, at all events, the comfort and consolation of knowing that if a Select Committee could be granted an inquiry would immediately follow, and they ventured to think that a time would come when some hon. Members opposite would regret that they had taken the course that night which would end in there being no inquiry into these shameful charges.

SIR ROBERT FOWLER (London) said, that the proposition of hon. Gentlemen opposite was that they should leave the decision of this question to a Committee of the House. But he believed it had been said by some hon. Gentlemen opposite that hon. Members on his side of the House had already made up their minds on the question. That might be so; and he did not think he would be very far wrong if he said that a great many hon. Gentlemen opposite had also already made up their minds. He would ask how it was possible that any Committee could arrive at a conclusion which would give satisfaction to the House; for everyone must feel certain that the result of an inquiry by Committee would be a majority and a minority Report. For his own part, he might say that he would certainly be unfit to serve on any such Committee, and if he were nominated for it, the hon. Member for East Mayo (Mr. Dillon) would be perfectly justified in challenging his nomination. It was said by hon. Gentlemen opposite that a Committee of the ~~se would be a more impartial tribunal t' °n a Middlesex jury. As representing Metropolitan constituency, he thoug he was only doing justice to his con tuents when he said that it would be easier to find 12 impartial jurymen than it would be to find 16 impartial men in that

Mr. Mac Innes

House. It was also said that juries in London and Middlesex were prejudiced by what they read in the Press. He would remind hon. Members, however, that the Press advocated two sides of this question. There was an able portion of the Press which strongly supported the views entertained by the right hon. Member for Mid Lothian (Mr. W. E. Gladstone) and the hon. Member for Cork (Mr. Parnell). On the other hand, there was, doubtless, a large number of powerful newspapers which advocated the views held by Conservative Members. The men who would sit on a jury would be comparatively impartial for this reason—that they only knew the hon. Member for Cork and the hon. Member for East Mayo, and other Members of the Irish Party, as public men. They had read their speeches in the Press, but they had no personal acquaintance with those hon. Gentlemen. He maintained that such a tribunal would be more prepared to give an impartial consideration to this question than hon. Members of the House, who, night after night, had been brought into hostile conflict with hon. Gentlemen opposite. He did not wish to say anything uncourteous, but there could be no doubt that hon. Members, on his own side of the House especially, were brought night after night into personal hostility with hon. Members from Ireland; and, that being the case, he did not think that hon. Members who differed from the hon. Member for Cork and his followers— and who were subject to interruptions in debate and exclamations which were not altogether pleasant to hear—were likely to give such an impartial verdict as 12 jurors who had no personal knowledge of these hon. Gentlemen, and who could come to the consideration of the matter with fresh minds. To appoint a Committee meant that the hon. Member for East Mayo was to be the absolute judge of the tribunal by whom he was to be tried. That was a concession which the House could not grant to anyone. They must all form their opinions as to which tribunal would be the most impartial to try a question of this kind. As he unhesitatingly believed that the matter would be more likely to be fairly, justly, and truly tried by a jury than it could be by those whose minds were prejudiced by the stormy conflicts in the

House, he should vote for the Motion of the hon. and learned Gentleman the Solicitor General.

Mr. LABOUCHERE (Northampton) said, there was nothing so beautiful as modesty. He could assure the hon. Baronet that they had a far better opinion of him on that side of the House than he had of himself. They had also a better opinion of hon. Gentlemen who sat on the Ministerial side of the House than the hon. Baronet appeared to have, and they did not consider that it was impossible to find 16 men who could give a fair verdict upon this question. He could assure the hon. Baronet that if he were put upon the Committee the Irish Members would willingly accept him. The hon. Baronet told the House that he would not be a fair man to appoint on the Committee because he would be prejudiced by the fact that occasionally hon. Members on the Opposition side of the House interrupted him. He was sure the hon. Baronet had exaggerated when he said that. The hon. Baronet then said that the Committee would take a considerable time to investigate these charges. He thought it possible that the Committee would take some time; but when the hon. Baronet said that it must take a considerable time because the Committee would not sit *de die in diem*, the Committee appointed to inquire into the corrupt practices of the City of London not having sat from day to day, he would point out, in reply, that there was an arrangement for the general convenience that that Committee should not sit from day to day. In this particular case, however, everyone would be so anxious to have the matter settled that the Committee would sit probably from day to day. He was not surprised that the hon. Baronet had so high an opinion of Middlesex juries. He pointed out that the Sheriffs of Middlesex were Sheriffs of the City of London, and there was not the slightest doubt that the next most virtuous man in the whole world to a juryman in the City of London was a juryman of Middlesex. When the hon. and gallant Member for North Armagh (Colonel Saunderson) began his speech he was under the impression that the hon. and gallant Member was going to vote in favour of a Committee being appointed, because he said the charges of *The Times* must be taken

notice of by the House of Commons. But how did he propose to do this? By bandying accusations backwards and forwards from one side of the House to the other? The hon. and gallant Member was so Irish that he wished to convert the House into an Irish faction fight. The hon. and gallant Member said that his main objection to a Committee was that its scope would be too narrow; but since the hon. and gallant Member had spoken a telegram had been received from the hon. Member for Cork (Mr. Parnell), in which he stated that he was perfectly ready to enlarge the scope of the inquiry and, if it was desired, that the forged letter should be submitted to the Committee in the same way as the article complained of. In these circumstances, he thought they had a right to claim the vote of the hon. and gallant Member for North Armagh. He was an honourable man, and he had no doubt that he would recognize their claim and vote with the Opposition on this matter, especially since the receipt of this telegram. It was remarkable that no one on the Treasury Bench had addressed the House except the legal Members of the Government. When a private individual got into a great mess and did not know how to get out of it he consulted his lawyers. However reasonable this might be on the part of a private individual, it was hardly fitting conduct on the part of a Government in a great Parliamentary and national question like this, in which the honour of a Member of the House and the honour of the House of Commons itself was involved. Not only did the Government consult their lawyers, but up to the present time their lawyers only had spoken for them. This had been carried so far that the Liberal Unionist supporters of the Government on his own side of the House put forward an ex-Attorney General. What had been the result of this consultation of the lawyers and the speeches they had made? It was that the House affirmed the previous night that the charge of falsehood against an hon. Member was not a Breach of the Privileges of the House. It was afterwards urged that, while it was admitted that this was not a Breach of Privilege, the House should prosecute *The Times* for having committed what was not a Breach of Privilege. On what possible grounds except

[Fourth Night.]

that it was a Breach of Privilege should hon. Gentlemen say that the public Exchequer ought to be called upon to pay for one side of this prosecution, and that *The Times* — he was no friend of *The Times*—should be called upon to incur this vast expense for doing what the great majority of hon. Members on the opposite side of the House said it did most properly and righteously. The Attorney General said that it was monstrous to say that this prosecution would be a bogus one. He quite agreed with him; he did not believe it would be a bogus prosecution. He would tell the hon. and learned Gentleman what was bogus however. The bogus proposed was that there should be a prosecution at all. Before that proposal was made, it was perfectly well known to hon. Gentlemen opposite that the Irish Members and the hon. Member for East Mayo would have refused it. Those charges had been made again and again, and it was not likely that hon. Members from Ireland would be forced into a prosecution now simply because the Government offered to pay the expense, as if the honour of Irish Members was a question of pounds, shillings, and pence. He considered the Irish Members were perfectly right in declining the proposal, and they had been perfectly right not to begin a prosecution against *The Times*. His reason for saying so was that, notwithstanding what had fallen from the hon. Baronet the Member for the City of London (Sir Robert Fowler), they would have no sort of chance of a fair trial before a Middlesex jury. They had heard a great deal of clap-trap about trial by jury in the course of that debate. The Gentleman who indulged most in it was the right hon. and learned Gentleman the Member for Bury (Sir Henry James). The right hon. and learned Gentleman spoke of trial by jury in terms which must have almost made Lord Erskine turn in his grave. He spoke of it in terms which he had no doubt many and many a time addressed to that noble institution. But hon. Members were called upon to believe that it was perfectly monstrous on the part of the Irish Members to doubt and hesitate whether they would obtain justice from a Middlesex jury. He need not point out to Gentlemen who were lawyers that there was nothing more common in this country

than for an individual who wanted to bring an action or defend an action to be told that he would not get justice from the jury. Had they never heard of a change of venue on the ground of a prejudice existing on the one side or the other? Had they not heard of the difference between an ordinary and a special jury? Why did persons ask for a special jury? He had done it himself, and had had to pay £12 12s., because he believed he should be more likely to get justice from a special jury than an ordinary jury. It might be said that was a reflection on the character of a jury. Certainly it was. No one would deny that there was on the part of a great number of persons in Middlesex a very strong prejudice against the Irish. It was proved at the last Election. He was in a suburban train the other day, and happening to be in a first-class carriage—perhaps he should have heard better sentiments if he had been in a third-class one—he found four or five gentlemen discussing the Irish Question. They all seemed to disagree, but upon one thing they entirely agreed—namely, that it would do good to the country if the hon. Member for Cork were incontinently hanged. This jury would have to decide whether *The Times* was criminal or not. If it was, then, by the law, the right hon. Gentleman the Leader of the House was equally criminal. The man who sold the newspaper was equally liable for its contents with the man who printed it. The law was an absurd one, but so it was. The right hon. Gentleman the Leader of the House, the head of the Conservatives, was deservedly popular. Would not the jury hesitate—particularly if they were taken from the Strand Division— to bring in a verdict against *The Times*, when its effect might be to put the man whom they deservedly respected in the dock on the same charge? He did not say that Middlesex juries were packed, but he maintained they could be packed. How was a Middlesex jury chosen? The Sheriffs of London were elected by the Corporation of London.

SIR ROBERT FOWLER: Not by the Corporation.

MR. LABOUCHERE: Who are they, then?

SIR ROBERT FOWLER: The Livery of the City of London.

MR. LABOUCHERE said, he believed the Livery were a shade worse. By the fact of their being Sheriffs of London they were Sheriffs of Middlesex. They appointed Under Sheriffs; these in turn had their subordinates, who went to some particular district and always took the jury from one particular district. The selection of the panel was absolutely and entirely in their hands, and they might act fairly or they might act unfairly. They knew the Livery of London was Conservative, and they knew that, as a general rule, it was well to stand well with their employers. With these facts before them, the Irish Members would be foolish, indeed, to submit their case to a Middlesex jury. It was not only the jury who would be prejudiced. A considerable number of the Judges were prejudiced. Mr. Justice Stephen undoubtedly would do justice; but he had a bias in his mind, and had written letters to *The Times* very much in the strain of those which were the subject of discussion. He asked any reasonable men whether, if a jury were taken from the Strand Division, and if Mr. Justice Stephen were to be the Judge on the case, the Court would command entire confidence? A jury of that House would be selected by the Committee of Selection, honourable and experienced men whom no one suspected would not be able to act honestly and justly. Hon. Gentlemen opposite believed themselves so entirely prejudiced that they could not express an unbiased opinion on the case; but he had a better opinion of them than they had of themselves. He was not a Conservative, and he did not agree with them; but he did not believe they were such a Sodom that one could not find half-a-dozen honest men among them. Now, when it was urged that in a political issue Members of the House of Commons were never impartial, he might almost call Mr. Speaker as his witness. Some 20 years ago he was returned as Member for Windsor. Someone brought a Petition against him. One of his agents had infringed the law in some little trifling matter; he did not remember what it was. The Committee appointed was a Liberal Committee, the present Speaker being one of the Liberals upon it, and they voided the Election. [*Laughter.*] He could assure those hon. Gentlemen who laughed that all the Members who served on that Committee were not such prejudiced scoundrels as they seemed to imagine. Once or twice occasionally there was a certain bias, but in the main the decisions were perfectly fair—as fair as he had not the slightest doubt the decision was in his own case. He wanted to know how possibly it could be asserted that a jury of Middlesex would not be prejudiced, and yet that Members of this House would be prejudiced? There was a very good and sound reason why everybody should prefer a Committee of the House to any jury. It was because in a matter of libel it was always an advantage to the defendant and a disadvantage to the bringer of the action, and for this reason, that the man who brought the action had to bet 12 to 1 on himself. He had had actions brought against him in which the plaintiffs had had to bet 12 to 1; but they had lost their actions. He had been libelled more than once, but he had never been such a fool as to bring an action. In the case of a Committee, however, the betting would be even, the decision being by a majority, and that was an important feature in this matter. Hon. Gentlemen opposite had come to the conclusion that in Ireland Irishmen ought not to be tried by juries, because juries would be unfair, but that they should be tried by these half-pay captains who were appointed Resident Magistrates. Irishmen said—"We object to be tried by English juries;" and he thought that the two tribunals would be equal in fairness. The noble Lord the Member for South Paddington (Lord Randolph Churchill) had said that the Irish Members would not accept the finding of a Committee of the House of Commons. But if they would not accept the finding of a Committee, would they accept the finding of a jury? They distinctly said they objected to a London jury, but not to a Committee of the House of Commons. Obviously they would place themselves in a most contemptible position if, after electing to have their case examined by a Committee, they refused to accept the verdict. They would honestly accept the finding of the Committee. What was the reason the Government were pursuing this foolish and suicidal course? He knew that they would do it. He had been asked in the Lobby why he knew it, and he replied that he knew it because he had read an article in *The Times* that morning, saying—"We do not think that the House will be well advised in dealing with the question as one of Privilege." He knew that the Government had received their orders. He knew that their orders were in substance—"On every occasion, at any cost, at any risk, at any sacrifice, even of honour, evade, for Heaven's sake, this inquiry." No wonder that the Government should obey *The Times*; *The Times* was their trusted ally, and the Conservatives had adopted its views. What would be said of Conservative and Unionist Gentlemen who had scattered these charges broadcast if no proof were adduced of these charges? They would be regarded as persons even meaner than *The Times*, because the person who hired a bravo was even meaner than the bravo himself. There was a saying—"Set a thief to catch a thief;" but he had never heard of a receiver of stolen goods being anxious that there should be a fair investigation into the theft. He considered that the Irish Members had been perfectly right in treating with contempt the accusations levelled against them by *The Times*. What did *The Times* say? It said that it would simply have to place Mr. Dillon's denial side by side with extracts from *The Irish World*, *The Freeman's Journal*, and *United Ireland*. That was to say that *The Times*, when confronted, did not pretend that it had any fresh evidence. All these articles which it had been swaggering and boasting about were merely a re-hash of accusations made again and again, and despised and refuted again and again by the Irish Members. The Irish Members had not brought this matter before the House—it had been brought forward by a Conservative—but they had said that they were ready to accept any investigation by a Committee into their conduct. After that he thought they ought to treat with redoubled contempt any further lies, false letters, and accusations on the part of *The Times*, however much it might choose to misrepresent them. What was *The Times* that any such accusations should be treated as of importance? *The Times* was no Divine oracle sent down from Heaven; *The Times* was merely Mr. Walter. He had sat in that House with Mr. Walter, who was a quiet, decent, respectable man, no doubt; but he had never heard

Mr. Labouchere

of anybody who had paid the slightest attention to any single word that Mr. Walter had said in that House. [*Laughter, and Ministerial cries of* "No!"] No? Well, he congratulated Mr. Walter on the fact that there were three Gentlemen who had paid attention to his words; his followers were small in number, though, no doubt, important. The Irish Members had good authority and good precedent for treating with contempt everything that fell from *The Times*. *The Times* had attacked Mr. Cobden and the right hon. Member for Birmingham (Mr. John Bright) in a series of the most atrocious articles, and Mr. Cobden had written to the editor of *The Times* asking—

"Is it seriously contended that as often as you choose to pervert the sense of our speeches, and to charge us with a scheme of public robbery, the onus lies with us to disprove the imputation, and that we have no right to complain if we do not do so that we are henceforth to be treated as robbers?"

The Times had progressed since then; it now called people the associates of assassins; but the system was the same and ought to be treated in the same way, and he trusted that hon. Members below the Gangway would act as the right hon. Member for Birmingham and Mr. Cobden had acted. The fact was that the Tory Party were thoroughly in a bog. They might be dragged out of it by the brute force of their majority; but they would come out of it discredited and bespattered. This debate had been most useful to those sitting on the Opposition side of the House. It had clearly shown what was the meaning of all the vapourings about a desire for investigation, and it now appeared that neither *The Times* nor the Government dared to face an investigation. ["Oh, oh!" *and cheers.*] Hon. Gentlemen opposite laughed. Did they dare to face the investigation? Would they change their minds now at the eleventh hour, and allow the investigation to take place? This debate might also teach hon. and right hon. Gentlemen opposite a useful lesson—namely, never to pay in advance for political services. If they were wise they would learn experience by what had occurred. In future they would probably never make their Baronets at the commencement of a Parliament. They would wait till the end. They might rest assured that the recipient of promotion so prematurely conferred would be extremely anxious to make it believed that he was made a Baronet on his own merits. He would be sure to take an opportunity of acting against his own Party in order to show what an independent man he was. While he condoled with hon. Members opposite for the Baronet they had made, and for the cruel return they had received, they on the Opposition side of the House were sincerely and truly thankful to the hon. Baronet for having done them an inestimable service by enabling them to repel these charges which had been brought against their Friends in Ireland, and by showing that when they were perfectly ready to face an investigation, hon. Members opposite ran away.

MR. OSBORNE MORGAN (Denbighshire, E.) said the hon. baronet the Member for North Antrim had certainly managed to bring about a debate which had been most damaging to the Government, and this was the opinion of their own journal, *The Standard*. There were two points that distinguished this case from that of any precedent that had been quoted. The charges complained of did not appear in an isolated article. There had been a series of articles blackening and maligning the character of five-sixths of the Irish Representatives, and those articles were written not merely for the purpose of influencing public opinion, but for the deliberate purpose of influencing the votes of certain Members upon a certain measure before the House. They were intended, as had been well said, to make the weak-kneed Liberal Unionists stick to their guns and to bind them closer to the Ministerial chariot. The House had already declared that these charges did not constitute a Breach of Privilege, but if they did not, what in Heaven's name did? The right hon. and learned Gentleman the Member for Bury had said that Privilege was a rusty sword. If that Resolution was to hold good, it was, it would seem, something even worse—it was a Government cutlass. It seemed now that the whole idea of Breach of Privilege, which had lasted these hundreds of years, was at the bidding of a Conservative Government, to vanish like a dream. The Ministerial decision was enough to make some of the Speaker's Predecessors turn in their graves. It amounted to this—that the

foulest and blackest and most unfounded charges might be brought, not only against one Member but against some 80 or 90 Members, and that when those charges were solemnly denied in this House, that denial was made an occasion for restating the charges, and the hon. Members who denied them were branded as liars, and yet that was not a matter of Privilege. An hon. Member had said that the House was the guardian of its own honour. All he could say was the present views held by the majority of the House on the question of Privilege that guardianship would be the merest sinecure ever imposed on a great assembly. The noble Lord the Member for South Paddington (Lord Randolph Churchill) had urged that the Members attacked should bring, what he once called, "a more or less collusive action in a Court of Law. In the meantime, however, they were to be assumed to be guilty. This was a strange perversion of the old English maxim, that a man was to be presumed to be innocent until he was proved to be guilty—a privilege which we conceded to the meanest criminal at the bar, but which we denied to the chosen representatives of the Irish nation. But since the House had decided that this was not a Breach of Privilege, what right had the Government to spend public money in prosecuting a newspaper which had not committed a Breach of Privilege? The hon. Member for East Mayo refused, and quite rightly, to enter any such prosecution. He would go into Court with all the prejudices against him due to the fact that this House had refused him the protection which the House usually afforded to its Members. The right hon. and learned Member for Bury (Sir Henry James) said that fact would not be before the jury. But of course it would be in the minds of the jury. The right hon. and learned Gentleman also denied that there would be any delay, and he said the whole matter could be decided in six weeks. Would he contend that it was possible to instruct counsel and get the witnesses from America in six weeks? Reference had also been made to the Judges. He would not say a word in disparagement of the present members of the Judicial Bench; but judges were men, and it was well known that one of them at least had spoken on this Irish Question in terms of extreme bitterness and acrimony. He did not for a moment suggest that there would not be a fair trial before Mr. Justice Stephen; but a Judge, like Cæsar's wife, ought to be above suspicion; and what would those who throughout the country sympathized with the hon. Member for East Mayo think of a trial before that learned Judge? As to the jury, that was an unknown quantity. For his own part he very much doubted whether any Irish Home Ruler would get a fair trial before a Special Jury of London stockbrokers. And there was this essential difference between a jury and a Committee of this House—that one juror could render the trial abortive. It was said that Party feeling was so strong that it would not be possible to get an impartial Committee; but he considered it a gross reflection on the character of the House to say that out of its 670 Members it would not be possible to select 15 or 16 English and Scotch Gentlemen who would do their duty. The noble Lord the Member for South Paddington said that the House of Commons was powerless against the Press, that all the House could do was to grovel before this many-headed and many-tongued monster. That was the most humiliating position to take up. Would the noble Lord have taken that view if the character of 86 Conservative Members had been at stake? The result of the action of the Government would be that the opinion would grow up in the country, and it would be very difficult to disprove it, that the application of the law of Privilege depended, like so many other questions, upon considerations of nationality and race. The country would get the idea that as the Government were determined to establish two standards of crime, one for Englishmen and another for Irishmen, so they were determined to establish two standards of Privilege, one for English Members and another for Irish Members. He appealed to the Liberal Unionists, who were so anxious to have one and the same law for England and Ireland, and who, he supposed, managed to reconcile that wish with their votes in support of coercion—he appealed to them to support the right hon. Member for Mid Lothian in the approaching Division. Of this he was sure, that nothing could do

more to widen the breach between the two nations, which, Heaven knew, was wide enough already, and to precipitate the crisis which they were anxious to avert, than the course which the Government, with the aid of their mechanical majority, were pursuing.

Mr. ANDERSON (Elgin and Nairn) said, he would warn the House to be careful before they rushed to admiration of British juries in a political case. He would take up the challenge of the right hon. and learned Member for Bury to produce a case which showed that they could not be trusted in times of political excitement. In 1881 six persons were charged with bribery committed at the recent Boston election. The cases were tried before Mr. Justice Stephen at the Lincoln Assizes, and the defendants were all acquitted. Describing the result of one of the Boston cases, *The Times*, which was so much in favour with the Party opposite, said that after a long deliberation the jury returned a verdict of "Not Guilty." After the verdict there was a loud outburst of applause, especially on the two front benches, which were reserved for the jurymen in waiting. That was a specimen of the independence of juries on political matters. The Judge then ordered "the man with the red face," as *The Times* described one of these expectant jurymen, to be brought forward, and he turned out to be a farmer of 200 or 300 acres, and fined him £5. The Judge was then informed that the delinquent was one of the jurors in the next case. The Judge then expressed his opinion that the public should be informed of this state of things, and ordered that that particular juror should not be called upon. This was the sort of jury to which the Irish Members were told to go. He hoped he had met the challenge of the right hon. and learned Gentleman. *The Times* commented in the most caustic terms on the sympathy of Lincolnshire jurymen with bribers, and said that grave dissatisfaction would be generally felt at the existence of such a state of things. *The Times* further said that the person charged with perjury and acquitted was charged practically on his own confession, and that in refusing to convict the Lincolnshire jury had, perhaps, only done what other juries had done all over the country in political cases, that the juryman who was fined £5 was probably

Mr. Osborne Morgan

neither better nor worse than his fellows, and that they only shared in the common local feeling. What had been the course of the Government in this matter? The hon. Baronet brought forward his Motion. A conference then took place between the Leaders of the Government and the Law Officers, and the decision was arrived at not to accept the hon. Baronet's Motion. The offer of the Government was that the case should be tried before a jury by means of a criminal information. Did the Government, in making that offer, honestly believe that it would be accepted? They knew perfectly well, for they had heard it over and over again, that the Irish Members would decline to go before a jury. The Solicitor General knew it, the Attorney General knew it, and every Member of the Government knew it. The Government had found themselves in a corner. They found that the hon. Baronet (Sir Charles Lewis) had played a card honestly as far as he was concerned, but a very false one so far as the Government were concerned, and they wanted to get out of the difficulty, so they resorted to another card trick. [*Cries of* " Oh, oh! " *from the Ministerial Benches.*] He called it the card trick— [*Cries of* " Oh, oh ! "]—not in any offensive sense. [*Renewed cries of* "Oh, oh!" *and a Voice*, "Certainly not."] There were so many games of cards, and he was referring to innocent games, playful games. [*Cries of* " Withdraw ! " *from the Ministerial Benches, and* " No, no!" *from the Opposition.*]

THE SOLICITOR GENERAL (Sir EDWARD CLARKE) (Plymouth): I rise to Order, Mr. Speaker. I wish to ask whether the hon. Member is within the bounds of courtesy and Order in saying that the Attorney General and the Solicitor General had resorted to another card trick?

MR. SPEAKER: It is not a Parliamentary expression, and I hope the hon. and learned Member will withdraw it.

MR. ANDERSON said, he willingly withdrew the expression, but he thought he had conveyed to the House that he did not use it in any offensive sense, but only in the way it was used every day. What he wished to convey to the House was that the Government in proposing that there should be a criminal prosecution must have known that their proposal would not be accepted, as the Irish Members had already refused to take such a course. This was not playing the game fairly. The Government had been most unfair; they knew that a prosecution could not be confined to the Dillon article of the 2nd of May, but must extend to a far larger field. Their proposal, however, simply included the Dillon article, and had no reference to the alleged forged letter. Perhaps the Government had found that the latter could not be substantiated. They knew that if they went before a jury that letter would be excluded; but if a Committee were granted it might inquire into the alleged forged letter and all the charges which had been brought against hon. Members below the Gangway. [Sir EDWARD CLARKE: Read the Amendment.] Perhaps that was another technical objection. He supposed that it was possible to amend the Amendment so as to include any charge which had ever been made against hon. Members below the Gangway. He hoped the Chancellor of the Exchequer would get up and say that he would accept a general inquiry, because he felt certain that nothing less than such an inquiry would be satisfactory to the country.

THE CHANCELLOR OF THE EXCHEQUER (Mr. GOSCHEN) (St. George's, Hanover Square): Mr. Speaker, the hon. and learned Member who has just sat down (Mr. Anderson) has indirectly criticized the Amendment which is submitted to us by the right hon. Gentleman the Member for Mid Lothian (Mr. W. E. Gladstone). He has asked the Government why they cannot extend this matter to a general inquiry into all the charges which have been made against hon. Members who represent the Nationalist Party in Ireland? Why has he not addressed that question to his own Leader? I suppose it is because, as yet, his own Leader has not re-appeared in the House, and is not at present sitting on the Bench opposite. [*Cries of* "Oh!" *from the Irish Members.*] Yes; it is an absence which I regret. I am aware that right hon. Gentlemen opposite have expected a Member of Her Majesty's Cabinet to intervene at this moment in the debate; and, if so, I think that we might also fairly claim—[*Cries of* " Oh ! "]—I think that we might fairly claim the presence of my right hon.

Friend; and I will say why, and will leave hon. Members themselves to determine whether they think it is best that the right hon. Gentleman should be criticized in his absence or in his presence. It will be my duty to comment upon some of the statements of my right hon. Friend; and, at all events, it will not be my fault, if I do not see him before me in this House and able to accept or to contradict the construction which I shall put on certain of the expressions which he has addressed to us. But the hon. and learned Member who has just sat down taunts the Government with attempting to limit this inquiry. Do I interpret him rightly? Why, he has also vanished from the House; and I am, therefore, unable to elicit a reply from him. [*Cries of* "Oh!" *from the Irish Members.*] I do not understand the remonstrance which comes from hon. Members below the Gangway opposite. Do they not think that I am entitled to ask what was the effect of the speech of the hon. and learned Member? What was the effect of that speech? I say that, as regards the Amendment which is now before the House, the Government have absolutely no responsibility whatever. I admit the objection which my right hon. Friend has made to the proposition I am laying down. The hon. Baronet the Member for North Antrim (Sir Charles Lewis) submitted a limited Motion to this House. The hon. and learned Solicitor General has moved that this case is not a Breach of Privilege. On that, my right hon. Friend the Member for Mid Lothian confines his Amendment to this one particular point of the alleged falsehood charged against the hon. Member for East Mayo (Mr. Dillon). If the issue is limited, it is not the fault of the Government, and I feel sure that right hon. Gentlemen opposite are perfectly aware that I am stating the case correctly and fully. Whether the Amendment is to be extended or not does not rest with Her Majesty's Government. It rests with those who have chosen to submit this Amendment now before the House, for the appointment of a Select Committee. It rests with the right hon. Gentleman the Member for Mid Lothian to determine what scope he will give to his own Motion, and it is rather hard upon the Government, on the fourth night of this

debate, to have it thrown in their teeth that they do not know what the scope of that Motion is, and that we are attempting to limit it. Do the Opposition stand by the Motion which they have made, or do they wish to change it on the fourth night of this debate? Do they wish to change the issue after they have been fighting upon this particular issue for the last three nights? They are silent upon that point; but, perhaps, at a later hour of the evening, we may hear what course they intend to pursue, though I think it will be rather late for them to make a change of front. Now, Mr. Speaker, I would wish to make a remark which I should have preferred to make in the presence of my right hon. Friend the Member for Mid Lothian. I wish he were present in his capacity of Leader of Her Majesty's Opposition and of the united Party who sit above the Gangway and below the Gangway. Let me recall the attention of the House to a painful incident, if I may call it so. Let me recall to the notice of the House the observations which fell from the hon. and learned Member for North Longford (Mr. T. M. Healy) with regard to the Leader of this House—to the personalities which the hon. and learned Member chose to pour out with regard to the Leader of this House and the Leader of the Conservative Party. Well, Sir, I think my right hon. Friend (Mr. W. H. Smith) can well afford to pass by the observations which were made by the hon. and learned Member, and the House, though it felt it was a painful thing to listen to that flood of personalities, will also pass them by; but I should have liked to know what was the feeling of the Leader of the Opposition when he heard that new style from his allies below the Gangway. [An hon. MEMBER: He was not here.] [An hon. MEMBER on the Ministerial side: He cheered them.] My right hon. Friend the Member for Derby (Sir William Harcourt) was not present, and I can tell him that the Leader of the Opposition was present, and I felt for my right hon. Friend. [*Cries of* "Oh!" *from the Irish Members.*] Yes; I am not surprised at the scoffs from hon. Members below the Gangway, for they do not know how my right hon. Friend has been the guardian of the best traditions of this House, and with what pain expressions and personalities

Mr. Goschen

such as proceeded from the hon. and learned Member for North Longford must have fallen on the ears of a man who has been the associate of a Palmerston, of a Russell, and of all the great statesmen of his time. Mr. Speaker, the Law Officers of the Crown have placed before this House, and with conspicuous ability, the case of the precedents which govern this matter, and they have not been overthrown by hon. Gentlemen opposite. [*Cries of "Oh!" from the Irish Members.*] I do not know whether all the Members of this House were present when the right hon. Member for East Wolverhampton (Mr. Henry H. Fowler) admitted that there was no precedent analogous to the present situation. But leaving the more legal and technical part of the case to the Law Officers of the Crown, I am anxious to establish, and I believe I can undertake to establish, that this case is totally different from any other of the alleged precedents where there have been Committees of Inquiry or Votes of this House in regard to Breach of Privilege. I can undertake to show that there are considerations in this matter that are totally different, and which remove this case entirely from the region of precedent, even if it were possible to establish formal precedents in this instance. One word I may perhaps be allowed to say in regard to the precedents that have been alleged. It has been shown by my right hon. and learned Friend the Member for Bury (Sir Henry James), that in almost every instance the precedents which have been quoted, and alleged to govern this case, have been cases in which the conduct of a Member has been impugned in his capacity of acting in the particular service of the House. To-night a new precedent has been quoted—but a precedent not with regard to the proposal of an inquiry, but on the point of Breach of Privilege; and I ask the House to draw a distinction between the case of an examination by a Committee and a Vote of the House as regards Privilege. A new case has been cited with regard to my right hon. Friend the Member for Birmingham (Mr. John Bright), where the House took action, and where there was a Vote of the House in reference to words spoken by my right hon. Friend. Does the right hon. Member for East Wol-

verhampton say that that bears on the present case? He is silent.

MR. HENRY H. FOWLER (Wolverhampton, E.): It certainly bears upon the present case. I simply said that it went to show that Members of the present Administration are inconsistent in saying that a charge against Members of this House of being in alliance with murderers and assassins is not a Breach of Privilege. In the case of the right hon. Member for Birmingham, they voted that being in alliance with the Irish Rebels was a Breach of Privilege.

MR. GOSCHEN: Have we asserted that a Breach of Privilege has not been committed? Has that been the object of hon. Members on this side of the House? [*Ironical cheers from the Irish Members, and interruption.*] My right hon. Friend opposite, who objects to so great an extent to interruptions from this side—and I believe my hon. Friends on this side of the House are probably still smarting from the castigation which he has administered to them sometimes for their interruption—will now be able to judge, from the conduct of his allies below the Gangway, to what extent example may be infectious. I am not quite so sensitive as some right hon. Gentlemen to interruptions. They seem to me to be often a tonic and a stimulus to a speaker. At the same time, I ask hon. Gentlemen opposite—as followers of my right hon. Friend who objects to continuous interruption—to give me a fair, if not a very patient, hearing during the observations which I feel it my duty to address to the House. Sir, I was speaking of the precedent of my right hon. Friend the Member for Birmingham, and the right hon. Member for East Wolverhampton says that it is an analogous case to this.

MR. HENRY H. FOWLER: No.

MR. GOSCHEN: Then it is not analogous?

MR. HENRY H. FOWLER: No.

MR. GOSCHEN: Then I think that the right hon. Gentleman has wasted his time. But if his observations should have any effect on any Members in this House, or on the public outside, let me, in a sentence, point out the great difference between the two cases. In the case of my right hon. Friend the Member for Birmingham, it was a Member

[*Fourth Night.*]

of this House who uttered the alleged libel, and he was amenable to the jurisdiction of this House; and, in the next place, that libel, if it was a libel, was not uttered against any particular person who might have brought an action in a Court of Law, but uttered against a body of men, in which case no action would lie. And that is the great distinction in all these cases. These precedents and these cases, where there has been no other Court open than a Court of Inquiry by this House, are not analogous to this case, and cannot guide us on this occasion. Our position in this case is this—and it governs the whole situation and the whole issue— namely, that there are tribunals open to those who have a complaint to make —the tribunals of the land, and that in most of the cases where an alleged analogy is sought to be found, there was no such appeal to any other tribunal. I will not labour this question of precedents, because I am prepared to contend, that whatever precedents may be quoted, there are none really similar to the present situation, and that we must be guided, apart from precedents, by higher considerations in this matter. In some of the cases that have been cited, the libellers, the defendants, have been summoned to the Bar of the House, and, refusing to apologize, have been committed to prison. And I remember a most eloquent passage in a speech of the hon. Member for East Mayo (Mr. Dillon), in which he said he should like to see his antagonist—that foul liar, he called him—standing at the Bar of the House, face to face with him. But what object would the hon. Member have achieved if the object of his denunciation, his opponent, had been standing at the Bar of the House? No inquiry would have been possible; and the result, judging by most of the precedents that have been quoted, would simply have been that, without any inquiry, the defendant at the Bar would have been committed to prison. Is not that the teaching of the precedents which have been quoted? Then what is the good of heroics, and saying that you will meet your accuser at the Bar of the House, if the encounter that would take place must be entirely barren of any result whatever? I have said that I would not dwell upon precedents. We have to deal with this mat-

Mr. Goschen

ter, as is now acknowledged on both sides of the House, apart from precedents; but before I pass on to make good the contention I seek to establish, that this is a case perfectly different from any other that has ever arisen, I wish to ask the House whether, notwithstanding the gravity of the charges which are at issue—and the right hon. Member for Mid Lothian was in error if he thought we do not admit the gravity of them— I wish to ask whether these charges, however grave they may be, ought to be tried, as suggested, as a matter of Privilege? It is scarcely necessary for me to insist on a point that was so eloquently treated by my right hon. and learned Friend the Member for Bury earlier in the evening, as to the danger and inexpediency of extending the doctrine of Privilege and the practice of inquiry on important public matters of general interest by what I may call the domestic tribunal of this House. My right hon. Friend the Member for Mid Lothian charged the Leader of the House with being indifferent to the honour of its Members. It is a charge that is most undeserved, and a charge which will be repudiated, not only by Members sitting on this side of the House, but, I am convinced, by a large proportion of hon. Members sitting on that (the Opposition) side of the House also. But the Leader of the House has other functions, besides that of looking to the honour of individual Members of the House. He has to see that we do not, by claiming too much Privilege, imperil the authority of the House of Commons on questions which are at issue between this House and others who are outside its walls. I am surprised to see that the Leaders and the chief bulwarks of the Liberal Party are prepared to vote in a direction which will curtail freedom of speech on the part of the Press. That has not been the line which they have taken in those past cases which have been quoted; and when the right hon. Member for East Wolverhampton charges Members sitting on this side of the House with inconsistency, he, at the same time, refers to cases where his hon. Friends voted against the extension of Privilege, and on the very ground that we ought not by any hasty action to restrain the greatest freedom on the part of the Press. We heard from the hon. and learned Member for Dumfries (Mr. R. T. Reid), the other night, that the Liberal Party expected a political advantage from the refusal by this House of the Committee which is asked for. ["Hear, hear!" *from the Irish Members.*] Is it for the sake of that political advantage that they are acting? [*Cries of* "No!"] Let hon. Members below the Gangway reconcile their cheers with those of hon. Members above the Gangway. Will they take up a totally different position from that which they took up on almost every other occasion in recent years when the question of Privilege has been discussed? It is for hon. Members who are better conversant with the precedents and the legal aspect of the question than I am to argue the case; but I would ask, is it wise in these days to take up the position we are now asked to take up in all cases where Members of this House are libelled by the Press, or by anyone outside it? I think if we were to take up that position, we might as well establish at once a permanent Committee for the examination of libels. Why, look at the Irish Press. If we were to take up the position, that when the characters of Members are attacked, they are to be taken charge of by this House, it would be necessary for us to have the editor of *United Ireland* in permanent attendance at the Bar of this House. And, indeed, Sir, it is a very interesting sight to see the owners of and the writers in the Irish Press indignantly fulminating against the wicked slanders of *The Times.* What time would be occupied by this House if we were to undertake this new duty which my right hon. Friend the Member for Mid Lothian thinks ought to be discharged by the Leader of the House. [Mr. W. E. GLADSTONE: I did not say anything of the kind.] What! Did not my right hon. Friend complain of the Leader of the House for not being more sensitive with regard to the honour of its Members? Well, but there are other hon. Members whose honour is attacked in the Irish Press. ["Name, name!"] "Name?" yes, you shall have names. Did my right hon. Friend treat as matters of Privilege the articles in which Lord Spencer and Sir George Trevelyan were assailed by the Irish Press? I only wish the cartoons in *United Ireland* could be circulated to every Member of this House and sown broadcast through this country, and then we should know what slanders and libels are. And it is in these conditions, and with this license of the Press constantly going on, and habitually tolerated, that we are asked to interfere upon this particular occasion. See what the demand is that is made on us. It was well put by my right hon. and learned Friend the Member for Bury; but I will put it again, because we have had a most interesting illustration of this very practice to-night. My right hon. and learned Friend has pointed out that certain things are said in this House—certain charges are made against Members, not as Members of this House. These charges are denied in this House. The persons who are responsible for the original assertions say that the denial is false, and then their conduct is to be inquired into by a Committee of this House. That is the claim which is made by hon. Members opposite. Now, what I want to know is this. Do we claim as our Privilege this, that we may denounce persons outside this House, and that if they deny the assertions made by us, they are to be brought up before a Committee of this House? The hon. and learned Member for North Langford uttered serious allegations against *The Times*, which I can perfectly conceive *The Times* might consider to be extremely slanderous. I do not use the word myself; but I think *The Times* might consider them to be slanderous, and to-morrow morning, under this new doctrine of Privilege, or under the exercise of the Privilege now claimed by the Liberal Party, I presume *The Times* might have a blank column side by side with the hon. Member's speech, and might say—"We cannot declare that the hon. Member has uttered slanders against us; because, if we did so, we might bring ourselves within the doctrine of Privilege, the printer might be summoned to the Bar, and a Committee of Inquiry might be appointed—a domestic tribunal of Members of the House of Commons—to investigate whether we were justified in denying what we consider to be slanders upon ourselves." Slanders may be uttered by Members of this House, as well as against Members, and the best tribunal to decide what is or is not slander is a Court of Law. Now, I will

[Fourth Night.]

undertake to endeavour to show to the House that the present case differs from all other cases which have come before the House, and which are alleged to be precedents in a certain sense. What is the present case? It is a charge brought against a particular Member; but in this case the Members of the Irish Party associate themselves with that hon. Member, and the hon. and learned Member for North Longford has stated, boldly and bravely, and I think another hon. Member has made the same assertion, that they associate themselves entirely with the hon. Member for East Mayo. ["Hear, hear!" *from the Irish Members.*] Thus we are to try, not this particular charge, but the character of 86 Members of this House. [*Cries of* "If you like!"] If we like. I wish to know whether, in some of the speeches which have been made, the association has not been absolute. Hon. Members have asserted that what we should be really trying by a Committee would be the character of the Irish National Party, and the hon. Member went further than that, and he said that the character of the Liberal Party would also be at stake. I do not deny it, nor, in frankness be it conceded, was it repudiated by my right hon. Friend the Member for East Wolverhampton. He said—"Our character is at stake," and he immediately proceeded to ask that the Members whose character is impugned should be made the judges in their own cause. After having established that the character of the Liberal Party was deeply involved, and that this trial which is to take place of the 86 Members for Ireland, would involve also the trial of the whole of their allies, he said—"We are the best tribunal, I assure you, in the world to try this case." I can quite understand the view of my right hon. Friend.

Mr. HENRY H. FOWLER: I did not say so. ["Hear, hear!" *from the Irish Members.*]

Mr. GOSCHEN: A few spasmodic cheers approve of the statement of my right hon. Friend, that he did not say so. I think he will admit that at least he implied so, when he made that eloquent and impassioned appeal to which I listened, but to which a great many of those who cheered him did not listen, that the best tribunal in the world for trying the character of the Irish Party and their allies was a tribunal of which, of necessity, a large number of right hon. and hon. Members opposite would be a constituent part. Does he deny it?

Mr. HENRY H. FOWLER: Certainly.

Mr. GOSCHEN: Then, what did my right hon. Friend say? He will not deny that he said the tribunal was an excellent one.

Mr. HENRY H. FOWLER: I said that a Select Committee of this House was an excellent one, and the best tribunal.

Mr. GOSCHEN: Why, I am speaking of a Select Committee of this House. Although we have had generous offers from hon. Members below the Gangway, that for this occasion, and this occasion only, they would have confidence in Members on this side; yet they have taken good care, in asking for a Committee, to denounce the character of some of those who might sit upon it. I presume that the whole of the Committee would not be composed of hon. Members on this side of the House, but that a large number—as is the usual way, would be taken from that Party which my right hon. Friend adores. Well, I stand by my proposition, that, after having stated that the character of his Friends was involved, he said the character of the Liberal Party was at stake. [*Cries of* "No, no!"] Will my right hon. Friend do me the favour to contradict the statement of his hon. Friends behind him? Did he not say that the character of the Liberal Party was at stake? My right hon. Friend admits that it was so.

Mr. HENRY H. FOWLER: I said the character of the Liberal Party, and the character of the House.

Mr. GOSCHEN: Well, my right hon. Friend knows the point that was made by the hon. and learned Member for North Longford; it was a good point, and I entirely agree with it. I thought it was an admirable point. He said—

"We do not care about our characters being cleared; there is a much more important question; our characters are such that we do not care what becomes of them."

Mr. T. C. HARRINGTON (Dublin, Harbour): Our character is as good as yours, and much higher in the estima tion of the Irish people. He said that it was yours that required to be cleared.

MR. GOSCHEN : Cannot hon. Members below the Gangway endure for a moment any kind of attack upon themselves, when their attacks upon us are so fierce? I trust they will endeavour to exercise the self-control which, although sometimes, I must confess, under great provocation, we have endeavoured to use. And this reminds me of another point to which I desire to call attention before I forget it. The hon. Member alluded to the constituencies of Great Britain; he said he would appeal from this House to the constituencies. It was to the constituencies and not to a jury his eloquent appeals were to be made—to the country and not to twelve men selected to sit in a jury-box, and sworn on their oath to give a true deliverance according to the evidence. I was led aside by the doubt thrown upon my statement, that it was alleged, truly or untruly, that the character of the Liberal Party was at stake. Now, let me ask the House seriously to consider among all the declarations which have been made, what is the issue to be tried before a Committee, and who are to be the judges to try it? I said that this did not resemble any of the other cases that had been brought before us. And why? It is not a case of investigating a particular offence. It is not as the hon. Member for North Longford said, a question of investigating the conduct of a particular man; but a Party, he says, is to be tried; 86 Members of this House are to be tried. [An hon. MEMBER: Nonsense!] That was the statement made by the hon. Member for North Longford. I wish to know where we are. [*Cries of* "Hear, hear!"] Yes, you cheer that statement; but is it so or not? I wish to know where we are. Am I right in saying that the hon. Member for North Longford stated that it was the character of the 86 Members from Ireland?

MR. T. M. HEALY (Longford, N.): If the right hon. Gentleman wants to know, I meant to convey that we did not take our stand on any narrow technicality in reference to the charge made against the hon. Member for East Mayo. I added that we repudiated the idea of taking our stand upon any technicality, and I said that if there was any specific charge against any one of us, or against 50 Members of the Party, we were quite willing that any specific allegation against us, as well as the specific allegation against the hon. Member for East Mayo, should be fully gone into by a Committee of this House.

MR. GOSCHEN: Yes, but my memory is absolutely certain that these very words were used. I will not be certain they were used by the hon. Member for North Longford—" We associate ourselves (the whole Party) with the case of the hon. Member for East Mayo." And the whole was based on the assumption that it was not a simple issue or a small fact that was in dispute; but that it was the character of a Party. Well, such a matter has never in the history of this country been submitted to a Select Committee of this House. We are to try a Party. On such a Commtttee by whom is that Party to be tried? By the Representatives of two other Parties in this House, of which one has, on its own admission, its own character at stake, and the other has been denounced beforehand as incapable of giving an impartial judgment. I do not know whether hon. Members will remember the words of the hon. Member for the Scotland Division of Liverpool (Mr. T. P. O'Connor). What did he say of the Judges whom he invited to try the case? What did he say of hon. Members on this side of the House? The hon. Member said—

"I say that there is scarcely a Gentleman on those Benches who has not made himself a partner of and a fellow conspirator with the libellers against whom we protest."

[*Cheers.*] Hon. Gentlemen opposite, below the Gangway generally cheer a sentiment of this kind; but they did not cheer it when I read it out, because they see how fatal it is to their case. Well, if this trial is to take place who are to be the judges? " Fellow conspirators the libellers against whom we now protest" —that is to be one side of the tribunal and the other is to be the Representatives of the Party whose character is as much impugned as that of the hon. Member for East Mayo. A pretty tribunal to try the case, men denounced in advance as partizans, and men whose own character is said to be at stake. The hon. Member for the Scotland Division of Liverpool, speaking of a right hon. Member on

1203 *Privilege* (*Mr. Dillon and* {COMMONS} "*The Times*" *Newspaper*). 1204

this side of the House, said that he ought to be in the dock with the editor of *The Times*, and then we are to take people who ought to be in the dock and put them on the Select Committee. But, Mr. Speaker, I would call the serious attention of the House. [*An ironical cry of* "Hear, hear!"] I am glad to get that cheer from my right hon. Friend. Does not my right hon. Friend think that the argument I put forward deserves serious consideration? Does he think that the verdict of a Select Committee composed, as it must be composed under the circumstances of men denounced in advance by his Friends below the Gangway. [*Cries of* "No, no!"] Well, if hon. Gentlemen do not call such words as "fellow conspirators" a denunciation I do not know what a denunciation is. My right hon. Friend must see the serious importance of a case of this kind. Who can tell what the verdict of such a tribunal would be? I assume that we do not know—that hon. Members on that side of the House and hon. Members on this side of the House do not at the present moment know, and have not formed, a definite opinion as to the guilt or innocence of either Party concerned. But looking to the fact that while hon. Members say they will trust a Committee of this kind, other hon. Members of their Party have denounced hon. Gentlemen on this side of the House, and called them "fellow conspirators," what effect —and I ask my right hon. Friend's attention to this point—what effect is the verdict of the Committee likely to have? If the verdict should be a verdict of acquittal of the hon. Member for East Mayo and his Friends, then I admit they will be satisfied; but if the verdict should be a verdict of guilty, then they will fall back on the condemnation which has already been pronounced in advance on the Benches which are to supply the Judges. This is a most serious point to contemplate, and does not deserve any sneers from my right hon. Friend. And, again, what would be the position of hon. Members on this side who might be appointed to serve on that Committee? I ask hon. Members opposite—in fairness to consider the point I am going to put before them. I assume and the House must assume, that the guilt or innocence of either Party is still in dispute, and it is possible

Mr. Goschen

that either *The Times* or the hon. Member for East Mayo may be guilty. Then hon. Members on this side of the House who have been in violent opposition to the hon. Member for East Mayo and the whole Party of Irish Members, are to select men from themselves who are to go upstairs and sit in a Committee room. They are expected to shed all their political passions, and when they arrive in the Committee room they are to find themselves in an impartial atmosphere. Well, looking at the judicial inquiries which have been made by the House in the past, I am sorry to think that in many judicial cases the votes have been given according to Party interests. I believe that hon. Members would do their utmost to give an impartial verdict, and I believe this, too—that there would be an internal struggle in the breasts of hon. Members upstairs between their feelings as generous and honourable opponents, and their sense of the duty of a stern and impartial Judge. I fear they would be in the greatest possible difficulties. [*Cries of* "No, no!"] I hear a murmur of dissent. What, cannot hon. Members realize the position of a man who has been vilified and stung to the last degree by such words as sometimes fall from the hon. Member for North Longford and others, if, sitting on the Committee, he were to see such an opponent on his trial before him, who seemed to him on the brink of a precipice, and whom by two or three more searching questions he might push over the brink? I say that an hon. opponent might feel himself in the greatest embarrassment—might shrink from that final course of cross-examination. Can you not see—can you not appreciate when you yourselves say you will trust the honour of English gentlemen—the intolerable difficulty in which he might be placed? Are hon. Members to undertake the tremendous duty of cross-examination on a question of life or death to other hon. Members when they consider that they must meet afterwards in this House under the ordinary amenities of debate? Are you going to put this tremendous responsibility upon any hon. Member who might be selected to serve on such a Committee. Hon. and right hon. Gentlemen opposite have been extremely chary in explaining the *modus operandi* of a Committee of this kind.

Who is to conduct the cross-examination? Is it to be counsel? I think I heard words fall from the right hon. Member for Mid Lothian that Members of this House who were to be advocates from either side. Are hon. Members to undertake that tremendous duty, and are the incriminated parties to have no other counsel? [*Interruption.*] Are not the parties to this great issue, whose whole character and vital interests are at stake, to be at liberty to choose their own counsel who are to cross-examine the witnesses, and to guide them in their conduct of the case? I cannot believe for a moment that hon. and right hon. Gentlemen opposite will contend that they should not be allowed to have counsel, and if they are to be allowed to have counsel, then all that irrelevancy to which right hon. Gentlemen opposite object so much in a Court of Law will occur in the Committee as it occurs in a Court of Law. The Report of the Committee in Mr. Butt's case shows that it is as difficult for the Chairman of a Committee to check all irrelevancy and idle gossip as it is for a Judge of the land. Nay, it will be all the more difficult to check that irrelevancy, from the inexperience of Members of the Committee, in the conduct of trials of this nature. And this is the tribunal to which hon. and right hon. Members opposite wish to relegate a case of this enormous importance. And how do they arrive at the conclusion that they ought to select a Committee of that kind? They arrive at it by denouncing the tribunals of the land. Hon. and right hon. Members opposite have spent a great portion of their time in this debate in showing that juries cannot be trusted, and that Judges may possibly not be impartial. That is the dilemma into which they are driven in this case, and I am not sure whether this line of argument was not inaugurated by my right hon. Friend the Member for Mid Lothian. In the right hon. Gentleman's advocacy of the case of Home Rule it has become his duty, or what he considers to be his duty, to fall foul of many of the institutions of the land. Do right hon. Gentlemen opposite remember the attacks of the right hon. Gentleman upon the Irish Judges? Do they remember the attack upon the Irish Bench and upon the *dicta* of the Irish Bench?

And now it has fallen to the right hon. Gentleman to impugn the character of British juries and of British Judges. [*Cries of* "No, no!"] Yes; I say most distinctly that he has done that, and he has been followed in that course by the right hon. Gentleman the Member for East Wolverhampton (Mr. Henry H. Fowler), and by the hon. and learned Member for Elgin and Nairn, who preceded me in this debate (Mr. Anderson). They have thought it necessary to impugn the character of the Courts of Law, in order to attempt to drive this case before a less competent tribunal—namely, a Committee of this House. [*Cries of* "No!"]

MR. HENRY H. FOWLER (Wolverhampton, E.): I rise to Order. I never impugned the character of the Courts of Law. I distinctly declared the contrary. The right hon. Gentleman is not justified in his position. His statements are absolutely unfounded. [*Cries of* "Withdraw!"]

MR. GOSCHEN: I am not thinking of withdrawing. What was the object of the right hon. Gentleman in referring to the case of Lord Ellenborough? I think that there were other cases to which the right hon. Gentleman alluded to show the fallibility of juries.

MR. HENRY H. FOWLER: That is not impugning Judges.

MR. GOSCHEN: I say that he was impugning the Courts of Law, because, certainly, juries form a part of the Courts of Law.

MR. HENRY H. FOWLER: I said juries were not infallible.

MR. GOSCHEN: I am not surprised at the warmth of the right hon. Gentleman, because it is a very serious thing to be taxed with impugning British justice as it is administered in our Courts of law. But that is their argument. [*Cries of* "No!"]. The Irish Party have been invited not to go into our Courts of Law, because they were less likely to find adequate justice there than in a Committee of this House. Can that be denied? Is not the argument of hon. and right hon. Members opposite that hon. Members are less likely to find justice in a British Court of Law than before a Committee of this House? You will mark the silence of hon. Members opposite. We have had fair notice that we are to be accused before the country of shrinking from an inquiry. We are

[*Fourth Night.*]

to be charged with refusing an inquiry before a Committee of the House of Commons. I give fair notice to hon. and right hon. Members opposite that the country will be informed that they have thrown discredit upon British justice, and that they have done so in order to bring this case before a less competent tribunal, less well equipped with the necessary machinery for dealing with such a question, and having a less trained president. They have thrown, I say again, discredit upon the tribunals of the country. It is a court of honour which hon. Members below the Gangway are now anxious to avail themselves of — a court of honour, not a Court of Law—and the right hon. Member for Mid Lothian is prepared on this occasion only to have confidence in the intelligence of English gentlemen, and to appeal from the masses to the classes. No jury for us, taken from the ordinary masses of the population, but a domestic tribunal composed of the classes in the House. So that I think we can well afford to meet our opponents upon that ground. We are still prepared to say that we have confidence in the tribunals of the land. Exception has been taken to the course which we have proposed to take for giving facilities and providing for a trial in the Courts of Law; and do hon. Members scoff at the Courts of Law? [*Ironical Irish cheers.*] Every cheer which they utter clinches my argument.

MR. E. HARRINGTON (Kerry, W.): We are not afraid of your Courts of Law if you bring any charge against us before them.

MR. GOSCHEN: I am extremely grateful for the patience hon. Members below the Gangway opposite have shown me, although it has been my duty to speak somewhat strongly.

AN IRISH MEMBER: Do not mention it.

MR. GOSCHEN: I say that every cheer—yes, and every sneer—which is directed against the proposal Her Majesty's Government have made, strengthens the case I am anxious to put forward—that we are ready for inquiry and anxious to facilitate any inquiry which we can feel sure will be properly conducted. The right hon. Member for Mid Lothian said that ours was an unexampled offer. Yes; I admit that

Mr. Goschen

we have gone out of our way to make it. I admit that we have gone out of our way, but we have done so because we realize too full the gravity of the crisis. My right hon. Friend spoke in solemn words towards the end of his eloquent speech of the gravity of the question; and what did he call it? He called it an "International Question." My right hon. Friend is already borrowing largely from the vocabulary of the Nationalist Party, and is representing a difficulty and a difference between two portions of Her Majesty's subjects as an "International" Question—an adjective which hitherto, and I think my right hon. Friend's experience will confirm me, has been applied only to differences between foreigners and ourselves. The adjective struck strangely, I must admit, on my ear, falling from the lips of my right hon. Friend. But I admit the gravity of the charges which have been made, and it is because we are sensible of the gravity of those charges that we, as I say, have gone out of our way to offer to create a precedent, if you like to call it so—I say we have gone out of our way to create a precedent, because we consider it to be of Imperial importance that this matter should be cleared up. The difference between us is not as to whether there should be an inquiry or there should not We have for a long time felt that there should be an inquiry; but we think if there is to be one, it is the duty of this House to look to it that the inquiry should be of the most authoritative and searching character, such as would be conducted by those tribunals to which all classes of Her Majesty's subjects have been accustomed to look up, and that truth and justice will best be attained by having recourse to the Courts of Law of the Queen.

MR. DILLON (Mayo, E.): I do not propose to occupy the time of the House for more than a few moments. I have risen to take part in this debate simply because I thought it would not be convenient that this House should go to a Division without a few words from, and on behalf of, those hon. Members who sit by me on these Benches. We have all listened with attention—at least I know I have—to the right hon. Gentleman who has just spoken, and I dare say that many of us have admired the force and brilliancy of his speech; but, although brilliant and forcible, it seems to me it was throughout an attempt to conceal from this House the real issues which are before it, and it was all the more objectionable on account of the extraordinary debating power and brilliancy the right hon. Gentleman has at his command. In the very few words I ask permission of the House to address to it, I shall confine myself strictly to endeavouring to lay before the House what the position in which we stand is. What is the real position in which we stand? The right hon. Gentleman, in one of the loftiest flights and most brilliant passages of that eloquent speech, asked—"Is this the first time that hon. Members of this House have been libelled by the Press?" and he recalled to the recollection of hon. Members the days when *United Ireland* used to assail in a manner which I fully admit was exceedingly violent the Gentlemen who were responsible for the Government of Ireland. Does the right hon. Gentleman mean to pretend that there is any parallel between the assaults of *United Ireland* and the assaults committed upon us. One would suppose, to listen to the right hon. Gentleman, that he had forgotten what he was in the habit of doing—what the Chair would not allow us to do—of reading out in this House the assaults made in the columns of *United Ireland* on the character of hon. Members, and I doubt very much whether they were anything like as grievous as the assaults made in *The Times* upon us. We are not in the habit of reading out those assaults in this House, and this is a matter which is complained of in this instance. Let me for a moment, in reply to the statement of the right hon. Gentleman, and in reply to the right hon. Gentleman the Member for Bury (Sir Henry James), recall to the memory of the House exactly what has occurred, and answer the question which was asked by the right hon. Gentleman when he said—"I wish to know where we stand?" Some right hon. Gentlemen compared us to women who, having scratched out the eyes of our adversaries, then fly to our friends and ask them for protection. Sir, what has happened in this matter? This *Times* newspaper has pursued us not

for months, as has been stated, but for years. There is not a charge, as the right hon. Gentleman ought to remember, with the solitary exception of the forged letter—there is not a single charge in "Parnellism and Crime" which has not done duty over and over again. Not one solitary new fact is stated, not one single charge that we have not been accustomed to read *ad nauseam* in the columns of the newspaper, and did I appeal to this House for protection; did I invoke the Privilege of this House? No; I said, *The Times* may go on repeating those charges till the Day of Judgment, and I would not invoke the Privileges of the House. What did I do? When these charges were read in the House, I simply got up in my place and denied them; but I did not ask for Privilege. I denied the charges, trusting that the usual courtesy of the House would be extended even to an Irish Member, and that my denial would be accepted. But that was not all. Two days afterwards appeared in *The Times* the article which is now the subject of the debate. Did I then appeal to the House and ask for protection against *The Times*? Nothing of the sort; and if it had been left to my judgment, this House would have been spared the four days which have been spent on this matter. I did not appeal to the House for protection even when they made that assault, though I should have been entitled to do so; but when an hon. Baronet—a Member of this House—came down and used these articles here to charge me with being—to use strong language, though the only language that can adequately describe what was done—to charge me with having in this House deliberately told lies, and I will also say cowardly lies, I did then think that the period had arrived, having regard not to my own character, but to the character of the House, and having regard to the warm and sympathetic friends whom I have found in England, I did think that the time had arrived when I was bound, as a Member of this House—little as I care for the opinion of *The Times* newspaper —to take some action to put a stop to what had become a growing and persistent scandal—namely, the repetition of these charges within these walls. I say that this controversy had not its origin from these Benches. It was forced upon us, and I say that if I had not then accepted the challenge, and appealed to this House for protection, I should have been taunted with being a craven and a coward. When it has been said from those Benches that I am afraid to face a Committee of Inquiry, I thought, Sir, that the time had then come when, if necessary, as I had said already, in the interests of the honour of this House, these matters should be investigated—not of my own honour and interests, because, where is it that I care for my reputation? I care for my reputation in a country where *The Times* newspaper can never assail it. Every Englishman in this House looks at this matter from a different standpoint to myself. In Ireland *The Times* has no influence, and no matter what *The Times* says it could have no effect on my reputation. In what I did I considered that I was bound, as a Member of this House, to take that action, in order to protect the House from a repetition of the scenes which have been a disgrace to the Parliament of England during the past month. ["Oh, oh!"] Yes. Who originated those scenes? Is it your code of honour that we are to sit on these Benches, silent and cowering, while you call us liars across the Floor of the House? Sir, I thought the time had arrived when, in the interests of this House, this matter ought to be thoroughly gone into. Looking at it from the standpoint of English Members, if I wanted confirmation of that position, surely the scene which took place to-night, when I had to stand up and appeal, Sir, to your protection against that process which is reducing this House to little better than a bear garden, and when you intervened and expressed your opinion that the time had come when this business ought to end—I say if I wanted confirmation, I think the action of the hon. and gallant Member for North Armagh (Colonel Saunderson) has fully confirmed me. What I want to know, Sir, is this— Where is to be the end of this matter? We are going now to vote on the question whether there shall be an investigation or not, and do not let hon. Gentlemen allow themselves to be deceived by the rhetoric of the Chancellor of the Exchequer. The question you have got to decide to-night is—shall there be an

investigation, or shall there not? I do not propose to enter any more into the question of the relative merits of the proposals. That matter has been amply discussed. But supposing, for the sake of argument, I were to admit that the Courts of Law are competent—which I do not admit, and I have stated it over and over again—to deal with this matter, in the Courts of Law it will not be investigated. The question, therefore, you have got to decide to-night is—shall there be any investigation, or shall there not? Whatever our reasons may be, in the laws of duelling, be they good or be they bad, the old doctrine used to be, that the man who was challenged had the right to the choice of weapons; and let me point out that of all the arguments that were put from that Bench opposite, not one went to show that in this House we should go before a tribunal prejudiced in our favour. We have got two tribunals to select from— the Courts of Law and a Select Committee of this House, and if we say we feel more confidence in the capacity, in the competence, and in the fair play of a Committee of this House, ought not our decision to be final? But whether it ought to be, or ought not to be final, our decision is made, and by your vote to-night you will decide, I suppose, for ever, and I hope for ever—for I trust the House of Commons will not allow itself to be again led by any Tory Baronet into spending four days in discussing the question of Dillon and Sheridan—I trust you will decide for ever; and remember, the question is whether this matter shall be investigated or not. I do trust, I confess, to the honourable feeling of at least the majority of the Party opposite, that after what has occurred during the last four days, they will, out of respect for the House, if not from any respect they bear us, cease, at least within the walls of this House—they can do what they like in the Primrose League—from persisting in and repeating charges which must, if they are repeated here, lead to disorderly and disgraceful scenes in this House. We have offered, and I now repeat that offer for the last time, to consent that the reference to the Committee shall not be narrowed to the question which is brought before the House by the Amendment. We are willing that the refer-

Mr. Dillon

ence shall be widened so as to include the question of the authenticity of the letter attributed to my hon. Friend the Member for Cork (Mr. Parnell), and widened so as to include every other charge which any Member opposite can select from "Parnellism and Crime." We believe, whether from good reasons or from bad reasons, that a Committee of this House is the most competent machinery by which the whole of the business can be thoroughly investigated, and the whole of the truth made clear; and I now deliberately allege, on behalf of my Colleagues, as well as on my own behalf, that we have now in our hands clues which we have good reason to hope would enable us to trace the forgers of the forged letter, and to expose the entire of this conspiracy in its nakedness to the British public. We appeal to you as honourable men, and as Gentlemen, not to deny us this opportunity. We appeal to you, not for our own sakes, I say once more—because I am willing to defy *The Times* and all its legion of forgers and of liars—but we appeal to you for your own sakes, for your own reputation as honourable men, as gentlemen and Englishmen with a spirit of fair play—we appeal to you for the sake, if it be dear to you, of the future relations of the people of Ireland and of England, whether they live under a system of Home Rule—[An hon. MEMBER on the Ministerial side : Never.] —or under a Unionist Government—we appeal to you, as you look to a future in which these two peoples shall cease to hate and distrust one another, to take this opportunity—which every man of you has said he was anxious to get— to allow us to clear our characters, not before our own people, but before your people ; to take this opportunity of removing what, if it be left, must inevitably prove a festering and poisonous sore. In going into the Lobby to-night remember the question upon which you are voting; and those who vote against this Amendment must remember that they will have resting upon their heads the full responsibility if this whole business be never investigated.

SIR WILLIAM HARCOURT (Derby): The Chancellor of the Exchequer asked us where we stood. I think, after the speech and the appeal which has just been made by the hon. Member for East

Mayo. [*Ministerial laughter.*] I am astonished that any hon. Gentleman should jeer. It shows the sort of spirit that actuates hon. Gentlemen on the other side of the House—I should have thought that an appeal of that kind, whether accepted or not, might have been treated with respect. But, at all events, whatever may be the case with Gentlemen who sit on the Benches opposite, of this I am certain that the people of this country will regard that appeal as a serious one that requires to be seriously considered and dealt with. Let me very briefly—for the hour is late—endeavour to show how it seems to me this question comes before the House. In the first place, this question of *The Times* newspaper was introduced in the House of Commons by a Member sitting on the opposite side of the House. He claimed that it should be treated as a question of Privilege. The Government having, in the first place, expressed a doubt whether it was a question of Privilege or not, instead of being taken up by the Leader of the House and treated upon his own responsibility—as I have heard questions of Privilege treated before—it was handed over to the Law Officers of the Crown to be treated, not according to the great traditions of Parliament, but by what I can only call most extraordinary special pleading. But, Sir, the remarkable part of it is that after the hon. and learned Solicitor General had argued that this was not a question of Privilege at all, he had not the courage of his own opinions ; because, in the Motion he has made, he has not ventured to say that it is not a question of Privilege. He said a very different thing ; he said the House should refuse to treat it as a question of Privilege. Why is this ? To assert that it is not a question of Privilege is to assert a thing which I venture to say, after this debate, no man can pretend. No such a case or anything like it has ever been brought before the House of Commons which has not been admitted to be a question of Privilege. The noble Lord the Member for South Paddington (Lord Randolph Churchill), though he calls it a technical matter, admits that it is so. My right hon. and learned Friend the Member for Bury (Sir Henry James) has not denied that it is a question of Privilege. But, says the Chancellor of the Exchequer — "How can you deal with it as a question of Privilege, when it is a question of a whole Party?" Has that never arisen before? Why, Sir, what is the case which was introduced by the hon. and learned Solicitor General I think in this debate? There was the opinion given by Mr. Disraeli when Leader of the House upon a question of Privilege. What was that? It was an attack by an hon. Member upon a whole Party. There was no allegation as to the conduct of any individual with reference to any particular act which came within any of the fanciful and original categories of the hon. and learned Solicitor General. It was a statement that the Liberal Party consorted with a disreputable gang of Irish Members. Is that Privilege, or is it not? Let me read the words of Mr. Disraeli—

"I am not here to deny that it is a Breach of Privilege to speak of any Members of this House in their capacity as such in terms which simply disgrace, or, as the hon. Gentleman said, ignominy."—(3 *Hansard*, [222] 330.)

I want to know whether you, on that side of the House, accept that definition of Privilege or not? But what is the consequence of that? These are the words of Mr. Disraeli—["Irish Members were entitled to receive satisfaction for such a statement as that, and if no apology was made, they would treat it as a matter of Privilege."] Well, therefore, that disposes of the whole of the categories of the hon. and learned Solicitor General. There is no charge of corruption here; there were none of the qualifications to which he referred; and I will pass from the question of precedents. Then, the Government say, first of all, that is not a question of Privilege at all. That they have been utterly unable to prove, but they decline to deal with it in the form of action against *The Times* newspaper—such action as is taken in some cases upon matters of Privilege. I will not argue that now. I should hardly be in Order after the Division which has been taken in the House in entering upon it; but they made a proposal for a prosecution by the Attorney General as a substantive Motion. I am sorry I do not see the hon. and learned Gentleman the Attorney General here, because he complained last night of my absence, and invited me to be here to answer for my

Sir William Harcourt

words at Southampton. He was very indignant with me for what I said, and exercised a right which belongs to his Office, the right of challenge. He invited me to meet him on the other side of the Solent. I should be very happy to meet the hon. and learned Gentleman anywhere, if he will allow me to make it a friendly meeting. Somewhere about August—at the Cowes meeting—I should be very happy to meet him there. But he objects to the language I used when I referred, in speaking of the Government proposition, to the story of Little Red Riding Hood. I thought that was very appropriate. A prosecution of this kind conducted by the Attorney General was, I pointed out, an absurd and monstrous proposition. How was this thing announced to the House? They are shamed out of it now. When the First Lord of the Treasury announced the course that was to be taken, these were his words—

"The Attorney General coupled with any Queen's counsel whom they may select, shall be instructed to prosecute *The Times* newspaper."

I do not think this hostile meeting in the Isle of Wight, which the Attorney General proposes to me, is really at all necessary, because we are both agreed. I think it would be most improper, not on account of anything personal to the Attorney General, but on account of his position with reference to the question, that this prosecution should be conducted by him. Well, he thinks so, too. He takes immense credit for saying that he is only to be nominally connected with the affair in which the prosecution is to be in his name, and why? Because he sees impropriety, as everyone must see impropriety, in the position in which the Government have taken up in his having anything really to do with this prosecution at all. And it is quite plain that in the situation in which this matter stands, one would much rather be prosecuted by the Attorney General, looking at his attitude towards the Irish Members, than be defended by him. The Attorney General practically disavows all connection with this prosecution, and then we are told that this prosecution that you offer is founded on the precedents of prosecution for Breach of Privilege, and for attacks on Members of this House. When has there been such a prosecution in which the Attorney General disavowed his connection with the case? Why, Sir, every prosecution has been a prosecution by the Government which condemned the action of the person prosecuted, and instituted the prosecution for the purpose of obtaining a conviction. But is that the fact now? Why, they are obliged to disavow their connection. And what is to be the effect upon the tribunals of the country to which the Chancellor of the Exchequer appeals? What is the effect upon a jury when the leading counsel throws up his brief? What is the statement on the part of the Attorney General except this—I am not fit, on account of the attitude of the Government with reference to this prosecution, to take the ordinary part which the Attorney General should take, and always has taken, in every prosecution so instituted by the House of Commons. Why, it is as much as to tell the jury, and it is intended to tell the jury—[*loud cheers, which prevented the end of the sentence being heard*]—and that is the natural and inevitable result of their severing the Law Officers of the Crown from the conduct of a prosecution which they are entrusted to undertake by the House of Commons. Well, now, Sir, it is a most remarkable circumstance in this case, with reference to this prosecution, that the challenge of my right hon. Friend the Member for Mid Lothian has never been taken up by anybody on that side of the House. The Attorney General had not a word to say upon it, and the Chancellor of the Exchequer has not answered it. My right hon. Friend has stated—and stated without contradiction —that there never has been a prosecution ordered by the House of Commons which was not preceded by a declaration that a false and scandalous libel had been uttered against a Member of this House. Then my right hon. and learned Friend the Member for Bury (Sir Henry James) says that you are going to take that course. We have a right to know whether the right hon. and learned Member for Bury is well instructed upon that. Do you say, are you going to vote, that you order a prosecution on the ground of false and scandalous libels having been uttered against a Member of this House? If not, you are flying in the face of every precedent on which

you pretend to rely, because there is no precedent of a prosecution without such a declaration as that; I defy you to produce one. They were all founded on the allegation of a Breach of Privilege. [Sir EDWARD CLARKE: No.] Well, do not be in a hurry—that does not alter the fact. You have, in some cases, allegations of a Breach of Privilege where the House did not intend to take it into its own hands. Where you have a vote of this House that a false and scandalous libel has been uttered, that involves a Breach of Privilege. But why were these prosecutions not undertaken in the old days? Was it because the House thought itself incapable of acting? Not at all. It was because they desired that a heavier punishment should be obtained in a Court of Law than the House could inflict. No doubt, that was the cause; but now let me ask why these proceedings have been discontinued for practically the whole of this century? I will tell the House why, and the reason for it has a close bearing on the question of an appeal to the tribunal of a jury of which we have heard so much from the Chancellor of the Exchequer. What would the prosecution be in this case? It would be a criminal prosecution for a political libel. Now, my right hon. and learned Friend the Member for Bury has said—"Who will say that any prosecution of this character has failed before a British jury?" I will tell him why, in his recollection, no such prosecution has failed. It is because no such prosecution, in my belief, has been brought within the memory of any living lawyer in this House. Criminal prosecutions for political libels were brought in the earlier part of the century and constantly failed, and they were discontinued from the absolute knowledge that prosecutions for political libels were certain to fail. That is my answer to the Chancellor of the Exchequer. When he talks of our attacking and vilifying the tribunals of the country, when he says that we have attacked the juries of this country for not having done justice, I reply that we did nothing of the kind. What we say is that criminal prosecutions for political libel are prosecutions which are not favoured, but which are disliked and almost certain to fail in this country. What is it that you offer? You offer to

Irish Members who have been calumniated a criminal prosecution on a criminal information for a political libel—a thing that no Government would venture upon in its own case, a thing you know perfectly well, by experience of former trials in this country, is almost certain under any circumstances to fail. It is a delusive and an illusory offer, and the Government—and nobody better than the Law Officers of the Crown—knows that a criminal prosecution for political libel is destined from the very nature of the case to fail. That is the whole allegation we make with regard to the trial you offer. Now, Sir, we have demanded that this matter should be investigated by a Committee of the House of Commons. You declare that a Committee of the House of Commons is incapable to inquire into this matter. Have any of your Predecessors in former Parliaments been of that opinion? Where can you give a single example where a Member of this House who conceived his character and his honour to be impeached has asked for a Committee and it has been refused? The House of Commons in which you command a majority is, for the first time, to declare itself incapable of doing that which you say a jury can do. All those fine declamations in favour of juries—from which I do not differ—of their capacity, impartiality, and justice, might equally be addressed to a Committee of this House; and I ask you whether you will deny the capacity, the impartiality, and the justice of the English House of Commons? That is the line you take up. I say that is a line which is not for the honour and dignity of this House. Objections have been taken that the scope of this inquiry is too limited. You say, and you say justly, that it is not a question merely about the article in *The Times*, but that an inquiry is wanted into the general character and conduct of the Nationalist Party. But how can you inquire into that before a jury? If you go before a jury you must have a specific incident or subject as the matter of inquiry. There is no tribunal such as a Judge and jury which can inquire into the general question. You cannot inquire into the character of a Party. Can you indict a Party before a jury? You know perfectly well that nothing of the kind can be done. A Committee of this House is the tribunal

Sir William Harcourt

where the truth and the whole truth upon the whole matter can be gone into, and where none of the technical objections which often prevail in the case of criminal indictments can be raised—where the whole matter can be heard from beginning to end. That is the inquiry which the country wants, and which you can supply and ought to supply; but which you refuse to supply. It has been said that the inquiry suggested in the Amendment of my right hon. Friend the Member for Mid Lothian is too limited, and that it will only raise the question between the hon. Member for East Mayo and *The Times*; but you have heard the distinct offer of the hon. Member for East Mayo. He asks you to inquire not into this matter of the question of his veracity in this House alone, he has offered distinctly that the inquiry shall include not only this, but also the authenticity of the letter alleged to have been written by Mr. Parnell, and the truth of all the charges that have appeared under the heading of "Parnellism and Crime." The responsibility rests upon you of refusing that inquiry before the only tribunal that can fully and completely inquire into these charges. To refute such an inquiry would, I think, be a most unwise and unjust course. We believe that your refusal will be condemned by the country. The right hon. Gentleman the Chancellor of the Exchequer (Mr. Goschen) said that we desired a tribunal of the classes, instead of one of the masses. But we shall appeal from the refusal of the classes in this House to the masses in the country. I wish to say nothing inconsistent with personal respect for the right hon. Gentleman the First Lord of the Treasury, and I hope he will consider that I have never spoken of or treated him otherwise than with respect; but I must point out that the position of the Leader of the House is very different from that of the Leader of any Party. My right hon. Friend has said, and said truly, that the Leader of the House is charged not only with the interests of his Party, but that he ought to use his position and power for the protection of every Member of the minority where their character is unduly impugned and attacked. He ought to do that which his Predecessors have never failed to do, and which I have pointed out that Mr. Disraeli did on behalf of some

Irish Members—which I have pointed out that Sir Stafford Northcote claimed, not for an individual, but for the whole of the Conservative Party in minority, when he said they were unjustly assailed. That, I contend, is the duty which the Leader of this House should discharge towards every individual and every Party in this House. It is a duty which no Leader of the House has hitherto declined to perform, whether in maintaining the dignity of this House on the point of Privilege, or in the granting of a Committee. The right hon. Gentleman has no right whatever to employ his majority to vote down the request for a Committee, or to maintain such a refusal as he now makes. That refusal, as I understand, is founded on the alleged inherent incapacity of this House to deal with the question. I think it would be much more accurate to say that it arises out of the profound unwillingness of the Party he leads to have this matter sifted to the bottom; because, otherwise, they would be deprived of the opportunity of insinuating that which they dare not allege. From whatever cause that refusal arises, however, I venture to say that it is one which is inconsistent with the dignity and honour of the House, and entirely incompatible with all the traditions which have hitherto governed the Leaders of this House.

THE FIRST LORD OF THE TREASURY (Mr. W. H. SMITH) (Strand, Westminster): Sir, I will not detain the House for more than two or three minutes; but the right hon. Gentleman who has just sat down has made an allusion to my duty to which I must refer. It is suggested that in the discharge of my duty I am influenced by a feeling on this side of the House of profound unwillingness to have this question sifted to the bottom. ["Hear, hear!"] Hon. Members below the Gangway opposite cheer. It is, therefore, clearly their view that hon. Members who sit on this side of the House do not want this question to be sifted. Here, then, we have evidence of the complete distrust of the good faith of the tribunal which is invoked to decide this question. The Members of that tribunal are charged beforehand with a profound unwillingness to have this question sifted. This is the temper that prevails when we are called upon to enter into a deliberate examination of these grave charges. I wish to say to hon. and right hon. Gentlemen opposite that we fully recognize the duty which rests upon those who lead the House of Commons to guard the honour and dignity and reputation of every Member in this House, and every Party in this House. But I am asked to be a party to an inquiry which I believe would be illusory, which I believe would bring this House into greater difficulties, and imperil its reputation more, than any which could possibly arise from any mistake which we could make by refusing to commit this grave subject to an inquiry before a Committee. I am bound to do my best to preserve the regularity of the proceedings and the honour of this House. My right hon. Friend sitting on my left has given, I think, conclusive reasons against referring this question to a Committee of the House of Commons, whether it be limited, as proposed by the right hon. Member for Mid Lothian, or extended, as the hon. Member for East Mayo proposes. [*Laughter and cheers.*] There is, on our side, the strongest desire that an inquiry, as impartial and as complete as possible, should be undertaken under the authority of Parliament. If the right hon. Gentleman will undertake the responsibility of moving for such an inquiry in a form which would command the confidence of the people of this country, and give assurance to his hon. Friends who sit around him that justice would be done, we should certainly put no difficulties in his way. [*Laughter.*] Here, again, we have evidence of the complete mistrust which hon. Members opposite have of the good faith of our statements, and consequently of the verdict which we might be called upon to give. Is there any consistency between the remarks and cheers of hon. Members and their declaration that they will trust a Committee consisting of a majority of Gentlemen sitting on this side of the House? ["No!"] Let us meet this question with the gravity which it demands, and endeavour to find a solution which shall be creditable to this House and to the people of the United Kingdom of Great Britain and Ireland; but do not let us be led into the adoption of a proposal which must be illusory, and must involve this House in questions which cannot fail to excite passion and Party prejudice. [*Laughter.*] Here, again, I say, is evidence of the incapacity of hon. Members to treat as serious and real any expression of opinion which comes from this side of the House. I earnestly hope that some method will be found by which an inquiry can be conducted. If so, the best assistance of the Government will be given to the hon. Member for East Mayo in his exposition of his view of the questions at issue. No exertions will be spared on our part; but we cannot consent to the reference of the question to a partizan Committee —["Oh!"]—composed of those who have already expressed an opinion on one side or the other, and who, as my right hon. Friend has said, by merely walking up the stairs to the Committee Room, will not be able to divest themselves of the prejudices and opinions which they have expressed inside this House and out of it.

MR. JOHN MORLEY (Newcastle-on-Tyne): I do not rise with an intention of prolonging the debate, or keeping the House more than a moment from going to the Division. I rise because my right hon. Friend the Member for Mid Lothian (Mr. W. E. Gladstone) is precluded from saying something which is important, and which should be very clearly understood. My hon. Friend the Member for East Mayo (Mr. Dillon) expressed his willingness and that of his Friends to extend the Reference mentioned in the Amendment of the right hon. Member for Mid Lothian, so as to include not only the charge made against the hon. Member, but also the subject of the letter imputed to the hon. Member for Cork (Mr. Parnell), and any other specific and definite charges which can be extracted from the articles called " Parnellism and Crime." Now, Sir, I only rise for the purpose of saying, on behalf of my right hon. Friend the Member for Mid Lothian, that he accepts definitely and fully that extension of the terms of his own Amendment. There should, therefore, be no mistake as to the length and breadth of the issue upon which we are now going to vote. What is submitted to the House is a proposal by which the whole body of charges made by *The Times* newspaper against the Irish Members shall be submitted

Mr. W. H. Smith

to the judgment of a Committee of this House.

Question put.

The House *divided:*—Ayes 317; Noes 233: Majority 84.

AYES.

Agg-Gardner, J. T.
Ainslie, W. G.
Allsopp, hon. G.
Allsopp, hon. P.
Amherst, W. A. T.
Anstruther, Colonel R. H. L.
Anstruther, H. T.
Ashmead-Bartlett, E.
Baden-Powell, G. S.
Baggallay, E.
Bailey, Sir J. R.
Baird, J. G. A.
Balfour, rt. hon. A. J.
Balfour, G. W.
Banes, Major G. E.
Baring, Viscount
Barnes, A.
Barry, A. H. Smith-
Bartley, G. C. T.
Barttelot, Sir W. B.
Bass, H.
Bates, Sir E.
Baumann, A. A.
Beach, W. W. B.
Beadel, W. J.
Beaumont, H. F.
Beckett, E. W.
Bective, Earl of
Bentinck, Lord H. C.
Bentinck, rt. hn. G. C.
Bentinck, W. G. C.
Beresford, Lord C. W. de la Poer
Bethell, Commander G. R.
Biddulph, M.
Bigwood, J.
Birkbeck, Sir E.
Blundell, Colonel H. B. H.
Bond, G. H.
Bonsor, H. C. O.
Boord, T. W.
Borthwick, Sir A.
Bridgeman, Col. hon. F. C.
Bright, right hon. J.
Bristowe, T. L.
Brodrick, hon. W. St. J. F.
Brookfield, A. M.
Brooks, Sir W. C.
Brown, A. H.
Bruce, Lord H.
Burdett-Coutts, W. L. Ash.-B.
Burghley, Lord
Caine, W. S.
Caldwell, J.
Campbell, Sir A.
Campbell, J. A.

Campbell, R. F. F.
Chaplin, right hon. H.
Charrington, S.
Churchill, rt. hn. Lord R. H. S.
Clarke, Sir E. G.
Cochrane-Baillie, hon. C. W. A. N.
Coddington, W.
Coghill, D. H.
Colomb, Capt. J. C. R.
Commerell, Adml. Sir J. E.
Compton, F.
Corbett, A. C.
Corbett, J.
Corry, Sir J. P.
Cotton, Capt. E. T. D.
Cross, H. S.
Crossley, Sir S. B.
Crossman, Gen. Sir W.
Cubitt, right hon. G.
Currie, Sir D.
Curzon, Viscount
Curzon, hon. G. N.
Dalrymple, C.
Davenport, H. T.
Davenport, W. B.
Dawnay, Colonel hon. L. P.
De Lisle, E. J. L. M. P.
De Worms, Baron H.
Dickson, Major A. G.
Dimsdale, Baron R.
Dixon, G.
Dixon-Hartland, F. D.
Donkin, R. S.
Dorington, Sir J. E.
Dugdale, J. S.
Duncan, Colonel F.
Duncombe, A.
Eaton, H. W.
Edwards-Moss, T. C.
Egerton, hon. A. J. F.
Elliot, hon. A. R. D.
Elliot, Sir G.
Elliot, G. W.
Ellis, Sir J. W.
Elton, C. I.
Evelyn, W. J.
Ewart, W.
Ewing, Sir A. O.
Farquharson, H. R.
Feilden, Lt.-Gen. R. J.
Fellowes, W. H.
Fergusson, right hon. Sir J.
Fielden, T.
Finch, G. H.
Finch-Hatton, hon. M. E. G.

Finlay, R. B.
Fisher, W. H.
Fitzgerald, R. U. P.
Fitzwilliam, hon. W. J. W.
Fitz - Wygram, Gen. Sir F. W.
Fletcher, Sir H.
Forwood, A. B.
Fowler, Sir R. N.
Fraser, General C. C.
Fry, L.
Fulton, J. F.
Gardner, R. Richardson-
Gathorne-Hardy, hon. A. E.
Gathorne-Hardy, hon. J. S.
Gedge, S.
Gent-Davis, R.
Gibson, J. G.
Giles, A.
Gilliat, J. S.
Godson, A. F.
Goldsmid, Sir J.
Goldsworthy, Major-General W. T.
Goschen, rt. hn. G. J.
Gray, C. W.
Green, Sir E.
Greenall, Sir G.
Greene, E.
Grimston, Viscount
Grotrian, F. B.
Gunter, Colonel R.
Hall, A. W.
Hall, C.
Hambro, Col. C. J. T.
Hamilton, right hon. Lord G. F.
Hamilton, Lord C. J.
Hamilton, Col. C. E.
Hamley, Gen. Sir E. B.
Hanbury, R. W.
Hardcastle, E.
Hardcastle, F.
Hartington, Marq. of
Havelock - Allan, Sir H. M.
Heath, A. R.
Heathcote, Capt. J. H. Edwards-
Herbert, hon. S.
Harvey, Lord F.
Hill, right hon. Lord A. W.
Hill, Colonel E. S.
Hoare, S.
Hobhouse, H.
Holland, right hon. Sir H. T.
Holloway, G.
Holmes, rt. hon. H.
Hornby, W. H.
Houldsworth, W. H.
Howard, J.
Hozier, J. H. C.
Hubbard, E.
Hughes, Colonel E.
Hughes - Hallett, Col. F. C.

Hulse, E. H.
Hunt, F. S.
Hunter, Sir W. G.
Isaacs, L. H.
Isaacson, F. W.
Jackson, W. L.
James, rt. hon. Sir H.
Jarvis, A. W.
Jennings, L. J.
Johnston, W.
Kelly, J. R.
Kennaway, Sir J. H.
Kenrick, W.
Kenyon, hon. G. T.
Kenyon - Slaney, Col. W.
Ker, R. W. B.
Kimber, H.
King, H. S.
King - Harman, right hon. Colonel E. R.
Knatchbull-Hugessen, H. T.
Knightley, Sir R.
Knowles, L.
Lafone, A.
Lambert, C.
Laurie, Colonel R. P.
Lawrance, J. C.
Lawrence, Sir J. J. T.
Lawrence, W. F.
Lea, T.
Lechmere, Sir E. A. H.
Legh, T. W.
Loighton, S.
Lethbridge, Sir R.
Lewisham, right hon. Viscount
Llewellyn, E. H.
Low, M.
Lowther, hon. W.
Lowther, J. W.
Lymington, Viscount
Macartney, W. G. E.
Macdonald, right hon. J. H. A.
Maclean, F. W.
Maclean, J. M.
Maclure, J. W.
M'Calmont, Captain J.
M'Garel-Hogg, Sir J. M.
Makins, Colonel W. T.
Malcolm, Col. J. W.
Mallock, R.
Manners, rt. hon. Lord J. J. R.
March, Earl of
Marriott, rt. hn. W. T.
Maskelyne, M. H. N. Story-
Maxwell, Sir H. E.
Mayne, Admiral R. C.
Mildmay, F. B.
Mills, hon. C. W.
Milvain, T.
More, R. J.
Morgan, hon. F.
Morrison, W.
Mount, W. G.
Mowbray, right hon. Sir J. R.
Mowbray, R. G. C.

Mulholland, H. L.
Muntz, P. A.
Murdoch, C. T.
Newark, Viscount
Noble, W.
Norris, E. S.
Northcote, hon. H. S.
Norton, R.
O'Neill, hon. R. T.
Paget, Sir R. H.
Parker, hon. F.
Pearce, W.
Pelly, Sir L.
Penton, Captain F. T.
Pitt-Lewis, G.
Plunket, rt. hn. D. R.
Plunkett, hon. J. W.
Pomfret, W. P.
Powell, F. S.
Price, Captain G. E.
Puleston, J. H.
Rankin, J.
Ridley, Sir M. W.
Ritchie, rt. hn. C. T.
Robertson, J. P. B.
Robinson, B.
Rollit, Sir A. K.
Ross, A. H.
Rothschild, Baron F. J. de
Round, J.
Russell, Sir G.
Salt, T.
Sandys, Lt.-Col. T. M.
Saunderson, Col. E. J.
Sclater-Booth, rt. hn. G.
Sellar, A. C.
Selwin - Ibbetson, rt. hon. Sir H. J.
Selwyn, Captain C. W.
Seton-Karr, H.
Shaw-Stewart, M. H.
Sidebotham, J. W.
Sidebottom, T. H.
Sinclair, W. P.

NOES.

Acland, A. H. D.
Acland, C. T. D.
Allison, R. A.
Anderson, C. H.
Asher, A.
Asquith, H. H.
Atherley-Jones, L.
Austin, J.
Balfour, Sir G.
Barbour, W. B.
Biggar, J. G.
Blake, J. A.
Blake, T.
Blane, A.
Bolton, J. C.
Bolton, T. D.
Bradlaugh, C.
Bright, Jacob
Bright, W. L.
Brown, A. L.
Bruce, hon. R. P.
Bryce, J.
Buchanan, T. R.
Buxton, S. C.
Byrne, G. M.

Smith, right hon. W. H.
Smith, A.
Stanhope, rt. hon. E.
Stanley, E. J.
Stewart, M.
Swetenham, E.
Sykes, C.
Talbot, J. G.
Taylor, F.
Temple, Sir R.
Theobald, J.
Thorburn, W.
Tollemache, H. J.
Tomlinson, W. E. M.
Tottenham, A. L.
Townsend, F.
Trotter, H. J.
Verdin, R.
Vernon, hon. G. R.
Walsh, hon. A. H. J.
Waring, Colonel T.
Watson, J.
Webster, Sir R. E.
Webster, R. G.
Weymouth, Viscount
Wharton, J. L.
White, J. B.
Whitley, E.
Whitmore, C. A.
Williams, J. Powell-
Wilson, Sir S.
Winn, hon. R.
Wodehouse, E. R.
Wolmer, Viscount
Wood, N.
Wortley, C. B. Stuart-
Wright, H. S.
Wroughton, P.
Yerburgh, R. A.
Young, C. E. B.

TELLERS.

Douglas, A. Akers-
Walrond, Col. W. H.

Cameron, J. M.
Campbell, H.
Campbell-Bannerman, right hon. H.
Carew, J. L.
Chance, P. A.
Channing, F. A.
Childers, right hon. H. C. E.
Clancy, J. J.
Clark, Dr. G. B.
Cobb, H. P.
Cohen, A.
Coleridge, hon. B.
Commins, A.
Connolly, L.
Conway, M.
Conybeare, C. A. V.
Corbet, W. J.
Cossham, H.
Cox, J. R.
Cozans-Hardy, H. H.
Craig, J.
Crawford, D.
Crawford, W.

Cremer, W. R.
Crossley, E.
Dillon, J.
Dillwyn, L. L.
Dodds, J.
Duff, R. W.
Ellis, J.
Ellis, J. E.
Ellis, T. E.
Esmonde, Sir T. H. G.
Esslemont, P.
Evershed, S.
Farquharson, Dr. R.
Fenwick, C.
Ferguson, R. C. Munro-
Finucane, J.
Flower, C.
Flynn, J. C.
Foley, P. J.
Foljambe, C. G. S.
Forster, Sir C.
Foster, Sir W. B.
Fowler, rt. hon. H. H.
Fox, Dr. J. F.
Fry, T.
Fuller, G. P.
Gane, J. L.
Gardner, H.
Gaskell, C. G. Milnes-
Gilhooly, J.
Gill, H. J.
Gill, T. P.
Gladstone, rt. hn. W. E.
Gladstone, H. J.
Gourley, E. T.
Graham, R. C.
Gray, E. D.
Grove, Sir T. F.
Gully, W. C.
Haldane, R. B.
Hanbury-Tracy, hon. F. S. A.
Harcourt, rt. hn. Sir W. G. V. V.
Harrington, E.
Harrington, T. C.
Hayden, L. P.
Hayne, C. Seale-
Healy, M.
Healy, T. M.
Holden, I.
Hooper, J.
Howell, G.
Hoyle, I.
Hunter, W. A.
Illingworth, A.
Jacoby, J. A.
James, hon. W. H.
Joicey, J.
Jordan, J.
Kay-Shuttleworth, rt. hon. Sir U. J.
Kennedy, E. J.
Kenny, C. S.
Kenny, M. J.
Labouchere, H.
Lalor, R.
Lawson, Sir W.
Lawson, H. L. W.
Leahy, J.
Leake, R.
Lefevre, right hon. G. J. S.

Lewis, T. P.
Lyell, L.
Macdonald, W. A.
Mac Innes, M.
Mac Neill, J. G. S.
M'Arthur, A.
M'Cartan, M.
M'Carthy, J.
M'Carthy, J. H.
M'Donald, P.
M'Donald, Dr. R.
M'Ewan, W.
M'Kenna, Sir J. N.
M'Lagan, P.
Mahony, P.
Maitland, W. F.
Mappin, Sir F. T.
Marum, E. M.
Mason, S.
Mayne, T.
Menzies, R. S.
Molloy, B. C.
Montagu, S.
Morgan, rt. hon. G. O.
Morgan, O. V.
Morley, rt. hon. J.
Mundella, right hon. A. J.
Murphy, W. M.
Nolan, Colonel J. P.
Nolan, J.
O'Brien, J. F. X.
O'Brien, P.
O'Brien, P. J.
O'Connor, A.
O'Connor, J. (Kerry)
O'Connor, J. (Tippry.)
O'Connor, T. P.
O'Doherty, J. E.
O'Hanlon, T.
O'Hea, P.
O'Kelly, J.
Palmer, Sir C. M.
Parker, C. S.
Paulton, J. M.
Peacock, R.
Pease, Sir J. W.
Pickersgill, E. H.
Pinkerton, J.
Playfair, rt. hon. Sir L.
Plowden, Sir W. C.
Portman, hon. E. B.
Potter, T. B.
Powell, W. R. H.
Power, P. J.
Power, R.
Price, T. P.
Priestley, B.
Provand, A. D.
Pugh, D.
Pyne, J. D.
Quinn, T.
Rathbone, W.
Redmond, W. H. K.
Reed, Sir E. J.
Reid, R. T.
Rendel, S.
Roberts, J.
Roberts, J. B.
Robertson, E.
Robinson, T.
Roe, T.

Roscoe, Sir H. E.
Rowlands, W. B.
Rowntree, J.
Russell, Sir C.
Russell, E. R.
Samuelson, Sir B.
Schwann, C. E.
Sexton, T.
Shaw, T.
Sheehan, J. D.
Sheehy, D.
Sheil, E.
Shirley, W. S.
Smith, S.
Stack, J.
Stanhope, hon. P. J.
Stansfeld, right hon. J.
Stevenson, F. S.
Stevenson, J. C.
Stuart, J.
Sullivan, D.
Sullivan, T. D.
Summers, W.
Swinburne, Sir J.
Talbot, C. R. M.

Tanner, C. K.
Thomas, A.
Tuite, J.
Vivian, Sir H. H.
Wallace, R.
Wardle, H.
Warmington, C. M.
Watt, H.
Wayman, T.
Whitbread, S.
Will, J. S.
Williams, A. J.
Williamson, J.
Williamson, S.
Wilson, C. H.
Wilson, H. J.
Wilson, I.
Woodall, W.
Woodhead, J.
Yeo, F. A.

TELLERS.
Marjoribanks, rt. hon. E.
Morley, A.

Words *added*.

Main Question, as amended, put.

Resolved, That this House declines to treat the publication of the article headed "Parnellism and Crime" in *The Times* of the 2nd of May as a Breach of the Privileges of this House.

MUNICIPAL CORPORATIONS ACTS (IRELAND) AMENDMENT (No. 2) BILL.

(Sir James Corry, Mr. Ewart, Mr. Johnston.)

[BILL 176.]　SECOND READING.

Order for Second Reading read.

SIR JAMES CORRY (Armagh, Mid): I rise in fulfilment of a pledge which I gave some days ago to the hon. Member for West Belfast (Mr. Sexton), that I would take the first opportunity which presented itself of asking the House to read this Bill a second time, so that it may be proceeded with and brought to an issue. A considerable number of hon. Members were opposed to the scope of this Bill, and I have had great difficulty in getting the blocks removed; but I have at last succeeded in so arranging matters that if the measure is read a second time, when we get into Committee the extension of the municipal franchise will be limited to the borough of Belfast, and we shall be able to dispose of the Bill at once. The question is, therefore, of interest to Belfast alone. By so limiting it, I desire to give effect to the wish which has been expressed not only by the hon. Member for West Belfast, but also by the other Members for the borough. We were anxious that this extension of the franchise should be applied to all the boroughs of Ireland; but we found that it would be impossible to carry the Bill in that way. We have, therefore, decided that an Amendment should be accepted, confining the extension of the municipal franchise to the borough of Belfast. I beg to move that the Bill be now read a second time.

Motion made, and Question proposed, "That the Bill be now read a second time."—(*Sir James Corry.*)

MR. T. M. HEALY (Longford, N.): The hon. Baronet need not have wasted so many words as he did on the question of the second reading of this Bill, because the measure is one which has passed through this House 50 times, I suppose, but which has always been killed "over the way." The hon. Baronet has made a most extraordinary proposition, and one to which I, for one, can never consent—that is to say, that this Bill, which is to extend to Ireland the franchise which is enjoyed by the English people, shall, in Committee, be so restricted as to apply to Belfast alone. Are we to put a stigma, a mark of degradation, on all the rest of Ireland? Are we to consent, and do the Government consent, that this Bill, which now applies to the whole of Ireland, shall in Committee be amended so as to apply to Belfast alone? I see opposite to me hon. Gentlemen who were very indignant at being considered "conspirators" with anyone or for anything. Well, I wish to ask the right hon. and learned Gentleman the Attorney General for Ireland (Mr. Holmes), who is so soon to be made an Irish Judge, and who is to deal out impartial justice to all Her Majesty's subjects, whether he is willing to be a party to the second reading of a Bill to extend the municipal franchise to the whole of Ireland, intending to lend his support to the hon. Baronet in Committee when the hon. Baronet proposes to confine the Bill to Belfast? Is it only in Belfast in which the municipal franchise is to be extended—the law-abiding and loyal borough of Belfast, where they only kill policemen and do not get hanged for it; where 40 of Her Majesty's subjects during the past 12 months have been murdered. Of all the cool and audacious and extraordinary proposals that I ever heard made, this is the coolest, most audacious, and most extraordinary. And are we to do this

without a word of explanation? What has Ireland done, that she should not have the principle of this Bill applied to her generally? The principle of the Bill has, as I say, been affirmed in this House over and over again. What is the Act of Union for? Are you Unionists not professing the desirability of applying to Ireland equal laws with England and Scotland; and is it, forsooth, for you who are dying to give my countrymen the benefit of the English connection, to propose to limit the measure of justice contained in this Bill to the borough of Belfast? I suppose this limitation was the price given to the hon. Baronet the authority on Privilege (Sir Charles Lewis) for taking off his block to the Bill. Are we to understand that the Government assent to this proposal? I see a long array of authorities opposite to me. I see on the Front Bench opposite the hon. and gallant Gentleman the Member for the Isle of Thanet (Colonel King-Harman). He, no doubt, would like to exclude every part of Ireland but Belfast. Are all the Loyalists outside Belfast to be excluded—all those who are longing to expire on the altar of the throne? Are not other loyal boroughs, such as Enniskillen, Banbridge, Down, Coleraine, to be included? Is there no corn in Egypt for any place but Belfast? Was ever anything so grotesque ever heard of in the whole range of Parliamentary proposals? And this is a proposal which emanates from a man who has been kicked out of Belfast. What are the Loyalists of Armagh to think of this proposal? Are they not to be put on an equal footing with English and Scotch constituencies? Her Majesty's Government are ready to humour their followers, who are eager to make sidelong attacks upon Bills which the Government pass in this House, knowing that they are sure to get knifed in the other. We shall be delighted to let this Bill go through, subject to some few Amendments, to make the franchise in Ireland what it is in England. We do not wish to extend it one bit beyond what it is in England. If we allow this Bill to go through in its present form, will they give us an understanding that, in the House of Lords, they will not add a provision to confine it to Belfast? I am surprised that Tory Gentlemen, who tell us so much about their love for Ireland, and their desire to see her prosper, and their anxiety to see equal laws in the three countries, and to see extended to Ireland every privilege they enjoy themselves—I am surprised that, on this occasion, they should allow a Bill to be passed on the understanding that it shall apply to Belfast alone. I will not move the adjournment of the debate; but if we do not get an understanding from the Government there will be plenty of my hon. Friends who are left to do it. Unless we are told that it is intended to extend to the whole of Ireland the privileges which the hon. Baronet has said he wishes to confine to the single city of Belfast, this Bill will be opposed. It is no answer to us to tell us that the Belfast Main Drainage Bill contains a provision of this character. Almost every Drainage Bill that has been passed for Ireland has contained one. There was one in the Rathmines Bill of 1885; and to come down to the Pembroke Bill, to the Clontarf Bill, to the Galway, Kingston, and Bray Bills, they all contained that provision. There is one in every Bill which creates a municipal authority in Ireland. I thought we had knocked the Chairman of Committees out of time on that question, so much so that we got a majority of this House to support us. The provision was proposed in this Bill by Sir Charles Dilke, and the Chairman of Ways and Means, to use his own expression, said that the Rathmines Clause had been passed *per incuriam*. Every Irish Private Bill, dealing with municipal authority, from Galway to Bray, and from Clontarf to Kilmainham, has contained this clause. We voted down the Chairman of Ways and Means, and carried the Bill against him, just as we had carried the principle in the Rathmines Bill against the hon. and gallant Member for the Isle of Thanet, by the aid of Sir Charles Dilke. That being so, it cannot be said that because we have taken advantage of separate Private Bills to adopt this provision, we need not necessarily apply the principle to more than one place in a Public Bill. The plain answer to hon. Gentlemen opposite is, either take this Belfast provision and swallow it as if it were all gall, or postpone this legislation until you receive from on High power to extend to all towns in Ireland the privileges it is proposed to confer on Belfast. We take advantage of the Belfast Private Bill, as we did of other Drainage Bills, to

Mr. T. M. Healy

insert Franchise Clauses to that town; but it would be monstrous to confine the powers of a Public Bill to one town.

THE ATTORNEY GENERAL FOR IRELAND (Mr. HOLMES) (Dublin University): My right hon. Friend the Chief Secretary (Mr. A. J. Balfour) would certainly have been in his place, if he had thought that this Bill would have come on for discussion to-night. I myself had no idea that the second reading would be moved to-night. It certainly would be a very unusual thing at this hour, a quarter past 1 in the morning, to proceed to the second reading of a Bill to extend the municipal franchise to a considerable number of boroughs in Ireland. The Government have said, again and again, that they intend, on the earliest opportunity, to deal with this question of Local Government generally. I may call the attention of the House to the fact that, even if this Bill were carried as it stands, it would not have the effect that the hon. and learned Gentleman who has spoken seems to think it would, of extending the franchise in such towns as Coleraine, Down, Enniskillen, or the other places mentioned. We are not prepared to give a pledge that we can accept the principle of a Bill like this, when we have stated on more than one occasion that it is our intention, on the earliest opportunity that the Business of the House will permit, to introduce a Bill dealing with Local Government. I think it would be inconvenient to continue the discussion at this hour, and I would suggest that the debate be adjourned to a time when the Chief Secretary will be in his place, and we should have an opportunity of expressing our views on this subject. I beg to move the adjournment of the debate.

Motion made, and Question proposed, "That the Debate be now adjourned." —(*Mr. Attorney General for Ireland.*)

MR. JOHNSTON (Belfast, S.): I am afraid I can scarcely enter into the subject-matter of this Bill on the Motion for the adjournment of the debate. I have great respect for the right hon. and learned Gentleman who moved the Motion, but I hope the House will not assent to it. We who have introduced this Bill, and have waited anxiously for an opportunity to pass it since the commencement of the Session, are most desirous of availing ourselves of this chance. We desire to take the sense of the House upon it. The hon. Member for Mid Cork (Dr. Tanner) challenged the Bill at an earlier period of the Session, and when his block was removed the hon. Baronet the Member for North Antrim (Sir Charles Lewis) put down another block. If hon. Gentlemen on the other side of the House had allowed the Bill to proceed when it was introduced, it would have had a second reading by this time, and probably would have been passed before the hon. Member for North Antrim came back to the House. For my part, I do not desire to be a party to restricting this Bill to Belfast alone. I think the proposal to extend to the Parliamentary boroughs of Ireland the same privilege in regard to Municipal Corporations as is enjoyed by similar boroughs in England is a good one. For my part, I trust the Bill will be passed, and that the House to-night will give it a second reading.

MR. O'DOHERTY (Donegal, N.): As a burgess of Derry, I have only to say that I hope this Bill will be passed, and that the right hon. and learned Gentleman will not persist in this Motion. It is a Bill which we are all anxious to pass. I do not hear a word from the place I represent in opposition to the extension of the principle contained in this Bill to all the boroughs of Ireland, and I trust that the Government will allow it to pass, seeing that similar measures have been adopted for the past 40 years.

MR. EWART (Belfast, N.): I will not occupy the House for more than a few moments; but I just wish to say that the Motion of the hon. Baronet (Sir James Corry) is, in effect, carrying out a compromise proposed by the hon. Gentleman the Chairman of Ways and Means, to which compromise the hon. Member for West Belfast (Mr. Sexton) was a party. That compromise was on the basis of a Bill being brought forward, or, rather, being continued, so as to deal only with the franchise in Belfast. This Bill is for the whole of Ireland; but it is now proposed to put it actually and really in the place of a Bill which was indicated on a former occasion—that is, the Bill introduced by the hon. and gallant Member for North Armagh (Colonel Saunderson). I think

we have some reason to complain that the hon. Member for West Belfast has not carried out the arrangement which was made a few days ago, whereby the Bill extending the municipal franchise in Belfast would have been carried. I think we have some reason to complain that he has not adhered to that arrangement.

MR. SEXTON (Belfast, W.): I have no power on any occasion to control the individual action of every Member of the Party to which I belong. My position in this matter is peculiar, inasmuch as it affects the relations between myself and my constituents. As the House is aware, I have endeavoured, on several occasions, to relieve the people of Belfast from the burden sought to be imposed upon them by an extensive system of main drainage being carried into law, without power being given to them to elect representatives on the Corporation. As the House is also aware, I, at length, succeeded in putting a Franchise Clause into the Belfast Main Drainage Bill; but the Lords struck it out. It becomes a question whether this action on the part of the Lords should be submitted to or not, and on the 20th instant the House will be asked to consider the position of the Lords in the matter. I said, in the discussion which took place, that on any Bill which contained a clause conferring the municipal franchise to the people of Belfast I should be willing to allow it to pass into law. It is obvious that my objection to the Belfast Main Drainage Bill must disappear, if, in either a Private Bill or a Public Bill, a clause for the extension of the franchise is inserted. I wish now to say that I shall vote for the second reading of this Bill, whatever shape it assumes. Even if it assumes the shape of extending the municipal franchise to Belfast alone, I shall be obliged to vote for it in discharge of my duty to my constituents; but I say, at the same time, that the Mover of the Bill has given very unsatisfactory grounds to the House for the proposal he makes. He says one of the grounds was the necessity of removing blocks. Well, we are not in any way responsible for those blocks, after that of my hon. Friend the Member for Mid Cork (Dr. Tanner) was removed. The other ground was the impossibility of passing a full Bill; but I am not aware of such an impossibility. I think I have made my personal position clear to the House, and that I have not been guilty of any breach of arrangement.

MR. HOLMES: My Motion, that the debate should be adjourned, arose from the circumstances that I understood from the hon. and learned Gentleman the Member for North Longford (Mr. T. M. Healy) that unless a pledge was given by the Government that they would support the Bill as it is framed in all its stages, the hon. and learned Member and his Friends would be obliged to oppose it. I have shown that I could not do that, the Chief Secretary for Ireland not being here; but if it is a question of the second reading merely, I will agree to that, and will withdraw my Motion for the adjournment of the debate. It will, however, have to be understood that the Government do not give any pledge as to the principle of the Bill.

MR. T. M. HEALY: I must say it is a most remarkable thing, looking at the very small amount of Business of a private nature in reference to Ireland that the Chief Secretary for Ireland has to attend to, if he could not foresee that, the block being taken off this Bill, No. 21 on the Paper, it would in all likelihood be moved by one of his supporters. The right hon. Gentleman appears to me to be wanting in his duty to this House, if he does not choose to come down when there is Irish Business before the House. He has altogether deserted the House at Question time, and leaves it at the mercy of the right hon. and gallant Gentleman opposite (Colonel King-Harman). The right hon. and gallant Gentleman was here when the second reading of the Bill was moved, and if he is able to take the place of the Chief Secretary at Question time, surely he is able to take it now. The right hon. and learned Gentleman opposite has now withdrawn his opposition.

MR. HOLMES: We did not oppose the Bill.

MR. T. M. HEALY: But the right hon. and learned Gentleman moved the adjournment of the debate, which was tantamount to killing the Bill, because, of course, our hon. Friend of Privilege fame after to-night would put the block on. I see the hon. and learned Gentleman the English Attorney General in the House. We have always found him a

Mr. Sexton

courteous, fair, and friendly opponent, and very liberal-minded. I would submit to him that it is most unfair to Irish Members to leave us alone with Orange officials, when these Bills are brought in, so that there is no Englishman interposed between us and the worst form of Orangeism, whether you take it as represented by the right hon. and gallant Gentleman (Colonel King-Harman), or I would say, in spite of his disclaimers, by the right hon. and learned Gentleman the Irish Attorney General. I trust that the next time this Bill comes on the right hon. Gentleman the Chief Secretary will find himself able to be in his place. I hope the Bill will be allowed to pass now, on the understanding that we shall have some English protection, even of a Tory character, when the Bill comes on at the next stage. I trust, as I say, that on the next occasion the right hon. Gentleman the Chief Secretary will be here to answer the very reasonable demand we make—namely, that this Bill shall be allowed to pass in its entirety, and apply to Ireland as a whole.

Motion, by leave, *withdrawn.*

Original Question again proposed.

DR. TANNER (Cork Co., Mid): The hon. Gentleman the Member for South Belfast (Mr. Johnston) appears to have expressed considerable dissatisfaction at my having blocked this Bill at an earlier period of the Session. My principal reason for doing that was simply and solely, Sir, that the Bill was promoted by a Gentleman who is a Member of a Party who have blocked every Irish Bill we are seeking to pass this Session. I may say that, were it not that my hon. Friend the Member for West Belfast (Mr. Sexton) came and spoke to me on the subject, I should have made it a personal matter, and should have declined to remove the block. I wish to correct the hon. Gentleman opposite, and say that it was merely in consequence of the appeal of my hon. Friend the Member for West Belfast that I removed my Notice of opposition to the Bill.

Original Question put, and *agreed to.*

Bill read a second time, and *committed* for *Tuesday* next.

TRUCK BILL.—[BILL 109.]

(Mr. Bradlaugh, Mr. Warmington, Mr. John Ellis, Mr. Arthur Williams, Mr. Howard Vincent, Mr. Esslemont.)

COMMITTEE.   [*Progress 5th May.*]

Bill *considered* in Committee.

(In the Committee.)

MR. D. CRAWFORD (Lanark, N.E.): I feel that I am under a great disadvantage in asking the attention of the Committee to my Amendments on this important Bill at so very late an hour (1.30 A.M.) But the questions involved are questions which concern my constituents very nearly. They affect not only the electors in my own constituency, which is a mining constituency, but also mining constituencies in many parts of the country. I will endeavour, as briefly as I can, to explain the object of this Amendment. The original Truck Act of 1831, which this Bill is intended to amend, dealt, I believe, with two points. The first point was, that wages were to be paid in current coin of this Realm; and there were various clauses which endeavoured to protect the workman from evasion of that part of the Bill. And the second point dealt with was a provision for certain deductions from wages for certain purposes, justified by public policy, such as education, medical assistance, and so forth. Experience has shown that the original Act requires considerable amendment. The Bill which is at present before the House, and which has already made considerable progress—the Bill of the hon. Member for Northampton—certainly proposes some very salutary changes in the law; the Committee have already agreed, for example, that the original Truck Act, which was restricted to certain trades only, shall now be extended to all trades. That is a great change for the better, but it will not much affect the constituency which I have the honour to represent. Secondly, the Bill before the House, in a clause which has been partially under discussion, proposes a most advantageous change as to the method and time of paying wages, abolishing the system of poundage or interest which now prevails, and establishing in principle that the wages shall be paid weekly. That, however, has not yet been accepted by the Committee.

But, assuming that this is also passed, I can only say that the evils under which my constituency and constituencies similar to mine labour will not, at least to the extent of one-half, be removed. Now, I should like to recall very briefly the attention of the Committee to the principle on which the Truck Act of 1831 proceeds. It prohibits the payment of wages in kind. That is a very considerable interference with the liberty of dealing between man and man; and yet, at so early a date as 1831, and, I believe, anterior to that, it was found necessary to make such an interference. I should be very sorry, any further than is absolutely necessary, to extend the principle of interference with the dealings between man and man. An hon. Member who sits on this side of the House—a very large employer of labour, and a respected Member of this House—said to me, a few days ago, that if he had liberty to pay his workmen in kind, they would get their food better and 20 per cent cheaper than they can at present. That may be so. I should be glad to see the day when such protective legislation as truck legislation has become entirely unnecessary, and I think it may possibly be that the day is not so very distant; but, in the meantime, I think no one at all acquainted with the subject can doubt that the existing Truck Act is still necessary for the protection of workmen; and all that my Amendment proposes is that the Act should be not merely a Statute on paper, liable to continual evasion. The reason on which any legislation of the kind cannot be dispensed with is, that the employers and workmen do not deal entirely on equal terms. It has been found necessary, therefore, to assist the workman in the object which he has at heart—namely, that he shall have the spending of his own wages; that his wages should not be subject to a second profit to be made by the master, compulsorily and against the workman's will—a profit beyond the fair profit derived from the legitimate exercise of the trade. The Committee has already passed clauses intended to give additional protection to the workman against any compulsion in respect of the payment of wages. It would be impossible for me to trespass on the patience of the Committee by going into each

detail of the subject; but I may say
that my contention is, that the new
clauses do little or nothing to strengthen
the present Act. I think my interpretation will be confirmed by the Attorney
General when he looks into the matter,
because I have no doubt that the Government will treat it in a judicial
spirit, and with a desire to do justice
to the interests concerned. I say that
the clauses of the Truck Act are as
strong on paper as they can be made.
The 1st and 2nd clauses of that Act
provide that no contract is to be lawful which stipulates that the workman is to spend his wages in any particular place and in any particular manner;
and then the definition of the word contract is so wide that I think—on paper
—it is sufficient to cover any attempt on
the part of the master to compel the
workman to spend his wages in a particular way. The definition is, that the
term "contract" is to include every
understanding . . . every agreement
or arrangement, direct or indirect. It
is evident that the framers of the Truck
Act of 1831 were very much in earnest
in making these provisions as stringent
as possible. I am afraid, although I
welcome the clause introduced, that it
does not materially improve the position
of the workman. Now, how far were
the clauses of the Act of 1831 effectual,
which provided that a workman should
be at liberty to spend his own wages? In
former days they proved to be very ineffectual, and the loud complaints which
were made throughout the country came
to a climax about 17 years since. A
Royal Commission was appointed to
consider the question, and they collected
a quantity of valuable information which
showed that the existing provisions of
the Truck Act were entirely ineffectual
in a great many places; that the masters
practically compelled their workmen to
deal at their stores, or at stores let to
others, or held by them in another name;
that those stores were very often spirit
shops; that this produced a demoralizing
effect upon the workmen; and that the
men were practically deprived of the
benefit of their own wages. The Royal
Commission consisted of an eminent
Judge and of a Gentleman who is now a
Member of this House, and their Report
was presented in 1872. They reported
that great evils existed, and they made
recommendations on the subject. Since

Mr. D. Crawford

then no legislation has taken place, although legislation was proposed in the
following Session by the Liberal Government, and a Bill went so far as to
be sent to a Select Committee and to be
reported with Amendments. I am far
from saying the evils are now so great
as then; because the attention which
was drawn to the subject by the issuing
of the Commission, and the publicity
given to the evidence given before the
Commission, had, no doubt, a very considerable effect. I will read a very few
lines from the Report of the Commission.
I should have liked to read a great deal
more if the time had been more favourable. The passage I will quote is from
page 82 of the Report; and the general
manager referred to is a gentleman with
whom I am well acquainted. I have
had no communication with him on
the subject at all. He is now retired
from business, but is a man of great
ability and experience, and what he says
may be fairly taken as an illustration of
what generally exists in my constituency.
The gentleman was the manager of one
of the largest works in my constituency,
and the Report says—

"The general manager expressed unqualified
disapproval of the store system. 'It is,' he
said, 'a disagreeable system to work, and I
think it has the effect of interfering with proper
men coming to the works generally. The
workmen do not like it. They generally disapprove of works where stores are, and do not
care about going to these works. It has a
tendency, I think, rather to demoralize the
people. Most of the people that I see who
deal in the store get into a state of poverty
from the working of the system. They are a
bad lot, I find generally, as compared with
others. They do not improve. They begin at
the bottom and stay at the bottom. The people
who spend their money in that sort of way are
rather degraded.'"

If it be said, as it may fairly be said,
that, to some extent, there has been an
improvement since that time, I would
like to read one or two letters I have
received from workmen with whom I
am personally acquainted. They are
not long letters, but they are written in
simple and effective language, and are
written by modest and respectable men
personally well known to me. One man
writes to me as follows:—

"Dear Sir,—In this district truck is carried
on to a great extent. Each coalmaster has a
store attached to his works, where his workmen
must take all his goods from. Every article
they sell is double the price that it is anywhere
else, and, besides, the worst of rubbish. In

fact, they think anything's good enough for their serfs. At a deal of the cash offices they have a system of giving their workmen money every night, or a line over to the store. So far, it's for their interest to give them it every night. It keeps the workmen in poverty, that they cannot wait for more than a day at a time; so, besides the fear of dismissal, they would get no money the following night. But, of course, that does not apply to all the workmen; there's some lets their money remain in the office till the pay. Supposing I had £2 for my fortnight's pay, and going into the store and leaving £1 8s. on Monday, the manager would tell me I must spend all my money in the store, or I would know the consequences. When they are dismissing workmen they do not say what it's for; but they can draw their own inferences from it. I myself was taking all I required, but that was not enough. I must take goods to correspond with the money I got. Suppose I was to let them go to waste, there is a messenger goes between the store and the office to let them know what each spends; they will say you have no excuse; they sell everything you require; there is always a spirit shop attached."

Now, if that is a true statement, it shows a lamentable state of matters, and I can vouch for the respectability of my informant. Here is another short letter—

"Sir,—The truck system is carried out in this way, where the employer keeps a grocery and spirit shop. The *employés* are paid their wages in full; but if they fail to leave their wages in the shop, they are simply dismissed without any reason being given except through some under-official. If the man asks him, he will be told he ought to know himself, for he has done nothing for the store. Now, dismissal from work means being turned out of house and home; because, where the employer has a shop, the men's houses belong to the employer. It is when work is scarce that the greatest pressure is brought to bear on the poor men."

Here is an extract from another letter—

"I beg to state that the stores is no convenience to the men; they would only be too glad to spend their money where they could make most of it. The men want the masters to be forbidden by law to have stores, especially grocery stores, no doubt. They do not care whether we eat or drink our money if they get it back, so long as they are allowed to have the profits of the stores. Our wages are not our own, and there should be none except on the co-operative principle."

That man expresses, in plain language, the principle in this case. So long as the men are obliged to deal with the stores their wages are not their own. In this Amendment I am not proposing anything of an extreme or violent nature. I am only proposing to carry out the principle of the existing Truck Act, which prohibits workmen being compelled to spend their money in any particular place, or in any particular man-

ner. I know it to be a fact that, in some instances, these stores have been established with a view to the convenience of the men. I am ready to admit they are often managed with the intention of benefiting the workmen; but I assert, with the utmost confidence, that, as far as my own constituency is concerned, and other constituencies from whom I have had communications, the men unanimously desire to have these stores prohibited, because they consider that, as long as such places exist, there is a practical compulsion upon them to deal at them. There is no hardship whatever upon the masters in prohibiting these stores, for the very reason that is stated, practically, in one of the letters I have read—namely, that while a man is entitled to a legitimate profit in his own trade, he is not entitled, against the will and desire of his workmen, to make a second profit out of the workmen's wages. That is the principle of this Amendment.

New Clause—

(Prohibition of Stores.)

"No spirits or other intoxicating drink, or groceries, or other provisions of any kind, or clothing, shall be sold by any employer, or any agent of an employer, to a workman in the employment of such employer.

"Provided that this enactment shall not apply to the supply of provisions to any workman living in the same house with his employer.

"For the purposes of this section, a person who is tenant of a store, shop, or other premises belonging to an employer, and who sells any of the aforesaid things to a workman in the employment of such employer, shall be deemed to be the agent of such employer, unless he shows that he is only an ordinary tenant, and that the employer does not directly or indirectly derive any profit from the store, shop, or premises beyond such reasonable rent as would be paid for a store, shop, or other premises of the same character held under another owner,"—(*Mr. D. Crawford,*)

—*brought up,* and read the first time.

Motion made, and Question proposed, "That the Clause be read a second time."

THE ATTORNEY GENERAL (Sir RICHARD WEBSTER) (Isle of Wight): I really must ask the Committee to report Progress. We have had a very interesting speech, occupying nearly half-an-hour, from the hon. Member; but it is impossible, at this hour of the night (1.45), to debate the question raised. This is a clause which must lead to considerable discussion, and, therefore, I hope the Committee will now report Progress.

Motion made, and Question proposed, "That the Chairman do report Progress, and ask leave to sit again," — (*Mr. Attorney General.*)

MR. BRADLAUGH (Northampton): I certainly shall not oppose a Motion to report Progress. It is quite clear a great deal of debate must arise upon this Amendment.

Motion *agreed to.*

Committee report Progress; to sit again upon *Monday* next.

House adjourned at ten minutes before Two o'clock till Monday next.

HOUSE OF LORDS,

Monday, 9th May, 1887.

MINUTES.]—PUBLIC BILLS—*Second Reading*—Smoke Nuisance Abatement (Metropolis) (43).
Committee—Customs Consolidation Act (1876) Amendment * (71).
PROVISIONAL ORDER BILLS — *First Reading* — Local Government (Highways) * (87); Local Government (Poor Law) * (88); Local Government (Poor Law) (No. 2) * (89).
Committee—Report—Local Government * (70).

ENDOWED SCHOOLS ACT, 1869, AND AMENDING ACTS—THE DAUNTSEY TRUST.

HER MAJESTY'S ANSWER TO THE ADDRESS.

THE LORD STEWARD OF THE HOUSEHOLD (The Earl of MOUNT-EDGCUMBE) *reported* the Queen's Answer to the Address of Tuesday, the 29th day of March last, as follows:—

"I have received your Address, praying that I will withhold my assent from the schemes of the Charity Commissioners relating to (1) the Foundation for a school and almshouses, and for other purposes, in the parish of West Lavington, otherwise Bishop Lavington, in the county of Wilts, founded under the will of Alderman William Dauntsey, dated 10th March 1542, and since further endowed; and (2) for dealing with the Endowment of the Wilts County School in the county of Wilts:

"I will comply with your advice."

IRISH LAND LAW BILL.

QUESTION. OBSERVATIONS.

LORD FITZGERALD said, he wished to put a Question, of which he had given

Sir Richard Webster

private Notice to the noble Earl opposite (Earl Cadogan), in reference to a very important Bill which stood for Committee on Thursday next—he alluded to the Irish Land Law Bill. The noble Earl would recollect that, in the course of the debate on the second reading, suggestions were made from various parts of the House for the amendment of the measure, and that the noble and learned Lord the Lord Chancellor of Ireland (Lord Ashbourne), as well as the noble Earl opposite himself, said that those suggestions would be considered by the Government, with a view to their being embodied in such Amendments as they might deem advisable. The Amendments to be proposed by the Government were not yet in the hands of their Lordships; but he understood they might expect to receive them some time to-morrow, and he thought that if the Committee were to be proceeded with on Thursday there would be but a very short interval allowed to their Lordships for considering the Amendments, which would require to be most carefully examined. He asked the noble Earl, therefore, Whether it would be inopportune to postpone, for some short time beyond Thursday next, the Committee stage of the Bill? He could assure the noble Earl that there was no desire in any part of the House to obstruct or delay that measure, but only an anxious wish to make it as perfect as possible. As the Bill was intended to amend the Act of 1881, by removing many of the inequalities and difficulties in applying that measure, he thought that a reasonable time should be given to consider these Amendments.

THE LORD PRIVY SEAL (Earl CADOGAN), in reply, said, he had received Notice only a few minutes ago of the noble and learned Lord's Question, and he was afraid he was unable to give him an immediate answer, as he had not been able to consider the matter, or to consult with his Colleagues upon it. He might, however, state that he was about to lay on the Table that evening the Amendments which the Government would propose in the Bill, and he hoped that they would be in the hands of noble Lords to-morrow. In regard to the Question of the noble and learned Lord as to the postponement of the Committee on the Bill, the Government were exceedingly anxious to proceed with the Bill without delay. They had already given an interval of three weeks between the second reading and the Committee stage, and he himself would be very unwilling to accede to any further delay. At the same time, as that appeal came from so influential a quarter, and was deserving of consideration, he would ask the noble and learned Lord to be kind enough to repeat his Question to-morrow.

THE DUKE OF ARGYLL, in supporting the request for a further postponement, said, that if the Amendments of the Government were of an extensive character, it appeared to him that Thursday was rather a shorter interval than was usual in a matter of such great importance.

EARL GRANVILLE said, that if the Amendments to be proposed by the noble Earl on behalf of the Government were of such a nature as to change the character of the measure, it would be necessary to consider it in its altered shape. If, however, the Government proposed to go on as arranged, there was scarcely time enough to consider them. He could not object to the answer to the Question being postponed under the circumstances; but he desired to impress on the noble Earl (Earl Cadogan) the great importance of the matter.

EARL CADOGAN said, that when the noble and learned Lord repeated his Question to-morrow he would answer those Questions.

Subsequently,

EARL CADOGAN said, he had consulted the Prime Minister, and also the noble Earl opposite (Earl Granville), and he was in a position to state that the Irish Land Bill would be put down for Committee on Monday next.

SMOKE NUISANCE ABATEMENT (ME-TROPOLIS) BILL.

(*The Lord Stratheden and Campbell.*)

(NO. 43.)   SECOND READING.

Order of the Day for the Second Reading, read.

Moved, "That the Bill be now read 2ᵃ." —(*The Lord Stratheden and Campbell.*)

THE DUKE OF WESTMINSTER, in supporting the Motion, said, he would recall their Lordships' attention to their action in 1884 when the same Bill was carried on a Division. He would also point out that several Committees had dealt with this question from the beginning of the century, and that Acts were passed in 1833 and 1856 for abating the smoke of furnaces and steamers. The provisions of these Acts, however, were now insufficient, as, owing to the great extension of London, they did not cover the area. It was, therefore, proposed by the Bill to extend the provisions to the Metropolis as defined by the Metropolis Management Act of 1855 to the area of police, and to give further powers as to dwelling houses. In that district there were 700,000 houses, with a population of 5,000,000, which was more than double the population and 10 times the number of houses of the next largest capital. More than half the present area of London had been built within the last 30 years. The rate of building was strikingly illustrated by comparing decennial periods. From 1854 to 1864 there were 28 new houses built each working day; from 1864 to 1874 there were 45; and from 1874 to 1884 there were 60. An extension of area having, therefore, been rendered necessary, the amount of smoke—as coal and no wood was burnt—might be imagined, but was hardly appreciated. The Smoke Abatement Committee of 1880, the Exhibition at South Kensington in 1881 of smoke-abatement apparatus, and the Smoke Abatement Institute of 1883 had evoked interest in the public mind, and the movement generally had excited very great attention. Experiments had been made and various apparatus had been tested, the result being that there was far greater knowledge of the principles of combustion than formerly. A series of experiments was recently made in a house in the Strand, to test the system of heating by one smokeless fire at the basement, as compared with the ordinary heating by open fires with the following results —the more equal distribution of heat throughout the building, with one smokeless fire, instead of 14 emitting smoke almost continuously. The cost of fuel was only one-seventh and the labour involved was only a hundredth part, calculating the attention to fires alone, and omitting the labour of carrying coals to, and ashes from, 14 fires instead of one. The question of properly housing the industrial classes was intimately connected with that of heating their dwellings. They would be enor mously benefited by an improved system of heating. This could be done at less than one-tenth of the present cost of fuel, with an absence of smoke, and with the advantage of giving facilities for cooking, drying clothes, &c. By an avoidance of dirt from smoking chimneys, by a saving of fuel for which they often paid 1*s.* to 2*s.* per week, and by a saving of labour, great advantage would be gained to the health, comfort, and general well-being of the people. Ventilation, too, did not, and need not, depend upon open grates. In consequence of the attention to the subject, there was a much greater use made of improved construction in grates, with a consequent greater economy in the use of fuel and with very much less smoke. But clubs and hotels were great offenders. In connection with this point he earnestly asked the First Commissioner of Works to consider the question of heating in the case of the new Government Offices. After all, legislation without the support and co-operation of the whole community was of not much avail. It seemed to him that the evil was not sufficiently appreciated; too much was taken for granted; but they hoped that people were more alive to the great and destructive agencies to health, vegetation, buildings, and other things, than they were formerly. The difficulty of enforcing the provisions of the Public Health Act of 1875 in the country consisted in the fact that the administration of the law was largely in the hands of producers of smoke. He thought power might be vested in stipendiaries where they existed. There had been considerable laxity on the part of the magistrates in enforcing the law, as the following Returns proved—In the administration of the Smoke Nuisance Acts in 1885, the total number of cases in which proceedings were taken was 124, total number of convictions 120, total amount of fines inflicted £275 10*s.*, average fine £2 5*s.* 11*d.* The number of cases in which fines below the minimum of 40*s.* provided by the Acts were inflicted was 66. Those figures showed—

"(1) That the number of cases in which proceedings are taken is very small and can include only a percentage of the cases in which a nuisance is created; (2) That when proceedings are taken, and convictions obtained, the penalties inflicted by the magistrates do not comply with the Acts of 1853 to 1856, and are in many

The Duke of Westminster

cases practically inoperative as a deterrent, being in 55 per cent of the cases below the minimum of 40*s.* One fine of £40 was inflicted, and seven of £10 each : the remaining 112 were all of less amount. No proceedings whatever appear to have been taken to enforce the conditions of the Acts as regards steamers on the River Thames, and this is a point which is considered of special importance."

At a meeting of the Metropolitan magistrates last year, under the presidency of Sir James Ingham, it was, however, decided to increase the fine in all cases. The Bill gave power to Local Authorities to make bye-laws, prohibiting the emission of smoke from buildings, and to the Metropolitan Board of Works to make bye-laws as to fireplaces, &c., in new buildings. Their Lordships lived, as a general rule, in pure air, and he asked them to give a second reading to the Bill, on the ground that it would be conferring a boon on those who were constrained to pass the bulk of their lives in an atmosphere greatly contaminated by smoke.

LORD MOUNT TEMPLE said, if there was one subject on which unanimity of opinion might be expected it was such a reform in the atmosphere of London as would prevent half of the burnt coal from polluting the air and entering the nostrils and throats of Londoners. One-half of the fuel was not producing heat at all, but only rising up into the atmosphere, and forming a dense and obscure canopy. We had, nevertheless, gone on for a number of years doing nothing effectual in the matter at all. London, in respect of amusements, conveniences, and so forth, compared favourably with the great cities of the Continent; but its atmosphere was its disgrace. Lord Palmerston's Act of 1853 went as far as public opinion and knowledge at the time justified; but science had now accomplished the avoidance of dense smoke. The difficulty was the punishment of individuals for their share of a collective injury. The Bill imposed on the smaller Local Authorities a duty which had been neglected by the more important Local Authorities, and they might effect a closer observance of the law within their narrow jurisdiction, supported as they would be by public opinion.

THE PRIME MINISTER AND SECRETARY OF STATE FOR FOREIGN AFFAIRS (The Marquess of SALISBURY) said, that Her Majesty's Government were not able to resist the Motion for the second reading, but he hoped the noble Lord (Lord Stratheden and Campbell) would allow sufficient time to elapse before the stage of Committee to enable the metropolitan authorities to take cognizance of the Bill.

EARL GRANVILLE said, he would suggest whether it would not be better, on the whole, after the second reading, to refer the Bill to a Select Committee.

THE MARQUESS OF SALISBURY: We shall consider the suggestion.

LORD STRATHEDEN AND CAMPBELL: My Lords, I do not rise to detain the House at any length. Having discussed the Bill, together with its object, on three separate occasions, I may claim exemption from the task of urging much upon it, after has fallen from the noble Duke (the Duke of Westminster) and the noble Lord who have so ably defended it. The noble Duke is well qualified to guide us by his Metropolitan authority, and also by his special knowledge. The approbation of the noble Lord who followed him, is singularly valuable, since to some extent at least he represents Lord Palmerston, whose well-known enactments against smoke it is intended merely to develop and improve upon. The noble Marquess at the head of the Government (the Marquess of Salisbury) suggests delay, that the Bill may become better known to the local bodies. There is no objection to delay, if the noble Marquess urges it. But the Bill, during the three preceding Sessions, has been made sufficiently familiar to the local bodies who, in the event of its becoming law, will be required to administer it. It may be convenient that I should now point out, in a few words, the mode in which its clauses ought to be divided. The essential clauses give the local bodies power to act against domestic smoke under the veto of the Home Office, and also give the Metropolitan Board power to insist in new constructions on a better heating apparatus. Thus it is proposed to deal with actual smoke, and to anticipate incoming smoke. These principles are vital. The subsidiary clauses enable the authorities to proceed at once against smoke of unusual density, although not coming from a factory, and they enlarge the area in which the Acts of Lord Palmerston are valid. These clauses might be given up

without destruction to the objects of the measure. As to the suggestion of the noble Earl the Lord Warden of the Cinque Ports, to refer the Bill to a Select Committee, its framers would not shrink from that ordeal. It would, however, be unfavourable to despatch, and there is no clear reason for resorting to such cumbrous machinery. The point may be reserved, if the House will have the goodness to repeat its former judgments, and to read the Bill a second time this evening.

Motion agreed to ; Bill read 2ª

ELECTION TO THE LOCAL BOARD OF HEALTH, CHATHAM — FORGERY OF VOTING PAPERS.

QUESTION.   OBSERVATIONS.

LORD MONKSWELL, in rising to call attention to the wholesale forgery of signatures to voting papers alleged to have taken place at Chatham at the recent election to the Local Board of Health ; and to ask, Whether the Local Government Board will inquire into the conduct of that election, said, that on this Board, previous to the recent election, all the members had been Conservatives, and he thought he would be able to show that the Party had been determined to maintain their monopoly. So fully, in fact, did the authorities at Chatham act on the American principle of "the spoils to the victor" that there was not in connection with the Chatham Board of Health a single officer, official, or clerk belonging to the Liberal Party. Suspicion being aroused, owing to hundreds of the voting papers being signed in the same handwriting, and to the fact that the votes taken from "the Chairman's bag" were, and had been at previous elections, mostly cast for the whole Conservative ticket, the names of 30 persons were, taken down during the counting of the votes who were alleged to have voted, but could not possibly have done so, some of them being dead, while others whose names appeared on the paper were not able to write. On the voting papers being examined, 220 were found to be signed in the same handwriting, but purporting to be signed by different ratepayers, many of whom had left Chatham and could not be found, while the others declared that they had had no voting papers left at their houses. The Conservatives had obtained the signatures of two or three of those alleged to have signed to papers acknowledging their signatures, but the handwriting on the acknowledgment was quite different from that on the voting papers. These 220 papers must have been forged at the Office of the Local Board of Health, as papers which could not be left at houses, owing to there being no one to receive them, were taken back to the Office. Votes recorded at the Office were put into what was known as "the Chairman's bag," and it was found that the great majority of the votes in it had been cast for the Conservative Party. With regard to a remedy for this state of things, he thought that the Report of the Select Committee of 1878 had been right in suggesting that the present system of voting by voting papers was bad, and ought to be amended. In the second place, it was desirable that some sort of provision should be made for the representation of large minorities, such as some modification of the system of cumulative voting. What they wanted in this case, was not to prosecute some clerk who had been used as a catspaw, but to get hold of those who were pulling the strings. The matter was something more than of mere local importance, and he hoped that the noble Lord who represented the Local Government Board would see his way to granting the inquiry which was asked for. In doing so, he (Lord Monkswell) could assure him he would be acting in accordance with the wishes of a large body of the ratepayers of Chatham.

Lord BALFOUR (A Lord in Waiting), in reply, said, that in putting that Question, the noble Lord had travelled over a wide field of subjects, from the election of Representative Peers in Scotland down through cumulative voting to the discharge of *employés* from Chatham Dockyard, and into those matters he would not attempt to follow him. With regard to the point as to whether the Local Government Board would institute an inquiry into this case, he had to say that the Board had no power or jurisdiction to make such an inquiry as the noble Lord had suggested. They were confined, under Section 293 of the Public Health Act, to making inquiries concerning the public health, and there was no statutory power whatever to make any other inquiry. He would remind the noble Lord, however,

that any of the parties aggrieved had a remedy which he (Lord Balfour) thought even the Liberals of Chatham, in the present state of feeling there, would think highly satisfactory—a remedy which left no reason whatever for an appeal to the Local Government Board. Schedule 2 of the Act provided that anyone guilty of the offence of fabricating, in whole or in part, any voting paper, could be proceeded against by anyone who was aggrieved, when fines of not exceeding £20, or, in default, three months' imprisonment, could be inflicted upon the offenders.

Lord MONKSWELL said, that it was charged that the signatures were forged.

Lord BALFOUR said, he understood that the noble Lord charged someone with fabricating the voting papers, and under another Act the penalty was even more substantial, for the fine was £100, with a disability from taking part in any election for five years. He could not help thinking that, if the facts were so well known to the Liberals of Chatham, as the noble Lord had appeared to indicate, no time ought to be lost by them in enforcing the statutory powers. If these practices had really occurred, the proper course was for those who alleged them to put the law in force, and not to appeal to the Local Government Board, who had no power in the matter. Such an inquiry as the noble Lord asked for could only take place with the witnesses on oath, whereas even if the Local Government Board were to institute the inquiry asked for they could not treat witnesses on oath. With regard to the stigma which the noble Lord had cast upon the clerks in the Office of the Local Board of Chatham, he thought the charge was one which ought not to have been put forward unless he had very clear and distinct evidence as to its truth. The statement of these alleged practices throw a certain amount of suspicion on some officials, and cast an unfair reflection upon them, unless they were afforded an opportunity of cross-examining those who brought forward these allegations. The noble Lord would not expect him to enter upon the subject of cumulative voting. There was no desire on the part of the Local Government Board to throw a screen over any persons guilty of the practices alleged, and the refusal of the Local Government Board to hold the inquiry suggested was based on the fact that the Statute provided the proper remedy, and it was beyond their power to enter upon it.

LAW AND JUSTICE (IRELAND)—EQUITABLE POWERS OF COUNTY COURT JUDGES.—OBSERVATIONS.

THE DUKE OF ARGYLL, in rising to call the attention of the House to certain recent rulings of a County Court Judge in Ireland, at Killarney Quarter Sessions, and to the nature of the equitable jurisdiction apparently involved therein, said, the main difficulty before them, upon which many very different opinions had been expressed, was as to how far it would be expedient or necessary to give more arbitrary powers to the Magistracy and County Court Judges in Ireland, as it was proposed to do by the Bill they had read a second time, and upon which they were going into Committee next week. The question depended a good deal upon two questions —first, as to the state of existing society in Ireland in regard to which they were to apply these increased powers; and, secondly, what were the existing powers, and how far they would be allowed to work? Upon these questions the transactions that had recently taken place at the Killarney Quarter Sessions threw an important light. First, he wished to call attention to the evidence they had of the state of society in the South-West of Ireland. In the evidence which was given before Lord Cowper's Commission, at page 37, Mr. Warburton, the Resident Magistrate of Bantry, said he thought there were some tenants who really had not got the money; but the majority of them, he thought, could pay. In reply to a further question which was asked by Lord Cowper to this effect—"And as to those who have not got the money, does it arise from their improvidence?" the same witness said he was of opinion that the tenants, not having had to pay for so long a time, when they had the money, spent it on drink, and the women on dress, and, consequently, when they came to be pressed, they had no money at all. He (the Duke of Argyll) was much struck by that passage when he read it; but he did not quote it in the course of the debate on the second reading of the Land Law Bill, for he knew that it was now the fashion in some quarters to pooh-pooh the evidence of Judges and Resident Magistrates in Ireland if it happened to be opposed to certain views; but here they had a Resident Magistrate examined before a Royal Commission, who gave it as his distinct opinion that, as regards the South-West of Ireland, the tenantry had, to a large extent, bad money, and had been spending it on drink. Judge O'Brien had made a speech on the same subject at the Clare Assizes in March last, in which he stated that he was greatly concerned to observe that, in addition to the crime that found its way into the Court of Assizes, there was a very large increase in the offences of intoxication, which tended to show a progressive and continual demoralization among the people. In entire conformity with that was the testimony of Mr. Edward Guinness, who was largely connected with the Munster Bank for many years, who, therefore, might be assumed to have considerable knowledge of the financial condition of the Irish tenantry, and whose evidence was to be found in the Appendix to the Report of the Commission. According to this witness there was a far greater difference and distance between the thrifty and the unthrifty tenant than there was between the fair and unfair rent. It would, he said, be absurd to deny that a very large percentage of those who were unable to meet their obligations had nobody to blame for it but their own unthrifty, wasteful, and idle habits. That was the state of society which they must consider when weighing the difficulties with which Judges had to deal in the exercise of an equitable jurisdiction. With respect to the transactions at Killarney, to which he wished to call the attention of their Lordships, a report of them had been sent to him by a friend of his who was now in Ireland. The Judge in question was Mr. John Curran, Q.C., a man of great eminence in Ireland, intimately known to his (the Duke of Argyll's) noble Friend the late Lord Lieutenant (Earl Spencer), and who had been employed by that noble Lord in many arduous duties. He was a man who was not only on intimate relations with the tenantry, but had a very warm affection for them. From a report which appeared in *The Kerry Post* of March 26th last, he found that applications were made for some new public-house licences. The Chief Constable objected very much to any increase in the number of licences, and pleaded with Mr. Curran that these applications should not be granted. Mr. Curran said the magistrates would not take it as a reflection upon them; but he must say that he found more public-houses in every town in Kerry than in any other county in Ireland. How this came about he did not know; but the number of public-houses in the villages and towns in Kerry was very large; and it was no wonder to him that the people of Kerry were impoverished and unable to pay their rents, without speaking of their ordinary debts. It was next to impossible for a countryman of Kerry to carry home the produce of the sale of a calf or a pig; it was next to impossible for him to go home sober. The dicta of Judges, when they were speaking in charges, had been represented "elsewhere" as speeches to which they need pay no particular attention; but it had not yet been alleged that the dicta of Judges, in dealing with particular cases, could be so lightly treated; and he had no doubt that a man of Mr. Curran's eminence would not have expressed himself so strongly if he had not agreed with the evidence of other witnesses, to which he (the Duke of Argyll) had just referred, as to the existing state of society in the South-West of Ireland. The case he wished to bring under their Lordships' notice was one in which Mr. Curran, after expressing the above decided opinions, stayed the proceedings in an ejectment where the rent was two and a-half years in arrear, on condition that the tenant should pay a gale's rent up to the 17th April. The landlord, not wishing to be hard on the tenant, said he did not object to this arrangement, provided that the tenant would pay that and the costs, he would not execute the decree before the 17th April. Mr. Curran then said there should be a stay put to further proceedings until August or September. The landlord said he had no objection to that, and Mr. Curran remarked—"Whether you have any objection to it or not, I will make the rule." In this case the Judge assumed that he had power to stay such proceedings absolutely according to his own discretion, and he did so in this action of ejectment for 2½ years' rent, upon condition that the tenant should pay one

half-year's rent. He did not question the discretion of the Judge, but it was a pure act of discretion. It was the exercise of the very power which the noble Lord opposite proposed to give to all County Court Judges by the Government Land Bill. It was impossible, however, not to express some surprise at this particular ruling. Mr. Curran had just expressed his belief that, for the most part, the tenants would be able to pay their rents if they did not drink the money they ought to have paid to their landlords; but the difficulty was that he did not know it in regard to this particular tenant. That was just the difficulty the magistrates would always have, and he did not see how they were to deal with it. They, in common with Mr. Curran, knew the general fact that the whole or a part of the population were thus thoroughly demoralized; but they did not know it as regards A. B., the tenant before the Court. That was a difficulty with which all the magistrates in Ireland would be confronted if the Legislature extended their powers to any considerable extent with regard to the non-payment of rent. All the County Court Judges might know perfectly well that the rents were withheld either from improvidence or from the pressure put upon them by the Land League; but they might be unable to prove it in a particular case, and the discretion was, therefore, one which it would be most difficult for them to exercise. In another case, Mr. Curran expressed himself on the general state of the country in equally strong terms, and he dealt with the case in a similar way. It was impossible to read the speeches of Judges and the evidence of witnesses before Lord Cowper's Commission without seeing that they had to deal in Ireland with a society which was thoroughly demoralized. The great proportion of the people seemed to have no idea of the principles upon which private or public virtue depends. How, then, were they to be dealt with? Let his noble Friend (Earl Spencer) not imagine that the alternative which the Government had taken of seeking to give a discretionary power to the magistrate and the County Court Judge was the only one open to objection. After reading those speeches and that evidence, it was impossible for him not to feel that to enlarge very widely the discretion of

The Duke of Argyll

Judges in Ireland in the present condition of society, was to put them into a position in which it would be almost impossible for them to fulfil their duty to the country. At the same time, he hoped they would remember that the quack medicine of Home Rule would only operate in the direction of making matters still worse. In Judge Curran they had a gentleman of high character; and though they might doubt his discretion, at least, he spoke out bravely against the evils he observed in the existing condition of society. But if they had a local Executive in Ireland, appointed under the advice of those who constitute the Land League, they would have far worse rulings than this of Mr. Curran, and they would have none of his honest denunciations. The evidence given before the Royal Commission showed that on Lord Kenmare's estate there was an organized society ordering the tenants not to pay their rents under any conditions; and so great was the violence employed that tenants were dragged out of their beds and shot in the legs for having paid their rents. Everything had gone to the dogs altogether, and was as bad as it ever had been; so bad, indeed, was the condition of affairs that, at one time, tenants had gone and paid their rents in secret, and had asked that notices of ejectment might be issued against them, because that would be a protection to them, being the only means of concealing from the Land League that they had paid their rents. This showed how desperate was the state of society from the corruption of the people and the intimidation of the League. It was all very well for his noble Friend (Lord Spencer) to go about the country and say that none of these things touched him now, because he had changed his mind about Home Rule. He (the Duke of Argyll) had absolute confidence in his noble Friend's integrity; but he wanted to know, and he thought they were entitled to know, why he thought that that powerful Land League, which was now exercising so demoralizing and so criminal an influence upon the people, should cease to do so when Home Rule was set up? That raised the whole question and put it in a nutshell. He quite understood the line that had been taken by noble Lords opposite. They had brought forward their Land Bill, by which they

proposed to extend so greatly the discretion of County Court Judges, because they felt that the people of this country, too indolent to investigate the facts, would not tolerate evictions unless it could be proved in each separate case that eviction was just and necessary. He feared that no law which could be devised could carry such views into practical operation. It was, he held, of the highest importance that the people of this country ought to understand that, since the passing of the Act of 1881, the tenantry of Ireland had a large amount of protection, such as no other tenantry in the world had; and, what with voluntary abatements given by the landlords and occasional suspensions in the Courts, as in the case decided by Mr. Curran, the difficulties which had arisen from the excessive fall in prices might be easily got over. He hoped both Parties in the House would consider the state of things with which they had to deal. They had to do in Ireland, as he had said, with a society which was thoroughly demoralized; and it would be all the more demoralized if it were found that both Parties in England were abusing each other and thinking very little about how they could introduce a better system into a land which was so unhappy. He hoped, therefore, that the interests of that unfortunate country would not be sacrificed to Party spirit.

LORD FITZGERALD said, he most decidedly deprecated anticipating, in discussions of this nature, topics which most shortly come before their Lordships when the Irish Land Law Bill reached Committee. He would point out that there was no ground of complaint against his learned Friend, Judge Curran, for having stayed proceedings against a tenant in a case where the landlord objected. But as to the question whether a Judge had the right to do so, quite irrespective of the will of the landlord, if Mr. Curran had said he had this power, then he (Lord Fitzgerald) thought his friend had, to some extent, erred. He thought that Mr. Curran, who was a man of great benevolence, and, at the same time, of strict impartiality, must have stayed proceedings in the cases referred to, on condition of the payment by a certain date of part of the rent, by the consent of the landlord; otherwise, he doubted whether the Judge would have had jurisdiction to do so. There was an equitable jurisdiction given by the Act of 1881 for the payment of a reduced sum until a judicial rent was fixed, and for the stay of eviction proceedings in the meantime. But that was confined to cases of applications for fair rent to the Commissioners. There was also a power under one of the Rules published under the County Court Act of 1876, which authorized the Judge to stay proceedings, under certain conditions, in an action of ejectment. But it was commonly believed by the Profession in Ireland that that Rule was *ultra vires.* He hoped the Government would give some discretionary power of the sort to the County Court Judges in the Bill which was to come before the House next week, in lieu of the Bankruptcy Clauses, to which such strong exception had been taken.

House adjourned at Six o'clock,
till To-morrow, a quarter
past Ten o'clock.

HOUSE OF COMMONS,

Monday, 9th May, 1887.

MINUTES.]—Select Committee—Saving Life at Sea, Viscount Kilcoursie *disch.; Mr.* Gourley *added.*
Public Bills—*Second Reading* — Oaths [104], *debate adjourned;* Licensed Premises (Earlier Closing) (Scotland) * [153].
Committee—Criminal Law Amendment (Ireland) [217] [*Fourth Night*]—R.P.; Incumbents of Benefices Loans Extension Act (1886) Amendment * [230] — R.P.; Pauper Lunatic Asylums (Ireland) (Superannuation) * [62]—R.P.

QUESTIONS.

EVICTIONS (IRELAND) — THE SKINNERS' ESTATE, NEAR DRAPERSTOWN, CO. DERRY.

Mr. M'CARTAN (Down, S.) asked the Chief Secretary to the Lord Lieutenant of Ireland, Whether, at the recent evictions on the Skinners' Estate, near Draperstown, County Derry, on the 19th April last, a tenant named Frank Haughey, his wife, and 11 children (including a baby three months old), were evicted from their home on the mountain top, and left there without food or shelter; whether he is

Lord Fitzgerald

aware that when Haughey purchased the holding it was a mere waste, without even a fence, and that all the improvements had been made by the tenant at his own expense; and, whether, in such cases, the Government will, pending legislation on the subject, continue to assist in the execution of decrees of ejectment? The hon. Gentleman explained that by the third paragraph of his Question he meant would the Government assist in cases where the rent was proved to have been exorbitant?

The PARLIAMENTARY UNDER SECRETARY (Colonel King-Harman) (Kent, Isle of Thanet) (who replied) said: The Irish Government are not aware that Haughey and his family were left as alleged, nor do they consider it probable that they were, as the relieving officer doubtless received the necessary notice of the intended eviction as required by law, and had due provision made to admit them to the workhouse if they had no other shelter. As to the improvements of the tenant, he is entitled under the existing law to obtain full compensation from the landlord for them, no matter what their value may be, and whether he is evicted for nonpayment of rent or not. The Irish Government have nothing to add to the statements already made in the House as to the affording protection to Sheriffs while engaged in the execution of decrees.

Mr. M'CARTAN asked, if the right hon. and gallant Gentleman had made any inquiries about the matter?

Colonel KING-HARMAN said, the Government had made full inquiries respecting the evictions, and they could not find that there had been any case of special hardship. The Board of Guardians had received no complaint of the relieving officer having neglected his duty.

EDUCATION DEPARTMENT — NON-ATTENDING CHILDREN AT BOARD SCHOOLS.

Mr. AINSLIE (Lancashire, N., Lonsdale) asked the Vice President of the Committee of Council on Education, If he is aware that there are at least 100,000 children who still escape the notice of the attendance officers of the School Board; whether most of these children are of the very poorest class, and, owing to their extreme wretchedness, unable or unfit to attend the existing schools; and, whether he will consider the advisability of establishing numerous small schools similar to dame's schools in localities where these children are to be found; and, whether it is his opinion that the ragged schools, which particularly deal with these children, have been crushed out by the Board schools?

THE VICE PRESIDENT (Sir WILLIAM HART DYKE) (Kent, Dartford), having elicited from the hon. Member that the first part of the Question did not refer to London alone, but referred to the country generally, said that he believed even so there were no grounds for supposing that so large a number of children evaded the vigilance of the attendance officers. He did not think it would be expedient or practicable to re-introduce dame's schools for the purpose of dealing with such children. School Boards had ample powers for meeting the difficulty; and he believed the School Board for Birmingham had adopted a system of free orders. As to the last Question, he really did not wish to hazard a statement on what was, after all, a matter of opinion upon a branch of a large question.

MR. COBB (Warwick, S. E., Rugby) inquired whether the right hon. Gentleman would consider the advisability of establishing a system of free education in public elementary schools?

SIR WILLIAM HART DYKE: I think the hon. Member is leading me rather far afield.

PETITIONS—VIOLATION OF RULES—
PETITION FROM CARDIGANSHIRE—
IRREGULARITY OF SIGNATURES.

MR. BOWEN ROWLANDS (Cardiganshire) asked the Chairman of the Committee on Public Petitions, Whether his attention has been called to a Petition against the Disestablishment of the Church in Wales, presented to this House from inhabitants of Llanon and other places, Cardiganshire; whether the Petition contains a large number of signatures in the same handwriting; and, whether the following names occur in the Petition:—Mary Catherine Gwendolen Davies; Henry Basil Davies, Rosehill; Mary Jane Davies, Rosehill; R. E. B. Jones, Cadivor Villa; Dorothy Anne Catherine Jenkins; and whether the Committee is aware that these are the names of children aged respectively

two and a-half years, two years, four months, 18 months, and eight months?

MR. LEWIS (Anglesey) also asked, Whether the hon. Baronet's attention has been called to a Petition against the Disestablishment of the Church in Wales, presented to this House by the hon. Member for East Bradford (Mr. Byron Reed), from the inhabitants of Llaneilian, County of Anglesey; whether the following names occur in the Petition:—Ellen Owen, Cae Lôn; John Owen, Cae Lôn; William Owen, Cae Lôn; and, whether the Committee is aware that these are the names of children, aged respectively four years, 30 months, seven months; and that the Petition contains the names of numerous other children below school age?

THE CHAIRMAN (Sir CHARLES FORSTER) (Walsall), in reply, said, that his attention had been called to the Petition mentioned in the first Question, and it did contain many signatures in the same handwriting. Of course, such signatures had not been counted. The same answer applied to the second Question. But as to the latter part of the Question, the Committee had no means of obtaining information as to the ages of those whose names were attached to the Petition. Accepting as facts the statements in the Questions, he had no hesitation in saying that such facts were a direct violation of the Rules of the House, and cast great discredit on the Petitioners.

CENTRAL ASIA—AFGHANISTAN AND HERAT.

SIR HENRY TYLER (Great Yarmouth) asked the Under Secretary of State for India, What is the latest information he is able to give in regard to the position of affairs in Afghanistan, and the conditions as regards defence of Herat; and, whether any measures have been taken for extending the railway in the direction of Candahar?

THE UNDER SECRETARY OF STATE (Sir JOHN GORST) (Chatham): The insurrection of Ghilzais is still proceeding, and engagements have taken place in which each side has claimed the victory; but there is no reason to think that the Ameer is not holding his own. The defences of Herat have recently been strengthened by the Ameer. No plan for extending the Quetta Railway to Candahar has yet been adopted.

REGISTER HOUSE (SCOTLAND) — REPORT OF THE DEPARTMENTAL COMMITTEE, 1881.

Mr. FRASER-MACKINTOSH (Inverness-shire) asked the Lord Advocate, Whether he has any objection to lay upon the Table of the House the Report of the Departmental Committee on the Register House, Scotland, in 1881, or such portion of said Report as deals with the votes and accounts of the several officers included in the Lord Clerk Register's Department?

The SECRETARY to the TREASURY (Mr. Jackson) (Leeds, N.) (who replied) said: The Report referred to was of a confidential character. The question of laying it on the Table was considered in 1882; and so much of it as could properly be presented was laid upon the Table in August of that year. (House of Commons Paper, 3,337.) I am afraid that I cannot agree to present any further portion.

WEST INDIA ISLANDS—MR. L. D. POWLES, MAGISTRATE OF NASSAU.

Mr. ATKINSON (Boston) asked the Secretary of State for the Colonies, If his attention has been given to a statement in *The Nassau Times* of the 2nd April last, to the effect that Mr. L. D. Powles, one of the Police and Circuit Magistrates in the Colony, has said "that he would not believe a d——d Methodist on oath;" and, whether he will inquire into the truth, or otherwise, of the statement thus publicly made in a leader of *The Nassau Times?*

The SECRETARY of STATE (Sir Henry Holland) (Hampstead): I have read the statement referred to by the hon. Member, and will at once direct the Governor to make formal inquiry, and to take such steps as may be necessary, should the facts be as stated, and to report to me upon the matter.

FINANCE, &c.—LISTS OF HOLDERS OF NATIONAL SECURITIES.

Sir EDWARD WATKIN (Hythe) asked Mr. Chancellor of the Exchequer, Whether there is any reason why lists of the names and addresses of the holders of National securities, with some note against the names of holders of (say) over £2,000, should not be annually printed and published, and be purchaseable by holders of such securities, or by others, especially considering that Parliament has already imposed upon the holders of Railway property, possessing a total capital larger than the "National Debt," a similar obligation?

The CHANCELLOR of the EXCHEQUER (Mr. Goschen) (St. George's, Hanover Square): The case of the holders of Government Securities is not analogous to that of the holders of railway property, the latter being partners, whose interest it is to assure themselves as to the position and solvency of their co-partners, a necessity which does not apply to the case of persons holding Government Stocks. Under these circumstances, I do not see that there is any public object to be attained by the suggestion of the hon. Baronet which would be sufficient to justify the expense and trouble of preparing the information: and I am informed that the information, if furnished, would facilitate frauds and forgeries. Thus, as at present advised, I cannot undertake to give effect to the suggestion.

WAR OFFICE — CRIMEAN QUARTERMASTER SERGEANTS.

Sir HENRY TYLER (Great Yarmouth) asked the Secretary of State for War, Whether he will consider further the question of placing Quartermaster Sergeants, retired under previous Regulations, and who have done good service in the Crimea, on the same footing, as regards pension, with those more recently retired, having regard to the fact that Quartermaster Sergeants recently retired receive on retirement a large sum of money in addition to a larger pension; and, what would be the total amount required to confer such a benefit on Quartermaster Sergeants, who served in the Crimea and retired under the then existing Regulations, by merely increasing their pension, without giving them any additional emolument?

The SECRETARY of STATE (Mr. E. Stanhope) (Lincolnshire, Horncastle): It has always been a recognized principle that Warrants creating new rates of retired pay or pension cannot be made retrospective as far as persons already retired are concerned. Under these circumstances, I cannot possibly re-open the case of Quartermaster Sergeants pensioned before the recent Regulations came into force.

WAR OFFICE—REDUCTION OF HORSE ARTILLERY BATTERIES—FIELD ARTILLERY — FORMATION OF AMMUNITION COLUMNS.

GENERAL FRASER (Lambeth, N.) asked the Secretary of State for War, in view of the statement in his letter to the signatories appealing against the Horse Artillery reductions, that the first object for such reduction and conversion is an increase to the number of Field Artillery Batteries, in which this country is especially deficient, and consequently in the number of our more powerful and effective field guns, He still proposes to adhere to his decision that 14 batteries of Field Artillery in excess of the number required for two Army Corps—

" Will be utilized for the purpose of forming an ammunition column in the event of the Army Corps being called upon service ? "

CAPTAIN COTTON (Chesire, Wirral) also asked, Whether it is the fact that it is proposed, in the new scheme for the organization of two Army Corps, to form 14 ammunition columns by breaking up for this purpose 14 four gun field batteries; whether this arrangement will deprive the Service, on the outbreak of war, of some 32 guns of Field Artillery, in which, as he states, in his letter of the 26th ultimo, "this country is especially deficient;" and, whether these guns are now reckoned on the effective strength of the Royal Artillery ?

THE SECRETARY OF STATE (Mr. E. STANHOPE) (Lincolnshire, Horncastle): Batteries, whether of Horse or Field Artillery, would, in time of war, be absolutely useless without ammunition columns. We have at present not one of these columns, nor any organization for furnishing them, on the outbreak of hostilities. They have, therefore, to be provided; and the question is, whether entirely new *cadres* are to be created, or whether they are to be furnished out of existing organizations? The first course would cause very great additional expense; whereas the latest addition to the Field Artillery makes it possible to form ammunition columns, as proposed, and yet leave batteries sufficient for two Army Corps. This latter plan has,

therefore, been adopted; and, I may add that, so far from diminishing our fighting strength by 32 guns, it makes efficient the whole of the batteries of two Army Corps which, otherwise, could not have taken the field.

BOARD OF WORKS (IRELAND)—LOAN FOR NENAGH TOWN HALL.

MR. P. J. O'BRIEN (Tipperary, N.) asked the Chief Secretary to the Lord Lieutenant of Ireland, Whether the Town Commissioners of Nenagh, County Tipperary, having resolved to build a Town Hall, took, in the year 1884, the necessary steps under "The Irish Reproductive Loan Fund Amendment Act, 1883," and made due application to the Board of Works for a loan for that purpose out of the fund then lying to the credit of the County of Tipperary under the provisions of the said Act; whether, after Correspondence on the subject, the Board of Works assented to a loan of £2,000 for said Town Hall; whether the first set of plans, specifications, and estimates submitted by the Town Commissioners were rejected, on the ground that the estimate was too high; whether a second set of amended plans, &c., by the same architect having been again rejected by the Board, the Town Commissioners employed (at additional expense) another architect, and forwarded new plans; whether the original estimate submitted by this architect would, according to the calculation of the Board of Works themselves, entail an expenditure of only £1,980, out of a proposed loan of £2,000, and whether, by the elimination of one item by the architect, at the suggestion of the Board, this estimate was reduced by £100; whether the Board of Works first intimated that these plans were unacceptable, on the ground that the estimate of £1,980 was too high; whether, after the reduction above referred to, they have now rejected the plans, on the ground that the estimate is too low; and, whether, under these circumstances, he will request the Board of Works to re-consider their decision, and grant the required loan; and, if not, whether he will consent to have the entire Correspondence in relation to this matter laid upon the Table?

THE SECRETARY TO THE TREASURY (Mr. JACKSON) (Leeds, N.) (who replied) said, the facts were as stated in the first paragraph of the Question. As to the second paragraph, the Board of Works agreed to recommend a loan of £2,000 for the erection of a Town Hall on certain conditions, one of which was that they should be satisfied that the work would be properly carried out for that amount. The plans first submitted were rejected as unsuitable, and they manifestly could not have been carried out for anything approaching the amount of the loan. The second plans were rejected because they could not have been carried out for £2,000. The third plans, as originally submitted, could have been carried out for £1,980; and by the omission of fittings, as suggested by the architect of the Town Commissioners, a saving of £100 could have been effected on the estimate. The objection made by the Board of Works was not that the estimate was too high, but was owing to the imperfect specifications prepared for the work. The Town Commissioners having failed to have the necessary amendments made, the Board were unable to recommend the loan for sanction to the Treasury. If a revised specification were submitted, on which it would be safe for the Town Commissioners to proceed to carry out the work, the Board of Works would be prepared to recommend the granting of the loan.

INDIA — PROSECUTION OF CHINNA NARRAIN—THE CHINGLEPUT CASE.

MR. J. F. X. O'BRIEN (Mayo, S.) asked the Under Secretary of State for India, Under what circumstances Chinna Narrain, a Monegar in the Chingleput District, is now on his trial for embezzling 700 rupees, Government money, in 1882, though this charge, after most careful inquiry, was at the time dismissed by a competent Court as false; and, whether two other cases connected with the notorious Chingleput scandal of 1882 have lately been re-opened by Government?

THE UNDER SECRETARY OF STATE (Sir JOHN GORST) (Chatham): The case alluded to in the first paragraph appears to be proceeding before the regular judicial tribunals; and the Secretary of State has no official information respecting it. Of the two cases referred to in the second paragraph the Secretary of State knows nothing.

Mr. Jackson

ISLANDS OF THE SOUTH PACIFIC—TONGA.

MR. CAINE (Barrow-in-Furness) (for Mr. S. SMITH) (Flintshire) asked the Under Secretary of State for Foreign Affairs, Whether his attention has been drawn to the following statement in *The Pall Mall Gazette* of the 5th May, regarding *The Reign of Terror in Tonga*, wherein it was alleged that the British Consul was fired upon:—

"On the following day, February 3, it leaked out that six more men had been found guilty of complicity in the business, and were to be shot. Among them was David Fenan, an ordained Wesleyan minister. Thirty more, it was reported, were being tried, and would probably share the same fate. . . . . The British residents protested strongly, and the British Consul protested on behalf of our Government. Dr. Bucklands was one of the protesting parties, and it was reported that Baker's reply to him was that if anybody dared to lay a finger on him every white man in the Island should be killed. Several British residents were, in fact, fired upon, the British Consul being amongst the number. On one occasion, as the Consul and Mr. Moulton were walking in the College grounds, a bullet passed quite close to them. The bullet was found, and identified as a Government bullet. The cool determination everywhere displayed by Mr. W. E. Giles, the British pro-Consul, has won universal admiration among all classes, European and Native;"

and, whether it is the intention of Her Majesty's Government to take any steps in regard thereto?

THE SECRETARY OF STATE FOR THE COLONIES (Sir HENRY HOLLAND) (Hampstead) (who replied) said: I have already twice stated that Her Majesty's High Commissioner for the Western Pacific is now holding an inquiry into these transactions (or has completed it), and that it is necessary to await his Report, and not to accept as strictly accurate the *ex parte* statements which have appeared in the Press. But I will send out the three articles in *The Pall Mall Gazette* by the next mail to Sir Charles Mitchell.

COAL MINES, &c. REGULATION BILL—FEMALE LABOUR AT THE PIT'S BANK.

MR. M'LAREN (Cheshire, Crewe) asked the Secretary of State for the Home Department, Whether, in view of the Amendments on the Notice Paper to be moved in Committee on the Coal, Mines, &c. Regulation Bill, to prohibit future labour by women and girls at the pit's bank, he will consent to receive a deputation of those opposed to such prohibition; and, whether he will postpone the Committee on the Bill for at least a week, in order to give the women who work at the pit's bank an opportunity of making their views known?

THE UNDER SECRETARY OF STATE (Mr. STUART-WORTLEY) Sheffield, Hallam) (who replied) said: The Secretary of State will have much pleasure in receiving a deputation of those opposed to the prohibition of labour by women and girls at the pit bank. He will undertake that discussion on the clauses of the Bill in Committee shall be postponed for a week; but will avail himself of the earliest opportunity to take the general discussion before going into Committee, which is desired by some hon. Members.

MERCHANT SHIPPING—WRECK OF THE CHANNEL STEAMER "VICTORIA."

MR. ISSACS (Newington, Walworth) asked the Secretary to the Board of Trade, Whether he is in a position to inform the House the reason given by the French Maritime Authorities for the non-sounding of the fog-horn at the lighthouse at Point D'Ailly, on the occasion of the Channel Steamer *Victoria* striking on a rock off that point, on the 13th of April last, during the fog then prevailing?

THE SECRETARY (Baron HENRY DE WORMS) (Liverpool, East Toxteth): Not at present, Sir. The Report of the Court of Inquiry will, when received, be transmitted to the Foreign Office, with a view to its being communicated to the French Maratime Authorities.

NORTH SEA FISHERIES — DEPREDATIONS BY FOREIGN FISHERMEN.

SIR SAVILE CROSSLEY (Suffolk, Lowestoft) asked the Under Secretary of State for Foreign Affairs, What steps have been taken by Her Majesty's Government to carry out the recommendations of the Board of Trade Committee, appointed to inquire into the depredations committed by foreign fishermen in the North Sea; and, whether those recommendations can be carried out before the commencement of the autumn fishing season, in order to prevent a recurrence of the outrages which have been so disastrous in past years?

THE UNDER SECRETARY OF STATE (Sir JAMES FERGUSSON) (Manchester, N.E.): As far as the Foreign Office is concerned, the Report of the Committee was sent on April 13 to Her Majesty's Representatives in the countries which are parties to the North Sea Convention of 1882. Belgium is the only country much concerned; and a reply has been received from Her Majesty's Minister at Brussels that the Belgian Government are seriously considering the Report, and are fully alive to the existing evils and to the occasion for remedies. The Governments of France and of the Netherlands have thanked Her Majesty's Government for transmitting the Report. No replies have been received from Germany and Denmark; but those countries are hardly at all concerned.

EVICTIONS (IRELAND)—EVICTIONS ON LORD GRANARD'S ESTATE.

MR. CHANCE (Kilkenny, S.) asked the Parliamentary Under Secretary to the Lord Lieutenant of Ireland, Whether any Statement has been received from Lord Granard or his representatives as to the allegation of Messrs. Roe, that the mortgagees of Lord Granard's estates were responsible for the impending evictions on such estates, or as to the allegation that the authorities of Maynooth College are the mortgagees; and, whether he will lay such Statement upon the Table of the House?

THE PARLIAMENTARY UNDER SECRETARY (Colonel KING-HARMAN) (Kent, Isle of Thanet): Sir, the Irish Government have nothing to add to my reply given to a Question on this subject on Thursday last, beyond saying that they have received convincing assurances that the authorities of Maynooth College are the mortgagees of Lord Granard's Drumlish property for a considerable sum, and that they have been pressing —and naturally pressing—for the interest due.

MR. CHANCE: By the indulgence of House, as this is a matter of some importance, I wish to make a short statement. On Thursday night, the right hon. and gallant Gentleman, in reply to a Question, said the Government were informed that the agents had stated that it was the mortgagees who were pressing the matter to eviction, that the agents were Messrs. Roe, and the mortgagees

Maynooth College. I hold in my hand a statement from the President of Maynooth College, in which he says neither the authorities nor any other person connected with the College are responsible, directly or indirectly, for originating or pressing these evictions, and that the first he heard of them was in the newspapers. I hold in my hand a copy of a letter written on the 7th instant by Lord Granard to the President of Maynooth College, in which he expresses his surprise at the statement of the right hon. and gallant Gentleman, and characterizes it as utterly erroneous. I have now to ask the right hon. and gallant Gentleman who is the informant of the Government in this matter; and, whether he will lay the information he has received before the House?

COLONEL KING-HARMAN: The information the Government received on this question with regard to the mortgagees was obtained from the officials engaged in the administration of the law in County Longford. The House will remember that I did not state the name of the mortgagees until specially asked the question by the hon. and learned Member for North Longford (Mr. T. M. Healy). I particularly refrained from doing so. My informants with regard to the College authorities being the mortgagees were Messrs. Darley and Roe; and I have received information from them that not only that Maynooth did hold the mortgage, but as to the sum and the conditions of the mortgage.

MR. CHANCE: Will the right hon. and gallant Gentleman inform the House whether he has received any information from Lord Granard on the subject; and whether he still states that the Trustees or authorities of Maynooth College are, directly or indirectly, party or privy to these transactions?

COLONEL KING-HARMAN: I am not aware, nor did I ever state, that Maynooth College were. [*Cries of* "You did!" *from the Irish Benches.*] What I stated was that the agents had made no secret of the matter that Lord Granard was not in the least anxious to treat his tenants harshly, but for the action of the mortgagees, as I have said just now, in pressing—and very naturally and properly pressing—for the interest due on the mortgage, which obliged the landlord to

Mr. Chance

have recourse to proceedings against the tenants.

MR. T. M. HEALY (Longford, N.): He states now that it was the mortgagees who were responsible for these evictions; and I wish to ask has his attention been called——

COLONEL KING-HARMAN: I never made use of the words the hon. and learned Gentleman used.

MR. T. M. HEALY said, that the right hon. and gallant Gentleman wished to imply that the authorities of Maynooth were responsible for these evictions; and he would like to ask him if his attention had been called to a letter which had been published in *The Longford Independent* of the 26th ultimo, which was addressed to the clerk at the Mohill Union, and which was a follows:—

"In reference to the statement made by you that the above estate, on which the evictions took place, is out of Lord Granard's hands, and in the hands of a receiver, we must ask you to contradict this statement at the next meeting of the Board. His Lordship's estate is not, nor never has been in the hands of a receiver.— Yours, &c., Darley and Roe."

He (Mr. Healy) wished to ask the right hon. and gallant Gentleman, as Messrs. Darley and Roe were the agents of Lord Granard, how it was he had drawn in the name of Maynooth College in order to prejudice a seminary for the education of Catholic priests?

MR. CHANCE: I wish to remind the right hon. and gallant Gentleman of his words on Thursday night.

MR. SPEAKER: Order, order! The hon. Gentleman is not entitled to debate this Question. The Question has been asked, and it is for the right hon. and gallant Gentleman to answer if he sees fit.

MR. T. M. HEALY: I wish to ask the First Lord of the Treasury, whether, in these matters, it is part of the instructions of the Government that the right hon. Gentleman the Chief Secretary to the Lord Lieutenant deliberately abstains from coming into the House until Questions are over; because, if that be the case, I will draw attention to it as a matter of urgent public importance.

THE FIRST LORD (Mr. W. H. SMITH) (Strand, Westminster): I think that is a Question which really ought not to be put to me. The exigencies of Public

Business require, under certain circumstances, that the Chief Secretary should devote himself to urgent business of his Department ; and, in the meanwhile, my right hon. and gallant Friend (Colonel King-Harman) answers the Questions, and the duties to the public and the House are adequately discharged.

MR. T. M. HEALY: I wish to give Notice that if the Chief Secretary continues to absent himself, and leaves us to the mercy of this Orangeman, I shall call attention— —

MR. SPEAKER: Order, order! The interposition of the hon. and learned Gentleman is most un-Parliamentary.

LAW AND JUSTICE (IRELAND)—SENTENCE ON ROBERT COMERFORD.

MR. M'CARTAN (Down, S.) asked the Chief Secretary to the Lord Lieutenant of Ireland, in reference to the case of Robert Comerford, who was sentenced by magistrates at Belfast in July last to 29 months' imprisonment with hard labour on conviction of an offence which, if committed in England, could not be punished with a longer period than six months' imprisonment, Whether the Government will consider the advisability of extending to Ireland the provisions which make six months' imprisonment the extreme penalty in England for assaults committed on the same occasion ; whether, in view of the dissimilarity of the laws in England and Ireland he will advise His Excellency the Lord Lieutenant of Ireland to re-consider the claim on his clemency in Comerford's case ; and, whether in England, on conviction of any felony or misdemeanour, a prisoner is ever sentenced by a Judge of Assize to hard labour for a longer period that two years?

THE PARLIAMENTARY UNDER SECRETARY (Colonel KING-HARMAN) (Kent, Isle of Thanet): The circumstances of this case have, on a recent occasion, been brought under the notice of the Government. I have also gone carefully into the case, and I find that five assaults were committed on five different occasions, and, in addition, that two rescues were made. Mr. Comerford is a man of bad character, who has undergone 15 previous convictions.

MR. M'CARTAN asked if the different assaults were not committed at the same time?

COLONEL KING-HARMAN: No; they were not. The three assaults were committed a considerable time apart, and there was something like two months between the three first assaults and the two second ones.

IRELAND—LETTER OF MR. EGAN.

MR. T. M. HEALY (Longford, N.) asked the Parliamentary Under Secretary to the Lord Lieutenant of Ireland, If he will state what answer has been returned to the letter of Mr. Egan, in which he offers to return to Dublin and take his trial if a criminal charge is formulated against him, provided the venue is not removed from Dublin ?

THE PARLIAMENTARY UNDER SECRETARY (Colonel KING-HARMAN) (Kent, Isle of Thanet): No Sir ; no answer has been returned to that letter, because no such letter has been received.

POST OFFICE — TELEGRAMS FROM LIVERPOOL TO BREMEN AND HAVRE *vid* NEW YORK.

MR. BADEN - POWELL (Liverpool, Kirkdale) asked the Postmaster General, Whether he is aware that Liverpool merchants and brokers at present send telegrams from Liverpool to Bremen and Havre *vid* New York, because they thereby save from one and a-half to two hours of the time ordinarily occupied by telegrams passing over the direct Government line and Submarine Telegraph Company's cable, and that the increased expense and delay is a serious impediment to business ; and, whether he can now state that any steps have been taken to remedy this in accordance with the terms of the letter from the General Post Office, of 1st February 1887, to the Liverpool Chamber of Commerce?

THE POSTMASTER GENERAL (Mr. RAIKES) (Cambridge University): Since the hon. Member's question was placed on the Notice Paper, I have ascertained upon inquiry that the Commercial Cable Company have accepted from merchants in Liverpool messages for Havre, and that such messages have been paid for at the tariff from England to America and from America to France. This practice is contrary to the agreement between the Department and the Company, and is not followed by any other American Cable Company. The average time taken in the transmission of messages between Havre and Liverpool is under an hour ; and there would, therefore, appear to be some mistake in supposing that the saving can be as stated in the hon. Member's Question. I am informed by the American Telegraph Companies that they have no knowledge of messages for Bremen having been sent over their lines. The whole question of the telegraphic communication between England and the neighbouring continental countries is at the present time receiving my earnest consideration.

INDIA—PRIZE MONEY.

MR. E. ROBERTSON (Dundee) asked the Under Secretary of State for India, Whether there is any objection to lay upon the Table of the House a short Return showing the amounts realised by the Indian Government, since 1857, from movable property belonging to the ex-Sovereigns or Princes of Lucknow, Jhansi, Kirwee, and Mandalay, not distributed as prize money to the troops?

THE UNDER SECRETARY OF STATE (Sir JOHN GORST) (Chatham): The Returns of July 5, 1869, and July 23, 1874, give full information respecting the Kirwee and Lucknow prize money. No question has arisen respecting that at Jhansi, which is all distributed; and no distribution of prize money from Mandalay has been made. The Return suggested is therefore, in the opinion of the Secretary of State, inexpedient.

SITTINGS AND ADJOURNMENT OF THE HOUSE—THE WHITSUNTIDE RECESS.

MR. ESSLEMONT (Aberldeen, E.) asked the First Lord of the Treasury, Whether, in consideration of the shortness of the Recess at Easter, the Government will consider and inform the House on an early day as to the date and probable duration of the adjournment at Whitsuntide?

THE FIRST LORD (Mr. W. H. SMITH) (Strand, Westminster): I must remind the hon. Gentleman that we are still at some distance from Whitsuntide; and, in the present state of Public Business, it is not in my power to make the statement which he desires. I hope to be in a position to make a statement next Monday, if in the interval, as I trust, substantial progress may have been made with Public Business.

MR. ESSLEMONT: I will repeat the Question on Monday.

Mr. Raikes

MR. ARTHUR O'CONNOR, MEMBER FOR EAST DONEGAL.

PERSONAL EXPLANATION.

MR. ARTHUR O'CONNOR(Donegal, E.): Sir, I ask the indulgence of the House while I make an observation of a personal character. Hon. Members will have noticed that in the articles copied from *The Times* which under your direction were circulated with the Votes and Proceedings of this House my name was more than once mentioned. It may be in the knowledge of many Members of this House, also that at the date of the suppression of the Land League I was in charge of the Land League offices and that there was, at that date, a warrant issued for my arrest. Nevertheless, since that time, Her Majesty's Government, in the year 1885, did not think it unfitting that they should invite me to act as a Member of the Royal Commission on the Depression of Trade. Again, last year, Her Majesty's present Advisers thought fit to nominate me to another Royal Commission to inquire into the administration of the Civil Services of the country. Under these circumstances, when these articles—which as long as they merely appeared in a newspaper I was perfectly content to treat with contempt—were brought formally under the notice of the House by the Motion of the hon. Baronet opposite (Sir Charles Lewis) I watched with considerable interest the attitude of the Government. It appears to me from their conduct on Friday last, and from the decision they ultimately came to, that they were perfectly willing to make Party capital out of allegations and insinuations such as have appeared in these articles. Under these circumstances, I do not consider it becoming either to myself or proper in the discharge of my duties to my constituents or to my Colleagues in this House any longer to serve on that Royal Commission, and I have intimated to the Chairman my desire that he should take such steps as may be necessary to cause my name to be removed from the list of Commissioners.

BUSINESS OF THE HOUSE.

THE FIRST LORD OF THE TREASURY (Mr. W. H. SMITH) (Strand, Westminster): I think I am under an engagement to right hon. Gentlemen opposite to state what the course of Public Business will be this week. We propose to continue the discussion of the Criminal Law Amendment (Ireland) Bill until Thursday, and on Thursday to take as the first Order the Duke of Connaught's Leave Bill; and the Vote for the Abbey, for the funds necessary to celebrate the Jubilee Service, as the second Order. The third Order will be the Customs and Inland Revenue Bill, which, we hope, will be reached at an early hour.

LORD RANDOLPH CHURCHILL (Paddington, S.): Will the right hon. Gentleman state when the Motion for referring the Army and Navy Estimates to a Parliamentary Committee will be made?

MR. W. H. SMITH: My noble Friend is aware that the Notice has been on the Paper for several weeks, if not months, and we have been exceedingly anxious to get it accepted without debate, as the condition of Public Business is such as to make it impossible to give an opportunity for debate. My noble Friend is aware that one of the conditions on which the Government put it down on the Paper was that it should be so accepted. But it has been blocked, and it has not been reached on any occasion before half-past 12 since it has been put on the Paper. Under these circumstances, it rests with those Gentlemen who oppose the Motion, for reasons unknown to me, to take the steps necessary to enable it to be made, and the inquiry to be undertaken by a Committee, which the Government are most anxious should be done without any loss of time.

LORD RANDOLPH CHURCHILL: May I ask whether we are to understand that Her Majesty's Government attach greater importance to getting the small sum of money necessary for the decoration of Westminster Abbey than to the far more important question of referring the Army and Navy Estimates to a Parliamentary Committee?

MR. W. H. SMITH: No; I do not attach more importance to that question; but I do also attach importance to the principle of not spending money until it has been voted by this House. It is a question with regard to the Jubilee, which the noble Lord will recognize ought not to be postponed. I should be very glad, indeed, if we reach that Motion before 8 o'clock on Thursday.

MR. CHILDERS (Edinburgh, S.): I rise to make a suggestion to the right hon. Gentleman. It is, that after the Duke of Connaught's Leave Bill the Motion for a Parliamentary Committee on the Army and Navy Estimates should be the next Order, Supply will have already lost its privilege by not being the first order.

MR. W. H. SMITH: I will consider the suggestion.

MR. RATHBONE (Carnarvonshire, Arfon): Do the Government intend to continue to take the private Members' nights on Tuesdays and Fridays?

MR. W. H. SMITH: Most certainly, until the Criminal Law Amendment (Ireland) Bill is through.

MR. LABOUCHERE (Northampton): May I ask the right hon. Gentleman. with regard to the observation which has just fallen from him, that he objects to spending money before the money is voted, who is at present paying the workmen now employed in the Abbey?

[No reply.]

ORDERS OF THE DAY.

CRIMINAL LAW AMENDMENT (IRELAND) BILL.—[BILL 217.]
(*Mr. A. J. Balfour, Mr. Secretary Matthews, Mr. Attorney General, Mr. Attorney General for Ireland.*)

COMMITTEE. [*Progress 3rd May.*]

[FOURTH NIGHT.]

Bill *considered* in Committee.
(In the Committee.)
PRELIMINARY INQUIRY.

Clause 1 (Inquiry by order of Attorney General).

MR. ANDERSON (Elgin and Nairn): I beg to move the omission in line 10 of the words "although no person may be charged before him with the commission of such crime." The words which I propose to leave out are very important words, and very much extend the scope of the preliminary inquiry which the Resident Magistrate is to undertake. Hon. Members will remember that this is called a Preliminary Inquiry Clause, but it is in reality a clause for the permanent establishment in Ireland of the inquisition. Bearing that fact in mind, hon. Members, I am sure, will see the importance of limiting that inquisition as much as possible. As the clause is at present drawn, it will be possible for any Resident Magistrate when put in force by the Attorney General to summon before him any number of persons, although nobody is charged with or accused of having committed any offence. That is the nature of the clause as it stands at present, and I wish to point out to the Committee that that is a condition of things which does not exist in any other part of the United Kingdom, but is altogether unknown. [The LORD ADVOCATE dissented.] The Lord Advocate seems surprised at that statement, but I am perfectly correct. Under the clause as it is now drawn, not only may people be summoned without any offence being charged, but they will be compelled to answer questions which may criminate themselves. I think the right hon. and learned Lord Advocate will see that under no circumstances, even in Scotland, is that the law. Therefore I think I am justified in saying that this clause as it is now drawn, is wholly unknown both to the law of Scotland and the rest of the United Kingdom. I think the Committee will see the importance of limiting the inquiry, because as it now stands—take the case of some combination to obtain a reduction of rent, or anything of that kind—it would be in the power of a Resident Magistrate to examine persons in a very general kind of way in regard to matters for which they might themselves be subsequently punished, and without any person being accused of an offence. I maintain that unless those words are omitted, we shall be establishing in short a kind of inquisition in which every person will be bound to answer the questions which will be put to him, whether they are incriminatory or not.

THE CHAIRMAN: I have waited to hear the explanation given by the hon. and learned Member of his Amendment. The Amendment has in my opinion been already negatived. It was proposed as a proviso, that the provisions of the clause should not be put in operation unless a person had been made amenable to such an offence. The actual words I think were "Provided that such person has not been made amenable for such offence." Those words were negatived, and therefore the Committee have already laid down that it is not necessary for any person to be made amenable. Under these circumstances, I am of opinion that

Mr. Anderson

the Amendment moved by the hon. and learned Member is not regular.

MR. ANDERSON: My Amendment is to strike out the words "although no person may be charged before him with the commission of such crime." I maintain that that is not the same question as that which you, Mr. Courtney, have put —namely, that it is not necessary that any person should be made amenable.

THE CHAIRMAN: I must say I do not see the distinction which the hon. and learned Member attempts to draw.

MR. ANDERSON: The distinction is that the words "that no person has been made amenable" would not apply to the case of a person who was actually in custody. The strict meaning of the words "made amenable" are pretty well understood in ordinary criminal proceedings, and are very different from the words "although no person may be charged before a magistrate with the commission of such crime." Under these words, it would not be necessary that any person should have been taken into custody. If you rule that the two expressions are identical, of course I cannot proceed further; but I would submit to you, with great respect, that "made amenable" and "not charged" have each a clear and distinct meaning. I believe there is no legal definition of what "made amenable" is, and I imagine that a person charged has a much larger and wider definition than "a person made amenable." I would suggest that, although no person may be charged before the Resident Magistrate, the commission of a crime is a different thing from the examination before a magistrate where there has been no person made amenable.

THE CHAIRMAN: The person accused of an offence may not have been charged before a magistrate. I am obliged to rule that the question already decided was analogous to the question now raised by the hon. and learned Member. Of course, before a person is proceeded against for the commission of an offence, he must be charged some where.

MR. ANDERSON: Of course, if you rule that the Amendment is irregular, I am bound to abide by your ruling. I do not for a moment suggest that I am able to carry the matter further.

THE CHAIRMAN: I only waited to hear from the hon. and learned Member how he distinguished between the two cases; and having heard the hon. Member's explanation, if he is unable to carry it further I am bound to rule that the question involved in his Amendment has already been decided.

MR. T. M. HEALY (Longford, N.): I had an Amendment on the Paper, but I gave way to the hon. and learned Member for Elgin (Mr. Anderson). I propose to omit the words "although no person may be charged" in order to insert the words "until some person has been charged." That Amendment, I apprehend, will be in Order. My object is to prevent the Government from empowering the Resident Magistrate to conduct a secret inquiry, and to call various persons before him where no person had been actually charged with a specific crime. Under these circumstances, if you, Mr. Courtney, rule that I am in Order, I will move to insert the words "until some person has been charged," instead of the words "although no person may be charged before him with the commission of such crime." The Government will have full power to hold an inquiry either in public or in private, and, in my opinion, there ought to be this protection—that an inquiry should not be taken until some person is charged with the commission of some offence. I presume that the necessity of the clause arises from the fact that it is desirable to make some person amenable, and when you have some person who can be made amenable, it will not be contended that this provision is required. Why, I would ask, under such circumstances, do you want a secret inquiry? You have already got your man, and you have full power under the Petty Sessions Act of holding an inquiry. Therefore, I cannot see any advantage that is to be derived from giving the Government the power of holding a secret inquiry.

THE CHAIRMAN: I think the proposed Amendment would be in Order, because it does not run side by side with the Amendment which has already been negatived, to provide that some person should be made amenable. It is a different thing to provide that when some person has been made amenable and charged with an offence this special power should cease. I understand the proposal of the hon. and learned Member to be that when any person has

been arrested for a crime, no such inquiry shall take place except in the presence of the accused. If that is the point which the hon. and learned Member desires to raise, he is at liberty to do so.

MR. T. M. HEALY: I must call attention to the slipshod way in which we are proceeding. We have now got beyond the word "crime." The Government proposed that when this word was reached, the word "offence" should be substituted for "crime;" and yet they have now allowed the matter to go by. They do not seem to take the slightest interest in their own Bill. Certainly, they have not taken the smallest trouble to make the two words coincide; and, as the clause now stands, we have in one part of it the words "such offence," and afterwards the words "such crime."

THE CHIEF SECRETARY FOR IRELAND (MR. A. J. BALFOUR) (Manchester, E.): The hon. and learned Gentleman has alluded to a conversation which took place some days ago, when the Government intimated that they had no objection to substitute the word "offence" for the word "crime." I have no hesitation in saying that it would have been far better drafting to have substituted the word "offence" for "crime," and I stated that I was quite ready to do so. But how was that declaration on the part of the Government met? The right hon. Gentleman the Member for Mid Lothian (Mr. W. E. Gladstone) told us that he would oppose the alteration to the best of his power. Therefore, I was apprehensive that the right hon. Gentleman, in resisting the alteration, would put his argument forward in an extremely powerful form, that it would probably give rise to a prolonged discussion—not, perhaps, on the part of the right hon. Gentleman himself, but a discussion which, having been initiated by him, the right hon. Gentleman would have no power to control. As a matter of fact, I was apprehensive that the right hon. Gentleman would let loose a waterflood which might overwhelm us. We regard this as a purely verbal alteration—a drafting Amendment, as the words mean exactly the same thing; and considering the amount of time which has already been devoted to the consideration of the Bill, and the extraordinarily slow progress we have hitherto made, the Government do not think they can incur the responsibility of initiating a discussion which must be prolonged, and which, in their opinion, is altogether unnecessary.

THE CHAIRMAN: I must point out that at the present moment there is no Motion before the Committee.

MR. W. E. GLADSTONE (Edinburgh, Mid Lothian): Perhaps by the indulgence of the Committee I may be allowed to say that, as far as I am concerned, I have no desire to raise any point which has been argued before. At the same time, the right hon. Gentleman is quite right in saying that I objected to this alteration.

MR. T. M. HEALY: I wish to point out that the Government are themselves to blame for the continual discussions which take place in the endeavour to make one part of the Bill square with another. It is the bad drafting of the Bill by the Government which has led to that result.

MR. A. J. BALFOUR: Shall I be out of Order if I say that the alteration which the hon. and learned Gentleman now seeks to make is altogether contrary to his own argument on a previous occasion ?

MR. T. M. HEALY: I beg to give Notice that on the Report stage I shall move, in the first part of the clause, to strike out the word "offence," and insert "crime."

MR. CLANCY (Dublin Co., N.): I rise for the purpose of moving an Amendment which stands in the name of the hon. Member for Roscommon (Dr. Commins)—namely, in line 11, after "crime," to insert "publicly." The object of the Amendment is to require that all these preliminary inquiries shall be held in public. We have been told that one of the objects of this clause is to assimilate the law in Ireland to that which exists in Scotland; but I maintain that there is a very material difference between the law of Scotland and what is proposed here. I have been given to understand that before a preliminary inquiry can take place in Scotland, not only must there be an accused person charged, but that there must have been a public preliminary examination before the Sheriff.

THE LORD ADVOCATE (Mr. J. H. A. MACDONALD) (Edinburgh and St. Andrew's Universities): Not at all.

MR. CLANCY: The right hon. and learned Lord Advocate will probably get up later on, and explain how the matter stands. But I certainly read in his own book, only a few nights ago, that that was the practice in Scotland— namely, that proceedings of this nature are initiated by the Procurator Fiscal, and that the next step is to go before the Sheriff, and lay a *primâ facie* case publicly before him.

MR. J. H. A. MACDONALD : Nothing of the kind.

MR. CLANCY: I am only stating what I read in the book to which I refer, and I repeat it certainly asserts that the first step is for the Procurator Fiscal to go before the Sheriff, and make out a *primâ facie* case, before any preliminary private inquiry can take place at all. It is only with the permission of the Sheriff that a preliminary inquiry can take place. Now, I maintain that if we are to have this preliminary inquiry, we are entitled to demand that the law of Scotland shall be substantially followed; and, in the second place, to ask that the inquiry shall be public. It must be borne in mind that the preliminary inquiry is to be made under the *régime* of the Resident Magistrate, and it is well known that most extraordinary things now take place in Ireland under the auspices of that body of functionaries—things which would, at any rate, certainly appear most extraordinary to the English public. In confirmation of that assertion, I should like to draw attention to what occurred only a few days ago, at an inquiry in the County of Cork at a place called Ardarn. Two Emergency men were brought before the Court on a summons, charged by a man with having attacked his house and presented a revolver at him.

THE CHAIRMAN : The remarks of the hon. Member are scarcely relevant to the Amendment he is moving, which is simply to provide that the preliminary inquiry shall be public.

MR. CLANCY : I was only going to mention this incident in support of the Amendment that the inquiry should be public; and I was going to argue that if such things can be done in open Court, what may we not expect in a private inquiry ? If such things can be done in the green wood, what may not be done in the dry ?

THE CHAIRMAN: I do not think that the observations of the hon. Member are at all relevant to the Amendment.

MR. CLANCY: Then I will content myself with the statement that, in my opinion, the substitution of a secret inquiry for a public trial in Ireland will result in scandalous perversions of justice. If there is to be no publicity in regard to these proceedings, the Resident Magistrates will simply follow the guidance of Dublin Castle. I think we are entitled to presume and predict, that, infamous as the acts have been, which have characterized the proceedings of the Executive in the past, still more infamous things are likely to be perpetrated if a private inquiry is substituted for a public examination. Moreover, the Irish people will be fully justified in arriving at the conclusion that things which can only be done in private cannot be defended. Are we to have any guarantee that the proceedings at these private investigations will ever come to the knowledge of the public at all? I am aware that a proviso is intended to be inserted requiring that notes of these private proceedings shall be furnished. But I am not sure that such reports will be laid regularly on the Table of this House. Of course, if that were done, it would to some extent mitigate the evils of which I complain, and would act as some check upon the Resident Magistrates. But I do not understand that the shorthand writers' notes will be laid regularly on the Table, or that they will be accessible at any time to Members of Parliament, or any other person who may be desirous of seeing them. In view of that state of things, we are entitled to ask that the preliminary inquiry shall be public, and that it shall not be held in secret—that these Resident Magistrates shall act in the face of the public, and upon their full responsibility. We believe that as the clause stands their responsibity will be a sham responsibility. Their only responsibility would be their own sweet will, and that of the landlords by whom they are surrounded and supported. Under these circumstances, I hope the Government will consider that this Amendment is not an unreasonable one, nor that it will defeat the object of any preliminary inquiry held under it. There can be no doubt that if a preliminary investigation takes place in private, any person who is examined will take very good care, when the examination is over, to inform his friends and neighbours of all that has passed. The additional guarantee which will be provided by the Amendment is this, that any blackguard or rascal who may court these inquiries, or who may give evidence casting serious imputations upon his neighbours, may be deterred by the fact that every statement he may make will be made in the hearing of those who will be able to contradict him if anything he states is untrue. I shall listen with some curiosity for the reasons which the Government may give for refusing the Amendment, should they refuse it, but I sincerely hope that it will be accepted.

Amendment proposed, in page 1, line 11, after "crime" insert "publicly."— (*Mr. Clancy.*)

Question proposed, "That the word 'publicly' be there inserted."

MR. A. J. BALFOUR: I hope the hon. Gentleman will pardon me if I fail altogether to satisfy the curiosity he has expressed. The hon. Member must be aware that the whole discussion of every Amendment upon this clause has proceeded upon the basis that the inquiry to which the clause relates is to be a secret inquiry. That is the very essence of the clause.

MR. CLANCY: A private inquiry.

MR. A. J. BALFOUR: Yes, a private inquiry; that is the essence of the clause. If the hon. Member dissents from that view—which he has a perfect right to do—he ought to refrain from moving this Amendment, which would stultify the whole clause, and then, when the clause is put from the Chair, he will be at liberty to ask the Committee to divide against it.

MR. T. M. HEALY: I think it would save the time of the Committee if the Government would say what Amendments they are prepared to accept. I can assure the Government that if they would intimate what concessions they are prepared to make, a great deal of waste of time might be avoided; but so far as we have gone at present it would appear that the Government have no desire except that of rejecting our Amendments *en masse.* The Irish Attorney General stated when the Bill was last under consideration that shorthand writers' notes would be taken of the proceedings. If that is so, may I ask what the good of the shorthand writers' notes of the proceedings will be, if they are to be kept secret? I think the right hon. Gentleman has made the matter still worse by dwelling on the word "secret." I had hoped that when the depositions were taken they would be accessible in some way to the person charged. It certainly will be a monstrous waste of public money to have shorthand writers' notes taken at the public expense, and then to deny the persons who are accused the opportunity of ascertaining what it is that has been given in evidence against them. I think we are entitled to know what the secrecy is for, and what is to be done with the shorthand writers' notes when they are taken. I would further ask the Government to tell us which of our Amendments they are going to accept, so that we may come to some sort of compromise with them. How do they propose to conduct these secret inquiries? Are they to take place at midnight, or are they to be restricted between the hours of 10 a.m. and 6 p.m.? When the right hon. Gentleman the Member for Derby (Sir William Harcourt) was conducting a similar Bill three years ago he conducted it in an entirely different manner. His tone was invariably conciliatory, and the treatment which the Irish Members received was altogether different from that which they are receiving now. I do not say that the right hon. Gentleman opposite has lost his temper as yet; nevertheless, we have only been three nights in Committee, and he is already complaining of the enormous waste of time which has taken place. I must remind the right hon. Gentleman that we are here in the discharge of our duty; and if the Government will evince a disposition to consider our Amendments in a proper spirit, I think the right hon. Gentleman will have no cause to complain that substantial progress is not made.

MR. A. J. BALFOUR: The hon. and learned Gentleman says that the temper displayed by the right hon. Gentleman the Member for Derby in discussing the clauses of a previous Bill was very much more conciliatory than that which has been displayed by the Government on this occasion.

Mr. T. M. Healy

MR. T. M. HEALY: I said that the right hon. Member for Derby never lost his temper.

MR. A. J. BALFOUR: Nor have we lost our temper; and I must remind the hon. and learned Gentleman that the right hon. Gentleman the Member for Derby got through the clause in his Bill which corresponds with this clause in one day, whereas we have only got through 11 lines of ours in four days. Therefore, if the precedent of 1882 is to be quoted, it will certainly not bear out the suggestion of the hon. and learned Member, at any rate so far as the progress made with the Bill is concerned. I do not propose to discuss the point which is raised by the Amendment; I will only point out that if we were to accept it, it would entirely destroy the whole principle of the clause. The hon. and learned Member asks the Government to say what concessions they are prepared to make, and he tells us that time would in that way be saved; but, so far, I would ask what advantage has the Government gained by taking hon. Gentlemen into their confidence? The Government told hon. Members they were willing to accept the Amendment as to shorthand writers, and the sole result of that has been that hon. Gentlemen have used that concession as a peg on which to hang a long criticism of the whole conduct of the Government. I cannot see what good purpose can be secured by discussing beforehand the merits of Amendments which have not yet been reached. When we do reach them I shall be happy to discuss them, and the Government will do in the future as they have done in the past—namely, put into their Bill any suggestion which will either improve it, or not materially alter it for the worse.

MR. CHANCE: I cannot quite understand the attitude which the Government have taken up on this question. I do not consider it possible to imagine how the evidence of witnesses brought before this tribunal and examined by a Resident Magistrate can be kept secret. When a witness has been examined, I presume that he will be allowed to go back to his home. He is not, I suppose, to be shut out from all intercourse with the civilized world until the trial is over. Then, of course, when he goes back he will naturally tell his friends and neighbours everything that he has stated in the preliminary inquiry. Therefore, I think, if only to prevent misrepresentation, that it is in the highest degree necessary that there should be publicity in this matter. I recollect a trial which occurred in Dublin not very long ago, in which I heard a Resident Magistrate make a very curious admission in reference to some depositions which he had taken. This Resident Magistrate happened to be a shorthand writer, and in examining the witnesses he took down their evidence in shorthand. Having done so, he retired to a private room, where he wrote out those portions of the evidence which he considered necessary to be reproduced on the trial; but he left out most essential statements which tended to prove the innocence of the prisoner. Now, if such things are not to occur again, it is highly desirable that a certain amount of publicity ought to be allowed. The Chief Secretary has told the Committee that a similar clause to this, which was contained in the Bill of 1882, passed in a couple of nights.

Mr. A. J. BALFOUR: No; in one night.

Mr. CHANCE: I would remind the right hon. Gentleman that the corresponding clause in the Bill of 1882 was altogether different in principle from this clause. In the Bill of 1882 it will be found that the application of this power did not depend on the Lord Lieutenant of Ireland, or the Attorney General, or on the issue of any Proclamation; but it depended upon the action of some private individual who went before a Resident Magistrate in open day with a deposition stating that a certain crime had been committed, and that he demanded an inquiry. There is, therefore, a very great distinction between this clause and the corresponding clause of the Act of 1882; and, under these circumstances, I think we are entitled to ask that this provision of the present Bill should be materially modified. We ask the Government to assist us in saving the time of the Committee. It is quite agreed, all over the country, that the Government are not saving time by the short and decisive method they have adopted of opposing all the Amendments which are submitted to them. We ask the Government to tell us what Amendments they will adopt, and what they are not prepared to adopt. A declaration upon that point from Her Majesty's Government would undoubtedly save a considerable deal of time. If the Government will not do that; if they will give us no information as to what they intend to do; if they insist upon fighting every point submitted to them, we are bound to adhere to all the Amendments we have placed upon the Table, although we are informed that when we may be fighting out the provisions of the measure before perfectly empty Benches at half-past 12 o'clock at night, the First Lord of the Treasury may come down upon us and move the clôture. I wish to know whether that is the manner in which we are likely to be dealt with by the Government?

Mr. A. J. BALFOUR: The only Amendment of a substantial kind in this sub-section which the Government are prepared to accept is that which proposes to omit the words "police station" as one of the places where a preliminary inquiry may be held.

Mr. MAURICE HEALY: I think we are entitled to complain that the right hon. Gentleman should get up from the Treasury Bench and describe a speech of two and a-half minutes as a waste of time, and an unnecessary prolongation of the discussion. I venture to tell the right hon. Gentleman that he will not facilitate the passing of this clause by pursuing a course of that kind towards the Amendment of my hon. Friend. All that the right hon. Gentleman did in reply to the speech of my hon. Friend was simply to say that the Amendment strikes at the whole principle of the clause, and that, therefore, he declines to discuss it. Now, I venture to tell the right hon. Gentleman that, if I understand the principle of the clause at all, my hon. Friend has done nothing of the kind. The principle of the clause is not the secrecy which the right hon. Gentleman has laid such stress upon, but the principle of the clause is to give power to the Resident Magistrates to hold a preliminary inquiry in reference to an offence which may have been committed, although no individual has been made amenable for it, or has been charged with the commission of any such offence. What are the reasons we urge in favour of our view of the case? We say, in the first place, that having regard to what we know of the class of officials to whom the administration of the law will be delegated, we

[Fourth Night.]

have the strongest reasons to apprehend that those gentlemen, when they obtain the power and privilege which this clause proposes to confer upon them, will grossly and gravely misuse the powers given to them. We are justified in taking that view, to some extent, from what we know in connection with a certain famous inquiry which took place under a previous Act. I have no doubt that the right hon. Gentleman opposite has heard of an inquiry which Judge Curran held in Dublin Castle. I know it is claimed that what Judge Curran did on that occasion was instrumental in bringing about the conviction of the persons who were afterwards hung for the Phœnix Park murders, and that that fact amply justifies any irregularities which may have been committed by Judge Curran on that occasion. The charge made against Judge Curran—and I am not aware that it has ever been denied—is that he used the most improper means in conducting that inquiry. He offered large sums of money to the witnesses who were brought before him on that occasion, and he made use of all kinds of threats and intimidation to extort admissions of complicity in that crime. If that is so, it may be quite true that Judge Curran was successful in obtaining the object he desired; but I maintain that information obtained in that way reflects most strongly upon Judge Curran, and the Government who employed him. There is another reason why I support the Amendment of my hon. Friend. We have had a considerable amount of experience in reference to the criminal investigations which have taken place in Ireland in the past. It frequently happens that the Crown Authorities get into their possession some important piece of evidence relating to a case which tells in favour of the person accused, and they invariably suppress that evidence for fear the prisoner might be acquitted. That was a charge which was preferred against the Government in the Maamtrasna case, and it was not denied, and the same thing occurred in another case where a man was hung at Cork. In that case Judge O'Brien refused to hear certain evidence on the first trial, but it was produced on the second trial, with the result I have mentioned. If an inquiry of this kind is

held secretly it is almost certain that the Government will only make use of the information obtained in the preliminary inquiry against the persons accused, and that they will suppress any scrap of information which may tell in their favour. There is this further consequence—that the prisoners when brought to trial will have no means of finding out what the nature of the evidence is. It is somewhat hard to argue against what the right hon. Gentleman has said, because he has, in point of fact, refused to discuss the question with my hon. Friend, on the pretext that the Amendment strikes at the principle of the clause; but, as my hon. Friend has pointed out, there can be no good and satisfactory reason for having an inquiry of this nature held in private. Anyone who considers the question for a moment must see that no more good can possibly result from holding the inquiry in private than would equally result from holding it in public. They cannot shut the mouths of the witnesses they may bring up, or prevent them from going among their neighbours and repeating what they have stated to the magistrate, together with everything that may have happened at the inquiry. That being so, it is perfectly hopeless for the Government to suppose that they can keep what happens at the inquiry perfectly secret. The only argument which can possibly be put forward on the other side is, that if you make the inquiry private the evidence may not come to the ears of those who are implicated, and who, if it did reach them, might take advantage of the opportunity to escape before they were arrested. There is no provision whatever in this clause which enables the Government to detain any person who has given evidence, although we know that in the past they have frequently detained witnesses and have done so illegally, and without having an atom of power to do it after the witnesses had given their evidence. I should like the Government to explain how, by holding an inquiry in secret, they propose to prevent any information, the publication of which might be dangerous, from getting into the possession of the persons who may be implicated. Under all the circumstances, I do not see what possible good can result from the secrecy of the investiga-

Mr. Maurice Healy

tion, and I entertain great fears that a public danger may be involved in this secrecy and privacy.

MR. CLANCY : I will ask the leave of the Committee to withdraw this Amendment; but, in doing so, I wish to say one or two words in reference to the lecture which the right hon. Gentleman the Chief Secretary delivered to me. The right hon. Gentleman not only lectured me, but, by implication, the Party to which I belong. Now, I need no lecture from the right hon. Gentleman, nor do I want to be taught Parliamentary or any other manners by the Chief Secretary. I see nothing inconsistent in opposing this clause of the Bill altogether, and in striving to mitigate its harshness and injustice. I may add that after having striven to take the venom out of this clause, I propose to accept the right hon. Gentleman's advice in one particular, and to do the best I can to get the clause rejected altogether at the proper time.

Amendment, by leave, withdrawn.

MR. J. E. ELLIS (Nottingham, Rushcliffe): I have now to move in line 11, after the word "sit," to leave out "at a police court or a petty sessional courthouse, or police-station." and to insert "at the place where petty sessions for the district are usually held." The clause provides that—

"The Resident Magistrate directed to hold the inquiry shall sit at a police court or petty sessional courthouse, or police station."

I propose to leave out those words, for the purpose of securing that the place of inquiry shall be the place where the district petty sessions is usually held. I think it will be allowed that the words of the clause as the Bill is printed are extremely wide. The Chief Secretary has already intimated that he is prepared to omit the words "police station;" but I did not understand him to make the same concession in regard to the holding of the inquiry at a police court or petty sessional court. My object in proposing this Amendment is to ensure that the proceedings and the supposed offence in connection with which they are held shall have the usual geographical relation. As the clause stands the words "police court or petty sessional court" may mean any court of the kind throughout the whole of Ireland, quite irrespective of the district in which the

offence has been committed. Hon. Members will remember an expression used by the Prime Minister last week in regard to what is going on in Ireland at present. The noble Marquess used an extensive phrase. He said that "a land war" is going on, and that it is necessary that an Act of Parliament should be speedily passed in order to secure the due administration of the law. We have been told this evening that much time has been lost in respect of this Bill, and the right hon. Gentleman the First Lord of the Treasury, in an after-dinner speech on Saturday, used the same sort of language. Now, in view of our proceedings in Committee, such insinuations appear to me baseless. I think that what has taken place in regard to this clause affords ample justification for all the Amendments which have been proposed, for not only have words been left out, but other words have been added, and the 60 words agreed to up to the present moment are essentially diverse from the 40 which stood in their place when the clause was introduced. I believe that no more complete justification of the action which has been taken on this side of the House could have been adduced.

Amendment proposed,

In page 1, line 11, after "sit," leave out "at a police court or petty sessional courthouse, or police station," and insert "at the place where petty sessions for the district are usually held."—(*Mr. J. E. Ellis.*)

Question proposed, "That the words proposed to be left out stand part of the Clause."

THE ATTORNEY GENERAL FOR IRELAND (Mr. HOLMES) (Dublin University): My right hon. Friend has already said that the Government are ready to accept the Amendment as far as leaving out the words "police station" is concerned. As to the words proposed to be inserted, the result of introducing them would be that if the offence were committed in Dublin no inquiry could be held, for the reason that Dublin is not a petty sessional district. There are police courts in Dublin, but there are no police courts out of Dublin. Throughout the country there are petty sessional courts; and what I propose is this—to omit the words "at a police court or petty sessional courthouse, or police station," in order to insert these words—

[Fourth Night.]

" At a police court or at a place where the petty sessions for the petty sessional district in which the said offence has been committed are usually held."

Those words are in the Acts of 1882 and 1883, and I am quite ready to substitute them for the words as they now stand in the clause.

MR. CHANCE: The words " police court" did not occur at all in the Act of 1882.

MR. HOLMES: Those were practically the words that were used in the Act of 1882, the only difference being that in that Act the words " police office" were used. The Government were of opinion that the words " police court" had a narrower application, and for that reason they proposed to introduce them. I may remind the hon. Member that inquiries were held in the police office in Castle Yard, in Dublin.

MR. T. M. HEALY: The proceedings which took place at Dublin Castle under the Act of 1882 were grossly illegal. At the same time, I would advise my hon. Friend the Member for Nottinghamshire (Mr. J. E. Ellis) above the Gangway to accept the proposal of the Attorney General for Ireland. The only object is to secure that the inquiry should be held in the district where the offence is committed.

MR. CHANCE: Why should not the police court jurisdiction be confined to Dublin, which is the only place where there are police courts?

An hon. MEMBER: There is a police court also in Belfast.

MR. HOLMES: Belfast and Cork are in a petty sessional district, and Dublin is the only place which is an exception, and where there are only police courts.

MR. CHANCE: I would move to add to the Amendment these words—"And in the case of Dublin, at the police court."

THE CHAIRMAN: That would not be altogether relevant to the Amendment now before the Committee.

MR. CHANCE: Then, if the Amendment is accepted, I will move an additional Amendment to add the words I have suggested.

THE CHAIRMAN: The only Amendment now before the Committee is the Amendment which has been moved by the hon. Member for Nottinghamshire.

MR. HOLMES: I have no objection to an Amendment in the form I propose—namely,

Mr. Holmes

" That an inquiry shall be held at a police court in Dublin, or at a place where the petty sessions for the petty sessional district in which the offence has been committed are usually held."

MR. CLANCY: These words will not do at all. Under them it seems to me that it will be quite possible to hold all the inquiries in Dublin, which would be intolerable.

MR. MAURICE HEALY: I think that the Amendment which stands in my name next on the Paper, in these words—to leave out " at a police court or," and insert—

"As regards any district where any building used as a police court exists, in such building, and elsewhere in a petty sessional courthouse,"

would exactly carry out the intention of the Attorney General for Ireland.

MR. HOLMES: I should prefer the words which I have myself suggested. I think there can be no doubt whatever that if these words are inserted the Act will apply to Dublin.

THE CHAIRMAN: Does the hon. Member for Nottinghamshire withdraw his Amendment?

MR. J. E. ELLIS: Yes.

Amendment, by leave, *withdrawn.*

Amendment proposed,

In page 1, line 11, to leave out the words " or petty sessional courthouse or police station," in order to insert the words " when an offence has been committed in Dublin or in the place where the petty sessions for the petty sessional district in which the offence has been committed are usually held." — (*Mr. Attorney General for Ireland.*)

Question, " That those words be there inserted," put, and *agreed to.*

MR. T. M. HEALY: I have now to propose, in line 12, to insert, after the word " and," the words " at any time between 10 a.m. and 6 p.m." I presume it is not necessary that I should say anything about the Amendment.

Amendment proposed, in page 1, line 12, after " and," insert " at any time between 10 a.m. and 6 p.m."—(*Mr. T. M. Healy.*)

Question proposed, "That those words be there inserted."

MR. A. J. BALFOUR: I think the hon. and learned Member will see that the Amendment he suggests would not be in the interest of the witness himself, who might find it necessary to come up for examination again. Suppose that an examination commenced at half-past 5, if this Amendment were adopted, it could not be continued after 6 o'clock.

MR. T. M. HEALY: Then make it midnight.

MR. A. J. BALFOUR: Under this Amendment, the inquiry would have to be cut short at 6, and a more inconvenient course could not be conceived, both as regards the persons the hon. and learned Member desires to protect and the magistrates. It would be clearly not for the convenience of the magistrate that he should be called upon to depart from the ordinary course; and the result of adopting this Amendment would be, in many instances, to occasion great delay, and probably subject the witnesses themselves to hardship. Therefore, I hope the hon. and learned Gentleman will not press the Amendment.

Mr. T. M. HEALY: Surely there ought to be some limit, and I would remind the right hon. Gentleman that we ourselves are placed under the half-past 12 o'clock Rule. The right hon. Gentleman says it is to the interest of the witnesses themselves that there should be no limit as to the hour of inquiry. I do not think that it is to the interest of anybody to be dragged out of his bed at midnight. I have no doubt that the Government will make this Bill, as they have made similar measures, an instrument of torture. That is what the Bill is, and, therefore, I am of opinion that these exceptional powers should not be employed except at a reasonable hour.

MR. A. J. BALFOUR: I am quite ready to accept words to provide that no examination shall begin except between the hours of 10 a.m. and 6 p.m.

MR. T. M. HEALY: I will withdraw the Amendment.

Amendment, by leave, *withdrawn.*

On the Motion of Mr. T. M. HEALY, Amendment made, in page 1, line 13, by leaving out " witness," and inserting " person."

MR. T. M. HEALY: My next Amendment is to provide that—

" The magistrate shall examine on oath concerning any alleged offence witnesses summoned before him in the prescribed manner."

This Amendment is of very great importance, and if the Government desire to work the provisions of the measure in a reasonable manner they will certainly accept it. I may be told that the Petty Sessions Act makes provision for all this; but I say that it does not. When the Grand Committee which sat upstairs, under the Presidency of the right hon. and learned Member for Bury (Sir Henry James), to consider the Bill for the Amendment of the Criminal Law, care was taken to have a prescribed form for everything that was done. In that Bill a considerable number of forms were included in a Schedule; and, in this case, I think it is only right to provide that the summons shall be in a prescribed form. The Government, later on in the clause, deal with the matter in a very insidious way. They say, in the 2nd sub-section—

" The enactments relating to the compelling of the attendance of a witness before a justice shall apply for the purpose of this section,"

and so on. As the clause now stands, the Government, in a cruel and atrocious manner, provide that a contumacious witness shall be subjected to the same penalty for an ordinary offence as if it were an indictable crime. For instance, under the Petty Sessions Act, a contumacious witness in a case of Boycotting could only receive one month's imprisonment; but if the case were treated as one which relates to an indictable crime, the contumacious witness would be rendered liable to a heavy sentence of penal servitude—even penal servitude for life. I think that everything done under the Act should be done regularly. In the first place, the offence of which a man is charged should be specified, and the witness should be informed of the nature of the subject upon which he is asked to give evidence, so that no irrelevant question may be put to him. For instance, if a person is summoned to give evidence in regard to an offence against coining, it should not be legal, when he goes before a magistrate, to put questions to him in regard to other offences. The magistrate should not have power to range over a whole series of questions. I am glad that the Government have, for the first time, numbered the Amendments on the Paper, which is a matter of great convenience to hon. Members. I would refer the Chief Secretary or the Attorney General to Amendment No. 45, which stands on the Paper in my name. That Amendment provides that—

" No witness shall be compelled to attend except upon a summons, stating the place of inquiry, the name of the magistrate authorized to hold it, and the crime with regard to which his evidence is desired, nor shall any witness be questioned on any matter not relating to the crime with respect to which he has been summoned."

I think that is a very fair Amendment to insert.

Amendment proposed, in page 1, line 13, leave out after " witness," and insert " summoned in the prescribed manner."—(*Mr. T. M. Healy.*)

Question proposed, "That those words be there inserted."

Mr. HOLMES : If these words are inserted it would be impossible for the Government to bring up witnesses before this tribunal except by the ordinary method of summons. The Government are not prepared to accept that proposal. A law passed for England in 1847, and extended to Ireland in 1851, provides that where depositions have been taken against a person charged with an offence under ordinary circumstances witnesses must be summoned, and the Schedule contains various forms of summonses. It has sometimes been found—I will not say that it happens often—but certainly it has sometimes happened, that the serving of a summons upon a witness has enabled him to put himself out of the jurisdiction of the Court—to conceal himself, and not go before the Court at all. If the magistrate is satisfied upon information that a witness is not likely to appear, then, instead of issuing a summons, he can issue a warrant for the purpose of bringing the witness before the Court that he may be examined. As he would be discharged as soon as he has been examined, I do not see that any injury would result. It might so happen, if it were made necessary to issue a summons, that you would place in the power of the man whose evidence you desire to obtain the very means which would induce him to go somewhere where he could not be reached, and could not, consequently, be called as a witness at all. I have pointed out that this is in no way an exceptional provision ; and, therefore, I hope the Committee will not consent to the Amendment.

Mr. T. M. HEALY: What we now understand the Government is going to do is this. They are going to place all the people in the whole of the countryside under arrest. That is the confession

which the right hon. and learned Gentleman has made. No witnesses are to be summoned, but a *posse* of police are to go down and throw a net or draw a cordon over the whole district, and then " beat " the people they succeed in catching into the police station. That is exactly what the right hon. and learned Gentleman has proposed. The witnesses are not to be summoned ; but they are to be hunted for by the police, and are not to receive half-an-hour's notice. Let me take a case. Suppose the right hon. and learned Gentleman were at work in the Four Courts, and a policeman were to pat him on the shoulder and say that he was wanted elsewhere. Would the right hon. and learned Gentleman like to be taken off without a moment's notice ? I say that a more monstrous proposal was never made. Surely the right hon. Gentleman the First Lord of the Treasury has his eyes open to the enormous mischief such a provision must produce. The Government appear to be carrying out the provisions of this Bill as though they were in Upper Burmah with a drum-head court martial, instead of legislating for a civilized country. I never heard of anything like it. Where is your Scotch law ? Where are the Liberal Unionists who have hitherto been so ready to tell us what is done in Scotland. Without even a *viaticum*, people are to leave their business at a moment's notice, whether they may be sick or suffering, or whatever their position may be. The right hon. and learned Gentleman's words are certainly a revelation to the House, for no one could have had any information that anything of this kind was intended. I do beseech the Government, if they wish to extract anything like good out of this clause, to render it something more tolerable to the people among whom it will have to be worked. I declare that unless the law is rendered somewhat more reasonable, the Irish Members ought to go among the Irish people, the moment the Bill is passed, and tell them at all risks to defy the law, and be prepared to go to prison rather than to obey a law so inhuman and iniquitous.

Mr. CHANCE : The Act of 1882 has been constantly quoted as a justification for this clause, but there is nothing contained in that Act about sending up a *posse* of police to capture witnesses, and drag them up before a magistrate upon

Mr. T. M. Healy

a warrant obtained behind their backs. You have quoted the Act of 1882 against us, and I think we are entitled to show how much more harshly this clause will bear upon the Irish people.

MR. O'DOHERTY (Donegal, N.): No distinction whatever is made in this Bill with regard to the power of obtaining evidence, whether the offence dealt with is an indictable offence, or one which may be tried summarily before a Court of Petty Sessions. I know that there have been cases where witnesses have been brought before a magistrate without a formal summons; but it has always been where the crime committed was an indictable offence, and even in that case a notice had to be handed into the Court in writing that there was a probability of the witness not attending unless steps were taken to compel him to do so. That, however, is not the case which the right hon. and learned Gentleman the Attorney General for Ireland has referred to. He has spoken of cases in which it is probable that if a summons were served the person receiving it would levant. The provisions of the Petty Sessions Act refer to a totally different circumstance—namely, where persons are unwilling to come forward unless they are forced to do so. I think this is a proper time to refer to the whole scope of the Bill. The explanation of the right hon. and learned Gentleman shows clearly that although the words at the end of the 1st clause show that the intention at the time the Bill was drafted was to confine these powers to indictable offences, and not to ordinary offences, it is intended now very materially to enlarge the scope of the measure. If hon. Members will refer to the 2nd clause, they will see that the offences there dealt with are indictable offences. My opinion is that no witness should be required to attend before the Resident Magistrate for examination except upon a summons, and that the summons itself should be in a prescribed form except in such a case as the right hon. and learned Gentleman has mentioned, where there is reason to believe that the person summoned would be likely to disappear without appearing before the Court at all, and would have time to do so. In that case a proviso may be inserted directing a warrant to be issued in a prescribed form after information upon oath has been given to the magistrate.

MR. HOLMES: My argument has been altogether misstated by the hon. and learned Member for North Longford. I did not say anything in my observations about drawing the cordon round the district, and dragging the people into a police station. What I referred to is only the existing law, both of England and Ireland—namely, that the justices may, in certain circumstances, issue a warrant.

MR. T. M. HEALY: For an indictable offence.

MR. HOLMES: Certainly, in the case of an indictable offence. But it is stated that a witness will not attend unless he is compelled to do so. A warrant may be issued for the arrest of such person, but it is merely a warrant to bring the person before the justices for the purpose of examination. It does not enable the magistrates to detain him for a moment longer, or to commit him to prison in any way. Reference has been made by the hon. Member for Donegal (Mr. O'Doherty) to the 2nd clause. That clause extends the summary jurisdiction and specifies the offences which may be proceeded against before a Court of Summary Jurisdiction under the provisions of this measure.

MR. CHANCE: We have had an interesting statement of the law of England and Ireland from the right hon. and learned Attorney General for Ireland; but the law he has referred to relates only to indictable offences, and he has taken no notice of the fact that in this section he does not deal with indictable offences, but with ordinary offences, and he provides a tribunal for dealing exceptionally with those offences for the first time by this Bill. Will the right hon. and learned Gentleman accept words to this effect—that a witness may be examined on oath upon a summons or warrant issued in the prescribed form?

MR. T. M. HEALY: I think that is a reasonable suggestion, and it would enable the Government to get all the power they desire. My hon. Friend suggests that the words should be—

"Examined on oath concerning such offence any witness appearing before him on a summons or warrant issued in the prescribed manner."

In that case there must either be a summons in the prescribed manner or a warrant in the prescribed manner.

[Fourth Night.]

MR. HOLMES: I think that if the suggestion of the hon. and learned Member were adopted it would make the clause much more stringent than it is now. I would strongly advise the Committee to retain the provision as it appears in the Bill itself.

MR. T. M. HEALY: The answer to that is, that provision would have to be made later on in regard to the prescribed form, fixing the time for the attendance of a witness, the place in which it will be necessary for him to appear, where he is to give his evidence, and the crime with regard to which he is to give evidence. These words involve, I think, all the essential elements of a summons—namely, that a man should be told where he is to go, when he is to appear, who he is to appear before, and what is the charge upon which he is to give evidence.

MR. EDWARD HARRINGTON (Kerry, W.): The conversation which has occurred justifies the view I took all along of the Amendment of my hon. and learned Friend. The previous Amendment proposed by my hon. and learned Friend limited the hours during which this secret investigation could be held. As the clause now stands, an investigation can commence before 6 o'clock in the evening and be continued all through the night; and if in the examination of a witness who may, perhaps, be a most untruthful man, and perhaps a criminal at heart, he may, in order to protect himself, criminate any respectable member of the community, who in that case can be hauled out of his bed at any hour of the night. Therefore, I think that what the hon. Member for Kilkenny has suggested is not unfair—namely, that a witness should appear after due notice by summons or warrant. If it should appear that a man incriminated by the evidence of a witness is likely to get out of the way, then, of course, a warrant would be valuable; but I think it is too bad to leave it in the power of any witness, under a cross-examination, to incriminate another person, and render him liable to be aroused out of his bed at a most unreasonable hour of the night. I may say that if this part of the clause is to be adhered to the other concessions which have been made by the Government are altogether valueless and illusory.

MR. O'DOHERTY: Sub-section 2 of this clause says—

"The enactments relating to the compelling of the attendance of a witness before a justice, and to a witness attending before a justice and required to give evidence concerning the matter of an information or complaint for an indictable offence, shall apply for the purposes of this section as if they were re-enacted herein, and in terms made applicable thereto."

I admit the force of giving exceptional powers in the case of an indictable offence; but this sub-section provides that all the enactments which at present exist shall apply as if they were re-enacted.

MR. HOLMES: The offences to which an extension of summary jurisdiction is applied are specified in the 2nd clause.

MR. MAURICE HEALY: I understand that this 2nd sub-section of the clause we are now considering applies to offences under the Petty Sessions Act. What I understand to be the complaint of the Attorney General for Ireland is, that the provisions of the Petty Sessions Act relating to indictable offences should apply to the case of indictable offences only, and that the provisions of the Act relating to summary procedure should apply only to the commission of an ordinary offence.

MR. HOLMES: I understand the hon. Member for Donegal to ask whether I am prepared to insert in the proper place—which I think would be the 2nd sub-section—a proviso that a warrant shall not be issued except in the case of an indictable offence. Surely it is quite enough to deal with the Amendment now before the Committee without entering into other matters.

MR. CHANCE: All I have to say is that hon. Members on this side of the House will feel it their duty to fight this Amendment, unless they clearly understand that it is the intention of the Government to abandon the power to issue warrants in cases of non-indictable offences. They have here a double power. Not only can they issue warrants for offences which may be proceeded against summarily, but they can send persons to prison for an indefinite period.

MR. MAURICE HEALY: There is another point arising out of this Amendment which I think is very material, and which I do not think has been referred to—namely, that not only does this section, as it is drawn, permit a person to be examined as a witness, but it justifies his being arrested summarily without a warrant. The power to keep him under arrest is practically indefinite. Inquiries under this section, we know very well, cannot be finished in the course of a day. The inquiries which took place in reference to the Phœnix Park murders occupied weeks and months. What may happen here is that before an inquiry commences, and before a single atom of evidence has been obtained, the Government may arrest in advance every man they may think capable of giving evidence. Such an investigation may occupy weeks and months, and they may keep the man they have arrested in prison under the pretext that the stage of the inquiry has not yet arrived when they ought to be examined. I think that is a very important matter. It means that the Government, under this provision, will have the power of imprisoning a man indefinitely.

MR. HOLMES: What we propose to do is this. As regards procuring the attendance of witnesses, and insuring that they shall give evidence, we retain the law as it stands now in reference to indictable offences, and also retain the existing law as to summary jurisdiction. In other words, the *modus operandi* will be the same as now in the case of indictable offences, and also the same as now in offences liable to be dealt with summarily. We provide, by a slight amendment in the drafting of the clause later on, to give all the protection that is needed.

MR. MAURICE HEALY: I admit the importance of the statement which has been made by the right hon. and learned Gentleman; but it does not quite meet our views. He says that, in regard to indictable offences, the procedure will be the procedure at present provided for the case of indictable offences when a prisoner is charged before the magistrates. I quite admit that that statement has met the point raised by my hon. Friend; but, as the section stood, a man could be arrested in the first instance, although the offence inquired into was an offence punishable summarily. But the point I am raising is a different point. The point I make is this. At present, when a preliminary examination takes place before the magistrates relating to an indictable offence, what may happen is

that the examination may only last a short time; but it is unquestionably in the power of the magistrate to arrest any witness and keep him in custody until the time arrives for examining him. That may be perfectly reasonable where you have a prisoner charged, and where, therefore, it is presumed that the hearing of the charge will only occupy a short time; but it would be grossly unreasonable, as has happened in secret inquiries before, if such inquiries are to last for weeks and months. When an inquiry is likely to last for an indefinite period of time, it is unreasonable that the Government should have such a power to arrest all witnesses in advance, and retain every one of them in custody until the prisoner has been arrested and charged. The fact is that a day may be fixed for the commencement of the inquiry, and, having fixed a day, the Government may immediately arrest every person they contemplate examining, and the inquiry may then last for weeks and months, as the preliminary inquiry concerning the Phœnix Park murders did. It is unreasonable that, during all that time, they should have power to keep every witness in custody under the pretext that the stage of the inquiry had not yet arrived at which it would be convenient to examine them. What I would suggest is that where the Government arrest a witness, and when they do not propose to examine him immediately, they may give such witness the option of entering into recognizances, with proper security, to come up at any stage of the investigation they may want his evidence. In that way they would dispense with the necessity of keeping him in custody for any length of time.

MR. J. O'CONNOR (Tipperary, S.): Before this Amendment is disposed of, I wish to express my dislike to the use of the word "warrant" altogether. I do not see why the Government should not accept the words of the Amendment proposed by the hon. and learned Member for North Longford. Reference has been made to the Act of 1883, and the words in that Act are "in the prescribed form." All the witnesses were to be summoned "in the prescribed form," and if any hon. Member has any doubt upon the subject, I am in a position to furnish him with a copy of the prescribed form in that respect. This Bill, when

it becomes an Act, will be successful, or a failure, in proportion to the confidence which the people have in its administration; and I will say this—that if a general power of arrest is retained in the Act, it will have the effect of defeating the object of the Act itself. It will inspire witnesses with a certain amount of alarm, and will be looked upon as a regular system of body-snatching. Indeed, the Bill might be fittingly termed a "Body-snatching Bill," and the Government might employ Buffalo Bill and his Indians with their lassoes to hunt down the unfortunate people of Ireland whom they desire to use as witnesses. A witness, if he gets a proper summons in a prescribed form, will be able to guard against being taken from his daily labour at an inconvenient moment; whereas, if he is arrested by warrant, and brought before a Resident Magistrate, and kept in durance even for only a limited period,
• he might lose his employment. This, I am afraid, would generally be the case under the operation of the clause as it now stands. I can say, from my experience of the past, that the issue of a summons in a prescribed form would be very much better than to give the Government the unlimited power of arrest which they are anxious to obtain. I must say that, until the right hon. and learned Attorney General for Ireland had delivered himself of his first speech on this clause, I certainly did not understand that it was to take the form in which it now presents itself. I hope that my hon. and learned Friend will persist in his Amendment, because I am sure that it will give the people some kind of confidence in the operation and administration of the Act; whereas, if it is allowed to remain in its present shape, it will undoubtedly have the effect of defeating the object the Government have in view.

MR. T. M. HEALY: The Act of 1882 provided that in all cases the attendance of witnesses should be procured by summons. The Attorney General for Ireland says the Government are not prepared to include a similar provision in the present Bill, and yet he has boasted of the magnificent success of the Act of 1882 in the case of the Phœnix Park murders. That being the case, and the proceeding under that Act having been by summons, I think we are justified in

demanding that at least the provisions of this Bill should be placed on a level with those of the Act of 1882. My proposal is to insert the words "summoned in the prescribed manner," and then we might have the same guarantee that everything would be right. I ask the right hon. and learned Gentleman why he is not willing to give us now what was considered sufficient in the Act of 1882?

THE ATTORNEY GENERAL (Sir RICHARD WEBSTER) (Isle of Wight): I admit that it will require words to be added, in order to show that the procedure applicable to indictable offences is to be extended to offences punishable by summary jurisdiction. Perhaps the hon. and learned Gentleman will remember that Section 13 of the Petty Sessions (Ireland) Act provides a certain mode of procedure in cases punishable upon summary conviction, and a certain other mode of procedure where the offence is an indictable offence. It certainly seems to me that, inasmuch as we have got the two classes of offences, the right course is to apply both modes of procedure, whether it may be by summons or warrant, in order to provide that both indictable offences, and offences capable of being dealt with by summary jurisdiction, shall be treated in the corresponding manner.

MR. T. M. HEALY: We have often heard this Bill paralleled with the Bill of the right hon. Member for Derby, and therefore it is only reasonable that we should seek to have it safeguarded by putting into it the same provision. Will hon. Members observe the way in which the 3rd sub-section is drawn, at line 24—

"A witness examined under this section shall not be excused from answering any question on the ground that the answer thereto may criminate, or tend to criminate, himself; but any statement made by any person in answer to any question put to him on any examination under this section shall not, except in the case of an indictment, or other criminal proceeding for perjury, be admissible in evidence against him in any proceeding, civil or criminal."

Every protection which was afforded by the Act of 1882 is omitted from this section. I say that the proposals of the Government are most unreasonable, and I regret that our objections to this clause should have been met in this way. We ask that a witness shall receive a summons before he is brought up before a magistrate, in the same way as was provided in the Act of 1882. Why should we have a less amount of safeguard and security here in a Bill which is to be permanent in its operation than we had in a measure which was only to be in operation for three years? I admit that although in the Act of 1882 the safeguard of a summons was provided, this safeguard itself was most terribly abused, and that the grossest irregularities were committed under the Act. It is because such mischief and irregularity were committed that we desire to introduce precautions. Surely it is unreasonable that there should be less safeguards in regard to the permanent law of the country than those which were intended to apply to a temporary Act of the Legislature?

MR. ANDERSON: I must protest against the way in which the Act of 1882 has been used. It was stated, at a political banquet on Saturday night, that three weeks had been expended in discussing the first eight lines of this clause, which are identical with the Act of 1882. That statement was made by the Prime Minister; but nobody knows better than the Prime Minister that, as far as the Act of 1882 is concerned, one-half of the Members of this House were not Members at the time it passed, and are in no way responsible for its provisions. I cannot conceive why, in the face of that fact, and also of the fact that that Act was for a temporary purpose and to last only for three years, and that it is sought to make this Bill a permanent measure imposing a rigid system of permanent inquisition, the Prime Minister could have been induced to make the observations he is reported to have made. Further than that, a new constituency has been created, which was pledged at the last election to oppose a Coercion Bill. We have heard, over and over again, that this clause has been drawn in conformity with the Act of 1882. What, then, is their possible excuse for endeavouring to make its provisions so much more stringent than those of the Act of 1882? Their whole course is indefensible, and I trust the Attorney General for Ireland will feel that there is no justification for making this measure so much more stringent than the Act of 1882.

MR. CHANCE: I must complain of the way in which this clause of the Bill has been drafted. It does not seem that the ordinary method of drafting a Bill has been followed in this case; but it would appear that a special method has been followed, with a view of concealing what the real object of the clause is. The clause, as drafted, was made to appear to be as innocent as possible, so that when it was read by Members who did not happen to be English and Irish legal Members, they would naturally say —"Well, there is nothing much in this clause, for it is practically identical with the existing Scotch law." But there is hardly a word in it which is intelligible to any man who is not a lawyer, and the power of imprisoning witnesses under the Petty Sessions Act for non-indictable offences seems to have been scarcely appreciated. If hon. Members will look at the Petty Sessions Act, they will find that the form of summons is prescribed, and not only that the name of the prisoner is stated, but that the nature of the evidence is very clearly set out. That cannot be done when there is no prisoner in custody. I can well understand why the Government object to have anything done under this Bill in a prescribed form. We know that the generality of Resident Magistrates are drawn from stupid and unsuccessful half-pay military and naval officers, and we can imagine the way in which they may be induced to fill up a warrant. It is for the purpose of preventing these men from having the real responsibility which ought to attach to a Justice of the Peace in issuing a summons or warrant that the Government fight so shy of anything like a prescribed form. If there is anything the Irish people like it is law, let alone justice. If you are to deprive them of justice, at any rate they like some form of law to justify you in doing so, because they have an idea that they are entitled to take advantage of any mistake of the law. The Government desire to give them no excuse of that kind, but to empower a Resident Magistrate, at 10 or 11 o'clock at night, after he may have been boozing with the land agent, to scribble his signature on a warrant! We want to have something beyond that —something which may, when the powers of the magistrate have been wrongfully exercised, be used to obtain judgment against a half-pay military and naval officer, or a full-pay Constabulary officer, who may have done something that is illegal.

[Fourth Night.]

Mr. CLANCY (Dublin Co., N.): The excuse which has been made for this part of the clause is that witnesses in Ireland, if summoned to attend before a magistrate, would run away. I should like to know whether the experience which the Government have obtained in Ireland bears out that assertion? I have yet to learn that any witness whom it was proposed to examine under the Act of 1882 actually ran away. It is desirable, at the same time, to draw attention to a remark of the Attorney General for Ireland, that this clause is to be extended not only to serious crimes, such as murder and attempt to murder, but to the Plan of Campaign. What the Attorney General virtually asserts is that the priests of Ireland would run away from this inquiry. I do not wish to misrepresent him. The right hon. and learned Gentleman has implied in this House that persons who have taken part in advocating the Plan of Campaign, including the priests of Ireland, the leading farmers, and other persons who are engaged in industrial occupations, will run away from this inquiry. I think that that is an insult to the Irish priests, and that the allegation ought not to be passed over without some notice being taken of it. The charge itself is perfectly absurd and ridiculous. The priests of Ireland who have taken part in the Plan of Campaign will not flinch one inch from any inquiry the Government may think fit to institute. We know what will take place. Say a meeting takes place of delegates from particular estates in the town hall of some place. A list will be taken of all the priests, laymen, and Members of Parliament who attend that meeting. Each of them will be served with a warrant, when the landlords have had time to consult the authorities of Dublin Castle and to make arrangements by which a *posse* of police may be sent to their houses, under the pretence that their evidence may be necessary in a preliminary inquiry. I certainly regard the defence of the clause as a greater insult to the Irish people than the clause itself.

Mr. W. H. SMITH: No allusion has been made either as to priests, or to the propriety of drawing a cordon around a district, and arresting every person within it. The Government have simply given an answer to an argument which has been advanced with considerable force by hon. Gentlemen opposite, and I would venture to ask the Committee to come now to a decision upon this Amendment, which has been fully argued upon both sides, and upon which the Government feel it their duty to take a stand. I trust that the Committee will be allowed to come to a decision upon the question which has been raised by the hon. and learned Member for North Longford.

Mr. T. M. HEALY: I propose to withdraw the Amendment, and move to insert words providing for the examination of witnesses appearing on summons.

Amendment, by leave, withdrawn.

Amendment proposed, in page 1, line 13, at the end of the last Amendment, to insert the words "on summons."—(*Mr. T. M. Healy.*)

Question proposed, "That those words be there inserted."

Mr. W. E. GLADSTONE: I am in favour of some provision being introduced to meet the separate point as to the possibility of indefinite detention. I think, however, that the First Lord of the Treasury is quite justified in saying that the matter has been fully argued. We have heard all that the Government wish to say, and I hope the Committee will now be disposed to go to a Division.

Question put.

The Committee *divided:*—Ayes 139; Noes 226: Majority 87.—(Div. List, No. 113.)

On the Motion of Mr. HENRY H. FOWLER, Amendment made, in page 1, line 13, by leaving out "appearing before him," and inserting "whom he has reason to believe to be capable of giving material evidence concerning such offence."

Mr. T. M. HEALY: I propose to leave out the word "may" in line 13, and substitute for it the word "shall." This Amendment, although a matter of verbiage, is of the greatest importance when we come to consider its effect with regard to the person accused. I wish the magistrate to be compelled to take the depositions, in writing, of the witnesses examined at the preliminary inquiries, because the witness is entitled to have the benefit of any admission that may be made. The noble Lord the

Member for South Paddington (Lord Randolph Churchill), the Under Secretary for India, and the Solicitor General for England will remember that on a former occasion they voted against us on the question with regard to the Maamtrasna trials on the ground that the informations had been suppressed. Our case in the Maamtrasna debate was that there were certain depositions taken which were in the prisoners favour, and which were suppressed by George Bolton and others. In this case, if the deposition is taken at all the least thing we can ask is that the prisoner shall have the advantage of the depositions. It would be a most unreasonable thing to allow the magistrate to ransack the entire country side, to take evidence from all kinds of persons which may perhaps tend in favour of the accused person unless the evidence is put on record, because if it be not put on record the prisoner will get no benefit from the inquiry at all. Surely what we want to do is to test the guilt or innocency of the accused—to arrive at the truth. But the object of the Government in Ireland is not to get at the truth, but to prove a case against a particular individual, and that is what the Gentlemen I have mentioned voted against on a former occasion. They voted against the suppression of the depositions. Now, I think it is only reasonable when men are examined, and it would conduce to the interests of justice if the magistrates were compelled to take, the deposition of everyone whom they summoned. This is certainly not an unreasonable proposal, and if it were adopted the Government could not be accused of doing what was done in the Maamtrasna case. It is only a matter of detail, and having thus placed it before the minds of the Government, I trust that the Attorney General for England will see his way to agree to the Amendment which I now move.

Amendment proposed, in page 1, line 13, leave out "may," and insert "shall." —(*Mr. T. M. Healy.*)

Question proposed, "That the word proposed to be left out stand part of the Clause."

SIR RICHARD WEBSTER: This Amendment does not commend itself to us. It would be wrong to impose beforehand on the magistrate the obliga-

tion to taking the deposition of a witness about whom he would know nothing. [Mr. T. M. HEALY: Why should he call them?] It would, of course, be impossible to say beforehand who should be called and who not, and in our opinion, therefore, this is a matter which should be left to the magistrate.

MR. T. M. HEALY: Suppose that a witness maintains that he knows nothing about the matter in question at the examination; and then suppose, on the other hand, that he says afterwards—"I know something about it," because he has got £100 from the Resident Magistrate, the person accused is not to have the benefit of the original statement of the witness. A man may have £10, £50, or £100 given him after the inquiry and then come forward and swear as in the Maamtrasna case. We want to get his original, his untainted statement placed on record. Surely it is not too much to ask that the prisoner shall have the benefit of the man's confession of ignorance. The Government says it is giving too much trouble to the Resident Magistrate to require that he should place the evidence on record; but, if it is not too much trouble for him to summon the man, it is not too much trouble for him to take down his original statement of ignorance. Here is an important Amendment, and its importance was confessed by the Solicitor General for England when he voted in reference to the Maamtrasna inquiry. Persons may make a statement which they afterwards enlarge and amplify, and if the original statement were introduced at the trial, it would, perhaps, be found that they had contradicted their former statement. What we ask is, that the statement made at the initial stage shall, in some shape or form, be recorded; yet the Government refuse this. Is it in the interest of truth that they refuse it? I think this Amendment ought to approve itself to the minds of hon. Members who do not want these convictions to be the result of blood-money. I thought that the Maamtrasna trial would have burned itself into the hearts of Tory Members— I thought it would have fixed itself in the minds of the Solicitor General for England, the noble Lord the Member for Paddington, and the Under Secretary for India. There was a distinct case where, if the original depositions had been introduced, a number of men would not have been hung and sent to penal servitude. The Government withheld those depositions, and they were condemned for so doing by the Solicitor General; and now our request is refused that the original as well as the subsequent statement of witnesses should be introduced. I must say that it is not in the interest of justice, but in the interest of injustice that this Amendment is rejected.

MR. CLANCY (Dublin Co., N.): In confirmation of what has been said by my hon. Friend, the Member for North Longford, I wish to point out that only a short time ago, a policeman named O'Halloran, in the County of Clare, attempted to bribe a man into giving manufactured evidence by giving him a ten pound note, and the money is now in the hands of the Irish Party. We have no doubt that this kind of thing will be often done when this Act comes into operation.

MR. MOLLOY: I am somewhat astonished at the way in which the Attorney General for England met this Amendment. First of all he shirked the question altogether. He said that the witness might give evidence which shows that he knows nothing about the case. But that is not the point; our point is that he may give evidence which will show the innocence of the accused. But I go further than this. The Attorney General said that because a witness may know nothing about the subject of inquiry it is of no use to take the deposition of such a man. How can the Attorney General, or anyone else, tell what the value of the evidence may be to the other side. The fact that a man brought up for examination has clearly shown that he knows nothing of the case, may be of the most vital importance to the person accused.

SIR RICHARD WEBSTER : This Amendment is of so little importance to the clause that I do not think Her Majesty's Government will offer further opposition to it.

Question put, and *negatived*.

MR. T. M. HEALY: I think the word deposition should be inserted in line 13.

SIR RICHARD WEBSTER: I will consider whether the word "deposition" should be inserted hereafter. In the meantime I think it would be desirable to substitute the word "statement."

Mr. T. M. Healy

Amendment proposed, to leave out "deposition" and insert "statement."

Question proposed, "That the word proposed to be left out stand part of the Clause."—(*Sir Richard Webster*.)

MR. T. M. HEALY: I have no objection if the Government provide that these depositions will be available in Court, and that the word "statement" should be reserved.

Question put, and *negatived*.

On the Motion of Mr. MARUM, Amendment made, in page 1, line 14, after "witness," by inserting "other than any person confessing himself or herself to be the offender, or the husband or wife of such person."

On the Motion of Mr. T. M. HEALY, Amendment made, in page 1, line 14, after "by," by inserting "his own."

MR. MARUM (Kilkenny, N.): I propose after the word "recognizance" in line 17 to insert the words "provided that any witness so appearing shall be entitled to have present at any such examination or other proceeding counsel or attorney on his or her behalf." I point out that this is permissible in the case of witnesses under the 20 and 21st of *Vict.* in the Probate Court. It may be alleged that these are civil and not criminal proceedings. But as they may lead to criminal proceedings, I say that they are analogous to cases under this clause. The clause is of so severe a character that I propose to limit it by the introduction of these words. I will read a very short extract from the work of Mr. Best, a high authority on evidence, to show the inquisitorial nature of the proceedings and the danger that it involves—

"In the mediæval tribunals of the Civil and Canon laws, the inquisitorial principle was essentially dominant. And this has so far survived that in many Continental tribunals at the present day every criminal trial commences with a rigorous interrogation of the accused by the Judge or other presiding officer. Nor is this interrogation usually conducted with fairness towards the accused. Facts are garbled or misrepresented, questions assuming his guilt are not only put, but pressed and repeated in various shapes; and hardly any means are left untried to compel him either directly or by implication, to avow something to his prejudice. This is no chimerical danger. By artful questioning and working on their feelings, weak-minded individuals can be made to confess or impliedly admit almost anything; and to resist continued importunities to acknowledge even falsehood, requires a mind of more than average firmness."

Mr. Best gives an instance of the trial of the Duke de Praslin, before the Chamber of Peers in France, in 1847, which, with the permission of the committee, I will read. The Duke was charged with the murder of his wife, and the following is part of his interrogation by the President—

"Was she (the deceased) not stretched upon the floor when you struck her for the last time?
"Why do you ask me such a question?
"You must have experienced a most distressing moment when you say upon entering the chamber that you were covered with the blood which you had just shed, and which you were obliged to wash off?
"Those marks of blood have been altogether misinterpreted. I did not wish to appear before my children with the blood of their mother upon me.
"You are very wretched to have committed this crime? (The accused makes no answer, but appears absorbed).
"Have you received bad advice which impelled you to this crime?
"I have received no advice. People do not give advice on such a subject."

I give you this instance of procedure on the other side of the water, to show that there be some protection for the persons who come under the operation of this clause. The Attorney General knows that this is the very reverse of our procedure, and that there is not a syllable of our jurisprudence that does not shout against it. Again, I remind the Committee that torture was permitted by the Scotch law down to the year 1708, and I bring this clause forward as an instance of the Government having reverted to that Scotch law. I do not propose that the witness should be represented by counsel, although that appears to be pointed at in the Amendment of the right hon. Gentleman the Member for Wolverhampton (Mr. Henry H. Fowler). I simply ask that counsel shall be present at the examination. Under the Bankruptcy Acts attornies are permitted to attend, and under the Petty Sessions Act the Justices cannot exclude counsel. I have had some experience in this matter; I have investigated a number of cases, and I tell Her Majesty's Government that this clause, in my opinion, will be perfectly useless. What you want here is not the discovery of persons who have committed offences, but the discovery of evidence for the purpose of prosecution. And I remind the Government that the name of "informer" is odious in Ireland. I myself committed a man a year ago for a social murder of a bad type. Before the depositions were completed I told the prisoner that if he wished to ask any questions he might do so; he turned to me and said—"At all events, I am not an informer." We have been told that the Irish people are supposed to have received "a double dose of original sin," and that this is the reason why they declined to give evidence. But it is not so. It is the effect of your penal laws. Where a son is required to give evidence against his father, and a daughter against her mother, it is felt that social life is invaded, and it is from that cause that the objection to give information arises. I ask if you can remedy that by this clause? The only way you can remedy it is by giving the people confidence in the administration of justice—not abstract, but actual justice. Your tribunals, so far from giving confidence in the administration of justice, will increase tenfold the objection of the people to give information, and therefore I say you are beginning at the wrong end by enacting this inquisitorial clause. You say that you were aided in the case of the Phœnix Park murder by the Crimes Act; but that is not a fact. There was an objection to give evidence, and I say that this Bill will intensify rather than remove the feeling which exists in the breasts of the people of Ireland. It is because I see that the Government are obstinately bent on carrying this Bill that I am trying to cut down and limit the operation of the clause; because, undoubtedly—and I say it in the interest of justice—if you attempt to obtain evidence by these inquisitorial means you will certainly compel the people to withhold evidence, which would not be the case if your tribunals were such as to inspire them with confidence. I have given Notice of my intention to move the rejection of the clause altogether; but I put this Amendment formally, and I ask the Government to make the small concession that that which is enacted by the Petty Sessions Act shall be applicable to this clause.

Amendment proposed,

In page 1, line 17, at the end of the foregoing Amendment, to insert the words "provided that any witness so appearing shall be entitled to have present at any such examination or other proceeding counsel or attorney on his or her behalf."—(*Mr. Marum.*)

Question proposed, "That those words be there inserted."

Sir RICHARD WEBSTER: I will endeavour to make it clear why it is impossible for us to accept the Amendment proposed by the hon. Gentleman. In the Act to which I believe he has referred the attendance of counsel is allowed for the prisoner alone. There is no power for counsel or attorney to be present on behalf of any witness. I do not want to go back on the arguments already used; but I think I may say, *à fortiori*, if there is no charge made against any person the necessity for the presence of counsel is less than when a person is charged. The Committee will be aware that the statements made before the magistrates are not to be used against the witness in any shape or form except in the case of a prosecution for perjury; they cannot be used in cross-examination for the purpose of showing that the witness has made a statement and afterwards gone back from that statement. That has been stated more than once by the Attorney General for Ireland, and we intend to make it clear that these depositions shall not be used in any way except in the case of a prosecution for perjury. Therefore, it cannot be urged that there is no protection for a witness who is examined under this clause by the magistrates. The first objection of the hon. Member is founded on the 31st section of the Probate (Ireland) Act, which I believe corresponds with the English Act; but if the Committee remembers why this was enacted, they will see that there is no connection between the two cases. The other objection of the hon. Gentleman is founded on the practice in bankruptcy. Now, a bankrupt is supposed in many cases to be the enemy of all his creditors; it may be that he is concealing part of his estate, and that there are a number of actions pending against him, and therefore when a bankrupt is being examined, inasmuch as all the creditors are to have a shot at him, so to speak, it is thought right that he should have counsel or attorney attending in his behalf. But, taking the whole range of the Criminal and Civil Law, except in these two instances there is no authority or precedent for counsel or attorney being present on behalf of a witness. They are not allowed to take any part, and when counsel are present it is without the knowledge of the Court. Again, seeing that these inquiries are for the purpose of getting at the truth, and not for the purpose of proving the guilt of individuals, I say it would be very undesirable that a third person should be present. On the other hand, their presence is not required for the protection of the persons examined, as has been shown. It is therefore impossible that Her Majesty's Government can accept this Amendment, which, while it is not required for the protection of witnesses, would interfere with the operation of the clause.

Mr. ANDERSON: I think the hon. and learned Gentleman who has just sat down has not quite covered the whole of this question, because there is another case in which witnesses are entitled to have counsel and solicitors to protect them. I refer to examinations under the Companies' Act. Under the 115th section of that Act this is provided for where information is sought with regard to the winding up of Companies. The section is to the effect that the Court may summon before it any officer of the Company or person known to have in his possession the names of persons who are supposed to be indebted to the Company, and the Court may also summon any person whom the Court may deem capable of giving information as to the effects of the Company. As I have said, under that section the witness is entitled to be protected by solicitor or counsel, and this is of daily occurrence. Further, in bankruptcy examinations, it is customary not only for the bankrupt but witnesses to be protected in this way. This, also, is the everyday practice in the Bankruptcy Court. The hon. and learned Gentleman says there is no precedent of this kind in criminal cases; but the object of the clause, as I understand it, is the obtaining of information, not the conviction of witnesses. I cannot understand where will be the difficulty of getting information if the witness is allowed to be protected by counsel or attorney—on the contrary, I think the adoption of this Amendment might facilitate the getting of information. Again, these powers are to be exercised by persons who have no great experience in legal matters, and, that being so, I do not understand why we should object to counsel or attorney being present to assist them and see that there is fair play. I shall regret to find that, after

Mr. Marum

further consideration, the Attorney General still objects to this Amendment. I believe he will see that it will not at all interfere with the operation of the clause, the object of which is to get information. It is not sought to convict anyone on the evidence taken under this clause, but it may nevertheless occur that something may be got out of a witness in the examination which may be prejudicial to him. You may get something out of a witness with regard to the Plan of Campaign, for instance, and although you do not want to use his deposition against him, you will be able through his evidence to summon someone else. For these reasons, I regard the clause as most dangerous, and trust that the Amendment of the hon. Member for Kilkenny will be accepted by the Government.

MR. MOLLOY: The hon. and learned Gentleman has said that this Amendment is unnecessary because a witness does not require protection; but I think there will be cases in Ireland where this protection will be necessary. Suppose that a landlord at the present time has a civil action against some of his tenants, and suppose that a near relative of the landlord is a Resident Magistrate. In that case the landlord may set this clause in motion against his tenants, and obtain this inquisitorial examination. The landlord wants evidence against the tenants in civil actions against them. You will probably have a near relative of a landlord carrying out this inquisitorial examination; and if the witness called before this person has no one to protect him, questions affecting a civil action may be asked, and information also may be obtained, which has nothing whatever to do with the question of crime or offences—questions which would be used merely for the purpose of assisting the landlord in some action against his tenants. Well, the Attorney General says that a witness does not require anyone to assist him. It seems to me that the witness most decidedly does require this assistance. If there was a solicitor or counsel attending on behalf of a witness, he would not interfere so long as the examination was a genuine and honest one for the purpose of obtaining evidence with regard to a particular crime, and such protection to the witness would do no harm to the object we have in view. In the case I have mentioned—and I take that as one

example within my own knowledge, and no doubt there are many such in Ireland—this Act would be used, not for a legitimate purpose, but simply and solely for the purpose of exacting evidence from the witness to be used on a future occasion by the landlord against the tenants. The Government think counsel should not attend on behalf of the witness, then will they tell me how the witness is to be protected under the circumstances I have mentioned? The Government cannot say that I wish these powers to be exercised in such a dishonest manner as I have indicated, and, therefore, if they will not allow counsel or solicitor to attend on behalf of a witness, will the Attorney General for Ireland state in what way the witness is to be protected in that which is solely his private interest? I hope the Attorney General will give some hint or suggestion as to how a witness is to be protected under these circumstances.

MR. WARMINGTON (Monmouth, W.): I suppose the Government, in proposing this section, desire that it should be worked. If the object of the Government is that the section should be worked, they should take steps to see that it is worked in some reasonable way. I was rather surprised to hear the Attorney General say that the examination will not be used against the person examined. Why, Sir, it will be used in a most serious manner. It will be used in this way—supposing the person who has been examined is thought by the Government to have stated what is untrue, that person for that statement so made in examination can be charged with perjury. If a man has to give evidence on the chance of being hereafter charged with perjury, is it not reasonable that he should take steps to have that examination made in a proper manner, and to see that proper questions are put to him—that questions are not put to him in a leading form, and that questions are put to him which concern the precise offence in respect of which he is examined? Surely a witness has the greatest possible interest in having his examination conducted in a reasonable and legal manner, and directed to the precise point, and the precise point only, which is mentioned in his summons. Therefore, I maintain to say that the witness has no interest in the matter, or in what he states in his examination is simply begging the question. The very object of a witness having to be examined on oath is that the evidence may be used against him hereafter on a charge of perjury.

MR. FINLAY (Inverness, &c.): I hope the Government will resist this Amendment. If it is introduced the whole section will be rendered useless. How would it work in practice? Why, what would happen would be this—in many cases if this Amendment were introduced, a professional gentleman would appear at the inquiry for every witness, and would object to every question which was put, and raise an argument upon every question. In this way the object of the section, which is to obtain information, would be absolutely defeated.

MR. T. M. HEALY: I think that Liberal Unionist Gentlemen might very well hold their tongues upon this matter. It goes without saying that they are opposed to all our Amendments, and, therefore, their intervention in this discussion becomes nothing more nor less than Obstruction. We know beforehand what they would say, consequently the only effect of their speaking is to waste time. The hon. and learned Gentleman the English Attorney General has not dealt with this most important question as to the asking of irrelevant questions, and the whole matter turns upon whether the man who puts a question to a witness is to be at the same time the judge of its propriety, and, if it is not answered to his satisfaction, be the person to send that witness to gaol? That was the question raised in the Bankruptcy Court in the case of Father Keller. What Father Keller was put in gaol for was this. He was asked—"Were you in a madhouse in Youghal on a particular day at a particular hour?" He replied—"I decline to answer." He might have been asked with equal propriety whether he had taken a bath, or whether he had indulged in a walk by the seaside on a certain day. The question raised in Court was that the inquiries addressed to the witnesses should be relevant to the issue. The Bankruptcy Judge departed from his usual practice, and had allowed a barrister to be in attendance to watch the interests of the witness. The Counsel objected to this question as an irrelevant one. If the Government do not assent to this

Amendment, which seems to me to be a very reasonable one, I would put down an Amendment that if a witness considers a question irrelevant, and the magistrate insists upon an answer, the witness shall have an appeal to the Attorney General for Ireland or to a Court as to whether the question is irrelevant or not, and whether he ought to be required to answer it. It seems to me that when hon. Gentlemen connected with Scotland ask the Government to stand to their guns, they should remember that in Scotland the Procurator Fiscal presides over the inquiry, and that another gentleman asks the questions. ["No, no!"] Well, it is so laid down in all the books of authority. The Irish Chief Secretary has not written a book on the question; but there is a book written by "Mr. Macdonald" (the Lord Advocate), and we have had the temerity to look into that book, and have found that what I say is stated there. It may be bad law, but it is so stated in that book. I ask, will the Government do anything to remedy this defect? We are told a great deal about the law of Scotland, and that law of Scotland has been the ground upon which this section has been, to a large extent, supported. We are entitled to anticipate something of the kind I have mentioned occurring between the person who puts the question and the person who answers. Questions that are irrelevant some witnesses will refuse to answer, and we contend that there should be someone at the inquiry to decide as to the legality of the line of examination. If the Resident Magistrate chooses to ask a child whether it has been vaccinated, and the child refuses to answer, he might send it to prison. We complain that the Government have not addressed themselves to that question. We have a right to know who is to decide, when an important question is put, as to whether or not it is relevant and legal that a proper one ought to be put.

MR. J. E. ELLIS (Nottingham, Rushcliffe): I merely rise to recall for a moment what the object of this Bill really is. The right hon. Gentlemen who sits on the Front Bench opposite always use the word "crime" in connection with it; but we have the word of a much more important person than anyone who sits on the Front Bench opposite as to what it is intended to cope with by this

Mr. Warmington

measure. I refer to Lord Salisbury. The noble Marquess says—"We have offered a measure to the other House to put a stop to certain combinations." In view of that most authoritative declaration that this Bill is meant to put a stop to certain combinations of tenants, which have been declared by an equally high authority to be their salvation, I think we cannot be too careful in dealing with the Amendments we are considering. I think the Amendment now before us is one that the Government ought in common justice to accept, looking at the object for which this Bill is brought forward.

MR. P. J. POWER (Waterford, E.): As has been pointed out repeatedly, the gentlemen to be entrusted with the administration of this Act are gentlemen in whom we have and can have no confidence. They are political opponents to us, and we know from experience how the Act will be administered. Many of my hon. Friends have experience of the manner in which the Crimes Act was administered within the last three or four years. We had at that time a Government which had some pretence to being just; but I do not think that that term could in any way be applied to the Government we have now. We know that, when this Act is put in force, it will not be put in force to resist real criminals, but that it will be put in force to grapple with political opponents, and, consequently, I think that every safeguard should be used to prevent a gross abuse of these powers. Now, as the Bill at present stands, this clause will apply not only to proclaimed districts where serious crime does exist, but also to unproclaimed districts. Witnesses may be summoned from any part of Ireland to give evidence before this inquisitorial Court, and it is certainly most reasonable that witnesses should be prevented from being insulted by Stipendiary Magistrates, who are only too prone to insult them. As has been pointed out by the hon. and learned Member for one of the Divisions of King's County, questions may be put to witnesses in this inquisitorial Court which may seriously affect the civil relations of the witnesses. He has given instances, and I venture to say that most of us, in our different constituencies, could give instances, where civil actions are pending against men against whom the provisions of this Bill

will certainly be enforced. It is assumed that leading questions will not be asked. I should like the Committee to tell me how ignorant men will be able to discriminate between questions which are leading and questions which are not leading, or how they will be able to tell what questions will injure them in their private affairs, and which will not. No matter how this question is looked at, we think that, for the safeguarding of the interests of the witnesses who are to be examined before these inquisitorial Courts, it is absolutely necessary that these witnesses should be provided with the protection of either an attorney or a counsel.

MR. FLYNN (Cork, N.): The right hon. and learned Gentleman the Attorney General for England has quoted the Petty Sessions Act in support of the Government proposal; but I venture to say that nothing contained in that Act with regard to the non-attendance of counsel or witnesses is a precedent for the Star Chamber inquiry contemplated by this measure. There is not the least analogy between the Petty Sessions Act and these Star Chamber inquiries. It must be remembered that these will be held with closed doors. There will be no reporters present, and there will be no possibility of anyone knowing what is going on. In the Petty Sessions Court, however, reporters are in attendance, so that everyone knows perfectly well what is going on. If witnesses are subjected to unfair pressure there is the adequate protection of public opinion to deal with the case. Therefore that argument of the Attorney General for England does not hold water. He says, further, that in his view no protection is required for witnesses. Now, this is a very strong assumption, totally unwarranted and unsupported by the present state of things in Ireland. It is totally unwarranted and unsupported by what has occurred under the Crimes Act, 1882, for the past four or five years; it is totally unwarranted and unsupported by the character and reputation of the men who are to administer this Act. No protection, forsooth, for the witnesses! Why, where inquiries have been held in Cork we have had respectable men examined, on whom no possible suspicion of criminality could rest—gentlemen of as high a character, nay, a far higher character than the men who tried them. We have had gentlemen in Cork examined who were taken away from their business for five or six days together, large traders, and others of all kinds; and irrelevant and tedious and impertinent questions have been put to them. I know of cases in which insulting questions were asked of a man, which had no relevancy to the point at issue. We knew perfectly well at the time that the object of the investigation was not to discover crime, but to find out the secrets of the National League; and as sure as this Act is before the Committee at the present moment, so surely will this clause be put into operation for similar purposes. This present clause, I feel confident, will be put into operation not for the purpose of detecting crime or so-called offences, but, as an hon. Member above the Gangway a short time ago stated—quoting a very high authority—for the purpose of putting down combinations. The hon. and learned Gentleman the Attorney General for England knows nothing whatever about the condition of things in Ireland, or he would not have said that there is no protection required for witnesses who will be examined under this clause. In view of what has occurred already in Ireland, in view of what has occurred under the Crimes Act of 1882, and in view of the fact that witnesses will be examined by hostile people on information supplied by spies, and in view of the fact that they will be examined hostilely and sternly, and by anything but a fair and impartial Judge presiding on the Bench, it is utterly impossible that questions unfair and altogether irrelevant will not be asked. We distrust the impartiality of the tribunal, and we say if these inquiries are to be held, if at the present time the Government think it necessary to revive these powers, which are a disgrace to civilization and which are pointed out by historians of to-day as one of the blots on the former civilization of this and other countries—if these powers are to be revived in Ireland under a Government notoriously hostile and unfriendly to the population and to combinations of the people, we ask that, at any rate, those unfortunate people who may not have committed any offence or crime shall be afforded that protection which this clause does not afford, and that their ignorance shall be defended by the presence of some competent legal

Mr. Flynn

advocate in Court to watch the course of the inquiry.

THE FIRST LORD OF THE TREASURY (Mr. W. H. SMITH) (Strand, Westminster): Once more I would make an appeal to hon. Gentlemen opposite. I fully admit their right to make a protest in a matter of this kind; but the Government have stated the ground upon which they feel it impossible to accept the Amendment, and I venture to think that the arguments which have since been addressed to them are not of sufficient weight to induce us to alter our determination. The constant repetition of arguments against the attitude of the Government will not advance the view that hon. Gentlemen take. Hon. Gentlemen are simply repeating again and again statements which have already been presented to us sufficiently and eloquently by the hon. Gentleman below the Gangway. I trust, therefore, that we may be allowed to divide without devoting any more time to this discussion.

MR. MAURICE HEALY (Cork): I think the success the right hon. Gentleman met with when he made his last appeal has induced him somewhat to abuse his position. When the right hon. Gentleman, on the last occasion, appealed to us to come to a Division, we had had speech after speech from the Gentlemen sitting on the Front Bench opposite, and what is more important, we had a promise of concessions made on the matter under discussion, therefore that is no parallel to the present case, and what has already taken place I think somewhat detracts from the appeal which the right hon. Gentleman makes. It is an important matter, and one that should be somewhat further pressed on the Government, who at present have only put forward one of their Members to reply to the repeated arguments that have been pressed upon them from this side of the House. The relevancy and propriety of this Amendment appears to me to depend upon two considerations. The first is this, there is a necessity for the protection of witnesses who may be examined on these inquiries that they should be represented at these inquiries in some legal way, and consequently the granting of such a protection cannot in any way detract from the results which may be expected from the holding of these inquiries. It appears to me that both these questions may be properly answered in a way favourable to the Amendment. In the first place, could any good reason be urged, or any proper grounds put forward, for the proposition that some protection is required for witnesses who may be examined on these inquiries. Speaker after speaker has got up on this side of the House, and has pointed out that very serious dangers indeed may arise to witnesses from the want of such protection. Let me call attention to this fact that the Government have already admitted, by accepting an Amendment from this side of the House to the effect that if a witness is a person who has committed a crime, or is the wife of a person who has committed a crime, it shall not be competent for the magistrate to proceed further with the examination, and that the witness should be immediately discharged therefrom. I ask, therefore, what good object is to be served by resisting the insertion of these words in the clause, and by refusing to give these persons the protection which has been pointed out against the power of the magistrates holding the inquiry. There is nothing to prevent a magistrate proceeding in his inquiry after the witness has admitted that he has been party to an offence, notwithstanding what the Government has said. It must be remembered that witnesses who may be examined may be ignorant persons who have not made a study of this Bill, and who may not know what their rights are—persons who would, therefore, be absolutely at the mercy of the Resident Magistrates holding the inquiry. Therefore it would, in this state of things, be in the power of any ignorant, incompetent, or malignant Resident Magistrate to proceed in the teeth of the Act, and examine persons under these circumstances though the House has solemnly declared that such examination should not be pursued. Let us take the case that an hon. Friend of mine mentioned, in which it would be in the power of the Resident Magistrate holding the inquiry under this clause to abuse his position for the purpose of extracting from witnesses evidence not at all relevant to the offence being inquired into, but which could be used against the witness in civil proceedings. That appears to me to be a most impor-

tant case, and upon the question which it involves the right hon. Gentleman the First Lord of the Treasury has omitted to notice that we have received no reply from any of his Colleagues sitting on that Bench. I venture to say that dozens of cases could be mentioned in which it would be in the power of a presiding magistrate to act in a manner grossly unfair, and to put question after question improperly to witnesses against which witnesses would and could have no protection such as would be conferred upon them by the attendance of a solicitor or counsel to watch over their interests. I think, as I have said, that this is a very important question, and before we go to a Division, as the right hon. Gentleman wishes, I think we are entitled to some answer from the Front Bench opposite. As to the question that arises—namely, would a court of justice suffer any defeat or detriment from the acceptance of this Amendment, or would any benefit which might be assumed to result from the adoption of this clause in its present form be in any way militated against by the witnesses being allowed to have an advocate present— I would point out that the right hon. Gentleman is the only Member of the Government who told us what the view of the Government is on this matter. I would venture to suggest that no such interference would take place. He has not attempted to show how the presence of a solicitor or barrister could in any way militate against the success of the inquiry; he has not ventured to allege that the presence of such a person could be used in a way to prevent the course of justice, or to prevent this inquiry being held, or in any way to defeat the object with which such an inquiry would be held. He has contented himself with this one argument, that the proposal contained in this Amendment is contrary to precedent. Well, unfortunately the whole of the proposals of this Bill are of such a nature as will make it distinctly difficult to find precedents bearing upon them. The proposals of this measure are novel and unprecedented, and therefore it would be very hard to find any precedent for the Amendment we propose. Our proposals are unprecedented, because the provisions we are asking the Committee to amend are themselves unprecedented. I therefore contend that this Committee cannot take such

[*Fourth Night.*]

an answer as that as conclusive on the Amendment.

Mr. CHANCE (Kilkenny, S.) : Hon. Gentlemen are in the habit of coming in about half-past 12 o'clock at night and sitting like mutes at a funeral until someone, without having heard a word of the debate, moves the clôture, when they go into the Lobby against us, we having throughout the early portion of the evening been speaking in support of our Amendments to empty Benches. Such a process seems to be taking place at the present moment. The right hon. Gentleman says we are not to repeat our statements; but I would remind him that, owing to the mental construction of hon. Gentleman opposite, it needs five or six repetitions of an argument to hammer it into their heads. It is necessary to repeat our arguments over and over again before we can get anything from the Government. I think in a matter such as this we have a right to argue our case fully. The power contained in this clause in its present form is one which will enable the Resident Magistrates of Ireland to torture every witness that may be brought before them, and subject them to an inquisitorial investigation. Our proposal is that witnesses brought before these Resident Magistrates, should, before this torture is inflicted on them, have the benefit of legal advice, and we call upon the Government to put forth whatever shreds of argument they may have to justify their opposition to this reasonable demand. There is no reason why we should not discuss this matter. We desire, in discussing this proposal of the Government, to give to witnesses the benefit of professional advice and assistance, and that proposal of ours is opposed as unwarrantable by the Government who defend this clause by a number of legal advocates—seven, I think—who have spoken for them on this matter. Well, if the Government found it difficult to defend this clause except by calling in to their aid seven legal gentlemen who are paid large sums out of the pockets of the taxpayers; I think the unfortunate people who will be brought for examination have as good a right to a legal opinion, for which they will pay out of their own pockets. Do the Government think that the liberties of witnesses can be more safely entrusted to Resident Magis-

trates without legal assistance, than their arguments in favour of the clause can be presented to the House without legal assistance? I think the Resident Magistrate is at least as much likely to be benefited by an advocate appearing for the witnesses as the government is benefited by several legal gentlemen appearing in support of their proposals. I think the liberties of the Irish people are of more importance to this Committee than the dinners of hon. Members, and therefore we are determined to debate this question to the utmost.

Mr. W. BOWEN ROWLANDS (Cardiganshire) : It seems to me that the Government would do well to accede to the wishes of the Irish Members in this matter. This is confessedly an exceptional proposal as far as the law of England and the practice of the law in Ireland are concerned, and it seems to me desirable in that state of things that every precaution should be taken to ensure that no unfair use should be made of the powers which are to be entrusted to gentlemen who in the main are absolutely without knowledge of legal matters. I should have thought that the hon. Gentlemen opposite, so far as their principles are identical with the professed aims of the Government, would have been satisfied that this Amendment should have been introduced. I have had considerable experience of matters of this kind professionally, and I would ask what harm can be done by accepting this Amendment? If proper questions are asked by the magistrates, to whom these powers are given, of the witnesses before them, then the counsel or attorney appearing for such witnesses would have no right to interfere; and if improper questions are put them, it seems to me that the person whose evidence is to be made use of for the purpose of launching some case against some other person should have an opportunity of having competent advice afforded him. It need not necessarily follow that counsel should be employed in every case. I would appeal to the experience of English Law Officers of the Crown whether, in regard to bankruptcy inquiries, though it by no means follows that counsel appearing for persons are entitled to make a speech, or even entitled to cross-examine, there

Mr. Maurice Healy

is not a great protection in having the advice of a legal gentleman as to the relevancy and propriety of questions which are put to witnesses. It is found to be very essential to have such advice in order that the witnesses may be satisfied that the investigation is being pursued in a manner within the scope of the Act. If, as we have been told, and as my own experience teaches me is likely to be the case, witnesses are called upon to give evidence who belong to the less educated and ignorant classes, what will be the state of things? Is it not necessary that they should have the protection of legal advice? I do not wish to protract this debate unduly, but I would press upon the Government the necessity of saying why they oppose this Amendment, or what harm the introduction of the words suggested would do to the legitimate operation of the Act. Here you have a Court inquiring into matters which are not within the limits of a specific indictment or the subject of a direct or specific charge. The inquiry under the clause will be a fishing inquiry, and as I have said, the only analogy in our law as to the inquiry is the inquiry which takes place under the law of bankruptcy, and there the attendance of an advocate, although his power is restricted, is admitted. As I have said, he is not allowed to speak, and he may not be allowed to cross-examine; but his presence is permitted, and he is allowed to give advice, and the mere fact of such advice being permitted is an encouragement to the witness, and also a protection. As the proceedings under this clause are of a private character, it is more than ever desirable that some person should be in attendance who would be able to carry out-of-doors a proper account of what took place before the magistrate. Of course we may take it for granted that respectable practitioners would be engaged for the witnesses, and it seems to me that the presence of such professional gentleman would be most desirable. I am at a loss to see what harm could accrue from the adoption of this Amendment, and I am extremely desirous that when exceptional legislation of this kind is adopted, all necessary precautions should be taken to secure its being administered in a fair manner. It is particularly essential, it seems to me, that every opportunity should be given

for making a true statement out-of-doors of what takes place at this private inquiry; and I am sorry that the Government have not been able, in any way, to accede to the proposal which has now been made to them. In the case of a Division, I shall feel myself bound to vote against the Government.

MR. O'DOHERTY: I should have liked to have asked the Government to consider one point in the examination with reference to which it is plainly desirable that a solicitor should be allowed to be present. I mean when the warrant for the committal is about to be made out. The Amendment says a solicitor should be present at the examination from beginning to end; but I would suggest, to meet the objections of the right hon. Gentlemen opposite, who say that the presence of a solicitor or a barrister would put an end to that privacy and secrecy which they think to be the essence of the whole clause, that the period at which the committal is about to be made out is the time above all others when it would be necessary that a counsel should be present representing the witness. Remember that these witnesses are not criminals. They are not brought up for trial, and they are, therefore, persons over whom the Committee should try to throw some protection. Take it that a time has come when a witness, who has been answering every question fairly and fully, says—"You are going too far," and refuses to say anything more. Take it that a time has come when he may say—"This is a matter involving my property or my character," or "This is an insulting question, and before I go any further I should like to consult a legal adviser," or "I think this is a question which should not be put, and I would like it to be put in the presence of a solicitor." If the Government cannot see their way to accept the spirit of the Amendment of my hon. Friend, I think this is a time when they ought to indicate it. What are the powers of these gentlemen sitting there in absolute secrecy? To use the words of the right hon. Gentleman the Chief Secretary— "If the witness refuses to answer a question the magistrate may commit him." But supposing a question is put to him which he should not be called upon to answer. Without this Amendment there would be no possibility of

[Fourth Night.]

the witness arguing with the magistrate. The mere fact that the magistrate has put a question and that the witness refuses to answer it, will be sufficient to ensure his committal. There will be no access so far as the witness and his friends are concerned, to the shorthand writers' notes. I ask, therefore, is it not fair that a witness should have some means of examining into the right, in certain instances, of exercising this immense power of committal. I would put it to the Committee, would it not be fair to give the witness a chance of saying, at a certain point—"Have you the right of exercising this power of committal? What have I done?" A man has no right to be troubled at all to give evidence unless he is supposed to have knowledge of guilt and is concealing it. This man should have a right to legal protection—it is a liberty which everybody possesses. Under this measure, a magistrate will have power to call upon witnesses to produce all kinds of papers and documents; and I want to know where this power will end, if we have not an Amendment such as this inserted in the clause? What may not a witness be asked to produce? He may be asked to produce his love letters. I know of nothing, as the clause is framed, to stop the course of the inquiry. The refusal to produce a single one of his private letters would enable a magistrate to send him to gaol. And surely in such a matter as that a man should have the right to ask that he may have counsel, through whom he can say—"Have I not a right to refuse to produce these things?" It must be borne in mind that these witnesses will be examined before local people, in the different localities, and upon information supplied locally. They may be examined by the agents of their own landlords; and I want to ask if it is not right that they should have some protection against malice, against ill-will, against unfair questions, and against questions put with an ulterior motive. If the Government do not agree with the Amendment as proposed, let them adopt it in the modified form I have suggested. Surely, if the Head of the Government comes in and finds that we are so reasonable, we shall not, when in future he makes his strong appeals to the House, have strength enough to resist him. He speaks with such earnestness, when he gets in that humour, that

Mr. O'Doherty

we are bound to accede to his wishes. I think that the right hon. Gentleman ought to be able to accept the Amendment qualified in the way I propose.

Mr. J. BRYN ROBERTS (Carnarvonshire, Eifion): It appears to me that the 3rd sub-section of this clause will have an important influence on the opinions of the Committee in deciding on this Amendment. I would wish to discuss the sub-section as far as it bears on the importance of the admission of a solicitor or advocate to defend a witness. It might be urged that because—

"A witness examined under this sub-section shall not be excused from answering any question on the ground that the answer thereto may criminate, or tend to criminate, himself,"

that, therefore, there is less necessity for the presence of an advocate; but I would point out that that sub-section is not passed, and may not be passed. It is not a fair method, in discussing a certain provision, to look ahead to another provision, and say that a certain course must be taken in order to avoid prejudicing what is to follow. We are entitled, I contend, to discuss this matter as though the 3rd sub-section were not in the Bill at all, and as if it were quite on the cards that it will not be passed. If then it should not be passed it would be a monstrous proposition that a witness, although not legally bound to answer a question which would criminate himself, yet should not have the right of having counsel to defend him from irrelevant questions. Whether the 3rd sub-section is rejected or not, the question is whether irrelevant questions should be permitted. It is impossible for a witness to protect himself against a Resident Magistrate. It requires a qualified person, skilled in the practice of the law, to see what questions are proper and relevant, and what are not. As one practising in the Legal Profession, it has frequently been my duty to attend police courts before unpaid magistrates, and I can say, with the greatest confidence, there is no branch of the law on which these gentlemen have greater difficulty than on questions of the relevancy of evidence. All other matters they can get into, and do get into, very well. They can consider Acts of Parliament, and, to some extent, judge of cases put before them; but the rules of evidence, especially as to what questions are relevant and what are not, they are singularly unable to deal with. Unpaid magistrates do not seem to have the slightest glimmer of capacity for dealing with such subjects. A case came within my own knowledge, only a short time ago, where a principal witness against the accused was asked whether there was not a bitter feud existing between him and his family on the one hand, and the accused on the other, and the magistrate would not allow that question to be put on the ground that it was not relevant, though, of course, anyone knowing anything of the law, would know that it was most relevant to the credibility of the witness. Fortunately, there was a solicitor engaged in the case, and he insisted upon his right to put the question; and owing solely to his presence and his persistency the question was allowed to be put. But equally before these inquiries irrelevant questions will be put if a solicitor or a barrister is not allowed to be present. In passing a Coercion Bill of this kind into law, we ought always to bear in mind how previous Coercion Bills have been exercised in Ireland. This is a consideration that ought never be absent from our minds. We ought to consider how the Act of 1881 was worked —in fact, how all these Acts are worked. The Act of 1881 was worked upon information supplied by local partizans of the landlord and Conservative Party in the districts in which the Act was in operation. In one of the debates on that Bill I heard the hon. Member for Cork give an illustration of a number of tenants who had applied in a body for a reduction of rent; and the spokesman of the party was told by the agent—"I will have you in Kilmainham by to-morrow night." The hon. Member for Cork said that, as a matter of fact, that man was put into gaol within 24 hours.

Mr. T. M. HEALY: Was his name Crosbie?

Mr. J. BRYN ROBERTS: Yes; that was the name. That was one of the cases in which Mr. Forster said that the Act could never be used. Mr. Forster, when he was granting his permission to arrest that man, did not know but that it was a proper case for arrest. No doubt he believed, when he gave his permission, that the man was one of those "village ruffians" of whom he had spoken. Therefore, we must take it that the information supplied him by some local partizan was that Mr. Crosbie was a village ruffian, and that Mr. Forster acted honestly on the dishonest information so supplied him. How can such occurrences as that be avoided in the future? Under this clause, witnesses will be summoned on the information of local partizans, who will give onesided information as a groundwork for examining a witness; and when that is so, I think it is most important that so un-English a proceeding as secret examination—the torturing of a witness in private—should not be adopted without professional advice being afforded such witness. I, therefore, think this clause should not be passed into law without the Amendment which has been proposed.

Mr. EDWARD HARRINGTON (Kerry, W.): I think we ought not to be expected to respond so readily to the appeal of the right hon. Gentleman the First Lord of the Treasury. We take a great interest in this matter; and on the presumption that the Government are attacking the liberties of the Irish people, and the liberties of the Leaders of the Irish people, we should not be expected to be so generous as to pay out this Crimes Bill fathom by fathom whenever the right hon. Gentleman chooses to stand up and make an appeal to us. This is what is before the Committee; and let English gentlemen understand it. We give you— I do not say readily, but you outvote us, and we give you—the power of calling witnesses at any hour of the day or night out of their beds, if you like; we give you power to bring up persons who have not been accused of any crime, and to examine them upon anything with this one reservation—that we ask that these persons shall have by them, sitting at their sides, a legal adviser who will be prepared to direct them as to whether questions are relevant or not, and as to whether, in a certain line of answer, they are not likely to criminate themselves. I think it is not too much to ask Her Majesty's Government that they should accept the Amendment. Sir, the right hon. and learned Gentleman, who spoke a-while ago from the Front Bench opposite, seemed not to know—and that is what we complain of generally against the Members of Her Majesty's Government, that they do not know what they themselves mean. They say that there should be no third party between the magistrate and the witness; but we have it already from them that there is to be some recorder present —some shorthand writer or some one to record the proceedings. Our desire is simply that the witness shall be protected from the asking of impertinent and irrelevant questions. Hon. Gentlemen on this side—at least, my hon. and learned Friend the Member for the King's County (Mr. Molloy), who spoke this evening, called attention to a case, and it was not an empty one. It was a case in which it was pointed out that there may be civil actions pending between a friend of the magistrate and certain civil litigants. Where the magistrate is a friend of the landlord, he could bring up persons, affect to examine them for the investigation of crime—a crime not named or specified—and could elicit most material evidence to be used on some future occasion in the civil cases of his friend the landlord. The Government should give us some assurance that they will set their several legal heads together, and, giving us the benefit of their knowledge and attainments in this matter, devise some means for the protection of witnesses. You are not to suppose that the persons summoned before these Courts are persons who are criminals. That is not the assumption at all. No one who pretends to know Ireland would hold that assumption. I tell you that the persons who will hold these investigations will have brought before them priests, Members of Parliament, and large traders—the leaders of thought in the small towns—and they will take advantage of local and petty disputes, for they will not be able to pretend that they are anything else—for the purpose of exercising their powers, and having exercised them, they will ask the witnesses all sorts of unnecessary and all sorts of impertinent questions. Hon. Members are anxious to give the Resident Magistrates powers which will conduce to the discovery of crime, but will they say that there should be no limitation as to importance and relevance in the questions that may be asked? It is because we feel these things very keenly that we have time after time to ring the changes in these debates. We have to persist in order to extract infor-

mation from hon. Gentlemen, and I say that no amount of appeals and platitudes that come from Her Majesty's Government, who do not know what the work to which they have put their hands is, will have the slightest influence upon us so long as we consider it necessary to lay our case before the Committee.

MR. P. J. POWER: I must say that we on this side of the House have a right to complain of the conspiracy of silence which prevails on the Ministerial Benches. We, on these Benches, have placed before the Government most important points—points that we know are important — and Gentlemen above the Gangway on this side of the House have also endeavoured to impress upon the Government the importance of these matters. But there is no impressing the Government it appears. I should think it would be far more seemly for hon. and right hon. Gentlemen opposite to get up from time to time and answer the questions we address to them, than for them to sit yawning there the whole evening. I know from sad experience, and my hon. Friends sitting around me know from sad experience, that this Coercion Act will be used like all previous Coercion Acts, not for the detection of real criminals, but for the choking-off of political opponents. Under these circumstances are we unreasonable in demanding that Her Majesty's Government should give us some explanation of the points which we endeavour to urge? The Committee will recollect that when different Governments at different periods endeavoured to pass different Coercion Acts, they merely asked for these powers for a limited time. The cases are not parallel. We have now before us the most drastic Coercion Act that any Government ever introduced, and they are asking for these powers, not for a limited time, but in perpetuity. Is it unreasonable, therefore, that we should ask the Government to give us some explanation on the points we endeavour to make? We have heard, in connection with this Amendment and this clause, that notes are to be taken of the proceedings which are to be conducted in private; and I wish to ask the right hon. and learned Gentleman the Attorney General for Ireland who is to have access to these notes? If we are to have access to them, how long will it be be after they are published? Perhaps the Government would condescend to answer so small a question as that. The Leader of the House came in and asked us to come to a Division on the Amendment as speedily as possible. I think we have rather spoiled the right hon. Gentleman by giving him Amendment after Amendment to-night. I do not think that even the most grasping of Her Majesty's Government's supporters can allege that we have not made good progress to-night. The progress we have made is really marvellous. This House has already been teaching the Irish people to think that they need not expect justice from it, and I think the manner in which our reasonable proposals are received to-night will confirm them in that opinion. We know how these laws will be brought to bear, and, so far as lies in our power, we will endeavour to thwart Her Majesty's Government at every step in the administration of this Act. We know that it is not levelled at real criminals, but at a Constitutional organization, whose only object has been to stop the rack-renting of the landlords. I would ask how this clause will work with reference to the Plan of Campaign? We know that the proposal——

THE CHAIRMAN : The hon. Gentleman is now travelling beyond the limits of the Amendment.

MR. J. O'CONNOR (Tipperary, S.): I thought, Mr. Courtney, we were getting on very well with this clause. Any person who observed the progress of the Business this evening must have seen with satisfaction Amendment after Amendment swept away; the Government, the Opposition, and my Colleagues who sit below the Gangway, seemed to understand each other pretty well. In fact, the Government were very plausible this evening, and I thought we would have continued doing Business for the balance of the evening in a very pleasant way. But the First Lord of the Treasury (Mr. W. H. Smith) made a sudden incursion into the House, and not satisfied, in company with the Prime Minister, in bullying Members of this House outside by speeches at banquets and soirées— [The CHAIRMAN: Order, order!] Well, Sir, the First Lord of the Treasury comes into the House—and I hope I am not out of Order in saying—tries to intimidate Members of this House in the per-

formance of their duty. What is it to us, Sir, if the First Lord of the Treasury threatens to put on the closure, to exercise those extreme powers which the House has conferred upon him. Nevertheless, with all these threats, with all these pains and penalties in view, we shall endeavour, without any passion, without any feeling of resentment, if we possibly can suppress it—we shall endeavour to perform our duty, and to discuss these Amendments according as the requirements of the case demand, and according as our experience compels us to. Well, Sir, I am very sorry that the Government seems to have abandoned its plausible mood, and that it will not accept this very important Amendment. I hold, Mr. Courtney, that the importance of this Amendment has been proved this evening. The Amendment has been called for, because we know, from our experience, that the magistrates in whose hands the administration of the Act of 1882 was placed used that Act for purposes for which the Act was never intended. A magistrate in administering that Act of Parliament always felt it to be his duty to ask irrelevant questions. Why did he do that? Because he was not a magistrate merely sent for the purpose of administering the law, but he was a man sent especially for the purpose of incriminating somebody, and he did not much mind whether the questions asked were relevant to the subject set forth in the summons, or had ulterior objects in view. The magistrates who usually are engaged in the administration of Coercion Acts are men who desire to please their employers—that is their first duty to themselves. It is always with that amount of self-interest in view that they perform their duties; therefore, if they can incriminate somebody, no matter whether the offence committed by the incriminated person has any bearing on the case they were sent to investigate, and if it pleases their employers, they are perfectly satisfied. We ask that an unfortunate witness, or, as he has been described this evening, an unfortunate person, who may be brought up before one of these Courts of Inquiry, shall have the assistance of a solicitor or barrister-at-law. We believe that a witness, no matter whether he be a very ignorant man or an ordinary man of business, will require such assistance

[Fourth Night.]

as a man of legal training can afford him, otherwise he will have no protection from the irrelevant questions that one of these magistrates will put to him. I was very much struck with a case in point, quoted by the Mover of this Amendment, from the practice of the French Courts. Certainly, it bore out strongly what I can very easily conceive to have been the practice of Courts that have been already held in Ireland under the old Act. But, not only does the witness require protection from the magistrate in regard to irrelevant questions, but he requires protection from the insults of the magistrate engaged in carrying on the inquiry; he requires protection from the very terror a magistrate tries to instil into him. Imagine one of these magistrates vested with authority, as he has been in Ireland, authority that he has been in the habit of exercising to the detriment of the people who hold him in absolute terror—imagine an investigating magistrate, whose anger has been aroused by a witness declining to answer an irrelevant question, jumping up from the table, pacing up and down the floor of the room in which the inquiry may be held, and looking daggers at the unfortunate witness, threatening him with all sorts of pains and penalties, threatening to put him into prison for six months, defying him to dare the law, asking him to leave the country, and using all the methods a magistrate practices, studies, and employs, in order to terrorize an unfortunate witness into giving evidence of some sort or other, evidence which has very often served to make himself commit perjury. Well, Sir, a witness would require some legal help in order to protect him from this terrorism which has been practised by these magistrates in the performance of their duties in the past, and which will undoubtedly be practised by them in the future. I am sure it can easily be imagined by this Committee that if an investigating magistrate is sitting in Court in the presence of a man of legal training, he will conduct himself with more dignity than he otherwise would. I am not drawing upon my imagination in describing the conduct of these magistrates; I have seen them act in the manner I have described. It was by a system of bullying, terrorism, and the asking of irrelevant questions, that they succeeded, in some respects, in driving

people into awkward positions and into gaol, rather than perjure themselves at the bidding of any Court whatever. Now, not only with regard to magistrates, should this safeguard be placed in the hands of the people, but also in regard to their assistants. I will give a case in point to the Committee. I believe that, according to an Amendment that has already been passed, a magistrate will have the assistance of some professional person, of the Petty Sessions Clerk, I think. Now, the Petty Sessions Clerks in Ireland are a class of men against whom the people require protection as much as they do from the magistrates themselves. Petty Sessions Clerks are usually appointed by the local gentry, or upon the recommendation of the local gentry. Now, under the Crimes Act of 1882, a celebrated case was tried in the town of Bandon, County Cork, and as the result of that case the present Mayor of Cork, a gentleman named Mr. Mahoney, and my hon. Friend the Member for West Cork (Mr. Gilhooly), were committed for terms of imprisonment ranging from two to three months. These hon. and distinguished men had to lie for months on plank beds. Well, Sir, the Petty Sessions Clerk of that district omitted to take down material evidence—wilfully omitted to take down material evidence —evidence that would have gone far to acquit my hon. Friend the Member for West Cork and his companions; and it was only after a very long wrangle, introduced and provoked by the hon. Gentleman who now sits for the City of Cork (Mr. Maurice Healy), that the magistrate consented to have this material evidence taken down; but although this was done, this evidence, however, was not allowed to be used at the trial. Not only did this Petty Sessions Clerk omit to take down material evidence, but he actually connived at witnesses who had made material and important statements leaving the Court and town without signing their depositions. Well, Sir, that is the course of conduct on the part of a class of people who are to play an important part in the carrying out of this Criminal Law Amendment Act, and in taking down depositions under this clause. What I have said, Mr. Courtney, is only a sample of many other unfair proceedings that may be quoted to this Committee, in

Mr. J. O'Connor (Tipperary)

order to prove the contention that I am endeavouring to urge. I maintain, Sir, that upon every ground upon which we can discuss this question, from every point of view that we can look at it, it is of the greatest possible importance to the people of Ireland who will be affected by this clause, that they should be protected at these inquiries by the presence of some legally-trained person. By reason of the manner in which they are appointed, the magistrates themselves will desire to serve their masters in the best way they can. They will not stand upon ceremony, they will not stand upon the mere Act of Parliament, they will not hesitate to put irrelevant questions, they will not hesitate to insult and terrorize witnesses so long as it pleases their employers and gets them a step of promotion, and a possible retention on the staff. An enormous number of appointments will be made under this Bill when it becomes law; we know the class of men who will be called upon to fill the various posts that will necessarily be created by this Bill; we know that they will be men who will scarcely know a line of the Act of Parliament which they will be asked to administer; broken down soldiers and promoted policemen will be called upon to administer this Act. They will study rather the intention of those above them than the lines of the Act of Parliament that have been so well considered in this House, and have been carried so strenuously and so plausibly by the Government. I say that, upon all these grounds, this Amendment is the most important that has been proposed for the consideration of this Committee to-night, and I must express my regret that the Government have abandoned the plausible mood in which they begun the Business of the evening, and that they stand firm against the acceptance of this most important Amendment. I look upon it as a bad augury. They have rejected every Amendment proposed on this side of the House night after night, and the rejection of this and other Amendments clearly shows what is the mind of the Government. They desire not only to draft a stringent Act of Parliament, but to carry it out in the most stringent manner they possibly can. Their conduct is susceptible of no other reading than that it is their intention to administer the Act in the same spirit in

which it has been conceived; and, notwithstanding many protestations to the contrary, it is clearly the intention of the Government to break up all those combinations, those legal and just combinations having for their object the reduction of unjust rents, and the benefit of the people generally.

MR. H. J. WILSON (York, W.R., Holmfirth): Mr. Courtney, I think we really have great reason to complain of the conduct of the Government in not giving any reply whatever to the question, asked over and over again, why they object to this Amendment? I have listened to Irish Member after Irish Member putting this question, and I have heard two Gentlemen from these Benches, both of them representing constituencies in Wales, one belonging to the higher and the other to the lower branch of the Legal Profession in this country, put this question very plausibly to the Government, yet the Government seem to think it is a fine thing to sit in silence and pay no heed to the arguments advanced in favour of the Amendment. If there is some good reason why these witnesses should not have legal assistance, why not get up and give it to us? In the absence of a given reason, the only conclusion we can come to is that it is desired to keep Irish witnesses more and more within the power of their enemies. I am not anxious to obtrude in this debate, and hitherto have taken no part in it. Some of the points are of a complicated kind, and need some knowledge of law and some knowledge of Ireland; but this is a perfectly clear and straightforward matter. I remember that, when I was a great deal younger than I am now, an eminent minister, who used to officiate in a chapel not far from where we now are, told me that if the Angel Gabriel came to him with a legal document he would not look at it until he had seen his solicitor. Surely, if a Resident Magistrate is vested with these extraordinary powers, a witness is entitled to have some protection from the abuse of those powers. One hon. Gentleman has spoken to-night of lay magistrates, and of their knowledge of the Law of Evidence. Well, I can corroborate all he has stated, because I am myself a lay magistrate. What the hon. Gentleman said may not be very complimentary to us, but it is, nevertheless, perfectly true; we are very often at sea as to what is real evidence and what is not. I think that we are really entitled to demand that the Government shall give us, and give us civilly, a reason why they think a witness should not be afforded the protection contemplated by this Amendment.

THE ATTORNEY GENERAL FOR IRELAND (Mr. HOLMES) (Dublin University): I do not know whether the hon. Member (Mr. Wilson) was in the House when my hon. and learned Friend the Attorney General (Sir Richard Webster) spoke a short time ago. If he had been in the House he would have heard very strong reasons given why this Amendment should not be adopted. Since my hon. and learned Friend spoke, each speech delivered from the Benches below the Gangway opposite has been a repetition of the preceding one, and the simple reason why the Government have not intervened is that they cannot add anything to the clear statement made by my hon. and learned Friend.

MR. H. J. GILL (Limerick): I think the reasons given by the Government for not accepting this Amendment are extremely weak. From every point of view that rational and sensible men can look upon this Bill, I think that the Government ought to accept this Amendment, inasmuch as it affords some security against this Act being administered in a tyrannical manner towards witnesses. The Government have promised to allow shorthand reports to be taken of the proceedings at these secret investigations; but what on earth is the good of the shorthand reports, unless they can be made use of. These proceedings will be carried on by magistrates, as we distinctly say, perfectly ignorant of the law, and we all know the class of men whom the Government will employ as shorthand reporters. It was said, I think, that there were no shorthand reporters employed during the administration of the Crimes Act of 1882. A right hon. Gentleman on the Government Bench said that the reason that they would accept the Amendment to have shorthand reporters was that such persons were plentiful now, and that they were very scarce at the time the last Crimes Act was in operation. But what kind of reporters do they intend to use? By their own admission they intend to use what we in Ireland know to be Con-

stabulary reporters, and the vast bulk of these gentlemen know very little about reporting. It has been proved over and over again that they were unable to write out their own notes, and that they had to make use of the reports in the daily papers in order to help them to transcribe their notes. Well, as this is to be a secret inquiry, they will get no assistance whatever from reports in the daily papers. These very clever gentlemen, therefore, will be thrown on their own resources, and I question very much whether one out of 10 of them will be able to write out on one day the shorthand notes taken on the previous day. Unless there is some legal gentleman, either a barrister or a solicitor, watching the case for the witness, how can we trust to the accuracy of these shorthand reports, which may afterwards be produced. There is no doubt of it but that when these transcripts are brought before the Court afterwards, there will 'be no witness, as regards their accuracy, except the shorthand reporter himself, and, as we all know very well, in Ireland these shorthand reporters are not at all to be depended upon, and, in fact, very many of them know little or nothing of shorthand writing. I admit the Government is in a great dilemma. If they want this proposal of theirs to be of any use, or to be looked upon with any amount of confidence by the people of Ireland, they should either allow a solicitor or barrister to be present and watch the proceedings, or they should allow the accused, or the witnesses, to have a shorthand writer of their own, so that his report might be compared with that of the Government reporter. I think that, from every point of view, this is a most reasonable Amendment, and should not be refused by the Government.

MR. T. P. O'CONNOR (Liverpool, Scotland): Mr. Courtney, we have no desire to prolong the discussion of this Amendment any further; yet, at the same time, I feel bound to enter the strongest and the most solemn protest I can against the whole action of the Government in regard to this Amendment. I am glad that my hon. Friend the Member for the Holmfirth Division of Yorkshire (Mr. H. J. Wilson) called attention to the discourtesy, and the incivility, and the decidedly unParliamentary action of the hon. Gen-

Mr. H. J. Wilson

tlemen who, for the moment, represent Her Majesty's Government. I suppose that, if these Gentlemen held some higher positions in the Government to which they belong, their conduct would be a little more rational and a little more civil. I always observe that the incivility of Members of the Government is in adverse proportion to their positions in the Government. My second protest is to these periodical visitations of the First Lord of the Treasury (Mr. W. H. Smith). The right hon. Gentleman is in the habit of making visits to this Committee, about which the only thing angelic is that they are few and far between. I protest most strongly against the First Lord of the Treasury coming in and saying that an Amendment has been sufficiently debated, when the right hon. Gentleman has not had the advantage of hearing one single syllable of the argument. Why, Sir, it is disrespectful to the Committee that the Leader of the House, taking no part whatever in the debates of the House, not even hearing these debates, should come in, and, in his lofty and Olympian manner, declare—as if, in the recesses of his room outside this House, he had been able, by inspiration, to discover it —that an Amendment had been sufficiently debated. And the third protest I wish to make is in reference to the position in which a person is placed who is examined under this clause. Now, Sir, it is perfectly clear that the way the Government intend to work this clause is by terror. I remember the time when every Englishman would be indignant at the idea that we would transfer to this country that system of interrogation, that system of putting an unfortunate person on the rack, which is to be considered the characteristic, and, in a certain sense, the shame of the French judiciary. By this clause we shall transfer to Ireland, and for ever, the very worst principles and the most shameful and the most exceptional practice of the French judiciary. My hon. Friend below me (Mr. Chance), who is learned in the law, which I am not, tells me that what is proposed is very much worse than what exists in France. It is perfectly clear that the Government do not intend these unfortunate men should have fair play; they want to bring them into Court alone; they want to terrorize them; they want

to leave them without counsel, or advice, or assistance; they want to take advantage of their unguarded moments, of their ignorance, of their want of acquaintance with legal and judicial forms —in other words, this is the modern equivalent of the ancient council. For these reasons, Mr. Courtney, I think, without further prolonging the discussion, we shall be perfectly justified in going to a Division.

Question put.

The Committee *divided:*—Ayes 131; Noes 193: Majority 62.—(Div. List, No. 114.)

MR. T. M. HEALY (Longford, N.): Mr. Courtney, I beg to move to insert, after the word "recognizance," in page 1, line 17, the words—

"The authority of the Attorney General for the holding of such inquiry shall remain in force for fourteen days, and no longer, but may be renewed by the Attorney General by warrant under his hand from time to time."

My object, of course, in moving this Amendment is that the orders issued by the Attorney General shall not remain in force for an indefinite length of time; I think that is only a reasonable proposition. Supposing the existing Attorney General went out of Office, or should be happily made a Judge— which, I understand, he is to be in a very short time—I think it is only right that these orders should be brought before his successor. I think, too, it is only right that a magistrate down in the country should consider every fortnight whether he wants fresh powers or not. I do think that the Committee will recognize that some period of time should be fixed when these inquiries and the powers under them should be completed. That being so, whether you take a fortnight, as suggested by me, or three weeks—if the Government would prefer three weeks or a month, I have no objection—at any rate, some time ought to come when the purposes of an inquiry would be served, and the Resident Magistrate should no longer have power to hold an inquiry. If a magistrate wants fresh powers, all he will have to do will be to write to the Attorney General; and as that right hon. and learned Gentleman will probably get a large fee of 10 guineas every time he signs his name, I do not think he would object. I think my Amendment affords the Government an opportunity of making a graceful concession.

Amendment proposed,

In page 1, line 17, after "recognizance," insert " the authority of the Attorney General for the holding of such inquiry shall remain in force for fourteen days and no longer, but may be renewed by the Attorney General by warrant under his hand from time to time."—(*Mr. T. M. Healy.*)

Question proposed, "That those words be there inserted."

THE ATTORNEY GENERAL FOR IRELAND (Mr. HOLMES) (Dublin University) : Mr. Courtney, hundreds of Amendments of this character might be suggested, and our answer to them all would be that they are altogether unnecessary, and would be overloading the Bill with unnecessary provisions. It may be assumed that an inquiry of this character will be held within a reasonable time of the date of the order. I certainly think that the Resident Magistrate to whom the order is sent should have the opportunity of choosing his own time for the holding of that inquiry. I cannot think that there would be any abuse of the power given to Resident Magistrates by the order.

MR. T. M. HEALY : It seems to me that the only objection that the right hon. and learned Gentleman the Attorney General for Ireland (Mr. Holmes) has to my Amendment is that it would cover too much paper. That is a very small matter to the taxpayers ; therefore, I hope the Government will accept my proposition. It will do them no harm, but will give us some satisfaction.

MR. HOLMES : I think it would be exceedingly inconvenient if fresh powers were to be sought for by Resident Magistrates every two or three weeks or a month. The hon. and learned Gentleman may be assured that no improper or undue use will be made of this power.

MR. T. M. HEALY : The right hon. and learned Gentleman the Attorney General for Ireland seems to me to leave out from the purview of his consideration the fact that these powers can be renewed at any time. All a Resident Magistrate has to do is to expend a penny stamp in forwarding a letter to the Attorney General asking to have the power of holding an inquiry renewed. All I wish to provide is that at some period, some moment of time, the power of holding an inquiry shall come to an end, and that if a magi-

strate wants the power renewed he can obtain its renewal. Is this unreasonable.? There is the First Lord of the Treasury (Mr. W. H. Smith) listening to the debate with great interest, and I put it to him is it unreasonable that some moment of time shall be fixed—you may make it a month or two months if you like—when a magistrate shall seek a renewal of the power given to him ? My Amendment is of a most elastic character, and I would accept any suggestion from the Government in the way of amending it. Where is the harm done by this Amendment ? I will pay all the penny stamps a Resident Magistrate may be out of pocket if it is desired. But it cannot be on the ground of expense that the Attorney General resists my Amendment ; it is on the ground that the right hon. and learned Gentleman does not want to appear reasonable. While he was out at dinner, the English Attorney General (Sir Richard Webster) made several concessions which led to great progress. He did so for the purpose of shortening debate. After having resisted one Amendment he immediately afterwards accepted it. [Mr. HOLMES : May and shall.] But it was a most important Amendment according to our view. I trust the Government will see their way to accept this reasonable Amendment.

MR. J. O'CONNOR (Tipperary, S.) : I give the Attorney General for Ireland (Mr. Holmes) credit for good intentions ; but when he says that an Act like this would not be used for any purpose but what it was intended for, and would not be used unduly, I think that was a very unfortunate phrase to use. We have been treated to that statement before over and over again with regard to this and other Acts. We know that Attorney Generals do not always remain in the same position, they are very likely to be promoted to the Bench, and the present Attorney General may possibly have some successor who would not be bound by the statement of the present Attorney General. Now, Sir, it is a very great hardship to keep any district in a state of tension, and once the Attorney General issues an order for an inquiry the whole district will certainly be in a state of tension and uncertainty. In that state of uncertainty it is quite possible that the people who thought they would be attacked would seek to leave the country. I can conceive a state of things occurring, when the Attorney General, acting for the Executive Government in Ireland, would proclaim a district for no other purpose than that of terrorizing the people into leaving that district. Now, if it be found, after a time, that this state of things has been brought about, that the desirable result has been accomplished, that those whom the Government do not wish to have in a district have been scared away, why not allow the edict to drop, and thereby restore persons to their usual and normal state of mind. I hold it is quite feasible for the Attorney General to bring about a state of uncertainty in a district which would be detrimental to the peace of men, and to the peace of all the families in the district. This Amendment is a very reasonable one, and the Government will do well to accept it. If, as my hon. and learned Friend (Mr. T. M. Healy) says, the Amendment provides that the power may be renewed upon application by the magistrate, it would be but a gracious thing for the Attorney General and the Government to accept the proposition.

MR. T. M. HEALY : I will not waste the time of the Committee if the Government are determined not to accept the Amendment. I beg to withdraw it.

Amendment, by leave, withdrawn.

MR. T. M. HEALY (Longford, N.): I presume the Government will not accept the two next Amendments that stand in my name, and therefore it is no use my moving them. I beg to move, however, Amendment number 47—namely, to insert after " recognizance," in line 17, the words—

" A witness may decline to answer, on the ground that the subject of inquiry is not a crime within the meaning of this Act, and shall not be committed for so refusing until a Judge of the High Court certifies that the inquiry is lawfully holden."

This Amendment, Mr. Courtney, deals somewhat with the burning question of the Plan of Campaign. Suppose it is alleged that there is a conspiracy on foot, and that a meeting is to be held at a town hall. As is always done in these cases, the Attorney General will send the warrants in blank, and every magistrate will have a pile of blanks forms of warrants already signed, and he will only have to fill in the dates. Now, if, as I say, a meeting of tenantry is held, a

magistrate will have it in his power to order every man to appear before him who has attended the meeting. All I wish to provide is that if any particular witness says that no conspiracy has taken place he may decline to answer, on the ground that the warrants have been signed in blank by the Attorney General. If no crime has been committed in the district, you have no authority under these blank warrants to hold a court. Under these circumstances, I do ask that the Government should give us some guarantee that such things will not be allowed to take place; that if a witness says that the meeting was a *bond fide* one and not a conspiracy at all, the inquiry shall not be held without some kind of restriction in the way of a second mind being brought to bear on the subject. I think that is a most reasonable suggestion, and I do not think warrants ought to be filled in in blank; but, of course, they will be. The Government are filled with good intentions, but, somehow or other, good intentions seem to leave them when they are dealing with Ireland. I do really think the Government should tell us exactly when these inquiries will be held, and whether they are only to be held in regard to some real crime, whether a witness will be protected from answering questions of an impertinent character, and the questions confined to matters relating to some real crime, such as murder, arson, firing into dwellings, manslaughter, or something that would really come within the definition of a serious crime.

THE CHAIRMAN : The clause, as it at present stands, authorizes inquiries where information has been laid that any offence to which this section applies has been committed. I think this Amendment would be out of Order, unless for the words " within the meaning of this Act " were substituted the words "to which this section applies."

MR. T. M. HEALY : I will submit to your suggestion, Mr. Courtney.

Amendment proposed—

In page 1, line 17, after "recognizance" insert —" a witness may decline to answer, on the ground that the subject of inquiry is not a crime to which this section applies, and shall not be committed for so refusing until a Judge of the High Court certifies that the inquiry is lawfully holden."—(*Mr. T. M. Healy.*)

Question proposed, " That these words be there inserted."

[*Fourth Night.*]

THE ATTORNEY GENERAL (Sir RICHARD WEBSTER) (Isle of Wight): The hon. and learned Gentleman seemed to suggest that the whole of these proceedings would be illegal; that a magistrate will have a number of blank warrants, and fill them up when required. I agree that if such irregularities are to be assumed, the position of the hon. and learned Gentleman is perfectly just. But we have many times pointed out that the inquiry is to be directed by the Attorney General upon sworn information, after an offence to which this section applies has been committed in a proclaimed district. I must say that it is scarcely fair to assume that this section would be worked illegally; that the Attorney General, without sworn information or the exercise of any discretion, would direct a magistrate to hold an inquiry at will. Then, again, the hon. and learned Member will recollect that in any question arising out of the refusal of a witness to answer, we have undertaken that in the warrant there shall appear the question put to him, so that the legality of the question can be ascertained. We cannot allow a witness to raise the point contemplated by the hon. and learned Gentleman, and thereby stop the inquiry at his pleasure.

MR. CHANCE (Kilkenny, S.): I should like to point out that an inquiry can be very easily stopped, and I have no doubt many will be stopped by the very simple and expeditious means of refusing to answer. The fact that witnesses can be sent to gaol will not prevent the stoppage of inquiries. I trust the Amendment will be pushed to a Division, unless we get some more cogent argument against it than that advanced by the Attorney General for England, a Gentleman who naturally has not the slightest conception of the way in which things are carried on in Ireland.

MR. MOLLOY (King's Co., Birr): I should like to put a question to the hon. and learned Gentleman the Attorney General (Sir Richard Webster). I mentioned a case earlier in the evening of a landlord in Ireland who has a civil action against some of his tenants. That landlord is a very near relative of one of the Resident Magistrates. Now, supposing an inquiry takes place under the mandate of the Attorney General, and the inquiry goes on in regard to an alleged offence or crime in the district, and this Resident Magistrate proceeds to make inquiries which may be used in the civil action, will the Attorney General tell me what protection there is for witnesses in such a case? The Attorney General will admit that if questions are addressed in regard to matters connected with the civil action, they will be entirely without the purview of the Bill. If a witness, under these conditions, declines to answer a question which has been put to him, which deals only—of course the Attorney General must assume my case—which deals only with the civil action, and which has nothing to do with the alleged crime in the district, will he, or will he not, be punished? If he is punished, is there any appeal? Will the Attorney General say in what way a witness will be able to protect himself from the unjust use of this section by a Resident Magistrate. I shall be glad if the hon. and learned Gentleman will answer my question.

SIR RICHARD WEBSTER: This Amendment really does not meet the point the hon. and learned Gentleman (Mr. Molloy) has called attention to. The Amendment refers to a witness declining to answer a question in regard to a crime to which this section applies. It has nothing to do with any question which a magistrate puts to him upon a totally irrelevant point.

MR. COX (Clare, E.): I entirely agree with the statement of my hon. and learned Friend the Member for North Longford (Mr. T. M. Healy), that warrants in large numbers will be signed in blank and sent to the magistrates from Dublin Castle, and I believe that if the hon. Members opposite were as well acquainted with the practice of the Castle as we are, they would not be quite so prejudiced against the Amendment of my hon. and learned Friend. I myself have had experience of the working of the former Act. I had the honour of being arrested and put in gaol under the Act of Mr. Forster. At that time, I read the debates which went on in this House, and in which it was over and over again stated by Mr. Forster that no one was arrested under that Act in the absence of a proper warrant. I was arrested on the 20th of June, charged with having incited the people to do what I believe they were entitled to do. Twelve months afterwards I came across the warrant under which I was arrested.

As I have said, I was arrested on the 20th of June for a speech made at Liverpool, and to my astonishment I found that the warrant was dated in the month of May previously. No doubt, the right hon. and learned Gentleman the Attorney General for Ireland will be astonished at that statement, but I have the warrant still; I have had it framed, and I shall have much pleasure in showing it to him, the date on which it was signed being the 20th or 21st of May. My experience, therefore, fully bears out the statement of my hon. and learned Friend the Member for North Longford. We know that blank warrants at that time were sent out in sheaves; the names of the persons for whom they were used were put in afterwards; they were signed by the Lord Lieutenant, Lord Cowper; the offence was put in afterwards, and when it suited the authorities at the Castle, the man was arrested. Now, Sir, we have every reason to believe that the same thing will take place under the present Act. As my hon. and learned Friend the Member for North Longford has stated, these blank warrants will be sent to the magistrates; and it is because we know, from our experience, what will be the working of the Act that we desire to insert this provision. I certainly hope my hon. Friends will press this Amendment on the Committee to the end.

MR. W. REDMOND (Fermanagh, N.): I also hope my hon. and learned Friend the Member for North Longford will divide the Committee on this Amendment, because it seems to me that, unless it is accepted, the unfortunate men who are called from their homes and from their businesses, to give evidence before this secret tribunal, will have no guarantee that they will not be committed to prison for what is practically no offence at all. The only thing which the Amendment provides is that the witness shall not be imprisoned by the Resident Magistrate without some good cause, and it is quite possible that a witness should be asked questions which, although the Resident Magistrate may consider them appropriate to the matter of the inquiry, may be altogether inappropriate.

THE CHAIRMAN: The hon. Member is speaking on a subject which is not at all relevant to the Amendment before the Committee.

MR. W. REDMOND: I am supporting the Amendment, No. 47, of my hon. and learned Friend, which says—

"A witness may decline to answer, on the ground that the subject of inquiry is not a crime to which this section applies, and shall not be committed for so refusing until a Judge of the High Court certifies that the inquiry is lawfully holden."

Well, Sir, I hold that this Amendment is absolutely necessary, and that it should be agreed to by the Government, inasmuch as it merely gives a witness a Court of Appeal to which he may have recourse in the event of his being committed to prison by the magistrate for refusing to answer a question, on the ground that the subject of inquiry is not a crime within the meaning of the Act.

MR. MAURICE HEALY (Cork): I think the hon. and learned Gentleman cannot have read this Amendment very carefully, inasmuch as in his reply he appears to me to have considered it from a point of view entirely different from that in which we regard it. His objection to the Amendment is founded on the assumption that the Attorney General had done an illegal act and had ordered an inquiry which was not within the meaning of the Act. But that is not the fact. The motion of the Attorney General under this clause is by an *ex parte* information; it may or may not be justified by facts. The Attorney General in directing inquiry may be quite wrong, and the danger, therefore, is that this section may be used for the purpose of inquiring, not about an offence which has been committed, but to enable the magistrate to find out whether an offence has been committed at all. Let me take a case arising under another portion of the Act. Say, that it is alleged that the tenants on a certain estate have combined to compel the landlord to take a certain course; say, that the landlord has come to the conclusion that a combination exists among the tenants, and for that reason desires that an inquiry should take place. He will go to the next magistrate and tell the story; he will want to convince the local Resident Magistrate that persons in the district will tell the truth, and that, on inquiry, he may be convinced that such and such a state of things exists. Now, notwithstanding that it may be believed that this combination

on the part of the tenants exists, and
that it is criminal, it may still be that
the combination is of a perfectly innocent character, and constitutes no offence
at all. I say that the danger which is
struck at by this Amendment is, that
whereas the section should really only
be worked for the purpose of finding
out offences which have been committed,
and bringing the perpetrators of those
offences to justice, there is a danger,
under the clause as it at present stands,
that the section, instead of being confined to that use, may be used to find
out whether or not an offence has been
committed.   Under the circumstances
which I have stated—namely, that on
the suggestion of a local landlord, you
may try to find out what is the real state
of facts, the clause may become a very
dangerous engine. I do not think the
right hon. and learned Gentleman has
met that point. He has dealt with the
Amendment on a wrong basis. He has
assumed that there can be no question
that an offence has been committed; but
that is not the fact, inasmuch as statements to that effect may be made by the
landlords, and no offence whatever may
have been committed. It is to guard
against that danger that the Amendment of my hon. and learned Friend
the Member for North Longford is proposed.

MR. T. M. HEALY: I do not want
to prolong this discussion; but I am
bound to say that I thought I should
have had the support of the right hon.
Gentleman the Chancellor of the Exchequer, who objected, on a memorable
occasion, to give a blank cheque to Lord
Salisbury.   We are asked to give a
blank cheque to Her Majesty's Government for holding these inquiries of an
official character. No one can say whether a conspiracy exists or does not
exist; it is a matter lying in the minds
of two or three people, although, of
course, I can understand you will get a
person to make an affidavit that he believes a conspiracy exists among tenants
—say, on the estate of Colonel King-
Harman, or an estate of that kind—but
as the Government have no intention to
meet us on this point, I ask leave to
withdraw my Amendment.

Amendment, by leave, withdrawn.

MR. T. M. HEALY (Longford, N.):
I shall not move the next Amendment

relating to the expenses of witnesses;
but I hope the Government will accept
my proposal to insert, after the word
" recognizance," the words—

" Should a witness refuse to answer any lawful question touching the subject of the inquiry, the magistrate shall forward such inquiry to the Attorney General, who, by warrant under his hand, may authorize such
magistrate to commit such witness should he
persist in such refusal."

I venture to say that this is a reasonable Amendment, inasmuch as it provides that no person shall be sent to
gaol for not answering an unlawful inquiry. I do not think the Government
will be able to resist this appeal. Surely
the Attorney General has enough respect for law to satisfy himself, on the
facts submitted to him, as to whether
the question put by the magistrate to
the witness is lawful or unlawful. We
are only asking for protection against
unlawful inquiries, and I sincerely hope
the Government will consent to the introduction of these words.

THE ATTORNEY GENERAL FOR
IRELAND (Mr. HOLMES) (Dublin University : I must point out that, although
the Government desire to meet every
just and reasonable Amendment, the
present proposal of the hon. Member is
not one which we can insert in the
clause. It is proposed that the magistrate shall forward a statement to the
Attorney General as to the questions refused to be answered by the witness,
and that the Attorney General may, by
warrant under his hand, authorize the
committal of the witness should he persist in his refusal. It is my opinion
that this Amendment is both valueless
in itself and proposes something beyond
the functions of the Attorney General.
It asks that an officer who has not been
present at the inquiry should, on a mere
statement, issue his warrant for the
committal of a witness. For these reasons the Government cannot accept the
Amendment of the hon. and learned
Member.

Amendment, by leave, withdrawn.

On the Motion of Mr. T. M. HEALY,
the following Amendment made :—In
page 1, after the word " recognizance,"
insert—

" Provided, also, a shorthand writer shall be
in attendance at such inquiries, and shall take
down the questions of the magistrates, and the
answers of each witness."

MR. T. M. HEALY (Longford, N.): The Government have agreed to the last Amendment. I presume they will have no objection to the one I now move.

Amendment proposed,

In page 1, line 17, after "recognizance" insert "upon any person being accused of a crime, respecting which an inquiry under this section has been held, such accused person, or his solicitor, upon being returned for trial, shall forthwith be supplied with copies of all depositions taken at any inquiry under this section."—(*Mr T. M. Healy.*)

Question proposed, "That those words be there inserted."

THE CHIEF SECRETARY FOR IRELAND (Mr. A. J. BALFOUR) (Manchester, E.): We propose to introduce an Amendment towards the end of the clause, to make it quite clear that, except in a single instance—namely, where there is a prosecution for perjury—the information taken under the section shall not be used either against or for the prisoner, that it shall not be produced in any action or shown to anybody connected therewith.

MR. T. M. HEALY: That is perfectly diabolical. To hold an inquiry and say that the prisoner shall not have the benefit of the result of that inquiry, is absolutely hateful. You put a man named Clark and his wife on trial for murder; they were acquitted, and I remember the Attorney General holding up that acquittal as a most infamous thing. No sooner did that take place, than two other men were arrested; you put them on their trial, and, like the others, they were acquitted also. That was under the Crimes Act. Supposing these men had been brought before this secret inquiry, they would not have been able to use the depositions. The Government have accepted my Amendment, providing that shorthand writers should take down the questions of the magistrates and the answers of the witnesses. But what is the good of that, if you will not give us access to the depositions? Am I to understand that I am moving Amendments for the benefit of Her Majesty's Government? It certainly amounts to this—you accept an amendment that a shorthand writer shall attend the inquiry, and take down the questions of the magistrates and the answers of the witnesses, and now you tell us that the prisoner and his advocate shall get

no benefit from it. There is no reason in the action of the Government. When you have provided for the holding of secret inquiries, and have abolished Petty Session indictments, there will be no such thing as Petty Session depositions. The Crown brief will be made up on the result of these secret investigations, and yet you say the prisoner and his counsel are not to be supplied with copies of the depositions. At the present time, the prisoner's counsel is entitled to a copy of the Crown brief, almost as a matter of course in Ireland, although it may not be so in England. If you abolish the Petty Session depositions, there will be practically no depositions taken except those depositions taken at the secret inquiry. [Mr. A. J. BALFOUR dissented.] The right hon. Gentleman shakes his head. But I must ask him if he means to contend that if the Law Officers of the Crown have had the secret depositions before them, they will not allow them to be used by the prisoner; do they mean to waste the money of the public in getting these depositions taken, and yet not allow the prisoner or his counsel to have advantage therefrom? You will make the secret inquiry stand in lieu of indictment by the system of taking depositions before the magistrates, and I say it is absolutely necessary that the evidence taken should not be withheld from the prisoner. I trust, therefore, that the Government will see the justice of this Amendment.

THE ATTORNEY GENERAL FOR IRELAND (Mr. HOLMES) (Dublin University): I think that the hon. and learned Gentleman will see that if the statements made before the magistrate were the same as those which would be used at the trial, it might be right that this Amendment should be accepted. But such a thing was never done under the Act of 1882, and no such thing will be done under this Act. The clause provides that the witnesses shall be bound on recognizance to give evidence. Their depositions will be taken in the ordinary way. It will be impossible to have any person returned for trial unless the depositions are so taken, and the accused will have every opportunity of referring to those depositions. The Attorney General for England has said not merely that these depositions will not be used against a man who is examined, but that they ought not to be in

[*Fourth Night.*]

any proceedings of the kind, and there is an Amendment on the Paper, which the Government will accept, for the purpose of preventing these depositions being used for any purpose, except in the case of a prosecution for perjury. It is therefore perfectly clear that there is no wish whatever to use the depositions on the trial of any person except in the case I have referred to. The hon. and learned Member asks why, if the Government refuse to accept this Amendment, they have agreed to the Amendment which provides that a shorthand writer shall be in attendance to take down the questions of the magistrates and the answers of the witnesses? That Amendment has been agreed to, because, for the sake of example, if a person were examined and sent to prison for refusing to answer a question put by the magistrate, it would very likely be the subject of a charge made in this House that the magistrate had asked questions which he had no right to ask, and was not justified in taking action under this section. In such a case as that, hon. Members will see that the shorthand notes would be a check upon the action of the Resident Magistrate.

Mr. ANDERSON (Elgin and Nairn): I do not think that the right hon. and learned Gentleman the Attorney General for Ireland appreciates the point taken by the hon. and learned Member for North Longford. As the clause is drawn at present, it will be in the power of the Attorney General to make use of knowledge which has been denied to the prisoner's counsel. I am sure that the Attorney General for England will see how unfair that would be, because you are in this position—you call the witness on this private inquiry, he makes a statement, he is afterwards called before a magistrate, where he makes a contrary statement, and no one but the Law Officers of the Crown know that he has contradicted himself. I do not assume that the right hon. and learned Gentleman opposite would be the prosecuting counsel on the trial; because I am sure he would not call a witness who has previously contradicted his statement, but there are cases in which the prosecution will be handed over to somebody else. Now the fact that a witness has made contradictory statements would, in the hand of a cross-examining counsel for the prisoner, be of the most vital

importance. This is quite distinct from the question of the witnesses' statements being used against him on the trial; the great thing is for the cross-examining counsel to have the knowledge that the witness has made a statement which he subsequently contradicted, and I impress upon the Attorney General for England the desirability of accepting this Amendment.

Mr. ATHERLEY JONES (Durham, N.W.): I venture to think that this Amendment is an extremely reasonable one, and I will endeavour to put before the Committee the reasons why I consider it to be so. This Bill gives power to the Crown to prosecute for perjury, in the event of a witness having stated in his deposition something that is different to that stated at this private inquiry. That is a privilege which is solely preserved for the Crown lawyer if the clause is allowed to stand as at present; because the prisoner would not be permitted to use the depositions, and, therefore, he would not be able to compare them with the evidence which may be given at the trial. Therefore, I venture to say that this is an unfair advantage given to the Crown. Now, a great deal has been said about there being a similarity to the law of Scotland in this respect. With the greatest respect for the Attorney General for Ireland, I venture to point out that the law of Scotland provides that the depositions of a witness may be destroyed, and shall be destroyed, if required. The deposition of a witness under this clause is to be perpetuated for purposes of the Crown, not for the purpose of the witness. It is a cardinal point of the administration of justice in this country that greater favour should be shown to the prisoner than is shown to the Crown; but, in this case, greater favour is shown to the Crown than to the prisoner. I point out that it will be absolutely out of the power of a prisoner to check any of the evidence which may be given by a witness on the trial, by comparing it with what he may have spoken previously. Therefore, I respectfully suggest that it is reasonable and fair, and in accordance with the ordinary course of proceedings in this country, that this Amendment should be accepted.

Mr. MAHONY (Meath, N.): I should like to offer a suggestion which I trust will meet the approval of the right hon.

Mr. Holmes

and learned Gentleman the Attorney General for Ireland. Will the right hon. and learned Gentleman consent that the depositions which have been made by the persons examined at the secret inquiry shall be afterwards brought forware at the trial, so that the witnesses for the Crown may be confronted with the statements they have previously made? I do not know whether the hon. and learned Gentleman who moved the Amendment will be satisfied with this concession or not; but with regard to the importance of some such provision I would mention a fact with which, in all probability, the right hon. and learned Gentleman the Attorney General for Ireland is acquainted—namely, that some of the chief witnesses at the Phœnix Park murders trial, when first examined, gave totally different evidence to that which they gave at the trial. I make this statement on very good authority, and I ask the Committee to bear it in mind. If the prisoners had had the benefit of the evidence those witnesses gave in the first instance, when examined at the secret inquiry, it would have thrown great light on the character of the persons by whom it was given. The effect of my statement is this—that the witnesses brought forward on behalf of the Crown had perjured themselves on the occasion of their examination at the secret inquiry.

An hon. MEMBER: I would put it to the hon. and learned Gentleman the Attorney General for England whether he will accept the suggestion that has just been made, and allow the statements—I will not call them depositions—that are made by persons examined at the preliminary inquiry to be brought forward at the trial? When a man is brought before a justice of the peace in connection with any charge his statement will be taken down by the shorthand writer, and ought, according to the principles of fair play, to be put before the jury if necessary in the interests of the accused. When a number of persons are brought before a Resident Magistrate some may make statements incriminating A, and others may make statements incriminating B; but when B is brought before the magistrate, or, rather, when he is placed upon his trial, he ought to be able to see that statements have been made incriminating someone else. Therefore, I

would, in all sincerity, venture to suggest that the Government should adopt this proposal, which I submit is fully in accord with the spirit of our criminal procedure. If we are to enter upon these odious inquiries which I am sure the hon. and learned Attorney General dislikes quite as much as we do, he ought to take care that the principle of fair play is applied all round.

THE ATTORNEY GENERAL (Sir RICHARD WEBSTER) (Isle of Wight): I am very much surprised to hear what the hon. Gentleman opposite (Mr. Mahony) has stated about the Phœnix Park murders—namely, that the men convicted of those murders ought not to have been found guilty.

MR. MAHONY: What I suggested was that some of the witnesses at the trial of the persons accused of the Phœnix Park murders had made statements at the secret inquiry which were totally opposed to the evidence they afterwards gave.

SIR RICHARD WEBSTER: Then the hon. Gentleman's point is that the witnesses were not entitled to credit, because they made different statements at the preliminary examination to those which they made at the trial—statements which were contradictory of the evidence they subsequently gave. I should like to know on what authority the hon. Member makes such a statement. I would merely point out to the Committee that the preliminary inquiry is to be instituted for the purpose of obtaining information under circumstances in which evidence cannot ordinarily be obtained. When prisoners are brought up they will be charged in a proper way, and depositions being taken before they can be committed for trial, they will be entitled to copies of those depositions, just as is the case under the existing practice; but Her Majesty's Government are certainly of opinion that these statements made before the Resident Magistrates for preliminary purposes in aid of justice ought not to be made public. This matter having now been amply discussed, I trust the Committee will be allowed to divide upon it.

SIR CHARLES RUSSELL (Hackney): Before a Division is taken I think there are a few words which ought to be said in favour of this Amendment, and I trust my hon. and learned Friends on the other side of the Table will give me

[*Fourth Night.*]

their attention for a very brief interval. I may say that I have taken very little part in the discussion of this 1st clause in Committee for reasons which I explained to the House when I addressed it during the debate on the second reading of the Bill; and I do not hesitate to say that, if we could fairly rely on the just administration of the clause, I think it is a provision that might very well be embodied in the ordinary law. But a great deal of distrust has been expressed with regard to this clause, and much anxiety has been displayed as to whether it will be safeguarded in a reasonable way. I do not think my right hon. and learned Friend opposite the Attorney General for Ireland has really met the point at issue in regard to this Amendment. I concede to my hon. and learned Friend that there may be a difficulty in requiring that a copy of the whole proceedings before a magistrate should be given to a particular prisoner charged with a particular offence; but I want to know why that prisoner is not to be entitled to the earlier deposition which a witness may have made at the private or secret inquiry, in the event of the same witness having to be called against him at the trial. The witness A is called before the Resident Magistrate and makes a detailed statement before him, and upon the basis of the information that person has thus given on oath, the matter is taken up by another and an independent magistrate, before whom the depositions are regularly taken, and the prisoner is charged and committed for trial. A is examined both before the Resident Magistrate at the private inquiry, and also before the magistrate who returns the prisoner for trial. Why should not the statement made by A at the earlier examination be brought forward so that it may be compared with the deposition he makes at the later inquiry on which the prisoner is committed for trial? I believe my right hon. and learned Friend the Attorney General for Ireland if such a case came before him as that of a witness having made upon oath two inconsistent statements, one of which must be known to the prisoner, because it has been taken before the committing magistrate, and the other of which was not known to the prisoner, because it was taken at the private inquiry, would think he was bound in fairness and in justice to communicate to the

Sir Charles Russell

prisoner the fact that that particular witness, who might be the most important witness in the case, had made two distinct and contradictory statements. I am sure the right hon. Gentleman the First Lord of the Treasury (Mr. W. H. Smith) will give me credit for only desiring to press matters to a reasonable and fair conclusion. I would therefore move as an Amendment to the proposed Amendment, the insertion of the words "of any witness to be called against him," so that the Amendment would read—

"Upon any person being accused of a crime respecting which an inquiry under this section has been held, such accused person, or his solicitor, upon his being returned for trial, shall forthwith be supplied with copies of all depositions taken at any inquiry under this section of any of the witnesses called against him."

Mr. HOLMES: I have no objection to the Amendment proposed by the hon. and learned Gentleman. But having regard to the fact that we have already agreed that the depositions should not be used on any trial, either against the man who made them, or any other person, the result of this Amendment renders it impossible to carry out this arrangement; and as the depositions can be used in cross-examination by the prisoner, they must also be used for the same purpose by the Crown.

Amendment proposed to proposed Amendment, after the word "section," insert the words "of any witness to be called against him."—(*Sir Charles Russell.*)

Question, "That those words be added to the proposed Amendment," put, and *agreed to.*

Sir RICHARD WEBSTER: It is a little difficult to take the clause exactly as it is with the words that have been added. I think it would be necessary to add some such words as these—"as far as the same relates to the offence with which the accused person is charged." It is quite clear that in the statements made, a number of other matters may have been gone into and a number of other persons may have been referred to. I will move that these words be inserted.

Further Amendment proposed to proposed Amendment, at end add the words —"as far as the same relates to the offence with which the accused person is charged."—(*Mr. Attorney General.*)

Question proposed, "That those words be there added."

SIR CHARLES RUSSELL: I understand the words the hon. and learned Gentleman proposes to add to be "as far as the same relates to the offence," but I should like to know what is the meaning of "relates to the offence." Does the hon. and learned Gentleman mean that if a witness at the secret or private inquiry inculpates some third person, or made a statement that he had suspicions as to some third person, that that also would be included? I should say that the depositions taken at the court of secret or private inquiry ought to be communicated to the prisoner or his solicitor.

MR. MAURICE HEALY (Cork): It appears to me that the hon. and learned Gentleman the Attorney General in moving to add these words to the Amendment, completely justifies the position we have all along taken with regard to the proposed inquiry. Those words seem to me to make it possible that in an inquiry regarding one offence, it will be competent to the magistrate holding the inquiry to so enlarge the scope of his inquisition that it may include almost any conceivable matter. Any inquiry held by a magistrate will be confined to the offence in respect of which he holds it, or it will not; and every word uttered by a witness before him will be of importance at the trial. The presumption is that if the Amendment of the hon. and learned Attorney General is accepted, it will be possible for a magistrate holding an inquiry to take evidence not relating to the offence to which it refers, and consequently there would be the utmost danger that the magistrates would be induced to enlarge the scope of their investigations far beyond the particular matter intended to be inquired into. We ought, therefore, to insist on a clear understanding on this point. Does the hon. and learned Gentleman mean to say that it would be competent to a magistrate inquiring into one offence to take evidence with regard to another offence? If he does not mean that, the words he proposes are illusory.

SIR RICHARD WEBSTER: I only desired, as far as possible, to see that justice was done, and also that statements might not be communicated to a prisoner as to a particular charge which is not intended to be brought against

him. I am afraid it is not clear that I have exactly succeeded in hitting the difficulty, and hon. Members who know anything of our Criminal Law will see that this is not a very easy thing to do. I am therefore willing to withdraw these words at the present moment, but I will consider the matter before the Report stage. Her Majesty's Government would not be justified in accepting the Amendment in the form in which it now stands; but I am willing that, for the present, the words of my Amendment should be withdrawn as being amenable to some of the criticism they have received.

Amendment to proposed Amendment, by leave, withdrawn.

MR. MAURICE HEALY: I wish it to be clearly understood that we are no parties to any bargain to the effect that because the Government agree that statements made at these private inquiries may be used on behalf of the prisoners, therefore they may be used in favour of the Crown. I do not admit it to be logical that because they may be used for the prisoner, they may, therefore, be used for the Crown. Things may happen similar to that what occurred before Mr. Justice O'Brien in regard to an agrarian offence in Kerry. Several witnesses had come forward against the accused person at the Petty Sessions, and had made such a case against him that, on their evidence, he was returned for trial. When the case was heard before Mr. Justice O'Brien, the same witnesses stated that all the evidence they had given against the prisoner before the magistrates was perjury, and had not a word of truth in it, the result being that the case completely broke down, not one of the witnesses swearing to an incriminating fact against the man. Counsel for the Crown were allowed to cross-examine those witnesses from their own depositions, for the purpose of showing that they were committing perjury. They pursued that line of cross-examination at some length, and all the witnesses persisted in their allegation that what they had stated at the preliminary inquiry was perjury, and that the evidence they were then giving was the truth; and, in the absence of any other evidence, the Judge directed that the jury might find the prisoner guilty, and the prisoner was found guilty, and sentenced to two years'

[Fourth Night.]

imprisonment. I submit that it would be monstrous to tolerate this sort of thing, and I certainly protest against it.

MR. CHANCE: I quite agree with what has just fallen from my hon. Friend (Mr. Maurice Healy).

MR. EDWARD HARRINGTON (Kerry, W.) (who was received with cries of "Divide!"): I can readily conceive that hon. Gentlemen opposite should cry "Divide!" when hon. Gentlemen around me are so impatient. I desire to point out that the Crown and the prisoner are not in the same position with regard to these depositions. All we ask is that the counsel representing the prisoner shall receive a copy of the depositions which are placed in the hands of the Crown. [*Cries of* "Agreed, agreed!"]

Proposed Amendment *agreed to.*

MR. WARMINGTON (Monmouth, W.): I beg to move the Amendment standing in my name—namely, to insert, after the word "recognizance" in line 17, the words—

"Provided, always, that the examination shall be conducted in such a manner only as it would be conducted if such person examined were giving evidence in support of a charge against some person for committing the offence in respect of which the inquiry shall be held."

My first object in moving this Amendment is this—that the examination shall be strictly confined to the offences mentioned in the Attorney General's order; my second object is, that the examination shall be confined to those matters which are evidence, and shall be conducted in such a way as would be observed if the examination were against a person accused of the offence which is mentioned in the Attorney General's order. If this is done, a Resident Magistrate will not be able to cross-examine a person who is summoned, or will he be able to put questions which are catching questions, but examine him exactly in the same way as the Attorney General would himself examine the same person if that person were giving evidence in support of a charge for the offence. I know that the Act of 1882 will probably be quoted against my Amendment; but may I point out to the Committee that it is a very strange thing that, in this Bill, one word which the right hon. Gentleman the Member for Derby (Sir William Harcourt) expressly put into his Act of Parliament is de-

signedly omitted from this; it is a strange thing that in this section the word evidence does not occur. The phrase used in this Bill is "may examine on oath concerning such offence," which, of course, is using as loose and as wide language as can possibly be employed; in the Act of 1882 the words used were —"a person who can give material evidence in connection with the offence." What is the object of this Bill? It is to allow the Government to become possessed of evidence. Why should they not take it in such a way as would commend itself to the people of Ireland? This is supposed to be a perpetual amendment of the Criminal Law of Ireland; it is not confined, as the Act of 1882 was confined, to a limited period; but it is to be put for ever upon the Statute Book with regard to Ireland. As has been already pointed out, there was a special Preamble to the Act of 1882, which justified the passing of that Act for a limited time; but in this Bill there is no Preamble, unless it be that the Government are prepared to accept this position—that the mention of the word "Ireland" is a sufficient Preamble for departing from the ordinary course with regard to criminal procedure. I beg to move the Amendment standing on the Paper in my name.

Amendment proposed,

In page 1, line 17, after "recognizance," insert —"Provided, always, that the examination shall be conducted in such a manner only as it would be conducted if such person examined were giving evidence in support of a charge against some person for committing the offence in respect of which the inquiry shall be held." –(*Mr. Warmington.*)

Question proposed, "That those words be there inserted."

THE ATTORNEY GENERAL FOR IRELAND (Mr. HOLMES) (Dublin University): As I understand, the hon. and learned Gentleman (Mr. Warmington) desires these words to be inserted for two purposes. One is, that the examination shall be concerning the offence mentioned in the order. If he looks at the portion of the clause that has already passed through Committee, he will find the examination is described as one relating to the offence. That, certainly, is much more specific than anything the hon. and learned Gentleman proposes in his Amendment. Then, the

Mr. Maurice Healy

hon. and learned Gentleman desires that the examination shall be conducted as if there was a person accused. It is wholly impossible that the examination can be taken in that way. The Laws of Evidence in this country are all relative to the particular matter and the particular person concerned in the case, and these inquiries cannot be conducted as if there was a person charged with an offence. The present words of the clause seem to me to be quite sufficient to guide the magistrate as to the character of the questions to be asked. The hon. and learned Gentleman has attributed to the Government some very deep object in not using the word "evidence," which was in the clause of 1882. There could not be any deep or hidden object in that, because the Government very readily accepted the Amendment proposed by the right hon. Gentleman the Member for East Wolverhampton (Mr. Henry H. Fowler)—namely, to insert the words "whom he has reason to believe to be capable of giving material evidence concerning such offence."

MR. CHANCE (Kilkenny, S.): I must confess I am unable to follow the argument of the right hon. and learned Gentleman (Mr. Holmes). The object of the hon. and learned Gentleman (Mr. Warmington), in proposing this Amendment, is to prevent the putting of misleading or catching questions— surely a very proper thing to prevent. The Attorney General for Ireland, however, desires to retain for the magistrates the power of putting totally irrelevant questions. Every day and every hour we discuss on this Bill, we get further evidence of the real intentions of the Government. We know it is very generally alleged that, at some secret inquiries held under the Act of 1882, witnesses were asked questions totally unconnected with any particular offence, and in some cases bribed to answer. We desire to safeguard this section as much as possible. If the right hon. and learned Gentlemen who, at the present moment, advises the Treasury Bench, have a leg to stand on, why do they not get up and argue the point?

SIR CHARLES RUSSELL (Hackney, S.): In order to save discussion, may I suggest that my hon. and learned Friend (Mr. Warmington) should look at Amendment No. 59, which is to add at the end of line 17—

"Such witness may only be examined concerning such offence, and shall not be examined concerning any other matter or subject whatsoever."

I recognize the contention of the Government, that the inquiry cannot be conducted as if it was an inquiry into the guilt of a particular person charged with a particular offence; but I think there ought to be some provision of a negative character—some provision that the inquiry shall not be a roving inquiry by a magistrate, but shall be confined to the offence, or the matter in relation to which the inquiry is held. Are the Government prepared to accept the Amendment No. 59, or an Amendment in substantially similar words? If so, I would suggest to my hon. and learned Friend that he should consider whether he should persist in his Amendment.

SIR RICHARD WEBSTER: Before this discussion arose, we had considered Amendment No. 59, in connection with this Amendment, and we had decided to accept Amendment No. 59, with modifications. We think the negative words of the Amendment are too stringent. We would accept the Amendment if it ran somewhat like this—

"Such witness can only be examined as to matters which, in the opinion of the magistrate holding the inquiry, relate to the offence and subject matter of the inquiry."

If those words were accepted, I think the view which the hon. and learned Gentleman the Member for Hackney (Sir Charles Russell) has expressed, would be attained. We cannot, however, agree to such a general Amendment as that proposed by my hon. and learned Friend (Mr. Warmington).

SIR CHARLES RUSSELL: But the words of the Attorney General would leave the matter absolutely to the discretion of the Resident Magistrate. Suppose that a Magistrate puts an utterly unreasonable question, having no relation to the particular offence or the particular subject, my hon. and learned Friend the Attorney General says—that at this juncture the shorthand notes will come in and play a very important part, because thereupon we should have the question and answer set forth, and if the question was not a proper one to be put to the witness and he had been committed to prison for not answering the question, he would have his remedy. Now, if the suggestion of the Attorney General is accepted, the witness would not have a remedy, because the magistrate would hold and find as a fact that it was in his opinion right and proper that the question should be put, because it related to the subject-matter of the inquiry. The witness would be entirely without protection and the magistrate would be without any check. I therefore submit for the Attorney General's further consideration, although I admit it is a little premature I interposed for the purpose of trying to shorten the discussion—that the words "and shall not be examined concerning any other matter or subject whatever" should be allowed to remain. If these words are allowed to remain and the proper exercise of judgment comes into question, the Court can judge whether the magistrate was or was not within his right.

MR. WARMINGTON : I am afraid I cannot except the suggestion just made. My objection is not simply with regard to the scope of the inquiry, but it is to undue examination. I desire that the examination should be restricted, so that only evidence shall be extracted in a proper way; that the Resident Magistrate shall not be at liberty to put leading questions, or to cross-examine a person who is summoned before him. Therefore, to limit the Amendment in the way suggested will not in any way meet my objection. I cannot withdraw my Amendment, or agree to its being limited as suggested.

MR. MAURICE HEALY (Cork): What the Attorney General suggests amounts to this—that the Government agree that a question not relevant to the inquiry shall not be asked, unless the Resident Magistrate says it is relevant to the inquiry; that is practically the offer the hon. and learned Gentleman makes to us. Of course, that does not directly arise on the Amendment of my hon. and learned Friend (Mr. Warmington), in regard to which Amendment I wish to know whether the Government insist that to these secret inquiries that none of the ordinary rules of evidence which prevail in Courts of Law shall apply? Let me give an example. In a Court of Law, hearsay evidence is not admissible. Is such evidence to be admissible at these inquiries? The Attorney General for Ireland (Mr. Holmes) says that an inquiry under this section cannot

Sir Charles Russell

be conducted as an inquiry would, if there was a person charged with the offence. Is it to be contended that, at an inquiry of this kind, a magistrate can ask questions such as this—" Did you ever hear A B murdered so and so?" I respectfully submit that the Committee should insist that there should be a check of some kind imposed upon the action of the magistrate. The whole contention of the Treasury Bench in the discussion upon this clause is that they will not put any check whatever on the magistrate. Everything is to be subjected to the discretion of the Resident Magistrates. Our experience of these gentlemen prompts us not to accept the view of the Government that the magistrates should have absolute discretion in matters of this kind.

MR. MAHONY (Meath, N.) : It appears to me it is all the more important to press some such Amendment as that now before the Committee, because it is perfectly clear the Government do intend that these inquiries should go beyond matters relating to actual offences. The Government have evinced a desire to revise the shorthand notes before they are made public. If during these secret inquiries, merely crime is to be inquired into, there can be no possible reason for revising the Amendment No. 52 which has been agreed to, yet the Attorney General (Sir Richard Webster) has distinctly reserved to himself the right to propose some Amendment to that Amendment.

MR. O'DOHERTY (Donegal, N.) : With reference to the words proposed to be added by the Attorney General (Sir Richard Webster), allow me to call attention to the words of the section as it originally stood, and ask the hon. and learned Gentleman as a lawyer, whether or not the protection of the witness is not greater under the section than under the words he proposes. The words of the section are, "and examine on oath concerning such offence."

THE CHAIRMAN : The hon. Member is anticipating the Amendment No. 59. We are considering Amendment No. 53.

MR. O'DOHERTY : Many remarks sprang out of the proposal of the hon. and learned Gentleman the Member for South Hackney (Sir Charles Russell). Now, Amendment 53 merely provides that the magistrate holding the inquiry must examine a witness upon oath concerning the offence, and that he must in the examination observe the ordinary rules of evidence. Why there should be any objection, in the case of a semi-legal tribunal of this sort, to putting the fullest possible instructions before the mind of the person conducting the inquiry I cannot understand. I think the Committee would do well to adopt the Proviso contained in this Amendment, and thus afford only proper protection to a witness summoned before this Court.

SIR WILLIAM HARCOURT (Derby): I can see the force of what the Attorney General for Ireland has said— that you cannot confine this inquiry to the same strict rule that it would be confined, if one individual were charged. But there are certain rules of evidence which would be observed whoever was charged. Suppose a magistrate has a witness before him whom he wishes to examine, and he says—"Now do you know anything about this offence; do you know who did it, or anything concerning the doing of it?" The man says, "No, I do not." Then the magistrate might ask him, "Did you ever hear anybody else say anything about it?" That is a question which would not be admissible where a person was charged. I should like to ask the Attorney General, whether questions of that character would be admissible at the inquiry.

MR. T. M. HEALY (Longford, N.): It is quite evident, by a subsequent Amendment, that the Government intend that the Crown should use hearsay evidence. Was anything more absurd ever provided? These inquiries ought to be conducted in a lawyer-like manner and according to the rules of evidence. Once you depart from this course, you embark upon a sea of trouble. These inquiries, although conducted by cavalry men, half-pay officers, militiamen, and horse marines, should be conducted with some regard to the ordinary decencies of judicial life. Of course, you cannot expect a horse marine to take the same view of legal questions as a legally trained man; but, at any rate, we are entitled to know whether the Government intend that hearsay evidence shall be accepted. But, if so, these judicial inquiries would be reduced to a farce.

MR. HOLMES: I think it would be perfectly legitimate that a question of the nature suggested by the right hon. Gentleman (Sir William Harcourt) should be put. It ought to be borne in mind that there is no accused person before the tribunal, and that it is the duty of the person presiding over the inquiry to put any question which will, in any way, lead to the detection of the crime. I quite admit that the Question put must be concerning the crime in respect of which the inquiry is held; and, of course, on the trial of a prisoner, no Judge would permit hearsay evidence to be used against any person whatever.

MR. ANDERSON (Elgin and Nairn): The other day the Committee was told by the Solicitor General for Scotland (Mr. J. P. B. Robertson) that the procedure provided by this section was part of the Constitutional Law of Scotland. That was loudly cheered by hon. Members opposite; but now we hear from the Attorney General for Ireland (Mr. Holmes), what he means by this Constitutional Law of Scotland. This inquiry is to be held secretly, and carried on in every way contrary to what we understand is the Constitutional Law of this country and of Scotland too in regard to evidence. [Mr. J. H. A. MACDONALD dissented.] The Lord Advocate (Mr. J. H. A. Macdonald) has thrown a good deal of light upon this discussion, for he has shaken his head when statements have been made with regard to the Law of Scotland. I trust, however, that this debate will be enlivened by some observations from the right hon. and learned Gentleman. Anyhow, we heard from the Solicitor General for Scotland, that this practice is not really the law of Scotland, but there is some sort of trace or form of it. The power has never been used, so said the Solicitor General for Scotland. [Mr. J. H. A. MACDONALD again dissented.] The Lord Advocate shakes his head again; but I have got a very valuable work here, by a person of the name of Macdonald.

THE CHAIRMAN: Order, order! The hon. and learned Gentleman must speak to the Amendment before the Committee.

MR. ANDERSON: I beg your pardon, Mr. Chairman. I am afraid I have been led astray by the silence of the Lord Advocate. We are discussing two most important questions, and it is right we should have some guidance from one of the Law Officers who are assisting the Crown in respect to this measure—the Law Officers for England, Ireland, and Scotland. By this Amendment a most important point is raised. The statement we have heard from the Attorney General for Ireland lets us into the secret that there is to be a private inquiry, and, that the rules of evidence are not to be observed in any way—that, in fact, persons are to be subjected to a regular inquisition. That is the object of the inquiry. | "No, no!"] The Lord Advocate seems to dissent from that. Will he get up and tell us that this has its origin in a Statute? I ask him further—[*Interruption, continued for some time.*] I beg, Sir, to move that you report Progress.

Motion made, and Question proposed, "That the Chairman do report Progress and ask leave to sit again."—(*Mr. Anderson.*)

Mr. A. J. BALFOUR: I hope the hon. and learned Member will not press——

Mr. T. M. HEALY: Keep your gang quiet then.

Mr. A. J. BALFOUR: The hon. and learned Gentleman makes a long speech on the Amendment—[An hon. MEMBER: Two minutes.]—which had already been fully discussed, and without rhyme or reason he concludes the speech by moving the adjournment of the discussion. Does the Committee think that that Motion is justified by any enormous progress with Public Business that we have made to-night, or has anything else happened in to-night's discussion which renders it desirable that we should report Progress? I do not think so, and it is perfectly impossible for us to accede to the Motion.

SIR WILLIAM HARCOURT (Derby): In asking that this Motion may not be pressed, I must say that I do not agree with the Chief Secretary for Ireland that we have made no progress. While I have been present to-night, a great many Amendments have been disposed of, a large number being assented to by the Government. I cannot, therefore, agree that we have not made progress, neither could I agree with anyone who contended that our Business had not been conducted in a satisfactory manner. I am sure my hon. and learned Friend behind me (Mr.

Mr. Anderson

Anderson) will not proceed at greater length than is necessary, if he is allowed to finish his speech.

Mr. T. M. HEALY: We have disposed of 33 Amendments in the absence of hon. Members opposite. We do not require the attendance of those hon. Gentlemen here at all, speaking of them collectively, and if they are impatient I would recommend them to go away. All they seem to do is to prevent speeches being heard in this direction. We, on our part, desire that this debate should be proceeded with in a regular manner, as it has hitherto gone on to-night, before the hon. Gentlemen opposite came in from their dinner. If this Motion is withdrawn, I hope they will be kept quiet.

Mr. ANDERSON: I do not wish to waste time by pressing on this Motion. I will point out that I was discussing, I hope not at undue length, this clause—I was referring to a matter which I think has not yet been mentioned in this Committee, and one which is of the greatest importance. Though it may not be of interest to hon. Gentlemen on the opposite side of the House, who have just come in, and who are anxious to go to bed, yet they must remember that we have a duty to perform. We do not wish to perform that duty to the extent of wearying the Committee, however. My point is this—and I think every fair-minded man in the Committee will see how important it is—will the Lord Advocate who brings forward this clause as part of the law of Scotland tell us whether it is founded upon any Statute? Will he tell us whether it was founded on the civil law or common law? I venture to think that it is not founded in any way upon these two. I will venture to tell the right hon. and learned Gentleman what it is founded upon. It is founded upon the canon law established for the purpose of bringing the Roman Inquisition into power. We are now told that it is to be introduced into the law of Ireland for the purpose of carrying on the Inquisition in that country which it used to carry on in Rome. I hope this Amendment will be carried to a Division unless the Government give way, and that I sincerely trust they will do.

Motion, by leave, *withdrawn.*

Original Question again proposed.

MR. ASHER (Elgin, &c.): I hope my hon. and learned Friend (Mr. Warmington) will press this Amendment. It appears to me to be directed to establishing a rule in connection with the preliminary examination on oath contemplated by this clause which cannot fail to be advantageous. My hon. and learned Friend who has just sat down (Mr. Anderson) has referred to the law of Scotland. Well, the position of the law of Scotland in regard to this matter has been frequently explained to the Committee. It has been frequently stated that a preliminary inquiry on oath is competent in Scotland; but, at the same time, such inquiries are not of common occurrence in Scotland now. I think it right to say that at no time, so far as I know, was this practice of preliminary examination upon oath ever permitted according to the law of Scotland, except on the lines set out in this Amendment. The Amendment of my hon. and learned Friend is intended to produce this result, that in a preliminary examination upon oath only such questions shall be put to the witness as could competently be put to a witness if he were being examined as a witness on a trial. Now that, undoubtedly, has always been the law of Scotland; but I should be sorry to allow that to rest entirely upon my statement, and, with the permission of the Committee, I will read a passage from Sir Archibald Alison's *Practice of the Criminal Law in Scotland,* the authority of which I am sure the Lord Advocate will acknowledge. Sir Archibald Alison, in dealing with this matter, speaking of the preliminary examination on oath, says—

"In discharging this delicate duty of compelling witnesses to appear and depone in a precognition, and of putting them on oath, or committing them to prison if they refuse to take the oath or to answer questions, it is the duty of the Judge as nearly as possible to walk by the rules of evidence which will ultimately be followed at the trial. There seems, therefore, no authority which can justify a Magistrate in tendering an oath to a wife against her husband or against any party with whom he is implicated in one common offence, or to a husband against a wife in similar circumstances, or to an adult child who refuses to depone against its parent, or to any child under the age when it can be legally sworn, or in compelling a child under that age to declare against its parent. As such proceedings would be illegal if attempted in open Court and when the accused is on his trial, so they seem to be equally exceptionable in the secret but equally regular and important investigations which precede that event: not to mention the prejudice which would accrue to the accused if information were thus to be extracted from his nearest and dearest relations which could not be brought against him directly from them when on trial for the crime; and the opinion of the prosecutors in determining on the case, were to be liable to the bias unavoidably incurred by reading important depositions which cannot ultimately be brought against him. No steps of coercion should therefore be adopted against witnesses in a precognition, except such persons and in relation to such questions as are competent to be examined or put at the trial. It is quite a different matter examining such witnesses when they come forward voluntarily or, though cited, state no objection to emitting their declaration."

The Amendment of my hon. and learned Friend would, I think, effect this—that in the case of the preliminary inquiry on oath, it would not be in the power of the magistrate to put any question to a witness which it would not have been competent to put to him if he were being examined as a witness, giving evidence at a trial. The clause, I understand, is intended merely to secure that evidence shall be obtained from persons who will not voluntarily make their statements—persons possessed of knowledge which they are withholding—and it is difficult to see why the magistrates should have the power of getting anything more than legal evidence from witnesses put on oath before them, seeing that when the trial comes on, all that can be done is to put to the witness such questions as the ordinary Law of Evidence will allow.

THE LORD ADVOCATE (Mr. J. H. A. MACDONALD) (Edinburgh and St. Andrews Universities): I am very unwilling to join in this discussion, knowing, from having read his speech in the papers, that the Solicitor General for Scotland has stated the law of Scotland with great accuracy and clearness in this House already. I do not desire to put in my word merely to take up the time of the House in repeating a statement which I believe to have been perfectly correct, and which nothing that my hon. and learned Friend has said impugns in the slightest degree; and though I must say that Alison, to whom my hon. and learned Friend has referred, has not always been looked upon as the best and most accurate authority at the time at which he wrote on our Criminal Law, there is nothing in the general statement which he made in the passage which my hon. and learned Friend has read out to which I take any exception—certainly not any serious exception—at all. In conducting these inquiries in private the Laws of Evidence in regard to witnesses whom it is competent to examine at a trial are the same as at a trial. It would not be possible to bring the wife of a man to be accused of a crime to give evidence against him—it would not be possible to take a man's wife and put her on oath and examine her in reference to that crime; but my hon. and learned Friend seems to forget that we are not dealing here with the case in which a husband is charged or a wife is charged with a crime, or in which a question can be raised whether the wife can be examined against her husband, or the husband can be examined against his wife. We are dealing with the case in which no person is yet charged. [An hon. MEMBER : But persons may be charged.] We are dealing with an inquiry for the purpose of finding out whether anybody can be charged, and if so what person it is. Well, in making that inquiry you can apply no such rules of evidence as those my hon. and learned Friend has referred to, because if you hear of a woman who is said to know something about a crime that has been committed, you cannot, by any possibility, tell before you examine her whether it may not turn out that when you are examining somebody else after her that her husband will be the person to be charged with the crime. Therefore, the case my hon. and learned Friend quotes is not a case in point at all ; because the case in Alison is the case of an inquiry conducted where some person is already charged with a crime. You are not in such a case to examine a man's wife on oath, or if it is a woman who is charged, you are not to examine her husband on oath ; but in what Alison says—that you are in a judicial proceeding to conduct the inquiry according to the Laws of Evidence, I concur thoroughly, and I am sure my hon. and learned Friend and other members of the Legal Profession will agree with me—that that is a sound statement of the law. Still, it is quite common in these inquiries, as my hon. and learned Friend knows well enough, to ask questions of witnesses which it might be incompetent to put in Court. For instance, it is perfectly competent in such an inquiry to ascertain from witnesses, by what is called "hearsay," whether any other

person has been heard speaking about the case for the purpose of ascertaining whether it is necessary to have other witnesses summoned and brought up in order to be examined. The evidence is taken, not for the purpose of conducting a trial, but for aiding or perhaps conducting an inquiry to discover witnesses who will be sufficient to prove the case. There is nothing at all inconsistent with what the hon. and learned Solicitor General for Scotland said on a previous occasion, in what has been read by my hon. and learned Friend opposite, nor is there anything in the latter to justify the proposition which is contained in the Amendment of the hon. and learned Member — namely, that the whole inquiry must necessarily be conducted as if a person were under charge. Let me point out that if the examination of a person is to be conducted as though someone was under charge, it would be a great deal worse for the person who would be under examination, because if complete examination were to take place, as would be the case at a trial, the character of the examination would be unfair to a person giving evasive answers. An inquiry of this kind should be conducted in a calm and quiet manner, and not in the least in the manner in which examinations take place before a Judge. My hon. and learned Friend opposite knows perfectly well how examinations take place at a trial, and he must see that inquiries under this clause must be conducted in a manner very different to such cross-examinations, for instance, as I know hon. Gentlemen below the Gangway opposite would be inclined to subject hostile witnesses to in a Court of Law. No pressure ought to be used upon a witness, and in Scotland no pressure is used. I venture to say, without the least fear of contradiction, that such an accusation as that one of the Public Prosecutors in Scotland in making one of these preliminary inquiries has unduly pressed a witness, is a thing so extremely rare that if it exists at all it is just the exception which proves the rule. No administration can be absolutely perfect; but I believe that the working of this system is one of the most perfectly fair exercises of the right of examination in private which could possibly be, and for the hon. Gentleman opposite to compare it to proceedings of the Inquisition—which he has done twice to-night in the course of two speeches he has made—certainly shows the extravagance of those who are not perfectly familiar with the working of our present system. I am sure the late hon. and learned Solicitor General for Scotland does not for one moment mean to suggest as a general rule—notwithstanding that there may be small exceptions with which those who are in the position of looking after Scotland have to find fault—that precognitions are not conducted with great fairness. They are conducted with a desire to obtain a fair statement of what the witness is to depone to, and it is only in very rare cases where there is reason to believe that persons are withholding their statements that people are put on oath. I wish to take this opportunity of correcting a statement made in this House some time ago to the effect that putting a person on oath in a precognition is a thing not known in Scotland. I contradict that distinctly. I say that in recent years, and that under the late Lord Advocate and late Solicitor General for Scotland, sitting opposite to me, it has been done by their own Deputes, when thought to be necessary. I know it also from a Judge now on the Bench that he and another Judge have both put it in practice during the past 25 years.

SIR WILLIAM HARCOURT: I am sure we are very much indebted to the Lord Advocate for his very clear and satisfactory statement as to the law of Scotland and its administration. I understand that the object of this Amendment is to, as nearly as possible, assimilate the law in this Bill to that which he has laid down as the practice in Scotland. Now, the illustration which he has given of the incompetence of the magistrates at an inquiry to take the statement of a wife against her husband, where the latter is charged with an offence, does not apply, according to his argument, because I understand him to say that if no person is charged, then that evidence may be practically got against the same person—that is to say, against the husband of the wife. It may not be usual, but it may be competent to get it. Suppose a person is suspected of an offence, and his wife is called to give evidence, because the man is not actually charged is the woman to be compelled to say everything she knows about him, because, if that is so,

you practically get the evidence of the woman against her husband? You get the evidence of the woman against the man because no actual charge is made, which you would not be allowed to do if a charge was made. I gather from the Lord Advocate that that would not be allowed in Scotland. I understand that the wife would not be capable of being examined against her husband if a charge were made, and that she would not be allowed to be examined against her husband, as even though no charge is made the husband may be suspected of a crime. As I understand the object of this Amendment, it is to provide in these words, or in some other words equivalent to them, that examinations before Resident Magistrates in Ireland shall, like the examinations under the Scotch law be governed by the general and fundamental Laws of Evidence. That is really the principle. We wish for some intimation from the Government that the persons who use the powers contained in this Bill shall be governed by the general and fundamental Laws of Evidence. I understand, though I do not think the Lord Advocate mentioned it—it was mentioned in a former debate by the hon. Member for Elgin, I think —that in Scotland this power is exercised under check, that is to say, that the Procurator Fiscal, who would conduct the examination, would conduct it in the presence of the Sheriff. I am told that that is so, and that the Sheriff would see that no irregularities took place in reference to the evidence that is permitted. Now, if that is so——

MR. J. H. A. MACDONALD: The Sheriff is responsible when the charge is made; but in our practice the Procurator Fiscal takes these precognitions without the presence of the Sheriff, who only comes in when it is necessary to compel witnesses.

SIR WILLIAM HARCOURT: I understood my right hon. and learned Friend to say—and I do not understand my right hon. and learned Friend to dissent from that—that the Sheriff is the controlling officer, and that the Procurator Fiscal is acting under his directions very much as the Solicitor to the Treasury acts for our Attorney General. That is so; then I do not think there is any material difference. What you want is some form of words which will indicate to persons very few of whom may be lawyers—who, in fact, are not, in general, lawyers—that they ought to govern themselves in the exercise of these powers by the general Law of Evidence, and not travel out of it.

MR. ATHERLEY-JONES: I only wish to add one observation in this very dry discussion on Scotch law. There seems to me, with great respect for the Attorney General for Ireland, to be a fundamental distinction to be drawn between what is known as precognition in Scotland and this inquiry in Ireland. I point this out, because I hope that that fairness which generally characterizes the right hon. and learned Gentleman will now operate in his mind. When a man is examined in Scotland, he is entitled to insist that the deposition he has given on precognition shall be destroyed. He cannot be prosecuted, under any circumstances, for perjury. Now, this Bill, as I find at the end of the 1st clause, provides that the statement of any person under the section—

"Shall not, except in the case of an indictment or other criminal proceeding for perjury, be admissible in evidence against him in any proceeding, civil or criminal."

I want to point out to the Attorney General for Ireland why I think it is of vital importance, for two reasons, that hearsay evidence should not be admissible. In the first place, if hearsay evidence be admissible in what I will term precognition by way of comparison, then evidence may be admitted of an extraneous character, which can be brought to bear upon a witness to a certain extent; and I do not think it is an exaggerated way of speaking to say that this evidence would be held *in terrorem* over him. Though that evidence might not be germane to the subject of inquiry, the witness might be proceeded against. It seems to me that the strict rules of evidence should be followed, as has been pointed out by the right hon. Gentleman who spoke on this side of the House. Sir Archibald Alison points out that every protection is given to witnesses against oppressive proceedings. He points out clearly that this inquiry has only been used in Scotland for the purpose of affording information to the Crown Officials for ulterior purposes of investigation; but here it is something more. A power is vested in the Crown for examination, which they may exer-

Sir William Harcourt

cise for the purpose of getting information from a witness which can be used against him. Therefore, I venture respectfully to differ from the right hon. Gentleman opposite, believing that there is a marked difference in this matter.

MR. MAHONY (Meath, N.): The right hon. and learned Lord Advocate for Scotland gave us a true picture of the law in Scotland. It is because we know, from past experience, what the administration of law in Ireland is, that we want to press this Amendment. The Lord Advocate has said that, in his opinion, no pressure should be applied; and he has added that in Scotland there is no power to prosecute for perjury in respect of evidence given on a precognition. Now, the threat of a prosecution for perjury is a very powerful weapon with which pressure can be brought to bear upon a witness. I will give an instance to show this. At one of the inquiries which took place under the Act of 1882, a witness was examined on one or two days. He gave evidence at great length and in great detail in answer to the questions put to him by Mr., now Judge, Curran. At the end of his evidence, Judge Curran told him that he had reason to know that his evidence was perfectly false, and that he had committed perjury, and therefore he gave him 24 hours to consider his position. At the end of the 24 hours, Judge Curran told him he would give him an opportunity of giving other evidence. The witness, accordingly, at the end of the 24 hours, or the specified time, appeared again before Judge Curran, and gave perfectly different evidence, and on that evidence the prisoners were prosecuted and convicted. If the Government do not accept my statement, I am sure that Judge Curran, who was then Mr. Curran, will confirm it.

MR. MAURICE HEALY: This Amendment is of great importance, and its importance is greatly enhanced by the declaration of the Government that they intend that any declarations taken at a secret inquiry shall afterwards be used to confront the witnesses at the trial. The Attorney General for Ireland has declared that questions which would be excluded as hearsay evidence on an ordinary trial are proper evidence at an inquiry under this section. The effect of that would be that hearsay evidence might be used at the trial of a prisoner charged with an offence. How would that happen? In this way. If a witness on the trial of an accused person were confronted with his own deposition at the previous inquiry, and it should turn out that the deposition was inconsistent with the evidence, that deposition might be put in evidence; and if the deposition be put in evidence for that purpose, the whole of the deposition may be, and must be, read against the prisoner. Therefore, it comes to this— we will take it that a witness makes a statement incriminating A B. That witness is afterwards examined on the trial of A B. Then he makes certain statements inconsistent with the evidence given in his deposition. The deposition is then put in to contradict the evidence given at the trial, and in that way is made evidence against the prisoner. The effect is that not merely that portion of the deposition which contradicts the evidence of the witness given at the trial is evidence against the prisoner, but the whole deposition is admitted, including any hearsay evidence which the Resident Magistrate may have admitted. That makes this Amendment one of an exceedingly important character. I do not think anyone would assert that it is reasonable or proper that hearsay evidence should be put in against a prisoner at a trial; and if this clause, as it is drawn, enables that to be done, it is a reason why it should be rejected or amended.

Original Question put.

The Committee *divided*:—Ayes 193; Noes 272: Majority 79.—(Div. List, No. 115.)   [12.40 A.M.]

MR. BRADLAUGH (Northampton): I beg to move, Sir, that you report Progress, and I beg to appeal to the right hon. Gentleman the Leader of the House to accede to that Motion.

Motion made and Question proposed, "That the Chairman do report Progress, and ask leave to sit again." — (*Mr. Bradlaugh.*)

THE FIRST LORD OF THE TREASURY (Mr. W. H. SMITH) (Strand, Westminster): I shall be very glad to report Progress as soon as we get to the end of this 1st sub-section of the clause. I trust that it may not take more than a very few minutes to dispose of.

MR. T. M. HEALY (Longford, N.) I should like to know, as regards the possibility of finishing this 1s sub-section to-night, how many of our Amendments the Government are going to accept? If they do not accept our Amendments, we shall take some time; but if they take my Amendments in a batch, we may soon finish.

MR. T. P. O'CONNOR (Liverpool, Scotland): I am rather surprised at the proposal of the right hon. Gentleman the Leader of the House, for, on looking at the Paper, I find no less than nine Amendments still on the Paper with regard to this 1st sub-section of the clause. It is ridiculous to propose that we should, at 1 in the morning, run hastily through them—every one of them being of considerable importance. I think the right hon. Gentleman does not meet the Committee in anything like a fair spirit. To-night we have got through a larger number of Amendments than we have done at any previous Sitting; and I could even go further, and say that we have gone through more Amendments this evening than were ever got through in respect of a Coercion Bill in the same time. The right hon. Gentleman shows very little gratitude for the very generous and forbearing spirit in which the Committee have met him to-night. There has not been a single Amendment discussed, I will not say at undue length— I will even say that our debates on several important Amendments have been curtailed to meet the right hon. Gentleman in a spirit of give and take, so as not to give him a decent excuse for saying that the debates have unduly delayed the Business of the House. If he perseveres, he is the master of many legions, and will overcome our opposition; but if we do proceed, we shall consider it our duty to discuss these Amendments in proportion to their importance, and with no regard to the hour of the night.

SIR WILLIAM HARCOURT (Derby): I hope the harmony of the evening is not going to be disturbed. I should rather gather, from the remarks of the right hon. Gentleman the Leader of the House, anticipating that in a very short time this sub-section will be finished, that he and his Friends will take a favourable view of the eight or nine Amendments on the Paper. I

[*Fourth Night.*]

think we might go on and see how far
those Amendments are likely to be accepted. I believe my hon. and learned
Friend the Member for South Hackney
(Sir Charles Russell) has an Amendment with regard to the Law of Evidence that might very likely displace
some other Amendments. At all events,
we might see how we got on, instead of
coming to a conflict on the question of
reporting Progress.

MR. BRADLAUGH : I have no wish
to press the Motion for reporting Progress now, though there is another
matter which I hope I shall have an
opportunity of discussing.

Motion, by leave, *withdrawn*.

MR. T. M. HEALY (Longford, N.):
I now propose, in page 1, line 17, at the
end, to insert—

"The summons served on a witness under
this section shall set forth the date and nature
of the offence respecting which information is
sought, the name of the person who alleges that
the witness can furnish information thereupon,
the hour and place at which the inquiry is to be
holden, and the magistrate who is to conduct
it."

This Amendment will, no doubt, have
to be modified to render it consistent
with previous determinations at which
the Committee have arrived; but I
think it cannot be denied that there
are certain cases in which a summons
ought to issue, and that this summons
should contain certain information.
You have negatived, I admit, the
principle that a summons shall, in all
cases, issue, since the Government have
pointed out that a summons may not
be issued in all cases; because a warrant may be issued in some cases. My
proposition is that when a summons is
issued—and there are certain cases in
which a summons will issue—it should
provide for certain things and contain
information on certain points. I should
like to hear what the Attorney General
for Ireland has to say on the subject.

THE ATTORNEY GENERAL FOR
IRELAND (Mr. HOLMES) (Dublin University : To remove any doubt on this
point, I will move, at the proper time,
to insert in a Schedule to the Bill the
form of summons we propose, and which
will, I hope, fulfil the object the hon.
and learned Gentleman has in view.

MR. T. M. HEALY: In that case, I
beg to withdraw the Amendment.

Amendment, by leave, *withdrawn*.

Sir William Harcourt

MR. T. M. HEALY (Longford, N.) :
I will now propose, in page 1, line 17, at
the end, to insert—

"No witness shall be kept waiting more than
two hours without being examined; and, if so
detained without examination, may depart
without further liability to being summoned in
reference to the same offence."

I propose this Amendment, because I
do not think that a witness should be
kept waiting an unreasonable time before
being examined. What happens? You
summon men in clusters, and keep them
waiting; taken from their employment
without reason or necessity. I do not
think you ought to attempt to do more
than a day's work in a day. You should
not summon more witnesses than you
want or can examine. If the Government will give an assurance that they
will not allow a whole country side to
be summoned from their work at once,
and without there being any possibility
of them all being examined in a reasonable time, then I will not press this
Amendment; but there is a real necessity for some provision that witnesses
should not be kept from their work an
unreasonable time without having an
opportunity to go away.

Amendment proposed,

In page 1, line 17, at end, insert—"No witness shall be kept waiting more than two hours
without being examined; and, if so detained
without examination, may depart without further liability to being summoned in reference
to the same offence."—(*Mr. T. M. Healy.*)

Question proposed, "That those words
be there inserted."

THE ATTORNEY GENERAL (SIR
RICHARD WEBSTER) (Isle of Wight):
This is one of the things which must be
left to the discretion of the Resident
Magistrate. It is impossible to say that
a witness must not be kept in attendance
more than a certain time; because it may
easily happen that the examination of a
previous witness or witnesses lasts longer
than was expected, and in that case it
may be necessary to detain a subsequent
witness until he can be examined. It
would be very inconvenient in such a
case if he was allowed to go away because a fixed time had elapsed.

MR. T. M. HEALY: In the case put
by the hon. and learned Attorney General, the magistrate may give a fresh
summons. [*Some cries of* "Oh, oh!"]
It is easy to cry "Oh;" but how do Gen-

tlemen like being kept here now? Are hon. Members opposite ready to remain here two hours longer? All I say is, that witnesses ought to be allowed to depart, just as hon. Gentlemen below the Gangway may be allowed to depart. Because these people are poor and wear frieze coats, why are they to be treated with less care than persons who are created Baronets by Her Majesty's Government? I am very fond of Baronets, but I do not see why we should treat poor people with more discourtesy than any other class of Her Majesty's subjects. I have suggested that the limit should be two hours; but the principle of the thing is the point to which I attach importance, and if four hours is preferred, I should not object to it. We ought, however, to have some limit put in.

MR. CONYBEARE (Cornwell, Cambourne): My experience of magistrates, especially of the great unpaid in this country, leads me to the conviction that this Amendment is very necessary. Certainly, it is necessary if it is held to apply to the case of magistrates keeping witnesses waiting, when they come two hours late, a circumstance which frequently happens in this country. I should like to see an Amendment going a great deal beyond this one. I should like to see an Amendment requiring magistrates to take their seats punctually, and not keep witnesses waiting, and I should be inclined to add a Proviso, that if the magistrate did keep witnesses or others waiting for two hours, or even for half-an-hour at the commencement of the proceedings, he should be guilty of misdemeanour, and punished accordingly. I think that if the Government refuse to admit the principle for which we contend of this Amendment it will be desirable, at any rate, to provide that the witnesses shall be compensated for the waste of time to which they are all subjected. The hon. and learned Member who has just spoken reminded the House that these witnesses are, in all probability, poor men, and it will also be recollected that their means of subsistence depends upon the amount of work they can do in the day. This is not the case with hon. Members opposite, and although it may be amusing to them, it is a matter of the utmost moment to these poor men. [*Cries of "Divide!"*]

THE CHAIRMAN: Order, order!

MR. CONYBEARE: It is of the greatest moment. [*Renewed cries of "Divide!"*] — Mr. Courtney, I beg leave to move to report Progress.

THE CHAIRMAN: Does the hon. Member move to report Progress?

MR. CONYBEARE: I do, Sir.

Motion made, and Question proposed, "That the Chairman do report Progress and ask leave to sit again."—(*Mr. Conybeare.*)

THE FIRST LORD OF THE TREASURY (Mr. W. H. SMITH) (Strand, Westminster): I trust the hon. Gentleman will not put the Committee to the trouble and loss of time incurred by a Division. The Government cannot consent to report Progress, and the Motion will therefore only expose the Committee to great delay.

SIR CHARLES RUSSELL (Hackney, S.): I hope I may be allowed to make this observation. I quite appreciate the object of the hon. and learned Gentleman the Member for North Longford (Mr. T. M. Healy) in moving his Amendment; but I would point out that it is not really practicable in my judgment to introduce such a provision. However fairly and honestly the Act may be administered, it is impossible to avoid some inconvenience to witnesses, either on account of the unexpected prolongation of the examination of a previous witness, or from other causes. The only means of checking abuses of this Act would be to call public attention to them in this House. I would suggest to the hon. and learned Member for North Longford whether he could not withdraw his Amendment.

MR. CONYBEARE: I moved to report Progress in consequence of the unruly conduct of supporters of Her Majesty's Government. I think it is perfectly well understood in this House that when I get up to speak, I intend to speak, and that under no circumstances will I allow myself to be howled down. All I can say is this—that if the conduct which we have seen and heard from that side of the House is continued without any reason whatever, and if the Government do not take the trouble to keep their own supporters in order, I shall invariably move to report Progress. If I desire to speak on any other subject this evening, and find I am interrupted in the same way, I

[Fourth Night.]

shall move to report Progress in the same way, and if it becomes necessary for me to again make a Motion of this kind, I shall not do what I am now asked to be allowed to do, to withdraw the Motion.

Motion, by leave, *withdrawn*.

Mr. T. M. HEALY: The hon. and learned Gentleman the Member for South Hackney (Sir Charles Russell) has spoken with some slight freedom in regard to this Amendment. I wonder if he is acquainted with the provisions of the Petty Sessions Act, which provides that if the magistrate is not in attendance at the proper time, the Clerk may adjourn the proceedings. It is all very well for the hon. and learned Member to say the thing is impracticable. I tell him that I have not proposed any Amendment in the nature of anything like Obstruction, nor any Amendment except an Amendment required in the nature of the case; and I do think it is a little hard on us who have sat down and sweated over this Bill, and spent hours drafting Amendments to it in order to mitigate the severity of its provisions, to be told that our Amendments are impracticable. I must say this sort of thing makes a man tired. If there are hon. Gentlemen on the Front Opposition Bench not pleased to support our Amendments they should be pleased not to condemn them. I say this Amendment is a perfectly reasonable Amendment. The principle of it is already embodied in the Petty Sessions Act, which provides that if the magistrate does not turn up in time the witnesses shall not be kept waiting; and knowing what we do of the magistrates in Ireland, I submit that there is no reason why it should not be adopted.

The ATTORNEY GENERAL for IRELAND (Mr. HOLMES) (Dublin University): The form of summons proposed to be issued to witnesses will be included in a Schedule to the Bill, and one of the things mentioned in the summons will be the hour of attendance. If the magistrate does not put in an appearance at the time stated he will certainly be guilty of neglect of duty. It is, however, quite possible that a witness may be kept waiting more than two hours, for the examination of the first witness may not be concluded in that time; but I would point out that we

have accepted an Amendment that the examination of witnesses shall not begin after 6 o'clock, so that they cannot be kept waiting long after that hour. I would ask the hon. and learned Member to withdraw this Amendment, and to consider under those circumstances, that we have given him real protection.

Dr. CLARK (Caithness): I would call the attention of the House to the fact that in Scotland we sometimes have some very curious conditions of things. I happened to be down in the Hebrides during the Easter Recess, and a crofter complained bitterly to me that after going some distance to attend a Sheriff's Court, he had to wait until midnight to get his case tried, the reason for the delay being that the Sheriff went out shooting. I trust the hon. and learned Member will keep to his Amendment.

Mr. CHANCE (Kilkenny, S.): If the form of the summons really enabled a witness to go away, I think the Government would welcome this Amendment, as it would give them two hours grace. But the fact is, the witnesses will be pitched into the police court, and kept there all day, and at six o'clock in the evening they will be taken to the police station and kept there all night, to be served up afresh the next morning. It will be disgraceful if such a power is given.

Mr. MAURICE HEALY (Cork City): The right hon. and learned Gentleman the Attorney General for Ireland has overlooked the fact that this section applies not merely to witnesses summoned, but also to witnesses who are arrested. It is all very well in regard to witnesses who are summoned; but what about witnesses who are arrested. We have had no answer about them. What will happen to them? May I further call the attention of the Committee to the fact that it is not merely a question of hours. Under this question, a witness may be detained for days and weeks to suit the convenience of the Resident Magistrate. If the Government object to the limit of two hours proposed in the Amendment, or to that of four hours, to which the Member for North Longford is willing to extend it, will they be content to detain witnesses a day or a week? Let us have some limit, at all events, to the powers which the Resident Magistrates will have under this clause. It is not candid to deal with this matter

Mr. Conybeare

as if it only related to witnesses who had been summoned.

MR. JOHN MORLEY (Newcastle-on-Tyne): I quite agree with the view that has been taken by my hon. and learned Friend the Member for North Longford, as to the possibility of considerable hardship arising under the operation of this clause. Still, I think my hon. and learned Friend must admit that the position taken up by the hon. Gentleman the Member for South Hackney (Sir Charles Russell) is a sound one. It is impossible, under all circumstances, to prevent cases of hardship arising; but if the light of public opinion is thrown upon these transactions, they would have to be carefully investigated. When advice in this sense is given by one who is so experienced in these affairs as my hon. and learned Friend near me, and who is so anxious that all safeguards should be adopted, I think great weight should be attached to his opinion. The Attorney General for Ireland has told us that we are to have in a Schedule, or at some other time, the form and manner in which the summonses will be issued. It may be that when the form comes before the Committee we shall find some pro s n to meet the objection of the honviaird learned Member. In that view I trust the hon. and learned Member will consent to withdraw his Amendment.

MR. T. M. HEALY: I have so much respect for the right hon. Gentleman the Member for Newcastle-on-Tyne that any suggestion from him would meet with my acceptance, even against my own judgment. I confess on the present occasion, it is against my judgment. I say the Amendment is an admirable one, although I am the author of it; nevertheless, I wish to withdraw it. We have a duty to perform here, and all I can say is that performing it and satisfying my own conscience is a great deal more to me than the opinions of hon. Members opposite.

COLONEL NOLAN (Galway, N.): We might now report Progress. I would ask some of the Members on this side of the House, if it is not now time for them to use their influence with the Government to allow us to enter on the consideration of the subject next on the Paper.

MR. CONYBEARE: I do not know exactly where we are. I do not know whether my hon. and learned Friend the Member for North Longford has withdrawn his Amendment, or whether my hon. and gallant Friend the Member for North Galway has moved to report Progress. Therefore, I wish to take a stand of my own. I move this Amendment.

THE CHAIRMAN: The Amendment of the hon. and learned Member for North Longford is still before the Committee. He has asked leave to withdraw it; but leave has not yet been given. When he has withdrawn it, there are several Amendments on the same point which must take precedence. Then you can move your Amendment.

MR. CHANCE (Kilkenny, S.): I wish to ask whether the discussion on the subsequent Amendments to which you have referred would prevent me moving an Amendment in reference to women and children being locked up in a police station under the powers taken by this clause? This is no Party Question, but a Question of purity and decency; and I trust the House will not be so degraded as to assent to this bringing of women and children away from their husbands and friends, and locking them up at night. It would be a disgrace to this Committee and to the House.

THE CHAIRMAN: The withdrawal of the present Amendment would not stop the hon. Member from moving the Amendment to which he refers.

MR. CHANCE: The moving of the subsequent Amendment might.

THE CHAIRMAN: The moving of subsequent Amendments on the same subject might. I am not aware that such Amendments would be moved.

MR. CONYBEARE: I find the proper way will be for me to move an Amendment to this Amendment. It is as follows:—

"That all the words after 'no' be omitted in order to insert 'no two witnesses shall be summoned for the same hour.'"

I am perfectly——

THE CHAIRMAN: The hon. Member cannot evade the Rules of the House in that way.

Amendment, by leave, withdrawn.

MR. ARTHUR O'CONNOR (Donegal, E.): I rise to a point of Order, Sir. Is the Committee to understand that it is not open to any Member to move an Amendment to any Amendment?

[Fourth Night.]

THE CHAIRMAN : It is in order to move a *bonâ fide* Amendment to an Amendment.

MR. CONYBEARE: I say it is *bonâ fide*.

THE CHAIRMAN : Order, order !

Motion made, and Question proposed, "That the Chairman do report Progress and ask leave to sit again."

MR. BRADLAUGH (Northampton): I respectfully repeat my appeal. Half-an-hour has elapsed since I made the last appeal, and I renew it in no spirit of obstruction.

THE FIRST LORD OF THE TREA-SURY (Mr. W. H. SMITH) (Strand, Westminster): I am very sensible of the spirit in which the hon. Member makes the appeal, but I must remark to him and to the House that these are Amendments which might be disposed of in a very few minutes indeed. They are Amendments of a character which, assuming that the clause is to be passed at all, could be disposed of very rapidly indeed, and looking to the time occupied at this stage, I regret to say that I must ask the Committee to finish the sub-section.

MR. T. P. O'CONNOR (Liverpool, Scotland): I am really very much astonished at the attitude of the right hon. Gentleman. I cannot see what complaint he has to make. We have only spent a few minutes on my hon. Friend's Amendment, and he has offered to withdraw it in order to expedite Business. I would in future take care never to withdraw any Amendment whatever. All I can say is, that if my hon. Friend in future proposes to with-draw any well-considered Amendment, I shall endeavour to dissuade him from such a course, and oppose such a with-drawal if the Government maintain their present attitude.

MR. ILLINGWORTH (Bradford, W.): I think the Committee is entitled to know what is considered a reasonable hour to adjourn these proceedings. I am sure we have spent a full night in a thoroughly business-like disposition making progress with the Bill. I pro-test that when an Amendment is brought forward, as was this of the hon. and learned Member, which really sought to meet the position of women and chil-dren who, it may be assumed, might under this section be summoned and de-tained over-night, it was nothing but reasonable that it should be submitted to the consideration of the Committee. Having regard to the fact that we are are giving extraordinary power to the Government to deal with what they call extraordinary offences in Ireland, the Committee ought to have regard to the interest of the innocent people who might be brought up wholesale by these Re-sident Magistrates. [*Cries of "* Ques-tion ! "] I am replying to the observa-tions of the right hon. Gentleman the Leader of the House on the point, and I think nothing has been done against which any complaint of obstruction can reasonably be made. Now, when the hon. Member for Northampton makes an appeal on behalf of an important Bill that is to follow in the order of Busi-ness, I think the interest of the greatest number of Members would be consulted, that it would be pressing matters too far to expect us to go further, that all ends would be served by allowing us now to report Progress.

MR. T. M. HEALY (Longford, N.): The Government have acted reasonably on several occasions to-night, and we have marked our sense of that reason-able spirit by being brief in our speeches, and by withdrawing a number of Amend-ments after short discussions. We have fully repaid the Government for their reasonable attitude by the speed of our progress. We have got over 33 Amend-ments, which is a large number. Why, I remember, during the discussions of the Crimes Act of 1882, during which I remember, too, that the right hon. Mem-ber for Derby (Sir William Harcourt) never once lost his patience for the two months or so those discussions continued, I recollect that we kept him all one night upon two or three Amendments. True, we were all suspended at the end of it ; but that was because we had come to the end of a very considerable debate in Committee. Now, I appreciate there are good reasons for the position the right hon. Gentleman has taken up ; but he must admit our position also. We say it is not fair to conduct debate under these conditions. [*Cries of "* Divide ! "] I beg hon. Gentlemen to believe that when the House is more thinly attended, when we have only the English Attorney General present with a few of his Friends, we get on admirably ; but when hon. Members return in numbers and cry

"Divide!" as soon as we get into a little entanglement, there is no hope of making progress. These discussions necessarily take a conversational form, these debates have a sort of undress character, which lessens their interest to many hon. Members. We are now long past 1 o'clock, and if hon. Gentlemen will go away from the House and be prepared to return when the Division Bell rings, we may be able to discuss Business in a calm temper, and get on as we never can if they make a clamour and interrupt us with cries of "Divide!" I think the Government will find that the spirit displayed by the hon. and learned Attorney General has led to substantial progress. If the Government intend to go .on—and personally I do not greatly mind if they do—let us do so in peace. Let us know whether the Government can meet us. Permit me to observe that as to the next two Amendments, so far as they have previouly been discussed, the Government have declared it is not possible to make any concession. As to the next, the right hon. Gentleman the Chief Secretary will deal with it. Now, I make this, which I consider a fair offer. I will not move the next two Amendments, but proceed to No. 58, which is a Proviso that the authority of the Attorney General for the holding of an inquiry shall name the witnesses to be examined. I am not going to discuss this Amendment on a Motion to report Progress; but I think it will be seen it is an Amendment having substance and bottom, and one that might fairly be considered by the Government.

SIR WILLIAM HARCOURT (Derby): May I venture to offer a suggestion. There is a very important Amendment I know my right hon. and learned Friend the Member for South Hackney (Sir Charles Russell) intends to move in reference to the examination of witnesses; but according to the rules of debate he could not move this until after No. 61; but if hon. Gentlemen who have Amendments before that had no objection, I imagine it might be moved now, and that would not preclude them from moving their Amendments afterwards if they thought fit. But if the Amendment of my right hon. and learned Friend is accepted, it will go a long way to remove the necessity for other Amendments; at all events, it is worth considering, and

might facilitate progress to the end of the section.

MR. T. M. HEALY: Of course, we are unable to say anything about the Amendment of the right hon. and learned Member for South Hackney, because it is not on the Paper.

Question put, and *negatived.*

THE CHAIRMAN: Does the hon. and learned Member for North Longford (Mr. T. M. Healy) move this Amendment?

MR. T. M. HEALY: I understand that the right hon. and learned Member for South Hackney is going to move an Amendment.

MR. CONYBEARE (Cornwall, Camborne): I rise to Order. If the right hon. and learned Member for South Hackney (Sir Charles Russell) puts his Amendment, which I understand would come after that standing in the name of the hon. and learned Member for the Brigg Division of Lincolnshire (Mr. Waddy), would the latter be able to move his Amendment afterwards?

THE CHAIRMAN: Yes; the power to move that Amendment will not be gone.

SIR CHARLES RUSSELL (Hackney, S.): I will read the words of my Amendment, which would come in after the word "recognizance"—

"Provided always that the examination shall be conducted as far as practicable in accordance with the ordinary rules of evidence, and such witnesses may be examined concerning such offences only, and shall not be examined concerning any other matter or subject whatsoever."

THE CHAIRMAN: I consider this Amendment covers exactly the same point as that moved by the hon. and learned Member for West Monmouth (Mr. Warmington), from which it differs only by the addition of the words "so far as practicable." That does not make a sufficient distinction between the Amendments.

SIR CHARLES RUSSELL: May I say, on a point of Order, that the objection made to the Amendment of the hon. and learned Member was that the examinations might, in some instances, take a form and be attended by circumstances in which it would not be possible to apply strictly the ordinary rules of evidence, inasmuch as there would be no definite person against whom an accusation was pointed? There is, therefore, a material distinction between this and the Amendment of my hon. and learned Friend. It is provided in my Amendment that the rules of evidence shall be applied so far as is practicable in the circumstances of the particular examination.

THE CHAIRMAN: The only variation is in the reference to a charge against some person; and practically I think it is the same Amendment.

SIR CHARLES RUSSELL: Then I presume I shall be in Order in moving the latter part of the Amendment, which is the same as that standing in the name of the hon. and learned Member for Brigg (Mr. Waddy), providing that such witness may be examined concerning such offences only, and shall not be examined concerning any other matter or subject whatsoever?

THE CHAIRMAN: There is an Amendment in the name of the hon. and learned Member for North Longford (Mr. T. M. Healy); but, of course, with his consent, this Amendment may come first.

MR. T. M. HEALY: I will assent to anything; but the Amendment I propose to move now is that standing in my name relating to a frivolous summons. It provides that any person frivolously summoned or needlessly detained under this section shall be compensated. Now, the right hon. and learned Attorney General for Ireland (Mr. Holmes) has assured us that the Act in this respect will be used reasonably, and, therefore, my Amendment is but a reasonable one, for if a man is not needlessly detained then my Amendment will not arise. If he is unreasonably detained, which the Government say is not what they desire and expect, then my Amendment comes in. It is only reasonable, I think, and consonant with fair play—even British fair play—that a man should be compensated for time needlessly taken from him.

Amendment proposed,

In page 1, line 17, at the end of the words last inserted, to add—"Provided also any person previously summoned or needlessly detained under this section may maintain an action for loss of time, unless suitably compensated against the magistrate conducting the inquiry."—(Mr. T. M. Healy.)

THE ATTORNEY GENERAL FOR IRELAND (Mr. HOLMES) (Dublin University): I have already stated, in reference to another Amendment, that we shall make provision for the reasonable expenses of witnesses for their loss of time. Beyond that I do not think we can go. You cannot leave a magistrate open to actions, which would probably be brought in any case, whether a man were only detained a few minutes or longer.

MR. T. M. HEALY: Who is to be the judge of a reasonable amount of compensation? Suppose a magistrate has summoned a number of men, and in the course of examination gets out of temper, having an idea they have information they declare they have not. He may thereupon dismiss them with 6d. for their expenses, when they consider themselves entitled to 6s., but he bids them go about their business. My proposition is that there should be a reasonable sum given, and that someone should be liable for the payment. If the Government think that their magistrates should be protected, and should not be made the subjects of action, then let the action lie against the Attorney General—he is a good mark—only let someone be liable. But who are to be the judges else of reasonable compensation? Is there to be a Treasury Schedule? Or by what means is it to be settled?

MR. CHANCE (Kilkenny, S.): I do not see how the compensation is provided. If a man is taken from agricultural work in winter time probably a small amount will compensate him; but suppose he is summoned from his work in the middle of harvest time, and only receives 6d. or 1s. in return, much harm will be done to him. I really do not see why Resident Magistrates in Ireland should be elevated into a species of demi-gods. They have no such position here, and I do not see why ordinary laws should not apply to them. They are men liable to go wrong, and the fact of their being under the control of the Lord Lieutenant and the Chief Secretary is no guarantee that they will not go wrong; and we object to the Government, in this Bill, setting up these men as a tribunal that will be subject to no law, civil or criminal action, or anything else. We know perfectly well that if an action is taken against one of these men for assault, for an outrage on a woman, or any offence, however serious, there is the power of the Law Officers, and the money of the taxpayers, at their back for defence, and affidavits ready to be sworn to. It is no argument to say that these gentlemen might be put to inconvenience by such actions. Surely a procedure that applies to us all is good enough for Resident Magistrates? I trust the Amendment will be pressed to the very last; and I ask hon. Members to recollect what gigantic powers are to be given to these men; and that they are set up as authorities that cannot possibly go wrong. If that is so, then there is no fear of danger of them from this Amendment, especially as they would have the assistance of the Law Officers of the Crown.

MR. JOHN O'CONNOR (Tipperary, S.): I desire to present a couple of reasons why this Amendment should be accepted. The magistrate who will hold these inquiries relies entirely on the police of the district to furnish him with the names of persons to be summoned; and as it invariably happens that the police have a dislike to certain people in the district, they will, from these, furnish the magistrate with names indiscriminately, having no regard to their ability to give material evidence, but simply for purposes of persecution. I have known such cases to occur more than once in connection with similar provisions in the Prevention of Crimes Act of 1882. I know a case in which a young man was marked out by the police for such persecution, and they managed to attach so much suspicion and hardship to his position that eventually he was discharged from his employment, and an amount of injury inflicted upon him for which he could get no compensation. I have known young men summoned to these inquiries who had long forsaken politics, and who held high social positions among their fellows, so marked out for prosecution by the police that they have been compelled to throw up their employment and leave the country. Now, this Amendment would provide for some such chance of compensation, and, what is more, will be some surety against the indiscriminate and capricious use of the Act by magistrates, and will curb the over-zeal of policemen. These are solid and substantial reasons, drawn from my own experience of such provisions in a Coercion Act, to encourage the Committee to entertain the Amendment of my hon. and learned Friend, and I trust the Committee will give it that consideration it deserves.

MR. MARUM (Kilkenny, N,): Under the Crimes Prevention Act compensation was provided by the Attorney General. Will the latter say upon what scale it was given, and that he will provide the same here? Possibly that might meet our views.

MR. HOLMES: I am not aware that there was any scale in the Act to which the hon. Gentleman refers; but I propose in this case that there should be a reasonable sum paid for loss of time, having regard to the position in life of the witness.

MR. T. M. HEALY: Will the right hon. and learned Gentleman tell us how much money was given to any witness, or to any body of witnesses, under the Act of 1882?

MR. HOLMES: I had nothing to do with the operation of that Act; but I may say that I have seen accounts since I came into Office, and I know that considerable sums were paid to witnesses——

MR. T. M. HEALY: To informers!

MR. HOLMES: Paid to witnesses, or, at any rate, paid to their solicitors.

MR. T. M. HEALY: The right hon. and learned Gentleman says payments were made to solicitors. Now, there are no solicitors for witnesses under this Act, and I am speaking of these witnesses—what is the use of trying to humbug us? [*Cries of* "Order!"] I do not wish to use an offensive word. I withdraw it. What is the use of trying to deceive us—that, I believe, is a Parliamentary expression—in regard to expenses of these persons by alluding to payments made to solicitors? The sneer, too, of the right hon. and learned Attorney General, suggesting a doubt whether Irish solicitors paid their witnesses, is unworthy of him. Time was he was dependent upon solicitors, and would not then have sneered at them; but now he is to be a Judge, and will be dependent upon them no longer. My experience of solicitors does not lead me to pay any heed to the sneer, though I have heard some complaint against the Crown Solicitor, on the ground of non-payment of witnesses. But I know no ground why solicitors as a body should be attacked even by a Judge *in posse*.

MR. HOLMES: I trust that, whatever may be said on the other side, I may preserve the courtesies of debate. I answered a specific question. The hon. Member asked me had any money been paid to witnesses under the Act of 1882, and my answer was, that I had nothing to do with the administration of that Act, but that I knew that money was paid, because three or four accounts happened to come under my notice, and these were accounts furnished by solicitors, and included expenses of witnesses. A considerable sum was paid to solicitors in this way. This was the only matter raised in my answer to a specific question.

MR. T. M. HEALY (Longford, N.): That shows how right I was. You have negatived the Amendment which provided that the solicitor should be employed for the protection of the witnesses; therefore, how can you say that any solicitor got money under this section? No provision was ever made under this section of the Act of 1862 for paying witnesses' expenses. The hon. and learned Attorney General for Ireland says the expenses were paid to the solicitor of the prisoner. Now, he knows very well that he negatived the provision providing that the solicitor should be in attendance; and therefore, Sir, I say that he was wrong when he said that the expenses were paid to this solicitor. Now, I must ask who is to decide what are reasonable expenses for witnesses? Is it to be left to the Resident Magistrate to say? If it is, then he will make it a species of bribery. He will say—"You will not get your expenses unless you answer the question;" and he may also add—"Instead of giving you 5s., I will give you £5 for your expenses," so that the money will be paid in the shape of blood-money unless you provide some check in the form of the liability of the Resident Magistrates, on behalf of the Crown, for the damages being paid to witnesses in case they are frivolously detained. I also think you should declare what sum should be paid to witnesses.

MR. JAMES STUART (Shoreditch, Hoxton): I beg to move, Sir, that you report Progress.

THE FIRST LORD OF THE TREASURY (Mr. W. H. SMITH) (Strand, Westminster): I am very sorry, Sir, that this should be moved again. The Amendments to this section remaining to be discussed ought to be got rid of in a very few minutes; and I think hon. Members will admit that it is only reasonable that we should ask that this sub-section should be finally disposed of before the House adjourns. I cannot go back from what I said on this matter. We must dispose of these Amendments before the Government can agree to report Progress. I must say that I recognize, to the fullest extent, the reasonableness of the appeal which has been made to us by the hon. Member for Northampton (Mr. Bradlaugh). I have not the slightest wish to put any obstacle in the way of the discussion of the measure in which he takes so deep an interest. I will do nothing, so far as I am concerned, to put any obstacle in the way of the consideration of it; but I must remind the House that I am not delaying the Business. I have represented to the House the necessity of making progress with the Business of the House; and I appeal to right hon. and hon. Gentlemen opposite whether the amount of progress we have thought it our duty to insist on this evening is either excessive or unreasonable. I say, again, that if hon. Gentlemen below the Gangway will simply put the Amendments which they desire to take the verdict of the House upon them, having regard to the fact that the Government feel it necessary to ask for the powers which they have asked for under this section, they may surely be satisfied with allowing the Committee to go at once to a Division upon them. Of course, if hon. Gentlemen insist upon debating those Amendments they may delay the measure of the hon. Member for Northampton; but it is my duty, and I am sure I shall be supported by hon. Members, when I ask the House to dispose of these Amendments before progress is reported.

MR. JOHN MORLEY (Newcastle-upon-Tyne): The right hon. Gentleman has admitted very fairly that the appeal of my hon. Friend the Junior Member for Northampton (Mr. Bradlaugh) is a reasonable appeal, and the ground upon which he declines to accede to that proposal is that he insists upon getting to the end of certain sections of the clause now before the Committee. Well, Sir, my right hon. Friend the Member for Derby (Sir William Harcourt) said, about half or three-quarters of an hour ago, that at that time it was not unreasonable. But now I will ask the right hon. Gentleman whether what has hap-

Mr. Holmes

pened since then gives us any reason to hope that we shall, except at a very late hour in the morning, arrive at the point at which he desires to arrive. I must remind the hon. Gentleman opposite that we have been sitting in this House since 5 o'clock. I have been here myself most of the time from 5 until 2 this morning, with some short interruptions. The right hon. Gentleman has made a most extraordinary suggestion—that these proposals and Amendments should be put without any debate. Why, if we go on that principle, should not every other Amendment on the Paper be put, and not be debated? If we do that, we are simply abdicating the rights of the House and of hon. Members. I must say I think the appeal is a most reasonable one, considering the long time we have been sitting deliberating these clauses, and I do hope that the right hon. Gentleman will accede to it.

MR. W. H. SMITH: Right hon. Gentlemen opposite have already admitted that the contention of the Government is a very reasonable one. The right hon. Gentleman the Member for Derby said so, and so, also, did the hon. and learned Gentleman the Member for South Hackney——

SIR CHARLES RUSSELL (Hackney, S.): I did not say so.

MR. W. H. SMITH: Then I withdraw the statement that the hon. and learned Gentleman did say so; but I think he admitted it generally. What I wish to point out is this. The argument is that what was reasonable half-an-hour ago is not reasonable now, because there has been protracted discussion since that period. Now, Sir, I very greatly regret that there should be any difference of opinion upon this point. My desire is, as far as possible, to act in accordance with the good feeling and good sense of both sides of the House in the course which I intend to pursue. But, Sir, is Parliament to make progress with the Business of the country, or is it not? If discussion is to be carried on to the length to which the right hon. Gentleman thinks it may be reasonable, then Parliament breaks down her legislative machine.

MR. JOHN MORLEY: I did not say what length I thought would be reasonable.

MR. W. H. SMITH: I understand the right hon. Gentleman thought it reasonable that those Amendments should be discussed at the length at which these Amendments had been debated.

MR. JOHN MORLEY: No; I said that we should discuss the Amendments at reasonable length.

MR. W. H. SMITH: Then I leave it to the right hon. Gentleman to interpret what a reasonable length is. We have been discussing this sub-section, which consists of 17 lines, for three nights and a-half.

MR. T. M. HEALY (Longford, N.): And it ought to have been discussed three months.

MR. W. H. SMITH: I say again, that I very much regret that I cannot consent now to report Progress. I admit the reasonableness of the request of the junior Member for Northampton; but I would suggest that if he will use his influence with hon. Members sitting around him it may be possible for us soon to report Progress.

MR. JOHN MORLEY: One word of reply to what has just fallen from the right hon. Gentleman. It is quite true that we have discussed a very considerable number of Amendments; but I must point out that upon nearly every one of these Amendments the Government have given some sort of concession.

THE CHIEF SECRETARY FOR IRELAND (Mr. A. J. BALFOUR) (Manchester, E.): I must say that the return the Government have received for having made these concessions is a very extraordinary one. We have stretched every point we could, in order to conciliate the Opposition, and the only reward we get now is that our concessions are thrown in our teeth, and we are told that if we concede a thing we admit that it was right and proper that the matter should be brought forward.

MR. LABOUCHERE (Northampton): The right hon. Gentleman seems to forget that it takes a very long time indeed to induce the Government to make these very small concessions that they do. I can tell the House that we are not going to be bullied by the slaves of the Government. [*Long and continued interruption.*] We perfectly understand what these obstructive tactics mean. If the Bill of my hon. Friend and Colleague

(Mr. Bradlaugh) were not on the Paper for to-night, hon. Members opposite would have been perfectly ready to adjourn at 1 o'clock. Why do they, then, not agree to adjourn now? It is because the Bill of my hon. Friend does not happen to be blocked. I say that these perpetual appeals of the right hon. Gentleman the Leader of the House to do Business are a farce, and are an insult to this House. I say, the obstructives are there on the other side of the House. We understand Parliamentary tactics. We understand how Gentlemen want to talk out the Bill of my hon. Friend. They have promised their constituents to do two things; they have promised to vote for it, and they have also promised to vote against it, and they do not see how they can reconcile their two pledges, so they want to shirk the matter altogether. They may make up their minds to this—that not one line more, not one additional word of this Bill, shall, if I can help it, be allowed to pass to-night, and I will stay here until to-morrow morning if no one else does, and keep on moving to report Progress.

Mr. CHAPLIN (Lincolnshire, Sleaford) then rose to speak, and for nearly five minutes was unable to obtain a hearing.

Mr. SEAGER HUNT (Marylebone, N.) also rose; but the cries of "Divide, divide!" were so loud that neither could be heard.

The CHAIRMAN: Order, order! The hon. Member for North Fermanagh (Mr. W. Redmond) is continually interrupting the speaker. I must warn him that if he continues I shall have to draw attention to his conduct. I call upon Mr. Chaplin.

Mr. CHAPLIN again rose, and again was unable to obtain a hearing.

The CHAIRMAN: Order, order! I have already told the hon. Member for North Fermanagh that I have observed him continually interrupting the speaker. I shall have to bring him under the notice of the House.

Mr. W. REDMOND (Fermanagh, N.): I have not interrupted. [*Loud cries of* "Oh, oh!"]

The CHAIRMAN: Order, order! I must ask hon. Gentlemen to be good enough to observe order themselves. [*Loud Opposition cheers.*] I address this to all sections of the House.

Mr. Labouchere

Mr. W. REDMOND: I am very much obliged to you, Sir, for making that statement. If hon. Members opposite had not interrupted me, they would have heard what I was about to say. I did not interrupt hon. Members in the slightest degree more than hon. Members opposite interrupted hon. Members on this side of the House. Sir, I draw your attention to the fact, which cannot have escaped your attention, that hon. Members opposite commence these scenes.

The CHAIRMAN: Order, order! The conduct of the hon. Member was very conspicuous.

Mr. CHAPLIN (Lincolnshire, Sleaford): I will not detain the Committee for more than a single moment. I was merely about to observe that the right hon. Gentleman the Member for Newcastle (Mr. John Morley) put a question to the Government as to whether it was conceivable that we could conclude this section within a reasonable time in the morning. Now, I would point out that everything that can be said in support of the remaining Amendments has already been said over and over again within the last three-quarters of an hour. The hon. Gentleman the senior Member for Northampton (Mr. Labouchere) informed us a few moments ago that no further progress whatever should be made unless the clôture was applied, and that we should amuse ourselves by walking through the Lobbies during the rest of the night. I venture, Sir, to say, with all respect for the hon. Gentleman, that that is a menace and a threat which he has no right to address to the House of Commons; and if that is the way in which the reasonable appeals of my right hon. Friend the Leader of the House are met, I hope that he will resort to all the Forms of the House to enable him to carry out his proposal. I say I agree that the appeal made by the hon. Member for Northampton (Mr. Bradlaugh) is a reasonable one, and I willingly recognize the moderation of his language. I will exonerate him, at all events, from obstruction; but I wish to point this out—that when he has already twice appealed to my right hon. Friend, he would now do well to appeal to his Friends on his own side of the House who are obstructing the progress of the Bill; for in their hands, and in the hands of his Colleague, rests entirely the question when the necessary stage will be reached.

MR. T. P. O'CONNOR (Liverpool, Scotland): I can assure the right hon. Gentleman who last addressed the Committee that there is every desire on these Benches to extend to him that courtesy which his long services in this House entitle him to; and if the right hon. Gentleman were interrupted at all, I can assure him that the interruption was not directed against him personally. It was a form of retaliation forced on hon. Members on this side of the House by the manner in which his Colleagues treated hon. Members on this side. Now, Mr. Courtney, I hope that we have done with these scenes, and that we may be able to go on discussing these Amendments in that spirit of fair play and good humour which should characterize all our proceedings in this House. I object very strongly to the manner in which the right hon. Gentleman the Leader of the House (Mr. W. H. Smith) deals with this question. I object to this system of debate—to his plan of measuring the value of clauses from the point of view of a carpenter measuring wood by inches. The right hon. Gentleman says that this clause, consisting of only 17 lines, has already occupied three nights and-a-half; but I venture to say that the importance of a clause does not turn upon the exact number of lines in it. Why, one line in a clause of a Bill may be more important than 1,000 Acts of Parliament consisting of 10,000, or even 1,000,000 lines. The proper way to measure the importance of a clause is not by the number of words or lines which it contains, but by the principles which underlie the words; and I venture to suggest that three and a-half nights is the very scantiest allowance of time which could have been bestowed upon a clause of this importance. The second proposal laid down by the right hon. Gentleman is that we must get to the end of a certain sub-section—that we must go by a sort of rule of thumb in measuring out what Business is to be transacted in a given time. We are not to study the importance of the clause; we are simply to look to the number of lines dealt with. His third proposition is a most extraordinary one, and I must say I never heard a more astounding proposition made to this House. He says that if hon. Members on these Benches would only put their Amendments without any discussion, then we could soon get to the point he wishes to arrive at. But as my right hon. Friend the Member for Newcastle (Mr. John Morley) says, if we adopt that policy the House will be abdicating its functions; it will be admitting that there are no arguments to be advanced in support of the proposals which we have made. I say, Sir, that this is a monstrous proposition. It would mean an entire transformation of this Assembly and its deliberative character into a mere Chamber to record whatever decisions may recommend themselves to the Ministerial majority for the time being. I must say the right hon. Gentleman seems grossly to misconceive the whole purpose of this Assembly, and to suggest that we should adopt a course which no Party with any sense of duty, and with any self-respect, could accept. I am sorry the Oaths Bill is delayed, and I am willing to give the First Lord of the Treasury credit for his good intentions; but I cannot help being exceedingly suspicious when I find that the master of a majority, with his Whips, officials, and means of maintaining his authority, should allow discussion to be prolonged, which has had the effect of diminishing the numerical strength of the supporters of the Oaths Bill. If the right hon. Gentleman was anxious to defeat the Bill or prevent discussion upon it, he could not have adopted a course more adapted to that end. For my part, I think we might now divide on the Motion to report Progress. My hon. and learned Friend (Mr. T. M. Healy) has undertaken, I understand, to withdraw two of his Amendments, and only desires a short discussion of the third, but his fair proposal met with no response. If we had been allowed to proceed, we might have cleared the Paper of several Amendments by this time, even though we did not arrive at the end of the sub-section.

Question put.

The Committee *divided*:—Ayes 176; Noes 249: Majority 73.—(Div. List, No. 116.)   [2.40 A.M.]

Question again proposed, "That those words be there inserted."

MR. T. M. HEALY (Longford, N.): The Government might, I think, tell us exactly what the scale and method of compensation would be. How is the money to be paid? Under ordinary circumstances, it would be paid to a solicitor; but here you have neither Crown Solicitor or solicitor for the witness. I object to the payment being from the magistrate direct to the witness, for I think it would open wide possibilities of corruption. If we are to discuss this matter at this late hour, let us do so seriously, with a sense of duty and a desire to make progress. Therefore, I put this reasonable point when I say let us know who is to pay this money, and on what scale is it to be paid. That, I think, is a reasonable demand to make before we go further with the discussion.

MR. W. H. SMITH: An answer has already been given. I beg to move that the Question be now put.

Question put accordingly, "That the Question be now put."

The Committee *divided:*—Ayes 249; Noes 170: Majority 79.—(Div. List, No. 117.)   [2.50 A.M.]

Question put, "That those words be there inserted."

The Committee *divided:*—Ayes 150; Noes 250: Majority 100.—(Div. List, No. 118.)   [3.0 A.M.]

Motion made, and Question put, "That the Chairman do report Progress, and ask leave to sit again."—(*Mr. Labouchere.*)

The Committee *divided:*—Ayes 170; Noes 248: Majority 78.—(Div. List, No. 119.)   [3.10 A.M.]

Motion made, and Question proposed, "That the Chairman do now leave the Chair."—(*Mr. Wallace.*)

MR. CONYBEARE (Cornwall, Camborne): It appears to me desirable that we should take stock of the situation. Not that I have any desire to review in detail the whole of the proceedings of to-night; but it must be apparent to every *habitué* of this Assembly, and as there are rather more *habitués* on this than on the other side of the House, this affords the opportunity of teaching them what is likely to go on. It must be obvious that if the Government do not see the desirability of allowing us to go home very shortly, we shall certainly not get on with any other Business.

MR. W. H. SMITH rose in his place, and claimed to move, "That the Question be now put."

Mr. T. M. Healy

Question put accordingly, "That the Question be now put."

The Committee *divided:*—Ayes 248; Noes 160: Majority 88.—(Div. List, No. 120.)   [3.35 A.M.]

Question put, "That the Chairman do now leave the Chair."

The Committee *divided:*—Ayes 162; Noes 245: Majority 83.—(Div. List, No. 121.)   [3.50 A.M.]

The FIRST LORD of the TREASURY and Mr. ESSLEMONT (Aberdeen, E.) rose simultaneously, and The CHAIRMAN called upon the FIRST LORD of the TREASURY.

MR. CHANCE (Kilkenny, S.): I rise to a point of Order, Sir. I beg to say the hon. Member for East Aberdeen first rose.

THE CHAIRMAN: I have given my decision for Mr. Smith.

MR. W. H. SMITH rose in his place, and claimed to move that the Question "That the words 'the enactments,' in page 1, line 18, stand part of the Clause, be now put."

THE CHAIRMAN: The Question put in my hands is that the words down to "enactment," in line 18, be now put. If that Amendment were put, Amendments Nos. 57, 58, 59, 60, 61, and 62 on the Paper, besides two others in manuscript, would be passed over. As far as I can judge by viewing these Amendments, Amendments 59 and 60 possibly deserve some discussion and a vote. I am unwilling, therefore, to put the Question until some further time has been given and an opportunity afforded, not necessarily of a long character, during which hon. Members who have put on the Paper these Amendments, to which I have signified that I attach little importance, may allow the other Amendments to be discussed and a vote taken upon them. Therefore, for the present, I do not put the Question.

MR. CHANCE: I rise, Sir, to a point of Order.

MR. T. M. HEALY (Longford, N.): Dry up. Sit down.

MR. CHANCE: My point of Order, Sir, is that I have an Amendment which is not on the Paper. Do I understand that you rule my Amendment out of Order?

THE CHAIRMAN: I said besides those on the Paper there are two Amendments in manuscript, one of which is in the name of the hon. Member.

MR. T. M. HEALY: May I ask, Sir, which is the Amendment of mine to which you attach importance?

THE CHAIRMAN: The Amendment standing in the name of the hon. Member to which I attach importance is No. 60. I will ask the hon. Member if he intends to propose Nos. 57 and 58?

MR. T. M. HEALY: Do I gather, Sir, that you say Nos. 57 and 58 are not to be moved?

THE CHAIRMAN: I intimated that I attached myself very little importance to them.

MR. T. M. HEALY: In deference to that, Sir, I will not move them.

SIR CHARLES RUSSELL (Hackney, S.): I have to move, Mr. Courtney, the Amendment which stands in the name of my hon. and learned Friend the Member for the Brigg Division of Lincolnshire (Mr. Waddy); but I venture to make a slight alteration—namely—

"Provided always that such witness may be examined concerning such offence only, and shall not be examined concerning any other matter or subject whatsoever."

Now, Sir, I understand from what has passed in the early part of the evening that the Government admit the substance of the Amendment, but their objection is that it is unnecessary, because they say its object is already provided for, and covered by a part of the clause which has already been passed. They found that argument on the provision in line 10. I am quite prepared to admit that if their inference from these words is a correct one that the Amendment is not necessary, but my object in moving it is to make it explicit. I want to make it clear that the examination of the magistrate shall be conversant only with the one offence, and that he shall not have power to conduct a fishing examination or inquiry outside the subject-matter of the offence alleged. At this hour of the morning I do not propose to trouble the Committee further; but I do hope the right hon. Gentleman the First Lord of the Treasury will see his way to accept my Amendment.

Amendment proposed,

In page 1, line 17, at the end of the foregoing Amendment, to add the words "such witness may only be examined concerning such offence, and shall not be examined concerning any other matter or subject whatsoever."—(*Sir Charles Russell.*)

Question proposed, "That those words be there added."

THE ATTORNEY GENERAL (Sir RICHARD WEBSTER) (Isle of Wight): I submit, Sir, that there is no necessity whatever for these words. The power given to the magistrate is distinct that he shall examine as to such offence. If the first part of this Amendment is inserted it will really be a repetition of the words preceding it, and in my opinion it might lead to misconstruction. I do not think that any magistrate could possibly misunderstand his functions under the clause as it stands, and, therefore, I regret that it is not in my power to accept the Amendment.

SIR CHARLES RUSSELL: I wish by this Amendment to make it clear to magistrates—a body of men not particularly well skilled in these matters, and in whose administration of this Act, as the Committee will see, there is no great amount of confidence felt by the Irish people—I wish, as I say, to give them a clear indication that they shall not be entitled to go beyond matters concerning the offence which is being inquired into. I will put it to the Committee—my hon. and learned Friend the Attorney General says that these words are unnecessary. If so, they can do no harm, and I humbly submit that they will do good. Therefore, I urge the Committee to accept them.

MR. T. P. O'CONNOR (Liverpool, Scotland): I am unwilling to prolong the debate, especially after the scenes we have just had; but I take it that, although the Amendment is a plain one, the answer of the hon. and learned Attorney General was utterly irrelevant. So I think it is our duty to press the Government a little further. The hon. and learned Attorney General said that the Amendment of the hon. and learned Member for South Hackney (Sir Charles Russell) would undoubtedly limit the authority of the magistrate, who might think, if these words were inserted, that he would be deprived of the power of examining the person before him with regard to other persons charged with the offence. I will put it this way. The magistrate has a man brought before him. He asks him if "A" committed the crime. The answer being in the negative, the magistrate puts another question, and this time asks him if "B" committed the crime. The hon.

and learned Attorney General says— "Oh, but the magistrate would be precluded from asking whether 'B' committed the crime if these words are put in." How on Heaven can he make that out? The words of the Amendment would not prevent the magistrate from asking questions with regard to the particular offence, or with regard to any particular person who might be involved in it. That is the only objection, so far as I can understand, that the hon. and learned Gentleman has to make to the Amendment. Does the hon. and learned Gentleman really mean to say that if these words were inserted a magistrate would not have the right of examining upon matters brought before him with regard to every person and every circumstance affecting it? I am astonished at the unreasonable attitude taken up, and I am still more astonished at the absurd arguments that a man of his acuteness has put before us.

DR. CLARK (Caithness): This is one of the cases in which officers in Scotland have somewhat similar powers; and when we come to the stage of Supply, I shall bring before the House a great number of cases where Procurators Fiscal in Scotland, in making inquiries regarding crimes, have asked political questions with regard to political meetings. In my own county the Procurator Fiscal called together the members of my committee, and asked them questions regarding my meetings, and what took place at them. When we come into Supply I will bring a number of these cases before the House, and I shall move to reduce the salaries of these Procurators Fiscal. I think we should have a limit to the exercise of similar powers in Ireland.

MR. BRADLAUGH (Northampton): The condition imposed by the right hon. Gentleman the Leader of the House, that the Amendments should be taken without debate, can, to my mind, hardly have been a fair condition in view of the decision which has recently been given from the Chair.

Question put.

The Committee *divided:*—Ayes 165; Noes 242: Majority 77.—(Div. List, No. 122.) [4.15 A.M.]

MR. T. M. HEALY (Longford, N.): Earlier in the night I deferred moving this Amendment, and had some hope

Mr. T. P. O'Connor

the Government would meet me with a concession. I now move it without another word.

Amendment proposed,

In page 1, line 17, after the words last inserted, add—" Provided also when any person has been arrested for the crime to which such inquiry relates, no further examinations of witnesses shall take place under this section except in the presence of the accused, who may examine or cross-examine them either by himself or by counsel or solicitor."—(*Mr. T. M. Healy.*)

Question proposed, "That those words be there added."

THE CHIEF SECRETARY FOR IRELAND (Mr. A. J. BALFOUR) (Manchester, E.): There are good reasons why the inquiry should go on, and, unless there is evidence for the prosecution obtained, no reason why the inquiry should cease, or take place under conditions the Committee had already rejected.

MR. T. M. HEALY: The Government would stultify themselves, I suppose, if they accepted the Amendment. I will not attempt now to convince anybody—even the right hon. Gentleman the First Lord of the Treasury—but will take an opportunity of raising the question in another form. I withdraw the Amendment.

Amendment, by leave, *withdrawn.*

MR. W. H. SMITH rose in his place, and claimed to move that the Question, "That the words 'the enactments' in page 1, line 18, stand part of the Clause."

MR. T. M. HEALY: Is there any objection to my moving the Amendment, which I think the Government might accept, providing that notice of every inquiry should be published in *The Dublin Gazette?*

THE CHAIRMAN: The hon. and learned Member would not be in Order, after this Motion is made, in raising any discussion at all.

MR. T. M. HEALY: This is the Closure Motion?

THE CHAIRMAN: Yes, it is.

Question put accordingly, and *agreed to.*

MR. T. M. HEALY (speaking seated and with head covered): On a point of Order, Sir, seeing that it is the intention of the Government to dispose of the subsection, will not the carrying of the first word of the following line answer their purpose?

THE CHAIRMAN: It will be competent for the hon. and learned Member to move Amendments after the word "enactment."

MR. CONYBEARE (speaking seated and with head covered): Were there not Amendments handed in to you in manuscript that might be put?

THE CHAIRMAN: These were referred to in my previous observations.

Committee report Progress; to sit again *To-morrow.*

OATHS BILL.—[BILL 104.]

(Mr. Bradlaugh, Sir John Simon, Mr. Courtney Kenny, Mr. Burt, Mr. Coleridge, Mr. Illingworth, Mr. Richard, Mr. Jesse Collings.)

SECOND READING.

Order for Second Reading read.

Motion made, and Question proposed, "That the Bill be now read a second time."—(*Mr. Bradlaugh.*)

MR. DE LISLE (Leicestershire, Mid): I beg leave to move that the House do now adjourn. In making this Motion I do not wish to be uncourteous, or intend to be unfair, towards the hon. Member for Northampton (Mr. Bradlaugh), who is specially interested in this Bill. Let me say I am equally interested in the matter, and I do not think it is reasonable to enter upon a measure of such importance at such an hour (4.30 A.M.). Its importance has been acknowledged by the Party opposite below the Gangway, for though I was not in the House I remember that, a few years ago, they voted against a Bill not so comprehensive as this Bill—the Parliamentary Oaths Bill—for substituting an Affirmation for the usual Oath at that Table. The Bill is of great importance, and is so felt to be by the great body of my constituents. I beseech the House to defer the consideration of it to a more reasonable time, and let us now retire to our rest.

Motion made, and Question proposed, "That this House do now adjourn."— (*Mr. De Lisle.*)

MR. BRADLAUGH (Northampton): No one doubts the great interest of the hon. Member who has moved the adjournment of the House in the measure now before us; he has shown that interest by blocking the Bill. The hon. Member says he desires to be courteous towards me. I have no desire he should be courteous towards me, but I have a desire that he should be fair towards this measure. I quite agree that at this hour it would be an absurdity to discuss a measure, however insignificant. I do not, therefore, intend to oppose the Motion beyond testing—by the votes of hon. Members present, without any long debate on the adjournment —opinion on the Bill; and I will ask those who are voting for the adjournment to remember that they are really voting against the Bill. If a Division could have been taken some few hours earlier there would have been more votes on this side. I trust the hon. Member, with his professions of courtesy, will show it by not blocking the measure in the future; for I feel sure he would not have professed courtesy now if he had already handed in a block to prevent it coming on again. I will not, then, put the Bill down again for to-day, but will leave some time longer for its consideration.

THE SOLICITOR GENERAL (Sir EDWARD CLARKE) (Plymouth): I may remind the House that earlier in the Sitting my right hon. Friend the First Lord of the Treasury (Mr. W. H. Smith) said he had no desire to use his influence to prevent the Bill being brought forward for second reading; and after the statement now made by the hon. Member for Northampton, I hope hon. Members will not think it necessary to go through the form of a Division, for this reason—that before any decision upon its principle be taken it should be fairly discussed. There is one aspect in which I am certainly anxious to see the Bill passed; it would certainly, whatever else it does—it would harmonize judicial procedure in this country in regard to juries, witnesses, and——

MR. BRADLAUGH: I rise to Order, Sir. I carefully refrained from going into the merits of this Bill myself, and I ask, is the hon. and learned Solicitor General in Order in going into the provisions of the Bill on a Motion for Adjournment?

MR. SPEAKER: The Motion before the House is the Motion for Adjournment.

SIR EDWARD CLARKE: I was aware of the Motion; but I did not think I was trespassing on the Rules in pointing out reasons for not pressing the

Motion now. I hope the hon. Member for Mid Leicestershire will not persist. The hon. Member for Northampton has fairly earned the step for the Bill at this hour of the morning, and I think it might be taken, it being quite understood that the discussion will be taken on the next stage.

DR. CAMERON (Glasgow, College): May I point out that the hon. Member, if he carried his Motion for Adjournment, would shut out all other Bills on the Orders? If he would confine his Motion to an adjournment of the debate he would not prejudice other Bills.

MR. STANLEY LEIGHTON (Shropshire, Oswestry): I hope my hon. Friend the Member for Mid Leicestershire will go to a Division, that we may make a protest against the weakness of the Government in not either bringing in a Bill of this sort themselves or else opposing this Bill. If the Government think such a Bill should be brought forward, let them undertake it; if not, let them stand to their guns and oppose the change. Where is the Leader of the House? Where are the Cabinet? They have all fled precipitately in a body. They have left the conduct of the debate to their Solicitor General. Questions of morality are ill-handled by practising barristers. The late Prime Minister used to resign the Leadership whenever a vote on this question was taken, though he always remained in the House. But the First Lord of the Treasury evidently considers that in such a crisis absence of body is better than presence of mind.

MR. T. M. HEALY (Longford, N.): Let me point out that if this Motion is carried now there will be a double wrong. I understand that the Question for second reading is put?

MR. SPEAKER: Yes; but it was followed by an amending Motion, that this House do now adjourn.

MR. T. M. HEALY: If the Motion is carried, the Bill becomes a dropped Order, and the hon. Member for Northampton could not move his Bill another night without a Motion to set it up again, which might be opposed by the hon. Member for Mid Leicestershire.

COMMANDER BETHELL (York, E.R., Holderness): I must take exception to the statement that Members voting for the adjournment are voting against the Bill. I shall vote for the adjournment, but I should have voted for the Bill.

Sir Edward Clarke

MR. T. P. O'CONNOR (Liverpool, Scotland): Yes; but by voting for the adjournment now the hon. and gallant Member votes for the destruction of the Bill, for this is not simply a Motion for the adjournment of the debate, the carrying of which would give him an opportunity of voting for the Bill on another occasion. If this Motion is carried, all chance of voting upon the Bill itself will be lost. In passing allusion to the remark of the hon. Member for the Oswestry Division of Shropshire (Mr. Stanley Leighton), in which he called on the Government, if they intended to see a Bill of this kind passed, to bring it in themselves, I beg to say that the worst chance for passing a Bill was to entrust it to a Government, the Leader of which is discredited.

THE SECRETARY TO THE TREASURY (Mr. JACKSON) (Leeds, N.): The observation of the hon. Gentleman is a little misleading. I understood him to say that if this Motion were carried it would involve the destruction of the Bill.

MR. T. P. O'CONNOR: For this Session.

MR. JACKSON: I understand that the Bill might be set down to-morrow, for the Thursday, at the same stage; therefore it would not mean the destruction of the Bill.

MR. BRADLAUGH: On the question of Order, may I ask what would be the effect if the Motion for the adjournment were carried, you, Sir, having put the Question for the second reading?

MR. SPEAKER: The effect of the Motion being carried would be that the Bill would be dropped from the Order Book. It could be revived on Notice, to-morrow, by an ordinary Motion.

MR. BRADLAUGH: On the question of Order, may I ask whether that Motion could be made the subject of a "block?"

MR. SPEAKER: It would be subject to the same condition as now.

MR. T. M. HEALY: It would be competent to oppose the Motion to set up the Bill?

MR. SPEAKER: Yes; the block might be interposed at any moment.

Question put.

The House *divided:*—Ayes 104; Noes 195: Majority 91.—(Div. List, No. 123.)

[4.40 A.M.]

Original Question again proposed.

THE UNDER SECRETARY OF STATE FOR FOREIGN AFFAIRS (Sir JAMES FERGUSSON) (Manchester, N.E.): The Division which has taken place indicates a good deal of cross voting; but I hope before the Bill is read we shall take a Division on the Main Question, when I, for one, shall certainly vote against the second reading, for I think it would be unworthy of the House of Commons, and unworthy of the Party to which I belong, not to take the opportunity of asserting at least once their desire to keep in public Affirmations an appeal to the Supreme Being, in token of fidelity to our engagements.

COLONEL HUGHES (Woolwich): I was at first under the impression that this Bill related only to Parliamentary Oaths; but I find that it relates to our whole system of law, and witnesses and anyone else may make an Affirmation, omitting the appeal to the Deity on the truth of their statements. This, I think, would be a great misfortune for our country and for the course of justice. It is a very important matter, indeed, too important for the House to pass lightly over, coming to a Division almost without debate, probably even passing the second reading, at the end of a long Sitting devoted to other Business, at 5 in the morning. I hope we have sufficient knowledge of our duty in this Christian country to press the importance of this upon hon. Members of the House. I have listened frequently and with great pain to quotations from Scripture used to point a joke or sarcasm, but I think there are deeper feelings that will make themselves felt, and should have a definite way of expressing themselves. Certainly, to pass this Bill now without full debate would be a most imprudent thing for the Conservative Party to do. I shall oppose such a course, and would, if it were the best means of doing so, move an adjournment of the debate.

Motion made, and Question proposed, "That the Debate be now adjourned." —(*Mr. Byron Reed.*)

MR. BRADLAUGH (Northampton): I feel that I should be in the highest degree unwise, on the Motion for Adjournment, to allow myself to be influenced by words which have no relation whatever to the measure before the House. I deeply regret this opposition to the second reading, and I specially regret it if any act of mine should have given a Party colour to the Division which has just been taken, because I quite feel that a large number of hon. Members on the other side of the House who have voted did so with the intention of supporting what they considered to be a reasonable change in the law apart from any Party conflict. I shall ask the House to divide on the Question of the adjournment of the debate. I quite feel it is in the power of hon. Members opposite to hinder further discussion, but it is due to hon. Members that I should take at least one Division on it.

MR. GEDGE (Stockport): I really have a good deal to say on this subject, not on religious grounds, but on the practical grounds of obtaining the truth in Courts of Justice, of which I have had considerable experience. I shall be prepared to speak on this subject, even at this hour in the morning, if hon. Members will listen to me; but, seeing that the House has now been sitting over 12 hours, it is scarcely likely we can go into the subject as it deserves. Therefore, I must support the Motion for Adjournment, because I wish to insure a full discussion of this important Bill on its second reading.

MR. ILLINGWORTH (Bradford, W.): I wish to make an appeal to hon. Members opposite. I think it is necessary in order to clear the Government supporters from the suspicion that the protracted debate on an earlier measure was carried on for the purpose of preventing this Bill being read a second time. If the Bill is read a second time, I believe my hon. Friend the Member for Northampton (Mr. Bradlaugh) will give an undertaking not to press it further until the House has had a fair opportunity of discussing it. I make this appeal to withdraw the Motion in the interests of the hon. and learned Gentleman the Solicitor General, and I would point out that a very large number of hon. Members have stayed behind for this Bill, thus showing the deep interest they feel in it. I hope we shall make some progress with it.

MR. BARTLEY (Islington, N.): Although I sit on this side of the House, I strongly support the Motion of the hon. Member for Northampton (Mr. Bradlaugh). I do trust hon. Members on this side of the House will not press this

Motion to a Division. I like to be as fair and as square as I can; and it seems to me that this is simply an obstructive Motion. We have just had a Division, there has been an overwhelming majority, and even if I were opposed to the Bill, I should say the vote should be taken as settling the question. When we object to factious opposition, and to fictitious Amendments coming from the other side of the House, we certainly ought not to imitate those tactics. I, therefore, urge most strongly that this further Motion for Adjournment should not be pressed, and that we should go to a Division on the Main Question.

COLONEL BLUNDELL (Lancashire, S.W., Ince): The opposition to this Bill is no factious opposition; the question is whether the evidence of witnesses given on oath is more reliable than evidence not given on oath. I think that anyone who has seen witnesses being sworn before giving evidence, and has noticed how some witnesses have attempted to kiss the thumb and so avoid kissing the Book, will have formed a strong opinion as to whether testimony on oath is necessary to insure eliciting the truth, but no stronger confirmation of the importance of evidence being given on oath than was furnished only the other day by the hon. Member who brought in this Bill.

MR. SPEAKER: Order, order! The Motion before the House is the adjournment of the debate. The hon. Member is not entitled to go into other matters.

MR. JOHNSTON (Belfast, S.): I think a fair course now to be taken is for the Motion for the adjournment to be withdrawn. Let us take a Division on the second reading. I am entirely opposed to the Bill, and shall vote against it. I think we should have a fair and square debate upon it.

MR. DE LISLE (Leicestershire, Mid): I have no wish to prolong the debate; but I wish it to be understood that before the Bill goes to a second reading I shall certainly claim the privilege of an independent Tory Member of this House, and give my reasons for voting against it.

Question put.

The House *divided:*—Ayes 87; Noes 191: Majority 104.—(Div. List, No. 124.) [5.20 A.M.]

Mr. Bartley

Original Question again proposed.

MR. J. G. HUBBARD (London): It is quite evident that a majority of the House desire the second reading. This professes to be a Bill to amend the law relating to oaths, and it should, therefore, give an increased value to oaths and affirmations either as promissory declarations or as evidence in Courts of Law; but would that be its effect? If we assent to the second reading now, it is with the distinct understanding that the Bill has careful consideration in its future stages. I do not deny that there may be certain cases in which an alteration of the law may tend to promote the interests of justice; but, at the same time, I say, although we may accept it now, it will not be allowed to proceed without prolonged and careful consideration, for its provisions are of a very sweeping character, and we may find it necessary to introduce large and important Amendments in Committee.

MR. BRADLAUGH (Northampton): I will only say that I quite accept this statement in the spirit in which it is made, and it is in accord with what was said earlier by the Solicitor General— that the fullest discussion should be taken at another stage.

MR. GEDGE (Stockport): I do not understand how we can assent to the second reading of a Bill without thereby admitting its principle, and I am not prepared to do that. I am sorry to take up time at this late hour, and that I have to do so without that preparation I should have liked to give to the subject. I am not going to argue the question on religious grounds, as that has been done already by others; and I may say at once that, so far as promissory oaths are concerned, I set very little value by them. I know there is a strong feeling in favour of them in many parts of the House; but, at the same time, I must admit that those who take promissory oaths of allegiance to Her Majesty are no better subjects than those who do not, nor is there any difference in the result in the Army between privates who do and officers who do not take the oath. I doubt very much whether any promissory oath of allegiance ever prevented a man from becoming a traitor to his Sovereign or his country when so inclined. On the other hand, when we come to deal with oaths in a Court of Justice, experience shows that we cannot attach the same value to evidence whether sworn to or not, and to point the distinction I may refer to the action of the hon. Member for Northampton (Mr. Bradlaugh) himself, who, when a short time ago he desired an inquiry to be made into transactions connected with the Corporation of London, was anxious to have witnesses examined upon oath. I do not at all believe that this was done merely in order that those who gave evidence should render themselves liable to the penalty attaching to perjury.

MR. BRADLAUGH: I said it was proposed solely for the purpose of being able to proceed with a prosecution for perjury.

MR. GEDGE: I did not hear that, and should be sorry to impute to the hon. Member that for which I had no warrant. We do not believe that the sanctity given to the truth when a witness takes an oath springs entirely from the fear of punishment for perjury. There is a feeling that when a man calls upon God to witness the truth of his statement, he, if that statement is false, commits a greater sin than if he was merely telling a lie. I do not say that the feeling has very much weight with me, yet, having had experience for years in Courts of Justice, I am bound to acknowledge the difference there is between the affirmative statement and the giving of evidence on oath. Over and over again I have had to notice this difference. In the first instance, a solicitor takes a careful note of a statement for the instruction of counsel, and afterwards you take down the statement in a more precise way in the form in which it is to be presented in Court; and I have continually found with even educated people, religious people, that when reminded that the statement will be made on oath there comes a pause, and the witness, drawing a long breath, says—"Yes; I said that, but if I am to swear to it "—then he begins to think about it, and finally the statement becomes more accurate. I do not say this would be so with enlightened minds of hon. Members in this House; but I say it is the continual experience of those who have to take the evidence of ordinary people. You may say that a man may object to taking an oath against his conscientious scruples; but these are the people who would not think of telling a lie at which the unscrupulous man would not hesitate, in either case. Has anyone seen a Jew of low class give evidence? I do not for a moment say that Jews are less scrupulous than other people. Has it not been known for a Jew to lift his hat off when taking the oath in order to take it in such a manner that he may flatter himself that any want of truth in his statement will be less important, because the oath is not binding, in his opinion, unless he keeps his hat on in the proper fashion. Again, I recollect an important case in Chancery in which Sir John Karslake was engaged as my counsel; it was necessary to prove that a certain claimant was legitimate. That the father and mother were married there was no doubt, but there was a shrewd suspicion that the father was married before, and that his wife was living at the time of the second marriage. Affidavits were filed on either side, and the attempt was made to establish the inference that there had been a Scotch marriage between the husband and his first wife, and several Scotch witnesses had made affidavits to the effect that the first wife was living at the time of the second marriage. These witnesses had sworn to these affidavits in the English form—that is, they signed their names and kissed a Testament—they were brought up to London to be cross-examined, and took the oath in the Presbyterian fashion, holding up the right hand; each in turn, when cross-examined by Sir John Karslake, swore diametrically opposite to the facts in his affidavit. He swore he was a God-fearing man, and when he was confronted with his name to the affidavit, he said—"That is my name; but I did not swear to that as I do now, and it is not equally binding on my conscience." And said Sir John Karslake—"You call yourself a God-fearing man?"—"Yes."—"Then you may leave the box." I might give other illustrations to show the effect upon some minds of going through the ceremony of taking an oath. In Criminal Courts we know that care is taken that a witness shall not kiss his thumb instead of the book. However superstitious this may be, we have to take account of these things and their effect upon our endeavours to elicit the truth. There is a vast difference in the minds of people—not always among the most ignorant classes—between lying and perjuring themselves, quite apart from the punishment that attaches to the latter. However foolish that may be, however we may look forward to the time when it shall cease to be, I say, at the present time, we cannot leave it open to a witness to exercise his option whether he will swear or not, for if he intends to lie he will not swear, and will salve his conscience with the idea that a lie unsworn to does not matter. Therefore, I must vote against the second reading of the Bill.

Mr. MARK STEWART (Kirkcudbright): From a deep sense of personal duty, and feeling sure that my feeling is one that animates a large number in and outside the House, I must protest against proceeding with such a measure at 6 o'clock in the morning. It is absolutely ridiculous to attempt to do so. To attempt to discuss the bearings of the question now is sheer nonsense. It is due to the country that the matter should be fully discussed, and I, therefore, move the adjournment of the House.

Mr. TOMLINSON (Preston): I second that Motion.

Motion made, and Question proposed, "That this House do now adjourn."— (*Mr. Mark Stewart.*)

Mr. BRADLAUGH: I should not do wisely to attempt to prolong a series of Divisions. I admit that the offer of the hon. and learned Gentleman the Solicitor General (Sir Edward Clarke) was an exceedingly fair one, and the Government have given evidence of their desire to carry it out by voting in each of the Divisions with me. [An hon. Member: No; not all the Government.] Well, some Members of the Government did. I do not wish to imply more. A very large majority has twice expressed a clear declaration in favour of the principle of the Bill. [*Cries of* "No, no!"] Each Division was specially challenged by myself on that principle. I will merely repeat that, and add nothing more, believing I should best consult the wishes of the House by agreeing to an adjournment, being content with a moral victory.

The SOLICITOR GENERAL (Sir Edward Clarke) (Plymouth): I would just like to say that what has been done this evening is not intended to indicate the action of the Government on the one

side or the other. It was not a matter on which the Government intended to call upon their supporters to act. Some hours before the Bill came on the matter was discussed, and, having regard to the circumstances of the time, some of us thought it would be better to postpone the real discussion to a later stage.

Mr. BRADLAUGH: If the hon. Member will withdraw this Motion, I offer no opposition to the adjournment of the debate.

Mr. DE LISLE (Leicestershire, Mid): It is my intention to offer determined opposition to the Bill, and I shall renew the block which by accident failed last night. I merely ask, is it competent for me to put a block on the Paper before I leave the House renewing my opposition to the Bill?

Mr. SPEAKER signified assent.

Mr. BRADLAUGH: It will be competent, but not courteous.

Motion, by leave, *withdrawn.*

Original Question again proposed.

Debate arising;

Debate *adjourned* till *Thursday.*

LICENSED PREMISES (EARLIER CLOSING) (SCOTLAND) BILL.—[BILL 153.]

(*Dr. Cameron, Mr. Robert Reid, Mr. Mark Stewart, Mr. Donald Crawford, Mr. Lyell, Mr. Provand.*)

SECOND READING. [ADJOURNED DEBATE.]

Order read, for resuming Adjourned Debate on Question [7th March], "That the Bill be now read a second time."

Question again proposed.

Debate *resumed.*

Dr. CAMERON (Glasgow, College): On the last occasion when the Bill was before the House, all the Scotch Members voted in its favour, with the exception of three who are Members of the Government. That being so, I hope there will be now no opposition to the second reading.

Sir HERBERT MAXWELL (A Lord of the Treasury) (Wigton): At this hour it is not proposed to oppose the Motion for Second Reading; but in assenting to that stage the Government reserve the right to move important Amendments in Committee. The Government are aware that in some parts of the country it will be convenient to have an earlier hour for the closing of public-houses,

Mr. Gedge

and in deference to the view of the majority of Scotch Members, expressed on the last occasion, we do not now oppose the second reading.

Question put, and *agreed to.*

Bill read a second time, and *committed* for *Thursday.*

> House adjourned at ten minutes before Six o'clock in the morning.

HOUSE OF LORDS,

Tuesday, 10th May, 1887.

MINUTES.]—PUBLIC BILLS—*First Reading*— Crofters Holdings (Scotland) * (90) ; Dog Owners * (91).
Second Reading — Bankruptcy Offices (Sites) (76).
Report — Customs Consolidation Act (1876) Amendment * (71).
PROVISIONAL ORDER BILLS — *First Reading* — Elementary Education (Christchurch) * (92) ; Elementary Education (Middleton St. George) * (93) ; Elementary Education (London) * (94); Local Government (Ireland) (Dublin, &c.) * (95).
Third Reading—Local Government * (70), and *passed.*

BANKRUPTCY OFFICES (SITES) BILL.

(The Lord Henniker.)

(NO. 76.) SECOND READING.

Order of the Day for the Second Reading read.

Moved, "That the Bill be now read 2ª." —(*The Lord Henniker.*)

LORD HERSCHELL suggested that a Petition having been presented against the Bill it should be referred to a Select Committee.

LORD HENNIKER said, the First Commissioner of Works had no objection whatever, although the time had expired for presenting Petitions, to allow the Petition to go to the Select Committee. The Bill was a hybrid one, and as there was already a Petition against it, it would go, as a matter of course, before a Select Committee. He might mention that there was an agreement between the Office of Works and Clement's Inn with respect to a footway to take the place of the one to be moved. This agreement would be considered as honourably binding on the Government ; but if it was desired, the First Commissioner had no objection to insert a clause in the

Bill to carry out the agreement. Perhaps this statement might meet the objection of the noble and learned Lord.

THE CHAIRMAN OF COMMITTEES (The Duke of BUCKINGHAM and CHANDOS) pointed out that the Committee could not be appointed before Whitsuntide. As to the Petition, he thought the proper course would be to give Notice for Thursday that Standing Order No. 93 should be considered with the view of its being suspended in order to admit the Petition being received.

Motion *agreed to ;* Bill read 2ª accordingly, and *committed :* The Committee to be proposed by the Committee of Selection.

ENDOWED SCHOOLS ACT (1869) AND AMENDING ACTS (ARCHBISHOP HOLGATE'S GRAMMAR SCHOOL AT HEMSWORTH).

MOTION FOR AN ADDRESS.

THE ARCHBISHOP OF YORK, in rising to move—

" That an humble address be presented to Her Majesty praying Her Majesty to withhold her consent from the Scheme of the Charity Commissioners for England and Wales for the management of the Free Grammar School founded by Archbishop Holgate in the parish of Hemsworth in the county of York, the Hospital founded by Archbishop Holgate in the above-named parish of Hemsworth commonly known as Hemsworth Hospital, the Grammar School founded by Thomas Keresford in the borough of Barnsley in the county of York, and of the endowment attached to the last-named grammar school, and the gift of Phœbe Locke, so far as such Scheme affects the said grammar school and hospital at Hemsworth, and which Scheme is now lying on the Table of the House pursuant to the Endowed Schools Acts of 1869 and Amending Acts,"

said, he presented Petitions from the inhabitants of the neighbourhood, who had signed to the number of 3,482 persons, from the rural clergy, from the Board of Guardians, and from the Rural Sanitary Authority at Hemsworth and the Poor Law Union against the scheme of the Charity Commissioners. Those Petitions, he thought, fairly represented the public opinion of the whole locality against the scheme. In moving his Resolution, he submitted that the facts of the case were somewhat complicated by a Memorial from the Department dated 3rd May, 1867, in which the position of the Department was strongly described, but he thought more strongly than accurately. In the first place, they were told that the Commissioners were encouraged to take the course which they had taken with respect to this foundation by the patron and visitors, the Lord Archbishop of York and the trustees. The school of Hemsworth was in the year 1879 in considerable straits. They had the misfortune which might happen to any school—that of having a master who was somewhat supine, and the governors decided to get rid of him. They took such steps as they were advised, but it proved impossible to remove him, unless some charge of immorality or misbehaviour was preferred against him. In other words, it was not enough that the duties were imperfectly performed; there must be some specific charge which would justify the removal. At that time, no doubt, there was an opinion, the population being somewhat small and the difficulties of the school in the past having been considerable, that some other site might be found, or that it might be united with some other foundation. But an expressed opinion at that time in the early stages ought not in their view to be now binding. He ventured to hold that it was the publication of the scheme which drew forth that public opinion which enabled a right decision to be arrived at; and when the Commissioners complained that they were led by the preliminary opinion of the trustees and the visitors into what they seemed to regard as a false position, they ought also to remember that the publication of the scheme was not a final act, but rather a preliminary and first step towards ascertaining the opinion of the locality. Of the opinion of the locality there could not be the slightest doubt, as the Petitions laid upon the Table covered the whole ground. With regard to the reference which has been made to himself, he did not believe he was a visitor, and he was only patron in a very limited sense. In 1857, according to his reading of the Act, the office of visitor was done away with by ordering that the trustees should appoint a committee to visit the foundation and report to them. That took away the visitorial power from the Archbishop of York, which power had never been restored. Under the scheme of the Court of Chancery of 1861 it was provided that the Archbishop should be the patron to appoint the Head Master, provided he

did it within 20 days, but it was impossible to exercise that patronage under those conditions; therefore, virtually, the patronage was taken away from the Archbishop, hence his connection with the hospital was of the slightest description. But not only was he made responsible by the trustees in their statement, but he found it was alleged that what he had written on the subject tended to raise a religious difficulty. He denied that that construction was to be put upon anything he had written. The only point he had wished to raise was whether an endowed school of this kind could be properly dealt with by being removed to another site. The only question he wished to place before their Lordships was that here was an endowment of the net value of £450. It was an endowment of a high school among a population of about 20,000, which was largely increasing. The history of Barnsley for the last 50 or 60 years showed how the population had increased, and it was possible that Hemsworth would largely develop in the near future, its mines being by no means exhausted. He might instance the case of Middlesborough, situate at the north edge of Yorkshire, which was a few years ago a mere village, but now a large borough, returning a Member to Parliament and having a Municipal Corporation, and all the elements of civic life. He contended that before this endowment was irrevocably diverted they should consider that the time might come, and in the next 20 years, when Hemsworth, like Middlesbrough, would become a large and thriving place, and require this money for its own educational purposes. This £450 a-year it was now proposed to take to Barnsley, to which place, owing to the defective railway accommodation, there was considerable difficulty for the school children of Hemsworth to get to. He really was at a loss to find any reason for this removal. It was not only a question of geography, but it was to some extent a matter of sentiment, for Barnsley was in another diocese, and he protested against a school founded by one of his Predecessors being transferred to another diocese without some valid reason. He pleaded for a suspension of operations in regard to this foundation, submitting that in course of time the trustees would be able to establish an efficient school,

The Archbishop of York

and that in making their demand they were asking nothing that was not reasonable and wise. They asked for two years to set their house in order, and they wished for permission to establish scholarships and endowments as an encouragement to the school. The Commissioners refused that and threatened the institution, which fact, he reminded their Lordships, was bound to have a bad effect on the school. The most rev. Prelate concluded by submitting the Motion of which he had given Notice.

VISCOUNT MIDLETON, in seconding the Motion, said, that he had examined into this matter in all its bearings on the spot. He considered that the scheme propounded by the Charity Commissioners in this case was needless, unwise, and unjust. The neighbourhood was a growing one; it had doubled within the last 10 years, and would be doubled again in the next 10 years. The scheme would take away from this rising neighbourhood the very thing which it needed—a good secondary school. They were now being called upon to sweep away every intention of the original founder, although the reasons for which it had been created were five times as strong as they had then been, and to transfer it to a manufacturing town eight miles off, which had no facilities of access, and which had not even asked for it. There were sufficient educational facilities at present existing in Barnsley, and he could not conceive a place more unfitted for the transfer of such a foundation as that under consideration. The income also of the school was almost entirely derived from the surrounding people. The sum of £300 a-year had been given for a certain length of time, after which the question was to be reconsidered. As the whole income of the school was only about £500 a-year, he thought that they might at all events wait until that time came if anything had to be done. The scheme had only been settled 20 years ago; it had been practically revised 10 years ago, and it was now proposed to revise it again. He admitted that it was within the legal power of the Charity Commissioners to frame a scheme which took away the benefits of the charity from the district to which it had originally been granted; but the Report of the Select Committee of the House of Commons on Endowed Schools, which

had just been published, had recommended that these provisions should only be applied in cases where population was decreasing, and where, therefore, the need for any such accommodation was likely to lessen rather than to increase. In the present instance exactly the converse was the case, as the neighbourhood was a rising one, and there was a large amount of property which was being further developed. The school also met the wants of a class of parents who wished for something better than the national schools for their children, and could not afford the expense of a public school. If this scheme were adopted the Hemsworth school building, which had cost £5,000, would be a White Elephant, for it was incapable of being turned into cottages, and it was unsaleable for residential purposes. The scheme unsettled everything, and settled nothing. A great deal more good might be achieved by leaving matters as they were. He hoped that in deciding this question their Lordships would not be guided by any Party question, but follow their own judgment.

Moved, "That an humble address be presented to Her Majesty praying Her Majesty to withhold her consent from the Scheme of the Charity Commissioners for England and Wales for the management of the Free Grammar School founded by Archbishop Holgate in the parish of Hemsworth, in the county of York, the Hospital founded by Archbishop Holgate in the above-named parish of Hemsworth commonly known as Hemsworth Hospital, the Grammar School founded by Thomas Keresford in the Borough of Barnsley in the county of York, and of the endowment attached to the last-named grammar school, and the gift of Phœbe Locke, so far as such Scheme affects the said grammar school and hospital at Hemsworth, and which Scheme is now lying on the Table of the House pursuant to the Endowed School Act of 1869 and Amending Acts."—(*The Lord Archbishop of York.*)

EARL SPENCER said, he entirely sympathized with the last sentence of the noble Lord, and sincerely trusted that their Lordships would carefully weigh and consider all the arguments that might be adduced for and against the proposal of the most rev. Prelate. This scheme, after passing through its various stages, had been submitted in due course to the Education Committee of the Privy Council last summer. It had come before him as Lord President of the Council, and after carefully going through it he had signed his approval. Subsequently various Memorials were presented to the Judicial Committee of the Privy Council, drawing attention to the legal aspects of the case. The case was disposed of by the Judicial Committee, who had given their opinion in favour of the promoters of the scheme. It had then come before Her Majesty in Council, and had been laid on the Table of the House. He believed that their Lordships had all read the clear statement submitted to them from the Charity Commissioners, and also the judgment of the Judicial Committee of the Privy Council. He did not wish to go through these arguments at any length, but he would like shortly to explain why he had thought it right to give his approval to the scheme. It had been shown on most conclusive evidence that this school, which had been founded in the Reign of Henry VIII., had been, certainly in recent years, a failure. It was to be noted that the words of the original Charter, granted in 1548, stated the object to be the encouragement of education in England, but there was no mention of any special locality in which this was to be done. Schools, however, were established, a grammar school in Hemsworth, and elementary schools in surrounding villages, each of which received about £40 a-year towards its elementary school. With regard to the grammar school there was a long chain of evidence showing how entirely it had failed. In 1828 Lord Brougham's Commission pointed out that it did not appear that the school had been carried on with success, and that there was not a sufficient number of boys in the neighbourhood who required a classical education to make the school a success. Lord Taunton's Commission, in 1865, reported very much to the same effect. In these villages, the Report said, no day scholars could be expected who required a classical instruction, or more than an elementary education. In 1878 one of the Assistant Commissioners of the Charity Commission, Mr. Fearon, now the Secretary, went down to make an inquiry, and he came to the conclusion that it was of little or no use to maintain the school at Hemsworth. "No day scholars can be expected to avail themselves of the classical instruction." The Commissioners before this had been opposed to the moving of the school, but after learning the result of this inquiry they came to the conclusion that they

Earl Spencer

ought to exercise their undoubted power and remove the school to some other locality. They accordingly invited the attention of the trustees and patrons to this point. The most rev. Prelate then wrote a letter, dated April 10, 1879, in which he said—

"In my judgment the grammar school is not much needed in its present position, and I fear that so long as it remains at Hemsworth it will languish."

The trustees, however, asked for some delay, to give the school a fair trial under the new head master, and to this the Commissioners agreed, and a delay of two years was allowed. After this further trial, the head master himself wrote saying that he did not think that the school could succeed. Further correspondence took place between the trustees and the Commissioners, in which the trustees, while practically agreeing to the removal, made certain stipulations —that the town to which the school was removed should find £5,000, that the head master should be provided for, and other small matters of this kind. All these points had been met by the Commissioners, but the trustees were not satisfied. Since then, a Committee of the House of Commons had inquired into the whole matter, and, after hearing all the evidence against the scheme, they approved the scheme, without even calling upon the Charity Commission to support it. It was said that Barnsley was a dirty, smoky town, but that surely was no reason why it should be denied the advantages of a grammar school. If the school were established in a rural district like Hemsworth, enormous expenditure would have to be incurred in the erection of boarding-houses for the scholars. The scheme had been approved by a Committee of the House of Commons, on which two Vice Presidents of the Council, Sir Lyon Playfair and Sir Henry Holland, served. It would be a serious disaster if the idea should go forth that the scheme was opposed on grounds of religious difference. In the interests of the Church of England itself it was greatly to be hoped that nothing approaching to sectarian acrimony would be caused in connection with the matter before their Lordships. He earnestly trusted that the House would not agree to the Memorial presented by the most rev. Prelate.

LORD GRIMTHORPE said, he objected to the scheme on the ground that neither the founder's wishes nor the wishes of the locality had been regarded. In Hemsworth itself and the neighbourhood there was absolute unanimity in opposition to the scheme. Even the head master, Mr. Butler, might be considered an opponent of the scheme, as his objection in 1881 to the school remaining at Hemsworth was solely based on the absence of scholarships which the Charity Commissioners refused to found in the old school, but founded further new ones. Hemsworth was admirably suited, according to the testimony of a late master of Malvern College, and other competent authorities, to be the site of a school of this character. It was the centre of a growing district of over 20,000 inhabitants, and was certainly a much better place than " Black Barnsley," as that town had always been called. The climate was good, and Hemsworth and its neighbourhood were an oasis amid the surrounding blackness. The scheme had been very imperfectly advertised, and was but little known in the district. It was not the case that the opponents of the scheme wished the school to be reduced to the level of an elementary school. But it would do good service as a middle or second grade school, though it could not be expected to compete with the great public schools. The paper which had been circulated a few days ago was full of misstatements and suppressions most discreditable to whoever had drawn and issued it. It first suppresses the fact that the Archbishop of York had, so far back as 1881, objected to the removal of the school, and said that he should be particularly unwilling to have it removed out of the diocese. It represents the trustees as having been willing at first to have it removed. They had never voted anything of the kind, but only that if it was to be removed (which they supposed the Commissioners to have power to do) it should not be removed to Barnsley but to Pontefract, therefore the Commissioners were not justified in saying that they were encouraged either by the patron or by the trustees to go on with the scheme for the removal of the school; and the statements which had been put forth on that subject were misleading. Mr. Fearon was evidently very anxious to prove that the school was a failure; and how did he try to make that out? He gave the results of his inquiries during two visits, on both of which he found that there were very few boys at the school. But when was that? The latest of those occasions was in 1878, and in 1886 that gentleman made an affidavit for the information of the Privy Council; but he did not tell them what had happened since 1878, when the new master came to the school. How could the school be said to have failed? Reference had been made to the House of Commons Committee of last year, which was said to have been satisfied of the goodness of the scheme. Mr. Fearon had given evidence, and two of the Commissioners had also done so, and had said all that they wanted to say about the school. Sir George Young said that there were two, and perhaps only two, classes of cases where the removal of a school ought to be persisted in in spite of opposition, one of them being where the school sought to be removed had been a failure where it stood, and was proved to be so by a long-continued experience, and not only by what it was eight years ago under a different master; and the other was where it was not fulfilling the desire of the founder, and where they did not see their way in the same place to turn it into anything that would do good upon the principle upon which they acted in such matters. Another of the Commissioners gave evidence that a complete change of locality was very rare, and that, in fact, the circumstances would have to be very strong to justify it. The paper of reasons suppresses another letter from the Archbishop in 1883, a considerable time before the scheme was published, which only means circulated. It was not true that the Commissioners had entered into no engagements of any kind with Barnsley before then, as the paper asserted. Pointing out further inaccuracies in the statements put forward in support of the scheme, the noble Lord asked how it could be said that that school had failed? It had been built for 40 boys, and a year ago there were 37 boys in it. The numbers were stated to have fallen, and the noble Lord below (Lord Middleton) had given a very sufficient reason for it in the unsettled state of things caused by the Commissioners;

the school was as good as it was intended or expected to be. The noble Earl had referred to the school as it was 60 years ago, and had also read another report about its state 23 years ago; and that was the way in which it was sought to show that it was a failure now. He contended that the school was not a failure, and that the Commissioners had not made out a case. Hemsworth had a moral right to the school remaining where it was, and it should not be taken away. The compensation professed to be given by scholarships at other places is no real compensation to inhabitants of that neighbourhood. He would only add, that he concurred with the views of the most rev. Prelate, and hoped that their Lordships would agree to the Address.

THE LORD PRESIDENT OF THE COUNCIL (Viscount CRANBROOK) said, he came first to the consideration of this case with a mind quite open, and, perhaps, he should say with a feeling against the unnecessary removal of a school from the place in which it was originally founded. But the more he looked into the matter the more satisfied did he become that the most rev. Prelate (the Archbishop of York) was right in the statement he made in 1879 that the school was not likely to answer in the place in which it existed. When removal was spoken of it had to be borne in mind that this was not a removal in the ordinary sense of the term. It was the removal of a school to a place in the immediate neighbourhood, and so far as the district generally was considered, the proposed place to which the school was to be removed was a better locality than Hemsworth. Royston contained about half the population of the district, and was nearer to Barnsley than was Hemsworth. To make the school successful, it was necessary that a certain amount of money should be spent on it, and no one supposed that Hemsworth could supply that money. It was said that there were 37 boys attending the school at one time. He found, on the contrary, that on May 4 the entire number was 22 scholars, three of whom were boarders and 13 paying scholars, only five of the boys belonging to Hemsworth. No doubt, when Archbishop Holgate founded the three schools in different parts of Yorkshire he had ambitious ideas, and believed that they

would grow up to much larger institutions, but that had not been the case at Hemsworth. In a district of such a kind it was not to be expected that the class of school provided would succeed. In 1881 the trustees themselves were prepared, subject to a satisfactory provision being made to preserve the interests of the parishes concerned, to consent to the removal of the school. All the conditions which they laid down had been fulfilled by the Charity Commission, and the only question was as to the difference between Barnsley and Pontefract. He was not going to argue that Pontefract was not a much pleasanter place than Barnsley; but Pontefract was, if anything, a declining place; while Barnsley was swarming with a thronging and increasing population of some 80,000 people. No doubt the people there were subject to all the influences of a crowded population in a smoky atmosphere; but, while admitting that, he did not see that there was the less necessity to encourage the languishing grammar school there. If the school remained at Hemsworth, a large sum would have to be raised, as was admitted by the main advocate of the present site, and must come out of and bring very low the endowments, whereas at Barnsley the needful money was to be provided and buildings secured. Anything objectionable in the shape of cottages too near was to be removed, and two endowments which at present existed at Barnsley were to be given to the school. He was surprised to hear a noble Lord say that Barnsley was well supplied with schools, because that was not the case. It was said, however, that Barnsley had not asked for the removal of the school. The Committee on Endowed Schools which inquired into the question pointed out that Barnsley had a population of 80,000 persons, and that there was a great want of provision for higher education. The Charity Commissioners had made no secret of their intentions since 1879, nor had there been a word to lead anyone to suppose that Mr. Fearon had misled those interested. In 1879 the case was practically given up for Hemsworth as a place suited for the kind of school wanted. A grammar school in the midst of that population was unsuited to the condition of the people. On the other hand, they had in their power the means of benefiting

Lord Grimthorpe

the large population of Barnsley. The most rev. Prelate very lately contemplated removal, as he spoke of other languishing schools needing aid. By adopting the scheme of the Commissioners, they were acting in accordance with the wishes of the founder, and were also increasing the capabilities for usefulness of the institution. He, therefore, trusted their Lordships would concur with him in the opinion which the Charity Commissioners had come to, and in regard to which he himself had come to the same conclusion as the noble Earl opposite (Earl Spencer), and two different Vice Presidents of the Council —namely, that the scheme ought to be confirmed.

LORD ST. OSWALD, as one of the trustees of the school, said, the trustees were all against the removal of the school to Barnsley. They considered Hemsworth was the place where the school ought to be, and that, even if there had not been occasions for it in 1879, there was ample occasion for it now. The population of Hemsworth had increased enormously, and was still increasing, and it would be a great injustice to take the school away. No doubt, in past years, the school had not come up to the expectations formed of it; but in future years there would be a better system of management. The inhabitants of the parish were absolutely and unanimously against its removal. He admitted it was true that the school had gone down in attendance last year; but the sole reason for that, as told him the other day by the headmaster, Mr. Butler, was the circulation of a report that the school was going to be removed to Barnsley. Looking at all the circumstances of the case, he hoped the House would not sanction the scheme.

LORD COLCHESTER said, that, before touching upon the principles involved in this question, he must take occasion to protest most emphatically against the attack made by the noble Lord (Lord Grimthorpe) on Mr. Fearon, who was one of the most useful men in the Public Service. He thought that very often the spirit of the original intention of a founder was best carried out by not adhering too rigidly to the letter of his instructions when circumstances had changed. In order to carry

out their great object, founders of institutions had sometimes insisted on some minor point which, in altered circumstances, interfered with the carrying out of their intentions. It would not be fair to reject this scheme, except for exceptional reasons, which in the present case had not been shown. No scheme had been rejected since 1874, except one withdrawn by the Education Department. He thought the power of rejection should only be used where a broad principle was marked out, on the ground of a number of local details which the majority of the House could hardly pronounce upon. He trusted, therefore, that the House would take the advice of the noble Viscount the President of the Council and reject the Motion of the most rev. Prelate.

LORD DENMAN (who had some difficulty in obtaining a hearing) said: The Archbishop, being a native of Hemsworth, would never have wished students to go to Barnsley (seven miles off) even if a railway went the whole distance. He would have desired that they should have the best education that an educated man could give them, near their own home. As the House wished to "Divide," the sooner their Lordships did so the better.

On Question? Their Lordships *divided:*—Contents 38; Not-Contents 61: Majority 23.

CONTENTS.

NOT-CONTENTS.

Canterbury, L. Archp.
Halsbury, L. (*L. Chancellor.*)
Cranbrook, V. (*L. President.*)
Cadogan, E. (*L. Privy Seal.*)

Bedford, D.
Grafton, D.
Manchester, D.
Marlborough, D.

Ripon, M.
Salisbury, M.

Camperdown, E.
Derby, E.
Fortescue, E.
Granville, E.
Harrowby, E.
Kimberley, E.
Lindsay, E.
Lovelace, E.
Milltown, E.
Morley, E.
Northbrook, E.
Onslow, E.
Spencer, E.
Strafford, E.

Oxenbridge, V.
Torrington, V.

London, L. Bp.
Southwell, L. Bp.

Balfour of Burley, L. [*Teller.*]
Belper, L.
Boyle, L. (*E. Cork and Orrery.*)

Brougham and Vaux, L.
Colchester, L.
De Mauley, D.
de Ros, L.
Elgin, L. (*E. Elgin and Kincardine.*)
Foxford, L. (*E. Limerick.*) [*Teller.*]
Hamilton of Dalzell, L.
Harris, L.
Hartismere, L. (*L. Henniker.*)
Herschell, L.
Hobhouse, L.
Hopetoun, L. (*E. Hopetoun.*)
Houghton, L.
Kensington, L.
Ker, L. (*M. Lothian.*)
Lingen, L.
Lovat, L.
Lyttleton, L.
Macnaghten, L.
Monk-Bretton, L.
Monkswell, L.
Montagu of Beaulieu, L.
Northington, L. (*L. Henley.*)
O'Neill, L.
Poltimore, L.
Rosebery, L. (*E. Rosebery.*)
Saltersford, L. (*E. Courtown.*)
Stanley of Preston, L.
Thring, L.
Winmarleigh, L.

Resolved in the *negative.*

CREMATION.

MOTION FOR A PAPER.

LORD FORBES, in moving for a Return of the number of cremations that had taken place in England within the last five years, and asking by what authority and under what regulations they were permitted, said, that this question was of importance from a social point of view, because it was necessary that precautions should be insisted upon by which any poison could be detected before a body was cremated.

Moved, "That there be laid before this House Return of the number of cremations that have taken place in England within the last five years."—(*The Lord Forbes.*)

THE PRIME MINISTER AND SECRETARY OF STATE FOR FOREIGN AFFAIRS (The Marquess of SALISBURY) said, that the Government would have been willing to give such a Return if it

had been in their power; it was impossible, however, for them to do so, because, as cremation was a matter of individual discretion and not an official proceeding, no records were kept, or at least none that were accessible to the Government. He did not know whether the danger referred to by the noble Lord was real or not, as he was not well informed on that matter; but he doubted whether the traces of mineral poisons would be absolutely obliterated. The practice was scarcely sufficiently common at present to call for any Parliamentary interference, and as to the information which the noble Lord desired, the Home Office were unable to supply it.

THE EARL OF MILLTOWN said, he might point out that cremation did not require any official sanction. It was perfectly legal, unless so conducted as to be a nuisance or offensive to public decency.

LORD HERSCHELL said, the noble Lord would find that this matter had been fully discussed in a debate in the House of Commons, in the Session of 1884 or 1885, when it was proposed to legislate.

Motion (by leave of the House) *withdrawn.*

TITHE RENT-CHARGE BILL.

QUESTION.

THE DUKE OF MARLBOROUGH asked the Prime Minister, Whether it would be convenient to somewhat postpone the Committee stage of the Tithe Rent-charge Bill, so as to allow a fuller consideration of the Amendments that had been put down on the Paper?

THE PRIME MINISTER AND SECRETARY OF STATE FOR FOREIGN AFFAIRS (The Marquess of SALISBURY) said, the only other day available was Monday week, the day on which the House rose before the Queen's birthday. He might take this opportunity of stating that he had received a great number of communications with regard to the clause in the Bill which provided for the reduction of 5 per cent by the landowner, and he felt that this would in many cases inflict an injustice on the titheowner, where, for instance, the landowner now paid his own tithe, where the landowner was in occupation, and where the titheowner was in the habit of collecting the tithe himself. He, therefore, proposed to drop the clause.

CROFTERS HOLDINGS (SCOTLAND) BILL [H.L.]

Was *presented* by The Marquess of Lothian; read 1ª. (No. 90.)

DOG OWNERS BILL [H.L.]

Was *presented* by The Lord Mount-Temple; read 1ª. (No. 91.)

ELEMENTARY EDUCATION PROVISIONAL ORDER CONFIRMATION (CHRISTCHURCH) BILL [H.L.] (NO. 92.)

ELEMENTARY EDUCATION PROVISIONAL ORDER CONFIRMATION (MIDDLETON ST. GEORGE) BILL [H.L.] (NO. 93.)

ELEMENTARY EDUCATION PROVISIONAL ORDER CONFIRMATION (LONDON) BILL [H.L.] (NO. 94.)

Were *presented* by The Lord President; read 1ª.

LOCAL GOVERNMENT (IRELAND) PROVISIONAL ORDER (DUBLIN, &c.) BILL [H.L.]

Was *presented* by The Lord Privy Seal; read 1ª. (No. 95.)

House adjourned at a quarter past Seven o'clock, to Thursday next, a quarter past Ten o'clock.

HOUSE OF COMMONS,

Tuesday, 10th May, 1887.

MINUTES.] — SELECT COMMITTEE — Town Holdings; Mr Crilly *disch.*; Dr. Fox *added.*

PUBLIC BILLS—*First Reading*—Sheriffs (Consolidation) * [262].

Second Reading—Deeds of Arrangement Registration [231].

Committee—Criminal Law Amendment (Ireland) [217] [*Fifth Night*]—R.P.; First Offenders (*re-comm.*) [189]—R.P.

Committee—'*Report — Third Reading* — Incumbents of Benefices Loans Extension Act (1886) Amendment * [230], and *passed.*

Considered as amended—Colonial Service (Pensions) * [251].

PROVISIONAL ORDER BILLS — *Ordered — First Reading*—Local Government (Gas) * [259]; Local Government (Poor Law) (No. 3) * [260]; Local Government (No. 2) * [261].

PARLIAMENT—PETITIONS—FICTITIOUS SIGNATURES.

MR. WEBSTER (St. Pancras, E.): I have a Petition to present from the Anti-Wine and Coal Dues Association, East St. Pancras, against the continuance of the Coal and Wine Dues. I regret to inform the House that although I am cognizant of the fact that a large number of the signature are *bonâ fide*

signatures of the inhabitants of that district of London, yet I have received information, which I consider to be trustworthy, that a great many of these signatures are forgeries, and that some of them purport to be the signatures of persons who, as far as I can find out, do not exist. I, therefore, present the Petition, having given that information to the House.

MR. SPEAKER: The best course will be for the hon. Member to present the Petition, and it can then be referred to the Committee now sitting to inquire into the presentation of several other Petitions.

MR. W. LOWTHER (Westmoreland, Appleby): I wish to know, Sir, whether the Petition can go before the Committee if it is not presented, and in the possession of the House? I did not understand you to order it to lie on the Table.

MR. SPEAKER: If the hon. Member will bring it up, it will be ordered to lie on the Table, and it will be for the Committee of the House now sitting to deal with it.

Petition *brought up*, and *ordered* to lie on the Table.

QUESTIONS.

WAR OFFICE—AEROSTATIC BALLOONS —INVENTIONS OF WILLIAM HOWSON.

MR. SHIRLEY (Yorkshire, W.R., Doncaster) asked the Secretary of State for War, Whether some valuable inventions and recommendations in regard to aerostatic balloons have been communicated to the War Office by one William Howson, of Mexborough, in Yorkshire; whether the War Office has availed itself of some of such inventions and recommendations without rewarding or recognizing the services of the said William Howson, and would he state what negotiations have taken place between the War Office and the said William Howson; whether he is aware that the said William Howson professes to be the possessor of a valuable secret for destroying armies, and has offered to make experiments at Woolwich for the purpose of testing the value of his secret; and, whether the War Office will cause such experiments to be made?

THE SURVEYOR GENERAL OF ORDNANCE (MR. NORTHCOTE) (Exeter)

(who replied) said : Mr. Howson's proposals have been before the War Office since 1878; but they have been considered impracticable, and have been declined. The War Office has not availed itself of any of Mr. Howson's recommendations, nor has there been any connection between his proposals and certain balloon experiments which have taken place.

ALLOTMENTS EXTENSION ACT, 1882— "POORS CLOSE" CHARITY, GREAT EASTON.

MR. J. ELLIS (Leicestershire, Bosworth)(for Mr. CHANNING)(Northampton, E.) asked the Secretary of State for the Home Department, Whether his attention has been drawn to the following facts—that in the village of Great Easton, in the County of Leicester, a statutory notice, to put into operation the Allotments Extension Act of 1882, has been duly served on the administrators of the "Poors Close" Charity; that the said "Poors Close" is about three-fourths of a mile from the village, has a good road to it, and is more conveniently situated than the present allotments, and that the latter are insufficient for the acquirements of the village; that the overseers have refused to put "The Allotments Extension Act, 1882," in force, and that, though notified that the Charity Commissioners have been appealed to in the matter, they re-let the field for another year; and, whether, taking all the circumstances into consideration, he will direct any steps to be taken to compel the administrators of the "Poors Close," at Great Easton, to carry out the Allotments Extension Act?

THE UNDER SECRETARY OF STATE (Mr. STUART-WORTLEY) (Sheffield, Hallam) (who replied) said : The Charity Commissioners were informed by a correspondent writing on behalf of certain applicants for allotments on the 21st of April and 2nd instant to the effect stated in the first three paragraphs of the Question. The Commissioners have already called upon the overseers, who appear to administer the Charity, to take steps to carry out the Allotments Extension Act, 1882, and are making inquiries. Pending the result of those inquiries, the Commissioners are unable to say whether any proceedings on their part to compel the overseers to carry out the Act will be necessary. The overseers

have expressed to the Secretary of State the opinion that the land is quite unsuitable for allotments.

EDUCATION DEPARTMENT—THE NEW CODE, 1887—"SPECIFIC SUBJECTS."

MR. HOWARD VINCENT (Sheffield, Central) asked the Vice President of the Committee of Council on Education. What other specific subjects other than algebra, Euclid and mensuration, mechanics, chemistry, physics, animal physiology, botany, principles of agriculture, Latin, French, and domestic economy are sanctioned by the Department, as entitling a school to a grant of 4s. in respect of each passed scholar; why book-keeping, commercial correspondence, epistolary style, English composition, commercial history, commercial geography, shorthand, or German are not enumerated; how many schools in Great Britain provided last year a graduated scheme of teaching approved by the Inspector in any of such last-named subjects, and which of them; how many scholars in Great Britain were submitted last year for examination in each such subject, and how many earned the grant; and, if it is possible to add these commercial subjects, or some of them, to the list given in Clause 15 of the Education Code of 1887, with a view to directing the studies of the senior classes of Board Schools into a practical channel?

THE VICE PRESIDENT (Sir WILLIAM HART DYKE) (Kent, Dartford) : If my hon. Friend will refer to the answer given to the hon. Member for Merioneth (Mr. T. E. Ellis) on the 17th of March he will see what specific subjects other than those mentioned in Article 15 of the Code have, from time to time, been sanctioned by the Department. They include book-keeping and German; while English composition and epistolary style form part of the ordinary course of instruction in the upper Standards, and commercial history and geography are necessarily taught whenever history and geography are taken as class subjects. I have not the detailed information asked for in the third and fourth parts of the Question; but I can assure my hon. Friend that any suitable scheme of teaching subjects important to those likely to be engaged in commerce will meet with every encouragement from the Department, and if such subjects were adopted to any extent the results would

Mr. Northcote

be separately tabulated in the General Report.

EDUCATION DEPARTMENT — HOUSE VISITATION BY SCHOOL MANAGERS.

MR. BEACH (Hants, Andover) asked the Vice President of the Committee of Council on Education, Whether an Inspector of Schools has a right to make a manager of a school go to every house in the parish (rich and poor), ask the number of persons in each house, and send a Report thereof to him; and whether (as the case is) the grant due to Newtown Schools, Hants, can be refused to be paid by Government until the order of the Inspector (with regard to the above) has been carried out?

THE VICE PRESIDENT (Sir WILLIAM HART DYKE) (Kent, Dartford): No, Sir; an Inspector has no such right as that suggested. But an Inspector is bound to require the managers of a school who claim a special grant under Article 3 to establish that claim by reasonable evidence. In this case I am informed by the Inspector that the correspondent actually agreed to supply the "list of inhabited houses with the number of souls in each." But when the correspondent afterwards objected, the Inspector at once accepted the half-yearly statement of the Guardians, upon which he understood the Returns in previous years to have been based.

WAR OFFICE—HORSE ARTILLERY RE-DUCTION—FIELD ARTILLERY GUNS.

GENERAL FRASER (Lambeth, N.) asked the Secretary of State for War, In view of the statement in his letter to the signatories of the appeal against the Horse Artillery reductions, quoted from the distinguished General's Minute, in discrediting the value of that arm, that—

"At present the bulk of Horse Artillery is armed with a 9-pounder, a very poor gun; whilst our Field Batteries are armed with an admirable 13-pounder, or the old pattern 16-pounder, a good but unwieldy gun;"

and, if it is the fact that there are 53 batteries of Field Artillery also armed with a 9-pounder gun, and that there are only 13 batteries out of the whole number of 84 batteries of Field Artillery armed with the 13-pounder, and 15 batteries with the 16-pounder?

THE SURVEYOR GENERAL OF ORDNANCE (Mr. NORTHCOTE) (Exeter) (who replied) said: My hon. and gallant Friend's figures are substantially cor-

rect; but I am glad to say that rapid progress is being made in re-armament during the present financial year. The new guns for two more batteries are now being prepared for issue to Field Artillery; those for 10 more will follow at the rate of two per month, and for nine more the guns will be ready during the year. My hon. and gallant Friend should also remember that 42 of the batteries named by him are in India, and their armament rests with the Indian Government.

INDIA—INDIAN FAMINE INSURANCE FUND.

SIR THOMAS ESMONDE (Dublin Co., S.) asked the Under Secretary of State for India, If it is a fact, as reported in *The Bengalee* of Calcutta, that the Indian Famine Insurance Fund has practically ceased to exist, as it has been devoted to the Burmese War; and, if so, what steps are being taken by the Indian Government to meet the eventuality of famine in India in future?

THE UNDER SECRETARY OF STATE (Sir JOHN GORST) (Chatham): It is not true that the Famine Insurance Fund has been devoted to the Burmese War; but there is no surplus for 1887-8 out of which the Famine Grant can be paid. The Government of India seeks to protect the country against famine by completing the protective system of railways as rapidly as financial considerations will allow.

LAW AND JUSTICE (IRELAND)—NON-DELIVERY OF SUBPŒNAS.

SIR THOMAS ESMONDE (Dublin Co., S.) asked the Chief Secretary to the Lord Lieutenant of Ireland, If it is a fact that Mr. Hazley, Postmaster of Blackrock, County Dublin, has recently had a law-suit with a Mr. Edward Little, cab-owner of Blackrock; and, if it is a fact that subpœnas issued by Mr. Little's Counsel, Mr. Gerald Byrne, to witnesses for the defence, were posted on Thursday, April 14th, and instead of being delivered the same day were not delivered until the following Saturday afternoon, too late for the witnesses to attend the Court, whereby Mr. Hazley won the case; and, if so, what is the explanation of the delay, and who is responsible for keeping the summonses in the post office so long undelivered?

THE PARLIAMENTARY UNDER SECRETARY (Colonel KING-HARMAN)

(Kent, Isle of Thanet) (who replied) said: The Irish Government have no knowledge of the law-suit alluded to. With regard to the latter portion of the Question, I have already stated, in reply to a similar Question put by the hon. Member for South Armagh (Mr. Blane) on Friday last, that in the case of any alleged irregularities on the part of Post Office officials, the proper course is for the person feeling aggrieved to communicate with the Postmaster General.

CRIME AND OUTRAGE (IRELAND)—ALLEGED MUTILATION OF CATTLE AT RATHFARNHAM.

SIR THOMAS ESMONDE (Dublin Co., S.) asked the Chief Secretary to the Lord Lieutenant of Ireland, Whether, in the case of the recently reported outrage at Rathfarnham, County Dublin, whereby six of Colonel Rowley's cattle had their tails cut off, it was discovered, upon examination, that only one of the beasts had lost its tail; if, upon further examination, the missing tail was found in the farmyard, where it had dropped off, eaten away by disease; and, whether this outrage forms one of those enumerated in the last Return of Irish crime laid upon the Table of the House, or will form one of those enumerated in the next?

THE PARLIAMENTARY UNDER SECRETARY (Colonel KING-HARMAN) (Kent, Isle of Thanet) (who replied) said, it was reported to the police at Rathfarnham, on 27th ultimo, that the tail of one cow—not six as mentioned in the Question, Colonel Rowley having but two—had been cut off the previous night. The police at once visited the place, and on examination found that the loss of the tail had been occasioned through disease. No outrage having occurred the case does not, and will not, appear in any Return.

ROYAL IRISH CONSTABULARY—SUB-INSPECTOR SUMMERVILLE AND CONSTABLE WARD.

MR. T. M. HEALY (Longford, N.) asked the Chief Secretary to the Lord Lieutenant of Ireland, Whether Sub-Inspector Summerville and Constable Ward, released on bail after a verdict of wilful murder, have resumed police duty.; are they since in the receipt of pay, or what is their position; and, do

the Government intend to prosecute them?

THE PARLIAMENTARY UNDER SECRETARY (Colonel KING-HARMAN) (Kent, Isle of Thanet) (who replied) said, the officer and constable are on leave of absence, and not on duty. They are both in receipt of pay, and will return to duty on the expiration of their leave, as the Attorney General sees no grounds to advise a prosecution.

COURT OF BANKRUPTCY—(IRELAND).

MR. P. M'DONALD (Sligo, N.) asked Mr. Attorney General for Ireland, Whether the existing staff of the Court of Bankruptcy in Ireland (with two exceptions) from the Judges downwards are Protestants, and if no Catholic has received any promotion, place, or employment in that Court for several years; and, whether the Government will now make an exception to the rule so rigidly observed, and appoint a Catholic to the office of official assignee now vacant?

THE ATTORNEY GENERAL FOR IRELAND (Mr. HOLMES) (Dublin University): I do not know the religion of the officials of the staff of the Court, and I should not feel justified in making inquiries on the subject. Neither the Government, nor any Member of the Government, have anything to do with the appointment of official assignees, or any other official of the Court.

OPEN-AIR MEETINGS (METROPOLIS)—ACTION OF THE POLICE.

MR. PICTON (Leicester) asked the Secretary of State for the Home Department, Whether an intended open-air meeting in Sancroft Street was prevented on Sunday, 8th May, by a body of police, who occupied the ground before the conductors of the meeting arrived; whether this was done by the orders of the Chief Commissioner of Police; whether the prohibition of the meeting has the approval of the Secretary of State; whether the conductors of the meeting proceeded from Sancroft Street to the Thames Embankment, and carried out their programme without any disturbance of the peace; and, whether the prohibition of the meeting was due to any exceptional reasons, which can be stated to the House, or is it intended to be repeated in the case of all open-air meetings called by Socialists and their supporters?

MR. JAMES STUART (Shoreditch, Hoxton) also asked, Whether the police prevented the holding of a public meeting at Sancroft Street, Kennington Road, London, on Sunday last; and, what were the instructions under which they acted in dealing with this proposed meeting?

MR. PICKERSGILL (Bethnal Green, S.W.) also asked, Whether the Home Secretary is aware that for a long time past meetings have been held in Sancroft Street, Kennington Road; whether, on Sunday last, the police prevented a meeting being held there; and, if so, upon what grounds and by what authority; and, whether two persons, named respectively Chapman and Kemp, were arrested by the police; and, if so, by what authority and for what offence in each case?

THE UNDER SECRETARY OF STATE (Mr. STUART-WORTLEY) (Sheffield, Hallam) (who replied) said: I am informed by the Commissioner of Police that, as is usual in cases of an anticipated breach of the peace, the police were on the ground at the time and place in question in double patrols, but that no attempt was made to hold a meeting. It appears that a certain number of persons did go from Sancroft Street to the Embankment; but that they did not hold any meeting. I am informed that meetings have been held in Sancroft Street on Sundays for about six months past. Chapman and Kemp were arrested on a warrant issued on the 4th of May by a magistrate sitting at Lambeth Police Court, charging them, I believe, with unlawful assembly. I have before informed the House that the police have no special instructions to prevent Socialist meetings as such; and I am assured that no such instructions, nor any special instructions at all, were given in the case of last Sunday's meeting. The Secretary of State gave no orders at all concerning it.

MR. PICTON asked, whether the hon. and learned Member would inform the House what reason the Commissioner of Police had to anticipate any breach of the peace; and, whether any breach of the peace had occurred at previous meetings on the same spot?

MR. STUART-WORTLEY: I can only suppose that the Commissioner of

Police anticipated a breach of the peace for good reasons.

BUSINESS OF THE HOUSE—EMPLOYERS' LIABILITY BILL.

MR. BROADHURST (Nottingham, W.) asked the Secretary of State for the Home Department, Whether he can inform the House when he proposes to introduce the Employers' Liability Bill?

THE UNDER SECRETARY OF STATE (Mr. STUART-WORTLEY) (Sheffield, Hallam) (who replied) said: I have already informed the House that the Secretary of State will introduce this Bill at the earliest possible opportunity. The provisions of the Bill have been remodelled in many particulars since my last answer; and it has, therefore, been again in the hands of the draftsman, who has returned it to-day.

DUKE OF CONNAUGHT'S LEAVE BILL—CHARGE ON INDIAN REVENUE.

MR. BUCHANAN (Edinburgh, W.) asked the Under Secretary of State for India, Whether any additional charge, directly or indirectly, will be imposed upon the Revenues of India in the event of the Duke of Connaught's Leave Bill becoming law?

THE UNDER SECRETARY OF STATE (Sir JOHN GORST) (Chatham): There will be no additional charge, direct or indirect, on the Revenues of India in the event of the Duke of Connaught's Leave Bill becoming law and being acted on. There will, on the contrary, be an appreciable saving in salaries.

ARMY (AUXILIARY FORCES) — THE VOLUNTEER FORCE—THE NEW REGULATIONS.

MR. LAWSON (St. Pancras, W.) asked the Secretary of State for War, Why the issue of the new Regulations has been delayed until half of the Volunteer year has elapsed; and, what will be the position of those Corps who have commenced their musketry course on the old system?

THE SURVEYOR GENERAL OF ORDNANCE (Mr. NORTHCOTE) (Exeter) (who replied) said: My right hon. Friend the Secretary of State for War desires me to say that he is personally responsible for the delay in issuing the new Volunteer Regulations. He kept them back partly at the request of some hon. Friends behind him, in order that he might have time to consider what modifications could be introduced to meet their objections, and the changes he proposed had also to obtain the approval of the Treasury.

LAW AND POLICE — SEVERE SENTENCE AT THE MARYLEBONE POLICE COURT.

MR. W. A. MACDONALD (Queen's Co., Ossory) asked the Secretary of State for the Home Department, Whether it is true, as stated in *The Daily News* of Saturday, that on the previous day at the Marylebone Police Court, a woman named Fowles, who had acted as cook in a gentleman's family for over two years, and had hitherto borne a good character, was sentenced by the magistrate, Mr. Cooke, to three months' imprisonment, with hard labour, for giving a poor woman named Box, a halfpenny bundle of wood, a beetroot, and a basin of soup, the property of her master; and, whether he will inquire into the circumstances of the case, with a view, if possible, of mitigating the severity of the sentence?

THE UNDER SECRETARY OF STATE (Mr. STUART-WORTLEY) (Sheffield, Hallam) (who replied) said: It appears that the newspaper account of this case incompletely states the facts. The magistrate was satisfied that the particular theft charged, though small in itself, was not the first of which the prisoner had been guilty, but was one of a systematic series of small robberies from her master. Under these circumstances, the Secretary of State sees no reason to interfere with the sentence.

EVICTIONS (IRELAND)—EVICTIONS ON THE MARQUESS OF LANSDOWNE'S ESTATE AT LUGGACURRAN.

MR. W. A MACDONALD (Queen's Co., Ossory) asked the Chief Secretary to the Lord Lieutenant of Ireland, Whether it is true that the police at Borris-in-Ossory, Queen's County, have torn down all the osters announcing a collection in aid of the Marquess of Lansdowne's evicted tenants at Luggacurran; and, if so, whether he will inform the House, by virtue of what Act of Parliament the police took this course?

Mr. Northcote

THE PARLIAMENTARY UNDER SECRETARY (Colonel KING-HARMAN) (Kent, Isle of Thanet) (who replied) said: I regret that I have been unable to obtain the necessary reply for this Question as it is down without Notice, and involves a local reference.

LAW AND POLICE—OUTRAGE AT A MEETING AT AUDLEM, CHESHIRE.

MR. M'LAREN (Cheshire, Crewe) asked the Secretary of State for the Home Department, Whether his attention has been called to the account in the papers of an attempt, on May 6th, to break up a meeting, in favour of Home Rule, in Audlem, in the Eddesbury Division of Cheshire, to the following effect :—

"That, while Mr. Walter M'Laren, M.P., was speaking, some person placed under the door behind the platform a lighted fusee, attached to a bag containing cayenne pepper and other strong smelling powder. That the room soon became full of dense and poisonous smoke, and every one was nearly suffocated, while it had a most injurious effect on their throats and lungs;"

whether he will offer a reward for the discovery of the perpetrators of this outrage; and, if they are discovered, whether he will prosecute them?

THE UNDER SECRETARY OF STATE (Mr STUART-WORTLEY) (Sheffield, Hallam) (who replied) said: The Secretary of State's attention has not been called, otherwise than by the hon. Member's Question, to the newspaper report referred to. The preservation of order, and the detection of crime in the County of Cheshire are duties incumbent upon the County Police. The Secretary of State has discontinued the practice of offering rewards.

LAW AND JUSTICE—EXCLUSION FROM THE POLICE COURTS.

MR. CUNNINGHAME GRAHAM (Lanark, N.W.) asked the Secretary of State for the Home Department, If the police were justified in excluding from the Lambeth Police Court, on Monday, 2nd May, J. Kemp, G. Morris, W. Mahony, G. Chapman, T. Griffiths, Mrs. Andrews, and Miss Andrews, who went for the purpose of hearing Blackwell's examination; and, whether the police are to exclude at their discretion any persons who conduct themselves properly?

THE UNDER SECRETARY OF STATE (Mr. STUART WORTLEY) (Sheffield, Hallam) (who replied) said: The police magistrate reports that on Monday, the 2nd of May, the Court was crowded from its first opening. The officer who was on duty at the door reports that, though many persons were of necessity kept waiting in the lobby until others left the Court, no application for admission was made to him by any persons expressing themselves interested in Blackwell's case.

MR. BRADLAUGH (Northampton) asked, whether the hon. and learned Gentleman meant to say that in all cases of summary prosecution the police court was not an open court, to which any members of the public had a right of access?

MR. STUART WORTLEY: That is a question that had better be addressed to the Attorney General.

INLAND REVENUE—THE STAMP ACTS LEGISLATION.

MR. CRAIG SELLAR (Lanarkshire, Partick) asked Mr. Chancellor of the Exchequer, If it is his intention to consider the question of the Stamp Acts, with the view of introducing a measure next Session to deal with the anomalies now existing in these Acts?

THE CHANCELLOR OF THE EXCHEQUER (Mr. GOSCHEN) (St. George's, Hanover Square): It is somewhat early to ask me what measures I shall see my way to introduce next Session; but certainly it would be my desire, so far as it is possible to do so, to review the many anomalies that exist in the Stamp Acts, and I will give my best attention to the subject, including the point which I know the hon. Member is interested in with regard to stamps upon leases, and other documents of that description.

OPEN-AIR MEETINGS (METROPOLIS)— PROPOSED MEETING AT KENNINGTON—CRITICISM OF THE POLICE.

MR. CONYBEARE (Cornwall, Camborne) asked the Secretary of State for the Home Department, Whether the chief officer at the Kennington Road Police Station is correctly reported as having given the following reply to a request, on the part of the promoters of a public meeting, for protection, on Sunday last—namely—

"If you assemble here and attract opposition, I shall hold you responsible, and deal with you. If you hold no meeting there can be no disturbance; if you do hold one, and opposition arrives, I shall hold you responsible for attracting that opposition, and I shall have you moved on pretty quickly;"

and, if this report is accurate, will he state under what authority the police were acting on this occasion?

THE UNDER SECRETARY OF STATE (Mr. STUART WORTLEY) (Sheffield, Hallam) (who replied) said: I am informed by the Chief Commissioner of Police that Superintendent Brennan, who was chief officer on the occasion to which the hon. Member refers, states that he made no such reply, nor used any words to that effect, and that the report is entirely incorrect.

THE MAGISTRACY (IRELAND)— CAPTAIN SHAW, R.M.

DR. TANNER (Cork Co., Mid) asked Mr. Attorney General for Ireland, Which of the two men, named respectively Daniel Falvey and Timothy Buckley, was charged before the Aghadillane Bench of Magistrates, on the night of the 27th of April, with attacking a dwelling house, was proved to have had in his possession a revolver; who were the witnesses that proved Buckley, the man in question, drew the said revolver upon an old man named Twomey, the owner of the dwelling house attacked, and his two young daughters; whether the licence to carry arms was granted to Falvey in his capacity of an *employé* of the Cork Landlords' Defence Union; whether Daniel Falvey has undergone a confinement for the term of five years at the Upton Reformatory, County Cork, for housebreaking; whether Captain Stokes, R.M., admitted that, from the evidence given, he was both satisfied and sorry that the emergency *employés* had committed the offence with which they were charged; what reasons have been given by Captain Stokes, R.M., for disagreeing with his fellow magistrate, and in marking "No rule" in the case; and, whether Captain Stokes will be one of the magistrates to whom it is proposed to give discretionary power under the Crimes Act, 1887?

THE ATTORNEY GENERAL FOR IRELAND (Mr. HOLMES) (Dublin University), in reply, said, he had already stated, in reply to the same Question, that neither of the men had a revolver in his possession. No reference was made at the hearing of the case to the fact that Falvey had undergone a term of confinement in Upton Reformatory for housebreaking; and if it had been made he would have considered it most objectionable. Captain Stokes did not make the admission referred to in the Question; and he (the Attorney General for Ireland) would not discuss the Criminal Law Amendment Bill with the hon. Member.

Mr. MAURICE HEALY (Cork) asked, what exactly was the provocation Falvey had received?

Mr. HOLMES said, he had already answered the Question on the Paper; and if any further information was wanted on the subject, a Question should be put on the Paper.

Dr. TANNER: I will call attention to it in another form.

AUSTRALIA (NORTH-WEST COAST)— DISASTER AT SEA—THE PEARL FISHING FLEET.

Mr. JOICEY (Durham, Chester-le-Street) asked the Secretary of State for the Colonies, If he can give any information as to the recent disaster to the Pearl Fishing Fleet on the North West Coast of Australia, and state the number of British lives lost; and whether, considering the number of British sailors employed in the fleet whose families are anxious about them, he will endeavour to ascertain and publish the names of those whose lives have been lost by the disaster?

The SECRETARY of STATE (Sir Henry Holland) (Hampstead): I have not yet received any details with regard to this disaster; but it appears from telegrams that some of the boats supposed to have been lost have escaped. The pearling vessels are, for the most part, manned by Natives, and it is hoped that there were very few White men lost. The Governor will be desired, by telegraph, to give the names as far as known.

NEW GUINEA—THE COLONY OF QUEENSLAND.

Mr. W. H. JAMES (Gateshead) asked the Secretary of State for the Colonies, Whether the Government has come to any understanding with the Colony of Queensland as to the future administra-

Mr. Holmes

tion of New Guinea; and, if so, what stipulations have been made on behalf of the Native inhabitants of the Protected Territory?

The SECRETARY of STATE (Sir Henry Holland) (Hampstead): The scheme proposed by Her Majesty's Government with respect to the government of New Guinea has been laid before the Delegates at the Colonial Conference, and approved by them; but the sanction of the different Colonial Governments and Legislatures is, of course, required. Till communications have been made to those Governments it is not desirable to enter into details; but I can assure the hon. Member that full protection has been given to Native interests.

ADMIRALTY CONTRACTS — CONSTRUCTION OF ENGINES.

Mr. BARBOUR (Paisley) asked the First Lord of the Admiralty, If it is true, as stated in *The Standard* of Friday last, that when a vessel is laid down in any of the Dockyards, it has been decided to obtain from the chief of the steam branch of such Dockyard an estimate for the engines, to consider such estimate in connection with the tenders from private firms, and, should the comparison be favourable to the official estimate, that the engines will then be constructed in the Dockyard; and, what security the House will have that the engines will be actually constructed and supplied within the terms of the estimates so submitted to the Admiralty?

The FIRST LORD (Lord George Hamilton) (Middlesex, Ealing): The statement is only true so far as it refers to the machinery of two gunboats of the *Rattler* class about to be built at Devonport. The officers of the engineering staff of the Admiralty and Dockyards will be responsible that the engines are constructed and supplied within the terms of the estimates.

POST OFFICE (SCOTLAND) — POSTAL SERVICE IN INVERNESS-SHIRE.

Dr. CLARK (Caithness) asked the Postmaster General, Whether it is the case that letters from Loch Lochy to Inverness, a distance of 15 miles, take 55 hours in delivery, and whether letters from Invergarry to Achnacarry, a distance of eight miles, are carried 360 miles before delivery; and, whether he intends to adopt measures to remedy the defective postal communication along the line of the Caledonian Canal, and to directly connect Inverness, Invergarry, and Fort William?

THE POSTMASTER GENERAL (Mr. RAIKES) (Cambridge University), in reply, said, it would be necessary to make inquiries before he could give any satisfactory reply to the Question of the hon. Member, and he should give directions for such inquiry to be made.

POST OFFICE (SCOTLAND)—SERVICE BETWEEN PERTH, ABERDEEN, AND KEITH.

DR. CLARK (Caithness) asked the Postmaster General, The average weight of the mails from Perth to the North by the 12.40 a.m. train, and from Aberdeen to Keith by the 3.35 a.m. train, also the sums paid for the conveyance of each of those mails?

THE POSTMASTER GENERAL (Mr. RAIKES) (Cambridge University), in reply, said, he would call for an account if the hon. Member desired it; but without taking an account he was unable to answer the Question. The remuneration for the conveyance of this particular mail from Perth to the North was included in the total payment under the contract with the Railway Company.

THE MAGISTRACY (IRELAND)—CAPTAIN STOKES, R.M.

DR. TANNER (Cork Co., Mid) asked Mr. Attorney General for Ireland, If his attention has been directed to the conduct of Captain Stokes, R.M., on the Bench of Magistrates at Ballyvourney, at the last Monthly Sessions; whether, in the case of William Connell, junior, a process server and assistant of Mr. Hegarty, J.P., *versus* John Casey, the language made use of by Captain Stokes was as reported, "the old gentleman Casey appears to have been a fighting old rascal;" whether the evidence tendered by an Irish speaking witness in behalf of Casey was stated in and before the Court to have been improperly interpreted; whether Leghare, the interpreter, was a fellow bailiff of the complainants; whether Leghare was fined subsequently by the same Bench for assaulting an aged man by striking him violently with a whip; whether the Go-

vernment will recommend that Casey's fine be remitted; whether Michael Connell, a brother of the process server, was in the employment of Mr. Hegarty; whether he was fined by Captain Stokes and Mr. Hegarty on the day in question for deliberately throwing stones at and severely injuring a horse, the property of the honorary secretary of the National League; and, what steps the Government propose to take in the matter?

THE ATTORNEY GENERAL FOR IRELAND (Mr. HOLMES) (Dublin University), in reply, said, no rule was entered in this case. Captain Stokes, R.M., did not use the expression attributed to him. His answer to paragraphs five and eight was "yes;" but subject to the qualification that the assault was not an aggravated one. He had no information with regard to paragraph seven. The Government did not intend to take any steps in the matter.

SCOTLAND—THE CROFTERS COMMISSION—VISIT TO SOLITOTE, ISLE OF SKYE.

DR. CLARK (Caithness) asked the Lord Advocate, If the following report of the visit of the Crofters Commission to the township of Solitote in *The Scotsman* of 6th May was correct:—

"Without exception, Solitote is the most miserable place which the Commissioners have yet visited, the patches of ground which the tenants cultivate vary in size from three roods to two acres. The township has no right of grazing. There are 17 families in the township and only three cows, and two of these are fed with grass purchased from the tenants of Conista, while the third picks up its living at the roadside. . . . The visit of the Commission caused a great deal of excitement in the township; the people crowded out to meet them, and followed them from croft to croft with long tales of their grievances. At various points of the inspection the Commissioners were met by groups of men, who urged them to give them more land. They pointed to the green fields of the sheep farms lying around, and asked why they should be huddled together while so much of the best land in Skye was under sheep. It was in vain that the Commissioners pointed out that under the present Act they had no power to create new crofts, even if the land were available;"

and, whether the Government will introduce a measure to empower the Crofters Commissioners to form new holdings or townships to relieve such congested townships as Solitote?

THE LORD ADVOCATE (Mr. J. H. A. MACDONALD) (Edinburgh and St.

Andrew's Universities): The Question which the hon. Member has put to me varies slightly from the Notice I received. It is quite impossible on short notice to express an opinion on a newspaper report regarding the condition of a distant part of the Highlands; but assuming the report is correct, Her Majesty's Government are not prepared to introduce a measure inconsistent with the provisions of an Act deliberately passed in a recent Session.

BUSINESS OF THE HOUSE.

MR. CHILDERS (Edinburgh, S.): I should like to ask the First Lord of the Treasury, Whether he could now say what the Business will be on Thursday?

THE FIRST LORD (Mr. W. H. SMITH) (Strand, Westminster): It is proposed to take the Duke of Connaught's Leave Bill first on Thursday, and the Motion for the Committee on the Army and Navy Estimates second, and then Supply, in the hope of getting the Jubilee Vote, and after that will come the Inland Revenue Bill.

MR. MARK STEWART (Kirkcudbright) asked what Business would be taken on Friday?

MR. W. H. SMITH: I can hardly expect that the Criminal Law Amendment Bill will be through Committee before then.

MR. LABOUCHERE (Northampton) asked why the additional Estimate, ordered to be printed on the 20th of April, and promised at the commencement of this week, and to be taken on Thursday, was not yet in the hands of Members?

THE SECRETARY TO THE TREASURY (Mr. JACKSON) (Leeds, N.) said, that had it not been for the rather late Sitting last night the Estimate would have been in the hands of Members that morning; but it would be in the hands of Members to-morrow morning. It was simple, and would be easily understood.

MR. LABOUCHERE: Sir, should the amount proposed to be voted for the celebration of the service in Westminster Abbey exceed the sum of £2,000, I shall move that it be reduced to that sum. I wish also to ask you, Sir, whether, in the event of a Motion being made to go into Committee of Supply in order to vote an additional Civil Service Esti-

Mr. J. H. A. Macdonald

mate, the Rule which allows a Motion to be made before you leave the Chair on first going into Committee of Supply on the Civil Service Estimates will be applicable?

MR. SPEAKER: The ordinary Rule will apply. Motions may be made on the Question, "That I now leave the Chair."

MR. LABOUCHERE said, he had understood the Speaker to rule that if a Motion were made on such an occasion the discussion could not be continued beyond one Sitting.

MR. SPEAKER said, the hon. Gentleman was in error. He had never ruled that a debate could not be continued if not concluded on the first day that the Motion was made that he should leave the Chair.

MR. CHILDERS said, he presumed that Supply not being the first Order on Thursday, Motions on going into Committee would be taken in the same way?

MR. SPEAKER: Certainly; that is the case.

MR. HENRY H. FOWLER (Wolverhampton, E.) asked when it was intended to take the Vote on Account of the Civil Service Estimates?

MR. W. H. SMITH said, it would be taken on Monday.

COAL MINES, &c. REGULATION BILL.

In reply to Sir JOSEPH PEASE (Durham, Barnard Castle),

THE FIRST LORD OF THE TREASURY (Mr. W. H. SMITH) (Strand, Westminster) said, he wished to arrange, if possible, for the consideration of this measure at a time which would be most convenient to hon. Members. He understood that it was the desire of hon. Gentlemen to discuss its provisions on going into Committee. The Government would endeavour to arrange for a time convenient to hon. Members; and until such arrangement was made the Bill would not be brought forward.

DUKE OF CONNAUGHT'S LEAVE BILL.

SIR GEORGE CAMPBELL (Kirkcaldy, &c.) asked, Whether it was necessary to proceed with the Bill granting leave to the Duke of Connaught to attend the Jubilee festivities, as it was only necessary for the Duke to give up his command, and then at the end of the celebrations it would be quite in the power of the Executive to re-appoint him at any moment?

THE FIRST LORD OF THE TREASURY (Mr. W. H. SMITH) (Strand, Westminster) said, it would be more consistent with the order and regularity of Public Business, when it was intended that His Royal Highness the Duke of Connaught should obtain leave to come home, that the legal obstacles, the legislative obstacles, which existed to that course should be removed by Parliament itself. It would be giving the go-by to Parliament if they adopted the course suggested by the hon. Gentleman, without having previously taken the opinion of Parliament on the subject.

PRIVATE BILL LEGISLATION.

MR. T. M. HEALY (Longford, N.) said, there had appeared on the Paper that morning, for the first time a Motion standing in the name of the First Lord of the Treasury in regard to Private Bill Legislation as follows:—

"That a Committee of Five Members of this House be appointed, to join with a Committee of The Lords, to consider the best means of relieving Parliament from the duties now discharged by Private Bill Committees, and making other provisions in lieu thereof."

Had that Notice anything to do with the Home Rule Question; and was it the intention of the Government to take the Motion that night?

THE FIRST LORD OF THE TREASURY (Mr. W. H. SMITH) (Strand, Westminster) said, certainly not. If it was the desire of hon. Members to discuss this question, an opportunity would be given them to do so.

PARLIAMENT—PRIVILEGE—MR. MOLLOY AND "THE TIMES"—PERSONAL EXPLANATION.

MR. MOLLOY (King's Co., Birr): I wish to make, Sir, a personal explanation. I desire to read the copy of a letter which I have addressed to the noble Viscount the Secretary of State for India—

"9th May, 1887.

"The Right Hon. Viscount Cross, G.C.B., Chairman of the Royal Commission on Education.

"My Lord,—I have the honour to inform you of the resignation of my seat at the Board of the Royal Commission on Education. In deference to my Colleagues upon that Commission, I feel it necessary to state the causes of such resignation. In 1885, when the Conservative Government was in close alliance with the Irish Nationalist Party, I was named one of the Royal Commissioners on Education by Her Majesty on the recommendation of the then Conservative Government. Previous to this recommendation a number of scandalous anonymous libels had been published against the Irish Nationalist Members of the House of Commons. Since the advent to power of the present Conservative Administration, composed of the same gentlemen as those of the previous one, the same anonymous libels have been reproduced by *The Times* newspaper and issued as a pamphlet. This pamphlet has been used and circulated, as I believe, for political purposes by Members of the present Government. When the Government was challenged in a late debate to afford an opportunity for refuting these infamous accusations by the appointment of a Committee of the House, the Government, although publishing and using such charges, declined to afford this facility. Since this refusal Members of the Government continue to use and circulate these libels in the same manner and for the same purpose as hitherto. Under these circumstances, my self-respect compels me to resign my position as a Member of the Royal Commission on Education, since it was conferred upon me on the recommendation of these very Gentlemen whose conduct I have above described. I have the honour to be, my Lord, your obedient servant,

"BERNARD C. MOLLOY."

MUNICIPAL CORPORATIONS ACTS (IRELAND) AMENDMENT (No. 2) BILL.

MR. SEXTON (Belfast, W.) said, he saw by the Paper that this Bill was blocked by both the hon. Member for North Antrim (Sir Charles Lewis) and the hon. Member for Wigton (Sir Herbert Maxwell), two supporters of the Government; and he wished to know did the Government intend to take any action in reference thereto?

THE FIRST LORD OF THE TREASURY (Mr. W. H. SMITH) (Strand, Westminster) said, the Chief Secretary for Ireland, who was responsible for the government of Ireland, was the only Minister who could answer the question; and he would see what the views of the right hon. Gentleman were on the subject.

CRIMINAL LAW AMENDMENT (IRELAND) BILL.—[BILL 217.]

(*Mr. A. J. Balfour, Mr. Secretary Matthews, Mr. Attorney General, Mr. Attorney General for Ireland.*)

COMMITTEE. [*Progress* 9*th May.*]

[FIFTH NIGHT.]

Bill *considered* in Committee.

(In the Committee.)

[*Fifth Night.*]

PRELIMINARY INQUIRY.

Clause 1 (Inquiry by order of Attorney General).

MR. T. M. HEALY (Longford, N.), in moving, as an Amendment, in page 1, line 18, after "enactments," to insert—

"Viz. sections eleven, twelve, and thirteen of the Act of the fourteenth and fifteenth Victoria, chapter ninety-three,"

said: I desire to know from the Government exactly what it is they propose to do by means of this sub-section. We sometimes hear a great deal about the difficulty of making progress with this measure; but I should like to call the attention of the Committee to the fact that in the half-a-dozen lines of which the sub-section consists the Government have imported three entire sections of an Act of Parliament of enormous length, which, if published—as they ought to be published—in the Bill, would take up four or five pages of the measure. My complaint is that in this way they are endeavouring to hoodwink the Committee. The Amendment I propose is a very trifling alteration indeed; but I wish to show what the sections are which the Government are endeavouring to import into the measure. I do not say that I approve of the importation of these sections at all; and all I desire is that we should know whether these are the sections which the Government propose to import, or whether they are not? The sections of the Petty Sessions (Ireland) Act which I propose to embody are—first, Section 11, which is a section of considerable length, and which relates to the person against whom an information has been laid. It provides that—

"In all cases of indictable crimes and offences where an information that any person has committed the same shall have been taken in writing or on oath, the justice shall issue a warrant to arrest and bring such person before him or some other justice of the same county to answer to the complaint made in the information—and which warrant may be issued and executed on a Sunday or any other day—or if he should think that the course of justice would be thereby sufficiently answered it should be lawful for him, instead of issuing such warrant, to issue a summons, in the first instance, to such person requiring him to appear and answer to the said complaint."

I object altogether to the justices having power to hold an inquiry on a Sunday, and of thus desecrating the Sabbath; and I hope to have the support of hon. Members who, although they may have been scheduled for corrupt practices in connection with elections, nevertheless warmly protest against anything like the desecration of the Sabbath. It does appear to me that the power given to the justices to issue warrants in this manner at their discretion is not sufficiently defined. I think the Government ought to let us know in what cases they think a summons should be issued, and in what cases a warrant should be issued. It is a monstrous thing to give the magistrates illimitable power of issuing warrants up and down the country without strictly defining their powers. This section was never intended to apply to these cases, but was simply intended to apply to indictable offences; and yet the Government propose to apply this clause to ordinary cases, other than indictable offences. They propose to apply provisions, intended to meet the case of indictable offences, to ordinary cases, which can be dealt with summarily, and which include very small offences indeed. The section goes on to say—

"But nothing herein contained shall prevent any justice from issuing a warrant for the arrest of such person at any time before or after the time mentioned in such summons for his appearance."

That is certainly a very nice provision. A man may be arrested at any time; he may be taken out of his bed to answer any questions that may be put to him without a summons; he may be arrested at any time, and although a summons may have been issued to compel his appearance, he may be arrested in spite of that summons. The summons may require him to appear before the magistrates at 3 o'clock in the afternoon; but under a warrant he may be arrested at midnight. We are attacked by the newspapers for opposing the provisions of this Bill. Personally I pay very little attention to what ignorant men, who do not know what they are talking about, may say. I maintain that when we are endeavouring to expose these monstrous and iniquitous proceedings in the House of Commons we ought to receive some reasonable consideration, instead of being met by Motions—"That the Question be now put." The section goes on to say—

"And whenever such person shall afterwards appear or be brought before any such justice he shall proceed according to the provisions hereinafter contained."

That section of the clause deals altogether with indictable offences. Conspiracy is an indictable offence. If men combine against a landlord for a reduction of rent that is conspiracy; and a magistrate would be justified in taking them out of their beds at any time by means of a warrant, and without a summons. The 2nd section of the clause relates to cases of summary jurisdiction. It says—

"In all cases of summary jurisdiction the justice may issue his summons direct to such person, requiring him to appear in person in answer to the complaint, and it shall not be necessary that such justice shall be the justice, or one of the justices, by whom the complaint shall be afterwards heard and determined."

I defy anybody to make sense of that, yet it is proposed that this provision is to be put in force by ignorant military and naval officers, who know nothing whatever about the law, and will have to work out the meaning of the clause in their own intelligent brains.

"It shall not be necessary that such justice shall be the justice, or one of the justices, by whom the complaint shall be afterwards heard and determined."

In the next place, any justice may, in spite of the issue of a summons, issue a warrant for the appearance of any man without reference to the requirements of the Resident Magistrate; and the section goes on to say—

"And in all cases of offences where such person shall not appear at the required time and place, and it shall be proved on oath, either that he was personally served with such summons, or that he is keeping out of the way of such service, the justice may issue a warrant to arrest and bring such person before him, or some other justice of the same county, to answer to the said complaint."

It then goes on to provide—

"That the warrant or summons is to be signed, but not in blank, and that the summons or warrant may run into an adjoining county."

The next clause is No. 12, which relates to the service of the summons. I do not know how far the Government intend to import Section 12 into this Bill.

THE ATTORNEY GENERAL FOR IRELAND (Mr. HOLMES) (Dublin University): We do not import it at all.

MR. T. M. HEALY: Is Clause 13 imported?

MR. HOLMES: A portion of it.

MR. T. M. HEALY: I should be glad to learn what portion of that sec-

tion the Government propose to include in this clause. The sub-section now under discussion states that the enactments relating to the compelling of the attendance before a justice shall apply as if they were re-enacted. Section 11 provides what the justices are to do. The right hon. and learned Gentleman says that he does not propose to include Section 12; but when I put a question to him in reference to Section 13 he said that he proposes to include a portion of it. How is a justice to know what portion of that section is included? I myself may presume to have some small knowledge of the law, and I confess that I cannot tell by reading this section what part of it the right hon. and learned Gentleman intends to incorporate in the present Bill. I shall be glad if the right hon. Gentleman will tell us exactly what it is that he proposes, and how much of the section is intended to include. I am quite ready to give way to the right hon. and learned Gentleman; so that the Committee may hear what he has to say.

THE CHAIRMAN: It would be necessary, in the first instance, for the hon. and learned Member to make a Motion.

MR. T. M. HEALY: I make the Motion standing on the Paper in my name.

Amendment proposed,

In page 1, line 18, after " enactments." insert " viz., sections eleven, twelve, and thirteen of the Act of the fourteenth and fifteenth Victoria, chapter ninety-three."—(*Mr. T. M. Healy.*)

Question proposed, "That those words be there inserted."

MR. HOLMES: At this stage of the Committee it is, perhaps, too much to express surprise at anything that may happen; but I must protest against the speech of the hon. and learned Member, which surprises me more than I had believed I could be surprised. I believe that the Bill pretty clearly expresses, in the 2nd sub-section of the clause, what is proposed to be done. It provides that—

" The enactments relating to the compelling of the attendance of a witness before a justice, and to a witness attending before a justice and required to give evidence concerning the matter of an information, or a complaint for an indictable offence, shall apply for the purposes of this section as if they were re-enacted herein, and in terms made applicable thereto."

I think that is sufficiently definite and clear for such purposes, and yet, that being so, I am asked by the hon. and learned Member, who is himself acquainted, I presume, with the interpretation of statutes, and who certainly ought to be acquainted with the provisions of such a statute as the Petty Sessions (Ireland) Act, to explain the meaning .of these clauses of that Act. Now, according to my recollection, there is not a line in the 11th section of the Petty Sessions (Ireland) Act which deals in any way with enforcing the attendance of witnesses. The 11th section deals with an entirely different matter. It deals with the compelling of a person against whom a criminal charge is made—which is wholly different from compelling a witness—to attend. If the hon. and learned Member looks at the marginal note attached to that section, he will find that it is described as "process to enforce appearance in cases of indictable offences." All these provisions refer to the case of a person against whom a charge is made, and it provides the means by which such person may be compelled to come into Court. There is nothing whatever in the section about compelling the attendance of a witness. The section which compels the attendance of a witness is the 13th section. If the hon. and learned Member will look at that section, he will find that the marginal note is that " the justice may force witnesses to attend and give evidence." The clause is divided into different sub-sections. The first provides for the issue of a summons for the attendance of a witness to give evidence in a case which may be disposed of by summary jurisdiction. In that particular case a summons is issued to the witness, and he is naturally obliged to attend in compliance with the summons; if he does not attend, a warrant may then be issued for the purpose of bringing the witness before the Justice of the Peace in the same way as in the case of an indictable offence. The summons must be issued in the first instance ; but if that summons is disobeyed, then the person disobeying it may be arrested forthwith. The section goes on to specify what persons shall be competent witnesses, and to provide that witnesses may be examined on oath, and the information or complaint is required to be in writing or on oath. The refusal or

neglect of any person summoned to appear at the time and place appointed by such summons justifies the justice in bringing him before the Court under a warrant. A further sub-section deals with witnesses who are contumacious, and provides that a witness declining to answer a question or refusing to take the oath may be committed by the justice or justices for any period not exceeding eight days. He may then be brought up again, and if he still declines to answer proper questions or to be sworn, he may be further imprisoned, provided that no such imprisonment shall, in any case of summary jurisdiction, exceed one month in the whole. What we propose to do in this section is to incorporate those provisions. Our attention, however, has been called to the circumstance that the clause, as it has been drafted, might make the procedure applicable to a summons or warrant for an indictable offence applicable also to a person summoned for summary jurisdiction, and for the purpose of removing that doubt it will be necessary to insert an Amendment. The House must bear in mind that nothing is proposed in this clause which is new in our ordinary procedure in regard to criminal cases; and, under these circumstances, the Government cannot possibly accept the Amendment of the hon. and learned Gentleman, because, if they did, they would be incorporating in the Bill a number of provisions which can have no possible application to the particular cases in question.

MR. T. M. HEALY: The only object of my Amendment was to define clearly the powers which the Government propose to take. I have no desire by this Amendment to extend the powers which the Government themselves propose to take. I will, therefore, only ask them to accept my Amendment so far as Section 13 is concerned. *Quo ad* Section 13, I only wish the Government to define this part of the clause. Nevertheless, I maintain that my construction of the section is perfectly correct, and, if necessary, I could point out reasons for arriving at that conclusion. What I am afraid of is that no sooner will this Act be put into operation than the magistrates will take advantage of the powers given under Section 11, although the Government say that Section 11 is not to apply at all. If that is the case, I think the Government ought to make it clear that Section 11 does not apply. Are they prepared to do that? No, Sir; the Government will do nothing of the kind; and there, I am afraid, is the dodge of the whole matter. I dispute the sincerity of the Government. The provisions of this Bill will be put in force by magistrates who are as incapable of reading an Act of Parliament as a body of horse marines. If I, who may be presumed to understand the law, fail to see that the section may not be made to apply, how much more likely would a horse marine be to jump at the same conclusion? Section 11 provides that—

"Whenever information shall be given to any justice that any person has committed, or is suspected to have committed, any treason, felony, misdemeanour, or other offence within the limits of the jurisdiction of such justice, it shall be lawful for such justice to receive such information or complaint, and to proceed in respect of the same."

By this provision a man may be sent to gaol if he is suspected of having committed any offence whatever; and the clause provides that such person shall be punishable either by indictment or upon a summary conviction, and then, if any person has committed, or is suspected to have committed, any crime or offence, certain things are to happen which are intended to secure his appearance before a Court. I ask the right hon. and learned Gentleman the Attorney General to give his attention to Sub-section 1 of Section 10, which states—

"Whenever it is intended that a summons only shall be issued to require the attendance of any person, the information or complaint may be made either with or without oath, in writing or not, according as the justice may see fit."

That is to say, that such information or complaint may be made even when an offence has been committed. But what is an offence? A police constable may be altogether ignorant of the law; and, therefore, what I want the Government to do is to define what the sections of this Act are which they are taking power to incorporate. To say that Section 10 will not apply is, I maintain, treating the matter in an illusory manner, unless it is specifically provided that it shall not apply. It says that whenever a summons is issued certain things are to happen. Whenever it is intended that a warrant shall be issued the information or complaint is to be in

writing, and then there is a further provision in regard to summary proceedings. It is in that way that Section 10 will come in, and the marginal note to the section is "process to enforce appearance." The right hon. and learned Gentleman says that no power is taken to incorporate Section 11, and, if so, I hope the right hon. and learned Gentleman will have the goodness to declare that in the clause itself in express terms. What I am afraid of is that this is an attempt to take powers by a side wind. It will be impossible to do that if the Government consent to accept my Amendment, and therefore I ask the right hon. and learned Gentleman to take my Amendment *quo ad* every portion of the sections he desires to incorporate. I hope the Committee will receive a full explanation as to what it is Her Majesty's Government really propose to do.

SIR GEORGE CAMPBELL (Kirkcaldy, &c.): As I understand this subsection, it provides that the law in regard to the attendance of a witness before the justices in an indictable offence shall be extended to the case of witnesses summoned under the Summary Jurisdiction Act. I presume that when the law of Ireland requires a witness to attend to be examined in an indictable offence he is ordinarily examined in public, and I gather that the object of this extension of the law is to provide that the same powers should be conferred upon the Resident Magistrate in the case of the examination of a witness in connection with an offence. Now we are told that the examination is to be in private. I do not say that that is wrong, but it does not appear on the face of the clause. One would rather suppose that the Resident Magistrate is to sit in open court to examine the witness who is to be summoned, and that the law is to be the same in regard to his attendance as if it were an indictable offence. I think we ought to have some explanation from the Government as to how the secrecy under such circumstances is to be brought about. We are quite aware that the examination before the Sheriff in Scotland, at the instance of the Procurator Fiscal, is a private examination.

THE CHAIRMAN: The hon. Gentleman is re-opening a question which has already been discussed, and which is not pertinent to the Amendment now before the Committee.

Mr. BRADLAUGH (Northampton): May I be allowed to point out that last night the words which commenced this sub-section—namely, "the enactments" —were carried. Now, I do not find in the Bill any definition of those words. What is meant by "the enactments?" Are the words intended to apply to some specific enactments? The words contained in the 2nd clause, which refer to the Whiteboy Acts, are definite. The right hon. and learned Attorney General for Ireland has given an explanation which, if it formed part of the Bill itself, would be perfectly satisfactory, except that a certain portion of it seems to be inconsistent with the wording of the clause. I do not quite see that "the enactments" are limited by any means of construction which are known to an ordinary Court, and this Act is to guide a Court of very limited experience. I notice that the hon. and learned Gentleman the Attorney General (Sir Richard Webster) seems to think that that is a very absurd position to take. I beg the hon. and learned Gentleman's pardon for confusing the Attorney Generals together. It was the right hon. and learned Attorney General for Ireland (Mr. Holmes) who seemed to consider that that was an absurd construction to put upon the matter; but, nevertheless, I venture to maintain that it is the clear wording of the section as it stands. It applies to a witness attending before a justice, and being required to give evidence concerning the matter of an information or complaint for an indictable offence; and, therefore, it rules the words "the enactments," which are to apply to witnesses giving evidence against some person charged with the commission of a crime? They are to be "the enactments concerning the examination of witnesses." Now, I am not fully conversant with what Irish enactments are, but some of them I know are on all fours with English enactments, and I am of opinion that this provision would be absolutely inconsistent with the procedure which the right hon. and learned Attorney General for Ireland has told us is meant to be pursued. I would suggest that the Committee ought not to let the words "the enactments," be left as they are without any definition, without knowing

The Chairman

what it is that the Government really desire to do, and only with an explanation of what may be in the mind of the right hon. and learned Attorney General for Ireland. We must remember that the mind of the Attorney General is no part of the Statute, and what the Committee require is that there should be a clear definition of the provisions of the Statute which the Government propose to enforce.

Mr. HOLMES: Although the words appear to me to be perfectly plain, and have been used in former Statutes, yet, if it is thought that it would make the meaning more clear, I have no objection whatever to correct the section in this way—

"The enactments contained in the Petty Sessions (Ireland) Act of 1851 in Section 13 relating to the attendance of witnesses before justices."

I do not think that anything will be done by that Amendment which has not been done before; but I am willing to insert it, although, in the clause as it has been drawn, I have followed the words of the former Act.

Mr. T. M. HEALY: I beg to thank the right hon. and learned Gentleman and to withdraw the Amendment.

Amendment by leave, *withdrawn.*

Amendment proposed,

After the word "enactments," to insert "contained in Section 13 of the Petty Sessions (Ireland) Act of 1851 relating to the attendance of witnesses before justices."—(*Mr. Attorney General for Ireland.*)

Question, "That those words be there inserted," put, and *agreed to.*

Mr. O'DOHERTY (Donegal, N.): I have an Amendment on the Paper to leave out the words "for an indictable offence," which appear in the fourth line of this sub-section. The sub-section would then read in this way—

"The enactments relating to the compelling of the attendance of a witness before a justice, and to a witness attending before a justice and required to give evidence concerning the matter of an information or complaint, shall apply for the purposes of this section as if they were re-enacted herein, and in terms made applicable thereto."

That I apprehend would be taken distributively.

The ATTORNEY GENERAL (Sir Richard Webster) (Isle of Wight): The Amendment which follows this, and which is in the name of the right hon. and learned Attorney General for Ireland, deals with that matter,

MR. O'DOHERTY : I am quite aware of that, and I think that the words of the right hon. and learned Gentleman are a fair attempt to meet the engagement he gave the other day; but I wish to call attention to the word "complaint," because a complaint is not an information. The word "complaint" is applied where a case is dealt with summarily. The question I wish to raise is, whether the power of compelling the witness to give evidence before a Court where the case is being heard should be applied in all its nakedness to a witness who is not known to be able, but is merely suspected of being able, to give evidence. In other words, I desire to secure that there should be no power to compel a man to attend by arrest who would attend if summoned. I wish the Committee to understand clearly what sort of oath has to be made before a summary process is put in force to compel the attendance of a witness on an indictable offence. Its contents would simply be that there is a probability that such person would not attend to give evidence without being compelled to do so. There are two forms of compulsion—one by means of physical force, and another by moral compulsion; and what I complain of here is that, as the clause now stands, any man would be liable to be arrested at any hour of the night without the magistrate having been informed on oath by the constable, or the person laying the information, that there was any suspicion that he would. levant if he got a summons. Therefore, I think it is better not to apply in all its nakedness the extreme power of the Petty Sessions Act to the case of offences which may be tried summarily by a magistrate. I admit that the object of any Amendment is fairly met by the Amendment of the right hon. and learned Attorney General for Ireland; but I would call the attention of the Committee to the fact that the oath which is required to be taken before the issue of a warrant is not exactly what the right hon. and learned Gentleman specifies in his description.

THE CHAIRMAN : I must remind the hon. Member, that, at the present moment, there is no Motion before the Committee. Does the right hon. and learned Attorney General for Ireland move the Amendment which is on the Paper in his name?

MR. HOLMES : Yes.

Amendment proposed,

In page 1, line 21, after "offence," insert "or concerning the matter of an information in respect of an offence punishable upon summary conviction, as the case may be."—(*Mr. Attorney General for Ireland.*)

Question proposed, "That those words be there inserted."

MR. MAURICE HEALY (Cork): I doubt whether the Amendment which has been moved by the Attorney General for Ireland quite covers the undertaking which was given by the hon. and learned Attorney General for England (Sir Richard Webster). The Government undertook that in applying the provisions of the Petty Sessions (Ireland) Act to proceedings under this clause, the provisions of that Act which relate to indictable offences only should be applied, and that the clauses of the Petty Sessions Act which relate to summary jurisdiction shall only apply when summary offences are under consideration. I do not think that the Amendment of the Attorney General for Ireland entirely carries out that undertaking, although, no doubt, it does partially. Perhaps I may be permitted to point out that it deals with two sets of enactments. In the first place, to the enactments relating to compelling the attendance of a witness before a justice. That is one set of enactments. But the point I wish to raise is this—that Section 13 of the Petty Sessions Act applies to two different things. It applies, in the first place, to the process of compelling the attendance of a witness before a justice; and, in the second place, to the process by which a witness attending before a justice may be compelled to give evidence. If the Amendment of the right hon. and learned Gentleman is agreed to, the clause will run in this way—

"The enactments relating to the compelling of the attendance of a witness before a justice, and to a witness attending before a justice and required to give evidence concerning the matter of an information or complaint for an indictable offence, or concerning the matter of an information in respect of an offence punishable upon summary conviction, as the case may be, shall apply for the purposes of this section as if they were re-enacted herein, and in terms made applicable thereto."

It is perfectly plain that the words the right hon. and learned Gentleman proposes to insert are only qualified

[*Fifth Night.*]

by the words "a witness attending before a justice and required to give evidence." I think it ought to be made perfectly clear that in the case of summary offences to be dealt with under this clause only that part of Section 13 of the Petty Sessions Act which relates to summary offences is to apply; but if the section is permitted to stand as it is at present, it will empower a magistrate to issue a warrant to compel the attendance of a witness in the first instance, although the offence may be one which is simply punishable summarily.

MR. HOLMES: I do not think the hon. and learned Member is correct. It so happens that my hon. and learned Friend the Attorney General for England and myself made independent drafts of the proposed Amendment, and there was only one unimportant word of difference between us. I do not think there can be any serious doubt as to the Amendment having the meaning intended to be given to it.

MR. MAURICE HEALY: I contend with great respect that the Amendment can only be read in one manner, and that is the manner which I have pointed out. The right hon. and learned Gentleman says that he and the hon. and learned Gentleman the Attorney General for England are agreed upon the point; but this is a matter which we wish to have made perfectly clear, and I will ask if the Government are willing to accept an Amendment in the form of a Proviso to provide that Section 13 is to be applied only in the case of indictable offences where the procedure relates to indictable offences, and in the case of summary offences to such offences only as those to which summary jurisdiction applies?

THE ATTORNEY GENERAL (Sir RICHARD WEBSTER) (Isle of Wight): I am afraid that if we were to add a Proviso such as that which the hon. Gentleman has suggested we should make a double enactment which would stultify the clause as it stands. The governing words of this section are—

"The enactments relating to the compelling of a witness before a justice, and to a witness attending before a justice and required to give evidence concerning the matter of an information or complaint for an indictable offence."

Then come in the words proposed to be

Mr. Maurice Healy

inserted by my right hon. and learned Friend—

"or concerning the matter of an information in respect of an offence punishable upon summary conviction, as the case may be."

Consequently, two alternatives are put, and then comes the distribution of the words "as the case may be." We have endeavoured to draft the Amendment to the best of our ability, and, in my opinion, I do not think it necessary to change the phraseology we have proposed.

MR. MAURICE HEALY: I trust that neither the right hon. and hon. and learned Gentlemen for a moment think I intend to impute any desire on their part to act unfairly; but this appears to me to be altogether a question of grammar. The word "concerning" in the sense in which it is used in the clause is an adjective, and together with the second word "concerning" proposed to be introduced into the section, it must, according to the contention of the Government, be read in conjunction with the word "enactments." Now, I maintain that it is to be read only in connection with the word "evidence." As the right hon. and learned Attorney General for Ireland puts the matter, the word "concerning" is made to apply to another word two lines off—namely, the second word in the sub-section; whereas the grammatical construction shows that it applies to the word immediately preceding it—namely, "evidence." I have no desire to press the matter unduly, but I would ask the right hon. and learned Attorney General for Ireland to give some attention to the point I have raised. It is to be regretted that we have not the exact words on the Paper, which would show how the clause would stand with this Amendment inserted in it. The right hon. and learned Gentleman says he is satisfied, and in that case I presume there is no getting over the matter. I would further ask him, when he sees a reprint of the Bill and has the whole clause in type, to examine it carefully, and I think he will come to a different conclusion.

MR. WALLACE (Edinburgh, E.): I would suggest to the right hon. and learned Gentleman the Attorney General for Ireland that he should substitute the words "which concern" instead of "concerning." They may appear to be clumsy, but I think they would be perfectly unambiguous.

Question, "That those words be there substituted," put, and *agreed to.*

Amendment, as amended, *agreed to.*

MR. T. M. HEALY (Longford, N.): I have now to move an Amendment by which I seek to provide that every person committed for contempt under the enactments referred to in the sub-section shall be treated as a first-class misdemeanant. It appears to me that the Government ought to consent to make the punishment of persons sent to prison for disobedience to this sub-section as light as possible. Of course, the Government may say that the offence may be of a serious character; but, after all, the punishment for it cannot amount to more than mere detention, and my point is that, even under the most favourable condition of the prison regulations, detention in gaol is a very severe discipline indeed. We very often complain that we are detained in this House at considerable inconvenience; but what must be the condition of a person in confinement in a prison who is locked up in his cell every night at 6 o'clock, and kept there until 8 o'clock in a morning. That, I believe, applies to the case of a first-class misdemeanant, and will, I think, be held to be sufficiently severe, whereas, if a man is not treated as a first-class misdemeanant, he is liable to be locked up in a cell in solitary confinement for 23 out of the 24 hours. I maintain that this is a most inhuman punishment. A man is locked up in a cell not bigger than that table, and is confined there for 23 hours out of the 24, and it must also be borne in mind that the great majority of persons who will be dealt with under this Act will be farmers and others who have been accustomed all their lives to the open air. Surely this would be a most monstrous punishment, even if the prisoners should not be compelled to sleep on a plank bed. Mr. Forster's Act was a humane Act compared what this is likely to be, and even under the stringency of the provisions of that Act several persons went out of their mind, and others died. A good many suffered from a variety of diseases; their eyes and teeth got bad, and all those parts of the body which it is necessary to keep in motion in order to maintain physical vigour went out of order. As a matter of fact, hundreds of persons suffered more or less from the restraint imposed upon them, and the punishment inflicted upon them was beyond all comprehension. More than 500 of the men who were imprisoned under that Act left the prison with their lives practically shortened by eight or 10 years. I contend that, under this section, it is a most unreasonable thing, when you are confining men for the mere purpose of detention, to keep them in prison for an inordinate length of time, and to subject them to unnecessary cruelty and hardship. I trust the Government will see their way to the acceptance of my Amendment.

Amendment proposed,

In page 1, line 23, after the word "thereto," to insert the words "with this exception, that every person committed for contempt, under the said enactments, shall be treated as a first class misdemeanant."—(*Mr. T. M. Healy.*)

Question proposed, "That those words be there inserted."

THE CHIEF SECRETARY FOR IRELAND (Mr. A. J. BALFOUR) (Manchester, E.): I wish to point out to the hon. and learned Gentleman that however severe the punishment may be, even if it comes up to the highly-coloured description he has given of it, it will be in the power of the prisoner, under this section, at any time to relieve himself from the pains and penalties of the clause by answering certain questions. And, further, the maximum time during which a witness can be imprisoned, without being again brought up and again asked questions, is eight days. With regard to the general policy of the Government on this question, we do not consider that this is a proper occasion on which to alter the law as it applies now to witnesses who refuse to answer. There is no reason why a witness detained under this clause should receive either better or worse treatment than a witness committed for contempt under the ordinary law. Therefore, taking our stand on a broad principle, the Government feel compelled to disagree both with this Amendment and with the next one which stands in the name of the hon. and learned Member for North Longford, and which proposes to provide that no person, for an offence against these enactments, shall be sentenced to more than seven days' imprisonment.

MR. HENRY H. FOWLER (Wolverhampton, E.): I am very sorry to hear the proposition laid down by the right hon. Gentleman the Chief Secretary for Ireland that there is no difference in the case of a witness brought up under a preliminary inquiry, and of a witness committed for contempt under the ordinary law. The right hon. Gentleman says that the two cases stand on the same footing. I think that there is an essential difference. In the case of a public inquiry in the ordinary administration of the law, the witness has the protection of being advised as to whether he is compelled to answer a question. It must be remembered that a legal adviser has a right to be present in the one case, but that he is expressly precluded from being present in the other. You may have an ignorant peasant brought up as a witness who knows nothing of the law or of the effect of the questions put to him, and he may foolishly refuse to answer. It is quite probable that if the questions had been put in public he would have been advised to answer them, although, on the other hand, questions might be put to him in a secret inquiry which he would be advised not to answer if they were put to him in public. If he refuses to answer, he is liable to be sent to prison. Now, I am not going to raise any question as to general prison treatment, although I believe that the prison treatment in this country is atrociously severe; and when the Government have time to attend to other matters than those which concern Ireland, they may, perhaps, look into that question. I do not see why a man who refuses to answer a question ought to be punished in the same way as a prisoner who has committed a crime. The right hon. Gentleman says that he may, by answering the question put to him, get out of prison. That argument will apply to the case of the Rev. Mr. Cox, or to any other prisoner who refuses on conscientious grounds to comply with the laws. To take an Irish farmer from his outdoor life, and to confine him in a gaol because he refuses to answer some questions, is, in all conscience, punishment enough for the offence he has committed without subjecting him to all the rigours of the imprisonment inflicted upon a criminal. To subject him to the same punishment as a man who has committed a crime, and to treat him as a criminal prisoner, is, I think, unneces-

Mr. Henry H. Fowler

sarily harsh and severe. I believe there are hon. Members here who know what such a terrible ordeal is, and I do not see why the Government should not make this decent concession which the hon. and learned Member for North Longford asks for. I would, therefore, ask the Government to reconsider the matter. All they can want is to get at the evidence, and I believe they would be able to get at it quite as well by administering the law humanely, as they can by administering it cruelly.

SIR RICHARD WEBSTER: As far as the argument of the right hon. Gentleman the Member for East Wolverhampton goes, I am quite ready to answer it fairly, although I am bound to refuse the concession which he asserts to be a matter of decency. The right hon. Gentleman has argued from premises which are altogether founded on a mistake. He has stated, in the first place, that the object with which a witness is called is to get evidence, and that, in the event of his refusal to answer the questions put to him, he may be committed for contempt of Court. He says that it is a great protection to the witness to have the proceedings in such a case conducted in an open Court, where the witness can have the benefit of legal advice. I do not think the right hon. Gentleman could have been present last night when we were discussing a similar point. Both in England and Ireland justices who may be taking preliminary evidence with regard to a sworn information before them have the power of excluding everybody from the Court, and to treat the inquiry as a private one. I believe that that practice does prevail when it is found to be necessary for the proper administration of justice.

MR. HENRY H. FOWLER: I would ask the hon. and learned Gentleman whether he is aware of a single instance in which that course has been taken?

SIR RICHARD WEBSTER: Most unquestionably; at the time of the Fenian trials it was constantly done, and I could mention other cases in which it has been done to my own knowledge. It has been the law of England for 40 years, and of Ireland since 1851. I merely mention the fact; I am not discussing the policy of the matter. Therefore there is no weight to be attached to the argument of the right hon. Gentleman in regard to the course of procedure when evidence is taken in an open Court. The right hon. Gentleman has said that at the present moment a witness who is called upon to give evidence, and who may be an unwilling witness, is entitled to have a counsel or solicitor.

MR. HENRY H. FOWLER: That rule applies to inquiries held in open Court.

SIR RICHARD WEBSTER: That is not so. I have paid great attention to everything the right hon. Gentleman has said, but I would ask him to be sure of his law before he lays it down. At the present moment, the only person in Court who is entitled to have a counsel or solicitor is the prisoner. A witness who may be called upon to give evidence may be an unwilling witness brought into Court by summons or even by means of a warrant, but he is not entitled to be represented either by counsel or by a solicitor. The only person entitled to have counsel or a solicitor is the prisoner. Therefore, the second public protection which the right hon. Gentleman has referred to does not exist at the present moment. Then the right hon. Gentleman states that, as the law now stands, evidence cannot be extracted from an unwilling witness or by a process of law, except where some person is in charge. Now, the inquiry proposed by this Bill, and by the Act of 1882—namely, a preliminary inquiry—already exists, and may be entered into before a person is charged, and many Members of the House have expressed a wish that the power of holding a preliminary inquiry should become part of the permanent law of the land. Assuming that it is right to have a preliminary inquiry, and that it is proper to have a preliminary inquiry although no person may be charged, what difference ought we to make in the way in which a witness is to be treated and punished if he refuses to answer the question put to him whether a person is charged or not? In both cases the proceedings would probably be on sworn information that a crime had been committed. The only difference would be that in the one case a person is charged, whereas in the other it is alleged that some person or persons unknown have been guilty of crime. In the interest of a real desire to get at the truth, which I am certain actuates the right hon. Gentleman as much as anybody else, what difference ought there to be in the treatment of an unwilling witness? We submit that, inasmuch as we have assimilated the proceedings in the case of indictable offences to those which are punishable by summary conviction, the usual consequences should follow in both cases, and that the change ought to make no difference in regard to the obligations of a witness to answer a question or the punishment of an unwilling or recalcitrant witness. I submit to the Committee that the three grounds which have been put forward by the right hon. Gentleman are entirely without foundation, if he will allow me respectfully to say so—that the deduction which he draws is one which ought not to be drawn, and that this is certainly not the time to alter the law either as regards the punishment or the treatment of a witness.

MR. JOHN O'CONNOR (Tipperary, S.): I am very much surprised that the Government should stick by this portion of the clause. As a matter of fact, my breath has been almost taken away by the speech of the hon. and learned Gentleman the Attorney General (Sir Richard Webster). Why does he not apply the torture at once; why does he not go over to Lambeth and get a thumb-screw and a rack, and all the old instruments of torture, and apply them? The proposal of the Government is absolutely monstrous. Under the last Coercion Act, I think I am right in saying that a recalcitrant witness was treated as a first-class misdemeanant, and, although he was retained in solitary confinement for a certain number of hours out of the 24, he was allowed to have his own bed, and, if he chose, to have his own doctor. It will be altogether different under the provisions of this Bill. There may be a number of men put in prison, but they will not be allowed to associate or come together, or take exercise together, but will be compelled, as far as I understand the provisions of the Bill, to take their exercise with ordinary criminals, or, at least, with untried criminals. I remember what occurred to myself when I was in prison under similar circumstances. I was compelled to take an hour's exercise at 6 o'clock in the morning, and on one occasion I was required at a couple of paces' distance to follow a little boy who had been brought in the day before. That child was one mass of sores, from head to foot; his eyes were almost melting out of his head, his shoes were slipping from his feet, and he displayed one mass of sores all over his body. I was compelled to walk round the prison yard behind him until I became sick, and absolutely fell to the ground. I protested over and over again, but my protests were unheeded until I fell down, and the doctor was sent for to revive me. Under the prison regulations, I was compelled to take my exercise daily with every criminal who might have been brought in the night before, and for what? The hon. and learned Attorney General may say that crime must have been committed. Had I committed a crime? No, Sir; I had not, and yet this is the punishment I received, and what I presume the Government now propose to award again. In my case they drew no distinction between a man who had committed no crime and the most hardened criminal. I had refused to disclose to the magistrate what I was absolutely ignorant of. I contend that treatment of that sort is simply monstrous. When I read the Amendment I thought the Government would have no hesitation in acceding to it, for I felt it would be an act of barbarity to retain the clause in its present shape. As a matter of fact, it is going back to the tortures of olden times, which were resorted to to compel prisoners to answer the questions put to them at the inquisition. It is nothing short of torture to attempt to compel men to disclose facts of which they know nothing whatever, as it was in my case. I desire to make no appeal whatever to the Government, because I believe that it would be in vain. I am sure that they and their officials in Ireland revel in acts of injustice just as swine revel in mire. The Government, in order to support the acts of their officials in Ireland, reduce themselves to the same condition. I will not, therefore, indulge in the language of appeal, and demean myself or humble myself before them in order to entreat them to do that which in no civilized country ought to be refused. I said to myself when I read the Amendment—"Surely the Government do not propose to adhere to their proposition." I have not been present during the whole of this discussion, but knowing as I do the temper of the men who superintend these prisons, and the way in which Acts of Parliament are

used for the persecution of political opponents instead of the prevention of crime, I have very little expectation that a Tory Government will accept such an Amendment as this. I am personally too indignant to argue the matter in anything like good temper. If the Government adhere to a clause of this nature, I say that they will make themselves part and parcel of this system of government, and of that system of officialism in Ireland, which is a disgrace to any civilized country.

MR. HENRY H. FOWLER: I only desire to point out that the hon. and learned Gentleman the Attorney General misunderstood and misinterpreted me. The hon. and learned Gentleman said that I based my argument on three points, the principal one. of which was that the proposed inquiry differs from any other inquiry in being held in private instead of in open Court. He added that I ought to know that at the present moment there exists a power to exclude the public during a preliminary investigation. Now, I have the honour to be a Justice of the Peace, and, acting in that capacity, I never knew a case in which a preliminary inquiry was conducted in private and the witnesses ordered out of Court. The hon. and learned Gentleman alluded to certain cases in connection with Fenianism; but I have no recollection of there having been any deviation from the ordinary course, unless under those exceptional circumstances. With regard to my second point, the hon. and learned Gentleman the Attorney General somewhat twisted what I said. I did not speak as a lawyer, but as a Member of the House of Commons; and he says that I spoke of the right of a witness not to be left entirely without protection, but to have a legal adviser present. I never dreamt of saying anything of the kind; but I said that there were always present representatives of persons who were accused, who took care that no improper questions were put. The Committee have been asked to insert a clause to provide that witnesses called up for examination in secret should have the right of having a legal adviser present; but the Committee refused to accept that proposition. The hon. and learned Attorney General has said that it would do no harm if the clause were extended to crimes in England. I candidly confess to the hon. and

Mr. John O'Connor (Tipperary)

learned Attorney General that I am one of those who think that that might be so, if it were extended to crimes, but to crimes only, and not to political offences. I believe that in such cases a great many crimes, which now go undiscovered, would be detected. What I protest against in regard to this clause is, that not only accused persons, but witnesses who are asked to give evidence against them will be subjected to a much more severe punishment than their offence warrants.

MR. T. FRY (Darlington): I hope the Government will reconsider the matter. The answer of the right hon. Gentleman the Chief Secretary for Ireland (Mr. A. J. Balfour) is precisely the answer which might have been given 300 years ago, in the time of Queen Mary, when persons were sent to prison because they declined to answer questions which were put to them, and were subjected to torture in an attempt to make them answer. There are often questions which it is impossible for a man to answer without incriminating himself or his nearest friends. I think the Amendment is one which ought to commend itself to every Member of the House, and I really believe that it would do so, if hon. Members on the opposite Benches did not believe that they were bound to follow their Party. We are now told that when the witnesses answer the questions put to them they will be set free. But that was precisely what was said by the inquisitors centuries ago. I trust that Her Majesty's Government will reconsider the attitude they have taken with regard to the Amendment.

MR. O'HEA (Donegal, W.): I feel bound to protest against the cold-blooded and brutal attitude which Her Majesty's Government have taken up. There are hon. Members of this House who know from previous experience in Ireland what prison discipline is, and the brutality which is exercised towards prisoners in the Irish gaols. It ought to be borne in mind that the prisoners to whom this Amendment applies are not malefactors who have been found guilty, but simply men summoned to give evidence, and various motives may prompt and actuate them in regard to the evidence sought to be extorted from them in a preliminary inquiry. It might so happen that some of my hon. Friends and myself might be called upon to give evidence as to the action of my hon. Friend the Member for East Mayo (Mr. Dillon), and his connection with the Plan of Campaign. Personally, I should certainly refuse to give any evidence, good, bad, or indifferent. I should undoubtedly be prepared to endure all the horrors and the tortures Her Majesty's Government might be prepared to inflict upon me, for a refusal to give evidence in such a case and under such circumstances. I trust that the Amendment will be pressed to a Division. Hon. Members will then see how much of the milk of human kindness is to be found in the breasts of Her Majesty's Ministers and of hon. Gentlemen who sit on the opposite Benches, as well as their Friends and Colleagues, the Liberal Unionists, who sit on these Benches.

MR. FINLAY (Inverness, &c.): One would imagine that the hon. Member who has just spoken thinks that the proposition of the Government is to treat those who refuse to answer questions in an inquiry of this kind as if they were the greatest criminals and were to be treated in some way different from those who refuse to answer questions in any other inquiry. Nothing can be more absolutely opposed to the actual state of the facts. As I understand the clause, it merely means that a witness who refuses to answer questions in an inquiry of this kind will be treated in precisely the same way as would a witness who refuses to answer questions when anyone is accused may now be treated. Can it be seriously alleged that it is a less heinous offence, or an offence of a different complexion, for a witness to refuse to answer in an inquiry of this kind than for a witness to refuse to answer when there is a person accused? It may be a question whether an inquiry of this kind should be held at all; but we are not discussing that issue now, and a great deal of the argument of the right hon. Gentleman the Member for East Wolverhampton (Mr. Henry H. Fowler) seemed to be levelled at the general question whether it is desirable to hold inquiries of this kind with regard to a particular kind of offence. That is not the question we are discussing; but it is whether we are to treat witnesses who are contumacious in these inquiries in any way different from that which is applicable to other cases. To my mind, that is a question which does not admit of argument. With regard to the general question of prison discipline, no doubt there is a great deal to be said. There is a great deal in our prison discipline which certainly demands reform, and I would cordially join in any movement to relax severities which are wholly uncalled for; but I think it would be improper for the House, in passing a section to provide for inquiries of this kind, to say that witnesses who are contumacious shall be put on a different platform from other witnesses who are contumacious.

SIR CHARLES RUSSELL (Hackney, S.): I do not think that my hon. and learned Friend the Member for Inverness has done complete justice, or, indeed, anything like justice, to the argument of my right hon. Friend the Member for East Wolverhampton (Mr. Henry H. Fowler). I am sorry, also, that my hon. and learned Friend's first intervention in Committee should be to resist an attempt to mitigate some of the possible inconveniences to individuals from the operation of this exceptional legislation. The first thing to bear in mind is that the Government profess to justify the introduction of this process, which is one hitherto unknown to the English law, by a reference to the analogy of the Scotch law. But we have heard from Scotch lawyers that the practice there only applies to voluntary witnesses. This is one difference which my hon. and learned Friend has overlooked. The witness in Scotland can claim the right of having the depositions returned to him, or, in other words, of destroying a record of the evidence. We are now dealing with a witness who does not come forward voluntarily. He may be a witness who is under suspicion himself, and yet he is obliged to answer, even although his answer should criminate himself, any questions relating to the offence as to which the inquiry is being held. It seems to me that my hon. and learned Friend has lost sight of this further difference between this enactment and the provisions of the Scotch law — the almost obsolete and unused provisions of the Scotch law in regard to which this Bill is supposed to afford some analogy. That difference is this—that under the Scotch system the witness is brought before the Sheriff, at the instance of the Procurator Fiscal, who is the person who collects the *data* on which the wit-

Mr. Finlay

ness is examined. The magistrate is not an active party to the inquiry; he is rather there for the protection of the witness; whereas, under this Bill, the magistrate will be a party to the inquiry, which will assume an inquisitorial character rather than that of a protection. I think that my hon. and learned Friend, when he spoke with that high tone of severity which he adopts of the fearful act of contumacy committed by a man who refuses to give evidence, might have borne these facts in mind, as well as the fact that the principle is unknown to the general law of England. You will also be dealing with a class of witnesses who do not know and cannot be expected to know what the law is. You propose to deprive the witness of the protecting influence of Judge, counsel, or solicitor, and it may be reasonably expected that a man without any desire to commit contumacy, as my hon. and learned Friend calls it, may honestly refuse to answer the questions put to him, believing that he is justified in so refusing. This is altogether a different offence from that of frustrating a criminal inquiry, and I think there is clear ground for drawing a distinction between those who are and those who are not voluntary witnesses.

THE CHIEF SECRETARY FOR IRELAND (Mr. A. J. BALFOUR) (Manchester, E.): I do not rise to add anything to the statement of the case of the Government which has been made by my hon. and learned Friend near me, and by the hon. and learned Member for Inverness (Mr. Finlay). I rise simply for the purpose of correcting an error in the statement made by the hon. and learned Gentleman who has just sat down (Sir Charles Russell) on a matter of law. The hon. and learned Gentleman said that the procedure introduced into this Bill is unknown to the law of England. In that he is in error, as he will find, if he will refer to the Explosives Act.

SIR CHARLES RUSSELL: I said the general law of England. I was perfectly aware of that particular Act dealing with a particular crime.

MR. A. J. BALFOUR: I quite accept that; but the phrase used by the hon. and learned Gentleman was that it was unknown to the law of England.

SIR CHARLES RUSSELL: I meant the general law.

MR. A. J. BALFOUR: I wish to point out that it is now part of the law of England, having been made so two years ago. Right hon. Gentlemen opposite introduced the principle into their Explosives Act of 1882, and if it is a gross injustice, let them get out of their own Act.

MR. W. E. GLADSTONE (Edinburgh, Mid Lothian): The right hon. Gentleman the Chief Secretary for Ireland has discovered one particular English Act containing a procedure of this kind, and it is the Explosives Act, which has regard to offences that are only in a high degree criminal, but are anti-social and almost unnatural, going beyond the lines of human nature and beyond the lines of human crime. It is from an Act of this kind that this method of procedure is taken; and it is now to be adopted in a case in which a man is called upon to give evidence as to whether someone has induced some other person to take or not to take a particular part, or to deal or not to deal with some other person. That is the parallel the right hon. Gentleman has given, and the advantage he has derived from the study of the English law.

MR. A. J. BALFOUR: The right hon. Gentleman appears to be of opinion that one ought to protect a witness in a case of ordinary crime, but to leave him unprotected if the crime is serious. I do not understand that what the right hon. Gentleman said is relevant to the discussion at all. If witnesses deserve to be protected at all, they deserve to be protected always. It is wholly irrelevant to say that the Act cited dealt with what the right hon. Gentleman called anti-social crimes. The ground taken by the right hon. Gentleman differs from the ground taken by the two preceding speakers. They rested their objections on the ground that witnesses were unprotected. I believe that witnesses would be as amply protected as they are under the existing law. The right hon. Gentleman has taken new ground in speaking not of the protection of witnesses, but of the character of the crime, which will be dealt with at a later stage of the clause. The right hon. Gentleman can limit the clause if he likes, but do not let him drag in now an argument which is wholly irrelevant.

MR. MOLLOY (King's Co., Birr): I contend that the confusion is with the right hon. Gentleman the Chief Secretary, who never seems able to see any point, however plainly it may be put before him, and who, in this case, fails to see the difference between a severity of treatment which may be meted out to a person guilty of a very small offence, and an obdurate witness under the Explosives Act, who is properly deemed guilty of an anti-social crime. The right hon. Gentleman has missed that point altogether, and the whole of his indignation falls to the ground, as it did on a previous occasion two or three nights ago. The hon. and learned Gentleman the late Attorney General (Sir Charles Russell) made one mistake in the observations he addressed to the Committee. He spoke of the hon. and learned Unionist Member for Inverness (Mr. Finlay) as having spoken for the first time on this Bill. I beg to inform him that the hon. and learned Gentleman spoke on another occasion, although his speech was not in the cause of humanity, but to prop up the Government in carrying out the measure now before the Committee in the severest possible manner. The hon. and learned Unionist Member informed the Committee that, although he supports this clause, he is prepared to consider the question hereafter under certain conditions. He, therefore, fully admits the impropriety of this severe treatment. All he says is—" Why introduce a new law now?" I will tell him why. It is because the Government are introducing a new law altogether, to which, I maintain, we have no right to tack on a condition of circumstances which does not attach to the action of the Courts and the action of justice in the law as it now stands in regard to other matters. The hon. and learned Attorney General for England asked why there should be any difference in the treatment of a witness who comes under the action of the law as it exists now and another witness who will come under the action of this measure? The reason is very simple. Under the laws that exist now the examination of a witness is in public. The witness is, therefore, protected; and it is childish to compare the secret inquiry now proposed to be held before a Justice of the Peace with an inquiry in open Court under present circumstances. The Government are introducing a system of secret inquisitorial examination,

[Fifth Night.]

and they are putting extraordinary powers in the hands of men who have had no judicial training, and who are totally unfit to exercise powers one-half as strong as these. Let me give an instance of an inquisitorial examination which may take place to-day. It will take place under the auspices of a man thoroughly trained in the traditions and customs of the law, whereas, when this Bill is passed, these secret inquiries will take place before a half-pay military or naval officer with no judicial training whatever. If the power were placed in the hands of an ordinary non-official man, there might not be the same objection as now exists, because, in all probability, he would exercise the power placed in his hands justly and fairly. But is there any Member of this House, either on one side or the other, who dares to express an independent opinion, who will say he believes that in one single instance the powers given to a Resident Magistrate under this Bill will be exercised fairly and justly in the case of any unfortunate man who may be brought before him? We know perfectly well, from our past experiences of the manner in which these Resident Magistrates have exercised their power, and in which they are daily exercising that power now, that it is exercised not only for the purpose of punishing criminals, but in many cases for purposes which are highly improper, and would never for a moment receive the sanction of this House. The great probability is, that these Resident Magistrates, when they obtain these powers, will put questions to witnesses which they have no right to put, and which an unfortunate and ignorant peasant brought before them cannot discuss or argue, but which, from a sort of natural instinct, he will decline to answer. Is it humane, then, on the part of the Government to refuse the concession that is now asked? We have heard a good deal of learned language on the subject; but let us get back to the point at which we started. When all the learned language which has been used on the part of the Government is got rid of, it will be seen that the only demand which is made upon them is that a witness sent to prison under this clause shall receive some treatment more humane than that which the Government propose. All the pious indignation which has been used

Mr. Molloy

on this occasion on the part of the Government, and which is used nowadays about a dozen times a night, is simply directed against the Amendment. In asking for a little more humanity in the administration of the law, we are simply demanding that these prisoners shall have a little more fresh air than they will get under the clause as it now stands. The whole refusal of the Government, based on high-flown arguments, is directed against that one concession, that the men sent to prison under the clause shall be able to spend two or three hours in the fresh air. As the clause now stands, a man may be sent to prison, perhaps, for refusing to answer a question which never ought to have been put to him, and which he may have been perfectly justified in not answering. He has, however, no means of protecting himself, and when in prison he is to be allowed only an hour and a-half a-day of fresh air. I ask the Committee to imagine what that means in the case of a man in a healthy condition, who has been accustomed to an out-door life, and who finds himself penned up in a cell little bigger than a band-box? All we ask is, that he shall have a little better treatment in order to enable him to endure his imprisonment; and, in imprisoning a man under such circumstances, is it not right that we should give him some small chance of preserving his health and life? Let any one of the pious Gentlemen on the Treasury Bench ask himself this question: What would be his condition if he were compelled to spend three or four months in a small cell, with scarcely any light, no books to read, and only an hour and a-half a-day for exercise in the fresh air, and that only in the courtyard of the prison? In what condition would he find himself at the end of that time? Be it remembered, too, that this treatment is to be meted out to men who have been guilty of no crime or offence themselves, but who simply decline to answer questions which they consider to be unfair. Is this anything more than the re-introduction of the thumb-screw? You are acting on a man's mind in a way which must weaken his mental powers as well as destroy him physically. The right hon. Gentleman the Chief Secretary says that a witness may only have to remain in prison for eight days, and that he can get out then if he consents to answer the questions put to him. It may, however, be taken for granted that the man would act again upon the same principle, and he is more likely to remain in prison for eight months than to come out at the end of eight days. This treatment, therefore, simply amounts to torture. Is it calculated to do the Government any good, or to do good to the cause of justice, law, and order? Is it calculated to raise the Government in the opinion of those Conservative working classes to whom they are so fond of appealing outside this House, when it is said that unfortunate men who have been guilty of no crime, but who, from a feeling of generosity, or it may be folly, refuse to answer questions which probably they were perfectly entitled to refuse to answer, are not to have this small modicum of humanity extended towards them, but they are to be treated in a manner worthy only of the days of the rack and the thumb-screw?

MR. CLANCY (Dublin Co., N.): I cannot help making one observation in regard to the speech of the hon. and learned Member for Inverness (Mr. Finlay). We now know the precise extent to which the Liberal Unionists are prepared to go in support of the present Government. Whenever there is a piece of dirty work to be done, or an especially brutal act to be defended, we are sure to find one of the 76 Unionist Members coming in with all the learned eloquence he can command to do it or to defend it. Unlike most of my Colleagues, I have not been in prison myself, but I have acquainted myself, nevertheless, with the treatment to which prisoners under this section will be subjected. What is that treatment? A prisoner is required to get up at 6 o'clock in the morning; he is allowed one hour for exercise; he is then to go back and scrub his cell, empty the slops, and after that is done, stop inside all day with the exception of an hour for dinner, and then go to bed and stay there until 6 o'clock next morning. He gets six ounces of bread in the morning, and a pint of something like ditch-water. He is provided with 10 or 12 potatoes at dinner, and a piece of meat like cow's ear. This is the humane treatment advocated for untried prisoners by the Liberal Unionist Member for Inverness! And to whom is it to be applied? It is intended to apply to a good many of the Irish priests and respectable farmers and labourers in Ireland. I cannot help congratulating the right hon. Gentleman the Chief Secretary on the humanity he has displayed in the course of this debate. For some days past we have been wondering what particular functions the right hon. Gentleman has to perform in connection with his duty as Chief Secretary. We now find out that his chief duty here and in Ireland will be to act as Chief Gaoler. His work will be confined to putting men in prison, and treating them there as inhumanly as possible. The right hon. Gentleman says that a man need only be in prison for eight days. I should very much like to see the right hon. Gentleman after undergoing eight days' imprisonment of this nature. But I must remind him that after having been confined in prison for eight days there would be nothing to prevent a man from being re-imprisoned if he still refused to answer the questions put to him. As a matter of fact, he might be re-committed again and again for all the days of his life, because we know that this Bill is to last for ever. He says the prisoner can get out, if he likes, by answering the questions. That reminds me of what Cromwell is asserted to have said, when the Papists complained of the harsh treatment to which they were subjected. They were told—"You have only to turn Protestant and forswear the Mass." It is the argument of the highway robber, who says to his victim that he has only to give up his money to escape with his life. That is practically what the right hon. Gentleman the Chief Gaoler of Ireland recommends in this case. I think the speech of the right hon. Gentleman throws a great light on the spirit in which this measure will be administered. We have now received the first important indication which has yet been given of the spirit in which the measure has been conceived, and the manner in which it is likely to be carried out. We have to-night had an exhibition of cynical brutality for which I was not prepared, although I was afraid that a good deal of it was likely to be exhibited in the course of this discussion. All I can say is that if this brutality is to be exercised in the administration of this Bill, the Government will produce a good deal more disorder in Ireland than is found to exist there now, and will probably make things much worse than they found them when they entered into Office. The attitude of the right hon. Gentleman the Chief Secretary, in this matter, is characteristic of all his acts in this House. I do not recollect a single speech of his, or a single answer to a Question put to him in this House, in which he has not betrayed the same spirit — the same indifference to the sufferings of the Irish people, and the same contempt for their opinions and desires. I can assure the right hon. Gentleman that his attitude is being closely watched in Ireland, and I believe that not only in Ireland, but in England also, his attitude is condemned.

MR. PICTON (Leicester): I am anxious to say a word or two in support of the Amendment. The wickedest vice of this most intolerable Bill is that it is intended to persecute cruelly the Irish people for their loyalty to one another. Who are the witnesses specially aimed at in this clause? I do not think it is, in the main, witnesses who are called in to testify as to murders and real crimes, because there appear to be scarcely any of those kind of crimes committed in Ireland; indeed, they are much fewer than in Great Britain; but the witnesses aimed at are those who happen to possess the confidence of their fellows, and who, in circumstances of great difficulty, have been aggrieved by a cruel system of rackrent. It is witnesses who know anything of combinations not to pay excessive rents who are specially aimed at. I am not prepared to say that in some circumstances the reticence of a witness may not be a virtue rather than a vice. In times past, when other unjust laws oppressed the people of this country, it has been so regarded when unjust laws were directed against the combination of labour; it was regarded as a virtue on the part of the oppressed to withhold their testimony against their fellows either under threats or hopes of reward. So, also, I can easily conceive that there may be circumstances in Ireland in which I myself would very much prefer to shut my mouth and resolve to say nothing whatever, rather than gain some little temporary reward or freedom from personal suffering by telling all I knew of the circumstances under which my fellow men had combined. I think it is a great mistake in the relations of the British Government with Ireland that constant attacks should be made upon

Mr. Clancy

the loyalty of the Irish people one to another. If Great Britain had only known how to appreciate the faithfulness of the Irish people one to the other in times gone by, we might have been a happy and United Kingdom now. Because the Amendment tends to lessen the vice of the Bill I shall most heartily support it. It may be said that the magistrate will have no power of discriminating between one reticent witness and another, but I am not at all inclined to trust to the discretion of any magistrates as to men who ought to be committed to prison. It appears to me that the Resident Magistrates will always have the interests of the landlord class at heart, and that they will regard as a most unpardonable crime any combination against that class. As the Government tell us that this Bill is aimed at crime and not at political combination, I hope they will prove the sincerity of their words by allowing this Amendment to pass.

MR. T. M. HEALY (Longford, N.): There is one suggestion I desire to make. I think no man ought to be kept in solitary confinement for more than 20 hours, at any rate, out of the 24. Even the Liberal Unionists will hardly object to that. My object is to give these unfortunate men something like exercise. To restrict people who have been accustomed to farming work and out-door exercise, and to keep them in solitary confinement for 20 hours out of the 24, is a refinement of cruelty which I imagine the Committee will scarcely approve. Surely it is not too much to ask that no man shall be kept in solitary confinement for more than 20 hours a-day. It is absolutely essential that some reasonable amount of exercise should be allowed to men who are placed in these unfortunate circumstances.

MR. A. J. BALFOUR: The whole question of prison regulations will be looked into and considered, and if anything in the nature of harshness or brutality exists we will do our best to cure it. But the Government most distinctly take their stand upon the position which has already been sufficiently explained to the Committee, and they make no difference between witnesses imprisoned under this Act and witnesses imprisoned under the existing law.

MR. T. P. O'CONNOR (Liverpool, Scotland): I must express my great astonishment that when the hon. and learned Member for Inverness (Mr. Finlay) interferes in this debate it is only for the purpose of encouraging the Government in brutality, and not for the purpose of mitigating the severity of the Bill. I have listened with astonishment. I may almost say that I have listened with disgust, and with an indignation I can scarcely control, to the arguments and speeches I have heard in support of this clause. I suppose it will be news to the right hon. Gentleman the Chief Secretary for Ireland and the hon. and learned Member for Inverness to know that this is almost the only country which retains a want of distinction between ordinary offences and political offences. There is nothing in the whole history of Ireland that has left more dark and more bitter memories than the manner in which political prisoners have been treated in Ireland. I have here an extract from the Report of Dr. Macdonald in regard to the treatment of prisoners arrested under the suspension of the Habeas Corpus Act. That gentleman, who was then physician of Mountjoy Prison, states that one prisoner—Thomas Burke—showed undoubted symptoms of insanity; that another named Finigan gave way to paroxysms brought on by confinement; that another named Feeny was considered altogether unfit to be subjected to prison discipline; and that a fourth named Burnes was considered unfit to go away from the prison without someone in charge of him. Dr. Macdonald says that he had no doubt that the severe prison discipline had produced these results, and he adds that in some cases there was a probability of the prisoners committing suicide. He, therefore, recommended a relaxation of the prison discipline, especially in regard to untried prisoners. As a matter of fact, the result was that a large number of these men did become insane; and I am speaking within the knowledge of hon. Members around me when I say that more than one of the prisoners met his death by his own hand in consequence of the mental disturbance created by the confinement to which he had been subjected. Martin Carey was driven to insanity by treatment such as the Government propose to enact by this Bill, and Martin Carey found his death in the Liffey. I think it will be found that the leaders of the dynamite conspiracy are mostly men whose reason has been unhinged, and whose appreciation of right and wrong has been obliterated by the cruelties practised upon them in confinement in Ireland. Insanity has in many cases been the result. There is nothing which an Irishman resents so bitterly as the injustice and cruelty of the treatment he has been subjected to in this way, and yet the hon. and learned Member for Inverness gets up and says that he hopes no distinction will be made between the treatment provided under this and under any other Act of Parliament. Does the hon. and learned Gentleman, in that omniscience of his, know that we have on the Table of this House the Report of a Committee presented this Session on the accommodation in Court-houses for prisoners awaiting trial at the Assizes and Sessions? There has not been a single newspaper in the country which has not taken up that Report and declared that the revelations contained in it are a disgrace to and a blot upon the civilization of the country. The 12th paragraph of the Report of the Committee is to the effect that it does not seem right to submit prisoners awaiting trial to physical or moral discomfort of any kind, and that it appeared that a large percentage of prisoners awaiting trial have been subjected for many hours to the severest mental and physical discomfort, such as exposure to damp, and being kept for hours in the dark. Now, that is the Report of a Committee on the treatment of untried prisoners in England. But the hon. and learned Member for the Inverness Burghs (Mr. Finlay), although he says he is willing to vote in favour of reform with regard to the treatment of prisoners in England, is not willing to vote in favour of the small reform which we now ask in the case of persons committed for contempt under this clause. It is trifling with the intelligence of the Committee for the hon. and learned Member to put forward such reasons as he has in his speech on this Amendment. The reason why he will not vote in favour of the Amendment is because Irish political prisoners will get some little benefit by it. I am glad, however, that the hon. and learned Gentleman intends to vote in this way, because it will afford an excellent opportunity of bringing the fact before the people of this country, that when we are discussing where barbarity is on one side, and civilization is on the other, the hon. and learned Gentleman allows the weight of his small voice to be heard in favour of the former. My hon. and learned Friend the Member for North Longford (Mr. T. M. Healy) said that this clause would deal with the peasants of Ireland. I think my hon. and learned Friend here forgot his usual acuteness, because the Bill would deal with a large class of people other than peasants. The clause is meant to work against men who will not dishonour themselves and dishonour their cloth and their country by putting at the mercy of the Government the secrets of a combination which have been intrusted to them through the confidence of their fellow countrymen. I ask what would be thought of this clause, if, under its operation, Father Kelleher, having refused to give evidence with regard to the Plan of Campaign, for instance, were kept for 22 hours in his cell and required to turn his face to the wall every time his excellency the warder came by; if he were compelled to empty the slops in his cell every morning and to be put to all the miserable and shameful degradations which are reserved, in every country but Ireland, for the lowest and most ignorant of mankind! Sir, we shall persevere on this question; I have spoken once upon it and I shall speak upon it again. I am glad to see that the system of gag which the Government are endeavouring to force upon us cannot always be successfully applied to the House of Commons. Is there a man in this Committee who thinks that the treatment of untried prisoners in England is just? Why, it is one of the blots on the civilization of the country. Under the present system it is just as bad to be accused of crime as to be guilty of crime. We go on repeating in our self-complacency that every man is supposed to be innocent until he is proved to be guilty. But the truth is, that every man from the time that he is taken into custody is supposed to be guilty until he has proved his innocence, and it is this barbarity which the right hon. Gentleman the Chief Secretary for Ireland (Mr. A. J. Balfour) wants to retain in this Act, and that which the hon. and learned Gentleman above the Gangway, who disgraces the name of Liberal, wishes to help him in retaining. I hope my hon. Friends will discuss this question fully,

Mr. T. P. O'Connor

and bring before the mind of the country the attitude which the Liberal Unionists have taken up with reference to the Amendment.

MR. BRADLAUGH (Northampton): So far as the Law in England is concerned, the words "first-class misdemeanants" have ceased to have the meaning which they had some 12 years ago, although it is perfectly true that in some gaols, I presume with the consent of the Commissioners of Prisons, regulations are occasionally made with reference to particular prisoners which are analogous to those which used to be applied to first-class misdemeanants. I think the use of the phrase and the practice with regard to first-class misdemeanants has ceased to exist in England since 1878. I assume that what is meant by the Amendment is what was meant by that phrase in England prior to that time. I will draw the attention of the Committee to what is meant by ordinary imprisonment without any kind of hard labour, unless there is some order made by the authorities of the gaol or by the Commissioners of Prisons to the contrary. On one occasion, a gentleman of fair education who was undergoing this kind of imprisonment had to appear in Court; the present Lord Chief Justice of England was so shocked at the effect of the imprisonment on him that he adjourned the trial and made an order that the prisoner should have a reasonable amount of food and sleep, and access to some literature, so as to relieve the mental strain, at the effects of which he— Lord Coleridge—expressed himself to be somewhat horrified. The first-class misdemeanant used to have access to books, if his friends could supply them, and he used to have food beyond the prison dietary, if his friends had the means to get it for him; but the present first-class misdemeanant is shut out from the whole world. I do not know what the period of solitary confinement is, but certainly it is for 18 hours a-day at the very least. [An hon. MEMBER: 22 hours.] I do not know what the period is. I always try to limit my statement to something incapable of contradiction. It is impossible to conceive anything more horrible than solitary confinement, and I say that the present regulations should be enforced with great care. Because, against whom do you propose to enforce them? Against persons who have refused, as they think honestly, to give information with regard to a combination of tenants, as you call it, for the non-payment of rents which are legally due to their landlords. If the Committee will permit me, I will take a case in British history; and I speak of the time when the Society of Friends refused to pay Church rates. Those Church rates were as legal as any rents which landlords are entitled to receive in Ireland. Could it be maintained, in the present century, that it would have been possible to send a member of the Society of Friends to solitary confinement for refusing to give information? I think it is said that the combination with regard to rent is of a very shocking nature. I have heard it put that this is not only a combination of tenants who cannot pay, but also a combination of those tenants who can pay, but will not pay. I suggest that the tenants who cannot pay do not want much persuasion on the subject, and that among those who can pay there are honest men who urge those who can pay not to pay, so that they may procure the support of their miserable co-tenants in their endeavour to resist exorbitant rent. And however much you may determine to punish them, surely you will not try to deal with people—who refuse to give information—with the severity of punishment which becomes torture to them. We are occasionally, in this country, fond of denouncing the severity of punishment in other lands; but I know of no punishment conceivably more severe than to take an individual used to ordinary life, to shut him out from people with whom he has been in the habit of associating, to deny him any access to books and papers, and leave to him simply the blank walls of his cell. It is so absolutely shocking that I appeal to every Member, without reference to politics, to make some alteration here. As far as I can understand, the provision under this clause is much worse than the arrangement under Mr. Forster's Act. I will not trouble the Committee further; but I should not have done my duty had I not called attention to this subject.

THE FIRST LORD OF THE TREASURY (Mr. W. H. SMITH) (Strand, Westminster): I think there is a good deal to be said as to the rules which concern the regulations of prisons; and

my right hon. Friend has given an undertaking on the part of the Government that if there is any unnecessary harshness in the treatment of witnesses who have been imprisoned, it would be the duty of the Government to review the regulations. But I submit to the Committee that this part of the clause has been very fully discussed, and that it would be consistent with the convenience of the Committee that we should now come to a decision by dividing on the Amendment.

MR. W. E. GLADSTONE (Edinburgh, Mid Lothian): I agree fully with the right hon. Gentleman that regard should be had to the promise given with reference to the review of the prison regulations, because I believe it to be made in all sincerity. But the time when it would come about it is extremely difficult to predict. And even if it were to come about at once, I own I have, in my own mind, the greatest difficulty with regard to placing in the same category the man who refuses to assist the known ends of public justice as handed down to us, and the man who may be called possibly to give evidence against his father, and to say whether his father has been concerned in the advising of another not to let or hire a farm. I agree with the right hon. Gentleman that this subject has been well and fully argued. I quite admit that there remains the all-important question of the limitation or non-limitation of the clause; but if the Government are determined not to move on the subject, if I might offer a suggestion to the Committee, it would be the same as that given by the right hon. Gentleman opposite.

Question put.

The Committee *divided:*—Ayes 144; Noes 195: Majority 51.—(Div. List, No. 125.)

MR. T. M. HEALY (Longford, N.): Looking at the result of the Division which has just taken place, I hope that, although the Government may not be inclined to modify the character of the imprisonment, they will, at all events, shorten its duration. Under the Petty Sessions Act, it is provided that whenever a person shall appear as witness, and shall be required to answer questions by the justice, and refuse to be examined on oath, or refuse to take such oath, or refuse to answer the question concerning the matter in question, or refuse to give an account of papers or documents, the justice may adjourn the proceedings, and may by warrant commit the said witness to gaol unless he shall consent to be sworn. And it further provides that if such witness again refuses to be sworn, or to produce accounts, papers, or documents, as the case may be, the said justice may again adjourn the proceedings and commit him to prison, and so on from time to time until he shall consent to be sworn and produce the accounts, papers, and documents. It provides also that in all cases, other than the case of summary jurisdiction, there shall be no limit to the duration of imprisonment. Let me call attention to the fact that the Bill was introduced into the House of Lords, and passed by that ancient and venerable Assembly, reducing the term of imprisonment to three months. That Bill came down to the House of Commons, and the House of Commons refused to pass it on the ground that it had not time to do so. If the House of Lords passed that Bill restricting the term of imprisonment to three months, how much more should this House of Commons be ready to put some limit to the period of imprisonment? Suppose the case is one of murder; the murderer may have been hanged; but if the witness refuses to produce books and accounts, although the purpose of the inquiry had been served, yet the punishment for contempt will continue if the man still refuses to answer. There is in this scheme, which is embodied in the Bill, one very objectionable provision; it is not that a man may refuse to answer—because he may give all the verbal information in his power—but if he does not produce accounts, books, documents, papers, although he may have discharged his mind with regard to the crime, he is to be committed to prison. Suppose, for instance, my hon. Friend the Member for East Mayo (Mr. Dillon) were examined with reference to the Plan of Campaign, he might refuse to give up his banking account on the ground that it was not necessary for the purpose of the inquiry, his refusal would be contempt under this section, and my hon. Friend would be committed to prison for an unlimited period, although he had given all the information in his power concerning the matter in question.

Mr. T. M. Healy

Now, I ask if it is reasonable that—the House of Lords, having agreed to reduce the term of imprisonment to three months—the Government should be at this time of day continuing the provisions of the Petty Sessions Act. I will not at the present moment go into the question of the treatment of these prisoners; but surely, when you refuse to treat them with anything like consideration, you should, at all events, shorten the period of their incarceration. I do not say that the acceptance of this Amendment by the Government would meet the whole case; but it would, at all events, be some concession to the justice of our demands.

Amendment proposed,

In page 1, line 23, insert "Provided that no person shall be imprisoned for an offence against the said enactments for a period exceeding seven days."—(*Mr. T. M. Healy.*)

Question proposed, "That those words be there inserted."

THE ATTORNEY GENERAL FOR IRELAND (Mr. HOLMES) (Dublin University): The power which is given of holding a preliminary inquiry, can never be exercised unless there is some penalty attached to refusal to give evidence. The effect of the Amendment of the hon. and learned Member, which provides that the period of imprisonment should not be more than seven days would, in my opinion, render the power nugatory. The Government do not ask for any alteration of the Law, but simply that the Law, as it at present exists in England and Ireland, shall be applied to these preliminary inquiries. As the Law at present stands, in cases of summary jurisdiction, the imprisonment is limited to a month, and during that month the prisoner must be brought up four times before the magistrate, so that he has four opportunities of purging his contempt. If when he is brought up he repeats the original contumacy he may be imprisoned for seven days more. That is the Law in England and the Law in Ireland. Although the hon. and learned Member has referred to the Bill introduced into the House of Lords, I should be surprised to find that it contains any provision to reduce the term of imprisonment in the case of a witness who may be committed for the contempt of refusing to answer. [Mr. T. M. HEALY: I have sent for the Bill.] If a warrant is issued against a witness for refusing to answer a question, that warrant must state on the face of it the question which he declined to answer and on account of which he is committed. That gives the prisoner at any moment an opportunity of having the legality of his committal tested either by a writ of Habeas Corpus or otherwise, and I do not think that any magistrate would be likely to run the risk of the penalty which would be applied in the case of wrongful committal, but would take great care that it was only in extreme cases that he committed a witness at all. I think it would be exceedingly inconvenient as well as exceedingly improper to change the Law on this subject as regards the particular penalty under this Bill. If there be any reason for altering the provision of the Law as it now stands let that alteration be made, but we have said from the first that having asked the House for the power of holding these preliminary investigations, we think that the ordinary penalties which attach under the ordinary Law should attach in this particular instance.

SIR WILLIAM HARCOURT (Derby): The right hon. and learned Attorney General for Ireland has stated what is the Law of England and Ireland on this subject, but he omitted to inform the Committee that under the existing Law witnesses are so safeguarded that they cannot be pressed or asked to answer questions which are not within the rules of evidence. The right hon. and learned Attorney General last night refused to admit that the Government did not mean to apply the rules of evidence in this case. I put this question to the right hon. and learned Attorney General— If a witness is asked whether he knows anything about the matter, and he says he knows nothing, that is one thing, but suppose he is asked whether he has heard anyone else say anything about it and he says "Yes," his answer might tend to incriminate another party. Now, any person would be justified by the Law in England or Ireland in refusing to answer that question, but under this Bill he would be asked that question and he may be sent to prison for refusing to answer it. An English Court of Law would sustain him in his refusal. The right hon. and learned Attorney General says you may appeal to the Court above; but what is the use of that? The Court above cannot give any redress, because

this tribunal is superior. You have declared that it shall be unrestricted in this inquiry by the ordinary laws of justice and evidence which bind the highest Courts of Law in the land. I put the case of hearsay evidence, and I have put the case of the competency of the witness. I was consulting recently one of the most eminent of the Scotch Judges on the subject, and he says that he should never dream of allowing a question to be put to a witness which could not be put in a Court of Law. The Government have declared that their object is that the magistrates should put questions which would not be allowed, and send witnesses to prison for not answering them. Besides the question of the Law of Evidence as I have said there is that of the competency of the witnesses; for instance a wife might be asked to answer questions concerning an offence with which her husband might afterwards be charged, and if she were to refuse to answer on the ground that she believed her husband was about to be charged in connection with the offence, she would in a Court of Law be sustained in that. Therefore, I ask what is the use of appealing to the practice in the English or Irish Courts of Justice? That practice relates only to men who are under the protection of the regular Law of Evidence, but you are applying your clause to men who are to be asked questions under circumstances in which that practice will not be applied. If I were asked a question on this subject—if I were asked whether I knew anything about the crime, and knew nothing about it, I should say so; but if the magistrate asked me if I had known anything about it, I should refuse to answer. Why am I—in a case of murder of which I know nothing—to be compelled to reveal all the gossip I have heard on the subject, and which may bring a man in peril of his life. I should say—"No, this is far too grave a matter; I will give my evidence according to my conception of the Law of Evidence, but with regard to what I have heard whispered, it may be with the object of injuring another man, I will not answer." It is for making such an answer as that that a man is under this clause to be sent to prison for contempt. Therefore, I say you have destroyed the efficacy of this method of inquiry in the conception of every man who has a respect for justice by refusing the witness that protection which belongs to the Rules and Law of Evidence. If you say you will punish a man who will not give legal evidence on a matter of which he knows something, then I am with you. I would punish that man in England, Scotland, or Ireland; but if you are proposing to punish a man because he will not state all the hearsay slanders and calumnies which he has no reason to believe, then I say it is one of the most wicked acts and one of the most incompatible with justice which it is possible to conceive. I am bound to say that I think the right hon. Gentleman will not ultimately refuse to screen this proceeding, and that he will see that the character of the inquiry should be such that would demand nothing of a man in the position of a witness in these cases which would not be sanctioned by the Rules of Evidence. I am sure the right hon. and learned Attorney General must see the infinite danger of putting this clause into the hands of a man far less responsible and far less skilled than a judge. It is quite capable of being abused, and this very thing shows the force of the contention that the matter should be settled according to the Rule and Law of Evidence; and I trust that the Government will say that this power shall be safeguarded in accordance therewith.

THE ATTORNEY GENERAL FOR IRELAND (Mr. HOLMES) (Dublin University): I think the right hon. Gentleman has overlooked the great safeguard and protection which this Bill affords, and for which the Government are indebted to the right hon. Gentleman himself—that is, the protection which a witness has that nothing he may say can be used against him under any circumstances, or in any subsequent proceedings, except those for perjury. We now repeat that assurance, and whatever may be said upon the subject, this is a very important and a very great safeguard.

SIR WILLIAM HARCOURT (Derby): My objection does not apply to the witness being made to suffer hardships for the evidence given. My objection is to the punishment of a witness for not giving a particular class of evidence; and I put to the right hon. and learned Attorney General for Ireland the case of a man refusing from the most honourable motives to retail conversation which

might be injurious to another, who may be ultimately a prisoner. A man's character may be injured; he may be damaged in this private examination by people being asked to say what they do not know to be true, and what, if it were said, would be no evidence at all. That is my point, and the protection to which the right hon. and learned Gentleman has referred is no protection against the danger of being sent to prison for refusing to answer questions which he is not able to answer. All I can say is, that if I were in the position I have described, I should refuse to answer, and take the consequences. You must remember that this is a thing which has no parallel in the Courts of Law, and I hope the Government will think again before they decide against the Amendment.

THE CHIEF SECRETARY FOR IRELAND (Mr. A. J. BALFOUR) (Manchester, E.): If I may give my opinion on this point, I would say that the right hon. Gentleman had laid down a principle of evidence with which I cannot agree. He says under no circumstances whatever would he repeat to anybody hearsay evidence, even if it would lead to the discovery of murder.

SIR WILLIAM HARCOURT : Not in judicial cases.

MR. A. J. BALFOUR : In other words if a person told him he had seen a man murdered in the next street, the right hon. Gentleman would consider himself bound by the Law of Honour and Evidence not to communicate that to the Judicial Authorities, by whom ultimately, the criminal, on the statement being made to them, might be brought to justice. That seems to me to be an extraordinary principle to lay down. But I wish to ask who it is that is not protected by the clause as it now stands. Is it the witness or the criminal? The witness is sufficiently protected by the fact that anything which he says cannot be used against him; and clearly the criminal is protected by the fact that nothing that the witness may say, and which does not come within the description of the evidence which can be used in a Court of Law can be brought up against him. A witness may say something in his examination which may put the Crown on the trace of crime; that is what may happen, and what we desire to happen; but nothing which the witness says can be brought up against an accused person unless it is strictly in conformity with the rules of the Courts of Justice with regard to evidence.

SIR WILLIAM HARCOURT: The point is not what may happen after the witness has said something; it is that a man may be committed for refusing to answer a question which any man may properly refuse to answer.

MR. A. J. BALFOUR: My reply to the right hon. Gentleman is that no statement of the witness can hurt the prisoner, except that it may lead to the production of evidence. The right hon. Gentleman speaks of stealing away a man's character. But can the witness steal away a man's character unless by giving evidence which leads to the apprehension of someone. The investigations would be perfectly secret, and nobody's character will be touched. Although I do not wish to introduce unnecessarily controversial matter, but when the right hon. Gentleman exhausts the whole vocabulary in attacking this clause, he surely might recollect that he has twice enriched the law with a similar clause. The right hon. Gentleman may change his opinion about Irish Government, but that which he said did not apply to the clause in 1883 does not surely apply to it in 1887. The right hon. Gentleman allowed this provision to be on the Statute Book then and he cannot consistently say that it is harsh in the present case. I do not wish to push this argument against the right hon. Gentleman.

SIR WILLIAM HARCOURT: It is the only argument you have used.

MR. A. J. BALFOUR: I do not think it is a bad argument, at all events, to say that we are simply repeating in this Bill one of the provisions of an Act passed during the last five years with the full assent of the Liberal Party in both Houses of Parliament.

MR. ANDERSON (Elgin and Nairn): I think it is clear that on this point we are to have no mercy from the right hon. Gentleman the Chief Secretary for Ireland. The way in which he speaks of the penal character of the clause seems to show that he rather enjoys it. I know that if we had a shorthand writer here to take down the words he used we should find that instead of witnesses he talks of the "accused." The right hon. Gentleman seems to think that every

unfortunate witness under this Act is guilty. That idea seems to pervade the mind of the Government; they seem to think that because a man is connected with a district in which there is some agrarian difficulty he is a guilty person. It seems to be the whole fallacy of the Government with respect to this clause. I agree that when you are legislating in regard to the ordinary law that you should be consistent, and I think this should be the case in regard to the law of contempt. But are you going to apply the ordinary law of contempt to ordinary offences? This ordinary law is intended to be applied to ordinary crimes; but you introduce by this Act of Parliament new crimes, a new procedure, and a new kind of examination of witnesses of an extraordinary character; and it is no argument to say that you are going to apply the ordinary law of contempt when you are about to make a new offence under this Act. I must say that the argument used by the Government seems to me entirely to fail to meet the difficulty which has been put forward on this side of the House. The argument is that there is nothing in the clause that is not in the Act of 1882, and beyond that there is no argument at all. But I wish to point out that the right hon. Gentleman the Attorney General for Ireland is entirely mistaken when he says that the witness is protected. The witness is not protected. The fact that the statement he makes cannot be used against him is no protection whatever. You get out in examination what you want; you get the secrets of a man's life, and the fact that the statement is not to be used does not prevent that. You ask a man these questions; he is bound to answer any question asked; you have your shorthand writer to take down his answer. This is a means of getting a man to convict himself by a system which has no limit. The hon. and learned Solicitor General for Scotland (Mr. J. P. B. Robertson)—whom I am glad to see in his place—has not told us anything lately about the law of Scotland. The people of Scotland do not like to hear it said that three-fourths of this Bill is the law of Scotland. I ask the Scotch Law Officers to tell us which part of the Bill is Scotch Law, and whether it is ever exercised? I trust the Government will accept this Amendment. It cannot hurt the Government; it cannot interfere with the object they have in view; and I appeal to them to make some concession which will at any rate let the people feel that a concession has been made, and that the clause will not have that possibly cruel effect which it will have if it is allowed to stand as at present.

Mr. O'HEA (Donegal, W.): The speeches of the right hon. and learned Gentleman the Attorney General for Ireland (Mr. Holmes) and the right hon. Gentleman the Chief Secretary for Ireland (Mr. A. J. Balfour) were enough, I think, to show that Her Majesty's Government intend to punish, by making them witnesses, those who are their political opponents in Ireland. Under this clause a person may be summoned as witness in respect of some crime which only exists in the mind of a police constable or magistrate, and, as the hon. and learned Member for North Longford (M. T. M. Healy) said, when a person is summoned to give evidence, because he may refuse to produce his books and banking account, and reveal his private and domestic affairs, he can be kept in gaol as long as Her Majesty's Government think fit. To say that this Bill is not intended to cover a wider scope than that which is expressed in the 2nd section, is nothing more than a pretence. The persons who will be dealt with under this Act are those who will be punished under the Summary Jurisdiction Clause by a term of imprisonment not exceeding six months. Supposing an offence to be committed in a district; a person who is, perhaps, Chairman of the Poor Law Board, or acting in some public capacity, may be summoned as a witness, while a number of others may be able to give a great deal more information with regard to the matter in question; this person may be kept in prison for an unlimited time, although he is not charged with any offence under the section, because of his refusal to give evidence. That, I contend, is the view which may be deduced from the action of Her Majesty's Government and the attitude of the right hon. and learned Attorney General and the right hon. Gentleman the Chief Secretary for Ireland. While one person in respect of the offence is undergoing imprisonment, another man may be kept in solitary confinement for refusing to reveal what may be altogether

foreign to the Act and the subject-matter of the inquiry.

Mr. MOLLOY (King's Co., Birr): The right hon. and learned Gentleman the Attorney General for Ireland has stated that when a witness is committed for contempt of Court he will have the right of appeal, and sue out a writ of Habeas Corpus. But is it not a fact that under the Bill the Resident Magistrate can ask any question he likes? Of course, if he is able to ask any question, he may go very wide of the subject in the warrant. That being so, how are you to sue out a writ of Habeas Corpus to test whether the witness has been wrongfully committed or not? Would not the Court say that under the powers of the Bill the magistrate had a right to ask any question he might think proper, and that he has power to commit a witness to prison if he refused to answer? Would not the Court answer that it had no power to interfere since the Resident Magistrate had acted strictly within the limits of the power conferred upon him by the Act? There has been an argument used by the right hon. and learned Attorney General which I should like to put an end to once for all. The right hon. and learned Gentleman said that witnesses summoned before the magistrates are protected as no witnesses have been protected before by any rule of law, and because nothing that a witness says can be produced against him. But, under the ordinary law, if you ask a witness a question which may criminate him, he makes that excuse at once and declines to answer. Now, I ask where is the force of the argument of the right hon. and learned Gentleman? Now, there has been put by my hon. and learned Friend the Member for North Longford a question which ought to be answered. He has asked that a limit should be put to imprisonment under this clause. The right hon. and learned Attorney General for Ireland did not touch that question in the least degree; nor did the right hon. Gentleman the Chief Secretary for Ireland in the observations he made in reply to the right hon. Gentleman the Member for Derby (Sir William Harcourt). Supposing that a witness is committed for the contempt of not answering a question, on the ground that the question is unusual and has nothing whatever to do with the subject-matter

Mr. Anderson

of the inquiry; on the supposition that he committed the crime, will that person then be entitled to his dismissal from prison as regards his contempt of Court? These are questions which I should be glad if the right hon. and learned Attorney General would answer, more especially that with regard to sueing out the writ of Habeas Corpus.

MR. T. M. HEALY (Longford, N.): I have here the Bill to which I referred as having been passed by the House of Lords, and as to which the right hon. and learned Attorney General for Ireland expressed some doubt. It provides that every sentence or order for attachment or commitment to prison for contempt "shall operate and be in force for such time not exceeding three months." I ask the Government to give us the law as the House of Lords agreed to it, and I think that is not an unreasonable request. The right hon. and learned Attorney General for Ireland says that if there is a wrongful commitment there will be a full check upon it, because the particulars will have to be set out in the warrant; but I point out that the Government have not even taken the trouble to put on the Paper their own views. They tell us what their views are; but if we had them on the Paper we should be able to give them our views as to whether they were carrying out the intention they have expressed. I do hope that the Government will be persuaded to agree not to have this continuous punishment inflicted under the Act.

THE ATTORNEY GENERAL FOR IRELAND (Mr. HOLMES) (Dublin University): With regard to our not putting down the Amendment referred to by the hon. and learned Gentleman, it will be seen that there are some Amendments which have to be disposed of before the Amendment of my right hon. Friend can be dealt with. With regard to this Amendment, I cannot assent to the limit proposed by the hon. and learned Gentleman. If I remember rightly, the Bill referred to by the hon. and learned Gentleman related to ordinary commitments, but it had no reference to what is contemplated in this Bill.

MR. T. M. HEALY: I think the right hon. and learned Gentleman is mistaken. I am sorry the Government do not see their way to accept my Amendment, and I shall feel it my duty to divide the Committee upon the question.

MR. MAURICE HEALY (Cork): I cannot agree with what the right hon. and learned Attorney General for Ireland says with reference to the witness having the right of appeal; but even if he could sue out a writ of Habeas Corpus I cannot agree that it would be the smallest protection to persons examined under this clause. We know that the persons who will be sent to prison are those who belong largely to the poorer portion of the peasant class, to whom the cost would render it impossible that they should sue out the writ. The cost of a provisional order for a writ of Habeas Corpus would be from £10 to £20, and that 99 out of 100 of the class I have referred to could not pay, and those who were sent to gaol would have to remain there indefinitely unless this Amendment is accepted. I call the attention of the right hon. and learned Attorney General to the fact that in the Bill, as it at present stands, in the case of a large class of the offences detailed in the 2nd section, it will be in the power of the Government to treat these offences as punishable summarily, and that when they want to get evidence they can refuse to treat them so, and imprison witnesses for refusing to answer. They will be treated summarily when the Government want to get two Resident Magistrates speedily to convict a prisoner; but they will be indictable whenever a man is brought up under the clause and refuses to answer. Take the offences described in the 2nd section of the Bill—taking part in any criminal conspiracy and Boycotting—for what I say will also apply to them, and let us see what will be the state of things with regard to that class of offences. The Bill does not provide that they are to cease to be indictable offences. They are to remain indictable offences; but what the Bill does is to enable the Resident Magistrates to deal with them summarily. Therefore, I say that injustice will be perpetrated, and that so to speak the Government will be able to play the game of "Heads I win, tails you lose," according as they want to send a man to prison indefinitely or otherwise. I submit that this is most unfair, and that no one who considers the matter will regard it in any other light. I appeal to the Government at least to say whe-

[*Fifth Night.*]

ther they will be prepared to accept an Amendment providing that an offence punishable summarily under clause 2 shall not be treated as an indictable offence for the purpose of the 1st clause of the Bill. That I think is a fair offer. If we are not to get any concession with regard to the period of imprisonment. I think we are entitled to some reply on this point. Now, the right hon. and learned Attorney General for Ireland, who I regret is not in his place, in his usual manner in dealing with this Amendment spoke of the period of one week as the principal point which we were contending for. But we do not stick on that point. We do not ask that the imprisonment should be limited to a week, although a great many reasons could be urged in favour of the view that a week would not be too short a period; but we ask that in no case shall a Resident Magistrate have the indefinite power of imprisoning which the clause implies. Let some limit be placed to this. Let the Government take, for instance, a month in the case of an indictable offence, and if that will not satisfy them let them put down two months. I respectfully submit that we are entitled to some limit, because under the clause as it stands a man may be put in prison for refusing to answer a question, for a longer period than he would get in Court if he were found guilty of an indictable offence. There are hundreds of cases in which it would not be dreamt of giving a longer term of imprisonment than of four, five, or six months. Is it to be said that, though in ordinary cases of contempt the man found guilty would not be sentenced by a Judge to a longer period of imprisonment than a couple of months, magistrates under this section should have the power of imprisonment indefinitely. Such a state of things cannot be defended by reason and argument, and I do not think that we are doing anything unreasonable in asking that some limit, at all events, should be imposed upon the power of imprisonment conferred by this section. The right hon. Gentleman the Member for Derby (Sir William Harcourt) has adverted to a large number of cases in which witnesses might come to the conclusion that they were bound in honour not to answer the question which a magistrate might put to them. The right hon. Gentleman

pointed out that the effect of compelling a witness to answer as regards hearsay matters, as regards tittle-tattle, might be to make him a party to taking away the character of a person who might be as innocent of the charge as the witness was himself. Thereupon, the right hon. Gentleman the Chief Secretary for Ireland (Mr. A. J. Balfour) rose in his place and made a great point, by saying that no one would hear what was said except the magistrate holding the inquiry, and that the information would not be afterwards used for any purpose. Do the Government mean to tell us that a magistrate holding an inquiry will be sworn to secrecy; and will there be anything to prevent a magistrate who holds an inquiry from going about the country telling this man and that man what somebody said when brought up at an inquiry? Why, Sir, these inquiries might be made a gigantic machine for taking away the character of respectable persons in Ireland: Magistrates will hold inquiries in some little towns in reference to some offences which have been committed, and, no doubt, some unscrupulous person will be ready to come forward and to say—"I do not know anything about this offence, but I heard so-and-so say that John Smith committed it." Because there are unscrupulous persons ready to make these assertions, is it to be within the power of a magistrate to retail this tittle-tattle; is it to be within the power of a magistrate holding an inquiry to retail all over the country-side the slanders he has heard repeated in the privacy of these inquiries? It is all very well to tell us that magistrates will not do this kind of thing. We know what these gentlemen are; we know that when they get their legs under the mahogany of some county club, every atom of the evidence given at these inquiries will be retailed for the benefit of the landlords and agents who frequent the place. There is no justification whatever for the allegation that there will be any special secrecy about these inquiries. The magistrate who holds them will not be bound to secrecy. Perhaps I am trespassing too long upon the Committee; if so I must apologize for doing so, and I will only advert to one other matter, which I will make relevant to this question of hearsay evidence. It has been submitted to you, Sir, and I think very properly, that a

Mr. Maurice Healy

large number of cases may arise, in which it would be unjust that a Resident Magistrate should have the power to commit, indefinitely, a person who might consider himself bound in honour to refrain from answering as to the gossip which he has casually heard, and about which he really knows nothing. "Oh," says the right hon. Gentleman (Mr. A. J. Balfour), "it can do no harm at all that he should tell at these inquiries, because what he says at these inquiries can never be put in evidence against anybody." I have made a point already in regard to that statement, and it has never been answered. I maintain that gossip may be given in evidence, and I put a case in point, and no learned Gentleman on the Treasury Bench will attempt to challenge it. Let me take this case. The Government have now announced that, in consideration of an alleged concession made on an Amendment of ours, they intend to permit the depositions taken at these inquiries to be used by the Crown in case any witness examined at the inquiries should go back on what he said, or, upon cross-examination, declare that what he said at the inquiry was false. If the Government carry out that intention it will be in the power of the prosecuting counsel, if anyone of the Crown witnesses says anything different from what he has sworn at the inquiry to confront him with his own deposition, and to put that deposition in evidence, to use it for the purpose of contradicting the witness. What I insist upon is this, that when a deposition is so used in evidence, not merely will the portions which relate to what is within the knowledge of the witness be put in, but every bit of the deposition containing, perhaps, such gossip as I have mentioned, such hearsay evidence as would not, under ordinary circumstances, be admissible; every atom of the deposition, no matter how irrelevant and how illegal some of them may be, will be put in evidence against the prisoner. These considerations, Mr. Courtney, make it all the more important that the Resident Magistrate holding these inquiries should have some limit placed upon his powers. It may be that the Government contend that no consideration of that kind should prevent a witness from helping the administration of justice by answering any questions put to him. That may be so; the Govern-

ment may be right in that, but what we maintain is that, whether they are right or not, it is conceivable that a case can arise in which a witness might consider himself justified from conscientious motives in refusing to answer. And we say that a Court constituted under this section should not have the power of indefinitely imprisoning a witness who, upon conscientious grounds, objects to answer certain questions.

MR. HANDEL COSSHAM (Bristol, E.): Mr. Courtney, I will not intervene for more than a couple of minutes between the Committee and the Division; but I want to point out that there is one hopeful side about this discussion. The occupants of the Tory Benches, except the Front Government Bench, are silent, and I hope I may assume that hon. Gentlemen who sit upon those Benches are disposed to look favourably upon the Amendment now before the Committee. If I am right in my surmise, I think that we shall find that there is yet courage enough on the part of hon. Gentlemen on that side of the House to give expression to their views. There are two points on which the Government rely, as far as I can gather from their arguments, for the carrying of this clause. The first is that the witness is protected by the fact that he cannot be indicted for anything he professes by his evidence. But the whole value of that is destroyed by the fact that a magistrate has power to imprison a man perpetually, whether the evidence is against himself or not. If the Government brought this man to justice, in all probability he would be likely to get a less severe punishment than would be inflicted upon him by magistrates under this section. I contend that the Government are seeking to obtain power to perpetually imprison a man for no criminal act at all, but simply because a man declines to give any evidence, or is not honourably able to give evidence. Then there was another point very much relied upon by the right hon. Gentleman the Chief Secretary for Ireland (Mr. A. J. Balfour), and that was, that in the Act of 1882 there was power to imprison witnesses in connection with criminal offences. But the Government lose sight of the fact, or 'if they do not lose sight of it they try to evade it, that the offences contemplated by this Bill are not criminal offences at all, but political. It is a very different thing, as the right hon. Gentleman the Member for Mid Lothian (Mr. W. E. Gladstone) pointed out, to imprison a man for refusing to give evidence where a great crime has been committed, and imprisoning a man for refusing to give evidence in connection with political offences. I hope the day will never come when political offences in this country will be placed in the same category as offences against the Criminal Law. There is one thing which has struck me very much during this debate, and that is that, while during the last 50 years we have been continually improving the Criminal Law in this country, and have improved it with so much advantage, we are now in regard to Ireland going back in legislation, and we are actually making a Criminal Law so oppressive, and I believe so utterly disliked by the people, that instead of having their sympathy on the side of law and order, we have their sympathy invoked against the administration of the law. On these grounds, I disapprove of the clause which is now before the Committee, but if it is to be adopted I shall support the Amendment of my hon. and learned Friend the Member for North Longford (Mr. T. M. Healy).

MR. EDWARD HARRINGTON (Kerry, W.): Mr. Courtney, it is the contention of the Government that the power of commitment will not be improperly exercised; but, judging from experience, we are unable to put much faith in such a declaration. The Committee is in possession of certain statistics as regards commitments for contempt by the Irish Bankruptcy Court, and I venture to draw the attention of the Government to what has already been done in Ireland almost unnoticed. Our contention is that every law intended for civil administration in Ireland is diverted into a political channel by which to inflict suffering on the people, and the proceedings of the Irish Bankruptcy Court illustrates this strongly. A Return was recently presented to the House, showing the number of commitments by the Bankruptcy Court for contempt. It will be maintained by anyone who attends the Irish Bankruptcy Court, or watches its proceedings, that the most singular means are taken to arrive at the truth. An agrarian complexion is given to the dealings with all those who are brought before the Court, and we allege that

this clause will be worked to carry out the agrarian views of the Government. If it is possible in the case of one man, why should it not be possible for many men to be committed for an indefinite period for contempt of Court. Michael —— was committed by the Bankruptcy Court for contempt on the 19th of January, 1886, and he is still in prison. If it is possible to keep that man in gaol from January, 1886, until the present moment for what is considered unsatisfactory answering, how much more likely is it that this clause and this Bill will be used in a more severe and drastic way towards persons in Ireland who are suspected of political offences, or towards farmers who are accused of not paying impossible rents to the landlords, the friends of the magistrates? In the case of this man it is a melancholy fact that he is incapable of taking steps to obtain his release. My hon. Friend the junior Member for the City of Cork (Mr. Maurice Healy) has pointed out that the vast majority of the men who will be committed for contempt will not have the means of taking steps to extricate themselves from prison. Michael —— has been in gaol since January, 1886, and his wife and children are in the workhouse as a consequence of his committal for unsatisfactory answering. In the Return, it is shown that two men named Howard are lingering in prison for contempt. I am assured that these men are absolutely idiots. There is a grosser case, which does not appear at all in the Return. It is the case of two men of the county of Kerry. A once Member of this House — the O'Donoghue — has a property in Kerry, which is a burden to himself and to every one who lives upon it. The two men in question applied for a reduction of rent; but the agent refused it. They fell into arrears and were evicted; when they saw there was no one to prevent them they went back to their huts. The Sheriff was armed with authority to arrest the men; he came out and arrested one of the men, lodged him in gaol, where he was kept for two years, until, in fact, the Motion for this Return was made, when the Government thought it better to overhaul the account. The Resident Magistrate is, virtually, the gamekeeper and bailiff of the local landlord; and if Judges of the land commit indefinitely for con-

Mr. Handel Cossham

tempt, what can be expected from these local despots?

Mr. OSBORNE MORGAN (Denbigh-shire, E.): I know something of the power of imprisonment for contempt. I have seen a good deal of it in my professional career; and I must say that a more barbarous mode of enforcing the law does not exist. In recent times we have restricted the time of imprisonment; but, as a general rule, where a man is imprisoned for contempt of the Supreme Court of Justice, he is discharged on payment of costs; that, however, means that the man is possessed of money. I really put it to the Government whether it would not be possible—I do not want to restrict myself to the period of seven days—to impose some limit upon that practically unlimited power which they are giving to Summary Courts. The legislature has found it necessary to impose a limit in the case of the Supreme Court; therefore, I really think the Government might fairly see their way to propose some limitation in the case of inferior Courts.

Mr. MURPHY (Dublin, St. Patrick): I understand the Government refuse any concession upon this point on the ground that there will be no abuse of the power of commitment proposed to be conferred on the Resident Magistrates. I have, however, personal knowledge of at least three cases of persons committed for an indefinite period. In two of the cases the men are mentally unfit to plead. I do not know what will be considered unsatisfactory answering; but I can quite conceive there will be great abuse of the power of commitment for contempt. I trust that if the Government cannot accept this Amendment, they will, at all events, make some compromise in the matter.

Dr. TANNER (Cork Co., Mid): I have to call your attention, Mr. Courtney, to the fact that there are not 40 Members present.

Committee counted; and 40 Members being found present,

Mr. WALLACE (Edinburgh, E.): I shall not detain the Committee many minutes, and I should not have addressed them at all, except that I wish to explain to the Committee the reason why I feel myself unable to accept the principle upon which it seems to me the Go-

vernment steadily refuse Amendments of the nature of that which is now before the Committee. Their refusal in this case is precisely on the same ground as their refusal in the preceding case, and the Amendments are kindred in nature. The principle on which they go, as I understand it, is that there is no difference, in point of moral turpitude, on the part of a witness who refuses to be sworn, or to give evidence in a trial under the existing law, and the refusal of a witness to answer questions put to him at these preliminary inquiries. That argument has been stated over and over again by the Government, and was also well put in point of form by the hon. and learned Gentleman the Member for the Inverness Burghs (Mr. Finlay). I am unable to say that that principle is sound. It seems to me that it is vitiated by a fatal fallacy, and that is in not distinguishing between the circumstances of the two cases, which create a totally different moral position for a witness, in the one case, from what he occupies in the other case. Take the case of the refusal of a witness to give testimony in a regular trial under the present law. Now, it seems to me that there is a far greater degree of moral turpitude in the refusal of a witness in a trial under the present law, from what there would be in the case of a witness in the inquiries proposed to be created by this Bill. The witness at present who refuses may be committing, is almost certain to be committing, something which is morally indefensible. A fellow-creature is on his trial, it may be for his life, it must be, at all events, for his infamy, or his loss. A witness who then refuses to state what he knows may be incurring the guilt of allowing a fellow-creature who is innocent to be unrighteously condemned. On the other hand, if the prisoner who is on trial is guilty, the witness, by his refusal to give evidence, is declining to protect his country from a clearly ascertained enemy—a pest in that way. I say he cannot but have clearly forced home upon his mind the consciousness that he is acting against his duty in refusing to give his testimony as a contribution to the cause of justice, either on the behalf of an innocent and maligned fellow-being, or on behalf of the country and society. The whole surroundings of the trial tend to give the man a clearness of mental vision in regard to his

[Fifth Night.]

duty in the matter. He is made a party to the whole proceedings, he hears the explanation of the charge, he understands the risk to which society is exposed, he sees the individual, he becomes acquainted with the individual, and gets into new moral and personal relations with the individual whose fate may be depending upon his giving or withholding his testimony, and therefore I say that the distinctness of the understanding with reference to his duty which is forced home to his mind can hardly be exceeded, he is left without an excuse. But in the case of the proposed preliminary inquiry, the conditions are so totally different, that they are almost totally reversed. The whole thing is vague— there is no person with whom he is made acquainted, whose fate is made evident to him as depending upon his conduct. The Resident Magistrate has arbitrary power, requiring him to answer questions on this, that, or the other matter, the bearing of which upon any particular individual or element of public welfare is totally concealed from his mind. I say that, under these circumstances, nothing could be more completely calculated to produce vagueness and indistinctness of mental vision with respect to a man's duty in the matter of witness-bearing than this preliminary inquiry. If it had been ingeniously contrived to obfuscate a man's sense of his duty, it could not have been more successfully constructed. Therefore, I say, the obligation upon a witness in a regularly constituted trial at law under the present system, and the obligation upon a proposed witness in this preliminary investigation, do not stand upon the same level at all, and do not carry with them the same correlative moral obligation. To tell me, therefore, that a person who refuses to give testimony at a preliminary inquiry stands upon the same basis of guiltiness, and merits the same primitive treatment, as a person who refuses to give evidence at an ordinary trial at law, is to tell me something which is ridiculous. As far as I am able to understand the principle upon which the Government go, it is an untenable one, it is an endeavour to identify positions which are totally distinct. Upon this point a very subtle argument was advanced by the right hon. Gentleman the Member for Derby (Sir William Harcourt); that argument has not been

Mr. Wallace

answered as yet from the other side ; and, in fact, hon. Gentlemen opposite hardly seem to perfectly comprehend the force of the argument. I make no allusion to the hon. and learned Gentleman the Attorney General. (Sir Richard Webster), because he did not deal with the argument of the right hon. Gentleman the Member for Derby ; I only speak of those who did affect to deal with it. The argument of the right hon. Gentleman (Sir William Harcourt) was simply this—that the moral guilt of a witness who refuses, in the case of a regular trial, according to the standard established by the Laws of Evidence, is necessarily totally distinct from the guilt of a witness who refuses to answer under the entirely new standard of evidence which is set up in regard to this preliminary inquiry. The Laws of Evidence are understood to be an absolutely perfect instrument for getting out truth and gaining justice, and anything that differs from that, or contradicts the established Rules of Evidence, must to that extent be an instrument of injustice. It is one thing to refuse to use the instrument of justice, and another, and a totally different thing, to refuse to use the instrument of injustice. What the witness in the proposed preliminary inquiry refuses to use is not the instrument of justice, but, by the hypothesis, is the instrument of injustice. It is extremely hard upon Irish witnesses, in the peculiar circumstances of their situation, to propose to deal with them in this way. They have a sense of political wrong, which naturally creates in their minds a feeling that they are not justified in making contribution to information that may be useful to a Government which they regard as their enemy. The relationship between the Irish people and the Government is totally different from the relationship between the people of this country and the British Government. There is a relationship of friendliness between the people of this country and the British Government, even although there may not be agreement in Party politics ; but there is no such relationship between the Irish people and Dublin Castle. We can see every day, illustrated across the floor of this House, the relationship between these two Parties—a relationship which, I venture to say, is one of mutual hatred. [" Oh, oh !" *and Irish cheers.*]

I am speaking only of the impression made on my mind by the evidence before me. It seems to me that the Irish nation hates Dublin Castle just as heartily as Dublin Castle hates the Irish nation, and that being so, the feeling that is necessarily created in the mind of the average Irish witness must be that he is not only entitled, but even bound in honour and in national duty, to keep back what he knows from the enemy, or even to mislead him, or send him upon the wrong track. The position is one of war—it may be a bloodless and Constitutional war—but still it is war, and war, we know, suspends ordinary moral relations and duties. The state of mind of the average Irish witness is one in which he feels himself not only authorized, but even morally bound, to do what he can to prevent the secrets of his own political side from being revealed to the enemy, so as to enable them to strike down his friends. I say, in such a condition of feeling, it is peculiarly hard and oppressive that the average Irish witness should be subject to the treatment to which this legislation proposes to subject him. Now, these are the reasons which have induced me to trespass, somewhat reluctantly, upon the attention of the Committee at this time. I think there is a fallacy in the position taken up by the Government in identifying the positions and demerits of the two classes of witnesses; and I think, further, there is an excuse for the refusal on the part of Irish witnesses to give evidence in connection with political crimes that ought to be considered even by a Government that feels itself related towards them not as a friendly protector, but as a baffled tyrant—a Government that is trying, by a difficult and ever-increasingly difficult means, to establish its unauthorized tyranny over the people.

Question put.

The Committee *divided:*—Ayes 111; Noes 138: Majority 27.—(Div. List, No. 126.)

THE CHAIRMAN: Several Amendments follow in the name of the hon. Member for the City of Cork (Mr. Maurice Healy). Some of them refer to the 3rd sub-section, and others constitute Provisos; but they are mixed together. The Provisos must come first. The 1st Proviso, No. 69, has been already decided, therefore, it will fall upon the hon. Gentleman to move Proviso No. 71.

MR. MAURICE HEALY (Cork): I do not know whether the Government are disposed to look on this Amendment favourably or not; but I cannot think there is anything in it to which they can reasonably object. The Committee has decided that it is to be in the power of a Resident Magistrate to arrest a witness in the first instance. The Petty Sessions Act provides that before a witness can be arrested without summons, an information must be sworn, the witness can command a copy of the sworn information, and has a right to redress if a wrong has been inflicted upon him. It is supposed that many witnesses will probably leave the country the moment they receive an information that they will be summoned; and we apprehend that, in some districts of Ireland, the police will exercise this power of arresting a person, though there is no necessity whatever for such a proceeding, and we want to provide that the party by whom the wrong is inflicted may be brought to justice. We think that a witness should be entitled to obtain a copy of the information on which the warrant for his arrest is founded. A policeman, or other person, may maliciously go to a magistrate and say, "So-and-so can give important evidence in relation to the offence that has been committed; but if he is simply summoned, he will probably leave the country, therefore a warrant should be issued for his arrest." If a policeman, or other person, does this maliciously, and does it in a case where there is no necessity for it, surely the aggrieved party ought to have some means of obtaining redress. The first step in obtaining redress, I apprehend, would be to ascertain on whose information the warrant for his arrest was issued. There could be no objection whatever to affording the information, if the policeman, or other person, had nothing to conceal. I should be glad to hear what the right hon. Gentleman the Attorney General for Ireland has got to say upon this point. I beg to move the Amendment which stands in my name.

Amendment proposed,

In page 1, line 23, after "thereto," insert—"Provided, that in case a warrant shall be issued for the arrest of any witness in the first instance, and without any summons having previously been served and disobeyed, such witness shall, on demand, be entitled to receive from the resident magistrate holding the inquiry a copy of the information or complaint on which the warrant for his arrest was issued."—(*Mr. Maurice Healy.*)

Question proposed, "That those words be there inserted."

THE ATTORNEY GENERAL FOR IRELAND (Mr. HOLMES) (Dublin University): I quite agree with the hon. Gentleman (Mr. Maurice Healy) that nothing is more reasonable, if a man is arrested, than that he should be entitled to a copy of the information upon which his arrest is founded; but, probably, the hon. Gentleman is aware that at present it is an invariable practice that if a person is arrested on warrant, he can, upon application, get a copy of the information upon which the warrant is issued. As far as the Amendment is concerned, I have not the smallest objection to it; but it is just possible there may be some danger in its acceptance, and that it will injuriously affect the present practice.

MR. MOLLOY (King's Co., Birr): The right hon. and learned Gentleman the Attorney General for Ireland's (Mr. Holmes) explanation is satisfactory as far as it goes; but he has pointed out that, if this Amendment is inserted in the Bill, it will endanger the right which now exists by custom of law. [Mr. HOLMES: Practice.] Does the right hon. and learned Gentleman not think it worth while, in accepting this Amendment, to add some qualifying words to show this is no more than an extra precaution in consequence of the extraordinary character of this Bill? [Mr. HOLMES: No.] Why not; surely the position which the Attorney General for Ireland takes up is an extraordinary one, because, he says, that under the law, as it exists, a person arrested is entitled to the information upon which the warrant for his arrest has been issued.

MR. HOLMES: I am willing to accept the Amendment.

MR. MOLLOY: We are very much obliged to the right hon. and learned Gentleman for accepting the Amendment; but I am pointing out that he has said that the acceptance of this Amendment would endanger the right which now exists in all other cases. Surely, if

he accepts the Amendment, but thinks that it may endanger the present custom and right, there is no difficulty in putting in some words to make the matter clear. I presume that, in the acceptance of this Amendment, there is no intention to endanger the right which exists in all the three countries. Is there anything irrational or unreasonable in adding some qualifying words or amending the Amendment, so that there shall be no danger to the right which is acknowledged to exist?

MR. HOLMES: The hon. and learned Gentleman is under some misapprehension. I did not say there was a right; but I said there was, as far as I am aware, a practice that a copy of the warrant and information should always be given. I merely pointed out that the acceptance of this Amendment might endanger the present practice; but said that, if the hon. Gentleman (Mr. Maurice Healy) desired to have this special provision here, the Government had no objection to it.

MR. LOCKWOOD (York): May I point out what really is the practice in England. There can be no infringement of the practice now existing by the acceptance of this Amendment. So far as the practice of England exists at the present time, there is no section in any Act of Parliament under which a witness can be examined in the terms of the section which it is now asked shall become law, and, therefore, by acceding to this Amendment, there will be no infringement of any practice hitherto. If the right hon. Gentleman accedes to this Amendment he will not in any way jeopardize the practice as it exists at present.

MR. HOLMES: I quite agree with the hon. and learned Gentleman.

Question, "That these words be there inserted," put, and *agreed to.*

THE CHAIRMAN: The next Provisos which stand in the name of the hon. Member for Cork (Mr. Maurice Healy), and which are numbered 73 and 74, have already been decided, and the next Amendment to be submitted to the Committee is 75b; 75a is a separate sub-section, and will come after the Provisos as a new clause.

MR. MAURICE HEALY (Cork): Then I will move 75b, which is in the following terms:—

"Where a warrant has been issued to bring up a person under arrest for examination at an inquiry under this section, the warrant shall specify a place and a day and hour at which such examination is to take place, and such person shall be forthwith released on his entering into recognisance with sufficient sureties conditioned to attend for examination at such time or place."

This Amendment is drawn to meet a point I have already adverted to. The Committee is aware that the Government have insisted that the court of inquiry under this clause should have the right to arrest a witness in the first instance without a summons. I have pointed out that the result of this proceeding will be this—these inquiries, in many cases, are not finished in a day, or in a week; some of them have lasted months, and have extended for a very long time indeed, and my point is that in the case of an inquiry extending for a long time it will be competent, under this clause, for the authorities to arrest an intended witness at the beginning of the month and keep him in custody for the whole month, or until the point of the inquiry arrives at which it would please the Resident Magistrate, or whoever has charge of the investigation, to examine him. I maintain that that is not reasonable, and I say that consistently with the powers which the Government say the authorities should have, my Amendment might very well be accepted. Admitting that it may be necessary to arrest a witness, if he says to the Resident Magistrate, "I am willing to enter into my recognizance or to give sureties to appear at any day or any hour to be subjected to examination, I can give sufficient security that I will not leave the country, as you say there is danger of my doing." If a witness says that, I maintain that it is unreasonable and unjust to keep him in custody for any lengthened period.

Amendment proposed,

In page 1, line 23, after "thereto," insert— "Where a warrant has been issued to bring up a person under arrest for examination at an inquiry under this section, the warrant shall specify a place and a day and hour at which such examination is to take place, and such person shall be forthwith released on his entering into recognisance with sufficient sureties conditioned to attend for examination at such time or place."—(*Mr. Maurice Healy.*)

Question proposed, "That those words be there inserted."

Mr. HOLMES: If the hon. Member considers the mode in which this will work he will see that the acceptance of this Amendment would leave the witness in a much worse position than he would be under the clause as it now stands. Under the clause the magistrate may receive information that there is danger of a witness leaving the country, and he may issue a warrant to have that person brought before him forthwith for examination. The magistrates will have no power either to commit such person to prison, or to detain him in custody. It will be necessary for him then and there to examine the witness, or he will be obliged to dismiss him. The case the hon. Member has put of an examination lasting over a week or a month does not imply that a witness will be kept in custody for that period. Under the Act the magistrate will have no power to detain a witness. If he can examine then and there, well and good, but if he cannot he will have to let the witness go about his business. ["No, no!"] Will the hon. Member show me anywhere where the magistrate has power to keep a man in custody, or power to place him under recognizances to appear. It would be a very extraordinary thing if, under any circumstances, power were given to a Resident Magistrate to send a man to gaol for a week, or a fortnight, or a month, seeing that he is only engaged in an inquiry. I can assure the hon. Member that he is altogether mistaken —that no such power exists—and I can assure the Committee that I am at a loss to imagine why the Amendment has been moved.

Mr. MAURICE HEALY: I never, for a moment, suggested that it would be in the power of a Resident Magistrate to remand a witness arrested under these circumstances; but I say that Section 13 of the Petty Sessions Act, taken in connection with this clause, will provide that when the authorities arrest a man under the powers this law gives them, they will be able to keep him in custody until such period as he has been examined. [The Attorney General for Ireland dissented.] The right hon. and learned Gentleman shakes his head, but if he will make it clear to me that I am wrong I shall be very happy to withdraw my Amendment and resume my seat. The Government have rejected an Amendment limiting the time they can keep a man in custody. They have rejected a Proviso that the authorities, when they have arrested a man, shall not keep him in custody beyond a certain time, and they have argued in rejecting it, and given as a reason for rejecting it, that, perhaps, when a man had been arrested and brought before the magistrates, it might not be convenient for them to examine him at that particular time. The right hon. and learned Gentleman challenges me to show him anything in the Act which would give the magistrates authority to detain a witness under these circumstances. I would refer him to Section 13, which enables the authorities to arrest a man and, I presume, to keep him in custody until he has been examined. Does the right hon. Gentleman contend that it would be the duty of the magistrate to drop all other business when a man is arrested, and to proceed to examine him, although he might have 30 or 40 others to examine, or a great many other functions to perform? I do not see anything of that kind in the section. I see that, as a Court of Justice, considering this section and the section of the Petty Sessions Act to which I have referred, the authorities will fairly conclude that the intention of the Legislature was that when the man had been arrested, it was to be in the power of the Government or the Executive to keep him in custody until a convenient time came to examine him. If the Government will make it clear that it will be the duty of the magistrate to examine a man the moment he is brought up in custody, I shall be satisfied; but either of these two things is necessary—namely, that this Amendment should be accepted, or that some Proviso should be inserted declaring that a man should be examined the moment he is brought up in custody before the Resident Magistrate who is conducting the inquiry.

MR. HOLMES: The section of the Petty Sessions Act to which the hon. Member refers, and under which the procedure he is describing takes place, has been the law of the land for 36 years, and during the whole of that time, so far as I know, no complaint has been made of its operation. I venture to say that during these 36 years it would be impossible to point to a case where a man has been detained over night under the circumstances described. The magis-

trate has the power to issue a warrant and to arrest a person, and to have him examined before him. I do not mean to say that the magistrate must examine him immediately, but he must examine him within a short time of his arrest, and if he is not able to conduct that examination, he has no power on earth to do anything but to direct the man's discharge. I challenge the hon Gentleman to give an instance during the last 35 or 36 years in which that which he complains of has been done. Of course, I do not mean to say that the law may not have been abused and that wrong may not have been done in some individual instances; but, of course, we cannot provide against action on the part of those who may choose to break the law. They will be amenable to the punishments which are provided against infringements of Acts of Parliament. I may point out that the English and Irish law upon this point is exactly the same.

COLONEL NOLAN (Galway, N.): I cannot understand the object of the right hon. and learned Gentleman the Attorney General for Ireland refusing the acceptance of this Amendment. I will show how inconveniently his plan works out, and how much more convenient will be found that suggested by the hon. Member for Cork. I do not mean to say that it will be more convenient for the magistrate, but that it will certainly be so for the unfortunate man who is brought up to give evidence. Suppose a man is brought up in the vicinity of Glenbeigh, he would have to be taken over 25 miles for the purpose of giving evidence, and he probably would not come before the magistrate before 6 o'clock at night. It would then be too late to examine him that day, and what I want to know is what would be done under such circumstances —would the man be discharged then and there? If he were discharged, then what would be the use of arresting him? Under this Amendment the course adopted would be to take the witness before the nearest local magistrate, and not necessarily to take him before the magistrate conducting the inquiry in the first instance. Before the local magistrate he would be bound over or enter into his recognizances to appear before the magistrate conducting the inquiry at a time and place mentioned. Then there is this to bear in

Mr. Maurice Healy

mind, the police might get instructions to arrest a man for the purpose of examination, and might not be able to find him until an hour in the evening, at any rate, not before 5 o'clock, and when they bring him up it might be too late for the magistrate to examine him. I maintain that the witness would be saved a great deal of unnecessary annoyance and trouble by the acceptance of this Amendment.

MR. HOLMES: My point is that while this Amendment is altogether unnecessary, it would impose a burden upon the unfortunate man hon. Members are anxious to protect. It would impose upon him the necessity of entering into his recognizances, while, under the provision as it stands, it will be necessary to discharge him if the magistrate is not in a position to examine him at once.

MR. JOICEY (Durham, Chester-le-Street): I scarcely understand the opposition of the Government in this matter, but so far as I can make out the practice in England is this, that usually a warrant is only issued in the event of a summons not being attended to. Is it the intention of the Government that a summons should be issued for a witness to attend at the Court, and in the event of that not being obeyed that a warrant shall be issued, or is it intended that a warrant shall be issued in the first instance?

MR. HOLMES: The hon. Member cannot I think have been present during the discussion which has taken place upon this point, or he would have heard my explanation, that the law upon this subject is precisely the same in England and Ireland.

MR. MAURICE HEALY: The right hon. and learned Gentleman has challenged me to give him an instance of the exercise of the Petty Sessions Act, in a sense unfavourable to the position which he has taken up. I am not in a position to give him any such case, but the reason I cannot give a precedent is because there is no precedent for the action of the Government. I never heard of an Executive attempting to put in force this extraordinary power to arrest a witness in the first instance on a warrant, without some person being charged with an offence. I must also point out that, because the administration of the ordinary law appears to

have been conducted in an unobjectionable manner it does not follow that the magistrates to whom the administration of the new coercive law will be entrusted will not exercise their powers in a harsh and oppressive manner. The question to be decided by the Committee is this, would the Government, as the section at present stands, have the power to detain a witness for, practically speaking, an indefinite time—so long as the summons was continued? With great respect for the right hon. and learned Gentleman the Attorney General for Ireland, I hold that there is great danger that the Irish Courts will hold that such power exists under this Act. The right hon. and learned Gentleman says "No"—he says it is not the intention of the Government that such powers should exist. If he does not wish them to exist, and if it is not the intention of the Government that this shall be the law, I ask him to make his intention plain. I ask him to make it clear within the four corners of the Act, that it is not the intention of the Government, who are the framers of this Bill, that this power should be conferred upon the magistrates. If that is done, I will cease to press my Amendment—I will sit down in a moment. The right hon. and learned Gentleman says, it is not the intention of the Government that a witness shall be detained over night. Will he then insert a Proviso in this section to the effect, that if a witness is not examined on the day of his arrest, he shall be discharged? If he does that I will withdraw my Amendment in favour of his Proviso. I should be glad to accept any such Amendment as that—will he propose it?

THE ATTORNEY GENERAL (Sir RICHARD WEBSTER) (Isle of Wight): Really, if we are to deal with all these questions, we might as well set about writing a text-book on criminal practice. I cannot agree with the hon. Gentleman opposite, who does not seem to me to have a proper appreciation of the clause as it at present stands. Where it is shown that a certain individual is likely to be able to give information of a valuable character, a warrant may be issued, and if the inquiry is not complete that day the witness will have to attend at the next sitting. That is the practice in this country with regard to summonses. My view of the matter is that it will do considerable harm and no good whatever to endeavour to make a special point in Acts of this kind of provisions which are in operation, and which are very well known. All I can say is that it is much better to adhere to an Act which has existed, as the Act of 1851, for 36 years, in respect of which the practice is perfectly well known. I cannot see any authority for putting a man in prison simply because he has not been examined. There is no parallel whatever between that case and the case of a man who is committed for contempt. I can only repeat what my right hon. and learned Friend the Attorney General for Ireland has said—namely, that no reason has been shown for the admission of this Amendment. If there was any ground for it I should admit it at once. I am anxious to put in what is necessary, but I do not think we should attempt to incorporate in a measure rules and practices which already exist.

Mr. MAURICE HEALY: Unfortunately the practice in Ireland is not at all as well settled as the right hon. and learned Gentleman would have us believe, and, with the greatest respect, I venture to differ from him as to the law as it at present exists. I cannot accept it as he has laid it down. The Government say that under the Petty Sessions Act as it stands at present, if the authorities thought it necessary to arrest a witness under a warrant, if they had brought him for examination, and if the examination had not terminated on the day he was arrested, they would be bound to discharge him and re-arrest him on another day.

Sir RICHARD WEBSTER: If he did not come forward again.

Mr. MAURICE HEALY: Yes; if he did not come forward again. I contend that the Courts in Ireland will, without the slightest hesitation, if the authorities think it necessary to arrest a witness at all under these circumstances—I mean where it is declared that there is danger of a witness absconding and running away in order to avoid giving information—I say the Courts would not have the slightest hesitation in taking measures to prevent a man running away when his evidence was only half given. As the law stands, under the Petty Session Act, it is plain that if a witness is brought in under arrest, the authorities

have decided to arrest him, and not summon him, if his depositions are not completed on the day he is arrested, they have abundant power to keep him in custody until the depositions are completed. That is the state of things under the existing law, and I say that it will be greatly aggravated under this new law.

Mr. J. O'CONNOR (Tipperary, S.): I desire to point out what seems to me to be one reason why this Amendment is necessary. We have been dealing, so far, with a single case during this discussion—of the possible single case of one witness being brought up for examination; but let us suppose a case where many witnesses will be examined. Let us suppose a case of alleged conspiracy, and that an investigation is opened for the purpose of getting information concerning that conspiracy. Let us suppose also that the authorities of the district imagine that a number of witnesses are likely to abscond in order to avoid being examined. Naturally, under these circumstances, the magistrate, desiring to get information, would issue summonses for the attendance, it might be of 30, 40, or 50 persons. It is reasonable to suppose that these 30, 40, or 50 persons could not be examined in one day. Then what is to be done? I contend that it is to the advantage of the Government themselves that they should have the power to arrest these men under warrant, and to allow them to go about their business on sufficient security being given that they will attend for examination at the time and place mentioned in the warrant. This will be an advantage to the Government, and it will also be an advantage to the witnesses themselves. If the Government have not the power, and do not take the power, to issue these warrants, where it is quite on the cards and probable that 49 out of the 50 men may abscond, they will have to put up with whatever information one man can afford them. But if they take the power, and the safeguard is not put in that these men are to be allowed out on bail, they can detain in custody and put in prison the 49 men, and they would inflict great inconvenience upon these people. There is another way in which it might be worked. It very often happens in the administration of such an Act as this that policemen and officials and the Executive generally use it in a capricious fashion. Very often the names of the people as witnesses are put in by policemen in a bundle, and this is done by policemen for the purpose of inflicting injury upon persons against whom they have a grudge. It might be in the power of a policeman to inflict a serious and possibly a permanent injury upon a man in his business or profession by taking him up and putting him in prison, and keeping him from his family and his employment for a long period. I think there is good and sufficient reason established for inserting this Amendment, having due regard, as I say, to the interests of the Government, and also to the safety of witnesses who may be injured in their employment or otherwise. I think, therefore, that the hon. Member for Cork would be fully justified in forcing this Amendment on the consideration of the Government. I admit that in the carrying of measures of this kind we very often have assurances from the Front Ministerial Bench that they will not be used capriciously. They have the best intentions in the world, no doubt; they are very plausible; no doubt they do all they can to get Bills passed without a murmur. But what do all these good intentious amount to when the law comes to be administered by the officials in Ireland? We have often had the characters of these officials before Committees and before this House. The character of these people in Ireland is well known to the House, and in regard for its own legislation it ought to safeguard the proper administration of the Acts it passes. I say, that taking these things into account—bearing in mind the defective administration of the law in our country—we are entitled to throw very grave doubt on good intentions, at any rate to look with a serious amount of suspicion upon the good intentions expressed by the Government during the passage of these measures. The Attorney General for England, the Attorney General for Ireland, and the Government generally may have credit given to them for the good intentions they express; but we ought not to be satisfied with these expressions, and we should avail ourselves of the power while it is in our hands of amending this Act as we conceive it requires to be amended. I

trust my hon. Friend the Member for Cork will press his Amendment.

MR. CHANCE (Kilkenny, S.): I hope my hon. Friend will take a Division upon this Amendment, and that we shall have that Division very soon. I admit that when we deal with the Attorney General for England we always get a straightforward and fair answer, and that every argument that he has he states fairly and openly. We know after he has expressed his opinion it is no use debating with him further; we know that he has nothing at the back of his head that he has refrained from putting before the Committee. On what grounds has he refused this Amendment? Because it merely states what the existing procedure is. According to the Attorney General for Ireland, if a warrant is issued, it will only apply to the examination of the witness on the day for which the warrant is issued, and would have no application if it was necessary to examine the man on a second day. Well, even admitting for the purpose of argument that this Amendment does embody the existing law, I would ask the Committee to recollect that this Act is to be administered by Resident Magistrates, who are for the most part altogether ignorant of law. These gentlemen are very largely taken from professions in which very little knowledge of the law exists. The nature of their lives has precluded them from acquiring any such knowledge, and we must remember that the only power we shall have of checking these gentlemen will be by going before the Court of Criminal Appeal, which means going before the Court of Queen's Bench in Ireland. Well, Sir, I know it is against the Order of this House for a Member to say any thing derogatory to the Judges, or to express an adverse opinion of our legal tribunals. I regret that that is the fact, but I am bound to obey that rule, and, therefore, I will refrain from characterizing the Court of Queen's Bench in Ireland by terms which I should be inclined to use were it competent for me to express my opinion openly. I will only say that the appeal will lie in a Court which we regard as having very little sympathy with the mass of the population of Ireland, and a Court which cannot be said to have the least claim to popularity. If, as the

[Fifth Night.]

Government say, the provisions contained in this clause are already in the existing law, I would impress upon them the necessity of laying down distinctly and clearly the extent of these provisions, so that the Resident Magistrate may not be able to misunderstand them.

MR. MOLLOY (King's Co., Birr): I think, with reference to the statement which has just now been made by the Attorney General, that it goes far to settle this question. I do not wish to discuss the legal point with the hon. and learned Gentleman whose criminal knowledge must necessarily be much more extensive than mine. I merely wish to ask him for a decided statement upon this point. Will the warrant be spent at the end of the first examination—supposing the witness is brought up under a warrant—at 6 o'clock when the Court closes? Will the witness be free or will he not? If he will, we shall be perfectly satisfied. But if, on the other hand, the warrant does not end at 6 o'clock, or if it is not spent in one day's examination and extends over to the next day, what will become of the witness between the hour of 6 o'clock in the evening of the first day and 10 o'clock of the morning of the next day? I am bringing the point down to the very smallest compass. We want to know during the interval between the examination on the first day and the second day whether the witness will be set at liberty or kept in custody under the authority of the warrant. If the witness is kept in custody between the hours of 6 o'clock at night and 10 o'clock in the morning, is there any reason for saying that the same process will not go on from day to day until the witness becomes practically a prisoner? Is there to be any limit in point of time, or are the Resident Magistrates to be allowed to keep witnesses in custody just as long as they may think it necessary to keep on the examinations? I ask the Attorney General for England to answer me upon this point. I desire an answer from him, although in saying so I do not wish to appear discourteous to the right hon. and learned Gentleman the Attorney General for Ireland. But I have been discussing this matter with the English Attorney General, whose knowledge of law, as I say, is necessarily much more extensive than my own. Of course, if the virtue of the warrant is not spent

Mr. Chance

on the first day, then our contention is that the witness virtually becomes a prisoner for an unlimited period, and that accordingly the Bill requires amendment.

MR. HOLMES: It does not require a very extensive knowledge of law to answer the hon. Member's question.

MR. MOLLOY: I did not say you could not answer it.

MR. HOLMES: I have answered this question more than once. There is no power whatever vested in a magistrate who has a witness brought before him to do more than examine him. The moment the examination ceases, the magistrate must discharge the witness. If, for instance, he ceases to examine at 6 or half-past 6 in the evening, the witness may walk away perfectly free, the magistrate having no right to detain him. No doubt the magistrate will have the power, if necessary, to continue the examination after 6 o'clock, because as hon. Members are aware, we have taken care to provide for cases in which it may not be possible for examinations to commence before 6 o'clock, and where it may be absolutely necessary that they should be continued over that hour. It is certain that a magistrate having begun an examination must go on with it. When an examination ceases either permanently or for a time the magistrate has no power to detain the witness.

MR. MOLLOY: The warrant is spent.

MR. HOLMES: Entirely spent.

SIR JOSEPH M'KENNA (Monaghan, S.) : Is it competent for the authorities to issue a warrant on the day the man is to be examined, or is it necessary that the warrant should be issued on a day before the examination is to take place? It may not be possible for the witness to be examined on the day he is taken up; and I think, therefore, the Amendment ought to be inserted in order to enable the witness to get his liberty if it is impossible for the examination to take place on the day the warrant is issued.

MR. CHANCE: Will the Government agree to insert words in this clause on Report to make the view they have expressed to-day perfectly clear? When we recollect the character of tribunal, we shall see the necessity of having everything put right. We know the Secretary to the Lord Lieutenant is laughing in his sleeve at us, and that makes it necessary for us to scan every line of this measure, and to take care that the good intentions of the Government shall be carried out, and that the course to be followed by the gentlemen who will preside upon the Judicial Bench shall be very clearly marked out.

Mr. P. J. POWER (Waterford, E.): I should like to know if the examination is to be continued on the second day, whether it will be necessary for a second warrant to be issued.

Mr. HOLMES: I think that the general experience we have had of the working of the ordinary law shows that witnesses who attend upon a warrant if their examination is not finished on the first day put in an appearance on a second day as a matter of course. If, however, under this Bill a witness should not appear on the second day, it will be necessary to enforce his attendance with a second warrant.

Mr. MAURICE HEALY: Could he abscond in the meantime?

Mr. HOLMES: No doubt he could if he chose.

Mr. MAURICE HEALY: After what the right hon. and learned Gentleman has said it would be idle for me to go to a Division. At the same time I would ask the right hon. and learned Gentleman to consider the desirability of introducing words into the clause to make the matter perfectly clear. This Act, as has been frequently pointed out, will have to be administered by the Resident Magistrates and the Courts of Law, and it is by no means clear that they would take the same view of this subject as the right hon. and learned Gentleman.

THE CHAIRMAN: Does the hon. Member withdraw his Amendment?

Mr. MAURICE HEALY: Yes; I ask leave to withdraw.

Amendment, by leave, *withdrawn.*

Mr. MAURICE HEALY: Do you, Mr. Courtney, rule out my Amendment 75a—

"Where at the date when any inquiry under this section is held any person shall be charged with the offence in reference to which such inquiry has been held, such person or his solicitor or counsel shall be entitled to attend such inquiry, and to cross-examine any witnesses examined thereat."

THE CHAIRMAN: Yes; it is a separate sub-section, and will form a new clause. The hon. Member can proceed with 75c, which is a Proviso.

Mr. MAURICE HEALY: Then, Sir, I beg leave to move in line 23, after "thereto," to insert—

"Provided that a warrant to commit any person to prison for refusing to answer any question or questions put to him at any inquiry under this section, shall specify the offence in reference to which the inquiry has been held, and shall set forth the question or questions for refusing to answer which such person has been committed to prison, and in any legal proceedings which may be taken by any such person in reference to or arising out of such warrant, or his committal to prison, it shall be competent for the court in which such proceedings are taken to examine into the circumstances under which such persons were committed to prison, and such warrant was issued, and to review the order of the resident magistrate holding such inquiry, and examine and ascertain whether he was warranted or authorised in committing any such person to prison, or whether such committal was a proper exercise of his discretion; and for such purpose the court may hear any legal evidence which may be offered, and, in particular, may refer to the shorthand notes of the inquiry."

This is an attempt to put into words the pledge the Attorney General has given us over and over again in these debates —one which has been relied upon frequently. I will not argue the matter, because I believe the right hon. and learned Gentleman the Attorney General for Ireland will accept the Amendment.

Amendment proposed,

In page 1, line 23, after "thereto," insert— "Provided that a warrant to commit any person to prison for refusing to answer any question or questions put to him at any inquiry under this section, shall specify the offence in reference to which the inquiry has been held, and shall set forth the question or questions for refusing to answer which such person has been committed to prison, and in any legal proceedings which may be taken by any such person in reference to or arising out of such warrant, or his committal to prison, it shall be competent for the Court in which such proceedings are taken to examine into the circumstances under which such person was committed to prison, and such warrant was issued, and to review the order of the resident magistrate holding such inquiry, and examine and ascertain whether he was warranted or authorised in committing any such person to prison, or whether such committal was a proper exercise of his discretion; and for such purpose the Court may hear any legal evidence which may be offered, and, in particular, may refer to the shorthand notes of the inquiry."—(*Mr. Maurice Healy.*)

Question proposed, "That these words be there inserted."

Mr. HOLMES: It is impossible to accept this Amendment. I will put on

[*Fifth Night.*]

the Paper this evening an Amendment to provide that the warrant shall specify the particular questions in respect of refusal to answer which the witness has been committed to prison. It will be in the hands of hon. Members to-morrow morning. Beyond that, it will be perfectly impossible for us to go. The Amendment I propose will give the Court above the opportunity of deciding whether the committal was within the jurisdiction of the magistrate who issued the warrant.

Mr. MAURICE HEALY: The alleged "concession" of the right hon. and learned Gentleman is perfectly illusory. According to his own statement, all this will do will be to express in a sub-section in this measure what is already the existing law. The right hon. and learned Gentleman says that when an inferior Court commits a person for contempt of that Court, it is necessary that the warrant should specify——

Mr. W. REDMOND (Fermanagh, N.): I wish, Mr. Chairman, to call your attention to the loud and continuous conversation and laughter of hon. Gentlemen opposite, which I can assure you, Sir, is greatly interfering with hon. Members on this side of the House who are endeavouring to hear and understand what is going on.

The CHAIRMAN: I am sure hon. Members will concur with me in thinking that the speaker ought to be heard.

Mr. MAURICE HEALY: I was saying, Sir, that, in my opinion, the concession of the Government amounted to no more than a promise that they would embody in this Bill that which is the existing law. The right hon. and learned Gentleman states that the existing law is that an inferior Court shall set forth in its warrant what its jurisdiction is, in order to commit for contempt. I contend, Sir, that a warrant which should show—that should necessarily show—the two great elements in my Amendment—namely, the nature of the inquiry that is to be held, and what the question was that the witness refused to answer. The object of the Amendment is that a person committed to prison should go behind the warrant and inquire into any legal evidence as to whether or not the magistrates had acted properly. I do not think the Attorney General has offered any argument against that being done. What is the value of

Mr. *Holmes*

the concession of the right hon. and learned Gentleman?

Mr. MAHONY (Meath, N.): I rise, Sir, to a point of Order; it is perfectly and absolutely impossible for us to hear what the hon. Member is saying. The conversation and interruption which is going on on the other side of the House is deliberate.

The CHAIRMAN: Perhaps the hon. Member for Cork (Mr. Maurice Healy) will speak a little louder?

Mr. MAURICE HEALY: My contention is this—the Government has accepted an Amendment from this quarter of the House providing that a shorthand writer shall attend, and shall take notes of what goes on at these secret inquiries; and what I say is, that that concession dwindles down to the smallest value if they step in now and say that, though they have these shorthand notes, the person committed to prison for refusing to answer shall not have the the power of making the smallest use of them. That is really the whole question at issue. Is a prisoner committed for refusing to answer questions under this clause to be in a position that the warrant of the Court which commits him to gaol is to be final and conclusive, and that no Court of Law is to have the power of going behind that warrant and ascertaining whether the Resident Magistrate has acted properly or not? Permit me to point out that nothing could be easier than for the Resident Magistrate holding an inquiry, no matter how illegally he had acted, to draw his warrant in such a form that no Court would go behind it and inquire into its propriety or illegality. All the Resident Magistrate would have to do in order to protect his warrant from investigation would be to say that the question put to the witness was a perfectly proper one, but that the witness had refused to answer it. Unless such an Amendment as this I now propose is put in, it will not be in the power of the Court to ascertain whether or not the Resident Magistrate was to blame; and we ask, seeing that the Government have provided for the taking of shorthand notes, that the person committed to prison for refusing to answer the Resident Magistrate shall have the opportunity of examining those notes, and of bringing them before the Court in which he questions the action of the Resident Magistrate. We claim that on going into the Court the witness may get whatever benefit it is possible to derive from the shorthand notes.

MR. O'DOHERTY (Donegal, N.): There is a vast difference between a trial in a public Court and one of these examinations, and between a witness refusing to answer in a private inquiry and refusing to answer questions put publicly. A person examined in secret may be committed to prison upon a warrant on its face perfectly right. No one will know what has taken place at a secret inquiry unless the shorthand notes are forthcoming. No one would dream of concocting a warrant; but I can imagine a witness exciting the anger of a Resident Magistrate, and I can imagine that Resident Magistrate committing a witness, and finding when he afterwards cooled down that he had gone a little too far in committing the witness, and I can then understand him in writing out the committal—the witness being in custody—putting a colour to the proceedings in order to justify his hasty action. In writing out a record of the proceeding it is plain that he may find that he has done something wrong, having acted in a passion, or in haste, or without due consideration. I ask are there no means of protecting witnesses? Is there no Court to which they can appeal to take all the circumstances into consideration, and to say whether or not they have been wrongly treated? If the Attorney General's Amendment is inserted then all the magistrate has to do is to be keen enough to state in his warrant that he has put certain questions. But he may have put other questions besides those he records, or the witness may have answered a particular question in another form. The witness himself may have got angry, and may have made some hasty observation, or may have acted hastily, and the magistrate may have committed him, although his offence was not one in any way warranting such a punishment. What we ask in this Amendment is not whether or not the warrant is right on the face of it, but whether the action of the magistrate in committing the witness to prison was a proper and right exercise of his discretion under the circumstances. For this purpose we ask not that the prisoner shall see the shorthand notes, but

that the Court shall have power to examine them. My hon. Friend's Amendment clearly mentions that it is only the Court that is to have power to examine the shorthand writer's notes. Undoubtedly, what is now proposed is an amendment of the existing law. Undoubtedly, if the warrant is right on the face of it, the Court before whom it comes for consideration should be able to go into the question of the discretion of the Resident Magistrate, and we do ask that a provision should be made to meet special and exceptional proceedings which may take place on one of these special and exceptional inquiries which would not occur in an open Court.

MR. HOLMES: I wish to make this matter as clear as I possibly can. The hon. Gentleman, so far as I understand it, has first of all suggested that the magistrate should make out a warrant which in form would be perfectly correct, but which would not correctly represent the circumstances of the inquiry. In such a case there would absolutely be no protection for the magistrate. If he wilfully falsified the facts and spread them out in a dishonest form, no Judge or jury would hesitate to declare that his conduct was improper. No Judge or jury would hesitate to condemn such a magistrate; therefore we have a protection against the evil the hon. Member wishes to provide against in the ordinary law as it stands. A case which may arise may be this. A magistrate may commit a man without having proper jurisdiction to do so—for instance, he might commit a man for refusing to answer a question which he had no right to ask. Now, the warrant, assuming that it has been properly prepared, will show the question that has been put, and it will be for the Court above to say whether or not the magistrate had jurisdiction to ask the question. Suppose that the warrant truthfully sets out the matter, and there is no ground for saying that the magistrate has acted maliciously; under these circumstances, the hon. Gentleman says that the Court above should review the discretion of the magistrates. I say that we should not accept any such Amendment as that. It would be contrary to the principle upon which all our law is based, and I do not think there is a single English lawyer in the House who would agree to it.

SIR WILLIAM HARCOURT (Derby): The difficulty I have in understanding the right hon. and learned Gentleman the Attorney General for Ireland is this, that it is supposed that the question put to the witness will be recorded in the warrant. I take it that that would be very valuable if there were any means by which the Court above could review the propriety of putting that question. As I understand it, there is no question which cannot be put so long as it is not entirely relative to a totally different matter to that under investigation. You are dealing with the analogy of a Court of Law when there are certain questions that are proper and others that are not proper according to the Law of Evidence. If the latter class of questions are put in a Court of Law, you can appeal to the Court above; but it is the very essence of this secret inquiry, that the Rules of Evidence do not apply to it. Therefore, I do not see what there is upon which you can appeal to the Court above. The right hon. and learned Gentleman the Attorney General for Ireland said just now that the Court will not be allowed to review the discretion of the magistrate; but, unfortunately, the discretion of the magistrate is extremely wide—in fact, there seems to be no limitation to it whatever, and, therefore, there will be no limitation to the questions the magistrate can put to the witness.

MR. MOLLOY (King's Co., Birr): Will the Government state what objection there can be to the Judge before whom a case is brought being allowed to see the shorthand notes? The fact of their being submitted to the Judge will not bring them before the public—the reporters will not see them; consequently, they will not be published, and they will not come to the knowledge of those people from whom it is desirable to withhold the information which has been obtained. Surely the Judge who has to try the case should be allowed to see the notes and the context of the particular sentence in regard to which the appeal is made. It is not very difficult for anyone here to state a case at once where it would be necessary for the Judge to see the shorthand notes in order to get at the context. If I gave the Committee an illustration of the point in question, both the Attorney Generals would see that a particular sentence and a particular phrase may not give the slightest information whatever to the Judge who has to try the case, and before whom the appeal is brought. What is the objection to making this concession? Will the Government state out frankly to the House what objection they have to allowing the Judge who has to try the case access to the whole of the evidence? Why do you say the case has to be tried, and then lay down that the Judge has not to have the whole of the evidence before him, but only such part of it as the particular magistrate whose conduct is in question chooses to send before him? This is very like a man being tried for a crime, and the accused laying down what information shall be placed before the Court. Will the Attorney General for Ireland say frankly what objection there is to the Judge seeing the shorthand notes if he thinks proper to do so? What objection is there to the Judge having all the information which, in his discretion, will enable him to come to a just decision? Will the right hon. and learned Gentleman answer that point? If he will, no doubt we shall be able to make further progress with the Bill.

MR. P. J. POWER (Waterford, E.): It is evident that the Government are afraid to allow the conduct of the Resident Magistrates to come under the review of any Court. We have contended that they are incompetent to undertake these powers, and the action of the Government confirms that. What is the object of going to the great expense of having complete shorthand notes and this inquisitorial inquiry if they are not to be seen by anyone? What is the object, if the Court of Queen's Bench, or any Court to which the appeal would lie, has not an opportunity of seeing these notes—what would be the use of them? It would be much better that they should never be taken at all.

MR. CHANCE (Kilkenny, S.): The Attorney General for Ireland should recollect the case of Father Kelleher. In the Court of Queen's Bench it was decided that since the question was taken down, on the face of the warrant, the Court had no power to inquire into the relevancy or irrelevancy of certain questions put under the Bankruptcy Act in open day. There was a protection in that case, because the whole body of public opinion could be brought to bear upon the matter. There is a great distinction to be drawn between that case and the present case. But the decision in Father Kelleher's case shows that the statement in the warrant will be no protection to the witness; so that, so far as that is concerned, the right hon. and learned Gentleman might have saved his breath, and might have refrained from proposing what he called a concession. It is clear that in the case of this inquiry into a crime committed by some person —or by no person, for there may be no one accused—there are no other means by which you can ascertain the relevancy of a question, and that, therefore, the Court should be allowed to consider what previous questions had been put, in order to discover the course which the inquiry ought to have taken, and to enable the Judge to say whether the magistrate's jurisdiction had been fairly exercised.

MR. STAVELEY HILL (Staffordshire, Kingswinford) : There are two points before us—one is what the warrant should contain, and the other is what the Superior Court should have before it. The right hon. Gentleman the Member for Derby (Sir William Harcourt) says the Superior Court should have before it, not only the warrant, but every point that can be brought before it in evidence. That is not the Amendment of the hon. Gentleman. [Mr. MAURICE HEALY : Yes, it is.] Anyone who can read the English language will say that what the Amendment provides is that the warrant should set forth the question. I agree with the right hon. Gentleman (Sir William Harcourt) that the Court should have before it the shorthand writer's notes of the evidence; but the suggestion that they should appear on the warrant is absurd.

MR. CHANCE (Kilkenny, S.): May I recall the hon. and learned Gentleman's (Mr. Staveley Hill's) attention to the Amendment—

"Provided that a warrant to commit any person to prison for refusing to answer any question or questions put to him at any inquiry under this section, shall specify the offence in reference to which the inquiry has been held, and shall set forth the question or questions for refusing to answer which," &c.

The other questions are not to be set forth; it is only the precise question for refusing to answer which he is sent to prison. That is conceded by the Law Officers of the Crown, and I now ask them to state whether it would be necessary to put anything on the warrant but the precise question and answer ?

MR. STAVELEY HILL: The Government have agreed that the question should be set forth on the warrant. I go with hon. Gentlemen opposite as far as that, but I do not agree with the Amendment that anything else should be set forth.

SIR WILLIAM HARCOURT : I think we may come to a very clear understanding that the warrant should contain nothing but the question and answer. Then the question is whether the Court which is to determine the imprisonment should have full seizing of all that has happened. I understand my hon. and learned Friend (Mr. Staveley Hill) to contend that the Court should have full possession of the circumstances attending the question in order to judge rightly; that the Court should not be in possession of the bare statement of the question only, but of the matters under which the question arose, and, in point of fact, of what took place in the Court of Inquiry. Everybody knows that in the case of an ordinary proceeding before a common tribunal, the shorthand notes or the Judge's notes would be available to show whether the evidence is admissible. That is all that is asked here. I understand that hitherto the Government have refused to consent that the shorthand writer's notes should go before the Court. In that case, they practically agree that the Court is not to know what has passed. How is the witness who is to be committed to prison to satisfy the Court above that he has not had justice done him ? Upon affidavit, is it ? If upon affidavit, why is not the affidavit to be accompanied by the most authentic document ? I should say that in any tribunal that would be the natural and proper course. It has been said, and said quite truly, that a magistrate—in repeating it I do not wish to attribute any evil motive to any magistrate—will fight very hard to maintain his decision, and unless you are able when you are appealing to a Court *in Banco* to bring before them everything that has occurred, you will have very little chance of success. You cannot judge of the whole transaction from the mere words of the warrant. You cannot judge what gave rise to the question how the magistrate came to put such a question, and what are the surrounding circumstances. The authentic evidence of that is the shorthand writer's notes. What are those notes for? Are they only for the Government to use when it suits them, and to disregard them when they are adverse to the Government's view? Why should they not be at the service of the witness who is affected by them, who is committed upon the transactions recorded in them? The Attorney General for Ireland made a very fair and proper concession in agreeing that the question should be put upon the warrant; but surely the complement of that is that if there is to be an appeal, the Court which is to hear it should know all the circumstances.

THE ATTORNEY GENERAL FOR IRELAND (Mr. HOLMES) (Dublin University): The right hon. Gentleman (Sir William Harcourt) knows as well as I do that a witness may apply for a writ of *certiorari*, and that if he can establish a case not only the warrant but the statements which are contained in the transcript of the shorthand writer's notes are at once removed. That is one remedy under the existing law. Another remedy is that he may bring an action against the magistrate if he thinks, of course, he has been unjustly treated. The reason why we object to the Amendment is that it deals with entirely different subject-matter. Let me read the last portion of the Amendment—

" And in any legal proceedings which may be taken by any such person in reference to or arising out of such warrant, or his committal to prison, it shall be competent for the court in which such proceedings are taken to examine into the circumstances under which such person was committed to prison, and such warrant was issued, and to review the order of the resident magistrate holding such inquiry, and examine and ascertain whether he was warranted or authorized in committing any such person to prison, or whether such committal was a proper exercise of his discretion."

Now, we entirely object to that, because we do not profess at all to give an appeal as regards the discretion of the magistrate. If a magistrate makes an illegal order it can be quashed by the High Court of Justice, and the shorthand writer's notes and the order can be made available according to certain legal rules now in existence. We take our stand upon that; we shall not go further.

Sir William Harcourt

MR. MAURICE HEALY (Cork): I am really amazed at the representation of what the existing law is that the right hon. and learned Gentleman the Attorney General for Ireland has ventured to give the Committee. He states, in the first place, that the man who is committed to prison for contempt would have a remedy by *certiorari*. If I read the provisions of the Justices' Protection Act aright, there is no remedy in such a matter as this unless the witness can show express malice. What is the use of a witness bringing an action if, when he has brought it, the magistrate pleads he acted in good faith and claims that the action shall be dismissed? I challenge the right hon. and learned Gentleman to show by any authority that the law is as he has stated. I assert, and I challenge contradiction, that it will not be competent for a witness who was committed to prison under this section to bring an action until he has by one procedure or another quashed the warrant under which he was committed to gaol. The right hon. and learned Gentleman says, that if the witness applies by *certiorari*, the order of the Court would be that not merely the warrant of committal, but the shorthand writer's notes, would be returned into the Queen's Bench. I challenge that statement. I assert such is not the case, and that my Amendment is drawn to provide that such should be the law. If a witness should proceed by *certiorari*, the only thing which the Court of Queen's Bench would have power to return into Court for the purpose of being inquired into would be the mere warrant of committal, and to obtain an order for *certiorari* the witness would have nothing but his individual affidavit, which would be valueless if contradicted by the shorthand writer's notes. The right hon. and learned Gentleman deals with the evidence raised by this Amendment as if it was solely a question of giving the man who was committed to prison the right of action. It is nothing of the kind. The important object of this Amendment is to enable a man committed to gaol to get out of gaol if the magistrate has acted improperly. The answer of the Attorney General for Ireland really amounts to this—that the Government do not intend that there shall be any appeal from the order of the Resident Magistrate. The Government are determined that the proceedings of the Resident Magistrates shall be open to no question and no review. They are determined not to submit to the light of day what goes on at these star-chamber inquiries through which all the people of a country side may be sent to gaol without any appeal. We have a right to expect that the Attorney General for Ireland should not, as I think he does, misrepresent to the Committee what the real state of the law is, and what the condition of the unfortunate witnesses committed to prison under this section would be.

MR. CHANCE (Kilkenny, S.): I deny that by *certiorari* the shorthand notes can be brought up, but even supposing they can, I ask the Attorney General (Sir Richard Webster) if he is of opinion that the notes can be used to contradict any statement whatever in the warrant? If a civil action were brought and an application were made for the production of the shorthand notes, every one knows perfectly well that the answer of the magistrate would be that the notes were not his property but of the Government, and they were privileged. it would be further said that the inquiry was strictly secret, and that by this Act it was not intended that everything taking place before the tribunal should see the light of day in other Courts. I cannot see what necessity there is for giving the magistrate the protection which is sought for him. I trust I shall receive an answer to the question I have asked, and that the hon. and learned Gentleman (Mr. Staveley Hill), who for the first time since this debate has opened has given us some assistance, will continue to give us his assistance and encourage us to fight our case.

MR. STAVELEY HILL: I assure the hon. Gentleman (Mr. Chance) I shall do all I can to prevent coercion being improperly applied to Ireland. But there is nothing sought to be given by the Amendment that is not given under the existing law. If I thought there was I should vote for the Amendment most heartily. I believe the witness has every protection under the existing law he can possibly have.

THE ATTORNEY GENERAL (SIR RICHARD WEBSTER) (Isle of Wight): In reply to the hon. Gentleman the Member for South Kilkenny (Mr. Chance), I have to say I am most distinctly of opinion that on *certiorari* the shorthand notes can be brought up and referred to. The practice is that an affidavit must be made setting forth that the warrant is bad for certain specified reasons. The deponent can make any statement he thinks fit, and then the Court will be able to judge whether the warrant has been properly framed. If *certiorari* is applied for all the proceedings will be returned. That is an entirely different matter from giving the Court power of review. It has nothing to do with the question whether or not a magistrate acted within his jurisdiction or beyond his jurisdiction. We do intend that when the question is one which it is competent for the magistrate to put, and the witness says—"I decline to answer," the magistrate shall be protected.

MR. CHANCE: Is the hon. and learned Gentleman of opinion that on *certiorari* the shorthand notes can be used as evidence to contradict or explain the statements in the warrant?

SIR RICHARD WEBSTER: Most certainly they could.

MR. O'DOHERTY (Donegal, N.): It is perfectly idle to tell the Committee that the writ of *certiorari* is open to a witness. It may be open to him to bring an action afterwards.

Question put.

The Committee *divided:*—Ayes 155; Noes 256: Majority 101. [Div. List, No. 127.]

MR. MAURICE HEALY (Cork): I rise to move to insert after "thereto"—

"Provided, That if at any inquiry held under this section it is proposed to commit any witness to prison for refusing to answer any question or questions, such witness shall thereupon be entitled to be heard by counsel or solicitor in case he shall so desire."

I have no desire to weary the Committee by arguing before it a matter which has been, at any rate, partly discussed on a previous Amendment. The Committee has decided that it will not allow a solicitor or barrister to represent a witness at an inquiry. I would, however, appeal to the Committee to allow a witness, before being committed to gaol, to be heard by counsel or solicitor, so that his case may be properly presented.

Amendment proposed,

In page 1, line 23, after "thereto," insert—"Provided, That if at any inquiry held under this section it is proposed to commit any witness to prison for refusing to answer any question or questions, such witness shall thereupon be entitled to be heard by counsel or solicitor in case he shall so desire."—(*Mr. Maurice Healy.*)

Question proposed, "That those words be there inserted."

THE ATTORNEY GENERAL FOR IRELAND (Mr. HOLMES) (Dublin University): I would point out to the Committee that it has already rejected an Amendment of a similar nature. The result of the adoption of the Amendment would be to give witnesses the power of delaying the proceedings by making application for the assistance of counsel, and by the arguments which counsel would be instructed to use. The whole proceedings would, in fact, be likely to be made ridiculous.

MR. T. M. HEALY (Longford, N.): The right hon. and learned Gentleman the Attorney General for Ireland seems suddenly to have got on a high horse. He says to give a witness the use of counsel would lead to long argument. One would have thought that before the liberty of Her Majesty's subjects is taken away, there should be some sort of argument; but now, forsooth, it is said that we are to go to gaol without argument. Was ever such a position taken up by a legal Gentleman? I can understand the Chief Secretary, who revels in this clause, and laves in it, and steeps himself in the idea of men being sent to gaol without argument, opposing this Amendment; but I must say that I am astonished at the position taken up by the Attorney General for Ireland, who is a lawyer. We say send a man to gaol if you like for refusing to answer reasonable and proper questions; but when you come to questions on which reasonable and proper debate can arise, let that debate take place, and let it be between competent debaters. Let the question as to whether or not you are to send a man to prison for declining to answer improper questions be decided by legal gentlemen. In Scotland, the gentleman who puts the questions, and the gentleman who decides on the propriety of the questions, are legal gentlemen. I ask the Attorney General for England to allow these questions to be decided on argument. The hon. and learned Gentleman objects to argument; but for him to say on behalf of the Government that they will send men to gaol without argument seems to me to be expressing an altogether irrational and uncivilized view.

THE ATTORNEY GENERAL (Sir RICHARD WEBSTER) (Isle of Wight): I have not the smallest objection to argument, but I really think we ought not to be pressed further on this matter when we have already decided that solicitors and barristers are not to be allowed to attend the inquiries held under this section, and when it has been pointed out by the right hon. Gentleman the Member for Derby (Sir William Harcourt) that it is necessary to give large discretion to the magistrates in the putting of questions. There is no limit to the questions that can be put, provided they have reference to the crime that has been committed. We shall be stultifying our previous decisions if we say now that a counsel or solicitor may be introduced; besides, the acceptance of this proposal will be a direct temptation to a witness to set the whole proceeding at defiance by causing adjournments to take place, and introducing proceedings which are not possible under other sections of the Bill.

Question put, and negatived.

MR. O'DOHERTY (Donegal, N.): The Amendment of which I have given Notice deals with the case of a person for whom, I think, the Committee has some regard—namely, a witness who has to be arrested in the first instance, without being summoned. I have observed all through a feeling of considerable hesitation in the Committee with reference to giving absolute discretion to stipendiary and other magistrates, with regard to the arrest of witnesses in the first instance. I observed, and took down carefully, the words of the Attorney General.

SIR RICHARD WEBSTER: Will the hon. Member read the Amendment.

MR. O'DOHERTY: It says—

"Provided always, That the warrant 'b.' in sub-section mentioned shall not issue i the first instance for the arrest of a witness u oath is made that it is probable that if serve with a summons such witness would remove from jurisdiction and would not be forthcoming at such inquiry."

The words are carefully framed, and I have adopted them with the view of meeting the case mentioned by the Attorney General.

Amendment proposed,

At the end of the last Amendment, to insert the words—" Provided always, That the warrant ' B.b.' in sub-section mentioned shall not issue in the first instance for the arrest of a witness until oath is made that it is probable that if served with a summons such witness would remove from the jurisdiction, and would not be forthcoming at such inquiry."—(*Mr. O'Doherty.*)

Question proposed, "That those words be there inserted."

SIR RICHARD WEBSTER: It seems to me that these words are altogether inconsistent with an Amendment already passed, which applies to these proceedings—Section 13 of the Petty Sessions Act of 1851. We put in that section, at the request of hon. Gentlemen below the Gangway opposite, and we think, as at present advised, that the present Amendment is inconsistent with that for which we have in that way provided.

MR. O'DOHERTY: I quite agree that if you take out Section 13 of the Petty Sessions Act, and read the words of it, you will perceive that this Amendment is inconsistent with it; but I seek to modify the oath having regard to that Section of the Petty Sessions Act. The information is to be laid before the issue of the warrant, that is to say, the oath is to be taken before the arrest of a person in the first instance, to the effect that it is probable that the witness will not attend to give evidence without being compelled so to do. That is in the 13th section of the Petty Sessions Act, and, as I say, if we consider that section as written out, it is inconsistent with my Amendment; but I think the hon. and learned Gentleman will admit that this Committee and Parliament have power to modify that oath by a Proviso. The reason why I am anxious that this alteration should be made is, that I do not believe it is intended by those in charge of the Bill to enable a warrant to issue where it should not. I believe they would be slow to allow power which might be abused, or might be exercised too harshly. I, therefore, took down the words of the Attorney General for Ireland when he mentioned the cases in which a warrant should issue in the first instance—namely, the danger of a witness not attending himself, the danger of a witness removing out of the jurisdiction of the magistrate, and the danger of his not attending without a warrant. These are the words of the Attorney General for Ireland in explaining to the Committee the cases in which a warrant should issue for the attendance of a

witness without a summons. I think that the people of Ireland, and especially persons called on to be examined before a tribunal of this sort, are *primâ facie* entitled to receive a summons. Many people might be seriously inconvenienced by being brought up under a warrant, and I, therefore, think that the ordinary right of witnesses to be summoned to the Court ought to apply. I admit that there are cases in which a person, if summoned, would fly from the jurisdiction of the magistrate, and would, therefore, not be available to give evidence at an inquiry; but those cases will be cases in which it will be made clear to the magistrate, on oath, that there is danger, if a summons is served, of a man absconding or not being forthcoming. Any words which will provide a better safeguard than that which is already contained in the Petty Sessions Act ought, I think, to be adopted by the Committee. I should like to tell the Committee what is the safeguard provided against the unjust and harsh exercise of this power of arresting a witness in the first instance, and what is the extent to which it goes in the original Act. A person may swear, for instance, that a witness will not attend without being compelled, though he may know very well that the witness will not run away. He may be able very well to swear that he does not believe the witness would attend, though he would not dream of swearing that the man would run away. He can also very well swear—I would even put this extreme case—to a sort of belief that the witness would not attend, although he might know that if the witness was served with a summons, he would attend, believing himself bound by some honourable obligation to do so—because I know, in my own practice, that there are many men who would submit to a summons, and who would be perfectly willing to give evidence, if summoned, who would not voluntarily attend before an inquiry to give evidence in a particular case. Therefore, it is open to a man to swear the oath in the 13th section of the Petty Sessions Act, and believe that the witness would attend on a summons. But it is altogether unfair not to require that the magistrate should be satisfied in his own mind that the witness will not attend on a summons before granting a warrant. I appeal to right hon. Gentlemen opposite whether there is really anything in my Amendment which, if adopted, would frustrate the operation of the Act. I am not wedded to these words; but I must say I do dislike the words in the 13th section of the Petty Sessions Act, which are really no safeguard to a witness.

SIR RICHARD WEBSTER: I really would appeal to the hon. Member to consider what it is he proposes. Remember we are dealing with a contumacious witness, and the hon. Gentleman proposes to limit the clause by inserting the words "will be removed from jurisdiction, and will not be forthcoming." The words are practically the same as the words "will not attend," but they are all governed by "removed from jurisdiction," and the witness who does not desire to give evidence may hide from the jurisdiction of a magistrate, and may decline to answer a summons and set the ordinary law at defiance; but unless he goes out of the jurisdiction there is no power to serve a warrant. It would be impossible for oath to be made that the witness would be removed from jurisdiction, or that the deponent should know that the man would not come, or that he said he would not come, or something of that kind. If the Act is to be put in force at all, witnesses who it is supposed can give material evidence must not be allowed to evade the inquiry. The Committee will remember that we have accepted the Amendment of the right hon. Member for East Wolverhampton (Mr. Henry H. Fowler), to the effect that the warrant should be issued in the case of a man whom the magistrate believed capable of giving material evidence, but whom he had reason to believe would not attend. That seems to me to be the proper test in this matter. If the hon. Member cuts that down by providing that, before a warrant shall issue, oath must be taken that the witness will be removed from jurisdiction, and will not be forthcoming, it will make the whole clause nugatory. Unless an affidavit could be made which, practically speaking, could not be made or would not be made in nine cases out of ten, the witnesses would not be forthcoming.

MR. O'DOHERTY: If it would render the Amendment more acceptable to the

Mr. O'Doherty

hon. and learned Gentleman, I would agree to these words—"will remove from jurisdiction or otherwise will not be forthcoming."

SIR RICHARD WEBSTER: The same objection applies.

MR. O'DOHERTY: I wish to provide that a warrant shall not be issued merely because a person chooses to think that a witness will not attend voluntarily.

MR. MAURICE HEALY (Cork): Mr. Courtney, the right hon. Gentlemen who sit on the Treasury Bench are very hard to please. When we draw up Amendments to try and meet their views they say we are endeavouring to turn the Bill upside down and to render it unworkable. The Irish Attorney General came forward and said he could not agree to one Amendment because there are a certain class of witnesses in Ireland who, the moment they got a summons, would abscond. On that proper argument the Committee agreed to allow a warrant to be issued, and all that we now ask is, that that being the reason on which the Committee agreed to allow the witness to be arrested in the first instance, the Committee shall express its reasons in the Bill, and say that only in those cases where there is a danger of the witness absconding a warrant shall be issued. I would press upon the Committee this consideration, that the words used in the Bill are words which would place in the hands of the officials in Ireland a power which they might very grossly abuse. We know very well what will happen if this clause passes as it stands. The Resident Magistrate will get down his warrant from the Attorney General, will go to the nearest sub-inspector, will make out a list of witnesses, and will hand it over to a constable, who will swear an affidavit in the common form, that he has reason to believe the witnesses will not attend, and, therefore, they will all be arrested. We know quite well what is going to happen, and we object that it should be in the power of officials in Ireland to bring about that state of things. The Attorney General for England says it will be impossible for any official to swear that witnesses are going to abscond, or that they will not be forthcoming. It is a great deal easier to say that than to prove it. On referring to the Petty Sessions Act, I find that it requires the officials to swear as to what is in a man's mind—that the police officer shall swear that a certain class of people have their minds made up not to attend. But all we ask is that the officer shall swear, not to what he cannot know, but to what he can know, see, and discover by the exercise of his intelligence—namely, that there is a danger that the witness will abscond if an opportunity is given to him and he is not arrested in the first instance. Now, Mr. Courtney, the Irish officials will have to face this difficulty—that there is the greatest reason to suppose that if the clause is worked as we have every reason to suppose it will be, there will be a very great indisposition among large classes of people in Ireland to come before these inquiries at all. It does not follow that there is any disposition on the part of these people to leave the country; all that it means is that, for certain reasons of a political or other nature, they have made up their minds not to facilitate the working of these inquiries, which they believe to be utterly abominable and detestable. Is it to be said that because they entertain these views any constable may swear "A, B, C, and D, I know, have objections to attend these inquiries, and therefore let them be arrested instead of being summoned?" That would be a gross injustice. If this power is to be exercised, let it be exercised for the reason which the Irish Attorney General gave as an inducement to the Committee to grant the power of arresting witnesses—namely, that there is a danger of the witness absconding and getting out of the jurisdiction of the Court, if he is able to get wind of the inquiry which is to be held. But do not put it on the general statement of some constable that certain persons have an indisposition to attend the inquiries, and that he believes they will not attend. Do not, in the terms of this Bill, enable the officials to arrest a whole country-side without first giving them the privilege of being summoned, and of saying whether or not they will attend the inquiries without arrest. It is quite bad enough that the authorities should have the power of arresting persons who may be quite as respectable as the Resident Magistrate holding the investigation. Do not let them be at the mercy of every ruffian magistrate or policeman who chooses to abuse his power in an offensive manner. Do not

let the power be exercised until the danger which the Attorney General for Ireland has pointed out arises—until there is some competent person who knows the facts prepared to swear that if the warrant is not issued there is a danger that the witness will abscond.

MR. EDWARD HARRINGTON (Kerry, W.): Mr. Courtney, this measure was introduced under false pretences, and it has been maintained upon them all along. It should be generally understood that, even in what is popularly called the loyal minority in Ireland, there is a strong and ingrained objection to give evidence at these tribunals, as in other cases. Therefore, in discussing this matter, we may set out with the assumption that every man, woman, and child in Ireland has an objection to give evidence, and therefore it may be taken that the condition of this warrant or thing—I am not a lawyer, and am, therefore, not aware of these technicalities—but the primary condition of this warrant is that witnesses will not attend unless they are compelled to do so. Under these circumstances, the whole argument turns on the meaning which is to be attached to the word "compelled." It has been very properly put by the hon. Member for North Donegal (Mr. O'Doherty) that the giving of a summons to a witness may be considered as "compelling." Anyone who has attended the Petty Sessions Courts in Ireland, as I have had to do myself on legal business for eight or nine years, knows what I have seen daily, that witnesses are allowed to come in and mix themselves up with cases where, even as witnesses, there is no suspicion against them. All we ask for is, that where there is a reasonable presumption that these witnesses will answer your summons on the receipt of it, you should not, in the first instance, issue a warrant. But we know very well what will be the alternative if the Government maintain their present attitude. It is that the Resident Magistrates will never put themselves to the trouble of issuing a summons. They will spare themselves that trouble, and will do that which will cause much annoyance in Ireland, and cause many a prolonged debate in this House. They will walk into the field where men are at their spring or harvest work, and tap them on the shoulder, and bring them before these secret tribunals, keeping them day after day, and, perhaps, committing them to prison for contumaciousness. Then there is another point to which I would like to call attention. The Irish people are often accused of being addicted to taking a drop of drink. Now, I ask, is it fair or reasonable that your policeman shall seize a farmer on a market night when he has been drinking, and shall lug him before a magistrate, when, for the purposes of this Bill, if he had been summoned a day or two before, he could have his mind clearly made up, and be able to say what he knows about the subject? The result of your action will be that you will be continually touching a very sore point by your administration of this Bill. The Government set out with a presumption that causes all this friction. They set out with the presumption that the magistrates are just, and will carry out the Bill in a spirit of justice. But we set out with a spirit of distrust. We may be right, or we may be wrong; but we act according to our experience, and we cannot believe in the justice of these magistrates from what we know of them. You cannot blame us when we have had cause to distrust them. Then why do you object to putting into an Act of Parliament words which crystallize your own sentiment as well as our objection? Why is it that you will not have in some form—either in the shape of this Amendment, or in some other form that you may devise yourselves—why is it that you will not be content to put into this Bill a safeguard that a man shall be summoned where it is presumable that he will attend, and why should you give to people whom we allege to be despots the right of exercising all their powers in a despotic spirit? It adds a great deal to the friction which prevails, and to the prolongation of debate night after night, that the Government constantly take up the position that the Resident Magistrates of Ireland are angels who have come down from Heaven. Even from that po nt of view they are fallen angels, and we ought to be more particular in dealing with them. Any assertion we make against them is not regarded. We allege that they are a class of men prone to tyranny and injustice, and you hold the opposite view. Why is it that you will not allow us the limitations and reservations which you

acknowledge are in the spirit of the Bill—why do you not put them in the letter so as to satisfy all objections?

Mr. O'DOHERTY (Donegal, N.): I will not detain the Committee for more than a minute, but I want to answer the right hon. Gentleman on one point. He put the case of a man having removed himself from the jurisdiction of the Court. In that case a warrant would issue, so that the very case referred to is met by the 13th section. I do not know where we are. I do not know of any possible objection that the right hon. Gentleman has urged against my proposition that is not met by the explanation that the existing law provides for the case. The Committee will decide now on the question whether or not a warrant is to issue at the discretion of the magistrate, without having any satisfactory information before him in regard to the disposition of the witness. This is a very hard position for the people of Ireland, for any person can at any moment be arrested at the instance of the officials of Dublin Castle. I put the distinction very clearly between these cases and indictable offences. In indictable cases it might be a very great public inconvenience if the witness were not in attendance at the Petty Sessions, because the Assizes might be coming on. I can thoroughly understand how it might be necessary to secure the attendance of a witness for a particular day in an indictable offence, but it is a very different thing where you appoint the day yourselves, and where the next day a warrant might issue if the witness were not forthcoming. These are points on which I ask the Committee to reflect before supporting the Bill as it now stands.

Question put.

The Committee *divided*:—Ayes 129; Noes 227: Majority 98.—(Div. List, No. 128.)

Mr. CHANCE (Kilkenny, S.): I beg to move the following Amendment, of which I have given private Notice :—

In page 1, line 23, after "thereto," insert— "Provided, That in no case shall a warrant be issued for the arrest of any female intended to be examined as a witness in the first instance, or until a summons has first been served on such female in manner as in said enactment provided, and disobeyed by her."

I trust that the Government will see the desirability of a provision of this kind, and will, at any rate, agree to make the neglect of a summons a necessary preliminary to the issue of a warrant in the case of a woman. I think you all agree that no woman, no matter how low she may be in the social scale, shall be permitted to suffer unnecessary indignities; but if the sub-section be adopted without any safeguard, such as that which I have proposed, she will be exposed to great hardship. It may, of course, be said that a woman would be able to evade a summons by getting out of the jurisdiction of the Court by which it is issued; but I would point out that it is not so easy a matter for a woman to get beyond the jurisdiction as it is for many men. In the case of married women, having children and other home ties, such a proceeding would be well-nigh impossible.

Amendment proposed,

At end of last Amendment, to insert the words—"Provided, That in no case shall a warrant be issued for the arrest of any female intended to be examined as a witness in the first instance, or until a summons has first been served on such female, in manner as in said enactment provided, and disobeyed by her."— *(Mr. Chance.)*

Question proposed, "That those words be there inserted."

THE CHIEF SECRETARY FOR IRELAND (Mr. A. J. BALFOUR) (Manchester, E.): I hope, Sir, the hon. and learned Gentleman will not think it necessary to put this question, which, I think, can hardly have been brought seriously before the notice of the Committee. I do not know of any case in our Criminal Law which furnishes a precedent for a provision of this kind, nor can I conceive of any reason being alleged why women should be placed in a different category to men in this connection. The object of the warrant is to prevent the escape of recalcitrant witnesses, and I have no reason to believe that women are less likely to prove recalcitrant than men. Certainly, experience has not shown this to be the case. In any case, I think hon. Gentlemen will agree that if there was a recalcitrant witness, the fact that she happened to be a woman would be no reason for not issuing a warrant against her. In regard to the argument of the hon. and learned Member, that women are not likely to get out of the jurisdiction of the Court for the purpose of evading

summonses, I would remind him that every woman has not got a family of children.

MR. CHANCE: I hope this Amendment will be divided upon. It is the very simple question of the nature of the procedure up to the present. It has been decided not to adopt the ordinary rules of procedure in the case of people generally, and this Amendment is but the logical corollary of that decision.

MR. MARUM (Kilkenny, N.): As I have an Amendment on the Paper somewhat in the same direction as that now before the Committee, perhaps I may be permitted to make a few observations in reply to the Chief Secretary. As the entire clause is derived from the Scottish jurisprudence, I think it not unnatural that I should make some reference to the enactments relating to that system; and I find that, in accordance with the Law of Scotland, women were not, until a recent period, admissible. Of course, I speak under correction from the Lord Advocate. I do not attempt to say whether that circumstance is owing to any psychological deduction, or whether it is accounted for by the fact of a woman having five ounces of brain matter less than a man; but, whatever the reason may be, certainly the Common Law of Scotland did attach disability to women as witnesses. Therefore, it is not unnatural that I should refer to the point, when we are going back on the Scottish Criminal Law for precedents. When this inquisitorial process was in existence in Scotland, women were practically excluded from its operation; and it was with the object of bringing that circumstance before the notice of the Committee that I intended to bring forward my Amendment.

MR. ANDERSON (Elgin and Nairn): We have now been several hours discussing the question of the treatment of witnesses, and I venture to think that, as we have to meet again at 12 o'clock, the Motion I propose to make is not unreasonable. We are now falling again into the meshes of the Scottish law, and it is inevitable that a discussion of this kind must take a great deal of time, and lead to wide controversy. I, therefore, beg to move to report Progress.

Motion made, and Question proposed, "That the Chairman do report Progress, and ask leave to sit again."—*(Mr. Anderson.)*

THE FIRST LORD OF THE TREA-SURY (Mr. W. H. SMITH) (Strand, Westminster): I understand that the hon. and learned Member who moved this Amendment is most desirous that a Division should be taken on it. Under those circumstances, I take it that the hon. and learned Member for Elgin and Nairn will not press his Motion.

MR. T. M. HEALY (Longford, N.): No sensible man should ever be out of bed after 1 o'clock. It seems to me that, bearing in mind the fact that we were here until 6 o'clock yesterday morning, and shall have to be in our places again at 12 o'clock to-day, the Motion is not an unreasonable one.

MR. W. H. SMITH: I say nothing about the hour. I wish to advance the Business of the Committee as much as possible; and as I understand that the hon. and learned Member for South Kilkenny is himself desirous that a Division should be taken on his Amendment, the withdrawal of the Motion to report Progress appears to be the natural course to be adopted.

MR. T. P. O'CONNOR (Liverpool, Scotland): I would suggest to my hon. and learned Friend above the Gangway (Mr. Anderson) that he should withdraw his Motion. We are prepared to go to a Division on the Amendment immediately; but I hope it will be the last taken during the present Sitting.

Motion, by leave, *withdrawn*.

MR. T. M. HEALY (Longford, N.): We originally proposed that these warrants should not be issued at all. The Act of 1882 has been thrown at us again and again and again by the noble Marquess the Member for Rossendale (the Marquess of Hartington), whom I am glad to see in his place this evening. The noble Marquess has been supporting the Bill on the ground that we were only re-enacting the measure of 1882; but the principle of that Bill was that the citation should only take place on a summons, or, in other words, that policemen should not be allowed to go into the houses of the people for the purpose of dragging their women before the Resident Magistrate at any hour of the day or night. I respectfully submit that when, under the Act of 1882, both for men and women summonses were required, the Liberal Unionists, at least, should abate some of their Toryism, and

not compel women to be brought up under this section, without summons, at any hour. If summonses are issued, you have this guarantee, at any rate—that the witnesses will have an intimation as to the time at which they are required to appear; whereas, if there is no safeguard of this kind, the Constabulary will be able to arrest women at any hour of the night, and a most deplorable state of things will ensue. This is really a system of inquisition by night; and I contend that, as far as women are concerned, it is not a reasonable thing that they should be arrested summarily upon a warrant.

COLONEL NOLAN (Galway, N.): I do not want to stand between the Committee and the Division; but I wish to say a few words in reference to the argument that there are no precedents of exceptions being made in the case of women. I contend that exceptions have been made. What you are doing now will be a shock and an indignity to the whole of the women in Ireland. Moreover, you are passing this Bill in opposition to the wishes of five-sixths of the Irish Members. It may happen that a warrant will be issued against a woman —a farmer's wife or daughter, for instance—in regard to whom there is not even a suspicion that she has infringed the law. Nevertheless, she will be liable to be marched off, at a moment's notice, to the nearest market town. A more shocking indignity to a respectable woman cannot be conceived. At the present time especial care should be taken in dealing with a question of this magnitude. Every word you say here goes to the United States, to Australia, and to New Zealand; and if it goes forth that you contemplate submitting the women of Ireland to these indignities, your position will not be a pleasant one. The game is not worth the candle. You are making a scandal which will bo brought up against you on many platforms in countries where the English language is spoken; and I do not think you will be backed up by the public opinion of Great Britain. Certainly, if you had women's suffrage you would have a large vote against it.

Original Question put.

The Committee *divided*:—Ayes 117; Noes 208: Majority 91.—(Div. List, No. 129.)

MR. ANDERSON (Elgin and Nairn): I beg again to move, Sir, that you report Progress.

Motion made, and Question proposed, "That the Chairman do report Progress, and ask leave to sit again."—(*Mr. Anderson.*)

THE CHIEF SECRETARY FOR IRELAND (Mr. A. J. BALFOUR) (Manchester, E.): I do not wish to take the Amendments which move that the whole sub-section be left out; but there is one in manuscript which, I believe, should come on later in the clause. There is Amendment No. 68, and the Amendment numbered 70. On these Amendments the Government will be prepared to make large concessions. Then there is an Amendment, 75a, on page 20, the principle of which was discussed last night, and I understood it to be withdrawn. I hope the Committee will see that there is no controversial matter before the Amendments to omit the sub-section, and that we may be allowed to go on with those as to which no difficulty is likely to arise.

MR. ANDERSON: I do not wish to stand in the way if the Committee desire to take Amendments as to which no difference of opinion is likely to arise; but I think that if there is any Amendment that will lead to controversy it is not desirable to proceed with that at this late hour.

SIR WILLIAM HARCOURT (Derby): I hope, after the declaration of the Chief Secretary for Ireland, that the Government propose to make concessions in regard to the Amendments 68 and 70, that the Government will be allowed to proceed with those Amendments.

MR. CONYBEARE (Cornwall, Camborne): I am not inclined to be let in by the Government, as is usually the case when we do not nail them down to definite concessions before we consent to withdraw a Motion to report Progress. I should like to know what these proposed concessions are. We have heard before a good deal as to the enormous concessions which the Government propose to grant; but they always turn out to be moonshine or smoke, and we shall, no doubt, find the concessions of which they now talk are just as bogus as we have hitherto found the former concessions of the Government. I am prepared to meet the concessions of the Government in a spirit of conciliation; but it is impossible that we should meet the Government in that spirit without being prepared at the same time to discuss these concessions, and put the case as we view it from our side of the House. Seeing that we were working here again till 6 o'clock this morning, and that many of us have been working in Committees since 12 o'clock to-day—although the Leader of the House has, I observe, taken a holiday to-night—I think it is not too much to ask that we should now report Progress. If, indeed, the Chief Secretary wishes to explain what his proposed concessions are, we shall be glad to hear him; but it would be better to postpone the detailed consideration of the Amendments to which they relate until 12 o'clock to-day. Therefore, I think we ought to persist in the Motion to report Progress.

SIR WILLIAM HARCOURT: It would not be in Order, on a Motion to report Progress, for the Chief Secretary to make a statement as to Amendments. The hon. Member who has just spoken will lose nothing by allowing the Motion to be withdrawn, and then permitting the Government to state what concessions they will make. If those concessions are not satisfactory, he can renew the Motion to report Progress. Therefore, I hope he will allow the Motion to report Progress to be withdrawn.

MR. T. M. HEALY: I am quite prepared to go on; but I see no prospect of concluding the discussion on the Amendments referred to at this late hour of the morning. As I have already said, I am quite prepared to go on; but I hope I may be allowed to say this—the hon. and learned Attorney General (Sir Richard Webster) has very courteously intimated to me the purport of the concessions which the Government are prepared to make; and I may say that, so far as Amendment 68 is concerned, there will be no discussion on it, for I agree that the concession which the hon. and learned Gentleman is prepared to make will avoid the necessity for a discussion on that Amendment. I cannot, however, say so much for Amendment 70. The discussion on that and the other Amendments might take three hours. Under these circumstances, and although I am prepared to go on with the discussion on Amendment, I see no advantage in doing so to-night.

MR. CONYBEARE: After what has fallen from my right hon. Friend (Sir William Harcourt), I am prepared to assent to the withdrawal of the Motion for reporting Progress, if the Government will stop after Amendment 68 has been disposed of.

MR. W. H. SMITH: The Government are anxious to make Progress with the Business of the House. I entirely agree with the observations of the right hon. Gentleman opposite (Sir William Harcourt). We wish to make progress with Business; for we think this is essential for the character and the reputation of the House. The right hon. Gentleman opposite has remarked that it is only reasonable that we should be permitted to explain the Amendments on which we are prepared to make concessions. If, however, hon. Gentlemen opposite think that these Amendments will take three hours in discussing them, although we are prepared to make concessions, we will not ask the House to continue a discussion which would be unprofitable and a waste of public time. I regret, however, that hon. Gentlemen should insist on reporting Progress when it appeared possible to make some progress.

MR. T. M. HEALY: The right hon. Gentleman has misinterpreted the remarks from our side. We said that we thought the Amendments would take time. [Several hon. MEMBERS: Three hours.] Well, suppose they did take three hours. At all events, it cannot be denied that we were perfectly frank with the Committee; and yet, because we say this, the right hon. Gentleman flashes out into a considerable passion, which was certainly entirely needless. I have always myself been in favour of late Sittings. They agree with me; and I have no objection to go on if the Government wish it. However, the Government seem tired, and I am not surprised at it; for, certainly, we are tired of the Government. And as the Government think it desirable to report Progress, perhaps it would be better to do so.

MR. CONYBEARE: The right hon. Gentleman has talked, as usual, about the honour and dignity of the House, and implied that it was owing to my action in this matter that the dignity and honour of the House were imperilled. I have only to say that if the dignity and honour of this House have been endangered at all, it has been by the introduction of this Bill.

Question put, and agreed to.

Committee report Progress; to sit again To-morrow.

DEEDS OF ARRANGEMENT REGISTRATION BILL.—[BILL 231.]

(Sir Bernhard Samuelson, Mr. Howard Vincent, Sir John Lubbock, Mr. Coddington, Mr. Lawson, Sir Albert Rollit.)

SECOND READING.

Order for Second Reading read.

SIR ALBERT ROLLIT (Islington, S.), in moving that the Bill be now read a second time, said, that it had the support of all political Parties, and of the Association of Chambers of Commerce of the United Kingdom, and had met with the approval of the various Trade Protection Societies, and of the commercial public generally. Under those circumstances, he thought it would be sufficient to move that it be now read a second time.

Motion made, and Question, "That the Bill be now read a second time,"—(Sir Albert Rollit,)—put, and agreed to.

Bill read a second time, and committed for Friday.

FIRST OFFENDERS (re-committed) BILL.

(Mr. Howard Vincent, Lord Randolph Spencer Churchill, Sir Henry Selwin-Ibbetson, Mr. Hoare, Mr. Addison, Mr. Hastings, Mr. Lawson, Mr. Molloy.)

[BILL 189.]   COMMITTEE.

[*Progress 5th May.*]

Bill *considered* in Committee.

(In the Committee.)

Clause 1 (Power to court to release upon probation of good conduct instead of sentencing to imprisonment).

MR. RADCLIFFE COOKE (Newington, W.): The questions involved in this Bill are very important, altering, as they do, the Criminal Law of the country to a considerable extent. The Bill raises serious questions of law, and, that being so, I do not think we should proceed with it now, and I will therefore move, Sir, that you do report Progress.

Motion made, and Question proposed, "That the Chairman do report Progress, and ask leave to sit again."—(Mr. Radcliffe Cooke.)

MR. HOWARD VINCENT (Sheffield, Central): I do hope that some prógress will be made with this Bill. It passed through this House in the last Parliament, and was then fully discussed. It was before the Committee last week, and I trust the Committee will now allow progress to be made with it. Its provisions are well known to the Committee.

MR. T. M. HEALY (Longford, N.): I think it would be most unreasonable that we should now be asked to proceed with this Bill, if it were only for the sake of the officers of the House, and of the Chairman of Committees, who was in the Chair until 5 o'clock yesterday morning, and will have to take the Chair again at 12 o'clock to-day.

MR. HOWARD VINCENT: If the Committee is anxious to report Progress, I shall not, under the circumstances and at this hour, stand in the way.

Question put, and agreed to.

Committee report Progress; to sit again upon Friday.

FIRST OFFENDERS.
ADDRESS FOR A RETURN.

Order [5th April], for an Address for a Return relating to First Offenders read, and *discharged;* and, instead thereof—

Address for—

"Return of the number of persons convicted, either upon indictment or summarily, and not known to have been previously convicted, who shall, on the 31st day of May 1887, be undergoing sentence of imprisonment (whether imposed absolutely or in default of payment of a fine), or shall be undergoing sentence of penal servitude, such sentences being in either case for offences other than arson, burgulary, coining, uttering counterfeit coin, throwing corrosive fluid, extortion, forgery, larceny from the person with violence, murder or attempted murder, placing explosives so as to endanger life or property, or receiving stolen goods; stating the number of those convicted under the age of twenty, and of those who shall have received sentences of less than twelve months' imprisonment."—(*Mr. Hoare.*)

DR. TANNER (Cork Co., Mid.) said, he had observed that many of these Motions for Returns came on late at night, and appeared then to be assented to as a matter of course. He desired to know whether, if a Member rose in his place and objected to a Return, that would prevent the Motion being made, or being agreed to?

THE UNDER SECRETARY OF STATE FOR THE HOME DEPART-

MENT (Mr. STUART-WORTLEY) (Sheffield, Hallam): I hope the hon. Member will not oppose the Motion. This is a Return which has duly appeared on the Notice Paper. It has been fully considered by the House on a former occasion, and has been ordered by the House in the regular way. But it was found necessary to make a small alteration in it; and this required that the original Order should be discharged, and that the Return should be ordered in the present amended form.

Address agreed to.

MOTIONS
—o—

LOCAL GOVERNMENT PROVISIONAL ORDERS (GAS) BILL.

On Motion of Mr. Long, Bill to confirm certain Provisional Orders of the Local Government Board, under the provisions of "The Gas and Water Works Facilities Act, 1870," "The Gas and Water Works Facilities Act (1870) Amendment Act, 1873,"and "The Public Health Act, 1875,"relating to the LocalGovernment Districts of East Dereham and Meltham, *ordered* to be brought in by Mr. Long and Mr. Ritchie.

Bill *presented*, and read the first time. [Bill 259.]

LOCAL GOVERNMENT PROVISIONAL ORDER (POOR LAW) (NO. 3) BILL.

On Motion of Mr. Long, Bill to confirm an Order of the Local Government Board, under the provisions of "The Divided Parishes and Poor Law Amendment Act, 1876," as amended and extended by "The Poor Law Act, 1879," relating to the Parishes of Aldington, Saint Leonard, Hythe, and West Hythe, *ordered* to be brought in by Mr. Long and Mr. Ritchie.

Bill *presented*, and read the first time. [Bill 260.]

LOCAL GOVERNMENT PROVISIONAL ORDERS (NO. 2) BILL.

On Motion of Mr. Long, Bill to confirm certain Provisional Orders of the Local Government Board relating to the Local Government District of Abergele and Pensarn, the District of Bilston, the Boroughs of Bradford (Yorks.) and Evesham, the Improvement Act District of Leek, the Local Government Districts of Leyton and Wanstead, and the Borough of Ramsgate, *ordered* to be brought in by Mr. Long and Mr. Ritchie.

Bill *presented*, and read the first time. [Bill 261.]

House adjourned at half after One o'clock.

HOUSE OF COMMONS,

Wednesday, 11th May, 1887.

MINUTES.]—PUBLIC BILLS--*Committee*—Criminal Law Amendment (Ireland) [217] [*Sixth Night*]—R.P.
PROVISIONAL ORDER BILL—*Second Reading* — Water ° [250].

PRIVATE BUSINESS.

—o—

SHEFFIELD CORPORATION WATER BILL [*Lords*].
SECOND READING.

Order for Second Reading read.

Motion made, and Question proposed, "That the Second Reading be deferred till Tuesday, 14th June."—(*Mr. Dodds.*)

MR. KELLY (Camberwell, N.): I object to that proposal. I can see no advantage to be derived from postponing the Bill for so long a period, and it would certainly be exceedingly inconvenient to do so. All that the Corporation of Sheffield want is a little more time, and an adjournment for a week would be sufficient for their purpose. Why the adjournment should be for a month I cannot see.

MR. SPEAKER: The Bill must go over until another day.

MR. DODDS (Stockton): I have no authority to make any promise for another day, and I would remind the hon. Member that in the interval between now and the 14th of June there will probably be a Vacation of 14 days, for Whitsuntide, the Derby Day, and other matters, so that there would not be very much time left.

MR. KELLY: While I appreciate the necessity for postponing the second reading of the Bill, I have no wish to throw out the Bill for the Session, which I believe may be the result of postponing it until the 14th of June.

MR. SCHWANN (Manchester, N.): I beg to support the remarks of the hon. Gentleman. I think that an earlier day will meet the requirements of the case.

MR. SPEAKER: It will be competent for any hon. Member to move an earlier day for the second reading.

MR. KELLY: Then I will propose that the second reading be taken on Wednesday next, the 18th of May, instead of the 14th of June.

Amendment proposed, to leave out "Tuesday, 14th June," in order to insert "Wednesday next,"—(*Mr. Kelly,*) —instead thereof.

Question proposed, "That 'Tuesday, 14th June,' stand part of the Question."

THE CHAIRMAN OF COMMITTEES (Mr. COURTNEY) (Cornwall, Bodmin): I do not think that there would be any advantage obtained from deferring the second reading for a week. I understand that it is a Bill which excites a great deal of interest, although I confess that I am myself but imperfectly informed as to its provisions. I am informed that its progress has been arrested by an injunction from the Court of Chancery to restrain the promoters from going on with it in consequence of an informality in a meeting held under the Borough Funds Act. That informality is, I am told, that the meeting was held a day earlier than it should have been. It is proposed to correct that informality. I only mention this matter, in passing, as a reason why the Bill should be postponed until the 14th of June. I would remind the hon. Member for North Camberwell (Mr. Kelly) that should the postponement result in the loss of the Bill it would be only realizing the result which his own Motion, now standing on the Paper, is intended to secure.

MR. F. S. POWELL (Wigan): Perhaps I may be allowed to say that the decision of the Court of Chancery was directed against the payment of money by the Corporation, and had nothing to do either with the merits of the Bill or the proceedings in this House. The Court would not presume to interfere with the course of legislation.

MR. KELLY: May I make a brief explanation?

MR. SPEAKER: The hon. Member has already spoken. He would not be in Order in speaking again. Does the hon. Member wish to withdraw the Amendment?

MR. KELLY: No; I have no wish to do that. I desire that the Bill shall be taken on Wednesday next.

Question put, and *agreed to.*

Main Question put.

Second Reading *deferred* till *Tuesday* 14th June.

CRIMINAL LAW AMENDMENT (IRE-
LAND) BILL.—[BILL 217.]

(*Mr. A. J. Balfour, Mr. Secretary Matthews, Mr.
Attorney General, Mr. Attorney General for
Ireland.*)

COMMITTEE. [*Progress* 10*th May.*]

[SIXTH NIGHT.]

Bill *considered* in Committee.

(In the Committee.)

PRELIMINARY INQUIRY.

Clause 1 (Inquiry by order of Attorney General).

MR. MAURICE HEALY (Cork): I
rise to move, in page 1, line 23, after
"thereto," to insert—

"Provided, that in no case shall a summons
be issued, requiring any person to attend at an
inquiry under this section, unless by information on oath and in writing it has been made to
appear that there is good reason to suppose
that such person is able to give material evidence touching the subject of such matter of
such inquiry."

This is an Amendment to provide that
no summons requiring any person to
attend an inquiry unless, by information
on oath, it has been shown that there is
good reason to suppose that he is able
to give material evidence. Now, we all
know that in the working of the Crimes
Act there were a number of respectable
persons dragged up in a secret way, and
detained for no other purpose than to subject them to annoyance, seeing that they
were persons who could not possibly
know anything of the matters proposed
to be investigated. I think it ought not
to be in the power of any local Resident
Magistrate to go fishing for evidence,
and for that purpose to direct to appear
before him every person he may choose
to lay his hands upon. I am of opinion
that, previously to requiring any person to attend for examination before
this secret inquisition, an information
should be sworn that the person swearing has reason to believe that if a
certain person were examined valuable
evidence might be obtained from him.
I trust that it is not intended to
make this a Star Chamber Clause.
There would clearly be no difficulty in
complying with the conditions laid down
in this Amendment—namely, that before
any person is brought up for examina-

tion, some person worthy of belief should
express an opinion in writing and upon
oath that if the witness were brought up
he would be able to give evidence material to the inquiry. I can imagine
nothing more reasonable than such a
proposal, and if we are to have any concessions at all, this is a point upon which
I think the Government ought to give
way.

Amendment proposed,

In page 1, line 23, after "thereto," insert—
"Provided, that in no case shall a summons be
issued, requiring any person to attend at an
inquiry under this section, unless by information on oath and in writing it has been made to
appear that there is good reason to suppose
that such person is able to give material evidence touching the subject matter of such inquiry."—(*Mr. Maurice Healy.*)

Question proposed, "That those words
be there inserted."

THE ATTORNEY GENERAL FOR
IRELAND (Mr. HOLMES) (Dublin University): The Government have already
accepted an Amendment, proposed by
the right hon. Gentleman the Member
for Wolverhampton (Mr. Henry H.
Fowler), which substantially carries out
the suggestion of the hon. Member, and
affords sufficient protection—namely, that
the magistrate should examine witnesses
whom he has reason to believe capable
of giving material evidence concerning
such offence. We do not accept the
Amendment now proposed by the hon.
Member for Cork (Mr. Maurice Healy),
because the Committee must be aware
that the inquiries to be conducted under
this section must be kept within due
limits, and that there should be no
unnecessary mode of procedure which
would have the effect of delaying the
time when it might be absolutely necessary to hold the inquiry. If it were requisite to obtain affidavits from a number
of quarters, from persons who have good
reason for believing that a witness about
to be examined can give material evidence, there would be delay. It would
also be necessary to introduce a number
of other Amendments, which would
throw unnecessary obstacles in the way
of holding the inquiry which the Committee has again and again declared to
be essential.

MR. T. M. HEALY (Longford, N.):
The learned Attorney General for
Ireland has entirely forgotten that his
stock case is the Phœnix Park murders.

The right hon. and learned Gentleman says it is absolutely necessary to reject the Amendment, because, if it were accepted, it would prevent the expeditious working of the clause. Now, the case which the Government have made for the passing of this clause is based upon the assassinations in the Phœnix Park. But what is the fact? The Phœnix Park murders were committed in the month of May, and, as everyone knows, no inquiry took place until November; therefore, six months elapsed before anybody thought of holding an inquiry, and yet we are now told by the Irish Attorney General that the object of this clause is to enforce the same practice as was followed in the Phœnix Park case. When we propose an Amendment that no person shall be brought up needlessly without some proof that it is probable he may give material evidence, we are told that the ground of refusing that Amendment is that this provision of the Bill must be worked expeditiously. I maintain that the Government ought not only to use reasonable, but consistent arguments. The Irish Attorney General must be very well aware that if the Bill is passed without this provision inserted, it will entail enormous expense on the taxpayers of this country, and for this reason—I have already told the Committee that the carrying out of law and order in Ireland costs the British taxpayer ten times more than in England. It is proposed by this Bill that the expenses of witnesses shall be paid ·by the Crown, and there is no check against witnesses being brought up in undue number for no particular purpose. Whatever check there may have been hitherto is swept away at one blow. The right hon. and learned Gentleman has referred to affidavits. Now, the Amendment does not refer to affidavits, but to an information — an information on oath and in writing. I cannot see what difficulty there would be in getting a police constable to lay such information. Let me point out that the Government have at their disposal in every district in Ireland a large force of constabulary. English gentlemen may not believe it, but there is scarcely a square yard in the country where a policeman is not planted. Go up to any mountain and you will find a police barracks in the distance and a police station in every village. The police are spread all over

Mr. T. M. Healy

the country. I believe there are 12 policemen in Ireland for every one in England. It cannot, therefore, be from a want of persons to lay these informations that the Government object to the Amendment. What can be more reasonable, when the Government desire that the character of respectable men should be taken away, that they should be brought before Resident Magistrates, kept for long hours from their homes and occupations, and subjected to an inquisition of an unpleasant and degrading character— what can be more reasonable than that someone should be required to say on oath—"I believe this person will be a material witness?" We are told that we have been wasting the time of the Committee, and yet reasonable Amendments of a substantial nature are refused by Her Majesty's Government, with no plea except that their consideration may take up time, although I have pointed out that in the Phœnix Park case the inquiry was not made until six months after the murders. The Irish Attorney General opposes this Amendment on the ground that it would undoubtedly delay inquiry. I am sorry that the English Attorney General is not present; he does not seem so much imbued as his right hon. and learned Colleague with the idea that it is necessary to oppose all Amendments. All I can say is that in this instance the right hon. and learned Gentleman has given a very bad reason for opposing a very good Amendment.

MR. BRADLAUGH (Northampton): May I be permitted to ask whether it will be possible to present each day with the Paper of Amendments a copy of the clause already passed? It may be perfectly true that an Amendment proposed by the right hon. Member for Wolverhampton (Mr. Henry H. Fowler) meets this point; but as the clause stands on the Paper it does not enable me quite to follow the bearing of the Amendment which the Government accepted. I would suggest that the Government should print at the top of the Paper of Amendments, each day, that part of the clause which has already been passed.

THE CHIEF SECRETARY FOR IRELAND) (Mr. A. J. BALFOUR) (Manchester, E.): I think the suggestion is, in substance, a good one, and I will consult the authorities of the House in order to see whether there is any practical difficulty in carrying it out.

MR. MAURICE HEALY: I cannot imagine anything more reasonable or more necessary than the provision which this Amendment contains. I wish the Committee to understand what the *rationale* of the matter is. The Government come down to the House and say that, owing to the state of things in Ireland, the considerable number of crimes which are being committed, and the difficulty of obtaining the evidence necessary to procure a conviction, it is necessary to call in the assistance of the Resident Magistrates in order to hold a preliminary inquiry. For that reason they have provided the machinery contained in this clause, which enables a secret inquiry to be held, and any person to be summoned to give evidence before it. What follows from that? It follows that every man brought up before this secret inquiry will be under the necessary implication that he is seized with some personal knowledge in relation to an alleged crime, and that he is suppressing that knowledge for an improper reason. Therefore, he may be summoned to attend the inquiry, and the mere fact that he is summoned is, *ipso facto*, a slur on that man's character and a declaration that he is connected in some way with crime, and has some reason for suppressing what he knows about it. I think it is a very grave matter for the Government to insist that they should have power to cast that slur upon the character of respectable persons without, in the first instance, requiring the slight formality to be gone through of having a sworn information laid. The Attorney General for Ireland talks about an affidavit, as if the swearing of an affidavit or of an information is a most tremendous business. We know pretty well that in every police barracks there are hundreds of these informations, printed in a common form, ready to be sworn, and the swearing of them in any particular case would not take five minutes. One might be misled by the impression conveyed by the Attorney General that the swearing of an affidavit is a tremendous and cumbrous business. It is nothing of the kind. An affidavit might be sworn in two minutes. An affidavit of this kind is a common form of affidavit—an affidavit which could be printed in readiness to be filled up. All that would be necessary in reference to it would be to fill in the name of the person to be summoned, and to require the man laying the information to read it over, swear to its truth, and take it before the nearest Justice. It is monstrous to say that going through a slight formality of that kind would in any way impede the operation of the law or delay its administration. We are told that the Amendment which the Government have already accepted from the right hon. Member for Wolverhampton has got rid of the necessity for any further Amendment of this kind. Now, all that the Amendment of the right hon. Gentleman provides is that the Resident Magistrate should believe that the person who is to be summoned is an important witness. On what material is that belief to be founded? We know perfectly well that it takes very little to satisfy a Resident Magistrate. The whisper of a landlord, or of a land agent, or a conversation in a club, would be quite sufficient to satisfy a Resident Magistrate. What we want is that, before a man is degraded by being dragged before a secret inquiry of this sort, someone should have pledged his oath that a necessity for examining him existed, so that a needless degradation may not be inflicted upon him. The Amendment moved by the right hon. Member for Wolverhampton was a very proper one, but it is only one step in the matter. What I desire is not only that the Resident Magistrate should be satisfied, but that he should be satisfied by an information upon oath laid by some credible person who pledges his credit to the fact that the individual proposed to be summoned can give material evidence touching the subject-matter of inquiry. I say that it is trifling with the Committee to give reasons such as those which have been given by the Government for resisting Amendments of a fair and *bonâ fide* description. For goodness sake let us have some safeguards for the unfortunate people among whom the Resident Magistrates will be sent down to hold these secret inquiries. Let us have some guarantee that the whole population of a district will not be outraged by being dragged before a Resident Magistrate on the mere whisper of a landlord or a land agent. Let us have a pledge from some person, on oath, that there is a real necessity for taking this action. I say that it is trifling with the Committee to refuse the Amendment on the flimsy pretext which has been put forward by the Irish Attorney General.

MR. O'DOHERTY (Donegal, N.): I think the Committee will agree with me that the leading principle decided by almost the first Amendment which was accepted by the Government after we got into Committee on this Bill touches this very point. As the Bill originally stood, it provided that the Attorney General for Ireland should believe that an offence had been committed; but on the proposal of the right hon. Member for Wolverhampton that provision was amended, and it was declared that that belief should be founded on information upon oath. Why, then, should the belief of an officer so high as the Attorney General be required to be on the basis of an information on oath, while that of a person occupying a very inferior position, with far less responsibility, is to go round the district and issue warrants founded on his own mere belief? When we admit the principle that the belief of a judicial officer is to be acted upon it should be founded upon some sort of evidence, either sworn in Court or upon information on affirmation or oath. One principle we have already decided is that the belief of the officer in a certain matter is to be the basis on which the proceedings are to be taken, and that that belief shall be founded on information. I would go further; I think the right hon. and learned Attorney General for Ireland is mistaken in supposing that these things can be done with the lightning speed he anticipates. The Attorney General must first receive the information, and the information must detail the nature of the evidence. It is then sent to Dublin to be considered, and if Parliament is sitting it may have to be sent over here before it can reach the Attorney General. Therefore, it is ridiculous to say that these preliminary inquiries are likely to be instituted and completed with lightning speed. It will be well known when these persons are to go down to put the law in motion, and surely precautions can be taken to have the informations cut and dried and sworn before the local magistrates. I regret the manner in which the Amendment is opposed. The grounds for opposing it

Mr. Maurice Healy

are of the very slightest nature, and are not at all worthy of the right hon. and learned Gentleman, nor of the Government. I should like to ask the attention of the Attorney General for Ireland to some of the Amendments which appear further down on the Paper. The right hon. and learned Gentleman does not seem to be at present devoting much attention to the discussion.

MR. HOLMES: I can hear every word the hon. Member says.

MR. O'DOHERTY: I am very glad of it. There is an Amendment lower down on the Paper to which I wish to call attention now, so that if my hon. Friend fails to carry his Amendment, it may be provided that, at any rate, an information shall be made before any man is arrested upon a warrant.

MR. P. J. POWER (Waterford, E.): I wish to know exactly how we stand. By previous Amendments we have asked that some safeguards should be placed on the liberty of the subject, and that witnesses summoned to give evidence before a private inquiry should have the benefit of counsel. I have no intention of entering into that matter now. All I will say is that that demand was refused. We also ask that there should be a summons in cases that might be dealt with summarily, and that it should not be competent to arrest a witness by warrant. That, also, was refused, and we think it is only reasonable that we should now press the Government to accept the safeguard contained in this Amendment. We regard the whole of this clause as an insult to the well-conducted population of Ireland. It is aimed at the liberties of the people of Ireland, and I certainly think that the Amendment which is proposed by my hon. Friend the Member for the City of Cork is necessary, in order to prevent the entire community from being subjected to outrage and insult. It is the intention of most Nationalists who may be summoned before this inquisitorial Court to refuse to give evidence. We know what the consequence of that refusal to give evidence will be. If persons summoned before this Star Chamber refuse to give evidence, they will be committed to prison for contempt. Then we certainly say that before a person is summoned or arrested by a warrant to give evidence this safeguard should be provided, otherwise it might be a very easy mode of securing the imprisonment of the present Leaders of the Irish nation—namely, to summon them before an inquisitorial Court with the knowledge that they would refuse to give evidence, and then commit them immediately to prison for contempt. We certainly think that, before a witness is required to attend a Court, an information should be laid that the person intended to be summoned will be able to give material evidence. If some safeguard of that nature is not provided, it will be quite possible for the enemies of all Constitutional agitation in Ireland to ask the Attorney General, or any other person who happens to be in authority, to summon before the Resident Magistrates the whole of the local leaders, and especially such leaders as may have made themselves objectionable to the authorities. It is only reasonable, therefore, that before such men are to be summoned with the knowledge that they would refuse to give evidence, the Resident Magistrates should have some ground to go upon, and should be satisfied that the persons intended to be summoned as witnesses have really material information to give. The Amendment of the right hon. Gentleman the Member for Wolverhampton which was accepted by the Government does, to some extent, safeguard our interests; but most of those who sit on these Benches know, from sad experience, how this measure will be worked. We know that we are surrounded by powerful enemies, and, therefore, I submit that the Amendment of the right hon. Gentleman does not go far enough. I ask the Committee to go a step further, and to endeavour to protect us from what we believe to be a gross insult. The Committee should bear in mind that the clause, as it at present stands, does not merely deal with a district in which crime exists, but deals with the whole of the country. It is quite competent for Dublin Castle, if an information be laid before it that outrages exist in a certain district in Ireland, to summon witnesses from all parts of the country—not only from those parts where crime exists, but from those in which there has been no crime whatever for a considerable period. Therefore, in the interests of the whole community, it is absolutely necessary that some such Amendment as that proposed by my hon. Friend should be adopted, and I hope he

will continue to press the matter on the attention of the Government, and that he will take the sense of the Committee on the subject.

MR. O'HEA (Donegal, W.): This Amendment is in every respect an Amendment based upon reason and sound common sense, and it affords one of the only safeguards a person may claim who may be summoned before one of these inquisitorial Courts. I know very well how the rejection of the Amendment may work. Let me mention a certain matter that occurred in the Fenian times. Searches were frequently made for arms. The houses and places of business of respectable men were searched for arms or suspicious documents, solely upon the whisper and secret information of some rival in trade. I know of one instance where a man's house was ransacked from garret to basement in an endeavour to discover arms or treasonable documents. The person thus outraged protested strongly against the course pursued, but he was told by the constables, who knew the man to be a most respectable person, that they were obliged to carry out the search. It transpired afterwards that the search was made at the instance of a personal enemy who told the police that his rival was connected with the Fenian organization, and was suspected of conspiring with that organization for nefarious objects. There was ample proof that the man had nothing whatever to do with the Fenian organization, and that there was no ground whatever for the accusation. The same thing will happen again if this clause is passed as it stands. The Resident Magistrate will be earwigged by some bailiff or an estate or land agent; he may hear a whisper at some county club, or at some landlords' dinner, and he will at once rely upon it as an ample justification for putting the law in motion; whereas if he had exercised proper discretion, and had acted within the scope of his duty, he would have found that there were no grounds whatever for the insinuation. I consider that when persons may be subjected to great inconvenience, and their liberty interfered with, they should, at any rate, be afforded this safeguard—that information on oath should be required from some person or other sufficient to satisfy the authorities that there was a probability, if a witness were summoned, that he would be able to give material evidence touching the commission of some crime—evidence sufficient to satisfy the Resident Magistrate that it was possible to convict some other person charged with the commission of an offence. Unless this Amendment is accepted hundreds of persons will be summoned, and subjected to inconvenience and expense, without having the slightest remedy or redress, while the perjured informers who will be responsible for bringing them before this inquisitorial Court will go scot free. If, in the first instance, they were required to pledge their oath to the truth of the allegation, they would probably be altogether discouraged, and would be afraid to swear an information, for fear of the consequences which would be entailed if it were afterwards proved to be false. I maintain that this is the only safeguard which this measure can give to the respectable persons who may be summoned to give evidence from all parts of Ireland touching some imaginary and trumped-up crime or offence.

MR. J. O'CONNOR (Tipperary, S.): The Amendment proposed by the right hon. Member for Wolverhampton, and accepted by the Government, goes only to a certain length, and affects only a portion of the way in which we wish the Government to proceed. It is a very good Amendment as far as it goes, but we wish to enlarge the provision. If it were necessary I could point out instances to show that it is absolutely essential to afford some protection in the direction provided by the Amendment of my hon. Friend. The provisions of the Act will be administered not altogether by Resident Magistrates, who belong to the particular districts in which the crimes about to be investigated have occurred. In the administration of the old Act evidence was generally taken by magistrates who came from a distance. It is provided in the Bill that the Resident Magistrate is to act upon reasonable grounds of suspicion. What reasonable ground can a Resident Magistrate have who comes from a distance, and who knows nothing about the state of the district to which he is sent? He can only act upon information obtained from the police of the district, and what we want is to protect the people from the capricious exercise of the power placed in the hands of the police and

the Resident Magistrates by this Bill. In many instances either the police or the land agent, or others interested, may attempt to get these powers put in force, to the detriment of their neighbours. That is the main reason, in my mind, why this protection should be given. The protection itself is very simple, being merely to provide that no summons shall be issued unless, by information on oath and in writing, it has been made to appear that there is good reason to suppose the person required to be summoned is able to give material evidence touching the subject-matter of the inquiry. Let me point out further to the Government a case in which the provisions of this measure may be administered to the disadvantage of the people. I am acquainted with the case of a man —a Town Councillor—who was summoned before an inquiry of this kind, and it was strongly suspected that he was summoned on a certain day in order that he might be prevented from attending a meeting of the Town Council, where it was known that he intended to vote for a particular measure. What was the result in that case? This gentleman, instead of being detained upon that day only, when called before the magistrate, declined to be sworn, and was sent to prison. This is a case which may possibly occur again. I do not believe, however, that it would have occurred on that occasion if the person who gave the information had been compelled to swear upon oath that he had reason to believe the person summoned was able to give material evidence. In giving this case I am not drawing upon my imagination, and, if I am challenged, I am perfectly ready to give names. It has been pointed out by the Attorney General that there may be delay in requiring an information to be laid. Now, I believe that there will be no delay whatever; but if there were delay, why should there not be a little delay and inconvenience where you are striking at the prosperity, the liberty, and, it may be, the lives, of witnesses who may be brought before the inquiry? I maintain that the Government should be very careful as to the manner in which they exercise these great powers, so that injury may not be inflicted. That, however, is a point which seems to weigh very lightly on the consciences of the Government. The Government seem to

Mr. O'Hea

exist in Ireland for the purpose of tantalizing and annoying the subjects of the Queen, rather than to protect them from injury. Under this provision, a man who is daily engaged in business may be summoned. Let me suppose the case of a man who is very largely brought in contact with the public—a man who may reasonably be supposed sometimes to overhear conversations—let me take the case of a publican. Men who are likely to commit crime are men who will probably be found occasionally in the public-house. It would be impossible for a publican, however respectable, to keep out of his house all possible criminals. Let me suppose, then, that a particular publican overheard a conversation in front of his bar, and a police constable or detective conceived in his own mind that that publican could give material evidence. Well, he states that; he does not know it for a fact, nor would he, if he had any conscience at all, swear that it was so. He is altogether unable to swear that the man can give material evidence; but, as the clause is now drawn, he will be at liberty to go to the authorities and say he has reason to suspect that the man can give material evidence. What follows? Any reasonable publican having a due regard to his own interests would decline to be examined. Certainly he would so decline if he took my advice; and I heard it stated by a right hon. Gentleman the other night that, under certain circumstances, he himself would decline to be sworn. The matter is one which I have endeavoured to illustrate by the case of a publican. I say that a man in that position would be perfectly justified in refusing to be sworn. The evidence itself could only be hearsay evidence, which ought to be received with the very greatest caution by the magistrate himself. These are the reasons why, in addition to what has been said by my hon. Colleagues, I believe there is an absolute necessity for passing this Amendment. I am at a loss, however, to know why we should be troubling ourselves, and losing the valuable time of this House and of the country, by passing this law at all. I think the Government ought to reconsider their position. In reading *The Standard* this morning——

THE CHAIRMAN : The hon. Gentleman must not diverge into the general law; but he must confine himself to the specific Amendment before the Committee.

MR. J. O'CONNOR : I have already expressed the various reasons which occur to my mind for supporting the Amendment; and I hope they will have due weight with the Government. The Mover of the Amendment said that it was only a reasonable Amendment; but I am afraid the Government are indisposed to accept any Amendment, no matter how reasonable it may be. Hon. and right hon. Gentlemen opposite do not seem to have an open mind on the matter. No matter how reasonable the arguments are which are urged in favour of the Amendment, the Government are opposed to everything in the shape of concession. As a result, I believe that the Bill, when it becomes an Act, and an attempt is made to administer it in Ireland, will be treated as it deserves to be treated.

MR. P. J. O'BRIEN (Tipperary, N.): I would earnestly impress upon the Government the necessity of safeguarding the clause by this Amendment, or by some other Amendment drawn upon similar lines. I have some reason to know what the state of feeling in Ireland is in regard to this matter. It is felt that it will lead to any amount of abuse and injustice against private and innocent individuals. Unfortunately, we are too well aware in Ireland of the manner in which Coercion Acts have been carried out by the Resident Magistrates. I have had some painful experience of that myself. I had the honour of being arrested under a Coercion Act. Previous to my arrest I had been intimately known to the Resident Magistrate, and everybody knows how closely connected the Resident Magistrates were with the working of that Act. After being arrested I was taken away at a moment's notice, and when I was liberated this very Resident Magistrate, who, I have no doubt, had taken an active part in my arrest, came to actually "welcome me home," and told me "how sorry he was that I should have been arrested," and "how happy he was to find me released." I simply replied to him—"You knew quite as much about me before my arrest as you do now;" and I did not trouble myself to have further intercourse with him. This clause will enable the Resident Magistrates to bring persons before them as witnesses upon the most haphazard evidence possible, upon the ear-wigging of a policeman, or upon the *ipse dixit* of the Resident Magistrate himself. I am satisfied that such a provision will lead to any amount of abuse and injustice. I therefore hope that the Government will take the whole matter into their serious consideration, and allow the Amendment of my hon. and Friend to pass.

MR. FLYNN (Cork, N.) : Hon. Members on this side of the House naturally view this Bill from a very different standpoint from that in which the Government view it. I think, however, that the Government will admit that the provisions of this Bill should be carried into effect with the minimum of injury to the Irish people. The traders and farmers, and others who are likely to be affected, should be protected as far as possible. I do not think the Government would be doing anything unreasonable or anything inconsistent with the fair reading of this 2nd section if they were to accept the Amendment. It has been fully pointed out to the Committee by hon. Gentlemen sitting on these Benches how injury and injustice may probably arise. There cannot be a doubt that when these Courts of Inquiry come to be held, witnesses, in a large number of cases, will be brought up who know nothing whatever of the alleged crime or offence, and who could not possibly know anything of it. The local constables and the local officials will throw out as wide a net as possible ; they will make the meshes as close as possible, in order to haul in fish from every quarter, utterly regardless of the fact that the majority of those who may be summoned can know nothing whatever of any alleged crime. If this Amendment be accepted by the Government, it will, at least, be incumbent on the local officials and constables only to bring before the magistrates persons whom, on a sworn information, they reasonably believe to be capable of giving material evidence. Reference has been made to the inquiry which was held in Cork in 1883. I have some knowledge of the way in which that inquiry was conducted. I know that a large number of respectable traders and others were taken away from their occupations in the middle, perhaps, of their busiest days, often upon a Saturday or a market day, and they were kept away from their business in attendance

Mr. P. J. O'Brien

upon the tribunal for the entire day, hanging about the Court, and incurring great loss and injury, although many of them could not possibly have any knowledge of the matters which were being inquired into. I know that a number of respectable business men, some of them in a large way of business, were treated in that manner, and that a considerable number of labourers were thrown out of work in consequence. For instance, a foreman builder was compelled to attend one of these inquiries, and his absence for several days threw a large number of working men out of employment. If a sworn information is required, a large amount of this injury, inconvenience, and loss will be saved. I trust that the Government, in passing this stringent measure, will not avow a total and unblushing disregard for the convenience of the people of Ireland. I hope that, at any rate, they will arrive at the conclusion that the Bill ought to be carried out with a minimum of injury. They hope to get the maximum of result ; and, therefore, we are justified in asking them to provide that the minimum of injury, inconvenience, and loss shall be inflicted. I cannot see any reasonable ground which should induce them to refuse to accept this Amendment, which is in no way inconsistent with the spirit of the sub-section.

MR. MAURICE HEALY (Cork) : I feel bound to complain that the arguments addressed to the Committee by hon. Members sitting on these Benches have met with no answer from the Government. Perhaps I may be permitted to say that, although the Government may be perfectly satisfied, no conspiracy of silence on their part in refusing to answer our arguments, and the considerations put forward from this quarter of the House, will compel us, in any way, to bring the debate to an end one minute before the proper moment arrives. I will further express a hope that the attitude of hon. Members opposite upon this Amendment will not be the key-note of their attitude towards the remaining provisions of the Bill. I saw it stated the other day in a newspaper which supports the Government that the best way to pass this Bill was to refuse all concessions.

THE CHAIRMAN : Order, order ! The hon. Member must confine himself to the Question before the Committee.

MR. MAURICE HEALY: If you, Sir, consider that line of argument irrelevant, I will not continue it further, but will simply express a hope that, in considering other Amendments, the Government will take a more reasonable course.

SIR THOMAS ESMONDE (Dublin Co., S.): If these provisions are not amended, every honest man will be at the mercy of any malicious blackguard, who will have it in his power to affirm that persons who really know nothing about a particular offence can give evidence with respect to it. Suppose that one person has a grudge against another; there is nothing to prevent him from going in malice and stating that he has reason to believe that the man he accuses is able to give important evidence. Take the case of the Plan of Campaign. It would be very easy for a labourer who may have been dismissed from his employment to go to a police station, and say that he believes the farmer who has employed him can give important evidence about the Plan of Campaign. Whether he is able to do so or not, I do not see why the Government should reject this Amendment. I do not think that it would make much difference to the stringent character of the Bill. It would, however, provide a safeguard against some of the abuses which may follow if the clause is passed as it stands.

MR. H. GILL (Limerick): May I point out a matter in which even this House itself is interested. I believe that it will be possible, with the connivance of the Resident Magistrate, to use the powers conferred by the clause to prevent Members of the Nationalist Party from leaving Ireland at a time when important Divisions are expected in this House. We know that nearly all the Resident Magistrates are of one way of thinking, and that they are supporters of the Government and friends of the landlords, mixing up most intimately in the very matters which will have principally brought this Crimes Act into operation. What is there, I would ask, to prevent some very ardent and zealous supporter of Her Majesty's Government, when there is an important Division coming on hereafter on which, perhaps, the fate of the Government might depend, from summoning eight or ten Members of this House to appear before a Resident Magistrate to give evidence with regard to an alleged offence? He would easily be able to get people around him to say they believed that these hon. Members could give important information if they were examined. If it were necessary to require that these men should lay an information on oath, I think it would be difficult to induce them to do so, because they would know that they might hereafter be prosecuted for perjury. I do not think that this is an improbable case. We know very well that statesmen are not very scrupulous when the interests of their Party are at stake. We had an instance of that only the other day in the conduct of Members of the present Government in refusing the inquiry we asked for in regard to certain alleged charges which have been made against the Irish Party.

COLONEL WARING (Down, N.): I have no wish to delay the Committee; but I think it is necessary that I should deny that the Resident Magistrates are likely to make the bad use of their powers, which hon. Members opposite pretend to fear. As a matter of fact, the large majority of Resident Magistrates of Ireland owe their appointment to the Government of which the right hon. Member for Mid Lothian (Mr. W. E. Gladstone) was the Head. They are not, therefore, likely to be supporters of Her Majesty's Government, or to make use of the powers entrusted to them in any improper manner.

SIR THOMAS ESMONDE: In a debate which occurred in this House a very short time ago, letters were produced to show the unworthy grounds upon which Resident Magistrates have been appointed. In some cases application for a post appears to have been made on the ground that the candidate, if not appointed, would take to drink or some other evil course.

THE CHAIRMAN: Order, order! This discussion is very irregular, and the remarks of the hon. Baronet are not relevant to the Amendment.

DR. TANNER (Cork Co., Mid): After the remarks which have been made by the hon. and gallant Colonel the Member for North Down (Colonel Waring), I cannot help rising to say what I know about these Resident Magistrates.

THE CHAIRMAN: Order, order! I have already intimated that that would be totally irregular.

Question put.

The Committee *divided*:—Ayes 106; Noes 174: Majority 68.—(Div. List, No. 130.)

MR. MAURICE HEALY, in rising to move at the end of the last Amendment the insertion of the following words:—

"Provided that, in construing the said enactments, an offence for which a person may be prosecuted before a court of summary jurisdiction under this Act shall not be deemed to be an indictable offence;"

said: This is a very important Amendment, and one upon which I do hope the Government will yield us some concession. Any hon. Member who has studied this Bill will know that one of the most important principles contained in it is to be found in the 2nd clause—namely, that a large number of offences hitherto triable by jury are henceforward to be tried by two Resident Magistrates. These offences will be seen to include criminal conspiracy, intimidation, Boycotting, riot, unlawful assembly, taking forcible possession, assaulting the police, and the various offences that come under the Whiteboy Acts. These are what are called indictable offences, and have hitherto been triable only by jury, though they are, under the Bill, to be tried by two Resident Magistrates. Now, what we complain of is this—that whereas, for their own purposes when it suits them to do so, the Government make these summary offences, in the clause with which we are now dealing they make them indictable offences. Under this Star Chamber Clause there are two distinctions between summary offences and indictable offences. In indictable offences you can arrest a witness by warrant without summons. You cannot in summary offences; secondly, in the case of summary offences if a witness refuses to answer, you can only commit him to prison for a month or less, whereas, in the case of indictable offences, a man can be committed for an indefinite period. What we complain of is this—that, when it suits their own purpose, they make these offences, set forth in the 2nd clause, summary offences for the purpose of having them dealt with by two Resident Magistrates;

but in the clause we are upon for this Star Chamber inquiry these same are indictable offences. This I say is not fair, let these offences be summary offences, or let them be indictable offences; but do not let them vary, and be in the one category or the other just as it suits the Government purpose. It is a case of "heads I win, tails you lose," for the purpose of collecting evidence, these are indictable offences and when you want to convict a prisoner the case comes under summary jurisdiction. This is playing with loaded dice, it is using a marked card, and gives the Crown a most improper and unfair advantage. If the Government say there should be indictable offences let them be so, but do not let an unfortunate person be in this position the Government may shift their ground, treating the case for one purpose as one for summary proceedings, and for another purpose as an indictable offence.

Amendment proposed,

In page 1, line 23, after "thereto," insert the words—"Provided, That, in construing the said enactments, an offence for which a person may be prosecuted before a court of summary jurisdiction under this Act shall not be deemed to be an indictable offence."—(*Mr. Maurice Healy.*)

Question proposed, "That those words be there inserted."

THE ATTORNEY GENERAL FOR IRELAND (Mr. HOLMES) (Dublin University): The 13th section of the "Petty Sessions Act" of 1851, draws a very intelligible distinction between offences punishable by summary jurisdiction and indictable offences, and in the same sense this section must be regarded. If the case is one for summary jurisdiction, a summons issues and the provision is inserted; but if the charge is that of an indictable offence, then it comes under another provision, and we have introduced that provision here. The hon. Member asks us to introduce a further distinction, the effect of which would throw every Resident Magistrate in Ireland into hopeless perplexity, and render it impossible to use the section in anything like a reasonable way. There are certain criminal acts under the law as it stands at present which may be dealt with both by means of indictment or by summary process. Of course, as regards some of these acts the administrators of the law never think of treating them otherwise than as indictable, while, as regards others, no responsible person would deal with them otherwise than by summary jurisdiction; but the criminal act itself is capable of being made punishable either one way or the other. Now, what the hon. Member wants to do is to so construe the section that any offence, however criminal, shall be made subject to summary jurisdiction.

MR. MAURICE HEALY: Under this Act, not under any circumstances.

MR. HOLMES: In this Act. It extends summary jurisdiction as it now exists. As the hon. Member states the object of his Amendment is this—that any of these offences, no matter what the circumstances, shall be dealt with by process of summary jurisdiction; that the provisions of the 13th section of the Petty Sessions Act shall not apply at all. What would be the effect of this? In the 2nd section it will be observed we have a clause in reference to intimidation that extends very little indeed the law as it stands now under the Conspiracy Act of 1875, and is identical in form with a section in the Act of 1882. Any criminal act of the most serious character, such as attacking a dwelling house, an aggravated assault on an individual, such an offence as murder might be an act of intimidation under that section. I need hardly say that no Attorney General, or anyone who puts the law in force, would dream of treating that particular act as a matter to be punished by summary jurisdiction; but if this Amendment were adopted its effect would be to deprive Resident Magistrates of the power which the 13th section of the Petty Sessions Act of 1851 gives them in regard to dealing with indictable offences. As I understand the section it is clear and definite. There must be a summons or warrant issued, and it will bear on its face the instruction that the offence, whatever it is, shall be dealt with by summary jurisdiction or indictment. If it appears to be an offence for summary jurisdiction, then the rules of law applicable to the attendance of witnesses will be applied to it, and if from the document it appears that it is proposed to proceed with the offence as an indictable offence, then the rules applicable to that will apply. That is precisely the law now. Take the case of an assault on a policeman. If it is necessary to have recourse to a summons to bring witnesses to the preliminary examination, it is printed on the summons if the charge is to be dealt with by summary jurisdiction, and all the rules apply. If, on the other hand, it appears that the charge is so framed that it must be dealt with as an indictable offence, then there are rules to apply. This is reasonable; we propose to extend these provisions to the section, and the Government cannot accept the Amendment.

MR. MAURICE HEALY: We quite believe that the Resident Magistrates who will administer the clause are a puzzle-headed set of gentlemen; but we do not think they are quite so stupid as the Attorney General for Ireland would make them out to be. According to him these intelligent captains, colonels, and others do not know what is an indictable offence and what is not. Before he decries these gentlemen in this way, he might endeavour to point out what the difficulty of Resident Magistrates would be. If the right hon. and learned Gentleman appeared to have a mean opinion of the intelligence of Resident Magistrates, he appears to have a still meaner opinion of the intelligence of this Committee. For what is his argument? That certain offences may be summarily punished, or by way of indictment. He takes the case of a murder committed, and he says that may be an act of intimidation; and, when that is committed, a Resident Magistrate would not know whether to treat it as murder or an act of intimidation. Now, surely that is not an argument to address to this Committee. Does he mean to say that an official to whom he will entrust the working of this clause is so utterly dense, so utterly ignorant—I will not say of all legal principles—but of the commonest information that is to be found in any intelligent person, that he would not know how to treat a serious offence like murder, whether to treat it as the crime of murder or an act of intimidation? Special pleading of this character is hardly worth the attention of the Committee. The point I make is this. The Government have decided, under this Bill, to take for their purpose certain classes of offences as summarily punishable; they say these offences have been indictable in the past, but the character of Irish jurors is such that we cannot rely on them; we ask, therefore, that these offences shall be summarily punishable by two Resident Magistrates. Well, though asking the House to treat these offences as summarily punishable, they also seek, when it suits their own purpose in another direction, to regard these same offences as indictable. Take the example of a certain class of offences. Let us suppose, say after the passing of this Act, a Resident Magistrate in any district comes to the conclusion that there is a conspiracy among the tenants in the district of the nature of the Plan of Campaign. Let us suppose this takes place a few months after the passing of this Act, which enables the Government, if a conspiracy of the kind is started, to bring the parties concerned before Resident Magistrates, and to punish them summarily with six months' imprisonment. That being so, is it not the height of unfairness to leave at the same time in the hands of the Government the right to take evidence of that kind for the purposes of the Star Chamber Clause, as for an indictable offence? If it is an offence to be summarily punished, let it be so for all purposes, but do not let the Government blow hot and cold and use the offence for the purpose of fishing evidence to make up an indictment. The 2nd clause of the Bill says that a large and important class of offences shall cease absolutely to be indictable and become summary, and thereupon we know where we stand. There should not be this double category of indictable and summary offences as it may suit the Government. They have drawn this Bill in this cunning way— they do not say these shall be summary offences, but that the Government may regard them as such for the purpose of punishment by a Resident Magistrate, leaving them free to regard them as indictable for Star Chamber purposes. The Attorney General has not met my argument. It is idle to tell us that a Resident Magistrate, or any man with common intelligence, will not know when to treat an offence summarily and when to treat it as indictable. The right hon. and learned Gentleman says the warrant to hold the investigation will fix whether the offence is to be dealt with summarily or by indictment. Permit me to tell him that there is another

of those difficulties bungling draftsmanship has introduced into this unfortunate Bill. If he had taken the course of putting on the face of the Bill what the form of the warrant is to be, then we should know what is the value of his argument. But he does nothing of the kind. He does not present the form of the warrant in the Bill. He tells us here, without responsibility, that when, by-and-bye, the Lord Lieutenant comes to draw up an order, he will draw it up in a precise form. But we have no guarantee whatever that the Lord Lieutenant will draw up the warrant in a particular form—promises of this kind must be regarded as those that are speedily forgotten, and when this Bill passes the Committee we shall be left to the tender mercies of the junior barrister the Lord Lieutenant employs, and he will draft the forms of procedure under this Bill. I challenge the Attorney General for Ireland to meet the point I have put before the Committee, and, with great respect, I say he has not done so. Let him tell us how it is possible for even the most stupid Resident Magistrate not to know when an offence is murder and when it is an offence like intimidation. Let him put any conceivable case in which such a preposterous state of things can arise. Coming under the 2nd clause of the Bill everybody will know at once, the facts being ascertained what is the character of the offence. If the information is that a conspiracy, such as the Plan of Campaign is in existence, the Resident Magistrate will know at once, that it is an offence under the 2nd clause, and so, also, with a case of unlawful assembly, forcible possession, and all the other classes of offences coming under the 2nd clause. It is impossible to say any magistrate with ordinary intelligence can have any doubt on the subject. I say, the Attorney General has not met my argument on the point. It is unfair that the Government should have the double advantage of treating an offence as one deserving summary punishment, and when it suits them again to treat it as an indictable offence. Let us have some surety that officials in Ireland, shall not one day say an offence is punishable under the summary clause by six months' imprisonment, and then again be allowed to make

Mr. Maurice Healy

it an indictable offence with power to summon witnesses indiscriminately to get up evidence.

MR. O'DOHERTY (Donegal, N.): It will be recollected that we had a long discussion on an Amendment of my hon. Friend, with reference to a proposed Amendment of the Attorney General. My hon. Friend wished to leave out indictable offences, showing how the Act would add considerably to the power over witnesses, and that witnesses should be treated in the way provided for summary offences, not as for indictable offences. The Attorney General, I believe, did at the time intend to meet the objections we urged. I ask the Committee to read the Amendment inserted, it comes in immediately after the words "indictable offences," in relation to witnesses being ordered to attend to give evidence upon indictable offences, and, also, in respect to offences coming under summary jurisdiction. I defy any person to make any meaning of it but what my hon. Friend has stated. We accepted the Amendment of the Attorney General in that sense, and I believe at the time he fully intended to have it so understood by the Committee, and, that it was understood by himself, that when proceedings were taken under this Act for summary process, then the ordinary procedure for witnesses would be applicable. But he is clearly wrong in leaving it to the person who issues the summons to treat the offence as for summary jurisdiction and for indictment. Will it not be possible, as the section stands, for an over-zealous man, having first treated the case as an indictable offence, using the greater power over witnesses, and having collected evidence, than to proceed by process of summary jurisdiction? The right hon. Gentleman does not intend that. But there is the power to do so. He has to get information as to an indictable offence having been committed; but what we strongly object to, is that after the means of collecting this evidence is set in operation, it should be left to this official to adopt the method of dealing with the offence by summary process. You may, under the exceptional powers and penalties against witnesses, collect evidence because a man may not be prepared to undergo the punishment the Court of Inquiry can inflict; but you have this evidence collected by one machinery you cannot

put in force on the hearing of the case itself. Here is a plain contradiction in terms, and I ask the Attorney General to re-consider the matter. We talk in this Committee about summary jurisdiction and indictable offences, and sometimes, perhaps, these terms do not exactly convey our meaning to Gentlemen not conversant with criminal procedure. No offence can be tried and punished at Petty Sessions, that is by summary jurisdiction, that is not capable of being tried both there and also by a Judge and jury, and so almost every offence triable at Petty Sessions is, in that sense, an indictable offence; and if the Government wish to ride off upon that construction it is another matter. They have not given us that which it was understood they had given us. I ask the Attorney General's attention to this, that a case of the commonest assault can be tried by a Judge and jury as well as by a magistrate—in short, the whole panoply of the law can be brought to deal with a case of this kind. We called attention to this point at the earliest possible stage, and I only wish to say further that my firm belief is, that when my hon. Friend put down his Amendment, his meaning was the same as mine, and that, if I am deceived in this matter in any way, I know it was not his fault.

Question put.

The Committee *divided*:—Ayes 139; Noes 178: Majority 39.—(Div. List, No. 131.)

Amendment proposed,

In page 1, line 23, after "thereto," insert— "A resident magistrate, holding an inquiry under this section, shall himself conduct such inquiry, and shall not permit any other person to question or examine any witness or otherwise to take part in such inquiry."—(*Mr. Maurice Healy.*)

Amendment proposed to omit from the proposed Amendment the words, "or otherwise take part in such inquiry."—(*Mr. A. J. Balfour.*)

Amendment *agreed to.*

Amendment (*Mr. Maurice Healy*), as amended, *agreed to.*

MR. MAURICE HEALY (Cork): I rise to move an Amendment, the object of which is that in cases where a person is charged with the offence which is the subject of the inquiry, he or his solicitor or counsel shall be allowed to attend the inquiry and cross-examine witnesses. I think this is a very substantial point, and one which may be very reasonably discussed. The Committee has decided that inquiries under this clause may be held, although no person may be charged with the offence inquired into; they have also decided that they will not allow a solicitor or counsel to attend on the part of any witness summoned. My Amendment is, therefore, a very reasonable one; and I cannot imagine anything more important than that when one of these secret inquiries are being held, and a person is in custody, that person should have full knowledge of what is going on, and know what is being sworn against him; it is necessary to know that the inquiry is fairly conducted. The point is one on which, I think, some concession should be made, and I trust that the Government will consider the matter.

Amendment proposed,

In page 1, line 23, after "thereto," insert—"Where at the date when any inquiry under this section is held any person shall be charged with the offence in reference to which such inquiry has been held, such person or his solicitor or counsel shall be entitled to attend such inquiry, and to cross-examine any witnesses examined thereat."—(*Mr. Maurice Healy*.)

Question proposed, "That those words be there inserted."

The CHIEF SECRETARY for IRE-LAND (Mr. A. J. BALFOUR) (Manchester, E.): The hon. Member is, of course, quite within his right in moving this Amendment, but I remind him that an Amendment substantially similar was proposed the other evening by an hon. Member opposite, and, after discussion, withdrawn by him. I, therefore, hope the hon. Member will not raise the discussion again.

MR. MAURICE HEALY: I think the Chief Secretary for Ireland is quite wrong in supposing that the Amendment withdrawn by my hon. Friend is in substance the same as mine. If the Amendment of my hon. Friend had been accepted, the moment a person was charged with the offence the whole machinery of the secret inquiry would have ceased to operate. In that case the secret inquiry would be adjourned, and the prisoner would be brought before a magistrate; and the evidence would be subject to the ordinary rules of evidence. But that is quite a different point from that

Mr. Maurice Healy

of my Amendment. What my Amendment asks is that, the Government having decided that the inquiry should be continued, with regard to the prisoner in custody, the prisoner should be represented at the inquiry and know what is going on, so that this knowledge should be made use of for the purpose of his defence. I submit that the difference is a substantial one, and that if the Government do not accept it, they should give some reason for their refusal to do so.

MR. O'DOHERTY (Donegal, N.): I understood that it had been agreed that the proceedings at the private inquiry should be the same as if it were the trial of the offence; but now it turns out that the preliminary inquiry may go on as to an indictable offence, while, at the same time, the man may be tried summarily. My hon. Friend in this Amendment puts his finger on the weak spot in the policy of the Government. It is possible now for a magistrate holding a preliminary inquiry to issue a summons as for an indictable offence, in order to see what evidence he can collect under the machinery of the Bill, while, at the same time, another Court is dealing summarily with the same man and the same offence. I think I have brought the right hon. Gentleman face to face with the question whether it is not perfectly clear that the powers now given may be exercised by the magistrate with greater severity than by the Court before which the prisoner is actually on trial. When the hon. and learned Member for North Longford (Mr. T. M. Healy) proposed his Amendment, we imagined that the Government had put forward an Amendment by which the preliminary examination would be conducted as if a trial were going on; but it now appears to be altogether different, and it is possible for a magistrate to have a more far-reaching method of procedure than that on the trial of an individual. If a person were in custody, by the Amendment of the hon. and learned Member for North Longford, he would hear all the evidence long before the trial; and the Amendment would prevent, owing to the presence of counsel, anything wrong being put down. I wish to point out that the Committee has to consider whether or not this Amendment is absolutely necessary, inasmuch as there are two procedures, one of which is stronger than the other.

MR. HENRY H. FOWLER (Wolverhampton, E.): I understand the case to be this—when the private inquiry takes place the witness is bound over under recognizances to appear in Petty Sessions where a prisoner can be dealt with summarily, or where he will be committed for trial. The magistrate who has conducted the private inquiry cannot sit on the examination at Petty Sessions, and whatever evidence is to be used against the man on trial will be taken at the second inquiry, which will be conducted according to the ordinary rules of evidence, and no evidence given at the private inquiry can be used to convict or punish the man. If I am correct in my assumption, I must say it rather weakens the case of the hon. Member below the Gangway.

THE ATTORNEY GENERAL FOR IRELAND (Mr. HOLMES) (Dublin University): I have endeavoured to see whether there is any distinction between the Amendment now under discussion and that which was withdrawn on a former occasion; but on the whole I am unable to see that there is any difference in principle between them. We stated, on that occasion, our objections very fully, and I am unable to add anything further, especially bearing in mind what has been said by the right hon. Gentleman the Member for Wolverhampton with regard to the accused man—namely, that the depositions must be taken when he is charged in the form of law in which they are taken at the present moment. The man will then have the right to be represented by counsel. It will be upon the evidence taken then, and not upon the evidence taken at the inquiry under this clause, that the man will be tried.

MR. O'DOHERTY: We do not want to provide any protection for criminals, but for witnesses. I wish to draw the attention of the Attorney General for Ireland to this—that it is impossible to compel any witnesses to appear before a magistrate unless it be either by taking them by the neck and bringing them there, or by summons. My contention is, that in this case we desire to have a safeguard against the people being dragged by the neck before the magistrates. We are not endeavouring to prolong this discussion, we are en-deavouring to prevent a process of law being used under circumstances in which great and unnecessary inconvenience may be inflicted.

MR. ARTHUR O'CONNOR (Donegal, E.): I do not think the argument of the Chief Secretary for Ireland is well founded. No doubt the Amendment he referred to was before the House before it was withdrawn, with the view of bringing it forward at another point. I altogether demur to the statement of the Chief Secretary for Ireland. The chief mischief which this Amendment proposes to deal with is this—that the clause enables the Government or the Administration to do that which is perfectly repugnant to all ideas prevalent in this country with regard to the treatment of offenders under the Bill. Unless the Amendment is adopted the prosecution will be in a position in which they are able to take before a secret tribunal every one of the witnesses whom it is proposed to call, or whom it is likely will be called, in defence of the prisoner. The prosecution will be enabled in that way to ascertain the probable lines of the defence, and will practically get a knowledge of what is in the brief of the counsel for the prisoner. Now, I do not think that anything can be more repugnant than that to the feelings of the people of this country. I appeal to any Member whether anything of this kind has ever before been the practice, and whether it is not distinctly a breach of fairplay to treat a man thus, when he is charged with no offence whatever.

MR. W. REDMOND (Fermanagh, N.): I wish to point out to the Committee that, unless this Amendment is accepted, what will occur will be that the man will practically be tried behind his back, and that the subsequent examination before the magistrate will be nothing but a farce, the man having been examined before and practically tried by the Resident Magistrate without being represented by counsel in any way. It is all very well to say that the evidence procured at the secret inquiry will not be used at the trial which subsequently takes place; but it is a well-known fact that the character of evidence is frequently changed by cross-examination. Now, if this Amendment is not accepted, the witnesses will not be subjected to any cross-examination on the part of the accused persons, so that a man may be in custody for committing an offence, and before he is brought to trial and brought face to face with his accusers, the evidence will have been gone into before a tribunal where he was unrepresented. I think it is against the principles of the Constitution that a man should be tried behind his back, and I do not see what possible objection the Government can have to accept this Amendment, which is very simple and very limited in its scope, and which only asks, that where a man is under arrest, or charged with an offence, he shall be represented by counsel, so that the evidence brought against him may not be unfairly got.

MR. T. P. O'CONNOR (Liverpool, Scotland): I was rather alarmed when the right hon. Gentleman the Member for Wolverhampton (Mr. Henry H. Fowler) spoke against our Amendment, because I am satisfied he is favourable to its principle, and because of his great authority; but I think his suggestion would have been more acceptable if it were not for the way in which law is administered in Ireland. I wish to show that the protection which the right hon. Gentleman believes to be the rule would not be the rule in the present case. I speak, of course, with the greatest modesty on this subject, because I am not a lawyer; but, as I understand the position of the Government, it is that the inquiry should be entirely secret in order to the detection of crime. There I agree with them. But an inquiry might be held where no man has been arrested, and it might be held where a man has been arrested; and I maintain that there is a distinction between the necessity for secret inquiry, in the one case, and the necessity for secret inquiry in the other. I will assume that I am charged with a crime under this Bill, and that my hon. Friend below me is undergoing a process of secret inquiry. Surely I have a right, as I am standing on my trial, that nothing shall take place at the secret inquiry which should be prejudicial to my fair rights as a prisoner standing on my defence? I am entitled, when I am charged with a crime on which a secret inquiry is being held, to all the safeguards which are given in cases where a prisoner is on his trial. Now, my hon. Friend wants, that if I be charged with a crime, my interests shall be protected at the secret

inquiry, and that this shall be done by my legal representative being present on my behalf. But then comes in the objection of my right hon. Friend the Member for Wolverhampton, who says that the evidence given at the secret inquiry will not be used against me, and that, therefore, I do not require the protection which this Amendment is intended to afford. But that is not the case. Anything said by a witness may be brought against him by the way of testing his credibility. Am I correct in this? The Attorney General makes no answer. I will state the point again. I say that anything which a witness says at the secret inquiry may be used subsequently for the purpose of testing his credibility. Will the Chief Secretary for Ireland say whether I am right, because the Attorney General is now showing some traces of the fatigue he has undergone? I see also the Lord Advocate is begging to be let off. But, in consideration of the fact that it is difficult to get him to speak on Scotch law, I shall not waste my strength in asking him to speak on Irish law. I will ask the Attorney General, who may now be said to be "in evidence," whether I am right in stating that the evidence given by a witness at a secret inquiry may be used at the trial to test his credibility. If that be so, the evidence used to test his credibility would be upon my supposition, evidence against me. Well, then, if the witness at the secret inquiry stated that I had committed the crime, and afterwards said that I did not, surely his former statement would be used against me. But does my right hon. and learned Friend know that, in Ireland, under the Crimes Act, witnesses for the defence have been brought before secret inquiries, and that in that way the whole case has been discovered. If you allow the prosecution to discover the whole of the defence of the prisoner, you enormously decrease the amount of fair play and equality which he is entitled to have shown him when he is tried. I speak within the knowledge of my hon. Friends, possessed of legal knowledge, when I say that some of the witnesses for the defence of prisoners have been brought before secret inquiries, and by that means the whole ground has been cut from under them on their trial. Therefore, I think that, without the Amendment which my hon.

Mr. W. Redmond

Friend (Mr. Maurice Healy) proposes, this clause can be used against the rights of a prisoner, and the fair play to which he is entitled.

THE CHIEF SECRETARY FOR IRE-LAND (Mr. A. J. BALFOUR) (Manchester, E.): There are only two possible plans of dealing with the notes or records of the inquiry; they must either be used on the trial or not at all. Hon. Gentlemen opposite have strongly appealed to us to allow the prisoner to have a copy of the notes. Of course, if a copy is furnished, you must allow cross-examination upon them in Court.

MR. T. P. O'CONNOR: I do not deny that, that is my statement, and that is exactly the point at which the right hon. Gentleman comes in contact with my hon. Friends. My hon. Friend has pointed out that the depositions taken at the secret inquiry are going to be given to the prisoner, and, therefore, as the right hon. Gentleman properly says, they should also be given to the prosecuting counsel, and that it is right they should be used in cross-examination. Therefore, I say that in the defence of the prisoner, the protection for the prisoner to which my right hon. Friend has alluded entirely disappears. I wish to point out again, that if a witness can be cross-examined as to credibility, so far he is examined to the prejudice of the prisoner in whose behalf he has said something. Therefore, I think it right that when the secret inquiry is going on where proceedings are taken against me, I have the right to be safeguarded by my counsel.

MR. HENRY H. FOWLER (Wolverhampton, E.): Let me put this case. Suppose a murder has been committed; it may be absolutely necessary to arrest someone at the moment, or he may escape before the preliminary inquiry is taken. By this Amendment being adopted the whole object of the clause relating to crime would be defeated. I said last night that if this clause were confined to crime I would support it. I think it would be a great improvement in English jurisprudence if this were part of our law. I believe there have been many serious crimes committed in this country which would not have remained undetected had this clause been in force at the time they were committed. I can conceive a case in which the whole use of the preliminary inquiry would be swept away if the Amendment were accepted. It is clear that any evidence taken behind a man's back ought not to be used against him. But how is this evidence to be used? When the evidence is complete the witness is to be bound over to appear before another magistrate, and has there to repeat that evidence. Nothing he has said can be read at the second inquiry; it cannot be used against the prisoner. [An hon. MEMBER: Yes.] Can it be used against him?

THE ATTORNEY GENERAL FOR IRELAND (Mr. HOLMES) (Dublin University): No; and we have provided that the same magistrate shall not preside at the second inquiry.

MR. MAURICE HEALY: You have said it ought to be used.

MR. HENRY H. FOWLER: It cannot be used at all then. The witness will be put into the box, and have to repeat his evidence. But the hon. Member for the Scotland Division of Liverpool (Mr. T. P. O'Connor) says that you may use what has been said at the preliminary examination for the purpose of testing the credibility of the witness. The Government have admitted the principle that what is taken at the preliminary inquiry should be used for that purpose at the second inquiry, and the hon. Member for North Longford (Mr. T. M. Healy) moved that the evidence might be so used for the purpose of cross-examining the witness. I think my hon. Friend will admit that what is fair for the accused is fair for the Crown. Given the principle of the private inquiry, given the principle that the evidence taken upon that inquiry should never be used again except upon oath, and given that the House has decided unwisely, as I think, that the witness should not have the protection of professional advice on that inquiry, I do not see that the mere fact of anybody having been apprehended makes any substantial difference. I am as anxious as anyone that these proceedings should be conducted fairly.

MR. T. P. O'CONNOR (Liverpool, Scotland): What about the case I alluded to where witnesses, known to be for the defence, have been brought before a secret inquiry, by which means the whole plan of defence has been revealed?

[*Sixth Night.*]

MR. HENRY H. FOWLER: That is an argument against the clause. The Amendment will not touch that point.

MR. T. P. O'CONNOR: Oh, yes, it will.

MR. HENRY H. FOWLER: No doubt, it is a serious objection to the clause that witnesses for the defence may be examined before the prosecutor, who may find out what the defence is; but no provision you can insert regarding the presence of a professional man will prevent that. I do not see how the Amendment could remedy the evil. I will only say that I should be disposed to agree with my hon. Friend if I could follow him; but I think that, assuming the principle of the secret inquiry, and that the evidence given before it shall not be used, and that it is decided that the witness is not to have professional advice at the secret inquiry, I do not think that the mere distinction, in the fact of a person being apprehended, makes any substantial alteration in the condition of the question the Committee decided yesterday.

MR. MAURICE HEALY (Cork): I quite admit that the question incidentally raised in the course of the discussion of this Amendment—namely, the question as to how far the depositions taken at a secret inquiry can afterwards be used at the trial of the offence with reference to which the inquiry has taken place, has an important bearing on the Amendment before the Committee, and I should like to make it clear where we stand on that subject. The right hon. Gentleman the Member for East Wolverhampton has assumed that the Committee has already decided that the information taken at a secret inquiry is to be capable——

Notice taken, that 40 Members were not present; Committee counted, and 40 Members being present,

MR. MAURICE HEALY: I was saying that, in my opinion, the Committee has not decided this point, and that the right hon. Gentleman the Member for East Wolverhampton has assumed that the depositions taken at the secret inquiry will be used for or against the prisoner. The furthest step taken in that direction is this—the Committee has decided that a prisoner charged with any offence in reference to which a secret inquiry has been held shall be

entitled, if he so desires, to obtain copies of the depositions that have been taken at the secret inquiry. That is a very different thing to deciding that these depositions can be used for or against him at the trial. It is one thing to decide that he is entitled to these copies—it is only proper that they should be placed at the disposal of a prisoner charged with an offence—but, with great respect, I say that it is quite another thing to decide that, in addition to giving these copies, the authorities shall be able to use them against the prisoner at his trial. That I take to be the stage at which we stand on this question as to whether or not the depositions taken at the secret inquiry shall be used. Now, the right hon. Member for East Wolverhampton has assumed, and the right hon. and learned Attorney General for Ireland has assented to the assumption that the depositions taken at a secret inquiry can never be used against a prisoner. With great respect, I venture to differ from that opinion of the right hon. Gentleman the Member for East Wolverhampton, and from that opinion of the right hon. and learned Gentleman the Attorney General for Ireland, and perhaps I can best illustrate the position I take up by describing what occurred in a criminal case that was tried in my presence in Cork about two years ago. In that case the prisoner was charged with shooting at with intent to murder. The crime was committed in the county of Kerry, and the trial took place at the Cork Winter Assizes before Mr. Justice O'Brien. The sole evidence against the prisoner was the evidence of the man who was shot at, and that person had unquestionably swore at the preliminary investigation that the prisoner in the dock had fired the shot which struck him; but when the case came before Mr. Justice O'Brien, the man who had so sworn went to the back of what he had so sworn and declared to the jury that the prisoner was not the man who had fired the shot. Now, the position in which the case stood before the jury was this. There was not an atom of evidence to go to the jury to show that the prisoner in the dock was the man who fired the shot. The only evidence that the Crown could produce was the evidence of this man who swore that the prisoner was not the man who shot him, who swore to the features of the man who committed the offence, and said they were not like the features of the prisoner. Well, according to the statement of the law we have from the right hon. and learned Gentleman the Attorney General for Ireland, and from the right hon. Gentleman the Member for East Wolverhampton, the prisoner ought to have been immediately discharged from the dock. But what actually occurred? Why, the Crown, as they were entitled to do, put into the hand of the witness the deposition he had made at the preliminary investigation. They cross-examined him by means of that deposition. He admitted that he had made that deposition—he admitted that he had sworn that the prisoner in the dock was the man who had shot at him, but he now swore positively to the jury that in making that statement at the preliminary inquiry he had perjured himself, and that what he had said was not true. He declared that the prisoner was not the man who had shot him. If what the right hon. Gentleman the Member for East Wolverhampton and the right hon. and learned Gentleman the Attorney General for Ireland say is true, the prisoner in the dock, I say, ought to have been discharged, because though the witness was confronted with his own deposition, that deposition ought only to have been put in evidence for the purpose of contradicting him and showing that he was a person not worthy of credit on his oath. But the learned Judge, Mr. Justice O'Brien, reserved his judgment for the next day. He went over the matter and considered it carefully, and the next day he declared that he had found two authorities for the view, that when once a deposition was in evidence for one purpose it was in evidence for all purposes, and that it was competent for the jury, though the deposition was the sole scrap of evidence before them, to convict the prisoner. They did convict the prisoner, who was sentenced to two years' imprisonment. What, I ask, therefore, is the value of the statement of the right hon. and learned Attorney General for Ireland in face of a case of that kind? We say that that is exactly the sort of case which may arise out of these secret inquiries. We say that persons when brought up at these secret inquiries, unless protection is afforded by publicity, and when they are taken before the Resident Magis-

trates, and questioned and cross-hackled, and, perhaps, intimidated and bribed, may swear away the lives and liberties of innocent persons, and that it is possible when, afterwards, those persons are brought to trial—it is conceivable, I say—that the witness who in the Star Chamber inquiry has given certain evidence may admit that in giving that evidence he had been lying. The state of things appears to be this, that though that condition of things arises, that though the only scrap of evidence against the prisoner is the information of the man who makes the deposition at the secret inquiry, and who at the trial says that his statement was false and that he was perjuring himself and that the prisoner is innocent, it is to be possible to convict an innocent man upon a deposition afterwards declared by the deponent to be false. I say that that is an outrageous state of things, and I say very fortunately, Sir, this Committee has not yet decided that this information should be used in that manner. I say that when the time comes to discuss that matter, we in this quarter of the House shall vehemently oppose the use of information obtained under these circumstances for any purpose whatever. I challenge the right hon. and learned Gentleman the Attorney General for Ireland to contradict my statement of the law as laid down by Mr. Justice O'Brien. I do not know whether he is familiar with the case I have mentioned, but I can assure him it is one which has been alluded to at least half-a-dozen times in this House. It is a matter of notoriety amongst the Bench and Bar of Ireland. I was myself present at the trial and heard what took place. If that is the state of the case, is it not monstrous that an innocent man is to be convicted on the unsupported statement of a witness who at a secret inquiry swears away his life and liberty; is it not monstrous that an innocent man is to be convicted upon a statement which is declared by the person who made it when he has to give his evidence in the light of day before a Judge and jury to be false? No stronger argument could be used in favour of the Amendment before the Committee. I challenge the right hon. and learned Gentleman the Attorney General for Ireland to contradict the narrative of the case that I have given. I quite concede that if the Committee had once decided

[*Sixth Night.*]

that the information to be taken at the secret inquiry should not afterwards be used for any purpose, it might be a strong thing to provide that the person charged with the offence should have counsel before the inquiry; but so long as it is decided that hearsay statements full of the most illegal and improper evidence—statements which would be scouted if it was attempted to make them in any Court of Law—shall be admitted at this inquiry; so long as he is to be fettered by no rule of evidence, or of decency, or of common sense, we say that so long as that state of things exists there is the strongest necessity and urgency for providing that a prisoner who may be cruelly accused at this inquiry shall have the opportunity of knowing what is going on at the time and what slanders are being uttered against him.

Mr. T. M. HEALY (Longford, N.): I am sorry we have not the support of the right hon. Gentleman the Member for East Wolverhampton (Mr. Henry H. Fowler). I should like to put this point to him. Is he aware that there is an Irish Statute which states that in cases of murder, where witnesses are dead, their depositions may be used? I believe that is also the law in England that in a case of murder where a witness dies and there is an accused person, and some statement has been made by that deceased person, the deposition of the deceased is put in for all purposes as substantive evidence, although the accused person shall have had no opportunity of examination. The prisoner would have had an opportunity of examination if this inquiry took place before an ordinary magistrate. The prisoner would there be represented; but the Government now wish to use depositions given at a secret inquiry as substantive evidence as though they had been made in an ordinary manner.

The ATTORNEY GENERAL for IRELAND (Mr. Holmes) (Dublin University): Can the hon. and learned Member refer me to a single Statute in which what he states as being the law during the present century?

Mr. T. M. HEALY: Yes, I can. I could give you the exact Statute if I had time to go to my case and get it. As soon as I have done talking I will go out and get it. Speaking at this moment

Mr. Maurice Healy

from memory, I think the Statute is of George III., of the Irish Parliament. I think it is one of the Whiteboy Acts which sets forth that there is grave danger to the lives of witnesses and so on. It sets out that this thing which I have described should then happen. I say that it is a serious thing, if you are going to allow depositions taken at secret inquiries to be used as substantive evidence, not to give the accused an opportunity of cross-examination.

The ATTORNEY GENERAL (Sir Richard Webster) (Isle of Wight): The hon. and learned Gentleman I am sure does not wish to fix upon us an intention which we have disclaimed over and over again. We do not mean to make these statements evidence at all, certainly not as depositions. If the depositions were intended to be used as evidence cross-examination would be allowed. At the suggestion either of the hon. and learned Gentleman himself or of someone sitting near him, we agreed that if we were going to call evidence against a prisoner over again, as the right hon. Gentleman the Member for East Wolverhampton has pointed out, the statement made by the witness at the preliminary inquiry would be handed to the prisoner's counsel or solicitor in order that they, as well as the prosecution, might have the benefit of cross-examination; but at no stage of these proceedings have we ever proposed that a statement taken down or a deposition should be used as evidence at all, or should be put in or have the least validity as a deposition. The hon. and learned Member is quite mistaken as to the Law of England. He is mistaken in his opinion that it is permissible to use the statement of a dead man as evidence. The hon. and learned Member must be referring to a dying declaration.

Mr. T. M. HEALY: I did not assert it as a positive fact in regard to the Law of England. I do not gather from the hon. and learned Gentleman—whom I thank for being at all times anxious to assist the Committee—that he stated that in no case will these depositions be liable to be used by the Crown. Do I gather that? You see there is no answer. That is the way to test the matter. Do I gather—and, if so, I will sit down at once—that the Crown will put in and use these depositions?

SIR RICHARD WEBSTER: Certainly not.

MR. HOLMES : Statements have been made upon this point so frequently that I feel ashamed to answer the hon. and learned Member's question again. I would call his attention to what has already occurred. It has been stated more than once from this Bench that the view we take of these depositions is, and what we are prepared to do is, to provide that they should not be used in any legal proceeding against any person, except a person who might have been committed for perjury. But, yielding to the strongest pressure, after a debate which lasted two hours, we assented to give the depositions of any witness who might be called against a prisoner upon his trial to the counsel of that prisoner, for the purpose of being used in cross-examination. When that concession—for it was a concession—was made by us, I distinctly stated what everyone in the House must admit to be reasonable and fair—namely, that if the depositions were used for cross-examination by the prisoner's counsel, they should also be used for a similar purpose by the representative of the Crown. No one can understand that less clearly than we do. It has been repeated again and again, and if hon. Members complain of it it is their own fault, because it was at their suggestion that the arrangement was made.

MR. T. M. HEALY : The right hon. and learned Gentleman has not quite accurately stated what took place. What we asked was that the counsel for the prisoner should have copies of these depositions. If the counsel for the prisoner chooses to make them evidence by cross-examining out of them, then they would become substantive evidence, just as other depositions would. But what the Government wanted to do was this—when the Motion was carried that the prisoner's counsel should have copies of the depositions, they got up and said—"Then we will use them." That was what we objected to, and we object to it yet, and when the Government come to that Amendment, they will not make that proposal unless they want to create a long wrangle. I say the Judge shall rule that the prisoner is entitled to have copies of the depositions, and that if he uses them for purposes of cross-examination so also shall all parties. They

will have been put in definitely by the prisoner's counsel, and no one will be able to object. The depositions then could be used by the prisoner, and the evidence might be given over again. But what we object to is making these depositions, which will be full of hearsay evidence, substantive evidence at the trial, and that is the point of our case for the necessity of this Amendment. This is a remarkable thing, and shows how the views of the Government shift from time to time. When the case mentioned by the hon. Member for Cork (Mr. Maurice Healy) took place, I made a Motion on going into Committee of Supply, and pointed out that it was historically unparalleled, this man having been convicted upon a deposition which in Court was denied on oath by the man who made it—there being no evidence to go to the jury but the two contradictory statements of the same man. Well, what happened? After I had stated my case, Mr. Johnston, then Attorney General for Ireland, but now Mr. Justice Johnston—a gentleman for whose authority we all had and have great respect—got up and supported Mr. Justice O'Brien's ruling. But that is not all. The present Lord Chancellor —Lord Ashbourne—who was then leading the Opposition, got up and supported the proposition to allow a deposition to be used as substantive evidence. Well, then, you now have a Judge in the High Court of Appeal, you have a Judge in the Court of Queen's Bench, and also Mr. Justice Johnston, of pronounced opinion upon this point, and what result could you expect if anyone ventured to dispute the view of this triumvirate. I see the right hon. and learned Solicitor General for Ireland coming into his place. He very well knows the state of the law in Ireland on the point, as delivered by Mr. Justice O'Brien, because he was present during the trial of the case of Cornwell against O'Brien, where the same point arose, and where Mr. Justice O'Brien's attention was called to the decision he had given in Cork with regard to using depositions as substantive evidence. It was voted on his certificate, which he gave for the purpose of a new trial, that he had given this decision in Cork and now confirmed it. That statement of the fact cannot be contradicted. It is the case that in all civil matters you have your appeal;

but in criminal matters you have no appeal whatever. You are depending upon what is called the personal equasion of a particular Judge. He may state a case to the Court for Crown cases reserved, if he likes; but, generally speaking, he will not do so. Therefore, every Judge has you at his mercy in criminal matters; and what are you going to do? We heard from the right hon. Gentleman the Member for Derby (Sir William Harcourt) that, so far as he was concerned, he would give no hearsay evidence before the Court or before one of these secret tribunals, and that he would take the consequences and allow himself to be committed. But a poor Irish peasant will have no knowledge of the law, and will be examined, not in the Scotch fashion, with an assessor present to decide as to the legality of the questions put, but with the questioner being at the same time the judge of the legality of the question and the person to commit him to gaol for refusing to answer. Hearsay evidence will be extracted from him, and without a prisoner having any opportunity of cross-examining upon, or rebutting that evidence, it will in a moment become substantive evidence. Not only that; but all the witnesses for the defence may be examined. The Government have given us no guarantee that they will not do that, and this system is to continue after the prisoner has been committed for trial. The inquiry may go on, as in the case of the Phœnix Park trial. A private investigation may be going on in the Bar-room, whilst the trial is taking place in Green Street—an informal trial may be taking place at one end of the Court-house whilst the prisoner is in the dock at the other. Very well, the prisoner's witnesses will be examined. How will they get their names? The witnesses must supply their names to the Treasury Solicitor for the purpose of having their expenses paid. All the names of the witnesses will come under the notice of the Treasury Solicitor, who will summon every person whose name is returned as a witness for the defence; the Government will be enabled, by the Amendment they say they intend to pass, to use the statements they have extracted from the witnesses for the defence. If these witnesses refuse to answer they will be put in gaol, and will not be available for the prisoner at all. This is a pretty state of things! This is "Scotch

Mr. T. M. Healy

law," I presume? You will commit the witnesses for the defence, and they will not have an opportunity of giving evidence at all. I do hope, in view of the discussion that has taken place, the right hon. Gentleman the Member for East Wolverhampton will reconsider his position. I consider this matter of unparalleled importance. When a prisoner is accused of an offence, I think his liberty to cross-examine should ensue. I think the Government have not met us in a reasonable spirit, and if they continue by moving the Amendments the right hon. and learned Attorney General suggests, all I can say is, they will not get out of this Committee till Christmas; for I see an endless vista of mischief which, so far as we are concerned, we shall oppose to the bitter end. If you are going to put additional virus into the Bill we shall take objection to it, no matter what the result may be.

MR. T. P. O'CONNOR (Liverpool, Scotland): I have listened to the whole of this debate, except for a few moments when I was out of the House, and if my hon. Friend below me were to take a suggestion from me, he would not go to a Division on the Amendment, in view of the fact that we shall not have the assistance of the right hon. Gentleman the Member for East Wolverhampton, and the several Gentlemen who are acting with him. I cannot say that he has convinced me; but we are anxious not to take a Division in which we are not all taking up the same attitude. In this sense, I would ask my hon. Friend to rest satisfied with the very instructive discussion we have had. I would appeal to my hon. Friend to ask leave to withdraw the Amendment.

MR. MAURICE HEALY: Under the circumstances, I will withdraw. I do not see the use of going to a Division.

THE CHAIRMAN: Is it your pleasure that the Amendment be withdrawn? [*Cries of* "No!"]

Question put, "That those words be there inserted."

The Committee *divided:*—Ayes 141; Noes 241: Majority 100.—(Div. List, No. 132.)

MR. T. M. HEALY (Longford, N.): I wish to make an explanation in reply to a statement made by the right hon. and learned Gentleman the Attorney General for Ireland a few moments ago.

He said there was no Statute in existence applying to Ireland under which it is possible to take the depositions of a deceased person as substantive evidence. I refer him to the 15th *Geo.* III. c. 102, s 5, which fully sets out the fact I stated. I think the right hon. and learned Gentleman will see from this the necessity of being more slender in his correction.

MR. MAURICE HEALY (Cork): Before we pass to the subject-matter of the 3rd sub-section, I am anxious to obtain from Gentlemen sitting on the Front Bench opposite an undertaking as regards a matter that was discussed at some length. I am aware that a desultory discussion would not be in Order, and, if necessary, I will propose an Amendment dealing with the matter; but I think, for the sake of saving time, it may be convenient to allow me to ask a question of the Government. The Committee decided yesterday that persons committed to prison under this clause for refusing to answer shall not be treated as first-class misdemeanants. Now, I want some information from right hon. Gentlemen sitting on the Front Bench opposite as to how, in their opinion, persons so committed will be entitled to be treated. My impression has been, up to the present, that they should be treated in the same way as persons committed for contempt of Court; but, on reading the Petty Sessions Act, I find that it is not at all clear that that is so. The section of the Petty Sessions Act does not use the word "contempt," and does not use any expression that would make that result necessarily follow. My apprehension is this, that the authorities in Ireland would hold that this power of committing persons for refusing to be sworn, or for refusing to answer, is a proceeding entitling them to inflict such a punishment as would be inflicted for an ordinary offence. I am sure the Government do not mean that that should be so, but that they mean that the prisoner in this case should be committed as if for contempt. However, I should like to have an express declaration from the Government on this point.

THE CHIEF SECRETARY FOR IRELAND (Mr. A. J. BALFOUR) (Manchester, E.): The hon. Gentleman is not quite correct in stating that we made an assertion that prisoners committed under this section would not be treated as first-class misdemeanants. We made no statement of that kind at all. All we said was that we would make no distinction between the treatment of persons committed under this clause and the practice prevailing under the existing law in Ireland.

MR. MAURICE HEALY: As the answer of the right hon. Gentleman gives me no information at all, I am reluctantly compelled to move an Amendment. It is in these terms—Clause 1, page 1, after the sub-clause just added, to insert the additional sub-clause—

"A person committed to prison for refusing to be sworn, or refusing to answer at an inquiry held under this section, shall be deemed, for all purposes relating to prison discipline and regulation, a person committed to prison for contempt of court."

I will, Sir, hand that Amendment in to you.

THE CHAIRMAN: I am of opinion that we have passed the point when this could be properly introduced. It is really a Proviso affecting Sub-section 2. We have come to the end of the Provisos in connection with Sub-section 2, and we have proceeded to deal with Sub-sections 3 and 4. The appropriate moment has passed for the consideration of this Amendment therefore.

MR. MAURICE HEALY: I do not attempt to question your ruling, Sir; but may I ask whether it will not be competent for me to raise this question in some form at some subsequent stage of the Committee?

THE CHAIRMAN: I should be reluctant to give a ruling of that kind, but it certainly may be possible at some other stage of the Committee to adopt the Amendment. I cannot say when. I think it is non-admissible here as a separate sub-section, as it is a Proviso that should properly be attached to Sub-section 2.

MR. MAURICE HEALY:—["Order, order!"]—As a matter of courtesy I ask to be allowed to say a word. I do not wish to discuss the ruling of the hon. Gentleman, but may I ask Gentlemen sitting on the Front Ministerial Bench how they intend to treat prisoners under this section? That is not asking a great deal—I only want information on that point.

THE ATTORNEY GENERAL FOR IRELAND (Mr. HOLMES) (Dublin University): Prisoners committed under this section will be treated in precisely the same manner as prisoners committed under the 13th section of the Petty Sessions Act, 1851.

Mr. MAURICE HEALY: I am extremely reluctant to trespass on the Committee; but will the right hon. and learned Gentleman say whether prisoners committed under the 13th section of the Petty Sessions Act, 1851, are prisoners committed for contempt of Court? Surely that is the whole question.

Mr. HOLMES: I decline to answer further.

Mr. MAURICE HEALY: Does the right hon. and learned Gentleman decline to say?

The CHAIRMAN: The Question is wholly irregular. I must call on the hon. Gentleman who has the next Amendment on the Paper.

Mr. WALLACE (Edinburgh, E.): I wish to ask, in the name of my hon. Friend the Member for Elgin and Nairn (Mr. Anderson), whether on the Amendments you have called on being rejected, the clause will stand as a whole, and he will not have an opportunity of bringing on an Amendment to part of the section? He wishes to move to omit part of the clause.

The CHAIRMAN: The Amendment now about to be moved is to omit the whole sub-section; but the Question I shall put from the Chair will be "That the words 'a witness examined under this section' shall stand part of the Clause." Any Amendment which will come after those words will be open to discussion.

Mr. P. McDONALD (Sligo, N.): I propose to say a very few words in putting this Amendment. I may say that it is well understood that, according to the Law of England, statutory powers are given under which a witness cannot be forced to give an answer that may tend to criminate himself. This is the case, not merely as to grave offences, but it is equally applicable to all ordinary offences as well as crimes. If that be so as regards ordinary offences, how much more is it desirable that the witness should be protected in regard to matters of a political nature, as it is now pretty well understood that this Act will apply to political offences, as well as to grave and serious crimes.

Mr. Holmes

The CHAIRMAN: I am not quite sure from the hon. Member's remarks whether he is addressing himself to Amendment No. 76 or 79, each of which stands in his name?

Mr. P. McDONALD: I am addressing myself to No. 76. I may be answered that the witness is protected by the concluding portion of this sub-section by the fact that the defendant may not be called on to defend himself as regards any evidence that he may have given at the preliminary examination. But I consider that that is the gravest portion of our cause of complaint, inasmuch as I consider it merely as a machine for converting a witness into an informer. Therefore, Sir, I must enter my protest against the insertion of this sub-section in the Act. It is repugnant to all common sense, as well as repugnant to the Law of England, especially in view of the manner in which the Act will be administered in Ireland, and I shall, therefore, vote against its insertion in the Act.

Amendment proposed, in pages 1 and 2 to leave out sub-section (3).—(*Mr. Peter McDonald.*)

Mr. HUNTER (Aberdeen, N.): I am aware that the answer may be made on the part of the Government that this sub-section was substantially contained in the Act of 1882. For my own part, I would reply to any statement of that kind by saying that the Act of 1882 is no authority to me. I was not in Parliament when it was discussed, and if I had been, I should have opposed every line in it, from beginning to end. I object to this sub-section, Sir, because it is an idiotic proposal. It contains this absurd proposition, that a person examined as a witness is bound to criminate himself. Now, I should like the right hon. and learned Attorney General for Ireland, or any other hon. Gentleman on the opposite side of the House, to be good enough, when he defends this clause, to point to the laws of any civilized country in which any such proposition is contained. A great deal has been made of the Scotch Laws, and we have all felt considerably humiliated by the way in which Scotland has been dragged forward in this business, because there is nothing in the administration of the law of that country that at all justifies the proposition of the Government. Let me call the attention of the Government, as they are so enamoured of the Scotch Law, to what is the Scotch Law on this point. Allison says that it is competent for a Judge to put a witness on oath; in doing so, however, the Judge must keep in view that the person who has been put on oath in regard to any crime cannot be himself tried for its commission; consequently, if the Crown, or those acting in the public interest, have put any party on oath, it must be held that they have passed from all intention of putting him on his trial, and that the oath was taken on that implied condition; if, therefore, there is any doubt as to which of the persons in custody is to be selected for trial, which is very frequently the case in offences committed by large gangs of criminals, none of them should be put on oath except such as are certainly not the intended objects of punishment. That is the Scotch Law, it is the law of every country, and it is the law of common sense. Does the right hon. and learned Gentleman the Attorney General for Ireland imagine that any person who is examined as a witness will be such a fool as to criminate himself? Now, I will suppose the case of an inquiry into a murder, and that the police have accidentally called on one of these private inquiries the very man who committed the crime. He is examined; under this law he cannot excuse himself from answering questions on the ground that his answers may tend to criminate himself; but, of course, under these circumstances, he would answer with a bold negative from beginning to end, because, if he were committed, the utmost punishment he would get would be punishment for perjury, and that would be a doubtful and distant possibility. If he were to admit his guilt he would be hanged; and, therefore, the Government are in this absurd position—that they actually expect a person who is examined as a witness to prefer the greater punishment to the lesser, and to put his own neck in the noose by which he will be hanged. The same remark applies to all serious crimes; it applies to attempts to murder; it applies to all those crimes which are visited habitually with long terms of penal servitude; and it is only in cases of comparatively small offences that a man could not distinctly gain by per-

juring himself. Now, Sir, there is another consideration. If a man gives evidence which tends to criminate himself he at once exposes himself to punishment; but if he denies the charge he has a chance of getting off, there being only a remote possibility of his being prosecuted for perjury. That is the reason why in no civilized system of jurisprudence do you find this provision requiring a man to answer questions, when they tend to criminate himself. Now, Sir, I dare say there are parents who indulge in the practice of extorting confessions from their children by beating them. Well, any man who would treat his child in that fashion would be both a brute and a fool, because the only effect of such a mode of discipline is to teach his child to be a confirmed and justifiable liar. In the same way in regard to this inquiry, no man who is summoned as a witness will criminate himself, whatever the law may be. Where is the humanity, where is the common sense, where is the justice of a provision so absurd that can have no effect at all except to do mischief? For purposes of inquiry it is utterly useless. On the face of it, it is useless, and such a provision, therefore, is one that cannot be justified by humanity, which is utterly opposed to the law of every civilized country, including the law of England, and which, if adopted as the law of this country, would be useless, except for the purpose of creating irritation and mischief.

THE CHIEF SECRETARY FOR IRELAND (Mr. A. J. BALFOUR) (Manchester, E.): The hon. and learned Gentleman who has just sat down spoke in the interest of witnesses whom he thought would be injured by this provision; but he told us, in the course of his argument, that no witness would be such a fool as to give any evidence that would criminate himself, and, if that argument was worth anything at all, it went to show that this sub-section would not injure the witness. The hon. Gentleman seemed to think that because no witness would ever give any evidence criminating himself, that, therefore, this sub-section is totally useless. Has it not occurred to the hon. Gentleman that a witness may attempt to stop the whole of an examination by alleging falsely that to answer would be to criminate himself? Does he not see that a witness, knowing that such a reply will at once stop the questions, will say that he declines to answer, because the answer will criminate himself? The whole object of the inquiry might be entirely foiled without this sub-section. The hon. and learned Gentleman went on to tell us that this provision was absolutely idiotic. Well, it has been copied verbatim from the work of Gentlemen whom he does not usually regard as the authors of that which is idiotic. It is the work of the right hon. Gentleman the Member for Derby (Sir William Harcourt), the right hon. Gentleman the Member for Bury (Sir Henry James), and the right hon. Gentleman the Member for Mid Lothian (Mr. W. E. Gladstone). If the hon. and learned Member will look for it, he will find a subsection in the Corrupt and Illegal Practices Prevention Act which says—

"A person called as a witness respecting an election, at any election court, shall not be excused from answering any question relating to any offence at or in connection with any election, on the ground that the answer thereto may tend to criminate himself."

So that that provision, if it be idiotic, is one that, at all events, has been thought sufficiently sensible by successive Parliaments to be introduced into the Legislature. The arguments of the hon. Gentleman who moved the Amendment are not really relative to this Amendment, but are relative to another Amendment that stands on the Paper lower down. The second portion of the section has been introduced by us to prevent the abuse of this provision, and will be found a sufficient protection. If, however, the Amendment now before the Committee were carried, the result would be that hon. Members opposite would not only exclude the words to which they object, but would also exclude the last five lines of the sub-section, which simply afford protection to anyone from being made to suffer any ill consequences that might otherwise result from the evidence he may give. Therefore, I think that if hon. Members who support the Amendment had reserved their observations until we had got to the Amendments numbered 79 and 82, upon which their speeches would have been relevant, and had not directed them to the whole of the sub-section, a portion of which, as I have already shown, is in the interest of those who may be summoned as wit-

nesses under the clause, they would have taken a more desirable and a more consistent course.

Mr. ATHERLEY-JONES (Durham, N.W.): The right hon. Gentleman the Chief Secretary to the Lord Lieutenant of Ireland (Mr. A. J. Balfour) has told the Committee that if the sub-section is not passed as it stands, any witness who may be called upon to attend before a Resident Magistrate, for the purposes of the intended preliminary inquiry, might stultify the whole investigation by refusing to answer such questions as might be put to him, on the fallacious ground that the answers to those questions might incriminate, or have a tendency to incriminate him. May I ask the right hon. Gentleman whether he is aware of the discretionary power which is now exercised by the Judges in reference to the questions which may be put to witnesses, and the answer to which a witness may say would have a tendency to incriminate him? According to the argument of the right hon. Gentleman it would be equally in the power of any witness in any of our Courts of Law to refuse to answer any question put to him, and successfully to refuse to do so, by merely alleging as his reason for so doing that the answer to that question would tend to incriminate himself. I would point out with regard to the Corrupt Practices Prevention Act—although that Act is an exceptional measure—the right hon. Gentleman will find, if he looks into it, that as far as that Act is concerned it does not enable proceedings of the nature proposed by this Bill to be taken against any person examined as a witness as the result of his evidence. This measure would enable a witness, as the result of his confession, to be prosecuted for murder. Now, I venture to say that I think the Amendment we are considering is a very important one, and one that well deserves to receive the consideration, and the fair consideration, of every hon. Member of this House. The sub-section it proposes to omit is one which embodies a principle involving a total departure from a long recognized and valuable principle of the Criminal Law, not only of this, but of almost every other country. Let me remind the right hon. and learned Gentleman the Attorney General sitting opposite me, that the law has invariably been most tender in its dealings with witnesses, and that it

Mr. A. J. Balfour

was not until the Reign of George III. that any witness could, by Statute, be compelled to answer a question which might even have the effect of subjecting him to a civil action, that is to say, that the Courts have always thrown their protection around any witness who has said—"If I answer the question put to me I should be exposing myself to the risk of a civil action;" and even, at the present time, as the right hon. and learned Attorney General is well aware, a witness cannot be asked a question the answer to which might expose him to a forfeiture. Much less can any witness be compelled to answer a question which may tend to incriminate himself. With regard to the sub-section under discussion, I do not hesitate to say that the protection the right hon. and learned Attorney General for Ireland has pointed out as afforded by one portion of the provision is, in reality, no protection at all. All it amounts to is this—that a witness shall not be prosecuted by means of the evidence which his own confession would afford. The right hon. and learned Gentleman must know that a witness may be asked all sorts of questions, the answers to which might enable the Crown to fill in all the essential links in a chain of evidence against a person whose own confession they have obtained without being compelled to resort to the confession itself when they had decided upon bringing him to trial. Let us see how it would work. Here is a man put into the witness-box, unsupported by his friends, much less by a solicitor or counsel, without the slightest protection being afforded to him, and then, under fear of the punishment he may receive for contempt if he should refuse to answer the questions put to him, he is compelled to disclose every fact and circumstance in relation to the matter being inquired into, and thus place himself in a position in which he may be prosecuted for an offence known to the law. May I venture, before Her Majesty's Government plunge headlong into all the consequences of the passing of this clause, to remind them of the language used by such eminent legal authorities as Lord Mansfield and Lord Eldon. I do not give the exact words, but those two Judges pointed out that not only ought no witness to be asked a question which might directly incriminate him, but they also laid it down that no one

was entitled to ask a witness any question which might tend to incriminate him; thus not only enabling a witness to refuse to answer such questions, but positively forbidding such questions to be asked. In point of fact, they went even further than this, for Lord Mansfield said he refused to allow a witness to answer a question, although on the face of the question there was no appearance of its being likely to incriminate him, on the ground that it might afford a link in the chain of evidence which might be made to incriminate him. Lord Eldon also said a person should be protected from any question not only that had a direct tendency to incriminate him, but from any question that might operate or tend towards incrimination. On these grounds, I would respectfully submit to Her Majesty's Government that they would do well to hesitate before offering their resistance to the Amendment that has been brought forward. I say, speaking as a lawyer, that while I consider it to be the duty of Her Majesty's Government to bring forward such a measure as will secure the due administration of the law, and that the measure they are now promoting shall not be rendered totally inoperative; at the same time, they are asking this House to grant them, by means of this Bill, powers of a singularly questionable character. They are refusing to allow any adequate protection to the witnesses who may be examined under this clause; and they have also refused even to allow the shorthand notes, which will form the only record of the proceedings at these preliminary inquiries, and would be the only protection to the witnesses, to be brought forward at the trial on their behalf. I say Her Majesty's Government will do well to pause before sanctioning a course that will be a complete reversal of our present mode of criminal procedure.

THE CHAIRMAN: I would here point out that while the Amendment before the Committee is that which is numbered 76 upon the Paper, hon. Gentlemen have been addressing their arguments in reality to Amendments Nos. 78 and 79. If the debate is to be continued in that fashion, I must call on hon. Members who have set down Amendments 77 and 78, or proceed to Amendment 79.

SIR GEORGE CAMPBELL (Kirkcaldy, &c.): I desire, Sir, as far as the working of this clause is concerned, to address myself to Amendment No. 76. I am greatly in favour of a judicial examination and cross-examination of prisoners; but I think that if you are to put a witness on his oath, and compel him to give evidence in which he may say he has committed some crime, and, at the same time, provide that that admission may not be used again, it is practically impossible that such a power can be placed in the hands of the Government without inevitably leading to most objectionable results. It seems to me that there is a great distinction between what is here proposed and what takes place in Scotland at preliminary inquiries before the Procurator Fiscal, because the inquiry before that official is bound to be kept secret; but there is no provision in this section that the inquiry shall be secret. If a similar provision were made here, and the inquiry was to be kept wholly secret, I could understand the theory on which the Government have proceeded, though I doubt if it is possible in practice. I cannot find, from the statement of the right hon. and learned Attorney General for Ireland, that the inquiry under this section will necessarily be secret. It may be in the power of the Resident Magistrate to exclude the public from the Court; but so far as I can see by this section that is not necessarily so. I notice that the right hon. Gentleman the late Lord Advocate (Mr. J. B. Balfour) has given Notice of an Amendment to omit this sub-section from the clause, and I am sorry he is not now present, because I think that anything he might say upon this subject would be received by the Committee as having much weight and authority. At any rate, the fact that the right hon. Gentleman has put down an Amendment to omit this sub-section is sufficient to strengthen my belief that it would not be found to be a workable provision. I do, therefore, hope Her Majesty's Government will seriously consider whether it would not better for them at least to omit the first part of this sub-section.

THE ATTORNEY GENERAL FOR IRELAND (Mr. HOLMES) (Dublin University: I would point out to the Committee that by the second part of the sub-section it is provided that anything a witness may state at a preliminary inquiry before the Resident Magistrate cannot be given in evidence against him

Sir George Campbell

on any subsequent proceeding, except on a charge of perjury. I take it that this is a substantial protection to those persons who may be so examined. In the Bill of 1882, it will be remembered that a corresponding clause to that which we are now debating was introduced by the then Government, but without the safeguard which we have provided by means of the latter part of this sub-section. At that time hon. Members in various parts of the House called the attention of those who had charge of the Bill to the fact that under that clause a poor man and an ignorant man who might be called upon to give evidence, might be entirely damnified, and made to say unwillingly, under cross-examination, a great deal that would tend to incriminate himself without his knowing it, or having the slightest idea that he was subjecting himself to a possible prosecution for crime. But, Sir, in this Bill, we have provided a remedy for such a state of things, and it was to relieve a witness from the danger thus pointed out that the latter part of this sub-section was drafted. Why is it, I would ask, that the English Law enables a man to decline to answer questions of an incriminatory character? The reason is that the evidence he might otherwise give could be used against him, and he might consequently be convicted out of his own mouth. This seems to be the foundation for the English rule of law with regard to evidence to which the hon. and learned Gentleman opposite has called attention. In this sub-section, however, we have introduced a Proviso declaring that no answer a witness may make can ever be used as evidence against him, except on a charge of perjury; and, therefore, we say we afford him every reasonable protection.

MR. CHANCE (Kilkenny, S.): The first part of the sub-section we are now discussing will have the effect of compelling a man, for the first time in the history of the English Law, to incriminate himself, and the second part of the sub-section goes on to say that the statements he may make shall not be used as evidence against him. The first provision, we are all agreed, is a most serious one; and this is the first time such a proposal has ever been brought before the House of Commons. As to the second part of the sub-section, which provides that the statements of a witness at a preliminary inquiry shall not be used against him, that, I contend, is completely illusory; because, what would happen would be this—A man would come up to be cross-examined; he would be compelled to reveal the names of all those who might afterwards be called as witnesses against him, and generally to put into the hands of the Government officials a complete brief for his own prosecution, his only protection being that his own words shall not be used against him. Now, I would ask the Committee to remember how this subject was dealt with in a Bill brought in by the right hon. and learned Member for Bury (Sir Henry James), who is now a supporter of Her Majesty's Government—the Bill I refer to having been passed into law in 1883. There it was enacted that a witness might, under certain circumstances, be compelled to answer questions incriminating or tending to incriminate him, and the Act did not say that his statements were not to be used against him; but when they wanted honestly to give the witness protection, they gave it to him in very different words from those now employed. They provided that the witness who answered truly all questions put to him, should be entitled to receive a certificate of indemnity under the hand of the Court. Now, that is a substantial provision, and very different from the present proposal, because the witness got an absolute indemnity in consideration of his having truthfully disclosed to the Court even his own criminality. It may be said that this applied only to election offences; but the answer to that statement is this—If a person has committed a serious crime, in all probability the Government know something about it, and they need not call him as a witness, but can seek for evidence elsewhere. I hope the Committee will not allow a sub-section to pass which puts a witness under a very serious disadvantage, and gives him no effectual protection whatsoever. It may, however, be deemed an advantage to pass it, and, in doing so, they will doubtless have the very valuable assistance of the right hon. and learned Member for Bury.

MR. MAURICE HEALY (Cork): Hon. Members who may follow Her Majesty's Government into the Division Lobby on this question will find that they will not, by the course they are taking with regard to this Bill, long be assisting the Government to occupy the positions they now hold on the Treasury Bench. The arguments used by the Government in support of this sub-section have been blown to pieces by subsequent speakers. The right hon. Gentleman the Chief Secretary stated at one time that if a witness under this clause had the power to refuse to answer a question, on the ground that it might tend to incriminate himself, any witness would have the power to put a stop to the whole proceeding by raising that excuse for refusing to answer any question that might be put to him. But, as hon. Members have since pointed out, this is a thing which might occur on any judicial proceeding; and yet although Law Courts have been established in this country for 700 years, I am not aware of any serious mishap to English jurisprudence owing to the fact that this principle has been maintained. If this be so, I venture to think that this contemplated Star Chamber inquiry by the Resident Magistrates would have an equally long life if the sub-section we are now opposing were omitted. That was the first argument. The second argument was founded on the Corrupt Practices Act, to which I will not refer further, my hon. Friend the Member for South Kilkenny (Mr. Chance) having shown how disingenious that argument was. In taking up the position we occupy upon this Amendment, we are fighting for one of the oldest principles of English jurisprudence. It is a principle which has existed in these countries as long as the Courts of Justice have existed. It is a principle which has been laid down and defended by the whole of the English Judges, and it is laid down in law-books that so consonant was this principle with reason, so much did it commend itself to good sense and reason, that even the notorious Judge Jeffries upheld it in several cases which came before him, refusing to allow it to be departed from, when he was trampling on a great many other principles at the bidding of his Lord. What is the reason the Government endeavour to support the position they take up? Let me call the attention of the Committee to the position in which we stand in this matter. The Government have already accepted an Amendment of my hon. Friend the Member for

South Kilkenny, declaring that at these inquiries, no person who admits himself to be the perpretator of a crime shall be examined further, but they now maintain that though a man who admits himself the author of a crime shall not be further questioned, they wish to retain the power of compelling him to admit he is the author of the crime. On what principle of logic can that be justified? If it is a reasonable thing that a man who admits himself the author of a crime should not be further pressed on points of detail connected with the crime, is it not equally reasonable and just that he shall be protected from any questions at all which would incriminate himself? How can right hon. Gentlement opposite logically defend the position they take up on this Amendment. Now, Sir, let me call attention to another consideration. The right hon. Gentleman the Chief Secretary for Ireland (Mr. A. J. Balfour), in his usual jaunty manner, states that whoever is damnified by this Proviso being included in the Bill, the man who admits his guilt cannot be damnified, because the section goes on to provide that his admission shall not afterwards be used in evidence against him. What is the good of the admission if it cannot be used in evidence against him? If you start upon the principle that a man's admission, that he is the perpetrator of a crime, shall not be used against him, and, then, say that once a man makes such an admission, he shall not be further pressed upon points of detail, what is the use of keeping in the Bill a provision that a man may be asked questions which incriminate himself. I could quite understand the adoption by the Government of the broad and naked principle, that a man should be questioned, and that his statement should be used in evidence against him. A great many reasons might be urged in favour of such a provision; but I cannot understand the logic of the present position of the Government. You have I think, struck away all foundation for the admission of this clause in the Bill; because you have utterly deprived it of any use. But Sir, the facts are not exactly as the right hon. Gentleman stated. He said a man could not suffer, if he were examined under this clause and made certain admissions. Yes; he could. The clause goes on to provide that a man may

be prosecuted for perjury, if he is guilty of it, at these inquiries. It does appear to me that the sole effect of admitting this sub-section into the clause will be that these secret inquiries will simply be machinery for creating and perpetuating perjury in Ireland; because it is preposterous, as my hon. Friends have said, to expect that a man who has committed a grave crime will come up at one of these inquiries and make admissions, which will afterwards have the effect of convicting him. It is hopeless to expect that such a state of things will arise. We know perfectly well that a man who is guilty, will in the most bare-faced way deny any connection with the offence, and that, therefore the effect of this clause will be to produce unusual and indiscriminate perjury amongst the class at whom the law should strike— namely, the perpetrators of offences.

Mr. JAMES STUART (Shoreditch, Hoxton): Mr. Courtney; this sub-section is the most serious innovation of the Criminal Law which exists in the Bill. The Act of 1882 was a temporary measure; but this is intended to be permanent. You are introducing an absolutely new principle into the Criminal Code for Ireland, and that is a most important point. It is not for a specific or immediate purpose, that this serious innovation is being introduced in the law. The Attorney General for Ireland (Mr. Holmes) wishes us to believe that this provision is for the protection of liberties. That is a most extraordinary argument, and surely must have been used sarcastically. In this case a witness is to be compelled to answer, and we are to suppose his evidence cannot be used against him. I submit that that is a technical way of looking at the law. The object of the law does not seem to me to be merely to hinder the words of an accused person being brought in evidence against him at a trial, but to be this—that you are to prevent the authorities obtaining evidence against a man through compelling him to answer questions concerning his guilt. It is not a question whether you use the evidence, but whether you get a clue to that particular evidence. There is another point I wish to urge upon the attention of the Committee, and it is an important one; because under this clause you can say to a witness—" Are you guilty; did you do this?" and if he

Mr. Maurice Healy

says "No," and afterwards it is proved that he is guilty, he can be punished in addition for perjury. That is a great power to hold over a witness, to make him state what may incriminate himself. You have therefore got a screw to put on a witness. On these grounds I shall certainly support the Amendment, and I cannot conclude without saying how remarkable it does seem to me that these great innovations should be introduced into the Constitution of this country by Gentlemen on the other side of the House.

THE FIRST LORD OF THE TREASURY (Mr. W. H. SMITH) (Strand, Westminster): I venture to appeal most earnestly to hon. Gentlemen to conclude this particular debate. It will be in the knowledge of hon. Gentlemen below the Gangway opposite, and hon. Gentlemen above the Gangway opposite, that the arguments we have heard upon this Amendment are arguments that have been repeatedly used over and over again against this sub-section. I quite admit that hon. Gentlemen are within their right in opposing this sub-section; but I think that out of regard to the conduct of the Business in this House, it is necessary we should come to a decision upon this sub-section. The question involved has been argued at great length during the last four or five days, and I make this appeal in the hope that the Committee will listen to it, and allow a Division to be now taken.

MR. J. E. ELLIS (Nottingham, Rushcliffe): I rise to protest against the action of the right hon. Gentleman, and I wish to protest against it in the strongest manner consistent with courtesy. The right hon. Gentleman has absented himself, for reasons best known to himself, during the best part of the afternoon; and he then comes in from behind the Chair for a moment or two, and says the arguments have been repeated at great length. I have been sitting here for some time, and I can tell the right hon. Gentleman to his face that the arguments have not been repeated; and I say that the dignity of this Assembly is lowered by the right hon. Gentleman, occupying the position he does, using the language he does to hon. Gentlemen who sit on this side of the House. We are sent here by our constituents to perform a duty, and that duty we shall perform. The right hon. Gen-

tleman represents in this House the shopkeepers of the Strand; but he has no right to use the language of menace that he constantly does to Members on this side of the House, and I venture to say he will not improve the chance of this Bill making progress unless he very much alters his style.

MR. HOLMES: I have been in attendance during the entire course of the debate. The hon. Member had unquestionably heard a great many of the arguments used in reference to this clause, used again and again. ["No!"] I doubt very much if the hon. Member has been in the House one third of the time I have.

MR. J. E. ELLIS: I have been here since half-past two.

MR. HOLMES: I am speaking of the last five days. The point to which I wish to call the attention of the Committee is, that the observations made by hon. Gentlemen opposite may be very pertinent indeed to several Amendments on the Paper, but they seem to me to be in no way pertinent to the Amendment which is now before the Committee, which deals with the clause as a whole. I think we might now be allowed to go to a Division.

MR. W. H. SMITH: I rise to move that the words down to "shall," in line 24, stand part of the clause.

Question proposed, "That the Question that the words 'A witness examined under this section shall' stand part of the Clause be now put."—(*Mr. W. H. Smith.*)

MR. T. P. O'CONNOR: As a point of Order, Mr. Courtney, may I ask if you have put the Question in the terms handed to the Chair?

THE CHAIRMAN: Yes.

Question put.

MR. ANDERSON (Elgin and Nairn) (speaking sitting, with head covered): May I ask whether this proposal will exclude my Amendment No. 78a?

THE ATTORNEY GENERAL (Sir RICHARD WEBSTER) (Isle of Wight): It has been already decided in your absence.

MR. J. E. ELLIS: Order, order! You are not the Chairman.

THE CHAIRMAN: The Amendment 78a could not have been moved in any case; but the Amendments 79 and 80, which are really Amendments which have been discussed for the last hour, can still be taken.

MR. ANDERSON: May I ask if Amendment 82 can still be taken?

THE CHAIRMAN: 82 may still be taken.

The Committee *divided:*—Ayes 265; Noes 162: Majority 103.—(Div. List, No. 133.)

Question put, "That the words 'A witness examined under this section shall' stand part of the Clause."

The Committee *divided:*—Ayes 267; Noes 167: Majority 100.—(Div. List, No. 134.)

MR. P. McDONALD (Sligo): I beg to move to leave out the word "not" in line 24. Notwithstanding the result of the Division which has just been taken, I claim that it is contrary to the English idea of justice, and the English idea of the just administration of the law, that a witness should be obliged to give evidence that may criminate himself. Why apply to Ireland a provision which the English sense of honour and justice would not permit for a single day? Therefore it is I beg to move the omission of the word "not" from this sub-section.

Amendment proposed, in page 1, line 24, leave out the word "not."—(*Mr. P. McDonald.*)

Question proposed, "That the word 'not' stand part of the Clause."

THE CHIEF SECRETARY FOR IRELAND(Mr. A. J. BALFOUR)(Manchester, E.): The whole question of how far a witness should be obliged to give evidence tending to criminate himself was discussed on the question whether this sub-section should stand part of the Bill. The question has been fully debated, and I trust the Committee should come to a decision upon it. In any case, the Government feel they have nothing to add to the statement they have already made.

MR. T. P. O'CONNOR (Liverpool, Scotland): I will just show the Committee how the question was discussed. I do not like interrupting opponents when speaking; but I do regret I did not interrupt the right hon. Gentleman (Mr. A. J. Balfour) when he was making his previous speech, because he said the proposal contained in this sub-section

The Chairman

was exactly the same as one contained in several Acts of Parliament already in force. The right hon. Gentleman, by way of proving that statement—that grossly inaccurate statement—professed to read a section of the Corrupt Practices Prevention Act, 1883. I thought of asking the right hon. Gentleman not to stop reading at the point he did stop; but my memory, which was possibly a little blurred by what had happened, did not serve me at the moment. I did not think the right hon. Gentleman would have been—I was about to use an un-Parliamentary expression, but I will say I thought he would have been ingenuous, and frank, and honest enough to tell the Committee the whole meaning of the clause, and not leave upon the Committee a false impression. What did the right hon. Gentleman do? He only read two or three lines of the clause, in order to establish the proposition that, under existing laws, a man was bound to criminate himself. Why, Sir, if he had read the concluding portions of the clause, he would have been able to show to the Committee the very opposite to the proposition he was trying to lay down. He would have been able to show that, under the law which he quoted, a man was safeguarded in the most cautious manner from the very thing he is obliged to do under this Act—namely, criminate himself. The right hon. Gentleman read the following portion of the 59th section of the Corrupt Practices Prevention Act:—

"A person who is called as a witness respecting an election before any election court shall not be excused from answering any question relating to any offence at or connected with such election, on the ground that the answer thereto may criminate or tend to criminate himself, or on the ground of privilege."

Why was the right hon. Gentleman not honest enough to read the rest of the section? What are the other words?

"Provided that (a) the witness who answers truly all questions which he is required by the election court to answer shall be entitled to receive a certificate of indemnity under the hand of a member of the court, stating that such witness has so answered; and (b) an answer by a person to a question put by or before any election court shall not, except in the case of any criminal proceedings for perjury in respect of such evidence, be in any proceeding, civil or criminal, admissible in the evidence against him."

Not only is the witness who gives evidence under this clause saved from being prosecuted afterwards, but he is actually guaranteed his expenses, in case any prosecution is brought against him. Subsection 2 of the 59th clause of the Act says—

"Where a person has received such a certificate of indemnity in relation to an election, and any legal proceeding is at any time instituted against him for any offence under the Corrupt Practices Prevention Acts, or this Act committed by him previously to the date of the certificate at or in relation to the said election, the court having cognizance of the case shall on proof of the certificate"—

Now mark these words—

"stay the proceeding, and may in their discretion award to the said person such costs as he may have been put to in the proceeding."

It is in this state of things that the right hon. Gentleman the First Lord of the Treasury (Mr. W. H. Smith), without hearing the arguments, says the question has been sufficiently discussed. I must say that I never, in all my seven years' experience of this House, heard a Gentleman occupying so important a position as that of Chief Secretary for Ireland make so unfair and uncandid a use of a section in the Act as the right hon. Gentleman (Mr. A. J. Balfour) has done to-day. I do not know whether we are to be treated to another sudden incursion of the First Lord of the Treasury, who, in spite of the reproof you found it necessary to administer to him a night or two ago, seems determined to revolutionize by force the jurisprudence of the last seven centuries; but, nevertheless, I intend to stubbornly resist as long as I can this proposal, and make manifest to the country its real character and purpose.

MR. O'DOHERTY (Donegal, N.): Upon the proposition to leave out the word "not," I do not intend to weary the Committee by any long dissertation upon the history of this Bill, or upon its effect upon the British Constitution Several times the Attorney General for Ireland has said that the statement a witness may make cannot be used against him; but he never emphasized the proposed words, "used in evidence against him."

It being a quarter of an hour before Six of the clock, the Chairman left the Chair to report Progress; Committee to sit again upon *Friday*.

House adjourned at one minute to Six o'clock.

HOUSE OF LORDS,

Thursday, 12th May, 1887.

MINUTES.]—Public Bills—*Second Reading*—Markets and Fairs (Weighing of Cattle) (72).
Third Reading — Customs Consolidation Act (1876) Amendment * (71), and *passed*.

BANKRUPTCY OFFICES (SITES) BILL.

Ordered, That Standing Order No. 93 be suspended, and that any petitions praying to be heard against the Bill be received by this House which shall be deposited in the Private Bill Office before three o'clock in the afternoon on or before *Friday* the 20*th instant*.

MARKETS AND FAIRS (WEIGHING OF CATTLE) BILL.

(*The Earl of Camperdown.*)
(NO. 72.) SECOND READING.

Order of the Day for the Second Reading read.

THE EARL OF CAMPERDOWN, in moving that the Bill be now read a second time, said, it was a Bill to amend the law with respect to the weighing of cattle in markets and fairs. It was proposed to apply the Bill to all legal markets and fairs in which tolls were for the time being authorized to be taken by any Company, Corporation, or person, every such Company, Corporation, or person being called "the market authority." In every market or fair to which the Bill applied, the market authority should provide and maintain sufficient and proper buildings or places for weighing cattle brought for sale within the market or fair, and should keep therein machines and weights proper for that purpose, and should appoint proper persons to afford the use of such machines to the public for weighing cattle as might be from time to time required. If the market authority failed to comply with the provisions of this section, it should not be lawful for them to demand, receive, or recover any toll whatever in respect of any cattle brought to the market or fair for sale, so long as such failure continued. The cattle were to be weighed at the option of the seller or buyer, and persons appointed by the market authority to weigh cattle sold in the market or fair refusing to weigh cattle, or to give tickets specifying the true weight of the cattle weighed, should be liable on summary conviction to a fine not exceeding £5. It was unnecessary to take up their Lordships' time by going into details in regard to the Bill; but the question of the weighing of cattle had been for some time under the consideration of agriculturists in this country, and it had been satisfactorily adopted in the United States and elsewhere. During the severe agricultural depression, it had been found that, under the present system, farmers were very often unable to sell their cattle to advantage, and it was very desirable that the buyer and seller, if they wished it, should be able to know what exactly was the weight of the animals that were changing hands. This he could do, if he had the option, for a small toll, of weighing his cattle, as was done in America. The Central Chamber of Agriculture had discussed the matter, and passed a Resolution in favour of a measure of the sort; and the Royal Agricultural Society had determined to offer two prizes for the best machines for weighing cattle. He believed the Bill would be found of a very useful character, though it was not at all ambitious in appearance. The noble Earl concluded by moving the second reading.

Moved, "That the Bill be now read 2ᵃ."
—(*The Earl of Camperdown*.)

Lord BRAMWELL said, he was entirely opposed to the Bill, and hoped that their Lordships would not pass it. It was a proposal to put a duty and burthen on the owners of existing fairs and markets to which they were not liable. It applied to them provisions in the Fairs and Markets Clauses Act which were incorporated in every Bill that passed Parliament for the purpose of establishing a fair or market. When those clauses were so applied, they worked no injustice, because people came to Parliament for powers to establish a fair or market knowing on what terms they could have their market or fair if it was granted, and if they did not like those terms, they could leave the matter alone. But the Bill was to apply to fairs and markets already in existence, and which might have been in existence for 500 years. It would, therefore, impose upon market proprietors a duty to which they were not at present liable. Whether it was to be profitable or not to the person who owned the

market or fair, he had to provide, according to this Bill, sufficient and proper buildings for the weighing of cattle, and machines and weights for this purpose. Was it right that their Lordships should impose that duty on the market proprietor? If this Bill passed, the result might be that it might not be worth while for the proprietor to keep open his market or fair. If providing these machines would be compensated for by the tolls for the use of them, they would be provided without an Act of Parliament. On the other hand, if such machines would not pay their expenses, it would be unfair to put the burden of providing them upon the owner of the market. The Bill would apply to all markets—a fish market and a vegetable market, as well as to a cattle market; and he noticed that cattle included horses, asses, and so on, and why horses and asses required weighing he could not understand. The measure, as the noble Earl had said, though not ambitious, was unreasonable, and therefore he moved its rejection.

Earl SPENCER said, the principle of the Bill was of some importance. The noble and learned Lord (Lord Bramwell) had made some criticisms of great force which were well worthy of attention; but he was sure his noble Friend the Earl of Camperdown did not propose that the measure should apply to fish or butter markets. The Bill might be rather of too far a reaching nature in its present shape; and he hoped that, while supporting the second reading, it would be considerably amended in Committee. It was important that Parliament should not throw cold water on the growing desire which was finding expression among intelligent men connected with agriculture, that farmers should sell their cattle by live weight when they used the market. He (Earl Spencer) was strongly in favour of the principle enabling the farmer to adopt that system; because it eliminated one of the elements of uncertainty in the sale of cattle. He knew that many farmers entirely objected to that method, believing that they could judge of the weight of an animal much better than the butcher. But the fact was that the butcher, from his continual experience, was far better able than the farmer to estimate the weight of a live animal. He, therefore, considered it would be an immense advantage to the farmers of

The Earl of Camperdown

this country, if they fell in with the fashion of weighing their cattle, as was done in America, and by many agriculturists now in this country, who had found how valuable that system was. At the same time, he admitted that that was rather an early day to force such provisions as those contained in the Bill upon the proprietors of every market and fair. At present, the matter was in an experimental stage; but they wished to induce farmers to take it up. He thought it would be rather hard to ask every market, however small, to provide weighing places for cattle. At the same time, when public opinion advanced a little more, it would be found indispensable, he believed, that all large markets, where cattle were sold, should have the means of weighing the animals. He did not know whether it was possible to modify the Bill in such a manner as to withdraw from it some of the grave difficulties which he could see would be urged against it; but he should be sorry to see the Bill thrown out at the present stage. As far as he was concerned, therefore, while admitting that great difficulties and objections lay in the way, he hoped the Bill would be read a second time, in order that its provisions might be fairly considered by the agricultural world.

EARL NELSON said, that, as an instance of the hardship that would ensue upon the carrying out of the measure, he would put before their Lordships the case of a charity school supported by tolls levied on a particular fair. These tolls had fallen in recent years to about £30 a-year. That school would be practically disendowed if, in addition to the small number of cattle sold, the authorities of the fair were obliged to go to the expense of providing weighing machines, or, in default, to lose the tolls of the fair. He did not think the Bill, being merely a tentative measure, ought to touch small fairs at the present time, because great cases of hardship, such as he had shown, might be inflicted.

THE EARL OF POWIS said, he supported the second reading, and regarded the Bill as a not unreasonable extension of the existing law, which required weighing machines to be provided for all other commodities. It would be quite reasonable that a fee should be imposed for animals weighed.

It would be easy in Committee to protect the owners of the smaller markets.

THE EARL OF JERSEY, in reply to the objections urged by the noble and learned Lord opposite (Lord Bramwell), said, he would point out that the Bill was one which might very well be amended in Committee. He (the Earl of Jersey) was the owner of a market himself, and should not object to have the Bill applied to him. A few years ago the Privy Council compelled the owners of markets to pave their markets, and this was only another step in advance. He agreed with the view, that it would be a very good thing if public opinion could be advanced in this direction.

LORD LECONFIELD said, he trusted the Bill would be read a second time. Some time ago he sold a number of bullocks to a certain butcher for £19 each; but eight others, for which he was only offered £18 10s. per head, he retained. Ten days or a fortnight afterwards, he sent those eight bullocks to a Farmers' Supply Association, through whom, curiously enough, they found their way to the same butcher. Those bullocks were sold by live weight, and he realized for each animal £21 19s. 8d.

LORD STANLEY OF ALDERLEY also supported the second reading of the Bill. He knew of a market where heavy tolls were taken and no accommodation given of any kind; the open street was the market. In that district a farmer had provided himself with a weighing machine. At present, in the absence of weighing machines, farmers were at a great disadvantage with the butchers.

LORD BALFOUR (LORD in WAITING) said, he was authorized by the Local Government Board to ask their Lordships to allow the Bill to be read a second time, very much on the grounds mentioned by the noble Earl on the Bench opposite (Earl Spencer). At the same time it must be understood that it is not intended, by reading the Bill a second time, to approve of all the provisions it contained, or to go the whole length that it would go if it were passed exactly as it stood. There was no doubt whatever there were great complaints on the part of farmers and others connected with agriculture that they did not get the full value of their fat stock —for this reason, that those who bought from them had greater experience than they in estimating the weight of the cattle, and were apt to overreach—he used the word in no bad sense—and sometimes to take advantage of them. There was, at the same time, a growing public opinion among those interested in agriculture in favour of buying and selling more by live weight than had been the practice in the past. It would, therefore, be very undesirable if this House by its action were to do anything to prejudice the question or retard the advance of public opinion in that direction. He did not think the House was prepared to go the whole length that the noble and learned Lord opposite (Lord Bramwell) had gone in his opposition to the Bill; because it would not be reasonable that market proprietors should have the power to say that there should be no change. In asking the House to assent to the second reading, he would, at the same time, ask the noble Earl (the Earl of Camperdown) if he would be good enough to postpone the Committee stage for some time, in order to afford some opportunity for the consideration of its provisions. He would also suggest to him whether, for this year, his purpose would not be served by this discussion, and by the Bill being read a second time. He was informed that there was to be a Commission shortly to consider the whole question of markets and tolls, and, perhaps, it was desirable that the Legislature should allow the question to stand over until the Commission had examined the matter, and reported upon it.

The Earl of CAMPERDOWN, in reply, said, he hoped the noble and learned Lord (Lord Bramwell) would, upon further consideration, take a more favourable view of his proposals, and not push his opposition so far as to ask their Lordships not to read the Bill a second time. Nothing like confiscation of any rights was contemplated, and the proprietors of fairs and markets would be empowered to charge proper tolls for the accommodation afforded. With regard to what had been said by the noble Lord opposite, he readily admitted that the Bill, as it stood now, applying to all markets and fairs, was too wide; but if were thought desirable, small fairs and markets could be exempted from the provisions of the Bill, and he was perfectly willing, before going into Com-

Lord Balfour

mittee, to introduce words to exclude from its scope certain small fairs, which a charge of even £25 or £30 would probably kill. Such exemptions were, perhaps, specially necessary in regard to small fairs and markets in Ireland; but he understood that, in Dublin, the principle of the Bill was already in operation, and worked satisfactorily. In regard to postponing the Committee stage, he could not see the advantage of waiting until such time as the Commission which was not yet appointed had reported; but he was quite prepared to postpone the Committee stage for some weeks, at all events, in order to give agriculturists throughout the country an opportunity of expressing an opinion in regard to the measure.

Lord BRAMWELL said, that, having regard to the general current of the discussion, he should not persevere in his opposition to the second reading; but would content himself in expressing his regret that nobody seemed to think it a matter of any consequence that a burden should be put upon a man whether he liked it or not.

Motion *agreed to;* Bill read 2ª accordingly.

METROPOLIS (STREET IMPROVEMENTS) — THE COLONNADES OF BURLINGTON HOUSE, AND TEMPLE BAR.—QUESTION.—OBSERVATIONS.

The Earl of MILLTOWN, in rising to ask Her Majesty's Government, Why the colonnades of Burlington House, which were temporarily placed on the river terrace of Battersea Park many years ago, have been suffered to lie there ever since neglected and uncared for; and whether there was any intention of erecting these beautiful works of art, as originally proposed, in the Park; and, if so, when; also to ask what had become of Temple Bar, and whether that historic monument has met with a fate similar to that which had befallen the colonnades of Burlington House? said, that the façade of Burlington House, which had been described by an eminent authority as one of the finest architectural monuments in Europe, was still lying derelict on the banks of the Thames, Burlington House having been pulled down in 1866. Of this façade Horace Walpole had also said—"We have few examples of architecture more antique and imposing." It had been taken to Battersea Park, where it had been intended to erect it as a summer house; but it had been lying there utterly uncared for and exposed to every chance. Boys with hobnail boots ran from one end of the stones to the other; and, in consequence, the façade had been seriously injured, and in a short time would be absolutely destroyed. With regard to Temple Bar, it was nine years since that gross act of vandalism had been perpetrated by which Wren's beautiful arch had been taken down and the hideous griffin put in its place, which now disfigured and obstructed the thoroughfare. Where Temple Bar now was nobody seemed to know; probably, it had met with a fate similar to that of the colonnades. As one who had passed many years of his life almost under the shadow of Temple Bar, he ventured to hope that his noble Friend would assure him that the Government would allow it to be placed in the care of the Benchers of the Temple, who would be only too glad to take charge of it, and give it an appropriate home within their domains.

LORD HENNIKER, in reply, said, that the stones which formerly composed the colonnades of Burlington House—a colonnade of whose artistic merit the noble Earl had spoken so highly—were laid on the river bank at Battersea Park in 1868, and were there still. It was decided by Lord John Manners, then First Commissioner of Works, to save this valued architectural work, and it was absolutely necessary to remove it to make room for the new buildings. It was accordingly taken down with great care—each stone was marked so as to go into its proper place again—and it was removed, with the archway and the two lodges, at no small expense, to Battersea Park, as the only available place at the time. It was not removed, as the noble Lord supposed, with any definite plan for its re-erection. He must, however, remind the noble Earl that the structure had not been complete in itself; it depended greatly on the brick wall facing Piccadilly, which, of course, was not saved. When the colonnade was taken down, it was found that a great deal of it was useless; the balustrade was worn and broken, and a great part of it was carted away as rubbish. In fact, it would not have been possible to re-erect it without

considerable renovation. The question of re-erecting the colonnade and archway had been considered over and over again. Many proposals had been made, such as making it the river gateway to the Park, making a picturesque ruin of it, as the noble Lord had stated, making a summer house of it, and so on; but all the proposals had been rejected, not only on the ground of the expense they would involve, but also because they were unsuitable to the character of the architecture. It was even proposed to sell it, if a proper place could be found for it, rather than allow the stones to lie where they were. As a matter of fact, it had been designed for Burlington House, and it was most difficult to find any other suitable site for it now that Burlington House was rebuilt. Under these circumstances, the First Commissioner of Works did not propose at present to take any steps to re-erect the building. However, if his noble Friend would make any suggestion to the First Commissioner, he was quite ready to take any proposal which might be put before him by the noble Earl into consideration. As to Temple Bar, he could only repeat what his right hon. Friend the First Commissioner had said, last year, in the House of Commons. It was to the effect that Temple Bar was the property of the Corporation of the City of London, and that it was removed by them. Under these circumstances, he could not, of course, give the noble Earl the information he desired. He had been favoured, however, with the following letter from the Corporation of the City of London, in which they gave the desired information:—

"Guildhall, London, E.C.,
"May 11, 1887.

"Dear Sir,—With reference to Lord Milltown's Question, which appears in to-day's Lords' Minutes, I have the honour to inform you that Temple Bar was taken down in 1878, a careful key drawing was made, and the stones so numbered that they could be erected thereby in their original order. The stones were deposited on some vacant land belonging to the Corporation near Farringdon Street, and arranged in such a way as to be readily and continuously available for re-erection. Many different sites have been proposed for this purpose, but there have been objections to them all. The greatest care was taken to preserve the stones in their removal; but it was found, as a matter of fact, that the stones had suffered much more from atmospheric causes and decay, and were far more chipped and injured, than there was any reason to anticipate from the general appearance of the building when standing. This, of course, will very greatly increase the cost of re-erection. It is estimated that the cost of re-erecting the old materials would be about double the cost of a similar structure new, say about £2,000.

" I have the honour to remain,
    " Yours faithfully,
        " G. PRIOR GOLDNEY,
            " Remembrancer,

"To the Right Hon. D. R. Plunket, M.P.,
    " First Commissioner of Works."

He thought that that letter would give the nformat n required by the noble Earli   io

THE EARL OF MILLTOWN asked whether, if the Office of Works was unwilling, the Government would allow anyone else to make use of the colonnade ?

LORD HENNIKER said, he had already stated that the Office of Works had considered the proposal to sell the stones, but without effect; if, however, a proper offer were made, and a guarantee that a proper site was provided were given, the Government would be prepared to consider the matter.

THE EARL OF ROSEBERY asked, what the expense would be of repairing the colonnade of Burlington House ? He had reason to believe it was past praying for.

LORD HENNIKER said, he did not know that he could give the noble Earl opposite any better answer than that when a proposal had been made some years ago, to erect this building in Regent's Park, Mr. Taylor, the able architect of the Office of Works, with whom the noble Earl was no doubt well acquainted, had made an estimate, and had calculated that the expense of re-erecting it where it now was would be £2,500, and if it were removed some four miles, that was to say, to Regent's Park, £3,000.

House adjourned at half past Five o'clock, till To-morrow, a quarter past Ten o'clock.

HOUSE OF COMMONS,

Thursday, 12th May, 1887.

MINUTES.]—SELECT COMMITTEE—Army and Navy Estimates, *appointed.*
SUPPLY—*considered in Committee*—CIVIL SERVICE ESTIMATES; CLASS VII. — MISCELLANEOUS.

Lord Henniker

PUBLIC BILLS — *Ordered — First Reading —* East India Stock Commission * [263].
Second Reading—Duke of Connaught's Leave [228].
Committee—Municipal Corporations Acts (Ireland) Amendment (No. 2) * [176]—R.P.
Third Reading—Colonial Service (Pensions) * [251], and *passed.*
PROVISIONAL ORDER BILL—*Report*—Pier and Harbour * [222].

QUESTIONS.

EMIGRATION FROM IRELAND, JANUARY TO APRIL, 1887.

MR. J. E. ELLIS (Nottingham, Rushcliffe) asked the Chief Secretary to the Lord Lieutenant of Ireland, What was the number of emigrants from Ireland during each of the months of January, February, March, and April, 1887 ?

THE PARLIAMENTARY UNDER SECRETARY (Colonel KING-HARMAN) (Kent, Isle of Thanet) (who replied) said : The numbers of emigrants from Ireland during the period named appear to have been as follows :—January, 1,678 ; February, 2,749 ; March, 7,147 ; and April, 18,968.

INDIA—THE FOREST SERVICE—PENSION REGULATIONS.

MR. HOWARD VINCENT (Sheffield, Central) asked the Under Secretary of State for India, Why the Pension Regulations of the Forest Service in India are based on a considerably lower scale than those now obtaining in the Public Works Department ; and, if, having regard to the fact that the European officers in both Services are trained in an analogous manner, and that the duties of Foresters involve much hardship, solitude, and exposure, he will consider the advisability of taking steps to remove this distinction ?

THE UNDER SECRETARY OF STATE (Sir JOHN GORST) (Chatham) : I find, upon inquiry, that the Questions which the hon. Member has addressed to me are among those which the Government of India has submitted to the Public Service Commission. The attention of that Commission is specially directed to placing Departments, as regards recruitment and future conditions of service, upon a full satisfactory basis. Alleged existing grievances as to conditions of service and retirement in various Departments are being considered from this point of view. The Secretary of

State cannot, therefore, express any opinion upon the matter till the Report of the Commission is made.

THE CURRENCY COMMISSION.

COLONEL LLOYD ANSTRUTHER (Suffolk, Woodbridge) asked Mr. Chancellor of the Exchequer, Whether, having regard to the very considerable public interest taken in the matter, he will arrange that the proceedings of the " Currency Commission," of which Lord Herschell is Chairman, be public, and that it do not sit with closed doors, as was the case when Mr. Arthur Balfour was Chairman of the Commission ; and, whether he will arrange that the proceedings of the Commission, with the evidence already taken before it, be printed and circulated ?

THE CHANCELLOR of the EXCHEQUER (Mr. GOSCHEN) (St. George's, Hanover Square): The proceedings of Royal Commissions are invariably conducted in private, and it would be contrary to precedent to admit the public The accommodation at the disposal of the Commission would, moreover, be inadequate for such a purpose. I understand that the Commission purpose, at an early date, to make an interim Report to Her Majesty of their proceedings.

ARMY — AUXILIARY FORCES — REMOVAL OF THE WEXFORD MILITIA FOR TRAINING.

MR. W. REDMOND (Fermanagh, N.) asked the Secretary of State for War, If he will state why the Wexford Militia are to removed this year from the town of Wexford for their training ?

THE FINANCIAL SECRETARY, WAR DEPARTMENT (Mr. BRODRICK) (Surrey, Guildford) (who replied) said : The 3rd Battalion of the Royal Irish Regiment will this year be trained at Duncannon Fort instead of Wexford, because there is no suitable rifle range available at the latter place.

LAW AND JUSTICE—CULPABLE NEGLIGENCE—GENTLEMAN CADET WARD.

MR. SHIRLEY (Yorkshire, W.R., Doncaster) asked the Secretary of State for War, Whether it is intended to take any criminal proceedings against, or otherwise to secure the proper punishment of, Gentleman Cadet Ward, for the culpable negligence by which he

shot an errand boy, named William Vicars, at Woolwich, on Saturday, 7th May?

THE SECRETARY OF STATE (Mr. E. STANHOPE)(Lincolnshire, Horncastle): This matter has been somewhat exaggerated. The boy Vicars did not fall down insensible, and his injury is, fortunately, not dangerous. Compensation has been offered and accepted, and the police have withdrawn from interference. Although it has not been deemed necessary to detain Gentleman Cadet Ward in arrest he has been most seriously cautioned as to his future conduct. His behaviour has been hitherto most exemplary, and the recollection of his indescribable folly will be in itself a severe punishment to him.

ARMY MEDICAL SERVICE—RELATIVE RANK.

DR. CLARK (Caithness) asked the Secretary of State for War, Whether, considering the great dissatisfaction that exists amongst medical students and the Medical Profession generally at the abolition of relative rank, which dissatisfaction may seriously diminish the number of candidates for the Army Medical Service, he will advise Her Majesty to issue a Warrant conferring honorary rank on all medical officers, and place them at least in as good a position as the officers in the Commissariat, Ordnance, and Pay Departments?

THE SECRETARY OF STATE (Mr. E. STANHOPE)(Lincolnshire, Horncastle): I have said many times that the abolition of relative rank has not in any way altered the position or status of medical officers ; and I have no reason to suppose that these officers are desirous of being called by titles so dissociated from the duties of their honourable Profession as those of Colonel, Major, and Captain. These titles are, however, necessary in the case of other Departments, whose officers, unlike those of the Medical Department, do not belong to a recognized Profession.

LOSS OF LIFE AT SEA—THE SELECT COMMITTEE.

MR. FINLAY (Inverness, &c.) asked the Secretary to the Board of Trade, Whether he has ascertained that there is serious dissatisfaction with the limited scope of the inquiry to be conducted by the Select Committee on Loss of Life at Sea; and, whether that scope will be extended to include inquiry into loss of life and property cause by collision, and the prevention of such loss?

THE SECRETARY (Baron HENRY DE WORMS) (Liverpool, East Toxteth): In answer to my hon. Friend, I have to say that the Reference to the Select Committee has been enlarged, and now includes almost everything which is not within the scope of the Royal Commission to inquire into Loss of Life at Sea. The question of collisions involves international considerations as to possible modifications of the Rule of the Road at Sea. The advantages which might accrue from any such alterations would have to be carefully weighed against the possible disadvantage of changing Rules which are well known and adopted by all maritime countries, and by seamen in all parts of the world.

AUSTRALIAN COLONIES—NORTH QUEENSLAND.

MR. McDONALD CAMERON (Wick, &c.) asked the Secretary of State for the Colonies, What steps the Government propose to take in connection with the Separation Petition received from the people of North Queensland, advocating the formation of that part of Australia into a new Colony?

THE SECRETARY OF STATE (Sir HENRY HOLLAND) (Hampstead): I have fixed a day on which to receive and hear the views of the promoters of the separation of North Queensland; but I am advised that Her Majesty's Government can take no step without Imperial legislation, and I must add that such legislation could hardly be resorted to without some prior resolution, in favour of the change, being passed by the Colonial Legislature.

MR. McDONALD CAMERON asked if the right hon. Gentleman would present the Correspondence which had taken place on the matter?

SIR HENRY HOLLAND: At present I can see no objection; but I would rather defer an answer until I have seen the deputation.

THE MAGISTRACY (IRELAND) — MR. TURNER, R.M., DRUMSNA.

MR. COX (Clare, E.) (for Mr. O'KELLY) Roscommon, N.) asked the Chief Secretary to the Lord Lieutenant of Ireland, Whether his attention had been called to the refusal of Mr. Turner, R.M., to grant an information against Francis Cooke, a bailiff, charged with presenting a loaded revolver at Mr. Veich Simpson, of Drumsna; whether a number of witnesses swore that Francis Cooke and some companions had driven into the village of Drumsna and called out for Mr. Simpson; whether, when Mr. Simpson presented himself, Francis Cooke drew a revolver and presented it at Simpson; whether Mr. Turner, R.M., refused an information against Cooke, on the ground that—

"Though the revolver was produced and flourished by Cooke, to the danger of a crowd of persons near Mr. Dalrymple's door, still as there was no actual proof that he presented it at Simpson, he could not return Cooke for trial;"

and, whether the Government propose to take any further action in the matter?

THE PARLIAMENTARY UNDER SECRETARY (Colonel KING-HARMAN) (Kent, Isle of Thanet) (who replied) said: The Resident Magistrate reports that he did not refuse information on the ground alleged in the Question, but because there was no evidence to prove the charge. The three witnesses produced by Simpson in support of the charge denied that Cooke had presented the revolver at him or anybody else; and there was, therefore, no ground for returning information.

MR. COX asked, could no prosecution be taken for drawing a revolver in a crowd because he did not present the revolver at any individual in the crowd?

COLONEL KING-HARMAN said, there was no evidence to prove that the man presented the revolver at Simpson, or at anyone at all.

MR. COX: Will the right hon. and gallant Gentleman inquire into the truth of the statement that Cooke did draw his revolver in a crowd?

COLONEL KING-HARMAN: Will the hon. Gentleman put the Question down?

FRANCE — ASSIMILATION OF HOME AND COLONIAL CUSTOMS TARIFFS.

MR. KNOWLES (Salford, W.) asked the Under Secretary of State for Foreign Affairs, Whether the French Government have assimilated their Home and Colonial Customs Tariffs; and, whether such assimilation will

Mr. Finlay

shortly come into force in their Asiatic Settlements, and impose differential duties against British trade?

THE UNDER SECRETARY OF STATE (Sir JAMES FERGUSSON) (Manchester, N.E.): The French Government have not assimilated their Home and Colonial Tariffs. It is enacted that from and after June 1, 1887, the General Tariff of France shall be applied to all foreign goods imported into Cochin-China, Cambodia, Annam, and Tonquin, with such exceptions as may be considered advisable by the French Indo-Chinese Authorities, and be sanctioned by the French Council of State. French goods entering Indo-China will be free of duty, unless they come under the exceptional rates above-mentioned, whether they are imported under the French or a foreign flag. Since September 6, 1886, French ships entering ports in Annam and Tonquin have been liable to pay tonnage dues at the rate of 2 francs per ton for three months, or 50 centimes per ton per voyage. Foreign ships pay double—namely, 4 francs in the first case, and 1 franc in the second.

ADMIRALTY—EXAMINATION OF MIDSHIPMEN IN SEAMANSHIP.

MR. CRAIG SELLAR (Lanarkshire, Partick) asked the First Lord of the Admiralty, in reference to his statement regarding the examination of midshipmen in seamanship, If he can state the number of first class, second class, and third class certificates respectively which have been awarded since September, 1885; what proportion of the holders of these certificates served in the Training Squadron; and, how many first, how many second, and how many third classes respectively have been awarded by the Examiners in the Training Squadron during that period?

THE FIRST LORD (Lord GEORGE HAMILTON) (Middlesex, Ealing): Since September, 1885, there have been awarded to midshipmen at their seamanship examination 40 first class certificates, 35 second class certificates, 21 third class certificates, making in all 96. Of these 43 served in the Training Squadron. The officers of the Training Squadron examined 19 of the above number, with the following results:— Three first classes; nine second classes; seven third classes; making a total of

19. The remaining 24 of the 43 were examined by officers of other Squadrons.

CENTRAL AFRICA — TRANSIT TARIFF THROUGH PORTUGUESE TERRITORY.

MR. CRAIG SELLAR (Lanarkshire, Partick) asked the Under Secretary of State for Foreign Affairs, Whether it is a fact that the Portuguese Government has, for more than two years, suspended the 3 per cent. Transit Duty on goods passing through Portuguese territory to British Settlements on Lake Nyassa and the Shiré Highlands; and, if so, whether Her Majesty's Government have taken any steps to secure the advantages of the transit tariff arranged in 1877; and, whether Her Majesty's Government can safeguard British interests in that region by pressing for a permanent Transit Duty, which will not be liable (as is now the case) to suspension without British concurrence?

THE UNDER SECRETARY OF STATE (Sir JAMES FERGUSSON) (Manchester, N.E.): There is no arrangement as to the Transit Tariff between Great Britain and Portugal. The Mozambique Tariff of 1877 was imposed by Royal Decree, and was purely an act of internal administration. The temporary suspension of the Transit Duty was also put into operation by Decree. Her Majesty's Government have been assured that the suspension, which was owing to local causes, will be removed on the first suitable opportunity, due regard being had to fiscal interests. Her Majesty's Government, having no Treaty rights, cannot press the Portuguese Government in the sense suggested.

THE NEWSPAPER PRESS—THE LANGWORTHY MARRIAGE CASE IN "THE PALL MALL GAZETTE."

DR. CAMERON (Glasgow, College) asked the Secretary of State for the Home Department, Whether his attention has been called to the number of instances in which statements apparently obviously and wilfully false, have been made in affidavits quoted by *The Pall Mail Gazette*, in its narrative of the Langworthy marriage case; and, whether he will instruct the Public Prosecutor to inquire into the truth of the allegations therein contained, with a view, in the event of their proving true, to instituting proceedings for perjury against the guilty parties?

THE UNDER SECRETARY OF STATE (Mr. STUART-WORTLEY) (Sheffield, Hallam) (who replied) said, the Home Secretary had no intention of taking action in the matter. If those concerned were of opinion that proceedings for perjury should be instituted against anyone, it would be open to them to make an application to the Director of Public Prosecutions.

POST OFFICE—SAVINGS BANK DEPARTMENT IN QUEEN VICTORIA STREET.

DR. CAMERON (Glasgow, College) asked the Postmaster General, Whether he has yet been able to take any steps for ameliorating the accommodation of the Savings Bank *employés* in the Savings Bank Department in the temporary premises in Queen Victoria Street and Knightrider Street, or the mitigation of the annoyance of which they complain from the noise and vibration of adjacent machinery, and want of sufficient air, space, and ventilation?

THE POSTMASTER GENERAL (Mr. RAIKES) (Cambridge University): I have to state that the First Commissioner of Works has carried out measures for improving the ventilation in the premises in Queen Victoria Street temporarily occupied by a portion of the staff of the Savings Bank, and that it has been found possible to reduce the number of officers who are required to work there. Thus a considerable improvement has been effected. As regards the premises in Knightrider Street, I may say that I trust shortly to be able to obtain some other premises which will afford better accommodation. Meanwhile, an effort will be made to mitigate the effect of the vibration caused by adjacent machinery as far as possible.

POOR LAW (IRELAND) — BELFAST GUARDIANS—JOSEPH WATT, A RELIEVING OFFICER.

MR. LEAHY (Kildare, S.) asked the Chief Secretary to the Lord Lieutenant of Ireland, If it be true that the Belfast Poor Law Guardians, at their usual weekly meeting held on 3rd May, 1887, had under consideration the conduct of Joseph Watt, one of their relieving officers, who attended the Board Meeting in a drunken state without his diary for

Dr. Cameron

the week being duly written up; is it true that Watt had been sent home by Mr. Harkness, one of the Guardians, owing to his incapacity, and that he made a Report of Watt's condition to the Chairman and other members of the Board; was Watt absent from duty on the previous weekly meeting of the Board from the same cause; did the Guardians make any Report to the Local Government Board as to Watt's condition in the Minutes of their last day's proceedings; and, if not, why not; and, will Watt's services be now continued?

THE PARLIAMENTARY UNDER SECRETARY (Colonel KING-HARMAN) (Kent, Isle of Thanet) (who replied) said: It appears that Mr. Watt attended the meeting on the 3rd instant, but was obliged to retire, owing to his weak state of health, another relieving officer undertaking to discharge his duties. Mr. Harkness has stated that he did not advise Mr. Watt to retire, nor did he report his absence to the Board. Mr. Watt was absent from the previous meeting of the Board owing to illness, a medical certificate of which he has since furnished to the Guardians. An entry appeared in the Guardians' Minutes of the 3rd instant, to the effect that the Chairman did not sign Mr. Watt's diary, as that officer was unable to remain during the meeting. The Local Government Board do not consider that there is anything calling for their interference at present in the matter.

WAR OFFICE—PERMANENT FINANCIAL CONTROL.

SIR WILLIAM PLOWDEN (Wolverhampton, W.) asked the Secretary of State for War, Whether he will state, for the information of the House, the nature of the permanent financial control he proposes to establish at the War Office?

THE SECRETARY OF STATE (Mr. E. STANHOPE) (Lincolnshire, Horncastle): I explained to the House the other day the reason why, at present, I could make no further statement on this subject.

EDUCATION DEPARTMENT—PUPIL TEACHERS.

MR. MACLURE (Lancashire, S.E., Stretford) asked the Vice President of the Committee of Council on Education,

Whether instructions may be given that candidates and pupil teachers shall be informed, soon after their examination on paper, whether they have passed that part of their examination?

THE VICE PRESIDENT (Sir WILLIAM HART DYKE) (Kent, Dartford): The whole subject of the examination of pupil teachers is now under consideration, with a view to the alteration of the terms under which, so far as the Department is concerned, they are apprenticed; and, in the meantime, it will not be expedient to make any change in the Regulations.

THE MAGISTRACY (ENGLAND AND WALES)—CERRIG Y DRUIDION PETTY SESSIONS.

MR. T. E. ELLIS (Merionethshire) asked the Secretary of State for the Home Department, Whether his attention has been called to a paragraph in *The Carnarvon and Denbigh Herald* of 30th April, relating to the Petty Sessional Division of Cerrig y Druidion, County of Denbigh—

"An Abortive Petty Sessions. — Another Petty Sessions fell due here on Monday last, and although there were a few cases to be heard, no magistrate could be found to attend;" whether the repeated failure of the Monthly Petty Sessions at Cerrig y Druidion is due to the aversion of magistrates to sit with a gentleman recently made a Justice, and who is said to have associated himself with the anti-tithe agitation; and, whether he will take steps to procure a prompt administration of justice in this Petty Sessional Division?

THE UNDER SECRETARY OF STATE (Mr. STUART-WORTLEY) (Sheffield, Hallam) (who replied) said: There was an abortive Petty Sessions at Cerrig y Druidion in April last; and those Sessions have not been held regularly in the past in consequence of the difficulty of obtaining a quorum of Justices. This was not due, the Secretary of State is informed, to the cause suggested in the Question, but to the inaccessibility of the place, and the limited number of magistrates. The Lord Lieutenant has recently added one magistrate to the Bench of the district, and he hopes to find a second qualified person. By this increase of strength on the Bench the Lord Lieutenant anticipates that the regular attendance of a quorum will be secured.

WAR OFFICE—THE TWO ARMY CORPS —THE HORSE ARTILLERY.

MR. TOTTENHAM (Winchester) asked the Secretary of State for War, Whether the eight batteries of Horse Artillery of the two Army Corps about to be formed will be on the peace or war establishment, and if there has been any alteration in the latter establishment from that laid down by the War Office Equipment Regulations—namely, 175 men and 168 horses per battery; if no alteration, how it is proposed now, or on sudden emergency, to supply the deficiency of men and horses required to raise these batteries to their war strength; whether the full complement of horses in these eight batteries at war strength would be 1,344; whether the total number effective on 1st April of present year, in the whole of the 13 batteries then existing and before the reduction, was 980; and, whether it is now but 808 for the nine batteries which remain after the reduction has been carried out?

THE SECRETARY OF STATE (Mr. E. STANHOPE) (Lincolnshire, Horncastle): The Horse Artillery batteries will be on the peace establishment. The war establishment of a battery has not been altered. On full mobilization—that is, of two Army Corps, a Cavalry Division, and lines of communication—the batteries would be completed in men from the Reserve and in horses by purchase. At war strength the eight batteries would require 1,304 horses. On the 1st of April the effective number was 1,032. If the Horse Artillery batteries required for the two Army Corps were to be kept at full strength, to enable them to take the field instantly, we should require 568 more horses and 230 more men, and the extra cost the first year would be £51,000. I should be very glad if there were the least probability of such a proposal being accepted by the House; but I do not think it likely that they would approve an establishment far in excess of what other countries think of maintaining in peace time. I may add that the supply of horses for the Artillery forms part only of the much larger question of horse supply generally, about which I hope to be in a position before long to make proposals.

AFRICA (EAST COAST)—THE SLAVE TRADE ON THE MOZAMBIQUE COAST.

MR. A. E. PEASE (York) asked the Under Secretary of State for Foreign Affairs, Whether, in view of the concurrent and recent testimony borne by travellers, missionaries, and other residents to the great activity of the Slave Trade on the Mozambique Coast, in the Nyassa District, and on the Red Sea Littoral, Her Majesty's Government will lay upon the Table of the House such Reports as may have been received from Her Majesty's Consuls stationed at Mozambique, Lake Nyassa, Suakin, and Jeddah?

THE UNDER SECRETARY OF STATE (Sir JAMES FERGUSSON) (Manchester, N.E.): No Reports have been received showing that there is exceptional activity in Mozambique and the Nyassa District. Such Reports as have been received on the subject will be found in the annual Slave Trade Blue Book about to be presented.

WAR OFFICE (ORDNANCE DEPARTMENT)—DEFECTIVE WEAPONS—THE ROYAL HORSE GUARDS.

MR. HANBURY (Preston) asked the Secretary of State for War, Whether it is the fact that, in or about October of last year, an official was sent from Enfield to Regent's Park Barracks to test the swords belonging to the Royal Horse Guards; whether the swords so tested were the new pattern sword, and when were they issued; whether, out of 15 tested in one troop, only one passed; and, how many in all were so tested, and out of what total, and how many failed to stand the test?

THE SECRETARY OF STATE (Mr. E. STANHOPE) (Lincolnshire, Horncastle): I have not at present found any record of an official testing of the swords of the Royal Horse Guards in October last; but I am making further inquiries. In the previous January, however, 165 swords belonging to that regiment were examined, when a large proportion were found to be in bad condition, and all were reported as very old, and not worth the cost of repair. The regiment had had these swords for many years, and they had been obtained by purchase on the responsibility of the officers commanding the regiment, in accordance with the practice which formerly obtained in the regiments of Household Cavalry. All these swords were replaced by new ones when they were found to be in bad condition.

CEYLON — RAILWAY CONSTRUCTION.

MR. McDONALD CAMERON (Wick, &c.) asked the Secretary of State for the Colonies, Whether he is aware that the Ceylon Government have constructed 42 miles of railway between Nawalapitya and Nanuoya at a cost of £900,000; that it was the original intention of the Government to extend the line to Haputale, 25 miles further, in order to tap the traffic of the Uva District, which now goes by a long route of 150 miles to the sea; that two successive Governors have recommended the construction of the 25 miles alluded to; that it has been estimated that this extra expenditure would lead to a return of 6 per cent on the total capital of £1,400,000, whereas the traffic revenue from the 42 mile section already constructed is only sufficient to pay 3 per cent on the £900,000 expended upon it; and, whether the Imperial Government is prepared to recommend the construction of the 25 miles alluded to, and so obtain a greater revenue, besides conferring a highly desirable benefit on the planters and other inhabitants of the Uva District?

THE SECRETARY OF STATE (Sir HENRY HOLLAND) (Hampstead): The line to Nanuoya has been constructed; but it was sanctioned by the Government irrespective of any further extension. In the event, however, of the section to Nanuoya justifying expectations, Badulla, some 30 miles beyond Haputale, was looked to as the ultimate terminus. Two successive Governors recommended the extension; and estimates have been furnished, from time to time, purporting to show that the extension would be profitable, but the *data* given did not satisfy my Predecessors. In the face of the fact that the revenue for 1886 did not reach the estimate, and that the last few years have shown a constantly growing burden of debt, there would be considerable difficulty in varying the decision of my immediate Predecessor—namely, that the extension could not be undertaken by Government in the present financial condition of the Colony, but that a private Company would be at liberty to take it up. There is little to add to the answers given to the hon. Member in April last year, and to my hon. Friend the Member for North Kensington (Sir Roper Lethbridge) in March last; but I am to receive a deputation on the subject in the course of next week, and shall, of course, give careful consideration to any statements they bring before me.

Mr. McDONALD CAMERON asked, whether the Government would sanction the construction of the railway by a private Company?

Sir HENRY HOLLAND imagined that a private Company could start without the sanction of the Government.

FRANCE—THE PARIS EXHIBITION IN 1889.

Mr. J. G. HUBBARD (London) asked the Under Secretary of State for Foreign Affairs, Whether it be true, as stated in *The Morning Post* of Monday the 9th instant, that Her Majesty's Government have declined official participation in the proposed Exhibition to be held in Paris in 1889 to commemorate the capture of the Bastille and the triumph of the French Revolution?

The UNDER SECRETARY OF STATE (Sir JAMES FERGUSSON) (Manchester, N.E.): The French Government have been informed that Her Majesty's Government do not propose to take any official part in the Exhibition to be held in Paris in 1889; but that they will be happy to afford every facility to exhibitors who may be desirous of sending their goods, or of contributing in other respects to the undertaking.

WAR OFFICE — QUARTERMASTERS — THE WARRANT OF 1886.

Dr. CLARK (Caithness) asked the Secretary of State for War, Whether it is the intention of the Government to put in force, at any early date, the provisions of the Royal Warrant of 1886 regarding Quartermasters having honorary rank conferred upon them; and whether several Quartermasters have been strongly recommended by their Commanding Officers for the honorary rank of Major, but have not yet had the rank conferred upon them; and, whether it is the case that two Majors have been appointed in the Royal Artillery Coast Brigade whose total commission service is only 12 years, while there are Quartermasters and Ridingmasters of over 20 years' commission service not yet promoted?

The SECRETARY OF STATE (Mr. E. STANHOPE)(Lincolnshire, Horncastle): The grant of the honorary rank of Major to a limited number of Quartermasters has been decided on and will shortly take effect. Two Majors have recently been appointed in the Coast Brigade of Royal Artillery who had only 12 years' commissioned service, though they also had long service in the ranks; but the position is regimental, and dependent on the establishment of the corps. The promotion has no reference to the claims of Quartermasters or Ridingmasters, none of whom would have been eligible for the appointment.

THE HOUSE OF COMMONS — EXTRA ALLOWANCE TO THE POLICE CONSTABLES.

Mr. O'HANLON (Cavan, E.) asked Mr. Chancellor of the Exchequer, How many nights' extra duty have constables been engaged in and about the House for which they have not been paid any money; when they are to get these wages; and, how much per night he intends to give each man?

The UNDER SECRETARY OF STATE FOR THE HOME DEPARTMENT (Mr. STUART-WORTLEY) (Sheffield, Hallam)(who replied) said: The police have been employed longer than usual on two nights in this Session— namely, March 21 and May 9. The Chief Commissioner has recommended that for the former of these two occasions the men should receive 2*s.* 6*d.* each, and the Inspectors 5*s.* each, the messengers of the House having been granted an extra allowance for that occasion. It is understood that the messengers will not be granted any extra allowance for the 9th instant; and in order that there may be a uniformity in the allowances to messengers and police it is not proposed to grant an extra allowance to the police for that day.

EDUCATION—SECOND REPORT OF THE ROYAL COMMISSION ON EDUCATION.

Mr. SYDNEY BUXTON (Tower Hamlets, Poplar) asked the Vice President of the Committee of Council on Education, Whether some arrangement could be made whereby the Second Report of the Royal Commission on Education, just issued, could be sold at a more reasonable price, and not at one which is practically prohibitory to most of those desirous of purchasing the volume ?

THE SECRETARY TO THE TREASURY (Mr. JACKSON) (Leeds, N.) (who replied) said : I am afraid that I cannot agree to any reduction in the price fixed according to the established scale for the Report referred to.   The price is based only on the cost of paper and printing, and does not include the cost of setting up the type.

NEW ARMY MEDICAL WARRANT— HALF-PAY.

MR. W. J. CORBET (Wicklow, E.) asked the Secretary of State for War, Whether, in view of the proposed alterations in the New Warrant with reference to the Medical Department of the Army, the same privileges, as enjoyed at present by the Royal Engineers under paragraph 71, Clause 1, Army Circular, 1st January, 1887, would be extended to Medical Officers, namely—

"That an officer, placed on half-pay on ac count of ill-health incurred in and by the Service, may reckon time on half-pay, not exceeding one year, towards promotion, towards voluntary retirement, and towards retired pay ?"

THE FINANCIAL SECRETARY, WAR DEPARTMENT (Mr. BRODRICK) (Surrey, Guildford) (who replied) said : The general rule for all Departmental officers is that they do not reckon time on half-pay towards promotion or retirement.   Medical officers come under this rule, in common with those of all other Departments.

EDUCATION DEPARTMENT—THE INSTRUCTIONS TO INSPECTORS.

MR. J. G. TALBOT (Oxford University) asked the Vice President of the Committee of · Council on Education, Whether he could arrange that the Instructions to Inspectors should be issued earlier in the year, and nearer to the time when the Education Code is published, so as to avoid the anomaly, now existing, of having the Code of one year and the Instructions of another year in circulation at the same time ?

Mr. Sydney Buxton

THE VICE PRESIDENT (Sir WILLIAM HART DYKE) (Kent, Dartford): The form which the Instructions to Inspectors, if they undergo any change, finally take, depends, to some extent, upon the results of the Easter Conference between the Chief Inspectors.   It is the practice of the Department to issue the Instructions as soon as possible after the conclusion of the Conference.

EDUCATION DEPARTMENT—ELEMENTARY EDUCATION—THE RETURNS.

MR. J. G. TALBOT (Oxford University) asked the Vice President of the Committee of Council on Education, When the Returns as to Elementary Education, usually issued early in the year in advance of the Report, will be in the hands of Members ?

THE VICE PRESIDENT (Sir WILLIAM HART DYKE) (Kent, Dartford): The Returns will shortly be in the hands of Members.

EVICTIONS (IRELAND) — THE MARQUESS OF LANSDOWNE'S ESTATES, LUGGACURRAN — ACTION OF THE POLICE.

MR. W. A. MACDONALD (Queen's Co., Ossory) asked the Chief Secretary to the Lord Lieutenant of Ireland, Whether it is true that the police at Borrisin-Ossory, Queen's County, have torn down all the posters announcing a collection in aid of the Marquess of Lansdowne's evicted tenants at Luggacurran ; and, if so, whether he will inform the House by virtue of what Act of Parliament the police took this course ?

THE PARLIAMENTARY UNDER SECRETARY (Colonel KING-HARMAN) (Kent, Isle of Thanet) (who replied) said : Yes, Sir ; six placards, announcing a collection in aid of what was represented as the Luggacurran Campaign, were torn down by the police.   The placards directly, though not expressly, advocated the Plan of Campaign, and the Divisional Magistrate properly ordered their removal.

MR. W. A. MACDONALD: Will the right hon. and gallant Gentleman answer what is really the important part of the Question ; by virtue of what Act of Parliament the placards were torn down ?

COLONEL KING-HARMAN: The Divisional Magistrate acted in pursuance of his duty as an officer in charge of the district, and in the interests of peace.

THE SCOTCH UNIVERSITY BILL.

MR. MASON (Lanark, Mid) asked the Lord Advocate, When the Scotch University Bill is to be introduced, which was promised in the Queen's Speech?

THE LORD ADVOCATE (Mr. J. H. A. MACDONALD) (Edinburgh and St. Andrew's Universities): This Bill will be introduced as soon as the clauses which require the consent of the Lords of the Treasury have been adjusted.

DOGS—THE RABIES ORDER.

MR. COGHILL (Newcastle-under-Lyme) asked the Secretary of State for the Home Department, Whether, having regard to the recent increase in the number of mad dogs since the suspension of the "rabies" order issued by the police, he will give instructions for that order to be re-issued, and for other precautionary measures to be taken for the protection of the public; and, whether he has any information to show that, in Berlin, where all dogs are at all times compulsorily muzzled, rabies has almost completely disappeared?

THE UNDER SECRETARY OF STATE (Mr. STUART-WORTLEY) (Sheffield, Hallam) (who replied) said, the Commissioner of Police reports no abnormal increase of cases in April in the Metropolitan Police District. We have no official information as to the results of whatever may be the practice in Berlin.

POST OFFICE—CARRIAGE OF MAILS TO CORNWALL.

MR. CONYBEARE (Cornwall, Camborne) asked the Postmaster General, What are the terms of the existing Mail Contract with the Great Western Railway Company for the carriage of Mails for the County of Cornwall, relative to the power of the Company and of the Post Office respectively to stop its trains at various points; how long such contract has still to run; and, whether it can be terminated on the part of the Post Office by giving any, and, if so, what notice?

THE POSTMASTER GENERAL (Mr. RAIKES) (Cambridge University): The hours and stops of the mail trains on the Great Western Railway are de-termined by a Schedule attached to the Mail Contract. As regards these trains, the Postmaster General may require alterations of the time bill; but the Company have no power of making an alteration, except by consent of the Postmaster General. The contract is for a term of five years from December 1, 1883, and is determinable afterwards by notice of six months.

INDIA — INDIAN TELEGRAPH OFFICIALS.

MR. CONYBEARE (Cornwall, Camborne) asked the Under Secretary of State for India, Whether he is now in a position to state more definitely the intentions of the Government respecting the grievances complained of by the Indian Telegraph Officials; and, whether he can now,· or, if not, how soon, lay before the House the Correspondence on the subject with the Indian Government?

THE UNDER SECRETARY OF STATE (Sir JOHN GORST) (Chatham): I regret that I am not yet in a position to state definitely the intentions of the Government respecting the Indian Telegraph Department. The Correspondence is not yet complete, and it would be premature to lay it before the House.

POST OFFICE (IRELAND)—THE ANNUAL HOLIDAY.

SIR THOMAS ESMONDE (Dublin Co., S.) asked the Postmaster General, If the annual holiday of one month, referred to in the Post Office Circular of November 30, 1886, has been allowed to the overseers in the sorting branch of the General Post Office, Dublin?

THE POSTMASTER GENERAL (Mr. RAIKES) (Cambridge University): No, Sir; it has not. The case of the overseers in Dublin is being considered, with that of the corresponding officers in London and in Edinburgh, and the decision, when arrived at, will apply to all three offices in common.

FISHERY COMMISSIONERS (IRELAND)— TRAWLING IN DONEGAL BAY.

MR. T. M. HEALY (Longford, N.) (for Mr. MAC NEILL) (Donegal, S.) asked the Chief Secretary to the Lord Lieutenant of Ireland, Whether the Fishery Commissioners, who held inquiries last year in the towns of Donegal and Killybegs, have arrived at any, and, if so, what decision on the question of permitting trawling in Donegal Bay?

THE PARLIAMENTARY UNDER SECRETARY (Colonel KING-HARMAN) (Kent, Isle of Thanet) (who replied) said: I have been unable to obtain the necessary answer for this Question, as the Inspectors of Fisheries are absent from their headquarters on duty. But since I came down to the House I have received a telegram from Sir Thomas Brady to the effect that trawling is allowed on a part of Donegal Bay, and the Inspectors of Fisheries have come to no decision as to prohibiting it.

POST OFFICE (TELEGRAPH DEPARTMENT)—TELEGRAPH INSULATORS.

COLONEL HUGHES-HALLETT (Rochester) asked the Postmaster General, Whether the form of telegraph insulator now adopted by the Telegraph Department is the subject of letters patent; and, whether the patentee is in the service of the Department; and, if so, whether the Post Office pays royalty in respect of such insulators, or whether the insulators are purchased in the ordinary manner by open tender, and the price paid for such insulators?

THE POSTMASTER GENERAL (Mr. RAIKES) (Cambridge University): In reply to the hon. and gallant Member, I have to state that the form of telegraph insulator generally used by the Post Office is the subject of letters patent. The patentee is an officer of the Post Office; but no separate royalty is paid in respect of such insulator. The insulator can only be obtained from one firm, who are the sole makers of the article, and therefore open tenders cannot be called for. The price paid is 10¼d. per insulator.

EVICTIONS (IRELAND)—LORD GRANARD.

MR. T. M. HEALY (Longford, N.) for (Mr. CHANCE) (Kilkenny, S.) asked the Parliamentary Under Secretary to the Lord Lieutenant of Ireland, Whether any letter from Lord Granard has been published, denying that the authorities of Maynooth College are, either directly or indirectly, responsible for the evictions on his estate?

THE PARLIAMENTARY UNDER SECRETARY (Colonel KING-HARMAN) (Kent, Isle of Thanet) (who replied) said: A letter has appeared in *The Free-*

Mr. T. M. Healy

man's Journal of Tuesday last, addressed to Dr. Browne, the President of Maynooth College, which does not exactly tally with the suggestions contained in the hon. Member's Question, but in which Lord Granard describes himself as being "quite ready to assume the responsibility" for the evictions on his Drumlish estate.

MR. T. M. HEALY: I wish to ask the right hon. and gallant Gentleman, whether he proposes to make any apology to the authorities of Maynooth College for his insinuation that they were responsible for the evictions?

MR. SPEAKER: Order, order!

Subsequently,

COLONEL KING-HARMAN, in asking leave to make a personal explanation, said: The hon. and learned Member for North Longford (Mr. T. M. Healy) either insinuated or stated that I had brought a charge against the authorities of Maynooth College. I wish to explain. It will be in the recollection of the House that what I did say was that Lord Granard's agents stated that his Lordship did not desire to press the matter to the point of eviction; but that it was owing to the action of the mortgagees that this course had to be adopted. The hon. and learned Member for North Longford then demanded from me the names of the mortgagees. I had not intended to give them; but I was obliged, in reply to his Question, to mention that the mortgagees were the Trustees of Maynooth College. On the following Monday, the hon. Member for Kilkenny (Mr. Chance) read what purported to be a letter from Lord Granard's agents to the clerk of the Mohill Union, stating that his Lordship's estate had never been in the hands of a receiver. The hon. Member, probably from the excitement of the moment, did not read the end of the letter, which went on as follows:—

"We have, unfortunately, been obliged to press for payment of the rents now overdue. This is in consequence of charges on the estate, the principal one being the interest due to Maynooth College, and which the Trustees state they do not feel themselves justified in allowing to fall into arrears.

Yours obediently,
DARLEY AND ROE."

I think the House will see that I was justified in saying that the agents of Lord Granard's said that the mortgagees were the Trustees of Maynooth College.

MR. T. M. HEALY : After the statement of the right hon. and gallant Gentleman, to prevent further discussion, I think it is only right, speaking on behalf of the mortgagees to some extent, to say that it was the right hon. and gallant Gentleman himself who stated, in reply to my Question, that it was in consequence of the pressure of the mortgagees that these evictions occurred. I asked then who were the mortgagees, and the right hon. and gallant Gentleman said Maynooth College. It was the right hon. and gallant Gentleman's original statement that these evictions took place in consequence of the mortgagees that brought out the names of the mortgagees; and the right hon. and gallant Gentleman must now see, owing to the letter of Lord Granard and the statement of Maynooth College, that these evictions in no sense have taken place in consequence of the action of Maynooth College.

WAR OFFICE (ORDNANCE DEPARTMENT) — SMALL ARMS MANUFACTORY AT ENFIELD.

COLONEL HUGHES-HALLETT (Rochester) asked the Surveyor General of the Ordnance, How many reversed ratchet barrels have been manufactured at Enfield, approximately; what has been the rate of production a-week during January, February, March, and April of this year; and, how many Enfield Martini-Henry rifles have been manufactured, with short levers and half cook, similar in pattern to those issued experimentally?

THE SURVEYOR GENERAL (Mr. NORTHCOTE) (Exeter) : Upwards of 70,000 reversed-ratchet barrels have been made at Enfield, at the average rate, during the present year, of 1,668 per week. 21,875 Enfield-Martini rifles, similar to those issued experimentally, have been constructed. Some objections have been raised in detail to the experimental weapons; and arrangements are now in progress to alter the main supply, so as to meet those objections.

ROYAL IRISH CONSTABULARY—EXTRA POLICE IN THE NORTH RIDING OF TIPPERARY.

MR. P. J. O'BRIEN (Tipperary, N.) asked the Chief Secretary to the Lord Lieutenant of Ireland, At what date or dates the 43 men stated to be acting as extra police in the North Riding of Tipperary were appointed for that duty; whether these 43 men represent the exact number by which the Parliamentary quota in the district stands reduced; whether the district is at present acknowledged to be in a peaceful condition, and cannot, therefore, be "declared by proclamation to be in a state of disturbance" to warrant extra police; and, whether, having regard to these facts, the extra police will be withdrawn, and, if necessary, the Parliamentary quota restored to its original number, 309?

THE PARLIAMENTARY UNDER SECRETARY (Colonel KING-HARMAN) (Kent, Isle of Thanet) (who replied) said : On the 23rd of January, 1882, 64 police were sent to the North Riding of Tipperary, and on the 4th of August following 50 men. That force has been gradually reduced to the present number of 43. The question of extra police in counties comes under the consideration of the authorities yearly; and on the last occasion the matter was before them the Local Authorities responsible for the peace of the district of the North Riding could not advise the withdrawal of the force.

POST OFFICE (IRELAND) — UNSATISFACTORY ARRANGEMENTS IN TYRONE.

MR. M. J. KENNY (Tyrone, Mid) asked the Postmaster General, If his attention has been directed to the unsatisfactory postal arrangements at present existing at Fintona, County Tyrone; if the latest hour for posting letters is 6.50 p.m., although a train carrying the mails from surrounding towns passes Fintona without stopping at 10 p.m.; and whether he will in future cause the mails to be despatched by this train; if it is a fact that the latest hour for posting English letters is 10.30 a.m., although a train passes through Fintona at 2 p.m., connecting at Omagh with the regular English mail train; and, whether he will cause the incoming mails to be delivered at Fintona by the train which now passes that town without stopping at 3 a.m., but which carries the incoming mails to other towns further on?

THE POSTMASTER GENERAL (Mr. RAIKES) (Cambridge University) : My attention had not been previously directed to the postal arrangements at

Fintona as unsatisfactory. The letter box closes for the night mail as late as 6.40 p.m., the mail bag being despatched to Omagh by the 7.10 p.m. train. The arrival of the night mail in the morning is by the train due at 8.35 a.m. The trains to which the hon. Member refers as passing through Fintona at about 10 p.m. and about 3 a.m. respectively are trains recently put on for the conveyance of the Enniskillen night mail; and it seems to me unnecessary, considering the amount of correspondence from Fintona, to make special arrangements, and to incur additional expense, in order to give the very late despatch and the very early arrival now suggested. The day mail at present leaves Fintona at 10.30 a.m., so as to be available, not only for English letters, but for the down day mail from Omagh for Londonderry, and it is undesirable to withdraw the despatch at 10.30 a.m. Inquiry is, however, being made whether an additional despatch for the English letters from Fintona can be made by the train at 2 p.m.; and on receiving a Report on this point I will communicate further with the hon. Member.

WRECK COMMISSIONERS COURT — WRECK OF THE CHANNEL STEAMER "VICTORIA."

MR. CHANNING (Northampton, E.) asked the Secretary to the Board of Trade, Whether, in view of the findings of the Wreck Commissioners Court in the case of the loss of the *Victoria* near Dieppe, the Board of Trade will make any representations, through the Foreign Office or otherwise, to the French Authorities, as to the regulations for sounding fog-horns, and also as to the omission to send boats from the shore to rescue the passengers and crew of the *Victoria?*

THE SECRETARY (Baron HENRY DE WORMS) (Liverpool, East Toxteth): I would refer the hon. Gentleman to the reply I gave on Monday to the hon. Member for Walworth (Mr. Isaacs). The Report of the Court of Inquiry will be communicated to the Foreign Office, with a view to its being brought before the French Maritime Authorities.

FISHERIES (SCOTLAND)—LOSS OF LIFE FROM SHALLOW-DECKED BOATS.

MR. McDONALD CAMERON (Wick, &c.) asked the Secretary to the Board

of Trade, Whether his attention has been called to the frequent loss of life among the Scottish fishermen, owing to the shallow-decked boats now in use; that these shallow-decked boats have only a few inches between the deck and the top of the gunwale, and that such frequent loss of life could, in most instances, have been avoided by the owners of boats being compelled to adopt some kind of safety rail; and, whether it is within the power of the Department to make compulsory the adoption, by the owners of all shallow-decked fishing boats, of a safety rail?

THE SECRETARY (Baron HENRY DE WORMS) (Liverpool, East Toxteth): Representations have been made—which I believe to be true—that life is lost from the decks of the fishing boats referred to, and that the bulwarks are very low. The boats are built in a way to suit the requirements of the trade, and the Board of Trade have no power to make the adoption of a safety rail compulsory.

FISHERIES (SCOTLAND)—THE BRITISH FISHERY SOCIETY — NET - DRYING GROUNDS.

MR. McDONALD CAMERON (Wick, &c.) asked the Lord Advocate, Whether it is true that the British Fishery Society has appropriated, for agricultural purposes, certain lands in the neighbourhood of Pulteneytown, Wick, which at one time were used by the fishermen for drying and mending their nets?

THE LORD ADVOCATE (Mr. J. H. A. MACDONALD) (Edinburgh and St. Andrew's Universities): I have not as yet ascertained how the facts stand; but I may inform the hon. Member that fishermen who dry and mend their nets on waste lands free of charge under the Act 2 *Geo.* III., c. 31, do not thereby acquire any right to prevent land capable of cultivation from being utilized. The Act only gives them a privilege of free use of land which happens to be in a condition of waste.

INDIA—THE FAMINE GRANT.

SIR THOMAS ESMONDE (Dublin Co., S.) asked the Under Secretary of State for India, If it is owing to the military operations in Burmah that there is no surplus for 1887-8 out of which the Famine Grant can be paid; and, if there is any likelihood, if the occupation of Burmah continues, of there being a surplus available for the Famine Grant in 1888-9?

THE UNDER SECRETARY OF STATE (Sir JOHN GORST) (Chatham): It is not correct to say that it is owing to the military operations in Burmah that there is no surplus in 1887-8 out of which the Famine Grant can be paid. It is impossible, at present, to say whether there is likely to be a surplus available for the Famine Grant in 1888-9.

THE CONSTABULARY — CASE OF EX-POLICE SERGEANT ESKETT.

DR. CLARK (Caithness) asked the Secretary of State for the Home Department, Whether it is the case that ex-Police Sergeant Eskett, who has been compelled to retire in consequence of being permanently injured while on duty, has only been allowed a pension based on his length of service, while the custom is, under such conditions, to allow a full pension to all officers who are compelled to retire through being injured on duty; and, whether he will reconsider this case?

THE UNDER SECRETARY OF STATE (Mr. STUART-WORTLEY) (Sheffield, Hallam) (who replied) said, the ex-Police Sergeant referred to was not allowed a special pension, because the Home Secretary was not able to treat his case as one of disablement caused by injuries whilst on duty. He regretted that he could not alter that decision.

THE NATIONAL DEBT BILL.

MR. CHILDERS (Edinburgh, S.) asked Mr. Chancellor of the Exchequer, When he proposes to introduce the National Debt Bill?

THE CHANCELLOR OF THE EXCHEQUER (Mr. GOSCHEN) (St. George's, Hanover Square): I hope to-morrow.

THE SCOTCH CHURCH — CHURCH BUILDING IN PITSLIGO, ABERDEENSHIRE.

MR. ESSLEMONT (Aberdeen, E.) asked the Lord Advocate, Whether his attention has been directed to the circumstances in connection with a proposal to build a new church in the parish of Pitsligo, County Aberdeenshire, whereby, against the unanimous protests of the Heritors, the Presbytery, relying upon a very old and all but ob-

solete statute, propose to compel the erection of a building to accommodate 1,150 persons, practically the whole church-going population of the parish, notwithstanding that there are several other churches in the parish, and that the attendance at the old church, for which the new one is proposed to be substituted, never exceeds 250 persons; and, should he find the circumstances substantially as stated, is he able to take any steps to prevent this expenditure of public money?

THE LORD ADVOCATE (Mr. J. H. A. MACDONALD) (Edinburgh and St. Andrew's Universities): I do not think that a Presbytery can insist on a church being built to accommodate practically the whole church-going population of a parish; and the Courts of Law have jurisdiction to prevent any Court of Presbytery from overstepping its authority. It is not in the power of the Lord Advocate to take any action in such a matter.

INLAND REVENUE — FARMERS' RETURNS TO THE INCOME TAX.

MR. LLEWELLYN (Somerset, N.) asked Mr. Chancellor of the Exchequer, Whether he will sanction a form of balance sheet, similar to that now used in certain parts of England, for farmers submitting their accounts to the Commissioners?

THE CHANCELLOR OF THE EXCHEQUER (Mr. GOSCHEN) (St. George's, Hanover Square): I find that the Inland Revenue officers consider that there are considerable difficulties in the way of carrying out the suggestion made by my hon. Friend; but I will inquire further into the possibility of facilitating the task of farmers in submitting their accounts to the Commissioners of Income Tax.

PRISONS (ENGLAND AND WALES) — MILLBANK PRISON.

MR. FELL PEASE (York, N.R., Cleveland) asked the Secretary of State for the Home Department, If orders have been given to Colonel Lodge or any other official to have preparations made in Millbank Prison for the reception of first-class misdemeanants; and, if so, why he anticipates a large increase of such persons requiring first-class accommodation?

THE UNDER SECRETARY OF STATE (Mr. STUART-WORTLEY) (Sheffield, Hallam) (who replied) said : First-class misdemeanants used to be imprisoned in Coldbath Fields Prison, which is now closed. They are at present generally confined in Holloway Prison, where the accommodation is wanted for ordinary prisoners, who have constantly to be removed from thence for want of room. The Directors of Prisons have, with the approval of the Secretary of State, determined to place all first-class misdemeanants in Millbank Prison. The orders given to the Governor of Millbank have been to appropriate part of a Pentagon there, which is used for female prisoners, and is never full, to the use of male prisoners, both first-class misdemeanants and ordinary prisoners. The Secretary of State has no reason to anticipate an increase of first-class misdemeanants.

MR. BRADLAUGH (Northampton): Do I understand the hon. and learned Gentleman to say that the modification arrived at a few years ago, by which first-class misdemeanants were erased as a class, has since been changed?

MR. STUART-WORTLEY : I think the hon. Member had better give Notice of that Question.

POST OFFICE—TELEGRAMS FROM LIVERPOOL TO BREMEN, *via* NEW YORK.

MR. BADEN-POWELL (Liverpool, Kirkdale) asked the Postmaster General, Whether he is aware that Liverpool merchants and brokers at present send telegrams from Liverpool to Bremen and Havre, *via* New York, because they thereby save from one and a-half to two hours of the time ordinarily occupied by telegrams passing over the direct Government line and Submarine Telegraph Company's cable, and that the increased expense and delay is a serious impediment to business; and, whether he can now state that any steps have been taken to remedy this, in accordance with the terms of the letter from the General Post Office of 1st February, 1887, to the Liverpool Chamber of Commerce?

THE POSTMASTER GENERAL (Mr. RAIKES) (Cambridge University): Since the hon. Member's Question was placed on the Notice Paper, I have ascertained upon inquiry that the Commercial Cable Company has accepted from merchants in Liverpool messages for Havre, and that such messages have been paid for

at the tariff from England to America and from America to France. This practice is contrary to the agreement between the Department and the Company, and is not followed by any other American Cable Company. The average time taken in the transmission of messages between Havre and Liverpool is under an hour, and there would, therefore, appear to be some mistake in supposing that the saving can be as stated in the hon. Member's Question. I am informed by the American Telegraph Companies that they have no knowledge of messages for Bremen having been sent over their lines. The whole question of the telegraphic communication between England and the neighbouring Continental countries is at the present time receiving my earnest consideration.

WAYS AND MEANS—THE FINANCIAL RESOLUTIONS—THE TOBACCO DUTIES.

MR. HOOPER (Cork, S.E.) asked Mr. Chancellor of the Exchequer, Whether any, and, if so, what, steps were taken to ascertain the views of Irish tobacco manufacturers, in the same way as the views of other manufacturers were obtained, at a meeting of trade representatives, preceding the concession made recently to cigar manufacturers; whether, in the event of a rebate of 4*d.* per lb. being granted to Irish roll tobacco manufacturers on all stock on hand on the 21st instant, any loss would be likely to eventually result to the Revenue; and, whether any protests have been received against the granting of this suggested rebate; and, if so, from how many manufacturers in Ireland, Scotland, and England, respectively.

THE CHANCELLOR OF THE EXCHEQUER (Mr. GOSCHEN) (St. George's, Hanover Square): I have previously informed the House, I think, that the concession made to the cigar trade was not made in consequence of a meeting of manufacturers. I saw a deputation, mainly consisting of representatives of the working men engaged in the cigar trade, and I afterwards ascertained that the cigar trade could be treated separately. I have taken no steps myself, since the introduction of the Budget, to ascertain the views of any manufacturers, English or Irish; but representatives of various branches of the manufacturing trade pressed upon me to receive deputations. I received the deputations, but made no concessions, finding I could not make them. Loss would certainly accrue to the Revenue from granting a rebate on all stock in hand on the 21st instant. No protests have been received from any manufacturers against the grant of a rebate. No manufacturer would object to a proceeding which would benefit him at the expense of the Revenue.

In reply to Mr. CHILDERS (Edinburgh, S.),

MR. GOSCHEN said: What I understood was that the cigar trade might be treated on a separate footing from the rest of the tobacco trade without injustice being done to any portion of it.

MR. T. M. HEALY (Longford, N.): Can the right hon. Gentleman say what would be the total loss to the Revenue if the concession claimed by Irish roll manufacturers was made?

MR. GOSCHEN: I could not say without knowing what the stock would be. It would be impossible to make any concession to the Irish roll manufacturers that would not be made to the roll manufacturers of the whole of the United Kingdom.

POST OFFICE—MAIL BAGS FOR IRELAND ON SUNDAY EVENINGS.

MR. KENNEDY (Sligo, S.) asked the Postmaster General, Whether a mail bag is despatched from the Irish Office on Sunday evenings to Euston to catch the Irish Mail; and, if so, whether he will offer any facilities to the public, by establishing one central office, for despatch of Irish letters on Sundays, and thereby do away with great inconvenience felt by Irish residents and others in London.

THE POSTMASTER GENERAL (Mr. RAIKES) (Cambridge University): There is an arrangement by which a mail bag can be sent from the Irish Office when necessary; but, as a matter of fact, such a bag is not often sent. As regards the facilities for posting letters for Ireland by the public, as the hon. Member is, no doubt, aware, post offices in London are closed generally on Sunday; and I do not consider it necessary to make any change in this respect. There is, however, an arrangement by which letters for the Irish Mail (among other mails),

if prepaid with an extra halfpenny stamp, can be posted in a special letter-box at the Euston Railway Station all day up to 8.20 p.m. on Sunday, and this has hitherto been found sufficient to meet the requirements of the public.

OPEN AIR MEETINGS (METROPOLIS)— ARREST OF CHAPMAN AND KEMP.

MR. PICKERSGILL (Bethnal Green, S.W.) asked the Secretary of State for the Home Department, Whether the police applied for the warrant upon which Chapman and Kemp were arrested; and, if so, why they did not proceed against them by summons; why the warrant, which was issued on the 4th May, was not acted upon until the 8th May; whether Chapman and Kemp were arrested in Sancroft Street, where they had assembled with a number of other persons for the purpose of holding a meeting, as usual; whether, at the hearing of the charge, the police, in reply to the magistrate, stated that Chapman and Kemp were known to them, and that they would appear on remand; and, whether Chapman and Kemp were then released upon their own recognizances?

THE UNDER SECRETARY OF STATE (Mr. STUART-WORTLEY) (Sheffield, Hallam) (who replied) said: The police applied for a warrant because Chapman and Kemp could not be arrested at the time of the committing of the offence, and their addresses were not known. The hon. Member is aware that the issue of a warrant, in the first instance, is left to the discretion of a magistrate, and must be preceded by an information on oath. I understand that May 8 was the first day upon which Chapman and Kemp were seen after the issue of the warrants. Chapman was arrested in Kennington Road on the way to Sancroft Street. There were a number of persons assembled there at the time, and he did express himself to the effect that he had intended to address a meeting. He appeared, however, to be too late to do so. Kemp was arrested in Blackfriars Road. After being arrested Chapman and Kemp gave their addresses, and accordingly the police made at the hearing the statement set out in the hon. Member's fourth Question. They were released on their recognizances, the police offering no opposition, as the addresses had been given.

PUBLIC BILLS—BILLS RELATING TO PARLIAMENTARY ELECTIONS.

MR. HOWELL (Bethnal Green, N.E.) asked the First Lord of the Treasury, Whether, having regard to the numerous Bills now before this House dealing with various statutes and matters relating to Parliamentary Elections, and proposing amendments in the laws regulating elections in the United Kingdom, the Government will consent to the Second Reading of all such Bills *pro formâ*, with the view of their being considered by a Select Committee?

THE FIRST LORD (Mr. W. H. SMITH) (Strand, Westminster): As these Bills involve matters of principle as well as of detail, Her Majesty's Government do not think that they can give effect to the proposal of the hon. Gentleman that the second readings of the Bills should be taken without debáte.

QUESTIONS AND ANSWERS—MINISTERIAL RESPONSIBILITY — THE CHIEF SECRETARY FOR IRELAND.

MR. CAMPBELL - BANNERMAN (Stirling, &c.) asked the First Lord of the Treasury, Whether it is intended by the Government that Questions addressed to the Minister responsible to this House for the conduct of Irish Affairs shall be habitually answered by the right hon. and gallant Member for the Thanet Division of Kent, who has been appointed unpaid Under Secretary to the Lord Lieutenant; whether there is any precedent for such an arrangement; and, whether a similar delegation of duties will be applied to other Departments of State, of which the responsible Head and certain of his subordinate officers are simultaneously Members of the House?

THE FIRST LORD (Mr. W. H. SMITH) (Strand, Westminster): The arrangement to which the right hon. Gentleman refers has been made by my right hon. Friend and Colleague the Chief Secretary, to meet the pressing demands made upon his time at the present moment in connection with the discharge of his official duties. No inference must be drawn from that circumstance, either that the arrangement is intended to be permanent, or that it will affect any other

Mr. Stuart-Wortley

Department of Her Majesty's Government.

MR. T. M. HEALY (Longford, N.): May I ask the right hon. Gentleman whether the present Chief Secretary is more involved in Irish business than was the late Mr. Forster, or Mr. Trevelyan, or the late Chief Secretary?

MR. W. H. SMITH: I apprehend that the hon. Member is aware that the present Chief Secretary is greatly involved in work; but whether more so than the Gentlemen he has named I cannot say.

MR. CAMPBELL-BANNERMAN: Does the fact that another hon. Member of the Irish Administration is also a Member of the Cabinet, and resides in Ireland, diminish or increase the labours of the Chief Secretary?

MR. W. H. SMITH: I am surprised at the Question of the right hon. Gentleman. He is sufficiently aware of the mode in which Public Business is conducted to be able to answer the Question himself.

MUNICIPAL CORPORATIONS ACTS (IRELAND) AMENDMENT (No. 2) BILL.

MR. T. M. HEALY (Longford, N.): I wish to ask some Member of the Government to refer me to one of their Colleagues who can answer a Question put by my hon. Friend the Member for West Belfast (Mr. Sexton) the other night. There is a Bill down to-night in the name of the hon. Baronet the Member for Mid Armagh (Sir James Corry) from which the blocks have been withdrawn. I wish to know, whether it is the intention of the Government to support the hon. Baronet in restricting the Bill to Belfast alone; or, whether the Government will support the extension of the principle of the Bill to all Ireland?

THE FIRST LORD OF THE TREASURY (Mr. W. H. SMITH) (Strand, Westminster): My right hon. Friend and Colleague the Chief Secretary is the only Member of the Government who can answer that Question, and he is not in his place just now.

MR. T. M. HEALY: Will the right hon. Gentleman say why the Irish Chief Secretary cannot be in his place to answer a Question of this kind?

MR. W. H. SMITH: I am sure the right hon. Gentleman would be in his place had he the slightest notion that the Question would be asked,

Subsequently,

MR. T. M. HEALY said : I wish to ask the right hon. and gallant Gentleman the Member for the Isle of Thanet and Parliamentary Under Secretary to the Lord Lieutenant of Ireland, whether he can give the House any information, either from his conferences with the Irish Secretary or not, as to whether Her Majesty's Government will vote in support of the hon. Baronet the Member for Mid Armagh (Sir James Corry) in moving to restrict to Belfast the franchise which the Bill proposes to extend to the whole of Ireland ?

THE PARLIAMENTARY UNDER SECRETARY (Colonel KING-HARMAN) (Kent, Isle of Thanet) : The hon. Member for Mid Armagh has brought in the Bill to which the hon. and learned Member refers entirely on his own responsibility, and has taken the course which seems to him best calculated to effect his object.

MR. T. M. HEALY : That is not an answer to my Question. My Question is, whether he can inform the House if Her Majesty's Government intend to support the hon. Baronet the Member for Mid Armagh in restricting to one particular borough an Act for the whole of Ireland ?

COLONEL KING-HARMAN : When the hon. Member for Mid Armagh brings forward his Bill the hon. and learned Member will have an opportunity of seeing what course the Government will adopt.

PARLIAMENT — THE HALF - PAST TWELVE O'CLOCK RULE—" BLOCKING " OF SCOTCH BILLS.

MR. E. ROBERTSON (Dundee) : I wish to ask the First Lord of the Treasury a Question with reference to a large number of Blocking Notices which appear on the Paper to-day against Scotch Bills, in the name of the hon. Baronet the Member for Wigtonshire (Sir Herbert Maxwell). It will be convenient to know whether these Notices imply that the Government intends to oppose the Bills against which blocks have been placed ?

MR. HENRY H. FOWLER (Wolverhampton, E.) : I should also like to ask whether it was not laid down from the Chair two or three years ago that systematic blocking, by one Member, of a large number of Bills is a violation of the Rules of the House ?

THE FIRST LORD (Mr. W. H. SMITH) (Strand, Westminster) : I have not seen the Bills to which the hon. Member refers ; but if he will give me Notice, I shall put myself in a position to give him an answer. I should say, as a rule, that the blocks put on the Paper by Members of the Government are rather given in view of the necessity of discussing them at an hour when the Bills can be discussed than to be taken as a distinct Notice of opposition. As to the Question of the right hon. Member for East Wolverhampton (Mr. Henry H. Fowler), I am not aware whether such a ruling was given or not.

WITHDRAWAL OF MOTION.

ARMY—STORES AND MUNITIONS OF WAR (VOTES IN SUPPLY).

LORD RANDOLPH CHURCHILL (Paddington, S.) drew attention to a Return moved for by him showing—

"(1) The Annual Votes for Stores and Munitions of War from 1870.1 to 1886-7, exclusive of Votes of Credit ; (2) The amounts allotted out of Votes of Credit and Supplementary Estimates, during the same period, for purchase of Stores and Munitions of War ; (3) The amounts allotted to the Navy out of Annual Votes ; and (4) The amounts allotted to the Navy out of Votes of Credit and Supplementary Estimates."

The noble Lord said, that for some unaccountable reason a Notice of opposition had been placed against it by the hon. Member for Mid Cork (Dr. Tanner), and he now begged to move that the Motion for the Return be withdrawn and the Order discharged, for the reason that the Secretary of State for War had kindly promised to lay the information before Parliament on his own initiative.

MR. SPEAKER : The noble Lord has done all that is necessary in the matter.

Motion, by leave, *withdrawn*.

Order *discharged*.

ORDERS OF THE DAY.

DUKE OF CONNAUGHT'S LEAVE BILL.
(*Mr. William Henry Smith, Mr. Secretary Stanhope, Sir John Gorst.*)

[BILL 228.]   SECOND READING.

Order for Second Reading read.

THE UNDER SECRETARY OF STATE FOR INDIA (Sir JOHN GORST)

(Chatham), in rising to move that the Bill be now read a second time, said, there were no less than five Notices of objection to it. The terms in which the objections were expressed were so short and concise that he was unable to gather from them the reasons which actuated the hon. Members in giving those Notices. The only one which condescended to reasons was that of the hon. Member for Leicester (Mr. Picton). He (Sir John Gorst) would answer, as well as he could, such objections as he was able to find. He rather gathered, from a Question put to him by the hon. Member for Swansea, that there was in the hon. Member's mind—and he understood in the minds of some other hon. Members —a doubt as to whether such a Bill was necessary. It was rendered necessary by an old Statute, 53 *Geo.* III., which was repeated in the now operative Statute, the 3 and 4 *Will.* IV., c. 75, Clause 79 of which provides—

" That the return to Europe, or the departure from India with the intent to return to Europe, of any Governor General of India, Governor, Member of Council, or Commander-in-Chief, shall be deemed a resignation or voidance of his Office and employment."

Therefore, if His Royal Highness the Duke of Connaught left Bombay for the purpose of coming to this country, he would *ipso facto* lose his appointment. If he had been allowed to leave his appointment, and had then been re-appointed on his return, it would have been regarded by many persons as an improper evasion of the Statute he had just read. There was another objection —that the condition of India might be such that it would not be expedient that the Commander-in-Chief of the Bombay Army should be absent. The Bill did not enact that His Royal Highness the Duke of Connaught was to come home. The Bill would be permissive; and only provided that the Viceroy of India—who was responsible for the safety of India—might, should he think the circumstances of the time admitted it, grant such leave for three months to enable him to return to this country. He had gathered also that there was a feeling on the part of hon. Members that the Revenues of India might be burdened by the salary of an official not attending to his duties there. That was a misconception, as the effect of the Bill, if enacted, would only be to enable

Sir John Gorst

His Royal Highness to return to this country without resigning his command, but would not enable him to draw his salary during his absence.

SIR GEORGE CAMPBELL (Kirkcaldy, &c.): It is not in the Bill.

SIR JOHN GORST said, it was not there because it was not necessary. The section of the Act of Parliament to, which he had already referred, said that—

"If any of the specified officials should leave the Presidency, &c., to which he belonged, the salary and allowances belonging to his Office should not be paid or payable to any agent or person to his use."

The Act would not be disturbed by that Bill if passed ; therefore, no part of His Royal Highness's pay or allowances would become payable to him.

GENERAL SIR GEORGE BALFOUR (Kincardine): What about the pay as Member of the Council ?

SIR JOHN GORST said, he believed that His Royal Highness received no pay as a Member of the Council; but if he did, that would share the same fate under the Act. He did not think he need at that—or, indeed, at any—stage of the Bill argue the general question as to whether it was desirable that His Royal Highness should be present on such an occasion as the Queen's Jubilee. [*Cheers.*] He accepted that cheer as showing that the whole House agreed with him in what he had just indicated. He now came to another objection. He understood that the hon. Member for Leicester objected to the Bill as a measure specially relating to His Royal Highness the Duke of Connaught, and not a general Bill dealing with the clause in the Act of 1833. He admitted that there was a strong case for a general repeal of those provisions of the Act of 1833 which were referred to. When that Act was passed the only way a person could come to this country from India or return to India from this country was by sailing ship round the Cape of Good Hope; a passage which would occupy three or four, or even as much as nine months. It might be a very proper provision then ; but now when the passage was made—or would be made under the new contract with the Peninsular and Oriental Company—in 16 or 17 days, and had actually been done in 15 days; when it was possible also by means of the electric telegraph to recall an officer to his post at a few hours' notice, the House would see that the reasons which might have influenced Parliament to pass that Act no longer existed, at any rate in anything like the same degree. The fact of the Duke of Connaught desiring to come home for the Queen's Jubilee had, no doubt, raised the question as to whether Parliament ought not now to be asked to repeal that section of the old Act altogether. It had occurred to his mind, however, that if Her Majesty's Government had proceeded in that fashion, hon. Members might have accused the Government of trying to alter the law under cover of a Bill for an apparently different purpose; and although the Government did not often get credit for frankness and candour in their proceedings—[*laughter*]—he was sure that hon. Members would say that on that occasion, at all events, its procedure had been candid and frank. Therefore, if the Government had proceeded by a general Bill it might have been made matter of objection. But there was a more serious objection to a General Bill than that, and it was that in Indian legislation it was the practice of the Government at home to proceed with extreme caution, and not to tamper with the laws of India without consulting the Indian Government itself. It was a matter which took some time. On such a question the Government of India itself would not proceed rashly; it would refer the question to the provincial Government, and hear the opinion of that Government before it would form or indicate its own opinion to the Secretary of State; and that also would take a considerable amount of time. The course which the Government had adopted, and which he hoped would commend itself to the good judgment of the House, was in this particular case to proceed by special legislation for the purpose of giving statutory authority to the Viceroy of India on his own responsibility to give leave of absence to the Duke of Connaught. Having so dealt with this special case, at more leisure and when the time of Parliament was better able to be devoted to such a question, the Government intended to bring this old Statute under the consideration of Parliament, with a view to ascertaining whether the present law might be altered or not. He hoped the House

would consent to that course being adopted, and agree to the second reading of this Bill. He begged to move that the Bill be now read a second time.

Motion made, and Question proposed, "That the Bill be now read a second time."—(*Sir John Gorst.*)

MR. DILLWYN (Swansea, Town) in rising to move that the Bill be read a second time that day six months, said, that he had understood from the hon. and learned Gentleman the Under Secretary of State for India (Sir John Gorst) that the Government might have given His Royal Highness the Duke of Connaught leave to come home without initiating any special legislation, but that the Government on the whole considered it desirable that this Bill should be passed.

SIR JOHN GORST said, that he had said there was nothing to prevent His Royal Highness the Duke of Connaught coming home except the fact that by doing so he would have to resign his command, and that if he did so the Government might re-appoint him. The Government did not adopt that course, for the reason that it might be considered an evasion of the Statute.

MR. DILLWYN said, he quite understood what the hon. and learned Gentleman had said. He was glad to hear that there was no intention at present to repeal the Statute, which he considered a very salutary one. For many reasons he was extremely unwilling to bring forward this Resolution, and he only did so from a sense of duty. [*Cries of* "Oh!"] He considered it was advisable that those who were opposed to this measure should express their opinions frankly and fairly. There was a very strong feeling outside the House on this point, that there were many exalted personages in this country who received high appointments over the heads of other officers in consequence of their connection with the Throne—appointments which they would not have received otherwise. That was believed to be so, not only in the case of his Royal Highness, but in the case of other personages who had chief commands entrusted to them in this country. That, however, was not the ground on which he now moved the rejection of the Bill. In doing so he wished emphatically to declare to the House that it was not from any want of loyalty to Her Majesty or respect for His Royal Highness, whom he believed to be an estimable person and an excellent officer; but he contended that if these appointments were given to exalted personages they ought to hold them upon the conditions on which other persons held them. His Royal Highness—or whoever else was entrusted with the command in India—enjoyed high pay, great power, a good position, and many great privileges. What he said was this—and he thought a very large proportion of the country agreed with him—that those who had this great power and these great privileges, on account of their relationship to the Throne—which he did not complain of—should take the rough with the smooth — that they should not have all the good things, but should take the disabilities and the inconveniences which attached to the positions with which they were entrusted. That was his chief reason for moving the rejection of this Bill. He was bound to say that the House were asked to grant these special privileges to His Royal Highness at a very unseasonable time. [An hon. MEMBER: The Jubilee.] Mr. Dillwyn said he would say nothing about the year of Jubilee; but the political horizon of India was not so satisfactory that just now, of all other times, they should give to his Royal Highness leave to come home to see his respected mother. He almost doubted whether his Royal Highness himself would wish to leave India at this particular crisis. They had troops on the North-West Frontier, where they did not know what might turn up; and in Burmah, again, they had a considerable army. He had now stated, he hoped with all respect to Her Majesty and his Royal Highness, the reasons that had induced him to make this Motion. He repeated that it was a sense of duty only which impelled him to move the rejection of the Bill.

SIR JOHN SWINBURNE (Staffordshire, Lichfield), in seconding the Amendment, said, that high places in the Army and the Navy were being filled by exalted personages. He would refer to a few examples. He hoped the House would acquit him of any want of respect or loyalty to the Queen in the course he was taking. In the first place, His Royal Highness the

Duke of Cambridge—the Commander-in-Chief—had never served as ensign, lieutenant, captain, major, or lieutenant-colonel. [Cries of "Order!"]

MR. PULESTON (Devonport): I rise to Order. I wish to submit to you, Sir, whether the hon. Baronet is in Order, and is speaking to the Question before the House, in referring to the names of these Royal personages, who hold appointments in the Army, as he is proceeding to do?

MR. SPEAKER: The specific point of this Bill is the question of leave to His Royal Highness the Duke of Connaught. The hon. Member certainly appears to me to be travelling beyond the question before the House in discussing the position of the members of the Royal Family.

MR. E. ROBERTSON (Dundee): I wish to know, Sir, whether, in discussing this Bill, we shall not be at liberty to consider the practice of appointing to high positions in the Army and the Navy members of the Royal Family?

MR. SPEAKER: That would certainly be out of Order.

MR. ARTHUR O'CONNOR (Donegal, E.): On the question of Order, Mr. Speaker, I should like to ask you, whether you will be good enough to direct the Clerk at the Table to take down that ruling as a precedent?

MR. SPEAKER: I shall do nothing of the sort.

SIR JOHN SWINBURNE said, he brought the other cases forward as an illustration of his argument; but, in accordance with the Speaker's ruling, he should try to avoid them. But there were in the Army and Navy three or four of the highest positions held by exalted persons, and the consequence was that officers of the Army and Navy had been precluded from obtaining these high appointments. [Cries of "No, no!"] He would give as an illustration the case of the hon. and gallant Member for Southampton (Admiral Sir John Commerell)—one of the most gallant Admirals in the Navy—who found that his prospects of hoisting his flag as Commander of the Mediterranean Squadron were very materially diminished——

MR. SPEAKER: The clause of this Bill—and the only clause—relates to the return of His Royal Highness the Duke of Connaught without the resignation of his appointment, and the remarks of the hon. Baronet are not pertinent to that.

SIR JOHN SWINBURNE said, that in seconding the Amendment of the hon. Member for Swansea, he merely wished to suggest that an opportunity had occurred when His Royal Highness—finding his Royal duties incompatible with his military duties—might gracefully retire from the post he filled and allow some distinguished military officer to take his place. He would only refer for a moment to the enormous amount of ineffective service both in the Army and Navy in consequence of these positions being held by persons of exalted social rank. Our Army and Navy Estimates now amounted to £31,000,000, and one-sixth of that was for pay, pensions, and retirements, because naval and military officers could see no chance of promotion, or of obtaining these high positions. There were now some 600 or 700 lieutenants in the Royal Navy——

MR. SPEAKER: The hon. Member is palpably evading the ruling of the Chair.

As the hon. Baronet did not rise to continue his remarks,

MR. SPEAKER: Has the hon. Gentleman concluded by seconding the Motion?

SIR JOHN SWINBURNE said: I have great pleasure in seconding the Amendment.

Amendment proposed, to leave out the word "now," and at the end of the Question to add the words "upon this day six months."—(*Mr. Dillwyn.*)

Question proposed, "That the word 'now' stand part of the Question."

MR. CONYBEARE (Cornwall, Camborne) said, he wished to state the reasons which had induced him to put an Amendment to the Bill upon the Paper. He had not done so in any spirit of disloyalty—[*laughter*]—though some persons might look upon it in that light. He—like the hon. Member for Swansea, Mr. Dillwyn—had acted merely in discharge of a public duty. He objected to the Bill on the ground that it was special legislation, for which there was no necessity, and which did not affect any large section of the community. Although the occasion might be interesting, it could not be contended that it was a public duty for His Royal High-

ness to return to England; and he, therefore, protested against the proposed legislation. If the hon. and learned Gentleman the Under Secretary of State for India could say that such legislation would be undertaken with regard to Sir Frederick Roberts or Lord Wolseley, there might be some show of reason in proposing it. He thought the opportunity was a convenient one for protesting against His Royal Highness holding such an appointment as that in question. [*Cries of* "Question!"] He was arguing that if His Royal Highness had not been appointed at all the Bill would not be required, and now that he was appointed it was doubly unnecessary. He should like to know whether the Nation would be called upon to pay His Royal Highness's expenses home, for if the journey were undertaken the Nation, in the circumstances, certainly ought not to be called upon to pay the expense.

MR. BRADLAUGH (Northampton) said, that, with all due respect to the opinion given by the hon. and learned Gentleman the Under Secretary of State for India (Sir John Gorst) he (Mr. Bradlaugh) was inclined to think that Section 79 of the Statute 3 & 4 *Will.* IV. c. 85 merely provided that the salary of the Commander-in-Chief should cease as a consequence of what the Act declared to be a resignation and avoidance of the office. This Bill said that the departure of His Royal Highness should not be a resignation or avoidance of the office, and he would respectfully submit that if the resignation and avoidance were cleared away all the consequences attaching thereto would also be cleared away. He would suggest that Her Majesty's Government should distinctly state that there was no intention whatever to impose a burden. Even if his contention were not accepted by the Government, he thought it would be desirable to introduce words so as to clear up the legal doubt, and make the point quite clear.

MR. PICTON (Leicester), who had placed on the Paper the following Amendment—

"That in the opinion of this House it is unadvisable to pass a Bill for the purpose of conferring special or exceptional privilege on any commanding officer of Her Majesty's Forces, unless when such a measure is required for the due recognition of extraordinary personal services to the nation," said, he was as anxious as the most loyal subject of Her Majesty that His Royal Highness the Duke of Connaught should take his share in the rejoicings and ceremonies of this year; but he held that the Bill was unnecessary. His Royal Highness might have resigned and been re-appointed; or, he thought, power would have been found in the Government of India Act, which enabled Her Majesty, by Order in Council, to alter and regulate the terms and conditions of Service under which persons held their Commissions. But the real point was whether or not it was desirable, for purposes of mere personal convenience, to set the whole legislative machinery of the Empire in motion. This Bill was an illustration of the saying that the British Parliament was like an elephant's trunk, which could pick up a pin or rend an oak. By an act of its omnipotent power it could unite nations or dissolve a marriage between an ill-matched couple; and it had been recently suggested by the editor of an evening paper that its power might be used to declare two persons to be man and wife who had never been legally married. But he maintained that, as a general rule, the Imperial power of the Legislature should only be invoked for purposes affecting the interests of the whole commonwealth. There were, of course, sometimes cases of extraordinary suffering, or gross personal wrong, which did indirectly affect the commonwealth, and create a scandal of sufficient magnitude and public interest to require a special Act of Parliament to deal with it. There was, for instance, a case in which a special Act had been passed for the purpose of securing to a particular family the possession and enjoyment of certain estates that had been wasted by a malignant pretender. And it was suggested by the newspaper previously mentioned that the power of Parliament would be well employed in passing an Act to relieve the misery of an individual caused by the special brutality and villiany of one man, on the ground that such unpunished villiany was a public shame and scandal. He had no doubt, however, that very many hon. Members would object, in such a case, to the power of Parliament being invoked for what would be considered private ends. But if they were right in that objection, how could they support the Bill before

Mr. Picton

them for the mere private convenience of a Royal Prince, who wanted to be relieved of his public responsibilities in order that he might come to England to take a part in family rejoicings? He thought the legislative machinery should not be set in motion for a purely personal object. It would be said that an exception should be made, because this was the case of an illustrious Prince. The fact of His Royal Highness the Duke of Connaught being a Prince was just the reason for not passing this particular Bill, and making an exception in his favour. Persons of such high station ought to set an example of uncomplaining obedience to the law. The people liked to see persons in exalted stations taking the rough with the smooth, and setting the example of uncomplaining obedience to the law; and nothing endeared exalted persons to the public affection more than such an obedience. It was singular what little sacrifices in persons of high station were looked upon as heroic; for them to face a shower of rain out of good nature was thought almost as much of as for a common soldier to face a shower of grape. This Bill was an abuse of Parliamentary omnipotence. Seeing that popularity could be so easily obtained, he thought that responsibilities ought to be fearlessly accepted, and that for the Government to bring forward a Bill of this kind was unwise in the interest of that loyalty which they desired should be always cherished towards the Throne of this Realm.

Mr. CREMER (Shoreditch, Haggerston) said, he regretted that the hon. Member for Swansea (Mr. Dillwyn) should have felt it his duty to oppose the Bill, because the time of the House would be wasted in a somewhat useless discussion. Nevertheless, he intended to vote with the hon. Member, because he could not but regard the Bill as a piece of class legislation, for which there was no justification. If "Tommy Atkins"—whose interest was quite as dear to him as that of His Royal Highness—with his body covered with wounds received in the service of his country, had desired to return home to celebrate his father and mother's silver or golden wedding, or on the occasion of domestic affliction, the Government would not have undertaken to introduce such a Bill for his benefit. He was not aware of His Royal Highness having earned any special distinction, and he failed to see what the Duke of Connaught had done to justify such a measure. Had he not been fortunate enough to have been born Duke of Connaught he would not have been accorded such a privilege. He objected to special legislation of this kind, even when the person concerned was a son of Her Majesty.

GENERAL GOLDSWORTHY (Hammersmith) said, that the reason this Act was necessary for the Duke of Connaught was that he was Commander-in-Chief, whereas a private soldier could get leave without an Act of Parliament; but with reference to the argument about "Tommy Atkins," he protested —as one who had been a regimental and staff officer for many years — against the suggestion that the interests of private soldiers were not taken into consideration. On all occasions when there were domestic circumstances in the case of private soldiers requiring leave of absence, the commanding officer strained a point to give them leave.

MR. CREMER said, he should like to ask whether that privilege had ever been extended so far that private soldiers had been permitted to return from India for such purposes?

GENERAL GOLDSWORTHY said, similar cases could not arise; but he happened to know there had been cases where private soldiers had been allowed to return home from India. Of course there was the money difficulty for the passage; but commanding officers did consider the welfare of their men, and would strain a point, if a troop-ship were going home, and there was room for them, to obtain them a passage; whilst this Bill was necessary, because His Royal Highness the Duke of Connaught held the position of Commander-in-Chief in Bombay. He admitted that the Government had made a tactical mistake in calling it the "Duke of Connaught's Leave Bill," and should be glad if it were extended to all Commanders-in-Chief, which would probably have met the objections of hon. Members opposite. He (General Goldsworthy) had himself been Assistant Adjutant General of the District in the South of Ireland at the same time as His Royal Highness was serving there. It was a long time—[An hon. MEMBER: Six months.] — more than that. His Royal Highness was in

command of a battalion and performed his duties to the full satisfaction of the General, and as well as any officer could do. He (General Goldsworthy) himself could also bear testimony to the efficient way in which His Royal Highness performed his duties as an officer, and to the fact that he was never in the habit of taking advantage of his position as a Member of the Royal Family to ask for any special privilege which any other officer might not have asked for. He should support the Bill.

MR. CHILDERS (Edinburgh, S.) said, the state of the matter was this— that during the last century the voyage to and from India occupied not less than a year, or even a year and a-half. In 1833, when the voyage took nine months, or even a year, it was thought right by Parliament that there should be a distinct prohibition put upon a practice, in former days not very uncommon, under which officers appointed to very high positions in India spent a large amount of time in this country. The Act of Parliament provided that the officers holding certain high appointments in the Military and Civil Services in India — namely, the Governor General, the Governors of the Presidencies, the Commander-in-Chief, and the Commanders-in-Chief of the Presidencies, should not be permitted to leave their ¦posts without *ipso facto* vacating them. But what was the present position of the matter with respect to persons holding high offices, whether civil or military, in distant parts of the world? When he held the Office of First Lord of the Admiralty and Secretary for War, it was in his power to give leave of absence to persons holding the highest military and naval positions at greater distances than India. During his tenure of Office at the Admiralty, leave had been given to the Naval Commander-in-Chief in China, and to the Naval Commander-in-Chief in the Pacific. In the same way leave could be given by the Secretary of State for Foreign Affairs to Ambassadors, and by the Secretary for the Colonies to Colonial Governors. Only a few years ago it was proposed by a Royal Commission that the Commander-in-Chief of a Presidency should cease to be so designated, and should, for the future, be entitled, "the General commanding in the Presidency of Madras or Bombay." Now, if this proposal had been carried into effect, the officer holding the position filled by His

Royal Highness the Duke of Connaught could have obtained leave of absence from the Secretary of State for War. Under these circumstances, it would be altogether wrong to reject this measure, and for the House to lay down that an officer holding an appointment of that kind ought to be restrained from having leave, if the Governor General and the Secretary of State thought it right that he should have such leave; and more especially when officers holding similar appointments at a greater distance might obtain it. Then the question arose, was it reasonable to maintain a distinction by which one class of officers should be absolutely prohibited from leaving their commands, while others in similar or more important positions should be at liberty to do so? How should they deal with this particular Bill? It seemed to him that the clause in the Act of 1833 was altogether obsolete, and that it would be desirable, at the earliest possible moment, to bring in a Bill in order to repeal the restriction which he had pointed out and enable the Governor General and Secretary of State to grant leave to all the high officials whom he had already named. If the House was of that opinion, the next question they had to consider would be, whether they should pass the present Bill, or let it to be postponed with a view of passing within a short time a Bill repealing those restrictions. Considering the pressure of Business, he thought it would be inexpedient to substitute for this Bill a general measure; and if they received an assurance that the Government would, as soon as possible, bring in a Bill repealing altogether the clause in the Act of 1833, he could not see why the House, under all the circumstances, should reject the present proposal.

THE FIRST LORD OF THE TREASURY (Mr. W. H. SMITH) (Strand, Westminster): I rise at once in response to the appeal of the right hon. Gentleman. The Government will certainly introduce the Bill which the right hon. Gentleman has suggested. We feel that there is not only no objection to the course indicated, but that very great advantage is to be derived from it in the public interest. There are occasions on which the public interest is greatly served by an opportunity of consulting with officers high in command and holding positions of great responsibility in different parts of the world. In the

administration of Departments, I have found great advantage in being able to confer personally with officers who have some straight home from those commands, returning again to them. Therefore, the circumstances being so completely changed from what they were when the Act of 1833 was passed, render it advisable in the public interest that these officers in India should be in a position to be recalled home for a few weeks to confer with the Government, and to obtain that leave which every other officer subordinate to them is entitled to, and does obtain, at the present time. The hon. Member for Northampton has a doubt as to the application of the Act with regard to pay and allowances to His Royal Highness. I can give the hon. Gentleman the assurance that Her Majesty's Government are advised that the Act operates to prevent the pay and allowances being given; but, whether it does or not, I will undertake that His Royal Highness shall not draw either pay or allowances during the period of leave. It is hardly necessary that I should refer to the observations which have been made by hon. Gentlemen with regard to this measure. The Government have acted frankly in bringing it forward in the form in which it has been presented to the House; and we have not the slightest doubt that it will be accepted by the House as a reasonable and proper measure under the circumstances. The hon. Member for Leicester (Mr. Picton) referred to the fact that it was only reasonable to suppose that His Royal Highness should return to take part in an event which affords satisfaction to the whole of the United Kingdom. I think that any man who stands in the relation of parent to a family must feel that it is not only reasonable, but most fitting and desirable, that the Family of the Queen should be around her upon an occasion which is one of rejoicing, of satisfaction, and of happiness to the whole of Her Majesty's subjects. With regard to the observations of the hon. Member for Shoreditch (Mr. Cremer), there is no officer serving Her Majesty under the rank of Commander-in-Chief in India who is entitled to leave under circumstances such as these who does not get it with pay and allowances, and leave is given in every reasonable case if the exigencies of the Service permit. Reference has been made by the hon. Member for

Mr. Childers

Swansea (Mr. Dillwyn) to the condition of India and the duties of the Commander-in-Chief. I can say, without any hesitation whatever, that neither His Royal Highness nor the Governor General of India will be any party to the neglect of any duty which falls upon His Royal Highness. If the circumstances of the day are such as to render it at all desirable or necessary that His Royal Highness should remain in India when the time comes for his departure, we may regret the circumstances, but certainly His Royal Highness will not come home. There is, however, no reason to believe, from the events which are happening, that the departure of His Royal Highness will have to be postponed, or that any of the sinister forebodings in which the hon. Member has indulged will be fulfilled. I trust the House will not be put to the trouble of a Division on a question of this kind; and that, although there may be some difference of opinion on the subject, hon. Members will allow a measure of this character to be accepted by the House with that unanimity which is usually extended to proposals of this kind, which in themselves are reasonable and justifiable. and which, I am sure, will be accepted by the country as graceful and fitting under all the circumstances.

SIR WILFRID LAWSON (Cumberland, Cockermouth) said, he did not think this was so exciting a question as some of his hon. Friends around him seemed to think, nor did he consider it to be a matter of high Constitutional policy which need keep them there till 6 o'clock in the morning. The real point was whether the Bill was, on the whole, for the public good. Now, there were three parties to the Bill. First, there was the Duke of Connaught himself; secondly, there were the people of India; and thirdly, there were the people of England. With regard to the Duke of Connaught—[*cries of* "The Queen!" *from the Ministerial Benches.*] Some hon. Members opposite said "The Queen!" He begged to assure those hon. Members that it was a most unconstitutional practice to bring the name of the Sovereign into the debates of that House, and whatever might be done on the other side of the House he should scrupulously abstain from doing so. If the Duke of Connaught wanted to come home to the Jubilee, why should he not? It might be a pleasure to His Royal Highness, though, for his part, he should think it would be the greatest pleasure to keep away from such a performance. It appeared to him to be one of the most intolerable of nuisances. However, if His Royal Highness wished to come, and thought it a matter of duty, why should he not? Then there were the people of India. His hon. Friend below him seemed to be greatly alarmed at what might happen in India. But did his hon. Friend really think that the Duke of Connaught's presence in India would do anything to avert any danger which might be impending? That was a most extraordinary idea. There were plenty of officers who might be sent out to take his place. There was, for example, the hon. and gallant Member for Hammersmith (General Goldsworthy). The third party to be considered were the people of England. It had been solemnly declared from the Front Bench opposite that this step would not cost the people of this country one penny, and it would give them the great pleasure of bringing the Royal Duke home to be stared at when the Jubilee celebrations took place, and that was an amusement which the English people liked better than any other people in the world. Under these circumstances, he did not see any great objection to this Bill, and so he would vote against his hon. Friend.

SIR GEORGE CAMPBELL (Kirkcaldy, &c.) said, he did not so much object to the Bill as to the waste of the time of the House of Commons in introducing what he considered to be a totally unnecessary Bill, especially when there were many more important measures waiting to be discussed. He thought it would have been much less invidious if the Government had taken upon themselves the responsibility of saying that it was a reasonable thing that the Duke should be allowed to come away entirely without pay, and of re-appointing him. There were grave objections to the proposals of the right hon. Member for Edinburgh to introduce a general measure, which would lead to a still further waste of time.

MR. LABOUCHERE (Northampton) said, that they had seen the right hon. Member for Edinburgh (Mr. Childers) get up and propose some sort of transaction to the right hon. Gentlemen sitting opposite him. There was one sound rule in that House which he trusted would always be followed, at least in that part of the House where he sat. It was that whenever there was the slightest sign of a bargain or arrangement between the two Front Benches they ought invariably to upset it. He should not be surprised if the general Bill referred to by the right hon. Gentleman were blocked; a strong proof that the proposal was an improper one was that it was necessary to bring in a Bill to give effect to it. Whether it was desirable or undesirable that these great and lucrative places should be given to Royal Princes was open to question; but he thought when any of these places were given to a Royal Prince the holder of it should sink the Prince in the soldier. If any Governor General or Commander-in-Chief, who was not a Royal Prince, wished to come home to see his mother, or if his mother was anxious to see him, would anybody bring in a Bill to enable him to do so? He should say not. [*Ministerial cries of* "Divide!"] If there was any discussion on a Bill introduced by the Government, there was an immediate cry of Obstruction, and the Leader of the House began to lecture them. They were perpetually told by the right hon. Gentleman that they were obstructing the Coercion Bill—["Order, order!" *and* "Divide!"]—for which everything else was set aside. ["Divide!"] The action of the Government showed how hollow all their protests were against Obstruction, when they set aside important Business in order to bring forward this Bill. ["Divide!"] If hon. Members opposite persist in their interruptions, he would move the adjournment. He told them that he and his hon. Friends were not going to be crushed down by a Party who tried to break, destroy, and put an end to the debates in the House. ["Order, order!"]

MR. SPEAKER: The hon. Member is not speaking to the Question before the House.

MR. LABOUCHERE said, that he was about to invoke the Speaker's protection. Important Business was being delayed, and the House was asked to occupy itself with a Bill which was an obsequious and servile Bill, brought in to suit the private convenience of a Royal Prince. He would leave it to the country to judge between the Opposition and hon. Gentlemen on the other side as to who were most anxious that the

Mr. Labouchere

real and true Business of the country should be proceeded with.

SIR WILLIAM PLOWDEN (Wolverhampton, W.) said, that the First Lord of the Treasury had given them an undertaking that the Duke of Connaught would not draw any pay and allowances during his absence from duty. He wished to ask whether there was any objection to insert the words "without pay and allowances" in the Bill?

MR. W. H. SMITH: That is wholly unnecessary. Surely my undertaking is sufficient.

SIR WILLIAM PLOWDEN: I quite accept the right hon. Gentleman's undertaking. But this Bill is a precedent for the general measure now announced.

MR. SCHWANN (Manchester, N.) wished to know whether it was clearly understood that the travelling expenses of the return of the Duke of Connaught to this country and back to India would be defrayed by His Royal Highness or by the Treasury?

No audible answer being given,

DR. TANNER (Cork Co., Mid) said, he must complain of the want of courtesy of the right hon. Gentleman. The question put by the Member for Manchester ought to be answered. He considered that no sufficient reasons had been advanced in support of the Bill. The Chief Secretary for India had drawn attention to the dangers and difficulties that beset India; and was this a time when the Commander-in-Chief should evacuate his post? He thought they had not received the assurances from the Government that they were entitled to receive, and if they obtained those assurances, the Irish Members would agree to the Bill without a Division.

Question put.

The House *divided:*—Ayes 318; Noes 45: Majority 273.—(Div. List, No. 135.)

Main Question put, and *agreed to.*

Bill read a second time.

MR. W. H. SMITH: I think, Sir, I may now make an appeal to the House to pass this Bill through its remaining stages—[*Cries of* "No!" *from the Opposition Benches*]—if that is in accordance with the general sense of the House. [*Renewed cries of* "No!"] In dealing with a measure of this character, which is confined and limited, I think it is only reasonable and fitting that the House should expedite its passing.

["No!"] I beg to move, Sir, that you do now leave the Chair.

Motion made, and Question proposed, "That Mr. Speaker do now leave the Chair."—(*Mr. W. H. Smith.*)

MR. DILLWYN: I appeal to you, Sir, whether it is in Order for the right hon. Gentleman to take the remaining stages of the Bill now?

MR. SPEAKER: It is perfectly in Order for the right hon. Gentleman to make the Motion, if it is done with the general assent of the House.

MR. MAURICE HEALY (Cork): Can it be done without the unanimous assent of the House?

MR. SPEAKER: The general assent of the House is all that is necessary.

DR. TANNER (Cork Co., Mid): Notice has been given of opposition to the Motion for going into Committee upon the Bill.

MR. SPEAKER: That is impossible, the period for receiving Notices on that stage not having yet arrived.

DR. TANNER: I have just handed the Notice in.

Question put. [No, no!"]

MR. SPEAKER: I do not think that sufficient general assent has been given. What day does the right hon. Gentleman propose to fix for the Committee?

MR. W. H. SMITH: As the general assent of the House has not been given to the Motion I will put the Committee down for to-morrow.

Bill committed for *To-morrow.*

ARMY AND NAVY ESTIMATES.
MOTION FOR A SELECT COMMITTEE.
[ADJOURNED DEBATE.]

Order for resuming Adjourned Debate on Question [5th April],

"That a Select Committee be appointed to examine into the Army and Navy Estimates, and to report their observations thereon to the House."—(*Mr. William Henry Smith.*)

Question again proposed.

Debate *resumed.*

DR. CAMERON (Glasgow, College): I should like to know whether it is intended that the Committee shall have power to call for persons, papers, and records?

MR. W. H. SMITH: Certainly.

Question put, and *agreed to.*

Select Committee *appointed,* "to examine into the Army and Navy Estimates, and to report their observations thereon to the House."

SUPPLY.—COMMITTEE.

Order for Committee read.

Motion made, and Question proposed, "That Mr. Speaker do now leave the Chair."—(*Mr. W. H. Smith.*)

POST OFFICE PATRONAGE.
OBSERVATIONS.

MR. CONYBEARE (Cornwall, Camborne): Sir, in rising to call the attention of the House to the question of Post Office patronage, I feel it necessary to explain that I find myself placed in a position of some little difficulty. I am most anxious to proceed with the Motion which appears in my name on the Motion for going into Committee of Supply, and I am naturally all the more anxious, because, upon a former occasion, when it was expected that this question might be discussed, it was not reached until a very late hour of the night, and it was the general sense of the House on that occasion that so important a matter should not be proceeded with when there was no possibility of securing for it adequate discussion. In this instance, I have been called upon suddenly to proceed with the Motion, and the difficulty I find myself in is this—owing to the Division which took place a few minutes ago, I was hurriedly summoned into the Division Lobby from the dinner table; but I had understood that there would be some discussion on the Question which has been just put from the Chair on the first Motion upon the Paper in the name of the hon. Member for Canterbury (Mr. Henniker-Heaton), for cheapening and facilitating postal communication between all parts of the Empire. Believing that that discussion would take some time, I am obliged to admit that I have not got with me, at the present moment, the notes and papers which I had prepared, and which are necessary to enable me to go on with my Resolution. I have them in my locker. I do not wish hon. Members to suppose for a moment that I have any desire to shirk the matter. I am perfectly willing to deal with the matter as well as I am able without the assistance of my notes, if it is the desire of the House, although I should be in a much better position to do so if the House would allow me first to go to my locker. I only make this statement in order to explain the difficulty of the position in which I find myself placed. Having said this in order to explain the reasons why, under existing circumstances, it will be impossible for me to deal with the question as fully and completely as I should wish, I propose to give a brief and, I am afraid, only an imperfect outline of my complaint. There has been a good deal said in the public Press with regard to certain appointments which have been made by the Postmaster General during the present year. As I understand, the question resolves itself into two branches, the first of which has reference to the transference of certain clerks in a particular department of the Post Office from one class to another. It has been alleged that certain transferences have been made which have not been in accordance with the usual rule which prevails in the Post Office, and not in accordance with the information and advice supplied to the Postmaster General by the permanent heads of the department who are cognizant of the work done by the different clerks, and are, therefore, best able to judge of the propriety of the particular appointments made. It is alleged that the course which the Postmaster General has taken in this matter is not only a novel course, but is so opposed to the regulations which are issued in respect of competition for appointments in the public service relating to the Post Office as to constitute almost a breach of contract between the Post Office and those who have entered the service of the Post Office by means of public competition. I understand that, in one particular case, a gentleman has been promoted by the Postmaster General on his own responsibility, and against the wishes of the permanent officials of the Post Office, who were best able to judge whether he was the most competent person to be promoted to a higher position. There have been other and extraneous matters imported into the question; but I hope it will be clearly understood that I do not refer to the matter in order to make any personal charge against the Postmaster General. I say so because, in answer to a Question which was put to him, the right hon. Gentleman gave a firm denial to the charges which have been made. The allegation was that, in making these appointments, some regard was had by the right hon. Gentleman to the fact that the persons promoted were, in some

way or other, connected with him by family ties. The right hon. Gentleman took the earliest opportunity of denying those allegations, and I am glad that it was so. The right hon. Gentleman also stated, in answer to a Question addressed to him by myself, that he had no acquaintance with the gentlemen in regard to whose appointments these stories had been set afoot. That remark, however —that he had no acquaintance with the gentlemen he promoted—only goes to confirm the contention which is made, that he must have been unable to know whether he was appointing the best and most suitable men. The whole gist of the question is, that the right hon. Gentleman appointed persons in the teeth of the direct opposition of the permanent officials, who were the persons best qualified to judge of the fitness of the gentlemen promoted. If the right hon. Gentleman tells us that he made these appointments without knowing anything about the individuals, or the work they had been doing, we are certainly justified in our contention that it would have been much better if he had followed the practice which had previously prevailed. Another important point which I wish to raise is, that the right hon. Gentleman, in making appointments to Provincial postmasterships, has on various occasions made alterations in the amount of salaries, with the view of keeping these offices as a part of the political patronage of the Government of the day. I have had cases placed before me which fully bear out that allegation—cases in which the right hon. Gentleman has reduced the salary below £120, which is the amount beyond which the political patronage of the Post Office cannot be exercised in England; and in other cases below £100, which is the amount beyond which the political patronage of the Treasury cannot be exercised in Ireland and Scotland. I am not prepared to contend that it is solely with a view of indulging in political patronage, and for the sake of giving these appointments to the supporters of the Government, that these reductions have been made; but the fact remains that, in some cases, they have had the effect of making the offices to which they are attached a part of the political patronage of the Government; and there is this remarkable coincidence—that where these reductions of salary have been made appointments of a Tory rather than of

Mr. Conybeare

a Liberal or Radical complexion had taken place apparently as a consequence. The conclusion is, therefore, forced upon the public mind that the reductions have been made with the express purpose and intention of keeping these appointments in the hands of the Government of the day, and of turning them into political and Party appointments. If my contention is right, I have good reasons for bringing the matter before the House, and for complaining that such a state of things should exist, because I look upon it as introducing into our system of administration some of the worst features of the American Civil Service system, which have always been presented to us on this side of the Atlantic in the most odious light. Whenever anything is said of political corruption in America, the allegation is always coupled with a reference to the fact that whenever a change of Government is made in the United States every petty official throughout the country is changed at once. That is a system which we rightly regard as a mischievous system; and if I had no other ground, I should feel it my duty to resist any attempt on the part of a Minister in this country to introduce a system which could have the most remote resemblance to that mischievous example. I am not saying that this is so; but an impression has got hold of the mind of the public that it is so, and the facts which have been brought to light go a long way towards bearing out that impression. What we desire is that these appointments should be given to the most fit and proper persons. In appointing a postmaster in a country district, what is wanted is to secure the services of a person who has sufficient time at his disposal to enable him to discharge the duties properly, whose fitness is admitted, and whose character is above suspicion. If the appointments are to be given to the friends of this Party or of that, just as a Liberal or Tory Government happens to be in power, it will be impossible to prevent jobbery and scandal. I look upon this as the strongest part of my case; and I propose to make the Resolution I will venture to place before the House sufficiently wide to deal with the question not merely as a personal question relating to the administration of the Post Office by the right hon. Gentleman who now occupies the position of Postmaster General (Mr. Raikes), but in such a

form as to place on record that this House desires to see all these appointments kept carefully clear from Party jobbery. I do not use that expression as relating to one Party more than another; but I apply it to all Parties. What I desire is that these appointments should be kept clear altogether from Party influence, and that there should be some general principle laid down in regard to the administration of the Civil Service generally, and especially in regard to the Post Office. The Post Office is an institution which we have always regarded with pride. We have seen it attain gigantic dimensions; and it is one of the few paying institutions with which the Government have any connection. I hope it will long continue to be well administered; but I am afraid that if we once allow the minor appointments in the Post Office to be drawn into the whirlpool of Party strife, the result will be that the high character for efficiency which it has hitherto enjoyed will speedily vanish, and we shall have to regret the innovations which have apparently been introduced for the first time by the present Administration. In reference to the question of appointing partizans to these humble positions, I will only quote one case which has been brought to my notice. I refer to Appledore. A complaint has been laid before me by persons who say that the postmastership has been given to a particular individual who had been promised the post, even before a vacancy, by the secretary of the Tory local organization or society. That fact proves, to a great extent, the proposition I have advanced that there is a tendency in these days to place these appointments in the hands of persons connected with the Party in power, and that they are given as a piece of political patronage. I think the right hon. Gentleman the present Postmaster General would do well to signalize his holding of the Office by doing all he can to remove these appointments from the atmosphere of politics and Party influences. The Resolution I propose to place before the House is—

"That is is desirable, in the interests of the efficiency of the Post Office, that the present system of Post Office patronage, so far as it depends upon Party influence, should cease."

MR. SPEAKER: The hon. Gentleman is not entitled to move any Resolution inasmuch as he has given no Notice of it. The Order of the House is that a Resolution must be in the hands of Members, and due Notice must be given of it. The hon. Member cannot spring, so to speak, a Resolution upon the House.

MR. CONYBEARE: I am sorry if I have transgressed the Orders of the House; but your ruling, Sir, relieves me of a difficulty. I have called attention to the matter as I was bound to do, and, having done so, I will leave the matter in the hands of the House without moving any Resolution at all. I will only apologize to the House, not so much for having sprung a Resolution upon hon. Members, because I did not intend to do anything of the kind, and I was not aware that it was necessary to do more than give Notice of my Motion in the form I have done; but for having acquitted myself in a very feeble way in consequence of having the matter rather sprung upon myself, owing to the circumstance which I have already mentioned.

MR. M'LAREN (Cheshire, Crewe), in supporting the contention of the hon. Member (Mr. Conybeare), said, that persons who had been connected with the Post Office assured him, from their knowledge, that there had been cases since the right hon. Gentleman obtained control of the Department which tended to the well-founded belief that patronage in the Post Office was not exercised solely in the interest of the public, but very largely for Party ends. That remark applied specially to the appointment of medical officers. It was alleged that there was a decided tendency to fill these posts with gentlemen of Conservative principles. In that way, great political influence might from time to time be exercised. With regard to the charge that salaries of £120 in England had been reduced to £119, and of £100 in Scotland to £99, in order to bring the posts within the sphere of political influence, whether the motive alleged was the right one or not, it at any rate gave grounds for great suspicion, and while he did not mean to say that the Postmaster General wished to make those appointments for political purposes, he thought the House ought to protest against any such thing being done. He hoped the Postmaster General would declare, not only that such things had

Mr. Speaker

not been done, but that they would not be done for the future.

MR. ARTHUR O'CONNOR (Donegal, E.) said, he would not, at all events, be suspected of an undue leaning towards Her Majesty's present Advisers; but he was bound to state that he had never seen anything to justify the great outcry which had been made a little while ago with regard to the manner in which the present Postmaster General exercised the power entrusted to him. The right hon. Gentleman had a very difficult post to fill, and it appeared that the difficulties in his way had been exceptionally great. Certain appointments had been made, on the right hon. Gentleman's own responsibility, which did not meet with the approval of his subordinates, and something like a public scandal, something like an organized opposition to the Postmaster General by gentlemen who constituted his Staff, had been the result. His (Mr. Arthur O'Connor's) own experience of the Civil Service generally was that there was a great deal too much power in the hands of the permanent officials. He believed that, to a large extent, the excessive expenditure in connection with the Civil Service, and also of the Army and Navy, was due to the fact that the permanent Staff had too much power in their hands, and had been able to control the Parliamentary officials who, for some time after they came into office, were necessarily largely at the mercy of the permanent officials; and, after that, were to a great extent broken in to the established lines and modes of thought in the different Departments. The Postmaster General had dared, what few Ministers had dared, to think for himself; and, as a consequence, those who ought to be subordinate and obedient to him had opposed him. For his part, he was glad to see the dignified and firm attitude of the right hon. Gentleman. If Ministers were to be held responsible for the administration of their Departments, they must have the authority which should be concomitant with the responsibility; and it would never do for that House to deprive Ministers of the authority which was necessary to maintain and enforce their responsibility. The result of such interference would be that the permanent officials would have everything in their own hands. If Parliament allowed the higher portion of the permanent Staff to interfere with all parts of the organization, the country would have to pay for it. If we had Ministers responsible to Parliament, let them be held responsible for the expenditure and for every single detail; but, while we did so, let us have the justice to leave them with a free hand.

THE POSTMASTER GENERAL (Mr. RAIKES) (Cambridge University): I am sure the House will condole with the hon. Gentleman the Member for the Camborne Division of Cornwall (Mr. Conybeare) who has brought forward this subject on his misfortune in having been called in from his dinner, although they will probably have heard with some feeling of satisfaction that the hon. Member had left his papers behind. But I think we must commiserate the hon. Member even in a greater degree upon the misfortune that he has at last been brought to book. These charges have been hanging over for many weeks and months, and what is the position in which the House now finds itself? The hon. Member, who is so anxious to arraign the conduct of a Member of Her Majesty's Government, has had upon the Paper for something like two months a vague charge which he has never thought fit or never found himself able to put in any practical or articulate shape. When at last the hon. Member is called upon to substantiate his charges before the House, he has not even been able—although two months have been allowed to him—to put them in any practical form so that a vote may be taken upon it; and the House is now called upon to deal with this case in the absence of those precious memoranda which the hon. Member has found it convenient to leave elsewhere, and under circumstances in which the House cannot pronounce an opinion upon his statement. I venture to think that it has never before happened, in the history of this House, that a Minister has been called upon to reply to such a charge. I do not know really what the charge is. The hon. Member comes down to the House without materials, and he has failed to place on the Paper any Notice which it is possible to deal with in the form of argument or contradiction. Nevertheless, I feel that it is my duty to notice the very general statement the hon. Member has made in support of a Motion which he has been precluded from putting to the House in

a formal way. The hon. Member has dealt very largely in innuendo. I observe that that is a growing practice among certain classes of politicians in this country—namely, the practice of not making positive and categorical charges, but of insinuating that there may be something in some kind of charge. The hon. Member has talked about the transference of certain clerks. Can the hon. Member offer the slightest shadow of justification for the use of the plural in this case? There never has been any question of more than one particular appointment having been made against the wishes or advice of the permanent officials. Nevertheless, the hon. Member talked about certain clerks as if it were a general practice, insinuating that there has been a general departure from the usual practice of the Post Office in this matter. He has mentioned no name but one. A more unworthy manner of treating such a question as this could not have been adopted. In regard to the whole case the hon. Gentleman has mentioned only one person in reference to whom this preposterous mass of insinuation, innuendo, and suggestion has been brought forward. The hon. Gentlemen did not think fit to be present on a former occasion when a Question which stood upon the Paper in his name was reached, and when his accusation could have been properly met.

MR. CONYBEARE: I think I am entitled to say a word by way of explanation. I did explain to the right hon. Gentleman the Postmaster General on a former occasion that the only reason why I was not in my place on that occasion was because I had not intended to put the Question that evening. I gave you, Mr. Speaker, Notice of my intention not to put the Question, and I understood that you had marked the Question as one which was not to be put. As the right hon. Gentleman had not the courtesy to send me any reply to my note, but insisted upon answering it, although it was not put, I do not think I am to be blamed for not having been in my place.

MR. RAIKES: The statement made by the hon. Member is exactly what I was going to say myself. When the hon. Member talks of courtesy, I certainly cannot understand what his notion of courtesy is. The hon. Member placed a Notice on the Paper impugning the action of a Member of the Government, when the Question relating to the matter was reached. It is true that at the last moment he sent me a notice which I had no opportunity of replying to, or of acknowledging his note, intimating that it was not his intention to put the Question. That Notice only reached me after I had taken my place in the House on the night in question. No, Sir, in these circumstances, I cannot accept the explanation of the hon. Member as a satisfactory explanation. He has now repeated a matter which I think was sufficiently disposed of on a former occasion, when the hon. Member had an opportunity of bringing his Motion forward and dividing upon it, but did not think proper to do so. I am about to deal with the case of the one gentleman whose name has been given in connection with these charges. I have already stated in this House, and I will repeat the statement now, that the gentleman to whom reference has been made, and whose promotion has been called in question, was very nearly at the head of his class. As a matter of fact, he was second in his class, and there was no question whatever of the promotion of the gentleman who was first in the class, and who was the only clerk who was senior to him, seeing that he had been passed over upon at least 20 different occasions, and that, in fact, he was regarded as one who could not expect promotion. I believe that every one of the assistant secretaries in the Post Office had been promoted over the head of that gentleman. What was it that I was asked to do? I was asked to promote a gentleman who was much lower down in the class—a gentleman who was third or fourth in the class, and to place him over the heads of his colleagues. This I declined to do. I made inquiries in the office, and I found that the gentleman who was promoted was a meritorious officer who had discharged his duties with adequate ability, and, therefore, I thought there was no reason for promoting over his head, and over the heads of one or two other competent officers, a junior official who could well afford to wait his turn. I acted in the interests of the Public Service, and especially in the interests of the Department itself. The hon. Member still speaking in the plural number, went on to talk about some of the persons whom I had promoted being connected with me by family ties of some sort or other. I think I sufficiently exploded the groundlessness of that charge on another occasion. The gentleman who was promoted, although a connection of some relative of mine, was not a relative of my own, and so far from being influenced by considerations of that nature he was personally unknown to me, nor was I, nor am I, acquainted with his political opinions. I hope the House will not consider that it is necessary I should answer that charge further. I come now to a more important question —namely, the question of the appointment of persons upon political grounds to Provincial postmasterships to which the hon. Member has referred. It seems to be almost in vain to endeavour to beat into the heads of some politicians a solid and simple fact, and here, again, I have to meet what has already been contradicted, and to state that I have made no reductions in the salaries of provincial postmasters in order to gain patronage for political purposes. The country is, perhaps, not aware, although I think the hon. Member for Camborne (Mr. Conybeare) will be aware by this time, that the patronage of the Post Office is administered by the Postmaster General in cases where the salary exceeds £120 a-year in England, and £100 in Scotland and Ireland, and that all the lower appointments are in the gift of the Lords of the Treasury, and not of the Postmaster General. The allegation is that in certain cases I reduced the salaries in order to place the patronage in the hands of the Treasury. Now it is not the fact that I have reduced the salary of any postmaster, either in this country or in Scotland or Ireland, in any single instance, in order to bring the patronage into the hands of the Treasury. Then what does the hon. Gentleman mean by coming here and giving currency to statements which have not a single atom of truth to support them?

MR. CONYBEARE: There was the Pershore appointment.

MR. RAIKES: Does the hon. Member say that I reduced the salary in that case in order to take the patronage away from the Postmaster General and place it in the hands of the Treasury? Why I find that the salary of the Postmaster at Pershore was £80 when I went to the Post Office, and that it has been and he absented himself from his place raised to £110. That is a sample of the sort of facts which have found currency in the mind of the hon. Member. I hold in my hand a list of 35 appointments in which I have raised the salaries, since I have been in Office, above the Treasury limit, thereby bringing them within the patronage of the Postmaster General. I think, therefore, that I am entitled to complain of the loose way in which charges of this kind are preferred. Here are 35 cases in which I have raised the salaries, since I have been in Office, above a Treasury limit, and have placed the appointments in the gift of the Postmaster General — namely, 20 in England, 4 in Scotland, and 11 in Ireland. There are 16 other appointments in connection with which I have raised the salaries, although the salaries themselves have not reached the Treasury limit, and one of those is the Pershore case. In regard to every one of the 16 cases, of which 11 were in England, 4 in Scotland, and 1 in Ireland, I have made a substantial increase in the salary of the postmaster, and, while doing so, I have not thought it necessary or desirable to make a greater increase, because I believe that the increase allowed affords adequate and sufficient recognition of the services of the officer. The House is probably aware that, in regard to the offices in the gift of the Postmaster General, they are filled up by the appointment of persons already in the service of the Department. I think that in all important Post Offices it is exceedingly desirable that the postmaster shall be a person of actual experience and knowledge of the work of the Department. In very large and important towns that course is universally adopted; but in regard to the smaller towns, where the salaries are very small—rarely exceeding £120 or £125 a-year—I confess that I do not think that it is always for the public interests that the postmaster should be an officer who has no other means of livelihood than the £120 a-year that he gets from the Post Office. I am bound to say that in such circumstances, a respectable tradesman, who has a good shop and business, and who is respected and popular in the place in which he lives, is more likely to make an efficient public servant than some poor clerk, brought from a distance, entirely un-

connected with the neighbourhood, with a salary of little more than £2 or £2 10s. a-week, who has to fit up the premises with borrowed money, and has, in addition, to have recourse to some guarantee society for a security, thus making a further inroad upon his small salary, and who may be placed under extreme temptations in consequence of the inadequacy of the remuneration he receives to maintain him, and who is forbidden to increase his income by engaging in any other pursuit. I may be wrong, but I cannot help thinking that it is to the public interest, when we cannot make the salary such as would enable a man fairly to live upon it, and to maintain a position of respectability and responsibility, to leave the appointments as they are—in the gift of the Treasury, who fill them up by persons with a local connection, and who are able to improve their position by other means. My connection with the Post Office has tended to confirm the opinion which I previously entertained, that it is quite possible not to do any really good service to the neighbourhood, or to the men you appoint as postmasters, by an indiscriminate raising of the salaries above the Treasury limit, thus taking them out of the Treasury patronage, because in such places you would put men who have no other means of earning a livelihood in a position which they ought not to occupy in the town in which they live. It is a mistake to suppose that by raising the salaries of those who fill these appointments I secure any additional patronage either for myself or my Party, because no appointments will take place until vacancies arise. Although the Post Office may have obtained no increase of patronage from what has been done, the appointments under the new regulations are left to be filled up on the next vacancy, and probably by the time they arise another Government may be in Office. So far from exercising the patronage entrusted to me in the interests of the Party to which I belong, I have only been guided by two considerations in the matter; first, the convenience of the public; and, secondly, the propriety of recognizing the claims of the present holder of a particular office. There is no doubt that a good deal of inconvenience does arise in the filling up of the very small appointments. I believe they are sometimes conferred by the Treasury upon their political friends, and I may say that the very last person who applied to me to appoint a postmaster was the hon. Member for the Camborne Division of Cornwall himself. I received his letter only a few days ago. I have forwarded his letter to the Treasury in whose gift the appointment is, and not in mine. He also referred to a place called Appledore, the postmastership of which is not in my gift, but in that of the Treasury. I do not know who is the postmaster there, but the name submitted to me by them was, of course, sent down and reported upon to me by the surveyor of the district. The nominations to these appointments are made by the Treasury in the ordinary course, and checked by the permanent Post Office Authorities. I have no interest whatever in these appointments, not even so much as the hon. Member for North-West Cornwall appears to have himself.

Mr. CONYBEARE: I did not at all mention the case of Appledore with the intention of making any charge or complaint against the right hon. Gentleman. I think I was careful to explain that my remarks were directed against the system. In the particular instance referred to I was desired to make the application. I very much regret, that, in the performance of my duty to my constituents I should be required to make an application of such a nature. It is a kind of political patronage which I think ought to be abolished, and, for my own part, I would rather not be troubled with matters of that sort.

Mr. RAIKES: The hon. Member disclaims any personal object in connection with the case of Appledore. I will only say that it is difficult to see anything in the speech of the hon. Member in which he gave any fact to support the insinuations with which the speech itself abounded. I am inclined to agree with the opinion which I know has been expressed by some hon. Members of this House, that as regards the extremely small appointments, they might with advantage be preferred to the head postmaster of the locality in which they have to be made. Of course, we cannot guard altogether against favouritism or jobbery of some kind or other, and a local postmaster would probably be quite as likely to perpetrate a job as a Secretary to the Treasury. At the same time, I think it would be a convenience to the Treasury—I am speaking upon a matter with regard to which I have had no official communication with them—I think it would be a convenience if they were relieved of this tiresome duty of finding postmasters for these extremely small places. That would leave for the Treasury what I may call the lower middle-class appointments, and those, I think, ought not to be given to the Postmaster General, because he cannot have the local knowledge which would enable him to select the most proper men. I have only one word more to say, and that is in regard to the observations of the hon. Member for the Crewe Division of Cheshire (Mr. McLaren), who made some reference to medical officers. He spoke of the great political influence which medical officers can exercise; but, for my part, I do not know what form that influence can take, unless it is in the administration of drugs to particular persons to prevent them from attending the poll on particular days. These appointments are very small ones—worth from £20 to £50 a-year, and I do not see how a medical officer holding an appointment of even £50 a-year is likely to exercise any great amount of political influence. I may tell the hon. Member for Crewe that the only case with which I am acquainted in which an appointment has been in any way cavilled at by anybody on the spot, is a case in which a gentleman wrote to complain of an appointment I had made, and to say that he had voted for the Conservative candidate, and, therefore, thought it hard that he had not been appointed himself. That is the only complaint which has reached me in regard to the exercise of this patronage; but as I have said the value of these appointments is extremely small. I am always glad to obtain reliable information on the spot, and what I do generally is to get from the surveyor of the Post Office a list of candidates whom, on the whole, he may believe to be suitable for the appointment, and if I know anybody on the spot, I then refer to him in order that I may check the surveyor's report with an opinion obtained privately, and by that means secure the appointment of the most qualified person. I will undertake to say that no question of a Party nature has influenced any of these appointments; but that I have always endeavoured to obtain an unprejudiced opi-

Mr. Raikes

nion from the local surveyor, and any other information that it is in my power to obtain. The hon. Member for East Donegal (Mr. Arthur O'Connor) has alluded to a certain difference of opinion which existed some time ago between myself and some of the experienced and very able gentlemen who act as my professional advisers. I shall speak of them with all respect. The great services they have rendered to the country and their large experience entitles them to respect, and I should be extremely foolish were I not to recognize fully the value of their services. I am delighted to avail myself whenever I can of their matured opinion, but I claim for myself the right to differ from them when I consider it my duty to do so. I should be very sorry to hold my present Office for one day if I felt that I was bound to endorse every paper that is put before me. As long as I have the honour to serve Her Majesty in any capacity whatever, I shall endeavour to maintain the respect that is due to the experience and ability of the permanent officials; but I shall also have regard to that sense of public duty which ought to animate every public man who is placed in a position of trust.

MUSSEL BEDS IN TIDAL WATERS (SCOTLAND).—RESOLUTION.

MR. ANDERSON (Elgin and Nairn) said, he rose to call attention to the recent prosecution, by the Procurator Fiscal of Ross-shire, of Lossiemouth fishermen at Tain, for dredging for mussels to be used as bait; to the alleged existence of private rights in mussel beds in tidal waters; to the injury to the prosperity of the fishing industry caused by such alleged private rights; and to the advisability of vesting all mussel beds in the tidal waters of Scotland in the Scotch Fishery Board; and to move—

"That an humble Address be presented to Her Majesty, praying Her Majesty to appoint a Royal Commission to inquire as to the existence and extent of private rights in mussel beds in the tidal waters of Scotland, and to inquire generally as to the nature and value of such rights, and to report as to the advisability of compelling the transfer of all such rights to the Fishery Board for Scotland."

Notice taken, that 40 Members were not present; House counted, and 40 Members being found present,

MR. ANDERSON said, his Motion raised several of the most important

questions concerning the fishing industry in Scotland that could possibly be brought before Parliament. The prosecution mentioned in the Notice arose out of the fact that certain fishermen who resided at Lossiemouth, in Elginshire, were dredging for mussels for bait in the Dornoch Firth on the 25th of May, 1886, and took away about two tons of mussels which were lying below low-water mark, where one could suppose private rights of property could not exist. These men were summoned at the instance of Major Rose of Tarlogie, the charge being that they had stolen the mussels, which were alleged to be his property. The case was heard at considerable length in the Sheriff's Court, and the men were fined £10. It was stated at the trial that Major Rose had put buoys to warn people for infringing on the mussel beds in question, and that notices were published to the same effect. But fishermen had been in the habit of taking away mussels for 30 years, and at the trial they stated their willingness to pay for the mussels if Major Rose could establish his title. In such circumstances it was perfectly extraordinary that any conviction could have taken place; but the men had been convicted, and the verdict had been affirmed by the Court of Session.

THE LORD ADVOCATE (Mr. J. H. A. MACDONALD) (Edinburgh and St. Andrew's Universities) said, the question had been decided by the Justiciary Court.

MR. ANDERSON said, the matter was the subject of an appeal, and had been finally decided. They had heard of a good many startling claims made by lairds, but of all the rights they had succeeded in establishing in the Courts of Law, that, to his mind, was one of the most monstrous. The fishermen were dependent for their existence on getting cheap bait, and he maintained that, by all natural laws, they had a right to dredge for it in the deep sea. The fishing industry was a very precarious one. Owing to the difficulties connected with the conveyance of their fish to market the fishermen had often to sell their fish by auction, at a ridiculously small price, sometimes not realizing more than 3s. or 4s. for their take, and out of that small sum they had to pay the laird from 1s. 6d. to 2s. or more per basket for the mussels with which they baited their hooks. In the Western Highlands of Scotland the laird did not charge these poor men for the mussels, which were habitually gathered for local consumption without interference on the part of the proprietor or the factor. When they were collected for sale the right of purchase in some rare instances had been limited to particular agents paying rent to the proprietors. Thus that extravagant charge for bait was not made on the Western Coast of Scotland, but on the North Eastern Coast of Scotland it imposed a very heavy burden on the precarious industry of the fishermen. Indeed, so onerous was the charge made by the factors for those mussels on the East Coast of Scotland that the fishermen there had actually to get their bait from Glasgow and the Western Coast instead of from the mussel beds of their own districts. Those lairds thus compelled the fishermen to pay enormous railway rates, the freight being £1 per ton from Glasgow to Lossiemouth or Burghead, although coal was carried for 10s. a ton. These matters called for the interference of the House of Commons, and he could not imagine any case of greater importance. He had endeavoured to see his way to bring in a Bill to legislate on the subject. But it was necessary, in the first place, to ascertain the nature, extent, and value of these private rights in the mussel beds, and how it came to pass that the law of Scotland should have recognized anything of the kind. He had himself put questions on that subject, and he had been told that the Scotch Fishery Board could not give any information regarding it. It was natural that the lairds should give none. They were thus left completely in the dark as to the nature, extent, and value of those rights; and therefore it was necessary that there should be an inquiry instituted before any legislation was introduced on the subject. He did not propose that the Commission should lead to the confiscation of any rights of property which had been legitimately acquired; but he believed that in many cases those alleged rights did not legally exist. The Commission, however, would ascertain how that matter stood, and what sum, if any, was required for compensation. In the next place, he thought that those bait beds, instead of being left to the care of the proprietors or of persons who were not proprietors, should

be placed under some authority in the public interest who would look after their proper preservation. They were far more important than oyster beds. Many complaints had been made about the Scotch Fishery Board, but he understood that the Board was to be reconstituted and made efficient; and he could not think of any better way of using the Scottish Fishery Board than by vesting in it the right to all these bait beds. They had at present a staff of inspectors who received good pay, but had practically nothing to do; they might be usefully employed in looking after the mussel beds. Then the revenue which the Board would derive from the sale of mussels would be sufficient to recoup any expense which might be incurred for that purpose, and also pay the interest which might be necessary to meet the lairds' claims to compensation for any well-defined legal rights; while the poor fishermen would get their mussels at 6d. instead of 1s. 6d., 2s., or 2s. 6d. per basket. That was the scheme which he suggested, and he did not see what objection there could be to it. He was sorry to say he believed the Government were going to object to it. He had had communications on the subject with the present Chief Secretary for Ireland (Mr. A. J. Balfour) when he was Secretary for Scotland. That right hon. Gentleman had taken a great interest in the subject, had gone into it thoroughly, and had been satisfied that it was a case in which Parliament ought to interfere, and the right hon. Gentleman had agreed with him that the course he proposed was the proper one. He had even gone so far as to say that if a discussion were brought on there would not be much objection to the proposal. He had, therefore, received great encouragement from the late Secretary for Scotland, and had congratulated himself on the thing being done. But since that time several serious changes had taken place, one of them being the transfer of the right hon. Gentleman from the administration of Scotland to that of Ireland, to the disadvantage of both countries. He had addressed a communication to the present Secretary for Scotland, but, instead of receiving the answer he expected, Lord Lothian had sent him a letter in which he stated that he could not consent to any inquiry of the kind. It was most unfortunate that on an important ques-

Mr. Anderson

tion of this sort the Minister who had to decide whether this inquiry should be granted or not was not in the House of Commons to listen to the arguments adduced in support of it. In his opinion, it illustrated the inconvenience of having the Secretary for Scotland a Member of the House of Lords. He was sure if Lord Lothian had heard his statement he would have been satisfied that his proposal was a reasonable one. They had reason to complain of the manner in which Scottish Business was conducted in that House. Neither the First Lord of the Treasury nor any other Member of the Government who could give a satisfactory reply was present. The Lord Advocate had, no doubt, received his marching orders from Lord Lothian. This was not the way to treat Scotland, and Scottish Members were placed in a very great difficulty. He hoped, however, that before the debate was concluded they should hear something really hopeful from the Government, who could do nothing better than accept his proposal, if they really wanted to do anything that would conduce to the prosperity of the fishing industry. The hon. and learned Gentleman concluded by moving the Resolution which stood in his name.

MR. ESSLEMONT (Aberdeen, E.), in seconding the Resolution, said, he did not think any good purpose would be served by continuing the discussion at great length. He could not share the despairing feelings of his hon. and learned Friend in supposing that nothing was going to be done by the Government in regard to this question. That was a larger question than might be supposed. Although the mussel itself was of no apparent value, yet for the line fishing —on which thousands of people depend in Scotland—it was essential for the carrying on of the industry. The fishing on the coast of Aberdeen was a larger source of annual revenue than the whole of the land in the county—that was to say, that the produce of the sea around Aberdeenshire represented a greater value in money than the produce of the land. A great deal of attention was paid to the Land Laws and to the interests of agriculture; but the Legislature remained blind to the enormous interests involved in the fishing industry. He was of opinion that the object which his

hon. and learned Friend had in view could be attained without the expense of a Royal Commission. He could suppose no better business for the Scottish Fishery Board than to inquire into this subject, and there was no great necessity at the present stage for appointing a Royal Commission. The Scottish Fishery Board, if properly constituted, would have a greater knowledge of the fishing industry, and of the importance of this question, than any Royal Commission that could be appointed. Why not give to that Board the powers which his hon. and learned Friend asked for a Royal Commission? His hon. and learned Friend might disagree with him, but he (Mr. Esslemont) had been longer acquainted with the East Coast of Scotland than his hon. and learned Friend, and his hon. and learned Friend must not suppose that he had any superior information in regard to this question than he (Mr. Esslemont) claimed to have. On the other hand, he was quite sure that he represented as large a fishing interest as any Member in the House. But his purpose was to get the information they required with the least possible expense, and in the best form; and he hoped the Lord Advocate, if he would not agree to the appointment of a Royal Commission, would at least give them an assurance that the subject would receive the attention of the Government, and that he would communicate with the Fishery Board, and see by what means they could best bring about the result they all desired. In one fishing village in his own constituency, with about 14 boats, a sum of £224 was paid annually for the right of laying down mussels in the river Ythan and picking them up again. The right seemed to be leased to a firm, and was sub-let by them to the fishermen, who were practically obliged to pay that large sum or cease to carry on the industry of white fishing. He did not desire that any private rights should be violated, but only desired in the meantime full information. He begged to second the Resolution.

Amendment proposed,

To leave out from the word "That" to the end of the Question, in order to add the words "an humble Address be presented to Her Majesty, praying Her Majesty to appoint a Royal Commission to inquire as to the existence and extent of private rights in mussel beds in the tidal waters of Scotland, and to inquire generally as to the nature and value of such rights, and to report as to the advisability of compelling the transfer of all such rights to the Fishery Board for Scotland,"—(*Mr. Anderson,*) —instead thereof.

Question proposed, " That the words proposed to be left out stand part of the Question."

THE LORD ADVOCATE(Mr. J. H. A. MACDONALD) (Edinburgh and St. Andrew's Universities) said, that there were two points involved in the Motion of the hon. and learned Member—the first relating to the prosecution of the Lossiemouth fishermen at Tain, and the second affecting the general question. Now, as regarded the general question, there could be no doubt whatever that from far distant times legal rights had been established to mussel beds on the coasts of Scotland. Of that there could be no more substantial proof than the fact that an Act was passed under the Government of Lord John Russell in 1847, the Preamble of which set forth that certain rights had been established by law to mussel beds in Scotland, and that the Act was passed for the purpose of making the taking of mussels from such beds by persons who had no right to take them an act of theft. Therefore, about the general question that such rights had been recognized, not only by the Law Courts of Scotland, but also by Parliament, and that within recent times, there could be no question whatever. Whether that was a wise state of things was a different question, regarding which people could have their own opinions. So far as he knew, where such rights did exist, they were well-defined rights, and rights which could be ascertained by reference to documents and to practice. Even if the Government were prepared to assent to a Royal Commission on a matter of this kind, the last thing they would think of referring would be the question of law as to whether individual proprietors had those rights or not. It was quite plain that to set aside the Courts of Law which had to deal with those matters would be perfectly out of the question. For instance, the case of Tarlogie was a case in which, as regarded the legal right, there could be no question whatever, and no room for an inquiry, by Royal Commission or otherwise, as to whether the right existed or not. In regard to that case, the questions ap-

pealed to the Court of Justiciary were these—" Had Major Rose a good title to the mussel beds ? " and the answer was " Yes." The second question was —" Could said title be held in a question with the public to convey an exclusive right to mussel fishing below low-water mark ? " and the answer was also " Yes." It must be remembered that those mussel beds were in an estuary, and not in the open sea ; but whether below or above low-water mark, it was only right to say, in this public assembly, that, as regarded what was done by the fishermen who were put on their trial, he had not the slightest doubt that on the occasion in question their object was not to go surreptitiously and as knaves to take the mussels, but that they went openly in the face of day for the purpose of having the right tested, and that any theft committed was not a malicious or immoral theft ; and the decision having been against them, the fishermen had, so far as he knew, submitted to it, and had not again trespassed. He thought it due to them to say that. Having said that on their behalf, he was bound to say, on behalf of the proprietor, that he had taken pains and trouble to give intimation to those who might interfere with his rights as to the extent to which he claimed those rights, and the ground which they covered. It was perfectly well known that he asserted his right by letting out the mussel beds, and that the extent of them was carefully marked by buoys, about which there could be no mistake. The only remaining question, then, was whether the Government were to consent to the appointment of a Royal Commission upon this question. There was no doubt that the existence of a proper supply of mussels for fishermen on the coast of Scotland was a most important matter for their industry ; but he thought all who knew anything about it would bear him out in saying in all fairness that the existence of those mussel beds had, to a great extent, tended to keep up the supply of mussels. They knew perfectly well that fishermen in most places, and certainly in Scotland, were sometimes a little careless of the gifts of Nature when they had them in their own hands ; and that in the past, whatever might be advisable in the present, what was needful to the fishermen in the prosecution of their industry was, to a great extent, protected for them by the fact that there was some legislation regarding it. The question was whether now—he understood the Motion to go that length—it was advisable that all the mussel beds in Scotland at present possessed by private individuals should become the property of the nation, not, as the hon. and learned Member fairly said, by way of confiscation, but by taking them over, and giving compensation to the present owners. The hon. and learned Member asked for a Royal Commission to investigate the matter. Now, whatever the hon. and learned Member's individual conversations might have been with the late Secretary for Scotland, he did not know; but he would accept the hon. and learned Member's statement regarding them—namely, that the reading of those conversations was that a Royal Commission would be assented to if he made a good case in that House. But Her Majesty's Government were not prepared to assent to a Royal Commission, and that for two reasons. In the first place, they did not think it was necessary for the purpose of inquiring into this matter; and, in the second place, they thought that whatever inquiry was to take place could take place in a much cheaper and better way. At the same time, the Government did think that this was a matter which ought not to be overlooked; and he could assure the hon. and learned Member that they had not got to begin that work, because they had already been in communication with the Fishery Board, and had obtained some information and some of their views on the subject. He was glad the hon. Member for Aberdeen (Mr. Esslemont) agreed with him that the Fishery Board was a competent tribunal to look into this matter, and perfectly competent to advise the Secretary for Scotland, first, as to whether anything should be done, and, in the second place, as to what should be done. He could assure hon. Members that the matter would not escape the careful attention of the Government; and the Secretary for Scotland was quite alive to the necessity of full and accurate inquiry. He, therefore, hoped the House would not accept the Motion of the hon. and learned Member, but, after the statement he had made, would allow it to be negatived, and he was sure his

hon. and learned Friend would accept the assurances he had given on behalf of the Government.

DR. CLARK (Caithness) said, he had hoped they should have heard something more definite from the Lord Advocate in this matter. As to the suggestion to consult the Fishery Board, he did not think there was much confidence in that body amongst Members who represented fishing constituencies; but that Board was to be re-constituted this year, and if the new Board contained representatives of the fishermen and fish-curers, they would be glad to have the question referred to them. That Board might then have full control of the mussel beds, and where there were private rights they should be bought over. Whether there were private rights or not, it was most important that the mussel beds should be protected, or they would be altogether destroyed. Another matter which should be considered, either by the Fishery Board or by Commissioners, was the pollution of the mussel and oyster beds on the West Coast by sewage. The filth dredged from that great canal the River Clyde was carried down to the fertile mussel and other beds in the lochs at the foot of the Clyde, and these beds were destroyed by the malign substances deposited upon them, to the great injury and loss of the fishermen in those parts. In consequence of the destruction of mussel beds, supplies of mussel bait had to be brought over at great expense by steamer from Ireland to the North-East of Scotland. With regard to the right of private individuals to buoy out several acres of ocean, he thought that that was a matter which might be brought before the Crofter Commission when their duties extended to the whole of Scotland, as would soon be the case.

MR. COLERIDGE (Sheffield, Attercliffe) said, he regretted that Courts of Law had lent themselves to a process of constantly whittling down the effect of Magna Charta, which had made it illegal for the Crown to grant out to a private individual any rights of fishing in tidal waters that might belong to it. The provisions of the Oyster Fisheries Act sanctioned the marking out of oyster beds for miles along the coast, one being six miles long by half a mile in breadth. Poor people whose sole industry had been the collection of mussels were not allowed to take them from these oyster beds, and so were deprived of their means of existence.

Mr. BRADLAUGH (Northampton) said, he wished to draw the attention of the Lord Advocate to the great injury now being done to the mussel beds and fisheries in Loch Long and Loch Goil by the deposit of enormous quantities of silt. He supposed there was a difficulty in taking the dredging vessels used on the Clyde to where they would meet the real action of the sea; but he was told—he spoke without personal knowledge to justify an opinion—that if it was possible to take the whole of that silt down as far as Ailsa Craig, it would not come back to Loch Long and Loch Goil. He had seen long lines baited with mussels which, after lying through the night, were so coated with absolute filth as utterly to prevent the fishermen from earning a livelihood. These men were an industrious and sober body, and it was clear they had not been protected in this matter. They had no means of protecting themselves against a powerful Corporation, such as that which had the charge of the dredging of the Clyde; and he therefore trusted before these men were ruined that the Lord Advocate, or whoever was in a position to act, would be able to take some steps to prevent the utter annihilation of their industry on that part of the coast.

Mr. J. H. A. MACDONALD said, he could assure the hon. Member that this matter had been brought to the notice of the Government; it was undoubtedly an evil which required their attention.

Question put.

The House *divided:*—Ayes 130; Noes 108: Majority 22.—(Div. List, No. 136.)

Main Question proposed, "That Mr. Speaker do now leave the Chair."

MERCHANT SHIPPING—MEDICAL SERVICE ON BOARD TRANSATLANTIC LINERS.—OBSERVATIONS.

Dr. TANNER (Cork Co., Mid), in rising to call attention to the entirely insufficient medical requirements and supervision on board Transatlantic liners for emigrants and steerage passengers; also to invite inquiry into the great risks incurred by master mariners and seamen on board vessels making long voyages, in consequence of the former being obliged to act as physician and surgeon to the crew, in addition to his

Mr. Coleridge

other duties, said, the Irish people were leaving our shores in vast numbers, and, as an Irishman, he felt bound to try in the best way he could to safeguard those people when undergoing the horrors—because it was a fact that horrors did exist on board those steamers—on their passage across the Atlantic, notably in the inclement season of the early spring and in the winter. The medical men who were on board those steamers might practically be divided into separate classes. First, there were men who went on board those vessels, such as the White Star steamers and the American liners, for a certain period. During that period they hoped to enjoy themselves, and did not look for any pecuniary advantage. At the same time, they always tried, as most men did, to endeavour to make their responsibility as small as they possibly could. Then there were men who went on board those steamers, and who undertook the care of the passengers in course of transport across the Atlantic, as a means of livelihood. Unfortunately, the major portion of those medical men were men who could not always get other employment—they were men who possessed minor qualifications; and he maintained that if the hon. Gentleman the Secretary to the Board of Trade (Baron Henry De Worms) inquired into the qualifications of the medical officers on board most of those Transatlantic liners, he would find that, with the exception, of course, of some of the great Companies, and some of the excellent and super-excellent steamers, the major portion of the men so employed possessed qualifications which he would term totally inadequate to the responsibility entrusted to them. The position of the doctor was also very unsatisfactory. He was not treated as a gentleman, and had no authority. He wished to call the hon. Gentleman's attention to the fact that the doctors on those emigrant steamers, though appointed by the Board of Trade, practically speaking, were not allowed to report to the Board of Trade. The doctor on one of these ships ought, no doubt, to be subject to the authority of the captain; but he ought to have in his own department sufficient authority, and to be responsible to the Board of Trade. Only three years ago the Board of Trade issued a form, which required that all ships' surgeons should report any complaints made by passengers on the voyage. That Order had never been complied with; and why? Simply because, like many other Orders which had been formulated in that House, which had received the sanction of that House and of the responsible Government, the Government, and possibly the House, were not strong enough for the shipmasters. The owners of the vessels were practically too strong for them, and although the Order was given it had not been carried out. The Shipping Companies, in defiance of that Order, stated that the doctors who complied with the Order would be instantly dismissed the Companies' service. Now, he maintained that that in itself would certainly warrant him in calling attention to this subject. The letter of Dr. Irwin, which appeared in *The British Medical Journal* in February, 1884, first drew attention publicly to the matter under discussion. He stated that the average shipowners took a person whose qualifications complied with the minimum requirements of the law, and who could be judiciously silent when it might be inconvenient to speak and judiciously blind when not intended to see, but who would act as a buffer between negligence on the one hand and public indignation on the other when the health and interest of passengers came into opposition with the money interests of his employer. Dr. Irwin at the present time occupied a distinguished position in America, and it was stated in the medical journals of America that if the Government of this country did not pay attention to these facts it would become the duty of the American Government to fill up the gap. Dr. Irwin went on to state that practically the public did not see the danger; and what he (Dr. Tanner) maintained was, that in due course of time, if they did not safeguard the position, they would have a calamity which might be a very grave one on some of these ocean-going steamers, and a calamity which might be easily guarded against if they only paid attention to these facts which he brought under their attention. Dr. Irwin stated that his statistics were disregarded by the right hon. Gentleman the Member for West Birmingham (Mr. Joseph Chamberlain) when he was President of the Board of Trade. He (Dr. Tanner) sincerely hoped that the present occupant of that position would practically go in and win. Cargo ships were often sent to sea as emigrant vessels, and emigrants were condemned to wretched quarters which could be patched up on an emergency. A great number of vessels were sent from Liverpool to America with goods. They brought back cattle, and then, without being sufficiently cleansed, they received large numbers of emigrants. Ought not that to be seen to? Then, there were no interpreters on board these vessels. He also wished to draw the attention of the House to the fact that there was insufficient hospital accommodation on board these ocean-going steamers. If he were to take any hon. Member of that House into some of these little dens which were dignified by the name of hospitals, they would be surprised at the miserable inadequacy of the accommodation. The hospital was generally a small apartment not the size of the Table in that House, miserably fitted up, and totally inadequate to meet any emergency which might arise. Practically speaking, there was only one line of steamers—the White Star Line —which carried such a thing as a surgery. There ought to be ample accommodation on board every ocean-going steamer for treating cases of sickness, and a proper place where medicine and medicinal appliances could be made out and put at the disposition of the medical men. There should also be some isolated place set apart for the treatment of infectious cases. On one ship capable of carrying 1,500 steerage passengers there was only one water tank. The House could appreciate the danger of such a state of things. In many cases the accommodation for steerage passengers was wretched in the extreme, and passengers were huddled together in a manner which it would be horrible to describe in detail. He hoped the Government would give their earnest attention to this question, and take steps to bring about a better state of things.

THE SECRETARY TO THE BOARD OF TRADE (Baron HENRY DE WORMS) (Liverpool, East Toxteth): I have listened with attention to the remarks of the hon. Member for Mid Cork (Dr. Tanner), who has brought his professional knowledge to bear upon the subject; but the question was narrowed to much smaller limits than the speech of the hon. Member by the Notice which he placed upon the Paper, and which is—

"To call attention to the entirely insufficient medical requirements and supervision on board Transatlantic liners for emigrants and steerage passengers; also to invite inquiry into the great risks incurred by master mariners and seamen on board vessels making long voyages, in consequence of the former being obliged to act as physician and surgeon to the crew in addition to his other duties."

It is scarcely necessary for me to point out to the hon. Member that the regulations of the Board of Trade are simply the embodiment of the Act of Parliament which relates to the carriage of passengers on ships, and the sections which bear specially on the question are Nos. 41, 42, 43, and 44. These sections of the Passengers Act clearly lay down that every passenger ship must carry a duly qualified medical practitioner. I quite admit that the words "duly qualified" are somewhat elastic, and may be construed in one way by some persons, and in a different way by others. I would only point out that those particular cases in which practitioners have not proved themselves fit for the situation they occupied are not, as a rule, reported to the Board of Trade. In nine cases out of ten the Board of Trade are utterly unaware of the condition of things as stated by the hon. Gentleman. When a passenger ship leaves Liverpool with emigrants on board, it is accompanied by a doctor, and it is inspected, before it leaves, by an official from the Board of Trade, who inspects the ship in the first instance, goes down below and sees that the berths for the emigrants are in accordance with the rules laid down by the Passengers Act—for instance, that every passenger has so many cubic feet of air, and that there are proper divisions between the different sexes. The officer in charge of the emigrants has all the emigrants paraded before him for inspection, and if there is the slightest symptom or suspicion of infectious disease the emigrant is sent on shore. So far as the Board of Trade is concerned, every possible precaution is taken to prevent the spread of infectious disease on board ship, and to see that the regulations founded on the Act of Parliament are rigidly carried out. As to the qualifications of the medical officers, the Board of Trade have very little authority. A "duly qualified medical practitioner" is deemed to mean

Baron Henry De Worms

one who has taken a diploma as a doctor, or surgeon, or, in some cases, as an apothecary. I am bound to say that I do not think that an apothecary ought to be considered a duly qualified medical practitioner; and I hope that this view may be adopted generally on board passenger and other ships. With regard to doctors or surgeons, it is impossible for the Board of Trade to ascertain whether the officer is duly qualified or not. If a medical officer turns out to be incompetent, and his incompetence is brought to the notice of the Board of Trade, the Board would have a right to exercise the power of causing such person to be dismissed. I believe that in the large lines of Transatlantic steamers the proprietors do their utmost to procure the services of competent medical officers, but the difficulty is that there are a great many young medical men who are anxious to take a passage on board these steamers in the summer months, as a matter of pleasure, who go away when the more inclement season arrives. No doubt that circumstance does give rise to difficulty; but in dealing with that difficulty the Board of Trade are in no way called upon to assist the Steamship Company. We have nothing to do with the selection of medical officers, although we might interfere in a flagrant case of incompetency. It is in no way my province to provide medical officers for ships. As to the hospital accommodation, it is such as the proprietors of the steam ships deem adequate; but I am not prepared to say that it always is adequate. I am informed that in cases of infectious disease they are invariably isolated. No doubt the accommodation for such cases is occasionally inadequate, and certainly, so far as the Board of Trade is concerned, it is our endeavour to do all that is possible to improve the accommodation for emigrants, and to see that the rules as to cleanliness and hygiene are properly observed. The hon. Gentleman says that the accommodation for emigrants is insufficient in certain very important particulars. I believe that the hon. Member is right in that statement, although I know that in all new ships of the White Star, Inman, Cunard, and other great lines, those arrangements are being perfected and great improvements are being introduced. In every ship a list of drugs in store is required to be kept.

DR. TANNER: I said nothing about that. I merely spoke of the inadequate provision for the storing of drugs.

BARON HENRY DE WORMS: The Board of Trade is extremely particular, not only with regard to the storing of drugs, but to the general surgical accommodation.

DR. TANNER: The point I called attention to was the want of adequate surgical accommodation.

BARON HENRY DE WORMS: I do not think the hon. Member is correct in his objection to the arrangements in that respect.

DR. TANNER: In many cases there is not only inadequate surgical accommodation, but no proper place allotted for the storing of drugs.

BARON HENRY DE WORMS: There is a special cabin fitted up for surgery. In some of the largest steamers provision is made for every surgical appliance. The hon. Member will find, if he chooses to inquire, that every possible precaution is taken in the large ocean-going ships, and that they do fulfil, as far as possible, the requirements of the law. The Board of Trade have no further responsibility in the matter than to see that the requirements of the Passengers Act are thoroughly carried out, and I can assure him that so long as I have had the honour to be at the Board of Trade no charge of negligence or gross violation of the provisions of the Passengers Act on the part of a medical officer has been received. I can only say that if the hon. Member will bring forward any definite case that requires investigation it shall receive the fullest inquiry. It is our desire to see that the regulations are fully carried out, and that the rules which concern the comfort and well-being of the passengers and emigrants are fully carried out.

DR. TANNER: May I be permitted, by the indulgence of the House, to say one word? I am afraid that I did not sufficiently explain myself in regard to the difficulty in which ship doctors are placed. It unfortunately happens that their grievances cannot be brought forward properly on account of the paramount influence of the shipowners. If the ship doctors were to parade their grievances and the consequent grievances to which the emigrants are subjected, they would inevitably lose their place and their means of livelihood.

PUBLIC MEETINGS (METROPOLIS)—SOCIALIST MEETINGS ON OPEN SPACES.—OBSERVATIONS.

MR. JAMES STUART (Shoreditch, Hoxton): I rise to call attention to the interference with public meetings in open spaces in London. I do so at the present moment because there are very few opportunities for any private Member to call attention to a matter of this kind, and also because the present is a very apt opportunity for doing so, inasmuch as the old formula of grievance before Supply is particularly applicable in this instance. I believe that there is a real grievance in this matter, as I hope to be able to show to the House before I have done. I may also say, in my own behalf, and on the behalf of those for whom I speak, that I am not bringing forward this matter from any sympathy with the views of those who are most concerned in it—I mean the Socialists. It is the misfortune of those who have to contend for any important principle that they frequently have to contend for that principle in the persons of those with whom they do not agree. I do not propose to follow that point farther at the present moment. All I say is that the action of the Socialist body, which is mostly interested in what I have to deal with, has been as lately in Northumberland to the detriment of interests which I, for one, deem to be important. At the same time, I feel that I am bound to maintain, as far as I can, the right of public meeting when I believe that that right has been violated in any way. I believe that, whatever may be the views of any body of persons, there is great advantage to the community in allowing those views to have free expression, and that injury is done to the community if there is any prevention of, or even appearance of preventing, that free expression of opinion. I think, also, it is necessary to call attention to anything we may believe to be an interference with the right of public meeting in the open spaces of London on account of the peculiar situation of London itself, and of the few facilities which it affords for the holding of public meetings. There is no town in England so badly off in regard to facilities for the holding of public meetings as London. Take Bradford with its great St. George's Hall, capable of holding 5,000 or 6,000 persons, and used as a large meeting place for the people of that town. Go to the East End of London, and you will find that probably the biggest hall is that of Shoreditch, which is only capable of containing 2,000 persons, whereas the population drawn from on the occasion of a public meeting there may amount to six or seven times the population of the entire town of Bradford. I am sorry to say, also, that the School Board of London does not afford those facilities for the holding of public meetings in the board schools which is given by the authorities of Birmingham, Bradford, and other large towns. I merely mention this fact in order to show the importance of the question I am about to bring forward, and I may add that I have myself given Notice of my intention to move a Motion upon the subject of the application of board schools, under proper conditions, to the purposes of public meetings. I think that it is especially the duty of those hon. Members who, like myself, represent the populous districts of London, to draw the attention of the House to what has recently taken place with respect to meetings which have been held in the open spaces of London, and especially in regard to the relations of the police with such meetings. In the case of a meeting held at St. George's Hall, Bradford, the duty of the police is simply to protect the meeting, and not to interfere with it. What we desire is to be placed in a similar position in respect to the meetings which we are compelled to hold in the open spaces of the Metropolis, so long as such meetings do not interfere with the ordinary traffic. There is also another matter with respect to London to which it is necessary for me to call attention in connection with the right of public meeting. It is this —that whereas the police of other towns are under the government of the Municipality, and thereby under the government of the people themselves, the police of the Metropolis are in no sense whatever under the government of the ratepayers of the Metropolis. On the contrary, they are under the government of the Chief Commissioner, and are directly under the Home Office. The head of the police of London is, therefore, a member of a political Party in this House, and, therefore, he ought to avoid

the appearance of any partizanship with respect to the control of political meetings in London, as far as the interference of the police may be concerned. As a matter of fact, the Secretary of State for the Home Department is ultimately the responsible party for the action of the police in London, and that fact may be regarded as a further apology for my bringing this matter before the House. Whereas the ratepayers of other towns have an opportunity of appealing to their Town Council or their Watch Committee, in London, if they desire to raise a question of the kind, they are compelled to bring their complaint under the notice of this House. I will, however, pass from that point without further comment, in order to get to the special matter with which I desire to deal this evening, and I shall in no sense wander into the general question of the right of public meeting in London, but I will confine myself to one particular case. There have been several instances occurring lately in regard to such meetings, and I wish particularly to refer to two meetings which have been held in Sancroft Street, near the Kennington Road, on May 1 and 8. These were meetings of the Socialists, and I am informed that meetings of that body have been held for a considerable time on Sundays. Those meetings have not been disturbed until of late, when disturbances began to arise in consequence of the interference of a body calling themselves the Primrose Society. In an answer given by the hon. Gentleman the Under Secretary of State for the Home Department (Mr. Stuart-Wortley) to a Question put to him recently, he referred to the meeting which was held on the 8th of May, and spoke of two rival meetings being held. I have made what inquiry I could into the matter, and I have not been able to find that the society calling itself "The Primrose Society" has in any sense endeavoured to hold any public meeting at all. I am unable to trace their meetings as existing in any way other than as an endeavour to disturb the meetings which have been held by the Socialists. The principal mover, as far as I can make out, in the Primrose Society is a greengrocer and a boxing man, connected with a school of arms in Lambeth Walk, and I take it that the supporters of the society generally partake very much of the same character. The result of the interference of the Primrose Society with the meetings of the Socialists has been, that a disturbance has taken place on several Sundays between the two rival bodies, as they are called. In the week preceding the meeting of May 1 an application was made by the Socialists to the Lambeth Police Court in regard to an interference which had occurred at one of their meetings ; the case was reported full in *The Daily News* and *The Standard*, and the report says—

"A disturbance took place between the rival bodies on Sunday week, and during the week an application was made by a Socialist at the Lambeth Police Court with regard to the interference with their meetings, and Chief Inspector Chisholm then informed the magistrate, that in order to stop these disturbances, neither party would be permitted to hold these meetings."

There is a point to which I shall refer a little later on. But this is a statement made by Chief Inspector Chisholm in reference to the meeting of the 1st of May. A considerable gathering of Socialists took place in the Sancroft Road on that day, and Superintendent Brennan and Inspector Chamberlain were both present. After the meeting at the corner of Sancroft Street, where it joins the Kennington Road, there were seen marching down Sancroft Street from the other end a body of the Primrose Society with yellow favours and a large primrose-coloured banner with an inscription on it. It was known beforehand that they were coming, and it was perfectly well understood why they were coming. They approached quite close to the Socialists who had attended the meeting, and then orders were given by the Superintendent and Inspector to 100 police, stationed about 50 or 100 yards off, to come up to the place. This body of police charged the crowd, charging first against the body of Socialists. If the facts, as I state them, are wrong they can be easily contradicted. I am only stating them as they have been represented to me. *The Daily News* says—

"Finding it was impossible to quell the opposing force, Superintendent Brennan forced his way into the ranks of his men, and the police then charged in a compact body, scattering members of both bodies right down the street, and dispersing them in all directions. . . . Some of the leading Socialists were severely handled by the police, and one of their members, after a sharp chase down the Kennington Road, was taken into custody. Small bodies of men assembled in the Kennington Road, but were immediately dispersed by the police. The mem-

bers of the Primrose Society, however, succeeded in re-assembling in Regent Street, and forthwith marched to Saville Place, Lambeth Walk, where a large crowd had assembled, in the expectation that the Socialists would hold a meeting there. No meeting was held, but the members of the Primrose Society came across two Socialists and chased them down the Lambeth Road into Church Street. The men were overtaken and a fight ensued. One of the Socialists was knocked down and kicked, but the police put in an appearance, and the injured man was put in a cab and taken home with two fellow-Socialists."

This is what took place on the following Sunday, and here I quote again from *The Daily News*—

"Having regard to the possibility of a renewal of the previous Sunday's disturbance in Sancroft Street, Kennington Road, the police, under Mr. Superintendent Brennan, of the L Division, made ample arrangements yesterday to prevent a collision between the Socialists and their opponents, the Anti-Socialists. For some time past the Lambeth Branch of the Social Democratic Federation has held peaceful meetings at the head of the street. After the occurrence on the previous Sunday it was resolved to hold a meeting at the same place yesterday to protest against the conduct of the police. It would seem, however, that the proposal was abandoned. The Battersea Branch alone appeared in organized form, and, finding that access to the street for the purpose of a meeting was barred by the police, made no attempt to assert their claim."

Now, what I wish to point out is that, in my opinion, it would have been proper in regard to the first meeting on the previous Sunday for the police to have barred the approach of the threatening crowd in Sancroft Street. And this leads me to make the remark that we have here an instance of a meeting prohibited, practically, by the police, because, in addition to the newspaper report that no meeting was held, I find this report of it in the Socialists' own paper—

"We were not allowed to hold our meeting on Sunday morning at all. There was a strong force of the police and a good muster of our comrades and sympathizers, but we were kept continually moving. Chapman, on his arrival, was immediately arrested. Afterwards we made a move to the Albert Embankment, followed by mounted police and constables who emerged from the stable yard of the London Tramway Company. Arrived at the Embankment, Rossiter had no sooner mounted the box to open the meeting for Ward than we were hustled from our position. A temperance meeting was not interfered with, and a religious meeting was going on the whole time at the corner of a street at Vauxhall Cross. The police would give us no explanation. Bail for Chapman was refused."

And now let me refer the House to what

took place in 1882 at Weston-super-Mare when the Salvation Army was frequently assaulted by a body called the Skeleton Army. I quote from the case of "Beatty *v.* Gillbanks," reported in *The Law Journal* of 1883, vol. 51, page 117, which was an appeal by the Salvation Army against the decision of the magistrates. The report says—

"A riotous mob had assembled on the 23rd March, 1882, to prevent the Salvation Army meeting. This caused great terror and alarm in the minds of the peaceful inhabitants of the town, who believed, and had good reason to believe, that the procession would lead to a repetition of disturbance, and would endanger life, property, and the public peace ; and who in consequence brought the matter to the notice of the sergeant of police in charge of the town, and made divers complaints to him thereon. The Justices in consequence placarded a notice stating that, ' as there are reasonable grounds for apprehending a repetition of such riotous and tumultuous assembly in the public streets of Weston-super-Mare, we do hereby require order, and direct all persons to abstain from assembling to the disturbance of the public peace in the public streets.' "

In the appeal it is further stated that—

" The appellants intended to parade their procession through the principal streets and public places of the town and to collect on their march a large mob of persons to accompany them, and they had good reason to expect that they would come into collision with the Skeleton Army and the other persons antagonistic to themselves, and had good reason to expect that there would be the same fighting, stone throwing, and disturbance as there had been on previous occasions, and intended, on meeting such opposition, to force their way through the streets and places as they had done on previous occasions."

The hon. and learned Gentleman the present Solicitor General (Sir Edward Clarke) contended for the appellants that—

" There was no intention to commit an unlawful act, nor to do a lawful act in an unlawful way. No definition of an unlawful assembly goes so far as to include a case where the assembly is with a lawful intent, and not in its nature tumultuous or riotous, but where, by reason of the riotous conduct of others, a tumult is likely to ensue. An act which is right in itself does not become wrong by reason of the apprehension of misconduct in other persons."

In giving the judgment of the Court, Mr. Justice Field said—

"They certainly did assemble in great numbers, but such assembly to be unlawful must be tumultuous and against the peace. The finding of the Justices," the Court declared, " comes to this—that a man may be indicted for doing a lawful act if he knows that his doing it will cause another to do an unlawful act. There is no authority for such a proposi-

Mr. James Stuart

tion, and I, therefore, think the appeal must be allowed."

The result is that—

" A lawful assembly is not rendered unlawful by reason of the knowledge of those taking part in it that opposition will be raised to it, which opposition will in all probability give rise to a breach of the peace by those creating it."

I have already shown that in the case of the Salvation Army at Weston-super-Mare there was a formal proclamation by the Justices of the Peace, and that the endeavour to prevent the meeting in London was made by an application from the Superintendent of Police to the magistrate in the terms I have already read, when he "informed the magistrate that in order to stop these disturbances neither party would be permitted to hold these meetings." There had not in any sense been an offence committed, nor had it been hinted, in the reply to a Question given in this House by the hon. Gentleman the Under Secretary of State for the Home Department, that there was anything at all in the nature of a riotous proceeding in connection with the meetings of the Socialists in Sancroft Street, other than had arisen from the attacks made upon them by the Primrose Society as it is called. On the 5th of May the hon. Gentleman the Under Secretary of State for the Home Department, in reply to a Question put by the hon. Member for Northampton (Mr. Labouchere) said—

" The Commissioner of Police informs me that Inspector Chamberlain did not call upon the meeting held in Kennington last Sunday to break up, and that he did not direct the police to break it up. The mere contemplation of violence by Primrose Societies gives to the police no additional power of interference with peaceable meetings."

I take that to be a correct statement of the law. I put a further Question to the hon. Gentleman the Under Secretary of State on Friday last, and his reply to me was—

" Except a general police order, which has been public property for many years, and the substance of which is that the police are not to interfere with persons attending political meetings unless specially ordered by the Commissioner, there are no general instructions upon which the police are authorized to act in respect to public meetings in open spaces. Each case must depend on its own particular circumstances, and must be left to be dealt with according to the discretion of the Chief Commissioner."

On Tuesday last, in reply to a Question put by the hon. Member for Leicester (Mr.

Picton), the hon. Gentleman the Under Secretary stated—

"I have before informed the House that the police have no special instructions to prevent Socialist meetings as such, and I am assured that no such instructions, nor any special instructions at all, were given in the case of last Sunday's meeting."

Now, what I want to ask is this—that if no general instructions were given with regard to that meeting, and the Socialists were acting in accordance with what the Government admit to be the law, how was it that the police interfered to prevent the holding of a meeting when the only danger to the public peace arose from a possible attack upon it by other persons? In the same reply to the hon. Member for Leicester the hon. Gentleman the Under Secretary said—

"I am informed that meetings have been held in Sancroft Street on Sundays for about six months past. Chapman and Kemp were arrested under a warrant issued by a magistrate sitting at Lambeth Police Court charging them with unlawful assembly."

I maintain, judging from what I have quoted of the law, that the assembly was in no sense an unlawful assembly, and that it is a very dangerous thing indeed that the police of London should get into the habit—whether for Socialists or any body of persons—of considering an assembly to be rendered unlawful because of the knowledge of those taking part in it that opposition will be raised to it, which opposition will, in all probability, give rise to a breach of the peace. If the police hold this view, and act upon it, it is particularly dangerous to the general political life of the Metropolis. When, for instance, I stood for the borough which I now represent, I should think I am not wrong in saying that two-thirds of the meetings which I held had to be held in open spaces. Had a threat been held out by any opponent that these meetings would be disturbed, and the public peace endangered by their opposition, I should apparently have been in danger of having my meetings suspended. I take it, therefore, Sir, that, at any rate, I have a right to hope that, in the future, we may see given to the police of this Metropolis some directions in regard to their duty in the matter of public meetings in open spaces—some intimation that it is part of their duty to prevent interference with orderly public meetings in the open spaces of London, and that it is not their duty to prevent the holding of such meetings on account of threatened opposition, which may give rise to a breach of the peace by those creating it.

Mr. PICKERSGILL (Bethnal Green, S.W.): As a Metropolitan Member, and one, therefore, especially interested in this question, I desire to make a few remarks. It cannot be denied, I think, that the opinion very extensively prevails in the public mind that recently the police have unduly interfered with the right of public meeting in London, and also that the action of the police has been inspired from very high quarters. Of course, I accept most fully and implicitly the statements which have been made from the Treasury Bench, that in particular cases no explicit instructions have been given from the Home Office. It would be quite unnecessary that such instructions should be given, and, as it would be unnecessary, I can quite believe that to give them would be an indiscretion, and I am sure the right hon. Gentleman the Secretary of State for the Home Department (Mr. Matthews) would not be guilty of such indiscretion. But, Mr. Speaker, this suspicion in regard to the conduct of the police undoubtedly prevails, and—even though it should be ill-founded—the existence of it is mischievous, and justifies us in calling the attention of the House to this subject. I desire, Sir, to confine my attention to one particular case, and I am anxious not to put before the House any facts in regard to which there may be possibly a conflict of evidence. Now, in regard to the meeting of the 1st of May, in Sancroft Street, these facts were admitted in evidence by Chief Inspector Chamberlain. It is admitted, in the first place, that meetings have, for several months, been peaceably held in that street; it is admitted also that during the week preceding the 1st of May a gang of roughs had publicly threatened to break up the meeting on the following Sunday; it is admitted that just when the meeting was on the point of starting a gang of roughs, calling themselves the Primrose Society, were seen advancing, obviously with the intention of carrying their threat into execution. Then, it is admitted in the evidence of Chief Inspector Chamberlain that he called upon the Socialists to break up their meeting. I submit that that order, which Chief Inspector Chamberlain admitted in the Lambeth Police Court, was clearly illegal. The law was settled, as my hon. Friend the Member for the Hoxton Division of Shoreditch (Mr. James Stuart) has already informed the House, in several cases, of which the "Queen v. Beatty" is the most important, and in which the Salvation Army was concerned. This case most clearly decided that a lawful meeting does not become unlawful although it is certain to be resisted by force. I say, then, that to give the order which is admitted was given was illegal. These Socialists, who appear to be better acquainted with the law than are the Metropolitan Police, declined to disperse, and the police then cleared the street. Well, looking at the broad facts of this case, what do they amount to? They amount to this—that a gang of roughs publicly threatened that they would break up a peaceable meeting, and that, with the assistance of the police, they succeeded in effecting their purpose. How would it be possible, Sir, to give greater encouragement to rowdyism? The right of public meeting is no right at all, unless it is held to imply a right to protection in the exercise of that right of public meeting. In this case you have this gang of roughs, who had threatened to break up this meeting, who were at the time advancing—they had, in fact, begun to put their threat into execution—and I submit it was the clear duty of the police, under such circumstances, either to keep off the Primrose Society from the Socialist meeting, or, if it were necessary, to disperse the Primrose Society altogether. Now, I desire, Sir, to call attention to one consequence arising out of this business. I asked a Question to-day of the hon. Gentleman the Under Secretary of State for the Home Department (Mr. Stuart-Wortley) with regard to the arrest of two men. I admit that the reply that I received was perfectly courteous, as far as I was concerned; but it seemed to me very unsatisfactory as regards the police. Now, what are the facts as regards the man Chapman? Chapman, it is admitted, was present at the meeting on the 1st of May. For some reason—which, apparently, is not known to the hon. Gentleman the Under Secretary —he was not arrested on that day.

Nothing, in fact, was done in regard to him until the 4th of May. On the 4th of May a warrant was obtained against this man Chapman on a charge of having taken part in an unlawful assembly. Now, an unlawful assembly is only a misdemeanour, and a misdemeanour not of a very heinous character; and I submit that the natural, proper, and usual course would have been to take out a summons against this man Chapman. But, Sir, if the offence was so serious as to render it necessary that the police should take the somewhat extraordinary step of obtaining a warrant, one would naturally suppose that the police would have immediately put that warrant into effect; but they do nothing of the kind. Nothing was done in regard to this warrant until the 8th of May; and on the 8th of May, when Mr. Chapman was about to take part in the meeting in Sancroft Street, he was arrested. Well, now, what is the natural inference from that? I think it is that the warrant was obtained in order to be held *in terrorem* over the head of Mr. Chapman, and that a particular moment was chosen for putting the warrant into execution when the arrest of Mr. Chapman would be likely to strike terror into the minds of all those who, within the jurisdiction of the Metropolitan Police, might be disposed to exercise what I thought was a Constitutional privilege — the right of public meeting. The conduct of the police in itself is serious enough; but it does not stand alone. There are, upon many sides, indications of an attempt— which may be, perhaps, a last and despairing attempt—on the part of the privileged classes to put the people down. There is, if I may so express it, a spirit of coercion in the air, which finds its chief embodiment in a Bill upon which much of our time this Session has been expended, and which also takes on many other forms. We see it in the Boycotting and intimidation which is practised by the Primrose Party, and one cannot travel, even for a quarter of an hour in a carriage on a suburban railway, without hearing expressions of the same spirit in the terms in which the readers of *The Globe* and *The St. James's Gazette* refer to their fellow-citizens— terms which I do not hesitate to characterize as inhuman and most unwise. Well, Sir, in such circumstances as these, I conceive that it is peculiarly the

Mr. Pickersgill

duty of this House to maintain the right of public meeting, a right which has been, and is, one of the chief safeguards of the liberties of the people; and I think it is the duty of this House to guard that right all the more jealously, and all the more vigorously, in the persons of men from whose political opinion we may very widely dissent, and whose conduct in some respects we may condemn.

MR. CUNNINGHAME GRAHAM (Lanark, N.W.): Mr. Speaker, I claim the indulgence of this House for a few moments to say a few words on this question, which I consider a most important one, and I do so all the more readily as I am not in the habit of trespassing often, or at great length, upon the patience and time of this House. I can quite imagine hon. Gentlemen opposite will say—What is the good of making a row about a lot of poor devils of Socialists? I do not think that anything very serious has been charged against these Socialists, though your Socialist is a fearful wild fowl. It is not long ago that the hon. Gentleman the junior Member for Northampton (Mr. Bradlaugh) was looked upon as Lucifer or Beelzebub, and hon. Gentlemen opposite said they could never sit with him in this House. Now they manage to take their dinners with him, and digest them very well; and I dare say the day is not far distant when we shall see the hon. Gentleman the junior Member for Northampton occupying a place above the Gangway, and not below it. I believe that these Socialists have been dispersed in their meetings simply and solely because they are poor, because their doctrines are not popular, and because no one cares to stand up and incur the odium of speaking for them. England is a free country—thanks to Heaven! It is a free country for a man to starve in—that is a boon you can never take away from him—but it appears in the future it is not going to be a free country to hold public meetings in. What with the closure in the House of Commons, coercion in Ireland, and the suppression of meetings in London, we are getting to an almost Russian pitch of freedom. And, Sir, should we succeed in arriving at the priceless boon of that freedom, we cannot wonder if the people at last shake themselves clear of their apathy, and take the matter a little into their own hands; I think it is not unlikely that, while we are talking here, the people will make a determined effort to assert their undoubted rights. I do not suggest that the people of England are ripe for revolution yet; they will be soon enough, especially in face of the Bills which are now presented to this House; but I do say that I can see no just motive whatever that—because a man's doctrine, or political faith, differs in some measure from that held by the rest of the community—free speech, which has always been considered the birthright of an Englishman, should be denied to him. Neither do I say that the police have acted on their own motion in this matter; we know perfectly well who stands behind them; we know that by the way in which questions have been dealt with, by the paltry, shuffling manner in which they have been put off—and I am not here to say one word against the police of London; I consider them to be one of the finest bodies of men in the Kingdom; I am here to compassionate with them in having to do such dirty work as to break up meetings, and to behave in a manner which cannot but be repugnant to their feelings. Now, I think every hon. Member of this House knows Buffalo Bill — Colonel Cody — and I would suggest, very respectfully, to this House that a select deputation of the Unionist Party should wait upon Colonel Cody to ask him for the loan of a few thoroughbred Unionist Indians to coerce the people of London. As this House, after all, represents but a small portion of the community, and as nothing is gained nowadays without agitation, I hope the public will not let this matter rest, but will agitate and bring it before the attention of this House, so that we shall be obliged to concede freedom of speech and the right of meeting to every class of the community.

THE SECRETARY OF STATE FOR THE HOME DEPARTMENT (Mr. MATTHEWS) (Birmingham, E.): Mr. Speaker, I agreed with the hon. Gentleman the Member for the Hoxton Division of Shoreditch (Mr. James Stuart), when, in the temperate speech in which he introduced this subject to-night, he said that considerable inconvenience is felt in London from the want of suitable places of meeting. It is quite true, as the hon. Gentleman said, that open spaces are few and separated by considerable distances, and that there are very few halls which can accommodate large meetings, especially of the character of the Socialist gatherings to which people in all parts of the Metropolis are invited to attend. Now, Sir, it seems to have been assumed by some hon. Gentlemen opposite that there is at the Home Office, or in my mind, some particular animus against Socialist meetings. I assure the House that that is absolutely untrue; I have not troubled myself a bit about Socialist meetings, all that I know of them is from what I have read and heard. I have never given any directions of any sort or kind with regard to Socialist meetings. The only directions I have given have tended to prevent obstruction in the streets; and here let me point out one fallacy, if I may use the expression without discourtesy, entertained by the hon. Gentleman the Member for Shoreditch (Mr. Stuart). He said that Sancroft Street is an open space. It is nothing of the kind; it is an ordinary street. The hon. Member knows perfectly well that many of the open spaces of the Metropolis are vested in the Board of Works, and that the Parks are, by special regulations, appropriated to public meetings. As a rule, there can be no objection to large public meetings held in the Parks, because they do not tend to obstruct the ordinary traffic of the Metropolis. If any body of men, whether the Socialists or the Primrose Society, chose to hold large meetings in streets, and inconvenience arises, and interruption of traffic takes place, they ought to be dispersed.

Mr. JAMES STUART: I think I stated, Mr. Speaker, that there have been no complaints of these meetings interrupting the traffic, and that, what is more, the ground given for the opposition on the part of the police to their being held was not that of an interruption of traffic.

Mr. MATTHEWS: I do not think any ground was alleged by the police. Now, the hon. Member has said—and said, I believe, with truth—that for six months meetings have been held every Sunday in Sancroft Street, and not interfered with by the police, and not interfered with by anybody, and held in a perfectly peaceable manner. Sancroft Street is a street in which, I believe, on

Sunday mornings, there is very little traffic; consequently, these meetings for the last six months have not impeded the traffic, and, therefore, the police did not interfere. The meetings were held peaceably and quietly; but, unhappily, on the 1st of May, that happened which the hon. Gentleman the Member for North-West Lanark (Mr. Cunninghame Graham) described in very classical language—namely, that the people took the matter into their own hands. The people living in Kennington, strongly opposed to the views of those who form the Socialist meetings, disliking their eloquence, and disliking the presence of these Socialists in their midst, determined to take the matter into their own hands, and not to allow the meetings; and, accordingly, on the 1st of May what occurred was this—that a crowd of 2,000 or 3,000 persons appeared, marching in a body on the Socialist meeting then assembled in Sancroft Street, with obviously hostile intentions. As I am informed, the police, seeing this body of men approaching with obviously hostile intentions, advanced and stopped them in their advance on Sancroft Street. Meanwhile the Socialists, very wisely, and with commendable prudence, withdrew from Sancroft Street down Kennington Lane, and the police having stopped and dispersed the people who call themselves the Anti-Socialist Primrose Society—[*Ironical cheers*]—I say they call themselves the Lambeth Anti-Socialist Primrose Society; but I know nothing of their composition; all I know is that they are inhabitants of the district and dislike the Socialists—having encountered and stopped the Anti-Socialists, the police followed, no doubt, in the rear of the Socialist meeting, always remaining between them and those who proposed to attack them. Upon that, I regret to say, some members of the gathering, which had originally been a Socialist meeting, became extremely violent to the police, and two men — Chapman and Kemp — called upon their followers and supporters to turn back and fight. The police, in preventing them doing this, were assaulted, and one man, as the hon. Member has stated, was taken up for assaulting the police in the riot which ensued in consequence of the incitements which were given by Chapman and Kemp to their followers, and one man named

Mr. Matthews

Blackwell. Warrants were forthwith applied for against Chapman and Kemp for the part they had taken in the riot. That is what occurred on the 1st of May. The police applied for the warrants, and the hon. Member for Bethnal Green (Mr. Pickersgill) has complained that that was an unusual procedure. Whether rightly or wrongly—I think rightly —the police applied for warrants instead of applying for summonses, because, as the hon. Member knows perfectly well, when a warrant is asked for, it is in the discretion of the magistrate to grant or to refuse it. An information on oath must be made, and the magistrate has an opportunity of hearing what is deposed upon oath, and exercising his judgment upon the case before anyone is called upon to appear at all. The police thought that would be a fair and proper course; they thought that in a case which might bear a political complexion the fairer course was to bring the facts before a magistrate in the first instance, before the defendants were called upon to answer the charge, and let the magistrate say whether it was a proper case to be brought before the Court. That is the reason why the police resorted to the process by warrants instead of by summons. The warrants were not executed at once, for the very simple reason that the residences of Messrs. Chapman and Kemp were not known to the police, and were not contained in any of the ordinary publications relating to residences. Therefore, the police were unable to execute the warrants until the 8th of May, when Mr. Chapman came again to address another meeting in the same locality. Under the circumstances, I put it to the fair and candid consideration of the hon. Members for Shoreditch and Bethnal Green, whether the police could have acted otherwise. In the interval between the 1st and the 8th of May the meetings were held of both parties. At the meeting of the Socialists it was announced that boxes of cartridges had been provided; that there would be a regular fight next Sunday; and that, if the people who had come the Sunday before for the purpose of attacking the Socialists came again, they would meet with a warmer reception. On the other hand, the Anti-Socialists, also meeting in Kennington, determined that non-residents of Sancroft Street and the locality

should not be allowed to meet there again. A Petition signed by 63 people living close to Sancroft Street, was presented to the First Commissioner of Police, objecting to these meetings in the street as being a great nuisance to them and praying him to prevent the gatherings. In consequence of that, I think, the First Commissioner of Police acted strictly in accordance with his duty in ordering double patrols to be on the spot the next Sunday. Accordingly, there were some 200 police sent down to Sancroft Street, and the street very soon became filled with an angry crowd which never assumed the character of a meeting on either side, because the Socialists and the anti-Socialists were more or less mixed. Accordingly, the police prohibited no meeting, and stopped no meeting; but they did what was a wise and sensible thing to do, they kept the crowd constantly on the move in order to prevent a conglomeration of persons on either side to take place on one spot, because there is no doubt that if these two bodies, so filled with inflammable material, had come together the consequences would have been terrible, for a breach of the peace would have been inevitable. This further occurred, that Chapman appeared on the scene; he was then got at for the first time by the police, who arrested him under the warrant they had. These are the simple facts as they are laid before me, and I think that if the state of things which I have described had been allowed to continue, the First Commissioner of Police and the Home Secretary would have deserved the severest censure. There has not been the slightest political bias in the action of the authorities; the same measure of justice has been meted out to the anti-Socialists as to the Socialists. The crowd was kept moving, and the intervention of the police was caused solely by the imminent danger of a breach of the peace if these hostile bodies had been allowed to come together. They certainly would have come to blows if the police had not interfered, and compelled the one party and then the other to move on. In any of the proceedings there has not been the slightest partiality shown on behalf of either party. The sole duty of the police is to keep the peace in the Metropolis; their duty is not to interfere,

I quite agree, with any public meeting held in a place where the traffic of the street, or the convenience of the inhabitants, are not interfered with. Of course, when they have such good and substantial grounds for believing that a serious breach of the peace is going to be committed, the police would be neglecting their primary duty if they did not take measures to prevent such an occurrence.

Mr. BRADLAUGH (Northampton): The subject of public meeting in the Metropolis is one in which I have taken considerable interest and made great exertions for some 40 years of my life. I will first put to the right hon. Gentleman the Secretary of State for the Home Department (Mr. Matthews) what I conceive to be the law on the subject. By the Metropolitan Police Act, I understand, that the Chief Commissioner of Police, and no other person, has the right to make such regulations as, in his discretion, he may think fit, for the regulation of traffic in every thoroughfare, making special regulations when he considers, from the processions announced, or from the probability of large assemblies of people, such regulations may be necessary. I do not understand that there is any other power whatever put by Statute in the Home Secretary or in any other person. As far as meetings in London are concerned—and when I speak of London I mean the Metropolis—I think I am right in saying that, with the exception of some few occasions when great feeling has been evoked in connection with some special question, large public meetings have been more orderly during the last 50 years than probably they have been in any other city in the world, and that the tendency of the people has been to preserve order. I would suggest that it is the interest of every Government in this country, whatever its politics may be, to allow the widest latitude with reference to holding reasonable public meetings, and that the exercise of this right constitutes a kind of safety-valve for the expression of public opinion. The House should bear in mind that there are many people who have taken part in such assemblies who would have been excluded from a meeting held in a public building by the mere impossibility of hiring a public building for the purpose, and I maintain that it is to the

advantage of the public peace that these persons should have reasonable opportunities of meeting and discussing any matters of grievance. There has been considerable difficulty in my mind in speaking on this matter, because I fear there are men who have during the last few years done much to imperil the right of public meeting by the needless provocation offered sometimes to the authorities and sometimes to persons with whom they disagreed. Although I regret that, I think it ought not, on the other hand, to influence our judgment in dealing with the general question, and I think that a great deal is due to the hon. Member for the Hoxton Division of Shoreditch (Mr. Stuart), who has raised the question this evening, and I would point out what seems to be a great want of attention to their duties as guardians of the peace on the part of the police. According to the statement which we have listened to, of the Home Secretary, I understand him to say that a number of inhabitants, hostile to the holding of meetings in Sancroft Street, took the law into their own hands and announced that they intended to prevent by force, if necessary, the holding of such a meeting. Now, the meeting was either lawful or unlawful. If the meeting was unlawful, these inhabitants were not the persons to declare the law and enforce it; if the meeting was lawful, the police had knowledge of it, and it was their duty to take steps in order to restrain those who threatened to break the peace. I do not go to the length to which the hon. Member for the Hoxton Division of Shoreditch went, who said that the right to public meeting involves the right of protection on the part of the police of the meeting. I cannot say that I accept this as a matter of law, or as a matter of policy. I am inclined to think that the less the police have in any way to do with public gatherings on political or social questions, until a breach of the peace has commenced, the better for all concerned. I have never needed the assistance of the police, and I have never given the police more trouble than I could help in connection with any meeting that I have held. I have always tried to keep within the law, and I hope that I have done so. Although I have sometimes disagreed with the Home Office as to what the law was, I have never admitted the right of the Home Office to interfere with a public meeting convened for a lawful purpose in London. I remember on one occasion, about 15 years ago, a meeting announced to be held in Trafalgar Square was forbidden by a proclamation from the Home Office. I replied to the Home Office proclamation by a notice to the Home Office and the Chief Commissioner of Police that I intended to hold that meeting, and that it was a lawful one, and that any attempt to interfere with it would be illegal and would be resisted. The meeting was held. The Chief Commissioner of Police was present, and I presume that he was satisfied with it, because I have never heard anything on the subject since. I am of opinion that any kind of interfering by the police in gatherings of this kind often provokes disorder which might otherwise be escaped. Although I have no love for those persons who call themselves Socialists—they are not complimentary to me—yet I am bound to say that since they have held their meetings in and about London, there has been a great deal of harsh treatment shown to them which has never been shown to street preachers, who very often assemble in places where they stop the traffic and cause inconvenience to the neighbourhood. I will undertake to drive the Home Secretary round in a Hansom cab next Sunday morning, and show him 200 or 300 such meetings in places where the traffic in the streets is certainly greatly impeded. While I am claiming the right of public meeting to the fullest extent, I would also claim a generosity of construction with regard to what may be the right to hold public meetings, and that it should not be tied down by exact legal technicality; because I think that if you give the public —especially the poorer classes of the public—any sort of notion that you deal a harsher measure to them than you do to other classes, you provoke feeling which otherwise would not exist, and you give them power which they would not otherwise command. The police in the East of London interfered with a meeting at a corner of Dodd Street; the conduct of the police was undoubtedly in that case, if their own expression may be judged, prompted somewhat by their disapproval of the opinions expressed there, and I suggest that this was no business of the police whatever. They

have nothing to do with the views expressed at meetings, whether by Socialists, or the Salvation Army, or by those people who habitually gather a number of persons around them to sing—whatever their opinions may be, it is no part of the duty of the police to consider them. At Dodd Street the audience used to number about 20; after the police interfered they increased rapidly to 2,000 or 3,000; and it is in this way that interference gives prominence to men who would otherwise have to stand or fall by their own arguments. What happened in Dodd Street will always be the result in similar cases of interference on the part of the police with public meetings. The meetings which have taken place since the Chartists' movement up to the present time may be said, on the whole, to have tended to make a people wiser, and better, and more law-abiding. There is, at the present moment, danger of contagion from abroad, where repressive laws have been resorted to against a class of people bearing the name of Socialists, and if those to whom that name is applied in this country are given the same ground of complaint, we shall be playing into the hands of a class of men, and assisting them in sowing the seeds of mischief among the people.

MR. J. ROWLANDS (Finsbury, E.): Having regard to the neighbourhoods in which public meetings are held, there are few questions of more importance than that of the right of public meeting in open places. There is, I believe, no one of us who represent East End constituencies on this side of the House who has not had to avail himself of open spaces in that district for the purpose of addressing his constituents. I am pleased to hear that the Home Secretary has given no directions whatever to the police with regard to these meetings, and the statement coming from him is one which we welcome with the utmost satisfaction. Meetings at street corners in London are not at all exceptional; you find them in streets where there is a small amount of traffic, and where, I venture to think, they do very little harm. The noticeable circumstance in the present case is that the party who wanted to break up the meeting alluded to by the hon. Member for the Hoxton Division of Shoreditch, and who succeeded in doing so, had no desire themselves to hold a meeting. They did not declare that they wanted to hold a meeting; but that they wanted to prevent the other side from doing so, and the moment the police kept the people on the move, they succeeded in their object. I think it would have been better to prevent the two parties coming together, and to have allowed one party to hold its meeting, rather than to keep both parties on the move. I do not think the police did well to give as a reason for applying for warrants against Mr. Chapman and Mr. Kemp, that their addresses could not be found. I find that when the case went before the magistrate, the detectives admitted that the men were well known to them, and that they were allowed to go away on bail without sureties; and I say it is an extraordinary thing, if they were so well known, that the police should have had any difficulty in tracing them. I do not know of one instance of such persons being out of the way when called upon by the authorities, and I have no doubt that the whereabouts of these men could easily have been ascertained by the police. I was sorry to notice, while my hon. Friend was seriously discussing the right of public meeting, a levity on the Ministerial Benches, which, I think, warrants us, as Members having the right of open-air meeting at heart, in thinking that it would be better at once to fight out this question in th House of Commons. There was an article which appeared in one of the public journals in relation to public meetings, which, among other things, said that this question was of so serious a nature that unless it was settled at once "we should find ourselves in the throes of a social revolution." That was said with reference to the Hyde Park demonstration that took place on Easter Monday, and which was one of the largest and most orderly gatherings ever drawn together in the country. If such language is written with regard to a meeting of that kind, I ask how long it would have taken writers in the public Press to inflame the people still more, if that meeting had been interfered with, and how long it would have been before they went one step further? I am bound to express my belief that the right of public meeting has in other times been the salvation of the country, and that the people should be allowed

to meet for the purpose of discussing their grievances in the light of day, because, under those circumstances, those who hold extreme opinions have those opinions modified, and in that way public attention is directed to grievances which exist. I believe that all hon. Members will admit that in this way the public weal is benefited. I hope we shall soon find that these disturbances in London will cease, and that the right of public meeting will remain as sacred in the future as it has been in the past.

MR. CREMER (Shoreditch, Haggerston): I have listened attentively to the observations addressed to the House by the right hon. and learned Gentleman the Home Secretary, and I am not so clear in my interpretation of his views, with regard to the instructions given to the police, as the hon. Member for East Finsbury (Mr. J. Rowlands) seems to be. I hope, however, that the interpretation which my hon. Friend has placed on those utterances is correct. And if the right hon. and learned Gentleman does not rise and deny them, we shall, of course, consider that his remarks were faithfully interpreted by my hon. Friend, and feel more secure that no attempts will be made hereafter to suppress the meetings of Socialists, or any other class of our fellow-citizens. I have no particular love for the doings of the Socialists, and I think that ought to be made clear, because, otherwise, we might hereafter be accused of sympathizing with their actions. Most of us on this side of the House, especially Members of the Party to which I belong, have been roundly and scandalously abused by the men who have been imprisoned through the action of the police, and who are now posing as martyrs. But this question of public meeting is dear to us, no matter whether it be in connection with street preachers, Socialists, the Salvation Army, or any other class of our fellow-citizens, and we shall feel bound to defend their right of meeting, because we have seen the beneficial results which have followed its exercise. I am surprised that the Government have not profited by past experience in this matter. It is not more than 23 years ago since a Tory Government entered upon a crusade of this kind against the people of London. We were not then enfranchised, and the masses were not represented in this House. It was in the year 1864 that a Tory Government attempted to put down a gathering of peaceable citizens on Primrose Hill. For a time they succeeded, and my ribs for weeks afterwards bore testimony to the efforts of the police engaged in that operation. The crusade continued until those famous riots occurred in Hyde Park. We know that the Government attempted to suppress the right of the people of London to meet in their open spaces and express their opinions with regard to the great Constitutional changes they desired ; we know that the people were shut out from Hyde Park, but that by some accident the railings fell down and the people went into the Park. The Government failed then to put down the meetings on Primrose Hill, in Hyde Park, and elsewhere. And what was the result ? An enormous impetus was given to the Reform movement of that day, and the people shortly afterwards entered upon their political heritage. If it had not been for the attempts to suppress the meetings on Primrose Hill and Hyde Park, we should have gone on toiling, year after year, to attain that position which the Government speedily secured for us by their hostility. The hon. Member for Northampton (Mr. Bradlaugh) has referred to the advertisement which the Government are giving week after week to the Socialist Party. In consequence of the action of the police, thousands of people now flock to hear what the Socialist have to say, and the result is, that a large number of converts are made to what some persons regard as very pernicious doctrines. If the Government do not want to continue this advertisement, they will certainly discontinue the prohibition of meetings in open spaces. They should remember the words of Scripture—"If this work be of man, it will come to nought"— and allow the Socialists to go on preaching to their hearts' content. The same result has followed the prohibition of public meetings in Germany. I have been present in Berlin, and have witnessed the efforts made there to suppress the right of public meeting ; and, during the last few years, I have seen the number of Socialists doubled and trebled through the efforts of Prince Bismarck to put down their meetings by force ; whereas, if they had been free to preach their doctrines, I venture to say, from practical acquaintance with the Leaders of the

Social Democracy in Germany, that the strength of the Party would not have increased as it has done. Now, Sir, I hope the right hon. and learned Gentleman the Home Secretary or some other Member of Her Majesty's Government will, before this debate concludes, give us distinctly to understand that these open air meetings will not be interfered with. A large number of our constituents who have not the slightest sympathy with the doings of the Socialists, knowing as they do that their object is to advertise themselves — to get upon a pedestal in order to propagate their doctrines, are nevertheless anxious that free speech should be preserved. I sincerely trust that we shall receive a distinct pledge from Her Majesty's Government that this persecution will cease. If they desire to prevent these men from propagating what they conceive to be pernicious views they will give the pledge for which I ask.

Main Question, "That Mr. Speaker do now leave the Chair," put, and *agreed to.*

SUPPLY—CIVIL SERVICE ESTIMATES

SUPPLY—*considered* in Committee.

(In the Committee.)

CLASS VII.—MISCELLANEOUS.

THE FIRST COMMISSIONER OF WORKS (Mr. PLUNKET) (Dublin University) : Sir, in submitting this Estimate, I am sure the Committee will allow me, and, indeed, expect from me that I should take this opportunity to give some further and fuller particulars of the services for which this £17,000 is asked than would have been possible to exhibit on the face of such a formal document as this. It is not necessary for me, and indeed it would be impertinent on my part, on this occasion, to dwell on the deep and respectful sympathy which we all feel for the desire which Her Majesty has expressed to signalize this Jubilee year of her reign by offering solemn and public thanksgiving for the prosperity and happiness with which Providence has blessed her and her people during 50 years of her life and of her rule. I am also sure that all will agree with me that it is right and fitting that this great National Thanksgiving should be made in Westminster Abbey, where Her Majesty and all her

Predecessors for well nigh 600 years have been crowned as Sovereigns of England. Sir, I do not think it necessary to say more on that subject, for I hope and believe, indeed I am confident, that upon it there will be an absolute unanimity of feeling amongst all the Members of this House. But I am very glad of this opportunity of explaining the nature of the preparations which it will fall to my duty, in conjunction with the Lord Chamberlain, to make on this occasion—and more especially as I know that some misapprehension - prevails amongst Members of this House, and, indeed, amongst some members of the public out-of-doors, with reference to the objects to which this Vote of £17,000 is to be applied. I think if the Committee will allow me to occupy its attention for a very few moments, that misapprehension I shall be easily able to dispel. Sir, the object of this Estimate is perfectly truly described as "for the preparation of Westminster Abbey," for this ceremony and nothing else. The necessity for this Vote of £17,000 springs from the simple fact that it takes a little money to make such arrangements as will enable that Abbey to contain 10,000 men in a space which usually accommodates, I suppose, about a third of that number, and especially when it is remembered that the Abbey is so full of very old sculpture and statues of priceless historical value, which might very easily be defaced, or even destroyed. Of course, if you were simply to open the doors of the Abbey and invite only the Members of the two Houses of Parliament to walk in, there would be very little expense; but it has been felt—and, I believe, the feeling will be shared universally—that on such a great and solemn and historical occasion all classes and all interests that together make up the people should, as far as possible, be represented, and that the representation should not be confined merely to the inhabitants of this country, but should also include Her Majesty's faithful subjects in the Colonies and the great dependency of India. Now, Sir, the first and principal item in this Estimate is a sum which has been estimated at £9,000 for the erection of galleries and the necessary staircases leading to them for the accommodation of this large number of people, and for the making of such structural alteration

as may be necessary for providing access to all parts of the building, and for other consequential expenses. I may say that this sum of £9,000 corresponds with the sum of £10,700 which was spent in 1872, when, as I suppose, a great many Members of this House recollect, there was a Thanksgiving Service at St. Paul's Cathedral for the recovery of the Prince of Wales. And before I pass away from that item, I should like to explain to the Committee exactly how we have arrived at the amount which it will be necessary to spend for this object. It was determined, as this was so large and important an occasion, it would be well to ask several of the leading firms of the builders and contractors in London to send in tenders for the work. We invited tenders from Messrs. Holland and Hannen, Messrs. Cubitt and Co., Messrs. George Trollope and Sons, and Messrs. Mowlem and Co. These four firms, as many Members of the House are doubtless aware, are amongst the most eminent in London. They sent in their estimates as we desired, according to a schedules of prices; and, of course, the estimate which was lowest—that of Messrs. Mowlem, which was 17 per cent. lower than either of the others—was accepted. The next principal item is also necessarily a large one, and it is as near as we can calculate it, £5,600. It is for the covering of seats with calico for the convenience of those who attend the ceremony and the carpeting of the passages. I may say at once that this work will be done on the most economical basis possible. We have endeavoured to make arrangements corresponding as nearly as possible, to those carried out on the occasion of the Thanksgiving Service for the recovery of the Prince of Wales, to which I have already referred. It is not easy to make an exact estimate of this item; but I have gone into the matter very carefully, and I hope it is more likely that we shall fall short, rather than exceed the Estimate I have given, and, in that case, the money we have over will be paid back into the Treasury. These two items together of £9,000 and £5,600 will amount to £14,600. Then there is the item of £1,300 for the Dean and Chapter. I know that it has been said that the Dean and Chapter will gain considerably by

Mr. Plunket

this ceremony, and that part of the money given under this Vote will go into their pockets. I am glad to have this opportunity to deny that statement; of course, it is not the fact—not one penny will go into the pockets of the Dean and Chapter. The item will be paid as insurance against such injuries as may be done to the Abbey in spite of the care that will be taken. [*Laughter.*] Well, if hon. Members will consider that the Abbey is very full of ancient, historical, and priceless statuary and sculpture, they will see that it is absolutely impossible to say that some slight damage may not be done, although we have taken the greatest precautions against that by shielding the monuments with wood. And so there is the sum of £500 allowed as an insurance against any such structural damage as we may, in spite of all our care, inflict upon the building. We also allow a sum of £250 for musical services and a sum of £300, their loss of fees during our occupation, which fees, I believe, are usually applied in payment of the guides. Finally, there is an item of £1,100 for the necessary printing and stationary and clerical assistance in the Lord Chamberlain's Department. We have adopted that figure from the corresponding item in the expenses that were incurred in 1872 on the occasion of the Thanksgiving for the recovery of the Prince of Wales. That was the sum actually spent in 1872 ; and, judging from the tide of correspondence already rushing in upon the Lord Chamberlain, I should not think that this item could well be put at less. These make together the £17,000 ; and I may say, in concluding this portion of my statement, that I hope the necessary arrangements will be fully covered by the Estimate. I assure the Committee that no effort will be wanting on my part to secure that result. I have taken into account the expenditure which has been incurred on similar occasions, and I believe this Estimate may be relied upon as correct. There is one other subject in which I am sure the Committee will be interested. I should like to satisfy everybody as to the accommodation which we will be able to provide, and as to the persons to be invited to attend the ceremony. For instance, it has, I am aware, been a burning question with Members of

this House as to whether they will be allowed to bring their wives. Only this evening a friend of mine said to me— " If you do not make room for Members' wives—if you do not settle this point in our favour—even your own Party will vote against you." I said—" Yes ; but if I do include Members' wives, no man of any Party will dare to vote against me." Well, I hope we shall be able to make satisfactory arrangements on this point. With regard to the accommodation, I may say that I to-day received a letter from the Lord Chamberlain, in which he says—

" It may be convenient for you to know the arrangements which I have been commanded to make for Her Majesty's Jubilee Thanksgiving Service in Westminster Abbey on the 21st of June."

I am glad to take this opportunity of saying, in my own defence, that I shall have nothing whatever to do with the giving away of seats, although applications for admission to the ceremony are falling upon me in showers.

" It is wished that it shall be of a thoroughly national and representative character; and I therefore propose, in the first place, to set apart the whole of the lower level of the transepts of the north and south of the Abbey for the Members of the two Houses of Parliament. I shall hope to provide here and in the Galleries above also for the wives of Members ; but this must, to some extent, depend on the number of Members who express their intention to be present. Upon this, however, I propose to consult the Lord Chancellor and the Speaker."

I have myself no doubt at all that we shall, on this point, be able to make satisfactory arrangements, and that it will be possible to avoid giving disappointment to hon. Members.

" In addition to these, I shall have to provide for the Corps Diplomatique and other distinguished foreigners ; for the representatives of the Army, the Reserve Forces, the Navy and Marines, and the Civil Service ; for representatives of the Colonies and India, the Lord Lieutenants and High Sheriffs of counties, the Mayors of the United Kingdom, as well as the representatives of trade, commerce, and agriculture who will be invited to attend. The Church will, of course, be provided for in communication with the Dean of Westminster, in addition to the Houses of Convocation ; and I am sure you will be glad to learn——"

This may be taken as an answer to a Question which was addressed to me the other day, and which I was only able at the time to answer in a general way—

" that I have already received an assurance that the various Nonconformist Bodies will wish to be represented, and that I shall not fail to reserve places for them."

I quote this with pleasure, as I have said, as an answer to the Question put to me the other day—

"I have not forgotten that on the occasion of the Thanksgiving for the Prince of Wales's recovery representatives of the working classes were provided for, and I shall most certainly follow that precedent on this occasion."

Then the Lord Chamberlain concludes—

"I may have omitted to enumerate some classes of Her Majesty's subjects. If I have done so, as time goes on I shall, no doubt, be reminded of them, for the innumerable applications that I daily receive show the extraordinary interest taken in all parts of Her Majesty's dominions in this interesting ceremony. I trust that you will soon be in a position to get the Vote for the preparations in the Abbey to enable me to proceed with the arrangements."

I have to thank the Committee for having allowed me to make this explanation, and I now beg to move the Vote, which I trust will be passed without serious opposition.

Motion made, and Question proposed,

"That a sum not exceeding £17,000, be granted to Her Majesty, to defray the Charge which will come in course of payment during the year ending on the 31st day of March 1888, for the Expenses in connection with the Celebration of the Jubilee of Her Majesty's Reign."

MR. LABOUCHERE (Northampton): I hope whatever decision the Committee may come to nobody will be induced to give a vote one way or the other owing to the "wife bribe" which has been put forward by the right hon. Gentleman. I do not propose to discuss for a moment whether or not there ought to be a Jubilee Service. It is decided upon, and it will take place. Nor will I discuss whether it should take place at Westminster Abbey or in St. Paul's Cathedral. I can understand the sentimental feeling, though I confess I do not share in it, which gives the preference to Westminster Abbey; but the real question is what ought this Jubilee Service to cost. I hold that the scale of arrangements is too costly, and that if it is adopted it will be open to the condemnation of being too reckless and expensive. The right hon. Gentleman has explained that there are to be a number of galleries, as I understand, throughout the Cathedral. Well, it seems to me that when you have a Cathedral with fine spaces in its interior,

you really spoil its structural advantages and its proportions by erecting galleries. You are perpetrating, in point of fact, an artistic blunder. What you are really going to do is this—with the best intentions—you are going to convert the noble aisle into a species of race-course stand, under the auspices of some West End upholsterer. I do not think any hon. Gentleman will assert this is essentially a religious function; it is rather a Court function. We understand from the right hon. Gentleman the First Commissioner of Works that positively a sum of money is to be paid over to the Dean and Chapter for what they will lose in the way of charges at services that will have to be suspended in consequence of this particular service. The arrangement is, as I have said, inartistic; but it seems to me that this expenditure is all the more objectionable, because, notwithstanding what the right hon. Gentleman has said, most undoubtedly the classes will be invited to the ceremony, and the masses will not. It is all very well to talk about representative Bodies, but I should like to know if one constituent happened to be hungry he would be satisfied if his representative in this House were to be given a good dinner at the public expense? The right hon. Gentleman says Members of the House of Commons may go to the Service. I doubt whether I shall go. Certainly, if I had any desire to go but was kept out I should not be satisfied if my Representative in Parliament were allowed to go. Now, we are to pay £9,000 for the erection of these high galleries, and £5,600 for cushioning the seats in the galleries. I estimated, while the right hon. Gentleman was speaking, that if there are 10,000 persons present, the expenditure will be at the rate of £1 14s. per head. Hon. Gentlemen know what is the average cost of seating people. The cost of seating people in a large hall or chapel—a permanent building—is £2 per head, only 6s. more than you propose for this one show. In addition to this expenditure for galleries and cushioning the seats you propose to grant £1,300 as a species of insurance—[Mr. PLUNKET: £500.]—£500. This sum is to be given to the Dean and Chapter. The right hon. Gentleman went on to say that the Abbey is filled with monuments, which are invaluable. Now, these monuments, if they are broken, cannot be replaced or mended, and the £500 will undoubtedly go into the pockets of the Dean and Chapter.

Mr. PLUNKET: I can assure the hon. Gentleman that not one penny will go to the Dean and Chapter. The £500 will go to the general fabric fund of the Cathedral.

Mr. LABOUCHERE: If we were asked to vote something to the fabric fund of the Cathedral, I could see that reasons might be urged in favour of the proposal. But here, under the guise of voting a sum of money for this Thanksgiving Service, we are called upon to contribute a sum of £500 to the fabric fund of the Cathedral. I think we really ought to object to that. £9,000 is far too much to spend upon wood. Let hon. Gentlemen consider what can be done in the way of building for £9,000; besides, it must be remembered that in this case this sum is only for the loan of the wood. I have seen the wood that is being taken into the Cathedral. It consists of battens and pieces cut into lengths for flooring. The greater portion of it will be precisely as good when it has been used as now; and, therefore, we are practically called upon to pay £9,000 for the loan of this wood for one day. The right hon. Gentleman says that he has put out a schedule to the various builders. I do not say it has occurred in this case, but has the right hon. Gentleman not heard of builders standing in ? When half - a - dozen builders are asked to tender for certain work, it is frequently the case that they agree amongst themselves not to cut each other out; and, although I say I do not know it of my own knowledge, I think there are evidences that there has been a little standing in in this case. The right hon. Gentleman has cited the case of the Thanksgiving Service in St. Paul's; and he seems to consider that if he can show a like expenditure previously, we ought to cordially and thankfully acknowledge that he does not propose to expend more than he ought. I asked the right hon. Gentleman, a few days ago, what was the total expenditure upon the Thanksgiving Service in St. Paul's, and he said that, in round figures, it was precisely the sum asked for now. One would suppose that £17,000 is the sum we are to be called upon to recognize as the par value of such Services as

these. I hope we shall establish a very different precedent. I propose to reduce the amount to the sum of £2,000. I consider this is amply sufficient. It seems to me that all that is wanted in the Cathedral—for everybody knows that the Cathedral itself is one of the finest buildings in the world—is a däis for Her Majesty and those in attendance upon her, and a few special seats for the Corps Diplomatique. I have seen a good deal of these Services abroad ; but I never heard of such reckless, such ridiculous expenditure as that proposed in this case. Those who will go to the Cathedral upon this occasion will not go for religious purposes, but to see and to be seen. If £17,000 is to be expended upon Jubilee festivities, it might be expended to better advantage in various other ways, because, in all these matters, the best way is that which will please the greatest number of people. I am not advocating for a moment any expenditure of this character ; but we have to deal with this positive fact, that there is to be this Jubilee Service, and the real point is, what is it to cost? Now, we are frequently asked to vote money after it has been spent; we are told we must vote it. But we have been told by the right hon. Gentleman the First Lord of the Treasury (Mr. W. H. Smith) that he would not think of spending 1*s.* of this money until it has been voted. It is quite true that a large quantity of wood is being taken into the Abbey; who, I wonder, is it who is paying for it ? Anyhow, we have the assurance that the right hon. Gentleman the Leader of the House would not for a moment countenance the idea of one farthing being spent before we vote the money. We are, therefore, perfectly free to say whether the money expended shall be £1,000 or £2,000, or whatever sum we think proper. Speaking broadly, I think that, considering the atrocious want of taste in the proposals of the right hon. Gentleman, considering that all these galleries will only be used one day, and that they will vanish like the

" Baseless fabric of a vision,"

considering the many better ways in which this money could be expended, considering the reckless extravagance which characterizes everything which the Lord Chamberlain and such people in anything they have to do with, considering that the right hon. Gentleman can offer no better reason for the expenditure of this money than that there was a like expenditure in St. Paul's, and considering that, if we do spend this money, future generations will be called upon occasionally to act similarly, we owe it, as a duty to the country and to ourselves, to protest against this expenditure. Although I have moved to reduce the Vote to £2,000, I do not want to stick at £5,000 one way or the other. Some Gentlemen think I am not proposing to reduce the Vote sufficiently; others may think I am proposing to reduce it too much. What I want to do is to reduce the Vote from £17,000 to something like £2,000. Perhaps we can make a bargain with the right hon. Gentleman. If, for instance, he is prepared to accept a Motion to reduce the Vote to £3,000, I will gladly move such a Motion. All I want is that, in a matter like this, we should say to the authorities—to the Lord Chamberlain and others—" Take £2,000 or £3,000; make the best of it, and give us as good a show as you can for the money." I beg to move that this Vote be reduced to £2,000.

Motion made, and Question proposed, "That a sum of £2,000 be granted for the said Service."—(*Mr. Labouchere.*)

THE FIRST LORD OF THE TREASURY (Mr. W. H. SMITH) (Strand, Westminster): Mr. Courtney, I understand the hon. Gentleman (Mr. Labouchere) to be distinctly of opinion that a Jubilee Service should be held in Westminster Abbey. [Mr. LABOUCHERE: I am not of that opinion. I accept the fact.] At all events, he recognizes the propriety of a Jubilee Service in Westminster Abbey; but he suggests that the Jubilee Service should be held under circumstances which would render it impossible for the Representatives of the Constitution of this country to take part in it. He proposes that only the sum of £2,000 should be spent, and that the galleries which he protests against as being an evidence of want of taste, and as being destructive of the architectural beauty of the building, should not be erected. The result of that would be, as I am sure the hon. Gentleman himself will realize, that, instead of 10,000 persons taking part in the ceremony, it would be utterly impossible for more than 2,000 persons at the most to be present to do so. And therefore all the people nominated by the Lord Chamberlain as representing the several elements of the Constitution could not be present. I do not think that that is a result which will be acceptable to the House of Commons. I believe that the House of Commons desires that opportunities should be afforded to the representatives of all classes of Her Majesty's subjects to take part in a ceremony which they regard with infinite satisfaction and pleasure, as one which reflects honour upon Her Majesty, honour upon the nation over which she reigns, and in which the people desire by their Representatives to show a lively and real interest. Sir, there is a universal feeling of thankfulness and gratitude that we have been permitted to see the 50th year of a Reign during which the country has advanced in prosperity, has advanced in liberty— ["Oh, oh!" *and ironical Home Rule cheers.*] I am sorry to say a single word upon an occasion like this which would afford the slightest opportunity for a difference of opinion. I thought I was fairly representing the views and the feelings of the great majority of the subjects of the Queen; but I will refrain from pursuing the topic. Perhaps I may express my own feeling, and that is that it is with infinite thankfulness that I have lived to see the accomplishment of a period which I believe will be memorable in the history of this great Empire, as a period in which certainly great advance has been made in the happiness and prosperity of all classes of the inhabitants of this great Empire. It would be only fitting and proper that an opportunity should be afforded to the Representatives of these classes to take part in a ceremony which fittingly and properly marks the occasion. Sir, the hon. Gentleman has referred to a sum of £500, which is included in this Vote, as a contribution to the fabric fund. I wish it to be distinctly understood that this is given precisely in the sense in which my right hon. Friend (Mr. Plunket) has referred to it. It is impossible, notwithstanding the greatest possible care used in the introduction of the timber, that some damage should not be done to the building. Any damage to the Abbey must be repaired out of the fabric fund, and therefore we felt that a

Mr. Labouchere

sum of £500 would not be an extensive contribution towards that fund. Not one single farthing of that money goes to any individual connected with the Abbey. If the amount is in excess of the cost of any repairs which will be necessary, the excess will simply go as a contribution towards the fund for maintaining a building which in itself is a great national monument. The hon. Gentleman (Mr. Labouchere) referred to the possibility of the builders standing in. The Office of Works took every precaution which it is possible to take, in order to satisfy themselves that the amount asked for was a reasonable amount. The chief portion of the £17,000 will be spent in labour, as unquestionably much labour will be expended in the fitting up of the proposed galleries. I do not think I need recommend this Vote to the House of Commons by any further remarks of my own. It has, however, been said that there is no precedent for this expenditure other than the expenditure upon the Thanksgiving Service for the recovery of the Prince of Wales. That is not the case. I find that £55,000 was spent upon the Duke of Wellington's funeral, apart altogether from the cost of the monument. If the hon. Member would trouble himself to obtain information as to the charges which are incurred in other countries under circumstances of a similar character, he would find that those charges are enormously greater than that which is now presented to the Committee. But that, after all, is not the ground on which I recommend this Vote to hon. Members. I recommend it because the country takes an interest in this ceremony, and desires that all classes of the community should be represented in the congregation. I, therefore, trust it will be voted very cordially by the Committee.

SIR JOSEPH PEASE (Durham, Barnard Castle): Mr. Courtney, I do not wish to find any fault with Her Majesty's Government in having this service in Westminster Abbey, but, on looking at this Estimate, I was struck, as I feel other Members of the House must have been struck, by the large amount of money which is to be spent upon the service; indeed, I very much doubt whether we shall get value for the £17,000 proposed to be expended; £17,000 is £1 14s. for every seat, as-

suming that 10,000 are provided. It has been said that a similar expenditure was incurred upon the occasion of the Thanksgiving Service in St. Paul's Cathedral for the recovery of the Prince of Wales; but surely hon. Members are perfectly aware that timber is down in price since that day something like 50 per cent, that working-men's wages are down 5 to 20 per cent. ["No, no!"] I am speaking of what I know. The Thanksgiving Service in St. Paul's was in 1872, a year in which the wages of the working classes ranged as high or higher than they have been for some years past. I will not say there has been any collusion between the builders who were invited to tender in this case; but it is well known that London tradesmen have a great propensity for "standing in" with each other. I dare say I know a great deal more about tendering than the right hon. Gentleman the First Commissioner of Works (Mr. Plunket). I certainly know how tendering is often done, and I cannot help thinking that we are asked to spend a great deal more than we ought to spend considering the accommodation which is to be provided. I have no doubt that the First Commissioner of Works adopted what he considered to be the best plan; but to me the course he took to obtain tenders seems most extraordinary, as I understand the process described. The Office of Works sent out a schedule of prices, and then asked the builders to say for how much below those prices they would tender. The tenders that I am in the habit of seeing go out with specifications and with quantities supplied by a professional man, and with schedules to be filled up with prices. A tenderer fills in his schedule with prices which ought to correspond with the gross amount of his contract, with such addition as he may make after by way of making the total sum even money. In this case, the schedule of prices should not have been sent out, but a blank schedule to be filled in with prices. I merely say this because I think it is our duty, however much we desire to celebrate Her Majesty's Jubilee, to endeavour to get a fair return for the taxpayers' money that we expend.

MR. ARTHUR O'CONNOR (Donegal, E.): Mr. Courtney, the right hon. Gentleman (Mr. Plunket) who introduced this Vote seemed to think it necessary to refer to precedent. Well, now, the precedent which occurs to my mind most readily in connection with this Jubilee celebration is the original Jubilee from which this takes its name. It takes its name from the Hebrew word *Yobel*, which signifies the name of a musical instrument, which every 50 years, according to the directions in Deuteronomy, was to sound throughout the land, in notes of triumph, proclaiming liberty, and in that 50th year each man of the Hebrew nation returned into his own possessions, free in the bosom of his family. If we could have such notes of jubilation in every part of the United Kingdom as those Hebrews who witnessed a Jubilee had, there might be little question about this £17,000, or seventeen times £17,000, to manifest the gratitude of the people, for what the right hon. Gentleman (Mr. Plunket) calls the blessings which Providence has showered upon Her Majesty's people during the last 50 years. In Scripture it is said that the multiplication of the people is the glory of the King, and in this country the last 50 years have witnessed an immense increase of the population. In the year 1837, the population of England and Wales was over 14,000,000; now it is 27,000,000. In 1837, the population of Ireland was over 8,000,000; now, after these 50 years of blessings, we have a population of just under 5,000,000. I wonder what the author of the Jubilee of old would have thought of these signs of blessings and of happiness of the people of one portion of the United Kingdom. Sir, when the right hon. Gentleman the First Lord of the Treasury talked about liberty, it appeared to me there was a tone of satire about his words, and he did well I think to drop the subject. But Sir, if the Jubilee is to be celebrated at all in a religious manner, if this is a just mode of celebrating it, perhaps it is just as well that Westminster Abbey should be chosen. It is a very interesting monument, full of the records of Royalty in this country. As Addison says in one of his essays in the *Spectator*—" When I consider in that place kings lie by those who have deposed them, I reflect with sorrow and astonishment upon the petty wrangles, quarrels, and debates of mankind." Well, Sir, we are to have this show, or this religious ceremony, in Westminster

Mr. Arthur O'Connor

Abbey at a cost of £17,000. In the Papers which were issued to Members this morning, there were two in juxtaposition. One was the Paper which set forth the amount of money to be demanded for this particular Service, and the other was the Paper I hold in my hand. It is headed "Deaths in the Metropolitan District." It is a Return of the number of deaths in the Metropolitan District in the year 1886, upon which the Coroners juries have returned verdicts of deaths from starvation, or deaths accelerated by privation. I find that in the Central Division there were 15 deaths from starvation, in the Eastern Division there were 16 deaths, and smaller numbers in other divisions, one of the divisions being the verge of the Royal Palaces. There was no death from starvation within the verge of the Royal Palaces; those who are there are in "purple or fine linen." You are asking for a sum of £17,000, while men are dying in this same city, in the immediate neighbourhood of Westminster Abbey—dying week after week of starvation; while men, hundreds and thousands of men, are unable to obtain work, when—I am tempted to go into a number of considerations which might perhaps be looked upon as somewhat foreign to the subject-matter of this Vote. But the fact is, that there is immense distress in this country, and what do we know besides? We know that Her Majesty the Queen is probably the richest person in the world. In Eastern countries, kings barbaric scatter pearls and gold upon such an occasion as this. In this country we do not find that the donations and bounties are in the same direction. It is the poor people who are to be taxed on this occasion. Now, I want to know what earthly good this Vote will do to the poor people of Great Britain or of London. If it will do good to the people of this country, why do you not have a similar expenditure in Ireland. Why are the Irish people to be taxed to contribute towards this £17,000 you propose to expend on this ceremony? Is it because the Government feel that there is no ground for jubilation over the past 50 years in Ireland; but if that is so, why do you expect us to contribute from the Irish resources towards this expenditure? I do not know, Sir, by what process it can be arranged that the money contributed on this occasion should be drawn entirely from those who care for this kind of thing; but there is one single expedient by which the difficulty might be met without any expenditure at all from the public purse, and that is by testing the loyalty of those deeply religious people who are to be furnished with cushioned seats at two guineas a-head, charge two guineas a-head for admission. You will get the money over and over again. The snobocracy of the suburbs of London will crowd to get in and you will be able to make a profit out of the transaction. Sir, this Estimate appears to be simply ridiculous. Admitting all the other items, how on earth can even a lavish Board of Works justify the charge of £1,100 for stationery in connection with this service? Are the tickets of admission to cost 2s. a-piece? Why you can get them printed by hundreds for half the money; £1,100 for stationery appears indicative of the character of this Estimate. It is perfectly plain it is inflated, and altogether beyond the requirements of the case. And then we are told, and this struck me as extraordinary, that the Abbey will hold, in ordinary times, 2,000 persons. You are going to put 10,000 persons in there. You will have to put them tier over tier, five deep. Now, what kind of galleries are you going to put in Westminster Abbey, by which you will increase its capacity five fold? There must be something wrong in the Estimate. I suspect the Estimate for standing or sitting accommodation is about as good as the Estimate for stationery. Under the circumstances, I shall certainly vote with my hon. Friend the Member for Northampton (Mr. Labouchere).

Mr. BROADHURST (Nottingham, W.): I should like to ask the right hon. Gentleman the First Commissioner of Works (Mr. Plunket) what he estimates will be the return in the resale of timber. He mentioned nothing about that in his statement to the Committee, and that is a matter of great importance. The timber will be almost as valuable for all practical purposes when it is taken down, as when it is first taken into the Abbey. [*Laughter*] Hon. Gentlemen laugh about a matter which they really do not understand. One expense in the matter of timber is the difficulty occasioned by the stacking of it for a length of time to dry. There you have a process of drying

going on to a certain extent, and to that extent the timber will be more valuable when it is taken away from the Abbey. [*Renewed laughter*.] These are matters about which I know something. I have one other remark to make with regard to the right hon. Gentleman's statements. He said that the Office of Works had invited tenders from Messrs. Holland and Hannen, Messrs. William Cubitt and Co., Messrs. George Trollope and Sons, and Messrs. Mowlem and Co. These are the four favoured firms of the Metropolis. There are at least 300 firms in the Metropolis equally as capable of doing this work as the firms mentioned. These are firms who have been in the habit of knowing each other perfectly well for a great number of years. The last mentioned, Messrs. Mowlem and Co., was only recently admitted to the inner circle of contractors, but the three other firms have been in the habit of contracting for Government work for the last 40 years at the very least. I see a right hon. Gentleman who perhaps will be able to give us some information on this point.

Mr. CUBITT (Surrey, Mid.): If the hon. Gentleman appeals to me, I should like to say that for the last 25 years neither I nor any relation of mine has had any part in the firm of Messrs. Cubitt and Co. I think it would be well if the hon. Gentleman would get up his facts better before he speaks.

Mr. BROADHURST: I am perfectly within my facts. The firm is carried on in the same place as of old, and it is carried on under the name of the hon. Gentleman. Well, there are at least within the Metropolis 300 firms who are equally as capable of doing work of this kind as any of the firms I have mentioned, and I am much dissatisfied myself with the exceedingly limited number of firms invited to contract for this work. Now, I have only one other remark to make, and that is in extenuation of the remarks of the hon. Baronet (Sir Joseph Pease). I am not surprised that a total sum of £17,000 is considered a very large sum indeed. I, myself, frequently worship in a Dissenting Chapel which has been recently built to accommodate from 800 to 1,000 people. The purchase of the ground and the erection of the building, which is a very handsome one indeed—there are very few buildings in London to surpass it—

cost £10,000. Now, that is a permanent building, accommodating nearly 1,000 worshippers, and it is very handsomely built outside, and well fitted inside. [*Laughter.*] I cannot say that the hilarity of hon. Gentlemen opposite displays any extraordinary knowledge on their part of the subject. I say that this permanent building has been erected for £10,000 or less.

MR. PLUNKET: I only rise for the purpose of answering the question addressed to me by the hon. Member. I have to say that work of this kind is always done by measure, and that the estimate includes the cost of putting up and taking away.

MR. T. P. O'CONNOR (Liverpool, Scotland): I conceive it to be my duty to join in the protest of the hon. Gentleman below me (Mr. Labouchere) against this proposal, and I join in his protest on the merits and the principle of his proposal as well as on the details. I must say that the two right hon. Gentlemen who have proposed this Vote invited, nay, I will say, even compelled criticism from this quarter of the House. I am surprised at this in the case of the right hon. Gentleman the First Commissioner of Works, who is so adroit as well as so eloquent and powerful a Speaker. I am not surprised that the First Lord of the Treasury should rather damage any cause he takes up and advocates. I deny altogether that this money will be expended in the manner the right hon. Gentleman declared. I deny that this money will be spent in the interests of the masses of the people. The number who this £17,000 will accommodate clearly shows the purpose for which it will be spent. The First Commissioner of Works told us that by this expenditure 10,000 people would be seated in the Abbey. Well, he might have added an adjective —he might have said "The Upper Ten Thousand." Both the right hon. Gentlemen said that it was their desire that all classes of Her Majesty's subjects should be represented at this ceremony. Well, I wonder how many working people will be provided with places to witness the proceedings? I understand that the procession to the Abbey is to be of the shortest and most private character, so that the humble subjects of Her Majesty will not have an opportunity of even seeing her face on the

Mr. Broadhurst

day on which this celebration takes place. I do, Sir, maintain that it is trifling with the intelligence of the House to declare that accommodation for 10,000 people does not mean accommodation for 10,000 people drawn from practically one class of society, and therefore to the exclusion of the masses of the people. That is my first objection to this Vote. I say nothing with regard to the amount of the expenditure on which criticism has already been offered by some of my hon. Friends; but I feel compelled to notice the observations as to the purpose of this celebration which were offered by the two right hon. Gentlemen. The right hon. Gentleman the First Commissioner of Works declared that this Jubilee was in celebration of the happiness and prosperity with which Providence had blessed Her Majesty and Her people. I suppose the right hon. Gentleman adheres to that as a statement of the purpose for which this celebration takes place. The other right hon. Gentleman declared that this celebration was for the purpose of manifesting thanks for the advance which had taken place in the "prosperity and liberty" of the subjects of the Queen. Now, I presume, when these two right hon. Gentlemen spoke thus, they did not mean to exclude Ireland from their consideration. I certainly believe that the right hon. Gentleman the First Commissioner of Works, of whom, as an Irishman, we are all proud, however much we may differ from him in politics, would be the last man in the world to exclude from his consideration, on an occasion like this, the thought of his own country. Therefore, I must assume, when he used the words to which I have referred, that he was of opinion that Irishmen are called upon to celebrate the Jubilee of the Queen in thanksgiving for the increase in the prosperity and the happiness of Ireland. Now, I take issue with the right hon. Gentleman altogether on that, and I commend to his consideration a few figures that are already familiar to this Committee and the country. They show what has been the advance of happiness and the advance of prosperity in Ireland during Her Majesty's reign. The figures are these—that during the 50 years of Her Majesty's reign, 3,600,000 people have been evicted; that during the period that has elapsed since Her Majesty came to the Throne, 4,186,000 people have been driven from their homes; that in the period of Her Majesty's reign 1,225,000 Irish people, men, women, and children, have been starved to death; and that in the same period of 50 years the population of Ireland has diminished from over 8,000,000 to under 5,000,000. Now, does the right hon. Gentleman, with those facts staring him in the face, really mean to ask Irishmen to go to Westminster Abbey and to offer thanks to Providence for 1,250,000 of their countrymen having been starved to death in the course of Her Majesty's reign—starved to death by the legislation of this Parliament? Why, Sir, if the right hon. Gentleman had proposed that on the 50th anniversary of the Queen we should have a day of humiliation and of general sorrow at the amount of destruction and desolation brought about by famine and by plague, and emigration and eviction in Ireland during this half-century, then we might not have grudged the £17,000 that is asked for. But it really is too much for him to ask us to thank Providence for a reign which has been more disastrous, according to the most rigid statisticians of our country, than the blood-stained and horrible reign of Elizabeth. There is an observation which I must make here. The First Lord of the Treasury had what I must, for Parliamentary reasons, call the courage to declare that we should offer our thanksgiving to Providence for "the advance in liberty" of the subjects of the Queen during the 50 years of her reign; and the right hon. Gentleman says that in the short interval of time between the debate of yesterday on a drastic Coercion Bill and the debate of to-morrow on the same measure. Why, Sir, the right hon. Gentleman, I think, wantonly insulted the Members on this side of the House when he said that. Coming fresh from a Motion gagging discussion in this House on a Bill depriving Ireland of the fundamental liberties of free subjects in a free country, he asks us to join him in thanking Providence for the advance in liberty of the subjects of the Queen. No, Sir; we shall vote against this proposal. We know we shall subject ourselves to misinterpretation in doing so. We are anxious not to do that, and we declined, many of us, to take part in the Division which took place at an earlier period of the evening on the Duke of Connaught's Leave Bill, in order to avoid that misinterpretation. But when, in the face of this House, we are asked to agree to the statement that we feel we have to thank Providence for happiness and prosperity in the midst of the terrible distress and starvation which has existed, and which is now taking place, and that we feel we ought to thank Providence for advance in the liberty when we have before us the drastic proposal of the Government for the coercion of our countrymen, we say it is too much to ask of us.

MR. CONYBEARE (Cornwall, Camborne): Though the hour is rather late, I should like to say a word on this matter, particularly as I shall not be here to-morrow. It is always entertaining to hear the right hon. Gentleman opposite (Mr. W. H. Smith) wax eloquent, and when he has so splendid a theme, which he is so capable of displaying his eloquence upon, it is really refreshing to listen to him, and I do not think his worst enemy will be dissatisfied with the manner in which he acquitted himself of the pleasing duty which fell to his lot this evening. But I cannot endorse some of his eloquent expressions as to the pleasure he thinks all classes of Her Majesty's subjects feel in passing this Vote. I will not venture to set up my experience against that of the right hon. Gentleman so far as the denizens of the Strand are concerned; but I must say, if my experience of the working classes of this country counts for anything at all, they do not care twopence-halfpenny about the whole business, and so far from allowing their Representatives in this House to vote huge sums of money for this sort of thing, when it has been shown that many of their class are starving in our streets, they would not assent to anything of the kind for a moment. When we are told, in those eloquent tones and strains which are familiar to us from Court circles, that we ought to be blessing Providence for the amount of prosperity and liberty and that sort of thing which has resulted to us from 50 years of the present reign, I would venture to ask—and I think it is a question which deserves an answer—who it is we have to thank for all the prosperity which has come to this nation in the course of the last half-century? Is it the intelligence, is it the labour, is it the energy of those who are the creators of wealth in this country, or is it the do-nothing, gilded luxury of the aristocracy, commencing with the Royal House itself, and descending to the lower grades of that aristocracy who simply batten on the labour of others and do not contribute one farthing in the promotion, or in the division, or in the creation of wealth? Why, Sir, if we calculate the burden which the Royal Family has been to this country during the last 50 years we find it amounts to £24,000,000; and when we are asked to put our hands in our pockets in order to provide for the interesting amusement of a few of the select aristocracy during an hour or two on a particular day, all I can say is that until we see some attempt made to reduce the vast expenditure that is going on for needless purposes in other parts of the country, I, for one, shall not consent, without a stern protest, to waste like this going on. If the right hon. Gentleman opposite wants to know what good this Vote will do, I will tell him. It will make the people very much dissatisfied with some of the institutions we are told most to reverence and venerate, and I shall not be surprised if, in a few years, the people of this country come to the conclusion that this shall be the last Jubilee celebration they will tolerate. [*Laughter.*] Well, some of us, no doubt, will be old men when the next Jubilee celebration takes place; but men may come and men may go, while the nation goes on for ever, and I sincerely hope that before another century has passed this nation will be a Republic and not a Monarchy. [*Cries of* "Order!"] I want to put one or two questions to the right hon. Gentleman who has to expend this money. I want to know whether provision will be made for the servants of this House to attend the ceremonial, as well as the Members of it? I think they have quite as hard if not harder work than we have, and I think they are entitled to be considered in this matter. We are told that all classes are to be represented; but we have not yet been informed how many of the poor people, how many of the starving people of this City are to be represented. Will the right hon. Gentleman go out into the highways and byeways and collect together a few specimens of the distressed and the starving on which Her Majesty may feast her

eyes on this solemn occasion? I think it would have a good effect if the Sovereign were once to be brought face to face with some of the realities of life in this country. The right hon. Gentleman is fond of quoting precedents when he wants some excuse for an intolerable and unnecessary Coercion Bill. "Oh!" he says, "it is founded on the precedent of those who preceded us—on precedents coming from your side of the House." Well, if these things are founded on precedents, we have a right to ask why should not those who go to enjoy the sunshine of Royal smiles on this occasion pay for the luxury? I will give the right hon. Gentleman a precedent for our contention that those who attend this ceremonial ought to be made to pay for it. There was a banquet in St. James's Palace the other day, and I believe the Representatives of our Colonies were invited; but they were invited also to pay for their dinner. I believe the attendance was rather small, much smaller than would otherwise have been the case. I think that that is a very valuable precedent; and I think it is one that ought to have been followed in this case. I think that those who attend Westminster Abbey ought to be charged, as has been suggested this evening, £2 2s. each for their enjoyment. There is one item, or rather, there are two items in the £17,000 I want to make a remark upon. I would, first, ask does this £17,000 include the cost of removing? [An hon. MEMBER: Yes.] I should like the right hon. Gentleman to say that, because this is a sort of thing on which we cannot tolerate any Supplementary Estimate on a future day. We are told that £500 is to go to insure "priceless treasures." I want to know what consolation this nation will be able to get out of that £500, if these priceless treasures are mutilated so as to be perfectly valueless? It is impossible that all this construction of galleries can take place in Westminster Abbey without considerable damage being done, or great danger of damage being done being incurred. I think this consideration alone ought to have been sufficient to prevent these ridiculous proceedings in the Abbey. There are priceless treasures in the building, besides sculpture and masonry—there are rusty swords, and helmets, and there is the stone upon

Mr. Conybeare

which the Kings of Scotland used to be enthroned. Will these be put away during the ceremonial, or will an opportunity be given to dishonest persons, if any should find their way the Abbey, to carry away some of these treasures? I think we should have an assurance from the right hon. Gentleman on that point. I see there is an item of £250 for musical services. I think we have a right to ask on what kind of musical service will this money be spent? Does the right hon. Gentleman propose that there should be a special Jubilee hymn on the part of Irish Members, and poems of thankful praise for their 86 Coercion Acts? We are in the habit of regarding Westminster Abbey with feelings of veneration, and even of awe and worship; but the proposed proceedings in that splendid building incline me to apply a text of Scripture—"My house shall be called a house of prayer, but ye have made it a den of thieves."

Mr. CREMER (Shoreditch, Haggerston): I only wish to say, Sir, that I sincerely hope the Vote will be reduced by the sum suggested by the hon. Member for Northampton (Mr. Labouchere). In case it should be, and Her Majesty's Government should find themselves in a difficulty, and not have the means at their disposition to enable them to pay for the fitting up of the Abbey, I suggest that they might not only charge for admission, but put up the seats to auction. By that means a very considerable sum would be obtained over and above that which is actually required for the purpose of fitting the Abbey for this ceremony. It would be a very good test of the loyalty of the wealthier classes of our country. For instance, the man who would pay £1,000 for a seat would be considered a thousand times more loyal than the man who only paid £1. There are plenty of people, I believe, who would be ready to do this. There is an enormous amount of wealth in this Metropolis; and the Government might apply any surplus of receipts over expenditure to another institution which has been sending round the hat for some months past—namely, the Imperial Institute.

Mr. W. REDMOND (Fermanagh, N.) (who was received with cries of "Divide!") said: I only wish to say a very few words upon this Vote, and I assure the Committee that in what I shall say, I shall not utter one word which can possibly be construed as disrespectful of those things which hon. Members opposite me regard with veneration. Sir, it is utterly impossible for the Irish Members to allow this Vote to pass by without some kind of a protest, and without pointing out the condition in which the people of Ireland are to-day when you are asking them to contribute towards this Jubilee celebration. Now, hon. Members opposite, Members who represent rich constituencies and are rich themselves, will not perhaps so easily understand the sentiments of men, very many of whose constituencies are among the poorest people in the United Kingdom, men who are intimate with the lives and sufferings of the poor. In Ireland to-day there are somewhere near 400,000 people in the workhouses or receiving out-door relief, that is nearly one-tenth of the whole population of our country, and under these circumstances, I think it is heartless in the extreme to expect that the people of Ireland will co-operate in a celebration of this kind which is to cost so enormous a sum of money. My hon. Friend the Member for the Scotland Division of Liverpool (Mr. T. P. O'Connor) has entered into the details of the history of Ireland during the past 50 years, and has pointed out how miserable the condition of the people has been in the course of that time. Therefore, Sir, it is not necessary further to point out why Irishmen, without any disrespect at all to the prejudices and the opinions of hon. Members opposite, may be expected to offer some protests against this Vote, when they are told that the celebration for which it is intended is to evince the sense of the people's satisfaction at the progress which their people and their country has made. But apart from the Irish point of view, and speaking in the interests of hon. Members who wish to celebrate the Queen's Jubilee, and I do not at all feel surprised that hon. Members who represent English constituencies should have a desire to celebrate the Jubilee of their Queen's reign, which has seen such an advance in the prosperity and greatness of England, I ask hon. Members whether, if they want to get the sympathy of their own people, they do not make their celebration in some form which will commend it to the people at large. There have been very many methods proposed to celebrate the Jubilee of Her Majesty. It has been proposed to establish an Institute; it has been proposed to erect statues, and it is proposed to hold on the 21st of June a costly celebration Service in Westminister Abbey. In the face of the poverty and misery of large masses of people in England, why do you not celebrate the Jubilee of Her Majesty by some work which will have for its object the benefiting of the people of the country who most need to be benefited. I am constantly hearing outside complaints from people, who are not averse to some sort of celebration, that no method of celebrating the Jubilee takes the form of establishing, or endowing, or helping some institution which would benefit the poor people. While £17,000 is to be spent on a service in Westminster Abbey, while large sums of money, hundreds of thousands of pounds are to be spent in erecting monuments in celebration of this year, not one shilling, as far as we know, is going by way of celebrating the Jubilee to a single hospital— ["Oh, oh!"]—or a single institution which has for its object the amelioration of the condition of the people. I do not deny that in certain localities, individual effort has been made to subscribe comparatively small amounts to some such institutions, but not one shilling of the money which is asked from this House, or from the people nationally, is to go to any such institution or object, and I must say, Sir, that if I were an Englishman anxious to celebrate this Jubilee in a proper manner. I would say that, instead of spending large sums of money on a ceremonial of a single day, these large sums of money should be spent in endowing deserving institutions for the purpose of helping the weak and the suffering and the poor. Apart from the Irish view of the subject, it is impossible for any person who has been through the poor parts of this city, and who has seen unfortunate men and women in bitter weather at night with little children in their arms cowering in sheds and in door ways—[*Cries of* "Question!"]—yes, it is a very burning question. I do not claim that hon. Members opposite who reside in the West End are so liable to see the suffering people as men who live in more humble quarters; but I say it is impos-

sible to see the streets filled with these poor and miserable people, and to vote away with a light heart such large sums of money for a ceremony of a single day. This celebration is to take place in Westminster Abbey—["Hear, hear!"] —yes, it is to take place in that Abbey, because it is considered that it will in consequence be all the more acceptable in the eyes of God, who has given the Queen 50 years of prosperity and of power. I do not think that, if the object is to signify gratitude 'to the Deity, you can do so better than by spending this money well in ameliorating the sufferings of the poor, instead of spending it in enabling the ladies and gentlemen of England to attend for a few hours in costly Court dresses at Westminster Abbey to celebrate the Jubilee of the Queen. I wish to say, in conclusion, that I have made these remarks in no spirit of factious opposition at all, not because I wish to be disrespectful at all to hon. Members in regard to this Bill which is really an English, and not an Irish subject.

MR. ILLINGWORTH (Bradford, W.): I wish to ask the right hon. Gentleman the First Commissioner of Works (Mr. Plunket) whether there will be any liability under this Vote beyond the £500 in case the damage is greater than that figure? [Mr. PLUNKET: No.] Well, if that be so, I must say I regard this as a most unbusiness-like transaction. It is said that the *personnel* of the Abbey are not to receive any pecuniary advantage from this Vote of the Committee; but, if that be so, why should not the £500 in question be reserved by the First Commissioner of Works, and if any injury is done, or very small injury, it be provided for out of the amount? There is a very important principle involved in this question. I hope that the House of Commons will not, by a side wind, consent to grant money to Westminster Abbey under its present management. Before sitting down, I must say I can easily understand that hon. and right hon. Gentlemen opposite have heard observations from this side of the House not at all in accordance with their feelings and expectations in regard to this Vote. There is to be a skeleton at the feast, I say, which amazed the right hon. Gentleman the Leader of the House, who ventured to put forward, in the presence of Irish

Mr. W. Redmond

Members, the opinion that this ceremony in Westminster Abbey is to take the form of thanksgiving for the increased liberty and prosperity of the people. I think the right hon. Gentleman (Mr. W. H. Smith) would have met the case more fairly if he had excepted Ireland from this suggestion. Sir, the opportunities have been very few in which private Members of this House have been enabled to express what they know to be the feeling of dissatisfaction and complaint in many parts of the country in regard to the celebration of the Jubilee, and hon. Gentlemen opposite must not be surprised that even at this untimely hour (2.20) this opportunity should be taken advantage of to express feelings which many people outside hold. For my own part, I could have wished that the Committee had been spared the proposal for this Vote. I shall go into the Lobby with my hon. Friend the Member for Northampton (Mr. Labouchere), as an expression of my opinion that it would have been much fairer, under the circumstances, that a charge should have been made to that eager crowd of people who will be anxious to visit the Abbey upon the occasion of this ceremony. It would be more fitting the House of Commons should have been spared a Vote of this character, and therefore I shall divide against it.

¦ SIR JOHN SWINBURNE (Staffordshire, Lichfield): A large quantity of dry timber is being taken into Westminster Abbey, and therefore I should like to ask the right hon. Gentleman the First Commissioner of Works (Mr. Plunket) what precautions he is taking against fire?

MR. PLUNKET: Every possible precaution has been taken, and assurances have been effected in case of loss by fire.

SIR JOHN SWINBURNE: Is that included in the £17,000 asked for?

MR. PLUNKET: Yes.

DR. TANNER (Cork Co., Mid): There is one point I should like to direct the right hon. Gentleman's attention to—it has been possibly overlooked up to the present time—and that is, that on these Benches there are 86 Members, and that of these 86 Members, I venture to say, none of them will attend this ceremony, for the reasons which have been most eloquently explained by the hon. Member for East Donegal (Mr. Arthur O'Connor) and the hon. Member for the Scotland Division of Liverpool (Mr. T. P. O'Connor). As we, with our wives —certainly I could not attend with my wife, because I have not got one—will not put in an appearance, I think that some amount of this expenditure might be curtailed. Then I would throw out the suggestion that, instead of providing this very large and sumptuous accommodation, very considerably smaller accommodation should be provided, and a ballot be resorted to in the same way as hon. Gentlemen are accustomed to ballot for places in the Ladies' Gallery of this House, and in this way provide the means of further curtailing the expenditure upon this ceremony. I merely throw out this suggestion in the hope that it will receive at the hands of the Government the consideration which it deserves.

Question put,

The Committee *divided* :—Ayes 84 ; Noes 208 : Majority 124.—(Div. List, No. 137.)

Original Question put, and *agreed to*.

Resolution to be reported *To-morrow*.

Committee to sit again *To-morrow*.

MUNICIPAL CORPORATIONS ACTS (IRELAND) AMENDMENT (No. 2) BILL.

(*Sir James Corry, Mr. Ewart, Mr. Johnston.*)

[BILL 176.] COMMITTEE.

Order for Committee read.

Motion made, and Question proposed, "That Mr. Speaker do now leave the Chair."—(*Sir James Corry.*)

MR. T. M. HEALY (Longford, N.): of course, we cannot expect that any pledge made by this Government will be kept. I shall say nothing on this very important Bill, as no Member of Her Majesty's Government is present; but I must say that after the statement of the First Lord of the Treasury (Mr. W. H. Smith) the absence of the responsible Minister is rather remarkable.

Question put, and *agreed to*

Bill *considered* in Committee.

(In the Committee.)

Motion made, and Question proposed, "That the Chairman do report Progress, and ask leave to sit again."— (*Sir James Corry.*)

MR. T. M. HEALY: I am very glad this Motion has been made, and I trust that the Government will remember that these 86 Irish Members belong to a particular Party who sometimes do expect some statement of policy from Her Majesty's Government.

Question put, and *agreed to*.

Committee report Progress; to sit again upon *Tuesday* next.

MOTION.

—o—

EAST INDIA STOCK CONVERSION BILL.

On the Motion of Sir John Gorst, Bill for giving facilities for the conversion of India Four Per Cent. Stock into India Three and a-half Per Cent. Stock; and for other purposes relating thereto, *ordered* to be brought in by Sir John Gorst and Mr. Jackson.

Bill *presented*, and read the first time. [Bill 263.]

House adjourned at a quarter before Three o'clock.

——————

HOUSE OF LORDS,

Friday, 13*th May*, 1887.

——————

MINUTES.]—PUBLIC BILLS—*First Reading*— Pluralities Act Amendment Act (1885) Amendment * (96); Duration of Speeches in Parliament (97); Colonial Service (Pensions) * (98).

DURATION OF SPEECHES IN PARLIAMENT BILL.

BILL PRESENTED. FIRST READING.

LORD DENMAN, in rising to call attention to the subject of noticing and limiting the duration of speeches in Parliament, and to present a Bill thereupon, said, that Mr. Caine, in his Amendment on Procedure, wished to allow such ordinary Members as himself (Lord Denman) in their Lordships' House a full hour and to give Privy Councillors unlimited time; but whilst he (Lord Denman) thought an hour too much for an ordinary speaker, he considered some notice of time necessary. He had no wish to speak disrespectfully of those who could enchain and delight either House by a three hours' speech; and, indeed, he had found in a letter by his lamented Predecessor, when a young barrister—"I had the pleasure of hearing myself speak for three hours." He (Lord Denman) deemed both Houses of Parliament to be one, for even if figures (in red ink or italics) were inserted in a Bill begun in the House of Lords, if the House of Commons accepted those figures, it became law. No one would wish to interrupt an able speaker in the midst of an argument, and if he were to sit down for a moment and no one to rise, he might continue his speech. He had himself been tied to a two minutes' speech, avoiding politics, and he believed a quarter of an hour might suffice for many in both Houses. At Derby, a party of 300 men at their breakfast, enjoyed an exposition of the Holy Scriptures by a minister, either an Independent, or Congregationalist, Wesleyan, or Presbyterian, for half-an-hour, and at the end of that time a musician began to play, and so harmoniously put an end to the discourse. In many speakers of ability agreeing to this Bill might be a "Self-Denying Ordinance." It was best for both Houses to consider this, and for the second reading to be postponed till after the Whitsuntide Vacation. The Bill might be the same as is used at Diocesan conferences. He (Lord Denman) had seen in *Punch* a caricature of a room, round which were telephones, through which Members of Parliament were speaking to their constituents, whilst others addressed the House of Commons. A suggestion had been made that they might write to newspapers; but he had no confidence in them, and they had made him appear to have uttered such nonsense that, but for Mr. Hansard, he would appear to the public as the stupidest man breathing.

Bill to ascertain and limit the duration of speeches in Parliament—*Presented* (The Lord DENMAN); read 1ª. (No. 97.)

PLURALITIES ACT AMENDMENT ACT (1885) AMENDMENT BILL [H.L.]

A Bill to amend the Pluralities Act Amendment Act, 1885—Was *presented* by The Lord Bishop of Bangor; read 1ª. (No. 96.)

House adjourned at a quarter before Five o'clock, to Monday next, a quarter before Eleven o'clock.

HOUSE OF COMMONS,

Friday, 13th May, 1887.

MINUTES.]—SUPPLY—*considered in Committee—Resolution* [May 12] *reported.*
PRIVATE BILL (*by Order*) — *Second Reading* — Burry Port and North Western Junction Railway.*
PUBLIC BILLS — *Ordered* — *First Reading* — Legal Proceedings (Reports) [264].
Committee— Criminal Law Amendment (Ireland) [217] [*Seventh Night*]—R.P.; Deeds of Arrangement Registration * [231] — R.P.; Truck [109] —R.P.
Committee—Report — Third Reading—Metropolis Management (Battersea and Westminster) (*re-comm.*) * [258], and *passed.*
PROVISIONAL ORDER BILL—*Considered as amended*—Pier and Harbour [222].*

PRIVATE BUSINESS.

—o—

PECKHAM AND EAST DULWICH TRAMWAYS.—RESOLUTION.

MR. DODDS (Stockton) (for Sir CHARLES FORSTER) (Walsall) moved—

"That the Resolution of the Standing Orders Committee of the 5th day of April last, with respect to the Peckham and East Dulwich Tramways Petition, together with the said Petition and the Bill annexed thereto, be referred back to the said Committee, and that they have power to inquire whether the parties be permitted to proceed with their Bill provided that so much of Clause 15 as relates to the widening of Rye Lane be struck out of the Bill."

MR. KELLY (Camberwell, N.): I wish to say a few words in reference to this particular clause.

MR. SPEAKER: If the hon. Member rises to oppose the Motion it must stand over.

MR. KELLY: I only wish to point out that this particular clause is a clause in which the inhabitants of Peckham take great interest. The Company obtained powers in 1882, 1883, and 1885, to construct tramways over which no tramcar has as yet ever run. The matter has now come on very suddenly without sufficient notice. The real opposition to the proposal is that it is proposed to strike out of the Bill that part of it which principally interests the people of Peckham. I therefore beg to move that the debate be adjourned for a week.

Motion made, and Question proposed, "That the Debate be adjourned till Friday, the 20th May."—(*Mr. Kelly.*)

MR. DODDS: I cannot consent to the suggestion of the hon. Member for North Camberwell, that the debate should be adjourned for a week; but I am quite willing to postpone it until Tuesday next. In the meantime, I may say that the right hon. Gentleman the Member for the University of Oxford (Sir John Mowbray) entirely approves of the Resolution I have moved. I beg to move that the debate be adjourned until Tuesday.

Motion, by leave, *withdrawn.*

Motion made, and Question proposed, "That the Debate be adjourned till Tuesday."—(*Mr. Dodds.*)

MR. KELLY: I trust, in accepting the proposal of the hon. Member, I may be allowed to say that I represent part of the district which is included within the provisions of this Bill, and that I am acting only in the interests of the inhabitants.

Question put, and *agreed to.*

Debate *adjourned* till *Tuesday* next.

QUESTIONS.

—o—

POOR LAW (IRELAND)—POOR'S RATE NEWRY UNION.

MR. BLANE (Armagh, S.) asked the Chief Secretary to the Lord Lieutenant of Ireland, What amount of Poor's Rate, being the last made rate of the Newry Union, is due by immediate lessors to that Union in respect of holdings of £4 and under, and what steps the Guardians have taken for the recovery of the last made rate from the immediate lessors since that rate was struck upon such holdings?

THE PARLIAMENTARY UNDER SECRETARY (Colonel KING-HARMAN) (Kent, Isle of Thanet) (who replied) said: The amount of rate so due and recoverable is £19. The rate collectors have been instructed to take proceedings for the recovery of the rate.

POOR LAW (IRELAND) — BELFAST GUARDIANS—JOSEPH WATT, RELIEVING OFFICER.

MR. BLANE (Armagh, S.) asked the Chief Secretary to the Lord Lieutenant of Ireland, If the attention of the Local Government Board has been directed to the proceedings of the Admission Committee of the Belfast Board of Guardians, at their meeting on 26th April, 1887, at which Joseph Watt, one of the relieving officers of the Union, was absent without previously obtaining leave from the Guardians; why was the book containing the usual entry of lines issued for the previous week not duly written up and presented for approval; what condition did the workhouse messenger find Watt in when he went to his residence, and was there any Report made to the Local Government Board on the subject; and, is Watt the same person who was formerly Master of the Belfast Workhouse, and who was obliged by the Local Government Board to resign his position, owing to inebriety and and gross irregularities in the management of the workhouse?

THE PARLIAMENTARY UNDER SECRETARY (Colonel KING-HARMAN) (Kent, Isle of Thanet) (who replied) said: Part of this Question was answered yesterday. In reply to the remainder of the Question I have to say that Mr. Watt explained to the Board of Guardians that his absence from the meeting was due to illness, and his failure to enter up his book the previous week was due to the same cause. Mr. Watt's explanation was supported by a medical certificate. The messenger sent to Mr. Watt by the Guardians informed them that he seemed to be in a very delicate state of health. Mr. Watt formerly held the office of Master of the Belfast Workhouse, which, however, he resigned upwards of 10 years ago, on receipt by the Guardians of an unfavourable Report in regard to the management and condition of the workhouse, and his resignation did not appear to have been due to any inebriety, as alleged, but to the fact that he was phisically unfit to discharge the duties of the situation.

NEW GUINEA — THE AUSTRALIAN COLONIES.

SIR GEORGE CAMPBELL (Kirkcaldy, &c.) asked the Secretary of State for the Colonies, Whether Her Majesty's Government propose to transfer the administration of the part of New Guinea claimed by this country to the Australian Colonies or to Queensland in particular; and, if so, whether, considering the magnitude of the question and its effect on the Native races, an opportunity will be given to Parliament to express an opinion before such a measure is carried

Mr. Blane

out; and, whether, in any case, the proposed scheme will be submitted for the sanction of the British Legislature, in the same way that it is to be submitted for the sanction of the Colonial Legislatures?

THE SECRETARY OF STATE (Sir HENRY HOLLAND) (Hampstead): The Government of New Guinea will be administered by an officer appointed by, and responsible to, Her Majesty's Government, and he will be guided by the instructions of the Governor of Queensland. The Governor of Queensland will be directed to consult his Government upon all matters relating to British New Guinea; but will not be absolutely bound by their opinions. The scheme will have to be approved by the Colonial Governments, and legislation will be necessary in Queensland. The details of the scheme will shortly be placed before Parliament so that an opinion may be expressed upon it before it is carried out; but the formal sanction of Parliament is not required. A vote will have to be taken in due course of time.

ADMIRALTY—NAVAL DEFENCE OF THE AUSTRALIAN COLONIES.

SIR GEORGE CAMPBELL (Kirkcaldy, &c.) asked the First Lord of the Admiralty, Whether any arrangement with the Australian Colonies for naval defence, which is made subject to the approval of the Colonial Parliaments, will also be submitted, without delay, for the approval of this House; and, if so, whether he can say when, and in what shape, the matter will be brought forward?

THE FIRST LORD (Lord GEORGE HAMILTON) (Middlesex, Ealing): I am glad to say that the Colonial Delegates agreed to an arrangement, subject to the approval of the Colonial and Imperial Parliament, which will conduce to the effective strength of the Navy, and establish a partnership in the expenditure connected with that force which did not before exist. Papers on the subject will be laid upon the Table of the House in due course, and so soon as the respective Colonial Parliaments have signified their acceptance of the scheme.

SIR GEORGE CAMPBELL: Is this House to have no opportunity of expressing an opinion until the Colonial Parliaments have done so?

LORD GEORGE HAMILTON: The hon. Gentleman must be aware that any proposal connected with expenditure must be laid before this House.

THE COLONIAL CONFERENCE—THE MINUTES.

MR. CHILDERS (Edinburgh, S.) asked the Secretary of State for the Colonies, When the Minutes of the Colonial Conference would be laid on the Table?

THE SECRETARY OF STATE (Sir HENRY HOLLAND)(Hampstead)(in reply) said, they were in course of revision. They would be laid as soon as he could do so.

CEYLON—THE POLICE FORCE.

SIR THOMAS ESMONDE (Dublin Co., S.) asked the Secretary of State for the Colonies, Whether complaints have reached him that the Ceylon Police are open to bribery, and that it is customary for would-be recruits to pay "admission fees" to the Police Superintendents; if the authorities are aware of the corruption of the Force; and, whether any steps will be taken to re-organize the Department?

THE SECRETARY OF STATE (Sir HENRY HOLLAND) (Hampstead): No reports of the kind have reached me; but I will make inquiry of the Governor.

POST OFFICE (IRELAND)—"HAZLEY v. LITTLE"—DELAY OF SUMMONSES.

SIR THOMAS ESMONDE (Dublin Co., S.) asked the Postmaster General, What explanation has Mr. Hazley, Postmaster of Blackrock, County Dublin, to offer for the delay which occurred in the delivery of the summonses to witnesses for the defence in the case of "Hazley v. Little," owing to which the summonses, which should have been delivered on Thursday, 14th April, were not delivered until the following Saturday?

THE POSTMASTER GENERAL (Mr. RAIKES) (Cambridge University): The delay in the delivery of the letter referred to was owing to its having accidentally slipped between the folds of a newspaper, and to its having thus been misdelivered. The postman concerned has been punished for his want of care?

INDIA—THE IRON FLOATING DOCK AT BOMBAY.

ADMIRAL FIELD (Sussex, Eastbourne) asked the Under Secretary of State for India, Whether he can inform the House of the original cost of the Iron Floating Dock at Bombay; when, and by whose authority and advice, this expenditure was incurred; whether any of Her Majesty's ships have ever been docked therein; whether he can explain the nature of the arrangement recently made with the Peninsular and Oriental Company for leasing the said dock to them; and, whether he has any information to show that the enlargement of existing docks in the Government Yard at Bombay, as recommended by successive Admirals in command of the Indian Station, might have been carried out at one-third of the cost of the aforementioned Floating Dock?

THE UNDER SECRETARY OF STATE (Sir JOHN GORST) (Chatham): (1.) £307,000. (2.) In 1868, by authority of the Secretary of State for India in Council, and by the advice of the Government of Bombay, backed by the Government of India. (3.) I am not aware of any ships of Her Majesty's Navy having been docked there. (4.) The dock has been leased to the Peninsular and Oriental Company for five years, at a nominal rent, the Company being under the obligation to keep it in proper repair. (5.) I have no information to the effect suggested in the Question.

INDIA—STATE OF MOHRBHANJ, IN ORISSA.

SIR ROPER LETHBRIDGE (Kensington, N.) asked the Under Secretary of State for India, Whether the State of Mohrbhanj in Orissa is regarded by the Government of India as British territory; whether the administration of the State during the minority of the present Raja has been put into the hands of an English gentleman, to the exclusion of the relatives of the minor; and, if so, under what authority this has been done; whether the relatives of the minor Raja (including his mother and uncles) have complained of this arrangement as disgraceful to the Raj family, preventing the marriage of its daughters, and causing other serious injury to its dignity; whether one of the uncles of the minor Raja had been entrusted by the late

Raja, his brother, with an important administrative charge in the State; and, whether the British Government has allowed any public independent inquiry to be made into the truth of any complaints that may have been made?

THE UNDER SECRETARY OF STATE (Sir JOHN GORST) (Chatham): (1.) No. (2.) Yes; under the authority of the Government of India. (3.) No such complaints have ever reached the Secretary of State. (4.) Yes; and in this charge he has been continued. (5.) No public inquiry has ever been made.

CIVIL SERVICE WRITERS—SERVICE ON THE CENSUS OF 1881.

MR. FLYNN (Cork, N.) asked Mr. Chancellor of the Exchequer, Whether applications from Civil Service Writers, who served on the Census of 1881, to have such services counted towards bonus and gratuity under the provisions of the Treasury Minute of December last, have been received at the Treasury, and that the Lords Commissioners have replied to them declining to consider the question; and, if he will, in accordance with his promise to examine further into the case of the writers, take this matter into favourable consideration, with a view to permitting such writers to count the services rendered by them to the State as Census clerks towards the benefits promulgated in such Treasury Minute?

THE CHANCELLOR OF THE EXCHEQUER (Mr. GOSCHEN) (St. George's, Hanover Square): I am informed that an application from one Civil Service copyist praying that non-copyist service should be counted as copyist service was received at the Treasury and refused, because the Treasury Minute of December was confined to copyist service. A claim that non-copyist service should count as copyist service would require very careful consideration. If such a claim were sent in to the Head of the Department in which the applicants gave such service it would have my attention; but I must not be understood thereby as implying any promise of compliance.

RAILWAYS (IRELAND)—DEBT OF THE DERRY CENTRAL RAILWAY.

MR. BIGGAR (Cavan, W.) asked the Secretary to the Treasury, How much

is due to the Treasury by the Derry Central Railway; what is the nature of the security; how much interest, if any, is due; and, when the last payment of interest was made?

THE SECRETARY (Mr. JACKSON) (Leeds, N.): The amount of principal due is £100,000. The security is a mortgage on the undertaking. The Advance, representing the loan capital of the Company, is the first charge on the net receipts. The interest due is £12,284 7s. 5d.; and the last payment of interest was made on the 23rd of February, 1887.

DRAINAGE (IRELAND)—RIVER FERGUS RECLAMATION SCHEME.

MR. BIGGAR (Cavan, W.) asked the Secretary to the Treasury, How much money has been advanced by the Treasury toward the River Fergus Reclamation Scheme; what is the present state of the works, and how much is expected it will cost to finish them; what is the extent of the property, and its estimated value; and, what is the present income derivable from it?

THE SECRETARY (Mr. JACKSON) (Leeds, N.): The amount advanced is £125,151. The works are nearly completed, and the embankment is expected to be fully closed this summer. The estimated cost of completion is £4,000. The extent of the property is about 1,300 statute acres, and the estimated value is £70,510. This value was estimated some years ago by the late Mr. John Kelly, who had considerable experience in such reclamations; but it is impossible to say what it would realize under the present circumstances of the Land Question in Ireland. The present income is *nil.*

THE MAGISTRACY (ENGLAND AND WALES)—THE FLINTSHIRE NONCONFORMISTS.

SIR THOMAS ESMONDE (Dublin Co., S.) asked the Secretary of State for the Home Department, If he will cause inquiries to be made with a view to ascertaining the number of Non-conformists qualified to hold the Commission of the Peace in Flintshire; and, if, in the event of Non-conformists being found qualified to hold the position, steps will be taken to place them upon the Bench?

THE UNDER SECRETARY OF STATE (Mr. STUART-WORTLEY) (Sheffield, Hallam) (who replied) said, the appointment of the magistrates rested with the Lord Chancellor, on the recommendation of the Lord Lieutenant of the county. It was no part of the duty of the Home Secretary to make inquiries in respect to the number of persons qualified to hold Commissions of the Peace, nor to suggest the appointment of magistrates from any particular class.

MR. T. E. ELLIS (Merionethshire) asked, whether there was any special Minister in the House who could answer Questions relating to the Welsh Magistracy?

THE FIRST LORD OF THE TREASURY (Mr. W. H. SMITH) (Strand, Westminster) said, if it was considered that a sufficient answer had not been given a Member of the Government would communicate with the Lord Chancellor on the subject.

LABOURERS (IRELAND) ACT — MACROOM BOARD OF GUARDIANS.

Dr. TANNER (Cork Co., Mid), who had the following Question on the Paper:—To ask the Chief Secretary to the Lord Lieutenant of Ireland, If he can state the reason why the Local Government Board have not ordered their arbitrator to proceed to Macroom, as requested by the Macroom Board of Guardians early last month; and, when the Government purpose sending the said arbitrator, for the purpose of valuing the sites for labourers' cottages? said, that as the Chief Secretary for Ireland was not in his place, and as he did not expect to get a satisfactory answer from the Parliamentary Under Secretary for Ireland, he would postpone the Question until next week.

PALACE OF WESTMINSTER — ELECTRIC LIGHTS IN THE HOUSE OF COMMONS.

DR. TANNER (Cork Co., Mid) asked the First Commissioner of Works, Whether it is a fact that, although a great portion of the offices could be more cheaply and efficiently lit by electricity, the present engine is inadequate to give the necessary supplement; whether, when the engine was first chosen, attention was called to its disproportionate size; whether a room, called the Ex-

chequer Room, can now be utilised to hold a larger engine of increased power; and, whether he will recommend the substitution of an engine which will give the requisite supply for the existing engine?

THE FIRST COMMISSIONER (Mr. PLUNKET) (Dublin University): I doubt whether the offices of the House of Commons could be more cheaply lighted by electricity than by gas, though in other respects the electric light is certainly preferable; but it is quite true that the present plant is inadequate to meet any further demands upon it. I have asked Dr. Percy to prepare for me a complete plan and estimate for a considerably increased plan for lighting the whole of the Palace with electricity, on the chance that I may some day find the House in a sufficiently generous mood to vote the additional expense; but small additions from time to time would, I am advised, be very expensive, and I could not recommend their adoption.

WAYS AND MEANS—THE FINANCIAL RESOLUTIONS—THE TOBACCO DUTY.

MR. MURPHY (Dublin, St. Patrick's) asked Mr. Chancellor of the Exchequer, Whether inquiries have been made, through the Inland Revenue Department, which have confirmed the statements that many workpeople in Ireland have been thrown out of employment owing to the change in the Tobacco Duty; and, whether he will re-consider his decision as to granting a drawback, or making some arrangement whereby manufacturers may re-employ their hands without suffering serious loss?

THE CHANCELLOR OF THE EXCHEQUER (Mr. GOSCHEN) (St. George's, Hanover Square): I have made inquiries not only as to the discharge of workpeople in Ireland, but also as to the amount of tobacco which has been taken out of bond. The allegation is that the manufacturers must wait till the 21st of May, when the reduced duty comes in, and that they must discharge their workpeople in the meantime. Now, it is a curious fact that the quantity of tobacco cleared for consumption in Dublin from the date of the Budget to the 6th instant was more than 10 per cent greater than during the corresponding period of last year. I am at a loss, therefore, to understand why, more tobacco having been taken out for working up, hands should have been discharged. I have heard that there has been a certain discharge of workpeople ; but do not know what proportion it bears to the whole number employed. In Dublin I hear that 381 were discharged ; in Belfast 11, and none by the great firms. I do not admit that manufacturers will necessarily "suffer serious loss." I have seen a Circular from one of the largest firms saying that they should not reduce the price to their customers for some weeks, thus clearly showing that it is possible to recoup themselves for the loss from the higher duty.

THE METROPOLITAN POLICE — THE CHIEF COMMISSIONER.

MR. O. V. MORGAN (Battersea) asked the Secretary of State for the Home Department, Whether his attention had been directed to an article in *The Globe* of 11th instant, in which it is stated—

" From all ranks of the Force, however, come complaints of the rigorous administration of the Chief Commissioner, who, it is alleged, orders the discharge or reduction in rank of men reported for comparatively slight offences, which in former times would have been dismissed with a caution ;"

and, whether there is any foundation for the report ?

THE UNDER SECRETARY OF STATE (MR. STUART-WORTLEY) (Sheffield, Hallam) (who replied) said : No, Sir ; the Secretary of State has no reason to believe that there is any foundation for this report. On the contrary, there is not wanting proof that the police service is gaining in popularity. The Secretary of State is informed by the Chief Commissioner that there has been no alteration in the mode of punishing minor or slight offences since he has been in office.

BUSINESS OF THE HOUSE — COMMITTEE ON THE COAL MINES, &c. REGULATION BILL.

MR. J. E. ELLIS (Nottingham, Rushcliffe) asked the Secretary of State for the Home Department, Whether, in view of the inconvenience to which the uncertainty in the matter is giving rise, he will now state definitely when the Motion to go into Committee on the Coal Mines, &c., Regulation Bill will be made ?

Mr. Goschen

THE UNDER SECRETARY OF STATE (MR. STUART-WORTLEY) (Sheffield, Hallam) (who replied) said : The Secretary of State regrets extremely that any inconvenience should have been caused in regard to the committal of this Bill. The Motion to go into Committee has been twice postponed at the request of hon. Members interested in the question. The Secretary of State will endeavour to arrange with my right hon. Friend the Leader of the House an opportunity for making this Motion before Whitsuntide ; but the hon. Member must see that, in the present state of Public Business, it is not possible to give a more definite reply.

POST OFFICE (IRELAND) — POSTMASTER AT BORRIS IN OSSORY, QUEEN'S CO.

MR. W. A. MACDONALD (Queen's Co., Ossory) asked the Postmaster General, Whether it is a fact that a man named Tynan is now a candidate for the office of Postmaster at Borris in Ossory, Queen's County ; whether the said Tynan is over 70 years of age, and can hardly be expected to discharge the duties in person ; and, whether a more suitable candidate cannot be found ?

THE POSTMASTER GENERAL (MR. RAIKES) (Cambridge University): Thomas Tynan has been nominated by the Treasury to the Post Office at Borris in Ossory. Inquiry is being made as to his fitness, and he will not be appointed unless he should be found to be a proper person for the office.

ARMY (AUXILIARY FORCES) — THE WEXFORD MILITIA.

MR. W. REDMOND (Fermanagh, N.) asked the Secretary of State for War, Whether he will order the Wexford Militia to be trained in the town of Wexford if it is found that there is good ground for rifle range in that locality ?

THE SECRETARY OF STATE (MR. E. STANHOPE) (Lincolnshire, Horncastle): Even if a suitable range for rifle practice could now be provided, it would be too late to make the necessary arrangements for the camp this year, as the battalion is to come out for training on the 30th instant. The Military Authorities consider a change in the place of training, from time to time, to be advantageous; but I will consider for next year the claims of Wexford to have the battalion trained there.

ADMIRALTY CONTRACTS — ENGINES FOR GUNBOATS.

MR. BARBOUR (Paisley) asked the First Lord of the Admiralty, If, in the event of the cost of producing the engines for the gunboats proposed to be constructed in Devonport Dockyard exceeding the estimate, whether the officers of the Departments concerned will be held pecuniarily responsible, to the extent of making good the difference?

THE FIRST LORD (Lord GEORGE HAMILTON) (Middlesex, Ealing): No, Sir; the officers in no shipbuilding yard are pecuniarily responsible if their estimates are exceeded; and we do not propose to introduce such an innovation in the Royal Dockyards.

SOUTH AFRICA—ZULULAND.

MR. M'ARTHUR (Leicester) asked the Secretary of State for the Colonies, Whether the Heads of the Zulu people have accepted the boundary fixed by the recent Convention with the Boers, together with the British Protectorate over East Zululand; and, whether he is able to communicate to the House any information as to the establishment of Law and order in Swaziland?

THE SECRETARY OF STATE (Sir HENRY HOLLAND) (Hampstead): No formal concurrence as to the boundary has been given by the Zulu Chiefs; but they are understood to have accepted it, now that they have been informed that the arrangement is final and cannot be altered. They received favourably the announcement that the supreme authority and protection of Her Majesty would be extended to Zululand. Her Majesty's Sovereignty will be declared over Zululand, which includes the Reserve and what has been called Eastern Zululand, and Residents will be appointed under the Governor of Natal, who will also be appointed Governor of Zululand, with power of legislating and establishing Courts by Proclamation. As to Swaziland, Her Majesty's Government are precluded, by Article 12 of the Convention with the South African Republic, from assuming the control of that territory, and nothing has occurred there to warrant active interference in its affairs. Assurances have been given by the Government of the South African Republic that they are mindful of the obligations resting upon them, as upon Her Majesty's Government, by the Convention to maintain the independence of Swaziland.

SIR GEORGE CAMPBELL (Kirkcaldy, &c.): Will the Boer Republic in Zululand be absolutely independent?

SIR HENRY HOLLAND: Certainly; because it is no longer a part of Zululand—it is carved out of Zululand.

PARLIAMENTARY ELECTIONS — BOSTON ELECTION PETITION — MR. FYDELL ROWLEY— DISQUALIFICATION FOR OFFICE.

MR. FINCH (Rutland) asked Mr. Attorney General, Whether Mr. Fydell-Rowley is, or is not, legally disqualified from holding any public office?

THE ATTORNEY GENERAL (Sir RICHARD WEBSTER) (Isle of Wight): In my opinion, Mr. Fydell-Rowley is not legally disqualified from holding any public office. The Report of the Commissioners does not of itself disqualify.

IRISH PETTY SESSIONS ACT—SECTION 13—COMMITTALS.

MR. MAURICE HEALY (Cork) asked Mr. Attorney General for Ireland, Under what category persons committed to prison under Section 13 of the Irish Petty Sessions Act, for refusing to answer or refusing to be sworn, are classed for the purposes of prison discipline; and, whether they are treated as convicted prisoners, or as persons committed for contempt of Court?

THE ATTORNEY GENERAL FOR IRELAND (Mr. HOLMES) (Dublin University): As misdemeanants of the first class.

MR. MAURICE HEALY wished to know how that was, considering that prisoners committed for contempt in civil cases in the Superior Courts, and in criminal cases in Quarter Sessions Courts, were treated differently from prisoners committed under the Petty Sessions Act?

MR. HOLMES said, he was not aware any such difference existed.

WAR OFFICE—QUARTERMASTER-GENERAL TO THE FORCES.

MR. TOTTENHAM (Winchester) asked the Secretary of State for War, If the post of Quartermaster General to the Forces is to be temporarily filled from 1st June to 1st October, 1887, by Major General Sir Robert Biddulph, and if Major General Sir Redvers Buller is to fill that post from the latter date; and, whether the post of Inspector General of Recruiting is to be temporarily filled till same date by an officer holding the rank of Colonel, with the intention that Sir Robert Biddulph should then return to that Department?

THE SECRETARY OF STATE (Mr. E. STANHOPE) (Lincolnshire, Horncastle): Sir Robert Biddulph has been appointed Quartermaster General from the 1st of June, and the vacancy so created will be filled by Colonel Rocke. I can give no other information on the subject.

WAR OFFICE—THE TWO ARMY CORPS AND CAVALRY DIVISION.

MR. TOTTENHAM (Winchester) asked the Secretary of State for War, If he can state when the two Army Corps and Cavalry Division, stated by him as about to be formed, will be so, and if they will be on the peace or war footing; what will be the number of Infantry Battalions, Cavalry Regiments, Horse and Field Batteries in each Corps, and the establishment of each; what will be the total effective strength of each Corps and Division, and where the head-quarters of each will be; and, whether it is proposed to assemble any, or all, of these Corps and Division at one or more points for exercise within the present year, and for what period?

THE SECRETARY OF STATE (Mr. E. STANHOPE)(Lincolnshire, Horncastle): The organization of the two Army Corps and Cavalry Division is worked out in detail, and I propose shortly to lay before Parliament a Paper which will fully answer my hon. Friend's Questions. To assemble all or any of these Corps would involve a large expenditure, which is not provided for in the present Estimates.

WAR OFFICE—ORGANIZATION OF THE TWO ARMY CORPS — SUPPLY OF HORSES.

GENERAL FRASER (Lambeth, N.) asked the Secretary of State for War, Whether, in view of the organization of two Army Corps ready to embark even

"before the necessary stores could be got on board ship," it is a fact that for the Royal Artillery and their ammunition columns alone it would be necessary to provide 3,702 horses over and above the whole number of horses estimated for in the Army Estimates of 1887, for the whole number of horses requisite for the Royal Artillery.

THE SECRETARY OF STATE (Mr. E. STANHOPE) (Lincolnshire, Horncastle): Substantially the figures quoted by my hon. and gallant Friend are correct.

CELEBRATION OF THE JUBILEE YEAR OF HER MAJESTY'S REIGN — A GENERAL AMNESTY IN IRELAND.

MR. NORRIS (Tower Hamlets, Limehouse) asked the First Lord of the Treasury, Whether, on the passing of the Criminal Law Amendment (Ireland) Bill, the Government will take into consideration to recommend to Her Majesty the Queen, in celebration of Her Jubilee year, a general amnesty in Ireland to all persons undergoing imprisonment for agrarian crime, excepting such as have been guilty of violence to the person?

THE FIRST LORD (Mr. W. H. SMITH) (Strand, Westminster): Her Majesty's Government are not in a position to enter into any engagement of the kind suggested by the hon. Gentleman.

THE COLONIAL CONFERENCE—THE MINUTES.

In reply to Mr. CHILDERS (Edinburgh, S.),

THE SECRETARY OF STATE FOR THE COLONIES (Sir HENRY HOLLAND) (Hampstead) said, that his former answer as to the publication of the Minutes of the Conference was not strictly correct. The Papers and Minutes would be revised; and it was possible that the proceedings referring to the New Hebrides and the negotiations with France might not be included; but no decision had yet been arrived at.

MR. CHILDERS: The Papers as to the naval arrangement will be included?

SIR HENRY HOLLAND: Absolutely.

SIR GEORGE CAMPBELL (Kirkcaldy, &c.): As also those relating to New Guinea?

SIR HENRY HOLLAND: Yes.

Mr. Tottenham

ISLANDS OF THE SOUTH PACIFIC—TONGA.

MR. W. H. JAMES (Gateshead) asked the Secretary of State for the Colonies, Whether any intelligence had been received at the Colonial Office confirming the report sent home appearing in *The Melbourne Argus*, to the effect that previously to the arrival of Sir Charles Mitchell in Tonga, peace had been established by the whole of the Wesleyan body having been exterminated?

THE SECRETARY OF STATE (Sir HENRY HOLLAND) (Hampstead): We have not got that information; but we have received a more satisfactory telegram, from which it appears that at least some Wesleyans are left. A telegram was received yesterday from Sir Charles Mitchell in the following words:—

"April 30.—Returned from Tonga to-day. Send report by next mail. Full inquiry showed report of religious persecution true to considerable extent. King promises make Chiefs observe Constitution as regards religious freedom in future and generally protect Wesleyans. All quiet now. Europeans in no case interfered with."

PARLIAMENT—PETITIONS—FICTITIOUS SIGNATURES.

MR. CODDINGTON (Blackburn), on private Notice, asked the hon. Member for North Westmoreland (Mr. W. Lowther), as a Member of the Committee on Public Petitions, Whether it was a fact that 108 Petitions, out of a total of 130, recently presented by the hon. Member for the Scotland Division of Liverpool (Mr. T. P. O'Connor) against the Criminal Law Amendment (Ireland) Bill had been impugned by that Committee on the ground that many of the signatures appeared to be in the same handwriting; and what further proceedings the Committee propose to take in the matter?

MR. W. LOWTHER (Westmoreland, N.) (for Sir CHARLES FORSTER) (Walsall) said, he believed it to be correct that 108 out of the 130 Petitions presented by the hon. Member for the Scotland Division of Liverpool had been impugned by the Public Petitions Committee. Hon. Members, on referring to their Papers, which were delivered this morning, would find the Petitions marked with a star and an explanation, stating that the Committee had, in the case of the Petitions marked, reported to the House the number of names appended thereto; but that they were of opinion that many of the names were in the same hand writing, and that the Orders of the House, which required that every Petition must be signed or marked by the parties whose names were appended thereto, and must be signed by no one else except in cases of incapacity by sickness, had not been complied with. It might be that the signatures to the Petitions were not forgeries. The people might have signed them for their children, or their belongings. The Committee would meet in a day or two, and would take into consideration the Petitions alluded to.

MR. T. E. ELLIS (Merionethshire) asked, whether the Committee would also take into consideration the Petitions against the disestablishment of the Church in Wales, which had been similarly impugned by the Public Petitions Committee?

MR. W. LOWTHER said, that if the hon. Member would call the attention of the Committee to the matter he had no doubt that they would attend to it.

THE IRISH LAND LAW BILL.

MR. T. M. HEALY (Longford, N.): I wish to ask the First Lord of the Treasury, If it is the fact that in "another place," without any comment at all, or any intimation of the kind from anybody, the Government have given Notice to omit from the Irish Land Law Bill five of its most important clauses, two of them entirely, and to substitute for the other three wholly new clauses; that is to say, the clauses dealing with the stay of evictions, the jurisdiction of the County Court, and the Bankruptcy Clauses. I wish further to ask whether, under these circumstances, the Government will postpone taking any such action in the House of Lords, and wait to propose their Amendments when the Bill comes down to the House of Commons, which is a more competent Chamber to deal with them?

THE FIRST LORD (Mr. W. H. SMITH) (Strand, Westminster): The hon. and learned . Gentleman has given me no Notice whatever of the Question which he has put to me. I am really not aware of the procedure of the other House of Parliament in the matter. I can give him this assurance, however, that nothing will be done that will invalidate the Irish Land Law Bill, with the consent of the Government, in the House of Lords.

MR. T. M. HEALY: Are we to understand that these Amendments have not been made a Cabinet matter, and that this is entirely the action of the Marquess of Salisbury?

MR. W. H. SMITH: The House will see that the Question which the hon. and learned Member puts to me is one which ought not to be put to me without ample Notice.

MUNICIPAL CORPORATIONS ACTS (IRELAND) AMENDMENT (No. 2) BILL.

MR. T. M. HEALY (Longford, N.) said, that notwithstanding the pledges given by the First Lord of the Treasury last night that the Chief Secretary for Ireland would be in his place to answer any Question in relation to the Municipal Corporations Acts (Ireland) Amendment (No. 2) Bill, when the Bill came on last night the Chief Secretary and the First Lord of the Treasury disappeared from the House just before the Motion was made that the Speaker do leave the Chair. There was no one present to answer any Question; and, therefore, the stage of the Bill was taken without any guarantee from the Government that the principle of the Bill would be extended to all Ireland.

THE FIRST LORD (Mr. W. H. SMITH) (Strand, Westminster): I was not really aware of the Bill coming on last night, as. the hour was so late; but I was under the impression that the Chief Secretary was in his place when I left the House.

MR. T. M. HEALY: He was; but he ran away.

EGYPT—RUMOURED EVACUATION.

MR. W. REDMOND (Fermanagh, N.) asked the Under Secretary of State for Foreign Affairs, Whether it was true, as stated in some of the newspapers that morning, that an agreement had been arrived at with regard to the evacuation of Egypt; and, whether it was true that the date of the evacuation had been fixed, with the consent of the Porte, at not less than two years from now, and not more than five years?

THE UNDER SECRETARY OF STATE (Sir JAMES FERGUSSON) (Man-

Mr. W. H. Smith

chester, N.E.): I am not able to inform the hon. Member respecting any details of the negotiations at Constantinople. I hope it will not be long before I can fully inform the House. I must not be understood to convey any inference respecting the particular statements in the newspapers referred to. They are quite inaccurate, and do not give any true description of the proposals.

MR. W. REDMOND asked, whether it was a fact that an agreement had been arrived at with regard to evacuation; and, if not, whether the hon. Gentleman would state, as soon as possible, after such an agreement had been come to, that it was intended to evacuate Egypt?

SIR JAMES FERGUSSON: I must ask the hon. Member to give Notice of the Question.

MR. W. REDMOND: Then I will ask the Question on Monday.

CRIMINAL LAW AMENDMENT (IRELAND) BILL.—[BILL 217.]

(Mr. A. J. Balfour, Mr. Secretary Matthews, Mr. Attorney General, Mr. Attorney General for Ireland.)

COMMITTEE. [*Progress* 11*th May.*]

[SEVENTH NIGHT.]

Bill *considered* in Committee.

(In the Committee.)

PRELIMINARY INQUIRY.

Clause 1 (Inquiry by order of Attorney General).

Amendment proposed, in page 1, line 24, to leave out the word "not."—(*Mr. Peter McDonald.*)

Question proposed, "That the word 'not' stand part of the Clause."

MR. O'DOHERTY (Donegal, N.): When the Committee adjourned on Wednesday, I was speaking of the effect of the Amendment then before the Committee. The general principle with regard to the English Law of Evidence, is that any witness can excuse himself from answering a question which, in his opinion, may tend to criminate himself. That principle is applicable in the trial of any case in this country, whether civil or criminal; it is applicable where there is a Judge sitting upon the bench, and the Court is an open Court, and it is also applicable wherever and whenever a witness may be called upon to give evidence. It is now proposed to alter that Law of Evidence in reference to secret tribunals, and to allow such questions to be put under the considerations contained in this clause, even when the answers may criminate the witness. I was proceeding on Wednesday to point out to the Committee that the protection which this sub-section purports to give to a witness, is simply to prevent any statement the witness may make from being used in evidence against him, but that it is perfectly competent for the Crown or the prosecutor to use it for any other purpose except as a confession or as a statement in evidence. I wished on that occasion to call the attention of the Committee to the extraordinary results to which the adoption of this principle may lead, supposing that the statement of the witness is not held to be sacred, and provision is not made that, so far as he is concerned, it cannot be used in any way against him.

THE CHAIRMAN: The hon. Member is anticipating an Amendment which comes later on. The only question now before the Committee is whether the word "not" shall stand part of the clause.

MR. O'DOHERTY: Of course the word "not" will regulate the whole of the sub-section. One of the excuses of the Government for altering the Criminal Law in this respect, is that although a witness may be called upon to criminate himself, in a subsequent part of the section provision is made that no harm shall happen to him. It is provided that any statement made by a witness in answer to a question put to him on examination, except in the case of an indictment, or any other criminal proceeding for perjury, shall not be admissible in evidence against him in any proceeding, civil or criminal. I was pointing out that that is an illusory concession in reference to the compelling of a witness to answer whether the answer may criminate him or not, and I was calling attention to the attempt which was made by the Chief Secretary to defend this provision. What was the point of the right hon. Gentleman? His point was this. We should constantly have cases occurring in which the witnesses would falsely allege that a particular answer would criminate themselves. But surely that is an obvious fact in reference to every

case to which the English Law of Evidence applies, because in any Court of Justice in which a witness may be asked to give evidence he may falsely allege that his answer would tend to criminate himself. Let me call attention to the manner in which such an important change in the law of the country is defended, and the grounds on which the Committee are asked to be satisfied with so enormous a change. No doubt a clause in the Act of 1882 was passed in almost exactly the same words as this sub-section; but the right hon. Gentleman for once sought to be original, and the original argument he used for changing the entire Law of Evidence for this country was this—That there would be this dilemma in regard to the witness— he would either be a true or a false witness. If he were a true witness in saying that an answer to the question would criminate himself, then that fact ought not to be against him, because if he were a true and honest witness, the answer he gave would undoubtedly criminate him. But according to the right hon. Gentleman, he may be a false witness, and, in that case, no reliance can be placed upon any answer he may choose to make, whether it tends to criminate himself or not. If you have a witness under examination who is a false witness, why compel that witness to give answers and make certain admissions which are to be used against other people. I must say that this argument seems to me to reduce to an absurdity the entire position of the Government in this matter in reference to a previous Amendment accepted by the Government. I want to know from the Attorney General in what way the confession of a man is to come in and to be made use of? How is the case of a confession previously made to be provided for? Take the case of a man coming in and saying to the magistrate—"I am not going to give any evidence about this case, because I committed the crime myself." That may take place without the witness having been called upon to answer any question on oath at all, and how is such a witness to be dealt with? Let me ask the Committee to remember that in this sub-section we are dealing with witnesses, and not with criminals. In this preliminary inquiry, as the clause stands, a man is called upon to tell the truth, even although his answer may

[*Seventh Night.*]

criminate himself. Now, the French system is very different. In France there is a preliminary examination for the purpose of eliciting the truth, and not for the purpose of compelling the witness to criminate himself. Sir James Stephen has commented with considerable force upon the French principle; but it is not the French principle which is proposed to be introduced here. In France the inquiry is conducted before a permanent judicial officer, and everything taken down goes before a superior Judge, who is able to see whether that judicial officer exceeded his power or exercised the torture of repeated remands in order to compel the person brought before him to make criminatory statements. In this case there are no means of correcting an examination, or of having it inquired into and considered by a superior Judge. There is no protection of that sort at all, and the magistrate who takes the examination is under no responsibility whatever, because the examination can never be commented upon by the Judge of a superior Court. A second and most important distinction between this case and the whole French principle, is that in proceeding against a man by interrogation in France, there must already have been some evidence laid before the Court which tended to criminate the person examined. He is already under a cloud of suspicion, whereas the witness in Ireland is presumed to be perfectly innocent. Under these circumstances, I cannot help thinking that the French system is infinitely to be preferred to that which the Government now seek to introduce. In deference to your ruling, Mr. Courtney, I will not, as I had intended, touch upon other matters. I presume that I shall have an opportunity of referring to them hereafter. Taking the clause from beginning to end, I maintain that it is in the highest degree objectionable, and may be converted into a trap to extort from the witness certain admissions as to the time and place and circumstances which may give a clue to the prosecution, and ultimately make the witness a criminal himself. Therefore, I contend that the system proposed to be introduced here is worse than the French system, and totally opposed to and inconsistent with the ancient traditions of law and evidence. What I want to know from the Government is, whether

Mr. O'Doherty

henceforward we are to have observed in Ireland the ancient spirit of the Law of Evidence, or whether we are to have imported into that country something infinitely worse than the French Code?

Mr. T. M. HEALY (Longford, N.): The worst part of this proposal is, in my opinion, the words which declare that the witness examined under this section shall not be excused from answering any question on the ground that the answer may criminate, or tend to criminate himself. Why do not the Government say—"lawful question?"—that the witness shall not be excused from answering "any lawful question." As the sub-section runs, the witness is not to be excused from answering "any question." I think there ought to be a definition of the word "question." The Government promised that there should be a definition; but the Amendment which has been put down by the Government simply provides that—

"Every warrant to commit a witness to prison for refusing to answer a question put to him on an examination held under this section shall set out the question which the witness refused to answer."

I am of opinion that the Amendment which appears in the name of the Attorney General does not tend to mitigate the severity of the clause in any way, and the promise of the Government to mitigate the severity of the provision has been proved to be entirely illusory. In my opinion, all that will be gained by inserting this clause will be an increase of perjury. That is recognized by the Government themselves, because they provide that the answer given by a witness to a question shall be admissible in evidence against such witness in any proceeding, civil or criminal, in case of an indictment for perjury. They must know this—that self-preservation is the first law of nature, and that a man if asked directly "Did you do so and so?" may commit perjury rather than criminate himself. I do not think that in England, with all your love of law and order, you would be able to induce a person who is liable to be convicted of burglary or murder to answer a direct question that criminates himself; and yet in this clause you provide that he may be punished for perjury if he answers falsely. The meaning of this is, that a man who is undoubtedly guilty of the first offence, having been found guilty, may possibly be hanged, and then, after being hanged, he may be prosecuted for perjury. That is one of the clear absurdities of this proposal. If a man's evidence will criminate him, he must be a criminal *ab initio*, and you may give him seven years' penal servitude, or hang him; and, having carried out that sentence, you may prosecute him for perjury. Can anything be more absurd? How can you prove that a man has committed perjury unless you show that he ought to have criminated himself? Having done that, you punish him for the original offence, and heap Pelion on Ossa. It is certainly one of the most extraordinary proposals which have been suggested, even by an Irish Attorney General.

MR. LABOUCHERE (Northampton): This proposal of the Government really goes far beyond anything that has ever been suggested in connection with the Law of Evidence in any other part of the world. Under the French Code a *Juge d'Instruction* may examine a person generally as to crime; but he has no right to compel the witness to answer. He can cross-examine him if he likes, but he must take the answer he gets, or accept the fact that the witness declines to answer. In no case can a man who has been examined be punished for perjury in consequence of any answer he may have given to the *Juge d'Instruction*. Such an inquiry is regarded as being of a strictly private nature, and it entails no penal consequences.

MR. HUNTER (Aberdeen, N.): I am surprised that the Government should persist with this section. It certainly contains the most revolutionary proposal which has ever been introduced into our jurisprudence. The other night I challenged the Government to produce from the law of any country any such power as they are asking for now—namely, to make a man criminate himself in the evidence he may be required to give before a magistrate. What was the answer given by the right hon. Gentleman the Chief Secretary for Ireland to the appeal made to him to amend this clause? The right hon. Gentleman read a portion of a sentence from the Corrupt and Illegal Practices Prevention Act, 1883, which provides that a person called as a witness respecting an election before an Election Court shall not be excused from answering any question relating to

the election on the ground that the question may tend to criminate himself. Strange to say, the right hon. Gentleman stopped there. I do not suppose the right hon. Gentleman intended to mislead the House, and I imagine that he acted from pure ignorance. He ought, however, to have continued his reading, when he would have found that the next part of the clause entirely destroyed the effect of his answer, because it is provided in that Act that a witness who answers a question properly shall be entitled to receive a certificate of indemnity, so that, in whatever respect he may have criminated himself, he is altogether relieved from any painful consequences. That is the only precedent that can be found in the English law; and, so far from supporting the view of the right hon. Gentleman, it entirely destroys his case. The effect of that provision is to make it to the interest of the witness to tell the truth; whereas, under the present Bill of the Government, it is manifestly the interest of the witness to tell a lie. It has been stated that a clause of a similar character was seriously considered in 1882, when the Crimes Act of that year was before the House. Now, I find, on looking at *Hansard*, that that clause was never considered at all. Curiously enough, there was no Amendment to that portion of the clause, and it seems to have slipped into the Bill entirely without consideration. That omission makes it even more necessary that on this occasion the Committee should direct its attention to a provision which is utterly inconsistent with every principle of our criminal jurisprudence, and calculated to destroy every principle of morality, because it is not likely that you will be able to induce a witness who is a criminal to criminate himself. Let me call the attention of the right hon. Gentleman the Chief Secretary for Ireland to the essential difference which exists between the Corrupt Practices Act and this Bill. In the case of the Corrupt Practices Act a man is asked to criminate himself only in respect of election offences, and if he tells the truth in regard to what he knows, he is entitled to receive a certificate of indemnity, and cannot be punished. Therefore, under the Corrupt Practices Act, a witness escapes the usual penalties which attach to bribery and other corrupt practices. Unfortunately, in regard to the offences dealt with by the Corrupt Practices Act, public opinion is not so stringent as the law. We all object to bribery in the abstract; but in the concrete hon. Gentlemen condemn it only when it is practised by the opposite Party. As far as corrupt practices go, that Act provides that if a person, when under examination, tells the truth he shall receive no punishment of any kind; but under this Bill, when a Resident Magistrate is making an inquiry into a serious crime, such as murder, that consideration does not apply, and the precedent afforded by the Corrupt Practices Act does not hold good in cases of this kind. If a witness, under the stress of examination, discloses to the magistrate the fact that he has committed a criminal offence, although there may be no means of proving it beyond the man's own confession, it is provided here that that confession shall not be admissible against him. But still, there is no statutory limitation in regard to criminal offences, and the witness may afterwards become liable to be prosecuted when other evidence is forthcoming. In giving evidence before this secret tribunal the witness will necessarily place himself in the hands of his enemies, and I do not think his enemies will feel themselves bound to keep his evidence secret. On the contrary, it may be a matter of common knowledge to Dublin Castle, to the parish priest, and to the magistrate, and may even become a subject of common gossip. Therefore, if the precedent of the Corrupt Practices Act were entirely satisfactory, it would afford no adequate reason for this particular piece of legislation. There is only one other point in the speech of the right hon. Gentleman to which I will refer. He stated that it was necessary to compel a witness to criminate himself, because otherwise he might falsely allege a claim of privilege, and refuse to answer on the false ground that his answer might criminate him. Did it not strike the right hon. Gentleman that that objection, if it is a good one, is clearly applicable in every case where a witness is called upon to give evidence in a Court of Justice? In a Court of Justice a witness may falsely raise the same plea; but I doubt whether he would do it successfully. I wonder what it was that put that idea into the mind of

Mr. Hunter

the right hon. Gentleman. I remember an inquiry which was held not long ago before a Coroner in Ireland into a case of stabbing by the police; and although on the first day of the inquest the police answered truthfully the questions put to them, on the second day, from some mysterious cause which was not disclosed, the police constables appeared to be animated by a desire to protect themselves, and they refused to answer the questions put to them on the ground that they might criminate themselves. The experience of the policemen who gave that answer was not very encouraging, because what happened to them was this—the Coroner made out a warrant for their committal for contempt in not answering the questions. It is perfectly easy for a Court to judge, in a large majority of cases, whether the answer to a question may or may not criminate a witness; and if a plea of privilege were falsely raised, a competent Court and a competent magistrate would disregard such false plea, and commit the witness who refused to answer it to prison. Therefore, I trust that, even at the last moment, the Government will strike this clause out of their Bill, or, at all events, accept the Amendment which I have put down on the Paper, and which will come on later.

MR. ANDERSON (Elgin and Nairn): I will ask the right hon. and learned Gentleman the Attorney General for Ireland whether he will accept an Amendment which appears in my name, and which is numbered in the Paper of Amendments as No. 124? It provides that—

"No person who is examined under this section shall be charged with the commission of the offence in respect of which he has been examined."

That would remove the necessity for arguing this sub-section further. Will the Government say whether they are prepared to accept that Amendment or not?

THE CHIEF SECRETARY FOR IRELAND (Mr. A. J. BALFOUR) (Manchester, E.): The Government will have no objection to accept, with some very slight modification, Amendment No. 83a, which stands on the Paper in the name of the hon. Member for Aberdeen (Mr. Hunter). They cannot accept the Amendment referred to by the hon. and learned Member for Elgin (Mr. Anderson). The

Amendment of the hon. Member for Aberdeen provides that—

"A witness who answers truly all questions which he is required to answer shall be entitled to a certificate of indemnity under the hand of the magistrate making such examination, stating that such witness has so answered, and such a certificate of indemnity shall be a bar to all criminal proceedings, and proceedings for the recovery of any penalty in respect of any offence as to which such person has been examined in such inquiry."

MR. ANDERSON : That is some concession which, I think, we ought to be thankful for; but I should be glad if the Government were prepared to go much further, and I hope the Attorney General for Ireland may be persuaded to do so.

THE ATTORNEY GENERAL FOR IRELAND (Mr. HOLMES) (Dublin University) : Certainly not.

MR. ANDERSON : I think it highly probable that the Government, on reconsideration, may see their way to accept my Amendment, which would get rid of all further discussion of the Amendment now before the Committee. What I wish to call the attention of the Committee to is this. In the course of these discussions we have heard a good deal about the law of Scotland. The right hon. and learned Lord Advocate (Mr. J. H. A. Macdonald), however, has not said a word on the matter; and, therefore, I ask him now to tell the Committee if the proposal here made to compel the witness to answer a question which might criminate himself is in accordance with the law of Scotland? The right hon. and learned Lord Advocate makes no sign; but I find in the right hon. and learned Gentleman's own book that it is not permitted by law to compel a witness, under any circumstances, to answer questions of this character. If that be so, and you cannot compel a witness to answer such questions either by the French law, the English law, or the Scotch law, I think there ought to be the very strongest grounds shown for the proposal to make it the law of Ireland before the Committee agree to accept this clause. I think we are entitled to ask from the right hon. and learned Lord Advocate, or from the hon. and learned Solicitor General for Scotland (Mr. J. P. B. Robertson), an explanation of what the Scotch law on the subject really is.

Question, "That the word 'not' stand part of the Clause," put, and *agreed to.*

THE CHAIRMAN : The next Amendment—81—which stands in the name of the hon. and learned Member for the Attercliffe Division of Sheffield (Mr. Coleridge), relates to a point which has already been decided.

MR. T. M. HEALY (Longford, N.) : I wish to move an Amendment which comes in after the word "any"—namely, the word "lawful," which will make the sub-section read—

" A witness examined under this section shall not be excused from answering any lawful question on the ground that the answer thereto may criminate, or tend to criminate, himself."

Surely the Government have no desire to have unlawful questions asked.

Amendment proposed, in page 1, line 25, after the word "any" to insert the word "lawful."—(*Mr. T. M. Healy.*)

Question proposed, "That the word 'lawful' be there inserted."

THE ATTORNEY GENERAL (Sir RICHARD WEBSTER) (Isle of Wight) : The hon. and learned Gentleman knows that the insertion of that word is not necessary. It adds nothing at all to the clause except another word.

MR. T. M. HEALY : Allow me to point out that I have taken the word from the Bankruptcy Act. We have it asserted by the hon. and learned Attorney General for England that the word is unnecessary; and, therefore, I inform him at once that I quote it directly from the Bankruptcy Act, which provides that a witness is not to be committed unless he has refused to answer a "lawful" question. Surely it is not proposed that unlawful questions shall be asked ? The Government either want proper questions to be asked, or they do not; and if they desire proper questions to be asked the introduction of the word "lawful" cannot possibly do any harm. I hope the Government will not put us to the trouble of a Division, because I shall certainly press the Amendment, believing it to be a matter of principle. As to the insertion of the word "lawful" in the Bankruptcy Act, I presume they will accept my statement of the fact.

MR. MAURICE HEALY (Cork) : I am afraid that the Government do not see the importance of this point. They have already laid upon the Table a Parliamentary Paper which shows the constitution and character of the gentlemen who will be entrusted with the administration of the law. It may be quite true that a Judge or a barrister with legal training would be aware that the word "question" implied "lawful question;" but we have no such guarantee in the case of the military and naval gentlemen who will have to administer this law in Ireland, and whose knowledge of the law, as we all know, is of the most superficial character. Is there any reason why this Amendment should not be adopted? It would certainly afford some guarantee that a proper check was imposed upon the gentlemen who would have to administer the Act. They would read the word and regard it to some extent as a safeguard, inasmuch as it attaches some limit to their discretion. If that word or some similar word is not contained in the provision, they will arrive at the conclusion that there is to be no limit to the questions asked, and that they may ask lawful or unlawful questions just as it suits them. The Government will also bear in mind that the word "lawful" is contained in the Irish Bankruptcy Act, and that no objection, up to the present moment, has been raised to its existence there. I trust that, as the Amendment involves very grave questions, the Government will give us some further reply than the brief rejoinder of the hon. and learned Attorney General for England.

Mr. CHANCE (Kilkenny, S.): I think it is perfectly understood that the Resident Magistrates will place their own interpretation upon the words of an Act of Parliament, and that it is, therefore, absolutely necessary to define clearly what the nature of their power is. If such clear definition is not given, I am afraid it will be necessary for the right hon. and learned Gentleman the Attorney General for Ireland to send down a code of instructions to the Resident Magistrates who will have to administer the Act. My view is that the necessary instructions with regard to an administration of an Act of Parliament, especially when it will have to be administered by such men as the Irish Resident Magistrates, had better be embodied in the Act itself rather than left to any instructions which the Attorney General for the time being may send

Mr. Maurice Healy

down. There is great reason to fear that, unless some Amendment of this kind is inserted, the Resident Magistrates will arrive at the conclusion that they may put what questions they choose, and that they will act in a grossly illegal manner.

Mr. M. J. KENNY (Tyrone, Mid): I think we are entitled to some answer from those who are responsible for the framing of the clause, and who may be presumed to intend that it shall be properly shaped. All we want to show is that the questions put to a witness examined under this section of the Bill must be lawful questions. Hon. Members will bear in mind that this is a secret and not a public examination, and that it would be most undesirable to allow the magistrate to extort answers to any questions he may choose to put. I quite admit that the word "question" in an ordinary Court of Law would be construed to mean "lawful question," and in open Court a witness is protected by an attorney or counsel, who would take care that no unlawful question was put. In most cases which now come before the Courts we see counsel constantly jumping up for the purpose of protecting a witness against an unfair question; and, therefore, I greatly regret the absence in this clause of any protection whatever against unfair questions being put. Looking at the sinister surroundings of the whole thing, and the way in which witnesses are to be dragged into a secret chamber before the presence of persons they may have never seen before, without anyone to watch over their interests, I think they ought to be afforded some real protection in the construction of the Act itself, so that they may refuse to answer questions which are totally irrelevant and illegal, and which would only be put for the purpose of entrapping them into statements which may be used against them in a criminal trial for perjury. I think we are entitled to some concession from the right hon. and learned Gentleman the Attorney General for Ireland, and it is absolutely necessary to insert some such word as this for the purpose of protecting witnesses from being entrapped or bullied, as they have been in former inquiries.

Mr. T. M. HEALY: I hope the Government will save the Committee the trouble of a Division, which will certainly waste a quarter of an hour. The words are simply "lawful question," and I will again ask the Government whether they want unlawful questions to be put? What we ask them is simply that a witness shall not be compelled to answer any but lawful questions.

MR. O'DOHERTY: I do not see that any harm can be done by the insertion of this word. The Resident Magistrate is to examine on oath concerning the offence, and he is only to examine a person who, in his opinion, can give material evidence. Therefore, it is simply implied in the section itself that the questions must be lawful questions, and I do not see what objection there can be to making use of the word "lawful."

MR. MAURICE HEALY: The hon. and learned Attorney General for England objected to the Amendment on the ground that it would mar the section by introducing a superfluous word. Now, that is a view we cannot take. Our position is this—that although the word may, as the hon. and learned Gentleman says, have no legal effect, it would have a very great moral effect upon the minds of the Resident Magistrates. If these gentlemen knew their business, no such word would be necessary; but, unfortunately, they do not know their business, and they need proper direction in order to restrain them within the strict lines of legality.

Question put.

The Committee *divided*:—Ayes 169; Noes 241: Majority 72.—(Div. List, No. 138.)

MR. ANDERSON (Elgin and Nairn): I have now to move, in line 27, after the word "himself," to insert the words—

"Every statement made under this section shall be cancelled before the person making it is called as a witness in support of any criminal charge."

THE CHAIRMAN: Order, order! I must point out to the hon. and learned Member that Amendments Nos. 82 and 83 must be taken together, and 82 can only be moved in conjunction with 83.

MR. ANDERSON: Then, in obedience to your ruling, I will move the omission of the rest of the sub-section—

"But any statement made by any person in answer to any question put to him on any examination under this section shall not, except in the case of an indictment or other criminal proceeding for perjury, be admissible in evidence against him in any proceeding, civil or criminal,"

for the purpose of inserting the words I have already read.

MR. MAURICE HEALY: Upon the point of Order, may I ask whether the adoption of this Amendment would exclude the moving of any other Amendment?

THE CHAIRMAN: I will put the Question in such a form as to safeguard everything.

MR. ANDERSON: The Amendment I propose is in page 1, line 26, after the word "himself," to leave out to the end of Sub-section 3, and to insert words to provide that every statement made by a witness shall be cancelled before the person making it is called as a witness in support of any other criminal charge. It has already been conceded, I think, that the copies of the examination of witnesses shall be at the disposal of the accused, and I shall be glad to hear from the Government any further explanation of the course which they propose to take.

Amendment proposed,

In page 1, line 26, leave out all the words after the word "himself" to end of the sub-section, in order to insert the words "every statement made under this section shall be cancelled before the person making it is called as a witness in support of any criminal charge."—(*Mr. Anderson.*)

Question proposed, "That the words proposed to be left out stand part of the Clause."

THE ATTORNEY GENERAL FOR IRELAND (Mr. HOLMES) (Dublin University): I am unable to accept the Amendment. We have already inserted a Proviso in the 1st sub-section—

"That any person accused of a crime respecting which an inquiry under this section has been held, such accused person, or his solicitor, upon being returned for trial, shall forthwith be supplied with copies of all depositions taken at any inquiry under this section of any witness to be called against him."

We have, therefore, accepted a proposition that copies of the depositions shall be supplied to an accused person. In point of fact, it has been stated again and again in the discussions which have taken place that the object of being supplied with copies of the depositions was that there should be some material for the cross-examination of a witness. The Amendment now before the Committee suggests that every statement made by the witness shall be cancelled before the person making it is called as a witness in support of any criminal charge. Speaking as a lawyer, I do not know what the word "cancelled" means. It is certainly not a term which has ever been applied to the examination of a witness. I am told that it has some signification in the Scotch law, and it is obvious that the hon. and learned Member is much better acquainted with the Scotch law than that of England. I take it that the meaning of "cancelled" is that, by some process or other, the instrument is destroyed and becomes useless for any legal purposes. It is wholly impossible that the Government can consent to a proposition of that kind, because the document may be required for use in some other way, and at any moment the original may be called for. If the original is destroyed, under such a provision as this, it would be quite impossible for a copy to be of any value. What is the object of holding this inquiry at all? It is for the purpose of getting information, and, if so, why is the information, when obtained, to be destroyed as soon as you have got it? If the information given in evidence is to be cancelled, I do not see any necessity for the trouble we propose to take. The Government certainly cannot accept the Amendment.

MR. ANDERSON: I am very sorry that the Government are indisposed to accept the Amendment. I thought the advisability of inserting it was so apparent that it was not necessary for me to take up any time in order to explain it. I thought the right hon. and learned Gentleman would feel that the words are not inconsistent with the words of the Amendment which was introduced the other day. The object of the Amendment the other day was to give the prisoner's counsel full information as to the statements made at the preliminary inquiry, by providing them with copies of the depositions containing the statements which had been made against the prisoner, thus affording the counsel for the prisoner the same information as that in the possession of the Crown. No doubt, this is directed to a totally different object. A statement cancelled cannot be used by the Crown Prosecutor against the witness, and that is the simple object of the Amendment. With regard to the term "cancelling," the right hon. and learned Gentleman says that it has no signification or meaning. If there is anything novel or peculiar in

it I hope that the right hon. and learned Lord Advocate will tell us. It is a very well understood term. The right hon. and learned Attorney General for Ireland professes not to understand the meaning of the word in connection with legal documents. What I mean by "cancelling" is that the statement of the witness cannot be used in evidence upon the trial of a criminal. That is the interpretation given to the term and printed in large letters in the book of the Lord Advocate, and perhaps the right hon. and learned Gentleman will tell us whether that is correct or not?

THE CHAIRMAN: Order, order! I think it is as well to point out that the Amendment of the hon. Member for Aberdeen (Mr. Hunter) relates to the same subject, and that the Government have intimated their intention of accepting it, with a slight modification. The hon. Member for Aberdeen proposes to omit the same words, and if the Government accept the words the hon. Member proposes to substitute, subsequent Amendments will become Amendments to those words. Probably the best course would be to put the Question at once, so far as it relates to the omission of the last part of the sub-section. The only question which can then arise is what words shall be substituted. Therefore, I will at once put the Question that the words proposed to be left out stand part of the clause, and the Committee will then come to the question of the words to be substituted.

Amendment proposed,

In page 1, line 26, leave out the words " but any statement made by any person in answer to any question put to him on any examination under this section shall not, except in the case of an indictment or other criminal proceeding for perjury, be admissible in evidence against him in any proceeding, civil or criminal."—(*Mr. Anderson.*)

Question, " That those words stand part of the Clause," put, and *negatived.*

Question proposed,

" That the words ' every statement made under this section shall be cancelled before the person making it is called as a witness in support of any criminal charge,' be there inserted."

MR. MAURICE HEALY: It has already been decided that any person who may be subsequently charged with any offence shall get copies of the information and of the depositions, but it has not yet been decided to what extent the Crown or the prisoner shall have the right of using the statements which may have been made. The Attorney General puts a dilemma in this form. He says that the depositions taken at this secret inquiry are to be used for some purpose, or they are not to be used; if they are not to be used, why should the Government object to cancel them? There can be no doubt that the Government, by holding on to these secret inquiries, hope to obtain certain information in reference to the commission of crime, which they hope will ultimately put them on the track of the perpetrators of such crime and enable them to bring the criminals to justice. All that we ask is that the prisoner and his counsel shall be put upon a footing of perfect equality with the Crown counsel at any trial which may take place, and that if the Government have any special knowledge gained in these secret inquiries the prisoner's counsel shall be placed in possession of that knowledge. That is a very different thing from saying that either party shall have the right to use the knowledge so obtained. The Amendment before the Committee appears to me to raise two different issues. In the first place, it apparently raises this issue, whether or not the person examined in one of these secret inquiries is to be liable afterwards to a prosecution for perjury for any statement he may have made. That is the first question raised. I apprehend that if the statement made by the witness is cancelled it should not be used for any purpose whatever. That is a very important issue. The second is, to what extent the depositions taken at these secret inquiries may be used against the person being tried. That being so, may I be permitted to point out that in moving this Amendment the hon. and learned Gentleman is simply moving words to give expression to the conclusion to which the Government originally came? In a previous part of this stage of the Bill, in connection with an Amendment proposed by my hon. Friend the Member for South Kilkenny (Mr. Chance), the Government were understood to pledge themselves that the depositions taken in these secret inquiries should not be used for any purpose whatever. There can be no doubt that the Government originally came to that conclusion. They state now that they have modified that conclusion in consequence of an Amendment which they were subsequently in-

duced to accept, compelling the Crown to hand over copies of the depositions of the examinations at these secret inquiries to the prisoner's counsel in the event of a trial. What I would press upon the Government is that there is really no inconsistency whatever in the two things. It is perfectly consistent to compel an inquiry and, at the same time, to cancel all the information given at it. The information may have been exceedingly useful to the Government in enabling them to get upon the track of the offender, and in bringing them to justice, although it may not be available in prosecuting the offender. But if the information can be made available to the Government in that way in the prosecution of the offenders, and in enabling them to get at the facts, is it to be pretended that it may not be equally useful to the prisoner's counsel? If a witness, who happens to be under examination in a criminal case, has knowledge of the fact that the counsel examining him has in his hand an attested copy of the depositions previously made by him, that fact would, no doubt, afford a powerful check in securing that the witness told the truth. It may be that the prisoner's counsel would not be in a position to use the original statement even should the witness perjure himself, but the mere knowledge that the statement is in the hands of the prisoner's counsel showing that on a previous occasion the witness had testified to a different state of facts would be, of itself, sufficient to induce the witness to consider carefully what he was saying, and to take care that in what he said he did not contradict himself. For my own part, if I had to choose between the cancellation of the depositions and the decision the Government have come to that copies of the depositions should be supplied, I would certainly vote for the Amendment of my hon. and learned Friend to provide that the statements contained in the depositions should be absolutely cancelled, and that they should not be able to be referred to by anyone.

Mr. M. J. KENNY (Tyrone, Mid): There has been an absolute change of front on the part of the Government in reference to this Amendment. We had an expression of opinion from the Government a short time ago, that the evidence taken at the secret inquiry should not be used subsequently against the prisoners. But now what they say is that the acceptance of the Amendment adopted at an earlier period has altogether changed the character of the clause. I am at a loss to see that there is any value whatever in the contention of the right hon. and learned Gentleman the Attorney General for Ireland as to the legal meaning of the word "cancellation." It is a mere evasion of the importance of the Amendment, and the right hon. and learned Gentleman did not seriously address himself to the question before the Committee. If the original document cannot be used, how can any copy be used? What we want is that neither the original deposition nor any copy shall be used, but that all shall be cancelled. The real object of the Amendment, in fact, is to prevent any statement which a witness may be compelled to make in the secret inquiry from being used afterwards in evidence. Now, I contend that the evidence which will be taken before this secret inquiry will be illegal evidence—generally hearsay evidence—but it will be beyond the ordinary discipline of the the Courts of Law, and will not be evidence that would be admitted in an open Court. We should, therefore, I think, be careful to exclude in open Court evidence which has been taken in a secret inquiry. The evidence which will be taken in these secret tribunals is evidence which will not be in accordance with the law, but which is altogether illegal. We are now asked to make such illegal evidence legal by Act of Parliament. The Government, in beginning the discussion of this clause, had the firmness to admit that it would be improper to receive any such evidence; but now, in consequence of the acceptance of an Amendment, they maintain that they have a right to make a change of front on this question. I would seriously ask them if they are of opinion that illegal evidence taken before a secret tribunal should be subsequently used in open Court to the prejudice of a prisoner? I maintain that that would be altogether improper, and that the Amendment of the hon. and learned Member ought to be accepted.

MR. T. P. O'CONNOR (Liverpool, Scotland): I would suggest to the Attorney General for Ireland that my hon. and learned Friend might be induced to withdraw his Amendment if the Government would make a concession which, I think, would make both sides agree. I concur with the right hon. and learned Gentleman that it is a somewhat strong proposal that the original deposition should be destroyed, and copies of it preserved. There is a certain amount of logical contradiction in that proposal; and I think the Attorney General for Ireland is right in saying that there is a certain amount of inconsistency in the proposal. An Amendment has been accepted by the Government which provides that copies of the depositions shall be given to the prisoner and his counsel. I listened carefully to the speech of my hon. Friend below me; and I think he pointed out the distinction on which the right hon. and learned Gentleman seems to proceed—namely, that, although we have decided that the prisoner's counsel shall get a copy of the depositions, the question is still open whether he or anybody else is to have the right to make use of them. The depositions given to a prisoner's counsel may serve either of two purposes—they may put the prisoner's counsel on an equality with regard to information with the prosecuting counsel, or they may serve another purpose in being used at the trial to test, on cross-examination, the credibility of a witness. Now, I am strongly prejudiced against the use of depositions obtained in this way for the latter of those two purposes. I think the Government would be well advised if they would follow the precedent of the Scotch law, and not use anything that takes place at a secret inquiry except for the purpose of obtaining information. I would suggest to the right hon. and learned Gentleman the Attorney General for Ireland that he should undertake to introduce words that will limit the use of the depositions to purposes of information, and preclude their use for any other purpose. If he will do that, I shall be strongly inclined to urge my hon. and learned Friend to withdraw his Amendment.

THE ATTORNEY GENERAL FOR IRELAND (Mr. HOLMES) (Dublin University): The demand made to the Government was that the prisoner should have the opportunity of getting the benefit of the evidence received at the preliminary inquiry, and there appeared to me to be a strong and powerful argument in favour of it. It was not merely suggested by hon. Members below the Gangway, but by hon. Members above the Gangway; and it certainly appeared to me to be a strong argument. It is said that if the depositions remain in possession of the Crown they may be used for some improper purpose; but we do not propose that they shall be used as evidence. They are to be used for the purpose of examination and cross-examination alone, and not as evidence.

MR. T. M. HEALY: They have been used as evidence, and you know it very well.

MR. HOLMES: I know nothing of the kind. The hon. and learned Member repeatedly makes use of observations of that character—observations which are not couched in the most courteous form. I know nothing of the kind.

MR. T. M. HEALY: Was it not so in the Kerry case?

MR. HOLMES: Not to my knowledge. And all I say now in regard to the Amendment is that, having accepted an Amendment on Tuesday, after full discussion, and in the belief that strong arguments had been employed in favour of the Amendment, it would be most unwise to alter on Friday what was done on Tuesday. If we were to do so, it is manifest that it will be impossible ever to come to the end of the Bill. So far as the observations of the hon. Member for the Scotland Division of Liverpool (Mr. T. P. O'Connor) are concerned, we must use these statements for one purpose, at all events, and that is for a prosecution for perjury. I can be no party to the insertion in this Bill of a provision that the penalties for perjury committed by a witness on oath shall not be put in force.

MR. T. M. HEALY: If the right hon. and learned Gentleman will put into the Bill that these depositions shall not be made the subject of evidence, but only be used for the purpose of crediting or discrediting evidence, and for protecting a prisoner, I shall be very glad. But what happened at the Cork Assizes? A Kerry prisoner named Welsh was tried at the Winter Assizes. A witness swore to particular facts, and Judge O'Brien called for the depositions of the witness, after having taken a night to consider the point. The present Lord Chancellor of Ireland—Lord Ashbourne

—has maintained that the Judge had a perfect right to do what he did. In that case it was a civil action, in which the Attorney General for Ireland represented *United Ireland*, although we now hear a great deal about the iniquitous character of *United Ireland*. A deposition having been made in London as to something done there, it was held that the witness might be cross-examined upon it. What I fear is that the memory of a witness may be jogged by a reference to the depositions, and that the matter may never find its way to a Court of Appeal, so that, practically, any Judge will have the decision of the matter in his own hands, and in the case of a subservient Judge, as most of the Judges are who are sent down to try these cases, he would refuse to grant a case for the Court of Crown Cases Reserved. Therefore, I maintain that it would be unfair to give the Crown the right to use these depositions, unless for the purpose of discrediting a witness. To put them in, with liberty to make them substantial evidence, is a thing we can never consent to. Will the Government consent to the insertion of a Proviso that the depositions are to be used only for the purpose of contradicting a witness?

MR. HOLMES: I have never suggested that the depositions can be used except for the purpose of testing the credibility of a witness.

MR. ANDERSON: I will give way to the Attorney General for Ireland on this point, in the hope that I may obtain some further concession on the point hereafter.

Amendment, by leave, *withdrawn.*

Amendment proposed,

In page 1, line 26, after "himself" leave out to end of sub-section, and insert—"Provided that—(a) A witness who answers truly all questions which he is required to answer shall be entitled to a certificate of indemnity under the hand of the magistrate making such examination, stating that such witness has so answered, and such a certificate of indemnity shall be a bar to all criminal proceedings, and proceedings for the recovery of any penalty in respect of any offence as to which such person has been examined in such inquiry; and (b) An answer by a person to a question put at such examination shall not, except in the case of any criminal proceeding for perjury in respect of any statements made by him on such examination, be, in any proceeding civil or criminal, admissible in evidence against him."—(*Mr. Hunter.*)

[*Seventh Night.*]

Question proposed, "That the words proposed to be left out stand part of the Clause."

THE ATTORNEY GENERAL (Sir RICHARD WEBSTER) (Isle of Wight): The Government have considered this matter most carefully after the long debate which took place upon it on Wednesday, and we are willing to insert this Proviso in order that it may be made clear on the face of the Bill. We propose, however, to omit the words "in respect of any statements made by him on such examination," in order to insert the words "committed at or after the holding of such inquiry." That would, we think, amply protect the witness in regard to statements which have no relevance to the inquiry. The proceedings must, of course, be limited to perjury committed at or after the inquiry. With this modification, we are prepared to accept the Amendment.

MR. T. M. HEALY: May I suggest an Amendment after the word "answer," so as to make the Proviso read—

"Any witness required to answer in respect to any offence as to which such person has been examined in such inquiry?"

SIR RICHARD WEBSTER: That is the same question the hon. and learned Member has already raised. The magistrate must inquire concerning the offence, and to insert other words might give rise to difficulty.

SIR GEORGE CAMPBELL (Kirkcaldy, &c.): If a witness, when under examination, says — "I committed a certain murder," is he to go scot free? There may be cases where a man is an approver, and has been granted a free pardon; but are you entitled to have sprung upon you, at any time, a declaration that the witness has committed a murder, and that he is to be freed from all the consequences of the crime?

MR. T. M. HEALY: In a previous part of the clause we have the words, "other than any person confessing himself or herself to be the offender."

SIR RICHARD WEBSTER: The hon. Member for Kirkcaldy (Sir George Campbell) seems to forget that we discussed the question a few nights ago, as to a confession being used against a witness.

MR. MAURICE HEALY: I wish to understand exactly what the position is. Does the hon. and learned Gentleman say that if a magistrate holds an inquiry he is to examine a witness with regard to some offence other than the offence which is the subject-matter of the inquiry, and that if the witness does not answer truly in regard to such offence this clause is to come into operation? Is that the position which the hon. and learned Gentleman takes up?

SIR RICHARD WEBSTER: I have already answered that question. I presume that the magistrate would do his duty and confine the questions to matters relative to the inquiry. Our Bill must be passed on the assumption that the magistrate does his duty.

MR. O'DOHERTY: I think the words ought to be so framed as to cover the case of a confession, and I would propose to insert words in the clause to that effect. I will move the insertion of the words "confession or," before the words "an answer by." The effect of the insertion of these words will be to provide that a person who has confessed to the commission of any offence will be entitled to an indemnity.

Amendment proposed to the said proposed Amendment, after the word "and," insert "confession or."—(*Mr. O'Doherty.*)

Question proposed, "That those words be there inserted."

MR. T. M. HEALY: This Amendment relates to section (b) of the Amendment. Will it not be better to put the whole of (a) first, and allow (b) to remain separate?

THE CHAIRMAN: Unless the two are put together it will be impossible for the hon. Member for Cork (Mr. Maurice Healy) to move his Amendment.

Question put, and *negatived.*

Original Question again proposed.

MR. T. M. HEALY: I would propose to omit the words, "except in the case of any criminal proceeding for perjury."

THE CHAIRMAN: Order, order! Do I understand that the hon. Member for Cork does not propose to move his Amendment?

MR. MAURICE HEALY: I intend to move the insertion of the words "to a question put," on the ground that if they are allowed to stand a witness would not be protected who volunteers a statement, because that would not be in answer to a question put. The words in the Amendment are, "an answer by a person to a question put at such examination." I understand that you have already put a Question to insert the words, "confession or in answer to," and that we have not got further yet than section (a). When section (a) has been adopted, I intend to move, instead of the words "a question put," to substitute the words "a statement made."

Amendment proposed to the said proposed Amendment, to leave out the words "a question put," in order to insert "a statement made."—(*Mr. Maurice Healy.*)

Question proposed, "That the words proposed to be left out stand part of the said proposed Amendment."

SIR RICHARD WEBSTER: The Government are able to accept that Amendment.

MR. MAURICE HEALY: We have already disposed of the point which relates to the putting of a question by the Resident Magistrate. My Amendment is directed to the fact that a witness may volunteer statements which are not directly made in answer to any questions put to him. The Committee have not yet decided that point. There is nothing to prevent a magistrate from putting questions at the beginning of an inquiry which may draw from the witness, in the form of a narrative, all he knows of a particular offence. Surely the hon. and learned Gentleman does not mean to say that a witness who, in answer to one question, gives the whole narrative, is to be liable for anything that may be extorted from him in that way, in regard to which, if it had been put as a question, he would have been protected?

MR. M. J. KENNY: I think it is only right to substitute the words, "a statement made by him on examination," instead of "in answer to a question put." That would cover both answers to questions put and statements made by any person in the course of an examination.

Question put, and *agreed to.*

Original Question again proposed.

MR. T. M. HEALY: I propose to move in sub-section (b) to omit the words which provide that the deposition of any witness may be used in a prosecution for perjury against him. You cannot prove perjury against a man unless you convict him of an offence, and it is repugnant to British ideas of justice to punish a man more than once for the same offence. Having punished him once, are you to proceed against him for perjury? You cannot convict him of perjury unless you prove the first offence, because the offence which entitles you to proceed against him for perjury must be the offence for which he has been convicted in the first instance. You cannot prove perjury against a witness unless you put in a record of his conviction, and I do not see how you are to do that.

Amendment proposed to the said proposed Amendment to omit the words, "except in the case of any criminal proceeding for perjury."—(*Mr. T. M. Healy.*)

Question proposed, "That the words proposed to left out stand part of the said proposed Amendment."

MR. HOLMES: The Government cannot accept the Amendment proposed by the hon. and learned Gentleman. The words are inserted for a very obvious reason—namely, that a witness who gives false testimony in these inquiries shall be treated in all respects like any other person who is guilty of perjury. The hon. and learned Member says that we render the witness liable for two offences; but what is said here is that a man who gives truthful evidence is entitled to an indemnity, but that, if he commits perjury, he shall be prosecuted as any other witness would be. If it can be proved that a witness swears he was not present on a particular occasion, and it can be proved that he was there, why should he not be prosecuted for perjury? I certainly do not understand the force of the argument of the hon. and learned Gentleman.

MR. CHANCE (Kilkenny, S.): I certainly object to the retention of the words "except in the case of any criminal proceeding for perjury." In an ordinary prosecution for perjury, it would be necessary to prove that the answers given by the witness were relevant to a particular offence. But in such a case you have a prisoner in custody charged with the commission of a crime, and it is in reference to that crime that you test the falsehood of the statement. But in this inquiry there may be no prisoner and no specific crime alleged; and, to my mind, there will be no standard by which you can test the relevancy of the answer. How can you possibly draw up an indictment for perjury committed in the course of such an inquiry? Therefore, to my mind, these words are altogether unnecessary and unreasonable.

MR. T. M. HEALY: To impute perjury where there is no issue before anybody is simply absurd, and nobody knows that better than the right hon. and learned Gentleman. In fact, a man might commit perjury from start to finish, and yet it would be impossible to prove perjury, because there must be a distinct issue in order to justify a charge of perjury. Here there is no issue at all. I maintain that such a provision would be a paralyzing provision, because it might render any witness who answered a simple question liable to two years' imprisonment for perjury.

Question put, and *agreed to.*

Original Question again proposed.

MR. T. M. HEALY: The whole point we have been fighting for from the beginning is the fear that the statements made before these secret tribunals may be used for some other purpose. The Government say they do not propose to use the depositions in a Court of Law. Then why not accept an Amendment to that effect? Here, however, they provide that the depositions of a witness may be used on all other occasions; and yet this is the very thing the Attorney General says he does not desire to do. In this Proviso he sets up these very depositions as substantive evidence.

MR. MAURICE HEALY: As a point of Order, I wish to know if the Attorney General for Ireland proposes to move the Amendment 88a after "perjury" insert "committed at or after the holding of such inquiry?"

THE CHAIRMAN: Those words have already been incorporated.

MR. T. M. HEALY: The Government have stated that in no case are the depositions to be used as substantive evidence; but, by putting in these words "against him," the depositions are set up, and may be used in a Court of Law. If the words "against him" are taken out, the depositions could only be used for the purpose of examination and cross-examination. Is it intended, as was done by Justice O'Brien in the case of the man Welsh, to put them in as substantive evidence?

Amendment proposed to the said proposed Amendment, to leave out the words "against him."—(*Mr. T. M. Healy.*)

Question proposed, "That the words proposed to be left out stand part of the said proposed Amendment."

MR. HOLMES: I take it that it has been clearly decided that the statements made by a witness are only to be used for the purpose of testing his credibility. What we say is that these depositions may be used for the purpose of cross-examining a witness. Possibly they might be used in an action against a magistrate for outstepping his jurisdiction, but they cannot be given in evidence at all in any proceeding under the Habeas Corpus Act. The hon. and learned Gentleman (Mr. T. M. Healy) does not seem to consider the fact that the depositions cannot be used against the man who makes the statements, except in a perfectly legitimate way. There is nothing that can make them substantive evidence, except in a trial to test the credibility of the witness.

MR. T. M. HEALY: I gathered from the remarks of the right hon. and learned Gentleman 10 minutes ago that the Government pledged themselves not to use the depositions as substantive evidence in a Court of Law. The statement he has just made is directly contrary to that undertaking, because he tells us that it may be necessary to use them in a criminal inquiry, altogether independent of the private inquiry in which the statements were made. If a prisoner is charged with perjury the Court will be told by counsel that under this section the depositions may be used as substantive evidence. The whole of the depositions from first to last may be used, and there will be no end to the irregularities which may be committed. The Government are now turning the whole practice of the Law Courts topsy-turvy.

MR. CHANCE: I am sorry that some of the English lawyers are not in their places, because I believe that the law of England is that the depositions of a

Mr. Chance

witness cannot be used subsequently as substantive evidence. They can only be used when a witness is in the witness-box for the purpose of cross-examination in order to bring him to his bearings. They may, also, be used for the purpose of cross-examination by the prisoner's counsel. In Ireland, however, doubt has been thrown upon this rule of law by the extraordinary decision of Judge O'Brien in violation of that principle at the Cork Assizes. Judge O'Brien held, in that case, that depositions taken in a preliminary inquiry were admissible in evidence if the witness prevaricated, and went back on his original statement. In that particular case, I believe, the witness was a woman who said she could not identify the prisoner, and this extraordinary thing happened—Judge O'Brien turned round upon her in a very unusual fashion and charged her with perjury. He then called for the depositions which were read in Court, and he committed the witness for perjury. We know that in England that could not have been done, and what we desire by this Amendment is to make the law of Ireland the same upon this point as the law of England. In the case of this clause as it stands, the depositions could be used as substantive evidence in prosecuting a witness for perjury, notwithstanding that the Attorney General for Ireland has said that it is not so, and that it has never been so intended. Having now reached the part of the clause which relates to that matter, the Attorney General for Ireland says we must retain these words, in order to give a power which he told us before was never intended to be exercised. I hope that the right hon. and learned Gentleman will not insist on retaining in this clause what amounts to a direct violation of the statement he made in this House, and which is reported in *Hansard*.

MR. R. T. REID (Dumfries, &c.): The case which has been referred to, in which use was made by a Judge of depositions taken in a private inquiry, was undoubtedly a gross violation of the law. I can hardly conceive anything more absurd. I should like to know if it is really the case that this circumstance occurred, and I will ask the Attorney General for Ireland to be good enough to say whether it is the case or not that depositions obtained in this way were

made use of before a jury? The second question I should like to put is this—assuming that that did occur, has there been any decision of the Superior Court declaring that what Judge O'Brien did was a violation of the law? because I understand that the Court of Appeal in Ireland has no criminal jurisdiction. It would be a most dangerous thing to leave a precedent of this kind unreserved, although it is only a precedent set by one Judge. There may be a danger of other Judges following the precedent in the future. I am satisfied that the Attorney General for Ireland cannot desire that such a precedent shall be followed; and, therefore, I hope he will take some effective steps to procure its reversal.

MR. HOLMES: There has been no report of the case as far as I know. I have no knowledge of the matter, except such as I have derived from the statements of hon. Members opposite. I believe there was a case which came before the same learned Judge, Mr. Justice O'Brien, in which the depositions were produced for the purpose of cross-examination. In the course of the examination a certain statement was made by the witness which directly contradicted a previous statement he had made. Mr. Justice O'Brien ruled that that was evidence which should go to the jury of the fact therein stated; but when the case was brought before the Court of Appeal the Court had no hesitation in declaring that the evidence had been improperly received for this purpose. That was a civil action, I believe; and although the hon. and learned Gentleman has told us that a Court of Appeal would not deal with criminal cases, I think it is well understood that the rules of evidence in both cases are the same. There is only this difference—that these rules are much more stringently enforced against the Crown than against the prisoner.

MR. CHANCE: The hon. and learned Gentleman the Solicitor General for Ireland (Mr. Gibson) was concerned in Cornwall's case. He acted as counsel for me, and I acted as solicitor. However illegally the Judge may have acted, the result, so far as the prisoner Welsh was concerned, was that he was detained in prison for a considerable period. When, however, the Crown official was concerned the decision was appealed against, and was reversed. In the other case, the man was kept in prison for two years, and no point was reserved.

MR. MAURICE HEALY: The Attorney General for Ireland seems to be ignorant of the fact that it was Judge O'Brien who tried both cases, and in trying the case of Cornwall I believe the learned Judge gave a certificate that he had given a previous decision to the same effect. Will the right hon. and learned Gentleman permit me to point out another fact? We have it now declared pretty plainly that in these secret inquiries the Resident Magistrates will be bound by no rules of evidence. We have this further declaration from the right hon. and learned Gentleman—that not only will it be legal, but proper for a Resident Magistrate to examine and cross-examine persons giving evidence before him as to matters of hearsay. What will be the effect of that? A witness will be examined on all sorts of matters, not only within his own knowledge, but things he may have heard. Is it the duty of the magistrate, in taking the deposition of a witness, to put down all the statements made, whether the statements themselves relate to matters of fact within the witness's own knowledge or to mere hearsay? What is to happen afterwards if statements on matters of hearsay are to be made substantive evidence? Are the Government to be entitled subsequently to use such depositions in a criminal trial, and to put another person on trial upon such evidence? When once the depositions are put in every word of them, from the first to the last, will be evidence, no matter how illegal the statements may be. The effect of what the Government are now doing may be that, in certain cases, a jury trying a prisoner may be influenced in a most serious manner by statements made on hearsay which are contained in the depositions. In that respect it appears to me that the most important and lamentable results may follow from the position the Government propose to take in this matter. In the jurisprudence of all other countries hearsay evidence has always been excluded from the consideration of juries, not only in criminal but in civil cases. The evidence is always confined to what the witness knows, and not to what he has heard. Among the many innovations which this Bill makes, we are to have this—that we are to introduce into the

Mr. Chance

jurisprudence of Ireland statements made by a witness, not upon his own personal knowledge, but what he may have heard at tenth-hand, which may seriously prejudice a prisoner.

MR. HENRY H. FOWLER (Wolverhampton, E.): We are agreed as to what the law in England is, and we are also agreed as to what the law in Ireland ought to be; but we are confronted with this difficulty—that it is alleged that there has been a decision which the right hon. and learned Gentleman the Attorney General for Ireland admits is in practical contradiction both to English and Irish law. It ought to be made perfectly clear that the statements made by a witness at the preliminary inquiry are not to be used again in any trial, civil or criminal, except, first, in case of indictment against him for perjury; and, secondly, in case the man who has been examined should bring an action against the magistrate. We are all agreed upon that. What is asked to be guarded against is the possibility of the witness's statement being used against anybody else in an indictment under Clause 2. I would ask the Attorney General for Ireland for an assurance that he will, before the Report, see if he cannot introduce some words which, without infringing on the two points I have referred to, would place it beyond doubt that this mischief cannot take place.

MR. HOLMES: I would certainly not have the smallest objection to consider the matter. I certainly have some personal doubts on the matter as to whether it is possible; but if the right hon. Gentleman would put upon Paper the form of words which he thinks would meet this point we will consider them.

Amendment, by leave, *withdrawn.*

Amendment (*Mr. Hunter*) amended, and *agreed to.*

MR. T. M. HEALY (Longford, N.): I trust the Government will agree to the Amendment I am about to move. We know very well that in these cases the witnesses for the defence have been examined, and it is to prevent that in future that my Amendment is proposed. I must say that it is a most reprehensible thing that the names of the witnesses for the defence should be got for the purpose of giving them their expenses, and that, having got them, counsel for the Crown should go to the magistrate and get the statement taken of every witness within the precincts of the Court. This has been done, and the Crown Counsel have had as part of their brief the brief of the counsel for the defence. I do not think that any such thing would be tolerated in any other country, certainly not in France. If the Government do not intend that the infamous practice of taking the case of the prisoner and putting it in the Crown brief shall continue, let them give the guarantee asked for in this Amendment.

Amendment proposed,

In page 2, line 4, after "criminal" insert— " Provided that if any person has been charged with the commission of the crime which is the subject of the inquiry, no witness shall be compelled to answer who shall state that he believes he is to be called to give evidence for the defence of such accused person."—(*Mr. T. M. Healy*.)

Question proposed, "That those words be there inserted."

Mr. HOLMES: The Government cannot accept this Amendment, inasmuch as it would defeat the object of the inquiry which is to take place, because there is no person accused of the crime. Without a person is accused, it is wholly impossible to know the witnesses for the defence. Our object in introducing this clause and asking for this power is to obtain the evidence of men who are unwilling to come forward. If the only thing a man had to do to avoid examination were to state that he believed he would be called as a witness for the defence when a person is charged, he might leave the Court without being asked a single question. It is clear, then, that the effect of this Amendment would be to make the whole section nugatory, and for that reason the Government cannot agree to the insertion of the words.

Mr. T. M. HEALY: I ask the hon. and learned Solicitor General (Sir Edward Clarke) if he will defend the practice of calling the witnesses for the defence, and examining them when a person is in custody, and is returned for trial? Will that practice be defended by any honest man in this House? Would the Attorney General for England (Sir Richard Webster), in a recent case, have liked his witnesses to be taken in hand by Mr. Poland and plied with leading questions, and is he sure that if that had been done Mrs. Bartlett would have got off? I ask if any lawyer would consent

to his witnesses for the defence being examined and their statement put into the Crown brief? The system is a loathsome one, and I say that it is one of those things which make the Government who proposes it hated by the people of Ireland. We are told that they want the laws of the three countries to be the same. Will anyone tell me that this is the law of any place in the world besides Ireland? Why, a Choctaw Indian, who burns his victim at the stake, would not entertain the idea. This plan was the invention of George Bolton. Will the hon. and learned Solicitor General get up and defend this practice, and will he, with his intellect and on his conscience, support the Government in their refusal to accept this Amendment? My Amendment may not be drafted with the skill of the famous draftsman in the Irish Office—I will not say of the draftsman of this Bill, for whoever drafted that is sufficiently discredited already—but, if you find fault with the words, bring in words of your own to insure that a witness for the defence shall not be examined at this inquiry when the prisoner is in the dock.

Mr. CHANCE (Kilkenny, S.): It is natural that the Solicitor General, who has gained his name and position by the defence of prisoners, should be silent on this point, and I can understand that the hon. and learned Gentleman has not the hardihood to stand up and defend the system in this House which my hon. and learned Friend has described. I wish to point out that this Amendment is altogether restricted to cases in which the perpetrator of the crime is supposed to have been caught. Do the Government intend to say that they propose to treat prisoners as persons on their trial before they are committed? Let me point out what will be the effect of this. Some person is brought up and charged with a crime; it very often happens that a person who is entirely innocent will be inclined, when before the magistrate, to enter on his defence; but he cannot do that now because, by entering on his defence and calling witnesses, he will supply the Crown with the names of his witnesses, and those witnesses will be called up under this clause and compelled by threats or bribes to criminate the prisoner, or else be sent to gaol. Now, the result will be, first, that the prisoner will be compelled by this, however innocent he may be, to reserve his defence; and, secondly, that he will be put in gaol as an untried prisoner for six, eight, or ten months, as the case may be, whereas in England the man would not be imprisoned for six minutes after his case had been heard by the magistrates. I say it is an abominable thing thus to compel a man to reserve his defence, and go to gaol as an untried prisoner, where he will get only two hours' exercise out of the 24, and be allowed to see only a limited number of visitors. The refusal of the Government to accept this Amendment will compel persons to do this rather than in a straightforward and manly way to come forward and meet the charge.

MR. R. T. REID (Dumfries, &c.): I have not much to say on this point, although I have a strong opinion on the subject. I do not think the Government, or any humane person experienced in the law, will say that when a person has been committed for the crime, the witnesses for the defence should be sent for and examined with reference to the subject-matter of the case. The spirit of this Amendment is to prevent any person being taken and treated in the manner I have described. I hope the Government will be able now, or at some future time, to prevent that which I think is a scandal, and which would be a gross thing if it were allowed to occur again in Ireland.

THE SOLICITOR GENERAL (Sir EDWARD CLARKE) (Plymouth): I do not think there is any difference of opinion with regard to this matter of the examination of witnesses for the defence, as stated by the hon. and learned Gentleman who has just sat down. Although, of course, I do not want to prolong the debate by always answering personal appeals made from the other side of the House. I have no hesitation whatever in saying, with regard to the allegation made as to the examination under this clause of witnesses who had been called for the defence in Ireland, that it would be most unjustifiable if such a thing were to occur under a process of this kind. I do not know anything of what is alleged to have taken place; but, with regard to this Amendment, I point out that the words are too large, because they would be in conflict with the decision already arrived at by the Committee. As to the witnesses who

have been called for the defence, there would be, as I have said, no justification for afterwards holding an inquiry beyond that at which they may have been examined; but, of course, it would be impossible to exempt from the operation of this section anybody who said he was going to be called for the defence, because to include these words would be to exclude from the section what it has already been decided to include. The effect would be that a guilty man might at once shut out from examination persons who might be very important witnesses indeed. Although there is practically an agreement on the principle of the Amendment, it will, for these reasons, be necessary to suggest more limited words to give effect to it.

MR. HUNTER (Aberdeen, N.): I think the Amendment might be made to run thus—

"No witness shall be compelled to answer who has given evidence or has received a *subpœna* to give evidence for the defence of such accused person."

I should like to point out to the Government that there would be no harm in taking the wider words "subpœnaed to give evidence." Although the person may be debarred from examination on oath, there would be nothing to hinder his being examined privately by the Crown officials. In Scotland it is not usual to employ the oath in inquiries at all; it is usual to ask the witness what he has to say on the subject of inquiry; the Procurator Fiscal can go to any person whether subpœnaed or not, and ask him what he knows about the case. I suggest as an Amendment to the Amendment the words I have indicated.

An hon. MEMBER: I think it would be wise to consider whether the first line of the Amendment might not run thus— "Provided that if any person has been returned for trial," and that then the words of the hon. and learned Member for Aberdeen should follow.

SIR EDWARD CLARKE: I think, perhaps, it would be better to substitute for the words "who shall state that he believes he is to be called," the words "who has been called to give evidence."

MR. CHANCE (Kilkenny, S.): If the witness is subpœnaed it would be perfectly competent for the prosecuting counsel to insist on the man being produced and put in the witness-box. When once a witness is subpœnaed he is in the hands of the Crown to cross-examine. What we want to prevent is the getting of a deposition from a witness under threats or bribes, as I have explained.

THE ATTORNEY GENERAL FOR IRELAND : It has been ruled according to Irish Law that the prisoner is allowed to call any witness. It would follow from the Amendment that the witnesses for the prosecution might be called and exempted from the operation of the section.

MR. MAURICE HEALY (Cork) : I do not know whether the right hon. and learned Attorney General for Ireland is aware that the Resident Magistrates refuse to hear any witnesses for the defence on these inquiries. Captain Plunket did that over and over again. He said that all a magistrate had to do at a police court was to satisfy himself that a *primâ facie* case had been made out. I do not agree that that is the law, but there can be no doubt that it will be done frequently. But will the right hon. and learned Gentleman allow me to say that it would be departing from the practice to compel the witnesses for the defence to be examined on this inquiry. I think no lawyer of experience in criminal cases would approve that. The concluding passage in the report of almost every examination of prisoners is that the prisoner "reserves his defence," and of course that is done for good reasons. I do not see why there should be any departure from what has always been the practice in Ireland—namely, when anything like a case is made out to allow the prisoner to reserve his defence. Allow me to point out what will probably happen if the clause is passed in its present form. I would not suggest that there is anything improper in the Crown having before a magistrate and examining any witness who can give evidence about the offence ; but it may be in many cases that the evidence of the witness is given in relation to the prisoner only, and not in relation to the commission of the offence, and in that case, I think, both sides of the House will agree that the examination of those witnesses under the circumstances would be eminently unfair. It very often happens that the only defence a prisoner has is an *alibi ;* and would it not be a monstrous thing, if the prisoner alleged that he was at another place when the offence was committed, that the Crown

should summon all the witnesses who could prove that ? For instance, a man may be charged with Moonlighting ; his defence is that he was in bed at the time. Would it not be a monstrous thing that the Crown should examine his father and mother, or the other members of the family, to get evidence so as to be in a position to confront him with any small discrepancy which might be found out in their evidence ?

MR. T. M. HEALY : I think the offer of the hon. and learned Solicitor General is a most reasonable one, and I am willing that the Amendment should be amended in accordance with his suggestion.

Amendment proposed, to leave out from the proposed Amendment, the words "he believes he is to be," in order to insert "he has been."

Question proposed, "That the words proposed to be left out stand part of the proposed Amendment," put, and *negatived.*

Question, "That the words 'he has been' be there inserted," put, and *agreed to.*

MR. T. M. HEALY (Longford, N.) : It has always been held that solicitors and barristers are privileged in respect of not being compelled to answer on matters within their knowledge professionally, and I presume the Government do not want to depart from that principle. But where you have the great body of the priesthood engaged in the agrarian movement in Ireland, I think you will be laying up for yourselves a large store of trouble if you do not also exempt clergymen from the operation of the clause. If this Bill is put forward harshly against Catholic priests in Ireland, the effect will be that the farmers will gather in the sacristy after mass on Sundays and pay their rents to the priests ; and the war will be carried on in that way. The Government have already two priests in prison ; and they have lately caught another who is in a position to go to prison. This question with regard to the priests has caused great trouble here and abroad, and it will have a most disastrous effect if you seek to get the priests in Ireland to break the seals of the Confessional ; but to send priests to prison for refusing to do it will, in my judgment, lead to the worst kind of war in Ireland—not civil war, but it would lead to all kinds of reprisals if priests are sent to prison in this way. I maintain that the Government do not want the priests to reveal the secrets of the Confessional; but you have in Ireland some magistrates who are Orangemen, and who are full of religious bigotry against the priesthood. Supposing Mr. Holt Waring were holding a meeting—he would be delighted to get an opportunity of committing a Catholic priest to gaol, and having done it he would thereby produce a state of things in Ireland which would lead to the worst possible complication. In India, where these religious difficulties arise, you are most delicate in the treatment of those concerned. It was only the other day that you allowed a person connected with a particular caste, who was sent to prison, to be accompanied by another person to cook his food, although the second man had not done anything at all. That is the case in India, where there is not a high-spirited people; but a population of 150,000,000 who have not much pluck, or they would not allow themselves to be governed as they are. In Ireland that is not the case. I am discussing this in an abstract spirit, and I say, if you send Catholic priests to gaol for refusing to break the seals of the Confessional, that government in Ireland will not be a very convenient or handy thing to carry on. I hope, therefore, in the interest of law and order, that the Government will accept the Amendment which I beg to move.

Amendment proposed, at the end of the foregoing Amendment, to insert the words—

"No barrister, solicitor, or clergyman shall be compelled to answer any question on any matter respecting which such person shall state he has acquired the information sought from him in the course of his professional duties."— (*Mr. T. M. Healy.*)

Question proposed, "That those words be there inserted."

THE CHIEF SECRETARY FOR IRE-LAND (Mr A. J. BALFOUR) (Manchester, E): The view of the Government is that the passage of this Bill through the House does not offer a proper opportunity for an alteration in the law with regard to privilege. We are not of opinion that any Proviso is necessary; but to make it clear that every privilege

which now exists will apply as under the ordinary law, we are prepared to move a Proviso to the effect that no witness examined under this section shall be required to answer any question which he may lawfully refuse to answer on the ground of privilege if he were being examined as a witness at the trial of a person accused of an offence alleged to have been committed.

MR. T. M. HEALY: That would not touch the priests.

MR. A. J. BALFOUR: The intention is to leave the Law of Privilege exactly where we find it, and that the witness examined under this section shall have all the same immunities as under the present law, "save as aforesaid," of course.

MR. T. M. HEALY: The present Primate of Armagh was sent to gaol for a long period for refusing to disclose the secrets of the Confessional.

MR. A. J. BALFOUR: When was that?

MR. T. M. HEALY: Twenty years ago; but the law has not been altered since.

MR. A. J. BALFOUR: We do not propose to alter the law; and the invariable custom in Ireland is to respect the secrets of the Confessional. The hon. and learned Member wants us to alter the law by putting into this clause what is already the custom. The effect of that would not be in the direction which he intends. The priests are already sufficiently protected by custom; and if the law were altered as the hon. Member proposes, in every case which is not covered by statute the custom would break down, and the protection be less efficient than before. I hope the hon. and learned Member will see that the Government have done all they can reasonably be asked to do, and that we are doing our best to carry out his intention.

MR. CHILDERS (Edinburgh, S.): I have not intervened in the legal questions which have been discussed in Committee on this Bill; but I think the present is one in which a layman may be allowed to express an opinion. We are now about to introduce into Irish Criminal Law a system of procedure which is absolutely unknown in England, which exists certainly in an obsolete form in Scotland, and which is only known to have been applied in Ireland in extraordinary cases. We are now going to deal permanently with a very grave form of law; and although there is nothing in the English, Irish, or Scotch practice to which we can have reference in deciding this delicate question, there is the practice of France, which has been established many years, of inquiry by the *Juge d'Instruction*, which is different from the process of taking evidence in Court. They are extremely careful in this matter in France, and it is laid down that there shall be exempted from examination all those who have acquired knowledge in the exercise of their profession with regard to the question proposed to be put to them. The classes exempted are surgeons, doctors, priests, barristers, solicitors, and notaries. Instead of having immunity in Court to which the right hon. Gentleman the Chief Secretary for Ireland (Mr. A. J. Balfour) has referred, I think it would be much better to have the practice which experience has very carefully built up in France. I do not venture to say more, but I would press upon the Committee to consider the French practice a good precedent in the present instance.

MR. A. J. BALFOUR: The right hon. Gentleman wishes us to assimilate our system of jurisprudence to the French system in this particular; but I understand the privilege of which he speaks extends not only to the preliminary inquiry, but over the whole French system; and, if so, I think the same privilege which extends to the statements of professional men before the *Juge d'Instruction* also extends to them in open Court. We do not think that this is the occasion for altering the law, nor do we think that the sanctity of the Confessional would be guarded, but rather the reverse, by the proposal which the right hon. Gentleman has made.

MR. CHILDERS: What I propose is to use, with regard to the professional persons of the classes named when examined on these inquiries, the same system as that which has been established in France in similar cases. I think the right hon. Gentleman is entirely mistaken in thinking that the evidence taken by the *Juge d'Instruction* is under the same rule as that taken in open Court, because the evidence in the former case is not taken on oath, and it cannot form the subject of a charge of perjury.

MR. GEDGE (Stockport): I wish to point out that the arguments of the hon. and learned Member for North Longford (Mr. T. M. Healy) go a great deal beyond the case put by the right hon. Gentleman; he proposes that "no clergyman" shall be compelled to answer with regard to information obtained in the course of his professional duties. A crime may have been committed in the presence of a clergyman, when engaged in the course of his professional duties in baptizing, visiting the sick, or celebrating the Mass, and yet this clause would protect him from giving any evidence on the subject. With regard to the point taken by the right hon. Gentleman opposite (Mr. Childers), I suggest that you can scarcely quote the one mild feature in the system in France of examining a prisoner before the *Juge d'Instruction* in the hope of making him commit himself as a reason why you should adopt that one mild part which happens to be the only mild one in that harsh system.

MR. MOLLOY (King's Co., Birr): The right hon. Gentleman the Chief Secretary for Ireland says that this is not the proper place to make this alteration in the law. Will the right hon. Gentleman tell us where is the proper place? This is surely the place, because you are now giving to a non-judicial body of men powers which are not exercised in any Court of Justice. It seems to me that as you are adding something absolutely new to the law of the country, it is time to put in all necessary safeguards. I can give the right hon. Gentleman a more recent instance than that of the Primate of Armagh who was sent to prison some 20 years ago. A question was put by a counsel to a priest, which he said he could not answer; but he gave as the reason why he could not answer that the information was one of the secrets of the Confessional. The Judge intimated to the counsel that it was not the custom to press these questions; but the counsel insisted on his right to put the question, and the Judge said—

"I am sorry I have not the power to compel the question not to be put; but I am bound by law as it stands at the present time, and I am compelled to punish the witness for not answering the question."

The priest was then imprisoned in his room for a quarter of an hour or so. That happened at one of the Courts at Westminster, where the Judge took a more judicial view of the question than would be taken by Resident Magistrates, who are for the most part half-pay officers. My hon. Friend said there are some magistrates who would press these questions. I am certain that there is a large number of them who would not do so; but I am satisfied that others would press these questions and take every possible advantage of the priests. Is it right to put this power in the hands of men of this character—men who are not trained to judicial functions? There is no one in this country or in this House who would not despise the priest who gave information under the circumstances. We want to avoid these conflicts in Court, and I say if a priest is put in prison for refusing to reveal the secrets of the Confessional, you will have such an agitation in Ireland as you have not known up to the present time. The right hon. Gentleman the Chief Secretary for Ireland says it is sufficient that the Government should declare their view of the matter, than a priest should not answer these questions; but if that is their view, what possible objection can they have to putting it in the Bill? Will it create any difficulty, or will it in any way interfere with the powers of the Bill? Certainly not. Well, then, if the Amendment is in accordance with the wishes of the people of Ireland, can you find a better time to lay down in law what you say distinctly is your own opinion and also the custom? I think, under the circumstances, the least that the Government can do is to agree to the Amendment proposed by my hon. and learned Friend the Member for North Longford.

SIR CHARLES RUSSELL (Hackney, S.): With regard to the remark of the right hon. Gentleman the Chief Secretary for Ireland that this is not the occasion for altering the law, I am of opinion that the introduction of this provision would not be an alteration of the law. It would be applying the Scotch Law to the clause. An hon. Member had asked what is the state of the Law in England. It is that a barrister or solicitor has the right to decline to answer questions with regard to matters conveyed to them in confidence by their clients. It is more strictly speaking the privilege of the client, and is so recognized by the law. But there is no similar protection with regard to communications which are made by an ordinary person to another professional or otherwise, and there is no such exemption in the case of clergymen. So far from that being so, I well recollect a case tried before Mr. Justice Hill some years ago at York. A clergyman was asked if he had not been the medium for making restitution of stolen property and from whom he had received it; he was called as a witness for the prosecution; he refused to answer, and the Judge committed him to prison, and he was kept there for a considerable time. I agree with the right hon. Gentleman the Chief Secretary for Ireland that this would not be allowed to take place in these days in our Courts. I am certain it would not; but I have not the same opinion with regard to Courts of the Resident Magistrates, who might press similar inquiries, and who might feel themselves justified in doing so, and in visiting the refusal to answer them with punishment. I do not see any reason, if on account of general policy it is right to extend the privilege of exemption to barristers and solicitors, why clergymen should not be placed in the same position, which is all that the Amendment asks for.

MR. A. J. BALFOUR: I think the hon. and learned Gentleman will hardly, by his suggestion, carry out the object in view. He admits that the ordinary Courts of Law in England and Ireland will not now abuse the existing laws in this matter; but he suggests that there are some Resident Magistrates who will do so. I am sorry to say that the hon. and learned Gentleman never loses an opportunity of speaking ill of the Resident Magistrates.

SIR CHARLES RUSSELL: I have never attacked the Magistrates. I said I was not certain that there might not be such Resident Magistrates.

MR. A. J. BALFOUR: Then I will not press the point. I point out that at the present time Resident Magistrates have the power of examining priests; but if you put into this Statute that there are special privileges guarding the secrecy of the Confessional, will not the Resident Magistrates immediately make the natural inference that when they are

Mr. Molloy

not examining under this Statute, but under the existing law, they may press the inquiries which it is the object of hon. Gentlemen opposite to prevent being pressed; and will not the result be that instead of putting up a barrier the Amendment will pull down one which already exists, and which might be perfectly effectual in guarding against the danger that is feared. I hope the hon. and learned Gentleman will look at the matter from this point of view, and give us, at all events, the opportunity of maintaining the practice which he admits to be general.

MR. HUNTER (Aberdeen, N.): I wish to invite the attention of the Government to the superior quality of the Scotch Law on this particular point. There is no doubt that under the English Law, clergymen are not privileged, but the Scotch Law has always taken a very reasonable view of the matter. Mr. Alison says—

"Our law latterly disowns any attempt to make a clergyman of any religious persuasion whatever divulge any confession made to him in the course of religious visits, or for the sake of spiritual consolation. . . . "

I suggest that the Government should take this opportunity of putting the law right where it is wrong, with regard to Ireland and England. It was the Canon Law that a clergyman should not divulge any confession made to him; but as bigotry is stronger than common sense, I suspect that there is an element of the former underlying the absence of this protection for clergymen in the ordinary law.

MR. T. M. HEALY (Longford, N.): The object of the Amendment is to provide for the Resident Magistrates a finger post to direct them. There is a distinct difference between the Courts of Law and the Courts of Inquiry. The Court of Inquiry is working in the dark, but in the Courts of Law everything goes on in daylight. A man may be summoned into the room of the Resident Magistrate, questioned, and sent to prison if he refuses to answer. The priest has no protection whatever. I remind the Committee of the words of the oath of the Orange Order—"You swear to extirpate Popery." [*Cries of* " No, no!"] That is part of the oath of the Orange Order. [An hon. MEMBER: Never.] I venture to say that that oath was sworn by the right hon. Gentleman

the Under Secretary to the Lord Lieutenant, when he joined the Order three years ago.

MR. JOHNSTON (Belfast, S.): I hope I may be allowed to give the statement of the hon. Member for North Longford my emphatic contradiction.

MR. T. M. HEALY: I have the greatest respect for the hon. Gentleman opposite. I believe his sincerity is so great that if he had lived 300 years ago he would have been burned at the stake, or would have burned somebody else. Now, this is a matter which ought to be treated by the Government on a serious basis. The Resident Magistrates in Ireland are dismissible at pleasure; they are not like the Judges, who can defend themselves; their salaries, and their increase of salary, depend on the will of the Executive. If you have a Tory Government in power, of course, when they have priests to deal with whom they think unruly subjects, the magistrates will endeavour to find some pretext for putting them in prison. Lord Palmerston, when he was hunting priests in Ireland, wrote a letter, in which there is this passage—

"I wish you could catch a priest amongst them, like a ptarmigan in a bag of grouse."

If that was written by Lord Palmerston in his calm moments in the secrecy of his closet, what may we expect from the administration of magistrates who are Orangemen, who, as Sir George Trevelyan tells us, will, under ordinary circumstances, tyrannize over and oppress the people. Seventy per cent of the Resident Magistrates in Ireland at the present moment are either promoted policemen or half-pay officers. The Primate of Ireland was sent to gaol, and remained there a long time, for refusing to answer a question touching the secrets of the Confessional. The Government say that occurred 20 years ago. Yes; but the law remains unaltered; and if a Judge in the Superior Courts in Ireland acted in that way with regard to a Prelate who is certainly as saintly a man as ever existed in the country, what would be the case with regard to red-hot Orangemen who are magistrates? Why do you break the seals of the Confessional? What has the unworthy profession to which I belong done that it should be singled out for special recognition? What are barristers that they should be protected?

[*Seventh Night.*]

What is that most mundane profession to that spiritual profession which appeals to men's consciences and hearts, and which, by your Bill, is to be left to the tender mercy of Resident Magistrates? This is the very case in which the Government can shut our mouths by the clôture; because, certainly as long as we have the right to protest we shall protest against priests being sent for to answer inquiries before Orange Magistrates, and being committed to prison for refusing to reveal things of which they can only derive any information through the discharge of their sacred duties.

MR. DE LISLE (Leicestershire, Mid): Perhaps, as a Catholic, I may be allowed to state my opinion that the Catholic priests of this country do not wish any exceptional legislation to be made on their behalf, especially on a matter which is so essentially a part of their sacred duty as confession. I speak with some trepidation upon this subject, because I see before me the right hon. Gentleman the Member for Mid Lothian (Mr. W. E. Gladstone), and it is not many years ago since he used all the arts of his rhetoric, and published some pamphlets to make out the case that the Catholic religion was dangerous to the State. Now, there has been raging in Germany, for several years past, a conflict called the *Cultur-kampf.* I was in Germany when that question was before the people, and the contention of Prince Bismarck was that the Catholic religion was necessarily such as to constitute a serious danger to the State. The Duke of Wellington held this opinion also, and he laid down that the Catholic religion was a most dangerous religion in the speech which he made against Catholic Emancipation in the House of Lords.

THE CHAIRMAN: I must invite the hon. Gentleman to confine himself more closely to the Amendment before the Committee.

MR. DE LISLE: I did not wish to wander from the point in dispute, but I wanted to show that owing to the prejudices which exist against us as a religious body, I do not believe it would be for the interest of religion if any exceptional legislation were passed, especially with regard to this question of confession, and for the reason that I believe our clergy, as a whole, rather than raise the prejudice which would be

Mr. T. M. Healy

created in the minds of men, would prefer that the law should remain as it is at present; and that they would, if they were compelled to suffer, think it better to go to prison, because it is part of their faith that those who suffer here for justice sake will receive their reward elsewhere. The Amendment of the hon. and learned Member for North Longford refers to clergymen without distinction.

MR. T. M. HEALY: It is because I did not wish to give offence to Protestant feeling in the House that I have not put other words on the Paper.

MR. DE LISLE: It seems to me that if the hon. and learned Member uses the words in his speech he might just as well put them on the Paper. I say that the clause, as it stands, will cover all that the clergymen of our Church wish to enjoy, which is the same amount of privilege and no more than is enjoyed by barristers, solicitors, and doctors; and I, for one, shall vote against any such exemption as that proposed by the hon. and learned Member.

MR. W. E. GLADSTONE (Edinburgh, Mid Lothian): Unfortunately, the discursive nature of the hon. Gentleman's speech has led him into an illustration of his argument which you, Sir, with the full assent of the Committee, at once checked. In deference to that judgment, I will not attempt to answer the hon. Gentleman. I will only observe that there was not a word which the hon. Gentleman said on the subject of my pamphlet that was accurate. This shows either that the hon. Gentleman has never read it—which is perfectly excusable—or that he has forgotten it, which is entirely natural and proper, or that he thought fit to refer to it on the chance of not being contradicted, which I cannot say is either natural or proper.

MR. DE LISLE: The right hon. Gentleman is mistaken in supposing that I have forgotten his pamphlets, because I had the pleasure of looking through them last night. The right hon. Gentleman will remember that I have a personal interest in the matter, inasmuch as the right hon. Gentleman spoke very kindly of my father's reply to the attack which was made upon his Church.

MR. W. E. GLADSTONE—[The CHAIRMAN: Order, order!]—I am not going to break your ruling, Sir, because I intend to confine myself strictly to contradictions. As the hon. Member refers to one whom I revere in common with himself, I say I am not aware of any reply to what he calls my attack on his Church.

MR. MOLLOY (King's Co., Birr): I protest against its being considered that the hon. Member for Mid Leicestershire (Mr. De Lisle) is expressing anything more than his personal sentiments upon this subject. I totally differ from the views of the hon. Gentleman upon this question. The Amendment of my hon. Friend the Member for North Longford (Mr. T. M. Healy) refers to the clergy of all denominations, although, as the hon. Member went on to say, that it did not refer to Catholics specially. I say, speaking with knowledge in this matter, that the Catholic priests will look upon this Amendment as a fair and honest protection to which they are entitled; and I point out that if hon. Members vote against this Amendment they will be voting against the opinions, not only of Catholic priests, but of the ministers of every Denomination in the country. Of course, if the hon. Gentleman says he he expresses simply his own individual opinion, that is another matter; but then I do not see the object of his getting up. We Catholics do look upon this as a most important Amendment. It is one which, I think, we are entitled to urge upon the Government, and, if the Government decline to accept it, it will be taken by the Catholics of the three Kingdoms as an indication of the intention of the Government to leave this power in the hands of men who we have every reason to fear will use it in the way we have indicated.

SIR CHARLES RUSSELL: I rise for the purpose of removing a misapprehension from the mind of the hon. Gentleman opposite (Mr. De Lisle). He said that the clergy of the Church to which he belongs, and to which I also belong, do not desire any special protection. But I point out that this Amendment applies equally to the clergy of all denominations. As my hon. Friend on these Benches has pointed out, the protection already exists under the Scotch Law; and, further, I wish to say that the exemption proposed to be given to clergymen of all Denominations rests not upon their sacerdotal character at all, but upon the fact that they are, in common with physicians, solicitors, and barristers, persons to whom confidential communications are likely to be made. It is, therefore, considered to be for the general interest of the community that they should be exempt from making disclosure of what is told them.

MR. JOHN O'CONNOR (Tipperary, S.): I wish to point out that it is possible for a priest to acquire information which he may consider confidential otherwise than in the Confessional. In the case of Father Keller, who is imprisoned for not answering questions put to him in Court, we obtained the opinion of a very celebrated lawyer in France. And, in reference to Father Keller's refusal to be examined, he stated that it was the practice of the Courts of preliminary inquiry in France to consider that all information which a priest may receive in his ordinary daily vocations should be respected in the same way as if they were received in confession. We do not desire to protect the Confessional, because there is no necessity for that, for no priest would answer with respect to information received in that way—the Confessional would be well defended without our assistance. We are asking this in the interest of the mothers and fathers of families who consult the priests on matters concerning their children. Again, there are parish matters which place information in the possession of the priest, and all these are held to be as sacred, or almost as sacred, by the priest as any communication made to him in confession, and he is quite ready to undergo any amount of inconvenience rather than divulge them. If the Government look to the occurrences which have recently taken place in Ireland, they will find that the police force, who have resisted every attempt hitherto made for the purpose of disaffecting them, have, the moment the Government laid hands on the priests, resigned in considerable numbers. Now, if this Bill goes into law in its present form, it will tend in the same direction, and I have no doubt there will be a large number of resignations in consequence. I am sorry to find that the Government will not accept this Amendment. I believe they are acting very unwisely in striking at the confidence which exists between the people and the priests in Ireland, which has done more for the maintenance of law and order than any Act which can be put in operation by the Government.

[*Seventh Night.*]

Mr. P. J. POWER (Waterford, E.): It is, I think, well for the Committee to understand the position with regard to this question. Previous to the last Division, we asked the Committee to say that no unlawful question should be asked, and we tried to get the word "lawful" inserted. The Committee were not of our opinion, and decided that any question, lawful or unlawful, may be asked a witness, and that the witness must answer the question. We are now asked to believe that the men who administer this Act will respect the position of the priests in Ireland. We know from sad experience that these Stipendiary Magistrates are not worthy of confidence, and we know well the nature of the questions they will put. They are to be the judges as to whether a question is a leading question or not. It is preposterous that the gentlemen who have to ask these questions should, at the same time, be the judges of whether the questions are leading or not. It is notorious that the vast majority of Resident Magistrates who will have to carry out these inquisitorial Courts are Orangemen, and we know that they can use the powers of the private inquiry to endeavour to extract answers from priests that would be injurious to the creed to which these Orange gentlemen are so much opposed. We will admit that there is a certain sprinkling of Catholics on the Bench in Ireland; but, as far as we are concerned, we prefer the Orangemen on the Bench to the "Cawtholics"—as we call them—who disgrace that Bench, and who cater to the prejudices of their opponents by trying to insult the religion to which they belong. So far as we are concerned, we should have no hesitation in saying that if a priest were brought before some of these private inquiries, he would receive more injustice at the hands of the Orangemen of the class of Gentlemen sitting opposite than he would from some of those "Cawtholics," who are a disgrace to their creed. It is evident from the remarks which have fallen from the Government side of the House, that they are going to grant this privilege to attorneys, barristers, and even to the police. We had an instance of that not long since, when a policeman at an inquiry refused to answer questions; and we submit that the privilege extended to attorneys, barristers, and police should be allowed to the priests of our Church. I think, under the circumstances, Sir, that the Government would do well to accept this Amendment, and not further to outrage the feelings of Catholic people by outraging the clergy to whom those people have proved their attachment through long centuries.

Mr. M. J. KENNY (Tyrone, Mid): I wish to point out to the Committee that there is really nothing in the Amendment we are discussing which brings out anything connected with sectarianism or anything connected with the Confessional or with Catholic priests. The Amendment affects all clergymen alike—the clergymen of the Protestant religion, as well as the clergymen of the Catholic religion. This Amendment will protect the hon. Member for South Belfast (Mr. Johnston)—who is a divine of his own Church—as well as Catholic priests. Besides, this Bill, if it becomes law, will exist for a considerable period. It may have to be put in force by an Irish Government; and if it were, we should find this clause a useful protection against the Kanes and the Hannas who disturbed the public peace in the North of Ireland. So that really raising the question of the Catholic religion in connection with this clause is beside the purpose. Of course, we are aware of this, that from time to time clergymen have been examined, principally Catholic clergymen, who are more numerous than others in Ireland. We are aware that they have been examined, and committed to prison for contempt of Court for refusing to answer certain questions put to them; but the ordinary law does not prevent these gentlemen from being sent to gaol. The ordinary law empowers magistrates to send them to prison. That is an open question, and has not been generally discussed or approached; but this is a definite law we are asked to pass, and these examinations are not conducted in open Court, but in secret. The circumstances are altogether different; and what may be good in the case of an examination in open Court, may be altogether bad and unsound in the case of a secret inquiry. These gentlemen will be brought into a room where the Officer who is presiding holds a secret inquiry, an inquiry from which all the public are excluded, and the only record of which will be made by a person appointed by the presiding magistrate, or by the person who appointed the presiding magistrate. That being the case, it is extremely desirable that the scope of the examination which this secret official should be entitled to pursue should be limited. The only objection I take to the Proviso under discussion is that it is not sufficiently complete. Under the French Law, physicians are protected from answering questions of this character, and I do not see why physicians in Ireland should not be similarly protected. I can understand some of the people of Ireland entrusting secrets to the hon. Member for Mid Cork (Dr. Tanner), and I do not see why he should not have protection. I certainly think we might extend this protection to others besides solicitors, barristers, and clergymen. I have pointed out the difference there is between the proposal of the Bill and the existing law under which these examinations take place in open Court; but the hon. Member for North Aberdeen (Mr. Hunter) has pointed out, very appropriately, as I think, the state of the Scotch Law. The Scotch Law affords absolute protection not only in private examinations, but also in public examinations, to all clergymen of any Denomination whatever, on grounds of public policy. It is considered unwise that clergymen who have secrets entrusted to them as clergymen, and not as citizens, should be dragged before a Court of Law, in order to have their secrets pumped out of them. I think the proposal to provide an exception of this kind in the Bill will commend itself to the common sense of the House generally. The Government should endeavour to make the question of privilege definite in the Bill. I do not think that their proposal is at all sufficient; besides, so far as it goes, I do not see anything inconsistent with it in the Amendment of my hon. Friend. I can only see, in the refusal of the Government to accept the Amendment, that which is observable in their refusal to accept all our Amendments—namely, the fault that it proceeds from a certain portion of the House. If it is attempted to confuse the issue by raising a debate on the conduct of the Catholic priest, I would point out that the Amendment has no more to do with the Catholic priest than it has to do with the Protestant clergyman or any other clergyman. It will

extend to Turks, Jews, Mahomedans, and the clergy of every other religious persuasion. I do not see what reason can be urged against the acceptance of this Proviso. The Government should not forget that it by no means invades the provisions of the ordinary law in Ireland or England in regard to examination in open Court, and that it is only meant for protection in secret Courts—Courts which are altogether unknown to English Law, which were only once temporarily established in Ireland, and which it is now sought to establish there permanently.

DR. TANNER (Cork, Co., Mid): I think the Government ought to give some consideration to this Amendment. This Bill that we have now under consideration is supposed to be a Bill for the promotion of law and order in Ireland. Goodness knows we have had these words often and often reiterated, stalely reiterated day after day. Then, surely, if they have any desire to promote law and order in the country, they will make the alteration in the Bill which this Amendment practically provides for. I was astonished to hear the remark which fell from the hon. Member for Mid Leicestershire (Mr. De Lisle). In the course of his remarks there was only one point that afforded me any consolation whatever, as regards the character of his remarks, and that was his German pronunciation, which was excellent. As regards the remarks themselves, I cannot congratulate the hon. Member upon them. He certainly brought a distinct charge of cowardly conduct against the clergy of his own religion. He said—I will quote his words, for I took them down—"rather than raise a prejudice against them they would sooner let the law remain where it was." He says, in effect, that the priests of his own country would suffer indignity rather than have a prejudice raised against them. If that is not charging the clergy of his own religion with cowardice I do not know what it is. I hope the hon. Gentleman will reconsider these words, and that he will retract and withdraw them. He spoke as if he were the Catholic representative of a Protestant constituency. Well, I happen to be a Protestant representative of an extremely ultra-Catholic constituency. The hon. Gentleman is always fond of posing as a Catholic champion. Just now he stated that he really did not intend to pose as a Catholic champion—as a Representative of Catholic opinion on that side of the House, but what did he say? He turned round to the few Gentlemen on those Benches and said they were not to be afraid of any of their Catholic constituents if they voted against this clause, they might take his word for it; and the extraordinary manner in which he subsequently proceeded to devour his words was more amusing than anything else. I trust the hon. Member when next he makes remarks will do so without indulging in that jocular spirit he indulged in just now. I have risen, however, not to take cognizance of the remarks of the hon. Gentleman to which I have directed the attention of the Committee, but to ask the Committee to consider the proposal now made. Hon. and right hon. Gentlemen should have seen what was the effect produced in Ireland, not in one part of Ireland, but from the Town of Youghal to the City of Dublin, when that reverend gentleman, Father Keller, was dragged up at Youghal and incarcerated in Kilmainham Prison—and, as I am informed, incarcerated on the order of an Orangeman. Is this sort of thing going to be carried on? I am informed that it will be carried on. I have known for a number of years a great many of these Stipendiary Magistrates. I do not wish to trespass on the time of this Committee—I do not like to overstep the lines that are laid down for the maintenance of proper debate; but I could tell you, if I liked, what actually many of these gentlemen have stated in different parts of Cork where I have met them. I am certain that when this Crimes Act is brought into play one of the first things that will be done by many of these people——

An hon. MEMBER: And done to you.

DR. TANNER: Yes; I know the hon. Member would only be too delighted if it were done to me. Perhaps his wish may be gratified; and if it is he may rest assured that I shall be perfectly satisfied. I say this, that one of the first things which will be done—if the pluck of the Government continues, and their stern fortitude does not ooze out at their finger tips, as I believe it will, for I know the stuff they are made of—will be to incarcerate a considerable number of the Catholic clergy. I say every one of the maintainers of true law and order—

[*Laughter.*] Well, of course, I know that the hon. Gentleman who laughs at me considers the stirring up of hostility and strife in the North of Ireland law and order. It may be law and order according to his notion of law and order. I feel no hostility to the hon. Gentleman or any of his followers. I maintain that in Ireland the proper plan of proceeding and of gaining the confidence of the people, instead of going on in that way, stirring up faction and opposition, and Orange riots, is to give them the system of government they want, and which they are sure to get in the end. The Government should pay attention to this Amendment, and not only pass it in its present form, but in an extended form, in view of the remarks of the hon. Gentleman who spoke from these Benches, and who clearly pointed out what is the law in France— that not only barristers, solicitors, and clergymen are excluded from examination into the secrets confided to them in their professional capacity, but doctors also. In Ireland, also, these gentlemen should be protected against being forced to divulge any information which they may have obtained in the course of their professional duties. I feel perfectly certain that in this matter there is involved, morally speaking, not merely a legal rule, but a far higher rule, a grand, unwritten code of honour, by which every professional man, whether barrister, solicitor, physician, or, highest of all, clergyman, will feel himself bound. Whether the Government accepts this Amendment or not, professional gentlemen will be bound by that code of honour, aye, even though, in their loyalty to it, they break the law of the land.

MR. W. REDMOND (Fermanagh, N.): I hope no hon. Member on the other side of the House will be induced to record a vote against this Amendment under a wrong impression. There is nothing easier than to make hon. Members representing English constituencies believe that it is the desire of Members in this quarter of the House to hold Catholic clergymen in Ireland excused from the liabilities and responsibilities of ordinary citizens in the country. People have repeatedly attempted to show that we desire to make priests in Ireland free from the ordinary responsibilities of citizenship; and, therefore, I can conceive that it is quite likely that hon. Members opposite may be induced to vote against this clause, under the impression that we are in reality endeavouring to free, unduly, the Catholic priesthood in Ireland from the responsibilities which they owe to the country as citizens. Now, nothing more erroneous could possibly be conceived. We do not for a single moment wish to maintain that the priests in Ireland are not as liable as any other citizens in the country to help in the maintenance of law and order, and in the affairs of the State. We should be very sorry from these Benches—and it would be contrary to the liberal views that we hold with regard to religious matters—to attempt for a single moment to argue that a man, because he was a Catholic priest, should be freed from the ordinary responsibilities of citizens of the country. Therefore, that is not what the Amendment proposes at all; and that argument, I think, should not induce any hon. Member opposite to record a vote against this proposal which deals with quite a different matter. Sir, all that this Amendment proposes is that when a secret inquiry is held, a clergyman, whether he be Catholic or Protestant, shall not be unduly——

Notice taken, that 40 Members were not present; Committee counted, and 40 Members being found present,

MR. W. REDMOND: When I was interrupted by the Motion for a Count, I was saying that I hoped hon. Members opposite would not be induced to vote against this Amendment under the impression that we wish to excuse the Catholic priest in Ireland from his ordinary duties and responsibilities as a citizen. Nothing is more erroneous than that idea, and that idea is not the foundation of the Amendment proposed by the hon. and learned Gentleman the Member for North Longford (Mr. T. M. Healy). The Amendment simply means that when the secret inquiry is making its investigation, the priest or clergyman, whether Protestant or Catholic, shall be excused from answering questions with regard to information which may have come to him whilst exercising his office amongst the people. Now, nobody objects in the slightest degree to a clergyman, whether Catholic or Protestant, being asked to throw light upon any investigation having for its object

the finding out of criminals and the putting down of crime; and I am quite certain that so far from objecting to help in the investigation of crime in the country, the Catholic priesthood would be very glad to do so, inasmuch as they have always done everything in their power to put down crime in Ireland, and to induce the people to confine themselves to lawful courses of action in struggling for their rights and their reforms. This being so, nobody for a moment will attempt to maintain that there would be any disinclination on the part of the clergyman, any more than on the part of any other citizen, to do what he fairly and reasonably could to help in the investigation of crime. What this Amendment is framed for is this—to prevent a magistrate who calls a clergyman before him at a secret inquiry from being able to send him to prison for refusing to answer a question which the clergyman feels his conscience will not allow him to answer. I can quite understand hon. Gentlemen opposite, whose information regarding Ireland is extremely small, being loath to believe that there are any men in the country, either Resident Magistrates or any class of the community, who would so far forget themselves as to basely endeavour to get information by unworthy means from a clergyman, and at the cost of that clergyman's self-respect. But, Sir, we, who know what occurs in Ireland, know very well that there is nothing in the wide world which certain people in that country, and, to a large extent, what magistrates in that country, both Resident and ordinary Magistrates, will not do in order to inconvenience, and, in very many cases, absolutely to insult the clergy of the country, particularly, and almost exclusively, the Catholic clergy. Now, I will just relate what occurred at an Election in the constituency which I represent, and I believe, Sir, that the relation of this fact will do much to illustrate what it is that we fear when we propose this Amendment for the purpose of safeguarding the clergymen of Ireland from unfair persecution and cross-examination under the secret inquiry of the Resident Magistrates of the country. I represent a constituency, Sir, which is equally composed of Catholics and Protestants; and, representing such a constituency, I do not hesitate to say that I believe both my

[Seventh Night.]

Catholic and Protestant constituents would highly, and do highly, approve of this Amendment, which has for its object the safeguarding of Protestant clergymen as well as Catholic clergymen. I know very well that while the great bulk of the Protestant constituency I represent, and, I believe, the great bulk of the Protestants in Ireland, are disposed to treat Catholic clergymen as equals, and as gentlemen, and as fellow-citizens; and while I freely acknowledge that with pleasure, I am also obliged to say that there are in the North of Ireland certain men bound up in the meshes of Orangeism who will stop at nothing to humiliate and insult Catholics —Catholic clergymen especially. Why, Sir, in the campaign conducted by the Orange Committee in the County of Fermanagh against my Election last year, it was freely stated over and over again, in the most unblushing manner, that the priests who were supporting me at that Election were responsible for the outrages and crimes which have stained the history of the country during recent years; and it was, moreover, stated that if there was any power which could make a priest divulge the secrets of the Confessional in Ireland, it would be the means of bringing to justice a great many of the criminals. Well, Sir, I need hardly say that, from beginning to end, that was a most outrageous and infamous and groundless statement, and that, as such, it was taken, not alone by the Catholics, but by the Protestant people of my constituency. I know very well that a great many Protestants were quite as indignant as the Catholics at such a thing being said against their fellow-citizens in the Catholic Church. But this goes to prove that there is in the Province of Ulster a minority which goes, to some extent, over the other Provinces—a minority which is so embittered and filled with so much hatred against the Catholic religion, that there is nothing they will stop at to humiliate the ministers of that religion in the eyes of the people; and this I say, Sir, goes to prove that it is necessary that there should be some safeguard for clergymen when they are unceremoniously dragged before this secret inquisition presided over by the Resident Magistrate. It has been stated that a great many of the Resident Magistrates of

Mr. W. Redmond

Ireland are Orangemen. There are some few Catholics amongst them; but the great bulk of them, if they are not Orangemen themselves, are influenced in their surroundings by Orangemen; and I am certain that, more especially in the Province of Ulster, every Resident Magistrate who holds a secret inquiry court will be more or less influenced by the surrounding landlords, and the circumstances in which they pass their daily lives. Whether they are intense Orangemen or not, they will be compelled to call up indiscriminately—right, left, and centre—the Catholic priests of the country, to question them upon matters not relating to crime at all, and to endeavour to insult them by asking them questions as to matters upon which they could not give information except in the way of their calling. That is a thing the Government ought to safeguard against. In the first place, it is infamous that the priests in Ireland—men whose lives are blameless, and have done everything in their power to put down crime—should be called before a secret inquisition and examined in private just as if they were in sympathy with crime, and would not come and give information openly as to criminal matters if they had such information to give. The very fact of considering it necessary to bring them before this secret investigation is more than an insult; but if you wish to prevent the insult going further, make some provision by which neither Catholic nor Protestant clergy — make no distinction at all between them— will be saved from being asked questions. [*Laughter.*] I do not feel in the least degree surprised that hon. Members opposite should not hesitate to laugh at this. They pass lightly what I conceive to be most disastrous provisions in this Bill containing within them absolute insults to our priests. We are endeavouring to defend our clergymen, whom we know to be men of honest and blameless lives, and our protests are met by laughter. All I can say is, that while the laughter of hon. Gentlemen opposite will not deter us from doing our duty, most certainly it will not help the Government in meeting the difficulty they will have to encounter in their attempts to pass this Bill through the House. Now, I leave the hon. Member who thinks it desirable to laugh at our protests on behalf of the Catholic clergy of Ireland, and I say again that I hope the Government will recognize the necessity for this clause and will accept it. Why, it is a perfectly monstrous thing, on the face of it, to say that you will exempt barristers and attorneys from cross-examination with regard to matters which have come to their knowledge professionally, but that you will not extend the same exemption to the clergy in Ireland. I cannot conceive how anyone can think that information which comes professionally to an attorney or a barrister is likely to be more secret, or that these gentlemen are likely to consider themselves more bound to secrecy than a clergyman who receives, in the course of his sacred calling, information which is intended for his ear, and his ear alone. I warn the Government most seriously and earnestly, as a Representative of a constituency where Catholics and Protestants are now living, I am happy to say, peaceably and quietly together as fellow-citizens in one country—I warn them that if they do not accept this Amendment, but leave clergymen in Ireland open to be badgered and questioned in regard to every matter which a Resident Magistrate is prompted to inquire into by any landlord or agent in the district in which he holds his inquiry, he will see a large number of the Irish priests sent to prison. This will be the effect of refusing to pass this Amendment to safeguard the Irish priests from this cross-examination. I ask every hon. Member in this House, whether English or Irish, if he is desirous to see some sort of an end put to the strife that is going on between the two countries, whether he thinks it will be likely to help us to arrive at a settlement of the Irish Question to have priests sent to prison day after day in Ireland? You have already got a couple of priests in prison in Ireland, men of the highest possible character, men who not only never committed crime, but never hesitated to condemn crime on every possible occasion. Why, Sir, are these men in prison? It is because you insisted, through your authorities, on questioning them in regard to matters on which they said they had no information except such as they had received in the course of their profession—information which, because of that, they

could not divulge in a Court of Law. These men are imprisoned to-day because they refused to divulge to you information which they got in the course of their lives as ministers of God's Word in Ireland. These men were examined and bullied, and they refused to give evidence in open Court, and, as a result, they were committed to prison. Well, if, as the result of an open investigation, these priests were sent to prison and are in prison now, I want to know is it not all the more likely that priests will be sent to prison when brought before a secret inquiry at which the magistrate will use as much power as the Czar of Russia? Do hon. Members think that a clergyman under this Bill will be treated more tenderly than by Judge Boyd? I should think not. I should think that, seeing that as a result of Judge Boyd's action in Ireland you have now two most respectable priests in prison, it is certain, if you do not accept this Amendment, these priests, who are respected beyond everything by the people of Ireland, will be dragged before these secret inquiries. They will be brought before the Resident Magistrates, who, prompted by the landlords, will ask them all manner of questions as to their relations with their flocks. If you allow this to be done time after time, you will have priests refusing to answer questions asked by the Resident Magistrate, and, as a result, you will see them day after day sent off to prison. I ask the Government, as an act of simple justice—if justice is to be expected of them, and I fear it is not—I ask them as a matter of justice, even as a matter of expediency, and as a thing which will make their work and duty in Ireland all the more light and easy, and as a means of promoting peace and putting down strife, of which we have quite enough, to accept this Amendment, and not allow the Catholic priesthood and the people of Ireland to read in the newspapers to-morrow that you refuse to extend to the Irish clergy the same protection and consideration which you extend to attorneys and barristers, and that you refuse to protect clergyman from being heckled by Resident Magistrates about matters they know nothing of except through the Confessional, if they be Catholic, and, if not, in the ways of their lives as ministers generally. If the Government do not accept this Amendment there will be indignation throughout the country. The people of Ireland will be greatly incensed, because they will take it as a further proof that you not only want to pass a Coercion Bill, but that you want to pass it in the roughest and most inconsiderate manner possible. In this manner you will double and redouble the opposition of the Irish people to your measure, because they will see that, not content with outraging the liberty of the Irish people, you would attempt to outrage the priests of the Church.

MR. FLYNN (Cork, N.): I am astonished that the Government have not looked upon this Amendment as most reasonable. The Government could easily ascertain—through their sources of information in Ireland—the feelings with which this matter will be regarded—and properly enough regarded — by the people of Ireland, unless safeguarded in the manner proposed by the Amendment. The Amendment proposes nothing revolutionary and nothing inconsistent, even from a Government point of view, with the scope and tendency of the measure. What it does propose is that, in certain circumstances, certain classes of people, that is to say, gentlemen engaged in a sacred calling, shall be preserved from the indignity, and, oftentimes, outrage, to which they would be subjected if brought before these secret inquiries and put under a cross-examination to which they could not in conscience submit. I do not appeal to the Committee as an Irish Catholic Member. I do not speak in a sense either Catholic or Protestant. I appeal to the honourable feeling of the Committee to accept this Amendment, or to support us in this Amendment. I cannot understand the reason of the Government refusal to accept this Amendment. We know very well that the Government are cognizant, and that the Committee are cognizant, of the fact that quite recently two Catholic clergymen were arrested for refusing in open Court to answer questions, because they considered it was utterly inconsistent with their duty, and utterly inconsistent with that sense of confidence which ought to exist between a pastor and his people for them to do so. I should like to point out this additional reason why this Amendment should be passed, and why it is essential that the Committee should accept it. In

the case in which the two clergymen I refer to—namely, Fathers Keller and Ryan, were arrested—they were brought before the open Court, and deeming a question put by the Judge in Bankruptcy inconsistent with their sacred duty, and inconsistent with the confidence which ought to exist between clergymen and people, and which does exist to a paramount degree between the Irish priests and their flocks, they thought it their duty to refuse to answer the question. They accepted the penalty and alternative, and are now undergoing imprisonment. Well, Sir, if in open Court they found it their duty to take such a stand as that, the condition of things will be very much worse when you have secret Courts of Inquiry established all over the country, because, at least, in open Court the public had the satisfaction of knowing that though they might regret the manner in which Judge Boyd interpreted the provisions of the Bankruptcy Law, he interpreted it according to his view of the regulations of the Court as laid down by Statute, and as subject to public criticism and before the public eye. But coming before the Resident Magistrates, whom it is a matter of common notoriety are utterly incompetent to deal with nice points of legal evidence, and utterly incompetent to preside over tribunals at which delicate points of law must arise, we say that extra safeguards are necessary for the protection of clergymen. We say that when this law comes into operation and this clause comes to be put in force, large numbers of clergymen will be brought before the Courts of Inquiry, that in discharge of their duty they will feel it incumbent upon them to refuse to answer questions, and that they will be sent to prison. Is that a pleasant thing for the Government to contemplate? You will add to the state of exasperation and to the elements of disorder which are already sufficiently abundant in Ireland, by this Measure which you bring forward in support of law and order. The law will not be vindicated by the imprisonment of clergymen for refusing to answer unjust, irrelevant, and unfair questions. Nor will order be advanced, but will be still further seriously imperilled, and the condition of things will be worse under your Courts of Inquiry than it is at the present time. I do not desire, in speaking in Committee on a particular measure, and in referring to an Amendment of which we desire to talk in a reasonable and rational tone —I do not desire, I say, to refer to the past history of the Irish priesthood ; but even the most cursory students of Irish history, the most thoughtless reader of the history of Ireland for the past five or six years, will recognize that if there is one point on which the Government are more certain to break down than another it is when they seek to run a-muck against the rights and privileges of the sacred profession of the priest-hood, whether Catholic or Protestant. I would urge these reasons in what I believe to be a temporary and reasonable spirit. I say that if the Government are reasonable and seriously desirous, as they allege they are, of main-taining order in Ireland it will be absolutely necessary for them to insert this Amendment in the clause. They must do that if they wish, as far as possible, to remove sources of friction in the future and to make the clause opera-tive from their point of view.

MR. P. McDONALD (Sligo, N.): I regret I was not present actually in the House when the debate upon this Amendment commenced, and I must congratulate the Committee upon the great rapidity of its progress during the portion of the evening that I was un-avoidably absent. I consider this to be one of the most important Amendments which have yet been discussed. I under-stand the position in which we find our-selves to be this. The Amendment proposes that this privilege of not answering questions respecting informa-tion which has been obtained in the discharge of professional duty should be extended to barristers, solicitors and clergymen. Already, however, it has been discovered that barristers and solicitors are protected by the existing law, so that the question is virtually narrowed down to the case of clergymen, and the question which this Committee has now to consider is this—whether this privilege of not replying to ques-tions on matters communicated to clergy-men in a professional capacity should be conceded to them or not. Now it does seem to me that if the Government really desire to make this Bill absolutely inoperative for all useful purposes they will refuse to accept this Amend-ment, and will rush blindly into the pit-

fall which they have dug for themselves. For what is the actual fact with regard to the priests in Ireland—and I speak as a Protestant—and I do say that Englishmen — and I think this is a remarkable proof of the impossibility of one country governing another, of Eng-land governing Ireland—do not in gene-ral in the least understand the intimate character of the relations which subsist between the priests of Ireland and the people committed to their charge. Those relations have been expressed in various ways. They are to some extent repre-sented by the term "Father"—father and son—which implies the closest pos-sible intimacy of feeling and sympathy, and the Catholic priests, we know, are especially bound by all the most solemn obligations of their oaths not to com-municate anything that may be told them in confession. Now I suppose it is not the intention even of the present Government, advised by the Parliamen-tary Under Secretary with his anti-Catholic proclivities, to require Catholic priests to communicate to these secret tribunals what has been stated to them in the Confessional. I cannot believe that even the present Government can go as far as that, but, as I understand it, this section is aimed not merely against crime in the proper sense of the word, but also against what are called "offences," and one of the offences against which it is directed is conspiracy —namely, the conspiracy of the Plan of Campaign. Now I have no doubt whatever that in various parts of the country the priests have been consulted by their people as to what is their duty in reference to the Plan of Campaign, and no doubt the priests would be able to give information on this subject if they chose to do so ; but I say it most deliberately as a Protestant Representa-tive, that they would be false to all that is truest in the traditions of their Church, and false to their sacred posi-tion and to their influence with their people, if they were to divulge matters of this sort and were thereby to break the link which binds the people and priests. I believe that if the priests were to communicate these secrets they would lose all the legitimate influence which they now exercise amongst the people, not only in matters of faith, but also in matters of every day life ; and I say that if they lost that influence it would be a terrible misfortune to those who would have to govern the Irish people; and I say, in conclusion, that I feel no doubt as to what the result of your refusing to pass this Amendment will be. The priests will be asked to give information before these secret tribunals; they will refuse to give it, and they will be sent to prison in crowds—and they would be false to all that is best in their history if they did not go to prison And when you have sent them to prison in large numbers will you be one whit nearer the pacification of the country? Will Her Majesty's Government find that law and order are more respected? Will not they and the country find that there will be a gulf wider and deeper than ever between the people of Ireland and the Government?—because if there is one thing that the people of Ireland love and revere it is their religion. The people of Ireland reverence the men who labour amongst them, who feel for them in all the circumstances of their lives, and are their friends and companions religiously and politically. I warn the Government of the danger they will run if they refuse this Amendment.

Question put.

The Committee *divided:*—Ayes 121; Noes 183: Majority 62.—(Div. List, No. 139.)

MR. T. M. HEALY (Longford, N.): Mr. Courtney, the next Amendment which stands in my name I propose in order to meet the case of Ulster, where whenever a Catholic is murdered no person is ever brought to justice. The murder of Catholics in the North of Ireland is merely child's-play. Take the case of Philip Maguire. In that case the late Government made no real substantial attempt to punish the offender, and what I wish to provide for is this. That as the Attorney General for Ireland under a Tory Administration will always be an Orange partizan, the deceased person's relatives, or his kindred, in some way should have the power to compel the Attorney General, on their requisition and sworn information, to hold an investigation. Now, the records of the Orange Party in Ireland are simply the records of crime. It is but reasonable that in cases of serious crime you should be able to compel the Government to hold inquiries on the requisition either of the deceased's rela-

Mr. P. McDonald

tives, or, if the injured person has not died from his wounds, on the requisition of the injured person himself. I do not see how the Government, if they are really anxious to quell crime in Ireland, can resist an Amendment of this kind, which is directed against crime.

Amendment proposed,

In page 2, line 4, after "criminal," insert "the Attorney General shall direct an inquiry under this section in the case of any crime, whether committed in a proclaimed district or not, upon sworn information made to him by any injured person, or the next of kin of such persons, or of any deceased person."—(*Mr. T. M. Healy.*)

Question proposed, "That those words be there inserted."

THE ATTORNEY GENERAL FOR IRELAND (Mr. HOLMES) (Dublin University): Mr. Courtney, the hon. and learned Gentleman himself, or one of his Friends, submitted, at an earlier period of the discussion, an Amendment which we accepted—namely, to the effect that the Attorney General may direct an inquiry "if he thinks fit." At the present time these words stand part of the clause. The intention of the Government and the Committee was that it should not be compulsory on the Attorney General to direct an inquiry of this kind. He is an officer who is responsible to this House; he is an officer who may be called to account at any time, and we consider it necessary to vest in him a discretion. In the same way, a discretion is vested in a Resident Magistrate. This Amendment, which is proposed on the ground that the Attorney General cannot be trusted to act properly in certain parts of the country, will certainly not be accepted by Her Majesty's Government. The hon. and learned Member has said that when a Tory Government is in Office, the Attorney General for Ireland is always an Orange partizan. I desire to give the most emphatic contradiction to such an assertion. I have no sympathy with crime, whether it be committed by Orangemen or by any other members of the population. I have no more sympathy with outrage and disorder, and with disturbance, if the authors of it be Orangemen, than I have if the authors of it are Nationalists.

MR. T. M. HEALY: What about Giffen?

MR. HOLMES: In every case which has come before my notice, I have endeavoured, as far as possible, to hold the balance evenly between Parties, and in so doing I have only followed the steps of all my Predecessors. As I have already said, we have accepted the suggestion that the words " if he thinks fit" shall be inserted in the clause. We have also accepted the words "in a proclaimed district," and we do not intend to alter the clause in the direction the hon. and learned Member desires. It will make no difference whether an outrage is committed in the North, South, East, or West of Ireland. If it is necessary that a district shall be proclaimed, it will be proclaimed, no matter in what part of Ireland it is. Where it is necessary to have an inquiry an inquiry will be held. It will be directed to be held by the Attorney General acting upon his discretion, and the Attorney General in acting in the matter will be directly responsible to this House, and be ready at any time to account for his action. I must entirely repudiate the assertion that there is any foundation for the allegation that the Law Officers of the Crown, either in this or in any other Conservative Government, have, or have had, any sympathy with disorder, no matter from what particular faction, if I may use the expression, the disorder may come.

MR. T. M. HEALY: I suppose the right hon. and learned Gentleman has not forgotten that he said the blood of Giffen was on the head of Lord Spencer. That expression of his was reported in *The Dublin Daily Express*, and it distinctly proves that the right hon. and learned Gentleman is a sympathizer with the Orange faction. He never repudiated his language ; I believe he did attempt, in reply to one of the Members for Donegal, to make out that his language was not capable of the meaning we attribute to it. It was so reported in *The Daily Express*, and it has remained in record for three years, uncontradicted by the right hon. and learned Gentleman. He had been a Law Officer of the Crown a short time before that, and the language was reported by an Orange reporter in an Orange organ, and, further, was published, as I understand, in the official report of the proceedings. As I have said, the right hon. and learned Gentleman has never contradicted the language. I should say he is capable of anything, if he is capable of contra-

dicting now a report in this newspaper three years old, having allowed it to rest in the meantime. Now, what is this Amendment ? This Amendment is aimed at the detection of crime. It proceeds, no doubt, on the supposition that Her Majesty's Government in Ireland will mainly be represented by Orange partizans. Instance me a case of an Orangeman who, having murdered a Catholic, was ever hanged. Two or three Orangemen have been convicted of murder, but not one has ever been hanged. I need not go into the numberless cases of murder ; but in the case of Philip Maguire we know how the Government transferred the venue to Dublin, how an Orange jury acquitted the man, and how the Judge pointed out to the authorities that they were challenging Mr. Mackintosh, who he said had no sympathy with crime, and how Mackintosh was thereupon left on the jury and acquitted Maguire. Show me the case of an Orangeman who has ever been hanged in Ireland. You cannot do it. If the petty jurors do not do their business, the grand jurors will do it for them. We want, when these crimes are committed against our people, to have some guarantee that inquiries will be held. You tell us you are responsible to this House. What is the good of that ? The Government have taken all the time of the House, and I suppose that if we ever did get a day for a Motion of ours they would think it right to clôture us. This House has no sympathy for Irish Business, except it be Irish Business in the shape of a Crimes Act. To say that you are responsible to this House is to use a perfectly illusory expression. You are responsible to the Orange Party in this House. They are the only people you look to—your King-Harmans and your Tottenhams—you have more regard for the little finger of one of them than you have for the whole 86 Members of the Irish Nationalist Party put together. The Government boast of their anxiety to put down crime in Ireland ; but when we ask them that an injured party or the next-of-kin of a deceased person shall have the right to demand one of these inquiries they refuse us, because their Attorney General is so ethereal, so devoid of partizanship, that he will be certain to order an inquiry.

MR. HOLMES: I am exceedingly glad that the hon. and learned Gentleman, by the observations he has just made, has given me an opportunity of explaining a matter which I have desired to explain for some time. It has been referred to once or twice in the debates on this Bill; but, unfortunately, on each occasion it was referred to it was after I had already spoken, and when I could not again interpose in the debate. The right hon. Gentleman the Member for Derby (Sir William Harcourt) referred to the matter; but when challenged by my hon. and learned Colleague (Mr. Gibson) he said he made no charge—he was merely quoting. Now, the speech which the hon. and learned Member (Mr. T. M. Healy) has referred to was a speech which was, according to my recollection, delivered in the month of January, 1884, and I am quite prepared to submit the whole of that speech to the candid judgment of hon. Gentlemen, because they will see the connection between the various parts of it. The circumstances under which that speech was made were these — the Crimes Act of 1882 was at that time in force, and in that Act there was a provision which enabled the Lord Lieutenant to prohibit any public meeting which would, in his opinion, tend to endanger the public peace. He had made use of that power to prohibit a number of public meetings in the South and West of Ireland. Towards the end of 1883 he had made use of that power on several occasions. About the same period the Nationalist Party of Ireland announced their intention of holding meetings in Ulster, and it was represented to the Lord Lieutenant that if meetings in the South of Ireland held by the Nationalist Party were calculated to endanger the public peace they were more likely to do so in the North, because in the North of Ireland there was a much stronger feeling between the two factions than there was in the South. That was represented to the Lord Lieutenant from more than one quarter. The first meeting was announced to be held at Rosslea, in County Monaghan. The Lord Lieutenant did not prohibit the meeting, and he did not prohibit it even when a counter-meeting was announced. He prohibited neither one meeting nor the other, and the result was that there was as nearly as anything could be a serious breach of the public peace. In the month of January following—that

was in the month of January, 1884—a meeting was called by the Nationalists at Dromore, County Tyrone. Shortly after that meeting was called a meeting was called by the people describing themselves as the Loyalists of that part of the country, to be held the same day at the same place. I was one of those who conceived that those meetings should have been proclaimed in the cause of public order, and for the purpose of preventing public disturbance. That view was also taken by gentlemen of moderate views. It was pressed on the Government of the day; but, notwithstanding that, the Government of the day allowed both meetings to proceed. The result of that was what might naturally be expected. There was a disturbance, and in the course of the disturbance a man named Giffen lost his life. It is not the fact that Giffen fired at any policeman; but, at the same time, I never said that the circumstances under which Giffen's life was taken might not make the homicide justifiable or excusable. On the contrary, I remember stating that I thought the matter was one which ought to be investigated. I certainly do not for a moment say that the circumstances, so far as the authorities were concerned, did not justify the action which cost Giffen his life. At a meeting in Dublin, not a meeting of the Orange Party — it was hardly a very strong Party meeting—I made a speech and referred to this question. I called attention to the various facts which I have now enumerated. I said that the Government of Ireland were culpable in allowing these meetings to take place in the North, having been vested with power to prohibit meetings which were calculated to disturb the public peace, and having used this power in other parts of Ireland, where it was much less likely the peace would be disturbed; and then I used language which has been frequently used in this House in reference to many cases in which, owing to the adoption of a particular policy on the part of the Government, lives have been lost. I said the blood which was shed there rested on the head of the Irish Executive. [*Cries of* "Lord Spencer!"] Yes; he was Lord Lieutenant at the time. It was not because I conceived there was anything criminal in what had taken place; for, on the contrary, as I said, it was perfectly

Mr. Holmes

possible and probable that the action of the authorities was justifiable; but the policy pursued by the Government was a policy which, if there had been any foresight, any consideration, must have been known by the Government of the day would lead to a breach of the peace. That is the explanation I give. I withdraw no observation I made; but what I ask the Committee, or any Members of it who choose to discuss this, to do is to read all the observations I made, and then let them say whether my words were not perfectly justified by way of criticism. So far with regard to this personal matter. I say again, as far as the enforcement of public justice in Ireland against Orangemen or any other persons is concerned, there is no distinction of any kind drawn. The hon. Member has asked me when was any Orangeman hanged. I really cannot answer that question. [*Home Rule cheers.*] If he asked me also when any Nationalist was hanged, I could not answer the question. Can the hon. Gentleman point to any case in the North of Ireland where life has been lost or injury inflicted, and where evidence was not forthcoming? This section is devised with the object of getting evidence, and if it should turn out that in any part of the North of Ireland it is necessary to put this section in force for the purpose of obtaining evidence, either against Orangemen or any other persons, it will be put in force. I would not maintain my present Office in this Government for one moment if the section were not enforced under such circumstances.

SIR WILLIAM HARCOURT(Derby): I think the right hon. and learned Gentleman the Attorney General for Ireland might have spared the explanation, or, rather, the reiteration which he has chosen to make of his declaration, which I hoped he might have said was an ill-considered declaration—namely, that the blood of this man was on the head of Lord Spencer. Notwithstanding the position which he occupied at the time, the Attorney General for Ireland has shown that his principal object was, as I am bound to say, for Party purposes, to inflame the passions of the Irish people. Considering the task which Lord Spencer was then engaged in performing, doing his duty, as I understand, according to the best of his ability, I am afraid that it is setting an example

to Ireland which will be evil in its consequences, that a man who is now Attorney General for Ireland should stand up in this House and say that he did deliberately charge Lord Spencer with having the blood of a man upon his head, or that to-day, during the passing of this Crimes Act, he should reiterate that charge. How can he expect that the Executive Government which he represents will be treated in a different way to that in which he treated Lord Spencer in those days? I have heard the language of the right hon. and learned Gentleman with the deepest regret. What is his charge against Lord Spencer? It is that having had, under the Crimes Act, the power to prevent all public meetings, he exercised that power according to his discretion, with as little intention to restrain public meetings as he thought consistent with the public interest. That is what Sir George Trevelyan referred to in his letter the other day. He said that the object of Lord Spencer and himself, in the administration of justice in Ireland, had been to use the powers which were given to them as little as possible in restraint of public liberty, and it is because they so used these powers that this charge was brought by the right hon. and learned Gentleman, and reiterated to-day after an interval of three years.

THE CHIEF SECRETARY FOR IRELAND (Mr. A. J. BALFOUR) (Manchester, E.): The right hon. Gentleman the Member for Derby (Sir William Harcourt) might have recollected that if my right hon. and learned Friend the Attorney General for Ireland (Mr. Holmes) has revived what might well have been a forgotten contest, it was not because he desired to do so, but because reiterated accusations on the Benches opposite, backed up by the references of the right hon. Gentleman himself on the second reading of this Bill, gave him no choice whatever but to explain and defend—and, in my opinion, he has successfully defended—the action he then took. Well, I do not blame the right hon. Gentleman the Member for Derby for rising to defend Lord Spencer. I think he was bound to do so; but he need not be afraid that the example which he thinks may be of such serious import in future will have any bad effect upon the conduct of hon. Gentlemen below the Gangway opposite.

I am sure they do not require any leading in that direction. [*Loud cries of* "Oh!" *and* "Speak for yourself!"] I know I was not in Office a week before I was accused, and the Government I represent was also accused, of deliberately getting up outrages for the purpose of passing a Coercion Bill, and not only so, but I was deliberately charged by hon. Gentlemen in this House, and by people whom they represent, with having promoted murder. I hope that this incident may now be considered to have come to an end, an incident which I am bound to say was not provoked from this side of the House. I trust that the hon. and learned Gentleman (Mr. T. M. Healy) who has moved this Amendment will recollect, in the first place, that we have a great deal of work before us to-night, and also recollect, in the second place, that if his Amendment were carried it would have the effect of extending the operation of this clause, which he and his Friends have persistently opposed all along, to non-proclaimed districts—[Mr. T. M. HEALY: Ulster.]—to non-proclaimed districts, whether in Ulster or out of Ulster. And I would ask with what consistency they can really support an Amendment which has the effect of materially extending the clause, every sentence of which, every word of which, and every line of which they have opposed to the best of their ability? I hope hon. Gentlemen will now allow us to proceed to a Division upon this Amendment.

MR. W. E. GLADSTONE (Edinburgh, Mid Lothian): I must say that I marvel a little at the appeal of the right hon. Gentleman (Mr. A. J. Balfour) for a peaceable progress of this discussion, when he has himself by interfering in it done everything he can to widen the field and exasperate his opponents, and not for the first time, nor for the first time by a great many, in the course of the discussions on this Bill. I make no reply to the right hon. Gentleman; but I must refer to the speech of the right hon. and learned Gentleman the Attorney General for Ireland, which I heard with grave concern. It appears that the right hon. and learned Gentleman has done one thing in this House and another thing in Ireland. I was astonished, I must say, when I——

THE CHAIRMAN: Order, order! This discussion is travelling very wide

Mr. A. J. Balfour

of the Question before the Committee. The right hon. and learned Gentleman the Attorney General for Ireland made a reply to the hon. and learned Member for North Longford, and the right hon. Gentleman the Member for Derby has replied to the Attorney General for Ireland. I think it would be consistent with the course of Business if this subject were now allowed to drop.

MR. W. E. GLADSTONE: I can only express my regret that the Chief Secretary to the Lord Lieutenant chose to lengthen and prolong the discussion. I might, perhaps, have ascertained——

THE CHAIRMAN: I understood the right hon. Gentleman to say that he was not going to reply to the right hon. Gentleman the Chief Secretary for Ireland, but only to comment on the speech of the Attorney General for Ireland.

MR. COX (Clare, E.): May I ask the Attorney General for Ireland one question? He has given an explanation to-night, or an attempted explanation, of his speech at the Rotunda in Dublin. May I ask him to say how it was he came on the second reading of this Bill to declare he never made use of the expression which has been referred to?

MR. T. M. HEALY: I think it is not right that a wrong impression should go abroad on the matter raised by me. On the occasion in question a meeting took place in a purely Catholic district, and those who came in and were bayonetted by the police were men belonging to another county altogether. I admit I am trespassing on the indulgence of the Committee, but I think it is right I should be permitted to explain. I will not trouble the Committee by going to a Division if I am allowed to explain, and in that way it is possible 10 minutes of the time of the Committee will be saved. The meeting was held at Dromore, County Tyrone, and the man who was killed came from Portadown, County Armagh. Lord Spencer permitted the meeting to take place in the middle of a Catholic district, and what he was blamed by the Attorney General for Ireland for doing was this— that when interlopers from another county 100 miles away, having had their train fares paid by the Orange Society, said they meant to upset the meeting. he did not proclaim the meeting. Giffen, the man who was killed and whose blood, according to the Attorney General for Ireland, was on the head of Lord Spencer, was proved to be something in the linen trade, and to have come by his death 100 miles away from his place of birth and work. In the face of the declaration of the Attorney General for Ireland in regard to this Amendment, I certainly do not feel myself warranted in taking a Division. I take note, however, and the people of Ireland will also take note, of the declaration of Her Majesty's Government, that they will punish the perpetrators of all crimes in Ireland; that they will hold inquiries into crimes, irrespective of whether they are committed under Orange auspices or not. I will rest satisfied, for the present at any rate, or until I see a reason to change my mind, with that declaration, and under the circumstances I ask leave to withdraw my Amendment.

Amendment, by leave, *withdrawn.*

MR. T. M. HEALY (Longford, N.): I beg to move the next Amendment standing in my name.

Amendment proposed,

In page 2, line 4, after "criminal," insert "except with the consent of the witness under examination, no person other than the magistrate and his shorthand clerk shall be present at such inquiry."—(*Mr. T. M. Healy.*)

Question proposed, "That those words be there inserted."

THE ATTORNEY GENERAL (Sir RICHARD WEBSTER) (Isle of Wight): The Committee will remember that the Government have accepted an Amendment to the effect that the Resident Magistrate holding the inquiry under this section should himself conduct the inquiry, and should not permit any person to question or examine the witness. What is now proposed is that no person should be in the room except the magistrate and the shorthand clerk. It is quite possible to conceive that there will be times when it will be necessary for the magistrate to communicate with others; indeed, it would be impossible to conduct an inquiry if the magistrate has not some means of communicating with persons concerned. Her Majesty's Government cannot possibly accept an Amendment of this kind.

MR. CHANCE (Kilkenny, S.): When it comes to a question of badgering a witness, or of obtaining publicity of an official character, a policeman and others can be brought in. I admit there is a certain amount of reason in the objection taken to this Amendment—namely, that during an examination it may be necessary for the magistrate to consult with others. But it seems to me that it would be only reasonable, under such circumstances, to suspend the examination for a few minutes. Perhaps the Government may be inclined to accept the Amendment if it were made to read— "Present during such actual examination."

MR. T. M. HEALY: I think it is reasonable we should ask that the landlord or his agent should not be present during the inquiry. These inquiries will be aimed at so-called conspiracies; and, therefore, it will be most unreasonable to allow the landlord to be present. Will the Government accept the Amendment with any modification? Allow the police to be present, if you like; but will you keep out the local Bench of Magistrates, who, of course, will be the landlord and agent? Will the Government make us any concession in the matter?

THE ATTORNEY GENERAL FOR IRELAND (Mr. HOLMES) (Dublin University): It must be quite evident to hon. Gentlemen below the Gangway that certain officials must be present.

MR. T. M. HEALY: Will the Government accept the words—"No person other than the magistrate and official persons?" That will get over the difficulty. The Chief Secretary to the Lord Lieutenant is in his place. I think he ought to lubricate this Committee by a little concession.

THE CHIEF SECRETARY FOR IRELAND (Mr. A. J. BALFOUR) (Manchester, E.): I have no objection to that.

Amendment proposed to the proposed Amendment, to leave out "his shorthand clerk," and insert "other official persons."—(*Mr. T. M. Healy.*)

Question, "That the words 'his shorthand clerk' stand part of the proposed Amendment," put, and *negatived.*

Question, "That the words 'other official persons' be there inserted," put, and *agreed to.*

Question, "That those words, as amended, be there inserted," put, and *agreed to.*

MR. T. M. HEALY (Longford, N.): I beg to move Amendment No. 100.

[Seventh Night.]

Amendment proposed,

To add after the Amendment last adopted, "Before beginning the examination of any witness the magistrate shall read to him the words of this section."—(*Mr. T. M. Healy.*)

Question proposed, "That those words be there inserted."

THE ATTORNEY GENERAL FOR IRELAND (Mr. HOLMES) (Dublin University): Surely it is not wise that this clause should be unduly long.

MR. T. M. HEALY: I withdraw the Amendment.

Amendment, by leave, *withdrawn.*

MR. T. M. HEALY (Longford, N.): I now move the next Amendment standing in my name.

Amendment proposed,

To add after the Amendment last adopted, the words "reasonable adjournment shall be granted to any witness who shall apply for same in order to consult his legal advisers."— (*Mr. T. M. Healy.*)

Question proposed, "That those words be there inserted."

THE ATTORNEY GENERAL (Sir RICHARD WEBSTER) (Isle of Wight): The Committee will remember that we have discussed, on two or three occasions, the desirability of a witness having a counsel or solicitor present at the inquiry. The Committee negatived the suggestion; and, therefore, it is clear that if they adopted this Amendment they would simply stultify themselves.

SIR CHARLES RUSSELL (Hackney, S.): The hon. and learned Gentleman should understand that what is asked for is a reasonable adjournment. The Resident Magistrate will be the Judge in the matter, and if he is of opinion there is no ground for the adjournment asked for he will not grant it.

MR. T. M. HEALY: I hope the Government will agree. that the word "reasonable" really governs this matter. The Amendment will leave the matter in the hands of the Resident Magistrate. If he does not think an adjournment reasonable, he will refuse it. The Government might fairly entrust their agent with the power to grant an adjournment. Surely the Government will admit that a man should be allowed some little time within which to consult his friends or a solicitor. The police will have him under surveillance the whole of the time.

MR. MAURICE HEALY (Cork): I think this is the very least concession

we can ask. We asked that a witness should be protected by having a counsel or solicitor present, and the Government refused that. Then we asked that before a witness is committed to prison under this section, he should have the right to be heard by counsel or solicitor, and the Government refused that. Now, we ask the very lowest form of protection that a witness can get, and that is that if a difficulty arises and a witness finds himself embarrassed, he should, before the inquiry proceeds further, have an opportunity of taking advice. It is hard to see what the Government can say against such a proposition. It is perfectly idle to say it would in any way frustrate the inquiry, or baffle the course of justice. The matter is left absolutely in the discretion of the Resident Magistrate; he can say what is reasonable and what is not; in his hands the whole matter rests. The granting of a reasonable adjournment cannot, in any way, seriously interfere with the holding of the inquiry. Unless a witness is to be wholly and absolutely at the mercy of the official holding the inquiry, the Government must insert some Amendment of this kind.

MR. T. M. HEALY: The Government made me a little concession some time ago; if they will not accept this Amendment, I will not detain the Committee by pressing it further.

Amendment, by leave, *withdrawn.*

MR. T. M. HEALY: Will the Government now insert the words they propose?

THE CHIEF SECRETARY FOR IRELAND (Mr. A. J. BALFOUR): Yes; I beg to move to insert the following words as a new sub-section:—

"A witness who is examined under this section shall not be required to answer any question which he might legally refuse to answer on the ground of privilege if he were examined as a witness at the trial of an accused person."

Question, "That those words be there inserted," put, and *agreed to.*

MR. MAURICE HEALY (Cork): The Amendments 104 and 105 have been already decided. I therefore beg to move No. 106—namely, to insert the words—

"An inquiry under this section shall not be held on Sunday, Good Friday, or Christmas Day."

I presume it is not necessary to expatiate upon the Amendment. Let us have a close time for witnesses.

Amendment proposed, to add, after the Amendment last adopted—

"(4.) An inquiry under this section shall not be held on Sunday, Good Friday, or Christmas Day."—(*Mr. Maurice Healy.*)

Question proposed, "That those words be there inserted."

THE ATTORNEY GENERAL FOR IRELAND (Mr. HOLMES) (Dublin University): The Government cannot assent to this Amendment, because we can well understand that an inquiry may be urgent. I have a very strong opinion that if there had been power to hold an inquiry the morning after the Phœnix Park murders, and thus to examine the persons who were known to be in the Park on the day of the murders, the offenders would have been discovered earlier. If a day or week is allowed to pass before an inquiry is held into the circumstances of a crime, we might just as well allow four or five months to transpire.

MR. MAURICE HEALY: I cannot agree with the right hon. and learned Gentleman that any case can possibly arise in which the lapse of a day would make an enormous difference in the discovery of the perpetrators of a crime. He has one class of case in mind, and we have another. We have a case in mind in which respectable witnesses may, under this section, be harassed and annoyed by being brought away from their homes at all times and seasons. Now, no legal act can be done on Sunday, and no legal offices are open on Sunday either in England or Ireland. It is not reasonable that witnesses should be dragged away from their homes on such days as mentioned in the Amendment, and I do not think the Government are acting at all reasonably in opposing the Amendment.

MR. T. M. HEALY: Even a Tory Parliament, during the famine in 1848, provided that no eviction should take place on Good Friday.

Question put, and *negatived*.

MR. WARMINGTON (Monmouth, W.): I beg leave, in page 2, line 4, at the end, to insert—

"Every person examined under this section shall be entitled, on demand made to the clerk of the court before which the examination is held, and on payment of the usual charges, to have delivered to him a copy of his examination."

It seems to me only fair that a man who has been examined, and may be put upon his trial, should have before him an authentic copy of the statements he himself has made, so that he may know the charges he has to meet.

Amendment proposed,

In page 2, line 4, at the end, insert—" Every person examined under this section shall be entitled, on demand made to the clerk of the court before which the examination is held, and on payment of the usual charges, to have delivered to him a copy of his examination."
—(*Mr. Warmington.*)

Question proposed, "That those words be there inserted."

THE ATTORNEY GENERAL (Sir RICHARD WEBSTER) (Isle of Wight): I think my hon. and learned Friend should remember that the acceptance of this Amendment would enable an improper use to be made of a witness's examination. We have already decided that an accused person respecting whom an inquiry under this section has been held, or his solicitor, shall, upon his return for trial, be supplied with copies of all depositions taken at any inquiry under this section of any witnesses to be called against him. But now my hon. Friend proposes that every person examined under this section shall be entitled to a copy of his examination. That would put an end altogether to the privacy and secrecy of the inquiry, because everything a man had said would be put into his hands. I do not see how such information could be of any use to a witness. He knows what he has said, and what statements, if any, can be charged against him; and I do not see what could be the object of giving him a copy of his examination.

MR. O'DOHERTY (Donegal, N.): I think the hon. and learned Member the Attorney General does not quite appreciate the object with which this Amendment is brought forward. It seems to me only desirable that a witness should have an opportunity of correcting the shorthand notes, seeing the danger there is of a charge of perjury being brought against him. I think that it is extremely desirable that a copy of his examination should be supplied to the witness from that point of view. Of course, the statement would only be sent or supplied to the man who had been examined. Supposing there were several witnesses, they would not receive copies of each other's examinations, but each would receive a copy of his own examination. Even if a witness choose to publish his statement, I do not see what objection there could be to his doing so—I do not see how it could affect any other person. He could tell what his examination had been by word of mouth; and what harm could there be in putting forward an absolutely correct statement? It seems to me desirable that a witness should have a copy of the shorthand writer's transcript of his examination, in order that, if necessary, he might make corrections. He should be allowed to do that for the purpose of preventing mistakes. We all know that shorthand writers, however expert, are always apt to make mistakes in transcribing their notes. No harm would arise from sending a draft of a witness's examination to that witness for correction. I would suggest that perhaps it would be well to allow the witness to return to the Court for the purpose of making such correction. My contention is that no person would be safe if, on an incorrect copy of evidence given by him by word of mouth in a secret inquiry, he is to be open subsequently to a charge of perjury in respect of what may appear in a transcript of a shorthand writer's notes. The matter upon which he is charged might possibly be owing to the mistake of a clerk, or the shorthand writer who had taken down the notes of his evidence.

MR. T. M. HEALY (Longford, N.): In all cases of inquiry in Magisterial Courts depositions are read over to the witnesses, and signed by them. In this clause, however, we have no provision for the reading over of depositions to the witnesses. I would ask the Government to make some provision for that being done.

SIR WILLIAM HARCOURT(Derby): I think that is a very reasonable suggestion. It appears to me to be only just and reasonable that a witness should have an opportunity of verifying the accuracy of the report of his examination.

THE ATTORNEY GENERAL FOR IRELAND (Mr. HOLMES) (Dublin University): I would point out to the Committee that as the matter originally stood in our clause the wording adopted was different. We said the magistrate might "take the deposition of such

witness;" but it was suggested that the word "statement" would be better than "deposition." The word "deposition" would imply that the evidence should be read over and signed by the witness; but I do not know that the same can be said of the word "statement." However, we will undertake to consider the matter, and introduce such words as will insure that the witness's evidence shall be read over and signed.

MR. T. M. HEALY: The right hon. and learned Gentleman is mistaken in saying that the word "deposition" has been omitted, and replaced by the word "statement." In the first part of this clause we have "and shall take the statement of such witness," and towards the end of the 1st section we have words amongst which the word "deposition" occurs. It will, therefore, be seen that the word "deposition" was left out in one place, and put in in another.

MR. HOLMES: The word "statement" was inserted.

MR. T. M. HEALY: But, as I pointed out, the word "deposition" was still left in the section. We have agreed to the following Proviso:—

"Provided also, that upon any person being accused of a crime respecting which an inquiry under this section has been held, such accused person or his solicitor, upon being returned for trial, shall forthwith be supplied with copies of all depositions taken at any inquiry under this section of any witnesses to be called against him."

MR. HOLMES: We will see that the alteration I have referred to is made on Report.

MR. J. O'CONNOR (Tipperary, S.): We have provided in the 1st section of this clause that a magistrate may bind a witness in his own recognizances to appear and give evidence at the next Petty Sessions, or when called upon within three months of the date of such recognizances. Well, unless a witness is supplied with copies of his depositions, there may be discrepancies between his public evidence and the statement taken before the private inquiry, and then he would be liable to a charge of perjury.

THE CHAIRMAN: Does the hon. and learned Member (Mr. Warmington) withdraw his Amendment?

MR. WARMINGTON: I understand that the Government now propose that the examination shall be read over to the witness, and signed by him. That being so—as the right hon. and learned

Mr. O'Doherty

Gentleman undertakes to introduce amending words into the Bill—I withdraw my Amendment.

Amendment, by leave, *withdrawn.*

MR. T. M. HEALY: I beg to move the insertion in page 2, line 6, after "offence," of the words, "or who has read the depositions taken at such examination." It is provided in the 4th sub-section of this clause that the magistrate who conducts the examination shall not take part in the hearing and determination of the charge concerning any offence which has been inquired into, and shall not, if such offence is an indictable offence, take part in the committing for trial of such person for such offence. Now, it appears to me that not only the magistrate who conducts this examination should be placed under this disability, but that magistrates who have read the depositions taken at the examination should be included in the category. It seems to me to be the same thing to conduct the examination, and to know how the examination has been conducted. Any magistrate who reads over the depositions will come subsequently to the trial with the same idea of the prisoner as he would have had if he had been conducting the examination. It appears to me that the magistrate who hears and determines the charge, and takes part in the committing for trial, should come to the consideration of the case with a virgin mind. I think that the Government will see that my suggestion in this matter is a fair and reasonable one, especially when it is remembered that we are not dealing with what are properly speaking crimes, but only agrarian matters. If a magistrate comes to the consideration of a Boycotting case with his mind poisoned through reading over all the depositions, he will, under the circumstances, have already prejudged the case. I trust the Government will exclude from the Bench, not only the persons who hold these inquiries, but anyone who knows anything about them. In conducting a trial, the Government, by their solicitor or counsel, will have these depositions in their hands, and I should think that would be quite sufficient for them, without wishing to have the case decided by a magistrate whose mind is already poisoned against the prisoner.

Amendment proposed, in page 2, line 6, after "offence," insert "or who has read the depositions taken at such examination."—(*Mr. T. M. Healy.*)

Question proposed, "That those words be there inserted."

THE ATTORNEY GENERAL FOR IRELAND (Mr. HOLMES) (Dublin University): I am afraid it will be impossible for the Government to accept the Amendment.

MR. T. M. HEALY: I am sorry the right hon. and learned Gentleman is unable to accept this, as I considered it a very hopeful Amendment. However, as I should not be likely to be successful in pressing it, I will withdraw it.

Amendment, by leave, *withdrawn.*

Amendment proposed,

In page 2, line 10, after "offence," insert "or the hearing or determining summarily, or the taking depositions against or committing for trial of any person charged, either in conjunction with such person or separately, as principal or accessory in the commission of such offence."—(*Mr. T. M. Healy.*)

Question proposed, "That those words be there inserted."

THE ATTORNEY GENERAL FOR IRELAND (Mr. HOLMES) (Dublin University): We could not accept this Amendment.

Amendment, by leave, *withdrawn.*

MR. T. M. HEALY (Longford, N.): I beg now to move the following Amendment:—In page 2, line 10, after "offence," insert—

"An accused person may require any magistrate, before whom he is summoned, to state upon oath that he is not within the prohibitions of this sub-section.

"The rules of evidence shall apply to examinations under this section, and leading questions shall not be put, but, if put, need not be answered.

"Any person committed under this section shall have the right of appeal to the next going Judge of Assize, and shall not be imprisoned pending appeal."

I would ask the Government whether, in the case of a committal of a prisoner, they do not mean to give him some appeal beyond the bringing of an action against the magistrate, which would be a very expensive process, and one that a poor peasant would be unable to afford? I think a person committed should have power to appeal in order to see whether the committal was reasonable or not. The appeal may not be to Judges of Assize; but, at any rate, let it be to some tribunal or other.

Amendment proposed,

In page 2, line 10, after "offence," insert—
"an accused person may require any magistrate before whom he is summoned to state upon oath that he is not within the prohibitions of this sub-section.
"The rules of evidence shall apply to examinations under this section, and leading questions shall not be put, but, if put, need not be answered.
"Any person committed under this section shall have the right of appeal to the next going Judge of Assize, and shall not be imprisoned pending appeal."—(*Mr. T. M. Healy.*)

Question proposed, "That those words be there inserted."

THE ATTORNEY GENERAL FOR IRELAND (Mr. HOLMES) (Dublin University): I do not think it will be possible to show, on any principle of our law, that a person should have a right of appeal on a question of contempt. The Committee, in cases of this kind, must depend upon the discretion of the person holding the inquiry.

MR. T. M. HEALY: The right hon. and learned Gentleman may not have heard of an appeal on a question of contempt; but he has heard, no doubt, that under the Bankruptcy Law there was an appeal as to whether a question put at an examination of a witness, for refusing to answer which that witness was commanded, was a proper question or not. The appeal was conducted in the case I refer to under the form of a Habeas Corpus, which was a very expensive one. That is a process which it would be well to avoid in connection with proceedings under this Bill. The Government say that commitments under the existing law for contempt are without provision for appeal, but I would remind them that they are not now dealing with the existing law. I think it very necessary that an appeal should be given in cases under this clause, because the Resident Magistrates may act very stupidly, and may make serious mistakes. I submit that it would be a great saving of time and trouble to grant this appeal. It would be a saving of time to the Lord Lieutenant himself and to this House, as I will show. If no appeal of the kind is allowed, if the magistrate has

Mr. T. M. Healy

acted wrongfully, the prisoner will send up his memorial to the Lord Lieutenant, and the result will be that we, in this House, shall question the Chief Secretary, who may say that these things are in the hands of the Courts of Law, and that the Executive cannot deal with them. We know that that will be the course of events—we have all these things off by heart. If you allow the appeal you will save this round about process, and the result will be much more satisfactory to everyone concerned. I would press this Amendment upon the Government in the hope that they may see their way to promise us something. If they like, let the appeal go to the County Court Judge. I admit that the Judge of Assize would be the better tribunal; but he does not sit probably often enough to render reference to him convenient. He only holds his Assizes once every four months, and to appeal to him would necessarily cause considerable delay. That, however, would not be the case if the appeal were granted to the County Court Judge, who sits very much oftener. I do not feel by any means the same amount of satisfaction with the discretion of the Resident Magistrate as does the right hon. and learned Gentleman opposite. I trust that some appeal will be given against the discretion of these gentlemen, particularly when we remember that 70 out of 80 of them are half-pay officers, and know nothing about law.

MR. ARTHUR O'CONNOR (Donegal, E.): It must be remembered that all commitments for contempt in England and Ireland have hitherto necessarily taken place in open Court. They will not take place in open Court, however, under this Bill. In England it has always been recognized that a Judge hearing a case *in camerâ* cannot commit for contempt of Court. Under this clause you will have cases heard *in camerâ*, and you propose to give a power which is altogether unknown to the law. Under these circumstances, it appears to me to be altogether beside the mark to say that you cannot interfere with the discretion of the magistrate in committing for contempt.

MR. MAURICE HEALY (Cork): There is not the smallest analogy to be drawn between the commitment under this clause and commitment under the ordinary law. Under the ordinary law a commitment takes place during the course of an action, and the fact of a witness being committed for contempt does not prevent the case being concluded. Evidence will be given by other parties, the Judge will arrive at an opinion, the suit will terminate, and in a short time, and as the case has come to an end, the person committed will be discharged. But the commitment under this Bill will be altogether different. The answer the witness refuses to give will probably go to the root of the whole inquiry, and the offence will go on indefinitely, because you have no such termination as you would have in the case of an action between two parties. It is altogether misleading the Committee to pretend that there is any analogy between the existing law and this clause.

Question put, and *negatived.*

MR. MAURICE HEALY (Cork): I wish to know if the Government will accept the Amendment which stands next on the Paper in my name?

Amendment proposed,

In page 2, line 10, after "offence," insert— "(5) In case any witness examined under this section shall not speak English, the interpreter employed shall not be a policeman or other person in the service of the Crown otherwise than as an interpreter."—(*Mr. Maurice Healy.*)

Question proposed, "That those words be there inserted."

THE CHIEF SECRETARY FOR IRELAND (Mr. A. J. BALFOUR)(Manchester, E.): Yes; the Government are prepared to accept the Amendment down to the word "policeman." Inconvenience would arise from the adoption of the remaining part of the Amendment.

Question,

"That the words '(5) In case any witness examined under this section shall not speak English, the interpreter employed shall not be a policeman' be there inserted,"

—put, and *agreed to.*

MR. MAURICE HEALY (Cork): The next Amendment is in my name. It is a very important Amendment, and one that I hope the Committee will agree to. In the course of the administration of the Crimes Act, the gravest charges were brought against the Resident Magistrates. Witnesses

who were brought up were browbeaten and intimidated; all species of threats were thrown out against them, and pecuniary inducements to a very large amount were offered to them if they would only give that class of evidence which would suit the authorities who examined them. I think a state of things like that is a very great evil, and I think that such a danger is one that we ought to guard against when we are establishing this machinery. I do not imagine that the Government will defend the practice of either threatening witnesses with any kind of legal consequences or of holding out pecuniary inducements to them to give evidence of a particular kind. There is a danger that something of the kind may happen, therefore I think some safeguard should be adopted.

Amendment proposed,

In page 2, line 10, after "offence," insert —"(5) A resident magistrate holding an inquiry under this section shall not induce, or attempt to induce, any witness examined thereat to give evidence by any promise of pecuniary or other reward, or by any threat or menace, and any resident; magistrate acting in contravention of this provision shall be guilty of a misdemeanour."—(*Mr. Maurice Healy.*)

Question proposed, "That these words be there inserted."

THE ATTORNEY GENERAL (Sir RICHARD WEBSTER) (Isle of Wight): I think that if magistrates were to be guilty of such practices as are suggested by the hon. Member in his Amendment they would commit a very grave offence. I must be allowed distinctly to point out that, whatever the views of hon. Members opposite with regard to Resident Magistrates may be, we emphatically decline to frame this Bill on the assumption that those persons who will have to administer it are going to be guilty of gross misconduct, such as bribery, menace, and things of that kind. We are framing this Bill on the assumption that those persons who will have to administer it will, at any rate, do their duty honestly, so far as this kind of charge is concerned, and that they will not be guilty of corruption. If they should be guilty of corruption or other improper proceedings they will bring themselves within the range of the law, and no doubt will receive adequate

[*Seventh Night.*]

punishment; but we must decline to insert in this measure any words that would presume that the magistrates are likely to be guilty of misconduct.

MR. T. M. HEALY (Longford, N.): The speech of the hon. and learned Gentleman the Attorney General is a very noble speech no doubt. Nothing strikes me more forcibly than the way in which the Government suppose that every one of their subordinates is a most admirable person, never likely to do wrong. Of course, the way in which the English people have won their liberty is to be always admiring their Sovereigns; to be bowing down before them at all times, and worshipping them as angelic beings; and this House of Commons has won its position, I suppose, as a temple of liberty, and the whole Constitution has been framed on the principle that the King can do no wrong, and neither can any of his Ministers. We have had a Return presented to us with regard to the Resident Magistrates of Ireland. We have seen who they are. Hon. Members on the Conservative side of the House have not read that Return, and there is nothing to be surprised at in that, because we know from Mr. Disraeli that the aristocratic Party in this country never read anything. Even if they have taken to reading, it is too much to assume that they have read a Return relating to Ireland. When we know that at the inquiries held under the Crimes Act every witness was either bribed or bullied, or sought to be bribed or bullied, it is rather too much to tell us that, under a Conservative *régime*, the state of things will be very much better than it was under the Liberal *régime*. I am sorry the right hon. and learned Gentleman the Home Secretary (Mr. Matthews) is not in his place. [*Interruption.*] I think that if hon. Members who insist on preparing their letters for *The Times* audibly in this House would go out into the Lobby and do it there, it would be much more convenient. I say, I am sorry that the Home Secretary for England is not in his place. He has abandoned as a portion of the system of thief-catching or criminal-catching the offering of rewards. That practice was relinquished by the Liberal Home Secretary, and the Tory Home Secretary has followed the example. Well, while

you will not offer bribes in England in order to bring about the detection of criminals, in Ireland, where the people have no confidence in your administration of justice, you still practise corruption, and hold out bribes to the people to give evidence. Now, in England, the classes and the masses are not divided in so keen a way as they are in Ireland, yet you have found it necessary to abandon altogether a portion of your system of police administration here. In Ireland you ask us to say that the magistrates are such admirable persons that there is no foundation for the idea that any possible suspicion could rest upon them. All I can say is, that the Government will soon find out, by a system of criticism in this House, that their magistrates in Ireland are not the perfect persons they suppose them to be. Then, I have no doubt we shall see letters in *The Times* complaining that not only have we, the Irish Members, exhaustively discussed the Bill in its birth, but continue to discuss it after it has become law. So that not only are we occupying time with this Bill now, but a great deal of time may be wasted in the future in discussing matters relating to it, if you refuse to give us such proper Amendments as this we are now asking for. Unless this appeal is granted, we may have hereafter to call attention to the abuse of the discretionary powers granted to the Resident Magistrates, and an endless series of letters may have to be written to that excellent newspaper *The Times.*

MR. GEDGE (Stockport): If all that the hon. and learned Member opposite says were perfectly true, even then there would be no occasion for accepting this Amendment. If the object of the examination were to bring a person to a conviction by means of false evidence, then it is conceivable that the magistrates might offer rewards to get that false evidence; but as the object of the inquiry is preliminary, to enable the magistrates to get further facts to bring criminals to justice, and as none of the facts can be used against the person who gives the evidence, it is clear that nothing will be more likely to defeat the ends of the examination than for the magistrates to get evidence by means of bribes. They want facts, not fictions, which would be useless for their purpose. It seems to

Sir Richard Webster

me that this is an utterly useless Amendment, and that, therefore, it ought to be rejected.

MR. EDWARD HARRINGTON (Kerry, W.) : The hon. Gentleman who has just sat down does not know anything about the Irish Resident Magistrates. He does not know what they have done; he is not as familiar with their filthy work as we are. But we know what disreputable methods they have adopted, and we it is who know how they have been promoted for such work. There is a certain Resident Magistrate who worked the secret inquiry business in Ireland, and one of his favourite stories over the dinner table was, how, when he was conducting the inquiry, he had beside him a pile of sovereigns covered by a table cloth, and how he used occasionally to lift up a corner of the cloth in order to let the witness see the money in the hope that it would operate on his cupidity. A Resident Magistrate is elevated to the position of a County Court Judge. I could give a number of instances in which these matters have been brought up in the public Press at the time they occurred, and the magistrates, in place of being censured, have been rewarded. It is our experience of the past that causes us to make this protest. This Amendment is certainly one upon which we are justified in taking a Division.

MR. J. O'CONNOR (Tipperary, S.) : The hon. Gentleman opposite (Mr. Gedge) can scarcely be acquainted with the discussions which have taken place in this House in relation to this question. Has the hon. Gentleman ever heard of the Barbavilla case—a case which has been worked up close to the wind? Does he not know that the Government officials have boasted, and praised each other for working cases close to the wind? Our experience is that it is not for the purpose of ascertaining facts that these inquiries are held, but for the purpose of procuring, if necessary, false evidence. Not only have public officials in Ireland sought to procure false evidence, but they have been known to suppress the truth, when the truth contradicts statements that have been already made in secret inquiries. Not only is it by bullying that magistrates in Ireland seek to procure false testimony, but it is also by holding out the probability of the witness, who does not do

as they wish, being sent away to the Cape of Good Hope or to Australia, or some other remote part of Her Majesty's Dominions. It is in order to put it out of the power of these unscrupulous magistrates either to bully or to bribe that this Amendment has been proposed, and I trust the Government will accept it.

MR. MAURICE HEALY (Cork) : No doubt it is because the Irish officials present know a little about the matter that the hon. and learned Attorney General for England (Sir Richard Webster) was put up to reply to this Amendment. One would imagine that, after the whitewashing they have received, the Irish Resident Magistrates would be the most immaculate body of men on earth. Our experience is that, notwithstanding the severe process of purification they have gone through, they are still as black as they can well be. I admit it is a serious thing for Members of the House to suggest that Government officials are capable of the conduct we attribute to the Resident Magistrates of Ireland; but I can assure right hon. Gentlemen opposite, and especially English right hon. Gentlemen who are not familar with the devious ways of Irish administration, that there is good reason to believe that our fears and suspicions are well founded. Some two or three years ago I was concerned in a political libel case. An Irish journal was indicted for what is called a " seditious " libel, and one of the strongest passages in that libel was one in which the Government were charged with the very malpractice suggested in this Amendment—namely, that of offering large rewards to witnesses for the purpose of obtaining evidence. The general rule is, that the person charged in a case of libel is not allowed to justify or to prove the truth of the libel; but it was suggested by one of the counsel concerned that, under one section of the Newspaper Libel Act, it was possible that evidence of the truth of the charges made in the article might be allowed. To enable my client to give such evidence, it was necessary I should make some inquiries as to what took place at one of the secret inquiries. At the hearing of the case I was prepared to offer the evidence of 10 or 20 witnesses, every one of whom had been brought up at an inquiry, every one of whom had been

[*Seventh Night.*]

threatened, bullied, browbeaten, and intimidated in the manner pointed out in the article, and nearly every one of whom had been offered money rewards in consideration of giving evidence. In the face of these facts, I can assure right hon. Gentlemen opposite it is quite out of our power to accept these statements as to the character of Irish Resident Magistrates.

MR. MOLLOY (King's Co., Birr): I understand that the Attorney General (Sir Richard Webster) objects to this Amendment, because it casts a slur upon the Resident Magistrates of Ireland. I can quite understand him taking the course he does, if he really thinks the Amendment amounts to a slur upon the Resident Magistrates, some of whom are the nominees of his own Government. But the object of this Amendment is simply to lay down a strict rule which those magistrates shall observe. The Attorney General can only object to the wording of the Amendment; if he would word the Amendment in such a way that it would not, in his opinion, cast a slur upon these magistrates, and still give us the benefit of the Amendment as it stands, we shall be perfectly satisfied.

Question put, and *negatived*.

MR. MURPHY (Dublin, St. Patrick's): I beg to move Amendment No. 114b which stands in my name.

Amendment proposed,

In page 2, line 10, after "offence," insert— "The Lord Lieutenant shall cause to be published in *The Dublin Gazette*, once in every month, a Return of all persons who have been committed to prison at any inquiry held under this section, and who may be still detained in prison, on a date one week preceding each such publication. Such Return shall contain the name, address, and description of each prisoner, together with the date of his commitment, and the cause of committal, and, if he was subsequently brought up for examination, the date on which he was last remanded." — (*Mr. Murphy.*)

Question proposed, "That those words be there inserted."

THE ATTORNEY GENERAL FOR IRELAND (Mr. HOLMES) (Dublin University): The Government cannot assent to prepare a monthly Return; but they are quite prepared to lay one upon the Table of the House at the opening of every Session of Parliament.

MR. MOLLOY (King's Co., Birr): I do not see what object there can be

in keeping these committals secret; indeed, the Government are prepared to make a Return yearly. But I should like to ask the Chief Secretary for Ireland what is the use of a Return presented at the beginning of each Session? Take the case of a man who has been committed to prison under this section —say, for three months. What can be the object of making a Return of his committal nine months afterwards? This is not a matter which affects the principle or the working of the Bill; and, therefore, I think that we ought to have a Return presented at least once a month.

THE CHIEF SECRETARY FOR IRELAND (Mr. A. J. BALFOUR) (Manchester, E.): The hon. Gentleman (Mr. Molloy) will see it is no protection to the prisoner at all that a Return should be presented monthly, quarterly, or yearly. The protection to be given is that Parliament should have some knowledge of the working of the section, and that knowledge would be obtained from a Return presented yearly.

MR. T. M. HEALY: It is our opinion that witnesses would find very substantial protection in the knowledge by the British public of what was going on. I do feel the Government might reasonably agree not to exclude even from the knowledge of the Primrose Dames the number of persons who are committed to gaol under this section. This is an Amendment which does not at all touch the principle of the clause. It only provides that information should be given to the country. If the Government will not give a Return monthly, will they do it quarterly?

MR. BRADLAUGH (Northampton): I venture to appeal to the Government, as I understand them to be practically making a concession in this matter, not to make it in a grudging fashion. The preparation of this Return cannot be a serious matter; therefore, why waste time as to the number of times it shall be presented?

MR. A. J. BALFOUR: I trust the hon. Gentleman (Mr. Murphy) will not persevere with this Amendment. This Return has never been introduced in any Bill of this kind. [Mr. T. M. HEALY: Yes; Forster's Act.] We shall make a Return yearly, and will put Parliament in full possession of all that Parliament really wants to know. If other Returns are wanted, hon. Members can, of course, move for them.

Mr. BRADLAUGH: I only speak from memory; but I think that a Return was laid on the Table under the Act of 1881.

Mr. COX (Clare, E.): Will the right hon. Gentleman tell the Committee that such Returns as are now asked for were not issued quarterly under the Act of 1881, and published in *The Dublin Gazette*, and from that copied in all the Irish newspapers? It is quite clear that the Government wish to make Bastiles of the Irish gaols.

Mr. T. M. HEALY: Perhaps I may enlighten the Committee upon this point. Mr. Forster's Act, I see, provided that a list of persons for the time being detained in prison under it, with a statement of each person's name, address, and prison in which he was detained, and the ground of the warrant, should be laid before Parliament in the course of the first seven days of every month when Parliament was sitting, and should be published in *The Dublin Gazette*, when Parliament was not sitting, in the course of the first seven days of every month.

Mr. M. J. KENNY (Tyrone, Mid): The Chief Secretary to the Lord Lieutenant of Ireland (Mr. A. J. Balfour) says this is no protection for prisoners who are arrested. He is labouring under a mistake. It is not many years ago when a man named Casey was four years in gaol, and was altogether forgotten. It is quite possible that even now a Resident Magistrate might run a man into gaol, and then find some reason to forget him. I think it is as well that the Return asked for should be published in *The Dublin Gazette*. Papers which are laid on the Table of the House are generally forgotten; whereas if they are published in *The Dublin Gazette* they are immediately copied into the general Press of the country, and they attract attention. I can quite understand why this Government does not wish the proceedings of the Resident Magistrates to be published; but I think, seeing that there is a precedent for the making of this Return—namely, a similar provision to this in Mr. Forster's Act of 1881, the Government should now accept the Amendment before the Committee.

Mr. MAURICE HEALY (Cork): I should like to know what is the real reason of the attitude of the Government

upon this most reasonable Amendment? Upon what ground can they refuse it? The publication cannot do any conceivable harm. The right hon. and learned Gentleman the Attorney General for Ireland says that he will give us an annual Return. What is the meaning of that? It means that he will inform the public of the number of persons who have been arrested under this clause; but he will inform them of it when the people have got out of gaol. That is the real meaning of the offer of the Government; because it is inconceivable they should keep any man in gaol, under this clause, for so long as twelve months. The inevitable result of merely publishing this information in the form of a Parliamentary Return is that nine out of every ten men whose names will be contained in the Return will have been long since released. The Chief Secretary has said that witnesses will find a protection in the knowledge by Parliament of how this clause has been worked. We have no confidence whatever that this Parliament will make any effort to see that this clause is properly worked. Our hope is not in this House, but in the opinion of the masses of the British people; and it is in order to bring information home to them that we ask for this Return. The Government are carrying out a policy of suppression and concealment, and therefore are determined that this information shall not be given. It is our duty to see that the Committee is not misled by the illusory and, I might almost say, absurd suggestion of the right hon. and learned Gentleman the Attorney General for Ireland.

Mr. CHANCE (Kilkenny, S.): Under this section a magistrate has full power by day and by night to catch any unfortunate person who he thinks knows anything about an offence—drag him from one end of Ireland to the other, bring him before a secret Court without any publicity, and then, if he thinks proper, cast him into gaol. How is the prisoner to get his witness, when no one knows in what gaol he is lodged? If this Return is made once a month, it will be seen where a man is, and with what offence he is charged. It is quite evident that the Government desire that witnesses should have no opportunities afforded them of defending themselves. I trust the Committee will see that justice is done by these men.

[Seventh Night.]

Mr. MURPHY: The Government seem to decide, before they come down to the House, on what points they will make any concessions, and on what points they will refuse them. In this case they seem to have made up their minds under the impression that the Act of 1881 did not contain any provision of this sort. Now, Sir, as it has been shown that the Act of 1881 contained a provision substantially the same as that I now propose. I think the Government will be only consistent if they accept my Amendment.

Mr. O'DOHERTY (Donegal. N.): In any case *The Dublin Gazette* will have to be used for the purpose of publishing notices proclaiming districts. There, therefore, can be no reason whatever why the Government should not use *The Gazette* for the purpose of showing what persons have been sent to gaol under the section.

Mr. ROWNTREE (Scarborough): Surely it is a most modest and reasonable request that the country should be placed in a position to follow the working of this Act. If the Government will not consent to furnish us with this Return oftener than once a-year, I hope the Amendment will be pressed to a Division.

Sir WILLIAM HARCOURT (Derby): I trust we may be spared a Division. What objection can there be to the Government making this Return once a quarter? The object of the publication of the Return is to inform the public as to the working of the Act—an Act that is exceptional in its character, and in the working of which the people are naturally much interested. The Return will not be very voluminous; therefore, I trust the Government may at least consent to its being made once a quarter.

Mr. A. J. BALFOUR: It is suggested that we should insert in a permanent Act a provision for a quarterly Return. There is no reason why this Return should be made every quarter. When any hon. Gentleman thinks a Return is desirable, let him move for it. ["How can we during the Recess?"] Do not let us embody in the provisions of a permanent Statute anything so absurd and unnecessary as a quarterly Return.

Mr. T. P. O'CONNOR (Liverpool, Scotland): I appeal to the First Lord of the Treasury (Mr. W. H. Smith) to indulge in his favourite pastime, and to

close this discussion; but to do so by impressing on his Colleagues the desirability of making a concession upon such a small point as this. The right hon. Gentleman the Chief Secretary practically gives up the whole case, when he says this Return can be moved for. Why should we be put to the trouble of moving periodically for this Return? Why should the furnishing of a piece of information like this be at the mercy of any Member of the House who chooses to put down a block to the Motion for the Return? Why should the Government refuse to give us a Return? When we are told the Returns can be moved for when wanted, I would point out that it is quite customary to block official Returns, even of the most simple character. What I want to impress on the minds of the Committee is this—that the demand we make is in strict accordance with all the precedents. When Mr. Forster's Act was passed in 1881, a similar Return was provided for; but we do not press for a monthly Return; we should be quite satisfied with a quarterly one. I heard someone say that there were quarterly Returns under the Land Act, but that is contrary to my recollection, which is that the Returns were monthly under that Act. Does the Chief Secretary mean to say that there is no reason in what is going on in Ireland for such a Return? I am reminded of cases in which persons were sent to prison, and kept there for months and even years, until everybody seemed to have forgotten them. The hon. Member for Tyrone (Mr. M. J. Kenny) has drawn attention to a case in which a man was actually kept in prison for four years without anyone knowing of it except his nearest friends.

Mr. A. J. BALFOUR: The Government are willing to accept the Amendment, No. 130, which stands in the name of the hon. and learned Gentleman the Member for North Longford (Mr. T. M. Healy).

Mr. T. M. HEALY: I will just read to the Committee the section of the Act of 1881 which has been already referred to. The section provides that a Return shall be laid on the Table of the House every week while Parliament is sitting, and be published in *The Dublin Gazette* every month during the remainder of the year of all persons arrested under the Act.

MR. T. P. O'CONNOR: I understand the right hon. Gentleman the Chief Secretary to say that the Government accept the Amendment of my hon. and learned Friend the Member for North Longford, No. 130, which says—

"There shall be laid before Parliament, at the beginning of every Session, a Return showing the number of inquiries held since the preceding Session, the number of summonses issued, the number of witnesses examined, the names of, and the sentences on, the persons committed for contempt, and the result, if any, of each inquiry."

May I ask the right hon. and learned Attorney General for Ireland whether he has read this Amendment.

THE ATTORNEY GENERAL FOR IRELAND (Mr. HOLMES) (Dublin University): I have done so carefully.

MR. T. P. O'CONNOR: Will the right hon. and learned Gentleman allow me to point out that the Amendment of my hon. Friend (Mr. Murphy), and that of my other hon. and learned Friend (Mr. T. M. Healy) are essentially distinct. The first proposal is, that there should be a Return published every month, and it should be confined to persons who have been committed to prison under the Bill, while the Amendment of the hon. and learned Member for North Longford is that there shall be laid before Parliament at the beginning of every Session a Return showing the number of inquiries held since the preceding Session, the number of witnesses examined, the names of and the sentences on the persons committed for contempt, and the result, if any, of each inquiry. That is a totally distinct thing from the other proposal. The Committee ought to know definitely from the right hon. and learned Gentleman the Attorney General for Ireland what it is that the Government accept.

MR. HOLMES: The Government believing that something in the nature of the information asked for should be given, have looked over the Amendments on the Paper, and agreed to accept that of the hon. and learned Member for North Longford (Mr. T. M. Healy).

MR. J. E. ELLIS (Nottingham, Rushcliffe): I should like to ask the Government whether the Amendment of the hon. and learned Member for North Longford covers the period during which Parliament is in Session?

MR. A. J. BALFOUR: Yes; Certainly.

MR. T. W. RUSSELL (Tyrone, S.): I think the proposal is a most reasonable one, and I hope the Government will accept it.

MR. T. M. HEALY: The Government ought to bear in mind the case of Patrick Casey, who was imprisoned under the Westmeath Act. Although that man was unconvicted of any offence, he was kept in prison for four years. when, at length, Mr. Roebuck called attention to the case in Parliament, and the man was immediately released. That man had never been tried for any offence, and his release was granted by Mr. Disraeli's Government. What we want to do is to prevent the recurrence of such cases.

THE ATTORNEY GENERAL (Sir RICHARD WEBSTER) (Isle of Wight): What the hon. and learned Member opposite seems to think possible could never happen under the present Bill, because those who are sent to prison must be brought before the Court and questioned every eight days. Therefore, the prospect of their being allowed to languish in gaol, without ever being seen or heard of, is quite out of the question.

MR. BRADLAUGH: There is no reason, that I can see, which would justify the Government in refusing the Amendment. As was the case in 1881, Parliament, in giving power to commit men to gaol under this clause, naturally wants to know how that power is exercised. I cannot understand why the Government waste the time of the Committee in discussing a matter of this kind. If it is right to refuse the proposal before the Committee let the Government refuse it; but to haggle about the Question as to whether a Return should be made once a month, or at longer intervals, is monstrous, and I feel bound to enter my protest against it.

MR. CHILDERS (Edinburgh, S.): May I be allowed to suggest to the Committee that the return should be made once a-quarter. I hope this will meet the views of hon. Members below the Gangway.

THE FIRST LORD OF THE TREASURY (Mr. W. H. SMITH) (Strand, Westminster): The Government accept that suggestion.

THE CHAIRMAN: Does the hon. Gentleman (Mr. Murphy) withdraw his Amendment?

MR. MURPHY: Yes.

SIR JOSEPH PEASE (Durham, Barnard Castle): I want to point out that I think the wording of Amendment No. 130 could not possibly carry out all that is required.

MR. W. H. SMITH: I will undertake that the wording shall be carried out as stated.

Amendment, by leave, *withdrawn*.

MR. LOCKWOOD (York): In rising to move the Amendment which stands in my name I do not intend to trouble the Committee at any great length at this late hour, and I hope that if only a short time is taken in moving this Amendment hon. Members will not suppose that that result is due to a want of appreciation of its importance. I am willing to admit that this Amendment proposes seriously to modify both the stringency and the scope of the section to which it relates; but if I correctly appreciate the position of the Government in regard to this section, it is that they are fully alive to the extraordinary character of the powers they ask for under it, and are honestly willing to apply those powers only when urgent occasion for their exercise arises. Under the Indictable Offences Act of 1883, Clause 12 deals with the same matter as is dealt with by this section of the present Bill. I have no doubt that Clause 12 of that Act is familiar to hon. and learned Gentlemen opposite, and, if so, they will see that without some such modification as I now propose, the Government will be extending to the Resident Magistrates powers of an almost unlimited description. I am sure the framers of this Bill have had the intention of modifying the stringency and scope of this section. Anyone need only look at this 1st section, in the second line, where the word "offence" is used, and then look at the subsequent lines, where the word "crime" is used, in order to see that the section has undergone at one time or another a process of modification. If, however, that process of modification had been perfect, no doubt the word "crime" would have been corrected, and the word "crime" would have been used in the first instance. Now, I ask the Government to continue the process of modification in the same spirit as that in which it was at first adopted. Let them just imagine what will be the nature of the inquiries the Resident Magistrates would be entitled to make under this section, if it be allowed to remain as it is at present. Here is one offence—If any person shall encourage any other person to take part in a conspiracy with a third person to induce a fourth person not to work for a fifth person in the ordinary course of trade. Surely the Government do not intend to ask the Committee to give the Residential Magistrates power to apply such an extraordinary provision as this. I appeal to the hon. and learned Gentleman the Attorney General (Sir Richard Webster) for an assurance on this point. Then we have any person who shall incite another to interfere with the ordinary operation of the law. Suppose an inflammatory speech should be made in this House, charging the high crime of murder against any Member of Her Majesty's Government, would not that be an interference with the ordinary operation of the law? I say it would be a most serious interference; but is it to be suggested that the section was intended to apply to an offence of that description? I trust the Government will give the section their earliest consideration, with a view to its further modification. I will only further detain the Committee in order to tell them that I have taken the extraordinary crimes mentioned in the 4th section of this Bill as those which are regarded by the Government as being the most heinous crimes which the section is intended to meet; and I now ask the Government, in a spirit of moderation, to accede to my Amendment, and accept the words I propose.

Amendment proposed,

In page 2, line 11, to leave out from the word "are" to end of Clause, and insert the words—"(*a*) Murder or manslaughter. (*b*) Attempt to murder. (*c*) Aggravated crime of violence against the person. (*d*) Arson by statute or common law. (*e*) Breaking into, firing at or into, or otherwise assaulting, or injuring a dwelling house, however such crime may be described in an indictment."—(*Mr. Lockwood.*)

Question proposed, "That the words 'any felony' stand part of the Clause."

THE ATTORNEY GENERAL (Sir RICHARD WEBSTER) (Isle of Wight): I appreciate the fair way in which the hon. and learned Member for York (Mr. Lockwood) has brought this Amendment before the Committee; but I must point out to the Committee why it is impossible for Her Majesty's Government to accept this Amendment. I would, first, say one word, by way of criticism, upon the word "offence" occurring in one line, and the word "crime" occurring four or five lines down. My hon. and learned Friend the Member for York has assumed that because these two words occur, it was the result of some scheme by which offence should be taken as meaning something lighter than crime. He must permit me to say he is quite mistaken in what he assumes. For the purposes of this section Her Majesty's Government could not allow any distinction between offence and crime; where they wished to draw a distinction, they have done it in another way. As the Chief Secretary for Ireland has pointed out, where "offence" and "crime" have both occurred it has been through inadvertence, and there is no desire to make any distinction between the two. The word "crime" accidentally crept into the Bill; and I admit that it was a bad and careless piece of drafting. We have, therefore, now to consider, putting aside this criticism, whether or not this Inquiry section, as it is called, ought to be applied only to the more heinous crimes enumerated by the hon. and learned Member, murder or manslaughter, attempt to murder, and so on. I would first say I do not think this question is decided by the application of Sub-section 5, because it might apply to a light offence under the earlier part of the section. That would be an argument, if it is one at all, for limiting or altering the words in Sub-section 5 and Clause 2. But that is not the object of the hon. and learned Member's Amendment, the real point of which is that he proposes to limit the inquiry only to that class of offences enumerated in his Amendment. To that Her Majesty's Government could not for one moment accede. If there is one crime or offence—I care not which it is—which requires this Inquiry section to be put in operation more than another, it is the crime or offence—as I have said, I care not which it is—of the conspiracy to Boycott. [*Laughter.*] I think the hon. and learned Members below the Gang-

way know by this time we are quite accustomed to their receiving our arguments with laughter. It is impossible for us to regard Boycotting as a matter to be laughed at. We have recommended in this House, for reasons we have put before the House, that the crime of Boycotting deserves to be dealt with strongly and with a firm hand. I do not suppose hon. Members will deny this is a matter in which the most valuable work of the Inquiry section will be done, because persons dare not give evidence openly with respect to Boycotting. This is a test case, to which, without going further, I call the attention of the hon. and learned Member for York. This is the test case for which the principle is contended. I am not now discussing whether there should be any modification of Clause 2; but we consider there are offences punishable under Clause 2 of this Bill which would require to be inquired into under Clause 1, and therefore we cannot assent to the proposal that the Inquiry Clause should be limited to those the hon. and learned Member has mentioned. I have now sufficiently indicated the principle on which we are prepared to stand—namely, that this power of inquiry shall not be limited, but shall include all substantial offences under the Bill.

MR. T. P. O'CONNOR (Scotland, Liverpool): Let me first inform the hon. and learned Gentleman that he rather misapprehended the laugh that came from this quarter; it was a cheer rather than a laugh, and the cheer was not at the argument of the hon. and learned Gentleman—for I confess I was unable to find any argument in his remarks—but the cheer was meant that at last we had the Government letting the cat out of the bag. I very much regret that I did not think of bringing along with me a Western newspaper, which contained a report of a speech of a Member of the Unionist Liberal Party, delivered in the St. Austell Division of Cornwall, I think by the hon. Member for Barrow (Mr. Caine). There have been very many distinguished Unionists down in that neighbourhood; but, I think, as the speech was so absurd and exaggerated, that I am right in attributing it to the hon. Member for Barrow. And what did he say?—

" The Liberal Unionists are denounced for supporting the Coercion Bill of the Government;

but what is it for? It is for putting down murderers."

If it were only for that purpose the Bill would have passed in three days in this House, with not one word more of dissent from this part of the House than from any other. The hon. Gentleman in this speech said—

> "We are supporting the Bill of the Government, because we believe it is for the purpose of putting down murderers, moonlighters, and houghers of cattle."

Now, we have the hon. and learned Gentleman the Attorney General telling us that one of the most stringent and exhaustive powers is not merely for putting down murderers, moonlighters, and houghers of cattle, but is for putting down conspiracy to Boycott. ["Hear, hear!"] I wish to make my meaning clear, even to hon. Gentlemen on the opposite side of the House who say "hear, hear." It may be right or wrong that this Bill should put down conspiracy to Boycott; but it is obviously not accurate to describe a Bill which proposes to put down conspiracy to Boycott as exclusively aimed at murderers, moonlighters, and houghers of cattle, which is the description given by Liberal Unionists. The hon. and learned Gentleman the Attorney General devoted some portion of his speech to meeting the point of "offence" used in one part of the clause, and "crime" in the other, and rather unnecessarily laboured the point, for the purpose of showing that crime and offence meant the same things in the mind of the Government. We know perfectly well that offence and crime mean the same in this Bill in the eyes of the Government, for there is the same machinery for the detection and punishment of the lightest offence as for the gravest crime; therefore, they mean the same except upon election platforms, when Liberal Unionists and Tories say little of the offence and speak largely of the crime. The hon. and learned Gentleman said it was not fair to bring the consideration of the 2nd clause of this Bill into the consideration of the 1st clause. I altogether traverse that proposition of the hon. and learned Gentleman. The clause, if it be allowed to stand as it is, will bring under its purview every slight offence created by this Bill if committed after the passing of the Act—that is the

one limitation. Every offence created by this Act——

Sir RICHARD WEBSTER: I have an Amendment down upon the Paper.

Mr. T. P. O'CONNOR: I know, and I have read it; but what I may call the more trivial offences, or those created by this Act, will not come under this secret inquiry unless committed after the passing of the Act, and in a proclaimed district. That is the distinction made; accordingly, every single offence which is an offence under the 2nd clause of this Act, and in a proclaimed district, after the Proclamation, comes under the survey of the secret inquiry. The hon. and learned Gentleman treated the matter perfectly unfairly, and, from a logical point of view, very uncandidly, in confining his observations to conspiracy to Boycott; he ought to be able to prove to the Committee that the Government were justified in bringing the secret inquiry to bear upon every offence under the clause. We are entitled to expect that everything that becomes an offence under the 2nd clause of this Bill will be brought under review of the secret inquiry. What does that imply? My hon. and learned Friend the Member for York gave one case; I will give another. Suppose I went down to the property of the Marquess of Clanricarde, and I said to the tenants upon that property—"My friends, I find that you have not paid your rent, and that the landlord is threatening you with eviction, and you are not taking any means whatever to prevent that; you are unable to pay, and yet you are taking no means for the purpose of producing a reduction of your rent;" suppose I further said—"If you look to another portion of the property of the Marquess of Clanricarde, you will find the tenants there were prudent enough to go into the Land Court and get a 30 per cent reduction, every penny of which the Marquess exacts from you;" and if I then said—"It is your duty to combine together to see if, by combining, you can get a reduction of your rents equal to the reduction in the case of your fellow-tenants," under the 2nd clause of this Act I would be interfering, not to compel, but interfering by power of persuasion with persons in the letting, hiring, usage, or occupation of land, and, therefore, guilty of an offence under this Bill. [An hon. MEMBER: Sub-section 5 of Clause 2.] Yes; Sub-section 5 of Clause 2, which is—

"Any person who, by words or acts, shall incite, solicit, encourage, or persuade any other person to commit any of the offences herein-before mentioned."

You cannot make a speech, you cannot write an article, or hold a conversation which may not be interpreted into per-suading a person to do a certain act; and if you hold a conversation at a private dinner-table interfering with the relations of landlord and tenant, you are guilty of an offence under the 2nd clause; and a Resident Magistrate would have the power to drag you, to drag the host, to drag every one of your fellow-guests before a secret inquiry, and in that way to submit to examination every single act done that had any reference, nigh or remote, to the relations of land-lord and tenant. I submit the question to the Government—is not that a great abuse, and an inexcusable extension of the power of the secret inquiry? Under these circumstances, that is a question we have really to argue very strenuously and emphatically. I am convinced that even if Tories outside in the constitu-encies were to know that secret inquiry was not for the purpose of tracking murder, but for the purpose of dragging into the authority, terrorism, and in-timidation of secret inquiry, every com-bination of tenants against landlords' evictions and rack-renting, I am sure a large number of Tories would have enough of the English love of liberty to protest against it. I see the Chief Se-cretary is anxious to get up—["No, no!"]—and I will not longer stand be-tween him and the Committee. Activity is so unusual a sign of the right hon. Gentleman, that I do not wish to de-prive the Committee of this unusual phenomenon. I could say much more; but at this hour, a quarter to 1 o'clock, I do not wish to take up more time; still, I must say I think we are now really testing the meaning of the Bill and the *bona fides* of the Government.

SIR WILLIAM HARCOURT (Derby): I wish to call the attention of the Go-vernment to the great difference of the offence of conspiracy in regard to this inquiry from any other offences. At all events, they cannot take shelter in this matter under the Act of 1882; there was no inquiry into any question of the character of conspiracy under the Act of 1882; all those subjects which could be inquired into there were matters which were overt acts. When a murder takes place, there is the body of the murdered man, a house broken into, those are overt acts; but what is the character of a conspiracy? It consists in the agree-ment, the secret agreement, and there need not be any overt act whatever in order to charge conspiracy. What are you going to inquire into privately? You are going to inquire into privately some secret agreement which this inquiry is alone going to reveal, and, in point of fact, you may start this inquiry with-out there being any offence at all; there-fore, no one is safe, because the Resi-dent Magistrate may surmise there is an agreement, of which there is no evi-dence, and may proceed to a secret inquiry to find the evidence of that agreement of which there is no other proof. That is a most dangerous and unheard-of proceeding. We ought to be extremely careful in this matter, because there is no book on the law that does not warn us of the extreme danger of giving this power of inter-pretation, even to the most learned mind, of the Law of Conspiracy. I speak of conspiracy now, because the Attorney General has rendered his whole case upon it; it is the thing for which this clause is required. I venture to urge on the Committee that inquiry of this character ought never to be allowed. I am not speaking of the conspiracy to Boycott merely; but I would like to inquire what that ambiguous word means. If it is a conspiracy merely to agree, like in a trades union, not to work except at particular wages, then there is no overt act at all, and the use of the words "conspiracy to Boycott" is meaningless. I would draw the atten-tion of the Committee to the seriousness of giving a power of this kind in such a vague and undefined thing as the Law of Conspiracy. What is the Law of Conspiracy? I am speaking in the presence of lawyers, and they will not deny what I say, that the Law of Con-spiracy is that which any Judge may hold to be morally wrong or socially inexpedient. You are going to leave that which it has been proved is not safe in the hands of any but safe Judges to the Resident Magistrates, for them to create an offence out of their own conscience by determining it to be an act of conspiracy. Let me read this sentence from Roscoe's *Criminal Law*—

"Conspiracy is defined as an agreement to do an unlawful act."

Roscoe further says—

"But the word 'unlawful,' on which it turns, is ambiguous, and appears to be used in definition in a sense in which it is nowhere else used. It has no precise meaning, and the definition is, in reality, no definition at all."

That is the power you are going to give into the hands of these Magistrates, and on which they are to found a universal inquiry. There is no one that you could not surmise to have entered into an overt act. This writer goes on to say—

"The vagueness of these propositions leaves so broad a discretion in the hands of the Judges, that it is hardly too much to say that plausible means may be found for declaring it to be a crime to combine to do almost anything which the Judge may regard as morally wrong, or politically dangerous. The power which the vagueness of the Law of Conspiracy puts into the hands of the Judges, is something like the power which the vagueness of the Law of Libel puts into the hands of the juries."

That is the Law of Conspiracy, and you are going to leave the Resident Magistrates to declare at Common Law anything he regards to be morally wrong, or politically dangerous, to be a conspiracy, and, having assumed that, to make use of this inquiry to any extent he may desire. The writer goes on to say—

"Another remarkable circumstance connected with the Law of Conspiracy is that it renders it possible, by a sort of fiction, to convert an act innocent in itself into a crime, by charging in the indictment, as an overt act of conspiracy, of what there is no other evidence but the act itself."

In that instance there is the protection of a jury; but here you are going to give this dangerous implement, without the protection of a jury, to a man who is not a Judge. The writer continues—

"In other words, if the jury choose to impute bad motives to an act *primâ facie* innocent, they can convict those who combine to do it of conspiracy."

I undertake to say that under this subsection, even with the words the Attorney General proposes to insert, that what the Judge may choose to hold as being a conspiracy may be so held, although Parliament has been previously obliged to step in and put an end

Sir William Harcourt

to a decision of that character. It is of this sort of proceeding that Baron Rolfe said—

"It never is satisfactory, though, undoubtedly, it is legal."

Cockburn said—

"This course operates, it is manifest, unfairly and unjustly against the parties accused. The prosecutors are thus enabled to combine in one indictment a variety of offences which, if treated individually, as they ought to be, exclude the possibility of giving evidence against one defendant to the prejudice of others, and deprive defendants of calling their co-defendants as witnesses."

That is the answer to the hon. and learned Attorney General's point—it is never satisfactory, though undoubtedly legal, and Chief Justice Cockburn says this operates unjustly and unfairly against the person accused and to the advantage of the prosecution. That is exactly this case. You could have up the whole village on a surmise and charge of conspiracy, have every one up on an overt act, and charge the agreement as a conspiracy. Agreement has been laid down to be the overt act; therefore, you may have the whole village up on a surmise of conspiracy, and embrace the whole of them in the conspiracy. I gather from the Attorney General that is the very object with which this clause is framed. In the year 1842, which was a period when there was great disturbance in this country, and there were many combinations proceeded against, it was thought necessary to revise the jurisdiction of the Courts of Quarter Sessions, and an Act was passed, 5 & 6 *Vict.*, c. 38, by which the power of dealing with these combinations and conspiracies was expressly taken away from Quarter Sessions, and now that which the English Parliament would not allow an English Court of Quarter Sessions to deal with on account of the character of the offence, you are going to give to Resident Magistrates. I think I have given the Government very considerable authorities why such a course should not be taken. I will give one more, and that is the Commission on the Criminal Code. The Commission on the Criminal Code, consisting of the most eminent Judges now living on the Bench, said Section 5 will have the effect of preventing indictments at Common Law for conspiracy, and they absolutely considered it necessary to put an end to this dangerous and mischievous doctrine of Common Law Conspiracy. They said—

"An agreement to do unlawful acts has been said to be a conspiracy. No definition is to be found of what constitutes unlawfulness; it seems to be unsatisfactory that there should be any indictable offence of which the elements should be left to uncertainty."

That is their decision on the question of the Law of Conspiracy, and they accordingly recommended its adoption in the Criminal Code introduced by the Attorney General of the Conservative Government. Is it possible to have a more overwhelming mass of authority in favour of restricting the operation of this clause, and of putting an end to legislation containing this mischievous doctrine of Common Law Conspiracy? And yet it is just that doctrine which Section 2 of this Bill establishes. Under that section you make this conspiracy an offence, and you apply to it the whole of this inquisitorial inquiry. That seems to me to be a most dangerous and unjustifiable thing, and one which is certain to cause extreme irritation. There is absolutely no limit to it. The magistrate can treat as conspiracy whatever he likes. Take the 1st sub-section of Section 2—

"Any person who shall take part in any criminal conspiracy to compel or induce any person or persons either not to fulfil his or her legal obligations, or not to let, hire, use, or occupy any land, or not to deal with, work for, or hire any person or persons in the ordinary course of trade, business or occupation, or to interfere with the administration of the law."

Under this sub-section a Resident Magistrate may take up half-a-dozen men in a village. There may be some land to let, and he may say—"I suspect you have entered into an agreement about this land; have you done anything about this land; have you talked about this land; have you formed any intention about this land; have you agreed with anybody else about this land?" Such questions would be perfectly proper under this section. It will be a criminal proceeding for three men to meet together and to enter into an agreement not to occupy certain land, except at a particular price. I hope now-a-days that such an action would not be treated as criminal—I hope that no Judge would so treat it—but if any Judge should do so, there is no one who could say that there are not decisions

which would justify him in so doing. ["No, no!"] Well, we shall have to discuss that more fully in connection with Section 2. What is the history of the whole of the trades unions' decisions? The history of the whole of the trades unions' decisions was that trades unionism was looked upon as an illegal conspiracy. It was regarded as an illegal conspiracy for half-a-dozen men to agree not to work for certain wages. That was the doctrine for years, until an Act of Parliament put an end to it. That doctrine is revived under Clause 2, and being under that clause an offence, it is subject to inquiry under this 1st clause, and I contend that under this doctrine of conspiracy every matter that relates to a man's social and domestic life may be inquired into. If this clause were acted upon in Ireland it would make life absolutely intolerable. You can have no restriction whatever on the magistrate on what he might surmise to be conspiracy with reference to land, or with reference to a man's ordinary trade or business occupation. I hope the Government will make some limitation in this clause, or, at all events, that they will not include in it this vague, loose law of conspiracy.

THE CHIEF SECRETARY FOR IRELAND (Mr. A. J. BALFOUR) (Manchester, E.): I do not intend to go into the question of conspiracy as the right hon. Gentleman has done. I think, indeed, that the right hon. Gentleman's speech would have been more appropriate on the 2nd clause. I can only say that the instances given by him and by the hon. Member for the Scotland Division of Liverpool would not constitute an illegal act, and I do not think there is a single lawyer in the Committee who will disagree with me in that opinion. I would make a suggestion to the Committee. The Amendment we are now considering in common with a good many other Amendments, and notably that of the right hon. Gentleman himself, though they differ in many respects, all agree in this fundamental fact, that they restrict the operation of this clause to certain offences—only to those offences dealt with in the Bill and in the speech which the hon. and learned Gentleman opposite the Member for York (Mr. Lockwood) delivered in moving his Amendment. The speech of the hon. and learned

Gentleman would have been perfectly applicable to the Amendment of the right hon. Gentleman, and would not have been less applicable to the Amendments of other hon. Members opposite. It would shorten the debate considerably, and it would be much more convenient to hon. Members if we could take this discussion upon one Amendment to be selected by the hon. Gentleman opposite. We, on our part, feel bound to resist every Amendment which refuses inquiry into an offence punishable under this Act. That is the principle we laid down at the outset, and if hon. Members will select which Amendment they will fight that principle upon, it will, I say, be convenient to the Committee.

Sir WILLIAM HARCOURT: I, for my part, should be glad to do anything that would tend to shorten the proceedings; but it is obvious that there are a good many subjects between the crimes mentioned in the Amendment of the hon. and learned Gentleman the Member for York and the clause of the Government.

Mr. A. J. BALFOUR: If the Committee would consent to divide upon this Amendment, and then debate the principle of the Amendment of the right hon. Gentleman opposite (Sir William Harcourt), I should think that everyone would be satisfied.

Mr. T. P. O'CONNOR: I interpret the right hon. Gentleman's proposal in such a way as to make it a just one. I think it undesirable that an Amendment of such enormous importance as that moved by my hon. and learned Friend should be discussed at this hour of the night, when not only we on these Benches, but Gentlemen on the Treasury Bench, are exhausted after many hours of discussion, and after many hours of an attention to this clause, which, I must say, speaking for myself, was as severe an intellectual trial as one could possibly go through. At the same time, I think the right hon. Gentleman is reasonable in asking that we should not discuss the same principle on different Amendments. I think the fair way to get out of the difficulty is this— let us now report Progress; I am sure the hon. and learned Gentleman the Member for York will have no desire to repeat on this Amendment any of the considerations which have been used in the speeches that have already been

made. Thus, by the time the Bill came on again, we might find an opportunity of comparing the different Amendments on this clause, and of weeding out those which cover the same ground. I think my hon. Friends around me would have no desire to have more than one discussion—that discussion being a serious one on the central principle as to whether this clause should be confined in its operation to serious and grave crime, or whether it should be extended to what we call offences and combinations. I respectfully submit to the First Lord of the Treasury that this course which I suggest would be the proper one. On our part, I think we should have no difficulty in giving an undertaking that we shall take the discussion on one Amendment. I think we should be allowed between this and the next discussion to select the ground we would take up, and the Government, I am sure, would lose nothing by the delay.

The FIRST LORD of the TREASURY (Mr. W. H. SMITH) (Strand, Westminster): I am glad to recognize the desire that appears to exist in the Committee on both sides of the House to limit the discussion of this important question; but it would appear to me to be possible to come to a decision on the Amendment of the hon. and learned Member for York this evening. We have all had the benefit of hearing the able arguments upon this particular Amendment which have come from the other side, and if we now divide upon it I think the suggestion of the hon. Member for the Scotland Division of Liverpool might very well be acted upon. We might put in some of the Amendments which follow in the name of the Attorney General, and which, I believe, will be accepted by the Committee without opposition. We should then arrive at the point at which the right hon. Gentleman the Member for Derby could move his Amendment, if that is the one upon which hon. Gentlemen opposite rely, and that Amendment could be discussed at the next sitting of the Committee.

Sir WILLIAM HARCOURT: I think that a very reasonable proposal, and it would probably now be convenient for the Committee to take a Division on the Amendment of the hon. and learned Member for York. That Division will probably decide that the clause shall not be limited to these particular offences.

Well, we should endeavour after that to, what I may call, consolidate the Amendments in order to put the question in to as short and as simple a form as possible.

MR. MAURICE HEALY (Cork): Do I understand the right hon. Gentleman (Mr. W. H. Smith) to say that after disposing of the Amendment of the hon. and learned Member for York, we should proceed to dispose of the Amendments in the name of the Attorney General? The Amendment which stands in my name would merely limit the question of time. If that were disposed of, whether it were adopted or negatived, it would be open to the Committee to discuss further words limiting the clause to certain offences. What I believe would be the best course to pursue would be to dispose of this Amendment of the hon. and learned Member for York, to take the decision of the Committee upon my Amendment, and to leave the Committee free for the discussion as to whether there should be any further limitation of this clause or not.

SIR WILLIAM HARCOURT: I understand that it is proposed that we should take a Division upon the Amendment of the hon. and learned Member for York, that we should then put in for discussion the Attorney General's Amendments, and that we should then report Progress, and consider what should be done in the future.

MR. T. P. O'CONNOR: I think we all mean the same thing, so that we can discuss this matter with perfect equanimity on both sides. I do not object to the Division being taken on the Amendment of the hon. and learned Gentleman (Mr. Lockwood); but I think there is some difficulty in disposing of the Amendment of the hon. and learned Gentleman the Attorney General. I am not a lawyer; but I must say that it appears to me, from reading the Amendment, that it was prejudicing the question which we wish to hold over. I think the right hon. Gentleman the First Lord of the Treasury would lose nothing by consenting to report Progress after the Division about to be taken.

THE ATTORNEY GENERAL (Sir RICHARD WEBSTER) (Isle of Wight): I think it is desirable to get rid of the Amendments which now it merely formal and do not raise di   would save

time. May I point out to hon. Members that the right hon. Gentleman the Member for Derby has put his Amendment into the shape of a Proviso. He says—

"Provided that no examination under this section shall be held in respect of any matters relating to public meetings, or transactions relating to the letting, hiring, or occupation of land, or the dealing with, working for, or hiring of any persons in the ordinary course of trade, business, or occupation."

It seems to me that this is open to any hon. Member who desires to limit the operation of the clause, after we have disposed of Amendment 115 and my Amendment, to move any further Amendment in the shape of a Proviso in regard to the operation of the clause.

MR. MAURICE HEALY: I would ask Her Majesty's Government not to insist on getting further in the debate tonight. It appears to me the Amendment of the Attorney General places a totally distinct issue before us. There are two issues to be decided—the first is what class of offences committed before the passing of this Act shall be included in this clause; and, secondly, what class of offences committed after the passing of this Act shall be included. The Amendment of the Attorney General is in these words—

"Clause 1, page 2, line 12, at end, add—'committed in a proclaimed district, whether committed before or after the passing of this Act, provided that no inquiry should be held under this section concerning any offence punishable under this Act commenced in any district before the proclamation of such district, unless such offence would have been indictable if this Act had not passed.'"

If we pass this Amendment the Act will apply to all offences committed after the passing of the Act save those stated in the Amendment. That is the contentious matter. We have on the Paper, Amendments limiting the scope of the Act in a different direction to that indicated in the Amendment of the hon. and learned Gentleman. We should desire to discuss the question raised by this Amendment, and I would, therefore, ask the Government not to press on that discussion tonight. I need not point out what these Amendments are; I think there is one in my own name, but, be they few or many, they certainly raise contentious matter. They are not in any way involved in the Amendment now before the Committee, and I would therefore ask that they also should be postponed until Tuesday.

[Seventh Night.]

Mr. T. P. O'CONNOR: Perhaps this would meet the view of the Government. I think we, on these Benches, could undertake, that on Tuesday we will do all in our power to assist the Government to get to the discussion of the Amendment of the right hon. Gentleman the Member for Derby at the earliest hour possible. The hon. and learned Gentleman the Attorney General therefore need have no apprehension that, if he allows his Amendment to be put off, anything but the briefest time would be occupied in its consideration.

Mr. W. H. SMITH: Agreed.

Mr. MILVAIN (Durham): I feel somewhat surprised to hear from the right hon. Gentleman the Member for Derby that we ought to be most careful as to the hands into which we entrust the Law of Conspiracy. I am also surprised that he has quoted the Act in which the Law of Conspiracy is taken out of the hands of the Court of Quarter Sessions. I am sure the right hon. Gentleman must have forgotten that the Act of the 38th & 39th *Vict.*, regarding conspiracy in restraint of trade, gives a Court of Summary Jurisdiction power to deal with such conspiracies. [*Interruption.*]

Question put.

The Committee *divided*:—Ayes 257; Noes 170: Majority 87.—(Div. List, No. 140.)

Amendment proposed,

In page 2, line 12, at end, add " committed in a proclaimed district, whether committed before or after the passing of this Act, provided that no inquiry shall be held under this section concerning any offence punishable under this Act committed in any district before the proclamation of such district, unless such offence would have been indictable if this Act had not passed."—(*Mr. Attorney General.*)

Question proposed, " That those words be there inserted."

THE CHIEF SECRETARY FOR IRELAND (Mr. A. J. BALFOUR) (Manchester, E.): Mr. Courtney, I beg to move that you do now report Progress.

Motion made, and Question proposed, " That the Chairman do report Progress, and ask leave to sit again."—(*Mr. A. J. Balfour.*)

Mr. T. M. HEALY (Longford, N.): I suppose it will be competent to move an Amendment to this Amendment, providing that the offence must be committed since the dropping of the Crimes Act?

THE CHAIRMAN: The words, being additional, can, of course, be amended.

Question put, and *agreed to.*

Committee report Progress; to sit again upon *Tuesday* next.

TRUCK BILL.—[BILL 109.]
(*Mr. Bradlaugh, Mr. Warmington, Mr. John Ellis, Mr. Arthur Williams, Mr. Howard Vincent, Mr. Esslemont.*)

COMMITTEE. [*Progress 6th May.*]

Bill *considered* in Committee.

(In the Committee.)

Clause (Prohibition of Stores,)—(*Mr. Donald Crawford,*)—*brought up,* and read the first time.

Question proposed, "That the Clause be read a second time."

THE ATTORNEY GENERAL (Sir RICHARD WEBSTER) (Isle of Wight): I do not know whether it is possible to deal with this clause to-night. I have not the smallest objection to sit a little longer if hon. Gentlemen think it right to do so. ["No, no!"] This certainly is a clause which will raise considerable discussion.

SIR JOSEPH PEASE (Durham, Barnard Castle): Mr. Courtney, I beg to move that you report Progress, and ask leave to sit again. I have no wish at all to interfere with the proper progress of this Bill. I think it is a very important Bill, a Bill to which some time ought to be alloted, in order that the difficult questions with which it deals, involving as they do enormous sums of money and matters of great importance to the working classes, should be fairly and properly discussed. Certainly, a Bill of this excellent but complicated character should not be taken at 10 minutes to 2 o'clock in the morning. Some of us were here until half-past 3 o'clock yesterday morning. It is really more than human nature can endure, that we should go on with Bill after Bill after 2 o'clock in the morning.

Motion made, and Question proposed, " That the Chairman do report Progress, and ask leave to sit again.—(*Sir Joseph Pease.*)

MR. BRADLAUGH (Northampton): I trust that [...] decide that the discussion; it [...] ed, [...] d to these p[...]

but that if it is reported, it will be reported with some distinct understanding on the part of the Government that reasonable facilities will be afforded for the discussion of the provisions of the Bill. I have tried my best during this week to consult the convenience of the House by not pressing the Bill unduly upon its attention. This is a Bill which it is admitted on both sides of the House ought to be carried, and, therefore, I hope the Government will afford some facilities for its passage.

Sir RICHARD WEBSTER: I do not think the hon. Member for Northampton (Mr. Bradlaugh) means to suggest that Her Majesty's Government have any desire to obstruct the progress of the Bill. This is a private Bill; but the Government will endeavour to give its clauses the best consideration we can. The difficulty is this—very important Amendments have been put down by independent Members, Amendments which do not arise on the Bill as originally framed. It is impossible for Her Majesty's Government to give any pledge as to affording facilities for the discussion of the Bill; but, as far as we possibly can, we shall see that the Bill is fairly and properly discussed. Certainly, clauses such as that proposed by the hon. Gentleman opposite (Mr. Donald Crawford) cannot be adequately discussed at this time of the night.

Mr. BRADLAUGH: If I consent to report Progress now, and a similar Motion to this is made when the Bill again comes before the Committee, I shall do my best, believing I have a very large amount of support on both sides of the House, to resist Progress being reported. I admit that the Government have done their best to facilitate the passing of the Bill; and that I have received assistance from Members on both sides of the House. I do not want at such time of the morning, and when hon. Members are jaded with their labours, to press the Bill on.

Mr. D. CRAWFORD (Lanarkshire, N.E.): One word in support of the appeal of the hon. Member for Northampton (Mr. Bradlaugh). There are a great many Members on this side of the House, and I dare say on the other, who stay night after night until 2 and 3 o'clock to take part in the discussion of this Bill. I know it is difficult for the Government to make special arrangements for the Bill; but I am convinced, that almost any arrangement would be better for the despatch of Public Business than allowing the Bill to drag on in this way. Amendments accumulate night after night, and hon. Gentlemen are detained here at great inconvenience.

Mr. BRADLAUGH: May I make one suggestion? A large number of clauses have now been carried through Committee. It would simplify matters if the Bill were reprinted as far as it has gone. Many hon. Members do not understand the position in which the Bill is, and Amendments are suggested to me which are beside the question, because we have already passed them.

Mr. TOMLINSON (Preston): Many Amendments have been put down. It would simplify future discussion if hon. Gentleman would consider whether the Amendments they have suggested are entirely germane to Truck.

Mr. CHANCE (Kilkenny, S.): I quite agree with the hon. Member for Northampton (Mr. Bradlaugh), that it would be a great convenience to Members who desire to take some intelligent part in the proceedings on this Bill, that these clauses should be reprinted. At present, we do not know where we are.

The SECRETARY to the TREASURY (Mr. JACKSON) (Leeds, N.): I am afraid there are difficulties in the way of reprinting the Bill at this stage.

The UNDER SECRETARY of STATE for the HOME DEPARTMENT (Mr. STUART-WORTLEY) (Sheffield, Hallam): We have our own private reprint which any Gentleman can see. It shows what Amendments have been made in the Bill.

Question put, and *agreed to.*

Committee report Progress; to sit again upon *Monday* next.

LEGAL PROCEEDINGS (REPORTS) BILL

LEAVE.	FIRST READING.

Motion made, and Question proposed,

"That leave be given to bring in a Bill to amend the Law as to Reports of Proceedings in Courts of Law."—(*Mr. Finlay.*)

Mr. CHANCE (Kilkenny, S.): I beg to move that this debate be now adjourned. I do not think the people who are brought into the Divorce Court should be saved the shame of exposure. The reports in newspapers need not be indecent; but I should be sorry to prevent a certain amount of publicity being given to the cases brought in the Divorce Court.

Motion made, and Question proposed, "That the Debate be now adjourned." —(*Mr. Chance.*)

MR. SPEAKER: It is rather irregular to make such a Motion. The hon. Member has not yet seen the Bill.

MR. CHANCE: This is rather a thin House in which to challenge a Division,

and therefore I will not press my objection.

Motion, by leave, *withdrawn.*

Original Question put, and *agreed to.*

Bill *ordered* to be brought in by Mr. Finlay, Mr. Egerton Hubbard, Mr. Lockwood, Mr. Samuel Smith, Mr. Bryce, Mr. Robert Reid, and Mr. Asquith.

Bill *presented*, and read the first time. [Bill 264.]

House adjourned at Two o'clock till Monday next.

PROTEST.

—o—

HOUSE OF LORDS, FRIDAY, 22ND APRIL, 1887.

———

AGAINST THE SECOND READING OF THE IRISH LAND LAW BILL.

"*DISSENTIENT:*

"1. Because the Amendment to the Motion for the Second Reading of the "Bill was not submitted to the vote of their Lordships, and no permission was "given to the Mover of it to withdraw it.

"2. Because during the progress of the Bill the First Lord of the Treasury "had received a deputation of persons who, having paid for their holdings with "borrowed money, at the rate of 27 years' purchase, had been unable to pay the "high rate of interest, and desired a reduction of it.

"3. Because the adoption of the Bright Clauses of the Land Act, 1870, had "been inserted in this Bill.

"4. Because, although the Land Purchase Act of 1885, adding 14 years to "the time of payment, prevented tenants from at once crippling their power to "purchase implements and stock, yet, as in the Writer's Protest in 1870, "purchasers would be obliged to crave indulgence from the State in order to "prevent foreclosure.

"5. Because, although the State, having the first claim for repayment, would "become owners of the land, yet their caretaker or tenant would be in danger of "encountering the opposition of those who have carried by *violence* the advice ' to "take a firm grip of the land.'

"6. Because the purchasing tenants would wish to have—and would right-"fully own—all the powers of which the Bill seeks to deprive the landlords on "becoming landlords themselves.

"7. Because it was stated truly that this Bill, in its present shape, would be "very injurious to landlords.

"8. Because tenants, being obliged to borrow money as in the Act of 1870, "or as in the Act of 1885, prove by their want of money their incapacity to "improve their land.

"9. Because the "gombeen man" would be the owner of every farm for which, "whether by the State or a private scrivener, money had been advanced to men "incapable of paying their instalments.

"10. Because the statement that the Duke of Wellington consented to the "Emancipation Act through fear of civil war is not true, as His Grace's only "apprehension was, that a sense of the injustice of Romanists paying for two "Establishments might induce a belief on their part that they would be right "in resistance.

"DENMAN."

[INDEX.

INDEX

TO

HANSARD'S PARLIAMENTARY DEBATES,

VOLUME CCCXIV.

FIFTH VOLUME OF SESSION 1887.

EXPLANATION OF THE ABBREVIATIONS.

Bills, Read 1°, 2°, 3°, or 1ª, 2ª, 3ª, Read the First, Second, or Third Time.—In Speeches 1R., 2R., 3R., Speech delivered on the First, Second, or Third Reading.—*Amendt.*, Amendment.—*Res.*, Resolution.—*Comm.*, Committee.—*Re-Comm.*, Re-Committal.—*Rep.*, Report.— *Consid.*, Consideration.—*Adj.*, Adjournment or Adjourned.—*cl.*, Clause.—*add. cl.*, Additional Clause.—*neg.*, Negatived.—*M. Q.*, Main Question.—*O. Q.*, Original Question.—*O. M.*, Original Motion.—*P. Q.*, Previous Question.—R. P., Report Progress.—*A.*, Ayes.—*N.*, Noes.—*M.*, Majority.—1*st. Div.*, 2*nd. Div.*, First or Second Division.—*l.*, Lords.—*c.*, Commons.
When in this Index a * is added to the Reading of a Bill, it indicates that no Debate took place upon that stage of the measure.
When in the Text or in the Index a Speech is marked thus *, it indicates that the Speech is reprinted from a Pamphlet or some authorised Report.
When in the Index a † is prefixed to a Name or an Office (the Member having accepted or vacated office during the Session) and to Subjects of Debate thereunder, it indicates that the Speeches on those Subjects were delivered in the speaker's private or official character, as the case may be.
Some subjects of debate have been classified under the following "General Headings:"— ARMY — NAVY — INDIA — IRELAND — SCOTLAND — PARLIAMENT— POOR LAW—POST OFFICE— METROPOLIS — CHURCH OF ENGLAND — EDUCATION — CRIMINAL LAW — LAW AND JUSTICE— TAXATION, under WAYS AND MEANS.

ACLAND, Mr. C. T. D., *Cornwall, Launceston*
Truck, Comm. *cl.* 3, 306, 308 ; *add. cl.* Amendt. 834, 837, 1091, 1099

Accountant General's Department—Greenwich Hospital Branch
Question, Mr. W. H. James ; Answer, The First Lord of the Admiralty (Lord George Hamilton) *May 5*, 955

Accumulations Bill
(*Mr. Cozens-Hardy, Mr. Bryce, Mr. Haldane*)
c. Committee ; Report *May 3*, 676 [Bill 31] Read 3° * *May 4*
l. Read 1ª * (*Lord Herschell*) *May 5* (No. 81)

Admiralty—see *Navy*

ADMIRALTY—First Lord (*see* HAMILTON, Right Hon. Lord G. F.)

ADMIRALTY—Secretary to (*see* FORWOOD, Mr. A. B.)

ADMIRALTY—A Lord of (*see* ASHMEAD-BARTLETT, Mr. E.)

ADVOCATE, The LORD (*see* MACDONALD, Right Hon. J. H. A.)

Afghanistan—Reported Disturbances
Question, The Earl of Fife ; Answer, The Secretary of State for India (Viscount Cross) *May 5*, 930 ; Ministerial Statement, The Secretary of State for India (Viscount Cross) *May 6*, 1109 [See title *Central Asia*]

Africa (Central)
Transit Tariff through Portuguese Territory, Question, Mr. Craig-Sellar ; Answer, The Under Secretary of State for Foreign Affairs (Sir James Fergusson) *May 12*, 1666

Africa (East Coast)
The Slave Trade on the Mozambique Coast,
Question, Mr. A. E. Pease: Answer. The
Under Secretary of State for Foreign Affairs
(Sir James Fergusson) *May* 12, 1671

Africa (South)
Republic of South Africa (Transvaal)—
Flogging of Native Women, Question, Sir
Robert Fowler: Answer, The Secretary of
State for the Colonies (Sir Henry Holland)
April 26, 9
Zululand, Questions, Mr. M'Arthur, Sir George
Campbell ; Answers, The Secretary of State
for the Colonies (Sir Henry Holland) *May* 13,
1813

AINSLIE, Mr. W. G., *Lancashire, N.
Lonsdale*
Education Department—Non-Attending Child-
ren at Board Schools, 1260

Allotments Extension Act, 1882—" Poors
Close" Charity, Great Easton
Question, Mr. J. Ellis ; Answer, The Under
Secretary of State for the Home Department
(Mr. Stuart-Wortley) *May* 10, 1451

ANDERSON, Mr. C. H., *Elgin and Nairn*
Criminal Law Amendment (Ireland), Comm.
cl. 1, Amendt. 362, 363. 384, 442, 603, 813,
1278, 1280, 1309, 1320, 1363 ; Motion for
reporting Progress, 1378, 1380. 1517, 1574,
1577, 1646, 1647, 1828, 1829 ; Amendt. 1832,
1834, 1835, 1842
Ireland—Prevention of Crime Act, 1882—Examinations under Section 16, 12 ;—Returns,
248
Parliament—Privilege (Mr. Dillon and " The
Times " Newspaper), Res. 1188, 1189
Scotland—Scotch Fishery Board—Trawling in
the Moray Firth, 555, 556
Scotland—Mussel Beds in Tidal Waters, Res.
1729, 1730

ANSTRUTHER, Colonel R. H. L., *Suffolk,
Woodbridge*
Currency Commission, 1661

ARGYLL, Duke of
Ireland—Irish Land Law. 1245
Law and Justice — Equitable Powers of
County Court Judges, 1253
Ireland—Land Improvement, Motion for a
Paper, 524
Sheffield Corporation Water, 3R. 162

ARMY   (Questions)
Aërostatic Balloons—Inventions of William
Howson, Question, Mr. Shirley; Answer,
The Surveyor General of Ordnance (Mr.
Northcote) *May* 10, 1450
Cameron Highlanders, The, Question, Mr.
Finlay ; Answer, The Secretary of State for
War (Mr. E. Stanhope) *April* 28, 247

[cont.

ARMY—cont.
Horse Artillery Batteries, Reduction of—Field
Artillery — Formation of Ammunition
Columns, Questions, General Fraser, Captain
Cotton ; Answers, The Secretary of State
for War (Mr. E. Stanhope) *May* 9, 1265 ;—
Field Artillery Guns, Question, General
Fraser ; Answer. The Surveyor General of
Ordnance (Mr. Northcote) *May* 10, 1453
Medical Service—Relative Rank, Question, Dr.
Clark ; Answer, The Secretary of State for
War (Mr. E. Stanhope) *May* 12, 1662
Medical Warrant, The New – Half-Pay, Ques-
tion, Mr. W. J. Corbet; Answer, The
Financial Secretary, War Department (Mr.
Brodrick) *May* 12, 1675
Military Prisons—Report on Discipline and
Management (1885), Question, Sir Robert
Fowler ; Answer, The Secretary of State for
War (Mr. E. Stanhope) *May* 3, 691
Permanent Financial Control, Question, Sir
William Plowden ; Answer, The Secretary
of State for War (Mr. E. Stanhope) *May* 12,
1668
Stores and Munitions of War (Votes in Supply),
Motion for a Return, Lord Randolph
Churchill *May* 12, 1694 ; Motion withdrawn ;
Order discharged

The Two Army Corps and Cavalry Division
Organisation, Question, Mr. Henniker Heaton :
Answer, The Secretary of State for War (Mr.
E. Stanhope) *April* 26, 14
The Horse Artillery, Question, Mr. Tottenham ;
Answer, The Secretary of State for War
(Mr. E. Stanhope) *May* 12, 1670
Cavalry Division, Question, Mr. Tottenham :
Answer, The Secretary of State for War (Mr.
E. Stanhope) *May* 13, 1815
Supply of Horses, Question, General Fraser ;
Answer, The Secretary of State for War (Mr.
E. Stanhope) *May* 13, 1815

Personnel
Captains, Promotion of—The Amended War-
rant—The Jubilee Year, Question, Colonel
Hughes-Hallett ; Answer, The Secretary of
State for War (Mr. E. Stanhope) *May* 6,
1123
Royal Engineers, Promotions in the, Question,
Mr. Bradlaugh ; Answer, The Secretary of
State for War (Mr. E. Stanhope) *April* 28,
232
Commissariat and Transport Corps, The,
Question, Captain M'Calmont ; Answer,
The Secretary of State for War (Mr. E.
Stanhope) *April* 29, 349
Crimean Quartermaster Sergeants, Question,
Sir Henry Tyler ; Answer, The Secretary of
State for War (Mr. E. Stanhope) *May* 9,
1264
Quartermasters—The Warrant of 1886, Ques-
tion, Dr. Clark ; Answer, The Secretary of
State for War (Mr. E. Stanhope) *May* 12,
1673
Quartermaster General to the Forces, Question,
Mr. Tottenham ; Answer, The Secretary of
State for War (Mr. E. Stanhope) *May* 13,
1814
Soldiers at Political Meetings—The Royal
Irish Regiment at Gosport, Question, Mr.
Labouchere ; Answer, The Secretary of
State for War (Mr. E. Stanhope) *May* 5, 957

[cont.

[*cont.*

[cont.

[cont.

INDIA—Secretary of State (*see* CROSS, Viscount)

INDIA—Under Secretary of State (*see* GORST, Sir J. E.)

INDIA (*Questions*)

Chinna Narrain, Prosecution of—The Chingleput Case, Question, Mr. J. F. X. O'Brien; Answer, The Under Secretary of State for India (Sir John Gorst) *May* 9, 1267

Distribution of Prize Money for the Capture of Jhansi, Questions, Mr. E. Robertson; Answers, The Under Secretary of State for India (Sir John Gorst) *May* 2, 548; *May* 9, 1275

Education Department — Directorships of Public Instruction, Question, Sir Roper Lethbridge; Answer, The Under Secretary of State for India (Sir John Gorst) *April* 29, 351

Indian Famine Insurance Fund, Questions, Sir Thomas Esmonde; Answers, The Under Secretary of State for India (Sir John Gorst) *May* 10, 1454; *May* 12, 1684

Public Civil Service, Report of the Commission on the, Question, Mr. King; Answer, The Under Secretary of State for India (Sir John Gorst) *May* 2, 543

State of Mohrbhanj, in Orissa, Question, Sir Roper Lethbridge; Answer, The Under Secretary of State for India (Sir John Gorst) *May* 13, 1806

Telegraph Officials, Question, Mr. Conybeare; Answer, The Under Secretary of State for India (Sir John Gorst) *May* 12, 1678

The Forest Service—Pension Regulations, Question, Mr. Howard Vincent; Answer, The Under Secretary of State for India (Sir John Gorst) *May* 12, 1660

The Hindoo Law of Marriage—Infant Marriages, Question, Mr. J. G. Talbot; Answer, The Under Secretary of State for India (Sir John Gorst) *April* 28, 236; *The Punjaub Civil Code*, Question, Mr. Cozens-Hardy; Answer, The Under Secretary of State for India (Sir John Gorst) *May* 2, 532

The Maharajah Dhuleep Singh, Question, Sir George Campbell; Answer, The Under Secretary of State for India (Sir John Gorst) *May* 3, 687

The North-Western Frontier — The Quetta Railway, Question, The Earl of Kimberley; Answer, The Secretary of State for India (Viscount Cross) *May* 2, 496

BENGAL

Manufacture and Sale of Strong Drink, Question, Mr. S. Smith; Answer, The Under Secretary of State for India (Sir John Gorst) *April* 29, 350

Pay of Native Officials, Question, Sir Roper Lethbridge; Answer, The Under Secretary of State for India (Sir John Gorst) *April* 29, 352

BOMBAY

The Iron Floating Dock at Bombay, Question, Admiral Field; Answer, The Under Secretary of State for India (Sir John Gorst) *May* 13, 1806

[*cont.*

INDIA—*cont.*

MADRAS

The Gunpowder Factory at Madras, Question, Mr. Mallock; Answer, The Under Secretary of State for India (Sir John Gorst) *May* 3, 683

Violation of the Civil Service Covenant, Question, Mr. Buchanan; Answer, The Under Secretary of State for India (Sir John Gorst) *April* 29, 356

IRELAND (*Questions*)

Arms (Ireland) Act—Emergency Caretaker, Roscommon Co., Question, Mr. Hayden; Answer, The Parliamentary Under Secretary for Ireland (Colonel King-Harman) *April* 29, 347

The Ancient Laws of Ireland — Editing and Republication, Question, Mr. T. P. Gill; Answer, The Parliamentary Under Secretary for Ireland (Colonel King-Harman) *May* 2, 544

Belfast — Strike of Shipwrights, Questions, Mr. Sexton; Answers, The Parliamentary Under Secretary for Ireland (Colonel King-Harman), The Secretary of State for the Home Department (Mr. Matthews) *May* 2, 553; Question, Mr. Sexton; Answer, The Under Secretary of State for the Home Department (Mr. Stuart-Wortley) *May* 3, 697; Question, Mr. M'Cartan; Answer, The Parliamentary Under Secretary for Ireland (Colonel King-Harman) *May* 5, 964

Boycotting and Intimidation—Circular Letter to the Chiefs of Police, Question, Dr. Tanner; Answer, The Parliamentary Under Secretary for Ireland (Colonel King-Harman) *May* 3, 700

Emigration from Ireland, January to April, 1887, Question, Mr. J. E. Ellis; Answer, The Parliamentary Under Secretary for Ireland (Colonel King-Harman) *May* 12, 1660

Industrial Schools—The Cappoquin Industrial School, Waterford, Question, Mr. Pyne; Answer, The Parliamentary Under Secretary for Ireland (Colonel King-Harman) *April* 28, 236

Irish Petty Sessions Act—Section 13—Committals, Questions, Mr. Maurice Healy; Answers, The Attorney General for Ireland (Mr. Holmes) *May* 13, 1814

Letter of Mr. Egan, Question, Mr. T. M. Healy; Answer, The Parliamentary Under Secretary for Ireland (Colonel King-Harman) *May* 9, 1274

Local Government—Supply of Water to Rathmines, Question, Mr. P. M'Donald; Answer, The Parliamentary Under Secretary for Ireland (Colonel King-Harman) *April* 29, 355

Prevention of Crime (Ireland) Act, 1882—Examinations under Section 16, Questions, Mr. Anderson, Mr. Sexton; Answers, The Parliamentary Under Secretary for Ireland (Colonel King-Harman) *April* 26, 12;—*Returns*, Question, Mr. Anderson; Answer, The Parliamentary Under Secretary for Ireland (Colonel King-Harman) *April* 28, 243

The Cattle Trade—The Rathdown Union—Pleuro-Pneumonia, Questions, Mr. Murphy, Mr. J. W. Barclay; Answers, The Parliamentary Under Secretary for Ireland (Colonel King-Harman) *April* 26, 7

[*cont.*

MAXWELL, Sir H. E. (A Lord of the Treasury). *Wigton*
Colonial Service (Pensions). Comm. 675; cl. 3, 676; cl. 4, Amendt. 824, 825; cl. 5, 830; cl. 6, Amendt. 833; *add. cl.* 833
Licensed Premises (Earlier Closing) (Scotland), 2R. 1433

Merchandise Marks Act (1862) Amendment Bill   (*Baron Henry De Worms, Mr. Attorney General*)
s. Select Comm., Mr. Lane *disch.*, Mr. Peter M'Donald *added May* 2   [Bill 142]

Merchant Shipping
Loss of Life at Sea—The Select Committee, Question, Mr. Finlay; Answer, The Secretary to the Board of Trade (Baron Henry De Worms) *May* 12, 1662
Medical Service on board Transatlantic Liners, Observations, Dr. Tanner; Reply, The Secretary to the Board of Trade (Baron Henry De Worms) *May* 12, 1739
Merchant Shipping Act, 1876—Denmark—Deck Cargoes, Question, Mr. Caldwell; Answer, The Under Secretary of State for Foreign Affairs (Sir James Fergusson) *April* 26, 14
Russian Bills of Health at Constantinople, Question, Mr. Conybeare; Answer, The Under Secretary of State for Foreign Affairs (Sir James Fergusson) *May* 2, 553
Saving Life at Sea, Select Committee appointed and nominated *May* 2; List of the Committee, 681
Saving Life at Sea—The Line-Throwing Gun, Question, Mr. Hoare; Answer, The Secretary to the Board of Trade (Baron Henry De Worms) *May* 3, 684
The Loo Rock, Baltimore Harbour, Question, Mr. Gilhooly; Answer, The Secretary to the Board of Trade (Baron Henry De Worms) *May* 2, 541
Wreck Commissioners Court—Wreck of the Channel Steamer "Victoria," Question, Mr. Isaacs; Answer, The Secretary to the Board of Trade (Baron Henry De Worms) *May* 9, 1269; Question, Mr. Channing; Answer, The Secretary to the Board of Trade (Baron Henry De Worms) *May* 12, 1683

Merchant Shipping (Fishing Boats) Acts Amendment Bill
(*The Lord Stanley of Preston*)
l. Royal Assent *April* 28   [50 Vict. c. 4]

Meteorology—Storm Warnings—Mr. B. A. Collins
Question, Mr. Henniker Heaton; Answer, The Secretary to the Board of Trade (Baron Henry De Worms) *May* 5, 959

METROPOLIS   (*Questions*)
Open Air Meetings
Instructions to the Police, Question, Mr. James Stuart; Answer, The Under Secretary of State for the Home Department (Mr. Stuart-Wortley) *May* 6, 1124

[*cont.*

METROPOLIS—*cont.*
Action of the Police, Questions, Mr. Picton, Mr. James Stuart, Mr. Pickersgill; Answers, The Under Secretary of State for the Home Department (Mr. Stuart-Wortley) *May* 10, 1456;—*Arrest of Chapman and Kemp*, Question, Mr. Pickersgill; Answer, The Under Secretary of State for the Home Department (Mr. Stuart-Wortley) *May* 12, 1690
Meeting at Kennington—Interference by the Police, Question, Mr. Labouchere; Answer, The Under Secretary of State for the Home Department (Mr. Stuart-Wortley) *May* 5, 950
Letter of Chief Officer at Kennington Road Police Station, Question, Mr. Conybeare; Answer, The Under Secretary of State for the Home Department (Mr. Stuart-Wortley) *May* 10, 1461
Socialist Meetings on Open Spaces, Observations, Mr. James Stuart; Reply, The Secretary of State for the Home Department (Mr. Matthews); short debate thereon *May* 12, 1746   [See title *Law and Police*]
Open Spaces—The Churchyard Bottom Wood, Hornsey, Question, Mr. J. Rowlands; Answer, Sir Henry Selwin-Ibbetson *May* 2, 552
Street Improvements—The Colonnades of Burlington House, and Temple Bar, Question, Observations, The Earl of Milltown; Reply, Lord Henniker; Question, The Earl of Rosebery; Answer, Lord Henniker *May* 12, 1656

Metropolis Management Acts Amendment (No. 2) Bill   (*Mr. Octavius Morgan, Mr. Gilliat, Mr. Kimber*)
c. Report * *May* 6   [Bill 166]

Metropolis Management Acts Amendment (Westminster) Bill
(*Mr. Burdett-Coutts, Mr. John Talbot, Mr. Tomlinson, Mr. Seager Hunt*)
c. Read 2°, and committed to the Select Committee on the Metropolis Management Acts Amendment (No. 2) Bill *April* 26, 99
Report * *May* 6   [Bill 208]

Metropolis Management Acts Amendment (No. 2) Bill
Metropolis Management Acts Amendment (Westminster) Bill   }
Consolidated into

Metropolis Management (Battersea and Westminster) Bill
c. Report * *May* 6   [Bill 258]
Committee * (*on re-comm.*); Report; read 3° *May* 13

Metropolitan Police, The
Case of Ex-Police Sergeant Eskett, Question, Dr. Clark; Answer, The Under Secretary of State for the Home Department (Mr. Stuart-Wortley) *May* 12, 1685

[*cont.*

[*cont.*   [*cont.*

[cont.

SCOTLAND (Questions)

Church of Scotland—Church Building in Pitsligo, Aberdeenshire, Question, Mr. Esslemont; Answer, The Lord Advocate (Mr. J. H. A. Macdonald) May 12, 1685

Holidays for the Agricultural Population, Question, Mr. Thorburn; Answer, The Lord Advocate (Mr. J. H. A. Macdonald) April 28, 240

Register House—Reports of the Departmental Committee, 1881, Question, Mr. Fraser-Mackintosh; Answer, The Secretary to the Treasury (Mr. Jackson) May 9, 1263

Scotch University Bill, Question, Mr. Mason; Answer, The Lord Advocate (Mr. J. H. A. Macdonald) May 12, 1677

Sea-Fishing Boats (Scotland) Act, 1886, Question, Mr. Macdonald Cameron; Answer, The Lord Advocate (Mr. J. H. A. Macdonald) May 5, 945

The Crofters' Commission—Visit to Solitote, Isle of Skye, Question, Dr. Clark; Answer, The Lord Advocate (Mr. J. H. A. Macdonald) May 10, 1466

EDUCATION DEPARTMENT (SCOTLAND)

School Board Elections—Cumulative Voting, Question, Mr. Shiress Will; Answer, The Solicitor General for Scotland (Mr. J. P. B. Robertson) April 29, 347

The Gaelic Language, Question, Dr. Cameron; Answer, The Lord Advocate (Mr. J. H. A. Macdonald) May 6, 1115

The Garnethill and Hutcheson Schools in Glasgow, Question, Mr. Caldwell; Answer, The Lord Advocate (Mr. J. H. A. Macdonald) April 28, 239

FISHERIES (SCOTLAND)

Loss of Life from Shallow-Decked Boats, Question, Mr. Macdonald Cameron; Answer, The Secretary to the Board of Trade (Baron Henry De Worms) May 12, 1693

Scotch Fishery Board—Trawling in the Moray Firth, Questions, Mr. Anderson; Answers, The Lord Advocate (Mr. J. H. A. Macdonald), The First Lord of the Treasury (Mr. W. H. Smith) May 3, 555

The British Fishery Society — Net-Drying Grounds, Question, Mr. Macdonald Cameron; Answer, The Lord Advocate (Mr. J. H. A. Macdonald) May 12, 1684

White Herring Fishery, Wick and Pulteneytown, Question, Mr. Macdonald Cameron; Answer, The Solicitor General for Scotland (Mr. J. P. B. Robertson) April 29, 345

LAW AND JUSTICE (SCOTLAND)

Case of —— Ferrie, at Hamilton, Question, Mr. Mason; Answer, The Lord Advocate (Mr. J. H. A. Macdonald) April 28, 241

Sending "Deeds for Adjudication" by Post, Questions, Mr. J. C. Bolton; Answers, The Solicitor General for Scotland (Mr. J. P. B. Robertson) April 29, 345

LAW AND POLICE (SCOTLAND)

Outrages at Duthil, Inverness-shire, Question, Mr. Fraser-Mackintosh; Answer, The Lord Advocate (Mr. J. H. A. Macdonald) May 2, 539

SCOTLAND—cont.

POST OFFICE (SCOTLAND)

Postal Service in Inverness-shire, Question, Dr. Clark; Answer, The Postmaster General (Mr. Raikes) May 10, 1464

Service between Perth, Aberdeen, and Keith, Question, Dr. Clark; Answer, The Postmaster General (Mr. Raikes) May 10, 1465

Scotland—Mussel Beds in Tidal Waters

Amendt. on Committee of Supply, May 12, to leave out from "That," add "an humble Address be presented to Her Majesty, praying Her Majesty to appoint a Royal Commission to inquire as to the existence and extent of private rights in mussel beds in the tidal waters of Scotland, and to inquire generally as to the nature and value of such rights, and to report as to the advisability of compelling the transfer of all such rights to the Fishery Board for Scotland " (Mr. Anderson) v., 1729; Question proposed, "That the words, &c.;" after short debate, Question put; A. 130, N. 108; M. 22 (D. L. 136)

SELBORNE, Earl of

Railway and Canal Traffic, 3R. Amendt. 931
Tithe Rent-Charge, 2R. 173

SELLAR, Mr. A. C., Lanarkshire, Partick

Admiralty—Examinations in Seamanship of Midshipmen for Rank of Lieutenants, 329, 1665

Africa (Central) — Transit Tariff through Portuguese Territory, 1666

Inland Revenue—Stamp Acts—Legislation, 1461

Private Bill Legislation, 2R. 490, 495

SELWIN-IBBETSON, Right Hon. Sir H. J., Essex, Epping

Church Estates Commissioners—Vacant Land, Bream's Buildings, Chancery Lane, 1114
Open Spaces (Metropolis)—The Churchyard Bottom Wood, Hornsey, 552

SEXTON, Mr. T., Belfast, W.

Belfast Main Drainage, Lords' Amendts. Consid., 185; Amendt. 186, 193, 194, 199, 203, 204, 206

Ireland—Questions

Criminal Law Amendment, 250
Prevention of Crime Act, 1882—Examinations under Section 16, 12
Trade and Commerce—Strike of Shipbuilders at Belfast, 553, 697

Municipal Corporations Acts (Ireland) Amendment (No. 2), 2R. 1234, 1470

Parliament — "Offices of Profit under the Crown" — Disqualifications under the 6th Anne, 233

Parliament—Privilege (Mr. Dillon and "The Times" Newspaper), Res. 716, 717, 719, 753; Amendt. 754, 872, 898

Primrose League, Bournemouth — Criminal Law Amendment (Ireland), 15

[··nt

[cont.

[o nt.

WEMYSS, Earl of
Sheffield Corporation Water, 3R. Amendt. 150, 168

West India Islands—Mr. L. D. Powles, Magistrate of Nassau
Question, Mr. Atkinson ; Answer, The Secretary of State for the Colonies (Sir Henry Holland) May 9, 1263

West Lancashire Railway Bill (by Order)
c. Read 3°, after short debate April 27, 100

WESTMINSTER, Duke of
Smoke Nuisance Abatement (Metropolis), 2R. 1245

WHITBREAD, Mr. S., Bedford
Parliament—Privilege (Mr. Dillon and " The Times " Newspaper), Res. 746

WHITMORE, Mr. C. A., Chelsea
Police Force Enfranchisement, Comm. 98

WILL, Mr. J. S., Montrose, &c.
Scotland — Education Department — School Board Elections—Cumulative Voting, 347

WILLIAMS, Mr. Powell J., Birmingham, S.
Hong Kong—Punishment of Flogging, 1118

WILSON, Sir S., Portsmouth
Civil Service Writers—The Bonus Scheme, 967
Greenwich Hospital — Investment of Funds, 554

WILSON, Mr. H. J., York, W.R., Holmfirth
Criminal Law Amendment (Ireland), Comm. cl. 1, 1346
Jubilee Year of Her Majesty's Reign, Celebration of—Service in Westminster Abbey, 952

WINTERBOTHAM, Mr. A. B., Gloucester, Cirencester
Inland Revenue—Payments to the Legacy and Succession Duty Department, 350

WOLMER, Viscount, Hants, Petersfield
Criminal Law Amendment (Ireland), Comm. 47 ; cl. 1, 483

Woods and Forests, Commissioners of—Crown Rents in Wales
Question, Mr. Kenyon ; Answer, The Secretary to the Treasury (Mr. Jackson) May 6, 1117

WORKS—First Commissioner (see PLUNKET, Right Hon. D. R.)

WORTLEY, Mr. C. B. STUART- (Under Secretary of State for the Home Department), Sheffield, Hallam
Allotments Extension Act, 1882 —." Poors Close " Charity, Great Easton, 1451
Burial Act—Fees—Vicar of Long Compton, 344
Coal Mines, &c. Regulation Bill—Female Labour at the Pit's Bank, 1269
Dogs—Rabies Order, 1677
Extraordinary Tithe Rent-Charge—Capital Value, 1118
First Offenders, Address for a Return, 1581
First Offenders, Comm. cl. 1, 1083, 1090
Incumbents of Benefices Loans Extension Act (1886) Amendment, 2R. 490
Law and Justice (England and Wales)—Questions
    Lambeth Police Court—Exclusion of the Public, 1461 ; — Southampton Borough Police Court, 959
    Magistracy—Cerrig-y-Druidion Petty Sessions, 1869 ;—Flintshire Nonconformists, 1809
    Public Prosecutions—A Solicitor to the Treasury, 694
Law and Police (England and Wales)—Questions
    Case of Ex-Police Sergeant Eskett, 1685
    Disturbances at Kennington, 695
    Metropolitan Police — Chief Commissioner, 1811
    Outrage at a Meeting at Audlem, Cheshire, 1460
    Personal Searches by the Police, 968
    Salvation Army, 968
    Severe Sentence at the Marylebone Police Court, 1459
    Socialist Meetings—Instructions to the Police, 693
Newspaper Press—The Langworthy Marriage Case in " The Pall Mall Gazette," 1667
Open Air Meetings (Metropolis)—Questions
    Arrest of Chapman and Kemp, 1690
    Instructions to the Police, 1124, 1457
    Proposed Meeting at Kennington—Criticism of the Police, 1462
Parliament—Questions
    Business of the House—Coal Mines, &c. Regulation, 235, 1124, 1812
    House of Commons—Extra Allowance to the Police Constables, 1674
    Public Business — Employers' Liability, 353, 1458
Parliamentary Elections—Habitation of the Primrose League, Birmingham, 353
Prisons (England and Wales) — Millbank Prison, 1686, 1687
Public Meetings—Interference by the Police, 950
    Salvationist or Socialist Meetings and the Police, 961
Quarries, Comm. 824
Trade and Commerce—Strike of Shipbuilders at Belfast, 698
Trade and Manufacture—" Sweating System," 13
Truck, Comm. cl. 1, Amendt. 304 ; cl. 2, Amendt. ib. ; cl. 3, Amendt. 305, 677 ; cl. 5, Amendt. ib., 678 ; cl. 6, Amendt. ib.; cl. 7, Amendt. ib. ; cl. 8, Amendt. 679 ; cl. 9,

[cont.

Lightning Source UK Ltd.
Milton Keynes UK
UKHW021830281118
333125UK00009B/317/P